# Street by Street

**KU-596-936**

# GREATER LONDON

**Reprinted April 2011**
5th edition April 2010
© AA Media Limited 2011

Original edition printed May 2001

Published by AA Publishing (a trading name of AA Media Limited, whose registered office is Fanum House, Basing View, Basingstoke, Hampshire RG21 4EA. Registered number 06112600).

Produced by the Mapping Services Department of The Automobile Association. (A04678)

A CIP Catalogue record for this book is available from the British Library.

Printed by Oriental Press in Dubai

The contents of this atlas are believed to be correct at the time of the latest revision. However, the publishers cannot be held responsible or liable for any loss or damage occasioned to any person acting or refraining from action as a result of any use or reliance on any material in this atlas, nor for any errors, omissions or changes in such material. This does not affect your statutory rights. The publishers would welcome information to correct any errors or omissions and to keep this atlas up to date. Please write to Publishing, The Automobile Association, Fanum House (FH12), Basing View, Basingstoke, Hampshire, RG21 4EA. E-mail: *streetbystreet@theaa.com*

Ref: GS040w

| | |
|---|---|
| Key to map pages | ii–iii |
| Key to map symbols | iv–1 |
| Enlarged map pages | 2–19 |
| Main map pages | 20–285 |
| Index – towns & villages | 286–287 |
| Index – streets | 288–377 |
| Index – featured places | 377–398 |
| Acknowledgements | 398 |

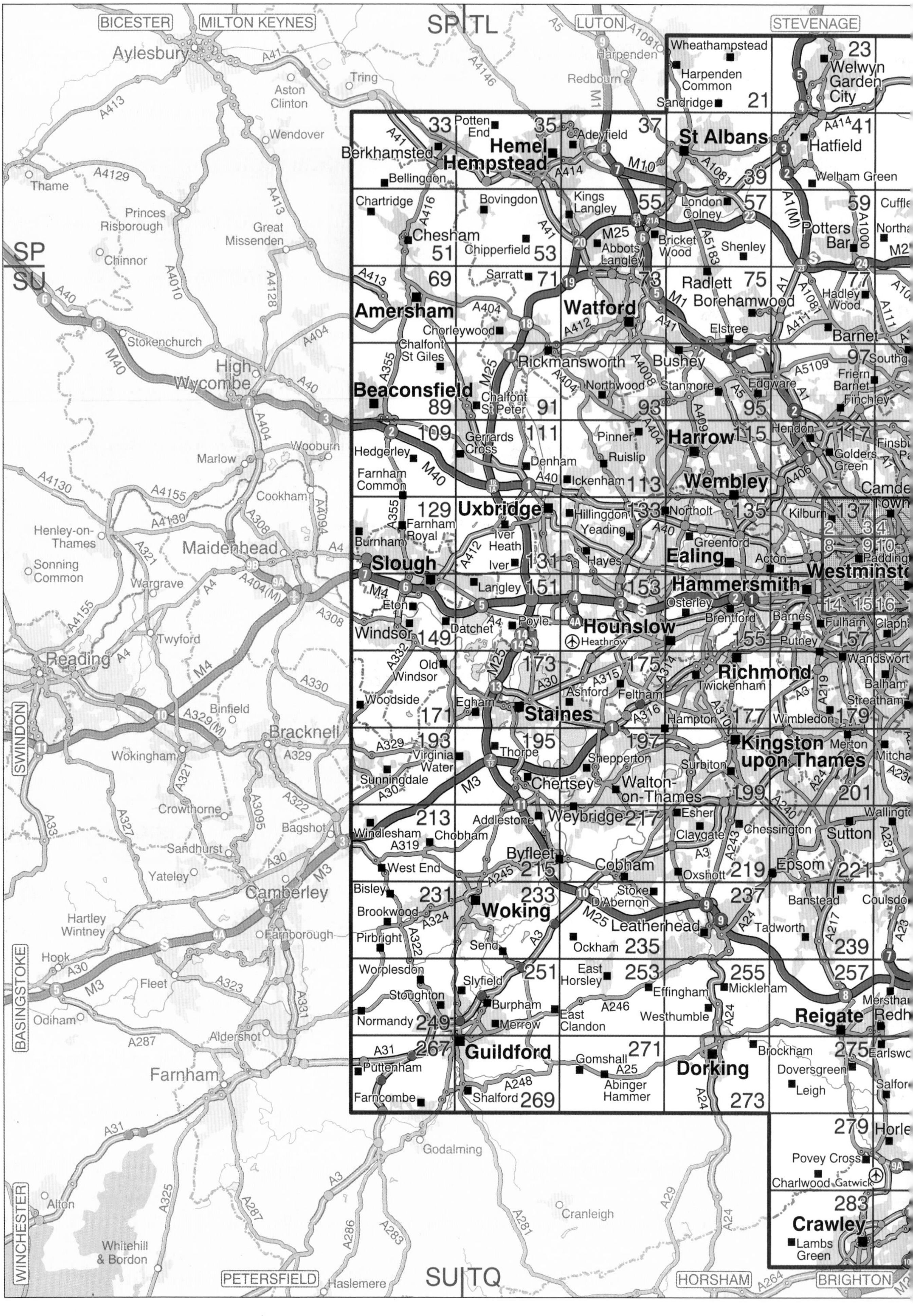

BICESTER | MILTON KEYNES | SP TL | LUTON A1081 | STEVENAGE

Aylesbury
Aston Clinton
Tring
Wendover
Thame
A4129
A41
A4146
A5
M1
Harpenden
Redbourn
Wheathampstead
Harpenden Common
Sandridge
23
Welwyn Garden City
21
Berkhamsted
Bellingdon
Chartridge
Bovingdon
Kings Langley
Adeyfield
St Albans
London Colney
Hatfield
Welham Green
41
39
57
59
Cuffle
Northa
M2
Potters Bar
33
35
37
55
Hemel Hempstead
Chesham
Chipperfield
Sarratt
Abbots Langley
Bricket Wood
Shenley
Radlett
Borehamwood
Elstree
75
77
Hadley Wood
Barnet
51
53
69
71
73
Amersham
Chorleywood
Rickmansworth
Bushey
Stanmore
Edgware
Hendon
97
Southg
Friern Barnet
Finchley
Golders Green
Camde
Beaconsfield
Chalfont St Giles
Chalfont St Peter
Gerrards Cross
Northwood
Pinner
Ruislip
Harrow
Wembley
115
117
Finsb Pa
89
91
93
95
109
111
113
Hedgerley
Farnham Common
Denham
Ickenham
Hillingdon
Yeading
Hayes
Greenford
Northolt
Acton
Ealing
Kilburn
135
137
Uxbridge
129
131
133
Westminst
Slough
Burnham
Farnham Royal
Iver Heath
Iver
Langley
Eton
Datchet
Poyle
Hounslow
Osterley
Brentford
Barnes
Putney
Hammersmith
Fulham
Clapha
Richmond
Twickenham
Wimbledon
155
157
Windsor
149
151
153
Heathrow
Old Windsor
Woodside
Egham
Ashford
Feltham
Hampton
Wandswoth
Balham
Streatham
177
179
173
175
171
Staines
Virginia Water
Thorpe
Shepperton
Surbiton
Kingston upon Thames
Merton
Mitcha
193
195
197
199
201
Sunningdale
Chertsey
Walton-on-Thames
Esher
Claygate
Chessington
Sutton
Wallingt
Windlesham
Chobham
Addlestone
Weybridge
217
Oxshott
Epsom
219
221
West End
Byfleet
Cobham
Banstead
Coulsdo
213
215
Bisley
Brookwood
Pirbright
Woking
Stoke D'Abernon
Leatherhead
Tadworth
237
239
231
233
235
Worplesdon
Stoughton
Send
Slyfield
Burpham
Merrow
East Horsley
Effingham
Mickleham
Westhumble
Reigate
Mersth
Redh
251
253
255
257
Normandy
249
Guildford
Puttenham
Gomshall
East Clandon
Abinger Hammer
Dorking
Brockham
Doversgreen
Leigh
Earlsw
Salfor
267
271
273
275
Farncombe
Shalford
269
Godalming
Cranleigh
Povey Cross
Charlwood Gatwick
279
Horle
9A
Crawley
Lambs Green
283

WINCHESTER | PETERSFIELD | SU TQ | HORSHAM | BRIGHTON

Scale of enlarged map pages 1:10,000 6.3 inches to 1 mile

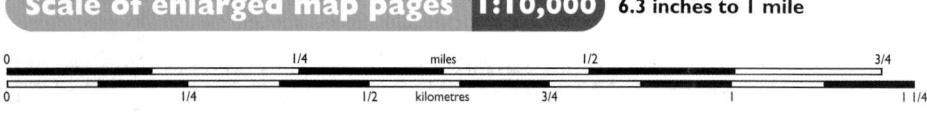

| 0 | 1/4 | miles | 1/2 | 3/4 |
| 0 | 1/4 | kilometres | 3/4 | 1 | 1 1/4 |

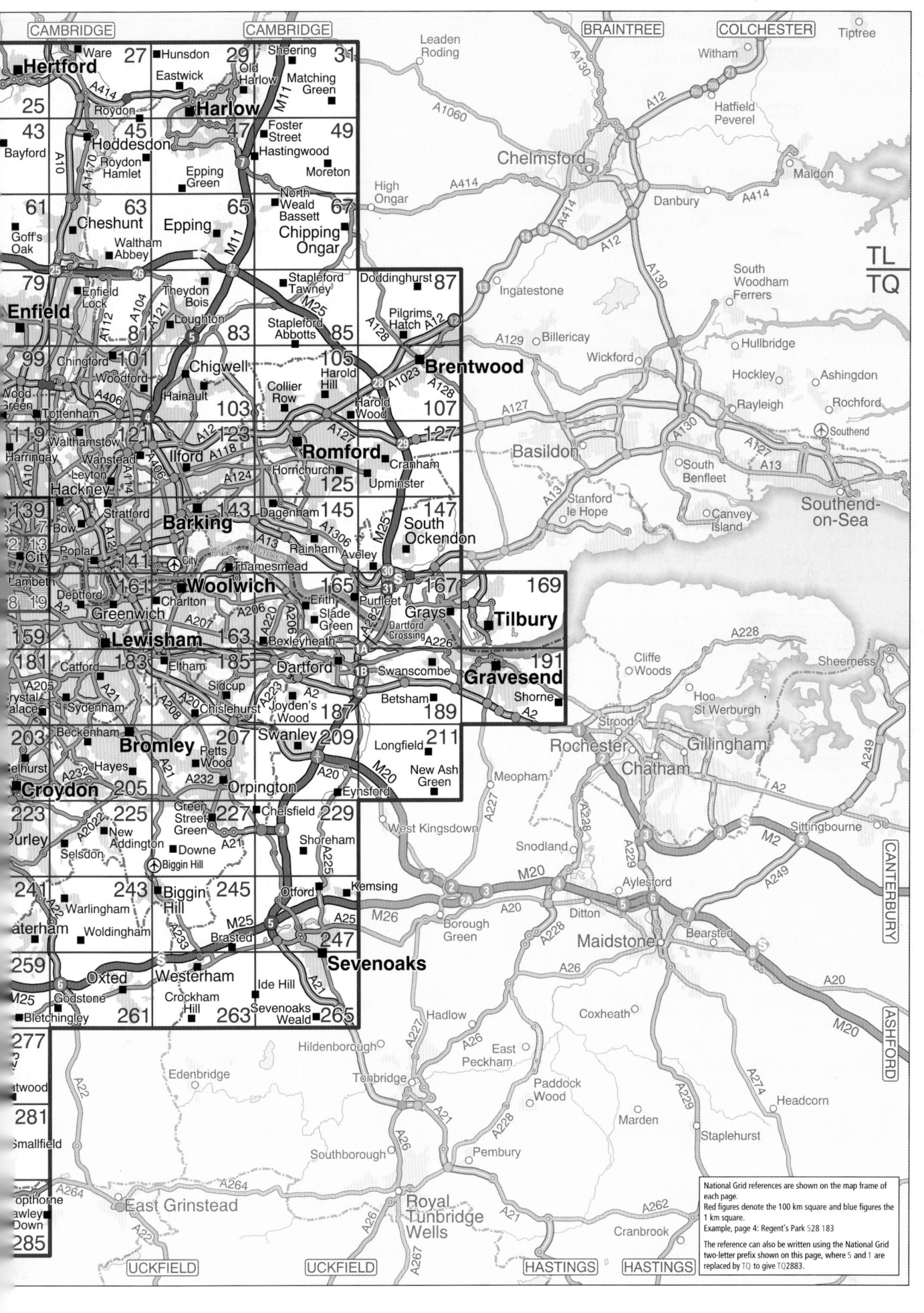

3.2 inches to 1 mile

**Scale of main map pages** 1:20,000

National Grid references are shown on the map frame of each page.
Red figures denote the 100 km square and blue figures the 1 km square.
Example: page 4: Regent's Park 528 183

The reference can also be written using the National Grid two-letter prefix shown on this page, where 5 and 1 are replaced by TQ to give TQ2883.

| | |
|---|---|
| **Junction 9** | Motorway & junction |
| **Services** | Motorway service area |
| **J58** | Primary road single/dual carriageway & junction |
| **Services** | Primary road service area |
| | A road single/dual carriageway |
| | B road single/dual carriageway |
| | Other road single/dual carriageway |
| | Minor/private road, access may be restricted |
| ← ← | One-way street |
| | Pedestrian area |
| | Track or footpath |
| | Road under construction |
| | Road tunnel |
| **30** **V** | Speed camera site (fixed location) with speed limit in mph or variable |
| **40** **V** | Selection of road with two or more fixed camera sites; speed limit in mph or variable |
| **50→ ←50** | Average speed (SPECS™) camera system with speed limit in mph |
| **P** | Parking |
| **P+** | Park & Ride |
| | Bus/coach station |
| | Railway & main railway station |
| | Railway & minor railway station |

| | |
|---|---|
| ⊖ | Underground station |
| ⊖ | Docklands Light Railway (DLR) station |
| ⊖ | Light railway & station |
| ⊖ | London Overground station |
| *LC* | Level crossing |
| •—•—•—•—• | Tramway |
| - - - - - - - | Ferry route |
| ·············· | Airport runway |
| —·—·—·—· | County, administrative boundary |
| | Congestion Charging Zone * |
| | Low Emission Zone (LEZ) (visit **theaa.com** for further information) |
| | Charge-free route through the Charging Zone |
| **151** | Page continuation 1:20,000 |
| **17** | Page continuation to enlarged scale 1:10,000 |
| | River/canal, lake, pier |
| | Aqueduct, lock, weir |
| | Beach |
| | Woodland |
| | Park |
| | Cemetery |
| | Built-up area |

\* The AA central London congestion charging map is also available

Industrial / business building

Castle

Leisure building

Historic house or building

Retail building

Wakehurst Place (NT)    National Trust property

Other building

Museum or art gallery

City wall

Roman antiquity

**A&E** Hospital with 24-hour A&E department

Ancient site, battlefield or monument

**PO** Post Office, public library

Industrial interest

*i* Tourist Information Centre, seasonal

Garden

Petrol station, 24 hour
Major suppliers only

Garden Centre
Garden Centre Association Member

† Church/chapel

Garden Centre
Wyevale Garden Centre

Public toilets, with facilities for the less able

Arboretum

**PH** Public house
AA recommended

Farm or animal centre

Restaurant
AA inspected

Zoological or wildlife collection

Madeira Hotel    Hotel
AA inspected

Bird collection

Theatre or performing arts centre, cinema

Nature reserve

Golf course

Aquarium

▲ Camping
AA inspected

Visitor or heritage centre

Caravan site
AA inspected

Country park

Camping & caravan site
AA inspected

Cave

Theme park

Distillery, brewery or vineyard

Abbey, cathedral or priory

Windmill

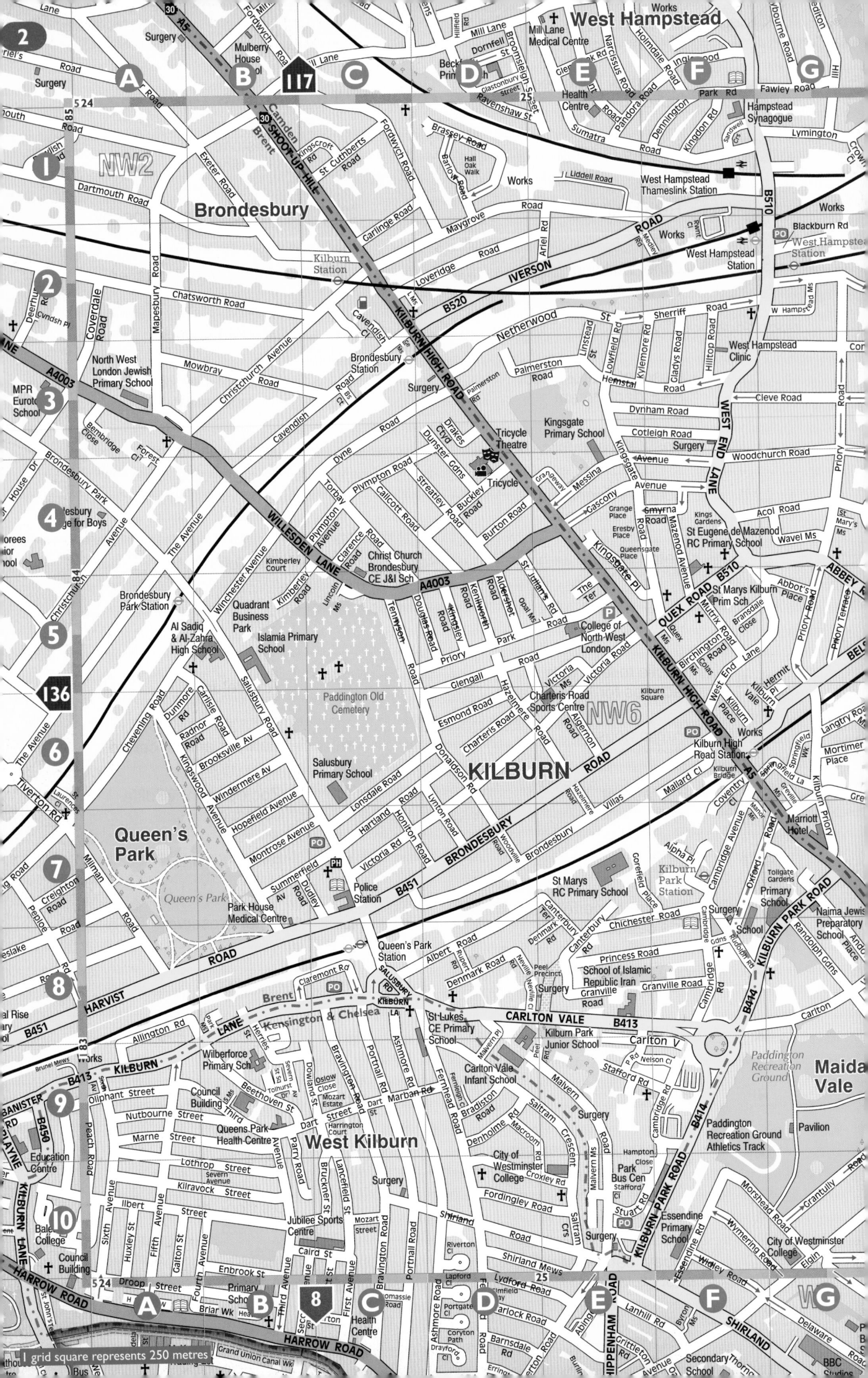

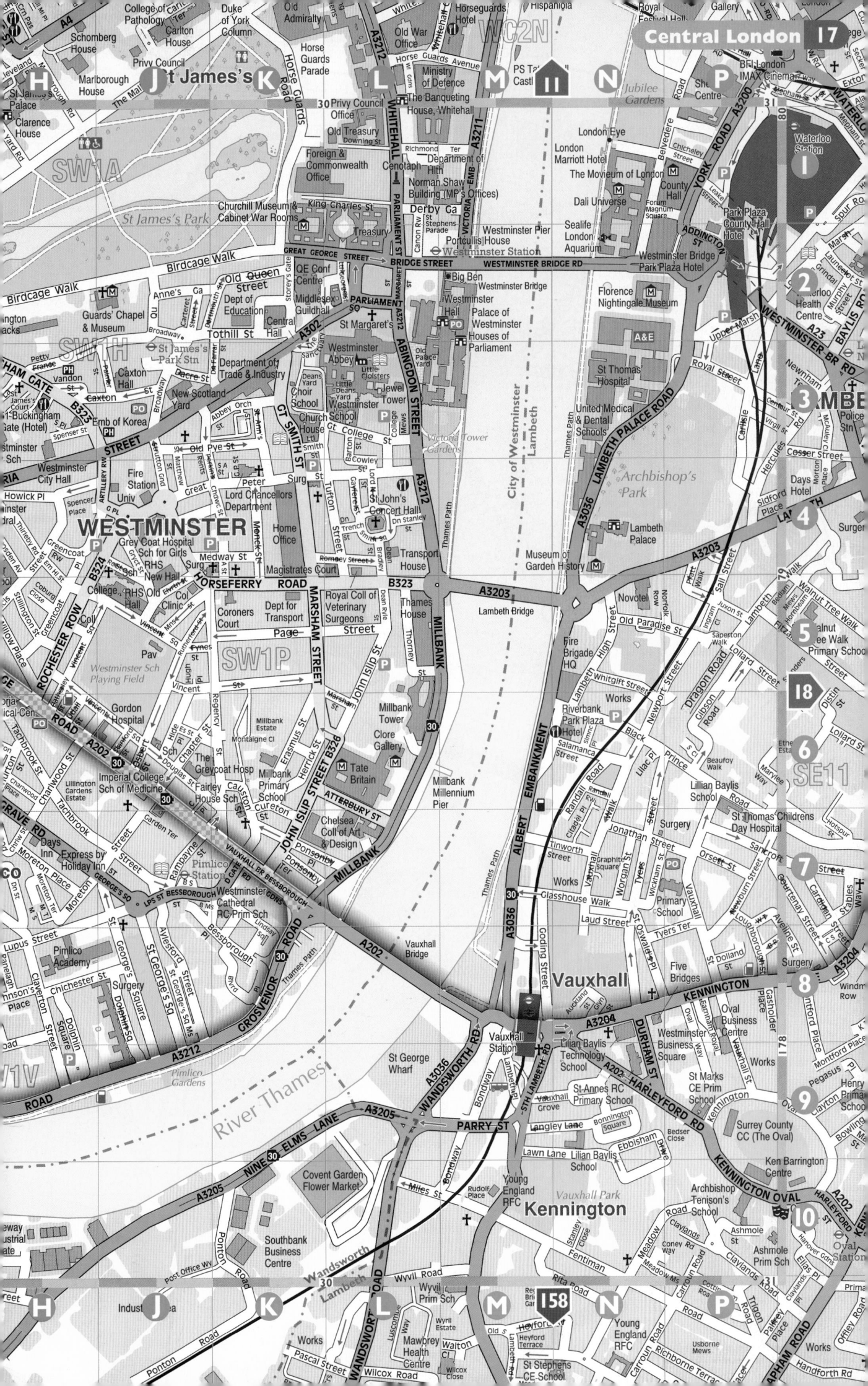

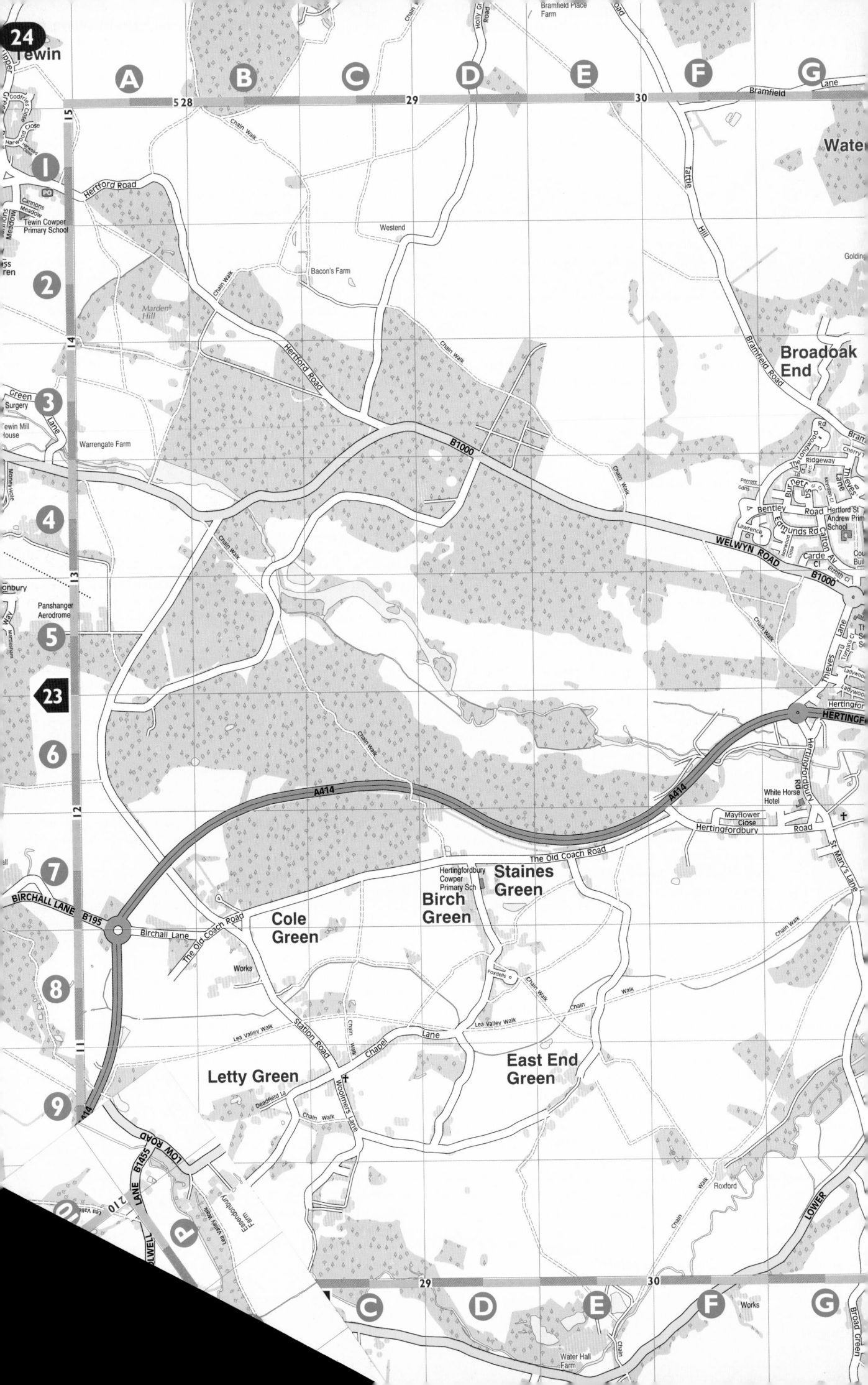

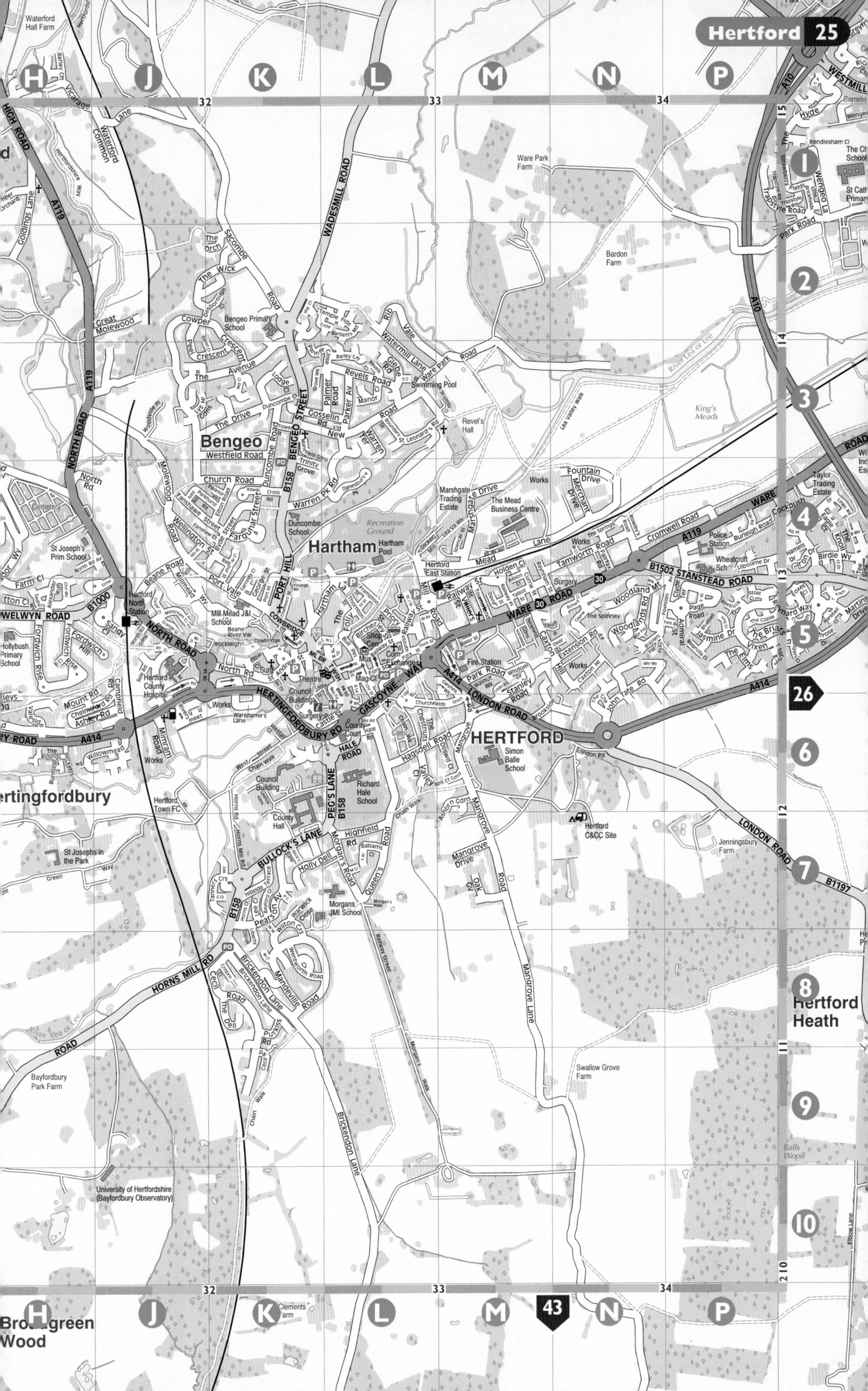

H  J  K  L  M  N  P

39  40  41  15

1

Hunsdon

2

3

4

Hunsdonbury

5

28

6

7

8

9

10

Roydon

H  J  K  L  M  N  P

39  45  40  41

Morley Hall

Wareside Primary School

B1004

Harcamlow Way

Watersplace Farm

Mardocks Farm

Newgate Wood

Easneye

Hollycross Road

Little Briggens

Newlands

Capell Lane

Chapelfields

Mill Race

Abbotts Way

St Andrews Primary School

Crofters Way

Woodcock Avenue

St Margarets Station

HIGH ST

ROYDON

South St

Miller's La

STATION RD

Works

Lawrence Av

Rush

Lee Ct

The Maltings Industrial Estate

Marsh Lane

Thele Av

Netherfield La

ROAD

Netherfield House

Works

HUNSDON

Stanstead Abbotts

Cat's Hill

B181

Robin Close

Lawrence Av

The Granary

Ryegate Farm

A414

Rye Meads

RSPB Reserve

Lea Valley Walk

Toll

Rye

Road

Ryde Park Ind Est

Rye House Stadium

Rye House Station

Plumpton Road

Fillets Farm

Harcamlow Way

Harcamlow Way

B180

Bonningtons

Halfway House

HUNSDON ROAD

B180

Olives Farm

Home Farm Industrial Estate

Harcamlow Way

Lord's Wood

EASTWICK ROAD

50 50

A414

Briggen

Stanstead Lodge

Harcamlow Way

Roydon Station

LC

Hertfordshire County

Essex County

LC

B181

Smake Mead

HIGH STREET

Farm Cl

Church

Roydon

Stort Valley Way

Three Forests Way

River Stort

Harlow Road

Cranee La

Beaumont Dr

Bakery Close

Roydon CP School

Lightfoots

Hansells Mead

Widford Road

Widford Rd

Paddock Close

Chestnut Close

HIGH ST

PO

PH

Tanners Way

Rectory Close

Tudor Cl

14

Acorn Street

Gt Oak Ct

Spellers

Nine Acres

Works

13

12

11

10

Cow
Roast

A4251

A41

Hastoe

Wigginton
Bottom

Buckland
Common

Cholesbury

Heath End

Bellingdon

A   B   C   D   E   F   G

1 grid square represents 500 metres

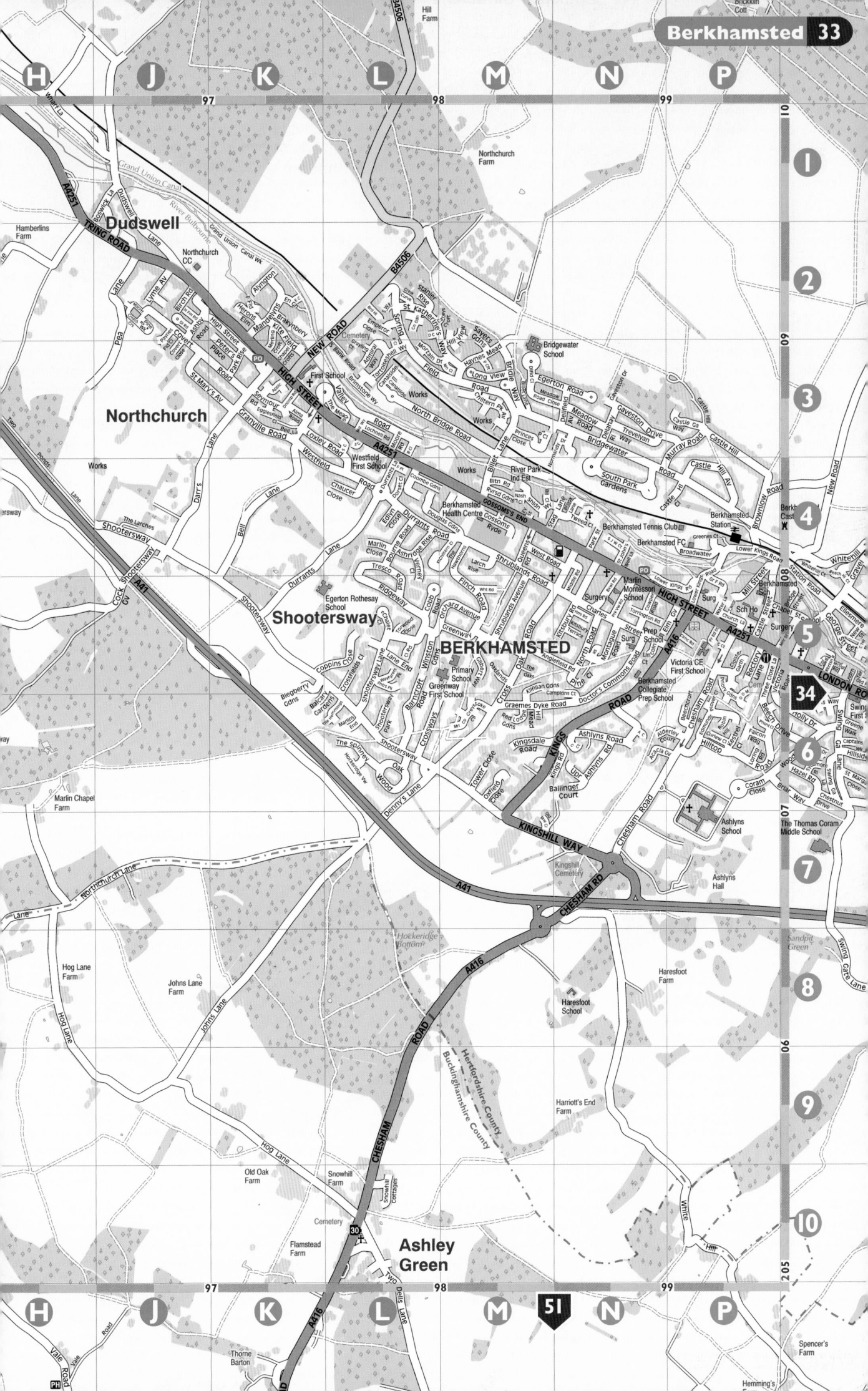

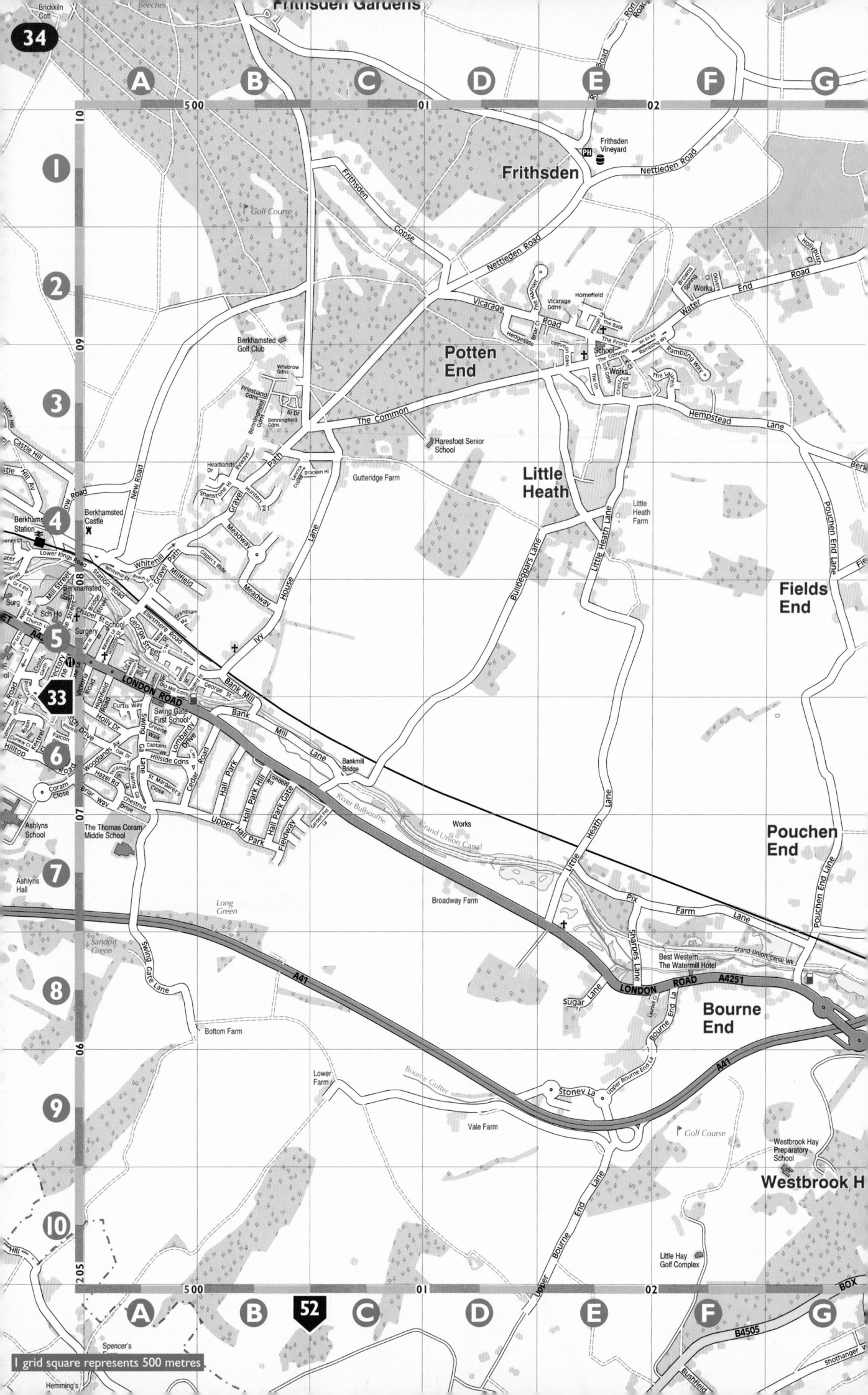

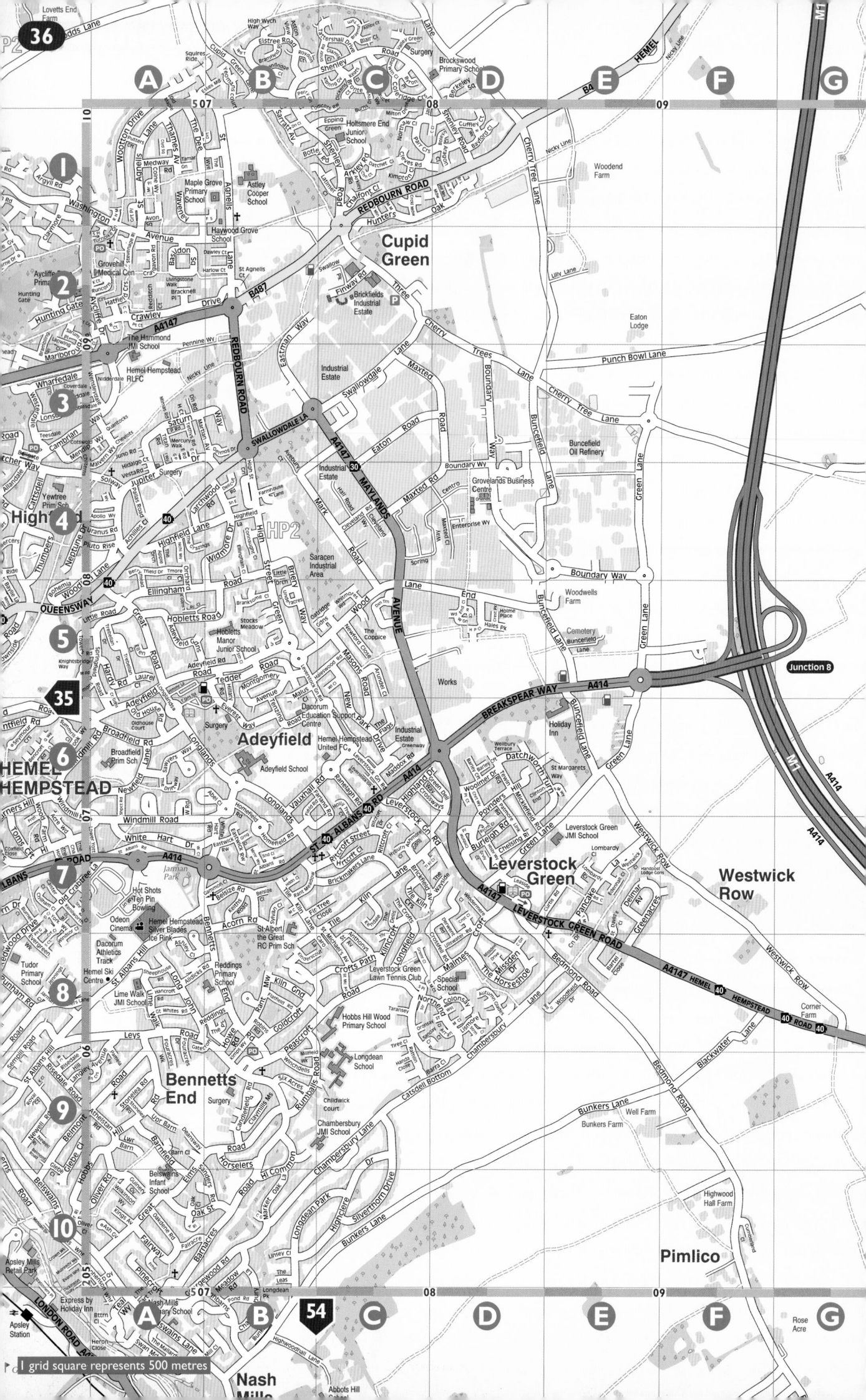

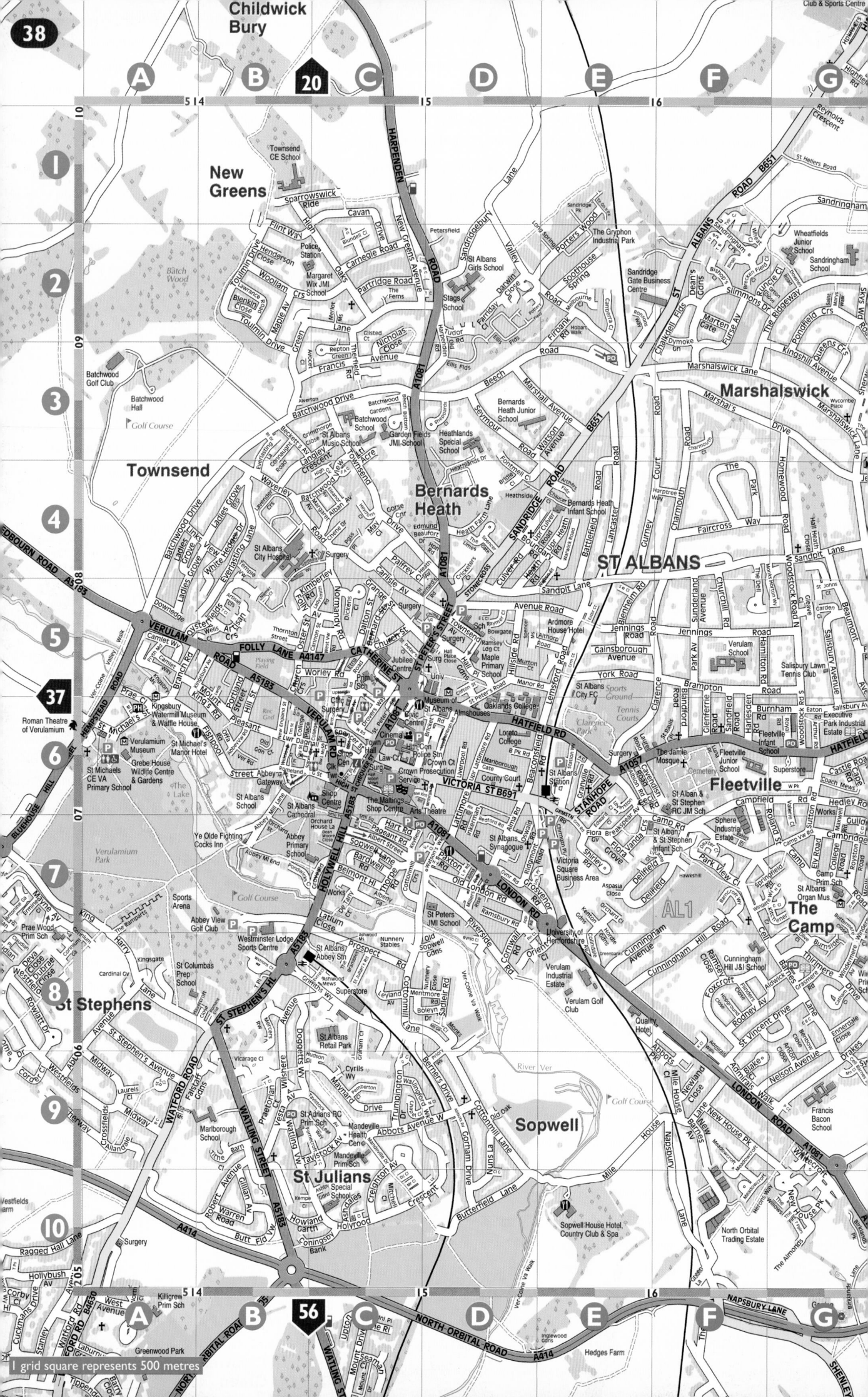

24

A   B   C   D   E   F   G

528   29   30

Holwell Court

Lea Valley Walk

HOLWELL LANE B1455

Lea Valley Walk

LOW ROAD

B158

1

Essendonbury Farm

ESSENDON HILL B158

2

Howe Green

Kennel Hall Farm

Water Hall Farm

Lwr Hatfield Rd

Chain Walk

Chain Walk

3

Essendon

Glebe Cottages

School Lane

Essendon Primary School

Bedwell Avenue

Chain Walk

Culverwood House

Bayford Hall

Bayford Wood

Bayfor

HIGH ROAD

Bedwellpark Farm

Bedwell Av

Stockings Lane

Bayford Primary School

Ashendene Roa

4

80

Robins West Hill

5

Essendon Place

Bedwell Park

Little Berkhamsted

Little Berkhamsted La

Church Road

Orchard Close

The Boundary

Goodyards

Bucks Alley

Bucks Farm

Bucks Aly

The 'Clyd

Hatfield London Country Club

Golf Course

41

07

6

Little   Berkhamsted   Lane

Bedwell Lodge Farm

Chain   Walk

Bush Farm

Ashendene Farm

7

Cucumber Hall Farm

Cucumber Lane

rnbeam   Lane

Woodcock Lodge

Epping House School

Chain Walk

8

06

Woodfield Lane

Woodcock Lodge Farm

Tylers Causeway

Tylers   Causeway

Epping Green

Newgate Street Village

9

Coldharbour Farm

Ponsbourne Park Hotel

10

Barbers Lodge Farm

Ponsb

New Park Farm

New Pk Rd

New   Park   Road

Newgate Street

Ponsb Tunnel

Ponsbourne St Marys Primary School

PO

Newgate Street Village

205

528   29   30

A   B   C   D   E   F   G

60

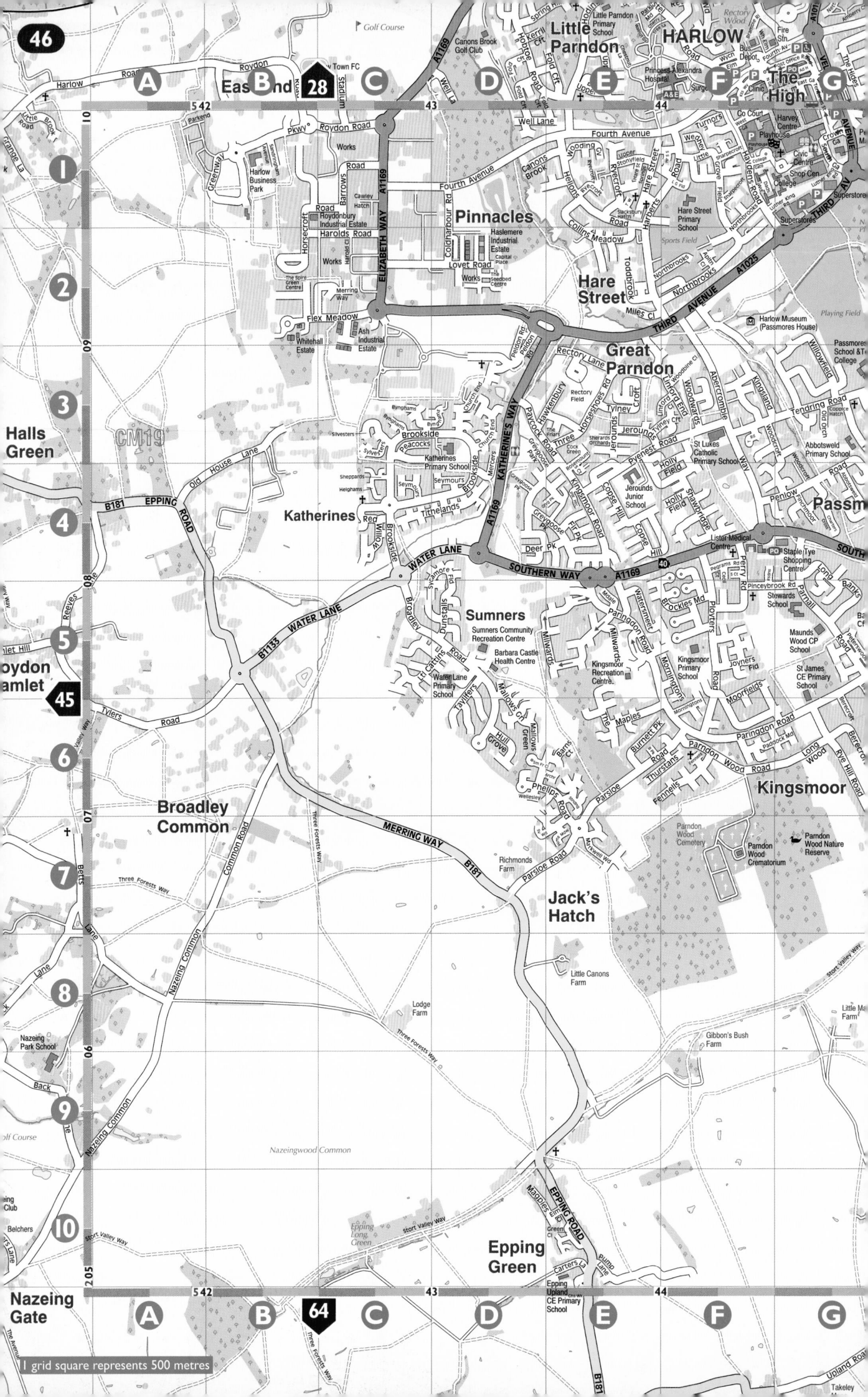

48

Hobbs
Cross

Loyter's
Green

A  B  30  C  D  E  F  G

549  50  51  Faggotters  Faggo
Lane  Farm

CM17  New  Way  Lane  Great
Wilmores

Roffey
Hall

I
Hubbard's Hall
Denby  Crabtree
Old  Hall
Ridgeways  Mallinson  New Way

Chelsea Gdns
Doulton Cl
Davenport  Malkin Dr
Malkin Dr  Weldon  Gra

2
Threshers
Bush

Foster
Street

Green Lane

Foster Street  Tilegate Green

Works  School Lane  Tilegate Road

3
Works  Magdalen
Laver

Mill  Street  Tilegate Road

4
Wynter's
Farm

Rolls
Farm

Hall
Farm

Stort Valley Way

Spencers
Farm

Willow  Hastingwood Road

5
Wynter's
Grange

47
Hastingwood

Humphreys

Greens
Farm

Stort

6
Shanks Brook
Paris
Hall

Stort Valley Way  Sewalds
Hall Farm  Weald Lodge

Glovers
Farm

07

7
Kents  Lane

Stort Valley Way

8
Canes
Farm

Canes  Lane  Weald
Bridge

Ashlyns Lane

Ashlyns

Weald Bridge Road

06  Golf Course

9
Little
Weald
Hall

North Weald
Golf Club  A414

Wyldingtree

Brook

Ravley  Lane

10
New House
Farm

Tower
Close  Bluemans
End

Tyler's
Green  Bovi

Weald
Hall

Merlin Way  Vicarage  Lane  Vicarage  Lane

A414  St Andrews Cl  Bluemans
Hows
Mead  Travelodge  A414

EPPING

Weald Hall Lane

549

A  B  66  C  D  E  F  G

50  51

St Andrews
CE Primary

HIGH ROAD  B181

ROAD

Princes Green Lane  Beamish Close

Princes
Close  Queens Road

1 grid square represents 500 metres

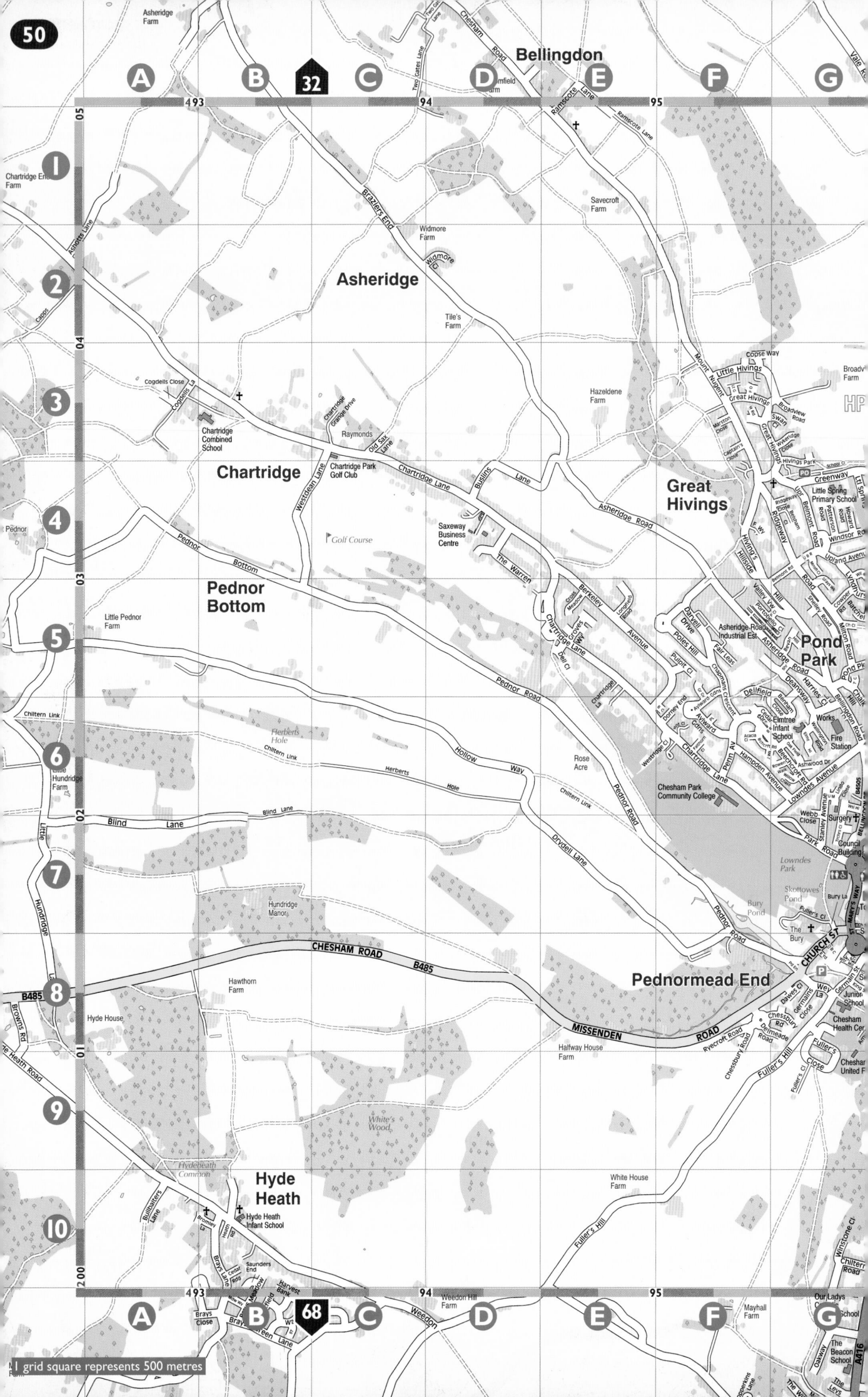

58

A  B  40  C  D  E  F  G

521      22      A1(M)      23

I  Coursers Road
   Coursers Farm
                                                    Potterells
                                                    Medical Centre
                                                    Potterells

2  River Colne
   Walsingham Wood                    North Mymms CC    Water End    Bradmore Lane
                                                                     Br St

3                                                    Abdale Lane

4  Cobs Ash                                          Royal Vete College
                                                     New Cottages

5  Redwell Wood Farm    Potwells
   Redwell Wood                       Mymmshall Wood

57 Crossoaks Lane                     Hawkshead Wood
   Shenley Lodge

6  Manor Lodge School   Ridgehill    M25  BLACKHORSE  LANE  B556    The Grange    Warrengate Farm
                                     Blackhorse Lane                              Mymms Hall

7  Packhorse Lane    Southridge      ST ALBANS ROAD                Cecil Road    B556  30  Deepdene
   Rectory Lane                                     Brookside                    Windmore Avenue  Wroxham Gardens
                                                    B556  Gascoyne Close         Ranworth Gdns  The Wroxham School
                                                                                Ormesby Drive

8  Rabley Park Farm    Catharine    Bourne         South Mimms                  Oulton Crescent
                                    Blanche Lane                                 Bridgefoot
                                    Frowycke Crs   St Giles Primary School  St Giles' Avenue    Kimptons Close
9  Mimms Lane    Earls Lane         Hamilton Close                              Kimptons Mead
   Deeves Hall   Earl's Farm        Old Earls La   Greyhound Lane
   Deeves Hall Lane                 Blanche Lane   Bignell's Corner   Swanland Road
                                                                      Days Inn
10 Crossoaks Lane    Ridge          Blanche Farm   A1(M)              South Mimms Service Area
                                    Blanche Farm   M25                Junction 1/23

2 00      521      22      A1(M)      23

A  B  76  C  D  E  St ALBANS ROAD  F  G
   Crossoaks Farm    Summerswood                              Dancers Hill A108
                     Summerswood Farm

I grid square represents 500 metres

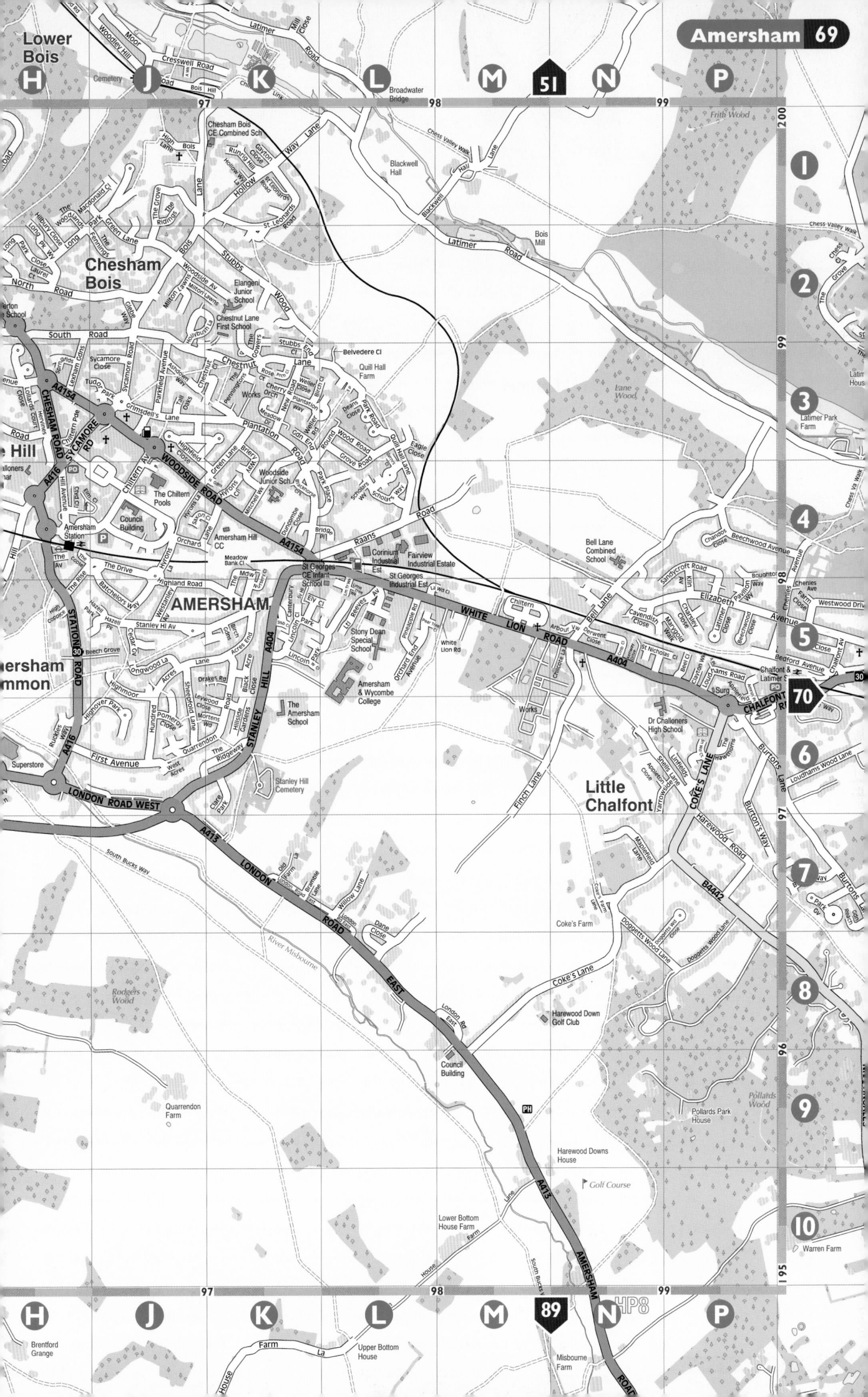

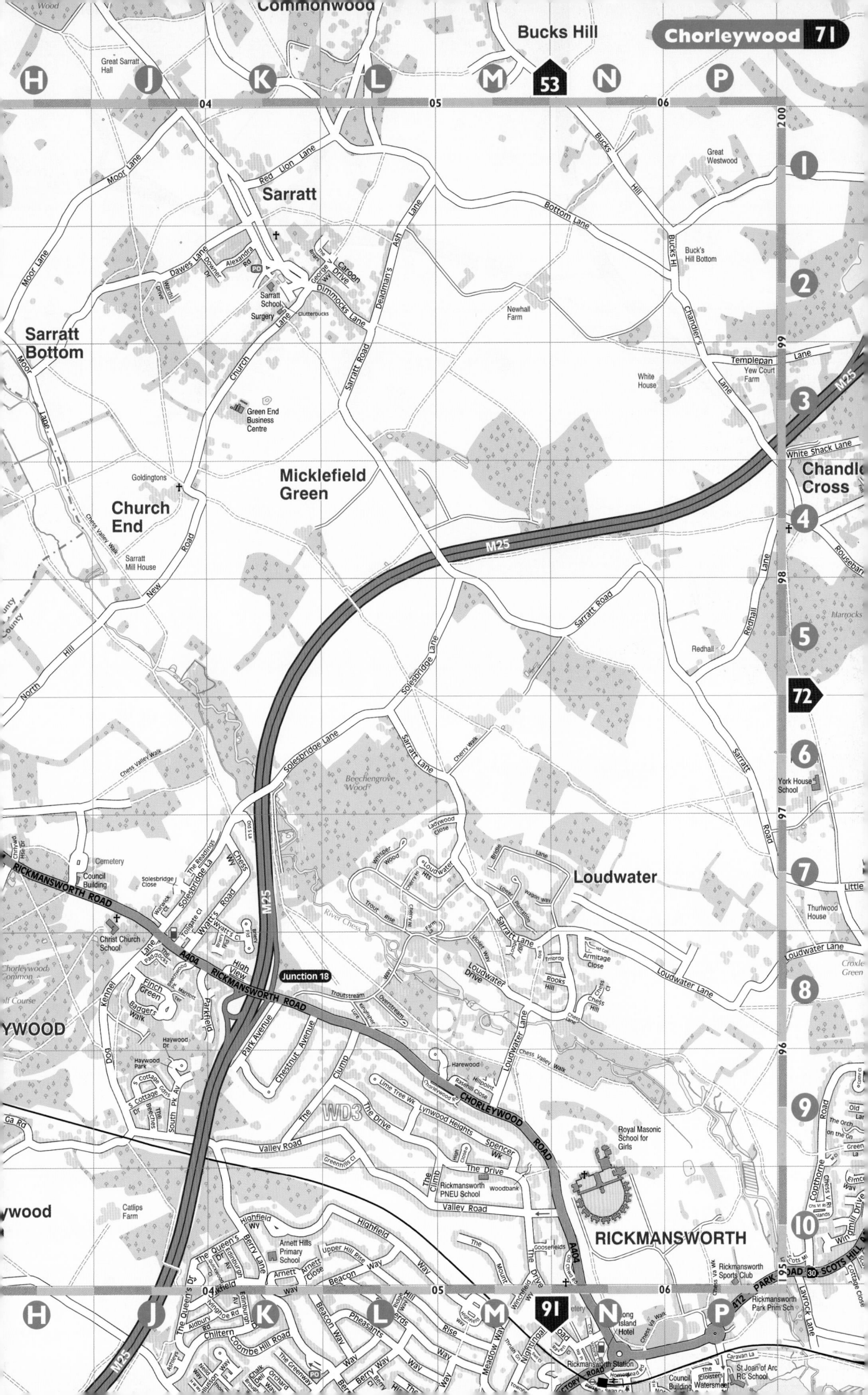

1 grid square represents 500 metres

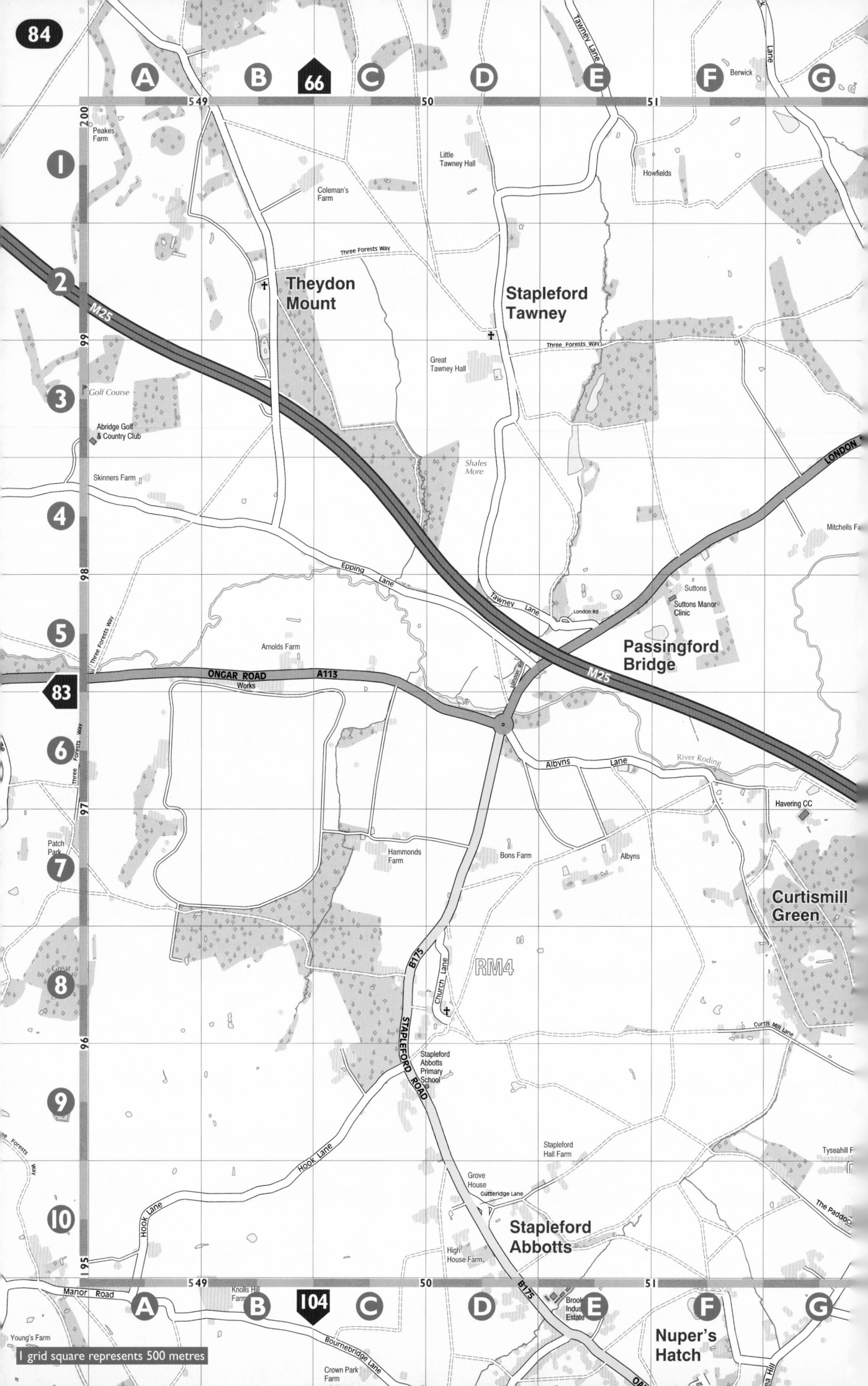

H    J    K    L    M  69  N    P

97    98    99

HP8

Lower Bottom House Farm

Warren Farm

Brentford Grange

The Vache

I

Bottom

Upper Bottom House

Misbourne Farm

Stratton Chase

2

NIGHTINGALES LANE

Bottom

Works

Hill Farm House

Works

Kings Close    Cherry Rd    Goreelands    Highfield

3

B4442    VACHE LANE

Works    Kings    Ashwell Way    High View

Hill    Farm    Lane    La    Stratton    Mill    Lane    Chase    Drive    South Bucks Way    Silver Hill    Up Cnr    Pheasant Hill    High St

Hodgemoor Woods    Bottom House Farm    Bottrells    Lane    Dodds    Lane    South Bucks Way

CHALFONT ST GILES

Grayburn Close    White Hart    Chalfont St Giles Infant School    Milton Fields    PO    Cromwell    Outlook Drive    Stylecroft    The Brow

4    Woodbank Drive

Three Households    PH    Sycamore Road    Rose    Dean Way    Bowler's Orch    Bramble Mead    Narcot Road    Palliser Road    Chalfont St Giles Junior School    The    Aran Hts    Milton's Cottage    Deanway    Silsden Hill    Gordon Way    Crossleys    Surgery

Rawlings    Lane    Widmer    Meadow    Three    Households    Narcot    Way    To Cook Close    Samsoul    Middle Meadow    Bowbridge Lane    Cemetery

93    A413    AMERSHAM

Widmer Farm    Newbarn    Lane    Tickels Cnr    Oakland Park Golf Club    Golf Course    Lagger    Dibden Hill

5    South Bucks Wy

Butlers Cross    Newbarn    Dibden Hill    90

Rawlings Farm    Newbarn    6

Highlands Road    Chalfont Rd    Sportsfield Approach    Manor Rd    Manor Place    Austens    Bowstridge    Lane    Bowstridge    92

Howard Crescent    Howard Road    Hearnes    Meeting House    Wilton    Lane    Long    Wd Dr    Grove Farm    Chalfont Grove    Windmill Farm

7

Gurneis Road    Orchard Road    Raeside Close    PO    Hall Place    Jordans School    Jordans La    Long    Wd    Drive

Long Grove    Wood Pond    Farmers Way    Greenwood Close    Cemetery    Puers La    Gn N Rd    Jordans Way    Chalfont St Peter Infant School    Pinetree    Lovel End    8    Field Way

Barracks Way    Wicks    School Lane    Seer Mead    PO    Green E Rd    Meadowside    Lovel Mead    Pennington Road    The Chalfonts Community College    Lovel    End    Lansdowne    Laurel Rd    Chalfont St Peter Junior Sc

Seer Green CE Combined School    Vicarage Close    Bayne Hl    Bayne Hill    Seer Green    La    Copse    Lane    Beech    Lane    Wilton    Jordans    Lane    Jordans    Welders    Lane    Chalfont Leisure Centre    Calcot Medical Centre    Hamdrden Rd    9

Seer Green Station    Beech    Lane    Jordans    Glebe Road    Nicol    Eleanor Rd    Market    Clinic    Church

Beaconsfield Golf Club    Dean Wood Rd    Farm    Lane    Grove    Nicol    Road    Orchard Grove    Hill Rd    Gold Hill North    East

Porklin    Lane    Stone Dean Farm    Leachcroft    Weston    Cl    Leachcroft    Grove Cl    Pond    Layters Green    Layters Av    Gold Hill    Meadowcroft    10

London    50    Road    A40    Porklin    Lane    Stampwell Farm    Mumfr    109    Austenwood    St Josephs RC Combined School    Priory Rd    The Rowans    Lewins Rd

Layters    Green    Farmers Place    Austenwood    Lane    90 Rd    Austenwood

Maltmans Green School    Maltmans Lane

90

A  B  70  C  D  E  F  G

Roughwood Park

1  2  3  4  5  6  7  8  9  10

Warren

The Swillett

Heronsga

Heronsgate Road

Old Shire Lane

Piggy Lane

Bullsland County

Long Lane

The Vache

NIGHTINGALES LANE

Deadhearn Lane

Philipshill Wood

Buckinghamshire County

Hertfordshire County

Bottom Wood

Works

VACHE LANE

R4442

Gorelands Lane

Gorelands Lane

Chiltern Open Air Museum

Bucks Chilterns University College

Newland Park

Chalfont Road

Shrubs Woods

Gorelands

Gorelands Lane

Gorelands Lane

Shire Lane

LONDON ROAD

Ashwell's Farm

Chesham Lane

Shire Horse Centre

Brawlings Farm

Horn Hill Court

Maple Cross

Chalfont Road

Woodbank Drive

Gables Close

Micholls Avenue

Chesham Lane

89

Brallings

Horn Hill

Hornhill Road

Beechen Wood

Dibden Hill

AMERSHAM ROAD

Felpen Way

Micholls Avenue

Chalfont Common

Robert's Farm

Bowstridge Lane

Tate Road

Penn Gaskell Lane

Rickmansworth

By-Wood End

Roberts Lane

Bowstridge

The Paddock

Misbourne

Copper Ridge

Ravensmead

Nortoft Road

Windmill Farm

Old Mead

Rickmansworth Lane

Denham Lane

Gravel Hill

Robertswood Combined School

West Hyde Lane

M25

Chalfont Lane

Chalfont St Peter Infant S

Lower End

Elms Road

Highlands Close

CHALFONT ST PETER

Garden of Rest Cemetery

Chalfont Leisure Centre

Chalfont St Peter FC

Hillfield Road

30

Denham Lane

Warren Farm

Glebe Road

Calcot Medical Cen

Market Place

Joiners

Lewis Lane

Chiltern Hill

Hogtrough Wood

St Josephs CE Combined School

Orchard Grove

Works

Linden Drive

Mopes Farm

South Bucks Way

A413

Maltmans Green

Lewins Rd

Austenwood Lane

SL9

110

Gerrards Cross Golf Club

Chalfont

Hertfordshire County

Buckinghamshire County

M25

Chalfont Lane

A  B  110  C  D  E  F  G

Kingscote Pre-Preparatory School

Chalfont Park

Golf Course

Old Shire

1 grid square represents 500 metres

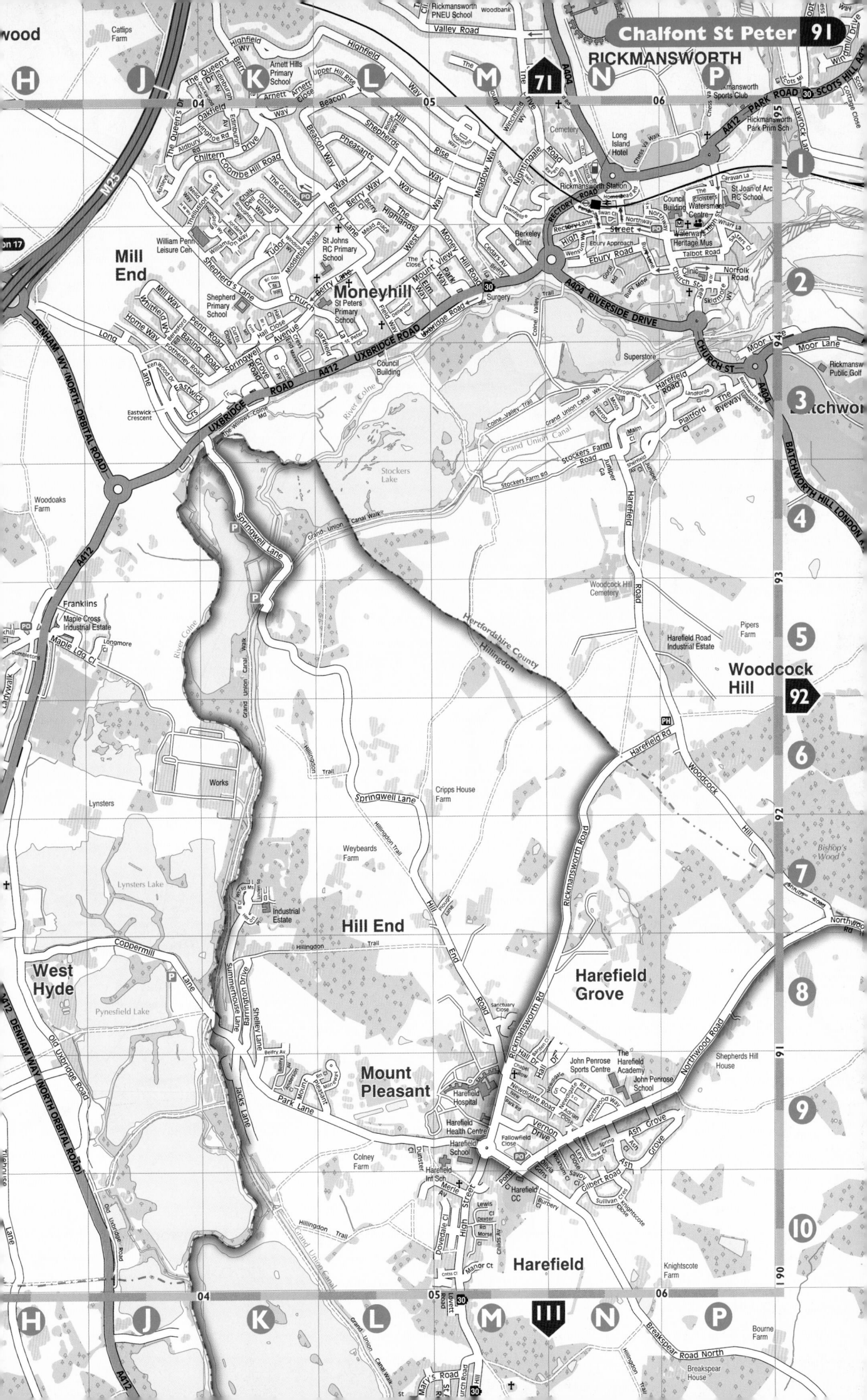

A   B   86   C   D   E   F   G

1

**St Vincent's Hamlet**

2

3

4

5

105

6

7

**Harold Park**

8

9
**Harold Wood**

10

A   B   126   C   D   E   F   G

**South Weald**

**Brook Street**

**Great Warley**

**BRENTWO**

Weald Country Park

Junction 28

Essex County Havering

M25

A12

A1023

COLCHESTER ROAD

Weald Road

LONDON ROAD

WARLEY ROAD

GREAT WARLEY STREET

Dark Lane

Green Lane

Dagnam Park

Maylands Golf Club

Tylers Common

Harold Court

Shepherds Hill

H  J  K  L  M  **89**  N  P

97  98  99

**Austenwood**

St Josephs
CE Combined
School

The
Rowans

Porklin
Lane

Stampwell
Farm

Maltmans
Green
School

Maltmans Lane

DON 50 ROAD  A40

Gayhurst
School

Bull Lane

Milton
Avenue

Austenwood
Close

Latchmoor Avenue

Greenway

Acrefield
Way

Orchehill Avenue

South
View
Road

Layters Way

Way

1

M40

Mumfords
Lane

Mumfords
Farm

The Manor
House

OXFORD ROAD  A40

Bull 68

Bentinck
Close

Bulstrode

2

3

Main Drive

Main Dr

Valley Way

Woodhill

Portland Av

Chiltern
Hundreds

Siblet's
Woods

Bulstrode
Park

4

Slade Farm

Hedgerley Lane

Wapseys

Wapseys Lane

Lane

**Hedgerley
Green**

Moat
Farm

**GERRARDS
CROSS**

Camp Road

BA16

5

Village Lane

Church Wood
RSPB Reserve

PH

**Hedgerley**

Hill View

Kiln  Lane

Andrew Hill La

Beaconsfield Common Lane

Farm

Hedgerley Lane

Stoneyfield

WINDSOR RD

Wayside

**110**

Gerrards
Sports

Meadway Par

6

Dukes Wo

The
Spinney

Dukes Wood Drive

High

Birchdale

Beeches

7

Howards Thicket

Howards Wood Dr

**Hedgerley
Hill**

Stevenson Road

Gregory Rd

Robert

Elkins Road

James View Way

Old Nursery
Court

Cottage Park
Road

Hedgerley

PO

Longfield

Copse Way

Hedgerley
Park

Mount Hill Lane

Dukes Valley

Low
Farm

M40

8

Parish Lane

Timberwood

Collum Green Road

Wood End
Close

Colley Hill Lane

Tara

Cemetery

Fulmer
Chase

The Pickeridge

Framewood

86

Christmas Lane

Woodland
Glade

Romsey
Drive

Heathercroft Gdns

Asherton Walk

Crispin Way

Stoke
Wood

A355

Stoke Wood Lane

Stoke Common Road

**Fulmer**  9

Mount
Close

Farnham Common
Junior School

Farnham Common
Middle School

Sherbourne
Walk

Mayflower Way

Bracken Cl

Templewood La

Grange Gdns

Templewood Lane

Larchmoor
Park

Beeches Way

Stoke
Common

Windmill Road

10

Oakridge

Common
Wood

Scott
Close

Pin One

Temple Way

Rownhurst Rd

Templewood Dr

Fryerpane Rd

Orchard Close

Dell Cl

rosewood Way

nham Wk

Brockhurst
Wood

Templewood Lane

B416

GERRARDS CROSS ROAD

Duffield Lane

185

186

**H**  **Farnham
Com J n**  **K**  **L**  **M**  **I29**  **N**  **P**

Meadow

Lane

97

Forge

Beeches Way

Parson

Close

Rickman's Lane

Hazel Lane

Neville Close

Vine Road

Clevehurst Close

Elderfield Road

Firfort Close

ans Close

98

99

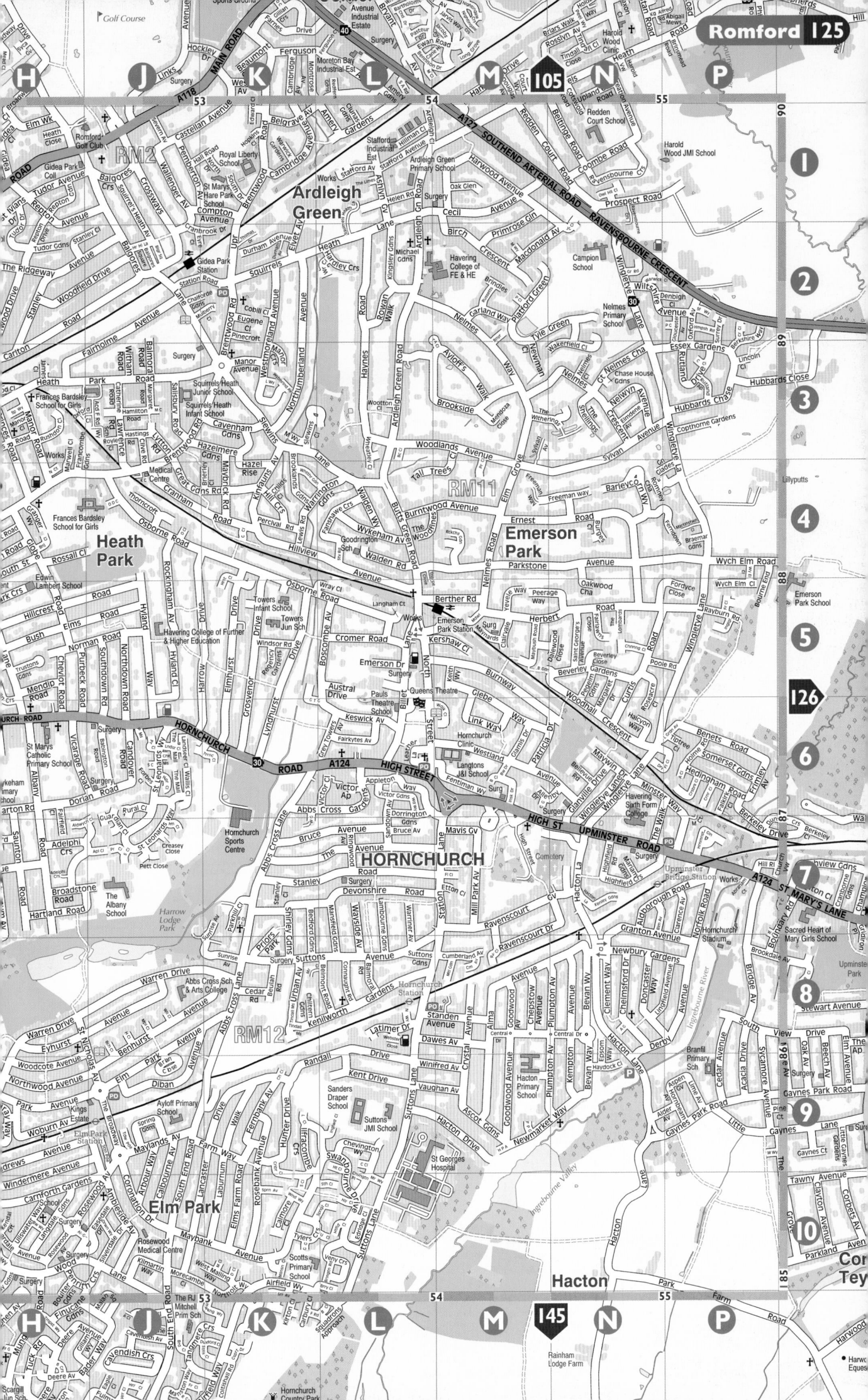

H J K L M 107 N P

Little Warley

Roses Farm

Warley Park Golf Club

Golf Course

60 61 62 90

I

Childerditch Industrial Park

Rectory Chase

Childerditch Hall Drive

Childerditch Hall Dr

Childerditch Street

Childerditch Lane

2

Woodlands Preparatory School

Crossways

Little Warley Hall Lane

Kelrose Swimming Pool Centre

SOUTHEND ARTERIAL ROAD

A127

Thorndon Avenue

89

3

Nuttys Farm

West Horndon Primary School

ARTERIAL ROAD A127

Great Warley Hall

Church Lane

Little Warley Hall Lane

West Horndon

Cadogan Avenue

Clayview Pretoria Ave

4

PO

Dunmow Gdns

Fyfield Cl Birchwell

Freshwell Gdns

88

Works

Horndon Industrial Park

West Horndon Station

Upminster Trading Park

St Mary's Lane

5

Monks Farm

St Mary's Lane

Field House

6

Old Englands Farm

Puddle Dock

Tillingham Hall

87

Works

7

Dunnings Lane

Bury Farm

Thurrock Havering

8

Clay Tye Farm

Blankets Farm

9

Fen Lane

RM14

Home Farm

White Post Farm

Stone Hall

Harrow Rd

10

185

Corner Farm

Fen Lane

Golf Course

Fen Lane

Ockendon

Top Meadow Golf Club

60 61 62

H J K L M 147 N P

CLAY TYE ROAD

B186

WARLEY STREET

B186

OCKENDON ROAD

A B 128 C D E F G

Cippenham

**I**

Lake End

M4

**2**

Dorney

Jubilee River (Maidenhead, Windsor & Eton Flood Alleviation Scheme)

**3**

COMMON ROAD B3026

Slough
Buckinghamshire County

Dorney Common

Eton Wick

**4**

South Field

**5**

Eton College Rowing Lake

Boveney Court

Boveney Lock

Boveney

Lock Path

Thames Path

River Thames

Royal Windsor Racecourse

**6**

Buckinghamshire County
Windsor & Maidenhead

WINDSOR ROAD A308

Thames Path

Windsor Marina

Willows Riverside Park

Maidenhead Road

A308 MAIDENHEAD ROAD

Marina

Sutherland Grange

Racecourse Yacht Basin

Clewer Village

A308

**7**

OAKLEY GREEN ROAD

Oakley Green Cemetery

Dedworth

St Edwards Royal Free Ecumenical Sch

The Windsor Boys School

**8**

DEDWORTH ROAD

Wyvale Garden Centre

Fairacres Industrial Estate

Dedworth County Middle School

Dedworth Green First School

DEDWORTH ROAD

B3025

CLARENCE ROAD

Clewer New Town

**9**

Oakley Green

Alexander First School

Tarbay Farm

Clewer Green

St Leonard's Hill

Clewer Green C.E. First School

IMPERIAL ROAD

Windsor Girls Sch

B3022

**10**

St Leonards Farm

St Leonards

SL4

Woodland Avenue

WINKFIELD ROAD

B3022

A B 170 C D E F G

Legoland Windsor

I grid square represents 500 metres

H J K L M **131** N P

I

Fairway Avenue

Warwick Rd

04   05   06   80

Iver Station

Thorney

Golf Course

Richings Park Sports Club

St James Walk

Thorney House

Thorney Park Golf Club

Richings

St Leonards Walk

The Poynings

Junction 15/4b

M25

Thorney Ml Rd

Thorney Mill Road

Buckinghamshire County

Hillingdon

West Drayton

Works

Donkey La

West Drayton CC

St Catherines RC J&I Sch

Medical Centre

Church

Police Station

West Drayton Prim School

Longmead Primary School

The Closes Recreation Ground

West Drayton Cemetery

Laurel Lane

Harmondsworth

Brambles

Wordsworth Way

Coleridge Way

Keats Way

1

2

3

4

M4

Old Slade La

Colne Valley Way

Slough

Hillingdon

Lakeside Industrial Estate

Lakeside Industrial Estate

River Colne

Harmondsworth

Saxon Way

Moor Lane

Accommodation Lane

Tarmac Way

Duke of Northumberland's River

Hatch Lane

Harmondsworth Lane

Sips

A3044

Candover Close

**152**

Airport Business

5

6

Coln Industrial Estate

Colnbrook Sports Club

M25

Speedbird Way

Speedbird Wy

COLNBROOK BY-PASS

A4

Skyport Dr

Zealand Av

Pinglestone Close

BATH ROAD

Bath Road

Newton Road

Newbury Rd

50

7

Britannia Industrial Est

Mckay Trading Est

Trident Industrial

Junction 14

Polygon Business Centre

Blackthorne Crs

Stanwell Moor Road

Heathrow

Works

Longford

Thistle Hotel

Northern Perimeter Rd (West)

Northern Perimeter Road

Northern

8

River Colne

Horton Rd

Junction 14

A3113 AIRPORT WAY

M25

Horton

Spout Lane

Silverbeck Wy

Vine

Leylands La

Spout Lane North

Works

Woodcock

Burrows Hill Cl

A3044

Western Perimeter Road

STANWELL MOOR ROAD

Windsock Way

Wayfarer Road

STANWELL

Western Perimeter Road

Heathrow Terminal 5 Station

Terminal 5

Bedfont Court

9

10

Term

H J K L M **173** N P

04   05   06

I 75

Southern Perimeter Road

Heathrow World Cargo Centre

Shoreham Rd (West)

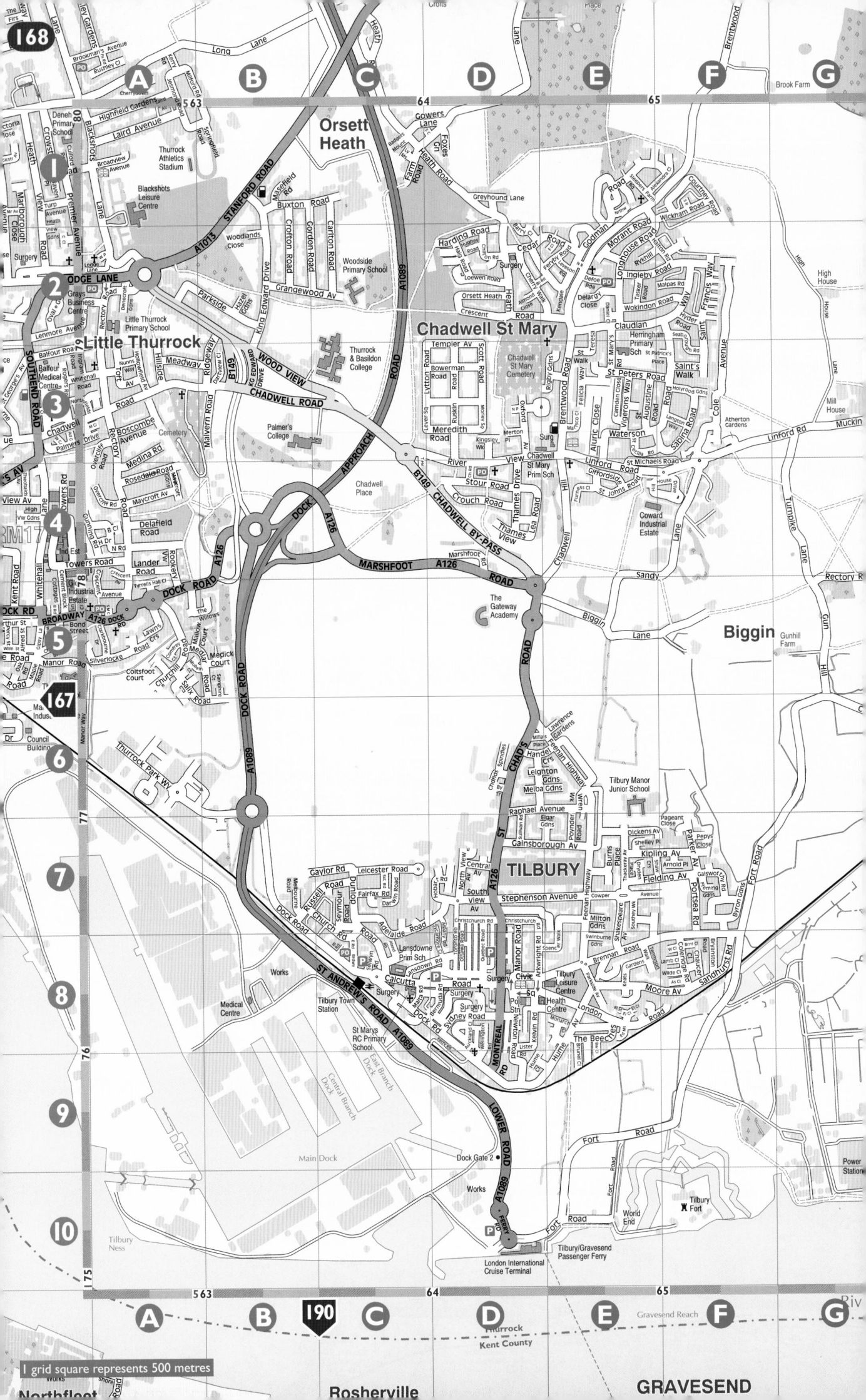

H  J  K  L  M  N  P

67  68  69  80

1
2
3
4
5
6
7
8
9
10

79
78
77
76
175

Holford Road

Holford Road

**Linford**

Northumberland Road
Essex Gdns
Tilbury Road
Somerset Road
Stafford Close
Lower Crescent
Meadow
East Gdns

**Muckingford**

Becksland

Muckingford Road

Halt Drive
Brindley
Beechcroft
Stanning AV
LC

East Tilbury Station

**East Tilbury**

Alexandra Way
Severn
Queen Elizabeth Avenue
King George VI AV
Thomas Bata AV
Princess Margaret Road
Buff
Waldon
Solway
Colne
Hayle
Surgery
Coronation
Clyde
Tweed
Avenue
Arun
Trent
Farm Road
BATA Medical Centre
Queen Mary AV
Surgery
Gloucester AV
Bata AV
PO
Coronation AV
Princess
Birch

**Thames Industrial Park**

Tilbury Industrial Park

East Tilbury Infant School

**West Tilbury**

**Low Street**

church Road
Low Street Lane
Shaw Road
LC
LC
Works

Industrial Estate

Station Road

Love Lane

Buckland

Bowaters Farm

RM18

West Tilbury Marshes

East Tilbury Marshes

Princess Margaret Road
Linley
Gordon Close

Coalhouse Fort
P

Coalhouse Point

Works

King Marshes

Walton's Hall Road

67  68  69

H  J  K  L  M  N  P

**191**

148

A   B   C   D   E   F   G

SL4

Windsor & Eto

WINKFIELD ROAD

B3022

1

2

WINKFIELD

Windsor Forest

3  Winkfield Place

Barton Lodge

Cranbourne Chase

Drift Road

4

Forest Road

Cranbourne Tower

Ranger's Lodge

B3022

B383

5  Cranbourne

Light Industrial Estate

Kingsmead

Windsor Great Park

Forest Road

Forest Lodge

Hatchet Lane

MOUNTS HILL

Forest Gate

Lime Avenue

6

Fernhill Park

Forest Farm

A332 SHEET STREET ROAD

Holly Walk

The Village

Hatchet Lane

WINDSOR RD

7

Sandpit Gate

D A330

B3034 LOVEL LANE  Woodside

WINDSOR ROAD A332

A332

South Forest

Bracknell Forest
Windsor and Maidenhead

Windsor Great Park

Duke's L

8

Woodside Road

Windsor Lodge

SUNNINGHILL

MOUNTS HILL

Wood End

PH

9

Home Farm

ROAD

B383

Three Castles Path

WINDSOR ROAD

A332

10  Onslow drive

A330

WINKFIELD ROAD A330

WINKFIELD

A   B   C   D   E   F   G

192

Three Castles Path

SUNNINGHILL ROAD

Cheapside CE Primary School

Water Splash

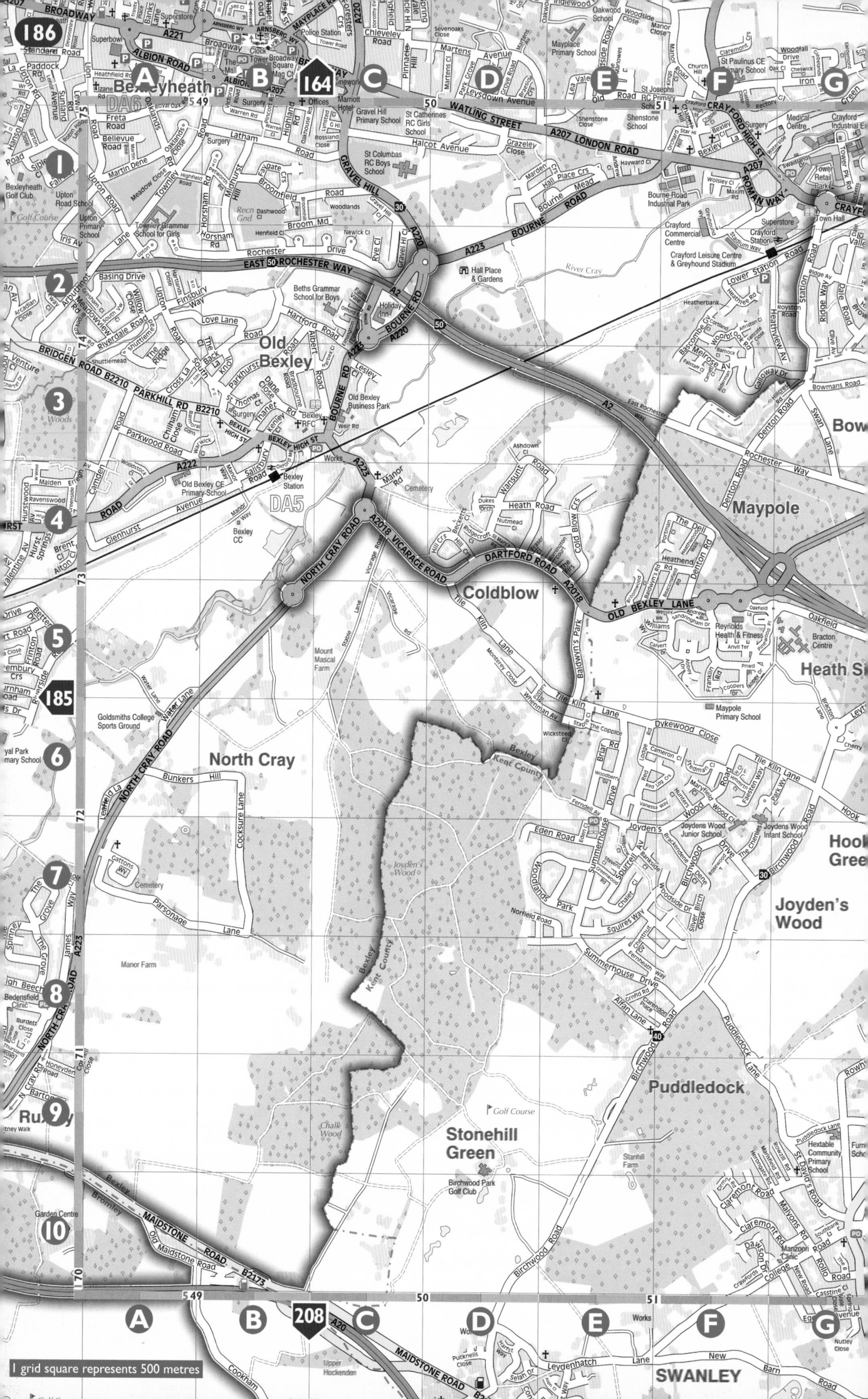

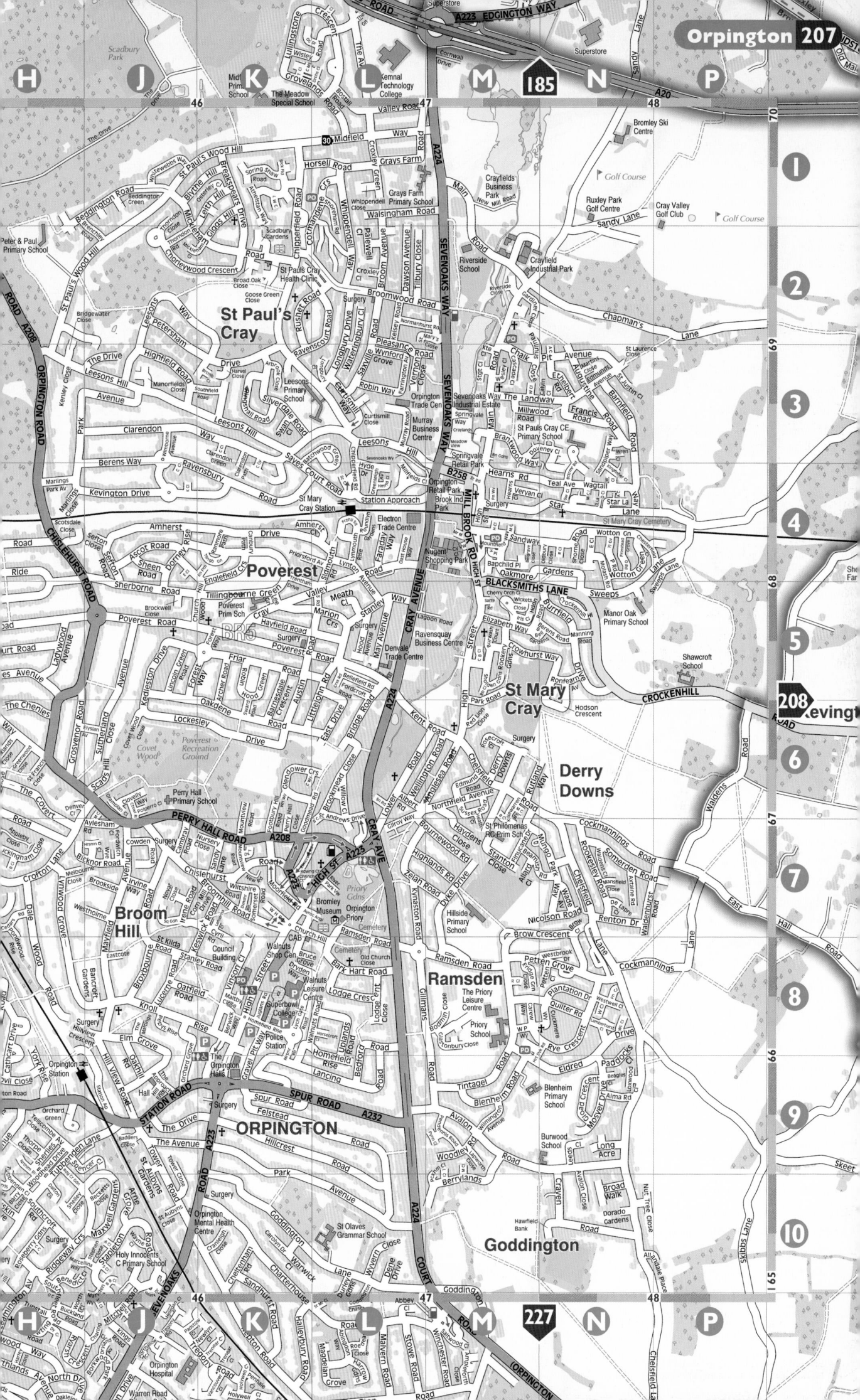

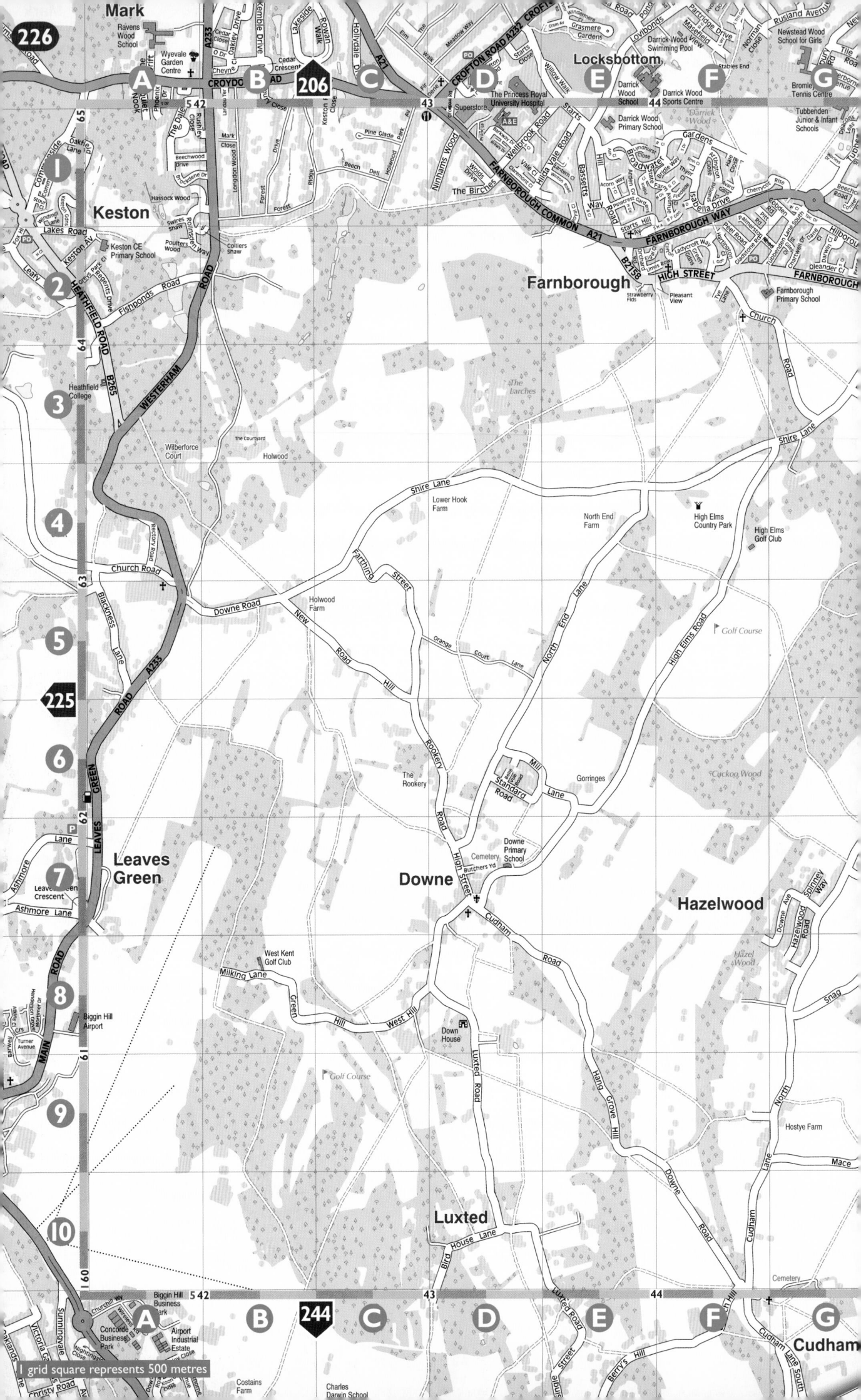

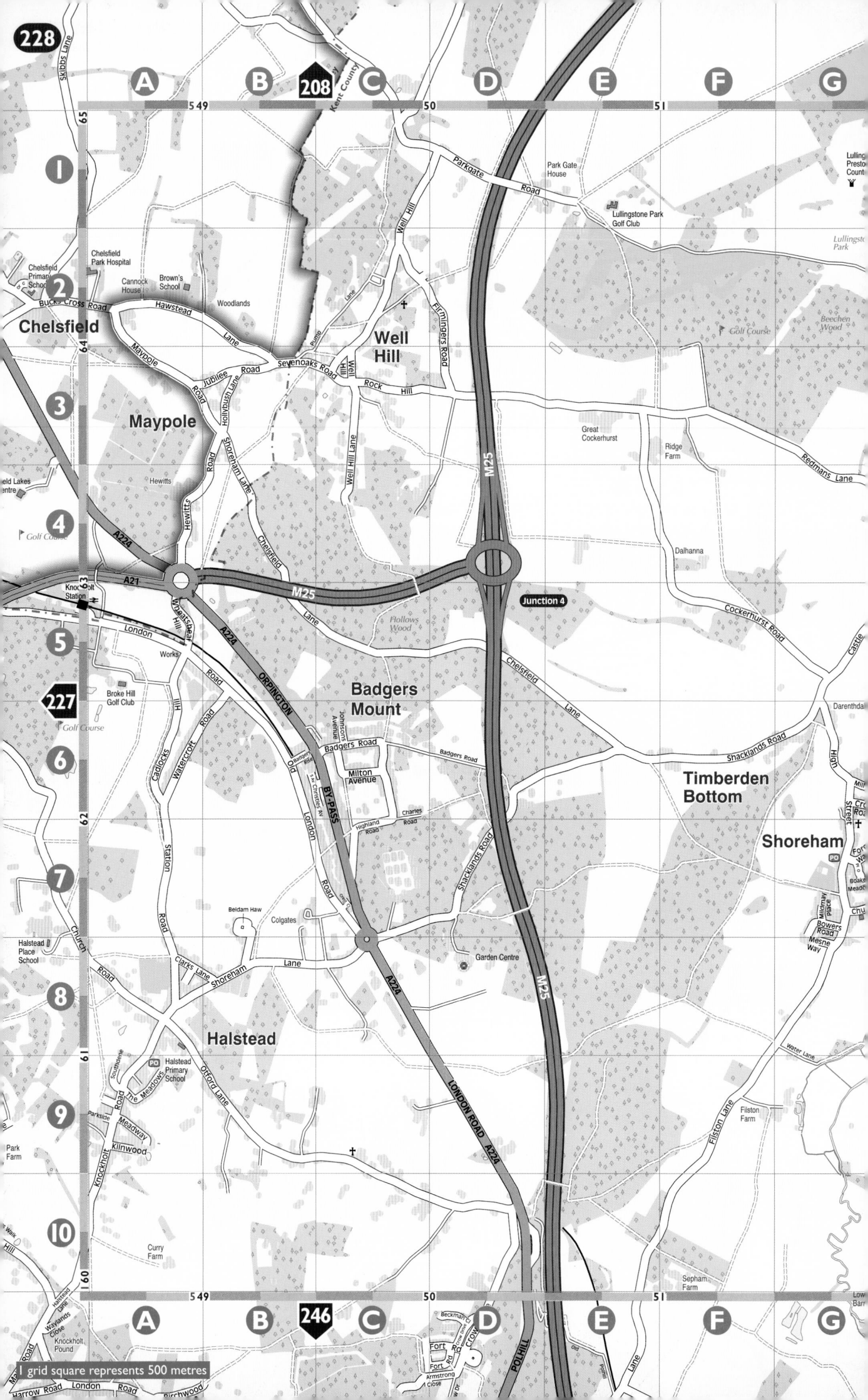

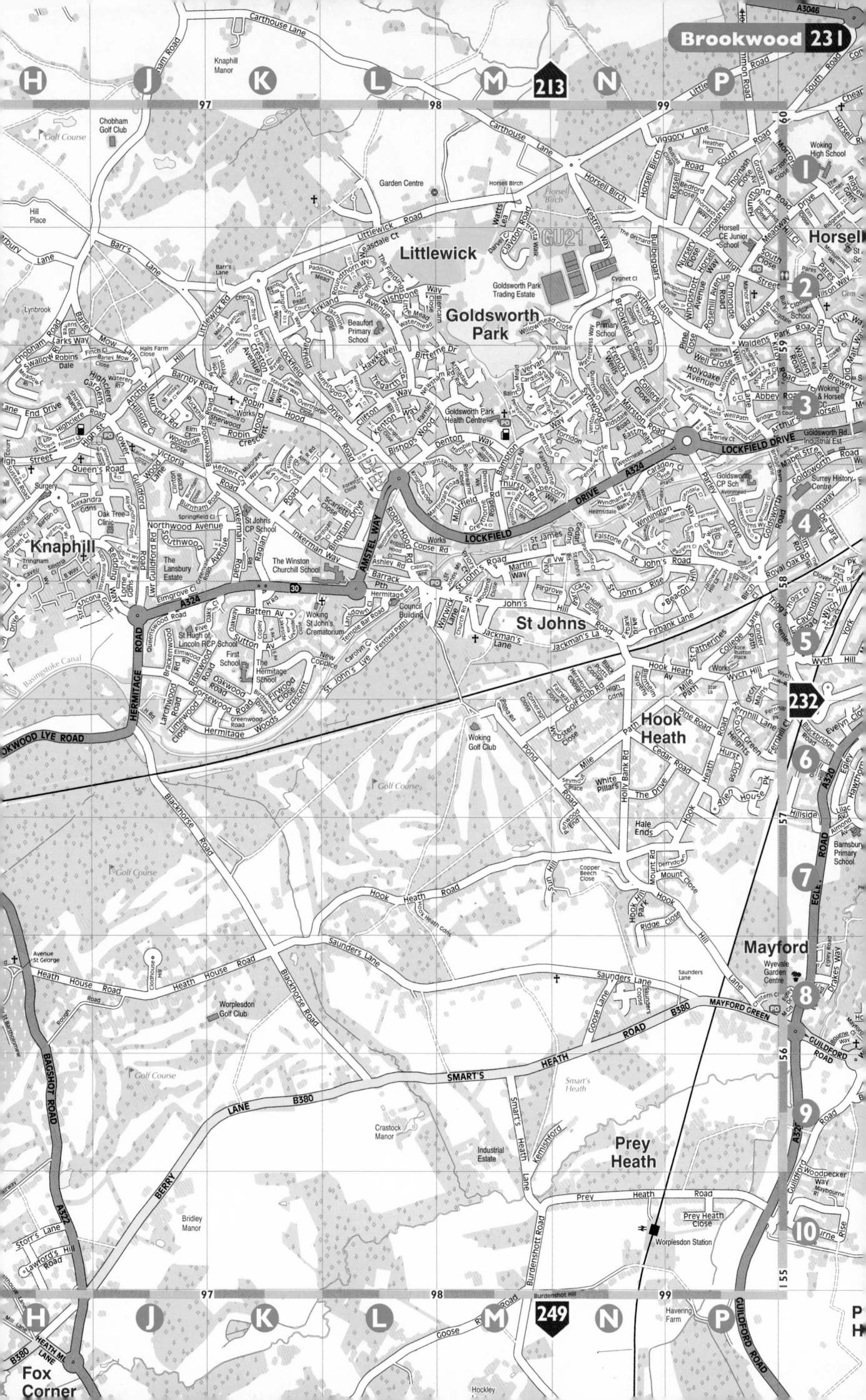

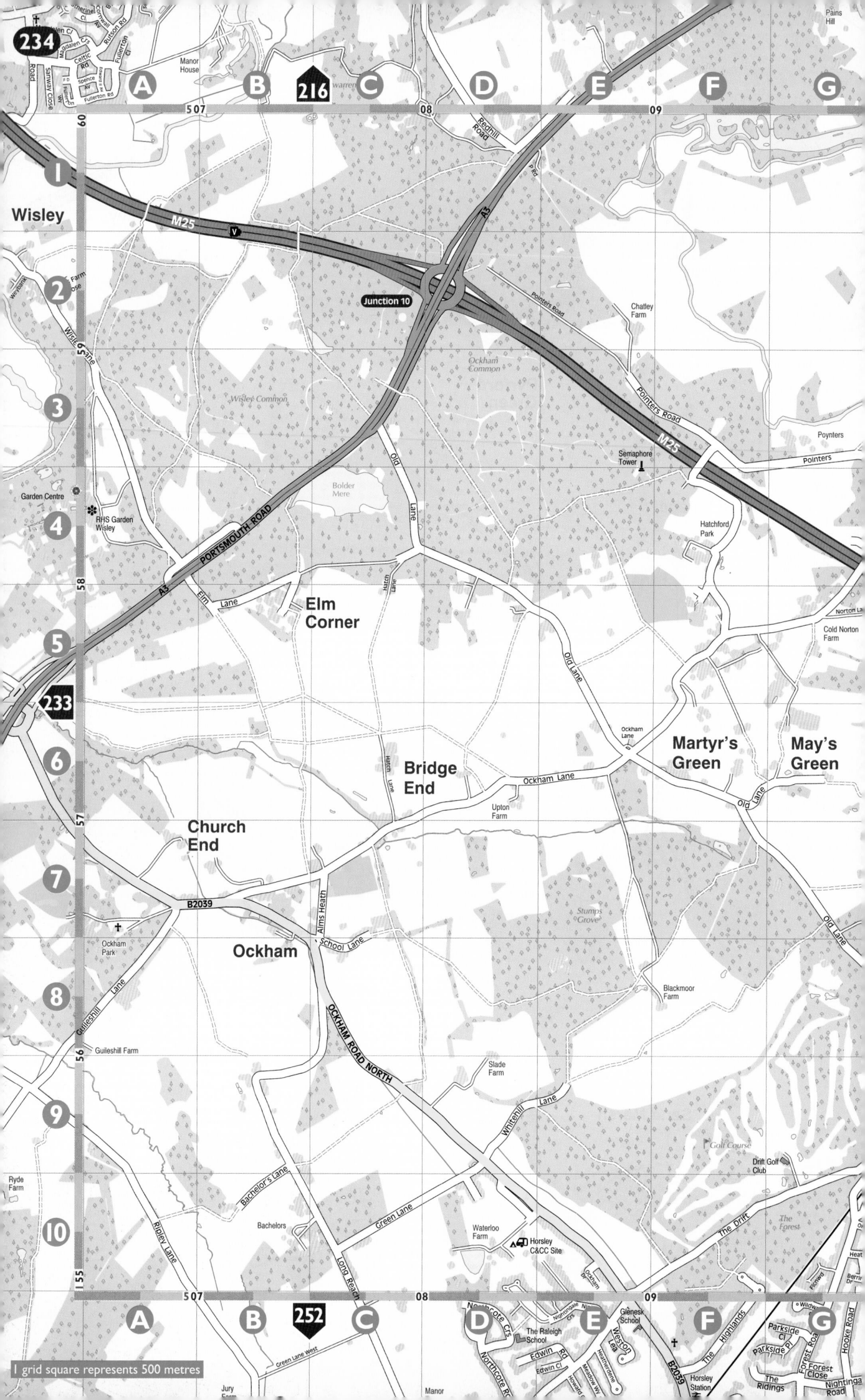

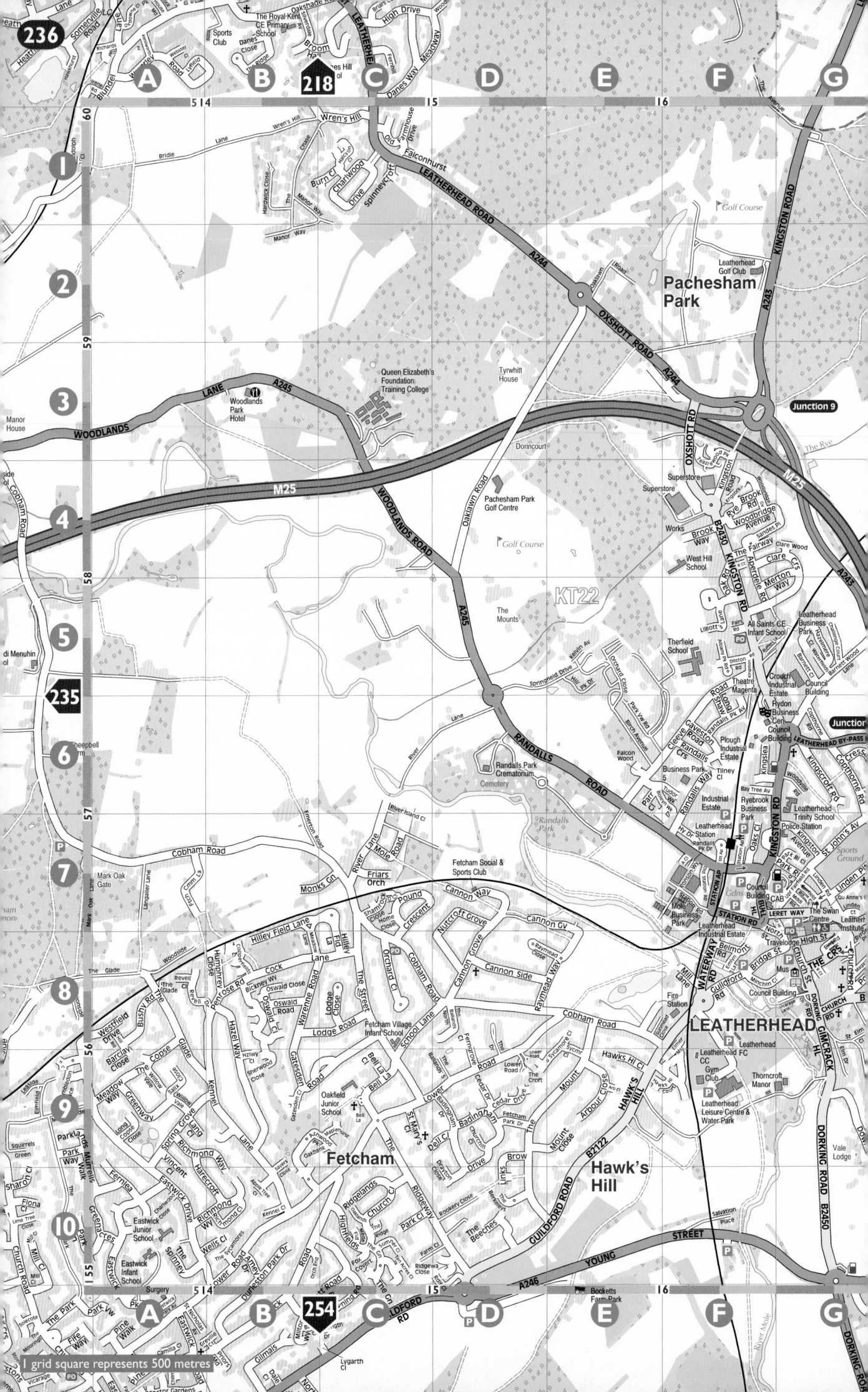

Fickleshole

H High Hill J Road K L Skid 40 M N 225 P 41 60 Churchill Wy
39

Scotshall Lane
Fairchildes Road

Church Lane
✝

Heslers Road

Heslers Hill

Court Road
Chelsham

Chelsham Court Farm
Beech Farm Rd

Lane

Broom Bank

Beddlestead

Beech Farm Road

Beech Farm

Beddlestead Lane

Beddlestead Farm

Cheverells Farm

B269 CROYDON ROAD

Clarks Lane Farm

Approach Road

B2024 CLARKS LANE
North Downs Way
White Lane
B269

TITSEY HILL
North Downs Way
Pilchmor Lane
Downs Way

Titsey Place

Vanguard Way

Flint House

Titsey

H J K The Ridge L M 261 N Titsey P
39 40 41

Skid Hill Farm

Oaklands Junior School
Oaklands Infant Sch
Norheads Lane
Chalock Close
Highfield Road
Beech Road
Kings Road
Hillingdale
Melody Road
Scarborough Close
Swievelands Road
Bromley Road
Alexandra Road
Bridlington Close
Ramscroft Close
Willey Close

Norheads Lane
Grand View Av
East

Victoria Gardens
Oaklands Lane
Christy Road
Arthur Road
Sunningvale Avenue

Concorde Bus
Biggin Business Park

Sopwith Av
Sunningvale Close
Camelot Close
Lancaster
Keymer
Melrose Road
Mount Pleasant
Lebanon Gdns
Falcon Close
Hillcrest Road
Forcefield Road

A233 MAIN ROAD

PO Rosehill Road
Steeple Hts Dr
Charton Close

Timberton Road
Treetops Dr
Valley View
Lillie Road
Foley
Everglade Mewsend
St Mary's Close Upper Drive
Springholm Close
Wood Road
Wakeley Close
Greenwell

Surrey County
Beech Avenue
Kemble

Lusted Hall Lane
Lusted Hall Farm

244 Ta

Costfield Road
Shaw Road
Greenway
Westmore
Crossways Cotts
Crossways
The Close
Whitewood
Grove
Bedmo Rd
The
Westmore Road

Paynesfield Road
Edgar Road
Maesmaur Road
Barnfield
Jol
George
Long's

Ninehams Road
Ship Hill
PO
Ship Field Close
Surgery
Approach
Still Hill
Borough Road
Edgar Road

Church Hill

Clarks Lane Farm

8

9

Pilgrims Farm
Pilgrims Lane

10

55 56 57 58 59 60
2 3 4 5 6 7 8 9 10
I

**Luxted**

**244**

A    B    **226**    C    D    E    F    G

60
Churchill Wy
Biggin Hill Business Park
Concorde Business Park
Airport Industrial Estate
Crossley Close
Costains Farm
Charles Darwin School
Darwin Leisure Centre
Cudham CE Primary School

**Cudham**

Cemetery

Church Hill
Cudham Lane South

**1**
Christy Road
Arthur Road

**2**
Lunar Close
Magnolia
Acer Road
Spruce Road
**BIGGIN HILL**
Biggin Hill Primary School
Old Tye Avenue
Juniper Close

**Berry's Green**

Cherry Lodge Golf Club
Berry's Green Road

New Barn Farm

**3**
Church Road
Nelson Close
Village Green Road
Aperfield Road

**Aperfield**

Golf Course

**4**
Moselle Road
St Winifred's Road
Belvedere Road
Clarence Road
Woodbury Close
Edward Road
Foxearth Close

Surrey County

**5**
**Tatsfield**

Cudham Road

**South Street**

A233 MAIN ROAD

Southwood
Bombers Farm

**243**

**6**
Crossways
Paynesfield Road
Manor Road
Maesmaur Road

Buckhurst Road

Cudham Grange
Grays

Silversted La

**7**
Edgar Road
Borough Road
Old Lane
Rag Hill Road
Parkwood Road
Tatsfield Lane

Grays Road
Hawley's Corner
Buckhurst Road

**Bromley Kent County**

Grays Farm

Pilgrim House

**8**
Clarks Lane Farm
Park Wood Golf Club
Church Hill
Chestnut Avenue
The Avenue
Betsom's Hill
Chestnut Avenue
The Avenue

WESTERHAM HILL
North Downs Way

**TN16**

Hill Park
Hill School

**9**
North Downs Way
Rectory Lane
Tatsfield Court Farm
**B2024**

The Avenue
Pilgrims Way
Betsoms Farm

A233 LONDON ROAD

**10**
Pilgrims Farm
Pilgrims Lane
Clacket Lane

Gaysham Farm

Force Green

55

**A**    **B** **262**    **C**    **D**    **E**    **F**    **G**

sey
Clacket Lane Service Area

Westerham Wood
Court Lodge
Churchill CE Primary School

I grid square represents 500 metres

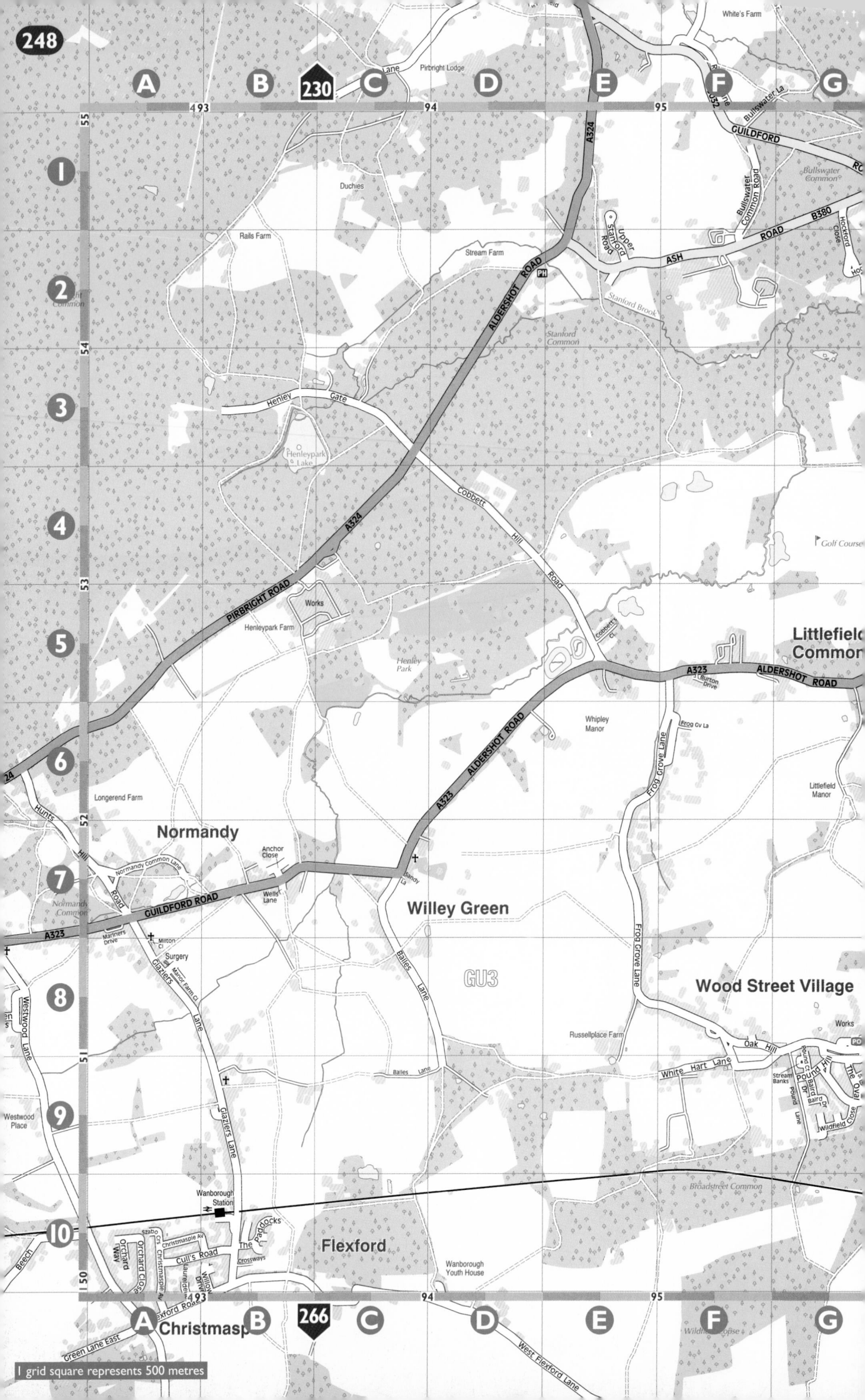

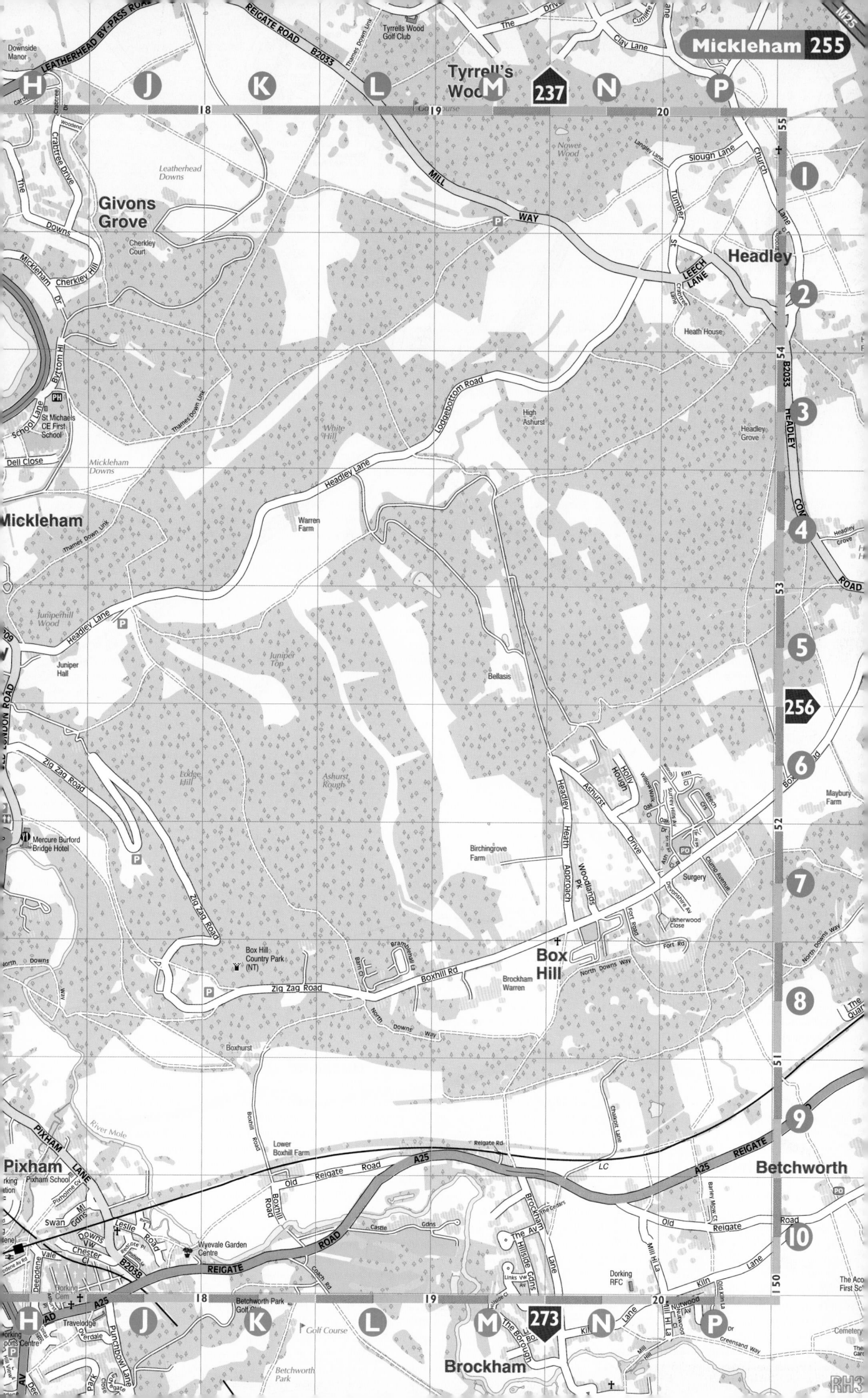

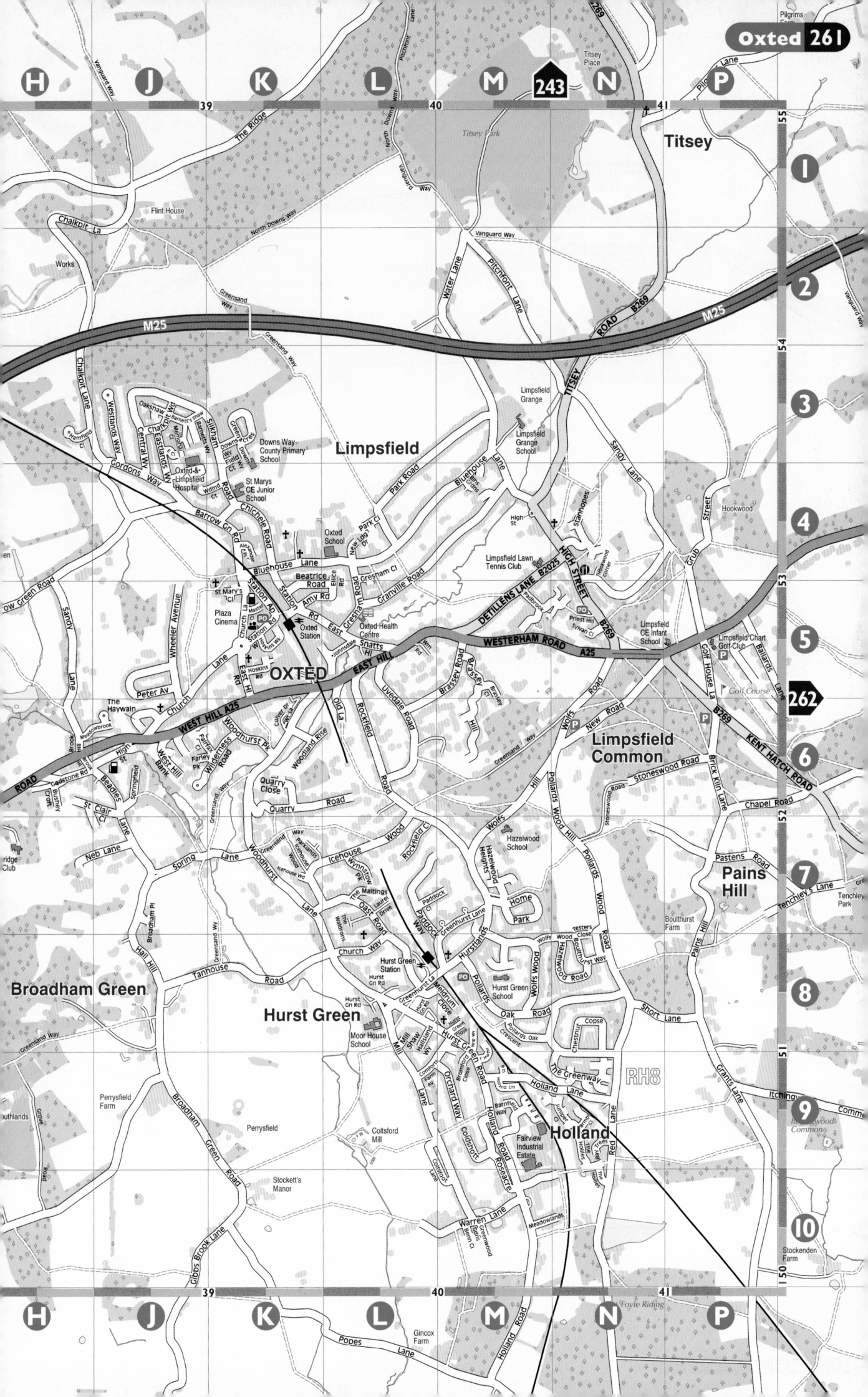

244

261

I grid square represents 500 metres

Brasted

Sundridge

H J K L M N P

**245**

WESTERHAM ROAD A25

BRASTED ROAD

Chart Lane

Church Road

New Road

Manor Road

Woodside Road

Greystone Park

Church Road

Penn Lane

Sundridge & Brasted CE Primary School

Lodge Farm

Park Farm

Watermill Close

The Mill Works

High St

West End

Surgery

Heversood

Colinette Farm

Birchfield Farm

Penn Farm

Westerham Golf Club

Valence School

Golf Course

Dunsdale

Piper's La

Pipers Lane

Vines Gate

Foxwold

Pipers Lane

Brasted Chart

Piper's Green Road

Quornden

Core Farm

Great Nor of Far

**264**

Norman Street

Hosey Common Road

French Street

Horns Hill

Hosey Common Lane

Greensand Way

Canons VW

Canons VW

The Phillippines

The Chart

Emmetts Road

Emmetts Garden (NT)

Scords Wood

Ide Hill

Ide Hill CE Aided Primary Sch

Camberwell Lane

Camberwell La

PO

Greensand Way

Toy's Hill

PH

Mapleton Road

Chartwell (NT)

Chartwell

Puddledock Lane

Bardogs Farm

Scords Lane

Canon Close

Toy's Hill

Puddledock

HILL ROAD

B2042

Oakwood Lodge

Henden Manor

Tan House

Obriss Farm

Ha Ba

Boons Park

Maple

H J K L M N P

1 2 3 4 5 6 7 8 9 10

46 47 48

54 53 52 51 50 55

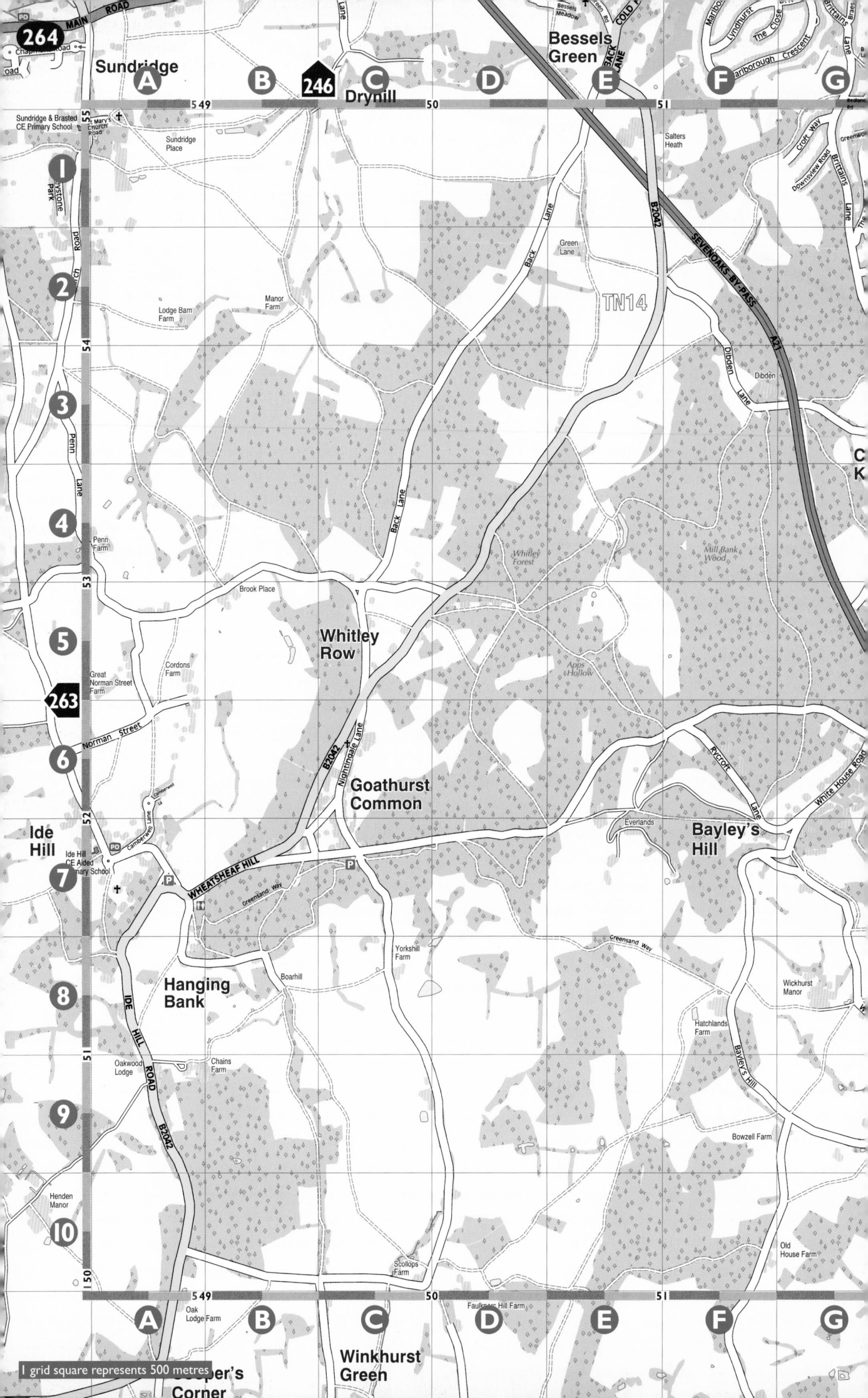

PO

MAIN ROAD

Sundridge

**A**   **B**   246   **C**   Drynill   **D**   Bessels Green   **E**   **F**   **G**

5 49   55   50   51

Chapman Road

Sundridge & Brasted CE Primary School

St Mary's Church Road

Sundridge Place

Salters Heath

Keystone Park

**I**

Green Lane

TN14

Lodge Barn Farm

Manor Farm

54

**2**

Back Lane

Penn Lane

B2042

SEVENOAKS BY-PASS

A21

Dibden Lane

Dibden

**3**

Penn Farm

53

**4**

Whitley Forest

Mill Bank Wood

C K

Brook Place

Whitley Row

**5**

Cordons Farm

Apps Hollow

Great Norman Street Farm

263

Norman Street

B2042

Nightingale Lane

**6**

52

Camberwell

Goathurst Common

Rycroft Lane

Everlands

White House Road

Bayley's Hill

**Ide Hill**

Ide Hill CE Aided Primary School

PO

Camberwell Lane

WHEATSHEAF HILL

P

P

Greensand Way

**7**

Yorkshill Farm

Greensand Way

Wickhurst Manor

Hanging Bank

Boarhill

**8**

IDE HILL ROAD

Hatchlands Farm

51

Oakwood Lodge

Chains Farm

B2042

Bayley's Hill

**9**

Bowzell Farm

Henden Manor

**10**

Old House Farm

1 50   55   49   50   51

**A**   Oak Lodge Farm   **B**   **C**   Winkhurst Green   **D**   Faulkners Hill Farm   Scollops Farm   **E**   **F**   **G**

Cooper's Corner

Flexford

**248**

Christmaspie

Wanborough

HOG'S BACK

A31

Puttenham

Compton

Shackleford

Hurtmore

Norney

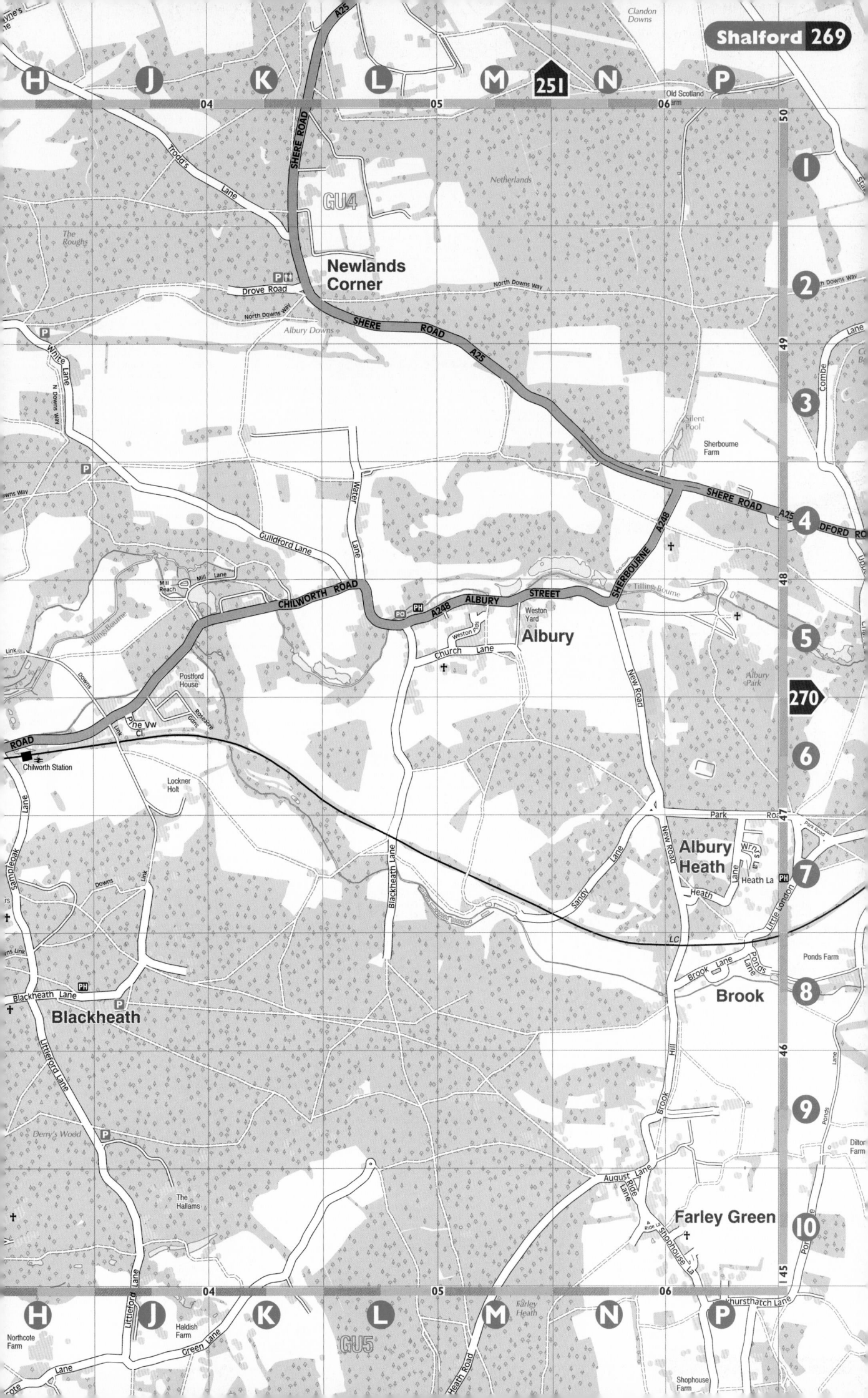

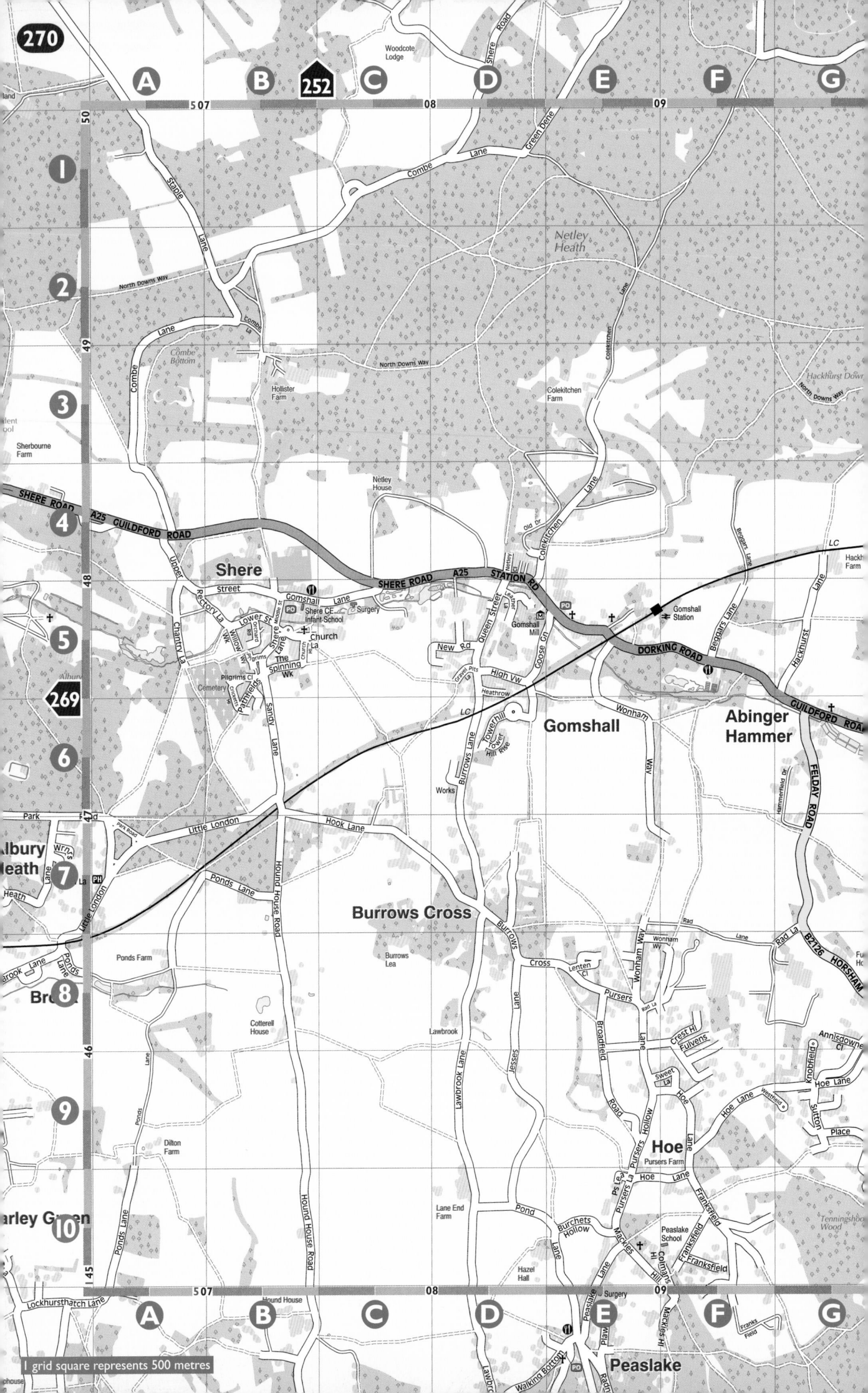

H  J  K  L  M  253  N  P

Works
Dunley Hill Farm
High Barn Road
Crocknorth Road
Hood
North Downs Way
11  12  13

50
**1**  Landbarn Farm

Oaken Grove
**2**  Rokefield
Hoe Hill Road
Lane

White Downs
North Downs Way
Stockman's Coomb Farm
Batchins
49
**3**  Westcot

Deerleap Road
Sandrock Road

Park Farm
Vale Farm
Coast Hill Lane
COAST HILL  A25
48
**4**  Westcott Heath
Rookery Drive
The Rookery
Greensand

Leasers Barn
Deerleap Wood
COAST HILL

Westlane Barn
West Lane
Wotton
Sheephouse Lane
Sheephouse Gn
**5**

**272**
GUILDFORD ROAD  A25
Crossways Farm
Manor Farm
47
**6**

Paddington Farm
Raikes Lane
Brickyard Lane
Hollow Lane
Wotton Drive
Wotton House
Greensand Way
Wolvens Lane
**7**  Logmore Green
Wolvens Lane

Abinger Lane

**8**

Raikes Farm
Abinger Common First School
Donkey Lane
46
Sutton Abinger
PH
Abinger Common
Street
Noons Corner Road
**9**  Broadmoor
Water Lane
Sutton Lane
Friday Street
PH
Woodhouse Lane
Friday Street

B2126
Radnor Lane
Felbury House
Glebe Lane
Abinger Common
Sheephouse Lane
**10**

Pasture Wood Road
Leith Hill Road
Lemon's Farm Road
Abinger Bottom
Sewer's Farm Road
Shootlands

45
H  J  K  L  M  N  P
11  12  13

Belmont Preparatory
Parkhurst

REIGATE

WEST STREET

HIGH STREET

CHURCH ST

A25 REIGATE ROAD

**H** **J** **K** **L** **M** **257** **N** **P**

**I**

South Park

Woodhatch

**Mead Vale**

South Earlswood

**2**

**3**

**4**

**5**

RH2

**Doversgreen**

**276**

**6**

BRIGHTON ROAD

WOODHATCH ROAD

DOVERS GREEN ROAD

A217

Sidlow

**7**

Irons Bottom

**8**

IRONSBOTTOM

**9**

River Mole

REIGATE ROAD

**10**

**H** **J** **K** **L** **M** **279** **N** **P**

Bletchingley

Coneybury

Rabies Heath Road

H    J    K    L    M    **259**    N    P

Greensand Way

Sandhills

Coldharbour Farm

32     33     34     50

**1**

Cooper's Hill Road

M23

Sandhills Farm

Greensand Way

South Park Lane

Wychcroft House

**2**

49

Nutfield Pk

Cucksevs Farm

South Park Farm

South Park Lane

**3**

Lyttel all

Cooper's Hill Rd

Kennels Farm

La Bu Pa

Henshaw Farm

Outwood Lane

**4**

Cooper's Hill Road

48

**5**

Burstow Park Farm

Lower South Park

**6**

47

Carlton Road

Wales Road

Lodge Farm

**7**

Brown's Hill

Harewood House

**8**

Prince of

46

Tile Barn

beard's

**9**

Outwood Common

Brickfield Road

Outwood Lane

Lane

Cayhouse

Outwood Windmill

Wasp Green Lane

Scott's Hill

**Outwood**

Daysey's Hill

Bellwether Lane

Miller's Lane

Miller's Copse

Miller's La

**Wasp Green**

Hornecourt Hill

Whitewood

**10**

45

Jarv Farr

Whitewood

H    J    K    L    M    **281**    N    P

Rookery Farm

Old Hall Farm

Hornecourt Manor Farm

Whitewood House Farm

Rookery

Wilmots Lane

32     33     34

Nalderswood

Mynthurst

Grove Farm

A   521   B   274   C   22   D   E   23   F   G

Smalls Hill Road

45

Brook Farm

1

Ewood Lane

Ewood Lane

Norwood Place Farm

Mill Lane

Broad Lane

Parkhouse Farm

Deanoak Brook

Rose Cott Farm

2

44

Hammond's Copse

Chantersluer Farm

Becket Wood

Norwood Hill

3

Parkgate

PH

Partridge Lane

Hales Bridge

Rickettswood Farm

43

Cidermill Road

4

Blanks Lane

Red House

Highworth Farm

5

Hatchetts

Sturtwood Farm

Pudding Lane

M. Laundry P.

Stanhill Court Hotel

6

42

Cudworth Lane

Burnt Oak Lane

Cudworth

The Greenings

Beggarshouse Lane

Stan Hill

7

Green Lane

The Stables Cudworth

Manor House

Burnt Oak Lane

8

Beam Brook

Glover's Rd

41

Home Farm

Partridge Lane

Cidermill Farm

Glover's Wood

Russ Hill Road

Ockley Lodge

Duke's Road

Lowfield Heath Windmill

9

Duke's Road

Russ Hill

10

Newhouse Farm

Duke's Rd

Boothlands Farm

Charlwood La

Russ Hill

40

A   521   B   282   C   22   D   E   23   F   G

Upper Prestwood Farm

1 grid square represents 500 metres

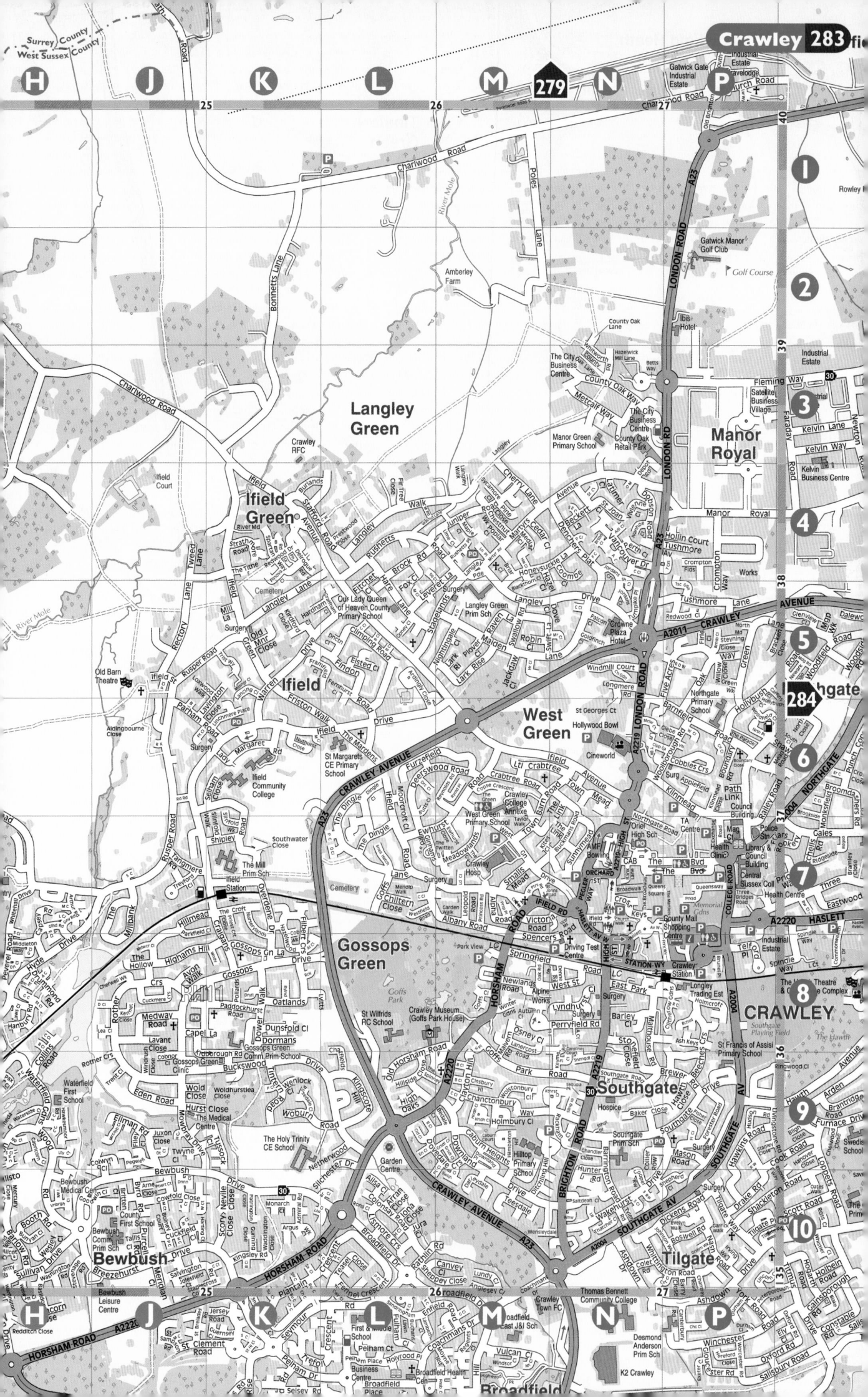

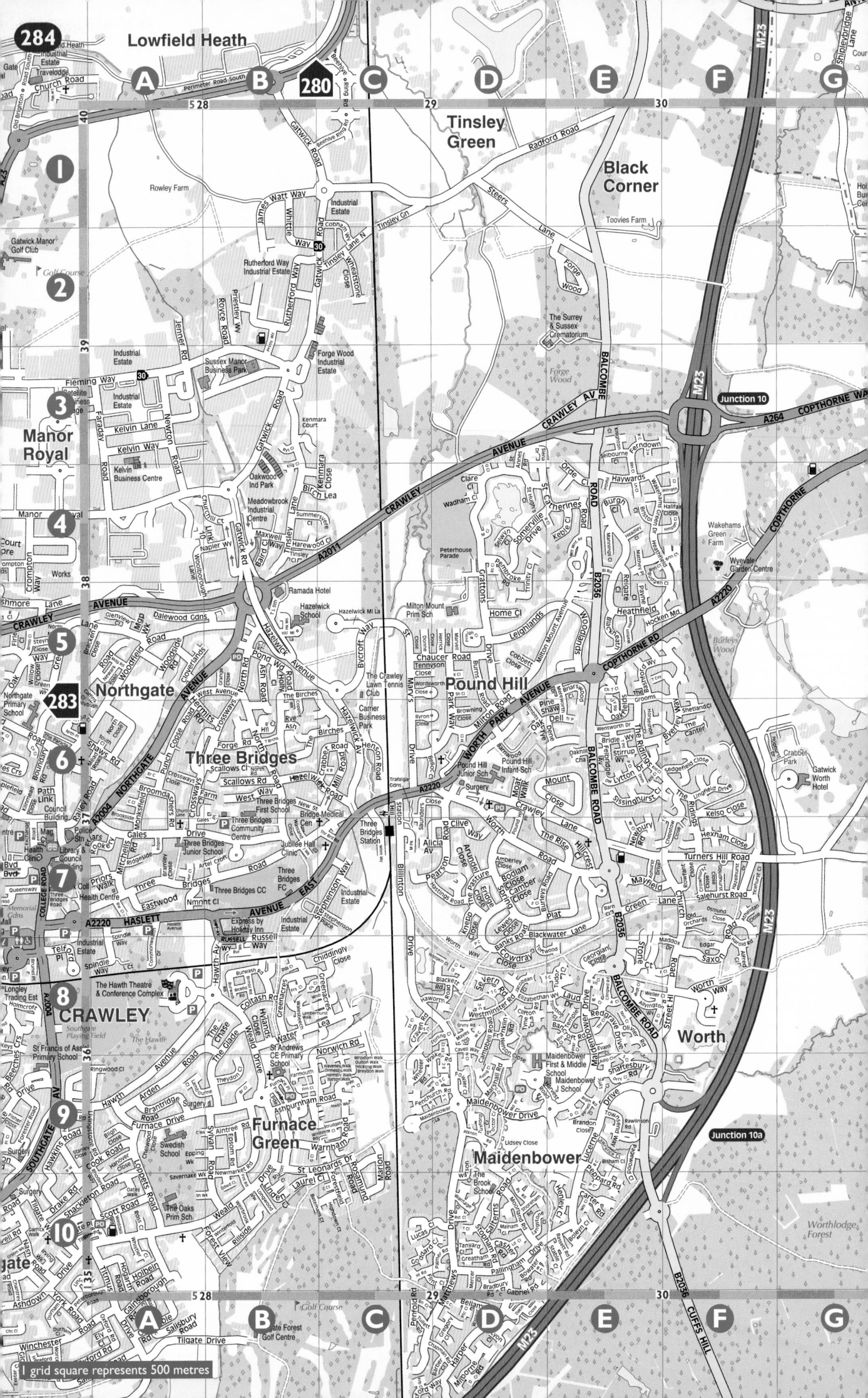

| Place | Page | Grid |
|---|---|---|
| Abbey Mead | 195 | L6 |
| Abbey Wood | 163 | L3 |
| Abbots Langley | 54 | F8 |
| Abbotswood | 250 | C8 |
| Abinger Common | 271 | L9 |
| Abinger Hammer | 270 | F6 |
| Abridge | 83 | L8 |
| Acton | 135 | P10 |
| Acton Green | 156 | A4 |
| Addington | 224 | F3 |
| Addiscombe | 203 | N7 |
| Addlestone | 215 | M2 |
| Addlestonemoor | 195 | M9 |
| Adeyfield | 36 | B6 |
| Aimes Green | 63 | L4 |
| Albury | 269 | M5 |
| Albury Heath | 269 | P7 |
| Aldenborough Hatch | 123 | H2 |
| Aldenham | 74 | A3 |
| Aldersbrook | 121 | P6 |
| Alperton | 135 | K3 |
| Amersham | 69 | J5 |
| Amersham Common | 69 | H5 |
| Amersham Old Town | 68 | G8 |
| Amersham on the Hill | 68 | G3 |
| Amwell | 21 | H4 |
| Anerley | 203 | P2 |
| Anthonys | 214 | D8 |
| Aperfield | 244 | C3 |
| Apsley | 35 | N10 |
| Ardleigh Green | 125 | K1 |
| Ardley End | 31 | J2 |
| Arkley | 76 | E9 |
| Artington | 267 | N5 |
| Ascot | 192 | B2 |
| Asheridge | 50 | C2 |
| Ashford | 174 | B7 |
| Ashford Common | 174 | E9 |
| Ashley Green | 33 | L10 |
| Ashley Park | 197 | H10 |
| Ashtead | 237 | K4 |
| Austenwood | 109 | N1 |
| Aveley | 146 | C9 |
| Avery Hill | 184 | F2 |
| Ayot Green | 22 | C3 |
| Ayres End | 20 | E6 |
| Badgers Mount | 228 | C5 |
| Baker's Wood | 111 | H6 |
| Balham | 180 | A3 |
| Bandonhill | 222 | E2 |
| Banstead | 239 | L1 |
| Barking | 142 | G2 |
| Barkingside | 122 | E1 |
| Barnehurst | 164 | E6 |
| Barnes | 156 | E7 |
| Barnes Cray | 165 | J10 |
| Barnet | 77 | J10 |
| Barnet Gate | 76 | B10 |
| Barnsbury | 5 | N3 |
| Barwell | 219 | H4 |
| Batchworth | 92 | A4 |
| Batchworth Heath | 92 | B5 |
| Batlers Green | 74 | F7 |
| Battersea | 158 | A6 |
| Bayford | 42 | A4 |
| Bayley's Hill | 264 | F7 |
| Bayswater | 9 | J7 |
| Beaconsfield | 88 | B10 |
| Bean | 188 | G6 |
| Beckenham | 204 | F2 |
| Beckton | 142 | C8 |
| Becontree | 123 | N10 |
| Beddington | 202 | C9 |
| Beddington Corner | 202 | B7 |
| Bedford Park | 156 | C2 |
| Bedmond | 54 | E7 |
| Belgravia | 16 | C5 |
| Bell Bar | 41 | K10 |
| Bell Common | 64 | C8 |
| Bell Green | 182 | E6 |
| Bellfields | 249 | P7 |
| Bellingdon | 32 | D10 |
| Bellingham | 182 | F7 |
| Belmont | 94 | F10 |
| Belmont | 221 | K5 |
| Belsize | 53 | L4 |
| Belvedere | 164 | C4 |
| Bengeo | 25 | J5 |
| Benhilton | 201 | L10 |
| Bennetts End | 36 | A4 |
| Bentley | 86 | D7 |
| Bentley Heath | 77 | J1 |
| Berkhamsted | 33 | M5 |
| Bermondsey | 19 | N2 |
| Bernards Heath | 38 | C4 |
| Berryllands | 199 | J6 |
| Berry's Green | 244 | D2 |
| Bessels Green | 246 | E10 |
| Betchworth | 255 | P9 |
| Bethnal Green | 140 | A5 |
| Betsham | 189 | L17 |
| Bewbush | 283 | J10 |
| Bexley | 163 | M10 |
| Bexleyheath | 164 | A10 |
| Bickley | 206 | B2 |
| Biggin | 168 | F5 |
| Biggin Hill | 244 | A2 |
| Binscombe | 267 | H9 |
| Birch Green | 24 | D7 |
| Birchwood | 40 | E2 |
| Bishopsgate | 171 | L7 |
| Bisley | 230 | F2 |
| Black Corner | 284 | E1 |
| Blackbrook | 273 | K7 |
| Blackfen | 185 | J2 |
| Blackheath | 161 | L8 |
| Blackheath | 269 | H6 |
| Blackheath Park | 161 | M10 |
| Blacknest | 193 | H5 |
| Blackwall | 141 | J9 |
| Bletchingley | 259 | L10 |
| Bloomsbury | 11 | J3 |
| Bobbingworth | 49 | L2 |
| Borehamwood | 75 | K2 |
| Botany Bay | 78 | E2 |
| Botley | 51 | M7 |
| Bourne End | 34 | A6 |
| Boveney | 148 | B5 |
| Bovingdon | 52 | C5 |
| Bovingdon Green | 52 | C5 |
| Bovinger | 48 | G2 |
| Bow | 140 | F4 |
| Bow Common | 140 | F6 |
| Bowes Park | 98 | F2 |
| Bowmans | 186 | G8 |
| Box Hill | 255 | N8 |
| Boxmoor | 35 | L8 |
| Brands Hill | 150 | E6 |
| Brasted | 245 | L10 |
| Brasted Chart | 263 | L4 |
| Brays Grove | 47 | K2 |
| Brentford | 155 | J5 |
| Brentford End | 154 | G6 |
| Brentwood | 106 | C3 |
| Brewer Street | 259 | F4 |
| Brick Hill | 213 | H1 |
| Brickendon | 43 | K5 |
| Bricket Wood | 55 | N1 |
| Bridge End | 250 | C6 |
| Brimsdown | 30 | E5 |
| Britwell | 128 | F6 |
| Brixton | 159 | H10 |
| Broad Colney | 57 | J4 |
| Broad Green | 203 | J7 |
| Broadford | 267 | P7 |
| Broadgreen Wood | 43 | H4 |
| Broadham Green | 261 | N8 |
| Bradley Common | 48 | A6 |
| Broadmoor | 272 | A9 |
| Broadoak End | 24 | G3 |
| Brockham | 273 | M1 |
| Brockham Park | 273 | P3 |
| Brockley | 182 | E1 |
| Bromley | 140 | G4 |
| Bromley | 205 | N2 |
| Bromley Common | 206 | A6 |
| Bromley Park | 205 | K1 |
| Brondesbury | 2 | B1 |
| Brondesbury Park | 136 | C3 |
| Brook | 269 | P8 |
| Brook Green | 156 | F2 |
| Brook Street | 106 | D5 |
| Brooklands | 216 | A5 |
| Brookmans Park | 59 | H2 |
| Brookwood | 230 | F6 |
| Broom Hill | 207 | J7 |
| Broomhall | 192 | G7 |
| Broxbourne | 44 | A4 |
| Broxhill | 98 | B4 |
| Buckhurst Hill | 101 | P4 |
| Buckland | 256 | D9 |
| Bucks Hill | 53 | M10 |
| Bullen's Green | 40 | B8 |
| Bulls Cross | 79 | P2 |
| Buistrode | 53 | H4 |
| Bumble's Green | 45 | M10 |
| Bunce Common | 274 | A7 |
| Burgh Heath | 238 | G5 |
| Burnham | 84 | A8 |
| Burnt Oak | 96 | A8 |
| Burntcommon | 251 | J1 |
| Burpham | 250 | D6 |
| Burrows Cross | 270 | C7 |
| Burstow | 281 | H8 |
| Burwood Park | 217 | H2 |
| Bury Green | 62 | A7 |
| Bush Hill Park | 79 | M10 |
| Bushbury | 273 | M5 |
| Bushey | 94 | D1 |
| Bushey Heath | 94 | D1 |
| Bushey Mead | 200 | G3 |
| Bushy Hill | 250 | E8 |
| Butlers Cross | 89 | L5 |
| Byfleet | 215 | N9 |
| Caldecote Hill | 94 | E1 |
| Camberwell | 159 | N7 |
| Camden Town | 4 | D4 |
| Campions | 30 | A6 |
| Canary Wharf | 140 | F10 |
| Canning Town | 141 | N7 |
| Cannon Hill | 200 | G4 |
| Canonbury | 6 | E3 |
| Canons Park | 95 | K8 |
| Carpenders Park | 93 | N3 |
| Carshalton | 221 | P1 |
| Carshalton Beeches | 221 | P5 |
| Carshalton on the Hill | 222 | A4 |
| Cartbridge | 232 | E8 |
| Carter's Green | 47 | J9 |
| Castle Green | 143 | M5 |
| Castle Green | 213 | K9 |
| Caterham | 241 | M9 |
| Catford | 183 | H4 |
| Chadwell Heath | 123 | N3 |
| Chadwell St Mary | 168 | C2 |
| Chafford Hundred | 167 | K2 |
| Chaldon | 241 | J10 |
| Chalfont Common | 90 | C5 |
| Chalfont Grove | 89 | N7 |
| Chalfont St Giles | 89 | L3 |
| Chalfont St Peter | 90 | D8 |
| Chalk | 191 | K4 |
| Chalvey | 149 | H1 |
| Chandler's Cross | 72 | A4 |
| Charlton | 162 | A4 |
| Charlton | 196 | D2 |
| Charlwood | 279 | J8 |
| Chartridge | 50 | B4 |
| Chase Cross | 104 | F7 |
| Chattern Hill | 174 | C7 |
| Chaulden | 34 | G7 |
| Cheam | 221 | H2 |
| Cheapside | 192 | D2 |
| Chelsea | 15 | M8 |
| Chelsfield | 227 | P2 |
| Chelsham | 242 | F3 |
| Chenies | 70 | F4 |
| Chertsey | 195 | K7 |
| Chertsey Meads | 195 | P8 |
| Chesham | 71 | J1 |
| Chesham Bois | 69 | H2 |
| Cheshunt | 62 | A6 |
| Chessington | 219 | K3 |
| Chessmount | 51 | K8 |
| Chevening | 246 | F4 |
| Chigwell | 102 | E3 |
| Chigwell Row | 103 | L3 |
| Childerditch | 127 | L2 |
| Child's Hill | 117 | H7 |
| Childsbridge | 247 | N5 |
| Childwick Bury | 20 | B10 |
| Childwick Green | 20 | A1 |
| Chilworth | 268 | F6 |
| China Town | 11 | K7 |
| Chingford | 101 | J2 |
| Chingford Green | 101 | L2 |
| Chingford Hatch | 101 | K5 |
| Chipperfield | 53 | L7 |
| Chipping Barnet | 77 | H9 |
| Chipping Ongar | 67 | M4 |
| Chipstead | 240 | B5 |
| Chipstead | 246 | D8 |
| Chislehurst | 184 | F10 |
| Chislehurst West | 184 | D9 |
| Chiswell Green | 55 | N1 |
| Chiswick | 156 | C3 |
| Chobham | 213 | J6 |
| Cholesbury | 32 | B7 |
| Chorleywood | 70 | C8 |
| Chorleywood Bottom | 70 | C10 |
| Chorleywood West | 70 | D9 |
| Christmaspie | 266 | A1 |
| Church End | 71 | H6 |
| Church End | 97 | K10 |
| Church End | 136 | C2 |
| Church End | 234 | A7 |
| Church Langley | 47 | N1 |
| Church Town | 260 | D8 |
| Churchgate | 62 | A5 |
| Churchgate Street | 30 | A8 |
| Cippenham | 128 | C10 |
| City of London | 12 | D7 |
| Clapham | 158 | C8 |
| Clapham Park | 180 | C2 |
| Clapton Park | 120 | E9 |
| Claremont Park | 217 | P4 |
| Clatterford End | 67 | J6 |
| Claverhambury | 63 | N3 |
| Clay Hill | 79 | N3 |
| Claygate | 218 | E3 |
| Clayhall | 102 | C10 |
| Clement Street | 187 | L19 |
| Clerkenwell | 11 | A1 |
| Clewer Green | 148 | D9 |
| Clewer New Town | 148 | C8 |
| Clewer Village | 148 | F8 |
| Clock House | 222 | D10 |
| Cobham | 217 | H10 |
| Cockfosters | 77 | P3 |
| Cockmore | 51 | K6 |
| Codicote | 10 | E1 |
| Coldblow | 186 | D5 |
| Coldharbour | 165 | H3 |
| Cole Green | 24 | D7 |
| Coleman Green | 21 | M6 |
| Coles Meads | 258 | A4 |
| Coleshill | 68 | E10 |
| Colham Green | 132 | A6 |
| Colindale | 116 | B1 |
| College Park | 136 | D5 |
| Collier Row | 104 | B4 |
| Colliers Hatch | 66 | D6 |
| Collier's Wood | 179 | N10 |
| Colnbrook | 150 | F7 |
| Colney Hatch | 98 | A4 |
| Colney Heath | 39 | H6 |
| Colney Street | 56 | D6 |
| Commonwood | 53 | K10 |
| Compton | 266 | F6 |
| Coney Hall | 225 | K1 |
| Coombe | 178 | B10 |
| Cooper's Green | 39 | N1 |
| Cooper's Hill | 172 | A6 |
| Coopersale Common | 65 | N5 |
| Coopersale Street | 65 | M7 |
| Copse Hill | 178 | D10 |
| Copthall Green | 64 | A9 |
| Copthorne | 285 | J2 |
| Corbets Tey | 126 | A10 |
| Cottenham Park | 200 | A1 |
| Counters End | 35 | K6 |
| Cowley | 131 | M6 |
| Cowley Peachy | 131 | M8 |
| Coxtie Green | 86 | C9 |
| Cranbourne | 170 | A5 |
| Cranbrook | 122 | D5 |
| Cranford | 153 | H6 |
| Cranham | 126 | D5 |
| Cranley Gardens | 118 | B2 |
| Crawley | 283 | P8 |
| Crayford | 187 | H1 |
| Creekmouth | 143 | H7 |
| Crews Hill | 79 | J1 |
| Cricklewood | 116 | D9 |
| Crockenhill | 208 | D6 |
| Crockham Hill | 262 | F9 |
| Crofton | 206 | G9 |
| Cromer-Hyde | 21 | P6 |
| Crooked Billet | 178 | E9 |
| Cross Keys | 264 | G3 |
| Crouch End | 118 | D4 |
| Crow Green | 86 | F7 |
| Croxley Green | 72 | B9 |
| Croydon | 35 | P10 |
| Crystal Palace | 181 | P9 |
| Cubitt Town | 161 | H5 |
| Cudham | 244 | G1 |
| Cudworth | 278 | B7 |
| Cuffley | 60 | G4 |
| Cupid Green | 36 | C2 |
| Curtismill Green | 84 | C7 |
| Custom House | 142 | B9 |
| Dagenham | 144 | C2 |
| Dalston | 7 | M2 |
| Dancers Hill | 76 | F1 |
| Darenth | 188 | B3 |
| Dartford | 187 | K3 |
| Dartmouth Park | 118 | B7 |
| Datchet | 149 | N7 |
| Datchet Common | 149 | P8 |
| Dawesgreen | 274 | B6 |
| De Beauvoir Town | 7 | J5 |
| Deacons Hill | 75 | M10 |
| Dean Bottom | 210 | G3 |
| Dean Street | 82 | F4 |
| Debden Green | 148 | C7 |
| Deepdene | 273 | J2 |
| Denbies | 254 | C10 |
| Denham | 111 | K7 |
| Denham Green | 111 | H4 |
| Denton | 191 | H3 |
| Deptford | 160 | E5 |
| Derry Downs | 207 | N6 |
| Digswell | 22 | C2 |
| Digswell Park | 23 | K1 |
| Digswell Water | 23 | J2 |
| Doddinghurst | 86 | G3 |
| Dollis Hill | 116 | E8 |
| Donkey Town | 212 | C9 |
| Dorking | 272 | G3 |
| Dormer's Wells | 134 | A9 |
| Dorney | 148 | A2 |
| Doversgreen | 275 | L4 |
| Down Park | 285 | P4 |
| Downe | 226 | F8 |
| Downend | 183 | J8 |
| Downside | 235 | J5 |
| Dryhill | 246 | C10 |
| Ducks Island | 96 | G1 |
| Dudden Hill | 116 | D10 |
| Dudswell | 33 | J2 |
| Dulwich | 181 | N5 |
| Dulwich Village | 181 | M3 |
| Dunton Green | 246 | F5 |
| Ealing | 135 | H9 |
| Earl's Court | 14 | E6 |
| Earlsfield | 179 | M4 |
| Earlswood | 276 | A2 |
| East Acton | 136 | C9 |
| East Barnet | 97 | N1 |
| East Bedfont | 174 | C3 |
| East Burnham | 128 | E3 |
| East Clandon | 251 | P7 |
| East Dulwich | 181 | P1 |
| East End | 28 | B10 |
| East End | 220 | G6 |
| East Ewell | 220 | G6 |
| East Finchley | 117 | N1 |
| East Ham | 142 | B4 |
| East Horsley | 252 | A5 |
| East Molesey | 198 | B5 |
| East Sheen | 178 | A1 |
| East Tilbury | 169 | L3 |
| East Wickham | 163 | K7 |
| Eastbury | 92 | C5 |
| Eastcote | 113 | J5 |
| Eastcote Village | 113 | J3 |
| Eastwick | 28 | E7 |
| Eden Park | 204 | E4 |
| Edgware | 95 | N5 |
| Edmonton | 99 | M5 |
| Effingham | 253 | M3 |
| Egham | 172 | D9 |
| Egham Hythe | 172 | C9 |
| Egham Wick | 171 | L10 |
| Ellenbrook | 39 | P5 |
| Elm Corner | 234 | B5 |
| Elm Park | 125 | J10 |
| Elmers End | 204 | C3 |
| Elmstead | 184 | B8 |
| Elstree | 75 | K10 |
| Eltham | 184 | B2 |
| Emerson Park | 125 | M4 |
| Enfield | 79 | K8 |
| Enfield Highway | 80 | G6 |
| Enfield Island Village | 80 | G4 |
| Enfield Lock | 80 | E5 |
| Enfield Town | 79 | L7 |
| Enfield Wash | 80 | D4 |
| Englefield Green | 171 | N10 |
| Epping | 65 | K6 |
| Epping Green | 42 | E8 |
| Epping Green | 46 | D10 |
| Epping Upland | 64 | F2 |
| Epsom | 219 | F10 |
| Erith | 164 | G10 |
| Esher | 218 | B1 |
| Essendon | 42 | A5 |
| Eton | 149 | H5 |
| Eton Wick | 148 | D5 |
| Ewell | 220 | D5 |
| Eynsford | 209 | M9 |
| Fair Cross | 123 | J10 |
| Fairlands | 249 | J7 |
| Fairlop | 103 | H3 |
| Fairmile | 217 | N8 |
| Falconwood | 163 | H10 |
| Fanns | 153 | H2 |
| Farleigh Court | 224 | E10 |
| Farley Green | 269 | P10 |
| Farnborough | 226 | D3 |
| Farncombe | 267 | J9 |
| Farnham Common | 129 | H3 |
| Farnham Park | 129 | H3 |
| Farnham Royal | 129 | H4 |
| Farningham | 209 | P7 |
| Fawkham Green | 210 | C10 |
| Feltham | 175 | K6 |
| Felthamhill | 174 | F9 |
| Fernhill | 280 | E10 |
| Ferndale | 236 | C9 |
| Fickleshole | 225 | K10 |
| Fiddlers Hamlet | 65 | M8 |
| Field Common | 197 | N7 |
| Fields End | 34 | G5 |
| Finchley | 97 | L3 |
| Finsbury | 6 | H9 |
| Finsbury Park | 118 | F2 |
| Flamstead End | 62 | A4 |
| Flaunden | 52 | D8 |
| Fleet Downs | 188 | D3 |
| Fleetville | 38 | F6 |
| Fletcher's Green | 265 | L10 |
| Flexford | 248 | G10 |
| Foots Cray | 185 | L9 |
| Force Green | 245 | H10 |
| Forest Gate | 141 | L5 |
| Forest Hill | 182 | C4 |
| Forestdale | 224 | D5 |
| Fortis Green | 118 | A2 |
| Forty Hill | 79 | N5 |
| Foster Street | 48 | A2 |
| Fox Corner | 249 | H1 |
| Fox Hatch | 86 | E4 |
| Foxbury | 184 | G8 |
| Fredley | 254 | C5 |
| Freezy Water | 80 | D2 |
| French Street | 263 | H4 |
| Friday Hill | 101 | J4 |
| Friday Street | 271 | N9 |
| Friern Barnet | 97 | P5 |
| Frithsden | 34 | D1 |
| Froghole | 262 | G8 |
| Frogmore | 56 | D4 |
| Fulham | 156 | G6 |
| Fullwell Cross | 102 | G9 |
| Fulmer | 110 | A9 |
| Furnace Green | 284 | B9 |
| Furzedown | 180 | B5 |
| Gadbrook | 274 | A4 |
| Gadebridge | 35 | P4 |
| Gallows Corner | 105 | L9 |
| Gants Hill | 122 | C4 |
| Ganwick Corner | 77 | L1 |
| Garston | 73 | K1 |
| Gatton | 258 | A6 |
| George Green | 130 | B7 |
| Gerrards Cross | 110 | A4 |
| Gidea Park | 104 | C10 |
| Giggshill | 198 | F7 |
| Gilston | 28 | E5 |
| Gilston Park | 28 | F5 |
| Gilwell Park | 81 | H7 |
| Givons Grove | 255 | J1 |
| Globe Town | 140 | C5 |
| Goathurst Common | 264 | C6 |
| Goddington | 207 | M10 |
| Godstone | 260 | A7 |
| Goff's Oak | 61 | K4 |
| Goldsworth Park | 231 | M2 |
| Gomshall | 270 | D6 |
| Goodley Stock | 262 | E6 |
| Goodmayes | 123 | L7 |
| Goose Green | 44 | B2 |
| Gorhambury | 37 | K5 |
| Gospel Oak | 118 | B10 |
| Gossops Green | 283 | L8 |
| Grange Hill | 102 | C7 |
| Grange Park | 79 | H9 |
| Gravel Hill | 90 | C7 |
| Gravesend | 191 | J8 |
| Grays | 167 | L6 |
| Great Amwell | 26 | D5 |
| Great Bookham | 254 | A2 |
| Great Burgh | 238 | F3 |
| Great Hivings | 50 | A4 |
| Great Parndon | 46 | E3 |
| Great Warley | 126 | G6 |
| Greatness | 247 | L6 |
| Green End | 35 | J7 |
| Green Street | 75 | M3 |
| Green Street Green | 188 | F7 |
| Green Street Green | 227 | H4 |
| Greenford | 134 | C6 |
| Greenhill | 114 | B8 |
| Greenhithe | 166 | E10 |
| Greensted | 67 | J4 |
| Greensted Green | 67 | J4 |
| Greenwich | 161 | J8 |
| Grove Park | 156 | A7 |
| Grove Park | 183 | P6 |
| Grovehill | 35 | N3 |
| Grubb Street | 210 | C1 |
| Guildford | 267 | M1 |
| Guildford Park | 267 | M1 |
| Hackbridge | 202 | C9 |
| Hackney | 7 | J1 |
| Hackney Wick | 140 | F1 |
| Hacton | 125 | N10 |
| Hadley | 77 | H7 |
| Hadley Wood | 77 | N4 |
| Haggerston | 7 | M7 |
| Hailey | 26 | E3 |
| Hainault | 103 | J8 |
| Haldens | 23 | K1 |
| Hale End | 101 | J7 |
| Half Acre | 23 | L7 |
| Hall Grove | 45 | P5 |
| Halstead | 228 | B8 |
| Hamm Moor | 215 | N1 |
| Hammer | 35 | L6 |
| Hammersmith | 156 | E5 |
| Hammond Street | 61 | K2 |
| Hampstead | 117 | L3 |
| Hampstead Garden Suburb | 117 | L3 |
| Hampton | 198 | A1 |
| Hampton Hill | 176 | B7 |
| Hampton Wick | 198 | G1 |
| Hamsey Green | 241 | M3 |
| Handside | 22 | E6 |
| Hanging Bank | 264 | A8 |
| Hanwell | 134 | C10 |
| Hanworth | 175 | L6 |
| Hare Street | 46 | E2 |
| Harefield | 91 | N10 |
| Harefield Grove | 91 | N8 |
| Harlesden | 136 | B4 |
| Harlington | 152 | D5 |
| Harlow | 28 | F10 |
| Harmondsworth | 151 | M5 |
| Harold Hill | 105 | M6 |
| Harold Park | 106 | A7 |
| Harold Wood | 105 | P9 |
| Harpenden Common | 20 | A4 |
| Harringay | 119 | J3 |
| Harrow | 114 | C6 |
| Harrow on the Hill | 114 | D6 |
| Harrow Weald | 94 | D8 |
| Hartham | 25 | K4 |
| Hartley | 211 | K5 |
| Hartley Green | 211 | K5 |
| Hastingwood | 48 | A5 |
| Hatch End | 93 | M8 |
| Hatfield | 40 | C5 |
| Hatfield Garden Village | 23 | B10 |
| Hatfield Hyde | 23 | J8 |
| Hatton | 152 | F10 |
| Hatton Hill | 212 | C1 |
| Havering-atte-Bower | 104 | F4 |
| Hawk's Hill | 236 | G10 |
| Hawley | 187 | M8 |
| Hayes | 132 | C1 |
| Hayes | 205 | N7 |
| Hayes End | 132 | C6 |
| Hayes Town | 133 | K10 |
| Hazelwood | 226 | F7 |
| Headley | 255 | P2 |
| Headstone | 114 | A2 |
| Heath End | 32 | F7 |
| Heath Park | 125 | J4 |
| Heath Side | 186 | D5 |
| Hedgerley | 109 | J6 |
| Hedgerley Green | 109 | K7 |
| Hedgerley Hill | 109 | J7 |
| Hemel Hempstead | 35 | P6 |
| Hendon | 116 | D3 |
| Herne Hill | 181 | K2 |
| Heronsgate | 90 | C1 |
| Hersham | 217 | K2 |
| Hertford | 25 | M6 |
| Hertford Heath | 26 | A8 |
| Hertingfordbury | 25 | H6 |
| Heston | 153 | N6 |
| Hextable | 187 | N10 |
| High Barnet | 76 | F7 |
| High Beach | 81 | N5 |
| High Cross | 74 | C2 |
| High Laver | 49 | J3 |
| High Wych | 29 | J1 |
| Higham Hill | 100 | D10 |
| Highams Park | 100 | G8 |
| Highbury | 119 | J10 |
| Highgate | 118 | A5 |
| Highwood Hill | 96 | C3 |
| Hill End | 91 | L7 |
| Hill Park | 244 | E9 |
| Hillingdon | 132 | A3 |
| Hillingdon Heath | 132 | C7 |
| Hilltop | 51 | J5 |
| Hinchley Wood | 198 | E10 |
| Hither Green | 183 | K2 |
| Hobbs Cross | 30 | D10 |
| Hobbs Cross | 83 | N2 |
| Hockenden | 208 | C3 |
| Hoddesdon | 44 | D3 |
| Hoe | 270 | E9 |
| Hogpits Bottom | 52 | E8 |
| Holborn | 11 | N4 |
| Holders Hill | 96 | G9 |
| Holland | 261 | M9 |
| Hollybush Hill | 129 | N2 |
| Holmethorpe | 258 | C8 |
| Holtspur | 88 | C10 |
| Holyfield | 63 | H4 |
| Holywell | 72 | F10 |
| Homerton | 140 | C1 |
| Honor Oak | 182 | C2 |
| Honor Oak Park | 182 | D2 |
| Hook | 219 | K2 |
| Hook End | 87 | H1 |
| Hook Green | 186 | C7 |
| Hook Green | 189 | L3 |
| Hook Heath | 231 | N6 |
| Hookwood | 279 | M5 |
| Hooley | 240 | B8 |
| Horley | 280 | C2 |
| Horn Hill | 90 | E3 |
| Hornchurch | 125 | L7 |
| Horne | 281 | H7 |
| Horns Cross | 188 | E2 |
| Horns Green | 245 | H5 |
| Hornsey | 118 | F2 |
| Hornsey Vale | 118 | G3 |
| Horsell | 232 | A2 |
| Horseman Side | 85 | M8 |
| Horton | 150 | D9 |
| Horton Kirby | 210 | C4 |
| Hosey Hill | 263 | H4 |
| Housham Tye | 30 | G9 |
| How Wood | 56 | B5 |
| Hoxton | 7 | J8 |
| Hubbard's Hill | 265 | J6 |
| Hulberry | 209 | J9 |
| Hunsdon | 27 | P2 |
| Hunsdonbury | 27 | P5 |
| Hunton Bridge | 54 | C9 |
| Hurst Green | 261 | K8 |
| Hurst Park | 198 | B2 |
| Hurtmore | 266 | F10 |
| Huston | 87 | F10 |
| Hutton | 107 | N2 |
| Hutton Mount | 107 | M2 |
| Hyde Heath | 50 | B10 |
| Hythe End | 172 | E6 |
| Ickenham | 112 | B8 |
| Ide Hill | 263 | P7 |
| Ifield | 283 | K5 |
| Ifield Green | 283 | K4 |
| Ifieldwood | 282 | C4 |
| Ilford | 122 | E8 |
| Ingrave | 107 | P7 |
| Irons Bottom | 275 | K8 |
| Isle of Dogs | 161 | H3 |
| Isleworth | 154 | C5 |
| Islington | 6 | A5 |
| Istead Rise | 190 | B10 |
| Iver | 131 | J8 |
| Iver Heath | 130 | C3 |
| Ivy Chimneys | 65 | H8 |
| Jack's Hatch | 46 | E7 |
| Jacobs Well | 249 | P5 |
| Jordans | 89 | J1 |
| Joyden's Wood | 186 | G7 |
| Katherines | 46 | B4 |
| Kelvedon Hatch | 86 | C5 |
| Kemsing | 247 | N3 |
| Kenley | 241 | M10 |
| Kennington | 17 | M10 |
| Kensal Green | 136 | F4 |
| Kensal Town | 8 | G4 |
| Kensington | 14 | F4 |
| Kentish Town | 4 | F1 |
| Kenton | 115 | H3 |
| Keston | 206 | A1 |
| Keston Mark | 206 | C1 |
| Kevingtown | 208 | A6 |
| Kew | 155 | J3 |
| Keysers Estate | 44 | C8 |
| Kidbrooke | 161 | P3 |
| Kilburn | 2 | D6 |
| Kingfield | 232 | B6 |
| Kings Farm | 190 | F6 |
| Kings Langley | 54 | B4 |
| Kingsbury | 115 | N4 |
| Kingsland | 7 | J3 |
| Kingsmoor | 46 | F6 |
| Kingston upon Thames | 199 | H3 |
| Kingston Vale | 178 | A2 |
| Kingswood | 55 | J10 |
| Kingswood | 239 | J7 |
| Kippington | 265 | H2 |
| Kitt's End | 77 | H4 |
| Knaphill | 231 | H4 |
| Knight's Hill | 181 | K4 |
| Knightsbridge | 15 | P1 |
| Knockhall | 188 | G1 |
| Knockholt | 245 | K3 |
| Knotty Green | 88 | B5 |
| Knowle Green | 173 | J2 |
| Knowle Hill | 193 | N7 |
| Ladywell | 160 | F10 |
| Lake End | 148 | A5 |
| Lakeside | 167 | J5 |
| Laleham | 195 | M3 |
| Laleham Burway | 195 | L5 |
| Lambeth | 18 | A3 |
| Lambourne | 103 | M1 |
| Lambourne End | 103 | J4 |
| Lambs Green | 282 | C7 |
| Lampton | 154 | C7 |
| Lane End | 188 | G8 |
| Langley | 131 | K3 |
| Langley Corner | 130 | C1 |
| Langley Green | 284 | E8 |
| Langley Vale | 238 | A6 |
| Langleybury | 54 | C10 |
| Latchmore Heath | 74 | C6 |
| Latimer | 70 | F3 |
| Latton Bush | 47 | K5 |
| Layters Green | 89 | N7 |
| Lea Bridge | 120 | C8 |
| Leashes Bridge | 20 | F1 |
| Leatherhead | 236 | F10 |
| Leaves Green | 225 | N4 |
| Leavesden Green | 54 | F10 |
| Lee | 183 | L1 |
| Leigh | 274 | F9 |
| Lemsford | 22 | C6 |
| Lessness Heath | 164 | C5 |
| Letchmore Heath | 74 | D5 |
| Lett's Green | 245 | J2 |
| Letty Green | 24 | B9 |
| Leverstock Green | 36 | D7 |
| Lewisham | 161 | N10 |
| Ley Hill | 51 | H6 |
| Leyton | 121 | J6 |
| Leytonstone | 121 | L6 |
| Lightwater | 212 | G4 |
| Limehouse | 140 | D9 |
| Limpsfield | 261 | L9 |
| Limpsfield Chart | 262 | C7 |
| Limpsfield Common | 261 | M9 |
| Linford | 169 | J1 |
| Lippitts Hill | 81 | L6 |
| Lisson Grove | 10 | B3 |
| Little Berkhamsted | 42 | B5 |
| Little Bookham | 253 | P4 |
| Little Chalfont | 69 | N6 |
| Little End | 67 | M10 |
| Little Heath | 34 | D4 |
| Little Heath | 59 | L5 |
| Little Heath | 123 | M4 |
| Little Heath | 217 | N10 |
| Little Ilford | 122 | A6 |
| Little Laver | 49 | P1 |
| Little Missenden | 68 | D2 |
| Little Parndon | 28 | E10 |
| Little Stanmore | 95 | L8 |
| Little Thurrock | 167 | P3 |
| Little Warley | 107 | L4 |
| Littlewoodcote | 222 | B7 |
| Littlefield Common | 248 | C5 |
| Littleton | 196 | C3 |
| Littleton | 267 | M6 |
| Littleton Common | 174 | C10 |
| Littleton | 231 | L2 |
| Littleworth Common | 108 | C8 |
| Lockbottom | 206 | E10 |
| Logmore Green | 272 | A7 |
| London Colney | 57 | K2 |
| Long Ditton | 198 | G3 |
| Longcross | 193 | N10 |
| Longfield | 211 | L3 |
| Longford | 151 | L7 |
| Longford | 246 | E6 |
| Longlands | 184 | F6 |
| Loudwater | 71 | N7 |
| Loughton | 82 | C8 |
| Love Green | 130 | C7 |
| Low Street | 169 | J4 |
| Lower Ashtead | 237 | H5 |
| Lower Bobbingworth Green | 49 | J3 |
| Lower Bois | 51 | H10 |
| Lower Clapton | 99 | M3 |
| Lower Edmonton | 99 | M3 |
| Lower Feltham | 174 | F7 |
| Lower Green | 198 | A9 |
| Lower Halliford | 196 | F2 |
| Lower Holloway | 118 | C10 |
| Lower Kingswood | 257 | K2 |
| Lower Nazeing | 45 | J9 |
| Lower Place | 135 | P4 |
| Lower Sheering | 30 | A2 |
| Lower Sunbury | 197 | H3 |
| Lower Sydenham | 182 | C7 |
| Lower Woodside | 41 | J8 |
| Lowfield Heath | 280 | A10 |
| Loxford | 122 | F10 |
| Loyter's Green | 30 | C10 |
| Lucas End | 61 | K7 |
| Lucas Green | 230 | C1 |
| Luxted | 226 | D10 |
| Lye Green | 51 | L4 |
| Magdalen Laver | 48 | E4 |
| Maida Vale | 2 | G9 |
| Maidenbower | 284 | D9 |
| Maidenhead Court | 4 | A1 |
| Maiden Rushett | 218 | G8 |
| Manor Park | 122 | B9 |
| Manor Park | 129 | H6 |
| Manor Royal | 283 | P7 |
| Mantles Green | 68 | F4 |
| Manwood Green | 31 | M6 |
| Maple Cross | 90 | G5 |
| Marden Ash | 67 | N6 |
| Margery | 257 | K5 |
| Mark Hall North | 29 | K9 |
| Mark Hall South | 29 | K9 |
| Marks Gate | 103 | P10 |
| Marshalswick | 38 | F3 |
| Marshmoor | 40 | G8 |
| Martyr's Green | 234 | F5 |
| Marylebone | 10 | C4 |
| Matching | 31 | N7 |
| Matching Green | 31 | L8 |
| Matching Tye | 30 | G8 |
| Maybury | 232 | E3 |
| Mayfair | 10 | E8 |
| Mayford | 231 | P8 |
| Maypole | 186 | F4 |
| Maypole | 228 | A3 |
| May's Green | 234 | G6 |
| Mead Vale | 275 | M3 |
| Meadgate | 279 | N2 |
| Meriden | 73 | M2 |
| Merrow | 250 | F9 |
| Merry Hill | 94 | A2 |
| Merstham | 258 | C6 |
| Merton | 201 | K1 |
| Merton Park | 201 | J2 |
| Mickleham | 255 | H4 |
| Mickleham Green | 255 | H4 |
| Mid Holmwood | 273 | G8 |
| Middle Green | 130 | B9 |
| Mile End | 140 | D6 |
| Mill End | 91 | J2 |
| Mill Green | 41 | H1 |
| Mill Hill | 96 | D6 |
| Mill Meads | 141 | L4 |
| Milton | 190 | G2 |
| Mimbridge | 213 | N9 |
| Mitcham | 201 | J6 |
| Mogador | 256 | C5 |
| Moneyhill | 91 | J2 |
| Monken Hadley | 77 | H6 |
| Monks Orchard | 204 | B7 |
| Moor Park | 92 | D5 |
| Moorhouse Bank | 262 | D4 |
| Morden | 201 | K6 |
| Morden Park | 201 | H6 |
| Moreton | 49 | K7 |
| Mortlake | 155 | P8 |
| Motspur Park | 200 | D5 |
| Mottingham | 183 | P5 |
| Mount End | 64 | C6 |
| Mount Hermon | 232 | C5 |
| Mount Pleasant | 91 | J9 |
| Muckingford | 169 | M3 |
| Mugswell | 257 | L1 |
| Muswell Hill | 98 | B1 |
| Naldenswood | 274 | F10 |
| Nash | 225 | N3 |
| Nash Mills | 54 | B1 |
| Navestock Heath | 85 | K6 |
| Navestock Side | 85 | L4 |
| Nazeing | 45 | M7 |
| Nazeing Gate | 45 | L9 |
| Nazeing Long Green | 63 | N1 |
| Nazeing Mead | 45 | J4 |
| Neasden | 116 | A9 |
| Netherne on the Hill | 240 | C8 |
| Nettleswell | 28 | C10 |
| New Addington | 225 | J4 |
| New Ash Green | 211 | N9 |
| New Barn | 211 | N2 |
| New Barnet | 77 | N3 |
| New Beckenham | 182 | D9 |
| New Charlton | 162 | A3 |
| New Cross | 160 | D8 |
| New Cross Gate | 160 | C8 |
| New Denham | 131 | K1 |
| New Eltham | 184 | D4 |
| New Greens | 38 | B1 |
| New Haw | 215 | M4 |

New House 190 B5
New Malden 200 C3
New Southgate 98 D5
New Town 187 N2
Newbury Park 122 G4
Newgate Street 42 F10
Newington 18 B4
Newlands Corner 269 L2
Newman's End 30 G6
Newtown 51 H5
Newyears Green 112 B5
Noah's Arks 247 P5
Noak Hill 105 M3
Noel Park 99 J10
Nomansland 21 H5
Norbiton 199 L2
Norbury 203 J2
Nork 238 G2
Normandy 248 A7
North Acton 135 P6
North Cheam 200 G10
North Cray 186 D6
North End 117 M6
North End 164 G7
North Feltham 175 J1
North Finchley 97 M7
North Harrow 113 N4
North Hillingdon 132 C2
North Holmwood 272 G7
North Hyde 153 M3
North Kensington 136 G7
North Looe 220 F9
North Ockendon 126 G10
North Sheen 155 N8
North Stifford 147 K9
North Watford 73 J3
North Weald Bassett 66 C3
North Wembley 114 G6
North Woolwich 162 B1
Northaw 60 B6
Northchurch 33 J3
Northfleet 189 P1
Northfleet Green 189 P8
Northgate 284 A5
Northolt 133 P2
Northumberland Heath 164 D6
Northwood 92 D9
Northwood Hills 92 E10
Norwood Green 153 P3
Norwood Hill 279 H4
Norwood New Town 181 L9
Notting Hill 8 B7
Nunhead 160 B10
Nuper's Hatch 104 F1
Nutfield 258 G10
Oakhurst 265 P9
Oakleigh Park 97 N3
Oakwood 78 E10
Oatlands Park 216 F1
Ockham 234 B8
Old Bexley 186 B3
Old Coulsdon 241 J6
Old Ford 140 D3
Old Harlow 29 N7
Old Hatfield 40 G3
Old Malden 200 A7
Old Oak Common 136 C6
Old Windsor 171 N2
Old Woking 232 E6
Onslow Village 267 K2
Orchard Leigh 51 N3
Orpington 207 K9
Orsett Heath 168 C1
Osidge 98 D3
Osterley 154 B6
Otford 247 H3
Ottershaw 214 F2
Otterspool 73 N3
Outwood 277 K9
Oxhey 73 L10
Oxlease 40 E5
Oxshott 218 B9
Oxted 261 K5
Pachesham Park 236 F2
Paddington 9 L4
Pains Hill 261 P7
Palmers Green 98 F4
Panshanger 23 K4
Park Barn 249 K9
Park Langley 205 H6
Park Royal 135 M5
Park Street 56 B2
Parkgate 278 A3
Parrock Farm 190 G6
Parsons Green 157 K8
Passingford Bridge 84 E5
Passmores 46 G4
Patchetts Green 74 B5
Peartree 23 H6
Peartree Green 87 J3
Peasmarsh 267 P8
Peckham 160 A8
Pedlars End 49 J7
Pednor Bottom 50 B5
Pednormead End 50 E8
Penge 182 B10
Penn Street 68 A8
Pentonville 5 P7
Perivale 135 H3
Perry Street 190 C3
Petersham 177 K4
Petts Wood 206 G4
Piccotts End 35 M2
Piercing Hill 82 G1
Pilgrims Hatch 86 G8
Pimlico 16 G7
Pimlico 36 F10
Pinnacles 46 D1
Pinner 113 L2
Pinner Green 93 K10
Pinnerwood Park 93 K8
Pirbright 230 E9
Pitch Place 249 L5
Pixham 255 H9
Plaistow 141 L5
Plaistow 183 M9
Plashet 142 A1
Plumstead 162 F4
Plumstead Common 163 J5
Pond Park 50 G5
Ponders End 80 B9
Poplar 140 F9
Potten End 34 D3
Potter Street 47 N3
Potters Bar 59 P8
Potters Crouch 37 L10
Pouchen End 34 G7
Pound Hill 284 D5
Poverest 207 K4
Povey Cross 279 M6
Poyle 151 H7
Pratt's Bottom 227 L6
Presdales 26 D4
Preston 115 J6
Prey Heath 231 N9
Primrose Hill 4 D6
Puddledock 186 E9
Puddledock 263 K9
Pudds Cross 52 B4
Purfleet 165 P4
Purley 223 H8
Putney 178 G1
Putney Heath 178 F3
Putney Vale 178 D6
Puttenham 266 A4
Pyle Hill 250 A1
Pyrford 233 J1
Pyrford Green 233 L3
Pyrford Village 233 H4
Queen's Park 2 A7
Queensbury 115 K1
Radlett 75 H1
Rainham 145 J5
Ramsden 207 M8
Ranmore Common 254 B9
Rayners Lane 113 N6
Raynes Park 200 F3
Redbridge 121 P3
Redhill 258 B8
Regent's Park 4 F8
Reigate 257 J10
Reigate Hill 257 J8
Richings Park 151 H2
Richmond 177 K1
Richmond Hill 177 K2
Rickmansworth 71 N10
Ridge 58 C10
Ridge Green 276 F3
Ripley 233 L7
Rise Park 104 F9
Riverhead 246 E8
Riverview Park 191 K7
Roe Green 40 D4
Roehampton 178 C1
Roestock 40 A9
Romford 124 D3
Romney Street 229 N8
Rose Hill 272 F2
Rosedale 61 N4
Rosehill 201 L8
Rosherville 190 C1
Rotherhithe 160 C2
Round Bush 74 C4
Roundshaw 222 G3
Row Town 215 J3
Rowley Green 76 C8
Roxeth 114 B7
Roydon 27 N10
Roydon Hamlet 45 P5
Rucklers Lane 53 P2
Ruislip 112 F4
Ruislip Common 112 D2
Ruislip Gardens 112 F8
Ruislip Manor 113 H7
Rush Green 26 B5
Rush Green 124 E5
Rushmore Hill 227 M9
Russ Hill 278 F10
Russell Hill 222 G6
Ruxley 185 P9
Rydens 197 K9
Rydeshill 249 J8
Rye Meads 27 J10
Rye Park 44 C2
Sabine's Green 85 L6
Salfords 276 C8
Salt Hill 129 J10
Sanderstead 223 P7
Sandridge 21 H10
Sands End 157 M7
Sarratt 71 K1
Sarratt Bottom 71 H2
Sawbridgeworth 29 L1
Scotswood 192 C8
Seal 247 P7
Seer Green 88 G7
Seething Wells 198 G6
Selhurst 203 L5
Selsdon 224 B6
Send 232 G9
Send Grove 250 E2
Send Marsh 233 J9
Seven Kings 123 H6
Sevenoaks 247 K10
Sevenoaks Common 265 H5
Sevenoaks Weald 265 H8
Sewardstone 81 H6
Sewardstonebury 81 K9
Shackleford 266 C10
Shacklewell 119 P9
Shadwell 140 B9
Shalford 268 C7
Sheering 30 E3
Sheerwater 214 F9
Sheets Heath 230 E5
Shelley 49 P10
Shellwood Cross 274 B9
Shenfield 107 K1
Shenley 57 L10
Shenleybury 57 J7
Shepherd's Bush 136 E10
Shepperton 196 B6
Shepperton Green 196 B4
Shere 270 B4
Sherrardspark 22 E3
Shipley Bridge 280 G9
Shirley 204 B9
Shooters Hill 162 F7
Shootersway 33 K5
Shoreditch 7 H10
Shoreham 228 F7
Shorne 191 P8
Shorne Ridgeway 191 N10
Shortlands 205 K3
Shreding Green 132 E8
Shrubs Hill 193 H6
Sidcup 185 L7
Sidlow 275 L7
Silvertown 161 P1
Singlewell 190 F9
Sipson 152 A4
Slade Green 165 H8
Sleapshyde 39 P7
Slough 129 M10
Slyfield 250 A7
Smallfield 281 H5
Smallford 39 N5
Smug Oak 56 A6
Soho 11 J6
Somers Town 5 J8
Sopwell 38 D9
South Beddington 222 E3
South Bromley 141 J8
South Croydon 223 J3
South Darenth 210 C1
South Earlswood 275 P5
South Field 148 G4
South Hackney 140 B3
South Hampstead 3 K3
South Harefield 111 N2
South Harrow 114 A8
South Hatfield 40 E7
South Hornchurch 144 E3
South Kensington 15 J6
South Lambeth 158 F6
South Merstham 258 E6
South Mimms 58 E8
South Norwood 203 L3
South Nutfield 276 F2
South Ockendon 147 H6
South Oxhey 93 J4
South Park 275 H3
South Ruislip 113 L9
South Stifford 167 J4
South Street 244 C5
South Tottenham 119 M3
South Weald 106 D3
South Wimbledon 179 M8
South Woodford 101 M10
Southall 153 L1
Southborough 206 C6
Southend 183 H7
Southfields 179 K4
Southfleet 189 N9
Southgate 98 F2
Southgate 283 N9
Speed Gate 210 E9
Spital 148 G10
Spitalbrook 44 F5
Spitalfields 13 L3
Spring Grove 154 C7
Spring Park 204 F9
St Albans 38 E4
St George in the East 13 P8
St George's Hill 216 D5
St Giles 11 K5
St Helier 201 M8
St James's 11 J10
St Johns 160 F8
St Johns 231 M5
St John's 247 H8
St John's Wood 3 K6
St Julians 38 B10
St Luke's 12 F1
St Margarets 26 F7
St Margarets 177 H2
St Mary Cray 207 M5
St Pancras 5 M10
St Paul's Cray 207 K2
St Stephens 37 P8
St Vincent's Hamlet 105 P2
Staines 173 J7
Staines Green 24 D7
Stamford Hill 119 N5
Stanborough 22 C8
Stanford Rivers 67 J9
Stanmore 94 G6
Stanstead Abbotts 27 K7
Stanwell 173 N2
Stanwell Moor 173 K2
Stapleford Abbotts 84 D10
Stapleford Tawney 84 D2
Stepney 140 B7
Stewards 47 H6
Steward's Green 65 L8
Stockwell 158 F9
Stoke D'Abernon 235 M1
Stoke Green 129 M6
Stoke Newington 119 N7
Stoke Poges 129 K2
Stone 188 E1
Stonebridge 273 J5
Stonehill 214 B3
Stonehill Green 186 D9
Stoneleigh 220 C2
Stonewood 189 J6
Stoughton 249 N7
Strand 11 L7
Stratford 141 H2
Stratford Marsh 140 G3
Stratford New Town 141 H1
Strawberry Hill 176 C6
Streatham 180 F8
Streatham Hill 180 F4
Streatham Park 180 D7
Streatham Vale 180 C10
Stroud Green 119 H4
Stroude 194 C2
Sudbury 114 E10
Summerstown 179 N5
Sumners 46 D5
Sunbury 196 F1
Sunbury Common 174 G10
Sundridge 183 P9
Sundridge 246 A10
Sunningdale 192 F5
Sunninghill 192 C5
Sunnymeads 150 B10
Surbiton 199 H8
Sutton 150 F4
Sutton 221 M2
Sutton Abinger 271 J9
Sutton at Hone 187 P10
Sutton Green 250 C1
Swallows Cross 87 L3
Swanley 208 F1
Swanley Bar 59 L4
Swanley Village 209 H2
Swanscombe 189 L1
Swiss Cottage 3 M5
Sydenham 182 C8
Tadworth 238 F8
Tandridge 260 F9
Tatling End 110 E6
Tatsfield 244 A6
Teddington 176 C9
Temple Fields 29 K7
Temple Hill 165 L10
Temple Mills 120 G10
Thames Ditton 198 F7
Thamesmead 143 K9
The Borough 18 F2
The Camp 38 G7
The Chart 263 L6
The Folly 20 G1
The Frythe 22 D1
The Grove 72 D3
The High 28 F10
The Hyde 116 C3
The Ridgeway 60 C3
The Rise 192 D6
The Rookery 93 H1
The Ryde 40 F1
The Swillett 90 F1
The Village 170 G6
The Wells 219 L10
The Wrythe 201 P9
Theydon Bois 82 G3
Theydon Garnon 83 M2
Theydon Mount 84 B2
Thong 191 K9
Thorney 151 L1
Thornton Heath 203 J3
Thornwood Common 65 L1
Thorpe 194 F3
Thorpe Green 194 D4
Thorpe Lea 172 F10
Three Bridges 284 A6
Three Households 89 L4
Threshers Bush 48 B2
Tilbury 168 D7
Tilegate Green 48 E3
Tilgate 283 N10
Timberden Bottom 228 F6
Tinsley Green 284 D1
Titsey 261 P1
Tittenhurst 192 F4
Tokyngton 135 N1
Tolmers 60 F2
Tolworth 199 M8
Toot Hill 66 G6
Tooting 180 A8
Tooting Graveney 179 N8
Tottenham 99 M10
Tottenham Hale 119 N1
Totteridge 97 J2
Totteridge Green 96 F2
Tower Hill 53 J5
Tower Hill 272 G4
Townsend 38 A4
Toy's Hill 263 M8
Trumpsgreen 193 P6
Tufnell Park 118 D9
Tulse Hill 181 J4
Turners Hill 285 P9
Turnford 62 D1
Twickenham 176 D4
Twitton 246 F2
Two Waters 35 M9
Tye Green 46 G3
Tylers Causeway 42 C8
Tyler's Green 48 E10
Tyler's Green 260 A6
Tyler's Hill 51 M7
Tyrrell's Wood 237 M10
Tyttenhanger 39 K9
Underhill 77 K10
Underriver 265 P6
Upminster 126 B7
Upper Clapton 119 P6
Upper Edmonton 99 P5
Upper Elmers End 204 E5
Upper Halliford 196 E4
Upper Holloway 118 D6
Upper Norwood 203 L1
Upper Shirley 224 B1
Upper Sydenham 181 P7
Upper Tooting 179 P6
Upper Walthamstow 121 H2
Upshire 63 P8
Upton 141 N2
Upton 149 M2
Upton Lea 129 M8
Upton Park 141 P3
Uxbridge 131 M3
Uxbridge Moor 131 L3
Vale of Health 117 N8
Valley End 212 F2
Vauxhall 17 M8
Venus Hill 52 E7
Virginia Water 193 P3
Waddon 202 F9
Walham Green 157 K7
Wallend 142 D3
Wallington 222 B2
Waltham Abbey 63 J8
Waltham Cross 62 B9
Walthamstow 120 E2
Walton on the Hill 238 C10
Walton-on-Thames 197 H8
Walworth 18 F8
Wanborough 266 A3
Wandle Park 203 H9
Wandsworth 157 K10
Wanstead 121 N5
Wapping 140 A10
Ware 26 E1
Warley 106 G6
Warlingham 242 C4
Warners End 35 H5
Warwick Wold 259 H5
Wasp Green 277 K10
Water End 58 F2
Waterdale 55 K6
Waterend 21 P3
Waterford 24 G1
Waterhales 85 L10
Waterside 51 J9
Watford 72 G7
Watford Heath 93 M1
Watton's Green 85 J10
Wealdstone 114 F1
Weatherhill 281 H3
Welham Green 40 E9
Well End 75 P4
Well Hill 228 C2
Welling 163 L9
Welsh Harp 116 A6
Welwyn Garden City 23 L3
Wembley 115 K9
Wembley Park 115 M8
Wennington 145 M9
West Acton 135 M8
West Barnes 200 F5
West Bedfont 174 A3
West Brompton 14 G9
West Byfleet 215 L9
West Clandon 251 L5
West Court 191 H5
West Drayton 151 N2
West Dulwich 181 L5
West Ealing 134 F10
West End 21 N4
West End 212 E10
West End 217 N2
West Ewell 220 A3
West Green 119 K1
West Green 283 M6
West Hampstead 117 K10
West Harrow 114 B5
West Heath 117 L7
West Heath 163 N5
West Hendon 116 D5
West Hill 179 H3
West Horndon 127 P4
West Horsley 252 D4
West Hyde 91 H8
West Kensington 156 G4
West Kilburn 2 B9
West Molesey 197 N4
West Norwood 181 K7
West Ruislip 112 D6
West Thurrock 166 F4
West Tilbury 169 H5
West Watford 73 H9
West Wickham 205 J8
West Yoke 211 J10
Westbourne Green 8 D2
Westbrook Hay 34 F10
Westcott 272 A3
Wested 208 F7
Westerham 262 G5
Westfield 232 C8
Westhumble 254 F7
Westminster 17 H4
Weston Green 198 D8
Westwick Row 36 F7
Westwood 189 H10
Wexham Street 129 P3
Weybridge 216 B1
Wheathampstead 21 J2
Whelpley Hill 52 A2
Whetstone 97 L3
Whippendell Bottom 53 M6
White Oak 208 F2
Whitebushes 276 C5
Whitechapel 13 M7
Whiteley Village 216 G5
Whiteley Row 264 C5
Whitton 176 B2
Whyteleafe 241 N4
Widmore 206 A2
Wigginton Bottom 32 D1
Wildernesse 247 M8
Wildhill 41 M7
Willesden 136 D1
Willesden Green 136 E2
Willey Green 248 C7
Willowbank 111 M10
Wilmington 187 J7
Wilton Park 88 G9
Wimbledon 179 H8
Winchmore Hill 88 C1
Winchmore Hill 99 J2
Windlesham 212 A3
Windsor 149 K7
Wisley 233 P1
Woking 232 C4
Woldingham 242 F9
Woldingham Garden Village 242 E7
Wonersh 268 F10
Wood End 132 F8
Wood End 170 B9
Wood End Green 132 F7
Wood Green 63 P10
Wood Green 99 H9
Wood Street Village 248 F8
Woodbridge Hill 249 M8
Woodcock Hill 91 P5
Woodcote 222 F7
Woodcote 238 A2
Woodcote Green 222 C6
Woodford 101 N7
Woodford Bridge 102 C8
Woodford Green 101 M8
Woodford Wells 101 N4
Woodhall 23 H7
Woodham 215 K6
Woodhatch 275 K3
Woodlands 154 C9
Woodmansterne 239 N1
Woodrow 68 B8
Woodside 41 K7
Woodside 55 J8
Woodside 65 N2
Woodside 170 A7
Woodside 203 P6
Woodside Park 97 K5
Woollensbrook 26 C10
Woolwich 162 D2
Worcester Park 200 E9
World's End 79 H8
Wormley 44 D10
Wormley West End 43 P8
Wormleybury 44 A9
Worplesdon 249 J3
Worth 284 F8
Wotton 271 M5
Wray Common 257 N8
Wraysbury 172 C2
Yeading 133 K6
Yiewsley 131 P9

# USING THE STREET INDEX

Street names are listed alphabetically. Each street name is followed by its postal town or area locality, the Postcode District, the page number, and the reference to the square in which the name is found.

Standard index entries are shown as follows:

**1 Av** *WOOL/PLUM* SE18 **162** E2

Street names and selected addresses not shown on the map due to scale restrictions are shown in the index with an asterisk:

**Abbeville Ms** *CLAP* SW4 * **180** E1

Entries in red indicate streets located within the London Congestion Zone. Refer to the map pages for the location of the Zone boundary

# GENERAL ABBREVIATIONS

| | |
|---|---|
| ACC | ACCESS |
| ALY | ALLEY |
| AP | APPROACH |
| AR | ARCADE |
| ASS | ASSOCIATION |
| AV | AVENUE |
| BCH | BEACH |
| BLDS | BUILDINGS |
| BND | BEND |
| BNK | BANK |
| BR | BRIDGE |
| BRK | BROOK |
| BTM | BOTTOM |
| BUS | BUSINESS |
| BVD | BOULEVARD |
| BY | BYPASS |
| CATH | CATHEDRAL |
| CEM | CEMETERY |
| CEN | CENTRE |
| CFT | CROFT |
| CH | CHURCH |
| CHA | CHASE |
| CHYD | CHURCHYARD |
| CIR | CIRCLE |
| CIRC | CIRCUS |
| CL | CLOSE |
| CLFS | CLIFFS |
| CMP | CAMP |
| CNR | CORNER |
| CO | COUNTY |
| COLL | COLLEGE |
| COM | COMMON |
| COMM | COMMISSION |
| CON | CONVENT |
| COT | COTTAGE |
| COTS | COTTAGES |
| CP | CAPE |
| CPS | COPSE |
| CR | CREEK |
| CREM | CREMATORIUM |
| CRS | CRESCENT |
| CSWY | CAUSEWAY |
| CT | COURT |
| CTRL | CENTRAL |
| CTS | COURTS |
| CTYD | COURTYARD |
| CUTT | CUTTINGS |
| CV | COVE |
| CYN | CANYON |
| DEPT | DEPARTMENT |
| DL | DALE |
| DM | DAM |
| DR | DRIVE |
| DRO | DROVE |
| DRY | DRIVEWAY |
| DWGS | DWELLINGS |
| E | EAST |
| EMB | EMBANKMENT |
| EMBY | EMBASSY |
| ESP | ESPLANADE |
| EST | ESTATE |
| EX | EXCHANGE |
| EXPY | EXPRESSWAY |
| EXT | EXTENSION |
| F/O | FLYOVER |
| FC | FOOTBALL CLUB |
| FK | FORK |
| FLD | FIELD |
| FLDS | FIELDS |
| FLS | FALLS |
| FM | FARM |
| FT | FORT |
| FTS | FLATS |
| FWY | FREEWAY |
| FY | FERRY |
| GA | GATE |
| GAL | GALLERY |
| GDN | GARDEN |
| GDNS | GARDENS |
| GLD | GLADE |
| GLN | GLEN |
| GN | GREEN |
| GND | GROUND |
| GRA | GRANGE |
| GRG | GARAGE |
| GT | GREAT |
| GTWY | GATEWAY |
| GV | GROVE |
| HGR | HIGHER |
| HL | HILL |
| HLS | HILLS |
| HO | HOUSE |
| HOL | HOLLOW |
| HOSP | HOSPITAL |
| HRB | HARBOUR |
| HTH | HEATH |
| HTS | HEIGHTS |
| HVN | HAVEN |
| HWY | HIGHWAY |
| IMP | IMPERIAL |
| IN | INLET |
| IND EST | INDUSTRIAL ESTATE |
| INF | INFIRMARY |
| INFO | INFORMATION |
| INT | INTERCHANGE |
| IS | ISLAND |
| JCT | JUNCTION |
| JTY | JETTY |
| KG | KING |
| KNL | KNOLL |
| L | LAKE |
| LA | LANE |
| LDG | LODGE |
| LGT | LIGHT |
| LK | LOCK |
| LKS | LAKES |
| LNDG | LANDING |
| LTL | LITTLE |
| LWR | LOWER |
| MAG | MAGISTRATES' |
| MAN | MANSIONS |
| MD | MEAD |
| MDW | MEADOWS |
| MEM | MEMORIAL |
| MI | MILL |
| MKT | MARKET |
| MKTS | MARKETS |
| ML | MALL |
| MNR | MANOR |
| MS | MEWS |
| MSN | MISSION |
| MT | MOUNT |
| MTN | MOUNTAIN |
| MTS | MOUNTAINS |
| MUS | MUSEUM |
| MWY | MOTORWAY |
| N | NORTH |
| NE | NORTH EAST |
| NW | NORTH WEST |
| O/P | OVERPASS |
| OFF | OFFICE |
| ORCH | ORCHARD |
| OV | OVAL |
| PAL | PALACE |
| PAS | PASSAGE |
| PAV | PAVILION |
| PDE | PARADE |
| PH | PUBLIC HOUSE |
| PK | PARK |
| PKWY | PARKWAY |
| PL | PLACE |
| PLN | PLAIN |
| PLNS | PLAINS |
| PLZ | PLAZA |
| POL | POLICE STATION |
| PR | PRINCE |
| PREC | PRECINCT |
| PREP | PREPARATORY |
| PRIM | PRIMARY |
| PROM | PROMENADE |
| PRS | PRINCESS |
| PRT | PORT |
| PT | POINT |
| PTH | PATH |
| PZ | PIAZZA |
| QD | QUADRANT |
| QU | QUEEN |
| QY | QUAY |
| R | RIVER |
| RBT | ROUNDABOUT |
| RD | ROAD |
| RDG | RIDGE |
| REP | REPUBLIC |
| RES | RESERVOIR |
| RFC | RUGBY FOOTBALL CLUB |
| RI | RISE |
| RP | RAMP |
| RW | ROW |
| S | SOUTH |
| SCH | SCHOOL |
| SE | SOUTH EAST |
| SER | SERVICE AREA |
| SH | SHORE |
| SHOP | SHOPPING |
| SKWY | SKYWAY |
| SMT | SUMMIT |
| SOC | SOCIETY |
| SP | SPUR |
| SPR | SPRING |
| SQ | SQUARE |
| ST | STREET |
| STN | STATION |
| STR | STREAM |
| STRD | STRAND |
| SW | SOUTH WEST |
| TDG | TRADING |
| TER | TERRACE |
| THWY | THROUGHWAY |

TNL ... TUNNEL
TOLL ... TOLLWAY
TPK ... TURNPIKE
TR ... TRACK
TRL ... TRAIL
TWR ... TOWER
U/P ... UNDERPASS
UNI ... UNIVERSITY
UPR ... UPPER
V ... VALE
VA ... VALLEY
VIAD ... VIADUCT
VIL ... VILLA
VIS ... VISTA
VLG ... VILLAGE
VLS ... VILLAS
VW ... VIEW
W ... WEST
WD ... WOOD
WHF ... WHARF
WK ... WALK
WKS ... WALKS
WLS ... WELLS
WY ... WAY
YD ... YARD
YHA ... YOUTH HOSTEL

# POSTCODE TOWNS AND AREA ABBREVIATIONS

ABLGY ... Abbots Langley
ABR/ST ... Abridge/Stapleford Abbotts
ABYW ... Abbey Wood
ACT ... Acton
ADL/WDHM ... Addlestone/Woodham
ALP/SUD ... Alperton/Sudbury
AMS ... Amersham
AMSS ... Amersham south
ARCH ... Archway
ASC ... Acsot
ASHF ... Ashford (Surrey)
ASHTD ... Ashtead
BAGS ... Bagshot
BAL ... Balham
BANK ... Bank
BAR ... Barnet
BARB ... Barbican
BARK ... Barking
BARK/HLT ... Barkingside/Hainault
BARN ... Barnes
BAY/PAD ... Bayswater/Paddington
BCTR ... Becontree
BEAC ... Beaconsfield
BECK ... Beckenham
BELMT ... Belmont
BELV ... Belvedere
BERK ... Berkhamsted
BERM/RHTH ... Bermondsey/Rotherhithe
BETH ... Bethnal Green
BF/WBF ... Byfleet/West Byfleet
BFN/LL ... Blackfen/Longlands
BFOR ... Bracknell Forest/Windlesham
BGR/WK ... Borough Green/West Kingsdown
BGVA ... Belgravia
BH/WHM ... Biggin Hill/Westerham
BKHH ... Buckhurst Hill
BKHTH/KID ... Blackheath/Kidbrooke
BLKFR ... Blackfriars
BMLY ... Bromley
BMSBY ... Bloomsbury
BNSTD ... Banstead
BORE ... Borehamwood
BOW ... Bow
BRKHM/BTCW ... Brockham/Betchworth
BRKMPK ... Brookmans Park
BROCKY ... Brockley
BROX ... Broxbourne
BRW ... Brentwood
BRWN ... Brentwood north
BRXN/ST ... Brixton north/Stockwell
BRXS/STRHM ... Brixton south/Streatham Hill
BRYLDS ... Berrylands
BTFD ... Brentford
BTSEA ... Battersea
BUSH ... Bushey
BXLY ... Bexley
BXLYHN ... Bexleyheath north
BXLYHS ... Bexleyheath south
CAMTN ... Camden Town
CAN/RD ... Canning Town/Royal Docks
CANST ... Cannon Street station
CAR ... Carshalton
CAT ... Catford
CAVSQ/HST ... Cavendish Square/Harley Street
CDALE/KGS ... Colindale/Kingsbury
CDW/CHF ... Chadwell St Mary/Chafford Hundred
CEND/HSY/T ... Crouch End/Hornsey/Turnpike Lane
CFSP/GDCR ... Chalfont St Peter/Gerrards Cross
CHARL ... Charlton
CHCR ... Charing Cross
CHDH ... Chadwell Heath
CHEAM ... Cheam
CHEL ... Chelsea
CHERT ... Chertsey
CHES/WCR ... Cheshunt/Waltham Cross
CHESW ... Cheshunt west
CHIG ... Chigwell
CHING ... Chingford
CHOB/PIR ... Chobham/Pirbright
CHONG ... Chipping Ongar
CHSGTN ... Chessington
CHST ... Chislehurst
CHSWK ... Chiswick
CITYW ... City of London west
CLAP ... Clapham
CLAY ... Clayhall
CLKNW ... Clerkenwell
CLPT ... Clapton
CMBW ... Camberwell
COB ... Cobham
CONDST ... Conduit Street
COUL/CHIP ... Coulsdon/Chipstead
COVGDN ... Covent Garden
CRAWE ... Crawley east
CRAWW ... Crawley west
CRICK ... Cricklewood
CROY/NA ... Croydon/New Addington
CRW ... Collier Row
CSHM ... Chesham
CSTG ... Chalfont St Giles
CTHM ... Caterham
DAGE ... Dagenham east
DAGW ... Dagenham west
DART ... Dartford
DEN/HRF ... Denham/Harefield
DEN/HRF ... Denham/Harefield
DEPT ... Deptford
DORK ... Dorking
DTCH/LGLY ... Datchet/Langley
DUL ... Dulwich
E/WMO/HCT ... East & West Molesey/Hampton Court
EA ... Ealing
EBAR ... East Barnet
EBED/NFELT ... East Bedfont/North Feltham
ECT ... Earl's Court
ED ... Edmonton
EDEN ... Edenbridge
EDGW ... Edgware
EDUL ... East Dulwich
EFNCH ... East Finchley
EGH ... Egham
EHAM ... East Ham
EHSLY ... East Horsley
ELTH/MOT ... Eltham/Mottingham
EMB ... Embankment
EMPK ... Emerson Park
EN ... Enfield
ENC/FH ... Enfield Chase/Forty Hill
EPP ... Epping
EPSOM ... Epsom
ERITH ... Erith
ERITHM ... Erith Marshes
ESH/CLAY ... Esher/Claygate
EW ... Ewell
EYN ... Eynsford
FARR ... Farringdon
FBAR/BDGN ... Friern Barnet/Bounds Green
FELT ... Feltham
FENCHST ... Fenchurch Street
FITZ ... Fitzrovia
FLKWH/TG ... Flackwell Heath/Tylers Green
FLST/FETLN ... Fleet Street/Fetter Lane
FNCH ... Finchley
FRIM ... Frimley
FSBYE ... Finsbury east
FSBYPK ... Finsbury Park
FSBYW ... Finsbury west
FSTGT ... Forest Gate
FSTH ... Forest Hill
FUL/PGN ... Fulham/Parsons Green
GDMY/SEVK ... Goodmayes/Seven Kings
GDST ... Godstone
GFD/PVL ... Greenford/Perivale
GINN ... Gray's Inn
GLDGN ... Golders Green
GNTH/NBYPK ... Gants Hill/Newbury Park
GNWCH ... Greenwich
GODL ... Godalming
GPK ... Gidea Park
GRAYS ... Grays
GSTN ... Garston
GT/LBKH ... Great Bookham/Little Bookham
GTDUN ... Great Dunmow
GTMIS/PWD ... Great Missenden/Prestwood
GTPST ... Great Portland Street
GU ... Guildford
GUW ... Guildford west
GVE ... Gravesend east
GVW ... Gravesend west
GWRST ... Gower Street
HACK ... Hackney
HAMP ... Hampstead
HARH ... Harold Hill
HARP ... Harpenden
HART ... Hartley
HAT ... Hatfield
HAYES ... Hayes
HBRY ... Highbury
HCH ... Hornchurch
HCIRC ... Holborn Circus
HDN ... Hendon
HDTCH ... Houndsditch
HERT/BAY ... Hertford/Bayford
HERT/WAT ... Hertford/Watton at Stone
HEST ... Heston
HGDN/ICK ... Hillingdon/Ickenham
HGT ... Highgate
HHNE ... Hemel Hempstead northeast
HHOL ... High Holborn
HHS/BOV ... Hemel Hempstead south/Bovingdon
HHW ... Hemel Hempstead west
HLW ... Harlow
HLWE ... Harlow east
HLWS ... Harlow south
HLWW/ROY ... Harlow west/Roydon
HMSMTH ... Hammersmith
HNHL ... Herne Hill
HNWL ... Hanwell
HOD ... Hoddesdon
HOL/ALD ... Holborn/Aldwych
HOLWY ... Holloway
HOM ... Homerton
HOR/WEW ... Horton/West Ewell
HORL ... Horley
HORS ... Horsham
HPTN ... Hampton
HRW ... Harrow
HSLW ... Hounslow
HSLWW ... Hounslow west
HTHAIR ... Heathrow Airport
HYS/HAR ... Hayes/Harlington
IL ... Ilford
ING ... Ingatestone
IS ... Islington
ISLW ... Isleworth
IVER ... Iver
KENS ... Kensington
KGLGY ... Kings Langley
KIL/WHAMP ... Kilburn/West Hampstead
KTBR ... Knightsbridge
KTN/HRWW/WS ... Kenton/Harrow Weald/Wealdstone
KTTN ... Kentish Town
KUT/HW ... Kingston upon Thames/Hampton Wick
KUTN/CMB ... Kingston upon Thames north/Coombe
KWD/TDW/WH ... Kingswood/Tadworth/Walton on the Hill
LBTH ... Lambeth
LCOL/BKTW ... London Colney/Bricket Wood
LEE/GVPK ... Lee/Grove Park
LEW ... Lewisham
LEY ... Leyton
LHD/OX ... Leatherhead/Oxshott
LING ... Lingfield
LINN ... Lincoln's Inn
LOTH ... Lothbury
LOU ... Loughton
LSQ/SEVD ... Leicester Square/Seven Dials
LTWR ... Lightwater
LVPST ... Liverpool Street
MANHO ... Mansion House
MBLAR ... Marble Arch
MDHD ... Maidenhead
MEO ... Meopham
MFD/CHID ... Milford/Chiddingfold
MHST ... Marylebone High Street
MLHL ... Mill Hill
MNPK ... Manor Park
MON ... Monument
MORT/ESHN ... Mortlake/East Sheen
MRDN ... Morden
MTCM ... Mitcham
MUSWH ... Muswell Hill
MV/WKIL ... Maida Vale/West Kilburn
MYFR/PICC ... Mayfair/Piccadilly
MYFR/PKLN ... Mayfair/Park Lane
NFNCH/WDSPK ... North Finchley/Woodside Park
NKENS ... North Kensington
NOXST/BSQ ... New Oxford Street/Bloomsbury Square
NRWD ... Norwood
NTGHL ... Notting Hill
NTHLT ... Northolt
NTHWD ... Northwood
NWCR ... New Cross
NWDGN ... Norwood Green
NWMAL ... New Malden
OBST ... Old Broad Street
ORP ... Orpington
OXHEY ... Oxhey
OXSTW ... Oxford Street west
OXTED ... Oxted
PECK ... Peckham
PEND ... Ponders End
PGE/AN ... Penge/Anerley
PIM ... Pimlico
PIN ... Pinner
PLMGR ... Palmers Green
PLSTW ... Plaistow
POP/IOD ... Poplar/Isle of Dogs
POTB/CUF ... Potters Bar/Cuffley
PUR ... Purfleet
PUR/KEN ... Purley/Kenley
PUT/ROE ... Putney/Roehampton
RAD ... Radlett
RAIN ... Rainham (Gt Lon)
RBRW/HUT ... Rural Brentwood/Hutton
RBSF ... Rural Bishop's Stortford
RCH/KEW ... Richmond/Kew
RCHPK/HAM ... Richmond Park/Ham
RDART ... Rural Dartford
RDKG ... Rural Dorking
REDBR ... Redbridge
REDH ... Redhill
REGST ... Regent Street
REIG ... Reigate
RFNM ... Rural Farnham
RGUE ... Rural Guildford east
RGUW ... Rural Guildford west
RKW/CH/CXG ... Rickmansworth/Chorleywood/Croxley Green
ROM ... Romford
ROMW/RG ... Romford west/Rush Green
RPLY/SEND ... Ripley/Send
RSEV ... Rural Sevenoaks
RSLP ... Ruislip
RSQ ... Russell Square
RTON ... Rural Tonbridge
RYLN/HDSTN ... Rayners Lane/Headstone
RYNPK ... Raynes Park
SAND/SEL ... Sanderstead/Selsdon
SBW ... Sawbridgeworth
SCUP ... Sidcup
SDTCH ... Shoreditch
SEV ... Sevenoaks
SEVS/STOTM ... Seven Sisters/South Tottenham
SHB ... Shepherd's Bush
SHGR ... Shamley Green
SHPTN ... Shepperton
SKENS ... South Kensington
SL ... Slough
SLH/COR ... Stanford-le-Hope/Corringham
SLN ... Slough north
SNWD ... South Norwood
SOCK/AV ... South Ockendon/Aveley
SOHO/CST ... Soho/Carnaby Street
SOHO/SHAV ... Soho/Shaftesbury Avenue
SRTFD ... Stratford
STA ... Staines
STAL ... St Albans
STALE/WH ... St Albans east/Wheathampstead
STALW/RED ... St Albans west/Redbourn
STAN ... Stanmore
STBT ... St Bart's
STHGT/OAK ... Southgate/Oakwood
STHL ... Southall
STHWK ... Southwark
STJS ... St James's
STJSPK ... St James's Park
STJWD ... St John's Wood
STKPK ... Stockley Park
STLK ... St Luke's
STMC/STPC ... St Mary Cray/St Paul's Cray
STNW/STAM ... Stoke Newington/Stamford Hill
STP ... St Paul's
STPAN ... St Pancras
STRHM/NOR ... Streatham/Norbury
STWL/WRAY ... Stanwell/Wraysbury
SUN ... Sunbury
SURB ... Surbiton
SUT ... Sutton
SWCM ... Swanscombe
SWFD ... South Woodford
SWLY ... Swanley
SYD ... Sydenham
TEDD ... Teddington
THDIT ... Thames Ditton
THHTH ... Thornton Heath
THMD ... Thamesmead
TIL ... Tilbury
TOOT ... Tooting
TOTM ... Tottenham
TPL/STR ... Temple/Strand
TRDG/WHET ... Totteridge/Whetstone
TRING ... Tring
TWK ... Twickenham
TWRH ... Tower Hill
UED ... Upper Edmonton
UPMR ... Upminster
UX/CGN ... Uxbridge/Colham Green
VW ... Virginia Water
VX/NE ... Vauxhall/Nine Elms
WAB ... Waltham Abbey
WALTH ... Walthamstow
WALW ... Walworth
WAN ... Wanstead
WAND/EARL ... Wandsworth/Earlsfield
WAP ... Wapping
WARE ... Ware
WARL ... Warlingham
WAT ... Watford
WATN ... Watford north
WATW ... Watford west
WBLY ... Wembley
WBPTN ... West Brompton
WCHMH ... Winchmore Hill
WCHPL ... Whitechapel
WDGN ... Wood Green
WDR/YW ... West Drayton/Yiewsley
WDSR ... Windsor
WEA ... West Ealing
WELL ... Welling
WEST ... Westminster
WESTW ... Westminster west
WEY ... Weybridge
WFD ... Woodford
WGCE ... Welwyn Garden City east
WGCW ... Welwyn Garden City west
WHALL ... Whitehall
WHTN ... Whitton
WIM/MER ... Wimbledon/Merton
WKENS ... West Kensington
WLGTN ... Wallington
WLSDN ... Willesden
WLYN ... Welwyn
WNWD ... West Norwood
WOKN/KNAP ... Woking north/Knaphill
WOKS/MYFD ... Woking south/Mayford
WOOL/PLUM ... Woolwich/Plumstead
WOT/HER ... Walton-on-Thames/Hersham
WPK ... Worcester Park
WTHK ... West Thurrock
WWKM ... West Wickham
YEAD ... Yeading

# Index - streets



## 1

1 Av WOOL/PLUM SE18 ... 162 E2
1st Av KWD/TDW/WH KT20 ... 257 H1
2nd Av KWD/TDW/WH KT20 ... 257 H1
3rd Av KWD/TDW/WH KT20 ... 257 H1
4th Av KWD/TDW/WH KT20 ... 257 H1
5th Av KWD/TDW/WH KT20 ... 257 H1
6th Av KWD/TDW/WH KT20 ... 257 H1
7th Av KWD/TDW/WH KT20 ... 257 H1
8th Av KWD/TDW/WH KT20 ... 257 H2
9th Av KWD/TDW/WH KT20 ... 257 H1
10th Av KWD/TDW/WH KT20 ... 257 H2
11th Av KWD/TDW/WH KT20 ... 257 H1
12th Av KWD/TDW/WH KT20 ... 257 H2
13th Av KWD/TDW/WH KT20 ... 257 H2
14th Av KWD/TDW/WH KT20 ... 257 H2
15th Av KWD/TDW/WH KT20 ... 257 J2
16th Av KWD/TDW/WH KT20 ... 257 H2

## A

Aaron Hill Rd EHAM E6 ... 142 D7
Abberley Ms BTSEA SW11 ... 158 C9
Abbess Cl BRXS/STRHM SW2 ... 181 J4
Abbeville Ms CLAP SW4 * ... 180 E1
Abbeville Rd CEND/HSY/T N8 ... 118 E2
CLAP SW4 ... 180 D2
Abbey Av ALP/SUD HA0 ... 135 K4
STALW/RED AL3 ... 37 P9
Abbey Cha CHERT KT16 * ... 195 L6
Abbey Cl HYS/HAR UB3 ... 133 J10
NTHLT UB5 ... 133 N5
ORP BR6 ... 227 L1
PIN HA5 ... 113 J1
ROM RM1 ... 124 G4
SL SL1 ... 128 D9
WOKS/MYFD GU22 ... 233 H2
Abbey Ct CHERT KT16 * ... 195 L7
WAB EN9 ... 62 G10
Abbey Crs BELV DA17 ... 164 B3
Abbey Dale Cl HLWE CM17 ... 47 M2
Abbeydale Rd ALP/SUD HA0 ... 135 L3
Abbey Dr ABLGY WD5 ... 55 H8
STA TW18 ... 195 M3
TOOT SW17 ... 180 B8
Abbeyfield Cl MTCM CR4 ... 201 P2
Abbeyfield Est
BERM/RHTH SE16 ... 160 B3
Abbeyfield Rd
BERM/RHTH SE16 ... 160 B3
Abbeyfields Cl WLSDN NW10 ... 135 M5
Abbey Gdns BERM/RHTH SE16 ... 19 P5
CHERT KT16 ... 195 K6
CHST BR7 ... 206 D1
HMSMTH W6 ... 14 A10
STJWD NW8 ... 3 J8
Abbey Gn CHERT KT16 ... 195 K6
Abbey Gv ABYW SE2 ... 163 L3
Abbeyhill Rd BFN/LL DA15 ... 185 M4
Abbey La BECK BR3 ... 182 F10
SRTFD E15 ... 141 H4
Abbey Mdw CHERT KT16 ... 195 M7
Abbey Ms ISLW TW7 ... 154 G7
STA TW18 * ... 195 M3
STAL AL1 * ... 38 C7
WALTH E17 ... 120 F3
Abbey Mill End
STALW/RED AL3 ... 38 B7
Abbey Mill La STALW/RED AL3 ... 38 B7
Abbey Mt BELV DA17 ... 164 A4
Abbey Orchard St WEST SW1P ... 17 K3
Abbey Pk BECK BR3 ... 182 F10
Abbey Park La SL SL1 ... 108 D7
Abbey Pl CHERT KT16 ... 195 K3
DART DA1 * ... 187 L1
Abbey Rd BARK IG11 ... 142 E3
BELV DA17 ... 163 N3
BXLYHN DA7 ... 163 P10
CHERT KT16 ... 195 L7
CHES/WCR EN8 ... 62 D10
CROY/NA CR0 ... 203 J10
EN EN1 ... 79 M9
GNTH/NBYPK IG2 ... 122 G3
GVE DA12 ... 191 H4
KIL/WHAMP NW6 ... 2 G5
SAND/SEL CR2 ... 224 C6
SHPTN TW17 ... 196 B8
SRTFD E15 ... 141 J4
STJWD NW8 ... 3 J6
SWCM DA10 ... 189 H1
VW GU25 ... 194 A5
WIM/MER SW19 ... 179 M10
WLSDN NW10 ... 135 N4
WOKN/KNAP GU21 ... 231 P3
Abbey St PLSTW E13 ... 141 M6
STHWK SE1 ... 19 L3
Abbey Ter ABYW SE2 ... 163 M2
Abbey Vw MLHL NW7 ... 96 C4
RAD WD7 ... 74 E1
Abbeyview WAB EN9 ... 62 G9
Abbey View Rd
STALW/RED AL3 ... 38 B6
Abbey Wk E/WMO/HCT KT8 ... 198 A3
Abbey Wd ASC SL5 ... 192 F7
Abbey Wood La RAIN RM13 ... 145 L4
Abbey Wood Rd ABYW SE2 ... 163 L3
Abbot Cl BF/WBF KT14 ... 215 N6
RSLP HA4 ... 113 L8
STA TW18 ... 173 N10
Abbot Rd GU GU1 ... 268 A2
Abbots Av HOR/WEW KT19 ... 219 M7
STAL AL1 ... 38 D9
Abbots Av West STAL AL1 ... 38 C9
Abbotsbury Cl SRTFD E15 ... 141 H4
WKENS W14 ... 14 C2
Abbotsbury Gdns PIN HA5 ... 113 K4
Abbotsbury Ms PECK SE15 ... 160 B9
Abbotsbury Rd MRDN SM4 ... 201 L4
NTGHL W11 ... 14 B1
WWKM BR4 ... 205 L9
Abbots Cl BRWN CM15 ... 107 M2
RAIN RM13 ... 145 K4
STMC/STPC BR5 ... 206 F8
Abbot's Cl GUW GU2 ... 267 K3
Abbots Dr RYLN/HDSTN HA2 ... 113 P7
VW GU25 ... 193 P4
Abbotsfield Rd CRAWW RH11 ... 282 G8
Abbotsford Av
SEVS/STOTM N15 ... 119 K2
Abbotsford Cl
WOKS/MYFD GU22 ... 232 D3
Abbotsford Gdns WFD IG8 ... 101 M8
Abbotsford Rd
GDMY/SEVK IG3 ... 123 K7
Abbots Gdns EFNCH N2 ... 117 N2
Abbots Gn CROY/NA CR0 ... 224 C3
Abbotshade Rd
BERM/RHTH SE16 * ... 140 C10
Abbotshall Av STHGT/OAK N14 ... 98 D4
Abbotshall Rd CAT SE6 ... 183 J4
Abbots Hl HHS/BOV HP3 * ... 54 C1
Abbots La PUR/KEN CR8 ... 241 K2
Abbotsleigh Cl BELMT SM2 ... 221 L4
Abbotsleigh Rd
STRHM/NOR SW16 ... 180 D7
Abbots Mnr PIM SW1V ... 16 E7
Abbots Manor Est PIM SW1V ... 16 E7
Abbotsmede Cl TWK TW1 ... 176 E5
Abbots Pk BRXS/STRHM SW2 ... 181 H4
STAL AL1 ... 38 E8
Abbots Pl BORE WD6 ... 75 N4
Abbot's Pl KIL/WHAMP NW6 ... 2 G5
Abbots Ri KGLGY WD4 ... 54 A3
Abbots Rd ABLGY WD5 ... 54 D7
EDGW HA8 ... 96 A8
EHAM E6 ... 142 A3
Abbots Ter CEND/HSY/T N8 ... 118 F4
Abbotstone Rd
PUT/ROE SW15 ... 156 F9
Abbot St HACK E8 ... 7 L1
Abbots Vw KGLGY WD4 ... 54 A2
Abbots Wk CTHM CR3 ... 242 A8
KENS W8 * ... 14 G4
Abbot's Wk WDSR SL4 ... 148 D8
Abbots Wy BECK BR3 ... 204 D5
CHERT KT16 ... 195 J7
Abbot's Wy GU GU1 ... 250 G9
Abbotsweld HLWS CM18 ... 46 G4
Abbotswell Rd BROCKY SE4 ... 182 E1
Abbotswood GU GU1 ... 250 C8
Abbotswood Cl BELV DA17 ... 163 P2
GU GU1 ... 250 C7
Abbotswood Dr WEY KT13 ... 216 E6
Abbotswood Gdns CLAY IG5 ... 122 C1
Abbotswood Rd EDUL SE22 ... 159 M10
STRHM/NOR SW16 ... 180 E6
Abbotswood Wy
HYS/HAR UB3 ... 133 J10
Abbott Av RYNPK SW20 ... 200 G2
Abbott Cl HPTN TW12 ... 175 M9
NTHLT UB5 ... 133 N1
Abbott Rd POP/IOD E14 ... 141 H7
Abbotts Cl IS N1 * ... 6 E3
ROMW/RG RM7 ... 124 C1
SWLY BR8 ... 209 H4
THMD SE28 ... 143 M9
Abbott's Cl UX/CGN UB8 ... 131 N7
Abbotts Ct WARE SG12 ... 27 J7
Abbotts Crs CHING E4 ... 101 J5
ENC/FH EN2 ... 79 J6
Abbotts Dr ALP/SUD HA0 ... 114 G7
WAB EN9 ... 63 M10
Abbotts Md
RCHPK/HAM TW10 * ... 177 H7
Abbotts Park Rd LEY E10 ... 121 H5
Abbotts Ri REDH RH1 ... 258 B8
WARE SG12 ... 27 J7
Abbotts Rd BAR EN5 ... 77 L8
CHEAM SM3 ... 221 H1
MTCM CR4 ... 202 D4
STHL UB1 ... 133 M10
Abbotts Tilt WOT/HER KT12 ... 197 M10
Abbotts V CSHM HP5 ... 51 H4
Abbott's Wk BXLYHN DA7 ... 163 N6
Abbotts Wy SL SL1 ... 128 C10
WARE SG12 ... 27 J7
Abbs Cross Gdns HCH RM12 ... 125 K6
Abbs Cross La HCH RM12 ... 125 K8
Abchurch La MANHO EC4N ... 13 H7
Abdale La BRKMPK AL9 ... 58 E3
Abdale Rd SHB W12 ... 136 E10
Abel Cl HHNE HP2 ... 36 B6
Abelia Cl CHOB/PIR GU24 ... 212 D9
Abenberg Wy
RBRW/HUT CM13 ... 107 M3
Aberavon Rd BOW E3 ... 140 D5
Abercairn Rd
STRHM/NOR SW16 ... 180 D10
Aberconway Rd MRDN SM4 ... 201 L3
Abercorn Cl MLHL NW7 ... 97 H8
SAND/SEL CR2 ... 224 C8
STJWD NW8 ... 3 J8
Abercorn Crs
RYLN/HDSTN HA2 ... 114 A6
Abercorn Dell BUSH WD23 ... 94 B3
Abercorn Gdns CHDH RM6 ... 123 L4
KTN/HRWW/WS HA3 ... 115 J5
Abercorn Gv RSLP HA4 ... 112 E2
Abercorn Ms
RCHPK/HAM TW10 ... 177 L1
Abercorn Pl STJWD NW8 ... 3 J9
Abercorn Rd MLHL NW7 ... 97 H8
STAN HA7 ... 95 H8
Abercorn Wk STJWD NW8 ... 3 J9
Abercorn Wy STHWK SE1 ... 19 N7
WOKN/KNAP GU21 ... 231 M4
Abercrombie Dr EN EN1 ... 79 P5
Abercrombie St BTSEA SW11 ... 157 P8
Abercrombie Wy
HLWW/ROY CM19 ... 46 F3
Aberdale Gdns POTB/CUF EN6 ... 59 J9
Aberdare Cl WWKM BR4 ... 205 H9
Aberdare Gdns
KIL/WHAMP NW6 ... 3 H4
MLHL NW7 ... 96 G8
Aberdare Rd PEND EN3 ... 80 B8
Aberdeen Av SL SL1 ... 128 F9
Aberdeen Cots STAN HA7 * ... 95 H8
Aberdeen La HBRY N5 ... 119 J10
Aberdeen Pde UED N18 * ... 100 A6
Aberdeen Pk HBRY N5 ... 119 J10
Aberdeen Pl BAY/PAD W2 ... 9 L2
Aberdeen Rd CROY/NA CR0 ... 223 K1
HBRY N5 ... 119 K9
KTN/HRWW/WS HA3 ... 94 E10
UED N18 ... 99 P6
WLSDN NW10 ... 116 C10
Aberdeen Ter BKHTH/KID SE3 ... 161 J8
Aberdour Rd GDMY/SEVK IG3 ... 123 L8
Aberdour St STHWK SE1 ... 19 J5
Aberfeldy St POP/IOD E14 ... 141 H8
Aberford Gdns
WOOL/PLUM SE18 ... 162 B7
Aberford Rd BORE WD6 ... 75 M6
Aberfoyle Rd
STRHM/NOR SW16 ... 180 E10
Abergeldie Rd LEE/GVPK SE12 ... 183 N2
Abernethy Rd LEW SE13 ... 161 K10
Abersham Rd HACK E8 ... 119 N10
Abery St WOOL/PLUM SE18 ... 163 H3
Abigail Ms HARH RM3 ... 105 P10
Abingdon Cl CAMTN NW1 ... 5 J2
HGDN/ICK UB10 ... 132 A3
WIM/MER SW19 ... 179 M9
WOKN/KNAP GU21 ... 231 N4
WPK KT4 ... 200 E10
Abingdon Pl POTB/CUF EN6 ... 59 L8
Abingdon Rd FNCH N3 ... 97 M10
KENS W8 ... 14 F4
STRHM/NOR SW16 ... 202 F1
Abingdon St WEST SW1P ... 17 L2
Abingdon Vls KENS W8 ... 14 E4
Abingdon Wy ORP BR6 ... 227 L1
Abinger Av BELMT SM2 ... 220 F5
Abinger Cl BMLY BR1 ... 206 B3
CROY/NA CR0 ... 225 H3
GDMY/SEVK IG3 ... 123 K9
RDKG RH5 ... 273 H6
WLGTN SM6 ... 222 F2
Abinger Common Rd
RDKG RH5 ... 271 M10
Abinger Dr NRWD SE19 ... 181 K10
REDH RH1 ... 275 P2
Abinger Gdns ISLW TW7 ... 154 D9
Abinger Gv DEPT SE8 ... 160 E5
Abinger La RDKG RH5 ... 271 K8
Abinger Ms MV/WKIL W9 ... 8 E1
Abinger Rd CHSWK W4 ... 156 C2
REDH RH1 ... 275 P3
Abinger Wy RGUE GU4 ... 250 E5
Ablett St BERM/RHTH SE16 ... 160 B4
Abney Park Ter
STNW/STAM N16 * ... 119 N7
Aboyne Dr RYNPK SW20 ... 200 D2
Aboyne Rd TOOT SW17 ... 179 M6
WLSDN NW10 ... 116 B8
Abraham Cl OXHEY WD19 ... 93 J5
Abraham Ct UPMR RM14 ... 125 P7
Abridge Cl CHES/WCR EN8 ... 80 C1
Abridge Gdns CRW RM5 ... 104 B7
Abridge Rd CHIG IG7 ... 83 H10
Abridge Wy BARK IG11 ... 143 L4
Abyssinia Cl BTSEA SW11 ... 157 P10
Abyssinia Rd BTSEA SW11 * ... 157 P10
Acacia Av BTFD TW8 ... 154 G6
HCH RM12 ... 124 G7
HYS/HAR UB3 ... 132 G8
RSLP HA4 ... 113 H6
SHPTN TW17 ... 196 B5
STWL/WRAY TW19 ... 150 B10
TOTM N17 ... 99 L8
WBLY HA9 ... 115 K10
WDR/YW UB7 ... 132 A9
WOKS/MYFD GU22 ... 232 A6
Acacia Cl ADL/WDHM KT15 ... 215 J6
CHESW EN7 ... 61 M3
CSHM HP5 ... 50 F6
DEPT SE8 ... 160 D3
STAN HA7 ... 94 D7
STMC/STPC BR5 ... 206 G5
Acacia Dr ADL/WDHM KT15 ... 215 J7
BNSTD SM7 ... 220 G10
CHEAM SM3 ... 201 J8
UPMR RM14 ... 125 P9
Acacia Gdns STJWD NW8 ... 3 M7
UPMR RM14 ... 126 E5
WWKM BR4 ... 205 H9
Acacia Gv BERK HP4 ... 33 N6
DUL SE21 ... 181 L5
NWMAL KT3 ... 200 B3
Acacia Ms WDR/YW UB7 ... 151 N5
Acacia Pl STJWD NW8 ... 3 M7
Acacia Rd ACT W3 ... 135 P9
BECK BR3 ... 204 E3
ENC/FH EN2 ... 79 L5
GU GU1 ... 250 A10
HPTN TW12 ... 175 P9
MTCM CR4 ... 202 B2
RDART DA2 ... 188 D2
STA TW18 ... 173 L8
STJWD NW8 ... 3 M7
STRHM/NOR SW16 ... 202 F1
WALTH E17 ... 120 D4
WAN E11 ... 121 K7
WDGN N22 ... 99 H9
The Acacias EBAR EN4 * ... 77 N9
Acacia St HAT AL10 ... 40 D7
Acacia Wk HARP AL5 ... 20 C5
Acacia Wy BFN/LL DA15 ... 185 J3
Academia Wy TOTM N17 ... 99 M7
Academy Fields Rd GPK RM2 ... 125 J3
Academy Gdns CROY/NA CR0 ... 203 N8
NTHLT UB5 ... 133 L4
Academy Pl ISLW TW7 ... 154 D6
WOOL/PLUM SE18 ... 162 C7
Academy Rd
WOOL/PLUM SE18 ... 162 C6
Acanthus Dr STHWK SE1 ... 19 N7
Acanthus Rd BTSEA SW11 ... 158 B9
Accommodation La
WDR/YW UB7 ... 151 M5
Accommodation Rd
CHERT KT16 ... 214 B1
GLDGN NW11 ... 117 J5
Ace Pde CHSGTN KT9 ... 199 K10
Acer Av RAIN RM13 ... 145 L5
YEAD UB4 ... 133 M6
Acer Dr CHOB/PIR GU24 ... 212 E9
Acer Rd BH/WHM TN16 ... 244 A2
Acers LCOL/BKTW AL2 ... 56 B4
Acfold Rd FUL/PGN SW6 ... 157 L7
Achilles Cl HHNE HP2 ... 36 A4
STHWK SE1 ... 19 P7
Achilles Pl WOKN/KNAP GU21 ... 231 P3
Achilles Rd KIL/WHAMP NW6 ... 117 K10
Achilles St NWCR SE14 ... 160 D6
Acklam Rd NKENS W10 ... 8 C3
Acklington Dr
CDALE/KGS NW9 ... 96 B9
Ackmar Rd FUL/PGN SW6 ... 157 K7
Ackroyd Dr BOW E3 ... 140 E7
Ackroyd Rd FSTH SE23 ... 182 C3
Acland Cl WOOL/PLUM SE18 ... 162 G6
Acland Crs CMBW SE5 ... 159 L10
Acland Rd CRICK NW2 ... 136 E1
Acle Cl BARK/HLT IG6 ... 102 E9
Acme Rd WATN WD24 ... 73 H4
Acock Gv NTHLT UB5 ... 114 A9
Acol Crs RSLP HA4 ... 113 J10
Acol Rd KIL/WHAMP NW6 ... 2 F4
Acorn Cl CHING E4 ... 100 G6
CHST BR7 ... 184 F8
DTCH/LGLY SL3 ... 150 E4
ENC/FH EN2 ... 79 H5
HORL RH6 ... 280 D3
HPTN TW12 ... 176 A9
STAN HA7 ... 94 G8
Acorn Gdns ACT W3 ... 136 A7
NRWD SE19 ... 203 N1
Acorn Gv HYS/HAR UB3 ... 152 G6
KWD/TDW/WH KT20 ... 239 J10
RSLP HA4 ... 112 G9
WOKS/MYFD GU22 * ... 232 B7
Acorn La POTB/CUF EN6 ... 60 F5
Acorn Pde PECK SE15 * ... 160 A6
Acorn Pl WATN WD24 ... 73 H3
Acorn Rd DART DA1 ... 186 G1
HHS/BOV HP3 ... 36 B7
The Acorns HORL RH6 ... 281 J4
SEV TN13 ... 247 H9
STALE/WH AL4 * ... 39 J6
Acorn St WARE SG12 ... 28 A4
Acorns Wy ESH/CLAY KT10 ... 218 B2
Acorn Wy BECK BR3 ... 205 H5
FSTH SE23 ... 182 C6
ORP BR6 ... 226 E1
Acre Dr EDUL SE22 ... 159 P10
Acrefield Rd CFSP/GDCR SL9 ... 110 A2
Acre La BRXS/STRHM SW2 ... 158 G10
CAR SM5 ... 222 B1
Acre Rd DAGE RM10 ... 144 C2
KUTN/CMB KT2 ... 199 K1
WIM/MER SW19 ... 179 N9
Acres Av CHONG CM5 ... 67 N2
Acres End AMSS HP7 ... 69 K5
Acres Gdns
KWD/TDW/WH KT20 ... 238 F5
Acre Wy NTHWD HA6 ... 92 G9
Acre Wd HHNE HP2 ... 35 P6
Acrewood Wy STALE/WH AL4 ... 39 L6
Acris St WAND/EARL SW18 ... 179 M1
Acton Cl CHES/WCR EN8 ... 62 D7
ED N9 ... 99 P3
Acton Hill Ms ACT W3 * ... 135 N10
Acton La CHSWK W4 ... 155 P2
Acton Ms HACK E8 ... 7 L5
Acton St FSBYW WC1X ... 5 N10
Acuba Rd WAND/EARL SW18 ... 179 L5
Acworth Cl ED N9 ... 100 B1
Acworth Pl DART DA1 * ... 187 K2

| Name | Area | Page | Grid |
|---|---|---|---|
| Ada Cl | *FBAR/BDGN* N11 | 98 | A4 |
| Ada Gdns | *POP/IOD* E14 | 141 | J8 |
| | *SRTFD* E15 | 141 | L1 |
| Adair Cl | *SNWD* SE25 | 204 | A3 |
| Adair Gdns | *CTHM* CR3 | 241 | K7 |
| Adair Rd | *NKENS* W10 | 8 | B2 |
| | *FSTH* SE23 | 182 | E1 |
| | *SL* SL1 | 128 | F10 |
| Adam & Eve Ms | *KENS* W8 | 14 | C4 |
| Adam Cl | *CAT* SE6 | 182 | E7 |
| | *FNCH* N3 | 97 | K8 |
| | *WBLY* HA9 | 115 | N7 |
| Adam Ct | *CBIST* EC1N | 13 | L5 |
| Adams Ct | *CHOB/PIR* GU24 | 230 | B6 |
| Adams House | *HLW* CM20 | 28 | G10 |
| Adams Ms | *TOOT* SW17 | 180 | A5 |
| | *WDGN* N22 | 98 | G8 |
| Adamson Rd | *CAN/RD* E16 | 141 | J6 |
| | *HAMP* NW3 | 3 | M3 |
| Adams Pl | *HOLWY* N7 | 118 | G10 |
| Adamsrill Cl | *EN* EN1 | 79 | L10 |
| Adamsrill Rd | *SYD* SE26 | 182 | C7 |
| Adams Rd | *BECK* BR3 | 204 | D5 |
| | *TOTM* N17 | 99 | H1 |
| Adam's Rw | *MYFR/PKLN* W1K | 10 | D8 |
| Adam St | *BXLYHS* DA6 | 163 | J5 |
| Adams Wk | *KUT/HW* KT1 | 199 | K2 |
| Adams Wy | *CROY/NA* CR0 | 203 | N6 |
| Adam Wk | *FUL/PGN* SW6 | 156 | F6 |
| Ada Pl | *BETH* E2 | 7 | P6 |
| Ada Rd | *STRHM/NOR* SW16 | 181 | M6 |
| | *ALP/SUD* HA0 | 115 | H8 |
| | *CMBW* SE5 | 159 | M6 |
| Ada St | *HACK* E8 | 140 | A3 |
| Adderley Gdns | *ELTH/MOT* SE9 | 183 | M5 |
| Adderley Rd | *KTN/HRWW/WS* HA3 | 94 | E9 |
| Adderley Gv | *BTSEA* SW11 | 180 | B1 |
| Adderley St | *POP/IOD* E14 | 141 | N8 |
| Adderley Dr | *NFNCH/WDSPK* N12 | 97 | N7 |
| Addington Cl | *WDSR* SL4 | 148 | F8 |
| Addington Gv | *SYD* SE26 | 182 | D7 |
| Addington Rd | *BOW* E3 | 140 | F5 |
| | *CAN/RD* E16 | 141 | K6 |
| | *CROY/NA* CR0 | 203 | H8 |
| | *FSBYPK* N4 | 119 | H5 |
| | *SAND/SEL* CR2 | 223 | P7 |
| | *WWKM* BR4 | 225 | H1 |
| Addington Sq | *STHWK* SE5 | 159 | K6 |
| Addington Village Rd | *CROY/NA* CR0 | 224 | E3 |
| Addis Cl | *PEND* EN3 | 80 | C5 |
| Addiscombe Av | *CROY/NA* CR0 | 203 | P7 |
| Addiscombe Cl | *KTN/HRWW/WS* HA3 | 115 | H3 |
| Addiscombe Court Rd | *CROY/NA* CR0 | 203 | M8 |
| Addiscombe Gv | *CROY/NA* CR0 | 203 | M9 |
| Addiscombe Rd | *WATW* WD18 | 73 | J3 |
| Addison Av | *HSLW* TW3 | 154 | B7 |
| | *NTGHL* W11 | 8 | A10 |
| | *STHGT/OAK* N14 | 78 | C10 |
| Addison Bridge Pl | *WKENS* W14 | 14 | B5 |
| Addison Cl | *CTHM* CR3 | 241 | L8 |
| | *IVER* SL0 | 131 | H9 |
| | *NTHWD* HA6 | 93 | H9 |
| | *STMC/STPC* BR5 | 206 | F6 |
| Addison Ct | *EPP* CM16 | 65 | J10 |
| Addison Crs | *WKENS* W14 | 14 | B5 |
| Addison Gdns | *BRYLDS* KT5 | 199 | L4 |
| | *WKENS* W14 | 156 | G2 |
| Addison Gv | *CHSWK* W4 | 156 | C1 |
| Addison Pl | *NTGHL* W11 | 8 | A10 |
| Addison Rd | *BARK/HLT* IG6 | 102 | F3 |
| | *CSHM* HP5 | 51 | H5 |
| | *CTHM* CR3 | 241 | L7 |
| | *GU* GU1 | 268 | C2 |
| | *HAYES* BR2 | 206 | A5 |
| | *PEND* EN3 | 80 | B5 |
| | *SNWD* SE25 | 203 | P4 |
| | *TEDD* TW11 | 176 | C9 |
| | *WALTH* E17 | 120 | G3 |
| | *WAN* E11 | 121 | M4 |
| | *WKENS* W14 | 14 | B2 |
| Addison's Cl | *CROY/NA* CR0 | 204 | A9 |
| Addison Ter | *CHSWK* W4 | 155 | P3 |
| Addison Wy | *GLDGN* NW11 | 117 | J1 |
| | *HYS/HAR* UB3 | 133 | H8 |
| | *NTHWD* HA6 | 92 | G9 |
| Addle Hl | *BLKFR* EC4V | 12 | D7 |
| Addlestone Moor | *ADL/WDHM* KT15 | 195 | M9 |
| Addlestone Pk | *ADL/WDHM* KT15 | 215 | L2 |
| Addlestone Rd | *ADL/WDHM* KT15 | 215 | P1 |
| Addle St | *CITYW* EC2V | 12 | F5 |
| Adecroft Wy | *E/WMO/HCT* KT8 | 198 | B1 |
| Adela Av | *NWMAL* KT3 | 200 | E5 |
| Adelaide Av | *BROCKY* SE4 | 160 | F10 |
| Adelaide Cl | *CRAWR* RH11 | 283 | N4 |
| | *EN* EN1 | 79 | M4 |
| | *SL* SL1 | 148 | F1 |
| | *STAN* HA7 | 94 | F5 |
| Adelaide Gdns | *CHDH* RM6 | 123 | P4 |
| Adelaide Gv | *SHB* W12 | 136 | D10 |
| Adelaide Pl | *WEY* KT13 | 216 | E1 |
| Adelaide Rd | *ASHF* TW15 | 173 | N8 |
| | *CHST* BR7 | 184 | E8 |
| | *HAMP* NW3 | 3 | M3 |
| | *HEST* TW5 | 135 | M7 |
| | *IL* IG1 | 122 | E7 |
| | *LEY* E10 | 121 | H8 |
| | *NWDGN* UB2 | 153 | M3 |
| | *PUT/ROE* SW15 | 155 | K1 |
| | *RCH/KEW* TW9 | 155 | L10 |
| | *STJWD* NW8 | 3 | L4 |
| | *SURB* KT6 | 199 | K5 |
| | *TEDD* TW11 | 176 | E9 |
| | *TIL* RM18 | 168 | C7 |
| | *WDSR* SL4 | 146 | E3 |
| | *WEA* W13 | 154 | F1 |
| | *WOT/HER* KT12 | 197 | H10 |
| Adelaide Sq | *STALW/RED* SL4 | 149 | J8 |
| Adela St | *NKENS* W10 | 8 | C1 |
| Adelina Gv | *WCHPL* E1 | 140 | E7 |
| Adelina Ms | *BAL* SW12 | 180 | G2 |
| Adeline Pl | *RSQ* WC1B | 11 | K4 |
| Adeliza Cl | *BARK* IG11 | 142 | C1 |
| Adelphi Crs | *HCH* RM12 | 125 | J1 |
| | *YEAD* UB4 | 132 | G4 |
| Adelphi Gdns | *SL* SL1 | 149 | K5 |
| Adelphi Rd | *EW* KT17 | 220 | H3 |
| Adelphi Ter | *CHCR* WC2N | 11 | M8 |
| Adelphi Wy | *YEAD* UB4 | 132 | G5 |
| Adeney Cl | *HMSMTH* W6 | 156 | G5 |
| Adenmore Rd | *CAT* SE6 | 182 | E5 |
| Aden Rd | *IL* IG1 | 122 | C3 |
| | *PEND* EN3 | 80 | D8 |
| Adeyfield Gdns | *HHNE* HP2 | 36 | A5 |
| Adeyfield Rd | *HHNE* HP2 | 35 | N6 |
| Adhara Rd | *NTHWD* HA6 | 50 | C10 |
| Adie Rd | *HMSMTH* W6 | 137 | H8 |
| Adine Rd | *PLSTW* E13 | 141 | M3 |
| Adlers La | *RDKG* RH5 | 254 | F7 |
| Adler St | *WCHPL* E1 | 13 | P5 |
| Adley St | *CLPT* E5 | 120 | D1 |
| Adlington Cl | *UED* N18 | 99 | L6 |


| Name | Area | Page | Grid |
|---|---|---|---|
| Admaston Rd | *WOOL/PLUM* SE18 | 162 | G1 |
| Admiral Ms | *NKENS* W10 | 136 | C6 |
| Admiral Ms | *BERM/RHTH* SE16 | 140 | D10 |
| Admiral Rd | *CRAWE* RH10 | 283 | K10 |
| Admirals Cl | *STALE/WH* AL4 | 40 | E9 |
| | *SWFD* E18 | 121 | N2 |
| Admirals Ga | *GNWCH* SE10 | 160 | C10 |
| Admiral Seymour Rd | *ELTH/MOT* SE9 | 162 | C10 |
| Admiral's Ga | *GNWCH* SE10 | 160 | C10 |
| Admiral St | *DEPT* SE8 | 160 | F7 |
| | *HERT/BAY* SG13 | 25 | P5 |
| Admirals Wk | *HOD* EN11 | 33 | L6 |
| | *HAMP* NW3 | 117 | M8 |
| | *POP/IOD* E14 | 160 | F1 |
| | *WDR/YW* UB7 | 131 | P10 |
| Admiralty Rd | *TEDD* TW11 | 176 | E9 |
| Admiralty Wy | *TEDD* TW11 | 176 | E9 |
| Admiral Wk | *MV/WKIL* W9 | 137 | M4 |
| Adnams Wk | *RAIN* RM13 | 125 | H10 |
| Adolf St | *CAT* SE6 | 182 | F7 |
| Adolphus Rd | *FSBYPK* N4 | 119 | J7 |
| Adolphus St | *DEPT* SE8 | 160 | E6 |
| Adomar Rd | *BCTR* RM8 | 123 | N8 |
| Adpar St | *BAY/PAD* W2 | 9 | L3 |
| Adrian Av | *CRICK* NW2 | 82 | G10 |
| Adrian Cl | *BAR* EN5 | 76 | G10 |
| | *DEN/HRF* UB9 | 91 | N9 |
| Adrian Ms | *WBPTN* SW10 | 15 | H9 |
| Adrians Wk | *ABLGY* WD5 | 54 | F7 |
| Adrienne Av | *STHL* UB1 | 133 | N6 |
| Adstock Ms | *CFSP/GDCR* SL9 | 90 | A9 |
| Adstock Wy | *GRAYS* RM17 | 167 | L3 |
| Advance Rd | *WNWD* SE27 | 181 | K7 |
| Advent Wy | *UED* N18 | 100 | C6 |
| Advice Av | *CDW/CHF* RM16 | 167 | M3 |
| Adys Lawn | *CRICK* NW2 | 136 | E1 |
| Adys Rd | *PECK* SE15 | 159 | N9 |
| Aerodrome Rd | *CDALE/KGS* NW9 | 116 | C1 |
| Aerodrome Wy | *HEST* TW5 | 153 | K5 |
| Aeroville | *CDALE/KGS* NW9 | 96 | B10 |
| Affleck St | *IS* N1 | 5 | P8 |
| Afghan Rd | *BTSEA* SW11 | 157 | J8 |
| Aftab Ter | *WCHPL* E1 | 140 | A6 |
| Afton Dr | *SOCK/AV* RM15 | 146 | G8 |
| Agamemnon Rd | *KIL/WHAMP* NW6 | 117 | J10 |
| Agar Cl | *SURB* KT6 | 199 | L9 |
| Agar Gv | *CAMTN* NW1 | 5 | K3 |
| Agar Pl | *CAMTN* NW1 | 5 | H4 |
| Agars Pl | *DTCH/LGLY* SL3 | 149 | M5 |
| Agar St | *CHCR* WC2N | 11 | L7 |
| Agate Cl | *CAN/RD* E16 | 142 | A8 |
| Agate Rd | *HMSMTH* W6 | 156 | F2 |
| Agates La | *ASHTD* KT21 | 237 | J4 |
| Agaton Rd | *ELTH/MOT* SE9 | 184 | F5 |
| Agave Rd | *CRICK* NW2 | 116 | F9 |
| Agdon St | *FSBYE* EC1V | 12 | C1 |
| Agincourt Pl | *ASC* SL5 | 192 | B3 |
| Agincourt Rd | *HAMP* NW3 | 118 | A9 |
| Agister Rd | *CHIG* IG7 | 103 | K6 |
| Agnes Av | *IL* IG1 | 122 | D9 |
| Agnes Cl | *EHAM* E6 | 142 | D9 |
| Agnesfield Cl | *NFNCH/WDSPK* N12 | 97 | P7 |
| Agnes Gdns | *BCTR* RM8 | 123 | N9 |
| Agnes Riley Gdns | *CLAP* SW4 | 180 | D3 |
| Agnes Rd | *ACT* W3 | 137 | H5 |
| Agnes Scott Ct | *WEY* KT13 | 196 | C10 |
| Agnes St | *POP/IOD* E14 | 140 | E8 |
| Agnew Rd | *FSTH* SE23 | 182 | D3 |
| Agraria Rd | *GUW* GU1 | 267 | N1 |
| Agricola Pl | *EN* EN1 | 79 | N9 |
| Aidan Cl | *BCTR* RM8 | 123 | P9 |
| Ailsa Av | *TWK* TW1 | 176 | F1 |
| Ailsa Cl | *CRAWW* RH11 | 283 | L10 |
| Ailsa Rd | *TWK* TW1 | 176 | C1 |
| Ailsa St | *POP/IOD* E14 | 141 | H7 |
| Ainger Rd | *HAMP* NW3 | 4 | B4 |
| Ainsdale Cl | *ORP* BR6 | 206 | E4 |
| Ainsdale Crs | *PIN* HA5 | 113 | P1 |
| Ainsdale Dr | *STHWK* SE1 | 19 | N8 |
| Ainsdale Rd | *EA* W5 | 135 | J6 |
| | *OXHEY* WD19 | 93 | K4 |
| Ainsdale Wy | *WOKN/KNAP* GU21 | 231 | M3 |
| Ainsley Av | *ROMW/RG* RM7 | 124 | D4 |
| Ainsley Cl | *ED* N9 | 99 | M2 |
| Ainslie Wood Crs | *CHING* E4 | 100 | C6 |
| Ainslie Wood Gdns | *CHING* E4 | 100 | C5 |
| Ainslie Wood Rd | *CHING* E4 | 100 | A6 |
| Ainsty St | *BERM/RHTH* SE16 | 160 | B5 |
| Ainsworth Cl | *CMBW* SE5 | 159 | M8 |
| | *CRICK* NW2 | 116 | D3 |
| Ainsworth Rd | *CROY/NA* CR0 | 203 | J8 |
| | *HOM* E9 | 140 | E2 |
| Ainsworth Wy | *STJWD* NW8 | 3 | J1 |
| Aintree Av | *EHAM* E6 | 142 | A3 |
| Aintree Cl | *DTCH/LGLY* SL3 | 151 | H1 |
| | *GVE* DA12 | 190 | E6 |
| | *UX/CGN* UB8 | 132 | C8 |
| Aintree Crs | *BARK/HLT* IG6 | 102 | F10 |
| Aintree Rd | *UPMR* RM14 | 125 | M6 |
| | *CRAWE* RH10 | 284 | B9 |
| | *GFD/PVL* UB6 | 134 | G4 |
| Aintree St | *FUL/PGN* SW6 | 157 | H6 |
| Airco Cl | *CDALE/KGS* NW9 | 115 | P1 |
| Airdrie Cl | *IS* N1 | 5 | M1 |
| | *YEAD* UB4 | 133 | M4 |
| Airedale Av | *CHSWK* W4 | 156 | C4 |
| Airedale Av South | *CHSWK* W4 | 156 | C4 |
| Airedale Cl | *RDART* DA2 | 188 | B4 |
| Airedale Rd | *BAL* SW12 | 180 | A3 |
| | *EA* W5 | 155 | H2 |
| Aire Dr | *SOCK/AV* RM15 | 146 | G6 |
| Airfield Wy | *GSTN* WD25 | 54 | G10 |
| | *WOKN/KNAP* GU21 | 232 | C1 |
| Airlie Gdns | *IL* IG1 | 121 | P5 |
| | *KENS* W8 | 8 | B10 |
| Airport Wy | *HORL* RH6 | 280 | B7 |
| | *STWL/WRAY* TW19 | 151 | K10 |
| Air St | *REGST* W1B | 11 | H8 |
| Airthrie Rd | *GDMY/SEVK* IG3 | 123 | L3 |
| Aisgill Av | *WKENS* W14 | 14 | B8 |
| Aisher Rd | *THMD* SE28 | 143 | H9 |
| Aisher Wy | *SEV* TN13 | 246 | F7 |
| Aislibie Rd | *LEE/GVPK* SE12 | 161 | K1 |
| Aiten Pl | *HMSMTH* W6 | 156 | F1 |
| Aitken Cl | *HACK* E8 | 7 | N5 |
| | *MTCM* CR4 | 202 | A7 |
| Aitken Rd | *BAR* EN5 | 76 | F9 |
| | *CAT* SE6 | 182 | C7 |
| Aitman Dr | *BTFD* TW8 | 155 | M4 |
| Ajax Av | *CDALE/KGS* NW9 | 116 | A1 |
| | *SL* SL1 | 128 | B3 |
| Ajax Rd | *KIL/WHAMP* NW6 | 117 | J9 |
| Akabusi Cl | *CROY/NA* CR0 | 203 | P6 |
| Akehurst Cl | *CRAWE* RH10 | 285 | H2 |
| Akehurst La | *SEV* TN13 | 265 | K11 |
| Akehurst St | *PUT/ROE* SW15 | 178 | D2 |
| Akeman Cl | *BXLY* DA5 | 164 | F6 |
| Akenside Rd | *HAMP* NW3 | 117 | N10 |
| Akerman Rd | *BRXN/ST* SW9 | 159 | J7 |
| | *SURB* KT6 | 199 | H6 |
| Alabama St | *WOOL/PLUM* SE18 | 162 | G6 |
| Alacross Rd | *EA* W5 | 155 | H1 |
| Alamein Cl | *BROX* EN10 | 44 | C6 |
| Alamein Gdns | *RDART* DA2 | 188 | C3 |
| Alamein Rd | *SWCM* DA10 | 189 | J3 |
| Alanbrooke Cl | *WOKN/KNAP* GU21 | 230 | D9 |
| Alan Cl | *DART* DA1 | 165 | K10 |


| Name | Area | Page | Grid |
|---|---|---|---|
| Alandale Dr | *PIN* HA5 | 93 | J9 |
| Alander Ms | *WALTH* E17 | 120 | G2 |
| Alan Dr | *BAR* EN5 | 77 | H10 |
| Alan Gdns | *ROMW/RG* RM7 | 124 | B5 |
| Alan Hilton Cl | *CHERT* KT16 * | 214 | G3 |
| Alan Hocken Wy | *SRTFD* E15 | 141 | K4 |
| Alan Rd | *WIM/MER* SW19 | 179 | H8 |
| Alanthus Cl | *LEE/GVPK* SE12 | 183 | M1 |
| Alan Turing Rd | *GUW* GU2 | 249 | J10 |
| Alan Wy | *DTCH/LGLY* SL3 | 130 | B8 |
| Alaska St | *STHWK* SE1 | 12 | A10 |
| Alba Cl | *YEAD* UB4 | 133 | L6 |
| Albacore Crs | *LEW* SE13 | 182 | G3 |
| Alba Gdns | *GLDGN* NW11 | 117 | H4 |
| Albain Crs | *ASHF* TW15 | 173 | K5 |
| Alban Hwy | *STALW/RED* AL3 | 38 | C1 |
| Alban Crs | *BORE* WD6 | 75 | N5 |
| | *EYN* DA4 | 209 | P8 |
| Alba Pk | *STALE/WH* AL4 * | 39 | L6 |
| Albans Vw | *GSTN* WD25 | 55 | J9 |
| Albany Cl | *BUSH* WD23 | 74 | C10 |
| | *BXLY* DA5 | 185 | M3 |
| | *ESH/CLAY* KT10 | 217 | P5 |
| | *HGDN/ICK* UB10 | 112 | B10 |
| | *MV/WKIL* W9 | 137 | M1 |
| | *SEVS/STOTM* N15 | 119 | N10 |
| Albany Cots | *HNWL* W7 * | 134 | D10 |
| Albany Ct | *EPP* CM16 | 65 | L7 |
| Albany Ctyd | *MYFR/PICC* W1J | 10 | G8 |
| Albany Crs | *EDGW* HA8 | 95 | M8 |
| | *ESH/CLAY* KT10 | 218 | D3 |
| Albany Ms | *BMLY* BR1 | 183 | M9 |
| | *IS* N1 | 6 | B3 |
| | *KUTN/CMB* KT2 | 177 | J9 |
| | *LCOL/BKTW* AL2 | 58 | P3 |
| | *SUT* SM1 | 221 | L2 |
| | *WARE* SG12 | 26 | D2 |
| Albany Pde | *BTFD* TW8 | 155 | K5 |
| | *PEND* EN3 | 80 | C4 |
| Albany Park Av | *PEND* EN3 | 80 | B5 |
| Albany Park Rd | *KUTN/CMB* KT2 | 177 | J9 |
| | *LHD/OX* KT22 | 236 | F5 |
| Albany Pl | *BTFD* TW8 | 155 | J5 |
| | *EGH* TW20 | 172 | D7 |
| Albany Rd | *BELV* DA17 | 164 | A5 |
| | *BRWN* CM15 | 86 | C10 |
| | *BTFD* TW8 | 155 | J5 |
| | *BXLY* DA5 | 185 | M3 |
| | *CHDH* RM6 | 124 | A4 |
| | *CHST* BR7 | 184 | E8 |
| | *CMBW* SE5 | 19 | J9 |
| | *CRAWE* RH11 | 283 | M7 |
| | *FSBYPK* N4 | 118 | G4 |
| | *HCH* RM12 | 125 | H6 |
| | *LEY* E10 | 120 | F5 |
| | *MNPK* E12 | 122 | A9 |
| | *PEND* EN3 | 80 | C5 |
| | *RCHPK/HAM* TW10 * | 177 | L1 |
| | *TIL* RM18 | 168 | D7 |
| | *UED* N18 | 100 | A6 |
| | *WALW* SE17 | 19 | J9 |
| | *WDSR* SL4 | 149 | J8 |
| | *WEA* W13 | 134 | G9 |
| | *WCCE* AL7 * | 23 | H5 |
| | *WIM/MER* SW19 | 179 | L8 |
| | *WOT/HER* KT12 | 217 | L1 |
| The Albanys | *REIG* RH2 | 257 | K7 |
| Albany St | *CAMTN* NW1 | 4 | F3 |
| Albany Ter | *RCHPK/HAM* TW10 * | 177 | L1 |
| The Albany | *KUTN/CMB* KT2 | 177 | J9 |
| Albany Vw | *BKHH* IG9 | 101 | M2 |
| Alba Pl *NTGHL* W11 | | 8 | D1 |
| Albatross Cl | *EHAM* E6 | 142 | C6 |
| Albatross Gdns | *SAND/SEL* CR2 | 224 | C7 |
| Albatross St | *WOOL/PLUM* SE18 | 163 | H6 |
| Albatross Wy | *HAT* AL10 | 40 | A4 |
| Albemarle Ap | *GNTH/NBYPK* IG2 | 122 | B8 |
| Albemarle Av | *CHES/WCR* EN8 | 62 | B4 |
| | *POTB/CUF* EN6 | 59 | L9 |
| | *WHTN* TW2 | 175 | N4 |
| Albemarle Gdns | *GNTH/NBYPK* IG2 | 122 | B8 |
| | *NWMAL* KT3 | 200 | A4 |
| Albemarle Pk | *BECK* BR3 | 204 | A5 |
| | *STAN* HA7 | 95 | H4 |
| Albemarle Rd | *BECK* BR3 | 204 | A4 |
| | *EBAR* EN4 | 97 | P1 |
| Albemarle St | *CONDST* W1S | 10 | G8 |
| Albeny Ga | *STAL* AL1 | 38 | C7 |
| Alberon Gdns | *GLDGN* NW11 | 117 | J2 |
| Alberta Av | *SUT* SM1 | 221 | H1 |
| Alberta Est | *WALW* SE17 | 18 | E8 |
| Alberta Rd | *EN* EN1 | 79 | N10 |
| | *ERITH* DA8 | 164 | D7 |
| Alberta St | *WALW* SE17 | 19 | K7 |
| Albert Av | *CHERT* KT16 | 195 | K3 |
| | *CHING* E4 | 100 | F5 |
| | *VX/NE* SW8 | 158 | G6 |
| Albert Br | *CHEL* SW3 | 15 | P10 |
| Albert Bridge Rd | *BTSEA* SW11 | 157 | P6 |
| Albert Carr Gdns | *STRHM/NOR* SW16 | 181 | K8 |
| Albert Cl | *CDW/CHF* RM16 | 167 | P2 |
| | *HOM* E9 | 140 | A3 |
| | *WDGN* N22 | 98 | B9 |
| Albert Cots | *WCHPL* E1 * | 13 | N1 |
| Albert Crs | *CHING* E4 | 100 | F5 |
| Albert Dr | *STA* TW18 | 173 | J8 |
| | *WIM/MER* SW19 | 179 | H1 |
| | *WOKN/KNAP* GU21 | 232 | F1 |
| Albert Emb | *STHWK* SE1 | 17 | N7 |
| Albert Gdns | *HLWE* CM17 | 47 | N2 |
| | *WCHPL* E1 | 140 | G8 |
| Albert Ga | *KTBR* SW1X | 16 | E1 |
| Albert Gv | *RYNPK* SW20 | 200 | G1 |
| Albertine Cl | *EW* KT17 | 238 | E2 |
| Albertine St | *HLWE* CM17 | 29 | N9 |
| Albert Ms | *BROCKY* SE4 * | 160 | E10 |
| | *FSBYPK* N4 | 118 | E6 |
| | *POP/IOD* E14 * | 140 | G10 |
| Albert Murray Cl | *GVE* DA12 | 190 | F3 |
| Albert Pl | *FNCH* N3 | 97 | K9 |
| | *KENS* W8 * | 15 | H1 |
| | *WDSR* SL4 | 148 | F4 |
| Albert Rd | *ADL/WDHM* KT15 | 195 | N10 |
| | *ASHF* TW15 | 174 | A8 |
| | *ASHTD* KT21 | 237 | L4 |
| | *BCTR* RM8 | 124 | A6 |
| | *BELV* DA17 | 164 | A4 |
| | *BKHH* IG9 | 102 | A3 |
| | *CAN/RD* E16 | 142 | B5 |
| | *CAR* SM5 | 222 | B10 |
| | *CSHM* HP5 | 51 | H7 |
| | *DAGE* RM10 | 124 | D4 |
| | *EA* W5 | 134 | G6 |
| | *ED* N9 | 99 | H3 |
| | *EDUL* SE22 | 159 | M9 |
| | *EHAM* E6 | 142 | A2 |
| | *EN* EN1 | 79 | H1 |
| | *FSBYPK* N4 | 118 | E6 |
| | *HAYES* BR2 | 206 | A5 |
| | *HDN* NW4 | 116 | C2 |
| | *HOR/WEW* KT19 | 220 | A6 |
| | *HPTN* TW12 | 175 | L10 |
| | *HSLW* TW3 | 155 | H8 |
| | *HYS/HAR* UB3 | 152 | F2 |
| | *IL* IG1 | 122 | F8 |
| | *KIL/WHAMP* NW6 | 2 | D1 |
| | *KUT/HW* KT1 | 199 | G1 |
| | *LEY* E10 | 121 | H7 |
| | *MLHL* NW7 | 96 | C6 |
| | *MTCM* CR4 | 202 | A3 |
| | *NWMAL* KT3 | 200 | D3 |
| | *ORP* BR6 | 227 | K2 |
| | *PGE/AN* SE20 | 182 | C10 |
| | *RCHPK/HAM* TW10 | 177 | L1 |
| | *REDH* RH1 | 258 | D5 |
| | *ROM* RM1 | 124 | G4 |
| | *RYLN/HDSTN* HA2 | 114 | B1 |
| | *SEVS/STOTM* N15 | 119 | M4 |
| | *SNWD* SE25 | 204 | A4 |
| | *SRTFD* E15 | 141 | K4 |
| | *SUT* SM1 | 221 | N2 |
| | *SWCM* DA10 | 189 | H5 |
| | *SWFD* E18 | 121 | N1 |
| | *TEDD* TW11 | 176 | E9 |
| | *WALTH* E17 | 120 | C5 |
| | *WDGN* N22 | 98 | F9 |
| | *WDR/YW* UB7 | 131 | P10 |
| | *WLSDN* NW10 | 119 | H8 |


| Name | Area | Page | Grid |
|---|---|---|---|
| | *IL* IG1 | 122 | F8 |
| | *KIL/WHAMP* NW6 | 2 | D1 |
| | *KUT/HW* KT1 | 199 | G1 |
| | *LEY* E10 | 121 | H7 |
| | *MLHL* NW7 | 96 | C6 |
| | *MTCM* CR4 | 202 | A3 |
| | *NWMAL* KT3 | 200 | D3 |
| | *ORP* BR6 | 227 | K2 |
| | *PGE/AN* SE20 | 182 | C10 |
| | *PECK* SE15 | 159 | L6 |
| | *SL* SL1 | 128 | E10 |
| Alderbury Rd | *BARN* SW13 | 156 | D5 |
| Alderbury Rd West | *DTCH/LGLY* SL3 | 150 | C1 |
| Alder Cl | *EGH* TW20 | 172 | B8 |
| | *HOD* EN11 | 44 | E2 |
| | *PECK* SE15 | 159 | H5 |
| | *SL* SL1 | 128 | E10 |
| Aldercombe La | *CTHM* CR3 | 259 | M3 |
| Alder Cft | *COUL/CHIP* CR5 | 240 | F2 |
| Alder Gv | *CRICK* NW2 | 116 | D7 |
| Alderholt Wy | *PECK* SE15 | 159 | H6 |
| Alderman Av | *BARK* IG11 | 143 | K5 |
| Aldermanbury | *CITYW* EC2V | 12 | F5 |
| Aldermanbury Sq | *CITYW* EC2V | 12 | F4 |
| Alderman Cl | *BFN/LL* DA15 | 185 | H1 |
| Alderman Judge Ml | *KUT/HW* KT1 | 199 | K2 |
| Alderman's Hl | *PLMGR* N13 | 98 | K2 |
| Aldermary Rd | *BMLY* BR1 | 205 | M1 |
| Aldermoor Rd | *CAT* SE6 | 182 | C9 |
| Alderney Gdns | *NTHLT* UB5 | 133 | N2 |
| Alderney Ms | *STHWK* SE1 | 19 | L3 |
| Alderney Rd | *ERITH* DA8 | 165 | H10 |
| | *WCHPL* E1 | 140 | G6 |
| Alderney St | *PIM* SW1V | 16 | E8 |
| Alder Rd | *DEN/HRF* UB9 | 131 | L1 |
| | *MORT/ESHN* SW14 | 156 | A9 |
| | *SCUP* DA14 | 186 | H6 |
| Alders Av | *WFD* IG8 | 101 | K7 |
| Aldersbrook Av | *EN* EN1 | 79 | M6 |
| Aldersbrook Dr | *KUTN/CMB* KT2 | 177 | L9 |
| Aldersbrook La | *MNPK* E12 | 121 | P7 |
| Aldersbrook Rd | *MNPK* E12 | 121 | P7 |
| Alders Cl | *EA* W5 | 155 | J2 |
| | *EDGW* HA8 | 95 | P6 |
| | *WAN* E11 | 121 | N1 |
| Aldersey Gdns | *BARK* IG11 | 142 | C1 |
| Aldersey Rd | *GU* GU1 | 250 | C10 |
| Aldersford Cl | *BROCKY* SE4 | 160 | C10 |
| Aldersgate St | *CITYW* EC2V | 12 | E3 |
| Aldersgrove | *E/WMO/HCT* KT8 | 198 | C5 |
| Aldersgrove Av | *ELTH/MOT* SE9 | 183 | J8 |
| Aldershot Rd | *CHOB/PIR* GU24 | 248 | D2 |
| | *GUW* GU2 | 249 | L8 |
| | *KIL/WHAMP* NW6 | 2 | D5 |
| | *RGUW* GU3 | 248 | F5 |
| Aldershot Ter | *WOOL/PLUM* SE18 * | 162 | D6 |
| Alderside Wk | *EGH* TW20 | 172 | B8 |
| Aldersmead Av | *CROY/NA* CR0 | 204 | G6 |
| Aldersmead Rd | *BECK* BR3 | 183 | H10 |
| Alderson Pl | *NWDGN* UB2 | 134 | B10 |
| Alderson St | *NKENS* W10 * | 8 | C1 |
| Alders Rd | *EDGW* HA8 | 95 | P6 |
| | *REIG* RH2 | 257 | L8 |
| Aldersted La | *REDH* RH1 | 258 | E1 |
| The Alders | *BF/WBF* KT14 | 215 | M8 |
| | *DEN/HRF* UB9 | 131 | M1 |
| | *FELT* TW13 | 175 | M8 |
| | *HEST* TW5 | 135 | N5 |
| | *STRHM/NOR* SW16 | 180 | D7 |
| | *WCHMH* N21 | 79 | H10 |
| | *WWKM* BR4 | 204 | G10 |
| Alders Wk | *SBW* CM21 | 29 | P1 |
| Alderton Cl | *BRWN* CM15 | 86 | G9 |
| | *WLSDN* NW10 | 116 | A9 |
| Alderton Crs | *HDN* NW4 | 116 | E3 |
| Alderton Hall La | *LOU* IG10 | 82 | B6 |
| Alderton Hill | *LOU* IG10 | 82 | C9 |
| Alderton Ri | *LOU* IG10 | 82 | D9 |
| Alderton Rd | *CROY/NA* CR0 | 203 | N7 |
| | *HNHL* SE24 | 159 | N8 |
| Alderton Wy | *HDN* NW4 | 116 | E3 |
| | *LOU* IG10 | 82 | C9 |
| Alder Wk | *GSTN* WD25 | 73 | J1 |
| | *IL* IG1 | 122 | C5 |
| Alder Wy | *SWLY* BR8 | 208 | E2 |
| Alderwick Dr | *HSLW* TW3 | 155 | L8 |
| Alderwood Cl | *CTHM* CR3 | 259 | M1 |
| Alderwood Dr | *ABR/ST* RM4 | 83 | L7 |
| Alderwood Ms | *EBAR* EN4 | 77 | M4 |
| Alderwood Rd | *ELTH/MOT* SE9 | 184 | C2 |
| Aldford St | *MYFR/PKLN* W1K | 10 | C8 |
| Aldgate | *FENCHST* EC3M | 13 | K6 |
| Aldgate Barrs | *WCHPL* E1 * | 13 | N5 |
| Aldgate High St | *TWRH* EC3N | 13 | L6 |
| Aldham Dr | *SOCK/AV* RM15 | 146 | G5 |
| Aldin Av North | *SL* SL1 | 149 | M1 |
| Aldin Av South | *SL* SL1 | 149 | M1 |
| Aldine St | *SHB* W12 | 157 | H1 |
| Aldingbourne Cl | *CRAWW* RH11 | 283 | J6 |
| Aldingham Gdns | *HCH* RM12 | 125 | L1 |
| Aldington Cl | *CHDH* RM6 | 105 | P10 |
| Aldington Rd | *CHARL* SE7 | 162 | A2 |
| Aldis Ms | *PEND* EN3 | 80 | A5 |
| | *TOOT* SW17 | 180 | E8 |
| Aldis St | *TOOT* SW17 | 180 | E8 |
| Aldock | *WGCE* AL7 | 23 | K7 |
| Aldred Rd | *KIL/WHAMP* NW6 | 117 | K10 |
| Aldren Rd | *TOOT* SW17 | 180 | A4 |
| Aldrich Crs | *CROY/NA* CR0 | 225 | H5 |
| Aldriche Wy | *CHING* E4 | 101 | H2 |
| Aldrich Gdns | *CHEAM* SM3 | 201 | K9 |
| Aldrich Ter | *WAND/EARL* SW18 | 179 | L6 |
| Aldridge Av | *EDGW* HA8 | 95 | N4 |
| | *PEND* EN3 | 80 | G1 |
| | *RSLP* HA4 | 113 | J6 |
| | *STAN* HA7 | 95 | P7 |
| Aldridge Ri | *NWMAL* KT3 | 200 | B7 |
| Aldridge Rd Vls | *NTGHL* W11 | 8 | D1 |
| Aldridge Wk | *STHGT/OAK* N14 | 77 | P8 |
| Aldrington Rd | *STRHM/NOR* SW16 | 180 | D8 |
| Aldsworth Cl | *MV/WKIL* W9 | 2 | B10 |
| Aldwick Cl | *ELTH/MOT* SE9 | 184 | C6 |
| Aldwick Rd | *CROY/NA* CR0 | 202 | G10 |
| Aldworth Gv | *LEW* SE13 | 183 | H1 |
| Aldworth Rd | *SRTFD* E15 | 141 | L7 |
| Aldwych | *HOL/ALD* WC2B | 11 | N6 |
| Aldwych Av | *BARK/HLT* IG6 | 122 | F1 |
| Aldwych Cl | *HCH* RM12 | 125 | H7 |
| Aldykes | *HAT* AL10 | 40 | A6 |
| Alers Rd | *BXLYHS* DA6 | 185 | H1 |
| Alesia Cl | *WDGN* N22 | 98 | A6 |
| Alestan Beck Rd | *CAN/RD* E16 | 142 | C9 |
| Alexander Av | *WLSDN* NW10 | 119 | K7 |
| Alexander Cl | *BFN/LL* DA15 | 185 | J8 |
| | *EBAR* EN4 | 77 | L3 |
| | *HAYES* BR2 | 205 | N10 |
| | *NWDGN* UB2 | 134 | B10 |
| | *TWK* TW1 | 176 | G1 |
| Alexander Crs | *CTHM* CR3 | 241 | K7 |
| Alexander Evans Ms | *FSTH* SE23 | 182 | G3 |
| Alexander Fleming Rd | *GUW* GU2 | 267 | J1 |
| Alexander Godley Cl | *ASHTD* KT21 | 237 | L8 |
| Alexander La | *BRWN* CM15 | 87 | M9 |
| Alexander Ms | *BAY/PAD* W2 | 8 | F6 |
| Alexander Pl | *OXTED* RH8 | 261 | K4 |
| | *SKENS* SW7 | 15 | N4 |
| Alexander Rd | *ARCH* N19 | 118 | E3 |
| | *BXLYHS* DA6 | 163 | H10 |
| | *CHST* BR7 | 184 | G2 |
| | *COUL/CHIP* CR5 | 240 | C3 |
| | *HERT/WAS* SG14 | 25 | J1 |
| | *LCOL/BKTW* AL2 | 57 | H1 |
| | *REIG* RH2 | 275 | K3 |
| Alexander Sq | *CHEL* SW3 | 15 | N5 |
| Alexander Ter | *ABYW* SE2 * | 163 | L4 |
| Alexandra Av | *BTSEA* SW11 | 158 | A6 |
| | *RYLN/HDSTN* HA2 | 113 | N9 |
| | *STH* UB1 | 133 | N9 |
| | *SUT* SM1 | 201 | K10 |
| | *WARL* CR6 | 227 | P5 |
| | *WDGN* N22 | 98 | B9 |
| Alexandra Cl | *ASHF* TW15 | 174 | E10 |
| | *CDW/CHF* RM16 | 168 | E1 |
| | *RYLN/HDSTN* HA2 | 113 | N9 |
| | *STA* TW18 | 173 | N9 |
| | *SWLY* BR8 | 208 | F2 |
| | *WOT/HER* KT12 | 197 | H9 |
| Alexandra Cots | *NWCR* SE14 | 160 | E2 |
| Alexandra Crs | *BMLY* BR1 | 183 | M8 |
| Alexandra Dr | *BRYLDS* KT5 | 199 | M6 |
| | *NRWD* SE19 | 181 | L3 |
| Alexandra Gdns | *CAR* SM5 | 222 | B10 |
| | *HSLW* TW3 | 155 | H6 |
| | *MUSWH* N10 | 118 | C2 |
| | *WOKN/KNAP* GU21 | 231 | H4 |
| Alexandra Ms | *EFNCH* N2 | 118 | A1 |
| | *WAT* WD17 | 73 | H6 |
| Alexandra Palace Wy | *CEND/HSY/T* N8 | 118 | D2 |
| Alexandra Pde | *RYLN/HDSTN* HA2 | 114 | A9 |
| Alexandra Park Rd | *MUSWH* N10 | 98 | C10 |
| | *SNWD* SE25 | 268 | C2 |
| | *STJWD* NW8 | 3 | K5 |
| Alexandra Rd | *ADL/WDHM* KT15 | 215 | N10 |
| | *ASHF* TW15 | 174 | E10 |
| | *BH/WHM* TN16 | 243 | N5 |
| | *BORE* WD6 | 76 | A4 |
| | *BTFD* TW8 | 155 | J5 |
| | *CEND/HSY/T* N8 | 119 | H1 |
| | *CHDH* RM6 | 123 | N4 |
| | *CHSWK* W4 | 156 | B1 |
| | *CROY/NA* CR0 | 203 | M8 |
| | *ED* N9 * | 100 | A1 |
| | *EGH* TW20 | 171 | P9 |
| | *EHAM* E6 | 142 | C3 |
| | *ERITH* DA8 | 164 | C10 |
| | *EW* KT17 | 220 | C9 |
| | *GVE* DA12 | 191 | H3 |
| | *HDN* NW4 | 116 | C2 |
| | *HHNE* HP2 | 35 | M10 |
| | *HSLW* TW3 | 154 | A8 |
| | *KCLGY* WD4 | 53 | K6 |
| | *KCLGY* WD4 | 35 | K8 |
| | *KUTN/CMB* KT2 | 177 | M10 |
| | *LEY* E10 | 120 | F2 |
| | *MORT/ESHN* SW14 | 156 | A9 |
| | *MUSWH* N10 | 98 | C9 |
| | *PEND* EN3 | 80 | C5 |
| | *PGE/AN* SE20 | 182 | G9 |
| | *RCH/KEW* TW9 | 155 | L8 |
| | *RKW/CH/CXG* WD3 | 71 | K2 |
| | *ROM* RM1 | 124 | G3 |
| | *SEVS/STOTM* N15 | 119 | L3 |
| | *SL* SL1 | 149 | J2 |
| | *STAL* AL1 | 38 | D6 |
| | *STJWD* NW8 | 3 | J3 |
| | *SWFD* E18 | 121 | N1 |
| | *TIL* RM18 | 168 | C8 |
| | *TWK* TW1 | 176 | D3 |
| | *UX/CGN* UB8 | 149 | J4 |
| | *WALTH* E17 | 120 | C5 |
| | *WARL* CR6 | 242 | D3 |
| | *WAT* WD17 | 73 | H6 |
| | *WDSR* SL4 | 146 | E3 |
| | *WIM/MER* SW19 | 179 | K8 |
| Alexandra Sq | *MRDN* SM4 | 201 | K5 |
| Alexandra St | *CAN/RD* E16 | 141 | P6 |
| | *NWCR* SE14 | 160 | D6 |
| Alexandra Ter | *GU* GU1 | 268 | B1 |
| Alexandra Wy | *EYN* DA4 * | 210 | C2 |
| Alexandria Rd | *CHES/WCR* EN8 | 62 | E10 |
| | *WEA* W13 | 134 | F9 |
| Alexia Sq | *POP/IOD* E14 | 160 | G1 |
| Alexis St | *BERM/RHTH* SE16 | 159 | N3 |
| Alfan La | *RDART* DA2 | 188 | A7 |
| Alfearn Rd | *CLPT* E5 | 138 | F1 |
| Alford Cl | *RGUE* GU4 | 250 | C7 |
| Alford Gn | *CROY/NA* CR0 | 225 | J3 |
| Alford Pl | *IS* N1 * | 6 | F8 |
| Alford Rd | *ERITH* DA8 | 164 | D4 |
| Alfoxton Av | *SEVS/STOTM* N15 | 119 | J2 |
| Alfred Cl | *CHSWK* W4 | 156 | B3 |
| | *CRAWE* RH10 | 284 | F6 |
| Alfred Gdns | *STHL* UB1 | 133 | H6 |
| Alfred Ms | *GWRST* WC1E | 11 | J3 |
| Alfred Pl | *GWRST* WC1E | 11 | J3 |
| Alfred Rd | *ACT* W3 | 135 | P10 |
| | *BAY/PAD* W2 | 8 | F3 |
| | *BELV* DA17 | 164 | A4 |
| | *BKHH* IG9 | 102 | A3 |
| | *BRW* CM14 | 107 | J3 |
| | *FELT* TW13 | 173 | J2 |
| | *GVW* GU1 | 190 | F3 |
| | *KUT/HW* KT1 | 199 | K3 |
| | *SNWD* SE25 | 203 | P5 |
| | *SRTFD* E15 | 141 | L10 |
| | *SUT* SM1 | 221 | M2 |
| Alfred's Gdns | *BARK* IG11 | 143 | H4 |
| Alfred St | *BOW* E3 | 140 | H5 |
| | *GRAYS* RM17 | 167 | K7 |
| Alfred's Way (East Ham & Barking By-Pass) | *BARK* IG11 | 142 | G4 |
| Alfreton Cl | *WALTH* E17 * | 120 | G4 |
| Alfriston *WIM/MER* SW19 | | 178 | G6 |
| Alfriston Av | *CROY/NA* CR0 | 202 | F4 |
| | *RYLN/HDSTN* HA2 | 113 | P4 |
| Alfriston Cl | *BRYLDS* KT5 | 199 | M4 |
| | *DART* DA1 | 171 | H4 |
| Alfriston Rd | *BTSEA* SW11 | 180 | A1 |
| Algar Cl | *ISLW* TW7 | 154 | G8 |
| Algarve Rd | *WAND/EARL* SW18 | 179 | M4 |
| Algernon Rd | *HDN* NW4 | 116 | A4 |
| | *KIL/WHAMP* NW6 | 2 | C1 |
| | *LEW* SE13 | 160 | G9 |
| Algers Cl | *LOU* IG10 | 82 | A9 |
| Algers Rd | *LOU* IG10 | 82 | A9 |
| Alghers Md | *LOU* IG10 | 82 | A9 |
| Algiers Rd | *LEW* SE13 | 160 | G10 |
| Alguin Ct | *STAN* HA7 * | 95 | H7 |
| Alibon Gdns | *DAGE* RM10 | 124 | B10 |
| Alibon Rd | *DAGE* RM10 | 124 | B10 |
| Alice Cl | *BAR* EN5 * | 76 | G4 |
| | *SL* SL1 | 128 | A6 |
| Alice Ruston Pl | *WOKS/MYFD* GU22 | 231 | P5 |
| Alice St | *STHWK* SE1 | 19 | K4 |
| Alice Thompson Cl | *LEE/GVPK* SE12 | 183 | P3 |
| Alice Walker Cl | *HNHL* SE24 * | 158 | A10 |
| Alicia Av | *CRAWE* RH10 | 285 | H10 |
| | *KTN/HRWW/WS* HA3 | 114 | C2 |
| Alicia Cl | *KTN/HRWW/WS* HA3 | 114 | C2 |
| Alicia Gdns | | | |
| | *KTN/HRWW/WS* HA3 | 114 | C2 |
| Alie St | *WCHPL* E1 | 13 | M6 |

Alington Crs CDALE/KGS NW9 ... 115 P6
Alington Gv WLGTN SM6 ... 222 E5
Alison Cl CROY/NA CRO ... 204 C8
  EHAM E6 ... 142 D8
  WOKN/KNAP GU21 ... 232 B1
Aliwal Ms BTSEA SW11 ... 157 H10
Aliwal Rd BTSEA SW11 ... 157 H10
Alkerden La SWCM DA10 ... 189 N2
Alkerden Rd CHSWK W4 ... 156 N6
Alkham Rd STNW/STAM N16 ... 119 N7
Allan Barclay Cl SEVS/STOTM N15 ... 119 N3
Allandale HHNE HP2 ... 35 N4
  STALW/RED AL3 ... 38 A9
Allandale Av FNCH N3 ... 117 H5
Allandale Cl POTB/CUF EN6 ... 59 H8
Allandale Pl ORP BR6 ... 207 N10
Allandale Rd EMPK RM11 ... 124 C5
  PEND EN3 ... 80 C2
Allan Wy ACT W3 ... 135 P7
Allard Cl STMC/STPC BR5 ... 207 H4
Allard Crs BUSH WD23 ... 94 E5
Allard Wy BROX EN10 ... 44 D7
Allardyce St CLAP SW4 ... 158 G10
Allbrook Cl TEDD TW11 ... 176 D8
  EBED/NFELT TW14 ... 174 G4
Allcot Cl CRAWW RH11 ... 283 H10
  EBED/NFELT TW14 ... 174 G4
Allcroft Rd KTTN NW5 ... 4 C1
Alder Wy HHS/BOV HP3 ... 36 A8
Alldicks Rd HHS/BOV HP3 ... 36 A8
Allenby Av SAND/SEL CR2 ... 223 K5
Allenby Crs GFD/PVL UB6 ... 133 P5
Allenby Crs GRAYS RM17 ... 167 N4
Allenby Dr EMPK RM11 ... 125 M6
Allenby Rd BH/WHM TN16 ... 244 B3
  FSTH SE23 ... 182 D6
  STHL UB1 ... 133 P8
  WOOL/PLUM SE18 ... 162 F2
Allen Cl HAT AL10 * ... 40 E6
  MTCM CR4 ... 180 B9
  RAD WD7 ... 57 K8
  STALE/WH AL4 ... 21 J4
  SUN TW16 ... 197 J1
Allen Ct HAT AL10 * ... 40 E6
Allendale Av STHL UB1 ... 133 P8
Allendale Cl CMBW SE5 ... 159 L8
  RDART DA2 ... 188 C4
  SYD SE26 ... 182 C8
Allendale Rd GFD/PVL UB6 ... 134 C3
Allen Edwards Dr VX/NE SW8 ... 158 K7
Allen House Pk WOKS/MYFD GU22 ... 231 P6
Allens Md GVE DA12 ... 191 J4
Allens Rd PEND EN3 ... 80 B9
Allen St KENS W8 ... 14 C3
Allensbury Pl CAMTN NW1 ... 5 L4
Allens Rd PEND EN3 ... 80 B9
Allenswood KUTN/CMB KT2 * ... 176 B10
Allenswood Rd ELTH/MOT SE9 ... 162 B9
Allerds Rd SLN SL2 ... 128 E3
Allerford Ct HRW HA1 ... 114 A3
Allerford Rd CAT SE6 ... 182 G7
Allerton Cl BORE WD6 ... 75 L4
Allerton Rd BORE WD6 ... 75 K4
  STNW/STAM N16 ... 119 K7
Allerton St IS N1 ... 7 H6
Allestree Rd FUL/PGN SW6 ... 157 H6
Alleyn Crs DUL SE21 ... 181 L5
Alleyndale Rd BCTR RM8 ... 123 M7
Alleyn Pk DUL SE21 ... 181 L5
  NWDGN UB2 ... 153 N4
Alleyn Rd DUL SE21 ... 181 L6
Allfarthing La WAND/EARL SW18 ... 179 M2
Allgood Cl MRDN SM4 ... 200 E6
Allgood St BETH E2 ... 7 N8
Allhallows La CANST EC4R * ... 12 G8
Allhallows Rd EHAM E6 ... 142 B8
All Hallows Rd TOTM N17 ... 99 M10
Alliance Cl ALP/SUD HA0 ... 115 N1
  HSLWW TW4 ... 175 N1
Alliance Rd ACT W3 ... 135 N6
  PLSTW E13 ... 141 P6
  WOOL/PLUM SE18 ... 163 K5
Allied Wy ACT W3 ... 156 B1
Allingham Cl HNWL W7 ... 134 F4
Allingham Rd REIG RH2 ... 275 K3
Allington Av TOTM N17 ... 99 M7
Allington Cl GFD/PVL UB6 ... 134 B2
  WIM/MER SW19 ... 178 G8
Allington Rd HDN NW4 ... 116 E3
  NKENS W10 ... 2 A9
  ORP BR6 ... 207 H8
  RYLN/HDSTN HA2 ... 114 B3
Allington St BGVA SW1W ... 16 C4
  WESTW SW1E ... 16 C4
Allis Ms HLWE CM17 ... 29 M10
Allison Cl GNWCH SE10 ... 161 H7
  WAB EN9 ... 63 N4
Allison Gv DUL SE21 ... 181 M4
Allison Rd ACT W3 ... 135 P8
  CEND/HSY/T N8 ... 97 J1
Allitsen Rd STJWD NW8 ... 3 L4
Alkins Ct WDSR SL4 ... 149 J8
Allmains Cl WAB EN9 ... 63 N1
Allnutts Rd EPP CM16 ... 65 K9
Allnutt Wy CLAP SW4 ... 180 L1
Alloa Rd DEPT SE8 ... 160 C4
  GDMY/SEVK IG3 ... 123 L7
Allonby Dr RSLP HA4 ... 112 C5
Allonby Gdns WBLY HA9 ... 115 H6
Allotment La SEV TN13 ... 255 H9
Alloway Rd BOW E3 ... 139 K5
Allport Ms WCHPL E1 * ... 140 E7
All Saints Cl BRWN CM15 ... 86 G2
  CHIG IG7 ... 103 L4
  SWCM DA10 ... 189 L1
All Saints' Cl ED N9 ... 99 N3
Allsaints Crs GSTN WD25 ... 55 L1
All Saints Dr BKHTH/KID SE3 ... 161 L8
  SAND/SEL CR2 ... 223 N8
All Saints La RKW/CH/CXG WD3 ... 72 B10
All Saints Ms STAN HA7 ... 94 D7
All Saints Pas WAND/EARL SW18 ... 179 K1
  NTGHL W11 ... 8 C4
  SUT SM1 ... 201 L10
  WIM/MER SW19 ... 179 M10
All Saints' Rd ACT W3 ... 155 P2
  SUT SM1 ... 190 C4
All Saints St IS N1 ... 5 N7
Allsop Pl CAMTN NW1 ... 10 B1
All Souls Av CHOB/PIR GU24 ... 99 N3
All Souls Pl WLSDN NW10 ... 136 E4
All Souls' Pl REGST W1B ... 10 D2
Allum Cl BORE WD6 ... 75 K5
Allum La BORE WD6 ... 75 J4
Allwood Cl SYD SE26 ... 182 G7
Allwood Rd CHESW EN7 ... 46 D1
Allyington Wy CRAWE RH10 ... 284 E8
Alryn Cl STA TW18 ... 173 H8
Alma Av CHING E4 ... 101 M4
  HCH RM12 ... 125 M8
Alma Cl WOKN/KNAP GU21 ... 231 K3
Alma Cut STAL AL1 ... 39 H4
Alma Gv STHWK SE1 ... 19 M6
Alma Pl NRWD SE19 ... 181 N10
  THHTH CR7 ... 203 H5
  WLSDN NW10 ... 136 H5
Alma Rd BERK HP4 ... 185 K6
  BFN/LL DA15 ... 185 K6
  CAR SM5 ... 221 D2
  CSHM HP5 ... 51 L6


ESH/CLAY KT10 ... 198 D8
MUSWH N10 ... 98 B4
PEND EN3 ... 80 D9
REIG RH2 ... 257 J7
STAL AL1 ... 38 D7
STHL UB1 ... 133 M8
STMC/STPC BR5 ... 207 N4
SWCM DA10 ... 189 K1
WAND/EARL SW18 ... 179 N1
WATW WD18 ... 148 E3
Alma Rw
  KTN/HRWW/WS HA3 * ... 94 G1
Alma Sq STJWD NW8 ... 3 H3
Alma St KTTN NW5 ... 4 E2
  SRTFD E15 ... 141 J6
Alma Ter BOW E3 ... 140 E3
  KENS W8 ... 14 F4
  WAND/EARL SW18 ... 179 N3
The Alma GVE DA12 * ... 191 J7
Almeida St IS N1 ... 6 C1
Almeric Rd BTSEA SW11 ... 158 A10
Almer Rd RYNPK SW20 ... 178 D10
Almington St FSBYPK N4 * ... 6 A1
Almond Av CAR SM5 ... 202 A8
  EA W5 ... 155 K2
  HGDN/ICK UB10 ... 112 C8
  WDR/YW UB7 ... 152 B2
  WOKS/MYFD GU22 ... 232 G5
Almond Cl CDW/CHF RM16 ... 168 D2
  CRAWW RH11 ... 283 K8
  EGH TW20 ... 171 N9
  FELT TW13 ... 175 H4
  GU GU1 ... 250 A6
  HAYES BR2 ... 206 D7
  HYS/HAR UB3 ... 132 C2
  PECK SE15 ... 159 P8
  RSLP HA4 ... 112 C8
  SHPTN TW17 ... 196 D2
  WDSR SL4 ... 148 A8
Almond Gv BTFD TW8 ... 154 B7
Almond Rd BERM/RHTH SE16 ... 160 A3
  HOR/WEW KT19 ... 220 A7
  RDART DA2 ... 188 C3
  SL SL1 ... 128 A4
  TOTM N17 ... 99 P8
Almonds Av BKHH IG9 ... 101 M3
The Almonds STAL AL1 ... 38 G10
Almond Wy BORE WD6 ... 75 N4
  HAYES BR2 ... 206 D7
  MTCM CR4 ... 202 E5
  RYLN/HDSTN HA2 ... 113 N1
Almorah Rd HEST TW5 ... 153 L7
  IS N1 ... 6 E1
Almsgate RGUW GU3 ... 267 J7
Alms Heath RPLY/SEND GU23 ... 234 C7
Almshouse La CHSGTN KT9 ... 219 H5
  EN EN1 ... 80 A2
Alnwick Gv MRDN SM4 ... 201 L4
Alnwick Rd CAN/RD E16 ... 141 P8
  LEE/GVPK SE12 ... 183 K5
Alnwick Ter LEE/GVPK SE12 ... 183 N5
Alperton La ALP/SUD HA0 ... 135 J5
Alperton St NKENS W10 ... 8 D1
Alphabet Gdns CAR SM5 ... 201 N6
Alpha Cl CAMTN NW1 ... 3 L7
Alpha Est CTHM CR3 ... 241 P4
Alpha Est HYS/HAR UB3 * ... 152 F1
Alpha Gv POP/IOD E14 ... 160 L1
Alpha Pl CHEL SW3 ... 15 P9
  KIL/WHAMP NW6 ... 2 E4
Alpha Rd BRYLDS KT5 ... 199 L6
  CHING E4 ... 100 F4
  CHOB/PIR GU24 ... 213 L6
  CRAWW RH11 ... 283 M7
  CROY/NA CRO ... 203 M8
  HGDN/ICK UB10 ... 132 C6
  NWCR SE14 ... 160 E7
  PEND EN3 ... 80 D8
  TEDD TW11 ... 176 C8
  UED N18 ... 99 P7
  WOKS/MYFD GU22 ... 232 G2
Alpha St PECK SE15 ... 159 P8
Alpha St North SL SL1 ... 149 M1
Alpha St South SL SL1 ... 149 L2
Alpha Wy EGH TW20 ... 194 F1
Alphea Cl WIM/MER SW19 ... 179 P10
Alpine Av CROY/NA CRO ... 203 M10
Alpine Cl CROY/NA CRO ... 203 K1
Alpine Copse BMLY BR1 ... 206 D2
Alpine Rd BERM/RHTH SE16 ... 160 B3
  LEY E10 ... 120 C7
  REDH RH1 ... 258 B7
  WOT/HER KT12 ... 197 N1
Alpine Vw CAR SM5 ... 221 P2
Alpine Wk BUSH WD23 ... 94 D3
Alpine Wy EHAM E6 ... 142 C7
Alresford Rd GUW GU2 ... 267 N1
Alric Av NWMAL KT3 ... 200 B3
  WLSDN NW10 ... 136 G4
Alroy Rd FSBYPK N4 ... 119 H5
Alsace Rd WALW SE17 ... 19 M4
Ascot Dr STHWK SE1 ... 19 M4
Alscot Rd STHWK SE1 ... 19 N3
Alscot Wy STHWK SE1 ... 19 M4
Alsike Rd ERITHM DA18 ... 165 L6
Alsom Av WPK KT4 ... 200 C1
Alsop Cl LCOL/BKTW AL2 ... 57 K4
Alston Cl SURB KT6 ... 198 G12
Alston Rd BAR EN5 ... 77 H2
  HHW HP1 ... 35 K7
  TOOT SW17 ... 180 A8
  UED N18 ... 100 A6
Altair Cl TOTM N17 ... 99 N7
Altair Wy NTHWD HA6 ... 92 D9
Altash Wy ELTH/MOT SE9 ... 184 C5
Altenburg Av WEA W13 ... 154 C4
Altenburg Gdns BTSEA SW11 ... 183 A10
Alterton Cl WOKN/KNAP GU21 ... 231 N10
Alt Gv WIM/MER SW19 ... 178 C9
Altham Gdns OXHEY WD19 ... 92 G3
Altham Rd PIN HA5 ... 93 M6
Althea St FUL/PGN SW6 ... 157 P7
Althorne Gdns SWFD E18 ... 121 K2
Althorne Rd REDH RH1 ... 276 B2
Althorne Wy DAGE RM10 ... 124 B2
Althorp Cl BAR EN5 ... 96 C1
Althorpe Gv BTSEA SW11 ... 158 D8
Althorpe Rd HRW HA1 ... 114 A3
Althorp Rd STAL AL1 ... 180 A4
  TOOT SW17 ... 180 A4
Altior Ct HGT N6 ... 96 B4
Alton Av STAN HA7 ... 94 E8
Alton Cl BXLY DA5 ... 185 K10
  ISLW TW7 ... 135 H4
Alton Gdns BECK BR3 ... 182 G1
  TWK TW1 ... 176 C2
Alton Rd CROY/NA CRO ... 203 H10
  PUT/ROE SW15 ... 177 K1
  RCH/KEW TW9 ... 155 K9
Alton St POP/IOD E14 ... 140 L7
Altwood Cl SL SL1 ... 128 C3
Altwood Rd MPK HA1 ... 20 C2
Altyre Cl BECK BR3 ... 204 E5
Altyre Rd CROY/NA CRO ... 203 E5
Altyre Wy BECK BR3 ... 204 D5
Aluric Cl CDW/CHF RM16 ... 168 G2
Alvanley Gdns KIL/WHAMP NW6 ... 117 L10
Alva Wy OXHEY WD19 ... 93 H5
Alverstone Av EBAR EN4 ... 97 N1
  WAND/EARL SW18 ... 179 N5
Alverstone Gdns ELTH/MOT SE9 ... 184 F4
Alverstone Rd MNPK E12 ... 141 N1
  NWMAL KT3 ... 200 D2
  WALTH E17 ... 119 J3
  WBLY HA9 ... 115 L6


Alverston Gdns SNWD SE25 ... 203 M5
Alverton STALW/RED AL3 ... 38 D1
Alverton St DEPT SE8 ... 160 E4
Alveston Av KTN/HRWW/WS HA3 ... 114 G1
Alveston Sq SWFD E18 * ... 101 N10
Alvey Rd WALW SE17 ... 19 J7
Alvia Gdns SUT SM1 ... 221 N1
Alvington Crs HACK E8 ... 119 N10
Alvista Av MDHD SL6 ... 128 A8
Alway Av HOR/WEW KT19 ... 219 P2
Alwen Gv SOCK/AV RM15 ... 146 F2
Alwin Pl WATW WD18 ... 72 F8
Alwold Crs LEE/GVPK SE12 ... 183 P2
Alwyn Av CHSWK W4 ... 156 A4
Alwyne Av BRWN CM15 ... 87 L10
  CROY/NA CRO ... 224 G4
Alwyn Cl BORE WD6 ... 75 L10
  CROY/NA CRO ... 224 G4
Alwyne La IS N1 ... 6 D1
Alwyne Pl IS N1 ... 6 E1
Alwyne Rd HNWL W7 ... 134 D9
  IS N1 ... 6 E1
  WIM/MER SW19 ... 179 J9
Alwyne Sq IS N1 ... 6 E1
Alwyne Vls IS N1 ... 6 C1
Alwyn Gdns ACT W3 ... 135 N8
  HDN NW4 ... 116 D2
Alwyns Cl CHERT KT16 ... 195 K6
Alwyns La CHERT KT16 ... 195 J6
Alyn Bank CEND/HSY/T N8 * ... 118 K2
Alyngton BERK HP4 ... 33 K7
Alyth Gdns GLDGN NW11 ... 117 J4
Alzey Gdns HARP AL5 ... 20 C3
Amalgamated Dr BTFD TW8 ... 154 A7
Amanda Cl CHIG IG7 ... 102 G3
Amanda Ct DTCH/LGLY SL3 ... 150 B3
Amanda Ms ROMW/RG RM7 ... 124 D3
Amar Ct WOOL/PLUM SE18 ... 163 J3
Amardeep Ct WOOL/PLUM SE18 ... 163 J4
Amazon St WCHPL E1 ... 140 A8
Ambassador Cl HSLW TW3 ... 153 M8
Ambassador Gdns EHAM E6 ... 142 B6
Ambassador Sq POP/IOD E14 ... 160 M3
Amber Cl BARK/HLT IG6 ... 121 H3
  CHES/WCR EN8 ... 62 C4
  RGUW GU3 ... 248 B7
Ambercroft Wy COUL/CHIP CR5 ... 241 H5
Amberden Av FNCH N3 ... 117 K1
Ambergate St WALW SE17 ... 18 F8
Amber Gv CRICK NW2 ... 116 C6
Amberley Cl CRAWE RH10 ... 284 D7
  HARP AL5 ... 20 A1
  ORP BR6 ... 227 J2
  PIN HA5 ... 113 N1
  RPLY/SEND GU23 ... 251 J1
  SCUP DA14 ... 185 M8
Amberley Ct CRAWW RH11 * ... 283 J8
  SCUP DA14 ... 185 M8
Amberley Dr ADL/WDHM KT15 ... 215 L5
Amberley Gdns
  HOR/WEW KT19 ... 220 C1
  Gv CROY/NA CRO ... 203 N7
Amberley Gv CROY/NA CRO ... 203 N7
  SYD SE26 ... 182 A7
Amberley Rd ABYW SE2 ... 164 N5
  BARK IG11 ... 143 N1
  BKHH IG9 ... 101 P2
  EN EN1 ... 99 N1
  LEY E10 ... 120 F5
  MV/WKIL W9 ... 8 F3
  PLMGR N13 ... 98 G3
  SLN SL2 ... 128 D7
Amberley Wy HGDN/ICK UB10 ... 131 P4
  HSLWW TW4 ... 175 K1
  MRDN SM4 ... 201 J7
  ROMW/RG RM7 ... 124 C2
Amberry Ct HLW CM20 ... 28 G10
Amber St SRTFD E15 ... 141 J7
Amberside Cl ISLW TW7 ... 176 C2
Amberwood Cl WLGTN SM6 ... 222 F5
Amberwood Ri NWMAL KT3 ... 200 B6
Amblecote COB KT11 ... 231 H8
Amblecote Cl LEE/GVPK SE12 ... 183 N6
Amblecote Meadow
  LEE/GVPK SE12 ... 183 N6
Amblecote Mdw
  LEE/GVPK SE12 ... 183 N6
Amblecote Rd LEE/GVPK SE12 ... 183 N6
Ambler Rd FSBYPK N4 ... 119 J3
Ambleside BMLY BR1 ... 183 J9
  EPP CM16 ... 65 K7
  HARP AL5 ... 20 C1
Ambleside Av BECK BR3 ... 204 D5
  HCH RM12 ... 125 J10
  STRHM/NOR SW16 ... 180 E7
  WOT/HER KT12 ... 197 K8
Ambleside Cl CRAWW RH11 ... 282 D8
  HOM E9 ... 120 H6
  LEY E10 ... 120 A4
  REDH RH1 ... 276 B5
Ambleside Crs PEND EN3 ... 80 C7
Ambleside Dr
  EBED/NFELT TW14 ... 174 C4
Ambleside Gdns BELMT SM2 ... 221 M3
  REDBR IG4 ... 122 B2
  SAND/SEL CR2 ... 224 C6
  WBLY HA9 ... 115 J6
Ambleside Rd BXLYHN DA7 ... 164 A8
  WLSDN NW10 ... 136 C2
Ambleside Wy EGH TW20 ... 172 E10
Ambrey Wy WLGTN SM6 ... 222 G6
Ambrook Rd BELV DA17 ... 146 A9
Ambrosden Av WEST SW1P ... 17 H4
Ambrose Av GLDGN NW11 ... 116 C2
Ambrose Cl DART DA1 ... 164 G10
  ORP BR6 ... 207 M2
Ambrose St BERM/RHTH SE16 ... 160 A3
Ambrose Wk BOW E3 * ... 139 L1
Ambulance Rd WAN E11 ... 121 J3
Amelia Cl ACT W3 ... 135 N10
Amelia St WALW SE17 ... 18 G8
Amen Cnr STP EC4M * ... 12 D6
  TOOT SW17 ... 180 B9
Amen Ct STP EC4M ... 12 D5
America Sq TWRH EC3N ... 13 L7
America St STHWK SE1 ... 19 H9
Amerland Rd PUT/ROE SW15 ... 179 J2
Amersham Av UED N18 ... 99 U3
Amersham Cl HARH RM3 ... 105 M7
Amersham Dr HARH RM3 ... 105 M7
Amersham Gv NWCR SE14 ... 160 E8
Amersham Pl AMSS HP7 ... 69 P5
Amersham Rd AMS HP6 ... 51 H10
Amersham Rd AMS HP6 ... 70 B5
  CFSP/GDCR SL9 ... 50 A5
  CFSP/GDCR SL9 ... 90 A5
  CROY/NA CRO ... 203 M6
  CSTG HP8 ... 69 N10
  DEN/HRF UB9 ... 70 H6
  HARH RM3 ... 105 M7
  NWCR SE14 ... 160 E7
Amersham V NWCR SE14 ... 160 E6
Amersham Wy AMS HP6 ... 71 H1
Amery Gdns GPK RM2 ... 124 F1
  WLSDN NW10 ... 137 K1
Amery Rd HRW HA1 ... 114 G8
Amesbury Av
  BRXS/STRHM SW2 ... 180 A4
Amesbury Cl WPK KT4 ... 201 H1
Amesbury Dr CHING E4 ... 87 J8
Amesbury Rd BMLY BR1 ... 184 C6
  DAGW RM9 ... 143 P1
  EPP CM16 ... 65 K9
  FELT TW13 ... 174 E5
Ames Cots POP/IOD E14 * ... 140 C7
Amethyst Rd CRICK NW2 ... 136 D1
Amethyst Rd SRTFD E15 ... 121 K9
Amey Dr GT/LBKH KT23 ... 236 D10
Amherst Av WEA W13 ... 135 H8


Amherst Cl STMC/STPC BR5 ... 207 K4
Amherst Dr STMC/STPC BR5 ... 207 J4
Amherst Gdns WEA W13 * ... 135 H8
Amherst Hl SEV TN13 ... 246 F8
Amherst Rd SEV TN13 ... 247 J8
  WEA W13 ... 135 H8
Amhurst Pde STNW/STAM N16 * ... 119 N5
Amhurst Pk STNW/STAM N16 ... 119 M5
Amhurst Rd HACK E8 ... 119 M5
Amhurst Ter STNW/STAM N16 ... 119 M5
Amicia Gdns BCTR RM8 ... 123 L2
Amidas Gdns BCTR RM8 ... 123 H3
Amies St BTSEA SW11 ... 158 E4
Amina Wy BERM/RHTH SE16 ... 159 N4
Amis Av ADL/WDHM KT15 ... 215 K7
  HOR/WEW KT19 ... 219 M3
Amity Gv RYNPK SW20 ... 200 F1
Amity Rd SRTFD E15 ... 141 L8
Ammanford Gn
  CDALE/KGS NW9 * ... 116 B4
Amner Rd BTSEA SW11 ... 180 A1
Amor Rd HMSMTH W6 ... 156 E7
Amott Rd PECK SE15 ... 159 P9
Ampere Wy CROY/NA CRO ... 202 F7
Ampleforth Cl ORP BR6 ... 227 M1
Ampleforth Rd ABYW SE2 ... 165 L1
Ampthill Est CAMTN NW1 ... 5 H8
Ampthill Sq CAMTN NW1 ... 5 H8
Amroth Cl FSTH SE23 ... 182 A5
Amroth Gn CDALE/KGS NW9 * ... 116 B4
Amstel Gv POP/IOD E14 ... 141 H2
Amsterdam Rd POP/IOD E14 ... 161 N2
Amwell Cl ENC/FH EN2 ... 79 L1
  GSTN WD25 ... 56 B2
Amwell Common WGCE AL7 ... 23 L5
Amwell End WARE SG12 ... 26 B1
Amwell Hl WARE SG12 ... 26 B1
Amwell La STALE/WH AL4 ... 20 D4
Amwell St CLKNW EC1R ... 6 A9
  HOD EN11 ... 44 F2
Amyand Cots TWK TW1 * ... 176 C3
Amyand Park Gdns TWK TW1 ... 176 C4
Amyand Park Rd TWK TW1 ... 176 B4
Amy Cl WLGTN SM6 ... 222 F6
Amy Rd OXTED RH8 ... 261 K5
Amyruth Rd BROCKY SE4 ... 182 A1
Amy Warne Cl EHAM E6 ... 142 B7
Anatola Rd ARCH N19 ... 118 C7
Ancaster Cl NWMAL KT3 ... 200 D6
Ancaster Ms BECK BR3 ... 204 C3
Ancaster Rd BECK BR3 ... 204 C3
Ancaster St WOOL/PLUM SE18 ... 163 N4
Anchorage Cl WIM/MER SW19 ... 179 K6
Anchor & Hope La CHARL SE7 ... 161 N2
Anchor Bvd RDART DA2 ... 168 D4
Anchor Cl BARK IG11 ... 143 L3
  CHES/WCR EN8 ... 62 C4
  RGUW GU3 ... 248 B7
Anchor Hl WOKN/KNAP GU21 ... 231 H9
Anchor Ms CLPH SW4 * ... 158 B10
Anchor Rd RAIN RM13 ... 145 J5
Anchor Rd MNPK E12 ... 122 G10
Anchor Ter WCHPL E1 * ... 140 C6
Anchor Yd FSBYE EC1V * ... 7 H9
Ancill Cl HMSMTH W6 ... 157 H6
Ancona Rd WLSDN NW10 ... 136 D3
  WOOL/PLUM SE18 ... 162 G4
Andace Park Gdns BMLY BR1 * ... 184 D6
Andalus Rd BRXN/ST SW9 ... 158 F9
Ander Cl ALP/SUD HA0 ... 115 J9
Andermans WDSR SL4 * ... 148 A7
Anderson Cl ACT W3 ... 136 A8
  CHEAM SM3 ... 201 K8
  DEN/HRF UB9 ... 91 K9
  HOR/WEW KT19 ... 219 N8
  UED N18 ... 100 C1
Anderson Dr ASHF TW15 ... 157 N6
Anderson Pl HSLW TW3 ... 154 A10
Anderson Rd HOM E9 ... 139 H3
  WEY KT13 ... 196 E10
  WFD IG8 ... 122 A1
Anderson's Pl HSLW TW3 ... 154 A10
Anderson Sq IS N1 ... 6 C6
Anderson St CHEL SW3 ... 15 P7
Andover Av CAN/RD E16 ... 142 A9
Andover Cl EBED/NFELT TW14 ... 174 A4
  GFD/PVL UB6 ... 133 P4
  HOR/WEW KT19 ... 220 A7
  UX/CGN UB8 ... 131 K4
Andover Pl KIL/WHAMP NW6 ... 2 E1
Andover Rd HOLWY N7 ... 118 F1
  ORP BR6 ... 207 M3
  WHTN TW2 ... 176 C6
Andover Ter HMSMTH W6 * ... 156 F8
Andre St HACK E8 ... 120 A10
Andrew Borde St
  LSQ/SEVD WC2H * ... 11 K5
Andrew Cl BARK/HLT IG6 ... 102 F3
  DART DA1 ... 186 E1
  RAD WD7 ... 57 L9
Andrewes Gdns EHAM E6 ... 142 B8
Andrew La SLN SL2 ... 109 H6
Andrew Pl VX/NE SW8 ... 158 A7
Andrews Cl BKHH IG9 ... 101 M3
  HNHE HP2 ... 35 M4
  HRW HA1 ... 114 D6
  STMC/STPC BR5 ... 207 N3
  WPK KT4 ... 201 J1
Andrew's Cl EW KT17 ... 220 C10
Andrewsfield WGCE AL7 ... 23 M5
Andrews La CHESW EN7 ... 61 M4
Andrews Rd BETH E2 ... 140 A3
  STALE/WH AL4 ... 21 H10
Andrew St POP/IOD E14 ... 140 N8
Andromeda Cl CRAWW RH11 ... 283 P6
Andwell Cl ABYW SE2 ... 165 L10
Anelle Ri HHS/BOV HP3 ... 35 P5
Anerley Gv NRWD SE19 ... 181 H9
Anerley Hl NRWD SE19 ... 181 J9
Anerley Pk PGE/AN SE20 ... 182 C10
Anerley Park Rd PGE/AN SE20 ... 182 D10
Anerley Rd PGE/AN SE20 ... 182 D10
Anerley Station Rd
  PGE/AN SE20 ... 182 D10
Anerley V NRWD SE19 ... 181 M10
Anfield Cl BAL SW12 ... 180 D2
Angas Ct WEY KT13 ... 216 D2
Angela Carter Cl
  BRXN/ST SW9 ... 158 F9
Angel Aly WCHPL E1 ... 13 N3
Angel Cl HPTN TW12 ... 174 G10
  UED N18 ... 99 M7
Angel Corner Pde UED N18 * ... 99 P7
Angel Ct LOTH EC2R ... 13 H5
Angelfield HSLW TW3 ... 175 H9
Angel Ga GU GU1 ... 268 A4
Angel Gdns GU GU1 ... 250 A6
  MTCM CR4 ... 180 B7
Angelica Cl WDR/YW UB7 ... 132 A2
Angelica Dr EHAM E6 ... 142 H1
Angel La HYS/HAR UB3 ... 132 A4
  SRTFD E15 ... 141 J6
Angell Park Gdns
  BRXN/ST SW9 ... 158 G10
Angell Rd BRXN/ST SW9 ... 158 G10
Angel Ms IS N1 ... 6 B6
Angel Pas CANST EC4R ... 12 G8
Angel Pl BORO SE1 ... 19 J2


Angel Pl REIG RH2 * ... 275 L2
Angel Rd HRW HA1 ... 114 E5
  THDIT KT7 ... 198 F8
Angel Road (North Circular)
  UED N18 ... 99 P6
Angel Sq FSBYE EC1V * ... 6 C8
Angel Wk HMSMTH W6 ... 156 F9
Angelwood Cl RAIN RM13 ... 124 F8
Angerstein La BKHTH/KID SE3 ... 161 K6
Angle Cl HGDN/ICK UB10 ... 132 A2
Anglefield Rd BERK HP4 ... 33 M5
Angle Rd WTHK RM20 ... 167 J5
Anglers La KTTN NW5 ... 4 E2
Anglers Reach SURB KT6 ... 199 J5
Anglesea Ms
  WOOL/PLUM SE18 ... 162 G3
Anglesea Pl CVW DA11 ... 190 E2
Anglesea Rd KUT/HW KT1 ... 199 J4
  STMC/STPC BR5 ... 207 M6
  WOOL/PLUM SE18 ... 162 E3
Anglesey Cl ASHF TW15 ... 157 L8
  CRAWW RH11 ... 283 M10
Anglesey Court Rd CAR SM5 ... 222 B5
Anglesey Dr RAIN RM13 ... 145 K6
Anglesey Gdns OXHEY WD19 ... 93 K6
Anglesmede Crs PIN HA5 ... 113 N1
Anglesmede Wy PIN HA5 ... 113 N1
Angles Rd STRHM/NOR SW16 ... 180 F7
Anglia Cl TOTM N17 ... 100 A8
Anglian Cl WATN WD24 ... 73 K6
Anglian Rd WAN E11 ... 121 P5
Anglo Rd BOW E3 ... 139 K8
Angus Dr RSLP HA4 ... 113 A9
Angus Gdns CDALE/KGS NW9 ... 96 A9
Angus Rd PLSTW E13 ... 141 N2
Angus St NWCR SE14 ... 160 C6
Anhalt Rd BTSEA SW11 ... 157 P6
Ankerdine Crs
  WOOL/PLUM SE18 ... 162 E7
Anlaby Rd TEDD TW11 ... 175 D8
Anley Rd HMSMTH W6 ... 156 H5
Anmersh Gv STAN HA7 ... 95 J9
Annabel Cl POP/IOD E14 ... 140 N8
Anna Cl HACK E8 ... 7 M5
Annaele Neagle Cl FSTGT E7 ... 121 K8
Annandale Gv HGDN/ICK UB10 ... 112 D8
Annandale Rd BFN/LL DA15 ... 185 H3
  CHSWK W4 ... 156 B3
  CROY/NA CRO ... 204 D9
  GNWCH SE10 ... 161 J3
  GUW GU2 ... 267 N2
Anna Neagle Cl FSTGT E7 ... 121 K8
Annan Wy ROM RM1 ... 104 D7
Anne Boleyn's Wk
  CHEAM SM3 ... 220 G4
  KUTN/CMB KT2 ... 177 K8
Anne Case Ms NWMAL KT3 * ... 200 A3
Anne Compton Ms
  LEE/GVPK SE12 ... 183 J3
Anne Heart Cl CDW/CHF RM16 ... 167 J3
Anners Cl EGH TW20 ... 194 F3
Annesley Av CDALE/KGS NW9 ... 96 A1
Annesley Cl WLSDN NW10 ... 117 H8
Annesley Dr CROY/NA CRO ... 204 E10
Annesley Rd BKHTH/KID SE3 ... 161 N7
Annesmere Gdns
  BKHTH/KID SE3 ... 162 A9
Anne St PLSTW E13 ... 141 M6
Annett Cl SHPTN TW17 ... 196 F4
Annette Cl
  KTN/HRWW/WS HA3 ... 94 D10
Annette Rd HOLWY N7 ... 118 F9
Annett Rd WOT/HER KT12 ... 197 H7
Anne Wy BARK/HLT IG6 ... 102 F3
Annie Besant Cl BOW E3 * ... 139 K7
Annie Brookes Cl STA TW18 ... 172 G6
Anningsley Pk CHERT KT16 ... 214 E6
Anning St WCHPL E1 ... 13 K1
Annington Rd EFNCH N2 ... 118 A1
Annisdowne Cl RDKG RH5 ... 270 G8
Annis Rd HOM E9 ... 140 D1
Ann Moss Wy
  BERM/RHTH SE16 ... 160 B2
Ann's Cl KTBR SW1X ... 16 B2
Ann St WOOL/PLUM SE18 ... 162 G3
Annsworthy Av THHTH CR7 ... 203 L5
Annsworthy Crs SNWD SE25 ... 203 L4
Ansar Gdns WALTH E17 ... 120 D2
Anscuif Rd SLN SL2 ... 128 A5
Ansdell Rd PECK SE15 ... 161 L1
Ansdell St KENS W8 ... 14 F3
Ansdell Ter KENS W8 * ... 14 F3
Ansell Gv CAR SM5 ... 202 A8
Ansell Rd DORK RH4 ... 272 G4
  TOOT SW17 ... 179 M6
Anselm Cl CROY/NA CRO ... 204 A1
Anselm Rd FUL/PGN SW6 ... 14 B10
  PIN HA5 ... 93 M7
Ansford Rd BMLY BR1 ... 183 H8
Ansleigh Pl NTGHL W11 ... 136 D7
Ansley Cl SAND/SEL CR2 ... 224 D9
Anslow Gdns IVER SL0 ... 130 C4
Anslow Pl SL SL1 ... 129 N2
Anson Cl HHS/BOV HP3 ... 52 C3
  PUR/KEN CR8 ... 241 L6
  ROMW/RG RM7 ... 104 E1
  STAL AL1 ... 38 C8
  STALE/WH AL4 ... 21 H10
Anson Rd ARCH N19 ... 118 D9
  CRICK NW2 ... 116 G3
Anson Wk NTHWD HA6 ... 92 D5
Anstead Dr RAIN RM13 ... 144 G8
Anstey Rd PECK SE15 ... 159 H4
Anstice Cl CHSWK W4 ... 156 C6
Anstridge Rd ELTH/MOT SE9 ... 184 D3
Antelope Av CDW/CHF RM16 ... 167 H6
Antelope Rd
  WOOL/PLUM SE18 ... 162 G4
Anthony Cl MLHL NW7 ... 96 E2
  OXHEY WD19 ... 92 L2
  SEV TN13 ... 246 F7
Anthony Rd BORE WD6 ... 75 K6
  GFD/PVL UB6 ... 134 B3
  SNWD SE25 ... 203 P4
  WELL DA16 ... 163 P4
Anthony's Cl WAP E1W ... 15 L9
Anthony St WCHPL E1 ... 140 B8
Anthony Wy SL SL1 ... 128 B9
Anthus Ms NTHWD HA6 ... 92 D7
Antill Rd BOW E3 ... 139 L6
  SEVS/STOTM N15 ... 119 P5
Antill Ter WCHPL E1 ... 140 E8
Antlands La HORL RH6 ... 280 C9
Antlands La East HORL RH6 ... 280 F9
Antlands La West HORL RH6 ... 280 E9
Antlers Hl CHING E4 ... 87 P9
Antoinette Ct ABLGY WD5 * ... 56 D2
Anton Crs SUT SM1 ... 201 K10
Antoneys Cl PIN HA5 ... 93 L10
Antonine Ga STALW/RED AL3 ... 37 P7
Anton Pl WBLY HA9 ... 115 P3
Anton Rd SOCK/AV RM15 ... 146 G6
Anton St HACK E8 ... 7 K1
Antrim Gv HAMP NW3 ... 4 B1
Antrobus Cl SUT SM1 ... 221 L3
Antrobus Rd CHSWK W4 ... 155 P3
Anvil Cl STRHM/NOR SW16 ... 180 D10
Anvil La COB KT11 ... 217 H10
Anvil Pl LCOL/BKTW AL2 ... 59 H1
Anvil Rd SUN TW16 ... 195 J3
Anworth Cl WFD IG8 ... 101 H6
Anyards Rd COB KT11 ... 216 F10
Anzio Gdns CTHM CR3 ... 241 K2
Aostle Wy STRHM/NOR SW16 ... 181 J10
Apeldoorn Dr WLGTN SM6 ... 222 F5


Aperdele Rd LHD/OX KT22 ... 236 D1
Aperfield Rd BH/WHM TN16 ... 244 B3
  ERITH DA8 ... 164 G5
Apers Av WOKS/MYFD GU22 ... 232 C7
Apex Cl BECK BR3 ... 204 G1
Apex Pde MLHL NW7 * ... 96 A5
Apex Point BRKMPK AL9 * ... 40 F8
Apex Rd HTWD SL6 ... 128 B6
Apley Rd REIG RH2 ... 275 K6
Apollo Av BMLY BR1 ... 205 N1
  NTHWD HA6 ... 93 H6
Apollo Cl HCH RM12 ... 125 J3
Apollo Pl WAN E11 ... 121 K8
  WBPTN SW10 * ... 157 N9
  WOKN/KNAP GU21 ... 231 M5
Apollo Wy ERITH DA8 ... 164 G3
  HHNE HP2 ... 35 P4
  THMD SE28 ... 163 J10
Apothecary St BLKFR EC4V * ... 12 C6
Appach Rd BRXS/STRHM SW2 ... 181 H1
Apperlie Dr
  BRKHM/BTCW RH3 ... 273 P1
Apple Blossom Ct
  VX/NE SW8 * ... 158 C6
Appleby Cl CHING E4 ... 101 H1
  SEVS/STOTM N15 ... 119 L3
  STMC/STPC BR5 ... 207 H3
  UX/CGN UB8 ... 132 D8
  WHTN TW2 ... 176 C5
Appleby Gdns
  EBED/NFELT TW14 ... 174 A4
Appleby Rd CAN/RD E16 ... 141 M8
  HACK E8 ... 7 K2
Appleby St BETH E2 ... 7 L1
  CHESW EN7 ... 61 M2
Apple Cells HHS/BOV HP3 ... 52 D3
Applecroft BERK HP4 ... 33 J2
  LCOL/BKTW AL2 ... 58 G4
Applecroft Rd WCCW AL8 ... 22 E5
Appledore Av BXLYHN DA7 ... 164 D7
  RSLP HA4 ... 113 J8
Appledore Cl EDGW HA8 ... 95 M4
  HARH RM3 ... 105 K9
  HAYES BR2 ... 205 L5
  TOOT SW17 ... 180 A5
Appledore Crs SCUP DA14 ... 185 H6
Appledore Wy MLHL NW7 ... 96 C8
Appledown Ri COUL/CHIP CR5 ... 240 D1
Appledfield AMSS HP7 * ... 69 P5
  CRAWE RH10 ... 283 P6
Appleford's Cl NKENS W10 ... 8 D9
Appleford's Cl BTFD TW8 ... 155 J8
Applegarth CROY/NA CRO ... 224 G4
  ESH/CLAY KT10 ... 218 G2
Applegarth Av GUW GU2 ... 249 J10
Applegarth Dr
  GNTH/NBYPK IG2 ... 123 J2
Applegarth Rd THMD SE28 ... 143 J10
  WKENS W14 ... 156 G2
Apple Ga BRW CM14 ... 86 F9
Apple Gv CHSGTN KT9 ... 219 K1
  EN EN1 ... 79 M7
Apple Ldg ALP/SUD HA0 * ... 115 H8
Apple Market KUT/HW KT1 ... 199 J2
Apple Orch SWLY BR8 ... 208 E4
The Apple Orch HHNE HP2 ... 36 A4
Apple Rd WAN E11 ... 121 K6
Appletree Cl EBAR EN4 ... 77 P8
  HLWW/ROY CM19 ... 46 F7
Appletree Gdns EBAR EN4 ... 78 A4
Apple Trees Pl
  WOKS/MYFD GU22 * ... 231 P5
Appletree Wk CSHM HP5 ... 51 J10
  GSTN WD25 ... 56 C2
Apple tree Yd STJS SW1Y ... 11 H9
Applewood Cl CRICK NW2 ... 116 H8
  HGDN/ICK UB10 ... 111 P9
  TRDG/WHET N20 ... 97 P2
Applewood Dr PLSTW E13 ... 141 M6
Appleyard Ter PEND EN3 * ... 80 B3
Appold St ERITH DA8 ... 164 G5
Apprentice Gdns NTHLT UB5 ... 133 N6
Apprentice Wy CLPT E5 ... 120 G5
Approach La MLHL NW7 ... 97 H6
The Approach ACT W3 ... 136 B6
  BETH E2 ... 140 B4
  BH/WHM TN16 ... 243 P6
  E/WMO/HCT KT8 ... 197 P5
  EBAR EN4 ... 77 M6
  PUR/KEN CR8 ... 223 H8
  RYNPK SW20 ... 200 F2
  STAL AL1 ... 38 D7
Appspond La LCOL/BKTW AL2 ... 37 K10
Aprey Gdns HDN NW4 ... 116 C2
April Cl ASHTD KT21 ... 237 L4
  FELT TW13 ... 174 D7
  HNWL W7 ... 134 D9
  ORP BR6 ... 227 M2
April Dn FSTH SE23 ... 182 G6
April St HACK E8 ... 119 N10
Aprilwood Cl ADL/WDHM KT15 ... 215 H3
Apsley Cl HRW HA1 ... 114 B3
Apsley La NWMAL KT3 ... 199 N3
  SNWD SE25 ... 204 A4
Apsley Wy CRICK NW2 ... 116 G7
Aquarius TWK TW1 * ... 176 C4
Aquarius Wy NTHWD HA6 ... 93 H8
Aquila Cl LHD/OX KT22 ... 237 K7
Aquila St STJWD NW8 ... 3 M1
Aquinas St STHWK SE1 ... 12 B10
Arabella Dr PUT/ROE SW15 ... 156 B10
Arabia Cl CHING E4 ... 88 B10
Arabin Rd BROCKY SE4 ... 161 N1
Araby Cnr STNW/STAM N16 ... 196 D6
Aragien Av SOCK/AV RM15 ... 146 G2
Aragon Av EW KT17 ... 220 G6
  THDIT KT7 ... 198 C4
Aragon Cl CROY/NA CRO ... 205 K9
  ENC/FH EN2 ... 78 G1
  HAYES BR2 ... 206 D4
  LOU IG10 ... 89 J10
  SUN TW16 ... 174 D9
Aragon Ct HHS/BOV HP3 ... 52 D3
Aragon Dr BARK/HLT IG6 ... 103 H2
  RSLP HA4 ... 113 K5
Aragon Pl MRDN SM4 ... 201 H5
Aragon Rd KUTN/CMB KT2 ... 177 H7
  MRDN SM4 ... 200 G6
Aran Ct WEY KT13 * ... 197 L6
Aran Dr STAN HA7 ... 95 K2
Aran Hts CSTG HP8 ... 89 P4
Arandora Crs CHDH RM6 ... 123 J5
Aran Ms HOLWY N7 * ... 118 G1
Arbery Rd BOW E3 ... 139 K8
Arbor Cl BECK BR3 ... 204 G2
Arbor Ct STNW/STAM N16 ... 119 M9


Angel Pl REIG RH2 *... (already above)
...
Arbour Rd PEND EN3 ... 81 K2

Arbour Sq *WCHPL E1* . . . . . 140 C8
The Arbour *CODL GU7* . . . . . 266 E8
HERT/BAY SG13 . . . . . . . . 25 L7
Arbroath Gn *OXHEY WD19* . . . 69 N5
Arbroath Rd *ELTH/MOT SE9* . . 162 B9
Arbrook La *STMC/STPC BR5* . . 207 N3
Arbrook Ct *HERT/CLAY KT10* . . 218 C3
Arbuthnot La *BXLY DA5* . . . . 185 P7
Arbuthnot Rd *REDH RH1* . . . . 160 C8
Arbutus Rd *REDH RH1* . . . . . 275 M2
Arbutus St *HACK E8* . . . . . . 7 K5
Arcade Chambers
  *ELTH/MOT SE9* . . . . . . . 184 D2
Arcade Pde *CHSGTN KT9* . . . . 219 K1
The Arcade *BEAC HP9* . . . . . 88 D9
  *ELTH/MOT SE9* . . . . . . . 184 D2
  *LVPST EC2M* . . . . . . . . 13 J4
  *REDH RH1* . . . . . . . . . 258 B9
  *WALTH E17* . . . . . . . . . 120 F2
Arcadia Av *FNCH N3* . . . . . . 97 K5
Arcadia Cl *CAR SM5* . . . . . . 222 B1
Arcadian Av *BXLY DA5* . . . . . 185 P2
Arcadian Cl *BXLY DA5* . . . . . 185 P2
Arcadian Pl *WAND/EARL SW18* . 179 J7
Arcadian Rd *BXLY DA5* . . . . . 185 P5
Arcadia St *POP/IOD E14* . . . . 140 F8
Arcany Rd *SOCK/AV RM15* . . . 146 G6
Archangel St
  *BERM/RHTH SE16* . . . . . 160 C1
Archates Av *CDW/CHF RM16* . . 167 M2
Archbishop's Pl
  *BRXS/STRHM SW2* . . . . . 180 G2
Archdale Pl *NWMAL KT3* . . . . 199 N3
Archdale Rd *EDUL SE22* . . . . 176 B3
Archel Rd *WKENS W14* . . . . . 14 C9
Archer Cl *BAR EN5* . . . . . . . 77 J10
  *KGLGY WD4* . . . . . . . . . 54 C1
  *KUTN/CMB KT2* . . . . . . . 177 K10
Archer Ct *FELT TW13* . . . . . 175 H4
Archer Ms *HPTN TW12* . . . . . 176 B9
Archer Rd *SNWD SE25* . . . . . 204 A8
  *STMC/STPC BR5* . . . . . . 207 K6
Archers Hlww/ROY CM19 . . . . 46 D6
Archers Cl *HERT/WAT SG14* . . 25 K4
Archers Dr *PEND EN3* . . . . . 30 J6
Archers Rds *STAL AL1* . . . . . 38 E4
Archers Green La *WLYN AL6* . . 23 N3
Archers Ride *STAL AL1* . . . . . 23 L7
Archers Sq *NWCR SE14* . . . . 160 B5
Archer St *SOHO/SHAV W1D* . . 11 J7
Archer Wy *SWLY BR8* . . . . . 208 G2
  *KTN/HRWW/WS HA3* . . . . 114 C1
The Arches *ELTH/MOT SE9* . . 184 C1
  *KTN/HRWW/WS HA3* . . . . wait

The Arches *CHCR WC2N* *. . . . 11 J7
  *RYLN/HDSTN HA2* . . . . . . 114 A7
  *WDSR SL4* *. . . . . . . . . 149 H7
Archery Cl *BAY/PAD W2* . . . . 9 G7
  *KTN/HRWW/WS HA3* . . . . 114 C1
Archfield *WGCE AL7* . . . . . . 23 H2
Archibald Cl *PEND EN3* . . . . 80 C2
Archibald Rd *HARH RM3* . . . . 105 P9
  *HOLWY N7* . . . . . . . . . 118 A3
Archibald St *BOW E3* . . . . . 140 F5
Archie Cl *WDR/YW UB7* . . . . 132 E1
Arch Rd *WOT/HER KT12* . . . . 197 L10
Arch St *STHWK SE1* . . . . . . 18 E4
Archway Cl *ARCH N19* *. . . . 118 D7
  *NKENS W10* . . . . . . . . . 136 C7
  *WIM/MER SW19* . . . . . . . 179 L7
  *WLGTN SM6* . . . . . . . . . 202 F10
Archway Ms *DORK RH4* . . . . 272 F1
Archway Rd *HGT N6* . . . . . . 118 A3
Archway St *SW13* . . . . . . . 158 B9
Arcola St *HACK E8* . . . . . . 7 J1
Arctic St *KTTN NW5* . . . . . . 119 N10
Arcturus Rd *CRAWW RH11* . . . 283 H9
Arcus Rd *BMLY BR1* . . . . . . 183 K9
Ardbeg Rd *HNHL SE24* . . . . . 181 C2
Arden Cl *BUSH WD23* . . . . . 94 E1
  *HHS/BOV HP3* . . . . . . . . 52 D4
  *HRW HA1* . . . . . . . . . . 114 C8
  *REIG RH2* . . . . . . . . . . 275 L4
  *THMD SE28* . . . . . . . . . 143 N8
  *WHTN TW2* . . . . . . . . . 175 N3
Arden Court Gdns *EFNCH N2* . 97 H5
Arden Crs *DAGW RM9* . . . . . 143 N2
  *POP/IOD E14* . . . . . . . . 160 F5
Arden Est *IS N1* . . . . . . . . 7 H8
Arden Gv *HARP AL5* . . . . . . 20 A2
  *ORP BR6* . . . . . . . . . . 226 E1
Arden Mhor *PIN HA5* . . . . . . 113 J2
Arden Rd *CRAWE RH10* . . . . 284 A9
  *FNCH N3* . . . . . . . . . . 117 H1
  *WEA W13* . . . . . . . . . . 135 N9
Ardens Marsh *STALE/WH AL4* . 39 J4
Arden Wy *STALE/WH AL4* . . . 39 J4
Ardent Cl *SNWD SE25* . . . . . 203 M8
Ardesley Wd *WEY KT13* . . . . 216 F1
Ardfern Av *STRHM/NOR SW16* . 203 H1
Ardfillan Rd *CAT SE6* . . . . . 183 H1
Ardgowan Rd *CAT SE6* . . . . 183 K4
Ardilaun Rd *HBRY N5* . . . . . 119 K9
Ardingly Cl *CRAWW RH11* . . . 283 L5
  *CROY/NA CRO* . . . . . . . 204 C10
Ardleigh Cl *EMPK RM11* . . . . 125 L1
Ardleigh Ct *BRWN CM15* . . . . 107 L1
Ardleigh Gdns *CHEAM SM3* . . 201 K8
Ardleigh Green Rd
  *EMPK RM11* . . . . . . . . 125 L1
  *IS N1* . . . . . . . . . . . . 7 J2
  *WALTH E17* . . . . . . . . . 100 E9
Ardleigh Ter *WALTH E17* . . . . 100 E9
Ardley Cl *CAT SE6* . . . . . . . 182 D7
  *WLSDN NW10* . . . . . . . . 116 B8
Ardley Crs *RBSF CM22* . . . . 31 J1
Ardlui Rd *WNWD SE27* . . . . 162 D8
Ardmay Gdns *SURB KT6* . . . . 199 K5
Ardmere Av *GFD/PVL UB6* . . . wait

Ardmere Rd *LEW SE13* . . . . . 183 J2
Ardmore Av *GU GU2* . . . . . . 249 N8
Ardmore La *BKHH IG9* . . . . . 101 N1
Ardmore Pl *BKHH IG9* . . . . . 101 N1
Ardmore Rd *SOCK/AV RM15* . . 146 G6
Ardmore Wy *GU GU2* . . . . . 249 N8
Ardoch Rd *CAT SE6* . . . . . . 183 G5
Ardra Rd *ED N9* . . . . . . . . 100 C4
Ardrossan Cl *SLN SL2* . . . . . 129 J3
Ardrossan Gdns *WPK KT4* . . . 200 F2
Ardross Av *NTHWD HA6* . . . . 92 F6
Ardshiel Cl *PUT/ROE SW15* . . 159 G9
Ardshiel Dr *REDH RH1* . . . . . 275 P7
Ardwell Av *BARK/HLT IG6* . . . 122 F3
Ardwell Rd *BRXS/STRHM SW2* . 180 F5
Ardwick Rd *CRICK NW2* . . . . 117 H1
Arena Est *FSBYPK N4* *. . . . . 5 M1
The Arena *STKPK UB11* *. . . . 132 D10
Arethusa Pl *SWCM DA10* *. . . 166 G10
Arewater Gn *LOU IG10* . . . . 236 E1
Argall Av *LEY E10* . . . . . . . 101 G6
Argall Wy *LEY E10* . . . . . . . 120 C6
Argenta Wy *WLSDN NW10* . . . 135 K2
Argent Cl *EGH TW20* . . . . . 192 B9
Argent St *SURB KT6* . . . . . . 199 M10
Argles Cl *RDART DA2* . . . . . 188 F1
Argon Ms *FUL/PGN SW6* . . . . 157 A9
Argon Rd *UED N18* . . . . . . 100 G4
Argosy Gdns *STA TW18* . . . . 173 N9
Argosy La *STWL/WRAY TW19* . 173 N9
Argus Cl *ROMW/RG RM7* . . . 104 C9
Argus Wk *CRAWW RH11* . . . . 283 K10
Argus Wy *NTHLT UB5* . . . . . 133 M5
Argyle Av *HSLW TW3* . . . . . 175 G1
Argyle Cnr *WEA W13* . . . . . 134 G2
Argyle Cl *WATW WD18* . . . . 72 G2
Argyle Rd *BAR EN5* . . . . . . 76 A5
  *CAN/RD E16* . . . . . . . . 141 M9
  *GFD/PVL UB6* . . . . . . . 134 E5

**Column 2**

HSLW TW3 . . . . . . . . . . 176 A1
IL IG1 . . . . . . . . . . . . . 122 D7
NFNCH/WDSPK N12 . . . . . 97 K5
RYLN/HDSTN HA2 . . . . . . 114 A4
SEV TN13 . . . . . . . . . . 265 J11
SRTFD E15 . . . . . . . . . . 121 K9
TOTM N17 . . . . . . . . . . 99 P9
WCHPL E1 . . . . . . . . . . 14 A1
WEA W13 . . . . . . . . . . 134 F8
Argyle Sq *IS N1* . . . . . . . . 5 M3
Argyle St *CAMTN NW1* . . . . . 5 L4
Argyle Wk *CAMTN NW1* . . . . 5 L5
Argyll Av *STHL UB1* . . . . . . 134 A10
Argyll Cl *BRXN/ST SW9* . . . . 158 A9
Argyll Gdns *EDGW HA8* . . . . 96 D8
Argyll Rd *GRAYS RM17* . . . . 191 M7
  *HHNE HP2* . . . . . . . . . 35 J7
  *KENS W8* . . . . . . . . . . 14 E2
  *WOOL/PLUM SE18* . . . . . 162 F2
Argyll St *SOHO/SHAV W1D* . . 10 G6
Archie St *STHWK SE1* . . . . . 19 K2
Arica Rd *BROCKY SE4* . . . . . 160 D10
Ariel Cl *DAGE RM10* . . . . . . 191 J7
Ariel Rd *KIL/WHAMP NW6* . . . 2 E1
Ariel Wy *HSLWW TW4* . . . . . 153 J9
  *SHB W12* . . . . . . . . . . 156 F10
Arisdale Av *SOCK/AV RM15* . . 146 C2
Aristotle Rd *CLAP SW4* . . . . 158 E9
Ark Av *CDW/CHF RM16* . . . . 167 M2
Arkindale Rd *CAT SE6* . . . . . 183 H6
Arklay Cl *UX/CGN UB8* . . . . 132 A6
Arkley Cl *WALTH E17* . . . . . 120 E3
Arkley Dr *BAR EN5* . . . . . . 76 B3
Arkley Cl *BAR EN5* . . . . . . . 76 D7
Arkley Rd *HHNE HP2* . . . . . 36 C1
  *WALTH E17* . . . . . . . . . 120 E3
Arkley Vw *BAR EN5* . . . . . . 76 B3
Arkwright Rd *NWCR SE14* . . . 160 E5
Arkwright Rd *DTCH/LGLY SL3* . 151 H4
  *HAMP NW3* . . . . . . . . . 117 M10
  *SAND/SEL CR2* . . . . . . . 223 N6
  *TIL RM18* . . . . . . . . . . 168 D8
Arkwrights *HLW CM20* . . . . . 29 J10
Arlesford Rd *BRXN/ST SW9* . . 158 F9
Arlingford Rd
  *BRXS/STRHM SW2* . . . . . 181 J4
Arlington *NFNCH/WDSPK N12* . 97 K4
Arlington Av *IS N1* . . . . . . . 6 F3
Arlington Cl *BFN/LL DA15* . . . 185 H3
  *LEW SE13* . . . . . . . . . . 183 J1
  *SUT SM1* . . . . . . . . . . 201 K9
  *TWK TW1* . . . . . . . . . . 177 J2
Arlington Crs *CHES/WCR EN8* . 62 D10
Arlington Dr *CAR SM5* . . . . . 202 A9
  *RSLP HA4* . . . . . . . . . . 113 G10
Arlington Gdns *CHSWK W4* . . 155 P4
  *HARH RM3* . . . . . . . . . 105 M3
  *IL IG1* . . . . . . . . . . . . 122 C5
Arlington Ldg *WEY KT13* . . . . 216 C1
Arlington Pde
  *BRXS/STRHM SW2* *. . . . . 158 G10
Arlington Rd *ASHF TW15* . . . . 174 A8
  *CAMTN NW1* . . . . . . . . 4 B1
  *STHGT/OAK N14* . . . . . . 98 C3
  *TEDD TW11* . . . . . . . . . 176 E7
  *WEA W13* . . . . . . . . . . 134 G8
  *WFD IG8* . . . . . . . . . . 101 M9
Arlington Sq *IS N1* . . . . . . 6 F3
Arlington St *MYFR/PICC W1J* . 10 C9
Arlington Wy *CLKNW EC1R* . . 6 A6
Arliss Wy *NTHLT UB5* . . . . . 133 K3
Arlow Rd *WCHMH N21* . . . . . 99 H8
Armadale Cl *TOTM N17* . . . . 120 A2
Armadale Rd
  *EBED/NFELT TW14* . . . . . 175 H1
  *FUL/PGN SW6* . . . . . . . 157 K6
  *WOKN/KNAP GU21* . . . . . 231 M3
Armada St *DEPT SE8* . . . . . 160 F5
Armada Wy *CAN/RD E16* . . . . 142 F3
Armagh Rd *BOW E3* . . . . . . 140 E3
Armand Cl *WAT WD17* . . . . . 72 A9
Armfield Crs *MTCM CR4* . . . . 202 A4
Armfield Rd *ENC/FH EN2* . . . 79 L5
Arminger Rd *SHB W12* . . . . . 136 E10
Armistice Gdns *SNWD SE25* . . 203 P3
Armitage Cl
  *RKW/CH/CXG WD3* . . . . 71 N3
Armitage Ct *ASC SL5* . . . . . 192 B6
Armitage La *LVPST EC2M* . . . 13 K4
  *SHB W12* . . . . . . . . . . 136 D8
Armitage Rd *GLDGN NW11* . . 117 H6
  *GNWCH SE10* . . . . . . . . 161 L3
Armor Rd *PUR RM19* . . . . . 166 C2
Armour Cl *HOLWY N7* . . . . . 5 N1
Armoury Dr *GVE DA12* . . . . . 191 P8
Armoury Rd *DEPT SE8* . . . . . 160 G8
Armoury Wy
  *WAND/EARL SW18* . . . . . 179 K1
Armstead Wk *DAGE RM10* . . . 144 B2
Armstrong Av *WFD IG8* . . . . 101 J7
Armstrong Cl *BCTR RM8* . . . . 123 N5
  *BMLY BR1* . . . . . . . . . . 206 B3
  *BORE WD6* . . . . . . . . . 75 P7
  *EHAM E6* . . . . . . . . . . 142 C8
  *LCOL/BKTW AL2* . . . . . . 57 K3
  *RSEV TN14* . . . . . . . . . 246 C1
  *RSLP HA4* . . . . . . . . . . 113 H3
  *WOT/HER KT12* . . . . . . . 197 H6
Armstrong Crs *EBAR EN4* . . . 77 N3
Armstrong Gdns *RAD WD7* . . . 57 K8
Armstrong Pl *HHW HP1* . . . . 35 M4
Armstrong Rd *ACT W3* . . . . . 136 C10
  *EGH TW20* . . . . . . . . . 171 P9
  *FELT TW13* . . . . . . . . . 175 M8
  *WLSDN NW10* . . . . . . . . 136 D2
Armstrong Wy *WDGN N22* . . . 99 J6
Armytage Rd *HEST TW5* . . . . 153 L6
Arnal Crs *WAND/EARL SW18* . 179 H3
Arncliffe Cl *FBAR/BDGN N11* . 98 A5
Arncliffe *IS N1* . . . . . . . . . wait

Arndale Wy *EGH TW20* . . . . . 172 B9
Arne Cl *CRAWW RH11* . . . . . 283 J11
Arne Gv *HORL RH6* . . . . . . 279 P2
  *ORP BR6* . . . . . . . . . . 207 J3
Arne St *LSQ/SEVD WC2H* . . . 11 M6
Arnett Cl *RKW/CH/CXG WD3* . 71 K4
Arnett Sq *RKW/CH/CXG WD3* . 71 K5
Arnett Wy *RKW/CH/CXG WD3* . 71 K4
Arneways Av *CHDH RM6* . . . . 123 N2
Arneway St *WEST SW1P* . . . . 17 L4
Arnewood Cl *HLW/OX KT22* . . 218 A10
  *PUT/ROE SW15* . . . . . . . 178 D4
Arney's La *MTCM CR4* . . . . . 202 B6
Arngask Rd *CAT SE6* . . . . . . 183 J3
Arnheim Pl *POP/IOD E14* . . . 160 F2
Arnhem Pl *POP/IOD E14* . . . . 160 F2
Arnhem Dr *CROY/NA CRO* . . . 225 J7
Arnison Rd *E/WMO/HCT KT8* . 198 C7
Arnold Av East *PEND EN3* . . . 80 H4
Arnold Av West *PEND EN3* . . . 80 A4
Arnold Circ *BETH E2* *. . . . . 7 K9
Arnold Cl *KTN/HRWW/WS HA3* . 115 M5
Arnold Crs *ISLW TW7* . . . . . 176 A1
Arnold Dr *CHSGTN KT9* . . . . 219 K5
Arnold Est *STHWK SE1* . . . . 19 M2
Arnold Gdns *PLMGR N13* . . . 99 H5
Arnold Pl *TIL RM18* . . . . . . 168 G7
Arnold Rd *BOW E3* . . . . . . 140 F5
  *DAGW RM9* . . . . . . . . . 144 B4
  *GVE DA12* . . . . . . . . . 190 F5
  *NTHLT UB5* . . . . . . . . . 133 G5
  *SEVS/STOTM N15* . . . . . 119 N1
  *STA TW18* . . . . . . . . . . 173 H10
  *TOOT SW17* . . . . . . . . . 180 A9
  *WAB EN9* . . . . . . . . . . 81 H6
Arnolds Av *BRWN CM15* . . . . 87 P2
Arnolds Cl *BRWN CM15* . . . . 87 P2
Arnolds La *EYN DA4* . . . . . . 187 P6

**Column 3**

EHAM E6 . . . . . . . . . . . 142 C5
GVW DA11 . . . . . . . . . . 190 E6
SEVS/STOTM N15 . . . . . . 119 L3
STMC/STPC BR5 . . . . . . . 207 L4
TOOT SW17 . . . . . . . . . 180 B9
UED N18 . . . . . . . . . . . 99 P5
WATW WD18 . . . . . . . . . 72 A9
Ascots La *BRKMPK AL9* . . . . 23 H10
  *TOOT SW17* . . . . . . . . . 180 A8
Ascot Av *UX/CGN UB8* . . . . . 132 B5
Ascot Cl *BARK/HLT IG6* . . . . 103 H5
  *BORE WD6* . . . . . . . . . 75 N5
Ashanti Ms *HACK E8* . . . . . . 140 A1
Ascot Dr *MNPK E12* . . . . . . 122 A6
Ascot Gdns *WBLY HA9* . . . . . 115 J5
  *STHL UB1* . . . . . . . . . . 114 C10
Ascot Ms *WLGTN SM6* . . . . . 222 D7
Ascot Rd *BROX EN10* . . . . . 44 E2
  *EA W5* . . . . . . . . . . . . 135 J6
  *EBED/NFELT TW14* . . . . . 173 L6
  *NFNCH/WDSPK N12* . . . . 97 L5
  *ORP BR6* . . . . . . . . . . 226 C1
  *STHGT/OAK N14* . . . . . . 98 D4
  *TOOT SW17* . . . . . . . . . 180 B9
Ashbourne Rd *COUL/CHIP CR5* . 240 D4
  *EA W5* . . . . . . . . . . . . 135 G3
  *MTCM CR4* . . . . . . . . . 180 B9
Ashbourne Av *BXLYHN DA7* . . 164 B10
  *EFNCH N2* . . . . . . . . . 117 L2
  *RYLN/HDSTN HA2* . . . . . 114 C7
  *SWFD E18* . . . . . . . . . 102 A10
  *WALTH E17* . . . . . . . . . wait


Arnould Av *CMBW SE5* . . . . . 159 L5
Arnsberg Wy *BXLYHN DA7* . . . 164 B10
Arnside Gdns *WBLY HA9* . . . . 115 J1
Arnside Rd *BXLYHN DA7* . . . . 164 B7
Arnside St *WALW SE17* . . . . 18 F9
Arnulf St *CAT SE6* . . . . . . . 182 G7
Arnull's Rd *STRHM/NOR SW16* . 181 J9
Arodene Rd
  *BRXS/STRHM SW2* . . . . . 180 G2
Arosa Rd *TWK TW1* . . . . . . 177 J2
Arragon Gdns
  *STRHM/NOR SW16* . . . . . 180 F10
  *WWKM BR4* . . . . . . . . . 204 C10
Arragon Rd *EHAM E6* . . . . . 142 A5
  *TWK TW1* . . . . . . . . . . 176 F3
  *WAND/EARL SW18* . . . . . 179 K4
Arran Cl *CRAWW RH11* . . . . 283 L10
  *ERITH DA8* . . . . . . . . . 164 E5
  *HHS/BOV HP3* . . . . . . . 36 B8
  *WLGTN SM6* . . . . . . . . . 222 D1
Arran Dr *MNPK E12* . . . . . . 122 A6
  *STAN HA7* . . . . . . . . . . 95 J1
Arran Ms *EA W5* . . . . . . . . 135 U10
Arranmore Ct *BUSH WD23* . . . 73 M8
Arran Rd *CAT SE6* . . . . . . . 182 C5
Arran Wk *IS N1* . . . . . . . . 6 E3
Arran Wy *ESH/CLAY KT10* . . . 198 A9
Arras Av *MRDN SM4* . . . . . . 201 M5
Arretine Cl *STALW/RED AL3* . . 38 A2
Arreton Md *WOKN/KNAP GU21* . 214 B10
Arrivals Rd *HORL RH6* . . . . . 280 A7
Arrol Rd *BECK BR3* . . . . . . 202 G1
Arrow Rd *BOW E3* . . . . . . . 140 G5
Arrowsmith Rd *CHIG IG7* . . . . 103 J6
Arsenal Rd *ELTH/MOT SE9* . . 162 D1
Arsenal Wy *WOOL/PLUM SE18* . 162 F3
Artel Cft *CRAWE RH10* . . . . . 284 A7
Artemis Cl *GVE DA12* . . . . . 191 H3
Artemis Pl *WAND/EARL SW18* . 179 H3
Arterberry Rd *RYNPK SW20* . . 178 F10
Arterial Road North Stifford
  *CDW/CHF RM16* . . . . . . 167 J1
Arterial Road Purfleet
  *PUR RM19* . . . . . . . . . 166 B3
Arterial Road Purfleet
  *SOCK/AV RM15* . . . . . . . 165 P2
Arterial Road (West Thurrock)
  *WTHK W20* . . . . . . . . . 166 G2
Arterial Road West Thurrock
  *WTHK W20* . . . . . . . . . 166 G2
Artesian Cl *ROM RM1* . . . . . 124 G4
  *WLSDN NW10* . . . . . . . . 136 A2
Artesian Gv *BAR EN5* . . . . . 77 M8
Artesian Houses
  *BAY/PAD W2* *. . . . . . . 8 E6
Arthingworth St *SRTFD E15* . . 141 K3
Arthurdon Rd *BROCKY SE4* . . 182 F1
Arthur Gv *WOOL/PLUM SE18* . 162 F3
Arthur Rd *BH/WHM TN16* . . . 243 P11
  *CHDH RM6* . . . . . . . . . 123 M5
  *CRAWW RH11* . . . . . . . 283 H7
  *ED N9* . . . . . . . . . . . . 99 N3
  *EHAM E6* . . . . . . . . . . 142 C4
  *HOLWY N7* . . . . . . . . . 118 C9
  *KUTN/CMB KT2* . . . . . . . 177 N5
  *NWMAL KT3* . . . . . . . . . 200 E5
  *RSLP HA4* . . . . . . . . . . 113 H7
  *WIM/MER SW19* . . . . . . . 179 L7
Arthur's Bridge Rd
  *WOKN/KNAP GU21* . . . . . 231 P3
Arthur St *BUSH WD23* . . . . . 73 L7
  *CANST EC4R* . . . . . . . . 13 H8
  *ERITH DA8* . . . . . . . . . 164 G6
  *GRAYS RM17* . . . . . . . . 167 P5
  *GVW DA11* . . . . . . . . . 190 D3
Arthur St West *GVW DA11* . . . 190 D3
Artichoke Dell
  *RKW/CH/CXG WD3* . . . . 71 H8
Artichoke HI *WAP E1W* . . . . . 140 A9
Artichoke Pl *CMBW SE5* *. . . . 159 L7
Artillery Cl *GNTH/NBYPK IG2* . 122 F7
Artillery La *LVPST EC2M* . . . . 13 K4
  *SHB W12* . . . . . . . . . . 136 D8
Artillery Pas *WCHPL E1* *. . . . 13 K4
Artillery Rd *GU GU1* . . . . . . 268 A5
Artillery Rw *GVE DA12* . . . . . 190 F3
  *WEST SW1P* . . . . . . . . . 17 H4
Artington Wk *GU GU1* . . . . . 250 A10
Arundel Av *EW KT17* . . . . . . 220 E6
  *MRDN SM4* . . . . . . . . . 201 J4
  *SAND/SEL CR2* . . . . . . . 223 P6
Arundel Cl *BTSEA SW11* . . . . 179 P1
  *BXLY DA5* . . . . . . . . . . 186 A2
  *CHES/WCR EN8* . . . . . . 62 A4
  *CRAWE RH10* . . . . . . . . 284 D7
  *CROY/NA CRO* . . . . . . . 203 J10
  *HHNE HP2* . . . . . . . . . 36 B5
  *HPTN TW12* . . . . . . . . . 176 A6
  *SRTFD E15* . . . . . . . . . 121 M3
Arundel Ct *HYS/HAR UB3* . . . 133 H5
  *NFNCH/WDSPK N12* . . . . 97 L5
Arundel Dr *BORE WD6* . . . . . 75 P3
  *RYLN/HDSTN HA2* . . . . . 113 P8
  *WFD IG8* . . . . . . . . . . 101 M7
  *WOKS/MYFD GU22* . . . . . 232 D6
Arundel Gdns *EDGW HA8* . . . 96 E2
  *GDMY/SEVK IG3* . . . . . . 123 J1
  *NTGHL W11* . . . . . . . . . 8 D1
  *WCHMH N21* . . . . . . . . 99 H7
Arundel Gv *STNW/STAM N16* . 120 A10
Arundel Pk *ASC SL5* . . . . . . 192 F10
Arundel Pl *IS N1* . . . . . . . . 5 P1
Arundel Rd *ABLGY WD5* . . . . 54 A3
  *BAR EN5* . . . . . . . . . . 77 G2
  *BELMT SM2* . . . . . . . . . 221 H7
  *CROY/NA CRO* . . . . . . . 203 M7
  *DART DA1* . . . . . . . . . . 171 G4
  *DORK RH4* . . . . . . . . . 272 F7
  *EBAR EN4* . . . . . . . . . . 77 N2
  *GDMY/SEVK IG3* . . . . . . 123 J1
  *HODN N20* . . . . . . . . . .
  *HSLWW TW4* . . . . . . . . 153 L4
  *KUT/HW KT1* . . . . . . . . 199 J1
  *UX/CGN UB8* . . . . . . . . 131 L4
Arundel Sq *HOLWY N7* . . . . . 5 P1
  *STALW/RED AL3* . . . . . . 38 C1
Arundel St *TPL/STR WC2R* . . . 11 P7
Arundel Ter *BARN SW13* . . . . 156 E7
Arvon Rd *HBRY N5* . . . . . . 118 G1
Asbaston Ter *IL IG1* . . . . . . 122 F7
Ascalon St *VX/NE SW8* . . . . 158 A6
Ascension Rd *CRW RM5* . . . . 104 C10
Ascham Dr *CHING E4* . . . . . 100 A1
Ascham End *WALTH E17* . . . . 100 B10
Ascham St *KTTN NW5* . . . . . 118 D1
Aschurch Rd *CROY/NA CRO* . . 203 N10
Ascot Cl *BARK/HLT IG6* . . . . 103 H5

**Column 4**

HGDN/ICK UB10 . . . . . . . 132 B5
KUT/HW KT1 . . . . . . . . . 199 K2
PEND EN3 . . . . . . . . . . 80 B7
REIG RH2 . . . . . . . . . . . 276 A6
WLSDN NW10 . . . . . . . . 136 B5
Ashdown Wy *AMS HP6* . . . . . 69 U3
  *TOOT SW17* . . . . . . . . . 180 A7
Ash Dr *HAT AL10* . . . . . . . 40 G7
  *REDH RH1* . . . . . . . . . 275 K8
Ashen *EHAM E6* . . . . . . . . 142 D2
Ashendene Rd *CLPT E5* . . . . 120 D10
  *HERT/BAY SG13* . . . . . . 25 K1
Ashenden Rd *CLPT E5* . . . . . 120 E3
Ashenden Wk *SLN SL2* . . . . 109 J9
Ashen Gv *WIM/MER SW19* . . . 179 K6
Ashen V *SAND/SEL CR2* . . . . 224 C5
Asher Loftus Wy
  *FBAR/BDGN N11* . . . . . . 98 A7
Asher Wy *WAP E1W* . . . . . . 140 A8
Ashfield Av *BUSH WD23* . . . . 74 A10
  *FELT TW13* . . . . . . . . . 174 A4
Ashfield Cl *ASHTD KT21* . . . . 237 K5
  *BECK BR3* . . . . . . . . . . 183 G5
  *RCHPK/HAM TW10* . . . . . 177 K4
Ashfield La *CHST BR7* . . . . . 184 F9
Ashfield Rd *ACT W3* . . . . . . 136 C10
  *CEND/HSY/T N8* . . . . . . 99 G5
  *WCHMH N21* . . . . . . . . 99 L5
Ashfields *GU GU2* *. . . . . . . 249 L10
Ashfield St *WCHPL E1* . . . . . 140 C7
Ashfield Yd *WCHPL E1* *. . . . 140 C7
Ashford Av *ASHF TW15* . . . . 174 A8
  *CEND/HSY/T N8* . . . . . . 99 G6
  *HYS/HAR UB4* . . . . . . . . 133 N6
Ashford Cl *ASHF TW15* . . . . 174 A8
  *WALTH E17* . . . . . . . . . 120 E4
Ashford Crs *ASHF TW15* . . . . 173 N6
  *PEND EN3* . . . . . . . . . . 80 B1
Ashford Gdns *PIN HA5* . . . . . 113 M2
Ashford Ms *TOTM N17* . . . . . 99 P9
Ashford Pk *ASHF TW15* . . . . 173 N7
Ashford Rd *ASHF TW15* . . . . 174 C9
  *CRICK NW2* . . . . . . . . . 116 F2
  *EHAM E6* . . . . . . . . . . 142 C1
  *FELT TW13* . . . . . . . . . 173 K7
  *IVER SL0* . . . . . . . . . . 130 F2
  *STA TW18* . . . . . . . . . . 173 H9
  *SWFD E18* . . . . . . . . . . 101 N10
Ashgrove Rd *ASHF TW15* . . . . 174 C9
  *BMLY BR1* . . . . . . . . . . 183 J8
  *GDMY/SEVK IG3* . . . . . . 123 J9
Ash Gn *DEN/HRF UB9* . . . . . 131 J1
Ash Gv *ALP/SUD HA0* . . . . . 135 J5
  *AMS HP6* . . . . . . . . . . 68 D7
Ashgrove *SUT SM1* no.
Ashgrove Rd continues:
Ashgrove *RSEV TN14* . . . . . 245 P11
Ash Gv *CRICK NW2* . . . . . . 116 C1
  *DEN/HRF UB9* . . . . . . . . 91 H9
  *EA W5* . . . . . . . . . . . . 135 L1
  *EBED/NFELT TW14* . . . . . 174 A1
  *EN EN1* . . . . . . . . . . . 90 M1
  *GUW GU2* . . . . . . . . . . 249 M10
  *HACK E8* . . . . . . . . . . 140 A3
  *HEST TW5* . . . . . . . . . 153 L6
  *HHS/BOV HP3* . . . . . . . 36 A10
  *HYS/HAR UB3* . . . . . . . . 132 A10
  *MUSWH N10* . . . . . . . . . 118 C2
  *PGE/AN SE20* . . . . . . . . 200 B2
  *PLMGR N13* . . . . . . . . . 99 K4
  *SLN SL2* . . . . . . . . . . . 129 L2
  *STA TW18* . . . . . . . . . . 173 M9
  *STALE/WH AL4* . . . . . . . 21 G7
  *STHL UB1* . . . . . . . . . . 133 P7
  *WDR/YW UB7* . . . . . . . . 132 B1
  *WWKM BR4* . . . . . . . . . 205 H8
Ashgrove Cl *EGH TW20* . . . . 192 B9
  *ORP BR6* . . . . . . . . . . 227 N1
Ash Hill Cl *BUSH WD23* . . . . 73 N7
Ash Hill Dr *PIN HA5* . . . . . . 113 K1
Ashingdon Cl *CHING E4* . . . . 100 A1
Ashington Rd *FUL/PGN SW6* . . 157 J8
Ashlake Rd *STRHM/NOR SW16* . 180 F7
Ashland Pl *MHST W1U* . . . . . 10 B3
Ashlar Pl *WOOL/PLUM SE18* . . 162 L3
Ashlea Rd *CFSP/GDCR SL9* . . 90 A1
Ashleigh Av *EGH TW20* . . . . 172 F10
Ashleigh Cl *HORL RH6* . . . . . 280 A12
Ashleigh Gdns *SUT SM1* . . . . 201 L8
  *UPMR RM14* . . . . . . . . . 105 P10
Ashleigh Rd
  *MORT/ESHN SW14* . . . . . 156 B9
  *PGE/AN SE20* . . . . . . . . 200 D5
Ashley Av *BARK/HLT IG6* . . . . 102 G10
  *EPSOM KT18* . . . . . . . . 238 A3
  *MRDN SM4* . . . . . . . . . 201 L5
Ashley Cl *GT/LBKH KT23* . . . . 253 N1
  *HDN NW4* . . . . . . . . . . 96 F10
  *HHS/BOV HP3* . . . . . . . 36 A7
  *PIN HA5* . . . . . . . . . . . 93 H3
  *SEV TN13* . . . . . . . . . . 247 J10
  *WOT/HER KT12* . . . . . . . 197 H6
Ashley Cots *ASHTD KT21* *. . . 237 H6
Ashley Crs *BTSEA SW11* . . . . 158 B10
  *WPK KT4* . . . . . . . . . . 197 G4
Ashley Ct *HAT AL10* . . . . . .
Ashley Dr *BNSTD SM7* . . . . . 221 K10
  *BORE WD6* . . . . . . . . . 75 G5
  *ISLW TW7* . . . . . . . . . . 154 D5
  *WHTN TW2* . . . . . . . . . 175 L5
  *WOT/HER KT12* . . . . . . . 197 H6
Ashley Gdns *ORP BR6* . . . . . 227 G8
  *PLMGR N13* . . . . . . . . . 99 K3
  *RCHPK/HAM TW10* . . . . . 176 G7
  *WBLY HA9* . . . . . . . . . . 115 P9
Ashley Green Rd *CSHM HP5* . . 51 J3
Ashley La *CROY/NA CRO* . . . . 223 J2
  *HDN NW4* . . . . . . . . . . 96 F10
Ashley Park Av
  *WOT/HER KT12* . . . . . . . 197 G8
Ashley Park Crs
  *WOT/HER KT12* . . . . . . . 197 H8
Ashley Park Rd
  *WOT/HER KT12* . . . . . . . 197 H9
Ashley Ri *WOT/HER KT12* . . . 197 H10
Ashley Rd *ARCH N19* . . . . . 118 E6
  *CHING E4* . . . . . . . . . . 101 N7
  *DORK RH4* . . . . . . . . . 272 G3
  *EPSOM KT18* . . . . . . . . 238 B1
  *FSTGT E7* . . . . . . . . . . 141 N1
  *HPTN TW12* . . . . . . . . . 175 G2
  *PEND EN3* . . . . . . . . . . 80 E1
  *RCH/KEW TW9* . . . . . . . 156 K9
  *SEV TN13* . . . . . . . . . . 247 K10
  *STAL AL1* . . . . . . . . . . 38 B2
  *THDIT KT7* . . . . . . . . . . 198 A8
  *THHTH CR7* . . . . . . . . . 204 G1
  *TOTM N17* . . . . . . . . . 119 P3
  *UX/CGN UB8* . . . . . . . . 148 H1
  *WALTH E17* . . . . . . . . . 119 N3
  *WIM/MER SW19* . . . . . . . 179 L3
  *WOKN/KNAP GU21* . . . . . 231 M1
  *WOT/HER KT12* . . . . . . . 196 B6
Ashleys *RKW/CH/CXG WD3* . . 71 G5
Ashley Wy *CHOB/PIR GU24* . . 212 C10
Ashlin Rd *SRTFD E15* . . . . . 121 J2
Ashling Rd *CROY/NA CRO* . . . 204 C9
Ashlone Rd *PUT/ROE SW15* . . 157 G10
Ashlyn Cl *BUSH WD23* . . . . . 73 G1
Ashlyn Gv *EMPK RM11* . . . . 105 K5
Ashlyns Ct *BERK HP4* *. . . . . 35 N6

**Column 5**

Ashlyns La *CHONG CM5* . . . . 48 G7
Ashlyn's Pk *BERK HP4* . . . . . 217 M9
Ashlyns Rd *BERK HP4* . . . . . 35 N6
  *EPP CM16* . . . . . . . . . . 65 J6
Ashmead *CHSGTN KT9* . . . . . 219 J3
Ashmead Rd *ROMW/RG RM7* . 104 C3
  *TOOT SW17* . . . . . . . . . 78 D9
Ash Dr *HAT AL10* . . . . . . . 40 G7
Ashmead Dr *DEN/HRF UB9* . . 111 K4
Ashmead Ga *BMLY BR1* . . . . 205 P1
Ashmead Pl *DEN/HRF UB9* . . 111 K4
Ashmead Rd *AMSS HP7* . . . . 69 P5
  *DEPT SE8* . . . . . . . . . . 181 N2
  *EBED/NFELT TW14* . . . . . 174 A4
Ashmere Av *BECK BR3* . . . . . 205 A2
Ashmere Cl *CHEAM SM3* . . . . 220 G2
Ashmere Gv
  *BRXS/STRHM SW2* . . . . . 158 F10
Ash Ms *EPSOM KT18* . . . . . 220 B8
  *KTTN NW5* *. . . . . . . . . 118 D10
Ashmill St *STJWD NW8* . . . . 9 N3
Ashmole Cl *WASH E17* . . . . . 17 P10
Ashmore Cl *PECK SE15* . . . . 159 P10
Ashmore Gdns *GVW DA11* . . . 36 C7
Ashmore La *HAYES BR2* . . . . 225 P7
  *MV/WKIL W9* . . . . . . . . 2 G1
Ashmore Rd *WELL DA16* . . . . 162 G9
Ashmount Crs *SLSL1* . . . . . 148 F1
Ashmount Rd *ARCH N19* . . . . 118 D5
  *SEVS/STOTM N15* . . . . . 119 N3
Ashmour Gdns *ROM RM1* . . . 104 H10
Ashmead Gdns *GVW DA11* . . . wait
Ashneal Gdns *HRW HA1* . . . . 114 C8
Ashness Gdns *GFD/PVL UB6* . . 134 G1
Ashness Rd *BTSEA SW11* . . . 180 A1
Ash Platt Rd *BGR/WK TN15* . . 247 N6
Ash Ride *ENC/FH EN2* . . . . . 79 H1
Ashridge Cl *HHS/BOV HP3* . . . 52 D4
  *KTN/HRWW/WS HA3* . . . . 115 H4
Ashridge Crs
  *WOOL/PLUM SE18* . . . . . 162 F6
Ashridge Dr *LCOL/BKTW AL2* . 58 M6
  *OXHEY WD19* . . . . . . . . 93 K6
Ashridge Gdns *PIN HA5* . . . . 113 M2
  *PLMGR N13* . . . . . . . . . 98 F6
Ashridge La *CSHM HP5* . . . . 52 A7
Ashridge Ri *BERK HP4* . . . . . 35 G4
Ashridge Wy *MRDN SM4* . . . . 193 K9
  *SUN TW16* . . . . . . . . . . 175 J10
Ash Rd *BH/WHM TN16* . . . . . 262 C11
  *CHEAM SM3* . . . . . . . . . 201 H8
  *CHOB/PIR GU24* . . . . . . 248 F2
  *CRAWE RH10* . . . . . . . . 284 D5
  *CROY/NA CRO* . . . . . . . 204 F9
  *GVE DA12* . . . . . . . . . . 190 F7
  *HART DA3* . . . . . . . . . . 211 K7
  *ORP BR6* . . . . . . . . . . 227 N4
  *SHPTN TW17* . . . . . . . . 196 B4
  *SRTFD E15* . . . . . . . . . 121 K10
  *STMC/STPC BR5* . . . . . . wait
Ash Rw *HAYES BR2* . . . . . . 205 D6
Ashstead Woods Rd
  *ASHTD KT21* . . . . . . . . 237 H10
Ashton Cl *SUT SM1* . . . . . . 201 K1
  *WOT/HER KT12* . . . . . . . 217 J11
Ashton Gdns *CHDH RM6* . . . . 153 N10
  *HSLWW TW4* . . . . . . . . 153 N10
Ashton Rd *HARH RM3* . . . . . 105 N7
  *PEND EN3* . . . . . . . . . . 80 D2
  *SRTFD E15* . . . . . . . . . 121 J10
  *WOKN/KNAP GU21* . . . . . 231 L3
Ashton St *POP/IOD E14* . . . . 141 H9
Ashtree Av *MTCM CR4* . . . . . 201 N2
Ash Tree Cl *CROY/NA CRO* . . . 204 D6
  *SURB KT6* . . . . . . . . . . 199 K8
Ashtree Cl *ORP BR6* . . . . . . 226 D1
Ash Tree Cl *SURB KT6* . . . . . 199 K8
Ashtree Ct *STAL AL1* . . . . . 38 E6
Ash Tree Dell *CDALE/KGS NW9* . 115 H3
Ash Tree Fld *HLW CM20* . . . . 28 D9
Ash Tree Rd *WATN WD24* . . . 73 J2
Ashtree Wy *HHW HP1* . . . . . 35 H4
Ashtrees *CROY/NA CRO* . . . . 204 D5
Ashurst Cl *DART DA1* . . . . . 164 G9
  *LHD/OX KT22* . . . . . . . . 236 F7
  *NTHWD HA6* . . . . . . . . 92 F8
  *PGE/AN SE20* . . . . . . . . 200 B4
  *PUR/KEN CR8* . . . . . . . 241 L1
Ashurst Dr *CRAWE RH10* . . . . 284 A9
  *CNTH/NBYPK IG2* . . . . . . 122 E6
  *KWD/TDW/WH KT20* . . . . 255 N6
  *SHPTN TW17* . . . . . . . . 195 M5
Ashurst Gdns
  *BRXS/STRHM SW2* . . . . . 181 H4
Ashurst Pk *ASC SL5* *. . . . . . 192 C3
Ashurst Pl *DORK RH4* . . . . . 273 H1
Ashurst Rd *EBAR EN4* . . . . . 78 A5
  *KWD/TDW/WH KT20* . . . . 255 N6
  *NFNCH/WDSPK N12* . . . . 97 P4
Ashurst Wk *CROY/NA CRO* . . . 204 E7
Ashvale Dr *UPMR RM14* . . . . 126 D7
Ashvale Gdns *CRW RM5* . . . . 104 E4
  *UPMR RM14* . . . . . . . . . 126 D7
Ashvale Rd *TOOT SW17* . . . . 180 A8
Ashview Cl *ASHF TW15* . . . . 173 H9
Ashview Gdns *ASHF TW15* . . . 173 H9
Ashville Rd *WAN E11* . . . . . . 121 F3
Ash Wk *ALP/SUD HA0* . . . . . 114 A7
  *SOCK/AV RM15* . . . . . . . 147 J5
Ashwater Rd *LEE/GVPK SE12* . 183 M4
Ashwell Pl *HARP AL5* . . . . . 20 C2
Ashwells Rd *BRWN CM15* . . . 87 G5
Ashwells Rd *BRWN CM15* . . . 73 C5
Ashwells Wy *STALW/RED AL3* . 38 D5
Ashwick Cl *CTHM CR3* . . . . . 259 P1
Ashwin St *HACK E8* . . . . . . 7 J1
Ashwood *WARL CR6* . . . . . . 242 H6
Ashwood Av *RAIN RM13* . . . . 145 J3
  *UX/CGN UB8* . . . . . . . . 152 G6
Ashwood Gdns *CROY/NA CRO* . 224 G3
  *HYS/HAR UB3* . . . . . . . . 152 D3
Ashwood Rd *STAL AL1* . . . . . 38 C6
  *WOKS/MYFD GU22* . . . . . 232 D4
Ashworth Cl *CMBW SE5* . . . . 159 M6
Ashworth Pl *GU GU2* . . . . . . 249 G1
  *HLWE CM17* . . . . . . . . . 47 K2
Ashworth Rd *MV/WKIL W9* . . . 3 H9
Askern Cl *BXLYHS DA6* . . . . 163 N10
Aske St *IS N1* . . . . . . . . . 7 H7
Askew Crs *SHB W12* . . . . . . 156 C1
Askew Rd *NTHWD HA6* . . . . . 32 C2
  *SHB W12* . . . . . . . . . . 156 C1
Askews Farm La *GRAYS RM17* . 167 K5
Askew Vls *PLMGR N13* *. . . . 99 J4
Askill Dr *PUT/ROE SW15* . . . . 59 D6
Askwith Rd *RAIN RM13* . . . . 144 G4
Asland Rd *SRTFD E15* . . . . . 141 J9
Aslett St *WAND/EARL SW18* . . 179 L3
Asmara Rd *CRICK NW2* . . . . 117 L2
Asmar Cl *COUL/CHIP CR5* . . . 240 F11
Asmuns Hl *GLDGN NW11* . . . 117 J4
Asmuns Pl *GLDGN NW11* . . . 117 H4
Asolando Dr *WALW SE17* . . . 18 F6
Aspasia Cl *STAL AL1* . . . . . . 39 J5
Aspdin Rd *GVW DA11* . . . . . 190 B7
Aspen Cl *COB KT11* . . . . . . 233 M4
  *EA W5* . . . . . . . . . . . . 155 L1
  *LCOL/BKTW AL2* . . . . . . 58 M6
  *ORP BR6* . . . . . . . . . . 227 G2
  *RGUE GU4* . . . . . . . . . . 252 C5
  *SLN SL2* . . . . . . . . . . . 128 G2
  *STA TW18* . . . . . . . . . . 173 J6
  *SWLY BR8* . . . . . . . . . . 208 B1
Aspen Copse *BMLY BR1* . . . . 206 G2

Aspen Ct *RBRW/HUT* CM13 . 107 M4
Aspen Dr *ALP/SUD* HA0 . 114 F8
Aspen Gdns *ASHF* TW15 . 174 B5
　*MTCM* CR4 . 202 B5
Aspen Gn *ERITHM* DA18 . 164 A10
Aspen Gv *PIN* HA5 . 112 G1
　*UPMR* RM14 . 125 P9
Aspen La *NTHLT* UB5 . 133 M5
Aspenlea Rd *HMSMTH* W6 . 156 G5
Aspen Park Dr *GSTN* WD25 . 73 J1
Aspen Pl *HHW* HP1 . 35 J9
Aspen Sq *WEST* E13 . 196 E10
Aspen V *CTHM* CR3 . 241 N4
Aspen Wy *BNSTD* SM7 . 220 G10
　*FELT* TW13 . 175 J6
　*PEND* EN3 . 80 C1
　*POP/IOD* E14 . 141 M9
　*SOCK/AV* RM15 . 147 J5
　*WCCE* AL7 . 23 M4
Aspern Gv *HAMP* NW3 . 117 P10
Aspfield Rw *HHW* HP1 . 35 L4
Aspinall Rd *BROCKY* SE4 . 160 C9
Aspinden Rd
　*BERM/RHTH* SE16 . 160 A3
Aspley Rd *WAND/EARL* SW18 . 179 L1
Asplins Rd *TOTM* N17 . 99 P9
Asplins VIs *TOTM* N17 * . 99 P9
Asprey Gv *CTHM* CR3 . 241 P10
Asprey Ms *BECK* BR3 . 204 E5
Asquith Cl *BCTR* RM8 . 123 M6
Assam St *WCHPL* E1 . 6 D7
Assata Ms *IS* N1 * . 6 J3
Assembly Pas *WCHPL* E1 . 140 B7
Assembly Wk *CAR* SM5 . 201 P7
Assher Rd *WOT/HER* KT12 . 197 M10
Assheton Rd *BEAC* HP9 . 88 C7
Ass House La
　*KTN/HRWW/WS* HA3 . 94 C3
Astall Cl *KTN/HRWW/WS* HA3 . 94 C3
Astbury Rd *PECK* SE15 . 160 B7
Astede Pl *ASHTD* KT21 . 237 L4
Astell St *CHEL* SW3 . 61 L4
The Asters *CHESW* EN7 . 6 C3
Asteys Wv *IS* N1 . 6 C3
Astleham Wy *SHPTN* TW17 . 195 P3
Astle St *BTSEA* SW11 . 158 F8
Astley *GRAYS* RM17 . 167 L5
Astley Av *CRICK* NW2 . 116 F10
Astley Rd *HHW* HP1 . 35 M6
Aston Cl *ASHTD* KT21 . 237 H4
　*BUSH* WD23 . 74 B10
　*SCUP* DA14 . 185 K6
　*WATN* WD25 . 73 K6
Aston Gra *HERT/WAT* SG14 . 25 L3
Aston Av *HSLWW* TW4 . 153 K8
Aston Md *WDSR* SL4 . 148 D7
Astonplace *STRHM/NOR* SW16 . 181 J9
Aston Rd *EA* W5 . 135 J4
　*ESH/CLAY* KT10 . 218 G2
　*RYNPK* SW20 . 200 F2
Astons Rd *NTHWD* HA6 . 92 D4
Aston St *POP/IOD* E14 . 140 D8
Aston Ter *BAL* SW12 * . 180 C2
Astonville St
　*WAND/EARL* SW18 . 179 K4
Aston Wy *EPSOM* KT18 . 238 C2
　*POTB/CUF* EN6 . 59 N8
Astor Av *ROMW/RG* RM7 . 124 C4
Astor Cl *ADL/WDHM* KT15 . 215 N1
　*KUTN/CMB* KT2 . 177 N9
Astoria Pde *ASHF* TW15 * . 174 B7
　*STRHM/NOR* SW16 . 181 F6
Astoria Wk *BRXN/ST* SW9 . 159 H9
Astra Ct *HCH* RM12 . 145 J1
Astra Dr *GRAVS* DA12 . 191 H8
Astrop Ms *HMSMTH* W6 . 156 F2
Astrop Ter *HMSMTH* W6 . 156 F2
Astwick Av *HAT* AL10 . 40 C1
Astwood Ms *SKENS* SW7 . 15 H5
Asylum Arch Rd *REDH* RH1 . 276 A3
Asylum Rd *PECK* SE15 . 160 A6
Atalanta Cl *PUR/KEN* CR8 . 223 H6
Atalanta St *FUL/PGN* SW6 . 151 H6
Atbara Rd *TEDD* TW11 . 176 C9
Atcham Rd *HSLW* TW3 . 154 B10
Atcost Rd *BARK* IG11 . 143 K7
Atfield Gv *BFOR* GU20 . 212 C3
Atheldene Rd
　*WAND/EARL* SW18 . 179 L4
Athelney St *CAT* SE6 . 182 F6
Athelstane Gv *BOW* E3 . 139 L1
Athelstane Ms *FSBYPK* N4 . 119 H6
Athelstan Gdns
　*KIL/WHAMP* NW6 . 2 B1
Athelstan Rd *HARH* RM3 . 105 N9
　*HHS/BOV* HP3 . 35 H9
　*KUT/HW* KT1 . 199 L4
Athelstan Wk North
　*WGCE* AL7 . 23 H6
Athelstan Wk South
　*WGCE* AL7 . 22 G6
Athelstone Rd
　*KTN/HRWW/WS* HA3 . 94 C10
　*RYLN/HDSTN* HA2 . 114 C2
Athena Cl *KUT/HW* KT1 . 199 L4
　*RYLN/HDSTN* HA2 . 114 C2
Athenaeum Pl *MUSWH* N10 . 118 C1
Athenaeum Rd
　*TRDG/WHET* N20 . 97 M2
Athena Pl *NTHWD* HA6 * . 92 D9
Athenia Cl *CHESW* EN7 . 61 J5
Athenlay Rd *PECK* SE15 . 161 K3
Athens Gdns *MV/WKIL* W9 * . 8 E2
Atherden Rd *CLPT* E5 . 120 B9
Atherfield Rd *REIG* RH2 . 275 M3
Atherford Rd *BRXN/ST* SW9 . 158 F9
Atherley Wy *HSLWW* TW4 . 175 N3
Atherstone Ms *SKENS* SW7 . 15 H5
Atherton Cl *RGUE* GU4 . 268 B6
Atherton Dr *WIM/MER* SW19 . 178 C2
Atherton Gdns
　*CDW/CHF* RM16 . 168 F8
Atherton Hts *CAN/RD* E16 . 135 H1
Atherton Ms *FSTGT* E7 . 141 F5
Atherton Pl *RYLN/HDSTN* HA2 . 114 B1
　*STHL* UB1 . 133 P6
Atherton Rd *BARN* SW13 . 156 D6
　*CLAY* IG5 . 102 B10
　*FSTGT* E7 . 121 L4
Atherton St *BTSEA* SW11 . 157 H8
Athlone *ESH/CLAY* KT10 . 218 D3
Athlone Cl *CLPT* E5 . 120 A10
　*RAD* WD7 * . 74 G2
Athlone Rd *WALTH* E17 . 121 J1
Athlone Rd *BRXS/STRHM* SW2 . 180 C3
Athlone St *KTTN* NW5 . 4 A1
Athol Cl *PIN* HA5 . 93 J9
Athol Gdns *PIN* HA5 . 93 J9
Atholl Rd *GDMY/SEVK* IG3 . 123 K5
Athol Rd *ERITH* DA8 . 164 D4
Athol Sq *POP/IOD* E14 . 141 M8
Athol Wy *HGDN/ICK* UB10 . 132 B2
Atkins Cl *BH/WHM* TN16 . 225 P8
Atkins Dr *WWKM* BR4 . 205 J10
Atkinson Cl *ORP* BR6 . 227 N4
Atkinson Rd *HORL* RH6 . 280 C5
Atkinson Rd *CAN/RD* E16 . 141 P7
　*CRAWE* RH10 . 284 D9
Atkins Rd *BAL* SW12 . 180 C2
　*LEY* E10 . 120 C4
Atlanta Bvd *ROM* RM1 . 124 F4
Atlantic Cl *SWCM* DA10 . 189 N1
Atlantic Rd *BRXN/ST* SW9 . 159 H10
Atlantis Av *CAN/RD* E16 . 142 F4
Atlantis Cl *BARK* IG11 . 143 L5
Atlas Gdns *CHARL* SE7 . 161 G3
Atlas Ms *HACK* E8 . 7 M1
Atlas Rd *DART* DA1 . 171 N5


　*FBAR/BDGN* N11 . 98 B7
　*PLSTW* E13 . 141 M10
　*WBLY* HA9 . 115 P9
　*WLSDN* NW10 . 136 B5
Atley Rd *BOW* E3 . 140 F3
Atlip Rd *ALP/SUD* HA0 . 135 K3
Atney Rd *PUT/ROE* SW15 . 157 H10
Atria Rd *NTHWD* HA6 . 93 H6
Attenborough Cl
　*OXHEY* WD19 . 93 M4
Atterbury Cl *BH/WHM* TN16 . 262 G10
Atterbury Rd *FSBYPK* N4 . 119 H4
Atterbury St *WEST* SW1P . 17 K6
Attewood Av *WLSDN* NW10 . 116 E5
Attewood Rd *NTHLT* UB5 . 133 M1
Attfield Cl *TRDG/WHET* N20 . 97 M3
Attimore Cl *WGCW* AL8 . 22 C6
Attimore Rd *WGCW* AL8 . 22 C6
Attlee Cl *HGDN/ICK* UB10 . 132 B4
　*THHTH* CR7 . 203 K6
Attlee Ct *GRAYS* RM17 . 167 M2
Attlee Dr *DART* DA1 . 171 M2
Attlee Rd *THMD* SE28 . 143 J6
　*YEAD* UB4 * . 133 H5
Attlee Ter *WALTH* E17 . 120 D2
Attneave St *FSBYW* WC1X . 12 A1
Attwell Cl *SAND/SEL* CR2 . 224 A10
Atwell Pl *THDIT* KT7 . 198 F8
Attwell Rd *PECK* SE15 . 159 P8
Atwood *GT/LBKH* KT23 . 235 M10
Atwood Av *RCH/KEW* TW9 . 155 M8
Atwood Rd *HMSMTH* W6 . 156 E3
Aubert Cl *HOD* EN11 . 26 E10
Aubert Pk *HBRY* N5 . 119 J9
Aubert Rd *HBRY* N5 . 119 J9
Aubrey Cl *LCOL/BKTW* AL2 . 57 J7
Aubrey Pl *STJWD* NW8 . 8 D1
Aubrey Rd *CEND/HSY/T* N8 * . 118 F3
　*KENS* W8 . 8 A10
　*WALTH* E17 . 120 F1
Aubreys Rd *HHW* HP1 . 35 H1
Aubries Wl *KENS* W8 . 8 A10
Aubrietia Cl *HARH* RM3 . 105 M9
Auburn Cl *NWCR* SE14 . 160 D6
Aubyn HI *WNWD* SE27 . 181 K7
Aubyn Sq *PUT/ROE* SW15 . 156 D10
Auckland Cl *CRAWW* RH11 . 283 N4
　*EN* EN1 . 80 A3
　*NRWD* SE19 . 203 N1
　*TIL* RM18 . 168 D8
Auckland Gdns *NRWD* SE19 . 203 N1
Auckland Ri *NRWD* SE19 . 203 M1
Auckland Rd *BTSEA* SW11 . 157 P10
　*CTHM* CR3 . 241 M8
　*IL* IG1 . 122 F6
　*KUT/HW* KT1 . 199 L4
　*LEY* E10 . 120 C8
　*NRWD* SE19 . 203 N1
　*POTB/CUF* EN6 . 58 G8
Auckland St *LBTH* SE11 . 17 K8
Aucuba VIs *WELL* DA16 * . 164 A10
Audax *CDALE/KGS* NW9 * . 96 C10
Auden Dr *BORE* WD6 . 75 N4
Auden Pl *CAMTN* NW1 . 4 C1
　*CHEAM* SM3 * . 220 F1
Audleigh Pl *CHIG* IG7 . 102 D7
Audley Cl *ADL/WDHM* KT15 . 215 N10
　*BORE* WD6 . 75 M2
　*BTSEA* SW11 . 158 B9
　*MUSWH* N10 . 98 C8
Audley Ct *PIN* HA5 . 121 L10
Audley Dr *CAN/RD* E16 . 141 N10
　*WARL* CR6 . 242 B1
Audley Firs *WOT/HER* KT12 . 197 N11
Audley Gdns *GDMY/SEVK* IG3 . 123 J7
　*LOU* IG10 . 82 G6
　*WAB* EN9 . 63 H10
Audley Pl *BELMT* SM2 . 221 L4
Audley Rd *EA* W5 . 135 L7
　*ENC/FH* EN2 . 79 J6
　*HDN* NW4 . 116 D4
　*RCHPK/HAM* TW10 . 177 L1
Audley Sq *MYFR/PKLN* W1K * . 10 D9
Audley St *BETH* E2 * . 7 N7
Audric Cl *KUTN/CMB* KT2 . 199 M1
Audwick Cl *CHES/WCR* EN8 . 62 C4
Augur Cl *STA* TW18 . 173 J8
Augurs La *PLSTW* E13 . 141 N5
Augusta Cl *E/WMO/HCT* KT8 . 197 M3
Augusta Rd *WHTN* TW2 . 176 B5
Augustine Cl *STMC/STPC* BR5 . 185 N10
Augustine Ct *WAB* EN9 . 62 D3
　*HMSMTH* W6 . 156 G2
　*KTN/HRWW/WS* HA3 . 94 A3
　*STMC/STPC* BR5 . 207 N3
August La *SHGR* GU5 . 265 K10
Augustus Cl *BTFD* TW8 . 155 J6
　*SHB* W12 * . 156 E1
　*STAN* HA7 . 95 K4
Augustus Rd *WIM/MER* SW19 . 178 C4
Augustus St *CAMTN* NW1 . 4 F1
Aukingford Gdns *CHONG* CM5 . 67 M3
Aukingford Gn *CHONG* CM5 . 67 N3
Aultone Wy *CAR* SM5 . 202 A10
　*SUT* SM1 . 201 L9
Aurelia Gdns *CROY/NA* CR0 . 202 C5
Aurelia Rd *CROY/NA* CR0 . 202 C6
Auriel Av *DAGE* RM10 . 144 F1
Auriga Ms *IS* N1 . 119 L10
Auriol Cl *WPK* KT4 . 200 B10
Auriol Dr *CFD/PVL* UB6 . 134 C2
　*HGDN/ICK* UB10 . 132 C1
Auriol Park Rd *WPK* KT4 . 200 B10
Auriol Rd *WKENS* W14 . 14 A6
Aurum Cl *HORL* RH6 . 280 C5
Austell Gdns *MLHL* NW7 . 96 B4
Austen Cl *LCOL/LBTW* AL2 . 58 F3
　*SWCM* DA10 . 189 J7
　*THMD* SE28 . 143 L10
　*TIL* RM18 . 168 F8
Austen Rd *ERITH* DA8 . 164 C6
　*GU* GU1 . 268 C1
　*RYLN/HDSTN* HA2 . 114 A7
Austin Friars *OBST* EC2N . 13 H5
Austin Av *BTSEA* SW11 . 158 B7
Austin Cl *COUL/CHIP* CR5 . 241 J4
　*FSTH* SE23 . 182 D3
　*TWK* TW1 . 177 H1
Austins Md *HHS/BOV* HP3 . 52 E4
Austins Pl *HHW* HP1 * . 35 L4
Austral Cl *BFN/LL* DA15 . 185 J6
Austral Dr *EMPK* RM11 . 125 K7
Australia Rd *SHB* W12 . 137 J6
　*SL* SL1 . 149 M3
Austral St *LBTH* SE11 . 18 C6
Austyn Gdns *BRYLDS* KT5 * . 199 P7
Autumn Cl *CRAWW* RH11 . 283 N4
　*EN* EN1 . 80 A3
　*SL* SL1 . 148 G4
　*WIM/MER* SW19 . 179 N9
Autumn Dr *BELMT* SM2 . 221 J5


Autumn Glades *HHS/BOV* HP3 . 36 D8
　*WCCE* AL7 . 23 L7
Autumn St *BOW* E3 . 140 F3
Avalon Cl *ENC/FH* EN2 . 79 H6
　*GSTN* WD25 . 55 M8
　*ORP* BR6 . 207 N9
　*RYNPK* SW20 . 201 N2
　*WEA* W13 . 135 J7
Avard Gdns *ORP* BR6 . 226 F1
Avarn Rd *TOOT* SW17 . 180 A9
Avebury *SL* SL1 . 128 F10
Avebury Ct *HHNE* HP2 . 36 B3
Avebury Pk *SURB* KT6 . 199 J6
Avebury Rd *ORP* BR6 . 206 G10
　*WAN* E11 . 121 J4
　*WIM/MER* SW19 . 201 J1
Aveley St *IS* N1 . 6 G6
Aveley Rd *UPMR* RM14 . 146 A2
　*SOCK/AV* RM15 . 146 B9
Aveley Cl *ERITH* DA8 . 164 C5
　*SOCK/AV* RM15 . 146 C10
Aveley Rd *UPMR* RM14 . 146 A2
Aveline St *LBTH* SE11 . 17 P7
Aveling Cl *CRAWE* RH10 . 284 D9
　*PUR/KEN* CR8 . 222 G9
Aveling Park Rd *WALTH* E17 . 100 F10
Avenell Rd *HBRY* N5 . 119 J8
Avening Rd *WAND/EARL* SW18 . 179 K3
Avening Ter *WAND/EARL* SW18 . 179 K3
Avenons Rd *PLSTW* E13 . 141 M7
Avenue All Hallows
　*WOKS/MYFD* GU22 . 230 A10
Avenue All Saints
　*WOKS/MYFD* GU22 . 230 G8
Avenue Ap *KGLGY* WD4 . 54 B6
Avenue C *ADL/WDHM* KT15 . 195 P10
Avenue Cl *HARH* RM3 . 105 N8
　*HEST* TW5 . 153 J7
　*KWD/TDW/WH* KT20 . 238 E8
　*STHGT/OAK* N14 . 78 D10
　*STJWD* NW8 . 3 P6
　*WDR/YW* UB7 . 151 N2
Avenue Crs *ACT* W3 . 155 N1
　*HEST* TW5 . 153 J7
Avenue De Cagny
　*CHOB/PIR* GU24 . 230 G8
Avenue Dr *DTCH/LGLY* SL3 . 130 C7
Avenue Elmers *SURB* KT6 . 199 K5
Avenue Gdns *ACT* W3 . 155 N1
　*HEST* TW5 . 153 H6
　*HORL* RH6 . 280 C5
　*MORT/ESHN* SW14 . 156 B9
　*SNWD* SE25 . 203 P3
　*TEDD* TW11 . 176 E10
Avenue La *LOU* IG10 . 81 P3
Avenue Ldg *GRAYS* RM17 * . 167 H4
Avenue Ms *MUSWH* N10 . 118 C1
Avenue One *ADL/WDHM* KT15 . 215 P1
Avenue Pde *SUN* TW16 . 197 J3
　*WCHMH* N21 * . 99 L1
Avenue Ri *BUSH* WD23 . 73 P9
Avenue Rd *ACT* W3 . 155 N1
　*BELMT* SM2 . 221 K6
　*BH/WHM* TN16 . 244 B6
　*BNSTD* SM7 . 239 L1
　*BRW* CM14 . 107 H5
　*BTFD* TW8 . 155 H4
　*BXLYHN* DA7 . 163 P9
　*CEND/HSY/T* N8 . 118 E4
　*CHDH* RM6 . 123 L5
　*COB* KT11 . 235 L2
　*CTHM* CR3 . 241 L8
　*EPP* CM16 . 82 G2
　*EPSOM* KT18 . 220 A10
　*ERITH* DA8 . 164 D6
　*ERITH* DA8 . 164 F5
　*FELT* TW13 . 174 G6
　*FSTGT* E7 . 121 N9
　*HAMP* NW3 . 3 L3
　*HARH* RM3 . 105 N8
　*HGT* N6 . 118 B5
　*HOD* EN11 . 45 J5
　*HPTN* TW12 . 198 A1
　*ISLW* TW7 . 154 D7
　*KUT/HW* KT1 . 199 K3
　*NFNCH/WDSPK* N12 . 97 J3
　*NWMAL* KT3 . 200 B1
　*PGE/AN* SE20 . 204 B1
　*PIN* HA5 . 113 M1
　*RYNPK* SW20 . 200 F2
　*SEV* TN13 . 247 K10
　*SNWD* SE25 . 203 P2
　*STA* TW18 . 172 G8
　*STHGT/OAK* N14 . 78 D10
　*STHL* UB1 . 133 N10
　*STJWD* NW8 . 3 M4
　*STRHM/NOR* SW16 . 202 D1
　*TEDD* TW11 . 176 F10
　*WFD* IG8 . 101 P7
　*WLGTN* SM6 . 222 B8
　*WLSDN* NW10 . 136 C4
Avenue St Andrew
　*CHOB/PIR* GU24 . 230 G7
Avenue St Barnabas
　*CHOB/PIR* GU24 . 230 F8
Avenue St Bartholomew
　*WOKS/MYFD* GU22 . 230 H8
Avenue St Chad
　*WOKS/MYFD* GU22 . 231 H10
Avenue St David
　*WOKS/MYFD* GU22 . 230 H8
Avenue St George
　*WOKS/MYFD* GU22 . 230 G10
Avenue St Margaret
　*WOKS/MYFD* GU22 . 230 G7
Avenue St Mark
　*CHOB/PIR* GU24 . 230 G8
Avenue St Saviour
　*CHOB/PIR* GU24 . 230 G7
Avenue South *SURB* KT6 . 199 L7
　*BRYLDS* KT5 . 199 P6
Avenue Ter *NWMAL* KT3 . 199 P3
　*OXHEY* WD19 . 93 M10
The Avenue *ADL/WDHM* KT15 . 215 N6
　*AMSS* HP7 . 36 A1
　*BAR* EN5 . 77 H7
　*BECK* BR3 . 204 C1
　*BELMT* SM2 . 221 A5
　*BH/WHM* TN16 . 244 B6
　*BKHH* IG9 . 101 J2
　*BMLY* BR1 . 206 A3
　*BRKHM/BTCW* RH3 . 255 M10
　*BRYLDS* KT5 . 199 L8
　*BUSH* WD23 . 73 N8
　*BXLY* DA5 . 163 K7
　*CAR* SM5 . 222 C7
　*CEND/HSY/T* N8 . 119 H1
　*CHING* E4 . 101 J7
　*CHOB/PIR* GU24 . 213 G5
　*CHSWK* W4 . 156 B1
　*CLAP* SW4 . 180 A1
　*COUL/CHIP* CR5 . 240 E1
　*CROY/NA* CR0 . 203 M10
　*CTHM* CR3 . 241 P5
　*DTCH/LGLY* SL3 . 149 N7
　*EGH* TW20 . 150 E7
　*EW* KT17 . 218 D3
　*FBAR/BDGN* N11 . 98 C4
　*FNCH* N3 . 97 K10
　*GNWCH* SE10 . 161 K1
　*GVW* DA11 . 190 C4
　*HCH* RM12 . 125 J4
　*HEST* TW5 . 153 J7
　*HGDN/ICK* UB10 . 132 B2
　*HHW* HP1 . 35 H5


　*HOD* EN11 . 44 E5
　*HORL* RH6 . 280 A5
　*HPTN* TW12 . 175 N9
　*HSLW* TW3 . 176 A1
　*KIL/WHAMP* NW6 . 2 A4
　*KTN/HRWW/WS* HA3 . 94 E9
　*KWD/TDW/WH* KT20 . 238 E8
　*LHD/OX* KT22 . 218 E7
　*LOU* IG10 . 82 G10
　*MUSWH* N10 . 98 D10
　*NTHWD* HA6 . 92 D7
　*ORP* BR6 . 207 N9
　*PIN* HA5 . 93 N7
　*POTB/CUF* EN6 . 59 J6
　*RAD* WD7 . 56 F10
　*RBRW/HUT* CM13 . 107 L7
　*RCH/KEW* TW9 . 155 N8
　*REDH* RH1 . 276 E3
　*RGUW* GU3 . 267 H8
　*ROM* RM1 . 124 E2
　*SLN* SL2 . 108 G10
　*STA* TW18 . 195 L1
　*STMC/STPC* BR5 . 185 L10
　*STWL/WRAY* TW19 . 150 A9
　*SUN* TW16 . 197 J2
　*SWCM* DA10 . 166 G10
　*TOTM* N17 . 121 L5
　*TWK* TW1 . 177 H1
　*UX/CGN* UB8 . 131 M8
　*WAB* EN9 . 63 P1
　*WAT* WD17 . 73 H6
　*WBLY* HA9 . 115 K6
　*WDSR* SL4 . 171 N1
　*WEA* W13 . 134 G9
　*WPK* KT4 . 200 C9
　*WWKM* BR4 . 205 J7
Aylesbury Crs *SL* SL1 . 129 J8
Aylesbury End *BEAC* HP9 . 88 D10
Aylesbury Est *WALW* SE17 . 19 H8
Aylesbury Rd *HAYES* BR2 . 205 M3
　*WALW* SE17 . 19 H8
　*WLSDN* NW10 . 116 A2
Aylesford Av *BECK* BR3 . 204 D5
Aylesford St *PIM* SW1V . 17 J7
Aylesham Cl *MLHL* NW7 . 96 D7
Aylesham Rd *ORP* BR6 . 207 H7
Ayles Rd *YEAD* UB4 . 133 J3
Aylestone Av
　*KIL/WHAMP* NW6 . 136 G2
Aylesworth Av *SLN* SL2 . 108 G5
Aylesworth Sp *WDSR* SL4 . 171 N1
Aylett Rd *ISLW* TW7 . 154 D8
　*SNWD* SE25 . 204 A4
　*UPMR* RM14 . 126 B7
Ayliffe Cl *KUT/HW* KT1 . 199 M2
Aylmer Cl *STAN* HA7 . 95 H2
Aylmer Dr *STAN* HA7 . 95 H2
Aylmer Pde *EFNCH* N2 . 118 A2
Aylmer Rd *BCTR* RM8 . 123 P8
　*EFNCH* N2 . 117 P3
　*SHB* W12 . 156 C1
　*WAN* E11 . 121 L5
Ayloffe Rd *DAGW* RM9 . 144 A1
Ayloffs Cl *EMPK* RM11 . 125 M2
Aylofls Wk *EMPK* RM11 . 125 M3
Aylsham Cl *HARH* RM3 . 105 N5
Aylsham Dr *HGDN/ICK* UB10 . 112 D7
Aylsham La *HARH* RM3 . 105 N5
Aylton Est *BERM/RHTH* SE16 * . 160 B1
Aylward Gdns *CSHM* HP5 . 50 B3
Aylward Rd *FSTH* SE23 . 182 G5
　*RYNPK* SW20 . 201 J2
Aylwards Ri *STAN* HA7 . 95 H2
Aylward St *WCHPL* E1 . 140 C8
Aymer Cl *STA* TW18 . 195 H1
Aymer Dr *STA* TW18 . 195 H1
Aynhoe Rd *WKENS* W14 . 14 A2
Aynho St *WATW* WD18 . 73 J9
Aynscombe Angle *ORP* BR6 . 207 M5
Aynscombe La
　*MORT/ESHN* SW14 . 156 A9
Ayot Little Green La *WLYN* AL6 . 22 C4
Ayot St *PLSTW* E13 . 141 M5
Ayres Crs *WLSDN* NW10 . 136 A2
Ayres End La *HARP* AL5 . 20 C7
Ayres St *STHWK* SE1 . 19 H2
Ayr Gn *ROM* RM1 . 104 F3
Ayron Rd *SOCK/AV* RM15 . 146 C6
Ayrsome Rd *STNW/STAM* N16 . 119 M8
Ayrton Rd *SKENS* SW7 . 15 H3
Ayr Wy *ROM* RM1 . 104 F3
Aysgarth Rd *DUL* SE21 . 162 A9
Aytoun Pl *BRXN/ST* SW9 . 158 F8
Aytoun Rd *BRXN/ST* SW9 . 158 E8
Azalea Cl *HNWL* W7 . 134 E10
　*IL* IG1 . 142 B3
　*LCOL/BKTW* AL2 . 57 H3
Azalea Ct *WFD* IG8 * . 101 P6
　*WOKS/MYFD* GU22 . 232 A5
Azalea Dr *SWLY* BR8 . 186 C8
Azalea Wy *DTCH/LGLY* SL3 . 130 B8
Azania Ms *KTTN* NW5 . 116 C10
Azenby Rd *PECK* SE15 . 159 N8
Azof St *GNWCH* SE10 . 161 K3

## B

Baalbec Rd *HBRY* N5 . 119 J10
Baas Hill *BROX* EN10 . 44 D7
Baas Hill Cl *BROX* EN10 . 44 D7
Baas La *BROX* EN10 . 44 D7
Babbacombe Gdns *CHSGTN* KT9 . 219 J2
Babbacombe Rd *REDBR* IG4 . 122 B8
Babbacombe Rd *BMLY* BR1 . 205 N1
Baber Dr *EBED/NFELT* TW14 . 175 K2
Babington Ri *WBLY* HA9 . 135 M1
Babington Rd *BCTR* RM8 . 123 M10
　*HCH* RM12 . 125 J6
　*HDN* NW4 . 116 B2
　*STRHM/NOR* SW16 . 180 M8
Babmaes St *STJS* SW1Y . 11 H1
Babylon La
　*KWD/TDW/WH* KT20 . 257 D5
Bacchus Wk *IS* N1 . 7 K2
Bachelors Acre *WDSR* SL4 . 149 P1
Bachelor's La
　*RPLY/SEND* GU23 . 234 B10
Bache's St *IS* N1 . 7 H6
Back Church La *WCHPL* E1 . 6 N6
Back Gn *WOT/HER* KT12 . 217 K3
Back La *BGR/WK* TN15 . 247 P10
　*BTFD* TW8 . 155 J6
　*BXLY* DA5 . 186 B5
　*CDW/CHF* RM16 . 169 J6
　*CEND/HSY/T* N8 . 118 E4
　*CHDH* RM6 . 123 K4
　*EDGW* HA8 . 96 E5
　*GSTN* WD25 . 55 P9
　*HAMP* NW3 . 117 M9
　*KTN/HRWW/WS* HA3 . 114 C1
　*MORT/ESHN* SW14 . 156 A9
　*PLMGR* N13 . 99 H3
　*SAND/SEL* CR2 . 223 K3
　*SEVS/STOTM* N15 . 119 J5
　*WALTH* E17 . 121 J1
　*WELL* DA16 . 164 C3
　*WIM/MER* SW19 . 179 L8
Backs *CSHM* HP5 . 51 H4
The Back *BERK* HP4 . 32 A6
Bacon Gv *STHWK* SE1 . 19 L5
Bacon La *CDALE/KGS* NW9 . 115 N2
　*EDGW* HA8 . 96 B5
Bacon Link *CRW* RM5 . 104 G6
Bacons Dr *POTB/CUF* EN6 . 59 M3
Bacon St *BETH* E2 . 7 M5
Bacon Ter *BCTR* RM8 . 123 H6
Badburgham Ct *WAB* EN9 . 63 P1
Baddeley Cl *PEND* EN3 . 80 F2
Baddow Cl *DAGE* RM10 . 144 B3
　*WFD* IG8 . 101 K9
Baden Cl *STA* TW18 . 173 K10
Baden Dr *HORL* RH6 . 280 A4
Baden Pl *STHWK* SE1 . 19 H2
Baden Powell Cl *DAGW* RM9 . 143 P5
　*SURB* KT6 . 199 M10
Baden Powell Rd *SEV* TN13 . 246 F5
Baden Rd *CEND/HSY/T* N8 . 118 C4
　*GU* GU1 . 249 M8
　*IL* IG1 . 142 B6
Bader Cl *PUR/KEN* CR8 . 241 K1
　*WGCE* AL7 . 23 M5
Bader Gdns *SL* SL1 . 148 B4
Bader Wk *GVW* DA11 . 190 G7
Badger Cl *FELT* TW13 . 175 M5
　*GU* GU1 . 249 N5
　*HSLWW* TW4 . 153 H7
Badgers Cl *ASHF* TW15 * . 175 L6
　*BORE* WD6 . 75 L4
　*ENC/FH* EN2 . 79 M1
　*GODL* GU7 . 267 J3
　*HRW* HA1 . 114 D6
　*HSHAM* RP13 . 137 M10
　*WOKN/KNAP* GU21 . 231 P3


Badgers Copse *ORP* BR6 . 207 P3
　*WPK* KT4 . 200 C9
Badgers Ct *WPK* KT4 . 200 C9
Badgers Cft *BROX* EN10 . 44 D7
　*ELTH/MOT* SE9 . 184 D6
　*HHNE* HP2 . 36 E7
　*TRDG/WHET* N20 . 97 H1
Badgers La *WARL* CR6 . 242 B5
Badgers Mt *CDW/CHF* RM16 . 168 G4
Badgers Ri *RSEV* TN14 . 228 B6
Badgers Rd *RSEV* TN14 . 228 C6
Badgers Wk *CTHM* CR3 . 241 N4
　*NWMAL* KT3 . 200 B2
　*PUR/KEN* CR8 . 222 D7
　*RKW/CH/CXG* WD3 . 71 J4
Badger Wy *HAT* AL10 . 40 C6
Badlingham Dr *LHD/OX* KT22 . 236 D10
Badlis Rd *WALTH* E17 . 100 F10
Badlow Cl *ERITH* DA8 . 164 F6
Badminton Cl *BORE* WD6 . 75 M6
　*HRW* HA1 . 114 D2
　*NTHLT* UB5 . 133 P7
Badminton Ms *BROX* E16 . 141 M10
Badminton Pl *BROX* EN10 . 44 D6
Badminton Rd *BAL* SW12 . 180 C1
Badsworth Rd *CMBW* SE5 . 159 K6
Bafton Gu *HAYES* BR2 . 205 N8
Bagden Hl *RDKG* RH5 . 254 C6
Bagley Cl *WDR/YW* UB7 . 151 P1
Bagley House
　*WOOL/PLUM* SE18 * . 162 B7
Bagley's La *FUL/PGN* SW6 . 157 L2
Bagleys Spring *CHDH* RM6 . 123 P2
Bagot Cl *ASHTD* KT21 . 237 L2
Bagshot Ct
　*WOOL/PLUM* SE18 * . 162 D7
Bagshot Rd *ASC* SL5 . 192 A8
　*CHOB/PIR* GU24 . 212 G7
　*ECH* TW20 . 171 P10
　*EN* EN1 . 79 N10
　*WOKN/KNAP* GU21 . 230 G5
Bagshot St *WALW* SE17 . 19 K8
Bahram Rd *HOR/WEW* KT19 . 220 A6
Baigents La *BFOR* GU20 . 212 C3
Baildon St *DEPT* SE8 . 160 E6
Bailes La *RGUW* GU3 . 248 C9
Bailey Cl *FBAR/BDGN* N11 . 166 C3
　*OXHEY* WD19
　*THMD* SE28 . 143 H10
　*WDSR* SL4 . 148 F8
Bailey Cots *POP/IOD* E14 * . 140 D7
Bailey Crs *CHSGTN* KT9 . 219 J4
Bailey House
　*WOOL/PLUM* SE18 * . 162 B6
Bailey Ms *BRXS/STRHM* SW2 . 181 N6
　*CHSWK* W4 . 155 N5
Bailey Pl *SYD* SE26 . 182 G2
Bailey Rd *DORK* RH4 . 272 B3
Baillie Cl *RAIN* RM13 . 145 J6
Baillie Rd *GU* GU1 . 268 C1
Bainbridge Rd
　*RCHPK/HAM* TW10 . 177 K8
Bainbridge Rd *DAGW* RM9 . 124 A9
Bainbridge St
　*NOXST/BSQ* WC1A . 11 K5
Baines Cl *SAND/SEL* CR2 . 223 L2
Bainton Md
　*WOKN/KNAP* GU21 . 231 M3
Baird Av *STHL* UB1 . 134 A9
Baird Cl *BUSH* WD23 . 74 A10
　*CDALE/KGS* NW9 . 115 P4
　*CRAWE* RH10 . 284 B4
　*LEY* E10 . 120 F6
　*SL* SL1 . 148 G1
Baird Dr *RGUW* GU3 . 248 G9
Baird Gdns *NRWD* SE19 . 181 M7
Baird Memorial Cots
　*STHGT/OAK* N14 * . 98 E3
Baird Rd *EN* EN1 . 80 A7
Baird St *STLK* EC1Y . 12 F1
Bairstow Ct *BORE* WD6 . 75 K5
Baizdon Rd *BKHTH/KID* SE3 . 161 K6
Bakeham La *EGH* TW20 . 171 P10
Bakehouse Rd *HORL* RH6 . 280 C2
Baker Cl *CRAWE* RH10 . 283 N9
Baker Hill Cl *GVW* DA11 . 190 C7
Baker La *MTCM* CR4 . 202 B2
Baker Ms *ORP* BR6 . 227 J3
Baker Pl *HOR/WEW* KT19 . 219 P5
Baker Rd *WLSDN* NW10 . 136 B3
　*WOOL/PLUM* SE18 . 162 B6
Bakers Av *WALTH* E17 . 120 G4
Bakers Ct *SNWD* SE25 . 203 L2
Bakerscroft *CHES/WCR* EN8 . 62 C1
Bakers End *RYNPK* SW20 . 201 H2
Bakers Fld *HOLWY* N7 . 118 G8
Bakers Gdns *CAR* SM5 . 202 B9
Bakers Hl *CLPT* E5 . 120 A6
Bakers La *EPP* CM16 . 65 J6
Bakers Md *GDST* RH9 . 260 B6
Bakers Meadow *BRWN* CM15 . 87 H3
Baker's Ms *MHST* W1U . 10 C5
Bakers Rents *BETH* E2 . 7 L3
Bakers Rw *CHESW* EN7 . 62 A6
　*SRTFD* E15 . 141 K1
Baker's Rd *UX/CGN* UB8 . 131 N2
Baker's Rw *CLKNW* EC1R . 12 A2
Baker St *BAR* EN5 . 77 H1
　*CAMTN* NW1 . 10 B1
　*EN* EN1 . 79 L6
　*HERT/BAY* SG13 . 25 M5
　*MHST* W1U . 10 C4
　*POTB/CUF* EN6 . 59 J9
　*WEY* KT13 . 216 B1
Bakers Wd *DEN/HRF* UB9 . 110 G6
Bakery Cl *BRXN/ST* SW9 . 158 G6
　*HLWW/ROY* CM19 . 45 P1
Bakery Ms *SURB* KT6 . 199 M8
Bakewell Wy *NWMAL* KT3 . 200 B2
Balaams La *STHGT/OAK* N14 . 98 E3
Balaam St *PLSTW* E13 . 141 M5
Balaclava Rd *SURB* KT6 . 199 H6
　*STHWK* SE1 . 19 M6
Bala Gn *CDALE/KGS* NW9 * . 96 B10
Balcary Gdns *BERK* HP4 . 32 A6
Balcaskie Rd *ELTH/MOT* SE9 . 184 C1
Balchier Rd *EDUL* SE22 . 182 B1
Balchins La *DORK* RH4 . 271 J6
Balcombe Cl *BXLYHS* DA6 . 163 N10
Balcombe Gdns *HORL* RH6 . 280 D6
Balcombe St *CAMTN* NW1 . 3 N10
Balcon Wy *BORE* WD6 . 75 N2
Balcorne St *HOM* E9 . 139 H2
Balder Ri *LEE/GVBK* SE12 . 183 M2
Balderton St *OXSTW* W1C . 10 C6
Baldocks La *EPP* CM16 . 83 M1
　*WARE* SG12 . 26 C1
Baldock St *WARE* SG12 . 26 C1
Baldock Wy *BORE* WD6 . 75 L3
Baldry Gdns
　*STRHM/NOR* SW16 . 180 F9
Baldwin Cl *CRAWE* RH10 . 285 L7
Baldwin Crs *CMBW* SE5 . 159 H7
　*RGUE* GU4 . 268 E3
Baldwin Gdns *HSLW* TW3 . 154 B7
Baldwin Rd *BTSEA* SW11 . 180 A1
　*SL* SL1 . 128 B7
Baldwins *WGCE* AL7 . 23 L5
Baldwin's Gdns *FSBYW* WC1X . 12 A3
Baldwin's La
　*RKW/CH/CXG* WD3 . 71 L4
Baldwins Store *WDSR* SL4 . 149 L5
Baldwin St *FSBYE* EC1V . 7 H6
Baldwin Ter *IS* N1 . 6 E2

| Name | Page | Grid |
|---|---|---|
| Baldwyn Gdns ACT W3 | 135 | P9 |
| Baldwyn's Pk BXLY DA5 | 186 | E5 |
| Baldwyn's Rd BXLY DA5 | 186 | E5 |
| Bale Rd WCHPL E1 | 140 | D7 |
| Balfern Gv CHSWK W4 | 156 | B5 |
| Balfern St BTSEA SW11 | 157 | P8 |
| Balfe St IS N1 * | 5 | M8 |
| Balfont Cl SAND/SEL CR2 | 223 | J8 |
| WOKS/MYFD GU22 | 232 | B8 |
| Balfour Av HNWL W7 | 134 | E10 |
| Balfour Ms ED N9 | 99 | P4 |
| HHS/BOV HP3 | 52 | C5 |
| MYFR/PKLN W1K * | 10 | D9 |
| Balfour Pl MYFR/PKLN W1K | 10 | C9 |
| PUT/ROE SW15 | 156 | E10 |
| Balfour Rd ACT W3 | 135 | P7 |
| CAR SM5 | 222 | A4 |
| GRAYS RM17 | 167 | N3 |
| HAYES BR2 | 206 | A2 |
| HBRY N5 | 119 | K9 |
| HRW HA1 | 114 | C4 |
| HSLW TW3 | 154 | A9 |
| IL IG1 | 122 | A2 |
| NWDGN UB2 | 153 | L2 |
| SNWD SE25 | 203 | P4 |
| WEY W13 | 154 | C1 |
| WEY KT13 | 216 | A1 |
| WIM/MER SW19 | 179 | L10 |
| Balfour St HERT/WAT SG14 | 25 | K4 |
| STHWK SE1 | 18 | G5 |
| Balgonie Rd CHING E4 | 101 | J2 |
| Balgores Crs GPK RM2 | 125 | J2 |
| Balgores La GPK RM2 | 125 | J3 |
| Balgores Sq GPK RM2 | 125 | J3 |
| Balgowan Cl NWMAL KT3 | 200 | B2 |
| Balgowan Rd BECK BR3 | 204 | D3 |
| Balgowan St WOOL/PLUM SE18 | 163 | J8 |
| Balham Gv BAL SW12 | 180 | C4 |
| Balham High Rd BAL SW12 | 180 | C4 |
| Balham Hl BAL SW12 | 180 | C3 |
| Balham New Rd BAL SW12 | 180 | C3 |
| Balham Park Rd BAL SW12 | 180 | A3 |
| Balham Rd ED N9 | 99 | P3 |
| Balham Station Rd BAL SW12 | 180 | B4 |
| Balham Wk WAP E1W * | 140 | C1 |
| Balladier Wk POP/IOD E14 | 140 | G7 |
| Ballamore Rd BMLY BR1 | 183 | M6 |
| Ballance Rd HOM E9 | 140 | C1 |
| The Ballands North LHD/OX KT22 | 236 | D8 |
| The Ballands' South LHD/OX KT22 | 236 | C9 |
| Ballantine St WAND/EARL SW18 | 157 | M10 |
| Ballantyne Cl ELTH/MOT SE9 | 184 | B1 |
| Ballantyne Dr KWD/TDW/WH KT20 | 239 | J7 |
| Ballard Cl KUTN/CMB KT2 | 178 | A10 |
| Ballards Cl DAGE RM10 | 144 | D6 |
| Ballards Farm Rd SAND/SEL CR2 | 223 | P3 |
| Ballards Gn KWD/TDW/WH KT20 | 239 | H5 |
| Ballards La FNCH N3 | 97 | L8 |
| OXTED RH8 | 261 | M7 |
| Ballards Ms EDGW HA8 | 96 | B1 |
| Ballards Ri SAND/SEL CR2 | 223 | P3 |
| Ballards Rd CRICK NW2 | 116 | F2 |
| DAGE RM10 | 144 | C3 |
| Ballards Wy SAND/SEL CR2 | 223 | P3 |
| Ballast Quay GNWCH SE10 | 161 | J4 |
| Ballater Cl OXHEY WD19 | 93 | K3 |
| Ballater Rd BRXS/STRHM SW2 | 158 | F10 |
| SAND/SEL CR2 | 223 | N2 |
| Ballencrieff Rd ASC SL5 | 192 | B7 |
| Ballina St FSTH SE23 | 182 | C5 |
| Ballingdon Rd BTSEA SW11 | 181 | H4 |
| Ballinger Ct BERK HP4 | 33 | M6 |
| Ballinger Wy NTHLT UB5 | 133 | M6 |
| Balliol Av CHING E4 | 101 | L5 |
| Balliol Cl CRAWE RH10 | 284 | D5 |
| Balliol Rd NKENS W10 | 136 | F9 |
| TOTM N17 | 99 | P8 |
| WELL DA16 | 163 | L8 |
| Balloch Rd CAT SE6 | 183 | J4 |
| Ballogie Av WLSDN NW10 | 116 | F8 |
| Ballow Cl CMBW SE5 * | 159 | L6 |
| Ball's Pond Pl IS N1 * | 7 | J1 |
| Balls Pond Rd IS N1 | 7 | J1 |
| Balmain Cl EA W5 | 135 | K1 |
| Balmer Rd BOW E3 | 140 | L4 |
| Balmes Rd IS N1 | 7 | J1 |
| Balmoral Av BECK BR3 | 204 | D4 |
| FBAR/BDGN N11 | 98 | B7 |
| Balmoral Cl CHES/WCR EN8 | 62 | C10 |
| PUT/ROE SW15 * | 178 | G5 |
| SL1 | 128 | C8 |
| Balmoral Crs E/WMO/HCT KT8 | 197 | P3 |
| Balmoral Dr BORE WD6 | 76 | B3 |
| STHL UB1 | 133 | N6 |
| WOKS/MYFD GU22 | 232 | G5 |
| YEAD UB4 | 132 | F6 |
| Balmoral Gdns BXLY DA5 | 186 | A6 |
| SAND/SEL CR2 | 223 | L6 |
| WDSR SL4 | 149 | J8 |
| WEA W13 * | 154 | F2 |
| Balmoral Ms SHB W12 | 156 | C2 |
| Balmoral Rd ABLGY WD5 | 55 | N8 |
| BRWN CM15 | 86 | C9 |
| CRICK NW2 | 136 | E1 |
| EYN DA4 | 187 | P9 |
| FSTGT E7 | 121 | P9 |
| GPK RM2 | 125 | J2 |
| KUT/HW KT1 | 199 | L4 |
| PEND EN3 | 80 | C2 |
| RYLN/HDSTN HA2 | 113 | P9 |
| WATN WD24 | 75 | K4 |
| WPK KT4 | 200 | E10 |
| Balmoral Wy BELMT SM2 | 221 | K6 |
| Balmore Crs EBAR EN4 | 78 | B9 |
| Balmore St ARCH N19 | 118 | C7 |
| Balmuir Gdns PUT/ROE SW15 | 156 | F10 |
| Balnacraig Av WLSDN NW10 | 116 | F8 |
| Balquhain Cl ASHTD KT21 | 237 | J3 |
| Balsams Cl HERT/BAY SG13 | 25 | J1 |
| Baltic Pl IS N1 * | 7 | K5 |
| Baltic St East STLK EC1Y | 12 | C1 |
| Baltic St West STLK EC1Y | 12 | C1 |
| Baltimore Pl WELL DA16 | 163 | J8 |
| Balvaird Pl PIM SW1V | 17 | K8 |
| Balvernie Gv WAND/EARL SW18 | 179 | J3 |
| Bamber Rd PECK SE15 | 159 | N7 |
| Bamborough Gdns SHB W12 | 156 | F1 |
| Bamford Av WBLY HA0 | 136 | A5 |
| Bamford Rd BMLY BR1 | 183 | J8 |
| BARK IG11 | 104 | C6 |
| Bampfylde Cl WLGTN SM6 | 202 | D10 |
| Bampton Dr MLHL NW7 | 96 | G7 |
| Bampton Rd FSTH SE23 | 182 | C6 |
| HARH RM3 | 105 | M8 |
| Bampton Wy WOKN/KNAP GU21 | 231 | M4 |
| Banavie Gdns BECK BR3 | 204 | D1 |
| Banbury Av SL SL1 | 128 | E7 |
| Banbury Cl ENC/FH EN2 | 79 | J5 |
| Banbury Ct BELMT SM2 * | 221 | K6 |
| COVGDN WC2E * | 11 | J7 |
| Banbury Rd HOM E9 | 140 | C2 |
| WALTH E17 | 100 | D8 |
| Banbury St BTSEA SW11 * | 157 | P8 |
| WATW WD18 | 73 | M4 |
| Banbury Vls MEO DA13 | 189 | J10 |
| Banchory Rd BKHTH/KID SE3 | 161 | L5 |
| Bancroft Av EFNCH N2 | 117 | P3 |
| Bancroft Cha ASHF TW15 * | 174 | B7 |

| Name | Page | Grid |
|---|---|---|
| Bancroft Ct NTHLT UB5 | 133 | K3 |
| REIG RH2 | 257 | L10 |
| Bancroft Gdns KTN/HRWW/WS HA3 | 94 | B3 |
| ORP BR6 | 207 | J8 |
| Bancroft Rd CRAWE RH10 | 284 | B8 |
| KTN/HRWW/WS HA3 | 94 | B10 |
| REIG RH2 | 257 | K10 |
| WCHPL E1 | 140 | B6 |
| Banders Ri GU GU1 | 250 | B10 |
| Band La EGH TW20 | 172 | C8 |
| Bandon Cl HGDN/ICK UB10 | 132 | A4 |
| Bandon Ri WLGTN SM6 | 222 | E2 |
| Banes Down WAB EN9 | 45 | K8 |
| Banfield Rd PECK SE15 | 160 | A9 |
| Bangalore St PUT/ROE SW15 | 156 | G5 |
| Bangor Cl NTHLT UB5 | 114 | A10 |
| Bangors Cl IVER SL0 | 131 | J8 |
| Bangors Rd North IVER SL0 | 130 | G3 |
| Bangors Rd South IVER SL0 | 131 | H6 |
| Banim St HMSMTH W6 | 156 | E7 |
| Banister Rd NKENS W10 | 136 | G1 |
| Bank Av MTCM CR4 * | 201 | N2 |
| Bank End STHWK SE1 * | 12 | E9 |
| Bankfoot GRAYS RM17 | 167 | L3 |
| Bankfoot Rd BMLY BR1 | 183 | K7 |
| Bank On CSHM HP5 | 32 | B9 |
| Bankhurst Rd CAT SE6 | 182 | E5 |
| Bank La BGR/WK TN15 | 265 | P8 |
| CRAWE RH10 | 283 | N7 |
| KUTN/CMB KT2 | 177 | K10 |
| PUT/ROE SW15 | 178 | B3 |
| Bank Ms SUT SM1 | 221 | M3 |
| Bankmill BERK HP4 * | 34 | B5 |
| Bank Mill La BERK HP4 | 34 | B6 |
| Bank Pl BRW CM14 * | 107 | H3 |
| Bank Prec CRAWE RH10 * | 284 | B4 |
| Banksia Rd UED N18 | 100 | B6 |
| Bankside ENC/FH EN2 | 79 | J5 |
| GVW DA11 | 189 | N2 |
| SAND/SEL CR2 | 223 | N3 |
| SEV TN13 | 246 | E12 |
| STHL UB1 | 133 | L10 |
| STHWK SE1 * | 12 | E8 |
| Bankside Av LEW SE13 * | 161 | N4 |
| NTHLT UB5 * | 133 | H4 |
| Bankside Cl BH/WHM TN16 | 243 | P4 |
| BXLY DA5 | 186 | E7 |
| CAR SM5 | 221 | P2 |
| DEN/HRF UB9 | 91 | K7 |
| ISLW TW7 | 154 | E10 |
| Bankside Down RKW/CH/CXG WD3 * | 71 | N10 |
| Bankside Dr THDIT KT7 | 198 | C9 |
| Bankside Rd IL IG1 | 122 | F10 |
| Bank's La EHSLY KT24 | 235 | J8 |
| Banks Rd BORE WD6 | 75 | P6 |
| CRAWE RH10 | 284 | D8 |
| Banks Sp SL SL1 | 148 | G1 |
| Bank St GVW DA11 | 190 | B2 |
| Banks Wy MNPK E12 | 122 | G9 |
| RGUE GU4 | 250 | C7 |
| Bankymead HEST TW5 | 153 | N5 |
| Bank Ter CRAWE RH10 * | 283 | N8 |
| The Bank ARCH N19 * | 285 | P9 |
| HGT N6 | 118 | C6 |
| Bankton Rd BRXS/STRHM SW2 | 159 | N10 |
| Bankwell Rd LEW SE13 | 161 | K10 |
| Bann Cl SOCK/AV RM15 | 146 | C9 |
| Banner Cl PUR RM19 | 166 | C3 |
| Banner St STLK EC1Y | 12 | F2 |
| Banning St GNWCH SE10 | 161 | K4 |
| Bannister Cl BRXS/STRHM SW2 | 181 | H4 |
| DTCH/LGLY SL3 | 150 | B1 |
| GFD/PVL UB6 | 114 | C10 |
| Bannister Dr RBRW/HUT CM13 | 87 | P10 |
| Bannister Gdns STMC/STPC BR5 | 207 | M3 |
| Bannister's Rd GUW GU2 | 267 | L2 |
| Bannockburn Rd WOOL/PLUM SE18 | 163 | N8 |
| Bannow Cl HOR/WEW KT19 | 220 | B2 |
| Banson's La CHONG CM5 | 67 | P4 |
| Bansons Wy CHONG CM5 | 67 | N4 |
| Banstead Ct SHB W12 * | 136 | C9 |
| Banstead Gdns ED N9 | 99 | L4 |
| Banstead Rd BNSTD SM7 * | 239 | N6 |
| CAR SM5 | 221 | N4 |
| CTHM CR3 | 241 | L8 |
| EW KT17 | 220 | F8 |
| PUR/KEN CR8 | 223 | H7 |
| Banstead Rd South BELMT SM2 | 221 | M6 |
| Banstead Wy WLGTN SM6 | 222 | F4 |
| Banstock Rd EDGW HA8 | 95 | N7 |
| Banting Dr WCHMH N21 | 78 | D9 |
| Banton Cl EN EN1 | 80 | A6 |
| Bantry St CMBW SE5 | 159 | L6 |
| Banwell Rd BXLY DA5 | 185 | L6 |
| Banyard Rd BERM/RHTH SE16 | 141 | L9 |
| Banyards EMPK RM11 | 125 | M3 |
| Bapchild Pl STMC/STPC BR5 | 207 | M4 |
| Baptist Gdns KTTN NW5 | 4 | C1 |
| Barandon Wk NTGHL W11 * | 136 | C6 |
| Barbara Castle Cl FUL/PGN SW6 * | 14 | D10 |
| Barbara Cl SHPTN TW17 | 196 | C5 |
| Barbara Hucklesbury Cl WDGN N22 | 99 | J10 |
| Barbaraville Camp BRKMPK AL9 * | 41 | J1 |
| Barbauld Rd STNW/STAM N16 | 119 | N8 |
| Barbel Cl CHES/WCR EN8 | 62 | F10 |
| Barberry Cl HARH RM3 | 105 | K3 |
| Barberry Rd HHW HP1 | 35 | K6 |
| Barbers Rd SRTFD E15 | 140 | G5 |
| Barbican Rd GFD/PVL UB6 | 134 | A8 |
| Barb Ms HMSMTH W6 | 156 | G6 |
| Barbon Aly LVPST EC2M | 13 | L4 |
| Barbon Cl BMSBY WC1N | 11 | L1 |
| Barbot Cl ED N9 | 100 | D2 |
| Barchard St WAND/EARL SW18 | 179 | L1 |
| Barchester Cl HNWL W7 | 134 | F1 |
| UX/CGN UB8 | 132 | A9 |
| Barchester Rd DTCH/LGLY SL3 | 150 | A2 |
| KTN/HRWW/WS HA3 | 94 | C9 |
| Barchester St POP/IOD E14 | 140 | G7 |
| EN EN1 | 80 | A1 |
| MTCM CR4 | 180 | E10 |
| WARL CR6 | 242 | C5 |
| Barclay Cl FUL/PGN SW6 * | 157 | K6 |
| HERT/BAY SG13 | 26 | A7 |
| LHD/OX KT22 | 236 | A9 |
| WATW WD18 | 73 | H6 |
| Barclay Ov HOD EN11 | 44 | F4 |
| Barclay Ov WOKN/KNAP GU21 | 101 | M5 |
| Barclay Rd CROY/NA CRO | 203 | L10 |
| FUL/PGN SW6 | 157 | K6 |
| PLSTW E13 | 141 | K6 |
| UED N18 | 99 | J2 |
| WALTH E17 | 121 | H3 |
| WAN E11 * | 121 | L1 |
| Barclay Wy WTHK RM20 | 166 | E4 |
| Barcombe Av BRXS/STRHM SW2 | 181 | P5 |
| Barcombe Cl STMC/STPC BR5 | 207 | H3 |
| Barden St WOOL/PLUM SE18 | 163 | N6 |
| Bardeswell Av BRW CM14 | 107 | M2 |
| Bardney Rd MRDN SM4 | 201 | L4 |
| Bardolph Av CROY/NA CRO | 224 | D5 |
| Bardolph Rd HOLWY N7 | 118 | D10 |
| RCH/KEW TW9 | 155 | N7 |
| Bard Rd NKENS W10 | 136 | E3 |
| Bards Cnr HHW HP1 | 35 | L5 |

| Name | Page | Grid |
|---|---|---|
| Bardsey Pl WCHPL E1 | 140 | B6 |
| Bardsey Wk IS N1 * | 6 | F1 |
| Bardsley Cl CROY/NA CRO | 203 | N10 |
| Bardsley La GNWCH SE10 | 161 | N5 |
| Bardwell Ct STAL AL1 | 38 | C7 |
| Bardwell Rd STAL AL1 | 38 | C7 |
| Barfett St NKENS W10 | 138 | B4 |
| Barfield EYN DA4 | 210 | A1 |
| Barfield Av TRDG/WHET N20 | 98 | A3 |
| Barfield Rd BMLY BR1 | 206 | D3 |
| WAN E11 * | 121 | L1 |
| Barfields LOU IG10 | 82 | D8 |
| REDH RH1 | 259 | J9 |
| Barfields Gdns LOU IG10 | 82 | D8 |
| Barfields Pth LOU IG10 | 82 | D8 |
| Barford Cl HDN NW4 | 96 | A10 |
| Barford St IS N1 | 5 | M5 |
| Barforth Rd PECK SE15 | 160 | A9 |
| Barfreston Wy PGE/AN SE20 | 204 | A1 |
| Bargate Cl NWMAL KT3 | 200 | D7 |
| WOOL/PLUM SE18 | 163 | J4 |
| Barge Ct SWCM DA10 | 167 | H10 |
| Barge House Rd STHWK SE1 | 12 | B9 |
| Bargery Rd CAT SE6 | 182 | G4 |
| Barge Wk KUT/HW KT1 | 199 | J3 |
| Bargrove Av PGE/AN SE20 | 181 | P10 |
| Bargrove Cl PGE/AN SE20 | 181 | P10 |
| Bargrove Crs CAT SE6 | 182 | E5 |
| Barham Av BORE WD6 | 75 | L7 |
| CHST BR7 | 184 | E8 |
| GVE DA12 | 191 | J4 |
| HAYES BR2 | 206 | B8 |
| ROMW/RG RM7 | 104 | C10 |
| WEY KT13 | 216 | C5 |
| Barham Cl ALP/SUD HA0 | 135 | H1 |
| CHST BR7 | 184 | E8 |
| RYNPK SW20 | 178 | D10 |
| SAND/SEL CR2 | 223 | K1 |
| WIM/MER SW19 | 178 | C9 |
| Baring Cl LEE/GVPK SE12 | 183 | M5 |
| Baring Rd BEAC HP9 | 88 | B3 |
| CROY/NA CRO | 203 | P8 |
| EBAR EN4 | 77 | N7 |
| LEE/GVPK SE12 | 183 | N5 |
| Baring St IS N1 | 6 | G4 |
| Barkantine Shaw OXTED RH8 | 261 | J14 |
| Barker Cl CHERT KT16 | 195 | H1 |
| NTHWD HA6 | 92 | G8 |
| NWMAL KT3 | 199 | N4 |
| Barker Dr CAMTN NW1 | 5 | H4 |
| Barker Rd CHERT KT16 | 195 | H7 |
| Barker St WBPTN SW10 | 15 | J9 |
| Barker Wk STRHM/NOR SW16 | 180 | E6 |
| Barkham Rd TOTM N17 | 99 | L8 |
| Bark Hart Rd ORP BR6 | 207 | L8 |
| Barking Rd EHAM E6 | 142 | A4 |
| POP/IOD E14 | 141 | K8 |
| Bark Pl BAY/PAD W2 | 8 | B7 |
| Barkston Gdns ECT SW5 | 14 | G6 |
| Barkway Dr ORP BR6 | 226 | D1 |
| Barkwood Cl ROMW/RG RM7 | 124 | D3 |
| Barkworth Rd BERM/RHTH SE16 | 159 | N4 |
| Barlby Gdns NKENS W10 | 136 | F7 |
| Barlby Rd NKENS W10 | 136 | F7 |
| Barle Gdns SOCK/AV RM15 | 146 | C9 |
| Barley Brow GSTN WD25 | 55 | J7 |
| Barley Cl ALP/SUD HA0 | 115 | J9 |
| BUSH WD23 | 74 | A9 |
| CRAWE RH10 | 282 | B1 |
| Barleycorn Wy EMPK RM11 | 125 | N4 |
| POP/IOD E14 | 140 | E9 |
| Barley Cft HERT/WAT SG14 | 25 | J5 |
| HHNE HP2 | 36 | D6 |
| WAB EN9 | 46 | C5 |
| Barleycroft Gn WCGW AL8 | 22 | F5 |
| Barleycroft Rd WCGW AL8 | 22 | F6 |
| Barley Fld BRWN CM15 | 86 | E5 |
| Barley La GDMY/SEVK IG3 | 123 | K4 |
| Barley Mow Ct BRKHM/BTCW RH3 | 255 | P10 |
| WOKN/KNAP GU21 | 231 | J3 |
| Barley Mow Pas CHSWK W4 | 156 | B4 |
| ESBYE EC1V | 12 | E1 |
| Barley Mow Rd EGH TW20 | 171 | P8 |
| Barley Mow Wy SHPTN TW17 | 196 | B6 |
| Barlow Cl WLGTN SM6 | 222 | G6 |
| Barlow Dr BKHTH/KID SE3 | 162 | B7 |
| Barlow Pl MYFR/PICC W1J | 10 | D8 |
| Barlow Rd ACT W3 | 135 | N10 |
| CRAWW RH11 | 283 | H10 |
| HPTN TW12 | 175 | P10 |
| KIL/WHAMP NW6 | 2 | B1 |
| Barlow St WALW SE17 | 19 | H5 |
| Barlow Wy RAIN RM13 | 144 | E9 |
| Barlow Wy South RAIN RM13 | 144 | E9 |
| Barmeston Rd CAT SE6 | 182 | G5 |
| Barmor Cl RYLN/HDSTN HA2 | 94 | A10 |
| Barmouth Av GFD/PVL UB6 | 134 | A1 |
| Barmouth Rd CROY/NA CRO | 204 | A10 |
| WAND/EARL SW18 | 179 | M2 |
| Barnabas Rd HOM E9 | 121 | H9 |
| Barnaby Cl RYLN/HDSTN HA2 | 114 | A4 |
| Barnaby Pl SKENS SW7 | 16 | B3 |
| Barnaby Wy CHIG IG7 | 102 | D4 |
| Barnacres Rd HHS/BOV HP3 | 53 | L6 |
| Barnard Cl CHST BR7 | 205 | H7 |
| SUN TW16 | 175 | L10 |
| WLGTN SM6 | 222 | F6 |
| WOOL/PLUM SE18 | 162 | D4 |
| Barnard Gdns NWMAL KT3 | 200 | D2 |
| YEAD UB4 | 133 | J6 |
| Barnard Gn WGCE AL7 | 23 | J6 |
| Barnard Hl MUSWH N10 | 98 | C10 |
| Barnard Ms BTSEA SW11 | 157 | P10 |
| Barnardo Dr BARK/HLT IG6 | 122 | G1 |
| Barnardo Gdns WCHPL E1 * | 140 | E8 |
| Barnardo Pl WCHPL E1 * | 140 | E8 |
| Barnard Rd BTSEA SW11 | 157 | P10 |
| EN EN1 | 80 | A6 |
| MTCM CR4 | 180 | B7 |
| WARL CR6 | 242 | C5 |
| Barnards Wy HHS/BOV HP3 | 35 | P7 |
| Barnato Cl BF/WBF KT14 | 215 | P8 |
| Barnby Sq SRTFD E15 | 140 | D1 |
| Barnby St CAMTN NW1 | 5 | H7 |
| SRTFD E15 | 140 | C1 |
| Barncroft CWL UB8 | 132 | A9 |
| Barn Cl ASHF TW15 | 174 | A8 |
| BNSTD SM7 | 239 | N1 |
| CRAWE RH10 | 284 | E7 |
| EPP CM16 | 70 | A2 |
| HHS/BOV HP3 | 36 | A9 |
| KTTN NW5 * | 118 | E10 |
| RAD WD7 | 74 | F1 |
| SLN SL2 | 130 | B3 |
| WGCW AL8 | 22 | F5 |

| Name | Page | Grid |
|---|---|---|
| Barneby Cl WHTN TW2 | 176 | D4 |
| Barnehurst Av BCTR RM8 | 123 | N6 |
| Barnehurst Cl ERITH DA8 | 164 | D7 |
| Barnehurst Rd BXLYHN DA7 | 164 | E7 |
| Barnes Av BARN SW13 | 156 | D6 |
| CSHM HP5 | 32 | D5 |
| NWDGN UB2 | 153 | N3 |
| Barnes Br CHSWK W4 | 156 | B5 |
| Barnes Cl MNPK E12 | 122 | A9 |
| Barnes Cray Rd DART DA1 | 165 | H10 |
| Barnes End NWMAL KT3 | 200 | D5 |
| Barnes High St BARN SW13 | 156 | C8 |
| Barnes La KGLGY WD4 | 53 | M4 |
| Barnes Ri KGLGY WD4 | 54 | A3 |
| Barnes Rd GODL GU7 | 267 | K9 |
| IL IG1 | 122 | F10 |
| UED N18 | 99 | P1 |
| Barnes St POP/IOD E14 | 140 | D8 |
| Barnes Ter DEPT SE8 | 140 | F10 |
| Barnes Wallis Ct EHSLY KT24 | 253 | L3 |
| Barnes Wallis Dr BF/WBF KT14 | 215 | P7 |
| Barnes Wy IVER SL0 | 131 | K9 |
| Barnet By-Pass BORE WD6 | 76 | B9 |
| Barnet Dr HAYES BR2 | 206 | B10 |
| Barnet Gate La BAR EN5 | 76 | C10 |
| Barnet Gv BETH E2 | 7 | N9 |
| Barnet Hl BAR EN5 | 76 | F4 |
| Barnet La BORE WD6 | 75 | L1 |
| TRDG/WHET N20 | 97 | J2 |
| Barnet Rd BAR EN5 | 76 | B1 |
| LCOL/BKTW AL2 | 57 | K3 |
| POTB/CUF EN6 | 59 | L10 |
| Barnet Rd ERITH DA8 | 164 | G8 |
| Barnet Trd Est BAR EN5 | 76 | F2 |
| SHGR GU5 | 268 | F9 |
| Barnett Cl LHD/OX KT22 | 236 | G5 |
| RYLN/HDSTN HA2 * | 114 | A9 |
| Barnett La SHGR GU5 | 268 | E10 |
| Barnett Rd RGUE GU4 | 250 | A5 |
| Barnett Way (Barnet By-Pass) MLHL NW7 | 96 | A1 |
| Barnet Wood Rd HAYES BR2 | 205 | P9 |
| HAYES BR2 | 206 | B9 |
| Barney Cl CHARL SE7 | 161 | J4 |
| Barnfield EPP CM16 | 65 | K4 |
| GVW DA11 | 190 | D5 |
| HAMP NW3 | 118 | A10 |
| IVER SL0 | 131 | H8 |
| NWMAL KT3 | 200 | B4 |
| SL SL1 | 128 | C10 |
| Barnfield Av CROY/NA CRO | 204 | B8 |
| KUTN/CMB KT2 | 177 | K8 |
| MTCM CR4 | 180 | G7 |
| Barnfield Cl COUL/CHIP CR5 | 241 | K5 |
| CEND/HSY/T N8 | 118 | E2 |
| CHEAM SM3 | 201 | H7 |
| CRAWE RH10 | 285 | N9 |
| DORK RH4 | 272 | F5 |
| LOU IG10 | 82 | F7 |
| SWLY BR8 | 208 | D10 |
| TOOT SW17 | 180 | C6 |
| WAB EN9 | 46 | A9 |
| Barnfield Gdns KUTN/CMB KT2 | 177 | K8 |
| WOOL/PLUM SE18 | 162 | G8 |
| Barnfield Pl POP/IOD E14 | 160 | C1 |
| Barnfield Rd BELV DA17 | 164 | A5 |
| BH/WHM TN16 | 244 | A6 |
| CRAWE RH10 | 285 | N6 |
| EA W5 | 135 | H3 |
| EDGW HA8 | 96 | D3 |
| HARP AL5 | 20 | B9 |
| SAND/SEL CR2 | 223 | N5 |
| SEV TN13 | 246 | F12 |
| STMC/STPC BR5 | 207 | M3 |
| WOOL/PLUM SE18 | 162 | E7 |
| Barnfield Wd Rd BECK BR3 | 205 | J6 |
| Barnham Dr GFD/PVL UB6 | 134 | B5 |
| Barnham St STHWK SE1 | 19 | M1 |
| Barnhill PIN HA5 | 111 | N3 |
| Barnhill Av HAYES BR2 | 205 | P1 |
| Barn Hl HLWW/ROY CM19 | 45 | N9 |
| Barnhill La YEAD UB4 | 133 | J3 |
| Barnhill Rd WBLY HA9 | 115 | N8 |
| YEAD UB4 | 133 | J3 |
| Barnhurst Pth OXHEY WD19 | 93 | K6 |
| Barningham Wy CDALE/KGS NW9 | 115 | P4 |
| Barn Lea RKW/CH/CXG WD3 | 91 | K2 |
| Barnlea Cl FELT TW13 | 175 | H5 |
| Barn Md BRWN CM15 | 87 | H2 |
| Barnmead CHOB/PIR GU24 | 213 | L6 |
| EPP CM16 | 70 | B6 |
| Barn Md HLWS CM18 | 46 | G3 |
| Barnmead Gdns DAGW RM9 | 124 | A3 |
| Barnmead La GT/LBKH KT23 | 235 | N10 |
| Barnmead Rd BECK BR3 | 183 | N6 |
| DAGW RM9 | 124 | A3 |
| Barn Ri WBLY HA9 | 96 | A10 |
| Barnsbury Cl NWMAL KT3 | 199 | P3 |
| Barnsbury Crs BRYLDS KT5 | 199 | P6 |
| Barnsbury Est IS N1 | 5 | M4 |
| Barnsbury Gv HOLWY N7 | 5 | N1 |
| Barnsbury La BRYLDS KT5 | 199 | N8 |
| Barnsbury Pk IS N1 | 5 | M3 |
| Barnsbury Rd IS N1 | 6 | A4 |
| Barnsbury Sq IS N1 | 5 | M3 |
| Barnsbury St IS N1 | 5 | M3 |
| Barnsbury Ter IS N1 | 5 | L3 |
| Barnscroft RYNPK SW20 | 200 | E2 |
| Barnsdale Av POP/IOD E14 | 160 | C3 |
| Barnsdale Rd MV/WKIL W9 | 137 | N3 |
| Barnsfield Pl UX/CGN UB8 | 131 | N2 |
| Barnsford Crs CHOB/PIR GU24 | 212 | F10 |
| Barnside Ct WGCW AL8 | 22 | E2 |
| Barnsley Rd HARH RM3 | 105 | N6 |
| Barnsley St WCHPL E1 | 140 | C6 |
| Barnstaple La LEW SE13 | 161 | H10 |
| Barnstaple Rd RSLP HA4 | 113 | M4 |
| Barnston Wy BRWN CM15 | 87 | J1 |
| Barn St STNW/STAM N16 | 119 | N8 |
| The Barn GRAYS RM17 * | 167 | N3 |
| Barnway EGH TW20 | 172 | A9 |
| Barn Wy WBLY HA9 | 115 | N1 |

| Name | Page | Grid |
|---|---|---|
| Baron Gv MTCM CR4 | 201 | P4 |
| Baron Rd BCTR RM8 | 123 | N6 |
| Barons Cl IS N1 * | 6 | A7 |
| Baron's Court Rd WKENS W14 | 14 | A1 |
| Baronsfield Rd TWK TW1 | 176 | G2 |
| Barons Ga EBAR EN4 | 77 | P10 |
| Baron's Hurst EPSOM KT18 | 237 | P2 |
| Barons Md HRW HA1 | 114 | D2 |
| Baronsmead Rd BARN SW13 | 156 | C6 |
| Baronsmede EA W5 | 155 | L1 |
| Baronsmere Ct BAR EN5 * | 77 | H8 |
| Baronsmere Rd EFNCH N2 | 117 | J2 |
| Baron's Pl STHWK SE1 | 12 | B11 |
| The Barons TWK TW1 | 176 | G2 |
| Baron St IS N1 | 6 | A6 |
| Barons Wk CROY/NA CRO | 204 | D6 |
| Baron's Wy REIG RH2 | 267 | K4 |
| Barque Ms DEPT SE8 | 160 | E5 |
| Barrack Pth WOKN/KNAP GU21 | 231 | J4 |
| Barrack Rd GUW GU2 | 249 | M8 |
| HSLWW TW4 | 153 | L10 |
| Barrack Rw GVW DA11 | 190 | C2 |
| Barracks La BAR EN5 * | 76 | C3 |
| Barra Cl HHS/BOV HP3 | 88 | E1 |
| Barra Hall Rd HYS/HAR UB3 | 132 | F9 |
| Barrards Wy BEAC HP9 | 89 | H7 |
| Barrass Cl PEND EN3 | 80 | F3 |
| Barratt Av WDGN N22 | 98 | G10 |
| Barratt Wy KTN/HRWW/WS HA3 | 114 | C1 |
| Barrenger Rd MUSWH N10 | 98 | A9 |
| Barrens Brae WOKS/MYFD GU22 | 232 | D5 |
| Barrens Cl WOKS/MYFD GU22 | 232 | D4 |
| Barrens Pk WOKS/MYFD GU22 | 232 | D4 |
| Barrett Cl HARH RM3 | 105 | J3 |
| Barrett Rd LHD/OX KT22 | 236 | E5 |
| WALTH E17 | 121 | H2 |
| Barrett's Green Rd WLSDN NW10 | 135 | P4 |
| Barrett's Gv STNW/STAM N16 | 119 | M10 |
| Barretts La SEV TN13 | 246 | E6 |
| Barrett Wood La LHD/OX KT22 | 236 | G5 |
| Barricane WOKN/KNAP GU21 | 232 | A7 |
| Barriedale NWCR SE14 | 160 | D7 |
| Barrie Cl COUL/CHIP CR5 | 240 | D2 |
| Barrier Point Rd CAN/RD E16 | 141 | P10 |
| Barringer Sq TOOT SW17 | 180 | F7 |
| Barrington Cl CLAY IG5 | 102 | A9 |
| KTTN NW5 | 118 | B10 |
| LOU IG10 | 83 | L1 |
| Barrington Ct DORK RH4 | 272 | F3 |
| DEN/HRF UB9 | 91 | K8 |
| Barrington Dr DEN/HRF UB9 | 91 | K8 |
| Barrington Rd BXLYHS DA6 | 163 | P9 |
| CEND/HSY/T N8 | 118 | D4 |
| CHEAM SM3 | 201 | K8 |
| CRAWE RH10 | 285 | N10 |
| DORK RH4 | 272 | F2 |
| LOU IG10 | 82 | F7 |
| SL SL1 | 128 | C5 |
| Barrington Vls WOOL/PLUM SE18 | 162 | G1 |
| Barrington Wk NRWD SE19 * | 181 | M9 |
| Barron's Cl CHONG CM5 | 67 | N3 |
| Barrow Av CAR SM5 | 221 | P4 |
| Barrow Cl WCHMH N21 | 99 | H1 |
| Barrowdene Cl PIN HA5 | 93 | M10 |
| Barrowell Gn WCHMH N21 | 99 | H1 |
| Barrow Gdns REDH RH1 | 258 | G5 |
| Barrow Green Rd OXTED RH8 | 260 | F6 |
| Barrow Hedges Cl CAR SM5 | 221 | P4 |
| Barrow Hedges Wy CAR SM5 | 221 | P4 |
| Barrow Hill WPK KT4 | 200 | B9 |
| Barrow Hill Cl WPK KT4 | 200 | B9 |
| Barrow Hill Rd STJWD NW8 | 3 | N8 |
| Barrow La CHESW EN7 | 61 | M2 |
| Barrow Point Av PIN HA5 | 93 | M10 |
| Barrow Point La PIN HA5 | 93 | M10 |
| Barrow Rd CROY/NA CRO | 223 | H3 |
| STRHM/NOR SW16 | 180 | C9 |
| Barrowsfield SAND/SEL CR2 | 242 | A1 |
| Barrow Wy HLWW/ROY CM19 | 45 | N8 |
| Barrs Av NWDGN UB2 | 153 | K4 |
| Barrsbrook Farm Rd CHERT KT16 | 195 | H8 |
| Barr's La WOKN/KNAP GU21 | 231 | J2 |
| Barr's Rd MDHD SL6 | 128 | C1 |
| Barry Av BXLYHN DA7 | 163 | P6 |
| SEVS/STOTM N15 | 99 | L8 |
| WDSR SL4 | 148 | G3 |
| Barry Cl CDW/CHF RM16 | 146 | G5 |
| CRAWE RH10 | 283 | P10 |
| LCOL/BKTW AL2 | 56 | A1 |
| ORP BR6 | 207 | K10 |
| Barry Pde EDUL SE22 * | 181 | P2 |
| EHAM E6 | 142 | B2 |
| WLSDN NW10 | 135 | P2 |
| Barry Ter ASHF TW15 * | 174 | A5 |
| Barset Rd PECK SE15 | 160 | B3 |
| Barsons Cl PGE/AN SE20 | 182 | E10 |
| The Bars GU GU1 | 6 | C3 |
| Barston Rd WNWD SE27 | 181 | K5 |
| Barstow Crs BRXS/STRHM SW2 | 180 | G4 |
| Bartel Cl HHS/BOV HP3 | 36 | C2 |
| Bartelotts Rd BARN SW13 | 128 | C6 |
| Barter St NOXST/BSQ WC1A | 11 | M4 |
| Barth Ms WOOL/PLUM SE18 | 163 | N8 |
| Bartholomew Cl STBT EC1A | 12 | D4 |
| WAND/EARL SW18 | 157 | M10 |
| Bartholomew Dr HARH RM3 | 105 | L10 |
| Bartholomew La OBST EC2N | 13 | J5 |
| Bartholomew Pl STBT EC1A * | 12 | D4 |
| Bartholomew Rd KTTN NW5 | 4 | E2 |
| Bartholomew Sq FSBYE EC1V | 12 | F1 |
| WCHPL E1 | 140 | C5 |
| Bartholomew St STHWK SE1 | 19 | H3 |
| Bartholomew Vs KTTN NW5 | 4 | E2 |
| Bartholomew Wy SWLY BR8 | 208 | E9 |
| Bartle Av EHAM E6 | 141 | P7 |
| Bartle Rd NTGHL W11 | 136 | D6 |
| Bartlett Cl POP/IOD E14 | 140 | F8 |
| Bartlett Ct FLST/FETLN EC4A * | 11 | P5 |
| Bartlett Rd BH/WHM TN16 | 244 | B5 |
| GVW DA11 | 190 | D6 |

| Name | Page | Grid |
|---|---|---|
| Barton Wk CRAWE RH10 | 284 | C9 |
| Barton Wy BORE WD6 | 75 | M4 |
| RKW/CH/CXG WD3 | 72 | C9 |
| Bartram Cl UX/CGN UB8 | 132 | D1 |
| Bartram Rd BROCKY SE4 | 182 | C1 |
| Bartrams La EBAR EN4 | 77 | M4 |
| Bartrip St HOM E9 | 140 | D1 |
| Bartrop Cl CHESW EN7 | 61 | L4 |
| Barts Cl BECK BR3 | 204 | F5 |
| Barwell Crs CHSGTN KT9 | 219 | H4 |
| Barwell Dr BR/WHM TN16 | 225 | P9 |
| Barwell La CHSGTN KT9 | 219 | H4 |
| Barwick Dr UX/CGN UB8 | 132 | C2 |
| Barwick Rd FSTGT E7 | 121 | N1 |
| Barwood Av WWKM BR4 | 204 | G8 |
| Bascome St BRXS/STRHM SW2 | 181 | H1 |
| Basden Gv FELT TW13 | 175 | P5 |
| Basedale Rd DAGW RM9 | 143 | L2 |
| Baseing Cl EHAM E6 | 142 | D9 |
| Basevi Wy DEPT SE8 | 160 | F5 |
| Basford Wy WDSR SL4 | 148 | C9 |
| Bashford Wy CRAWE RH10 | 284 | G5 |
| Bashley Rd WLSDN NW10 | 136 | A5 |
| Basil Av EHAM E6 | 141 | P8 |
| Basildene Rd HSLWW TW4 | 153 | L9 |
| Basil Gdns CROY/NA CRO | 204 | A10 |
| WNWD SE27 | 181 | K8 |
| Basil Ms HLWE CM17 | 29 | M1 |
| Basilon Rd BXLYHN DA7 | 164 | A6 |
| Basin Ap CAN/RD E16 | 142 | A9 |
| POP/IOD E14 | 140 | D8 |
| Basing Ap THDIT KT7 | 198 | C9 |
| Basing Cl THDIT KT7 | 198 | C9 |
| Basing Ct PECK SE15 | 159 | N7 |
| Basingdon Wy CMBW SE5 | 159 | L10 |
| Basing Dr BXLY DA5 | 186 | A2 |
| Basingfield Rd THDIT KT7 | 198 | C9 |
| Basinghall Av CITYW EC2V | 12 | G5 |
| Basinghall St CITYW EC2V | 12 | G5 |
| Basing Hill GLDGN NW11 | 117 | K6 |
| WBLY HA9 | 115 | L7 |
| Basing Pl BETH E2 | 7 | L6 |
| Basing Rd BNSTD SM7 | 221 | P10 |
| RKW/CH/CXG WD3 | 91 | J2 |
| Basing St NTGHL W11 | 136 | F6 |
| Basing Wy FNCH N3 | 117 | K1 |
| THDIT KT7 | 198 | C9 |
| Basire St IS N1 | 6 | E4 |
| Baskerville Gdns WLSDN NW10 | 116 | B9 |
| Baskerville Rd WAND/EARL SW18 | 179 | P4 |
| Basket Gdns ELTH/MOT SE9 | 184 | B1 |
| Baslow Cl KTN/HRWW/WS HA3 | 94 | C9 |
| Baslow Wk CLPT E5 | 120 | C9 |
| Basnett Rd BTSEA SW11 | 158 | B9 |
| Bassano St EDUL SE22 | 181 | N1 |
| Bassant Rd WOOL/PLUM SE18 | 163 | J5 |
| Bassein Park Rd SHB W12 | 156 | C1 |
| Basset Dr REIG RH2 | 257 | K9 |
| Bassett Cl BELMT SM2 | 221 | L5 |
| Bassett Gdns EPP CM16 | 66 | C2 |
| ISLW TW7 | 154 | B6 |
| Bassett Rd CRAWE RH10 | 284 | C10 |
| NKENS W10 | 136 | E7 |
| UX/CGN UB8 | 131 | M2 |
| WOKS/MYFD GU22 | 232 | F2 |
| Bassetts Cl ORP BR6 | 226 | E1 |
| Bassetts Wy ORP BR6 | 226 | E1 |
| Bassett Wy GFD/PVL UB6 | 134 | A3 |
| Bassil Rd HHNE HP2 | 35 | N7 |
| Bassingbourne Cl BROX EN10 | 44 | E6 |
| Bassingham Rd ALP/SUD HA0 | 135 | P1 |
| WAND/EARL SW18 | 179 | M3 |
| Basswood Cl PECK SE15 | 160 | A9 |
| Bastable Av BARK IG11 | 143 | J4 |
| Baston Rd HAYES BR2 | 205 | H7 |
| Baston Manor Rd WWKM BR4 | 205 | N10 |
| HAYES BR2 | 205 | N9 |
| Bastwick St FSBYE EC1V | 12 | D1 |
| Basuto Rd FUL/PGN SW6 | 157 | K7 |
| Bata Av TIL RM18 | 169 | L4 |
| Batavia Ms NWCR SE14 | 160 | D6 |
| Batavia Rd NWCR SE14 | 160 | D6 |
| SUN TW16 | 197 | J1 |
| Batchelor St IS N1 | 6 | A7 |
| Bachelors Wy AMSS HP7 | 69 | J5 |
| CSHM HP5 | 47 | J3 |
| Batchwood Dr STALW/RED AL3 | 38 | A4 |
| Batchwood Gdns STALW/RED AL3 | 38 | C3 |
| Batchwood Gn STMC/STPC BR5 | 207 | K4 |
| Batchwood Vw STALW/RED AL3 | 38 | B4 |
| Batchworth Hl RKW/CH/CXG WD3 | 91 | P3 |
| Batchworth Hill London Rd RKW/CH/CXG WD3 | 91 | P3 |
| Batchworth La NTHWD HA6 | 92 | D6 |
| Bateman Cl BARK IG11 | 142 | F1 |
| Bateman Ct CRAWE RH10 * | 284 | D10 |
| Bateman Rd CHING E4 | 100 | F7 |
| RKW/CH/CXG WD3 | 72 | B10 |
| Bateman's Blds SOHO/SHAV W1D * | 11 | J6 |
| Bateman's Rw SDTCH EC2A | 13 | L1 |
| Batemans Rw SDTCH EC2A | 13 | K1 |
| Bates Crs CROY/NA CRO | 223 | H5 |
| STRHM/NOR SW16 | 180 | D10 |
| Bateson Wy WOKN/KNAP GU21 | 214 | F10 |
| Bates Rd HARH RM3 | 105 | P8 |
| Bate St POP/IOD E14 | 140 | E8 |
| Bateup Rd ADL/WDHM KT15 | 215 | M5 |
| Batford Cl WGCE AL7 | 23 | L6 |
| Batford Rd HARP AL5 * | 20 | C1 |
| Bath Cl PECK SE15 | 160 | A6 |
| Bathgate Rd WIM/MER SW19 | 178 | G5 |
| Bath Gv BETH E2 | 7 | N8 |
| Bath House Rd CROY/NA CRO | 202 | F8 |
| Bath Pas KUT/HW KT1 | 199 | J2 |
| Bath Pl BAR EN5 | 76 | F4 |
| SDTCH EC2A * | 7 | J9 |
| Bath Rd CHSWK W4 | 156 | B3 |
| DTCH/LGLY SL3 | 151 | H2 |
| ED N9 | 100 | A3 |
| FSTGT E7 | 142 | C1 |
| HSLWW TW4 | 153 | H8 |
| SL SL1 | 128 | B3 |
| WDR/YW UB7 | 152 | C4 |
| Baths Ap FUL/PGN SW6 | 157 | J6 |
| Bath St FSBYE EC1V | 12 | E1 |
| GVE DA12 | 190 | C2 |
| Bathurst Av WIM/MER SW19 | 178 | C9 |
| Bathurst Gdns WLSDN NW10 | 136 | E1 |
| Bathurst Ms BAY/PAD W2 | 8 | C6 |
| Bathurst Rd HHNE HP2 | 35 | N3 |
| IL IG1 | 122 | C6 |
| Bathway WOOL/PLUM SE18 | 162 | G2 |
| Batley Cl MTCM CR4 | 202 | A8 |
| Batley Pl STNW/STAM N16 | 119 | N9 |
| Batley Rd ENC/FH EN2 | 79 | L2 |
| STNW/STAM N16 | 119 | N9 |
| Batman Cl SHB W12 | 136 | C10 |
| Baton Cl PUR RM19 | 166 | G5 |

Batoum Gdns HMSMTH W6 ... 156 F2
Batson St SHB W12 ... 156 D1
Batsworth Rd MTCM CR4 ... 201 N3
Batten Cl EHAM E6 ... 142 C4
Batten Cots POP/IOD E14 * ... 140 D7
Batten Cl SE1 ... 157 F9
Batterdale BRKMPK AL9 ... 30 C1
Battersby Rd CAT SE6 ... 183 J5
Battersea Br WBPTN SW10 ... 157 N6
Battersea Bridge Rd BTSEA SW11 ... 157 P6
Battersea Church Rd BTSEA SW11 ... 157 N7
Battersea High St BTSEA SW11 ... 157 N8
Battersea Park Rd BTSEA SW11 ... 158 B7
Battersea Ri BTSEA SW11 ... 179 H5
Battersea Sq BTSEA SW11 * ... 157 P6
Battery Rd THMD SE28 ... 143 J10
Battishill St IS N1 ... 6 C4
Battle Bridge La STHWK SE1 ... 13 J1
Battle Cl WIM/MER SW19 ... 179 M9
Battledean Rd HBRY N5 ... 119 J10
Battlefield Rd STAL AL1 ... 38 E4
Battle Rd ERITH DA8 ... 164 D3
Battlers Green Dr RAD WD7 ... 74 D3
Battleview STALE/WH AL4 ... 21 K3
Batts Hl REIG RH2 ... 257 N6
Batty St WCHPL E1 ... 13 L3
Baudwin Rd CAT SE6 ... 183 K5
Baugh Rd SCUP DA14 ... 185 M8
The Baulk WIM/MER SW19 ... 179 K3
Bavant Rd STRHM/NOR SW16 ... 202 A2
Bavaria Rd ARCH N19 ... 118 E1
Bavdene Ms HOM E9 ... 116 C2
Bavent Rd CMBW SE5 ... 159 K8
Bawdale Rd EDUL SE22 ... 181 N1
Bawdsey Av GNTH/NBYPK IG2 ... 123 J2
Bawtree Cl BELMT SM2 ... 221 M6
Bawtree Rd NWCR SE14 ... 160 D6
  UX/CGN UB8 ... 131 N1
Bawtry Rd TRDG/WHET N20 ... 98 A2
Baxendale TRDG/WHET N20 ... 97 M3
Baxendale St BETH E2 ... 7 M9
Baxter Av REDH RH1 ... 257 P10
  HGDN/ICK UB10 ... 132 C5
  NWDGN UB2 ... 154 A2
  SL SL1 ... 149 K2
Baxter Rd CAN/RD E16 ... 141 P8
  IL IG1 ... 122 E10
  IS N1 ... 7 H2
  UED N18 ... 100 A5
Bayards WARL CR6 ... 242 B4
Bay Cl HORL RH6 ... 279 P1
Bay Ct EA W5 * ... 155 K2
Baycroft Cl PIN HA5 * ... 113 K1
Bayeux KWD/TDW/WH KT20 ... 238 C8
  HORL RH6 ... 279 P1
Bayford Cl HERT/BAY SG13 ... 43 H3
  HHNE HP2 ... 36 D1
Bayford La HERT/BAY SG13 ... 42 C1
Bayford Ms HACK E8 * ... 140 A2
Bayford Rd WLSDN NW10 ... 138 C5
Bayford St HACK E8 ... 140 A2
Baygrove Ms KUT/HW KT1 ... 199 H1
Bayham Pl CAMTN NW1 ... 4 E3
  MRDN SM4 ... 201 M4
  SEV TN13 ... 247 K9
  WEA W13 ... 134 G9
Bayham St CAMTN NW1 ... 4 C5
Bayhorne La HORL RH6 ... 280 C7
Bayleaf Cl NTHWD HA6 ... 92 G7
Bayleaf Cl HPTN TW12 ... 176 C8
Bayley Hall Ms HERT/WAT SG14 ... 25 L6
Bayley Md HHW HP1 * ... 35 L8
Bayley's Hl RSEV TN14 ... 264 F8
Bayleys Md RBRW/HUT CM13 ... 107 P3
Bayley St FITZ W1T ... 11 J3
Baylie Ct HHNE HP2 ... 35 P5
Baylie La HHNE HP2 ... 35 P5
Baylis Ms TWK TW1 ... 176 F3
Baylis Rd SL SL1 ... 129 J8
  STHWK SE1 ... 12 A1
Bayliss Av THMD SE28 ... 143 L9
Bayliss Cl ENC/FH EN2 ... 78 N9
Bayliss Ct GU GU1 ... 267 P5
Bay Manor La WTHK RM20 ... 166 C5
Baymans Wd BRWN CM15 ... 107 K3
Bayne Cl EHAM E6 ... 142 C4
Bayne Hl BEAC HP9 ... 89 J8
Bayne Hill Cl BEAC HP9 ... 89 J8
Baynes Cl EN EN1 ... 79 P5
Baynes Ms HAMP NW3 ... 3 M1
Baynes St CAMTN NW1 ... 4 D1
Baynham Cl BXLY DA5 ... 186 A2
Baynton Rd WOKS/MYFD GU22 ... 232 B6
Bayonne Rd HMSMTH W6 ... 14 A10
Bays Cl SYD SE26 ... 182 B8
Baysfarm Cl WDR/YW UB7 ... 151 M7
Bayshill Ri NTHLT UB5 ... 133 K6
Bayston Rd STNW/STAM N16 ... 119 N8
Bayswater Rd BAY/PAD W2 ... 9 J8
Baythorne St BOW E3 ... 140 E4
Baythorn La HORL RH6 ... 280 D7
Bay Tree Cl LHD/OX KT22 ... 236 F6
  LCOL/BKTW AL2 ... 75 J2
Bay Tree Ct SL SL1 ... 128 B5
Bay Tree Cl BRXS/STRHM SW2 ... 158 G10
Bay Trees OXTED RH8 ... 261 N9
Bay Tree Wk WAT WD17 ... 72 G4
Baywood Sq CHIG IG7 ... 103 N5
Bazalgette Cl NWMAL KT3 ... 199 M5
Bazalgette Gdns NWMAL KT3 ... 200 A3
Bazely St POP/IOD E14 ... 141 N4
Bazes Shaw HART DA3 ... 211 L9
Bazile Rd WCHMH N21 ... 79 H10
Beacham Cl CHARL SE7 ... 162 A4
Beachborough Rd BMLY BR1 ... 183 H7
Beachcroft Rd WAN E11 ... 121 K8
Beach Gv FELT TW13 ... 175 P6
Beachy Rd BOW E3 ... 140 F2
Beacon Cl BNSTD SM7 ... 238 G2
  CFSP/GDCR SL9 ... 90 C7
  UX/CGN UB8 ... 111 N10
Beacon Ct DTCH/LGLY SL3 ... 150 C4
  HERT/BAY SG13 * ... 26 B1
Beacon Dr DART DA2 ... 189 H6
Beaconfield Av EPP CM16 ... 65 J5
Beaconfield Rd EPP CM16 ... 65 J5
Beaconfields SEV TN13 ... 264 C2
Beaconfield Wy EPP CM16 ... 65 J5
Beacon Ga NWCR SE14 ... 160 G6
Beacon Hl HOLWY N7 ... 118 C1
  PUR RM19 ... 166 G4
  WOKN/KNAP GU21 ... 231 P5
Beacon Hill Rd BRW CM14 ... 86 B3
Beacon Ri SEV TN13 ... 265 H2
Beacon Rd ERITH DA8 ... 165 K4
  HTHAIR TW6 ... 174 B2
  LEW SE13 ... 183 L1
  WARE SG12 ... 26 C1
Beaconsfield Cl BKHTH/KID SE3 ... 161 M5
  WIM/MER SW19 ... 155 P4
Beaconsfield Common La SLN SL2 ... 109 J5
Beaconsfield Cots TRDG/WHET N20 * ... 97 K4
Beaconsfield Ct HAT AL10 * ... 40 F1
Beaconsfield Gdns ESH/CLAY KT10 ... 218 D4

Beaconsfield Pl EW KT17 ... 220 B8
Beaconsfield Rd BKHTH/KID SE3 ... 161 M5
  BMLY BR1 ... 206 A3
  CAN/RD E16 ... 141 L6
  CHSWK W4 ... 156 A2
  CROY/NA CR0 ... 156 H1
  EA W5 ... 155 H1
  ED N9 ... 99 P4
  ELTH/MOT SE9 ... 184 B5
  ELTH/MOT SE9 ... 184 B6
  EPSOM KT18 ... 238 A10
  ESH/CLAY KT10 ... 218 D4
  HAT AL10 ... 40 F1
  LEY E10 * ... 121 H8
  NWMAL KT3 ... 200 A2
  PEND EN3 ... 80 C3
  SEVS/STOTM N15 ... 119 M2
  SLN SL2 ... 129 H3
  STAL AL1 ... 38 D6
  SURB KT6 ... 199 J8
  TRDG/WHET N20 ... 98 A4
  TWK TW1 ... 176 C3
  WALTH E17 ... 120 E4
  WALW SE17 ... 19 H8
  WLSDN NW10 ... 136 C1
  WOKS/MYFD GU22 ... 232 C6
  YEAD UB4 ... 133 N3
Beaconsfield Wk FUL/PGN SW6 ... 157 J7
The Beacons LOU IG10 ... 82 D4
Beacontree Av WALTH E17 ... 101 J9
Beacontree Rd WAN E11 ... 121 L5
Beacon Wy BNSTD SM7 ... 238 G2
  RKW/CH/CXG WD3 ... 91 K1
Beadles La OXTED RH8 ... 261 J6
Beadlow Cl CAR SM5 ... 201 N6
Beadman St WNWD SE27 ... 181 J4
Beadman Pl WNWD SE27 * ... 181 J7
Beadnell Rd FSTH SE23 ... 182 C4
Beadon Rd HAYES BR2 ... 205 M4
  HMSMTH W6 ... 156 F3
Beads Hall La BRWN CM15 ... 86 G8
Beaford Gv RYNPK SW20 ... 201 H3
Beagle Cl FELT TW13 ... 175 J7
  RAD WD7 ... 74 E3
Beagles Cl STMC/STPC BR5 ... 207 N6
Beal Cl WELL DA16 ... 148 B2
Beale Cl PLMGR N13 ... 99 J6
Beale Pl BOW E3 ... 140 E4
Beale Rd BOW E3 ... 140 E3
Beales La GT/LBKH KT25 ... 254 E10
Beales La WEY KT13 ... 196 C10
Bealings End BEAC HP9 ... 88 C6
Beal Rd IL IG1 ... 122 D7
Beam Av DAGE RM10 ... 144 C3
Beames Rd WLSDN NW10 ... 136 A3
Beaminster Gdns BARK/HLT IG6 ... 122 E1
Beamish Cl EPP CM16 ... 66 D1
Beamish Dr BUSH WD23 ... 94 B2
Beamish Rd ED N9 ... 99 P2
  STMC/STPC BR5 ... 207 M7
Beamway DAGE RM10 ... 144 G2
Beanacre Cl HOM E9 ... 140 E1
Beane River Vw HERT/WAT SG14 ... 25 K5
Beane Rd HERT/WAT SG14 ... 25 J5
Bean La RDART DA2 ... 188 F5
Bean Rd BXLYHS DA6 ... 163 N10
  SWCM DA10 ... 188 G2
Beanshaw ELTH/MOT SE9 ... 184 D7
Beansland Gv CHDH RM6 ... 103 P10
Bear Cl ROMW/RG RM7 ... 124 C2
Beardell St NRWD SE19 ... 181 N9
Beardow Gv STHGT/OAK N14 * ... 78 D10
Beard Rd KUTN/CMB KT2 ... 176 G6
Beardsfield PLSTW E13 ... 141 M8
Beard's HI HPTN TW12 ... 197 J1
Beard's Hill Cl HPTN TW12 ... 197 J1
Beardsley Wy ACT W3 ... 156 A1
Beards Rd ASHF TW15 ... 174 F9
Bearfield Rd KUTN/CMB KT2 ... 177 K10
Bear Gdns STHWK SE1 ... 12 E9
Bearing Cl CHIG IG7 ... 103 K5
Bearing Wy CHIG IG7 ... 103 K5
Bear La STHWK SE1 ... 12 D9
Bear Rd FELT TW13 ... 175 L7
Bears Den KWD/TDW/WH KT20 ... 239 J8
Bearstead Ri BROCKY SE4 ... 182 B1
Bearstead Ter BECK BR3 * ... 204 F1
Bear St LSQ/SEVD WC2H ... 11 K7
Bearswood End BEAC HP9 ... 88 D7
Bearwood Cl ABLGY WD5 * ... 215 K3
  POTB/CUF EN6 ... 59 N7
Beasant House WATN WD24 * ... 73 L6
Beasley's Ait SUN TW16 ... 196 C6
Beasley's Ait La SUN TW16 ... 196 C6
Beaton Cl SWCM DA10 ... 166 G10
Beatrice Av STRHM/NOR SW16 ... 202 C3
  WBLY HA9 ... 115 K10
Beatrice Cl PIN HA5 ... 113 H2
  PLSTW E13 ... 141 M6
Beatrice Pl KENS W8 ... 14 C4
Beatrice Rd ED N9 ... 100 B1
  FSBYPK N4 ... 119 H5
  OXTED RH8 ... 261 K4
  RCHPK/HAM TW10 ... 177 L1
  STHL UB1 ... 133 N10
  STHWK SE1 ... 19 P5
  WALTH E17 ... 120 E3
Beattie Cl EBED/NFELT TW14 ... 174 A3
  GT/LBKH KT23 ... 235 N10
Beattock Ri MUSWH N10 ... 118 C2
Beatty Av GU GU1 ... 250 D9
Beatty Rd CHES/WGN EN8 ... 62 E10
  STAN HA7 ... 95 H7
  STNW/STAM N16 ... 119 N1
Beatty St CAMTN NW1 ... 4 C2
Beattyville Gdns CLAY IG5 ... 122 G1
Beauchamp Gdns RKW/CH/CXG WD3 ... 91 K2
Beauchamp Pl CHEL SW3 ... 15 H4
Beauchamp Rd BTSEA SW11 ... 157 N10
  E/WMO/HCT KT8 ... 198 A3
  FSTGT E7 ... 141 K1
  NRWD SE19 ... 203 L1
  STHL UB1 ... 133 N10
  SUT SM1 ... 221 P4
  TWK TW1 ... 176 F3
Beauchamps WGCE AL7 ... 23 L4
Beauchamp St HCIRC EC1N ... 12 A4
Beauchamp Ter STRHM/NOR SW16 ... 156 E10
Beauclare Cl LHD/OX KT22 ... 237 J2
Beauclerc Rd HMSMTH W6 ... 156 F1
Beauclerk Cl FELT TW13 ... 142 D7
Beaufort EHAM E6 ... 142 D7
Beaufort Av ALP/SUD HA0 ... 114 A3
Beaufort Cl CDW/CHF RM16 ... 167 L2
  EA W5 ... 135 L2
  EPP CM16 ... 66 B3
  PUT/ROE SW15 ... 178 F4
  REIG RH2 ... 257 J9
  ROMW/RG RM7 ... 124 D2
  WOKS/MYFD GU22 ... 232 F2
Beaufort Ct RCHPK/HAM TW10 ... 177 H7
Beaufort Dr GLDGN NW11 ... 117 K2
  HARH RM3 ... 105 P6
Beaufort Gdns BCVA SW1X ... 15 J2
  CEND/HSY/T N8 ... 118 E4
  CHING E4 ... 101 N2
  HSLWW TW4 ... 175 K2
Beaufort St CHEL SW3 ... 15 L9

Beaufort Rd EA W5 ... 135 L2
  KUT/HW KT1 ... 199 H5
  RCHPK/HAM TW10 ... 176 G7
  REIG RH2 ... 257 J9
  RSLP HA4 ... 112 C9
  TWK TW1 ... 176 D4
  WOKS/MYFD GU22 ... 232 D7
Beauforts EGH TW20 ... 171 P8
Beaufort St CHEL SW3 ... 15 L9
Beaufort Wy EW KT17 ... 220 D4
Beaufoy Rd TOTM N17 ... 99 M8
Beaufoy Wk LBTH SE11 ... 17 P6
Beaulah Rd WLSDN NW10 ... 170 A5
Beaulieu Av CAN/RD E16 ... 141 N6
  SYD SE26 ... 182 A7
Beaulieu Cl CDALE/KGS NW9 ... 116 D2
  CMBW SE5 ... 159 L9
  DTCH/LGLY SL3 ... 149 N7
  HSLWW TW4 ... 175 H1
  MTCM CR4 ... 202 B1
  OXHEY WD19 ... 93 K2
  TWK TW1 ... 177 J2
Beaulieu Dr PIN HA5 ... 113 J6
  WAB EN9 ... 62 G8
Beaulieu Gdns WCHMH N21 ... 99 K1
Beaulieu Pl CHSWK W4 ... 155 P1
Beauly Ct ROM RM1 ... 104 F9
Beauly Wy ROM RM1 ... 104 F9
Beaumaris Gn CDALE/KGS NW9 ... 116 B4
Beaumayes Cl HHW HP1 * ... 35 L7
Beaumont Av ALP/SUD HA0 ... 115 H10
  RCH/KEW TW9 ... 155 N9
  RYLN/HDSTN HA2 ... 114 A4
  STAL AL1 ... 38 A4
  WKENS W14 ... 14 C7
Beaumont Cl CRAWW RH11 ... 283 H8
  KUTN/CMB KT2 ... 177 K7
  RAIN RM13 ... 145 J4
Beaumont Crs RAIN RM13 ... 145 J4
  WKENS W14 ... 14 C7
Beaumont Dr ASHF TW15 ... 174 E8
  WPK KT4 ... 200 E8
Beaumont Gdns HAMP NW3 ... 117 K7
  RBRW/HUT CM13 ... 87 P10
Beaumont Ga RAD WD7 ... 74 F1
Beaumont Gv WCHPL E1 ... 140 E6
Beaumont Ms MHST W1U * ... 10 D3
Beaumont Park Dr HLWW/ROY CM19 ... 45 N1
Beaumont Pl BAR EN5 ... 77 J5
  FITZ W1T ... 11 K2
  ISLW TW7 ... 176 A1
Beaumont Ri ARCH N19 ... 118 E6
Beaumont Rd BROX EN10 ... 43 N10
  CHSWK W4 ... 155 P2
  LEY E10 ... 120 G5
  NRWD SE19 ... 181 K9
  PLSTW E13 ... 141 N5
  PUR/KEN CR8 ... 223 H9
  SLN SL2 ... 129 J7
  STMC/STPC BR5 ... 206 C6
  WDSR SL4 ... 146 A6
  WIM/MER SW19 ... 179 H3
Beaumonts REDH RH1 ... 276 A8
Beaumont Sq WCHPL E1 ... 140 E8
Beaumont Ter LEW SE13 * ... 183 K5
Beaumont Vw CHESW EN7 ... 61 L2
Beaumont Wk HAMP NW3 ... 4 A1
Beauvais Ter NTHLT UB5 ... 133 L1
Beauval Rd EDUL SE22 ... 181 N2
Beaverbank Rd ELTH/MOT SE9 ... 184 C4
Beaver Rd BARK/HLT IG6 ... 103 M6
Beavers Cl RGUW GU3 ... 249 K9
Beavers Crs HSLWW TW4 ... 153 L10
Beavers La HSLWW TW4 ... 153 K9
Beaverwood Rd CHST BR7 ... 185 H6
Beazley Cl WARE SG12 ... 26 D1
Bebbington Rd WOOL/PLUM SE18 * ... 143 K8
Beblets Cl ORP BR6 ... 227 J2
Beccles Dr BARK IG11 ... 143 J1
Beccles St POP/IOD E14 ... 140 L8
Bec Cl RSLP HA4 ... 113 L8
Beck Ct BECK BR3 ... 203 J1
Beckenham Gdns ED N9 ... 99 M4
Beckenham Gv HAYES BR2 ... 205 J2
Beckenham Hill Rd BECK BR3 ... 182 G5
Beckenham La HAYES BR2 ... 205 K2
Beckenham Place Pk BECK BR3 ... 182 G5
Beckenham Rd BECK BR3 ... 204 D1
  WWKM BR4 ... 204 C1
Beckenshaw Gdns BNSTD SM7 ... 239 P1
Becket Av EHAM E6 ... 142 C3
Becket Cl RBRW/HUT CM13 ... 107 P5
  SNWD SE25 ... 203 P6
  WIM/MER SW19 ... 201 L1
Becket Fold HRW HA1 * ... 114 E3
Becket Rd UED N18 ... 100 B5
Becketts Pl RSEV TN14 ... 247 K2
Becketts Wk BERK HP4 * ... 33 N6
Becket St STHWK SE1 * ... 18 G3
Beckett Av PUR/KEN CR8 ... 241 J1
Beckett Cl STRHM/NOR SW16 ... 181 N4
  WKENS W14 ... 14 D6
Beckett Cha DTCH/LGLY SL3 ... 150 C4
Beckett Rd CLAY IG5 ... 122 F1
Beckford Dr STMC/STPC BR5 ... 206 G3
Beckford Pl WALW SE17 * ... 18 F8
Beckford Rd CROY/NA CR0 ... 203 N6
Beckham Pl GUW GU2 ... 249 M9
Beck La BECK BR3 ... 204 B1
Beckley Cl SHB W12 ... 156 A3
Becklow Ms SHB W12 ... 156 B3
Becklow Rd SHB W12 ... 156 B3
Beck River Pk BECK BR3 ... 204 F1
Beck Rd HACK E8 ... 140 B3
  MTCM CR4 ... 202 A6
Becks Rd SCUP DA14 ... 185 J6
Beckton Rd CAN/RD E16 ... 141 K6
Beck Wy BECK BR3 ... 204 E3
Beckway Rd STRHM/NOR SW16 ... 202 A9
Beckway St WALW SE17 ... 19 H6
Beckwell Rd SL SL1 ... 149 H1
Beckwith Rd HNHL SE24 ... 162 C4
Beclands Rd TOOT SW17 ... 180 A6
Becmead Av KTN/HRWW/WS HA3 ... 114 A1
  STRHM/NOR SW16 ... 181 P8
Becondale Rd NRWD SE19 ... 181 M8
Becontree Av BCTR RM8 ... 123 J9
Bective Rd FSTGT E7 ... 121 N9
  PUT/ROE SW15 ... 157 P9
Becton Pl ERITH DA8 ... 164 C1
Bedale Rd ENC/FH EN2 ... 79 N4
  HARH RM3 ... 105 N6
Bedale St STHWK SE1 ... 12 G10
Bedale Wk RDART DA2 ... 188 B3

Beddington Cross CROY/NA CR0 ... 202 E7
Beddington Farm Rd CROY/NA CR0 ... 202 G7
Beddington Gdns CAR SM5 ... 222 A5
Beddington Gn STMC/STPC BR5 ... 207 J3
Beddington Gv WLGTN SM6 ... 222 E4
Beddington La CROY/NA CR0 ... 202 D6
Beddington Path STMC/STPC BR5 ... 207 J3
Beddington Rd GDMY/SEVK IG3 ... 123 J8
  STMC/STPC BR5 ... 207 J2
Beddington Ter BRXS/STRHM SW2 ... 180 G2
Beddlestead La WARL CR6 ... 243 L4
Bede Cl PIN HA5 ... 93 L9
Bedens Rd SCUP DA14 ... 185 P9
Bedevere Rd ED N9 ... 100 C4
Bedfont Cl EBED/NFELT TW14 ... 174 D4
  MTCM CR4 ... 202 B2
Bedfont Court Est STWL/WRAY TW19 ... 151 L10
Bedfont Green Cl EBED/NFELT TW14 ... 174 D4
Bedfont La EBED/NFELT TW14 ... 174 A2
Bedfont Rd STWL/WRAY TW19 ... 174 A2
Bedford Av BAR EN5 ... 77 J9
  RSQ WC1B ... 11 K4
  SL SL1 ... 128 B8
  YEAD UB4 ... 133 J8
Bedfordbury CHCR WC2N ... 11 K8
Bedford Cl CHSWK W4 ... 156 B5
  MUSWH N10 ... 98 B8
  RKW/CH/CXG WD3 ... 70 E4
  WOKN/KNAP GU21 ... 231 P1
Bedford Cnr CHSWK W4 * ... 156 B5
Bedford Crs PEND EN3 ... 80 D1
Bedford Dr SLN SL2 ... 108 G10
Bedford Gdns HCH RM12 ... 125 K7
  KENS W8 ... 8 E10
Bedford Hl BAL SW12 ... 180 C5
  ASC SL5 ... 192 G5
Bedford Ms CAT SE6 ... 182 G5
Bedford Pk CROY/NA CR0 ... 203 L8
Bedford Park Rd STAL AL1 ... 38 D6
Bedford Pl CROY/NA CR0 ... 203 L8
  RSQ WC1B ... 11 J2
Bedford Rd BFN/LL DA15 ... 185 H6
  ASC SL5 ... 192 G5
  CHSWK W4 ... 156 A2
  CLAP SW4 ... 158 F10
  ED N9 ... 100 A1
  EFNCH N2 ... 117 J2
  EHAM E6 ... 142 D3
  GRAYS RM17 ... 167 N4
  GU GU1 ... 267 P1
  GWW DA11 ... 190 C5
  HRW HA1 ... 114 D4
  IL IG1 ... 122 D8
  MLHL NW7 ... 96 B3
  NTHWD HA6 ... 92 A6
  ORP BR6 ... 207 L9
  RSLP HA4 ... 112 G9
  SEVS/STOTM N15 ... 119 L2
  STAL AL1 ... 38 D7
  SWFD E18 ... 101 M10
  WALTH E17 ... 101 H3
  WDGN N22 ... 98 F9
  WEA W13 ... 134 G9
  WHTN TW2 ... 176 C6
  WPK KT4 ... 200 F9
Bedford Rw GINN WC1R ... 11 P3
Bedford Sq RSQ WC1B ... 11 K4
Bedford St BERK HP4 ... 34 A5
  COVGDN WC2E ... 11 L7
  WATN WD24 ... 73 J5
  WCGE AL7 ... 23 H7
Bedford Vis KUT/HW KT1 * ... 199 J2
Bedford Wk WAB EN9 * ... 81 J1
Bedgebury Gdns WIM/MER SW19 ... 179 H5
Bedgebury Rd ELTH/MOT SE9 ... 183 M6
Bedlam Ms LBTH SE11 ... 17 P5
Bedlow Cl STJWD NW8 ... 9 M2
Bedlow Wy CROY/NA CR0 ... 222 G1
Bedmond La ABLGY WD5 ... 55 L1
  LCOL/BKTW AL2 ... 37 K10
Bedmond Rd ABLGY WD5 ... 54 E5
  HHS/BOV HP3 ... 36 E9
Bedonwell Rd BELV DA17 ... 164 A5
  BELV DA17 ... 163 P5
  BXLYHN DA7 ... 164 B5
  BXLYHN DA7 ... 164 A7
Bedser Cl LBTH SE11 ... 17 P9
  THHTH CR7 ... 203 K3
  WOKN/KNAP GU21 ... 232 D1
Bedser Dr GFD/PVL UB6 ... 114 C10
Bedster Gdns E/WMO/HCT KT8 ... 198 A2
Bedwardine Rd NRWD SE19 ... 181 M10
Bedwell Av BRKMPK AL9 ... 42 M4
Bedwell Cl WGCE AL7 ... 23 H6
Bedwell Gdns HYS/HAR UB3 ... 152 A3
Bedwell Rd BELV DA17 ... 164 B2
  TOTM N17 ... 99 N9
Beeby Rd CAN/RD E16 ... 141 N7
Beech Av ACT W3 ... 136 F5
  BFN/LL DA15 ... 185 K3
  BH/WHM TN16 ... 244 A5
  BRW CM14 ... 86 B3
  EFNCH N2 ... 117 J2
  ENC/FH EN2 ... 79 H1
  RAD WD7 ... 56 F1
  RBRW/HUT CM13 ... 107 L4
  RSLP HA4 ... 113 H6
  RYLN/HDSTN HA2 ... 113 N8
  STAL AL1 ... 38 G4
  SUN TW16 ... 175 P9
  THHTH CR7 ... 203 J4
  UX/CGN UB8 ... 132 A4
  WEY KT13 ... 216 F1
Beechbank Rd HAMP NW3 * ... 69 P5
  CHESW EN7 ... 61 M2
  HERT/BAY SG13 ... 43 N5
  MLHL NW7 ... 96 B6
  SURB KT6 ... 199 H4
  WEY KT13 ... 216 F1
  WOKN/KNAP GU21 ... 231 K4
Beechwood Cl AMS HP6 ... 69 P5
  CHESW EN7 ... 61 M2
  ENC/FH EN2 * ... 118 J2
  HERT/BAY SG13 ... 43 N5
  MLHL NW7 ... 96 B6
  SURB KT6 ... 199 H4
  WEY KT13 ... 216 F1
  WOKN/KNAP GU21 ... 231 K4
Beechwood Crs BXLYHN DA7 ... 163 N9
  PGE/AN SE20 ... 204 B1
Beechwood Dr COB KT11 ... 217 P7
  HAYES BR2 ... 226 A1
  WFD IG8 ... 101 L6
Beechwood Gdns CLAY IG5 ... 241 P8
  CTHM CR3 ... 145 J7
  RAIN RM13 ... 145 J7
  RYLN/HDSTN HA2 ... 114 A8
  SL SL1 ... 149 K8
Beechwood Gv ACT W3 ... 136 B5
  WARL CR6 ... 242 D5
Beechwood Mnr WEY KT13 ... 216 F1
Beechwood Ms ED N9 ... 99 P3
Beechwood Pk HHS/BOV HP3 ... 35 J10
  LHD/OX KT22 ... 237 J2
  SWFD E18 ... 101 M1
Beechwood Ri CHST BR7 ... 184 F1
  WATN WD24 ... 73 J2
Beechwood Rd BEAC HP9 ... 88 B9
  CEND/HSY/T N8 ... 118 C2
  CTHM CR3 ... 241 P8
  HACK E8 ... 7 L1
  SAND/SEL CR2 ... 223 M5
  SLN SL2 ... 129 J7
  VW GU25 ... 193 N7
  WOKN/KNAP GU21 ... 231 K4
Beechworth Vls REDH RH1 ... 285 B10
Beechworth Cl HAMP NW3 ... 117 J1
Beechy Lees Rd RSEV TN14 ... 247 L5
Beecot La WOT/HER KT12 ... 197 K5
Beecroft La BROCKY SE4 ... 182 B1
Beecroft Ms BROCKY SE4 ... 182 B1
Beecroft Rd BROCKY SE4 ... 182 B1
Beehive Cha BRWN CM15 ... 87 J1
Beehive Cl BORE WD6 ... 75 L3
  HGDN/ICK UB10 ... 132 A2
Beehive La REDBR IG4 ... 122 C3
  WCCE AL7 ... 23 K8
Beehive Pl BRXN/ST SW9 ... 159 H9
Beehive Ring Rd HORL RH6 ... 280 C10
Beehive Rd CHESW EN7 ... 61 J4
  STA TW18 ... 173 J8
Beehive Wy REIG RH2 ... 275 L4
Beeken Dene ORP BR6 ... 226 F1
Beeleigh Rd MRDN SM4 ... 201 L4
Beesfield La EYN DA4 ... 209 P8
Beeston Cl HACK E8 ... 119 P10
  OXHEY WD19 ... 93 L5
Beeston Dr CHES/WGN EN8 ... 62 C3
Beeston Pl BGVA SW1W ... 16 E4
Beeston Rd EBAR EN4 ... 77 N10
Beethoven Rd BORE WD6 ... 95 H1
Beethoven St NKENS W10 ... 2 B8
Beeton Cl PIN HA5 ... 93 P8
Begbie Rd BKHTH/KID SE3 ... 161 P7
Beggars Bush La WATW WD18 ... 72 E9
Beggarshouse La HORL RH6 ... 278 C10
Beggars La BH/WHM TN16 ... 262 C1
  CHOB/PIR GU24 ... 213 H7
  RDKG RH5 ... 270 F5
Beggars Roost La SUT SM1 ... 221 K5
Begonia Cl EHAM E6 ... 142 F1
Begonia Pl HPTN TW12 ... 175 P9
Behenna Cl CRAWW RH11 ... 282 C3
Beira St BAL SW12 ... 180 C3
Beken Ct WATN WD25 ... 73 K1
Bekesbourne St POP/IOD E14 * ... 140 G8
Belcher Rd HOD EN11 ... 44 F2
Belchers La NWE EN9 ... 81 L10
Belcroft Cl BMLY BR1 ... 183 L10
Beldam Bridge Rd CHOB/PIR GU24 ... 212 F9
Beldam Haw RSEV TN14 ... 228 B7
Beldham Gdns E/WMO/HCT KT8 ... 198 A3
Belfairs Dr CHDH RM6 ... 123 M5
Belfairs Gn OXHEY WD19 ... 93 L3
Belfast Av SL SL1 ... 129 H8
Belfast Rd SNWD SE25 ... 204 A4
  STNW/STAM N16 ... 119 N5
Belfield Rd HOR/WEW KT19 ... 220 A5
Belford Gv WOOL/PLUM SE18 ... 162 G3
Belford Rd BORE WD6 ... 75 K8
Belfort Rd PECK SE15 ... 161 L1
Belfour Ter WCHMH N21 * ... 99 H2
Belfry Av HGDN/ICK UB10 ... 132 A2
Belfry Cl BERM/RHTH SE16 ... 159 M4
Belfry La RKW/CH/CXG WD3 ... 91 M2
Belfry Rd MNPK E12 ... 122 A7
The Belfry REDH RH1 ... 258 A6
Belgrade Rd HPTN TW12 ... 175 P7
  STNW/STAM N16 ... 119 N1
Belgrave Av ACT W3 ... 125 K1
  MLHL NW7 ... 96 A6
  STALE/WH AL4 ... 78 D9
  STHGT/OAK N14 ... 96 C10
  STMC/STPC BR5 ... 217 J1
  WAT WD18 ... 72 F6
Belgrave Crs SUN TW16 ... 197 H8
Belgrave Dr KGLGY WD4 ... 54 D2
Belgrave Gdns STAN HA7 ... 95 K4
  STJWD NW8 ... 3 H2
  STJWD NW8 ... 3 J1
Belgrave Mnr WOKS/MYFD GU22 ... 232 B5
Belgrave Ms South KTBR SW1X ... 16 D3
Belgrave Ms West KTBR SW1X ... 16 C3
Belgrave Pde KTBR SW1X * ... 16 C5
Belgrave Pl KTBR SW1X ... 16 D3
Belgrave Rd BARN SW13 ... 156 G10
  HSLWW TW4 ... 175 H5
  IL IG1 ... 122 C6
  LEY E10 ... 121 H6
  MTCM CR4 ... 201 N3
  PIM SW1V ... 16 F6
  PLSTW E13 ... 141 P2
  SL SL1 ... 129 H7
  SNWD SE25 ... 203 N3
  SUN TW16 ... 197 H8
  WALTH E17 ... 120 E2
  WAN E11 ... 121 N6
Belgrave St WCHPL E1 ... 140 C7
Belgrave Wk MTCM CR4 ... 201 N3
Belgravia Cl BAR EN5 ... 77 K3
Belgravia Gdns KUT/HW KT1 ... 199 K3
Belinda Rd BRXN/ST SW9 ... 159 H9
Belitha Vls IS N1 ... 5 L1
Bellamaine Cl THMD SE28 ... 163 H1
Bellamy Cl EDGW HA8 ... 96 D6

HGDN/ICK UB10 112 B8
POP/IOD E14 160 F1
WAT WD17 73 H5
WKENS W14 14 D8
Bellamy Dr STAN HA7 94 G9
Bellamy Rd CHES/WCR EN8 62 D5
CHING E4 100 G7
ENC/FH EN2 * 79 L6
Bellamy St BAL SW12 180 C3
Bel La FELT TW13 175 M6
Bellarmine Cl THMD SE28 143 J10
Bellasis Av BRXS/STRHM SW2 180 F4
Bell Av HARH RM3 105 J9
WDR/YW UB7 152 A2
Bell Bridge Rd CHERT KT16 195 J8
Bellchambers Cl
LCOL/BKTW AL2 57 H2
Bell Cl ABLGY WD5 54 G3
PIN HA5 113 K1
RDART DA2 188 E1
SLN SL2 129 N7
Bellclose Rd WDR/YW UB7 151 P1
Bell Common EPP CM16 65 H8
Bell Crs COUL/CHIP CR5 240 C7
Bell Dr WAND/EARL SW18 179 H3
Bellefield Rd STMC/STPC BR5 207 L5
Bellefields Rd BRXN/ST SW9 158 G9
Bellegrove Cl WELL DA16 163 J8
Bellegrove Rd WELL DA16 163 H8
Bellenden Rd PECK SE15 159 N8
Belle Staines Pleasaunce
CHING E4 100 F3
Belleville Rd BTSEA SW11 179 P1
Belle Vue GFD/PVL UB6 134 C3
Belle Vue Cl STA TW18 195 K1
Belle Vue La BUSH WD23 94 C2
Bellevue Pk THHTH CR7 203 K3
Belle Vue Pl SL SL1 * 149 L2
Bellevue Pl WCHPL E1 * 140 B6
Bellevue Rd EMPK RM11 125 N6
FBAR/BDGN N11 98 B5
KUT/HW KT1 199 K3
TOOT SW17 180 A3
WARE SG12 26 D2
WEA W13 134 G6
BARN SW13 156 D8
BXLYHS DA6 186 A1
Belle Vue Rd CRW RM5 104 D7
HDN NW4 116 G2
ORP BR6 226 D6
WALTH E17 101 J10
Belle Vue Ter DEN/HRF UB9 * 91 K8
Bellew St TOOT SW17 179 M6
Bell Farm Av DAGE RM10 124 D8
Bellfield CROY/NA CR0 224 D5
Bellfield Av
KTN/HRWW/WS HA3 94 C7
Bellfield Cl BKHTH/KID SE3 161 N6
Bellfield Gdns HLWE CM17 47 M2
Bellfields Rd GU GU1 250 A7
Bell Gdns LEY E10 * 120 F6
STMC/STPC BR5 207 M5
Bellgate HHNE HP2 35 P3
Bellgate Ms KTTN NW5 118 C9
Bell Gn HHS/BOV HP3 * 52 E3
SYD SE26 182 E7
Bell Green La SYD SE26 182 E8
Bellhouse La BRW CM14 86 D9
Bell House Rd ROMW/RG RM7 124 D6
Bellina Ms KTTN NW5 118 C9
Bellingdon Rd CSHM HP5 50 G7
Bellingham Dr REIG RH2 257 J10
Bellingham Gn CAT SE6 182 F6
Bellingham Rd CAT SE6 183 H6
Bell La ABLGY WD5 55 H3
AMSS HP7 69 N5
BERK HP4 33 K4
BRKMPK AL9 41 K10
BROX EN10 44 D7
CAN/RD E16 141 L10
HDN NW4 116 G2
HERT/WAT SG14 25 L5
HOD EN11 44 F3
LCOL/BKTW AL2 57 K5
LHD/OX KT22 236 C9
PEND EN3 80 C4
TWK TW1 176 F4
WBLY HA9 * 115 J7
WCHPL E1 13 L4
WDSR SL4 148 E3
Bell Lane Cl LHD/OX KT22 236 C9
Bellman Av GVE DA12 191 H4
Bellmarsh Rd
ADL/WDHM KT15 215 L1
Bell Md SBW CM21 29 P1
Bell Meadow GDST RH9 260 B8
NRWD SE19 181 M7
Bellmount Wood Av
WAT WD17 72 F5
Belloc Cl CRAWE RH10 284 C6
Bello Cl HNHL SE24 181 J4
Bellot St GNWCH SE10 161 K4
Bell Pde HSLW TW3 * 154 A10
WWKM BR4 * 205 H9
Bellridge Pl BEAC HP9 88 A5
Bellring Cl BELV DA17 164 B5
Bell Rd E/WMO/HCT KT8 198 C5
EN EN1 79 L5
HSLW TW3 154 A9
The Bell Rbt LCOL/BKTW AL2 57 M3
Bells Hl BAR EN5 76 G8
SLN SL2 129 M3
Bells Hill Gn SLN SL2 129 M2
Bells La DTCH/LGLY SL3 150 E9
Bell St BAY/PAD W2 9 N3
REIG RH2 257 K10
SBW CM21 29 P1
WOOL/PLUM SE18 162 B7
Bellswood La IVER SL0 130 E7
Belltrees Gv
STRHM/NOR SW16 180 G8
Bell Vw STALE/WH AL4 39 J6
WDSR SL4 148 E9
Bell View Cl WDSR SL4 148 E8
Bell Water Ga
WOOL/PLUM SE18 162 D2
Bellweir Cl STWL/WRAY TW19 172 E5
Bellwether La REDH RH1 277 J9
Bell Wharf La CANST EC4R 12 F8
Bellwood Rd PECK SE15 160 C10
Bell Yd LINN WC2A 12 A6
Bell Yard Ms STHWK SE1 19 K2
Belmont SLN SL2 128 F7
Belmont Av ALP/SUD HA0 135 L3
EBAR EN4 78 A9
ED N9 99 P2
GUW GU2 249 L7
NWDGN UB2 153 M2
NWMAL KT3 200 D5
PLMGR N13 98 F6
UPMR RM14 125 N7
WELL DA16 163 H8
Belmont Cir
KTN/HRWW/WS HA3 * 94 G9
Belmont Cl CHING E4 101 J6
CLAP SW4 158 D9
EBAR EN4 78 A8
TRDG/WHET N20 97 L2
UX/CGN UB8 131 N1
WFD IG8 101 N5
Belmont Gv CHSWK W4 156 A3
LEW SE13 161 J9
Belmont Hl LEW SE13 161 J9
STAL AL1 38 C7
Belmont La CHST BR7 184 F8
STAN HA7 95 H8
Belmont Pde CHST BR7 * 184 E8
GLDGN NW11 * 117 J3
Belmont Pk LEW SE13 161 J10
Belmont Park Cl LEW SE13 161 K10
Belmont Park Rd LEY E10 120 G4
Belmont Ri BELMT SM2 221 J4
Belmont Rd BECK BR3 204 D2
BELMT SM2 221 K6
BUSH WD23 73 M8
CHST BR7 184 E8
CLAP SW4 158 D9
CSHM HP5 50 G4
ERITH DA8 164 C6
ERITH DA8 164 B6
GRAYS RM17 167 L4
HCH RM12 125 L8
HHS/BOV HP3 35 P9
IL IG1 122 F8
KTN/HRWW/WS HA3 114 E1
LHD/OX KT22 236 F8
REIG RH2 275 M1
SEVS/STOTM N15 119 K2
SNWD SE25 204 A5
UX/CGN UB8 131 N2
WHTN TW2 176 C5
WLGTN SM6 222 D2
Belmont St CAMTN NW1 4 D3
Belmont Ter CHSWK W4 156 A3
Belmor BORE WD6 75 M9
Belmore Av
WOKS/MYFD GU22 232 G2
YEAD UB4 133 H8
Belmore La HOLWY N7 118 E10
Belmore St VX/NE SW8 158 E7
Beloe Cl PUT/ROE SW15 156 D10
Belsham Cl CSHM HP5 50 G4
Belsham St HOM E9 140 B1
Belsize RKW/CH/CXG WD3 * 52 G9
Belsize Av HAMP NW3 3 N1
PLMGR N13 98 G7
WEA W13 154 G2
Belsize Cl HHS/BOV HP3 36 B7
STALE/WH AL4 39 H1
Belsize Court Gdns
HAMP NW3 117 N10
Belsize Crs HAMP NW3 117 N10
Belsize Gdns SUT SM1 221 L1
Belsize Gv HAMP NW3 3 P1
Belsize La HAMP NW3 3 L2
Belsize Pk HAMP NW3 3 L2
Belsize Park Gdns HAMP NW3 3 N1
Belsize Park Ms HAMP NW3 * 3 M1
Belsize Pl HAMP NW3 117 N10
Belsize Rd HHS/BOV HP3 36 B7
KIL/WHAMP NW6 3 K4
KTN/HRWW/WS HA3 94 C8
Belsize Sq HAMP NW3 3 M2
Belsize Ter HAMP NW3 3 M1
Belson Rd WOOL/PLUM SE18 162 C3
Belswains La HHS/BOV HP3 35 P10
Beltana Dr GVE DA12 191 H7
Beltane Dr WIM/MER SW19 178 G6
Belthorn Crs BAL SW12 180 D3
Beltinge Rd HARH RM3 125 N1
Beltona Gdns CHES/WCR EN8 62 C3
Belton Rd BERK HP4 33 M4
FSTGT E7 141 N2
SCUP DA14 185 K7
TOTM N17 119 M1
WAN E11 121 K9
WLSDN NW10 136 D1
Belton Wy BOW E3 140 F7
Beltran Rd FUL/PGN SW6 157 L8
Beltwood Rd BELV DA17 164 D3
Belvedere Av CLAY IG5 102 E10
WIM/MER SW19 179 H8
Belvedere Blds STHWK SE1 18 D2
Belvedere Cl AMS HP6 69 L3
ESH/CLAY KT10 218 A2
GUW GU2 249 N8
GVE DA12 190 F4
TEDD TW11 176 D8
WEY KT13 216 B2
Belvedere Ct BELV DA17 164 A2
OXHEY WD19 73 L10
Belvedere Dr WIM/MER SW19 179 H8
Belvedere Gdns
E/WMO/HCT KT8 197 N5
LCOL/BKTW AL2 55 N3
Belvedere Gv WIM/MER SW19 179 H8
Belvedere Ms PECK SE15 160 B9
Belvedere Pl
BRXS/STRHM SW2 158 G10
Belvedere Rd ABYW SE2 143 N10
BH/WHM TN16 244 C4
BRW CM14 106 E4
BXLYHN DA7 164 A9
HNWL W7 154 D2
LEY E10 120 D6
NRWD SE19 181 N10
STHWK SE1 17 N1
Belvedere Sq WIM/MER SW19 179 H8
Belvedere Strd
CDALE/KGS NW9 96 C10
The Belvedere WBPTN SW10 * 157 M7
Belvedere Wy
KTN/HRWW/WS HA3 115 K4
Belvoir Rd EDUL SE22 181 P3
Belvue Cl NTHLT UB5 133 P2
Belvue Rd NTHLT UB5 133 P2
Bembridge Cl
KIL/WHAMP NW6 2 A3
Bembridge Gdns RSLP HA4 112 E7
Bembridge Pl GSTN WD25 * 55 H9
Bemerton Est IS N1 5 N5
Bemerton St IS N1 5 N5
Bemish Rd PUT/ROE SW15 156 G9
Bempton Dr RSLP HA4 113 J7
Bemsted Rd WALTH E17 120 E1
Benares Rd WOOL/PLUM SE18 163 J3
Benbow Cl STAL AL1 38 G8
Benbow Moorings
UX/CGN UB8 * 131 M7
Benbow Rd HMSMTH W6 156 E2
Benbow St DEPT SE8 160 F5
Benbow Wy UX/CGN UB8 131 M7
Benbrick Rd GUW GU2 267 M1
Benbury Cl BMLY BR1 183 H8
The Bence EGH TW20 194 E3
Bench Fld SAND/SEL CR2 223 N3
Benchleys Rd HHW HP1 35 J7
Bench Manor Crs
CFSP/GDCR SL9 89 P10
The Bench
RCHPK/HAM TW10 * 177 H6
Bencombe Rd PUR/KEN CR8 223 H10
Bencroft CHESW EN7 61 P2
Bencroft Rd HHNE HP2 35 P6
STRHM/NOR SW16 180 D10
Bencurtis Pk WWKM BR4 205 J10
Bendall Ms CAMTN NW1 9 P3
Bendemeer Rd
PUT/ROE SW15 156 G9
Bendish Rd EHAM E6 142 B2
Bendmore Av ABYW SE2 163 K4
Bendon Va WAND/EARL SW18 179 L3
Bendysh Rd BUSH WD23 73 M7
Benedict Cl ORP BR6 207 H10
Benedict Dr
EBED/NFELT TW14 174 E3
Benedictine Ga
CHES/WCR EN8 62 D3
Benedict Rd BRXN/ST SW9 158 G9
MTCM CR4 201 N3
Benedict Wy EFNCH N2 * 117 M1
Benedict Whf MTCM CR4 201 P3
Benenden Gn HAYES BR2 205 M5
Benen-Stock Rd
STWL/WRAY TW19 173 K2
Benets Rd EMPK RM11 125 P6
Benett Gdns
STRHM/NOR SW16 202 F2
Benfleet Cl COB KT11 217 M8
SUT SM1 201 M10
Benfleet Wy FBAR/BDGN N11 98 B3
Benford Rd HOD EN11 44 E5
Bengal Rd IL IG1 122 E9
Bengarth Dr
KTN/HRWW/WS HA3 94 C10
Bengarth Rd NTHLT UB5 133 L3
Bengeo Mdw
HERT/WAT SG14 * 25 K2
Bengeo Ms HERT/WAT SG14 * 25 K2
Bengeo St HERT/WAT SG14 25 K4
Bengeworth Rd CMBW SE5 159 K9
HRW HA1 114 F7
Ben Hale Cl STAN HA7 94 F6
Benham Cl CHSGTN KT9 219 H3
COUL/CHIP CR5 241 J4
CSHM HP5 50 G5
Benham Gdns HSLWW TW4 175 N1
Benham Rd HNWL W7 134 D7
Benhams Dr HORL RH6 280 B2
Benhill Av SUT SM1 221 L1
Benhill Rd CMBW SE5 159 L6
SUT SM1 201 N10
Benhill Wood Rd SUT SM1 221 M1
Benhilton Gdns SUT SM1 201 L10
Benhurst Av HCH RM12 125 J9
Benhurst Cl SAND/SEL CR2 224 C6
Benhurst Gdns SAND/SEL CR2 224 B6
Benhurst La
STRHM/NOR SW16 181 H8
Beningfield Dr
LCOL/BKTW AL2 56 F6
Benin St LEW SE13 183 J3
Benjafield Cl UED N18 100 A5
Benjamin Cl EMPK RM11 125 H4
HACK E8 7 P5
Benjamin La SLN SL2 129 N6
Benjamin Ms BAL SW12 180 D3
Benjamin Rd CRAWE RH10 284 E9
Benjamin St FARR EC1M 12 C3
Ben Jonson Rd WCHPL E1 140 D7
Benledi St POP/IOD E14 141 J8
Benn Cl OXTED RH8 261 M10
Bennelong Cl SHB W12 136 E9
Benner La CHOB/PIR GU24 212 E8
Bennerley Rd BTSEA SW11 179 P1
Bennet Cl KUT/HW KT1 199 H1
Bennetsfield Rd STKPK UB11 132 C10
Bennet's Hl BLKFR EC4V 12 D7
Bennett Cl COB KT11 217 H9
HSLWW TW4 175 M1
NTHWD HA6 92 G8
WELL DA16 163 K8
WGCE AL7 23 J9
Bennett Gv LEW SE13 160 G7
Bennett Pk BKHTH/KID SE3 161 L9
Bennett Rd BRXN/ST SW9 159 H8
CHDH RM6 123 P4
PLSTW E13 141 P6
Bennetts CSHM HP5 51 J6
Bennetts Av CROY/NA CR0 204 D9
GFD/PVL UB6 134 D3
Bennett's Castle La BCTR RM8 123 M9
Bennetts Cl MTCM CR4 202 C1
SL SL1 128 F10
STALE/WH AL4 40 A9
TOTM N17 99 N7
Bennetts Copse CHST BR7 184 B9
Bennetts End Cl
HHS/BOV HP3 * 36 A8
Bennetts End Rd
HHS/BOV HP3 36 A7
Bennetts Farm Pl
GT/LBKH KT23 253 N1
Bennett St CHSWK W4 156 B5
WHALL SW1A 10 G9
Bennetts Wy CROY/NA CR0 204 D9
Bennetts Yd UX/CGN UB8 * 131 N2
Bennett Wy RDART DA2 188 C7
RGUE GU4 251 K5
Benning Cl WDSR SL4 148 C9
Benningfield Gdns BERK HP4 34 B3
Benningholme Rd EDGW HA8 96 B7
Bennington Dr BORE WD6 75 L5
Bennington Rd TOTM N17 99 M9
WFD IG8 * 101 K8
Bennions Cl HCH RM12 145 L1
Bennison Dr HARH RM3 105 L10
Benn St HOM E9 140 D1
Benrek Cl BARK/HLT IG6 102 F8
Bensbury Cl PUT/ROE SW15 178 E3
Bensham Cl THHTH CR7 203 K4
Bensham Gv THHTH CR7 203 K2
Bensham La CROY/NA CR0 203 J7
Bensham Manor Rd
THHTH CR7 203 K4
Benskin Rd WATW WD18 73 H9
Benskins La ABR/ST RM4 105 L2
Bensley Cl FBAR/BDGN N11 98 A6
Ben Smith Wy
BERM/RHTH SE16 19 P3
Benson Av PLSTW E13 141 P4
Benson Cl HSLW TW3 153 P10
SLN SL2 129 M10
UX/CGN UB8 131 P7
Benson Quay WAP E1W 140 B9
Benson Rd CROY/NA CR0 203 H10
FSTH SE23 182 B4
GRAYS RM17 167 N5
Benthall Gdns PUR/KEN CR8 241 K2
Benthal Rd STNW/STAM N16 119 N7
Bentham Av
WOKN/KNAP GU21 214 F10
Bentham Rd HOM E9 140 C1
THMD SE28 143 L10
Ben Tillet Cl BARK IG11 143 K2
CAN/RD E16 * 142 C10
Bentinck Cl CFSP/GDCR SL9 110 A3
Bentinck Ms MHST W1U 10 D5
Bentinck Rd WDR/YW UB7 131 N10
Bentinck St MHST W1U 10 D5
Bentley Cl HART DA3 211 P3
WIM/MER SW19 179 K6
Bentley Dr CRICK NW2 117 J8
GNTH/NBYPK IG2 122 F4
HLWE CM17 47 M2
WEY KT13 216 B5
Bentley Heath La BAR EN5 77 H1
Bentley Ms EN EN1 79 L10
Bentley Pk SL SL1 128 C4
Bentley Rd HERT/WAT SG14 24 F4
IS N1 7 K2
SL SL1 128 E10
Bentley's Meadow
BGR/WK TN15 247 N6
Bentley St GVE DA12 190 F2
Bentley Wy STAN HA7 94 F6
WFD IG8 101 M4
Benton Rd IL IG1 122 G6
OXHEY WD19 93 L6
Bentons WAB EN9 * 45 K8
Benton's La WNWD SE27 181 K7
Benton's Ri WNWD SE27 181 L8
Bentry Cl BCTR RM8 123 P7
Bentry Rd BCTR RM8 123 P7
Bentsbrook Cl RDKG RH5 272 G6
Bentsbrook Pk RDKG RH5 272 G6
Bentsbrook Rd RDKG RH5 272 G6
Bentsley Cl STALE/WH AL4 38 G2
Bentworth Rd SHB W12 136 E8
Benwell Ct SUN TW16 * 197 H1
Benwell Rd CHOB/PIR GU24 230 E6
HOLWY N7 119 H9
Benwick Cl BERM/RHTH SE16 160 A3
Benwood Ct SUT SM1 201 M10
Benworth St BOW E3 140 E5
Benyon Ct SOCK/AV RM15 147 H4
Benyon Pth SOCK/AV RM15 147 H4
Benyon Rd IS N1 7 H5
Benyon Whf IS N1 7 K5
Beomonds Rw CHERT KT16 * 195 K7
Berberis Cl GU GU1 249 P8
Berberis Wk WDR/YW UB7 151 P3
Berber Pde WOOL/PLUM SE18 162 B7
Berber Rd BTSEA SW11 * 180 A1
Berceau Wk WAT WD17 72 F5
Bercta Rd ELTH/MOT SE9 184 F5
Bere Cl SWCM DA10 189 H1
Berecroft HLWS CM18 46 G5
Beredens La RBRW/HUT CM13 106 E10
Berefeld HHNE HP2 35 N4
Berengers Pl DAGW RM9 143 L1
Berenger Wk WBPTN SW10 * 157 N6
Berens Rd STMC/STPC BR5 207 M5
WLSDN NW10 136 G5
Berens Wy CHST BR7 207 J4
Beresford Av ALP/SUD HA0 135 M3
BRYLDS KT5 199 N8
HNWL W7 134 C7
SLN SL2 129 P9
TRDG/WHET N20 98 A3
TWK TW1 177 H2
Beresford Dr BMLY BR1 206 A3
WFD IG8 101 P5
Beresford Gdns CHDH RM6 123 P3
EN EN1 79 M8
HSLWW TW4 175 N1
Beresford Rd BELMT SM2 221 J4
CEND/HSY/T N8 119 H3
CHING E4 101 K2
DORK RH4 272 G2
EFNCH N2 117 P1
GVW DA11 190 B3
HBRY N5 119 L10
HRW HA1 114 C3
KUTN/CMB KT2 199 L1
NWMAL KT3 199 P4
RKW/CH/CXG WD3 91 J2
STAL AL1 39 H7
STHL UB1 133 L9
WALTH E17 100 G9
Beresford Sq
WOOL/PLUM SE18 162 E3
Beresford St
WOOL/PLUM SE18 162 E2
WOOL/PLUM SE18 162 F2
Beresford Ter HBRY N5 119 K10
Berestede Rd HMSMTH W6 156 C4
Bere St WAP E1W 140 C9
Bergenia Ct CHOB/PIR GU24 212 D9
Berger Cl STMC/STPC BR5 206 G6
Berger Rd HOM E9 140 C1
Berghem Ms WKENS W14 156 G2
Bergholt Av REDBR IG4 122 B3
Bergholt Crs STNW/STAM N16 119 M5
Bergholt Ms CAMTN NW1 5 H4
Bericot Wy WGCE AL7 23 M5
Bering Sq POP/IOD E14 160 F4
Bering Wk CAN/RD E16 142 A8
Berisford Ms
WAND/EARL SW18 179 M2
Berkeley Av BXLYHN DA7 163 N7
CLAY IG5 102 D10
CRW RM5 104 D8
CSHM HP5 50 E5
GFD/PVL UB6 134 D1
HSLWW TW4 153 H7
Berkeley Cl ABLGY WD5 54 G8
BORE WD6 75 M9
CSHM HP5 50 F6
EMPK RM11 126 A7
KUTN/CMB KT2 177 K10
POTB/CUF EN6 59 H8
RSLP HA4 112 G8
STMC/STPC BR5 207 H7
STWL/WRAY TW19 172 G5
WARE SG12 26 B1
Berkeley Ct
RKW/CH/CXG WD3 * 72 E9
WEY KT13 196 E9
WLGTN SM6 202 D10
Berkeley Crs EBAR EN4 77 N9
Berkeley Dr E/WMO/HCT KT8 197 N3
EMPK RM11 125 P6
WDSR SL4 170 A4
Berkeley Gdns BF/WBF KT14 215 J10
ESH/CLAY KT10 218 F4
KENS W8 8 F10
WCHMH N21 99 L1
WOT/HER KT12 196 G7
Berkeley Ms MBLAR W1H 10 B5
SUN TW16 197 K3
Berkeley Pl EPSOM KT18 238 A1
WIM/MER SW19 178 G9
Berkeley Rd BARN SW13 156 D7
CDALE/KGS NW9 115 M2
CEND/HSY/T N8 118 E3
HGDN/ICK UB10 132 D2
MNPK E12 122 B10
Berkeley Sq MYFR/PICC W1J 10 F8
The Berkeleys LHD/OX KT22 236 D10
SNWD SE25 * 203 P4
Berkeley St MYFR/PICC W1J 10 F8
Berkeley Ter TIL RM18 168 D6
Berkeley Waye HEST TW5 153 M6
Berkhampstead Rd
BELV DA17 164 B4
CSHM HP5 51 H6
Berkhamsted Av WBLY HA9 135 L1
Berkhamsted Rd HHW HP1 34 G4
Berkley Av CHES/WCR EN8 62 C10
Berkley Cl STALE/WH AL4 39 H2
WHTN TW2 * 176 D6
Berkley Ct GU GU1 250 B10
Berkley Gv CAMTN NW1 4 C4
Berkley Pl CHES/WCR EN8 * 62 C10
Berkley Rd BEAC HP9 88 C5
CAMTN NW1 4 B4
GVE DA12 190 E2
Berkley Rw GVE DA12 * 190 E2
Berks Hl RKW/CH/CXG WD3 70 F9
Berkshire Av SL SL1 128 G8
Berkshire Cl CTHM CR3 241 L8
Berkshire Gdns PLMGR N13 99 H7
UED N18 100 A6
Berkshire Rd HOM E9 140 E1
Berkshire Wy EMPK RM11 125 P3
MTCM CR4 202 F4
Bermans Wy WLSDN NW10 116 B9
Bermer Rd WATN WD24 73 K5
Bermondsey St STHWK SE1 19 J3
Bermondsey Wall East
BERM/RHTH SE16 19 P2
Bermondsey Wall West
STHWK SE1 19 N1
Bermuda Rd TIL RM18 168 D8
Bernal Cl THMD SE28 143 N9
Bernard Ashley Dr CHARL SE7 161 N4
Bernard Av WEA W13 154 G2
Bernard Cassidy St
CAN/RD E16 141 L7
Bernard Gdns WIM/MER SW19 179 J8
Bernard Gv WAB EN9 62 G9
Bernard Rd ROMW/RG RM7 124 D5
SEVS/STOTM N15 119 N3
WLGTN SM6 222 B2
Bernards Cl BARK/HLT IG6 102 F8
Bernard St BMSBY WC1N 11 L2
GVE DA12 190 E2
STALW/RED AL3 38 C5
Bernays Cl STAN HA7 95 H7
Bernay's Gv BRXN/ST SW9 158 G10
Bernel Dr CROY/NA CR0 204 E10
Berne Rd THHTH CR7 203 J5
Berners Cl SL SL1 128 D9
Berners Dr STAL AL1 38 C9
WEA W13 134 F9
Berners Ms FITZ W1T 11 H4
Berners Pl FITZ W1T 11 H5
Berners Rd IS N1 6 C6
WDGN N22 99 H9
Berners St FITZ W1T 11 H4
Berners Wy BROX EN10 44 E9
Berner Ter WCHPL E1 * 13 N6
Berney Rd CROY/NA CR0 203 L7
Bernhardt Crs STJWD NW8 9 N1
Bernhart Cl EDGW HA8 95 P8
Bernice Cl RAIN RM13 145 K6
Bernwell Rd CHING E4 101 K4
Berridge Gn EDGW HA8 95 M8
Berridge Ms KIL/WHAMP NW6 117 K10
Berridge Rd NRWD SE19 181 L8
The Berries STALE/WH AL4 38 F2
Berriman Rd HOLWY N7 118 G8
Berrington Dr EHSLY KT24 234 G10
Berriton Rd RYLN/HDSTN HA2 113 N6
Berry Av WATN WD24 73 J2
Berrybank Cl CHING E4 101 H3
Berry Cl DAGE RM10 124 B10
HCH RM12 125 K10
RKW/CH/CXG WD3 91 L1
WCHMH N21 99 J2
Berry Cots POP/IOD E14 * 140 D8
Berry Ct HSLWW TW4 175 N1
Berrydale Rd YEAD UB4 133 M6
Berry Fld SLN SL2 129 P8
Berryfield Cl BMLY BR1 206 B1
Berry Field Cl WALTH E17 120 G2
Berry Field Pk AMS HP6 68 G3
Berryfield Rd WALW SE17 18 D7
Berrygrove La GSTN WD25 73 P5
Berry Grove La WATN WD24 73 M4
Berryhill ELTH/MOT SE9 162 E10
Berry Hl STAN HA7 95 J5
Berryhill Gdns ELTH/MOT SE9 162 E10
Berrylands BRYLDS KT5 199 M5
HART DA3 211 M6
ORP BR6 207 M10
RYNPK SW20 200 F3
Berrylands Rd BRYLDS KT5 199 L6
Berry La DUL SE21 181 L7
RGUW GU3 231 J10
RKW/CH/CXG WD3 70 G10
Berryman Cl BCTR RM8 123 M8
Berryman's La SYD SE26 182 C7
Berrymead HHNE HP2 36 A4
Berry Meade ASHTD KT21 237 L3
Berry Meade Cl ASHTD KT21 237 L3
Berrymead Gdns ACT W3 135 P10
Berrymede Rd CHSWK W4 156 A2
Berry Pl FSBYE EC1V 6 D10
Berryscroft Rd STA TW18 173 M10
Berry's Green Rd
BH/WHM TN16 244 E2
Berry's Hl BH/WHM TN16 244 E1
Berry's La BF/WBF KT14 215 N7
Berry St FSBYE EC1V 12 D2
Berry Wk ASHTD KT21 237 L5
Berry Wy EA W5 155 K2
RKW/CH/CXG WD3 91 L1
Bersham La GRAYS RM17 167 L3
Bertal Rd TOOT SW17 179 N7
Berther Rd EMPK RM11 125 M5
Berthold Ms WAB EN9 62 G9
Berthons Gdns WALTH E17 * 121 J3
Berthon St DEPT SE8 160 F6
Bertie Rd SYD SE26 182 C9
WLSDN NW10 136 D1
Bertram Rd EN EN1 79 P8
HDN NW4 116 D4
KUTN/CMB KT2 177 M10
Bertram St KTTN NW5 118 C8
Bertrand St LEW SE13 160 G9
Bertrand Wy THMD SE28 143 L9
Bert Rd THHTH CR7 203 K5
Bert Wy EN EN1 79 N8
Berwick Av SL SL1 128 G9
YEAD UB4 133 L8
Berwick Cl BEAC HP9 88 G10
CHES/WCR EN8 62 F10
STAN HA7 94 E7
WHTN TW2 175 P4
Berwick Crs BFN/LL DA15 185 H2
Berwick Gdns SUT SM1 201 M10
Berwick La CHONG CM5 66 F9
Berwick Pond Cl RAIN RM13 145 L4
Berwick Pond Rd RAIN RM13 145 M4
Berwick Rd BORE WD6 75 L4
CAN/RD E16 141 N8
RAIN RM13 145 L4
WDGN N22 99 J9
WELL DA16 163 L7
Berwick St SOHO/CST W1F 11 H6
Berwick Wy ORP BR6 207 K8
RSEV TN14 247 J7
Berwyn Av HSLW TW3 154 A7
Berwyn Rd HNHL SE24 181 J4
RCHPK/HAM TW10 155 N10
Beryl Av EHAM E6 142 B7
Beryl Rd HMSMTH W6 156 G4
Berystede KUTN/CMB KT2 177 N10
Besant Cl CRICK NW2 * 117 H8
Besant Pl EDUL SE22 159 N9
Besant Rd CRICK NW2 117 H9
Besant Wy WLSDN NW10 115 P10
Besley St STRHM/NOR SW16 180 D9
Bessant Dr RCH/KEW TW9 155 N6
Bessborough Gdns PIM SW1V 17 K7
Bessborough Pl PIM SW1V 17 J8
Bessborough Rd HRW HA1 114 C6
PUT/ROE SW15 178 D4
Bessborough St PIM SW1V 17 J7
Bessels Green Rd SEV TN13 246 E9
Bessels Meadow SEV TN13 246 E10
Bessemer Cl DTCH/LGLY SL3 150 C4
Bessemer Rd CMBW SE5 159 K8
WGCW AL8 23 H1
Bessie Lansbury Cl EHAM E6 142 D8
Bessingby Rd RSLP HA4 113 H7
Besson St NWCR SE14 160 B7
Bessy St BETH E2 * 140 B5
Bestobell Rd SL SL1 129 H8
Best Ter SWLY BR8 * 208 D5
Bestwood St DEPT SE8 160 C3
Beswick Ms KIL/WHAMP NW6 117 L10
Betam Rd HYS/HAR UB3 152 E1
Beta Rd CHOB/PIR GU24 213 L6
WOKS/MYFD GU22 232 E2
Beta Wy EGH TW20 194 F1
Betchworth Cl SUT SM1 221 N2
Betchworth Rd
GDMY/SEVK IG3 123 H7
Betchworth Wy CROY/NA CR0 225 H5
Betenson Av SEV TN13 246 G8
Betham Rd GFD/PVL UB6 134 C5
Bethany Cl HCH RM12 125 K7
Bethany Pl
WOKN/KNAP GU21 * 232 A4
Bethany Waye
EBED/NFELT TW14 174 F3
Bethecar Rd HRW HA1 114 D3
Bethel Cl HDN NW4 116 G3
Bethell Av CAN/RD E16 141 L6
IL IG1 122 D5
Bethel Rd SEV TN13 247 K9
WELL DA16 163 M9
Bethersden Cl BECK BR3 182 E10
Bethnal Green Rd BETH E2 13 M1
Bethune Av FBAR/BDGN N11 98 A5
Bethune Cl CRAWE RH10 284 E8
Bethune Rd STNW/STAM N16 119 L5
WLSDN NW10 136 A6
Bethwin Rd CMBW SE5 159 J6
Betjeman Cl CHESW EN7 61 P4
COUL/CHIP CR5 240 G3
HARP AL5 * 20 B2
RYLN/HDSTN HA2 113 P2
Betjeman Ct WDR/YW UB7 * 131 N10
Betjeman Gdns
RKW/CH/CXG WD3 70 G8
Betjeman Wy CHONG CM5 67 N2
HHW HP1 35 L4
Betley Ct WOT/HER KT12 197 J10
Betony Cl CROY/NA CR0 204 C8
Betoyne Av CHING E4 101 K5
Betsham Rd ERITH DA8 164 G6
MEO DA13 189 K8
Betstyle Rd FBAR/BDGN N11 98 C5
Betterton Dr SCUP DA14 185 P5
Betterton Rd RAIN RM13 144 F4
Betterton St LSQ/SEVD WC2H 11 L6
Bettles Cl UX/CGN UB8 131 M4
Bettons Pk SRTFD E15 141 K3
Bettridge Rd FUL/PGN SW6 157 J8
Betts Cl BECK BR3 204 D2
Betts La WAB EN9 45 P7
Betts Ms WALTH E17 120 E4
Betts Rd CAN/RD E16 141 N8
Betts St WAP E1W 140 A9
Betts Wy CRAWE RH10 283 N3
PGE/AN SE20 204 A2
SURB KT6 198 G8
Betula Cl PUR/KEN CR8 241 L1
Betula Ter CHES/WCR EN8 * 62 D8
Between Streets COB KT11 217 H10
Beulah Av THHTH CR7 * 203 K2
Beulah Cl EDGW HA8 95 N4
Beulah Crs THHTH CR7 203 K2
Beulah Gv CROY/NA CR0 203 K6
Beulah Hl NRWD SE19 181 J9
Beulah Rd EPP CM16 65 K5
HCH RM12 125 K8
SUT SM1 221 K1
THHTH CR7 203 K3
WALTH E17 120 G3
WIM/MER SW19 179 J10
Beulah Wk CTHM CR3 242 D6
Beult Rd DART DA1 165 H9
Bevan Av BARK IG11 143 K2
Bevan Cl HHS/BOV HP3 35 N8
Bevan Ct CROY/NA CR0 223 H2
Bevan Hl CSHM HP5 50 G5
Bevan House WATN WD24 73 L6
Bevan Pk EW KT17 220 C7
Bevan Pl SWLY BR8 208 G4
Bevan Rd ABYW SE2 163 L4
EBAR EN4 78 A8
Bevans Cl SWCM DA10 189 H2
Bevan St IS N1 6 F6
Bevan Wy HCH RM12 125 N8
Bev Callender Cl VX/NE SW8 158 C9
Bevenden St IS N1 7 H9
Beveridge Rd WLSDN NW10 136 B2
Beverley Av BFN/LL DA15 185 J3
HSLWW TW4 153 N10
RYNPK SW20 200 C1
Beverley Cl ADL/WDHM KT15 215 N2
BARN SW13 156 D8
BTSEA SW11 157 N10
CHSGTN KT9 219 H1
EMPK RM11 125 N5
EW KT17 220 F7
WCHMH N21 99 K2
WEY KT13 196 F9
Beverley Ct BROCKY SE4 160 E9
Beverley Crs WFD IG8 101 N9
Beverley Dr EDGW HA8 115 L1
Beverley Gdns BARN SW13 156 C9
CHESW EN7 61 N7
EMPK RM11 125 M5
GLDGN NW11 117 H5
STALE/WH AL4 39 J2
STAN HA7 94 F9
WBLY HA9 115 L6
WGCE AL7 23 M5
WPK KT4 200 D8
Beverley Hts REIG RH2 257 L8
Beverley La KUTN/CMB KT2 178 B10
Beverley Ms CRAWE RH10 284 B8
Beverley Rd BARN SW13 156 C9
BXLYHN DA7 164 D8
CHING E4 101 J7
CHSWK W4 156 C4
CTHM CR3 241 M3
DAGW RM9 123 P9
EHAM E6 142 A5
HAYES BR2 206 B9
KUT/HW KT1 199 H1
MTCM CR4 202 E4
NWDGN UB2 153 M3
NWMAL KT3 200 D4
PGE/AN SE20 204 A2
RSLP HA4 113 J7
SUN TW16 196 C1
WPK KT4 200 F9
Beverley Wy KUTN/CMB KT2 200 C1
RYNPK SW20 200 C1
Beverley Way (Kingston
By-Pass) NWMAL KT3 200 C2
Beverly Cl BROX EN10 44 D7
Beversbrook Rd ARCH N19 118 E8
Beverstone Rd
BRXS/STRHM SW2 180 G1
THHTH CR7 203 H4
Beverston Ms MBLAR W1H 10 A4
Bevill Allen Cl TOOT SW17 180 A9
Bevill Cl SNWD SE25 203 P3
Bevin Cl BERM/RHTH SE16 140 D10
Bevington Rd BECK BR3 204 G2
NKENS W10 8 B3
Bevington St
BERM/RHTH SE16 19 P2
Bevin Rd YEAD UB4 133 H5
Bevin Sq TOOT SW17 180 A6
Bevin Wy FSBYW WC1X 6 A8
Bevis Cl RDART DA2 188 B3
Bevis Marks HDTCH EC3A 13 K5
Bewbush Dr CRAWW RH11 283 J10
Bewcastle Gdns ENC/FH EN2 78 F8
Bewdley Cl HARP AL5 20 C5
Bewdley St IS N1 6 A3
Bewick Ms PECK SE15 160 A6
Bewick St VX/NE SW8 158 C8
Bewley Cl CHES/WCR EN8 62 C7
Bewley St WCHPL E1 140 A9
WIM/MER SW19 179 M9
Bewlys Rd WNWD SE27 181 J8
Bexhill Cl FELT TW13 175 M5
Bexhill Dr GRAYS RM17 167 K5
Bexhill Rd BROCKY SE4 182 E2
FBAR/BDGN N11 98 E6
MORT/ESHN SW14 155 P9
Bexley Gdns CHDH RM6 123 L3
ED N9 99 L4
Bexley High St BXLY DA5 186 B3
Bexley La SCUP DA14 185 M5
SCUP DA14 185 M7
ELTH/MOT SE9 184 G1
Bexley Rd ELTH/MOT SE9 184 D2
ERITH DA8 164 D6
ERITH DA8 * 164 G4
Bexley St WDSR SL4 148 G7
Beyers Gdns HOD EN11 26 F10
Beyers Prospect HOD EN11 26 F10
Beyers Ride HOD EN11 26 F10
Beynon Rd CAR SM5 222 A2
Bianca Rd PECK SE15 19 M10
Bibsworth Rd FNCH N3 97 J10
Bibury Cl PECK SE15 19 K10
Bicester Rd RCH/KEW TW9 155 M9
Bickenhall St MHST W1U 10 B3
Bickersteth Rd TOOT SW17 180 A9
Bickerton Rd ARCH N19 118 C7
Bickles Yd STHWK SE1 19 K2
Bickley Crs BMLY BR1 206 B4
Bickley Park Rd BMLY BR1 206 C3
Bickley Rd BMLY BR1 206 A2
LEY E10 120 G5
Bickley St TOOT SW17 179 P8
Bicknell Cl GU GU1 250 A9
Bicknell Rd CMBW SE5 159 K9
Bickney Wy LHD/OX KT22 236 B8
Bicknoller Cl BELMT SM2 221 L6
Bicknoller Rd EN EN1 79 N5
Bicknor Rd ORP BR6 207 H7
Bidborough Cl HAYES BR2 205 L5
Bidborough St STPAN WC1H 5 L10
Biddenden Wy ELTH/MOT SE9 184 D7
Biddenham Turn GSTN WD25 73 K1
Bidder St CAN/RD E16 141 K7
Biddestone Rd HOLWY N7 118 G9
Biddles Cl SL SL1 128 D10
Biddulph Rd MV/WKIL W9 3 H10
SAND/SEL CR2 223 K5
Bideford Av GFD/PVL UB6 134 G5
Bideford Cl EDGW HA8 95 M9
FELT TW13 175 N6
HARH RM3 105 K9
Bideford Gdns EN EN1 99 M1
Bideford Rd BMLY BR1 183 L6
PEND EN3 80 E4
RSLP HA4 113 J8
WELL DA16 163 L6
Bideford Sp SLN SL2 128 G5
Bidhams Crs
KWD/TDW/WH KT20 238 F7
Bidwell Gdns FBAR/BDGN N11 98 D9
Bidwell St PECK SE15 * 160 A7
The Bield REIG RH2 275 K2
Big Common La REDH RH1 259 J9
Biggerstaff Rd SRTFD E15 141 H3
Biggerstaff St FSBYPK N4 119 H7
Biggin Av MTCM CR4 202 A1
Biggin Cl CRAWW RH11 283 M9
Biggin Hl NRWD SE19 181 J10
Biggin La CDW/CHF RM16 168 E5
Biggin Wy NRWD SE19 181 J10

| Street | Area | Page | Grid |
|---|---|---|---|
| Bigginwood Rd STRHM/NOR SW16 | | 181 | J10 |
| Biggs Grove Rd CHESW EN7 | | 61 | M3 |
| Biggs Rw PUT/ROE SW15 | | 156 | G9 |
| Big Hl CLPT E5 | | 120 | A6 |
| Bigland St WCHPL E1 | | 140 | A8 |
| Bignell Rd WOOL/PLUM SE18 | | 162 | K4 |
| Bignells Cnr POTB/CUF EN6 | | 58 | E10 |
| Bignold Rd FSTGT E7 | | 121 | M9 |
| Bigwood Rd GLDGN NW11 | | 117 | G9 |
| Biko Cl UX/CGN UB8 | | 131 | M8 |
| Bilberry Cl CRAWW RH11 | | 283 | L10 |
| Billesden Rd CHOB/PIR GU24 | | 230 | B7 |
| Billet Cl BARK IG11 | | 33 | M3 |
| DTCH/LGLY SL3 | | | |
| EMPK RM11 | | 125 | L6 |
| IVER SL0 | | 130 | E5 |
| Billet Rd CHDH RM6 | | 123 | M1 |
| WALTH E17 | | 100 | C9 |
| Billets Hart Cl HNWL W7 | | 154 | D11 |
| Billingford Cl BROCKY SE4 | | 160 | C10 |
| Billing Pl WBPTN SW10 | | 157 | L6 |
| Billing Rd WBPTN SW10 | | 157 | L6 |
| Billings HART DA3 | | 211 | L6 |
| Billing St DAGW RM9 | | 143 | M2 |
| Billington Hl CROY/NA CRO | | 203 | L9 |
| Billington Rd NWCR SE14 | | 160 | C6 |
| Billinton Dr CRAWE RH10 | | 284 | F10 |
| Billiter Sq FENCHST EC3M | | 13 | K6 |
| Billiter St FENCHST EC3M | | 13 | K6 |
| Bill Nicholson Wy TOTM N17 | | 99 | M8 |
| Billockby Cl CHSGTN KT9 | | 219 | L3 |
| Bilson St POP/IOD E14 | | 161 | H3 |
| Billy Lows La POTB/CUF EN6 | | 59 | G3 |
| Bilton Cl BERK HP4 | | 165 | H6 |
| GFD/PVL UB6 | | 134 | C3 |
| Bilton Wy HYS/HAR UB3 | | 153 | J1 |
| PEND EN3 | | 80 | E5 |
| Bina Gdns ECT SW5 | | 15 | A5 |
| Bincote Rd ENC/FH EN2 | | 78 | C7 |
| Binden Rd SHB W12 | | 156 | C2 |
| Binfield Rd BF/WBF KT14 | | 215 | P8 |
| CLAP SW4 | | 158 | F7 |
| SAND/SEL CR2 | | 223 | N2 |
| Bingfield St IS N1 | | 5 | M5 |
| Bingham Cl HHW HP1 | | 35 | J4 |
| SOCK/AV RM15 | | 146 | G8 |
| Bingham Dr IS N1 | | 6 | D3 |
| Bingham Dr STA TW18 | | 173 | N10 |
| WOKN/KNAP GU21 | | 231 | G4 |
| Bingham Pl CAMTN NW1 | | 10 | C2 |
| MHST W1U | | 10 | C2 |
| Bingham Rd CROY/NA CRO | | 203 | P8 |
| IS N1 | | 6 | C1 |
| Bingley Rd CAN/RD E16 | | 141 | L9 |
| GFD/PVL UB6 | | 134 | B6 |
| HOD EN11 | | 45 | H5 |
| SUN TW16 | | 175 | H10 |
| Binney Ct CRAWE RH10 | | 284 | F4 |
| Binney St MYFR/PKLN W1K | | 10 | C7 |
| Binns Rd CHSWK W4 | | 156 | B4 |
| Binscombe CODL GU7 | | 267 | J9 |
| Binscombe Crs GODL GU7 | | 267 | J8 |
| Binscombe La GODL GU7 | | 267 | J9 |
| Binsey Wk ABYW SE2 | | 163 | M1 |
| Binstead Ct CRAWW RH11 | | 283 | M7 |
| YEAD UB4 | | 133 | M7 |
| Binyon Crs STAN HA7 | | 94 | E6 |
| Birbetts Rd ELTH/MOT SE9 | | 184 | C5 |
| Birchall La HERT/WAT SG14 | | 23 | J1 |
| Birchall Rd WCCE AL7 | | 23 | M6 |
| Birchanger Rd SNWD SE25 | | 203 | L5 |
| Birch Av CTHM CR3 | | 241 | L10 |
| LHD/OX KT22 | | 236 | E6 |
| PLMGR N13 | | 99 | K4 |
| WDR/YW UB7 | | 132 | A8 |
| Birch Cir GODL GU7 | | 167 | L9 |
| Birch Cl ADL/WDHM KT15 | | 215 | N5 |
| AMS HP6 | | 69 | K3 |
| BKHH IG9 | | 102 | A4 |
| BNSTD SM7 | | 221 | H10 |
| BTFD TW8 | | 154 | C6 |
| CAN/RD E16 | | 141 | M7 |
| EYN DA4 | | 209 | L10 |
| HART DA3 | | 211 | P2 |
| HSLW TW3 | | 154 | C9 |
| IVER SL0 | | 130 | C4 |
| ROMW/RG RM7 | | 124 | C1 |
| RPLY/SEND GU23 | | 251 | J1 |
| SEV TN13 | | 247 | J9 |
| SOCK/AV RM15 | | 147 | J6 |
| TEDD TW11 | | 176 | B7 |
| WOKN/KNAP GU21 | | 231 | G3 |
| Birch Copse LCOL/BKTW AL2 | | 55 | M6 |
| Birch Ct WLGTN SM6 | | 222 | C1 |
| Birch Crs EMPK RM11 | | 125 | M2 |
| HGDN/ICK UB10 | | 112 | C6 |
| SOCK/AV RM15 | | 147 | J5 |
| Birchcroft Cl CTHM CR3 | | 259 | L4 |
| Birchdale CBF/WBF KT14 | | 215 | L10 |
| Birchdale Cl BF/WBF KT14 | | 215 | K8 |
| Birchdale Gdns CHDH RM6 | | 123 | N5 |
| Birchdale Rd FSTGT E7 | | 121 | P10 |
| Birchdene Dr THMD SE28 | | 143 | K10 |
| Birch Dr HAT AL10 | | 40 | D5 |
| RKW/CH/CXG WD3 | | 90 | G6 |
| Birchen Cl CDALE/KGS NW9 | | 116 | A7 |
| Birchend Cl SAND/SEL CR2 | | 223 | L3 |
| Birchen Gv CDALE/KGS NW9 | | 116 | A7 |
| Bircherley Ct | | | |
| HERT/WAT SG14 * | | 25 | L5 |
| Bircherley St HERT/WAT SG14 | | 25 | L5 |
| Birches Cl EPSOM KT18 | | 238 | B1 |
| MTCM CR4 | | 202 | A3 |
| PIN HA5 | | 113 | M3 |
| The Birches BUSH WD23 | | 74 | B9 |
| CHARL SE7 * | | 161 | N5 |
| CHBW SE27 | | 159 | M9 |
| CRAWE RH10 | | 284 | F8 |
| EHSLY KT24 | | 252 | F2 |
| EPP CM16 | | 66 | C2 |
| HHS/BOV HP3 | | 35 | J9 |
| HSLWW TW4 | | 175 | M3 |
| ORP BR6 | | 226 | D1 |
| RBRW/HUT CM13 | | 107 | K4 |
| SWLY BR8 | | 208 | F2 |
| WAB EN9 | | 63 | L10 |
| WCHMH N21 | | 98 | G5 |
| WOKS/MYFD GU22 | | 232 | C4 |
| Birchfield CDW/CHF RM16 | | 167 | J1 |
| Birchfield Cl ADL/WDHM KT15 | | 215 | L1 |
| COUL/CHIP CR5 | | 240 | G2 |
| Birchfield Est HORL RH6 * | | 282 | C11 |
| Birchfield Gv EW KT17 | | 220 | H6 |
| Birchfield St POP/IOD E14 | | 62 | A5 |
| Birch Gdns AMSS HP7 | | 69 | K5 |
| Birchgate Ms | | 124 | D4 |
| KWD/TDW/WH KT20 * | | 238 | F7 |
| Birch Gn HHW HP1 | | 35 | J5 |
| STA TW18 | | 173 | J7 |
| Birch Gv ACT W3 | | 135 | M10 |
| COB KT11 | | 217 | K10 |
| GU GU1 * | | 249 | P7 |
| KWD/TDW/WH KT20 | | 239 | H10 |
| LEE/GVPK SE12 | | 183 | L3 |
| POTB/CUF EN6 | | 59 | N2 |
| SHPTN TW17 | | 196 | F2 |
| SLN SL2 | | 128 | C2 |
| WAN E11 | | 121 | K8 |
| WDSR SL4 | | 148 | C3 |
| WOKS/MYFD GU22 | | 232 | C1 |
| Birch HI CROY/NA CRO | | 224 | C2 |
| Birchin Cross Rd | | | |
| BGR/WK TN15 | | 229 | P10 |
| RSEV TN14 | | 247 | M1 |
| Birchington Rd BXLYHN DA7 | | 165 | K6 |
| Birchington Rd BRYLDS KT5 | | 199 | L7 |
| CEND/HSY/T N8 | | 118 | E6 |
| KIL/WHAMP NW6 | | 2 | B1 |
| WDSR SL4 | | 148 | B3 |
| Birchin La BANK EC3V | | 13 | H6 |

| Street | Area | Page | Grid |
|---|---|---|---|
| Birchlands Av BAL SW12 | | 180 | A3 |
| Birchlea Cl GDALE/PIR GU24 | | 212 | C10 |
| HHS/BOV HP3 | | 52 | H9 |
| PUR/KEN CR8 | | 222 | F7 |
| Birch Lea CRAWE RH10 | | 284 | E4 |
| Birch Levs HHNE HP2 | | 36 | D1 |
| Birchmead BAL SW12 | | 80 | B6 |
| Birchmead WAT WD17 | | 72 | G4 |
| Birchmead Av PIN HA5 | | 113 | K2 |
| Birchmead Cl | | | |
| STALW/RED AL3 * | | 38 | C3 |
| Birchmere Rw BKHTH/KID SE3 | | 161 | H3 |
| Birchmore Wk HBRY N5 | | 119 | K8 |
| Birch Pk KTN/HRWW/WS HA3 | | 94 | B8 |
| Birch Pl PDART DA2 | | 188 | D2 |
| Birch Platt CHOB/PIR GU24 | | 212 | C9 |
| Birch Rd BERK HP4 | | 33 | J2 |
| BFOR | | 212 | D3 |
| FELT TW13 | | 175 | L8 |
| GODL GU7 | | 267 | L9 |
| ROMW/RG RM7 | | 124 | C1 |
| Birch Tree Av HAYES BR2 | | 206 | D7 |
| Birch Tree Gv CSHM HP5 | | 51 | N6 |
| Birch Tree Rd WWKM BR4 | | 225 | L2 |
| Birch Tree Wk WAT WD17 | | 72 | F1 |
| Birch V COB KT11 | | 217 | P9 |
| Birch Wk BORE WD6 | | 75 | M5 |
| MTCM CR4 | | 202 | C1 |
| Birchway HAT AL10 | | 40 | D2 |
| HYS/HAR UB3 | | 133 | H10 |
| Birchway HAT AL10 | | 40 | D2 |
| FELT TW13 | | | |
| GODL GU7 | | 267 | L9 |
| ROMW/RG RM7 | | 124 | C1 |
| Birch Wy LCOL/BKTW AL2 | | 57 | J3 |
| Birchway REDH RH1 | | 276 | C2 |
| Birch Wy WARL CR6 | | 242 | D4 |
| Birchwood RAD WD7 | | 57 | M10 |
| Birchwood Av BECK BR3 | | 204 | E4 |
| HAT AL10 | | 40 | D2 |
| MUSWH N10 | | 118 | B1 |
| SCUP DA14 | | 185 | L6 |
| WLGTN SM6 | | 202 | B10 |
| Birchwood Cl CRAWE RH10 | | 284 | D10 |
| HAT AL10 | | 40 | D2 |
| HORL RH6 | | 280 | C3 |
| MRDN SM4 | | 201 | L4 |
| Birchwood Dr BF/WBF KT14 | | 215 | K8 |
| HAMP NW3 | | 117 | L8 |
| LTWR GU18 | | 212 | B6 |
| Birchwood Gv HPTN TW12 | | 175 | P9 |
| Birchwood La CTHM CR3 | | 259 | J1 |
| ESH/CLAY KT10 | | 218 | C5 |
| RSEV TN14 | | 246 | A1 |
| Birchwood Park Av SWLY BR8 | | 208 | F3 |
| Birchwood Rd BF/WBF KT14 | | 215 | K8 |
| RDART DA2 | | 187 | P4 |
| STMC/STPC BR5 | | 206 | C4 |
| SWLY BR8 | | 186 | D10 |
| TOOT SW17 | | 180 | C8 |
| Birchwood Ter SWLY BR8 * | | 208 | D1 |
| Birchwood Wy | | | |
| LCOL/BKTW AL2 | | 56 | A4 |
| Birdbrook Cl DAGE RM10 | | 144 | D2 |
| RBRW/HUT CM13 | | 87 | N10 |
| Birdbrook Rd BKHTH/KID SE3 | | 161 | M3 |
| Birdcage Wk WESTW SW1E | | 17 | H2 |
| Birdcroft Rd WGCW AL8 | | 22 | G6 |
| Birdham Cl BMLY BR1 | | 206 | B5 |
| CRAWW RH11 | | 283 | L5 |
| Bird House La ORP BR6 | | 226 | D11 |
| Birdhurst Av SAND/SEL CR2 | | 223 | L1 |
| Birdhurst Gdns SAND/SEL CR2 | | 223 | L1 |
| Birdhurst Ri SAND/SEL CR2 | | 223 | M2 |
| Birdhurst Rd SAND/SEL CR2 | | 223 | M2 |
| WIM/MER SW19 | | 179 | P9 |
| Birdie Wy HERT/BAY SG13 | | 26 | A4 |
| Bird in Bush Rd PECK SE15 | | 159 | P6 |
| Bird-in-Hand La BMLY BR1 | | 206 | A2 |
| Bird-in-Hand Ms FSTH SE23 | | 182 | B5 |
| Bird-in-Hand Pas FSTH SE23 | | 182 | B5 |
| Bird La RBRW/HUT CM13 | | 107 | H10 |
| UPMR RM14 | | 126 | C3 |
| Birds Cl WGCE AL7 | | 23 | L7 |
| Birds Farm Av CRW RM5 | | 104 | C9 |
| Birdsfield La BOW E3 | | 129 | N8 |
| Birds Cv WOKN/KNAP GU21 | | 230 | G4 |
| Birds Hill Dr LHD/OX KT22 | | 218 | C2 |
| Birds Hill Ri LHD/OX KT22 | | 218 | C3 |
| Birds Hill Rd LHD/OX KT22 | | 218 | C3 |
| Bird St MHST W1U | | 10 | D6 |
| Birdswood Dr | | | |
| WOKN/KNAP GU21 | | 231 | K5 |
| Bird Wk WHTN TW2 | | 175 | N4 |
| Birdwood Av DART DA1 | | 165 | P8 |
| LEW SE13 | | 183 | L5 |
| Birdwood Cl SAND/SEL CR2 | | 224 | C7 |
| TEDD TW11 | | 176 | D7 |
| Birkbeck Av ACT W3 | | 135 | P9 |
| GFD/PVL UB6 | | 134 | B3 |
| Birkbeck Gdns WFD IG8 | | 89 | K11 |
| Birkbeck HI DUL SE21 | | 181 | J5 |
| Birkbeck Ms ACT W3 * | | 136 | A9 |
| HACK E8 | | 119 | N10 |
| Birkbeck Pl DUL SE21 | | 181 | J4 |
| Birkbeck Rd ACT W3 | | 136 | B9 |
| BECK BR3 | | 204 | B3 |
| CEND/HSY/T N8 | | 117 | N1 |
| EA W5 | | 155 | H3 |
| ENC/FH EN2 | | 79 | L4 |
| GNTH/NBYPK IG2 | | 122 | G5 |
| HACK E8 | | 119 | N10 |
| MLHL NW7 | | 96 | C6 |
| NFNCH/WDSPK N12 | | 97 | H3 |
| ROMW/RG RM7 | | 124 | C6 |
| SCUP DA14 | | 185 | K6 |
| TOTM N17 | | 99 | L8 |
| WIM/MER SW19 | | 179 | L8 |
| Birkbeck St BETH E2 | | 140 | A5 |
| Birkbeck Wy ACT W3 * | | 134 | C3 |
| Birkdale Av HARH RM3 | | 105 | P3 |
| PIN HA5 | | 113 | N1 |
| Birkdale Cl BERM/RHTH SE16 * | | 160 | A4 |
| ORP BR6 | | 206 | G7 |
| THMD SE28 | | 143 | P4 |
| Birkdale Dr CRAWW RH11 | | 282 | C11 |
| Birkdale Gdns CROY/NA CRO | | 224 | C1 |
| OXHEY WD19 | | 112 | B3 |
| Birkdale Rd ABYW SE2 | | 163 | K5 |
| EA W5 | | 135 | K6 |
| Birkenhead Av | | | |
| KUTN/CMB KT2 | | 199 | L2 |
| Birkenhead St CAMTN NW1 | | 5 | M9 |
| Birkett Wy CSTG HP8 | | 70 | A2 |
| Birkhall Rd CAT SE6 | | 183 | J4 |
| Birkheads Rd REIG RH2 | | 257 | N9 |
| Birklands La LCOL/BKTW AL2 | | 38 | C10 |
| Birklands Pk STAL AL1 | | 38 | C10 |
| Birkwood Cl BAL SW12 | | 180 | G1 |
| Birley Rd SL SL1 | | 129 | J8 |
| TRDG/WHET N20 | | 97 | M3 |
| Birley St BTSEA SW11 | | 158 | F8 |
| Birling Rd ERITH DA8 | | 164 | E6 |
| Birnam Rd FSBYPK N4 | | 118 | C7 |
| Birnham Cl RPLY/SEND GU23 | | 233 | K10 |
| Birse Crs WLSDN NW10 | | 116 | E9 |
| Birstal Gn OXHEY WD19 | | 93 | L5 |
| Birstal Rd SEVS/STOTM N15 | | 119 | P7 |
| Birtchnell Cl BERK HP4 | | 33 | M4 |
| Biscay Rd HMSMTH W6 | | 156 | G4 |
| Biscoe Cl HEST TW5 | | 153 | P5 |
| Biscoe Wy LEW SE13 * | | 161 | L11 |
| Bisenden Rd CROY/NA CRO | | 203 | M9 |
| Bisham Cl CAR SM5 | | 202 | A7 |
| CRAWE RH10 | | 284 | H9 |
| Bisham Gdns HGT N6 | | 118 | A6 |
| Bishop Butt Cl ORP BR6 | | 207 | H10 |
| Bishop Duppas Pk | | | |
| SHPTN TW17 | | 196 | F6 |
| Bishop Fox Wy | | | |
| E/WMO/HCT KT8 | | 197 | N4 |
| Bishop Ken Rd | | | |
| KTN/HRWW/WS HA3 | | 94 | E10 |

| Street | Area | Page | Grid |
|---|---|---|---|
| Bishop King's Rd WKENS W14 | | 14 | B5 |
| Bishop Rd STHGT/OAK N14 | | 98 | C1 |
| Bishops Av BMLY BR1 | | 205 | P3 |
| BORE WD6 | | 95 | L1 |
| CHDH RM6 | | 123 | M4 |
| NTHWD HA6 | | 92 | F5 |
| PLSTW E13 | | 141 | N3 |
| Bishop's Av FUL/PGN SW6 | | 156 | G8 |
| The Bishops Av EFNCH N2 | | 117 | N4 |
| Bishop's Bridge Rd | | | |
| BAY/PAD W2 | | 9 | H5 |
| Bishops Cl BAR EN5 | | 76 | C10 |
| CHSWK W4 | | 155 | P4 |
| ELTH/MOT SE9 | | 184 | F5 |
| EN EN1 | | 80 | A6 |
| HAT AL10 | | 40 | C1 |
| RCHPK/HAM TW10 | | 177 | H6 |
| SUT SM1 | | 201 | K10 |
| Bishop's Cl ARCH N19 | | 118 | C10 |
| COUL/CHIP CR5 | | 241 | H4 |
| HGDN/ICK UB10 | | 132 | B4 |
| STALW/RED AL3 | | 38 | F2 |
| WALTH E17 | | 120 | C2 |
| Bishops Ct CHES/WCR EN8 * | | 62 | A1 |
| RDART DA2 | | 188 | D1 |
| Bishops Dr FELT TW13 | | 153 | L9 |
| NTHLT UB5 | | 133 | H11 |
| Bishops Farm Cl WDSR SL4 | | 148 | A8 |
| Bishopsfield HLWS CM18 | | 47 | M3 |
| Bishopsford Rd MRDN SM4 | | 201 | M7 |
| Bishopsgate LVPST EC2M | | 13 | J3 |
| Bishopsgate Ar LVPST EC2M | | 13 | J4 |
| Bishopsgate EGH TW20 | | 171 | M6 |
| Bishops Gn BMLY BR1 * | | 205 | P1 |
| Bishops Gv BFOR GU20 | | 212 | B3 |
| EFNCH N2 | | 117 | N4 |
| HPTN TW12 | | 175 | H8 |
| Bishop's Hall KUT/HW KT1 | | 199 | J2 |
| Bishop's Hall Rd BRWN CM15 | | 86 | G10 |
| Bishops HI WOT/HER KT12 | | 197 | N4 |
| Bishops Md CMBW SE5 * | | 159 | K6 |
| HHW HP1 | | 35 | J4 |
| Bishopsmead Cl EHSLY KT24 | | 252 | C4 |
| HOR/WEW KT19 | | 220 | A6 |
| Bishopsmead Pde EHSLY KT24 * | | 252 | C5 |
| Bishops Orch SLN SL2 | | 128 | C5 |
| Bishops Park Rd | | | |
| STRHM/NOR SW16 | | 202 | F1 |
| Bishop's Park Rd FUL/PGN SW6 | | 156 | C8 |
| Bishop's Pl SUT SM1 | | 221 | M2 |
| Bishop Sq HAT AL10 | | 40 | B3 |
| Bishops Ri HAT AL10 | | 40 | B3 |
| Bishops Rd CROY/NA CRO | | 203 | J7 |
| FUL/PGN SW6 | | 157 | J7 |
| HGT N6 | | 99 | P11 |
| HNWL W7 | | 154 | D1 |
| HYS/HAR UB3 | | 133 | H8 |
| Bishop's Ter LBTH SE11 | | 18 | E6 |
| Bishopsthorpe Rd SYD SE26 | | 182 | E7 |
| Bishop St IS N1 | | 6 | E2 |
| Bishops Wk BRWN CM15 | | 107 | L5 |
| CHST BR7 | | 206 | F1 |
| CROY/NA CRO | | 224 | C2 |
| Bishop's Wy BETH E2 | | 140 | B4 |
| Bishops Wd | | | |
| WOKN/KNAP GU21 | | 231 | L3 |
| Bishopswood Rd HGT N6 | | 118 | A5 |
| Biskra WATW WD18 * | | 73 | H5 |
| Bisley Cl CHES/WCR EN8 | | 62 | C9 |
| WPK KT4 | | 200 | H11 |
| Bispham Rd WLSDN NW10 | | 135 | L3 |
| Bisson Rd SRTFD E15 | | 141 | H4 |
| Bittacy Cl MLHL NW7 | | 96 | F4 |
| Bittacy HI MLHL NW7 | | 96 | F4 |
| Bittacy Park Av MLHL NW7 | | 96 | F4 |
| Bittacy Rd MLHL NW7 | | 96 | G4 |
| Bittams La CHERT KT16 | | 214 | C1 |
| Bittern Cl CHESW EN7 | | 61 | J1 |
| CRAWW RH11 | | 282 | G8 |
| HHS/BOV HP3 | | 35 | J9 |
| YEAD UB4 | | 133 | L7 |
| Bitterne Dr WOKN/KNAP GU21 | | 231 | L5 |
| Bittern Pl WDGN N22 | | 98 | D10 |
| Bittern St STHWK SE1 | | 18 | E2 |
| The Bit AMSS HP7 * | | 68 | E10 |
| Bittoms Ct KUT/HW KT1 * | | 199 | J3 |
| Bixley Cl NWDGN UB2 | | 153 | N3 |
| Black Acre Cl AMSS HP7 | | 69 | K5 |
| Blackacre Rd EPP CM16 | | 83 | H3 |
| Blackbird Cl SDTCH EC2A | | 135 | H8 |
| Blackberry Cl GU GU1 * | | 249 | N7 |
| SHPTN TW17 | | 196 | F4 |
| Blackberry Farm Cl HEST TW5 | | 153 | M6 |
| Blackberry Fld | | | |
| STMC/STPC BR5 | | 207 | K1 |
| Blackbird HI WBLY HA9 | | 115 | P7 |
| Blackbird La GSTN WD25 | | 56 | B10 |
| Blackbird Yd BETH E2 | | 7 | M9 |
| Blackborne Rd DAGE RM10 | | 144 | C4 |
| Blackborough Cl REIG RH2 | | 257 | N10 |
| Blackborough Rd REIG RH2 | | 257 | N10 |
| Black Boy La | | | |
| SEVS/STOTM N15 | | 119 | K3 |
| Black Boy Wd LCOL/BKTW AL2 | | 55 | N7 |
| Blackbridge Rd | | | |
| WOKS/MYFD GU22 | | 232 | A6 |
| Blackbrook La HAYES BR2 | | 206 | D5 |
| Blackbrook Rd RDKG RH5 | | 273 | K7 |
| Blackburne's Ms | | | |
| MYFR/PKLN W1K | | 10 | C7 |
| Blackburn Rd | | | |
| KIL/WHAMP NW6 | | 2 | C2 |
| The Blackburn GT/LBKH KT23 | | 235 | N10 |
| Blackbury Cl POTB/CUF EN6 | | 59 | M2 |
| Blackbush Av CHDH RM6 | | 123 | N3 |
| Blackbush Spring HLW CM20 | | 29 | K10 |
| Blackcap Cl CRAWW RH11 | | 283 | M9 |
| Black Cut STAL AL1 | | 38 | D3 |
| Blackdale CHESW EN7 | | 61 | P3 |
| Black Ditch Rd WAB EN9 | | 81 | H2 |
| Black Dog Wk CRAWE RH10 | | 283 | P5 |
| Blackdown Av | | | |
| WOKS/MYFD GU22 | | 233 | H1 |
| Blackdown Cl EFNCH N2 | | 97 | M10 |
| WOKS/MYFD GU22 | | 232 | F7 |
| Blackdown Ter | | | |
| WOOL/PLUM SE18 * | | 162 | C7 |
| Black Eagle Cl BH/WHM TN16 | | 262 | F6 |
| Blackenham Rd TOOT SW17 | | 180 | F7 |
| Blackett Cl STA TW18 | | 195 | H2 |
| Blackett St CRA TN19 | | 156 | H4 |
| Blacketts Wood Dr | | | |
| RKW/CH/CXG WD3 | | 70 | G8 |
| Black Fan Cl ENC/FH EN2 | | 79 | K5 |
| Black Fan Rd WGCE AL7 | | 23 | M3 |
| Blackfen Pde BXLY DA15 * | | 185 | K2 |
| Blackfen Rd BFN/LL DA15 | | 185 | J1 |
| Blackford Rd CRAWE RH10 | | 284 | B8 |
| Blackford Rd OXHEY WD19 | | 93 | L6 |
| Blackfriars Br STHWK SE1 | | 12 | C7 |
| Black Friars La BLKFR EC4V | | 12 | D5 |
| Blackfriars Pas BLKFR EC4V | | 12 | C7 |
| Blackfriars U/P BLKFR EC4V | | 12 | C7 |
| Black Green Wood Cl | | | |
| LCOL/BKTW AL2 | | 56 | A3 |
| Blackhall La RSEV TN14 | | 247 | N9 |
| Blackheath Av CRAWE RH10 | | 285 | H4 |
| Blackheath Av GNWCH SE10 | | 161 | J1 |
| Blackheath Gv BKHTH/KID SE3 | | 161 | J3 |
| Blackheath La RGUE GU4 | | 269 | H11 |
| SHGR GU5 | | 268 | D4 |

| Street | Area | Page | Grid |
|---|---|---|---|
| Blackheath Pk BKHTH/KID SE3 | | 161 | L9 |
| Blackheath Ri LEW SE13 | | 161 | H8 |
| Blackheath Rd GNWCH SE10 | | 160 | G1 |
| Blackheath V BKHTH/KID SE3 | | 161 | J3 |
| Blackhills ESH/CLAY KT10 | | 217 | N5 |
| Black Horse Av CSHM HP5 | | 51 | L5 |
| Black Horse Cl WDSR SL4 | | 148 | C8 |
| Blackhorse Crs AMS HP6 | | 69 | K6 |
| Blackhorse La CROY/NA CRO | | 203 | P7 |
| EPP CM16 | | 66 | E1 |
| KWD/TDW/WH KT20 | | 257 | L5 |
| POTB/CUF EN6 | | 58 | A6 |
| WALTH E17 | | 120 | C1 |
| Black Horse Pde PIN HA5 * | | 113 | J3 |
| Black Horse Rd SCUP DA14 | | 185 | K7 |
| Blackhorse Rd DEPT SE8 | | 160 | D5 |
| UX/CGN UB8 | | 131 | L3 |
| WALTH E17 | | 119 | P1 |
| Blackhorse Rd WALTH E17 | | 120 | C2 |
| WOKN/KNAP GU21 | | 231 | J6 |
| Blacklands Dr YEAD UB4 | | 132 | D6 |
| Blacklands Meadow | | | |
| REDH RH1 | | 258 | F9 |
| Blacklands Rd CAT SE6 | | 183 | H7 |
| Blacklands Ter CHEL SW3 | | 16 | F6 |
| Blackley Cl WATT WD17 | | 72 | G3 |
| Black Lion Ct HLWE CM17 * | | 29 | P7 |
| Black Lion Ga BAY/PAD W2 | | 9 | H8 |
| Black Lion HI HAMP NW3 | | 57 | K8 |
| Black Lion La HMSMTH W6 | | 156 | D3 |
| Blackman's La WARL CR6 | | 225 | K10 |
| Blackmans Yd WCHPL E1 * | | 13 | M1 |
| Blackmead SEV TN13 | | 246 | F7 |
| Blackmoor Av WLSDN NW10 | | 135 | N2 |
| Blackmoor Rd BKHH IG9 | | 102 | B1 |
| BRWN CM15 | | 86 | D4 |
| Blackmore Av STHL UB1 | | 134 | C10 |
| Blackmore Cl SAB EN9 | | 63 | M9 |
| Blackmore Crs | | | |
| WOKN/KNAP GU21 | | 214 | F10 |
| Blackmore Rd WLSDN NW10 | | 135 | N2 |
| Blackmore Rd BKHH IG9 | | 102 | B1 |
| BRWN CM15 | | 86 | D4 |
| GRAYS RM17 | | 167 | P4 |
| Blackmore's Gv TEDD TW11 | | 176 | D2 |
| Blackmores AL7 | | | |
| WOKS/MYFD GU22 | | 232 | B5 |
| Blacknest Gate Rd ASC SL5 | | 192 | C5 |
| Blacknest Rd ASC SL5 | | 193 | J3 |
| Blackness Cots HAYES BR2 * | | 226 | A5 |
| Blackness La HAYES BR2 | | 226 | A6 |
| WOKS/MYFD GU22 | | 232 | B5 |
| Blache La BAR EN5 | | 76 | C6 |
| POTB/CUF EN6 | | 58 | C10 |
| Blanche St CAN/RD E16 | | 141 | H6 |
| Blanchland Rd MRDN SM4 | | 201 | L5 |
| Blanchman's Rd WARL CR6 | | 242 | D4 |
| Blandfield Rd BAL SW12 | | 180 | B2 |
| WHTN TW2 | | | |
| Blandford Cl CROY/NA CRO | | 202 | F10 |
| Blandford Cl ROM RM1 | | 117 | M3 |
| EFNCH N2 | | 117 | M3 |
| ROMW/RG RM7 | | 123 | N6 |
| WOKS/MYFD GU22 | | 232 | E3 |
| Blandford Crs CHING E4 | | 101 | H1 |
| Blandford Ms REIG RH2 | | 257 | N10 |
| Blandford Rd BECK BR3 | | 204 | B3 |
| CHSWK W4 | | 156 | B2 |
| EA W5 | | 155 | J3 |
| NWDGN UB2 | | 153 | P3 |
| STAL AL1 | | 38 | F1 |
| TEDD TW11 | | 176 | B7 |
| Blandford Rd North | | | |
| DTCH/LGLY SL3 | | 150 | A2 |
| Blandford Rd South | | | |
| DTCH/LGLY SL3 | | 150 | A2 |
| Blandford Sq CAMTN NW1 | | 9 | P2 |
| Blandford St MHST W1U | | 10 | B5 |
| Blandford Waye YEAD UB4 | | 133 | K8 |
| Bland St ELTH/MOT SE9 | | 162 | A10 |
| Blaney Crs EHAM E6 | | 142 | E9 |
| Blanford Rd REIG RH2 | | 275 | M1 |
| Blanks La HORL RH6 | | 278 | D4 |
| Blanmerle Rd ELTH/MOT SE9 | | 184 | E4 |
| Blann Cl ELTH/MOT SE9 | | 184 | A5 |
| Blantyre St WBPTN SW10 | | 157 | N6 |
| Blantyre Wk WBPTN SW10 * | | 157 | N6 |
| Blashford St LEW SE13 | | 183 | L5 |
| Blattner Cl BORE WD6 | | 75 | H4 |
| Blawith Rd HRW HA1 | | 114 | D2 |
| Blaydon Cl RSLP HA4 | | 112 | F5 |
| TOTM N17 | | 100 | A8 |
| Blays Cl ECH TW20 | | 171 | P9 |
| Blay's La EGH TW20 | | 171 | N9 |
| Bleak Hill La | | | |
| WOOL/PLUM SE18 | | 163 | J5 |
| Blean Gv PGE/AN SE20 | | 182 | B10 |
| Bleasdale Av GFD/PVL UB6 | | 134 | F4 |
| Blechynden Gdns NKENS W10 | | 136 | B9 |
| Blechynden St NKENS W10 | | 136 | A9 |
| Bledlow Cl THMD SE28 | | 143 | M9 |
| Bledlow Rd GFD/PVL UB6 | | 134 | B4 |
| Bleeding Heart Yd | | | |
| HCIRC EC1N * | | 11 | P11 |
| Blegberry Gdns BERK HP4 | | 33 | K6 |
| Blegborough Rd | | | |
| STRHM/NOR SW16 | | 180 | D9 |
| Blencarn Cl WOKN/KNAP GU21 | | 231 | M2 |
| Blendon Dr BXLY DA5 | | 185 | N3 |
| Blendon Rd BXLY DA5 | | 185 | N3 |
| Blendon Ter | | | |
| WOOL/PLUM SE18 | | 162 | F4 |
| Blendworth Wy PECK SE15 | | 159 | M6 |
| Blenheim CDALE/KGS NW9 | | 96 | C10 |
| Blenheim Av GNTH/NBYPK IG2 | | 122 | E4 |
| Blenheim Cl BF/WBF KT14 | | 215 | J9 |
| CRAWE RH10 | | 285 | H4 |
| GFD/PVL UB6 | | 134 | C3 |
| LEE/GVPK SE12 | | 184 | B1 |
| OXHEY WD19 | | 93 | K1 |
| ROMW/RG RM7 | | 124 | C1 |
| RYNPK SW20 | | 200 | F3 |
| UPMR RM14 | | 126 | D6 |
| WCHMH N21 | | 99 | J7 |
| WLGTN SM6 | | 222 | D6 |
| WOKS/MYFD GU22 | | 231 | N5 |
| Blenheim Ct ARCH N19 | | 118 | E11 |
| BFN/LL DA15 | | 185 | H7 |
| SAND/SEL CR2 * | | 223 | P8 |
| Blenheim Crs NTGHL W11 | | 8 | A7 |
| RSLP HA4 | | 94 | B11 |
| SAND/SEL CR2 | | 223 | L5 |
| Blenheim Dr WELL DA16 | | 165 | J1 |
| Blenheim Gdns | | | |
| BRXS/STRHM SW2 | | 180 | C2 |
| CRICK NW2 | | 117 | H2 |
| KUTN/CMB KT2 | | 177 | N10 |
| SAND/SEL CR2 | | 223 | P7 |
| WBLY HA9 | | 115 | N2 |
| WLGTN SM6 | | 222 | D6 |
| WOKS/MYFD GU22 | | 231 | N5 |
| Blenheim Gv PECK SE15 | | 159 | H8 |
| Blenheim Park Rd | | | |
| SAND/SEL CR2 | | 223 | K5 |
| Blenheim Pl TEDD TW11 * | | 176 | B8 |
| Blenheim Ri | | | |
| SEVS/STOTM N15 * | | 119 | N2 |
| Blenheim Rd BAR EN5 | | 76 | C1 |
| BFN/LL DA15 | | 185 | M4 |
| BMLY BR1 | | 206 | B1 |
| BRWN CM15 | | 86 | F3 |
| CHSWK W4 | | 156 | A4 |
| DTCH/LGLY SL3 | | 150 | A3 |
| EHAM E6 | | 142 | A3 |
| HOR/WEW KT19 | | 220 | A5 |
| NTHLT UB5 | | 134 | A3 |
| ORP BR6 | | 207 | N6 |
| PGE/AN SE20 | | 182 | F11 |
| PIN HA5 | | 93 | L11 |
| RYNPK SW20 | | 200 | F3 |
| STAL AL1 | | 38 | C5 |
| STJWD NW8 | | 2 | G1 |
| SUT SM1 | | 201 | K10 |
| WALTH E17 | | 120 | C1 |

| Street | Area | Page | Grid |
|---|---|---|---|
| YEAD UB4 | | 132 | E4 |
| Blakeden Dr ESH/CLAY KT10 | | 218 | E4 |
| Blakefield Gdns | | | |
| COUL/CHIP CR5 | | 240 | G2 |
| Blake Gdns DART DA1 | | 165 | N10 |
| FUL/PGN SW6 | | 157 | N7 |
| Blakehall Rd CAR SM5 | | 222 | A5 |
| Blake Hall Rd CHONG SE19 | | 67 | H1 |
| WAN E11 | | 121 | M6 |
| Blakemere Rd WGCW AL8 | | 22 | G4 |
| Blakemore Rd BCH SE13 | | 43 | K7 |
| STRHM/NOR SW16 | | 180 | F6 |
| THHTH CR7 | | 202 | G5 |
| Blakemore Wy BELV DA17 | | 163 | P2 |
| Blakeney Av BECK BR3 | | 204 | E1 |
| Blakeney Cl CAMTN NW1 | | 5 | J1 |
| HACK E8 | | 119 | P10 |
| HOR/WEW KT19 | | 220 | A7 |
| TRDG/WHET N20 | | 97 | M2 |
| Blakeney Rd BECK BR3 | | 204 | E1 |
| Blakeney Cl CHARL SE7 * | | 161 | K5 |
| Blake Rd CAN/RD E16 | | 141 | L6 |
| CROY/NA CRO | | 203 | M9 |
| MTCM CR4 | | 202 | B3 |
| PLMGR N11 | | 98 | D3 |
| Blaker Rd SRTFD E15 | | 141 | H5 |
| Blakes Av NWMAL KT3 | | 200 | D3 |
| Blake's Gn WWKM BR4 | | 204 | F11 |
| Blakes La NWMAL KT3 | | 200 | D3 |
| Blake's La EHSLY KT24 | | 252 | A7 |
| Blakesley Av EA W5 | | 135 | K4 |
| Blake's Rd PECK SE15 | | 159 | M6 |
| Blakes Ter NWMAL KT3 | | 200 | E3 |
| Blakesware Gdns ED N9 | | 99 | L1 |
| Blakewood Cl FELT TW13 | | 175 | H7 |
| Blanchedowne CMBW SE5 | | 159 | L10 |
| Blanche La BAR EN5 | | 76 | D1 |
| POTB/CUF EN6 | | 58 | C10 |
| Blanche St CAN/RD E16 | | 141 | H6 |
| Blanchland Rd MRDN SM4 | | 201 | L5 |
| Blanchman's Rd WARL CR6 | | 242 | D4 |
| Blandfield Rd BAL SW12 | | 180 | B2 |
| Blandford Av BECK BR3 | | 203 | L7 |
| WHTN TW2 | | 176 | A4 |
| Blandford Cl CROY/NA CRO | | 202 | F10 |
| EFNCH N2 | | 117 | M3 |
| ROMW/RG RM7 | | 123 | N6 |
| WOKS/MYFD GU22 | | 232 | E3 |
| Blandford Crs CHING E4 | | 101 | H1 |
| Blandford Ms REIG RH2 | | 257 | N10 |
| Blandford Rd BECK BR3 | | 204 | B3 |
| CHSWK W4 | | 156 | B2 |
| EA W5 | | 155 | J3 |
| NWDGN UB2 | | 153 | P3 |
| STAL AL1 | | 38 | F1 |
| TEDD TW11 | | 176 | B7 |
| Blandford Sq CAMTN NW1 | | 9 | P2 |
| Blandford St MHST W1U | | 10 | B5 |
| Blandford Waye YEAD UB4 | | 133 | K8 |
| Bland St ELTH/MOT SE9 | | 162 | A10 |
| Blaney Crs EHAM E6 | | 142 | E9 |
| Blanford Rd REIG RH2 | | 275 | M1 |
| Blanks La HORL RH6 | | 278 | D4 |
| Blanmerle Rd ELTH/MOT SE9 | | 184 | E4 |
| Blann Cl ELTH/MOT SE9 | | 184 | A5 |
| Blantyre St WBPTN SW10 | | 157 | N6 |
| Blantyre Wk WBPTN SW10 * | | 157 | N6 |
| Blashford St LEW SE13 | | 183 | L5 |
| Blattner Cl BORE WD6 | | 75 | H4 |
| Blawith Rd HRW HA1 | | 114 | D2 |
| Blaydon Cl RSLP HA4 | | 112 | F5 |
| TOTM N17 | | 100 | A8 |
| Blays Cl ECH TW20 | | 171 | P9 |
| Blay's La EGH TW20 | | 171 | N9 |
| Bleak Hill La | | | |
| WOOL/PLUM SE18 | | 163 | J5 |
| Blean Gv PGE/AN SE20 | | 182 | B10 |
| Bleasdale Av GFD/PVL UB6 | | 134 | F4 |
| Blechynden Gdns NKENS W10 | | 136 | B9 |
| Blechynden St NKENS W10 | | 136 | A9 |
| Bledlow Cl THMD SE28 | | 143 | M9 |
| Bledlow Rd GFD/PVL UB6 | | 134 | B4 |
| Bleeding Heart Yd | | | |
| HCIRC EC1N * | | 11 | P11 |
| Blegberry Gdns BERK HP4 | | 33 | K6 |
| Blegborough Rd | | | |
| STRHM/NOR SW16 | | 180 | D9 |
| Blencarn Cl WOKN/KNAP GU21 | | 231 | M2 |
| Blendon Dr BXLY DA5 | | 185 | N3 |
| Blendon Rd BXLY DA5 | | 185 | N3 |
| Blendon Ter | | | |
| WOOL/PLUM SE18 | | 162 | F4 |
| Blendworth Wy PECK SE15 | | 159 | M6 |
| Blenheim CDALE/KGS NW9 | | 96 | C10 |
| Blenheim Av GNTH/NBYPK IG2 | | 122 | E4 |
| Blenheim Cl BF/WBF KT14 | | 215 | J9 |
| CRAWE RH10 | | 285 | H4 |
| GFD/PVL UB6 | | 134 | C3 |
| LEE/GVPK SE12 | | 184 | B1 |
| OXHEY WD19 | | 93 | K1 |
| ROMW/RG RM7 | | 124 | C1 |
| RYNPK SW20 | | 200 | F3 |
| UPMR RM14 | | 126 | D6 |
| WCHMH N21 | | 99 | J7 |
| WLGTN SM6 | | 222 | D6 |
| WOKS/MYFD GU22 | | 231 | N5 |

| Street | Area | Page | Grid |
|---|---|---|---|
| WAN E11 | | 121 | K9 |
| Blenheim St CONDST W1S | | 10 | E6 |
| Blenheim Ter STJWD NW8 | | 3 | J1 |
| ISLW TW7 | | 154 | F7 |
| Blenhiem Ct WGCE AL7 | | 23 | M4 |
| Blenhiem Rd ABLGY WD5 | | 55 | H9 |
| Blenkin Cl STALW/RED AL3 | | 38 | B2 |
| Bleriot Rd HEST TW5 | | 153 | K6 |
| Blessbury Rd EDGW HA8 | | 95 | P5 |
| Blessington Rd LEW SE13 | | 161 | L11 |
| Blessing Wy BARK IG11 | | 143 | M4 |
| Bletchingley Cl REDH RH1 | | 258 | C5 |
| THHTH CR7 | | 203 | J4 |
| Bletchingley Rd GDST RH9 | | 259 | P7 |
| REDH RH1 | | 258 | D5 |
| Bletchley St IS N1 | | 6 | F8 |
| Bletchmore Cl HYS/HAR UB3 | | 152 | A1 |
| Bletsoe Wk IS N1 | | 6 | F6 |
| Bligh Cl CRAWE RH10 | | 284 | A9 |
| Bligh Rd GRAYS RM17 | | 190 | D2 |
| Blighs Rd SEV TN13 | | 265 | J3 |
| Blighs Wk SEV TN13 * | | 265 | J3 |
| Blincoe Cl WIM/MER SW19 | | 179 | G5 |
| Blinco La DTCH/LGLY SL3 | | 130 | B9 |
| Blind La CTMIS/PWD HP16 | | 50 | A7 |
| Blindley Rd CRAWE RH10 | | 284 | E4 |
| Blindman's La CHES/WCR EN8 | | 62 | C6 |
| Blissett St GNWCH SE10 | | 161 | H7 |
| Bliss Ms NKENS W10 * | | 2 | B9 |
| Blisworth Cl YEAD UB4 | | 133 | M6 |
| Blithbury Rd DAGW RM9 | | 143 | L1 |
| Blithdale Rd ABYW SE2 | | 163 | K3 |
| Blockley Rd ALP/SUD HA0 | | 114 | C7 |
| Bloemfontein Av SHB W12 | | 136 | G10 |
| Bloemfontein Rd SHB W12 | | 136 | G9 |
| Blomfield Rd MV/WKIL W9 | | 9 | H3 |
| Blomfield Rd SHB W12 | | 136 | G9 |
| Blomville Rd BCTR RM8 | | 123 | P8 |
| Blondell Cl WDR/YW UB7 | | 151 | N5 |
| Blondel St BTSEA SW11 | | 158 | F8 |
| Blondin Av EA W5 | | 135 | H5 |
| Blondin St BOW E3 | | 140 | A1 |
| Bloomfield Cl | | | |
| WOKN/KNAP GU21 | | 231 | K4 |
| Bloomfield Crs | | | |
| GNTH/NBYPK IG2 | | 122 | E4 |
| Bloomfield Pl | | | |
| MYFR/PKLN W1K | | 10 | F7 |
| Bloomfield Rd CHESW EN7 | | 61 | K1 |
| HAYES BR2 | | 206 | A5 |
| HGT N6 | | 118 | A3 |
| KUT/HW KT1 | | 199 | K4 |
| WOOL/PLUM SE18 | | 162 | E4 |
| Bloomfield Ter BGVA SW1W | | 16 | C7 |
| Bloom Gv WNWD SE27 | | 181 | J6 |
| Bloomhall Rd NRWD SE19 | | 181 | L8 |
| Bloom Park Rd FUL/PGN SW6 | | 157 | J6 |
| Bloomsbury Cl EA W5 | | 135 | L9 |
| HOR/WEW KT19 | | 220 | A6 |
| Bloomsbury Pl | | | |
| NOXST/BSQ WC1A | | 11 | M4 |
| Bloomsbury Sq | | | |
| NOXST/BSQ WC1A | | 11 | M4 |
| Bloomsbury St GWRST WC1E | | 11 | J3 |
| Bloomsbury Wy | | | |
| NOXST/BSQ WC1A | | 11 | L4 |
| Blore Cl VX/NE SW8 | | 158 | E7 |
| Blossom Cl DAGW RM9 | | 144 | A5 |
| EA W5 | | 155 | K1 |
| SAND/SEL CR2 | | 223 | N2 |
| Blossom La ENC/FH EN2 | | 79 | K5 |
| Blossom Wy HGDN/ICK UB10 | | 132 | A3 |
| WDR/YW UB7 | | 152 | B3 |
| Blossom Waye HEST TW5 | | 153 | M5 |
| Blount St POP/IOD E14 | | 140 | G8 |
| Bloxam Gdns ELTH/MOT SE9 | | 184 | B1 |
| Bloxhall Rd LEY E10 | | 120 | E6 |
| Bloxham Crs HPTN TW12 | | 197 | H1 |
| Bloxworth Cl WLGTN SM6 | | 202 | D10 |
| Blucher Rd CMBW SE5 | | 159 | H5 |
| Blucher St CSHM HP5 | | 50 | C7 |
| Blue Anchor La | | | |
| BERM/RHTH SE16 | | 19 | P5 |
| TIL RM18 | | 169 | H3 |
| Blue Anchor Yd WCHPL E1 | | 13 | N7 |
| Blue Ball La EGH TW20 | | 172 | C8 |
| Blue Ball Yd WHALL SW1A | | 10 | G10 |
| Blue Barn La WEY KT13 | | 216 | B7 |
| Bluebell Av MNPK E12 | | 122 | A11 |
| Bluebell Cl CRAWW RH11 | | 283 | L10 |
| HERT/BAY SG13 | | 25 | L5 |
| HHW HP1 * | | 35 | H7 |
| HOM E9 | | 140 | B3 |
| LCOL/BKTW AL2 | | 58 | N1 |
| NTHLT UB5 | | 133 | N1 |
| ORP BR6 | | 206 | G11 |
| ROMW/RG RM7 | | 124 | F7 |
| SYD SE26 | | 182 | B8 |
| WLGTN SM6 | | 202 | C10 |
| Bluebell Dr WOKS/MYFD GU22 | | 53 | G3 |
| CHESW EN7 | | 61 | L4 |
| Bluebell La EHSLY KT24 | | 252 | E7 |
| Bluebell Rd LTWR GU18 | | 212 | A4 |
| Bluebell Wk SBW CM21 | | 29 | L2 |
| Bluebell Wy HAT AL10 | | 22 | C10 |
| IL IG1 | | 142 | E1 |
| Blueberry Cl STALW/RED AL3 | | 38 | C2 |
| WFD IG8 | | 100 | M7 |
| Blueberry Gdns | | | |
| COUL/CHIP CR5 | | 240 | G2 |
| Blueberry La RSEV TN14 | | 245 | M2 |
| Bluebird Wy LCOL/BKTW AL2 | | 58 | N5 |
| THMD SE28 | | 162 | C1 |
| Bluebridge Av BRKMPK AL9 | | 59 | H3 |
| Blue Bridge Rd BRKMPK AL9 | | 59 | H2 |
| Blue Cedars BNSTD SM7 | | 222 | G10 |
| Blue Cedars Pl COB KT11 | | 217 | L3 |
| Bluecoats Av HERT/WAT SG14 | | 25 | L5 |
| Bluefield Cl HPTN TW12 | | 175 | K7 |
| Bluegates EW KT17 | | 220 | D4 |
| Bluehouse Gdns OXTED RH8 | | 261 | M4 |
| Bluehouse Hill Hemel | | | |
| Hempstead Rd | | | |
| STALW/RED AL3 | | 37 | P7 |
| Bluehouse La OXTED RH8 | | 261 | L4 |
| Bluehouse Rd CHING E4 | | 101 | K4 |
| Blue Leaves Av | | | |
| COUL/CHIP CR5 | | 240 | G8 |
| Blue Lion Pl STHWK SE1 * | | 19 | K3 |
| Bluemans End EPP CM16 | | 48 | E10 |
| Bluemans EPP CM16 | | 48 | E10 |
| Blue Riband Est | | | |
| CROY/NA CRO * | | 203 | J9 |
| Bluett Rd LCOL/BKTW AL2 | | 58 | C2 |
| Bluewater Pkwy RDART DA2 | | 188 | G4 |
| Blundell Av HORL RH6 | | 280 | A4 |
| Blundel La COB KT11 | | 235 | J1 |
| Blundell Cl HACK E8 | | 119 | P6 |
| STALW/RED AL3 | | 38 | B1 |
| Blundell Rd EDGW HA8 | | 96 | B5 |
| Blundell St HOLWY N7 | | 5 | L2 |
| Blunden Cl BCTR RM8 | | 123 | M6 |
| Blunden Dr DTCH/LGLY SL3 | | 150 | D2 |
| Blunesfield POTB/CUF EN6 | | 59 | N1 |
| Blunt Rd SAND/SEL CR2 | | 223 | M3 |
| Blunts Av WDR/YW UB7 | | 152 | C5 |
| Blunts La LCOL/BKTW AL2 | | 55 | M3 |
| Blunts Rd ELTH/MOT SE9 | | 184 | D4 |
| Blurton Rd CLPT E5 | | 120 | E1 |
| Blyth Cl POP/IOD E14 | | 161 | H3 |
| TWK TW1 | | 176 | G2 |
| Blythe Cl CAT SE6 | | 182 | G1 |
| IVER SL0 | | 131 | K4 |
| Blythe Hill CAT SE6 | | 182 | G1 |
| Blythe Hill La CAT SE6 | | 182 | G1 |

**Column 1**

Blythe Hill Pl *FSTH SE23* * ... 182 D3
Blythe Ms *WKENS W14* * ... 156 C2
Blythe Rd *HOD EN11* ... 45 J5
  *WKENS W14* ... 14 A5
Blythe St *BETH E2* * ... 140 A5
Blytheswood Pl *STRHM/NOR SW16* ... 180 G7
Blyth Rd *BMLY BR1* ... 205 E4
  *HYS/HAR UB3* ... 152 L1
  *THMD SE28* ... 143 M9
  *WALTH E17* ... 120 C6
Blyth's Whf *POP/IOD E14* * ... 140 D9
Blythwood Rd *GDMY/SEVK IG3* ... 123 K6
Blyth Wk *UPMR RM14* ... 126 D5
Blythway *WGCE AL7* ... 23 J2
Blythwood Rd *FSBYPK N4* ... 118 F5
  *PIN HA5* ... 93 J6
Blyton Cl *BEAC HP9* ... 88 C7
Boadicea Cl *SL SL1* ... 128 D3
Boadicea St *IS N1* ... 5 N6
Boakes Cl *CDALE/KGS NW9* ... 115 J1
Boakes Meadow *RSEV TN14* * ... 228 C2
Boardman Av *CHING E4* ... 80 G9
Boardman Cl *BAR EN5* ... 77 H9
Boardman Rd *BRW CM14* ... 106 C4
Board School Rd *WOKN/KNAP GU21* ... 232 C2
Boardwalk Pl *POP/IOD E14* ... 141 C2
Boar Hl *DORK RH4* ... 272 D8
Boarlands Cl *SL SL1* ... 114 B9
Boathouse Wk *PECK SE15* ... 159 N6
  *RCH/KEW TW9* ... 155 L7
Boat Lifter Wy *BERM/RHTH SE16* ... 160 D3
Boat Quay *CAN/RD E16* ... 141 K9
Bob Anker Cl *PLSTW E13* ... 141 M5
Bobbin Cl *CLAP SW4* ... 158 D9
Bobbingworth Mi *CHONG CM5* ... 49 H10
Bob Dunn Wy *DART DA1* ... 165 P10
Bob Marley Wy *HNHL SE24* ... 159 H10
Bockhampton Rd *KUTN/CMB KT2* ... 177 L10
Bocking St *HACK E8* ... 140 A3
Boddicott Cl *WIM/MER SW19* ... 179 H5
Bodell Cl *CDW/CHF RM16* ... 167 N1
Bodiam Cl *CRAWE RH10* ... 284
  *EN EN1* ... 79 L6
Bodiam Rd *STRHM/NOR SW16* ... 202 E1
Bodiam Wy *WLSDN NW10* ... 135 L5
Bodicea Ms *HSLWW TW4* ... 172 N2
Bodle Av *SWCM DA10* ... 189 K2
Bodley Cl *EPP CM16* ... 65 J5
  *NWMAL KT3* ... 200 B5
Bodley Rd *NWMAL KT3* ... 200 B6
Bodmin Cl *RYLN/HDSTN HA2* ... 113 N8
  *STMC/STPC BR5* ... 207 M8
Bodmin Gv *MRDN SM4* ... 201 L4
Bodnant Gdns *RYNPK SW20* ... 200
Bodney Rd *CLPT E5* ... 120 A10
Bodwell Cl *HHW HP1* ... 5
Boeing Wy *NWDGN UB2* ... 155 J2
Bofors House *CHARL SE7* * ... 162 B6
Bognor Gdns *OXHEY WD19* * ... 93 K6
Bognor Rd *WELL DA16* ... 153
Bohemia *HHW HP2* ... 35
Bohemia Pl *HACK E8* ... 140
Bohn Rd *WCHPL E1* ... 140
Bohun Gv *EBAR EN4* ... 77 P10
Boileau Rd *BARN SW13* ... 156 C4
  *EA W5* ... 135 L8
Bois Av *AMS HP6* ... 68 C2
Bois Hall Rd *ADL/WDHM KT15* ... 215 N1
Bois La *AMS HP6* ... 69 J1
Bois Mi *CSHM HP5* * ... 69 M2
Bois Moor Rd *CSHM HP5* ... 51 K10
Boissy Rd *STALE/WH AL4* ... 39 K7
Bolberry Rd *PEND EN3* ... 104 E6
Bolden St *DEPT SE8* ... 160 G8
Bolderwood Wy *WWKM BR4* ... 204 D9
Bolding House La *CHOB/PIR GU24* ... 212 D10
Boldmere Rd *PIN HA5* ... 113 K5
Boleyn Av *EN EN1* ... 80 A5
  *EW KT17* ... 220 B6
Boleyn Cl *CDW/CHF RM16* ... 167 L2
  *CRAWE RH10* ... 284 E10
  *HHW HP2* ... 35
  *LOU IG10* ... 82 B10
  *STA TW18* ... 173 H8
  *WALTH E17* ... 120 F2
Boleyn Dr *E/WMO/HCT KT8* ... 197 N3
  *RSLP HA4* ... 113 L7
  *STAL AL1* ... 38 C8
Boleyn Gdns *DAGE RM10* ... 144 D2
  *RBRW/HUT CM13* ... 107 M4
  *WWKM BR4* ... 204 G9
Boleyn Rd *BGR/WK TN15* ... 247 N5
  *EHAM E6* ... 141 M2
  *FSTGT E7* ... 141 M1
  *STNW/STAM N16* ... 119 M10
Boleyn Wk *WALTH E17* ... 236 E6
  *BARK/HLT IG6* ... 77 M7
  *SWCM DA10* ... 189
Bolina Rd *BERM/RHTH SE16* ... 160 B4
Bolingbroke Gv *BTSEA SW11* ... 179 H1
Bolingbroke Rd *WKENS W14* ... 156 G2
Bolingbroke Wk *BTSEA SW11* ... 157 N6
Bolingbrook *HYS/HAR UB3* ... 132 D4
Bolingbrook *STALE/WH AL4* ... 38 F2
Bollo Bridge Rd *ACT W3* ... 155 N2
Bollo La *ACT W3* ... 155 N2
Bolney Ct *CRAWW RH11* ... 283 J10
Bolney Gdns *SKENS SW7* ... 15 L6
Bolney St *VX/NE SW8* ... 158 G6
Bolsover Gv *REDH RH1* ... 268 C5
Bolsover St *GTPST W1W* ... 10 F2
Bolstead Rd *MTCM CR4* ... 202 E1
Bolster Gv *WDGN N22* ... 98
Bolt Ct *FLST/FETLN EC4A* ... 12
Bolters La *BNSTD SM7* ... 221 J10
Bolters La *HORL RH6* ... 288 G7
Bolters Rd South *HORL RH6* ... 280 A2
Boltmore Cl *HDN NW4* ... 116 C1
Bolton Av *WDSR SL4* ... 149 H3
Bolton Cl *CHSGTN KT9* ... 219 J5
Bolton Crs *CMBW SE5* ... 158 E6
  *WDSR SL4* ... 149 H3
Bolton Dr *MRDN SM4* ... 201 M4
Bolton Gdns *BMLY BR1* ... 183 P8
  *ECT SW5* ... 15 H7
  *TEDD TW11* ... 159 F9
  *WLSDN NW10* ... 136 G4
Bolton Gardens Ms *WBPTN SW10* ... 15 H7
Bolton Pl *IS N1* *
Bolton Rd *CHSGTN KT9* ... 156 C4
  *CHSWK W4* ... 155 P6
  *HRW HA1* ... 114 B2
  *SRTFD E15* ... 141 L6
  *STJWD NW8* ... 3 H1
  *UED N18* ... 99
  *WDSR SL4* ... 149 H3
  *WLSDN NW10* ... 136 G5
The Boltons *HYS/HAR UB3* * ... 114
  *WFD IG8* * ... 101 M5
Bolton St *MYFR/PICC W1J* ... 10
Bombay St *BERM/RHTH SE16* ... 160 A3
Bombers La *BH/WHM TN16* ... 244 G5

**Column 2**

Bomer Cl *WDR/YW UB7* ... 152 B6
Bomore Rd *NTGHL W11* ... 8 A7
Bonaparte Ms *PIM SW1V* ... 17 J7
Bonar Pl *CHST BR7* ... 184 D10
Bonar Rd *PECK SE15* ... 159 P6
Bonaventure Cl *GVE DA12* ... 191 K7
Bonchester Cl *CHST BR7* ... 184 D10
Bonchurch Cl *BELMT SM2* ... 221 L4
Bonchurch Rd *NKENS W10* ... 8 A3
  *WEA W13* ... 134 D10
Bond Cl *IVER SL0* ... 130 C2
  *RSEV TN14* ... 245 N1
  *WDR/YW UB7* ... 132 A8
Bond Gdns *WLGTN SM6* ... 222 D1
Bond Rd *MTCM CR4* ... 202 A2
  *SURB KT6* ... 199 L9
  *WARL CR6* ... 242 C4
Bond's La *RDKG RH5* ... 272 C10
Bond St *EA W5* ... 135 J9
  *ECH TW20* ... 171 N9
  *GRAYS RM17* ... 167 P5
  *SRTFD E15* ... 121 K10
Boneta Rd *WOOL/PLUM SE18* ... 162 C2
Bonfield Rd *LEW SE13* ... 161 N10
Bonham Gdns *BCTR RM8* ... 123 N7
Bonham Rd *BCTR RM8* ... 123 N7
  *BRXS/STRHM SW2* ... 180 C1
Bonham Wy *CHSWK W4* ... 189 P4
Bonheur Rd *CHSWK W4* ... 156 A1
Bonhill St *SDTCH EC2A* ... 13 H2
Boniface Gdns *KTN/HRWW/WS HA3* ... 94 A8
Boniface Rd *HGDN/ICK UB10* ... 112 C8
Boniface Wk *KTN/HRWW/WS HA3* ... 94 A8
Bonington Rd *HCH RM12* ... 125 J3
Bonita Ms *PECK SE15* ... 160 C9
Bonks Hl *SBW CM21* ... 29
Bonner Hill Rd *KUT/HW KT1* ... 199 L3
Bonner Rd *WOKS/MYFD GU22* ... 232 C8
Bonnersfield Cl *HRW HA1* ... 114 F4
Bonnersfield La *HRW HA1* ... 114 F4
Bonner St *BETH E2* ... 140 B4
Bonner Wk *CDW/CHF RM16* * ... 167
Bonnetts La *CRAWW RH11* ... 283 K2
Bonneville Gdns *CLAP SW4* ... 180 C1
Bonney Gv *CHESW EN7* ... 61 N6
Bonney Wy *SWLY BR8* ... 208 F2
Bonningtons *BRW CM14* ... 107
Bonnington Sq *VX/NE SW8* ... 17 L6
Bonnys Rd *REIG RH2* ... 256 C10
Bonny St *CAMTN NW1* ... 4 C2
Bonser Rd *TWK TW1* ... 176 E5
Bonser Cl *WOKS/MYFD GU22* ... 232 B7
Bonsey's La *CHOB/PIR GU24* ... 214 E5
Bonsor Dr *KWD/TDW/WH KT20* ... 239 H10
Bonsor St *CMBW SE5* ... 159 M6
Bonville Gdns *HDN NW4* ... 116 D2
Bonville Rd *BMLY BR1* ... 183 L8
Booker Rd *UED N18* ... 99 P6
Bookham Ct *GT/LBKH KT23* ... 235 N9
Bookham Gv *GT/LBKH KT23* ... 254 A2
Bookham Rd *COB KT11* ... 235 L6
Boones Rd *LEW SE13* ... 161 K10
Boord St *GNWCH SE10* ... 141 K8
Boothby Rd *ARCH N19* ... 118 E7
Booth Cl *HOM E9* ... 139 M8
  *THMD SE28* ... 143 L10
Booth La *BLKFR EC4V* ... 12 E7
Booth Rd *CDALE/KGS NW9* ... 96 A5
  *CRAWW RH11* ... 283 H10
  *CROY/NA CR0* * ... 203 J9
Booths Cl *BRKMPK AL9* ... 40 G10
Boot Pde *EDGW HA8* * ... 95 M7
Boot St *FSBYE EC1V* ... 7 J10
Borage Cl *CRAWW RH11* ... 283 K10
Bordars Rd *HNWL W7* ... 134 D7
Bordars Wk *HNWL W7* ... 134 D7
Borden Av *EN EN1* ... 79 L10
Border Cha *CRAWE RH10* ... 285 H3
Border Cdns *CROY/NA CR0* ... 224 C1
Border Ga *MTCM CR4* ... 201 P9
Border Rd *SYD SE26* ... 182 A8
Borderside *SLN SL2* ... 129 J8
Borders La *LOU IG10* ... 82 D8
Bordesley Rd *MRDN SM4* ... 201 L4
Bordon Wk *PUT/ROE SW15* ... 178 D3
Boreham Av *CAN/RD E16* ... 141 M8
Boreham Cl *WAN E11* ... 121 H6
Boreham Ms *HOD EN11* ... 26 F10
Boreham Rd *WDGN N22* ... 99 M3
Borers Arms Rd *CRAWE RH10* ... 285 J1
Borers Cl *CRAWE RH10* * ... 285 K2
Borgard Rd *WOOL/PLUM SE18* ... 162 D6
Borgard Rd *WOOL/PLUM SE18* ... 162
Borkwood Pk *ORP BR6* ... 227 H1
Borkwood Wy *ORP BR6* ... 227 H1
Borland Cl *RDART DA2* ... 188 D1
Borland Rd *PECK SE15* ... 160 B10
  *TEDD TW11* ... 176 D2
Bornedene *POTB/CUF EN6* ... 59 H7
Borneo St *PUT/ROE SW15* ... 156 G9
Borough High St *STHWK SE1* ... 18 F3
Borough Hd Mj *CROY/NA CR0* ... 205 J10
Borough Rd *BH/WHM TN16* ... 244 A7
  *ISLW TW7* ... 154 D7
  *KUTN/CMB KT2* ... 199 M1
  *MTCM CR4* ... 201 P2
  *STHWK SE1* ... 18 C3
Borough Sq *STHWK SE1* ... 18 E2
The Borough *BRKHM/BTCW RH3* ... 273 M1
  *CHONG CM5* ... 67 N5
Borough Wy *POTB/CUF EN6* ... 59 H8
Borrell Cl *BROX EN10* ... 44 D6
Borrett Cl *WALW SE17* ... 18 F8
Borrodaile Rd *WAND/EARL SW18* ... 179 L2
Borrowdale Av *KTN/HRWW/WS HA3* ... 94 F10
Borrowdale Cl *CRAWW RH11* ... 283 J10
  *EFNCH N2* ... 97 M10
  *EGH TW20* ... 172 C10
  *REDBR IG4* ... 122 B2
  *SAND/SEL CR2* ... 223 N8
Borrowdale Ct *WAN E11* * ... 121 K9
Borthwick Ms *WAN E11* * ... 121 K9
Borthwick Rd *CDALE/KGS NW9* ... 116 C4
  *SRTFD E15* ... 121 K10
Borthwick St *DEPT SE8* ... 160 F4
Borwick Av *WALTH E17* ... 120 C1
Bosanquet Cl *UX/CGN UB8* ... 131 N5
Bosanquet Rd *HOD EN11* ... 45 H1
Bosbury Rd *CAT SE6* ... 183 H6
Boscastle Rd *KTTN NW5* ... 118 C6
Boscobel Cl *BMLY BR1* ... 206 C2
Boscobel Pl *BCVA SW1W* ... 16
Boscobel St *BAY/PAD W2* ... 9 M3
Boscombe Av *EMPK RM11* ... 125 N4
  *GRAYS RM17* ... 168 A3
  *LEY E10* ... 121 H1
Boscombe Cl *CLPT E5* ... 120 D3
  *EGH TW20* ... 194
Boscombe Rd *SHB W12* ... 156
  *TOOT SW17* ... 180 B9
  *WIM/MER SW19* ... 179 N9
  *WPK KT4* ... 200 H1
Bose Cl *FNCH N3* ... 97 H1
Bosgrove *CHING E4* ... 80 A2
Bosham Rd *CRAWE RH10* ... 284 D10

**Column 3**

Bosman Dr *BFOR GU20* ... 192 A10
Boss St *STHWK SE1* ... 19 L1
Bostall Heath *ABYW SE2* ... 163 M4
Bostall Hill *ABYW SE2* ... 163 L4
Bostall La *ABYW SE2* ... 163 L3
Bostall Manorway *ABYW SE2* ... 163 L3
Bostall Park Av *BXLYHN DA7* ... 163 P6
Bostall Rd *STMC/STPC BR5* ... 185 L10
Boston Gdns *BTFD TW8* ... 154 F3
  *CHSWK W4* ... 156 B5
Boston Gv *RSLP HA4* ... 112 A4
Boston Manor Rd *BTFD TW8* ... 154 D3
Boston Pde *HNWL W7* * ... 154 F5
Boston Park Rd *BTFD TW8* * ... 154 A1
Boston Rd *CROY/NA CR0* ... 202 G6
  *EDGW HA8* ... 95 P8
  *EHAM E6* ... 142 B5
  *HNWL W7* ... 134 D10
  *WALTH E17* ... 120 F4
Bostonthorpe Rd *HNWL W7* * ... 154 E1
Boston Vis *BTFD TW8* * ... 154 E2
Bosville Dr *SEV TN13* ... 247 H9
Bosville Rd *SEV TN13* ... 247 H9
Boswell Cl *RAD WD7* ... 57 K8
  *STMC/STPC BR5* ... 207 M6
Boswell Ct *BMSBY WC1N* ... 11 M3
Boswell Rd *CRAWE RH10* ... 283 P10
  *THHTH CR7* ... 203 K4
Boswick La *BERK HP4* ... 33 J1
Bosworth Cl *WALTH E17* ... 100 C2
Bosworth Rd *BAR EN5* ... 77 K7
  *DAGE RM10* ... 124 C7
  *FBAR/BDGN N11* ... 98 E2
  *NKENS W10* ... 8 B2
Botany Bay La *CHST BR7* ... 206 F2
Botany Cl *EBAR EN4* ... 77 P8
Botany Ter *PUR RM19* * ... 165 N4
Boteley Cl *CHING E4* ... 101 J3
Botery's Cross *REDH RH1* ... 259 J9
Botham Cl *EDGW HA8* ... 95 P8
Botham Dr *SL SL1* ... 149 K2
Botha Rd *PLSTW E13* ... 141 N7
Bothwell Cl *CAN/RD E16* ... 141 M7
Bothwell Rd *CROY/NA CR0* ... 225 M7
Bothwell St *HMSMTH W6* ... 156 G5
Botley La *CSHM HP5* ... 51 M6
Botley Rd *CSHM HP5* ... 51 K6
  *HHNE HP2* ... 36
Botleys Pk *CHERT KT16* ... 214 F2
Botolph Aly *MON EC3R* ... 13 J8
Botolph La *MON EC3R* ... 13 J8
Botsford Rd *RYNPK SW20* ... 201 H2
Bottom House Farm La *CSTG HP8* ... 89 J7
Bottom La *BEAC HP9* ... 89 H7
  *KGLGY WD4* ...
Bottrells La *CSTG HP8* ... 89 L3
Bott's Ms *BAY/PAD W2* ... 8 F6
Bouchier Cl *SEV TN13* ... 265 H3
Bouchier St *SOHO/SHAV W1D* ... 11 J7
Bourdon Pl *MYFR/PKLN W1K* ... 10 C7
Bourdon Rd *PGE/AN SE20* ... 182 G4
Bourdon St *MYFR/PKLN W1K* ... 10 C7
Bourke Cl *CLAP SW4* ... 180 C1
  *WLSDN NW10* ... 137 H2
Bourke Hl *COUL/CHIP CR5* ... 240 A4
Bourlet Cl *GTPST W1W* ... 10 F4
Bournbrook Rd *BKHTH/KID SE3* ... 162 C4
Bourne Av *CHERT KT16* ... 195 K3
  *HYS/HAR UB3* ... 152 D2
  *RSLP HA4* ... 113 H10
  *WCHMH N21* ... 99 J7
  *WOT/HER KT12* ... 197 J9

**Column 4**

  *STHGT/OAK N14* ... 98 F3
  *WDSR SL4* ... 149 L9
Bowbridge La *ABR/ST RM4* ... 70 A4
  *BROX EN10* ... 44 E6
  *ISLW TW7* ... 154 D9
  *RGUE GU4* ... 268 B2
  *THDIT KT7* ... 198 B9
  *WARE SG12* ... 26 C1
Bourne Ct *BF/WBF KT14* * ... 215 P9
  *RSLP HA4* ... 113 J9
Bourne Dr *MTCM CR4* ... 201 N2
Bourne End *EMPK RM11* ... 125 P5
Bourne End La *HHW HP1* ... 34 F8
Bourne End Rd *NTHWD HA6* ... 92 F5
Bourne Est *HCIRC EC1N* * ... 12 A2
Bournefield Rd *CTHM CR3* ... 241 N4
Bourne Gdns *CHING E4* ... 100 G5
Bourne Gv *ASHTD KT21* ... 237 J5
Bournehall Av *BUSH WD23* ... 73 P9
Bournehall La *BUSH WD23* ... 73 P10
Bournehall Rd *BUSH WD23* ... 73 P10
Bourne Hl *PLMGR N13* ... 98 C3
Bourne Hill Cl *PLMGR N13* * ... 98 D3
Bourne La *CTHM CR3* ... 241 L7
Bournemead *BUSH WD23* ... 73 P10
Bournemead Av *NTHLT UB5* ... 133 H5
Bournemead Cl *NTHLT UB5* ... 133 H5
Bourne Meadow *EGH TW20* ... 193 M10
Bournemouth Cl *PECK SE15* ... 159 K9
Bournemouth Rd *PECK SE15* ... 159 K9
  *WIM/MER SW19* ... 201 K1
Bourne Pde *BXLY DA5* * ... 186 C3
Bourne Park Cl *PUR/KEN CR8* ... 241 M2
Bourne Rd *ASHTD KT21* ... 237 J5 (?)
  *BERK HP4* ... 33 L4
  *BUSH WD23* ... 73 P9
  *BXLY DA5* ... 186 C2
  *BXLY DA5* ... 186 C2
  *CEND/HSY/T N8* ... 118 E4
  *GODL GU7* ... 267 J9
  *GVE DA12* ... 191 J7
  *HAYES BR2* ... 206 B1
  *REDH RH1* ... 258 F5
  *SL SL1* ... 149 H1
  *VW GU25* ... 195 A4
  *WAN E11* ... 121 H1
Bourneside *VW GU25* ... 195 M7
Bourneside Crs *STHGT/OAK N14* ... 98 H2
Bourneside Gdns *CAT SE6* ... 183 H8
Bourneside Rd *ADL/WDHM KT15* ... 215 N2
  *CROY/NA CR0* ... 205 P3
Bourne Ter *BAY/PAD W2* ... 8 G3
The Bourne *HHS/BOV HP3* ... 52 D3
  *WCHMH N21* ... 98 E3
  *WARE SG12* ... 26 C1
Bourne V *HAYES BR2* ... 205 M7
Bournevale Rd *STRHM/NOR SW16* ... 180 D7
Bourne Vw *GFD/PVL UB6* ... 134 C1
  *PUR/KEN CR8* ... 241 L1
Bourne Wy *ADL/WDHM KT15* ... 215 M9
  *HAYES BR2* ... 205 M9
  *HOR/WEW KT19* ... 219 P1
  *SUT SM1* ... 221 J2
  *SWLY BR8* ... 208 D3
  *WOKS/MYFD GU22* ... 232 A8
Bournewood Rd *STMC/STPC BR5* ... 207 L1
  *WOOL/PLUM SE18* ... 163 P8
Bournville Rd *CAT SE6* ... 182 D5
Bournwell Cl *EBAR EN4* ... 78 A6
Bourton Cl *HYS/HAR UB3* ... 133 H10
Bousfield Rd *NWCR SE14* ... 160 C5
Bousley Ri *CHERT KT16* ... 214 G3
Boutflower Rd *BTSEA SW11* ... 157 P10
Boutique Hall *LEW SE13* * ... 161 N10
Bouverie Gdns *KTN/HRWW/WS HA3* ... 115 J4
  *PUR/KEN CR8* ... 222 F10
Bouverie Ms *STNW/STAM N16* ... 119 M7
Bouverie Pl *BAY/PAD W2* ... 9 M5
Bouverie Rd *COUL/CHIP CR5* ... 240 C5
  *HRW HA1* ... 114 B1
  *STNW/STAM N16* ... 119 M7
Bouverie St *EMB EC4Y* ... 12 B6
Bouverie Wy *DTCH/LGLY SL3* ... 150 B4
Bouvier Rd *PEND EN3* ... 80 A6
Boveney Cl *SL SL1* ... 148 B5
Boveney New Rd *WDSR SL4* ... 148 B3
Boveney Rd *FSTH SE23* ... 182 B3
  *WDSR SL4* ... 148 B3
Boveney Wy *SOCK/AV RM15* ... 146 G2
Bovey Wy *SOCK/AV RM15* ... 146 G2
Bovill Rd *FSTH SE23* ... 182 B3
Bovingdon Av *WBLY HA9* ... 135 N3
Bovingdon Cl *ARCH N19* ... 118 C1
Bovingdon La *CDALE/KGS NW9* ... 96 B9
Bovingdon Rd *FUL/PGN SW6* ... 157 L7
Bovingdon Sq *MTCM CR4* ... 202 E2
Bow Arrow La *DART DA1* ... 188 A2
Bowater Cl *BRXS/STRHM SW2* ... 180 A2
  *CDALE/KGS NW9* ... 96 F2
Bowater Gdns *SUN TW16* ... 197 K1
Bowater Pl *BKHTH/KID SE3* ... 162 A7
Bowater Rd *WOOL/PLUM SE18* ... 146 A6
  *WBLY HA9* ... 116 B9
Bow Bridge Est *BOW E3* ... 139 N6
Bow Churchyard *STP EC4M* ... 12 F6
Bow Common La *BOW E3* ... 139 P8
Bowden Cl *EBED/NFELT TW14* ... 153 K9
Bowden Dr *EMPK RM11* ... 125 N2
Bowden Rd *ASC SL5* ... 192 A5
Bowden St *LBTH SE11* ... 18 B8
Bowditch *DEPT SE8* ... 160 G4
Bowdon Rd *WALTH E17* ... 120 E2
Bowen Dr *DUL SE21* ... 181 N1
Bowen Rd *HRW HA1* ... 114 A5
Bowen St *POP/IOD E14* ... 140 G9
Bowens Wd *CROY/NA CR0* ... 224 D9
Bower Av *GNWCH SE10* ... 161 K7
Bower Cl *CRW RM5* ... 104 B1
  *NTHLT UB5* ... 133 G1
Bowerdean St *FUL/PGN SW6* ... 157 N7
Bower Farm Rd *ABR/ST RM4* ... 70 A1
Bower Hill *EPP CM16* ... 65 K8
Bower Hill Cl *REDH RH1* ... 276 G10
Bower Hill La *REDH RH1* ... 276 D9
Bower La *EYN DA4* ... 209 M10
Bowerman Av *NWCR SE14* ... 160 G7

**Column 5**

Bowes Wd *HART DA3* ... 211 L10
Bowfell Rd *HMSMTH W6* ... 156 F5
Bowford Av *BXLYHN DA7* ... 163 P7
Bowgate *STAL AL1* ... 38 D5
Bowhay *RBRW/HUT CM13* ... 107 N3
Bowhill Cl *BRXN/ST SW9* ... 158 H6
Bowie Cl *CLAP SW4* ... 180 E3
Bowland Rd *CLAP SW4* ... 158 E10
  *WFD IG8* ... 101 P7
Bowland Yd *KTBR SW1X* * ... 16 B2
Bow La *NFNCH/WDSPK N12* ... 97 F6
  *STP EC4M* ... 12 F6
Bowl Ct *WCHPL E1* ... 13 K2
Bowler's Orch *CHIG IG7* ... 102 E7
Bowles Gdn *EN EN1* ... 80 A2
Bowley Cl *NRWD SE19* ... 181 N9
Bowley La *NRWD SE19* ... 181 N8
Bowley St *POP/IOD E14* ... 140 E9
Bowling Cl *HGDN/ICK UB10* ... 132 A3
Bowling Green Cl *PUT/ROE SW15* ... 178 F6
Bowling Green La *CLKNW EC1R* ... 12 B2
Bowling Green Pl *STHWK SE1* ... 18 G1
Bowling Green Rd *CHOB/PIR GU24* ... 213 K5
Bowling Green Rw *WOOL/PLUM SE18* ... 146 D7
Bowling Green St *LBTH SE11* ... 18 A9
Bowling Green Wk *IS N1* ... 7 J9
  *WARE SG12* ... 26 D2
Bowls Cl *STAN HA7* ... 95 H4
Bowls The *WARL CR6* ... 242 C5
Bowman Av *CAN/RD E16* ... 141 J9
Bowman Ct *CRAWE RH10* * ... 283 N6
Bowman Ms *WAND/EARL SW18* ... 179 J4
Bowmans Cl *POTB/CUF EN6* ... 59 M8
  *SL SL1* ... 128 A3
  *WEA W13* ... 134 G10
Bowmans Lea *FSTH SE23* ... 182 B3
Bowman's Meadow *WLGTN SM6* ... 202 C10
Bowman's Ms *WCHPL E1* ... 13 N7
  *HOLWY N7* ... 118 C1
Bowmead *ELTH/MOT SE9* ... 184 C5
Bowmont Cl *CAMTN NW1* ... 5 K4
Bowness Cl *HACK E8* ... 7 M1
Bowness Crs *PUT/ROE SW15* ... 178 A9
Bowness Dr *HSLWW TW4* ... 172 A9
Bowness Rd *BXLYHN DA7* ... 164 B3
  *CAT SE6* ... 182 G3
Bowness Wy *HCH RM12* ... 125 L10
Bowood Rd *CLAP SW4* ... 158 E10
  *PEND EN3* ... 80
Bowring Gn *OXHEY WD19* ... 93 K6
Bow Rd *BOW E3* ... 139 N6
Bowrons Av *ALP/SUD HA0* ... 135 J2
Bowry Dr *STWL/WRAY TW19* ... 152 C2
Bowsley Ct *FELT TW13* ... 175 P5
The Bowsprit *COB KT11* ... 235 K1
Bowstridge La *CSTG HP8* ... 89 P7
Bowyer Cl *EHAM E6* ... 142 C7
Bowyer Dr *SL SL1* ... 128 D9
Bowyer Pl *CMBW SE5* ... 159 K5
Bowyers *HHNE HP2* ... 35
Bowyer's Cl *ASHTD KT21* ... 237 L4
Bowyer St *CMBW SE5* ... 159 K6
Bow Yd *BARK IG11* ... 143 L4
Boxall Rd *DUL SE21* ... 181 M2
Boxelder Cl *EDGW HA8* ... 95 P6
Boxfield *WGCE AL7* ... 23
Boxford Cl *SAND/SEL CR2* ... 224 C8
Boxgrove Av *GU GU1* ... 250
Boxgrove La *GU GU1* ... 250
Boxgrove Rd *ABYW SE2* ... 163 L1
  *GU GU1* ... 250 D9
Boxhill *HHNE HP2* ... 35 K10
Boxhill Rd *DORK RH4* ... 245 K10
Boxhill Wy *BRKHM/BTCW RH3* ... 273 N4
Box La *BARK IG11* ... 143 L4
  *HHS/BOV HP3* ... 52 C1
  *HOD EN11* ... 44 B3
Boxley Rd *MRDN SM4* ... 201 M4
Boxley St *CAN/RD E16* ... 141 M1
Boxmoor Rd *CRW RM5* ... 104 D6
  *KTN/HRWW/WS HA3* ... 114 C2
Boxoll Rd *DAGW RM9* ... 124 A8
Box Ridge Av *PUR/KEN CR8* ... 222 G8
Boxted Cl *BKHH IG9* ... 102 B2
Boxted Rd *HHW HP1* ... 35 H4
Box Tree La *CSHM HP5* ... 51 J9
Boxtree La *KTN/HRWW/WS HA3* ... 94 C8
Boxtree Rd *KTN/HRWW/WS HA3* ... 94 C8
Box Tree Wk *REDH RH1* ... 275 M3
Boxwell Rd *BERK HP4* ... 33 N5
Boxwood Cl *WDR/YW UB7* ... 152 A1
Boxwood Wy *WARL CR6* ... 242 C5
Boxworth Cl *NFNCH/WDSPK N12* ... 97 N6
Boxworth Gv *IS N1* ... 5 P5
Boyard Rd *WOOL/PLUM SE18* ... 162 G6
Boyce St *BORE WD6* ... 75 K5
Boyce Wy *PLSTW E13* ... 141 M3
Boycroft Av *CDALE/KGS NW9* ... 115 P4
Boyd Cl *KUTN/CMB KT2* ... 177 M10
Boydell Ct *STJWD NW8* ... 3 J4
Boyd Rd *WIM/MER SW19* ... 179 P9
Boyd St *WCHPL E1* ... 140 B8
Boyfield St *STHWK SE1* ... 18 D2
Boyland Rd *BMLY BR1* ... 183 N4
Boyle Av *STAN HA7* ... 95 G5
Boyle Cl *HGDN/ICK UB10* ... 132 A4
Boyle Farm Rd *THDIT KT7* ... 198 B9
Boyne Av *HDN NW4* ... 116 C1
Boyne Rd *DAGE RM10* ... 124 B7
  *LEW SE13* ... 161
Boyne Terrace Ms *NTGHL W11* ... 8 B9
Boyson Rd *WALW SE17* ...
Boyton Cl *CEND/HSY/T N8* ... 97 P9
  *WCHPL E1* ... 140
Boyton Rd *CEND/HSY/T N8* ... 97 P9
Brabazon Av *WLGTN SM6* ... 223 H5
Brabazon Rd *HEST TW5* ... 153 M6
  *NTHLT UB5* ... 133 N1
Brabazon St *POP/IOD E14* ... 140 M8
Brabourne Cl *NRWD SE19* ... 181 M8
Brabourne Crs *BXLYHN DA7* ... 147 P10
Brabourne Hts *MLHL NW7* ... 96 A9
Brabourne Ri *BECK BR3* ... 203 K4
Brabourn Gv *PECK SE15* ... 160 B8
Brace Cl *CHESW EN7* ... 60 E1
Bracebridge Ct *HAYES BR2* * ... 205 P8
Bracewell Av *GFD/PVL UB6* ... 114 E10
Bracewell Rd *NKENS W10* ... 8 A4
Bracewood Gdns *CROY/NA CR0* ... 3 N10
Bracey Ms *FSBYPK N4* * ... 118 E1
Bracey St *FSBYPK N4* ... 118 E1
Bracken Av *BAL SW12* ... 180 B1
  *CROY/NA CR0* ... 206 F10
Brackenbridge Dr *RSLP HA4* ... 113 M8
Brackenbury Gdns *HMSMTH W6* ... 156 F6
Brackenbury Rd *EFNCH N2* ... 117 H1
  *HMSMTH W6* ... 156
Bracken Cl *BORE WD6* ... 75 M5
  *CRAWE RH10* ... 285
  *EHAM E6* ... 142
  *GT/LBKH KT23* ... 235 N10
  *LOU IG10* ... 82 E5

**Column 6**

  *SLN SL2* ... 109 J9
  *SUN TW16* ... 174 G9
  *WHTN TW2* ... 175 P3
  *WOKS/MYFD GU22* ... 232 E9
Brackendale *POTB/CUF EN6* ... 59 G9
  *WCHMH N21* ... 98 C5
Brackendale Cl *EGH TW20* ... 171 P9
  *HSLW TW3* ... 154 A10
Brackendale Gdns *UPMR RM14* ... 126 B9
Brackendene *LCOL/BKTW AL2* ... 55 N6
  *WOKN/KNAP GU21* ... 232 D2
Bracken Dr *CHIG IG7* ... 102 E7
Bracken End *ISLW TW7* ... 176 F4
Brackenforde *DTCH/LGLY SL3* ... 149 P1
Bracken Gdns *BARN SW13* ... 156 D4
Bracken Hl *BERK HP4* ... 34 B4
Brackenhill *COB KT11* ... 217 P6
  *RSLP HA4* ... 113 M9
Bracken Hill Cl *BMLY BR1* ... 205 L1
Bracken Hill La *BMLY BR1* ... 205 L1
Brackenlea *GODL GU7* ... 267 J10
Bracken Ms *ROM/RG RM7* ... 124 B4
Bracken Pth *EPSOM KT18* ... 219 N9
Brackens *BECK BR3* ... 183
The Brackens *EN EN1* ... 99 N1
  *HHNE HP2* ... 35 N5
  *ORP BR6* ... 227 K2
The Bracken *CHING E4* ... 101 N3
Bracken Wy *CHOB/PIR GU24* ... 213 L6
  *RGUW GU3* ... 249 G8
Brackenwood *SUN TW16* ... 197 N1
Brackenwood Rd *WOKN/KNAP GU21* ... 231 J5
Brackley *WEY KT13* ... 216 D2
Brackley Av *PECK SE15* ... 160 B9
Brackley Cl *WLGTN SM6* ... 222 F4
Brackley Rd *BECK BR3* ... 182 E10
  *CHSWK W4* ... 156 B3
Brackley Sq *WFD IG8* ... 102 A8
Brackley St *BARB EC2Y* ... 12 F3
Brackley Ter *CHSWK W4* ... 156 B3
Bracklyn St *IS N1* ... 6 G1
Bracknell Cl *WDGN N22* ... 99 H9
Bracknell Gdns *HAMP NW3* ... 117 L10
Bracknell Hl *HHNE HP2* ... 35 N4
Bracknell Wy *HAMP NW3* ... 117 L9
Bracondale *ESH/CLAY KT10* ... 218 B2
Bracondale Av *ABYW SE2* ... 163 K3
Bracton La *RDART DA2* ... 186 G5
Bradbery *RKW/CH/CXG WD3* ... 90 C4
Bradbourne Park Rd *SEV TN13* ... 247 H9
Bradbourne Rd *BXLY DA5* ... 186 E8
  *GRAYS RM17* ... 167 N5
  *SEV TN13* ... 247 J8
Bradbourne Vale Rd *SEV TN13* ... 246 G8
Bradbourne St *FUL/PGN SW6* ... 157 K8
Bradbury Cl *BORE WD6* ... 75 N5
  *NWDGN UB2* ... 153 N3
Bradbury Rd *CRAWE RH10* ... 284 D10
Bradbury St *STNW/STAM N16* ... 119 M10
Bradd Cl *SOCK/AV RM15* ... 147 N5
Braddock Cl *CRW RM5* ... 104 A1
  *ISLW TW7* ... 154 E9
Braddon Ct *BAR EN5* * ... 77 H7
Braddon Rd *RCH/KEW TW9* ... 155 L9
Braddyll St *GNWCH SE10* ... 161 K4
Bradenham Av *WELL DA16* ... 163 N1
Bradenham Cl *WALW SE17* ... 18 C9
Bradenham Rd *KTN/HRWW/WS HA3* ... 114 C2
  *YEAD UB4* ...
Bradenhurst Cl *CTHM CR3* ... 259 N2
Bradfield Cl *RGUE GU4* ... 250 D7
  *WOKS/MYFD GU22* ... 232 B4
Bradfield Dr *BARK IG11* ... 123 K10
Bradfield Rd *CAN/RD E16* ... 161 K1
  *RSLP HA4* ... 113 M10
Bradford Cl *HAYES BR2* ... 206 C8
  *SYD SE26* ... 182
  *TOTM N17* ... 99 N7
Bradford Dr *HOR/WEW KT19* ... 220 C5
Bradford Rd *ACT W3* ... 156 B1
  *IL IG1* ... 122 C6
  *RKW/CH/CXG WD3* ... 90 F1
  *SL SL1* ... 128 F8
Bradgate *POTB/CUF EN6* ... 60 B3
Bradgate Rd *CAT SE6* ... 182 D10
Brading Crs *WAN E11* ... 121 N7
Brading Rd *BRXS/STRHM SW2* ... 180 A1
  *CROY/NA CR0* ... 202 G2
Brading Ter *SHB W12* ... 156 D4
Bradiston Rd *MV/WKIL W9* ... 2 D8
Bradleigh Av *GRAYS RM17* ... 167 P3
Bradley Cl *BELMT SM2* ... 221 J4
  *HOLWY N7* ... 5 M2
Bradley Gdns *WEA W13* ... 134 G8
Bradley La *RDKG RH5* ... 254 C8
Bradley Rd *NRWD SE19* ... 181 L2
  *PEND EN3* ... 80 D2
  *SL SL1* ...
  *WAB EN9* ... 81 H1
Bradley's Cl *IS N1* ... 5 M6
Bradley Stone Rd *EHAM E6* ... 142 C8
Bradman Rw *EDGW HA8* * ... 96 C3
Bradmead *VX/NE SW8* ... 157 P7
Bradmore Gn *BRKMPK AL9* ... 59 J2
Bradmore Park Rd *HMSMTH W6* ... 156 E2
Bradmore Wy *BRKMPK AL9* ... 59 J2
  *COUL/CHIP CR5* ... 240 G6
Bradshaw Cl *WDSR SL4* ... 148 D7
  *WIM/MER SW19* ... 179 K9
Bradshaw Cots *POP/IOD E14* * ... 140 D8
Bradshaw Dr *MLHL NW7* ... 96 F6
Bradshaw Rd *CDW/CHF RM16* ... 167 M10
  *WATN WD24* ... 75 K5
Bradshaws *HAT AL10* ... 40
Bradshaws Cl *SNWD SE25* ... 203 P3
Bradstock Rd *EW KT17* ... 220 E2
  *HOM E9* ... 139 K7
Brad St *STHWK SE1* ... 12 B10
Bradwell Av *DAGE RM10* ... 124 B1
Bradwell Cl *HCH RM12* ... 143 P1
  *WAN E11* ... 121 J1
Bradwell Gn *RBRW/HUT CM13* ... 87 P10
Bradwell Ms *UED N18* * ... 99 P5
Bradwell Rd *BKHH IG9* ... 102 B2
Brady Av *LOU IG10* ... 82 G2
Brady Dr *BMLY BR1* ... 206 A5
Bradymead *EHAM E6* ... 142 D4
Brady St *WCHPL E1* ... 140 C6
Braebourne Cl *CRAWE RH10* ... 284 A6
Braemar Av *ALP/SUD HA0* ... 135 J7
  *BXLYHN DA7* ... 164 D10
  *SAND/SEL CR2* ... 223 K6
  *THHTH CR7* ... 203 H6
  *WDGN N22* ...
  *WIM/MER SW19* ... 179 K4
  *WLSDN NW10* ... 117 H10
Braemar Gdns *BFN/LL DA15* ... 164 C4
  *CDALE/KGS NW9* ... 95 K10
  *EMPK RM11* ... 125 L5
  *SL SL1* ... 148 F1
  *WWKM BR4* ... 204 A1
Braemar Rd *BTFD TW8* ... 155 H7
  *PLSTW E13* ...
  *SEVS/STOTM N15* ... 119 M3
  *WPK KT4* ... 200 E10
Braes Md *REDH RH1* ...
Braeside *ADL/WDHM KT15* ... 215 L10
  *BECK BR3* ... 182 G2
Braeside Av *RYNPK SW20* ... 200 E5
  *SEV TN13* ... 246 G10
Braeside Cl *PIN HA5* ... 94 A6
  *SEV TN13* ... 246 G9
Braeside Crs *BXLYHN DA7* ... 164 D10
Braeside Rd *STRHM/NOR SW16* ... 180 G10

Braes Md REDH RH1 276 F1
Braes St IS N1 6 D4
Braesyde Cl BELV DA17 164 A3
Brafferton Rd CROY/NA CRO 223 K1
Braganza St WALW SE17 18 C9
Bragg Cl BCTR RM8 143 L1
Bragg Rd TEDD TW11 176 D10
Bragmans La RKW/CH/CXG WD3 52 C9
Braham St WCHPL E1 13 M6
Braid Av ACT W3 136 B8
Braid Cl FELT TW13 175 N5
The Braid CSHM HP5 51 K6
Braidwood Rd CAT SE6 183 J4
Braidwood St STHWK SE1 13 J10
Brailsford Cl WIM/MER SW19 179 P10
Brailsford Rd BRXS/STRHM SW2 181 H2
Brain Cl HAT AL10 40 E3
Brainton Av EBED/NFELT TW14 175 J3
Braintree Av REDBR IG4 122 B3
Braintree Rd DAGE RM10 124 B1
RSLP HA4 113 J4
Braintree St BETH E2 * 140 E1
Braithwaite Av ROMW/RG RM7 124 B5
Braithwaite Gdns STAN HA7 95 H9
Braithwaite Rd PEND EN3 30 B1
Brakefield Rd MEO DA13 189 N9
Brakey HI REDH RH1 259 M10
Brakynbery BERK HP4 33 K7
Brailings La CFSP/GDCR SL9 90 C5
Bramalea Cl HGT N6 118 B4
Bramall Cl SRTFD E15 121 L10
Bramber Cl CRAWE RH10 283 N7
Bramber Ct EA W5 155 K3
SL SL1 128 F10
Bramber Rd NFNCH/WDSPK N12 97 P6
WKENS W14 14 C9
Bramber Wy WARL CR6 242 E2
Bramble Av RDART DA2 189 H6
Bramble Banks CAR SM5 222 B5
Bramblebury Rd WOOL/PLUM SE18 162 G6
Bramble Cl BECK BR3 205 H5
CFSP/GDCR SL9 90 B2
CHIG IG7 132 F2
CRAWE RH10 285 J2
CROY/NA CRO 224 F1
GSTN WD25 73 H1
OXTED RH8 261 N9
REDH RH1 276 B2
RGUW GU3 249 K6
SEVS/STOTM N15 119 J2
SHPTN TW17 196 F6
STAN HA7 95 J8
UX/CGN UB8 132 A7
Bramble Cft ERITH DA8 164 D3
Brambledene Cl WOKN/KNAP GU21 231 N5
Brambledown HART DA3 211 L4
Brambledown Rd WWKM BR4 205 K6
CAR SM5 222 B6
SAND/SEL CR2 223 M4
Bramblefield Cl HART DA3 211 K3
Bramble Gdns SHB W12 136 C9
Brambling La KWD/TDW/WH KT20 255 L8
Bramble Hall La KWD/TDW/WH KT20 * 255 L8
Bramble La AMSS HP7 69 K7
HPTN TW12 175 N9
SEV TN13 265 J4
UPMR RM14 146 B3
Bramble Ms CSTG HP8 89 M4
HLW CM20 20 E3
Brambles Cl CHRT SE14 241 M8
ISLW TW7 154 F6
Brambles Farm Dr HGDN/ICK UB10 132 A6
The Brambles CHES/WCR EN8 62 B1
CHIG IG7 102 F7
GODL SU7 267 J10
STAL AL1 38 C8
SUT SM1 201 N9
WDR/YW UB7 151 N4
WIM/MER SW19 * 179 J8
Brambletye Park Rd REDH RH1 276 A4
Brambletye Rd CRAWE RH10 284 E6
Bramble Wk EPSOM KT18 219 N10
REDH RH1 * 276 B2
Bramble Wy RPLY/SEND GU23 233 J10
Bramblewood Cl CAR SM5 258 F9
Brambling Cl BUSH WD23 73 M8
RDART DA2 188 F2
Brambling Ri HHNE HP2 35 P3
The Bramblings CHING E4 101 J5
Bramcote Gv BERM/RHTH SE16 160 B4
Bramcote Rd PUT/ROE SW15 156 E10
Bramdean Crs LEE/GVPK SE12 183 M4
Bramdean Gdns LEE/GVPK SE12 183 M4
Bramerton Rd BECK BR3 204 E3
Bramfield CHELS SW3 15 N4
Bramfield Rd GSTN WD25 55 M10
HERT/WAT SG14 24 B1
Bramford Rd WAND/EARL SW18 157 M10
Bramham Ct NTHWD HA6 92 B4
Bramham Gdns CHSGTN KT9 219 J3
ECT SW5 14 C7
Bramhope La CHARL SE7 161 N5
Bramlands Cl BTSEA SW11 157 P9
Bramleas WATW WD18 72 E4
Bramley Av COUL/CHIP CR5 240 C5
Bramley Cl CHERT KT16 195 H7
CRAWE RH10 284 A7
HYS/HAR UB3 133 H9
MEO DA13 190 C10
MLHL NW7 96 B4
ORP BR6 206 E8
PIN HA5 112 G1
REDH RH1 275 P2
SAND/SEL CR2 223 J2
STA TW18 173 K9
STHGT/OAK N14 78 C9
SWLY BR8 208 F4
WALTH E17 100 G10
WFD IG8 101 P8
WHTN TW2 176 B2
Bramley Ct GSTN GNTH/NBYPK IG2 122 D4
VX/NE SW8 158 C6
Bramley Gdns OXHEY WD19 93 K7
Bramley Hl SAND/SEL CR2 223 K5
Bramley House Ct ENC/FH EN2 79 L1
Bramley Hyrst SAND/SEL CR2 * 223 K5
Bramley Ldg ALP/SUD HA0 114 A5
Bramley Pde STHGT/OAK N14 78 D5
Bramley Pl DART DA1 165 H10
Bramley Rd BELMT SM2 220 C7
EA W5 155 H3
NKENS W10 136 C10
STHGT/OAK N14 78 C9
SUT SM1 221 N4
Bramley Shaw WAB EN9 63 N1
Bramley Wy HORL RH6 280 D6
HSLWW TW4 175 H1
STALE/WH AL4 39 H1
WWKM BR4 204 B8
Brammas Cl SL SL1 149 H2

Brampton Cl CHESW EN7 61 P4
CLPT E5 120 A2
HARP AL5 20 C2
Brampton Gdns WOT/HER KT12 217 J5
Brampton Gv HDN NW4 116 G2
KTN/HRWW/WS HA3 114 C2
WBLY HA9 115 M6
Brampton La HDN NW4 116 G2
Brampton Park Rd WDGN N22 119 H1
BXLYHN DA7 163 K6
BXLYHN DA7 163 N9
BXLYHN DA7 163 P6
CDALE/KGS NW9 115 M2
CROY/NA CRO 203 N7
EHAM E6 142 A6
HGDN/ICK UB10 132 C4
OXHEY WD19 93 H4
SEVS/STOTM N15 119 K3
STAL AL1 38 C11
Brampton Ter BORE WD6 * 75 M4
Bramshaw Gdns OXHEY WD19 93 K6
Bramshaw Ri NWMAL KT3 200 B6
Bramshaw Rd HOM E9 140 G1
Bramshill Gdns KTTN NW5 118 C4
Bramshill Rd WLSDN NW10 136 B4
Bramshot Av CHARL SE7 161 N5
Bramshot Wy OXHEY WD19 93 H5
Bramston Cl BARK/HLT IG6 103 J1
WLSDN NW10 136 A10
Bramston Rd MTCM CR4 180 A10
WLSDN NW10 136 A10
Bramwell Cl SUN TW16 197 L2
Bramwell Ms IS N1 5 N1
Brancaster Dr MLHL NW7 96 D8
Brancaster La PUR/KEN CR8 223 L7
Brancaster Rd KTN/HRWW/WS HA3 115 J1
BARK/HLT IG6 103 J3
GNTH/NBYPK IG2 122 G4
STNW/STAM N16 119 N6
Branch Cl HAT AL10 40 F2
Branch HI HAMP NW3 117 M8
Branch Pl IS N1 7 H5
Branch Rd BARK/HLT IG6 103 J3
LCOL/BKTW AL2 56 C3
POP/IOD E14 140 C3
STALW/RED AL3 38 A5
Branch St CMBW SE5 159 M6
Brancker Rd KTN/HRWW/WS HA3 115 J1
Brancroft Wy PEND EN3 80 D1
Brandesbury Sq WFD IG8 102 F3
Brandlehow Rd PUT/ROE SW15 157 J10
Brandon Cl CDW/CHF RM16 167 L1
CHESW EN7 61 M2
CRAWE RH10 284 E9
Brandon Est WALW SE17 18 C10
Brandon Groves Av SOCK/AV RM15 147 H5
Brandon Ms BARB EC2Y * 12 F3
HOLWY N7 5 L3
NWDGN UB2 153 N4
SUT SM1 221 L1
WALTH E17 121 L2
Brandon Rd GVW DA11 190 B5
WALW SE17 18 F5
Brandram Ms LEW SE13 * 161 K10
Brandram Rd LEW SE13 161 K9
Brandreth Ct HRW HA1 114 F4
Brandreth Rd EHAM E6 142 C8
TOOT SW17 180 C5
The Brandries WLGTN SM6 202 E10
Brands Hatch Pk HART DA3 210 E10
Brands Hatch Rd HART DA3 210 F10
Brandsland REIG RH2 275 L4
Brand St GNWCH SE10 161 N6
Brandville Gdns BARK/HLT IG6 122 E2
Brandville Rd WDR/YW UB7 151 P1
Brandy Wy BELMT SM2 221 K4
Branfill Rd UPMR RM14 126 C5
Brangbourne Rd BMLY BR1 183 H8
Brangton Rd LBTH SE11 17 P8
Brangwyn Crs WIM/MER SW19 201 N1
Branksea St FUL/PGN SW6 157 N6
Branksome Av UED N18 99 N7
Branksome Cl HHNE HP2 36 B5
TEDD TW11 176 B5
WOT/HER KT12 197 N5
Branksome Rd BRXS/STRHM SW2 180 F1
WIM/MER SW19 201 K1
Branksome Wy KTN/HRWW/WS HA3 115 N3
NWMAL KT3 199 P2
Bransby Rd CHSGTN KT9 219 K4
Branscombe Gdns WCHMN N21 99 H1
Branscombe St LEW SE13 160 G9
Bransdale Cl KIL/WHAMP NW6 2 F5
Bransgrove Rd EDGW HA8 95 L9
Branston Crs STMC/STPC BR5 206 C9
Branstone Rd RCH/KEW TW9 155 L7
Branton Rd RDART DA2 188 A6
Brantbridge Rd CRAWE RH10 284 A9
Brants Wk HNWL W7 135 L2
Brantwood Av ERITH DA8 164 D6
ISLW TW7 154 B3
Brantwood Cl BF/WBF KT14 215 J9
WALTH E17 120 G1
Brantwood Gdns RYLN/HDSTN HA2 114 A9
ENC/FH EN2 77 N1
REDBR IG4 122 B3
Brantwood Rd BXLYHN DA7 164 C1
NWTH SE24 181 K1
SAND/SEL CR2 223 K5
THHTH CR7 99 P7
Brantwood Wy STMC/STPC BR5 207 M3
Brasenose Dr BARN SW13 156 F5
Brasher Cl GFD/PVL UB6 114 C10
Brassey Cl EBED/NFELT TW14 * 175 H4
OXTED RH8 261 M5
Brassey HI OXTED RH8 261 M5
Brassey Rd KIL/WHAMP NW6 2 D1
OXTED RH8 261 M5
Brassey Sq BTSEA SW11 158 F3
Brassie Av ACT W3 136 B8
Brasted Cl BELMT SM2 221 K6
BXLYHS DA6 185 N1
SYD SE26 182 B1
Brasted Hill Rd BH/WHM TN16 245 J4
Brasted La RSEV TN14 245 K5
Brasted Rd BH/WHM TN16 245 K5
ERITH DA8 164 C6
Brathway Rd WAND/EARL SW18 179 K3
Bratley Wd SEV TN13 265 N2
Braund Av GFD/PVL UB6 134 A6
Braunston Dr YEAD UB4 133 M6
Bravington Cl SHPTN TW17 196 A5
Bravington Pl MV/WKIL W9 * 8 A1
Bravington Rd MV/WKIL W9 8 C1
Bravingtons Wk IS N1 5 M8
Braxfield Rd BROCKY SE4 160 A1
Braxted Pk STRHM/NOR SW16 180 G9
Brayard's Rd PECK SE15 160 A1
Braybourne Cl UX/CGN UB8 131 M1
Braybourne Dr ISLW TW7 136 C8
Braybrooke Gdns NRWD SE19 181 M10
Brayburne Av VX/NE SW8 158 D7
Bray Cl BORE WD6 75 K2
Bray Crs BERM/RHTH SE16 160 G1

Braydon Rd STNW/STAM N16 119 N6
Bray Dr CAN/RD E16 141 L10
Brayfield Ter IS N1 6 A4
Brayford Sq WCHPL E1 * 140 B8
Bray Gdns WOKS/MYFD GU22 233 H1
Bray Ldg CHES/WCR EN8 * 62 D3
Bray Pl CHEL SW3 15 L6
Bray Rd COB KT11 235 N2
GUW GU2 267 N1
MLHL NW7 96 G1
Brays Green La AMS HP6 68 A1
Brays Md HLWS CM18 47 J3
Brays Meadow AMS HP6 68 B1
Brayton Gdns ENC/FH EN2 78 E8
Braywood Av ECH TW20 172 C9
Braywood Rd ELTH/MOT SE9 162 G10
Brazier Crs NTHLT UB5 133 N6
Braziers Fld HERT/BAY SG13 25 N5
Brazil Cl CROY/NA CRO 202 F7
RBRW/HUT CM13 107 N6
ROM RM1 124 C4
Brereton Rd TOTM N17 99 N8
Bressay Dr MLHL NW7 96 D8
Bressenden Pl WESTW SW1E 16 F3
Bressey Av EN EN1 78 C9
Bressey Gv SWFD E18 101 L10
Bretlands Rd CHERT KT16 195 H9
Brett Cl NTHLT UB5 133 L5
STNW/STAM N16 119 M7
Brett Gdns DAGW RM9 143 P2
Brettell St WALW SE17 19 H8
Brettenham Av WALTH E17 101 J9
Brettenham Rd UED N18 99 P5
WALTH E17 100 F10
Brettgrave HARL CM19 283 H10
Brett Pas HACK E8 120 A1
Brett Pl WATN WD24 73 H3
Brett Rd BAR EN5 75 P5
HACK E8 120 A1
Brett Vis ACT W3 * 202 F7
Brevet Cl PUR RM19 166 C3
Brewer Rd CRAWW RH11 282 G11
Brewer St REDH RH1 259 K2
REGST W1B 11 H7
Brewery Cl ALP/SUD HA0 114 F10
Brewery La BF/WBF KT14 215 P9
SEV TN13 265 J1
Brewery Rd HAYES BR2 206 B10
HOD EN11 44 F3
HOLWY N7 5 L2
WOKN/KNAP GU21 232 A3
WOOL/PLUM SE18 162 C2
Brewhouse Hi STAL/WH AL4 9 L10
Brewhouse La HERT/WAT SG14 25 K5
WAP E1W 140 A10
Brewhouse Rd BRKHM/BTCW RH3 297 N4
WOOL/PLUM SE18 142 E10
Brewhouse St PUT/ROE SW15 157 H10
Brewhouse Wk BERM/RHTH SE16 141 J5
Brewhouse Yd FSBYE EC1V * 12 D1
GVE DA12 191 P7
Brewood Rd BCTR RM8 143 J2
Brewster Gdns NKENS W10 136 F7
Brewster Rd LEY E10 120 C6
Breydon Wk CRAWE RH10 284 C9
Brian Av SAND/SEL CR2 223 M8
Brian Cl HCH RM12 125 J9
Briane Rd HOR/WEW KT19 218 A9
Brian Rd CHDH RM6 123 N3
Briants Cl PIN HA5 93 N9
Briant St NWCR SE14 160 C7
Briar Av STRHM/NOR SW16 180 A10
Briar Bank CAR SM5 222 B9
Briarbank Rd WEA W13 135 H5
Briarcliff HHW HP1 35 H5
Briar Cl BERK HP4 33 K4
BF/WBF KT14 215 C2
BKHH IG9 102 A3
CHES/WCR EN8 62 B5
CRAWW RH11 283 M4
EFNCH N2 97 M10
HPTN TW12 175 H7
ISLW TW7 172 A1
MDHD SL6 128 A1
PLMGR N13 99 P3
WARL CR6 242 F7
Briar Ct BXLY DA5 186 E6
CRICK NW2 * 135 M4
HARH RM3 105 K4
KTN/HRWW/WS HA3 115 H3
RPLY/SEND GU23 233 H9
SHPTN TW17 196 A5
STALE/WH AL4 39 H6
STRHM/NOR SW16 * 202 F3
Briardale Gdns HAMP NW3 117 K8
Briarfield Av BKHTH/KID SE3 161 P8
Briarfield Cl BXLYHN DA7 164 B6
Briar Gdns HAYES BR2 205 L8
Briar Gv SAND/SEL CR2 223 M9
Briar Hl PUR/KEN CR8 222 F7
Briar La CAR SM5 222 C1
CROY/NA CRO 224 C1
Briarleas Gdns UPMR RM14 126 D5
Briarley Cl BROX EN10 44 A6
Briar Rd BXLY DA5 186 E6
CRICK NW2 135 M4
HARH RM3 105 K4
KTN/HRWW/WS HA3 115 H3
RPLY/SEND GU23 233 H9
SHPTN TW17 196 A5
STRHM/NOR SW16 199 N2
WATN WD24 73 H1
Briars Cl HAT AL10 40 C4
Briars Ct LHD/OX KT22 216 C10
The Briars CHES/WCR EN8 62 D7
DTCH/LGLY SL3 150 A8
HART DA3 210 B10
HLWS CM18 47 N4
RKW/CH/CXG WD3 71 K2
Briars Wd HAT AL10 40 C4
Briars Wy HART DA3 211 M5
Briarswood CHESW EN7 61 N1
Briarswood Wy ORP BR6 227 J3
Briarwood CROY/NA CRO 224 F4
Briarwood Cl CDALE/KGS NW9 115 P4
FELT TW13 175 K1
Briar Wood Cl HAYES BR2 206 B10
Briarwood Dr NTHWD HA6 93 H10
Briarwood Rd CLAP SW4 181 H1
EW KT17 220 D3
Briary Cl EDGW HA8 95 P5
Briary Ct SCUP DA14 186 G2
Briary Gdns BMLY BR1 184 B5
Briary La ED N9 99 N6
Brickbarn Cl WBPTN SW10 * 14 B9
Brick Cl EMB EC4Y * 12 A6
GRAYS RM17 167 N5
Brickcroft BROX EN10 43 N6
Brickcroft Hoppit HLWE CM17 47 P1
Brickenden Ct WAB EN9 63 N1
Brickendon La HERT/BAY SG13 25 K8
RAD EN6 59 M11
Brickett Cl RSLP HA4 95 H5
Brick Farm Cl RCH/KEW TW9 155 N7
Brickfield Av HHS/BOV HP3 36 C7
Brickfield Cl BTFD TW8 155 P6
Brickfield Cots WOOL/PLUM SE18 163 J5
Brickfield Farm Gdns ORP BR6 227 J3
Brickfield La BAR EN5 76 A4
HAYES BR2 205 P7
Brickfield Rd BOW E3 140 A4
THHTH CR7 181 L6
WIM/MER SW19 178 A3
Brickfields RYLN/HDSTN HA2 114 D7
Brickfields La EPP CM16 65 N5
Brickfields Wy WDR/YW UB7 152 B1
Brick Kiln Cl OXHEY WD19 73 M10

Brick Kiln La OXTED RH8 261 P6
Brick Knoll Pk STAL AL1 39 H7
Brick La BETH E2 8 M10
EN EN1 80 A6
NTHLT UB5 133 N5
PEND EN3 80 A3
STAN HA7 95 J8
WCHPL E1 13 M2
Brickmakers La HHS/BOV HP3 36 C7
Brickstock Furze BRWN CM15 * 107 M2
Brick St MYFR/PKLN W1K 10 E10
Brickwall Cl WLYN AL6 22 D3
Brickwall La RSLP HA4 112 F6
Brickwood Cl SYD SE26 182 A6
Brickwood Rd CROY/NA CRO 205 M9
Brickyard La RDKG RH5 271 L7
Brideake Cl CRAWW RH11 283 K10
Brideale Cl PECK SE15 19 M10
Bride La EMB EC4Y 12 B6
Bridel Ms FSBYE EC1V 6 C8
Bride St HOLWY N7 5 P2
Bridewain St STHWK SE1 19 L3
Bridewell Pl BLKFR EC4V 12 C6
WAP E1W 140 A10
Bridford Ms GTPST W1W 10 E3
Bridge Ap CAMTN NW1 4 C3
Bridge Av HMSMTH W6 156 G10
HNWL W7 134 C7
UPMR RM14 125 P8
Bridge Barn La WOKN/KNAP GU21 231 P3
Bridge Cl BF/WBF KT14 216 A2
EN EN1 80 A6
NKENS W10 136 B10
RBRW/HUT CM13 107 K4
RDART DA2 166 C9
ROMW/RG RM7 124 F4
SL SL1 128 F8
STA TW18 173 H7
WOKN/KNAP GU21 231 P3
WOT/HER KT12 196 G5
Bridge Dr PLMGR N13 98 G5
Bridge End WALTH E17 101 H9
Bridge End Cl KUTN/CMB KT2 199 N11
Bridgefield Cl BNSTD SM7 238 F11
Bridgefield Rd SUT SM1 221 K3
Bridge Foot WARE SG12 * 26 C2
Bridge Gdns ASHF TW15 174 D10
E/WMO/HCT KT8 198 C4
Bridge Ga WCHMN N21 99 K1
Bridgeham Cl WEY KT13 236 C5
Bridgeham Wy HORL RH6 281 J5
Bridge Hi EPP CM16 65 P5
Bridgehill Cl GUW GU2 249 M8
ALP/SUD HA0 114 B5
Bridge House Quay POP/IOD E14 141 H10
Bridgeland Rd CAN/RD E16 140 G9
Bridgelands CRAWE RH10 284 G2
Bridgelands Cl BECK BR3 182 E10
Bridge La BTSEA SW11 158 D1
HDN NW4 116 G2
VW GU25 194 B6
Bridgeman Dr WDSR SL4 148 F8
Bridgeman Rd IS N1 5 M1
TEDD TW11 176 B5
Bridge Mdw NWCR SE14 160 C5
Bridgeman St STJWD NW8 3 M8
Bridgen Rd BXLY DA5 185 P3
Bridgenhall Rd EN EN1 78 B2
Bridgen Rd BXLY DA5 185 P5
Bridge Pde STRHM/NOR SW16 * 180 F8
WCHMN N21 * 99 K1
Bridge Pl CROY/NA CRO 203 N10
PIM SW1V 16 E5
WAT WD17 23 H5
Bridgepoint Pl HGT N6 118 C8
Bridgeport Pl WAP E1W * 13 P9
Bridger Cl GSTN WD25 59 G12
Bridge Rd ASC SL5 192 C5
BECK BR3 183 J1
BXLYHN DA7 163 P9
CHERT KT16 195 J7
CHONG CM5 67 L11
CHSGTN KT9 219 K2
COB KT11 235 L2
E/WMO/HCT KT8 198 A4
ED N9 100 D1
EHAM E6 142 D5
HORL RH6 280 A4
KWD/TDW/WH KT20 222 F10
PUR/KEN CR8 222 G7
RSLP HA4 94 A7
SAND/SEL CR2 223 K5
STNW/STAM N16 119 M9
SURB KT6 199 H6
WATN WD24 73 H4
Bridge Rd East WCCE AL7 23 H4
Bridge Rw CROY/NA CRO * 203 E6
Bridges Cl HORL RH6 280 E6
Bridges Ct BTSEA SW11 157 N9
Bridges Dr DART DA1 188 C1
Bridges La CROY/NA CRO 222 G1
Bridges Ms WIM/MER SW19 * 179 L9
Bridges Pl FUL/PGN SW6 157 J6
Bridges Rd STAN HA7 95 G11
WIM/MER SW19 179 L9
Bridges Road Ms WIM/MER SW19 * 179 L9
Bridge St BERK HP4 33 M8
CHSWK W4 138 B10
GU GU1 6 E5
HDN NW4 116 G2
PIN HA5 113 J1
RCH/KEW TW9 177 J1
STA TW18 173 J2
TWK TW1 177 J2
WALTH E17 101 J2
WEST SW1P 17 J2
Bridge Ter LEW SE13 * 161 J10
SRTFD E15 121 J6
The Bridge EA W5 * 135 P5
KTN/HRWW/WS HA3 114 E1
Bridgeview HMSMTH W6 157 H1
Bridge Vw ASC SL5 192 D5
Bridgewater Cl STMC/STPC BR5 207 N4
Bridgewater Ct DTCH/LGLY SL3 150 A9
Bridgewater Gdns EDGW HA8 95 K9
Bridgewater Rd ALP/SUD HA0 114 B5
BERK HP4 33 N3
RSLP HA4 113 J2
WEY KT13 216 E4
Bridgewater Sq BARB EC2Y 12 F3
Bridgewater St BARB EC2Y 12 F3
Bridgewater Ter WDSR SL4 149 J5
Bridgewater Wy BUSH WD23 73 N9
GRAYS RM17 167 N5
WDSR SL4 149 J5
Bridge Wy COUL/CHIP CR5 239 P6
GLDGN NW11 117 J3

HGDN/ICK UB10 112 C10
WHTN TW2 176 B3
Bridgeways HOD EN11 44 G3
Bridgeway St CAMTN NW1 5 H8
Bridge Whf CHERT KT16 195 M7
Bridge Whf Rd ISLW TW7 154 C9
Bridgewood Cl PGE/AN SE20 182 A10
Bridgewood Rd STRHM/NOR SW16 180 G10
WPK KT4 220 D1
Bridgford St WAND/EARL SW18 179 M6
Bridgman Rd CHSWK W4 155 P2
Bridgwater Rd HARH RM3 105 K6
RSLP HA4 113 H9
Bridgwater Wk HARH RM3 105 L6
Bridle Cl HOD EN11 44 G3
HOR/WEW KT19 219 P6
KUT/HW KT1 199 J4
PEND EN3 80 E3
STALW/RED AL3 38 D4
SUN TW16 197 H3
Bridle La COB KT11 236 A1
RKW/CH/CXG WD3 71 M7
SOHO/CST W1F 11 H7
TWK TW1 176 G2
Bridle Pth CROY/NA CRO 223 H2
WAT WD17 73 J6
The Bridle Pth EW KT17 220 F6
WFD IG8 101 K8
Bridlepath Wy EBED/NFELT TW14 174 F3
Bridle Rd CROY/NA CRO 224 F1
ESH/CLAY KT10 218 G3
EW KT17 220 C9
PIN HA5 113 K4
The Bridle Rd PUR/KEN CR8 222 G7
Bridle Wy BERK HP4 33 M8
CRAWE RH10 284 E6
CROY/NA CRO 224 F2
HOD EN11 26 F10
ORP BR6 226 F1
WARE SG12 26 F5
Bridleway (North) HOD EN11 26 F9
Bridle Way (South) HOD EN11 26 F10
The Bridle Wy WLGTN SM6 222 F6
Bridlington Cl BH/WHM TN16 283 H5
Bridlington Rd ED N9 100 A11
OXHEY WD19 93 J3
Bridlington Sp SL SL1 148 G2
Bridport Av ROMW/RG RM7 124 C4
Bridport Pl IS N1 7 H6
Bridport Rd GFD/PVL UB6 134 A3
THHTH CR7 203 H1
UED N18 99 M6
Bridport Wy SLN SL2 128 C5
Bridstow Pl BAY/PAD W2 8 F3
Brief St BRXN/ST SW9 159 J7
Brier Lea KWD/TDW/WH KT20 257 J2
Brierley CROY/NA CRO 224 C3
Brierley Av ED N9 100 B2
Brierley Cl EMPK RM11 125 K4
SNWD SE25 203 P4
Brierley Rd BAL SW12 180 F3
WAN E11 121 J9
Brierly Cl GUW GU2 249 M8
Brierly Gdns BETH E2 * 140 E4
Briery Ct RKW/CH/CXG WD3 71 K7
The Briers POTB/CUF EN6 59 L8
Briery Fld RKW/CH/CXG WD3 71 K7
Briery Wy AMS HP6 69 K3
HHNE HP2 36 B4
Brigade Cl RYLN/HDSTN HA2 114 C7
Brigade St BKHTH/KID SE3 * 161 L8
Brigadier Av ENC/FH EN2 79 K5
Brigadier Hl ENC/FH EN2 79 K4
Briggs Cl MTCM CR4 202 C2
Bright Cl BELV DA17 163 N10
Brightfield Rd LEE/GVPK SE12 183 K1
Bright Hl GU GU1 268 A2
Brightlands GVW DA11 190 B7
Brightlands Rd REIG RH2 257 M8
Brightlingsea Pl POP/IOD E14 140 E9
Brightman Rd WAND/EARL SW18 179 N4
Brighton Av WALTH E17 121 J2
Brighton Cl ADL/WDHM KT15 215 M2
HGDN/ICK UB10 132 C2
Brighton Dr NTHLT UB5 113 M5
Brighton Rd ADL/WDHM KT15 215 M1
BELMT SM2 221 L6
BNSTD SM7 239 J2
CRAWE RH10 283 N10
EFNCH N2 97 M10
EHAM E6 142 D5
HORL RH6 280 A4
KWD/TDW/WH KT20 222 F10
PUR/KEN CR8 222 F10
REDH RH1 276 A2
SAND/SEL CR2 223 K5
STNW/STAM N16 119 M9
SURB KT6 199 H6
WATN WD24 73 H1
Brighton Sp SLN SL2 128 G6
Brighton Ter BRXN/ST SW9 158 G10
Brights Av RAIN RM13 145 J6
Brightside Rd LEW SE13 183 J2
The Brightside PEND EN3 80 C5
Bright St POP/IOD E14 140 G8
Brightview Cl LCOL/BKTW AL2 55 N5
Brightwell Cl CROY/NA CRO 203 H8
Brightwell Crs TOOT SW17 180 A4
Brightwen Gv STAN HA7 94 F3
Brig Ms DEPT SE8 160 C4
Brigstock Rd BELV DA17 164 C3
COUL/CHIP CR5 240 C1
THHTH CR7 203 J5
Brill Pl CAMTN NW1 5 K8
Brimfield Rd PUR RM19 166 B3
Brim HI EFNCH N2 117 H2
Brimpsfield Cl ABYW SE2 163 L2
Brimsdown Av PEND EN3 80 G5
Brimshot La CHOB/PIR GU24 213 K5
Brimstone Cl ORP BR6 227 L7
Brimstone La RDKG RH5 33 L3
Brindle Ga BFN/LL DA15 185 H6
Brindles EMPK RM11 125 K4
Brindles Cl RBRW/HUT CM13 107 K3
SLH/COR SL7 169 K3
The Brindles BNSTD SM7 239 J3
Brindley Cl ALP/SUD HA0 135 M1
BXLYHN DA7 164 B2
Brindley St BROCKY SE4 160 C2
Brindley Wy BMLY BR1 183 P3
STHL UB1 134 A6
Brindwood Rd CHING E4 101 J4
Brinkburn Cl ABYW SE2 162 A2
EDGW HA8 115 N1
Brinkburn Gdns EDGW HA8 115 M1
Brinkley Rd WPK KT4 200 F10
Brinklow Crs STALW/RED AL3 38 A9
Brinklow Crs WOOL/PLUM SE18 162 G6
Brinkworth Rd CLAY IG5 121 L2
Brinkworth Wy HOM E9 140 E1
Brinley Cl CHES/WCR EN8 62 C7
Brinsdale Rd HDN NW4 116 B2
Brinsley Rd KTN/HRWW/WS HA3 94 C10
Brinsley St WCHPL E1 * 140 A8
Brinsmead FBAR/BDGN N11 98 D7
Brinsmead Rd HARH RM3 105 P10
Brinsworth Cl WHTN TW2 176 C5
Briscoe Cl WAN E11 122 A9? 
Brisbane Av WIM/MER SW19 178 C3
Brisbane Ct WOOL/PLUM SE18 162 E5
Brisbane Rd EA W5 154 E2
IL IG1 122 D2
LEY E10 120 G7

Brisbane St CMBW SE5 159 L6
Briscoe Cl HOD EN11 44 E1
  WAN E11 121 L7
Briscoe Rd HOD EN11 44 E1
  RAIN RM13 145 K4
  WIM/MER SW19 179 M1
Briset Rd ELTH/MOT SE9 162 A9
Briset St FARR EC1M 12 C5
Brisson Cl ESH/CLAY KT10 217 H5
Bristol Cl CRAWE RH10 284 E4
  HSLWW TW4 175 P5
  STWL/WRAY TW19 222 F5
Bristol Gdns MV/WKIL W9 9 K2
Bristol Ms MV/WKIL W9 9 K2
Bristol Park Rd WALTH E17 120 D2
Bristol Rd FSTGT E7 141 P1
  GFD/PVL UB6 134 A2
  GVE DA12 190 G6
  MRDN SM4 201 M5
Bristol Wy SL SL1 129 K10
Briston Gv CEND/HSY/T N8 118 F4
Bristow Rd BXLYHN DA7 163 P7
  CROY/NA CRO 227 H2
  HSLW TW3 154 A9
  NRWD SE19 181 M8
Britannia Cl CLAP SW4 158 E10
  ERITH DA8 164 C8
  NTHLT UB5 133 L5
Britannia Ga CAN/RD E16 141 K4
Britannia La WHTN TW2 176 B3
Britannia Rd BRW CM14 107 H6
  BRYLDS KT5 199 L1
  CHES/WCR EN8 62 C10
  CSHM HP5 51 H5
  FUL/PGN SW6 157 L6
  IL IG1 122 E8
  NFNCH/WDSPK N12 97 M4
  POP/IOD E14 160 F5
Britannia Rw IS N1 6 B1
Britannia Wk IS N1 5 N9
Britannia Wy FUL/PGN SW6 157 L6
  STWL/WRAY TW19 173 N3
  WLSDN NW10 135 L4
British Est BOW E3 140 E5
British Gv HMSMTH W6 148 E4
British Grove Pas CHSWK W4 * 156 C4
British Legion Rd CHING E4 101 L3
Briton Cl SAND/SEL CR2 223 M7
Briton Crs SAND/SEL CR2 223 M7
Briton Hill Rd SAND/SEL CR2 223 M6
Brittage Rd WLSDN NW10 136 C2
Brittain Rd BCTR RM8 123 P8
Brittains La SEV TN13 264 C2
Britten Cl BORE WD6 75 J10
  CRAWW RH11 282 E2
  GLDGN NW11 117 L6
Brittenden Pde ORP BR6 * 227 J3
Britten Dr STHL UB1 133 P8
Brittens Cl GUW GU2 249 M5
Britten St CHEL SW3 15 M8
Brittidge Rd WLSDN NW10 * 136 E2
Britton Av STALW/RED AL3 38 C6
Britton Cl CAT SE6 183 H1
Britton St FARR EC1M 12 C2
Britwell Dr BERK HP4 34 B3
Brixham Crs RSLP HA4 113 H6
Brixham Gdns GDMY/SEVK IG3 125 H10
Brixham Rd WELL DA16 163 N7
Brixham St CAN/RD E16 142 C10
Brixton Hill BRXS/STRHM SW2 180 G2
Brixton Hill Pl BRXS/STRHM SW2 180 F3
Brixton Ov BRXS/STRHM SW2 159 H10
Brixton Rd BRXN/ST SW9 159 M1
  LBTH SE11 18 A10
  WATW WD18 23 G3
Brixton Station Rd BRXN/ST SW9 159 H9
Brixton Water La BRXS/STRHM SW2 180 G1
Broad Acre LCOL/BKTW AL2 55 M6
Broadacre STA TW18 22 B9
Broadacre Cl HGDN/ICK UB10 112 C8
Broad Acres GODL GU7 267 K9
  HAT AL10 40 C1
Broadacres RGUW GU3 249 K8
Broadbent Cl HGT N6 66 B6
Broadbent St MYFR/PKLN W1K * 10 E7
Broadberry Ct UED N18 100 A6
Broad Bridge Cl BKHTH/KID SE3 161 M6
Broadbridge La HORL RH6 281 H5
Broad Cl WOT/HER KT12 197 L10
Broad Common Est STNW/STAM N16 119 P6
Broadcoombe SAND/SEL CR2 224 C4
Broad Ct COVGDN WC2E * 11 M6
  WGCE AL7 23 H5
Broadcroft HHNE HP2 35 N4
Broadcroft Av STAN HA7 95 J10
Broadcroft Rd STMC/STPC BR5 206 G7
Broad Ditch Rd MEO DA13 189 P10
Broadeaves Cl SAND/SEL CR2 223 M4
Broadfield HLW CM20 29 H10
Broadfield Cl CRICK NW2 116 A3
  KWD/TDW/WH KT20 238 F6
  ROM RM1 124 G3
Broadfield Ct BUSH WD23 94 D3
Broadfield Dr CRAWW RH11 283 H10
Broadfield La CAMTN NW1 5 J1
Broadfield Pde EDGW HA8 * 95 H3
Broadfield Pl WGCW AL8 22 E6
Broadfield Rd CAT SE6 183 H1
  HHNE HP2 35 N4
Broadfield Sq EN EN1 29 L2
Broadfields ESH/CLAY KT10 198 C6
  E/WMO/HCT KT8 197 H5
  RYLN/HDSTN HA2 94 A10
  SBW CM21 29 L2
Broadfields Av EDGW HA8 95 H3
  WCHMN N21 99 H1
Broadfields Hts EDGW HA8 * 95 H3
Broadfields La OXHEY WD19 93 J2
Broadfield Wy BKHH IG9 101 N4
Broadford La CHOB/PIR GU24 213 N8
Broadford Pk RGUE GU4 268 A3
Broadford Rd RGUE GU4 268 A2
Broadgates Av EBAR EN4 77 L5
Broadgates Rd WAND/EARL SW18 179 N4
Broad Gn CHES/WCR EN8 62 C1
Broad Green Av CROY/NA CRO 203 J7
Broadgreen Rd CHESW EN7 61 L2
Broad Green Wd HERT/BAY SG13 42 G1
Broadham Green Rd OXTED RH8 261 J9
Broadham Pl OXTED RH8 261 J8
Broadhead Strd CDALE/KGS NW9 96 C10
Broadheath Dr CHST BR7 184 G1
Broad Hwy COB KT11 217 H10
Broadhinton Rd CLAP SW4 158 C9
Broadhurst ASHTD KT21 237 K6
Broadhurst Av EDGW HA8 95 N5
  GDMY/SEVK IG3 123 J9
Broadhurst Cl KIL/WHAMP NW6 3 J1
Broadhurst Gdns KIL/WHAMP NW6 3 H2
  REIG RH2 275 L3
  RSLP HA4 113 H6

Broadhusrt Cl RCHPK/HAM TW10 177 L1
Broadlake Cl LCOL/BKTW AL2 57 L3
Broadlands FELT TW13 175 N6
  GRAYS RM17 167 L4
  HORL RH6 280 D3
Broadlands Av CSHM HP5 51 H6
  PEND EN3 80 A7
  SHPTN TW17 196 D6
  STRHM/NOR SW16 180 F5
Broadlands Cl HGT N6 66 A9
  PEND EN3 80 A7
  STRHM/NOR SW16 180 F5
Broadlands Dr ASC SL5 192 B7
  WARL CR6 242 B5
Broadlands Rd BMLY BR1 183 N1
  HGT N6 118 A1
Broadlands Wy NWMAL KT3 200 C5
Broad La CEND/HSY/T N8 118 C2
  HPTN TW12 175 N10
  RDKG RH5 278 A2
  SEVS/STOTM N15 119 N3
Broad Lawn ELTH/MOT SE9 184 D1
Broadlawn Pde KIL/WHAMP NW6 * 3 K2
Broadwick St SOHO/CST W1F * 11 J1
Broadmead GVW DA11 190 E8
Broadmead Av WPK KT4 200 E6
Broad Oak SLN SL2 129 K6
  SUN TW16 174 C9
  WFD IG8 101 N6
Broadoak Av PEND EN3 80 C1
Broad Oak Cl CHING E4 100 F6
Broad Oak Cl EYN DA4 187 P9
Broad Oak Cl STMC/STPC BR5 207 K2
Broadoak Rd ERITH DA8 164 E6
Broad Oaks SURB KT6 199 N8
Broad Oaks Cl BF/WBF KT14 215 L10
Broad Oaks Wy HAYES BR2 205 L5
Broad Platts DTCH/LGLY SL3 150 A3
Broad St DAGE RM10 144 B2
  HHNE HP2 35 N2
  TEDD TW11 176 E9
Broad Street Av LVPST EC2M 13 H4
Broad Street Pl LVPST EC2M 13 H4
Broadstone Pl MHST W1U 10 C4
Broadstone Rd HCH RM12 144 A2
Broadstrood LOU IG10 82 D9
Broadview CDALE/KGS NW9 115 M4
Broadview Av GPK RM2 104 G9
Broadview Rd STRHM/NOR SW16 180 E4
Broad Wk CTHM CR3 * 107 M5
Broadwalk RYLN/HDSTN HA2 114 A3
  SWFD E18 121 L1
Broadwalk La GLDGN NW11 117 J5
The Broad Walk (North) RBRW/HUT CM13 107 M5
The Broadwalk (South) RBRW/HUT CM13 107 M5
The Broad Wk BAY/PAD W2 9 H9
  KENS W8 15 J1
Broadwall STHWK SE1 12 B9
Broadwater BERK HP4 33 P4
  POTB/CUF EN6 59 L6
Broadwater Gdns DEN/HRF UB9 111 K4
  ORP BR6 226 E1
Broadwater La DEN/HRF UB9 * 111 K4
Broadwater Pk DEN/HRF UB9 * 111 K4
Broadwater Ri GU GU1 268 E8
Broadwater Rd THMD SE28 147 L9
  TOOT SW17 179 P7
  TOTM N17 99 M10
  WGCW AL8 22 G6
Broadway BARK IG11 142 C7
  BXLYHS DA6 164 B10
  CDALE/KGS NW9 115 M4
  CEND/HSY/T N8 118 D2
  CFSP/GDCR SL9 90 B3
  CHEAM SM3 221 L5
  CRW RM5 104 C8
The Broadway ACT W3 155 J1

  CSHM HP5 50 G7
  EA W5 135 J9
  ED N9 99 P4
  FBAR/BDGN N11 * 98 A3
  HCH RM12 125 J9
  KTN/HRWW/WS HA3 94 D10
  LOU IG10 82 F7
  MLHL NW7 96 B6
  PIN HA5 93 N8
  PLSTW E13 141 M3
  POTB/CUF EN6 59 J8
  RYLN/HDSTN HA2 * 114 C7
  STA TW18 195 M3
  STAL AL1 38 C2
  STAN HA7 95 K4
  SUT SM1 221 M1
  THDIT KT7 198 D8
  WAT WD17 73 K7
  WFD IG8 101 N7
  WIM/MER SW19 179 J9
  WOKN/KNAP GU21 232 C3
Brocas Cl HAMP NW3 3 P3
Brocas St WDSR SL4 149 J6
Brocas Ter WDSR SL4 149 H6
Brockdene Dr HAYES BR2 226 A1
Brockdish Av BARK IG11 123 J10
Brockenhurst E/WMO/HCT KT8 197 J6
Brockenhurst Av WPK KT4 200 B8
Brockenhurst Cl WOKN/KNAP GU21 214 C10
Brockenhurst Gdns IL IG1 122 F6
  MLHL NW7 96 B6
Brockenhurst Ms UED N18 99 P5
Brockenhurst Rd CROY/NA CRO 204 B8
Brockenhurst Wy STRHM/NOR SW16 202 E2
Brocket Cl CHIG IG7 103 J5
Brocket Rd HOD EN11 44 F3
  WGCE AL7 22 C7
Brockett Cl WGCW AL8 22 C6
Brockett Rd CDW/CHF RM16 168 D2
Brocket Wy CHIG IG7 103 H6
Brockham Cl WIM/MER SW19 178 A1
Brockham Crs CROY/NA CRO 225 J4
Brockham Dr BRXS/STRHM SW2 180 G3
  GNTH/NBYPK IG2 122 F4
Brockham Hill Pk KWD/TDW/WH KT20 255 P7
Brockhamhurst Rd BRKHM/BTCW RH3 273 N7
Brockham La BRKHM/BTCW RH3 255 M10
Brockham St STHWK SE1 19 H3
Brockhill WOKN/KNAP GU21 231 M3
Brockhurst Cl STAN HA7 94 E7
Brockhurst Rd CSHM HP5 51 H5
Brockill Crs BROCKY SE4 160 D10
Brocklebank Rd CHARL SE7 161 N3
  WAND/EARL SW18 160 A3
Brocklehurst St NWCR SE14 160 C6
Brocklesbury Cl WATN WD24 75 K7
Brocklesby Rd SNWD SE25 202 E4
Brockles Md HLWW/ROY CM19 46 F5
Brockley Av STAN HA7 95 K4
Brockley Cl STAN HA7 95 K5
Brockley Combe WEY KT13 216 E2
Brockley Crs CRW RM5 104 D8
Brockley Cross BROCKY SE4 160 D9
Brockley Gv BROCKY SE4 181 K2
  RBRW/HUT CM13 107 M2
Brockley Hall Rd BROCKY SE4 181 J3
Brockley Hl STAN HA7 95 J3
Brockley Ms BROCKY SE4 181 J2
Brockley Pk FSTH SE23 162 A10
Brockley Ri FSTH SE23 182 A2
Brockley Rd BROCKY SE4 181 J3
Brockley Vw FSTH SE23 162 A10
Brockley Wy FSTH SE23 181 M4
Brockman Ri BMLY BR1 184 E3
Brock Pl BOW E3 140 C6
Brock Rd CRAWW RH11 283 L4
  PLSTW E13 141 K3
Brocks Dr CHEAM SM3 201 H10
Brockshot Cl BTFD TW8 155 J5
Brock St PECK SE15 160 B9
Brockswood La WGCW AL8 22 E4
Brockton Cl ROM RM1 124 C2
Brock Wy CU GU1 250 B8
Brockway Cl WAN E11 121 K7
Brockwell Av BECK BR3 202 E4
Brockwell Cl STMC/STPC BR5 207 J5
Brockwell Park Gdns HNHL SE24 181 J3
Brockwell Park Rw BRXS/STRHM SW2 181 H3
Brockworth Cl PECK SE15 19 J9
Broderick Gv EYN DA4 187 P9
Brodewater Rd BORE WD6 75 N3
Brodia Rd STNW/STAM N16 119 M9
Brodie Rd CHING E4 101 K4
  ENC/FH EN2 29 J4
  GU GU1 268 E1
Brodie St STHWK SE1 19 M7
Brodlove La WAP E1W 140 G9
Brodrick Gv ABYW SE2 163 K3
  GT/LBKH KT23 253 P2
Brodrick Rd TOOT SW17 179 P5
Brograve Gdns BECK BR3 204 G2
Broke Ct RGUE GU4 250 G3
Broke Farm Dr ORP BR6 227 M5
Broken Furlong WDSR SL4 148 D3
Broken Gate La DEN/HRF UB9 110 C2
Broken Wharf BLKFR EC4V * 12 E6
Brokes Crs REIG RH2 257 L2
Brokesley St BOW E3 140 L6
Brokes Rd REIG RH2 257 L2
Broke Wk HACK E8 * 7 J3
Bromar Rd CMBW SE5 159 N9
Bromborough Gn OXHEY WD19 93 K6
Bromefield STAN HA7 95 K9
Bromefield Ct WFD IG8 * 101 K4
Brome House CHST BR7 * 95 H2
Bromell's Rd CLAP SW4 158 D10
Bromet Cl WAT WD17 72 C4
Bromfelde Rd CLAP SW4 158 E9
Bromfield St IS N1 6 B3
Bromford Cl OXTED RH8 261 J9
Bromhall Rd DAGW RM9 143 L4
Bromhedge ELTH/MOT SE9 184 C1
Bromholm Rd ABYW SE2 148 E10
Bromleigh Cl CHES/WCR EN8 * 62 D1
Bromley Av BMLY BR1 183 K10
Bromley Common HAYES BR2 205 K10
Bromley Ct BMLY BR1 183 J5
Bromley Crs HAYES BR2 205 P2
  RSLP HA4 113 H6
Bromley Gdns HAYES BR2 205 P2
Bromley Hall Rd POP/IOD E14 141 N6
Bromley High St BOW E3 140 B8
Bromley Hl BMLY BR1 183 L4
Bromley La CHST BR7 185 J3
Bromley La AMS HP6 50 A10

  CHST BR7 184 F10
Bromley Rd BECK BR3 204 F1
  CAT SE6 182 G6
  CHST BR7 206 A3
  CHST BR7 184 F10
  HAYES BR2 205 K2
  LEY E10 120 G6
  UED N18 99 L5
  WALTH E17 120 F1
Bromley St WCHPL E1 140 G7
Brompton Ar CHEL SW3 * 16 A2
Brompton Cl HSLWW TW4 175 N10
Brompton Dr ERITH DA8 165 J6
Brompton Gv EFNCH N2 117 P2
Brompton Park Crs FUL/PGN SW6 14 F10
Brompton Pl CHEL SW3 15 P5
Brompton Rd CHEL SW3 15 P4
Brompton Sq CHEL SW3 15 N3
Brompton Ter WOOL/PLUM SE18 * 162 D7
Bromwich Av HGT N6 118 A1
Bromyard Av ACT W3 136 B10
Bromycroft Rd SLN SL2 128 C5
Brondesbury Ms KIL/WHAMP NW6 * 2 E4
Brondesbury Pk KIL/WHAMP NW6 136 F2
Brondesbury Rd KIL/WHAMP NW6 2 D7
Brondesbury Vis KIL/WHAMP NW6 2 D7
Bronhill Ter TOTM N17 99 P9
Bronsart Rd FUL/PGN SW6 157 H6
Bronson Rd RYNPK SW20 200 A3
Bronte Cl ERITH DA8 164 C6
  FSTGT E7 * 121 M9
  GNTH/NBYPK IG2 122 D2
  SL SL1 149 K1
  TIL RM18 168 F8
Bronte Gv DART DA1 165 N10
Bronti Cl WALW SE17 18 F7
Bronze Age Wy BELV DA17 164 D2
Bronze St DEPT SE8 160 F6
Brook Av DAGE RM10 144 C2
  EDGW HA8 95 N7
  WBLY HA9 115 L8
Brookbank Av HNWL W7 134 C7
Brookbank Rd LEW SE13 160 F11
Brook Cl ACT W3 135 M10
  BORE WD6 75 N5
  DORK RH4 255 H10
  GPK RM2 104 G9
  HOR/WEW KT19 220 B5
  RSLP HA4 112 F5
  RYNPK SW20 200 E5
  STWL/WRAY TW19 174 A3
  TOOT SW17 180 A3
Brook Ct BECK BR3 * 204 E1
  BRW CM14 106 G4
Brooke Av RYLN/HDSTN HA2 114 B8
Brooke End RAD WD7 56 F9
Brookend Rd BFN/LL DA15 185 N7
Brooker Rd WAB EN9 63 H10
Brookers Cl ASHTD KT21 237 H3
Brooke Rd SEV TN13 265 M4
  STNW/STAM N16 119 N7
  WALTH E17 121 H2
Brooke's Ct HCIRC EC1N 12 A3
Brooke's Market HCIRC EC1N * 12 A3
Brooke St HCIRC EC1N 12 A3
Brookfield CHIG IG7 103 K6
  GODL GU7 267 M9
  WOKN/KNAP GU21 231 K5
Brookfield Av EA W5 135 J3
  MLHL NW7 96 E3
  SUT SM1 201 P10
  WALTH E17 121 H1
Brookfield Cl ASHTD KT21 237 H3
  CHERT KT16 214 G3
  MLHL NW7 96 E3
  REDH RH1 276 B6
Brookfield Ct GFD/PVL UB6 133 N2
  KTN/HRWW/WS HA3 114 A3
Brookfield Crs KTN/HRWW/WS HA3 115 K3
  MLHL NW7 96 E3
Brookfield Gdns CHES/WCR EN8 62 C3
  ESH/CLAY KT10 218 D3
Brookfield La East CHES/WCR EN8 62 C3
Brookfield La West CHES/WCR EN8 62 B3
Brookfield Pk KTTN NW5 118 B4
Brookfield Pth WFD IG8 101 N1
Brookfield Pl COB KT11 235 M1
Brookfield Rd CHSWK W4 156 A4
  ED N9 100 E1
  HOM E9 140 D1
Brookfields EN EN1 30 E4
Brookfields Av MTCM CR4 201 P5
Brook Gdns BARN SW13 156 C9
  CHING E4 100 C1
  KUTN/CMB KT2 199 M1
Brook Green HMSMTH W6 148 G3
Brookhill Cl EBAR EN4 77 M4
  WOOL/PLUM SE18 162 F9
Brookhill Rd CRAWE RH10 285 H3
  EBAR EN4 77 M4
  WOOL/PLUM SE18 162 F9
Brookhouse Gdns CHING E4 100 E1
Brooking Rd FSTGT E7 121 M10
Brookland Cl GLDGN NW11 117 H2
Brookland Garth GLDGN NW11 117 J2
Brookland Hl GLDGN NW11 117 H2
Brookland Ri GLDGN NW11 117 H2
Brooklands Ap ROM RM1 104 F10
Brooklands Av BFN/LL DA15 184 B8
  WIM/MER SW19 178 G2
Brooklands Cl COB KT11 235 M1
  ROMW/RG RM7 104 F10
  SUN TW16 196 B8
Brooklands Ct KUTN/CMB KT2 * 159 H10
  RAIN RM13 145 J7
Brooklands Dr GFD/PVL UB6 135 J1

Brooklands Gdns EMPK RM11 125 K3
  POTB/CUF EN6 59 H8
Brooklands La ROMW/RG RM7 124 A8
  WEY KT13 216 A2
Brooklands Pk BKHTH/KID SE3 161 M9
Brooklands Pl HPTN TW12 176 A8
Brooklands Rd ROMW/RG RM7 124 A8
  THDIT KT7 198 B8
  WEY KT13 216 A3
Brooklands Ter SUN TW16 * 197 H4
The Brooklands ISLW TW7 * 154 A7
Brook La BERK HP4 33 L4
  BKHTH/KID SE3 161 L8
  BMLY BR1 183 P8
  BRW CM15 91 P9
  BXLY DA5 185 N2
Brook La North BTFD TW8 135 L5
Brooklea Cl CDALE/KGS NW9 96 A5
Brookleys CHOB/PIR GU24 213 L6
Brooklyn Av LOU IG10 82 B8
  SNWD SE25 204 A4
Brooklyn Cl CAR SM5 201 P9
  WOKN/KNAP GU21 232 B5
Brooklyn Gv SNWD SE25 204 A4
Brooklyn Rd HAYES BR2 205 K2
  SNWD SE25 204 A4
  WOKN/KNAP GU21 232 B4
Brooklyn Wy WDR/YW UB7 151 N2
Brookman's Av BRW CM15 86 F10
Brookmans Cl UPMR RM14 126 D5
Brookmans Park Dr UPMR RM14 126 D3
Brook Md HOR/WEW KT19 220 B3
Brookmead Av HAYES BR2 206 C3
Brookmead Cl STMC/STPC BR5 207 L6
Brook Meadow NFNCH/WDSPK N12 97 L5
Brook Meadow Wy WAB EN9 63 K7
Brookmead Rd CROY/NA CRO 202 G3
Brook Ms North BAY/PAD W2 * 9 J1
Brook Park Cl WCHMN N21 79 J8
Brook Pth SL SL1 128 G8
  LOU IG10 82 B9
Brook Pl BAR EN5 77 K9
Brook Ri CHIG IG7 102 G4
Brook Rd BKHH IG9 101 M2
  BORE WD6 75 M5
  BRW CM14 106 G4
  CEND/HSY/T N8 118 F2
  CRICK NW2 116 D7
  EPP CM16 105 J1
  GPK RM2 104 G10
  GVW DA11 190 G4
  LOU IG10 82 B9
  REDH RH1 276 A1
  REDH RH1 258 D4
  RGUE GU4 268 F6
  SURB KT6 199 K9
  SWLY BR8 208 E3
  THHTH CR7 203 K4
  TWK TW1 176 F2
  WDGN N22 97 P10
Brook Rd South BTFD TW8 155 J4
Brooks Av EHAM E6 142 C6
Brooksbank St HOM E9 140 C1
Brooksby Ms IS N1 6 A3
Brooksby St IS N1 6 A3
Brooksby's Wk HOM E9 120 C10
Brooks Cl WEY KT13 216 F6
Brooks Ct HERT/WAT SG14 * 24 C4
Brookscroft CROY/NA CRO 224 E8
Brookscroft Rd WALTH E17 100 G9
Brooksfield WGCE AL7 23 L4
Brookshill KTN/HRWW/WS HA3 94 D7
Brookshill Av KTN/HRWW/WS HA3 94 C6
Brookshill Dr KTN/HRWW/WS HA3 94 C6

Brookside CAR SM5 222 C8
  CHERT KT16 195 H7
  CRAWE RH10 285 H2
  CRAWW RH11 284 A6
  DTCH/LGLY SL3 150 F6
  EBAR EN4 77 H10
  EMPK RM11 125 M3
  HAT AL10 40 C4
  HERT/BAY SG13 23 M6
  HGDN/ICK UB10 132 A2
  HLWW/ROY CM19 46 A6
  HOD EN11 44 D5
  ORP BR6 207 J1
  POTB/CUF EN6 58 D4
  RGUE GU4 250 A5
  WAB EN9 63 K8
  WATN WD24 75 L2
  WCHMN N21 78 G10
Brookside Av ASHF TW15 173 H8
  STWL/WRAY TW19 150 B9
Brookside Cl BAR EN5 76 C10
  FELT TW13 173 N4
  KTN/HRWW/WS HA3 115 K3
  RSLP HA4 113 M9
Brookside Crs POTB/CUF EN6 59 H8
  WPK KT4 200 F8
Brookside Gdns EN EN1 80 A3
Brookside Rd ED N9 99 P4
  GLDGN NW11 117 H4
  HYS/HAR UB3 133 K5
  MEO DA13 190 C10
  OXHEY WD19 93 H7
  YEAD UB4 133 L2
Brookside South EBAR EN4 97 H1
Brookside Wy CROY/NA CRO 204 C6
Brooks La CHSWK W4 155 M5
Brook's Ms MYFR/PKLN W1K 10 D7
Brooks Rd CHSWK W4 155 M5
  PLSTW E13 141 K5
Brook St BAY/PAD W2 9 M7
  BELV DA17 164 D2
  BRW CM14 106 G4
  ERITH DA8 164 D5
  KUTN/CMB KT2 199 H1
  MYFR/PKLN W1K 10 D7
  TOTM N17 99 N10
  WDSR SL4 149 J4
Brooksville Av KIL/WHAMP NW6 2 B6
Brook Va RDKG RH5 272 G8
Brookview CRAWE RH10 285 H2
Brookview Rd STRHM/NOR SW16 180 E7
Brookville Rd FUL/PGN SW6 157 J6
Brook Wk EDGW HA8 96 D2
  NFNCH/WDSPK N12 97 H4
Brook Wy CHIG IG7 102 G6
Brookway BKHTH/KID SE3 161 K3
  LHD/OX KT22 274 D4
  RAIN RM13 145 J7
Brookwood RAIN RM13 145 J7
Brookwood Av BARN SW13 156 C9
Brookwood Cl HAYES BR2 205 L4

Brookwood Lye Rd CHOB/PIR GU24 231 H6
Brookwood Pk HORL RH6 280 C5
Brookwood Rd HSLW TW3 154 A8
  WAND/EARL SW18 179 J4
Broom Av STMC/STPC BR5 207 L4
Broom Bank WARL CR6 243 H5
Broom Cl CHESW EN7 61 P3
  ESH/CLAY KT10 217 H5
  HAYES BR2 206 B3
  TEDD TW11 177 J10
Broom Cnr HARP AL5 * 5 H5
Broomcroft Av NTHLT UB5 133 K5
Broomcroft Cl WOKS/MYFD GU22 232 G2
Broomcroft Dr WOKS/MYFD GU22 232 G1
Broomdashers Rd CRAWE RH10 284 A6
Broome Cl EPSOM KT18 256 A6
Broome Rd HPTN TW12 175 P7
Broomer Pl CHES/WCR EN8 62 A2
Broome Wy CMBW SE5 159 L6
Broomfield GUW GU2 249 K9
  HLW CM20 29 L8
  LCOL/BKTW AL2 56 B3
  SUN TW16 197 H1
  WALTH E17 120 E4
Broomfield Av BROX EN10 82 C10
  LOU IG10 82 C10
  PLMGR N13 98 G5
Broomfield Cl ASC SL5 192 E6
  RGUW GU3 249 K8
Broomfield Cots WEA W13 * 134 C4
Broomfield Ct WEY KT13 216 B5
Broomfield Ga SLN SL2 128 C6
Broomfield La PLMGR N13 98 F5
Broomfield Pk ASC SL5 192 E6
  DORK RH4 272 B5
Broomfield Pl WEA W13 * 134 C4
Broomfield Ride LHD/OX KT22 218 C10
Broomfield Ri ABLGY WD5 54 E8
Broomfield Rd ADL/WDHM KT15 215 L7
  BECK BR3 204 D4
  BXLYHS DA6 186 B1
  CHDH RM6 123 N5
  PLMGR N13 98 F6
  RCH/KEW TW9 155 L7
  SURB KT6 199 L8
  SWCM DA10 189 K2
  TEDD TW11 177 H9
  WEA W13 134 C4
Broomfields ESH/CLAY KT10 218 B2
Broomfield St POP/IOD E14 141 K7
Broom Gdns CROY/NA CRO 204 F2
Broom Gv WAT WD17 23 H1
Broomgrove Gdns EDGW HA8 95 M9
Broomgrove Rd BRXN/ST SW9 159 L8
Broomhall End WOKN/KNAP GU21 232 C6
Broomhall La WOKN/KNAP GU21 232 C6
Broomhall Rd SAND/SEL CR2 223 L5
  WOKN/KNAP GU21 232 C6
Broom Hl HHW HP1 35 H7
Broomhill Ri BXLYHS DA6 186 B1
Broomhill Rd DART DA1 171 J4
  GDMY/SEVK IG3 123 K7
  ORP BR6 207 J1
  WAND/EARL SW18 179 K1
  WFD IG8 101 M7
Broomhills MEO DA13 189 K7
Broomhouse La FUL/PGN SW6 157 K8
Broomhouse Rd FUL/PGN SW6 157 K8
Broomhurst Ct DORK RH4 272 G4
Broomlands La OXTED RH8 262 B3
Broom La CHOB/PIR GU24 213 K5
Broomleys STALE/WH AL4 39 J1
Broomloan La SUT SM1 201 K9
Broom Lock TEDD TW11 * 177 J9
Broom Md BXLYHS DA6 186 B2
Broom Pk TEDD TW11 177 H9
Broom Rd CROY/NA CRO 204 F2
  TEDD TW11 176 G8
Broom Water TEDD TW11 177 H8
Broom Water West TEDD TW11 177 H8
Broomwood Cl BXLY DA5 186 E5
  CROY/NA CRO 204 C5
Broomwood Gdns BRW CM15 86 F10
Broomwood Rd BTSEA SW11 158 G8
  STMC/STPC BR5 207 L2
Broseley Gdns HARM RM3 105 M5
Broseley Gv SYD SE26 182 D8
Broseley Rd HARM RM3 105 M5
Broster Gdns SNWD SE25 203 N3
Brougham Rd ACT W3 135 J8
  HACK E8 7 P5
Broughinge Rd BORE WD6 75 N4
Broughton Av FNCH N3 117 H1
  RCHPK/HAM TW10 176 D3
Broughton Dr BRXN/ST SW9 159 H10
Broughton Gdns HGT N6 66 C3
Broughton Rd FUL/PGN SW6 157 P8
  ORP BR6 226 G1
  RSEV TN14 247 H2
  THHTH CR7 204 D4
  WEA W13 134 C9
Broughton Road Ap FUL/PGN SW6 158 A8
Broughton St VX/NE SW8 158 C8
Broughton Wy RKW/CH/CXG WD3 91 K1
Brouncker Rd ACT W3 135 P5
Brow Crs STMC/STPC BR5 207 N7
Brow Va STMC/STPC BR5 207 M8
Browells La FELT TW13 154 B9
Browne Ct BRW CM14 106 G2
  WOKS/MYFD GU22 232 E6
Brownfield St POP/IOD E14 141 M8
Browngraves Rd HYS/HAR UB3 152 D6
Brown Hart Gdns MYFR/PKLN W1K 10 D7
Browning Av CAR SM5 222 D7
  HNWL W7 134 F5
  SUT SM1 221 P2
  WPK KT4 201 K6
Browning Cl CRAWE RH10 284 D6
  HPTN TW12 175 J6
  MV/WKIL W9 9 K2
  WALTH E17 121 H2
  WELL DA16 163 N7
Browning Ms CAVSQ/HST W1G 10 D4
Browning Rd DART DA1 165 N10
  ENC/FH EN2 29 N1
  HARP AL5 5 H2
  LHD/OX KT22 273 H7
  MNPK E12 141 L2
  WALTH E17 121 L1
Browning St WALW SE17 18 F7
Brownlea Gdns GDMY/SEVK IG3 123 K7

Brownlow Cl *EBAR* EN4 ... 77 N9
Brownlow Ms *BMSBY* WC1N ... 11 P1
Brownlow Rd *BERK* HP4 ... 33 P4
  *BORE* WD6 ... 75 N8
  *CROY/NA* CRO ... 223 M1
  *FBAR/BDGN* N11 ... 98 F1
  *FNCH* N3 ... 97 L8
  *FSTGT* E7 ... 121 N9
  *HACK* E8 ... 7 M5
  *REDH* RH1 ... 257 P10
  *WEA* W13 ... 134 F10
  *WLSDN* NW10 ... 136 B2
Brownlow St *HHOL* WC1V ... 11 P4
Brownrigg Rd *ASHF* TW15 ... 174 H3
Brown Rd *GVE* DA12 ... 191 H5
Brown's Hi *REDH* RH1 ... 277 L7
Browns La *EHSLY* KT24 ... 253 L3
Brownspring Dr
  *ELTH/MOT* SE9 ... 184 E6
Brown's Rd *BRYLDS* KT5 ... 199 L2
  *WALTH* E17 ... 120 F1
Brownswell Rd *EFNCH* N2 ... 97 N10
Brownswood Rd *BEAC* HP9 ... 88 C3
  *FSBYPK* N4 ... 119 K7
Broxash Rd *BTSEA* SW11 ... 180 B3
Broxbourne Av *SWFD* E18 ... 121 N2
Broxbourne Rd *FSTGT* E7 ... 121 N8
Broxbourne House *BOW* E3 ... 140 C4
  *ORP* BR6 ... 207 J8
Broxburn Cl *SOCK/AV* RM15 ... 146 C9
Broxburn Dr *SOCK/AV* RM15 ... 146 C9
Broxhill Rd *ABR/ST* RM4 ... 105 H4
Broxholm Cl *SNWD* SE25 ... 203 L4
Broxholm Rd *WNWD* SE27 ... 181 H6
Brox La *CHERT* KT16 ... 214 C5
Brox Rd *CHERT* KT16 ... 214 F4
Broxted Rd *CAT* SE6 ... 182 E5
Broxwood Wy *STJWD* NW8 ... 3 P6
Bruce Av *HCH* RM12 ... 125 K7
  *SHPTN* TW17 ... 196 F6
Bruce Castle Rd *TOTM* N17 ... 99 N9
Bruce Cl *BF/WBF* KT14 ... 215 N9
  *NKENS* W10 ... 136 C7
  *SL* SL1 ... 128 F10
  *WELL* DA16 ... 148 D2
Bruce Dr *SAND/SEL* CR2 ... 224 C5
Bruce Gdns *TRDG/WHET* N20 ... 98 A4
Bruce Gv *ORP* BR6 ... 207 K8
  *TOTM* N17 ... 99 N10
  *WATN* WD24 ... 73 J4
Bruce Hall Ms *TOOT* SW17 ...
Bruce Rd *BAR* EN5 ... 77 H7
  *BOW* E3 ... 140 C5
  *KTN/HRWW/WS* HA3 ... 94 D10
  *MTCM* CR4 ... 180 D10
  *SNWD* SE25 ... 203 L4
  *WLSDN* NW10 ... 136 K2
Bruces Wharf Rd *GRAYS* RM17 ... 167 M5
Bruckner St *NKENS* W10 ... 2 C10
Brudenell *WDSR* SL4 ... 148 E9
Brudenell Rd *TOOT* SW17 ... 180 A6
Bruffs Meadow *NTHLT* UB5 ... 133 M1
Bruford Ct *DEPT* SE8 ... 160 F5
Bruges Pl *CAMTN* NW1 ... 5 H4
Brumana Cl *WEY* KT13 ... 216 E4
Brumfield Rd *HOR/WEW* KT19 ... 219 P2
Brunel Cl *HEST* TW5 ... 153 J6
  *NRWD* SE19 ... 181 N9
  *NTHLT* UB5 ... 133 N1
  *ROM* RM1 ... 124 F2
  *TIL* RM18 ... 168 E8
Brunel Est *BAY/PAD* W2 ... 8 E4
Brunel House
  *WOOL/PLUM* SE18 * ... 162 B6
Brunel Ms *NKENS* W10 ... 136 C5
Brunel Pl *CRAWE* RH10 ... 283 P8
Brunel Rd *ACT* W3 ... 136 B7
  *BERM/RHTH* SE16 ... 160 B1
  *WALTH* E17 ... 120 D4
  *WFD* IG8 ... 102 C4
Brunel St *CAN/RD* E16 ... 141 L8
Brunel Wk *WHTN* TW2 ... 175 P3
Brunel Wy *SL* SL1 ... 129 L10
Brune St *WCHPL* E1 ... 13 L1
Brunner Cl *GLDGN* NW11 ... 117 L3
Brunner Ct *CHERT* KT16 ... 214 F2
Brunner Rd *EA* W5 ... 135 J6
  *WALTH* E17 ... 120 E3
Bruno Pl *CDALE/KGS* NW9 ... 115 P7
Brunswick Av
  *FBAR/BDGN* N11 ... 98 A3
  *UPMR* RM14 ... 126 D5
Brunswick Cl *BXLYHS* DA6 ... 163 N10
  *CRAWE* RH10 ... 284 E6
  *PIN* HA5 ... 113 M4
  *THDIT* KT7 ... 198 E8
  *WHTN* TW2 ... 176 C6
  *WOT/HER* KT12 ... 197 K9
Brunswick Ct *STHWK* SE1 ... 19 L4
Brunswick Crs
  *FBAR/BDGN* N11 ... 98 B4
Brunswick Dr *CHOB/PIR* GU24 ... 230 C10
Brunswick Gdns
  *BARK/HLT* IG6 ... 102 F8
  *EA* W5 ... 135 K5
  *KENS* W8 ... 8 B10
Brunswick Gv *COB* KT11 ... 217 K10
  *FBAR/BDGN* N11 ... 98 B4
Brunswick Ms *MBLAR* W1H ... 10 B5
  *STRHM/NOR* SW16 ... 180 E9
Brunswick Pk *CMBW* SE5 ... 159 L7
Brunswick Park Gdns
  *FBAR/BDGN* N11 ... 98 B3
Brunswick Park Rd
  *FBAR/BDGN* N11 ... 98 B4
Brunswick Pl *CAMTN* NW1 ... 10 B1
  *IS* N1 ... 7 H10
  *NRWD* SE19 ... 181 P10
Brunswick Quay
  *BERM/RHTH* SE16 ... 160 A4
Brunswick Rd *BXLYHS* DA6 ... 163 N10
  *CHOB/PIR* GU24 ... 230 C7
  *EA* W5 ... 135 J6
  *KUTN/CMB* KT2 ... 199 L1
  *LEY* E10 ... 121 H6
  *PEND* EN3 ... 15 M1
  *SEVS/STOTM* N15 ... 119 M2
  *SUT* SM1 ... 221 L1
Brunswick Sq *BMSBY* WC1N ... 11 M1
  *TOTM* N17 ... 99 N6
Brunswick St *WALTH* E17 ... 121 H3
Brunswick Vis *CMBW* SE5 ... 159 K6
Brunswick Wy *GVE* DA12 ... 190 G2
Brunswick Wy
  *FBAR/BDGN* N11 ... 98 C3
Brunton Pl *POP/IOD* E14 ... 140 D8
Brushfield St *WCHPL* E1 ... 13 L1
Brushfield Wy
  *WOKN/KNAP* GU21 ... 231 H4
Brushmakers Ct *CSHM* HP5 ... 51 H6
Brushrise *WATN* WD24 ... 73 H3
Brushwood Cl *POP/IOD* E14 ... 140 G7
Brushwood Dr
  *RKW/CH/CXG* WD3 ... 70 F8
Brussels Rd *BTSEA* SW11 ... 157 N10
Bruton Cl *CHST* BR7 ... 184 C10
Bruton La *MYFR/PICC* W1J ... 10 F8
Bruton Pl *MYFR/PICC* W1J ... 10 F8
Bruton Rd *MRDN* SM4 ... 201 M4
Bruton St *MYFR/PICC* W1J ... 10 F8
Bruton Wy *WEA* W13 ... 134 F7
Bryan Av *WLSDN* NW10 ... 136 G1
Bryan Cl *SUN* TW16 ... 175 H10
Bryanston Av *WHTN* TW2 ... 176 A5
Bryanston Cl *NWDGN* UB2 ... 153 L5
Bryanstone Av *GUW* GU2 ... 249 L5
Bryanstone Gv *GUW* GU2 ... 249 L6


Bryanstone Rd
  *CEND/HSY/T* N8 ... 118 C2
  *CHES/WCR* EN8 ... 62 E10
Bryanston Ms East
  *MBLAR* W1H ... 10 A4
Bryanston Ms West
  *MBLAR* W1H ... 10 A4
Bryanston Pl *MBLAR* W1H ... 10 A4
Bryanston Rd *TIL* RM18 ... 168 F8
Bryanston Sq *MBLAR* W1H ... 10 A5
Bryanston St *MBLAR* W1H ... 10 A6
Bryanswood Rd *HOLWY* N7 ... 119 H10
Bryant Av *HARH* RM3 ... 105 L10
  *SLN* SL3 ... 129 J7
Bryant Cl *BAR* EN5 ... 77 J9
Bryant Rd *NTHLT* UB5 ... 133 K5
Bryant Rw *HARH* RM3 ... 105 K3
Bryant St *SRTFD* E15 ... 141 J2
Bryantwood Rd *HOLWY* N7 ... 119 H10
Brycedale Crs *STHGT/OAK* N14 ... 98 E1
Bryce Rd *BCTR* RM8 ... 123 M9
Bryden Cl *SYD* SE26 ... 182 A10
Brydges Pl *CHCR* WC2N ... 11 J8
Brydges Rd *SRTFD* E15 ... 121 J10
Brydon Wk *IS* N1 ... 5 N1
Bryer Pl *WDSR* SL4 ... 148 C9
Bryett Rd *HOLWY* N7 ... 118 F8
Brymay Cl *BOW* E3 ... 140 B1
Brympton Cl *DORK* RH4 ... 272 F4
Brymford Cl *WOKN/KNAP* GU21 ... 232 B1
Brynmaer Rd *BTSEA* SW11 ... 158 F6
Bryn Wy *STALE/WH* AL4 ... 39 J8
Bryn-Y-Mawr Rd *EN* EN1 ... 79 N8
Bryony Cl *LOU* IG10 ... 82 E8
  *UX/CGN* UB8 ... 132 A7
Bryony Gv *GU* GU1 ... 250 E7
  *SHB* W12 ... 136 D9
Bryony Wy *SUN* TW16 ... 175 H9
Bubblestone Rd *RSEV* TN14 ... 247 J3
Bulsby Ms *KTTN* NW5 ... 5 J1
Buccleuch Rd *DTCH/LGLY* SL3 ... 149 M6
Buchanan Cl *SOCK/AV* RM15 ... 146 A9
  *WCHMH* N21 ... 78 C9
Buchanan Ct *BORE* WD6 ... 75 P6
Buchanan Gdns *WLSDN* NW10 ... 136 L4
Buchan Cl *UX/CGN* UB8 ... 131 M5
Buchan Rd *PECK* SE15 ... 160 B9
Bucharest Rd
  *WAND/EARL* SW18 ... 179 M3
Buckden Cl *LEE/GVPK* SE12 ... 183 M2
Buckfastleigh La *BORE* WD6 ... 76 A3
Buckfast Rd *MRDN* SM4 ... 201 L4
Buckfast St *BETH* E2 ... 7 N10
Buckham Thorns Rd
  *BH/WHM* TN16 ... 262 F2
Buckhold Rd
  *WAND/EARL* SW18 ... 179 K2
Buckhurst Av *CAR* SM5 ... 201 P8
  *SEV* TN13 ... 265 K1
Buckhurst La *ASC* SL5 ... 192 E2
Buckhurst St *WCHPL* E1 ... 140 A6
  *BH/WHM* TN16 ... 244 E6
Buckhurst Wy *BKHH* IG9 ... 102 A4
Buckingham Av
  *E/WMO/HCT* KT8 ... 198 A2
  *EBED/NFELT* TW14 ... 175 J2
  *GFD/PVL* UB6 ... 134 F3
  *THHTH* CR7 ... 203 H1
  *TRDG/WHET* N20 ... 97 H1
  *WELL* DA16 ... 163 H10
Buckingham Av East *SL* SL1 ... 129 H8
Buckingham Cl *CHST* BR7 ... 184 E8
Buckingham Gdns
  *E/WMO/HCT* KT8 ... 198 A2
  *SL* SL1 ... 149 L1
  *STAN* HA7 ... 95 H4
  *THHTH* CR7 ... 203 H2
Buckingham Ga *HORL* RH6 ... 280 D7
  *WESTW* SW1E ... 16 G3
Buckingham Gv
  *HGDN/ICK* UB10 ... 132 B4
Buckingham Ms *EA* W5 ... 135 H7
  *WESTW* SW1E * ... 16 G3
  *WLSDN* NW10 ... 136 C4
Buckingham Palace Rd
  *BGVA* SW1W ... 16 E5
Buckingham Pde
  *CFSP/GDCR* SL9 * ... 90 B9
  *STAN* HA7 * ... 95 H6
Buckingham Pl *WESTW* SW1E ... 16 G3
Buckingham Rd *BORE* WD6 ... 76 A8
  *EDGW* HA8 ... 95 L8
  *GVW* DA11 ... 190 A3
  *HPTN* TW12 ... 175 N7
  *HRW* HA1 ... 114 C3
  *IL* IG1 ... 122 C7
  *IS* N1 ... 7 J2
  *KUT/HW* KT1 ... 199 L4
  *LEY* E10 ... 120 C8
  *MTCM* CR4 ... 202 F5
  *RCHPK/HAM* TW10 ... 177 J5
  *RDKG* RH5 ... 273 H10
  *SRTFD* E15 ... 121 L10
  *SWFD* E18 ... 101 P5
  *WAN* E11 ... 121 N2
  *WATN* WD24 ... 73 K3
  *WDGN* N22 ... 99 H10
  *WLSDN* NW10 ... 136 C4
Buckingham St *CHCR* WC2N ... 11 M8
Buckland Av *DTCH/LGLY* SL3 ... 149 N7
Buckland Crs *HAMP* NW3 ... 3 L4
Buckland Gdns *BELMT* SM2 ... 220 F6
  *CHSGTN* KT9 ... 219 L2
  *KWD/TDW/WH* KT20 ... 257 J4
  *LEY* E10 ... 121 H1
  *ORP* BR6 ... 227 N1
  *RH2* RH2 ... 256 D8
Bucklands *OXHEY* WD19 * ... 35 J4
Bucklands Rd *TEDD* TW11 ... 177 H9
Buckland St *IS* N1 ... 7 H8
Bucklands Whf *KUT/HW* KT1 * ... 199 P1
Buckland Wk *MRDN* SM4 ... 201 M4
Buckland Wy *WPK* KT4 ... 200 H9
Buck La *CDALE/KGS* NW9 ... 115 L3
Buckleigh Av *RYNPK* SW20 ... 201 J5
Buckleigh Rd
  *STRHM/NOR* SW16 ... 180 H9
Buckleigh Wy *NRWD* SE19 ... 203 H1
Bucklers' Wy *CAR* SM5 ... 202 F2
Buckles La *SOCK/AV* RM15 ... 147 N1
Buckle St *WCHPL* E1 ... 13 M5
Buckley Cl *DART* DA1 ... 164 G6
  *FSTH* SE23 ... 163 N11
Buckley Pl *CRAWE* RH10 ... 285 P5
Buckman's Rd *KIL/WHAMP* NW6 ... 2 F1
Buckmans Rd *CRAWW* RH11 ... 283 N7
Buckmaster Rd *BTSEA* SW11 ... 158 E4
Bucknalls Cl *GSTN* WD25 ... 55 N1
Bucknalls Dr *LCOL/BKTW* AL2 ... 55 M4
Bucknalls La *GSTN* WD25 ... 55 N1
Bucknall St *NOXST/BSQ* WC1A ... 11 J3
Bucknall Wy *BECK* BR3 ... 202 G1
Bucknell Cl *BRXS/STRHM* SW2 ... 158 F10
Buckner Rd *BRXS/STRHM* SW2 ... 158 F10
Buckrell Rd *EPSOM* KT18 ... 219 P10
Buckrell Rd *CHING* E4 ... 104 C7
Bucks Aly *HERT/BAY* SG13 ... 42 E5


Buck's Aly *HERT/BAY* SG13 ... 42 F5
Bucks Av *OXHEY* WD19 ... 93 M1
Bucks Cl *BF/WBF* KT14 ... 215 L10
Bucks Cross Rd *GVW* DA11 ... 190 G6
  *ORP* BR6 ... 227 P2
Bucks Hl *KGLGY* WD4 ... 55 M9
Bucks Cl *FSTH* SE23 ... 182 B2
Buckstone Rd *ED* N18 ... 99 P7
Buck St *CAMTN* NW1 ... 4 F3
Buckswood Dr *CRAWW* RH11 ... 283 K9
Buckters Rents
  *BERM/RHTH* SE16 ... 140 D10
Buckthorne Rd *BROCKY* SE4 ... 182 D2
Buckton Rd *BORE* WD6 ... 75 L4
Budd Cl *NFNCH/WDSPK* N12 ... 97 H1
Buddcroft *WGCE* AL7 ... 23 L4
Buddings Cir *WBLY* HA9 ... 115 P8
Budebury Rd *STA* TW18 ... 173 J8
Budge La *MTCM* CR4 ... 202 A7
Budgen Cl *CRAWE* RH10 ... 284 E4
Budgen Dr *REDH* RH1 ... 258 B7
Budge Rw *MANHO* EC4N ... 12 G7
Budgin's Hi *ORP* BR6 ... 227 L8
Budleigh Crs *WELL* DA16 ... 163 M7
Budoch Dr *GDMY/SEVK* IG3 ... 123 K7
Buer Rd *FUL/PGN* SW6 ... 157 H8
Bug Hl *WARL* CR6 ... 242 F6
Bugsby's Wy *GNWCH* SE10 ... 161 L3
Bulbourne Cl *BERK* HP4 ... 33 P4
  *HNWL* W7 * ... 35 K7
Bulganak Rd *THHTH* CR7 ... 203 K4
Bulinca St *WEST* SW1P ... 17 J6
Bulkeley Av *WDSR* SL4 ... 148 G9
Bulkeley Cl *EGH* TW20 ... 171 P8
Bullace Cl *HHW* HP1 ... 35 J5
Bullace Rw *CMBW* SE5 ... 159 L7
Bullard Rd *TEDD* TW11 ... 176 D9
Bullards Pl *BETH* E2 ... 140 C5
Bullbaiters La *AMS* HP6 ... 50 A10
Bullbanks Rd *BELV* DA17 ... 164 D3
Bullbeggars La *BERK* HP4 ... 34 D5
  *GDST* RH9 ... 260 B8
  *WOKN/KNAP* GU21 ... 231 N2
Bull Cl *CDW/CHF* RM16 ... 167 L1
Bulleid Wy *BGVA* SW1W ... 16 F6
Bullen's Green La
  *STALE/WH* AL4 ... 40 B9
Bullen St *BTSEA* SW11 ... 157 P8
Buller Cl *PECK* SE15 ... 159 P6
Buller Rd *BARK* IG11 ... 143 H2
  *THHTH* CR7 ... 203 L3
  *TOTM* N17 ... 99 P10
  *WDGN* N22 ... 99 H10
  *WLSDN* NW10 ... 136 C5
Bullers Cl *SCUP* DA14 ... 185 P8
Bullers Wood Dr *CHST* BR7 ... 206 B1
Bullescroft Rd *EDGW* HA8 ... 95 M4
Bullfinch Cl *HORL* RH6 ... 279 P3
  *SEV* TN13 ... 246 E8
Bullfinch Dene *SEV* TN13 ... 246 E8
Bullfinch La *SEV* TN13 ... 246 E8
Bullfinch Rd *SAND/SEL* CR2 ... 224 C6
Bull Hl *EYN* DA4 ... 210 B4
  *LHD/OX* KT22 ... 236 F7
Bullivant Cl *RDART* DA2 ... 188 F1
Bullivant St *POP/IOD* E14 ... 141 H9
Bull La *CFSP/GDCR* SL9 ... 110 A1
  *CHST* BR7 ... 184 C10
  *DAGE* RM10 ... 124 C8
  *RGUE* GU4 ... 250 A2
  *STALE/WH* AL4 ... 20 F5
  *UED* N18 ... 99 M6
Bullock's La *HERT/BAY* SG13 ... 25 K7
Bull Pin *HERT/WAT* SG14 ... 25 L3
Bull Rd *SRTFD* E15 ... 141 L1
Bullrush Cl *CAR* SM5 ... 201 P9
  *CROY/NA* CRO ... 203 M6
  *HAT* AL10 ... 40 F4
Bulls Aly *MORT/ESHN* SW14 * ... 156 A9
Bulls Br *NWDGN* UB2 ... 153 H2
Bulls Bridge Rd *NWDGN* UB2 ... 153 H2
Bullsbrook Rd *YEAD* UB4 ... 133 K10
Bull's Cross *IS* N1 ... 79 P2
Bulls Cross Ride *CHESW* EN7 ... 61 P10
Bull's Gdns *CHEL* SW3 ... 15 P5
Bullsland Gdns
  *RKW/CH/CXG* WD3 ... 70 G10
Bullsland La
  *RKW/CH/CXG* WD3 ... 70 G10
Bulls La *BRKMPK* AL9 ... 40 G10
Bullsmoor Gdns
  *CHES/WCR* EN8 ... 80 A1
Bullsmoor La *ENC/FH* EN2 ... 79 P1
Bullsmoor Ride
  *CHES/WCR* EN8 ... 80 B1
Bullsmoor Wy *CHES/WCR* EN8 ... 80 B1
Bull Stag Gn *BRKMPK* AL9 ... 40 F2
Bulmer Gdns
  *KTN/HRWW/WS* HA3 ... 115 J5
Bulmer Ms *NTGHL* W11 ... 8 A9
Bulstrode Av *HSLW* TW3 ... 153 N9
Bulstrode Gdns *HSLW* TW3 ... 153 H9
Bulstrode La *KGLGY* WD4 ... 53 H5
  *MHST* W1U ... 10 D3
Bulstrode Wy *CFSP/GDCR* SL9 ... 110 B5
Bulwer Court Rd *WAN* E11 ... 121 N8
Bulwer Gdns *BAR* EN5 ... 77 M8
Bulwer Rd *BAR* EN5 ... 77 M8
  *UED* N18 ... 99 M6
  *WAN* E11 ... 121 N8
Bulwer St *SHB* W12 ... 136 F10
Bumbles Green La *WAB* EN9 ... 63 N1
Bunbury Wy *EW* KT17 ... 238 C2
Bunby Rd *SLN* SL3 ... 129 J8
Bunce Common Rd *REIG* RH2 ... 274 D9
Bunce Dr *CTHM* CR3 ... 241 L9
Buncefield La *HHNE* HP2 ... 36 C5
Buncefield Terminal
  *HHNE* HP2 * ... 36 E4
Bunces Cl *WDSR* SL4 ... 148 G4
Bunces La *WFD* IG8 ... 102 A4
Bundys Wy *STA* TW18 ... 173 J9
The Bungalows
  *RYLN/HDSTN* HA2 ... 113 N8
  *STRHM/NOR* SW16 ... 180 C10
  *RDKG* RH5 ... 166 F5
Bunhill Rw *STLK* EC1Y ... 12 G1
Bunhouse Pl *BGVA* SW1W ... 16 C7
Bunkers Hl *GLDGN* NW11 ... 117 M3
  *SCUP* DA14 ... 186 A6
Bunker's La *HHS/BOV* HP3 ... 54 B1
Bunning Wy *HOLWY* N7 ... 5 M3
Bunnsfield *WGCE* AL7 ... 23 N3
Bunn's La *MLHL* NW7 ... 96 H3
Bunsen St *BOW* E3 ... 140 D4
Buntan Meade *SL* SL1 ... 128 G4
Buntingbridge Rd
  *BARK/HLT* IG6 ... 122 G3
Bunting Cl *ED* N9 ... 100 G3
  *MTCM* CR4 ... 202 A4
Bunton St *WOOL/PLUM* SE18 ... 162 A5
Bunyan Cl *CRAWW* RH11 ... 283 H7
Bunyan Rd *WALTH* E17 ... 120 D1
Bunyard Dr *WOKN/KNAP* GU21 ... 232 D2
Burbage Cl *CHES/WCR* EN8 ... 80 D3
  *HYS/HAR* UB3 ... 132 D7
  *STHWK* SE1 ... 19 H4


Burbage Rd *HNHL* SE24 ... 181 L2
Burbeach Cl *CRAWW* RH11 ... 283 L10
Burberry Cl *NWMAL* KT3 ... 200 D9
Burberry Cl *DEN/HRF* UB9 ... 91 M10
Burbidge Rd *SHPTN* TW17 ... 196 M4
Burbridge Wy *TOTM* N17 ... 123 P9
Burcham St *POP/IOD* E14 ... 140 G8
Burcharbro Rd *ABYW* SE2 ... 163 N5
Burchell Rd *BUSH* WD23 ... 94 B1
  *LEY* E10 ... 120 C6
  *PECK* SE15 ... 159 M7
Burcher Gale Gv *PECK* SE15 ... 159 M6
Burchets Hollow *SHGR* GU5 ... 270 C7
Burchetts Wy *SHPTN* TW17 ... 196 C6
Burchwall Cl *CRW* RM5 ... 104 D8
Burcote *WEY* KT13 ... 216 F5
Burcott Gdns
  *ADL/WDHM* KT15 ... 215 N3
Burcott Rd *PUR/KEN* CR8 ... 241 J5
Burden Cl *BTFD* TW8 ... 155 H4
Burdenshott Av
  *RCHPK/HAM* TW10 ... 157 N9
Burdenshott Rd *RGUW* GU3 ... 231 M10
Burden Wy *GUW* GU2 ... 249 N5
  *WAN* E11 ... 121 N3
Burder Cl *IS* N1 ... 7 K1
Burder Rd *IS* N1 ... 7 K1
Burdett Av *GVE* DA12 ... 191 P7
  *RYNPK* SW20 ... 200 C2
Burdett Cl *CRAWE* RH10 ... 284 E8
  *SCUP* DA14 ... 185 P8
Burdett Ms *BAY/PAD* W2 ... 8 E6
Burdett Rd *CROY/NA* CRO ... 223 N5
  *POP/IOD* E14 ... 140 D7
  *RCH/KEW* TW9 ... 155 L8
Burdock Cl *CROY/NA* CRO ... 204 C9
  *LTWR* GU18 ... 212 A7
Burdock Rd *TOTM* N17 ... 119 P2
Burdon La *BELMT* SM2 ... 221 J5
Burdon Pk *BELMT* SM2 ... 221 J6
Bure *HLWE* HP2 ... 35 L7
Burfield Cl *HAT* AL10 ... 40 D2
  *TOOT* SW17 ... 179 P8
Burfield Dr *WARL* CR6 ... 242 B5
Burfield Rd *RGUW* GU3 ... 249 M11
  *WDSR* SL4 ... 148 C9
Burford Cl *BARK/HLT* IG6 ... 122 F2
  *DAGW* RM9 ... 123 P8
  *HGDN/ICK* UB10 ... 111 P9
Burford La *KT17* KT17 ... 220 A1
Burford Ms *BMLY* BR1 ... 206 B4
Burford Pk *HLWW/ROY* CM19 ... 46 B5
Burford Rd *BMLY* BR1 ... 206 B4
  *BTFD* TW8 ... 155 K4
  *CAT* SE6 ... 182 B10
  *EHAM* E6 ... 142 A3
  *SRTFD* E15 ... 141 J2
  *SUT* SM1 ... 201 N3
  *WPK* KT4 ... 200 C5
Burford Wk *FUL/PGN* SW6 * ... 157 P4
Burford Wy *CROY/NA* CRO ... 225 L4
Burgage La *WARE* SG12 * ... 26 E1
Burgage La *WARE* SG12 ... 26 E1
Burgate Cl *DART* DA1 ... 166 G9
Burges Cl *EMPK* RM11 ... 125 M4
Burges Gv *BARN* SW13 ... 156 E6
Burges Rd *EHAM* E6 ... 142 C2
  *STA* TW18 ... 163 H10
Burgess Av *CDALE/KGS* NW9 ... 116 A4
Burgess Cl *CHESW* EN7 ... 61 K1
  *FELT* TW13 ... 175 H3
Burgess Hi *CRICK* NW2 ... 117 L9
Burgess Ms *WIM/MER* SW19 ... 179 L9
Burgess Rd *SRTFD* E15 ... 121 K9
  *SUT* SM1 ... 221 L1
Burgess St *POP/IOD* E14 ... 140 F7
Burgess Wood Gv *BEAC* HP9 ... 88 A9
Burgess Wood Rd South
  *BEAC* HP9 ... 88 A10
Burge St *STHWK* SE1 ... 19 H4
Burges Wy *STA* TW18 ... 173 K8
Burgett Rd *SL* SL1 ... 148 D2
Burgh Cl *CRAWE* RH10 ... 284 E4
Burghfield Rd *MED* DA13 ... 190 C10
Burgh Heath Rd *EW* KT17 ... 238 C6
Burghill Rd *SYD* SE26 ... 182 C7
Burghley Av *BORE* WD6 ... 76 B4
  *NWMAL* KT3 ... 200 A9
Burghley Hall Cl
  *WIM/MER* SW19 * ... 179 H4
Burghley Pl *MTCM* CR4 ... 202 A3
Burghley Rd *BRXN/ST* SW9 ... 158 G8
  *FSBYPK* N4 ... 119 H4
  *SUN* TW16 ... 174 C9
  *WIM/MER* SW19 ... 179 H4
  *WTHK* RM20 ... 166 G6
Burgh Mt *BNSTD* SM7 ... 239 J7
Burgh St *IS* N1 ... 6 E6
Burgh Wd *BNSTD* SM7 ... 239 H7
Burgon St *BLKFR* EC4V ... 12 E6
Burgos Cl *CROY/NA* CRO ... 223 H5
Burgos Gv *GNWCH* SE10 ... 160 E4
Burgoyne Rd *BRXN/ST* SW9 ... 158 F9
  *FSBYPK* N4 ... 119 H4
  *SNWD* SE25 ... 203 H3
  *SUN* TW16 ... 174 C9
Burham Cl *PGE/AN* SE20 ... 182 B10
Burhill Gv *PIN* HA5 ... 93 L10
Burhill Rd *WOT/HER* KT12 ... 217 H9
Burke Cl *PUT/ROE* SW15 ... 156 E1
Burkes Cl *BEAC* HP9 ... 108 A1
Burkes Ct *BEAC* HP9 * ... 88 C9
Burke St *CAN/RD* E16 ... 141 L6
Burket Cl *NWDGN* UB2 ... 153 H3
Burland Rd *BRWN* CM15 ... 107 M2
  *BTSEA* SW11 ... 180 D1
  *CRW* RM5 ... 104 F1
Burlands *CRAWW* RH11 ... 283 H4
Burlea Cl *WOT/HER* KT12 ... 197 L2
Burleigh Av *BFN/LL* DA15 ... 185 J1
  *WLGTN* SM6 ... 202 B10
Burleigh Cl *ADL/WDHM* KT15 ... 215 L2
  *ROMW/RG* RM7 ... 124 C5
Burleigh Gdns *ASHF* TW15 ... 175 H7
  *STHGT/OAK* N14 ... 98 E4
  *WOKN/KNAP* GU21 ... 232 C5
Burleigh Pde
  *STHGT/OAK* N14 * ... 98 E4
Burleigh Pk *COB* KT11 ... 217 M8
Burleigh Pl *PUT/ROE* SW15 ... 178 B1
Burleigh Rd *ADL/WDHM* KT15 ... 215 M3
  *CHEAM* SM3 ... 201 M8
  *CHES/WCR* EN8 ... 62 A1
  *EN* EN1 ... 79 N8
  *HERT/BAY* SG13 ... 42 B4
  *HGDN/ICK* UB10 ... 132 C3
  *HHNE* HP2 ... 8 G6
  *STAL* AL1 ... 38 C5
Burleigh St *COVGDN* WC2E ... 11 M7
Burleigh Wk *CAT* SE6 ... 183 H4
Burleigh Wy *ENC/FH* EN2 ... 79 M9
  *POTB/CUF* EN6 ... 60 D1
Burley Cl *CHING* E4 ... 101 N5
  *STRHM/NOR* SW16 ... 202 G1
Burley Hl *HLWE* CM17 ... 47 N1
Burley Rd *CAN/RD* E16 ... 141 M8
Burleys *CRAWE* RH10 ... 285 K6
Burlingham Cl *RGUE* GU4 ... 250 A6
Burlings La *RSEV* TN14 ... 245 H5
Burlington Ar *CONDST* W1S ... 10 G7
Burlington Av *RCH/KEW* TW9 ... 155 P5
  *ROMW/RG* RM7 ... 124 A1
Burlington Cl *EBED/NFELT* TW14 ... 174 E3


  *EHAM* E6 ... 142 B8
  *MV/WKIL* W9 ... 8 A1
  *ORP* BR6 ... 206 G8
  *PIN* HA5 ... 113 J1
Burlington Ct *SL* SL1 ... 149 K1
Burlington Gdns *CHDH* RM6 ... 123 M5
  *CHSWK* W4 ... 155 P4
  *CONDST* W1S ... 10 G8
  *FUL/PGN* SW6 ... 157 J7
Burlington La *CHSWK* W4 ... 155 P6
Burlington Ms *ACT* W3 ... 135 P10
Burlington Pde *CRICK* NW2 * ... 116 G9
Burlington Pl *FUL/PGN* SW6 ... 157 J7
  *REIG* RH2 ... 257 K9
  *WFD* IG8 ... 101 M4
Burlington Ri *EBAR* EN4 ... 97 P2
Burlington Rd *CHSWK* W4 ... 155 P4
  *ENC/FH* EN2 ... 79 M10
  *FUL/PGN* SW6 ... 157 H8
  *ISLW* TW7 ... 154 C7
  *MUSWH* N10 ... 118 B1
  *NWMAL* KT3 ... 200 D4
  *SL* SL1 ... 128 A2
  *THHTH* CR7 ... 203 L3
  *TOTM* N17 ... 99 P9
Burman Cl *RDART* DA2 ... 188 C5
Burma Rd *CHERT* KT16 ... 215 H5
  *STNW/STAM* N16 ... 119 L9
Burmar Rd *NRWD* SE19 * ... 181 M11
Burmester Rd *TOOT* SW17 ... 179 M6
Burnaby Crs *CHSWK* W4 ... 155 P5
Burnaby Gdns *CHSWK* W4 ... 155 N5
Burnaby St *WBPTN* SW10 ... 157 M6
Burnbrae Cl
  *NFNCH/WDSPK* N12 ... 97 L7
Burnbury Rd *BAL* SW12 ... 180 D4
  *GSTN* WD25 ... 74 C8
Burncroft Av *PEND* EN3 ... 80 B6
Burndell Wy *YEAD* UB4 ... 133 L8
Burnell Av *RCHPK/HAM* TW10 ... 177 H8
  *WELL* DA16 ... 163 K8
Burnell Gdns *STAN* HA7 ... 95 L10
Burnell Rd *SUT* SM1 ... 221 L2
Burnell Wk *RBRW/HUT* CM13 ... 107 H7
Burnels Av *EHAM* E6 ... 142 B2
Burness Cl *HOLWY* N7 ... 5 N1
  *UX/CGN* UB8 ... 131 N4
Burne St *CAMTN* NW1 ... 9 N3
Burnet Cl *CHOB/PIR* GU24 ... 212 D9
Burnet Gv *HOR/WEW* KT19 ... 219 P9
Burnett Cl *HMSMTH* W6 ... 137 H8
Burnett La *BARK/HLT* IG6 ... 102 E8
Burnett Pk *HLWW/ROY* CM19 ... 46 D5
Burnett Rd *ERITH* DA8 ... 165 J6
  *LEY* E10 ... 120 C6
Burnett Sq *HERT/WAT* SG14 ... 24 G4
Burnetts Rd *WDSR* SL4 ... 148 D7
Burney Av *BRYLDS* KT5 ... 199 L5
Burney Cl *LHD/OX* KT22 ... 254 B1
Burney Dr *LOU* IG10 ... 82 F7
Burney Rd *RDKG* RH5 ... 254 F7
Burney St *GNWCH* SE10 ... 161 N6
Burnfoot Av *FUL/PGN* SW6 ... 157 H7
Burnham Av *BEAC* HP9 ... 108 D1
  *HGDN/ICK* UB10 ... 112 D9
Burnham Cl *EN* EN1 ... 79 M4
  *KTN/HRWW/WS* HA3 ... 114 F2
  *MLHL* NW7 ... 96 B8
  *STHWK* SE1 ... 19 M4
  *WDSR* SL4 ... 148 G8
  *WOKN/KNAP* GU21 ... 231 J4
Burnham Crs *DART* DA1 ... 165 K10
  *WAN* E11 ... 121 P2
Burnham Dr *REIG* RH2 ... 257 K9
  *WPK* KT4 ... 201 K7
Burnham Gdns *CROY/NA* CRO ... 203 N7
  *HSLWW* TW4 ... 153 J5
  *HYS/HAR* UB3 ... 152 E2
Burnham La *SL* SL1 ... 128 C2
Burnham Rd *BEAC* HP9 ... 108 D4
  *CHING* E4 ... 101 J1
  *DAGW* RM9 ... 143 H3
  *DART* DA1 ... 165 K10
  *MRDN* SM4 ... 201 M5
  *ROMW/RG* RM7 ... 124 F1
  *SCUP* DA14 ... 185 P5
  *STAL* AL1 ... 38 F6
  *WOKN/KNAP* GU21 ... 231 J4
Burnhams Rd *GT/LBKH* KT23 ... 235 M10
Burnham St *BETH* E2 ... 140 B5
  *KUTN/CMB* KT2 ... 199 M1
Burnham Ter *DART* DA1 * ... 187 L3
Burnham Wy *SYD* SE26 ... 182 G8
  *WEA* W13 ... 154 A3
Burnhill Rd *BECK* BR3 ... 204 E3
Burnley Cl *OXHEY* WD19 ... 55 N10
Burnley Rd *BRXN/ST* SW9 ... 158 G8
  *WLSDN* NW10 ... 116 G10
  *WTHK* RM20 ... 166 G6
Burnsall St *CHEL* SW3 ... 15 P7
Burns Av *BFN/LL* DA15 ... 185 J5
  *CHDH* RM6 ... 123 M5
  *EBED/NFELT* TW14 ... 153 P11
  *STHL* UB1 ... 133 M7
Burns Cl *CAR* SM5 ... 220 D10
  *WOKN/KNAP* GU21 ... 232 A2
Burns Ct *WLGTN* SM6 ... 222 D7
Burnside *ASHTD* KT21 ... 237 L4
  *HERT/WAT* SG14 ... 25 H6
  *HOD* EN11 ... 44 E5
  *SBW* CM21 ... 29 N1
  *STAL* AL1 ... 38 F8
Burnside Av *CHING* E4 ... 100 G6
Burnside Cl *BAR* EN5 ... 77 K7
  *BERM/RHTH* SE16 ... 140 C10
  *TWK* TW1 ... 176 B6
Burnside Crs *ALP/SUD* HA0 ... 135 P4
Burnside Rd *BCTR* RM8 ... 123 H6
Burns Pl *TIL* RM18 ... 168 F8
Burns Rd *ALP/SUD* HA0 ... 136 A4
  *BTSEA* SW11 ... 158 A10
  *WEA* W13 * ... 154 A2
Burn's Rd *WLSDN* NW10 ... 136 G1
Burns Wy *HEST* TW5 ... 152 G6
  *NOXST/BSQ* WC1A ... 11 K3
Burnt Ash Hl *LEE/GVPK* SE12 ... 183 K9
  *LEE/GVPK* SE12 ... 183 K10
Burnt Ash La *BMLY* BR1 ... 183 P8
  *LEE/GVPK* SE12 ... 183 L6
Burnt Ash Rd *LEE/GVPK* SE12 ... 183 J5
Burnt Common Cl
  *RPLY/SEND* GU23 ... 251 K1
Burnt Common La
  *RPLY/SEND* GU23 ... 251 L1
Burntfarm Ride *ENC/FH* EN2 ... 61 J10
Burnt House La *HORS* RH12 ... 282 D1
Burnthwaite Rd
  *FUL/PGN* SW6 ... 157 J6
Burnt Ml *HLW* CM20 ... 28 E1
Burntmill La *HLW* CM20 ... 28 D2
Burnt Oak Broadway
  *EDGW* HA8 ... 95 N8
Burnt Oak Fids *EDGW* HA8 ... 95 P8
Burnt Oak La *BFN/LL* DA15 ... 185 K2
  *BFN/LL* DA15 ... 185 L3
  *RDKG* RH5 ... 278 F9
Burnt Pollard La *LTWR* GU18 ... 212 D10
Burntwood Av *EMPK* RM11 ... 125 M4
Burntwood Cl *CTHM* CR3 ... 241 N7
  *WAND/EARL* SW18 ... 179 N4
Burntwood Grange Rd
  *WAND/EARL* SW18 ... 179 N4
Burntwood La *CTHM* CR3 ... 241 N6
  *TOOT* SW17 ... 179 N5


Burntwood Rd *SEV* TN13 ... 265 L10
Burntwood Vw *NRWD* SE19 * ... 181 N6
Burnway *EMPK* RM11 ... 125 M5
Burnwood Park Rd
  *WOT/HER* KT12 ... 217 L2
Burrage Gv *WOOL/PLUM* SE18 ... 147 L3
Burpham La *RGUE* GU4 ... 250 D5
Burrage Gv *WOOL/PLUM* SE18 ... 162 F3
Burrage Pl *WOOL/PLUM* SE18 ... 162 G4
Burrage Rd *REDH* RH1 ... 258 B8
  *WOOL/PLUM* SE18 ... 162 F3
Burrard Rd *CAN/RD* E16 ... 141 M8
  *KIL/WHAMP* NW6 ... 117 K10
Burr Bank Ter *RDART* DA2 * ... 187 K7
Burr Cl *BXLYHN* DA7 ... 164 A9
  *LCOL/BKTW* AL2 ... 59 J5
  *WAP* E1W ... 13 N9
Burrell Cl *CROY/NA* CRO ... 204 D6
  *EDGW* HA8 ... 95 N3
Burrell Rw *BECK* BR3 ... 204 F2
Burrell St *STHWK* SE1 ... 12 C9
Burrells Wharf Sq
  *POP/IOD* E14 ... 160 G4
The Burrell *DORK* RH4 ... 272 C6
Burrells Whf *POP/IOD* E14 * ... 140 A8
The Burren *AMS* HP6 * ... 69 J5
Burrfield Dr *STMC/STPC* BR5 ... 207 M5
Burr Hill La *CHOB/PIR* GU24 ... 213 K5
Burritt Rd *KUT/HW* KT1 ... 199 M2
Burroughs Cots
  *POP/IOD* E14 * ... 140 D7
Burroughs Gdns *HDN* NW4 ... 116 G2
The Burroughs *HDN* NW4 ... 116 E2
Burroway Rd *DTCH/LGLY* SL3 ... 150 E2
Burrow Cl *BARK/HLT* IG6 ... 123 H1
Burrowfield *WGCE* AL7 ... 22 C7
Burrow Gv *CHIG* IG7 ... 103 J6
Burrow Hill Grn
  *CHOB/PIR* GU24 ... 213 J5
Burrow Rd *CHIG* IG7 ... 103 K6
  *EDUL* SE22 ... 159 M10
Burrows Cha *WAB* EN9 ... 81 J2
Burrows Cross *SHGR* GU5 ... 270 D7
Burrows Hill Cl
  *STWL/WRAY* TW19 ... 151 L10
Burrows La *SHGR* GU5 ... 270 C6
Burrow Wk *DUL* SE21 * ... 161 P10
Burr Rd *WAND/EARL* SW18 ... 179 K4
Bursar Wy *STHWK* SE1 ... 13 J9
Bursdon Cl *BFN/LL* DA15 ... 185 J5
Burses Wy *RBRW/HUT* CM13 ... 107 M7
Bursland Rd *PEND* EN3 ... 80 C8
Burslem Av *BARK/HLT* IG6 ... 103 K7
Burslem St *WCHPL* E1 ... 13 N5
Burstead Cl *COB* KT11 ... 217 L9
Burstock Rd *PUT/ROE* SW15 ... 157 H10
Burston Dr *LCOL/BKTW* AL2 ... 56 B4
Burston Rd *PUT/ROE* SW15 ... 178 A2
Burstow Rd *RYNPK* SW20 ... 201 H1
Burtenshaw Rd *THDIT* KT7 ... 198 F7
Burtley Cl *FSBYPK* N4 ... 119 K6
Burton Av *WATW* WD18 ... 73 H4
Burton Bank *IS* N1 * ... 6 G4
Burton Cl *CHSGTN* KT9 ... 219 J4
  *HOD* EN11 ... 280 A5
  *THHTH* CR7 ... 203 L8
Burton Dr *PEND* EN3 ... 80 F3
  *RGUW* GU3 ... 249 F5
Burton Gdns *HEST* TW5 ... 153 J6
Burton Gv *WALW* SE17 ... 18 G8
Burtonhole Cl *MLHL* NW7 ... 96 C5
Burtonhole La *MLHL* NW7 ... 96 G5
Burton La *BRXN/ST* SW9 * ... 158 H8
  *CHESW* EN7 ... 61 M4
Burton Ms *BGVA* SW1W ... 16 C6
Burton Pl *STPAN* WC1H ... 11 J1
Burton Rd *BRXN/ST* SW9 ... 158 H8
  *KIL/WHAMP* NW6 ... 2 D1
  *KUTN/CMB* KT2 ... 177 K10
  *LOU* IG10 ... 82 F7
  *SWFD* E18 ... 121 N1
Burtons Ct *SRTFD* E15 ... 141 J2
Burtons La *CSTG* HP8 ... 69 P6
Burton's Rd *HPTN* TW12 ... 176 B7
Burton St *STPAN* WC1H ... 11 K1
Burton Vw *CSTG* HP8 ... 69 M6
Burton Wy *WDSR* SL4 ... 148 D9
Burt Rd *CAN/RD* E16 ... 141 P10
Burtwell La *WNWD* SE27 ... 181 M6
Burwash Ct *STMC/STPC* BR5 ... 207 M5
Burwash Rd *CRAWE* RH10 ... 284 E8
  *WOOL/PLUM* SE18 ... 162 G4
Burway Cl *SAND/SEL* CR2 ... 223 A4
Burway Crs *CHERT* KT16 ... 195 K4
Burwell Av *GFD/PVL* UB6 ... 134 C3
Burwell Cl *WCHPL* E1 ... 140 C6
Burwell Rd *LEY* E10 ... 120 C6
Burwood Av *HAYES* BR2 ... 205 N9
  *PIN* HA5 ... 113 K3
  *PUR/KEN* CR8 ... 223 J10
Burwood Cl *GU* GU1 ... 250 F9
  *REIG* RH2 ... 257 N10
  *SURB* KT6 ... 199 M8
  *WOT/HER* KT12 ... 217 K9
Burwood Gdns *RAIN* RM13 ... 144 G5
Burwood Pl *BAY/PAD* W2 ... 9 P5
  *EBAR* EN4 ... 77 H1
Burwood Rd *WEY* KT13 ... 216 G4
  *WOT/HER* KT12 ... 217 H4
Bury Av *RSLP* HA4 ... 112 A4
  *YEAD* UB4 ... 132 G1
Bury Cl *BERM/RHTH* SE16 ... 140 C10
  *WOKN/KNAP* GU21 ... 232 A2
Bury Ct *HDTCH* EC3A ... 13 K4
Burycroft *WGCE* AL7 ... 23 K2
Burydell La *LCOL/BKTW* AL2 ... 59 J1
Bury Farm *AMS* HP7 ... 267 P2
Bury Fids *GUW* GU2 ... 6 C8
Bury Green Rd *CHESW* EN7 ... 61 N5
Bury Gv *MRDN* SM4 ... 201 L5
Bury Hl *HHW* HP1 ... 35 M5
Bury Hill Cl *HHW* HP1 ... 35 M5
Bury Holme *BROX* EN10 ... 44 H1
Bury La *CHESW* EN7 ... 61 L3
  *EPP* CM16 ... 64 G6
  *RKW/CH/CXG* WD3 ... 70 C4
  *WOKN/KNAP* GU21 ... 231 P2
Bury Mdw *RKW/CH/CXG* WD3 ... 70 C5
Bury Pl *BLOOMSBY* WC1A ... 11 K3
Bury Rd *CHING* E4 ... 88 J1
  *DAGE* RM10 ... 124 D10
  *EPP* CM16 ... 65 H7
  *HAT* AL10 ... 41 J5
  *HHW* HP1 ... 35 M5
  *HLWE* CM17 ... 29 P7
  *WDGN* N22 ... 99 M10
Buryside Cl *GNTH/NBYPK* IG2 ... 123 K3
Bury St *ED* N9 ... 99 M1
  *GUW* GU2 ... 6 C8
  *HDTCH* EC3A ... 13 K4
  *RSLP* HA4 ... 112 A3
  *STJS* SW1Y ... 10 G9
Bury St West *ED* N9 ... 99 M1
The Bury *CSHM* HP5 ... 51 H8
Bury Wk *CHEL* SW3 ... 15 P6
Burwick Ct *BAR* EN5 * ... 77 M5
Busby Pl *KTTN* NW5 ... 5 H1
Busch Cl *ISLW* TW7 ... 154 C7
Bushbaby Cl *STHWK* SE1 ... 19 J4
Bushberry Rd *HOM* E9 ... 139 M1
Bushbury La *BRKHM/BTCW* RH3 ... 273 M5
Bushby Av *BROX* EN10 ... 44 A8
Bush Cl *ADL/WDHM* KT15 ... 215 M2
  *GNTH/NBYPK* IG2 ... 122 G4
Bush Cots *WAND/EARL* SW18 * ... 179 J3
Bush Elms Rd *EMPK* RM11 ... 124 G4
Bush Fair *HLW* CM18 ... 28 C4
Bushell Cl *BRXS/STRHM* SW2 ... 180 A2
Bushell Gn *BUSH* WD23 ... 94 D1
Bushell Wy *CHST* BR7 ... 184 D8

Bush Elms Rd EMPK RM11 125 H5
Bushetts Gv REDH RH1 258 C5
Bushey Av STMC/STPC BR5 206 G7
SWFD E18 121 L1
Bushey Cl CHING E4 101 H4
HGDN/ICK UB10 112 B7
PUR/KEN CR8 241 N2
WGCE AL7 23 L6
Bushey Cft HLWS CM18 47 H3
OXTED RH8 261 H6
Bushey Gn WGCE AL7 23 L6
Bushey Grove Rd BUSH WD23 73 L8
Bushey Hall Dr BUSH WD23 73 M8
Bushey Hall Pk BUSH WD23 * 73 M8
Bushey Hall Rd BUSH WD23 73 L8
Bushey Hill Rd CMBW SE5 159 N7
Bushey La SUT SM1 201 K10
Bushey Lees BFN/LL DA15 * 185 J2
Bushey Ley WGCE AL7 23 L6
Busheymill Br WATN WD24 73 M4
Bushey Mill Crs WATN WD24 73 K2
Bushey Mill La WATN WD24 73 K3
Bushey Rd CROY/NA CR0 204 F9
HGDN/ICK UB10 112 B7
HYS/HAR UB3 152 F3
PLSTW E13 141 P4
RYNPK SW20 200 E3
SEVS/STOTM N15 119 M4
SUT SM1 221 K1
Bushey Wy BECK BR3 205 J6
Bushfield Cl EDGW HA8 95 N3
Bushfield Crs EDGW HA8 95 N3
Bushfield Dr REDH RH1 276 B5
Bushfield Rd HHS/BOV HP3 52 F1
Bushfields LOU IG10 82 D9
Bush Gv CDALE/KGS NW9 115 P5
STAN HA7 95 J8
Bushgrove Rd BCTR RM8 123 N9
Bush Hall La BRKMPK AL9 40 G1
Bush Hl WCHMH N21 99 K1
Bush Hill Pde ED N9 * 99 L1
Bush Hill Rd
KTN/HRWW/WS HA3 115 L4
WCHMH N21 79 L10
Bush House
WOOL/PLUM SE18 * 162 B6
Bush La CANST EC4R 12 G7
RPLY/SEND GU23 232 G10
Bushmead Cl
SEVS/STOTM N15 * 119 N2
Bushmoor Crs
WOOL/PLUM SE18 162 E6
Bushnell Rd TOOT SW17 180 C5
Bush Rd BKHH IG9 102 A5
DEPT SE8 160 C3
HACK E8 140 A3
RCH/KEW TW9 155 L5
SHPTN TW17 196 A5
WAN E11 121 L5
Bushway BCTR RM8 123 N9
Bushwood WAN E11 121 L6
Bushwood Cl BRKMPK AL9 40 E9
Bushwood Dr STHWK SE1 19 M6
Bushwood Rd RCH/KEW TW9 155 M5
Bushy Cl CRW RM5 104 E7
Bushy Hill Dr GU GU1 250 E8
Bushy Lea CHONG CM5 67 P5
Bushy Park Gdns HPTN TW12 176 C8
Bushy Park Rd TEDD TW11 176 G10
Bushy Rd LHD/OX KT22 236 A8
TEDD TW11 176 D9
Bushy Shaw ASHTD KT21 237 H3
Buslins La CSHM HP5 50 D4
Butcher Rw WAP E1W 140 C8
Butchers La BGR/WK TN15 211 J9
Butchers Rd CAN/RD E16 141 M8
Butchers Yd ORP BR6 226 D7
Bute Av RCHPK/HAM TW10 177 K5
Bute Gdns HMSMTH W6 156 G3
RCHPK/HAM TW10 * 177 K4
WLGTN SM6 222 D2
Bute Gdns West WLGTN SM6 222 D2
Bute Ms GLDGN NW11 117 L3
Bute Rd BARK/HLT IG6 122 E3
CROY/NA CR0 203 H8
WLGTN SM6 222 D1
Bute St SKENS SW7 15 L5
Bute Wk IS N1 6 G2
Butler Av HRW HA1 114 C5
Butler Cl EDGW HA8 95 N10
Butler Rd BCTR RM8 123 L9
HRW HA1 114 B5
WLSDN NW10 136 C2
Butlers Cl AMS HP6 68 F3
HSLWW TW4 153 N10
WDSR SL4 148 C8
Butlers & Colonial Whf
STHWK SE1 19 M1
Butlers Court Rd BEAC HP9 88 C10
Butlers Dene Rd CTHM CR3 242 E6
Butlers Dr CHING E4 81 H4
Butlers Farm Cl
RCHPK/HAM TW10 177 J7
Butlers Hl EHSLY KT24 252 C6
Butlers Pl BGR/WK TN15 * 211 K10
Butler St BETH E2 * 140 B5
HGDN/ICK UB10 132 C6
Buttell Cl GRAYS RM17 168 A4
Buttercross La EPP CM16 * 65 K6
Buttercup Cl HARH RM3 105 L9
HAT AL10 22 C10
NTHLT UB5 133 N1
Buttercup Sq
STWL/WRAY TW19 * 173 N4
Butterfield Cl
BERM/RHTH SE16 19 P2
TOTM N17 99 K7
TWK TW1 176 E2
Butterfield House
CHARL SE7 * 162 B6
Butterfield La STAL AL1 38 D10
Butterfield Ms
WOOL/PLUM SE18 162 E5
Butterfield Rd STALE/WH AL4 21 H4
Butterfields WALTH E17 121 H3
Butterfield Sq EHAM E6 142 C8
Butterfly La BORE WD6 74 G7
ELTH/MOT SE9 184 E2
Butterfly Wk CMBW SE5 * 159 L7
WARL CR6 242 B6
Butter Hl CAR SM5 202 B10
DORK RH4 272 F2
Butteridges Cl DAGW RM9 144 A3
Butterly Av DART DA1 * 187 N5
Buttermere Av SL SL1 128 B7
Buttermere Cl
EBED/NFELT TW14 174 G4
MRDN SM4 200 G6
SRTFD E15 121 J9
STAL AL1 38 G7
STHWK SE1 19 L6
Buttermere Dr
PUT/ROE SW15 179 H1
Buttermere Gdns
PUR/KEN CR8 223 L9
Buttermere Pl GSTN WD25 * 55 H9
Buttermere Rd
STMC/STPC BR5 207 N4
Buttermere Wk HACK E8 7 M2
Buttermere Wy EGH TW20 172 E10
Buttersweet Ri SBW CM21 29 P2
Butterwick GSTN WD25 73 M2
HMSMTH W6 156 F3
Butterworth Gdns WFD IG8 101 M7
Buttery Ms STHGT/OAK N14 98 F4
Buttesland St IS N1 7 H9
Buttfield Cl DAGE RM10 144 C1
Butt Field Vw STAL AL1 38 B10
Buttlehide
RKW/CH/CXG WD3 90 G6
Buttmarsh Cl
WOOL/PLUM SE18 162 E4
Buttondene Crs BROX EN10 44 G8
Button Rd GRAYS RM17 167 L3
Button St SWLY BR8 209 K4
Buttsbury Rd IL IG1 122 F10
Butts Cl CRAWW RH11 283 L6
Butts Crs FELT TW13 175 P6
Butts End HHW HP1 35 K5
Butts Green Rd EMPK RM11 125 L4
Buttsmead NTHWD HA6 92 D8
Butts Piece NTHLT UB5 133 J4
Butts Rd BMLY BR1 183 K8
WOKN/KNAP GU21 232 B4
The Butts BROX EN10 44 D10
BTFD TW8 155 J5
RSEV TN14 247 J3
Buxhall Crs HOM E9 140 E1
Buxted Rd EDUL SE22 159 M10
HACK E8 7 L3
NFNCH/WDSPK N12 97 P6
Buxton Av CTHM CR3 241 M7
Buxton Cl HOR/WEW KT19 219 N7
STALE/WH AL4 39 J3
WFD IG8 102 A7
Buxton Crs CHEAM SM3 221 H1
Buxton Dr NWMAL KT3 200 A2
WAN E11 121 K2
Buxton Gdns ACT W3 135 N9
Buxton La CTHM CR3 241 M7
Buxton Ms CLAP SW4 158 E8
Buxton Pth OXHEY WD19 * 93 K4
Buxton Pl CTHM CR3 241 L6
Buxton Rd ARCH N19 118 E6
ASHF TW15 173 N8
CDW/CHF RM16 168 B1
CHING E4 101 J1
CRICK NW2 136 E1
EHAM E6 142 B5
EPP CM16 83 H2
ERITH DA8 164 E6
GNTH/NBYPK IG2 123 H4
MORT/ESHN SW14 156 B9
SRTFD E15 121 K10
THHTH CR7 203 J5
WAB EN9 63 M8
WALTH E17 120 D2
Buxton St WCHPL E1 13 M2
Byam St FUL/PGN SW6 157 M8
Byards Cft
STRHM/NOR SW16 202 E1
Bybend Cl SLN SL2 128 G3
Bychurch End TEDD TW11 * 176 E8
Bycliffe Ms GVW DA11 * 190 C3
Bycliffe Ter GVW DA11 * 190 C3
Bycroft Rd STHL UB1 133 P7
Bycroft St PGE/AN SE20 182 C10
Bycroft Wy CRAWE RH10 284 C5
Byculiah Av ENC/FH EN2 79 J7
Byculiah Rd ENC/FH EN2 79 J6
Byde St HERT/WAT SG14 25 K4
Byelands Cl
BERM/RHTH SE16 140 C10
Byerley Wy CRAWE RH10 284 F6
Byers Cl POTB/CUF EN6 59 M10
The Bye ACT W3 136 B8
Byewaters WATW WD18 72 D10
Bye Ways WHTN TW2 176 A6
The Byeways BRYLDS KT5 199 M5
The Bye Wy
KTN/HRWW/WS HA3 94 D9
The Byeway
MORT/ESHN SW14 155 P9
RKW/CH/CXG WD3 91 P3
Byfeld Gdns BARN SW13 156 D7
Byfield WGCW AL8 23 H2
Byfield Cl BERM/RHTH SE16 160 D1
Byfield Ct RBRW/HUT CM13 * 127 P4
Byfield Rd ISLW TW7 154 F9
Byfleet Rd ADL/WDHM KT15 215 N5
COB KT11 216 C8
Byford Cl SRTFD E15 141 K2
Bygrove CROY/NA CR0 224 G3
Bygrove Rd WIM/MER SW19 179 N9
Bygrove St POP/IOD E14 140 G8
Byland Cl ABYW SE2 163 L2
CAR SM5 201 M7
STHGT/OAK N14 98 G1
Bylands WOKS/MYFD GU22 232 D4
Byne Rd CAR SM5 201 P9
SYD SE26 182 B9
Bynes Rd SAND/SEL CR2 223 L4
Byng Dr POTB/CUF EN6 59 K7
Bynghams HLWW/ROY CM19 46 C3
Byng Pl GWRST WC1E 11 K2
Byng Rd BAR EN5 76 G7
Byng St POP/IOD E14 160 F1
Bynon Av BXLYHN DA7 163 P9
Byrd Rd CRAWW RH11 283 J10
Byrefield Rd GUW GU2 249 L7
Byre Rd STHGT/OAK N14 78 B10
Byrne Cl CROY/NA CR0 203 J6
Byrne Rd BAL SW12 180 C4
Byron Av BORE WD6 75 M9
CDALE/KGS NW9 115 N2
COUL/CHIP CR5 240 F1
HSLWW TW4 153 J8
MNPK E12 142 B1
NWMAL KT3 200 D5
SUT SM1 221 N1
SWFD E18 121 L1
WATN WD24 73 L5
Byron Av East SUT SM1 221 N1
Byron Cl CHESW EN7 61 N3
CRAWE RH10 284 C6
HACK E8 7 N5
HPTN TW12 175 N7
PGE/AN SE20 * 204 A3
SYD SE26 * 182 D7
THMD SE28 143 M10
WOKN/KNAP GU21 231 K3
WOT/HER KT12 197 M8
Byron Ct ENC/FH EN2 79 J6
WDSR SL4 148 F9
Byron Dr EFNCH N2 117 N4
ERITH DA8 164 C6
Byron Gdns SUT SM1 221 N1
TIL RM18 168 F7
Byron Hill Rd
RYLN/HDSTN HA2 114 C6
Byron Ms HAMP NW3 117 P10
MV/WKIL W9 8 F1
Byron Pde HGDN/ICK UB10 * 132 C6
Byron Pl LHD/OX KT22 236 G8
Byron Rd ADL/WDHM KT15 215 N1
ALP/SUD HA0 115 H7
CRICK NW2 116 E7
DART DA1 166 A10
EA W5 135 L10
HRW HA1 114 D4
KTN/HRWW/WS HA3 94 E10
LEY E10 120 G6
MLHL NW7 96 D6
SAND/SEL CR2 224 A6
WALTH E17 120 F1
Byron St POP/IOD E14 141 H8
Byron Ter ED N9 * 100 B1
Byron Wy HARH RM3 105 K9
NTHLT UB5 133 M5
WDR/YW UB7 152 A3
YEAD UB4 132 F6
Bysouth Cl CLAY IG5 102 E9
SEVS/STOTM N15 119 L2
By The Wood OXHEY WD19 93 L3
Bythorn St BRXN/ST SW9 158 G9
Byton Rd TOOT SW17 180 A9
Byttom Hl RDKG RH5 255 H3
Byward Av
EBED/NFELT TW14 175 K2
Byward St MON EC3R 13 K8
Bywater Pl BERM/RHTH SE16 140 D10
Bywater St CHEL SW3 16 A7
Byways BERK HP4 34 B4
The Byway BELMT SM2 221 N5
HOR/WEW KT19 220 C1
POTB/CUF EN6 59 K9
Bywell Pl GTPST W1W * 10 G4
Bywood Av CROY/NA CR0 204 B6
Bywood Cl BNSTD SM7 239 J3
PUR/KEN CR8 241 J1
By-Wood End
CFSP/GDCR SL9 90 D6

# C

Cabbell Pl ADL/WDHM KT15 215 M1
Cabbell St CAMTN NW1 9 N4
Cabell Rd GUW GU2 249 K9
Caberfeigh Cl REDH RH1 257 P10
Caberfeigh Pl REDH RH1 * 257 N10
Cabinet Wy CHING E4 100 E7
Cable Pl GNWCH SE10 161 H7
Cables Cl ERITH DA8 164 D2
Cable St WCHPL E1 13 P7
Cable Trade Pk CHARL SE7 * 161 M4
Cabot Sq POP/IOD E14 140 F10
Cabot Wy EHAM E6 142 A3
Cabrera Av VW GU25 194 A5
Cabrera Cl VW GU25 193 P6
Cabul Rd BTSEA SW11 157 P8
Caburn Ct CRAWW RH11 283 M9
Caburn Hts CRAWW RH11 283 M9
Cacket's La RSEV TN14 244 G1
The Cackstones
CRAWE RH10 * 284 E6
Cactus Cl CMBW SE5 * 159 M8
Cadbury Cl ISLW TW7 154 F7
SUN TW16 174 F10
Cadbury Rd SUN TW16 174 F10
Cadbury Wy
BERM/RHTH SE16 19 M4
Caddington Cl EBAR EN4 77 P9
Caddington Rd CRICK NW2 117 H8
Caddis Cl STAN HA7 * 94 E8
Caddy Cl EGH TW20 172 D8
Cade La SEV TN13 265 K4
Cadell Cl BETH E2 7 M8
Cade Rd GNWCH SE10 161 J7
Cader Rd WAND/EARL SW18 179 M2
Cadet Dr STHWK SE1 19 M7
Cadet Pl GNWCH SE10 161 K4
Cadiz Rd DAGE RM10 144 D2
Cadiz St WALW SE17 18 F8
Cadlocks Hl RSEV TN14 228 A6
Cadman Cl BRXN/ST SW9 159 J6
Cadmer Cl NWMAL KT3 200 B4
Cadmore La CHES/WCR EN8 62 D4
Cadmus Cl CLAP SW4 158 E10
Cadogan Av RDART DA2 188 C3
Cadogan Cl HOM E9 * 140 E2
RYLN/HDSTN HA2 114 A9
TEDD TW11 176 D8
Cadogan Ct BELMT SM2 221 L3
Cadogan Gdns CHEL SW3 16 B5
FNCH N3 * 97 L9
SWFD E18 121 N1
WCHMH N21 79 H9
Cadogan Ga KTBR SW1X 16 B5
Cadogan La KTBR SW1X 16 C3
Cadogan Pl KTBR SW1X 16 B3
PUR/KEN CR8 241 K3
Cadogan Rd SURB KT6 199 J5
WOOL/PLUM SE18 162 F2
Cadogan Sq KTBR SW1X 16 A4
Cadogan St CHEL SW3 16 A6
Cadogan Ter HOM E9 140 E1
Cadoxton Av
SEVS/STOTM N15 119 N4
Cadwallon Rd ELTH/MOT SE9 184 E5
Caedmon Rd HOLWY N7 118 G9
Caenshill Pl WEY KT13 * 216 B4
Caenshill Rd WEY KT13 216 B4
Caenswood Hl WEY KT13 216 B6
Caenwood Cl WEY KT13 216 B3
Caen Wood Rd ASHTD KT21 237 H4
Caerleon Cl ESH/CLAY KT10 218 G4
SCUP DA14 185 M8
Caernarvon Cl EMPK RM11 125 P6
HHNE HP2 35 N6
MTCM CR4 202 F3
Caernarvon Dr CLAY IG5 102 D9
Caesars Rd STALE/WH AL4 21 J3
Caesars Wk MTCM CR4 202 A5
Caesar's Wy SHPTN TW17 196 E6
Caffins Cl CRAWE RH10 283 P5
Cage Farm Cots OXTED RH8 * 260 G10
Cage Pond Rd RAD WD7 57 M9
Cages Wood Dr SLN SL2 108 G9
Cage Yd REIG RH2 * 257 K10
Cahill St STLK EC1Y * 12 F2
Cahir St POP/IOD E14 160 G3
Caillard Rd BF/WBF KT14 215 N7
Cain's La EBED/NFELT TW14 174 E1
Caird St NKENS W10 2 B10
Cairn Av EA W5 135 J10
Cairndale Cl BMLY BR1 183 L10
Cairnfield Av CRICK NW2 116 B8
Cairngorm Cl TEDD TW11 176 F8
Cairns Av WFD IG8 102 C7
Cairns Cl STALE/WH AL4 39 J7
Cairns Rd BTSEA SW11 179 P1
Cairn Wy STAN HA7 94 E7
Cairo New Rd CROY/NA CR0 203 J9
Cairo Rd WALTH E17 * 120 F2
Caishowe Rd BORE WD6 75 N5
Caister Cl HHNE HP2 35 P7
Caister Ms BAL SW12 180 C3
Caistor Park Rd SRTFD E15 141 L3
Caistor Rd BAL SW12 180 C3
Caithness Dr EPSOM KT18 220 A10
Caithness Gdns BFN/LL DA15 185 J2
Caithness Rd MTCM CR4 180 C10
WKENS W14 156 G2
Calabria Rd HBRY N5 6 C1
Calais Cl CHESW EN7 61 L2
Calais St CMBW SE5 159 J7
Calbourne Av HCH RM12 125 J10
Calbourne Rd BAL SW12 180 A3
Calbroke Rd SLN SL2 128 E6
Calbury Cl STAL AL1 38 G7
Calcott Cl BRW CM14 106 G2
Calcroft Av SWCM DA10 189 H1
Calcutta Rd TIL RM18 168 C8
Caldbeck WAB EN9 63 J10
Caldbeck Av WPK KT4 200 E9
Caldecot Av CHESW EN7 61 N5
Caldecote Gdns BUSH WD23 74 D10
Caldecote La BUSH WD23 94 E1
Caldecot Rd CMBW SE5 159 K8
Caldecott Wy CLPT E5 120 C8
Caldecot Wy BROX EN10 44 E8
Calder Av BRKMPK AL9 59 K2
GFD/PVL UB6 134 E4
Calder Ct DTCH/LGLY SL3 150 C4
Calderdale Cl CRAWW RH11 283 L9
Calder Gdns EDGW HA8 115 M1
Calderon Rd WAN E11 121 H9
Calder Rd MRDN SM4 201 M5
Caldervale Rd CLAP SW4 180 E1
Calder Wy DTCH/LGLY SL3 151 H9
Calderwood GVE DA12 191 H9
Calderwood Pl EBAR EN4 77 L5
Calderwood St
WOOL/PLUM SE18 162 D3
Caldew St CMBW SE5 159 L6
Caldicote Gn
CDALE/KGS NW9 * 116 B4
Caldwell Rd BFOR GU20 212 C2
OXHEY WD19 93 L5
Caldwell St BRXN/ST SW9 158 G6
Caldy Rd BELV DA17 164 C2
Caldy Wk IS N1 6 F2
Caledonian Cl
GDMY/SEVK IG3 * 123 L6
Caledonian Rd HOLWY N7 118 G10
IS N1 5 N4
Caledonian Sq CAMTN NW1 5 J1
Caledonian Wy HORL RH6 * 280 C7
Caledonian Wharf Rd
POP/IOD E14 161 J3
Caledonia Rd
STWL/WRAY TW19 173 P4
Caledonia St IS N1 5 M8
Caledon Pl RGUE GU4 250 D7
Caledon Rd BEAC HP9 88 D8
EHAM E6 142 C3
LCOL/BKTW AL2 57 H2
WLGTN SM6 222 B1
Calendar Ms SURB KT6 199 J6
Cale St CHEL SW3 15 N7
Calfstock La EYN DA4 209 M4
Calidore Cl
BRXS/STRHM SW2 * 180 G2
California Cl BELMT SM2 221 K6
California La BUSH WD23 94 C2
California Rd NWMAL KT3 199 P4
Caling Cft HART DA3 211 L8
Caliph Cl GVE DA12 191 J6
Callaby Ter IS N1 6 G2
Callaghan Cl LEW SE13 161 K10
Callaghan Cots WCHPL E1 * 140 B7
Callander Rd CAT SE6 182 G5
The Callanders BUSH WD23 * 94 D2
Callan Gv SOCK/AV RM15 147 H9
Callard Av PLMGR N13 99 J6
Callcott Rd KIL/WHAMP NW6 2 C4
Callcott St KENS W8 8 E9
Callendar Rd SKENS SW7 15 L3
Calley Down Crs
CROY/NA CR0 225 J6
Callingham Cl POP/IOD E14 140 E7
Callingham Pl BEAC HP9 88 D8
Callis Farm Cl
STWL/WRAY TW19 173 P2
Callisons Pl GNWCH SE10 161 K4
Callis Rd WALTH E17 120 E4
Callisto Cl CRAWW RH11 283 H10
Callisto Ct HHNE HP2 36 A3
Callow Fld PUR/KEN CR8 223 H9
Callow Hl VW GU25 193 P2
Callowland Pl WATN WD24 73 J4
Callow St CHEL SW3 15 L9
Calluna Ct WOKS/MYFD GU22 232 C4
Calluna Dr CRAWE RH10 285 H3
Calmington Rd CMBW SE5 19 K8
Calmont Rd BMLY BR1 183 J9
Calmore Cl HCH RM12 125 K10
Calne Av CLAY IG5 102 E9
Calonne Rd WIM/MER SW19 178 G7
Calshot Av CDW/CHF RM16 167 K1
Calshot Rd HTHAIR TW6 152 C8
Calshot St IS N1 5 N7
Calshot Wy ENC/FH EN2 79 J7
HTHAIR TW6 152 B8
Calthorpe Gdns EDGW HA8 95 L6
SUT SM1 201 M10
Calthorpe St FSBYW WC1X 11 P1
Calton Av DUL SE21 181 M2
HERT/WAT SG14 24 G4
Calton Rd BAR EN5 77 M10
Calumet BEAC HP9 88 C8
Calverley Cl BECK BR3 182 G9
Calverley Crs DAGE RM10 124 B7
Calverley Gv ARCH N19 118 E6
Calverley Rd EW KT17 220 D3
Calvert Av WCHPL E1 7 K10
Calvert Cl BELV DA17 164 B3
SCUP DA14 185 P9
Calvert Crs DORK RH4 254 G10
Calvert Dr RDART DA2 186 E5
Calverton Rd EHAM E6 142 D3
Calvert Rd BAR EN5 76 G6
DORK RH4 254 G10
EHSLY KT24 253 J4
GNWCH SE10 161 L4
Calvert St CAMTN NW1 4 C5
Calvin Cl STMC/STPC BR5 207 N3
Calvin St WCHPL E1 13 L2
Calydon Rd CHARL SE7 161 N4
Calypso Crs PECK SE15 159 M6
Calypso Wy BERM/RHTH SE16 160 E2
Camac Rd WHTN TW2 176 C4
Camarthen Gn
CDALE/KGS NW9 * 116 B4
Cambalt Rd PUT/ROE SW15 178 G1
Camber Cl CRAWE RH10 284 D7
Camberley Av EN EN1 79 M8
RYNPK SW20 200 E2
Camberley Cl CHEAM SM3 200 G10
Camberley Pl HARP AL5 20 C5
Camberley Rd HTHAIR TW6 152 B9
Cambert Wy BKHTH/KID SE3 161 N10
Camberwell Church St
CMBW SE5 159 L7
Camberwell Glebe CMBW SE5 159 L7
Camberwell Gn CMBW SE5 159 L7
Camberwell Gv CMBW SE5 159 L7
Camberwell La RSEV TN14 264 A6
Camberwell New Rd
CMBW SE5 159 J6
LBTH SE11 18 A10
Camberwell Rd CMBW SE5 18 F10
Camberwell Station Rd
CMBW SE5 159 K7
Cambeys Rd DAGE RM10 124 D10
Camborne Av HARH RM3 105 M8
WEA W13 154 G1
Camborne Cl HTHAIR TW6 152 B9
Camborne Crs HTHAIR TW6 152 B9
Camborne Dr HHNE HP2 35 P2
Camborne Ms
WAND/EARL SW18 179 K3
Camborne Rd BELMT SM2 221 K4
CROY/NA CR0 203 P7
MRDN SM4 200 G6
SCUP DA14 185 M6
WAND/EARL SW18 179 K3
WELL DA16 163 H8
Camborne Wy HARH RM3 105 N8
HEST TW5 153 P7
HTHAIR TW6 152 B9
Cambourne Av ED N9 100 C1
Cambourne Ms NTGHL W11 8 A6
Cambourne Wy HARH RM3 105 M8
Cambray Rd BAL SW12 180 D4
ORP BR6 207 J7
Cambria Cl BFN/LL DA15 184 G4
HSLW TW3 153 P10
Cambria Ct EBED/NFELT TW14 175 J3
Cambria Crs GVE DA12 191 H7
Cambria Gdns
STWL/WRAY TW19 173 P3
Cambrian Av GNTH/NBYPK IG2 123 H3
Cambrian Cl WNWD SE27 181 J6
Cambrian Gn CDALE/KGS NW9 116 B3
Cambrian Gv GVW DA11 190 D3
Cambrian Rd LEY E10 120 F5
RCHPK/HAM TW10 177 L2
Cambrian Wy HHNE HP2 35 P3
Cambria Rd CMBW SE5 159 K9
Cambria St FUL/PGN SW6 157 L6
Cambridge Av GFD/PVL UB6 114 E10
GPK RM2 105 K10
KIL/WHAMP NW6 2 F7
NWMAL KT3 200 B2
SL SL1 128 A4
WELL DA16 163 J10
Cambridge Barracks Rd
WOOL/PLUM SE18 162 C3
Cambridge Circ
SOHO/SHAV W1D 11 K6
Cambridge Cl CHES/WCR EN8 62 B5
EBAR EN4 98 B2
HSLWW TW4 153 M10
RYNPK SW20 200 E1
WALTH E17 120 E4
WDGN N22 * 99 H9
WDR/YW UB7 151 N5
WLSDN NW10 115 P8
WOKN/KNAP GU21 231 L4
Cambridge Crs BETH E2 140 A4
TEDD TW11 * 176 F8
Cambridge Dr LEE/GVPK SE12 183 M1
POTB/CUF EN6 59 H7
RSLP HA4 113 K7
Cambridge Gdns
CDW/CHF RM16 * 168 D3
EN EN1 79 P6
KIL/WHAMP NW6 2 F7
KUT/HW KT1 199 M2
MUSWH N10 98 B9
NKENS W10 8 B5
TOTM N17 99 L8
WCHMH N21 99 L1
Cambridge Ga CAMTN NW1 4 E10
Cambridge Gate Ms
CAMTN NW1 4 F10
Cambridge Gn ELTH/MOT SE9 184 E4
Cambridge Gv HMSMTH W6 156 E3
PGE/AN SE20 * 204 A1
Cambridge Grove Rd
KUT/HW KT1 199 M2
Cambridge Heath Rd BETH E2 140 A5
Cambridge Lodge Pk
HORL RH6 * 280 B1
Cambridge Pde EN EN1 * 79 P6
Cambridge Pk TWK TW1 177 H3
Cambridge Park Rd WAN E11 121 L5
Cambridge Pas HOM E9 140 B2
Cambridge Pl KENS W8 * 15 H2
Cambridge Rd ASHF TW15 174 D10
BARK IG11 142 F2
BARN SW13 156 C8
BEAC HP9 88 B9
BMLY BR1 183 M10
BTSEA SW11 158 A7
CAR SM5 221 P3
CHING E4 101 J2
E/WMO/HCT KT8 197 N4
GDMY/SEVK IG3 123 H6
HLW CM20 29 M5
HNWL W7 154 E1
HPTN TW12 175 N10
HSLWW TW4 153 M10
KIL/WHAMP NW6 2 F8
KUT/HW KT1 199 M2
MTCM CR4 202 D3
NWMAL KT3 200 A4
PGE/AN SE20 203 P3
RCH/KEW TW9 155 M6
RYLN/HDSTN HA2 113 P3
RYNPK SW20 200 E1
SCUP DA14 185 H7
STAL AL1 38 G7
STHL UB1 * 133 N10
TEDD TW11 176 F7
TWK TW1 177 J2
UX/CGN UB8 131 N1
WAN E11 121 M4
WATW WD18 * 73 K8
WOT/HER KT12 197 J6
Cambridge Rd North
CHSWK W4 155 N4
Cambridge Rd South
CHSWK W4 155 N4
Cambridge Rw
WOOL/PLUM SE18 162 E4
Cambridge Sq BAY/PAD W2 9 N5
REDH RH1 276 B3
Cambridge St PIM SW1V 16 F7
Cambridge Ter BERK HP4 34 A5
CAMTN NW1 4 E10
ED N9 * 99 N1
Cambridge Terrace Ms
CAMTN NW1 * 4 F10
Cambridge Yd HNWL W7 * 154 E1
Cambus Cl YEAD UB4 133 M7
Cambus Rd CAN/RD E16 141 M7
Camdale Rd
WOOL/PLUM SE18 163 J6
Camden Av FELT TW13 175 K5
YEAD UB4 133 K9
Camden Cl CDW/CHF RM16 168 E3
CHST BR7 206 F1
GVW DA11 189 P4
Camden Gdns CAMTN NW1 4 F4
SUT SM1 221 L2
THHTH CR7 203 J3
Camden Gv CHST BR7 184 E9
Camden High St CAMTN NW1 4 F4
Camden Hill Rd NRWD SE19 181 M9
Camdenhurst St POP/IOD E14 140 D8
Camden Lock Pl CAMTN NW1 4 E4
Camden Ms CAMTN NW1 5 J3
Camden Park Rd CAMTN NW1 5 K1
CHST BR7 184 C10
Camden Pas IS N1 6 C7
Camden Rd BXLY DA5 186 A4
CAMTN NW1 4 G4
CDW/CHF RM16 167 K2
SEV TN13 247 J8
SUT SM1 221 L2
WALTH E17 120 E4
WAN E11 121 N4
Camden Road (Permanent
Way) CAMTN NW1 * 5 J6
Camden Rw BKHTH/KID SE3 161 K8
PIN HA5 * 113 K1
Camden Sq CAMTN NW1 5 J2
Camden St CAMTN NW1 4 F4
Camden Ter CAMTN NW1 5 J2
Camden Wk IS N1 6 C6
Camden Wy CHST BR7 184 C10
THHTH CR7 203 J3
Camelford Wk NTGHL W11 8 A6
Camel Gv KUTN/CMB KT2 177 J8
Camellia Cl HARH RM3 105 M9
Camellia Ct CHOB/PIR GU24 212 E9
Camellia Pl WHTN TW2 176 A3
Camellia St VX/NE SW8 158 F6
Camelot Cl BH/WHM TN16 243 P2
THMD SE28 162 G1
WIM/MER SW19 179 J7
Camel Rd CAN/RD E16 142 A10
Camera Pl WBPTN SW10 15 L10
Cameron Cl BRW CM14 107 H5
BXLY DA5 186 E6
TRDG/WHET N20 97 P3
UED N18 100 A5
Cameron Ct WARE SG12 26 C1
Cameron Crs EDGW HA8 95 N9
Cameron Dr CHES/WCR EN8 62 C10
DART DA1 165 N8
Cameron Pl
STRHM/NOR SW16 181 H5
Cameron Rd CAT SE6 * 182 E5
CROY/NA CR0 203 J6
CSHM HP5 51 H6
GDMY/SEVK IG3 123 H6
HAYES BR2 205 M4
Cameron Sq MTCM CR4 201 P1
Cameron Ter LEE/GVPK SE12 * 183 N6
Camerton Cl HACK E8 7 M2
Camfield WGCE AL7 23 J9
Cam Gn SOCK/AV RM15 146 G8
Camilla Cl GT/LBKH KT23 254 A1
SUN TW16 * 174 G9
Camilla Dr RDKG RH5 254 F6
Camilla Rd BERM/RHTH SE16 160 A3
Camille Cl SNWD SE25 203 P3
Camlan Rd BMLY BR1 183 L7
Camlet St BETH E2 13 L1
Camlet Wy EBAR EN4 77 K6
STALW/RED AL3 38 A5
Camley St CAMTN NW1 5 J4
Camm Av WDSR SL4 148 D9
Camm Gdns KUT/HW KT1 * 199 L2
THDIT KT7 198 D7
Camomile Av MTCM CR4 202 A1
Camomile St OBST EC2N 13 J5
Camomile Wy WDR/YW UB7 131 P8
Camomile Rd ROMW/RG RM7 124 E7
Campana Rd FUL/PGN SW6 157 K7
Campbell Av BARK/HLT IG6 122 F2
WOKS/MYFD GU22 232 C7
Campbell Cl BF/WBF KT14 215 N7
HLWE CM17 47 L2
ROM RM1 104 F7
RSLP HA4 113 H4
STRHM/NOR SW16 * 180 E8
WHTN TW2 176 C4
WOOL/PLUM SE18 162 D7
Campbell Cots MTCM CR4 * 202 B2
Campbell Cft EDGW HA8 95 M6
Campbell Gordon Wy
CRICK NW2 116 E9
Campbell Rd BOW E3 140 F5
CRAWE RH10 284 D9
CROY/NA CR0 203 J7
CTHM CR3 241 L7
EHAM E6 142 B3
GVW DA11 190 C4
HNWL W7 134 D9
SRTFD E15 121 K9
TOTM N17 99 N9
WALTH E17 120 E2
WEY KT13 216 B4
WHTN TW2 176 C5
Campbell Wk IS N1 * 5 M5
Campdale Rd HOLWY N7 118 E8
Campden Crs ALP/SUD HA0 114 G8
BCTR RM8 123 M9
Campden Gv KENS W8 14 F1
Campden Hl KENS W8 14 E1
Campden Hill Gdns KENS W8 8 E9
Campden Hill Pl NTGHL W11 8 D9
Campden Hill Rd KENS W8 14 E1
Campden Hill Sq KENS W8 8 D10
Campden House Cl KENS W8 14 E1
Campden House Ter
KENS W8 * 8 F10
Campden Rd HGDN/ICK UB10 112 A8
SAND/SEL CR2 223 M2
Campden St KENS W8 8 E10
Campden Ter CHSWK W4 * 156 B4
Campden Wy BCTR RM8 123 L9
Campen Cl WIM/MER SW19 179 H5
Camp End Rd WEY KT13 216 C8
Camperdown St WCHPL E1 13 M6
Campfield Rd ELTH/MOT SE9 184 A3
HERT/WAT SG14 25 J5
STAL AL1 38 F6
Camphill Ct BF/WBF KT14 215 K8
Camphill Rd BF/WBF KT14 215 K8
Campine Cl CHES/WCR EN8 62 C4
Campion Cl CROY/NA CR0 223 M1
DEN/HRF UB9 111 K8
EHAM E6 142 C9
GSTN WD25 55 H9
GVW DA11 190 B7
KTN/HRWW/WS HA3 115 L4
ROMW/RG RM7 124 E7
UX/CGN UB8 132 A7
Campion Ct ALP/SUD HA0 * 135 K4
Campion Dr
KWD/TDW/WH KT20 238 E6
Campion Gdns WFD IG8 101 M6
Campion Pl THMD SE28 143 L10
Campion Rd HAT AL10 22 C10
HHW HP1 35 H7
ISLW TW7 154 E7
LEY E10 120 G5
PUT/ROE SW15 156 F10
Campions EPP CM16 65 K4
LOU IG10 82 D4
Campions Ct BERK HP4 33 M6
The Campions BORE WD6 75 L4
Campion Ter CRICK NW2 116 G8
Campion Wy EDGW HA8 95 P5
Cample La SOCK/AV RM15 146 F9
Camplin Rd
KTN/HRWW/WS HA3 115 K3
Camplin St NWCR SE14 160 C6
Camp Rd CFSP/GDCR SL9 110 A5
CTHM CR3 242 D7
STAL AL1 38 E7
WIM/MER SW19 178 E8
Campsbourne Pde
CEND/HSY/T N8 * 118 F2
Campsbourne Rd
CEND/HSY/T N8 118 F1
The Campsbourne
CEND/HSY/T N8 118 F2
Campsey Gdns DAGW RM9 143 L2
Campsey Rd DAGW RM9 143 L2
Campshill Pl LEW SE13 183 H1
Campshill Rd LEW SE13 183 H1
Campus Rd WALTH E17 120 E4
The Campus HHNE HP2 * 36 C4
LOU IG10 82 E8
WGCW AL8 22 G4
Camp Vw WIM/MER SW19 178 E8
Camp View Rd STAL AL1 38 G7
Cam Rd SRTFD E15 141 J3
Camrose Av EDGW HA8 95 L10
ERITH DA8 164 C5
FELT TW13 175 J7
STAN HA7 95 K10
Camrose Cl CROY/NA CR0 204 D7
MRDN SM4 201 K4
Camrose St WOOL/PLUM SE18 163 K4
Canada Av REDH RH1 276 B4
UED N18 99 K7
Canada Crs ACT W3 135 P7
Canada Dr REDH RH1 276 B4
Canada Farm Rd EYN DA4 210 G5
Canada La BROX EN10 62 D1
Canada Park Pde EDGW HA8 * 95 N9
Canada Rd ACT W3 135 P7
BF/WBF KT14 215 N7
COB KT11 217 K9
ERITH DA8 165 J6
SL SL1 149 N1
Canada Sq POP/IOD E14 140 G10
The Canadas BROX EN10 62 D2
Canada St BERM/RHTH SE16 160 C1
Canada Wy SHB W12 136 E9
Canadian Av CAT SE6 182 G4
Canal Ap DEPT SE8 160 D4
Canal Basin GVE DA12 190 G2
Canal Bvd CAMTN NW1 5 J1
Canal Cl NKENS W10 136 G6
WCHPL E1 140 D6
Canal Est DTCH/LGLY SL3 * 150 D1
Canal Gv PECK SE15 19 P9
Canal Pth BETH E2 7 L6
Canal Rd GVE DA12 190 F2
Canalside BERK HP4 33 L3
REDH RH1 258 C7
Canal St CMBW SE5 18 G10
Canal Wk CROY/NA CR0 203 M6
IS N1 7 H5
WLSDN NW10 * 135 P2
Canal Wy NKENS W10 136 G6
Canal Whf DTCH/LGLY SL3 150 D1
GFD/PVL UB6 * 134 F3
Canal Yd NWDGN UB2 * 153 J3
Canberra Cl CRAWW RH11 283 N4
DAGE RM10 144 E2
HCH RM12 125 K9
HDN NW4 116 D1
STALW/RED AL3 38 E2
Canberra Crs DAGE RM10 144 E2
Canberra Dr NTHLT UB5 133 K5
Canberra Rd HTHAIR TW6 152 B9
ABYW SE2 163 N5
CHARL SE7 161 P5
EHAM E6 142 C3
HTHAIR TW6 152 B9
WEA W13 134 F10
Canberra Sq TIL RM18 * 168 D8
Canbury Av KUTN/CMB KT2 199 L1
Canbury Ms SYD SE26 181 P6
Canbury Park Rd
KUTN/CMB KT2 199 K1
Canbury Pth STMC/STPC BR5 207 K4
Cancell Rd BRXN/ST SW9 159 H7
Candahar Rd BTSEA SW11 157 P8
Cander Wy SOCK/AV RM15 146 G9
Candlefield Rd HHS/BOV HP3 36 B9
Candle Gv PECK SE15 160 A9
Candlelight Ct SRTFD E15 141 L1
Candlemas La BEAC HP9 88 D9
Candlemas Md BEAC HP9 88 D9
Candler Ms TWK TW1 176 F3
Candler St SEVS/STOTM N15 * 119 L4
Candlerush Cl
WOKS/MYFD GU22 232 E3
Candover Cl WDR/YW UB7 151 N6
Candover Rd HCH RM12 125 J6
Candover St GTPST W1W * 10 G4
Candy Cft GT/LBKH KT23 254 A2
Candy St BOW E3 140 E3
Cane Hl HARH RM3 105 L10
Canes La HLWE CM17 47 P8

Canewden Cl WOKS/MYFD GU22 . 232 B5
Caney Ms CRICK NW2 . 116 G7
Canfield Dr RSLP HA4 . 113 J10
Canfield Gdns KIL/WHAMP NW6 . 3 H3
Canfield Pl KIL/WHAMP NW6 . 3 H3
Canfield Rd RAIN RM13 . 144 C3
WFD IG8 . 102 B8
Canford Av NTHLT UB5 . 133 M3
Canford Cl ENC/FH EN2 . 79 H6
Canford Gdns ADL/WDHM KT15 . 195 M3
Canford Gdns NWMAL KT3 . 200 B6
Canford Pl TEDD TW11 . 177 H9
Canford Rd CLAP SW4 . 158 E10
Cangels Cl HHW HP1 . 35 K8
Canham Rd CHSWK W4 . 156 B1
SNWD SE25 . 203 M5
Can Hatch KWD/TDW/WH KT20 . 239 H4
Canmore Gdns STRHM/NOR SW16 . 180 D10
Cann Hall Rd WAN E11 . 121 F6
Canning Crs WDGN N22 . 98 G5
Canning Cross CMBW SE5 . 159 M8
Canning Pas KENS W8 * . 15 J5
Canning Pl KENS W8 . 15 J5
Canning Place Ms KENS W8 * . 15 J5
Canning Rd CROY/NA CRO . 203 N9
HBRY N5 . 119 J8
KTN/HRWW/WS HA3 . 115 J1
SRTFD E15 . 141 K4
WALTH E17 . 120 E1
Cannington Rd DAGW RM9 . 143 M1
Cannizaro Rd WIM/MER SW19 . 178 F3
Cannonbury Pk PIN HA5 . 113 L4
Cannon Cl HPTN TW12 . 176 A9
RYNPK SW20 . 200 F3
Cannon Crs CHOB/PIR GU24 . 213 K7
Cannon Ga SLN SL2 . 129 P9
Cannon Gv LHD/OX KT22 . 236 D7
Cannon Hl KIL/WHAMP NW6 . 2 F1
STHGT/OAK N14 . 98 E4
Cannon Hill La RYNPK SW20 . 200 C5
Cannon Hill Ms STHGT/OAK N14 . 98 E4
Cannon La HAMP NW3 . 117 N8
PIN HA5 . 113 M5
Cannon Ms WAB EN9 . 62 G9
Cannon Pl CHARL SE7 . 51 J9
Cannon Pl CHARL SE7 . 162 B4
HAMP NW3 . 117 N8
Cannon Rd BXLYHN DA7 . 163 P7
STHGT/OAK N14 . 98 F4
WATW WD18 . 73 K9
Cannon Side LHD/OX KT22 . 236 C7
STHGT/OAK N14 . 98 F4
Cannons Meadow WLYN AL6 . 23 P1
Cannon St RKW/CH/CXG WD3 * . 12 E6
STALW/RED AL3 . 38 C5
Cannon Street Rd WCHPL E1 . 140 A8
Cannon Wy E/WMO/HCT KT8 . 197 N4
LHD/OX KT22 . 236 D7
Canon Av CHDH RM6 . 123 M5
Canon Beck Rd BERM/RHTH SE16 . 160 B7
Canonbie Rd FSTH SE23 . 182 B3
Canonbury Crs IS N1 . 6 E3
Canonbury Gv IS N1 . 6 E3
Canonbury La IS N1 . 6 E2
Canonbury Pk North IS N1 . 6 E2
Canonbury Pk South IS N1 . 6 E2
Canonbury Pl IS N1 . 6 D2
Canonbury Rd EN EN1 . 79 M5
IS N1 . 6 D1
Canonbury Sq IS N1 . 6 D3
Canonbury St IS N1 . 6 E3
Canonbury Vls IS N1 . 6 D4
Canonbury Yd East IS N1 * . 6 E3
Canon Mohan Cl STHGT/OAK N14 . 78 B10
Canon Rd BMLY BR1 . 205 P3
STALW SW1A . 17 L2
Canons Brook HLWW/ROY CM19 . 46 D1
Canons Cl EDGW HA8 . 95 L7
EFNCH N2 . 117 N5
RAD WD7 . 74 C1
REIG RH2 . 257 J9
Canons Cots EDGW HA8 * . 95 L7
Canons Dr EDGW HA8 . 95 L7
Canons Fld STALE/WH AL4 . 21 J2
Canons Ga CHES/WCR EN8 . 62 E2
HLW CM20 . 28 D9
Canon's Hl COUL/CHIP CR5 . 241 H4
Canons La KWD/TDW/WH KT20 . 239 H5
Canonsleigh Rd DAGW RM9 . 143 L2
Canons Rd WARE SG12 . 26 B1
Canon St IS N1 . 6 E6
Canons Wk BH/WHM TN16 . 263 H6
Canon's Wk CROY/NA CRO . 204 C10
Canopus Wy NTHWD HA6 . 95 F6
Canopy La HLWE CM17 . 173 P3
Canrobert St BETH E2 . 140 A4
Cantelowes Rd CAMTN NW1 * . 5 L1
Canterbury Av BFN/LL DA15 . 185 M5
IL IG1 . 122 B5
SLN SL2 . 129 H6
UPMR RM14 . 126 E6
Canterbury Cl AMSS HP7 . 69 K5
BECK BR3 . 204 G1
CHIG IG7 . 103 J4
CMBW SE5 . 159 K8
EHAM E6 . 142 G8
GFD/PVL UB6 . 134 A7
NTHWD HA6 . 95 G6
Canterbury Ct DORK RH4 * . 272 F1
Canterbury Crs BRXN/ST SW9 . 159 H8
Canterbury Gv WNWD SE27 . 181 H6
Canterbury Pde SOCK/AV RM15 . 147 N5
Canterbury Pl WALW SE17 . 18 D6
Canterbury Rd BORE WD6 . 75 M6
CROY/NA CRO . 202 G7
FELT TW13 . 175 M5
GUW GU2 . 249 L8
GVE DA12 . 190 F5
KIL/WHAMP NW6 . 2 E1
LEY E10 . 121 N5
MRDN SM4 . 201 M6
RYLN/HDSTN HA2 . 114 A3
WAT WD17 . 73 J6
Canterbury Ter KIL/WHAMP NW6 . 2 E7
Canterbury Wy RBRW/HUT CM13 . 107 H7
RKW/CH/CXG WD3 . 72 G1
WTHK RM20 . 166 D6
The Canter CRAWE RH10 . 284 F6
Cantley Gdns GNTH/NBYPK IG2 . 122 F4
NRWD SE19 . 203 N1
Cantley Rd HNWL W7 . 154 F2
Canton St POP/IOD E14 . 140 F8
Cantrell Rd BOW E3 . 140 F6
Cantwell Rd WOOL/PLUM SE18 . 162 G6
Canute Cl CRAWW RH11 . 283 M10
Canvey Cl CRAWW RH11 . 283 N4
Canvey St STHWK SE1 * . 12 A6
Capability Wy SWCM DA10 . 167 H10
Cape Cl BARK IG11 . 142 G2
Capel Av WLGTN SM6 . 222 G4
Capel Cl HAYES BR2 . 206 B8
TRDG/WHET N20 . 97 M4
Capel Crs STAN HA7 . 94 F1
Capel Gdns GDMY/SEVK IG3 . 123 L3
PIN HA5 . 113 N5
Capella Rd NTHWD HA6 . 92 G3
Capell Av RKW/CH/CXG WD3 . 70 G9
Capell Cl RKW/CH/CXG WD3 . 70 G9
Capell Wy RKW/CH/CXG WD3 . 70 G9
Capel Rd EBAR EN4 . 77 P10

EN EN1 . 80 A2
FSTGT E7 . 121 H3
OXHEY WD19 . 73 L10
Capelvere Wk WAT WD17 . 72 F5
Capeners Cl KTBR SW1X . 16 B2
Capern Rd WAND/EARL SW18 . 179 M4
Cape Rd STAL AL1 . 38 G6
Cape Yd WAP E1W . 13 P9
Capital Interchange Wy BTFD TW8 . 155 M4
Capital Pl HLWW/ROY CM19 . 46 D2
Capitol Wy CDALE/KGS NW9 . 115 P1
Capland St STJWD NW8 . 9 M1
Caple Pde WLSDN NW10 * . 136 C4
Caple Rd WLSDN NW10 . 136 C4
Caponfield WGCE AL7 . 23 L7
Cappell La WARE SG12 . 27 H6
Caprea Cl YEAD UB4 . 133 L7
Capricorn Cl CRAWW RH11 . 283 H9
Capri Rd CROY/NA CRO . 203 N7
Capsey Rd CRAWW RH11 . 283 M5
Capstan Cl CHDH RM6 . 123 L4
Capstan Ct RDART DA2 . 166 B10
Capstan Dr RAIN RM13 . 145 H7
Capstan Ms WLSDN NW10 * . 2 F7
Capstan Ride ENC/FH EN2 . 79 H6
Capstan Rd DEPT SE8 . 160 L5
Capstan Sq POP/IOD E14 . 161 H1
Capstan Wy WOKN/KNAP GU21 . 231 L4
Capstone Rd BMLY BR1 . 183 L7
Captains Cl BERM/RHTH SE16 . 140 D10
Captains Cl BMLY BR1 . 183 L7
Captain's Cl CSHM HP5 . 52 F1
Captain's Wk BERK HP4 . 34 A6
Capthorne Av RYLN/HDSTN HA2 . 113 M6
Capuchin Cl STAN HA7 . 94 C7
Capulet Ms CAN/RD E16 . 141 M10
Caractacus Cottage Vw WATW WD18 . 93 H1
Caractacus Gn WATW WD18 . 72 E10
Caradoc Cl BAY/PAD W2 . 8 E5
Caradoc St GNWCH SE10 . 161 K4
Caradon Cl WOKN/KNAP GU21 . 231 N6
Caradon Cl WAN E11 . 121 K6
Caradon Wy SEVS/STOTM N15 . 119 L2
Caravan La RKW/CH/CXG WD3 . 91 P1
The Caravan Site PUR RM19 . 166 C2
Caravel Cl CDW/CHF RM16 . 167 L2
POP/IOD E14 . 160 F2
Caravel Ms DEPT SE8 . 160 F5
Caraway Cl PLSTW E13 . 141 N7
Caraway Pl GUW GU2 . 249 M5
WLGTN SM6 . 202 C10
Carberry Av ASC SL5 . 192 A3
Carberry Rd NRWD SE19 . 181 M9
Carbery Av ACT W3 . 155 L1
Carbis Cl CHING E4 . 101 J2
Carbis Rd POP/IOD E14 . 140 E8
Carbone Hl POTB/CUF EN6 . 60 E7
Carburton St GTPST W1W . 10 F3
Carbury Cl HCH RM12 . 145 K1
Cardale St POP/IOD E14 . 161 K1
Cardamom Cl GUW GU2 . 249 M6
Carde Cl HERT/WAT SG14 . 24 G4
Carden Rd PECK SE15 . 104 F8
Cardiff Cl CRW RM5 . 104 E8
Cardiff Rd HNWL W7 . 154 F2
PEND EN3 . 80 A8
WATW WD18 . 73 J10
Cardiff St WOOL/PLUM SE18 . 163 M5
Cardigan Cl SL SL1 . 128 E9
WOKN/KNAP GU21 . 231 K4
Cardigan Gdns GDMY/SEVK IG3 . 123 K7
Cardigan Pl LEW SE13 * . 161 L2
Cardigan Rd BARN SW13 . 156 D8
BOW E3 . 140 E4
RCHPK/HAM TW10 . 177 K2
WIM/MER SW19 . 179 M9
Cardigan St LBTH SE11 . 18 A8
Cardigan Wk IS N1 * . 6 F3
Cardinal Av BORE WD6 . 75 N7
KUTN/CMB KT2 . 177 K8
MRDN SM4 . 201 H6
Cardinal Bourne St STHWK SE1 * . 19 H4
Cardinal Cl CHESW EN7 . 61 N2
CHST BR7 . 206 G1
EDGW HA8 . 95 P8
MRDN SM4 . 201 H6
SAND/SEL CR2 . 223 P9
WPK KT4 . 220 D1
Cardinal Crs NWMAL KT3 . 199 P2
Cardinal Dr BARK/HLT IG6 . 102 F7
WOT/HER KT12 . 197 L6
Cardinal Gv STALW/RED AL3 . 38 A8
Cardinal Hinsey Cl WLSDN NW10 . 136 D4
Cardinal Pl LCOL/BKTW AL2 . 56 C7
PUT/ROE SW15 . 178 G1
SUN TW16 . 196 G10
Cardinal's Wk HPTN TW12 . 176 C4
Cardinal Wy KTN/ARCH N19 . 118 C1
RAIN RM13 . 145 L1
Cardine Ms PECK SE15 . 160 A1
Cardingham WOKN/KNAP GU21 . 231 M3
Cardington Sq HSLWW TW4 . 153 L10
Cardington St CAMTN NW1 * . 5 H9
Cardozo Rd HOLWY N7 . 118 E9
Cardrew Av NFNCH/WDSPK N12 . 97 H4
Cardross St HMSMTH W6 . 156 E8
Cardwell Crs ASC SL5 . 192 D6
Cardwell Rd HOLWY N7 . 118 D7
Cardwells Keep GUW GU2 . 249 M5
Cardwell Ter HOLWY N7 * . 118 D7
Cardy Rd HHW HP1 . 35 M4
Career Cl CDW/CHF RM16 . 167 K2
COUL/CHIP CR5 . 241 J5
HOLWY N7 . 118 D7
Carew Cl HOLWY N7 . 118 D7
Carew Rd ASHF TW15 . 174 F9
MTCM CR4 . 202 B2
NTHWD HA6 . 92 H7
THHTH CR7 . 99 P10
TOTM N17 . 99 P10
WEA W13 . 155 H1
WLGTN SM6 . 222 D5
Carew Wy OXHEY WD19 . 93 N4
STMC/STPC BR5 . 207 N6
Carey Cl WDSR SL4 . 146 C9
Carey Gdns VX/NE SW8 . 158 D7
Carey La CITYW EC2V * . 12 D2
Carey Pl PIM SW1V . 17 H7
Careys Cl DAGW RM9 . 281 J3
Careys Copse HORL RH6 * . 281 J2
Careys Cft BERK HP4 . 33 L2
Carey's Fld LINN WC2A . 11 L2
Carey St LINN WC2A . 11 L2
Carey Wy WBLY HA9 . 136 D2
Carfax Pl CLAP SW4 . 158 F10
Carfax Rd HCH RM12 . 144 B5
HYS/HAR UB3 . 153 H4
The Carfax SYD SE26 * . 182 B5
Carfree Cl IS N1 . 6 B1
Cargill Rd WAND/EARL SW18 . 179 L5
Cargo Forecourt Rd HORL RH6 . 279 N8
Cargo Rd HORL RH6 . 279 N7

Cargreen Rd SNWD SE25 . 203 N4
Carholme Rd FSTH SE23 . 182 B4
Carisbrook Cl EN EN1 . 79 N5
Carisbrooke Cl HSLWW TW4 . 175 H4
STAN HA7 . 114 E1
Carisbrooke Ct NTHLT UB5 * . 133 N5
SL SL1 . 129 L9
Carisbrooke Gdns PECK SE15 . 159 N6
Carisbrooke Rd HARP AL5 . 20 B1
HAYES BR2 . 205 N4
MTCM CR4 . 202 F4
WALTH E17 . 120 D2
Carisbrook Rd BRWN CM15 . 86 G10
LCOL/BKTW AL2 . 57 J3
Carker's La KTTN NW5 . 118 C10
Carleton Av WLGTN SM6 . 222 E6
Carleton Cl ESH/CLAY KT10 . 198 D4
Carleton Ct ARCH N19 * . 118 D10
Carleton Pl EYN DA4 . 210 B4
Carleton Rd CHES/WCR EN8 . 62 C1
HOLWY N7 . 118 E9
Carlina Gdns WFD IG8 . 101 N6
Carlingford Rd HAMP NW3 . 117 J1
MRDN SM4 . 200 G6
SEVS/STOTM N15 . 119 J1
Carlisle Av ACT W3 . 136 B8
STALW/RED AL3 . 38 C4
TWRH EC3N . 13 K6
Carlisle Cl KUTN/CMB KT2 . 199 M1
PIN HA5 . 113 M5
Carlisle Gdns IL IG1 . 122 B8
KTN/HRWW/WS HA3 . 115 J5
Carlisle La STHWK SE1 . 17 M3
WEST SW1P . 16 G4
Carlisle Ms CDALE/KGS NW9 . 115 H10
Carlisle Rd FBAR/BDGN N11 . 98 C5
HPTN TW12 . 176 A10
KIL/WHAMP NW6 . 2 B3
LEY E10 . 120 F6
ROM RM1 . 124 E1
SL SL1 . 129 J9
SUT SM1 . 221 J3
Carlisle St SOHO/SHAV W1D . 11 H3
Carlisle Wk HACK E8 . 7 L1
Carlisle Wy TOOT SW17 . 180 B8
Carlos Pl MYFR/PKLN W1K . 10 B5
Carlow St CAMTN NW1 . 4 G1
Carlton Av EBED/NFELT TW14 . 175 K2
FELT TW13 . 176 D2
KTN/HRWW/WS HA3 . 114 G3
RDART DA2 . 188 D2
SAND/SEL CR2 . 223 L4
STHGT/OAK N14 . 97 J4
Carlton Av East WBLY HA9 . 115 J7
Carlton Av West ALP/SUD HA0 . 114 C7
Carlton Bank HARP AL5 . 20 A2
Carlton Cl BORE WD6 . 76 A4
CHSGTN KT9 . 219 J3
EDGW HA8 . 95 M6
HAMP NW3 . 117 F7
UPMR RM14 . 126 A7
WOKN/KNAP GU21 . 214 C10
Carlton Crs CHEAM SM3 . 221 H1
Carlton Dene EW KT17 * . 220 E2
Carlton Dr BARK/HLT IG6 . 122 G1
PUT/ROE SW15 . 178 G1
Carlton Ga MV/WKIL W9 . 8 G1
Carlton Gdns EA W5 . 135 J4
Carlton Gn REDH RH1 . 257 F5
Carlton Gv PECK SE15 . 160 F6
Carlton Hl STJWD NW8 . 3 H7
Carlton House Ter STJS SW1Y . 11 J7
Carlton Ms KIL/WHAMP NW6 * . 2 E1
Carlton Pde WBLY HA9 * . 116 K10
Carlton Pk EW KT17 . 220 E4
Carlton Pl WEY KT13 . 195 L8
Carlton Park Av RYNPK SW20 . 200 F2
Carlton Rd CDW/CHF RM16 . 168 C1
CHSWK W4 . 156 A1
EA W5 . 135 H9
ERITH DA8 . 164 C5
FBAR/BDGN N11 . 98 B6
FSBYPK N4 . 119 H4
GPK RM2 . 124 K3
MNPK E12 . 122 A9
MORT/ESHN SW14 . 156 E8
NWMAL KT3 . 200 B8
REDH RH1 . 258 A7
REIG RH2 . 257 N4
SAND/SEL CR2 . 223 L4
SCUP DA14 . 185 J8
SLN SL2 . 129 J3
SUN TW16 . 196 C10
WALTH E17 . 119 L2
WAN E11 . 121 L6
WELL DA16 . 163 H1
WOKN/KNAP GU21 . 214 C10
WOT/HER KT12 . 197 L6
Carlton Sq WCHPL E1 * . 140 E3
Carlton St STJS SW1Y . 11 H5
Carlton Ter SYD SE26 . 182 B7
UED N18 . 99 M1
WAN E11 . 121 N1
Carlton Tower Pl KTBR SW1X . 16 B3
Carlton V KIL/WHAMP NW6 . 2 F2
Carlwell St TOOT SW17 . 179 P8
Carlyle Av BMLY BR1 . 206 A1
Carlyle Cl E/WMO/HCT KT8 . 198 A2
STHL UB1 . 133 N9
Carlyle Ct E/WMO/HCT KT8 . 117 M4
EFNCH N2 . 117 N4
WLSDN NW10 . 136 D3
Carlyle Gdns STHL UB1 . 133 N9
Carlyle Pl PUT/ROE SW15 . 157 J9
Carlyle Rd CROY/NA CRO . 203 P9
EA W5 . 154 G5
MNPK E12 . 122 H3
STA TW18 . 172 F6
THMD SE28 . 143 J10
Carlyle Sq CHEL SW3 . 15 M8
Carlyon Av RYLN/HDSTN HA2 . 113 N6
Carlyon Cl ALP/SUD HA0 . 136 A6
Carlyon Rd ALP/SUD HA0 . 136 A7
HYS/HAR UB4 . 133 K5
Carlys Cl BECK BR3 . 203 P1
Carmalt Gdns PUT/ROE SW15 . 156 F10
WOT/HER KT12 . 217 K2
Carmarthen Rd SL SL1 . 129 K3
Carmel Cl WOKS/MYFD GU22 * . 232 B4
Carmel Ct KENS W8 * . 14 G1
Carmelite Cl KTN/HRWW/WS HA3 . 94 B9
Carmelite Rd KTN/HRWW/WS HA3 . 94 B9
Carmelite St EMB EC4Y . 11 N5
Carmelite Wy RCH/KEW TW9 * . 155 N8
Carmen St POP/IOD E14 . 140 G8
Carmichael Av SWCM DA10 . 167 H10
Carmichael Cl BTSEA SW11 * . 158 C2
RSLP HA4 . 113 N9
Carmichael Ms WAND/EARL SW18 . 179 N3
Carmichael Rd SNWD SE25 . 203 P5
Carminia Rd TOOT SW17 . 180 C5
Carnaby Rd BROX EN10 . 40 D6
Carnaby St SOHO/CST W1F * . 10 F4
Carnac St WNWD SE27 . 181 F1
Carnanton Rd WALTH E17 . 101 N9
Carnarvon Av EN EN1 . 80 D3
Carnarvon Dr HYS/HAR UB3 . 152 D2
Carnarvon Rd BAR EN5 . 76 C4
LEY E10 . 121 N4
SRTFD E15 . 141 M6
SWFD E18 . 101 P10
Carnation Cl ROMW/RG RM7 . 124 C1
Carnation St ABYW SE2 . 163 L4

Carnbrook Rd BKHTH/KID SE3 . 162 A9
Carnecke Gdns ELTH/MOT SE9 . 184 B1
Carnegie Cl PEND EN3 . 80 C4
SURB KT6 . 199 L9
Carnegie Pl WIM/MER SW19 . 178 G6
Carnegie Rd STALW/RED AL3 . 38 C2
Carnegie St IS N1 . 5 M3
Carnet Cl DART DA1 . 186 F5
Carnforth Cl HOR/WEW KT19 . 219 N3
Carnforth Gdns HCH RM12 . 144 A9
Carnforth Rd STRHM/NOR SW16 . 180 E10
Carnoustie Cl THMD SE28 . 143 N8
Carnoustie Dr IS N1 . 5 M1
Carnwath Rd FUL/PGN SW6 . 157 K9
Caro La HHS/BOV HP3 . 36 M5
Carol Cl HDN NW4 . 116 C4
Carolina Cl SRTFD E15 . 121 L1
Carolina Rd THHTH CR7 . 203 J2
Caroline Cl BAY/PAD W2 . 9 K5
CROY/NA CRO . 223 M1
ISLW TW7 . 154 C8
MUSWH N10 . 98 C10
STRHM/NOR SW16 . 181 K4
WDR/YW UB7 . 151 N1
Caroline Ct ASHF TW15 . 174 C9
CRAWW RH11 . 283 K6
STAN HA7 . 95 G5
Caroline Dr BETH E2 . 7 J9
Caroline Pl BAY/PAD W2 . 8 G5
BTSEA SW11 . 158 B8
HYS/HAR UB3 . 152 E6
OXHEY WD19 . 73 M10
Caroline Place Ms BAY/PAD W2 * . 9 H8
Caroline Rd WIM/MER SW19 . 178 G3
Caroline St WCHPL E1 . 140 E8
Caroline Ter BGVA SW1W . 16 C6
Caroline Wk FUL/PGN SW6 . 14 A10
Carol St CAMTN NW1 . 4 G5
Carolyn Cl WOKN/KNAP GU21 . 231 J3
Carolyn Rd ORP BR6 . 207 K10
Caroon Dr RKW/CH/CXG WD3 . 71 L2
Carpenders Av OXHEY WD19 . 93 M4
Carpenter Cl EW KT17 . 220 E6
Carpenter Gdns WCHMH N21 . 99 J3
Carpenters Arms La EPP CM16 . 65 L10
Carpenters Cl BAR EN5 . 77 H10
Carpenters Ms HOLWY N7 * . 5 M1
Carpenters Pl CLAP SW4 . 158 E10
Carpenters Rd EN EN1 . 80 B2
SRTFD E15 . 141 H7
Carpenter St MYFR/PKLN W1K . 10 C6
Carpenters Wood Dr RKW/CH/CXG WD3 . 70 E8
Carrara Cl BRXN/ST SW9 . 159 M9
Carrara Whf FUL/PGN SW6 . 157 H9
Carr Cl STAN HA7 . 94 C4
Carre Ms CMBW SE5 . 159 J7
Carr Gv WOOL/PLUM SE18 . 162 B3
Carriage Dr North BTSEA SW11 . 158 A6
Carriage Dr South BTSEA SW11 . 158 A7
Carriage Dr West BTSEA SW11 . 158 A6
Carriage Ms IL IG1 . 122 F7
The Carriageway BH/WHM TN16 . 245 N10
Carrick Cl ISLW TW7 . 154 F9
Carrick Dr BARK/HLT IG6 . 102 F9
SEV TN13 . 247 L6
Carrick Gdns TOTM N17 . 99 P6
Carrick Ga ESH/CLAY KT10 . 198 B10
Carrick Ms DEPT SE8 . 160 F5
Carrill Wy BELV DA17 . 163 N5
Carrington Av BORE WD6 . 75 N5
HSLW TW3 . 176 A1
Carrington Cl BAR EN5 . 65 N6
CROY/NA CRO . 204 D7
REDH RH1 . 258 A9
WIM/MER SW19 . 178 G6
Carrington Pl ESH/CLAY KT10 * . 218 A1
Carrington Rd RCHPK/HAM TW10 . 155 M10
SL SL1 . 129 K9
Carrington St KTN/HRWW/WS HA3 . 94 B9
Carrington St MYFR/PICC W1J . 10 D10
Carrol Cl KTTN NW5 . 118 C9
Carroll Av GU GU1 . 250 D10
Carroll Cl SRTFD E15 . 121 L10
Carroll Hl LOU IG10 . 82 C7
Carronade Pl THMD SE28 . 162 F2
Carroun Rd VX/NE SW8 . 158 G6
Carroway La GFD/PVL UB6 . 134 C5
Carrow Rd DAGW RM9 . 143 L2
WOT/HER KT12 . 197 L10
Carr Rd NTHLT UB5 . 134 A1
WALTH E17 . 101 H10
Carrs La WCHMH N21 . 79 L7
Carr St POP/IOD E14 . 140 D7
Carshalton Gv SUT SM1 . 221 N1
Carshalton Park Rd CAR SM5 . 222 A5
Carshalton Pl CAR SM5 . 222 C5
Carshalton Rd BNSTD SM7 . 222 B5
CAR SM5 . 202 A5
MTCM CR4 . 202 B5
SUT SM1 . 222 A4
Carslake Rd PUT/ROE SW15 . 178 F2
Carson Rd CAN/RD E16 . 141 K3
DUL SE21 . 181 P5
EBAR EN4 . 78 A4
Carstairs Rd CAT SE6 . 183 H6
Carston Cl LEE/GVPK SE12 . 183 H8
Carswell Cl REDBR IG4 . 122 A2
Carswell Rd CAT SE6 . 183 H6
Cartbridge Cl RPLY/SEND GU23 . 232 C8
Carter Cl CDALE/KGS NW9 . 116 A4
CRW RM5 . 104 C1
WLGTN SM6 . 222 E6
Carteret St STJSPK SW1H . 17 H2
Carteret Wy DEPT SE8 . 160 D3
Carterhatch La EN EN1 . 79 N1
Carterhatch Rd PEND EN3 . 80 D6
Carter La BLKFR EC4V . 12 B3
Carter Pl WALW SE17 . 19 F8
Carter Rd CRAWE RH10 . 284 D10
PLSTW E13 . 141 N4
WIM/MER SW19 . 180 A2
Carters Cl GU GU1 . 250 D6
KTTN NW5 . 4 G1
WPK KT4 . 201 J10
Cartersfield Rd WAB EN9 . 63 H10
Carters Hill Cl ELTH/MOT SE9 . 183 N4
Carters La EPP CM16 . 65 L5
WOKS/MYFD GU22 . 232 E6
Carters Md HLWE CM17 . 47 L6
Cartersmead Cl HORL RH6 . 280 D6
Carter St WALW SE17 . 238 C1
Carters Yd STAL AL1 . 38 D5
Carthew Rd HMSMTH W6 . 156 F6
Carthew Vis HMSMTH W6 . 156 G6
Carthouse La WOKN/KNAP GU21 . 213 H10
Carthusian St FARR EC1M . 12 C1
Carting La TPL/STR WC2R . 11 L6
Cart La CHING E4 . 101 J2
Cartmel CAMTN NW1 * . 4 C6
Cartmel Cl REIG RH2 . 257 P6
TOTM N17 . 99 P6
Cartmel Ct NTHLT UB5 . 133 H5
Cartmel Gdns MRDN SM4 . 201 N5
Cartmel Rd BXLYHN DA7 . 164 D2
Cart Pth GSTN WD25 . 59 K6
The Cart Tr HHS/BOV HP3 . 36 A10
Cartwright Gdns STPAN WC1H . 5 K10

Cartwright St WCHPL E1 . 13 M7
Cartwright Wy BARN SW13 . 156 E6
Carve Ley WCCE AL7 . 23 L6
Carver Cl CHSWK W4 . 155 P2
Carver Rd HNHL SE24 . 181 J1
Carville Crs BTFD TW8 . 155 A3
Cary Rd WAN E11 . 121 K9
Carysfort Rd CEND/HSY/T N8 . 118 E1
STNW/STAM N16 . 119 L8
Cary Wk RAD WD7 . 56 C10
Cascade Av MUSWH N10 . 118 D2
Cascade Cl STMC/STPC BR5 . 207 M3
Cascade Rd BKHH IG9 . 102 A3
Cascades CROY/NA CRO . 224 C6
Caselden Cl ADL/WDHM KT15 . 215 M2
Casella Rd NWCR SE14 . 160 C6
Casewick Rd WNWD SE27 . 181 J8
Casey Cl STJWD NW8 . 3 M10
Casher Rd CRAWE RH10 . 284 D10
Casimir Rd CLPT E5 . 120 A8
Casino Av HNHL SE24 . 181 K1
Caspian Cl PUR RM19 . 165 P4
Caspian St CMBW SE5 . 159 J4
Caspian Wk CAN/RD E16 . 142 A8
Caspian Wy PUR RM19 . 165 P4
SWCM DA10 . 189 J1
Cassandra Cl NTHLT UB5 . 114 C9
Cassandra Ga CHES/WCR EN8 . 62 G1
Casselden Rd WLSDN NW10 . 136 A2
Cassidy Rd FUL/PGN SW6 . 157 K6
Cassilda Rd ABYW SE2 . 163 K5
Cassilis Rd POP/IOD E14 . 160 F1
TWK TW1 . 176 G2
Cassiobridge Rd WATW WD18 . 72 F8
Cassiobury Av EBED/NFELT TW14 . 174 G3
Cassiobury Dr WAT WD17 . 72 F5
Cassiobury Park Av WATW WD18 . 72 F7
Cassiobury Rd WALTH E17 . 120 C3
Cassio Pl WATW WD18 . 72 E8
Cassio Rd WATW WD18 . 73 J8
Cassland Rd HOM E9 . 140 C2
THHTH CR7 . 203 L4
Cassiee Rd CAT SE6 . 182 E5
Casson St WCHPL E1 . 140 A1
Casstine Cl SWLY BR8 . 208 G1
Castellain Rd MV/WKIL W9 . 8 G1
Castellan Av GPK RM2 . 124 K3
Castellane Cl STAN HA7 . 94 B8
Castello Av PUT/ROE SW15 . 178 F1
Castell Rd LOU IG10 . 82 F5
Castelnau BARN SW13 . 156 E6
Casterbridge Rd BKHTH/KID SE3 . 161 N6
Casterton St HACK E8 . 140 A1
Castile Gdns KUTN/CMB KT2 . 50 A5
Castile Rd WOOL/PLUM SE18 . 162 D3
Castillon Rd CAT SE6 . 183 K5
Castlands Rd CAT SE6 . 182 E5
Castle Av CHING E4 . 101 K3
EW KT17 . 220 E5
Castle Baynard St BLKFR EC4V . 12 C4
Castlebrook Cl LBTH SE11 . 18 E6
Castle Cl ACT W3 . 155 N1
BUSH WD23 . 74 A10
HARH RM3 . 105 K4
HAYES BR2 . 205 K3
HOD EN11 . 27 H10
REDH RH1 . 289 P9
REIG RH2 . 275 L4
SUN TW16 . 176 D10
WIM/MER SW19 . 178 G6
Castlecombe Dr WIM/MER SW19 . 178 G3
Castlecombe Rd ELTH/MOT SE9 . 184 B8
Castle Ct BANK EC3V * . 13 H3
SYD SE26 . 182 G7
Castledine Rd PGE/AN SE20 . 182 A10
Castle Dr BGR/WK TN15 . 247 M3
HORL RH6 . 280 D6
REDBR IG4 . 122 B4
REIG RH2 . 275 K4
Castle Farm Rd RSEV TN14 . 228 G3
Castleford Av ELTH/MOT SE9 . 184 E6
Castleford Cl BORE WD6 . 75 N1
TOTM N17 . 99 P6
Castle Gdns DORK RH4 . 255 L10
Castlegate RCH/KEW TW9 . 155 L9
Castle Gate Wy BERK HP4 . 33 K2
Castle Gn WEY KT13 . 195 P1
Castle Grove Rd CHOB/PIR GU24 . 213 G5
Castlehaven Rd CAMTN NW1 . 4 D1
Castle Hl BERK HP4 . 33 M4
GU GU1 . 268 A2
HART DA3 . 211 J5
WDSR SL4 . 146 C10
Castle Hill Av BERK HP4 . 33 M4
CROY/NA CRO . 224 C5
Castle Hill Pde WEA W13 * . 135 J5
Castle Hill Rd EGH TW20 . 171 N7
Castle La WESTW SW1E . 16 G3
Castleleigh Ct ENC/FH EN2 . 79 L2
Castlemaine Av EW KT17 . 220 F5
SAND/SEL CR2 . 223 N2
Castlemaine St WCHPL E1 . 140 A7
Castle Md CMBW SE5 . 159 K6
Castle Mead Gdns HERT/WAT SG14 . 25 K5
Castle Ms HART DA3 . 34 A5
CROY/NA CRO * . 97 M6
Castle Pde EW KT17 * . 220 D4
Castle Pl CAMTN NW1 . 4 D1
CHSWK W4 * . 156 C2
Castle Rd ADL/WDHM KT15 . 239 M6
CAMTN NW1 . 4 D1
DAGW RM9 . 143 L3
EPSOM KT18 . 234 B8
EYN DA4 . 210 B4
GRAYS RM17 . 167 K5
HOD EN11 . 27 H10
ISLW TW7 . 154 A7
NFNCH/WDSPK N12 . 97 H4
NWDGN UB2 . 153 H2
PEND EN3 . 80 D5
STAL AL1 . 38 E4
WEY KT13 . 195 P1
WOKN/KNAP GU21 . 214 C10
Castle Row CHSWK W4 * . 156 A4
Castle St BERK HP4 . 33 M4
CBW/CH GUW GU1 * . 249 L8
CHSGT KT9 . 219 H8
DART DA1 . 187 K2
EHAM E6 . 141 N9
GU GU1 . 268 A3
HERT/WAT SG14 . 25 L4
KUT/HW KT1 . 199 K1
REDH RH1 . 259 K6
SL SL4 . 149 L6
SWCM DA10 . 189 J1
WEY KT13 . 195 P1
Castleton Av BXLYHN DA7 . 164 F1
WBLY HA9 . 115 N8
Castleton Cl BNSTD SM7 . 239 K11
CROY/NA CRO . 204 D6

Castleton Dr BNSTD SM7 . 239 K1
Castleton Gdns WBLY HA9 . 115 N8
Castleton Rd ELTH/MOT SE9 . 184 A4
GDMY/SEVK IG3 . 123 L6
MTCM CR4 . 202 K4
RSLP HA4 . 114 C6
WALTH E17 . 101 J10
Castletown Rd WKENS W14 . 14 A4
Castleview Av WKENS W14 . 119 K6
Castleview Gdns IL IG1 . 122 K8
Castleview Rd DTCH/LGLY SL3 . 149 P3
WEY KT13 . 216 C5
Castle Vls CRICK NW2 * . 136 C1
Castle Wy EW KT17 . 220 E6
FELT TW13 . 175 K7
WIM/MER SW19 . 178 E1
Castlewood Rd EBAR EN4 . 77 N4
STNW/STAM N16 . 119 P4
Castle Yd HGT N6 . 118 B5
RCH/KEW TW9 . 177 J1
STHWK SE1 . 12 B7
Castor La POP/IOD E14 . 140 G9
Catalina Cl CDW/CHF RM16 . 167 L1
Catalina Rd HTHAIR TW6 . 152 C9
Catalpa Ct LEW SE13 . 183 J2
Catena Ri LTWR GU18 . 212 A6
Cater Gdns RGUW GU3 . 249 K8
Caterham Av CLAY IG5 . 103 N2
Caterham-By-Pass CTHM CR3 . 242 C10
Caterham Ct CHOB/PIR GU24 . 230 D7
Caterham Dr COUL/CHIP CR5 . 241 J5
Caterham Rd LEW SE13 . 161 N1
Catesby St WALW SE17 . 19 H6
Catford Broadway CAT SE6 . 182 G5
Catford Hl CAT SE6 . 182 C5
Catford Island CAT SE6 * . 182 E4
Catford Rd CAT SE6 . 182 E4
Cathall Rd WAN E11 . 121 K8
Catham Cl STAL AL1 . 38 G8
Catharine Cl CDW/CHF RM16 . 167 L1
Cathay St BERM/RHTH SE16 . 160 A1
Cathcart Dr ORP BR6 . 207 H9
Cathcart Hl ARCH N19 . 118 D9
Cathcart Rd WBPTN SW10 . 15 H8
Cathcart St KTTN NW5 . 4 E1
Cathedral Cl GUW GU2 . 267 N1
Cathedral Hl GUW GU2 . 249 M9
Cathedral Vw GUW GU2 . 249 L10
Catherall Rd HBRY N5 . 119 K6
Catherine Cl BF/WBF KT14 . 215 P10
BRWN CM15 . 86 F9
HHNE HP2 . 35 M2
LOU IG10 . 82 C7
Catherine Dr RCH/KEW TW9 . 155 N10
SUN TW16 . 176 C10
Catherine Gdns HSLW TW3 . 154 G10
Catherine Griffiths Ct CLKNW EC1R * . 12 B1
Catherine Gv GNWCH SE10 . 160 G2
Catherine Howard Ct WEY KT13 * . 196 C10
Catherine Pl HRW HA1 . 114 E3
WESTW SW1E . 16 G3
Catherine Rd GPK RM2 . 125 J3
PEND EN3 . 80 C3
SURB KT6 . 199 J5
Catherines Cl WDR/YW UB7 * . 151 N1
Catherine St HOL/ALD WC2B * . 11 L5
STALW/RED AL3 . 38 C5
Catherine Vls RYNPK SW20 . 178 G10
Catherine Wheel Aly LVPST EC2M * . 13 K2
Catherine Wheel Rd BTFD TW8 . 155 J7
Catherine Wheel Yd WHALL SW1A . 10 G10
Cathles Rd BAL SW12 . 180 C2
Cathnor Rd SHB W12 . 156 E1
Cathrow Ms HOD EN11 . 26 F10
Catisfield Rd PEND EN3 . 80 D3
Catkin Cl HHW HP1 . 35 L4
Catlin Crs SHPTN TW17 . 196 E5
Catling Cl FSTH SE23 . 182 B6
Catlin's La PIN HA5 . 113 J1
Catlin St BERM/RHTH SE16 . 159 M4
HHS/BOV HP3 . 36 B1
Cator Cl CROY/NA CRO . 225 K7
Cator Crs CROY/NA CRO . 225 L7
Cator La BECK BR3 . 203 J1
Cato Rd CLAP SW4 . 158 F2
SYD SE26 . 182 G9
Cator Rd CAR SM5 . 222 A2
SYD SE26 . 182 G9
Cator St PECK SE15 . 159 M6
Catsdell Bottom HHS/BOV HP3 . 36 C9
Catsey La BUSH WD23 . 94 B1
Catsey Wd BUSH WD23 . 94 B1
Catterick Cl FBAR/BDGN N11 . 98 A6
Catterick Wy BORE WD6 . 75 L1
Cattistock Rd ELTH/MOT SE9 . 184 D8
Cattlegate Rd POTB/CUF EN6 . 60 E7
Cattley Cl BAR EN5 . 77 J4
Cattlins Cl CHESW EN7 . 61 N1
Catton St RSQ WC1B . 11 L1
Cattsdell HHNE HP2 . 35 K4
Caudwell Ter WAND/EARL SW18 * . 179 N5
Caulfield Rd EHAM E6 . 142 G2
PECK SE15 . 160 A4
Causeway Br PUR RM19 . 166 D2
Causeway Cl POTB/CUF EN6 . 60 F7
The Causeway BELMT SM2 . 221 N8
CAR SM5 . 202 B10
CHSGTN KT9 . 219 H4
EFNCH N2 . 117 N2
ESH/CLAY KT10 . 218 E4
POTB/CUF EN6 . 59 M7
STA TW18 . 172 F7
TEDD TW11 . 176 D2
WAND/EARL SW18 . 157 L10
WIM/MER SW19 . 178 C2
Causeyware Rd ED N9 . 90 F7
Causton Cots POP/IOD E14 * . 140 D7
Causton Rd HGT N6 . 118 C6
Causton Sq DAGE RM10 . 144 B2
Causton St WEST SW1P . 17 H7
Cautherly La WARE SG12 . 26 E6
Cautley Av CLAP SW4 . 180 A1
Cavalier Cl CHDH RM6 . 123 P4
Cavalier Gdns HYS/HAR UB3 . 152 L6
Cavalry Crs HSLWW TW4 . 154 G10
WDSR SL4 . 148 D9
Cavalry Gdns PUT/ROE SW15 . 179 H1
Cavan Dr STALW/RED AL3 . 38 G1
Cavan Pl PIN HA5 * . 94 B10
Cavaye Pl WBPTN SW10 . 15 H6
Cavell Crs DART DA1 . 165 L9
Cavell Dr ENC/FH EN2 . 79 H5
Cavell Rd CHESW EN7 . 61 N1
TOTM N17 . 99 P6
Cavell St WCHPL E1 . 140 A7
Cavell Wy CRAWE RH10 . 285 M7
HOR/WEW KT19 . 219 N7
WOKN/KNAP GU21 . 231 H4
Cavendish Av BFN/LL DA15 . 185 K5
ERITH DA8 . 164 D5
FNCH N3 . 97 H7
HCH RM12 . 145 J1
HRW HA1 . 114 D7
NWMAL KT3 . 200 E3
RSLP HA4 . 113 P9
STJWD NW8 . 3 L7
WBLY HA9 . 136 B1
WELL DA16 . 163 J9

| | | |
|---|---|---|
| WFD IG8 | 101 | N8 |
| Cavendish Cl AMS HP6 | 69 | N5 |
| KIL/WHAMP NW6 | 2 | C2 |
| STJWD NW8 | 3 | M9 |
| SUN TW16 | 174 | C9 |
| UED N18 * | 100 | A6 |
| YEAD UB4 | 132 | F7 |
| Cavendish Ct | | |
| RKW/CH/CXG WD3 * | 72 | E9 |
| SUN TW16 | 174 | E9 |
| HCH RM12 | 75 | M8 |
| Cavendish Dr BORE WD6 | 75 | M8 |
| HCH RM12 | 145 | J1 |
| Cavendish Dr EDGW HA8 * | 95 | L7 |
| ESH/CLAY KT10 | 218 | D2 |
| WAN E11 | 121 | J6 |
| Cavendish Gdns BARK IG11 | 123 | J10 |
| CHDH RM6 | 123 | P9 |
| CLAP SW4 * | 180 | D2 |
| IL IG1 | 122 | D6 |
| REDH RH1 | 258 | B9 |
| Cavendish Meads ASC SL5 | 192 | C6 |
| Cavendish Ms SUT SM1 | 201 | M9 |
| Cavendish Ms North | | |
| GTPST W1W * | 10 | F3 |
| Cavendish Ms South | | |
| GTPST W1W * | 10 | F4 |
| Cavendish Pde CLAP SW4 * | | |
| HSLWW TW4 * | 153 | M8 |
| Cavendish Pl BMLY BR1 | 206 | C3 |
| CRICK NW2 | 10 | F5 |
| CAVSQ/HST W1G * | 136 | G1 |
| Cavendish Rd BAL SW12 | 180 | D4 |
| BAR EN5 | 76 | F7 |
| BELMT SM2 | 221 | M4 |
| CHDH E4 | 101 | H7 |
| CHSWK W4 | 155 | P7 |
| CLAP SW4 | 180 | C2 |
| CROY/NA CR0 | 203 | J8 |
| CSHM HP5 | 51 | J8 |
| FSBYPK N4 | 119 | J4 |
| KIL/WHAMP NW6 | 2 | B3 |
| NWMAL KT3 | 200 | C5 |
| REDH RH1 | 258 | B10 |
| STAL AL1 | 38 | C6 |
| SUN TW16 | 174 | C9 |
| UED N18 | 100 | A6 |
| WEY KT13 | 216 | C5 |
| WIM/MER SW19 | 179 | P10 |
| WOKS/MYFD GU22 | 232 | A5 |
| Cavendish Sq CAVSQ/HST W1G * | 10 | F3 |
| HART DA3 | 211 | J3 |
| Cavendish St IS N1 | 6 | G8 |
| Cavendish St BOW E3 * | 140 | E5 |
| FELT TW13 * | 175 | H5 |
| Cavendish Wk | | |
| HOR/WEW KT19 | 219 | N7 |
| Cavendish Wy HAT AL10 * | 40 | C4 |
| WWKM BR4 | 204 | C8 |
| Cavenham Cl | | |
| WOKS/MYFD GU22 | 10 | A5 |
| IL IG1 | 122 | C8 |
| Caverleigh Wy WPK KT4 | 200 | D8 |
| Caverley Gdns | | |
| KTN/HRWW/WS HA3 | 115 | J5 |
| Cave Rd PLSTW E13 | 141 | M1 |
| RCHPK/HAM TW10 | 176 | F7 |
| Caversham Av CHEAM SM3 | 201 | H9 |
| PLMGR N13 | 41 | G10 |
| Caversham Rd KTTN NW5 | 4 | G1 |
| KUT/HW KT1 | 199 | L2 |
| SEVS/STOTM N15 | 119 | K2 |
| Caversham St CHEL SW3 | 16 | A9 |
| Caverswall St SHB W12 | 136 | F8 |
| Cawcott Dr WDSR SL4 | 148 | D7 |
| Cawdor Av SOCK/AV RM15 | 146 | F9 |
| Cawdor Crs WDR/YW UB7 | 154 | F3 |
| Cawley Hatch | | |
| HLWW RCM19 | 46 | C1 |
| Cawnpore St NRWD SE19 | 181 | M8 |
| WALTH E17 | 100 | F9 |
| Cawsey Wy WOKN/KNAP GU21 | 232 | B3 |
| Caxton Av ADL/WDHM KT15 | 215 | K5 |
| Caxton Cl CRAWE RH10 | 283 | N10 |
| Caxton Dr UX/CGN UB8 | 131 | M4 |
| Caxton Gdns GUW GU2 | 249 | N9 |
| Caxton Gv BOW E3 | 140 | E5 |
| Caxton Hl HERT/BAY SG13 | 25 | M5 |
| Caxton La OXTED RH8 | 262 | B7 |
| Caxton Ms BTFD TW8 | 155 | K6 |
| Caxton Ri REDH RH1 | 258 | B9 |
| Caxton Rd HOD EN11 | 26 | C9 |
| NWDGN UB2 | 153 | L2 |
| SHB W12 | 136 | G10 |
| WDGN N22 | 99 | M8 |
| WIM/MER SW19 | 179 | P8 |
| The Caxtons BRXN/ST SW9 * | 159 | J3 |
| Caxton St STJSPK SW1H | 17 | H3 |
| Caxton St North CAN/RD E16 | 141 | L8 |
| Caxton St ROM RM1 | 124 | F2 |
| WATW WD18 | 92 | E1 |
| Cayenne Ct STHWK SE1 | 13 | L10 |
| Caygill Cl HAYES BR2 | 205 | L4 |
| Cayley Rd NWDGN UB2 | 154 | A2 |
| Cayton Rd COUL/CHIP CR5 | 240 | D8 |
| GFD/PVL UB6 | 134 | D4 |
| Cayton St FSBYE EC1V | 6 | G10 |
| Cazenove Rd STNW/STAM N16 | 119 | N7 |
| WALTH E17 | 101 | P9 |
| Cearn Wy COUL/CHIP CR5 | 240 | G3 |
| Cecil Av BARK IG11 | 142 | G2 |
| CDW/CHF RM16 | 167 | L1 |
| EMPK RM11 | 125 | M1 |
| EN EN1 | 79 | N8 |
| WBLY HA9 | 115 | L10 |
| Cecil Cl ASHF TW15 | 174 | D10 |
| CHSGTN KT9 | 219 | J1 |
| EA W5 * | 135 | J7 |
| Cecil Ct BAR EN5 | 76 | C3 |
| HLWS CM18 | 46 | E1 |
| LSO/SEVD WC2H | 11 | K8 |
| Cecil Crs HAT AL10 | 40 | E2 |
| Cecil Pk PIN HA5 | 47 | J2 |
| Cecilia Cl EFNCH N2 | 117 | M1 |
| Cecilia Rd HACK E8 | 119 | N10 |
| Cecil Manning Cl | | |
| GFD/PVL UB6 | 134 | F3 |
| Cecil Pk PIN HA5 | 113 | M2 |
| Cecil Pl MTCM CR4 | 194 | C2 |
| Cecil Rd ACT W3 | 135 | P7 |
| ASHF TW15 | 174 | D10 |
| CDALE/KGS NW9 | 116 | A1 |
| CHDH RM6 | 123 | N5 |
| CHES/WCR EN8 | 62 | A4 |
| CROY/NA CR0 | 202 | F6 |
| ENC/FH EN2 | 79 | J4 |
| GVW DA11 | 190 | C4 |
| HERT/BAY SG13 | 25 | K9 |
| HOD EN11 | 45 | H1 |
| HSLW TW3 | 135 | B9 |
| IL IG1 | 122 | E9 |
| IVER SL0 | 131 | H8 |
| KTN/HRWW/WS HA3 | 114 | D1 |
| MUSWH N10 | 98 | C10 |
| PLSTW E13 | 141 | M10 |
| POTB/CUF EN6 | 59 | K6 |
| STAL AL1 | 38 | E6 |
| STHGT/OAK N14 | 98 | C2 |
| SUT SM1 | 221 | J3 |
| WALTH E17 | 100 | F9 |
| WAN E11 | 121 | K7 |
| WIM/MER SW19 | 179 | L10 |
| WLSDN NW10 | 137 | H4 |
| Cecil St WATN WD24 | 73 | J4 |
| Cecil Wy HAYES BR2 | 205 | L4 |
| SLN SL2 | 128 | E6 |
| Cedar BFN/LL DA15 | 185 | K3 |
| CHDH RM6 | 123 | P9 |
| CHES/WCR EN8 | 62 | A4 |
| EBAR EN4 * | 97 | P2 |
| HYS/HAR UB3 | 133 | H8 |
| PEND EN3 | 80 | B6 |
| RSLP HA4 | 113 | K10 |
| UPMR RM14 | 125 | P2 |
| WDR/YW UB7 * | 132 | A10 |


| | | |
|---|---|---|
| WHTN TW2 | 176 | A2 |
| Cedar Cl BKHH IG9 | 102 | A3 |
| BOW E3 | 140 | A8 |
| BRXS/STRHM SW2 | 222 | A3 |
| CRAWW RH11 | 283 | N4 |
| CSHM HP5 | 51 | K5 |
| DORK RH4 | 272 | G2 |
| DUL SE21 | 181 | N4 |
| ESH/CLAY KT10 | 217 | N4 |
| EW KT17 | 220 | C10 |
| HAYES BR2 | 206 | B10 |
| HERT/WAT SG14 | 111 | G10 |
| IL IG1 | 122 | G10 |
| IVER SL0 | 130 | F3 |
| KUTN/CMB KT2 | 178 | A7 |
| POTB/CUF EN6 | 59 | K6 |
| REIG RH2 | 275 | M7 |
| ROMW/RG RM7 | 124 | D2 |
| SBW CM21 | 29 | P2 |
| STA TW18 | 195 | M2 |
| SWLY BR8 | 208 | D2 |
| WARE SG12 | 26 | C3 |
| WARL CR6 | 242 | F10 |
| Cedar Copse BMLY BR1 | 206 | C2 |
| Cedar Ct CHARL SE7 * | 161 | P5 |
| ECH TW20 | 172 | D7 |
| ELTH/MOT SE9 | 184 | B2 |
| STALE/WH AL4 | 39 | J4 |
| WIM/MER SW19 | 178 | G6 |
| Cedar Crs HAYES BR2 | 206 | B10 |
| Cedarcroft Rd CHSGTN KT9 | 219 | L1 |
| Cedar Dr ASC SL5 | 192 | F7 |
| CSHM HP5 | 50 | F6 |
| EFNCH N2 | 117 | P2 |
| EYN DA4 | 210 | A2 |
| GLDGN NW11 | 117 | K2 |
| LHD/OX KT22 | 236 | D9 |
| LOU IG10 | 82 | E6 |
| PIN HA5 | 93 | P7 |
| Cedar Gdns BELMT SM2 | 221 | M3 |
| CHOB/PIR GU24 | 213 | L6 |
| UPMR RM14 | 126 | B8 |
| BXLY DA5 | 185 | N2 |
| Cedar Gv AMSS HP7 | 69 | J5 |
| BXLY DA5 | 185 | N2 |
| CHOB/PIR GU24 | 230 | F1 |
| CSHM HP5 | 32 | C9 |
| EA W5 | 155 | J2 |
| STHL UB1 | 133 | P7 |
| WEY KT13 | 216 | D1 |
| Cedar Hts RCHPK/HAM TW10 | 177 | K4 |
| Cedar Lawn Av BAR EN5 | 77 | H9 |
| Cedar Ms ELTH/MOT SE9 | 184 | A4 |
| Cedarne Rd FUL/PGN SW6 | 157 | K6 |
| Cedar Pk CTHM CR3 | 241 | M7 |
| Cedar Park Gdns CHDH RM6 | 122 | G1 |
| WIM/MER SW19 | 178 | G6 |
| Cedar Park Rd ENC/FH EN2 | 79 | K4 |
| Cedar Pl CHARL SE7 | 161 | P4 |
| Cedar Rd BELMT SM2 | 221 | M3 |
| BERK HP4 | 34 | A6 |
| BMLY BR1 | 205 | P2 |
| CDW/CHF RM16 | 168 | D2 |
| COB KT11 | 217 | J10 |
| CRICK NW2 | 70 | A4 |
| CROY/NA CR0 | 203 | M9 |
| E/WMO/HCT KT8 | 198 | D4 |
| EBED/NFELT TW14 | 174 | E4 |
| ENC/FH EN2 | 79 | J4 |
| ERITH DA8 | 165 | H7 |
| HART DA3 | 211 | K10 |
| HCH RM12 | 125 | K8 |
| HSLWW TW4 | 153 | M8 |
| OXHEY WD19 | 73 | K10 |
| ROMW/RG RM7 | 124 | D2 |
| TEDD TW11 | 176 | B7 |
| TOTM N17 | 99 | M9 |
| WEY KT13 | 216 | D1 |
| WOKS/MYFD GU22 | 231 | N6 |
| Cedars BNSTD SM7 | 222 | A10 |
| WAB EN9 | 81 | P1 |
| Cedars Av MTCM CR4 | 202 | B4 |
| RKW/CH/CXG WD3 | 91 | M2 |
| WALTH E17 | 120 | F1 |
| Cedars Cots PUT/ROE SW15 * | 178 | D2 |
| Cedars Ct ED N9 | 99 | M3 |
| GU GU1 * | 250 | D7 |
| Cedars Dr HGDN/ICK UB10 | 132 | B4 |
| Cedars Ms CLAP SW4 * | 158 | G10 |
| Cedars Rd BARN SW13 | 156 | C5 |
| BECK BR3 | 204 | D2 |
| CHSWK W4 | 155 | P5 |
| CLAP SW4 | 158 | G9 |
| CROY/NA CR0 | 202 | F10 |
| ED N9 | 99 | P3 |
| KUT/HW KT1 | 199 | H1 |
| MRDN SM4 | 201 | L4 |
| SRTFD E15 | 141 | K1 |
| WCHMH N21 | 99 | J4 |
| The Cedars BERK HP4 * | 34 | B5 |
| BF/WBF KT14 | 216 | A8 |
| BKHH IG9 | 101 | M2 |
| BRKHM/BTCW RH3 | 255 | M10 |
| GU GU1 * | 250 | D7 |
| HARP AL5 * | 20 | A2 |
| HOM E9 * | 140 | C2 |
| LHD/OX KT22 | 237 | J7 |
| REIG RH2 * | 255 | N10 |
| SLN SL2 | 128 | E5 |
| SRTFD E15 * | 141 | L4 |
| TEDD TW11 | 176 | B7 |
| Cedar Ter RCH/KEW TW9 | 159 | L6 |
| Cedar Terrace Rd SEV TN13 | 247 | K9 |
| Cedar Tree Gv WNWD SE27 | 181 | J8 |
| Cedarville Gdns | | |
| STRHM/NOR SW16 | 180 | G9 |
| Cedar Wk ESH/CLAY KT10 | 218 | E3 |
| KWD/TDW/WH KT20 | 78 | J7 |
| PUR/KEN CR8 | 241 | K2 |
| Cedar Wy BERK HP4 | 34 | A5 |
| CAMTN NW1 | 5 | J4 |
| DTCH/LGLY SL3 | 150 | B3 |
| GU GU1 | 249 | P7 |
| SUN TW16 | 174 | B8 |
| Cedar Wood Dr GSTN WD25 | 73 | J1 |
| Cedarwood Dr | | |
| STALE/WH AL4 | 39 | J6 |
| Cedric Av ROM RM1 | 124 | F1 |
| Cedric Rd ELTH/MOT SE9 | 184 | F6 |
| Celadon Cl PEND EN3 | 80 | D7 |
| Celandine Cl POP/IOD E14 | 140 | J5 |
| SOCK/AV RM15 | 147 | H6 |
| Celandine Dr HACK E8 | 7 | L1 |
| THMD SE28 | 143 | L10 |
| Celandine Rd WOT/HER KT14 | 218 | B6 |
| Celandine Wy SRTFD E15 | 141 | K4 |
| BAY/PAD W2 | 8 | B3 |
| Celbridge Ms BAY/PAD W2 | | |
| Celedon Cl CDW/CHF RM16 | 167 | K1 |
| Celendine Gdns HACK E8 | 161 | L10 |
| Celia Crs ASHF TW15 | 173 | H5 |
| Celia Rd ARCH N19 | 118 | C1 |
| Cell Barnes Cl STAL AL1 | 38 | G8 |
| Cell Barnes La STAL AL1 | 38 | G9 |
| Cell Farm Av WDSR SL4 | 171 | N1 |
| Cement Block Cots | | |
| GRAYS RH17 * | 167 | P4 |
| Cemetery Hl HHW HP1 | 35 | M7 |
| Cemetery La CHARL SE7 | 162 | C7 |
| SHPTN TW17 | 196 | C7 |


| | | |
|---|---|---|
| Cemetery Pales | | |
| CHOB/PIR GU24 | 230 | A7 |
| Cemetery Rd ABYW SE2 | 163 | N1 |
| FSTGT E7 | 121 | L10 |
| TOTM N17 | 99 | M8 |
| Cenmaes Court Rd HHW HP1 | 35 | M5 |
| Cenmaes Meadow HHW HP1 | 35 | N6 |
| Cenacle Cl HAMP NW3 | 117 | K8 |
| Centaur Ct BTFD TW8 * | 155 | K4 |
| Centaur St STHWK SE1 | 17 | P3 |
| Centaurus Sq LCOL/BKTW AL2 | 56 | D3 |
| PEND EN3 | 80 | B8 |
| Centenary Rd EN EN1 | 79 | N6 |
| Centenary Wk CHING E4 | 101 | K6 |
| LOU IG10 | 81 | M7 |
| MNPK E12 | 122 | A4 |
| WAN E11 | 121 | K2 |
| WFD IG8 | 102 | B9 |
| Centennial Ct BORE WD6 | 98 | C1 |
| Centennial Pk BORE WD6 | 95 | H1 |
| Central Av ASHF TW15 * | 174 | A7 |
| E/WMO/HCT KT8 | 197 | N5 |
| ED N9 | 99 | M4 |
| EFNCH N2 | 97 | N10 |
| EN EN1 | 79 | P6 |
| GVE DA12 | 190 | E5 |
| HSLW TW3 | 155 | J3 |
| HYS/HAR UB3 | 152 | C1 |
| PIN HA5 | 113 | N4 |
| SOCK/AV RM15 | 166 | B1 |
| TIL RM18 | 168 | D7 |
| WAN E11 | 121 | J4 |
| WELL DA16 | 163 | K8 |
| WLGTN SM6 | 222 | G4 |
| WTHK RM20 | 166 | A4 |
| Central Blds EA W5 * | 135 | J9 |
| Central Circ HDN NW4 * | 116 | E3 |
| Central Ct CHIG IG7 | 103 | H6 |
| Central Dr HCH RM12 | 125 | M8 |
| SL SL1 | 128 | E9 |
| STAL AL1 | 39 | H5 |
| WELGLY AL7 | 23 | J3 |
| RKW/CH/CXG WD3 | 70 | E9 |
| Central Gdns MRDN SM4 | 201 | M5 |
| STAL AL1 | 39 | H5 |
| Central Hall Blds | | |
| ARCH N19 * | 118 | D7 |
| Central Hl NRWD SE19 | 181 | M8 |
| Central La WDSR SL4 | 170 | A4 |
| Central Pde ACT W3 * | 155 | P1 |
| BFN/LL DA15 * | 185 | M5 |
| CROY/NA CR0 | 225 | H6 |
| E/WMO/HCT KT8 * | 197 | N4 |
| GFD/PVL UB6 * | 134 | C2 |
| HORL RH6 * | 280 | B5 |
| HRW HA1 | 114 | F3 |
| PEND EN3 * | 80 | C2 |
| PGE/AN SE20 * | 182 | C10 |
| STRHM/NOR SW16 * | 180 | F7 |
| SURB KT6 * | 199 | P3 |
| WALTH E17 * | 120 | F2 |
| Central Park Av EHAM E6 | 142 | A4 |
| Central Park Est | | |
| HSLWW TW4 * | 153 | L10 |
| Central Pl SNWD SE25 * | 203 | P4 |
| Central Rd ALP/SUD HA0 | 114 | C10 |
| DART DA1 | 165 | M10 |
| HLW CM20 | 29 | K7 |
| MRDN SM4 | 201 | L5 |
| WPK KT4 | 200 | D10 |
| Central Sq E/WMO/HCT KT8 | 197 | N4 |
| GLDGN NW11 | 117 | K4 |
| Central St FSBYE EC1V | 6 | E9 |
| EPP CM16 | 65 | J8 |
| Central Ter BECK BR3 * | 204 | C3 |
| Central Wy CAR SM5 | 221 | P4 |
| EBED/NFELT TW14 | 175 | J1 |
| NTHWD HA6 | 92 | B3 |
| OXTED RH8 | 261 | J3 |
| THMD SE28 | 143 | H9 |
| WLSDN NW10 | 135 | P5 |
| Centre Av ACT W3 | 135 | A10 |
| EPP CM16 | 65 | J8 |
| Centre Common Rd CHST BR7 | 184 | F10 |
| Centre Dr EPP CM16 | 65 | J8 |
| Centre Rd DAGE RM10 | 144 | C2 |
| HART DA3 | 211 | K10 |
| WAN E11 | 121 | J4 |
| Centre St BETH E2 | 140 | A6 |
| Centre Wy ED N9 | 100 | A4 |
| Centric Cl CAMTN NW1 * | 4 | B5 |
| Centurion Cl IS N1 | 5 | M2 |
| Centurion La BOW E3 | 139 | P10 |
| Centurion Sq | | |
| WOOL/PLUM SE18 | 162 | B7 |
| Centurian Wy ERITH DA18 | 164 | G2 |
| Centurion Cl HOLWY N7 | 5 | L1 |
| Centurion La BOW E3 | 139 | P10 |
| Centurion Sq CHARL SE7 * | 162 | A1 |
| Century Cl HDN NW4 | 116 | F3 |
| WOKN/KNAP GU21 | 232 | C2 |
| Century Ms CLPT E5 | 120 | B9 |
| Century Pk WAT WD17 * | 73 | K9 |
| Century Rd EGH TW20 | 172 | B7 |
| HOD EN11 | 44 | F2 |
| WALTH E17 | 120 | D1 |
| WARE SG12 | 26 | C1 |
| Cephas Av WCHPL E1 | 140 | D7 |
| Cephas St WCHPL E1 | 140 | D7 |
| Ceres Rd WOOL/PLUM SE18 | 163 | N6 |
| Cerise Rd PECK SE15 | 159 | J8 |
| Cerne Cl YEAD UB4 | 133 | H4 |
| Cerne Rd GVE DA12 | 191 | H7 |
| MRDN SM4 | 201 | M6 |
| Cerney Ms BAY/PAD W2 | 9 | M6 |
| Cerotus Pl CHERT KT16 | 195 | J7 |
| Cervantes Ct BAY/PAD W2 * | 9 | M6 |
| NTHWD HA6 | 92 | G8 |
| Cervia Wy GVE DA12 | 191 | M6 |
| Cestreham Crs CSHM HP5 | 51 | J5 |
| Cezanne Rd GSTN WD25 | 14 | A4 |
| Cezanne Rd GSTN WD25 | 73 | L2 |
| Chabot Dr PECK SE15 | 160 | A9 |
| Chace Av POTB/CUF EN6 | 59 | N6 |
| Chacombe Rd BEAC HP9 | 88 | B6 |
| Chadacre Av CLAY IG5 | 122 | C1 |
| Chadacre Rd EW KT17 | 220 | E2 |
| Chadbourn St POP/IOD E14 | 140 | M4 |
| Chad Crs ED N9 | 100 | B4 |
| Chadd Dr BMLY BR1 | 206 | C3 |
| Chadfields TIL RM18 | 168 | E5 |
| Chadhurst Cl RDKG RH5 | 273 | J3 |
| Chadville Gdns CHDH RM6 | 123 | N5 |
| Chadway DAGW RM9 | 123 | N7 |
| Chadwell WARE SG12 | 26 | B3 |
| Chadwell Av CHDH RM6 | 123 | L5 |
| CHES/WCR EN8 | 62 | B4 |
| Chadwell By-Pass | | |
| CDW/CHF RM16 | 168 | D4 |
| Chadwell Heath La CHDH RM6 | 123 | J4 |
| Chadwell Hl CDW/CHF RM16 | 168 | E4 |
| Chadwell La CEND/HSY/T N8 | 118 | E1 |
| Chadwell Rd GRAYS RM17 | 167 | P5 |
| Chadwell St CLKNW EC1R * | B9 | |
| Chadwick Av CHING E4 | 101 | N2 |
| WCHMH N21 | 78 | G9 |
| WIM/MER SW19 | 179 | B5 |
| Chadwick Cl GVW DA11 | 190 | B5 |
| PUT/ROE SW15 | 176 | F4 |
| TEDD TW11 | 176 | D1 |
| Chadwick Rd HARH RM3 | 105 | L10 |
| NWDGN UB2 | 153 | N3 |
| PECK SE15 | 159 | H8 |
| WAN E11 | 121 | L3 |
| WLSDN NW10 | 136 | G1 |
| Chadwick St WEST SW1P | 17 | J4 |
| Chadwin Rd PLSTW E13 | 141 | N4 |
| Chadworth Wy | | |
| ESH/CLAY KT10 | 218 | C2 |
| Chaffers Md ASHTD KT21 | 237 | L5 |
| Chaffinch Av CROY/NA CR0 | 204 | C6 |
| Chaffinch Cl CRAWW RH11 | 283 | N5 |
| CROY/NA CR0 | 204 | C6 |
| ED N9 | 100 | C2 |


| | | |
|---|---|---|
| SURB KT6 | 199 | M10 |
| Chaffinch Cl ORP BR6 | 207 | K5 |
| Chaffinch La WATW WD18 | 92 | G1 |
| Chaffinches Gn HHS/BOV HP3 | 36 | B10 |
| Chaffinch Rd BECK BR3 | 204 | D1 |
| Chaffinch Wy HORL RH6 | 279 | P3 |
| Chafford Wy CDW/CHF RM16 | 147 | M10 |
| CHDH RM6 | 123 | M2 |
| Chagford St CAMTN NW1 | 9 | N1 |
| Chagrin Ct TOTM N17 | 7 | N10 |
| Chailey Av EN EN1 | 79 | N6 |
| Chailey Cl CRAWW RH11 | 283 | K10 |
| HEST TW5 | 153 | L7 |
| Chailey Pl ESH/CLAY KT12 | 217 | M1 |
| Chailey St CLPT E5 | 120 | B8 |
| Chain Wk CHESW EN7 | 61 | N7 |
| Chalbury Wk IS N1 | 5 | P7 |
| Chalcombe Rd ABYW SE2 | 163 | L2 |
| Chalcot Cl BELMT SM2 | 221 | K4 |
| Chalcot Crs CAMTN NW1 | 4 | C3 |
| Chalcot Gdns HAMP NW3 | 3 | P1 |
| Chalcot Ms | | |
| STRHM/NOR SW16 | 180 | F6 |
| Chalcot Rd CAMTN NW1 | 4 | C2 |
| Chalcot Sq CAMTN NW1 | 4 | C1 |
| Chalcott Gdns SURB KT6 | 199 | H8 |
| Chalcroft Rd LEW SE13 | 183 | K1 |
| Chaldon Cl REDH RH1 | 275 | P2 |
| Chaldon Common Rd | | |
| CTHM CR3 | 241 | K10 |
| Chaldon Rd CTHM CR3 | 241 | K10 |
| FUL/PGN SW6 | 157 | H6 |
| Chaldon Wy COUL/CHIP CR5 | 240 | F5 |
| Chale Rd BRXS/STRHM SW2 | 180 | A5 |
| Chalet Cl BERK HP4 | 33 | H3 |
| BXLY DA5 | 186 | E7 |
| Chalet Est MLHL NW7 | 97 | H2 |
| Chalfont Av WBLY HA9 | 136 | B5 |
| Chalfont Cha | | |
| REDH RH1 * | 257 | P3 |
| Chalfont Cl HHNE HP2 | 36 | C1 |
| Chalfont Gn ED N9 | 99 | M4 |
| Chalfont La RKW/CH/CXG WD3 | 70 | E9 |
| Chalfont Ms | | |
| WAND/EARL SW18 | 179 | J4 |
| BFN/LL DA15 | 38 | M6 |
| Chalfont Pl STAL AL1 | 38 | C1 |
| Chalfont Rd BEAC HP9 | 89 | J6 |
| HORL RH6 | 280 | B5 |
| HYS/HAR UB3 | 133 | N10 |
| PEND EN3 | 80 | C1 |
| PGE/AN SE20 | 182 | C10 |
| STRHM/NOR SW16 | 180 | F7 |
| SURB KT6 | 199 | P4 |
| WALTH E17 * | 120 | F2 |
| Chalfont Wk PIN HA5 | 93 | K10 |
| Chalfont Wy WEA W13 | 154 | A1 |
| Chalford Cl E/WMO/HCT KT8 | 197 | P4 |
| Chalford Gdns CRK RM2 | 125 | J2 |
| Chalford Rd DUL SE21 | 181 | L7 |
| Chalford Wk WFD IG8 | 102 | A9 |
| Chalforde Gdns GPK RM2 | 124 | F3 |
| Chalgrove WCCE AL7 | 23 | H4 |
| Chalgrove Av MRDN SM4 | 201 | K5 |
| Chalgrove Crs CLAY IG5 | 102 | F10 |
| Chalgrove Gdns FNCH N3 | 116 | F6 |
| Chalgrove Rd BELMT SM2 | 221 | N6 |
| HACK E8 | 120 | A6 |
| TOTM N17 | 100 | E4 |
| Chalice Cl WLGTN SM6 | 223 | H4 |
| Chalice Wy RDART DA2 | 188 | D1 |
| Chalk Ct GRAYS RM17 | 167 | M5 |
| Chalk Cl WCCE AL7 | 23 | L4 |
| Chalk Dell RKW/CH/CXG WD3 | 91 | K1 |
| Chalkdell Flds STALE/WH AL4 | 39 | P4 |
| Chalkdell Hl HHNE HP2 | 35 | P6 |
| Chalkenden Cl PGE/AN SE20 | 182 | A10 |
| Chalk Farm Pde HAMP NW3 * | 4 | A1 |
| Chalk Farm Rd CAMTN NW1 | 4 | C3 |
| Chalk Hl AMSS HP7 | 88 | E1 |
| Chalk Hill Rd HMSMTH W6 | 156 | H10 |
| Chalkhill Rd WBLY HA9 | 115 | M8 |
| Chalklands WBLY HA9 | 115 | P8 |
| Chalk La ASHTD KT21 | 237 | M5 |
| EBAR EN4 | 78 | A4 |
| EHSLY KT24 | 252 | F7 |
| EPSOM KT18 | 238 | A6 |
| Chalkley Cl MTCM CR4 | 202 | A2 |
| Chalkmill Dr EN EN1 | 80 | B2 |
| Chalk Paddock EPSOM KT18 | 238 | A1 |
| Chalk Pit Av STMC/STPC BR5 | 207 | P1 |
| Chalkpit La BRKHM/BTCW RH3 | 254 | F10 |
| DORK RH4 | 261 | H3 |
| OXTED RH8 | 261 | H3 |
| Chalk Pit La SL SL1 | 128 | A3 |
| GT/LBKH KT23 | 253 | N3 |
| Chalk Pit Rd BNSTD SM7 | 239 | K3 |
| EPSOM KT18 | 238 | A3 |
| SUT SM1 * | 221 | M2 |
| Chalkpit Ter DORK RH4 | 254 | F10 |
| Chalkpit Wd OXTED RH8 | 261 | J3 |
| Chalk Rd GVE DA12 | 191 | K4 |
| PLSTW E13 | 141 | L4 |
| Chalkstone Cl WELL DA16 | 163 | H1 |
| Chalkways GR/WK TN15 | 247 | M5 |
| Chalkwell Park Av EN EN1 | 79 | N8 |
| Chalky Bank GVE DA12 | 190 | G7 |
| Chalky La CHSGTN KT9 | 219 | J5 |
| Challacombe Cl | | |
| RBRW/HUT CM13 | 107 | N2 |
| Challenge Cl GVE DA12 | 191 | J7 |
| WLSDN NW10 | 136 | B3 |
| Challenge Rd ASHF TW15 | 174 | A7 |
| Challice Wy BRXS/STRHM SW2 | 180 | A5 |
| Challin St PGE/AN SE20 | 204 | B1 |
| Challinor HLWE CM17 | 47 | P1 |
| Challis Rd BTFD TW8 | 155 | J4 |
| Challock Cl BH/WHM TN16 | 283 | P2 |
| Challoner Cl EFNCH N2 | 97 | N10 |
| Challoner Crs WKENS W14 | 14 | B9 |
| Challoners Cl E/WMO/HCT KT8 | 198 | C4 |
| Challoner St WKENS W14 | 14 | B9 |
| Chalmers Ct HORL RH6 | 279 | H5 |
| Chalmers Rd ASHF TW15 | 174 | C7 |
| BNSTD SM7 | 239 | M1 |
| Chalmers Rd East ASHF TW15 | 174 | C7 |
| Chalmers Wy | | |
| EBED/NFELT TW14 | 175 | J1 |
| TWK TW1 | 154 | G10 |
| Chalsey Rd BROCKY SE4 | 160 | A10 |
| Chalton Dr EFNCH N2 | 117 | M4 |
| Chalton St CAMTN NW1 | 5 | J7 |
| Chalvey Gv SL SL1 | 148 | G2 |
| Chalvey Rd SL SL1 | 149 | H1 |
| Chalvey Rd East SL SL1 | 149 | K1 |
| Chalvey Rd West SL SL1 | 148 | G1 |
| Chamberlain Cl HLWE CM17 | 47 | N1 |
| IL IG1 | 122 | F1 |
| THMD SE28 | 163 | K1 |
| Chamberlain Cots | | |
| CMBW SE5 | 159 | J7 |
| Chamberlain Gdns HSLW TW3 | 154 | B7 |
| Chamberlain La PIN HA5 | 113 | H2 |
| Chamberlain Pl WALTH E17 | 101 | H1 |
| Chamberlain St HAMP NW3 | 3 | P2 |
| Chamberlain Wy PIN HA5 | 113 | J1 |
| SURB KT6 | 199 | K7 |
| Chamberlayne Rd | | |
| WLSDN NW10 | 136 | G1 |
| Chamberlens Garages | | |
| HMSMTH W6 * | 156 | G3 |
| Chambers Av SCUP DA14 | 185 | P9 |
| Chambersbury La | | |
| HHS/BOV HP3 | 54 | B1 |
| Chambers Cl RDART DA2 | 188 | F1 |
| Chambers Gdns EFNCH N2 | 97 | M10 |
| Chambers Gv WCCE AL7 | 23 | H8 |
| Chambers La WLSDN NW10 | 136 | M1 |


| | | |
|---|---|---|
| Chambers Pl SAND/SEL CR2 | 223 | L4 |
| Chambers Rd HOLWY N7 | 118 | F9 |
| Chambers St | | |
| BERM/RHTH SE16 | 25 | K5 |
| Chamber St WCHPL E1 | 13 | M7 |
| Chambon Pl HMSMTH W6 | 156 | D3 |
| Chambord St BETH E2 | 7 | P10 |
| Champa Cl TOTM N17 | 99 | G2 |
| Champion Crs SYD SE26 | 182 | D7 |
| Champion Down EHSLY KT24 | 252 | G7 |
| Champion Gv CMBW SE5 | 159 | L5 |
| Champion Hill CMBW SE5 | 159 | L5 |
| Champion Pk CMBW SE5 | 159 | L5 |
| Champion Rd SYD SE26 | 182 | D7 |
| Champions Cl BORE WD6 | 75 | N3 |
| Champions Wy HOD EN11 | 26 | F10 |
| CDALE/KGS NW9 | 96 | E10 |
| Champneys Cl BELMT SM2 | 221 | J3 |
| Champneys OXHEY WD19 | 93 | M3 |
| Champneys Cl DTCH/LGLY SL3 | 150 | D9 |
| Chance Cl CHF/CHF RM16 | 167 | L2 |
| Chancellor Gdns | | |
| SAND/SEL CR2 | 223 | J6 |
| Chancellor Gv DUL SE21 | 181 | K5 |
| Chancellor Rd CLD/KGS NW9 | 96 | A10 |
| Chancellors AMSS HP7 | 69 | J3 |
| Chancellors Rd HMSMTH W6 | 156 | G4 |
| Chancellors St HMSMTH W6 | 156 | G4 |
| Chancellors Whf HMSMTH W6 * | 156 | G4 |
| Chancelot Rd ABYW SE2 | 163 | L3 |
| Chancel St STHWK SE1 | 12 | C9 |
| Chancery La BECK BR3 | 204 | A2 |
| LINN WC2A | 11 | P4 |
| Chancery La BECK BR3 | 13 | L1 |
| Chanctonbury Cha | | |
| REDH RH1 | 276 | F1 |
| Chanctonbury Cl | | |
| ELTH/MOT SE9 | 184 | E6 |
| Chanctonbury Dr ASC SL5 | 192 | D7 |
| Chanctonbury Gdns | | |
| BELMT SM2 | 221 | L4 |
| Chanctonbury Wy | | |
| CRAWW RH11 | 283 | M9 |
| NFNCH/WDSPK N12 | 97 | J3 |
| Chandler Av CAN/RD E16 | 141 | M7 |
| Chandler Cl CRAWE RH10 | 283 | N7 |
| HPTN TW12 | 175 | P7 |
| Chandler Rd LOU IG10 | 83 | H1 |
| Chandlers Cl E/WMO/HCT KT8 | 198 | A5 |
| EBED/NFELT TW14 | 173 | N3 |
| Chandlers Ct LEE/GVPK SE12 * | 183 | M3 |
| Chandlers Dr ERITH DA8 | 164 | E3 |
| Chandler's La | | |
| RKW/CH/CXG WD3 | 71 | P2 |
| Chandlers Ms POP/IOD E14 | 160 | F1 |
| Chandlers Rd STALE/WH AL4 | 39 | H3 |
| Chandlers Wy WAP E1W | 140 | A10 |
| HERT/WAT SG14 | 25 | J3 |
| ROM RM1 | 124 | F3 |
| Chandler Wy PECK SE15 | 19 | K10 |
| RDKG RH5 | 273 | H4 |
| Chandos Av EA W5 | 155 | H3 |
| STHGT/OAK N14 | 98 | C4 |
| TRDG/WHET N20 | 97 | N2 |
| WALTH E17 * | 100 | F9 |
| Chandos Cl AMS HP6 | 69 | K3 |
| BKHH IG9 | 101 | K5 |
| Chandos Crs EDGW HA8 | 95 | J8 |
| Chandos Gdns COUL/CHIP CR5 | 241 | J5 |
| Chandos Pde CHCR WC2N | 11 | L8 |
| Chandos Rd BORE WD6 | 75 | L6 |
| CRICK NW2 | 116 | F10 |
| EFNCH N2 | 97 | N10 |
| HRW HA1 | 114 | B3 |
| PIN HA5 | 113 | J5 |
| SRTFD E15 | 121 | J10 |
| STA TW18 | 172 | G8 |
| TOTM N17 | 99 | M10 |
| WLSDN NW10 | 136 | B6 |
| Chandos St | | |
| CAVSQ/HST W1G | 10 | E1 |
| Chandos Wy GLDGN NW11 | 117 | L1 |
| Chanlock Pth SOCK/AV RM15 | 146 | F9 |
| Channel Cl HEST TW5 | 153 | P7 |
| Channel Gate Rd | | |
| WLSDN NW10 | 136 | B5 |
| Channelsea Rd SRTFD E15 | 141 | J3 |
| Channing Cl EMPK RM11 | 125 | N5 |
| Channings WOKN/KNAP GU21 | 232 | B3 |
| Chanton Dr BELMT SM2 | 220 | F6 |
| Chantress Cl DAGE RM10 | 144 | D3 |
| Chantrey Cl ASHTD KT21 | 237 | H5 |
| Chantrey Rd BRXN/ST SW9 | 158 | G9 |
| Chantry Cl ENC/FH EN2 | 79 | K1 |
| EPSOM KT18 | 283 | P10 |
| HRW HA3 | 114 | A4 |
| KTN/HRWW/WS HA3 | 96 | A10 |
| RGUE GU4 | 268 | G6 |
| Chantry East ASHF TW15 | 174 | C7 |
| Chantry La HAT AL10 | 40 | C5 |
| HAYES BR2 | 206 | A5 |
| LCOL/BKTW AL2 | 57 | J7 |
| SHGR GU5 | 270 | A5 |
| Chantry Pl | | |
| KTN/HRWW/WS HA3 | 94 | A9 |
| SEV TN13 | 246 | G8 |
| Chantry Rd CHERT KT16 | 195 | L8 |
| CHSGTN KT9 | 219 | L2 |
| KTN/HRWW/WS HA3 | 94 | B9 |
| RGUE GU4 | 268 | G6 |
| Chantry Rd East ASHF TW15 | 174 | C7 |
| Chantry Sq KENS W8 | 14 | G4 |
| Chantry St IS N1 | 6 | C6 |
| The Chantry CHING E4 | 101 | H2 |
| HLW CM20 | 29 | K9 |
| UX/CGN UB8 | 132 | A5 |
| Chantry View Rd GU GU1 | 250 | E8 |
| Chantry Wy MTCM CR4 | 201 | N3 |
| Chant Sq SRTFD E15 * | 141 | J7 |
| Chant St SRTFD E15 * | 141 | J7 |
| Chapel Av ADL/WDHM KT15 | 215 | H7 |
| Chapel Cl GUW GU2 | 230 | G2 |
| MNPK E12 | 122 | A4 |
| STAL AL1 | 38 | C9 |
| WTHK RM20 | 166 | D2 |
| Chapel Cots HHNE HP2 | 35 | H5 |
| Chapel Ct DORK RH4 * | 272 | F4 |
| EFNCH N2 | 117 | P1 |
| STHWK SE1 | 18 | G1 |
| Chapel Cft CFSP/GDCR SL9 | 90 | A10 |
| Chapel Crofts BERK HP4 | 33 | H3 |
| Chapel End CFSP/GDCR SL9 * | 90 | A10 |
| HOD EN11 | 44 | C2 |
| Chapel Farm Rd | | |
| ELTH/MOT SE9 | 184 | E4 |
| Chapel Flds HLWE CM17 | 47 | M3 |
| Chapelfields WARE SG12 | 27 | J6 |
| Chapel Gdns ADL/WDHM KT15 | 215 | L10 |
| EPSOM KT18 | 238 | C5 |
| Chapel Hl DART DA1 | 164 | G10 |
| EHSLY KT24 | 253 | L8 |
| MYFR/PICC W1J | 10 | E9 |


| | | |
|---|---|---|
| CRAWE RH10 | 285 | N1 |
| DORK RH4 | 272 | B3 |
| GT/LBKH KT23 | 254 | B4 |
| HERT/WAT SG14 | 24 | C9 |
| HLWE CM17 | 47 | M3 |
| PIN HA5 | 113 | L1 |
| RDKG RH5 | 254 | E7 |
| SLN SL2 | 129 | N2 |
| UX/CGN UB8 | 132 | B8 |
| Chapel Market IS N1 | 5 | P6 |
| Chapel Mill Rd KUT/HW KT1 | 199 | L3 |
| Chapel Park Rd | | |
| ADL/WDHM KT15 | 215 | L1 |
| IS N1 | 6 | B7 |
| STAL AL1 | 38 | C9 |
| TOTM N17 | 99 | N8 |
| Chapel Rd BXLYHN DA7 | 164 | B10 |
| EPP CM16 | 65 | J6 |
| HORL RH6 | 279 | H8 |
| HSLW TW3 | 154 | A9 |
| IL IG1 | 122 | C9 |
| KWD/TDW/WH KT20 | 238 | F9 |
| OXTED RH8 | 261 | L3 |
| REDH RH1 | 258 | A10 |
| TWK TW1 | 176 | C3 |
| WARL CR6 | 242 | C4 |
| WEA W13 | 134 | G10 |
| WNWD SE27 | 181 | J7 |
| Chapel Rw DEN/HRF UB9 | 91 | K9 |
| Chapels Cl SL SL1 | 128 | D10 |
| Chapel Side BAY/PAD W2 | 8 | G7 |
| Chapel Sq VW GU25 | 194 | B3 |
| Chapel St BAY/PAD W2 | 9 | M3 |
| BERK HP4 | 33 | P5 |
| ENC/FH EN2 | 79 | K7 |
| GU GU1 | 268 | A2 |
| HHNE HP2 | 35 | N5 |
| KTBR SW1X | 16 | D3 |
| WOKN/KNAP GU21 | 232 | C3 |
| Chapel Vw SAND/SEL CR2 | 224 | B4 |
| Chapel Wy COUL/CHIP CR5 | 240 | E8 |
| EPSOM KT18 | 238 | F5 |
| Chapel Wd HART DA3 | 211 | K9 |
| Chapel Wood Rd HART DA3 | 211 | K9 |
| Chaplaincy Gdns EMPK RM11 | 125 | M6 |
| Chaplemount Rd WFD IG8 * | 102 | C7 |
| Chaplin Cl ALP/SUD HA0 | 135 | J1 |
| STHWK SE1 | 18 | B1 |
| Chaplin Crs SUN TW16 | 174 | P7 |
| Chaplin Rd ALP/SUD HA0 | 135 | H1 |
| CRICK NW2 | 136 | D1 |
| SRTFD E15 | 141 | K4 |
| TOTM N17 | 119 | N1 |
| Chapman Av CRAWE RH10 | 285 | M7 |
| KTN/HRWW/WS HA3 | 152 | A2 |
| Chapman Crs | | |
| KTN/HRWW/WS HA3 | 115 | K3 |
| Chapman Rd BELV DA17 | 164 | B4 |
| CROY/NA CR0 | 203 | H8 |
| HOM E9 | 140 | C1 |
| Chapmans Crs CSHM HP5 | 50 | F5 |
| Chapmans Gn WDGN N22 * | 99 | M9 |
| Chapman's La STMC/STPC BR5 | 207 | N2 |
| SAND WIM/MER SW19 | 178 | G5 |
| Chapmans Pk RSEV TN14 | 245 | P10 |
| Chapman Sq WIM/MER SW19 | 178 | G5 |
| Chapman St WCHPL E1 | 140 | C8 |
| Chapone Pl SOHO/SHAV W1D | 11 | J6 |
| Chapter Cl CHSWK W4 | 155 | P2 |
| HGDN/ICK UB10 | 132 | B2 |
| Chapter Ms WDSR SL4 | 149 | J6 |
| Chapter Rd CRICK NW2 | 116 | D10 |
| WALW SE17 | 18 | D8 |
| Chapter St WEST SW1P | 17 | J6 |
| Chapter Wy HPTN TW12 | 175 | P7 |
| WIM/MER SW19 | 201 | N1 |
| Chara Pl CHSWK W4 | 156 | A5 |
| Charcroft Gdns PEND EN3 | 80 | C8 |
| Chardia Ter CRES/WCR EN8 * | 62 | C6 |
| Chardins Cl HHW HP1 | 156 | B3 |
| Chardmore Rd | | |
| STNW/STAM N16 | 119 | P6 |
| Chardwell Cl EHAM E6 | 142 | B8 |
| Charecroft Wy WKENS W14 | 156 | G1 |
| Charford Rd CAN/RD E16 | 141 | M7 |
| Chargate Cl WOT/HER KT12 | 216 | G3 |
| Chargeable La PLSTW E13 | 141 | M6 |
| Chargeable St CAN/RD E16 | 141 | L4 |
| Chargrove Cl | | |
| BERM/RHTH SE16 | 160 | C1 |
| Charing Cl ORP BR6 | 227 | J1 |
| Charing Cross CHCR WC2N * | 11 | L9 |
| Charing Cross Rd | | |
| LSO/SEVD WC2H | 11 | K7 |
| Chariot Cl BOW E3 | 140 | F3 |
| Charlotts Pl WDSR SL4 * | 149 | J7 |
| Charkham Ms BRKMPK AL9 | 40 | F10 |
| Charlbert St STJWD NW8 | 3 | N7 |
| Charlbury Av STAN HA7 | 95 | M4 |
| Charlbury Cl HARH RM3 | 105 | K7 |
| Charlbury Gdns IL IG1 | 123 | J7 |
| Charlbury Gv EA W5 | 135 | H8 |
| Charlbury Rd | | |
| HGDN/ICK UB10 | 112 | A9 |
| Charldane Rd ELTH/MOT SE9 | 184 | A6 |
| Charlecote Gv SYD SE26 | 182 | A6 |
| Charlecote Rd DAGE RM10 | 123 | P8 |
| Charlecote Rd EHAM E6 | 142 | C5 |
| Charles Babbage Cl | | |
| CHSGTN KT9 | 219 | H4 |
| Charles Barry Cl CLAP SW4 | 158 | D9 |
| Charles Cl SCUP DA14 | 185 | L7 |
| Charles Cobb Gdns | | |
| CROY/NA CR0 | 223 | H2 |
| Charles Coveney Rd | | |
| CMBW SE5 | 159 | N7 |
| Charles Crs HRW HA1 | 114 | C5 |
| Charles Dickens Ter | | |
| PGE/AN SE20 * | 182 | B10 |
| Charlesfield ELTH/MOT SE9 | 183 | P6 |
| Charlesfield Rd HORL RH6 | 280 | A3 |
| Charles Flemwell Ms | | |
| CAN/RD E16 | 141 | M10 |
| Charles Gdns SLN SL2 | 129 | M8 |
| Charles Grinling Wk | | |
| WOOL/PLUM SE18 | 162 | D3 |
| Charles Haller St | | |
| BRXS/STRHM SW2 | 181 | H1 |
| Charles II Pl CHEL SW3 | 15 | P8 |
| Charles II St STJS SW1Y | 11 | J9 |
| Charles Pl CAMTN NW1 * | 5 | H10 |
| Charles Rd CHDH RM6 | 123 | L6 |
| DAGE RM10 | 144 | E1 |
| FSTGT E7 | 141 | P2 |
| RSEV TN14 | 228 | G2 |
| STA TW18 | 173 | N9 |
| WEA W13 | 134 | F4 |
| WIM/MER SW19 | 201 | K1 |
| Charles Sevright Dr | | |
| MLHL NW7 | 96 | G2 |
| Charles Sq IS N1 | 7 | H10 |
| Charles Square Est IS N1 * | 7 | H10 |
| Charles St BARN SW13 | 156 | B9 |
| BERK HP4 | 33 | N5 |
| CAN/RD E16 | 141 | P10 |
| CHERT KT16 | 195 | J8 |
| CROY/NA CR0 | 203 | K10 |
| EN EN1 | 79 | P8 |
| EPP CM16 | 65 | K5 |
| GRAYS RM17 | 167 | N5 |
| HGDN/ICK UB10 | 132 | C6 |
| HHW HP1 | 35 | M3 |
| HSLW TW3 | 153 | M8 |
| MYFR/PICC W1J | 10 | E9 |
| RDART DA2 | 188 | E1 |
| SL SL1 | 149 | H2 |
| WALW SE17 | 18 | F6 |
| Charleston Cl FELT TW13 | 175 | H6 |
| Charleston St WALW SE17 | 18 | F6 |
| Charleston Cl CRAWE RH10 | 284 | C10 |

**Column 1**

Charles Whincup Rd
 CAN/RD E16 ........ 141 N10
Charlesworth Cl
 HHS/BOV HP3 ........ 35 N8
Charleville Circ SYD SE26 ........ 181 P8
Charleville Rd WKENS W14 ........ 14 B8
Charlmont Rd TOOT SW17 ........ 179 P9
Charlock Wy GU GU1 ........ 250 E7
 WATW WD18 ........ 8 A2
Charlotte Av SLN SL2 ........ 129 L9
Charlotte Cl ASHF KT21 ........ 237 K4
 BXLYHS DA6 ........ 185 P1
 OXHEY WD19 ........ 93 K1
 STALE/WH AL4 ........ 39 K6
Charlotte Ct ESH/CLAY KT10 ........ 218 B2
Charlotte Despard Av
 BTSEA SW11 ........ 158 C7
Charlotte Gdns CRW RM5 ........ 104 C7
Charlotte Gv HORL RH6 ........ 281 H3
Charlotte Ms ESH/CLAY KT10 * ........ 218 A1
 FITZ W1T ........ 11 H5
 NKENS W10 ........ 136 U8
 WKENS W14 ........ 14 A5
Charlotte Pde FSTH SE23 * ........ 182 D5
Charlotte Park Av BMLY BR1 ........ 206 B3
Charlotte Pl FITZ W1T * ........ 11 H4
 PIM SW1V ........ 16 C6
 WTHK RM20 ........ 166 C7
Charlotte Rd BARN SW13 ........ 156 C7
 SDTCH EC2A ........ 7 J10
 WLGTN SM6 ........ 222 F5
Charlotte Rw CLAP SW4 ........ 158 D9
Charlotte Ter IS N1 ........ 5 P6
Charlow Cl FUL/PGN SW6 ........ 157 M8
Charlton AMS HP7 ........ 148 B8
Charlton Av WOT/HER KT12 ........ 217 J1
Charlton Church La
 CHARL SE7 ........ 161 P4
Charlton Cl HGDN/ICK UB10 ........ 112 C7
 HOD EN11 ........ 44 F3
 SL S1 ........ 148 C1
Charlton Crs BARK IG11 ........ 143 J4
Charlton Dene CHARL SE7 ........ 161 P6
Charlton Dr BH/WHM TN16 ........ 244 A3
Charlton Gdns COUL/CHIP CR5 ........ 240 F7
Charlton Kings WEY KT13 * ........ 161 K7
Charlton King's Rd KTTN NW5 ........ 118 E10
Charlton La CHARL SE7 ........ 162 A4
 SHPTN TW17 ........ 196 D3
Charlton Mead La HOD EN11 ........ 45 H4
 CHARL SE7 ........ 162 A5
Charlton Park La CHARL SE7 ........ 162 A6
Charlton Park Rd CHARL SE7 ........ 162 A5
Charlton Pl IS N1 ........ 6 C7
 CHARL SE7 ........ 161 M6
 ED N9 ........ 100 C2
 KTN/HRWW/WS HA3 ........ 115 J2
 SHPTN TW17 ........ 196 D2
 WLSDN NW10 ........ 136 J5
Charlton St WTHK RM20 ........ 167 J5
Charlton Wy GNWCH SE10 ........ 161 K1
 HOD EN11 ........ 44 F4
Charlwood CROY/NA CR0 ........ 224 E5
Charlwood Cl CRAWE RH10 ........ 285 J1
 GT/LBKH KT23 ........ 236 G10
 KTN/HRWW/WS HA3 ........ 94 D7
Charlwood Dr LHD/OX KT22 ........ 236 C1
Charlwood La RDKG RH5 ........ 278 D10
Charlwood Pl PIM SW1V ........ 17 H6
 REIG RH2 ........ 257 J10
Charlwood Rd CRAWW RH11 ........ 283 J5
 HORL RH6 ........ 279 M7
 PUT/ROE SW15 ........ 156 G9
Charlwood Ter PIM SW1V * ........ 16 C7
Charlwood Wk CRAWW RH11 ........ 283 L4
Charman Rd REDH RH1 ........ 257 P10
Charm Cl HORL RH6 ........ 279 P3
Charmian Av STAN HA7 ........ 115 J1
Charminster Av
 WIM/MER SW19 ........ 201 K2
Charminster Rd
 ELTH/MOT SE9 ........ 184 A7
 WPK KT4 ........ 200 E8
Charmouth Ct STAL AL1 ........ 38 F3
Charmouth Rd STAL AL1 ........ 38 F4
 WELL DA16 ........ 163 M7
Charnwood La ORP BR6 ........ 227 L6
Charnock SWLY BR8 ........ 208 F4
Charnock Rd CLPT E5 ........ 120 A8
Charnwood ASC SL5 ........ 192 G6
Charnwood Av
 WIM/MER SW19 ........ 201 K2
Charnwood Dr SWFD E18 ........ 121 N1
Charnwood Gdns
 POP/IOD E14 ........ 160 F3
Charnwood Pl
 TRDG/WHET N20 ........ 97 H2
Charnwood Rd EN EN1 ........ 80 A2
 HGDN/ICK UB10 ........ 132 B4
 SNWD SE25 ........ 203 L5
Charnwood St CLPT E5 * ........ 119 P7
Charnwood Vls SWFD E18 ........ 121 N1
Charrington Pl STAL AL1 ........ 38 E7
Charrington Rd CROY/NA CR0 ........ 203 J9
Charrington St CAMTN NW1 ........ 5 J7
Charsley Cl AMS HP6 ........ 69 M7
Charsley Rd CAT SE6 ........ 182 G5
Charta Rd EGH TW20 ........ 204 B6
Chart Cl CROY/NA CR0 ........ 205 K1
 HAYES BR2 ........ 225 L1
 MTCM CR4 ........ 202 A4
 RDKG RH5 ........ 273 H4
Chart Downs RDKG RH5 ........ 273 H4
Charter Av GNTH/NBYPK IG2 ........ 72 G6
Charter Cl SL S1 ........ 149 L2
Charter Crs HSLWW TW4 ........ 153 N10
Charter Dr BXLY DA5 ........ 185 P3
Charterhouse Av
 ALP/SUD HA0 ........ 115 H10
Charterhouse Blds
 FARR EC1M ........ 12 D2
Charterhouse Dr SEV TN13 ........ 247 H9
Charterhouse Ms FARR EC1M ........ 12 D3
 ORP BR6 ........ 207 K10
Charterhouse Sq HCIRC EC1N ........ 12 B4
The Charterhouse
 FARR EC1M ........ 12 D2
Charteris Rd FSBYPK N4 ........ 118 G6
 KIL/WHAMP NW6 ........ 2 D6
 WFD IG8 ........ 101 N1
Charter Pl STA TW18 ........ 173 K9
 UX/CGN UB8 ........ 131 K2
 WAT WD17 * ........ 73 J8
Charter Rd KUT/HW KT1 ........ 199 P2
 SL S1 ........ 128 C4
The Charter Rd WFD IG8 ........ 101 K7
Charters Cl NRWD SE19 ........ 181 N8
Charters Cross HLWS CM18 ........ 46 C9
Charters La ASC SL5 ........ 192 C5
Charter Sq KUT/HW KT1 ........ 199 N2
Charters Rd ASC SL5 ........ 192 E7
Charter Wy FNCH N3 ........ 117 J2
 STHGT/OAK N14 ........ 83 D10
Chartfield Av PUT/ROE SW15 ........ 178 A3
Chartfield Rd REIG RH2 ........ 275 M1
Chartfield Sq PUT/ROE SW15 * ........ 178 G2
Chart Gdns RDKG RH5 ........ 273 H5
Chartham Gv WNWD SE27 ........ 204 A3
Chartham Rd SNWD SE25 ........ 181 N6
Chart Hills Cl THMD SE28 ........ 143 P8
Chart La BH/WHM TN16 ........ 263 H4
 DORK RH4 ........ 272 F5
 REIG RH2 ........ 257 L10
Chart La South RDKG RH5 ........ 273 J4
Chartley Av CRICK NW2 ........ 116 B8
 STAN HA7 ........ 94 B7
Chartley Pde CRICK NW2 * ........ 116 B8

**Column 2**

Charton Cl BELV DA17 ........ 164 A5
Chartridge OXHEY WD19 * ........ 93 L3
Chartridge Cl BAR EN5 ........ 76 D9
 BUSH WD23 ........ 74 B10
Chartridge Grange Dr
 CSHM HP5 ........ 50 C3
Chartridge La CSHM HP5 ........ 50 C3
Chartridge Wy HHNE HP2 ........ 36 H9
Chart St IS N1 ........ 7 H9
Chartway REIG RH2 ........ 257 L10
 SEV TN13 ........ 247 K10
Chartwell Cl CROY/NA CR0 ........ 203 L8
 ELTH/MOT SE9 ........ 184 C1
 GFD/PVL UB6 ........ 134 A3
 WAB EN9 ........ 63 K9
Chartwell Dr ORP BR6 ........ 226 G2
Chartwell Gdns CHEAM SM3 ........ 201 H10
Chartwell Pl CHEAM SM3 ........ 221 H1
 EPSOM KT18 ........ 238 B10
Chartwell Rd NTHWD HA6 ........ 92 G7
Chartwell Wy PGE/AN SE20 ........ 204 A1
Chartwood Pl DORK RH4 ........ 272 F2
Charville La HGDN/ICK UB10 ........ 132 D5
Charville La West
 HGDN/ICK UB10 ........ 132 C5
Charwood STRHM/NOR SW16 ........ 181 H7
Chase Cl ENC/FH EN2 ........ 79 K7
Chasden Rd HHW HP1 ........ 35 J3
Chase Ct AMSS HP7 ........ 68 F9
Chase Ct RYNPK SW20 ........ 201 H2
Chase Court Gdns
 ENC/FH EN2 ........ 79 K7
Chase Cross Rd CRW RM5 ........ 104 D8
Chase End HOR/WEW KT19 ........ 220 A4
Chasefield Cl RGUE GU4 ........ 250 D7
Chasefield Rd TOOT SW17 ........ 180 A7
Chase Gdns CHING E4 ........ 100 F5
 WHTN TW2 ........ 155 P10
Chase Gn ENC/FH EN2 ........ 79 K7
 POTB/CUF EN6 ........ 60 F5
Chase Green Av ENC/FH EN2 ........ 79 J6
Chase Hl ENC/FH EN2 ........ 79 K7
Chase House Gdns
 EMPK RM11 ........ 125 N3
Chase La BARK/HLT IG6 ........ 122 G8
 CHIC IG7 ........ 103 K4
Chaseley Ct CHSWK W4 ........ 155 N4
Chaseley Dr SAND/SEL CR2 ........ 223 L6
Chasemore Cl MTCM CR4 ........ 202 A7
Chasemore Gdns
 CROY/NA CR0 ........ 223 H2
Chase Ridings ENC/FH EN2 ........ 79 H6
Chase Rd ACT W3 ........ 136 A6
 BRW CM14 ........ 107 H4
 HOR/WEW KT19 ........ 220 A4
 STHGT/OAK N14 ........ 78 D9
Chase Side ENC/FH EN2 ........ 79 K6
 STHGT/OAK N14 ........ 78 D9
Chase Side Av RYNPK SW20 ........ 201 H1
 ENC/FH EN2 ........ 79 K5
Chaseside Cl ROM RM1 * ........ 104 F7
Chaseside Crs ENC/FH EN2 ........ 79 K5
Chase Side Pl CHERT KT16 ........ 195 L7
Chaseside Rd RYNPK SW20 ........ 201 H1
The Chase ASHTD KT21 ........ 237 H4
 BGR/WK TN15 ........ 247 N2
 BMLY BR1 ........ 205 N3
 BRW CM14 ........ 106 C3
 BRW CM14 ........ 107 J4
 BXLYHN DA7 ........ 164 C5
 CHESW EN7 ........ 61 J4
 CHIC IG7 ........ 102 E5
 CLAP SW4 ........ 158 C9
 COUL/CHIP CR5 ........ 222 D10
 CRAWE RH10 ........ 284 B8
 CSHM HP5 ........ 50 A5
 EDGW HA8 ........ 95 N9
 EHSLY KT24 ........ 252 G2
 FSTGT E7 ........ 122 A3
 GPK RM2 ........ 105 L2
 HERT/BAY SG13 ........ 25 N6
 HGDN/ICK UB10 ........ 112 B10
 HHNE HP2 ........ 35 P7
 HLWE CM17 ........ 29 M10
 KWD/TDW/WH KT20 ........ 239 M7
 LHD/OX KT22 ........ 236 B1
 LOU IG10 ........ 101 P1
 ORP BR6 ........ 227 K7
 PIN HA5 ........ 113 K4
 RAD WD7 ........ 74 E1
 RBRW/HUT CM13 ........ 107 P6
 REIG RH2 ........ 275 N1
 ROM RM1 ........ 124 F1
 ROMW/RG RM7 ........ 124 E6
 STAN HA7 ........ 94 F7
 STRHM/NOR SW16 ........ 180 C10
 SUN TW16 ........ 195 J1
 UPMR RM14 ........ 126 D8
 WARE SG12 ........ 26 F5
 WATW WD18 ........ 72 F8
 WLGTN SM6 ........ 222 F2
 WTHK RM20 ........ 167 K5
Chaseville Pde WCHMH N21 * ........ 78 G9
Chaseville Park Rd
 WCHMH N21 ........ 78 G9
Chase Wy STHGT/OAK N14 ........ 98 C2
Chaseways SBW CM21 ........ 46 C3
Chasewood Av ENC/FH EN2 ........ 79 L6
Chasewood Pk HRW HA1 * ........ 114 D8
Chatelet Cl HORL RH6 ........ 280 C3
Chatfield SLN SL2 ........ 128 F7
Chatfield Cl CTHM CR3 ........ 241 L8
Chatfield Dr RGUE GU4 ........ 250 F4
Chatfield Rd BTSEA SW11 ........ 157 M9
 CROY/NA CR0 ........ 203 J8
Chatfields CRAWW RH11 ........ 283 L9
Chatham Av HAYES BR2 ........ 223 L9
Chatham Cl CHEAM SM3 ........ 201 J7
 GLDGN NW11 ........ 117 K3
 WOOL/PLUM SE18 ........ 162 E2
Chatham Hill Rd RSEV TN14 ........ 247 K7
Chatham Ms GUW GU2 ........ 249 M7
Chatham Pl HOM E9 ........ 140 E1
Chatham Rd BTSEA SW11 ........ 199 M2
 KUT/HW KT1 ........ 199 M2
 SWFD E18 ........ 101 L11
 WALTH E17 ........ 120 D1
Chatham St WALW SE17 ........ 18 G5
 WOOL/PLUM SE18 ........ 162 E2
Chatham Wy BRW CM14 ........ 107 J7
Chatsfield EW KT17 ........ 220 D6
Chatsfield Pl EA W5 ........ 135 K6
Chatsworth Av BFN/LL DA15 ........ 183 N6
 BMLY BR1 ........ 96 H1
 RYNPK SW20 ........ 201 H1
 WBLY HA9 ........ 96 A10
Chatsworth Cl BORE WD6 ........ 75 M7
 CHSWK W4 ........ 155 P5
 HDN NW4 ........ 116 A7
 WWKM BR4 ........ 96 F10
Chatsworth Crs HSLW TW3 ........ 154 C10
Chatsworth Dr EN EN1 ........ 99 P1
Chatsworth Est CLPT E5 * ........ 120 B1
Chatsworth Gdns ACT W3 ........ 135 N10
 NWMAL KT3 ........ 200 A4
 RYLN/HDSTN HA2 ........ 114 A6
Chatsworth Pl LHD/OX KT22 ........ 218 G6
 MTCM CR4 ........ 202 A2
 TEDD TW11 ........ 174 D8
Chatsworth Ri EA W5 ........ 135 L6
Chatsworth Rd CHEAM SM3 ........ 220 G1
 CHSWK W4 ........ 155 P5
 CLPT E5 ........ 120 B8
 CRICK NW2 ........ 119 J5
 CROY/NA CR0 ........ 223 J1
 DART DA1 ........ 165 K10
 EA W5 ........ 135 K4
 SRTFD E15 ........ 123 L2
 YEAD UB4 ........ 133 J4
Chatsworth Wy WNWD SE27 ........ 181 J6
Chatteris Av HARH RM3 ........ 105 K1

**Column 3**

Chattern Hl ASHF TW15 ........ 174 C7
Chattern Rd ASHF TW15 ........ 174 D7
Chatterton Ms FSBYPK N4 * ........ 119 J7
Chatterton Rd FSBYPK N4 ........ 119 J8
 HAYES BR2 ........ 206 A5
Chatton Rw CHOB/PIR GU24 ........ 230 F3
Chatto Rd BTSEA SW11 ........ 180 A1
Chaucer Av HSLWW TW4 ........ 153 J8
 RCH/KEW TW9 ........ 155 M8
 YEAD UB3 ........ 133 H7
Chaucer Cl BERK HP4 ........ 33 L4
 BNSTD SM7 ........ 221 H10
 FBAR/BDGN N11 ........ 98 D6
 STAL AL1 ........ 38 C4
 TIL RM18 ........ 168 F8
 WDSR SL4 ........ 149 J9
Chaucer Ct GUW GU2 * ........ 249 L8
Chaucer Dr STHWK SE1 ........ 19 M6
Chaucer Gdns SUT SM1 ........ 201 K10
Chaucer Pk DART DA1 ........ 204 A7
Chaucer Rd ACT W3 ........ 135 P10
 ASHF TW15 ........ 173 P7
 BFN/LL DA15 ........ 185 M4
 CRAWE RH10 ........ 284 C5
 FSTGT E7 ........ 141 M1
 GVW DA11 ........ 190 A6
 HARH RM3 ........ 105 J8
 HERN SE24 ........ 181 H1
 SUT SM1 ........ 221 K1
 WALTH E17 ........ 101 H9
 WAN E11 ........ 101 J9
 WELL DA16 ........ 163 J7
Chaucer Wy ADL/WDHM KT15 ........ 165 P10
 DART DA1 ........ 26 F9
 SL S1 ........ 129 L10
 WIM/MER SW19 ........ 179 N9
Chaulden House Gdns
 HHW HP1 ........ 35 J8
Chaulden La HHW HP1 ........ 35 H9
Chaulden Ter HHW HP1 ........ 35 J8
Chauncey Cl ED N9 ........ 99 N4
Chauncy Av POTB/CUF EN6 ........ 59 M4
Chaundrye Cl ELTH/MOT SE9 ........ 184 C2
Chauntler Rd CAN/RD E16 ........ 141 N9
Chave Cft EPSOM KT18 * ........ 238 B9
Chavecroft Ter EPSOM KT18 * ........ 238 F5
Chaworth Cl CHERT KT16 ........ 214 F3
Chaworth Rd CHERT KT16 ........ 214 F3
Cheam Cl KWD/TDW/WH KT20 ........ 238 E7
Cheam Common Rd WPK KT4 ........ 200 E9
Cheam Man CHEAM SM3 ........ 221 H5
Cheam Park Wy CHEAM SM3 ........ 221 H3
Cheam Rd EW KT17 ........ 220 D6
 SUT SM1 ........ 221 J3
Cheam St PECK SE15 * ........ 160 A9
Cheapside CITYW EC2V ........ 12 F6
 EFNCH N2 ........ 118 A1
 PLMGR N13 ........ 99 J5
 WDGN N22 ........ 119 H1
 WOKN/KNAP GU21 ........ 214 A10
Cheapside La DEN/HRF UB9 ........ 111 J7
Cheapside Rd ASC SL5 ........ 192 B3
Chedburgh WGCE AL7 ........ 23 N4
Cheddar Rd FBAR/BDGN N11 ........ 98 A3
Cheddar Wave YEAD UB4 ........ 133 J8
Cheddington Rd UED N18 ........ 99 M5
Cheelson Rd SOCK/AV RM15 ........ 147 M9
Cheeseman Cl HPTN TW12 ........ 175 M9
Cheesemans Ter WKENS W14 ........ 14 B8
Cheffins Rd HOD EN11 ........ 26 E10
Chelford Rd BMLY BR1 ........ 183 J8
Chelmer Cl HARL CM19 ........ 29 M10
Chelmer Crs BARK IG11 ........ 143 L4
Chelmer Dr SOCK/AV RM15 ........ 147 N4
Chelmer Rd CDW/CHF RM16 ........ 166 C10
 HOM E9 ........ 120 C10
 UPMR RM14 ........ 125 N8
Chelmsford Av CRW RM5 ........ 104 E8
Chelmsford Cl BELMT SM2 ........ 221 K5
 EHAM E6 ........ 142 C8
 HMSMTH W6 ........ 156 C5
Chelmsford Dr UPMR RM14 ........ 125 N8
Chelmsford Gdns IL IG1 ........ 122 B5
Chelmsford Rd BRWN CM15 ........ 87 M9
 HERT/WAT SG14 ........ 23 J1
 RBSF CM22 ........ 31 J1
 STHGT/OAK N14 ........ 98 D3
 SWFD E18 ........ 101 L9
 WALTH E17 ........ 101 L11
 WAN E11 ........ 121 J6
Chelmsford Sq WLSDN NW10 ........ 136 F1
Chelsea Br BGVA SW1W ........ 16 D9
Chelsea Bridge Rd
 BGVA SW1W ........ 16 C7
Chelsea Cl EDGW HA8 ........ 95 M10
 HPTN TW12 ........ 176 B8
 WLSDN NW10 ........ 136 A3
 WPK KT4 ........ 200 D7
Chelsea Crs CRICK NW2 * ........ 2 C1
 WBPTN SW10 * ........ 157 M7
Chelsea Emb CHEL SW3 ........ 16 A10
Chelsea Flds EN EN11 ........ 26 D5
Chelsea Gdns CHEAM SM3 ........ 221 H1
 HLWE CM17 ........ 47 P2
 WEA W13 ........ 135 H4
Chelsea Harbour Dr
 WBPTN SW10 ........ 157 M7
Chelsea Manor Gdns
 CHEL SW3 ........ 15 N9
Chelsea Manor St CHEL SW3 * ........ 15 N7
Chelsea Ms EMPK RM11 ........ 125 N4
Chelsea Park Gdns CHEL SW3 ........ 15 L9
Chelsea Sq CAR SM5 ........ 222 A5
 CHEL SW3 ........ 15 L8
Chelsea Village
 FUL/PGN SW6 * ........ 157 L6
Chelsfield Av ED N9 ........ 100 C1
Chelsfield Gdns SYD SE26 ........ 182 B6
Chelsfield Hl ORP BR6 ........ 227 N5
Chelsfield La ORP BR6 ........ 227 M5
 ORP BR6 ........ 227 P2
 STMC/STPC BR5 ........ 207 M5
Chelsfield Rd STMC/STPC BR5 ........ 207 M6
Chelsham Common Rd
 WARL CR6 ........ 242 F5
Chelsham Court Rd WARL CR6 ........ 243 H7
 SAND/SEL CR2 ........ 223 L4
Chelsing Ri HHNE HP2 ........ 36 D5
Chelston Rd RSLP HA4 ........ 113 H7
Chelsworth Dr HARH RM3 ........ 105 M9
 WOOL/PLUM SE18 ........ 162 E8
Cheltenham Av TWK TW1 ........ 176 B5
Cheltenham Cl GVE DA12 ........ 190 F8
 NTHLT UB5 ........ 134 A1
 NWMAL KT3 ........ 145 H4
 RAIN RM13 ........ 145 H4
Cheltenham Gdns EHAM E6 ........ 142 A9
 LOU IG10 ........ 88 B10
Cheltenham Pl ACT W3 ........ 155 P1
 KTN/HRWW/WS HA3 ........ 115 P1
Cheltenham Rd LEY E10 ........ 120 B5
 ORP BR6 ........ 207 K10
 PECK SE15 ........ 179 L2
Cheltenham Ter CHEL SW3 ........ 16 B7
Chelton Av MLHL NW7 ........ 96 C3
Chelverton Rd PUT/ROE SW15 ........ 156 G10
Chelveston WGCE AL7 ........ 23 N2
Chelwood Av HAT AL10 ........ 40 G3
Chelwood Cl CHING E4 ........ 87 M9
 COUL/CHIP CR5 ........ 240 G5
 CRAWE RH10 ........ 284 H9
 EW KT17 ........ 220 E9
 NTHWD HA6 ........ 92 B8
Chelwood Gdns
 RCH/KEW TW9 ........ 155 N8
Chenappa Cl PLSTW E13 ........ 2 A2
Chenduit Wy STAN HA7 ........ 94 E6
Chene Dr STALW/RED AL3 ........ 38 A1
Cheney Rw WALTH E17 ........ 101 H9
Cheneys Rd WAN E11 ........ 121 K6
Cheney St PIN HA5 ........ 113 J2
Chenies Av AMS HP6 ........ 51 J4
Chenies Ct HHNE HP2 ........ 36 C1

**Column 4**

Chenies Ms GWRST WC1E ........ 11 J2
Chenies Pde AMSS HP7 * ........ 69 P6
Chenies Pl CAMTN NW1 ........ 5 H3
Chenies Rd RKW/CH/CXG WD3 ........ 70 C6
Chenies St GWRST WC1E ........ 11 J3
The Chenies ORP BR6 ........ 207 M9
Cheniston Gdns WDSR SL4 ........ 92 H1
Cheniston Cl BF/WBF KT14 ........ 215 K9
Cheniston Gdns KENS W8 ........ 14 F3
Chennells HAT AL10 ........ 40 C5
The Chennies HARP AL5 * ........ 40 C7
Chepstow Av HCH RM12 ........ 125 M8
Chepstow Cl CRAWE RH10 ........ 284 F7
 PUT/ROE SW15 ........ 179 J1
Chepstow Cnr BAY/PAD W2 * ........ 8 A6
Chepstow Crs GDMY/SEVK IG3 ........ 123 H4
 NTGHL W11 ........ 8 A7
Chepstow Gdns STHL UB1 ........ 133 U8
Chepstow Pl BAY/PAD W2 ........ 8 A7
Chepstow Ri CROY/NA CR0 ........ 203 M10
Chepstow Rd BAY/PAD W2 ........ 8 B6
 CROY/NA CR0 ........ 203 M10
 HNWL W7 ........ 154 C3
Chepstow Vls NTGHL W11 ........ 8 A8
Chequers BKHH IG9 ........ 101 N2
 BRKMPK AL9 ........ 42 C7
 WGCE AL7 ........ 22 G7
Chequers Cl CDALE/KGS NW9 ........ 116 D1
 HORL RH6 ........ 280 D1
 KWD/TDW/WH KT20 ........ 256 D1
 STMC/STPC BR5 ........ 207 K10
Chequers Dr HORL RH6 ........ 280 D1
Chequersfield WGCE AL7 ........ 22 G8
Chequers La DAGW RM9 ........ 144 A6
 GSTN WD25 ........ 56 J6
 KWD/TDW/WH KT20 ........ 256 D1
Chequers Orch IVER SL0 ........ 131 J8
Chequers Pde PLMCR N13 * ........ 99 L6
 DORK RH4 ........ 272 C2
Chequers Rd HARH RM3 ........ 105 M3
 LOU IG10 ........ 82 D9
Chequers Wy PLMGR N13 ........ 99 M5
The Chequers PIN HA5 * ........ 113 L6
Chequer St STAL AL1 ........ 38 C6
 STLK EC1Y ........ 7 F5
Chequers Wy PLMGR N15 ........ 99 M5
Chequer Tree Cl
 WOKN/KNAP GU21 ........ 231 K2
Cherbury Cl THMD SE28 ........ 143 L10
Cherbury St IS N1 ........ 7 H8
Cherimoya Gdns
 E/WMO/HCT KT8 ........ 197 P8
Cherington Rd HNWL W7 ........ 134 E10
Cheriton Av CLAY IG5 ........ 72 A10
Cheriton Cl EA W5 ........ 135 H9
 EBAR EN4 ........ 78 A7
 STALE/WH AL4 ........ 39 J7
Cheriton Ct WOT/HER KT12 ........ 197 K8
Cheriton Dr WOOL/PLUM SE18 ........ 162 A4
Cheriton Sq TOOT SW17 ........ 180 B5
Cherkley Hl LHD/OX KT22 * ........ 255 J7
The Cherries SL S1 ........ 129 P8
Cherry Acre CFSP/GDCR SL9 ........ 90 A5
Cherry Av DTCH/LGLY SL3 ........ 150 A1
 RBRW/HUT CM13 ........ 107 L4
 STHL UB1 ........ 133 L10
 SWLY BR8 ........ 208 B3
Cherry Bank HHNE HP2 * ........ 36 B8
 BERK HP4 ........ 32 B8
 CSHM HP5 ........ 50 D8
 GTMS/PWID HP16 ........ 50 B6
 GU GU1 ........ 268 B1
Cherry Cl BNSTD SM7 ........ 220 G10
 BRXS/STRHM SW2 * ........ 181 H3
 CAR SM5 ........ 202 A9
 CDALE/KGS NW9 ........ 96 C10
 EA W5 ........ 155 J2
 MRDN SM4 ........ 201 H4
 RSLP HA4 ........ 112 C8
Cherry Crs BTFD TW8 ........ 154 G6
Cherry Dr RKW/CH/CXG WD3 ........ 72 B10
Cherry Gdns DAGW RM9 ........ 124 A10
 NTHLT UB5 ........ 134 A2
Cherry Garden St
 BERM/RHTH SE16 ........ 160 A1
Cherry Garth BTFD TW8 ........ 155 J2
Cherry Green Cl REDH RH1 ........ 276 C2
Cherry Gv HYS/HAR UB3 ........ 133 J10
 UX/CGN UB8 ........ 132 D7
Cherry Hl BAR EN5 ........ 94 D7
 KTN/HRWW/WS HA3 ........ 94 D7
 LCOL/BKTW AL2 ........ 55 P1
 RKW/CH/CXG WD3 ........ 71 C7
Cherry Hills OXHEY WD19 ........ 93 M6
Cherry Hollow ABLGY WD5 ........ 54 G7
Cherrylands
 CDALE/KGS NW9 ........ 115 P7
Cherry La AMSS HP7 ........ 68 B7
 CRAWW RH11 ........ 283 M4
 WDR/YW UB7 ........ 152 A3
Cherry Orch AMS HP6 ........ 69 K5
 CHARL SE7 ........ 161 P6
 HHW HP1 ........ 35 J4
 SLN SL2 ........ 129 L2
 STA TW18 ........ 173 K8
 WDR/YW UB7 ........ 151 P1
Cherry Orchard Cl
 STMC/STPC BR5 ........ 207 M5
Cherry Orchard Gdns
 CROY/NA CR0 ........ 203 L8
 E/WMO/HCT KT8 ........ 197 N2
Cherry Orchard Rd
 CROY/NA CR0 ........ 203 L8
 E/WMO/HCT KT8 ........ 197 N3
 HAYES BR2 ........ 206 A5
Cherry Ri CSTG HP8 ........ 90 A3
Cherry Rd EN EN3 ........ 80 B4
Cherry St ROMW/RG RM7 ........ 124 C3
 WOKN/KNAP GU21 ........ 232 B7
Cherry Tree Av ALP/SUD HA0 ........ 114 C7
 CRAWE RH10 ........ 284 G6
 HOM E9 ........ 140 B3
 RAIN RM13 ........ 145 H4
 RKW/CH/CXG WD3 ........ 90 P2
Cherry Tree Cl ALP/SUD HA0 ........ 114 C7
 CRAWE RH10 ........ 284 G6
 HOM E9 ........ 140 B3
 RAIN RM13 ........ 145 H4
 RKW/CH/CXG WD3 ........ 90 P2
Cherry Tree Cnr BEAC HP9 * ........ 89 J7
Cherry Tree Ct CHARL SE7 * ........ 161 P5
 COUL/CHIP CR5 ........ 240 G6
 GUW GU2 ........ 249 L8
 KTBR SW1X ........ 201 K9
Cherry Tree Dr
 STRHM/NOR SW16 ........ 180 F6
Cherry Tree Gn
 HERT/WAT SG14 ........ 24 C3
 SAND/SEL CR2 ........ 223 N7
Cherry Tree La EFNCH N2 ........ 117 H2
 IVER SL0 ........ 131 K5
 CFSP/GDCR SL9 ........ 90 A10
Cherry Tree La DTCH/LGLY SL3 ........ 150 D8
 GDST RG21 ........ 267 J9
 EPP CM16 ........ 36 E5
 SEV TN13 ........ 246 E8
 RAIN RM13 ........ 144 D2
 RKW/CH/CXG WD3 ........ 90 P2
Cherry Tree Ri BKHH IG9 ........ 101 K6
Cherry Tree Rd BEAC HP9 ........ 108 A1

**Column 5**

Cherry Tree Wk BECK BR3 ........ 204 E4
 CSHM HP5 ........ 51 J5
 STLK EC1Y ........ 12 F2
 WWKM BR4 ........ 214 A7
Cherry Tree Wy STAN HA7 ........ 94 C7
Cherrywood Av EGH TW20 ........ 171 N9
Cherrywood Cl BOW E3 ........ 139 J9
 KUT/HW KT1 ........ 159 G9
Cherrywood Dr PUT/ROE SW15 ........ 178 G2
Cherrywood La RYNPK SW20 ........ 201 H4
Cherston Gdns LOU IG10 ........ 82 D9
Cherston Rd LOU IG10 ........ 82 D9
Chertsey Bridge Rd
 CHERT KT16 ........ 195 N7
Chertsey Cl PUR/KEN CR8 ........ 241 J1
Chertsey Crs CROY/NA CR0 ........ 223 J7
Chertsey Dr CHEAM SM3 ........ 201 H9
Chertsey La HOR/WEW KT19 ........ 219 M8
 STA TW18 ........ 173 H10
Chertsey Rd ADL/WDHM KT15 ........ 195 L9
 ASHF TW15 ........ 174 E10
 BF/WBF KT14 ........ 215 N7
 BFOR GU20 ........ 212 D3
 FELT TW13 ........ 173 J9
 IL IG1 ........ 122 C9
 SHPTN TW17 ........ 195 P7
 SUN TW16 ........ 174 F9
 TWK TW1 ........ 176 B2
 WAN E11 ........ 121 J7
 WHTN TW2 ........ 176 B4
 WOKN/KNAP GU21 ........ 232 C3
Chertsey St GU GU1 ........ 268 D4
 TOOT SW17 ........ 180 B8
Chertsey Wk CHERT KT16 * ........ 195 K7
Chervil Cl FELT TW13 ........ 173 H6
Chervil Ms THMD SE28 ........ 143 L10
Cherwell Cl DTCH/LGLY SL3 ........ 150 B5
 RKW/CH/CXG WD3 ........ 72 B9
Cherwell Gv SOCK/AV RM15 ........ 147 G9
Cherwell Rd HNWL W7 ........ 134 E10
Cherwell Wy RSLP HA4 ........ 112 B3
Cheryls Cl FUL/PGN SW6 ........ 157 N7
Cheselden Rd GU GU1 ........ 268 E5
Cheseman St SYD SE26 ........ 182 A6
Chesfield Rd KUTN/CMB KT2 ........ 197 K8
Chesham Av STMC/STPC BR5 ........ 206 G5
Chesham Cl BELMT SM2 ........ 221 H6
 KTBR SW1X * ........ 16 C4
 ROMW/RG RM7 ........ 124 D3
Chesham Crs CFSP/GDCR SL9 ........ 90 B4
Chesham Ms GU GU1 ........ 268 B5
 KTBR SW1X ........ 16 C3
Chesham Pl KTBR SW1X ........ 16 C3
 AMS HP6 ........ 69 H5
 CSHM HP5 ........ 32 B8
 GTMS/PWID HP16 ........ 50 C8
 GU GU1 ........ 268 B1
Chesham Rd BELV DA17 ........ 164 B4
 DAGW RM9 ........ 124 A2
 NTHLT UB5 ........ 134 A2
Chesham Wash
 CHES/WCR EN8 ........ 62 D1
Chesilton Rd FUL/PGN SW6 ........ 157 J7
Chesil Wy YEAD UB4 ........ 132 G6
Chesley Gdns EHAM E6 ........ 142 A4
Chesney Crs CROY/NA CR0 ........ 225 H4
Chesney St BTSEA SW11 ........ 158 A7
Chestnut Av North WALTH E17 * ........ 119 N1
Chestnut Av South WALTH E17 ........ 119 N1
Chesterbrook RD
 STNW/STAM N16 ........ 119 H9
Chesterfield Cl ASHF TW15 ........ 174 D9

**Column 6**

Cheshnut Av ... (entries continued)
 STNW/STAM N16 ........ 119 M8
Chesham Ter WEA W13 ........ 154 G1
Chesham Wy WATW WD18 ........ 72 F10
Cheshire Cl CHERT KT16 ........ 214 C6
 EMPK RM11 ........ 125 P3
 MTCM CR4 ........ 202 F3
 WALTH E17 ........ 101 K9
Cheshire Dr GSTN WD25 ........ 54 C9
Cheshire Gdns CHSGTN KT9 ........ 219 J3
Cheshire Rd WDGN N22 ........ 98 G6
Cheshire St BETH E2 ........ 13 N1
Chesholm Rd
 STNW/STAM N16 ........ 119 M8
Cheshunt Rd BELV DA17 ........ 164 B4
 FSTGT E7 ........ 141 N2
Cheshunt Wash
 CHES/WCR EN8 ........ 62 D1
Chesil Ct BETH E2 * ........ 139 K4
Chesilton Rd FUL/PGN SW6 ........ 157 J7
Chesney Crs CROY/NA CR0 ........ 225 H4
Chesney St BTSEA SW11 ........ 158 A7
Chesnut Gv MNPK E12 ........ 123 H1
Chesnut Rd TOTM N17 ........ 119 M8
Chessell Cl THHTH CR7 ........ 203 J4
Chessfield Pk AMS HP6 ........ 70 B5
Chess Hl RKW/CH/CXG WD3 ........ 71 C8
Chessholme Ct ASHF TW15 ........ 174 D9
Chessington Av BXLYHN DA7 ........ 163 P6
 FNCH N3 ........ 117 J5
Chessington Cl
 HOR/WEW KT19 ........ 219 P3
Chessington Ct PIN HA5 * ........ 113 N2
Chessington Hall Gdns
 CHSGTN KT9 ........ 219 J6
Chessington Hill Pk
 CHSGTN KT9 ........ 219 M3
Chessington Pde
 CHSGTN KT9 ........ 219 J2
Chessington Rd
 HOR/WEW KT19 ........ 219 P4
Chess La RKW/CH/CXG WD3 ........ 71 G9
Chessmount Ri CSHM HP5 ........ 51 J9
Chesson Rd WKENS W14 ........ 14 C9
Chess Vale Ri
 RKW/CH/CXG WD3 ........ 72 C10
Chess Valley Wk AMS HP5 ........ 70 A4
 CSHM HP5 ........ 69 L1
Chess Wy RKW/CH/CXG WD3 ........ 71 F8
Chesswood Dr
 RKW/CH/CXG WD3 ........ 91 K7
Chesswood Wy PIN HA5 ........ 93 L10
Chester Av RCHPK/HAM TW10 ........ 177 G10
 UPMR RM14 ........ 126 D10
 WHTN TW2 ........ 175 M4
Chester Cl ASHF TW15 ........ 174 G9
 BAL SW12 ........ 180 B4
 BARK/HLT IG6 ........ 103 H2
 BRW CM14 ........ 107 H4
 EBAR EN4 ........ 78 B6
 HOD EN11 ........ 26 E10
 ISLW TW7 ........ 154 F7
 MTCM CR4 ........ 202 F3
 NWMAL KT3 ........ 200 A1
 RDART DA2 ........ 188 G10
 SAND/SEL CR2 ........ 224 B7
 STA TW18 ........ 173 M4
 WOKS/MYFD GU22 ........ 233 K4
Chester Cl North CAMTN NW1 ........ 4 F3
Chester Cl South CAMTN NW1 ........ 4 F10
Chester Crs HACK E8 ........ 119 N10
Chester Dr RYLN/HDSTN HA2 ........ 113 M8
Chesterfield Dr
 STMC/STPC BR5 ........ 207 N4
 DART DA1 ........ 186 F2
 ESH/CLAY KT10 ........ 198 F6
 SEV TN13 ........ 246 E8
Chesterfield Gdns
 GNWCH SE10 * ........ 161 L2
 MYFR/PICC W1J ........ 10 E8
 FSBYPK N4 ........ 119 H3
Chesterfield Gv EDUL SE22 ........ 181 N7
Chesterfield Hl
 MYFR/PKLN W1K ........ 10 B1
Chesterfield Ms ASHF TW15 ........ 173 P10
 FSBYPK N4 ........ 119 J3
Chesterfield Rd ASHF TW15 ........ 173 P10
 BAR EN5 ........ 76 B6
 CHSWK W4 ........ 155 P6
 FNCH N3 ........ 97 H10
 HOR/WEW KT19 ........ 220 A4

**Column 7**

 LEY E10 ........ 121 H5
 PEND EN3 ........ 80 D9
Chesterfield St
 MYFR/PICC W1J ........ 10 E9
Chesterfield Wy
 HYS/HAR UB3 * ........ 153 H1
 PECK SE15 ........ 160 B6
Chesterford Gdns HAMP NW3 ........ 117 J2
Chesterford Rd MNPK E12 ........ 122 C10
Chester Gdns MRDN SM4 ........ 201 N5
 PEND EN3 ........ 80 A10
 WEA W13 * ........ 134 G8
Chester Ga CAMTN NW1 ........ 4 C10
Chester Gibbons Gn ........
 LCOL/BKTW AL2 ........ 57 J2
Chester Ms KTBR SW1X ........ 16 E3
Chester Pl CAMTN NW1 ........ 4 E8
 NTHWD HA6 * ........ 92 F8
Chester Rd ARCH N19 ........ 118 C7
 BFN/LL DA15 ........ 185 H1
 BORE WD6 ........ 75 P7
 CAMTN NW1 ........ 4 C10
 CAN/RD E16 ........ 141 M4
 CHIG IG7 ........ 102 D4
 ED N9 ........ 100 A2
 FSTGT E7 ........ 142 A2
 GDMY/SEVK IG3 ........ 123 J4
 HSLWW TW4 ........ 153 J9
 HTHAIR TW6 ........ 152 B9
 LOU IG10 ........ 82 G7
 NTHWD HA6 ........ 92 G8
 SL S1 ........ 129 J8
 TOTM N17 ........ 119 L1
 WALTH E17 ........ 120 C3
 WAN E11 ........ 121 N1
 WATW WD18 ........ 73 M9
 WIM/MER SW19 ........ 178 F9
Chester Rw BGVA SW1W ........ 16 C4
Chesters HORL RH6 ........ 279 P2
Chester Sq BGVA SW1W ........ 16 D5
Chester Square Ms
 BGVA SW1W * ........ 16 E4
The Chesters NWMAL KT3 ........ 200 B3
Chester St BETH E2 ........ 13 P1
 KTBR SW1X ........ 16 D3
Chesterton Av HARP AL5 ........ 20 B2
Chesterton Cl CSHM HP5 ........ 50 C5
 GFD/PVL UB6 ........ 134 A4
 WAND/EARL SW18 ........ 179 K1
Chesterton Dr EA W5 * ........ 135 J4
 STWL/WRAY TW19 ........ 174 A4
Chesterton Gn BEAC HP9 ........ 88 D9
Chesterton Rd NKENS W10 ........ 8 A1
 PLSTW E13 ........ 141 M5
Chesterton Sq KENS W8 ........ 14 D5
Chesterton Sq KUT/HW KT1 * ........ 199 M2
 PLSTW E13 ........ 141 M5
Chester Wy LBTH SE11 ........ 18 A7
Chesthunte Rd TOTM N17 ........ 99 K9
Chestnut Aly FUL/PGN SW6 * ........ 14 D10
Chestnut Av ALP/SUD HA0 ........ 114 C10
 BH/WHM TN16 ........ 244 A6
 BKHH IG9 ........ 102 A4
 BTFD TW8 ........ 155 J4
 CDW/CHF RM16 ........ 167 N1
 CEND/HSY/T N8 ........ 118 P3
 CSHM HP5 ........ 51 J5
 DTCH/LGLY SL3 ........ 150 B1
 E/WMO/HCT KT8 ........ 198 E3
 EDGW HA8 ........ 95 K7
 ESH/CLAY KT10 ........ 198 C7
 FSTGT E7 ........ 121 N9
 GUW GU2 ........ 267 P4
 HCH RM12 ........ 124 D2
 HYS/HAR UB3 ........ 132 B7
 HYS/HAR UB3 ........ 152 C6
 KWD/TDW/WH KT20 ........ 239 K9
 SEV TN13 ........ 160 E7
 ORP BR6 ........ 227 K2
 REDH RH1 ........ 276 C2
 RPLY/SEND GU23 ........ 251 K1
 STHGT/OAK N14 ........ 78 D6
 STRHM/NOR SW16 ........ 119 J1
 SUN TW16 ........ 174 C9
 WARE SG12 ........ 26 A1

**Column 8**

 LEY E10 ........ 121 H5
 PEND EN3 ........ 80 D9
Chesterfield St
 MYFR/PICC W1J ........ 10 E9
Chestnut Av West
 HYS/HAR UB3 * ........ 153 H1
 PECK SE15 ........ 160 B6
Chestnut Cl ADL/WDHM KT15 ........ 215 N2
 AMS HP6 ........ 69 J3
 ASHF TW15 ........ 174 C7
 BERK HP4 ........ 34 E3
 BFN/LL DA15 ........ 185 K5
 BKHH IG9 ........ 102 A4
 CAR SM5 ........ 202 B7
 CAT SE6 ........ 183 M7
 CFSP/GDCR SL9 ........ 90 C10
 CROY/NA CR0 ........ 171 N9
 GVW DA11 ........ 190 C2
 HCH RM12 ........ 125 K6
 HYS/HAR UB3 ........ 132 F9
 HYS/HAR UB3 ........ 152 C6
 KWD/TDW/WH KT20 ........ 239 K9
 NWCR SE14 ........ 160 E7
 ORP BR6 ........ 227 K2
 REDH RH1 ........ 276 C2
 RPLY/SEND GU23 ........ 251 K1
 STHGT/OAK N14 ........ 78 D6
 STRHM/NOR SW16 ........ 181 L9
 SUN TW16 ........ 174 C9
 WARE SG12 ........ 26 A1
Chestnut Copse OXTED RH8 ........ 261 N4
Chestnut Cots
 TRDG/WHET N20 * ........ 97 H2
Chestnut Dr BERK HP4 ........ 34 A6
 BXLYHN DA7 ........ 165 K10
 EGH TW20 ........ 30 M4
 KTN/HRWW/WS HA3 ........ 94 F2
 PIN HA5 ........ 113 L4
 STAL AL1 ........ 38 G4
 WAN E11 ........ 121 M4
 WDSR SL4 ........ 148 D10
Chestnut Gln HCH RM12 ........ 124 D2
Chestnut Gv ALP/SUD HA0 ........ 114 C10
 BAL SW12 ........ 180 B2
 BARK/HLT IG6 ........ 103 H1
 BRW CM14 ........ 107 H4
 EA W5 ........ 155 J2
 EBAR EN4 ........ 78 A6
 HOD EN11 ........ 26 A9
 ISLW TW7 ........ 154 F9
 MTCM CR4 ........ 202 A2
 NWMAL KT3 ........ 200 A1
 RDART DA2 ........ 186 A5
 SAND/SEL CR2 ........ 224 A4
 STA TW18 ........ 173 M3
 WOKS/MYFD GU22 ........ 233 H6
Chestnut La SEV TN13 ........ 156 C2
 TRDG/WHET N20 ........ 97 H2
 WEY KT13 ........ 216 C2
Chestnut Manor Cl STA TW18 ........ 173 N9
Chestnut Pl ASHTD KT21 ........ 237 K5
 SYD SE26 ........ 182 A6
Chestnut Ri BUSH WD23 ........ 94 A1
 WOOL/PLUM SE18 ........ 143 M10
Chestnut Rd ASHF TW15 ........ 174 B7
 BEAC HP9 ........ 88 C2
 GU GU1 ........ 250 A10
 HORL RH6 ........ 280 B2
 KUTN/CMB KT2 ........ 177 C10
 PEND EN3 ........ 80 D2
 RYNPK SW20 ........ 200 G2
 WHTN TW2 ........ 176 B6
 WNWD SE27 ........ 181 J5
Chestnuts RBRW/HUT CM13 ........ 107 N4
The Chestnuts BECK BR3 * ........ 204 C3
 HERT/BAY SG13 ........ 25 J6
 HHS/BOV HP3 ........ 35 N8

PIN HA5 * 93 N8
WOT/HER KT12 197 L9
Chestnut Ter SUT SM1 221 L9
Chestnut Wk BGR/WK TN15 265 N4
  CFSP/GDCR SL9 * 90 A8
  CRAWW RH11 283 M4
  EPP CM16 64 E1
  SHPTN TW17 196 F5
  WATN WD24 73 H3
Chestnut Wy FELT TW13 175 M6
Cheston Av CROY/NA CR0 204 D8
Chestwood Gv
  HGDN/ICK UB10 132 A2
Chesworth Cl ERITH DA8 164 F7
Chettle Cl STHWK SE1 18 D5
Chetwode Dr EPSOM KT18 238 C4
Chetwode Rd EPSOM KT18 238 C4
  TOOT SW17 180 A6
Chetwynd Av EBAR EN4 98 A2
Chetwynd Dr HGDN/ICK UB10 132 A4
Chetwynd Rd KTTN NW5 118 C9
Chetwynd Vls KTTN NW5 118 C9
Chevalier Cl STAN HA7 35 J4
Cheval Pl SKENS SW7 15 J5
Cheval St POP/IOD E14 160 F2
Cheveley Gdns SL SL1 128 B4
Chevely Cl EPP CM16 65 N5
Cheveney Wk HAYES BR2 205 M3
Chevening La RSEV TN14 245 P2
Chevening Rd GNWCH SE10 161 L4
  KIL/WHAMP NW6 2 A6
  NRWD SE19 181 L10
  RSEV TN14 246 A3
The Chevenings SCUP DA14 185 L6
Cheverton Av ARCH N19 118 C6
Cheverton Rd ARCH N19 118 C6
Chevet St HOM E9 139 L6
Chevington CRICK NW2 * 2 C1
Chevington Pl HCH RM12 125 L10
Chevington Vls REDH RH1 259 N9
Chevington Wy HCH RM12 125 L9
Cheviot Cl BELMT SM2 221 N5
  BNSTD SM7 239 L5
  BUSH WD23 74 B10
  BXLYHN DA7 164 F6
  ENC/FH EN2 79 L6
  HYS/HAR UB3 152 C7
Cheviot Gdns CRICK NW2 116 C7
Cheviot Rd DTCH/LGLY SL3 150 D4
  EMPK RM11 142 B1
  WNWD SE27 181 H8
Cheviots HAT AL10 40 D7
  HHNE HP2 36 A3
Cheviot Wk CRAWW RH11 * 283 M4
Chevron Cl CAN/RD E16 141 K8
Chevy Rd NWDGN UB2 154 B1
Chewton Cl AFOR GU20 212 A1
Chewton Rd WALTH E17 120 D2
Cheyham Gdns BELMT SM2 220 G7
Cheyham Wy BELMT SM2 221 H6
Cheyne Cl SWFD E18 121 L1
  WHTN TW2 175 M4
Cheyne Ct BNSTD SM7 239 L1
  BUSH WD23 73 M8
Cheyne Gdns CHEL SW3 15 P10
Cheyne Hl BRYLDS KT5 191 L9
Cheyne Ms CHEL SW3 15 P10
Cheyne Park Dr WWKM BR4 205 H10
Cheyne Pth HNWL W7 134 E7
Cheyne Rd ASHF TW15 174 A9
Cheyne Rw CHEL SW3 15 P10
Cheyne Wk CHEL SW3 15 N10
  CROY/NA CR0 203 P9
  CSHM HP5 51 J7
  HORL RH6 280 B6
  WBPTN SW10 157 N6
  WCHMH N21 79 N9
Cheyneys Av EDGW HA8 95 N8
Chichele Gdns CROY/NA CR0 223 M1
Chichele Rd CRICK NW2 116 C2
  OXTED RH8 261 K4
Chicheley Rd
  KTN/HRWW/WS HA3 94 B8
Chicheley St STHWK SE1 17 P1
Chichester Cl BKHTH/KID SE3 161 P6
  CDW/CHF RM16 167 J3
  EHAM E6 142 B8
  HPTN TW12 175 N9
  SOCK/AV RM15 146 B10
  SL SL1 149 N2
  STAN HA7 94 F1
Chichester Gdns IL IG1 122 B5
Chichester Ri GVE DA12 190 C7
Chichester Rd BAY/PAD W2 9 H1
  CROY/NA CR0 203 M10
  DORK RH4 254 C9
  ED N9 99 E8
  KIL/WHAMP NW6 2 E8
  RDART DA2 188 C1
  WAN E11 128 C10
Chichester St PIM SW1V 17 H8
Chichester Wy
  EBED/NFELT TW14 175 K3
  GSTN WD25 55 M8
  POP/IOD E14 161 J3
Chichester Whf ERITH DA8 164 E4
Chicken La LCOL/BKTW AL2 57 J3
Chicksand Est WCHPL E1 13 N3
Chicksand St WCHPL E1 13 M4
Chiddingfold
  NFNCH/WDSPK N12 97 K4
Chiddingly Cl CRAWE RH10 284 D6
Chiddingstone Av
  BXLYHN DA7 164 A6
Chiddingstone Cl BELMT SM2 221 K6
Chiddingstone St
  FUL/PGN SW6 157 K8
Chieftan Dr PUR RM19 165 P3
Chieveley Pde BXLYHN DA7 * 164 C9
Chieveley Rd BXLYHN DA7 164 C10
Chiffinch Gdns GVW DA11 190 B6
Chignell Pl WEA W13 134 F10
Chigwell Hl WAP E1W 140 D8
Chigwell La LOU IG10 82 F10
Chigwell Park Dr CHIG IG7 102 D5
Chigwell Ri CHIG IG7 102 C3
Chigwell Rd SWFD E18 121 N1
  WFD IG8 102 A2
Chilberton Dr REDH RH1 258 D6
Chilbrook Rd COB KT11 235 H4
Chilcombe Cl PIN HA5 * 111 H2
Chilcote La AMSS HP7 35 P7
Chilcot Cl ALP/SUD HA0 115 H9
Chilcott Rd WATN WD24 72 F2
Childebert Rd TOOT SW17 180 C5
Childerditch Hall Dr
  RBRW/HUT CM13 127 L1
Childerditch La
  RBRW/HUT CM13 107 K9
Childerditch St
  RBRW/HUT CM13 127 L1
Childeric Rd NWCR SE14 160 D6
Childerley St FUL/PGN SW6 157 H7
Childers St DEPT SE8 160 G2
The Childers WFD IG8 102 C6
Child La GNWCH SE10 161 L2
Childs Av HGDN/ICK UB10 131 J1
Childsbridge La BGR/WK TN15 247 M4
Childs Cl EMPK RM11 125 L1
Childs Cl HYS/HAR UB3 133 H9
Childs Crs SWCM DA10 189 L2
Childs Hall Dr GT/LBKH KT23 253 N1
Childs Hall Rd GT/LBKH KT23 253 N1
Childs La NRWD SE19 * 181 M9
Child's Ms ECT SW5 * 14 G6

Child's Pl ECT SW5 * 14 F6
Child's St ECT SW5 * 14 F5
Child's Wk ECT SW5 * 14 F5
Childs Wy GLDGN NW11 117 J3
Childwick Ct HHS/BOV HP3 36 A3
Chilham Cl BXLY DA5 186 A3
  GFD/PVL UB6 134 F4
  HHNE HP2 35 P7
Chilham Rd ELTH/MOT SE9 184 B7
Chilham Wy HAYES BR2 205 M7
Chillerton Rd TOOT SW17 180 B8
Chillingham Wy
  TWK TW1 * 176 E5
Chillingworth Gdns
  TWK TW1 176 E5
Chillingworth Rd HOLWY N7 118 F10
Chilmans Dr GT/LBKH KT23 254 A5
Chilmark Gdns NWMAL KT3 200 D6
Chilmark Rd
  STRHM/NOR SW16 202 A2
Chiltern Av BUSH WD23 74 B10
  WHTN TW2 175 P4
Chiltern Cl BERK HP4 35 L6
  BORE WD6 75 L6
  BUSH WD23 74 A10
  BXLYHN DA7 164 F7
  CHESW EN7 61 J3
  CRAWW RH11 283 K11
  CROY/NA CR0 203 M10
  HGDN/ICK UB10 112 C7
  STA TW18 173 K8
  WATW WD18 72 C8
  WOKS/MYFD GU22 231 P8
  WPK KT4 200 F9
Chiltern Dene ENC/FH EN2 78 C8
Chiltern Dr BRYLDS KT5 191 J1
  RKW/CH/CXG WD3 91 J1
Chiltern Est WATN WD24 * 73 K5
Chiltern Gdns CRICK NW2 116 C8
  HAYES BR2 205 L4
Chiltern Hts AMSS HP7 69 M5
Chiltern Hill CFSP/GDCR SL9 90 B9
Chiltern Hills Rd BEAC HP9 88 B9
Chiltern Link CSHM HP5 50 B6
Chiltern Pde BERK HP4 35 L6
Chiltern Park Av BERK HP4 33 M5
Chiltern Pl CLPT E5 120 A7
Chiltern Rd AMS HP6 50 G10
  BELMT SM2 221 M6
  BOW E3 140 F6
  GNTH/NBYPK IG2 123 K5
  GVW DA11 190 B6
  PIN HA5 113 K5
  SL SL1 128 A7
  STALE/WH AL4 39 N1
Chilterns HAT AL10 40 D7
  HHNE HP2 35 P7
The Chilterns BELMT SM2 * 221 L5
Chiltern Vw MHST W1U 10 B3
Chiltern View Rd UX/CGN UB8 131 M4
Chiltern Wy WFD IG8 101 M4
Chilthorne Cl CAT SE6 182 C6
Chilton Av WEA W13 155 J3
Chilton Cl WCCE AL2 23 M5
Chilton Rd CDW/CHF RM16 168 D2
  CSHM HP5 51 H5
  EDGW HA8 95 M4
  RCH/KEW TW9 155 N9
Chiltons Cl BNSTD SM7 239 L1
Chilton St BETH E2 13 M1
Chilvers Cl WHTN TW2 176 B5
Chilver St GNWCH SE10 161 L10
Chilwell Gdns OXHEY WD19 93 K5
Chilwick Rd SL SL2 128 B6
Chilworth Gdns SUT SM1 201 M10
Chilworth Ms BROX EN10 44 A8
Chilworth Ms BAY/PAD W2 9 K3
Chilworth Rd SHGR GU5 269 K5
Chilworth St BAY/PAD W2 9 K3
Chimes Av PLMGR N13 99 H5
Chime Sq STALW/RED AL3 38 C5
China Hall Ms
  BERM/RHTH SE16 160 B8
China Ms BRXS/STRHM SW2 180 C3
Chinbrook Crs LEE/GVPK SE12 183 M6
Chinbrook Rd LEE/GVPK SE12 183 N6
Chinchilla Dr HSLWW TW4 153 M8
Chindit Cl BROX EN10 44 C6
Chindits La RBRW/HUT CM13 107 H6
The Chine ALP/SUD HA0 114 G10
  DORK RH4 * 272 G1
  MUSWH N10 98 B3
  WCHMH N21 79 J10
Chingdale Rd CHING E4 101 N4
Chingford Av CHING E4 100 F4
Chingford La WFD IG8 101 K5
Chingford Mount Rd
  CHING E4 100 E6
Chingford Rd CHING E4 100 F7
Chingley Cl BMLY BR1 183 K9
Ching Wy CHING E4 100 E7
Chinnery Cl EN EN1 79 N4
Chinnor Crs GFD/PVL UB6 133 M1
Chinthurst La RGUE GU4 268 B7
Chinthurst Ms COUL/CHIP CR5 240 D2
Chinthurst Pk RGUE GU4 268 B8
Chipka St POP/IOD E14 161 M1
Chipley St NWCR SE14 160 E6
Chipmunk Cha HAT AL10 40 A2
Chippendale Waye
  UX/CGN UB8 131 N2
Chippenham Cl PIN HA5 * 112 C2
Chippenham Gdns HARH RM3 105 L6
Chippenham Ms MV/WKIL W9 8 E2
Chippenham Rd HARH RM3 105 L7
  MV/WKIL W9 8 E1
Chipperfield Cl UPMR RM14 126 C6
  HHS/BOV HP3 35 M10
Chipperfield Rd HHS/BOV HP3 52 E6
  KGLGY WD4 53 N5
Chipping Cl BAR EN5 77 H7
Chippingfield HLWE CM17 27 M8
Chipstead Av THHTH CR7 203 J4
Chipstead Cl BELMT SM2 221 L6
  COUL/CHIP CR5 240 D1
  NRWD SE19 181 N10
  REDH RH1 276 A1
Chipstead Ct
  WOKN/KNAP GU21 231 J5
Chipstead Gdns CRICK NW2 116 A7
Chipstead La COUL/CHIP CR5 258 E2
  SEV TN13 246 E8
Chipstead Pk SEV TN13 246 E8
Chipstead Park Cl SEV TN13 246 D8
Chipstead Place Gdns
  SEV TN13 246 E9
Chipstead Station Pde
  ERITH DA8 164 E6
Chipstead St FUL/PGN SW6 157 K7
Chipstead Valley Rd
  COUL/CHIP CR5 240 D3
Chirk Cl YEAD UB4 133 J4
Chirton Wk WOKN/KNAP GU21 231 M4
Chisenhale Rd BOW E3 139 N5
Chisholm Rd CROY/NA CR0 203 M9
  RCHPK/HAM TW10 177 H5
Chislehurst Av
  NFNCH/WDSPK N12 97 H5
Chislehurst High St CHST BR7 184 D5
Chislehurst Rd BMLY BR1 206 B1
  ORP BR6 207 J7
  RCHPK/HAM TW10 177 H5

SCUP DA14 185 K8
STMC/STPC BR5 207 H4
Chislet Cl BECK BR3 182 F10
Chisley Rd SEVS/STOTM N15 119 M4
Chiswell Green La
  LCOL/BKTW AL2 55 L1
Chiswell Sq BKHTH/KID SE3 161 L1
Chiswell St CMBW SE5 159 L6
  STLK EC1Y 12 G3
Chiswick Br CHSWK W4 155 P9
Chiswick Cl CROY/NA CR0 202 G10
Chiswick Common Rd
  CHSWK W4 156 A3
Chiswick High Rd CHSWK W4 155 M4
Chiswick House Grounds
  CHSWK W4 156 A5
Chiswick La CHSWK W4 156 B4
Chiswick Gdns CHSWK W4 156 B4
Chiswick La South CHSWK W4 156 C4
Chiswick Mall CHSWK W4 156 C5
Chiswick Pk CHSWK W4 * 155 P2
Chiswick Pier CHSWK W4 * 156 C6
Chiswick Quay CHSWK W4 155 P7
Chiswick Rd CHSWK W4 155 P3
  ED N9 99 P3
Chiswick Sq CHSWK W4 * 156 B5
Chiswick Staithe CHSWK W4 * 155 P7
Chiswick Village CHSWK W4 155 M5
Chiswick Whf CHSWK W4 156 C5
Chithurst La CRAWE RH10 281 M8
Chittenden Cl HOD EN11 26 G10
Chitterfield Ga WDR/YW UB7 152 B3
Chitty's La BCTR RM8 123 N7
Chitty St FITZ W1T 11 H3
Chitty's Wk RGUW GU3 249 L6
Chivalry Rd BTSEA SW11 179 P1
Chivenor Gv KUTN/CMB KT2 177 J8
Chivenor Pl STALE/WH AL4 39 H8
Chivers Rd BRWN CM15 86 E1
  CHING E4 101 N1
Choats Manor Wy DAGW RM9 144 A4
Choats Rd BARK IG11 143 M4
Chobham Cl CHERT KT16 214 E3
Chobham Gdns
  WIM/MER SW19 178 C5
Chobham La CHERT KT16 193 M9
Chobham Park La
  CHOB/PIR GU24 213 M6
Chobham Rd ASC SL5 193 H9
  SRTFD E15 121 J10
  WOKN/KNAP GU21 213 J10
  WOKN/KNAP GU21 214 B1
  WOKN/KNAP GU21 230 G4
Choir Gn WOKN/KNAP GU21 231 K3
Cholesbury La CHESM HP5 32 B6
Cholesbury Rd TRING HP23 32 B6
Cholmeley Cl HGT N6 118 C5
Cholmeley Pk HGT N6 118 C5
Cholmley Gdns
  KIL/WHAMP NW6 117 K10
Cholmley Rd THDIT KT7 198 G6
Cholmley Ter THDIT KT7 * 198 G7
Cholmley Vls THDIT KT7 * 198 G7
Cholmondeley Av
  WLSDN NW10 136 D4
Chopwell Cl SRTFD E15 * 141 J2
Chorleywood Bottom
  RKW/CH/CXG WD3 70 C9
Chorleywood Cl
  RKW/CH/CXG WD3 91 N1
Chorleywood Crs
  STMC/STPC BR5 207 J2
Chorleywood House Dr
  RKW/CH/CXG WD3 71 H7
Chorleywood Rd
  RKW/CH/CXG WD3 71 L9
Choumert Gv PECK SE15 159 P8
Choumert Ms PECK SE15 159 P8
Choumert Rd PECK SE15 159 N9
Chow Sq HACK E8 * 119 N10
Chrisaline Cl
  STWL/WRAY TW19 173 N2
Chrisp St POP/IOD E14 140 G7
Christabel Cl ISLW TW7 154 D9
Christchurch Av
  ERITH DA8 164 E1
  KTN/HRWW/WS HA3 114 E3
  NFNCH/WDSPK N12 97 M7
  RAIN RM13 144 C4
  TEDD TW11 176 F8
Christchurch Cl ENC/FH EN2 79 K6
  NFNCH/WDSPK N12 97 M8
  WIM/MER SW19 179 N10
Christchurch Crs RAD WD7 74 F2
Christchurch Gdns
  KTN/HRWW/WS HA3 114 F2
  HOR/WEW KT19 219 N7
Christ Church Mt
  HOR/WEW KT19 219 N7
Christchurch Pk BELMT SM2 221 N7
Christ Church Rd BECK BR3 * 204 C1
  BRYLDS KT5 199 J2
  CEND/HSY/T N8 118 B1
  EPSOM KT18 219 K8
  GVE DA12 190 C7
  HOR/WEW KT19 219 N7
Christchurch Sq HOM E9 * 138 G3
Christchurch Ter CHEL SW3 * 16 A9
Christ Church Rd
  DEN/HRF UB9 111 M2
  HERT/BAY SG13 26 A7
  HRW HA1 114 D6
  LOU IG10 82 C7
  ORP BR6 207 K7
  PUR/KEN CR8 222 B8
  RDART DA2 188 D1
  REDH RH1 258 C2
  SHGR GU5 270 B5
  WALTH E17 120 F2
  WCHMH N21 98 D1
  WIM/MER SW19 179 J8
  WOKN/KNAP GU21 232 A3
  WOKS/MYFD GU22 233 J2
  WOOL/PLUM SE18 146 E10
Christchurch Gdns Rd
  PIM SW1V 16 G7
Christchurch Hi HAMP NW3 117 N9
Christchurch La BAR EN5 76 C2
Christchurch Pas HAMP NW3 117 N9
Christchurch Rd
  BFN/LL DA15 185 J4
  BRXS/STRHM SW2 180 A9
  HHNE HP2 35 N4
  IL IG1 122 E6
  PUR/KEN CR8 223 L9
  TW TW1 W25 194 M3
  VW GU25 212 A6
  VW GU25 193 M3
  WIM/MER SW19 179 N10
Christ Church Sq HOM E9 * 138 G3
Christ Church St CHEL SW3 16 A9
Christchurch Ter CHEL SW3 * 16 A9
Christchurch Wy GNWCH SE10 161 K3
  WOKN/KNAP GU21 232 C3
Christian Flds
  STRHM/NOR SW16 181 H10
Christian Fields Av GVE DA12 190 F10
Christian St WCHPL E1 13 N5
Christie Cl BROX EN10 44 F1
  GT/LBKH KT23 253 N1
  LTWR GU18 212 A6
Christie Ct WATW WD18 73 H9
Christie Dr CROY/NA CR0 203 P5
Christie Rd HOM E9 139 K6
  WAB EN9 80 G1
Christies Av RSEV TN14 228 G2
Christie Wk CTHM CR3 241 J8
Christina Sq FSBYPK N4 119 J6
Christina St SDTCH EC2A 13 J1
Christine Worsley Cl
  WCHMH N21 99 J2
Christmas Hi SHGR GU5 268 G8
Christmas La SLN SL2 109 H8
Christmaspie Av RGUW GU3 248 A10
Christopher Av HNWL W7 154 F3
Christopher Cl
  BERM/RHTH SE16 160 F6
  BFN/LL DA15 185 J1
  HCH RM12 125 L9
Christopher Ct WARE SG12 * 26 C2
Christopher Gdns DAGW RM9 143 P9
Christopher Pl CAMTN NW1 * 5 H4
  STALW/RED AL3 * 38 C5
Christopher Ms SDTCH EC1A 13 J1
Christopher's Ms NTGHL W11 8 A9
Christopher St SDTCH EC2A 13 H2
Christy Ter BRXS/STRHM SW2 180 A9
Chryssell Rd BRXN/ST SW9 159 H6
Chrystie La GT/LBKH KT23 254 A5
Chubworthy St NWCR SE14 160 G10
Chuck's La
  KWD/TDW/WH KT20 238 G10
Chudleigh Crs GDMY/SEVK IG3 123 H9

Chudleigh Gdns SUT SM1 201 M10
Chudleigh Rd BROCKY SE4 182 B1
  HARH RM3 105 M5
  KIL/WHAMP NW6 136 F2
  WHTN TW2 176 D2
Chudleigh St WCHPL E1 140 G9
Chudleigh Wy RSLP HA4 113 G5
Chulsa Rd SYD SE26 182 A8
Chumleigh St CMBW SE5 19 J9
Chumleigh Wk BRYLDS KT5 191 L4
Church Aly GVW DA11 * 190 E22
Church Ap DUL SE21 181 L6
  EGH TW20 194 F3
Church Av BECK BR3 204 F1
  CAMTN NW1 4 F1
  CHING E4 100 F5
  MORT/ESHN SW14 156 A10
  NWDGN UB2 153 M3
  PIN HA5 113 M4
  RSLP HA4 112 G6
  SCUP DA14 185 K8
Church Cl ADL/WDHM KT15 215 L1
  BRW CM14 86 C3
  CHOB/PIR GU24 230 E6
  EDGW HA8 96 D6
  EW KT17 220 B9
  HSLW TW3 153 N8
  HYS/HAR UB3 132 E7
  KWD/TDW/WH KT20 257 J3
  LHD/OX KT22 236 C10
  NTHWD HA6 92 G8
  POTB/CUF EN6 60 F5
  RAD WD7 74 F2
  STA TW18 195 M3
  TRDG/WHET N20 97 J3
  UX/CGN UB8 131 L4
  WDR/YW UB7 151 P2
  WDSR SL4 149 J5
Church Cft STALE/WH AL4 39 N8
Churchcroft Cl BAL SW12 * 180 B3
Churchdown BMLY BR1 183 K7
Church Dr CDALE/KGS NW9 116 A6
  RYLN/HDSTN HA2 114 A6
  WWKM BR4 205 K10
Church Elm La DAGE RM10 144 B1
Church End HNWL W7 116 E1
  HLWW/ROY CM19 46 D3
  STALE/WH AL4 21 H9
  WALTH E17 * 120 D1
Church Farm EBAR EN4 * 98 A1
Church Farm La CHEAM SM3 221 H4
Church Farm Wy GSTN WD25 74 A3
Church Fld EPP CM16 65 K5
  SEV TN13 246 C8
Churchfield HARP AL5 29 K9
Church Fld SEV TN13 246 C8
Church Field Pth
  CHES/WCR EN8 62 B5
Churchfield Av
  NFNCH/WDSPK N12 97 M7
Churchfield Cl HYS/HAR UB3 132 C6
  RYLN/HDSTN HA2 114 B2
Churchfield Ms SLN SL2 129 N8
Church Fields Av FELT TW13 175 H6
Churchfields BROX EN10 44 F1
  E/WMO/HCT KT8 197 P5
  GNWCH SE10 161 N5
  HERT/BAY SG13 25 J3
  LOU IG10 82 B7
  RGUE GU4 250 D5
  SWFD E18 102 B10
  WOKN/KNAP GU21 232 A2
  WEY KT13 216 B1
Churchfields Av FELT TW13 175 H6
  WEY KT13 216 C1
Churchfields La BROX EN10 44 F1
  BECK BR3 204 C1
Churchfield Wy
  NFNCH/WDSPK N12 97 M7
Church Gdns ALP/SUD HA0 114 F9
  EA W5 155 J1
Church Garth ARCH N19 * 118 D9
Churchgate CHES/WCR EN8 62 A6
Churchgate Rd
  CHES/WCR EN8 62 A5
Church Ga FUL/PGN SW6 157 H9
Churchgate St HLWE CM17 27 P7
Church Gn BRXN/ST SW9 159 H9
  HYS/HAR UB3 132 C8
  KWD/TDW/WH KT20 238 D10
  WOT/HER KT12 217 K3
Church Gv AMS HP6 70 B5
  DTCH/LGLY SL3 129 P7
  KUT/HW KT1 199 H1
  LEW SE13 160 C10
Church Hl ABLGY WD5 54 C1
  BH/WHM TN16 244 A8
  CAR SM5 222 A2
  CTHM CR3 241 N10
  DART DA1 164 D4
  DEN/HRF UB9 111 M2
  EPP CM16 65 K5
  HERT/BAY SG13 26 A7
  HRW HA1 114 D6
  LOU IG10 82 C7
  ORP BR6 207 K7
  PUR/KEN CR8 222 B8
  RDART DA2 188 D1
  REDH RH1 258 C2
  SHGR GU5 270 B5
  WALTH E17 120 F2
  WCHMH N21 98 D1
  WIM/MER SW19 179 J8
  WOKN/KNAP GU21 232 A3
  WOKS/MYFD GU22 233 J2
  WOOL/PLUM SE18 146 E10
Church Hill Rd CHEAM SM3 220 G1
  EBAR EN4 77 P10
  CHOB/PIR GU24 212 D6
  CHONG CM5 49 P10
  CRAWE RH10 285 N10
  CROY/NA CR0 203 K10
  CTHM CR3 241 H9
  DEN/HRF UB9 111 M2
  E/WMO/HCT KT8 197 P5
  EGH TW20 172 D9
  ESH/CLAY KT10 216 D2
  EW KT17 220 D9
  EYN DA4 199 M4
  FELT TW13 175 H6
  GNTH/NBYPK IG2 123 K5
  GT/LBKH KT23 253 N1
  GU GU1 258 B5
  GVE DA12 190 F7
  HART DA3 211 J3

Churchill Rd CAN/RD E16 141 P8
  CRICK NW2 136 E1
  DTCH/LGLY SL3 150 C3
  EDGW HA8 95 L7
  EYN DA4 210 B4
  GRAYS RM17 168 A5
  HOR/WEW KT19 219 M7
  HORL RH6 281 J4
  KTTN NW5 118 C9
  SAND/SEL CR2 223 K5
  STAL AL1 38 F4
Churchill Ter CHING E4 100 F5
Churchill Wk HOM E9 120 D10
Churchill Wy BH/WHM TN16 244 A1
  BMLY BR1 205 M2
  SUN TW16 175 P8
Churchin Cl BH/WHM TN16 225 P8
Churchlands Wy WPK KT4 200 G9
Church La ABR/ST RM4 83 N8
  ASC SL5 192 C4
  BERK HP4 33 P5
  BRKMPK AL9 40 F5
  BROX EN10 44 A8
  BRWN CM15 86 C3
  CDALE/KGS NW9 115 P6
  CEND/HSY/T N8 118 C2
  CFSP/GDCR SL9 90 A9
  CHES/WCR EN8 62 B5
  CHOB/PIR GU24 230 F1
  CHONG CM5 49 P10
  CHSGTN KT9 219 L3
  CHST BR7 206 F1
  COUL/CHIP CR5 240 B8
  CRAWE RH10 284 A6
  CRAWW RH10 285 H5
  CTHM CR3 241 H9
  DAGE RM10 144 C1
  DTCH/LGLY SL3 129 N6
  EA W5 155 H1
  ED N9 99 P3
  EFNCH N2 117 N1
  ENC/FH EN2 79 L7
  EPP CM16 66 B1
  EPSOM KT18 255 P1
  GDST RH9 260 C8
  GSTN WD25 74 A4
  GVE DA12 191 M5
  HAYES BR2 206 B8
  HHS/BOV HP3 52 E3
  HORL RH6 280 F9
  KGLGY WD4 54 B6
  KTN/HRWW/WS HA3 94 E9
  LOU IG10 81 N5
  OXTED RH8 261 J6
  PIN HA5 113 M1
  POTB/CUF EN6 60 A6
  PUR RM19 165 P4
  RAIN RM13 145 J4
  RBRW/HUT CM13 127 N4
  RBSF CM22 30 E3
  REDH RH1 259 L9
  RGUE GU3 249 K3
  RKW/CH/CXG WD3 71 K3
  ROM RM1 124 F2
  RPLY/SEND GU23 252 B8
  SEV TN13 246 G8
  SLN SL2 129 L6
  STALE/WH AL4 39 N8
  TEDD TW11 176 D7
  TIL RM18 168 B7
  TOTM N17 99 M9
  UX/CGN UB8 131 N6
  WALTH E17 100 D10
  WARL CR6 242 C3
  WAT WD17 73 H5
  WDR/YW UB7 151 N1
  WDSR SL4 171 N1
  WELL DA16 164 C3
  WOCW AL8 22 F5
  WIM/MER SW19 201 N2
  WLGTN SM6 202 D10
  WLSDN NW10 136 D1
  WOKN/KNAP GU21 231 M5
  WPK KT4 200 B8
Church Rw CHST BR7 206 F1
  CHST BR7 184 F10
  FUL/PGN SW6 157 L6
  HAMP NW3 117 M9
  NWDGN UB2 153 M3
  RPLY/SEND GU23 252 B3
  WAND/EARL SW18 179 N8
Church Row Ms CHST BR7 * 184 F10
Church Side EPSOM KT18 219 N9
Church Sq SHPTN TW17 196 C7
Church St AMSS HP7 68 G6
  BAY/PAD W2 9 J1
  BGR/WK TN15 247 P6
  BRKHM/BTCW RH3 274 B1
  BRKMPK AL9 41 P3
  CHSWK W4 156 B5
  COB KT11 235 J1
  CRAWW RH11 283 M7
  CROY/NA CR0 203 J10
  CSHM HP5 50 C7
  DAGE RM10 144 C2
  DORK RH4 272 F2
  ED N9 99 H1
  ENC/FH EN2 79 L7
  ESH/CLAY KT10 218 A1
  EW KT17 220 B9
  GRAYS RM17 167 P5
  GVW DA11 211 J3
  HART DA3 211 J3
  HERT/WAT SG14 25 J4
  HHNE HP2 35 N4
  HHS/BOV HP3 52 E3
  HPTN TW12 198 B1
  ISLW TW7 154 G9
  KUT/HW KT1 191 J2
  LHD/OX KT22 236 G8
  MEO DA13 189 N8
  REIG RH2 257 L10
  RKW/CH/CXG WD3 91 P2
  RSEV TN14 228 G2
  SBW CM21 29 P1
  SL SL1 128 B6
  SRTFD E15 141 K3
  STA TW18 172 G7
  STALW/RED AL3 21 J3
  SUN TW16 196 B1
  TWK TW1 176 A4
  WAB EN9 63 H9
  WARE SG12 25 N1
  WATW WD18 73 N4
  WDSR SL4 149 J7
  WIM/MER SW19 201 K1
  WOKS/MYFD GU22 232 F7
  WOT/HER KT12 197 H8
Church St East
  WOKN/KNAP GU21 232 E10
Church Street Est STJWD NW8 9 M2
Church St North SRTFD E15 141 K3
Church St West
  WOKN/KNAP GU21 232 E10
Church Ter BGR/WK TN15 247 N7
  BKHTH/KID SE3 161 J4
  FUL/PGN SW6 157 L8
  HDN NW4 116 E1
  RCHPK/HAM TW10 176 B10
  WDSR SL4 148 D8
Church V EFNCH N2 117 J1
Church V FSTH SE23 182 B5
Church Vw BROX EN10 182 E5
  FSTH SE23 182 B5
  SOCK/AV RM15 166 B1
  STALW/RED AL4 21 J3
Churchview Rd WHTN TW2 176 C4
Church Wk BTFD TW8 155 P7
  BUSH WD23 73 P10
  CDALE/KGS NW9 116 A6
  CRAWE RH10 283 N7
  CRICK NW2 117 J4
  CTHM CR3 241 P10
  GVE DA12 190 F7
  HORL RH6 280 F9
  HYS/HAR UB3 132 D3
  REIG RH2 257 L10
  RYNPK SW20 200 F5
  SBW CM21 29 P1
  STNW/STAM N16 119 N10
  STRHM/NOR SW16 198 D10
  THDIT KT7 190 C8
  WEY KT13 216 B10
  WOT/HER KT12 197 H8
Church Wy CAMTN NW1 5 H3
  EBAR EN4 98 C2
  OXTED RH8 261 L6
  SAND/SEL CR2 223 N6

HAYES BR2 226 A4
HDN NW4 116 C2
HERT/BAY SG13 42 D5
HERT/WAT SG14 25 J4
HEST TW5 153 P6
HGT N6 118 B4
HOR/WEW KT19 * 36 D5
HLWE CM17 47 M4
HNWL W7 154 D9
HOR/WEW KT19 220 A4
HORL RH6 281 H8
HORL RH6 279 P10
HORL RH6 281 N2
HYS/HAR UB3 132 G10
IS N1 6 F2
ISLW TW7 154 C7
IVER SL0 130 F4
KUT/HW KT1 199 L2
LEY E10 120 F6
LHD/OX KT22 236 G8
LOU IG10 81 M7
MEO DA13 190 G10
MNPK E12 122 A9
MTCM CR4 201 P3
NRWD SE19 181 M10
NTHLT UB5 133 L4
NTHWD HA6 92 G8
NWDGN UB2 153 N2
ORP BR6 227 N3
ORP BR6 226 F2
PEND EN3 80 B10
POTB/CUF EN6 59 L8
PUR/KEN CR8 222 F6
RCHPK/HAM TW10 177 K5
RCHPK/HAM TW10 188 D1
RDART DA2 188 D1
REDH RH1 275 P2
REIG RH2 257 P7
RSEV TN14 227 P7
RSEV TN14 263 P2
RSEV TN14 265 J8
SCUP DA14 185 K7
SHPTN TW17 196 C7
SLN SL2 129 H5
STAN HA7 94 G6
SURB KT6 199 H8
SWCM DA10 189 L2
SWLY BR8 209 L1
SWLY BR8 208 E7
TEDD TW11 176 D7
TIL RM18 168 B7
TOTM N17 99 M9
UX/CGN UB8 131 N6
WALTH E17 100 D10
WARL CR6 242 C3
WAT WD17 73 H5
WDR/YW UB7 151 N1
WDSR SL4 171 N1
WELL DA16 164 C3
WIM/MER SW19 201 N2
WLSDN NW10 136 D1
WOKN/KNAP GU21 231 M5
WPK KT4 200 B8
Churchway CAMTN NW1 5 H3
Churchwood Gdns WFD IG8 102 A3
Churchyard Rw LBTH SE11 18 E6
OXTED RH8 261 L6
SAND/SEL CR2 223 N6

| Name | Locality | Page | Grid |
|---|---|---|---|
| | TRDG/WHET N20 | 97 | P4 |
| Churchyard Rw LBTH SE11 | | 18 | D5 |
| Churston Av PLSTW E13 | | 141 | N3 |
| Churston Cl | | | |
| | BRXS/STRHM SW2 * | 181 | J4 |
| Churston Dr MRDN SM4 | | 200 | C5 |
| Churston Gdns | | | |
| | FBAR/BDGN N11 | 98 | D1 |
| Churston Av CHSWK W4 * | | 155 | N5 |
| | PIM SW1V | 17 | H6 |
| Churton St PIM SW1V | | 17 | H6 |
| Chuters Cl BF/WBF KT14 | | 216 | A8 |
| Chuters Gv EW KT17 | | 220 | C8 |
| The Chyne CFSP/GDCR SL9 | | 110 | C3 |
| Chyngton Cl BF/LL DA15 | | 185 | J6 |
| Cibber Rd FSTH SE23 | | 182 | C5 |
| Cicada Rd WAND/EARL SW18 | | 179 | M2 |
| Cicely Rd PECK SE15 | | 159 | P7 |
| Cidermill Rd RDKG RH5 | | 278 | B4 |
| Cilocks Cl HOD EN11 | | 44 | F2 |
| Cimba Wd GVE DA12 | | 191 | H7 |
| Cinderford Wy BMLY BR1 | | 183 | K1 |
| Cinema Pde EDGW HA8 * | | 95 | M7 |
| Cinnamon Cl CROY/NA CRO * | | 202 | F7 |
| | PECK SE15 | 159 | N6 |
| | WDSR SL4 | 148 | E7 |
| Cinnamon Gdns GUW GU2 | | 249 | M5 |
| Cinnamon St WAP E1W | | 140 | A10 |
| Cintra Pk NRWD SE19 | | 181 | H9 |
| Cippenham Cl SL SL1 | | 128 | E9 |
| Cippenham La SL SL1 | | 128 | E9 |
| | SL SL1 | 149 | H1 |
| Circle Gdns BF/WBF KT14 | | 216 | A8 |
| | WIM/MER SW19 | 201 | K3 |
| Circle Rd WOT/HER KT12 | | 216 | F6 |
| The Circle CRICK NW2 | | 116 | B8 |
| | MLHL NW7 | 96 | A7 |
| The Circuits PIN HA5 | | 113 | K2 |
| Circular Rd TOTM N17 | | 119 | N1 |
| Circular Wy WOOL/PLUM SE18 | | 162 | C5 |
| Circus Ms MBLAR W1H * | | 13 | H4 |
| Circus Pl LVPST EC2M * | | 13 | H4 |
| Circus St STJWD NW8 | | 3 | L9 |
| Circus St GNWCH SE10 | | 161 | H6 |
| The Circus LHD/OX KT22 * | | 236 | C6 |
| Cirencester St BAY/PAD W2 | | 8 | C3 |
| Cirrus Crs GVE DA12 | | 191 | H8 |
| Cissbury Hl CRAWW RH11 | | 283 | M9 |
| Cissbury Ring North | | | |
| | NFNCH/WDSPK N12 | 97 | J6 |
| Cissbury Ring South | | | |
| | NFNCH/WDSPK N12 | 97 | J6 |
| Cissbury Rd SEVS/STOTM N15 | | 119 | L3 |
| Citadel Pl LBTH SE11 | | 17 | N7 |
| Citizen Rd HOLWY N7 | | 119 | H8 |
| Citron Ter PECK SE15 * | | 160 | A9 |
| City Barracks SHB W12 * | | 136 | A6 |
| City Garden Rw IS N1 | | 6 | C4 |
| City Pk WCGE AL7 * | | 23 | K4 |
| City Rd FSBYE EC1V | | 6 | C6 |
| | STLK EC1Y | 13 | J3 |
| City Wk STHWK SE1 | | 19 | J3 |
| Civic Sq TIL RM18 | | 168 | B8 |
| Civic Wy BARK/HLT IG6 | | 122 | F2 |
| | RSLP HA4 | 113 | L10 |
| Clabon Ms KTBR SW1X | | 16 | A4 |
| Clacket La BF/WHM TN16 | | 244 | B10 |
| Clack Rd BERM/RHTH SE16 | | 160 | B1 |
| Clacton Rd TOTM N17 * | | 99 | N10 |
| | WALTH E17 | 120 | D4 |
| Claire Cswy RDART DA2 * | | 166 | D10 |
| Claire Cl RBRW/HUT CM13 | | 107 | M5 |
| Claire Gdns STAN HA7 | | 95 | H4 |
| Claire Pl POP/IOD E14 | | 160 | F2 |
| Clairvale EMPK RM11 | | 125 | M5 |
| Clairvale Rd HEST TW5 | | 153 | L7 |
| Clairview Rd | | | |
| | STRHM/NOR SW16 | 180 | C8 |
| Clairville Gdns HNWL W7 | | 134 | D10 |
| Clammas Wy UX/CGN UB8 | | 131 | M7 |
| Clancarty Rd FUL/PGN SW6 | | 157 | K8 |
| Clandon Av EGH TW20 | | 172 | A10 |
| Clandon Cl ACT W3 | | 155 | N1 |
| | EW KT17 | 220 | E3 |
| Clandon Gdns FNCH N3 | | 117 | K1 |
| | GU GU1 | 268 | B1 |
| | RGUE GU4 | 251 | K2 |
| Clandon St DEPT SE8 | | 160 | F8 |
| Clandon Ter RYNPK SW20 * | | 200 | G2 |
| Clanricarde Gdns | | | |
| | BAY/PAD W2 | 8 | B9 |
| Clapgate Rd BUSH WD23 | | 74 | A10 |
| Clapham Common North Side | | | |
| | CLAP SW4 | 158 | B10 |
| Clapham Common South Side | | | |
| | CLAP SW4 | 180 | C1 |
| Clapham Common West Side | | | |
| | BTSEA SW11 | 158 | A10 |
| Clapham Court Ter | | | |
| | CLAP SW4 * | 180 | F1 |
| Clapham Crs CLAP SW4 | | 158 | E10 |
| Clapham High St CLAP SW4 | | 158 | D9 |
| Clapham Manor Est CLAP SW4 * | | 158 | C9 |
| Clapham Park Est CLAP SW4 | | 158 | D10 |
| Clapham Park Rd CLAP SW4 | | 158 | D10 |
| Clapham Park Ter | | | |
| | BRXS/STRHM SW2 * | 180 | F1 |
| Clapham Rd BRXN/ST SW9 | | 158 | B8 |
| Clappers Ga CRAWE RH10 | | 283 | H6 |
| Clappers La CHOB/PIR GU24 | | 213 | H10 |
| Clapps Gate La EHAM E6 | | 142 | G1 |
| Clapton Common CLPT E5 | | 119 | P5 |
| Clapton Pas CLPT E5 | | 120 | B10 |
| Clapton Sq CLPT E5 | | 120 | B10 |
| Clapton Ter CLPT E5 | | 119 | P9 |
| Clapton Wy CLPT E5 | | 119 | P9 |
| Clara Pl WOOL/PLUM SE18 | | 162 | G9 |
| Clare Cswy RDART DA2 | | 166 | D10 |
| Clare Cl BF/WBF KT14 | | 215 | K9 |
| | BORE WD6 | 74 | D4 |
| | CRAWE RH10 | 284 | C4 |
| | EFNCH N2 | 117 | M1 |
| Clare Cnr ELTH/MOT SE9 | | 184 | H4 |
| Clare Ct CTHM CR3 | | 242 | F9 |
| | NTHWD HA6 | 92 | H4 |
| | SOCK/AV RM15 | 166 | B1 |
| Claredale St BETH E2 | | 7 | P8 |
| Clare Dr SLN SL2 | | 108 | C9 |
| Clare Gdns BARK IG11 | | 123 | L5 |
| | EGH TW20 | 172 | D8 |
| | FSTGT E7 | 121 | M9 |
| | NTGHL W11 | 8 | B6 |
| Clare Lawn Av | | | |
| | MORT/ESHN SW14 | 178 | A3 |
| Clare Ms CHONG CM5 | | 67 | H2 |
| | FUL/PGN SW6 | 157 | L6 |
| Claremont CHSWK EN7 | | 61 | N5 |
| | LCOL/BKTW AL2 | 55 | P7 |
| Claremont Av ESH/CLAY KT10 | | 217 | N3 |
| | KTN/HRWW/WS HA3 | 115 | N3 |
| | NWMAL KT3 | 200 | E5 |
| | SUN TW16 | 197 | J1 |
| | WOKS/MYFD GU22 | 232 | B5 |
| | WOT/HER KT12 | 217 | L1 |
| Claremont Cl | | | |
| | BRXN/ST SW9 | 180 | G4 |
| | CAN/RD E16 | 142 | D10 |
| | IS N1 | 167 | P2 (?) |
| | ORP BR6 | 226 | A1 |
| | SAND/SEL CR2 | 242 | A1 |
| | WOT/HER KT12 | 217 | L1 |
| Claremont Crs DART DA1 | | 164 | C2 |
| | RKW/CH/CXG WD3 | 50 | C7 |
| Claremont Dr ESH/CLAY KT10 | | 218 | A4 |
| | SHPTN TW17 | 196 | G6 |
| | WOKS/MYFD GU22 | 232 | B5 |
| Claremont End | | | |
| | ESH/CLAY KT10 | 218 | A3 |
| Claremont Gdns | | | |
| | GDMY/SEVK IG3 | 123 | H9 |
| | SURB KT6 | 199 | K4 |
| | UPMR RM14 | 126 | C6 |
| Claremont Gv CHSWK W4 | | 156 | B6 |
| | WFD IG8 | 101 | P7 |
| Claremont House | | | |
| | WATW WD18 * | 72 | E10 |
| Claremont La ESH/CLAY KT10 | | 218 | A2 |
| Claremont Pk FNCH N3 | | 97 | H9 |
| Claremont Park Rd | | | |
| | ESH/CLAY KT10 | 217 | P3 |
| Claremont Rd BF/WBF KT14 | | 215 | K8 |
| | BMLY BR1 | 206 | B4 |
| | CRICK NW2 | 116 | F5 |
| | EBAR EN4 | 77 | M4 |
| | ESH/CLAY KT10 | 218 | D4 |
| | FSTGT E7 | 121 | N10 |
| | GLDGN NW11 | 116 | B3 |
| | HGT N6 | 118 | C5 |
| | KTN/HRWW/WS HA3 | 94 | D10 |
| | MV/WKIL W9 | 2 | B8 |
| | REDH RH1 | 258 | B8 |
| | STA TW18 | 172 | G8 |
| | SURB KT6 | 199 | K4 |
| | SWLY BR8 | 186 | F10 |
| | TEDD TW11 | 176 | E8 |
| | WALTH E17 | 100 | D10 |
| | WAN E11 | 121 | J8 |
| | WDSR SL4 | 149 | H8 |
| | WEA W13 | 134 | F2 |
| Claremont Sq IS N1 | | 6 | A8 |
| Claremont Ter THDIT KT7 * | | 198 | G2 |
| Claremont Vls CMBW SE5 * | | 159 | L2 |
| | WKENS W14 * | 137 | K4 |
| Claremont Wy CRICK NW2 | | 116 | B8 |
| Claremount Cl EPSOM KT18 | | 238 | F3 |
| Claremount Gdns | | | |
| | EPSOM KT18 | 238 | F3 |
| Clarence Av BMLY BR1 | | 206 | B4 |
| | CLAP SW4 | 180 | E2 |
| | IL IG1 | 122 | C4 |
| | NWMAL KT3 | 199 | P2 |
| | UPMR RM14 | 125 | P7 |
| Clarence Cl BUSH WD23 | | 94 | L1 |
| | EBAR EN4 | 77 | N9 |
| | WOT/HER KT12 | 217 | J1 |
| Clarence Ct HORL RH6 | | 280 | F11 |
| | MLHL NW7 * | 96 | B6 |
| Clarence Crs CLAP SW4 | | 180 | E2 |
| | SCUP DA14 | 185 | L6 |
| | WDSR SL4 | 149 | H7 |
| Clarence Dr ECH TW20 | | 171 | P7 |
| | FNCH N3 | 4 | F10 |
| Clarence Gdns CAMTN NW1 * | | 4 | D2 |
| Clarence Ga CAMTN NW1 * | | 10 | B1 |
| Clarence Ms BERM/RHTH SE16 | | 140 | C10 |
| | CLPT E5 | 120 | A10 |
| | TOOT SW17 | 179 | M6 |
| Clarence Pas CAMTN NW1 * | | 5 | J1 |
| Clarence Pl CLPT E5 | | 120 | A10 |
| | GVE DA12 | 190 | E3 |
| Clarence Rd BERK HP4 | | 33 | L5 |
| | BH/WHM TN16 | 244 | C4 |
| | BMLY BR1 | 206 | B3 |
| | BRWN CM15 | 86 | C10 |
| | BXLYHS DA6 | 163 | P10 |
| | CAN/RD E16 | 141 | K6 |
| | CHSWK W4 | 155 | M4 |
| | CLPT E5 | 120 | A9 |
| | CROY/NA CRO | 203 | L7 |
| | DEPT SE8 | 160 | G5 |
| | ELTH/MOT SE9 | 184 | B5 |
| | GRAYS RM17 | 167 | M5 |
| | KIL/WHAMP NW6 | 2 | C4 |
| | MNPK E12 | 121 | P9 |
| | PEND EN3 | 30 | B9 |
| | RCH/KEW TW9 | 155 | L7 |
| | REDH RH1 | 275 | N3 |
| | SCUP DA14 | 185 | L6 |
| | SEVS/STOTM N15 | 119 | K3 |
| | STAL AL1 | 38 | F6 |
| | SUT SM1 | 221 | L1 |
| | TEDD TW11 | 176 | B9 |
| | WALTH E17 | 120 | C4 |
| | WDGN N22 | 98 | G10 |
| | WDSR SL4 | 148 | F8 |
| | WIM/MER SW19 | 179 | L9 |
| | WLGTN SM6 | 222 | C4 |
| | WOT/HER KT12 | 217 | J1 |
| Clarence Rw GVE DA12 | | 190 | E3 |
| Clarence St ECH TW20 | | 172 | C9 |
| | KUT/HW KT1 | 199 | J2 |
| | NWDGN UB2 | 153 | L2 |
| | RCH/KEW TW9 | 155 | L8 |
| | STHL TW13 (?) | 173 | H7 |
| Clarence Ter CAMTN NW1 * | | 10 | B1 |
| | HSLW TW3 | 154 | A10 |
| Clarence Vls KUT/HW KT1 * | | 199 | L2 |
| | WKENS W14 * | 137 | K4 |
| Clarence Wy CAMTN NW1 | | 4 | E3 |
| | HORL RH6 | 280 | E3 |
| Clarenden Flds | | | |
| | RKW/CH/CXG WD3 | 72 | A4 |
| Clarendon Cl BAY/PAD W2 * | | 9 | N5 |
| | HHNE HP2 | 35 | N5 |
| | HOM E9 | 140 | B2 |
| | STMC/STPC BR5 | 207 | K3 |
| Clarendon Crs WHTN TW2 | | 176 | B6 |
| Clarendon Gdns HDN NW4 | | 116 | D1 |
| | IL IG1 | 122 | C6 |
| | MV/WKIL W9 | 9 | K2 |
| | RDART DA2 | 188 | C3 |
| | WBLY HA9 | 115 | J8 |
| Clarendon Ga BAY/PAD W2 | | 9 | K4 |
| | CHERT KT16 | 214 | C3 |
| Clarendon Gn STMC/STPC BR5 | | 207 | J4 |
| Clarendon Gv MTCM CR4 | | 202 | A3 |
| | STMC/STPC BR5 | 207 | K4 |
| Clarendon Ms ASHTD KT21 | | 237 | K5 |
| | BAY/PAD W2 | 9 | K4 |
| | BORE WD6 * | 75 | M7 |
| Clarendon Pth | | | |
| | STMC/STPC BR5 | 207 | K4 |
| Clarendon Pl BAY/PAD W2 | | 9 | N7 |
| | RDART DA2 | 188 | C3 |
| | SEV TN13 * | 265 | H1 |
| Clarendon Ri LEW SE13 | | 161 | H1 |
| Clarendon Rd ASHF TW15 | | 174 | A7 |
| | BORE WD6 | 75 | M7 |
| | CEND/HSY/T N8 | 118 | C1 |
| | CHES/WCR EN8 | 62 | C5 |
| | CROY/NA CRO | 203 | J5 |
| | EA W5 | 135 | K2 |
| | GVE DA12 | 190 | F2 |
| | HRW HA1 | 114 | D4 |
| | HYS/HAR UB3 | 152 | C1 |
| | NTGHL W11 | 8 | B7 |
| | REDH RH1 | 258 | A9 |
| | SEV TN13 | 247 | H10 |
| | SEVS/STOTM N15 | 119 | J2 |
| | SWFD E18 | 121 | M1 |
| | UED N18 | 99 | M7 |
| | WALTH E17 | 100 | E3 |
| | WAN E11 | 121 | J6 |
| | WAT WD17 | 73 | J7 |
| | WDGN N22 | 98 | G10 |
| | WIM/MER SW19 | 179 | P10 |
| | WLGTN SM6 | 222 | D4 |
| Clarendon St PIM SW1V | | 16 | F8 |
| Clarendon Ter MV/WKIL W9 | | 9 | K1 |
| Clarendon Wy CHST BR7 | | 207 | J1 |
| | WCHMH N21 | 99 | K1 |
| Clare Pde GFD/PVL UB6 * | | 134 | C1 |
| Clare Pk AMSS HP7 | | 69 | K6 |
| Clare Rd GFD/PVL UB6 | | 134 | C1 |
| | HSLWW TW4 | 153 | N9 |
| | MDHD SL6 | 128 | B8 |
| | NWCR SE14 | 160 | E8 |
| | STWL/WRAY TW19 | 173 | N3 |
| | WAN E11 | 121 | J4 |
| | WLSDN NW10 | 136 | D2 |
| The Clares CTHM CR5 | | 241 | P10 |
| Clare St BETH E2 | | 140 | A4 |
| Claret Gdns SNWD SE25 | | 203 | M4 |
| Clareville Gv SKENS SW7 | | 15 | K6 |
| Clareville Rd CTHM CR3 | | 241 | P10 |
| | STMC/STPC BR5 | 206 | F9 |
| Clareville Sq SKENS SW7 | | 15 | K6 |
| Clare Wy BXLYHN DA7 | | 163 | P7 |
| | SEV TN13 | 265 | K3 |
| Clare Wd LHD/OX KT22 | | 236 | F4 |
| Clarice Wy WLGTN SM6 | | 222 | F6 |
| Claridge Rd BCTR RM8 | | 123 | N6 |
| Clarissa Rd CHDH RM6 | | 121 | P5 |
| Clarissa St HACK E8 | | 7 | L5 |
| Clarkbourne Dr GRAYS RM17 | | 168 | H1 |
| Clarke Cl CROY/NA CRO | | 202 | E4 |
| Clarke Ms CAVSQ/HST W1G | | 10 | D5 |
| Clarke's Rd HAT AL10 | | 40 | C2 |
| Clarkfield RKW/CH/CXG WD3 | | 91 | K2 |
| Clark Gv IL IG1 | | 123 | H9 |
| Clarkhill HLWS CM18 | | 47 | H4 |
| Clarks La EPP CM16 | | 65 | J7 |
| | OXTED RH8 | 243 | N9 |
| | RSEV TN14 | 228 | A10 |
| Clarks Md BUSH WD23 | | 94 | B1 |
| Clarkson Rd CAN/RD E16 | | 141 | A8 |
| Clarkson Rw CAMTN NW1 | | 4 | E5 |
| Clarkson St BETH E2 | | 140 | A5 |
| Clark's Rd IL IG1 | | 122 | G7 |
| Clark St WCHPL E1 | | 140 | B8 |
| Clarks Ter HEST TW5 | | 153 | L5 |
| Classon Cl WDR/YW UB7 | | 132 | B1 |
| Classon Cl DART DA1 | | 164 | F10 |
| Claude Monet Ct EDUL SE22 * | | 161 | J1 |
| Claude Rd LEY E10 | | 121 | H6 |
| | PECK SE15 | 160 | A8 |
| | PLSTW E13 | 141 | N3 |
| Claudian Pl STALW/RED AL3 | | 37 | P7 |
| Claudian Wy CDW/CHF RM16 | | 168 | L2 |
| Claudia Pl WIM/MER SW19 | | 179 | H4 |
| Claughton Rd PLSTW E13 | | 141 | P4 |
| Clauson Av NTHLT UB5 | | 114 | A10 |
| Clavell St GNWCH SE10 | | 161 | H5 |
| Claverdale Rd | | | |
| | BRXS/STRHM SW2 | 181 | J1 |
| Claverhambury Rd WAB EN9 | | 63 | L3 |
| Clavering Av BARN SW13 | | 156 | K6 |
| Clavering Cl TEDD TW11 | | 176 | F7 |
| Clavering Rd MNPK E12 | | 122 | A6 |
| Clavering Wy | | | |
| | RBRW/HUT CM13 | 87 | P10 |
| Claverley Gv FNCH N3 | | 97 | J3 |
| Claverley Vls FNCH N3 | | 97 | K3 |
| Claverton Cl HHS/BOV HP3 | | 52 | L5 |
| Clave St WAP E1W | | 140 | B10 |
| Claxton Gv HMSMTH W6 | | 156 | G4 |
| Clay Av MTCM CR4 | | 202 | C2 |
| Claybridge Rd LEE/GVPK SE12 | | 183 | P7 |
| Claybrook Cl EFNCH N2 | | 117 | N1 |
| Claybrook Rd HMSMTH W6 | | 156 | G4 |
| Clayburn Gdns SOCK/AV RM15 | | 146 | G10 |
| Claybury BUSH WD23 | | 94 | A1 |
| Claybury Rd WFD IG8 | | 102 | B8 |
| Clay Cnr CHERT KT16 | | 214 | G6 |
| Clay La BUSH WD23 | | 94 | D1 |
| | EPSOM KT18 | 237 | N10 |
| | REDH RH1 | 276 | D1 |
| | RGUE GU4 | 250 | A4 |
| | STWL/WRAY TW19 | 150 | F9 |
| Claymills Ms HHS/BOV HP3 | | 36 | B9 |
| Claymore HHNE HP2 | | 35 | P2 |
| Claymore Cl MRDN SM4 | | 201 | K7 |
| Claypit Hl WAB EN9 | | 78 | E1 |
| Claypole Dr HEST TW5 | | 153 | M7 |
| Claypole Rd SRTFD E15 | | 141 | H4 |
| Clayponds Av BTFD TW8 | | 135 | P8 |
| Clayponds Gdns EA W5 | | 155 | J3 |
| Clayponds La BTFD TW8 | | 155 | P7 |
| Clayside CHIG IG7 | | 102 | F6 |
| Clay's La LOU IG10 | | 82 | D5 |
| Clay St MHST W1U | | 10 | A3 |
| Clayton Av ALP/SUD HA0 | | 135 | N1 |
| | UPMR RM14 | 125 | P6 |
| Clayton Cl EHAM E6 | | 142 | C8 |
| Clayton Crs BTFD TW8 | | 135 | N6 |
| | IS N1 | 5 | N6 |
| Clayton Dr DEPT SE8 | | 160 | D4 |
| | GUW GU2 | 249 | L7 |
| | HHS/BOV HP3 | 52 | E10 |
| Clayton Fld CDALE/KGS NW9 | | 95 | B10 |
| Clayton Hl CRAWW RH11 | | 283 | M9 |
| Clayton Md GDST RH9 | | 260 | A6 |
| Clayton Pde DTCH/LGLY SL3 | | 129 | L10 |
| Clayton Rd CHSGTN KT9 | | 219 | H1 |
| | EW KT17 | 220 | B8 |
| | HYS/HAR UB3 | 153 | C1 |
| | ISLW TW7 | 154 | A8 |
| | PECK SE15 | 160 | A8 |
| | ROMW/RG RM7 | 124 | C4 |
| Clayton St LBTH SE11 | | 158 | C1 |
| Clayton Ter YEAD UB4 | | 133 | J4 |
| Claytonville Ter BELV DA17 * | | 147 | K2 |
| Clay Tye Rd UPMR RM14 | | 125 | P5 |
| Clay Wood Cl ORP BR6 | | 207 | H8 |
| Claywood La RDART DA2 | | 189 | H3 |
| Clayworth Cl BFN/LL DA15 | | 167 | L2 |
| Cleall Av WAB EN9 | | 78 | B10 |
| Cleanthus Cl | | | |
| | WOOL/PLUM SE18 | 162 | G1 |
| Cleanthus Rd | | | |
| | WOOL/PLUM SE18 | 162 | G1 |
| Clearbrook Wy WCHPL E1 | | 140 | D8 |
| Cleardene DORK RH4 | | 272 | G2 |
| Cleardown WOKS/MYFD GU22 | | 232 | E4 |
| Cleares Pasture SL SL1 | | 128 | A4 |
| The Clears REIG RH2 | | 257 | H8 |
| Clearwater Ter WKENS W14 * | | 156 | G1 |
| Clearwell Dr MV/WKIL W9 | | 9 | H2 |
| | ORP BR6 | 227 | H4 |
| Cleave Av HYS/HAR UB3 | | 152 | F3 |
| | ORP BR6 | 226 | F10 |
| Cleaveland Rd SURB KT6 | | 199 | J5 |
| Cleave Prior COUL/CHIP CR5 | | 239 | P5 |
| Cleaverholme Cl SNWD SE25 | | 204 | A6 |
| Cleaver Sq LBTH SE11 | | 18 | B7 |
| Cleaver St LBTH SE11 | | 18 | B7 |
| Cleeve Ct EBED/NFELT TW14 | | 174 | A6 |
| Cleeve Hl FSTH SE23 | | 182 | A4 |
| Cleeve Park Gdns SCUP DA14 | | 186 | C5 |
| The Cleeve GU GU1 | | 250 | D10 |
| Cleeve Wy PUT/ROE SW15 | | 178 | C2 |
| | SUT SM1 | 201 | L8 |
| Clegg St PLSTW E13 | | 141 | L1 |
| | WAP E1W | 140 | B10 |
| Cleland Pth LOU IG10 | | 82 | E5 |
| Clematis Cl HARH RM3 | | 124 | B2 |
| Clematis Cots SHB W12 * | | 136 | D9 |
| Clematis Gdns WFD IG8 | | 101 | M6 |
| Clematis St SHB W12 | | 136 | C5 |
| Clem Attlee Pde | | | |
| | FUL/PGN SW6 | 14 | D9 |
| Clemence St POP/IOD E14 | | 140 | D7 |
| Clement Av CLAP SW4 | | 158 | E10 |
| Clement Cl CHSWK W4 | | 146 | A3 |
| | KIL/WHAMP NW6 | 136 | F2 |
| | PUR/KEN CR8 | 241 | J2 |
| Clement Gdns HYS/HAR UB3 | | 152 | F3 |
| Clementhorpe Rd DAGW RM9 | | 143 | M1 |
| Clementina Rd LEY E10 | | 121 | H6 |
| Clementine Cl WEA W13 | | 154 | G1 |
| Clementine Wy HHW HP1 | | 35 | L8 |
| Clement Rd BECK BR3 | | 204 | C2 |
| | WIM/MER SW19 | 179 | H4 |
| Clements Av CAN/RD E16 | | 141 | M4 |
| Clements Cl | | | |
| | NFNCH/WDSPK N12 | 97 | L5 |
| | SL SL1 | 149 | N1 |
| Clements Inn LINN WC2A | | 11 | P4 |
| Clements La IL IG1 | | 122 | E8 |
| | MANHO EC4N | 13 | J5 |
| Clements Rd BERM/RHTH SE16 | | 19 | M9 |
| | WARE SG12 | 26 | D2 |
| Clement Sq SWLY BR8 | | 187 | L5 |
| Clement Wy UPMR RM14 | | 125 | N8 |
| Clenches Farm La SEV TN13 | | 265 | H4 |
| Clendon Wy | | | |
| | WOOL/PLUM SE18 | 162 | G3 |
| Clennam St STHWK SE1 * | | 19 | H2 |
| Clensham Ct SUT SM1 | | 201 | K9 |
| Clensham La SUT SM1 | | 201 | K9 |
| Clenston Ms MBLAR W1H | | 10 | A5 |
| Cleopatra Cl STAN HA7 | | 95 | J4 |
| Clephane Rd IS N1 | | 6 | F1 |
| Clephane Rd North IS N1 | | 6 | F1 |
| Clere St SDTCH EC2A | | 13 | H1 |
| Clerkenwell Cl CLKNW EC1R | | 12 | B1 |
| Clerkenwell Gn CLKNW EC1R | | 12 | C2 |
| Clerkenwell Rd CLKNW EC1R | | 12 | A2 |
| Clerks Cft REDH RH1 | | 259 | L9 |
| Clerks Piece LOU IG10 | | 82 | C7 |
| Clermont Rd HOM E9 | | 140 | B3 |
| Clevedon Cl STHGT/OAK N14 | | 98 | F5 |
| Clevedon Gdns CRICK NW2 * | | 115 | P2 |
| | HYS/HAR UB3 | 152 | E2 |
| Clevedon Rd KUT/HW KT1 | | 200 | C2 |
| | PGE/AN SE20 | 183 | L10 |
| | TWK TW1 | 177 | J2 |
| Clevehurst Cl SLN SL2 | | 129 | L1 |
| Cleveland Av CHSWK W4 | | 156 | C3 |
| | HPTN TW12 | 175 | N10 |
| | WIM/MER SW19 | 179 | J9 |
| Cleveland Crs BORE WD6 | | 75 | H4 |
| Cleveland Dr STA TW18 | | 195 | L2 |
| Cleveland Gdns BARN SW13 | | 156 | B5 |
| | BAY/PAD W2 | 8 | E5 |
| | CRICK NW2 | 116 | B4 |
| | SEVS/STOTM N15 | 119 | K3 |
| | WPK KT4 | 200 | B1 |
| Cleveland Gv WCHPL E1 | | 140 | E7 |
| Cleveland Ms FITZ W1T | | 10 | E1 |
| Cleveland Pk WALTH E17 * | | 120 | D1 |
| Cleveland Park Av | | | |
| | WALTH E17 | 120 | D1 |
| Cleveland Park Crs | | | |
| | WALTH E17 | 120 | D1 |
| Cleveland Pl STJS SW1Y | | 11 | H10 |
| Cleveland Ri MRDN SM4 | | 201 | H6 |
| Cleveland Rd BARN SW13 | | 156 | A5 |
| | CHSWK W4 | 155 | P2 |
| | ED N9 | 100 | C4 |
| | HHNE HP2 | 35 | P2 |
| | IL IG1 | 122 | C6 |
| | ISLW TW7 | 154 | A8 |
| | IS N1 | 6 | F1 |
| | NWMAL KT3 | 200 | C2 |
| | SWFD E18 | 121 | M1 |
| | UX/CGN UB8 | 131 | N6 |
| | WEA W13 | 134 | F7 |
| | WELL DA16 | 147 | P4 |
| | WPK KT4 | 200 | B1 |
| Cleveland Sq BAY/PAD W2 | | 8 | E5 |
| Cleveland St FITZ W1T | | 4 | D10 |
| Cleveland Ter BAY/PAD W2 | | 8 | E5 |
| Cleveland Wy HHNE HP2 | | 35 | P2 |
| | WCHPL E1 | 140 | E7 |
| Cleveley Crs EA W5 | | 135 | K4 |
| Cleveleys Rd CLPT E5 | | 120 | B10 |
| Cleverly Cl CHARL SE7 | | 162 | A3 |
| Cleverly Est SHB W12 | | 136 | D10 |
| Cleve Rd KIL/WHAMP NW6 | | 2 | B1 |
| | SCUP DA14 | 186 | E6 |
| Cleves Av CHOB/PIR GU24 | | 232 | B9 |
| | EW KT17 | 220 | E10 |
| Cleves Cl COB KT11 | | 217 | J10 |
| | LOU IG10 | 82 | B10 |
| Cleves Ct WDSR SL4 | | 148 | A5 |
| Cleves Crs CROY/NA CRO | | 225 | H10 |
| Cleves Rd BGR/WK TN15 | | 143 | A2 |
| | EHAM E6 | 142 | A2 |
| | HHNE HP2 | 35 | P2 |
| | RCHPK/HAM TW10 | 176 | A7 |
| Cleves Wy BARK/HLT IG6 | | 103 | L6 |
| | HPTN TW12 | 175 | J8 |
| | RSLP HA4 | 77 | H9 |
| | SUN TW16 | 174 | E7 |
| Cleves Wd WEY KT13 | | 196 | G4 |
| Clewer Av | | | |
| Clewer Court Rd WDSR SL4 | | 148 | A5 |
| Clewer Crs | | | |
| | KTN/HRWW/WS HA3 | 94 | C9 |
| Clewer Flds WDSR SL4 | | 148 | A5 |
| Clewer Hill Rd WDSR SL4 | | 148 | A6 |
| Clewer New Town WDSR SL4 | | 148 | A6 |
| Clewer Rd WDSR SL4 | | 148 | B4 |
| | PLSTW E13 | 141 | N5 |
| | CDW/CHF RM16 | 167 | K2 |
| | CRW RM5 | 104 | D8 |
| | EBED/NFELT TW14 | 174 | A6 |
| Clockhouse La East EGH TW20 | | 172 | E10 |
| Clockhouse La West | | | |
| | EGH TW20 | 172 | E10 |
| Clockhouse Md LHD/OX KT22 | | 218 | A10 |
| Clock House Pde | | | |
| | RKW/CH/CXG WD3 | 71 | N7 |
| Clockhouse Pl PUT/ROE SW15 | | 179 | H1 |
| Clock House Rd BECK BR3 | | 204 | D3 |
| Clock Pde ENC/FH EN2 * | | 79 | L9 |
| Clock Tower Crs HOLWY N7 | | 5 | L1 |
| Clocktower Ms HNWL W7 * | | 134 | D10 |
| Clock Tower Ms IS N1 | | 6 | D2 |
| Clock Tower Pl HOLWY N7 * | | 5 | L1 |
| Clock Tower Rd ISLW TW7 | | 154 | A8 |
| Clodhouse Hi | | | |
| | WOKS/MYFD GU22 | 231 | H8 |
| Cloister Cl HARH RM3 | | 145 | K6 |
| | TEDD TW11 | 176 | D2 |
| Cloister Gdns EDGW HA8 | | 95 | P6 |
| | SNWD SE25 | 204 | A6 |
| Cloister Garth BERK HP4 | | 33 | L5 |
| | STAL AL1 | 38 | D10 |
| Cloisters Av ACT W3 | | 135 | P7 |
| | CRICK NW2 | 117 | J8 |
| Cloister Rd ACT W3 | | 135 | P7 |
| | CRICK NW2 | 116 | C1 |
| The Cloisters HARP AL5 | | 20 | B5 |
| | HHS/BOV HP3 | 36 | B5 |
| | RKW/CH/CXG WD3 | 91 | P7 |
| | WGCW AL8 | 22 | C5 |
| | WOKS/MYFD GU22 | 232 | E7 |
| Cloister Wy HHNE HP2 | | 35 | N4 |
| | HAYES BR2 | 206 | C5 |
| | HHNE HP2 | 35 | N4 |
| Cloonmore Av ORP BR6 | | 227 | J2 |
| Clonard Wy PIN HA5 | | 94 | A5 |
| Clonbrock Rd STNW/STAM N16 | | 119 | P6 |
| Cloncurry St FUL/PGN SW6 | | 156 | G8 |
| Clonmel Cl ALP/SUD HA0 | | 114 | C6 |
| Clonmell Rd TOTM N17 | | 119 | L1 |
| Clonmel Rd FUL/PGN SW6 | | 157 | J6 |
| | TEDD TW11 | 176 | C7 |
| Clonmore Wy SL SL1 | | 128 | A3 |
| Clonmore St | | | |
| | WAND/EARL SW18 | 179 | J4 |
| Cloonmore Av ORP BR6 | | 227 | J2 |
| Clorane Gdns HAMP NW3 | | 117 | K8 |
| Closemead Cl NTHWD HA6 | | 92 | D7 |
| The Close ALP/SUD HA0 | | 135 | K1 |
| | BECK BR3 | 204 | D4 |
| | BF/WBF KT14 | 215 | K9 |
| | BH/WHM TN16 | 244 | E1 |
| | BRKHM/BTCW RH3 | 273 | N4 |
| | BRKMPK AL9 | 40 | C3 |
| | BRW CM14 | 107 | J4 |
| | BUSH WD23 * | 73 | P10 |
| | BXLY DA5 | 186 | B2 |
| | CAR SM5 | 221 | P5 |
| | CDW/CHF RM16 | 167 | N1 |
| | CHDH RM6 | 123 | P4 |
| | CHEAM SM3 | 201 | J7 |
| | CHING E4 | 101 | H8 |
| | EBAR EN4 | 78 | A10 |
| | GNTH/NBYPK IG2 | 123 | H4 |
| | HCDN/ICK UB10 | 131 | P2 |
| | HHS/BOV HP3 | 52 | F4 |
| | HORL RH6 | 280 | D6 |
| | ISLW TW7 | 154 | C8 |
| | IVER SL0 | 130 | F5 |
| | MTCM CR4 | 202 | A4 |
| | NWMAL KT3 | 199 | P2 |
| | PIN HA5 | 113 | K5 |
| | POTB/CUF EN6 | 59 | K8 |
| | PUR/KEN CR8 | 222 | G6 |
| | RAD WD7 | 56 | E9 |
| | RCH/KEW TW9 | 155 | N9 |
| | REIG RH2 | 275 | L1 |
| | RKW/CH/CXG WD3 | 91 | L2 |
| | SCUP DA14 | 185 | L8 |
| | SEV TN13 | 246 | F10 |
| | SHGR GU5 | 268 | G10 |
| | SL SL1 | 128 | C9 |
| | SNWD SE25 * | 203 | P6 |
| | STAL AL1 | 38 | E8 |
| | STMT/OAK N14 | 98 | E2 |
| | STMC/STPC BR5 | 199 | K7 |
| | SURB KT6 | 199 | K7 |
| | TRDG/WHET N20 | 97 | J3 |
| | VW GU25 | 194 | A5 |
| | WBLY HA9 | 115 | P8 |
| | WOKS/MYFD GU22 | 232 | E3 |
| Cloth Ct STBT EC1A | | 12 | D4 |
| Cloth Fair STBT EC1A | | 12 | D4 |
| Clothier St HDTCH EC3A | | 13 | L5 |
| Cloth St STBT EC1A | | 13 | H2 |
| Clothworkers Rd | | | |
| | WOOL/PLUM SE18 | 162 | G6 |
| Cloudberry Rd HARH RM3 | | 105 | J7 |
| Cloudesdale Rd TOOT SW17 | | 180 | C5 |
| Cloudesley Pl IS N1 | | 5 | P3 |
| Cloudesley Rd BXLYHN DA7 | | 164 | A7 |
| | ERITH DA8 | 164 | G7 |
| | IS N1 | 6 | A3 |
| Cloudesley Sq IS N1 | | 6 | A3 |
| Cloudesley St IS N1 | | 6 | A3 |
| Clouston Cl WLGTN SM6 | | 222 | F2 |
| Clova Rd FSTGT E7 | | 121 | N10 |
| Clove Crs POP/IOD E14 | | 141 | N8 |
| Clovelly Av CDALE/KGS NW9 | | 116 | C2 |
| | HGDN/ICK UB10 | 112 | D9 |
| | WARL CR6 | 242 | A4 |
| Clovelly Cl HGDN/ICK UB10 | | 112 | D9 |
| | PIN HA5 | 113 | J1 |
| Clovelly Gdns EN EN1 | | 90 | B1 |
| | ROMW/RG RM7 | 104 | C9 |
| Clovelly Rd BXLYHN DA7 | | 163 | P5 |
| | CEND/HSY/T N8 | 118 | B1 |
| | CHSWK W4 | 156 | A1 |
| | EA W5 | 155 | H1 |
| | HSLW TW3 | 153 | P8 |
| Clovelly Wy ORP BR6 | | 207 | K8 |
| | RYLN/HDSTN HA2 | 113 | N8 |
| | WCHPL E1 | 140 | D8 |
| Clover Cl WAN E11 * | | 121 | P2 |
| Clover Ct WOKS/MYFD GU22 | | 232 | A4 |
| Cloverdale Gdns BFN/LL DA15 | | 185 | J2 |
| Clover Fld HLWS CM18 | | 47 | K4 |
| Cloverfields HORL RH6 | | 280 | C2 |
| The Clover Fld BUSH WD23 | | 73 | N10 |
| Clover Hl COUL/CHIP CR5 | | 240 | C7 |
| Cloverland HAT AL10 | | 40 | A2 |
| Clover Lea GODL GU7 | | 267 | K3 |
| Clover Leas EPP CM16 | | 65 | J7 |
| Clover Ms CHEL SW3 | | 16 | A9 |
| Clover Rd CHONG CM5 | | 16 | A9 (?) |
| | GUW GU2 | 249 | K5 |
| The Clovers GVW DA11 | | 190 | B7 |
| Clover Wk SEV TN13 | | 265 | K8 |
| Clover Wy HHW HP1 | | 35 | L5 |
| | HORL RH6 | 281 | K4 |
| | WLGTN SM6 | 202 | B8 |
| Clove St PLSTW E13 | | 141 | M6 |
| Clowders Rd CAT SE6 | | 182 | G6 |
| Clowser Cl SUT SM1 * | | 222 | A2 |
| Cloyster Wd EDGW HA8 | | 95 | J3 |
| Club Gardens Rd HAYES BR2 | | 205 | M7 |
| Club Rw BETH E2 | | 13 | L1 |
| Clunas Gdns GPK RM2 | | 125 | L1 |
| Clunbury Av NWDGN UB2 | | 153 | N4 |
| Clunbury St IS N1 | | 7 | H6 |
| Cluny Est STHWK SE1 | | 14 | S6 (?) |
| Cluny Ms ECT SW5 | | 14 | E4 |
| Cluny Pl STHWK SE1 | | 19 | K3 |
| Clifford St CONDST W1S | | 10 | D7 |
| | CLAY IG5 | 102 | C9 |
| | RCH/KEW TW9 | 155 | M8 |
| | WLGTN SM6 | 222 | D6 |
| Clifford Wy WLSDN NW10 | | 116 | C10 |
| Clifton Gdns CHSWK W4 | | 156 | A3 |
| | WLSDN NW10 | 136 | D2 |
| Clifford Gv ASHF TW15 | | 174 | H4 |
| Clifford Manor Rd RGUE GU4 | | 268 | B4 |
| Clifford Rd ALP/SUD HA0 | | 135 | J3 |
| | BAR EN5 | 77 | L7 |
| | CAN/RD E16 | 141 | L6 |
| | CDW/CHF RM16 | 167 | M1 |
| | ED N9 | 80 | B10 |
| | HSLWW TW4 | 153 | M8 |
| | RCHPK/HAM TW10 | 177 | J5 |
| | SNWD SE25 | 203 | P6 |
| | WALTH E17 | 101 | H10 |
| Clifton Hatch HLWS CM18 | | 47 | K4 |
| Clifton Hl STJWD NW8 | | 3 | H3 |
| Clifton Lawns AMS HP6 | | 69 | H1 |
| Clifton Marine Pde GVW DA11 | | 190 | C2 |
| Clifton Ms SNWD SE25 | | 203 | M4 |
| Clifton Pde FELT TW13 * | | 175 | K7 |
| Clifton Park Av RYNPK SW20 | | 200 | F2 |
| Clifton Pl BAY/PAD W2 | | 9 | M7 |
| | BERM/RHTH SE16 | 160 | B5 |
| | BNSTD SM7 | 239 | K5 |
| | KUTN/CMB KT2 | 199 | M1 |
| Clifton Ri NWCR SE14 | | 160 | E8 |
| | WDSR SL4 | 148 | A6 |
| Clifton Rd AMSS HP6 | | 68 | C1 |
| | CAN/RD E16 | 141 | K7 |
| | CEND/HSY/T N8 | 118 | B3 |
| | COUL/CHIP CR5 | 240 | C1 |
| | CRAWE RH10 | 284 | D8 |
| | EMPK RM11 | 125 | M4 |
| | FNCH N3 | 97 | M9 |
| | FSTGT E7 | 142 | A1 |
| | GFD/PVL UB6 | 133 | P4 |
| | GNTH/NBYPK IG2 | 122 | E4 |
| | HTHAIR TW6 | 152 | C7 |
| | ISLW TW7 | 154 | D8 |
| | KTN/HRWW/WS HA3 | 115 | L3 |
| | KUTN/CMB KT2 | 199 | L1 |
| | LOU IG10 | 82 | B8 |
| | MV/WKIL W9 | 9 | K1 |
| | NWDGN UB2 | 153 | M3 |
| | PIN HA5 | 113 | K5 |
| | SCUP DA14 | 185 | P9 |
| | SL SL1 | 149 | H1 |
| | SNWD SE25 | 203 | P6 |
| | STMC/STPC BR5 | 206 | B5 |
| | SURB KT6 | 199 | K7 |
| | TEDD TW11 | 175 | N6 |
| | TRDG/WHET N20 | 97 | J3 |
| | VW GU25 | 194 | A5 |
| | WARE SG12 | 26 | D2 |
| | WBLY HA9 | 115 | P8 |
| | WOKS/MYFD GU22 | 232 | E3 |
| Clifton St SDTCH EC2A | | 13 | L1 |
| | STHWK SE1 | 12 | C8 |
| Clifton Ter FSBYPK N4 | | 119 | H7 |
| Clifton Vs MV/WKIL W9 | | 8 | G3 |
| Clifton Wk HMSMTH W6 | | 137 | H9 |
| Clifton Wy BORE WD6 | | 75 | H1 |
| | OXHEY WD19 | 73 | M2 |
| | PECK SE15 | 160 | B6 |
| | WOKN/KNAP GU21 | 231 | J3 |
| The Climb RKW/CH/CXG WD3 | | 71 | L10 |
| Climping Rd CRAWW RH11 | | 276 | D8 |
| Cline Rd FBAR/BDGN N11 | | 98 | D8 |
| | GU GU1 | 268 | C2 |
| Clink St STHWK SE1 | | 12 | G8 |
| Clinton Av E/WMO/HCT KT8 | | 198 | A2 |
| | WELL DA16 | 163 | H10 |
| Clinton Cl WEY KT13 | | 196 | C10 |
| | WOKN/KNAP GU21 | 231 | J4 |
| Clinton Crs BARK/HLT IG6 | | 103 | H7 |
| Clinton End HHNE HP2 | | 36 | C4 |
| Clinton Rd BOW E3 | | 139 | N6 |
| | FSTGT E7 | 121 | M9 |
| | LHD/OX KT22 | 237 | H9 |
| | SEVS/STOTM N15 | 119 | L2 |
| Clinton Ter DEPT SE8 * | | 160 | M1 |
| | SUT SM1 * | 222 | A2 |
| Clipper Bvd RDART DA2 | | 171 | J8 |
| Clipper Bvd West BERM/RHTH SE16 | | 160 | C1 |
| Clipper Cl BERM/RHTH SE16 | | 160 | C1 |
| Clipper Crs GVE DA12 | | 191 | J7 |
| Clipper Wy GVE SE13 | | 161 | H1 |
| Clippesby Cl CHSGTN KT9 * | | 219 | L3 |
| Clipstone Ms GTPST W1W | | 10 | E1 |
| Clipstone Rd HSLW TW3 | | 153 | P9 |
| Clipstone St GTPST W1W | | 10 | D1 |
| Clissold Cl EFNCH N2 | | 117 | P1 |
| Clissold Crs STNW/STAM N16 | | 119 | P10 |
| Clissold Rd STNW/STAM N16 | | 119 | N10 |
| Clitheroe Av RYLN/HDSTN HA2 | | 113 | P6 |
| Clitheroe Gdns OXHEY WD19 | | 93 | H2 |
| Clitheroe Rd BRXN/ST SW9 | | 158 | A8 |
| | CRW RM5 | 104 | D6 |
| Clitherow Av HNWL W7 | | 135 | H4 |
| Clitherow Rd BTFD TW8 | | 135 | L4 |
| Clitterhouse Crs CRICK NW2 | | 116 | B6 |
| Clitterhouse Rd CRICK NW2 | | 116 | B6 |
| Clive Av DART DA1 | | 190 | A3 |
| | UED N18 | 99 | P7 |
| Clive Cl POTB/CUF EN6 | | 59 | J2 |
| Cliveden Cl BRWN CM15 | | 107 | H1 |
| | NFNCH/WDSPK N12 | 97 | M5 |
| Cliveden Pl BGVA SW1W | | 16 | B5 |
| | SHPTN TW17 | 196 | G6 |
| Cliveden Rd CHING E4 | | 101 | P1 |
| | WIM/MER SW19 | 201 | J1 |
| Clivedon Ct WEA W13 * | | 134 | G1 |
| Clivedon Rd CHING E4 | | 102 | D1 |
| Clive Rd BELV DA17 | | 147 | J4 |
| | DUL SE21 | 181 | L6 |
| | EBED/NFELT TW14 | 175 | M1 |
| | EN EN1 | 30 | B3 |
| | ESH/CLAY KT10 | 217 | P4 |
| | GVW DA11 | 190 | F8 |
| | GVW DA11 | 190 | C2 |
| | RBRW/HUT CM13 | 107 | J3 |
| | TWK TW1 | 176 | C1 |
| | WDR/YW UB7 | 150 | C3 |
| | WIM/MER SW19 | 178 | F6 |
| Clive Wk DART DA1 | | | |
| | ESH/CLAY KT10 | 218 | D4 |
| Clockhouse La ASHF TW15 | | 174 | D5 |

**Column 1**

Clutterbucks RKW/CH/CXG WD3. 71 K2
Clutton St POP/IOD E14. 140 E6
Clydach Rd PEND EN1. 79 N8
Clyde TIL RM18. 169 H8
Clyde Av SAND/SEL CR2. 242 A1
Clyde Cir SEVS/STOTM N15. 119 M2
Clyde Ct REDH RH1. 258 B9
Clyde Crs UPMR RM14. 126 D2
Clyde Flats FUL/PGN SW6 *. 157 J6
Clyde Pl LEY E10. 120 C5
Clyde Rd CROY/NA CR0. 203 N9
HOD EN11. 45 J5
SEVS/STOTM N15. 119 M2
WATW/WRAY TW19. 173 N4
SUT SM1. 221 K2
WDGN N22. 98 E9
WLGTN SM6. 222 D8
Clydesdale PEND EN3. 80 C8
Clydesdale Av STAN HA7. 115 J3
Clydesdale Cl BORE WD6. 76 A3
ISLW TW7. 154 E9
Clydesdale Gdns RCHPK/HAM TW10. 155 N10
Clydesdale Pth BORE WD6 *. 76 A3
Clydesdale Rd EMPK RM11. 124 C5
NTGHL W11. 8 D1
Clyde Sq HHNE HP2. 36 A1
Clyde St DEPT SE8. 160 E6
Clyde Ter FSTH SE23. 182 B5
HERT/BAY SG13. 25 P5
Clyde V FSTH SE23. 182 B5
Clyde Wy ROM RM1. 104 F2
Clydon Cl ERITH DA8. 164 F5
Clyfford Rd RSLP HA4. 112 C9
Clyfton Cl BROX EN10. 44 E9
Clymping Dene EBED/NFELT TW14. 175 J3
Clyston Rd WATW WD18. 72 G10
Clyston St VX/NE SW8. 158 D8
Clyve Wy STA TW18. 195 H1
Coach & Horses Yd CONDST W1S. 10 F7
Coach House Ms HERT/WAT SG14 *. 25 K4
WIM/MER SW19. 178 C7
Coachhouse Ms HERT/WAT SG14. 25 K4
NWCR SE14 *. 160 F2
REDH RH1 *. 276 A1
Coach House Yd WAND/EARL SW18 *. 157 L10
Coachlads Av GUW GU2. 249 G5
Coach Ms STAL AL1. 38 G6
Coach Rd BRKHM/BTCW RH3. 273 M9
CHERT KT16. 255 K10
DORK RH4. 255 K10
HORL RH6. 280 C8
Coalecroft Rd PUT/ROE SW15. 156 F10
Coalport Ct HLWE CM17. 47 N6
Coal Post Ct ORP BR6 *. 227 J4
Coast Hl DORK RH4. 271 N4
Coast Hill La DORK RH4. 271 P4
Coates Av WAND/EARL SW18. 179 J4
Coates Cl THHTH CR7. 203 K3
Coates Dell GSTN WD25. 51 M9
Coates Hill Rd BMLY BR1. 206 D2
Coates Rd BORE WD6. 95 J1
Coate St BETH E2. 7 P8
Coates Wy GSTN WD25. 55 L8
Coat Wicks BEAC HP9. 89 H7
Cobalt Cl BECK BR3. 204 C4
Cobb Ct BORE WD6. 75 P9
DTCH/LGLY SL3. 150 A7
Cobbett Cl CRAWE RH10. 284 D5
PEND EN3. 80 B2
Cobbett Hill Rd RGUW GU3. 248 D6
GUW GU2. 249 K9
WHTN TW2. 175 P4
Cobbetts Av REDBR IG4. 122 A3
Cobbetts Cl WOKN/KNAP GU21. 231 N2
Cobbetts Crs GUW GU2. 248 E5
Cobbetts Farm CHOB/PIR GU24. 230 F1
Cobbetts Hl WEY KT13. 216 C3
Cobbetts Ms VX/NE SW8. 158 E7
Cobbetts Wk CHOB/PIR GU24. 230 F1
Cobb Gn GSTN WD25. 55 J8
Cobbinsbank WAB EN9 *. 63 J9
Cobbin's Br EPP CM16. 64 A3
Cobbinsend Rd WAB EN9. 64 A3
The Cobbins WAB EN9. 63 K8
Cobbins Wy HLWE CM17. 29 P7
Cobble La IS N1. 6 B3
Cobble Ms HBRY N5. 119 K8
Cobbles Crs SLN SL2. 128 C4
Cobbler's Wk TEDD TW11. 176 D10
Cobblers Wk CRAWE RH10. 283 P6
The Cobbles BRWN CM15. 107 K8
UPMR RM14. 141 L5
Cobble Wk WCHPL E1. 13 L5
Cobden Cl UXB/CGN UB8. 131 M3
Cobden Hl RAD WD7. 74 F1
Cobden Ms SYD SE26. 182 A8
Cobden Rd ORP BR6. 226 E1
SEV TN13. 247 K9
SNWD SE25. 203 P5
WAN E11. 121 P8
Cob Dr GVE DA12. 191 P8
Cobham Av NWMAL KT3. 200 G5
Cobham Cl BFN/LL DA15. 185 L2
BTSEA SW11. 179 P7
EDGW HA8. 95 N10
EN EN1. 79 P7
HAYES BR2. 206 F7
SL SL1. 128 E10
SWCM DA10. 188 G3
WLGTN SM6. 222 F3
Cobham Ms CAMTN NW1. 5 L2
Cobham Park Gdns GDMY/SEVK IG3. 235 L2
Cobham Park Rd COB KT11. 235 N8
Cobham Rd GDMY/SEVK IG3. 123 H7
HEST TW5. 153 G3
KUT/HW KT1. 199 J8
LHD/OX KT22. 236 A1
WALTH E17. 101 H9
WARE SG12. 26 E1
Cobill Cl GPK RM2. 125 K2
Cobland Rd LEE/GVPK SE12. 183 P7
Cobmead AL AL10. 40 G3
Cobnar Rd CRAWW RH11. 283 J9
Coborn Rd BOW E3. 140 G5
Coborn St BOW E3. 140 G5
Coburg St CAMTN NW1. 5 H3
Cobsdene GVE DA12. 190 G10
Coburg Crs BRXS/STRHM SW2. 180 A1
Coburg Dwellings WCHPL E1 *. 140 F7
Coburg Gdns CLAY IG5. 102 A10
Coburg Rd WDGN N22. 98 G10
Cob Wk CRAWW RH11. 283 H9
Cochrane Ms STJWD NW8. 3 K6
Cochrane Rd WIM/MER SW19. 178 A3
Cochrane St STJWD NW8. 3 K6
Cockaynes SG13. 25 L8
Cockcrow Hl SURB KT6 *. 199 N8
Cockerell Rd WALTH E17. 120 C2

**Column 2**

Cockerhurst Rd RSEV TN14. 228 F5
Cocker Rd BH EN1. 80 A2
Cockett Rd DTCH/LGLY SL3. 150 B2
Cockfosters Pde EBAR EN4 *. 78 B8
Cockfosters Rd EBAR EN4. 78 A7
Cock Gn HLWW/ROY CM19. 46 E3
Cock La BROX EN10. 44 K6
LHD/OX KT22. 236 B3
STBT EC1A. 12 C4
Cockle Wy RAD WD7. 57 K9
Cockmannings La STMC/STPC BR5. 207 N8
Cockmannings Rd STMC/STPC BR5. 207 N7
Cockpit La WLM CM20. 28 C4
Cocksett Av ORP BR6. 227 N3
Cockshot Hl REIG RH2. 275 L2
Cockshot Rd REIG RH2. 275 L2
Cockspur St STJS SW1Y. 11 K9
Cocksure La SCUP DA14. 186 B7
Codham Hall La RBRW/HUT CM13. 126 G3
Codicote Dr GSTN WD25. 55 L10
Codicote Rd STALE/WH AL4. 21 J2
Codicote Rw HHNE HP2. 36 B1
Codling La WAP E1W *. 13 P9
Codling Wy ALP/SUD HA0. 115 J9
Codmore Crs CSHM HP5. 51 K6
Codmore Wood Rd CSHM HP5. 51 L6
Codrington Ct WOKN/KNAP GU21. 231 L2
Codrington Crs GVE DA12. 190 F8
Codrington Gdns GVE DA12. 190 F8
Codrington Hl FSTH SE23. 182 B5
Codrington Ms NTGHL W11. 8 B6
Cody Rd CAN/RD E16. 141 J6
Cody Rd CAN/RD E16. 141 J6
Coe Av SNWD SE25. 203 P6
Coe's Aly BAR EN5. 77 H8
Coe Sp SL SL1. 130 D6
Coffey St DEPT SE8. 160 F6
Coftards SLN SL2. 129 P8
Cogan Av WALTH E17. 100 P9
Cogdells La CSHM HP5. 50 A3
Cogdells La CSHM HP5. 50 A3
Coin St STHWK SE1. 12 A9
Coity Rd KTTN NW5. 4 D1
Cokers La DUL SE21. 181 K4
Coke's Farm La CSTG HP8. 69 N7
Coke's La COT HP8. 69 K6
Colas Ms KIL/WHAMP NW6. 2 F1
Colbeck Ms SKENS SW7. 15 H6
Colbeck Rd HRW HA1. 114 B5
Colborne Wy WPK KT4. 200 F10
Colbrook Av HYS/HAR UB3. 152 A2
Colbrook Cl HYS/HAR UB3. 152 A2
Colburn Av CTHM CR3. 241 N10
PIN HA5. 93 M7
Colburn Crs RGUE GU4. 250 D7
Colburn Wy SUT SM1. 209 N10
Colby Rd NRWD SE19. 181 M8
WOT/HER KT12. 197 H8
Colchester Dr PIN HA5. 113 L3
Colchester Rd EDGW HA8. 95 N4
HARH RM3. 105 L9
LEY E10. 121 H5
NTHWD HA6. 93 H10
WALTH E17. 120 F4
Colchester St WCHPL E1. 13 N2
Cold Arbor Rd SEV TN13. 246 E10
Coldbath Sq CLKNW EC1R. 12 A2
Coldbath St LEW SE13. 160 G7
Cold Blow Crs BXLY DA5. 186 F6
Cold Blow La NWCR SE14. 160 C6
Coldershaw Rd WEA W13. 154 F1
Coldfall Av MUSWH N10. 98 A10
Coldham Gv PEND EN3. 80 D3
Coldharbour POP/IOD E14. 141 H10
Coldharbour EGH TW20. 194 B7
Coldharbour Crest ELTH/MOT SE9 *. 184 D6
Coldharbour La BRXN/ST SW9. 159 A10
BUSH WD23. 74 A10
CHOB/PIR GU24. 212 E9
DORK RH4. 272 E9
HYS/HAR UB3. 152 G1
PUR/KEN CR8. 223 H6
RAIN RM13. 145 H10
RAIN RM13. 165 K2
RAIN RM13. 165 J3
REDH RH1. 259 N10
WOKS/MYFD GU22. 233 J1
Coldharbour Pl CMBW SE5. 159 K8
Coldharbour Rd CROY/NA CR0. 223 H2
GVW DA11. 190 D3
HLWW/ROY CM19. 46 D1
WOKS/MYFD GU22. 233 J1
Coldharbour Wy CROY/NA CR0. 223 H2
Coldshott OXTED RH8. 261 M9
Coldstream Gdns WAND/EARL SW18. 179 J2
Coldstream Rd CTHM CR3. 241 K8
Colebeck Av IS N1. 6 D6
Colebert Av WCHPL E1. 140 B6
Colebrook CL MLHL NW7. 96 G8
Colebrooke Av WEA W13. 134 G4
Colebrooke Dr WAN E11. 121 N5
Colebrooke Rd REDH RH1. 257 P3
Colebrooke Rw IS N1. 6 C5
Colebrook Gdns LOU IG10. 82 E6
Colebrook La LOU IG10. 82 E6
Colebrook Ri HAYES BR2. 205 K2
Colebrook Rd STRHM/NOR SW16. 202 F1
Colebrook St ERITH DA8. 164 C5
Colebrook Wy FBAR/BDGN N11. 98 C6
Coleby Pth CMBW SE5 *. 159 L6
Cole Cl THMD SE28. 143 L6
Coledale Dr STAN HA7. 95 H9
Coleford Rd WAND/EARL SW18. 179 M1
Cole Gdns HEST TW5. 153 H6
Colegrave Rd SRTFD E15. 121 H9
Colegrave Rd WGCE AL7. 23 H3
Cole Green La HERT/WAT SG14. 25 J1
Colegrove Rd PECK SE15. 159 H10
Coleherne Ms WBPTN SW10. 14 G8
Coleherne Rd WBPTN SW10. 14 G8
Colehill Gdns FUL/PGN SW6 *. 157 H7
Colehill La FUL/PGN SW6. 157 H7
Colekitchen La SHGR GU5. 270 D4
Coleman Cl SNWD SE25. 203 P2
Coleman Flds IS N1. 6 E3
Coleman Green La STALE/WH AL4. 21 H8
Coleman Rd BELV DA17. 148 F2
CMBW SE5. 159 M6
Colemans Heath ELTH/MOT SE9. 184 D6
Coleman's La WAB EN9. 63 J2
Coleman St LOTH EC2R. 12 G2
Coleridge Wk RMY ... 
Colenso Dr MLHL NW7. 96 A4
Colenso Rd CLPT E5. 120 F1
GNTH/NBYPK IG2. 123 H4
Coleraine Rd CEND/HSY/T N8. 98 G9

**Column 3**

Colepits Wood Rd ELTH/MOT SE9. 184 G1
STALW/RED AL3. 38 C6
Coleraine Rd BKHTH/KID SE3. 161 L5
The College AV KT17. 238 D1
Coleridge Av MNPK E12. 142 B1
SUT SM1. 221 P1
Coleridge Cl CHESW EN7. 61 N5
VX/NE SW8. 158 C8
Coleridge Crs DTCH/LGLY SL3. 151 H7
Coleridge Gdns KIL/WHAMP NW6. 3 J1
WBPTN SW10. 157 M6
Coleridge La CEND/HSY/T N8. 98 E6
CROY/NA CR0. 204 B7
DART DA1. 165 P10
FSBYPK N4. 119 H6
HARH RM3. 105 J4
NFNCH/WDSPK N12. 97 M6
TIL RM18. 168 F8
WALTH E17. 120 E2
Coleridge Sq WEA W13. 134 F4
Coleridge Wk GLDGN NW11. 117 K2
RBRW/HUT CM13. 107 P1
Coleridge Wy BORE WD6. 95 K6
WDR/YW UB7. 151 P3
YEAD UB4. 133 P8
Cole Rd TWK TW1. 176 F2
WAT WD17. 73 J5
Colesburg Rd BECK BR3. 204 C4
Coles Cl CHONG CM5. 67 P2
Coles Crs RYLN/HDSTN HA2. 114 A7
Colescroft Hl PUR/KEN CR8. 241 H1
Coles Gn BUSH WD23. 74 E5
LOU IG10. 82 A5
Coles Green Rd CRICK NW2. 116 G3
Colesmead Rd REDH RH1. 258 A7
Colestown St BTSEA SW11. 157 P8
Cole St STHWK SE1. 18 F2
Colet Cl PLMGR N13. 99 J7
Colet Gdns WKENS W14. 156 G4
Colets Orch RSEV TN14. 247 J2
Coley Av WOKS/MYFD GU22. 232 D4
Coley Hl RDKG RH5. 273 J9
Coley La RKW/CH/CXG WD3. 70 C8
Coley Land RKW/CH/CXG WD3. 70 L8
Coley Manor Dr REIG RH2. 256 H9
Coley Wy REIG RH2. 256 H8
Collier Cl EHAM E6. 142 E9
HOR/WEW KT19. 219 M3
Collier Dr EDGW HA8. 95 M10
Collier Row La CRAWE RH10. 283 N10
Collier Row Rd CRW RM5. 104 D9
Colliers CTHM CR3. 259 P5
Colliers Cl WOKN/KNAP GU21. 231 M2
Colliers Shaw HAYES BR2. 226 B2
Collier St IS N1. 5 N8
Colliers Water La THHTH CR7. 203 H5
Collindale Av BFN/LL DA15. 185 K4
ERITH DA8. 148 A3
Collingbourne Rd SHB W12. 139 H1
Collingham Gdns ECT SW5. 15 H5
Collingham Pl ECT SW5. 15 H5
Collingham Rd ECT SW5. 15 H3
Collings Cl WDGN N22. 98 D6
Collington St GNWCH SE10 *. 161 H1
Collingtree Rd SYD SE26. 182 B7
Collingwood Av BRYLDS KT5. 199 P8
MUSWH N10. 98 B1
Collingwood Cl HORL RH6. 280 D3
PGE/AN SE20. 201 M2
WHTN TW2. 175 J3
Collingwood Crs GU GU1. 250 D3
Collingwood Dr LCOL/BKTW AL2. 59 J1
Collingwood Rd CRAWE RH10. 284 D8
MTCM CR4. 201 P2
RAIN RM13. 144 C2
SEVS/STOTM N15. 119 M2
SUT SM1. 209 L10
UX/CGN UB8. 131 M9
Collingwood St WCHPL E1. 140 A6
Collins Av STAN HA7. 95 K10
Collins Dr RSLP HA4. 113 K1
Collins Meadow HLWW/ROY CM19. 46 E1
Collinson St STHWK SE1. 18 E2
Collinson Wk STHWK SE1. 18 E2
Collins Rd HBRY N5. 119 K10
Collins Sq BKHTH/KID SE3 *. 161 K8
Collins St BKHTH/KID SE3. 161 K8
Collinswood Rd SLN SL2. 108 B7
Collinwood Av PEND EN3. 80 D2
Collinwood Gdns GNTH/NBYPK IG2. 122 C3
Collum Green Rd SLN SL2. 109 L8
Collyer Av CROY/NA CR0. 222 F1
Collyer Pl PECK SE15. 159 P7
Collyer Rd CROY/NA CR0. 222 F1
LCOL/BKTW AL2. 57 L1
Colman Cl EPSOM KT18. 238 D7
Colman Pde EN EN1 *. 79 M7
Colman Rd CAN/RD E16. 142 M1
Colmans Hl SHGR GU5. 270 F5
Colman Wy REDH RH1. 257 M9
Colmar Cl WCHPL E1. 140 D6
Colmer Pl KTN/HRWW/WS HA3. 94 D9
Colmer Ms PECK SE15. 160 A7
Colmore Ms PECK SE15. 159 P7
Colmore Rd PEND EN3. 80 C1
Coln Av OXHEY WD19. 73 J10
Colnbridge Cl STA TW18. 173 G9
Colnbrook Cl LCOL/BKTW AL2. 57 K5
Colnbrook St STHWK SE1. 18 C4
Coln Cl MTCM CR4. 202 B2
Colndale Rd DTCH/LGLY SL3. 151 H7
Colne Av OXHEY WD19. 73 J10
RKW/CH/CXG WD3. 50 B8
WATW/WRAY TW19. 173 G9
WDR/YW UB7. 151 M4
Colne Bank DTCH/LGLY SL3. 150 F9
Colnebridge Cl STA TW18. 173 G9
Colne Cl SOCK/AV RM15. 147 L10
Colne Ct HOR/WEW KT19. 219 P3
Colne Dr HARH RM3. 105 L3
WOT/HER KT12. 197 L10
Colne Gdns LCOL/BKTW AL2. 57 L1
Colne Md HLWW/ROY CM19. 46 E1
Colne Orch IVER SL0. 132 B8
Colne Reach STA TW18 *. 173 H5
Colne Rd CLPT E5. 120 G2
TRDG/WHET N20. 97 M4
WHTN TW2. 176 B5
Colne St PLSTW E13. 141 L2
Colne Va UPMR RM14. 126 D2
Colne Valley Trail HGDN/ICK UB10. 111 M8
RKW/CH/CXG WD3. 50 B5
Colne Valley Wy DTCH/LGLY SL3. 150 B8
IVER SL0. 132 B8
UED N18. 99 H6
WCHPL E1. 13 N1
Colne Wy HHNE HP2. 36 A1
STWL/WRAY TW19. 172 G6
WATN WD24 *. 73 J1
Colney Hatch La FBAR/BDGN N11. 97 N8
Colney Heath La STALE/WH AL4. 39 K7
STALW/RED AL3. 39 H1
Colombo Rd IL IG1. 122 F5
Colombo St STHWK SE1. 12 C10
Colomb St GNWCH SE10. 161 K4
Colonel's La CHERT KT16. 195 K6
Colonel's Wk ENC/FH EN2. 79 K3
Colonial Av WHTN TW2. 175 K5
Colonial Dr CHSWK W4. 147 P2
Colonial Rd EBED/NFELT TW14. 173 J4
SL SL1. 148 E2
Colonnade GWRST WC1E. 11 L1
Colonnade Wk BGVA SW1W. 16 G7
The Colonnades HAT AL10 *. 40 F3
BRXN/ST SW9 *. 158 A7
CHES/WCR EN8. 62 C4
DEPT SE8 *. 160 E3
STALW/RED AL3 *. 21 N3
SWLY BR8. 186 E10
TOTM N17. 99 P7
WALTH E17 *. 101 K4
WD/CM N21. 98 B5
WEA W13. 135 J6
WIM/MER SW19. 179 J4
WLSDN NW10. 137 H3
WOKS/MYFD GU22. 232 E4
Colonsay HHS/BOV HP3. 35 K8
Colosseum Ter CAMTN NW1 *. 10 E1
Colson Gdns LOU IG10. 82 C8
Colson Rd CROY/NA CR0. 203 J9
LOU IG10. 82 C8
Colson Wy STRHM/NOR SW16. 181 M6
Colsterworth Rd SEVS/STOTM N15. 119 N10

**Column 4**

Colston Crs CHESW EN7. 61 J3
Colston Rd FSTGT E7. 142 A1
MORT/ESHN SW14. 155 P10
COUL/CHIP CR5. 240 D6
Colt Hatch HLWE CM20. 28 E9
Colthurst Crs FSBYPK N4. 119 H5
Colthurst Dr ED N9. 100 A4
Colthurst Gdns HOD EN11. 45 J1
Coltishall Rd HCH RM12. 145 K1
Coltness Crs ABYW SE2. 163 H4
Colton Gdns TOTM N17. 99 N10
Colton Rd HRW HA1. 114 D3
Coltsfoot WGCE AL7. 23 L7
Coltsfoot Ct GRAYS RM17. 168 A5
Coltsfoot Dr WDR/YW UB7. 131 P8
Coltstead HART DA3. 191 K10
Coltsfoot La OXTED RH8. 261 L9
Coats Yd WAN E11. 121 P8
Columbas Dr HAMP NW3. 117 N7
Columbia Av EDGW HA8. 95 N9
RSLP HA4. 113 J6
WPK KT4. 200 C7
Columbia Rd BETH E2. 7 N6
BROX EN10. 62 D2
PLSTW E13. 141 L6
Columbia Wharf Rd GRAYS RM17. 167 M5
Columbine Av EHAM E6. 142 C9
SAND/SEL CR2. 241 J6
Columbine Wy HARH RM3. 105 M9
LEW SE13. 161 H7
Columbus Gdns NTHWD HA6. 93 H9
Colvers HLWE CM17. 31 K9
Colvestone Crs HACK E8. 119 N10
Colville Est IS N1. 7 H6
Colville Gdns LTWR GU18. 212 A7
NTGHL W11. 8 D6
Colville Houses NTGHL W11. 8 C5
Colville Ms NTGHL W11. 8 D6
Colville Pl FITZ W1T. 10 G1
Colville Rd ACT W3. 155 N2
ED N9. 100 A2
NTGHL W11. 8 D6
WALTH E17. 100 D10
WAN E11. 121 H8
Colville Sq NTGHL W11. 8 C6
Colville Square Ms NTGHL W11. 8 C5
Colville Ter NTGHL W11. 8 C6
Colvin Cl SYD SE26. 182 B8
Colvin Gdns BARK/HLT IG6. 122 C2
CHES/WCR EN8. 80 C1
CHING E4. 101 H4
SWFD E18. 121 N2
Colvin Rd EHAM E6. 142 A7
THHTH CR7. 202 G4
Colwall Gdns WFD IG8. 101 M6
Colwell Rd EDUL SE22. 181 N1
Colwick Cl HGT N6. 118 D5
Colwith Rd HMSMTH W6. 157 H5
Colwood Gdns WIM/MER SW19. 179 N10
Colworth Gv WALW SE17. 18 F6
Colworth Rd CROY/NA CR0. 203 P8
WAN E11. 121 K4
Colwyn Av GFD/PVL UB6. 134 C4
Colwyn Cl CRAWW RH11. 283 L9
STRHM/NOR SW16. 180 D8
Colwyn Crs HSLW TW3. 154 F7
Colwyn Gn CDALE/KGS NW9 *. 116 B3
Colwyn Rd CRICK NW2. 117 J1
Colyer Cl ELTH/MOT SE9. 184 E5
IS N1. 6 B6
Colyer Cl ERITH DA8. 164 C6
Colyers La ERITH DA8. 164 C7
ERITH DA8. 148 C9
Colyton Cl STRHM/NOR SW16. 180 D8
WELL DA16. 149 K7
WOKN/KNAP GU21. 231 P4
Colyton Rd EDUL SE22. 182 A1
Colyton Wy UED N18. 100 A4
Combe Av BKHTH/KID SE3. 161 K6
Combedale Rd GNWCH SE10. 161 M4
Combe La SHGR GU5. 270 A3
WOT/HER KT12. 216 C6
Combemartin Rd WAND/EARL SW18. 179 H3
Comber Cl CRICK NW2. 116 D7
Comber Gv CMBW SE5. 159 H5
Combermere Rd WDSR SL4. 148 G3
BRXN/ST SW9. 158 A9
MRDN SM4. 201 L6
Combe St DACW RM9. 144 A6
Comeragh Cl WOKS/MYFD GU22. 231 M5
Comeragh Ms WKENS W14. 14 C6
Comeragh Rd WKENS W14. 14 C6
Comerford Rd BROCKY SE4. 160 D10
Comet Cl GSTN WD25. 54 G10
MNPK E12. 122 C10
PUR RM19. 165 P5
WATN WD24. 54 G10
Comet Pl DEPT SE8. 160 F6
Comet Rd HAT AL10. 40 F6
STWL/WRAY TW19. 173 J5
Comet St DEPT SE8. 160 F6
Comet Wy HAT AL10. 40 D5
Comforts Farm Av OXTED RH8. 261 M9
Comfort St PECK SE15. 159 H5
Comfrey Ct GRAYS RM17. 168 A5
Commerce Rd BTFD TW8. 155 K7
WDGN N22. 98 G8
Commerce Wy CROY/NA CR0. 202 G10
Commercial Rd GU GU1. 248 G8
PUR RM19. 165 P5
STA TW18. 173 K9
UED N18. 99 H6
WCHPL E1. 13 N2
Commercial St WCHPL E1. 13 L2
Commercial Wy CMBW SE5. 159 N4
WLSDN NW10. 136 G2
WOKN/KNAP GU21. 231 P5
Commerell St GNWCH SE10. 161 J3
Commodore Pde STRHM/NOR SW16. 180 A10
Commodore St WCHPL E1. 140 C7
Common CI WOKN/KNAP GU21. 214 A10
Commonfield Rd BNSTD SM7. 221 K10
Commonfields CHOB/PIR GU24. 212 A9
Common Gate Rd RKW/CH/CXG WD3. 70 A5
Common La ASLWD/WDHM KT15. 215 G5
GSTN WD25. 74 D1
KGLGY WD4. 54 A4
NWDGN UB2. 153 L3
RAD WD7. 57 G7
Commons La HHNE HP2. 35 P5
The Commons WCGE AL7. 23 J4
The Common BERK HP4. 34 C5
EA W5. 135 L4
HAT AL10. 40 D3
KGLGY WD4. 53 K8
NWDGN UB2. 153 L3
RAD WD7. 57 G7
STAN HA7. 94 B3
WDR/YW UB7. 151 M4
Commonside GT/LBKH KT23. 235 P9
HAYES BR2. 225 P1
Commonside Cl BELMT SM2. 221 L8
COUL/CHIP CR5. ... 
Commonside East MTCM CR4. 202 B6
Commonside Rd HLWS CM18. 47 J5
Commonside West MTCM CR4. 202 B8
The Common BERK HP4. 34 C5

**Column 5**

College St CANST EC4R *. 12 F7
STALW/RED AL3. 38 C6
College Ter FNCH N3. 97 J9
The College AV KT17 *. 238 D1
College Vw ELTH/MOT SE9. 184 D7
College Wy ASHF TW15. 174 A7
HYS/HAR UB3. 133 H6
NTHWD HA6. 92 E7
College Yd KIL/WHAMP NW6 *. 2 B5
KTTN NW5 *. 118 C9
Collendean La HORL RH6. 279 J13
Collens Fld CHOB/PIR GU24. 230 D10
Collens Rd HARP AL5. 18 D3
Collet Cl CHES/WCR EN8. 62 B1
Collet Rd BERM/RHTH SE16. 159 P4
Collett Rd BGR/WK TN15. 247 M3
Collett Wy NWDGN UB2. 153 N7
Colley Land RKW/CH/CXG WD3. 70 L8
Colliard Cl PUR/KEN CR8. 241 L6
Collard Pl CAMTN NW1. 4 E1
College Ap GNWCH SE10 *. 161 H5
College Av EGH TW20. 172 E9
EW KT17. 238 C10
GRAYS RM17. 167 M3
KTN/HRWW/WS HA3. 94 D9
College Cl ADL/WDHM KT15. 215 N10
KTN/HRWW/WS HA3. 94 D8
LOU IG10. 82 D6
UED N18. 99 M6
WARE SG12. 26 C1
WHTN TW2. 176 A4
College Crs HAMP NW3. 3 K2
REDH RH1. 258 D9
SL SL4. 148 G8
College Cross IS N1. 6 B3
College Dr RSLP HA4. 113 H5
THDIT KT7. 198 A9
College East WCHPL E1 *. 13 M1
College Gdns CHING E4. 100 G5
ENC/FH EN2. 79 L3
NWMAL KT3. 200 D5
REDBR IG4. 122 A4
TOOT SW17. 179 P5
UED N18 *. 99 P4
College Gn HLW CM20. 46 F1
College Gv CAMTN NW1. 5 J6
College Hl CANST EC4R *. 12 F7
College Hill Rd KTN/HRWW/WS HA3. 94 D8
College La HAT AL10. 40 D8
KTTN NW5. 118 C9
WOKS/MYFD GU22. 231 P5
College Ms IS N1 *. 6 B3
WAND/EARL SW18 *. 179 L3
College Pde KIL/WHAMP NW6 *. 2 B5
College Park Cl LEW SE13. 161 H10
College Park Rd CAMTN NW1. 38 B6
College Rd ABLGY WD5. 55 J7
BH1 BR1 *. 205 P5
CHES/WCR EN8. 62 C4
CRAWE RH10. 283 P7
CROY/NA CR0. 2 E4
DUL SE21. 181 N1
ENC/FH EN2. 79 L2
EW KT17. 220 C10
GRAYS RM17. 167 N3
GU GU1. 268 A1
HARP AL5. 18 B1
HERT/BAY SG13. 26 B3
HRW HA1. 114 E2
ISLW TW7. 154 A6
KTN/HRWW/WS HA3. 94 D8
NRWD SE19. 181 N9
NWMAL KT3. 181 M10
SL SL1. 149 K9
STAL AL1. 38 G7
SWLY BR8. 186 F10
WBLY HA9. 115 N1
WCHPL E1 *. 13 M1
WIM/MER SW19. 179 L7
WLSDN NW10. 137 L2
WOKN/KNAP GU21. 231 P5
College Sq HLW CM20. 46 G1
College Slip BMLY BR1. 204 C5
College Vw SEV TN13. 247 H10
STALW/RED AL3. 38 B6
SWCM DA10. 190 D3
WALTH E17. 121 K1
WBPTN SW10 *. 157 M6
College Rd ABLGY WD5. 55 J7

**Column 6**

Colston Crs CHESW EN7. 61 J3
... (see Column 4 merged above)

Conferty / Conifer entries:
Commonwealth Av HYS/HAR UB3. 132 G8
SHB W12. 139 K7
Commonwealth Dr CRAWE RH10 *. 284 A8
Commonwealth Rd CTHM CR3. 241 P9
TOTM N17. 99 P8
Commonwealth Wy ABYW SE2. 163 L6
Common Wk HEST SG12. 26 D2
Common Wd SLN SL2. 109 H9
Community Cl HEST TW5. 153 J7
HGDN/ICK UB10 *. 112 C8
Community Rd GFD/PVL UB6. 134 B3
SRTFD E15. 121 J10
Community Wy RKW/CH/CXG WD3. 72 B9
Como Rd FSTH SE23. 182 G5
Como St ROMW/RG RM7. 124 E3
Compass Cl ASHF TW15. 174 D10
EDGW HA8. 95 L5
Compass Hl RCHPK/HAM TW10. 177 J2
Compassion Cl CRAWW RH11. 283 H6
Compayne Gdns KIL/WHAMP NW6. 2 E2
Comper Cl CRAWW RH11. 283 H9
Comport Gn CROY/NA CR0. 225 K8
Compton Av ALP/SUD HA0. 114 C9
EHAM E6. 142 A4
GPK RM2. 125 J1
HGT N6. 117 P5
IS N1. 6 C2
RBRW/HUT CM13. 107 P2
Compton Cl CAMTN NW1. 4 E2
ESH/CLAY KT10. 218 C3
GLDGN NW11. 116 G8
PECK SE15. 159 P6
WEA W13. 134 F4
Compton Crs CHSGTN KT9. 219 K5
CHSWK W4. 155 P5
NTHLT UB5. 133 J1
TOTM N17. 99 K8
Compton Gdns ADL/WDHM KT15. 215 K3
LCOL/BKTW AL2. 58 D6
Compton Hts RGUW GU3. 267 G8
Compton Pas FSBYE EC1V. 12 D1
Compton Pl ERITH DA8. 164 C5
OXHEY WD19. 93 M5
STPAN WC1H. ...
Compton Ri PIN HA5. 113 M3
Compton Rd CROY/NA CR0. 204 A9
HYS/HAR UB3. 132 F9
IS N1. 6 C2
WCHMH N21. 99 H2
WIM/MER SW19. 179 J3
WLSDN NW10. 136 G5
Compton St FSBYE EC1V. 12 C1
Compton Ter IS N1. 6 C2
WCHMH N21. 99 H2
Comreddy Cl ENC/FH EN2. 79 J1
Comus Pl WALW SE17. 19 J6
Comyne Rd WATN WD24. 72 G2
Comyn Rd BTSEA SW11. 157 P9
Comyns Cl CAN/RD E16. 141 L7
Comyns Rd DAGW RM9. 144 B2
The Comyns BUSH WD23. 94 B2
Conant Ms WCHPL E1. 13 N7
Conaways Cl EW KT17. 220 C6
Concanon Rd CLAP SW4. 158 G10
Concert Hall Ap STHWK SE1. 11 N10
Concord Cl NTHLT UB5. 133 L5
Concorde Cl HGDN/ICK UB10. 131 P4
HSLW TW3. 154 A8
Concorde Dr EHAM E6. 142 C7
Concorde Wy BERM/RHTH SE16. 160 C5
SL SL1. 149 J1
Concord Rd ACT W3. 135 N6
PEND EN3. 80 B2
Concord Wy BERM/RHTH SE16. 160 C5
Condell Rd VX/NE SW8. 158 D7
Conder St POP/IOD E14. 140 D8
Condor Cl GU GU1. 267 G2
Condor Rd STA TW18. 195 M5
Condover Crs WOOL/PLUM SE18. 162 G6
Condray Pl BTSEA SW11. 157 P5
Conduit La DTCH/LGLY SL3. 150 B5
HOD EN11. 44 C3
SAND/SEL CR2. 223 P2
UED N18. 100 B6
Conduit La East HOD EN11. 44 D3
Conduit Ms BAY/PAD W2. 9 J6
Conduit Rd WOOL/PLUM SE18. 162 G10
Conduit St CONDST W1S. 10 E7
The Conduit REDH RH1. 259 J5
Conduit Wy WLSDN NW10. 135 P2
Conegar Ct SL SL1. 129 K10
Conewood St HBRY N5. 119 J8
Coney Burrows CHING E4 *. 101 J10
Coney Gv HGDN/ICK UB10. 132 A5
Coneybury REDH RH1. 259 M10
Coneybury Cl WARC CR6. 242 A5
Coney Cl CRAWW RH11. 283 L5
Conedale WGCW AL8. 22 G3
Coney Gv HGDN/ICK UB10. 132 A5
Coney Hall Pde WWKM BR4. 205 K1
Coney Hill Rd WWKM BR4. 205 K9
Coneygate Ms CI CHING E4. 101 H3
Conference Cl CHING E4. 101 H3
Conference Rd ABYW SE2. 163 M3
Congleton Gv WOOL/PLUM SE18. 162 F4
Congo Dr ED N9. 101 H1
Congo Rd WOOL/PLUM SE18. 162 G4
Congress Rd ABYW SE2. 163 M3
Congreve Rd ELTH/MOT SE9. 162 G10
WAB EN9. 63 J9
Congreve St WALW SE17. 19 J6
Conical Cnr ENC/FH EN2. 79 K6
Conifer Av CRW RM5. 104 C6
Conifer Cl CHESW EN7. 61 L5
ORP BR6. 226 G1
REIG RH2. 257 K8
Conifer Dr BRW CM14. 107 K8
Conifer Gdns EN EN1. 80 A5
STRHM/NOR SW16. 180 A5
SUT SM1. 209 M7
Conifer La EGH TW20. 172 F8
Conifer Pk EW KT17. 220 C6
Conifers WEY KT13. 216 F2
Conifers Cl TEDD TW11. 176 E10
The Conifers GSTN WD25. 73 K5
HHS/BOV HP3 *. 35 J9
Conifer Wk WDSR SL4 *. 148 B6

**Column 1**

Conifer Wy ALP/SUD HA0 115 H8
  HYS/HAR UB3 133 H9
  SWLY BR8 208 D1
Coniger Rd FUL/PGN SW6 157 K8
Coningham Ms SHB W12 136 D10
Coningham Rd SHB W12 156 E1
Coningsby Av CDALE/KGS NW9 96 B10
Coningsby Bank STAL AL1 38 B10
Coningsby Ci BRKMPK AL9 40 F10
Coningsby Cots EA W5 155 K7
Coningsby Ct RAD WD7 74 F2
Coningsby Dr POTB/CUF EN6 59 N9
Coningsby Gdns CHING E4 155 H1
Coningsby Rd EA W5 155 H1
  HYS/HAR UB3 119 J5
  SAND/SEL CR2 223 M7
Conington Rd LEW SE13 160 C8
Conisbee Ct STHGT/OAK N14 78 D9
Conisborough Crs CAT SE6 183 H6
Coniscliffe Ci CHST BR7 206 D1
Coniscliffe Rd PLMGR N13 99 K4
Conista Ct WOKN/KNAP GU21 231 J2
Coniston Av BARK IG11 143 H3
  GFD/PVL UB6 134 G5
  PUR RM19 166 B5
  UPMR RM14 126 B9
  WELL DA16 163 H9
Coniston Ci BARN SW13 156 C6
  BXLYHN DA7 164 A7
  CHSWK W4 155 P7
  CRAWW RH11 282 C9
  ERITH DA8 164 F6
  HHS/BOV HP3 36 D7
  MRDN SM4 200 A6
Coniston Ct BAY/PAD W2 * 212 A6
  LTWR GU18 212 A6
Coniston Crs SL SL1 131 N2
Coniston Gv HOLWY N7 * 5 M3
Coniston Gdns BELMT SM2 * 221 N3
  CDALE/KGS NW9 116 A3
  ED N9 100 D2
  PIN HA5 113 H2
  REDBR IG4 122 B2
  WBLY HA9 115 H5
Coniston Rd BMLY BR1 183 K9
  BXLYHN DA7 164 A7
  COUL/CHIP CR5 240 D2
  CROY/NA CR0 203 P7
  KGLGY WD4 54 A4
  MUSWH N10 98 C10
  TOTM N17 99 P7
  WHTN TW2 176 A2
  WOKS/MYFD GU22 232 E6
Coniston Wk HOM E9 120 B10
Coniston Wy CHSGTN KT9 199 K10
  EGH TW20 172 C10
  HGT N6 125 H10
  REIG RH2 257 P9
Conlan St NKENS W10 8 A1
Conley Rd WLSDN NW10 136 B1
Conley St GNWCH SE10 161 K1
Connaught Av ASHF TW15 173 P7
  CDW/CHF RM16 167 K1
  CHING E4 101 J1
  EBAR EN4 98 A2
  EN EN1 79 N6
  HSLWW TW4 175 M1
  LOU IG10 82 A8
  MORT/ESHN SW14 155 P9
Connaught Br CAN/RD E16 142 A4
Connaught Ci BAY/PAD W2 * 9 N6
  EN EN1 79 N6
  HHNE HP2 36 B4
  LEY E10 120 D7
  SUT SM1 201 N9
  UX/CGN UB8 * 132 C7
Connaught Crs CHOB/PIR GU24 230 E6
Connaught Dr GLDGN NW11 117 K2
  WEY KT13 216 A7
Connaught Gdns BERK HP4 33 L2
  CRAWE RH10 283 N5
  MRDN SM4 201 M5
  MUSWH N10 118 C3
  PLMGR N13 99 J3
Connaught La LOU IG10 82 A8
Connaught La IL IG1 122 F7
Connaught Ms FUL/PGN SW6 * 157 H7
  HAMP NW3 * 117 P10
  WOOL/PLUM SE18 146 G10
Connaught Rd BAR EN5 76 C10
  CAN/RD E16 142 A10
  CHING E4 101 K1
  CHOB/PIR GU24 230 E6
  FSBYPK N4 119 H5
  HARP AL5 20 A1
  HCH RM12 125 L8
  IL IG1 122 C7
  KTN/HRWW/WS HA3 78 E9
  NWMAL KT3 200 B4
  RCHPK/HAM TW10 * 177 L7
  SL SL1 149 N1
  STALW/RED AL3 38 B4
  SUT SM1 201 N9
  TEDD TW11 176 C8
  WALTH E17 120 F8
  WAN E11 121 J4
  WEA W13 134 G9
  WLSDN NW10 136 A4
  WOOL/PLUM SE18 162 D4
Connaught Sq BAY/PAD W2 9 P6
Connaught St BAY/PAD W2 9 P6
Connaught Wy PLMGR N13 99 J3
Connect La BARK/HLT IG6 102 F7
Connell Crs WLSDN NW10 135 L6
Connemara Ci BORE WD6 * 75 J1
Connington Crs CHING E4 101 J4
Connop Rd PEND EN3 80 C2
Connor Ci BARK/HLT IG6 102 F9
  WAN E11 121 K6
Connor Rd DAGW RM9 124 A9
Connor St HOM E9 * 140 C2
Conolly Rd HNWL W7 134 D10
Conquerors HI STALE/WH AL4 21 K3
Conquest Rd ADL/WDHM KT15 215 K2
Conrad Ci CDW/CHF RM16 167 K1
Conrad Dr WPK KT4 192 G5
Conrad Gdns CDW/CHF RM16 167 K1
Consfield Av NWMAL KT3 200 D4
Consort Ci BRWM CM14 107 H6
  FBAR/BDGN N11 98 A6
Consort Ms ISLW TW7 176 C2
Consort Rd PECK SE15 160 A7
Consort Wy HORL RH6 280 D5
Consort Wy East HORL RH6 280 C5
Cons St STHWK SE1 * 18 B1
Constable Av SEVS/STOTM N15 119 P3
Constable Ci EDGW HA8 96 D2
  GLDGN NW11 117 L4
  YEAD UB4 133 J2
Constable Crs SEVS/STOTM N15 119 P3
Constable Gdns EDGW HA8 96 D2
  ISLW TW7 176 C1
Constable Ms BCTR RM8 123 L10
Constable Rd GVW DA11 190 B6
Constable Wk DUL SE21 181 M6
Constance Crs HAYES BR2 205 L8
Constance Rd CROY/NA CR0 223 M7
  EN EN1 79 M10
  SUT SM1 201 M1
  WHTN TW2 176 A1
Constance St CAN/RD E16 142 A10
Constantine Rd HAMP NW3 117 M7
Constitution HI GVE DA12 190 F4
  MYFR/PICC W1J 16 E1
  WOKS/MYFD GU22 232 B6
Constitution Ri WOOL/PLUM SE18 162 D7
Consul Av DAGE RM10 143 L4
  RAIN RM13 143 L4
Consul Gdns SWLY BR8 * 187 H10
Content St WALW SE17 18 F6

**Column 2**

Contessa Ci ORP BR6 227 H2
Control Tower Rd HORL RH6 279 N9
  HTHAIR TW6 152 B9
Convent Ci BECK BR3 183 H10
Convent Gdns EA W5 155 H5
  NTGHL W11 8 A7
Convent La NRWD SE19 181 K9
Convent Rd ASHF TW15 174 C8
  WDSR SL4 148 F8
Convent Wy NWDGN UB2 153 K5
Conway Ci RAIN RM13 145 L2
  STAN HA7 94 F7
Conway Crs CHDH RM6 123 L3
  GFD/PVL UB6 134 D4
Conway Dr ASHF TW15 174 D9
  BELMT SM2 221 L5
  HYS/HAR UB3 152 D2
Conway Gdns ENC/FH EN2 79 M3
  GRAYS RM17 167 N6
  MTCM CR4 202 E3
  WBLY HA9 115 H5
Conway Gv ACT W3 136 A7
Conway Ms FITZ W1T 10 G3
Conway Rd CRICK NW2 116 F7
  FELT TW13 175 J7
  HSLWW TW4 175 N5
  RYNPK SW20 200 F1
  SEVS/STOTM N15 119 J5
  STHGT/OAK N14 98 E2
  WOOL/PLUM SE18 162 G4
Conway St FITZ W1T 10 G3
Conway Wk HPTN TW12 * 174 G4
Conybeare HAMP NW3 * 3 J7
Conybury Ci WAB EN9 63 M8
Cony Ci CHESW EN7 61 M3
Conyers Ci WOT/HER KT12 217 L2
Conyers Rd STRHM/NOR SW16 180 E8
Conyer St BOW E3 139 L2
Conyers Wy LOU IG10 82 E7
Cooden Ci BMLY BR1 183 N10
Cooke Ci CDW/CHF RM16 167 K2
Cookes Ci WAN E11 121 L7
Cookes La CHEAM SM3 221 H5
Cookham Ci NWDGN UB2 154 A2
Cookham Dene Ci CHST BR7 206 C1
Cookham Rd SCUP DA14 186 D1
  SWLY BR8 186 D1
Cookhill Rd ABYW SE2 148 C1
Cook Rd CRAWE RH10 283 P9
Cook's Ci CRW RM5 104 D9
Cook's Ferry Rbt UED N18 100 D6
Cook's Hole Rd ENC/FH EN2 79 J4
Cooks Md BUSH WD23 74 A10
  HORS RH12 282 A6
Cooks Meadow HORS RH12 282 A6
Cookson Gv ERITH DA8 164 C6
Cook's Rd SRTFD E15 139 L3
  WALW SE17 17 B2
Cooks Spinney HLW CM20 29 K9
Cooks Vennel HHW HP1 35 K4
Cooks Wy HAT AL10 40 E6
Coolfin Rd CAN/RD E16 141 M8
Coolgardie Av CHIG IG7 102 D4
  CHING E4 101 K3
Coolgardie Rd ASHF TW15 174 D8
Coolhurst Rd HGT N6 118 C4
Cool Oak Br CDALE/KGS NW9 116 C5
Cool Oak La CDALE/KGS NW9 116 C5
Coomassie Rd MV/WKIL W9 8 C1
Coombe Av CROY/NA CR0 223 N1
  RSEV TN14 247 J6
Coombe Bank KUTN/CMB KT2 200 B1
Coombe Ci CRAWW RH11 283 J1
  EDGW HA8 95 P4
  HSLW TW3 155 P10
Coombe Cnr WCHMH N21 99 J2
Coombe Crs HPTN TW12 175 H10
Coombe Dr ADL/WDHM KT15 215 H9
  KUTN/CMB KT2 177 P8
Coombe End KUTN/CMB KT2 178 A10
Coombefield Ci NWMAL KT3 200 B5
Coombe Gdns BERK HP4 33 L4
  NWMAL KT3 200 C4
Coombe Hill Ct WDSR SL4 148 C10
Coombe Hill Gld KUTN/CMB KT2 178 B10
Coombe Hill Rd KUTN/CMB KT2 178 B10
  RKW/CH/CXG WD3 91 K1
Coombehurst Ci EBAR EN4 78 A6
Coombelands La ADL/WDHM KT15 215 K3
Coombe La ASC SL5 192 B4
  CROY/NA CR0 223 P5
  RGUW GU3 249 H4
  RYNPK SW20 200 C1
Coombe La West KUTN/CMB KT2 199 P1
Coombe Lea BMLY BR1 206 B3
Coombe Ldg CHARL SE7 161 P5
Coombe Mnr CHOB/PIR GU24 230 C1
Coombe Neville KUTN/CMB KT2 177 P10
Coombe Pk KUTN/CMB KT2 177 P8
Coombe Ridings KUTN/CMB KT2 177 P8
Coombe Rd BUSH WD23 94 B1
  CHSWK W4 156 B4
  CROY/NA CR0 223 K1
  GVE DA12 190 F5
  HARH RM3 105 L9
  HPTN TW12 175 H10
  KUTN/CMB KT2 199 M1
  NWMAL KT3 200 C3
  RSEV TN14 247 K1
  SAND/SEL CR2 223 M1
  SYD SE26 182 A7
  WDGN N22 99 H10
  WEA W13 154 D2
  WLSDN NW10 116 A8
Coomber Wy CROY/NA CR0 202 G7
Coombes Rd LCOL/BKTW AL2 57 H2
The Coombe BRKHM/BTCW RH3 256 A7
  CFSP/GDCR SL9 110 B5
Coombe Vis WAND/EARL SW18 179 K3
Coombe Wd BF/WBF KT14 216 A8
Coombewood Dr CHDH RM6 124 A4
Coombe Wood HI PUR/KEN CR8 223 K8
Coombe Wood Rd KUTN/CMB KT2 177 P8

**Column 3**

Coombs St IS N1 6 D3
Coomer Ms FUL/PGN SW6 157 J4
Coomer PI FUL/PGN SW6 14 C10
Coomer Rd FUL/PGN SW6 157 J4
The Coomings HOD EN11 26 F10
Coopers La LEW SE13 131 J7
Coopers Ci DAGE RM10 124 B10
  STHWK SE1 18 C1
Copping Ci CROY/NA CR0 223 M1
The Coppings HOD EN11 26 F10
Coppins La IVER SL0 131 J7
The Coppins CROY/NA CR0 224 C6
  KTN/HRWW/WS HA3 78 E1
Coppock Ci BTSEA SW11 157 P8
Coppsfield E/WMO/HCT KT8 197 P3
Copse Av HAYES BR2 205 M4
  WCHMH N21 99 J4
Copse Bank BGR/WK TN15 247 N6
Copse Ci CHARL SE7 161 N5
  NTHWD HA6 92 D7
  RGUE GU4 268 C6
  SL SL1 131 N4
  WDR/YW UB7 151 N2
Copse Crs CRAWW RH11 283 M6
Copse Edge RGE RH12 257 J10
Copse Gld SURB KT6 199 J8
Copse HI BELMT SM2 221 L4

**Column 4**

Corner Fielde BRXS/STRHM SW2 * 180 G4
Corner Gn BKHTH/KID SE3 161 M8
Corner Hall HHS/BOV HP3 35 N8
Corner Hall Av HHS/BOV HP3 35 N8
Corner Mead CDALE/KGS NW9 * 96 C1
Corner Meadow HLWS CM18 47 K5
Cornerside ASHF TW15 174 A3
Corney Reach Wy CHSWK W4 156 B5
Corney Rd CHSWK W4 156 B5
Cornfield Ci UX/CGN UB8 131 N4
Cornfield Rd BERK HP4 33 J2
  BUSH WD23 74 A8
Cornfields GODL GU7 267 L9
The Cornfields HHW HP1 35 M9
Cornflower La CROY/NA CR0 204 C8
Cornflower Ter EDUL SE22 182 A2
Cornflower Wy HARH RM3 105 M9
Cornford Ci HAYES BR2 205 M5
Cornford Gv BAL SW12 180 F3
Cornhill BANK EC3V 13 H6
Cornhill Ci ADL/WDHM KT15 195 L9
Cornhill Dr PEND EN3 80 G1
Cornhill Ct ED N9 * 100 A1
Cornish Gv PGE/AN SE20 204 A1
Corn Md WCCW AL8 22 F2
Cornmill WAB EN9 62 G9
Corn Mill Dr ORP BR6 207 J7
Cornmill La LEW SE13 160 C9
Cornmow Dr WLSDN NW10 116 C10
Cornshaw Rd BCTR RM8 123 N6
Cornsland BRW CM14 107 J4
Cornthwaite Rd CLPT E5 120 B8
Cornwall Av BETH E2 140 B5
  BF/WBF KT14 216 A10
  ESH/CLAY KT10 218 A4
  FNCH N3 97 K8
  SLN SL2 129 H6
  STHL UB1 133 N7
  WDGN N22 98 F3
  WELL DA16 163 P7
Cornwall Ci BARK IG11 143 J1
  CHES/WCR EN8 62 D9
  EMPK RM11 125 P2
  WDSR SL4 148 D4
Cornwall Crs NTGHL W11 * 8 B7
Cornwall Dr STMC/STPC BR5 185 M10
Cornwall Gardens Wk SKENS SW7 15 J4
Cornwall Gv CHSWK W4 156 B4
Cornwallis Av CHSWK W4 156 B4
  ED N9 100 A3
  ELTH/MOT SE9 184 G5
Cornwallis Ci CTHM CR3 241 K8
  ERITH DA8 150 B5
Cornwallis Gv ED N9 100 A3
Cornwallis Rd ARCH N19 118 F7
  DAGW RM9 123 P9
  ED N9 100 A3
  WALTH E17 120 C2
  WOOL/PLUM SE18 162 F5
Cornwallis Wk ELTH/MOT SE9 162 F9
Cornwall Ms South SKENS SW7 15 J4
Cornwall Ms West SKENS SW7 15 H4
Cornwall Rd BELMT SM2 221 J4
  BRWN CM15 86 C9
  CROY/NA CR0 203 J9
  DART DA1 170 A2
  ESB/STOTM N15 119 H5? 

Cornwall Rd HRW HA1 114 B4
  PIN HA5 94 A4
  RSLP HA4 112 G7
  SEVS/STOTM N15 119 J3
  STAL AL1 38 D8
  STHWK SE1 12 A9
  TWK TW1 176 F7
  UED N18 99 P8
  UX/CGN UB8 131 N4
  WALTH E17 101 A10
Cornwall Terrace Ms CAMTN NW1 10 B2
Cornwall Wy STA TW18 173 H9
Corn Wy WAN E11 121 J4
Cornwell Av GVE DA12 190 F5
Cornwood Ci EFNCH N2 117 J2
Cornwood Dr WCHPL E1 140 E8
Cornworthy Rd BCTR RM8 123 L5
Corona Rd LEE/GVPK SE12 183 M3
Coronation Av DTCH/LGLY SL3 150 B1
  TIL RM18 169 J7
Coronation Ci BARK/HLT IG6 122 A1
  BXLY DA5 185 H5
Coronation Dr HCH RM12 125 J10
Coronation Rd HYS/HAR UB3 152 G2
  PLSTW E13 141 M2
  WARE SG12 26 C1
  WLSDN NW10 135 N6
Coronation Vis WLSDN NW10 * 135 N6
Coronet Pde ALP/SUD HA0 * 135 K1
Coronet St IS N1 7 J10
The Coronet HORL RH6 280 F6
Corporation Av HSLWW TW4 153 M10
Corporation Rw CLKNW EC1R 12 B10
Corporation St HOLWY N7 118 F2
  SRTFD E15 141 K4
Corrance Rd BRXS/STRHM SW2 158 F10
Corran Wy SOCK/AV RM15 146 G9
Corri Av STHGT/OAK N14 98 E5
Corrib Dr SUT SM1 221 P2
Corrie Gdns VW GU25 235 P7
Corrie Rd ADL/WDHM KT15 215 L5
  WOKS/MYFD GU22 232 E6
Corrigan Av COUL/CHIP CR5 240 B5
Corrigan Ci HDN NW4 116 F1
Corringham Ct HDN NW4 116 F1
Corringham Rd GLDGN NW11 116 F1? 
  WBLY HA9 115 M7
Corringway GLDGN NW11 117 H2
  WEA W13 135 J7
Corris Gn CDALE/KGS NW9 * 96 C4
Corry Dr BRXN/ST SW9 159 J4
Corsair Rd STWL/WRAY TW19 173 P3
Corscombe Ci KUTN/CMB KT2 178 B7
Corsehill St STRHM/NOR SW16 180 C10
Corsellis Sq TWK TW1 153 K10
Corsham St IS N1 7 H8? 
Corsica St HBRY N5 6 D1
Cortayne Rd FUL/PGN SW6 157 J8
Cortina Dr DAGW RM9 144 D5
Cortis Ter PUT/ROE SW15 178 E4
Corunna Rd VX/NE SW8 158 C8
Corunna Ter VX/NE SW8 158 D7
Corwell Gdns UX/CGN UB8 132 A9
Corwell La UX/CGN UB8 132 A9
Coryton Pth MV/WKIL W9 * 137 P9
Cory-Wright Wy STALE/WH AL4 21 K3
Cosbycote Av HNHL SE24 181 J1
Cosdach Av WLGTN SM6 222 F5
Cosedge Crs CROY/NA CR0 223 H3
Cosgrove Ci WCHMH N21 99 K3
Cosmo PI RSQ WC1B 11 H3
Cosmur Ci SHB W12 156 C2

**Column 5**

Cosne Ms HARP AL5 20 B4
Cossall Wk PECK SE15 160 A7
Cossar Ms BRXS/STRHM SW2 181 H4
Cosser St STHWK SE1 18 A4
Costa St PECK SE15 159 P8
Costead Manor Rd BRW CM14 106 C1
Costells Meadow BH/WHM TN16 262 G4
Costons Av GFD/PVL UB6 134 C5
Costons La GFD/PVL UB6 134 C5
Cosway St CAMTN NW1 9 P3
Cotall St POP/IOD E14 140 F8
Coteford Ci LOU IG10 82 G6
  PIN HA5 113 H3
Coteford St TOOT SW17 180 A7
Cotelands CROY/NA CR0 203 M10
Cotesbach Rd CLPT E5 120 D8
Cotesmore Gdns BCTR RM8 123 M9
Cotesmore Rd HHW HP1 35 H9
Cotford Rd THHTH CR7 204 D2
Cotham St WALW SE17 18 F6
Cotherstone ROM/WEW KT19 212 A5
Cotherstone Rd BRXS/STRHM SW2 180 G4
Cotland Acres REDH RH1 275 N7
Cotlandswick LCOL/BKTW AL2 57 H1
Cotleigh Av BXLY DA5 184 F8
Cotleigh Rd KIL/WHAMP NW6 2 B1
  ROMW/RG RM7 124 A3
Cotman Ci GLDGN NW11 117 M4
  PUT/ROE SW15 178 G6
Cotman Gdns EDGW HA8 96 C5
Cotman Ms BCTR RM8 123 J6
Cotmans Ci HYS/HAR UB3 133 H10
Coton Rd WELL DA16 163 K9
Cotsford Av NWMAL KT3 199 P5
Cotswold Av BUSH WD23 74 B10
Cotswold Ci BXLYHN DA7 164 F7
  ESH/CLAY KT10 198 G3
  KUTN/CMB KT2 177 P9
  SL SL1 148 G3
  STA TW18 173 K8
  STALE/WH AL4 39 H1
  UX/CGN UB8 * 131 M4
Cotswold Gdns CRICK NW2 116 C2
  EHAM E6 141 J3
  GNTH/NBYPK IG2 122 C5
Cotswold Ga CRICK NW2 117 H6
Cotswold Gn ENC/FH EN2 78 G3
Cotswold Ms BTSEA SW11 157 N7
Cotswold Ri ORP BR6 207 J6
Cotswold Rd BELMT SM2 221 L6
  GVW DA11 190 B6
  HARH RM3 105 N10
  HPTN TW12 175 J7
  SUN TW16 * 173 P5? 
Cotswold St WNWD SE27 181 J7
Cotswold Wy ENC/FH EN2 78 G3
  WPK KT4 200 G10? 
Cottage Av HAYES BR2 206 B8
Cottage Ci CHERT KT16 214 F3
  RKW/CH/CXG WD3 72 A10
  RSLP HA4 112 C7
  RYLN/HDSTN HA2 114 C7
  WAT WD17 21 J2
Cottage Farm Wy EGH TW20 * 194 F3
Cottage Field Ci SCUP DA14 * 185 M4
Cottage Gn CMBW SE5 159 L6
Cottage Gv BRXN/ST SW9 158 D9
  SURB KT6 199 J6
Cottage Park Rd SLN SL2 130 A1
Cottage PI CHEL SW3 15 N3
  CRAWE RH10 285 N2
Cottage Rd HOLWY N7 5 N1
  ROM/WEW KT19 220 A4
The Cottages POP/IOD E14 * 140 G10
Cottage St POP/IOD E14 140 G10
Cottenham Dr CDALE/KGS NW9 116 C1
  RYNPK SW20 178 E10
Cottenham Park Rd RYNPK SW20 200 D1
Cottenham PI RYNPK SW20 178 D10
Cottenham Rd WALTH E17 120 D2
Cotterells HHW HP1 35 M8
Cotterill Rd SURB KT6 199 L9
Cottesbrooke Ci DTCH/LGLY SL3 150 B2
Cottesbrook St NWCR SE14 160 D6
Cottesloe Ci CHOB/PIR GU24 230 E2
Cottesmore Av CLAY IG5 102 C10
Cottesmore Gdns KENS W8 14 F3
Cottimore Av WOT/HER KT12 197 J7
Cottimore Crs WOT/HER KT12 197 J6
Cottimore La WOT/HER KT12 197 K7
Cottimore Ter WOT/HER KT12 197 J6
Cottingham Cha RSLP HA4 113 H7
Cottingham Rd PGE/AN SE20 182 G9
  VX/NE SW8 158 G6
Cottington Rd FELT TW13 175 H6
Cottington St LBTH SE11 18 B7
Cottis La EPP CM16 69 H4
Cotton Av ACT W3 136 A8
Cotton Ci DAGW RM9 143 P6
  WAN E11 121 K7
Cotton Dr HERT/BAY SG13 26 A3
Cotton Fld HAT AL10 40 E2
Cotton Gardens Est LBTH SE11 18 B6
Cottongrass Ci CROY/NA CR0 204 C8
Cottonham Ci NFNCH/WDSPK N12 97 N6
Cotton Hi BMLY BR1 183 J7
Cotton La RDART DA2 188 B1
Cottonmill Crs STAL AL1 38 C8
Cottonmill La STAL AL1 38 C8
Cotton Rd POTB/CUF EN6 59 M7
Cotton Rw BTSEA SW11 158 E9
Cottons Ap ROMW/RG RM7 124 E3
Cotton's Gdns BETH E2 7 K9
Cotton St POP/IOD E14 141 H10
Cotts Wood Dr RGUE GU4 250 D5
Couchmore Av CLAY IG5 102 C10
  ESH/CLAY KT10 198 C10
Coulgate St BROCKY SE4 160 D9
Coulsdon Court Rd COUL/CHIP CR5 240 G2
Coulsdon La COUL/CHIP CR5 240 C9
Coulsdon PI CTHM CR3 241 L4
Coulsdon Ri COUL/CHIP CR5 240 F4
Coulsdon Rd COUL/CHIP CR5 240 E3
  CTHM CR3 241 K7
Coulser Ci HHW HP1 35 M6
Coulson Ci BCTR RM8 123 M6
Coulson St CHEL SW3 15 P7
Coulson Wy SLN SL2 130 A8
Coulter Ci POTB/CUF EN6 60 A5
  YEAD UB4 133 L6
Coulter Rd HMSMTH W6 156 G1
Council Av GVW DA11 189 P4
Councillor St CMBW SE5 158 G6
Counters Ci HHW HP1 35 K6
Counter St STHWK SE1 13 J1
Countess Ci DEN/HRF UB9 91 H10
Countess Rd KTTN NW5 4 F1
Countisbury Av EN EN1 99 N1
Countisbury Gdns ADL/WDHM KT15 215 L2
Country Av FELT TW13 175 K8
County Ga BAR EN5 77 L9
  ELTH/MOT SE9 184 F5
County Gv CMBW SE5 158 G7
County Oak La CRAWW RH11 283 P3
County Oak Wy CRAWW RH11 283 N3
County Rd EHAM E6 142 C1
  THHTH CR7 180 C10
County St STHWK SE1 18 F4

**Column 6**

Cosne Ms HARP AL5 20 B4
(see column 5)

| Street | Area | Page | Grid |
|---|---|---|---|
| Coupland Pl | WOOL/PLUM SE18 | 162 | G1 |
| Courage Cl | EMPK RM11 | 125 | K4 |
| Courcy Rd | CEND/HSY/T N8 | 119 | H1 |
| Courier Rd | DAGW RM9 | 144 | D6 |
| Courland Gv | VX/NE SW8 | 158 | G7 |
| Courland Rd | ADL/WDHM KT15 | 195 | J10 |
| Courland St | VX/NE SW8 | 158 | G7 |
| Coursers Rd | LCOL/BKTW AL2 | 57 | M3 |
| The Course | ELTH/MOT SE9 | 184 | D6 |
| Courtauld Rd | ARCH N19 | 118 | E6 |
| Courtaulds | KGLGY WD4 | 53 | L5 |
| Courtaulds Cl | THMD SE28 | 143 | K10 |
| Court Av | BELV DA17 | 164 | A4 |
| Court Cl | CROY/NA CRO | 222 | C1 |
|  | HGDN/ICK UB10 | 132 | A3 |
|  | STAN HA7 | 95 | K5 |
|  | SUT SM1 | 221 | P1 |
| Courtenay Av | BELMT SM2 | 221 | K5 |
|  | HGT N6 | 117 | P5 |
|  | KTN/HRWW/WS HA3 | 94 | A3 |
|  | CDW/CHF RM16 | 167 | L2 |
| Courtenay Gdns | UPMR RM14 | 126 | B7 |
| Courtenay Ms | WALTH E17 | 120 | C3 |
|  | WOKN/KNAP GU21 | 232 | D2 |
| Courtenay Pl | WALTH E17 | 120 | D3 |
| Courtenay Rd | PGE/AN SE20 | 182 | C10 |
|  | WAN E11 | 121 | L8 |
|  | WBLY HA9 * | 115 | J8 |
|  | WOKN/KNAP GU21 * | 232 | D2 |
|  | WPK KT4 | 200 | F10 |
| Courtenay St | LBTH SE11 | 18 | A8 |
| Courtenay St | LBTH SE11 | 17 | P7 |
| Courten Ms | STAN HA7 * | 95 | H8 |
| Court Farm Av | HOR/WEW KT19 | 220 | A2 |
| Court Farm Cl | SL SL1 | 128 | C10 |
| Court Farm Gdns | HOR/WEW KT19 | 220 | A7 |
| Court Farm Pk | WARL CR6 * | 241 | P2 |
| Court Farm Rd | ELTH/MOT SE9 | 184 | A5 |
|  | NTHLT UB5 | 133 | P2 |
|  | WARL CR6 | 241 | P4 |
| Courtfield Av | HRW HA1 * | 114 | F3 |
| Courtfield Cl | BROX EN10 * | 44 | H6 |
| Courtfield Crs | HRW HA1 | 114 | E3 |
| Courtfield Gdns | DEN/HRF UB9 | 111 | K8 |
|  | ECT SW5 | 15 | H4 |
|  | RSLP HA4 | 112 | G7 |
|  | WEA W13 | 134 | F8 |
| Courtfield Ms | ECT SW5 | 15 | J5 |
| Courtfield Rd | ASHF TW15 | 174 | C9 |
|  | SKENS SW7 | 15 | J5 |
| Courtfields | HARP AL5 | 20 | C2 |
| Court Gdns | HOLWY N7 * | 6 | B2 |
| Courtgate Cl | MLHL NW7 | 96 | C7 |
| Court Green Hts | WOKS/MYFD GU22 | 231 | P6 |
| Court Haw | BNSTD SM7 | 239 | P7 |
| Courthill Rd | LEW SE13 | 161 | H10 |
| Court Hl | SAND/SEL CR2 | 223 | M8 |
|  | HAMP NW3 | 118 | A9 |
|  | WIM/MER SW19 | 179 | H8 |
| Courthope Vis | WIM/MER SW19 | 179 | H10 |
| Courthouse La | STNW/STAM N16 | 119 | M9 |
| Court House Rd | FNCH N3 | 97 | L7 |
| Courtland Av | CHING E4 | 101 | L3 |
|  | IL IG1 | 122 | C7 |
|  | MLHL NW7 | 96 | F10 |
|  | STRHM/NOR SW16 | 180 | C10 |
| Courtland Dr | CHIG IG7 | 102 | F4 |
| Courtland Gv | THMD SE28 | 143 | N9 |
| Courtland Rd | EHAM E6 | 142 | F4 |
| Courtlands | CHST BR7 | 184 | E10 |
|  | RCHPK/HAM TW10 | 177 | M1 |
| Courtlands Av | DTCH/LGLY SL3 | 150 | A3 |
|  | ESH/CLAY KT10 | 217 | N3 |
|  | HAYES BR2 | 205 | K8 |
|  | HPTN TW12 | 175 | N9 |
|  | LEE/GVPK SE12 | 183 | N1 |
|  | RCH/KEW TW9 | 155 | N8 |
| Courtlands Cl | RSLP HA4 | 112 | C5 |
|  | SAND/SEL CR2 | 223 | N6 |
|  | WATN WD24 | 72 | F1 |
| Courtlands Crs | BNSTD SM7 | 239 | K2 |
| Courtlands Dr | HOR/WEW KT19 | 220 | B5 |
|  | WAT WD17 | 72 | F2 |
| Courtlands Rd | BRYLDS KT5 | 199 | M7 |
| Court La | DUL SE21 | 181 | N3 |
|  | HOR/WEW KT19 | 219 | P9 |
|  | IVER SL0 | 131 | K10 |
|  | SL SL1 | 128 | C5 |
| Court Lane Gdns | DUL SE21 | 181 | M3 |
| Courtleas | COB KT11 | 217 | P9 |
| Courtleet Dr | BXLYHN DA7 | 164 | C7 |
| Courtleigh Av | EBAR EN4 | 77 | N4 |
| Courtleigh Gdns | GLDGN NW11 | 117 | H2 |
| Court Ldg | WD7 * | 57 | M10 |
| Court Lodge Rd | HORL RH6 | 280 | E10 |
| Courtman Rd | TOTM N17 | 99 | K8 |
| Court Md | NTHLT UB5 | 133 | N5 |
| Courtmead Cl | HNHL SE24 | 181 | K2 |
| Courtnell St | BAY/PAD W2 | 8 | B1 |
| Courtney Cl | NRWD SE19 | 181 | M9 |
| Courtney Crs | CAR SM5 | 222 | A4 |
| Courtney Pl | COB KT11 | 217 | N8 |
|  | CROY/NA CRO | 223 | H10 |
| Courtney Rd | CDW/CHF RM16 | 168 | F1 |
|  | CROY/NA CRO | 203 | H10 |
|  | HOLWY N7 | 6 | B2 |
|  | HTHAIR TW6 | 152 | B9 |
|  | WBLY HA9 | 115 | J8 |
|  | WIM/MER SW19 | 179 | P9 |
| Courtney Wy | HTHAIR TW6 | 152 | B9 |
| Courtoak La | HORL RH6 | 281 | K2 |
| Courtrai Rd | FSTH SE23 | 182 | D2 |
| Court Rd | BNSTD SM7 | 239 | K1 |
|  | CTHM CR3 | 241 | L9 |
|  | ELTH/MOT SE9 | 183 | L4 |
|  | ELTH/MOT SE9 | 184 | B5 |
|  | GDST RH9 | 260 | B7 |
|  | HGDN/ICK UB10 | 112 | C10 |
|  | NWDGN UB2 | 153 | N3 |
|  | RDART DA2 | 188 | D3 |
|  | SNWD SE25 | 203 | N2 |
| Court Road (Orpington By-Pass) | ORP BR6 | 207 | L10 |
| Courtside | HGT N6 | 118 | E4 |
|  | SYD SE26 * | 182 | B6 |
| The Courts | STRHM/NOR SW16 | 180 | A10 |
| Courtstreet | BMLY BR1 | 205 | M2 |
| Court St | WCHPL E1 | 140 | C6 |
| The Court | MUSWH N10 * | 118 | C2 |
|  | RSLP HA4 | 113 | M4 |
|  | WARL CR6 | 242 | D4 |
| Court Vw | HGT N6 * | 118 | C5 |
| Court Wy | ACT W3 | 135 | P7 |
|  | BARK/HLT IG6 | 122 | F1 |
|  | CDALE/KGS NW9 | 97 | H3 |
|  | HARH RM3 | 105 | M2 |
|  | WHTN TW2 | 176 | B3 |
| The Courtway | OXHEY WD19 | 93 | M3 |
| Court Wood La | CROY/NA CRO | 224 | G6 |
| Court Yd | ELTH/MOT SE9 | 184 | B2 |
| Courtyard Cl | AMS HP6 | 69 | H4 |
| Courtyard Ms | RAIN RM13 | 144 | C3 |
| The Courtyards | WATW WD18 * | 92 | H1 |
| The Courtyard | BF/WBF KT14 | 215 | K8 |
|  | BH/WHM TN16 * | 262 | G1 |
|  | BRKMPK AL9 | 42 | A5 |
|  | BRWN CM15 | 106 | C1 |
|  | CRAWE RH10 * | 283 | N8 |
|  | HHS/BOV HP3 | 53 | N6 |
|  | HLWE CM17 | 29 | N7 |
|  | IS N1 | 5 | P1 |
|  | STALE/WH AL4 | 39 | L6 |
| Cousin La | CANST EC4R | 12 | G7 |
| Cousins Cl | WDR/YW UB7 | 132 | C1 |
| Couthurst Rd | BKHTH/KID SE3 | 161 | N5 |
| Coutts Av | CHSGTN KT9 | 219 | K3 |
| Coutts Crs | KTTN NW5 | 117 | P1 |
| Couzins Wk | DART DA1 | 165 | N8 |
| Coval Gdns | MORT/ESHN SW14 | 155 | N10 |
| Coval La | MORT/ESHN SW14 | 155 | N10 |
| Coval Rd | MORT/ESHN SW14 | 155 | P10 |
| Coveham Crs | COB KT11 | 217 | H9 |
| Covelees Wall | EHAM E6 | 142 | B9 |
| Covent Gdn | COVGDN WC2 * | 11 | M7 |
| Covent Garden Piazza | COVGDN WC2E | 11 | M7 |
| Coventry Cl | EHAM E6 | 142 | A9 |
|  | KIL/WHAMP NW6 | 2 | F1 |
| Coventry Cross Est | BOW E3 | 141 | H6 |
| Coventry Rd | IL IG1 | 122 | E6 |
|  | SNWD SE25 | 203 | P4 |
|  | WCHPL E1 | 140 | A6 |
| Coverack Cl | CROY/NA CRO | 204 | D7 |
|  | STHGT/OAK N14 | 78 | D10 |
| Coverdale | HHNE HP2 | 35 | P3 |
| Coverdale Gdns | CROY/NA CRO | 3 | K6 |
| Coverdale Rd | CRICK NW2 | 2 | A1 |
|  | FBAR/BDGN N11 | 98 | B7 |
|  | SHB W12 | 136 | E10 |
| The Coverdales | BARK IG11 | 142 | C4 |
| Coverdale Wy | SLN SL2 | 128 | C6 |
| Coverley Cl | RBRW/HUT CM13 * | 107 | H9 |
|  | WCHPL E1 * | 13 | P3 |
| Covert Cl | BERK HP4 | 33 | J3 |
| Coverton Rd | TOOT SW17 | 179 | H7 |
| Covert Rd | BARK/HLT IG6 | 103 | J7 |
|  | BERK HP4 | 33 | J2 |
| The Covert | ASC SL5 | 192 | A7 |
|  | NRWD SE19 * | 181 | N10 |
|  | ORP BR6 | 207 | H6 |
| Covert Wy | EBAR EN4 | 77 | M6 |
| Covesfield | GVW DA11 | 190 | E3 |
| Covet Wood Cl | STMC/STPC BR5 | 207 | J6 |
| Covey Cl | WIM/MER SW19 | 201 | L2 |
| Covey Rd | WPK KT4 | 200 | G9 |
| The Covey | CRAWE RH10 | 284 | E5 |
| Covington Gdns | STRHM/NOR SW16 | 181 | J10 |
| Covington Wy | STRHM/NOR SW16 | 181 | H10 |
| Cowbridge La | BARK IG11 | 142 | C3 |
| Cowbridge Meadow | CHOB/PIR GU24 | 230 | E9 |
| Cowbridge Rd | KTN/HRWW/WS HA3 | 115 | J2 |
| Cowcross St | FARR EC1M | 12 | C3 |
| Cowdenbeath Pth | IS N1 | 5 | N5 |
| Cowden Rd | ORP BR6 | 207 | J7 |
| Cowden St | CAT SE6 | 182 | F7 |
| Cowdray Cl | CRAWE RH10 * | 284 | D6 |
| Cowdray Rd | HGDN/ICK UB10 | 132 | D3 |
| Cowdrey Cl | EN EN1 | 79 | M6 |
| Cowdrey Rd | WIM/MER SW19 | 179 | L3 |
| Cowen Av | HRW HA1 | 114 | C7 |
| Cowfold Cl | CRAWW RH11 | 283 | J10 |
| Cowgate Rd | GFD/PVL UB6 | 134 | C5 |
| Cowick Rd | TOOT SW17 | 180 | G7 |
| Cowings Md | NTHLT UB5 | 133 | N2 |
| Cowland Av | PEND EN3 | 80 | B8 |
| Cow La | BUSH WD23 * | 73 | P10 |
|  | GSTN WD25 | 73 | K2 |
| Cow Leaze | EHAM E6 | 142 | B8 |
| Cowleaze Rd | KUTN/CMB KT2 | 9 | J2 |
| Cowles | CHESW EN7 | 61 | N3 |
| Cowley Av | CHERT KT16 | 195 | J4 |
|  | RDART DA2 | 188 | E1 |
| Cowley Cl | SAND/SEL CR2 | 224 | B5 |
| Cowley Ct | WAN E11 * | 121 | K8 |
| Cowley Crs | UX/CGN UB8 | 131 | N7 |
|  | WOT/HER KT12 | 217 | K1 |
| Cowley Hl | BORE WD6 | 75 | M3 |
| Cowley La | WAN E11 * | 121 | K8 |
| Cowley Mill Rd | UX/CGN UB8 | 131 | L4 |
| Cowley Pl | HDN NW4 | 116 | F3 |
| Cowley Rd | ACT W3 | 136 | G5 |
|  | BRXN/ST SW9 | 159 | P1 |
|  | HARH RM3 | 105 | J3 |
|  | IL IG1 | 122 | C5 |
|  | MORT/ESHN SW14 | 156 | A9 |
|  | UX/CGN UB8 | 131 | N6 |
|  | WAN E11 | 121 | N1 |
| Cowley St | WEST SW1P | 17 | L4 |
| Cowling Cl | NTGHL W11 | 8 | J1 |
| Cowlins | HLWE CM17 | 29 | N7 |
| Coworth Cl | ASC SL5 | 192 | C5 |
| Coworth Pk | ASC SL5 | 193 | H3 |
| Coworth Rd | ASC SL5 | 192 | C5 |
| Cowper Av | EHAM E6 | 142 | B2 |
|  | SUT SM1 | 221 | P1 |
| Cox Cl | RAD WD7 | 57 | M10 |
| Coxdean | EPSOM KT18 | 238 | F10 |
| Coxe Pl | KTN/HRWW/WS HA3 | 114 | F2 |
| Coxes Av | SHPTN TW17 | 196 | F5 |
| Coxfield Cl | HHNE HP2 | 35 | P3 |
| Cox La | CHSGTN KT9 | 219 | L3 |
|  | HOR/WEW KT19 | 219 | P3 |
| Coxley Ri | PUR/KEN CR8 | 223 | K8 |
| Coxmount Rd | CHARL SE7 | 142 | C10 |
| Coxon Dr | CDW/CHF RM16 | 167 | K2 |
| Coxs Cots | WARL CR6 * | 225 | K10 |
| Coxson Wy | STHWK SE1 * | 19 | P2 |
| Coxtie Green Rd | BRW CM14 | 106 | A1 |
| Coxwell Rd | NRWD SE19 | 181 | N10 |
|  | WOOL/PLUM SE18 | 162 | G10 |
| Cozens La East | BROX EN10 | 44 | E8 |
| Cozens La West | BROX EN10 | 44 | E8 |
| Cozens Rd | WARE SG12 | 26 | E1 |
| Crabbe Crs | CHSH HP5 | 51 | J5 |
| Crabbet Rd | CRAWE RH10 | 285 | L5 |
| Crabbs Croft Cl | ORP BR6 * | 226 | F2 |
| Crab Hl | BECK BR3 | 183 | J10 |
| Crab La | STWL/WRAY TW19 | 56 | A10 |
| Crab Tree Cl | BEAC HP9 | 88 | A10 |
|  | CHDH RM6 | 123 | J4 |
| Crabtree Av | ALP/SUD HA0 | 135 | K4 |
|  | CHDH RM6 | 123 | P2 |
| Crabtree Cl | BETH E2 | 7 | J2 |
|  | BUSH WD23 | 74 | A9 |
| Crabtree Dr | HYS/HAR UB3 | 152 | A5 |
|  | LHD/OX KT22 | 276 | B5 |
| Crabtree La | FUL/PGN SW6 | 157 | G5 |
|  | HYS/HAR UB3 | 152 | A5 |
| Crabtree Manorway North | BELV DA17 | 164 | D1 |
| Crabtree Manorway South | ECH TW20 | 194 | D7 |
| Crabtree Wk | BROX EN10 | 44 | D5 |
| Crackley Meadow | HHNE HP2 | 36 | C5 |
| Cracknell Cl | EN EN1 | 80 | A3 |
| Craddock Rd | EN EN1 | 79 | N7 |
| Craddocks Av | ASHTD KT21 | 237 | L2 |
| Craddock's Cl | ASHTD KT21 | 237 | M2 |
| Craddock St | KTTN NW5 | 4 | C2 |
| Cradhurst Cl | DORK RH4 | 272 | B5 |
| Cradley Rd | ELTH/MOT SE9 | 184 | G4 |
| Cragg Av | RAD WD7 | 74 | E2 |
| Cragie Lea | MUSWH N10 * | 98 | C10 |
| Craigans | CRAWW RH11 | 283 | K7 |
| Craigavon Rd | HHNE HP2 | 36 | A3 |
| Craigdale Rd | EMPK RM11 | 124 | C4 |
| Craig Dr | UX/CGN UB8 | 132 | C8 |
| Craigen Av | CROY/NA CRO | 204 | A8 |
| Craigen Gdns | IL IG1 | 123 | H9 |
| Craigholm | WOOL/PLUM SE18 | 162 | D8 |
| Craiglands | CFSP/GDCR SL9 | 50 | A4 |
| Craig Mt | RAD WD7 | 74 | D1 |
| Craigmuir Pk | ALP/SUD HA0 | 135 | L3 |
| Craignair Rd | BRXS/STRHM SW2 | 180 | G3 |
| Craignish Av | STRHM/NOR SW16 | 202 | C2 |
| Craig Park Rd | UED N18 | 100 | A5 |
| Craigs Rd | RCHPK/HAM TW10 | 177 | H7 |
| Craigton Rd | ELTH/MOT SE9 | 162 | C10 |
| Craigweil Av | RAD WD7 | 74 | C1 |
| Craigweil Cl | STAN HA7 | 95 | J6 |
| Craigweil Dr | STAN HA7 | 95 | J6 |
| Craigwell Av | FELT TW13 | 175 | H6 |
| Craigwell Cl | STA TW18 | 195 | H1 |
| Crail Rw | WALW SE17 | 19 | H6 |
| Crakell Rd | REIG RH2 | 275 | N5 |
| Crakers Md | WDR/YW UB8 * | 73 | J7 |
| Cramer St | MHST W1U | 10 | A1 |
| Crammavill St | CDW/CHF RM16 | 147 | M10 |
| Crammond Cl | HMSMTH W6 * | 14 | A9 |
| Cramond Ct | EBED/NFELT TW14 | 174 | A4 |
| Crampshaw La | ASHTD KT21 | 237 | L6 |
| Crampton Rd | PGE/AN SE20 | 182 | B9 |
| Crampton's Rd | RSEV TN14 | 247 | M3 |
| Crampton St | NTHLT UB5 | 133 | L4 |
| Cranberry La | CAN/RD E16 | 141 | M5 |
| Cranbourne Av | NWDGN UB2 | 153 | J9 |
|  | SURB KT6 | 199 | M10 |
| Cranbourne Cl | HERT/BAY SG13 | 25 | K8 |
|  | POTB/CUF EN6 | 59 | J7 |
| Cranbourne Crs | POTB/CUF EN6 | 59 | J7 |
| Cranbourne Gdns | UPMR RM14 | 126 | A7 |
|  | WGCE AL7 | 23 | J6 |
| Cranbourne Pde | POTB/CUF EN6 * | 58 | G7 |
| Cranbourne Rd | BARK IG11 | 142 | G3 |
|  | CHES/WCR EN8 | 62 | C8 |
|  | HAT AL10 | 40 | E5 |
|  | HOD EN11 | 44 | E2 |
|  | POTB/CUF EN6 | 59 | H7 |
| Cranbourne Wk | CRAWE RH10 | 284 | A9 |
| Cranbourne Waye | YEAD UB4 | 133 | J9 |
| Cranbourn Pde | POTB/CUF EN6 * | 58 | G7 |
| Cranbrook Cl | HAYES BR2 | 205 | M6 |
| Cranbrook Dr | ESH/CLAY KT10 | 198 | B3 |
|  | GPK RM2 | 123 | P2 |
|  | STALE/WH AL4 | 39 | K6 |
|  | WHTN TW2 | 176 | A6 |
| Cranbrook La | FBAR/BDGN N11 | 98 | C5 |
| Cranbrook Ms | WALTH E17 | 120 | C5 |
| Cranbrook Pk | WDGN N22 | 99 | H9 |
| Cranbrook Ri | IL IG1 | 122 | C7 |
| Cranbrook Rd | BARK/HLT IG6 | 164 | A7 |
|  | BXLYHN DA7 | 164 | A7 |
|  | CHSWK W4 | 156 | B4 |
|  | DEPT SE8 | 160 | K8 |
|  | EBAR EN4 | 77 | N10 |
|  | GNTH/NBYPK IG2 | 122 | D4 |
|  | HSLWW TW4 | 153 | N10 |
|  | IL IG1 | 122 | C7 |
|  | THHTH CR7 | 203 | J4 |
|  | WIM/MER SW19 | 178 | A4 |
| Cranbrook St | BETH E2 | 140 | D7 |
| Cranbury Rd | FUL/PGN SW6 | 157 | L8 |
| Crandon Wk | EYN DA4 * | 210 | D2 |
| Cranes Dr | BRYLDS KT5 | 199 | M4 |
| Cranes Pk | BRYLDS KT5 | 199 | K4 |
| Cranes Park Av | BRYLDS KT5 | 199 | K4 |
| Cranes Park Crs | BRYLDS KT5 | 199 | M4 |
| Craneswater | HYS/HAR UB3 | 152 | G5 |
| Craneswater Pk | NWDGN UB2 | 153 | N4 |
| Cranes Wy | BORE WD6 | 75 | P9 |
| Crane Wy | WHTN TW2 | 176 | B3 |
| Cranfield Crs | POTB/CUF EN6 | 60 | B3 |
| Cranfield Dr | CDALE/KGS NW9 | 96 | G5 |
| Cranfield Rd | BROCKY SE4 | 160 | A12 |
| Cranfield Rd East | CAR SM5 | 222 | B5 |
| Cranfield Rd West | CAR SM5 * | 222 | B5 |
| Cranford Av | PLMGR N13 | 98 | F6 |
|  | STWL/WRAY TW19 | 173 | P5 |
| Cranford Cl | PUR/KEN CR8 | 223 | K9 |
|  | RYNPK SW20 | 178 | E10 |
|  | STWL/WRAY TW19 | 173 | P5 |
| Cranford Cots | ELTH/MOT SE9 * | 184 | F5 |
| Cranford Dr | HYS/HAR UB3 | 152 | C3 |
| Cranford La | HTHAIR TW6 | 152 | D2 |
|  | HYS/HAR UB3 | 152 | B5 |
| Cranford Park Rd | HYS/HAR UB3 | 152 | C3 |
| Cranford St | WCHPL E1 | 140 | G8 |
| Cranford Wy | CEND/HSY/T N8 | 118 | G2 |
| Cranham Gdns | UPMR RM14 | 126 | C5 |
| Cranham Rd | EMPK RM11 | 125 | J4 |
| Cranhurst Rd | CRICK NW2 | 118 | A3 |
| Cranleigh Cl | BXLY DA5 * | 186 | C2 |
|  | CHESW EN7 | 61 | N3 |
|  | ORP BR6 | 207 | K10 |
|  | PGE/AN SE20 | 204 | C3 |
|  | SAND/SEL CR2 | 223 | P8 |
| Cranleigh Dr | SWLY BR8 | 208 | A4 |
| Cranleigh Gdns | BARK IG11 | 142 | C2 |
|  | KTN/HRWW/WS HA3 | 115 | K3 |
|  | KUTN/CMB KT2 | 177 | K8 |
|  | LOU IG10 | 82 | C10 |
|  | SAND/SEL CR2 | 223 | P8 |
|  | SNWD SE25 | 203 | M3 |
|  | STHL UB1 | 133 | N6 |
|  | SUT SM1 | 201 | N10 |
|  | WCHMH N21 | 79 | H5 |
| Cranleigh Ms | BTSEA SW11 | 157 | P8 |
| Cranleigh Rd | ESH/CLAY KT10 | 198 | B2 |
|  | FELT TW13 | 174 | C7 |
|  | SEVS/STOTM N15 | 119 | K3 |
|  | WIM/MER SW19 | 201 | K3 |
| Cranleigh Ter | SHB W12 | 137 | H6 |
| Cranley Cl | GU GU1 | 250 | D10 |
| Cranley Dene | GU GU1 | 250 | D10 |
| Cranley Dr | GNTH/NBYPK IG2 | 122 | F5 |
|  | RSLP HA4 | 112 | C7 |
| Cranley Gdns | MUSWH N10 | 98 | C2 |
|  | PLMGR N13 | 98 | F2 |
|  | SKENS SW7 | 15 | H6 |
|  | WLGTN SM6 | 222 | D4 |
| Cranley Ms | SKENS SW7 | 15 | L6 |
| Cranley Pde | SKENS SW7 * | 15 | L6 |
|  | WOKN/KNAP GU21 * | 231 | J4 |
| Cranley Pl | SKENS SW7 | 15 | L6 |
| Cranley Rd | GNTH/NBYPK IG2 | 122 | F5 |
|  | GU GU1 | 250 | C10 |
|  | PLSTW E13 | 141 | N7 |
|  | WOT/HER KT12 | 216 | F2 |
| Cranley Ter | HDN NW4 * | 96 | C10 |
| Cranmer Av | WEA W13 | 154 | G2 |
| Cranmer Cl | MRDN SM4 | 201 | G6 |
|  | POTB/CUF EN6 | 59 | M6 |
|  | RSLP HA4 | 113 | L6 |
|  | STAN HA7 | 95 | H8 |
|  | WARL CR6 | 242 | D5 |
|  | WEY KT13 | 216 | B6 |
| Cranmer Ct | HPTN TW12 | 176 | A8 |
|  | KUTN/CMB KT2 | 177 | J7 |
| Cranmer Farm Cl | MTCM CR4 | 202 | A4 |
| Cranmer Gdns | DAGE RM10 | 124 | D9 |
|  | WARL CR6 | 242 | D5 |
| Cranmer Rd | BRXN/ST SW9 | 18 | E10 |
|  | CROY/NA CRO | 203 | J10 |
|  | EA W5 | 135 | K10 |
|  | EDGW HA8 | 96 | C8 |
|  | FSTGT E7 | 121 | J9 |
|  | HPTN TW12 | 176 | A8 |
|  | HYS/HAR UB3 | 133 | J7 |
|  | KUTN/CMB KT2 | 177 | K8 |
|  | MTCM CR4 | 202 | A4 |
|  | SEV TN13 | 246 | F9 |
| Cranmer Ter | TOOT SW17 | 179 | L9 |
| Cranmore Av | ISLW TW7 | 154 | B6 |
| Cranmore La | EHSLY KT24 | 252 | C5 |
| Cranmore Rd | BMLY BR1 | 183 | K6 |
|  | CHST BR7 | 184 | G4 |
| Cranmore Wy | MUSWH N10 | 118 | D2 |
| Cranston Cl | HGDN/ICK UB10 | 112 | C7 |
|  | HSLW TW3 | 153 | M8 |
|  | REIG RH2 | 275 | M5 |
| Cranston Gdns | CHING E4 | 101 | J2 |
| Cranston Rd | FSTH SE23 | 182 | B3 |
| Cranstoun Cl | RGUW GU3 | 249 | J6 |
| Cranswick Rd | BERM/RHTH SE16 | 160 | A4 |
| Crantock Rd | CAT SE6 | 183 | H5 |
| Cranwell Cl | BOW E3 | 140 | A3 |
| Cranwell Gv | SHPTN TW17 | 196 | A6 |
| Cranwells La | FNM GU9 | 9 | L1 |
| Cranwich Av | WCHMH N21 | 99 | L1 |
| Cranwich Rd | STNW/STAM N16 | 119 | M3 |
| Cranwood St | FSBYE EC1V | 7 | H10 |
| Cranworth Crs | CHING E4 | 101 | J2 |
| Cranworth Gdns | BRXN/ST SW9 | 159 | H9 |
| Craster Rd | BRXS/STRHM SW2 | 180 | A5 |
| Crathie Rd | LEE/GVPK SE12 | 183 | N1 |
| Cravan Av | FELT TW13 | 175 | J5 |
| Cravells Rd | HARP AL5 | 20 | B5 |
| Craven Av | EA W5 | 135 | N7 |
|  | STHL UB1 | 133 | N4 |
| Craven Cl | STNW/STAM N16 * | 119 | P5 |
|  | YEAD UB4 | 133 | J5 |
| Craven Gdns | BARK IG11 | 143 | H4 |
|  | BARK/HLT IG6 | 122 | G10 |
|  | SHPTN TW17 | 196 | A6 |
|  | STMC/STPC BR5 | 206 | B5 |
|  | WIM/MER SW19 | 179 | L4 |
| Craven Hill | BAY/PAD W2 | 9 | J7 |
| Craven Hill Gdns | BAY/PAD W2 | 9 | H7 |
| Craven Hill Ms | BAY/PAD W2 | 9 | J7 |
| Craven Ms | BTSEA SW11 | 158 | A5 |
| Craven Pk | WLSDN NW10 | 136 | B1 |
| Craven Park Ms | WLSDN NW10 | 136 | B1 |
| Craven Park Rd | SEVS/STOTM N15 | 119 | N4 |
|  | WLSDN NW10 | 136 | B3 |
| Craven Pas | CHCR WC2N | 11 | K9 |
| Craven Rd | BAY/PAD W2 | 9 | J7 |
|  | CROY/NA CRO | 204 | A8 |
|  | KUTN/CMB KT2 | 199 | L1 |
|  | ORP BR6 | 207 | N2 |
|  | WEA W13 | 135 | H5 |
|  | WLSDN NW10 | 136 | B3 |
| Craven St | CHCR WC2N | 11 | K8 |
| Craven Ter | BAY/PAD W2 | 9 | J7 |
| Craven Wk | CLPT E5 | 120 | C5 |
| Crawford Av | ALP/SUD HA0 | 115 | J10 |
|  | CDW/CHF RM16 | 147 | P10 |
| Crawford Cl | ISLW TW7 | 154 | A7 |
| Crawford Gdns | NTHLT UB5 | 133 | L3 |
|  | PLMGR N13 | 99 | J3 |
| Crawford Ms | MBLAR W1H * | 9 | N1 |
| Crawford Pas | CLKNW EC1R | 12 | A1 |
| Crawford Pl | MBLAR W1H | 9 | N2 |
| Crawford Rd | CMBW SE5 | 158 | F8 |
|  | HAT AL10 | 40 | C2 |
| Crawfords | SWLY BR8 | 186 | A10 |
| Crawford St | MBLAR W1H | 9 | N1 |
|  | WLSDN NW10 | 136 | F1 |
| Crawley Av | CRAWW RH11 | 283 | P9 |
| Crawley Goods Yd | CRAWE RH10 * | 284 | C5 |
| Crawley La | CRAWE RH10 | 285 | K3 |
| Crawley Rd | EN EN1 | 99 | M1 |
|  | LEY E10 | 120 | G6 |
|  | WDGN N22 | 99 | K10 |
| Crawley's La | TRING HP23 | 32 | D2 |
| Crawshaw Rd | CHERT KT16 | 214 | G3 |
| Crawshay Cl | SEV TN13 | 247 | H9 |
| Crawters Cl | CRAWE RH10 | 284 | H5 |
| Crawthew Gv | EDUL SE22 | 159 | N10 |
| Cray Av | ASHTD KT21 | 237 | K2 |
|  | ORP BR5 | 207 | L2 |
|  | STMC/STPC BR5 | 207 | L5 |
| Craybrooke Rd | SCUP DA14 | 185 | L2 |
| Crayburne | MEO DA13 | 189 | L8 |
| Craybury End | ELTH/MOT SE9 | 184 | F5 |
| Craydene Rd | ERITH DA8 | 165 | H9 |
| Crayford High St | DART DA1 | 164 | F10 |
| Crayford Rd | HOLWY N7 | 118 | C9 |
| Crayford Wy | DART DA1 | 165 | J10 |
| Craylands | STMC/STPC BR5 | 207 | N4 |
| Craylands La | SWCM DA10 | 189 | J1 |
| Craylands Sq | SWCM DA10 | 189 | J1 |
| Crayleigh Ter | SCUP DA14 * | 185 | M9 |
| Crayle St | SLN SL2 | 128 | C7 |
| Crayonne Cl | SUN TW16 | 196 | A9 |
| Cray Rd | BELV DA17 | 164 | B5 |
|  | SCUP DA14 | 186 | D6 |
|  | SWLY BR8 | 208 | D6 |
| Cray Valley Rd | STMC/STPC BR5 | 207 | M2 |
|  | ORP BR5 | 207 | M2 |
| Crealock Gv | WFD IG8 | 101 | P4 |
| Crealock St | WAND/EARL SW18 | 179 | L4 |
| Creasey Cl | EMPK RM11 | 125 | J4 |
| Creasy Cl | ABLGY WD5 | 54 | C3 |
| Crebor St | EDUL SE22 | 181 | P2 |
| Credenhill Dr | HAYES BR2 | 205 | P8 |
| Credenhill St | STRHM/NOR SW16 | 180 | D9 |
| Crediton Hl | KIL/WHAMP NW6 | 3 | L10 |
| Crediton Rd | WLSDN NW10 | 136 | G3 |
| Crediton Wy | ESH/CLAY KT10 | 218 | F2 |
| Credon Rd | BERM/RHTH SE16 | 160 | A4 |
|  | PLSTW E13 | 141 | N1 |
| Credo Wy | WTHK RM20 | 166 | C5 |
| Creechurch La | HDTCH EC3A | 13 | L5 |
| Creechurch Pl | HDTCH EC3A * | 13 | L5 |
| Creed Ct | STP EC4M * | 12 | E6 |
| Creek Cots | E/WMO/HCT KT8 * | 198 | A2 |
| Creek Rd | BARK IG11 | 143 | J5 |
|  | DEPT SE8 | 160 | E4 |
|  | E/WMO/HCT KT8 | 198 | A2 |
| Creekside | DEPT SE8 | 160 | E4 |
|  | RAIN RM13 | 144 | C6 |
| The Creek | GVW DA11 | 191 | H5 |
|  | SUN TW16 | 196 | B5 |
| Creek Wy | RAIN RM13 | 144 | B10 |
| Creeland Gv | CAT SE6 | 182 | C6 |
| Cree's Meadow | BFOR GU20 * | 212 | A2 |
| Crefeld Cl | HMSMTH W6 | 157 | H5 |
| Creffield Rd | EA W5 | 136 | A5 |
| Creighton Av | EFNCH N2 | 98 | A10 |
|  | EHAM E6 | 142 | A4 |
| Creighton Cl | SHB W12 | 137 | J6 |
| Creighton Rd | EA W5 | 135 | J2 |
|  | KIL/WHAMP NW6 | 137 | K1 |
|  | TOTM N17 | 99 | M8 |
| Cremer St | BETH E2 | 7 | L8 |
| Cremorne Gdns | HOR/WEW KT19 | 220 | A5 |
| Cremorne Rd | WBPTN SW10 | 157 | M6 |
| Crescent | TWRH EC3N | 13 | L7 |
| Crescent Av | HCH RM12 | 124 | C9 |
|  | GRAYS RM17 * | 168 | A4 |
| Crescent Cots | SEV TN13 | 246 | F6 |
| Crescent Ct | GRAYS RM17 * | 168 | A4 |
| Crescent Dr | BRWN CM15 | 107 | K2 |
| Crescent East | EBAR EN4 | 77 | J9 |
| Crescent Gdns | RSLP HA4 | 113 | J5 |
|  | SWLY BR8 | 186 | B9 |
|  | WIM/MER SW19 | 179 | K6 |
| Crescent Gv | CLAP SW4 | 158 | G10 |
|  | MTCM CR4 | 201 | P4 |
| Crescent La | CLAP SW4 | 158 | G10 |
| Crescent Pde | HGDN/ICK UB10 * | 132 | B5 |
| Crescent Ri | EBAR EN4 | 77 | N5 |
|  | FNCH N3 | 97 | J9 |
|  | WDGN N22 | 98 | F9 |
| Crescent Rd | BECK BR3 | 183 | K10 |
|  | BMLY BR1 | 183 | M10 |
|  | BRW CM14 | 106 | G5 |
|  | CEND/HSY/T N8 | 118 | C5 |
|  | CHING E4 | 101 | P1 |
|  | CTHM CR3 | 241 | P10 |
|  | DAGE RM10 | 124 | D4 |
|  | EBAR EN4 | 77 | N8 |
|  | ED N9 | 100 | F1 |
|  | EHAM E6 | 141 | P3 |
|  | ENC/FH EN2 | 79 | J6 |
|  | ERITH DA8 | 164 | A6 |
|  | FNCH N3 | 97 | J8 |
|  | FBAR/BDGN N11 | 98 | A5 |
|  | HHNE HP2 | 35 | N6 |
|  | KUTN/CMB KT2 | 177 | M10 |
|  | LEY E10 | 120 | C7 |
|  | PLSTW E13 | 141 | P5 |
|  | REDH RH1 | 259 | K9 |
|  | REIG RH2 | 275 | J4 |
|  | RYNPK SW20 | 200 | F1 |
|  | SEVS/STOTM N15 * | 119 | H5 |
|  | SHPTN TW17 | 196 | A6 |
|  | SOCK/AV RM15 | 166 | B1 |
|  | SWFD E18 | 103 | H10 |
|  | WDGN N22 | 98 | F9 |
|  | WOOL/PLUM SE18 | 145 | H9 |
| Crescent Rw | STLK EC1Y | 12 | E2 |
| Crescent St | IS N1 | 5 | P3 |
| The Crescent | ABLGY WD5 | 53 | P5 |
|  | ACT W3 | 136 | A5 |
|  | ALP/SUD HA0 | 114 | C10 |
|  | BAR EN5 | 77 | J2 |
|  | BARN SW13 | 156 | C9 |
|  | BECK BR3 | 183 | K9 |
|  | BELMT SM2 | 221 | K7 |
|  | BXLY DA5 | 165 | P10 |
|  | CHERT KT16 | 195 | M3 |
|  | CHOB/PIR GU24 | 230 | B8 |
|  | CRICK NW2 | 116 | C9 |
|  | CROY/NA CRO | 204 | A8 |
|  | E/WMO/HCT KT8 | 197 | N1 |
|  | EPP CM16 | 65 | J8 |
|  | EPSOM KT18 | 238 | B1 |
|  | FBAR/BDGN N11 | 98 | A4 |
|  | GNTH/NBYPK IG2 | 122 | B4 |
|  | GSTN WD25 | 74 | A3 |
|  | GUW GU2 | 250 | B7 |
|  | HART DA3 | 231 | H2 |
|  | HLWE CM17 | 29 | N4 |
|  | HORL RH6 | 280 | E8 |
|  | HYS/HAR UB3 | 133 | H10 |
|  | LCOL/BKTW AL2 | 55 | F5 |
|  | LHD/OX KT22 | 276 | D7 |
|  | LOU IG10 | 82 | G6 |
|  | NWMAL KT3 | 176 | F10 |
|  | REDH RH1 * | 275 | N1 |
|  | REIG RH2 | 275 | J2 |
|  | RKW/CH/CXG WD3 | 72 | C3 |
|  | RYLU/HDSTN HA2 | 114 | D2 |
|  | SCUP DA14 | 186 | A9 |
|  | SEV TN13 | 247 | L1 |
|  | SL SL1 | 149 | K1 |
|  | STHL UB1 | 153 | M1 |
| Crockford Cl | ADL/WDHM KT15 | 215 | M1 |
| SURB KT6 |  | 199 | K5 |
| SUT SM1 |  | 221 | N2 |
| SWCM DA10 |  | 189 | N2 |
| UPMR RM14 |  | 126 | D5 |
| WALTH E17 |  | 120 | C5 |
| WATW WD18 |  | 73 | K8 |
| WEY KT13 |  | 195 | K6 |
| WIM/MER SW19 |  | 179 | K6 |
| WWKM BR4 |  | 205 | K6 |
| Crescent Vw | LOU IG10 | 82 | A10 |
| Crescent Wk | SOCK/AV RM15 | 168 | B1 |
| Crescent Wy | BROCKY SE4 | 160 | B9 |
|  | HORL RH6 | 280 | B6 |
| Crescentway | NFNCH/WDSPK N12 | 97 | P7 |
| Crescent Wy | ORP BR6 | 227 | H2 |
|  | SOCK/AV RM15 | 146 | C10 |
|  | STRHM/NOR SW16 | 180 | C10 |
| Crescent West | EBAR EN4 | 77 | J4 |
| Crescent Wood Rd | SYD SE26 | 181 | P6 |
| Cresford Rd | FUL/PGN SW6 | 157 | L6 |
| Crespigny Rd | HDN NW4 | 116 | A4 |
| Cressage Cl | STHL UB1 | 133 | P6 |
| Cressall Cl | TEDD TW11 | 176 | C9 |
| Cressall Md | LHD/OX KT22 | 236 | C6 |
| Cress End | RKW/CH/CXG WD3 | 50 | D6 |
| Cresset Cl | STHL UB1 | 133 | P6 |
| Cresset Rd | HOM E9 | 139 | H5 |
| Cresset St | CLAP SW4 | 158 | E9 |
| Cressfield Cl | KTTN NW5 | 4 | A1 |
| Cressida Rd | ARCH N19 | 118 | D6 |
| Cressingham Gv | SUT SM1 | 221 | N3 |
| Cressingham Rd | EDGW HA8 | 96 | E1 |
|  | LEW SE13 | 161 | H10 |
| The Cressinghams | EPSOM KT18 | 220 | A9 |
| Cressington Cl | STNW/STAM N16 | 119 | M10 |
| Cress Rd | SL SL1 | 15 | G1 |
| Cresswell Gdns | ECT SW5 | 15 | J5 |
| Cresswell Pk | BKHTH/KID SE3 | 161 | L3 |
| Cresswell Pl | WBPTN SW10 | 15 | J10 |
| Cresswell Rd | CSHM HP5 | 51 | J10 |
|  | FELT TW13 | 175 | M6 |
|  | SNWD SE25 | 203 | P4 |
|  | TWK TW1 | 155 | P1 |
| Cresswell Wy | WCHMH N21 | 99 | H1 |
| Cressy Ct | HMSMTH W6 | 156 | F2 |
|  | WCHPL E1 | 140 | E7 |
| Cressy Houses | WCHPL E1 * | 140 | E7 |
| Cressy Pl | WCHPL E1 | 140 | E7 |
| Cressy Rd | HAMP NW3 | 118 | A10 |
| Cressys Cnr | HSLW TW3 * | 154 | A8 |
| Cresta Dr | ADL/WDHM KT15 | 215 | J6 |
| Crest Av | GRAYS RM17 | 167 | N6 |
| Crestbrook Av | PLMGR N13 | 99 | J6 |
| Crestbrook Pl | PLMGR N13 * | 99 | J6 |
| Crest Cl | RSEV TN14 | 228 | C7 |
| Crest Dr | PEND EN3 | 80 | B4 |
| Crestfield St | CAMTN NW1 | 5 | M9 |
| Crest Hl | SHGR GU5 | 270 | F6 |
| Cresthill Av | GRAYS RM17 | 167 | P4 |
| Creston Av | WOKN/KNAP GU21 | 231 | K3 |
| Creston Wy | WPK KT4 | 201 | K8 |
| Crest Pk | HHNE HP2 | 36 | D5 |
| Crest Rd | CRICK NW2 | 116 | D7 |
|  | HAYES BR2 | 205 | L7 |
|  | SAND/SEL CR2 | 224 | A4 |
| The Crest | BRYLDS KT5 | 199 | M5 |
|  | CHESW EN7 | 61 | J3 |
|  | HDN NW4 | 116 | F3 |
|  | HOLWY N7 * | 118 | E10 |
|  | PLMGR N13 | 99 | H1 |
|  | POTB/CUF EN6 * | 59 | M7 |
|  | SBW CM21 | 29 | N1 |
| Crest Vw | PIN HA5 | 93 | J10 |
|  | RDART DA2 | 166 | F10 |
| Crest View Dr | STMC/STPC BR5 | 206 | B5 |
| Crestway | PUT/ROE SW15 | 176 | G3 |
| Crestwood Wy | HSLWW TW4 | 175 | H1 |
| Creswell | WOKN/KNAP GU21 * | 231 | J3 |
| Creswell Dr | BECK BR3 | 204 | C3 |
| Creswick Ct | WGCE AL7 * | 22 | G6 |
| Creswick Rd | ACT W3 | 135 | N5 |
| Creswick Wk | GLDGN NW11 * | 116 | G1 |
| Crete Hall Rd | GVW DA11 | 190 | G4 |
| Creukhorne Rd | WLSDN NW10 | 136 | B2 |
| Crew Curve | BERK HP4 | 33 | G2 |
| Crewdson Rd | BRXN/ST SW9 | 158 | G6 |
|  | HORL RH6 | 280 | C4 |
| Crewe Pl | WLSDN NW10 | 136 | C5 |
| Crewe's Av | WARL CR6 | 242 | B2 |
| Crewe's Cl | WARL CR6 | 242 | B2 |
| Crewe's Farm La | WARL CR6 | 242 | C2 |
| Crewe's La | WARL CR6 | 242 | C1 |
| Crews Hl | ENC/FH EN2 | 60 | C10 |
| Crews St | POP/IOD E14 | 160 | C1 |
| Crewys Rd | CRICK NW2 | 117 | J2 |
|  | PECK SE15 | 160 | B1 |
| Crib St | WARE SG12 | 26 | C1 |
| Crichton Av | WLGTN SM6 | 222 | F4 |
| Crichton Rd | CAR SM5 | 222 | B8 |
| Crichton St | VX/NE SW8 * | 158 | D8 |
| Cricketers Arms Rd | ENC/FH EN2 | 79 | K6 |
| Cricketers Cl | CHSGTN KT9 | 219 | J2 |
|  | ERITH DA8 | 164 | F4 |
|  | STALW/RED AL3 | 38 | D1 |
|  | STHGT/OAK N14 | 98 | D1 |
| Cricketers La | BFOR GU20 | 212 | C2 |
| Cricketers Ms | BAL SW12 * | 180 | B1 |
|  | WAND/EARL SW18 | 179 | M5 |
| Cricketers Wk | SYD SE26 | 182 | B8 |
| Cricket Field Rd | UX/CGN UB8 | 131 | N5 |
| Cricketfield Rd | CLPT E5 | 120 | A10 |
|  | WDR/YW UB7 | 151 | M3 |
| Cricket Gn | MTCM CR4 | 202 | A3 |
| Cricket Ground Rd | CHST BR7 | 206 | E1 |
| Cricket Hl | REDH RH1 | 281 | B9 |
| Cricket La | BECK BR3 | 183 | J10 |
| Cricket Rw | EFNCH N2 * | 117 | P1 |
| Cricketts Hl | SHGR GU5 | 270 | E6 |
| Cricket Vw | WEY KT13 | 216 | C5 |
| Cricket Wy | WEY KT13 | 195 | P10 |
| Cricklade Av | BRXS/STRHM SW2 | 180 | A3 |
|  | HARH RM3 | 105 | L7 |
| Cricklewood Broadway | CRICK NW2 | 116 | C9 |
| Cricklewood La | CRICK NW2 | 117 | H8 |
| Cridland St | SRTFD E15 | 141 | H10 |
| Crieff Ct | TEDD TW11 | 177 | H10 |
| Crieff Rd | WAND/EARL SW18 | 179 | M5 |
| Criffel Av | BRXS/STRHM SW2 | 179 | M3 |
| Crimp Hl | WDSR SL4 | 173 | J1 |
| Crimscott St | STHWK SE1 | 19 | L4 |
| Crimsworth Rd | VX/NE SW8 | 158 | E6 |
| Crinan St | IS N1 | 5 | M7 |
| Cringle St | VX/NE SW8 | 158 | C5 |
| Cripplegate St | BARB EC2Y * | 12 | E3 |
| Cripsey Av | CHONG CM5 | 67 | N2 |
| Crispen Rd | FELT TW13 | 175 | J6 |
| Crispian Cl | WLSDN NW10 | 116 | D10 |
| Crispin Cl | BEAC HP9 | 88 | A2 |
|  | CROY/NA CRO | 202 | G10 |
| Crispin Crs | CROY/NA CRO | 202 | G10 |
| Crispin Rd | EDGW HA8 | 96 | E10 |
| Crispin St | WCHPL E1 | 13 | M2 |
| Crispin Wy | SLN SL2 | 129 | K1 |
|  | UX/CGN UB8 | 131 | J2 |
| Crisp Rd | HMSMTH W6 | 156 | G4 |
| Criss Gv | CFSP/GDCR SL9 | 89 | P10 |
| Criss La | CFSP/GDCR SL9 | 89 | P10 |
| Cristowe Rd | FUL/PGN SW6 | 157 | J8 |
| Criterion Ms | ARCH N19 | 118 | D7 |
| Critten La | RKW/CH/CXG WD3 | 275 | H5 |
| Crockenhill Hl | STMC/STPC BR5 | 207 | N9 |
| Crockenhill La | SWLY BR8 | 208 | B5 |
| Crockenhill Rd | STMC/STPC BR5 | 207 | N7 |
| Crockerton Rd | TOOT SW17 | 180 | A5 |
| Crockford Cl | ADL/WDHM KT15 | 215 | M1 |

Crockford Park Rd ADL/WDHM KT15 215 M2
Crockham Cl CRAWW RH11 283 M9
Crockham Wy ELTH/MOT SE9 184 D7
Crocknorth Rd EHSLY KT24 252 F6
Crocus Cl CROY/NA CR0 204 C8
Croffets KWD/TDW/WH KT20 238 G7
Croft Av DORK RH4 254 C10
WWKM BR4 205 H8
Croft Cl ABYW SE2 164 A4
CHST BR7 184 C8
HGDN/ICK UB10 132 B2
HYS/HAR UB3 152 D6
KGLGY WD4 53 K6
MLHL NW7 96 B4
Croft Ct BORE WD6 76 A7
HARP AL5 20 A2
RSLP HA4 112 C6
SUT SM1 201 N3
Croft End Rd KGLGY WD4 53 K6
Crofters Cl ISLW TW7 176 C1
REDH RH1 276 C2
Crofters Ct DEPT SE8 160 D3
Crofters Md NTHWD HA6 92 F5
The Crofters WDSR SL4 * 171 M2
Crofters Wy CAMTN NW1 5 J5
Croft Fld HAT AL10 40 D4
KGLGY WD4 53 K6
Croft Gdns HNWL W7 154 F1
RSLP HA4 112 C6
Crofthill Rd SLN SL2 128 C6
Croftleigh Av PUR/KEN CR8 241 H2
Croft La KGLGY WD4 53 K6
Croft Lodge Cl WFD IG8 101 N7
Croft Meadow KGLGY WD4 53 K6
Croft Ms NFNCH/WDSPK N12 97 M4
Crofton ASHTD KT21 257 K4
Crofton Av BXLY DA5 185 N3
CHSWK W4 155 P6
ORP BR6 206 F9
WOT/HER KT12 197 K10
Crofton Cl CHERT KT16 214 F4
Crofton Gate Wy BROCKY SE4 182 D7
Crofton Gv CHING E4 101 J5
Crofton La ORP BR6 207 N7
STMC/STPC BR5 206 G8
Crofton Park Rd BROCKY SE4 182 E2
Crofton Rd CDW/CHF RM16 159 M7
ORP BR6 206 D10
PLSTW E13 141 N3
Crofton Ter RCH/KEW TW9 155 N10
Crofton Wy BAR EN5 * 77 L10
ENC/FH EN2 79 H1
Croft Rd BH/WHM TN16 262 E2
BMLY BR1 183 N8
CFSP/GDCR SL9 90 B10
CTHM CR3 242 E8
PEND EN3 60 C2
STRHM/NOR SW16 181 N10
SUT SM1 221 N2
WARE SG12 26 B1
WIM/MER SW19 179 M10
Crofts Pth HHS/BOV HP3 36 C8
Crofts St WCHPL E1 13 N8
The Crofts HHS/BOV HP3 36 C7
SHPTN TW17 196 P4
Croft St DEPT SE8 160 D3
The Croft BH/SUD HA0 115 H10
BAR EN5 77 H8
BROX EN10 44 D9
CHING E4 101 K3
CRAWW RH11 283 K7
EA W5 135 K7
HEST TW5 153 H6
LCOL/BKTW AL2 55 P1
LHD/OX KT22 236 D9
LOU IG10 45 P4
PIN HA5 113 N5
RSLP HA4 113 K9
SWLY BR8 208 D3
WGCE AL7 23 J4
WLSDN NW10 136 C4
Croft Wy BFN/LL DA15 185 H6
RCHPK/HAM TW10 176 G6
SEV TN13 264 C1
Croftwell HARP AL5 20 E3
Crogsland Rd CAMTN NW1 4 C3
Croham Cl SAND/SEL CR2 223 M4
Croham Manor Rd SAND/SEL CR2 223 M4
Croham Mt SAND/SEL CR2 223 N4
Croham Park Av SAND/SEL CR2 223 N2
Croham Rd SAND/SEL CR2 223 L2
Croham Valley Rd SAND/SEL CR2 223 P3
Croindene Rd STRHM/NOR SW16 202 F1
Cromartie Rd ARCH N19 118 E3
Cromarty Rd EDGW HA8 95 N3
Cromarty Vls BAY/PAD W2 * 9 J7
Crombie Cl REDBR IG4 122 C3
Crombie Ms BTSEA SW11 * 157 P3
Crombie Rd BFN/LL DA15 184 C4
Cromer Cl UX/CGN UB8 132 C8
Cromer Hyde MRDN SM4 * 201 L5
Crome Rd WLSDN NW10 136 N1
Cromer Rd BAR EN5 * 77 M8
CHDH RM6 123 P4
EMPK RM11 125 L5
HTHAIR TW6 152 B9
LEY E10 121 J3
ROMW/RG RM7 124 D4
SNWD SE25 204 A3
TOOT SW17 180 B9
WATN WD24 73 K4
Cromer Rd West HTHAIR TW6 152 B9
Cromer St STPAN WC1H 5 M10
Cromer Ter HACK E8 * 119 D10
Cromer Villas Rd WAND/EARL SW18 179 J2
Cromford Cl ORP BR6 207 H10
Cromford Rd PUT/ROE SW15 179 J1
Cromford Wy NWMAL KT3 200 A1
Cromlix Cl CHST BR7 206 E2
Crompton Flds CRAWE RH10 283 P4
Crompton Pl PEND EN3 60 F4
Crompton St BAY/PAD W2 9 H2
Cromwell Av CRAWE RH10 283 P5
HAYES BR2 205 N3
HGT N6 118 C6
HMSMTH W6 156 H4
NWMAL KT3 200 D5
Cromwell Cl CHSWK W4 155 N4
CSTG N8 89 P4
EFNCH N2 117 N2
HAYES BR2 205 N4
STA TW18 39 J1
STALE/WH AL4 39 J1
WOT/HER KT12 197 J8
Cromwell Ct ALP/SUD HA0 135 K4
PEND EN3 80 C7
Cromwell Crs ECT SW5 14 F5
Cromwell Dr SL SL1 129 K8
Cromwell Gdns SKENS SW7 15 M5
Cromwell Gv CTHM CR3 241 K7
HMSMTH W6 156 F2
Cromwell Pde ALP/SUD HA0 * 135 K4
Cromwell Pl ACT W3 135 P10
HGT N6 118 C6
MORT/ESHN SW14 155 N4
Cromwell Rd ALP/SUD HA0 135 J4
ASC SL5 192 A4
BECK BR3 204 A5
BORE WD6 75 K5
BRW CM14 106 A3

BRXN/ST SW9 159 J7
CHSW E17 62 A4
CROY/NA CR0 203 L7
CTHM CR3 241 K7
ECT SW5 14 F5
FELT TW13 175 J4
FNCH N3 97 M10
FSTGT E7 141 P2
GRAYS RM17 167 M3
HERT/BAY SG13 25 N4
HSLW TW3 153 P10
HYS/HAR UB3 132 E8
KUTN/CMB KT2 199 K1
MUSWH N10 98 B9
REDH RH1 258 A10
SKENS SW7 15 H5
TEDD TW11 176 F9
WALTH E17 121 H3
WARE SG12 26 E2
WIM/MER SW19 179 K8
WK T4 200 A10
Cromwell St HSLW TW3 153 P10
Cromwell Ter HSLW TW3 * 153 P10
Crondace Rd FUL/PGN SW6 157 N3
Crondall St IS N1 7 H8
Cronin St PECK SE15 159 N6
Cronks Hi REIG RH2 275 N1
Cronks Hill Cl REDH RH1 275 N2
Crooked Billet Rbt CHING E4 100 C8
Crooked La GNWCH SE10 190 C2
Crooked Mile WAB EN9 63 H9
Crooked Usage FNCH N3 117 H1
Crooked Wy WAB EN9 45 K8
Crooke Rd DEPT SE8 160 D4
Crookham Rd FUL/PGN SW6 157 J7
Crookhams WGCE AL7 23 K3
Crook Log BXLYHS DA6 163 N9
Crookston Rd ELTH/MOT SE9 162 D9
ELTH/MOT SE9 184 A5
Croom's Hill GNWCH SE10 161 J6
Croom's Hill Gv GNWCH SE10 161 H6
Crop Common HAT AL10 40 C7
Cropley Ct IS N1 * 6 G7
Croppath Rd DAGE RM10 124 B1
Cropthorne Ct MV/WKIL W9 3 H10
Crosby Cl BEAC HP9 108 E1
FELT TW13 175 M7
STALE/WH AL4 39 J1
Crosby Rd DAGE RM10 144 C4
FSTGT E7 141 M1
Crosby Rw STHWK SE1 18 G1
Crosby Sq HDTCH EC3A 13 J6
Crosby Wk HACK E8 7 L1
Crosier Cl BKHTH/KID SE3 162 B7
Crosier Rd HGDN/ICK UB10 112 A6
Crosier Wy RSLP HA4 112 F8
Crosland Pl BTSEA SW11 158 F3
Crossacres WOKS/MYFD GU22 233 J1
Crossbow Pl CHIG IG7 103 N6
Crossbrook HAT AL10 40 B5
Crossbrook Rd CAN/RD E16 141 P6
Crossbrook St CHES/WCR EN8 62 C7
Cross Deep TWK TW1 176 F4
Cross Deep Gdns TWK TW1 176 F5
Crossfell Rd HHS/BOV HP3 36 D5
Crossfield Rd BRXN/ST SW9 158 G10
HAMP NW3 3 L2
Crossfields LOU IG10 81 K8
Crossfield St DEPT SE8 160 D7
Crossford St BRXN/ST SW9 158 G8
Crossgate EDGW HA8 95 M4
GFD/PVL UB6 134 C1
Crossing Rd EPP CM16 65 K4
Crossland Rd REDH RH1 258 B10
THHTH CR7 203 J6
Crosslands CHERT KT16 195 H10
Crosslands Av EA W5 135 L10
NWDGN UB2 153 N4
Crosslands Pde NWDGN UB2 * 153 N4
Crosslands Rd HOR/WEW KT19 220 A5
Cross La BEAC HP9 108 E1
BXLY DA5 186 A3
CEND/HSY/T N8 118 C2
CHERT KT16 214 E3
HARP AL5 20 B6
HERT/WAT SG14 25 J1
HORL RH6 281 K7
MON EC3R 13 J3
Cross La East GVE DA12 190 E5
Cross Lanes CFSP/GDCR SL9 90 C6
GU GU1 250 B10
Cross Lanes Cl CFSP/GDCR SL9 90 C6
Cross La West GVW DA12 190 D5
Crosslet St WALW SE17 19 H5
Crosslet V GNWCH SE10 160 E7
Crossley Cl BH/WHM TN16 244 A1
Crossleys HI CSTG N8 89 P4
Crossley St HOLWY N7 118 F2
Crossmead ELTH/MOT SE9 184 C4
OXHEY WD19 73 J10
Crossmead Av GFD/PVL UB6 133 P3
Cross Meadow CSHM HP5 50 C5
Crossness Rd BARK IG11 143 H3
Cross Oak WDSR SL4 148 F8
Cross Oak La REDH RH1 276 D10
Crossoaks La BORE WD6 58 A10
Crosspath CRAWE RH10 283 P6
The Crosspath RAD WD7 * 74 F2
Cross Rd ASC SL5
BELMT SM2 221 K6
CHDH RM6 123 M5
CHES/WCR EN8 62 D9
CHING E4 101 K2
CMBW SE5 159 M8
CROY/NA CR0 203 L8
EN EN1 79 M8
FBAR/BDGN N11 98 C4
FELT TW13 175 M4
GVW DA11 190 C2
HAYES BR2 205 K3
HERT/WAT SG14 25 K4
HRW HA1 114 C2
KTN/HRWW/WS HA3 114 J7
KWD/TDW/WH KT20 238 F9
OXHEY WD19 73 M10
PUR/KEN CR8 223 J9
ROMW/RG RM7 124 C2
RYLN/HDSTN HA2 113 P8
SCUP DA14 185 J7
STMC/STPC BR5 207 L5
SUT SM1 221 N2
WDGN N22 99 H7
WEY KT13 * 196 K10
WFD IG8 102 H2
Cross Roads LOU IG10 81 H7
The Crossroads EHSLY KT24 253 L4
Cross St BARN SW13 156 B8
ERITH DA8 164 F5
HPTN TW12 176 B8
IS N1 6 E1
STALW/RED AL3 11 D4
UED N18 99 P6
UX/CGN UB8 131 N2
WARE SG12 26 E1
Crossthwaite Av HNHL SE24 159 H8
Cross Wy HRW HA1 113 H1

Crossway BCTR RM8 123 M8
CDALE/KGS NW9 116 C2
CSHM HP5 51 K6
EN EN1 99 N1
HLWE CM17 29 N10
NFNCH/WDSPK N12 97 N7
NWMAL KT3 200 F4
PIN HA5 113 K9
RSLP HA4 113 K9
STMC/STPC BR5 206 G4
STNW/STAM N16 119 N10
THMD SE28 143 M8
WEA W13 134 E6
WCCW AL8 22 E1
WOT/HER KT12 197 J9
Crossway Pde WDGN N22 * 99 J8
Crossways BEAC HP9 88 G10
BELMT SM2 221 N10
BERK HP4 33 L6
BRW CM14 106 F10
BRWN CM15 284 A6
EGH TW20 172 G9
EHSLY KT24 253 L3
GPK RM2 125 J1
HHS/BOV HP3 36 C5
RGUW GU3 248 B10
SAND/SEL CR2 224 D4
SUN TW16 196 G1
Crossways Bvd RDART DA2 186 B10
RDART DA2 166 C8
Crossways La REIG RH2 257 M4
Crossways Rd BECK BR3 204 F4
MTCM CR4 202 C3
Crossways Ter CLPT E5 120 B9
The Crossways BRYLDS KT5 * 199 N8
COUL/CHIP CR5 240 C5
GUW GU2 267 L2
HEST TW5 153 N6
REDH RH1 258 C5
WAND/EARL SW18 179 J3
Crossway WD19 93 L5
Crowborough Cl WARL CR6 242 E6
Crowborough Dr WARL CR6 242 D4
Crowborough Pth OXHEY WD19 93 L5
Crowborough Rd TOOT SW17 180 B8
Crowden Wy THMD SE28 143 M9
Crowder Cl NFNCH/WDSPK N12 97 M8
Crowder St WCHPL E1 140 A9
Crow Dr RSEV TN14 246 C2
Crowfoot Cl HOM E9 120 B10
THMD SE28 143 H10
Crow Gn BRWN CM15 86 F8
Crow Green La BRWN CM15 86 F9
Crow Green Rd BRWN CM15 86 F9
Crowhurst Cl BRXN/ST SW9 159 H8
CRAWE RH10 284 F7
Crowhurst Md GDST RH9 260 B6
Crowhurst Wy STMC/STPC BR5 207 M5
Crowland Av HYS/HAR UB3 152 F3
Crowland Gdns STHGT/OAK N14 98 H1
Crowland Rd SEVS/STOTM N15 119 N3
THHTH CR7 203 L4
Crowlands Av ROMW/RG RM7 124 C4
Crowland Ter IS N1 6 G1
Crowland Wk MRDN SM4 201 L6
Crow La ROMW/RG RM7 124 A5
Crowley Crs CROY/NA CR0 223 H2
Crowline Wk IS N1 * 6 G1
Crowmarsh Gdns FSTH SE23 * 183 J2
Crown Ar KUT/HW KT1 * 199 J2
Crownbourne Ct SUT SM1 * 221 L1
Crown Cl BOW E3 140 A5
DTCH/LGLY SL3 150 F6
HYS/HAR UB3 152 G1
KIL/WHAMP NW6 2 G1
MLHL NW7 96 C3
ORP BR6 227 K1
RBSF CM22 30 D5
WOT/HER KT12 197 L8
Crown Ct HOL/ALD WC2B 11 K6
Crown Dr IS N1 DRWD SE19 181 K9
Crowndale Rd CAMTN NW1 5 H7
Crownfield BROX EN10 44 F7
Crownfield Av GNTH/NBYPK IG2 123 H3
Crownfield Rd SRTFD E15 121 J10
Crownfields SEV TN13 265 J1
Crown Ga HLW CM20 46 G1
Crown Gn GVE DA12 191 P7
Crown Green Ms WGLY HA9 115 K7
Crown Hts GU GU1 268 E5
Crown Hi CROY/NA CR0 * 203 K9
Crown Hill Ct ASC SL5 192 A5
Crown Hill Rd WLSDN NW10 136 C10
Crown La CHST BR7 206 F1
GVE DA12 191 P7
HAYES BR2 205 K3
MRDN SM4 201 K4
STHGT/OAK N14 98 D2
STRHM/NOR SW16 181 N9
VW GU25 194 A6
Crown Lane Gdns STRHM/NOR SW16 * 181 N9
Crown Lane Sp HAYES BR2 205 L4
Crown Meadow DTCH/LGLY SL3 150 E6
Crownmead Wy ROMW/RG RM7 124 C2
Crown Office Rw EMB EC4Y 12 G1
Crown Pde MRDN SM4 * 201 L4
STHGT/OAK N14 * 98 D2
Crown Pas STJS SW1Y 11 H10
Crown Pl KTTN NW5 4 F1
SDTCH EC2A 13 J1
Crown Ri CHERT KT16 195 H5
GSTN WD25 58 F8
Crown Rd BARK/HLT IG6 122 G2
BORE WD6 76 B1
BRW CM14 106 F9
EN EN1 79 P7
GRAYS RM17 167 M3
KUTN/CMB KT2 199 N2
MRDN SM4 201 K4
MUSWH N10 98 A7
NWDGN UB2 153 L1
RSLP HA4 113 L4
SUT SM1 221 N2
TWK TW1 176 G2

VW GU25 193 P6
WOKN/KNAP GU21 232 C3
Crownstone Rd BRXS/STRHM SW2 181 N10
Crown St ACT W3 135 N10
BRW CM14 107 H3
CMBW SE5 159 K6
DAGE RM10 144 D1
SOHO/SHAV W1D 11 H3
Crown Ter CRICK NW2 116 C9
RCH/KEW TW9 155 L10
STHGT/OAK N14 98 E2
Crowntree Cl ISLW TW7 154 E5
Crown Vis ACT W3 * 155 J7
Crown Wk HHS/BOV HP3 35 P10
WBLY HA9 115 L8
Crown Wy WDR/YW UB7 132 A10
Crown Woods La WOOL/PLUM SE18 162 E8
Crown Woods Wy ELTH/MOT SE9 184 G1
Crown Yd HSLW TW3 154 B9
Crow Piece La SLN SL2 128 C2
Crowshott Av STAN HA7 95 H4
Crows Rd BARK IG11 142 E1
BOW E3 141 J5
EPP CM16 65 J6
Crowstone Rd CDW/CHF RM16 167 P1
Crowther Av BTFD TW8 155 K4
Crowther Cl FUL/PGN SW6 157 N3
Crowther Rd SNWD SE25 203 P4
Crowthorne Cl WAND/EARL SW18 179 J3
Crowthorne Rd NKENS W10 136 B6
Croxdale Rd BORE WD6 75 L6
Croxden Cl EDGW HA8 116 A2
Croxden Wk MRDN SM4 201 N6
Croxford Gdns WDGN N22 99 J8
Croxley Cl STMC/STPC BR5 207 L2
Croxley Rd MV/WKIL W9 2 D10
Croxley Vw WATW WD18 72 F10
Croyde Av GFD/PVL UB6 133 P4
HYS/HAR UB3 152 F3
Croyde Cl BFN/LL DA15 184 C10
The Croydon F/O CROY/NA CR0 223 J1
Croydon Gv CROY/NA CR0 203 J8
Croydon La BNSTD SM7 221 L10
Croydon La South BNSTD SM7 221 L10
Croydon Rd BECK BR3 204 C5
BH/WHM TN16 262 E2
CROY/NA CR0 222 F1
CTHM CR3 241 P8
HAYES BR2 206 B10
MTCM CR4 202 C3
PGE/AN SE20 204 A2
PLSTW E13 141 L6
REIG RH2 257 M9
WARL CR6 242 C8
WLGTN SM6 222 C1
WWKM BR4 205 K10
Croyland Rd ED N9 99 J7
Croylands Dr SURB KT6 199 K7
Croysdale Av SUN TW16 197 H3
Crozier Dr SAND/SEL CR2 224 A6
Crozier Ter HOM E9 120 C10
Crucible Cl CHDH RM6 123 H5
Crucifix La STHWK SE1 19 J1
Cruden Rd GVE DA12 191 J6
Cruden St IS N1 6 D6
Cruick Av SOCK/AV RM15 147 H4
Cruikshank St FSBYW WC1X 6 A7
Cruikshank Rd SRTFD E15 121 K9
Crummock Cl SL SL1 128 B8
Crummock Gdns CDALE/KGS NW9 116 B4
Crumpsall St ABYW SE2 163 M3
Crundale Av CDALE/KGS NW9 115 M4
Crunden Rd SAND/SEL CR2 223 L4
Crusader Cl PUR RM19 155 P3
Crusader Gdns CROY/NA CR0 203 M1
Crusader Wy WATW WD18 72 C10
Crusoe Ms STNW/STAM N16 119 P7
Crusoe Rd ERITH DA8 164 F4
MTCM CR4 180 A10
Crutched Friars TWRH EC3N 13 K7
Crutchfield La HORL RH6 279 K1
WOT/HER KT12 197 J8
Crutchley Rd CAT SE6 183 K6
Crystal Av HCH RM12 125 K5
Crystal Palace NRWD SE19 * 181 P7
Crystal Palace Pde NRWD SE19 181 N9
Crystal Palace Park Rd SYD SE26 181 N9
Crystal Palace Station Rd NRWD SE19 181 P8
Crystal Ter NRWD SE19 181 N8
Crystal Wy BCTR RM8 123 P4
HRW HA1 114 E3
Cuba Dr PEND EN3 60 B6
Cuba St POP/IOD E14 160 A1
Cubitt Sq NWDGN UB2 * 154 B10
Cubitt St CLAP SW4 158 F2
Cubitt Ter CLAP SW4 158 D2
Cublands HERT/BAY SG13 26 A5
Cuckfield Cl CRAWW RH11 282 A8
Cuckmans Dr LCOL/BKTW AL2 55 P1
Cuckmere Crs CRAWW RH11 283 J8
Cuckmere Wy STMC/STPC BR5 207 N3
Cuckoo Av HNWL W7 134 C10
Cuckoo Dene HNWL W7 134 C10
Cuckoo Hall La PIN HA5 113 K1
Cuckoo Hi PIN HA5 113 K1
Cuckoo Hill Dr PIN HA5 113 K2
Cuckoo Hill Rd PIN HA5 113 L2
Cuckoo La CDW/CHF RM16 167 K1
CHOB/PIR GU24 212 C9
HNWL W7 134 C10
Cudas Cl WPK KT4 200 C10
Cuddington Av WPK KT4 200 C10
Cuddington Cl KWD/TDW/WH KT20 238 F6
Cuddington Gld HOR/WEW KT19 219 M8
Cuddington Park Cl BNSTD SM7 220 G8
Cudham Cl BELMT SM2 220 G8
Cudham Dr CROY/NA CR0 224 C6
Cudham La North ORP BR6 226 F10
RSEV TN14 226 F10
Cudham La South RSEV TN14 244 F1
Cudham Park Rd RSEV TN14 245 H3
Cudham Rd BH/WHM TN16 244 A10
ORP BR6 226 C7
Cudham St CAT SE6 183 H4
Cudworth Pk RDKG RH5 278 B3
Cudworth St WCHPL E1 140 C3
Cuff Crs ELTH/MOT SE9 184 A5
Cuffley Av GSTN WD25 55 L8
Cuffley Ct HHNE HP2 35 J1
Cuffley Hi CHESW EN7 61 M1
Cugley Rd RDART DA2 185 J4
Culcroft HART DA3 211 L4
Culford Gdns CHEL SW3 15 M5
Culford Gv IS N1 7 L1
Culford Ms IS N1 7 J1
Culford Rd CDW/CHF RM16 167 J1
IS N1 7 J2
Culgaith Gdns ENC/FH EN2 78 E4

Cullen Sq SOCK/AV RM15 147 H9
Cullera Cl NTHWD HA6 92 C7
Cullerne Cl EW KT17 220 C6
Cullesden Rd PUR/KEN CR8 241 J1
Culling Rd BERM/RHTH SE16 160 B2
Cullings Ct WAB EN9 63 J5
Cullington Cl KTN/HRWW/WS HA3 114 C2
Cullingworth Rd WLSDN NW10 116 E10
Culloden Cl BERM/RHTH SE16 159 P5
Culloden Rd ENC/FH EN2 79 P8
Culloden St POP/IOD E14 141 N8
Cull's Rd RGUW GU3 248 A10
Cullum St FENCHST EC3M 13 J7
Culmington Pde WEA W13 * 135 H5
Culmington Rd SAND/SEL CR2 223 K4
WEA W13 135 H6
Culmore Rd PECK SE15 160 A6
Culmstock Rd BTSEA SW11 180 B1
Culpepper Cl CHIG IG7 102 C7
UED N18 99 N5
Culross Cl SEVS/STOTM N15 119 K6
Culross St MYFR/PKLN W1K 10 B3
Culsac Rd SURB KT6 199 K9
Culverden Rd BAL SW12 180 D6
OXHEY WD19 93 J4
Culverden Ter WEY KT13 * 196 F10
Culver Dr OXTED RH8 261 K6
Culver Gv STAN HA7 95 H10
Culverhay ASHTD KT21 237 K2
Culverhouse Gdns STRHM/NOR SW16 181 N5
Culverlands Cl STAN HA7 94 C5
Culverley Rd CAT SE6 182 G4
Culver Rd STAL AL1 38 C5
Culvers Av CAR SM5 202 A8
Culvers Cft BEAC HP9 88 A4
Culverstone Cl HAYES BR2 205 L4
Culvers Wy CAR SM5 202 A8
Culvert La UX/CGN UB8 131 L4
Culvert Pl BTSEA SW11 158 G3
Culvert Rd BTSEA SW11 158 F2
SEVS/STOTM N15 119 M3
Culvey Cl HART DA3 211 K5
Culworth St STJWD NW8 3 N5
Cumberland Av GUW GU2 249 M5
GVE DA12 190 F5
NWDGN UB2 135 M10
WLSDN NW10 136 B2
Cumberland Cl AMSS HP7 69 N5
BARK/HLT IG6 102 F9
HACK E8 7 M1
HERT/WAT SG14 25 J1
HHS/BOV HP3 36 F10
HOR/WEW KT19 220 B6
TWK TW1 176 C10
Cumberland Crs WKENS W14 14 E5
Cumberland Dr BXLYHN DA7 163 P6
CHSGTN KT9 219 K10
DART DA1 185 K3
ESH/CLAY KT10 198 F2
Cumberland Gdns CAMTN NW1 5 N7
HDN NW4 95 N6
Cumberland House KUTN/CMB KT2 177 N10
Cumberland Market CAMTN NW1 4 F9
Cumberland Ms LBTH SE11 18 B8
Cumberland Pk ACT W3 135 P9
Cumberland Pl CAMTN NW1 4 E9
CAT SE6 183 L4
SUN TW16 197 H4
Cumberland Rd ACT W3 135 P9
ASHF TW15 173 H6
BARN SW13 156 D3
CDW/CHF RM16 167 K1
ED N9 99 J9
HAYES BR2 205 K4
HNWL W7 154 B2
HRW HA1 114 A4
MNPK E12 123 K10
PLSTW E13 141 L5
RCH/KEW TW9 155 N5
SNWD SE25 204 A6
STAN HA7 115 J3
WALTH E17 121 H1
WDGN N22 98 G10
Cumberlands PUR/KEN CR8 241 L1
Cumberland St PIM SW1V 16 F7
STA TW18 172 G8
Cumberland Ter CAMTN NW1 4 E8
PGE/AN SE20 * 182 A10
Cumberland Terrace Ms CAMTN NW1 * 4 E8
Cumberlow Av SNWD SE25 203 P3
Cumberton Rd TOTM N17 99 P10
Cumbrae Cl SLN SL2 128 D7
Cumbrae Gdns SURB KT6 199 J9
Cumbrian Av BXLYHN DA7 164 F8
Cumbrian Gdns CRICK NW2 116 B8
Cumbrian Wy UX/CGN UB8 131 N5
Cumley Rd CHONG CM5 66 H6
Cummings Hall La HARP AL5 20 C3
Cumming St IS N1 5 P5
Cumnor Cl BRXN/ST SW9 158 G8
Cumnor Gdns EW KT17 220 E7
Cumnor Rd PUR/KEN CR8 241 K3
Cumnor Rd BELMT SM2 221 M5
Cunard Crs WCHMH N21 79 L10
Cunard Rd WLSDN NW10 136 A5
Cundalls Rd WARE SG12 26 E1
Cundy Rd CAN/RD E16 141 N8
Cundy St BGVA SW1W 16 B6
Cunliffe Cl EPSOM KT18 237 N10
Cunliffe Rd HOR/WEW KT19 220 C1
Cunliffe St STRHM/NOR SW16 181 L9
Cunningham Av GU GU1 250 B3
Cunningham Hill Rd STAL AL1 38 C5
Cunningham Pk HRW HA1 114 C3
Cunningham Pl STJWD NW8 3 J9
Cunningham Rd BNSTD SM7 239 M1
CHES/WCR EN8 62 D3
SEVS/STOTM N15 119 P2
Cunnington St CHSWK W4 155 P5
Cupar Rd BTSEA SW11 158 G1
Cupola Cl BMLY BR1 183 B8
Cureton St WEST SW1P 17 J6
Curfew Bell Rd CHERT KT16 195 J8
Curfew La BERK HP4 33 N6
Curie Gdns CDALE/KGS NW9 115 B8
Curlew Cl BERK HP4 33 N6
SAND/SEL CR2 223 P8
THMD SE28 143 N9
Curlew Ct BROX EN10 44 E8
SURB KT6 199 L6
Curlew Gdns RGUE GU4 250 D8
The Curlews GVE DA12 190 G5
Curlew St STHWK SE1 19 N1
Curlew Wy YEAD UB4 133 H4
Curling Cl COUL/CHIP CR5 240 G6
Curling La GRAYS RM17 167 L4
Curness St LEW SE13 161 K1
Curnick's La WENWD SE27 181 M3
Curo Pk LCOL/BKTW AL2 56 B3
Curran Av BFN/LL DA15 184 A3
WLGTN SM6 202 B10
Curran Cl UX/CGN UB8 131 M6
Currey Rd GFD/PVL UB6 133 P1
Curricle St ACT W3 135 P5
Currie Hill Cl WIM/MER SW19 178 A10
Curriers Cl SL SL1 129 P5
Currie St HERT/BAY SG13 25 M4

Curry Ri MLHL NW7 96 G7
Cursitor St FLST/FETLN EC4A 12 A5
Curtain Pl SDTCH EC2A 7 K10
Curtain Rd SDTCH EC2A 13 J2
Curteys HLWE CM17 29 N6
Curthwaite Gdns ENC/FH EN2 78 E8
Curtis Cl RKW/CH/CXG WD3 91 K2
Curtis Dr ACT W3 135 A8
Curtis Field Rd STRHM/NOR SW16 180 G2
Curtis La ALP/SUD HA0 135 K1
Curtismill Cl STMC/STPC BR5 207 L3
Curtis Mill La ABR/ST RM4 84 F8
Curtismill Wy STMC/STPC BR5 207 L3
Curtis Rd DORK RH4 272 E1
EMPK RM11 125 N6
HHS/BOV HP5 36 F7
HOR/WEW KT19 219 P1
HSLWW TW4 175 J7
Curtis St STHWK SE1 19 L5
Curtis Wy BERK HP4 34 A6
STHWK SE1 19 L5
Curvan Cl EW KT17 220 C6
The Curve SHB W12 136 D6
Curwen Av FSTGT E7 121 N9
Curwen Rd SHB W12 156 D7
Curzon Av BEAC HP9 80 C9
STAN HA7 94 F9
Curzon Cl ORP BR6 226 G1
WEY KT13 216 B1
Curzon Crs BARK IG11 143 J5
WLSDN NW10 136 B2
Curzon Dr GRAYS RM17 167 P6
Curzon Pl PIN HA5 113 K3
Curzon Rd EA W5 134 G6
MUSWH N10 98 C10
THHTH CR7 203 H6
WEY KT13 216 B1
Curzon St MYFR/PKLN W1K 10 C7
Cusack Cl TWK TW1 176 E7
Cussons Cl CHESW EN7 61 P5
Custom House Reach BERM/RHTH SE16 160 E2
Cutcombe Rd CMBW SE5 159 K8
Cuthberga Cl BARK IG11 142 F2
Cuthbert Cl CHESW EN7 61 M5
Cuthbert Gdns SNWD SE25 203 M5
Cuthbert Rd CROY/NA CR0 203 J9
UED N18 99 P6
WALTH E17 121 H1
Cuthbert St BAY/PAD W2 9 L2
Cutlers Gardens Ar LVPST EC2M 13 K5
Cutler St HDTCH EC3A 13 K5
Cutmore Dr STALW/WH AL4 39 N8
Cutmore St GVW DA11 190 E3
The Cut STHWK SE1 18 B1
Cuttinglye La CRAWE RH10 285 P4
Cuttsfield Ter HHW HP1 35 J7
Cutty Sark Ct RDART DA2 188 F1
Cuxton Cl BXLYHS DA6 185 P1
Cwmbran Ct HHNE HP2 36 A2
Cyclamen Cl HPTN TW12 175 P9
Cyclamen Rd SWLY BR8 208 E4
Cyclamen Wy HOR/WEW KT19 219 P2
Cygnet Av EBED/NFELT TW14 175 K3
Cygnet Cl BORE WD6 76 D8
NTHWD HA6 116 A10
WOKN/KNAP GU21 231 N2
The Cygnets FELT TW13 175 J8
STA TW18 173 J8
Cygnet St WCHPL E1 13 M1
Cygnet Vw WHTN RH20 166 E2
Cygnet Wy YEAD UB4 133 L7
Cymbeline Ct HRW HA1 * 114 E4
Cynthia St IS N1 5 P9
Cypress Av ENC/FH EN2 79 N1
WGCE AL7 23 M6
WHTN TW2 176 B3
Cypress Ct VW GU25 194 C4
Cypress Gdns BROCKY SE4 182 C1
Cypress Gv BARK/HLT IG6 103 H1
Cypress Pl FITZ W1T 11 J1
Cypress Rd GU GU1 249 P2
KTN/HRWW/WS HA3 94 C10
SNWD SE25 203 M3
Cypress Tree Cl BFN/LL DA15 185 J4
Cyprus Av FNCH N3 116 G1
Cyprus Cl FSBYPK N4 119 H4
Cyprus Gdns FNCH N3 116 G1
Cyprus Pl BETH E2 140 E1
EHAM E6 142 D9
Cyprus Rd ED N9 99 N3
FNCH N3 116 G1
Cyprus St BETH E2 140 E1
Cyrena Rd EDUL SE22 182 B1
Cyril Rd BXLYHN DA7 163 P6
ORP BR6 207 K1
Cyrils Wy STAL AL1 38 C9
Czar St DEPT SE8 160 D5

## D

Dabbling Cl ERITH DA8 * 165 J6
Dabbs Hill La NTHLT UB5 113 N10
D'Abernon Cl ESH/CLAY KT10 217 P1
D'Abernon Dr COB KT11 235 M2
Dabin Crs GNWCH SE10 161 H7
Dacca St DEPT SE8 160 E5
Dace Rd BOW E3 140 F3
Dacorum Wy HHW HP1 35 M6
Dacre Av CLAY IG5 102 C10
SOCK/AV RM15 146 C10
Dacre Cl CHIG IG7 102 F5
GFD/PVL UB6 133 A4
Dacre Gdns BORE WD6 76 A9
CHIG IG7 102 F5
LEW SE13 161 K10
Dacre Pk LEW SE13 161 K10
Dacre Pl LEW SE13 161 K9
Dacre Rd CROY/NA CR0 202 F7
PLSTW E13 141 N3
WAN E11 121 L4
Dacres Est FSTH SE23 * 182 G10
Dacres Rd FSTH SE23 182 G10
Dade Wy NWDGN UB2 153 M4
Dads Wy HLW CM20 46 F1
Daerwood Cl HAYES BR2 206 C8
Daffodil Av BRWN CM15 86 G9
Daffodil Cl CROY/NA CR0 204 C8
HAT AL10 22 C10
HPTN TW12 175 P9
Daffodil Dr CHOB/PIR GU24 230 F2
Daffodil Gdns IL IG1 122 G10
Daffodil St SHB W12 136 C9
Dafforne Rd TOOT SW17 180 A6
Dagden Rd RGUE GU4 250 F5
Dagenham Av DAGW RM9 143 P9
Dagenham Rd DAGE RM10 124 D8
LEY E10 120 G6
RAIN RM13 144 F2
Dagger La BORE WD6 74 F10
Daggs Dell Rd HHW HP1 35 H4
Dagley La RGUE GU4 268 A5
Dagmar Av WBLY HA9 115 L9
Dagmar Gdns WLSDN NW10 136 G4
Dagmar Ms NWDGN UB2 153 L1
Dagmar Pas IS N1 * 6 E5
Dagmar Rd CMBW SE5 159 M7
DAGE RM10 144 D2

FSBYPK N4 119 H5
KUTN/CMB KT2 199 L1
NWDGN UB2 153 M2
SEVS/STOTM N15 119 L2
SNWD SE25 203 M4
WDGN N22 98 E9
WDSR SL4 149 J8
Dagmar Ter IS N1 6 D5
Dagnall Crs UX/CGN UB8 131 M7
Dagnall Pk SNWD SE25 203 M5
Dagnall Rd SNWD SE25 203 M5
Dagnall St BTSEA SW11 158 A8
Dagnam Park Cl HARH RM3 105 P6
Dagnam Park Dr HARH RM3 105 M6
Dagnam Park Gdns HARH RM3 105 P7
Dagnam Park Sq HARH RM3 105 P7
Dagnan Rd BAL SW12 180 C3
Dagonet Rd BMLY BR1 183 M6
Dagwood La BRWN CM15 86 G4
Dahlia Cl CHESW EN7 61 K1
Dahlia Dr SWLY BR8 208 G2
Dahlia Gdns IL IG1 142 E1
MTCM CR4 202 E4
Dahlia Rd ABYW SE2 163 L4
Dahomey Rd STRHM/NOR SW16 180 D9
Daiglen Dr SOCK/AV RM15 146 F9
Daimler Wy WLGTN SM6 222 F4
Daines Cl MNPK E12 122 C8
SOCK/AV RM15 146 F6
Dainford Cl BMLY BR1 183 J8
Daintry Cl KTN/HRWW/WS HA3 114 F2
Dairsie Rd ELTH/MOT SE9 162 D9
Dairy Cl BMLY BR1 * 183 N10
DORK RH4 272 B3
EYN DA4 188 A10
THHTH CR7 203 K2
WLSDN NW10 136 D3
Dairyfields CRAWW RH11 283 K8
Dairyglen Av CHES/WCR EN8 62 C7
Dairy La EDEN TN8 262 E10
WOOL/PLUM SE18 162 C3
Dairyman Cl CRICK NW2 116 G8
Dairymans Wk RGUE GU4 250 E5
Dairy Wy ABLGY WD5 54 G5
Daisy Cl CROY/NA CR0 204 C8
Daisy Dr HAT AL10 40 C1
Daisy La FUL/PGN SW6 157 K9
Daisy Meadow EGH TW20 172 D8
Daisy Rd SWFD E18 101 N10
Dakin Pl WCHPL E1 140 D7
Dakota Cl WLGTN SM6 222 G4
Dalberg Rd BRXS/STRHM SW2 181 H1
Dalberg Wy ABYW SE2 163 N2
Dalby Rd WAND/EARL SW18 157 M10
Dalbys Crs TOTM N17 99 M7
Dalby St KTTN NW5 4 E2
Dalcross Rd HSLWW TW4 153 M8
Dale Av EDGW HA8 95 L9
HSLWW TW4 153 M9
Dalebury Rd TOOT SW17 180 A5
Dale Cl ADL/WDHM KT15 215 L2
ASC SL5 192 F5
BAR EN5 77 L10
BKHTH/KID SE3 161 M9
GT/LBKH KT23 254 B1
PIN HA5 93 J9
SOCK/AV RM15 146 F8
Dale Ct GSTN WD25 * 55 H9
SBW CM21 29 N2
Dale Dr YEAD UB4 132 G6
Dale Gdns WFD IG8 101 N5
Dalegarth Gdns PUR/KEN CR8 223 L9
Dale Green Rd FBAR/BDGN N11 98 C4
Dale Gv NFNCH/WDSPK N12 97 M6
Daleham Av EGH TW20 172 D9
Daleham Dr UX/CGN UB8 132 C8
Daleham Gdns HAMP NW3 3 L1
Dale Lodge Rd ASC SL5 192 F5
Dalemain Ms CAN/RD E16 141 M10
Dale Park Av CAR SM5 202 A9
Dale Park Rd NRWD SE19 203 K1
Dale Rd KTTN NW5 118 B10
MEO DA13 189 M7
PUR/KEN CR8 223 H8
STHL UB1 134 A7
SUN TW16 * 174 G10
SUT SM1 221 J1
SWLY BR8 208 D3
WALW SE17 18 D10
WOT/HER KT12 196 G7
Dale Rw NTGHL W11 * 8 B6
Dale Side CFSP/GDCR SL9 110 B6
Daleside ORP BR6 227 K2
Daleside Cl ORP BR6 227 K3
Daleside Dr POTB/CUF EN6 59 J8
Daleside Gdns CHIG IG7 102 F4
Daleside Rd HOR/WEW KT19 220 A3
STRHM/NOR SW16 180 C8
Dales Pth BORE WD6 * 76 A9
Dales Rd BORE WD6 76 A9
Dalestone Ms HARH RM3 105 J7
Dale St CHSWK W4 156 B4
The Dale HAYES BR2 226 A1
WAB EN9 63 K10
Dale Vw BAR EN5 * 77 J7
EPSOM KT18 237 N9
ERITH DA8 165 H8
WOKN/KNAP GU21 231 M4
Dale View Av CHING E4 101 H3
Dale View Crs CHING E4 101 H4
Dale View Gdns CHING E4 101 J4
Daleview Rd SEVS/STOTM N15 119 M4
Dalewood HARP AL5 20 C2
WGCE AL7 23 N6
Dalewood Cl EMPK RM11 125 N5
Dalewood Gdns CRAWE RH10 284 A5
WPK KT4 200 E9
Dale Wood Rd ORP BR6 207 H7
Daley St HOM E9 140 C1
Daley Thompson Wy VX/NE SW8 158 C8
Dalgarno Gdns NKENS W10 136 F7
Dalgarno Wy NKENS W10 136 F6
Dalkeith Gv STAN HA7 95 J6
Dalkeith Rd DUL SE21 181 K4
HARP AL5 20 B1
IL IG1 122 F8
Dallas Rd CHEAM SM3 221 H3
EA W5 135 L7
HDN NW4 116 D5
SYD SE26 182 A7
Dallas Ter HYS/HAR UB3 152 G2
Dallega Cl HYS/HAR UB3 132 D9
Dallinger Rd LEE/GVPK SE12 183 L2
Dalling Rd HMSMTH W6 156 E3
Dallington Cl WOT/HER KT12 217 K3
Dallington Sq FSBYE EC1V 12 D1
Dallington St FSBYE EC1V 12 D1
Dallin Rd BXLYHS DA6 163 N10
WOOL/PLUM SE18 162 E6
Dalmain Rd FSTH SE23 182 C4
Dalmally Rd CROY/NA CR0 203 N7
Dalmeny Av HOLWY N7 118 E9
STRHM/NOR SW16 203 H2
Dalmeny Cl ALP/SUD HA0 135 H1
Dalmeny Crs HSLW TW3 154 C10
Dalmeny Rd BAR EN5 77 M10
CAR SM5 222 B4
ERITH DA8 164 C7
HOLWY N7 118 E9
WPK KT4 200 E10
Dalmeyer Rd WLSDN NW10 136 C1
Dalmore Av ESH/CLAY KT10 218 E3
Dalmore Rd DUL SE21 181 K5
Dalroy Cl SOCK/AV RM15 146 F8
Dalrymple Cl STHGT/OAK N14 78 E10
Dalrymple Rd BROCKY SE4 160 D10
Dalston Gdns STAN HA7 95 K9
Dalston La HACK E8 7 L1
Dalton Av MTCM CR4 201 P2
Dalton Cl ORP BR6 207 H10
YEAD UB4 132 E6
Dalton Gn DTCH/LGLY SL3 150 C4
Daltons Rd SWLY BR8 208 D9
Dalton St STALW/RED AL3 38 C5
WNWD SE27 181 J5
Dalton Wy WAT WD17 73 L9
Dalwood St CMBW SE5 159 M7
Dalyell Rd BRXN/ST SW9 158 G9
Damask Cl CHOB/PIR GU24 212 D9
Damask Crs CAN/RD E16 141 K6
Damask Gn HHW HP1 35 H7
Damer Ter WBPTN SW10 157 M6
Dames Rd FSTGT E7 121 M9
Dame St IS N1 6 E7
Damien St WCHPL E1 140 A7
Damigos Rd GVE DA12 191 J4
Damon Cl SCUP DA14 185 L6
Damsel Ct BERM/RHTH SE16 * 19 P2
Damson Dr HYS/HAR UB3 133 H9
Damson Gv SL SL1 149 H1
Damson Wy CAR SM5 222 A5
STALE/WH AL4 39 H4
Damsonwood Rd NWDGN UB2 153 P2
Danbrook Rd STRHM/NOR SW16 202 F1
Danbury Cl BRWN CM15 86 E9
CHDH RM6 123 N1
Danbury Crs SOCK/AV RM15 146 G8
Danbury Ms WLGTN SM6 222 C1
Danbury Rd LOU IG10 82 B10
RAIN RM13 144 G3
Danbury St IS N1 6 D7
Danbury Wy WFD IG8 101 P7
Danby St PECK SE15 159 N9
Dancer Rd FUL/PGN SW6 157 J7
RCH/KEW TW9 155 M9
Dancers Hill Rd BAR EN5 76 G2
Dandelion Cl ROMW/RG RM7 124 F7
Dando Crs BKHTH/KID SE3 161 N9
Dandridge Cl DTCH/LGLY SL3 149 P2
GNWCH SE10 161 L4
Danebury CROY/NA CR0 224 G3
Danebury Av PUT/ROE SW15 178 C3
Daneby Rd CAT SE6 183 H6
Dane Cl AMSS HP7 69 L7
BXLY DA5 186 B3
ORP BR6 226 G2
Dane Ct WOKS/MYFD GU22 233 J1
Danecourt Gdns CROY/NA CR0 203 N10
Danecroft Rd HNHL SE24 181 K1
Danehurst Cl EGH TW20 172 B9
Danehurst Gdns REDBR IG4 122 B3
Danehurst St FUL/PGN SW6 157 H7
Daneland EBAR EN4 78 A10
Danemead HOD EN11 26 F10
Danemead Gv NTHLT UB5 114 A10
Danemere St PUT/ROE SW15 156 F9
Dane Pl BOW E3 140 D4
Dane Rd ASHF TW15 174 D9
IL IG1 122 F10
RSEV TN14 246 F3
STHL UB1 133 M9
UED N18 100 B5
WARL CR6 242 C3
WEA W13 135 H9
WIM/MER SW19 201 M1
Danesbury Pk HERT/WAT SG14 25 L4
Danesbury Rd FELT TW13 175 J4
Danes Cl GVW DA11 189 P6
LHD/OX KT22 218 B10
Danescombe LEE/GVPK SE12 183 M4
Danescourt Crs SUT SM1 201 M9
Danescroft Av HDN NW4 * 116 G3
Danescroft Gdns HDN NW4 116 G3
Danesdale Rd HOM E9 140 D1
Danesfield RPLY/SEND GU23 233 J9
Danesfield Cl WOT/HER KT12 197 J10
Danes Ga HRW HA1 114 D1
Daneshill REDH RH1 257 P9
Danes Hl WOKS/MYFD GU22 232 E4
Daneshill Cl REDH RH1 257 P9
Danes Hill School Dr LHD/OX KT22 * 218 C10
Danesmead COB KT11 217 P7
Danes Rd ROMW/RG RM7 124 D5
The Danes LCOL/BKTW AL2 56 B4
Dane St GINN WC1R 11 N4
Danes Wy BRWN CM15 86 E9
LHD/OX KT22 218 C10
Daneswood Av CAT SE6 183 H6
Daneswood Cl WEY KT13 216 C2
Danethorpe Rd ALP/SUD HA0 135 J1
Danetree Cl HOR/WEW KT19 219 P4
Danetree Rd HOR/WEW KT19 219 P4
Danette Gdns DAGE RM10 124 A7
Daneville Rd CMBW SE5 159 L7
Dangan Rd WAN E11 121 M4
Daniel Bolt Cl POP/IOD E14 140 G7
CDW/CHF RM16 167 K1
Daniel Cl CDW/CHF RM16 168 E2
HSLWW TW4 175 N3
TOOT SW17 179 P9
UED N18 100 B5
Daniel Gdns PECK SE15 159 N6
Daniells WGCE AL7 23 K4
Daniell Wy CROY/NA CR0 202 F8
Daniel Pl HDN NW4 116 E4
Daniel Rd EA W5 135 L9
Daniels La WARL CR6 242 E2
Daniel's Rd PECK SE15 160 B9
Daniel Wy BNSTD SM7 221 L10
Dan Leno Wk FUL/PGN SW6 * 157 L6
Danses Cl RGUE GU4 250 G8
Dansey Pl SOHO/SHAV W1D 11 J7
Dansington Rd WELL DA16 163 K10
Danson Crs WELL DA16 163 L9
Danson La WELL DA16 163 L10
Danson Md WELL DA16 163 M9
Danson Rd BXLYHS DA6 185 N1
Danson U/P BFN/LL DA15 185 M2
Dante Rd LBTH SE11 18 C5
Danube Cl ED N9 100 B4
Danube St CHEL SW3 15 P7
Danvers Rd CEND/HSY/T N8 118 E2
Danvers St CHEL SW3 15 M10
Danvers Wy CTHM CR3 241 K9
Danyon Cl RAIN RM13 145 K4
Danziger Wy BORE WD6 75 P5
Dapdune Rd GU GU1 250 A10
Daphne Gdns CHING E4 101 H4
Daphne Jackson Rd GUW GU2 267 K1
Daphne St WAND/EARL SW18 179 M2
Daplyn St WCHPL E1 13 N3
Darblay Cl STALE/WH AL4 21 L6
D'Arblay St SOHO/CST W1F 11 H6
Darby Cl CTHM CR3 241 K8
Darby Crs SUN TW16 197 K2
Darby Dr WAB EN9 63 H9
Darby Gdns SUN TW16 197 K2
Darcy Av WLGTN SM6 222 D1
Darcy Cl CHES/WCR EN8 62 D7
COUL/CHIP CR5 241 J5
RBRW/HUT CM13 107 N1
TRDG/WHET N20 97 N3
D'Arcy Dr KTN/HRWW/WS HA3 115 J2
D'Arcy Gdns DAGW RM9 144 A3
KTN/HRWW/WS HA3 115 K2
Darcy Pl ASHTD KT21 237 L3
D'Arcy Pl HAYES BR2 205 M4
Darcy Rd ASHTD KT21 237 L3
ISLW TW7 154 F7
STRHM/NOR SW16 202 F2
D'Arcy Rd CHEAM SM3 220 G1
Darell Rd RCH/KEW TW9 155 M9
Darent Cl SEV TN13 246 D8
Darenth Dr GVE DA12 191 L4
Darenth Gdns BH/WHM TN16 262 G2
Darenth Hl RDART DA2 188 A8
Darenth La SEV TN13 246 F7
SOCK/AV RM15 146 F8
Darenth Park Av RDART DA2 188 C5
Darenth Pl RDART DA2 * 188 C8
Darenth Rd STNW/STAM N16 119 N5
WELL DA16 163 K7
Darenth Rd South RDART DA2 188 A7
Darenth Wy HORL RH6 280 A2
RSEV TN14 229 H7
Darenth Wood Rd RDART DA2 188 D4
Darent Md EYN DA4 210 A1
Darent Valley Pth DART DA1 187 M3
DART DA1 165 L10
ERITH DA8 165 L7
EYN DA4 209 J10
EYN DA4 229 J2
RDART DA2 188 B8
SEV TN13 246 C7
Darfield Rd BROCKY SE4 182 E1
RGUE GU4 250 D7
Darfield Wy NKENS W10 136 G9
Darfur St PUT/ROE SW15 156 G9
Dargate Cl NRWD SE19 181 N10
Darie Cl SL SL1 148 E1
Darien Rd BTSEA SW11 157 N9
Darkes La POTB/CUF EN6 59 K8
Dark La BRW CM14 106 E6
CHESW EN7 61 P6
HARP AL5 20 C4
RGUW GU3 266 A5
Darlands Dr BAR EN5 76 G9
Darlan Rd FUL/PGN SW6 157 J6
Darlaston Rd WIM/MER SW19 178 G10
Darley Cl ADL/WDHM KT15 215 M2
CROY/NA CR0 204 C6
Darley Cft LCOL/BKTW AL2 * 56 A4
Darleydale CRAWW RH11 283 M10
Darley Dene Ct ADL/WDHM KT15 * 215 M1
Darley Dr NWMAL KT3 200 A2
Darley Gdns MRDN SM4 201 L6
Darley Rd BTSEA SW11 180 A2
ED N9 99 N2
Darling Rd BROCKY SE4 160 F9
Darling Rw WCHPL E1 140 A6
Darlington Ct BRWN CM15 86 F10
Darlington Gdns HARH RM3 105 L6
Darlington Rd WNWD SE27 181 J8
Darlton Cl DART DA1 164 G8
Darmaine Cl SAND/SEL CR2 223 K4
Darndale Cl WALTH E17 100 E10
Darnets Fld RSEV TN14 246 G3
Darnicle Hl CHESW EN7 61 H1
Darnley Pk WEY KT13 196 C10
Darnley Rd GRAYS RM17 * 167 N5
GVW DA11 190 D4
HACK E8 140 A1
WFD IG8 101 M9
Darnley St GVW DA11 190 D3
Darnley Ter NTGHL W11 136 G10
Darns Hl SWLY BR8 208 D7
Darrell Cl DTCH/LGLY SL3 150 C3
Darrell Rd EDUL SE22 181 P1
Darren Cl FSBYPK N4 118 G5
Darrick Wood Rd ORP BR6 206 G9
Darrington Rd BORE WD6 75 K5
Darris Cl YEAD UB4 133 M6
Darr's La BERK HP4 33 J4
Darsley Dr VX/NE SW8 158 E7
Dart Cl DTCH/LGLY SL3 150 E5
UPMR RM14 126 C4
Dartfields HARH RM3 105 L7
Dartford Av ED N9 80 B10
Dartford Gdns CHDH RM6 123 L3
Dartford Rd BXLY DA5 186 D4
EYN DA4 209 N6
SEV TN13 247 K10
Dartford St WALW SE17 18 F9
Dart Gn SOCK/AV RM15 146 G8
Dartmoor Wk POP/IOD E14 * 160 F3
Dartmouth Av WOKN/KNAP GU21 214 F10
Dartmouth Cl NTGHL W11 8 D5
Dartmouth Gv GNWCH SE10 161 H7
Dartmouth Hl GNWCH SE10 161 H7
Dartmouth Park Av KTTN NW5 118 C8
Dartmouth Park Hl KTTN NW5 118 C8
Dartmouth Park Rd KTTN NW5 118 C8
Dartmouth Pl CHSWK W4 156 B5
FSTH SE23 182 B5
Dartmouth Rd CRICK NW2 2 A1
HAYES BR2 205 M7
HDN NW4 116 D4
RSLP HA4 113 H8
SYD SE26 182 A6
Dartmouth Rw GNWCH SE10 161 H8
Dartmouth St STJSPK SW1H 17 J2
Dartmouth Ter GNWCH SE10 161 J7
Dartnell Av BF/WBF KT14 215 M8
Dartnell Cl BF/WBF KT14 215 L8
Dartnell Ct BF/WBF KT14 215 M8
Dartnell Crs BF/WBF KT14 215 L8
Dartnell Park Rd BF/WBF KT14 215 L8
Dartnell Pl BF/WBF KT14 215 L8
Dartnell Rd CROY/NA CR0 203 N7
Dartrey Wk WBPTN SW10 * 157 M6
Dart St NKENS W10 2 B9
The Dart HHNE HP2 36 A1
Dartview Cl GRAYS RM17 168 B3
Darvel Cl WOKN/KNAP GU21 231 M2
Darvell Dr CSHM HP5 50 F5
Darvells Yd RKW/CH/CXG WD3 70 G8
Darville Rd STNW/STAM N16 119 N8
Darvill's La SL SL1 149 J1
Darwell Cl EHAM E6 142 D4
Darwin Cl FBAR/BDGN N11 98 C4
ORP BR6 226 G2
STALW/RED AL3 38 D2
Darwin Dr STHL UB1 134 A8
Darwin Gdns OXHEY WD19 93 K6
Darwin Rd DTCH/LGLY SL3 150 C1
EA W5 155 H4
TIL RM18 168 C7
WDGN N22 99 J9
WELL DA16 163 J9
Darwin St WALW SE17 19 H5
Daryngton Dr GFD/PVL UB6 134 C4
GU GU1 250 E10
The Dashes HLW CM20 29 H10
Dashwood Cl BF/WBF KT14 215 M8
BXLYHS DA6 186 B1
DTCH/LGLY SL3 149 P3
Dashwood Lang Rd ADL/WDHM KT15 215 P1
Dashwood Rd CEND/HSY/T N8 118 G4
GVW DA11 190 D4
Dassett Rd WNWD SE27 181 J8
Datchelor Pl CMBW SE5 * 159 L7
Datchet Cl HHNE HP2 36 C1
Datchet Pl DTCH/LGLY SL3 149 N7
Datchet Rd CAT SE6 182 E6
WDSR SL4 149 J6
Datchworth Turn HHNE HP2 36 D6
Date St WALW SE17 18 G8
Daubeney Gdns TOTM N17 99 K8
Daubeney Rd CLPT E5 120 D9
TOTM N17 99 K8
Dault Rd WAND/EARL SW18 179 M2
Davema Cl CHST BR7 206 D1
Davenant Rd ARCH N19 118 E7
Davenant St WCHPL E1 13 P4
Davenham Av NTHWD HA6 92 G5
Davenport HLWE CM17 47 P2
Davenport Cl TEDD TW11 * 176 F9
Davenport Rd CAT SE6 182 G2
SCUP DA14 185 N5
Daventer Dr STAN HA7 94 E8
Daventry Av WALTH E17 120 F4
Daventry Cl DTCH/LGLY SL3 151 J7
Daventry Gdns HARH RM3 105 K6
Daventry Rd HARH RM3 105 K6
Daventry St CAMTN NW1 9 N3
Davern Cl GNWCH SE10 161 L3
Davey Cl HOLWY N7 5 P2
PLMGR N13 98 G6
Davey Rd HOM E9 140 F2
Davey St PECK SE15 19 M10
David Av GFD/PVL UB6 134 D5
David Cl HYS/HAR UB3 152 E6
David Dr HARH RM3 105 P7
Davidge Pl BEAC HP9 88 B5
Davidge St STHWK SE1 18 C2
David Ms MHST W1U 10 B3
David Rd BCTR RM8 123 P7
DTCH/LGLY SL3 151 J8
Davidson Gdns VX/NE SW8 158 F6
Davidson Rd CROY/NA CR0 203 M8
DTCH/LGLY SL3 150 C4
Davidson Wy ROMW/RG RM7 124 F4
David's Rd FSTH SE23 182 B4
David St SRTFD E15 141 J1
Davids Wy BARK/HLT IG6 103 H8
David Twigg Cl KUTN/CMB KT2 199 K1
Davies Cl CROY/NA CR0 203 N6
GODL GU7 267 J10
RAIN RM13 145 K5
Davies La WAN E11 121 K7
Davies Ms MYFR/PKLN W1K 10 E7
Davies St HERT/BAY SG13 25 M5
MYFR/PKLN W1K 10 E7
Davies Wk ISLW TW7 154 C7
Davington Gdns BCTR RM8 123 L10
Davington Rd BCTR RM8 143 L1
Davinia Cl WFD IG8 102 C7
Davis Av GVW DA11 190 B4
Davis Cl SEV TN13 247 K8
Davis Ct STAL AL1 * 38 D6
Davison Cl CHES/WCR EN8 62 C4
Davison Dr CHES/WCR EN8 62 C4
Davis Rd ACT W3 136 C10
CDW/CHF RM16 167 K2
CHSGTN KT9 219 M1
SOCK/AV RM15 146 C10
WEY KT13 216 A6
Davis St PLSTW E13 141 N4
Davisville Rd SHB W12 156 D1
Davis Wy SCUP DA14 185 P9
Davos Cl WOKS/MYFD GU22 232 B5
Davys Cl STALE/WH AL4 21 K4
Davy's Pl GVE DA12 191 H9
Dawell Dr BH/WHM TN16 243 P3
Dawes Av HCH RM12 125 L8
ISLW TW7 176 F1
Dawes Cl CSHM HP5 50 G8
RDART DA2 188 E1
Dawe's Cl HGDN/ICK UB10 131 P4
Dawes Ct ESH/CLAY KT10 218 A1
Dawes East Rd SL SL1 128 B6
Dawes La RKW/CH/CXG WD3 71 J2
STALE/WH AL4 21 J2
Dawes Moor Cl SLN SL2 129 P8
Dawes Rd FUL/PGN SW6 157 J6
Dawe's Rd HGDN/ICK UB10 131 P4
Dawes St WALW SE17 19 H7
Dawley WGCE AL7 23 J2
Dawley Av UX/CGN UB8 132 C7
Dawley Ct HHNE HP2 36 A2
Dawley Gn SOCK/AV RM15 146 F8
Dawley Pde HYS/HAR UB3 132 D9
Dawley Ride DTCH/LGLY SL3 151 H7
Dawley Rd HYS/HAR UB3 152 E1
Dawlish Av GFD/PVL UB6 134 F4
PLMGR N13 98 F5
WAND/EARL SW18 179 L5
Dawlish Dr GDMY/SEVK IG3 123 J9
PIN HA5 113 M3
RSLP HA4 113 H7
Dawlish Rd CRICK NW2 136 G1
LEY E10 121 H7
TOTM N17 119 P1
Dawnay Gdns WAND/EARL SW18 179 N5
Dawnay Rd GT/LBKH KT23 254 A2
WAND/EARL SW18 179 M5
Dawn Cl HSLWW TW4 153 M9
Dawn Crs SRTFD E15 141 J3
Dawney Hl CHOB/PIR GU24 230 D7
Dawneys Rd CHOB/PIR GU24 230 D8
Dawn Redwood Cl DTCH/LGLY SL3 150 D9
Dawn Ri CRAWE RH10 285 H2
Dawpool Rd CRICK NW2 116 C7
Daws Hl CHING E4 81 H7
Daws La MLHL NW7 96 C6
Dawson Av BARK IG11 143 J2
STMC/STPC BR5 207 L2
Dawson Cl HYS/HAR UB3 132 E7
WDSR SL4 148 F8
WOOL/PLUM SE18 162 F3
Dawson Dr RAIN RM13 145 J2
SWLY BR8 186 F10
Dawson Gdns BARK IG11 143 J2
Dawson Pl BAY/PAD W2 8 E7
Dawson Rd BF/WBF KT14 215 N7
CRICK NW2 116 F10
KUT/HW KT1 199 L3
Dawson St BETH E2 7 M8
Dawson Ter ED N9 * 100 B1
Daybrook Rd WIM/MER SW19 201 L2
Dayemead WGCE AL7 23 L8
Daylesford Av PUT/ROE SW15 156 D10
Daylesford Gv SL SL1 148 E1
Daylop Dr CHIG IG7 103 L4
Daymer Gdns PIN HA5 113 K2
Daymerslea Rdg LHD/OX KT22 237 H7
Day's Acre SAND/SEL CR2 223 N6
Daysbrook Rd BRXS/STRHM SW2 180 G4
Days Cl HAT AL10 40 C4
Dayseys Hl REDH RH1 277 H9
Days La BFN/LL DA15 185 H3
BFN/LL DA15 185 J2
BRWN CM15 86 F8
Days Md HAT AL10 40 C4
Dayspring GUW GU2 249 N6
Dayton Dr ERITH DA8 165 L5
Dayton Gv PECK SE15 160 B7
Deacon Cl COB KT11 235 J5
PUR/KEN CR8 222 F5
STAL AL1 38 C10
The Deacon Est CHING E4 * 100 E7
Deacon Fld GUW GU2 249 M9
Deacon Ms IS N1 7 H4
Deacon Pl CTHM CR3 241 K9
Deacon Rd CRICK NW2 136 D1
KUTN/CMB KT2 199 L1
Deacons Cl BORE WD6 75 M8
PIN HA5 93 J10
Deaconsfield Rd HHS/BOV HP3 35 N9
Deacons Hts BORE WD6 75 M10
Deacons Hl OXHEY WD19 73 K10
Deacon's Hill Rd BORE WD6 75 L9
Deacons Leas ORP BR6 226 G1
Deacons Ri EFNCH N2 117 N3
Deacons Ter IS N1 * 6 F1
Deacons Wk HPTN TW12 175 P7
Deacon Wy WALW SE17 18 E5
WFD IG8 102 C8
Deadfield La HERT/WAT SG14 24 B9
Deadhearn La CSTG HP8 90 B2
Deadman's Ash La RKW/CH/CXG WD3 71 L2
Deakin Cl WATW WD18 92 F1
Deakins Ter ORP BR6 207 K7
Deal Av SL SL1 128 E8
Deal Porters Wy BERM/RHTH SE16 160 B2
Deal Rd TOOT SW17 180 B9
Deals Gtwy LEW SE13 160 G7
Deal St WCHPL E1 13 N3
Dealtree Cl BRWN CM15 86 G1
Dealtry Rd PUT/ROE SW15 156 F10
Deal Wk BRXN/ST SW9 159 H6
Deanacre Cl CFSP/GDCR SL9 90 B7
Dean Bradley St WEST SW1P 17 L4
Dean Cl BERM/RHTH SE16 140 C10
HGDN/ICK UB10 132 A2
HOM E9 120 B10
WDSR SL4 148 C9
WOKS/MYFD GU22 233 H2
Dean Ct ALP/SUD HA0 114 G8
GSTN WD25 * 55 L9
Deancroft Rd CFSP/GDCR SL9 90 B7
Deancross St WCHPL E1 140 B8
Dean Dr STAN HA7 95 K10
Deane Av RSLP HA4 113 J10
Deane Ct NTHWD HA6 * 92 F9
Deane Croft Rd PIN HA5 113 K4
Deanery Cl EFNCH N2 117 P2
Deanery Ms MYFR/PKLN W1K * 10 D9
Deanery Rd EDEN TN8 262 F10
SRTFD E15 141 K1
Deanery St MYFR/PKLN W1K 10 D9
Deane Wy RSLP HA4 113 J4
Dean Farrar St STJSPK SW1H 17 K3
Dean Fld HHS/BOV HP3 52 D3
Deanfield Gdns CROY/NA CR0 * 223 L1
Dean Gdns WALTH E17 121 J2
Deanhill Ct MORT/ESHN SW14 * 155 N10
Deanhill Rd MORT/ESHN SW14 155 N10
Dean La REDH RH1 240 D10
Dean Moore Cl STAL AL1 38 C7
Deanoak La REIG RH2 274 G10
Dean Rd CRICK NW2 136 F1
CROY/NA CR0 223 L1
HPTN TW12 175 P8
HSLW TW3 176 A1
THMD SE28 143 K9
Dean Ryle St WEST SW1P 17 L5
Deansbrook Cl EDGW HA8 95 P8
Deansbrook Rd EDGW HA8 95 N8
Dean's Blds WALW SE17 19 H6
Deans Cl ABLGY WD5 54 E8
AMS HP6 69 L3
CHSWK W4 155 N5
CROY/NA CR0 203 N10
EDGW HA8 95 P7
KWD/TDW/WH KT20 238 E10
SLN SL2 129 N3
Deans Ct BFOR GU20 212 C4
Dean's Ct STP EC4M 12 D6
Deanscroft Av CDALE/KGS NW9 115 P7
Deans Dr PLMGR N13 99 J7
Dean's Dr EDGW HA8 96 A6
Deansfield CTHM CR3 259 N1
Dean's Gdns STALE/WH AL4 38 F2
Deans Gate Cl FSTH SE23 182 C6
Deans La KWD/TDW/WH KT20 256 E1
REDH RH1 259 H9
Dean's La EDGW HA8 95 P7
Dean's Ms CAVSQ/HST W1G * 10 F5
Deans Rd BRW CM14 106 G4
REDH RH1 258 D6
SUT SM1 201 L10
Dean's Rd HNWL W7 154 E1
Dean Stanley St WEST SW1P 17 L4
Dean St FSTGT E7 121 M10
SOHO/SHAV W1D 11 J5
Deans Wk COUL/CHIP CR5 241 H4
Deans Wy EDGW HA8 95 P6
Deansway CSHM HP5 50 G5
ED N9 99 M4
EFNCH N2 117 N2
HHS/BOV HP3 36 A9
Deans Yd WEST SW1P 17 K3
Dean Trench St WEST SW1P 17 L4
Dean Vls COB KT11 * 217 K9
Dean Wk GT/LBKH KT23 254 A2
Deanway CSTG HP8 89 N4
Dean Wy CSTG HP8 89 M4
NWDGN UB2 154 A1
Dean Wood Rd BEAC HP9 89 J9
Dearne Cl STAN HA7 94 F6
De'Arn Gdns MTCM CR4 201 P3
Dearsley Rd EN EN1 79 P7
Deason St SRTFD E15 * 141 H3
De Barowe Ms HBRY N5 119 J9
Debden Cl CDALE/KGS NW9 96 B9
KUTN/CMB KT2 177 J8
WFD IG8 102 A8
Debden La LOU IG10 82 E4
Debden Rd LOU IG10 82 E4
De Beauvoir Crs IS N1 7 J5
De Beauvoir Est IS N1 7 J5
De Beauvoir Rd IS N1 7 J3
De Beauvoir Sq IS N1 7 K4
Debenham Rd CHESW EN7 62 A3
Debnams Rd BERM/RHTH SE16 160 B3
De Bohun Av STHGT/OAK N14 78 C10
Deborah Cl ISLW TW7 154 D7
Deborah Crs RSLP HA4 112 E5
Debrabant Cl ERITH DA8 164 E5
De Broome Rd FELT TW13 175 K4
De Burgh Gdns KWD/TDW/WH KT20 238 G5
De Burgh Pk BNSTD SM7 239 L1
Deburgh Rd WIM/MER SW19 179 M10
Decies Wy SLN SL2 129 M3
Decima St STHWK SE1 19 J3
Decimus Cl THHTH CR7 203 L4
Deck Cl BERM/RHTH SE16 140 C10
Decoy Av GLDGN NW11 117 H3
De Crespigny Pk CMBW SE5 159 L8
Dedisham Cl CRAWE RH10 284 B8
Dedswell Dr RGUE GU4 251 K5
Dedworth Dr WDSR SL4 148 D7
Dedworth Rd WDSR SL4 148 A8
Dee Cl UPMR RM14 126 C4
Deeley Rd VX/NE SW8 158 E7
Deena Cl ACT W3 135 L8
SL SL1 128 D9
Deep Acres AMS HP6 68 F2
Deepdale WIM/MER SW19 178 G7
Deepdale Av HAYES BR2 205 L4
Deepdale Cl FBAR/BDGN N11 98 B7
Deepdene POTB/CUF EN6 58 G7
Deepdene Av CROY/NA CR0 203 N10
RDKG RH5 273 H1
Deepdene Avenue Rd DORK RH4 255 H10
Deepdene Cl WAN E11 121 M2
Deepdene Ct WCHMH N21 79 J10
Deepdene Dr RDKG RH5 273 H1
Deepdene Gdns BRXS/STRHM SW2 180 G3
DORK RH4 272 G1
Deepdene Park Rd RDKG RH5 273 H1
Deepdene Pth LOU IG10 82 E8
Deepdene Rd HNHL SE24 159 K10
LOU IG10 82 D8
WELL DA16 163 K9
Deepdene V DORK RH4 255 H10
Deepdene Wd RDKG RH5 273 J2
Deep Fld DTCH/LGLY SL3 149 N6
Deepfields HORL RH6 280 A2
Deepfield Wy COUL/CHIP CR5 240 F2
Deep Pool La CHOB/PIR GU24 213 M9
Deeprose Cl GUW GU2 249 N6
Deepwell Cl ISLW TW7 154 F7
Deepwood La GFD/PVL UB6 134 C5
Deerbarn Rd GUW GU2 249 N9
Deerbrook Rd HNHL SE24 181 J4
Deer Cl HERT/BAY SG13 25 N5
Deerdale Rd HNHL SE24 159 K10
Deere Av RAIN RM13 145 H1
Deerfield Cl CDALE/KGS NW9 116 C3
WARE SG12 26 C1
Deerhurst Cl FELT TW13 175 H7
HART DA3 211 P3
Deerhurst Crs HPTN TW12 176 B8
Deerhurst Rd KIL/WHAMP NW6 136 G2
STRHM/NOR SW16 180 G8
Deerings Dr PIN HA5 113 H3
Deerings Rd REIG RH2 257 L10
Deerleap Gv CHING E4 80 G9
Deerleap La RSEV TN14 227 N9
Deerleap Rd DORK RH4 272 A3
Dee Rd RCH/KEW TW9 155 L10
WDSR SL4 * 148 B6
Deer Pk HLWW/ROY CM19 46 D4
Deer Park Cl KUTN/CMB KT2 177 N10
Deer Park Gdns MTCM CR4 * 201 N4
Deer Park Rd WIM/MER SW19 201 L2
Deer Park Wk CSHM HP5 51 K4
Deer Park Wy WAB EN9 80 G2
WWKM BR4 205 L9
Deers Farm Cl RPLY/SEND GU23 233 P2
Deerswood Av HAT AL10 40 E6
Deerswood Cl CRAWW RH11 283 L6
CTHM CR3 241 P10
Deerswood Rd CRAWW RH11 283 L6
Deeside Rd TOOT SW17 179 N6
Dee St POP/IOD E14 141 H8
The Dee HHNE HP2 36 A1
Deeves Hall La POTB/CUF EN6 58 B9
Dee Wy HOR/WEW KT19 220 B6
ROM RM1 104 F9
Defence Cl THMD SE28 143 H10
Defiant Wy WLGTN SM6 222 F4
Defoe Av RCH/KEW TW9 155 M6
Defoe Cl TOOT SW17 179 P9
Defoe Pde CDW/CHF RM16 168 E2
Defoe Pl TOOT SW17 179 P5
Defoe Rd BERM/RHTH SE16 160 E1
STNW/STAM N16 119 M7
Defoe Wy CRW RM5 104 B7
De Frene Rd SYD SE26 182 C7
Degema Rd CHST BR7 184 E8
Dehar Crs CDALE/KGS NW9 116 C5
De Haviland Dr WOOL/PLUM SE18 162 E4
Dehavilland Cl NTHLT UB5 133 L5
De Havilland Cl HAT AL10 40 C3
STALE/WH AL4 39 P5
De Havilland Ct IL IG1 122 G6
RAD WD7 * 57 K8
De Havilland Dr WEY KT13 215 P7
De Havilland Rd EDGW HA8 95 N10
HEST TW5 153 K6
De Havilland Wy ABLGY WD5 54 G8
STWL/WRAY TW19 173 N2
Deimos Dr HHNE HP2 36 B3
Dekker Rd DUL SE21 181 M2
Delabole Rd REDH RH1 258 F5
Delacourt Rd BKHTH/KID SE3 161 N6
Delafield Rd CHARL SE7 161 N4
GRAYS RM17 168 A4
Delaford Cl IVER SL0 * 131 J8
Delaford Rd BERM/RHTH SE16 160 A4
Delaford St FUL/PGN SW6 157 H6
Delagarde Rd BH/WHM TN16 262 F2
Delahay Ri BERK HP4 33 N3
Delamare Crs CROY/NA CR0 204 B6
Delamare Rd CHES/WCR EN8 62 E5
Delamere Gdns MLHL NW7 96 A6
Delamere Rd BORE WD6 75 N5
EA W5 135 K10
REIG RH2 275 L4
RYNPK SW20 200 G1
YEAD UB4 133 L9
Delamere St BAY/PAD W2 9 J4
Delamere Ter BAY/PAD W2 9 H3
Delancey Pas CAMTN NW1 4 F6
Delancey St CAMTN NW1 4 F6
Delaporte Cl EW KT17 220 B8
De Lapre Cl STMC/STPC BR5 207 N7
De Lara Wy WOKN/KNAP GU21 232 A4
Delargy Cl CDW/CHF RM16 168 E2
De Laune St WALW SE17 18 C8
Delaware Rd MV/WKIL W9 8 G1
Delawyk Crs HNHL SE24 181 L2
Delcombe Av WPK KT4 200 F8
Delderfield ASHTD KT21 237 J6
Delfont Cl CRAWE RH10 284 E9
Delhi Rd EN EN1 99 N1
Delhi St IS N1 5 M6
Delia St WAND/EARL SW18 179 L3
Delisle Rd THMD SE28 143 H10
Delius Cl BORE WD6 75 H10
Delius Gv SRTFD E15 141 H4
Della Pth CLPT E5 119 P8
Dellbow Rd EBED/NFELT TW14 175 J1
Dell Cl CSHM HP5 50 E5
LHD/OX KT22 236 C9
RDKG RH5 255 H3
SLN SL2 109 H10
SRTFD E15 141 J3
WFD IG8 101 N4
WLGTN SM6 222 D1
Dellcott Cl WGCW AL8 22 E4
Dellcut Rd HHNE HP2 36 B4
Dell Farm Rd RSLP HA4 112 E3
Dellfield CSHM HP5 50 F5
STAL AL1 38 E7
Dellfield Av BERK HP4 33 N3
Dellfield Cl BECK BR3 205 H1
BERK HP4 33 M3
RAD WD7 74 D1
WAT WD17 73 H6
Dellfield Crs UX/CGN UB8 131 M6
Dellfield Pde UX/CGN UB8 * 131 M6
Dellfield Rd HAT AL10 40 D4
Dell La EW KT17 220 D2
Dell Lees BEAC HP9 89 H7
Dellmeadow ABLGY WD5 54 F6
Dell Meadow HHS/BOV HP3 35 P10
Dellors Cl BAR EN5 76 G9
Dellow Cl GNTH/NBYPK IG2 122 G5
Dellow St WCHPL E1 140 A9
Dell Ri LCOL/BKTW AL2 56 A2
Dell Rd BERK HP4 33 J2
EW KT17 220 D3
GRAYS RM17 167 N3
PEND EN3 80 B4
WATN WD24 73 H3
WDR/YW UB7 152 A2
Dells Cl CHING E4 100 G1
TEDD TW11 176 E9
Dellside DEN/HRF UB9 111 M3
Dell Side WATN WD24 73 H3
Dell's Ms PIM SW1V * 17 H6
Dellsome La STALE/WH AL4 40 C9
The Dells HHS/BOV HP3 36 C7
Dellswood Cl HERT/BAY SG13 25 M6
Dells Wood Cl HOD EN11 26 E10
The Dell ABYW SE2 163 K4
ALP/SUD HA0 114 G10
BECK BR3 * 182 F10
BTFD TW8 155 H5
CFSP/GDCR SL9 90 B7
EBED/NFELT TW14 175 J3
HERT/BAY SG13 25 K8
HORL RH6 279 M2
KWD/TDW/WH KT20 238 F7
NRWD SE19 203 N1
NTHWD HA6 92 F3
PIN HA5 93 L10
RAD WD7 74 F2
RBRW/HUT CM13 106 G7
REIG RH2 * 257 K9
STAL AL1 38 F4
SWCM DA10 188 G1
WAB EN9 81 H2
WFD IG8 101 N4
WOKN/KNAP GU21 231 P5
Dell Wk NWMAL KT3 200 B2
Dell Wy WEA W13 135 H8
Dellwood RKW/CH/CXG WD3 91 L2
Dellwood Gdns CLAY IG5 122 D1
Delmar Av HHNE HP2 36 E7
Delmeade Rd CSHM HP5 50 F8
Delme Crs BKHTH/KID SE3 161 N8
Delmey Cl CROY/NA CR0 203 N10
Deloraine St DEPT SE8 160 F7
Delorme St HMSMTH W6 156 G5
Delrogue Rd CRAWW RH11 283 K4
Delta Cl CHOB/PIR GU24 213 L6
WPK KT4 200 B10
Delta Dr HORL RH6 280 B6
Delta Est BETH E2 * 7 N9
Delta Gain OXHEY WD19 93 L3
Delta Gv NTHLT UB5 133 L5
Delta Rd CHOB/PIR GU24 213 L6
WOKN/KNAP GU21 232 D2
WPK KT4 200 B10
Delta St BETH E2 7 N9
Delta Wy EGH TW20 194 F1

De Luci Rd ERITH DA8 164 D4
De Lucy St ABYW SE2 163 L3
Delvers Md DAGE RM10 124 D9
Delverton Rd WALW SE17 18 D7
Delves KWD/TDW/WH KT20 238 G7
Delvino Rd FUL/PGN SW6 157 K7
Demesne Rd WLGTN SM6 222 E1
Demeta Cl WBLY HA9 115 P8
De Montfort Pde STRHM/NOR SW16 * 180 F6
De Montfort Rd STRHM/NOR SW16 180 E5
De Morgan Rd FUL/PGN SW6 157 L9
Dempster Cl SURB KT6 199 H7
Dempster Rd WAND/EARL SW18 179 M1
Denbar Pde ROMW/RG RM7 124 D2
Denberry Dr SCUP DA14 185 L6
Denbigh Cl CHST BR7 184 C9
EMPK RM11 125 N2
HHNE HP2 35 P7
NTGHL W11 8 D7
STHL UB1 133 N8
SUT SM1 221 J2
Denbigh Dr HYS/HAR UB3 152 D1
Denbigh Gdns RCHPK/HAM TW10 177 L1
Denbigh Pl PIM SW1V 16 G7
Denbigh Rd EHAM E6 142 A5
HSLW TW3 154 A8
NTGHL W11 8 D7
STHL UB1 133 N8
WEA W13 134 G9
Denbigh St PIM SW1V 16 G6
Denbigh Ter NTGHL W11 8 D7
Denbridge Rd BMLY BR1 206 C2
Denby Gra HLWE CM17 47 P1
Denby Rd COB KT11 217 K8
Denchers Plat CRAWW RH11 283 N4
Dencliffe ASHF TW15 * 174 B8
Den Cl BECK BR3 205 J4
Dendridge Cl EN EN1 80 A3
Dendy St BAL SW12 180 B4
Dene Av BFN/LL DA15 185 L3
HSLW TW3 153 N9
Dene Cl BROCKY SE4 160 D9
COUL/CHIP CR5 239 P5
HAYES BR2 205 L8
HORL RH6 279 P2
WPK KT4 200 C9
Denecroft Crs HGDN/ICK UB10 132 C3
Denecroft Gdns GRAYS RM17 168 A2
Dene Dr HART DA3 211 N2
ORP BR6 207 L10
Denefield Dr PUR/KEN CR8 241 L1
Dene Gdns STAN HA7 95 H6
THDIT KT7 198 F9
Dene Holm Rd GVW DA11 190 A6
Denehurst Gdns ACT W3 135 N10
HDN NW4 116 F4
RCHPK/HAM TW10 155 M10
WFD IG8 101 N5
WHTN TW2 176 C3
Dene Pth SOCK/AV RM15 146 F8
Dene Pl WOKN/KNAP GU21 231 N4
Dene Rd ASHTD KT21 237 L5
BKHH IG9 102 B2
GU GU1 268 B1
NTHWD HA6 92 D7
TRDG/WHET N20 98 A2
Dene St DORK RH4 272 G2
Dene Street Gdns DORK RH4 272 G2
The Dene BELMT SM2 221 J7
CROY/NA CR0 224 C1
E/WMO/HCT KT8 197 N5
SEV TN13 265 J2
WBLY HA9 115 K9
WEA W13 134 G7
Dene Tye CRAWE RH10 284 D6
Dene Wk HART DA3 211 K3
Denewood BAR EN5 77 M9
EW KT17 * 220 B9
Denewood Cl WAT WD17 72 G3
Denewood Ms WAT WD17 72 G3
Denewood Rd HGT N6 117 P4
Denfield DORK RH4 272 G4
Dengie Wk IS N1 6 E5
Denham Av DEN/HRF UB9 111 J7
Denham Cl DEN/HRF UB9 111 K8
HHNE HP2 36 B1
WELL DA16 163 M9
Denham Court Dr DEN/HRF UB9 111 L8
Denham Crs MTCM CR4 202 A4
Denham Dr GNTH/NBYPK IG2 122 F4
Denham Garden Village DEN/HRF UB9 * 111 J4
Denham Green Cl DEN/HRF UB9 111 K5
Denham Green La DEN/HRF UB9 111 H3
Denham La CFSP/GDCR SL9 90 C8
Denham Ldg DEN/HRF UB9 * 131 M1
Denham Pde DEN/HRF UB9 * 111 J8
Denham Pl DEN/HRF UB9 * 111 K6
Denham Rd DEN/HRF UB9 111 J10
EBED/NFELT TW14 175 K3
EGH TW20 172 D7
EW KT17 220 C8
IVER SL0 130 G3
TRDG/WHET N20 98 A3
Denham Wk CFSP/GDCR SL9 90 C7
Denham Wy BARK IG11 143 H3
BORE WD6 75 P5
DEN/HRF UB9 111 K8
Denham Way (North Orbital Road) RKW/CH/CXG WD3 91 H8
Denholme Rd MV/WKIL W9 2 D9
Denholme Wk RAIN RM13 144 G1
Denholm Gdns RGUE GU4 250 D7
Denison Cl EFNCH N2 117 M1
Denison Rd EA W5 135 H6
FELT TW13 174 G7
WIM/MER SW19 179 N9
Deniston Av BXLY DA5 185 N4
Denleigh Gdns THDIT KT7 * 198 D6
WCHMH N21 99 H1
Denly Wy LTWR GU18 212 B6
Denman Dr ASHF TW15 174 C9
ESH/CLAY KT10 218 F2
GLDGN NW11 117 K3
Denman Dr North GLDGN NW11 117 K3
Denman Dr South GLDGN NW11 117 K3
Denman Rd PECK SE15 159 N7
Denmans CRAWE RH10 284 E6
Denman St SOHO/SHAV W1D 11 H8
Denmark Av WIM/MER SW19 179 H10
Denmark Ct MRDN SM4 201 K5
Denmark Gdns CAR SM5 202 A10
Denmark Gv IS N1 6 A7
Denmark Hl HNHL SE24 159 L10
Denmark Hill Dr CDALE/KGS NW9 116 D1
Denmark Rd BMLY BR1 205 N1
CAR SM5 202 A10
CEND/HSY/T N8 118 G2
CMBW SE5 159 K7
KIL/WHAMP NW6 2 D8
KUT/HW KT1 199 K3
SNWD SE25 204 A5
WEA W13 134 G9
WHTN TW2 176 C6
WIM/MER SW19 178 G9
Denmark St LSQ/SEVD WC2H 11 K6
PLSTW E13 141 N7
TOTM N17 100 A9
WAN E11 121 K8
WAT WD17 73 J6
Denmark Ter EFNCH N2 * 118 A1
Denmead Cl CFSP/GDCR SL9 110 B5
Denmead Rd CROY/NA CR0 203 J8
Dennan Rd SURB KT6 199 L8
Denne Rd CRAWW RH11 283 N8
Denner Rd CHING E4 100 F3
Denne Ter HACK E8 7 M6
Dennett Rd CROY/NA CR0 203 H7
Dennett's Gv NWCR SE14 160 C8
Dennettsland Rd EDEN TN8 262 F10
Dennett's Rd NWCR SE14 160 B7
Denning Av CROY/NA CR0 223 H2
Denning Cl HPTN TW12 175 N9
STJWD NW8 3 K9
Denning Ms BAL SW12 180 B2
Denning Rd HAMP NW3 117 N9
Dennington Park Rd KIL/WHAMP NW6 2 F1
The Denningtons WPK KT4 200 B9
Dennis Av WBLY HA9 115 L10
Dennis Cl ASHF TW15 174 E10
REDH RH1 257 P8
Dennises La UPMR RM14 146 D3
Dennis Gdns STAN HA7 95 H6
Dennis La STAN HA7 94 G5
Dennis Pde STHGT/OAK N14 * 98 E2
Dennis Park Crs RYNPK SW20 201 H1
Dennis Reeve Cl MTCM CR4 202 A1
Dennis Rd E/WMO/HCT KT8 198 B4
GVW DA11 190 D6
SOCK/AV RM15 146 F4
Dennis Wy CLAP SW4 158 E9
GU GU1 250 B5
SL SL1 128 C9
Denny Av WAB EN9 63 J10
Denny Crs LBTH SE11 18 B7
Denny Gdns DAGW RM9 143 L2
Denny Ga CHES/WCR EN8 62 E3
Denny Rd DTCH/LGLY SL3 * 150 C3
ED N9 100 A2
Denny's La BERK HP4 33 L7
Denny St LBTH SE11 18 B7
Den Rd HAYES BR2 205 J3
Densham Dr PUR/KEN CR8 223 H10
Densham Rd SRTFD E15 141 K3
Densley Cl WGCW AL8 22 F3
Densole Cl BECK BR3 * 204 D1
Densworth Gv ED N9 100 B3
Dent Cl SOCK/AV RM15 146 F8
Denton Cl BAR EN5 76 F9
REDH RH1 276 B5
Denton Court Rd GVE DA12 191 H4
Denton Gv WOT/HER KT12 197 M9
Denton Rd CEND/HSY/T N8 118 G3
TWK TW1 177 J2
UED N18 99 M5
WELL DA16 163 M6
Denton St GVE DA12 191 H3
WAND/EARL SW18 179 L2
Denton Ter BXLY DA5 * 186 F5
Denton Wy CLPT E5 120 C8
WOKN/KNAP GU21 231 M3
Denton Whf GVE DA12 * 191 J2
Dents Gv KWD/TDW/WH KT20 257 J4
Dents Rd BTSEA SW11 180 A2
Denvale Trade Pk MTCM CR4 201 N4
Denvale Wk WOKN/KNAP GU21 231 M4
Denver Cl ORP BR6 207 H6
Denver Rd STNW/STAM N16 119 M5
Denyer St CHEL SW3 15 P5
Denziloe Av HGDN/ICK UB10 132 C5
Denzil Rd GUW GU2 267 N1
WLSDN NW10 116 C10
Deodar Rd PUT/ROE SW15 157 H10
Deodora Cl TRDG/WHET N20 97 P4
Departures Rd HORL RH6 280 A7
Depot Ap CRICK NW2 116 G9
Depot Rd CRAWW RH11 283 N4
EW KT17 220 B9
HSLW TW3 154 C9
Depot St CMBW SE5 18 G10
Deptford Br DEPT SE8 160 F7
Deptford Broadway NWCR SE14 160 F7
Deptford Church St DEPT SE8 160 F5
Deptford Gn DEPT SE8 160 F5
Deptford High St DEPT SE8 160 F5
Deptford Whf DEPT SE8 160 E3
De Quincey Ms CAN/RD E16 141 M10
De Quincey Rd TOTM N17 99 L9
Derby Arms Rd EPSOM KT18 238 C3
Derby Av KTN/HRWW/WS HA3 94 C9
NFNCH/WDSPK N12 97 M6
ROMW/RG RM7 124 C4
UPMR RM14 125 N8
Derby Cl EPSOM KT18 238 E5
Derby Ga WHALL SW1A 17 L1
Derby Hl FSTH SE23 182 B5
Derby Hill Crs FSTH SE23 182 B5
Derby Rd BRYLDS KT5 199 M8
CROY/NA CR0 203 J9
FSTGT E7 142 A2
GFD/PVL UB6 134 A3
GUW GU2 249 L10
HOD EN11 45 J5
HOM E9 140 C3
HSLW TW3 154 A10
MORT/ESHN SW14 155 N10
PEND EN3 80 A9
SUT SM1 221 J3
SWFD E18 101 L9
UED N18 100 B6
UX/CGN UB8 131 M4
WAT WD17 73 K8
WIM/MER SW19 179 K10
Derby Road Br GRAYS RM17 167 N4
Derbyshire St BETH E2 7 P10
Derby Stables Rd EPSOM KT18 238 B3
Derby St MYFR/PICC W1J 10 D10
Dereham Pl CRW RM5 104 C7
SDTCH EC2A 13 K1
Dereham Rd BARK IG11 143 J1
Derek Av HOR/WEW KT19 219 M3
WBLY HA9 135 N2
WLGTN SM6 222 C1
Derek Cl HOR/WEW KT19 219 N2
Derek Walcott Cl HNHL SE24 * 181 J1
Derham Gdns UPMR RM14 126 B8
Deri Av RAIN RM13 145 J6
Dericote St HACK E8 7 P5
Deri Dene Cl STWL/WRAY TW19 * 173 P2
Derifall Cl EHAM E6 142 C7
Dering Pl CROY/NA CR0 223 K1
Dering Rd CROY/NA CR0 223 K1
Dering St OXSTW W1C 10 E6
Dering Wy GVE DA12 191 H3
Derinton Rd TOOT SW17 180 B7
Derisley Cl BF/WBF KT14 215 N8
Derley Rd NWDGN UB2 153 K2
Dermody Gdns LEW SE13 * 183 J1
Dermody Rd LEW SE13 183 J1
Deronda Rd HNHL SE24 181 J4
De Ros Pl EGH TW20 172 D9
Deroy Cl CAR SM5 222 A3
Derrick Av SAND/SEL CR2 223 K6
Derrick Gdns CHARL SE7 161 P2
Derrick Rd BECK BR3 204 E3
Derry Av SOCK/AV RM15 146 F7
Derrydown WOKS/MYFD GU22 231 N7
Derry Downs STMC/STPC BR5 207 M6
Derry Leys HAT AL10 40 B2
Derry Rd CROY/NA CR0 202 F10
Derry St KENS W8 14 G2
Dersingham Av MNPK E12 122 C9
Dersingham Rd CRICK NW2 117 H8
Derwent Av CDALE/KGS NW9 116 B3
EBAR EN4 98 A2
HGDN/ICK UB10 112 B7
MLHL NW7 96 A6
PIN HA5 93 M7
PUT/ROE SW15 178 B7
UED N18 99 L6
Derwent Cl ADL/WDHM KT15 215 N2
AMSS HP7 69 N5
CRAWW RH11 283 J8
EBED/NFELT TW14 174 C4
ESH/CLAY KT10 218 D3
GSTN WD25 55 K9
Derwent Crs BXLYHN DA7 164 B8
NFNCH/WDSPK N12 97 M4
STAN HA7 95 H10
Derwent Dr PUR/KEN CR8 223 L10
SL SL1 128 B7
STMC/STPC BR5 206 G7
YEAD UB4 132 F7
Derwent Gdns REDBR IG4 122 B2
WBLY HA9 115 H5
Derwent Gv EDUL SE22 159 N10
Derwent Ri CDALE/KGS NW9 116 B4
Derwent Rd EA W5 155 H2
EGH TW20 172 E9
HHS/BOV HP3 36 D7
LTWR GU18 212 A7
PGE/AN SE20 203 P2
PLMGR N13 98 G5
RYNPK SW20 200 G6
STHL UB1 133 N8
WHTN TW2 176 A2
Derwent St GNWCH SE10 161 K4
Derwentwater Rd ACT W3 135 P10
Derwent Wy HCH RM12 125 J10
Derwent Yd EA W5 * 155 H2
De Salis Rd HGDN/ICK UB10 132 D6
Desborough Cl HERT/WAT SG14 25 K2
SHPTN TW17 196 B7
WGCE AL7 23 L8
Desenfans Rd DUL SE21 181 M2
Deseronto Est DTCH/LGLY SL3 * 150 B1
Desford Rd CAN/RD E16 141 K6
Desford Wy ASHF TW15 174 A5
Desmond Rd WATN WD24 72 G2
Desmond St NWCR SE14 160 D5
Desmond Tutu Dr FSTH SE23 182 D4
De Soissons Cl WGCW AL8 22 E7
Despard Rd ARCH N19 118 D6
Desvignes Dr LEW SE13 183 J2
De Tany Ct STAL AL1 38 C7
Detillens La OXTED RH8 261 M5
Detling Cl HCH RM12 125 K10
Detling Rd BMLY BR1 183 M8
ERITH DA8 164 E6
GVW DA11 190 A4
Detmold Rd CLPT E5 120 A7
Deva Cl STALW/RED AL3 37 P8
Devalls Cl EHAM E6 142 D9
Devana End CAR SM5 202 A10
Devas Rd RYNPK SW20 200 F1
Devas St BOW E3 140 G6
Devenay Rd SRTFD E15 141 L2
Devenish La ASC SL5 192 C8
Devenish Rd ABYW SE2 163 K1
ASC SL5 192 C6
Deveraux Cl BECK BR3 205 H5
De Vere Cl WLGTN SM6 222 F4
De Vere Gdns IL IG1 122 C6
KENS W8 15 J2
Deverell St STHWK SE1 18 G4
De Vere Ms KENS W8 15 J3
Devereux Ct TPL/STR WC2R 12 A7
Devereux Dr WAT WD17 72 F4
Devereux La BARN SW13 156 E6
Devereux Rd BTSEA SW11 180 A2
CDW/CHF RM16 167 L2
WDSR SL4 149 J8
De Vere Wk WAT WD17 72 F6
Deverills Wy DTCH/LGLY SL3 150 F3
Deveron Gdns SOCK/AV RM15 146 F7
Deveron Wy ROM RM1 104 F9
Devey Cl KUTN/CMB KT2 178 C10
Devil's La EGH TW20 172 F9
Devitt Cl ASHTD KT21 237 M2
Devizes St IS N1 * 7 H6
Devoil Cl RGUE GU4 250 E6
Devoke Wy WOT/HER KT12 197 L9
Devon Av SL SL1 129 H8
WHTN TW2 176 B4
Devon Bank GUW GU2 267 P3
Devon Cl BKHH IG9 101 N3
GFD/PVL UB6 135 H3
HOR/WEW KT19 219 M8
PUR/KEN CR8 241 M2
TOTM N17 119 N1
Devon Ct STAL AL1 * 38 D7
Devon Crs REDH RH1 257 N10
Devoncroft Gdns TWK TW1 176 F3
Devon Gdns FSBYPK N4 119 J4
Devonhurst Pl CHSWK W4 * 156 A4
Devonia Gdns UED N18 99 K7
Devonia Rd IS N1 6 D7
Devon Man KTN/HRWW/WS HA3 * 115 H3
Devon Md HAT AL10 40 A2
Devonport Gdns IL IG1 122 C4
Devonport Ms SHB W12 * 136 E10
Devonport Rd SHB W12 156 E1
Devonport St WCHPL E1 140 B8
Devon Ri EFNCH N2 117 N2
Devon Rd BARK IG11 143 H3
BELMT SM2 221 H5
EYN DA4 210 A1
REDH RH1 258 D6
WATN WD24 73 L5
WOT/HER KT12 217 K1
Devons Est BOW E3 140 G5
Devonshire Av AMS HP6 68 G3
BELMT SM2 221 M4
KWD/TDW/WH KT20 255 P7
WOKN/KNAP GU21 214 F10
Devonshire Cl CAVSQ/HST W1G 10 E3
SRTFD E15 121 K9
Devonshire Ct FELT TW13 * 175 J5
Devonshire Crs MLHL NW7 96 G8
Devonshire Dr GNWCH SE10 160 G7
SURB KT6 199 J8
Devonshire Gdns CHSWK W4 155 P6
SLH/COR SS17 169 K1
TOTM N17 99 K7
WCHMH N21 99 K1
Devonshire Gn SLN SL2 128 G4
Devonshire Gv PECK SE15 160 A5
Devonshire Hill La TOTM N17 99 K7
Devonshire Ms CHSWK W4 156 B4
Devonshire Ms South CAVSQ/HST W1G 10 E3
Devonshire Ms West CAVSQ/HST W1G 10 D2
Devonshire Pl CAVSQ/HST W1G 10 D2
CRICK NW2 117 K8
KENS W8 * 14 G4
Devonshire Place Ms CAVSQ/HST W1G 10 D2
Devonshire Rd BELMT SM2 221 M4
BXLYHS DA6 163 P10
CAN/RD E16 141 N8
CAR SM5 222 B1
CDW/CHF RM16 167 K3
CHSWK W4 156 B4
CROY/NA CR0 203 L7
EA W5 155 H2
ED N9 100 B2
ELTH/MOT SE9 184 B5
FELT TW13 175 M6
FSTH SE23 182 C3
GNTH/NBYPK IG2 122 G5
GVW DA11 190 E4
HARP AL5 20 A1
HCH RM12 125 L7
HRW HA1 114 C4
MLHL NW7 96 G8
ORP BR6 207 K7
PIN HA5 113 K4
PLMGR N13 98 G5
STHL UB1 133 P7
TOTM N17 99 K7
WALTH E17 120 F4
WEY KT13 * 216 B1
WIM/MER SW19 179 P10
Devonshire Rw LVPST EC2M 13 K4
Devonshire Row Ms GTPST W1W 10 F2
Devonshire Sq HAYES BR2 205 N4
LVPST EC2M 13 K5
Devonshire St CAVSQ/HST W1G 10 D3
CHSWK W4 156 B4
Devonshire Ter BAY/PAD W2 9 K6
EDUL SE22 * 159 P10
Devonshire Wy CROY/NA CR0 204 E9
YEAD UB4 133 J8
Devons Rd BOW E3 140 F7
Devon St PECK SE15 160 A5
Devon Wy CHSGTN KT9 219 H1
HGDN/ICK UB10 132 A4
HOR/WEW KT19 219 N2
Devon Waye HEST TW5 153 N6
De Walden St CAVSQ/HST W1G 10 D4
Dewar Cl CRAWW RH11 * 283 H8
Dewar Sp DTCH/LGLY SL3 150 C5
Dewar St PECK SE15 159 P9
Dewberry Gdns EHAM E6 142 B7
Dewberry St POP/IOD E14 141 H8
Dewey La BRXS/STRHM SW2 181 H2
Dewey Rd DAGE RM10 144 D1
IS N1 6 A7
Dewey St TOOT SW17 180 A8
Dewgrass Gv CHES/WCR EN8 80 C1
Dewhurst Rd CHES/WCR EN8 62 B5
HMSMTH W6 156 G2
Dewlands GDST RH9 260 B7
Dewlands Av RDART DA2 188 A3
Dewsbury Cl PIN HA5 113 M4
Dewsbury Gdns HARH RM3 105 L7
WPK KT4 200 D10
Dewsbury Rd HARH RM3 105 M7
WLSDN NW10 116 D10
Dexter Cl GRAYS RM17 167 M2
STAL AL1 38 F7
Dexter Rd BAR EN5 76 G10
DEN/HRF UB9 91 M10
Deyncourt Gdns UPMR RM14 126 B7
Deyncourt Rd TOTM N17 99 K9
Deynecourt Gdns WAN E11 121 P2
D'Eynsford Rd CMBW SE5 159 L7
Dharam Marg GSTN WD25 * 74 D5
Diadem Ct SOHO/CST W1F 11 J5
Dial Cl SWCM DA10 189 H1
Diamedes Av STWL/WRAY TW19 173 N3
Diameter Rd STMC/STPC BR5 206 E7
Diamond Cl BCTR RM8 123 M6
CDW/CHF RM16 167 L2
Diamond Rd RSLP HA4 113 L9
SL SL1 149 M1
WATN WD24 73 H4
Diamond St CMBW SE5 159 M6
WLSDN NW10 136 A2
Diamond Ter GNWCH SE10 161 H7
Diana Cl CDW/CHF RM16 167 L2
DEPT SE8 160 E5
DTCH/LGLY SL3 130 B8
SCUP DA14 185 P5
SWFD E18 101 N9
Diana Gdns SURB KT6 199 L9
Diana Rd WALTH E17 120 E1
Dianne Wy EBAR EN4 77 P8
Dianthus Cl ABYW SE2 * 163 L4
CHERT KT16 195 H7
Dianthus Ct WOKS/MYFD GU22 232 A4
Diban Av HCH RM12 125 J9
Dibden Hl CSTG HP8 89 N5
Dibden La RSEV TN14 264 F3
Dibden St IS N1 6 E5
Dibdin Cl SUT SM1 201 K10
Dibdin Rd SUT SM1 201 K10
Diceland Rd BNSTD SM7 239 J2
Dicey Av CRICK NW2 116 F10
Dickens Av DART DA1 165 P10
FNCH N3 97 M9
TIL RM18 168 E7
UX/CGN UB8 132 C8
Dickens Cl ERITH DA8 164 C6
HART DA3 211 K5
HYS/HAR UB3 152 F3
RCHPK/HAM TW10 177 K5
STALW/RED AL3 38 C5
Dickens Dr ADL/WDHM KT15 215 J3
CHST BR7 184 F9
Dickens Est BERM/RHTH SE16 19 N3
Dickens La UED N18 99 M6
Dickens Ms FARR EC1M 12 C2
Dickenson Cl ED N9 99 P2
Dickenson Rd CEND/HSY/T N8 118 F5
FELT TW13 175 K8
Dickenson's La SNWD SE25 203 P6
Dickenson's Pl SNWD SE25 203 P6
Dickenson Wy WARE SG12 26 C2
Dickens Pl DTCH/LGLY SL3 151 H7
Dickens Ri CHIG IG7 102 D4
Dickens Rd CRAWE RH10 283 N10
EHAM E6 142 A4
GVE DA12 191 H4
Dickens Sq STHWK SE1 18 F3
Dickens St VX/NE SW8 158 C8
Dickens Wy ROM RM1 124 F2
Dickens Wood Cl NRWD SE19 181 J10
Dickerage La NWMAL KT3 199 P3
Dickerage Rd NWMAL KT3 199 P2
Dicker Mi HERT/BAY SG13 25 L4
Dickins Cl CHESW EN7 61 P3
Dickinson Av RKW/CH/CXG WD3 72 B10
Dickinson Quay HHS/BOV HP3 36 A10
Dickinsons Fld HARP AL5 20 B4
Dickinson Sq RKW/CH/CXG WD3 72 B10
Dickson CHESW EN7 61 N3
Dickson Fold PIN HA5 113 L2
Dickson House CHARL SE7 * 162 B6
Dickson Rd ELTH/MOT SE9 162 B9
Dick Turpin Wy EBED/NFELT TW14 152 G10
Didsbury Cl EHAM E6 142 C3
Digby Crs FSBYPK N4 119 K7
Digby Gdns DAGE RM10 144 B3
Digby Pl CROY/NA CR0 203 N10
Digby Rd BARK IG11 143 J2
HOM E9 140 C1
Digby St BETH E2 140 B5
Digby Wy BF/WBF KT14 216 A8
Dig Dag Hl CHESW EN7 61 N3
Digdens Ri EPSOM KT18 237 P1
Diggon St WCHPL E1 140 C7
Dighton Rd WAND/EARL SW18 179 M1
Dignum St IS N1 * 6 A7
Digswell Cl BORE WD6 75 M4
Digswell Hl WGCW AL8 22 D2
Digswell La WGCE AL7 23 J1
Digswell Ri WGCW AL8 22 G3
Digswell Rd WGCW AL8 22 G3
Digswell St HOLWY N7 6 B1
Dilhorne Cl LEE/GVPK SE12 183 N6
Dilke St CHEL SW3 16 B9
Dillwyn Cl SYD SE26 182 D7
Dilston Cl NTHLT UB5 133 K5
Dilston Rd LHD/OX KT22 236 F5
Dilton Gdns PUT/ROE SW15 178 D4
Dimes Pl HMSMTH W6 156 E3
Dimmock Dr GFD/PVL UB6 114 C10
Dimmocks La RKW/CH/CXG WD3 71 K2
Dimond Cl FSTGT E7 121 M9
Dimsdale Dr CDALE/KGS NW9 115 P6
EN EN1 99 P1
Dimsdale St HERT/WAT SG14 25 K5
Dimsdale Wk PLSTW E13 141 M3
Dimson Crs BOW E3 140 F6
Dinant Link Rd HOD EN11 44 F2
Dingle Cl BAR EN5 76 C10
CRAWW RH11 283 L6
Dingle Gdns POP/IOD E14 * 140 F9
Dingle Rd ASHF TW15 174 C8
The Dingle CRAWW RH11 283 L7
HGDN/ICK UB10 132 C5
Dingley La STRHM/NOR SW16 180 E5
Dingley Pl FSBYE EC1V 6 F10
Dingley Rd FSBYE EC1V 6 E10
Dingwall Av CROY/NA CR0 203 K9
Dingwall Gdns GLDGN NW11 117 K4
Dingwall Rd CAR SM5 222 A5
CROY/NA CR0 203 L9
WAND/EARL SW18 179 M3
Dinmont Est BETH E2 7 P7
Dinmont St BETH E2 140 A4
Dinmore HHS/BOV HP3 52 C4
Dinsdale Cl WOKS/MYFD GU22 232 C4
Dinsdale Gdns BAR EN5 77 L9
SNWD SE25 203 M5
Dinsdale Rd BKHTH/KID SE3 161 L5
Dinsmore Rd BAL SW12 180 C3
Dinton Rd KUTN/CMB KT2 177 L10
WIM/MER SW19 179 N9
Dione Rd HHNE HP2 36 A3
Diploma Av EFNCH N2 117 P2
Dippers Cl BGR/WK TN15 247 N3
Dirdene Cl EW KT17 220 C8
Dirdene Gdns EW KT17 220 C8
Dirdene Gv EW KT17 220 B8
Dirleton Rd SRTFD E15 141 L3
Dirtham La EHSLY KT24 253 J5
Disbrowe Rd HMSMTH W6 14 A10
Discovery Wk WAP E1W 140 A9
Dishforth La CDALE/KGS NW9 96 B9
Disney Pl STHWK SE1 18 F1
Disney St STHWK SE1 18 F1
Dison Cl PEND EN3 80 C5
Disraeli Cl THMD SE28 143 L10
Disraeli Ct DTCH/LGLY SL3 150 E5
Disraeli Pk BEAC HP9 88 C7
Disraeli Rd EA W5 135 J10
FSTGT E7 141 M1
PUT/ROE SW15 157 H10
WLSDN NW10 135 P4
Diss St BETH E2 7 L9
Distaff La BLKFR EC4V 12 E7
Distillery La HMSMTH W6 156 F4
Distillery Rd HMSMTH W6 156 F4
Distin St LBTH SE11 18 A6
District Rd ALP/SUD HA0 114 G10
Ditchburn St POP/IOD E14 141 H9
Ditches La COUL/CHIP CR5 240 E3
Ditchfield Rd HOD EN11 26 F10
YEAD UB4 133 M6
Ditchling Hl CRAWW RH11 283 M10
Dittisham Rd ELTH/MOT SE9 184 B7
Ditton Cl THDIT KT7 198 F7
Dittoncroft Cl CROY/NA CR0 223 M1
Ditton Grange Cl SURB KT6 199 J8
Ditton Grange Dr SURB KT6 199 J8
Ditton Hl SURB KT6 199 H8
Ditton Hill Rd SURB KT6 199 H8
Ditton Lawn THDIT KT7 198 F8
Ditton Park Rd DTCH/LGLY SL3 150 B5
Ditton Pl PGE/AN SE20 * 204 A1
Ditton Reach THDIT KT7 198 G6
Ditton Rd BXLYHS DA6 185 N1
DTCH/LGLY SL3 150 A7
NWDGN UB2 153 N4
SURB KT6 199 K8
Divot Pl HERT/BAY SG13 26 A4
Dixey Cots EFNCH N2 * 117 P3
Dixon Cl EHAM E6 142 C8
Dixon Dr WEY KT13 216 A6
Dixon Pl WWKM BR4 204 G8
Dixon Rd NWCR SE14 160 D7
SNWD SE25 203 M3
Dixons Ct WARE SG12 * 26 D3
Dixons Hill Cl BRKMPK AL9 58 E1
Dixons Hill Rd BRKMPK AL9 58 E1
Dixon Wy WLSDN NW10 136 B2
Dobbin Cl KTN/HRWW/WS HA3 94 F10
Dobbins Pl CRAWW RH11 282 G8
Dobb's Weir Rd HOD EN11 45 J4
Dobell Rd ELTH/MOT SE9 184 C1
Dobree Av WLSDN NW10 136 E2
Dobson Cl KIL/WHAMP NW6 3 L4
Dobson Rd CRAWW RH11 283 N4
GVE DA12 191 H8
Dock Approach Rd GRAYS RM17 168 B4
Dockers Tanner Rd POP/IOD E14 160 F3
Dockett Eddy La SHPTN TW17 196 A7
Dockett Moorings CHERT KT16 * 196 A8
Dockhead STHWK SE1 19 M2
Dock Hill Av BERM/RHTH SE16 160 C1
Dockland St CAN/RD E16 142 D10
Dockley Rd BERM/RHTH SE16 19 N4
Dock Rd BTFD TW8 * 155 J6
CAN/RD E16 141 L9
GRAYS RM17 168 A5
Dockside Rd CAN/RD E16 142 A9
Dock St WCHPL E1 13 N7
Dockwell Cl EBED/NFELT TW14 153 H10
Doctors Cl SYD SE26 182 B8
Doctor's Commons Rd BERK HP4 33 N6
Doctors La CTHM CR3 241 H10
Docwra's Blds IS N1 7 J1
Dodbrooke Rd WNWD SE27 181 H6
Doddinghurst Rd BRWN CM15 107 H1
BRWN CM15 87 H3
Doddington Gv WALW SE17 18 C9
Doddington Pl WALW SE17 18 C9
Dodds Crs BF/WBF KT14 215 L10
Doddsfield Rd SLN SL2 128 F5
Dodds La CSTG HP8 89 N3
HHNE HP2 35 M1
Dodd's La WOKS/MYFD GU22 215 K10
Dodds Pk BRKHM/BTCW RH3 273 N2
Dodsley Pl ED N9 100 B4
Dodson St STHWK SE1 18 B2
Dod St POP/IOD E14 140 F8
Dodwood WGCE AL7 23 L6
Doebury Wk WOOL/PLUM SE18 163 K5
Doel Cl WIM/MER SW19 179 M10
Doggett Rd CAT SE6 182 F3
Doggetts Ct EBAR EN4 77 P9
Doggetts Farm Rd DEN/HRF UB9 110 F5
Doggetts Wy STAL AL1 38 B8
Doggetts Wood Cl CSTG HP8 69 N8
Doggetts Wood La CSTG HP8 69 N7
Doghurst Av WDR/YW UB7 152 C6
Doghurst Dr WDR/YW UB7 152 C6
Doghurst La COUL/CHIP CR5 240 A6
Dog Kennel Hl CMBW SE5 159 M9
Dog Kennel La HAT AL10 40 D3
RKW/CH/CXG WD3 71 J9
Dog La WLSDN NW10 116 B9
Dognell Gn WGCW AL8 22 E4
Dog Rose Ramble YEAD UB4 133 H3
Dog Rose Ramble & Hillingdon Trail YEAD UB4 132 G4
Dogwood Cl GVW DA11 190 B7
Doherty Rd PLSTW E13 141 M6
Dolben Ct DEPT SE8 * 160 E3
Dolben St STHWK SE1 * 12 D10
Dolby Rd FUL/PGN SW6 157 J8
Dolby Ter HORL RH6 * 279 H9
Doldens Cots EYN DA4 * 210 A4
Dolland St LBTH SE11 17 P8
Dollary Pde KUT/HW KT1 * 199 N3
Dollis Av FNCH N3 97 J9
Dollis Cl CRAWE RH10 284 D8
Dollis Crs RSLP HA4 113 K6
Dollis Hill Av CRICK NW2 116 E8
Dollis Hill Est CRICK NW2 * 116 D8
Dollis Hill La CRICK NW2 116 C9
Dollis Pk FNCH N3 97 J9
Dollis Rd MLHL NW7 97 H9
Dollis Valley Dr BAR EN5 77 J9
Dollis Valley Green Wk FNCH N3 117 H2
TRDG/WHET N20 97 L4
Dollis Valley Wy EBAR EN4 77 N8
Dolman Cl FNCH N3 97 M10
Dolman Rd CHSWK W4 156 A3
Dolman St CLAP SW4 158 G10
Dolphin Ap ROM RM1 124 G2
Dolphin Cl BERM/RHTH SE16 160 C1
SURB KT6 199 J6
THMD SE28 143 M8
Dolphin Ct SL SL1 149 N1
STA TW18 173 K6
Dolphin Ct North STA TW18 * 173 K6
Dolphin Est SUN TW16 * 196 F1
Dolphin La POP/IOD E14 140 G9
Dolphin Rd NTHLT UB5 133 N4
SL SL1 149 N1
SUN TW16 196 F1
Dolphin Rd North SUN TW16 196 E1
Dolphin Rd South SUN TW16 196 E1
Dolphin Rd West SUN TW16 196 F1
Dolphin Sq CHSWK W4 * 156 B6
PIM SW1V 17 H8
Dolphin St KUT/HW KT1 199 K2
Dolphin Wy PUR RM19 166 D4
Dolphin Yd STAL AL1 * 38 C6
WARE SG12 * 26 C2
Dombey St BMSBY WC1N 11 N3
Dome Blds RCH/KEW TW9 * 177 J1
Dome Hl CTHM CR3 259 M2
Dome Hill Pk SYD SE26 181 N7
Dome Hill Peak CTHM CR3 259 M2
Domett Cl CMBW SE5 159 L10
Dome Wy REDH RH1 258 A9
Domingo St FSBYE EC1V 12 E1
Dominica Cl PLSTW E13 142 A5
Dominic Ct WAB EN9 62 G9
Dominion Cl HSLW TW3 154 C8
Dominion Dr CRW RM5 104 C7
Dominion Pde HRW HA1 * 114 E3
Dominion Rd CROY/NA CR0 203 N7
NWDGN UB2 153 M2
Dominion St LVPST EC2M 13 H3
Dominion Wy RAIN RM13 145 H5
Domonic Dr ELTH/MOT SE9 184 E6
Domville Cl TRDG/WHET N20 97 N3
Donald Biggs Dr GVE DA12 190 F4
Donald Dr CHDH RM6 123 M3
Donald Rd CROY/NA CR0 202 G6
PLSTW E13 141 N3
Donaldson Rd KIL/WHAMP NW6 2 D6
WOOL/PLUM SE18 162 D7
Donald Woods Gdns BRYLDS KT5 199 N9
Doncaster Dr NTHLT UB5 113 N10
Doncaster Gdns FSBYPK N4 * 119 K4
NTHLT UB5 113 N10
Doncaster Gn OXHEY WD19 93 K6
Doncaster Rd ED N9 100 A1
Doncaster Wk CRAWE RH10 * 284 B9
Doncaster Wy UPMR RM14 125 N8
Doncella Cl CDW/CHF RM16 167 H3
Donegal St IS N1 5 P8
Doneraile St FUL/PGN SW6 156 G8
Dongola Rd PLSTW E13 141 N5
TOTM N17 119 M1
WCHPL E1 140 D7
Dongola Rd West PLSTW E13 141 N5
Donington Av BARK/HLT IG6 122 F3
Donkey Aly EDUL SE22 181 P3
Donkey La EN EN1 79 P6
EYN DA4 210 A9
HORL RH6 280 E8
RDKG RH5 271 L9
WDR/YW UB7 151 M3
Donnafields CHOB/PIR GU24 230 F2
Donnay Cl CFSP/GDCR SL9 110 A4
Donne Cl CRAWE RH10 284 C5
Donnefield Av EDGW HA8 95 K7
Donne Gdns WOKS/MYFD GU22 233 H1
Donnella Cl CDW/CHF RM16 167 J2
Donne Pl CHEL SW3 15 P5
MTCM CR4 202 C4
Donne Rd BCTR RM8 123 M7
Donnington Ct CRAWW RH11 283 J10
Donnington Rd KTN/HRWW/WS HA3 115 J4
WLSDN NW10 136 E3
WPK KT4 200 D9
Donnybrook Rd STRHM/NOR SW16 180 D10
Donoghue Cots POP/IOD E14 * 140 D7
Donovan Av MUSWH N10 98 C10
Donovan Cl HOR/WEW KT19 220 A6
Donovan Pl WCHMH N21 78 G9
Don Phelan Cl CMBW SE5 159 L7
Don Wy ROM RM1 104 F8
Doods Park Rd REIG RH2 257 L9
Doods Pl REIG RH2 * 257 M9
Doods Rd REIG RH2 257 M9
Doods Wy REIG RH2 257 N9
Doone Cl TEDD TW11 176 F9
Doon St STHWK SE1 12 A9
Dorado Gdns ORP BR6 207 N10
Doral Wy CAR SM5 222 A2
Dorando Cl SHB W12 * 136 E9
Doran Dr REDH RH1 257 N10
Doran Gdns REDH RH1 * 257 N10
Doran Gv WOOL/PLUM SE18 163 H6
Dora Rd WIM/MER SW19 179 K8
Dora St POP/IOD E14 140 E8
Dora Wy BRXN/ST SW9 159 H8
Dorchester Av BXLY DA5 185 N4
HOD EN11 44 F1
PLMGR N13 99 K5
RYLN/HDSTN HA2 114 B4
Dorchester Cl ESH/CLAY KT10 198 E9
NTHLT UB5 114 A10
STMC/STPC BR5 185 L10
Dorchester Ct CRICK NW2 116 F8
HNHL SE24 181 K1
RKW/CH/CXG WD3 * 72 D9
STHGT/OAK N14 98 C1
WOKS/MYFD GU22 232 D2
Dorchester Dr EBED/NFELT TW14 174 F2
HNHL SE24 181 K1
Dorchester Gdns CHING E4 100 F5
GLDGN NW11 * 117 K2
Dorchester Gv CHSWK W4 156 B5
Dorchester Ms TWK TW1 177 H2
Dorchester Pde STRHM/NOR SW16 * 180 F5
Dorchester Rd GVE DA12 190 G6
MRDN SM4 201 L7
NTHLT UB5 114 A10
WEY KT13 196 C10
WPK KT4 200 F8
Dorchester Ter HDN NW4 * 96 G10
Dorchester Wy KTN/HRWW/WS HA3 115 L3
Dorchester Waye YEAD UB4 133 J8
Dorcis Av BXLYHN DA7 163 P8
Dordrecht Rd ACT W3 136 B10
Dore Av MNPK E12 122 D10
Doreen Av CDALE/KGS NW9 116 A6
Dore Gdns MRDN SM4 201 L7
Dorell Cl STHL UB1 133 N7
Doresa Cl ADL/WDHM KT15 215 K2
Dorian Ct WARL CR6 * 242 A5
Dorian Dr ASC SL5 192 D1
Dorian Rd HCH RM12 125 H6
Doria Rd FUL/PGN SW6 157 J8
Doric Dr KWD/TDW/WH KT20 239 J6
Doric Wy CAMTN NW1 5 J9
Dorie Ms NFNCH/WDSPK N12 97 L5
Dorien Rd RYNPK SW20 200 G2
Dorin Ct WARL CR6 * 242 A6
WOKS/MYFD GU22 233 H1
Doris Ashby Cl GFD/PVL UB6 134 F3
Doris Av ERITH DA8 164 D7
Doris Rd ASHF TW15 174 E9
FSTGT E7 141 M2
Dorking Cl DEPT SE8 160 E5
WPK KT4 200 G9
Dorking Ri HARH RM3 105 L5
Dorking Rd ASHTD KT21 237 N1
GT/LBKH KT23 254 A3

HARH RM3 105 L5
KWD/TDW/WH KT20 256 C7
LHD/OX KT22 236 C9
RGUE GU4 268 C6
SHGR GU5 270 E5
Dorking Wk HARH RM3 105 L5
Dorkins Wy UPMR RM14 126 D5
Dorlcote Rd WAND/EARL SW18 179 N14
Dorling Dr EW KT17 220 C8
Dorly Cl SHPTN TW17 196 F4
Dorman Pl ED N9 99 P5
Dormans CRAWW RH11 283 K6
Dormans Cl NTHWD HA6 92 B9
Dorman Wy STJWD NW8 3 L5
Dormay St WAND/EARL SW18 179 L1
Dormer Cl BAR EN5 76 C4
SRTFD E15 141 L1
Dormers HHS/BOV HP3 * 53 H3
Dormers Av STHL UB1 133 P8
Dormers Cl GODL GU7 267 J10
Dormers Ri STHL UB1 134 A9
Dormer's Wells La STHL UB1 133 P8
Dormie Cl STALW/RED AL3 38 B4
Dormywood RSLP HA4 112 C3
Dorney Cl BKHTH/KID SE3 161 M6
Dornberg Cl BKHTH/KID SE3 161 M6
Dorncliffe Rd FUL/PGN SW6 157 H7
Dornels SLN SL2 129 P8
Dorney End CSHM HP5 50 F6
Dorney Gv WEY KT13 196 C9
Dorney Hi North BEAC HP9 108 A7
Dorney Hi South SL SL1 108 F5
Dorney Rd STMC/STPC BR5 207 J4
Dorney Wy HSLWW TW4 175 M1
Dorney Wood Rd SL SL1 128 B3
Dornfell St KIL/WHAMP NW6 117 J10
Dornford Gdns COUL/CHIP CR5 241 K5
Dornton Rd BAL SW12 180 C5
SAND/SEL CR2 223 N8
Dorothy Av WBLY HA0 135 K2
Dorothy Evans Cl BXLYHN DA7 164 C10
Dorothy Gdns BCTR RM8 123 L9
Dorothy Rd BTSEA SW11 158 F2
Dorrell Pl BRXN/ST SW9 159 H9
Dorrien's Cft BERK HP4 33 L1
Dorrington Gdns HCH RM12 125 L6
Dorrington Wy BECK BR3 205 H5
Dorrit Crs RGUW GU3 249 K8
Dorrit Ms UED N18 99 N5
Dorrit St STHWK SE1 * 18 F1
Dorrit Wy CHST BR7 184 F9
Dorrofield Cl RKW/CH/CXG WD3 72 D9
Dors Cl CDALE/KGS NW9 116 A6
Dorset Av NWDGN UB2 153 P9
ROM RM1 124 E1
WELL DA16 163 P4
YEAD UB4 132 F5
Dorset Bldgs EMB EC4Y * 12 C3
Dorset Cl BERK HP4 33 L4
CAMTN NW1 10 A1
YEAD UB4 132 F5
Dorset Crs GVE DA12 191 H7
Dorset Dr EDGW HA8 96 A1
WOKS/MYFD GU22 232 E3
Dorset Gdns MTCM CR4 202 G4
Dorset Ms FNCH N3 97 K9
KTBR SW1X 16 A3
Dorset Ri SRTFD E15 141 L1
Dorset Rd ASHF TW15 173 N6
BECK BR3 204 C3
BELMT SM2 221 K6
EA W5 155 H2
ELTH/MOT SE9 184 B5
FSTGT E7 141 P2
HRW HA1 114 D4
MTCM CR4 201 P2
SEVS/STOTM N15 119 J6
VX/NE SW8 158 C6
WDGN N22 98 F3
WDSR SL4 149 H7
WIM/MER SW19 201 J1
Dorset Sq CAMTN NW1 10 A2
Dorset St MHST W1U 10 B2
WBY/WBF KT14 215 N7
HGDN/ICK UB10 132 A4
WHTN TW2 176 B4
Dorset Waye HEST TW5 153 N6
Dorton Cl PECK SE15 159 M6
Dorton Dr BGR/WK TN15 247 N6
Dorton Wy RPLY/SEND GU23 233 L7
Dorville Crs HMSMTH W6 156 E2
Dorville Rd LEE/GVPK SE12 183 K8
Dothill Rd WOOL/PLUM SE18 162 G6
Douai Gv HPTN TW12 198 B1
Doubleday Rd LOU IG10 82 F7
Doughty Ms BMSBY WC1N 11 N1
Doughty St BMSBY WC1N 11 N1
Douglas Av ALP/SUD HA0 135 K2
HARH RM3 105 M10
NWMAL KT3 200 A4
WALTH E17 100 F9
WATN WD24 73 L3
Douglas Cl BARK/HLT IG6 102 G2
CDW/CHF RM16 167 K2
EBAR EN4 77 N4
RGUE GU4 250 A4
STAN HA7 94 F5
WLGTN SM6 222 F4
Douglas Crs CTHM CR3 * 241 K8
Douglas Dr CROY/NA CRO 204 F10
Douglas Est IS N1 6 F2
Douglas Gdns BERK HP4 33 L4
Douglas Ms STWL/WRAY TW19 172 C5
CRICK NW2 117 H8
Douglas Pth POP/IOD E14 161 H8
Douglas Pl POP/IOD E14 161 H8
Douglas Rd ADL/WDHM KT15 195 M10
CAN/RD E16 141 M7
CHING E4 101 K1
ESH/CLAY KT10 198 A10
GDMY/SEVK IG3 123 K5
HSLW TW3 154 A9
IS N1 6 E1
KIL/WHAMP NW6 2 E1
KUT/HW KT1 199 J2
REIC RH2 257 K9
ROM RM1 124 G4
SLN SL2 129 J8
STWL/WRAY TW19 173 L2
SURB KT6 199 P1
WAN E11 90 G4
WELL DA16 163 L7
Douglas Rd North IS N1 6 F1
Douglas Rd South IS N1 6 F1
Douglas St WEST SW1P 17 J6
Douglas Ter WALTH E17 * 100 E8
Douglas Vls KUT/HW KT1 * 199 J2
Douglas Wy NWCR SE14 160 K9
WGCE AL7 23 M5
Doug Siddons Ct GRAYS RM17 * 167 P3
Doulton Cl HLWE CM17 47 P1
Doulton Ms KIL/WHAMP NW6 * 3 H1
The Doultons STA TW18 * 173 J8
Dounesforth Gdns WAND/EARL SW18 179 L4
Douro Pl KENS W8 15 L4
Douro St BOW E3 140 A1
Douthwaite Sq WAP E1W 13 N5
Dove Ap BARK IG11 142 F7
Dove Cl CDW/CHF RM16 167 K2
CRAWW RH11 283 M5
MLHL NW7 96 A6
NTHLT UB5 133 J5
SAND/SEL CR2 224 C7
WLGTN SM6 222 G4
Dovecot Cl PIN HA5 113 K3
Dovecote Cl WEY KT13 196 F5
Dove Ct BEAC HP9 88 C8

HAT AL10 40 D6
LOTH EC2R * 12 C6
Dovedale Av CLAY IG5 102 D10
KTN/HRWW/WS HA3 115 H4
Dovedale Cl DEN/HRF UB9 91 H10
RGUE GU4 250 D7
WELL DA16 163 K7
Dovedale Crs CRAWW RH11 283 L11
Dovedale Ri MTCM CR4 180 A10
Dovedale Rd EDUL SE22 182 A1
RDART DA2 188 B4
Dove House Cl STHGT/OAK N14 98 A3
Dove House Gdns CHING E4 100 F3
Dove House Pl WEY KT13 216 E1
Dovehouse Md BARK IG11 142 C4
Dovehouse St CHEL SW3 15 N8
Doveney Cl STMC/STPC BR5 207 M3
Dove Pk PIN HA5 93 N8
RKW/CH/CXG WD3 70 E10
Dover Cl CRICK NW2 116 C2
CRW RM5 104 D10
Dovercourt Av THHTH CR7 203 H4
Dovercourt Est IS N1 7 H1
Dovercourt Gdns STAN HA7 95 K6
Dovercourt La SUT SM1 201 M10
Dovercourt Rd DUL SE21 181 M4
Doverfield Rd BRXS/STRHM SW2 180 F2
RGUE GU4 250 D7
Dover Gdns CAR SM5 202 A10
Dover House Rd PUT/ROE SW15 156 G10
Doveridge Gdns PLMGR N13 99 J5
Dove Rd IS N1 7 H1
Dove Rw BETH E2 7 N7
Dove Park Dr PUT/ROE SW15 178 E2
Dover Patrol BKHTH/KID SE3 161 N8
Dover Rd ED N9 100 B3
MNPK E12 121 P7
NRWD SE19 181 L9
SL SL1 128 E8
WOOL/PLUM SE18 162 E3
Dover Rd East GVW DA11 190 E3
Dovers Green Rd REIC RH2 275 J9
Dover St CONDST W1S 10 D7
Dover Ter RCH/KEW TW9 * 155 M8
Dover Wy RKW/CH/CXG WD3 72 C8
Doves Cl HAYES BR2 206 B9
Doves Yd IS N1 6 A6
Doveton Rd SAND/SEL SE2 223 L2
Doveton St WCHPL E1 140 E6
Dowanhill Rd CAT SE6 183 J4
Dowd Cl FBAR/BDGN N11 98 B3
Dowdeswell Cl PUT/ROE SW15 156 B10
Dowding Cl HCH RM12 145 J2
Dowding Rd BH/WHM TN16 244 A11
HGDN/ICK UB10 132 A2
Dowding Wy GSTN WD25 54 C10
Dowdney Cl KTTN NW5 118 C10
Dower Av WLGTN SM6 222 C5
Dower Cl BEAC HP9 88 B6
Dower Pk WDSR SL4 148 E9
Dower Wk CRAWW RH11 283 K8
Dowgate Hi CANST EC4R 12 F6
Dowlands La HORL RH6 281 L5
Dowland St NKENS W10 2 B9
Dowlans Cl GT/LBKH KT23 253 P7
Dowlans Rd GT/LBKH KT23 254 A3
Dowlas St CMBW SE5 159 M6
Dowlerville Rd ORP BR6 227 J5
Dowley Wd WGCE AL7 23 J5
Dowling Ct HHS/BOV HP3 35 N9
Dowman Cl WIM/MER SW19 179 L10
Dowman Rd HDN NW4 96 A1
The Downage GVW DA11 190 D5
Downalong BUSH WD23 94 C2
Downbank Av BXLYHN DA7 164 E7
Down Barns Rd RSLP HA4 113 L9
Downbury Ms WAND/EARL SW18 179 L1
Downderry Rd BMLY BR1 183 J6
Downe Av RSEV TN14 226 C7
WELL DA16 163 N6
Downend WOOL/PLUM SE18 * 161 H8
Downer Dr RKW/CH/CXG WD3 70 C5
Downer Meadow GODL GU7 267 K9
Downe Rd HAYES BR2 226 A5
MTCM CR4 202 A1
ORP BR6 226 F10
Downer's Cots CLAP SW4 158 D10
Downes Cl TWK TW1 176 G2
Downes Ct WCHMH N21 99 H2
Downer Rd STALE/WH AL4 20 C8
Downfield WPK KT4 200 C8
Downfield Cl HERT/BAY SG13 26 B7
HERT/BAY SG13 26 B7
Downfields WGCW AL8 22 A5
Down Green La STALE/WH AL4 20 C1
Down Hall Rd KUT/HW KT1 199 J1
Downhall Rd RBSF CM22 31 J5
Downham Cl CRW RM5 104 B10
Downham La BMLY BR1 183 J3
Downham Rd IS N1 7 J1
Downham Wy BMLY BR1 183 M8
Downhills Av TOTM N17 119 K1
Downhills Park Rd TOTM N17 119 K1
Downhills Wy TOTM N17 99 K10
Downhurst Av MLHL NW7 96 F10
Downing Av GUW GU2 267 L11
Downing Cl RYLN/HDSTN HA2 114 A1
Downing Dr GFD/PVL UB6 134 D3
Downing Rd DAGW RM9 144 A3
Downings EHAM E6 142 D8
Downing St WHALL SW1A 17 L1
Downings Wd RKW/CH/CXG WD3 70 G6
Downland Cl COUL/CHIP CR5 222 C10
EPSOM KT18 238 C4
TRDG/WHET N20 97 M2
Downland Dr CRAWW RH11 283 H7
Downland Pl CRAWW RH11 283 M9
Downlands EPSOM KT18 238 C4
Downlands WAB EN9 63 K10
Downlands Rd PUR/KEN CR8 241 J7
Downlea Cl GDMY/SEVK IG3 123 H4
Down La RGUW GU3 266 C4
Downleys Cl ELTH/MOT SE9 183 P1
Downman Rd ELTH/MOT SE9 162 A5
Down Pl HMSMTH W6 156 F8
Downs Av CHST BR7 184 C1
PIN HA5 114 A6
Downs Bridge Rd BECK BR3 205 J9
Downs Court Pde HACK E8 * 120 A10
Downs Court Rd PUR/KEN CR8 223 J7
Downs Hill BECK BR3 183 N9
BECK BR3 204 A9
Downside BECK BR3 * 204 A9
CHERT KT16 195 H6

EPSOM KT18 220 B10
HHNE HP2 35 N5
SUN TW16 197 H1
WEA W13 176 B6
Downside Bridge Rd COB KT11 235 J1
Downside Common WIM/MER SW19 179 M9
Downside Common Rd COB KT11 235 J4
Downside Orch WOKS/MYFD GU22 232 D3
Downside Rd BELMT SM2 221 N3
COB KT11 235 J4
RGUE GU4 268 E1
Downs La CLPT E5 120 A9
HAT AL10 40 D6
LHD/OX KT22 236 C9
Downs Link SHGR GU5 268 C9
Downs Lodge Ct EW KT17 * 220 B10
Downs Park Rd HACK E8 119 P10
Downs Rd BECK BR3 204 C2
BELMT SM2 221 L1
CLPT E5 119 P9
COUL/CHIP CR5 240 G5
DTCH/LGLY SL3 150 A1
EN EN1 79 M8
EPSOM KT18 237 P6
MEO DA13 190 A8
PUR/KEN CR8 223 J7
THHTH CR7 203 K1
Downs Side BELMT SM2 221 J7
The Downs HAT AL10 40 D6
HLW CM20 47 N1
LHD/OX KT22 254 C1
RYNPK SW20 178 G10
Downs Vw DORK RH4 255 H10
ISLW TW7 154 A7
KWD/TDW/WH KT20 238 E7
Downsview Av WOKS/MYFD GU22 232 C7
Downs View Cl ORP BR6 227 M6
Downsview Ct SWLY BR8 208 C3
Downsview Gdns DORK RH4 272 C5
NRWD SE19 181 K10
Downs View Rd GT/LBKH KT23 254 B3
Downsview Rd NRWD SE19 181 K10
SEV TN13 264 C1
Downsway GU GU1 250 G10
SAND/SEL CR2 223 M7
CTHM CR3 241 K7
Downs Wy EPSOM KT18 238 C2
GT/LBKH KT23 254 B3
ORP BR6 227 H2
OXTED RH8 261 K3
Downsway Wy KWD/TDW/WH KT20 238 D7
The Downsway BELMT SM2 221 N5
Downswood REIG RH2 257 N8
Downton Av BRXS/STRHM SW2 180 G5
Downtown Rd BERM/RHTH SE16 160 D1
Downway NFNCH/WDSPK N12 97 P8
Down Wy NTHLT UB5 133 J3
Dowrey St IS N1 6 A5
Dowry Wk WAT WD17 72 C4
Dowsett Rd TOTM N17 99 P10
Dowson Cl CMBW SE5 159 L10
Doyce St STHWK SE1 18 E1
Doyle Cl ERITH DA8 164 F10
Doyle Gdns WLSDN NW10 136 E3
Doyle Rd SNWD SE25 203 P4
D'Oyley St BGVA SW1W 16 C5
Draco Ga PUT/ROE SW15 * 156 G2
Draco St WALW SE17 18 E9
Dragonfly Cl PLSTW E13 141 N5
Dragon Rd BECK BR3 216 D6
Dragon Rd HAT AL10 40 A8
LBTH SE11 17 P6
Dragoon Rd DEPT SE8 160 E4
Dragor Rd WLSDN NW10 135 P5
Drake Av CTHM CR3 241 K8
DTCH/LGLY SL3 150 A3
STA TW18 173 J8
Drake Cl BERM/RHTH SE16 160 C1
BRW CM14 105 M7
Drakefell Rd NWCR SE14 160 A4
Drakefield Rd TOOT SW17 180 B6
Drake Ms HAYES BR2 205 P4
HCH RM12 145 J2
Drake Rd BROCKY SE4 161 C10
CHSGTN KT9 219 M2
CRAWE RH10 285 P10
CROY/NA CRO 202 G10
HARH RM3 105 M7
MTCM CR4 202 B6
RYLN/HDSTN HA2 113 N7
Drakes Cl CHES/WCR EN8 62 C4
ESH/CLAY KT10 217 J7
Drakes Ctyd KIL/WHAMP NW6 2 D2
Drake St ENC/FH EN2 79 L5
FSBYW WC1X 11 N2
Drakes Wy WOKS/MYFD GU22 232 A8
Drakewood Rd STRHM/NOR SW16 180 D10
Draper Cl BELV DA17 164 A3
ISLW TW7 154 C8
Draper Est STHWK SE1 18 D5
Draper Pl IS N1 6 B1
Drapers Cnr CHONG CM5 * 67 K6
Drapers Rd ENC/FH EN2 79 J6
SRTFD E15 121 H9
TOTM N17 119 N3
Drappers Wy BERM/RHTH SE16 * 19 P5
Draven Cl HAYES BR2 205 P10
Drawell Cl WOOL/PLUM SE18 * 143 H10
Drax Av RYNPK SW20 178 D10
Draxmont WIM/MER SW19 178 A9
Draycot Rd SURB KT6 199 H5
WAN E11 121 H1
Draycott Av CHEL SW3 15 N5
KTN/HRWW/WS HA3 114 G3
Draycott Cl CMBW SE5 159 L6
CRICK NW2 117 K4
KTN/HRWW/WS HA3 114 G4
Draycott Ter CHEL SW3 16 A5
Draycott Rd KWD/TDW/WH KT20 238 E10
Draycroft Av HSLWW TW4 175 J3
Dray Ct ALP/SUD HA0 135 P1
GUW GU2 267 N1
Drayford Cl MV/WKIL W9 137 P2
Dray Gdns BRXS/STRHM SW2 180 B10
Drayman Ms PECK SE15 159 H8
Draymans Wy ISLW TW7 154 A9
Drayson Cl WAB EN9 63 J9
Drayton Av LOU IG10 82 C10
ORP BR6 226 G8
POTB/CUF EN6 59 H8
WEA W13 135 M9
Drayton Bridge Rd HNWL W7 135 N9
WEA W13 135 M9
Drayton Cl HSLWW TW4 * 175 H6
IL IG1 123 L5
LHD/OX KT22 236 D9
Drayton Ct WDR/YW UB7 * 152 A3
Drayton Gdns WBPTN SW10 15 K7

WDR/YW UB7 151 N1
WEA W13 135 F9
Drayton Green Rd WEA W13 135 G9
Drayton Gv WEA W13 135 F9
Drayton Pk HBRY N5 119 H10
Drayton Park Ms HOLWY N7 * 119 H10
Drayton Rd BORE WD6 75 M8
CROY/NA CRO 203 J9
TOTM N17 99 M10
WAN E11 90 G4
WEA W13 135 F8
WLSDN NW10 136 C3
Dreadnought Cl WIM/MER SW19 201 M2
Dreadnought St GNWCH SE10 161 K2
Drenon Sq HYS/HAR UB3 132 C9
Dresden Cl KIL/WHAMP NW6 3 H1
Dresden Rd ARCH N19 118 C8
Dressington Av BROCKY SE4 182 A2
Drew Av MLHL NW7 97 K6
Drewery Ct BKHTH/KID SE3 * 161 K9
Drew Gdns GFD/PVL UB6 134 E1
Drew Meadow SLN SL2 109 H9
Drew Pl CTHM CR3 241 L9
Drew Rd CAN/RD E16 142 B10
Drews Cots STRHM/NOR SW16 * 180 E5
Drews Pk BEAC HP9 88 B5
Drewstead Rd STRHM/NOR SW16 180 E5
The Drey CFSP/GDCR SL9 90 B2
Driffield Rd BOW E3 139 L8
Drift La COB KT11 235 N10
The Drift HAT AL10 40 A6
HAYES BR2 206 A10
Drift Rd WDSR SL4 146 A7
Drift Wy DTCH/LGLY SL3 150 A3
The Driftway BNSTD SM7 238 F7
HHNE HP2 35 H6
LHD/OX KT22 236 A6
MTCM CR4 180 B6
Driftwood Av LCOL/BKTW AL2 58 G1
Driftwood Dr PUR/KEN CR8 241 K3
Drill Hall Rd CHERT KT16 195 K8
Drinkwater Rd RYLN/HDSTN HA2 114 A2
Drive Cl EDGW HA8 * 95 P5
Drive Md COUL/CHIP CR5 222 F10
Drive Rd COUL/CHIP CR5 240 G10
Drive Sp KWD/TDW/WH KT20 239 L7
The Drive ACT W3 135 P8
AMSS HP7 69 J4
ASHF TW15 174 A11
BARK IG11 143 J2
BECK BR3 204 C2
BELMT SM2 221 J9
BKHH IG9 101 K4
BNSTD SM7 239 H7
BRKMPK AL9 59 L4
BXLY DA5 185 M2
CFSP/GDCR SL9 90 N10
CHESW EN7 61 J4
CHST BR7 185 P10
COB KT11 217 M10
COUL/CHIP CR5 222 F10
CRAWE RH10 285 K2
CRW RM5 104 E9
DTCH/LGLY SL3 149 N7
EBED/NFELT TW14 174 B6
ENC/FH EN2 79 L5
ERITH DA8 164 C6
ESH/CLAY KT10 198 B8
FNCH N3 97 K8
GLDGN NW11 117 H5
GUW GU2 267 L2
GVE DA12 190 G7
HARH RM3 105 M9
HART DA3 211 N3
HEST/BAY SG14 25 K5
HGDN/ICK UB10 132 B1
HGT N6 118 A3
HLW CM20 47 H1
HOD EN11 44 F1
HOLWY N7 5 P1
HOR/WEW KT19 220 C3
HORL RH6 275 K8
HSLW TW5 154 C10
IL IG1 122 B4
KUTN/CMB KT2 177 P10
KWD/TDW/WH KT20 * 239 K10
LCOL/BKTW AL2 58 E5
LHD/OX KT22 237 K9
LOU IG10 82 B7
MRDN SM4 201 P4
NTHWD HA6 92 C9
ORP BR6 207 L2
POTB/CUF EN6 59 J9
RAD WD7 56 F10
RBRW/HUT CM13 107 H6
RGUW GU3 267 N4
RKW/CH/CXG WD3 71 J4
RYLN/HDSTN HA2 113 P5
RYNPK SW20 178 F10
SBW CM21 29 P1
SCUP DA14 185 L6
SEV TN13 247 L10
STWL/WRAY TW19 172 A1
SURB KT6 199 L7
SWFD E18 121 N1
THHTH CR7 203 L1
VW GU25 194 C5
WALTH E17 72 F1
WAT WD17 72 D5
WBLY HA9 135 P5
WGCW AL8 22 B4
WKENS W14 149 M4
WLGTN SM6 222 E8
WOKS/MYFD GU22 232 A8
WWKM BR4 205 H7
The Driveway HHW HP1 35 H5
POTB/CUF EN6 60 F4
Dr Johnson Av TOOT SW17 180 D6
Drodges Cl SHGR GU5 270 D7
Droitwich Cl SYD SE26 181 M6
Dromey Gdns KTN/HRWW/WS HA3 94 E3
Dromore Rd PUT/ROE SW15 157 K2
Dronfield Gdns BCTR RM8 123 M10
Droop St NKENS W10 137 P2
Drop La LCOL/BKTW AL2 58 A7
Drove Rd RGUE GU4 269 K2
Drovers Pl PECK SE15 160 B7
Drovers Rd SAND/SEL CR2 223 P4
Drovers Wy ABLGY WD5 51 M2
BKHTH/KID SE3 161 N1
ENC/FH EN2 79 H5
FNCH N3 97 K8
HART DA3 211 N1
Drummond Av ROMW/RG RM7 124 D2

ROMW/RG RM7 124 D2
WAN E11 121 N4
Drummonds Pl RCH/KEW TW9 155 K10
The Drummonds EPP CM16 65 K6
Drummond St CAMTN NW1 10 C1
Drum St WCHPL E1 * 13 N3
Drury Cl CRAWE RH10 284 E9
Drury Crs CROY/NA CRO 202 G10
Drury La HOL/ALD WC2B 11 L5
WARE SG12 28 A2
Drury Rd HRW HA1 114 C6
Drury Wy WLSDN NW10 116 A10
Dryad St PUT/ROE SW15 * 156 E7
Dry Arch Rd ASC SL5 192 E7
Dryburgh Gdns CDALE/KGS NW9 115 M1
Dryburgh Rd PUT/ROE SW15 156 G10
Drycroft WGCE AL7 23 H9
Drydell La CSHM HP5 50 A7
Dryden Av HNWL W7 135 J6
Dryden Cl BARK/HLT IG6 103 J7
CLAP SW4 * 180 D1
Dryden Pl TIL RM18 168 B7
Dryden Rd EN EN1 79 M8
KTN/HRWW/WS HA3 94 E9
WELL DA16 163 J7
WIM/MER SW19 179 M9
Dryden St COVGDN WC2E 11 M6
Dryden Wy ORP BR6 207 K8
Dryfield Cl WLSDN NW10 135 P9
Dryfield Rd EDGW HA8 96 E1
Dryhill La RSEV TN14 246 C9
Dryhill Rd BELV DA17 164 A5
Dryland Av ORP BR6 227 J1
Drylands Rd CEND/HSY/T N8 118 E1
Drynham Rd WEY KT13 196 F10
Drysdale Av CHING E4 101 K10
Drysdale Cl NTHWD HA6 92 F8
Drysdale Dwellings HACK E8 * 119 N10
Drysdale Pl IS N1 7 K10
Drysdale St IS N1 7 K10
Duarte Pl CDW/CHF RM16 167 L2
Dublin Av HACK E8 7 P5
Dubrae Cl STALW/RED AL3 37 P8
Du Burstow Ter HNWL W7 135 M10
Ducal St BETH E2 7 M10
Du Cane Cl SHB W12 137 K6
Du Cane Rd SHB W12 136 F8
Duchess Cl FBAR/BDGN N11 98 C6
SUT SM1 221 N1
Duchess Ct WEY KT13 196 E10
Duchess Gv BKHH IG9 101 K9
Duchess Ms MHST W1U * 10 C3
Duchess of Bedford's Wk KENS W8 14 D2
Duchess St REGST W1B 10 D3
SNWD SE25 203 N3
Duchess' Wk BGR/WK TN15 265 M1
Duchy Rd EBAR EN4 77 N4
Duchy St STHWK SE1 11 N8
Ducie St CLAP SW4 158 F10
Duck Aly CSHM HP5 50 C8
Duckett Rd FSBYPK N4 119 H5
Ducketts Md KTN/HRWW/WS HA3 * 94 C9
Ducketts St WCHPL E1 140 C7
Ducking Stool Ct ROM RM1 124 F2
Duck La EPP CM16 65 M2
SOHO/CST W1F 11 H6
Duck Lees La PEND EN3 80 D8
Duckling La SBW CM21 29 P1
Ducks Hill Rd NTHWD HA6 92 B10
Du Cros Dr STAN HA7 95 L7
Du Cros Rd ACT W3 137 H9
Dudbrook Rd BRW CM14 85 G4
Dudden Hill La WLSDN NW10 136 C1
Dudden Hill Pde WLSDN NW10 * 116 C9
Duddington Cl ELTH/MOT SE9 184 A7
Dudley Av CHES/WCR EN8 62 C8
KTN/HRWW/WS HA3 114 G1
Dudley Cl ADL/WDHM KT15 195 L10
CDW/CHF RM16 167 K1
Dudley Ct HHS/BOV HP3 52 D1
Dudley Dr MRDN SM4 201 H9
RSLP HA4 113 J10
Dudley Gdns RYLN/HDSTN HA2 114 C6
WEA W13 154 C1
Dudley Gv EPSOM KT18 238 B9
Dudley Pl HYS/HAR UB3 152 C2
Dudley Rd ASHF TW15 173 M9
FNCH N3 97 M8
IL IG1 141 L10
KIL/WHAMP NW6 137 H1
KUT/HW KT1 199 L3
LHD/OX KT22 236 E7
NWDGN UB2 152 A1
RCH/KEW TW9 155 M8
RYLN/HDSTN HA2 114 A1
WALTH E17 100 F10
WIM/MER SW19 179 K9
WOT/HER KT12 197 H6
Dudley St BAY/PAD W2 * 9 L4
Dudley Wy IVER SL0 * 130 F10
Dudlington Rd CLPT E5 120 B7
Dudmaston Ms CHEL SW3 * 16 M7
Dudrich Cl NFNCH/WDSPK N12 98 A3
Dudrich Ms EDUL SE22 181 N1
Dudset La HEST TW5 153 M7
Dudswell Cl BERK HP4 * 33 H1
Dudswell Mi BERK HP4 * 33 H1
Dufferin Av STLK EC1Y 12 G1
Dufferin St STLK EC1Y 12 G1
Duffield Cl CDW/CHF RM16 167 K1
HRW HA1 114 E3
Duffield Dr SEVS/STOTM N15 119 K10
Duffield La SLN SL2 129 L5
Duffield Rd KWD/TDW/WH KT20 238 E10
Duffins Orch CHERT KT16 214 F6
Duff St POP/IOD E14 140 G8
Dufour's Pl SOHO/CST W1F 11 H6
Dugard Wy LBTH SE11 18 C5
Dugdale Hill La POTB/CUF EN6 59 H8
Dugdales RKW/CH/CXG WD3 72 B8
Duggan Dr CHST BR7 184 B9
Dugolly Av WBLY HA9 115 N9
Duke Humphrey Rd BKHTH/KID SE3 161 N1
Duke of Cambridge Cl WHTN TW2 176 D2
Duke of Edinburgh Rd SUT SM1 201 N10
The Duke of Wellington Av WOOL/PLUM SE18 162 G2
Duke of Wellington Pl KTBR SW1X 16 D2
Duke of York Sq CHEL SW3 15 P7
Duke of York St STJS SW1Y 11 H8
Duke Rd BARK/HLT IG6 103 J7
CHSWK W4 156 A4
Dukes Av EDGW HA8 95 P1
FNCH N3 97 N7
HRW HA1 114 D3
HSLWW TW4 154 A11
KTN/HRWW/WS HA3 114 C1
MUSWH N10 98 A11
NTHLT UB5 133 H5
NWMAL KT3 200 D2
PIN HA5 113 H7
RCHPK/HAM TW10 176 B7
Dukes Cl ASHF TW15 173 N9
HAMP NW3 117 M1
Duke's Dr GODL GU7 266 C10

Dukes Green Av EBED/NFELT TW14 175 H1
Dukes Hi CTHM CR3 242 D6
Dukes La CFSP/GDCR SL9 109 P7
Dukes La KENS W8 14 C1
Duke's La ASC SL5 170 F10
Dukes Ms MUSWH N10 118 C1
Duke's Ms MHST W1U 10 C4
Dukes Orch BXLY DA5 186 D4
Dukes Pth HLW CM20 29 J8
Duke's Pl HDTCH EC3A 13 L6
Dukes Point HGT N6 * 118 C6
Dukes Ride CFSP/GDCR SL9 110 B10
RDKG RH5 273 J5
Dukes Rd ACT W3 135 M6
EHAM E6 142 D5
WOT/HER KT12 217 L2
Duke's Rd CAMTN NW1 5 K10
RDKG RH5 278 A9
Duke's Yd MYFR/PKLN W1K * 10 B7
Dukesthorpe Rd SYD SE26 182 C7
Duke St HOD EN11 44 F2
MHST W1U 10 B5
RCH/KEW TW9 155 K8
SUT SM1 221 N1
WAT WD17 73 K7
WDSR SL4 148 G6
WOKN/KNAP GU21 232 C3
Duke Street Hi STHWK SE1 13 H9
Duke Street St James's MYFR/PICC W1J 11 H9
Dukes Va CFSP/GDCR SL9 109 N7
Dukes Wy BERK HP4 33 M3
UX/CGN UB8 131 L3
WBLY HA9 115 K10
WWKM BR4 205 K10
Dukes Wood Av CFSP/GDCR SL9 110 B5
Dukes Wood Dr CFSP/GDCR SL9 109 P6
Dulas St FSBYPK N4 118 G6
Dulford St NTGHL W11 8 A7
Dulka Rd BTSEA SW11 179 H5
Dulverton Rd ELTH/MOT SE9 184 F5
HARH RM3 105 L7
RSLP HA4 113 H7
SAND/SEL CR2 224 B6
Dulwich Common DUL SE21 181 L4
The Dulwich Oaks DUL SE21 * 181 N6
Dulwich Rd HNHL SE24 181 H1
Dulwich Village DUL SE21 181 L2
Dulwich Wy RKW/CH/CXG WD3 72 B9
Dulwich Wood Av NRWD SE19 181 M8
Dulwich Wood Pk NRWD SE19 181 M7
Dumbarton Av CHES/WCR EN8 62 C10
Dumbarton Rd BRXS/STRHM SW2 180 F2
Dumbleton Cl KUT/HW KT1 199 N1
Dumbletons RKW/CH/CXG WD3 91 H5
Dumbreck Rd ELTH/MOT SE9 162 D10
Dumfries Cl OXHEY WD19 93 H4
Dumont Rd STNW/STAM N16 119 N9
Dumpton Pl CAMTN NW1 4 C4
Dumville Dr GDST RH9 260 D4
Dunally Pk SHPTN TW17 196 F7
Dunbar Av BECK BR3 204 D4
DAGE RM10 124 B8
STRHM/NOR SW16 203 H1
Dunbar Cl SLN SL2 129 M9
YEAD UB4 133 H3
Dunbar Ct WOT/HER KT12 197 M8
Dunbar Gdns DAGE RM10 124 B10
Dunbar Rd FSTGT E7 141 M1
NWMAL KT3 199 P2
WDGN N22 99 H9
Dunbar St DUL SE21 181 K6
Dunblane Rd ELTH/MOT SE9 162 B9
Dunboe Pl SHPTN TW17 196 D7
Dunboyne Rd HAMP NW3 118 A10
Dunbridge St BETH E2 13 P1
Duncan Cl BAR EN5 77 M8
WGCE AL7 23 H6
Duncan Ct STA TW18 173 J8
Duncan Gdns STA TW18 173 K9
Duncan Gv ACT W3 136 B8
Duncannon Pde WDSR SL4 148 C9
Duncannon St CHCR WC2N 11 L8
Duncan Rd HACK E8 140 A2
RCH/KEW TW9 155 K8
Duncan St IS N1 6 C2
Duncan Ter IS N1 6 C1
Duncan Wy BUSH WD23 73 N6
Dunch St WCHPL E1 140 A8
Duncombe Cl AMS HP6 69 K4
HERT/WAT SG14 25 K3
Duncombe Hi FSTH SE23 182 B3
Duncombe Rd ARCH N19 118 D6
BERK HP4 33 K3
HERT/WAT SG14 25 K4
Duncrievie Rd LEW SE13 183 L5
Duncroft WOOL/PLUM SE18 163 M6
WOOL/PLUM SE18 163 H6
Duncroft Cl REIG RH2 257 J10
Duncton Cl CRAWW RH11 283 L6
Dundalk Rd BROCKY SE4 161 N9
Dundas Gdns E/WMO/HCT KT8 198 A3
Dundas Rd PECK SE15 160 B8
Dundee Rd PLSTW E13 141 N4
SNWD SE25 204 A3
Dundee St WAP E1W 140 B5
Dundee Whf POP/IOD E14 140 G10
Dundela Gdns WPK KT4 220 E1
Dundonald Cl EHAM E6 142 B8
Dundonald Rd WIM/MER SW19 179 J10
WLSDN NW10 136 G3
Dundrey Crs REDH RH1 258 F5
Dunedin Dr CTHM CR3 259 N6
Dunedin Rd IL IG1 122 F6
LEY E10 120 G9
RAIN RM13 144 G3
Dunedin Wy YEAD UB4 133 K6
Dunelm St WCHPL E1 140 E8
Dunfee Wy WBY/WBF KT14 215 P4
Dunfield Gdns CAT SE6 182 B7
Dunfield Rd CAT SE6 182 B7
Dunford Rd HOLWY N7 118 F10
Dungarvan Av PUT/ROE SW15 156 D10
Dunheved Cl THHTH CR7 203 H6
Dunheved Rd North THHTH CR7 203 H6
Dunheved Rd South THHTH CR7 203 H6
Dunheved Rd West THHTH CR7 203 H6
Dunholme Gn ED N9 99 N4
Dunholme La ED N9 99 N4
Dunholme Rd ED N9 99 N4
Dunkeld Rd BCTR RM8 123 J1
SNWD SE25 203 L4
Dunkellin Gv SOCK/AV RM15 146 F4
Dunkellin Wy SOCK/AV RM15 146 F3
Dunkery Rd ELTH/MOT SE9 184 B6
Dunkin Rd DART DA1 160 C3
Dunkirk Cl GVE DA12 191 L10
Dunkirk St WNWD SE27 * 181 L6
Dunleary Cl HSLWW TW4 175 H2
Dunley Dr CROY/NA CRO 225 L6
Dunlin Cl REDH RH1 275 P9
Dunlin Ri RGUE GU4 250 G8
Dunlin Rd HHNE HP2 35 H1
Dunloe Av TOTM N17 119 M3

Dunloe St BETH E2 7 L8
Dunlop Pl BERM/RHTH SE16 19 M4
Dunlop Rd TIL RM18 168 C7
Dunmail Dr PUR/KEN CR8 223 M10
SAND/SEL CR2 223 M9
Dunmore GUW GU2 249 J9
Dunmore Rd
KIL/WHAMP NW6 2 A6
RYNPK SW20 200 F1
Dunmow Cl CHDH RM6 123 M3
FELT TW13 * 175 M7
LOU IG10 82 B10
Dunmow Dr RAIN RM13 144 G3
Dunmow Rd SRTFD E15 121 J9
Dunmow Wk IS N1 * 6 E5
Dunnage Crs
BERM/RHTH SE16 160 D3
Dunnets WOKN/KNAP GU21 231 K3
Dunning Cl SOCK/AV RM15 146 F8
Dunningford Cl HCH RM12 124 G10
Dunnings La RBRW/HUT CM13 127 N7
Dunn Md CDALE/KGS NW9 96 C8
Dunnock Cl BORE WD6 75 M8
ED N9 100 C2
Dunnock Rd EHAM E6 142 B8
Dunn St HACK E8 119 N10
Dunny La RKW/CH/CXG WD3 53 J9
Dunnymans Rd BNSTD SM7 239 J1
Dunollie Pl KTTN NW5 118 D10
Dunollie Rd KTTN NW5 118 D10
Dunoon Gdns FSTH SE23 * 182 C3
Dunoon Rd FSTH SE23 182 B3
Dunottar Cl REDH RH1 275 N2
Dunraven Av REDH RH1 276 C8
Dunraven Dr ENC/FH EN2 79 H6
Dunraven Rd SHB W12 136 D10
Dunraven St MYFR/PKLN W1K 10 B7
Dunsany Rd HMSMTH W6 156 G2
Dunsbury Cl BELMT SM2 221 L5
Dunsdon Av GUW GU2 267 N1
Dunsfold Cl CRAWW RH11 283 K8
Dunsfold Ri COUL/CHIP CR5 222 E9
Dunsfold Wy CROY/NA CR0 224 G4
Dunsford Wy PUT/ROE SW15 178 E3
Dunsmore OXHEY WD19 * 93 L3
Dunsmore Cl BUSH WD23 74 C10
YEAD UB4 133 L6
Dunsmore Rd WOT/HER KT12 197 H6
Dunsmore Wy BUSH WD23 74 B10
Dunsmure Rd
STNW/STAM N16 119 M6
Dunspring La CLAY IG5 102 E10
Dunstable Ms CAVSQ/HST W1G 10 D3
Dunstable Rd
E/WMO/HCT KT8 197 N4
HARH RM3 105 L7
RCH/KEW TW9 155 K10
Dunstall Rd RYNPK SW20 178 E9
Dunstalls HLWW/ROY CM19 46 D5
Dunstall Wy E/WMO/HCT KT8 198 A3
Dunstall Welling Est
WELL DA16 * 163 L8
Dunstan Cl EFNCH N2 * 117 M1
Dunstan Gld STMC/STPC BR5 * 206 G6
Dunstan Houses WCHPL E1 * 140 B7
Dunstan Rd COUL/CHIP CR5 240 E3
GLDGN NW11 117 J6
Dunstan's Gv EDUL SE22 182 A2
Dunstan's Rd EDUL SE22 181 P3
Dunster Av MRDN SM4 200 G8
Dunster Cl BAR EN5 76 G8
CRW RM5 104 D10
DEN/HRF UB9 91 L9
Dunster Ct BORE WD6 76 A7
MON EC3R 13 J7
Dunster Crs EMPK RM11 125 P7
Dunster Dr CDALE/KGS NW9 115 P6
Dunster Gdns
KIL/WHAMP NW6 2 D3
SL SL1 128 F9
Dunsters Md WGCE AL7 23 K7
Dunsterville Wy STHWK SE1 19 H2
Dunster Wy RYLN/HDSTN HA2 113 M8
Dunston Rd BTSEA SW11 158 B8
HACK E8 7 L6
Dunston St HACK E8 7 K5
Dunton Cl SURB KT6 199 K8
Dunton Rd LEY E10 120 G5
ROM RM1 124 F2
STHWK SE1 19 L6
Duntshill Rd
WAND/EARL SW18 179 L4
Dunvegan Cl E/WMO/HCT KT8 198 A4
Dunvegan Rd ELTH/MOT SE9 162 C10
Dunwich Rd BXLYHN DA7 164 A7
Dunworth Ms NTGHL W11 8 C5
Duplex Ride KTBR SW1X 16 B2
Dupont Rd RYNPK SW20 200 G2
Duppas Av CROY/NA CR0 223 J1
Duppas Cl SHPTN TW17 196 E5
Duppas Hill Rd CROY/NA CR0 223 H1
Duppas Hill Ter CROY/NA CR0 203 J10
Duppas Rd CROY/NA CR0 203 H10
Dupre Cl CDW/CHF RM16 167 K2
SL SL1 148 D1
Dupree Rd CHARL SE7 161 N4
Dura Den Cl BECK BR3 182 G10
Durand Gdns BRXN/ST SW9 158 G7
Durand Wy WLSDN NW10 135 P2
Durant Rd SWLY BR8 187 H9
Durants Park Av PEND EN3 80 C8
Durants Rd PEND EN3 80 B8
Durant St BETH E2 7 N9
Durban Gdns DAGE RM10 144 D2
Durban Rd BECK BR3 204 E2
GNTH/NBYPK IG2 123 H6
SRTFD E15 141 K5
TOTM N17 99 M7
WALTH E17 100 E9
WNWD SE27 181 K7
Durban Rd East WATW WD18 73 H8
Durban Rd West WATW WD18 73 H8
Durbin Rd CHSGTN KT9 219 K1
Durdans Rd STHL UB1 133 N8
Durell Gdns DAGW RM9 123 N10
Durell Rd DAGW RM9 123 N10
Durfey Pl CMBW SE5 159 L6
Durfold Dr REIG RH2 257 M10
Durford Crs PUT/ROE SW15 178 D4
Durham Av GPK RM2 125 K2
HAYES BR2 205 L4
HEST TW5 153 N5
SL SL1 128 F8
WFD IG8 102 A6
Durham Cl GUW GU2 249 L8
SBW CM21 29 M2
WARE SG12 26 G6
Durham Hl BMLY BR1 183 L7
Durham House St
CHCR WC2N * 11 M8
Durham Pl CHEL SW3 16 A8
Durham Ri WOOL/PLUM SE18 162 F4
Durham Rd BORE WD6 75 P7
CAN/RD E16 141 K6
DAGE RM10 124 D10
EA W5 155 J2
EBED/NFELT TW14 175 K3
ED N9 99 P3
EFNCH N2 117 P1
HAYES BR2 205 M4
HOLWY N7 118 G7
HRW HA1 114 A3
MNPK E12 122 A9
RYNPK SW20 200 E1
SCUP DA14 185 L8
Durham Rw WCHPL E1 140 C7
Durham St LBTH SE11 17 N8
Durham Ter BAY/PAD W2 8 G5
PGE/AN SE20 * 182 A10
Durham Wharf Dr BTFD TW8 155 H6
Durham Yd BETH E2 * 140 A5
Duriun Wy ERITH DA8 165 J6
Durleston Park Dr
GT/LBKH KT23 254 B1
Durley Av PIN HA5 113 M4
Durley Gdns ORP BR6 227 L1
Durley Rd STNW/STAM N16 119 M5
Durlston Rd CLPT E5 119 P7
KUTN/CMB KT2 177 K9
Durndale La GVW DA11 190 B7
Durnell Wy LOU IG10 82 D7
Durnford St SEVS/STOTM N15 119 M3
Durning Rd NRWD SE19 181 L8
Durnsford Av WIM/MER SW19 179 K5
Durnsford Rd WDGN N22 98 E8
WIM/MER SW19 179 K6
Durpe Crs BEAC HP9 88 G10
Durrants Cl RAIN RM13 145 K4
Durrants Dr
RKW/CH/CXG WD3 72 D7
Durrants Hill Rd
HHS/BOV HP3 35 N9
Durrants La BERK HP4 33 K5
Durrants Rd BERK HP4 33 L4
Durrant Wy ORP BR6 226 G2
SWCM DA10 189 K3
Durrell Rd FUL/PGN SW6 157 H7
Durrell Wy SHPTN TW17 196 E6
Durrington Av RYNPK SW20 178 F10
Durrington Park Rd
RYNPK SW20 200 F1
Durrington Rd CLPT E5 120 D9
Dursley Cl BKHTH/KID SE3 161 P8
Dursley Gdns BKHTH/KID SE3 162 A7
Dursley Rd BKHTH/KID SE3 161 P8
Durward St WCHPL E1 13 P3
Durweston Ms MHST W1U * 10 B3
Durweston St MBLAR W1H 10 A4
Dury Falls Cl EMPK RM11 125 N6
Dury Rd BAR EN5 77 J5
Dutch Barn Cl
STWL/WRAY TW19 173 N2
Dutch Gdns KUTN/CMB KT2 177 N9
Dutch Yd WAND/EARL SW18 179 K1
Duthie St POP/IOD E14 141 H9
Dutton St GNWCH SE10 161 H7
Dutton Wy IVER SL0 131 H8
Duxberry Cl HAYES BR2 206 B5
Duxford Cl HCH RM12 145 J1
Duxhurst La REIG RH2 275 L10
Duxons Turn HHNE HP2 36 C5
Dwight Rd WATW WD18 92 E1
Dye House La BOW E3 140 F3
Dyer's Blds FLST/FETLN EC4A 12 A4
Dyer's Fld HORL RH6 281 J4
Dyers Hall Rd WAN E11 121 J7
Dyer's La PUT/ROE SW15 156 E9
Dyers Wy HARH RM3 105 H8
Dyke Dr STMC/STPC BR5 207 M7
Dyke La STALE/WH AL4 21 K4
Dykes Pth WOKN/KNAP GU21 232 F1
Dykes Wy HAYES BR2 205 L3
Dykewood Cl BXLY DA5 186 E6
Dylan Cl BORE WD6 * 95 J1
Dylan Rd BELV DA17 164 B2
HNHL SE24 159 J10
Dylways CMBW SE5 159 L10
Dymchurch Cl CLAY IG5 122 D1
ORP BR6 227 H1
Dymock St FUL/PGN SW6 157 L9
Dymoke Gn STALE/WH AL4 38 F3
Dymoke Rd ROM RM1 124 G5
Dymokes Wy HOD EN11 26 F10
Dyneley Rd LEE/GVPK SE12 183 P7
Dyne Rd KIL/WHAMP NW6 2 C4
Dynes Rd BGR/WK TN15 247 M3
Dynevor Pl RGUW GU3 249 H6
Dynevor Rd
RCHPK/HAM TW10 177 K1
STNW/STAM N16 119 M8
Dynham Rd KIL/WHAMP NW6 2 E3
Dyott St RSQ WC1B 11 K4
Dyrham La BAR EN5 76 D2
Dysart Av KUTN/CMB KT2 177 H8
Dysart St SDTCH EC2A 13 H2
Dyson Cl WDSR SL4 148 G9
Dyson Ct ALP/SUD HA0 114 F9
DORK RH4 * 272 F2
Dyson Rd SRTFD E15 141 L1
WAN E11 121 K4
Dysons Cl CHES/WCR EN8 62 C9
Dyson's Rd UED N18 100 A7
Dytchleys Rd BRW CM14 85 N8

# E

Eade Rd FSBYPK N4 119 K5
Eagans Cl EFNCH N2 * 117 N1
Eagle Av CHDH RM6 123 P4
Eagle Cl AMS HP6 69 L3
BERM/RHTH SE16 160 A4
HCH RM12 145 J1
PEND EN3 80 B8
WAB EN9 63 M10
WLGTN SM6 222 F3
Eagle Ct FARR EC1M 12 C3
HERT/BAY SG13 26 A4
Eagle Dr CDALE/KGS NW9 96 B10
Eagle Hl NRWD SE19 181 L9
Eagle House Ms CLAP SW4 180 D1
Eagle La BRWN CM15 86 D3
WAN E11 121 M2
Eagle Ms IS N1 7 J1
Eagle Pl SKENS SW7 15 K7
Eagle Rd ALP/SUD HA0 135 J2
GU GU1 268 A1
HTHAIR TW6 152 G9
Eagles Dr BH/WHM TN16 244 A4
Eaglesfield Rd
WOOL/PLUM SE18 162 E7
Eagles Rd RDART DA2 166 G10
Eagle St HHOL WC1V 11 N4
Eagle Ter WFD IG8 101 N8
Eagle Wy GVW DA11 189 M1
HAT AL10 40 D6
RBRW/HUT CM13 107 H7
Eagle Wharf Rd IS N1 6 F7
Eagling Cl BOW E3 140 F5
Ealdham Sq ELTH/MOT SE9 161 P10
Ealing Cl BORE WD6 76 A5
Ealing Golf Course
GFD/PVL UB6 * 134 F5
Ealing Gn EA W5 135 J10
Ealing Park Gdns EA W5 155 H3
Ealing Rd ALP/SUD HA0 135 K4
BOW E3 140 G5
EA W5 155 J3
NTHLT UB5 133 P2
Ealing Village EA W5 135 K8
Eamont Cl RSLP HA4 112 C5
Eamont St STJWD NW8 3 N7
Eardemont Cl DART DA1 164 G10
Eardley Crs ECT SW5 14 F7
Eardley Rd BELV DA17 164 B4
SEV TN13 247 J10
STRHM/NOR SW16 180 D9
Earl Cl FBAR/BDGN N11 98 C6
Earldom Rd PUT/ROE SW15 156 F10
Earle Gdns KUTN/CMB KT2 177 K10
Earleswood COB KT11 217 L8
Earleydene ASC SL5 192 A8
Earlham Gv FSTGT E7 121 L10
WDGN N22 98 G8
Earlham St LSQ/SEVD WC2H 11 K6
Earl Ri WOOL/PLUM SE18 162 G4
Earl Rd GVW DA11 190 B5
MORT/ESHN SW14 155 P10
Earlsbrook Rd REDH RH1 276 A2
Earls Cnr POTB/CUF EN6 * 58 D9
Earl's Court Gdns ECT SW5 14 G6
Earl's Court Rd KENS W8 14 E4
Earl's Court Sq ECT SW5 14 G7
Earls Crs HRW HA1 114 D2
Earlsferry Wy IS N1 5 M4
Earlsfield Rd
WAND/EARL SW18 179 M4
Earlshall Rd ELTH/MOT SE9 162 C10
Earls La POTB/CUF EN6 58 B8
SL SL1 128 D10
Earlsmead RYLN/HDSTN HA2 113 N9
Earlsmead Rd
SEVS/STOTM N15 119 N3
WLSDN NW10 136 F5
Earls Ms WAND/EARL SW18 179 M3
Earl's Pth LOU IG10 81 P7
Earls Ter KENS W8 14 D4
Earlsthorpe Ms BAL SW12 180 B2
Earlsthorpe Rd SYD SE26 182 C7
Earlstoke Est FSBYE EC1V 6 C9
Earlstoke St FSBYE EC1V 6 C9
Earlston Gv HOM E9 140 A3
Earl St SDTCH EC2A 13 J3
WAT WD17 73 K7
Earls Wk BCTR RM8 123 L9
KENS W8 14 E4
Earlswood Av THHTH CR7 203 H5
Earlswood Gdns CLAY IG5 122 D1
Earlswood Rd REDH RH1 276 A2
Earlswood St GNWCH SE10 161 K4
Early Commons CRAWE RH10 284 A6
Early Ms CAMTN NW1 4 F5
Earnshaw St
NOXST/BSQ WC1A 11 K5
Earsby St WKENS W14 14 B5
Easby Crs MRDN SM4 201 L6
Easebourne Rd BCTR RM8 123 M10
Easedale Dr HCH RM12 125 J10
Easington Pl GU GU1 268 C1
Easington Wy SOCK/AV RM15 146 F7
East Acton Ar ACT W3 * 136 C8
East Acton La ACT W3 136 B9
East Arbour St WCHPL E1 140 C8
East Av EHAM E6 142 B2
HYS/HAR UB3 152 G1
STHL UB1 133 N9
WALTH E17 120 G2
WLGTN SM6 222 G2
East Bank STNW/STAM N16 119 M5
Eastbank Rd HPTN TW12 176 B8
East Barnet Rd BAR EN5 77 M8
Eastbourne Av ACT W3 136 A8
Eastbourne Gdns
MORT/ESHN SW14 155 P9
Eastbourne Ms BAY/PAD W2 9 K5
Eastbourne Rd BTFD TW8 155 J4
CHSWK W4 155 P5
EHAM E6 142 D5
FELT TW13 175 L5
GDST RH9 260 B8
SEVS/STOTM N15 119 M4
SL SL1 128 F8
SRTFD E15 141 K3
TOOT SW17 180 B9
Eastbourne Ter BAY/PAD W2 9 K5
Eastbournia Av ED N9 100 A4
Eastbrook Av ED N9 100 B1
Eastbrook Cl DAGE RM10 124 D9
WOKN/KNAP GU21 232 D2
Eastbrook Dr ROMW/RG RM7 124 F8
Eastbrook Rd BKHTH/KID SE3 161 N7
WAB EN9 63 K9
Eastbrook Wy HHNE HP2 35 P6
East Burnham La SLN SL2 128 F3
East Burrowfield WGCE AL7 22 G7
Eastbury Av BARK IG11 143 H3
EN EN1 79 M5
NTHWD HA6 92 F6
Eastbury Ct OXHEY WD19 * 93 K1
STAL AL1 38 E5
Eastbury Gv CHSWK W4 156 B4
Eastbury La RGUW GU3 266 F6
Eastbury Rd EHAM E6 142 D6
KUTN/CMB KT2 177 K10
NTHWD HA6 92 F7
OXHEY WD19 93 K1
ROMW/RG RM7 124 E4
STMC/STPC BR5 206 G6
Eastbury Sq BARK IG11 143 J3
Eastbury Ter WCHPL E1 140 C6
Eastcastle St GTPST W1W 10 G5
Eastcheap FENCHST EC3M 13 H7
East Churchfield Rd ACT W3 136 A10
Eastchurch Rd HTHAIR TW6 152 F8
East Cl EA W5 135 M6
EBAR EN4 78 B8
GFD/PVL UB6 134 B4
LCOL/BKTW AL2 56 A1
RAIN RM13 145 J6
Eastcombe Av CHARL SE7 161 N5
East Common CFSP/GDCR SL9 110 B4
HARP AL5 20 B6
Eastcote ORP BR6 207 J8
Eastcote Av E/WMO/HCT KT8 197 N5
GFD/PVL UB6 114 F10
RYLN/HDSTN HA2 114 A7
Eastcote Dr HARP AL5 20 C5
Eastcote La NTHLT UB5 133 N1
Eastcote La North NTHLT UB5 133 N1
Eastcote Rd PIN HA5 113 L3
RSLP HA4 112 F5
RYLN/HDSTN HA2 114 B8
WELL DA16 162 G8
Eastcote St BRXN/ST SW9 158 F8
Eastcote Vw PIN HA5 113 K2
East Ct ALP/SUD HA0 115 H7
East Crs EN EN1 79 M9
FBAR/BDGN N11 98 A5
WDSR SL4 148 E7
Eastcroft SLN SL2 128 G6
Eastcroft Rd HOR/WEW KT19 220 B4
East Cross Route HOM E9 140 E1
Eastdean Av EPSOM KT18 219 N9
East Dene Dr HARH RM3 105 L6
Eastdown Pk LEW SE13 161 J10
East Dr CAR SM5 221 P5
GSTN WD25 73 J2
LCOL/BKTW AL2 56 G2
NTHWD HA6 92 F3
SBW CM21 29 P2
SLN SL2 129 K5
STALE/WH AL4 39 K5
STMC/STPC BR5 207 L6
VW GU25 193 N6
East Duck Lees La PEND EN3 80 D8
East Dulwich Gv EDUL SE22 181 M1
East Dulwich Rd EDUL SE22 159 N10
East End Rd FNCH N3 97 K10
East End Wy PIN HA5 113 M1
East Entrance DAGE RM10 144 C4
Eastergate BEAC HP9 88 B7
Eastern Av CHDH RM6 123 L2
CHERT KT16 195 K3
CHES/WCR EN8 62 E9
CHOB/PIR GU24 230 G7
GNTH/NBYPK IG2 122 F4
PIN HA5 113 L5
SOCK/AV RM15 166 B1
WAN E11 121 P4
Eastern Av East ROM RM1 124 E1
Eastern Av West CHDH RM6 123 P2
Eastern Gtwy CAN/RD E16 141 P9
Eastern Perimeter Rd
HTHAIR TW6 152 F8
Eastern Rd BROCKY SE4 160 F10
EFNCH N2 118 A1
PLSTW E13 141 N4
ROM RM1 124 F3
WALTH E17 121 H3
WDGN N22 98 F9
Eastern Vw BH/WHM TN16 243 P3
Easternville Gdns
GNTH/NBYPK IG2 122 F4
Eastern Wy ERITHM DA18 164 B1
GRAYS RM17 167 M5
THMD SE28 143 N10
THMD SE28 163 K1
East Ferry Rd POP/IOD E14 160 G3
Eastfield Av WATN WD24 73 L5
Eastfield Cl SL SL1 * 149 M2
Eastfield Ct STALE/WH AL4 39 J3
Eastfield Gdns DAGE RM10 124 B9
Eastfield Rd BRW CM14 107 J3
CEND/HSY/T N8 118 F1
CHES/WCR EN8 62 E8
DAGE RM10 124 B9
PEND EN3 80 C4
REDH RH1 276 C1
WALTH E17 120 F2
Eastfields PIN HA5 113 K3
Eastfields Av
WAND/EARL SW18 157 K10
Eastfields Rd ACT W3 135 P7
MTCM CR4 202 B2
Eastfield St POP/IOD E14 140 D7
East Flexford La RGUW GU3 266 E3
East Flint HHW HP1 35 H5
East Gdns TOOT SW17 179 P9
WOKS/MYFD GU22 232 F3
Eastgate BNSTD SM7 221 J10
East Ga HLW CM20 28 G10
Eastgate Cl THMD SE28 143 N8
Eastgate Ct GU GU1 * 268 B1
Eastgate Gdns GU GU1 268 A1
Eastglade NTHWD HA6 92 F6
East Hall La RAIN RM13 145 L8
East Hall Rd STMC/STPC BR5 207 P7
Eastham Cl BAR EN5 77 H9
East Ham Crs
RBRW/HUT CM13 107 M5
East Ham Manor Wy EHAM E6 142 D8
East Harding St
FLST/FETLN EC4A 12 B5
East Heath Rd HAMP NW3 117 N8
East Hl BH/WHM TN16 243 N4
EYN DA4 210 C1
OXTED RH8 261 L5
SAND/SEL CR2 223 M6
WAND/EARL SW18 179 M1
WBLY HA9 115 M7
WOKS/MYFD GU22 232 F2
East Hill La CRAWE RH10 281 L9
East Hill Rd OXTED RH8 261 K5
Eastholm GLDGN NW11 117 L2
East Holme ERITH DA8 164 E7
Eastholme HYS/HAR UB3 133 H10
East India Dock Rd
POP/IOD E14 140 F9
East India Wy CROY/NA CR0 203 N8
East Kent Av GVW DA11 189 P2
Eastlake Rd CMBW SE5 159 J8
Eastlands Cl OXTED RH8 261 J3
Eastlands Crs EDUL SE22 181 N2
Eastlands Wy OXTED RH8 261 J3
East La ABLGY WD5 55 H5
ALP/SUD HA0 115 H8
EHSLY KT24 252 D2
KUT/HW KT1 199 J3
STALE/WH AL4 21 J2
Eastlea Av GSTN WD25 73 M3
Eastlea Ms CAN/RD E16 141 K6
Eastleigh Av RYLN/HDSTN HA2 114 A7
Eastleigh Cl BELMT SM2 221 L4
CRICK NW2 116 B8
Eastleigh Rd BXLYHN DA7 164 D8
WALTH E17 100 E10
Eastleigh Wy
EBED/NFELT TW14 175 H4
East Lodge La ENC/FH EN2 78 E2
Eastman Rd ACT W3 156 A1
Eastman Wy HHNE HP2 36 B3
HOR/WEW KT19 219 N6
East Md RSLP HA4 113 L8
WGCE AL7 23 L8
Eastmead WOKN/KNAP GU21 231 N3
Eastmead Av GFD/PVL UB6 134 A5
Eastmead Cl BMLY BR1 206 B2
East Meads GUW GU2 267 L1
Eastmearn Rd WNWD SE27 181 K5
East Mi GVW DA11 190 C2
East Milton Rd GVE DA12 190 G3
East Mimms HHNE HP2 35 P5
Eastmont Rd ESH/CLAY KT10 198 E9
Eastmoor Pk HARP AL5 20 B5
Eastmoor Pl CHARL SE7 162 A2
Eastmoor St CHARL SE7 162 A2
WOOL/PLUM SE18 162 A3
East Mt STALE/WH AL4 21 J2
East Mount St WCHPL E1 * 140 A7
Eastney Rd CROY/NA CR0 203 J8
Eastney St GNWCH SE10 161 J4
Eastnor HHS/BOV HP3 52 D4
Eastnor Pl REIG RH2 * 275 K2
Eastnor Rd ELTH/MOT SE9 184 F4
REIG RH2 275 J2
Easton Gdns BORE WD6 76 B8
Easton St FSBYW WC1X 12 A1
Eastor WGCE AL7 23 K2
East Pk CRAWE RH10 283 N8
HLWE CM17 29 L8
SBW CM21 29 P2
East Park Cl CHDH RM6 123 N3
East Parkside GNWCH SE10 161 K1
WARL CR6 242 F2
East Pas STBT EC1A 12 E3
East Pl WNWD SE27 181 K7
East Pole Cots
STHGT/OAK N14 * 78 E8
East Poultry Av FARR EC1M 12 C4
East Rp HTHAIR TW6 152 C7
East Ridgeway
POTB/CUF EN6 60 F4
East Rd CHDH RM6 123 P3
CHEL SW3 16 C8
EBAR EN4 98 B2
EBED/NFELT TW14 174 E3
EDGW HA8 95 N9
HLW CM20 29 L7
IS N1 7 H9
KUTN/CMB KT2 199 K1
PEND EN3 80 B4
REIG RH2 257 J9
ROMW/RG RM7 124 E5
SRTFD E15 141 M3
WDR/YW UB7 152 A3
WELL DA16 163 L8
WEY KT13 216 E5
WIM/MER SW19 179 M9
East Rochester Wy
BFN/LL DA15 185 H1
BFN/LL DA15 185 M2
BXLY DA5 186 B2
DART DA1 186 E3
East Rw NKENS W10 8 B2
WAN E11 121 M4
Eastry Av HAYES BR2 205 L6
Eastry Rd ERITH DA8 164 B6
East Shalford La RGUE GU4 268 C5
East Sheen Av
MORT/ESHN SW14 156 A10
East Side SHB W12 * 156 F1
Eastside Rd GLDGN NW11 117 J2
East Smithfield WAP E1W 13 M8
East St BARK IG11 142 F2
BMLY BR1 205 M2
BTFD TW8 155 H6
BXLYHN DA7 164 B10
CSHM HP5 50 G8
EW KT17 220 B8
GT/LBKH KT23 254 A1
HHNE HP2 35 N6
HORS RH12 282 B6
WALW SE17 18 F7
WARE SG12 26 C2
WTHK RM20 167 K5
East Surrey Gv PECK SE15 159 N6
East Tenter St WCHPL E1 13 M6
East Ter BFN/LL DA15 * 185 H4
GVE DA12 190 F2
East Thurrock Rd
GRAYS RM17 167 N5
East Tilbury Rd SLH/COR SS17 169 K1
East Towers PIN HA5 113 L4
East V ACT W3 * 136 C10
East Vw BAR EN5 77 J6
BRKMPK AL9 42 A3
CHING E4 101 H6
Eastview Av
WOOL/PLUM SE18 163 H6
Eastville Av GLDGN NW11 117 J3
East Wk EBAR EN4 98 B2
HLW CM20 * 28 G10
HYS/HAR UB3 153 H1
REIG RH2 257 L10
East Wy CROY/NA CR0 204 D9
HYS/HAR UB3 133 H10
RSLP HA4 113 H6
WAB EN9 81 H2
Eastway BOW E3 140 D3
GUW GU2 249 L10
HAYES BR2 205 M7
HOM E9 140 E1
HOR/WEW KT19 219 P8
HORL RH6 280 C8
LEY E10 120 F9
MRDN SM4 200 G5
WAN E11 121 N3
WLGTN SM6 222 D1
Eastway Crs RYLN/HDSTN HA2 114 A7
Eastwell Cl BECK BR3 204 D1
Eastwick Crs
RKW/CH/CXG WD3 91 J3
Eastwick Dr GT/LBKH KT23 236 A10
Eastwick Hall La HLW CM20 28 D7
Eastwick Park Av
GT/LBKH KT23 236 A10
Eastwick Rd GT/LBKH KT23 254 A1
HLW CM20 28 E7
WARE SG12 27 N8
WOT/HER KT12 217 J2
Eastwick Rw HHNE HP2 36 B7
Eastwood CRAWE RH10 284 A7
Eastwood Cl HOLWY N7 119 H10
SWFD E18 101 M10
TOTM N17 * 100 A8
Eastwood Dr RAIN RM13 145 J8
Eastwood Ldg SHGR GU5 * 268 C10
Eastwood Rd GDMY/SEVK IG3 123 K5
MUSWH N10 98 B10
SHGR GU5 268 C10
SWFD E18 101 M10
WDR/YW UB7 152 B1
Eastwood St
STRHM/NOR SW16 180 D9
Eastworth Rd CHERT KT16 195 J8
Eatington Rd LEY E10 121 J3
Eaton Av SL SL1 128 B8
Eaton Cl BGVA SW1W 16 C5
STAN HA7 94 G5
Eaton Dr BRXN/ST SW9 159 J10
CRW RM5 104 C8
KUTN/CMB KT2 177 M10
Eaton Gdns BROX EN10 44 E8
DAGW RM9 143 P2
Eaton Ga BGVA SW1W 16 C5
NTHWD HA6 92 D7
Eaton La BGVA SW1W 16 F4
Eaton Ms North KTBR SW1X 16 D4
Eaton Ms South BGVA SW1W 16 D5
Eaton Ms West BGVA SW1W 16 D5
Eaton Pk COB KT11 217 M10
Eaton Park Rd COB KT11 217 M10
PLMGR N13 99 H3
Eaton Pl KTBR SW1X 16 C4
Eaton Ri EA W5 135 H7
WAN E11 121 P3
Eaton Rd BELMT SM2 221 N3
EN EN1 79 M7
HDN NW4 116 F3
HHNE HP2 36 C3
HSLW TW3 154 C10
SCUP DA14 185 N5
STAL AL1 38 G6
UPMR RM14 126 D7
Eaton Rw BGVA SW1W 16 E3
Eatons Md CHING E4 100 F3
Eaton Sq BGVA SW1W 16 D4
Eaton Ter BGVA SW1W 16 C5
BOW E3 * 140 D5
Eaton Terrace Ms BGVA SW1W 16 C5
Eatonville Rd TOOT SW17 180 A5
Eatonville Vls TOOT SW17 180 A5
Eaton Wy BORE WD6 75 L5
Eaves Cl ADL/WDHM KT15 215 M3
Ebba's Wy EPSOM KT18 237 N1
Ebberns Rd HHS/BOV HP3 35 P9
Ebbisham Cl DORK RH4 272 F2
Ebbisham Dr VX/NE SW8 17 N9
Ebbisham La
KWD/TDW/WH KT20 238 C7
Ebbisham Rd EPSOM KT18 219 N10
WPK KT4 200 F9
Ebbsfleet Rd CRICK NW2 117 H10
Ebdon Wy BKHTH/KID SE3 161 N9
Ebenezer St IS N1 6 G9
Ebenezer Wk
STRHM/NOR SW16 202 D1
Ebley Cl PECK SE15 19 L10
Ebner St WAND/EARL SW18 179 L1
Ebor St WCHPL E1 13 L1
Ebrington Rd
KTN/HRWW/WS HA3 115 J4
Ebsworth St FSTH SE23 182 C3
Eburne Rd HOLWY N7 118 F8
Ebury Ap RKW/CH/CXG WD3 91 N2
Ebury Br BGVA SW1W 16 E7
Ebury Bridge Rd BGVA SW1W 16 D8
Ebury Cl HAYES BR2 206 B10
NTHWD HA6 92 D6
Ebury Ms BGVA SW1W 16 D5
Ebury Ms East BGVA SW1W 16 E5
Ebury Rd RKW/CH/CXG WD3 91 N2
WAT WD17 73 L7
Ebury Sq BGVA SW1W 16 E6
Ebury St BGVA SW1W 16 D6
Ecclesbourne Cl PLMGR N13 99 H6
Ecclesbourne Gdns
PLMGR N13 99 H6
Ecclesbourne Rd IS N1 6 F4
THHTH CR7 203 K5
Eccles Hl RDKG RH5 273 H6
Eccles Rd BTSEA SW11 158 A10
Eccleston Cl EBAR EN4 77 P9
ORP BR6 * 206 G8
Eccleston Crs CHDH RM6 123 L5
Ecclestone Ct WBLY HA9 115 K10
Ecclestone Ms WBLY HA9 115 K10
Ecclestone Pl WBLY HA9 115 L10
Eccleston Ms KTBR SW1X 16 D4
Eccleston Pl BGVA SW1W 16 E4
Eccleston Rd WEA W13 134 F9
Eccleston Sq PIM SW1V 16 F6
Eccleston Square Ms
PIM SW1V 16 F6
Eccleston St BGVA SW1W 16 D4
Echelforde Dr ASHF TW15 174 B7
Echo Ct GVE DA12 190 F5
Echo Hts CHING E4 * 100 G2
Echo Pit Rd GU GU1 268 B4
Eckford St IS N1 6 A7
Eckstein Rd BTSEA SW11 157 P10
Eclipse Rd PLSTW E13 141 N7
Ecob Cl RGUW GU3 249 L6
Ecton Rd ADL/WDHM KT15 215 L1
Ector Rd CAT SE6 183 K5
Edans Ct SHB W12 156 C1
Edbrooke Rd MV/WKIL W9 8 E2
Eddington Crs WGCE AL7 22 G8
Eddinton Cl CROY/NA CR0 225 H3
Eddiscombe Rd FUL/PGN SW6 157 J8
Eddy Cl ROMW/RG RM7 124 C4
Eddystone Rd BROCKY SE4 182 D1
Eddy St BERK HP4 33 M4
Ede Cl HSLW TW3 153 N9
Edenbridge Cl
BERM/RHTH SE16 * 160 A4
STMC/STPC BR5 207 N4
Edenbridge Rd EN EN1 79 M10
HOM E9 * 140 C2
Eden Cl ADL/WDHM KT15 215 L6
ALP/SUD HA0 135 J3
BXLY DA5 186 E7
DTCH/LGLY SL3 150 D4
HAMP NW3 117 K7
KENS W8 14 F3
PEND EN3 80 F4
Edencourt Rd
STRHM/NOR SW16 180 C9
Edencroft SHGR GU5 268 D10
Edendale Rd BXLYHN DA7 164 E7
Edenfield Gdns WPK KT4 200 C10
Eden Gn SOCK/AV RM15 146 G7
Eden Gv HOLWY N7 118 G10
WLSDN NW10 136 E1
Eden Grove Rd BF/WBF KT14 215 P9
Edenhall Cl HHNE HP2 36 E7
Edenhall Rd HARH RM3 105 K6
Edenham Wy NKENS W10 8 C3
Edenhurst Av FUL/PGN SW6 157 J9
Eden Pde BECK BR3 * 204 D4
Eden Park Av BECK BR3 204 E4
Eden Pl GVE DA12 190 E3
Eden Rd BECK BR3 204 D4
BXLY DA5 186 D7
CRAWW RH11 283 J9
CROY/NA CR0 223 L1
WALTH E17 120 G3
WNWD SE27 181 J8
Edenside Rd GT/LBKH KT23 235 N10
Edensor Rd CHSWK W4 156 B6
Eden St KUT/HW KT1 199 J2
Edenvale CHESW EN7 62 A5
Edenvale Rd MTCM CR4 180 B10
Edenvale St FUL/PGN SW6 157 L8
Eden Wk KUT/HW KT1 * 199 K2
Eden Wy BECK BR3 204 F5
BOW E3 140 E3
WARL CR6 242 D4
Ederline Av STRHM/NOR SW16 202 G3
Edes Cots ASHTD KT21 * 237 J5
Edgar Cl CRAWE RH10 284 F8
SWLY BR8 208 G3
Edgar Kail Wy CMBW SE5 159 M9
Edgarley Ter FUL/PGN SW6 * 157 H7
Edgar Rd BGR/WK TN15 247 M3
BH/WHM TN16 244 A7
BOW E3 140 G5
HSLWW TW4 175 N3
SAND/SEL CR2 223 L6
WDR/YW UB7 131 P9
Edgars Ct WGCE AL7 23 H6
Edgar Wallace Cl PECK SE15 159 M6
Edgbaston Dr RAD WD7 57 K8
Edgeborough Ct GU GU1 * 268 C1
Edgeborough Wy BMLY BR1 206 A1
Edgebury CHST BR7 184 E7
Edge Cl WEY KT13 216 B4
Edgecombe Cl KUTN/CMB KT2 178 A10
Edgecoombe SAND/SEL CR2 224 C5
Edgecote Cl ACT W3 135 P10
Edgefield Av BARK IG11 143 J2
Edgefield Cl DART DA1 188 A4
REDH RH1 276 B5
Edge Hl WIM/MER SW19 178 G10
WOOL/PLUM SE18 162 E5
Edge Hill Av FNCH N3 117 K2
Edge Hill Ct WIM/MER SW19 178 G10
Edgehill Ct WOT/HER KT12 * 197 K8
Edgehill Gdns DAGE RM10 124 B9
Edgehill Rd CHST BR7 184 F6
MTCM CR4 202 C1
PUR/KEN CR8 223 H6
WEA W13 135 H8
Edgeley GT/LBKH KT23 235 M10
Edgeley La CLAP SW4 158 E9
Edgeley Rd CLAP SW4 158 D9
Edgell Cl VW GU25 194 C3
Edgell Rd STA TW18 173 J9
Edgel St WAND/EARL SW18 157 L10
Edge Point Cl
STRHM/NOR SW16 181 J8
Edge St KENS W8 8 F9
Edgewood Dr ORP BR6 227 J2
Edgewood Gn CROY/NA CR0 204 C8
Edgeworth Av HDN NW4 116 D3
Edgeworth Cl CTHM CR3 241 P4
HDN NW4 116 D3
Edgeworth Crs HDN NW4 116 D3
Edgeworth Rd EBAR EN4 77 P8
ELTH/MOT SE9 161 P10
Edgington Rd
STRHM/NOR SW16 180 E9
Edgington Wy SCUP DA14 185 M10
Edgwarebury Gdns
EDGW HA8 95 M6
Edgwarebury La EDGW HA8 95 L2
Edgware Rd BAY/PAD W2 9 L2
CDALE/KGS NW9 116 A1
Edgware Road High St
EDGW HA8 95 M7
Edgware Road The Hyde
CDALE/KGS NW9 116 B2
Edgware Road Wy
CRICK NW2 116 C7
Edgware Way (Watford By-Pass) EDGW HA8 95 K3
Edinburgh Av
RKW/CH/CXG WD3 71 K10
SL SL1 128 F8
Edinburgh Cl BETH E2 140 B4
HGDN/ICK UB10 112 C9
PIN HA5 113 M5
Edinburgh Ct KUT/HW KT1 * 199 K3
Edinburgh Crs CHES/WCR EN8 62 D9
Edinburgh Dr ABLGY WD5 55 H8
HGDN/ICK UB10 112 C9
STA TW18 173 N9
Edinburgh Gdns WDSR SL4 149 J8
Edinburgh Ga DEN/HRF UB9 111 J4
KTBR SW1X 16 A1
Edinburgh Ms TIL RM18 168 E8
Edinburgh Pl HLW CM20 29 K7
Edinburgh Rd HNWL W7 154 E1
PLSTW E13 141 N4
SUT SM1 201 M9
UED N18 * 99 P6
WALTH E17 120 F3
Edinburgh Wy HLW CM20 28 G8
HLWE CM17 29 M6
Edington Rd ABYW SE2 163 L2
PEND EN3 80 B6
Edison Av HCH RM12 124 G6
Edison Cl HCH RM12 124 G6
STALE/WH AL4 39 H7
WDR/YW UB7 152 A1
Edison Dr STHL UB1 134 A8
WBLY HA9 115 K7
Edison Gv WOOL/PLUM SE18 163 J6
Edison Rd CEND/HSY/T N8 118 E4
HAYES BR2 205 M2
PEND EN3 80 E5
WELL DA16 163 J7
Edis St CAMTN NW1 4 C5
Edith Cavell Wy
WOOL/PLUM SE18 162 B7
Edith Gdns BRYLDS KT5 199 N7
Edith Gv WBPTN SW10 15 J10
Edithna St BRXN/ST SW9 158 F9
Edith Nesbit Wk
ELTH/MOT SE9 162 B10
Edith Neville Cots
CAMTN NW1 5 J9
Edith Rd CHDH RM6 123 N5
EHAM E6 142 A2
FBAR/BDGN N11 98 E8
ORP BR6 227 K2
SNWD SE25 203 L5
SRTFD E15 121 J10
WIM/MER SW19 179 L9
WKENS W14 14 B6
Edith Rw FUL/PGN SW6 157 L7
Edith St BETH E2 7 M7
Edith Ter WBPTN SW10 * 157 M6
Edith Vls WKENS W14 14 C6
Edith Yd WBPTN SW10 157 N6
Edison Cl WALTH E17 120 F3
Edlyn Cl BERK HP4 33 L4
Edmansons Cl TOTM N17 99 N10
Edmeston Cl HOM E9 140 D1
Edmund Beaufort Dr
STALW/RED AL3 38 C4
Edmund Gv FELT TW13 175 N5
Edmund Halley Wy
GNWCH SE10 161 K1

Edmund Hurst Dr EHAM E6 ... 142 E7
Edmund Ms KGLGY WD4 ... 54 B5
Edmund Rd CDW/CHF RM16 ... 167 J1
MTCM CR4 ... 201 P3
RAIN RM13 ... 144 F5
STMC/STPC BR5 ... 207 M6
WELL DA16 ... 163 K9
Edmunds Av STMC/STPC BR5 ... 207 N3
Edmunds Cl YEAD UB4 ... 133 G4
Edmunds Rd HERT/WAT SG14 ... 24 C1
Edmund St CMBW SE5 ... 159 L6
Edmunds Wk EFNCH N2 ... 117 P2
Edna Av SWLY SL2 ... 90 D2
Edna Rd RYNPK SW20 ... 200 G2
Edon St BTSEA SW11 ... 157 P7
Edrick Rd EDGW HA8 ... 95 P7
Edrick Wk EDGW HA8 ... 95 P7
Edric Rd NWCR SE14 ... 160 C6
Edridge Cl BUSH WD23 ... 74 B9
HCH RM12 ... 125 L10
Edridge Rd CROY/NA CRO ... 203 J3
Edson Cl GSTN WD25 ... 54 A4
Eduif Rd BORE WD6 ... 75 N2
Edward Amey Cl GSTN WD25 ... 53 P5
Edward Av CHING E4 ... 100 G6
MRDN SM4 ... 201 N5
Edward Cl ABLGY WD5 ... 54 C8
CDW/CHF RM16 ... 167 J1
CRICK NW2 * ... 116 C9
ED N9 ... 99 N1
GPK RM2 ... 125 K1
HPTN TW12 ... 176 B8
STAL AL1 ... 38 E7
Edward Ct CAN/RD E16 ... 141 M7
HHS/BOV HP3 ... 35 N10
STA TW18 ... 173 M9
WAB EN9 ... 63 L9
Edwardes Pl KENS W8 ... 14 D4
Edwardes Sq KENS W8 ... 14 D4
Edward Gv EBAR EN4 ... 77 N9
Edward II Av BF/WBF KT14 ... 216 E10
Edward Mann Cl East WCHPL E1 * ... 140 C8
Edward Mann Cl West WCHPL E1 * ... 140 C8
Edward Ms CAMTN NW1 * ... 4 B1
Edward Pl DEPT SE8 ... 160 E5
Edward Rd BFOR GU20 ... 212 C3
BH/WHM TN16 ... 244 B4
BMLY BR1 ... 183 M1
CHDH RM6 ... 123 P6
CHST BR7 ... 184 B8
COUL/CHIP CR5 ... 240 E1
CROY/NA CRO ... 203 M7
EBAR EN4 ... 77 N9
EBED/NFELT TW14 ... 174 M1
HPTN TW12 ... 176 B8
NTHLT UB5 ... 133 K4
PGE/AN SE20 ... 182 C10
RYLN/HDSTN HA2 ... 114 B1
WALTH E17 ... 120 C2

Edwards Av RSLP HA4 ... 113 K10
Edward's Cots IS N1 * ... 6 A4
Edwards Dr FBAR/BDGN N11 ... 98 G6
Edwards Gdns SWLY SL2 ... 208 A4
Edward's La STNW/STAM N16 ... 119 L2
Edwards Ms IS N1 ... 6 B3
MHST W1U ... 10 C5
Edwards Pl FBAR/BDGN N11 ... 98 G6
Edwards Rd BELV DA17 ... 164 B3
Edward Sq IS N1 ... 5 N6
NWCR SE14 ... 160 C6
Edward's Wy BROCKY SE4 ... 182 H1
Edward Tyler Rd LEE/GVPK SE12 ... 183 N5
Edward Wy ASHF TW15 ... 174 H5
Edwina Gdns REDBR IG4 ... 122 B3
Edwin Av EHAM E6 ... 142 D4
Edwin Cl BXLYHN DA7 ... 164 A5
EHSLY KT24 ... 252 E1
RAIN RM13 ... 144 G5
Edwin Hall Pl LEW SE13 ... 183 J2
Edwin Petty Pl RDART DA2 * ... 188 B3
Edwin Pl CROY/NA CRO ... 203 L1
Edwin Rd EDGW HA8 ... 96 A1
EHSLY KT24 ... 252 C2
WHTN TW2 ... 176 D4
Edwin's Md HOM E9 ... 120 D9
Edwin St CAN/RD E16 ... 141 M7
GVE DA12 ... 190 K3
WCHPL E1 ... 140 B6
Edwin Ware Ct PIN HA5 ... 56 F10
Effie Pl FUL/PGN SW6 ... 157 K6
Effie Rd FUL/PGN SW6 ... 157 K6
Effingham Cl BELMT SM2 ... 221 L4
Effingham Common Rd EHSLY KT24 ... 253 K1
Effingham Ct WOKS/MYFD GU22 * ... 232 A8
Effingham La CRAWE RH10 ... 281 M10
Effingham Pl EHSLY KT24 ... 253 L3
Effingham Rd CEND/HSY/T N8 ... 119 J3
CROY/NA CRO ... 202 D7
HORL RH6 ... 281 N10
LEE/GVPK SE12 ... 183 K1
REIG RH2 ... 275 J1
SURB KT6 ... 198 G7
Effort St TOOT SW17 ... 179 P8
Effra Pde BRXS/STRHM SW2 ... 181 M1
Effra Rd BRXS/STRHM SW2 ... 181 M1
WIM/MER SW19 ... 179 L9
Egan Cl PUR/KEN CR8 ... 241 L6
Egan Wy HYS/HAR UB3 ... 132 F9
Egbert St CAMTN NW1 ... 4 B1
Egerton Av SWLY SL2 ... 208 C1
Egerton Cl PIN HA5 ... 113 H2
Egerton Crs CHEL SW3 ... 15 J5
Egerton Dr GNWCH SE10 ... 160 G7
Egerton Gdns CHEL SW3 ... 15 J4
GDMY/SEVK IG3 ... 123 J1
HDN NW4 ... 116 E2
WEA W13 ... 134 G8
WLSDN NW10 ... 137 L2
Egerton Gardens Ms CHEL SW3 * ... 15 J4
Egerton Pl CHEL SW3 * ... 15 J4
WEY KT13 ... 216 D3
Egerton Rd ALP/SUD HA0 ... 135 L2
BERK HP4 ... 33 M3
GUW GU2 ... 267 L6
NWMAL KT3 ... 200 D2
SNWD SE25 ... 203 M8
STNW/STAM N16 ... 119 N5
WEY KT13 ... 216 D3
WHTN TW2 ... 176 D3
Egerton Ter CHEL SW3 ... 15 J4
Egerton Wy HYS/HAR UB3 ... 152 C6
Egg Farm La KGLGY WD4 ... 54 D6
Egg Hall EPP CM16 ... 65 K5
Egglesfield Cl BERK HP4 ... 33 M3
Egham By-Pass STWL/WRAY TW20 ... 172 C7
Egham Cl CHEAM SM3 ... 201 H9
WIM/MER SW19 ... 178 F3
Egham Crs CHEAM SM3 ... 201 H10
Egham Hl EGH TW20 ... 172 A9
Egham Rd PLSTW E13 ... 141 M4
Eghams Cl BEAC HP9 ... 88 B3
Eghams Wood Rd BEAC HP9 ... 88 A3
Eglantine La EYN DA4 ... 210 A3
Eglantine Rd WAND/EARL SW18 ... 179 N4
Egleston Rd MRDN SM4 ... 201 L6
Eglington Ct WALW SE17 * ... 159 H1
Eglington Rd CHING E4 ... 101 J3
Egliston Ms PUT/ROE SW15 ... 156 F9
Egliston Rd PUT/ROE SW15 ... 156 F9

Egmont Park Rd KWD/TDW/WH KT20 ... 256 D1
Egmont Rd BELMT SM2 ... 221 N4
NWMAL KT3 ... 200 C3
SURB KT6 ... 199 L8
WOT/HER KT12 ... 197 J7
Egmont St NWCR SE14 ... 160 C6
Egmont Wy KWD/TDW/WH KT20 ... 239 L5
Egremont Gdns SL SL1 ... 128 F9
Egremont Rd WNWD SE27 ... 181 H6
Egret Wy YEAD UB4 ... 133 L8
Egypt La SLN SL2 ... 108 G8
Eider Cl SRTFD E15 ... 121 L10
Eight Acres SL SL1 ... 128 A6
Eighteenth Rd MTCM CR4 ... 202 F4
Eighth Av HYS/HAR UB3 ... 133 H10
KWD/TDW/WH KT20 ... 257 J2
MNPK E12 ... 122 F10
Eileen Rd SNWD SE25 ... 203 L5
Eindhoven Cl CAR SM5 ... 202 B8
Eisenhower Dr EHAM E6 ... 142 B7
Elaine Cl CMBW SE5 ... 159 J8
Eland St BTSEA SW11 ... 158 A9
CROY/NA CRO ... 203 J10
Elba Pl WALW SE17 * ... 18 F5
Elberon Av CROY/NA CRO ... 202 D6
Elborough Rd SNWD SE25 ... 203 P5
Elborough St WAND/EARL SW18 ... 179 K4
Elbow La HERT/BAY SG13 ... 26 A10
HOD EN11 ... 44 A7
Elbow Meadow DTCH/LGLY SL3 ... 151 J2
Elder Av CEND/HSY/T N8 ... 118 F3
Elderbeck Cl CHESW EN7 ... 61 P4
Elderberry Cl BARK/HLT IG6 ... 102 E8
Elderberry Rd EA W5 ... 155 L1
Elderberry Wy GSTN WD25 ... 73 J1
Elder Cl BFN/LL DA15 ... 185 J4
RGUE GU4 ... 250 D7
TRDG/WHET N20 ... 97 L3
WDR/YW UB7 ... 131 P9
Elder Ct BUSH WD23 ... 94 D3
Elderfield HLWE CM17 ... 29 N7
Elderfield Rd CLPT E5 ... 120 F3
SLN SL2 ... 129 L1
Elderfield Wk WAN E11 ... 121 L1
Elderflower Wy SRTFD E15 ... 141 K2
Elder Oak Cl PGE/AN SE20 ... 204 A1
Elder Rd CHOB/PIR GU24 ... 230 F1
WNWD SE27 ... 181 K8
Eldersley Cl REDH RH1 ... 258 A4
Eldersley Gdns REDH RH1 ... 258 A6
Elderslie Cl BECK BR3 ... 204 F6
Elderslie Rd ELTH/MOT SE9 ... 184 D1
Elder St WCHPL E1 ... 13 L3
Elderton Rd SYD SE26 ... 182 D7
Eldertree Pl MTCM CR4 ... 202 F4
Eldertree Wy MTCM CR4 ... 202 C1
Elder Wk IS N1 ... 6 D5
RDKG RH5 ... 273 H6

Elder Yd DTCH/LGLY SL3 * ... 150 C1
Eldon Av BORE WD6 ... 75 M6
CROY/NA CRO ... 204 B9
HEST TW5 ... 153 P6
Eldon Gv HAMP NW3 ... 117 N10
Eldon Pde WDGN N22 * ... 99 J9
Eldon Pk SNWD SE25 ... 204 A4
Eldon Rd CTHM CR3 ... 241 L7
ED N9 ... 99 P2
KENS W8 ... 14 D4
WALTH E17 ... 120 E2
WDGN N22 ... 99 J9
Eldon St LVPST EC2M ... 13 H1
Eldon Wy WLSDN NW10 ... 135 N4
Eldred Dr STMC/STPC BR5 ... 207 N9
Eldred Gdns UPMR RM14 ... 126 D5
Eldridge Cl EBED/NFELT TW14 ... 175 H4
Eleanora Ter SUT SM1 * ... 221 M2
Eleanor Av HOR/WEW KT19 ... 238 C4
STALW/RED AL3 ... 38 C4
Eleanor Cl BERM/RHTH SE16 ... 160 C1
SEVS/STOTM N15 ... 119 N1
Eleanor Cross Rd CHES/WCR EN8 ... 62 D10
Eleanor Gdns BAR EN5 ... 76 A7
BCTR RM8 ... 92 B9
HGDN/ICK UB10 ... 112 C8
Eleanor Rd CFSP/GDCR SL9 ... 89 P9
FBAR/BDGN N11 ... 98 F7
HACK E8 ... 140 A1
HERT/WAT SG14 ... 25 L4
SRTFD E15 ... 141 L1
Eleanor St BOW E3 ... 140 A10
Eleanor Wy BRW CM14 ... 107 J6
CHES/WCR EN8 ... 62 E10
Electra Av HTHAIR TW6 ... 152 C9
Electric Av BRXN/ST SW9 ... 159 N4
PEND EN3 ... 78 D1
Electric La BRXN/ST SW9 ... 159 N5
Electric Pde SURB KT6 * ... 199 J6
Elephant & Castle STHWK SE1 * ... 18 D3
Elephant La BERM/RHTH SE16 ... 160 B1
Elephant Rd WALW SE17 ... 18 E5
Elers Rd HYS/HAR UB3 ... 152 D3
WEA W13 ... 155 H1
Eleventh Av KWD/TDW/WH KT20 * ... 257 J2
Eley Rd UED N18 ... 100 C6
Elfindale Rd HNHL SE24 ... 181 H1
Elfin Gv TEDD TW11 ... 176 B8
Elford Cl BKHTH/KID SE3 ... 161 K9
Elfort Rd HBRY N5 ... 119 H6
Elfrida Crs CAT SE6 ... 182 F7
Elf Rw WAP E1W ... 140 E9
Elgal Cl ORP BR6 ... 226 G2
Elgar Av BRYLDS KT5 ... 199 N6
EA W5 ... 155 L1
STRHM/NOR SW16 ... 202 A3
WLSDN NW10 ... 137 H4
Elgar Cl BKHH IG9 ... 102 A3
BORE WD6 ... 95 H1
DEPT SE8 ... 160 H1
HGDN/ICK UB10 ... 112 B7
PLSTW E13 ... 141 J9
Elgar Gdns BERM/RHTH SE16 ... 160 H1
Elgar St BERM/RHTH SE16 ... 160 H1
Elgin Av ASHF TW15 ... 174 D9
HARH RM3 ... 106 J4
KTN/HRWW/WS HA3 ... 94 D10
MV/WKIL W9 ... 8 C1
Elgin Cl SHB W12 ... 156 L6
Elgin Crs CTHM CR3 ... 241 P8
HTHAIR TW6 ... 152 F8
NTGHL W11 ... 8 B5
Elgin Dr NTHWD HA6 ... 92 H4
Elgin Est MV/WKIL W9 * ... 8 C1
Elgin Gdns GU GU1 ... 250 D9
Elgin Ms NTGHL W11 ... 8 B5
Elgin Ms North MV/WKIL W9 ... 8 D1
Elgin Ms South MV/WKIL W9 ... 3 H9
Elgin Pl WEY KT13 ... 216 D5
Elgin Rd BROX EN10 ... 44 G10
CHES/WCR EN8 ... 62 D5

CROY/NA CRO ... 203 N9
GDMY/SEVK IG3 ... 123 H6
SUT SM1 ... 201 N10
WDGN N22 ... 98 D10
WEY KT13 ... 216 B5
WLGTN SM6 ... 222 D3
Elgiva La CHSGTN KT9 ... 50 C7
Elgood Av NTHWD HA6 ... 93 H7
Elgood Cl NTGHL W11 ... 8 A8
Elham Cl BMLY BR1 ... 184 A10
Elia Ms IS N1 ... 6 C8
Elias Pl VX/NE SW8 ... 18 A10
Elia St IS N1 ... 6 C8
Elibank Rd ELTH/MOT SE9 ... 162 A10
Elim St STHWK SE1 ... 19 J5
Elim Wy PLSTW E13 ... 141 L5
Eliot Bank FSTH SE23 ... 182 A5
Eliot Cl BAR EN5 ... 75 L5
Eliot Ct WFD IG8 ... 102 G8
Eliot Dr RYLN/HDSTN HA2 ... 114 A7
Eliot Gdns PUT/ROE SW15 ... 156 D10
Eliot Ms STJWD NW8 ... 3 J8
Eliot Pk LEW SE13 ... 161 K8
Eliot Rd BKHTH/KID SE3 ... 161 K8
DART DA1 ... 188 A1
Eliot V BKHTH/KID SE3 ... 161 H8
Elizabeth Av AMS HP6 ... 69 P5
ENC/FH EN2 ... 79 J7
IL IG1 ... 122 C7
IS N1 ... 6 F1
STA TW18 ... 173 M9
Elizabeth Barnes Ct FUL/PGN SW6 * ... 157 L8
Elizabeth Br BGVA SW1W ... 16 G7
Elizabeth Cl BAR EN5 ... 76 E7
HERT/WAT SG14 ... 24 G4
MV/WKIL W9 ... 9 K2
ROMW/RG RM7 ... 104 C9
SUT SM1 ... 221 J1
TIL RM18 ... 168 E8
WAB EN9 ... 45 J8
Elizabeth Clyde Cl SEVS/STOTM N15 ... 119 M2
Elizabeth Cots STAL/WH/RED AL3 ... 38 C2
Elizabeth Ct GODL GU7 ... 267 K10
HORL RH6 * ... 280 B6
STALE/WH AL4 ... 39 J3
WOOL/PLUM SE18 ... 161 H8
Elizabeth Dr EPP CM16 ... 83 H7
Elizabeth Fry Pl WOOL/PLUM SE18 ... 162 B7
Elizabeth Gdns ACT W3 ... 138 C10
ISLW TW7 ... 154 A9
STAN HA7 ... 95 K5
SUN TW16 ... 197 K3
Elizabeth Huggins Cots GVW DA11 ... 190 G5
Elizabeth Ms HAMP NW3 ... 3 P2
Elizabeth Pl EYN DA4 * ... 209 N6
SEVS/STOTM N15 ... 119 L2
Elizabeth Ride ED N9 ... 100 A1
Elizabeth Rd BRWN CM15 ... 106 G10
CDW/CHF RM16 ... 167 L2
EHAM E6 ... 141 P6
GODL GU7 ... 267 K10
RAIN RM13 ... 145 J2
SEVS/STOTM N15 ... 119 M3
Elizabeth Sq BERM/RHTH SE16 ... 140 D9
Elizabeth St BGVA SW1W ... 16 F6
RDART DA2 ... 188 D5
Elizabeth Ter ELTH/MOT SE9 ... 184 E6
Elizabeth Wy FELT TW13 ... 175 K7
HLW CM20 ... 6 C2
HLWW/ROY CM19 ... 46 C2
NRWD SE19 ... 181 L10
STMC/STPC BR5 ... 207 M5
Eliza Cook Cl SWCM DA10 ... 166 G10
Elkanette Ms TRDG/WHET N20 ... 97 M3
Elkington Rd PLSTW E13 ... 141 N6
Elkins Gdns RGUE GU4 ... 250 D7
Elkins Rd SLN SL2 ... 109 K7
The Elkins ROM RM1 ... 104 F10
Ellaline Rd HMSMTH W6 ... 156 M5
Ella Ms HAMP NW3 ... 118 A9
Ellanby Crs UED N18 ... 100 A6
Elland Cl BAR EN5 ... 77 H4
Elland Rd PECK SE15 ... 160 B10
WOT/HER KT12 ... 197 L8
Ella Rd CEND/HSY/T N8 ... 118 F5
Ellement Cl PIN HA5 ... 113 J3
Ellenborough Pl PUT/ROE SW15 ... 156 D10
Ellenborough Rd SCUP DA14 ... 185 N9
WDGN N22 ... 99 J9
Ellenbridge Wy SAND/SEL CR2 ... 223 M5
Ellenbrook Cl WATN WD24 * ... 73 K5
Ellenbrook Crs HAT AL10 ... 40 A4
Ellenbrook La HAT AL10 ... 40 A4
Ellen Cl BMLY BR1 ... 206 A5
HHNE HP2 ... 36 A5
Ellen Ct ED N9 ... 100 B3
Ellen Ms HHNE HP2 ... 36 A5
Ellen St WCHPL E1 ... 13 P6
Ellen Webb Dr KTN/HRWW/WS HA3 ... 114 D1
Elleray Rd TEDD TW11 ... 176 B9
Ellerby St FUL/PGN SW6 ... 156 G7
Ellerdale Cl HAMP NW3 ... 117 M10
Ellerdale Rd HAMP NW3 ... 117 M10
Ellerdale St LEW SE13 ... 160 E10
Ellerdine Rd HSLW TW3 ... 154 B7
Ellerker Gdns RCHPK/HAM TW10 ... 177 K2
Ellerman Av WHTN TW2 ... 175 N4
Ellerman Rd TIL RM18 ... 168 E8
Ellerslie GVE DA12 ... 190 C3
Ellerslie Rd SHB W12 ... 136 E10
Ellerton Gdns DAGW RM9 ... 143 M2
Ellerton Rd BARN SW13 ... 156 D6
DAGW RM9 ... 143 M2
RYNPK SW20 ... 178 F10
SURB KT6 ... 199 L9
WAND/EARL SW18 ... 179 N4
WIM/MER SW19 ... 178 F10
Ellery Rd NRWD SE19 ... 181 L10
Ellery St PECK SE15 ... 160 A1
Elles Av GU GU1 ... 250 E10
Ellesborough Cl OXHEY WD19 ... 93 K6
Ellesmere Av BECK BR3 ... 204 B5
MLHL NW7 ... 96 A4
Ellesmere Cl RSLP HA4 ... 113 L3
WAN E11 ... 121 L1
Ellesmere Gdns DAGW RM9 ... 143 M5
REDBR IG4 ... 121 P4
Ellesmere Gv BAR EN5 ... 77 J5
Ellesmere Pl WOT/HER KT12 ... 196 F7
Ellesmere Rd BERK HP4 ... 34 B1
BOW E3 ... 140 C6
GFD/PVL UB6 ... 134 B6
TWK TW1 ... 177 H2
WEY KT13 ... 216 D7
WLSDN NW10 ... 116 H10
Ellesmere St POP/IOD E14 ... 140 G8
Ellice Rd OXTED RH8 ... 261 L10
Ellies Ms ASHF TW15 ... 174 A5
Ellingfort Rd HACK E8 ... 140 A2
Ellingham Cl HHNE HP2 ... 36 A4
Ellingham Rd CHSGTN KT9 ... 219 L4
HMSMTH W6 ... 137 H9
SRTFD E15 ... 121 J9
Ellington Ct STHGT/OAK N14 ... 98 E3
Ellington Rd FELT TW13 ... 175 K7
HSLW TW3 ... 154 A5
MUSWH N10 ... 118 B3
Ellington St HOLWY N7 ... 119 G1
Ellington Wy EPSOM KT18 ... 238 E10
Elliot Cl CRAWE RH10 ... 284 A10
Elliot Rd STRFD E15 ... 141 K2

WFD IG8 ... 102 A7
Elliot Rd HDN NW4 ... 116 E4
STRHM/NOR SW16 ... 179 K4
Elliott Av RSLP HA4 ... 113 C2
Elliott Cl WGCE AL7 ... 22 G8
Elliott Ct WOKN/KNAP GU21 * ... 232 D2
Elliott Rd BRXN/ST SW9 ... 159 J6
CHSWK W4 ... 156 B3
HAYES BR2 ... 206 A4
STAN HA7 ... 94 F7
THHT CR7 ... 203 H9
Elliott's La BH/WHM TN16 ... 245 M10
Elliott's Pl IS N1 ... 6 D6
Elliott Sq HAMP NW3 ... 3 P5
Elliotts Rw LBTH SE11 ... 18 D5
Ellis Av CFSP/GDCR SL9 ... 90 C9
GUW GU2 ... 267 L2
RAIN RM13 ... 145 H7
SL SL1 ... 149 K5
Ellis Cl COUL/CHIP CR5 ... 240 G6
EDGW HA8 ... 96 C1
MTCM CR4 ... 202 A6
WCCW AL8 ... 22 C5
Ellis Farm Cl WOKS/MYFD GU22 ... 232 A8
Ellisfield Dr PUT/ROE SW15 ... 178 C3
Ellis Flds STAL/WH/RED AL3 ... 38 C2
Ellison Cl WDSR SL4 ... 148 B9
Ellison Gdns NWDGN UB2 ... 153 H3
Ellison Rd BARN SW13 ... 156 C5
BFN/LL DA15 ... 184 G2
STRHM/NOR SW16 ... 180 A5
Ellis Rd COUL/CHIP CR5 ... 240 G6
MTCM CR4 ... 202 A6
NWDGN UB2 ... 134 B10
Ellison Wy SUT SM1 ... 221 L1
Elliston Ms IS N1 ... 5 K4
Ellis St KTBR SW1X ... 16 E5
Ellis Waterton Cl SWLY BR8 ... 208 E4
Ellis Wy DART DA1 ... 187 N5
Elliswick Rd HARP AL5 ... 20 A1
Ellman Rd CRAWW RH11 ... 283 J9
Ellora Rd STRHM/NOR SW16 ... 180 E8
Ellsworth St BETH E2 ... 140 A5
Ellwood Gdns WATW WD18 ... 21 A5
Ellwood Pl CRAWW RH11 ... 283 J7
Ellwood Rd BEAC HP9 ... 88 A10
Elmar Gn SLN SL2 ... 128 F5
Elmar Rd SEVS/STOTM N15 ... 119 L2
Elm Av EA W5 ... 135 K10
OXHEY WD19 ... 93 M1
RSLP HA4 ... 113 H6
UPMR RM14 ... 125 M7
Elm Bank CHOB/PIR GU24 * ... 213 K7
STHGT/OAK N14 ... 98 F1
Elmbank Av BAR EN5 ... 76 A6
EGH TW20 ... 171 N10
Elmbank Dr BMLY BR1 ... 206 D1
Elm Bank Gdns BARN SW13 ... 156 B7
Elmbourne Dr BELV DA17 ... 164 F2
Elmbourne Rd TOOT SW17 ... 180 C6
Elmbridge HLWE CM17 ... 30 A8
Elmbridge Av BRYLDS KT5 ... 199 P6
Elmbridge Cl RSLP HA4 ... 113 H4
Elmbridge Dr RSLP HA4 ... 113 H4
Elmbridge La WOKS/MYFD GU22 ... 232 C5
Elmbridge Rd BARK/HLT IG6 ... 103 H3
Elmbridge Wk HACK E8 * ... 7 J1
Elmbrook Cl SUN TW16 ... 197 J1
Elmbrook Gdns ELTH/MOT SE9 ... 162 B10
Elmbrook Rd SUT SM1 ... 221 L1
Elmcote Wy RKW/CH/CXG WD3 ... 48 A10
Elm Cots MTCM CR4 * ... 202 A2
Elmcourt Rd WNWD SE27 ... 181 J5
Elm Crs EA W5 ... 155 K1
KUTN/CMB KT2 ... 199 K1
Elmcroft CEND/HSY/T N8 ... 118 F4
Elmcroft Av BFN/LL DA15 ... 185 H7
GLDGN NW11 ... 116 G5
Elm Ct WAT WD17 ... 21 J3

MTCM CR4 ... 202 B1
TEDD TW11 ... 176 E8
Elmfield Cl GVW DA11 ... 114 D7
HRW HA1 ... 114 D7
POTB/CUF EN6 ... 59 J9
RSEV TN14 ... 265 J9
Elmfield Pk BMLY BR1 ... 205 M5
Elmfield Rd BMLY BR1 ... 205 M5
CHING E4 ... 101 N1
EFNCH N2 ... 117 N1
NWDGN UB2 ... 153 M2
POTB/CUF EN6 ... 59 J9
TOOT SW17 ... 180 C5
WALTH E17 ... 120 C1
Elmfield Wy MV/WKIL W9 ... 8 C1
SAND/SEL CR2 ... 222 C1
Elm Friars Wk CAMTN NW1 ... 5 K4
Elm Gdns EFNCH N2 ... 117 M1
ENC/FH EN2 ... 79 L4
EPP CM16 ... 66 C2
EPSOM KT18 ... 238 F5
ESH/CLAY KT10 ... 219 H10
MTCM CR4 ... 202 F4
WCCW AL8 ... 22 C5
Elmgate Av FELT TW13 ... 175 J6
Elmgate Gdns EDGW HA8 ... 95 P6
Elm Gn ACT W3 ... 137 H5
Elmgreen Cl SRTFD E15 ... 141 K3
Elm Gv BERK HP4 ... 33 N5
CEND/HSY/T N8 ... 118 F4
CRICK NW2 ... 116 C9
CTHM CR3 ... 241 M8
EMPK RM11 ... 125 M4
EPSOM KT18 ... 219 P10
ERITH DA8 ... 164 E6
KUTN/CMB KT2 ... 199 K1
ORP BR6 ... 207 J8
PECK SE15 ... 159 P1
RYLN/HDSTN HA2 ... 113 P5
SUT SM1 ... 221 L1
WOR/PK KT4 ... 200 E9
Elm Grove Pde CAR SM5 ... 202 B10
Elm Grove Rd BARN SW13 ... 156 D8
COB KT11 ... 235 L2
Elmgrove Rd CROY/NA CRO ... 203 N6
HRW HA1 ... 114 D3
WEY KT13 ... 216 B1
Elm Hall Gdns WAN E11 ... 121 M4
Elm Hatch PIN HA5 ... 57 K8
Elmhurst BELV DA17 ... 163 P5
Elmhurst Av EFNCH N2 ... 117 N1
MTCM CR4 ... 180 B10
Elmhurst Crs EFNCH N2 ... 117 N1
Elmhurst Dr DORK RH4 ... 272 C4
SWFD E18 ... 121 M10
Elmhurst Rd DTCH/LGLY SL3 ... 150 D2
ELTH/MOT SE9 ... 184 D1
FSTGT E7 ... 141 K2
PEND EN3 ... 80 B3
TOTM N17 ... 99 P1
Elmhurst St CLAP SW4 ... 158 E9
Elmhurst Wy LOU IG10 ... 102 C1
Elington Ct BXLY DA5 ... 185 J6
Elmington Est CMBW SE5 ... 159 K6
Elmington Rd CMBW SE5 ... 159 K6
Elmira St LEW SE13 ... 160 E10
Elm La CAT SE6 ... 182 E6
RPLY/SEND GU23 ... 234 A5
Elm Lawn Cl STAL AL1 ... 38 E2
Elmlee Cl CHST BR7 ... 184 E4
Elmley Cl EHAM E6 ... 142 G8
Elmore Cl ALP/SUD HA0 ... 135 N4
Elmore Rd COUL/CHIP CR5 ... 240 B10
PEND EN3 ... 80 C5
WAN E11 ... 121 H6
Elmores LOU IG10 ... 102 G7
Elmore St IS N1 ... 6 F1
Elm Pde SCUP DA14 * ... 185 K7
Elm Pk ASC SL5 ... 210 D2
BRXS/STRHM SW2 ... 159 N9
STAN HA7 ... 95 K4
Elm Park Av HCH RM12 ... 125 H9
SEVS/STOTM N15 ... 119 M2
Elm Park Gdns HDN NW4 ... 116 B3
WBPTN SW10 ... 15 H8
Elmpark Gdns SAND/SEL CR2 ... 224 B6
Elm Park La CHEL SW3 ... 15 G8
Elm Park Rd CHEL SW3 ... 15 H9
FNCH N3 ... 97 J8
LEY E10 ... 121 H8
PIN HA5 ... 57 K9
SNWD SE25 ... 203 N9
WCHMH N21 ... 99 L8
Elmroyd Av POTB/CUF EN6 ... 59 H5
Elmroyd Cl POTB/CUF EN6 ... 59 H5
Elms Av HDN NW4 ... 116 B3
MUSWH N10 ... 118 C1
Elmscott Gdns WCHMH N21 ... 79 K10
Elmscott Rd BMLY BR1 ... 183 K6
Elms Ct ALP/SUD HA0 ... 135 K3
Elms Crs CLAP SW4 ... 180 D1
Elmscroft Gdns POTB/CUF EN6 ... 58 F1
Elmsdale Rd WALTH E17 ... 120 C2
Elmshaw Rd PUT/ROE SW15 ... 178 D2

WHTN TW2 ... 176 C5
Elmslie Cl EPSOM KT18 ... 219 P10
WFD IG8 ... 102 C7
Elms Park Av ALP/SUD HA0 ... 114 F9
Elms Rd CLAP SW4 ... 180 C1
KTN/HRWW/WS HA3 ... 94 D8
WARE SG12 ... 26 F1
Elmstead Av CHST BR7 ... 184 C8
WBLY HA9 ... 96 A9
Elmstead Cl HOR/WEW KT19 ... 220 B2
TRDG/WHET N20 ... 97 K3
Elmstead Gdns WPK KT4 ... 200 D10
Elmstead Gld CHST BR7 ... 184 B9
CHST BR7 ... 184 B9
Elmstead La CHST BR7 ... 184 B10
Elmstead Rd BF/WBF KT14 ... 215 G5
ERITH DA8 ... 164 F7
GDMY/SEVK IG3 ... 123 K3
The Elms BARN SW13 ... 156 C9
BORE WD6 * ... 75 P6
CHONG CM5 ... 67 P6
ESH/CLAY KT10 * ... 218 G4
HERT/BAY SG13 ... 25 P5
LOU IG10 ... 81 L6
NFNCH/WDSPK N12 ... 97 P6
TOOT SW17 ... 180 B6
WARL CR6 ... 242 B1
WLGTN SM6 ... 222 D1
Elmstone Ter STMC/STPC BR5 * ... 207 N4
Elmsway ASHF TW15 ... 174 A9
Elmswood GT/LBKH KT23 ... 235 N10
Elmsworth Av HSLW TW3 ... 154 A8
Elm Ter CRICK NW2 ... 116 K8
KTN/HRWW/WS HA3 ... 94 C8
WTHK RM20 ... 166 G5
Elmton Wy CLPT E5 ... 119 P9
Elm Tree Av ESH/CLAY KT10 ... 198 C2
Elmtree Cl BF/WBF KT14 ... 215 P9
Elm Tree Cl ASHF TW15 ... 174 C8
CHERT KT16 ... 195 J5
HORL RH6 ... 280 B3
NTHLT UB5 ... 133 N4
STJWD NW8 ... 3 L9
Elm Tree Ct CHARL SE7 * ... 161 P5
Elmtree Hl CSHM HP5 ... 176 H5
Elm Tree Rd STJWD NW8 ... 3 L9
Elm Tree Wk RKW/CH/CXG WD3 ... 71 J8
Elm Vls HNWL W7 * ... 134 D9
Elm Wk GPK RM2 ... 117 K7
HAMP NW3 ... 117 K7
ORP BR6 ... 206 C10
RAD WD7 ... 74 B2
RYNPK SW20 ... 200 F4
Elmway CDW/CHF RM16 ... 147 P9
Elm Wy BRW CM14 ... 106 F4
FBAR/BDGN N11 ... 98 B7
HOR/WEW KT19 ... 220 A2
RKW/CH/CXG WD3 ... 91 L2
WLSDN NW10 ... 116 B9
WPK KT4 ... 200 F10
Elmwood CHIG IG7 ... 102 G2
SBW CM21 ... 30 A2
WCCW AL8 ... 22 E6
Elmwood Av BORE WD6 ... 75 J6
FELT TW13 ... 175 J6
KTN/HRWW/WS HA3 ... 114 F3
PLMGR N13 ... 98 F6
Elmwood Cl ASHTD KT21 ... 237 J3
EW KT17 ... 220 G9
WLGTN SM6 ... 202 C9
Elmwood Crs CDALE/KGS NW9 ... 115 P2
EW KT17 ... 220 G9
Elmwood Gdns HNWL W7 ... 134 D1
Elmwood Rd CHSWK W4 ... 155 P5
CROY/NA CRO ... 203 J1
HNHL SE24 ... 160 H2
MTCM CR4 ... 202 A3
REDH RH1 ... 259 N5
SLN SL2 ... 129 N6
WOKN/KNAP GU21 ... 231 J5
Elmworth Gv DUL SE21 ... 181 L2
Elnathan Ms MV/WKIL W9 ... 8 E1
Elphinstone Rd WALTH E17 ... 119 L10
Elphinstone St HBRY N5 ... 119 J9
Elrick Cl ERITH DA8 ... 164 F5
Elrington Rd HACK E8 ... 7 N2
WFD IG8 ... 101 M6
Elruge Cl WDR/YW UB7 ... 151 N2
Elsa Cots POP/IOD E14 * ... 140 D7
Elsa Rd WELL DA16 ... 163 M8
Elsa St WCHPL E1 ... 140 E7
Elsdale St HOM E9 ... 140 B4
Elsden Rd TOTM N17 ... 99 N4
Elsenham St WAND/EARL SW18 ... 179 J4
Elsham Rd WAN E11 ... 121 K3
WKENS W14 ... 14 A2
Elsham Ter WKENS W14 * ... 14 A2
Elsiedene Rd WCHMH N21 ... 99 K1
Elsie Lane Ct BAY/PAD W2 ... 9 K1
Elsiemaud Rd BROCKY SE4 ... 182 K1
Elsie Rd EDUL SE22 ... 159 N10
Elsinge Rd EN EN1 ... 78 D5
Elsinore Av STWL/WRAY TW19 ... 173 P3
Elsinore Gdns CRICK NW2 ... 117 D8
Elsinore Rd FSTH SE23 ... 182 B6
Elsinore Wy RCH/KEW TW9 ... 155 A9
Elsley Rd BTSEA SW11 ... 158 A9
Elspeth Rd ALP/SUD HA0 ... 114 B5
BTSEA SW11 ... 158 A10
Elsrick Av MRDN SM4 ... 201 K5
Elstan Wy CROY/NA CRO ... 203 H5
Elsted Cl CRAWW RH11 ... 283 J6
Elsted St WALW SE17 ... 19 H6
Elstow Cl ELTH/MOT SE9 ... 143 J6
RSLP HA4 ... 143 L5
Elstow Gdns DAGW RM9 ... 143 L5
Elstow Rd DAGW RM9 ... 143 M5
Elstree Cl HCH RM12 ... 143 J2
Elstree Gdns BELV DA17 ... 143 J1
ED N9 ... 100 B10
IL IG1 ... 122 F10
Elstree Ga BORE WD6 * ... 75 P5
Elstree Hl BMLY BR1 ... 183 K10
Elstree Hl North BORE WD6 ... 75 J1
Elstree Hl South BORE WD6 ... 75 H2
Elstree Pk BORE WD6 ... 76 A10
Elstree Rd BUSH WD23 ... 94 C8
BSTEA SW11 ... 157 M8
Elswick Rd LEW SE13 ... 160 M10
Elswick St FUL/PGN SW6 ... 157 M8
Elsworth Cl EBED/NFELT TW14 ... 175 G6
Elsworthy THDIT KT7 ... 198 D6
Elsworthy Ri HAMP NW3 ... 3 N4
Elsworthy Rd HAMP NW3 ... 3 P5
Elsworthy Ter HAMP NW3 ... 3 P4
Elsynge Rd WAND/EARL SW18 ... 179 L4
Eltham Av SL SL1 ... 130 B3
Eltham Gn ELTH/MOT SE9 ... 183 M2
Eltham Green Rd ELTH/MOT SE9 ... 161 P10
Eltham Hl ELTH/MOT SE9 ... 184 A4
Eltham High St ELTH/MOT SE9 ... 184 D5
Eltham Palace Rd ELTH/MOT SE9 ... 183 P4
Eltham Park Gdns ELTH/MOT SE9 ... 162 D10

LEE/GVPK SE12 183 M1
Elthorne Rd FUL/PGN SW6 157 K7
Elthorne Av HNWL W7 116 E1
Elthorne Ct HNWL W7 175 L4
Elthorne Park Rd HNWL W7 154 E2
Elthorne Rd ARCH N19 118 C9
CDALE/KGS NW9 116 A5
UX/CGN UB8 131 N4
Elthorne Wy CDALE/KGS NW9 116 A4
Elthruda Rd LEW SE13 183 J2
Eltisley Rd IL IG1 122 E9
Elton Av ALP/SUD HA0 114 C10
BAR EN5 77 J9
GFD/PVL UB6 134 E1
Elton Cl KUT/HW KT1 177 H10
Elton Pk WAT WD17 73 H6
Elton Pl STNW/STAM N16 119 M10
Elton Rd HERT/WAT SE14 25 K4
KUTN/CMB KT2 199 L1
PUR/KEN CR8 222 D8
Eltringham St WAND/EARL SW18 157 M10
Elvaston Ms SKENS SW7 15 K4
Elvaston Pl SKENS SW7 15 H4
Elveden Cl WOKS/MYFD GU22 233 L3
Elveden Pl WLSDN NW10 135 M4
WOKS/MYFD GU22 * 233 L3
Elveden Rd COB KT11 217 K2
WLSDN NW10 135 M4
Elvendon Rd FBAR/BDGN N11 98 F7
Elver Gdns BETH E2 7 M2
Elverson Ms DEPT SE8 160 G8
Elverson Rd DEPT SE8 160 G8
Elverton St WEST SW1P 16 G5
Elvin Cl GPK RM2 125 K2
Elvington Gn HAYES BR2 200 A3
Elvington La CDALE/KGS NW9 96 B9
Elvino Rd SYD SE26 182 C8
Elvis Rd CRICK NW2 136 F1
Elwell Cl EGH TW20 172 D9
Elwick Rd WOT/AV RM15 147 H8
Elwill Wy BECK BR3 205 L6
Elwin St BETH E2 7 N9
Elwood LHLWE CM17 47 P2
Elwood St HBRY N5 119 H5
Elwyn Gdns LEE/GVPK SE12 183 M5
Ely Av SL SL1 129 H7
Ely Cl AMSS HP7 69 K5
ERITH DA8 164 C6
HAT AL10 40 C3
NWMAL KT3 200 D1
Ely Cots VX/NE SW8 158 G6
Ely Gdns BORE WD6 76 D5
DAGE RM10 124 D8
Elyne Rd FSBYPK N4 119 H4
Ely Pl CLGW GU2 * 12 B4
HCIRC EC1N 12 B4
WFD IG8 102 D2
Ely Rd CROY/NA CR0 203 L5
HSLWW TW4 155 K9
HTHAIR TW6 152 C8
LEY E10 121 H4
STAL AL1 38 C7
Elysan Pl SAND/SEL CR2 225 K9
Elysian Av STMC/STPC BR5 207 J1
Elysium Pl FUL/PGN SW6 157 J7
Elysium St FUL/PGN SW6 157 J7
Elystan Cl WLGTN SM6 222 D5
Elystan Pl CHEL SW3 15 N7
Elystan St CHEL SW3 15 N6
Elystan Wk IS N1 6 B1
Emanuel Av ACT W3 135 P3
Embankment PUT/ROE SW15 156 G9
Embankment Gdns CHEL SW3 16 B9
Embankment Pl CHCR WC2N 11 K8
The Embankment
STWL/WRAY TW19 171 P5
TWK TW1 176 F4
Embassy Ct SCUP DA14 185 N4
WLGTN SM6 * 222 E5
Emba St BERM/RHTH SE16 19 N2
Ember Cl ADL/WDHM KT15 215 K2
STMC/STPC BR5 206 F2
Embercourt Rd THDIT KT7 198 D6
Ember Farm Av
E/WMO/HCT KT8 198 C6
Ember Farm Wy
E/WMO/HCT KT8 198 C6
Ember Gdns THDIT KT7 198 C6
Ember La ESH/CLAY KT10 198 C7
Emberson Vw EPP CM16 66 G6
Emberton CRAWW RH11 * 283 N2
Emblem Ct STMC/STPC SE22 181 P1
Embleton Rd LEW SE13 160 G10
OXHEY WD19 93 H4
Embleton Rd LEW SE13 160 G10
Embry Dr STAN HA7 94 G7
Embry Cl STAN HA7 94 F7
Embry Wy STAN HA7 94 F7
Emden Cl WDR/YW UB7 152 B1
Emden St FUL/PGN SW6 157 N7
Emerald Cl CAN/RD E16 142 G8
Emerald Ct SL SL1 149 K1
Emerald Gdns BCTR RM8 124 B10
Emerald Sq NWDGN UB2 153 K2
Emerald St BMSBY WC1N 11 M1
Emerson Dr GPK RM2 125 M1
Emerson Gdns
KTN/HRWW/WS HA3 115 L4
Emerson Rd IL IG1 122 C8
Emersons Av SWLY BR8 186 F7
Emerson St STHWK SE1 12 E8
Emerton Cl BXLYHS DA6 163 P4
Emerton Gth BERK HP4 33 N4
Emerton Rd LHD/OX KT22 236 B1
Emery Hill St WEST SW1P 17 J4
Emery St STHWK SE1 18 A3
Emes Rd ERITH DA8 164 A8
Emilia Ct PEND EN3 80 A3
Emily Ct HARP AL5 33 K3
Emily Davison Dr EPSOM KT18 238 E10
Emily St CAN/RD E16 141 L8
Emley Rd ADL/WDHM KT15 195 L9
Emlyn La LHD/OX KT22 236 D4
Emlyn Rd HORL RH6 279 H1
REDH RH1 276 B8
SHB W12 156 B2
Emmanuel Cl GUW GU2 228 M7
Emmanuel Rd BAL SW12 180 D4
NTHWD HA6 92 D8
Emma Rd PLSTW E13 141 L4
Emmas Crs WARE SG12 26 C1
Emma St BETH E2 7 N4
Emmaus Wy CHIG IG7 102 D1
Emmets Cl WOKN/KNAP GU21 232 B4
Emmett Rd BH/WHM TN16 263 M6
Emmett Cl RAD WD7 57 J3
Emmott Av BARK/HLT IG6 103 J10
Emmott Cl CLDGN NW11 117 H4
WCHPL E1 140 D6
Emperor Pde HDN NW4 * 116 L2
Emperor's Ga SKENS SW7 15 H4
Empire Av UED N18 99 P6
WBLY HA9 * 115 P4
Empire Pde UED N18 * 99 P6
WBLY HA9 * 115 P4
Empire Rd GFD/PVL UB6 134 F1
Empire Sq HGT N6 * 117 P3
Empire Vls KWCM N10 167 P2
Empire Wy WBLY HA9 115 P4
Empire Wharf Rd
POP/IOD E14 161 H3
Empress Av CHING E4 100 D3
IL IG1 122 B7
MNPK E12 121 P5
WFD IG8 101 P7
Empress Dr CHST BR7 185 H2
Empress Pde CHING E4 * 100 C4
Empress Pl FUL/PGN SW6 14 E6
Empress Rd GVE DA12 191 N5
Empress St WALW SE17 18 F9
Empson St BOW E3 140 F10
Emsworth Cl CRAWE RH10 * 284 D10

ED N9 100 B2
Emsworth Rd BARK/HLT IG6 102 E10
Emsworth St BRXS/STRHM SW2 180 A5
Emu Rd VX/NE SW8 158 C8
Ena Rd STRHM/NOR SW16 202 E3
Enbrook St NKENS W10 2 B7
Endale Cl CAR SM5 202 D10
Endeavour Rd CHES/WCR EN8 62 D3
Endeavour Wy BARK IG11 143 K4
CROY/NA CR0 202 E7
WIM/MER SW19 179 L7
Enderby St GNWCH SE10 161 H7
Enderley Rd
KTN/HRWW/WS HA3 94 C9
Endersby Rd BAR EN5 76 F9
Enders Ct ENC/FH EN2 79 H4
Endersleigh Gdns HDN NW4 116 A9
Endlebury Rd CHING E4 101 H3
Endlesham Rd BAL SW12 180 B3
Endsleigh Cl SAND/SEL CR2 224 B6
Endsleigh Gdns IL IG1 122 C9
SURB KT6 199 H6
WOT/HER KT12 217 K2
WLSDN NW10 135 P8
Endsleigh Pl STPAN WC1H 11 J11
Endsleigh Rd NWDGN UB2 153 J2
REDH RH1 258 D3
WEA W13 134 F10
Endsleigh St STPAN WC1H 11 J11
Endway BRYLDS KT5 199 N4
Endwell Rd BROCKY SE4 160 G9
Endymion Cl HAT AL10 40 C3
Endymion Ms HAT AL10 40 C3
Endymion Rd
BRXS/STRHM SW2 180 C2
FSBYPK N4 119 H5
HAT AL10 40 C3
Energen Cl WLSDN NW10 136 A8
Enfield Cl UX/CGN UB8 131 M4
Enfield Rd ACT W3 155 P1
BTFD TW8 154 A6
ENC/FH EN2 78 F2
HTHAIR TW6 152 B10
IS N1 7 J1
Enford St CAMTN NW1 10 B1
Engadine Cl CROY/NA CR0 203 M2
Engadine St
WAND/EARL SW18 179 J3
Engate St LEW SE13 161 J7
Engayne Gdns UPMR RM14 126 C2
Engel Pk MLHL NW7 96 F7
Engineer Cl WOOL/PLUM SE18 146 P9
Engineers Wy WBLY HA9 115 N9
Englands La LOU IG10 82 G4
England's La HAMP NW3 4 A3
England Wy NWMAL KT3 199 N3
Englefield Cl CROY/NA CR0 203 L5
EGH TW20 171 M9
ENC/FH EN2 79 H1
STMC/STPC BR5 207 K1
Englefield Crs STMC/STPC BR5 207 K1
Englefield Pth
STMC/STPC BR5 207 K1
Englefield Rd IS N1 7 H1
WOKN/KNAP GU21 231 J3
Engleheart Dr
EBED/NFELT TW14 174 A1
Engleheart Rd CAT SE6 182 G6
Englehurst EGH TW20 171 M9
Englemere Pk COB KT11 218 B3
Englewood Rd BAL SW12 180 C2
English Gdns
STWL/WRAY TW19 150 C9
English St BOW E3 140 E9
Enid Cl LCOL/BKTW AL2 55 N5
Enid St BERM/RHTH SE16 19 N3
Enmore Av SNWD SE25 203 N3
Enmore Gdns
MORT/ESHN SW14 178 A1
Enmore Rd PUT/ROE SW15 156 F10
SNWD SE25 203 N3
STHL UB1 133 P6
Ennerdale Av HCH RM12 125 K9
STAN HA7 115 N1
Ennerdale Cl CRAWW RH11 283 N9
EBED/NFELT TW14 174 A1
STAL AL1 38 E5
SUT SM1 221 K3
Ennerdale Crs SL SL1 129 P6
Ennerdale Dr CDALE/KGS NW9 116 A3
Ennerdale Gdns WBLY HA9 115 J7
Ennerdale Rd BXLYHN DA7 164 B10
RCH/KEW TW9 155 M7
Ennersdale Rd LEW SE13 183 K4
Ennis Cl HARP AL5 20 E1
Ennismore Av CHSWK W4 156 D2
GFD/PVL UB6 134 D6
Ennismore Gdns SKENS SW7 15 M2
THDIT KT7 198 A6
Ennismore Gardens Ms
SKENS SW7 15 M3
Ennismore Ms SKENS SW7 15 M2
Ennismore St SKENS SW7 15 M3
Ennis Rd FSBYPK N4 119 H6
WOOL/PLUM SE18 162 A4
Ensign Cl HTHAIR TW6 152 E9
PUR/KEN CR8 223 K4
STWL/WRAY TW19 173 P1
Ensign Dr PLMGR N13 99 J2
Ensign St WCHPL E1 13 P7
Enslin Rd ELTH/MOT SE9 184 F4
Ensor Ms SKENS SW7 15 N5
Enstone Rd HGDN/ICK UB10 112 B4
PEND EN3 80 G1
Enterdent Rd GDST RH9 260 F8
Enterprise Cl CROY/NA CR0 203 H9
Enterprise Est GU GU1 * 250 B10
Enterprise Rw
SEVS/STOTM N15 119 N1
Enterprise Wy HHNE HP2 36 B1
TEDD TW11 176 B1
WAND/EARL SW18 157 K10
WLSDN NW10 136 D4
Enterprize Wy RGUW GU3 249 P10
Envis Wy RGUW GU3 249 H6
Envoy Av HTHAIR TW6 152 F9
Eothen Cl CTHM CR3 241 P10
Epcot Ms WLSDN NW10 136 D5
Epirus Ms FUL/PGN SW6 157 K6
Epirus Rd FUL/PGN SW6 157 K6
Epping Cl POP/IOD E14 160 G3
ROMW/RG RM7 124 C1
Epping Gld HHNE HP2 36 G1
Epping La ABR/ST RM4 83 P2
Epping New Rd BKHH IG9 101 N3
LOU IG10 81 P4
Epping Pl IS N1 6 B1
Epping Rd CHONG CM5 66 F5
EPP CM16 46 B8
HLWW/ROY CM19 45 K2
Epping Wy CHING E4 80 B9
Epple Rd FUL/PGN SW6 157 K6
Epsom Cl BXLYHN DA7 164 D2
NTHLT UB5 113 J4
Epsom College EW KT17 * 220 D6
Epsom La North EPSOM KT18 238 E8
Epsom La South
CHEAM SM3 201 H8
CROY/NA CR0 224 C1
EHSLY KT24 252 E5

EW KT17 220 C7
GDMY/SEVK IG3 123 J4
GU GU1 268 C1
LHD/OX KT22 236 C7
MRDN SM4 201 J6
RGUE GU4 250 D5
Epstein Rd THMD SE28 143 L10
Epworth Rd ISLW TW7 154 C6
Epworth St SDTCH EC2A 13 J1
Equity Sq BETH E2 * 7 M10
Erasmus St WEST SW1P 17 H6
Erconwald St SHB W12 136 C8
Erebus Dr THMD SE28 162 F2
Eresby Dr BECK BR3 204 F8
Eresby Pl KIL/WHAMP NW6 2 E4
Erica Cl CHOB/PIR GU24 212 D9
SL SL1 128 D9
Erica Ct WOKS/MYFD GU22 232 A4
Erica Gdns CROY/NA CR0 224 C1
Erica St SHB W12 136 D9
Erica Wy CRAWE RH10 284 G2
Eric Clarke La EHAM E6 142 G6
Ericson Cl WAND/EARL SW18 179 K1
Eric Est BOW E3 140 E6
Eric Rd CHDH RM6 123 N5
FSTGT E7 121 M9
WLSDN NW10 137 H6
Eric St BOW E3 140 E6
Eridge Green Cl
STMC/STPC BR5 207 M8
Eridge Rd CHSWK W4 156 A3
Erin Cl BMLY BR1 183 L8
Erindale WOOL/PLUM SE18 162 C5
Erindale Ter
WOOL/PLUM SE18 162 C5
Erin Ms WDGN N22 * 99 J9
Eriswell Crs WOT/HER KT12 216 G3
Eriswell Rd WOT/HER KT12 216 G3
Erith Ct PUR RM19 165 P3
Erith Crs CRW RM5 104 D9
Erith High St ERITH DA8 164 F4
Erith Rd BELV DA17 164 G4
BXLYHN DA7 164 C9
Erkenwald Cl CHERT KT16 195 H6
Erlanger Rd NWCR SE14 160 F10
Erlesmere Gdns HNWL W7 154 F2
Erlich Cots WCHPL E1 * 140 B7
Ermine Cl CHESW EN7 62 A7
HSLWW TW4 153 K8
STALW/RED AL3 37 P7
Ermine Rd LEW SE13 160 C9
SEVS/STOTM N15 119 N4
Ermine Side EN EN1 79 P9
Ermington Rd ELTH/MOT SE9 184 F5
Ermyn Cl LHD/OX KT22 237 J2
Ermyn Wy LHD/OX KT22 237 J2
Ernald Av EHAM E6 142 B4
Ernan Cl SOCK/AV RM15 146 A7
Ernan Rd SOCK/AV RM15 146 A7
Erncroft Wy TWK TW1 176 B2
Ernest Cl BECK BR3 204 D5
Ernest Gdns CHSWK W4 155 N5
Ernest Gv BECK BR3 204 E5
Ernest Rd EMPK RM11 125 M4
KUT/HW KT1 199 N2
Ernest St WCHPL E1 140 C6
Ernle Rd RYNPK SW20 178 E10
Ernshaw Pl PUT/ROE SW15 179 H1
Ernst Chain Rd GUW GU2 267 J1
Eripngham Rd PUT/ROE SW15 156 F9
Erridge Rd WIM/MER SW19 201 K2
Erriff Dr SOCK/AV RM15 146 F7
Errington Cl CDW/CHF RH16 70 B3
HAT AL10 40 B3
Errington Rd MV/WKIL W9 8 A1
Errol Gdns NWMAL KT3 200 D4
YEAD UB4 133 J6
Erroll Rd ROM RM1 124 G2
Erskine Cl SUT SM1 201 P10
Erskine Crs TOTM N17 120 A2
Erskine Hl GLDGN NW11 117 K2
Erskine Ms HAMP NW3 * 4 B4
Erskine Rd HAMP NW3 4 B4
SUT SM1 221 N1
WALTH E17 120 E2
Erwood Rd CHARL SE7 162 D4
Esam Wy STRHM/NOR SW16 181 H8
Escombe Dr GUW GU2 249 N5
Escot Rd SUN TW16 174 F10
Escott Pl CHERT KT16 214 F5
Escot Wy BAR EN5 76 F6
Escreet Gv WOOL/PLUM SE18 162 D3
Esdaile Gdns UPMR RM14 126 C5
Esdaile La HODD EN11 44 F4
Esher Av CHEAM SM3 200 G6
ROMW/RG RM7 124 D4
WOT/HER KT12 197 K4
Esher By-Pass
ESH/CLAY KT10 218 A2
Esher Crs HTHAIR TW6 152 E8
Esher Gdns WIM/MER SW19 178 A8
Esher Gn ESH/CLAY KT10 218 A1
Esher Green Dr
ESH/CLAY KT10 197 P9
Esher Ms MTCM CR4 202 B3
Esher Park Av ESH/CLAY KT10 218 A1
Esher Place Av ESH/CLAY KT10 217 P1
Esher Rd E/WMO/HCT KT8 198 C5
GDMY/SEVK IG3 123 J4
WOT/HER KT12 217 N1
Eskdale LCOL/BKTW AL2 57 J3
Eskdale Av NTHLT UB5 113 K6
Eskdale Cl DART DA2 168 A9
WBLY HA9 115 J7
Eskdale Gdns PUR/KEN CR8 223 L10
Eskdale Rd BXLYHN DA7 164 B10
UX/CGN UB8 131 L4
Eskley Gdns SOCK/AV RM15 146 A7
Eskmont Rdg NRWD SE19 181 N10
Esk Rd PLSTW E13 141 N6
Esk Wy ROM RM1 104 F8
Esmar Crs CDALE/KGS NW9 116 B4
Esmeralda Rd STHWK SE1 19 P6
Esmond Cl RAIN RM13 * 145 J2
Esmond Gdns CHSWK W4 156 A3
Esmond Rd CHSWK W4 156 A2
KIL/WHAMP NW6 2 D2
Esmond St PUT/ROE SW15 157 H10
Esparto St WAND/EARL SW18 179 L1
Essam Cl CTHM CR3 241 P10
Essendene Rd CTHM CR3 241 M9
Essenden Rd BELV DA17 164 B4
SAND/SEL CR2 224 A8
Essendine Rd MV/WKIL W9 8 F1
Essex Av ISLW TW7 154 D10
SLN SL2 129 H1
Essex Cl ADL/WDHM KT15 215 M1
MRDN SM4 200 D5
ROMW/RG RM7 124 C2
RSLP HA4 113 H6
WALTH E17 120 B6
Essex Ct BARN SW13 156 C3
EMB EC4Y 12 A6
Essex Gdns EMPK RM11 125 J5
FSBYPK N4 119 H5
Essex Park Ms ACT W3 136 C10
Essex Pl CHSWK W4 156 A2
Essex Place Sq CHSWK W4 * 156 A2
Essex Rd ACT W3 135 P3
BARK IG11 142 E7
BORE WD6 75 P1
CHDH RM6 123 K4
CHING E4 101 K2

CHSWK W4 156 A3
CSHM WG5 51 H5
DAGE RM10 124 D8
DART DA1 * 187 L2
ENC/FH EN2 79 L8
CVW DA11 190 D4
HART DA3 211 J2
HOD EN11 44 G2
IS N1 6 D1
LEY E10 121 H4
MNPK E12 122 B10
ROMW/RG RM7 124 D2
SWFD E18 101 N10
WALTH E17 120 C6
WAT WD17 73 H6
WLSDN NW10 137 H5
WTHK RM20 166 F5
Essex Rd South WAN E11 121 K5
Essex St FSTGT E7 121 M10
STAL AL1 38 D5
TPL/STR WC2R 12 A6
Essex Vls KENS W8 14 E2
Essex Wy CHONG CM5 66 F5
Essian St WCHPL E1 140 D7
Essoldo Wy EDGW HA8 115 L1
Estate Wy LEY E10 121 J6
Estcourt Rd FUL/PGN SW6 157 J6
SNWD SE25 204 A6
WAT WD17 73 K7
Estella Av NWMAL KT3 200 F3
Estelle Rd HAMP NW3 118 A9
Esterbrooke St WEST SW1P 17 H6
Este Rd BTSEA SW11 157 P9
Estfeld Cl HOD EN11 26 G10
Esther Cl WCHMH N21 99 H1
Esther Rd WAN E11 121 K5
Estoria Cl BRXS/STRHM SW2 181 H3
Estreham Rd
STRHM/NOR SW16 180 E9
Estridge Cl HSLW TW3 153 P10
Estuary Cl BARK IG11 143 L5
Eswyn Rd TOOT SW17 180 A7
Etchingham Pk Rd FNCH N3 97 L8
Etchingham Rd SRTFD E15 121 N9
Eternit Wk FUL/PGN SW6 156 F7
Etfield Gv SCUP DA14 185 L8
Ethel Bailey Cl
HOR/WEW KT19 219 M8
Ethelbert Cl BMLY BR1 200 B1
Ethelbert Gdns REDBR IG4 122 A8
Ethelbert Rd BMLY BR1 205 M5
ERITH DA8 164 E8
RYNPK SW20 200 D5
STMC/STPC BR5 207 N3
Ethelbert St BAL SW12 180 C2
Ethelburga Rd HARH RM3 105 N9
Ethelburga St BTSEA SW11 157 N9
Etheldene Av MUSWH N10 118 D2
Etheldene Rd SHB W12 136 E10
Ethelred Cl WGCE AL7 23 J6
Ethelred St WALW SE17 * 18 F7
Ethel Rd ASHF TW15 175 P8
CAN/RD E16 141 K9
Ethel St WALW SE17 18 E6
Ethel Ter ORP BR6 227 M5
Etheridge Rd CRICK NW2 116 F7
LOU IG10 83 J1
Etherley Rd SEVS/STOTM N15 119 K3
Etherow St EDUL SE22 181 P2
Etherstone Rd
STRHM/NOR SW16 181 H7
Ethnard Rd PECK SE15 160 A5
Ethronvi Rd BXLYHN DA7 164 A4
Etioe Rd LEY E10 121 P7
Etna Rd STALW/RED AL3 38 C5
Eton Av ALP/SUD HA0 115 H9
EBAR EN4 77 P10
HAMP NW3 3 M3
HEST TW5 153 N5
NFNCH/WDSPK N12 97 M8
NWMAL KT3 200 A5
Eton Cl DTCH/LGLY SL3 149 M5
WAND/EARL SW18 179 L3
Eton College Rd HAMP NW3 4 B3
Eton Ct STA TW18 173 J8
WBLY HA9 * 115 K7
Eton Garages HAMP NW3 * 3 P2
Eton Gv CDALE/KGS NW9 115 M1
LEW SE13 161 M1
Eton Hall HAMP NW3 * 4 B3
Eton Ri HAMP NW3 * 4 B3
Eton Rd DTCH/LGLY SL3 149 M5
HAMP NW3 4 B3
HYS/HAR UB3 152 A6
IL IG1 122 F9
ORP BR6 227 N4
Eton Sq WDSR SL4 149 J9
Eton St RCH/KEW TW9 177 J1
Eton Vls HAMP NW3 4 B3
Eton Wk DART DA1 165 K10
Eton Wick Rd WDSR SL4 148 B3
Etta St DEPT SE8 160 D5
Etton Cl HCH RM12 * 125 K10
Ettrick St POP/IOD E14 141 N8
Etwell St BRYLDS KT5 199 H7
Euclid Wy WTHK RM20 166 E3
Euesdon Cl ED N9 100 A4
Eugene Cl GPK RM2 125 K2
Eugenia Rd BERM/RHTH SE16 159 P8
Eunice Gv CSHM WG5 51 J9
Eureka Rd KUT/HW KT1 199 M2
Europa Pk WDSR SL4 149 P9
Europa Pl FSBYE EC1V 6 E10
Europa Rd GU GU1 229 P9
Europe Rd WOOL/PLUM SE18 146 C9
Eustace Pl WOOL/PLUM SE18 146 F3
Eustace Rd CHDH RM6 123 N5
EHAM E6 142 B4
FUL/PGN SW6 157 M6
RGUE GU4 250 D5
Euston Av WATW WD18 72 C3
Euston Centre CAMTN NW1 * 10 G1
Euston Rd CAMTN NW1 11 H1
CROY/NA CR0 203 H8
STPAN WC1H 11 J2
Euston Sq CAMTN NW1 11 H1
Euston St CAMTN NW1 11 H2
Euston Underpass
CAMTN NW1 11 H2
Evan Cook Cl PECK SE15 160 A2
Evandale Rd BRXN/ST SW9 158 B7
Evangelist Rd KTTN NW5 4 B1
Evans Cl GSTN WD25 72 G1
Evans Gv FELT TW13 173 H5
Evans Rd CAT SE6 183 H4
CHEAM SM3 201 J6
Evanston Av CHING E4 101 M3
Evanston Gdns REDBR IG4 122 A8
Evans Wf HHS/BOV HP3 35 P10
Evelina Rd PECK SE15 160 C2
PGE/AN SE20 182 G10
Eveline Lowe Est
BERM/RHTH SE16 19 N4
Eveline Rd MTCM CR4 202 A1
Evelyn Av CDALE/KGS NW9 116 A3
RSLP HA4 113 H4
Evelyn Cl WHTN TW2 176 A3
WOKS/MYFD GU22 232 G4
Evelyn Ct IS N1 * 7 H5
Evelyn Crs SUN TW16 195 J1
Evelyn Denington Rd
EHAM E6 142 A5
Evelyn Dr PIN HA5 93 M5

CHSWK W4 156 A3
SKENS SW7 15 K8
Evelyn Gv EA W5 135 L10
STHL UB1 133 N8
Evelyn Rd CAN/RD E16 143 K8
EBAR EN4 78 A8
RCH/KEW TW9 155 K9
RCHPK/HAM TW10 177 H5
RSEV TN14 247 K2
WALTH E17 120 E2
WIM/MER SW19 179 L8
Evelyns Cl UX/CGN UB8 131 L8
Evelyn Sharp Cl GPK RM2 * 125 L1
Evelyn St DEPT SE8 160 E5
GNWCH SE10 160 E5
Evelyn Ter RCH/KEW TW9 155 K9
Evelyn Wk CRAWE RH10 285 P10
IS N1 6 G7
Evelyn Wy COB KT11 230 N2
HOR/WEW KT19 219 M7
SUN TW16 196 C1
WLGTN SM6 222 E1
Evensford Wy WATW WD18 72 D10
Evenwood Cl
PUT/ROE SW15 157 M8
Everard Cl STAL AL1 38 C8
Everard Av HAYES BR2 199 N8
SL SL1 149 K1
Everatt Cl WAND/EARL SW18 * 179 J2
Everdon Rd BARN SW13 156 D5
Everest Cl GVW DA11 190 B6
Everest Pl POP/IOD E14 141 N7
SWLY BR8 208 A4
Everest Rd ELTH/MOT SE9 164 F10
STALW/WRAY TW19 173 N3
Everett Cl BUSH WD23 94 D2
CHESW EN7 61 K1
Everett Wk BELV DA17 * 164 C5
Everglade BH/WHM TN16 244 A4
Everglade Strd
CDALE/KGS NW9 96 C9
Evergreen Cl PGE/AN SE20 182 B10
Evergreen Oak Av WDSR SL4 149 M9
Evergreen Wk HHS/BOV HP3 35 P8
Everilda St IS N1 5 P6
Evering Rd STNW/STAM N16 119 N8
Everington Rd MUSWH N10 98 A10
Everington St HMSMTH W6 157 H6
Everitt Rd WLSDN NW10 136 A5
Everlands Cl
WOKS/MYFD GU22 232 B4
Everleigh St FSBYPK N4 118 G6
Eve Rd ISLW TW7 154 C6
SRTFD E15 141 K4
TOTM N17 119 M1
WAN E11 121 K5
WOKN/KNAP GU21 232 E1
Eversfield Gdns EDGW HA8 96 B6
Eversfield Rd RCH/KEW TW9 155 L8
REIG RH2 259 M5
Evershed Wk CHSWK W4 155 P2
Evershot St FSBYPK N4 118 G6
Eversleigh Rd BAR EN5 77 M9
BTSEA SW11 158 A10
EHAM E6 142 A8
FNCH N3 97 J3
Eversley Av BXLYHN DA7 164 G4
WBLY HA9 115 M7
Eversley Cl LOU IG10 82 F7
WCHMH N21 99 H4
Eversley Crs ISLW TW7 154 A7
RSLP HA4 112 F7
WCHMH N21 99 H4
Eversley Cross BXLYHN DA7 164 F8
Eversley Mt WCHMH N21 99 G10
Eversley Pk WIM/MER SW19 178 B8
Eversley Park Rd
WCHMH N21 99 H4
Eversley Rd BRYLDS KT5 199 L4
CHARL SE7 161 P5
NRWD SE19 181 N5
Eversley Wy CROY/NA CR0 204 F2
EGH TW20 194 F2
Everthorpe Rd PECK SE15 159 J3
Everton Bldgs CAMTN NW1 4 C10
Everton Dr STAN HA7 115 K3
Everton Rd CROY/NA CR0 203 P8
Evesham Av WALTH E17 101 H10
Evesham Cl BELMT SM2 221 J5
GFD/PVL UB6 134 B4
REIG RH2 259 L6
Evesham Gn MRDN SM4 201 L6
Evesham Rd FBAR/BDGN N11 98 C5
GVE DA12 190 G5
MRDN SM4 201 L6
SRTFD E15 141 L8
Evesham Rd North REIG RH2 259 L6
Evesham St NTGHL W11 136 G7
Evesham Ter SURB KT6 * 199 J5
Evesham Wk BRXN/ST SW9 158 B8
CMBW SE5 159 H8
Evesham Wy BTSEA SW11 158 A10
CLAY IG5 122 A1
Evette Ms CLAY IG5 122 A1
Evreham Rd IVER SL0 131 H3
Evry Rd SCUP DA14 186 C3
Ewald Rd FUL/PGN SW6 157 J7
Ewanrigg Ter WFD IG8 101 H3
Ewan Rd HARH RM3 105 N9
Ewart Gv WDGN N22 99 H9
Ewart Pl BOW E3 * 141 J1
Ewart Rd FSTH SE23 182 C3
Ewe Cl HOLWY N7 * 5 M1
Ewelands HORL RH6 280 D1
Ewell By-Pass EW KT17 220 D3
Ewell Court Av
HOR/WEW KT19 220 B3
Ewell Downs Rd EW KT17 220 D7
Ewell House Gv EW KT17 220 C7
Ewell House Gv EW KT17 * 220 C7
Ewell House Pde EW KT17 * 220 C7
Ewellhurst Rd CLAY IG5 103 P10
Ewell Park Gdns EW KT17 220 D5
Ewell Park Wy EW KT17 220 D3
Ewell Rd SURB KT6 199 N8
SURB KT6 199 M5
CHEAM SM3 201 H4
Ewelme Rd FSTH SE23 182 G3
Ewen Crs BRXS/STRHM SW2 180 B1
Ewer St STHWK SE1 12 E10
Ewhurst Av SAND/SEL CR2 224 C7
Ewhurst Cl BELMT SM2 220 F5
CRAWW RH11 282 D2
WCHPL E1 140 G7
Ewhurst Rd BROCKY SE4 183 L1
CRAWW RH11 282 D3
Exbury Rd CAT SE6 182 C6
Excalibur Cl CRAWW RH11 283 H7
Excel Ct LSQ/SEVD WC2H * 11 H7
Excel Marina CAN/RD E16 141 P2
Excel Waterfront CAN/RD E16 141 P2
Exchange Ar LVPST EC2M * 13 J3
Exchange Cl FBAR/BDGN N11 98 A3
Exchange Rd ASC SL5 219 J3
CRAWE RH10 285 H8
WATW WD18 23 F4
Exchange Sq SDTCH EC2A * 13 J3
Exchange St ROMW/RG RM7 124 C3
Executive Pk STAL AL1 * 38 G6
Exeforde Av ASHF TW15 174 B7

SKENS SW7 15 K8
Exeter Cl EHAM E6 142 C8
WATN WD24 73 K6
Exeter Gdns IL IG1 122 A7
Exeter Ms FUL/PGN SW6 157 L5
Exeter Pde CRICK NW2 * 2 E1
Exeter Pl GUW GU2 * 249 H5
Exeter Rd CAN/RD E16 141 M7
CRICK NW2 2 E1
CROY/NA CR0 203 M7
DAGE RM10 124 D1
ED N9 100 B3
FELT TW13 175 N6
GVE DA12 190 G6
HTHAIR TW6 152 F9
PEND EN3 80 G1
RYLN/HDSTN HA2 113 M7
STHGT/OAK N14 98 C2
WALTH E17 120 F3
WELL DA16 163 P3
Exeter St COVGDN WC2E 11 M7
Exeter Wy HTHAIR TW6 152 F9
NWCR SE14 160 L6
Exford Gdns LEE/GVPK SE12 183 N5
Exford Rd LEE/GVPK SE12 183 N5
Exhibition Rd SKENS SW7 15 H2
Exit Rd EFNCH N2 97 N10
Exmoor Cl BARK/HLT IG6 102 F9
Exmoor St NKENS W10 136 C6
Exmouth Market CLKNW EC1R 12 A1
Exmouth Ms CAMTN NW1 * 5 H10
Exmouth Pl HACK E8 140 A3
Exmouth Rd GRAYS RM17 167 N5
RSLP HA4 113 K8
WALTH E17 120 E3
WELL DA16 163 P1
YEAD UB4 132 F5
Exmouth St WCHPL E1 140 B8
Exning Rd CAN/RD E16 141 K6
Exon St WALW SE17 19 L6
Explorer Av STWL/WRAY TW19 173 P4
Explorer Dr WATW WD18 72 C10
Express Dr GDMY/SEVK IG3 123 L6
Extension Rd HERT/BAY SG13 25 N1
Exton Gdns BCTR RM8 123 N10
Exton Rd WLSDN NW10 135 P2
Exton St STHWK SE1 12 A10
Eybright Cl CROY/NA CR0 204 C9
Eyhurst Av EMPK RM11 125 H8
Eyhurst Cl CRICK NW2 116 F7
KWD/TDW/WH KT20 239 H10
Eyhurst Pk
KWD/TDW/WH KT20 * 239 J10
Eyhurst Sp
KWD/TDW/WH KT20 239 J10
Eylewood Rd WNWD SE27 181 K8
Eynella Rd DUL SE21 181 P4
Eynham Rd SHB W12 136 F8
Eynsford Cl STMC/STPC BR5 206 F2
Eynsford Crs BXLY DA5 164 G10
Eynsford Ri EYN DA4 199 H1
Eynsford Rd EYN DA4 209 N1
GDMY/SEVK IG3 123 J8
SWCM DA10 189 H1
SWLY BR8 208 F6
Eynsford Ter WDR/YW UB7 132 A8
Eynsham Dr ABYW SE2 163 L2
Eynswood Dr SCUP DA14 186 C4
Eyot Gdns HMSMTH W6 156 C4
Eyre Cl GPK RM2 125 J2
Eyre Street HI CLKNW EC1R 12 A2
Eyston Dr WEY KT13 216 B6
Eythorne Rd BRXN/ST SW9 159 H7
Ezra St BETH E2 7 M9

**F**

Faber Gdns HDN NW4 116 D3
Fabian Rd FUL/PGN SW6 157 J5
Fabian St EHAM E6 142 C6
The Facade FSTH SE23 * 182 B5
REIG RH2 * 257 K9
Fackenden La BGR/WK TN15 229 L6
Factory La CROY/NA CR0 203 H9
TOTM N17 99 N10
Factory Pl POP/IOD E14 160 F8
Factory Rd CAN/RD E16 142 B10
CVW DA11 189 P2
Factory Yd BEAC HP9 * 88 D10
HNWL W7 134 D10
Faggoters La CHONG CM5 49 H2
Faggots Cl RAD WD7 75 H1
Faggotters La HNWL W7 * 116 C1
Faggs Rd EBED/NFELT TW14 152 C10
Fagnall La AMSS HP7 48 B5
Fairacre ISLW TW7 * 154 A7
NWMAL KT3 200 B3
Fairacres COB KT11 217 L8
CROY/NA CR0 224 C5
Fair Acres HAYES BR2 200 B3
Fairacres KWD/TDW/WH KT20 238 C10
PUT/ROE SW15 156 C10
RSLP HA4 112 C5
Fairacres Cl POTB/CUF EN6 59 J9
Fairbairn Cl PUR/KEN CR8 223 J5
Fairbairn Gn BRXN/ST SW9 158 B6
Fairbank Av ORP BR6 226 E9
Fairbank Est IS N1 * 7 H5
Fairbanks Rd TOTM N17 119 P1
Fairbourne COB KT11 217 L9
Fairbourne
WOKN/KNAP GU21 231 M3
Fairbourne Cl CTHM CR3 * 241 M9
Fairbourne Rd TOTM N17 119 N1
Fairbridge Rd ARCH N19 118 E8
Fairbrook Cl PLMGR N13 99 H6
Fairburn Cl BORE WD6 75 H5
Fairby Hl HART DA3 211 K5
Fairby Rd LEE/GVPK SE12 183 N1
Fairchild Cl BTSEA SW11 157 N1
Fairchildes Av CROY/NA CR0 243 J1
Fairchildes Rd WARL CR6 243 J3
Fairchild Pl SDTCH EC2A * 13 K2
Fair Cl BUSH WD23 94 A1
Fairclough Cl NTHLT UB5 133 N3
Fairclough St WCHPL E1 13 P6
Faircroft SLN SL2 128 C5
Faircross Av BARK IG11 124 D8
CRW RM5 104 C8
Faircross Wy STAL AL1 38 F2
Fairdale Gdns HYS/HAR UB3 153 H1
PUT/ROE SW15 156 G2
Fairdene Rd COUL/CHIP CR5 240 G4
Fairey Av HYS/HAR UB3 152 G2
Fairey CDALE/KGS NW9 96 C10
Fairfax Av EW KT17 220 E9
REDH RH1 258 A9
Fairfax Cl OXTED RH8 261 J6
WOT/HER KT12 195 L9
Fairfax Gdns BKHTH/KID SE3 162 D2
Fairfax Ms CAN/RD E16 142 B10
CEND/HSY/T N8 * 117 P1
PUT/ROE SW15 156 G2
Fairfax Pl KIL/WHAMP NW6 2 B2
WKENS W14 * 3 G10
Fairfax Rd CEND/HSY/T N8 117 N1
CHSWK W4 156 B2
DART DA1 187 P2
GRAYS RM17 167 N4
HERT/BAY SG13 25 K3
KIL/WHAMP NW6 2 C2
TEDD TW11 176 A1
WOKS/MYFD GU22 232 E8
Fairfax Wy MUSWH N10 98 A6
Fairfield Ap STWL/WRAY TW19 172 F1
Fairfield Av CDW/CHF RH16 147 K2

DTCH/LGLY SL3 ... 149 P6
EDGW HA8 ... 95 N7
HDN NW4 ... 116 E4
HORL RH6 ... 280 D8
OXHEY WD19 ... 93 K4
RSLP HA4 ... 112 D5
STA TW18 ... 173 J7
UPMR RM14 ... 126 B8
WHTN TW2 ... 176 A4
Fairfield Cl BFN/LL DA15 ... 185 J2
  BGR/WK TN15 ... 247 P4
  GT/LBKH KT23 ... 254 A1
  GUW GU2 ... 249 C8
  HARP AL5 ... 20 C2
  HCH RM12 ... 125 H6
  HOR/WEW KT19 ... 220 B2
  MTCM CR4 ... 179 P10
  NFNCH/WDSPK N12 ... 97 N5
  PEND EN3 ... 80 C8
  RAD WD7 ... 74 D5
Fairfield Cnr KUT/HW KT1 * ... 199 L2
Fairfield Ct RSLP HA4 ... 112 E6
Fairfield Crs EDGW HA8 ... 95 N7
Fairfield Dr BROX EN10 ... 48 E10
  DORK RH4 ... 254 C10
  GFD/PVL UB6 ... 135 H3
  RYLN/HDSTN HA2 ... 114 B1
  WAND/EARL SW18 ... 179 L1
Fairfield East KUT/HW KT1 ... 199 K2
Fairfield Gdns
  CEND/HSY/T N8 ... 118 F3
Fairfield La CHARL SE7 ... 162 A5
Fairfield La COB/PIR GU24 ... 212 E6
  SL SL2 ... 128 C4
Fairfield North KUT/CMB KT2 ... 199 K2
Fairfield Pk COB KT11 ... 217 L10
Fairfield Pth CROY/NA CR0 ... 203 L10
Fairfield Pl KUT/HW KT1 ... 199 K3
Fairfield Ri GUW GU2 ... 249 L9
Fairfield Rd BECK BR3 ... 204 D2
  BMLY BR1 ... 183 M10
  BOW E3 ... 140 F4
  BRW CM14 ... 107 H4
  BXLYHN DA7 ... 164 A8
  CEND/HSY/T N8 ... 118 F3
  CHONG CM5 ... 67 N5
  CROY/NA CR0 ... 203 L10
  EPP CM16 ... 65 L5
  HOD EN11 ... 44 B7
  IL IG1 ... 142 E1
  KUT/HW KT1 ... 199 K2
  LHD/OX KT22 ... 236 G7
  SL SL1 ... 128 B5
  STHL UB1 ... 133 N8
  STMC/STPC BR5 ... 206 G6
  STWL/WRAY TW19 ... 172 A2
  UED N18 ... 99 P5
  UX/CGN UB8 ... 131 N1
  WALTH E17 ... 100 D10
  WDR/YW UB7 ... 132 P10
  WFD IG8 ... 101 M7
Fairfields CAT SE6 ... 182 G3
  CHERT KT16 ... 195 K8
Fairfields Cl CDALE/KGS NW9 ... 115 P5
Fairfields Crs CDALE/KGS NW9 ... 115 P5
Fairfield South KUT/HW KT1 ... 199 K3
Fairfield St WAND/EARL SW18 ... 179 L1
Fairfield Wk LHD/OX KT22 ... 236 G7
Fairfield Wy BAR EN5 ... 77 K4
  COUL/CHIP CR5 ... 222 E6
  HOR/WEW KT19 ... 220 B2
Fairfield West KUT/HW KT1 ... 199 K2
Fairfolds GSTN WD25 ... 73 M1
Fairford CAT SE6 ... 182 G3
Fairford Av BXLYHN DA7 ... 164 D7
  CROY/NA CR0 ... 204 C5
  HARH RM3 ... 106 A7
  REIG RH2 ... 257 M8
Fairford Cl BELMT SM2 * ... 221 L4
Fairford Gdns WPK KT4 ... 200 C10
Fairford Wy HARH RM3 ... 106 A7
Fairgreen EBAR EN4 ... 78 A7
Fairgreen East EBAR EN4 * ... 78 A7
Fairgreen Rd THHTH CR7 ... 203 J5
Fairham Av SOCK/AV RM15 ... 146 F9
Fairhaven EGH TW20 ... 172 C8
  LCOL/BKTW AL2 * ... 56 C3
Fairhaven Av CROY/NA CR0 ... 204 C6
Fairhaven Ct EGH TW20 ... 172 C8
Fairhaven Crs OXHEY WD19 ... 93 H4
Fairhaven Rd REDH RH1 ... 258 F5
Fairhazel Gdns KIL/WHAMP NW6 ... 3 J1
Fairhill HHS/BOV HP3 ... 36 A10
Fairholme EBED/NFELT TW14 ... 174 A3
Fairholme Av GPK RM2 ... 125 H3
Fairholme Cl FNCH N3 ... 117 H2
Fairholme Crs ASHTD KT21 ... 237 H3
  YEAD UB4 ... 132 G6
Fairholme Gdns FNCH N3 ... 117 H1
  UPMR RM14 ... 126 F8
Fairholme Rd ASHF TW15 ... 157 P8
  CROY/NA CR0 ... 203 H7
  HRW HA1 ... 114 D3
  IL IG1 ... 122 C5
  SUT SM1 ... 221 J3
  WKENS W14 ... 14 C8
Fairholt Rd STNW/STAM N16 ... 119 L6
Fairholt St SKENS SW7 ... 15 M3
Fairkytes Av EMPK RM11 ... 125 K4
Fairland Rd SRTFD E15 ... 141 L7
Fairlands Av BKHH IG9 ... 101 M3
  RGUW GU3 ... 249 J2
  SUT SM1 ... 201 K9
  THHTH CR7 ... 202 G4
Fairlands Rd RGUW GU3 ... 249 J1
Fair La COUL/CHIP CR5 ... 257 M5
Fairlawn CHARL SE7 ... 161 P6
  GT/LBKH KT23 ... 235 N10
  WEY KT13 ... 216 F2
Fairlawn Av BXLYHN DA7 ... 163 N8
  CHSWK W4 ... 155 P3
  EFNCH N2 ... 117 J2
Fairlawn Cl ESH/CLAY KT10 ... 218 E3
  FELT TW13 ... 175 N7
  KUTN/CMB KT2 ... 177 H7
  STHGT/OAK N14 ... 78 E10
Fairlawn Ct CHARL SE7 * ... 161 P6
Fairlawn Dr REDH RH1 ... 275 P2
  WFD IG8 ... 101 M8
Fairlawn Gdns STHL UB1 ... 133 N8
Fairlawn Gv BNSTD SM7 ... 221 N9
  CHSWK W4 ... 155 P3
Fairlawn Pk SYD SE26 ... 182 D8
  WOKN/KNAP GU21 ... 232 B1
Fairlawn Rd CAR SM5 ... 221 N9
  WIM/MER SW19 ... 179 J10
Fairlawns ADL/WDHM KT15 ... 215 J7
  HORL RH6 ... 280 C5
  PIN HA5 ... 93 K5
  SUN TW16 ... 197 H3
  TWK TW1 ... 176 A3
  WAT WD17 ... 72 C5
Fairlawns Cl EMPK RM11 ... 125 K5
  STA TW18 ... 173 L9
Fairlea Pl EA W5 ... 135 K4
Fair Leas CSHM HP5 ... 50 B6
Fairley Wy CHESW EN7 ... 62 A4
Fairlie Gdns FSTH SE23 ... 182 A5
Fairlie Rd SL SL1 ... 128 E4
Fairlight Av CHING E4 ... 101 L1
  WFD IG8 ... 101 K7
  WLSDN NW10 ... 137 H3
Fairlight Cl CHING E4 ... 101 L1
  WPK KT4 ... 220 F1
Fairlight Cross HART DA3 ... 211 N1
Fairlight Dr UX/CGN UB8 ... 131 K2
Fairlight Rd TOOT SW17 ... 179 N7
Fairlop Cl HCH RM12 ... 145 J2
Fairlop Gdns BARK/HLT IG6 ... 102 F8


Fairlop Pl STJWD NW8 ... 3 M10
Fairlop Rd BARK/HLT IG6 ... 102 F10
  WAN E11 ... 121 J3
Fairmark Dr HGDN/ICK UB10 ... 132 B2
Fairmead BMLY BR1 ... 206 C4
  BRYLDS KT5 ... 199 N8
  WOKN/KNAP GU21 ... 231 P4
Fairmead Av HARP AL5 ... 20 C4
Fairmead Cl BMLY BR1 ... 206 C4
  HEST TW5 ... 153 L6
  NWMAL KT3 ... 200 A3
Fairmead Crs EDGW HA8 ... 95 P5
Fairmead Gdns REDBR IG4 ... 122 A3
Fairmead Rd ARCH N19 ... 118 F8
  CROY/NA CR0 ... 203 H7
  LOU IG10 ... 81 N8
Fairmeads COB KT11 ... 217 M9
  LOU IG10 ... 82 E6
Fairmile Av COB KT11 ... 217 M10
  STRHM/NOR SW16 ... 180 E8
Fairmile Ct COB KT11 ... 217 N8
Fairmile La COB KT11 ... 217 L8
Fairmile Park Copse COB KT11 ... 217 N9
Fairmile Park Rd COB KT11 ... 217 N9
Fairmont Cl BELV DA17 ... 164 A4
Fairmount Rd BRXS/STRHM SW2 ... 180 C2
Fair Oak Cl LHD/OX KT22 ... 218 C7
Fairoak Cl PUR/KEN CR8 ... 241 J1
  STMC/STPC BR5 ... 206 B7
Fairoak Dr ELTH/MOT SE9 ... 184 G1
Fairoak La CHSGTN KT9 ... 218 D7
Fair Oak Pl BARK/HLT IG6 ... 102 F10
Fairoaks Gv PEND EN3 ... 80 C3
Fairs Rd LHD/OX KT22 ... 236 F5
Fairstead Wk IS N1 * ... 6 C1
Fairstone Ct HORL RH6 ... 280 C3
Fair St HSLW TW3 ... 19 K1
  STHWK SE1 ... 19 K1
Fairthorn Rd CHARL SE7 ... 161 M4
Fairtrough Rd ORP BR6 ... 227 L9
Fairview ERITH DA8 ... 164 C6
  EW KT17 ... 220 F7
  GDST RH9 ... 260 A4
  HART DA3 * ... 210 G10
Fair Vw POTB/CUF EN6 ... 59 J2
Fairview Av WOKN/KNAP GU21 ... 232 A6
  RAIN RM13 ... 145 L4
  WOKS/MYFD GU22 ... 232 A6
Fair View Cl WALTH E17 ... 100 D9
Fairview Cl CHIG IG7 ... 103 H5
  SYD SE26 ... 182 D8
  WOKS/MYFD GU22 ... 232 A6
Fairview Crs RYLN/HDSTN HA2 ... 113 P6
Fairview Dr CHIG IG7 ... 103 H5
  ORP BR6 ... 226 G1
  SHPTN TW17 ... 195 J4
  WAT WD17 ... 72 C2
Fairview Gdns WFD IG8 ... 101 N9
Fairview Pl BRXS/STRHM SW2 ... 180 A6
Fairview Rd CHIG IG7 ... 103 H5
  ENC/FH EN2 ... 79 M1
  EW KT17 ... 220 C7
  MEO DA13 ... 190 A10
  SEVS/STOTM N15 ... 119 N4
  SLN SL2 ... 128 F8
  STRHM/NOR SW16 ... 180 A2
  SUT SM1 ... 221 N2
Fairview Vs CHING E4 * ... 100 F8
Fairview Wy EDGW HA8 ... 95 M5
Fairwater Av WELL DA16 ... 163 K10
Fairwater Dr ADL/WDHM KT15 ... 215 P5
Fairway BXLYHS DA6 ... 185 P1
  CAR SM5 ... 221 M7
  CDW/CHF RM16 ... 147 N10
  CHERT KT16 ... 195 L8
  CRAWE RH10 ... 285 J4
  CRAWW RH11 ... 282 C6
  GU GU1 ... 250 C10
  HHS/BOV HP3 ... 35 P7
  RYNPK SW20 ... 200 F3
  SBW CM21 ... 30 A1
  STMC/STPC BR5 ... 206 C6
  WARE SG12 ... 26 B3
  WFD IG8 ... 101 P6
Fairway Av BORE WD6 ... 75 N6
  CDALE/KGS NW9 ... 115 N1
  WDR/YW UB7 ... 131 M10
Fairway Cl CRAWE RH10 ... 285 H3
  CROY/NA CR0 ... 204 D5
  GLDGN NW11 ... 117 M5
  HOR/WEW KT19 ... 219 P1
  HSLWW TW4 ... 175 K1
  LCOL/BKTW AL2 * ... 56 B3
  WLSDN NW10 * ... 119 P1
  WOKS/MYFD GU22 ... 231 N5
Fairway Dr GFD/PVL UB6 ... 134 A2
  RDART DA2 ... 188 A3
  THMD SE28 ... 143 N8
Fairway Gdns BECK BR3 ... 205 J6
  IL IG1 ... 122 F10
Fairways ASHF TW15 ... 174 B9
  CHES/WCR EN8 ... 62 C2
  ISLW TW7 ... 154 D7
  PUR/KEN CR8 ... 241 K3
  STAN HA7 ... 95 K10
  TEDD TW11 ... 177 J10
  WALTH E17 * ... 121 H2
The Fairways
  CHES/WCR EN8 * ... 62 C2
  WDGN N22 ... 275 N3
The Fairway ABLGY WD5 ... 54 E8
  ACT W3 ... 136 B8
  ALP/SUD HA0 ... 114 G7
  BAR EN5 ... 77 L10
  E/WMO/HCT KT8 ... 198 A3
  GVW DA11 ... 190 D5
  HAYES BR2 ... 226 C5
  HGDN/ICK UB10 ... 132 A5
  HLWS CM18 ... 6 A8
  HNWL W7 ... 134 D9
  LHD/OX KT22 ... 236 F4
  MLHL NW7 ... 96 A4
  NTHLT UB5 ... 134 B1
  NTHWD HA6 ... 92 F5
  NWMAL KT3 ... 200 A1
  PLMGR N13 ... 99 K4
  RGUW GU3 ... 231 H10
  RSLP HA4 ... 113 K9
  SL SL1 ... 128 B5
  STHGT/OAK N14 ... 98 C10
  UPMR RM14 ... 126 B5
  WEY KT13 ... 216 B7
Fairweather Cl
  SEVS/STOTM N15 ... 119 M2
Fairweather Rd
  STNW/STAM N16 ... 119 P4
Fairwell La EHSLY KT24 ... 252 C4
Fairwyn Rd SYD SE26 ... 182 D6
Faithfield BUSH WD23 * ... 73 M10
Faithorn Cl CSHM HP5 ... 50 B6
Fakenham Cl MLHL NW7 ... 96 C6
  NTHLT UB5 ... 133 P1
Fakruddin St WCHPL E1 ... 13 P1
Falaise EGH TW20 ... 172 B8
Falaize Av IL IG1 ... 122 D3
Falcon Av BMLY BR1 ... 206 A3
  GRAYS RM17 ... 167 N6
Falconberg Ct
  SOHO/SHAV W1D * ... 11 J5
Falcon Cl CHSWK W4 ... 155 N5
  CRAWW RH11 ... 282 C6
  DART DA1 ... 171 H4
  NTHWD HA6 ... 40 C6
  SBW CM21 ... 29 N2
Falcon Crs PEND EN3 ... 80 D8
Falconer Rd BARK/HLT IG6 ... 103 L1
  BUSH WD23 ... 73 P10


Falconers Pk SBW CM21 ... 29 N2
Falconhurst LHD/OX KT22 ... 236 C1
Falcon La BTSEA SW11 ... 157 P9
Falcon Rd BTSEA SW11 ... 157 P9
  GU GU1 ... 250 A10
  HPTN TW12 ... 175 N10
  PEND EN3 ... 80 F1
Falcons Cl BH/WHM TN16 ... 244 A5
Falcon St PLSTW E13 ... 141 M6
Falcon Ter BTSEA SW11 ... 157 P9
Falcon Wy CDALE/KGS NW9 ... 96 B10
  GSTN WD25 ... 55 M10
  KTN/HRWW/WS HA3 ... 115 K3
  POP/IOD E14 ... 160 G3
  SUN TW16 ... 196 F2
  WAN E11 ... 121 M2
  WCCE AL7 ... 25 H5
Falconwood EGH TW20 ... 172 B8
Falconwood Av WELL DA16 ... 162 G8
Falconwood Pde WELL DA16 ... 163 H10
Falconwood Rd CROY/NA CR0 ... 224 E5
Falcourt Cl SUT SM1 ... 221 L2
Falkirk Gdns OXHEY WD19 ... 93 L6
Falkirk St IS N1 ... 7 K3
Falkland Av FBAR/BDGN N11 ... 98 B5
  FNCH N3 ... 117 K8
Falkland Gv DORK RH4 ... 272 F3
Falkland Park Av SNWD SE25 ... 203 J8
Falkland Pl KTTN NW5 ... 118 D10
Falkland Rd BAR EN5 ... 77 H6
  CEND/HSY/T N8 ... 119 H2
  DORK RH4 ... 272 F3
  KTTN NW5 ... 118 D10
Falloden Wy GLDGN NW11 ... 117 K2
Fallow Court Av
  NFNCH/WDSPK N12 ... 97 M7
Fallowfield STAN HA7 ... 94 F1
  WCCE AL7 ... 23 H5
Fallowfield Cl DEN/HRF UB9 ... 91 M9
Fallowfield Ct STAN HA7 ... 94 F1
Fallow Flds LOU IG10 ... 101 P1
Fallowfield Dr
  NFNCH/WDSPK N12 ... 97 P7
Fallowfield Wy HORL RH6 ... 280 D7
Fallow Flds SAND/SEL CR2 ... 223 N7
Fallows Cl EFNCH N2 ... 97 N10
Fallsbrook Rd STRHM/NOR SW16 ... 180 C9
Falman Cl ED N9 ... 99 P2
Falmer Cl CRAWW RH11 ... 283 N9
Falmer Rd EN EN1 ... 79 M8
  SEVS/STOTM N15 ... 119 K3
  WALTH E17 ... 120 G1
Falmouth Av CHING E4 ... 101 J6
Falmouth Cl LEE/GVPK SE12 ... 183 L1
  WDGN N22 ... 98 C8
Falmouth Gdns REDBR IG4 ... 122 A2
Falmouth Rd SL SL1 ... 128 F8
  STHWK SE1 ... 18 F4
  WOT/HER KT12 ... 217 K1
Falmouth St SRTFD E15 ... 121 J10
Falstaff Gdns STAL AL1 ... 38 A9
Falstaff Ms HPTN TW12 ... 176 C8
Fambridge Cl SYD SE26 ... 182 F7
Fambridge Rd BCTR RM8 ... 124 B6
Famet Av PUR/KEN CR8 ... 223 K9
Famet Cl PUR/KEN CR8 ... 223 K9
Famet Wk PUR/KEN CR8 ... 223 K9
Fanhams Rd WARE SG12 ... 26 D1
Fanns Ri PUR RM19 ... 168 G5
Fann St FARR EC1M ... 12 C1
Fanshawe Av BARK IG11 ... 142 F1
Fanshawe Crs DAGW RM9 ... 123 P10
  EMPK RM11 ... 125 K1
Fanshawe Rd
  CDW/CHF RM16 ... 168 D2
  RCHPK/HAM TW10 ... 177 H7
Fanshaws La HERT/BAY SG13 ... 43 J4
Fanthorpe St PUT/ROE SW15 ... 156 F9
Fantail Cl THMD SE28 ... 143 M8
Fantasia Ct BRW CM14 ... 106 G6
Faraday Av SCUP DA14 ... 185 L5
Faraday Cl HOLWY N7 ... 5 P2
  WATW WD18 ... 72 E10
Faraday Pl E/WMO/HCT KT8 ... 135 P9
Faraday Rd ACT W3 ... 135 N4
  CRAWE RH10 ... 284 A5
  E/WMO/HCT KT8 ... 135 P9
  GU GU1 ... 249 P10
  NKENS W10 ... 8 A3
  SL SL2 ... 128 G2
  SRTFD E15 ... 141 L7
  STHL UB1 ... 134 A9
  WELL DA16 ... 163 K9
  WIM/MER SW19 ... 179 L9
Faraday Wy STMC/STPC BR5 ... 201 N5
  WOOL/PLUM SE18 ... 162 A2
Fareham Rd EBED/NFELT TW14 ... 175 K3
Fareham St SOHO/CST W1F ... 11 J3
Far End HAT AL10 ... 40 E7
Farewell Pl MTCM CR4 ... 201 N4
Faringdon Av HARH RM3 ... 106 A5
  HAYES BR2 ... 226 D7
Faringford Cl POTB/CUF EN6 ... 59 P1
Faringford Rd SRTFD E15 ... 141 K7
Faris Barn Dr
  ADL/WDHM KT15 ... 215 J8
Faris La ADL/WDHM KT15 ... 215 J7
Farjeon Rd BKHTH/KID SE3 ... 162 E1
Farland Rd HHNE HP2 ... 36 B6
Farleigh Court Rd
  CROY/NA CR0 ... 224 A9
Farleigh Dean Crs
  CROY/NA CR0 ... 224 E10
Farleigh Pl STNW/STAM N16 ... 119 M4
Farleigh Rd ADL/WDHM KT15 ... 215 J9
  STNW/STAM N16 ... 119 N9
  WARL CR6 ... 242 C4
Farleton Cl WEY KT13 ... 216 F5
Farley Dr GDMY/SEVK IG3 ... 123 H5
Farley La BH/WHM TN16 ... 262 G5
Farley Ms CAT SE6 ... 182 C5
Farley Nursery BH/WHM TN16 ... 262 F4
Farley Pl SNWD SE25 ... 203 P9
Farley Rd CAT SE6 ... 182 C6
  GVE DA12 ... 191 J7
  SAND/SEL CR2 ... 223 P5
Farleycroft BH/WHM TN16 ... 262 F5
Farley Rd SAND/SEL CR2 ... 224 A5
Farlington Pl PUT/ROE SW15 ... 178 G1
Farlow Cl GVW DA11 ... 191 M9
Farlow Rd PUT/ROE SW15 ... 156 G9
Farlton Rd WAND/EARL SW18 ... 160 A9
Farman Ter
  KTN/HRWW/WS HA3 * ... 115 J2
Farm Av ALP/SUD HA0 ... 135 H1
  CRICK NW2 ... 117 P8
  RYLN/HDSTN HA2 ... 113 P8
  STRHM/NOR SW16 ... 180 A6
  SWLY BR8 ... 187 K8
Farmborough Cl HRW HA1 ... 114 C5
Farm Cl AMS HP6 ... 35 L4
  ASC SL5 ... 192 A5
  BAR EN5 ... 76 F7
  BELMT SM2 ... 221 N8
  BF/WBF KT14 ... 216 A8


  BKHH IG9 ... 101 P4
  BORE WD6 ... 75 K4
  CHERT KT16 ... 194 D6
  CHES/WCR EN8 ... 62 B6
  COUL/CHIP CR5 ... 240 A6
  CRAWE RH10 ... 284 A6
  DAGE RM10 ... 144 D2
  EHSLY KT24 ... 252 B2
  FUL/PGN SW6 ... 157 K6
  HERT/WAT SG14 ... 25 H1
  HGDN/ICK UB10 ... 112 C8
  HLWW/ROY CM19 ... 27 N10
  LHD/OX KT22 ... 236 C10
  POTB/CUF EN6 ... 60 F3
  RAD WD7 ... 57 K6
  RBRW/HUT CM13 ... 107 P3
  RGUW GU3 ... 249 L5
  SHPTN TW17 ... 196 F2
  STA TW18 ... 173 H8
  WCCW AL8 ... 22 C5
  WLGTN SM6 ... 241 J4
  WWKM BR4 ... 205 K10
Farmcote Rd LEE/GVPK SE12 ... 183 M4
Farm Cots E/WMO/HCT KT8 * ... 198 A2
Farm Ct CRICK NW2 ... 117 H6
  SLN SL2 ... 129 N7
Farmcroft GVW DA11 ... 191 P9
Farmdale Rd CAR SM5 ... 221 J5
  GNWCH SE10 ... 161 K2
Farm Dr CROY/NA CR0 ... 204 E9
Farm End CHING E4 ... 81 K9
  WAB EN9 ... 63 M9
Farmer Rd LEY E10 ... 120 G6
Farmers Cl GSTN WD25 ... 89 P10
Farmers Rd CMBW SE5 ... 159 J6
  STA TW18 ... 173 H8
Farmer's Rd KTN/HRWW/WS HA3 ... 114 G3
Farmers Wy WAB EN9 ... 89 J1
Farmfield Dr HORL RH6 ... 279 J5
Farmfield Rd BMLY BR1 ... 183 K8
Farm Flds SAND/SEL CR2 ... 223 N7
Farm Gv BEAC HP9 ... 88 B6
Farm Hill Rd WAB EN9 ... 63 J10
Farmhouse Cl BROX EN10 * ... 62 E1
  WOKS/MYFD GU22 ... 232 C1
Farmhouse La HHNE HP2 ... 36 B7
Farmhouse Rd
  STRHM/NOR SW16 ... 180 C9
Farmilo Rd WALTH E17 ... 120 F5
Farmington Av SUT SM1 ... 201 N10
Farmlands ENC/FH EN2 ... 79 H5
  PIN HA5 ... 113 J4
The Farmlands NTHLT UB5 ... 133 N4
Farmleigh STHGT/OAK N14 ... 98 D7
Farm La ADL/WDHM KT15 ... 215 L5
  ASHTD KT21 ... 237 N4
  BEAC HP9 ... 35 M10
  CROY/NA CR0 ... 204 E9
  EHSLY KT24 ... 252 C4
  FUL/PGN SW6 ... 14 F10
  GDST RH9 ... 259 J6
  HOD EN11 ... 46 A1
  PUR/KEN CR8 ... 242 B7
  RKW/CH/CXG WD3 ... 71 J7
  RPLY/SEND GU23 ... 251 P5
  STHGT/OAK N14 ... 78 B10
Farmleigh Gv WOT/HER KT12 ... 216 C2
Farm Pl BERK HP4 ... 33 L4
  DART DA1 ... 165 H10
  KENS W8 ... 11 J7
Farm Rd ADL/WDHM KT15 ... 215 L5
  BELMT SM2 ... 221 M8
  CDW/CHF RM16 ... 168 C1
  EDGW HA8 ... 95 P6
  ESH/CLAY KT10 ... 197 M9
  HSLWW TW4 ... 175 M4
  MRDN SM4 ... 201 L5
  NTHWD HA6 ... 92 D6
  RAIN RM13 ... 145 K5
  RKW/CH/CXG WD3 ... 70 D3
  RSEV TN14 ... 231 K5
  STA TW18 ... 173 J9
  STAL AL1 ... 38 C5
  TIL RM18 ... 169 M3
  WARL CR6 ... 242 D5
  WCHMN N21 ... 99 K2
  WLSDN NW10 ... 136 A3
  WOKS/MYFD GU22 ... 232 E4
Farmstead Rd CAT SE6 ... 182 G4
  KTN/HRWW/WS HA3 ... 94 G7
Farm St MYFR/PICC W1J ... 10 C6
The Farm WIM/MER SW19 * ... 178 G2
Farm V BXLY DA5 ... 186 C2
Farmview COB KT11 ... 215 N4
Farm Wk GLDGN NW11 ... 117 J4
  GU GU1 ... 267 L2
Farmway BCTR RM8 ... 123 K9
Farm Wy BKHH IG9 ... 101 K9
  BUSH WD23 ... 74 A8
  HCH RM12 ... 125 K5
  NTHWD HA6 ... 40 C7
  STWL/WRAY TW19 ... 173 L3
  WPK KT4 ... 201 H1
Farm Yd WDSR SL4 ... 149 A9
Farnaby Dr SEV TN13 ... 264 F7
Farnaby Rd BMLY BR1 ... 183 K5
  ELTH/MOT SE9 ... 164 B10
Farnan Av WALTH E17 ... 100 F10
Farnan Rd STRHM/NOR SW16 ... 180 A8


  WIM/MER SW19 ... 179 K6
Farquharson Rd
  CROY/NA CR0 ... 205 K7
Farraline Rd WATW WD18 ... 73 J8
Farrance Rd CHDH RM6 ... 123 J4
Farrance St POP/IOD E14 ... 160 B8
Farrant Av WDGN N22 ... 99 H10
Farrant Cl ORP BR6 ... 227 K4
Farrant Wy BORE WD6 ... 75 K5
Farr Av BARK IG11 ... 143 K4
Farren Rd FSTH SE23 ... 182 B8
Farrer Ms CEND/HSY/T N8 ... 118 C4
Farrer Rd CEND/HSY/T N8 ... 118 C4
  KTN/HRWW/WS HA3 ... 115 J3
Farriday Cl STALW/RED AL3 ... 38 E1
Farrier Cl BMLY BR1 ... 206 A3
  SUN TW16 ... 196 D3
Farrier Pl SUT SM1 ... 201 L10
Farrier Rd NTHLT UB5 ... 133 N3
Farriers WARE SG12 ... 26 E1
Farriers Cl EW KT17 ... 220 B8
  GVE DA12 ... 191 M4
Farriers End BROX EN10 ... 62 E2
Farriers St CAMTN NW1 ... 4 A10
Farrier St CAMTN NW1 ... 4 B1
Farriers Wy BORE WD6 ... 75 N6
Farrier Wk WBPTN SW10 ... 15 H10
Farringdon La CLKNW EC1R ... 12 B2
Farringdon Rd CLKNW EC1R ... 12 B2
Farringdon St
  FLST/FETLN EC4A ... 12 C5
Farrington Cl CHST BR7 ... 184 G10
Farrington Acres WEY KT13 * ... 196 E10
Farrington Pl CHST BR7 ... 184 G10
Farrins Rents BERM/RHTH SE16 ... 141 N7
Farrow La NWCR SE14 ... 160 G8
Farrow Pl BERM/RHTH SE16 ... 141 M8
Farr Rd ENC/FH EN2 ... 79 L5
Farthingale Ct WAB EN9 ... 89 M10
Farthingale La WAB EN9 ... 89 M10
Farthingale Wk SRTFD E15 ... 141 H7
Farthing Aly STHWK SE1 ... 19 N2
Farthing Cl DART DA1 ... 171 K3
Farthing Flds WAP E1W * ... 140 D8
Farthing Green La SL SL2 ... 129 L1
Farthings WOKN/KNAP GU21 ... 231 N2
Farthings Cl CHING E4 ... 101 H1
  PIN HA5 ... 113 G4
The Farthings HHW HP1 ... 35 L6
  KUTN/CMB KT2 ... 199 L1
Farthing St HAYES BR2 ... 226 G7
Farthing Wy COUL/CHIP CR5 ... 240 G7
Farwell Rd SCUP DA14 ... 186 C8
Farwig La BMLY BR1 ... 184 A4
Fashion St WCHPL E1 ... 13 M2
Fassett Rd HACK E8 ... 7 N1
  KUT/HW KT1 ... 199 J5
Fassett Sq HACK E8 ... 7 N1
Fauconberg Rd CHSWK W4 ... 155 P5
Faulkner Cl BCTR RM8 ... 123 K5
Faulkner's Rd WOT/HER KT12 ... 217 L4
Faulkner St NWCR SE14 ... 160 G9
Fauna Cl CHDH RM6 ... 123 H6
  STAN HA7 ... 95 J4
Faunce St WALW SE17 ... 18 C10
Favart Rd FUL/PGN SW6 ... 157 N7
Faverolle Gn CHES/WCR EN8 ... 62 E2
Faversham Av CHING E4 ... 100 C10
  EN EN1 ... 79 K9
Faversham Cl CHIG IG7 ... 103 L2
Faversham Rd BECK BR3 ... 204 D2
  CAT SE6 ... 182 G5
  MRDN SM4 ... 201 L6
Fawcett Cl BTSEA SW11 ... 157 J9
  STRHM/NOR SW16 ... 180 G9
Fawcett Est CLPT E5 ... 119 P5
Fawcett Rd CROY/NA CR0 ... 203 J10
  WDSR SL4 ... 148 A5
  WLSDN NW10 ... 137 J5
Fawcett St WBPTN SW10 ... 15 J9
Fawcus Cl ESH/CLAY KT10 ... 218 E5
Fawe Park Rd PUT/ROE SW15 ... 157 L10
Fawe St POP/IOD E14 ... 140 G7
Fawkham Rd HART DA3 ... 211 P3
Fawkham Green Rd
  HART DA3 ... 211 P3
Fawley Rd KIL/WHAMP NW6 ... 117 M10
Fawnbrake Av HNHL SE24 ... 181 H1
Fawns Manor Cl
  EBED/NFELT TW14 ... 174 A4
Fawns Manor Rd
  EBED/NFELT TW14 ... 174 B4
Fawood Av WLSDN NW10 ... 136 G6
Faygate Crs BXLYHS DA6 ... 185 J3
Faygate Rd BRXS/STRHM SW2 ... 180 A4
Fay Gn ABLGY WD5 ... 54 D7
Fayland Av STRHM/NOR SW16 ... 179 N8
Faymore Gdns SOCK/AV RM15 ... 146 G9
Fays Pas GU GU1 * ... 267 P1
Feacey Down HHW HP1 ... 35 P6
Fearn Cl EHSLY KT24 ... 252 F5
Fearney Md RKW/CH/CXG WD3 ... 91 K2
Fearnley Crs HPTN TW12 ... 175 M8
Fearnley St WATW WD18 ... 73 J8
Fearns Md BRW CM14 ... 107 H4
Fearon St GNWCH SE10 ... 161 N1
Featherbed La ABLGY WD5 ... 53 N1
  HHS/BOV HP3 ... 35 M10
  SAND/SEL CR2 ... 224 C5
  WARL CR6 ... 224 F10
Feather Dell HAT AL10 ... 40 A2
Feathers La STWL/WRAY TW19 ... 172 G3
Feathers Pl GNWCH SE10 ... 161 M1
Featherstone Gdns
  BORE WD6 ... 76 A3
Featherstone Rd MLHL NW7 ... 96 C4
  NWDGN UB2 ... 153 M2
Featherstone St STLK EC1Y ... 12 G1
Featherstone Ter
  NWDGN UB2 ... 153 M2
Featley Rd BRXN/ST SW9 ... 158 C9
Federal Rd GFD/PVL UB6 ... 135 H1
Federal Wy WATN WD24 ... 73 N5
Federation Rd ABYW SE2 ... 163 J4
Fee Farm Rd ESH/CLAY KT10 ... 218 E6
Feenan Hwy TIL RM18 ... 169 N6
Feeny Cl WLSDN NW10 ... 119 J4
Felbridge Av STAN HA7 ... 95 G7
Felbridge Cl BELMT SM2 ... 221 M7
  STRHM/NOR SW16 ... 180 C6
Felbridge Rd GDMY/SEVK IG3 ... 123 P7
Felcott Cl WOT/HER KT12 ... 197 M7
Felcott Rd WOT/HER KT12 ... 197 M7
Felday Rd LEW SE13 ... 182 G1
  RDKG RH5 ... 270 G6
Felden Cl GSTN WD25 ... 89 L10
  PIN HA5 ... 93 L5
Felden Dr HHS/BOV HP3 ... 35 M8
Felden St FUL/PGN SW6 ... 157 J7
Feldon Cl ORP BR6 ... 206 A4


Felix Rd BRXS/STRHM SW2 ... 181 H1
  WEA W13 ... 134 H1
  WOT/HER KT12 ... 197 H6
Felixstowe Ct CAN/RD E16 ... 163 L4
  ED N9 ... 99 P4
  SEVS/STOTM N15 ... 119 N1
  WLSDN NW10 ... 136 E5
Felix St BETH E2 * ... 140 A1
Felland Wy REIG RH2 ... 275 N4
Felix Wy REIG RH2 ... 275 N4
Fellbrigg Rd EDUL SE22 ... 181 N1
Fellbrigg St WCHPL E1 ... 140 A6
Fellbrook RCHPK/HAM TW10 ... 176 G6
Fellmongers Yd CROY/NA CR0 * ... 203 K10
Fellowes Cl YEAD UB4 ... 133 L6
Fellowes Rd CAR SM5 ... 201 P10
Fellows Gn CHOB/PIR GU24 ... 212 C9
Fellow Green Rd
  CHOB/PIR GU24 ... 212 C9
Fell Pth BORE WD6 ... 76 A3
Fell Rd CROY/NA CR0 ... 2 E4
Felltram Ms CHARL SE7 * ... 161 P7
Felltram Wy CHARL SE7 ... 161 P7
Fell Wk EDGW HA8 ... 96 C1
Felmersham Cl CLAP SW4 ... 181 J1
Felmingham Rd PGE/AN SE20 ... 204 B2
Felmongers HLW CM20 ... 29 L9
Felsberg Rd BRXS/STRHM SW2 ... 180 F2
Fels Cl DAGE RM10 ... 124 C8
Fels Farm Av DAGE RM10 ... 124 D8
Felsham Ms PUT/ROE SW15 ... 156 G9
Felsham Rd PUT/ROE SW15 ... 156 G9
Felspar Cl WOOL/PLUM SE18 ... 163 J4
Felstead Av CLAY IG5 ... 102 D9
Felstead Cl RBRW/HUT CM13 ... 87 P10
Felstead Rd CHES/WCR EN8 ... 62 D8
  CRW RM5 ... 104 D7
  HOM E9 ... 140 F1
  HOR/WEW KT19 ... 220 A7
  LOU IG10 ... 102 B1
  ORP BR6 ... 207 N3
  WAN E11 ... 121 M5
Felstead St HOM E9 ... 140 E1
Felsted Rd CAN/RD E16 ... 142 F10
Feltham Av E/WMO/HCT KT8 ... 198 D3
Felthambrook Wy FELT TW13 ... 175 J8
Feltham Hill Rd ASHF TW15 ... 174 B8
Feltham Rd ASHF TW15 ... 174 B6
  MTCM CR4 ... 202 A2
  REDH RH1 ... 276 A5
Felton Cl BORE WD6 ... 75 K4
  STMC/STPC BR5 ... 206 G6
Felton Gra HLWE CM17 ... 47 M2
Felton Lea SCUP DA14 ... 185 J8
Felton Rd BARK IG11 ... 143 H4
  WEA W13 ... 155 H1
Felton St IS N1 ... 7 H2
Fencepiece Rd BARK/HLT IG6 ... 102 F7
Fenchurch Av FENCHST EC3M ... 13 J6
Fenchurch Blds FENCHST EC3M * ... 13 K6
Fenchurch Pl FENCHST EC3M * ... 13 J7
Fenchurch Rd CRAWE RH10 ... 284 C6
Fenchurch St FENCHST EC3M ... 13 J7
Fen Cl BRWN CM15 ... 87 P8
Fendall Rd HOR/WEW KT19 ... 219 P2
Fendall St STHWK SE1 ... 19 L5
Fendt Cl CAN/RD E16 ... 141 L8
Fendyke Rd BELV DA17 ... 163 N5
Fenelon Pl WKENS W14 ... 14 E1
Fengates Rd REDH RH1 ... 275 L10
Fen Gv BFN/LL DA15 ... 185 J2
Fenham Rd PECK SE15 ... 159 H6
Fen La UPMR RM14 ... 127 J10
Fenman Ct TOTM N17 ... 100 A9
Fenman Gdns GDMY/SEVK IG3 ... 123 N5
Fenn Cl BMLY BR1 ... 183 P10
Fennel Cl CAN/RD E16 ... 141 K6
  CROY/NA CR0 ... 204 C8
  GU GU1 ... 250 E3
Fennells CRAWW RH11 ... 285 L10
Fennells Md HOR/WEW KT19 * ... 46 D2
Fennel St WOOL/PLUM SE18 ... 162 G2
Fenner Cl BERM/RHTH SE16 ... 160 A3
Fenner Sq CDW/CHF RM16 * ... 167 J2
Fenners Marsh GVE DA12 ... 191 N5
Fenner Sq BTSEA SW11 * ... 157 N9
The Fennings AMS HP6 ... 69 J2
Fenning St STHWK SE1 ... 19 J1
Fennscombe Ct
  CHOB/PIR GU24 ... 212 D9
Fenns La WOKN/KNAP GU21 ... 232 C6
Fenn St HOM E9 ... 121 H10
Fenn's Wy WOKN/KNAP GU21 ... 232 B1
Fennycroft Rd HHW HP1 ... 35 P3
Fensomes Aly HHNE HP2 * ... 35 P4
Fensomes Cl HHNE HP2 ... 35 P5
Fenstanton Av
  NFNCH/WDSPK N12 ... 97 J3
Fen St CAN/RD E16 ... 141 L9
Fenswood Cl BXLY DA5 ... 187 H4
Fentiman Rd VX/NE SW8 ... 17 K10
Fentiman Wy EMPK RM11 ... 125 M6
  RYLN/HDSTN HA2 ... 114 A7
Fenton Cl BRXN/ST SW9 * ... 158 A8
  CHST BR7 ... 184 D8
  HACK E8 ... 7 N1
  REDH RH1 ... 258 B10
Fenton Rd CDW/CHF RM16 ... 258 B10
  TOTM N17 ... 99 K8
Fenton's Av PLSTW E13 ... 141 M1
Fenton St WCHPL E1 ... 140 C8
Fentum Rd WDGN N22 ... 249 D2
Fenwick Cl WOKN/KNAP GU21 ... 231 N4
  WOOL/PLUM SE18 ... 162 F8
Fenwick Gv PECK SE15 ... 159 J5
Fenwick Pl BRXN/ST SW9 ... 158 A9
  SAND/SEL CR2 ... 223 K5
Fenwick Rd PECK SE15 ... 159 J5
Ferdinand Pl CAMTN NW1 ... 4 A1
Ferdinand St CAMTN NW1 ... 4 A1
Ferguson Av BRYLDS KT5 ... 199 L5
  GPK RM2 ... 105 K1
  GVE DA12 ... 191 P7
Ferguson Cl BECK BR3 ... 202 D4
  POP/IOD E14 ... 160 C5
Ferguson Dr ACT W3 ... 136 E8
Ferguson Gv CHES/WCR EN8 ... 62 E1
Ferguson's Cl POP/IOD E14 ... 160 C5
Fergus Rd HBRY N5 ... 119 J3
Fermandy La CRAWE RH10 ... 285 N3
Ferme Park Rd
  CEND/HSY/T N8 ... 118 E4
Fermor Rd FSTH SE23 ... 182 B7
Fermoy Rd GFD/PVL UB6 ... 134 A4
  MV/WKIL W9 ... 8 B2
Fern Av MTCM CR4 ... 202 A2
Fernbank BKHH IG9 ... 101 J4
  EYN DA4 * ... 199 N9
Fernbank Av ALP/SUD HA0 ... 114 G9
  WOT/HER KT12 ... 197 N6
Fernbank Ms BAL SW12 ... 180 D2
Fernbank Rd ADL/WDHM KT15 ... 215 G2
Fernbrook Dr
  RYLN/HDSTN HA2 ... 114 A5
Fernbrook Rd LEW SE13 ... 183 J5
Fern Cl ERITH DA8 ... 164 G2
  IS N1 ... 7 J2
  WARL CR6 ... 242 D4
Fern Ct NWCR SE14 ... 160 G1
Ferncroft Av HAMP NW3 ... 117 J7
  NFNCH/WDSPK N12 ... 97 P7
  RSLP HA4 ... 113 K7
Ferndale BMLY BR1 ... 205 P1
  RGUW GU3 ... 249 K8
Ferndale Av CHERT KT16 ... 195 H10
  HSLWW TW4 ... 175 H6

WALTH E17 121 J3
Ferndale Rd BXLYHN DA7 163 P7
Ferndale Crs UX/CGN UB8 131 M5
Ferndale Rd ASHF TW15 173 N8
BNSTD SM7 239 J2
CLAP SW4 190 E5
CRW RM5 104 D10
FSTGT E7 141 N2
CVE DA12 190 E5
PEND EN3 80 D3
SEVS/STOTM N15 119 N4
SNWD SE25 204 A5
WAN E11 121 L7
WOKN/KNAP GU21 232 C2
Ferndale St EHAM E6 142 E9
Ferndale Ter HRW HA1 174 E2
Ferndale Wy ORP BR6 226 G2
Ferndell Av BXLY DA5 186 E6
Fern Dells HAT AL10 40 C5
Ferndene LCOL/BKTW AL2 55 N7
Fern Dene WEA W13 134 C1
Ferndene Rd HNHL SE24 159 N10
Fernden Ri GODL GU7 267 K10
Ferndown CRAWE RH10 284 E3
EMPK RM11 125 P4
HORL RH6 280 B2
NTHWD HA6 95 H10
Ferndown Av ORP BR6 206 G8
Ferndown Cl BELMT SM2 221 N3
GU GU1 268 D1
PIN HA5 93 M8
Ferndown Gdns COB KT11 217 K10
Ferndown Rd ELTH/MOT SE9 184 A3
OXHEY WD19 93 K4
Fern Dr HHS/BOV HP3 35 P7
MDHD SL6 128 A8
Fernecroft STAL AL1 38 B9
The Fernery STA TW18 173 H8
Fernes Cl UX/CGN UB8 131 M8
Ferney Rd BF/WBF KT14 215 N8
Ferney Meade Wy ISLW TW7 154 F8
Ferney Rd CHESW EN7 61 L2
EBAR EN4 98 B3
Ferngrove Cl LHD/OX KT22 236 D8
Fernhall Dr REDBR IG4 72 A7
Fernhall La WAB EN9 64 A7
Fernham Rd THHTH CR7 203 K3
Fernhead Rd MV/WKIL W9 8 D1
Fernheath Wy RDART DA2 186 E8
Fernhill CHIG CM18 47 N5
LHD/OX KT22 218 C10
Fernhill Cl WALTH E17 101 P6
Fernhill Ct WALTH E17 101 J8
Fernhill Gdns KUTN/CMB KT2 177 J8
Fern Hill La HLWS CM18 47 J5
Fernhill La WOKS/MYFD GU22 231 P6
Fernhill Pk WOKS/MYFD GU22 231 P6
Fernhill Rd HORL RH6 280 E8
Fernhills KGLGY WD4 54 E10
Fernhill St CAN/RD E16 142 C10
Fernholme Rd PECK SE15 182 C1
Fernhurst CRAWW RH11 283 L5
Fernhurst Gdns EDGW HA8 95 M7
Fernhurst Rd ASHF TW15 178 A7
CROY/NA CRO 203 P7
FUL/PGN SW6 157 H7
Fernihough Cl WEY KT13 216 B7
Fernlands Cl CHERT KT16 195 H10
Fern La HEST TW5 153 N4
Fernlea GT/LBKH KT23 236 A10
Fernlea Pl COB KT11 217 L8
Fernlea Rd BAL SW12 180 C4
MTCM CR4 202 B2
Fernleigh Cl CROY/NA CRO 223 H1
MV/WKIL W9 2 F1
WOT/HER KT12 197 J10
Fernleigh Ct RYLN/HDSTN HA2 94 A10
WBLY HA9 115 K6
Fernleigh Rd WCHMH N21 99 H3
Fernley Cl PIN HA5 113 H2
Fernleys STAL/WH AL4 39 H5
Fernsbury St FSBYW WC1X 6 A1
Ferns Cl PEND EN3 80 D2
SAND/SEL CR2 224 A6
Fernshaw Rd WBPTN SW10 15 J10
Fernside GLDGN NW11 117 K7
Fernside Av FELT TW13 175 J7
MLHL NW7 96 A4
Fernside Rd BAL SW12 180 A4
Fernsleigh Cl CFSP/GDCR SL9 90 B7
The Ferns STALW/RED AL3 38 C2
Fernthorpe Rd STRHM/NOR SW16 180 D9
Ferntower Rd HBRY N5 119 L10
Fern Towers CTHM CR3 259 P1
Fernville La HHNE HP2 35 N6
Fern Wk ASHF TW15 173 N8
BERM/RHTH SE16 19 P8
Fern Wy GSTN WD25 73 J1
Fernways IL IG1 122 E8
Fernwood Av ALP/SUD HA0 115 H1
STRHM/NOR SW16 180 E7
Fernwood Cl BMLY BR1 205 P2
Fernwood Crs TRDG/WHET N20 98 A4
Ferny Hl EBAR EN4 78 A4
Feroners Cl CRAWE RH10 284 E4
Ferranti Cl WOOL/PLUM SE18 162 A2
Ferraro Cl HEST TW5 153 P4
Ferrers Av WDR/YW UB7 151 N1
WLGTN SM6 222 E1
Ferrers Cl SL SL1 228 D9
Ferrers Rd STRHM/NOR SW16 180 B9? 
Ferrestone Rd CEND/HSY/T N8 118 G2
Ferrey Ms BRXN/ST SW9 159 N8
Ferriby Cl IS N1 6 A1
Ferrier St WAND/EARL SW18 157 L10
Ferriers Wy EPSOM KT18 238 F5
Ferring Cl RYLN/HDSTN HA2 114 B6
Ferrings DUL SE21 181 M5
Ferris Av CROY/NA CRO 223 H2
Ferris Rd EDUL SE22 159 P10
Ferron Rd CLPT E5 120 A8
Ferro Rd RAIN RM13 145 H6
Ferryhills Cl OXHEY WD19 93 K4
Ferry La BARN SW13 156 C5
BTFD TW8 155 L5
CHERT KT16 195 K6
GU GU1 268 D5
RAIN RM13 144 F8
SHPTN TW17 196 B8
STA TW18 195 M3
STWL/WRAY TW19 172 A5
TOTM N17 120 A2
Ferrymead Av GFD/PVL UB6 133 P4
Ferrymead Dr GFD/PVL UB6 133 P5
Ferrymead Gdns GFD/PVL UB6 134 B4
Ferrymoor RCHPK/HAM TW10 176 A5
Ferry Rd BARN SW13 156 G4
BF/WBF KT14 215 P4
E/WMO/HCT KT8 196 C2
TEDD TW11 176 D8
TWK TW1 176 C4
Ferry Sq BTFD TW8 155 M6
Ferry St POP/IOD E14 161 P5
Feryby Rd ABYW SE2 148 D10
Fesants Cft HLWE CM20 28 C4
Festing Rd PUT/ROE SW15 156 G3
Festival Cl BXLY DA5 185 M7
ERITH DA8 164 G6
HGDN/ICK UB10 132 B5


Festoon Wy CAN/RD E16 142 A9
Fetcham Common La LHD/OX KT22 236 A7
Fetcham Park Dr LHD/OX KT22 236 D9
Fetherstone Cl POTB/CUF EN6 59 N6
Fetter La FLST/FETLN EC4A 11 L3
Ffinch St DEPT SE8 160 F6
Fiddicroft Av BNSTD SM7 221 L10
Fiddle Bridge La HAT AL10 40 C3
Fiddlers Cl RDART DA2 166 G10
Fidgeon Rd BMLY BR1 206 D3
Fidler Pl BUSH WD23 74 A10
Field Cl ABR/ST RM4 83 L7
BKHH IG9 101 P4
BMLY BR1 206 E2
CHING E4 100 C10
CHSGTN KT9 219 H2
CRICK NW2 116 D7
CSHM HP5 51 K4
E/WMO/HCT KT8 196 A3
HARP AL5 20 C4
HYS/HAR UB3 152 C6
RGUE GU4 250 G8
RSLP HA4 76 A5
SAND/SEL CR2 224 A10
STALE/WH AL4 38 F2
Field Cots EFNCH N2 118 A1
FUL/PGN SW6 157 J8
Field Ct GINN WC1R 11 P4
GVW DA11 190 C5
OXTED RH8 261 K4
Field End BAR EN5 76 E8
COUL/CHIP CR5 222 E10
RSLP HA4 133 L1
Fieldend TEDD TW11 176 E7
Field End Cl OXHEY WD19 93 M1
Field End Rd PIN HA5 113 J3
Fieldend Rd STRHM/NOR SW16 202 D1
Fielders Cl EN EN1 79 M8
RYLN/HDSTN HA2 114 B6
Fielders Gn GU GU1 252 C2? 
Fielders Wy RAD WD7 57 K9
Fieldfare Rd THMD SE28 143 M9
Fieldfares LCOL/BKTW AL2 57 J3
Field Gdns CHONG CM5 67 M10
Fieldgate St WCHPL E1 13 M1
Fieldhouse Cl SWFD E18 101 N9
Fieldhouse Rd BAL SW12 180 D3
Field Hurst DTCH/LGLY SL3 150 A5
Fieldhurst Cl ADL/WDHM KT15 215 L2
Fielding Av TIL RM18 168 C6
WHTN TW2 176 B6
Fielding Gdns DTCH/LGLY SL3 149 P1
Fielding La HAYES BR2 205 P4
Fielding Ms BARN SW13 156 E3
Fielding Rd CHSWK W4 146 E5
WKENS W14 149 H1
The Fieldings BNSTD SM7 239 J3
FSTH SE23 182 A4
HORL RH6 280 C3
Fielding St WALW SE17 18 G5? 
Fielding Ter EA W5 136 B5
Fielding Wy RBRW/HUT CM13 87 P10
Field La BTFD TW8 155 L6
GODL GU7 267 L10
TEDD TW11 176 F8
Field Md CDALE/KGS NW9 96 B8
Fieldoaks Wy REDH RH1 258 G8
Fieldpark Gdns CROY/NA CRO 204 D8
Field Pl NWMAL KT3 200 D6
Field Rd DEN/HRF UB9 111 H4
EBED/NFELT TW14 175 J2
FSTGT E7 121 M9
HMSMTH W6 14 A8
OXHEY WD19 73 M10
SOCK/AV RM15 146 B10
TOTM N17 119 L1
Fields End La HHW HP1 34 C4
Fieldsend Rd CHEAM SM3 221 H4
Fields Est HACK E8 7 P1
Fieldside Cl ORP BR6 226 F1
Fieldside Cots TRDG/WHET N20 97 J1
Fieldside Rd BMLY BR1 183 J8
Fields Park Crs CHDH RM6 123 N3
Field St FSBYW WC1X 5 N9
Field Vw FELT TW20 172 F8
FELT TW13 174 E7
Fieldview WAND/EARL SW18 179 N4
Field View Cl ROMW/RG RM7 124 F1
Fieldview Cots STHGT/OAK N14 98 E3
Field View Ri LCOL/BKTW AL2 55 M5
Field View Rd POTB/CUF EN6 59 M5
Field Wk HORL RH6 281 K3
Fieldway BCTR RM8 123 J8
BERK HP4 34 B7
WARE SG12 26 C7
CDW/CHF RM16 147 N10
Field Wy CFSP/GDCR SL9 90 C3
CROY/NA CRO 224 G3
GFD/PVL UB6 133 P1
HHS/BOV HP3 52 D3
HOD EN11 26 G5
AMSS HP7 68 A7
RKW/CH/CXG WD3 91 L2
RPLY/SEND GU23 251 J1
RSLP HA4 112 D6
Fieldway STMC/STPC BR5 206 G6
Fieldway Crs HBRY N5 119 H10
Fiennes Cl BCTR RM8 123 N6
Fiennes Wy SEV TN13 265 K3
Fiesta Dr RAIN RM13 144 D6
Fifehead Cl ASHF TW15 173 H9
Fife Rd CAN/RD E16 141 M7
KUT/HW KT1 199 K2
MORT/ESHN SW14 177 P1
WDGN N22 99 J8
Fife Ter IS N1 5 P7
Fife Wy GT/LBKH KT23 253 P1
Fifield Pth FSTH SE23 182 C6
Fifteenth Av KWD/TDW/WH KT20 257 J2
Fifth Av KWD/TDW/WH KT20 257 J2
GSTN WD25 73 L1
HYS/HAR UB3 132 G10
KWD/TDW/WH KT20 257 J2
MNPK E12 122 G9
NKENS W10 5 K8? 
WTHK RM20 166 F5
Fifth Cross Rd WHTN TW2 176 D5
Fifth Wy WBLY HA9 115 N9
Figges Rd MTCM CR4 180 B10
Figgswood COUL/CHIP CR5 240 D8
Fig Tree Cl WLSDN NW10 136 B3
Figtree Hl HHW HP1 35 N5
Filbert Crs CRAWW RH11 283 J6
Filborough Wy GVE DA12 191 L4
Filby Rd CHSGTN KT9 219 L5
Filey Av STNW/STAM N16 119 L5
Filey Cl BELMT SM2 221 N5
BH/WHM TN16 245 H5
CRAWW RH11 283 J6
Filey Sp SL SL1 148 B3
Filey Wy RSLP HA4 113 H2
Fillebrook Av EN EN1 79 M6
Fillebrook Rd WAN E11 121 J6
Fillingham Wy HAT AL10 40 B2
Filmer Chambers FUL/PGN SW6 157 H7? 
Filmer La SEV TN14 247 M2
Filmer Rd FUL/PGN SW6 157 J6
WDSR SL4 148 C8
Filston La RSEV TN14 246 C7


Filton Cl CDALE/KGS NW9 96 B10
Finborough Rd TOOT SW17 180 A10
WBPTN SW10 15 H9
Finchale Rd ABYW SE2 163 K2
Fincham Cl HGDN/ICK UB10 113 N6
Finchdale Av WNWD SE27 181 L7
Finch Av WDSR SL4 121 L7? 
Finch Cl BAR EN5 77 H7
HAT AL10 40 D6
WOKN/KNAP GU21 231 H3
Finchdale HHW HP1 35 K6
Finchdean Wy PECK SE15 159 N7? 
Finches Ri GU GU1 250 E8
The Finches HERT/BAY SG13 26 A1
Finch Gdns CHING E4 100 F6
Finch Gn RKW/CH/CXG WD3 71 J8
Finchingfield Av WFD IG8 101 P8
The Finchinghfields BRWN CM15 86 D3
Finch La AMSS HP7 69 M6
BANK EC3V 13 H2
BEAC HP9 88 B6
BUSH WD23 73 P9
Finchley Pk NFNCH/WDSPK N12 97 N5
Finchley Pl STJWD NW8 3 L7
Finchley Rd GLDGN NW11 117 J5
GRAYS RM17 167 N5
HAMP NW3 3 J1
Finchley Vis NFNCH/WDSPK N12 97 N5
Finchley Wy FNCH N3 97 N5
Finch Ms PECK SE15 159 N7
Finchmoor HLWS CM18 46 C4
Finch Rd BERK HP4 33 N5
GU GU1 250 G10? 
Finch St POP/IOD E14 140 G9
Finden Rd FSTGT E7 121 N10
Findhorn Av YEAD UB4 133 J7
Findhorn St POP/IOD E14 141 N8
Findlay Dr RGUW GU3 249 L6
Findon Cl RYLN/HDSTN HA2 94 A10
WAND/EARL SW18 179 K2
Findon Gdns RAIN RM13 145 H7
Findon Rd CRAWW RH11 283 L5
ED N9 100 A2
SHB W12 148 A1
Fine Bush La DEN/HRF UB9 112 C4
Fingal St GNWCH SE10 161 L4
Finglesham Cl STMC/STPC BR5 207 N8
Finians Cl HGDN/ICK UB10 132 A2
Finland Rd BROCKY SE4 160 D9
Finland St BERM/RHTH SE16 160 F6? 
Finlay Gdns ADL/WDHM KT15 215 M2
Finlays Cl CHSGTN KT9 219 M2
Finlay St FUL/PGN SW6 156 G7
Finmart Ct WEY KT13 216 D1
Finney La ISLW TW7 154 F7
Finnis St BETH E2 140 D8
Finnymore Rd DAGW RM9 143 P9
Fir Tree Cl CRAWW RH11 283 L4
EA W5 135 K8
ESH/CLAY KT10 197 H5
EW KT17 238 F1
HHS/BOV HP3 36 B7
HOR/WEW KT19 220 B7
LHD/OX KT22 237 H8
ORP BR6 227 J2
ROM RM1 104 F1
STRHM/NOR SW16 180 D8
Fir Tree Gdns CROY/NA CRO 223 J3
Fir Tree Gv CAR SM5 222 A4
Fir Tree Hl RKW/CH/CXG WD3 72 B5
Fir Tree Pl ASHF TW15 174 B7
Fir Tree Rd BNSTD SM7 238 F2
EW KT17 238 F2
GU GU1 267 N4? 
HSLWW TW4 175 M3
LHD/OX KT22 237 H9
Fir Trees ABR/ST RM4 83 L7
Fir Trees Cl BERM/RHTH SE16 143 K10
Fir Tree Wk EN EN1 79 N4
REIG RH2 257 K7
Fir Wk CHEAM SM3 220 G3
Firbank Cl CAN/RD E16 142 A7
EN EN1 79 N4
Firbank Dr OXHEY WD19 93 M1
WOKN/KNAP GU21 231 N5
Firbank La WOKN/KNAP GU21 231 N5
Firbank Pl EGH TW20 171 N9
Firbank Rd CRW RM5 104 C6
PECK SE15 160 B1
STALW/RED AL3 38 E2
Fircroft Cl WOT/HER KT12 197 H7
WOKS/MYFD GU22 232 C4
Fircroft Gdns HRW HA1 114 D8
Fircroft Rd CHSGTN KT9 219 L1
TOOT SW17 180 A4
Firdene BRYLDS KT5 199 P8
Fir Dene ORP BR6 206 C10
Fireball Hl ASC SL5 192 C7
Fire Bell Aly SURB KT6 199 K6
Firebell Ms SURB KT6 199 K6
Firecrest Cl HART DA3 211 N5
Firecrest Dr HAMP NW3 117 L8
Firefly Cl WLGTN SM6 222 F4
Firefly Gdns EHAM E6 142 B6
Firemans Cots EFNCH N2 118 B1
Firethorn Cl EDGW HA8 95 P2
Firfield Rd ADL/WDHM KT15 215 K1
Firfields WEY KT13 216 C5
Fir Grange Av WEY KT13 216 C2
Fir Gv NWMAL KT3 200 D5
Firgrove WOKN/KNAP GU21 231 H5
Fir Grove Rd BRXN/ST SW9 159 N8
Firham Park Av HARP AL5 20 B1? 
Firhill Rd CAT SE6 182 F4
Firlands HORL RH6 280 C4
WEY KT13 216 F5
Firle Ct CRAWE RH10 283 M2? 
Firle Cl CRAWE RH10 283 M2
Firle Pl WAND/EARL SW18 179 M3
Firmingers Rd ORP BR6 228 D2
Fir Pk HLWW/ROY CM19 46 B4
Fir Rd CHEAM SM3 201 J8
FELT TW13 175 L1
Firs Av MORT/ESHN SW14 156 B7? 
MUSWH N10 48 A?
FBAR/BDGN N11 48 A11
WDSR SL4 148 B11? 
Firsby Av CROY/NA CRO 204 D8
Firsby Rd STNW/STAM N16 119 N7
Firs Cl DORK RH4 217 M10? 
ESH/CLAY KT10 197 H5
FSTH SE23 182 C5
IVER SL0 130 F2? 
MTCM CR4 202 C1? 
Firscroft PLMGR N13 99 K4
Firsdene Cl ADL/WDHM KT15 215 K2? 
Firs Dr DTCH/LGLY SL3 150 B10
HEST TW5 153 K5
LOU IG10 80 G2? 
Firs Gv CFSP/GDCR SL9 90 C3? 
First Av ACT W3 136 C4
ADL/WDHM KT15 215 J5? 
AMSS HP7 68 A7
BXLYHN DA7 163 H4? 
CHDH RM6 123 N5? 
DAGE RM10 144 B3? 
E/WMO/HCT KT8 197 P3? 
EN EN1 79 N8? 
Firs Wk NTHWD HA6 96 E7
First Park Av WCHMH N21 99 K1? 
First Park Gdns WCHMH N21 99 K1? 
The Firs Pk BRKMPK AL9 41 J5? 
Firs Rd PUR/KEN CR8 241 J8? 
First Av HAT AL10 40 E7? 
Firstway RYNPK SW20 200 F2
Firswood Av HOR/WEW KT19 220 C4
Firth Gdns FUL/PGN SW6 157 H7
Firtree Av MTCM CR4 202 B2
Fir Tree Av SLN SL2 129 L6
WDR/YW UB7 132 B7
Fir Tree Cl ESH/CLAY KT10 197 H5
Fire Tree Gv CAR SM5 222 A4
Fir Tree Pl ASHF TW15 174 B7
Fir Tree Rd BNSTD SM7 238 F2
EW KT17 238 F2
Fir Trees ABR/ST RM4 83 L7
Fir Tree Wk EN EN1 79 N4
REIG RH2 257 K7
Fir Wk CHEAM SM3 220 G3
Finsbury Av LVPST EC2M 13 H1
Finsbury Circ LVPST EC2M 13 H1
Finsbury Cots WDGN N22 98 F8
Finsbury Est CLKNW EC1R 6 D8? 
Finsbury Market SDTCH EC2A 13 J2
Finsbury Park Av FSBYPK N4 119 K4
Finsbury Park Rd FSBYPK N4 119 J7
Finsbury Pavement LVPST EC2M 13 H1
Finsbury Rd WDGN N22 98 G8
Finsbury Sq SDTCH EC2A 13 H1
Finsbury St STLK EC1Y 12 G1
Finsbury Wy BXLY DA5 186 A2
Finsen Rd CMBW SE5 159 K10
Finstock Rd NKENS W10 8 A2
Finucane Ct RCH/KEW TW9 155 H7? 
Finucane Gdns RAIN RM13 145 H1? 
Finucane Ri BUSH WD23 94 B5? 
Finway Ct WATW WD18 72 C9? 
Finway Rd HHNE HP2 36 C2? 
Fiona Cl GT/LBKH KT23 235 P10? 
Fiona Ct ENC/FH EN2 79 J7? 
Firbank WGCW AL8 22 F5? 
Firbank Cl CAN/RD E16 142 A7
Five Oaks HAT AL10 40 E7


GVW DA11 190 B4
HDN NW4 116 F2
HOR/WEW KT19 220 B5
HYS/HAR UB3 132 G10
MORT/ESHN SW14 156 A7
MNPK E12 122 B9
NKENS W10 8 C1
PLSTW E13 141 M5
UED N18 100 B5
WALTH E17 120 C3
WBLY HA9 115 J7
WOT/HER KT12 197 J6
WTHK RM20 166 F5
First Cl E/WMO/HCT KT8 196 C1
First Cross Rd WHTN TW2 176 D5
First Dr WLSDN NW10 136 G1
The Firs BF/WBF KT14 215 N8
BRWN CM15 86 F10
BXLY DA5 186 A6
CDW/CHF RM16 147 N10
CHESW EN7 61 M2
EBED/NFELT TW14 174 F2
EDGW HA8 96 C3
GT/LBKH KT23 254 A1
HARP AL5 20 C1
ORP BR6 228 B3
RGUW GU3 267 N4
STAL AL1 38 C10
TRDG/WHET N20 97 N2
Flanders Crs TOOT SW17 180 A10
Flanders Rd CHSWK W4 146 B3
EHAM E6 142 C4
Flanders Wy HOM E9 120 C1
Flank St WCHPL E1 13 N7
Flash La ENC/FH EN2 79 K3
Flask Wk HAMP NW3 117 M9
Flather Cl STRHM/NOR SW16 180 D9
Flatfield Ms HOR/WEW KT19 36 B8
Flather Cl HACK E8 101 L9? 
Flaunden Bottom CSHM HP5 70 B3
HHS/BOV HP3 52 C10
Flaunden Hl HHS/BOV HP3 52 E8
Flaunden La HHS/BOV HP3 52 G8
Flavell Ms GNWCH SE10 161 K4
Flaxen Cl CHING E4 100 D2? 
Flaxen Rd CHING E4 100 C4
Flaxley Rd MRDN SM4 201 L6
Flaxman Rd CMBW SE5 159 J8
Flaxman Ter STPAN WC1H 5 K10
Flaxton Rd WOOL/PLUM SE18 162 G10? 
Flecker Cl STAN HA7 94 E6
Fleece Dr ED N9 99 P5
Fleece Rd SURB KT6 199 H8
Fleece Wk HOLWY N7 5 M1
Fleeming Cl WALTH E17 100 E10
Fleeming Rd WALTH E17 101 H8? 
Fleet Av RDART DA2 188 B4
UPMR RM14 126 A4
Fleetdale Pde RDART DA2 188 B4
Fleethall Gv SRTFD E15 ...
Fleet Rd FLST/FETLN EC4A 11 L3? 
GVW DA11 190 A5? 
HAMP NW3 117 M10? 
RDART DA2 188 B4? 
Fleet Sq FSBYW WC1X 5 N10? 
Fleet St FLST/FETLN EC4A 11 L3
Fleet Street Hl WCHPL E1 13 L1
Fleet Ter CAT SE6 160 C10? 
Fleetway EGH TW20 194 A4? 
Fleetway Cl CAN/RD E16 142 H3? 
Fleetwood Cl CAN/RD E16 142 H3
CHSGTN KT9 219 J6
CROY/NA CRO 203 M1? 
CSTG HP8 ...
KWD/TDW/WH KT20 258 B3? 
Fleetwood Ct BF/WBF KT14 215 K9
WALTH E17 101 J3
Fleetwood Rd KUT/HW KT1 199 M3
SLN SL2 129 L2? 
WLSDN NW10 116 D10? 
Fleetwood St STNW/STAM N16 119 M7
Fleetwood Wy OXHEY WD19 93 L4
Fleming Cl CHESW EN7 61 K1? 
FARN/HRWW/WS HA3 94 F4? 
MV/WKIL W9 2 A6? 
Fleming Crs HERT/WAT SG14 25 L6? 
Fleming Dr WNWD SE27 181 M10? 
Fleming Gdns TIL RM18 168 F7? 
Fleming Md MTCM CR4 180 A10? 
Fleming Rd CDW/CHF RM16 167 P10? 
STHL UB1 134 A5? 
WAB EN9 62 A2? 
WALW SE17 18 E10? 
Flemings RBRW/HUT CM13 107 M7? 
Fleming Wy CRAWE RH10 284 D3? 
ISLW TW7 154 F6? 
THMD SE28 143 M5? 
Flemish Flds CHERT KT16 195 K7? 
Flemming Av RSLP HA4 113 J3? 
Fletcher Cl CHERT KT16 214 C3? 
CRAWE RH10 284 C8? 
EHAM E6 142 E5? 
Fletcher La LEY E10 102 B9? 
Fletcher Pth BROCKY SE4 160 E6? 
Fletcher Rd CHERT KT16 214 C3
CHIG IG7 103 M1? 
CHSWK W4 146 A3? 
Fletchers Cl HAYES BR2 205 K8? 
Fletcher St WCHPL E1 13 N4? 
Fletcher Wy HHNE HP2 35 L4? 
Fletching Rd CHARL SE7 162 A6? 
CLPT E5 120 E8? 
Fletton Rd FBAR/BDGN N11 99 H1? 
Fleur De Lis St WCHPL E1 13 J1? 
Fleur Gates WIM/MER SW19 178 G8? 
Flexford Rd RGUW GU3 266 A1? 
Flexley Wd WGCE AL7 23 L1? 
Flex Meadow HLWW/ROY CM19 46 A4? 
Flight Ap CDALE/KGS NW9 96 C9? 
Flimwell Cl BMLY BR1 183 J7? 
Flinders Cl STAL AL1 38 F5? 
Flint Cl BNSTD SM7 240 A3? 
CRAWE RH10 284 C10? 
GT/LBKH KT23 236 A10? 
ORP BR6 227 J2? 
REDH RH1 274 D2? 
SRTFD E15 141 L1? 
Flint Down Cl STMC/STPC BR5 207 K1? 
Flint Hill DORK RH4 272 G5? 
Flint Hill Cl DORK RH4 272 G5? 
Flintlock Cl STAI TW19 151 K10? 
Flintmill Crs BKHTH/KID SE3 162 G3? 
ELTH/MOT SE9 162 G3? 
Flinton St WALW SE17 19 K7? 
Flint St SOCK/AV RM15 147 K1? 
WALW SE17 19 K7? 
Flitcroft St LSQ/SEVD WC2H 11 J3? 
Floathaven Cl THMD SE28 143 K7? 
The Floats SEV TN13 246 F7? 
Flock Mill Pl WAND/EARL SW18 179 L4? 
Flockton St BERM/RHTH SE16 139 N7? 
Flodden Rd CMBW SE5 159 J8? 
Flood La TWK TW1 176 C4? 
Flood St CHEL SW3 15 N9? 
Flood Wk CHEL SW3 15 N9? 
Flora Cl POP/IOD E14 141 M8? 
STAN HA7 95 N2? 
Flora Gdns CHDH RM6 123 M4? 
CROY/NA CRO 205 P10? 
HMSMTH W6 148 E2? 


Five Oaks Cl WOKN/KNAP GU21 231 J5
Five Oaks La CHIG IG7 103 J5
Fiveways Cnr ELTH/MOT SE9 184 E5
Five Ways Jct HDN NW4 96 D9
Fiveways Rd BRXN/ST SW9 159 N8
Five Wents SWLY BR8 209 H2
Fladbury Rd SEVS/STOTM N15 119 L4
Fladgate Rd WAN E11 121 K4
Flag Cl CROY/NA CRO 204 G8
Flagstaff Cl WAB EN9 63 J9
Flagstaff Rd WAB EN9 62 G9
The Flags HHNE HP2 36 C6
Flag Wk PIN HA5 113 H4
Flambard Rd HRW HA1 114 F4
Flamborough Cl BH/WHM TN16 243 J8? 
Flamborough Rd RSLP HA4 113 L2? 
Flamborough Sp SL SL1 148 F1? 
Flamborough St POP/IOD E14 140 D8
Flamborough Wk POP/IOD E14 140 D8
Flamingo Wk HCH RM12 145 H5
Flamstead End Rd CHES/WCR EN8 62 A2
Flamstead Gdns DAGW RM9 143 P8? 
Flamstead Rd DAGW RM9 143 P8
Flamsted Av WBLY HA9 136 B3
Flamsteed Rd CHARL SE7 162 E3
Flanchford Rd REIG RH2 274 F5
First Avenue Mandela Av HLW CM20 28 J9
HLW CM20 198 A4
First Dr WLSDN NW10 136 D1? 
Flamsteed Rd CHARL SE7 162 E3
Flatford Ho PECK SE15 160 A5? 
Fleming Rd CROY/NA CRO 204 C1? 
Fleet Wk HCH RM12 145 H4? 
Fleming Ct CROY/NA CRO 223 H4? 
Fletcher Rd CHIG IG7 103 M1? 
CHSWK W4 146 A3? 
Fletchers Cl WCHPL E1 13 H1? 
Fletcher St WCHPL E1 13 N4? 
Fletching Rd CHARL SE7 162 A6? 
Fitzalan Rd ESH/CLAY KT10 218 D4
FNCH N3 117 H4
Fitzgeorge Av NWMAL KT3 200 A4? 
WKENS W14 149 J2
Fitzgerald Av MORT/ESHN SW14 156 A9? 
Fitzgerald Rd MORT/ESHN SW14 156 A9
THDIT KT7 197 P10? 
WAN E11 121 L2? 
Fitzhardinge St MBLAR W1H 10 B2? 
Fitzhugh Gv WAND/EARL SW18 179 P4? 
Fitzjames Av CROY/NA CRO 203 P9? 
WKENS W14 149 J3? 
Fitzjohn Av BAR EN5 76 B7? 
Fitzjohn's Av HAMP NW3 117 H10? 
Fitzmaurice Pl MYFR/PICC W1J 10 D7? 
Fitzneal St SHB W12 136 C8? 
Fitzrobert Pl EGH TW20 172 C6? 
Fitzroy Cl HGT N6 118 A6? 
Fitzroy Crs CHSWK W4 146 A6? 
Fitzroy Gdns NRWD SE19 181 M10? 
Fitzroy Ms FITZ W1T 10 G2? 
Fitzroy Pk HGT N6 118 A6? 
Fitzroy Pl REIG RH2 257 M10? 
Fitzroy Rd CAMTN NW1 4 C5? 
Fitzroy Sq FITZ W1T 10 F1? 
Fitzroy St FITZ W1T 10 G2? 
Fitzstephen Rd BCTR RM8 123 J10? 
Fitzwarren Gdns ARCH N19 118 C6? 
Fitzwilliam Av RCH/KEW TW9 155 P7? 
Fitzwilliam Cl TRDG/WHET N20 98 A2? 
Fitzwilliam Ms CAN/RD E16 141 M10? 
Fitzwilliam Rd CLAP SW4 159 H10? 
Fitzwilliams Ct HLWE CM17 29 P4? 
Fitzwygram Cl HPTN TW12 175 M8? 
Fiveacre Cl THHTH CR7 203 J4? 
Five Acres CDALE/KGS NW9 96 C10? 
CSHM HP5 51 H7? 
HLWS CM18 47 J4? 
KGLGY WD4 53 N1? 
LCOL/BKTW AL2 55 M4? 
Five Acres Av LCOL/BKTW AL2 55 M3? 
Five Ash Rd GVW DA11 191 N7? 
Fiveash Rd GVW DA11 191 N7
Five Elms Rd DAGW RM9 124 A7? 
HAYES BR2 205 P10? 
Five Fields Cl OXHEY WD19 93 P2? 
Five Oaks HAT AL10 40 E7? 
Flora Gv STAL AL1 38 E7? 


First Avenue Mandela Av HLW CM20 28 J9
HLW CM20 198 A4
First Crs CAN/RD E16 141 N6? 
First Cross Rd WHTN TW2 176 D5? 
First Dr WLSDN NW10 136 D1? 
First Quarter HOR/WEW KT19 220 B7? 
First St CHEL SW3 15 P5? 
Firstway RYNPK SW20 200 F2? 
Firswood Av HOR/WEW KT19 220 C4? 
Firs Wk NTHWD HA6 96 E7? 
WFD IG8 101 K9? 
Firth Gdns FUL/PGN SW6 157 H7? 
Firtree Av MTCM CR4 202 B2? 
Fir Tree Av SLN SL2 129 L6? 
WDR/YW UB7 132 B7? 
Fir Tree Cl CRAWW RH11 283 L4? 
EA W5 135 K8? 
ESH/CLAY KT10 197 H5? 
Flamborough Wk POP/IOD E14 140 D8? 
Flamingo Wk HCH RM12 145 H5? 
Flamstead End Rd CHES/WCR EN8 62 A2? 
Flamstead Gdns DAGW RM9 143 P8? 
Flamstead Rd DAGW RM9 143 P8? 
Flamsted Av WBLY HA9 136 B3? 
Flamsteed Rd CHARL SE7 162 E3? 
Flanchford Rd REIG RH2 274 F5? 
Flanders Crs TOOT SW17 180 A10? 
Flanders Rd CHSWK W4 146 B3? 
EHAM E6 142 C4? 
Flanders Wy HOM E9 120 C1? 
Flank St WCHPL E1 13 N7? 
Flash La ENC/FH EN2 79 K3? 
Flask Wk HAMP NW3 117 M9? 
Flather Cl STRHM/NOR SW16 180 D9? 
Flatfield Ms HOR/WEW KT19 36 B8? 
Flaxton Rd WOOL/PLUM SE18 162 G10? 
Fleeming Rd WALTH E17 101 H8? 
Fleet Av RDART DA2 188 B4? 
UPMR RM14 126 A4? 
Fleetdale Pde RDART DA2 188 B4? 
Fleethall Gv SRTFD E15 141 L7? 
Fleet Rd GVW DA11 190 A5? 
HAMP NW3 117 M10? 
RDART DA2 188 B4? 
Fleet Sq FSBYW WC1X 5 N10? 
Fleet St FLST/FETLN EC4A 11 L3? 
Fleet Street Hl WCHPL E1 13 L1? 
Fleetway EGH TW20 194 A4? 
Fleetway Cl CAN/RD E16 142 H3? 
Fleetwood Cl CAN/RD E16 142 H3? 
CHSGTN KT9 219 J6? 
CROY/NA CRO 203 M1? 
CSTG HP8 70 F4? 
KWD/TDW/WH KT20 258 B3? 
Fleetwood Ct BF/WBF KT14 215 K9? 
WALTH E17 101 J3? 
Fleetwood Rd KUT/HW KT1 199 M3? 
SLN SL2 129 L2? 
WLSDN NW10 116 D10? 
Fleetwood St STNW/STAM N16 119 M7? 
Fleetwood Wy OXHEY WD19 93 L4? 
Fleming Cl CHESW EN7 61 K1? 
FARN/HRWW/WS HA3 94 F4? 
MV/WKIL W9 2 A6? 
Fleming Crs HERT/WAT SG14 25 L6? 
Fleming Dr WNWD SE27 181 M10? 
Fleming Gdns TIL RM18 168 F7? 
Fleming Md MTCM CR4 180 A10? 
Fleming Rd CDW/CHF RM16 167 P10? 
STHL UB1 134 A5? 
WAB EN9 62 A2? 
WALW SE17 18 E10? 
Flemings RBRW/HUT CM13 107 M7? 
Fleming Wy CRAWE RH10 284 D3? 
ISLW TW7 154 F6? 
THMD SE28 143 M5? 
Flemish Flds CHERT KT16 195 K7? 
Flemming Av RSLP HA4 113 J3? 
Fletcher Cl CHERT KT16 214 C3? 
CRAWE RH10 284 C8? 
EHAM E6 142 E5? 
Fletcher La LEY E10 102 B9? 
Fletcher Pth BROCKY SE4 160 E6? 
Fletcher Rd CHERT KT16 214 C3? 
CHIG IG7 103 M1? 
CHSWK W4 146 A3? 
Fletchers Cl HAYES BR2 205 K8? 
Fletcher St WCHPL E1 13 N4? 
Fletcher Wy HHNE HP2 35 L4? 
Fletching Rd CHARL SE7 162 A6? 
CLPT E5 120 E8? 
Fletton Rd FBAR/BDGN N11 99 H1? 
Fleur De Lis St WCHPL E1 13 J1? 
Fleur Gates WIM/MER SW19 178 G8? 
Flexford Rd RGUW GU3 266 A1? 
Flexley Wd WGCE AL7 23 L1? 
Flex Meadow HLWW/ROY CM19 46 A4? 
Flight Ap CDALE/KGS NW9 96 C9? 
Flimwell Cl BMLY BR1 183 J7? 
Flinders Cl STAL AL1 38 F5? 
Flint Cl BNSTD SM7 240 A3? 
CRAWE RH10 284 C10? 
GT/LBKH KT23 236 A10? 
ORP BR6 227 J2? 
REDH RH1 274 D2? 
SRTFD E15 141 L1? 
Flint Down Cl STMC/STPC BR5 207 K1? 
Flint Hill DORK RH4 272 G5? 
Flint Hill Cl DORK RH4 272 G5? 
Flintlock Cl STAI TW19 151 K10? 
Flintmill Crs BKHTH/KID SE3 162 G3? 
ELTH/MOT SE9 162 G3? 
Flinton St WALW SE17 19 K7? 
Flint St SOCK/AV RM15 147 K1? 
WALW SE17 19 K7? 
Flitcroft St LSQ/SEVD WC2H 11 J3? 
Floathaven Cl THMD SE28 143 K7? 
The Floats SEV TN13 246 F7? 
Flock Mill Pl WAND/EARL SW18 179 L4? 
Flockton St BERM/RHTH SE16 139 N7? 
Flodden Rd CMBW SE5 159 J8? 
Flood La TWK TW1 176 C4? 
Flood St CHEL SW3 15 N9? 
Flood Wk CHEL SW3 15 N9? 
Flora Cl POP/IOD E14 141 M8? 
STAN HA7 95 N2? 
Flora Gdns CHDH RM6 123 M4? 
CROY/NA CRO 205 P10? 
HMSMTH W6 148 E2? 
Flora Gv STAL AL1 38 E7? 


Florence Cl GSTN WD25 73 H1
HCH RM12 125 M7
HLWE CM17 47 M3
WOT/HER KT12 197 J7
WTHK RM20 167 K5
Florence Dr ENC/FH EN2 79 M2
Florence Elson Cl MNPK E12 122 G9
Florence Gdns CHSWK W4 156 A1
STA TW18 173 L10
Florence Rd ABYW SE2 163 M2
BECK BR3 204 B2? 
BMLY BR1 205 M1? 
CHSWK W4 156 A2? 
EA W5 135 L1? 
EHAM E6 141 P5? 
FELT TW13 175 L4? 
FSBYPK N4 119 H2? 
FSTGT E7 141 M1? 
HDN NW4 116 F2? 
KUTN/CMB KT2 177 H2? 
NWCR SE14 161 K3? 
NWDGN UB2 153 L3? 
PLSTW E13 141 M4? 
SAND/SEL CR2 223 M5? 
WALTH E17 120 C3? 
WIM/MER SW19 179 M7? 
WOT/HER KT12 197 J7? 
Florence St CAN/RD E16 141 L6? 
HDN NW4 116 F2? 
IS N1 6 C1? 
Florence Ter NWCR SE14 161 K4? 
PUT/ROE SW15 176 E7? 
Florence Vis HGT N6 118 B6? 
Florence Wy BAL SW12 180 A4? 
UX/CGN UB8 131 M4? 
WOKN/KNAP GU21 231 H4? 
Florey Sq WCHMH N21 78 G9? 
Florfield Rd HACK E8 140 A1? 
Florian Av SUT SM1 221 P3? 
Florian Rd PUT/ROE SW15 157 H10? 
Florida Cl BUSH WD23 94 C3? 
Florida Rd RGUE GU4 268 B6? 
THHTH CR7 203 J1? 
Florida St BETH E2 140 C10? 
Florin Ct WD TK16 195 K5? 
Floris Pl CLAP SW4 158 D10? 
Floriston Av HGDN/ICK UB10 132 B2? 
Floriston Cl STAN HA7 94 G9? 
Floriston Gdns STAN HA7 94 G9? 
Floss St PUT/ROE SW15 156 G6? 
Flower & Dean Wk WCHPL E1 13 M1? 
Flowerfield RSEV TN14 246 A5? 
Flowerhill Wy MEO DA13 212 G5? 
Flower La MLHL NW7 96 G1? 
GSTN WD25 73 M4? 
Flower Ms GLDGN NW11 117 H7? 
Flowerpot Cl SEVS/STOTM N15 119 P8? 
Flowers Cl CRICK NW2 116 G2? 
Flowers Ms ARCH N19 118 B8? 
Flower Wk GUW GU2 267 P6? 
Floyd Rd CHARL SE7 161 P2? 
Floyds La WOKS/MYFD GU22 232 G3? 
Floyer Cl RCHPK/HAM TW10 177 J5? 
Fludyer St LEW SE13 161 N11? 
Flux's La EPP CM16 65 K9? 
The Flyers Wy BH/WHM TN16 262 D2? 
Fogerty Cl PEND EN3 80 G3? 
Fold Cft HLW CM20 28 D10? 
Foley Cl BEAC HP9 88 B7? 
Foley Ms ESH/CLAY KT10 218 C6? 
Foley Rd BH/WHM TN16 244 A4? 
ESH/CLAY KT10 218 C6? 
Foley St GTPST W1W 10 F1? 
Folgate St WCHPL E1 13 K1? 
Foliot St SHB W12 136 G8? 
Folkes La UPMR RM14 126 E3? 
Folkestone Ct DTCH/LGLY SL3 150 B2? 
Folkestone Rd EHAM E6 142 C1? 
UED N18 100 C10? 
WALTH E17 120 C1? 
Folkingham La CDALE/KGS NW9 96 A9? 
Folkington Cnr NFNCH/WDSPK N12 97 H3? 
Follet Cl WDSR SL4 171 P1? 
Follett Dr ABLGY WD5 54 C1? 
Follett St POP/IOD E14 141 P8? 
Folly Av STALW/RED AL3 38 D4? 
Follyfield Rd BNSTD SM7 221 K10? 
Folly Flds STALW/RED AL3 38 B5? 
Folly La RDKG RH5 273 J10? 
STALW/RED AL3 38 B5? 
WALTH E17 101 H2? 
Folly Pathway RAD WD7 74 G1? 
The Folly HERT/WAT SG14 25 L5? 
LTWR GU18 212 A8? 
Folly Vw WARE SG12 26 G6? 
Folly Wall POP/IOD E14 161 H1? 
Fontaine Rd STRHM/NOR SW16 180 C10? 
Fontana Cl CRAWE RH10 158 B10? 
Fontarabia Rd BTSEA SW11 158 B10? 
Fontayne Av CHIG IG7 103 K2? 
RAIN RM13 144 F10? 
ROM RM1 104 D1? 
Fontenoy Rd BAL SW12 180 A10? 
Fonteyne Gdns WFD IG8 102 A10? 
Fonthill Ms FSBYPK N4 118 F7? 
Fonthill Rd FSBYPK N4 118 F7? 
Font Hills EFNCH N2 97 M10? 
Fontley Wy PUT/ROE SW15 176 E3? 
Fontmell Cl ASHF TW15 173 K8? 
Fontmell Pk ASHF TW15 173 K8? 
Fontwell Cl KTN/HRWW/WS HA3 94 D8? 
NTHLT UB5 133 N5? 
Fontwell Dr HAYES BR2 205 H2? 
Fontwell Park Gdns HCH RM12 125 M7? 
Fontwell Rd CRAWE RH10 284 B10? 
Footbury Hill Rd ORP BR6 207 K10? 
The Footpath PUT/ROE SW15 178 D1? 
Foots Cray High St SCUP DA14 185 M9? 
Foots Cray La SCUP DA14 185 M4? 
Footscray Rd ELTH/MOT SE9 184 D2? 
Forbes Av POTB/CUF EN6 59 N3? 
Forbes Cl CRICK NW2 116 G1? 
EMPK RM11 125 P5? 
Forbes St WCHPL E1 13 N3? 
Forbes Wy RSLP HA4 76 F8? 
Forburg Rd STNW/STAM N16 119 P6? 
Force Green La BH/WHM TN16 244 G10? 
Fordbridge Cl CHERT KT16 195 M9? 
Fordbridge Rd ASHF TW15 173 J9? 
SUN TW16 196 B3? 
Ford Cl ASHF TW15 173 H9? 
BUSH WD23 74 B5? 
HRW HA1 114 D6? 
RAIN RM13 144 E6? 
SHPTN TW17 196 B5? 
THHTH CR7 203 K3? 
Fordcroft Rd STMC/STPC BR5 207 L5? 
Forde Av BMLY BR1 184 B10? 
Fordel Rd CAT SE6 183 H2? 
Ford End DEN/HRF UB9 111 J8? 
WFD IG8 101 K7? 
Fordham Rd EBAR EN4 77 M2? 
Fordham St WCHPL E1 13 N2? 
Fordhook Av EA W5 135 L4? 


Floral Dr LCOL/BKTW AL2 57 J7
Floral Pl IS N1 119 L10
Floral St COVGDN WC2E 11 M7? 
Flora St BELV DA17 164 A4? 
Florence Av ADL/WDHM KT15 215 J5? 
EN EN1 79 M8? 
MRDN SM4 201 P5? 
Florence Cl WAN E11 121 L7? 
Florence Dr ENC/FH EN2 79 M2? 
Florence Gdns CRW RM5 104 A10? 
Floral Dr LCOL/BKTW AL2 57 J7?

Fordingbridge Cl
  *CHERT* KT16 * — 195 L8
Fordingley Rd *MV/WKIL* W9 — 2 D10
Fordington Rd *HGT* N6 — 118 A2
Ford La *IVER* SL0 — 131 K8
  *RAIN* RM13 — 144 G2
Fordmill Rd *CAT* SE6 — 182 F5
Ford Rd *ASHF* TW15 — 174 H4
  *BOW* E3 — 140 D4
  *CHERT* KT16 — 195 L8
  *CHOB/PIR* GU24 — 230 E1
  *DAGW* RM9 — 144 A2
  *GVW* DA11 — 190 D4
  *WOKS/MYFD* GU22 — 232 E6
Fords Gv *WCHMH* N21 — 99 K2
Fords Park Rd *CAN/RD* E16 — 141 M8
Ford Sq *WCHPL* E1 — 140 D4
Ford St *BOW* E3 — 140 D4
Fordwater Rd *CHERT* KT16 — 195 L8
Fordwich Cl *HERT/WAT* SG14 — 25 H5
  *ORP* BR6 — 
Fordwich Hi *HERT/WAT* SG14 — 25 H5
Fordwich Ri *HERT/WAT* SG14 — 25 H5
Fordwich Rd *WCCW* AL8 — 23 G6
Fordwych Rd *CRICK* NW2 — 2 D1
Fordyce Cl *EMPK* RM11 — 125 P9
Fordyce Rd *LEW* SE13 — 183 H2
Fordyke Rd *BCTR* RM8 — 123 K9
Forebury Av *RSEV* TN14 — 30 A1
The Forebury *SBW* CM21 — 30 A1
Forefield *LCOL/BKTW* AL2 — 55 P5
Forelands Wy *CHAM* HP5 — 51 H8
Foreland St *WOOL/PLUM* SE18 — 162 G3
Foreland Wk *CSTN* HA7 — 
Foremark Cl *BARK/HLT* IG6 — 103 J7
Foreshore *DEPT* SE8 — 160 E4
Forest Ap *CHING* E4 — 101 K1
  *WFD* IG8 — 101 L8
Forest Av *CHING* E4 — 102 D8
  *CHING* E4 — 101 K1
  *HHS/BOV* HP3 — 35 M5
Forest Cl *CHST* BR7 — 206 D1
  *EHSLY* KT24 — 252 F6
  *KIL/WHAMP* NW6 — 2 A3
  *WAB* EN9 — 81 N5
  *WAN* E11 — 121 L1
  *WFD* IG8 — 101 N5
  *WOKS/MYFD* GU22 — 232 E5
Forest Ct *CHING* E4 — 101 L2
  *WAN* E11 — 121 K1
Forest Crs *ASHTD* KT21 — 237 N2
Forestdale *STHGT/OAK* N14 — 98 C5
Forest Dr *EPP* CM16 — 83 H2
  *HAYES* BR2 — 226 B3
  *KWD/TDW/WH* KT20 — 239 K7
  *MNPK* E12 — 122 A8
  *SUN* TW16 — 174 C10
  *WFD* IG8 — 101 J8
Forest Dr East *WAN* E11 — 121 J1
Forest Dr West *WAN* E11 — 121 J5
Forest Edge *BKHH* IG9 — 101 P4
Forester Rd *CRAWE* RH10 — 284 C9
  *GUW* GU2 — 
  *PECK* SE15 — 160 A10
Foresters Cl *CHESW* EN7 — 61 M1
  *WLGTN* SM6 — 222 E6
  *WOKN/KNAP* GU21 — 231 L4
Foresters Crs *BXLYHN* DA7 — 164 C10
  *WLGTN* SM6 — 222 E6
Foresters Dr *WALTH* E17 — 121 J2
  *WLGTN* SM6 — 222 E6
Forestfield *CRAWE* RH10 — 284 C9
Forest Gdns *TOTM* N17 — 99 N10
Forest Ga *CDALE/KGS* NW9 — 116 B2
Forest Gld *CHING* E4 — 101 K6
  *EPP* CM16 — 65 P3
  *WAN* E11 — 121 K4
Forest Gv *EPP* CM16 — 65 M2
  *HACK* E8 — 7 J1
Forest Hill Rd *WFD* IG8 — 101 J8
Forest Hts *WDSR* SL4 — 170 D2
Fore St *BARB* EC2Y — 12 E1
  *BRKMPK* AL9 — 40 F5
  *ED* N9 — 99 P5
  *HERT/WAT* SG14 — 25 L5
  *HLWE* CM17 — 29 M7
  *PIN* HA5 — 112 G2
  *UED* N18 — 99 P6
Forest Mount Rd *WFD* IG8 — 101 J8
Forest Pk *WDSR* SL4 — 170 D2
Fore St *BARB* EC2Y — 12 E1
  *ED* N9 — 99 P5
  *HERT/WAT* SG14 — 25 L5
  *HLWE* CM17 — 29 M7
  *PIN* HA5 — 112 G2
  *UED* N18 — 99 P6
Forest Ri *BECK* BR3 — 204 F5
  *HAYES* BR2 — 226 B1
Forest Ri *WALTH* E17 — 121 J2
Forest Rd *BARK/HLT* IG6 — 103 H9
  *CHEAM* SM3 — 201 K8
  *CHES/WCR* EN8 — 62 C5
  *ED* N9 — 100 A2
  *EHSLY* KT24 — 252 G2
  *EPP* CM16 — 82 D1
  *ERITH* DA8 — 165 H7
  *FELT* TW13 — 175 K5
  *FSTGT* E7 — 124 C9
  *GSTN* WD25 — 55 J9
  *HACK* E8 — 7 L2
  *LOU* IG10 — 82 A8
  *PEND* EN3 — 80 D2
  *RCH/KEW* TW9 — 155 N6
  *ROMW/RG* RM7 — 124 D2
  *TOTM* N17 — 120 B2
  *WAN* E11 — 121 H5
  *WDSR* SL4 — 170 A7
  *WFD* IG8 — 101 M4
Forest side *CHING* E4 — 101 L1
  *EPP* CM16 — 66 C9
  *FSTGT* E7 — 124 C9
  *WPK* KT4 — 200 C10
Forest St *FSTGT* E7 — 124 C10
The Forest *WAN* E11 — 101 K2
Forest Vw *CHING* E4 — 101 N1
  *WAN* E11 — 121 L5
Forest View Av *LEY* E10 — 121 J5
Forest View Rd *LOU* IG10 — 81 P7
  *MNPK* E12 — 123 J1
  *WALTH* E17 — 101 H9
Forest Wk *BUSH* WD23 — 73 N5
Forest Wy *ASHTD* KT21 — 237 N5
  *BFN/LL* DA15 — 184 G3
  *HLWE* CM17 — 30 C10
  *HLWE* CM17 — 31 H5
  *HLWS* CM18 — 31 J5
  *LOU* IG10 — 81 P7
  *STMC/STPC* BR5 — 207 J4
  *WAB* EN9 — 64 B7
  *WFD* IG8 — 101 N5
Forfar Rd *BTSEA* SW11 — 158 G7
  *WDGN* N22 — 99 J8
Forge Av *COUL/CHIP* CR5 — 241 H6
Forge Bridge La
  *COUL/CHIP* CR5 — 240 C8
Forge Cl *HAYES* BR2 — 205 N8
  *KGLGY* WD4 — 53 K7
Forge Cots *EA* W5 * — 135 J10
Forge Dr *ESH/CLAY* KT10 — 218 F4
  *SLN* SL2 — 129 H1
Forge End *LCOL/BKTW* AL2 — 55 P2
  *WOKN/KNAP* GU21 — 232 E6
Forgefield *BH/WHM* TN16 — 244 A2
Forge La *CHEAM* SM3 — 221 H8
  *CRAWE* RH10 * — 284 B6
  *EYN* DA4 — 210 B4
  *FELT* TW15 — 175 M4
  *GVE* DA12 — 191 J5
  *NTHWD* HA6 — 32 F6
  *RCHPK/HAM* TW10 — 177 K4
  *SUN* TW16 — 197 N4


Forge Rd *CRAWE* RH10 — 284 B6
The Forge *HORL* RH6 * — 279 H8
  *POTB/CUF* EN6 — 59 P6
Forge Wy *RSEV* TN14 — 228 G3
Forge Wd *CRAWE* RH10 — 284 E2
Formby Av
  *KTN/HRWW/WS* HA3 — 115 N1
Formby Cl *DTCH/LGLY* SL3 — 150 F3
Form Cl *RAD* WD7 — 57 K7
Formosa St *MV/WKIL* W9 — 9 H2
Formount Cl *CAN/RD* E16 — 141 L7
Forres Cl *HOD* EN11 — 44 B4
Forrester Pth *SYD* SE26 — 182 B7
Forresters Dr *WGCE* AL7 — 23 M7
Forrest Gdns
  *STRHM/NOR* SW16 — 202 G3
Forris Av *HYS/HAR* UB3 — 132 C10
Forset La *MBLAR* W1H — 9 P5
Forsiial Cl *HAYES* BR2 — 205 M3
Forster Rd *BECK* BR3 — 204 D3
Forster Rd *STRHM* SW2 — 180 G2
  *TOTM* N17 — 119 N1
  *WALTH* E17 — 120 D4
Forsters Cl *CHDH* RM6 — 124 A4
Forston St *IS* N1 — 6 F7
Forsyte Crs *NRWD* SE19 — 203 M1
Forsyth Gdns *WALW* SE17 — 18 D9
Forsythia Cl *IL* IG1 — 122 C10
Forsythia Pl *GU* GU1 * — 249 P8
Forsyth Pl *EN* EN1 — 79 M9
Forsyth Rd *WOKN/KNAP* GU21 — 214 F10
Fortescue Av *WHTN* TW2 — 176 B6
Fortescue Rd *EDGW* HA8 — 96 A9
  *WEY* KT13 — 216 A1
  *WIM/MER* SW19 — 179 N10
Fortess Gv *KTTN* NW5 — 180 H8
Fortess Rd *KTTN* NW5 — 118 C10
Fortess Wk *KTTN* NW5 — 118 C10
Forthbridge Rd *BTSEA* SW11 — 158 B10
Forth Rd *UPMR* RM14 — 126 C4
Fortin Cl *SOCK/AV* RM15 — 146 P3
Fortin Wy *SOCK/AV* RM15 — 146 P3
Fortis Cl *CAN/RD* E16 — 141 P8
Fortis Gn *EFNCH* N2 — 118 A1
Fortis Green Av *EFNCH* N2 — 118 B1
Fortis Green Rd *MUSWH* N10 — 118 A3
Fortismere Av *MUSWH* N10 — 118 A3
Fort La *REIG* RH2 — 257 L6
Fortnam Rd *ARCH* N19 — 118 C7
Fortnums Acre *STAN* HA7 — 94 E7
Fort Rd *GU* GU1 — 288 B6
  *KWD/TDW/WH* KT20 — 255 N7
  *NTHLT* UB5 — 133 P2
  *RSEV* TN14 — 246 D1
  *STHWK* SE1 — 19 M6
  *TIL* RM18 — 168 E10
Fortrose Cl *POP/IOD* E14 — 141 J8
Fortrose Gdns
  *BRXS/STRHM* SW2 — 180 F4
Fortrye Cl *GVW* DA11 — 190 B5
Fort St *CAN/RD* E16 — 141 N7
  *WCHPL* E1 — 13 K4
Fortuna Cl *HOLWY* N7 — 5 P1
Fortune Av *EDGW* HA8 — 95 N9
Fortune Green Rd
  *KIL/WHAMP* NW6 — 117 H3
Fortune Pl *STHWK* SE1 — 19 M8
Fortunes Md *NTHLT* UB5 — 133 M1
The Fortunes *HLWS* CM18 — 47 J3
Fortune St *STLK* EC1Y — 12 E5
Fortune Wy *WLSDN* NW10 — 136 D5
Forty Acre La *CAN/RD* E16 — 141 M7
Forty Av *WBLY* HA9 — 115 L8
Forty Cl *WBLY* HA9 — 115 L8
Fortyfoot Rd *LHD/OX* KT22 — 237 H7
Forty Green Rd *BEAC* HP9 — 88 A7
Forty Hi *ENC/FH* EN2 — 79 N3
Forty La *WBLY* HA9 — 115 N7
Forum Cl *BOW* E3 — 140 F3
Forum Magnum Sq
  *STHWK* SE1 — 17 L1
Forum Pl *HAT* AL10 * — 40 D3
Forumside *EDGW* HA8 — 95 M7
The Forum *E/WMO/HCT* KT8 — 198 A4
Forval Cl *MTCM* CR4 — 202 A5
Forward Dr
  *KTN/HRWW/WS* HA3 — 114 F2
Fosbury Ms *BAY/PAD* W2 — 9 H1
Foscote Ms *MV/WKIL* W9 — 8 F2
Foscote Rd *HDN* NW4 — 116 E4
Foskett Rd *FUL/PGN* SW6 — 157 J8
Foss Av *CROY/NA* CR0 — 223 H2
Fossdene Rd *CHARL* SE7 — 161 N4
Fossdyke Cl *YEAD* UB4 — 133 M7
Fosse Wy *BF/WBF* KT14 — 215 J9
  *WEA* W13 — 134 F7
Fossil Rd *LEW* SE13 — 160 F9
Fossington Rd *BELV* DA17 — 163 N10
Foss Rd *TOOT* SW17 — 179 N7
Fossway *BCTR* RM8 — 123 K9
Foster Av *WDSR* SL4 — 148 D9
Foster Cl *CHES/WCR* EN8 — 62 C6
Fosterdown *GDST* RH9 — 260 A5
Foster La *CITYW* EC2V — 12 E5
Foster Rd *ACT* W3 — 136 D5
  *CHSWK* W4 — 156 A4
  *HHW* HP1 — 35 N3
  *PLSTW* E13 — 141 M6
Fosters Cl *CHST* BR7 — 184 C4
  *SWFD* E18 — 101 N9
Fosters Gv *BFOR* GU20 — 212 A1
Fosters La *WOKN/KNAP* GU21 — 231 K5
Fosters Ms *HART* DA3 — 211 K5
Fosters Pth *SLN* SL2 — 128 E6
Foster St *HLWE* CM17 — 31 J5
Foster Wk *HDN* NW4 — 116 F2
Fothergill Cl *PLSTW* E13 — 141 M1
Fotherhill St *WCHMH* N21 — 78 F9
Fotheringay Gdns *SL* SL1 — 128 C6
Fotheringham Rd *EN* EN1 — 79 M9
Fotherley Rd
  *RKW/CH/CXG* WD3 — 91 J3
Foubert's Pl *SOHO/CST* W1F — 11 H9
Foulden Rd *STNW/STAM* N16 — 119 J9
Foulden Ter *STNW/STAM* N16 — 119 J9
Foulis Ter *SKENS* SW7 — 15 L6
Foulser Rd *TOOT* SW17 — 180 A6
Foulsham Rd *THHTH* CR7 — 203 K9
Foundry Ga *CHES/WCR* EN8 — 47 J3
Foundary Cl *DTCH/LGLY* SL3 — 150 F3
Foundry Ct *CHERT* KT16 — 195 K7
Foundry Ms *CAMTN* NW1 — 11 H7
Foundry Pl *WAND/EARL* SW18 — 179 L5
Founes Dr *CDW/CHF* RM16 — 167 M2
Fountain Cl *LUX/CGN* UB8 — 132 D7
Fountain Dr *CAR* SM5 — 222 A4
  *HERT/BAY* SG13 — 25 N4
  *NRWD* SE19 — 181 N1
  *WLGTN* SM6 — 222 F7
Fountain Farm *HLWS* CM18 — 47 J3
Fountain Gdns *WDSR* SL4 — 149 L8
Fountain Green Sq
  *BERM/RHTH* SE16 — 19 P7
Fountain Ms *HAMP* NW3 — 4 C1
Fountains Av *FELT* TW13 — 175 H8
Fountains Cl *CRAWW* RH11 — 283 P3
  *FELT* TW13 — 175 H8


FELT TW13 — 175 N5
Fountains Crs *STHGT/OAK* N14 — 98 F1
Fountain Rd *MV/WKIL* W9 — 276 B5
Fountayne Rd
  *STNW/STAM* N16 — 119 P7
Fount St *VX/NE* SW8 — 158 F6
Fouracres *PEND* EN3 — 80 D5
Four Acres *COB* KT11 — 217 M9
  *GU* GU1 — 250 F8
  *WGCE* AL7 — 23 H7
Fouracres Dr *HHS/BOV* HP3 — 36 A7
The Four Acres *SBW* CM21 — 30 B1
Fouracres Wk *HHS/BOV* HP3 — 36 A8
Fourdrinier Wy *HHS/BOV* HP3 — 35 P6
Fourland Wk *EDGW* HA8 — 95 P7
Four Limes *STALE/WH* AL4 — 21 J3
Four Oaks *BRWN* CM15 * — 107 K4
Four Seasons Cl *BOW* E3 — 140 F8
Four Seasons Crs *CHEAM* SM3 — 201 J9
Fourteenth Av
  *KWD/TDW/WH* KT20 * — 257 J2
Fourth Av *GSTN* WD25 — 73 L1
  *HLWN* CM20 — 28 F10
  *HLWW/ROY* CM19 — 46 D1
  *HYS/HAR* UB3 — 132 G10
  *KWD/TDW/WH* KT20 * — 257 J2
  *MNPK* E12 — 122 C9
  *NKENS* W10 — 8 A1
  *ROMW/RG* RM7 — 124 D6
  *WTHK* RM20 — 146 E6
Fourth Cross Rd *WHTN* TW2 — 176 C5
Fourth Dr *COUL/CHIP* CR5 — 240 E2
Fourth Wy *WBLY* HA9 — 115 N9
The Four Tubs *BUSH* WD23 — 94 C1
Four Wents *COB* KT11 — 217 J9
The Four Wents *CHING* E4 — 101 J3
Fovant Cl *HARP* AL5 — 20 F1
Fowey Av *REDBR* IG4 — 122 A3
Fowey Cl *WAP* E1W — 140 A10
Fox & Knot St *FARR* EC1M * — 12 C2
Foxacre *CTHM* CR3 — 241 M6
Foxberry Rd *BROCKY* SE4 — 160 D10
Foxboro Rd *REDH* RH1 — 258 C8
Foxborough Cl
  *DTCH/LGLY* SL3 — 150 D4
Foxborough Gdns
  *BROCKY* SE4 — 182 F2
Foxborough Hill Rd *SHGR* GU5 — 268 B9
Foxbourne Rd *TOOT* SW17 — 180 B5
Fox Burrow Rd *BARK/HLT* IG6 — 103 M6
  *CHIG* IG7 — 103 N5
Foxburrows Av *GUW* GU2 — 248 A10
Foxbury Av *CHST* BR7 — 184 C9
Foxbury Cl *BMLY* BR1 — 183 N9
  *ORP* BR6 — 227 K2
Foxbury Dr *ORP* BR6 — 227 K3
Foxbury Rd *BMLY* BR1 — 183 N9
Fox Cl *BORE* WD6 — 75 J10
  *BUSH* WD23 — 74 A9
  *CAN/RD* E16 — 141 M7
  *CRAWE* RH11 — 283 L5
  *CRW* RM5 — 104 C6
  *ORP* BR6 — 227 K2
  *WCHPL* E1 — 140 B6
  *WEY* KT13 — 216 E2
  *WOKS/MYFD* GU22 — 232 C1
Foxcombe *CROY/NA* CR0 — 224 C3
Foxcombe Rd *PUT/ROE* SW15 * — 178 C1
Fox Covert *LHD/OX* KT22 — 236 C10
  *ASC* SL5 — 192 B5
Foxcroft *STAL* AL1 — 38 F8
Foxcroft Rd
  *WOOL/PLUM* SE18 — 162 E7
Foxdell *NTHWD* HA6 — 32 C5
Foxdells *HERT/WAT* SG14 — 24 D8
Foxdell Wy *CFSP/GDCR* SL9 — 90 B6
Foxdene Cl *SWFD* E18 — 102 A6
Foxearth Cl *BH/WHM* TN16 — 244 B4
Foxearth Rd *SAND/SEL* CR2 — 224 A6
Foxearth Sp *SAND/SEL* CR2 — 224 A5
Foxenden Rd *GU* GU1 — 268 A5
Foxes Cl *HERT/BAY* SG13 — 26 A5
Foxes Di *BKHTH/KID* SE3 — 161 N1
  *HAYES* BR2 — 205 J3
Foxes Dr *CHESW* EN7 — 61 N5
Foxes Gn *CDW/CHF* RM16 — 168 D1
Foxes La *POTB/CUF* EN6 — 60 F4
Foxes Pde *WAB* EN9 * — 63 H9
Foxes Pth *RGUE* GU4 — 250 C2
Foxfield Cl *NTHWD* HA6 — 32 F5
Foxfield Rd *ORP* BR6 — 206 E9
Foxglove Cl *BF/LL* DA15 — 185 J5
  *ED* N9 — 100 B2
  *HAT* AL10 — 40 B3
  *HOD* EN11 — 27 H10
  *STHL* UB1 — 133 M1
  *STWL/WRAY* TW19 — 173 N4
Foxglove Gdns *PUR/KEN* CR8 — 242 C1
  *RGUE* GU4 — 250 F8
  *WAN* E11 — 121 P2
Foxglove La *CHSGTN* KT9 — 219 M1
Foxglove Pth *THMD* SE28 — 146 B1
Foxglove Rd *ROMW/RG* RM7 — 104 C10
  *SOCK/AV* RM15 — 147 H8
Foxglove St *SHB* W12 — 137 P1
Foxgloves Av *ACT* W3 — 136 A6
Foxglove Wy *WLGTN* SM6 — 202 D9
Foxgrove *STHGT/OAK* N14 — 98 E4
Fox Gv *WOT/HER* KT12 — 197 J3
Foxgrove Av *BECK* BR3 — 182 G10
Foxgrove Pth *OXHEY* WD19 — 93 L6
Foxgrove Rd *BECK* BR3 — 182 G10
Foxhall Rd *UPMR* RM14 — 126 E7
Foxham Rd *ARCH* N19 — 118 D8
Foxhanger Gdns
  *WOKS/MYFD* GU22 — 232 D2
Fox Hatch *BRWN* CM15 — 86 D3
Foxherne *DTCH/LGLY* SL3 — 149 P1
Fox Hi *HAYES* BR2 — 225 P1
  *NRWD* SE19 — 181 N10
Fox Hill Gdns *NRWD* SE19 — 181 N10
Foxhill Ms *CHERT* KT16 — 194 E10
Foxhills *WOKN/KNAP* GU21 — 231 H4
Foxhills Cl *CHERT* KT16 — 214 B1
Foxhollow Dr *BXLYHN* DA7 — 163 M7
Fox Hollow Cl
  *WOOL/PLUM* SE18 — 163 H4
Fox Hollow Dr *BXLYHN* DA7 — 163 M8
Foxhollows *HAT* AL10 — 40 E7
Foxhollows *SLN* SL2 — 109 H10
Foxholt Gdns *WLSDN* NW10 — 136 G2
Fox House Rd *BELV* DA17 — 164 C4
Foxlake Rd *BF/WBF* KT14 — 216 A8
Foxlands Cl *GSTN* WD25 — 55 H10
Foxlands Crs *DAGE* RM10 — 124 D10
Foxlands La *DAGE* RM10 — 124 D10
Foxlands Rd *DAGE* RM10 — 124 D10
Fox La *ASC* SL5 — 235 H10
  *HAYES* BR2 — 225 M8
  *PLMGR* N13 — 99 J4
  *REIG* RH2 — 257 P7
Fox La North *CHERT* KT16 — 195 J8
Fox La South *CHERT* KT16 * — 195 J8


Foxlees *ALP/SUD* HA0 — 114 F9
Foxley Cl *HACK* E8 — 119 P10
  *REDH* RH1 — 276 B5
Foxley Gdns *PUR/KEN* CR8 — 223 J8
Foxley Hill Rd *PUR/KEN* CR8 — 223 J7
Foxley Ms *CTHM* CR3 — 242 F6
Foxley Rd *CMBW* SE5 — 159 H6
  *PUR/KEN* CR8 — 223 J10
  *THHTH* CR7 — 203 J4
Foxleys *OXHEY* WD19 — 93 M4
Fox Manor Wy *WTHK* RM20 — 166 G5
Foxmead Ct *ENC/FH* EN2 — 78 G7
Foxmore St *BTSEA* SW11 — 158 A7
Foxoak Hi *WOT/HER* KT12 — 216 A3
Foxon Cl *CTHM* CR3 — 241 M7
Foxon La *CTHM* CR3 — 241 M7
Foxon Lane Gdns *CTHM* CR3 — 241 M7
Fox's La *BRKMPK* AL9 — 41 H10
Foxton Av *PEND* EN3 — 80 D5
Foxton Rd *HOD* EN11 — 44 B4
  *WTHK* RM20 — 167 J5
Foxwarren *ESH/CLAY* KT10 — 218 E5
Fox Wd *WOT/HER* KT12 — 216 G4
Foxwood Cl *FELT* TW13 — 174 B6
  *MLHL* NW7 — 96 B5
Foxwood Green Cl *EN* EN1 — 79 M10
  *ORP* BR6 — 227 M6
Foxwood Rd *BKHTH/KID* SE3 — 161 L10
  *RDART* DA2 — 188 G10
Foyle Dr *SOCK/AV* RM15 — 147 K5
Foyle Rd *BKHTH/KID* SE3 — 161 L5
  *TOTM* N17 — 99 P9
Frailey Cl *WOKS/MYFD* GU22 — 232 C4
Frailey Hi *WOKS/MYFD* GU22 — 232 C4
Framewood Rd
  *DTCH/LGLY* SL3 — 129 P2
  *SLN* SL2 — 129 J1
Framfield Cl *CRAWW* RH11 — 283 K5
  *NFNCH/WDSPK* N12 — 97 K5
Framfield Rd *HBRY* N5 — 119 J10
  *HNWL* W7 — 134 E8
  *MTCM* CR4 — 180 B10
Framlingham Crs
  *ELTH/MOT* SE9 — 184 B7
Frampton Cl *BELMT* SM2 — 221 K4
Frampton Park Rd *HOM* E9 — 140 A1
Frampton Rd *EPP* CM16 — 65 K4
  *HSLWW* TW4 — 175 M1
  *POTB/CUF* EN6 — 59 M6
Frampton St *HERT/WAT* SG14 — 25 L5
  *STJWD* NW8 — 9 M2
Francemary Rd *LEW* SE13 — 183 H1
Frances Av *CDW/CHF* RM16 — 167 H3
Frances Gdns *SOCK/AV* RM15 — 146 F9
Frances Rd *CHING* E4 — 101 M5
Frances St *CSHM* HP5 — 51 J6
  *WOOL/PLUM* SE18 — 146 D10
Franche Court Rd *TOOT* SW17 — 179 M6
Franchise St *CSHM* HP5 — 51 H6
Francis Av *BXLYHN* DA7 — 164 B8
  *FELT* TW13 — 175 H7
  *IL* IG1 — 122 C7
  *STALW/RED* AL3 — 38 C3
Francis Barber Cl
  *STRHM/NOR* SW16 — 180 G7
Francis Bentley Ms *CLAP* SW4 — 158 D9
Franciscan Rd *TOOT* SW17 — 180 B7
Francis Chichester Cl *ASC* SL5 — 234 B5
Francis Chichester Wy
  *BTSEA* SW11 — 158 A7
Francis Ct *GU* GU1 * — 249 N8
Francis Crick Rd *GUW* GU2 — 267 J1
Francis Ms *LEE/GVPK* SE12 * — 183 J2
Francis Rd *CROY/NA* CR0 — 203 J8
  *CTHM* CR3 — 241 N8
  *ERITH* N2 * — 118 A2
  *GFD/PVL* UB6 — 135 H4
  *HRW* HA1 — 114 F3
  *HSLWW* TW4 — 175 H5
  *LEY* E10 — 121 H7
  *PIN* HA5 — 113 K3
  *WLGTN* SM6 — 222 E6
Francis St *SRTFD* E15 — 123 C1
  *WEST* SW1P — 17 H5
Francis Ter *ARCH* N19 — 118 C8
Francis Wk *IS* N1 — 5 N1
Francis Yd *CSHM* HP5 — 50 J6
Francklyn Gdns *EDGW* HA8 — 95 M4
Francombe Gdns *ROM* RM1 — 124 E3
Franconia Rd *CLAP* SW4 — 158 A5
Frank Burton Cl *CHARL* SE7 — 161 M3
Frank Dixon Cl *DUL* SE21 — 181 M3
Frank Dixon Wy *DUL* SE21 — 181 M3
Frankfurt Rd *HNHL* SE24 — 160 L5
Frankham St *DEPT* SE8 — 160 L1
Frankland Cl
  *BERM/RHTH* SE16 — 160 A2
  *RKW/CH/CXG* WD3 — 92 B1
  *WFD* IG8 — 101 L2
Frankland Rd *CHING* E4 — 100 F6
  *RKW/CH/CXG* WD3 — 72 C10
  *SKENS* SW7 — 15 L4
Franklands Dr
  *ADL/WDHM* KT15 — 212 A5
Franklin Av *CHESW* EN7 — 61 N4
  *SLN* SL2 — 130 D2
  *WATW* WD18 — 73 H10
Franklin Cl *GU* GU1 — 249 L10
  *KUT/HW* KT1 — 199 M3
  *LEW* SE13 — 160 F9
  *STALE/WH* AL4 — 40 A6
  *TRDG/WHET* N20 — 97 M1
  *WNWD* SE27 — 181 L1
Franklin Crs *MTCM* CR4 — 180 E9
Franklin Rd *BXLYHN* DA7 — 164 A1
  *CRAWE* RH10 — 284 G4
  *GVE* DA12 — 190 G8
  *HCH* RM12 — 145 K1
  *PGE/AN* SE20 — 182 G2
  *WAT* WD17 — 73 J6
Franklin Sq *WKENS* W14 — 19 J1
Franklins *RKW/CH/CXG* WD3 — 91 H5
Franklins Ms *RYLN/HDSTN* HA2 — 114 C7
Franklin St *BOW* E3 — 140 G8
  *SEVS/STOTM* N15 — 119 N4
Franklin Wy *CROY/NA* CR0 — 202 G8
Franklyn Gdns *BARK/HLT* IG6 — 103 K2
Franklyn Rd *WLSDN* NW10 — 137 H2
  *WOT/HER* KT12 — 197 P3
Frank Martin Ct *CHESW* EN7 — 61 P6
Franks Av *NWMAL* KT3 — 199 P3
Franksfield *SHGR* GU5 — 270 D9
Franks La *EYN* DA4 — 209 P10
Franks Rd *GU* GU1 — 249 M1
Frank Sutton Wy *SL* SL1 — 129 H6
Franks Wood Av
  *STMC/STPC* BR5 — 206 D5
Frankswood Av *WDR/YW* UB7 — 113 J9
  *STMC/STPC* BR5 — 206 D5
Frankwell Dr *PLMGR* N13 — 99 H1
Franlaw Crs *PLMGR* N13 — 99 K3
Franmil Rd *HCH* RM12 — 124 G9
Fransfield Gv *SYD* SE26 — 182 A6
Franshams *BUSH* WD23 * — 74 F3
Frant Cl *PGE/AN* SE20 — 182 G1
Frant Rd *THHTH* CR7 — 203 L6
Fraser Cl *BXLY* DA5 — 186 A6
  *EHAM* E6 — 142 A3


Fraser Rd *CHES/WCR* EN8 — 62 D4
  *ED* N9 — 100 A4
  *ERITH* DA8 — 164 D4
  *GFD/PVL* UB6 — 135 H3
  *WALTH* E17 — 120 D5
Fraser St *CHSWK* W4 — 156 B4
Frating Crs *WFD* IG8 — 102 A6
Frays Av *WDR/YW* UB7 — 151 N1
Frays Cl *WDR/YW* UB7 — 151 N2
Fraysea Ux *UX/CGN* UB8 — 131 K4
Fray's Waye *UX/CGN* UB8 — 131 K3
Frazer Av *RSLP* HA4 — 113 K10
Frazer Cl *ROM* RM1 — 124 E5
Frazier St *STHWK* SE1 — 17 M3
Freda Corbett Cl *PECK* SE15 — 159 P6
Frederica Rd *CHING* E4 — 101 L2
Frederica St *HOLWY* N7 — 5 P3
  *SUT* SM1 — 221 J3
Frederick Cl *BAY/PAD* W2 — 9 P7
  *SUT* SM1 — 221 J3
Frederick Crs *BRXN/ST* SW9 — 159 J6
  *PEND* EN3 — 80 D2
Frederick Gdns *CROY/NA* CR0 — 203 J3
  *SUT* SM1 — 221 J2
Frederick Pl
  *WOOL/PLUM* SE18 — 162 E4
Frederick Rd *RAIN* RM13 — 144 A3
  *SUT* SM1 — 221 J4
  *WALW* SE17 — 18 D8
Frederick Sanger Rd
  *GUW* GU2 — 267 J1
Frederick's Pl *LOTH* EC2R * — 12 G6
  *NFNCH/WDSPK* N12 — 97 M5
Fredericks Pl
  *BERM/RHTH* SE16 — 140 D9
Frederick's Rw *FSBYE* EC1V — 6 C3
Frederick St *WALTH* E17 — 120 D5
Frederic Ms *KTBR* SW1X — 16 C2
Frederic St *WALTH* E17 — 120 D5
Fredora Av *YEAD* UB4 — 132 G4
Freeborne Gdns *RAIN* RM13 — 145 H1
Freedom Cl *WALTH* E17 — 120 D3
Freedom Rd *TOTM* N17 — 99 L10
Freedom St *BTSEA* SW11 — 158 E8
Freedown La *BELMT* SM2 — 221 L9
Freegrove Rd *HOLWY* N7 — 5 L1
Freeland Pk *HDN* NW4 — 97 H10
Freeland Rd *EA* W5 — 135 L7
Freelands Av *SAND/SEL* CR2 — 224 C5
Freelands Gv *BMLY* BR1 — 184 A4
Freelands Rd *BMLY* BR1 — 205 N1
  *COB* KT11 — 217 J10
Freeland Wy *ERITH* DA8 — 165 H7
Freeling St *IS* N1 * — 5 N4
Freeman Cl *NTHLT* UB5 — 133 J5
  *SHPTN* TW17 — 196 F6
Freeman Ct *SLN* SL2 — 129 L1
  *STHL* UB1 — 133 N6
Freeman Dr *E/WMO/HCT* KT8 — 197 K4
Freeman Rd *GVE* DA12 — 191 L8
  *MRDN* SM4 — 201 N5
Freemans Cl *SLN* SL2 — 129 L1
Freemans La *HYS/HAR* UB3 — 132 L1
Freemantle Av *PEND* EN3 — 80 E2
Freemantle St *WALW* SE17 — 19 J8
Freeman Wy *EMPK* RM11 — 125 M4
Freemasons Pl *CROY/NA* CR0 — 203 M8
Freemasons Rd *CAN/RD* E16 — 141 K8
  *CROY/NA* CR0 — 203 M8
Free Prae Rd *CHERT* KT16 — 195 K8
Freesia Cl *ORP* BR6 — 227 J2
Freestone Yd
  *DTCH/LGLY* SL3 * — 150 C6
Freethorpe Cl *NRWD* SE19 — 203 M1
Freezeland Wy
  *HGDN/ICK* UB10 — 132 B1
Freightmaster Est
  *RAIN* RM13 — 165 H3
Freke Rd *BTSEA* SW11 — 159 H5
Fremantle Rd *BARK/HLT* IG6 — 102 E10
  *BELV* DA17 — 163 J4
Fremont St *HOM* E9 — 140 A3
Frenchaye *ADL/WDHM* KT15 — 212 D8
French Gdns *COB* KT11 — 231 N1
Frenches Rd *REDH* RH1 — 258 B8
The Frenches *REDH* RH1 — 258 C8
French Gdns *COB* KT11 — 231 N1
French Horn La *WARE* SG12 * — 26 C2
French Horn La *HAT* AL10 — 40 E3
Frenchlands Hatch
  *EHSLY* KT24 — 252 F5
French Pl *SDTCH* EC2A — 7 K10
French's Cl *WARE* SG12 — 26 E1
French St *SUN* TW16 — 197 K2
French's Wls
  *WOKN/KNAP* GU21 — 231 N3
Frenchum Gdns *SL* SL1 — 128 D10
Frendsbury Rd *BROCKY* SE4 — 160 L1
Frensham *CHESW* EN7 — 61 N5
Frensham Cl *STHL* UB1 — 133 N6
  *PUR/ROE* SW15 — 178 D2
Frensham Dr *CROY/NA* CR0 — 225 J5
  *PUT/ROE* SW15 — 178 D2
Frensham Rd *ELTH/MOT* SE9 — 184 G10
  *PUR/KEN* CR8 — 223 J9
  *SEH* PECK SE15 — 19 P10
Frensham St *PECK* SE15 — 19 P10
Frensham Wy *PECK* SE15 — 19 P10
Frenshaw Dr *ELTH/MOT* SE9 — 184 G10
Fresco Dr *PIN* HA5 — 113 K5
Freshborough Ct *GU* GU1 * — 268 C1
Freshfield Av *HACK* E8 — 7 H1
Freshfield Cl *CRAWE* RH10 — 285 J1
  *LEW* SE13 — 161 L10
Freshfield Dr *STHGT/OAK* N14 — 98 C1
Freshfields *CROY/NA* CR0 — 204 P7
  *UPMR* RM14 — 126 A10
Freshford St *TOOT* SW17 — 179 J2
Fresh Mill La *STHL* UB1 — 133 P6
Freshmount Gdns
  *HOR/WEW* KT19 — 219 N7
Freshwater Cl *TOOT* SW17 — 180 C10
Freshwater Rd *BCTR* RM8 — 123 N6
  *TOOT* SW17 — 180 C10
Freshwaters *HLW* CM20 — 29 H10
Freshwell Av *CHDH* RM6 — 123 M2
Fresh Wharf Rd *BARK* IG11 — 142 A1
Freshwood Cl *BECK* BR3 — 204 G1
Freshwood Wy *WLGTN* SM6 — 222 D6
Freston Gdns *EBAR* EN4 — 78 B4
Freston Pk *FNCH* N3 — 97 H2
Freston Rd *NKENS* W10 — 136 G9
Freta Rd *BXLYHS* DA6 — 186 A1
Fretherne Chambers
  *WGCW* AL8 * — 22 G5
Fretherne Rd *WGCW* AL8 — 22 G5
Frewin Rd *WAND/EARL* SW18 — 179 M4
Friar Ms *WNWD* SE27 — 181 J10
Friar Rd *STMC/STPC* BR5 — 207 H3
  *YEAD* UB4 — 133 J3
Friars Av *PUT/ROE* SW15 — 178 A4
  *TRDG/WHET* N20 — 97 P4
Friars Cl *CHING* E4 — 101 L4


The Friars *CHIG* IG7 — 103 H5
  *HLWW/ROY* CM19 — 46 E1
Friars Av *ABYW* SE2 — 163 N4
  *STHGT/OAK* N14 — 98 C2
Friars Av *ACT* W3 — 135 N5
  *BUSH* WD23 — 73 N5
  *CHERT* KT16 — 195 K6
  *KGLGY* WD4 — 54 B6
Friars Av *WD/YW* UB7 — 224 D5
Friars Br *GU* GU1 — 267 P2
Friars Cl *NFNCH/WDSPK* N12 — 97 P6
Friars Cl *WOKN/KNAP* GU21 — 231 L4
Friars Est *PECK* SE15 — 159 P6
Friars Island
  *STWL/WRAY* TW19 — 171 J2
Friars Pk *NFNCH/WDSPK* N12 — 101 M5
Friars Pk
  *NFNCH/WDSPK* N12 — 97 P5
Friars Park Ct *ACT* W3 * — 135 N5
  *ASC* SL5 — 192 A6
Friars Rd *ACT* W3 — 135 N5
  *PECK* SE15 — 159 P6
  *STWL/WRAY* TW19 — 171 P2
The Friars *CHES/WCR* EN8 * — 62 C8
  *WDSR* SL4 — 171 P2
Friary Av *WLSDN* NW10 — 283 N8
  *NFNCH/WDSPK* N12 — 97 P5
Friday Hi *CHING* E4 — 101 K4
Friday Hi East *CHING* E4 — 101 L4
Friday Hi West *CHING* E4 — 101 K3
Friday Rd *ERITH* DA8 — 164 E4
  *MTCM* CR4 — 180 A10
  *WIM/MER* SW19 — 201 M9
Friday St *ROKG* RH5 — 291 M9
  *STP* EC4M — 12 E7
Frideswide Pl *KTTN* NW5 — 118 D10
Friendly Pl *LEW* SE13 — 160 G7
Friendly St *DEPT* SE8 — 160 F8
Friendly Street Ms *DEPT* SE8 — 160 F8
Friends Av *CHES/WCR* EN8 — 62 C8
Friendship Wy *SRTFD* E15 * — 141 H5
Friends Rd *PUR/KEN* CR8 — 223 J8
Friends' Rd *CROY/NA* CR0 — 223 L6
Friend St *FSBYE* EC1V — 6 C9
Friern Barnet La
  *TRDG/WHET* N20 — 97 N4
Friern Barnet Rd
  *FBAR/BDGN* N11 — 98 B6
Friern Cl *CHESW* EN7 — 61 M2
Friern Mount Dr
  *TRDG/WHET* N20 — 97 M1
Friern Pk *NFNCH/WDSPK* N12 — 97 N6
Friern Rd *EDUL* SE22 — 181 J2
Friern Watch Av
  *NFNCH/WDSPK* N12 — 97 N5
Frigate Ms *DEPT* SE8 — 160 F5
Frimley Av *EMPK* RM11 — 125 P6
  *WLGTN* SM6 — 222 F3
Frimley Cl *CROY/NA* CR0 — 225 H4
  *WIM/MER* SW19 — 179 H5
Frimley Ct *SCUP* DA14 — 186 E1
Frimley Crs *CROY/NA* CR0 — 225 H4
Frimley Gdns *MTCM* CR4 — 180 A10
Frimley Rd *CHSGTN* KT9 — 219 K11
  *GDMY/SEVK* IG3 — 123 H8
  *HHW* HP1 — 35 H5
Frimley Wy *WCHPL* E1 — 140 C6
Fringewood Cl *NTHWD* HA6 — 92 A9
Frinstead Gv *STMC/STPC* BR5 — 207 N4
Frinsted Rd *ERITH* DA8 — 164 E6
Frinton Cl *OXHEY* WD19 — 93 J3
Frinton Dr *WFD* IG8 — 101 J4
Frinton Ms *GNTH/NBYPK* IG2 — 122 C4
Frinton Rd *CRW* RM5 — 104 B8
  *EHAM* E6 — 141 P2
  *SCUP* DA14 — 185 P5
  *SEVS/STOTM* N15 — 119 M4
  *TOOT* SW17 — 180 B9
Friston Cl *FUL/PGN* SW6 — 157 J8
Friston Wk *CRAWW* RH11 — 283 K6
Friswell Pl *BXLYHN* DA7 — 164 B10
Fritham Cl *NWMAL* KT3 — 200 B6
Frith Cl *MLHL* NW7 — 97 H2
Frith Ct *MLHL* NW7 — 97 J7
Frith La *MLHL* NW7 — 97 J7
Frith Knowle *WOT/HER* KT12 — 217 J2
Frith La *MLHL* NW7 — 97 H7
Frith Manor Farm Cotts
  *MLHL* NW7 * — 97 H6
Frith Rd *CROY/NA* CR0 — 203 K9
  *WAN* E11 — 121 L6
Fritshden Copse *BERK* HP4 — 34 C1
Friths Dr *REIG* RH2 — 257 M4
Frithville Gdns *SHB* W12 — 136 F10
Frithwald Rd *CHERT* KT16 — 195 J7
Frithwood Av *NTHWD* HA6 — 32 D5
Frizlands La *DAGE* RM10 — 124 C6
Frobisher Cl *BUSH* WD23 — 73 P10
  *PIN* HA5 — 113 L5
  *PUR/KEN* CR8 — 241 K5
Frobisher Cl *BARB* EC2Y * — 12 F3
  *STWL/WRAY* TW19 — 173 P5
Frobisher Gdns
  *CDW/CHF* RM16 — 167 K2
  *GU* GU1 — 250 C4
  *LEY* E10 — 120 C4
Frobisher Ms *ENC/FH* EN2 — 79 L8
Frobisher Rd *CEND/HSY/T* N8 — 119 H2
  *EHAM* E6 — 142 C8
  *ERITH* DA8 — 165 H6
  *STAL* AL1 — 39 H6
Frobisher St *GVE* DA12 — 40 A1
  *HAT* AL10 — 40 A1
  *RDART* DA2 — 166 C10
Frog Grove La *RGUW* GU3 — 248 A6
Frogha Is La *HLW/HUF* UB9 — 110 D8
Froghole La *EDEN* TN8 — 263 N8
Frog La *RAIN* RM13 — 143 P8
  *RGUE* GU4 — 250 F8
Frogley Rd *EDUL* SE22 — 159 N10
Frogmoor La
  *RKW/CH/CXG* WD3 — 91 N3
Frogmore *LCOL/BKTW* AL2 — 56 D3
  *WAND/EARL* SW18 — 179 K1
Frogmore Av *HYS/HAR* UB3 — 215 N7
Frogmore Cl *CHEAM* SM3 — 221 H6
  *SL* SL1 — 130 C2
Frogmore Dr *WDSR* SL4 — 148 F1
Frogmore Gdns *CHEAM* SM3 — 221 H7
  *YEAD* UB4 — 132 G6
Frogmore Rd *HHS/BOV* HP3 — 35 M10
Frognal *HAMP* NW3 — 117 M10
Frognal Av *HRW* HA1 — 114 G4
  *SCUP* DA14 — 185 K9
Frognal Cl *HAMP* NW3 — 117 M10
Frognal Ct *HAMP* NW3 — 117 M10
Frognal Gdns *HAMP* NW3 — 117 M10
Frognal La *HAMP* NW3 — 117 L10
Frognal Man *HAMP* NW3 * — 3 J1
Frognal Pde *HAMP* NW3 * — 3 J1
Frognal Pl *SCUP* DA14 — 185 K9
Frognal Ri *HAMP* NW3 — 117 M8
Frognal Wy *HAMP* NW3 — 117 M9
Froissart Rd *ELTH/MOT* SE9 — 164 C10
Frome Rd *WDGN* N22 — 115 M2
Frome St *IS* N1 — 6 E6
Fromondes Rd *CHEAM* SM3 — 221 H4
Fromow Gdns *BFOR* GU20 — 212 A3
Fromows Cnr *CHSWK* W4 * — 156 A4
Front La *UPMR* RM14 — 126 D7
The Front *BERK* HP4 — 34 A2
Frostic Wk *WCHPL* E1 — 13 N3
Froude St *VX/NE* SW8 — 158 C8
Frowick Cl *BRKMPK* AL9 — 41 H10
Frowyke Crs *POTB/CUF* EN6 — 58 C5
Fruen Rd *EBED/NFELT* TW14 — 174 A2
Fryatt Rd *TOTM* N17 — 99 L8
Fry Cl *CRW* RM5 — 104 B1
Fryday Grove Ms *BAL* SW12 * — 180 B1
Fryent Cl *NFNCH/WDSPK* N12 — 116 B5
Fryent Crs *CDALE/KGS* NW9 — 116 B4
Fryent Flds *CDALE/KGS* NW9 — 116 B4

| | | |
|---|---|---|
| Fryent Gv CDALE/KGS NW9 | 116 | B4 |
| Fryent Wy CDALE/KGS NW9 | 115 | M3 |
| Fryer Cl CSHM HP5 | 51 | J9 |
| Fryern Wd CTHM CR3 | 241 | K10 |
| Frying Pan Aly WCHPL E1 | 13 | L6 |
| Frymley Vw WDSR SL4 | 148 | C3 |
| Fry Rd EHAM E6 | 142 | A2 |
| WLSDN NW10 | 136 | C3 |
| Fryston Av COUL/CHIP CR5 | 222 | C10 |
| CROY/NA CRO | 203 | P9 |
| Fryth Md STALW/RED AL3 | 38 | A5 |
| Fuchsia Cl ROMW/RG RM7 | 124 | F7 |
| Fuchsia St ABYW SE2 | 163 | L4 |
| Fuchsia Wy CHOB/PIR GU24 | 212 | D9 |
| Fuel Farm Rd HORL RH6 | 279 | P7 |
| Fulbeck Dr CDALE/KGS NW9 | 96 | F9 |
| Fulbeck Wy RYLN/HDSTN HA2 | 94 | B10 |
| Fulbourne Cl REDH RH1 | 257 | P8 |
| Fulbourne St WCHPL E1 | 140 | E1 |
| Fulbourn Rd WALTH E17 | 101 | H9 |
| Fulbrook Gv OXHEY WD19 | 93 | P4 |
| Fulford Rd CTHM CR3 | 241 | L7 |
| HOR/WEW KT19 | 220 | A4 |
| Fulford St BERM/RHTH SE16 | 160 | A1 |
| Fulham Broadway | | |
| FUL/PGN SW6 | 157 | K6 |
| Fulham Cl HGDN/ICK UB10 | 132 | D6 |
| Fulham Est SE2 | 163 | L4 |
| Fulham High St FUL/PGN SW6 | 157 | H8 |
| Fulham Palace Rd | | |
| FUL/PGN SW6 | 156 | G6 |
| Fulham Park Gdns | | |
| FUL/PGN SW6 | 157 | J8 |
| Fulham Park Rd | | |
| FUL/PGN SW6 | 157 | H8 |
| Fulham Rd FUL/PGN SW6 | 157 | H8 |
| WBPTN SW10 | 15 | K9 |
| Fullarton Crs SOCK/AV RM15 | 111 | K7 |
| Fullbrook Av ADL/WDHM KT15 | 215 | K7 |
| Fullbrooks Av WPK KT4 | 200 | C8 |
| Fuller Cl BETH E2 | 13 | M1 |
| BUSH WD23 | 94 | C1 |
| ORP BR6 | 227 | J2 |
| Fuller Gdns WATN WD24 | 73 | J3 |
| Fullerian Crs WATW WD18 | 72 | C8 |
| Fuller Rd BCTR RM8 | 123 | M8 |
| WATN WD24 | 73 | J3 |
| Fullers Av SURB KT6 | 199 | L3 |
| Fuller's Av SURB KT6 | 101 | L8 |
| Fullers Cl CRW RM5 | 104 | D8 |
| WAB EN9 | 63 | L9 |
| Fullers Hl BH/WHM TN16 | 262 | C9 |
| Fuller's Hl AMS HP6 | 50 | F10 |
| Fullers Md NHLW CM17 | 47 | M2 |
| Fullers Rd SWFD E18 | 101 | L9 |
| Fuller St HDNW4 | 116 | F2 |
| Fullers Wy North SURB KT6 | 199 | L10 |
| Fullers Wy South CHSGTN KT9 | 219 | K1 |
| Fullers Wood La REDH RH1 | 258 | D10 |
| Fullerton Dr BF/WBF KT14 | 216 | A10 |
| Fullerton Dr BF/WBF KT14 | 215 | P10 |
| CAR SM5 | 221 | P5 |
| CROY/NA CRO | 203 | M1 |
| WAND/EARL SW18 | 179 | M1 |
| Fullerton Wy BF/WBF KT14 | 215 | P10 |
| RKW/CH/CXG WD3 | 72 | B9 |
| Fullmer Wy ADL/WDHM KT15 | 215 | J4 |
| Fullwell Av CLAY IG5 | 102 | D9 |
| Fullwood Pl GINN WC1R | 11 | P4 |
| Fullwood's Ms IS N1 | 7 | H4 |
| Fulmar Cl CRAWW RH11 * | 282 | D8 |
| Fulmar Crs HHW HP1 | 35 | K7 |
| Fulmar Rd HCH RM12 | 145 | H2 |
| Fulmead St FUL/PGN SW6 | 157 | L7 |
| Fulmer Cl HPTN TW12 | 175 | M8 |
| Fulmer Common Rd | | |
| DTCH/LGLY SL3 | 130 | A1 |
| Fulmer Cnr CFSP/GDCR SL9 * | 110 | E2 |
| Fulmer Dr CFSP/GDCR SL9 | 110 | F3 |
| Fulmer La DTCH/LGLY SL3 | 110 | D5 |
| Fulmer PI DTCH/LGLY SL3 * | 110 | E3 |
| Fulmer Rd CAN/RD E16 | 142 | A7 |
| DTCH/LGLY SL3 | 110 | B9 |
| WEA W13 | 154 | G2 |
| Fulready Rd LEY E10 | 121 | J3 |
| Fulstone Cl HSLWW TW4 | 153 | N10 |
| Fulthorp Rd BKHTH/KID SE3 | 161 | L8 |
| Fulton Ms BAY/PAD W2 * | 9 | J7 |
| Fulton Rd WBLY HA9 | 115 | M8 |
| Fulvens SHGR GU5 | 270 | F9 |
| Fulwell Pk Av WHTN TW2 | 176 | B6 |
| Fulwell Rd TEDD TW11 | 176 | C2 |
| Fulwood Av ALP/SUD HA0 | 135 | L4 |
| Fulwood Gdns TWK TW1 | 176 | B2 |
| Fulwood Wk WIM/MER SW19 | 179 | H4 |
| Furber St HMSMTH W6 | 156 | F6 |
| Furham Fld PIN HA5 | 93 | P8 |
| Furley Rd PECK SE15 | 159 | P6 |
| Furlong Cl WLGTN SM6 | 202 | C8 |
| Furlong La DORK RH4 | 272 | E3 |
| HOLWY N7 | 84 | E3 |
| Furlongs HHW HP1 | 35 | K5 |
| The Furlongs ESH/CLAY KT10 | 198 | A10 |
| Furlong Wy HORL RH6 | 280 | A2 |
| WARE SG12 | 26 | E3 |
| The Furlough | | |
| WOKS/MYFD GU22 | 232 | D1 |
| Furmage St WAND/EARL SW18 | 179 | L3 |
| Furnace Dr CRAWE RH10 | 284 | G2 |
| Furnace Farm Rd | | |
| CRAWE RH10 * | 284 | B9 |
| Furnace Pde CRAWE RH10 | 284 | B9 |
| Furneaux Av WNWD SE27 | 181 | J8 |
| Furner Cl DART DA1 | 164 | G9 |
| Furness WDSR SL4 | 148 | B3 |
| Furness Cl CHDH RM6 | 168 | E4 |
| MRDN SM4 | 201 | L6 |
| RYLN/HDSTN HA2 | 114 | A5 |
| WLSDN NW10 | 136 | D4 |
| Furness Rd HCH RM12 | 125 | H10 |
| Fursby Av FNCH N3 | 97 | K7 |
| Furse Av STALW/WH AL4 | 24 | A4 |
| Further Acre CDALE/KGS NW9 | 96 | C9 |
| Furtherfield ABLGY WD5 | 58 | G5 |
| Furtherfield Cl CROY/NA CRO | 203 | H6 |
| Further Green Rd CAT SE6 | 183 | K3 |
| Furtherground HHNE HP2 | 35 | P7 |
| Furzebank ASC SL5 | 192 | C4 |
| Furzebushes La | | |
| LCOL/BKTW AL2 | 55 | N1 |
| Furze Cl HORL RH6 | 280 | E4 |
| OXHEY WD19 | 93 | K3 |
| REDH RH1 | 258 | F2 |
| Furzedown Dr TOOT SW17 | 180 | G8 |
| Furzedown Rd BELMT SM2 | 221 | N7 |
| TOOT SW17 | 180 | G8 |
| Furzefield CHES/WCR EN8 | 62 | A4 |
| CRAWW RH11 | 283 | H6 |
| Furze Fld LHD/OX KT22 | 218 | C3 |
| Furzefield Cl CHST BR7 | 184 | E4 |
| Furzefield Ct POTB/CUF EN6 * | 59 | H7 |
| Furzefield Rd BEAC HP9 | 275 | M2 |
| BKHTH/KID SE3 | 161 | N5 |

| | | |
|---|---|---|
| REIG RH2 | 275 | M2 |
| Furze Gv KWD/TDW/WH KT20 | 239 | J7 |
| Furzeham Rd WDR/YW UB7 | 151 | P1 |
| Furze Hl KWD/TDW/WH KT20 | 239 | J7 |
| PUR/KEN CR8 | 222 | F7 |
| Furzehill Rd BORE WD6 | 75 | M8 |
| Furze La GODL SU1 | 267 | L9 |
| PUR/KEN CR8 | 222 | F7 |
| Furzen Cl SLN SL2 | 128 | F5 |
| Furzen Crs HAT AL10 | 40 | C7 |
| Furze Pl REDH RH1 * | 258 | F2 |
| Furze Rd ADL/WDHM KT15 | 215 | J3 |
| HHW HP1 | 35 | H7 |
| THHTH CR7 | 205 | K3 |
| Furze St BOW E3 * | 140 | F3 |
| Furze Vw RKW/CH/CXG WD3 | 70 | F10 |
| Furzewood SUN TW16 | 197 | H1 |
| Fusedale Wy SOCK/AV RM15 | 146 | E9 |
| Fuzzens Wk WDSR SL4 | 148 | D3 |
| Fydlers Cl WDSR SL4 | 170 | A1 |
| Fye Foot La BLKFR EC4V * | 12 | E7 |
| Fyfe Wy BMLY BR1 | 205 | M2 |
| Fyfield Cl HAYES BR2 | 205 | J4 |
| Fyfield Dr SOCK/AV RM15 | 146 | E9 |
| Fyfield Rd BRXN/ST SW9 | 159 | H9 |
| CHONG CM5 | 49 | N6 |
| EN EN1 | 79 | M7 |
| RAIN RM13 | 144 | C3 |
| WALTH E17 | 121 | J1 |
| Fynes St WEST SW1P | 17 | J5 |

## G

| | | |
|---|---|---|
| Gabion Av PUR RM19 | 166 | C3 |
| Gable Cl ABLGY WD5 | 54 | F8 |
| PIN HA5 | 93 | P8 |
| Gable Ct SYD SE26 | 182 | A7 |
| Gable Ms HAYES BR2 | 206 | B9 |
| The Gables ASHF TW15 | 174 | A8 |
| BORE WD6 | 75 | L7 |
| Gables Cl CFSP/GDCR SL9 | 90 | B5 |
| CMBW SE5 | 159 | M7 |
| DTCH/LGLY SL3 | 149 | M5 |
| LEE/GVPK SE12 | 183 | M4 |
| WOKS/MYFD GU22 | 232 | C6 |
| The Gables BNSTD SM7 | 239 | J3 |
| CHONG CM5 | 67 | P2 |
| GRAYS RM17 | 167 | L3 |
| GUW GU2 | 249 | N7 |
| HART DA3 | 211 | P2 |
| LHD/OX KT22 | 218 | B8 |
| NWDGN UB2 | 203 | M1 |
| WBLY HA9 | 115 | J3 |
| WEY KT13 | 216 | D2 |
| Gables Wy BNSTD SM7 | 239 | J2 |
| Gabriel Cl CDW/CHF RM16 | 167 | H3 |
| CRW RM5 | 104 | D8 |
| FELT TW13 | 175 | M7 |
| Gabriel Gdns GVE DA12 | 191 | H8 |
| Gabrielle Cl WBLY HA9 | 115 | L8 |
| Gabrielspring Rd HART DA3 | 210 | P9 |
| Gabriel Spring Road (East) | | |
| HART DA3 | 210 | P9 |
| Gabriel St FSTH SE23 | 182 | C5 |
| Gabriel's Whf STHWK SE1 | 12 | A9 |
| Gadbrook Rd | | |
| BRKHM/BTCW RH3 | 273 | P4 |
| Gad Cl PLSTW E13 | 141 | N5 |
| Gaddesden Av WBLY HA9 | 135 | L4 |
| Gaddesden Crs WATN WD24 | 55 | L10 |
| Gaddesden Gv WGCE AL7 | 25 | L6 |
| Gade Bank RKW/CH/CXG WD3 | 72 | F8 |
| Gadebridge La HHW HP1 | 35 | L4 |
| Gadebridge Rd HHW HP1 | 35 | L3 |
| Gade CI HHW HP1 | 35 | L5 |
| HYS/HAR UB3 | 133 | J10 |
| WATW WD18 | 72 | F9 |
| Gadesden Rd HOR/WEW KT19 | 219 | P8 |
| Gade Valley Cl KGLGY WD4 | 54 | B4 |
| Gade View Gdns KGLGY WD4 | 54 | B4 |
| Gade View Rd HHS/BOV HP3 | 35 | M10 |
| Gadsbury Cl CDALE/KGS NW9 | 116 | C4 |
| Gadsden Cl UPMR RM14 | 126 | D4 |
| Gadswell Cl GSTN WD25 | 73 | M2 |
| Gadwall Cl CAN/RD E16 | 141 | M8 |
| Gage Rd CAN/RD E16 | 141 | K7 |
| Gage St BMSBY WC1N | 11 | M3 |
| Gainford Cl IS N1 * | 6 | A1 |
| Gainsboro Av GFD/PVL UB6 | 114 | D10 |
| Gainsborough Av MNPK E12 | 122 | F10 |
| STAL AL1 | 39 | H5 |
| TIL RM18 | 168 | G7 |
| Gainsborough Cl BECK BR3 | 182 | F10 |
| ESH/CLAY KT10 * | 198 | C10 |
| Gainsborough Ct SHB W12 | 156 | F1 |
| WOT/HER KT12 | 217 | H11 |
| Gainsborough Dr GVW DA11 | 190 | A6 |
| SAND/SEL CR2 | 223 | P9 |
| Gainsborough Gdns | | |
| EDGW HA8 | 95 | L10 |
| GLDGN NW11 | 117 | J5 |
| HAMP NW3 | 117 | N8 |
| HSLW TW3 | 176 | B1 |
| Gainsborough Ms DUL SE21 | 181 | N4 |
| SYD SE26 | 182 | A6 |
| Gainsborough Pl CHIG IG7 | 103 | M2 |
| COB KT11 | 235 | M1 |
| Gainsborough Rd BCTR RM8 | 123 | J8 |
| CHSWK W4 | 156 | C3 |
| HOR/WEW KT19 | 219 | P6 |
| NFNCH/WDSPK N12 | 97 | L6 |
| NWMAL KT3 | 200 | A6 |
| RAIN RM13 | 145 | H3 |
| RCH/KEW TW9 | 155 | L8 |
| SRTFD E15 | 141 | K5 |
| WAN E11 | 121 | K5 |
| WFD IG8 | 102 | B7 |
| YEAD UB4 | 133 | N4 |
| Gainsborough Sq BXLYHS DA6 | 163 | N9 |
| Gainsborough Ter | | |
| BELMT SM2 * | 221 | J4 |
| Gainsford Rd WALTH E17 | 117 | J2 |
| Gainsford St STHWK SE1 | 13 | L10 |
| Gainsthorpe Rd CHONG CM5 | 49 | H6 |
| Gainswood WGCE AL7 | 23 | H6 |
| Gairloch Rd CMBW SE5 | 159 | M8 |
| Gaisford St KTTN NW5 | 4 | G1 |
| Gaitskell Cl ELTH/MOT SE9 | 184 | F1 |
| Gaitskell Wy STHWK SE1 | 18 | F3 |
| Galahad Cl SL SL1 | 148 | A5 |
| Galahad Rd BMLY BR1 | 183 | M6 |
| CRAWW RH11 | 283 | H7 |
| ED N9 | 99 | P3 |
| Galata Rd BARN SW13 | 156 | D6 |
| Galatea Sq PECK SE15 | 160 | B6 |
| Galbraith St POP/IOD E14 | 161 | N1 |
| Galdana Av BAR EN5 | 77 | N2 |
| Galeborough Av WFD IG8 | 101 | J3 |
| Gale Cl HPTN TW12 | 175 | M9 |
| MTCM CR4 | 201 | N3 |
| Gale Crs BNSTD SM7 | 239 | K7 |
| Galena Rd HMSMTH W6 | 156 | F1 |
| Gale St BOW E3 | 140 | F4 |
| DAGW RM9 | 143 | P1 |
| Galey Gn SOCK/AV RM15 | 146 | F7 |
| Galgate Cl WIM/MER SW19 | 178 | A1 |

| | | |
|---|---|---|
| Gallants Farm Rd EBAR EN4 | 97 | P1 |
| Galleon Bvd DART DA2 | 166 | C10 |
| Galleon Cl BERM/RHTH SE16 | 160 | B1 |
| ERITH DA8 | 164 | E5 |
| Galleon Dr CDW/CHF RM16 | 167 | H3 |
| Galleons Dr BARK IG11 | 143 | K5 |
| Galleons La DTCH/LGLY SL3 | 130 | A5 |
| The Galleons AMSS HP7 * | 69 | H4 |
| The Galleria HAT AL10 * | 40 | C5 |
| The Galleries IS N1 * | 6 | C7 |
| Gallery Gdns NTHLT UB5 | 133 | L4 |
| Gallery Rd DUL SE21 | 181 | L4 |
| Galley Gn HERT/BAY SG13 | 26 | F9 |
| Galley Hl HART DA3 | 35 | K4 |
| Galley Hill Rd HART DA3 | 189 | L11 |
| Galleyhill Rd WAB EN9 | 63 | K9 |
| Galleyhill Rd WAB EN9 | 76 | D4 |
| Galleymead Rd | | |
| DTCH/LGLY SL3 | 151 | J7 |
| Galleywall Rd | | |
| BERM/RHTH SE16 | 160 | A3 |
| Galleywood Crs CRW RM5 | 104 | E7 |
| Galliard Rd ED N9 | 99 | J1 |
| Gallia Rd HBRY N5 | 119 | J10 |
| Gallions Cl BARK IG11 | 143 | K5 |
| Gallions Rd CHARL SE7 | 161 | P5 |
| Gallions Rd CHARL SE7 | 141 | P10 |
| Gallions View Rd THMD SE28 | 143 | M9 |
| The Gallop BELMT SM2 | 221 | N5 |
| SAND/SEL CR2 | 224 | A4 |
| Gallosson Rd | | |
| WOOL/PLUM SE18 | 143 | M10 |
| Galloway Cha SLN SL2 | 129 | M9 |
| Galloway Cl BROX EN10 | 62 | E2 |
| Galloway Pth CROY/NA CRO | 223 | L1 |
| Galloway Rd SHB W12 | 156 | D10 |
| Gallows Hl KGLGY WD4 | 54 | D8 |
| Gallows Hill La ABLGY WD5 | 58 | C1 |
| Gallus Cl WCHMH N21 | 78 | C10 |
| Gallus Sq BKHTH/KID SE3 | 161 | N9 |
| Gally's Rd WDSR SL4 | 148 | C7 |
| Galpin's Rd THHTH CR7 | 202 | F4 |
| Galsworthy Av CHDH RM6 | 123 | L5 |
| POP/IOD E14 | 140 | G7 |
| Galsworthy Cl THMD SE28 | 143 | L10 |
| Galsworthy Crs | | |
| BKHTH/KID SE3 | 161 | P7 |
| Galsworthy Rd CHERT KT16 | 195 | K7 |
| CRICK NW2 | 117 | H9 |
| KUTN/CMB KT2 | 199 | N1 |
| TIL RM18 | 168 | F7 |
| Galton Rd ASC SL5 | 192 | G6 |
| Galton St NKENS W10 | 2 | A10 |
| Galva Cl EBAR EN4 | 96 | D1 |
| Galveston Rd PUT/ROE SW15 | 179 | J1 |
| Galvin Rd SL SL1 | 149 | H2 |
| Galway Cl BERM/RHTH SE16 * | 160 | A4 |
| Galway St FSBYE EC1V | 7 | H8 |
| Gambetta St VX/NE SW8 | 158 | C8 |
| Gambia St STHWK SE1 | 12 | D9 |
| Gambles La RPLY/SEND GU23 | 251 | M1 |
| Gamble Rd TOOT SW17 | 179 | N7 |
| Games Rd EBAR EN4 | 77 | P7 |
| Gamlen Rd PUT/ROE SW15 | 156 | C10 |
| Gammon CI ACT W3 | 135 | M8 |
| Gammons Farm Cl | | |
| WATN WD24 | 72 | G2 |
| Gammons La WATN WD24 | 73 | H3 |
| Gamuel Cl WALTH E17 | 120 | E1 |
| Gander Green Crs HPTN TW12 | 197 | P1 |
| Gander Green La CHEAM SM3 | 201 | H9 |
| SUT SM1 | 221 | J3 |
| Ganders Ash GSTN WD25 | 55 | H9 |
| Gandhi Cl WALTH E17 | 120 | F4 |
| Gandolfi St PECK SE15 | 19 | L10 |
| Gangers Hl GDST RH9 | 260 | E5 |
| Ganghill GU GU1 | 250 | D8 |
| Gant Ct WAB EN9 | 63 | L10 |
| Ganton St REGST W1B | 10 | C6 |
| Ganton Wk OXHEY WD19 * | 93 | M5 |
| Gantshill Crs CNTH/NBYPK IG2 | 122 | D3 |
| Ganymede Pl HHNE HP2 * | 36 | A3 |
| Gap Rd WIM/MER SW19 | 179 | K3 |
| Garage Rd ACT W3 | 135 | M8 |
| Garbrand Wk EW KT17 | 220 | C5 |
| Garbutt PI MHST W1U * | 10 | A3 |
| Garbutt Rd UPMR RM14 | 126 | A4 |
| Garden Av BXLYHN DA7 | 164 | A9 |
| HAT AL10 | 40 | D7 |
| MTCM CR4 | 180 | C10 |
| Garden City EDGW HA8 | 95 | M7 |
| Garden Cl ADL/WDHM KT15 | 215 | N1 |
| ASHF TW15 | 174 | D9 |
| BAR EN5 | 76 | F3 |
| BH/WHM TN16 | 263 | M8 |
| BNSTD SM7 | 239 | K1 |
| CHING E4 | 101 | J2 |
| HPTN TW12 | 175 | M8 |
| LEE/GVPK SE12 | 183 | N6 |
| LHD/OX KT22 | 237 | H10 |
| NTHLT UB5 | 133 | J5 |
| PUT/ROE SW15 | 178 | E3 |
| RSLP HA4 | 112 | F7 |
| STAL AL1 | 38 | G5 |
| WAT WD17 | 72 | G2 |
| WLGTN SM6 | 222 | F1 |
| Garden Ct CHSWK W4 | 155 | P2 |
| EMB EC4Y * | 11 | N7 |
| HGDN/ICK UB10 | 113 | N8 |
| HPTN TW12 | 175 | M8 |
| SEV TN15 | 247 | L8 |
| STALE/WH AL4 | 21 | J2 |
| Garden End AMS HP6 | 69 | H5 |
| Gardeners Rd CROY/NA CRO | 203 | J8 |
| Gardener's Wk GT/LBKH KT23 * | 254 | A1 |
| Garden Field La BERK HP4 | 35 | K1 |
| Garden Flats HMSMTH W6 * | 156 | G5 |
| Gardenia Cl CHOB/PIR GU24 | 212 | E9 |
| Gardenia Rd BMLY BR1 | 206 | D5 |
| EN EN1 | 90 | B4 |
| Gardenia Wy WFD IG8 | 101 | M7 |
| Garden La BMLY BR1 | 183 | N9 |
| BRXS/STRHM SW2 | 180 | A3 |
| Garden Lodge Ct EFNCH N2 * | 117 | K1 |
| Garden PI HACK E8 | 7 | L5 |
| Garden Reach CSTG HP8 | 70 | A7 |
| Garden Rd ABLGY WD5 | 58 | G5 |
| BMLY BR1 | 183 | N10 |
| RCH/KEW TW9 | 155 | N9 |
| SEV TN13 | 247 | L8 |
| STJWD NW8 | 3 | H6 |
| WOT/HER KT12 | 197 | L6 |
| Garden Rw GVW DA11 | 190 | C6 |
| STHWK SE1 | 18 | C4 |
| The Gardens BECK BR3 | 183 | L5 |
| BRKMPK AL9 | 59 | H5 |
| BRWN CM15 | 86 | G2 |
| CEND/HSY/T N8 * | 67 | J10 |
| CHOB/PIR GU24 | 230 | B8 |
| CLPT E5 * | 99 | M10 |
| COB KT11 * | 234 | D5 |
| EBED/NFELT TW14 * | 153 | P10 |
| EDUL SE22 | 159 | J10 |
| ESH/CLAY KT10 | 217 | P1 |
| HCDN/ICK UB10 | 111 | M7 |
| HRW HA1 | 114 | F4 |
| PIN HA5 * | 113 | N3 |
| WAT WD17 | 72 | G1 |
| Garden St WCHPL E1 | 140 | G1 |
| Garden Studios BAY/PAD W2 * | 9 | K1 |
| Garden Ter PIM SW1V | 17 | J7 |
| Garden Terrace Rd | | |
| HLWE CM17 | 29 | M1 |
| Garden Vls ESH/CLAY KT10 * | 218 | A1 |
| Garden Wk BECK BR3 | 204 | E1 |
| SDTCH EC2A * | 13 | J1 |
| Garendon Gdns MRDN SM4 | 201 | L8 |
| Garendon Rd MRDN SM4 | 201 | L7 |
| Gareth Cl WPK KT4 | 201 | J1 |
| Gareth Gv BMLY BR1 | 183 | M7 |
| Garfield Ms BTSEA SW11 | 158 | G9 |
| Garfield Rd ADL/WDHM KT15 | 215 | M2 |
| BTSEA SW11 | 158 | G9 |
| CHING E4 | 101 | J2 |
| PEND EN3 | 80 | B8 |
| PLSTW E13 | 141 | L6 |
| TWK TW1 | 176 | A4 |
| WIM/MER SW19 | 179 | M1 |
| Garganey Wk THMD SE28 | 143 | M9 |
| Gargary Cl GVE DA12 | 191 | J4 |
| Garibaldi St REDH RH1 | 276 | A1 |
| Garibaldi St WOOL/PLUM SE18 | 143 | M10 |
| Garland Cl CHES/WCR EN8 | 62 | D7 |
| HHNE HP2 * | 35 | N5 |
| Garland Dr HSLW TW3 | 154 | B8 |
| Garland Rd STAN HA7 | 95 | P9 |
| WARE SG12 | 26 | D2 |
| WOOL/PLUM SE18 | 162 | G6 |
| Garlands La LHD/OX KT22 | 236 | C7 |
| Garlands Rd LHD/OX KT22 | 236 | C7 |
| REDH RH1 | 258 | A10 |
| Garland Wy CTHM CR3 | 241 | L8 |
| EMPK RM11 | 125 | M2 |
| Garlichill Rd EPSOM KT18 | 238 | E5 |
| Garlick Hl BLKFR EC4V | 12 | F7 |
| Garlies Rd FSTH SE23 | 182 | D6 |
| Garlinge Rd CRICK NW2 | 2 | C1 |
| Garman Cl UED N18 | 99 | L6 |
| Garman Rd TOTM N17 | 100 | A8 |
| Garnault Ms CLKNW EC1R * | 6 | B10 |
| Garnault Rd EN EN1 | 79 | N4 |
| Garner Cl BCTR RM8 | 123 | N6 |
| Garner Dr BROX EN10 | 62 | D2 |
| Garner Rd WALTH E17 | 101 | M8 |
| Garners Cl CFSP/GDCR SL9 | 90 | B7 |
| Garners End CFSP/GDCR SL9 | 90 | B7 |
| Garners Rd CFSP/GDCR SL9 | 90 | B7 |
| Garnet St SL SL1 | 148 | F1 |
| Garnet St WAP E1W | 140 | E9 |
| Garnett Cl ELTH/MOT SE9 | 162 | G9 |
| WATN WD24 | 73 | L2 |
| Garnett Dr LCOL/BKTW AL2 | 59 | L4 |
| Garnett Rd HAMP NW3 | 118 | A10 |
| Garnet Wk EHAM E6 | 141 | M8 |
| Garnham Cl STNW/STAM N16 * | 85 | M10 |
| Garnies Cl PECK SE15 | 159 | N6 |
| Garon St STNW/STAM N16 | 85 | N6 |
| Garrad's Rd | | |
| STRHM/NOR SW16 | 180 | E6 |
| Garrard Cl BXLYHN DA7 | 164 | B9 |
| CHST BR7 | 184 | B9 |
| Garrard Rd BNSTD SM7 | 239 | K2 |
| SLN SL2 | 128 | D6 |
| Garrard Wk WLSDN NW10 * | 136 | B9 |
| Garratt Cl CROY/NA CRO | 202 | G3 |
| Garratt La TOOT SW17 | 180 | A7 |
| WAND/EARL SW18 | 160 | A10 |
| Garratt Rd EDGW HA8 | 96 | B3 |
| Garratts La BNSTD SM7 | 239 | J2 |
| Garratt Ter TOOT SW17 | 180 | C7 |
| Garrett Cl ACT W3 | 136 | A7 |
| CRAWE RH10 | 284 | D11 |
| CSHM HP5 | 51 | H9 |
| Garretts Cl STLK EC1Y | 25 | K5 |
| Garrett St STLK EC1Y * | 7 | H10 |
| Garrick Av GLDGN NW11 | 117 | H4 |
| Garrick Cl EA W5 | 135 | L5 |
| RCH/KEW TW9 | 177 | H1 |
| STA TW18 | 173 | N10 |
| WOT/HER KT12 | 217 | J1 |
| Garrick Crs CROY/NA CRO | 3 | D9 |
| Garrick Dr HDN NW4 | 96 | F10 |
| THMD SE28 | 162 | G2 |
| Garrick Gdns E/WMO/HCT KT8 | 197 | P3 |
| Garrick Pk HDN NW4 | 116 | C1 |
| Garrick Rd CDALE/KGS NW9 | 116 | C4 |
| GFD/PVL UB6 | 133 | P3 |
| RCH/KEW TW9 | 155 | N8 |
| Garrick St COVGDN WC2E | 11 | J7 |
| Garrick Wy HDN NW4 | 116 | C1 |
| Garrick Yd CHCR WC2N * | 11 | J7 |
| Garrison Cl HSLWW TW4 | 175 | N1 |
| Garrison La CHSGTN KT9 | 219 | K4 |
| Garrolds Cl SWLY BR8 | 186 | E5 |
| The Garrones CRAWE RH10 * | 284 | F4 |
| Garron La SOCK/AV RM15 | 146 | E5 |
| Garrow HART DA3 | 211 | N3 |
| Garry Wy ROM RM1 | 104 | F8 |
| Garside Cl HPTN TW12 | 176 | C9 |
| THMD SE28 | 162 | A2 |
| Garsington Ms BROCKY SE4 | 161 | K10 |
| Garsmouth Wy GSTN WD25 | 73 | L2 |
| Garson Cl ESH/CLAY KT10 | 217 | J4 |
| Garson La STWL/WRAY TW19 | 173 | K2 |
| Garson Rd ESH/CLAY KT10 | 217 | J5 |
| Garston Dr GSTN WD25 | 55 | K10 |
| Garston La GSTN WD25 | 55 | L10 |
| PUR/KEN CR8 | 241 | L1 |
| The Garstons GT/LBKH KT23 | 255 | P6 |
| Garter Wy BERM/RHTH SE16 | 160 | D1 |
| Garth Cl KUTN/CMB KT2 | 177 | L8 |
| MRDN SM4 | 201 | J7 |
| RSLP HA4 | 113 | K6 |
| Garth Ms EA W5 * | 135 | K2 |
| Garthorne Rd FSTH SE23 | 162 | A5 |
| Garth Rd CHSWK W4 | 156 | A4 |
| CRICK NW2 | 82 | D7 |
| KUTN/CMB KT2 | 177 | L8 |
| MRDN SM4 | 201 | H7 |
| RSLP HA4 | 113 | K6 |
| The Garth ABLGY WD5 | 54 | E8 |
| COB KT11 | 234 | D5 |
| HHNE HP2 | 36 | A3 |
| Garthside RCHPK/HAM TW10 | 176 | G6 |
| Garthway | | |
| NFNCH/WDSPK N12 * | 97 | P5 |
| Garthway NFNCH/WDSPK N12 | 97 | P5 |
| Garthway WAT WD17 | 72 | G1 |
| Gartmoor Gdns | | |
| WIM/MER SW19 | 178 | C4 |
| Garton Cl CDMY/SEVK IG3 | 123 | H1 |
| Garton Pl WAND/EARL SW18 | 160 | A10 |
| Garvary Rd CAN/RD E16 | 141 | M9 |
| Garvin Av BEAC HP9 | 275 | P5 |
| Garvin Ms BEAC HP9 | 147 | H6 |
| Garway Rd BAY/PAD W2 | 8 | B6 |
| Gascoigne Cl TOTM N17 | 99 | P8 |

| | | |
|---|---|---|
| PEND EN3 | 80 | C10 |
| STMC/STPC BR5 | 202 | B6 |
| Gascoigne Gdns WFD IG8 | 101 | K8 |
| Gascoigne PI BETH E2 | 7 | L9 |
| Gedeney Rd TOTM N17 | 99 | K9 |
| Gedling Pl STHWK SE1 | 19 | L3 |
| Geere Rd SRTFD E15 | 141 | L9 |
| CROY/NA CRO | 225 | H6 |
| Gees Ct MHST W1U | 10 | B6 |
| Gee St FSBYE EC1V | 6 | G10 |
| Geffrye Est IS N1 * | 7 | K8 |
| Gascon Gv SLN SL2 | 128 | C6 |
| Geffrye St BETH E2 | 7 | L7 |
| Gascony Av KIL/WHAMP NW6 | 2 | D1 |
| Geisthorp Ct WAB EN9 | 63 | M9 |
| Gascony Cl HARH RM3 | 105 | L9 |
| Geldart Rd PECK SE15 | 160 | A6 |
| Gascoyne Dr DART DA1 | 164 | G9 |
| Geldeston Rd CLPT E5 | 119 | P7 |
| POTB/CUF EN6 | 58 | D8 |
| Gellatly Rd NWCR SE14 | 160 | B8 |
| Gascoyne Rd HOM E9 | 140 | G1 |
| Gelsthorpe Rd CRW RM5 | 104 | C8 |
| Gascoyne Wy HERT/WAS SG13 | 25 | L6 |
| Gemini Cl CRAWW RH11 | 282 | G9 |
| Gaselee St POP/IOD E14 | 141 | N9 |
| Gemmell Pl PUR/KEN CR8 | 222 | G10 |
| Gasholder Pl LBTH SE11 | 17 | P8 |
| Genas Cl BARK/HLT IG6 | 102 | E9 |
| Gaskarth Rd BAL SW12 | 180 | D2 |
| EDGW HA8 | 95 | P4 |
| General Gordon Pl | | |
| Gaskell Rd HGT N6 | 118 | A4 |
| WOOL/PLUM SE18 | 162 | G2 |
| Gaskell St CLAP SW4 | 158 | F9 |
| The Generals Wk PEND EN3 | 80 | D3 |
| Gaskin St IS N1 | 6 | C5 |
| General Wolfe Rd | | |
| Gaspar Cl ECT SW5 * | 15 | H5 |
| GNWCH SE10 | 161 | J7 |
| Gaspar Ms ECT SW5 * | 15 | H5 |
| Genesis Cl STWL/WRAY TW19 | 174 | A4 |
| Gassiot Rd TOOT SW17 | 180 | C7 |
| Genesta Gld CRAW DA12 | 191 | K8 |
| Gassiot Wy SUT SM1 | 201 | N10 |
| Genesta Rd WOOL/PLUM SE18 | 162 | G6 |
| Gasson Rd SWCM DA10 | 189 | N2 |
| Geneva Cl SHPTN TW17 | 196 | F2 |
| Gasson Wood Rd | | |
| Geneva Dr BRXN/ST SW9 | 159 | H10 |
| CRAWW RH11 | 283 | H9 |
| Geneva Gdns CHDH RM6 | 123 | P3 |
| Gastein Rd HMSMTH W6 | 157 | H4 |
| Geneva Rd KUT/HW KT1 | 199 | K4 |
| Gaston Bell Cl RCH/KEW TW9 | 155 | L9 |
| THHTH CR7 | 205 | K5 |
| Gaston Bridge Rd | | |
| Genever Cl CHING E4 | 100 | F6 |
| SHPTN TW17 | 196 | E5 |
| Genista Rd UED N18 | 100 | A6 |
| Gaston Rd MTCM CR4 | 202 | B3 |
| Genoa Av PUT/ROE SW15 | 178 | G11 |
| Gaston Wy SHPTN TW17 | 196 | E5 |
| Genoa Rd PGE/AN SE20 | 204 | B2 |
| Gataker St BERM/RHTH SE16 | 160 | A2 |
| Genotin Rd EN EN1 | 79 | L7 |
| Gatcombe Ms ARCH N19 | 118 | E8 |
| Gentleman's Rw ENC/FH EN2 | 79 | J8 |
| Gatcombe Wy EBAR EN4 | 78 | A5 |
| Genyn Rd GUW GU2 | 267 | N1 |
| Gate Cl BORE WD6 | 75 | P5 |
| Geoffrey Av HARH RM3 | 105 | P7 |
| Gatecroft HHS/BOV HP3 | 36 | A8 |
| Geoffrey Cl CMBW SE5 | 159 | M8 |
| Gate End NTHWD HA6 | 93 | H8 |
| Geoffrey Gdns EHAM E6 | 142 | B4 |
| Gateforth St STJWD NW8 | 9 | L2 |
| Geoffrey Rd BROCKY SE4 | 160 | A6 |
| Gatehill Rd NTHWD HA6 | 92 | G8 |
| George Avey Cft EPP CM16 | 66 | C2 |
| Gatehope Dr SOCK/AV RM15 | 146 | E5 |
| George Crs MUSWH N10 | 98 | B6 |
| Gatehouse Cl KUTN/CMB KT2 | 177 | P10 |
| George Downing Est | | |
| WDSR SL4 | 148 | G9 |
| STNW/STAM N16 | 119 | N7 |
| Gatehouse Ldg REDH RH1 | 276 | B11 |
| George Gange Wy | | |
| Gatehouse Sq STHWK SE1 | 12 | F9 |
| KTN/HRWW/WS HA3 | 114 | D1 |
| Gateley Rd BRXN/ST SW9 | 158 | G9 |
| George Green Dr | | |
| Gate Ms SKENS SW7 * | 16 | E2 |
| DTCH/LGLY SL3 | 130 | C8 |
| Gater Dr ENC/FH EN2 | 79 | N9 |
| George Green Rd | | |
| Gatesden Rd LHD/OX KT22 | 236 | B9 |
| DTCH/LGLY SL3 | 130 | B8 |
| Gates Green Rd WWKM BR4 | 205 | L10 |
| George Groves Rd | | |
| Gateshead Rd BORE WD6 | 75 | P5 |
| PGE/AN SE20 | 203 | P1 |
| Gateside Rd TOOT SW17 | 180 | A6 |
| George La HAYES BR2 | 205 | M8 |
| Gatestone Rd NRWD SE19 | 181 | M9 |
| LEW SE13 | 183 | H2 |
| Gate St LINN WC2A | 11 | N5 |
| SWFD E18 | 101 | M10 |
| Gateway WALW SE17 | 19 | H9 |
| George Lovell Dr PEND EN3 | 80 | D3 |
| Gateway Ar IS N1 * | 6 | C7 |
| George Mathers Rd | | |
| Gateway Gdns EHAM E6 | 142 | C5 |
| LBTH SE11 * | 18 | C5 |
| Gateway Ms FBAR/BDGN N11 | 98 | D7 |
| George Ms BRXN/ST SW9 | 159 | H8 |
| HACK E8 * | 7 | N10 |
| CAMTN NW1 | 4 | G10 |
| Gateway Pde FBAR/BDGN N11 | 98 | A7 |
| George Rd CHING E4 | 100 | F7 |
| Gateways GU GU1 | 268 | E1 |
| GODL GU7 | 267 | K10 |
| The Gateways CHESW EN7 * | 61 | L4 |
| GU GU1 | 250 | A10 |
| RCH/KEW TW9 * | 155 | J10 |
| KUTN/CMB KT2 | 177 | P10 |
| The Gateway WATW WD18 | 72 | F9 |
| NWMAL KT3 | 200 | C4 |
| WOKN/KNAP GU21 | 214 | G10 |
| George Rw BERM/RHTH SE16 | 19 | N2 |
| Gatfield Gv FELT TW13 | 175 | P5 |
| Georges Cl STMC/STPC BR5 | 202 | G4 |
| Gathorne Rd WDGN N22 | 98 | E7 |
| Georges Dr BRWN CM15 | 86 | E9 |
| Gathorne St BETH E2 | 140 | C1 |
| Georges Md BORE WD6 | 75 | K10 |
| Gatley Av HOR/WEW KT19 | 219 | P6 |
| George's Rd HOLWY N7 | 5 | N1 |
| Gatley Dr RGUE GU4 | 250 | C7 |
| George St BARK IG11 | 142 | F2 |
| Gatliff Rd BGVA SW1W | 16 | B8 |
| BERK HP4 | 34 | A5 |
| Gatling Rd ABYW SE2 | 163 | K4 |
| CAN/RD E16 | 141 | L8 |
| Gatonby St PECK SE15 | 159 | P7 |
| CROY/NA CRO | 203 | K9 |
| Gatting Wy UX/CGN UB8 | 131 | P1 |
| GRAYS RM17 | 167 | M5 |
| Gatton Bottom REIG RH2 | 258 | A4 |
| HERT/WAT SG14 | 25 | K4 |
| REIG RH2 | 257 | P1 |
| HNWL W7 | 135 | N10 |
| Gatton Cl BELMT SM2 | 221 | L5 |
| HSLW TW3 | 153 | N8 |
| Gatton Park Rd REIG RH2 | 257 | P2 |
| MBLAR W1H | 9 | M6 |
| Gatton Rd REIG RH2 | 257 | N5 |
| NWDGN UB2 | 153 | M3 |
| TOOT SW17 | 180 | A7 |
| RCH/KEW TW9 | 176 | A1 |
| Gattons Wy SCUP DA14 | 186 | A7 |
| ROM RM1 | 124 | G4 |
| Gatward Cl WCHMH N21 | 79 | J10 |
| STA TW18 | 173 | J7 |
| Gatward Gn ED N9 | 99 | M3 |
| STALW/RED AL3 | 38 | E4 |
| Gatwick Rd CRAWE RH10 | 284 | B10 |
| UX/CGN UB8 | 131 | N2 |
| GVE DA12 | 190 | E5 |
| WATW WD18 | 73 | J5 |
| WAND/EARL SW18 | 179 | H3 |
| George's Wood Rd | | |
| Gatwick Wy HORL RH6 | 258 | E11 |
| BRKMPK AL9 | 59 | K2 |
| STA TW18 * | 173 | J7 |
| Georgetown Cl NRWD SE19 | 181 | M8 |
| Gauden Cl CLAP SW4 | 158 | F7 |
| Georgette Pl GNWCH SE10 | 161 | H6 |
| Gauden Rd CLAP SW4 | 158 | F7 |
| George V Av PIN HA5 | 93 | N10 |
| Gaumont Ap WAT WD17 * | 8 | J7 |
| Georgeville Gdns | | |
| Gaumont Ter SHB W12 * | 156 | G1 |
| BARK/HLT IG6 | 122 | E2 |
| Gauntlet CRAWE RH10 | 284 | F4 |
| George V Wy GFD/PVL UB6 | 134 | C2 |
| Gauntlet Cl NTHLT UB5 | 133 | J5 |
| RKW/CH/CXG WD3 | 71 | K2 |
| Gauntlett Ct ALP/SUD HA0 | 114 | F10 |
| George Wk WARE SG12 | 26 | C2 |
| Gauntlett Rd SUT SM1 | 221 | N3 |
| Georgewood Rd | | |
| Gautrey Rd PECK SE15 | 160 | B8 |
| HHS/BOV HP3 | 54 | A1 |
| Gavell Rd COB KT11 | 217 | H9 |
| George Wyver Cl | | |
| Gavel St WALW SE17 * | 19 | K6 |
| WIM/MER SW19 | 179 | H3 |
| Gavenny Pth THMD SE28 | 143 | L6 |
| George Yd BANK EC3V | 13 | H6 |
| Gaverick Ms POP/IOD E14 | 160 | E4 |
| MYFR/PKLN W1K | 10 | B7 |
| Gaveston Dr BERK HP4 | 33 | N5 |
| Georgiana St CAMTN NW1 | 4 | E1 |
| Gaveston Rd LEE/GVPK SE12 | 183 | K3 |
| Georgian Cl CRAW RH10 | 284 | D8 |
| LHD/OX KT22 | 236 | F6 |
| HAYES BR2 | 205 | N8 |
| Gavestone Crs LEE/GVPK SE12 | 183 | L6 |
| HDGN/ICK UB10 | 111 | P9 |
| Gavestone Rd LEE/GVPK SE12 | 183 | L6 |
| STA TW18 | 173 | L7 |
| SLN SL2 | 129 | J4 |
| STAN HA7 | 94 | F8 |
| Gavina Cl MRDN SM4 | 201 | P5 |
| Georgian Ct WBLY HA9 | 135 | M1 |
| Gaviots Cl CFSP/GDCR SL9 | 110 | E4 |
| Georgian Wy HRW HA1 | 114 | C7 |
| Gaviots Gn CFSP/GDCR SL9 | 110 | E5 |
| Georgia Rd NWMAL KT3 | 199 | P2 |
| Gaviots Wy CFSP/GDCR SL9 | 110 | E4 |
| THHTH CR7 | 203 | P3 |
| Gawain Wk ED N9 | 100 | F4 |
| Georgina Gdns BETH E2 * | 7 | M9 |
| Gawber St BETH E2 | 140 | E2 |
| Geraint Rd BMLY BR1 | 183 | M6 |
| Gawdrey Cl CSHM HP5 | 51 | J9 |
| Geraldine Rd CHSWK W4 | 155 | N5 |
| Gawsworth Cl SRTFD E15 | 121 | L11 |
| WAND/EARL SW18 | 179 | M1 |
| Gawthorne Av MLHL NW7 | 97 | H6 |
| Geraldine St LBTH SE11 | 18 | C5 |
| Gawthorne Crs COUL/CHIP CR5 | 240 | D7 |
| Gerald Rd BCTR RM8 | 124 | A7 |
| Gay Cl CRICK NW2 | 81 | P10 |
| BGVA SW1W | 16 | B5 |
| Gayfere Rd CLAY IG5 | 122 | C1 |
| CAN/RD E16 | 141 | L6 |
| EW KT17 | 220 | D2 |
| GVE DA12 | 191 | H5 |
| Gayfere St WEST SW1P * | 17 | L4 |
| Gerald's Gv BNSTD SM7 | 220 | G10 |
| Gayford Rd SHB W12 | 156 | C1 |
| Gerard Av HSLWW TW4 | 175 | H2 |
| Gay Gdns DAGE RM10 | 124 | F10 |
| Gerald Gdns BARN SW13 | 144 | F2 |
| Gayhouse La REDH RH1 | 277 | M10 |
| Gerard Rd BARN SW13 | 156 | B7 |
| Gayhurst PECK SE15 * | 159 | N10 |
| HRW HA1 | 114 | G4 |
| Gayhurst Rd HACK E8 | 7 | N1 |
| Gerards Cl BERM/RHTH SE16 | 160 | A5 |
| Gayler Cl REDH RH1 | 258 | G11 |
| Gerda Rd ELTH/MOT SE9 | 184 | E5 |
| Gaymead NTHGT NW8 * | 3 | H3 |
| Germains Cl CSHM HP5 | 50 | G8 |
| Gaynes Ct UPMR RM14 | 126 | A4 |
| Germain St CSHM HP5 | 51 | G8 |
| Gaynesford Rd CAR SM5 | 221 | P3 |
| Germander Dr | | |
| FSTH SE23 | 182 | A5 |
| CHOB/PIR GU24 | 230 | F1 |
| Gaynes Hill Rd WFD IG8 | 103 | J6 |
| Germander Wy SRTFD E15 | 141 | L5 |
| Gaynes Park Rd UPMR RM14 | 125 | P9 |
| Gernon Cl RAIN RM13 | 145 | L4 |
| Gaynes Rd UPMR RM14 | 126 | A2 |
| Gernon Rd BOW E3 | 140 | G2 |
| Gay Rd SRTFD E15 | 141 | J4 |
| Gernon Vw CRICK NW2 | 116 | F7 |
| Gaysham Av GNTH/NBYPK IG2 | 122 | D3 |
| Gerpins La RAIN RM13 | 145 | N4 |
| Gay St PUT/ROE SW15 | 69 | J11 |
| Gerrard Crs BRWN CM15 | 86 | B3 |
| Gaysley Cl AMSS HP9 | 69 | K1 |
| Gerrard Gdns PIN HA5 | 113 | H3 |
| Gaysham Av GNTH/NBYPK IG2 | 122 | D3 |
| Gerrard Pl SOHO/SHAV W1D * | 11 | K6 |
| Gaywood Av CHES/WCR EN8 | 62 | C4 |
| Gerrards Cl STHGT/OAK N14 | 78 | D3 |
| Gaywood Rd ASHTD KT21 | 236 | B7 |
| Gerrards Cross Rd SLN SL2 | 129 | M1 |
| WALTH E17 | 120 | D1 |
| Gerrards Md BNSTD SM7 | 239 | J2 |
| Gaywood St STHWK SE1 | 18 | D4 |
| Gerrards Rd SOHO/SHAV W1D | 11 | J1 |
| Gaza St WALW SE17 | 158 | E1 |
| Gertrude Rd BELV DA17 | 163 | L3 |
| Gazelle Gld GVE DA12 | 191 | K8 |
| Gertrude St WBPTN SW10 | 15 | K10 |
| Gearies Cl | | |
| Gervaise Cl SL SL1 | 130 | A1 |
| GNTH/NBYPK IG2 | 122 | E2 |
| Gervase Cl WBLY HA9 | 116 | E8 |
| Gearing Cl TOOT SW17 | 181 | J6 |
| Gervase Rd EDGW HA8 | 96 | C5 |
| Geary Cl HORL RH6 | 280 | E7 |
| Gervase St PECK SE15 | 160 | B6 |
| Geary Rd WLSDN NW10 | 81 | J11 |
| Gew's Cnr CHES/WCR EN8 | 62 | B2 |
| Geary St HOLWY N7 | 84 | F3 |
| Ghent St CAT SE6 | 182 | E7 |
| Geary St BRW CM14 | 87 | J2 |
| Ghent Wy HACK E8 * | 7 | M1 |
| Geddes PI BXLYHS DA6 * | 164 | B10 |
| Ghyll Gdns BERK HP4 | 33 | J2 |
| Geddes Rd BUSH WD23 | 74 | C1 |
| Giant Arches Rd HNHL SE24 | 181 | J3 |
| Gedeling Rd HOD EN11 | 44 | G1 |
| Giant Tree Hi BUSH WD23 | 94 | C3 |
| Giffard Wy RGUW GU3 | 249 | H3 |
| Giffin St DEPT SE8 | 160 | G7 |
| Gibb Cft HLWS CM18 | 47 | H5 |
| Gibbfield Cl CHDH RM6 | 123 | P1 |

Gibbins Rd SRTFD E15 141 H2
Gibbon Rd ACT W3 136 B9
 KUTN/CMB KT2 199 K1
 PECK SE15 160 B8
Gibbons Cl BORE WD6 75 K5
 CRAWE RH10 284 D10
 STALE/WH AL4 21 H10
Gibbons Ms GLDGN NW11 117 J5
Gibbons Rd WLSDN NW10 136 A1
Gibbon Wk PUT/ROE SW15 156 D10
Gibb's Acre CHOB/PIR GU24 230 E9
Gibbs Av NRWD SE19 181 L9
Gibbs Brook La OXTED RH8 261 J10
Gibbs Cl CHES/WCR EN8 62 C5
 NRWD SE19 * 181 L8
Gibbs Couch OXHEY WD19 33 H3
Gibbs Gn EDGW HA8 95 P5
 WKENS W14 14 C7
Gibbs Green Cl WKENS W14 14 C7
Gibbs Rd UED N18 100 B5
Gibbs Sq NRWD SE19 * 181 L8
Gibraltar Cl RBRW/HUT CM13 107 H7
Gibraltar Crs HOR/WEW KT19 220 B6
Gibraltar Wk BETH E2 7 M10
Gibson Cl CHSGTN KT9 219 H12
 ISLW TW7 154 C9
 WCHMH N21 79 H10
 WCHPL E1 140 B6
Gibson Ct DTCH/LGLY SL3 150 C4
Gibson Gdns STNW/STAM N16 119 H7
Gibson Pl STWL/WRAY TW19 173 M2
Gibson Rd BCTR RM8 123 M6
 HGDN/ICK UB10 112 A9
 LBTH SE11 18 B5
 SUT SM1 221 L2
Gibson's Hl STRHM/NOR SW16 181 H10
Gibson Sq IS N1 6 B5
Gibson St GNWCH SE10 161 K4
Gidd Hl COUL/CHIP CR5 240 B2
Gidea Av GPK RM2 125 H1
Gidea Cl GPK RM2 125 H1
Gideon Ms EA W5 * 155 J1
Gideon Rd BTSEA SW11 158 B9
Gidian Ct LCOL/BKTW AL2 56 F8
Giesbach Rd ARCH N19 118 C7
Giffard Rd UED N18 99 M6
Giffard Wy GUW GU2 249 M7
Giffin St DEPT SE8 160 F6
Gifford Gdns HNWL W7 97 J6
Gifford Rd WLSDN NW10 136 E1
Giffordside CDW/CHF RM16 168 E4
Gifford St IS N1 5 M4
Giggs Hl STMC/STPC BR5 207 K2
Giggs Hills Gdns THDIT KT7 198 F8
Giggs Hill Rd THDIT KT7 198 F7
Gilbert Cl SWCM DA10 189 J2
 WIM/MER SW19 * 201 L1
 WOOL/PLUM SE18 162 C7
Gilbert Gv EDGW HA8 95 P9
Gilbert Pl NOXST/BSQ WC1A 11 L4
Gilbert Rd BELV DA17 164 B2
 BMLY BR1 183 M10
 CDW/CHF RM16 167 H2
 DEN/HRF UB9 91 N10
 LBTH SE11 18 B5
 PIN HA5 113 L2
 ROM RM1 124 C2
 WIM/MER SW19 181 M10
Gilbert Rw GVW DA11 * 190 B9
Gilbert St HSLW TW3 154 B9
 MYFR/PKLN W1K 10 C1
 PEND EN3 80 B3
 SRTFD E15 121 K9
Gilbert Wy BERK HP4 35 M4
Gilbert White Cl GFD/PVL UB6 134 F5
Gilbey Cl HGDN/ICK UB10 112 C9
Gilbey Rd TOOT SW17 179 P7
Gilbeys Yd CAMTN NW1 4 E1
Gilbourne Rd WOOL/PLUM SE18 163 J5
Gilda Av PEND EN3 80 D9
Gilda Crs STNW/STAM N16 119 M4
Gilda Hl RAD WD7 93 P8
Gildea Cl PIN HA5 93 P8
Gildea St GTPST W1W 10 F4
Gilden Crs KTTN NW5 118 A11
Gildenhill Rd SWLY BR8 187 K10
Gilden Wy HLWE CM17 29 N8
Gilders SBW CM21 29 N1
Gildersome St WOOL/PLUM SE18 162 D5
Giles Cl RAIN RM13 145 L4
 STALE/WH AL4 2
Giles Coppice NRWD SE19 181 N7
Giles Fld EGH TW20 191 J4
Giles Md EPSOM KT18 220 B10
Giles Travers Cl EGH TW20 194 F3
Gilfrid Cl UX/CGN UB8 133 L9
Gilham's Av BNSTD SM7 220 C8
Gilhams Cots BNSTD SM7 * 221 H8
Gilkes Crs DUL SE21 181 H3
Gilkes Pl DUL SE21 181 H3
Gillam Wy RAIN RM13 145 H1
Gillan Gn BUSH WD23 94 B3
Gillards Ms WALTH E17 120 D2
Gillards Wy WALTH E17 120 F2
Gill Av CAN/RD E16 141 M8
Gill Cl WATW WD18 72 D10
Gill Crs GVW DA11 190 C6
Gillender St BOW E3 141 H6
Gillespie Rd HBRY N5 119 H8
Gillies Cl EHAM E6 142 B4
Gillett Pl HACK E8 119 N10
Gillett Rd THHTH CR7 203 L4
Gillett St STNW/STAM N16 119 M10
Gillfoot CAMTN NW1 4 E2
Gillham Ter TOTM N17 99 P7
Gilliam Gv PUR/KEN CR8 223 L6
Gillian Av STAL AL1 38 D10
Gillian Crs GPK RM2 125 K1
Gillian Park Rd CHEAM SM3 201 J8
Gillian St LEW SE13 182 C1
Gillian Ter BRYLDS KT5 * 199 L6
Gilliat Dr RGUE GU4 250 D8
Gilliat Rd SL SL1 129 K9
Gilliat's Grn RKW/CH/CXG WD3 32 C3
Gilliatt Cl IVER SL0 131 H8
Gillies St KTTN NW5 118 B10
Gillingham Ms PIM SW1V 16 F6
Gillingham Rd CRICK NW2 117 H8
Gillingham Rw PIM SW1V 16 F6
Gillingham St PIM SW1V 16 F6
Gillison Wk BERM/RHTH SE16 159 P8
Gillman Dr SRTFD E15 141 L9
Gills Hl RAD WD7 74 E1
Gills Hill La RAD WD7 74 E1
Gills Hollow RAD WD7 74 E2
Gill's Rd EYN DA4 200 A2
Gill St POP/IOD E14 140 E8
Gillum Cl EBAR EN4 98 B1
Gilmais GT/LBKH KT23 254 B1
Gilman Crs WDSR SL4 146 C9
Gilmore Cl DTCH/LGLY SL3 149 L1
 HGDN/ICK UB10 112 B8
Gilmore Crs ASHF TW15 178 G8
Gilmore Rd LEW SE13 161 H11
Gilmour Cl CHESW EN7 77 L6
Gilpin Av MORT/ESHN SW14 156 A10
Gilpin Cl BAY/PAD W2 9 K4
 MTCM CR4 201 P2
Gilpin Crs UED N18 99 N12
 WHTN TW2 176 A3
Gilpin Gn HARP AL5 5 F2
Gilpin Rd CLPT E5 120 D9
 WARE SG12 26 C1
Gilpin's Gallop WARE SG12 26 C1
Gilpin's Ride BERK HP4 35 N4
Gilroy Cl RAIN RM13 144 C13
Gilroy Rd HHNE HP2 35 N5

Gilroy Wy STMC/STPC BR5 207 L7
Gilsland WAB EN9 81 K1
Gilsland Rd THHTH CR7 203 L4
Gilson Cl WDSR SL4 171 P3
Gilson Pl MUSWH N10 98 H9
Gilstead Rd FUL/PGN SW6 157 L8
Gilsted Rd FUL/PGN SW6 157 L8
Gilston Rd WBPTN SW10 15 K8
Gilton Pk HLW CM20 28 F4
Gilton Rd CAT SE6 183 K6
Giltspur St STBT EC1A 12 D5
Gimcrack Hl LHD/OX KT22 236 D8
Ginhams Rd CRAWH RH11 283 L2
Gippeswyck Cl PIN HA5 93 K8
Gipsy Hl NRWD SE19 181 M8
Gipsy La GRAYS RM17 167 P5
 PUT/ROE SW15 156 D10
 WNWD SE27 181 L8
Gipsy Road Gdns WNWD SE27 181 K7
Giralda Cl CAN/RD E16 142 A7
Giraud St POP/IOD E14 140 G8
Girdwood Rd WAND/EARL SW18 179 H3
Girling Wy EBED/NFELT TW14 153 M9
Girona Cl CDW/CHF RM16 167 H2
Gironde Rd FUL/PGN SW6 157 J6
Girtin Rd BUSH WD23 74 A6
Girton Av CDALE/KGS NW9 115 M1
Girton Cl NTHLT UB5 134 B1
Girton Gdns CROY/NA CR0 204 F10
Girton Rd NTHLT UB5 134 B1
 SYD SE26 182 C5
Girton Vw RKW/CH/CXG WD3 72 E10
Gisbourne Cl WLGTN SM6 202 G7
Gisburne Wy WATN WD24 73 H5
Gisburn Rd CEND/HSY/T N8 118 G2
Gissing Wk IS N1 6 A1
Gittens Cl BMLY BR1 183 L7
Glacier Wy ALP/SUD HA0 135 J4
Gladbeck Wy ENC/FH EN2 79 J8
Gladden Cl HLWS CM18 47 H5
Gladding Rd CHING E4 61 J1
 MNPK E12 122 D3
Glade Cl SURB KT6 * 199 J8
Glade Gdns CROY/NA CR0 204 D7
Glade La NWDGN UB2 154 A1
Glade Ms GU GU1 268 C5
Gladeside CROY/NA CR0 204 C5
 STALE/WH AL4 39 J3
 WCHMH N21 98 C1
Gladesmore Rd SEVS/STOTM N15 119 N4
Glade Sp KWD/TDW/WH KT20 239 L7
The Glades GVE DA12 190 C9
 HHW HP1 35 N2
The Glade ASC SL5 192 B5
 BELMT SM2 221 H5
 BF/WBF KT14 215 H9
 BMLY BR1 206 A2
 CFSP/GDCR SL9 110 A6
 CHARL SE7 161 K7
 CLAY IG5 102 C9
 COUL/CHIP CR5 241 H5
 CROY/NA CR0 204 B9
 ENC/FH EN2 79 H7
 EW KT17 220 D3
 HACK E8 7 L3
 KWD/TDW/WH KT20 239 L7
 LHD/OX KT22 235 P8
 NFNCH/WDSPK N12 97 N5
 RBRW/HUT CM13 107 N2
 SEV TN13 247 J9
 SHB W12 156 E1
 UPMR RM14 126 B10
 WCHMH N21 78 G10
 WFD IG8 101 N4
 WGCW AL8 22 F5
 WWKM BR4 204 G10
The Gladeway WAB EN9 63 J9
Gladiator St FSTH SE23 182 D2
Glading Ter STNW/STAM N16 119 M3
Gladioli Cl HPTN TW12 175 P9
Gladsdale Dr PIN HA5 94 A2
Gladsmuir Cl WOT/HER KT12 197 K9
Gladsmuir Rd ARCH N19 118 D6
 BAR EN5 77 H6
Gladstone Av EBED/NFELT TW14 175 L1
 MNPK E12 142 B2
 WDGN N22 99 H10
 WHTN TW2 176 C3
Gladstone Gdns HSLW TW3 154 A6
Gladstone Ms KIL/WHAMP NW6 2 D1
 PGE/AN SE20 182 B10
 WDGN N22 99 H10
Gladstone Pde CRICK NW2 * 116 F8
Gladstone Park Gdns CRICK NW2 116 F8
Gladstone Pl BAR EN5 76 C3
 E/WMO/HCT KT8 * 198 D5
Gladstone Rd ASHTD KT21 237 J4
 BKHH IG9 101 P2
 CHSWK W4 156 B7
 CROY/NA CR0 203 L7
 CSHM HP5 51 H7
 HOD EN11 44 C2
 KUT/HW KT1 199 M3
 NWDGN UB2 153 M1
 ORP BR6 226 F2
 SURB KT6 199 J9
 WARE SG12 26 B1
 WAT WD17 73 K7
 WIM/MER SW19 179 K10
Gladstone St STHWK SE1 18 C3
Gladstone Ter VX/NE SW8 * 158 C7
 WNWD SE27 * 181 K7
Gladstone Wy KTN/HRWW/WS HA3 114 D1
 SL SL1 148 F1
Gladwell Rd BMLY BR1 183 M9
 CEND/HSY/T N8 118 G4
Gladwin Wy HLW CM20 28 D4
Gladwyn Rd PUT/ROE SW15 156 G10
Gladys Rd KIL/WHAMP NW6 2 E1
Glaisher St DEPT SE8 160 F6
Glaisyer Wy IVER SL0 130 F4
Glamis Cl CHESW EN7 61 N5
Glamis Crs HYS/HAR UB3 152 D2
Glamis Dr EMPK RM11 125 M6
Glamis Pl HHNE HP2 35 P5
 WAP E1W 140 E6
Glamis Rd WAP E1W 140 E6
Glamis Wy NTHLT UB5 134 F6
Glamorgan Cl MTCM CR4 202 F2
Glamorgan Rd KUT/HW KT1 177 H10
Glandford Wy CHDH RM6 123 J3
Glanfield HHNE HP2 35 J5
Glanfield Rd BECK BR3 204 E4
Glanleam Rd STAN HA7 95 J5
Glanmor Rd SLN SL2 129 N9
Glanthams Rd BRWN CM15 107 N1
The Gianty MEO DA13 172 F9
Glanville Dr EMPK RM11 125 N7
Glanville Ms STAN HA7 95 H4
Glanville Rd BRXS/STRHM SW2 180 A4
 HAYES BR2 205 N3
Glasbrook Av WHTN TW2 175 N4
Glasbrook Rd ELTH/MOT SE9 164 A4
Glaserton Rd STNW/STAM N16 119 M3
Glasford St TOOT SW17 179 H10
Glasgow Rd PLSTW E13 141 N1
 SL SL1 128 B10
 UED N18 * 100 D4
Glasgow Ter PIM SW1V 16 E8
Glaskin Ms HOM E9 120 A10
Glasse Cl WEA W13 135 M3
Glasshill St STHWK SE1 18 D2
Glasshouse Cl UX/CGN UB8 132 C7

Glasshouse Flds WAP E1W 140 C9
Glasshouse St REGST W1B 11 H8
Glasshouse Wk LBTH SE11 17 M7
Glasshouse Yd FARR EC1M 12 E2
Glasslyn Rd CEND/HSY/T N8 118 E3
Glassmill La HAYES BR2 205 L2
Glass St BETH E2 140 A6
Glass Yd WOOL/PLUM SE18 162 D2
Glastonbury Av WFD IG8 102 A8
Glastonbury Cl STMC/STPC BR5 207 M8
Glastonbury Pl WCHPL E1 * 140 C7
Glastonbury Rd ED N9 99 P2
 MRDN SM4 201 K6
Glastonbury St KIL/WHAMP NW6 117 J10
Glaston Ct EA W5 * 135 J10
Glaucus St BOW E3 140 H3
Glazbury Rd WKENS W14 14 B6
Glazebrook Cl DUL SE21 181 L5
Glaziers La RGUW GU3 248 A6
Gleave Cl STAL AL1 38 G5
Glebe Av ENC/FH EN2 79 J7
 HGDN/ICK UB10 112 C8
 KTN/HRWW/WS HA3 115 K1
 MTCM CR4 201 P2
 WFD IG8 101 M7
Glebe Cl BKHTH/KID SE3 * 161 K9
 EA W5 * 135 J10
 GU GU1 250 C10
 HDN NW4 116 F2
 KTN/HRWW/WS HA3 115 K1
The Glebefield SEV TN13 246 C9
Glebe Gdns BF/WBF KT14 215 N10
 NWMAL KT3 200 B7
Glebe House Dr HAYES BR2 205 N8
Glebe Hyrst SAND/SEL CR2 223 N8
Glebelands CHIG IG7 103 J4
 CRAWE RH10 285 P5
 DART DA1 164 G10
 E/WMO/HCT KT8 198 D5
 ESH/CLAY KT10 218 E5
 HLW CM20 29 J8
Glebelands Av CNTH/NBYPK IG2 122 G5
 SWFD E18 101 M10
Glebelands Cl CMBW SE5 159 M9
 NFNCH/WDSPK N12 97 N5
Glebelands Rd EBED/NFELT TW14 175 J4
Glebe La BAR EN5 76 D3
 KTN/HRWW/WS HA3 115 K2
 RDKG RH5 271 L9
 SEV TN15 265 J2
Glebe Pth MTCM CR4 202 A3
Glebe Pl CHEL SW3 15 N9
Glebe Rd ASHTD KT21 237 J4
 BARN SW13 156 D8
 BELMT SM2 221 H5
 BMLY BR1 205 M4
 CAR SM5 222 A3
 CEND/HSY/T N8 118 G2
 CFSP/GDCR SL9 89 P4
 CHONG CM5 67 N5
 DAGE RM10 144 C3
 DORK RH4 272 E5
 FNCH N3 97 N4
 FSTGT E7 122 D3
 GVW DA11 190 C4
 HACK E8 7 L3
 HERT/WAT SG14 25 L3
 RAIN RM13 145 J5
 REDH RH1 240 B10
 RSEV TN14 265 J8
 STA TW18 173 L8
 STAN HA7 95 H6
 UX/CGN UB8 131 M4
 WARL CR6 242 C3
 WLSDN NW10 136 D1
Glebe Side TWK TW1 176 D5
Glebe Sp MTCM CR4 * 202 A3
Glebe St CHSWK W4 156 A4
The Glebe BKHTH/KID SE3 161 K9
 CHST BR7 206 F1
 CRAWE RH10 285 J2
 GSTN WD25 55 K9
 HLW CM20 29 H10
 HORL RH6 280 A4
 KGLGY WD4 54 B5
 REIG RH2 274 D7
 STRHM/NOR SW16 * 180 E7
 WDR/YW UB7 151 P3
 WPK KT4 200 C8
Glebe Wy AMS HP6 69 J2
 WWKM BR4 205 H9
Glebeway WFD IG8 101 P6
Gledhow Gdns ECT SW5 15 H5
Gledhow Wd KWD/TDW/WH KT20 239 M7
Gledstanes Rd WKENS W14 157 H3
Gledwood Av YEAD UB4 133 H7
Gledwood Crs YEAD UB4 133 H7
Gledwood Dr YEAD UB4 133 H7
Gledwood Gdns YEAD UB4 133 H7
Gleed Av BUSH WD23 94 C3
Gleeson Dr ORP BR6 227 J4
Glegg Pl PUT/ROE SW15 156 G10
Glemsford Dr HARP AL5 5 H1
Glenaffric Av POP/IOD E14 161 J1
Glen Albyn Rd WIM/MER SW19 178 G3
Glenalla Rd RSLP HA4 94 C5
Glenalmond Rd KTN/HRWW/WS HA3 115 K2
Glenalvon Wy WOOL/PLUM SE18 162 B9
Glena Mt SUT SM1 221 M1
Glenarm Rd CLPT E5 120 B9
Glen Av ASHF TW15 174 D7
Glenavon Cl ESH/CLAY KT10 218 F5
Glenavon Rd SRTFD E15 141 L8
Glenbarr Cl ELTH/MOT SE9 162 G12
Glenbow Rd BMLY BR1 183 N8
Glenbrook North ENC/FH EN2 78 G10
Glenbrook Rd KIL/WHAMP NW6 2 D1
Glenbrook South ENC/FH EN2 78 G10
Glenbuck Rd SURB KT6 199 J6
Glencairn Dr EA W5 135 J3
Glencairne Cl CAN/RD E16 142 C7
Glencairn Rd STRHM/NOR SW16 180 F10
Glen Cl KWD/TDW/WH KT20 239 H9
 SHPTN TW17 196 G1
Glencoe Av GNTH/NBYPK IG2 123 H5
Glencoe Dr DAGE RM10 124 B9
Glencoe Rd BUSH WD23 73 N9
 HYS/HAR UB3 133 L7
 WEY KT13 196 D10
Glencorse Gn OXHEY WD19 33 H5
Glen Crs WFD IG8 101 J5

Glendale HHW HP1 35 L6
 SWLY BR8 208 G5
Glendale Av CHDH RM6 123 M5
 EDGW HA8 95 M6
 WDGN N22 99 H8
Glendale Cl BRWN CM15 107 K2
 ELTH/MOT SE9 162 F10
Glendale Dr RGUE GU4 250 F6
 WIM/MER SW19 179 J8
Glendale Ms BECK BR3 204 G1
Glendale Ri PUR/KEN CR8 241 J1
Glendale Rd ERITH DA8 164 D3
Glendale Wy THMD SE28 143 M10
Glendall St BRXN/ST SW9 158 G9
Glendarvon St PUT/ROE SW15 * 156 G5
Glendene Av EHSLY KT24 252 G2
Glendevon Cl EDGW HA8 95 N4
Glendish Rd TOTM N17 99 P9
Glendor Gdns MLHL NW7 96 A5
Glendower Crs ORP BR6 207 K6
Glendower Gdns MORT/ESHN SW14 156 A9
Glendower Pl SKENS SW7 15 L5
Glendower Rd CHING E4 101 J2
 MORT/ESHN SW14 156 A9
Glendown Rd ABYW SE2 163 K4
Gleneagle Ms STRHM/NOR SW16 180 D8
Gleneagle Rd STRHM/NOR SW16 180 D8
Gleneagles STAN HA7 94 G7
Gleneagles Cl BERM/RHTH SE16 * 160 A5
 HARM RM3 105 N8
 OXHEY WD19 33 H5
 ORP BR6 206 G8
 STWL/WRAY TW19 173 M2
Gleneldon Ms STRHM/NOR SW16 180 F8
Gleneldon Rd STRHM/NOR SW16 180 F8
Glenelg Rd BRXS/STRHM SW2 180 F1
Glenesk Rd ELTH/MOT SE9 162 G10
Glenester Cl HOD EN11 26 F10
Glen Faba Rd HLWW/ROY CM19 45 L3
Glenfarg Rd CAT SE6 183 J4
Glenferrie Rd STAL AL1 38 F6
Glenfield Cl BRKHM/BTCW RH3 273 N3
Glenfield Rd ASHF TW15 174 C9
 BNSTD SM7 240 A4
 HNWL W7 135 N4
 STRHM/NOR SW16 180 F3
 WEA W13 154 C1
Glenfinlas Wy CMBW SE5 159 J6
Glenforth St GNWCH SE10 161 L3
Glengall Br POP/IOD E14 160 G2
Glengall Gv POP/IOD E14 160 G2
Glengall Pl STAL AL1 * 38 D9
Glengall Rd BXLYHN DA7 163 P9
 EDGW HA8 95 N4
 KIL/WHAMP NW6 2 D1
 PECK SE15 19 M9
 WFD IG8 101 M9
Glengall Ter PECK SE15 19 M9
Glen Gdns CROY/NA CR0 203 H10
Glengarnock Av POP/IOD E14 161 J4
Glengarry Rd EDUL SE22 159 M10
Glenham Dr GNTH/NBYPK IG2 122 G5
Glen Hazel Cl HLWE CM17 47 L1
Glenhaven Av BORE WD6 75 M7
Glenhead Cl ELTH/MOT SE9 162 G7
Glenheadon Rd LHD/OX KT22 237 J9
Glenhill Cl FNCH N3 97 J3
Glenhouse Rd ELTH/MOT SE9 164 D1
Glenhurst Av BXLY DA5 186 A4
 KTTN NW5 118 B9
 RSLP HA4 94 B5
Glenhurst Ct NRWD SE19 181 K10
Glenhurst Ri NRWD SE19 181 K11
Glenhurst Rd BTFD TW8 155 K5
 NFNCH/WDSPK N12 97 N5
Glenilla Rd HAMP NW3 3 N1
Glenister Park Rd STRHM/NOR SW16 180 E10
Glenister Rd CSHM HP5 51 H4
 GNWCH SE10 161 L3
Glenlea Rd ELTH/MOT SE9 164 D1
Glenlea Wk WOKS/MYFD GU22 231 P5
Glenloch Rd HAMP NW3 3 N1
 PEND EN3 80 B6
Glen Luce CHES/WCR EN8 62 C5
Glenluce Rd BKHTH/KID SE3 161 K5
Glenlyon Rd ELTH/MOT SE9 164 G12
Glenmere Av MLHL NW7 96 A5
Glenmere Rw LEE/GVPK SE12 175 L2
Glenmill HPTN TW12 175 H7
Glenmore Cl ADL/WDHM KT15 195 H7
Glenmore Gdns ABLGY WD5 55 H7
Glenmore Lawns WEA W13 135 J3
Glenmore Pde ALP/SUD HA0 * 135 P8
Glenmore Rd HAMP NW3 3 N1
 WELL DA16 163 M7
Glenmore Wy BARK IG11 143 J7
Glenn Av PUR/KEN CR8 223 J7
Glennie Rd WNWD SE27 180 G8
Glenny Rd BARK IG11 142 D7
Glenorchy Cl YEAD UB4 133 L3
Glenparke Rd FSTGT E7 141 N1
Glen Ri WFD IG8 101 N1
Glen Rd CHSGTN KT9 199 P6
 PLSTW E13 141 P1
 WALTH E17 120 B5
Glen Road End WLGTN SM6 223
Glenrosa St FUL/PGN SW6 158 B7
Glenrose Ct SCUP DA14 186 F5
Glenroy St SHB W12 137 L8
Glensdale Rd BROCKY SE4 160 A12
Glenshee Cl NTHWD HA6 32 B9
Glenshiel Rd ELTH/MOT SE9 164 G12
Glenside CHIG IG7 103 J4
Glenside Cl PUR/KEN CR8 241 L1
Glentanner Wy TOOT SW17 179
Glentham Cots BARN SW13 * 156
Glentham Gdns BARN SW13 156
Glentham Rd BARN SW13 156
Glenthorne Av CROY/NA CR0 204 B8
Glenthorne Cl CHEAM SM3 201 L8
Glenthorne Gdns BARK/HLT IG6 103 P5
 CHEAM SM3 201
Glenthorne Ms HMSMTH W6 156
Glenthorne Rd EFNCH N2 97 N9
 HMSMTH W6 156
 KUT/HW KT1 199
 WALTH E17 120
Glenthorpe Rd MRDN SM4 201 H9
Glenton Cl ROM RM1 104
Glenton Rd LEW SE13 161
Glenton Wy ROM RM1 104
Glentrammon Av ORP BR6 227 K6
Glentrammon Cl ORP BR6 227 K6
Glentrammon Gdns ORP BR6 227 K6
Glentrammon Rd ORP BR6 227 K6
Glentworth Pl SL SL1 129 H10

Glentworth St CAMTN NW1 10 D1
Glenure Rd ELTH/MOT SE9 164 D1
Glenview ABYW SE2 163 N5
Glen Vw GVE DA12 190 F6
Glenview Cl BRWN CM15 284
Glen View Rd BMLY BR1 206 A2
Glenview Ri HHW HP1 35 L6
Glenville Gv DEPT SE8 160 E6
Glenville Ms WAND/EARL SW18 179 J8
Glenville Rd KUTN/CMB KT2 199 M1
Glen Wy WAT WD17 72 F4
Glenwood BROX EN10 44 E5
 RDKG RH5 273 H4
 WGCE AL7 23 M6
Glenwood Av CDALE/KGS NW9 116 D2
 RAIN RM13 145 L6
Glenwood Cl HRW HA1 114 E3
Glenwood Dr GPK RM2 125 H3
Glenwood Gdns GNTH/NBYPK IG2 122 D3
Glenwood Gv CDALE/KGS NW9 115 P5
Glenworth Av POP/IOD E14 161 L4
Glevum Cl STALW/RED AL3 37 H8
Gliddon Dr CLPT E5 120 A9
Gliddon Rd WKENS W14 14 A7
Glimpsing Gn ERITH DA18 163 P2
Glisson Rd HGDN/ICK UB10 132 B2
Gload Crs STMC/STPC BR5 207 N9
Globe Cl HARP AL5 20 B2
Globe Pond Rd BERM/RHTH SE16 * 140 D10
Globe Rd BETH E2 140 B1
 EMPK RM11 125 J4
 SRTFD E15 121 L10
 WFD IG8 101 P7
Globe St STHWK SE1 18 G3
Globe Ter BETH E2 140 B1
Glory Md DORK RH4 273
Glossop Rd SAND/SEL CR2 223 L5
Gloster Rd NWMAL KT3 200 B8
Gloucester Av BFN/LL DA15 185 H5
 CAMTN NW1 4 C4
 CDW/CHF RM16 167 P1
 CHES/WCR EN8 62 D9
 SL SL1 129 H7
 TIL RM18 169 M4
 WELL DA16 185 J1
Gloucester Circ GNWCH SE10 161 H6
Gloucester Cl THDIT KT7 * 198 F8
 WLSDN NW10 136 A2
Gloucester Ct HAT AL10
 RCH/KEW TW9 155 M6
Gloucester Crs CAMTN NW1 4 E5
 STA TW18 173 N9
Gloucester Dr FSBYPK N4 119 J7
 GLDGN NW11 117 K2
 STA TW18 172 F6
Gloucester Gdns BAY/PAD W2 8 D6
 BNSTD SM7
 CRICK NW2
 EBAR EN4
 IL IG1
 SUT SM1
Gloucester Ga CAMTN NW1 4 D7
Gloucester Gate Ms CAMTN NW1 * 4 D7
Gloucester Gv EDGW HA8 96 A9
Gloucester Ms BAY/PAD W2 8 F7
Gloucester Ms West BAY/PAD W2 8 E6
Gloucester Pde BFN/LL DA15 * 185 K1
 HYS/HAR UB3 * 152 D2
Gloucester Pl CAMTN NW1 10 A1
 WDSR SL4 149
Gloucester Place Ms MHST W1U 10 A3
Gloucester Rd ACT W3 155 P1
 BAR EN5 77 L6
 BELV DA17 164 A4
 CROY/NA CR0 203 L7
 EA W5 155 H1
 ENC/FH EN2 79 K4
 FELT TW13 175 K4
 GUW GU2 249 L8
 GVE DA12 190 F7
 HPTN TW12 176 A10
 HRW HA1 114 A3
 HSLW TW4 153 M10
 KUT/HW KT1 200 A1
 LEY E10 120 C5
 MNPK E12 122 C8
 RCH/KEW TW9 155 M6
 REDH RH1 120 A6
 ROM RM1 124 F4
 SKENS SW7 14 F5
 TEDD TW11 176 D8
 TOTM N17 99 L10
 UED N18 100 A5
 WALTH E17 101 N12
 WAN E11 122
 WHTN TW2 176 A6
Gloucester Sq BAY/PAD W2 9 L6
 BETH E2 * 7 M6
Gloucester St PIM SW1V 16 E8
Gloucester Ter BAY/PAD W2 8 E6
 STHGT/OAK N14 * 98 E1
Gloucester Wk KENS W8 14 E1
Glover Cl ABYW SE2 163 M3
 THMD SE28
Glover Dr UED N18 100
Glover Rd PIN HA5 94 A5
Glovers Cl BH/WHM TN16 243 N2
 HERT/BAY SG13 25 K2
Glovers Fld BRWN CM15 86
Glovers La HLWE CM17
Glover's Rd HORL RH6 278
 REIG RH2 273
Gloxinia Rd MEO DA13 191
Glycena Rd BTSEA SW11 158
Glyn Av EBAR EN4 77 N3
Glyn Cl EW KT17 220 D5
 NRWD SE19 181
Glyn Ct STAN HA7 94
Glyn Davies Cl RDART DA2 187
Glyndebourne Pk ORP BR6 206 E10
Glynde Ms CHEL SW3 15
Glynde Rd BXLYHN DA7 163
Glynde St BROCKY SE4 181
Glyndon Rd WOOL/PLUM SE18
Glynfield Rd WLSDN NW10 136
Glyn Rd CLPT E5 120
 PEND EN3 80
 WPK KT4 201
Glyn St LBTH SE11 17
Glynswood CFSP/GDCR SL9 89 P9
Glynswood Pl NTHWD HA6 32
Glynwood Ct FSTH SE23 181
Goat La EN EN1
 SURB KT6
Goat Rd MTCM CR4
Goatsfield Rd BH/WHM TN16 243
Goatswood La ABR/ST RM4
Goat Whf BTFD TW8
Gobions Av CRW RM5
Gobions Wy POTB/CUF EN6 59
Goblins Gn WGCE AL7
Godalming Av WLGTN SM6 223
Godalming Rd POP/IOD E14 140
Godbold Rd SRTFD E15
Goddard Cl GSTN WD25

GUW GU2 249 M6
SHPTN TW17 196 A3
Goddard Pl ARCH N19 118 C9
Goddard Rd BECK BR3 204 C4
 CDW/CHF RM16 147 M10
Goddards Cl HERT/BAY SG13 42 D5
Goddards Wy IL IG1 122 C6
Goddington Cha ORP BR6 227 L6
Goddington La ORP BR6 207 K10
 ORP BR6 207 M10
Godfrey Av NTHLT UB5 133 M5
 WHTN TW2 176 C5
Godfrey Hl WOOL/PLUM SE18 162 B3
Godfrey Rd WOOL/PLUM SE18 162 C3
Godfrey St CHEL SW3 15 P7
 SRTFD E15 141 H4
Godfrey Wy HSLWW TW4 175 H5
Goding St LBTH SE11 17 J7
Godley Rd BF/WBF KT14 216 A9
 WAND/EARL SW18 179 N4
Godliman St BLKFR EC4V 12 E6
Godman Rd CDW/CHF RM16 168 A8
 PECK SE15 160 A8
Godolphin Cl BELMT SM2 221 J7
 PLMGR N13 99 J3
Godolphin Pl ACT W3 136 A9
Godolphin Rd BEAC HP9 82 B4
 SHB W12 156 E1
 SL SL1 129 J9
 WEY KT13 216 E3
Godric Crs CROY/NA CR0 225 J5
Godson Rd CROY/NA CR0 203 H10
Godson St IS N1 6 A4
Godstone Green Rd GDST RH9 260 D2
Godstone Mt PUR/KEN CR8 * 223 J8
Godstone Rd CTHM CR3 241 M4
 OXTED RH8 260 F7
 PUR/KEN CR8 241 M1
 REDH RH1 259 J9
 SUT SM1 221 M1
 TWK TW1 176 F2
Godstow Rd ABYW SE2 163 M4
Godwin Cl CHING E4 81 H4
 HOR/WEW KT19 219 P3
 IS N1 6 F1
Godwin Rd FSTGT E7 121 N9
 HAYES BR2 204 B3
Goffers Rd BKHTH/KID SE3 161 K7
Goff's Cl CRAWW RH11 283 H6
Goffs La CHESW EN7 61 P3
Goff's La CHESW EN7 61 J4
Goff's Oak Av CHESW EN7 61 J4
Goffs Park Rd CRAWW RH11 283 J6
Goffs Rd ASHF TW15 174 E9
Gogmore Farm Cl CHERT KT16 195 H7
Gogmore La CHERT KT16 195 J6
Goidel Cl WLGTN SM6 222 E1
Golborne Gdns NKENS W10 * 4 D2
Golborne Ms NKENS W10 * 4 C2
Golborne Rd NKENS W10 4 C2
Goldace GRAYS RM17 167 L5
Golda Cl BAR EN5 76 G10
Goldbeaters Gv EDGW HA8 96 D2
Goldcliff Cl MRDN SM4 201 K7
Gold Cl BROX EN10 44 D6
Goldcrest Cl CAN/RD E16 142 A7
 HORL RH6 279 N3
 THMD SE28 143 M9
Goldcrest Ms EA W5 * 135 J7
Goldcrest Wy BUSH WD23 94 B2
 CROY/NA CR0 225 J5
 PUR/KEN CR8 222 E6
Goldcroft HHS/BOV HP3 36 B8
Golden Cres HYS/HAR UB3 133 H7
Golden Cross Ms NTGHL W11 * 8 C5
Golden Dell WGCE AL7 23 J3
Golden Hind Pl DEPT SE8 * 160 E3
Golden Jubilee Br STHWK SE1 * 11 M8
Golden La STLK EC1Y 12 E2
Golden Lane Est STLK EC1Y 12 E1
Golden Mnr HNWL W7 135 N4
Golden Oak Cl SLN SL2 128 C1
Golden Pde WALTH E17 * 101 L12
Golden Plover Cl CAN/RD E16 141 M8
Golden Sq SOHO/CST W1F 11 H7
Golden Yd HAMP NW3 * 117 M9
Golders Cl EDGW HA8 96 B1
Golders Gdns GLDGN NW11 117 H5
Golders Green Crs GLDGN NW11 * 117 J5
Golders Green Rd GLDGN NW11 117 H4
Golders Hl HAMP NW3 * 117 L7
Goldersleigh GLDGN NW11 * 117 K6
Golders Manor Dr GLDGN NW11 116 G4
Golders Park Cl GLDGN NW11 117 K6
Golders Ri HDN NW4 116 G4
Golders Wy GLDGN NW11 117 H5
Goldfinch Cl CRAWW RH11 283 N5
 ORP BR6 227 K2
Goldfinch Gdns RGUE GU4 250 G2
Goldfinch Rd SAND/SEL CR2 223 N8
 THMD SE28 162 G2
Goldfinch Wy BORE WD6 75 M5
Goldhawk Ms SHB W12 * 156 E1
Goldhawk Rd HMSMTH W6 156 E1
Goldhaze Cl WFD IG8 101 P8
Gold Hl EDGW HA8 96 D1
Gold Hl North CFSP/GDCR SL9 89 A10
Gold Hl West CFSP/GDCR SL9 89 P9
Goldhurst Ter KIL/WHAMP NW6 3 H4
Golding Cl CRAWE RH10 284
Goldingham Av LOU IG10 29
Golding Rd SEV TN13 247
Goldings Crs HAT AL10
Goldings HI LOU IG10
Goldings La WARE SG12
Goldings Rd LOU IG10
The Goldings WOKN/KNAP GU21 231
Golding St WCHPL E1 140
Goldington Cl HOD EN11
Goldington Crs CAMTN NW1 5
Golding Ter WCHPL E1 * 140
Goldington St CAMTN NW1 5
Gold La EDGW HA8
Goldman Cl BETH E2
Goldney Rd MV/WKIL W9
Goldrill Dr FBAR/BDGN N11
Goldrings Rd LHD/OX KT22
Goldsboro Rd VX/NE SW8
Goldsborough Crs CHING E4
Goldsdown Cl PEND EN3
Goldsdown Rd PEND EN3
Goldsel Rd SWLY BR8
Goldsmith Av ACT W3
Goldsmith Av CDALE/KGS NW9 116 D3
 MNPK E12 142 B4
 ROMW/RG RM7 124 B5
Goldsmith Cl RYLN/HDSTN HA2 113 P6
Goldsmith La CDALE/KGS NW9 115
Goldsmith Pl KIL/WHAMP NW6 * 2
Goldsmith Rd ACT W3 136 A10
 FBAR/BDGN N11 98 A6
 LEY E10
 PECK SE15 159 J7
 WALTH E17 100 C10
Goldsmith's Rw BETH E2 7 L1
Goldsmith St CITYW EC2V 12 F5

Goldsmiths Whf GRAYS RM17 * ... 167 M6
Goldsmith Wy STALW/RED AL3. 38 B4
Goldstone Ct WARE SG12 ... 26 C1
Goldstone Farm Vw GT/LBKH KT23 ... 253 P3
Goldstone Orch WOKN/KNAP GU21 ... 231 M4
Goldsworth Rd WOKN/KNAP GU21 ... 231 P4
Goldsworthy Gdns BERM/RHTH SE16 ... 160 B8
Goldwell Rd THHTH CR7 ... 202 G4
Goldwing Cl CAN/RD E16 ... 141 M8
Gole Rd CHOB/PIR GU24 ... 230 C7
Golf Cl BUSH WD23 ... 73 L7
STAN HA7 ... 95 H8
THHTH CR7 ... 203 H1
WOKS/MYFD GU22 ... 215 H10
Golfe Rd IL IG1 ... 122 C8
Golf House La OXTED RH8 ... 281 P5
Golf Links Av GVE DA12 ... 190 E8
Golf Ride ENC/FH EN2 ... 79 N1
Golf Rd BMLY BR1 ... 206 D3
EA W5 ... 135 L8
PUR/KEN CR8 ... 241 L4
WHTN TW2 ... 176 C6
Golf Side BELMT SM2 ... 221 H7
WHTN TW2 ... 176 C6
Golf Side Cl TRDG/WHET N20 ... 97 P4
Gollogly Ter CHARL SE7 ... 141 J4
Gombards STALW/RED AL3 ... 38 C5
Gomer Gdns TEDD TW11 ... 176 F9
Gomer Pl TEDD TW11 ... 176 F9
Gomm Rd BERM/RHTH SE16 ... 160 B2
Gomms Wood Cl BEAC HP9 ... 88 A7
Gomshall Av WLGTN SM6 ... 222 F2
Gomshall Gdns PUR/KEN CR8 ... 241 M1
Gomshall La SHGR GU5 ... 270 F6
Gomshall Rd BELMT SM2 ... 220 F6
Gondar Gdns CRICK NW2 ... 217 J10
Gonson St DEPT SE8 ... 160 C5
Gonston Cl WIM/MER SW19 ... 179 H5
Gonville Av RKW/CH/CXG WD3 ... 72 C10
Gonville Crs NTHLT UB5 ... 134 A1
Gonville Rd THHTH CR7 ... 202 G5
Gonville St FUL/PGN SW6 ... 157 H9
Goodacre Cl POTB/CUF EN6 ... 59 L8
Goodall Rd WAN E11 ... 121 H8
Goodcare Cl WEY KT13 ... 216 D2
Gooden Ct HRW HA1 ... 114 C10
Goodenough Cl COUL/CHIP CR5 ... 241 H10
Goodenough Rd WIM/MER SW19 ... 179 J10
Goodenough Wy COUL/CHIP CR5 ... 240 G9
Goodey Rd BARK IG11 ... 143 J2
Goodge Pl FITZ W1T ... 11 H1
Goodge St FITZ W1T ... 11 H1
Goodhall Cl STAN HA7 ... 94 F7
Goodhall St WLSDN NW10 ... 136 B5
Goodhart Wy WWKM BR4 ... 205 K6
Gooding Cl NWMAL KT3 ... 199 P4
Goodinge Cl HOLWY N7 ... 118 F10
Goodinge Rd HOLWY N7 ... 5 L1
Goodison Cl BUSH WD23 ... 74 B9
Goodlake Ct DEN/HRF UB9 ... 111 J5
Goodley Stock Rd EDEN TN8 ... 262 E5
Goodman Ct ALP/SUD HA0 * ... 115 J9
Goodman Crs BRXS/STRHM SW2 ... 180 C5
CROY/NA CR0 ... 203 J6
Goodman Pk SLN SL2 ... 129 P10
Goodman Pl STA TW18 * ... 173 J2
Goodman Rd LEY E10 ... 121 H5
Goodman's Stile WCHPL E1 ... 13 P1
Goodman's Yd TWRH EC3N ... 13 M3
Goodmayes Av GDMY/SEVK IG3 ... 123 K6
Goodmayes La GDMY/SEVK IG3 ... 123 K9
Goodmayes Rd GDMY/SEVK IG3 ... 123 K6
Goodmead Rd ORP BR6 ... 207 N7
Goodrich Cl GSTN WD25 ... 73 H1
Goodrich Rd EDUL SE22 ... 181 N7
Goodson Rd WLSDN NW10 ... 136 B2
Goodway Gdns POP/IOD E14 ... 141 J8
Goodwin Cl BERM/RHTH SE16 ... 14 M4
CRAWW RH11 ... 283 H10
MTCM CR4 ... 201 N3
Goodwin Ct CHES/WCR EN8 ... 62 B4
Goodwin Dr SCUP DA14 ... 185 N5
Goodwin Gdns CROY/NA CR0 ... 223 J2
Goodwin Rd CROY/NA CR0 ... 223 J2
ED N9 ... 100 D3
SHB W12 ... 156 D1
SLN SL2 ... 128 C8
Goodwins Ct CHCR WC2N ... 11 L7
Goodwin St FSBYPK N4 ... 119 H7
Goodwood Av HCH RM12 ... 111 K5
PEND EN3 ... 80 B5
WATN WD24 ... 72 F1
Goodwood Cl CRAWE RH10 ... 284 B10
HOD EN11 ... 44 A4
MRDN SM4 ... 201 K4
STAN HA7 ... 95 J3
Goodwood Crs GVE DA12 ... 190 F9
Goodwood Dr NTHLT UB5 ... 133 P5
Goodwood Pde BECK BR3 * ... 204 D4
Goodwood Rd NWCR SE14 ... 160 D6
REDH RH1 ... 258 C8
Goodwood Rd REDH RH1 ... 258 C8
Goodwyn Av MLHL NW7 ... 96 B6
Goodwyns Pl DORK RH4 ... 272 G5
Goodwyn's V MUSWH N10 ... 98 B9
Goodyers Av RAD WD7 ... 56 E10
Goodyers Gdns HDN NW4 ... 116 C3
Goosander Wy THMD SE28 ... 162 G1
Goose Acre CSHM HP5 ... 51 M6
Gooseacre WGCE AL7 ... 23 J7
Gooseacre La KTN/HRWW/WS HA3 ... 115 J3
Goosecroft HHW HP1 ... 35 J5
Goosefields RKW/CH/CXG WD3 ... 71 M10
Goose Gn SHGR GU5 ... 270 D5
Goose Rye Rd RGUW GU3 ... 249 L2
Gooshays Dr HARH RM3 ... 105 M7
Gooshays Gdns HARH RM3 ... 105 M7
Goossens Cl SUT SM1 ... 221 N2
Gophir La CANST EC4R * ... 12 G7
Gopsall St IS N1 ... 7 H1
Goral Md RKW/CH/CXG WD3 ... 91 N2
Gordon Av CHING E4 ... 101 N2
HCH RM12 ... 124 D7
MORT/ESHN SW14 ... 156 B10
SAND/SEL CR2 ... 223 K7
STA TW18 ... 94 F7
TWK TW1 ... 176 F3
Gordonbrock Rd BROCKY SE4 ... 182 A1
Gordon Cl CHERT KT16 ... 195 H10
STA TW18 ... 173 J1
STAL AL1 ... 38 G7
TIL RM18 ... 169 J10
WALTH E17 ... 120 F4
Gordon Ct EDGW HA8 ... 95 N10
Gordondale Rd WIM/MER SW19 ... 179 K5
Gordon Dr CHERT KT16 ... 195 H10
SHPTN TW17 ... 195 L6

Gordon Gv CMBW SE5 ... 159 J8
Gordon HI ENC/FH EN2 ... 79 K5
Gordon House Rd KTTN NW5 ... 118 B9
Gordon Pr GVE DA12 ... 190 F2
KERS W6 ... 14 F1
Gordon Prom East GVE DA12 ... 190 G2
Gordon Rd ASHF TW15 ... 173 H6
BARK IG11 ... 143 H3
BECK BR3 ... 204 E3
BELV DA17 ... 164 D3
BFN/LL DA15 ... 185 H1
BRWN CM15 ... 107 M2
BRYLDS KT5 ... 199 L7
CAR SM5 ... 222 A5
CDW/CHF RM16 ... 168 B1
CHDH RM6 ... 124 A4
CHING E4 ... 101 K1
CHSWK W4 ... 155 N5
CSHM HP5 ... 51 H8
CTHM CR3 ... 241 L7
EA W5 ... 135 H9
ED N9 ... 100 A3
ENC/FH EN2 ... 79 L5
ESH/CLAY KT10 ... 198 A8
FNCH N3 ... 97 J8
GVW DA11 ... 190 B3
HRW HA1 ... 114 D2
HSLW TW3 ... 154 B10
IL IG1 ... 122 E8
KTN/HRWW/WS HA3 ... 114 D1
KUTN/CMB KT2 ... 199 L1
NWDGN UB2 ... 153 M3
PECK SE15 ... 159 L5
RCH/KEW TW9 ... 157 L8
REDH RH1 ... 258 B7
SEV TN13 ... 265 J1
SHPTN TW17 ... 196 E6
SRTFD E15 ... 121 H9
SWFD E18 ... 101 N9
WAB EN9 ... 62 F10
WAN E11 ... 121 M4
WDR/YW UB7 ... 131 P9
WIM/MER SW19 ... 178 B3
Gordon Sq STPAN WC1H ... 11 J1
STPAN WC1H ... 11 M5
Gordon St PLSTW E13 ... 141 M5
STPAN WC1H ... 11 J1
Gordons Wk HARP AL5 ... 20 B3
Gordon Wy BAR EN5 ... 77 J4
BMLY BR1 ... 205 M1
Gore Cl DEN/HRF UB9 ... 111 L2
Gorefield Pl KIL/WHAMP NW6 ... 2 C1
Gore HI AMSS HP7 * ... 68 G8
Gorelands La CSTG HP8 ... 90 A2
Gorell Rd BEAC HP9 ... 88 C10
Gore Rd HOM E9 ... 140 B5
RDART DA2 ... 188 C3
RYNPK SW20 ... 200 F2
SL SL1 ... 128 A5
Goresbrook Rd DAGW RM9 ... 143 K3
Gore St SKENS SW7 ... 15 H3
Gorham Dr STAL AL1 ... 38 D9
Gorham Pl NTGHL W11 ... 8 A3
Goring Cl CRW RM5 ... 104 D9
Goring Gdns BCTR RM8 ... 123 M9
Goring Rd DACW RM9 ... 144 E1
FBAR/BDGN N11 * ... 98 F7
STA TW18 ... 172 G8
Goring St HDTCH EC3A ... 13 L5
Gorle Cl GSTN WD25 ... 73 H1
Gorleston Rd SEVS/STOTM N15 ... 119 L3
Gorleston St WKENS W14 ... 14 B5
Gorling Cl CRAWW RH11 ... 283 H6
Gorman Rd WOOL/PLUM SE18 ... 162 C3
Gorringe Av EYN DA4 ... 210 C2
Gorringe Park Av MTCM CR4 ... 180 B10
Gorse Cl CAN/RD E16 ... 141 M8
CRAWE RH10 ... 285 J3
HAT AL10 ... 40 C7
KWD/TDW/WH KT20 ... 238 E6
Gorse Cnr HARP AL5 * ... 20 B5
Gorse Ct RGUE GU4 ... 250 F8
Gorse Dr HORL RH6 ... 281 J3
Gorse Hill La VW GU25 ... 194 A4
Gorse Hill Rd VW GU25 ... 194 A3
Gorselands HARP AL5 ... 20 A4
Gorse La CHOB/PIR GU24 ... 213 K4
Gorse Meade SL SL1 ... 128 C4
Gorse Ri TOOT SW17 ... 180 B8
Gorse Rd CROY/NA CR0 ... 204 F10
STMC/STPC BR5 ... 208 B9
Gorse Wk WDR/YW UB7 ... 131 P8
Gorseway ROMW/RG RM7 ... 124 D6
Gorse Wood Rd HART DA3 ... 211 L5
Gorsewood Rd WOKN/KNAP GU21 ... 231 J5
Gorst Rd BTSEA SW11 ... 180 A1
WLSDN NW10 ... 135 M3
Gorsuch Pl BETH E2 ... 7 M9
Gorsuch St BETH E2 ... 7 L9
Gosberton Rd BAL SW12 ... 180 A4
Gosbury Hl CHSGTN KT9 ... 219 K11
Gosden Cl CRAWE RH10 ... 284 B8
SHGR GU5 ... 268 C9
Gosden Hill Rd RGUE GU4 ... 250 F6
Gosden Rd CHOB/PIR GU24 ... 212 E9
Gosfield Rd BCTR RM8 ... 124 B6
HOR/WEW KT19 ... 220 A8
Gosfield St GTPST W1W ... 10 F1
Gosford Gdns REDBR IG4 ... 135 H4
Gosforth La OXHEY WD19 ... 33 H4
Gosforth Pth OXHEY WD19 ... 32 H4
Goshawk Gdns YEAD UB4 ... 132 F5
Goslett Yd SOHO/SHAV W1D ... 11 K5
Gosling Cl GFD/PVL UB6 ... 133 P5
Gosling Gn DTCH/LGLY SL3 ... 150 B1
Gosling Rd DTCH/LGLY SL3 ... 150 B1
Gosling Wy BRXN/ST SW9 ... 159 N7
Gospatrick Rd TOTM N17 ... 99 J8
Gosport Dr HCH RM12 ... 145 K1
Gosport Rd WALTH E17 ... 120 E5
Gosport Wy PECK SE15 ... 159 N6
Gossage Rd HGDN/ICK UB10 ... 132 A3
WOOL/PLUM SE18 ... 143 K10
The Gossamers GSTN WD25 ... 73 M2
Gosselin Cl HOD EN11 ... 45 K3
Gosselin Rd HERT/WAT SG14 ... 25 K3
Gosset St BETH E2 ... 7 N10
Gossington Cl CHST BR7 ... 184 F7
Gosshill Rd CHST BR7 ... 184 F7
Gostling Rd WHTN TW2 ... 175 N4
Goston Gdns THHTH CR7 ... 189 H9
Goswell HI WDSR SL4 ... 149 J7
Goswell Rd FSBYE EC1V * ... 6 D7
FSBYE EC1V ... 6 D10
WDSR SL4 ... 149 J7
Gothic Cl DART DA1 * ... 191 L4
Gothic Ct HYS/HAR UB3 * ... 152 C5
Gothic Rd WHTN TW2 ... 176 C5
Gottfried Ms KTTN NW5 ... 118 D9
Goudhurst Cl CRAWE RH10 ... 284 F11
Goudhurst Rd BMLY BR1 ... 183 N4
Gouge Av GVW DA11 ... 190 B4
Gough Rd EN EN1 ... 80 B1
SRTFD E15 ... 121 L3
Gough Sq FLST/FETLN EC4A ... 12 B5
Gough St FSBYW WC1X ... 11 N1
Gould Ct DUL SE21 ... 162 G10
RGUE GU4 ... 250 F8
Goulding Gdns THHTH CR7 ... 189 L7
Gould Rd EBED/NFELT TW14 ... 174 F3
WHTN TW2 ... 176 D4
Goulds Gn UX/CGN UB8 ... 132 C9
Gould Ter HACK E8 ... 120 K5
Goulston St WCHPL E1 ... 13 M1
Goulton Rd CLPT E5 ... 120 A10
Gourley Pl SEVS/STOTM N15 ... 119 M3
Gourley St SEVS/STOTM N15 ... 119 M3
Gourock Rd ELTH/MOT SE9 ... 184 D1
Govan St BETH E2 ... 7 N6
Government Rw PEND EN3 ... 80 F5
Governors Cl AMS HP6 * ... 68 L5
Govett Av SHPTN TW17 ... 196 D5
Govett Gv BFOR GU20 ... 212 C2
Gowan Av FUL/PGN SW6 ... 157 H7
Gowan Rd WLSDN NW10 ... 136 E2
Gower Ms GWRST WC1E ... 11 K4
Gower Pl FSTGT E7 ... 11 J3
GWRST WC1E ... 11 J3
Gower Rd HORL RH6 ... 279 P4
ISLW TW7 ... 154 E5
WEY KT13 ... 216 E3
Gowers Av CDW/CHF RM16 ... 168 C1
The Gowers AMSS HP6 ... 69 K3
Gower St GWRST WC1E ... 11 J2
Gower's Wk WCHPL E1 ... 13 N5
Gowings Gn SL SL1 ... 148 D1
Gowland Pl BECK BR3 ... 184 E2
Gowlett Rd PECK SE15 ... 159 P9
Gowland Cl CROY/NA CR0 ... 203 P7
Gowrie Pl CTHM CR3 ... 241 K8
Gowrie Rd BTSEA SW11 ... 159 K8
Graburn Wy E/WMO/HCT KT8 ... 198 C3
Gracechurch St BANK EC3V ... 13 H7
Grace Cl BARK/HLT IG6 ... 103 J7
BORE WD6 ... 75 H6
EDGW HA8 ... 95 P8
ELTH/MOT SE9 ... 184 A6
Grace Ct SL SL1 ... 129 H10
Gracedale Rd STRHM/NOR SW16 ... 180 C8
Gracefield Gdns STRHM/NOR SW16 ... 180 F6
Grace Jones Cl HACK E8 ... 7 M2
Grace Rd CROY/NA CR0 ... 203 K6
Grace's Al WCHPL E1 ... 13 N2
Grace's Ms STJWD NW8 * ... 3 K8
Grace's Ms CMBW SE5 ... 159 L8
Grace's Rd CMBW SE5 ... 159 M8
Grace St BOW E3 ... 140 C1
Gracious La SEV TN13 ... 265 H6
Gracious Lane Br BGR/WK TN15 ... 247 P2
Gracious Lane End RSEV TN14 ... 264 G6
Gracious Pond Rd CHOB/PIR GU24 ... 213 L4
The Gradient SYD SE26 ... 181 P7
Graduate Pl STHWK SE1 * ... 19 L3
Graeme Rd EN EN1 ... 79 M6
Graemesdyke Av MORT/ESHN SW14 ... 155 N9
Graemes Dyke Rd BERK HP4 ... 33 M6
Graffham Cl CRAWW RH11 ... 283 H5
Grafton Cl BF/WBF KT14 ... 215 J9
DTCH/LGLY SL3 ... 130 B8
HSLWW TW4 ... 175 M4
WEA W13 ... 134 F8
WPK KT4 ... 200 A1
Grafton Ct EBED/NFELT TW14 ... 174 E4
Grafton Crs CAMTN NW1 ... 4 B2
Grafton Gdns BCTR RM8 ... 123 P7
FSBYPK N4 ... 119 K4
Grafton Ms FITZ W1T ... 10 F2
Grafton Park Rd WPK KT4 ... 200 B9
Grafton Pl CAMTN NW1 ... 5 J10
Grafton Rd ACT W3 ... 135 P9
BCTR RM8 ... 123 P7
CROY/NA CR0 ... 223 H7
ENC/FH EN2 ... 78 G7
HRW HA1 ... 114 B3
KTTN NW5 ... 117 P3
NWMAL KT3 ... 198 D1
WPK KT4 ... 200 A10
Grafton Sq CLAP SW4 ... 158 D9
Grafton St CONDST W1S ... 10 E8
Grafton Ter HAMP NW3 ... 117 P3
Grafton Wy E/WMO/HCT KT8 ... 197 N4
FITZ W1T ... 10 G3
Grafton Yd KTTN NW5 ... 4 B1
Graham Av BROX EN10 ... 44 D6
MTCM CR4 ... 202 B1
WEA W13 ... 154 G1
Graham Cl CROY/NA CR0 ... 204 F9
RBRW/HUT CM13 ... 87 P9
STAL AL1 ... 38 E7
Grahame Park Wy MLHL NW7 ... 96 B8
Graham Gdns SURB KT6 ... 199 K8
Graham Rd BFOR GU20 ... 212 A10
BXLYHS DA6 ... 164 A10
CHSWK W4 ... 156 A2
HACK E8 ... 7 P1
HDN NW4 ... 116 A4
HPTN TW12 ... 175 J5
KTN/HRWW/WS HA3 ... 114 D1
MTCM CR4 ... 202 B1
PLSTW E13 ... 141 M5
PUR/KEN CR8 ... 223 H9
WIM/MER SW19 ... 178 C3
Graham St IS N1 ... 6 D8
Graham Ter BFN/LL DA15 * ... 185 L2
BGVA SW1W ... 16 C6
Grainger Cl NTHLT UB5 ... 114 B10
Grainger Rd ISLW TW7 ... 154 E8
WDGN N22 ... 99 K9
Grain Terminal TIL RM18 * ... 167 J2
Gramer Cl WAN E11 ... 121 M3
Grampian Cl BELMT SM2 ... 221 M4
HYS/HAR UB3 ... 152 A6
ORP BR6 ... 207 J6
Grampian Gdns CRICK NW2 ... 117 H6
Grampian Wy DTCH/LGLY SL3 ... 150 C6
Gramsci Wy CAT SE6 ... 182 G6
Granada St TOOT SW17 ... 180 F8
Granard Av PUT/ROE SW15 ... 178 E1
Granard Rd BTSEA SW11 ... 180 G5
The Granaries WAB EN9 ... 63 K10
Granary Cl ED N9 ... 100 E1
HORL RH6 ... 280 D8
STALE/WH AL4 ... 38 G1
Granary La HARP AL5 ... 20 C6
Granary Rd WCHPL E1 ... 13 P2
Granary St CAMTN NW1 ... 5 J6
The Granary HLWW/ROY CM19 ... 27 H8

Grand Pde CRAWE RH10 * ... 283 N7
FSBYPK N4 * ... 119 J4
MORT/ESHN SW14 * ... 155 P10
SURB KT5 * ... 199 M8
WBLY HA9 * ... 115 M8
Grand Stand Rd EPSOM KT18 ... 238 C3
Grand Union Canal Wk BERK HP4 ... 33 K2
DTCH/LGLY SL3 ... 150 A3
HHS/BOV HP3 ... 54 B2
NKENS W10 * ... 137 N6
Grand Union Cl MV/WKIL W9 ... 8 A2
Grand Union Crs HACK E8 ... 7 P5
Grand Union Wk CAMTN NW1 ... 4 F4
Grand View Av BH/WHM TN16 ... 243 P5
Grand Wk WCHPL E1 * ... 140 D6
Granfield St BTSEA SW11 ... 157 N7
Grange Av KTN/HRWW/WS HA3 ... 94 G10
SNWD SE25 ... 203 M1
TRDG/WHET N20 ... 97 H1
WFD IG8 ... 103 H5
WHTN TW2 ... 176 D5
Grangecliffe Gdns SNWD SE25 ... 203 M1
Grange Cl BFN/LL DA15 ... 185 K6
BH/WHM TN16 ... 262 G2
CRAWE RH10 ... 284 B5
E/WMO/HCT KT8 ... 198 A4
GUW GU2 ... 249 N6
HERT/WAT SG14 ... 25 J5
HEST TW5 ... 153 N4
HHNE HP2 ... 35 P2
HYS/HAR UB3 ... 132 A3
LHD/OX KT22 ... 257 J3
RBRW/HUT CM13 ... 107 P6
REDH RH1 ... 259 L9
REDH RH1 ... 258 C4
STWL/WRAY TW19 ... 172 B2
WAT WD17 ... 73 K3
WFD IG8 ... 101 M8
Grange Ct ALP/SUD HA0 ... 115 H10
BELMT SM2 ... 221 L4
EGH TW20 ... 172 C8
GUW GU2 ... 249 N6
HERT/WAT SG14 * ... 25 K4
HRW HA1 ... 114 B3
NTHLT UB5 ... 133 K5
PIN HA5 * ... 95 J8
WALTH E17 * ... 202 C10
WLGTN SM6 ... 222 D4
WOT/HER KT12 ... 197 N10
Grangecourt Rd STNW/STAM N16 ... 119 M6
Grange Crs CHIG IG7 ... 103 M6
RDART DA2 ... 188 A2
THMD SE28 ... 143 M8
Grangedale Cl NTHWD HA6 ... 32 D7
Grange Dr CHST BR7 ... 184 B9
ORP BR6 ... 227 M5
REDH RH1 ... 258 C4
WOKN/KNAP GU21 ... 232 B1
Grange End HORL RH6 ... 281 H4
Grange Farm Cl RYLN/HDSTN HA2 ... 114 B7
HSLW TW3 ... 175 P1
Grange Flds CFSP/GDCR SL9 ... 90 B9
Grangefields Rd RGUE GU4 ... 250 A4
Grange Gdns BNSTD SM7 ... 239 L5
HAMP NW3 ... 117 L8
PIN HA5 ... 95 L3
SLN SL2 ... 129 J7
SNWD SE25 ... 203 M1
Grange Gv IS N1 ... 6 F1
Grange Hl EDGW HA8 ... 96 C8
SNWD SE25 ... 203 M2
Grangehill Pl ELTH/MOT SE9 ... 162 C9
Grangehill Rd ELTH/MOT SE9 ... 162 C9
Grange Houses HBRY N5 * ... 119 J4
Grange La DUL SE21 ... 181 N1
GSTN WD25 ... 74 C5
HART DA3 ... 211 N7
HLWW/ROY CM19 ... 45 P7
Grange Meadow BNSTD SM7 ... 239 L2
Grange Ms FELT TW13 * ... 174 E6
Grangemill Rd CAT SE6 ... 182 F5
Grangemill Wy CAT SE6 ... 182 F5
Grangemount LHD/OX KT22 ... 237 J6
Grange Park Av WCHMH N21 ... 214 C10
Grange Park Pl RYNPK SW20 ... 178 F9
Grange Park Rd LEY E10 ... 121 H9
THHTH CR7 ... 203 H4
Grange Pl KIL/WHAMP NW6 ... 2 D1
STA TW18 ... 195 M2
WOT/HER KT12 ... 197 N10
Grange Rd ADL/WDHM KT15 ... 215 K6
BARK IG11 ... 142 C5
BELMT SM2 ... 221 L4
BORE WD6 ... 75 L9
BUSH WD23 ... 58 A7
CFSP/GDCR SL9 ... 90 A9
CHOB/PIR GU24 ... 212 C9
CHSGTN KT9 ... 219 K1
CHSWK W4 ... 155 P4
CRAWE RH10 ... 285 P6
CTHM CR3 ... 259 P3
E/WMO/HCT KT8 ... 198 A4
EDGW HA8 ... 96 C1
EGH TW20 ... 172 C8
GRAYS RM17 ... 167 N8
GUW GU2 ... 249 N6
HARH RM3 ... 105 J2
HRW HA1 ... 114 F4
HYS/HAR UB3 ... 133 H9
KUT/HW KT1 ... 199 K6
LEY E10 ... 121 J4
LHD/OX KT22 ... 237 J6
ORP BR6 ... 206 G10
PLSTW E13 ... 141 L5
RYLN/HDSTN HA2 ... 114 A2
SAND/SEL CR2 ... 223 K6
SEV TN13 ... 265 J2
SNWD SE25 ... 203 L4
STHGT/OAK N14 ... 98 E2
STHWK SE1 ... 19 M3
STRHM/NOR SW16 ... 180 D10
SWFD E18 ... 101 N10
THHTH CR7 ... 203 J4
TOTM N17 ... 99 N10
WALTH E17 ... 120 A5
WLSDN NW10 ... 137 J8
WOKN/KNAP GU21 ... 214 C10
WOKS/MYFD GU22 ... 232 D1

HART DA3 ... 211 L6
Grangeway HORL RH6 ... 281 H4
KIL/WHAMP NW6 ... 2 E1
NFNCH/WDSPK N12 ... 97 J10
WFD IG8 ... 101 L5
Grangeway Gdns REDBR IG4 ... 121 P2
Grangeways Cl GVW DA11 ... 190 C2
The Grangeway WCHMH N21 ... 99 J7
Grangewood BXLY DA5 ... 186 A4
DTCH/LGLY SL3 ... 150 B2
POTB/CUF EN6 ... 59 L6
Grangewood Cl CDW/CHF RM16 ... 168 B2
PIN HA5 ... 113 H3
RBRW/HUT CM13 ... 107 M4
Grangewood Dr SUN TW16 ... 195 N1
Grangewood La BECK BR3 ... 183 J8
Grangewood St EHAM E6 ... 142 A2
Grange Yd STHWK SE1 ... 19 L4
Granham Gdns ED N9 ... 99 N8
Granite St WOOL/PLUM SE18 ... 143 N9
Granleigh Rd WAN E11 ... 122 A3
Gransden Av HACK E8 ... 140 A2
Gransden Rd SHB W12 ... 156 C2
Grant Av SL SL1 ... 129 N3
Grantbridge St IS N1 ... 6 D2
Grantchester KUT/HW KT1 ... 199 M2
Grantchester Cl HRW HA1 ... 114 E8
Grant Cl SHPTN TW17 ... 196 C6
TOTM N17 ... 99 M10
Grantham Cl EDGW HA8 ... 95 K4
Grantham Gdns CHDH RM6 ... 124 A4
Grantham Gn BORE WD6 ... 75 P4
Grantham Ms BERK HP4 ... 33 M6
Grantham Pl MYFR/PKLN W1K ... 10 E10
Grantham Rd BRXN/ST SW9 ... 158 F9
CHSWK W4 ... 156 B6
MNPK E12 ... 123 K4
Grant Pl CROY/NA CR0 ... 203 M5
Grantock Rd WALTH E17 ... 102 A5
Granton Av UPMR RM14 ... 125 N7
Granton Rd GDMY/SEVK IG3 ... 123 K6
SCUP DA14 ... 186 G1
STRHM/NOR SW16 ... 180 D10
Grant Pl CROY/NA CR0 ... 203 N5
Grants Cl MLHL NW7 ... 96 F8
Grants La OXTED RH8 ... 261 P9
Grant St IS N1 ... 6 A1
PLSTW E13 ... 141 M5
Grant Ter STNW/STAM N16 * ... 119 P5
Grantully Rd MV/WKIL W9 ... 2 F2
Grant Wk ASC SL5 ... 192 D8
Grant Wy ISLW TW7 ... 154 F5
Grantwood Cl REDH RH1 ... 258 C6
Granville Ar BRXN/ST SW9 ... 159 H10
Granville Av ED N9 ... 100 B4
FELT TW13 ... 175 H6
HSLW TW3 ... 175 P1
SLN SL2 ... 129 J7
Granville Cl BF/WBF KT14 ... 216 H1
CROY/NA CR0 ... 203 M9
WEY KT13 ... 216 D3
Granville Dene HHS/BOV HP3 ... 52 D3
Granville Gdns HNWL W7 ... 135 H5
SNWD SE25 ... 203 N5
STRHM/NOR SW16 ... 180 A2
Granville Gv LEW SE13 ... 161 L9
Granville Ms SCUP DA14 ... 186 C10
Granville Pk LEW SE13 ... 161 K9
Granville Pl FUL/PGN SW6 ... 157 N6
MBLAR W1H * ... 9 N6
NFNCH/WDSPK N12 * ... 97 M8
PIN HA5 ... 113 J1
Granville Rd BAR EN5 ... 76 F8
BH/WHM TN16 ... 243 F2
CEND/HSY/T N8 ... 118 C4
CRICK NW2 ... 117 J2
EPP CM16 ... 65 L5
GVW DA11 ... 190 C3
HDN NW4 ... 116 C2
HGDN/ICK UB10 ... 132 C1
HYS/HAR UB3 ... 152 B8
IL IG1 ... 122 C2
KIL/WHAMP NW6 ... 2 B4
NFNCH/WDSPK N12 ... 97 N7
OXTED RH8 ... 261 L6
PLMGR N13 ... 99 H4
SCUP DA14 ... 186 C10
SEV TN13 ... 265 J2
SWFD E18 ... 102 A10
WALTH E17 ... 120 E1
WAT WD17 ... 21 M10
WELL DA16 ... 164 E4
WEY KT13 ... 216 C3
WIM/MER SW19 ... 178 A4
WOKS/MYFD GU22 ... 232 B5
Granville Sq PECK SE15 ... 159 H10
Granville St FSBYW WC1X ... 5 P10

Grassmere Rd EMPK RM11 ... 125 J3
Grassmount FSTH SE23 ... 182 A5
WLGTN SM6 ... 222 D8
Grass Pk FNCH N3 ... 97 J9
Grass Warren WLYN AL6 ... 23 P7
Grassway WLGTN SM6 ... 222 D1
Grassy Cl HHW HP1 ... 35 K5
Grassy La SEV TN13 ... 265 J3
Gravenor Av BAR EN5 ... 77 K10
Gratton Dr WDSR SL4 ... 148 D10
Gratton Rd WKENS W14 ... 14 A4
Grattons Dr CRAWE RH10 ... 284 D4
Gratton Ter CRICK NW2 ... 116 C8
Gravel Cl CHIG IG7 ... 103 K3
Graveley Av BORE WD6 ... 75 P4
Graveley Dell WGCE AL7 ... 23 L6
Gravel HI BXLYHS DA6 ... 186 C1
CFSP/GDCR SL9 ... 90 A5
CROY/NA CR0 ... 224 C3
FNCH N3 ... 97 H9
LHD/OX KT22 ... 236 F7
UX/CGN UB8 ... 111 N10
Gravel Hill Cl BXLYHS DA6 ... 186 C1
Gravel La CHIG IG7 ... 103 K3
HHW HP1 ... 35 K5
WCHPL E1 ... 13 L5
Gravelly HI CTHM CR3 ... 259 N4
Gravel Pth BERK HP4 ... 33 P5
Gravel Pits La SHGR GU5 ... 270 D5
Gravel Rd EYN DA4 ... 188 A10
HAYES BR2 ... 206 B9
WHTN TW2 ... 176 D4
Gravelwood Cl CHST BR7 ... 184 F6
Gravely Ct HHNE HP2 ... 36 D7
Gravenel Gdns TOOT SW17 * ... 179 P9
Graveney Gv PGE/AN SE20 ... 182 F2
Graveney Rd CRAWE RH10 ... 284 G5
TOOT SW17 ... 179 P7
Gravesend Rd GVE DA12 ... 191 P7
SHB W12 ... 136 D9
Gravetts La RGUW GU3 ... 249 K7
Gravetye Cl CRAWE RH10 ... 284 G5
Gray Av BCTR RM8 ... 124 A6
Grayburn Cl CSTG HP8 ... 89 M3
Gray Gdns RAIN RM13 ... 145 H1
Grayham Crs NWMAL KT3 ... 200 A4
Grayham Rd NWMAL KT3 ... 200 A4
Grayland Cl BMLY BR1 ... 205 K1
Graylands GRAYS RM17 ... 167 K5
WOKN/KNAP GU21 ... 232 B2
Graylands Cl WOKN/KNAP GU21 ... 232 B2
Grayling Cl CAN/RD E16 ... 141 K4
Grayling Ct BERK HP4 ... 33 L3
EA W5 ... 135 J2
Grayling Rd STNW/STAM N16 ... 119 L7
Grayling Sq BETH E2 ... 7 P9
The Graylings ABLGY WD5 ... 50 G7
Gray Pl CHERT KT16 ... 214 G5
Grays CH CHST BR5 * ... 207 M1
Grayscroft Rd STRHM/NOR SW16 ... 180 E10
Grays End Cl GRAYS RM17 ... 167 M2
Grays Farm Rd STMC/STPC BR5 ... 207 L1
Graysfield WGCE AL7 ... 23 K8
Grayshott Rd BTSEA SW11 ... 159 K8
Gray's Inn Rd FSBYW WC1X ... 5 M9
Grays La ASHF TW15 ... 173 J8
Gray's La ASHTD KT21 ... 237 L5
Grays Park Rd SLN SL2 ... 129 M5
Grays Pl SLN SL2 ... 129 L10
Grays Rd BH/WHM TN16 ... 244 E7
GODL GU7 ... 267 K10
SL SL1 ... 129 L10
Gray's Rd HGDN/ICK UB10 ... 131 P2
Grays Wk CHERT KT16 ... 195 J6
Grays Wd HORL RH6 ... 280 G5
Grayswood Ct RYNPK SW20 ... 200 E2
Gray's Yd MHST W1U * ... 10 C2
Graywood Ct NFNCH/WDSPK N12 ... 97 M8
Grazebrook Rd STNW/STAM N16 ... 119 L7
Grazeley Cl BXLYHS DA6 ... 186 D1
The Grazings HHNE HP2 ... 36 A4
Greatacre CRAWE RH10 ... 285 J6
Great Amwell La CEND/HSY/T N8 ... 118 C1
Great Benty WDR/YW UB7 ... 151 N3
Great Braitch La HAT AL10 ... 22 D1
Great Brays HLWS CM18 ... 47 K2
Great Break WGCE AL7 ... 23 L5
Great Brownings DUL SE21 ... 181 N7
Great Bushey Dr TRDG/WHET N20 ... 97 L2
Great Cambridge Jct PLMGR N13 * ... 99 K6
Great Cambridge Rd BROX EN10 ... 62 D2
CHES/WCR EN8 ... 80 A1
UED N18 ... 99 L6
Great Castle St REGST W1B ... 10 E5
Great Central Av RSLP HA4 ... 113 K10
Great Central St CAMTN NW1 ... 10 A3
Great Central Wy WBLY HA9 ... 115 P10
Great Chapel St SOHO/SHAV W1D * ... 11 J5
Great Chart St BTSEA SW11 ... 157 M9
Great Chertsey Rd CHSWK W4 ... 156 A7
FELT TW13 ... 175 N6
Great Church La HMSMTH W6 ... 156 G4
Great College St WEST SW1P ... 17 J3
Great Conduit WGCE AL7 ... 23 M4
Great Cross Av GNWCH SE10 ... 161 K6
Great Cullings ROMW/RG RM7 ... 124 F7
Great Cumberland Ms MBLAR W1H ... 10 A6
Great Cumberland Pl MBLAR W1H ... 10 A6
Great Dell WGCW AL8 ... 22 G3
Great Dover St STHWK SE1 ... 18 F3
Greatdown Rd HNWL W7 ... 134 E7
Great Eastern Rd BRW CM14 ... 107 H5
SRTFD E15 ... 141 J2
Great Eastern St SDTCH EC2A ... 7 J10
Great Eastern Whf BTSEA SW11 * ... 157 P5
Great Elshams BNSTD SM7 ... 239 K2
Great Elms Rd HAYES BR2 ... 205 N3
HHS/BOV HP3 ... 36 A10
Great Fld CDALE/KGS NW9 ... 95 J7
Greatfields Dr UX/CGN UB8 ... 142 J3
Greatfields Rd BARK IG11 ... 142 F1
The Great Fox Meadow BRWN CM15 ... 86 E3
Great Galley Cl BARK IG11 ... 143 L5
Great Ganett WGCE AL7 ... 23 L8
Great Gardens Rd EMPK RM11 ... 125 J4
Great Gatton Cl CROY/NA CR0 ... 204 D7
Great George St STJSPK SW1H ... 17 J2
Great Goodwin Dr RGUE GU4 ... 250 F6
Great Gregories La EPP CM16 ... 65 J3
Great Groves CHESW EN7 ... 62 B2
Great Guildford St STHWK SE1 ... 18 E1
Greatham Rd BUSH WD23 ... 73 L1
CRAWE RH10 ... 285 H6
Great Harry Dr ELTH/MOT SE9 ... 184 D4
Great Heart HHNE HP2 ... 35 P4
Great Heath HAT AL10 ... 40 A1
Great Hivings CSHM HP5 ... 51 J6
Great James St BMSBY WC1N ... 11 M1
Greatlake Cot HORL RH6 ... 280 G3
Great Lawn CHONG CM5 ... 48 H2

Great Ley WCCE AL7 .... 23 H7
Great Leylands HLWS CM18 .... 47 K2
Great Marlborough St
 REGST W1B .... 10 G6
Great Maze Pond STHWK SE1 .... 13 H10
Great Meadow BROX EN10 .... 44 F8
Great Molewood
 HERT/WAT SG14 .... 25 J2
Great Nelmes Cha
 EMPK RM11 .... 125 N3
Greatness La RSEV TN14 .... 247 K7
Greatness Rd RSEV TN14 .... 247 K7
Great New St
 FLST/FETLN EC4A * .... 12 B5
Great North Rd BAR EN5 .... 77 J6
 BRKMPK AL9 .... 59 L1
 EFNCH N2 .... 117 P2
 HAT AL10 .... 40 E5
 WCCW AL8 .... 22 D7
Great North Way (Barnet
 By-Pass) HDN NW4 .... 96 E9
Great Oak Ct WAB EN9 * .... 28 A4
Great Oaks CHIG IG7 .... 102 F5
 RBRW/HUT CM13 .... 87 N10
Great Oaks Pk RGUE GU4 .... 250 E6
Greatorex St WCHPL E1 .... 13 L2
Great Ormond St
 BMSBY WC1N .... 11 M3
Great Owl Rd CHIG IG7 .... 102 D4
Great Palmers HHNE HP2 .... 36 A1
Great Pk KGLGY WD4 .... 54 B6
Great Percy St FSBYW WC1X .... 5 P9
Great Peter St WEST SW1P .... 17 J4
Great Plumtree HLW CM20 .... 29 J9
Great Portland St GTPST W1W .... 10 F3
Great Pulteney St
 SOHO/CST W1F .... 10 F6
Great Quarry GU GU1 .... 268 A3
Great Queen St
 HOL/ALD WC2B .... 11 M5
Great Rd HHNE HP2 .... 36 A5
Great Ropers La
 RBRW/HUT CM13 .... 106 F7
Great Russell St RSQ WC1B .... 11 K5
Great St Thomas Apostle
 BLKFR EC4V * .... 12 F7
Great Scotland Yd
 WHALL SW1A .... 11 L10
Great Slades POTB/CUF EN6 .... 59 J9
Great Smith St WEST SW1P .... 17 J4
Great South-West Rd
 EBED/NFELT TW14 .... 174 D3
 HSLWW TW4 .... 153 J8
Great Spilmans EDUL SE22 .... 181 M1
Great Stockwood Rd
 CHESW EN7 .... 61 L2
Great Strd CDALE/KGS NW9 .... 96 C10
Great Sturgess Rd HHW HP1 .... 35 J6
Great Suffolk St STHWK SE1 .... 12 D10
Great Sutton St FSBYE EC1V .... 12 G2
Great Swan Aly LOTH EC2R * .... 12 G5
Great Tattenhams
 EPSOM KT18 .... 238 F4
Great Thrift STMC/STPC BR5 .... 206 F4
Great Till Rd RSEV TN14 .... 246 F2
Great Titchfield St
 GTPST W1W .... 10 F3
Great Tower St MON EC3R .... 13 J7
Great Trinity La BLKFR EC4V * .... 11 P4
Great Turnstile HHOL WC1V * .... 11 N5
Great Warley St
 RBRW/HUT CM13 .... 106 F9
Great Western Rd NTGHL W11 .... 8 D4
 HEST TW5 .... 153 M8
 HMSMTH W6 .... 156 A4
 ISLW TW7 .... 154 D6
Great West Rd BTFD TW8 .... 154 F6
Great West Road Chiswick
 CHSWK W4 .... 156 C4
Great West Road Ellesmere Rd
 CHSWK W4 .... 155 P5
Great West Road Hogarth La
 CHSWK W4 .... 156 A4
Great Westwood
 KGLGY WD4 * .... 71 P1
Great Whites Rd
 HHS/BOV HP3 .... 36 A8
Great Winchester St
 OBST EC2N .... 13 H5
Great Windmill St
 SOHO/SHAV W1D .... 11 J8
Greatwood CHST BR7 .... 184 D10
Greatwood Cl CHERT KT16 .... 214 F5
Great Woodcote Dr
 PUR/KEN CR8 .... 222 E6
Great Woodcote Pk
 PUR/KEN CR8 .... 222 F6
Greaves Cl BARK IG11 .... 142 E5
Greaves Cots POP/IOD E14 * .... 140 E8
Greaves Pl TOOT SW17 .... 179 P7
Grebe Av YEAD UB4 .... 133 L8
Grebe Cl BARK IG11 .... 143 K6
 FSTGT E7 .... 121 L10
 WALTH E17 .... 100 D8
Grebe Ct SUT SM1 .... 209 K3
Grebe Crest WTHK RM20 .... 166 F3
Grebe Ter KUT/HW KT1 * .... 199 L8
Grecian Crs NRWD SE19 .... 181 J9
Greding Wk RBRW/HUT CM13 .... 107 N3
Greek St
 WOKN/KNAP GU21 .... 231 J7
Greek St SOHO/SHAV W1D * .... 11 J6
Greenacre WDSR SL4 .... 148 D8
Greenacre Cl BAR EN5 .... 77 J4
 NTHLT UB5 .... 113 N10
 SWLY BR8 .... 208 F4
Greenacre Ct EGH TW20 .... 171 P9
Greenacre Gdns WALTH E17 .... 121 H2
Greenacre Pl WLGTN SM6 .... 202 C9
Greenacres BUSH WD23 .... 94 A3
 CRAWE RH10 .... 284 D6
Greenacres ELTH/MOT SE9 .... 184 F2
 GT/LBKH KT23 .... 235 P10
 HHNE HP2 .... 36 E8
 KWD/TDW/WH KT20 .... 257 N3
 OXTED RH8 .... 261 K3
Green Acres SCUP DA14 * .... 185 J1
 WCCE AL8 .... 23 J8
Greenacres Av
 HGDN/ICK UB10 .... 112 A8
Greenacres Cl ORP BR6 .... 226 F1
 RAIN RM13 .... 145 M5
Greenacres Dr STAN HA7 .... 94 G8
Greenacre Sq
 BERM/RHTH SE16 * .... 160 C1
Greenacre Wk
 STHGT/OAK N14 .... 98 E4
Greenall Cl CHES/WCR EN8 .... 62 D6
Green Arbour Ct STP EC4M .... 12 C5
Green Av MLHL NW7 .... 96 A5
 WEA W13 .... 154 A2
Greenaway Av UED N18 * .... 100 C6
Greenaway Gdns HAMP NW3 .... 117 L9
Greenbank CHES/WCR EN8 .... 62 A4
Green Bank
 NFNCH/WDSPK N12 .... 97 L5
 WAP E1W .... 140 A3
Greenbank Av ALP/SUD HA0 .... 113 N10
Greenbank Cl CHING E4 .... 101 N1
 HARH RM3 .... 105 L4
Greenbank Crs HDN NW4 .... 117 H2
Greenbanks DART DA1 .... 171 K8
 STAL AL1 .... 38 E8
 UPMR RM14 .... 126 D7
Greenbay Rd CHARL SE7 .... 162 A6
Greenberry St STJWD NW8 .... 3 M1
Greenbrook Av EBAR EN4 .... 77 M5
Greenbury Cl
 RKW/CH/CXG WD3 .... 70 F7
Green Chain Wk ABYW SE2 .... 163 L1
 BELV DA17 .... 164 A3
 BELV DA17 .... 164 A5
 BMLY BR1 .... 183 N3
 BMLY BR1 .... 184 A8
 CHARL SE7 .... 162 A3
 CHST BR7 .... 184 C8


 ELTH/MOT SE9 .... 184 B3
 ELTH/MOT SE9 .... 184 E1
 ELTH/MOT SE9 .... 184 A5
 ELTH/MOT SE9 .... 184 B5
 ELTH/MOT SE9 .... 162 A10
 ERITHM DA18 .... 163 N2
 LEE/GVPK SE12 .... 183 P5
 LEE/GVPK SE12 .... 183 P8
 SYD SE26 .... 182 C9
 WELL DA16 .... 162 F8
 WELL DA16 .... 163 K7
 WOOL/PLUM SE18 .... 162 C5
 WOOL/PLUM SE18 .... 162 E10
Green Ct BRKMPK AL9 .... 59 H2
 CAR SM5 .... 202 A3
 CDALE/KGS NW9 .... 115 P4
 CHES/WCR EN8 .... 62 D8
 EPP CM16 .... 46 E10
 FELT TW15 .... 175 M8
 GLDGN NW11 .... 117 M5
 HAYES BR2 .... 205 K3
 HNWL W7 .... 136 A1
Greencoates HERT/BAY SG13 .... 25 J3
Greencoat Pl WEST SW1P .... 17 H5
Greencoat Rw WEST SW1P .... 17 H5
Green Common La WDR/YW UB7 .... 108 C5
Green Court Av CROY/NA CR0 .... 204 A9
Green Court Gdns
 CROY/NA CR0 .... 204 A9
Greencourt Rd
 STMC/STPC BR5 .... 207 H5
Greencroft Av RSLP HA4 .... 113 K7
Greencroft Gdns EN EN1 .... 79 M7
 KIL/WHAMP NW6 .... 3 J5
Greencroft Rd HEST TW5 .... 153 N7
Green Curve BNSTD SM7 .... 239 J1
Green Dl EDUL SE22 .... 181 M1
Greendale Ms SLN SL2 .... 129 M9
Greendale Wk CVW DA11 .... 190 B6
Green Dell Wy HHS/BOV HP3 .... 36 C6
Green Dene EHSLY KT24 .... 270 D1
Green Dragon La BTFD TW8 .... 155 K4
Green Dragon Yd WCHPL E1 .... 13 N4
 RDKG RH5 .... 276 B5
 REDH RH1 .... 278 B5
 REDH RH1 .... 257 P8
 REIG RH2 .... 257 P10
 RGUE GU4 .... 251 K3
 RKW/CH/CXG WD3 .... 72 A5
 RPLY/SEND GU23 .... 234 C10
 SHPTN TW17 .... 196 D5
 SL SL1 .... 128 B5
 STA TW18 .... 195 H1
 STAL AL1 .... 38 B3
 STALW/RED AL3 .... 38 E3
 STAN HA7 .... 94 C5
 SUN TW16 .... 174 C10
 THHTH CR7 .... 203 J1
 UX/CGN UB8 .... 132 D7
 WAB EN9 .... 82 A1
 WDSR SL4 .... 148 F8
 WCCE AL8 .... 23 M7
 WAB EN9 .... 63 H10
 WAN E11 .... 121 P1
 WCHMN N21 .... 99 H1
 WOK/YW UB7 .... 151 N2
 WELL DA16 .... 163 H10
 WHTN TW2 .... 176 D4
 WIM/MER SW19 .... 178 G8
 WPK KT4 .... 200 B9
Green Lane Av WOT/HER KT12 .... 217 L6
Green Lane Cl BF/WBF KT14 .... 216 A8
 CHERT KT16 .... 195 H9
 HARP AL5 .... 20 C5
Green Lane Cots STAN HA7 * .... 94 C5
Green Lane Gdns THHTH CR7 .... 203 J3
Green Lanes FSBYPK N4 .... 119 J3
 HAT AL10 .... 40 C1
 HBRY N5 .... 119 K8
 HOR/WEW KT19 .... 220 B5
 SEVS/STOTM N15 .... 119 J2
 WCHMN N21 .... 99 K1
 WCCW AL8 .... 22 C7
Green La West EHSLY KT24 .... 252 C3
Greenlaw Ct EA W5 * .... 135 J5
Greenlaw Gdns NWMAL KT3 .... 200 C5
Greenlawn La BTFD TW8 .... 135 J3
Green Lawns
 NFNCH/WDSPK N12 * .... 97 L7
 RSLP HA4 * .... 113 K6
Greenlaw St
 WOOL/PLUM SE18 .... 162 G2
Greenlea Pk WIM/MER SW19 * .... 201 P1
Green Leas SUN TW16 .... 174 C10
Green Leas Cl ASHF TW15 * .... 174 C10
Greenleaf Av
 STMC/STPC BR5 .... 207 N4
Greenleaf Cl
 BRXS/STRHM SW2 * .... 181 H3
Greenleaf Ct DTCH/LGLY SL3 .... 149 M9
Greenleafe Dr BARK/HLT IG6 .... 122 E1
Greenleaf Rd EHAM E6 .... 141 P8
 WALTH E17 .... 120 C1
Greenleaf Wy
 KTN/HRWW/WS HA3 .... 115 K5
Greenlea Pk WIM/MER SW19 * .... 201 P1
Green Leas SUN TW16 .... 174 C10


Green La ADL/WDHM KT15 .... 195 L10
 AMS HP6 .... 69 J1
 ASC SL5 .... 192 D1
 ASHTD KT21 .... 237 H3
 BCTR RM8 .... 123 P3
 BF/WBF KT14 .... 216 A8
 BROX EN10 .... 44 C9
 BRW CM14 .... 106 A9
 BRW CM14 .... 106 B1
 BRWN CM15 .... 87 H10
 CDW/PRF RM16 .... 147 P7
 CHERT KT16 .... 195 H9
 CHIG IG7 .... 102 F2
 CHING E4 * .... 81 K7
 CHOB/PIR GU24 .... 213 L6
 CHSGTN KT9 .... 219 K5
 COB KT11 .... 217 M8
 COUL/CHIP CR5 .... 257 L1
 CRAWE RH10 .... 285 N1
 CRAWE RH10 .... 283 P5
 CSHM HP5 .... 51 N9
 DTCH/LGLY SL3 .... 149 N7
 E/WMO/HCT KT8 .... 198 A5
 EDGW HA8 .... 95 L5
 EGH TW20 .... 172 E7
 ELTH/MOT SE9 .... 184 D4
 FELT TW13 .... 175 M8
 GDMY/SEVK IG3 .... 123 K7
 GODL GU7 .... 267 K8
 GU GU1 .... 250 E10
 HDN NW4 .... 116 C3
 HHNE HP2 .... 36 D7
 HHS/BOV HP3 .... 52 C4
 HLWE CM17 .... 48 C2
 HNWL W7 .... 154 D1
 HORL RH6 .... 280 C9
 HSLWW TW4 .... 175 K1
 IL IG1 .... 122 G7
 KWD/TDW/WH KT20 .... 257 J2
 LHD/OX KT22 .... 237 J7
 MRDN SM4 .... 201 K6
 NTHWD HA6 .... 92 B8
 NWMAL KT3 .... 199 P5
 OXHEY WD19 .... 93 K2
 PGE/AN SE20 .... 182 C10
 RDKG RH5 .... 276 B5


Greenleaves AL7 .... 39 H7
Greensleeves Cl
 STALE/WH AL4 .... 39 H7
Greenstead SBW CM21 .... 29 P2
Greenstead Av WFD IG8 .... 101 P3
Greenstead Gdns
 PUT/ROE SW15 .... 178 D1
 WFD IG8 .... 101 P4
Greenstead Rd CHONG CM5 .... 67 H4
Greenstone Ms WAN E11 .... 121 M4
Green St BORE WD6 .... 75 M3
 FSTGT E7 .... 121 N10
 HLWE CM17 .... 29 N10
 MYFR/PKLN W1K .... 10 B7
 PEND EN3 .... 80 B6
 RKW/CH/CXG WD3 .... 70 F6
 SUN TW16 .... 197 H3
Green Street Green Rd
 RDART DA2 .... 188 G7
Greenstreet Hl NWCR SE14 * .... 210 G1
Greensward BUSH WD23 .... 74 A10
The Green ACT W3 .... 136 B8
 ASHF TW15 .... 173 N8
 BERK HP4 .... 34 E3
 BH/WHM TN16 .... 262 C2
 BKHH IG9 * .... 101 N2
 BXLYHN DA7 .... 164 B7
 CAR SM5 .... 202 B1
 CHES/WCR EN8 .... 62 B4
 CRAWE RH10 .... 285 J2
 CROY/NA CR0 .... 224 C5
 CTHM CR3 .... 242 F9
 ED N9 .... 99 P3
 ECH TW20 .... 171 P9
 EPP CM16 .... 82 G2
 EW KT17 .... 220 D8
 FELT TW13 .... 175 J5
 GDST RH9 .... 260 A8
 HARH RM3 .... 105 K4
 HAYES BR2 .... 205 M7
 HEST TW5 .... 153 N5
 HGDN/ICK UB10 .... 112 D7
 HRW HA1 .... 114 F7
 ISLW TW7 .... 154 D9
 MTCM CR4 .... 202 E5
 MRDN SM4 .... 201 H4
 NWDGN UB2 .... 153 N1
 NWMAL KT3 .... 199 P3
 ORP BR6 .... 227 M6
 RAIN RM13 .... 145 N9
 RCH/KEW TW9 .... 177 J1
 RDART DA2 .... 188 C5
 RKW/CH/CXG WD3 .... 72 A10
 SEV TN13 .... 247 L8
 SL SL1 .... 149 J1
 SRTFD E15 * .... 141 L1
Greg Cl LEY E10 .... 121 H4
Gregories Farm La BEAC HP9 .... 88 A8
Gregories Rd BEAC HP9 .... 88 A8
Gregor Ms BKHTH/KID SE3 .... 161 N6
Gregory Av POTB/CUF EN6 .... 59 M9
Gregory Cl WOKN/KNAP GU21 .... 231 P3
Gregory Dr WDSR SL4 .... 171 N2
Gregory Ms WAB EN9 .... 63 H3
Gregory Pl KENS W8 .... 14 C1
Gregson Cl BORE WD6 .... 75 P1
Gregson Gdns EHAM E6 .... 142 A8
Greig Cl CEND/HSY/T N8 .... 118 G5
Greig Ter WALW SE17 .... 18 D9
Grenaby Av CROY/NA CR0 .... 203 L7
Grenaby Rd CROY/NA CR0 .... 203 L7
Grenada Rd BKHTH/KID SE3 .... 161 P6
Grenade St POP/IOD E14 .... 140 E9
Grenadier Cl STALE/WH AL4 .... 39 H7
Grenadier Pl CTHM CR3 .... 241 K8
Grenadier Cl CAN/RD E16 .... 142 D10
Grenadine Cl CHESW EN7 .... 61 M5
Grena Gdns RCH/KEW TW9 .... 155 L10
Grena Rd RCH/KEW TW9 .... 155 L10
Grendon Cl HORL RH6 .... 280 A2
Grendon Gdns WBLY HA9 .... 115 M7
Grendon St STJWD NW8 .... 3 M5
Grenfell Av HCH RM12 .... 123 N10
Grenfell Cl BORE WD6 .... 75 P1
 MLHL NW7 * .... 96 E7
Grenfell Gdns
 KTN/HRWW/WS HA3 .... 115 K5
Grenfell Rd BEAC HP9 .... 88 B7
 MTCM CR4 .... 180 A5


Greenwich Church St
 GNWCH SE10 * .... 161 H5
Greenwich Crs EHAM E6 .... 142 B7
Greenwich Foot Tnl
 GNWCH SE10 .... 161 H4
Greenwich Hts CHARL SE7 * .... 162 C5
Greenwich High Rd
 GNWCH SE10 .... 160 C6
Greenwich House LEW SE13 .... 183 J2
Greenwich Park St
 GNWCH SE10 .... 161 J3
Greenwich Quay DEPT SE8 .... 160 G5
Greenwich South St
 GNWCH SE10 .... 160 C7
Greenwich Vw POP/IOD E14 .... 160 G2
Greenwood Av CHESW EN7 .... 62 A7
 DAGE RM10 .... 124 C9
 PEND EN3 .... 80 G1
Greenwood Cl ASC SL5 .... 193 H6
Greenwood Cots ASC SL5 * .... 193 H6
Greenwood Dr CHING E4 .... 101 H6
 GSTN WD25 .... 55 L10
 REDH RH1 .... 276 B5
Greenwood Gdns
 BARK/HLT IG6 .... 102 F8
 CTHM CR3 .... 259 P1
 OXTED RH8 .... 261 M10
 PLMGR N13 .... 99 H3
 RAD WD7 .... 57 K8
Greenwood Pk
 KUTN/CMB KT2 .... 178 B10
Greenwood Rd BXLY DA5 .... 186 A5
 CHIG IG7 .... 103 L5
 CHOB/PIR GU24 .... 230 A7
 CROY/NA CR0 .... 203 J7
 HACK E8 .... 7 P1
 ISLW TW7 .... 154 D9
 MTCM CR4 .... 202 E3
 PLSTW E13 .... 141 L4
 THDIT KT7 .... 198 F8
 WOKN/KNAP GU21 .... 231 K6
Greenwood Ter
 WLSDN NW10 .... 136 A3
The Greenwood GU GU1 .... 250 D10
The Greenwood Wy SEV TN13 .... 264 G1
Green Wrythe Crs CAR SM5 .... 201 N4
Green Wrythe La CAR SM5 .... 201 N6
Greenyard WAB EN9 .... 63 H9
Greer Rd KTN/HRWW/WS HA3 .... 94 B9
Greet St STHWK SE1 .... 12 B10
Greg Cl LEY E10 .... 121 H4
Gregory Rd CHDH RM6 .... 123 N2
 NWDGN UB2 .... 153 P2
 SLN SL2 .... 109 J7
Gregson Cl BORE WD6 .... 75 P1
Greig Cl CEND/HSY/T N8 .... 118 G5
Greig Ter WALW SE17 .... 18 D9
Grenaby Av CROY/NA CR0 .... 203 L7
Grenaby Rd CROY/NA CR0 .... 203 L7
Grenadier Pl CTHM CR3 .... 241 K8
Grenadier St CAN/RD E16 .... 142 D10
Grenadine Cl CHESW EN7 .... 61 M5
Grena Rd RCH/KEW TW9 .... 155 L10
Grendon Cl HORL RH6 .... 280 A2
Grendon Gdns WBLY HA9 .... 115 M7
Grendon St STJWD NW8 .... 3 M5
Grenfell Av HCH RM12 .... 123 N10
Grenfell Cl BORE WD6 .... 75 P1
Grenfell Gdns
 KTN/HRWW/WS HA3 .... 115 K5
Grenfell Rd BEAC HP9 .... 88 B7
 MTCM CR4 .... 180 A5
 NTGHL W11 .... 136 C6
Grennell Cl SUT SM1 .... 201 N10
Grennell Rd SUT SM1 .... 201 N10
Grenoble Gdns PLMGR N13 .... 99 H7
Grenside Rd WEY KT13 .... 196 C10
Grensville Rd PECK SE15 .... 161 J1
Grenville Av BROX EN10 .... 44 F8
 CHES/WCR EN8 .... 62 C8
 COB KT11 .... 217 K10
Grenville Cl BRYLDS KT5 .... 199 P8
 COB KT11 .... 217 K10
 FNCH N3 .... 97 J9
 SL SL1 .... 130 F10
Grenville Gdns WFD IG8 .... 101 P9
Grenville Ms ARCH N19 .... 118 F9
 HPTN TW12 .... 175 K7
Grenville Pl MLHL NW7 .... 96 A6
 SKENS SW7 .... 14 F6
Grenville Rd ARCH N19 .... 118 F9
 CDW/CHF RM16 .... 167 H4
 CROY/NA CR0 .... 225 K5
 MFD/CHID GU8 .... 266 C10


Greville Park Av ASHTD KT21 .... 237 K3
Greville Park Rd ASHTD KT21 .... 237 K4
Greville Pl KIL/WHAMP NW6 .... 3 H1
Greville Rd KIL/WHAMP NW6 .... 2 G6
 RCHPK/HAM TW10 .... 177 J10
 WALTH E17 .... 121 K1
Greville St HCIRC EC1N .... 12 B4
Grey Alders BNSTD SM7 .... 219 H7
Greycaine Rd WATW WD24 .... 75 L3
Grey Cl GLDGN NW11 .... 117 M4
Greycoat Pl WEST SW1P .... 17 J4
Greycoat St WEST SW1P .... 17 J4
Grey Eagle St WCHPL E1 .... 13 M2
Greyfell Cl STAN HA7 .... 94 G6
Greyfields Cl PUR/KEN CR8 .... 223 J6
Greyfriars Dr ASC SL5 .... 192 G6
Greyfriars Rd ASC SL5 .... 192 A6
 CHOB/PIR GU24 .... 231 H1
Greyfriars
 RPLY/SEND GU23 .... 233 K10
Greygoose Pk
 HLWW/ROY CM19 .... 46 B3
Greyhound Hl HDN NW4 .... 116 C1
Greyhound La CDW/CHF RM16 .... 168 C3
 POTB/CUF EN6 .... 59 M2
 STRHM/NOR SW16 .... 180 F9
Greyhound Rd HMSMTH W6 .... 157 H2
 SUT SM1 .... 221 N2
 TOTM N17 .... 119 N1
 WLSDN NW10 .... 136 E5
Greyhound Slip CRAWE RH10 .... 284 E6
Greyhound Ter
 STRHM/NOR SW16 .... 202 D1
Greyladies Gdns
 GNWCH SE10 .... 161 H8
Greys Park Cl HAYES BR2 .... 226 C6
Greystead Rd FSTH SE23 .... 182 B3
Greystoke Av PIN HA5 .... 113 P1
Greystoke Cl BERK HP4 .... 33 M6
Greystoke Cots EA W5 * .... 135 K6
Greystoke Dr RSLP HA4 .... 112 C4
Greystoke Gdns EA W5 .... 135 K6
 ENC/FH EN2 .... 78 E8
Greystoke Pk SLN SL2 .... 128 E7
Greystone Cl SAND/SEL CR2 .... 224 C9
Greystone Gdns BARK/HLT IG6 .... 102 F10
 KTN/HRWW/WS HA3 .... 115 H4
Greystones Dr REIG RH2 .... 257 M8
Greystones PK SEV TN14 .... 263 P1
Greystones Cl BGR/WK TN15 .... 247 N3
 REDH RH1 .... 275 N2
Greystones Dr REIG RH2 .... 257 M8
Greyswood Av UED N18 * .... 100 C6
Greyswood St
 STRHM/NOR SW16 .... 180 C9
Greythorne Rd
 WOKN/KNAP GU21 .... 231 M4
Grey Towers Av EMPK RM11 .... 125 L6
Grey Towers Gdns
 EMPK RM11 * .... 125 K6
Grice Av BH/WHM TN16 .... 225 N4
Gridiron Pl UPMR RM14 .... 126 A7
Grier Cl CRAWW RH11 .... 283 H8
Grierson Rd FSTH SE23 .... 182 A5
Grieves Rd GVW DA11 .... 190 C6
Griffin Av UPMR RM14 .... 126 D4
Griffin Cl SL SL1 .... 149 L1
 WLSDN NW10 .... 118 E10
Griffin Ct ASHTD KT21 * .... 237 K5
 GU GU1 * .... 117 H10
Griffin Manor Wy THMD SE28 .... 162 G2
Griffin Rd TOTM N17 .... 99 M10
 WOOL/PLUM SE18 .... 162 C4
Griffins Cl WCHMN N21 .... 99 M1
The Griffins CDW/CHF RM16 .... 167 N1
Griffin Wk RDART DA2 .... 188 E1
Griffith Cl CHDH RM6 .... 123 M1
Griffiths Rd WIM/MER SW19 .... 179 K10
Griffiths Wy STAL AL1 .... 38 E8
Griffon Wy GSTN WD25 .... 54 C10
Grifon Cl CDW/CHF RM16 .... 167 N2
Grifon Rd CDW/CHF RM16 .... 167 N2
Griggs Ap IL IG1 .... 122 F7
Griggs Cl IL IG1 .... 122 G2
Griggs Gdns HCH RM12 .... 125 K10
Grigg's Pl STHWK SE1 .... 19 K4
Griggs Rd LEY E10 .... 121 H4
Grimsby Gv CAN/RD E16 .... 142 G10
Grimsby St BETH E2 .... 13 M1
Grimsdells Cnr AMS HP6 * .... 69 J3
Grimsdell's La AMS HP6 .... 69 J3
Grimsdyke Crs BAR EN5 .... 76 F5
Grimsdyke Rd PIN HA5 .... 93 N8
Grimsel Pth CMBW SE5 .... 159 J6
Grimshaw Cl HGT N6 * .... 118 A6
Grimshaw Wy ROM RM1 .... 124 F3
Grimston Rd FUL/PGN SW6 .... 157 J8
 STAL AL1 .... 38 E6
Grimthorpe Cl STALW/RED AL3 .... 38 A2
Grimwade Av CROY/NA CR0 .... 203 P10
Grimwade Cl PECK SE15 .... 161 L2
Grimwood Rd TWK TW1 .... 176 C8
Grindall Cl CROY/NA CR0 .... 223 J1
Grindal St STHWK SE1 .... 18 A2
Grindcobbe Cl STAL AL1 .... 38 C9
Grindleford Av
 FBAR/BDGN N11 .... 98 B3
Grindley Gdns CROY/NA CR0 .... 203 N6
Grinling Pl DEPT SE8 .... 160 F5
Grinstead Rd DEPT SE8 .... 160 D4
Grisedale Cl CRAWW RH11 .... 284 B7
 PUR/KEN CR8 .... 223 M10
Grisedale Gdns PUR/KEN CR8 .... 223 M10
Grisle Cl ED N9 .... 100 A3
Grittleton Av WBLY HA9 .... 136 C4
Grittleton Rd MV/WKIL W9 .... 2 F8
Grizedale Ter FSTH SE23 .... 182 D3
Grobars Av WOKN/KNAP GU21 .... 231 P7
Grocers' Hall Ct LOTH EC2R * .... 12 G6
Groombridge Cl WELL DA16 .... 185 J1
 WOT/HER KT12 .... 217 J2
Groombridge Rd HOM E9 .... 140 G2
Groom Cl HAYES BR2 .... 205 N4
Groom Crs WAND/EARL SW18 .... 160 E9
Groomfield Cl TOOT SW17 .... 180 B7
Groom Pl KTBR SW1X .... 16 C3
Groom Rd BROX EN10 .... 62 G2
Grooms Cots CSHM HP5 * .... 50 A4
Grooms Dr PIN HA5 .... 113 H3
The Grooms CRAWE RH10 .... 284 E5
Grosmont Rd
 WOOL/PLUM SE18 .... 163 N3
Grosse Wy PUT/ROE SW15 .... 178 E2
Grosvenor Av CAR SM5 .... 222 A3
 HBRY N5 .... 119 K10
 KGLGY WD4 .... 54 D4
 MORT/ESHN SW14 .... 156 A2
 RCHPK/HAM TW10 .... 177 J10
 YEAD UB4 .... 133 K1
Grosvenor Br BRW SW1V .... 17 K6
Grosvenor Cots
 RKW/CH/CXG WD3 * .... 72 E9
Grosvenor Ct
 CDALE/KGS NW9 .... 115 M2
 HGDN/ICK UB10 .... 132 A3
 KTBR SW1X * .... 16 B2
Grosvenor Crescent Ms
 KTBR SW1X * .... 16 B2
Grosvenor Dr EMPK RM11 .... 125 K6
 LOU IG10 .... 82 E6
Grosvenor Gdns BGVA SW1W .... 16 E4
 CRICK NW2 .... 118 D3
 GLDGN NW11 .... 117 J3
 KUTN/CMB KT2 .... 177 J9
 MORT/ESHN SW14 .... 156 A1
 SEVS/STOTM N15 .... 119 K1
 STHGT/OAK N14 .... 98 E4
 UPMR RM14 .... 126 C1
 WFD IG8 .... 101 M7

WLGTN SM6 ... 222 D4
Grosvenor Gardens Ms East
  BCVA SW1W * ... 16 F3
Grosvenor Gardens Ms North
  BCVA SW1W ... 16 F4
Grosvenor Ga
  MYFR/PKLN W1K ... 10 D8
Grosvenor HI
  MYFR/PKLN W1K ... 10 E7
  WIM/MER SW19 ... 179 H9
Grosvenor Ms REIG RH2 ... 275 L3
Grosvenor Pde EA W5 * ... 135 M2
Grosvenor Ms CMBW SE5 ... 18 E10
Grosvenor Park Rd
  WALTH E17 ... 120 F3
Grosvenor Ri East WALTH E17 ... 120 F3
Grosvenor Ri East BCTR RM8 ... 124 A6
  BELV DA17 ... 164 A5
  BORE WD6 ... 75 M7
  BROX EN10 ... 44 E6
  BTFD TW8 ... 155 J5
  BXLYHS DA6 ... 185 N1
  CHOB/PIR GU24 ... 213 J9
  CHSWK W4 ... 155 P4
  ED N9 ... 100 A3
  EHAM E6 ... 142 A3
  EPSOM KT18 ... 238 E9
  FNCH N3 ... 97 J8
  FSTGT E7 ... 141 N1
  HNWL W7 ... 134 F10
  HSLWW TW4 ... 153 N9
  IL IG1 ... 121 H6
  LEY E10 ... 121 H6
  MLSWH N10 ... 98 C9
  NTHWD HA6 ... 92 C6
  NWDGN UB2 ... 153 N2
  PIM SW1V ... 16 F9
  RCHPK/HAM TW10 ... 177 K1
  ROMW/RG RM7 ... 124 E5
  SNWD SE25 ... 203 P4
  STA TW18 ... 173 K10
  STAL AL1 ... 38 D7
  STMC/STPC BR5 ... 207 H6
  TWK TW1 ... 176 F3
  WAN E11 ... 121 N8
  WAT WD17 ... 73 K8
  WLGTN SM6 ... 222 C3
  WWKM BR4 ... 204 C9
Grosvenor Sq HART DA3 * ... 211 K3
  KGLGY WD4 ... 54 D4
  MYFR/PKLN W1K ... 10 D7
Grosvenor St
  MYFR/PKLN W1K ... 10 D7
  HHW HP1 ... 35 K7
Grosvenor V RSLP HA4 ... 112 G7
Grosvenor Wharf Rd
  POP/IOD E14 ... 161 J3
Grote's Blds BKHTH/KID SE3 ... 161 K8
Grote's PI BKHTH/KID SE3 ... 161 K8
Groton Rd WAND/EARL SW18 ... 179 L5
Grotto Ct STHWK SE1 ... 18 L5
Grotto Pas MHST W1U ... 10 C3
The Grotto TWK TW1 ... 176 F5
  WEY KT13 ... 196 C10
Ground La HAT AL10 ... 40 D2
Grove Av EW KT17 ... 220 B9
  FNCH N3 ... 97 K8
  HARP AL5 ... 20 C4
  HNWL W7 ... 134 D8
  MUSWH N10 ... 98 D10
  PIN HA5 ... 113 M2
  SUT SM1 ... 221 K5
  TWK TW1 ... 176 F4
Grove Bank OXHEY WD19 * ... 93 L2
Grovebury Cl ERITH DA8 ... 165 P4
Grovebury Ct STHGT/OAK N14 ... 98 D1
Grovebury Gdns
  LCOL/BKTW AL2 ... 56 B3
Grovebury Rd ABYW SE2 ... 163 L1
Grove Cl CFSP/GDCR SL9 ... 89 P9
  FSTH SE23 ... 182 C4
  HAYES BR2 ... 205 N8
  HGDN/ICK UB10 ... 112 B10
  HOR/WEW KT19 ... 219 M6
  SL SL3 ... 149 M2
  STHGT/OAK N14 ... 98 C1
  WDSR SL4 ... 171 N3
Grove Cots CHEL SW3 ... 15 J5
  CHSWK W4 ... 156 B5
  COB KT11 * ... 235 G2
Grove Ct E/WMO/HCT KT8 ... 198 C5
  EA W5 ... 135 K10
  EGH TW20 ... 156 J9
  FELT TW13 ... 62 C9
Grove Crs CDALE/KGS NW9 ... 115 P2
  FELT TW13 ... 175 M7
  KUT/HW KT1 ... 199 K3
  RKW/CH/CXG WD3 ... 72 B8
  SWFD E18 ... 101 L10
  WOT/HER KT12 ... 197 J7
Grove Crescent Rd SRTFD E15 ... 141 J1
Grovedale Cl CHESW EN7 ... 61 N6
Grovedale Cl ARCH N19 ... 118 C7
Grove Dwellings WCHPL E1 ... 140 D2
Grove End CFSP/GDCR SL9 ... 89 P9
  KTTN NW5 ... 118 C9
  SWFD E18 ... 101 L10
Grove End La ESH/CLAY KT10 ... 198 C8
Grove End Rd STJWD NW8 ... 3 J3
Grove Farm Pk NTHWD HA6 ... 92 E6
Grove Footpath BRYLDS KT5 ... 199 K4
Grove Gdns HDN NW4 ... 116 D3
  PEND EN3 ... 80 C5
  STJWD NW8 ... 3 P10
  TEDD TW11 ... 176 F7
Grove Green Rd WAN E11 ... 121 H8
Grove Hall Rd BUSH WD23 ... 73 M8
Grove Heath La
  RPLY/SEND GU23 ... 233 M10
Grove Heath North
  RPLY/SEND GU23 ... 233 L8
Grove Heath Rd
  RPLY/SEND GU23 ... 233 L9
Groveherst Rd DART DA1 ... 165 N9
Grove HI CFSP/GDCR SL9 ... 89 P8
  HRW HA1 ... 114 D5
  SWFD E18 ... 101 L10
Grove Hill Rd CMBW SE5 ... 159 J9
  HRW HA1 ... 114 D5
Grovehill Rd REDH RH1 ... 257 P10
Grove House Rd
  CEND/HSY/T N8 ... 118 F2
Groveland Av
  STRHM/NOR SW16 ... 180 C10
Groveland Ct STP EC4M ... 12 F6
Groveland Rd BECK BR3 ... 204 E3
Grovelands E/WMO/HCT KT8 ... 197 P4
  HHW HP1 ... 36 D4
  LCOL/BKTW AL2 ... 56 A3
Grovelands Cl CMBW SE5 ... 159 M8
  RYLN/HDSTN HA2 ... 114 A8
Grovelands Ct
  STHGT/OAK N14 ... 98 E1
Grovelands Rd PLMGR N13 ... 98 G5
  PUR/KEN CR8 ... 115 J9
  STMC/STPC BR5 ... 185 K10
Grovelands Wy GRAYS RM17 ... 167 L4
Groveland Wy NWMAL KT3 ... 199 P5
Grove La CFSP/GDCR SL9 ... 89 P5
  CHIG IG7 ... 103 J4
  CMBW SE5 ... 159 L4
  COUL/CHIP CR5 ... 240 C11
  CSHM HP5 ... 51 L9
  EPP CM16 ... 65 K6
  KUT/HW KT1 ... 199 J4
  UX/CGN UB8 ... 132 C2
Grove Lea HAT AL10 ... 40 C3
Groveley Rd SUN TW16 ... 174 G6
Grove Market PI
  ELTH/MOT SE9 * ... 164 G2


Grove Md HAT AL10 ... 40 C4
Grove Meadow WGCE AL7 ... 23 M5
Grove Ms HMSMTH W6 ... 156 F2
Grove Mill La
  RKW/CH/CXG WD3 ... 72 C4
Grove Mill PI CAR SM5 ... 202 B10
Grove Pk CDALE/KGS NW9 ... 115 P2
  CMBW SE5 ... 159 M8
  WAN E11 ... 121 N3
Grove Park Av CHING E4 ... 100 C8
Grove Park Br CHSWK W4 ... 155 N6
Grove Park Gdns CHSWK W4 ... 155 N6
Grove Park Rd CHSWK W4 ... 155 N6
  ELTH/MOT SE9 ... 184 A6
  RAIN RM13 ... 149 M3
  SEVS/STOTM N15 ... 119 M2
Grove Park Ter CHSWK W4 ... 155 N6
Grove PI ACT W3 ... 135 P10
  BAL SW12 ... 180 C2
  BRKMPK AL9 ... 40 F10
  GSTN WD25 * ... 74 A5
  HAMP NW3 ... 117 N8
  WEY KT13 ... 216 D2
Grover Cl HHNE HP2 ... 35 N5
Grove Rd ACT W3 ... 135 P10
  AMS HP6 ... 69 L3
  ASHTD KT21 ... 237 L4
  BARN SW13 ... 156 C8
  BEAC HP9 ... 88 C9
  BELV DA17 ... 164 A5
  BGR/WK TN15 ... 247 P8
  BH/WHM TN16 ... 243 P6
  BORE WD6 ... 75 M5
  BOW E3 ... 140 C1
  BTFD TW8 ... 155 H4
  BXLYHN DA7 ... 164 D10
  CHDH RM6 ... 123 M5
  CHERT KT16 ... 195 J6
  CHING E4 ... 101 H4
  CRICK NW2 ... 136 F1
  EA W5 ... 135 J9
  EBAR EN4 ... 77 P7
  EDGW HA8 ... 96 B1
  ELTH/MOT SE9 ... 184 E6
  FBAR/BDGN N11 ... 98 C6
  GRAYS RM17 ... 167 P5
  GU GU1 ... 250 F10
  GVW DA11 ... 189 N1
  HARP AL5 ... 20 C4
  HHW HP1 ... 35 J4
  HOM E9 ... 140 C3
  HORL RH6 ... 279 P3
  HPTN TW12 ... 175 H3
  ISLW TW7 ... 154 D7
  MTCM CR4 ... 202 C2
  NFNCH/WDSPK N12 ... 97 N6
  NTHWD HA6 ... 92 C6
  OXTED RH8 ... 261 H9
  PIN HA5 ... 113 N3
  RCHPK/HAM TW10 ... 177 L2
  RKW/CH/CXG WD3 ... 91 K3
  RSEV TN14 ... 247 K7
  SEVS/STOTM N15 ... 119 M3
  SHPTN TW17 ... 196 D6
  SL SL1 ... 149 L9
  STAL AL1 ... 38 C7
  SURB KT6 ... 199 J3
  SUT SM1 ... 221 K5
  SWFD E18 ... 101 L10
  THHTH CR7 ... 203 H4
  UX/CGN UB8 ... 131 N2
  WALTH E17 ... 120 C3
  WAN E11 ... 121 L5
  WDSR SL4 ... 149 H6
  WIM/MER SW19 ... 179 M10
  WLGTN SM6 ... 222 C2
Grove Rd West PEND EN3 ... 80 B3
Grover Rd OXHEY WD19 ... 73 J10
Grovers Farm Cots
  ADL/WDHM KT15 * ... 215 H7
Groves Cl SOCK/AV RM15 ... 146 E3
Grove Shaw
  KWD/TDW/WH KT20 ... 239 H10
Groveside Gl ACT W3 ... 135 M8
Groveside Rd CHING E4 ... 101 K4
Grovestile Wave
  EBED/NFELT TW14 ... 174 L3
Grove St BERM/RHTH SE16 ... 160 L5
  UED N18 ... 99 N1
Groves Wy CSHM HP5 ... 50 E5
Grove Ter KTTN NW5 ... 118 C8
  STHL UB1 ... 133 P9
  TEDD TW11 ... 176 F7
Grove Terrace Ms KTTN NW5 ... 118 C8
The Grove ADL/WDHM KT15 ... 215 L2
  AMS HP6 ... 69 J1
  BH/WHM TN16 ... 244 A4
  BRKMPK AL9 ... 59 K3
  BRW CM14 ... 106 E5
  BXLYHS DA6 ... 163 N10
  CDALE/KGS NW9 ... 116 C3
  CHSWK W4 ... 155 N7
  COUL/CHIP CR5 ... 240 F1
  CRAWW RH11 ... 283 M7
  CSHM HP5 ... 70 A2
  CTHM CR3 ... 241 J7
  EA W5 ... 135 J10
  EDGW HA8 ... 95 N5
  EGH TW20 ... 172 B9
  ENC/FH EN2 ... 79 H6
  EW KT17 ... 220 B9
  FNCH N3 ... 97 K8
  FSBYPK N4 ... 118 G5
  GFD/PVL UB6 ... 134 B8
  GLDGN NW11 ... 117 H5
  GU GU1 ... 268 C2
  GVE DA12 ... 190 G3
  HARP AL5 ... 20 C4
  HGDN/ICK UB10 ... 112 B10
  HGT N6 ... 118 A6
  HORL RH6 ... 280 C5
  ISLW TW7 ... 154 B5
  KGLGY WD4 ... 53 M6
  PLMGR N13 ... 99 H5
  POTB/CUF EN6 ... 59 M8
  RAD WD7 ... 74 E2
  RKW/CH/CXG WD3 ... 72 B8
  SCUP DA14 ... 185 P7
  SL SL1 ... 149 M1
  SRTFD E15 ... 141 K2
  SWCM DA10 ... 189 K1
  SWLY BR8 ... 208 A5
  TEDD TW11 ... 176 F7
  UPMR RM14 ... 131 M6
  WALTH E17 ... 120 C3


Guardian Cl EMPK RM11 ... 125 J7
Guards Av CTHM CR3 ... 241 K8
Guards Ct ASC SL5 ... 192 C1
Guardsman Cl BRW CM14 ... 107 J6
Guards Rd WDSR SL4 ... 148 B8
Gubbins La HARH RM3 ... 105 N4
Gubyon Av HNHL SE24 ... 181 J1
Guernsey Cl HEST TW5 ... 153 P7
Guernsey Farm Dr
  WOKN/KNAP GU21 * ... 232 A1
Guernsey Gv HNHL SE24 ... 181 K3
Guernsey Rd IL IG1 ... 6 F2
  LEY E10 ... 121 J6
Guernsey Gv WGCW AL8 ... 22 F5
Guessens Ct WGCW AL8 ... 22 F5
Guessens Rd WGCW AL8 ... 22 F4
Guibal Rd LEE/GVPK SE12 ... 183 M3
Guildables La EDEN TN8 ... 262 B10
Guildcroft GU GU3 ... 250 D10

### H

Haarlem Rd WKENS W14 ... 156 G2
Haberdasher St IS N1 ... 7 H9
Haberdasher St IS N1 ... 7 H9
Habgood Rd LOU IG10 ... 82 B7
Habington Cl CMBW SE5 ... 159 L6
Habitat Cl PECK SE15 ... 160 A8
Haccombe Rd
  MER MER SW19 ... 179 M1
Hackbridge Park Gdns
  CAR SM5 ... 202 A9
Hackbridge Rd CAR SM5 ... 202 B9
Hacketts La ... 203 L6
  WOKS/MYFD GU22 ... 215 J10
Hackford Rd BRXN/ST SW9 ... 158 G7
Hackford Wk BRXN/ST SW9 ... 158 G7
Hackforth Cl BAR EN5 ... 76 B6
Hackhurst La RDKG RH5 ... 270 G5
Hackington Crs BECK BR3 ... 182 F9
Hackney Cl BORE WD6 ... 76 A4
Hackney Gv HACK E8 ... 140 A1
Hackney Rd BETH E2 ... 7 L9
Hackney Wick HOM E9 ... 140 B1
Hacton Dr HCH RM12 ... 124 M9
Hacton La UPMR RM14 ... 125 N5
Hadar Cl TRDG/WHET N20 ... 97 K2
Haddenham Cl ABYW SE2 ... 93 L4
Hadden Wy GFD/PVL UB6 ... 134 C1
Haddestoke Ga
  CHES/WCR EN8 ... 62 B2
Haddington Rd BMLY BR1 ... 183 J6
Haddon Cl BORE WD6 ... 75 M6
  EN EN1 ... 90 D1
  HHS/BOV HP3 ... 36 B7
  NWMAL KT3 ... 200 C5
  WEY KT13 ... 196 F10
Haddon Gv BFN/LL DA15 ... 185 K3
Haddon Rd RKW/CH/CXG WD3 ... 70 A3
  STMC/STPC BR5 ... 207 M5
  SUT SM1 ... 221 L1
Haddo St GNWCH SE10 ... 161 N5
Hadfield Cl STHL UB1 ... 133 N5
Hadfield Rd STWL/WRAY TW19 ... 173 N5
Hadland Cl HHS/BOV HP3 ... 36 B7
Hadleigh Cl RAD WD7 ... 57 J6
  WCHPL E1 ... 140 B6
Hadleigh Dr BELMT SM2 ... 221 K5
Hadley Cl BROX EN10 ... 44 B4
  ED N9 ... 100 A1
Hadley Cl BETH E2 ... 140 B5
Hadley Common BAR EN5 ... 77 H1
Hadley Gdns CHSWK W4 ... 156 A4
  NWDGN UB2 ... 153 N4
Hadley Gra HLWE CM17 ... 47 M1
Hadley Gn BAR EN5 ... 77 J7
Hadley Green West BAR EN5 ... 77 H6
Hadley Gv BAR EN5 ... 77 H6
Hadley Highstone BAR EN5 ... 77 H3
Hadley Pde BAR EN5 * ... 77 J7
Hadley Rdg BAR EN5 ... 77 J7
Hadley Rd BAR EN5 ... 77 L7
  BELV DA17 ... 164 A3
  MTCM CR4 ... 202 G4
  RKW/CH/CXG WD3 ... 90 F1
Hadlow Cl SL SL1 ... 129 H10
Hadlow Rd NRWD SE19 ... 185 K1
Hadley's Av SOCK/AV RM15 ... 146 G1
Hadrian Cl BOW E3 ... 190 B10
  STALW/RED AL3 ... 37 M4
  STWL/WRAY TW19 ... 173 N5
Hadrian's Ride EN EN1 ... 7 P8
Hadyn Park Rd SHB W12 ... 156 D1
Hafer Rd BTSEA SW11 ... 158 A10
Hafton Rd CAT SE6 ... 183 H1
Hagden La WATW WD18 ... 72 E5
Haggard Rd TWK TW1 ... 176 C4
Hagger Ct WALTH E17 ... 121 J1
Haggerston Rd BORE WD6 ... 75 H4
  HACK E8 ... 7 P1
Hagsdell Rd HERT/WAT SG14 ... 25 J2
Hague St BETH E2 ... 7 P10


Gwynne Whf CHSWK W4 ... 156 C5
Gwynn Rd GVW DA11 ... 189 M5
Gwynns Wk HERT/BAY SG13 ... 25 M5
Gylcote Cl CMBW SE5 ... 159 H4
Gyles Pk STAN HA7 ... 95 H9
Gyllyngdune Gdns
  GDMY/SEVK IG3 ... 123 J8
Gypsy Cl WARE SG12 ... 26 E7
Gypsy La KGLGY WD4 ... 54 E10
  SLN SL2 ... 109 K9
  WARE SG12 ... 26 E8
Gypsy Moth Av HAT AL10 ... 40 B2
Gwynne PI FSBYW WC1X ... 5 P10

### H

Halcyon Cl LHD/OX KT22 ... 236 C1
Halcyon Wy EMPK RM11 ... 125 N6
Haldane Cl MUSWH N10 ... 98 C8
  PEND EN3 ... 80 C4
Haldane Gdns GVW DA11 ... 189 J4
Haldane Rd WAND/EARL SW18 ... 179 L4
  EHAM E6 ... 142 A3
  FUL/PGN SW6 ... 157 J4
  STHL UB1 ... 134 B9
Haldan Rd CHING E4 ... 101 H7
Haldens WGCE AL7 ... 23 J1
Haldon Rd WAND/EARL SW18 ... 179 J4
Halebourne La
  CHOB/PIR GU24 ... 212 F6
Hale Cl CHING E4 ... 101 H4
  EDGW HA8 ... 96 D1
  ORP BR6 ... 226 F1
Hale Dr MLHL NW7 ... 96 F7
Hale End BXLYHN DA7 ... 164 F4
Hale End Cl RSLP HA4 ... 113 J7
Hale End Rd WALTH E17 ... 101 J10
  TOTM N17 ... 119 P1
Hale Gdns ACT W3 ... 135 M10
  TOTM N17 ... 119 P1
Hale Grove Gdns MLHL NW7 ... 96 A6
Hale House
  WOOL/PLUM SE18 * ... 162 B6
Hale La EDGW HA8 ... 95 P6
  MLHL NW7 ... 96 A6
  RSEV TN14 ... 265 H10
Hale Oak GT/LBKH KT23 ... 254 B2
Halesowen Rd MRDN SM4 ... 201 M9
Hales Pk HHNE HP2 ... 36 D5
Hales Park Cl HHNE HP2 ... 36 D5
Hales St DEPT SE8 ... 160 C9
Hale St POP/IOD E14 ... 140 G9
Halesworth Cl HARH RM3 ... 105 N1
Halesworth Rd HARH RM3 ... 105 M7
Haley Rd HDN NW4 ... 116 F4
Halfacre BTFD TW8 ... 155 J6
Half Acre Cl CFSP/GDCR SL9 ... 90 C9
Half Acre Ms BTFD TW8 ... 155 J6
Half Acre Rd HNWL W7 ... 134 D10
Halfhide La CHES/WCR EN8 ... 62 B2
Halfhides WAB EN9 ... 63 H9
Half Moon Crs IS N1 ... 5 P7
Half Moon La EPP CM16 ... 65 J7
  HNHL SE24 ... 181 K2
Half Moon Meadow
  HHNE HP2 ... 36 D1
Half Moon Ms STAL AL1 ... 38 C6
Half Moon Pas WCHPL E1 ... 13 M6
Halford Cl EDGW HA8 ... 96 B3
Halford Rd FUL/PGN SW6 ... 14 B10
  HGDN/ICK UB10 ... 112 B10
  LEY E10 ... 102 B4
  RCHPK/HAM TW10 ... 177 H7
Halfpenny Cl RGUE GU4 ... 268 G6
Halfpenny La ASC SL5 ... 192 F7
  GU GU1 ... 268 F5
Halfway Ct PUR RM19 ... 165 P3
Halfway Cn WOT/HER KT12 ... 197 J10
Halfway St BFN/LL DA15 ... 185 H4
Haliburton Rd TWK TW1 ... 176 F3
Haliday Wk IS N1 * ... 7 H1
Halidon Cl HOM E9 ... 120 F10
Halidon Ri HARH RM3 ... 106 A1
Halifax CRAWE RH10 ... 285 N5
  GSTN WD25 ... 54 C10
  LCOL/BKTW AL2 ... 55 N7
Halifax Rd ENC/FH EN2 ... 79 H6
  GFD/PVL UB6 ... 134 A3
  RKW/CH/CXG WD3 ... 90 F1
Halifax St SYD SE26 ... 182 A6
Halifax Wy WGCE AL7 ... 24 A5
Halifield Dr BELV DA17 ... 163 P2
Haling Down Pas
  PUR/KEN CR8 ... 223 K4
Haling Park Gdns
  SAND/SEL CR2 ... 223 J3
Haling Park Rd SAND/SEL CR2 ... 223 J3
Haling Rd SAND/SEL CR2 ... 223 L4
Halings La DEN/HRF UB9 ... 110 C2
Halkin Ar KTBR SW1X ... 16 C2
Halkingcroft DTCH/LGLY SL3 ... 149 P2
Halkin Ms KTBR SW1X ... 16 C3
Halkin PI KTBR SW1X ... 16 C3
Halkin St KTBR SW1X ... 16 C2
Hallam Cl BRWN CM15 ... 86 G5
  CHST BR7 ... 184 G8
  WATN WD24 ... 73 H6
Hallam Gdns PIN HA5 ... 93 M8
Hallam Ms GTPST W1W ... 10 F3
Hallam Rd BARN SW13 ... 156 E3
  SEVS/STOTM N15 ... 119 J2
Hallam St GTPST W1W ... 10 F3
Halland Cl CRAWW RH11 ... 284 D6
Halland Wy NTHWD HA6 ... 92 C7
Hallane Av SOCK/AV RM15 ... 146 B10
Hall Cl EA W5 ... 135 K2
  COOL GU27 ... 267 K10
  RKW/CH/CXG WD3 ... 91 K2
Hall Ct DTCH/LGLY SL3 ... 149 N6
  TEDD TW11 ... 175 P8
Hall Crs SOCK/AV RM15 ... 166 B1
Hall Dene Cl GU GU1 ... 250 F6
Hall Dr DEN/HRF UB9 ... 91 M9
  SYD SE26 ... 182 B8
Hall Farm Cl STAN HA7 ... 95 J3
Hall Farm Dr WHTN TW2 ... 176 B5
Hallfield Est BAY/PAD W2 ... 9 H3
Hall Gdns CHING E4 ... 100 G4
  STALW/RED AL3 ... 8 G10
Hall Ga STJWD NW8 ... 3 H10
Hall Gv WGCE AL7 ... 23 L2
Hall HI OXTED RH8 ... 261 J8
The Halliards WOT/HER KT12 ... 197 H6
Halliday Rd WD7 ... 57 K2
Halliday Sq NWDGN UB2 ... 135 H2
Hallifford St IS N1 ... 6 F1
Halliford Rd SHPTN TW17 ... 196 F3
  SUN TW16 ... 197 H1
Halliford St IS N1 ... 6 F1
Hallilo Valley Rd CTHM CR3 ... 242 D6
Halling HI HLW CM20 ... 29 J1
Hallington Cl
  WOKN/KNAP GU21 ... 231 N10
Halliwell Rd BRXS/STRHM SW2 ... 180 C2
Halliwick Court Pde
  NFNCH/WDSPK N12 * ... 98 A6
Halliwick Rd MUSWH N10 ... 98 B7
Hall La BRWN CM15 ... 87 K1
  CHING E4 ... 100 G4
  HDN NW4 ... 96 B10
  HYS/HAR UB3 ... 152 D6
  SOCK/AV RM15 ... 147 L4
  UPMR RM14 ... 126 B6
Hall Meadow SL SL1 ... 128 A5


Hall Oak Wk KIL/WHAMP NW6 ... 2 D1
Hallowell Av CROY/NA CR0 ... 222 F1
Hallowell Cl MTCM CR4 ... 202 B2
Hallowell Gdns THHTH CR7 ... 203 K2
Hallowes Cl GUW GU2 ... 249 N5
Hallowes Crs OXHEY WD19 ... 93 H4
Hallowfield Wy MTCM CR4 ... 201 N3
Hallows Gv SUN TW16 ... 174 C8
Hall Pk BERK HP4 ... 34 G6
Hall Pl BAY/PAD W2 ... 9 L2
  WOKN/KNAP GU21 ... 232 D2
Hall Place Crs BXLY DA5 ... 186 D5
Hall Place Dr WEY KT13 ... 216 F2
Hall Rd BARK/HLT IG6 ... 104 B8
  CHDH RM6 ... 123 M4
  EHAM E6 ... 142 C3
  GPK RM2 ... 125 J1
  HNHL SE24 ... 165 N10
  ISLW TW7 ... 176 C1
  MV/WKIL W9 ... 3 H9
  SHGR GU5 ... 268 C10
  SOCK/AV RM15 ... 166 B1
  SRTFD E15 ... 121 J9
  WLGTN SM6 ... 222 C5
Halls Farm Cl
  WOKN/KNAP GU21 ... 231 H3
Hallside Rd EN EN1 ... 79 N4
Hallslands Wy OXTED RH8 ... 261 J10
Halls Ter HGDN/ICK UB10 * ... 132 C6
Hall St FSBYE EC1V ... 6 D7
  NFNCH/WDSPK N12 ... 97 N6
Hallsville Rd CAN/RD E16 ... 141 L8
Hallswelle Pde GLDGN NW11 * ... 117 J3
Hallswelle Rd GLDGN NW11 ... 117 J3
Hall Ter SOCK/AV RM15 ... 166 C1
The Hall BKHTH/KID SE3 ... 161 M9
Hall Vw ELTH/MOT SE9 ... 184 A5
The Hall Wk BERK HP4 * ... 34 A5
Hallwood Crs BRWN CM15 ... 107 K1
Hallywell Crs EHAM E6 ... 142 C7
Hainaker Wk CRAWW RH11 * ... 283 J10
Halons Rd ELTH/MOT SE9 ... 184 D3
Halpin PI WALW SE17 ... 19 J6
Halsbrook Rd BKHTH/KID SE3 ... 161 P9
Halsbury Cl STAN HA7 ... 94 G6
Halsbury Rd SHB W12 ... 136 E10
Halsbury Rd East NTHLT UB5 ... 114 B7
Halsbury Rd West NTHLT UB5 ... 114 A10
Halse Dr SL SL1 ... 108 E9
Halsend HYS/HAR UB3 ... 133 J10
Halsey Dr HHW HP1 ... 35 J4
Halsey Pk LCOL/BKTW AL2 ... 57 L3
Halsey Rd WATW WD18 ... 73 J4
Halsey St CHEL SW3 ... 16 K5
Halsham Crs BARK IG11 ... 143 J1
Halsmere Rd CMBW SE5 ... 159 J7
Halstead Cl CROY/NA CR0 ... 203 K10
Halstead Ct EN EN1 ... 79 M4
Halstead Gdns WCHMH N21 ... 99 L2
Halstead La RSEV TN14 ... 245 P1
Halstead Rd EN EN1 ... 79 M8
  ERITH DA8 ... 164 F7
  WAN E11 ... 121 N3
  WCHMH N21 ... 99 L2
Halstead Wy
  RBRW/HUT CM13 ... 87 P10
Halston Cl BTSEA SW11 ... 180 A2
Halstow Rd GNWCH SE10 ... 161 M4
  WLSDN NW10 ... 136 G5
Halsway HYS/HAR UB3 ... 133 H10
Halt Dr SLH/COR SS17 ... 169 K3
Halter Cl BORE WD6 ... 76 A9
Halton Cl FBAR/BDGN N11 ... 98 A7
  LCOL/BKTW AL2 ... 55 N7
Halton Cross St N1 * ... 6 C1
Halton PI IS N1 * ... 6 E1
Halton Rd CDW/CHF RM16 ... 168 E2
  IS N1 ... 6 C1
  PUR/KEN CR8 ... 241 M6
Halt Robin Rd BELV DA17 ... 164 B3
Halt Robin Rd HAT AL10 ... 40 A5
Halwick Cl HHW HP1 ... 35 L5
Hambalt Rd CLAP SW4 ... 180 D1
Hamberlins La TRING HP23 ... 32 G2
Hamble Cl RSLP HA4 ... 113 J7
  WOKN/KNAP GU21 ... 231 M3
Hamble Ct UX/CGN UB8 ... 132 C6
Hambledon Av EA W5 * ... 135 K9
Hambledon Gdns SNWD SE25 ... 203 N3
Hambledon HI EPSOM KT18 ... 237 P2
Hambledon Pl DUL SE21 ... 181 N4
  GT/LBKH KT23 ... 235 P9
Hambledon Rd CTHM CR3 ... 241 L9
  WAND/EARL SW18 ... 179 J3
Hambledown Rd
  BFN/LL DA15 ... 184 G3
Hamble St FUL/PGN SW6 ... 157 P9
Hamble Wy HAYES BR2 ... 205 N6
Hambridge Wy BRXS/STRHM SW2 ... 180 B2
Hambro Av HAYES BR2 ... 205 N6
Hambrook Rd SNWD SE25 ... 204 A3
Hambro Rd CRAWW RH11 ... 107 J3
  STRHM/NOR SW16 ... 180 D9
Hambrough Rd STHL UB1 ... 133 N10
Hamburgh Ct CHES/WCR EN8 ... 62 C4
Ham Common
  RCHPK/HAM TW10 ... 177 J6
Ham Croft Cl FELT TW13 ... 175 J6
Hamden Crs DAGE RM10 ... 124 C8
Hamel Cl KTN/HRWW/WS HA3 ... 115 J2
Hamelin St POP/IOD E14 ... 161 H8
Hamel Cl HHS/BOV HP3 ... 52 D4
Hamerton Rd GVW DA11 ... 189 M1
Hameway EHAM E6 ... 142 D6
Ham Farm Rd
  RCHPK/HAM TW10 ... 177 J7
Hamfield Cl OXTED RH8 ... 261 H3
Hamfrith Rd SRTFD E15 ... 141 L1
Ham Gate Av
  RCHPK/HAM TW10 ... 177 K7
Hamhaugh Island SHPTN TW17 ... 196 B9
Hamilton Av BARK/HLT IG6 ... 122 E2
  CHEAM SM3 ... 201 H9
  COB KT11 ... 217 H9
  ED N9 ... 99 P1
  HOD EN11 ... 104 A10
  ROM RM1 ... 124 G2
  SURB KT6 ... 199 N9
  WOKS/MYFD GU22 ... 233 N2
Hamilton Cl BRW CM14 ... 105 M1
  HSLW TW3 ... 176 F1
  PLMGR N13 ... 98 F8
  RYLN/HDSTN HA2 ... 113 M10
Hamilton Ct EA W5 ... 135 K5
Hamilton Crs BRW CM14 ... 107 M4
  HSLW TW3 ... 176 F1
  PLMGR N13 ... 98 F3
  RYLN/HDSTN HA2 ... 113 M10
Hamilton Dr ASC SL5 ... 192 D7
  GUW GU2 ... 249 M6
  HARH RM3 ... 105 M10
Hamilton Gdns STJWD NW8 ... 3 H8
Hamilton Gordon Ct GU GU1 ... 249 N8

| | | |
|---|---|---|
| Hamilton Md HHS/BOV HP3 * | 52 | D3 |
| Hamilton Ms MYFR/PICC W1J | 16 | E1 |
| WEY KT13 * | 216 | B1 |
| Hamilton Pk HBRY N5 | 119 | J9 |
| Hamilton Pk West HBRY N5 | 119 | J9 |
| Hamilton Pl GUW GU2 | 249 | N5 |
| HORL RH6 | 280 | B5 |
| KWD/TDW/WH KT20 | 239 | J9 |
| MYFR/PKLN W1K | 10 | D10 |
| SUN TW16 | 175 | J10 |
| Hamilton Rd BERK HP4 | 33 | N5 |
| BTFD TW8 | 155 | J5 |
| BXLYHN DA7 | 163 | P8 |
| CHSWK W4 | 156 | B2 |
| EA W5 | 135 | K9 |
| EBAR EN4 | 77 | P8 |
| ED N9 | 99 | P1 |
| EFNCH N2 | 117 | M1 |
| FELT TW13 | 174 | C7 |
| GLDGN NW11 | 116 | C5 |
| GPK RM2 | 125 | J3 |
| HRW HA3 | 114 | D3 |
| ILS/HAR UB3 | 133 | J9 |
| IL IG1 | 72 | E9 |
| KGLGY WD4 | 54 | D9 |
| OXHEY WD19 | 93 | J4 |
| SCUP DA14 | 185 | K7 |
| SL SL1 | 128 | F8 |
| SRTFD E15 | 141 | K5 |
| STAL AL1 | 38 | F5 |
| STHL UB1 | 133 | N10 |
| THHTH CR7 | 203 | L3 |
| UX/CGN UB8 | 131 | N6 |
| WALTH E17 | 100 | D10 |
| WHTN TW2 | 176 | D4 |
| WIM/MER SW19 | 179 | L10 |
| WLSDN NW10 | 116 | D10 |
| WNWD SE27 | 181 | L7 |
| Hamilton Road Ms WIM/MER SW19 | 179 | L10 |
| Hamilton Sq NFNCH/WDSPK N12 * | 97 | M7 |
| Hamilton St DEPT SE8 | 160 | F5 |
| WATW WD18 | 73 | K9 |
| Hamilton Wy STJWD NW8 | 3 | J8 |
| FNCH N3 | 97 | K7 |
| Hamilton Wy FNCH N3 * | 97 | K7 |
| PLMGR N13 | 99 | J5 |
| WLGTN SM6 | 222 | E6 |
| Ham La EGH TW20 | 171 | N7 |
| WDSR SL4 | 149 | P10 |
| Hamlea Cl LEE/GVPK SE12 | 183 | M1 |
| Hamlet Cl CRW RM5 | 104 | B8 |
| LCOL/BKTW AL2 | 55 | N6 |
| LEW SE13 | 161 | K10 |
| Hamlet Gdns HMSMTH W6 | 156 | F3 |
| Hamlet Hl HLWW/ROY CM19 | 45 | N5 |
| Hamlet Rd CRW RM5 | 104 | B8 |
| NRWD SE19 | 181 | N10 |
| Hamlet Sq CRICK NW2 | 117 | H8 |
| Hamlets Wy BOW E3 | 140 | E6 |
| The Hamlet BERK HP4 | 34 | D2 |
| CMBW SE5 | 159 | L9 |
| Hamlet Wy STHWK SE1 | 19 | H2 |
| Hamlin Crs PIN HA5 | 113 | K3 |
| Hamlin Rd SEV TN13 | 246 | F7 |
| Hamlyn Cl EDGW HA8 | 95 | K4 |
| Hamlyn Gdns NRWD SE19 | 181 | M10 |
| Hammarskjold Rd HLW CM20 | 28 | F10 |
| Hamm Ct WEY KT13 | 196 | A10 |
| Hammelton Rd BMLY BR1 | 205 | M1 |
| Hammer La HHNE HP2 | 36 | A5 |
| Hammer Pde GSTN WD25 * | 55 | H9 |
| Hammers Ga LCOL/BKTW AL2 | 55 | P2 |
| Hammers La MLHL NW7 | 96 | D5 |
| Hammersmith Br HMSMTH W6 | 156 | E4 |
| Hammersmith Bridge Rd BARN SW13 | 156 | E4 |
| Hammersmith Broadway HMSMTH W6 | 156 | F3 |
| Hammersmith Emb HMSMTH W6 * | 156 | F5 |
| Hammersmith F/O HMSMTH W6 | 156 | F4 |
| Hammersmith Gv HMSMTH W6 | 156 | F2 |
| Hammersmith Rd HMSMTH W6 | 156 | G3 |
| Hammersmith Ter HMSMTH W6 | 156 | D4 |
| Hammerton Cl BXLY DA5 | 186 | F6 |
| Hammer Yd CRAWE RH10 * | 283 | N8 |
| Hammet Cl YEAD UB4 | 133 | L7 |
| Hammet St TWRH EC3N | 13 | L7 |
| Hamm Moor La ADL/WDHM KT15 | 215 | P2 |
| Hammond Av MTCM CR4 | 202 | C2 |
| Hammond Cl BAR EN5 | 77 | H9 |
| CHESW EN7 | 61 | N2 |
| GFD/PVL UB6 | 114 | C10 |
| HPTN TW12 | 197 | P3 |
| WOKN/KNAP GU21 | 231 | P1 |
| Hammond End SLN SL2 | 108 | C9 |
| Hammond Rd EN EN1 | 84 | C2 |
| NWDGN UB2 | 153 | M2 |
| WOKN/KNAP GU21 | 231 | P1 |
| Hammonds Cl BCTR RM8 | 123 | M8 |
| Hammonds La HAT AL10 | 21 | N8 |
| RBRW/HUT CM13 | 106 | C7 |
| STALE/WH AL4 | 21 | M8 |
| Hammond St CHESW EN7 | 4 | C1 |
| Hammondstreet Rd CHESW EN7 | 61 | J1 |
| Hammond Wy LTWR GU18 | 212 | A6 |
| Hamonde Cl EDGW HA8 | 95 | N3 |
| Hamond Sq IS N1 | 7 | J7 |
| Ham Pk Rd SRTFD E15 | 141 | L2 |
| Hampden Av BECK BR3 | 204 | B2 |
| CSHM HP5 | 50 | F6 |
| Hampden Cl CAMTN NW1 | 5 | K8 |
| CRAWE RH10 | 284 | F4 |
| EPP CM16 | 66 | B5 |
| SLN SL2 | 129 | M5 |
| Hampden Crs BRW CM14 | 107 | H6 |
| CHESW EN7 | 62 | A3 |
| Hampden Gurney St MBLAR W1H | 10 | E4 |
| WARE SG12 | 26 | E2 |
| Hampden Hl BEAC HP9 | 88 | A9 |
| WARE SG12 | 26 | E1 |
| Hampden Hill Cl WARE SG12 | 26 | E1 |
| Hampden Pl LCOL/BKTW AL2 | 56 | D5 |
| Hampden Rd ARCH N19 | 118 | D1 |
| BECK BR3 | 204 | D2 |
| CEND/HSY/T N8 | 119 | H2 |
| DTCH/LGLY SL3 | 150 | C2 |
| GRAYS RM17 | 167 | N4 |
| KTN/HRWW/WS HA3 | 94 | B9 |
| KUT/HW KT1 | 199 | M3 |
| MUSWH N10 | 99 | H8 |
| TOTM N17 | 99 | P8 |
| Hampden Wy STHGT/OAK N14 | 98 | F5 |
| WAT WD17 | 22 | C2 |
| Hampermill La OXHEY WD19 | 93 | H1 |
| Hampshire Av SL SL1 | 129 | H1 |
| Hampshire Cl UED N18 | 100 | F4 |
| Hampshire Gdns SLH/COR SS17 | 169 | K1 |
| Hampshire Hog La HMSMTH W6 * | 156 | E3 |
| Hampshire Rd EMPK RM11 | 125 | J2 |
| WDGN N22 | 98 | E5 |
| Hampshire St KTTN NW5 | 5 | J1 |
| Hampson Wy VX/NE SW8 | 158 | C2 |
| Hampstead Av WFD IG8 | 102 | G8 |
| THMD SE28 | 143 | K10 |
| Hampstead Gdns GLDGN NW11 | 117 | K4 |
| Hampstead Ga HAMP NW3 | 117 | M10 |
| Hampstead Gn HAMP NW3 | 117 | P10 |
| Hampstead Gv HAMP NW3 | 117 | M9 |
| Hampstead Hts EFNCH N2 | 117 | M2 |
| Hampstead Hill Gdns HAMP NW3 | 117 | P9 |
| HGT N6 | 118 | A5 |
| Hampstead La DORK RH4 | 272 | E3 |
| DORK RH4 | 272 | F3 |
| Hampstead Sq HAMP NW3 | 117 | M8 |
| Hampton Ms WKENS W14 | 156 | C1 |
| Hampton Wy GLDGN NW11 | 117 | K4 |
| Hampton Cl BORE WD6 | 75 | P4 |
| CDW/CHF RM16 | 167 | H2 |
| FBAR/BDGN N11 | 98 | B6 |
| KIL/WHAMP NW6 | 2 | E10 |
| RYNPK SW20 * | 178 | F10 |
| WOKN/KNAP GU21 | 230 | G5 |
| Hampton Ct IS N1 * | 6 | C2 |
| Hampton Court Av E/WMO/HCT KT8 | 198 | C6 |
| Hampton Court Crs E/WMO/HCT KT8 | 198 | C3 |
| Hampton Court Est E/WMO/HCT KT8 * | 198 | C3 |
| Hampton Court Rd HPTN TW12 | 198 | C2 |
| Hampton Court Wy ESH/CLAY KT10 | 198 | D9 |
| Hampton Crs GVE DA12 | 191 | H5 |
| Hampton Gdns SBW CM21 | 29 | L4 |
| Hampton La FELT TW13 | 175 | M7 |
| Hampton Ri KTN/HRWW/WS HA3 | 115 | K4 |
| Hampton Rd CHING E4 | 100 | E6 |
| CROY/NA CR0 | 203 | K6 |
| FSTGT E7 | 121 | N10 |
| IL IG1 | 122 | F9 |
| REDH RH1 | 276 | A5 |
| TEDD TW11 | 176 | C8 |
| WAN E11 | 121 | J6 |
| WHTN TW2 | 176 | C6 |
| WPK KT4 | 200 | D9 |
| Hampton Rd East FELT TW13 | 175 | N6 |
| Hampton Rd West FELT TW13 | 175 | M5 |
| Hampton St WALW SE17 | 18 | D6 |
| Ham Ridings RCHPK/HAM TW10 | 177 | L8 |
| Hamsey Green Gdns WARL CR6 | 242 | A2 |
| Hamsey Wy SAND/SEL CR2 | 242 | A1 |
| Ham Shades Cl BFN/LL DA15 | 185 | J6 |
| Hamstel Rd HLW CM20 | 28 | E9 |
| Hamstel La RCHPK/HAM TW10 | 177 | H5 |
| The Ham BTFD TW8 | 155 | H6 |
| Ham Vw CROY/NA CR0 | 203 | J7 |
| Ham Yd SOHO/SHAV W1D * | 11 | J7 |
| Hanameel St CAN/RD E16 | 141 | M10 |
| Hanbury Cl CHES/WCR EN8 | 62 | C5 |
| HDN NW4 | 116 | F1 |
| Hanbury Ct HRW HA1 * | 114 | F4 |
| Hanbury Dr BH/WHM TN16 | 225 | N10 |
| WAN E11 | 121 | L5 |
| Hanbury Ms IS N1 | 6 | G2 |
| Hanbury Path WOKN/KNAP GU21 | 231 | N1 |
| Hanbury Rd ACT W3 | 135 | N5 |
| TOTM N17 | 100 | A10 |
| Hanbury St WCHPL E1 | 13 | M1 |
| Hancock Ct BORE WD6 | 75 | P5 |
| Hancock Rd BOW E3 | 141 | H5 |
| NRWD SE19 | 181 | L9 |
| Hancocks Mt ASC SL5 | 192 | C6 |
| Hancroft Rd HHS/BOV HP3 | 36 | A7 |
| Handa Cl HHS/BOV HP3 | 36 | C9 |
| Handa Wk IS N1 * | 6 | F1 |
| Handcroft Rd CROY/NA CR0 | 203 | J7 |
| Handel Cl EDGW HA8 | 95 | N3 |
| Handel Crs TIL RM18 | 168 | D6 |
| Handel Pde EDGW HA8 * | 95 | M7 |
| Handel St BMSBY WC1N | 11 | L1 |
| Handel Wy EDGW HA8 | 95 | M8 |
| Handen Rd LEE/GVPK SE12 | 183 | K1 |
| Handforth Rd BRXN/ST SW9 | 159 | H6 |
| IL IG1 | 122 | C8 |
| Handl La SBW CM21 | 29 | M2 |
| Handley Page Rd WLGTN SM6 | 222 | G6 |
| Handley Page Wy LCOL/BKTW AL2 | 56 | E2 |
| Handley Rd HOM E9 | 140 | B2 |
| Handowe Cl HDN NW4 | 116 | D2 |
| Handpost Lodge Gdns HHNE HP2 | 36 | E7 |
| Handside Cl WGCW AL8 | 22 | D5 |
| WPK KT4 | 200 | G8 |
| Handside Gn WGCW AL8 | 22 | C4 |
| Handside La WGCW AL8 | 22 | B6 |
| Handsworth Av CHING E4 | 101 | J7 |
| Handsworth Rd TOTM N17 | 119 | L1 |
| Handtrough Wy BARK IG11 | 142 | A4 |
| Hanford Cl WAND/EARL SW18 | 179 | K4 |
| Hanford Rd SOCK/AV RM15 | 146 | B10 |
| Hangar Lane (North Circular Road) EA W5 | 135 | L2 |
| Hangar Ruding OXHEY WD19 | 93 | L1 |
| Hanger Cl HHW HP1 | 35 | L7 |
| Hanger Gn EA W5 | 135 | N6 |
| Hanger Hl WEY KT13 | 216 | C2 |
| Hanger Vale La EA W5 | 135 | K4 |
| Hanger View Wy ACT W3 | 135 | M8 |
| Hang Grove Hl ORP BR6 | 226 | G9 |
| Hanging Hill La RBRW/HUT CM13 | 107 | N4 |
| Hanging Sword Aly EMB EC4Y * | 12 | A7 |
| Hankey Pl STHWK SE1 | 19 | J2 |
| Hankins La MLHL NW7 | 96 | B3 |
| Hanley Pl BECK BR3 | 182 | G10 |
| Hanley Rd FSBYPK N4 | 118 | F6 |
| Hanmer Wk HOLWY N7 * | 118 | G3 |
| Hannah Cl BECK BR3 | 204 | G3 |
| WLSDN NW10 | 115 | P9 |
| Hannah Mary Wy STHWK SE1 * | 19 | P9 |
| Hannards Wy BARK/HLT IG6 | 105 | L8 |
| Hannay La ARCH N19 | 118 | B3 |
| Hannell Rd FUL/PGN SW6 | 157 | H6 |
| Hannen Rd WNWD SE27 | 181 | J5 |
| Hannibal Rd STWL/WRAY TW19 | 173 | P3 |
| WCHPL E1 | 140 | G7 |
| Hannibal Wy CROY/NA CR0 | 223 | H5 |
| Hanningfield Wy LOU IG10 | 39 | K5 |
| Hanover Av CAN/RD E16 | 141 | M10 |
| FELT TW13 | 175 | H4 |
| Hanover Cir HYS/HAR UB3 | 132 | D8 |
| Hanover Cl CHEAM SM3 | 221 | H1 |
| CRAWE RH10 | 284 | H1 |
| EGH TW20 | 171 | N9 |
| RCH/KEW TW9 | 155 | M6 |
| REDH RH1 | 258 | D4 |
| WDSR SL4 | 148 | G3 |
| Hanover Ct DORK RH4 | 272 | E4 |
| WOKS/MYFD GU22 | 232 | B5 |
| Hanover Dr CHST BR7 | 184 | F1 |
| Hanover Gdns ABLGY WD5 * | 54 | C1 |
| BARK/HLT IG6 | 102 | F8 |
| LBTH SE11 | 18 | A10 |
| Hanover Ga CAMTN NW1 | 3 | P8 |
| Hanover Gn WEA W13 | 134 | C5 |
| Hanover Hl HACK E8 | 139 | N2 |
| Hanover Md HLWW/ROY CM19 | 45 | M1 |
| Hanover Pk PECK SE15 | 159 | K8 |
| Hanover Pl BOW E3 | 140 | C6 |
| COVGDN WC2E * | 11 | M6 |
| Hanover Rd SEVS/STOTM N15 | 119 | N9 |
| WIM/MER SW19 | 179 | M10 |
| WLSDN NW10 | 136 | F1 |
| Hanover Sq CONDST W1S | 10 | F6 |
| Hanover Steps BAY/PAD W2 * | 9 | P6 |
| Hanover St CONDST W1S | 10 | F6 |
| CROY/NA CR0 | 203 | J10 |
| Hanover Ter CAMTN NW1 | 4 | A10 |
| Hanover Terrace Ms CAMTN NW1 | 3 | P9 |
| Hanover Wk HAT AL10 | 40 | C7 |
| WEY KT13 | 196 | E10 |
| Hanover Yd IS N1 * | 6 | D7 |
| Hansard Ms WKENS W14 | 156 | C1 |
| Hans Crs KTBR SW1X | 16 | A3 |
| Hanselin Cl STAN HA7 | 94 | E6 |
| Hansen Dr HLWW/ROY CM19 | 45 | M1 |
| Hansen Dr WCHMH N21 | 78 | G9 |
| Hanshaw Dr EDGW HA8 | 96 | A9 |
| Hansler Gv E/WMO/HCT KT8 | 198 | C5 |
| Hansler Rd EDUL SE22 | 181 | N1 |
| Hansol Rd BXLYHS DA6 | 185 | P1 |
| Hansom Ter BMLY BR1 * | 205 | N1 |
| Hanson Cl BAL SW12 | 180 | C5 |
| BECK BR3 * | 182 | G9 |
| MORT/ESHN SW14 | 156 | G10 |
| RGUE GU4 | 250 | C7 |
| WDR/YW UB7 | 152 | A2 |
| Hanson Dr LOU IG10 | 82 | F6 |
| Hanson Gdns STHL UB1 | 153 | M1 |
| Hans Pl KTBR SW1X | 16 | A3 |
| Hans Rd CHEL SW3 | 16 | A3 |
| Hans St KTBR SW1X | 16 | B4 |
| Hanway Pl FITZ W1T | 11 | J5 |
| SOHO/SHAV W1D | 11 | J5 |
| Hanway Rd HNWL W7 | 134 | C8 |
| Hanway St FITZ W1T | 11 | J5 |
| Hanworth La CHERT KT16 | 195 | J8 |
| Hanworth Rd FELT TW13 | 175 | J4 |
| HPTN TW12 | 175 | N7 |
| HSLW TW3 | 154 | A9 |
| HSLWW TW4 | 175 | N3 |
| REDH RH1 | 276 | A5 |
| SUN TW16 | 175 | H10 |
| Hanworth Ter HSLW TW3 | 154 | A9 |
| Hanyards La POTB/CUF EN6 | 59 | L1 |
| Hapgood Cl GFD/PVL UB6 | 114 | C10 |
| Harben Pde HAMP NW3 * | 3 | K3 |
| Harben Rd KIL/WHAMP NW6 | 2 | G1 |
| Harberson Rd BAL SW12 | 180 | C4 |
| SRTFD E15 | 141 | L3 |
| Harbet Rd BAY/PAD W2 | 9 | M4 |
| Harbex Cl BXLY DA5 | 185 | N5 |
| Harbinger Rd POP/IOD E14 | 160 | G3 |
| Harbledown Pl STMC/STPC BR5 | 207 | M4 |
| Harbledown Rd FUL/PGN SW6 | 157 | K7 |
| SAND/SEL CR2 | 223 | N7 |
| Harbord Cl CMBW SE5 | 159 | L8 |
| Harborne Cl OXHEY WD19 | 93 | J3 |
| Harborough Av BFN/LL DA15 | 185 | H5 |
| Harborough Rd STRHM/NOR SW16 | 180 | G7 |
| Harbour Av WBPTN SW10 | 157 | M7 |
| Harbour Cl MTCM CR4 | 202 | B7 |
| Harbour Rd PUT/ROE SW15 | 178 | C3 |
| Harbury Rd CAR SM5 | 221 | P5 |
| Harbut Rd BTSEA SW11 | 158 | D3 |
| Harcamlow Wy HLWE CM17 | 29 | N5 |
| HLWW/ROY CM19 | 27 | N9 |
| WARE SG12 | 27 | H1 |
| Harcastle Cl YEAD UB4 | 133 | M6 |
| Harcombe Rd STNW/STAM N16 | 119 | M8 |
| Harcourt Av E/WMO/HCT KT8 | 185 | P4 |
| EDGW HA8 | 96 | A9 |
| MNPK E12 | 122 | C9 |
| WLGTN SM6 | 222 | C1 |
| Harcourt Blds EMB EC4Y * | 12 | A7 |
| Harcourt Fld WLGTN SM6 | 222 | C1 |
| Harcourt Ms GPK RM2 | 124 | G3 |
| Harcourt Rd BROCKY SE4 | 160 | G10 |
| BUSH WD23 | 76 | E1 |
| BXLYHS DA6 | 163 | P10 |
| SRTFD E15 | 141 | L4 |
| THHTH CR7 | 202 | G6 |
| WDGN N22 | 98 | B9 |
| WIM/MER SW19 | 179 | K10 |
| WLGTN SM6 | 222 | C1 |
| Harcourt St MBLAR W1H | 9 | P4 |
| Harcourt Ter WBPTN SW10 | 15 | L9 |
| Hardcastle Cl CROY/NA CR0 | 203 | P6 |
| Hardcourts Cl WWKM BR4 | 224 | C1 |
| Hardel Ri BRXS/STRHM SW2 | 181 | H3 |
| Harden Farm Cl COUL/CHIP CR5 | 240 | D7 |
| Harden Rd GVW DA11 | 190 | D7 |
| Hardens Manorway WOOL/PLUM SE18 | 162 | A2 |
| Hardess St HNHL SE24 | 159 | K9 |
| Hardham Cl CRAWW RH11 | 283 | K5 |
| Hardie Cl WLSDN NW10 | 116 | A6 |
| Hardie Rd DAGE RM10 | 124 | D8 |
| Harding Cl CROY/NA CR0 | 203 | N10 |
| GSTN WD25 | 55 | N9 |
| KUTN/CMB KT2 | 199 | L1 |
| WALW SE17 | 18 | E9 |
| Hardinge Rd UED N18 | 99 | H6 |
| WLSDN NW10 | 136 | F3 |
| Hardinge St WCHPL E1 | 140 | B8 |
| WOOL/PLUM SE18 | 162 | F2 |
| Harding Pde HARP AL5 * | 20 | F3 |
| Harding Rd BXLYHN DA7 | 164 | A8 |
| CDW/CHF RM16 | 168 | D2 |
| CSHM HP5 | 51 | J6 |
| EPSOM KT18 | 238 | B5 |
| Hardings WGCE AL7 | 23 | P4 |
| Hardings La PGE/AN SE20 | 182 | G9 |
| Harding Sp DTCH/LGLY SL3 | 150 | C4 |
| Hardings Rw IVER SL0 | 131 | J1 |
| Hardley Crs EMPK RM11 | 125 | L2 |
| Hardman Rd CHARL SE7 | 161 | N1 |
| KUT/HW KT1 | 175 | H4 |
| Hardres Ter STMC/STPC BR5 * | 207 | K2 |
| Hardwick Cl LHD/OX KT22 | 235 | H7 |
| STAN HA7 | 95 | H4 |
| Hardwicke Av HEST TW5 | 153 | P7 |
| Hardwicke Gdns AMS HP6 | 35 | P7 |
| Hardwicke Ms FSBYW WC1X * | 5 | P10 |
| Hardwicke Pl LCOL/BKTW AL2 | 57 | J3 |
| Hardwicke Rd CHSWK W4 * | 155 | P3 |
| PLMGR N13 | 98 | F1 |
| RCHPK/HAM TW10 | 177 | H5 |
| REIG RH2 | 257 | K9 |
| Hardwick Gn WEA W13 | 134 | G4 |
| Hardwick St CLKNW EC1R | 6 | B10 |
| Hardwick's Wy WAND/EARL SW18 | 179 | K1 |
| RSLP HA4 | 113 | J10 |
| Hardy Cl BAR EN5 | 77 | H9 |
| BERM/RHTH SE16 | 160 | C1 |
| CRAWE RH10 | 284 | D6 |
| HORL RH6 | 279 | P4 |
| PIN HA5 | 113 | J5 |
| RDKG RH5 | 272 | C6 |
| SL SL1 | 128 | F10 |
| Hardy Cots GNWCH SE10 * | 161 | J5 |
| Hardy Gv DART DA1 | 165 | P10 |
| Hardy Ms UX/CGN UB8 | 131 | M4 |
| Hardy Rd BKHTH/KID SE3 | 161 | L5 |
| CHING E4 | 100 | E7 |
| WIM/MER SW19 | 179 | M3 |
| Hardy Wy ENC/FH EN2 | 79 | H5 |
| Harebell HLWE CM17 | 29 | N2 |
| Harebell Dr EHAM E6 | 142 | D7 |
| Harebell Hl COB KT11 | 217 | L10 |
| Hare & Billet Rd BKHTH/KID SE3 | 161 | L8 |
| The Harebreaks WATN WD24 | 73 | H3 |
| Hare Ct EMB EC4Y * | 12 | A6 |
| Harecourt Rd IS N1 | 6 | E1 |
| Harecroft DORK RH4 | 273 | H5 |
| LHD/OX KT22 | 236 | A9 |
| Haredale Rd HNHL SE24 | 159 | K10 |
| Haredon Cl FSTH SE23 | 182 | B3 |
| Harefield ESH/CLAY KT10 | 198 | G2 |
| HLW CM20 | 29 | K10 |
| Harefield Av BELMT SM2 | 221 | H5 |
| Harefield Ms BROCKY SE4 | 160 | G9 |
| Harefield Pl STALE/WH AL4 | 39 | J5 |
| Harefield Rd BROCKY SE4 | 160 | G9 |
| CEND/HSY/T N8 | 118 | E3 |
| RKW/CH/CXG WD3 | 91 | N6 |
| SCUP DA14 | 185 | N5 |
| STRHM/NOR SW16 | 180 | G10 |
| UX/CGN UB8 | 131 | N1 |
| Hareland Cl WOKN/KNAP GU21 | 231 | P3 |
| Hare La CRAWW RH11 | 283 | H9 |
| ESH/CLAY KT10 | 218 | C3 |
| HAT AL10 | 40 | E6 |
| Hare Marsh BETH E2 * | 13 | N2 |
| Harendon KWD/TDW/WH KT20 | 238 | G7 |
| Harepark Cl HHW HP1 | 35 | J5 |
| Harepark Ct SAND/SEL CR2 | 223 | J4 |
| Hares Rw BETH E2 | 140 | A4 |
| Haresfield Rd DAGE RM10 | 144 | B1 |
| Harestone Dr CTHM CR3 | 241 | N10 |
| Harestone Hill CTHM CR3 | 259 | N10 |
| Harestone La CTHM CR3 | 259 | M10 |
| Harestone Valley Rd CTHM CR3 | 259 | N10 |
| Hare St HLWW/ROY CM19 | 46 | A1 |
| WOOL/PLUM SE18 | 162 | D2 |
| Hare Street Springs HLWW/ROY CM19 | 46 | A1 |
| Hare Ter WTHK RM20 * | 167 | J4 |
| Hare Wk IS N1 | 7 | K8 |
| Harewood ADL/WDHM KT15 | 233 | L1 |
| Harewood Av CAMTN NW1 | 9 | P1 |
| NTHLT UB5 | 133 | H4 |
| Harewood Cl CRAWE RH10 | 284 | B4 |
| NTHLT UB5 | 133 | H5 |
| REIG RH2 | 257 | M8 |
| Harewood Dr CLAY IG5 | 102 | C10 |
| Harewood Gdns SAND/SEL CR2 | 242 | A1 |
| Harewood Hl EPP CM16 | 83 | H1 |
| Harewood Pl CONDST W1S | 10 | E6 |
| SL SL1 | 148 | D1 |
| Harewood Rd BRWN CM15 | 86 | G10 |
| CSTG HP8 | 69 | P6 |
| ISLW TW7 | 154 | F6 |
| OXHEY WD19 | 93 | J3 |
| SAND/SEL CR2 | 223 | M3 |
| WIM/MER SW19 | 180 | D2 |
| Harewood Rw CAMTN NW1 | 9 | P3 |
| Harewood Ter NWDGN UB2 | 152 | G3 |
| Harfield Gdns CMBW SE5 | 159 | L9 |
| Harfield Rd SUN TW16 | 197 | L2 |
| Harford Cl CHING E4 | 87 | P10 |
| Harford Dr WAT WD17 | 72 | F4 |
| Harford Ms ARCH N19 | 118 | D3 |
| Harford Rd CHING E4 | 100 | C1 |
| Harford St WCHPL E1 | 141 | J6 |
| Harford Wk EFNCH N2 | 117 | N2 |
| Harfst Wy SWLY BR8 | 186 | G10 |
| Harglaze Ter CDALE/KGS NW9 * | 96 | B10 |
| Hargood Cl KTN/HRWW/WS HA3 | 115 | N2 |
| Hargood Rd BKHTH/KID SE3 | 162 | A1 |
| Hargrave Pk ARCH N19 | 118 | C2 |
| Hargrave Pl KTTN NW5 | 118 | C7 |
| Hargrave Rd ARCH N19 | 118 | C2 |
| Hargreaves Av CHESW EN7 | 62 | A4 |
| Hargreaves Cl CHESW EN7 | 62 | A3 |
| Hargwyne St BRXN/ST SW9 | 158 | F8 |
| Haringey Pk CEND/HSY/T N8 | 118 | E6 |
| Haringey Rd CEND/HSY/T N8 | 118 | E4 |
| Harington Ter UED N18 * | 99 | J5 |
| Harkett Cl KTN/HRWW/WS HA3 | 114 | G1 |
| Harkness CHESW EN7 | 62 | A5 |
| Harkness Cl EW KT17 | 238 | F2 |
| HARH RM3 | 105 | N6 |
| Harkness Rd BTFD TW8 * | 155 | J6 |
| Harland Av BFN/LL DA15 | 185 | H5 |
| CROY/NA CR0 | 203 | N10 |
| Harland Cl WIM/MER SW19 | 201 | L3 |
| Harland Rd LEE/GVPK SE12 | 183 | L1 |
| Harlands Gv ORP BR6 | 226 | E1 |
| Harlech Gdns HEST TW5 | 153 | K5 |
| PIN HA5 | 113 | K5 |
| Harlech Rd ABLGY WD5 | 51 | H4 |
| STHGT/OAK N14 | 98 | K5 |
| Harlequin Av BTFD TW8 | 155 | G8 |
| Harlequin Cl ISLW TW7 | 176 | D1 |
| YEAD UB4 | 133 | H5 |
| Harlequin Rd TEDD TW11 | 176 | D3 |
| The Harlequin WAT WD17 * | 5 | H4 |
| Harlescott Rd PECK SE15 | 160 | D4 |
| Harlesden Gdns WLSDN NW10 | 136 | G5 |
| Harlesden La WLSDN NW10 | 136 | G5 |
| Harlesden Rd HARH RM3 | 105 | M8 |
| WLSDN NW10 | 136 | G5 |
| Harleston Cl CLPT E5 * | 120 | E10 |
| Harley Cl ALP/SUD HA0 | 135 | L5 |
| Harley Crs HRW HA1 | 114 | C2 |
| Harleyford BMLY BR1 | 205 | K6 |
| Harleyford Rd LBTH SE11 | 17 | M5 |
| Harleyford St LBTH SE11 | 17 | M6 |
| Harley Gdns ORP BR6 | 227 | H4 |
| WBPTN SW10 | 15 | H5 |
| Harley Gv BOW E3 | 140 | C5 |
| Harley Pl CAVSQ/HST W1G | 10 | D4 |
| Harley Rd HAMP NW3 | 3 | M4 |
| HRW HA1 | 114 | C2 |
| WLSDN NW10 | 136 | F3 |
| Harley St CAVSQ/HST W1G | 10 | D3 |
| Harley Vis WLSDN NW10 * | 136 | F3 |
| Harlinger St WOOL/PLUM SE18 | 162 | A2 |
| The Harlings HERT/BAY SG13 | 24 | A5 |
| Harlington Cl HYS/HAR UB3 | 152 | A3 |
| Harlington Rd BXLYHN DA7 | 163 | P9 |
| UX/CGN UB8 | 132 | B5 |
| Harlington Rd East EBED/NFELT TW14 | 175 | J3 |
| Harlington Rd West EBED/NFELT TW14 | 175 | J3 |
| Harlow Common HLWE CM17 | 47 | N4 |
| Harlow Ct HHNE HP2 | 35 | P4 |
| Harlow Gdns CRW RM5 | 104 | D7 |
| Harlow Rd CHONG CM5 | 65 | N9 |
| HLWE CM17 | 30 | D8 |
| HLWW/ROY CM19 | 27 | P10 |
| PLMGR N13 | 99 | L4 |
| RAIN RM13 | 144 | C3 |
| RBSF CM22 | 30 | C4 |
| SBW CM21 | 29 | N3 |
| Harlyn Dr PIN HA5 | 113 | J1 |
| Harman Av GVW DA11 | 190 | G8 |
| WFD IG8 | 101 | L8 |
| Harman Cl CRICK NW2 | 117 | J8 |
| STHWK SE1 | 19 | N9 |
| Harman Dr BFN/LL DA15 | 167 | H3 |
| CRICK NW2 | 117 | J8 |
| Harman Pl PUR/KEN CR8 | 223 | J7 |
| Harman Rd EN EN1 | 84 | C2 |
| Harmer St GVE DA12 | 191 | N9 |
| Harmondsworth La WDR/YW UB7 | 151 | P5 |
| Harmondsworth Rd WDR/YW UB7 | 151 | P2 |
| Harmony Cl CRAWW RH11 | 283 | H9 |
| HAT AL10 | 40 | D2 |
| WLGTN SM6 | 222 | F5 |
| Harmony Pl STHWK SE1 | 19 | M7 |
| Harmony Wy BMLY BR1 | 205 | M2 |
| HDN NW4 | 116 | F2 |
| Harmood Gv CAMTN NW1 * | 4 | E3 |
| Harmood St CAMTN NW1 | 4 | E3 |
| Harms Gv RGUE GU4 | 250 | F7 |
| Harmsworth Ms STHWK SE1 | 18 | C8 |
| Harmsworth St WALW SE17 | 18 | C8 |
| Harmsworth Wy TRDG/WHET N20 | 97 | J2 |
| Harness Rd THMD SE28 | 163 | K1 |
| Harness Wy STALE/WH AL4 | 39 | J3 |
| Harnetts Cl SWLY BR8 | 208 | E7 |
| Haroldstone Rd WALTH E17 | 122 | D1 |
| Harold Av BELV DA17 | 164 | A4 |
| HYS/HAR UB3 | 152 | G2 |
| Harold Cl HLWW/ROY CM19 | 46 | C2 |
| Harold Court Rd HARH RM3 | 106 | B4 |
| Harold Crs WAB EN9 | 63 | H8 |
| Harold Rd CEND/HSY/T N8 | 118 | G5 |
| CHING E4 | 101 | H4 |
| CRAWE RH10 | 284 | F8 |
| NRWD SE19 | 181 | L10 |
| PLSTW E13 | 141 | L10 |
| SEVS/STOTM N15 | 119 | M1 |
| SUT SM1 | 221 | N1 |
| SWFD E18 | 102 | B5 |
| WAN E11 | 121 | M9 |
| WLSDN NW10 | 136 | A5 |
| Harold Vw HARH RM3 | 105 | N10 |
| Harpenden Rd MNPK E12 | 121 | P7 |
| STALE/WH AL4 | 20 | C3 |
| STALW/RED AL3 | 38 | C1 |
| WNWD SE27 | 181 | J3 |
| Harper Cl CDW/CHF RM16 | 167 | H4 |
| La RAD WD7 | 56 | F7 |
| Harper Rd EHAM E6 | 142 | C8 |
| STHWK SE1 | 19 | H2 |
| Harpers La RBRW CM15 | 87 | J3 |
| Harpers Yd ISLW TW7 * | 154 | E8 |
| Harpesford Av VW GU25 | 193 | P5 |
| Harp Island Cl WLSDN NW10 | 115 | P1 |
| Harpley Sq WCHPL E1 | 140 | E5 |
| Harpour Rd BARK IG11 | 142 | F1 |
| Harpsden St BTSEA SW11 | 158 | A7 |
| Harpsfield Broadway HAT AL10 | 40 | C3 |
| Harps Oak La REDH RH1 | 258 | A1 |
| Harpswood Cl COUL/CHIP CR5 | 258 | D8 |
| Harptree Wy STALW/RED AL3 | 38 | E4 |
| Harpur Ms BMSBY WC1N | 11 | N3 |
| Harpurs KWD/TDW/WH KT20 | 238 | G7 |
| Harpur St BMSBY WC1N | 11 | N3 |
| Harraden Rd BKHTH/KID SE3 | 161 | P7 |
| Harrap Cha GRAYS RM17 | 167 | L4 |
| Harrier Cl HCH RM12 | 143 | P1 |
| Harrier Ms THMD SE28 | 162 | G1 |
| Harriers Cl EA W5 | 135 | K5 |
| Harrier Wy EHAM E6 | 142 | E7 |
| WAB EN9 | 63 | M10 |
| Harries Cl CSHM HP5 | 50 | G6 |
| Harriescourt WAB EN9 | 63 | K8 |
| Harriet Cl HACK E8 | 7 | N5 |
| Harriet Gdns CROY/NA CR0 | 203 | P10 |
| Harriet St KTBR SW1X | 16 | A2 |
| Harriet Tubman Cl BRXS/STRHM SW2 | 181 | H3 |
| Harriet Wk KTBR SW1X | 16 | A2 |
| Harriet Walker Wy RKW/CH/CXG WD3 | 91 | J8 |
| Harriet Wy BUSH WD23 | 94 | C1 |
| Harringay Gdns CEND/HSY/T N8 | 119 | J4 |
| Harringay Rd SEVS/STOTM N15 | 119 | J3 |
| Harrington Cl CROY/NA CR0 | 202 | F2 |
| REIG RH2 | 275 | L1 |
| WLSDN NW10 | 115 | N9 |
| Harrington Ct NKENS W10 * | 2 | C9 |
| Harrington Crs CDW/CHF RM16 | 147 | J10 |
| Harrington Gdns SKENS SW7 | 15 | H6 |
| Harrington Hl CLPT E5 | 120 | A6 |
| Harrington Rd SKENS SW7 | 14 | G5 |
| SNWD SE25 | 202 | B4 |
| WAN E11 | 121 | K4 |
| Harrington Sq CAMTN NW1 | 4 | G7 |
| Harrington St CAMTN NW1 | 4 | F8 |
| Harriott Cl GNWCH SE10 | 161 | K3 |
| Harriotts Cl ASHTD KT21 | 237 | H5 |
| Harriotts La ASHTD KT21 | 237 | H6 |
| Harris Cl CRAWW RH11 | 283 | J10 |
| ENC/FH EN2 | 79 | J8 |
| GVW DA11 | 191 | H8 |
| HARH RM3 | 105 | M8 |
| HSLW TW5 | 154 | C5 |
| Harris Gdns SL SL1 | 149 | H1 |
| Harris La RAD WD7 | 57 | M10 |
| Harrison Cl NTHWD HA6 | 32 | A9 |
| REIG RH2 | 275 | L1 |
| TRDG/WHET N20 | 97 | H4 |
| Harrison Rd DAGE RM10 | 144 | C1 |
| WLSDN NW10 | 136 | D1 |
| Harrison's Ri CROY/NA CR0 | 203 | J1 |
| Harrison St STPAN WC1H | 5 | M9 |
| Harrisons Whf PUR RM19 | 165 | P9 |
| Harris Rd BXLYHN DA7 | 163 | P9 |
| DAGW RM9 | 124 | A10 |
| GSTN WD25 | 73 | J1 |
| Harris St CMBW SE5 | 159 | L6 |
| WALTH E17 | 120 | C5 |
| Harris Wy SUN TW16 | 196 | A9 |
| Harrods On EDGW HA8 | 95 | M6 |
| Harrogate Ct DTCH/LGLY SL3 | 150 | D4 |
| Harrogate Rd OXHEY WD19 | 93 | K4 |
| Harrold Rd BCTR RM8 | 123 | L10 |
| Harrow Av EN EN1 | 79 | N10 |
| Harroway Rd BTSEA SW11 | 157 | N9 |
| Harrowband Rd HLWE CM17 | 30 | D8 |
| Harrow Bottom Rd VW GU25 | 195 | K6 |
| Harrowby Gdns GVW DA11 | 190 | D5 |
| Harrowby St MBLAR W1H | 9 | P5 |
| Harrowdene Cl ALP/SUD HA0 | 115 | J9 |
| Harrowdene Gdns TEDD TW11 | 176 | F10 |
| Harrowdene Rd ALP/SUD HA0 | 115 | J9 |
| Harrow Dr ED N9 | 99 | N2 |
| EMPK RM11 | 125 | K5 |
| Harrowes Meade EDGW HA8 | 95 | M4 |
| Harrow Fields Gdns HRW HA1 | 114 | E7 |
| Harrow Gdns ORP BR6 | 227 | L1 |
| WARL CR6 | 242 | E2 |
| Harrowgate Rd HOM E9 | 140 | D1 |
| Harrow Gn WAN E11 | 121 | K6 |
| Harrowlands Pk DORK RH4 | 272 | G3 |
| Harrow La GODL GU7 | 267 | K8 |
| POP/IOD E14 | 141 | H9 |
| Harrow Manor Wy ABYW SE2 | 163 | H10 |
| Harrow Pk HRW HA1 | 114 | D6 |
| Harrow Pl WCHPL E1 | 13 | K5 |
| Harrow Rd ALP/SUD HA0 | 114 | F9 |
| CAR SM5 | 221 | P5 |
| DTCH/LGLY SL3 | 150 | C2 |
| EBED/NFELT TW14 | 174 | B4 |
| IL IG1 | 122 | F9 |
| NKENS W10 | 2 | B1 |
| RSEV TN14 | 245 | P7 |
| UPMR RM14 | 121 | P10 |
| WAN E11 | 121 | L8 |
| WBLY HA9 | 115 | M10 |
| WLSDN NW10 | 136 | G5 |
| Harrow Road East DORK RH4 | 272 | G4 |
| Harrow Road F/O BAY/PAD W2 * | 9 | M4 |
| Harrow View HGDN/ICK UB10 | 132 | D5 |
| Harrow View Rd EA W5 | 134 | G6 |
| Harrow Wy OXHEY WD19 | 93 | M4 |
| SHPTN TW17 | 196 | D2 |
| Harrow Weald Pk KTN/HRWW/WS HA3 | 94 | C7 |
| Harry Cl THHTH CR7 | 202 | G6 |
| Harston Dr PEND EN3 | 80 | F4 |
| Hartcliff Ct HNWL W7 * | 154 | E1 |
| Hart Cl REDH RH1 | 259 | H9 |
| Hart Crs CHIG IG7 | 103 | K6 |
| Hartcroft Cl HHS/BOV HP3 | 36 | C7 |
| Hart Dyke Rd STMC/STPC BR5 | 207 | M9 |
| SWLY BR8 | 208 | E3 |
| Harte Rd HSLW TW3 | 153 | N8 |
| Hartfield Av BORE WD6 | 75 | M8 |
| NTHLT UB5 | 133 | H4 |
| Hartfield Cl BORE WD6 | 75 | M9 |
| Hartfield Crs WIM/MER SW19 | 179 | J10 |
| WWKM BR4 | 204 | G10 |
| Hartfield Gv PGE/AN SE20 | 182 | F4 |
| Hartfield Pl GVW DA11 | 190 | A5 |
| Hartfield Rd CHSGTN KT9 | 219 | J2 |
| WIM/MER SW19 | 179 | J9 |
| WWKM BR4 | 205 | M1 |
| Hartfield Ter BOW E3 | 140 | F2 |
| Hartford Av KTN/HRWW/WS HA3 | 114 | F1 |
| Hartforde Rd BORE WD6 | 75 | M6 |
| Hartford Rd BXLY DA5 | 186 | B2 |
| EW KT19 | 219 | N8 |
| HOR/WEW KT19 | 219 | N8 |
| Hart Gdns DORK RH4 | 272 | G4 |
| Hart Gv EA W5 | 135 | N6 |
| STHL UB1 | 133 | P7 |
| Harthall La KGLGY WD4 | 54 | C4 |
| Hartham Cl HOLWY N7 | 118 | F10 |
| ISLW TW7 | 154 | F7 |
| Hartham Common HERT/WAT SG14 | 25 | L4 |
| Hartham Rd HOLWY N7 | 118 | E10 |
| ISLW TW7 | 154 | F7 |
| TOTM N17 | 99 | P10 |
| Harting Ct CRAWW RH11 | 283 | J10 |
| Harting Rd ELTH/MOT SE9 | 184 | B7 |
| Hartington Cl HRW HA1 | 114 | D9 |
| ORP BR6 | 226 | F2 |
| REIG RH2 | 275 | M3 |
| Hartington Pl REIG RH2 | 257 | P6 |
| Hartington Rd CAN/RD E16 | 141 | N8 |
| CHSWK W4 | 155 | N6 |
| NWDGN UB2 | 152 | B1 |
| TWK TW1 | 176 | C6 |
| VX/NE SW8 | 17 | N9 |
| WALTH E17 | 120 | D4 |
| WEA W13 | 134 | G4 |
| Hartismere Rd FUL/PGN SW6 | 157 | J5 |
| Hartlake Rd HOM E9 | 140 | C1 |
| Hartland Cl ADL/WDHM KT15 | 215 | M6 |
| EDGW HA8 | 95 | J1 |
| SL SL1 | 129 | J10 |
| WCHMH N21 | 79 | M1 |
| Hartland Dr EDGW HA8 | 95 | J1 |
| RSLP HA4 | 113 | J8 |
| Hartland Rd ADL/WDHM KT15 | 215 | K4 |
| CAMTN NW1 | 4 | E3 |
| CHES/WCR EN8 | 62 | C6 |
| EPP CM16 | 65 | K7 |
| FBAR/BDGN N11 | 98 | A6 |
| HCH RM12 | 125 | L5 |
| HPTN TW12 | 176 | A7 |
| ISLW TW7 | 154 | F9 |
| KIL/WHAMP NW6 | 2 | C4 |
| MRDN SM4 | 201 | K7 |
| SRTFD E15 | 141 | L2 |
| Hartland Road Arches CAMTN NW1 * | 4 | D3 |
| Hartlands Cl BXLY DA5 | 186 | A2 |
| The Hartlands HEST TW5 | 153 | H4 |
| Hartland Wy CROY/NA CR0 | 204 | D9 |
| MRDN SM4 | 201 | J7 |
| Hartley Av EHAM E6 | 142 | B3 |
| MLHL NW7 | 96 | G1 |
| Hartley Bottom Rd HART DA3 | 211 | N8 |
| Hartley Cl BMLY BR1 | 206 | C2 |
| MLHL NW7 | 96 | G1 |
| Hartley Copse WDSR SL4 | 171 | N2 |
| Hartley Down PUR/KEN CR8 | 222 | G10 |
| Hartley Farm PUR/KEN CR8 | 240 | G1 |
| Hartley Hl PUR/KEN CR8 | 240 | G1 |
| Hartley Old Rd PUR/KEN CR8 | 240 | G1 |
| Hartley Rd BH/WHM TN16 | 162 | K1 |
| CROY/NA CR0 | 203 | K7 |
| WAN E11 | 121 | L6 |
| WELL DA16 | 148 | A7 |
| Hartley St BETH E2 | 140 | E5 |
| Hartley Wy PUR/KEN CR8 | 240 | G1 |
| Hartmann Rd CAN/RD E16 | 142 | A10 |
| Hartmoor Ms PEND EN3 | 81 | J2 |
| Hartnoll St HOLWY N7 | 118 | F10 |
| Harton Cl BMLY BR1 | 184 | C10 |
| Harton Rd ED N9 | 99 | H5 |
| Harton St DEPT SE8 | 160 | L2 |
| Hart Rd BF/WBF KT14 | 215 | P6 |
| DORK RH4 | 272 | G4 |
| Hartsbourne Av BUSH WD23 | 94 | B3 |

**Column 1**

Hartsbourne Cl BUSH WD23 94 C3
Hartsbourne Rd BUSH WD23 94 C3
Hartsbourne Wy HHNE HP2 36 D7
Harts Cl BUSH WD23 73 P6
Harts Gv GUW GU2 249 N7
Hart Shaw HART DA3 211 P2
Hartshill Cl HGDN/ICK UB10 132 B1
Hartshill Rd HGDN/ICK UB10 190 C5
Hartshorn Gdns EHAM E6 142 D6
Hartsland Rd SEV TN13 247 K9
Hart's La BARK IG11 142 E2
Hart's La NWCR SE14 160 D6
Hartslock Dr ABYW SE2 163 K1
Hartsmead Rd ELTH/MOT SE9 184 C5
Hartspiece Rd REDH RH1 276 B9
Hartspring La GSTN WD25 73 P6
Harts St MRDN SM4 * 201 L5
Hart St BRW CM14 107 P4
  MON EC3R 13 H7
Hartsway PEND EN3 80 A2
Hartswood RDKG RH5 273 P3
Hartswood Av REIG RH2 275 K4
Hartswood Cl BRW CM14 107 K5
  BUSH WD23 73 P6
Hartswood Gdns SHB W12 * 156 C2
Hartswood Gn BUSH WD23 94 C3
Hartswood Rd BRW CM14 107 K5
  SHB W12 156 C1
Hartsworth Cl PLSTW E13 141 L4
Hartville Rd WOOL/PLUM SE18 163 H3
Hartwell Cl BRXS/STRHM SW2 180 A3
Hartwell Dr BEAC HP9 88 C9
  CHING E4 101 J5
Hartwell St HACK E8 * 7 L1
Harty Cl CDW/CHF RM16 147 N10
Harvard Hl CHSWK W4 155 N4
Harvard Rd CHSWK W4 155 N4
  ISLW TW7 154 D7
  LEW SE13 183 H1
Harvel Cl CHST BR7 207 K3
Harvel Crs ABYW SE2 163 N4
Harvest Bank AMS HP6 50 B10
Harvest Ct STALE/WH AL4 39 K4
Harvest End GSTN WD25 73 L2
Harvester Cl ISLW TW7 176 C1
Harvesters Ms STALE/WH AL4 * 39 J2
Harvest La LOU IG10 102 A1
  THDIT KT7 198 F6
Harvest Md HAT AL10 40 E3
Harvest Rd BUSH WD23 74 A8
  CRAWE RH10 284 D9
  ECH TW20 171 P8
  FELT TW13 175 H7
Harvestside HORL RH6 280 E10
Harvey CDW/CHF RM16 167 N1
Harvey Dr HPTN TW12 198 A4
Harveyfields WAB EN9 63 H10
Harvey Gdns CHARL SE7 161 P4
  GU GU1 * 268 B1
  LOU IG10 82 A7
Harvey Rd CEND/HSY/T N8 118 C2
  CMBW SE5 159 L7
  GU GU1 268 B2
  HGDN/ICK UB10 175 N3
  HSLWW TW4 175 H5
  IL IG1 122 E10
  LCOL/BKTW AL2 57 H7
  NTHLT UB5 133 K2
  RKW/CH/CXG WD3 72 B10
  WAN E11 141 K3
  WOT/HER KT12 197 H7
Harvey's La ROMW/RG RM7 124 F2
Harvey St IS N1 7 H6
Harvill Rd SCUP DA14 185 N8
Harvil Rd DEN/HRF UB9 111 M2
Harvington Wk HACK E8 * 7 J1
Harwater Dr LOU IG10 82 C6
Harwell Cl RSLP HA4 112 B4
Harwich Rd SL SL1 128 F8
Harwood Av BMLY BR1 205 N8
  EMPK RM11 125 M1
  MTCM CR4 194 A1
Harwood Cl ALP/SUD HA0 115 J9
  NFNCH/WDSPK N12 97 P7
  WCCW AL8 23 P3
  WLYN AL6 23 P1
Harwood Dr HGDN/ICK UB10 132 A3
Harwood Gdns WDSR SL4 171 N3
Harwood Hall La UPMR RM14 146 A1
Harwood Hl WGCW AL8 23 H2
Harwood Ms FUL/PGN SW6 * 157 L6
Harwood Pk REDH RH1 276 B9
Harwood Rd FUL/PGN SW6 157 L6
Harwoods Rd WATW WD18 13 L7
Harwood Ter CMBW SE5 * 159 L7
Hasedines Rd HHW HP1 35 K5
Haselbury Rd UED N18 99 M5
Haseldine Mdw HAT AL10 40 C5
Haseldine Rd LCOL/BKTW AL2 57 J2
Haseley End FSTH SE23 * 182 B3
Haselrigge Rd CLAP SW4 158 E10
Haseltine Rd SYD SE26 182 G7
Haskard Rd DAGW RM9 123 J1
Hasker St CHEL SW3 15 P5
Haslam Av CHEAM SM3 201 H8
Haslam Cl HGDN/ICK UB10 112 D7
  IS N1 6 B3
Haslam St PECK SE15 159 N7
Haslemere Av EBAR EN4 98 A7
  HDN NW4 116 C4
  HEST TW5 153 K6
  HNWL W7 154 F2
  MTCM CR4 201 N2
  WAND/EARL SW18 179 L10
  WLGTN SM6 222 F9
Haslemere Gdns FNCH N3 117 J1
Haslemere Heathrow Est HSLWW TW4 * 153 J8
Haslemere Rd BXLYHN DA7 164 A6
  CEND/HSY/T N8 118 A5
  GDMY/SEVK IG3 123 J2
  THHTH CR7 203 J5
  WCHMH N21 99 J3
Hasler Cl THMD SE28 148 B3
Haslett Av CRAWE RH10 284 F4
Haslett Av East CRAWE RH10 284 F5
Haslett Av West CRAWE RH10 283 N6
Haslett Rd SHPTN TW17 196 F2
Haslewood Av HOD EN11 44 F2
Hasluck Gdns BAR EN5 77 N10
Hassard St BETH E2 7 M8
Hassendean Rd BKHTH/KID SE3 161 N5
Hassocks Cl SYD SE26 182 A6
Hassocks Rd STRHM/NOR SW16 202 E1
Hassop Rd CRICK NW2 116 B6
Hassop Wk ELTH/MOT SE9 * 184 E1
Hasted Cl SWCM DA10 190 F7
Hasted Rd CHARL SE7 162 A4
Hastings Av BARK/HLT IG6 122 F2
Hastings Cl ALP/SUD HA0 115 J9
  BAR EN5 80 D3
  GRAYS RM17 167 K5
  PECK SE15 * 160 A5
Hastings Dr SURB KT6 199 J6
Hastings Gdns CROY/NA CRO 203 H8
  FBAR/BDGN N11 98 E10
  GPK RM2 125 J6
  HAYES BR2 206 B8

**Column 2**

  TOTM N17 * 119 L1
  WEA W13 134 G9
Hastings Ter SEVS/STOTM N15 * 119 K3
Hastings Wy BUSH WD23 73 M8
  RKW/CH/CXG WD3 72 C1
Hastingwood Rd HLWE CM17 47 J8
Hastings Vls WOOL/PLUM SE18 162 F2
Hastoe Gt YEAD UB4 133 M6
Hatcham Park Ms NWCR SE14 160 C7
Hatcham Park Rd NWCR SE14 160 C7
Hatcham Rd PECK SE15 160 B5
Hatchard Rd ARCH N19 118 C7
Hatch Cl ADL/WDHM KT15 195 L10
Hatchcroft HDN NW4 116 E1
Hatch End BFOR GU20 212 B3
Hatchers Ms STHWK SE1 19 K2
Hatchet La WDSR SL4 170 A6
Hatchett Rd EBED/NFELT TW14 174 D7
Hatch Gdns KWD/TDW/WH KT20 238 G10
Hatchgate RDKG RH5 274 B1
Hatchgate Gdns SL SL1 128 C5
Hatch La BNSTD SM7 240 A1
  CHING E4 101 J5
  REDH RH1 276 C6
  RPLY/SEND GU23 253 J6
  WDSR SL4 151 N6
  WDSR SL4 148 F9
Hatch Pl KUTN/CMB KT2 177 L10
Hatch Rd BRWN CM15 86 P9
  STRHM/NOR SW16 202 F2
Hatch Side CHIG IG7 102 D6
The Hatch PEND EN3 80 C5
  WDSR SL4 148 B6
Hatchwoods WFD IG8 101 L5
Hatcliffe Cl BKHTH/KID SE3 161 J5
Hatcliffe St GNWCH SE10 161 L4
Hatfield Av HAT AL10 40 B1
Hatfield Cl BARK/HLT IG6 122 F1
  BELMT SM2 221 K5
  BF/WBF KT14 * 215 L8
  HCH RM12 125 L10
  MTCM CR4 * 201 N4
Hatfield Crs HHNE HP2 36 A2
Hatfield Ms DAGW RM9 141 P2
  WALTH E17 120 C2
Hatherleigh Gdns POTB/CUF EN6 59 J4
Hatherleigh Rd RSLP HA4 113 H1
Hatherleigh Wy HARH RM3 105 L9
Hatherley Crs BFN/LL DA15 185 K5
Hatherley Gdns EA W5 155 K2
  EHAM E6 142 A1
Hatherley Gv BAY/PAD W2 8 C5
Hatherley Ms WALTH E17 120 F2
Hatherley Rd RCH/KEW TW9 155 M5
  SCUP DA14 185 K6
  WALTH E17 120 C2
Hatherley St WEST SW1P 17 H6
Hathern Gdns ELTH/MOT SE9 184 D7
Hatherop Rd HPTN TW12 175 N10
Hathersham Cl HORL RH6 281 H3
Hathersham La HORL RH6 281 H2
Hatherwood LHD/OX KT22 237 J6
Hathorne Cl PECK SE15 160 A8
Hathorne Ter ARCH N19 * 118 E6
Hathway St PECK SE15 160 C7
Hatley Av BARK/HLT IG6 122 F2
Hatley Cl FBAR/BDGN N11 98 A9
Hatley Rd FSBYPK N4 118 F8
Hat & Mitre St FARR EC1M 12 D2
Hatteraick St BERM/RHTH SE16 160 E1
Hatters La WATW WD18 13 J4
Hatton Av SLN SL2 129 J6
Hatton Cl CDW/CHF RM16 167 M1
  WOOL/PLUM SE18 163 M3
Hatton Cross Est HTHAIR TW6 152 G10
Hatton Gdns HCIRC EC1N 12 A2
  MTCM CR4 202 A5
Hatton Gn EBED/NFELT TW14 153 P10
Hatton Hl BFOR GU20 212 B2
Hatton Pl HCIRC EC1N 12 A2
Hatton Rd CROY/NA CRO 203 H7
  EBED/NFELT TW14 173 M3
Hatton Rw STJWD NW8 9 M2
Hatton St STJWD NW8 9 M2
Hatton Wall HCIRC EC1N 12 A3
Haunch of Venison Yd OXSTW W1C * 10 E6
Havana Rd WIM/MER SW19 178 A5
Havannah St POP/IOD E14 160 E4
Havant Rd WALTH E17 121 J1
Havelock Cl SHB W12 * 136 E10
Havelock Pl HRW HA1 114 D4
Havelock Rd BELV DA17 165 H5
  CROY/NA CRO 203 P5
  GVW DA11 190 E7
  KGLGY WD4 54 A5
  KTN/HRWW/WS HA3 114 E5
  NWDGN UB2 153 H3
  TOTM N17 99 P9
  WIM/MER SW19 178 C7
Haven Cl BRYLDS KT5 * 199 N9
Havenhurst Ri ENC/FH EN2 79 M1
Haven La EA W5 135 L5
Haven Pl CDW/CHF RM16 167 N1
Havens Ms BOW E3 140 E3
Haven St CAMTN NW1 * 4 B1
Havenswood Ct KUTN/CMB KT2 177 N9
The Haven CDW/CHF RM16 168 C3

**Column 3**

  RCH/KEW TW9 155 M9
Havenwood WBLY HA9 115 N3
Havercroft Cl STALW/RED AL3 38 A3
Haverfield Est BTFD TW8 155 K5
Haverfield Gdns RCH/KEW TW9 155 M6
Haverfield Rd BOW E3 140 D5
Haverford Wy EDGW HA8 95 N5
Havergal Vls SEVS/STOTM N15 * 119 J2
Haverhill Rd BAL SW12 180 A3
  CHING E4 101 H2
Havering Dr ROM RM1 124 F2
Havering Gdns CHDH RM6 123 M3
Havering Rd ROM RM1 104 D10
Havering St WCHPL E1 140 C8
Havers Av WOT/HER KT12 197 L2
Haversham Cl CRAWE RH10 284 A7
  TWK TW1 * 177 J3
Haversham Pl HGT N6 117 P8
Haverstock Hl HAMP NW3 3 P1
Haverstock Pl FSBYE EC1V * 6 B7
Haverstock Rd KTTN NW5 118 B10
Haverstock St IS N1 6 D8
Haverthwaite Rd ORP BR6 206 G10
Havil St CMBW SE5 159 M7
Havisham Pl NRWD SE19 181 M8
Havisham Rd GPK RM2 124 K1
Hawarden Gv HNHL SE24 181 K5
Hawarden Hl CRICK NW2 116 D8
Hawarden Rd CTHM CR3 241 K7
  WALTH E17 120 C2
Haward Rd HOD EN11 45 H1
Hawbridge Rd WAN E11 121 J6
Hawes Cl NTHWD HA6 92 G8
Hawes La CHING E4 81 H4
  HAYES BR2 205 N1
  KWD/TDW/WH KT20 238 G6
Hawes St IS N1 6 C1
Haweswater Dr GSTN WD25 55 K9
Hawfield Bank ORP BR6 207 M10
Hawfield Gdns LCOL/BKTW AL2 56 C7
Hawgood St BOW E3 140 F7
Hawk Cl WAB EN9 63 M10
Hawkdene CHING E4 101 M1
Hawkenbury HLWW/ROY CM19 46 D3
Hawke Park Rd WDGN N22 119 J3
Hawke Pl BERM/RHTH SE16 * 160 C1
Hawke Rd NRWD SE19 181 L9
Hawker Pl WALTH E17 101 H10
Hawker Rd CROY/NA CRO 222 A1
Hawkesbury Cl BARK/HLT IG6 103 L5
Hawkesbury Rd PUT/ROE SW15 178 L1
Hawkes Cl GTCH/LGLY SL3 150 E2
  GRAYS RM17 167 N5
Hawkesfield Rd FSTH SE23 182 D5
Hawkesley Cl TWK TW1 176 F7
Hawkesley Ct RAD WD7 74 F1
Hawkesmoor Rd CRAWW RH11 283 H9
Hawkes Rd EBED/NFELT TW14 173 N5
  MTCM CR4 194 A9
Hawkewood Rd SUN TW16 197 H3
Hawkhirst Rd PUR/KEN CR8 241 L2
Hawkhurst Rd STRHM/NOR SW16 180 E10
Hawkhurst Wk CRAWE RH10 284 C9
Hawkhurst Wy NWMAL KT3 192 B3
  WWKM BR4 204 C9
Hawkins Av GVE DA12 191 K1
Hawkins Cl BORE WD6 75 P6
  EDGW HA8 96 A4
  HRW HA1 114 C5
Hawkins Dr CDW/CHF RM16 167 J1
Hawkins Rd CRAWE RH10 283 P9
  TEDD TW11 174 B2
Hawkins Wy CAT SE6 182 E9
Hawkley Gdns WNWD SE27 181 J5
Hawkridge Cl CHDH RM6 123 N4
Hawkridge Dr GRAYS RM17 168 A4
Hawksbrook La BECK BR3 204 B5
Hawkshaw Cl BRXS/STRHM SW2 180 A1
Hawkshead Cl BMLY BR1 183 K10
Hawkshead La BRKMPK AL9 59 H1
Hawkshead Rd CHSWK W4 156 B2
  POTB/CUF EN6 59 K5
  WLSDN NW10 136 C1
Hawkslade Rd PECK SE15 182 C1
Hawksley Rd STNW/STAM N16 119 N9
Hawksmead Cl PEND EN3 80 C2
Hawks Ms GNWCH SE10 * 161 L6
Hawksmoor Cl EHAM E6 144 B2
  WOOL/PLUM SE18 163 N4
Hawksmoor Ms WCHPL E1 140 D9
Hawksmoor St HMSMTH W6 156 G5
Hawksmouth CHING E4 100 G1
Hawkstone Est BERM/RHTH SE16 160 A3
Hawkstone Rd BERM/RHTH SE16 160 A3
Hawksview COB KT11 217 N10
Hawksway STA TW18 173 J6
Hawkswell WOKN/KNAP GU21 231 L3
Hawkswood Gv DTCH/LGLY SL3 130 C1
Hawkswood La DTCH/LGLY SL3 110 C10
Hawkwell Wk IS N1 * 6 F1
Hawkwood Crs CHING E4 80 G10
Hawkwood Dell GT/LBKH KT23 253 P2
Hawkwood La CHST BR7 205 K3
Hawkwood Mt CLPT E5 120 D6
Hawkwood Rd GT/LBKH KT23 253 P2
Hawlands Dr PIN HA5 113 M5
Hawley Cl HPTN TW12 175 H9
Hawley Crs CAMTN NW1 4 B1
Hawley Ms CAMTN NW1 * 4 B1
Hawley Rd CAMTN NW1 4 B1
  UED N18 100 C5
Hawley St CAMTN NW1 4 B1
Hawley Ter RDART DA2 * 187 P2
Hawley Vw ASHF TW15 174 B8
Haworth Rd CRAWE RH10 284 C6
Hawstead Cl ORP BR6 228 A2
Hawstead La ORP BR6 228 A3
Hawstead Rd CAT SE6 182 A2
Hawsted BKHH IG9 101 H1
Hawth Cl CRAWE RH10 284 E6
Hawthorn Av BCTR RM8 123 N8
  CAR SM5 222 C1
  PLMGR N13 98 H6
  RYNPK SW20 * 192 G1
  THHTH CR7 181 P9

**Column 4**

  THHTH CR7 203 J1
Hawthorn Cl ABLGY WD5 54 C3
  BNSTD SM7 221 N10
  CRAWW RH11 283 M4
  CVE DA12 * 190 E7
  HARP AL5 20 C7
  HEST TW5 153 H4
  HPTN TW12 175 H5
  IVER SL0 130 F5
  REDH RH1 276 B5
  STMC/STPC BR5 207 K5
  WAT WD17 72 A2
  WOKS/MYFD GU22 232 B6
Hawthorn Crs SAND/SEL CR2 224 D7
  TOOT SW17 180 B9
Hawthornden Cl NFNCH/WDSPK N12 97 P7
Hawthornden Gdns EDGW HA8 96 A4
Hawthorndene Cl HAYES BR2 205 L9
Hawthorndene Rd HAYES BR2 205 L10
Hawthorn Dr DEN/HRF UB9 131 M1
  RYLN/HDSTN HA2 113 P7
  WWKM BR4 225 K1
Hawthorne Av BRH/WHM TN16 244 A3
  BOW E3 140 E3
  CAR SM5 222 B4
  CHESW EN7 62 A1
  KTN/HRWW/WS HA3 114 F4
  MTCM CR4 201 N2
  RSLP HA4 113 J4
  WDSR SL4 170 A5
Hawthorne Cl BMLY BR1 206 C3
  CHESW EN7 62 A1
  IS N1 7 J1
Hawthorne Ct STWL/WRAY TW19 173 N3
Hawthorne Crs SL SL1 129 K8
  WDR/YW UB7 152 A1
Hawthorne Gv CDALE/KGS NW9 115 P5
Hawthorne Pl EW KT17 220 D8
  HYS/HAR UB3 133 H7
Hawthorne Rd BMLY BR1 206 C3
  RAD WD7 56 F10
  STA TW18 172 F8
  UED N17 99 N9
  WALTH E17 120 F1
Hawthorner Rd RDART DA2 187 N6
Hawthorne Wy ED N9 99 N5
  STWL/WRAY TW19 173 N3
Hawthorn Farm Av NTHLT UB5 133 M3
Hawthorn Gdns EA W5 155 M3
Hawthorn Gv ENC/FH EN2 79 L4
  PGE/AN SE20 182 E10
Hawthorn Hatch BTFD TW8 154 G6
Hawthorn La HHW HP1 35 L1
  SEV TN13 246 G8
  SLN SL2 128 E2
Hawthorn Ms MLHL NW7 97 H6
Hawthorn Pk SWLY BR8 209 H2
Hawthorn Pl ERITH DA8 164 D8
Hawthorn Rd BFN/LL DA15 185 J2
  BTFD TW8 154 F6
  BXLYHS DA6 * 164 A10
  CEND/HSY/T N8 118 C1
  FELT TW13 175 H6
  HOD EN11 44 C1
  RPLY/SEND GU23 233 J10
  SUT SM1 222 A3
  WDGN N22 99 J10
  WLGTN SM6 222 C6
  WLSDN NW10 136 D2
  WOKS/MYFD GU22 232 A6
Hawthorns HART DA3 211 L4
  HLWS CM18 47 J5
  WFD IG8 102 A2
The Hawthorns BERK HP4 33 M4
  CSTG HP8 69 P6
  DTCH/LGLY SL3 151 P2
  EW KT17 220 C3
  HHS/BOV HP3 35 J10
  OXTED RH8 261 M9
  RKW/CH/CXG WD3 90 C10
Hawthorn Ter BFN/LL DA15 185 H2
  WEY KT13 * 216 B7
Hawthorn Wk NKENS W10 8 A5
Hawthorn Wy ADL/WDHM KT15 215 L6
  CHOB/PIR GU24 230 F2
  CSHM HP5 51 J5
  LCOL/BKTW AL2 37 H10
  REDH RH1 276 C2
  SHPTN TW17 196 E4
Hawtrees RAD WD7 74 E1
Hawtrey Av NTHLT UB5 133 L4
Hawtrey Cl SL SL1 129 K8
Hawtrey Dr RSLP HA4 113 H5
Hawtrey Rd HAMP NW3 3 N4
  WDSR SL4 149 N4
Haxted Rd BMLY BR1 184 A10
Haybourn Cl HHW HP1 35 J1
Hayburn Wy HCH RM12 124 G6
Hay Cl BORE WD6 75 P6
  SRTFD E15 141 H7
Haycroft COUL/CHIP CR5 241 H4
Haycroft Gdns WLSDN NW10 137 J1
Haycroft Rd BRXS/STRHM SW2 180 A1
  SURB KT6 199 L3
Hay Currie St POP/IOD E14 140 C8
Hayday Rd CAN/RD E16 144 A1
Hayden Cl ADL/WDHM KT15 215 L6
Hayden Dell BUSH WD23 73 N10
Hayden Rd WAB EN9 81 H4
Haydens Cl STMC/STPC BR5 207 H2
Haydens Pl NTGHL W11 * 8 D6
Haydn Av PUR/KEN CR8 241 H1
Haydns Ms EA W5 135 N10
Haydock Av NTHLT UB5 133 N4
Haydock Gn NTHLT UB5 133 N4
Haydon Cl CDALE/KGS NW9 115 N3
  EN EN1 79 N10
  HARH RM3 105 J4
Haydon Dell Farm BUSH WD23 73 K9
Haydon Dr PIN HA5 112 G5
Haydon Park Rd WIM/MER SW19 178 C7
Haydon Pl GU GU1 268 A1
Haydon Rd BCTR RM8 123 N9
Haydon's Rd WIM/MER SW19 178 B8
Haydon Wk WCHPL E1 13 N3
Hayes Barton WOKS/MYFD GU22 232 G2
Hayes Cha WWKM BR4 205 L5
Hayes Cl HAYES BR2 205 N5
Hayes Ct BRXS/STRHM SW2 180 A2
  CHEAM SM3 220 G5
Hayes Crs CHEAM SM3 220 G5
  GLDGN NW11 117 H2
Hayes Dr RAIN RM13 145 J2
Hayes End Cl YEAD UB4 132 G2
Hayes End Dr YEAD UB4 132 F3
Hayes End Rd YEAD UB4 132 G2
Hayesford Park Dr HAYES BR2 205 N6
Hayes Gdn HAYES BR2 205 N6
Hayes Gv EDUL SE22 159 N10
Hayes Hill HAYES BR2 205 L5
Hayes Hill Rd HAYES BR2 205 M5
Hayes La BECK BR3 184 A10

**Column 5**

  RDART DA2 188 D3
Hayes St HAYES BR2 205 N5
Hayes Ter GVE DA12 * 191 P8
The Hayes EPSOM KT18 238 A5
Hayes Wy BECK BR3 204 C1
Hayes Wood Av HAYES BR2 205 N5
Hayfield Pas WCHPL E1 140 E7
Hayfield Rd STMC/STPC BR5 207 K5
Haygarth Pl WIM/MER SW19 178 A7
Hay Green La BRWN CM15 87 J1
Hay Hl MYFR/PICC W1J 10 E7
Hayland Cl CDALE/KGS NW9 116 A2
Hay La CDALE/KGS NW9 116 A2
  DTCH/LGLY SL3 130 A9
Hayle TN RM18 169 M2
Haylett Gdns KUT/HW KT1 * 191 K10
Hayley Cl CDW/CHF RM16 167 M1
Hayling Av FELT TW13 175 H6
Hayling Cl STNW/STAM N16 119 N10
Hayling Rd OXHEY WD19 92 G4
Hayman Crs YEAD UB4 132 E6
Haymarket ST/S SW1Y 11 H2
Haymeads Dr ESH/CLAY KT10 218 B3
Haymer Gdns WPK KT4 200 D10
Haymerle Rd PECK SE15 19 N10
Haymill Rd SL SL1 128 C6
Hayne Rd BECK BR3 183 P5
Haynes Cl BKHTH/KID SE3 161 K9
  DTCH/LGLY SL3 150 C4
  FBAR/BDGN N11 98 B4
  RPLY/SEND GU23 253 L8
  TOTM N17 100 A4
  WCCE AL7 23 K6
Haynes Dr ED N9 100 D2
Haynes La NRWD SE19 181 M9
Haynes Md BERK HP4 33 M3
Haynes Rd ALP/SUD HA0 135 K2
  EMPK RM11 125 N1
  GVW DA11 190 C6
Haynt Wk RYNPK SW20 193 H3
Haysoms Cl ROM RM1 124 F3
Haystall Cl YEAD UB4 132 E6
The Hays Wk BELMT SM2 * 220 G8
Hays Ms MYFR/PICC W1J 10 C1
Haywain OXTED RH8 * 261 M8
Hayward Cl DART DA1 187 H9
  WIM/MER SW19 178 A9
Hayward Dr DART DA1 187 N6
Hayward Gdns PUT/ROE SW15 178 F2
Hayward Rd THDIT KT7 198 B8
  TRDG/WHET N20 97 M3
Haywards Cl CHDH RM6 123 J3
Haywards Md WDSR SL4 148 A6
Hayward's Pl CLKNW EC1R * 12 C2
Haywood Cl PIN HA5 93 L10
Haywood Copse RKW/CH/CXG WD3 71 J9
Haywood Dr HHS/BOV HP3 35 J9
Haywood Pk RKW/CH/CXG WD3 71 J9
Haywood Ri ORP BR6 227 H2
Haywood Rd HAYES BR2 206 C2
Haywoods Dr HHS/BOV HP3 35 J9
Hazel Av WDR/YW UB7 152 B2
Hazelbank BRYLDS KT5 199 P2
Hazelbank Rd CAT SE6 183 H3
  CHERT KT16 195 H9
Hazelbourne Rd BAL SW12 180 C7
Hazelbrouck Gdns BARK/HLT IG6 102 G8
Hazelbury Av ABLGY WD5 54 C3
Hazelbury Cl WIM/MER SW19 193 L2
Hazelbury Gn ED N9 100 B3
Hazelbury La ED N9 100 B3
Hazel Cl BTFD TW8 154 G6
  CRAWW RH11 285 J6
  CROY/NA CRO 204 C7
  EGH TW20 171 N9
  HCH RM12 124 A8
  MTCM CR4 202 E2
  PLMGR N13 99 P1
  REIG RH2 275 M2
  TWK TW1 176 A7
Hazel Ct WDR/YW UB7 152 B2
Hazelcroft PIN HA5 93 P5
Hazelcroft Cl HGDN/ICK UB10 132 A5
Hazeldean Rd WLSDN NW10 137 H5
Hazeldell Link HHW HP1 35 H1
Hazeldell Rd HHW HP1 35 H1
Hazeldene ADL/WDHM KT15 215 L6
  CHES/WCR EN8 62 D8
Hazeldene Dr PIN HA5 113 H1
Hazeldene Gdns HGDN/ICK UB10 132 D3
Hazeldene Rd WELL DA16 165 M8
Hazeldon Rd BROCKY SE4 182 A1
Hazel Dr ERITH DA8 166 C1
  RPLY/SEND GU23 251 J1
  SOCK/AV RM15 151 K3
Hazeleigh RBRW/HUT CM13 107 N4
Hazeleigh Gdns WFD IG8 103 L5
Hazel End SWLY BR8 209 J6
Hazel Gdns EDGW HA8 96 B5
Hazelgreen Cl WCHMH N21 99 J7
Hazel Gv ALP/SUD HA0 135 K5
  CHDH RM6 123 P1
  EN EN1 90 C1
  FELT TW13 175 H4
  HYS/HAR UB3 133 J5
  ORP BR6 226 G1
  STA TW18 173 J9
  SYD SE26 183 L8
  SWLY BR8 208 B2
  VW GU25 194 A4

**Column 6**

Hazel Gv GSTN WD25 * 205 J2
  HORL RH6 * 280 B5
Hazelhurst BECK BR3 183 P5
Hazelhurst Cl RGUE GU4 250 E1
Hazelhurst Ct CAT SE6 * 205 J2
Hazelhurst Rd TOOT SW17 179 M7
Hazel La BARK/HLT IG6 122 B7
  RCHPK/HAM TW10 176 D4
Hazell Crs CRW RM5 104 A5
Hazell Pk AMSS HP7 50 F3
Hazellville Rd ARCH N19 118 D5
Hazelmead CI HLWE CM17 47 K2
Hazel Md BAR EN5 95 P5
  EPSOM KT18 220 A10
Hazel Pk SLN SL2 129 N10
Hazelmere CI EBED/NFELT TW14 173 N4
  LHD/OX KT22 236 A2
  NTHLT UB5 133 K5
Hazelmere Dr NTHLT UB5 133 L5
Hazelmere Rd KIL/WHAMP NW6 2 B1
  NTHLT UB5 133 L5
  STMC/STPC BR5 206 A1
Hazelmere Wk NTHLT UB5 133 M5
Hazelmere Wy HAYES BR2 205 N6
Hazel Pde LHD/OX KT22 * 236 B8
Hazel Rd BERK HP4 34 A6
  BF/WBF KT14 215 K10
  ERITH DA8 165 H1
  REIG RH2 275 M2
  SRTFD E15 * 121 K10
  WLSDN NW10 136 E5
Hazel Rw NFNCH/WDSPK N12 * 97 N6
The Hazels WLYN AL6 * 23 H7
Hazeltree La NTHLT UB5 133 M5
Hazel Tree Rd WATN WD24 73 H3
Hazel Wk HAYES BR2 206 D6
Hazel Wy CHING E4 100 C7
  COUL/CHIP CR5 240 B5
  LHD/OX KT22 236 B8
  STHWK SE1 19 L5
Hazelway Cl FUL/PGN SW6 157 H7
Hazelwick Av CRAWE RH10 284 B5
Hazelwick Ms CRAWE RH10 * 284 B5
Hazelwick Mill La CRAWE RH10 284 B5
Hazelwick Rd CRAWE RH10 284 C5
Hazelwood DORK RH4 * 272 C3
  SLH/COR SS17 169 K3
Hazelwood Av MRDN SM4 201 L4
Hazelwood Cl CLPT E5 * 120 D8
  CRAWE RH10 285 N10
  CSHM HP5 51 J5
  EA W5 155 K5
  RYLN/HDSTN HA2 113 J6
Hazelwood Ct SURB KT6 * 199 K6
  WLSDN NW10 * 93 J10
Hazelwood Crs PLMGR N13 99 H3
Hazelwood Dr PIN HA5 93 H4
Hazelwood Gdns BRWN CM15 107 H8
Hazelwood Gv SAND/SEL CR2 224 A10
Hazelwood Hts OXTED RH8 261 M7
Hazelwood La ABLGY WD5 54 E8
  COUL/CHIP CR5 240 C5
  PLMGR N13 99 H3
Hazelwood Park Cl CHIG IG7 103 P6
Hazelwood Rd EN EN1 90 C1
  OXTED RH8 261 N8
  RKW/CH/CXG WD3 72 D10
  RSEV TN14 246 B3
  WALTH E17 120 D3
  WOKN/KNAP GU21 231 K4
Hazlebury Rd FUL/PGN SW6 157 P7
Hazledean Rd CROY/NA CRO 203 L9
Hazledene Rd CHSWK W4 155 P5
Hazlemere Gdns WPK KT4 200 D10
Hazlemere Rd SLN SL2 129 N10
Hazlewell Rd PUT/ROE SW15 178 F1
Hazlewood Crs NKENS W10 * 8 B2
Hazlitt Cl FELT TW13 175 M7
Hazlitt Ms WKENS W14 * 14 A4
Hazlitt Rd WKENS W14 14 A4
Hazon Wy HOR/WEW KT19 220 A10
Heacham Av HGDN/ICK UB10 112 D8
Headcorn Rd BMLY BR1 183 N4
  THHTH CR7 204 C1
  UED N17 99 N8
Headfort Pl KTBR SW1X 16 B4
Headingley Cl CHESW EN7 61 N2
  RAD WD7 57 K8
Headlam Rd CLAP SW4 179 H1
Headlam St WCHPL E1 140 A6
Headlands Dr HARP AL5 34 B4
Headley Ap GNTH/NBYPK IG2 122 D4
Headley Av WLGTN SM6 223 L3
Headley Cha BRW CM14 107 H5
Headley Cl CHSGTN KT9 219 M3
  CRAWE RH10 284 E4
Headley Common RBRW/HUT CM13 106 C8
Headley Common Rd EPSOM KT18 238 A10
Headley Dr CROY/NA CRO 225 H4
  EPSOM KT18 238 E5
  GNTH/NBYPK IG2 122 D4
Headley Heath Ap KWD/TDW/WH KT20 238 B10
Headley La RDKG RH5 255 N6
Headley Pde LHD/OX KT22 * 238 A5
Headley Rd LHD/OX KT22 237 N8
Heads Ms NTGHL W11 8 C1
Headstone Dr HRW HA1 114 C2
Headstone Gdns RYLN/HDSTN HA2 114 B2
Headstone La RYLN/HDSTN HA2 94 A10
Headstone Pde HRW HA1 114 D3
Headstone Rd HRW HA1 114 D4
Head St WCHPL E1 140 E8
Headway Cl RCHPK/HAM TW10 176 G7
The Headway EW KT17 220 C10
Healey Rd WATW WD18 13 H7
Healey St CAMTN NW1 4 B1
Healy Dr ORP BR6 227 L4
Heanor Ct CLPT E5 * 120 F1
Hearne Rd CHSWK W4 155 H5
Hearnes Cl BRW CM15 87 H4
Hearne's Wy? WELL? 165 J9
Hearn Ri NTHLT UB5 133 H5
Hearn Rd ROM RM1 124 G4
Hearn's Bldgs WALW SE17 19 J7
Hearn's Cl STMC/STPC BR5 207 M4
Hearnshaw St POP/IOD E14 * 141 K8
Hearn St SDTCH EC2A 13 K2
Hearnville Rd BAL SW12 180 B4
Heathacre DTCH/LGLY SL3 * 151 L1

**Column 7**

  HORL RH6 * 280 B5
Hazelmere Wk NTHLT UB5 133 M6
Hazelmere Wy HAYES BR2 205 N6
Hazel Pde LHD/OX KT22 * 236 B8
Hazel Rd ERITH DA8 165 K10
  STHWK SE1 19 L5
Hazelway Cl LHD/OX KT22 236 B8
Hazel Wy COUL/CHIP CR5 240 A5
  LHD/OX KT22 236 B8
Hazledean Rd CROY/NA CRO 203 L9
Hazelwood Mill La CRAWE RH10 284 B5
Hazelwood La ABLGY WD5 54 E8
  COUL/CHIP CR5 240 C5
Hazelwood Gdns BRWN CM15 107 H8
Hazelwood Gv SAND/SEL CR2 224 A10
Hazelwood Hts OXTED RH8 261 M7
Hazelwood Park Cl CHIG IG7 103 P6
Heacham Av HGDN/ICK UB10 112 D8
Headcorn Pk WHTN TW2 176 A5
Headlam Rd CLAP SW4 179 H1
Hearnville Rd BAL SW12 180 B4
Heathbourne Rd BUSH WD23 94 D3
Heathbridge WEY KT13 216 B5
Heath Brow HAMP NW3 117 L8
Heath CI BNSTD SM7 221 L10
  EA W5 135 L4
  GLDGN NW11 117 J2
  GPK RM2 124 D1
  HARP AL5 20 A4
  HYS/HAR UB3 152 B2
  POTB/CUF EN6 59 L5
  SAND/SEL CR2 223 J5
  STMC/STPC BR5 206 G2
  STWL/WRAY TW19 172 A2
  SWLY BR8 187 L10
  VW GU25 194 A4
Heathcote KWD/TDW/WH KT20 239 H8
Heathcote Av CLAY IG5 102 C10
  HAT AL10 23 P9
Heathcote Gdns HLWE CM17 47 P1
Heathcote Gv CHING E4 101 P1
Heathcote Rd EPSOM KT18 238 A10
  TWK TW1 176 E8
Heathcote St BMSBY WC1N 11 N1
Heathcote Wy WDR/YW UB7 * 132 A10
Heathcroft EA W5 135 L3
  GLDGN NW11 117 J3
Heathcroft Av SUN TW16 176 C10
Heathcroft Gdns WALTH E17 * 101 P7
Heathdale Av HSLWW TW4 153 M9
Heathdene KWD/TDW/WH KT20 239 H5
Heathdene Dr BELV DA17 164 G4
Heathdene Mnr WAT WD17 * 72 G5
Heathdene Rd STRHM/NOR SW16 180 G10
  WLGTN SM6 222 C7
Heathdown Rd WOKS/MYFD GU22 232 G4

Heath Dr BELMT SM2 * 221 M5
CHOB/PIR GU24 230 F6
EPP CM16 83 H1
GPK RM2 105 H9
HAMP NW3 117 L9
POTB/CUF EN6 59 K6
RPLY/SEND GU23 232 E9
RYNPK SW20 200 F4
Heathdene SYD SE26 * 182 A10
Heather Av ROM RM1 104 E10
Heatherbank CHST BR7 206 D2
ELTH/MOT SE9 162 C8
Heatherbank CI COB KT11 217 L2
Heather CI ABLGY WD5 55 H8
ADL/WDHM KT15 215 L6
BRWN CM15 86 C9
CRAWE RH10 285 J3
EHAM E6 142 D8
GUW GU2 249 N8
HPTN TW12 197 N1
ISLW TW7 176 C1
KWD/TDW/WH KT20 239 H8
LEW SE13 183 J2
REDH RH1 258 F5
ROM RM1 104 E9
UX/CGN UB8 132 A7
VX/NE SW8
WOKN/KNAP GU21 231 P1
Heatherdale CI KUTN/CMB KT2 177 M9
Heatherdene EHSLY KT24 252 F6
Heatherdene CI MTCM CR4 201 N4
NFNCH/WDSPK N12 97 N3
Heatherden Gn IVER SL0 130 F3
Heather Dr ASC SL5 192 G7
ENC/FH EN2 79 J6
ROM RM1 104 E10
Heather End SWLY BR8 208 B5
Heatherfold Wy PIN HA5 112 G1
Heather Gdns BELMT SM2 221 K3
GLDGN NW11 117 H4
ROM RM1 104 E10
WAB EN9 81 H2
Heather Gln ROM RM1 104 H2
Heatherlands HORL RH6 * 280 D5
SUN TW16 175 H9
Heather La WDR/YW UB7 151 P8
Heatherlea Gv WPK KT4 200 F8
Heatherley Dr CLAY IG5 122 C1
Heather Park Dr ALP/SUD HA0 135 M2
Heather Park Pde ALP/SUD HA0 * 135 L2
Heather PI ESH/CLAY KT10 218 A2
Heather Rd BUSH WD23 73 N6
CHING E4 116 C2
CRICK NW2 116 C2
WGCW AL5 22 F7
Heatherset CI ESH/CLAY KT10 218 B2
Heatherset Gdns STRHM/NOR SW16 180 G10
Heatherside Dr GT/LBKH KT23 235 M10
Heatherside Dr VW GU25 193 M6
Heatherside Rd SLN SL2 109 J8
HOR/WEW KT19 220 A4
SCUP DA14 185 N4
Heatherside Rd HOR DA4 273 H5
The Heathers STWL/WRAY TW19 174 A3
Heatherton Pk AMS HP6 68 G2
Heathervale ADL/WDHM KT15 215 L6
Heathervale Wy ADL/WDHM KT15 215 M6
Heather Wk CHOB/PIR GU24 230 C2
EDGW HA8 95 N6
HORL RH6 281 K4
NKENS W10 8 B1
Heather Wy CHOB/PIR GU24 213 K4
HHNE HP2 35 N5
POTB/CUF EN6 59 J8
ROM RM1 104 E10
SAND/SEL CR2 224 C5
STAN HA7 94 C7
Heatherwood CI MNPK E12 121 N7
Heatherwood Dr YEAD UB4 132 B4
Heath Farm La STWL/RED AL3 38 D4
Heathfield CHING E4 101 H4
CHST BR7 184 F9
COB KT11 217 P10
CRAWE RH10 284 E4
HRW HA1 114 C6
Heathfield Av ASC SL5 192 D5
WAND/EARL SW18 179 N3
Heathfield CI ASHTD KT21 237 H5
CAN/RD E16 142 A7
HAYES BR2 225 P2
OXHEY WD19 93 K1
POTB/CUF EN6 59 L6
WOKS/MYFD GU22 232 D4
Heathfield Cots GRAYS RM17 * 167 M4
Heathfield Dr MTCM CR4 179 P10
REDH RH1 275 P4
Heathfield Gdns CHSWK W4 155 N4
CROY/NA CR0 * 223 K1
GLDGN NW11 116 F4
WAND/EARL SW18 179 N2
Heathfield La CHST BR7 184 F9
WEY KT13 216 F2
Heathfield North WHTN TW2 176 D3
Heathfield Pk CRICK NW2 116 A4
Heathfield Park Dr CHDH RM6 123 L3
Heathfield Ri RSLP HA4 112 D5
Heathfield Rd ACT W3 155 N1
BMLY BR1 183 L10
BUSH WD23 73 M8
BXLYHS DA6 136 A10
HAYES BR2 225 P2
SAND/SEL CR2 223 L2
SEV TN13 246 G8
WAND/EARL SW18 179 N2
WOKS/MYFD GU22 232 D4
WOT/HER KT12 217 M1
Heathfield South WHTN TW2 176 E3
Heathfield Sq WAND/EARL SW18 179 N3
Heathfield Ter CHSWK W4 155 P4
SWLY BR8 * 208 E2
WOOL/PLUM SE18 163 H5
Heathfield V SAND/SEL CR2 224 C5
Heath Gdns DART DA1 * 187 K4
TWK TW1 176 A4
Heathgate GLDGN NW11 117 L4
HERT/BAY SG13 26 A8
Heath Gv PGE/AN SE20 182 B10
SUN TW16 174 C10
Heath Hurst Rd HAMP NW3 117 P9
Heath La DORK RH4 272 C10
Heath House Rd WOKS/MYFD GU22 231 M8
Heathland Rd STNW/STAM N16 119 M6
Heathlands KWD/TDW/WH KT20 238 G10
CI SUN TW16 197 H2
HORL RH6 280 D5
WOKN/KNAP GU21 214 B10
Heathlands CI HSLWW TW4 175 M1
Heathlands Dr STALW/RED AL3 38 D4
Heathlands Rd HSLWW TW4 175 J2
HHW HP1 35 J8
SHGR GU5 269 P7
Heathlee Rd BKHTH/KID SE3 161 L10
Heathley End CHST BR7 184 F9
Heath Ldg BUSH WD23 * 94 C2
Heathman's Rd FUL/PGN SW6 157 J7
Heath Md WIM/MER SW19 178 C6


Heath Ms RPLY/SEND GU23 233 L9
Heath Mill La RGUW GU3 249 L6
Heathpark Dr BFOR GU20 212 D9
Heath Park Dr BMLY BR1 206 B3
Heath Park Rd GPK RM2 105 H9
Heath Ridge Gn COB KT11 217 P9
Heath Ri DORK RH4 272 B4
HAYES BR2 205 M6
PUT/ROE SW15 178 G2
Heath Rd RW GU6 * 194 A4
Heath Rd AMS HP6 50 B10
BXLY DA5 186 D4
CDW/CHF RM16 168 C1
CHDH RM6 123 N5
CTHM CR3 241 L9
HGDN/ICK UB10 132 D6
HRW HA1 114 B5
HSLW TW3 154 B10
THHTH CR7 203 K3
TWK TW1 176 A4
VX/NE SW8 141 J4
WEY KT13 216 B5
WOKN/KNAP GU21 232 C1
Heath Side SHGR GU5 270 D5
Heaths CI EN EN1 79 L6
Heathside ESH/CLAY KT10 198 D10
HAMP NW3 117 N9
HSLWW TW4 175 N3
STALE/WH AL4 39 N9
STALW/RED AL3 38 D4
Heath Side WOKN/KNAP GU21 232 C3
Heathside Av BXLYHN DA7 163 P8
Heathside CI ESH/CLAY KT10 198 D10
GNTH/NBYPK IG2 122 C3
NTHWD HA6 92 E6
Heathside Ct KWD/TDW/WH KT20 238 F10
Heathside Crs WOKS/MYFD GU22 232 E3
Heathside Gdns WOKS/MYFD GU22 232 C3
Heathside Park Rd WOKS/MYFD GU22 232 C4
Heathside Rd EPSOM KT18 238 C4
NTHWD HA6 92 E5
WOKS/MYFD GU22 232 C4
Heathstan Rd SHB W12 136 D8
Heath Vw EFNCH N2 117 M2
EHSLY KT24 252 C1
Heath View CI EFNCH N2 117 M2
Heath Vis WAND/EARL SW18 179 M4
WOOL/PLUM SE18 163 J4
Heathville Rd ARCH N19 118 F5
Heathwall St BTSEA SW11 158 A9
Heathway BKHTH/KID SE3 161 M6
CROY/NA CR0 204 E10
CTHM CR3 259 K1
DAGW RM9 124 A9
EHSLY KT24 252 C1
Heath Wy ERITH DA8 164 D7
IVER SL0 130 C4
Heathway NWDGN UB2 * 153 L3
Heath Wy WFD IG8 101 H5
Heathwood Gdns CHARL SE7 * 162 B3
SWLY BR8 208 D2
Heathwood Pde SWLY BR8 * 208 D2
Heaton Av HARH RM3 105 J8
Heaton CI CHING E4 101 H4
HARH RM3 105 K8
Heaton Grange Rd GPK RM2 104 G9
Heaton Rd MTCM CR4 180 B10
PECK SE15 160 A4
Heaton Wy HARH RM3 105 K8
Heaven Tree CI IS N1 119 K10
Heaver Rd BTSEA SW11 157 N9
Heavitree CI WOOL/PLUM SE18 162 G4
Heavitree Rd WOOL/PLUM SE18 162 G4
Heavy Hds WCCE AL7 23 M4
Hebden Ter TOTM N17 99 M7
Hebdon Rd TOOT SW17 179 P6
Heber Rd CRICK NW2 116 C10
EDUL SE22 181 N2
Hebron Rd HMSMTH W6 156 E2
Heckfield Pl FUL/PGN SW6 157 K6
Heckford St WAP E1W 140 F8
Hector CI ED N9 99 P3
Hector St WOOL/PLUM SE18 * 163 H5
Heddington Gv HOLWY N7 118 C10
Heddon CI ISLW TW7 154 A11
Heddon Court Av EBAR EN4 78 A9
Heddon Court Pde EBAR EN4 * 78 B9
Heddon St REGST W1S 10 G8
Hedge Hl ENC/FH EN2 79 J5
Hedge La PLMGR N13 99 J4
Hedgeley REDBR IG4 122 C2
Hedgemans Rd DAGW RM9 143 N5
Hedgemans Wy DAGW RM9 143 N2
Hedge Place Rd RDART DA2 188 D4
Hedgerley Ct WOKN/KNAP GU21 231 P3
Hedgerley Gdns GFD/PVL UB6 133 B4
Hedgerley Hl SLN SL2 109 J8
Hedgerley La BEAC HP9 44 A1
Hedgerley La BAL SL2 109 P7
Hedge Rw HHW HP1 35 K4
Hedgerow La ARK EN5 75 K4
The Hedgerows SBW CM21 30 A1
Hedgerows Wk CHES/WCR EN8 62 C1
Hedger St LBTH SE11 18 G8
Hedges CI HAT AL10 40 E5
Hedgeside BERK HP4 34 D2
Hedgeway GUW GU2 248 D6
Hedgewood Gdns CLAY IG5 122 C2
Hedingham CI IS N1 * 6 E1
Hedingham Rd BCTR RM8 123 K4
CDW/CHF RM16 167 N4
EMPK RM11 105 L10
Hedley Av WTHK RM20 167 N4
Hedley CI STAL AL1 11 F6
WHTN TW2 176 C4
Hedley Rw HBRY N5 119 H1
Hedworth Av CHES/WCR EN8 62 C9
Heenan CI BARK IG11 142 D8
Heene Rd ENC/FH EN2 79 J5
Heidegger Crs BARN SW13 156 E5
Heigham Rd EHAM E6 141 J6
Heighams HLWW/ROY CM19 46 A1
Heights CI BNSTD SM7 239 H7
The Heights BECK BR3 * 183 H10
CHARL SE7 162 A4
LOU IG10 89 H8
NTHLT UB5 113 N4
SEV TN13 * 246 F9


WAB EN9 63 N1
WEY KT13 * 216 B10
Heiron St WALW SE17 18 D10
Helby Rd CLAP SW4 180 A1
Helder Gv LEE/GVPK SE12 183 L5
Helder St SAND/SEL CR2 223 N4
Heldmann CI HSLW TW3 154 C10
Helegan St ORP BR6 227 J1
Helena CI EBAR EN4 77 N3
Helena PI HACK E8 * 140 A3
Helena Rd EA W5 135 J7
PLSTW E13 141 L4
WALTH E17 120 F3
WDSR SL4 36 B5
WLSDN NW10 116 E10
Helena Sq BERM/RHTH SE16 141 M3
Helen CI DART DA1 188 A3
E/WMO/HCT KT8 198 A1
EFNCH N2 117 M1
Helen Ga CHES/WCR EN8 62 E2
Helen Rd EBED/NFELT TW14 175 H1
Helen's PI BETH E2 140 B5
Helen St WOOL/PLUM SE18 * 162 G4
Helford CI RSLP HA4 112 B11
Helford Wk WOKN/KNAP GU21 231 M4
Helford Wy UPMR RM14 126 C4
Helgiford Gdns SUN TW16 174 F10
Helions Rd HLWW/ROY CM19 46 A1
Helios Rd WLGTN SM6 202 B8
Helix Gdns BRXS/STRHM SW2 180 A2
Helix Rd BRXS/STRHM SW2 180 A2
Helleborine GRAYS RM17 167 L4
Hellings St WAP E1W * 13 P10
Helm CI HOR/WEW KT19 219 M8
Helme CI WIM/MER SW19 178 F10
Helmet Rw FSBYE EC1V 12 F1
Helmore Rd BARK IG11 143 J2
Helmsdale WOKN/KNAP GU21 231 N4
Helmsdale CI ROM RM1 104 H6
YEAD UB4 133 M6
Helmsdale Rd STRHM/NOR SW16 202 D1
Helmsley PI HACK E8 140 A2
Helmsley St HACK E8 140 A2
Helperby Rd WLSDN NW10 116 B2
Helsinki Sq BERM/RHTH SE16 160 F2
Helston CI PIN HA5 93 N8
Helston Gv HHNE HP2 35 N1
Helston La WDSR SL4 148 G3
Helvellyn CI EGH TW20 172 C10
Helvetia St CAT SE6 182 E5
Hemans St VX/NE SW8 158 E6
Hemel Hempstead Rd HHS/BOV HP3 36 F8
HHW HP1 37 L8
LCOL/BKTW AL2 37 N9
Hemery Rd GFD/PVL UB6 114 C10
Hemingford CI NFNCH/WDSPK N12 97 N1
Hemingford Rd CHEAM SM3 220 F1
IS N1 5 P5
WAT WD17 72 F2
Heming Rd EDGW HA8 95 M7
Hemington Av FBAR/BDGN N11 98 A6
Hemlock CI KWD/TDW/WH KT20 239 H9
STRHM/NOR SW16 202 E2
Hemlock Rd SHB W12 136 C9
Hemmen La HYS/HAR UB3 133 J4
Hemming CI HPTN TW12 197 P1
Hemmings CI SCUP DA14 185 L5
Hemmingsmead HOR/WEW KT19 219 P3
The Hemmings BERK HP4 33 K6
Hemming St WCHPL E1 13 P2
Hemming Wy GSTN WD25 73 H1
SLN SL2 128 G5
Hemmingway CI KTTN NW5 118 A5
Hemnall St EPP CM16 65 J7
Hempshaw Av BNSTD SM7 240 A2
Hempson Av DTCH/LGLY SL3 149 P2
Hempstall WCCE AL7 23 L7
Hempstead La BRKHM RH3 274 F3
Hempstead Rd HHS/BOV HP3 35 H1
KGLGY WD4 54 A5
WALTH E17 121 J1
WAT WD17 72 E2
Hemp Wk WALW SE17 19 H5
Hemsby Rd CHSGTN KT9 219 L3
Hemsby Wk CRAWE RH10 285 J4
Hemstal Rd KIL/WHAMP NW6 2 E1
Hemsted Rd ERITH DA8 164 F7
Hemswell Dr CDALE/KGS NW9 96 A3
Hemsworth St IS N1 7 K1
Hemus PI CHEL SW3 16 E9
Henage La WOKS/MYFD GU22 232 G6
Henbit CI KWD/TDW/WH KT20 238 E5
Henbury Wy OXHEY WD19 93 L4
Henchley Dene RGUE GU4 250 D6
Henchman St SHB W12 136 C8
Hencroft St North SL SL1 149 L1
Hencroft St South SL SL1 149 L2
Hendale Av HDN NW4 95 P2
Henderson CI GUW GU2 249 N6
EMPK RM11 105 P7
WLSDN NW10 115 P6
Henderson Dr DART DA1 165 P10
STJWD NW8 9 L1
Henderson PI ABLGY WD5 54 G4
Henderson Rd CROY/NA CR0 204 C8
ED N9 100 A2
FSTGT E7 141 K4
WAND/EARL SW18 179 P3
YEAD UB4 133 L2
Hendham Rd TOOT SW17 179 P5
Hendon Av FNCH N3 96 G8
Hendon Gdns ROM RM1 104 C1
Hendon Gv HOR/WEW KT19 219 M5
Hendon Hall Ct HDN NW4 * 96 A5
Hendon La FNCH N3 96 G8
Hendon Park Rw GLDGN NW11 117 J4
Hendon Rd ED N9 100 C2
Hendon Ter ASHF TW15 174 B11
Hendon Wy CRICK NW2 116 C1
STWL/WRAY TW19 173 N1
Hendon Wood La MLHL NW7 96 C2
Hendren CI GFD/PVL UB6 114 C10
Hendre Rd STHWK SE1 19 L8
Hendrick Av BAL SW12 179 M5
Heneage Crs CROY/NA CR0 225 H4
Heneage La HDTCH EC3A
Heneage St WCHPL E1 13 M3
Henfield CI ARCH N19 118 D6
BXLY DA5
Henfield Rd WIM/MER SW19 201 H3
Henfold La RDKG RH5 291 K10
Hengelo Gdns MTCM CR4 201 N4
Hengist Rd ERITH DA8 164 D6
LEE/GVPK SE12 183 L5
Hengist Wy HAYES BR2 205 J8
Hengrave Rd FSTH SE23 181 P4
Hengrove Crs ASHF TW15 173 J6
Henhurst Rd GVE DA12 190 G9
Henley Av CHEAM SM3 219 M5
Henley Bank GUW GU2 248 D7
Henley CI BERM/RHTH SE16 * 140 B8
CRAWE RH11 284 B7
GFD/PVL UB6 114 D8
ISLW TW7 154 E7
Henley Ct CHOB/PIR GU24 230 B11
EFNCH N2 117 H3
Henley Cross BKHTH/KID SE3 162 B3
Henley Deane GVW DA11 190 G8
Henley Dr KUTN/CMB KT2 177 N9
STHWK SE1
Henley Ga CHOB/PIR GU24 230 A11
Henley Pk RGUW GU3
Henley Rd CAN/RD E16 162 A3
EN EN1 79
IL IG1 122 C9


SL SL1 128 D8
UED N18 99 H5
WLSDN NW10 116 A10
Henley Wy FELT TW13 175 L8
Henneker CI CRW RM5 104 D7
Hennel CI FSTH SE23 182 B6
Hennessy Ct WOKN/KNAP GU21 214 F9
Hennessy Rd ED N9 100 B3
Henniker Ms CHEL SW3 15 L9
Henniker Rd SRTFD E15 121 M2
Henningham Rd TOTM N17 99 P9
Henning St BTSEA SW11 157 P7
Henrietta CI DEPT SE8 160 F5
Henrietta Ms BMSBY WC1N 11 L1
Henrietta PI CAVSQ/HST W1G 10 C3
Henrietta St COVGDN WC2E 11 M7
SRTFD E15 121 H10
Henriques St WCHPL E1 13 P5
Henry CI ENC/FH EN2 79 M4
Henry Cooper Wy ELTH/MOT SE9 184 A6
Henry Darlot Dr MLHL NW7 96 A6
Henry De Grey CI GRAYS RM17 167 J3
Henry Dickens Ct NTGHL W11 136 D10
Henry Doulton Dr TOOT SW17 180 B7
Henry Jackson Rd PUT/ROE SW15 156 G9
Henry Macaulay Av KUTN/CMB KT2 177 K8
Henry Peters Dr TEDD TW11 176 F7
Henry Rd EBAR EN4 77 N9
EHAM E6 142 A4
FSBYPK N4 119 K6
SL SL1 149 J4
Henry's Av WFD IG8 101 L6
Henrys Grant STAL AL1 * 38 D7
Henryson Rd BROCKY SE4 182 A1
Henry St BMLY BR1 205 N6
GRAYS RM17 167 P5
HHS/BOV HP3 35 N10
Henry Tate Ms STRHM/NOR SW16 181 M8
Henry Wells Sq HHNE HP2 * 36 A2
Hensby Av OXHEY WD19 93 M10
Henshall St IS N1 7 H2
Henshaw Path CRAWW RH11 283 H10
Henshawe Rd BCTR RM8 123 N1
Henshaw St WALW SE17 18 C5
Henslowe Rd EDUL SE22 181 P5
Henslow Wy WOKN/KNAP GU21 214 C10
Henson Av CRICK NW2 116 A3
Henson CI ORP BR6 206 D10
Henson PI NTHLT UB5 133 H1
Henstridge PI STJWD NW8 3 J7
Hensworth Rd ASHF TW15 173 H9
Henty CI BTSEA SW11 158 E1
Henty Wk PUT/ROE SW15 178 E1
Henville Rd BMLY BR1 205 N1
Henwick Rd ELTH/MOT SE9 162 B11
Henwood Side WFD IG8 102 A7
Hepburn CI CDW/CHF RM16 167 J3
Hepburn Gdns HAYES BR2 205 L8
Hepple CI ISLW TW7 154 F8
Hepscott Rd HOM E9 140 A1
Hepworth Gdns BARK IG11 123 K10
Hepworth Rd STRHM/NOR SW16 180 F10
Hepworth Wy WOT/HER KT12 196 G8
Heracles CI LCOL/BKTW AL2 202 C10
Herald Gdns WLGTN SM6 202 C10
Herald St BETH E2 140 A4
Herald's PI LBTH SE11 18 F6
Herald Wk DART DA1 *
Herbal Hl CLKNW EC1R 11 P10
Herbert Crs KTBR SW1X 16 B5
WOKN/KNAP GU21 231 K4
Herbert Gdns CHDH RM6 123 K5
CHSWK W4 155 N5
WLSDN NW10 136 A1
Herbert Ms BRXS/STRHM SW2 * 180 B1
Herbert PI ISLW TW7 154 C8
WOOL/PLUM SE18 162 G5
Herbert Rd BXLYHN DA7 163 P8
CDALE/KGS NW9 116 D4
EMPK RM11 105 P7
FBAR/BDGN N11 98 F8
HAYES BR2 206 A5
IL IG1 122 C7
KUT/HW KT1 199 L5
MNPK E12 122 A1
SEVS/STOTM N15 119 L3
STHL UB1 133 J7
SWCM DA10 189 L7
SWLY BR8 208 E2
WALTH E17 120 E5
WIM/MER SW19 178 A3
WOOL/PLUM SE18 162 G6
Herberts Hole CSHM HP5 50 C6
Herbert St HHNE HP2 35 N5
KTTN NW5 4 C1
PLSTW E13 141 L1
Hercies Rd HGDN/ICK UB10 132 A1
Hercules PI HOLWY N7 * 118 D7
Hercules Rd STHWK SE1 17 P4
Hercules St HOLWY N7 118 D7
Hercules Wy GSTN WD25 54 C10
Hereford Av EBAR EN4 98 A2
Hereford CI EPSOM KT18 238 A4
GUW GU2 249 L8
STA TW18 195 L1
Hereford Copse WOKS/MYFD GU22 231 N5
Hereford Gdns IL IG1 122 B9
PIN HA5 113 M3
WHTN TW2 176 B1
Hereford Ms BAY/PAD W2 8 A5
Hereford PI NWCR SE14 * 160 F7
Hereford Retreat PECK SE15 159 J5
Hereford Rd ACT W3 135 P9
BAY/PAD W2 8 B4
BOW E3 139 N4
EA W5 154 A3
FELT TW13 175 M4
WAN E11 121 N1
Hereford Sq SKENS SW7 15 L6
Hereford St BETH E2 140 A4
Hereford Wy CHSGTN KT9 219 H11
Herent Dr CLAY IG5 122 C1
Hereward Av PUR/KEN CR8 223 N6
Hereward Gdns PLMGR N13 99 L6
Hereward Gn LOU IG10 89 L5
Hereward Rd TOOT SW17 179 P7
Herga Ct WAT WD17 72 E5
Herga Rd KTN/HRWW/WS HA3 114 F3
Herington Gv RBRW/HUT CM13 107 M13
Heriot Av CHING E4 101 J1
Heriot Rd CHERT KT16 195 K7
Heriots CI STAN HA7 94 F3
Heritage Av CDALE/KGS NW9 96 D4
Heritage CI STALW/RED AL3 * 38 D6
SUN TW16 197 H1
UX/CGN UB8 131 M6
Heritage Ct EGH TW20 172 G8
Heritage HI HAYES BR2 225 P4
Heritage Lawn HORL RH6 280 D5
Heritage PI WAND/EARL SW18 * 179 J3
WARE SG12 26 C3
WCCE AL7 23 N5
WLYN AL6


Hermes CI MV/WKIL W9 8 E2
Hermes Ct BRXS/STRHM SW2 * 180 A1
Hermes Wy WLGTN SM6 222 A8
Hermiston Av CEND/HSY/T N8 117 A8
DTCH/LGLY SL3 149 P2
ENC/FH EN2 79 J6
ESH/CLAY KT10 218 C1
RCHPK/HAM TW10 177 J1
SHPTN TW17 195 P4
SWFD E18 121 L2
Hermitage Cots STAN HA7 * 94 D6
Hermitage Ct POTB/CUF EN6 59 L3
Hermitage Gdns CRICK NW2 117 H3
NRWD SE19 181 K10
Hermitage La CRICK NW2 117 H3
CROY/NA CR0 203 N7
STRHM/NOR SW16 180 G10
UED N18 99 H5
WDSR SL4 148 F9
Hermitage Rd FSBYPK N4 119 H6
NRWD SE19 181 K10
WOKN/KNAP GU21 231 J5
Hermitage Rw HACK E8 * 119 P10
Hermitage St BAY/PAD W2 9 J2
Hermitage Wall WAP E1W 13 P10
Hermitage Wy STAN HA7 94 F9
Hermitage Woods Crs WOKN/KNAP GU21 231 J6
Hermit PI KIL/WHAMP NW6 2 C6
Hermit Rd CAN/RD E16 141 L6
Hermits PI FBAR/BDGN N4 284 A5
Hermit St FSBYE EC1V 6 C11
Hermon Gv HYS/HAR UB3 133 H10
Hermon HI WAN E11 121 M2
Herndon CI EGH TW20 172 D7
Herndon Rd WAND/EARL SW18 179 N4
Herne CI HYS/HAR UB3 133 H6
WLSDN NW10 116 A10
Herne Ct BUSH WD23 94 B2
Herne HI HNHL SE24 181 K4
Herne Hill Rd HNHL SE24 181 K9
Herne Ms UED N18 99 H5
Herne PI HNHL SE24 181 H9
Herne Rd BUSH WD23 94 A10
SURB KT6 199 J9
Herneshaw HAT AL10 40 C6
Herns La WCCE AL7 23 N3
Herns Wy WCCE AL7 23 N3
Heron CI BKHH IG9 101 M2
CRAWE RH11 283 H10
GUW GU2 249 N5
HAT AL10 40 C5
RKW/CH/CXG WD3 91 N5
WALTH E17 101 M11
WLSDN NW10 116 A10
Heron Ct BMLY BR1 205 H11
HAYES BR2 226 D1
KUT/HW KT1 199 K5
Heron Crs SCUP DA14 185 H7
Heron Dr ADL/WDHM KT15 215 M2
FSBYPK N4 119 K7
STHGT/OAK N14
Heron Flight Av HCH RM12 143 P4
Herongate Rd CHES/WCR EN8 62 C3
MNPK E12 121 P7
SWFD E18
Heron HI BELV DA17 163 P6
Heron Ms IL IG1 122 C7
Heron PI BERM/RHTH SE16 140 F10
DEN/HRF UB9
Heron Quays POP/IOD E14 140 F10
Herons, The CROY/NA CR0 * 224 C2
Heron Rd CROY/NA CR0
HNHL SE24 160 G11
TWK TW1 154 A11
Heron Sq RCH/KEW TW9 *
The Heronry WOT/HER KT12 216 D3
Herons CI CRAWE RH10 281 P10
Heronscourt LTWR GU18 212 B7
Herons Cft WEY KT13 216 D3
Herons Elm BERK HP4 33 K2
Heronsforde EDGW HA8 95 M6
Heronsgate EDGW HA8 95 M6
Herons Lea CRAWE RH10 281 P10
Heronslea WATN WD24 73 K2
Herons Lea HGT N6 117 G11
Heronslea Dr STAN HA7 95 N4
Herons PI ISLW TW7 154 E9
Herons Wd HLW CM20 28 A9
Heronswood PI PLMGR N13
Heronswood Rd HORL RH6 * 280 C5
Heron Wk NTHWD HA6 92 A9
Heron Wy EBED/NFELT TW14 153 H10
HAT AL10 40 C6
HLWW/ROY CM19 27 M10
UPMR RM14 126 D6
Heronway RBRW/HUT CM13 107 M13
WFD IG8 101 K3
Herrick Rd HBRY N5 119 J6
Herrick St WEST SW1P 17 H6
Herries St NKENS W10
Herringham Rd CHARL SE7 161 P7
Herrings La CHERT KT16 195 K5
Herrongate CI EN EN1 79 P6
Hersant CI WLSDN NW10 136 B1
Herschell Rd FSTH SE23 182 A5
Herschel St SL SL1 149 L1
Hersham CI PUT/ROE SW15 178 D6
Hersham Gdns WOT/HER KT12 217 M11
Hersham Rd WOT/HER KT12 217 L11
Hertford Av MORT/ESHN SW14 178 A1
Hertford CI EBAR EN4 77 N2
Hertford Ct STAN HA7 * 95 J11
Hertford End Ct NTHWD HA6 * 92 B11
Hertford PI FITZ W1T 10 F1
Hertford Rd BARK IG11 142 C11
BRXN/ST SW9
CHES/WCR EN8 62 D5
ED N9 100 D2
EBAR EN4 77 N2
ENC/FH EN2
GNTH/NBYPK IG2 122 G3
IS N1 7 K1
PEND EN3
WARE SG12
WCCE AL7
WLYN AL6
Hertford Road High St PEND EN3 * 80 B10
Hertfordshire Wy HERT/WAS SG14 25 H1
Hertford St MYFR/PICC W1J 10 E9


Hertford Wy MTCM CR4 202 F4
Hertingfordbury Rd HERT/WAT SG14 24 F7
Hertslet Rd HOLWY N7 118 D8
Hertsmere Rd POP/IOD E14 140 F9
Hertswood Ct BAR EN5 * 77 M4
Hervey CI FNCH N3 97 K9
Hervey Park Rd WALTH E17 120 D2
Hervines Ct AMS HP6 69 H5
Hervines Rd AMS HP6 68 G3
Hesa Rd HYS/HAR UB3 133 H8
Heseltine Rd SNWD SE25
Hesewall CI CLAP SW4 243 K5
Hesiers Av HARL CR6 243 K5
Hesiers Rd WARL CR6 243 K5
Hesketh Av RDART DA2 188 A4
Hesketh PI NTGHL W11 8 A11
Hesketh Rd FSTGT E7 121 H8
Heslop Rd BAL SW12 180 A4
Hesper Ms ECT SW5 14 G7
Hesperus Crs POP/IOD E14 160 G5
Hessel Rd WEA W13 154 F1
Hessel St WCHPL E1 140 A8
Hesselyn Dr RAIN RM13 145 J2
Hester Av WF KT7 220 C7
Hestercombe Av FUL/PGN SW6 157 J7
Hesterman Wy CROY/NA CR0 202 F8
Hester Rd BTSEA SW11 157 P6
UED N18 99 P6
Heston Av HEST TW5 153 N6
Heston Grange La HEST TW5 153 N5
Heston Rd HEST TW5 154 A5
REDH RH1 276 A5
Heston St NWCR SE14 160 F7
Heswell Gn OXHEY WD19 * 93 H4
Hetchleys HHW HP1 35 K3
Hetherington CI SLN SL2 128 E5
Hetherington Rd CLAP SW4 158 F10
SHPTN TW17 196 D2
Hetherington Wy HGDN/ICK UB10 111 P9
Hethersett CI REIG RH2 257 M7
Hetley Rd SHB W12 136 F10
Heton Gdns HDN NW4 116 D2
Hevelius CI GNWCH SE10 161 L4
Hever Court Rd GVE DA12 190 F9
Hever Gdns BMLY BR1 206 D2
Heveram Rd WOOL/PLUM SE18 163 H3
Hevers Av HORL RH6 280 A5
Heversham Rd BXLYHN DA7 164 B8
Hevingham Dr CHDH RM6 123 M3
Hewardine Ter HGDN/ICK UB10 132 D5
Hewens Rd HGDN/ICK UB10 111 P9
Hewers Wy KWD/TDW/WH KT20 238 G6
Hewett CI STAN HA7 94 G5
Hewett PI SWLY BR8 208 E4
Hewett St SDTCH EC2A 13 K2
Hewins CI WAB EN9 63 K8
Hewish Rd UED N18 99 H5
Hewison St BOW E3 140 A1
Hewitt Av WDGN N22 99 H10
Hewitt CI CROY/NA CR0 204 F10
STALE/WH AL4 21 J4
Hewitt Rd CEND/HSY/T N8 119 H3
Hewitts Rd ORP BR6 228 A4
Hewlett Rd BOW E3 140 D4
The Hexagon HGT N6 118 A6
Hexal Rd CAT SE6 183 H4
Hexham CI CRAWE RH10 284 F7
Hexham Gdns ISLW TW7 154 F6
Hexham Rd BAR EN5 77 J8
MRDN SM4 201 L8
WNWD SE27 181 K5
Hextalls La REDH RH1 259 L4
Heybourne Rd TOTM N17 100 A8
Heybridge STRHM/NOR SW16 180 G9
Heybridge Av STRHM/NOR SW16 180 G9
Heybridge Dr BARK/HLT IG6 122 G3
Heybridge Wy LEY E10 120 D5
Heydons CI STALW/RED AL3 38 C4
Heyford Av RYNPK SW20 200 H11
VX/NE SW8 158 F6
Heyford Rd LCOL/BKTW AL2 56 B4
MTCM CR4 201 P2
RAD WD7 74 B3
Heyford Ter VX/NE SW8 158 F6
Heygate Est WALW SE17 18 E5
Heygate St WALW SE17 18 C6
Heymede LHD/OX KT22 257 H9
Heynes Rd BCTR RM8 123 M9
Heysham Dr OXHEY WD19 93 K6
Heysham La HAMP NW3 117 J2
Heysham Rd SEVS/STOTM N15 119 L4
Heythorpe WOKN/KNAP GU21 231 L3
Heythorp St WAND/EARL SW18 179 J3
Heythrop Dr HGDN/ICK UB10 112 A9
Heywood Av CDALE/KGS NW9 96 B9
Heyworth Rd CLPT E5 139 P1
SRTFD E15 121 L3
Hibbert Rd KTN/HRWW/WS HA3 94 E10
WALTH E17 120 E5
Hibbert St BTSEA SW11 157 M9
Hibberts Wy CFSP/GDCR SL9 110 B1
Hibbs CI SWLY BR8 208 E2
Hibernia Dr GVE DA12 191 J6
Hibernia Rd HSLW TW3 153 P10
Hichisson Rd PECK SE15 182 B3
Hicken Rd BRXS/STRHM SW2 180 C11
Hickin CI CHARL SE7 162 A3
Hickin St POP/IOD E14 161 H1
Hickling Rd IL IG1 122 C10
Hickling Wk CRAWE RH10 284 C9
Hickman Av CHING E4 101 M11
Hickman CI BRXN E16 142 A7
CAN/RD E16 142 A7
Hickmans CI RDART DA2 188 A4
Hickmore Wy CHDH RM6 123 H6
Hickory CI ED N9 99 H7
Hicks Av GFD/PVL UB6 134 C5
Hicks CI BTSEA SW11 157 P9
Hicks St DEPT SE8 160 G4
Hidalgo Ct HHNE HP2 36 A2
Hidcote CI WOKS/MYFD GU22 232 G2
Hidcote Gdns RYNPK SW20 200 D4
The Hideaway ABLGY WD5 54 G7
Hide PI WEST SW1P 17 H7
The Hides HLW CM20 28 G10
Higgins Rd CHESW EN7 61 L3
Highacre DORK RH4 272 C5
High Acres ABLGY WD5 54 F5
Higham Hill Rd WALTH E17 120 C1
Higham Ms NTHLT UB5 133 N6
Higham PI WALTH E17 120 C2
Higham Rd TOTM N17 99 P10
WFD IG8 101 M4
Highams Hill Cots WARL CR6 * 225 M8
Highams Lodge Cots WARL CR6
Higham Station Av CHING E4 101 L11
The Highams WALTH E17 101 N10
High Ash CI SLH/COR SS17 169 K2
Highbanks CI WELL DA16 164 A11
Highbanks Rd PIN HA5 94 A4
Highbank Wy CEND/HSY/T N8 119 H2
High Barn Rd RDKG RH5 253 L10

Highbarrow Cl PUR/KEN CR8 .. 222 G6
Highbarrow Rd CROY/NA CR0 .. 203 N8
High Beech SAND/SEL CR2 .. 223 M4
High Beeches BNSTD SM7 .. 220 C10
  CFSP/GDCR SL9 .. 110 A6
  ORP BR6 .. 227 K3
  SCUP DA14 .. 185 P8
  WEY KT13 .. 216 F3
High Beeches Cl
  PUR/KEN CR8 .. 222 G6
High Beech Rd LOU IG10 .. 82 B8
High Bois La AMS .. 69 J1
Highbridge Rd BARK IG11 .. 142 E3
High Bridge St WAB EN9 .. 62 F10
Highbrook Rd BKHTH/KID SE3 .. 162 A9
High Broom Crs WWKM BR4 .. 204 C6
Highbury Av HOD EN11 .. 44 F7
  THHTH CR7 .. 205 H2
  WWKM BR4 .. 204 C9
Highbury Cnr IS N1 .. 6 C1
Highbury Crs HBRY N5 .. 119 H10
Highbury Dr LHD/OX KT22 .. 236 F5
Highbury Est HBRY N5 .. 119 K10
Highbury Gdns
  GDMY/SEVK IG3 .. 123 H7
Highbury Gra HBRY N5 .. 119 J10
Highbury Gv HBRY N5 .. 119 J10
Highbury New Pk HBRY N5 .. 6 D1
Highbury Pk HBRY N5 .. 119 J9
Highbury Pl HBRY N5 .. 6 C1
Highbury Qd HBRY N5 .. 119 K8
Highbury Rd WIM/MER SW19 .. 179 H8
Highbury Station Pde
  HBRY N5 * .. 6 C1
Highbury Station Rd IS N1 .. 6 B2
Highbury Ter HBRY N5 .. 119 J10
Highbury Terrace Ms
  HBRY N5 .. 119 J10
High Canons BORE WD6 .. 75 P3
High Cedar Dr RYNPK SW20 .. 178 C10
Highclere ASC SL5 .. 192 C5
  GU GU1 .. 250 D7
Highclere Cl PUR/KEN CR8 .. 241 K1
Highclere Ct
  WOKN/KNAP GU21 .. 231 H3
Highclere Dr HHS/BOV HP3 .. 36 C10
Highclere Rd NWMAL KT3 .. 200 A3
  WOKN/KNAP GU21 .. 231 H3
Highclere St SYD SE26 .. 182 D7
Highcliffe Dr PUT/ROE SW15 .. 178 C2
Highcliffe Gdns REDBR IG4 .. 122 B3
High Cl RKW/CH/CXG WD3 .. 71 N5
Highcombe CHARL SE7 .. 161 N5
Highcombe Cl ELTH/MOT SE9 .. 184 H4
High Coombe Pl
  KUTN/CMB KT2 .. 178 A10
Highcote La RGUE GU4 .. 251 K2
Highcroft CDALE/KGS NW9 .. 116 B3
Highcroft Av ALP/SUD HA0 .. 135 L2
Highcroft Ct GT/LBKH KT23 .. 235 P9
Highcroft Gdns GLDGN NW11 .. 117 J4
Highcroft Rd ARCH N19 .. 118 F5
  HHS/BOV HP3 .. 53 K1
Highcroft Trailer Gdns
  HHS/BOV HP3 * .. 52 E2
High Cross GSTN WD25 .. 74 C3
Highcross Rd MEO DA13 .. 189 J9
High Cross Rd TOTM N17 .. 119 P1
Highcross Wy PUT/ROE SW15 .. 178 D4
Highdaun Dr
  STRHM/NOR SW16 .. 202 A10
High Dells HAT AL10 .. 40 C5
High Down WPK KT4 .. 200 B9
Highdown Cl BNSTD SM7 .. 239 H2
Highdown Ct CRAWE RH10 .. 284 C10
High Down La PUT/ROE SW15 .. 178 E2
High Down Rd PUT/ROE SW15 .. 178 E2
High Dr CTHM CR3 .. 242 E8
  LHD/OX KT22 .. 218 C10
  NWMAL KT3 .. 199 P1
High Elms IG7 .. 103 H5
  UPMR RM14 .. 126 D6
  WFD IG8 .. 101 M6
High Elms Cl NTHWD HA6 .. 92 D7
High Elms La GSTN WD25 .. 55 J7
High Elms Rd ORP BR6 .. 226 F5
Higher Dr BNSTD SM7 .. 220 C9
  EHSLY KT24 .. 252 F5
  PUR/KEN CR8 .. 223 H4
Higher Gn EW KT17 .. 220 D9
Highfield BNSTD SM7 .. 239 H4
  CSTG HP8 .. 90 A3
  HLWS CM18 .. 47 K2
  KGLGY WD4 .. 53 H4
  OXHEY WD19 .. 93 N4
  RGUE GU4 ..
Highfield Av CDALE/KGS NW9 .. 115 P3
  ERITH DA8 .. 164 C5
  GFD/PVL UB6 .. 114 D10
  GLDGN NW11 .. 116 C3
  HARP AL5 .. 20 B3
  ORP BR6 .. 227 M5
  PIN HA5 .. 113 N3
  WBLY HA9 .. 115 P4
Highfield Cl CDALE/KGS NW9 .. 115 P3
  ERITH DA8 .. 164 C5
  GFD/PVL UB6 .. 114 D10
  GLDGN NW11 .. 116 C3
  HARP AL5 .. 20 B3
  ORP BR6 .. 227 M5
  PIN HA5 .. 113 N3
  WBLY HA9 .. 115 P4
Highfield Cl AMS HP6 .. 116 A3
  BF/WBF KT14 .. 215 K9
  CDALE/KGS NW9 .. 115 P3
  CRW RM5 .. 104 D7
  LEW SE13 .. 183 J2
  LHD/OX KT22 .. 218 C10
  NTHWD HA6 .. 92 D7
  SURB KT6 .. 199 H8
  WDGN N22 .. 99 H8
Highfield Cots RDART DA2 * .. 187 J9
Highfield Ct EGH TW20 .. 171 P9
  STHGT/OAK N14 ..
Highfield Crs HCH RM12 .. 125 N7
  NTHWD HA6 .. 92 F9
Highfield Dr BROX EN10 .. 44 D7
  HAYES BR2 .. 205 K4
  HGDN/ICK UB10 .. 111 P8
  HOR/WEW KT19 ..
  WWKM BR4 .. 204 G10
Highfield Gdns
  CDW/CHF RM16 .. 168 A1
  EPP CM16 .. 65 H7
  GLDGN NW11 .. 116 C3
Highfield Hl WNWD SE19 .. 181 L10
Highfield La HHNE HP2 .. 36 A1
  STALE/WH AL4 .. 39 H8
Highfield Link CRW RM5 .. 104 D7
Highfield Park Dr
  STALE/WH AL4 .. 39 H7
Highfield Pl EPP CM16 .. 65 H7
Highfield Rd ACT W3 .. 135 M10
  BERK HP4 ..
  BF/WBF KT14 .. 215 K9
  BGR/WK TN15 .. 247 M2
  BH/WHM TN16 .. 245 P5
  BMLY BR1 .. 206 D4
  BRYLDS KT5 .. 199 P7
  BUSH WD23 .. 73 M9
  BXLYHS DA6 .. 186 A1
  CHERT KT16 .. 195 K6
  CHESW EN7 .. 61 N2
  CHST BR7 .. 207 J3
  CRW RM5 .. 104 D7
  CSHM HP5 .. 50 C5
  CTHM CR3 .. 241 P9
  EGH TW20 .. 172 A9
  FELT TW13 .. 175 H4
  GLDGN NW11 * .. 117 H4
  HCH RM12 .. 125 N7
  HERT/BAY SG13 .. 25 L3
  ISLW TW7 .. 154 E7
  NTHWD HA6 .. 92 F9
  PUR/KEN CR8 .. 222 G6
  STALE/WH AL4 .. 39 H8
  SUT SM1 .. 196 G4
  SUT SM1 .. 221 P2
  WCHMH N21 .. 99 J3

WDSR SL4 .. 148 E9
WFD IG8 .. 102 H8
WOT/HER KT12 .. 197 H8
High Flds ASC SL5 .. 192 E5
Highfields ASHTD KT21 .. 237 J10
  EHSLY KT24 .. 252 C4
  KGLGY WD4 .. 53 H4
  LHD/OX KT22 .. 236 C10
  POTB/CUF EN6 .. 60 F4
  RAD WD7 .. 74 E1
Highfields Gv HGT N6 .. 118 B6
Highfield Wy POTB/CUF EN6 .. 59 J9
High Firs RAD WD7 .. 74 F1
  SWLY BR8 .. 208 F4
High Firs Crs HARP AL5 .. 20 C3
High Foleys ESH/CLAY KT10 .. 218 G4
Highgate Av HGT N6 .. 118 B5
High Garth ESH/CLAY KT10 .. 218 B3
Highgate Cl HGT N6 .. 118 C5
Highgate Edge EFNCH N2 * .. 117 J3
Highgate Gv SBW CM21 .. 29 N1
High Gv BMLY BR1 .. 205 P1
Highgate Hl ARCH N19 .. 118 B6
Highgate Rd KTTN NW5 .. 118 B8
Highgate Spinney
  CEND/HSY/T N8 * .. 118 A4
Highgate West Hl HGT N6 .. 118 B6
High Gv BMLY BR1 .. 205 P1
Highgrove BRWN CM15 .. 86 C10
Highgrove Cl CHST BR7 .. 206 A4
  FBAR/BDGN N11 .. 98 B6
Highgrove Ms CAR SM5 .. 201 P10
Highgrove Rd BCTR RM8 .. 123 M10
Highgrove Wy RSLP HA4 .. 113 H4
High Hill Ferry CLPT E5 .. 120 A6
High Hill Rd WARL CR6 .. 225 H10
High Holborn HHOL WC1V .. 11 M5
High House La TIL RM18 .. 168 C2
Highland Cots WLGTN SM6 * .. 222 C1
Highland Cft BECK BR3 .. 183 J8
Highland Dr BUSH WD23 .. 94 A1
  HHS/BOV HP3 .. 36 C10
Highland Pk FELT TW13 .. 174 C7
Highland Rd AMSS HP7 .. 69 J5
  BMLY BR1 .. 205 L1
  BXLYHS DA6 .. 164 B10
  HAYES BR2 .. 205 L2
  NRWD SE19 .. 181 M9
  NTHWD HA6 .. 93 H10
  PUR/KEN CR8 ..
  RSEV TN14 .. 228 C7
  WAB EN9 .. 45 K8
Highlands BRKMPK AL9 .. 40 F1
  OXHEY WD19 .. 93 K2
Highlands Av ACT W3 .. 135 M10
  LHD/OX KT22 .. 237 H8
  WCHMH N21 .. 78 G10
Highlands Cl CFSP/GDCR SL9 .. 90 C8
  FSBYPK N4 .. 118 C5
  LHD/OX KT22 .. 236 C10
Highlands End
  CFSP/GDCR SL9 .. 90 C8
Highlands Gdns IL IG1 .. 122 C6
Highlands Heath
  PUT/ROE SW15 .. 178 F3
Highlands La SWLY BR8 .. 209 H2
  CFSP/GDCR SL9 .. 90 C8
  WOKS/MYFD GU22 .. 232 B7
Highlands Pk BGR/WK TN15 .. 247 M7
Highlands Rd BAR EN5 .. 77 K9
  BEAC HP9 .. 89 H6
  LHD/OX KT22 .. 237 H8
  REIG RH2 .. 257 N9
  STMC/STPC BR5 .. 207 L7
The Highlands BAR EN5 .. 77 K9
  EDGW HA8 .. 95 N10
  EHSLY KT24 .. 252 F5
  POTB/CUF EN6 .. 59 M7
  RKW/CH/CXG WD3 .. 91 L1
  SLN SL2 .. 130 H9
Highland Ter LEW SE13 * .. 160 C9
High La CTHM CR3 .. 242 E5
  HNWL W7 .. 134 C8
  RBSF CM22 .. 30 F5
  WARL CR6 .. 242 E4
Highlea Cl CDALE/KGS NW9 .. 96 F5
High Level Dr SYD SE26 .. 181 P7
Highlever Rd NKENS W10 .. 136 F7
High Limes NRWD SE19 * .. 181 M9
High Md CHIG IG7 .. 102 F3
  WWKM BR4 .. 204 B9
Highmead WOOL/PLUM SE18 .. 163 A6
Highmead Crs ALP/SUD HA0 .. 135 L2
High Meadow Cl DORK RH4 .. 272 C6
  PIN HA5 .. 113 J2
High Meadow Crs
  CDALE/KGS NW9 .. 116 A3
High Meadow Pl CHERT KT16 .. 195 K6
High Mdw CHIG IG7 .. 102 C6
High Meads STALE/WH AL4 .. 21 H5
High Meads Rd CAN/RD E16 .. 142 A4
Highmoor AMSS HP7 .. 69 J5
Highmore Rd
  BKHTH/KID SE3 .. 161 K6
High Mt HDN NW4 .. 116 H4
High Oak Rd WARE SG12 .. 26 C1
High Oaks CRAWW RH11 .. 283 M10
  ENC/FH EN2 .. 78 C4
  STAL/WRAY AL3 .. 38 E1
High Oaks Rd WGCW AL8 .. 22 H4
High Pastures RBSF CM22 .. 30 F3
High Pth WIM/MER SW19 .. 201 L1
High Pewley GU GU1 .. 250 F10
High Pine Cl WEY KT13 .. 216 D2
The Pines WARL CR6 .. 242 F5
High Point ELTH/MOT SE9 .. 184 F6
Highpoint WEY KT13 .. 216 B2
High Rdg MUSWH N10 * .. 98 C9
Highridge Cl EPSOM KT18 * .. 238 E1
  RAD WD7 .. 56 D1

UX/CGN UB8 .. 131 M7
WBLY HA9 .. 115 K10
WDGN N22 .. 98 C9
WLSDN NW10 .. 136 B1
High Road Broxbourne
  BROX EN10 .. 44 E7
High Road Eastcote PIN HA5 .. 113 J3
High Road Ickenham
  HGDN/ICK UB10 .. 112 C8
High Road Leyton LEY E10 .. 120 C9
High Road Leytonstone
  WAN E11 .. 121 J3
High Road Turnford
  CHES/WCR EN8 .. 62 D2
High Road Woodford Gn
  SWFD E18 .. 101 M9
High Road Wormley
  BROX EN10 .. 44 E7
Highshore Rd PECK SE15 .. 159 N8
High Silver LOU IG10 .. 82 A8
High St IVER SL0 .. 131 J8
High Standing CTHM CR3 .. 259 K1
Highstead Crs ERITH DA8 .. 164 F3
Highstone Av WAN E11 .. 121 M4
High St ABLGY WD5 .. 54 C4
  ACT W3 .. 135 P10
  ADL/WDHM KT15 .. 215 L1
  AMSS HP7 .. 69 J5
  ASC SL5 .. 192 C5
  BAR EN5 .. 77 H7
  BARK/HLT IG6 .. 102 F10
  BECK BR3 .. 204 F1
  BELMT SM2 .. 221 M4
  BERK HP4 .. 33 G4
  BGR/WK TN15 .. 247 N7
  BH/WHM TN16 .. 262 F3
  BMLY BR1 .. 205 N7
  BMLY BR1 .. 183 M7
  BNSTD SM7 .. 239 K1
  BRW CM14 .. 107 H5
  BTFD TW8 .. 155 J5
  BUSH WD23 .. 73 P10
  CAR SM5 .. 222 A2
  CEND/HSY/T N8 .. 118 F2
  CFSP/GDCR SL9 .. 90 B2
  CHEAM SM3 .. 221 H3
  CHES/WCR EN8 .. 62 C9
  CHOB/PIR GU24 .. 212 D8
  COB KT11 .. 217 J10
  CRAWE RH10 .. 283 N7
  CROY/NA CR0 .. 203 K10
  CSHM HP5 .. 50 C7
  CSTG HP8 .. 89 P4
  CTHM CR3 .. 241 M9
  DART DA1 .. 187 M2
  DEN/HRF UB9 .. 91 M10
  DORK RH4 .. 272 C2
  DTCH/LGLY SL3 .. 149 N7
  E/WMO/HCT KT8 .. 197 P5
  EA W5 .. 135 J9
  EGH TW20 .. 172 C6
  EMPK RM11 .. 125 M7
  EPP CM16 .. 65 J7
  ESH/CLAY KT10 .. 218 A1
  EW KT17 .. 220 C5
  EYN DA4 .. 209 H4
  FBAR/BDGN N11 .. 98 C6
  FELT TW13 .. 174 A7
  GDST RH9 .. 260 A7
  GRAYS RM17 .. 167 M5
  GT/LBKH KT23 .. 254 A1
  GU GU1 .. 268 A1
  GUW GU2 .. 267 P2
  GVW DA11 .. 189 N2
  HARP AL5 .. 20 A3
  HCH RM12 .. 125 L6
  HEST TW5 .. 153 J5
  HHS/BOV HP3 .. 52 D3
  HHW HP1 .. 35 H5
  HLWE CM17 .. 29 M7
  HLWW/ROY CM19 .. 27 N10
  HOD EN11 .. 44 H1
  HOR/WEW KT19 .. 220 A9
  HORL RH6 .. 280 C4
  HPTN TW12 .. 198 A1
  HRW HA1 .. 114 D6
  HSLW TW3 .. 154 A9
  HYS/HAR UB3 .. 152 E5
  IVER SL0 .. 131 J8
  KGLGY WD4 .. 54 B5
  KTN/HRWW/WS HA3 .. 114 D1
  KUT/HW KT1 .. 199 H1
  KWD/TDW/WH KT20 .. 238 F10
  LCOL/BKTW AL2 .. 57 H1
  LHD/OX KT22 .. 236 C3
  MLHL NW7 .. 96 E6
  NTHWD HA6 .. 92 G9
  NWMAL KT3 .. 199 P1
  ORP BR6 .. 208 B7
  ORP BR6 .. 227 J2
  ORP BR6 .. 226 D7
  OXTED RH8 .. 261 A6
  PGE/AN SE20 .. 182 B10
  PIN HA5 .. 113 M1
  PLSTW E13 .. 141 M4
  POTB/CUF EN6 .. 59 L9
  PUR RM19 .. 169 H6
  PUR/KEN CR8 .. 223 H7
  RDART DA2 .. 188 E4
  REDH RH1 .. 258 A10
  REDH RH1 .. 258 G4
  REIG RH2 .. 257 K10
  RKW/CH/CXG WD3 .. 91 N2
  ROM RM1 .. 124 F3
  RPLY/SEND GU23 .. 233 M7
  RSEV TN14 .. 228 G6
  RSLP HA4 .. 112 F5
  SCUP DA14 .. 185 K7
  SEV TN13 .. 246 D8
  SHPTN TW17 .. 196 C6
  SL SL1 .. 149 H1
  SL SL1 .. 149 K1
  SNWD SE25 .. 203 N4
  SOCK/AV RM15 .. 146 B10
  SRTFD E15 .. 141 H4
  STA TW18 .. 173 J7
  STALE/WH AL4 .. 21 M4
  STAL/WRAY AL3 .. 38 G1
  STHGT/OAK N14 .. 98 C1
  STMC/STPC BR5 .. 207 M4
  STMC/STPC BR5 .. 207 H4
  STWL/WRAY TW19 .. 172 B2
  STWL/WRAY TW19 .. 173 J1
  SUT SM1 .. 221 P2
  SWCM DA10 .. 189 L1
  SWLY BR8 .. 208 F3
  TEDD TW11 .. 176 F8
  THDIT KT7 .. 197 P4
  THHTH CR7 .. 203 H4
  UX/CGN UB8 .. 131 M2
  WALTH E17 .. 120 E2
  WAN E11 .. 121 N4
  WARE SG12 .. 28 A2
  WAT WD17 .. 73 J2
  WBLY HA9 .. 115 L9
  WEY KT13 .. 216 B1
  WHTN TW2 .. 176 B3
  WIM/MER SW19 .. 178 C9
  WOKN/KNAP GU21 .. 231 H3
  WOKS/MYFD GU22 .. 232 D7
  WOT/HER KT12 .. 197 H8
  WWKM BR4 .. 204 C8
High Street Collier's Wd
  WIM/MER SW19 .. 179 N10
High Street Gn HHNE HP2 .. 36 B1
High Street Harlesden
  WLSDN NW10 .. 136 B3

High Street Harlington
  HTHAIR TW6 .. 152 E7
High Street Ms
  WIM/MER SW19 .. 179 H8
High St North EHAM E6 .. 142 B3
High St South EHAM E6 .. 142 C4
The High HLW CM20 * .. 28 E7
High Timber St BLKFR EC4V .. 12 E7
High Tor Cl BMLY BR1 * .. 184 B6
High Tree Cl ADL/WDHM KT15 .. 215 K2
High Trees BRXS/STRHM SW2 .. 162 B3
  CROY/NA CR0 .. 204 D8
  EBAR EN4 .. 77 P9
  RDART DA2 .. 188 E4
High Trees Cl CTHM CR3 .. 241 N6
High Trees Rd REIG RH2 .. 275 N1
Highview BNSTD SM7 .. 221 J3
  CSTG HP8 .. 90 A3
Highview CTHM CR3 .. 241 M10
High Vw HAT AL10 .. 40 C6
  PIN HA5 .. 113 K2
  RKW/CH/CXG WD3 .. 71 K8
  SHGR GU5 .. 270 D5
  WATW WD18 .. 73 H2
Highview Av EDGW HA8 .. 96 F8
  WLGTN SM6 .. 223 H3
High View Av LOU IG10 .. 82 C3
  NRWD SE19 .. 203 N2
Highview Ct REIG RH2 * .. 257 N10
Highview Crs
  RBRW/HUT CM13 .. 87 P10
  FBAR/BDGN N11 .. 98 D6
  FNCH N3 .. 115 N4
High View Gdns EDGW HA8 .. 96 F8
  GRAYS RM17 .. 167 P4
Highview Gdns
  POTB/CUF EN6 .. 59 M9
  STALE/WH AL4 .. 39 H1
  UPMR RM14 .. 126 A7
High View Rd GUW GU2 .. 267 J3
  NRWD SE19 .. 181 L9
Highview Rd SCUP DA14 .. 185 L7
  SWFD E18 .. 101 L10
Highview Rd WEA W13 .. 134 F8
High View Ter WEA W13 * ..
Highwaymans Rdg
  BFOR GU20 .. 212 A1
The Highway BELMT SM2 .. 221 N6
  ORP BR6 .. 227 L2
  STAN HA7 .. 94 F3
High Wickfield WGCE AL7 .. 23 M6
Highwold COUL/CHIP CR5 .. 240 B4
Highwood BUSH WD23 .. 73 N5
Highwood Cl BRW CM14 .. 106 G1
  ORP BR6 .. 226 F9
  PUR/KEN CR8 .. 241 K3
Highwood Dr ORP BR6 .. 226 F9
Highwood Gdns CLAY IG5 .. 122 B6
Highwood Gv MLHL NW7 .. 96 A6
Highwoodhall La
  HHS/BOV HP3 .. 54 B1
Highwood Hl MLHL NW7 .. 96 B1
Highwood La LOU IG10 .. 82 D10
High Wood Rd ARCH N19 .. 118 E6
Highwoods CTHM CR3 .. 259 N1
  LHD/OX KT22 .. 237 H7
High Worple
  RYLN/HDSTN HA2 .. 113 M5
Highworth FBAR/BDGN N11 .. 98 E7
Highworth St CAMTN NW1 * .. 9 P1
High Wych La SBW CM21 .. 29 H5
High Wych Rd SBW CM21 .. 29 J5
Hilary Av MTCM CR4 .. 202 B3
Hilary Cl ERITH DA8 .. 164 C7
  FUL/PGN SW6 * .. 157 L6
  HCH RM12 .. 125 L10
Hilary Rd SHB W12 .. 136 C9
  CEND/HSY/T N8 ..
Hilbert Rd CHEAM SM3 .. 201 H9
Hilborough Cl WIM/MER SW19 .. 179 M10
Hilborough Rd HACK E8 * .. 7 M4
Hilborough Wy ORP BR6 .. 226 G2
Hilda Lockett Wk
  BRXN/ST SW9 .. 159 J8
Hilda May Av SWLY BR8 .. 208 F3
Hilda Rd CAN/RD E16 .. 141 K6
  EHAM E6 .. 142 A4
Hilda Ter BRXN/ST SW9 .. 159 H8
Hilda Vale Cl ORP BR6 .. 226 D1
Hildenborough Gdns
  BMLY BR1 .. 183 K9
Hildenbrea Dr ERITH DA8 .. 165 A6
Hildenlea Pl HAYES BR2 .. 205 K2
The Hildens DORK RH4 .. 272 B6
The Hilders ASHTD KT21 .. 237 N3
Hildreth St BAL SW12 .. 180 F2
Hildyard Rd FUL/PGN SW6 .. 14 F9
Hiley Rd WLSDN NW10 .. 136 F5
Hilgay GU GU1 .. 250 C10
Hilgay Cl GU GU1 .. 250 C10
Hilgrove Rd KIL/WHAMP NW6 .. 3 K4
Hiliary Gdns STAN HA7 .. 94 H10
Hiljon Crs CFSP/GDCR SL9 .. 90 B10
Hillars Heath Rd
  COUL/CHIP CR5 .. 240 F1
Hillary Av GVW DA11 .. 190 B6
Hillhouse WAB EN9 .. 63 L6
Hill House Av STAN HA7 .. 94 H6
Hillary Crs WOT/HER KT12 .. 197 M6
Hillary Dr ISLW TW7 .. 154 E10
Hillary Rd DTCH/LGLY SL3 .. 150 B2
  NWDGN UB2 .. 133 P2
Hillbeck Cl PECK SE15 .. 160 B6
Hillbeck Wy GFD/PVL UB6 .. 134 C3
Hillborne Cl HYS/HAR UB3 .. 153 H4
Hillborough Av SEV TN13 .. 247 L8
Hillborough Cl
  WIM/MER SW19 .. 179 M10
Hillbrook Gdns WEY KT13 .. 216 B6
Hillbrook Rd TOOT SW17 .. 180 A6
Hill Brow BMLY BR1 .. 206 A1
  RDART DA2 .. 188 A4
Hillbrow NWMAL KT3 .. 200 C1
Hillbrow Cl BXLY DA5 .. 186 F6
  RGUW GU3 .. 248 G6
Hillbrow Rd BMLY BR1 .. 183 K10
  ESH/CLAY KT10 .. 218 B1
Hillbury Av
  KTN/HRWW/WS HA3 .. 114 C10
Hillbury Cl WARL CR6 .. 242 A4
Hillbury Gdns WARL CR6 .. 242 A4
Hillbury Rd TOOT SW17 .. 180 G6
  WARL CR6 .. 241 P3
Hill Cl BAR EN5 .. 76 F7
  CHST BR7 .. 184 C10
  COB KT11 .. 217 P8
  CRICK NW2 .. 82 C3
  GLDGN NW11 .. 117 H4
  HRW HA1 .. 114 E10
  MEO DA13 .. 190 D10
  PUR/KEN CR8 .. 223 K8
  STAN HA7 .. 94 A10
  WOKN/KNAP GU21 .. 232 A10
Hill Common HHS/BOV HP3 .. 36 E10
Hillcote Av STRHM/NOR SW16 .. 181 P4
Hillcourt Av
  NFNCH/WDSPK N12 .. 97 H6
Hillcourt Rd EDUL SE22 .. 181 A2
Hill Crs BRYLDS KT5 .. 199 M4
  BXLY DA5 .. 186 F6
  EMPK RM11 .. 125 L4
  HRW HA1 .. 114 E10
  TRDG/WHET N20 .. 97 H2
  WPK KT4 .. 200 F6

Hillcrest STALW/RED AL3 * .. 38 A8
  WCHMH N21 .. 99 H1
  WEY KT13 .. 216 C1
Hill Crest HAT AL10 .. 40 D5
  HGT N6 .. 118 B5
  NRWD SE19 .. 181 M9
Hillcrest Av CRICK NW2 .. 118 G1
  EDGW HA8 .. 96 C10
  GLDGN NW11 .. 117 L2
  PIN HA5 .. 113 J2
Hillcrest Cl BECK BR3 .. 204 E6
  EPSOM KT18 .. 238 C1
  SYD SE26 .. 182 B7
Hillcrest Dr RDART DA2 .. 188 F11
Hillcrest Gdns ESH/CLAY KT10 .. 198 E10
  FNCH N3 .. 115 L1
Hillcrest Rd ACT W3 .. 135 M10
  BH/WHM TN16 .. 244 A2
  BMLY BR1 .. 183 M7
  BRYLDS KT5 ..
  DART DA1 .. 186 F4
  EA W5 .. 135 J1
  EMPK RM11 .. 125 H5
  GUW GU2 .. 249 L9
  LOU IG10 .. 82 A10
  ORP BR6 .. 207 K9
  PUR/KEN CR8 .. 222 D9
  RAD WD7 .. 57 M9
  WALTH E17 ..
Hillcrest Vw BECK BR3 .. 204 E6
Hillcrest Wy EPP CM16 .. 65 K7
Hillcroft LOU IG10 .. 82 D6
Hillcroft Av PIN HA5 .. 113 N4
  PUR/KEN CR8 .. 222 C8
Hillcroft Crs EA W5 .. 135 J4
  OXHEY WD19 .. 93 J2
  RSLP HA4 .. 113 L9
  WBLY HA9 .. 115 L8
Hillcroft Rd CSHM HP5 .. 51 J5
Hillcroome Rd BELMT SM2 .. 221 N3
Hillcross Av MRDN SM4 .. 201 J6
Hilldale Rd SUT SM1 .. 221 J1
Hilldeane Rd PUR/KEN CR8 .. 223 J6
Hilldene Cl HARH RM3 .. 105 K4
Hilldown Rd HAYES BR2 .. 205 K8
  HHW HP1 .. 35 K4
  STRHM/NOR SW16 .. 180 F10
Hill Dr CDALE/KGS NW9 .. 115 N6
  STRHM/NOR SW16 .. 202 B5
Hilldrop Crs HOLWY N7 .. 118 C10
Hilldrop Est HOLWY N7 .. 118 D10
Hilldrop La HOLWY N7 .. 118 D10
Hilldrop Rd BMLY BR1 .. 183 N1
  HOLWY N7 .. 118 E10
Hill End ORP BR6 .. 207 H9
  WOOL/PLUM SE18 .. 162 D7
Hill End La STAL AL1 .. 39 H9
Hill End Rd DEN/HRF UB9 .. 91 L7
Hillersdon SLN SL2 .. 131 P4
Hillersdon Av BARN SW13 .. 156 D7
  EDGW HA8 .. 95 L6
Hillery Cl WALW SE17 .. 19 H6
Hilley Field La LHD/OX KT22 .. 236 B8
Hill Farm Av GSTN WD25 .. 55 L2
Hill Farm La CSTG HP8 .. 90 A2
Hill Farm Rd CFSP/GDCR SL9 .. 90 L2
  CSHM HP5 .. 51 J10
  NKENS W10 .. 136 F7
Hillfield HAT AL10 .. 40 F4
Hillfield Av ALP/SUD HA0 .. 135 K2
  CDALE/KGS NW9 .. 116 A3
  CEND/HSY/T N8 .. 117 F2
  MRDN SM4 .. 201 P6
Hillfield Cl GU GU1 .. 250 F8
  REDH RH1 .. 258 B10
  RYLN/HDSTN HA2 .. 114 B2
Hillfield Ct HHNE HP2 .. 35 P6
Hillfield La South BUSH WD23 .. 76 C3
Hillfield Ms CEND/HSY/T N8 .. 117 C3
Hillfield Pde MRDN SM4 .. 201 N6
Hillfield Pk MUSWH N10 .. 98 C1
  WCHMH N21 .. 99 H5
Hillfield Park Ms MUSWH N10 .. 98 C1
Hillfield Pl SEV TN13 .. 246 E6
Hillfield Rd CFSP/GDCR SL9 .. 90 B10
  HMPTN TW12 .. 175 J5
  HHNE HP2 ..
  KIL/WHAMP NW6 .. 2 E9
  REDH RH1 .. 276 B6
  SEV TN13 ..
Hillfield Sq CFSP/GDCR SL9 .. 90 B8
Hillfoot Av CRW RM5 .. 104 D8
Hillfoot Rd CRW RM5 .. 104 D8
Hill Gardens Craven
  BAY/PAD W2 * ..
Hillgate Pl BAL SW12 .. 180 C2
  KENS W8 .. 8 A5
Hillgate St KENS W8 .. 8 A5
Hillground Gdns
  SAND/SEL CR2 .. 223 P8
Hill Gv FELT TW13 .. 175 N5
  ROM RM1 .. 124 G5
Hillhampton ASC SL5 .. 192 E7
Hillhouse WAB EN9 .. 63 L6
Hill House Av STAN HA7 .. 94 H6
Hill House Cl CFSP/GDCR SL9 .. 90 B9
  WCHMH N21 .. 99 H6
Hill House Dr CDW/CHF RM16 .. 168 A1
  HPTN TW12 .. 175 J9
Hill House Rd RDART DA2 .. 188 D4
  STRHM/NOR SW16 .. 181 P8
Hilliard's Ct WAP E1W * .. 140 B10
Hilliards Rd UX/CGN UB8 .. 131 L10
Hillier Gdns CROY/NA CR0 .. 223 H4
Hillier Pl CHSGTN KT9 ..
Hillier Rd BTSEA SW11 .. 180 A2
  GU GU1 .. 250 D10
Hilliers Av UX/CGN UB8 .. 132 B5
Hilliers La CROY/NA CR0 .. 222 G2
Hillingdale BH/WHM TN16 .. 243 N4
Hillingdon Av SEV TN13 .. 247 N1
  STWL/WRAY TW19 .. 173 H4
Hillingdon Rd BXLYHN DA7 ..
  GVW DA11 .. 190 D5
  UX/CGN UB8 ..
Hillingdon St WALW SE17 .. 18 F11
Hillington Trail DEN/HRF UB9 ..
  HGDN/ICK UB10 ..
  HYS/HAR UB3 ..
  WOKN/KNAP GU21 .. 232 A10
Hill La KWD/TDW/WH KT20 .. 239 H10
  RSLP HA4 .. 94 A10
Hill Ley HAT AL10 .. 40 C4
Hill Leys POTB/CUF EN6 ..
Hillman Dr NKENS W10 .. 136 F11
Hillman St HACK E8 .. 7 P1
Hill Md BERK HP4 .. 33 M6
Hillmead CRAWW RH11 .. 283 J7
Hillmead Dr BRXN/ST SW9 .. 159 J3

Hillmead Dr BRXN/ST SW9 .. 159 J3
Hill Meadow AMSS HP7 .. 68 D8
Hillmont Rd ESH/CLAY KT10 .. 198 D3
Hillmore Gv SYD SE26 .. 182 C8
Hillmount WOKS/MYFD GU22 * .. 232 B7
Hill Pk LHD/OX KT22 * .. 236 B5
Hill Park Crt LHD/OX KT22 * .. 236 B5
Hill Pl CRAWW RH11 .. 283 M8
  SLN SL2 .. 128 G2
Hillpoint RKW/CH/CXG WD3 .. 71 M9
Hillreach WOOL/PLUM SE18 .. 162 C4
Hill Ri CFSP/GDCR SL9 .. 90 A10
  DORK RH4 .. 254 D10
Hillrise DTCH/LGLY SL3 .. 150 D5
Hill Ri ED N9 .. 80 A10
  ESH/CLAY KT10 .. 198 G9
  FSTH SE23 .. 182 A4
  GFD/PVL UB6 .. 134 B3
  GLDGN NW11 .. 117 L2
  POTB/CUF EN6 .. 60 E3
  POTB/CUF EN6 .. 59 M10
  RCHPK/HAM TW10 .. 177 H10
  RDART DA2 .. 188 C8
  RKW/CH/CXG WD3 .. 91 L1
  UPMR RM14 .. 125 D6
Hill Rd ALP/SUD HA0 .. 114 D8
  BRW CM14 .. 106 F4
  CAR SM5 .. 221 P4
  EPP CM16 .. 65 H3
  HRW HA1 .. 114 F5
  LHD/OX KT22 .. 236 A8
  MTCM CR4 .. 202 C1
  NTHWD HA6 .. 98 A9
  PIN HA5 .. 113 M4
  PUR/KEN CR8 .. 222 C8
  STJWD NW8 .. 3 G8
  SUT SM1 .. 221 M1
Hillsboro Rd EDUL SE22 .. 181 M1
Hillsborough Gn
  OXHEY WD19 * .. 93 H4
Hill's Chace BRW CM14 .. 107 H5
Hillsgrove Cl WELL DA16 .. 163 N6
Hill Shaw HARP AL5 .. 211 L6
Hillside BAR EN5 .. 192 M5
Hillside BAR EN5 * .. 76 D9
  BNSTD SM7 .. 239 H4
  CDALE/KGS NW9 .. 116 A2
  CSHM HP5 .. 50 C7
  DEN/HRF UB9 .. 111 M3
  ESH/CLAY KT10 * .. 218 A4
  EYN DA4 .. 209 N7
  GRAYS RM17 .. 168 A3
  HAT AL10 .. 40 D4
  HLWE CM17 .. 47 M3
  HOD EN11 .. 44 E2
  RDART DA2 .. 188 D8
  SL SL1 .. 149 H1
  VW GU25 .. 193 P6
  WARE SG12 .. 26 C3
  WGCE AL7 .. 23 L8
  WIM/MER SW19 .. 178 G9
  WLSDN NW10 .. 136 A3
  WOKS/MYFD GU22 .. 232 A6
Hillside Av BORE WD6 .. 75 N5
  CHES/WCR EN8 .. 62 C7
  FBAR/BDGN N11 .. 98 A6
  PUR/KEN CR8 .. 223 L8
  WBLY HA9 .. 115 P5
  WFD IG8 .. 101 P6
Hillside Cl ABLGY WD5 .. 54 F8
  BNSTD SM7 .. 239 H4
  BRKHM/BTCW RH3 .. 273 M1
  CFSP/GDCR SL9 .. 90 B7
  CRAWW RH11 .. 283 J9
  CSTG HP8 .. 89 N4
  MRDN SM4 .. 201 H4
  STJWD NW8 .. 3 H1
  WFD IG8 .. 101 P6
  WOKN/KNAP GU21 .. 231 J3
Hillside Cots BNSTD SM7 .. 222 A9
Hillside Crs CHES/WCR EN8 .. 62 A5
  ENC/FH EN2 .. 79 M3
  NTHWD HA6 .. 73 N10
  OXHEY WD19 .. 73 L10
  RYLN/HDSTN HA2 .. 114 A5
  WARE SG12 .. 26 G1
Hillside Dr EDGW HA8 .. 96 B1
Hillside Gdns ADL/WDHM KT15 .. 215 J9
  AMSS HP7 .. 69 K6
  BAR EN5 .. 76 B4
  BERK HP4 .. 34 A6
  BRKHM/BTCW RH3 .. 255 M10
  BRXS/STRHM SW2 .. 181 M5
  EDGW HA8 .. 95 L5
  FBAR/BDGN N11 * .. 98 C6
  HGT N6 .. 118 A5
  KTN/HRWW/WS HA3 .. 115 K5
  WALTH E17 .. 121 L1
  WLGTN SM6 .. 222 D5
Hillside La HAYES BR2 .. 205 P7
  WARE SG12 .. 26 C1
Hillside Pk ASC SL5 .. 192 E8
Hillside Ri NTHWD HA6 .. 92 B6
Hillside Rd ASHTD KT21 .. 237 L6
  BELMT SM2 .. 221 L5
  BGR/WK TN15 .. 247 N3
  BH/WHM TN16 .. 244 A4
  BRXS/STRHM SW2 .. 181 M5
  BUSH WD23 .. 73 M9
  COUL/CHIP CR5 .. 240 G6
  CROY/NA CR0 .. 223 H3
  CTHM CR3 .. 242 F6
  EA W5 .. 135 L4
  EW KT17 .. 220 C6
  HAYES BR2 .. 205 N7
  NTHWD HA6 .. 92 B6
  RAD WD7 .. 74 G1
  RKW/CH/CXG WD3 .. 71 M9
  SEV TN13 .. 247 H5
  SEVS/STOTM N15 .. 119 M3
  STAL AL1 .. 11 H5
  STHL UB1 .. 133 P4
Hillside Ter GVE DA12 .. 190 E4
  HERT/BAY SG13 .. 25 K7
The Hillside ORP BR6 .. 228 D3
Hillside Wk BRW CM14 .. 106 F4
Hillside Wy GODL GU7 .. 267 J10
Hills La NTHWD HA6 .. 92 B8
Hills Ms EA W5 * .. 135 K5
Hills Pl SOHO/SHAV W1D .. 10 E6
Hillspur Cl GUW GU2 .. 249 L9
Hillspur Rd GUW GU2 .. 249 L8
Hill's Rd BKHH IG9 .. 101 N2
Hillstowe St CLPT E5 .. 120 F8
Hill St MYFR/PICC W1J .. 10 B9
  RCH/KEW TW9 .. 177 J1
Hillswood Dr CHERT KT16 .. 214 F1
The Hill AMSS HP7 .. 68 G8
  CTHM CR3 .. 241 N10
  GVW DA11 .. 189 M7
  HLWE CM17 .. 29 M7
  STALE/WH AL4 .. 21 J4
Hillstrope Cl PUR/KEN CR8 .. 222 D8
Hill Top CHEAM SM3 .. 201 J7
  GLDGN NW11 .. 117 L2
  LOU IG10 .. 82 D6
  MRDN SM4 .. 201 L7
Hilltop WALTH E17 * .. 120 F2
Hilltop Av WLSDN NW10 .. 135 P2
Hilltop Cl ASC SL5 .. 192 D2

| Street | Area | Page | Grid |
|---|---|---|---|
| | CHESW EN7 | 61 | N2 |
| | LHD/OX KT22 | 237 | H9 |
| Hill Top Cl | LOU IG10 | 82 | D7 |
| Hilltop Ct | RGUW GU5 | 249 | L6 |
| Hilltop Cots | SYD SE26 * | 182 | A1 |
| | ORP BR6 | 207 | H9 |
| Hilltop Gdns | HDN NW4 | 96 | E10 |
| | ORP BR6 | 207 | H9 |
| Hilltop La | REDH RH1 | 259 | H2 |
| Hilltop Rd | GT/LBKH KT23 | 254 | E8 |
| | BERK HP4 | 33 | F3 |
| | CTHM CR3 | 241 | M1 |
| | KGLGY WD4 | 54 | E3 |
| | KIL/WHAMP NW6 | 2 | F3 |
| | REIG RH2 | 275 | L2 |
| | WTHK RM20 | 166 | F5 |
| Hill Top Vw | WFD IG8 * | 102 | C7 |
| Hilltop Wk | CTHM CR3 | 242 | D6 |
| | HARP AL5 | 20 | C3 |
| Hilltop Wy | STAN HA7 | 94 | H4 |
| Hill Tree Cl | SBW CM21 | 29 | N2 |
| Hillview | CTHM CR3 | 241 | N1 |
| | WMD SE28 | 178 | G10 |
| Hillvw | BERK HP4 | 33 | M3 |
| | CHOB/PIR GU24 * | 275 | H1 |
| | DORK RH4 | 275 | H1 |
| | SLN SL2 | 109 | J6 |
| Hillview Cl | EMPK RM11 | 125 | K4 |
| | KTN/HRWW/WS HA3 | 115 | K3 |
| Hillview Cl | PIN HA5 | 93 | N1 |
| | WBLY HA9 | 115 | L7 |
| Hill View Cl | KWD/TDW/WH KT20 | 238 | F7 |
| | PUR/KEN CR8 | 223 | J7 |
| Hillview Ct | WOKS/MYFD GU22 * | 232 | B8 |
| Hill View Crs | GUW GU2 | 249 | L8 |
| | ORP BR6 | 207 | H8 |
| Hillview Crs | IL IG1 | 122 | C4 |
| Hill View Dr | REDH RH1 | 276 | B1 |
| | WELL DA16 | 163 | H8 |
| Hill View Gdns | CDALE/KGS NW9 | 116 | A3 |
| Hillview Gdns | CHES/WCR EN8 | 62 | A1 |
| | HDN NW4 | 116 | C2 |
| | RYLN/HDSTN HA2 | 115 | P1 |
| Hill View Rd | COB KT11 | 217 | N9 |
| Hillview Rd | CHST BR7 | 184 | D8 |
| Hill View Rd | TWK TW1 | 176 | F2 |
| Hillview Rd | ESH/CLAY KT10 | 218 | F4 |
| | HART DA3 | 211 | N3 |
| Hill View Rd | MLHL NW7 | 96 | C5 |
| Hillview Rd | ORP BR6 | 207 | J8 |
| Hill View Rd | PIN HA5 | 93 | N1 |
| Hillview Rd | WOKS/MYFD GU22 | 232 | B8 |
| | STWL/WRAY TW19 | 172 | A2 |
| Hillview Rd | SUT SM1 | 201 | M10 |
| Hill Vw | WOKS/MYFD GU22 | 232 | B8 |
| Hill Vw | AMSS HP7 | 68 | G7 |
| Hillway | CDALE/KGS NW9 | 116 | B6 |
| | HGT N6 | 118 | B7 |
| Hill Waye | CFSP/GDCR SL9 | 110 | C4 |
| Hillwood Cl | RBRW/HUT CM13 | 107 | N2 |
| Hillwood Gv | RBRW/HUT CM13 | 107 | N2 |
| Hillworth | BECK BR3 * | 204 | G2 |
| Hillworth Rd | BRXS/STRHM SW2 | 181 | N1 |
| Hillyard Rd | HNWL W7 | 134 | D7 |
| Hillyard St | BRXN/ST SW9 | 159 | H4 |
| Hillybarn Rd | CRAWW RH11 | 282 | F4 |
| Hillydeal Rd | RSEV TN14 | 247 | L1 |
| Hilly Flds | HLWS CM18 | 47 | J5 |
| Hillyfield | WALTH E17 | 100 | E10 |
| Hillyfield Cl | HOM E9 | 120 | D10 |
| Hilly Flds | BROCKY SE4 * | 160 | F10 |
| Hillyfields | LOU IG10 | 82 | G6 |
| Hilly Flds | WGCE AL7 | 23 | M4 |
| Hilly Fields Crs | BROCKY SE4 | 160 | F10 |
| Hilmay Dr | HHW HP1 | 35 | L7 |
| Hilperton Rd | SL SL1 | 149 | K1 |
| Hilsea St | CLPT E5 | 120 | B9 |
| Hilton Av | NFNCH/WDSPK N12 | 97 | N6 |
| Hilton Cl | UX/CGN UB8 | 131 | L4 |
| Hilton Wy | SAND/SEL CR2 | 242 | A1 |
| Himalayan Wy | WATW WD18 | 72 | C10 |
| Himley Rd | TOOT SW17 | 179 | P8 |
| Hinchley Cl | ESH/CLAY KT10 | 198 | F10 |
| Hinchley Dr | ESH/CLAY KT10 | 198 | F10 |
| Hinchley Wy | ESH/CLAY KT10 | 198 | F10 |
| Hinckley Rd | PECK SE15 | 159 | P10 |
| Hind Cl | CHIG IG7 | 103 | K1 |
| Hind Crs | ERITH DA8 | 164 | D6 |
| Hinde Ms | MHST W1U * | 10 | D5 |
| Hindes Rd | HRW HA1 | 114 | D3 |
| Hinde St | MHST W1U | 10 | D5 |
| Hind Gv | POP/IOD E14 | 140 | F8 |
| Hindhead Cl | CRAWW RH11 | 283 | M9 |
| | UX/CGN UB8 | 132 | C7 |
| Hindhead Gdns | NTHLT UB5 | 133 | H3 |
| Hindhead Wy | WLGTN SM6 | 222 | G4 |
| Hindmans Rd | EDUL SE22 | 181 | H7 |
| Hindmans Wy | DAGW RM9 | 144 | A3 |
| Hindmarsh Cl | WCHPL E1 | 13 | P7 |
| Hindrey Rd | CLPT E5 | 115 | K3 |
| Hindsley's Pl | FSTH SE23 | 182 | B5 |
| Hind Ter | WTHK RM20 * | 167 | J5 |
| Hine Cl | COUL/CHIP CR5 | 240 | E8 |
| Hinkler Rd | KTN/HRWW/WS HA3 | 115 | J1 |
| Hinkley Cl | DEN/HRF UB9 | 111 | M2 |
| Hinksey Cl | DTCH/LGLY SL3 | 150 | E2 |
| Hinksey Pth | ABYW SE2 | 163 | N2 |
| Hinstock Rd | WOOL/PLUM SE18 | 162 | F6 |
| Hinton Av | HSLWW TW4 | 153 | L10 |
| Hinton Cl | ELTH/MOT SE9 | 184 | B4 |
| Hinton Rd | BRXN/ST SW9 | 159 | J9 |
| | SL SL1 | 128 | D9 |
| | UED N18 | 99 | M5 |
| | UX/CGN UB8 | 131 | M3 |
| | WLGTN SM6 | 222 | D3 |
| Hipkins Pl | BROX EN10 | 44 | B9 |
| Hipley St | WOKS/MYFD GU22 | 232 | B8 |
| Hippodrome Pl | NTGHL W11 | 8 | B9 |
| Hirst Crs | WBLY HA9 | 115 | K8 |
| Hispano Ms | ENC/FH EN2 | 80 | F3 |
| Hitcham Rd | WALTH E17 | 120 | C1 |
| Hitchcock Cl | SHPTN TW17 | 196 | A3 |
| Hitchens Cl | HHW HP1 | 35 | J5 |
| Hitches Yd | WARE SG12 * | 26 | C1 |
| Hitchin Cl | HARH RM3 | 105 | K5 |
| Hitchings Wy | REIG RH2 | 275 | K4 |
| Hithe Gv | BERM/RHTH SE16 | 160 | B2 |
| Hitherbaulk | WGCE AL7 | 22 | G7 |
| Hitherbroom Rd | HYS/HAR UB3 | 133 | H10 |
| Hitherbury Cl | GUW GU2 | 267 | P3 |
| Hither Farm Rd | BKHTH/KID SE3 | 161 | P9 |
| Hitherfield Rd | DAGE RM10 | 123 | P7 |
| | STRHM/NOR SW16 | 162 | C6 |
| Hither Green La | LEW SE13 | 183 | H1 |
| Hithermoor Rd | STWL/WRAY TW19 | 173 | H2 |
| Hitherway | WGCW AL8 | 22 | G1 |
| Hitherwell Dr | KTN/HRWW/WS HA3 | 94 | C10 |
| Hitherwood Cl | HCH RM12 | 125 | J3 |
| | REIG RH2 | 257 | N10 |
| Hitherwood Dr | NRWD SE19 | 181 | H7 |
| Hive Cl | BRW CM14 | 106 | F5 |
| | BUSH WD23 | 94 | C3 |
| Hive Rd | BUSH WD23 | 94 | C3 |
| Hiving's Hi | CSHM HP5 | 50 | F4 |
| Hivings Pk | CSHM HP5 | 50 | F4 |
| Hoadly Rd | STRHM/NOR SW16 | 180 | D3 |
| | YEAD UB4 | 133 | L6 |
| Hobart Dr | YEAD UB4 | 133 | L6 |
| Hobart Gdns | THHTH CR7 | 203 | L3 |
| Hobart La | YEAD UB4 | 133 | L6 |
| Hobart Pl | BCVA SW1W | 16 | E4 |
| | RCHPK/HAM TW10 | 177 | J3 |
| Hobart Rd | BARK/HLT IG6 | 102 | F10 |
| | DAGW RM9 | 123 | N9 |
| | TIL RM18 | 168 | D7 |
| | WPK KT4 | 200 | F1 |
| | YEAD UB4 | 133 | L6 |
| Hobart Wk | STALW/RED AL3 | 38 | E2 |
| Hobbayne Rd | HNWL W7 | 134 | C4 |
| Hobbes Wk | PUT/ROE SW15 | 178 | E1 |
| Hobbs Cl | BF/WBF KT14 | 215 | L5 |
| | CHES/WCR EN8 | 62 | C5 |
| | STALE/WH AL4 | 39 | K7 |
| Hobbs Cross Rd | EPP CM16 | 83 | N2 |
| Hobbs Gn | EFNCH N2 | 117 | M1 |
| Hobbs Hill Rd | HHS/BOV HP3 | 35 | P10 |
| Hobbs Pl | IS N1 | 7 | J6 |
| Hobbs Place Est | IS N1 * | 7 | J7 |
| Hobby Horse Cl | CHESW EN7 | 61 | L2 |
| Hobby St | PEND EN3 | 80 | C9 |
| Hobday St | POP/IOD E14 | 140 | G8 |
| Hoblands End | CHST BR7 | 185 | H9 |
| Hobletts Rd | HHNE HP2 | 36 | A5 |
| Hobson Cl | HNWL W7 | 134 | C4 |
| Hobsons Cl | ED N11 | 26 | E10 |
| Hobsons Pl | WCHPL E1 | 13 | N3 |
| Hobtoe Rd | HLW CM20 | 28 | D10 |
| Hobury St | WBPTN SW10 | 15 | K10 |
| Hockenden La | SWLY BR8 | 208 | B3 |
| Hocken Md | CRAWE RH10 | 284 | E5 |
| Hockering Gdns | WOKS/MYFD GU22 | 232 | E4 |
| Hockering Rd | WOKS/MYFD GU22 | 232 | D4 |
| Hocker St | BETH E2 * | 7 | L10 |
| Hockford Cl | CHOB/PIR GU24 | 248 | G2 |
| | RGUW GU5 | 248 | C1 |
| Hocklands | WGCE AL7 | 23 | M4 |
| Hockley Av | EHAM E6 | 142 | B4 |
| Hockley Dr | CPK RM2 | 105 | J3 |
| Hockley La | SLN SL2 | 129 | N2 |
| Hockley Ms | BARK IG11 | 143 | H4 |
| Hocroft Av | CRICK NW2 | 117 | P1 |
| Hocroft Rd | CRICK NW2 | 117 | P1 |
| Hocroft Wk | CRICK NW2 | 117 | P1 |
| Hodder Dr | GFD/PVL UB6 | 134 | C4 |
| Hoddesdon Rd | BELV DA17 | 164 | E3 |
| | WARE SG12 | 27 | H1 |
| Hodds Wood Rd | CSHM HP5 | 51 | H4 |
| Hodes Rw | HAMP NW3 | 2 | C1 |
| Hodford Rd | GLDGN NW11 | 117 | J6 |
| Hodge La | WDSR SL4 * | 149 | H10 |
| Hodgemoor Vw | CSTG HP8 | 89 | L4 |
| Hodges Cl | CDW/CHF RM16 | 167 | J4 |
| Hodges Wy | WATW WD18 | 73 | H10 |
| Hodgkin Cl | CRAWE RH10 | 284 | C8 |
| Hodgkins Cl | THMD SE28 | 143 | N9 |
| Hodgkins Ms | STAN HA7 | 94 | F4 |
| Hodgson Gdns | RGUE GU4 | 250 | D7 |
| Hodings Rd | HLW CM20 | 28 | C1 |
| Hodister Cl | CMBW SE5 | 159 | K6 |
| Hodnet Gv | BERM/RHTH SE16 | 160 | B5 |
| Hodson Cl | RYLN/HDSTN HA2 | 113 | N8 |
| Hodson Crs | STMC/STPC BR5 | 207 | N6 |
| Hodson Pl | PEND EN3 | 80 | F7 |
| Hoebrook Cl | WOKS/MYFD GU22 | 232 | A4 |
| Hoecroft | WAB EN9 | 45 | L8 |
| Hoe La | ABR/ST RM4 | 103 | N1 |
| | EN EN1 | 80 | A4 |
| | SHGR GU5 | 270 | G10 |
| | WAB EN9 | 45 | L8 |
| | WARE SG12 | 26 | C5 |
| Hoe Meadow | BEAC HP9 | 88 | B7 |
| Hoestock Rd | SBW CM21 | 29 | N1 |
| Hoe St | WALTH E17 | 120 | F3 |
| The Hoe | OXHEY WD19 | 93 | L3 |
| Hoffmann Gdns | SAND/SEL CR2 | 223 | P3 |
| Hoffman Sq | IS N1 * | 7 | J7 |
| Hogan Ms | BAY/PAD W2 | 9 | J1 |
| Hogarth Av | ASHF TW15 | 174 | D9 |
| | BRWN CM15 | 107 | K4 |
| Hogarth Cl | CAN/RD E16 | 142 | A7 |
| | EA W5 | 135 | K7 |
| | SL SL1 | 128 | C4 |
| | UX/CGN UB8 | 131 | M5 |
| Hogarth Crs | CROY/NA CR0 | 203 | K7 |
| | WIM/MER SW19 | 201 | N1 |
| Hogarth Gdns | HEST TW5 | 155 | P6 |
| Hogarth Hill | GLDGN NW11 | 117 | J2 |
| Hogarth Pl | ECT SW5 * | 14 | C6 |
| Hogarth Reach | LOU IG10 | 82 | C9 |
| Hogarth Rd | BCTR RM8 | 123 | L10 |
| | CDW/CHF RM16 | 147 | N10 |
| | CRAWE RH10 | 284 | A10 |
| | ECT SW5 | 14 | C6 |
| | EDGW HA8 | 95 | M10 |
| Hogarth Ter | CHSWK W4 * | 156 | A5 |
| Hogarth Wy | HPTN TW12 | 198 | B1 |
| Hogback Wood Rd | BEAC HP9 | 88 | A7 |
| Hogden La | RDKG RH5 | 253 | H8 |
| Hogden Rd | RDKG RH5 | 253 | J8 |
| Hogfair La | SL SL1 | 128 | B6 |
| Hogg End La | STALW/RED AL3 | 37 | H4 |
| Hogg La | BORE WD6 | 74 | F8 |
| | GRAYS RM17 | 167 | J4 |
| Hog Hill Rd | CRW RM5 | 104 | A3 |
| Hog La | CSHM HP5 | 32 | C8 |
| | GVW GU25 | 230 | A7 |
| Hogpits Bottom | HHS/BOV HP3 | 52 | D6 |
| Hog's Back | RGUW GU5 | 266 | C4 |
| Hogscross La | COUL/CHIP CR5 | 240 | A8 |
| Hogsdell La | HERT/BAY SG13 | 52 | A1 |
| Hogshead La | WAP E1W * | 140 | G2 |
| Hogshill La | COB KT11 | 217 | K10 |
| Hogsmill Wy | HOR/WEW KT19 | 219 | P2 |
| Hogtrough Hi | BH/WHM TN16 | 245 | K8 |
| Hogtrough La | OXTED RH8 | 260 | C8 |
| | REDH RH1 | 276 | E1 |
| Holden Av | CDALE/KGS NW9 | 115 | P6 |
| | NFNCH/WDSPK N12 | 97 | L6 |
| Holden Cl | BCTR RM8 | 123 | H9 |
| | HERT/BAY SG13 | 25 | M4 |
| Holden Gdns | BRW CM14 | 107 | J6 |
| Holdenhurst Av | FNCH N3 | 97 | L8 |
| Holden Rd | NFNCH/WDSPK N12 | 97 | L5 |
| Holden St | BTSEA SW11 | 158 | B8 |
| Holden Wy | UPMR RM14 | 126 | C6 |
| Holdernesse Rd | ISLW TW7 | 154 | F7 |
| | TOOT SW17 | 180 | A6 |
| Holderness Wy | WNWD SE27 | 181 | J8 |
| Holders Hill Av | HDN NW4 | 96 | C10 |
| Holders Hill Crs | HDN NW4 | 96 | C10 |
| Holders Hill Dr | HDN NW4 | 96 | C10 |
| Holders Hill Gdns | HDN NW4 | 96 | C10 |
| Holders Hill Pde | MLHL NW7 * | 96 | D10 |
| Holders Hill Rd | HDN NW4 | 96 | C10 |
| The Holdings | BRKMPK AL9 | 40 | G2 |
| Holecroft | WAB EN9 | 63 | K10 |
| Holford Ms | FSBYW WC1X * | 5 | N6 |
| Holford Rd | GU GU1 | 250 | F10 |
| | HAMP NW3 | 117 | M8 |
| | TIL RM18 | 168 | G3 |
| Holford Yd | FSBYW WC1X * | 5 | N5 |
| Holgate Av | BTSEA SW11 | 157 | N9 |
| Holgate Gdns | DAGE RM10 | 124 | B10 |
| Holgate St | CHARL SE7 | 162 | A2 |
| Holland Av | BELMT SM2 | 221 | K6 |
| | RYNPK SW20 | 200 | B1 |
| Holland Cl | BAR EN5 | 97 | N1 |
| | HAYES BR2 | 205 | L8 |
| | HOR/WEW KT19 | 219 | P7 |
| | REDH RH1 | 258 | A10 |
| | ROMW/RG RM7 | 124 | D3 |
| | STAN HA7 | 94 | G6 |
| Holland Crs | OXTED RH8 | 261 | M9 |
| Holland Dr | FSTH SE23 | 182 | D6 |
| Holland Gdns | BTFD TW8 | 155 | L4 |
| | ECH TW20 | 195 | J2 |
| | GSTN WD25 | 73 | K1 |
| | WKENS W14 | 14 | B3 |
| Holland Gv | BRXN/ST SW9 | 159 | H6 |
| Holland La | OXTED RH8 | 261 | M9 |
| Holland Pk | NTGHL W11 | 8 | B10 |
| Holland Park Av | NTGHL W11 | 8 | A10 |
| Holland Park Gdns | NTGHL W11 | 14 | A1 |
| Holland Park Ms | NTGHL W11 | 8 | C10 |
| Holland Park Rd | WKENS W14 | 14 | C1 |
| Holland Park Ter | NTGHL W11 * | 8 | C10 |
| Holland Pas | IS N1 * | 6 | E5 |
| Holland Pl | KENS W8 | 14 | C1 |
| Holland Rd | ALP/SUD HA0 | 135 | J1 |
| | EHAM E6 | 142 | C3 |
| | OXTED RH8 | 261 | M9 |
| | SNWD SE25 | 203 | P3 |
| | WKENS W14 | 14 | A2 |
| | WLSDN NW10 | 119 | K6 |
| Hollands Cft | WARE SG12 | 28 | A2 |
| The Hollands | WOKS/MYFD GU22 | 232 | B4 |
| | WPK KT4 | 200 | C8 |
| Holland St | KENS W8 | 14 | B1 |
| | STHWK SE1 | 12 | D9 |
| Holland Villas Rd | WKENS W14 | 14 | A1 |
| Holland Wk | STAN HA7 | 94 | F6 |
| Holland Wy | HAYES BR2 | 205 | L9 |
| | HLWE CM17 | 29 | N10 |
| Hollar Rd | STNW/STAM N16 | 119 | N8 |
| Hollen St | SOHO/CST W1F | 11 | H6 |
| Holles Cl | HPTN TW12 | 175 | P9 |
| Holles St | OXSTW W1C | 10 | E6 |
| Holley Rd | ACT W3 | 156 | B1 |
| Hollickwood Av | NFNCH/WDSPK N12 | 98 | A7 |
| Holliday Sq | BTSEA SW11 * | 158 | C1 |
| Hollidge Wy | DAGE RM10 | 144 | C1 |
| Hollie Cl | HORL RH6 | 281 | J5 |
| Holliers Wy | HAT AL10 | 40 | D4 |
| Hollies Av | BF/WBF KT14 | 215 | M2 |
| | BFN/LL DA15 | 185 | J5 |
| Hollies Cl | STRHM/NOR SW16 | 181 | L3 |
| | TWK TW1 | 176 | E5 |
| Hollies Ct | ADL/WDHM KT15 | 215 | M2 |
| Hollies End | MLHL NW7 | 96 | A5 |
| Hollies Rd | EA W5 | 155 | H5 |
| The Hollies | ADL/WDHM KT15 | 215 | M2 |
| | BAR EN5 * | 76 | D7 |
| | GVE DA12 | 190 | G9 |
| | HART DA3 | 211 | P3 |
| | HHS/BOV HP3 | 52 | D5 |
| | KTN/HRWW/WS HA3 | 114 | F2 |
| | OXTED RH8 | 261 | N10 |
| | STAL AL1 | 38 | D5 |
| | WOKN/KNAP GU21 | 231 | J3 |
| Hollies Wy | BAL SW12 * | 180 | B5 |
| | POTB/CUF EN6 | 59 | M7 |
| Holligrave Rd | BMLY BR1 | 205 | M1 |
| Hollin Ct | CRAWE RH10 | 283 | P4 |
| Hollingbourne Av | BXLYHN DA7 | 165 | K2 |
| Hollingbourne Gdns | WEA W13 | 134 | A7 |
| Hollingbourne Rd | HNHL SE24 | 181 | K1 |
| Hollingsworth Ms | GSTN WD25 | 53 | H5 |
| Hollingsworth Rd | CROY/NA CR0 | 224 | A3 |
| Hollington Crs | NWMAL KT3 | 200 | C6 |
| Hollington Rd | EHAM E6 | 142 | C3 |
| | TOTM N17 | 99 | P10 |
| Hollingworth Cl | E/WMO/HCT KT8 | 197 | N4 |
| Hollingworth Rd | STMC/STPC BR5 | 206 | E1 |
| Hollingworth Wy | BH/WHM TN16 | 262 | G2 |
| Hollins Cl | HARP AL5 | 20 | B3 |
| Hollis Pl | GRAYS RM17 * | 192 | B1 |
| Hollis Rw | REDH RH1 | 276 | D6 |
| Holloway Cl | WDR/YW UB7 | 152 | B4 |
| Holloway La | RKW/CH/CXG WD3 | 70 | E4 |
| | WDR/YW UB7 | 152 | A4 |
| Holloway Rd | ARCH N19 | 118 | E7 |
| | EHAM E6 | 142 | A2 |
| | HOLWY N7 | 118 | C2 |
| | WALTH E17 | 101 | J1 |
| | WAN E11 | 122 | C6 |
| Holloways La | BRKMPK AL9 | 40 | G5 |
| Hollow Cl | GUW GU2 | 267 | N1 |
| Hollowfield Av | GRAYS RM17 | 192 | C3 |
| Hollow Hill La | IVER SL0 | 132 | A10 |
| Hollow La | DTCH/LGLY SL3 | 150 | B2 |
| | IVER SL0 | 130 | D1 |
| | RDKG RH5 | 271 | L7 |
| The Hollow | CRAWW RH11 | 282 | B8 |
| | WFD IG8 | 102 | B1 |
| Hollow Wy Cl | HHNE HP2 | 35 | L3 |
| Holly Av | ADL/WDHM KT15 | 215 | L8 |
| | STAN HA7 | 95 | K2 |
| | WOT/HER KT12 | 197 | L8 |
| Hollybank | WOKS/MYFD GU22 | 231 | N6 |
| Holly Bank | MUSWH N10 | 98 | B1 |
| Hollybank Cl | HPTN TW12 | 175 | P7 |
| Holly Bank Rd | WOKS/MYFD GU22 | 231 | N6 |
| | OXHEY WD19 | 93 | K10 |
| | SEV TN13 | 247 | N10 |
| Hollybrake Cl | CHST BR7 | 185 | L3 |
| Hollybush Gdns | BETH E2 | 140 | A1 |
| Hollybush Hi | WAN E11 | 121 | L4 |
| Hollybush La | AMS HP6 | 69 | J3 |
| | ORP BR6 | 228 | B3 |
| | WGCE AL7 | 23 | H8 |
| Hollybush Rd | CRAWE RH10 | 285 | J6 |
| | KUTN/CMB KT2 | 177 | K8 |
| Hollybush Rw | WOKS/MYFD GU22 | 232 | C7 |
| Hollybush St | PLSTW E13 | 142 | C1 |
| Holly Bush V | HAMP NW3 * | 117 | M9 |
| Hollybush Wy | CHESW EN7 | 61 | M1 |
| Hollycroft Av | HAMP NW3 | 117 | K8 |
| | WBLY HA9 | 115 | P1 |
| Hollycroft Cl | SAND/SEL CR2 | 223 | M2 |
| | WDR/YW UB7 | 152 | A7 |
| Hollycroft Gdns | WDR/YW UB7 | 152 | A7 |
| Hollycross Rd | WARE SG12 | 28 | A2 |
| Hollydale Cl | NTHLT UB5 | 114 | A10 |
| Hollydale Dr | HAYES BR2 | 206 | C10 |
| Hollydale Rd | PECK SE15 | 160 | C1 |
| Holly Dell | WFD IG8 | 102 | A5 |
| Hollydown Wy | WAN E11 | 121 | J8 |
| Holly Dr | BERK HP4 | 34 | A6 |
| | CHING E4 | 88 | A10 |
| | EGH TW20 | 196 | A1 |
| | POTB/CUF EN6 | 59 | L9 |
| Holly Farm Rd | NWDGN UB2 | 153 | M4 |
| Hollyfield | ADL/WDHM KT15 | 215 | L6 |
| Hollyfield Av | FBAR/BDGN N11 | 97 | P8 |
| Hollyfield Rd | BRYLDS KT5 | 199 | L5 |
| Hollyfields Cl | BROX EN10 | 62 | D1 |
| Holly Gdns | BXLYHN DA7 | 164 | D10 |
| | WDR/YW UB7 | 152 | A1 |
| Hollygrove | BUSH WD23 | 94 | C3 |
| Holly Gv | CDALE/KGS NW9 | 115 | P6 |
| | PECK SE15 | 159 | H8 |
| | PIN HA5 | 93 | P10 |
| Hollygrove Cl | HSLW TW3 | 153 | N10 |
| Holly Hedge La | COB KT11 | 217 | J10 |
| Holly Hedge Ter | LEW SE13 | 183 | H1 |
| Holly Hill | HAMP NW3 | 117 | M9 |
| | WCHMH N21 | 98 | G1 |
| Holly Hill Rd | BELV DA17 | 164 | C4 |
| Holly Hock Dr | CHOB/PIR GU24 | 230 | F1 |
| Holly Hough | KWD/TDW/WH KT20 | 257 | L3 |
| Holly La | BNSTD SM7 | 239 | L3 |
| Holly La East | BNSTD SM7 | 239 | L4 |
| Holly La West | BNSTD SM7 | 239 | L4 |
| Holly Lea | RGUE GU4 | 249 | J5 |
| Holly Lodge | WOKN/KNAP GU21 * | 231 | K3 |
| Holly Lodge Gdns | HGT N6 | 118 | A6 |
| Holly Lodge (Mobile Home Park) | KWD/TDW/WH KT20 | 257 | L3 |
| Hollymead | CAR SM5 | 202 | A10 |
| Hollymead Rd | COUL/CHIP CR5 | 240 | B5 |
| Hollymeoak Rd | COUL/CHIP CR5 | 240 | C6 |
| Hollymoor La | HOR/WEW KT19 | 220 | A6 |
| Holly Mt | HAMP NW3 * | 117 | M9 |
| Hollymount Cl | GNWCH SE10 | 161 | H7 |
| Holly Pde | COB KT11 * | 235 | J1 |
| Holly Pk | FNCH N3 | 97 | J4 |
| | FSBYPK N4 | 98 | C10 |
| Holly Park Rd | FBAR/BDGN N11 | 98 | A10 |
| | HNWL W7 | 134 | C1 |
| Holly Rd | CHSWK W4 * | 156 | B1 |
| | DART DA1 | 171 | H4 |
| | HPTN TW12 | 175 | M7 |
| | HSLW TW3 | 155 | H9 |
| | ORP BR6 | 227 | P4 |
| | TWK TW1 | 176 | B6 |
| | WAN E11 | 121 | L3 |
| Holly St | HACK E8 | 7 | M2 |
| Hollytree Cl | CFSP/GDCR SL9 | 90 | B6 |
| | WIM/MER SW19 | 178 | G4 |
| Holly Tree Pde | SCUP DA14 * | 186 | A9 |
| Holly Tree Rd | CTHM CR3 | 241 | M8 |
| Holly Vw | CHING E4 | 101 | P4 |
| Holly Vls | HMSMTH W6 * | 156 | G7 |
| Holly Wk | ENC/FH EN2 | 79 | N1 |
| | HAMP NW3 | 117 | M9 |
| | RCH/KEW TW9 | 155 | M9 |
| Hollywood Gdns | YEAD UB4 | 133 | H5 |
| Hollywood Ms | WBPTN SW10 | 15 | H10 |
| Hollywood Rd | CHING E4 | 101 | J3 |
| | WBPTN SW10 | 15 | H10 |
| Hollywoods | CROY/NA CR0 | 224 | A8 |
| Hollywood Wy | ERITH DA8 | 165 | K3 |
| | WFD IG8 | 101 | L5 |
| Holman Cl | EW KT17 * | 220 | D5 |
| Holman Rd | BTSEA SW11 | 158 | C1 |
| | HOR/WEW KT19 | 219 | P5 |
| Holmbank Dr | SHPTN TW17 | 189 | H7 |
| Holmbridge Gdns | PEND EN3 | 80 | G1 |
| Holmbrook Dr | HDN NW4 | 116 | C2 |
| Holmbury Cl | BUSH WD23 * | 94 | D3 |
| Holme Cl | CHES/WCR EN8 | 62 | D7 |
| | HAT AL10 | 40 | C7 |
| Holme Ct | ISLW TW7 | 156 | A9 |
| Holmedale | SLN SL2 | 129 | P9 |
| Holmefield Pl | ADL/WDHM KT15 | 215 | L6 |
| Holme Lacey Rd | LEE/GVPK SE12 | 183 | J5 |
| Holme Pk | BORE WD6 | 75 | P1 |
| Holme Rd | EHAM E6 | 142 | B1 |
| | HHNE HP2 | 36 | D5 |
| Holmes Av | MLHL NW7 | 96 | G1 |
| | WALTH E17 | 120 | E1 |
| Holmes Cl | ASC SL5 | 192 | B6 |
| | EDUL SE22 | 159 | P10 |
| | PUR/KEN CR8 | 222 | G9 |
| | WOKS/MYFD GU22 | 232 | C7 |
| Holmesdale | CHES/WCR EN8 | 62 | A6 |
| Holmesdale Av | GU GU1 | 250 | D7 |
| | MORT/ESHN SW14 | 155 | N9 |
| | REDH RH1 | 258 | D7 |
| Holmesdale Cl | GU GU1 | 250 | D7 |
| | SNWD SE25 | 203 | N3 |
| Holmesdale Hi | EYN DA4 | 210 | C1 |
| Holmesdale Pk | REDH RH1 | 258 | G10 |
| Holmesdale Rd | BXLYHN DA7 | 163 | N8 |
| | CROY/NA CR0 | 202 | A5 |
| | EYN DA4 | 210 | B1 |
| | HGT N6 | 118 | C5 |
| | RCH/KEW TW9 | 155 | N9 |
| | RDKG RH5 | 272 | G6 |
| | REDH RH1 | 276 | D2 |
| | REIG RH2 | 257 | L9 |
| | SNWD SE25 | 202 | G5 |
| | TEDD TW11 | 177 | H10 |
| Holmesley Rd | FSTH SE23 | 182 | C2 |
| Holmes Meadow | HLWW/ROY CM19 | 46 | E7 |
| Holmes Rd | KTTN NW5 | 4 | A1 |
| | TWK TW1 | 176 | A5 |
| | WIM/MER SW19 | 179 | M10 |
| Holmes Ter | STHWK SE1 | 11 | N2 |
| Holme Wy | STAN HA7 | 94 | E7 |
| Holmewood Gdns | BRXS/STRHM SW2 | 181 | N1 |
| Holmewood Rd | BRXS/STRHM SW2 | 181 | N3 |
| | SNWD SE25 | 203 | M3 |
| Holmfield Av | HDN NW4 | 116 | G3 |
| Holmhurst Rd | BELV DA17 | 164 | C4 |
| Holmlea Rd | DTCH/LGLY SL3 | 150 | A7 |
| Holmlea Wk | DTCH/LGLY SL3 | 149 | P7 |
| Holmleigh Av | DART DA1 | 171 | H4 |
| Holmleigh Rd | STNW/STAM N16 | 119 | M6 |
| Holmoak Cl | PUR/KEN CR8 | 222 | G9 |
| Holm Oak Cl | PUT/ROE SW15 | 179 | J1 |
| Holm Oak Ms | CLAP SW4 * | 181 | K2 |
| Holmshaw Cl | SYD SE26 | 182 | D7 |
| Holmshill La | BORE WD6 | 76 | C3 |
| Holmside Ri | OXHEY WD19 | 93 | L10 |
| Holmside Rd | BAL SW12 | 180 | B2 |
| Holmsley Cl | NWMAL KT3 | 200 | D6 |
| Holmstall Av | EDGW HA8 | 95 | P10 |
| Holmstall Pde | EDGW HA8 * | 95 | P10 |
| Holmwood Av | BRWN CM15 | 107 | H1 |
| | SAND/SEL CR2 | 223 | N10 |
| Holmwood Cl | ADL/WDHM KT15 | 215 | K2 |
| | BELMT SM2 | 220 | D5 |
| | EHSLY KT24 | 253 | M10 |
| | NTHLT UB5 | 134 | A1 |
| | RYLN/HDSTN HA2 | 114 | B1 |
| Holmwood Gdns | FNCH N3 | 97 | K10 |
| | WLGTN SM6 | 222 | C5 |
| Holmwood Gv | MLHL NW7 | 96 | A6 |
| Holmwood Rd | BELMT SM2 | 220 | D5 |
| | CHSGTN KT9 | 219 | P6 |
| | GDMY/SEVK IG3 | 123 | K1 |
| | PEND EN3 | 80 | C2 |
| Holmwood Vls | CHARL SE7 | 161 | N4 |
| Holne Cha | EFNCH N2 | 117 | H4 |
| | MRDN SM4 | 201 | K6 |
| Holness Rd | SRTFD E15 | 140 | D6 |
| Holroyd Cl | ESH/CLAY KT10 | 218 | E5 |
| Holroyd Rd | ESH/CLAY KT10 | 218 | E6 |
| | PUT/ROE SW15 | 157 | N9 |
| Holsart Cl | KWD/TDW/WH KT20 | 258 | G10 |
| Holstein Av | WEY KT13 | 216 | B1 |
| Holstein Wy | ERITH DA18 | 147 | P4 |
| Holstock Rd | IL IG1 | 122 | F7 |
| Holsworth Cl | RYLN/HDSTN HA2 | 114 | B3 |
| Holsworthy Sq | FSBYW WC1X | 11 | M1 |
| Holsworthy Wy | CHSGTN KT9 | 219 | J10 |
| Holt Cl | BORE WD6 | 75 | N5 |
| | CHIG IG7 | 103 | L10 |
| | MUSWH N10 | 98 | B3 |
| | SCUP DA14 | 185 | P5 |
| | THMD SE28 | 143 | L10 |
| Holton St | WCHPL E1 | 140 | E6 |
| Holt Rd | ALP/SUD HA0 | 114 | C10 |
| | CAN/RD E16 | 142 | E6 |
| | HARH RM3 | 105 | M8 |
| Holtsmere Cl | GSTN WD25 | 53 | K1 |
| The Holt | BARK/HLT IG6 | 102 | F5 |
| | HHNE HP2 | 36 | C6 |
| | MRDN SM4 | 201 | M6 |
| | WGCE AL7 | 23 | N6 |
| | WLGTN SM6 | 222 | E3 |
| Holt Wy | CHIG IG7 | 103 | L10 |
| Holtwhite Av | ENC/FH EN2 | 79 | N5 |
| Holtwhite's Hi | ENC/FH EN2 | 79 | M5 |
| Holtwood Rd | LHD/OX KT22 | 216 | A10 |
| Holwell Pl | PIN HA5 | 93 | L1 |
| Holwood Park Av | ORP BR6 | 206 | E3 |
| Holwood Pl | CLAP SW4 | 181 | J1 |
| Holy Acre | HLWW/ROY CM19 | 27 | M10 |
| Holybourne Av | PUT/ROE SW15 | 178 | E7 |
| Holy Cross Hi | BROX EN10 | 43 | H7 |
| Holyfield Rd | WAB EN9 | 44 | B10 |
| Holyhead Cl | BOW E3 | 140 | A9 |
| | EHAM E6 | 142 | A8 |
| Holyhead Ct | KGLGY WD4 * | 54 | C7 |
| Holyoake Crs | WOKN/KNAP GU21 | 231 | N6 |
| Holyoake Ter | SEV TN13 | 247 | H10 |
| Holyoake Wk | EA W5 | 135 | J1 |
| | EFNCH N2 | 117 | H1 |
| Holyoak Rd | LBTH SE11 | 18 | D7 |
| Holyport Rd | FUL/PGN SW6 | 156 | G6 |
| Holyrood Av | RYLN/HDSTN HA2 | 113 | M10 |
| Holyrood Gdns | EDGW HA8 | 116 | B1 |
| Holyrood Ms | CAN/RD E16 | 141 | M4 |
| Holyrood Rd | BAR EN5 | 77 | H7 |
| Holyrood St | STHWK SE1 | 13 | L9 |
| Holywell Cl | BERM/RHTH SE16 | 159 | N5 |
| | ORP BR6 | 207 | H3 |
| | STWL/WRAY TW19 | 173 | H3 |
| Holywell La | SDTCH EC2A | 13 | L1 |
| Holywell Rd | WATW WD18 | 73 | H10 |
| Holywell Rw | SDTCH EC2A | 13 | J2 |
| Holywell Wy | STWL/WRAY TW19 | 173 | P4 |
| Home Cha | WEY KT13 | 216 | D5 |
| Home Cl | BROX EN10 | 44 | E10 |
| | CAR SM5 | 202 | A9 |
| | CRAWE RH10 | 284 | D5 |
| | HLW CM20 | 47 | L1 |
| | LHD/OX KT22 | 237 | H9 |
| | NTHLT UB5 | 133 | N10 |
| | VW GU25 | 194 | A6 |
| Home Ct | FELT TW13 * | 175 | H5 |
| | SURB KT6 * | 199 | J5 |
| Homecroft Gdns | LOU IG10 | 82 | G6 |
| Homecroft Rd | SEV TN13 * | 246 | D8 |
| | SYD SE26 | 182 | B8 |
| | WDGN N22 | 99 | J9 |
| Homedean Rd | SEV TN13 | 246 | D8 |
| Home Farm Cl | BRKHM/BTCW RH3 | 274 | B1 |
| | CHERT KT16 | 214 | D4 |
| | EPSOM KT18 | 238 | C5 |
| | ESH/CLAY KT10 | 198 | A3 |
| | SHPTN TW17 | 196 | F4 |
| | THDIT KT7 | 198 | E7 |
| Home Farm Gdns | WOT/HER KT12 | 197 | N10 |
| Home Farm Rd | BERK HP4 | 33 | J7 |
| | RKW/CH/CXG WD3 | 131 | K9 |
| Homefarm Rd | HNWL W7 | 134 | D8 |
| Home Farm Wy | DTCH/LGLY SL3 | 129 | P3 |
| Homefield | BERK HP4 | 34 | E2 |
| | HHS/BOV HP3 | 52 | E4 |
| | WAB EN9 | 63 | M8 |
| Homefield Av | GNTH/NBYPK IG2 | 123 | H3 |
| Homefield Cl | ADL/WDHM KT15 | 215 | H8 |
| | EPP CM16 | 65 | K5 |
| | HORL RH6 | 280 | C3 |
| | LHD/OX KT22 | 237 | H1 |
| | STMC/STPC BR5 | 207 | P2 |
| | SWLY BR8 | 208 | G3 |
| | WLSDN NW10 | 135 | P1 |
| | YEAD UB4 | 133 | K6 |
| Homefield Gdns | EFNCH N2 | 117 | N1 |
| | KWD/TDW/WH KT20 | 238 | F6 |
| | WIM/MER SW19 | 201 | M2 |
| Homefield Ms | BECK BR3 * | 204 | F1 |
| Homefield Pk | SUT SM1 | 221 | N4 |
| Homefield Ri | ORP BR6 | 207 | K8 |
| Homefield Rd | ALP/SUD HA0 | 114 | F9 |
| | BUSH WD23 | 75 | P5 |
| | CHSWK W4 | 156 | C3 |
| | COUL/CHIP CR5 | 241 | J6 |
| | EDGW HA8 | 96 | A7 |
| | HHNE HP2 | 36 | B6 |
| | RAD WD7 | 74 | E3 |
| | RKW/CH/CXG WD3 | 108 | D8 |
| | SEV TN13 | 246 | F8 |
| | WARE SG12 | 26 | D1 |
| | WARL CR6 | 242 | B5 |
| | WIM/MER SW19 | 178 | F8 |
| | WOT/HER KT12 | 197 | N7 |
| Homefield St | IS N1 * | 7 | J6 |
| The Homefield | MRDN SM4 * | 201 | K4 |
| Home Gdns | DAGE RM10 | 124 | D8 |
| Home Hi | SWLY BR8 | 186 | G10 |
| Homeland Dr | BELMT SM2 | 221 | L5 |
| Homelands | LHD/OX KT22 | 237 | H1 |
| Homelands Dr | NRWD SE19 | 181 | M10 |
| Home Lea | ORP BR6 | 227 | J2 |
| Homeleigh Ct | CHES/WCR EN8 | 62 | A6 |
| Homeleigh Rd | PECK SE15 | 183 | H1 |
| Home Ley | WGCE AL7 | 23 | H5 |
| Home Md | STAN HA7 | 95 | H9 |
| Home Mead Cl | GVE DA12 | 190 | E3 |
| Home Meadow | BNSTD SM7 | 239 | M2 |
| | SLN SL2 | 129 | H4 |
| | WGCE AL7 | 23 | H5 |
| Homemead | CROY/NA CR0 | 202 | D6 |
| | HAYES BR2 | 205 | C5 |
| Home Pk | OXTED RH8 | 261 | M7 |
| Home Park Ct | KUT/HW KT1 * | 199 | J4 |
| Home Park Mill Link Rd | KGLGY WD4 | 54 | C7 |
| Home Park Rd | WIM/MER SW19 | 179 | J7 |
| Home Park Ter | KUT/HW KT1 * | 199 | J4 |
| Home Park Wk | KUT/HW KT1 | 199 | J4 |
| Homer Cl | BXLYHN DA7 | 164 | D7 |
| Homer Dr | POP/IOD E14 | 160 | F5 |
| Home Rd | BTSEA SW11 | 157 | P8 |
| Homer Rd | CROY/NA CR0 | 204 | D6 |
| | HOM E9 | 120 | E9 |
| Homer Rw | CAMTN NW1 | 9 | P4 |
| Homersham Rd | KUT/HW KT1 | 199 | P4 |
| Homers Rd | WDSR SL4 | 148 | C7 |
| Homer St | MBLAR W1H | 9 | P4 |
| Homerswood La | WLYN AL6 | 22 | A1 |
| Homerton Gv | HOM E9 | 120 | C10 |
| Homerton High St | HOM E9 | 120 | C10 |
| Homerton Rd | HOM E9 | 120 | C10 |
| Homerton Ter | HOM E9 | 120 | B10 |
| Homesdale Cl | WAN E11 | 121 | M1 |
| Homesdale Rd | CTHM CR3 | 241 | L9 |
| | HAYES BR2 | 205 | P1 |
| | ORP BR6 | 207 | H7 |
| Homesfield | GLDGN NW11 | 117 | J3 |
| Homestall | GUW GU2 | 249 | J10 |
| Homestall Rd | EDUL SE22 | 181 | K4 |
| Homestead Cl | LCOL/BKTW AL2 | 23 | L6 |
| Homestead Ct | WGCE AL7 | 23 | L6 |
| Homestead Gdns | ESH/CLAY KT10 | 218 | D2 |
| Homestead La | WGCE AL7 | 23 | L6 |
| Homestead Paddock | STHGT/OAK N14 | 78 | C9 |
| Homestead Pk | CRICK NW2 | 116 | C8 |
| Homestead Rd | BCTR RM8 | 124 | A7 |
| | CTHM CR3 | 241 | J6 |
| | FUL/PGN SW6 | 157 | J6 |
| | HAT AL10 | 40 | C1 |
| | ORP BR6 | 227 | L4 |
| | RKW/CH/CXG WD3 | 91 | N1 |
| | STA TW18 | 173 | H10 |
| Homestead Wy | CROY/NA CR0 | 223 | N10 |
| Homewaters Av | SUN TW16 | 196 | C1 |
| Homeway | HARH RM3 | 105 | P1 |
| Home Wy | RKW/CH/CXG WD3 | 91 | J2 |
| Homewillow Cl | WCHMH N21 | 81 | J10 |
| Homewood | DTCH/LGLY SL3 | 149 | M1 |
| Homewood Av | POTB/CUF EN6 | 60 | F3 |
| Homewood Cl | HPTN TW12 | 175 | N9 |
| Homewood Crs | CHST BR7 | 185 | N6 |
| Homewood Gdns | SNWD SE25 * | 203 | M5 |
| Homewood La | POTB/CUF EN6 | 60 | G3 |
| Homewood Rd | STAL AL1 | 39 | J5 |
| Honduras St | FSBYE EC1V | 12 | E1 |
| Honeybourne Rd | KIL/WHAMP NW6 | 2 | L10 |
| Honeybourne Wy | STMC/STPC BR5 | 227 | N3 |
| Honey Brook | WAB EN9 | 45 | K9 |
| Honeybrook Rd | BAL SW12 | 180 | D3 |
| Honey Cl | BRWN CM15 | 87 | J1 |
| | DAGE RM10 | 144 | D1 |
| Honeycrock La | REDH RH1 | 276 | D7 |
| Honeycroft | LOU IG10 | 82 | D5 |
| | WGCW AL8 | 22 | F4 |
| Honeycroft Hi | UX/CGN UB10 | 131 | P2 |
| Honeycross Rd | HHW HP1 | 35 | J5 |
| Honeyden Rd | SCUP DA14 | 186 | F3 |
| Honey Hi | WAB EN9 | 45 | K9 |
| Honey Hl | HGDN/ICK UB10 | 132 | A2 |
| Honey La | WAB EN9 | 45 | K9 |
| Honeyman Cl | CRICK NW2 | 116 | G2 |
| Honeymeade | SBW CM21 | 29 | M4 |

Honeypot Cl CDALE/KGS NW9 115 L2
Honeypot La BRW CM14 106 F3
CDALE/KGS NW9 115 L2
STAN HA7 95 J9
WAB EN9 63 P10
Honeypots Rd
WOKS/MYFD GU22 232 A8
Honeysett Rd TOTM N17 99 N10
Honeysuckle Bottom
EHSLY KT24 252 F10
Honeysuckle Cl BRWN CM15 86 G9
HARH RM3 105 K7
HERT/BAY SG13 25 P5
HORL RH6 280 D3
IVER SL0 130 F8
STHL UB1 133 M9
Honeysuckle Fld CSHM HP5 51 H6
Honeysuckle Gdns
CROY/NA CR0 204 C7
HAT AL10 40 E5
Honeysuckle La CRAWW RH11 283 M4
Honeywell Rd BTSEA SW11 179 P2
Honeywood Cl POTB/CUF EN6 59 N9
Honeywood Rd ISLW TW7 * 154 F10
WLSDN NW10 136 C4
Honeywood Wk CAR SM5 222 A1
Honister Cl STAN HA7 94 G9
Honister Gdns STAN HA7 94 G8
Honister Hts PUR/KEN CR8 223 L10
Honister Pl STAN HA7 94 G9
Honiton Gdns MLHL NW7 96 G8
PECK SE15 * 160 B8
Honiton Rd KIL/WHAMP NW6 2 C7
ROMW/RG RM7 124 E4
WELL DA16 163 J8
Honley Rd CAT SE6 182 G3
Honnor Gdns ISLW TW7 154 C8
Honnor Rd STA TW18 173 N10
Honor Oak Pk FSTH SE23 182 B3
Honor Oak Ri FSTH SE23 182 B2
Honor Oak Rd FSTH SE23 182 B4
Honor St HLWE CM17 29 N10
Honours Md HHS/BOV HP3 * 52 D3
Hood Av MORT/ESHN SW14 177 P1
STHGT/OAK N14 78 C10
STMC/STPC BR5 207 L5
Hood Cl CROY/NA CR0 203 J8
Hoodcote Gdns WCHMH N21 99 J1
Hood Rd RAIN RM13 144 F3
RYNPK SW20 178 C10
Hood Wk ROMW/RG RM7 104 C9
Hook End Rd BRWN CM15 86 G1
Hooke Rd EHSLY KT24 252 G1
Hooker's Rd WALTH E17 120 C1
Hook Farm Rd HAYES BR2 206 A5
Hook Fld HLWS CM18 47 H3
Hookfield HOR/WEW KT19 219 P9
Hookfields GVW DA11 190 B6
Hook Ga EN EN1 80 A3
Hook Green Rd MEO DA13 189 K10
Hook Heath Av
WOKS/MYFD GU22 231 N5
Hook Heath Gdns
WOKS/MYFD GU22 231 L7
Hook Heath Rd
WOKS/MYFD GU22 231 L7
Hook Hl SAND/SEL CR2 223 M6
Hook Hill La
WOKS/MYFD GU22 231 N7
Hook Hill Pk
WOKS/MYFD GU22 231 N7
Hooking Gn RYLN/HDSTN HA2 114 A3
Hook La ABR/ST RM4 84 A10
CHOB/PIR GU24 212 B9
POTB/CUF EN6 60 A8
RGUW GU3 266 C6
SHGR GU5 270 C7
WELL DA16 163 J10
Hook Mill La LTWR GU18 212 C5
Hook Ri North SURB KT6 199 L10
Hook Ri South CHSGTN KT9 199 L10
Hook Rd CHSGTN KT9 219 J2
HOR/WEW KT19 219 P6
SURB KT6 199 K9
Hooks Hall Dr DAGE RM10 124 D8
Hookstone La CHOB/PIR GU24 212 E7
Hookstone Wy WFD IG8 102 A8
The Hook BAR EN5 77 N10
Hook Underpass (Kingston By-Pass) SURB KT6 199 J10
Hook Wk EDGW HA8 95 P7
Hookwood Cnr OXTED RH8 261 N4
Hooley La REDH RH1 276 A1
Hooper Dr UX/CGN UB8 132 C7
Hooper Rd CAN/RD E16 141 M8
Hoopers Ms BUSH WD23 94 A2
Hooper's Ms ACT W3 135 P10
Hooper St WCHPL E1 13 N6
Hoop La GLDGN NW11 117 J5
The Hoo HLWE CM17 29 M6
Hop Ct ALP/SUD HA0 * 135 H1
Hope Cl BTFD TW8 155 K4
CHDH RM6 123 N2
IS N1 6 F1
LEE/GVPK SE12 183 N6
SUT SM1 221 M2
Hopedale Rd CHARL SE7 161 N5
Hopefield Av
KIL/WHAMP NW6 2 B7
Hope Gdns ACT W3 155 N1
Hope Gn GSTN WD25 55 H9
Hope La ELTH/MOT SE9 184 E6
Hope Pk BMLY BR1 183 L10
Hope Rd SWCM DA10 189 L2
Hopes Cl HEST TW5 153 P5
Hope Sq LVPST EC2M 13 J4
Hope St BTSEA SW11 157 N9
Hope Ter WTHK RM20 * 167 J4
Hopetown St WCHPL E1 13 N4
Hopewell Cl CDW/CHF RM16 167 J4
Hopewell Dr GVE DA12 191 J8
Hopewell St CMBW SE5 159 L6
Hopewell Yd CMBW SE5 159 L6
Hopfield Av BF/WBF KT14 215 P8
Hopfield Cl RSEV TN14 247 K2
Hopgarden La SEV TN13 265 H4
Hop Gdns CHCR WC2N 11 L8
Hop Garden Wy GSTN WD25 55 K7
Hopgood St SHB W12 156 F1
Hopground Cl STAL AL1 38 F8
Hophurst Dr CRAWE RH10 284 F6
Hopkin Cl GUW GU2 249 N6
Hopkins Cl GPK RM2 125 K1
MUSWH N10 98 B8
Hopkins Crs STALE/WH AL4 20 G10
Hopkins Ms SRTFD E15 141 L3
Hopkinsons Pl CAMTN NW1 4 B5
Hopkins Rd LEY E10 120 G5
Hopkins St SOHO/CST W1F 11 H6
Hopkins Yd STAL AL1 38 D7
Hoppers Rd WCHMH N21 99 H3
Hoppett Rd CHING E4 101 K4
The Hoppety
KWD/TDW/WH KT20 238 G8
Hopping La IS N1 6 D2
Hoppingwood Av NWMAL KT3 200 B3
Hoppit Rd WAB EN9 62 G8
The Hoppitt CHONG CM5 49 K6
Hoppner Rd YEAD UB4 132 E4
Hop St GNWCH SE10 161 L3
Hopton Gdns NWMAL KT3 200 D6
Hopton Pde
STRHM/NOR SW16 * 180 F8
Hopton Rd STRHM/NOR SW16 180 F8
WOOL/PLUM SE18 162 E2
Hoptons Gdns STHWK SE1 * 12 D9
Hopton St STHWK SE1 12 D8
Hoptree Cl
NFNCH/WDSPK N12 * 97 L5
Hopwood Cl TOOT SW17 179 M6
WAT WD17 72 E2
Hopwood Rd WALW SE17 19 H9
Hopwood Wk HACK E8 * 7 P4
Horace Av ROMW/RG RM7 124 E6
Horace Rd BARK/HLT IG6 122 F1
FSTGT E7 121 N9
KUT/HW KT1 199 L3
Horatio Pl POP/IOD E14 161 H1
Horatio St BETH E2 7 M8
Horatius Wy CROY/NA CR0 222 G3
Horbury Crs NTGHL W11 8 E8
Horbury Ms NTGHL W11 8 D8
Horder Rd FUL/PGN SW6 157 H7
Hordle Gdns STAL AL1 38 E7
Hordle Prom East PECK SE15 159 N6
Hordle Prom North
PECK SE15 159 N6
Hordle Prom West PECK SE15 159 M6
Horksley Gdns
RBRW/HUT CM13 87 P10
Horley Cl BXLYHS DA6 186 B1
Horley Lodge La REDH RH1 276 A9
Horley Rd ELTH/MOT SE9 184 B7
HORL RH6 279 K8
REDH RH1 276 A5
Horley Rw HORL RH6 280 A3
Hormead Rd MV/WKIL W9 8 C2
Hornbeam Av UPMR RM14 125 P9
Hornbeam Cha
SOCK/AV RM15 147 J5
Hornbeam Cl BORE WD6 75 M5
EPP CM16 83 H3
IL IG1 122 G10
LBTH SE11 18 A5
MLHL NW7 96 C4
NTHLT UB5 113 N10
RBRW/HUT CM13 107 N4
Hornbeam Crs BTFD TW8 154 G6
Hornbeam Gdns
DTCH/LGLY SL3 149 M2
NWMAL KT3 200 D6
Hornbeam Gv CHING E4 101 K4
Hornbeam La BRKMPK AL9 41 P7
CHING E4 81 K9
Hornbeam Rd BKHH IG9 102 A4
EPP CM16 82 G3
GU GU1 249 P7
REIG RH2 275 M3
YEAD UB4 133 K7
Hornbeams LCOL/BKTW AL2 55 N6
WGCE AL7 * 23 L6
Hornbeams Av EN EN1 80 B1
Hornbeam Sq BOW E3 140 E3
Hornbeams Ri
FBAR/BDGN N11 98 B7
The Hornbeams HLW CM20 28 E9
Hornbeam Wy CHESW EN7 61 N5
HAYES BR2 206 D6
Hornbill Cl UX/CGN UB8 131 N8
Hornbuckle Cl
RYLN/HDSTN HA2 114 C7
Hornby Cl HAMP NW3 3 M3
Horncastle Cl LEE/GVPK SE12 183 M3
Horncastle Rd LEE/GVPK SE12 183 M3
Hornchurch Cl KUTN/CMB KT2 177 J8
Hornchurch Hl CTHM CR3 241 N3
Hornchurch Rd HCH RM12 125 H6
Horndean Cl CRAWE RH10 284 E3
PUT/ROE SW15 178 D4
Horndon Cl CRW RM5 104 D9
Horndon Gn CRW RM5 104 D9
Horndon Rd CRW RM5 104 D9
Hornecourt Hl HORL RH6 277 N10
Horne House CHARL SE7 * 162 B6
Horner La MTCM CR4 201 N2
Horne Rd SHPTN TW17 196 A4
The Hornets WATW WD18 73 J8
Horne Wy PUT/ROE SW15 156 F8
Hornfair Rd CHARL SE7 162 A5
Hornford Wy ROMW/RG RM7 124 F5
Hornhatch RGUE GU4 268 E7
Hornhatch Cl RGUE GU4 268 E6
Hornhatch La RGUE GU4 268 D6
Hornhill Rd RKW/CH/CXG WD3 90 F6
Horniman Dr FSTH SE23 182 A4
Horniman Gdns FSTH SE23 * 182 A4
Horning Cl ELTH/MOT SE9 184 B7
Horn La ACT W3 135 P10
GNWCH SE10 161 M3
WFD IG8 101 M7
Horn Link Wy GNWCH SE10 161 M2
Hornminster Gln EMPK RM11 125 P7
Horn Park Cl LEE/GVPK SE12 183 N1
Horn Park La LEE/GVPK SE12 183 N1
Horns Cl HERT/BAY SG13 25 K7
Hornscroft Cl BARK IG11 143 H2
Horns End Pl PIN HA5 113 K2
Hornsey Chambers CLPT E5 * 120 A7
Hornsey La HGT N6 118 D5
Hornsey Lane Est ARCH N19 * 118 E5
Hornsey Lane Gdns HGT N6 118 D5
Hornsey Park Rd
CEND/HSY/T N8 118 G1
Hornsey Ri ARCH N19 118 E5
Hornsey Rise Gdns ARCH N19 118 E5
Hornsey Rd ARCH N19 118 F6
Hornsey St HOLWY N7 118 G10
Hornsfield WGCE AL7 23 M4
Hornshay St PECK SE15 160 B5
Horns Mill Rd HERT/BAY SG13 25 J8
Horns Rd BARK/HLT IG6 122 F3
HERT/BAY SG13 25 K6
Hornton Pl KENS W8 14 F2
Hornton St KENS W8 14 F1
Horsa Gdns HAT AL10 40 A3
Horsa Rd ERITH DA8 164 D6
LEE/GVPK SE12 183 P3
Horseblock La CSHM HP5 32 D7
Horsebridges Cl DAGW RM9 143 P3
Horsecroft BNSTD SM7 239 J3
Horsecroft Cl ORP BR6 207 L8
Horsecroft Mdw BNSTD SM7 * 239 K2
Horsecroft Rd EDGW HA8 96 A8
HHW HP1 35 K8
HLWW/ROY CM19 46 B2
Horse Fair KUT/HW KT1 199 J2
Horseferry Pl GNWCH SE10 161 H5
Horseferry Rd POP/IOD E14 140 D9
WEST SW1P 17 J4
Horse Guards Av WHALL SW1A 11 L10
Horse Guards Rd WHALL SW1A 11 K10
Horse Hl CSHM HP5 52 A8
HORL RH6 279 L3
Horse Leaze EHAM E6 142 E8
Horselers HHS/BOV HP3 36 B9
Horsell Birch
WOKN/KNAP GU21 231 M1
Horsell Common Rd
WOKN/KNAP GU21 213 P10
Horsell Ct CHERT KT16 195 L7
Horsell Moor
WOKN/KNAP GU21 232 A3
Horsell Pk WOKN/KNAP GU21 232 A2
Horsell Park Cl
WOKN/KNAP GU21 232 A2
Horsell Ri WOKN/KNAP GU21 232 A1
Horsell Rise Cl
WOKN/KNAP GU21 232 A1
Horsell Rd HBRY N5 119 H10
STMC/STPC BR5 207 K1
Horsell V WOKN/KNAP GU21 232 B1
Horsell Wy WOKN/KNAP GU21 231 P2
Horselydown La STHWK SE1 19 L1
Horseman Ct BRWN CM15 86 D3
Horsemans Dr
LCOL/BKTW AL2 55 P2
Horseman Side BRW CM14 85 L10
Horsemoor Cl DTCH/LGLY SL3 150 D3
Horsemoor La AMSS HP7 68 A10
Horsenden Av GFD/PVL UB6 114 D10
Horsenden Crs GFD/PVL UB6 114 E10
Horsenden La North
GFD/PVL UB6 134 D1
Horsenden La South
GFD/PVL UB6 134 F3
Horseshoe Cl CRAWE RH10 284 E6
CRICK NW2 116 E7
POP/IOD E14 161 H4
WAB EN9 63 M10
Horse Shoe Crs NTHLT UB5 133 P4
Horseshoe Dr UX/CGN UB8 132 B8
Horseshoe Hl SL SL1 108 B9
WAB EN9 63 P9
Horseshoe La ENC/FH EN2 79 K7
GSTN WD25 55 J8
TRDG/WHET N20 96 C2
Horseshoe La East GU GU1 250 E9
Horseshoe La West GU GU1 250 E9
Horseshoe Ms
BRXS/STRHM SW2 158 F10
Horseshoe Rdg WEY KT13 216 D7
The Horseshoe BNSTD SM7 239 J1
COUL/CHIP CR5 222 E9
HHS/BOV HP3 36 D8
Horse Yd IS N1 6 D5
Horsfeld Gdns ELTH/MOT SE9 184 B1
Horsfeld Rd ELTH/MOT SE9 184 A1
Horsfield Cl RDART DA2 188 B3
Horsford Rd
BRXS/STRHM SW2 180 G1
Horsham Av
NFNCH/WDSPK N12 97 P6
Horsham Rd BXLYHS DA6 186 A2
CRAWW RH11 283 K10
DORK RH4 272 F3
EBED/NFELT TW14 174 D2
RDKG RH5 273 H10
RDKG RH5 270 G8
SHGR GU5 268 B8
Horsley Cl HOR/WEW KT19 220 A9
Horsley Dr CROY/NA CR0 225 H4
KUTN/CMB KT2 177 J8
Horsley Rd BMLY BR1 205 N1
CHING E4 101 H3
COB KT11 235 J5
Horsleys RKW/CH/CXG WD3 90 G6
Horsley St WALW SE17 18 G9
Horsmans Pl DART DA1 * 187 M3
Horsman St CMBW SE5 18 F10
Horsmonden Cl ORP BR6 207 H7
Horsmonden Rd BROCKY SE4 182 E1
Horticultural Pl CHSWK W4 156 A4
Horton Av CRICK NW2 117 H9
Horton Bridge Rd
WDR/YW UB7 132 A10
Horton Cl WDR/YW UB7 132 A10
Horton Crs HOR/WEW KT19 219 N7
Horton Gdns DTCH/LGLY SL3 * 150 C9
HOR/WEW KT19 219 P7
Horton Hl HOR/WEW KT19 219 P7
Horton La HOR/WEW KT19 219 M7
Horton Pde WDR/YW UB7 * 131 P10
Horton Pl BH/WHM TN16 262 C2
Horton Rd DTCH/LGLY SL3 149 P7
EYN DA4 210 B3
HACK E8 140 A1
WDR/YW UB7 131 P10
Horton St LEW SE13 160 G9
Hortons Wy BH/WHM TN16 262 C2
Horton Wy CROY/NA CR0 204 C5
EYN DA4 209 N7
Hortus Rd NWDGN UB2 153 N1
Horvath Cl WEY KT13 216 E1
Hosack Rd TOOT SW17 180 A5
Hoselands Vw HART DA3 211 K4
Hoser Av LEE/GVPK SE12 183 M5
Hosey Common La
BH/WHM TN16 263 H6
Hosey Common Rd
BH/WHM TN16 263 H5
Hosey Hl BH/WHM TN16 263 H3
Hosier La STBT EC1A 12 C4
Hoskins Cl HYS/HAR UB3 152 G4
Hoskin's Cl CAN/RD E16 141 P8
Hoskins Rd OXTED RH8 261 K5
Hoskins St GNWCH SE10 161 J4
Hoskins Wk OXTED RH8 261 K5
Hospital Bridge Rd
WHTN TW2 175 P3
Hospital Hl CSHM HP5 51 H8
Hospital Rd HSLW TW3 153 P9
LEY E10 121 J4
SEV TN13 247 K7
Hospital Wy LEW SE13 183 J2
Hotham Cl E/WMO/HCT KT8 197 P3
EYN DA4 187 P10
SWLY BR8 209 J1
Hotham Rd PUT/ROE SW15 156 F9
Hotham Road Ms
WIM/MER SW19 179 M10
Hotham St SRTFD E15 141 K3
Hothfield Pl BERM/RHTH SE16 160 B2
Hotspur Rd NTHLT UB5 133 P4
Hotspur St LBTH SE11 18 A7
Hottsfield HART DA3 211 K3
Houblon Rd
RCHPK/HAM TW10 177 K1
Houblons Hl EPP CM16 65 N7
Houghton Cl HACK E8 7 M2
HPTN TW12 175 M9
Houghton Rd CRAWE RH10 * 284 D10
SEVS/STOTM N15 119 N2
Houghton St LINN WC2A * 11 P6
Houlder Crs CROY/NA CR0 223 J2
Hound House Rd SHGR GU5 270 B10
Houndsden Rd WCHMH N21 78 G10
Houndsditch HDTCH EC3A 13 K5
Houndsfield Rd ED N9 100 A1
Houndswood Ga RAD WD7 56 F7
Hounslow Av HSLW TW3 176 A1
Hounslow Gdns HSLW TW3 176 A1
Hounslow Rd
EBED/NFELT TW14 175 J3
Housden Cl STALE/WH AL4 21 K4
Housefield Wy STALE/WH AL4 39 H9
House La STALE/WH AL4 21 H10
Houseman Wy CMBW SE5 159 L6
Housewood End HHW HP1 35 L3
Houston Rd FSTH SE23 182 D5
SURB KT6 198 G6
Hove Av WALTH E17 120 E3
Hove Cl GRAYS RM17 167 M5
RBRW/HUT CM13 107 P3
Hoveden Rd CRICK NW2 116 G10
Hove Gdns SUT SM1 201 L8
Hoveton Rd THMD SE28 143 M8
Howard Agne Cl
HHS/BOV HP3 52 D3
Howard Av BXLY DA5 185 M4
SLN SL2 129 J7
Howard Cl ACT W3 135 N8
ASHTD KT21 237 L4
BUSH WD23 94 D1
CRICK NW2 * 117 H9
EHSLY KT24 252 E1
FBAR/BDGN N11 98 B3
HPTN TW12 176 B10
KWD/TDW/WH KT20 256 C1
LHD/OX KT22 237 H9
LOU IG10 82 B10
STAL AL1 39 H9
SUN TW16 174 G9
WAB EN9 63 J10
WATN WD24 73 H3
Howard Crs BEAC HP9 89 H6
Howard Dr BORE WD6 76 A8
Howard Gdns GU GU1 250 D9
Howard Pl REIG RH2 257 K8
Howard Rdg RGUE GU4 250 D6
Howard Rd BARK IG11 142 G3
BEAC HP9 89 H6
BMLY BR1 183 M10
CDW/CHF RM16 167 H2
COUL/CHIP CR5 240 D1
CRICK NW2 116 G9
CSHM HP5 50 G4
DORK RH4 272 F2
EHAM E6 142 C4
EHSLY KT24 235 H8
GT/LBKH KT23 254 A3
IL IG1 122 E9
ISLW TW7 154 E9
NWMAL KT3 200 B3
PGE/AN SE20 204 B1
RDKG RH5 * 273 H6
REIG RH2 275 L1
SEVS/STOTM N15 119 M4
SNWD SE25 203 P5
STHL UB1 134 A8
STNW/STAM N16 119 L9
SURB KT6 199 L6
UPMR RM14 126 B7
WALTH E17 120 F1
WAN E11 121 K8
Howards Cl PIN HA5 * 93 J10
WOKS/MYFD GU22 232 D6
Howards Crest Cl BECK BR3 205 H2
Howards Dr HHW HP1 35 J3
Howardsgate WGCW AL8 22 G4
Howards La ADL/WDHM KT15 215 H3
Howard's La PUT/ROE SW15 156 F10
Howards Rd
WOKS/MYFD GU22 232 C6
Howard's Rd PLSTW E13 141 M5
Howards Thicket
CFSP/GDCR SL9 109 P7
Howard St THDIT KT7 198 G7
Howards Wood Dr
CFSP/GDCR SL9 110 A7
Howards Yd
WAND/EARL SW18 179 L3
Howard Wk EFNCH N2 117 M2
Howard Wy BAR EN5 76 G9
HLW CM20 29 J9
HLWS CM18 47 K1
Howarth Rd ABYW SE2 163 K4
Howberry Cl EDGW HA8 95 J7
Howberry Rd EDGW HA8 95 J7
THHTH CR7 203 L1
Howbury La ERITH DA8 165 H8
Howbury Rd PECK SE15 160 B9
Howcroft Crs FNCH N3 97 K8
Howcroft La GFD/PVL UB6 134 C5
Howden Cl THMD SE28 143 M9
Howden Rd SNWD SE25 203 N2
Howden St PECK SE15 159 P9
Howe Cl RAD WD7 57 K8
ROMW/RG RM7 104 B9
Howe Dell HAT AL10 40 E4
Howe Dr BEAC HP9 88 C6
CTHM CR3 241 L8
Howell Cl CHDH RM6 123 N3
Howell Hl BELMT SM2 * 220 F6
Howell Hill Cl EW KT17 220 F7
Howell Hill Gv EW KT17 220 F7
Howell Wk STHWK SE1 18 D6
Howerd Wy
WOOL/PLUM SE18 162 B7
Howe Rd HHS/BOV HP3 36 B8
Howes Cl FNCH N3 117 K1
Howfield Gn HOD EN11 26 E10
Howfield Pl TOTM N17 * 119 N1
Howgate Rd
MORT/ESHN SW14 156 A9
Howick Pl WESTW SW1E 17 H4
Howicks Gn WGCE AL7 23 K8
Howie St BTSEA SW11 157 P6
Howitt Cl HAMP NW3 3 N1
Howitt Rd HAMP NW3 3 P1
Howitts Cl ESH/CLAY KT10 217 P3
Howland Ct PIN HA5 * 93 P7
Howland Garth STAL AL1 38 B10
Howland Ms East FITZ W1T 11 H3
Howlands WGCE AL7 23 H8
Howland St FITZ W1T 11 H3
Howland Wy
BERM/RHTH SE16 160 D1
How La COUL/CHIP CR5 240 B4
Howletts La RSLP HA4 112 D4
Howletts Rd HNHL SE24 181 K2
Howley Pl BAY/PAD W2 9 K3
Howley Rd CROY/NA CR0 203 J10
Howse Rd WAB EN9 80 G1
Howsman Rd BARN SW13 156 D5
Hows Md EPP CM16 48 E10
Howson Rd BROCKY SE4 160 D10
Howson Ter
RCHPK/HAM TW10 * 177 K2
How's Rd UX/CGN UB8 131 M3
How's St BETH E2 7 L7
Howton Pl BUSH WD23 94 C2
How Wd LCOL/BKTW AL2 56 A4
Hoxton Market IS N1 7 J10
Hoxton Sq IS N1 7 J10
Hoxton St IS N1 7 J6
Hoylake Cl CRAWW RH11 282 G8
Hoylake Crs HGDN/ICK UB10 112 B6
Hoylake Gdns HARH RM3 105 P9
MTCM CR4 202 D3
OXHEY WD19 93 L5
RSLP HA4 113 J6
Hoylake Rd ACT W3 136 B8
Hoyland Cl PECK SE15 * 160 A6
Hoyle Rd TOOT SW17 179 P8
Hoy St CAN/RD E16 141 L8
Hoy Ter WTHK RM20 * 167 J4
Hubbard Dr CHSGTN KT9 219 H3
Hubbard Rd WNWD SE27 181 K7
Hubbards Cha EMPK RM11 125 P3
Hubbards Cl EMPK RM11 125 P3
UX/CGN UB8 132 C8
Hubbard's Hl RSEV TN14 265 J7
Hubbards Rd
RKW/CH/CXG WD3 70 G9
Hubbard St SRTFD E15 141 K3
Hubert Cl WIM/MER SW19 * 201 M1
Hubert Day Cl BEAC HP9 88 C8
Hubert Gv BRXN/ST SW9 158 F9
Hubert Rd BRW CM14 106 G4
DTCH/LGLY SL3 150 A2
EHAM E6 142 A5
RAIN RM13 144 G5
Hucknall Cl HARH RM3 105 N7
Huddart St BOW E3 140 E7
Huddleston Cl BETH E2 * 140 B4
Huddleston Crs REDH RH1 258 E4
Huddlestone Rd CRICK NW2 136 E1
FSTGT E7 121 L9
Huddleston Rd HOLWY N7 118 D8
Hudson Cl SHB W12 * 136 E9
STAL AL1 38 B9
WATN WD24 72 G2
Hudson Ct GUW GU2 249 L10
Hudson Pl DTCH/LGLY SL3 150 C4
WOOL/PLUM SE18 162 F4
Hudson Rd BXLYHN DA7 164 A8
CRAWE RH10 283 P9
HYS/HAR UB3 152 E5
Hudsons KWD/TDW/WH KT20 238 G7
Huesden Wy CFSP/GDCR SL9 110 C6
Huggens College GVW DA11 * 189 N1
Huggin Hl BLKFR EC4V 12 F7
Huggins La BRKMPK AL9 40 E9
Huggins Pl BRXS/STRHM SW2 180 G4
Hughan Rd SRTFD E15 121 J10
Hugh Dalton Av FUL/PGN SW6 14 C10
Hughenden Av
KTN/HRWW/WS HA3 114 G3
Hughenden Gdns NTHLT UB5 133 K5
Hughenden Rd SL SL1 129 J8
STALE/WH AL4 38 G3
WPK KT4 200 D7
Hughes Cl NFNCH/WDSPK N12 97 M6
Hughes Rd ASHF TW15 174 D10
CDW/CHF RM16 168 D2
HYS/HAR UB3 133 J9
Hughes Ter CAN/RD E16 * 141 L7
Hughes Wk CROY/NA CR0 203 K7
Hugh Gaitskell Cl
FUL/PGN SW6 14 C10
Hugh Ms PIM SW1V 16 F6
Hugh Pl WEST SW1P 17 J5
Hugh St PIM SW1V 16 F6
Hugo Cl WATW WD18 72 F8
Hugo Gdns RAIN RM13 144 G1
Hugon Rd FUL/PGN SW6 157 L9
Hugo Rd ARCH N19 118 D9
Huguenot Pl
WAND/EARL SW18 179 M1
WCHPL E1 13 M3
Huitt Sq BTSEA SW11 157 N9
Hullbridge Ms IS N1 6 G5
Hull Cl BERM/RHTH SE16 * 140 C10
CHESW EN7 61 L2
SL SL1 149 H1
Hullett's La BRWN CM15 86 E8
Hull Gn HLWE CM17 31 L9
Hull Gv HLWW/ROY CM19 46 D6
Hull St FSBYE EC1V 6 E10
Hulme Pl STHWK SE1 18 F2
Hulse Av BARK IG11 143 H1
ROMW/RG RM7 104 C9
Hulton Cl LHD/OX KT22 237 H9
Hulverston Cl BELMT SM2 221 L5
Humber Av SOCK/AV RM15 146 E8
Humber Cl WDR/YW UB7 131 N10
Humber Dr NKENS W10 136 G6
UPMR RM14 126 C4
Humber Rd BKHTH/KID SE3 161 M5
CRICK NW2 116 E7
Humberstone Rd PLSTW E13 141 P5
Humber Wy DTCH/LGLY SL3 150 D3
Humbolt Cl GUW GU2 249 K10
Humbolt Rd HMSMTH W6 14 A10
Hume Av TIL RM18 168 E9
Hume Cl TIL RM18 168 D9
Humes Av HNWL W7 154 E2
Hume Wy RSLP HA4 113 H4
Hummer Rd EGH TW20 172 D7
Humphrey Cl CLAY IG5 * 102 C9
LHD/OX KT22 236 B8
Humphrey St STHWK SE1 19 L7
Humphries Cl DAGW RM9 124 A9
Hundred Acre
CDALE/KGS NW9 96 C10
Hundred Acres
CHES/WCR EN8 * 62 F10
Hundred Acres La AMSS HP7 69 J6
Hungerdown CHING E4 101 H2
Hungerford Av SLN SL2 129 K7
Hungerford Sq WEY KT13 216 E1
Hungerford St WCHPL E1 * 140 A8
Hungry Hill La
RPLY/SEND GU23 251 M2
Hunsdon WGCE AL7 23 N5
Hunsdon Cl DAGW RM9 143 P1
Hunsdon Dr SEV TN13 247 J9
Hunsdon Rd NWCR SE14 160 C6
WARE SG12 27 K7
Hunslett St BETH E2 * 140 B4
Hunstanton Cl CRAWW RH11 282 G8
DTCH/LGLY SL3 150 F6
Hunston Rd MRDN SM4 201 L8
Hunt Cl BKHTH/KID SE3 * 161 M8
NTGHL W11 136 G10
STALE/WH AL4 39 J3
Hunter Av BRWN CM15 87 M10
Hunter Cl BAL SW12 180 B4
BORE WD6 75 P9
POTB/CUF EN6 59 L9
STHWK SE1 19 H4
WLGTN SM6 222 F4
Huntercombe Cl MDHD SL6 128 A8
Huntercombe La North SL SL1 128 B7
Huntercombe La South
MDHD SL6 128 A10
Hunter Ct CMBW SE5 * 159 L10
Huntercrombe Gdns
OXHEY WD19 93 K6
Hunter Dr HCH RM12 125 K9
Hunter Rd CRAWE RH10 283 N10
GU GU1 268 B1
RYNPK SW20 200 F1
THHTH CR7 203 L3
Hunters Cha CHONG CM5 67 P6
Hunters Cl CSHM HP5 50 F6
HHS/BOV HP3 52 D5
HOR/WEW KT19 219 P9
Hunters Ct RCH/KEW TW9 177 J1
Huntersfield Cl REIG RH2 257 L7
Hunters Ga REDH RH1 258 G9
Hunters Gv HYS/HAR UB3 133 H10
KTN/HRWW/WS HA3 115 H2
Hunter's Gv CRW RM5 104 C6
ORP BR6 226 F1
Hunters Hall Rd DAGE RM10 124 B9
Hunters Hl RSLP HA4 113 K8
Hunter's La GSTN WD25 54 G10
Hunters Meadow NRWD SE19 181 M7
Hunters Oak HHNE HP2 36 C1
Hunters Pk BERK HP4 34 B4
Hunters Reach CHESW EN7 61 N5
Hunters Ride LCOL/BKTW AL2 55 P7
Hunters Rd CHSGTN KT9 199 K10
IL IG1 122 E10
Hunters Sq DAGE RM10 124 B9
Hunter St BMSBY WC1N 11 M1
Hunters Wk RSEV TN14 227 P10
Hunters Wy CROY/NA CR0 223 M1
ENC/FH EN2 79 H5
SL SL1 128 D10
WGCE AL7 23 J8
Hunting Cl ESH/CLAY KT10 217 P1
Huntingdon Cl BROX EN10 44 D10
MTCM CR4 202 F4
NTHLT UB5 133 P1
Huntingdon Gdns CHSWK W4 155 P6
WPK KT4 200 F10
Huntingdon Rd ED N9 100 B2
EFNCH N2 117 P1
REDH RH1 258 A10
WOKN/KNAP GU21 231 K3
Huntingdon St CAN/RD E16 141 L8
IS N1 5 P3
Huntingfield CROY/NA CR0 224 E4
Huntingfield Rd
PUT/ROE SW15 178 D2
Huntingfield Wy EGH TW20 172 G10
Hunting Ga HHNE HP2 35 P2
Hunting Gate Cl ENC/FH EN2 79 H7
Hunting Gate Dr CHSGTN KT9 219 K4
Hunting Gate Ms WHTN TW2 * 176 D4
Huntings Rd DAGE RM10 144 B1
Huntington Pl DTCH/LGLY SL3 150 E2
Huntland Cl RAIN RM13 145 J7
Huntley Av GVW DA11 189 N2
Huntley Cl STWL/WRAY TW19 173 P3
Huntley St GWRST WC1E 11 H2
Huntley Wy RYNPK SW20 * 200 D2
Huntly Dr FNCH N3 97 K7
Huntly Rd SNWD SE25 203 M3
Hunton Bridge Hl KGLGY WD4 54 D9
Hunton St WCHPL E1 13 N3
Hunt Rd GVW DA11 190 B6
NWDGN UB2 153 P2
Hunts Cl BKHTH/KID SE3 161 M8
GUW GU2 249 J9
Hunt's La SRTFD E15 141 H4
Huntsman Cl FELT TW13 175 J7
Huntsman Rd BARK/HLT IG6 103 L7
Huntsmans Cl WARL CR6 242 B5
Huntsmans Dr UPMR RM14 126 B10
Huntsman St WALW SE17 19 J6
Hunts Md PEND EN3 80 C7
Hunts Medde Cl CHST BR7 184 B10
Huntsmill Rd HHW HP1 35 H7
Huntsmoor Rd
HOR/WEW KT19 220 A2
Huntspill St TOOT SW17 179 M6
Hunts Slip Rd DUL SE21 181 M5
Huntsworth Ms CAMTN NW1 10 A1
Hurdwick Pl CAMTN NW1 * 4 G7
Hurley Cl WOT/HER KT12 197 J9
Hurley Crs BERM/RHTH SE16 140 C10
Hurley Gdns RGUE GU4 250 D7
Hurley Rd GFD/PVL UB6 134 A7
Hurlford WOKN/KNAP GU21 231 M3
Hurlingham Gdns
FUL/PGN SW6 157 J9
Hurlingham Pk
FUL/PGN SW6 * 157 J9
Hurlingham Rd BXLYHN DA7 164 A6
FUL/PGN SW6 157 J8
Hurlingham Sq
FUL/PGN SW6 * 157 K9
Hurlock St HBRY N5 119 J8
Hurlstone Rd SNWD SE25 203 L5
Hurn Court Rd HSLWW TW4 153 L8
Hurnford Cl SAND/SEL CR2 223 M6
Huron Cl ORP BR6 227 H3
Huron Rd BROX EN10 62 D2
TOOT SW17 180 B5
Hurren Cl BKHTH/KID SE3 161 K9
Hurricane House
WOOL/PLUM SE18 * 162 B6
Hurricane Rd WLGTN SM6 222 F4
Hurricane Wy ABLGY WD5 55 H9
DTCH/LGLY SL3 150 E4
EPP CM16 66 A3
Hurry Cl SRTFD E15 141 K2
Hursley Rd CHIG IG7 103 J6
Hurst Av CHING E4 100 F4
HGT N6 118 D4
Hurstbourne ESH/CLAY KT10 218 E3
Hurstbourne Gdns BARK IG11 142 G1
Hurstbourne Rd FSTH SE23 182 D4
Hurst Cl CHING E4 100 F4
CHSGTN KT9 219 M2
CRAWW RH11 283 J9
EPSOM KT18 237 P10
GLDGN NW11 117 L4
HAYES BR2 205 L8
NTHLT UB5 133 N1
WGCE AL7 23 M6
WOKS/MYFD GU22 231 P6
Hurstcourt Rd SUT SM1 201 L8
Hurst Cft GU GU1 268 B3
Hurstdene Av HAYES BR2 205 L8
STA TW18 173 L9
Hurstdene Gdns
SEVS/STOTM N15 119 M5
Hurst Dr CHES/WCR EN8 62 C10
KWD/TDW/WH KT20 256 D2
Hurst Farm Rd RSEV TN14 265 J8
Hurstfield HAYES BR2 205 M5
Hurstfield Crs YEAD UB4 132 F7
Hurstfield Dr MDHD SL6 128 A8
Hurstfield Rd
E/WMO/HCT KT8 197 P3
Hurst Green Cl OXTED RH8 261 M8
Hurst Green Rd OXTED RH8 261 L8
Hurst Gv WOT/HER KT12 196 G8
Hurstlands OXTED RH8 261 M8
Hurstlands Cl EMPK RM11 125 K5
Hurst La ABYW SE2 163 N4
E/WMO/HCT KT8 198 B4
EGH TW20 194 C3
EPSOM KT18 238 A8
RSEV TN14 265 J9
Hurstleigh Cl REDH RH1 258 A8
Hurstleigh Dr REDH RH1 258 A8
Hurstleigh Gdns CLAY IG5 102 C9
Hurstlings WGCE AL7 23 L7
Hurst Park Av HCH RM12 125 M9
Hurst Pl ABYW SE2 163 M4
DART DA1 * 187 K2
NTHWD HA6 92 C9
Hurst Ri BAR EN5 77 K7
Hurst Rd BFN/LL DA15 185 L5
BKHH IG9 102 A2
BXLY DA5 185 P4
CROY/NA CR0 223 L2
E/WMO/HCT KT8 197 P3
EPSOM KT18 238 B9
ERITH DA8 164 D6
HOR/WEW KT19 220 A7
HORL RH6 279 P3
SL SL1 128 C7
WALTH E17 120 G1
WCHMH N21 99 H2
WOT/HER KT12 197 L4
Hurst Springs BXLY DA5 185 P4
Hurst St HNHL SE24 181 J2
Hurst View Rd SAND/SEL CR2 223 M4
Hurst Wy SAND/SEL CR2 223 M3
SEV TN13 265 K3
WOKS/MYFD GU22 215 H10
Hurstway Rd NTGHL W11 * 136 G9
Hurstway Wk NTGHL W11 * 136 G9
Hurstwood Av BRWN CM15 106 G1
BXLY DA5 185 P4
ERITH DA8 164 F7
SWFD E18 121 N2
Hurstwood Dr BMLY BR1 206 C3
Hurstwood Rd GLDGN NW11 117 H2
Hurtmore Cha GODL GU7 266 G9
Hurtmore Rd GODL GU7 266 E10
Hurtwood Rd WOT/HER KT12 197 N7
Hurworth Av DTCH/LGLY SL3 149 P2
Huson Cl HAMP NW3 3 N3
Hussain Cl HRW HA1 114 E9
Hussars Cl HSLWW TW4 153 M9
Husseywell Crs HAYES BR2 205 M8
Hutchingson's Rd
CROY/NA CR0 225 H7
Hutching's St POP/IOD E14 160 F1
Hutchings Wk GLDGN NW11 117 L2
Hutchins Cl HCH RM12 125 M8
SRTFD E15 141 H2
Hutchinson Ter WBLY HA9 115 J8
Hutchins Rd THMD SE28 143 K9
Hutchins Wy HORL RH6 280 A2
Hutton Cl BFOR GU20 212 C4
GFD/PVL UB6 114 C10
HERT/WAT SG14 25 H5
WFD IG8 101 N7
WOT/HER KT12 217 J2
Hutton Ga RBRW/HUT CM13 107 N1
Hutton Gv
NFNCH/WDSPK N12 97 L6
Hutton La
KTN/HRWW/WS HA3 94 B8
Hutton Pl RBRW/HUT CM13 87 N10
Hutton Rd BRWN CM15 107 L1
Hutton Rw EDGW HA8 95 P8
Hutton St EMB EC4Y 12 B6
Hutton Wk
KTN/HRWW/WS HA3 94 B8
Huxbear St BROCKY SE4 182 E1
Huxley UED N18 * 99 L6
Huxley Cl GODL GU7 267 J10
NTHLT UB5 133 M4
SLN SL2 129 N6
Huxley Dr CHDH RM6 123 L5
Huxley Gdns WLSDN NW10 135 L5
Huxley Pde UED N18 * 99 L6
Huxley Pl PLMGR N13 99 J5
Huxley Rd GUW GU2 267 J1
LEY E10 121 H7
UED N18 99 L5
WELL DA16 163 J9
Huxley Sayze UED N18 * 99 L6
Huxley St NKENS W10 2 A10
Hyacinth Cl HPTN TW12 175 P9
IL IG1 142 E1
Hyacinth Dr HGDN/ICK UB10 131 P2
Hyacinth Rd PUT/ROE SW15 178 D4
Hyatts Yd CSHM HP5 * 50 G8
Hyburn Cl HHS/BOV HP3 36 C7
LCOL/BKTW AL2 55 N6
Hycliffe Gdns CHIG IG7 102 F5
Hyde Av POTB/CUF EN6 59 L9
Hyde Cl BAR EN5 77 J7
CDW/CHF RM16 167 J2
CRW RM5 104 E7
PLSTW E13 141 M4
Hyde Crs CDALE/KGS NW9 116 B3
Hyde Dr CRAWW RH11 283 H8
STMC/STPC BR5 207 L4
Hyde Estate Rd
CDALE/KGS NW9 116 C3
Hyde Farm Ms BAL SW12 180 E4
Hydefield Cl WCHMH N21 99 L2
Hydefield Ct ED N9 99 M3
Hyde Gn BEAC HP9 88 E8
Hyde Gv DART DA1 165 N8
Hyde La BTSEA SW11 157 P7
HHS/BOV HP3 54 C3
HHS/BOV HP3 52 D3
LCOL/BKTW AL2 56 D4
Hyde Md WAB EN9 45 K9
Hyde Mdw HHS/BOV HP3 52 D4
Hyde Park Av WCHMH N21 99 K3
Hyde Park Cnr
MYFR/PICC W1J 16 D1
Hyde Park Crs BAY/PAD W2 9 N6

Hyde Park Gdns BAY/PAD W2 9 M7
WCHMH N21 99 K2
Hyde Park Gardens Ms BAY/PAD W2 9 M7
Hyde Park Ga SKENS SW7 15 J2
Hyde Park Gate Ms SKENS SW7 * 15 K2
Hyde Park Pl BAY/PAD W2 9 P7
Hyde Park Sq BAY/PAD W2 9 N6
Hyde Park Square Ms BAY/PAD W2 9 N6
Hyde Park St BAY/PAD W2 9 N7
Hyderabad Wy SRTFD E15 141 K2
Hyde Rd BXLYHN DA7 164 A8
IS N1 7 H6
RCHPK/HAM TW10 177 L1
SAND/SEL CR2 223 M9
WAT WD17 73 H7
Hyder Rd CDW/CHF RM16 168 F2
Hydeside Gdns ED N9 99 N3
Hyde's Pl IS N1 6 C3
Hyde St DEPT SE8 160 F5
Hyde Ter ASHF TW15 174 F9
The Hyde CDALE/KGS NW9 116 B3
WARE SG12 26 A1
Hydethorpe Av ED N9 99 N3
Hydethorpe Rd BAL SW12 180 D4
Hyde V GNWCH SE10 161 H6
Hyde Va WGCE AL7 23 J7
Hyde Wk MRDN SM4 201 K7
Hyde Wy ED N9 99 N3
HYS/HAR UB3 152 G3
WGCE AL7 23 H5
Hyland Cl EMPK RM11 125 J5
Hylands Cl CRAWE RH10 284 B8
Hylands Ms EPSOM KT18 237 P1
Hylands Rd EPSOM KT18 237 P1
WALTH E17 101 J10
Hyland Wy EMPK RM11 125 J5
Hylle Cl WDSR SL4 148 D7
Hylton Pl REDH RH1 258 D7
Hylton St WOOL/PLUM SE18 163 J3
Hyndewood FSTH SE23 * 182 C6
Hyndford Crs SWCM DA10 189 H1
Hyndman St PECK SE15 160 A5
Hynton Rd BCTR RM8 123 M7
Hyperion Ct CRAWW RH11 283 H9
HHNE HP2 36 A3
Hyperion Pl HOR/WEW KT19 220 A5
Hyrons Cl AMS HP6 69 K4
Hyrons La AMS HP6 69 J4
Hyrstdene SAND/SEL CR2 223 J1
Hyson Rd BERM/RHTH SE16 160 A4
Hythe Av BXLYHN DA7 163 P6
Hythe Cl STMC/STPC BR5 207 M4
UED N18 99 P5
Hythe End Rd STWL/WRAY TW19 172 D5
Hythe Field Av EGH TW20 172 G9
Hythe Park Rd EGH TW20 172 F8
Hythe Rd STA TW18 172 G8
THHTH CR7 203 L2
WLSDN NW10 136 C5
The Hythe STA TW18 173 H8
Hyver Hl BAR EN5 76 A10

## I

Ibbotson Av CAN/RD E16 141 L8
Ibbott St WCHPL E1 140 B6
Iberian Av WLGTN SM6 222 E1
Ibis La CHSWK W4 155 P7
Ibis Wy YEAD UB4 133 L8
Ibscott Cl DAGE RM10 144 D1
Ibsley Gdns PUT/ROE SW15 178 D4
Ibsley Wy EBAR EN4 77 P9
Icehouse Wd OXTED RH8 261 K7
Iceland Rd BOW E3 140 F3
Ickburgh Est CLPT E5 * 120 A7
Ickburgh Rd CLPT E5 120 A8
Ickenham Cl RSLP HA4 112 E7
Ickenham Rd RSLP HA4 112 E6
Ickleton Rd ELTH/MOT SE9 184 B7
Icklingham Ga COB KT11 217 K8
Icklingham Rd COB KT11 217 K8
Icknield Cl STALW/RED AL3 37 N8
Icknield Dr GNTH/NBYPK IG2 122 E3
Ickworth Park Rd WALTH E17 120 D2
Ida Rd SEVS/STOTM N15 119 L3
Ida St POP/IOD E14 141 H8
Ide Hill Rd RSEV TN14 264 A8
Iden Cl HAYES BR2 205 K3
Idlecombe Rd TOOT SW17 180 B9
Idleigh Court Rd HART DA3 211 N9
Idmiston Rd SRTFD E15 121 L10
WNWD SE27 181 K6
WPK KT4 200 C7
Idmiston Sq WPK KT4 200 C7
Idol La MON EC3R 13 J8
Idonia St DEPT SE8 160 E6
Iffley Cl UX/CGN UB8 131 N2
Iffley Rd HMSMTH W6 156 E2
Ifield Av CRAWW RH11 283 K4
Ifield Cl REDH RH1 275 P3
Ifield Dr CRAWW RH11 283 K6
Ifield Gn CRAWW RH11 283 K4
Ifield Pk CRAWW RH11 * 283 J7
Ifield Rd CRAWW RH11 283 L6
HORL RH6 279 H10
WBPTN SW10 15 H9
Ifield St CRAWW RH11 283 J5
Ifield Wy GVE DA12 190 G9
Ifield Wd CRAWW RH11 282 G4
Ifold Rd REDH RH1 276 B2
Ightham Rd ERITH DA8 164 B6
Ikona Ct WEY KT13 * 216 D2
Ilbert St NKENS W10 2 A10
Ilchester Gdns BAY/PAD W2 8 G7
Ilchester Pl WKENS W14 14 D3
Ilchester Rd BCTR RM8 123 L10
Ildersly Gv DUL SE21 181 L5
Ilderton Rd PECK SE15 160 B5
Ilex Cl EGH TW20 171 N10
SUN TW16 197 K2
Ilex Rd WLSDN NW10 136 C1
Ilex Wy STRHM/NOR SW16 181 H8
Ilford Hl MNPK E12 122 C9
Ilford La IL IG1 122 E9
Ilfracombe Crs HCH RM12 125 K9
Ilfracombe Gdns CHDH RM6 123 L5
Ilfracombe Rd BMLY BR1 183 L6
Iliffe St WALW SE17 18 D7
Iliffe Yd WALW SE17 18 D7
Ilkley Cl NRWD SE19 * 181 L9
Ilkley Ct FBAR/BDGN N11 98 B7
Ilkley Rd CAN/RD E16 141 P7
OXHEY WD19 93 L6
Illingworth WDSR SL4 148 D9
Illingworth Wy EN EN1 79 M9
Ilmington Rd KTN/HRWW/WS HA3 115 J4
Ilminster Gdns BTSEA SW11 157 P10
Imber Cl STHGT/OAK N14 98 D1
Imber Cross THDIT KT7 * 198 E7
Imber Gv ESH/CLAY KT10 198 C7
Imber Park Rd ESH/CLAY KT10 198 C8
Imber St IS N1 6 G6
Imperial Av STNW/STAM N16 * 119 M9
Imperial Cl CRICK NW2 116 E10
RYLN/HDSTN HA2 113 P4
Imperial College Rd SKENS SW7 15 L4
Imperial Ct WDSR SL4 148 F9
Imperial Crs FUL/PGN SW6 157 M8
Imperial Dr GVE DA12 191 J8
RYLN/HDSTN HA2 113 P5
Imperial Gdns MTCM CR4 202 C3
Imperial Ms EHAM E6 142 A4
Imperial Pk LHD/OX KT22 * 236 F6
Imperial Pl BORE WD6 * 75 N7
CHST BR7 206 D1
Imperial Rd EBED/NFELT TW14 174 F3
FUL/PGN SW6 157 L7
WDGN N22 98 F8
WDSR SL4 148 F9
Imperial Sq FUL/PGN SW6 157 L7
Imperial St BOW E3 141 H5
Imperial Wy CHST BR7 184 F6
CROY/NA CR0 222 G3
KTN/HRWW/WS HA3 115 K4
WATN WD24 73 K5
Imre Cl SHB W12 136 E10
Inca Dr ELTH/MOT SE9 184 E3
Ince Rd WOT/HER KT12 216 F4
Inchmery Rd CAT SE6 182 G5
Inchwood CROY/NA CR0 224 G1
Indells HAT AL10 40 C5
Independent Pl HACK E8 119 N10
Independents Rd BKHTH/KID SE3 161 L9
Inderwick Rd CEND/HSY/T N8 118 G4
Indescon Ct POP/IOD E14 160 G1
India Rd SL SL1 149 N1
India St TWRH EC3N 13 L6
India Wy SHB W12 136 E9
Indigo Ms POP/IOD E14 * 141 H9
STNW/STAM N16 119 L8
Indus Rd CHARL SE7 161 P6
Infant House WOOL/PLUM SE18 * 162 B6
Ingal Rd PLSTW E13 141 M6
Ingate Pl VX/NE SW8 158 C7
Ingatestone Rd MNPK E12 121 P6
SNWD SE25 204 A5
WFD IG8 101 N8
Ingelow Rd VX/NE SW8 158 C8
Ingels Md EPP CM16 65 J5
Ingersoll Rd PEND EN3 80 B4
SHB W12 136 E10
Ingestre Pl SOHO/CST W1F 11 H6
Ingestre Rd FSTGT E7 121 M9
KTTN NW5 118 C9
Ingham Cl SAND/SEL CR2 224 C5
Ingham Rd KIL/WHAMP NW6 117 K9
SAND/SEL CR2 224 B5
Inglebert St CLKNW EC1R 6 A9
Ingleboro Dr PUR/KEN CR8 223 L9
Ingleborough St BRXN/ST SW9 159 H8
Ingleby Dr HRW HA1 114 C8
Ingleby Gdns CHIG IG7 103 L4
Ingleby Rd CDW/CHF RM16 168 E2
DAGE RM10 144 C1
HOLWY N7 118 F8
IL IG1 122 E6
Ingleby Wy CHST BR7 184 D8
WLGTN SM6 222 E5
Ingle Cl PIN HA5 113 N1
Ingledew Rd WOOL/PLUM SE18 162 G4
Inglefield POTB/CUF EN6 59 K6
Inglefield Sq WAP E1W * 140 A10
Ingleglen EMPK RM11 125 P5
SLN SL2 108 G10
Inglehurst ADL/WDHM KT15 215 L6
Inglehurst Gdns REDBR IG4 122 C3
Inglemere Rd FSTH SE23 182 C6
TOOT SW17 180 A10
Ingles WGCW AL8 23 H2
Ingleside DTCH/LGLY SL3 151 H7
Ingleside Cl BECK BR3 182 F10
Ingleside Gv BKHTH/KID SE3 161 L5
Inglethorpe St FUL/PGN SW6 156 G7
Ingleton Av WELL DA16 185 K1
Ingleton Rd CAR SM5 221 P5
UED N18 99 P7
Ingleton St BRXN/ST SW9 159 H8
Ingleway NFNCH/WDSPK N12 97 N7
Inglewood CHERT KT16 195 J10
CROY/NA CR0 224 D5
SWLY BR8 * 208 F2
WOKN/KNAP GU21 231 N4
Inglewood Cl BARK/HLT IG6 103 J7
HCH RM12 125 L9
POP/IOD E14 160 F3
Inglewood Copse BMLY BR1 206 B2
Inglewood Gdns LCOL/BKTW AL2 56 E1
Inglewood Ms SURB KT6 199 M8
Inglewood Rd BXLYHN DA7 164 E10
KIL/WHAMP NW6 117 K10
Inglis Rd CROY/NA CR0 203 N8
EA W5 135 L9
Inglis St CMBW SE5 159 J7
Ingoldsby Rd GVE DA12 191 H4
Ingram Av GLDGN NW11 117 M5
Ingram Cl LBTH SE11 17 P5
STAN HA7 95 H6
Ingram Rd EFNCH N2 117 P2
GRAYS RM17 167 P3
THHTH CR7 203 K1
Ingrams Cl WOT/HER KT12 217 K2
Ingram Wy GFD/PVL UB6 134 C3
Ingrave Rd BRWN CM15 107 K4
ROM RM1 124 E2
Ingrave St BTSEA SW11 157 N9
Ingrebourne Gdns UPMR RM14 126 B6
Ingrebourne Rd RAIN RM13 145 J6
Ingress Park Av SWCM DA10 166 G10
Ingress St CHSWK W4 156 B4
Ingress Ter MEO DA13 * 189 L7
Ingreway HARH RM3 106 A7
Inholms La RDKG RH5 273 H6
Inigo Jones Rd CHARL SE7 162 A6
Inkerman Pde WOKN/KNAP GU21 * 231 K4
Inkerman Rd KTTN NW5 4 E1
STAL AL1 38 D7
WDSR SL4 148 E3
WOKN/KNAP GU21 231 K4
Inkerman Ter CSHM HP5 51 H9
Inkerman Wy WOKN/KNAP GU21 231 K4
Inks Gn CHING E4 101 H6
Inkwell Cl NFNCH/WDSPK N12 97 M4
Inman Rd WAND/EARL SW18 179 M3
WLSDN NW10 136 B3
Inmans Rw WFD IG8 101 M5
Inner Cir CAMTN NW1 4 C10
Inner Park Rd WIM/MER SW19 178 G5
Inner Ring East HTHAIR TW6 152 C9
Innes Cl RYNPK SW20 201 H2
Innes Ct HHS/BOV HP3 35 N8
Innes Gdns PUT/ROE SW15 178 E2
Innes St PECK SE15 159 M6
Innes Yd CROY/NA CR0 203 K10
Inniskilling Rd PLSTW E13 141 P4
Innovation Cl ALP/SUD HA0 135 K3
Innova Wy PEND EN3 80 E2
Inskip Cl LEY E10 120 G7
Inskip Dr EMPK RM11 125 M6
Inskip Rd BCTR RM8 123 N6
Institute Pl HACK E8 120 A10
Institute Rd DORK RH4 272 B3
EPP CM16 65 N5
Integer Gdns WAN E11 * 121 J5
International Av HEST TW5 153 K4
International Wy SUN TW16 196 F1
Inver Ct BAY/PAD W2 9 H6
Inveresk Gdns WPK KT4 200 C10
Inverforth Cl HAMP NW3 117 M7
Inverforth Rd FBAR/BDGN N11 98 C6
Inverine Rd CHARL SE7 161 N4
Invermore Pl WOOL/PLUM SE18 162 F3
Inverness Av EN EN1 79 M5
Inverness Dr BARK/HLT IG6 103 H7
Inverness Gdns KENS W8 8 G10
Inverness Ms BAY/PAD W2 9 H7
Inverness Pl BAY/PAD W2 9 H7
Inverness Rd HSLW TW3 153 N10
NWDGN UB2 153 M3
UED N18 100 A6
WPK KT4 200 G8
Inverness St CAMTN NW1 4 E5
Inverness Ter BAY/PAD W2 9 H8
WDGN N22 * 99 J9
Inverton Rd PECK SE15 160 C10
Invicta Cl CHST BR7 184 D8
EBED/NFELT TW14 174 G4
Invicta Gv NTHLT UB5 133 N5
Invicta Pde SCUP DA14 * 185 L7
Invicta Plaza STHWK SE1 12 C9
Invicta Rd BKHTH/KID SE3 161 M6
RDART DA2 188 A2
Inville Rd WALW SE17 19 H8
Inwood Av COUL/CHIP CR5 241 H6
HSLW TW3 154 B9
Inwood Cl CROY/NA CR0 204 D9
Inwood Rd HSLW TW3 154 B10
Inworth St BTSEA SW11 157 P8
Inworth Wk IS N1 * 6 E5
Iona Cl CAT SE6 182 F3
CRAWW RH11 283 L10
MRDN SM4 201 L7
Iona Crs SL SL1 128 D8
Ionian Wy HHNE HP2 36 A3
Ionia Wk GVE DA12 191 J6
Ion Sq BETH E2 * 7 N8
Ipswich Rd SL SL1 128 E8
TOOT SW17 180 B9
Ireland Cl EHAM E6 142 C7
Ireland Pl WDGN N22 98 F8
Irene Ms HNWL W7 * 134 E10
Irene Rd COB KT11 217 P10
FUL/PGN SW6 157 K7
ORP BR6 207 J7
Ireton Av WOT/HER KT12 196 G9
Ireton Cl MUSWH N10 98 B8
Ireton Pl GRAYS RM17 167 M3
Ireton St BOW E3 140 F6
Iris Av BXLY DA5 185 P2
Iris Cl BRWN CM15 86 G9
CROY/NA CR0 204 C8
EHAM E6 142 B7
STMC/STPC BR5 207 M5
SURB KT6 * 199 L7
Iris Crs BXLYHN DA7 164 A5
Iris Rd CHOB/PIR GU24 230 F1
HOR/WEW KT19 219 N2
Iris Wy CHING E4 100 E7
Irkdale Av EN EN1 79 N5
Iron Bridge Cl NWDGN UB2 134 B10
WLSDN NW10 116 B10
Iron Bridge Rd STKPK UB11 * 132 C10
Iron Bridge Rd North STKPK UB11 132 B10
Iron Bridge Rd South WDR/YW UB7 152 B1
Iron Dr HERT/BAY SG13 26 A4
Iron Mill La DART DA1 164 G10
Iron Mill Pl DART DA1 164 G10
WAND/EARL SW18 * 179 L2
Iron Mill Rd WAND/EARL SW18 179 L2
Ironmonger La CITYW EC2V 12 G6
Ironmonger Rw FSBYE EC1V 6 F10
Ironmongers Pl POP/IOD E14 160 F3
Ironsbottom REIG RH2 275 J10
Ironside Cl BERM/RHTH SE16 160 C1
Irons Wy CRW RM5 104 D8
Irvine Av KTN/HRWW/WS HA3 114 F1
Irvine Cl POP/IOD E14 140 G7
TRDG/WHET N20 97 P3
Irvine Gdns SOCK/AV RM15 146 E8
Irvine Pl VW GU25 194 B5
Irvine Wy ORP BR6 207 J7
Irving Av NTHLT UB5 133 L3
Irving Gv BRXN/ST SW9 158 G8
Irving Ms IS N1 6 E2
Irving Rd WKENS W14 156 G2
Irving St LSQ/SEVD WC2H 11 K8
Irving Wk CRAWE RH10 283 P10
Irving Wy CDALE/KGS NW9 116 C3
SWLY BR8 208 E2
Irwell Est BERM/RHTH SE16 * 160 B1
Irwin Av WOOL/PLUM SE18 163 H6
Irwin Cl HGDN/ICK UB10 112 B8
Irwin Gdns WLSDN NW10 136 E3
Irwin Rd GUW GU2 267 M1
Isaac Wy STHWK SE1 18 F1
Isabel Cl HOD EN11 44 G1
Isabel Ga CHES/WCR EN8 62 E2
Isabella Cl STHGT/OAK N14 98 D1
Isabella Ct RCHPK/HAM TW10 * 177 L2
Isabella Dr ORP BR6 226 F1
Isabella Ms IS N1 7 J1
Isabella Pl KUTN/CMB KT2 177 L8
Isabella Rd HOM E9 * 120 B10
Isabella St STHWK SE1 12 C10
Isabelle Cl CHESW EN7 61 K5
Isabel St BRXN/ST SW9 158 G7
Isambard Ms POP/IOD E14 161 H2
Isambard Pl BERM/RHTH SE16 140 B10
Isbells Dr REIG RH2 275 L2
Isenburg Wy HHNE HP2 35 N1
Isham Rd STRHM/NOR SW16 202 F2
Isis Cl PUT/ROE SW15 156 F10
RSLP HA4 112 D4
Isis Dr UPMR RM14 126 D4
Isis St WAND/EARL SW18 179 M5
Island Centre Wy PEND EN3 80 F4
Island Cl STA TW18 173 H7
Island Farm Av E/WMO/HCT KT8 197 N5
Island Farm Rd E/WMO/HCT KT8 197 N5
Island Rd BERM/RHTH SE16 160 C3
MTCM CR4 180 A10
Island Rw POP/IOD E14 140 E8
Isla Rd WOOL/PLUM SE18 162 F5
Islay Gdns HSLWW TW4 175 L1
Islay Wk IS N1 6 E2
Islay Whf POP/IOD E14 * 141 H7
Isledon Rd HOLWY N7 119 H8
Islehurst Cl CHST BR7 206 D1
Islington Gn IS N1 6 C6
Islington High St IS N1 6 C7
Islington Park Ms IS N1 6 C3
Islington Park St IS N1 6 B3
Islip Gdns EDGW HA8 96 A7
NTHLT UB5 133 M2
Islip Manor Rd NTHLT UB5 133 M2
Islip St KTTN NW5 118 D10
Ismailia Rd FSTGT E7 141 N2
Ismay Cl SLN SL2 * 129 K8
Isom Cl PLSTW E13 141 N5
Issa Rd HSLW TW3 153 N10
Istead Ri MEO DA13 190 C10
Itchingwood Common Rd OXTED RH8 261 P9
Ivanhoe Cl CRAWW RH11 283 N4
UX/CGN UB8 131 N7
Ivanhoe Dr KTN/HRWW/WS HA3 94 G10
Ivanhoe Rd CMBW SE5 159 N9
HSLWW TW4 153 L9
Ivatt Pl WKENS W14 14 D8
Ivatt Wy SEVS/STOTM N15 119 J1
Iveagh Av WLSDN NW10 135 M4
Iveagh Cl HOM E9 140 C3
NTHWD HA6 92 C9
WLSDN NW10 135 M4
Iveagh Rd GUW GU2 267 N1
Ivedon Rd WELL DA16 163 M8
Ive Farm Cl LEY E10 120 F7
Ive Farm La LEY E10 120 F7
Iveley Rd CLAP SW4 158 D8
Iverdale Cl IVER SL0 130 F9
Ivere Dr BAR EN5 77 L10
Iverhurst Cl BXLYHS DA6 185 N1
Iver La IVER SL0 131 L7
Iver Ldg IVER SL0 131 J7
Iverna Ct KENS W8 14 F3
Iverna Gdns EBED/NFELT TW14 174 E1
KENS W8 14 F3
Iverson Rd KIL/WHAMP NW6 2 D2
Ivers Wy CROY/NA CR0 224 G4
Ives Gdns ROM RM1 124 G2
Ives Rd CAN/RD E16 141 K7
DTCH/LGLY SL3 150 D2
HERT/WAT SG14 25 J4
Ives St CHEL SW3 15 P5
Ivimey St BETH E2 7 P9
Ivinghoe Cl EN EN1 79 M6
GSTN WD25 73 L1
STALE/WH AL4 39 H1
Ivinghoe Rd BCTR RM8 123 L10
BUSH WD23 74 C10
RKW/CH/CXG WD3 91 J1
Ivor Cl GU GU1 268 C1
Ivor Gv ELTH/MOT SE9 184 E4
Ivor Pl CAMTN NW1 10 A2
Ivor St CAMTN NW1 4 G4
Ivory Cl STALE/WH AL4 39 H8
Ivory Ct FELT TW13 175 H4
HHS/BOV HP3 35 P9
Ivorydown BMLY BR1 183 M7
Ivory Wk CRAWW RH11 283 H10
Ivy Bower Cl RDART DA2 188 G1
Ivybridge BROX EN10 44 F5
Ivybridge Cl TWK TW1 176 F2
Ivy Bridge Cl UX/CGN UB8 131 P5
Ivy Chimneys Rd EPP CM16 65 H8
Ivychurch Cl PGE/AN SE20 182 A10
Ivy Church La WALW SE17 * 19 L7
Ivy Cl GVE DA12 190 F7
PIN HA5 113 K5
RYLN/HDSTN HA2 113 N9
SUN TW16 197 K2
Ivy Cots HGDN/ICK UB10 * 132 B5
Ivy Crs CHSWK W4 155 P3
SL SL1 128 E9
Ivydale Rd CAR SM5 202 A9
PECK SE15 182 C1
Ivyday Gv STRHM/NOR SW16 180 G6
Ivydene E/WMO/HCT KT8 197 N5
WOKN/KNAP GU21 230 G4
Ivydene Cl REDH RH1 276 C5
SUT SM1 221 M1
Ivy Gdns CEND/HSY/T N8 118 F4
MTCM CR4 202 E3
Ivy House La BERK HP4 34 B5
SEV TN13 246 E3
Ivyhouse Rd DAGW RM9 143 N1
HGDN/ICK UB10 112 C8
Ivy La HSLWW TW4 153 N10
RSEV TN14 245 P2
WOKS/MYFD GU22 232 E4
Ivy Lea RKW/CH/CXG WD3 * 91 K2
Ivy Lodge La HARH RM3 106 B10
Ivy Mill Cl GDST RH9 260 A8
Ivy Mill La GDST RH9 259 P8
Ivymount Rd WNWD SE27 181 H6
Ivy Rd BROCKY SE4 160 E10
CAN/RD E16 141 M8
CRICK NW2 116 F9
HSLW TW3 154 A10
STHGT/OAK N14 98 D1
SURB KT6 * 199 M9
TOOT SW17 179 P8
WALTH E17 120 F4
Ivy St IS N1 7 J7
Ivy Ter HOD EN11 45 H1
Ivy Wk DAGW RM9 143 P1
NTHWD HA6 * 92 F9
Ixworth Pl CHEL SW3 15 N6
Izane Rd BXLYHS DA6 164 A10

## J

Jacaranda Cl NWMAL KT3 200 B3
Jacaranda Gv HACK E8 7 M3
Jackass La GDST RH9 260 E7
HAYES BR2 225 N3
Jack Clow Rd SRTFD E15 141 K4
Jack Cornwell St MNPK E12 122 D9
Jack Dash Wy EHAM E6 142 B6
Jackdaw Cl CRAWW RH11 283 M5
Jackdaws WGCE AL7 23 M5
Jackets La DEN/HRF UB9 92 B8
Jacketts Fld ABLGY WD5 54 G7
Jack Evans Ct SOCK/AV RM15 146 F8
Jack Jones Wy DAGW RM9 144 A3
Jackman Ms WLSDN NW10 116 B8
Jackman's La WOKN/KNAP GU21 231 M5
Jackman St HACK E8 140 A3
Jacks La DEN/HRF UB9 91 K9
Jackson Cl DTCH/LGLY SL3 150 B2
EMPK RM11 125 N2
EPSOM KT18 220 A10
HOM E9 140 C2
RDART DA2 188 E1
Jackson Rd BARK IG11 142 G3
EBAR EN4 77 N10
HAYES BR2 206 B9
HGDN/ICK UB10 131 P2
HOLWY N7 118 G9
Jacksons Cl CHONG CM5 * 67 P5
Jacksons Dr CHESW EN7 61 P4
Jackson's La HGT N6 118 B5
Jackson's Pl CROY/NA CR0 203 L8
Jackson St WOOL/PLUM SE18 162 D5
Jackson's Wy CROY/NA CR0 204 F10
Jackson Wy HOR/WEW KT19 219 M5
NWDGN UB2 154 A1
Jack Stevens Cl HLWE CM17 * 47 M3
Jack Walker Ct HBRY N5 119 J9
Jacob Cl WDSR SL4 148 D7
Jacobean Cl CRAWE RH10 284 D8
Jacobs Av HARH RM3 105 M10
Jacobs Cl DAGE RM10 124 C9
Jacob St STHWK SE1 19 M1
Jacob's Well Ms MHST W1U 10 D5
Jacobs Well Rd RGUE GU4 250 A5
Jacqueline Cl NTHLT UB5 133 M3
Jacqueline Creft Ter HGT N6 * 118 B4
Jacqueline Vls WALTH E17 * 121 H3
Jade Cl BCTR RM8 123 M6
CAN/RD E16 142 A8
CRICK NW2 116 G5
Jade Ter KIL/WHAMP NW6 * 3 K3
Jaffe Rd IL IG1 122 F6
Jaffray Rd HAYES BR2 206 A4
Jaggard Wy BAL SW12 180 A3
Jagger Cl RDART DA2 188 B3
Jago Cl WOOL/PLUM SE18 162 F5
Jago Wk CMBW SE5 159 L6
Jail La BH/WHM TN16 244 A1
Jakes Vw LCOL/BKTW AL2 56 B3
Jamaica Rd STHWK SE1 19 M2
THHTH CR7 203 J6
Jamaica St WCHPL E1 140 B7
James Av BCTR RM8 124 A6
CRICK NW2 116 F10
James Bedford Cl PIN HA5 93 K10
James Black Rd GUW GU2 267 J1
James Cl BUSH WD23 73 M9
GLDGN NW11 * 117 H4
GPK RM2 125 H3
PLSTW E13 141 M4
James Collins Cl MV/WKIL W9 8 C2
James Gdns TOTM N17 99 K8
James Joyce Wk BRXN/ST SW9 159 J10
James La WAN E11 121 H5
James Lee Sq PEND EN3 80 F4
James Martin Cl DEN/HRF UB9 111 K4
James Meadow DTCH/LGLY SL3 150 C5
Jameson St KENS W8 8 F9
James Pl TOTM N17 99 N8
James Rd RGUW GU3 267 P8
James St BARK IG11 142 F2
COVGDN WC2E 11 M7
EN EN1 79 N9
EPP CM16 65 J4
HSLW TW3 154 C9
MHST W1U 10 D6
WDSR SL4 149 J7
Jamestown Rd CAMTN NW1 4 E5
Jamestown Wy POP/IOD E14 141 J9
James Voller Wy WCHPL E1 140 B8
James Watt Wy CRAWE RH10 284 B1
ERITH DA8 164 F5
James Wy OXHEY WD19 93 L5
James Yd CHING E4 * 101 J7
Jamnagar Cl STA TW18 173 J9
Jamuna Cl POP/IOD E14 140 D7
Jane Cl HHNE HP2 36 C1
Jane St WCHPL E1 140 A8
Janet St POP/IOD E14 160 F2
Janeway Pl BERM/RHTH SE16 160 A1
Janeway St BERM/RHTH SE16 19 P2
Janmead RBRW/HUT CM13 107 N1
Janoway Hill La WOKN/KNAP GU21 231 P5
Janson Cl SRTFD E15 121 K10
WLSDN NW10 116 A8
Janson Rd SRTFD E15 121 K10
Jansons Rd SEVS/STOTM N15 119 M1
Japan Crs FSBYPK N4 118 G6
Japan Rd CHDH RM6 123 N4
Japonica Cl WOKN/KNAP GU21 231 P4
Jardine Rd WAP E1W 140 C9
Jarman Cl HHS/BOV HP3 35 P8
Jarman Wy HHNE HP2 36 A7
Jarrah Cots PUR RM19 * 166 C5
Jarrett Cl BRXS/STRHM SW2 181 J4
Jarrow Cl MRDN SM4 201 L5
Jarrow Rd BERM/RHTH SE16 160 B3
CHDH RM6 123 M4
TOTM N17 120 A2
Jarrow Wy HOM E9 120 E9
Jarvis Cleys CHESW EN7 61 N2
Jarvis Cl BAR EN5 76 G9
BARK IG11 142 G3
Jarvis Rd EDUL SE22 159 M10
SAND/SEL CR2 223 L3
Jarvis Wy HARH RM3 105 M10
Jasmin Cl NTHWD HA6 92 G9
Jasmine Cl IL IG1 122 E10
ORP BR6 206 E9
REDH RH1 276 B5
STHL UB1 133 M9
WOKN/KNAP GU21 231 L2
Jasmine Ct LEE/GVPK SE12 183 M2
Jasmine Dr HERT/BAY SG13 25 P5
Jasmine Gdns CROY/NA CR0 204 G10
HAT AL10 40 C2
RYLN/HDSTN HA2 113 P7
Jasmine Gv PGE/AN SE20 204 A1
Jasmine Rd HOR/WEW KT19 219 N3
ROMW/RG RM7 124 F7
Jasmine Ter WDR/YW UB7 152 B1
Jasmine Wk CSHM HP5 50 F6
Jasmin Rd HOR/WEW KT19 219 N2
Jasmin Wy HHW HP1 35 H5
Jason Cl REDH RH1 275 P5
WEY KT13 216 D2
Jasons Cl BRW CM14 106 E5
Jasons Dr RGUE GU4 250 F7
Jasons Hl CSHM HP5 51 N5
Jason Wk ELTH/MOT SE9 184 D7
Jasper Cl PEND EN3 80 B4
Jasper Rd CAN/RD E16 142 A8
NRWD SE19 181 N9
Javelin Wy NTHLT UB5 133 L5
Jay Av ADL/WDHM KT15 * 195 P10
Jaycroft ENC/FH EN2 79 H5
Jay Gdns CHST BR7 184 C7
Jay Ms SKENS SW7 15 K2
Jays Cl LCOL/BKTW AL2 55 P7
Jean Batten Cl WLGTN SM6 222 G4
Jebb Av BRXS/STRHM SW2 180 F2
Jebb St BOW E3 140 F4
Jedburgh Rd PLSTW E13 141 P5
Jedburgh St BTSEA SW11 158 B10
Jeddo Ms SHB W12 156 C1
Jeddo Rd SHB W12 156 C1
Jefferson Cl DTCH/LGLY SL3 150 D3
GNTH/NBYPK IG2 122 E3
WEA W13 154 G2
Jeffrey's Pl CAMTN NW1 4 G3
Jeffreys Rd CLAP SW4 158 F8
PEND EN3 80 E8
Jeffrey's St CAMTN NW1 4 F3
Jeffries Pas GU GU1 * 268 A1
Jeffries Rd EHSLY KT24 252 C6
WARE SG12 26 D2
Jeffs Cl HPTN TW12 * 176 A9
Jeffs Rd SUT SM1 221 J1
Jeger Av BETH E2 7 L6
Jeken Rd ELTH/MOT SE9 161 P10
Jelf Rd BRXS/STRHM SW2 181 H1
Jellicoe Av GVE DA12 190 F6
Jellicoe Cl SL SL1 148 G1
Jellicoe Gdns STAN HA7 94 E7
Jellicoe Rd TOTM N17 99 L8
WATW WD18 73 H10
Jemmett Cl KUTN/CMB KT2 199 N1
Jem Paterson Ct HRW HA1 * 114 D9
Jengar Cl SUT SM1 221 L1
Jenkins Av LCOL/BKTW AL2 55 M6
Jenkins Cl GVW DA11 190 C6
Jenkins La BARK IG11 142 E4
Jenkins Rd PLSTW E13 141 N6
Jenner Av ACT W3 136 A7
Jenner Cl SCUP DA14 185 K7
Jenner Dr CHOB/PIR GU24 212 F9
Jenner Pl BARN SW13 156 E5
Jenner Rd CRAWE RH10 284 A2
GU GU1 268 B1
STNW/STAM N16 119 N7
Jenner Wy HOR/WEW KT19 219 M5
Jennery La SL SL1 128 B5
Jennett Rd CROY/NA CR0 203 H10
Jennifer Rd BMLY BR1 183 L6
Jenningham Dr CDW/CHF RM16 147 M10
Jennings Cl ADL/WDHM KT15 215 M5
SURB KT6 199 H7
Jennings Rd EDUL SE22 181 N2
STAL AL1 38 E5
Jennings Wy BAR EN5 76 F7
HHS/BOV HP3 35 P8
HORL RH6 280 E4
Jenningtree Rd ERITH DA8 165 J6
Jenningtree Wy BELV DA17 164 D1
Jenny Hammond Cl WAN E11 121 L8
Jennys Wy COUL/CHIP CR5 240 D8
Jenson Wy NRWD SE19 181 N10
Jenton Av BXLYHN DA7 163 P7
Jephson Rd FSTGT E7 141 P2
Jephson St CMBW SE5 159 L7
Jephtha Rd WAND/EARL SW18 179 K2
Jeppo's La MTCM CR4 202 A4
Jepps Cl CHESW EN7 61 M3
Jerdan Pl FUL/PGN SW6 157 K6
Jeremiah St POP/IOD E14 140 G8
Jeremy's Gn UED N18 100 A5
Jermyn St STJS SW1Y 10 G9
Jerningham Av CLAY IG5 102 E10
Jerningham Rd NWCR SE14 160 D8
Jerome Dr STALW/RED AL3 37 P8
Jerome St WCHPL E1 13 L3
Jerounds HLWW/ROY CM19 46 E3
Jerrard St LEW SE13 160 G9
Jerrold St IS N1 * 7 K8
Jersey Av /HRWW/WS HA3 94 G10
Jersey Cl CHERT KT16 195 J10
HOD EN11 44 F2
RGUE GU4 250 E5
Jersey Dr STMC/STPC BR5 206 G6
Jersey La STAL AL1 38 G4
STALE/WH AL4 21 H10
Jersey Pl ASC SL5 192 C6
Jersey Rd CAN/RD E16 141 P7
HSLW TW3 154 A7
IL IG1 122 E9
LEY E10 121 J6
RAIN RM13 145 H2
TOOT SW17 180 C10
Jersey St BETH E2 140 A5
Jersey Vls HNWL W7 * 154 D1
Jerusalem Pas CLKNW EC1R 12 C2
Jervis Av PEND EN3 80 D1
Jerviston Gdns STRHM/NOR SW16 181 H9
Jervois House WOOL/PLUM SE18 * 162 B6
Jesmond Av WBLY HA9 135 L1
Jesmond Cl MTCM CR4 202 C3
Jesmond Dene HAMP NW3 * 3 J1
Jesmond Rd CROY/NA CR0 203 N7
Jesmond Wy STAN HA7 95 K6
Jessam Av CLPT E5 120 A6
Jessamine Pl RDART DA2 188 B3
Jessamine Rd HNWL W7 134 D10
Jessamine Ter SWLY BR8 * 208 D1
Jessamy Rd WEY KT13 196 B9
Jessel Dr LOU IG10 82 F6
Jesse Rd LEY E10 121 H6
Jesses La SHGR GU5 270 D9
Jessett Cl ERITH DA8 164 E3
Jessica Rd WAND/EARL SW18 179 M2
Jessiman Ter SHPTN TW17 196 B5
Jessop Av NWDGN UB2 153 N3
Jessop Sq POP/IOD E14 * 140 F10
Jessops Wy CROY/NA CR0 202 D6
Jessup Cl WOOL/PLUM SE18 162 F3
Jetstar Wy NTHLT UB5 133 M5
Jetty Wk GRAYS RM17 167 M5
Jevington Wy LEE/GVPK SE12 183 N4
Jewel Rd WALTH E17 120 F1
Jewels Hl WARL CR6 225 M8
Jewry St TWRH EC3N 13 L6
Jews Rw WAND/EARL SW18 157 L10
Jews Wk SYD SE26 182 A7
Jeymer Av WLSDN NW10 116 E10
Jeymer Dr GFD/PVL UB6 134 B3
Jeypore Rd WAND/EARL SW18 179 M3
Jillian Cl HPTN TW12 175 P10
Jim Bradley Cl WOOL/PLUM SE18 162 D3
Jim Veal Dr HOLWY N7 5 L1
The Jinnings WGCE AL7 23 L8
Joan Crs ELTH/MOT SE9 184 A3
Joan Gdns BCTR RM8 123 P7
Joan Rd BCTR RM8 123 P7
Joan St STHWK SE1 12 C10
Jocelyn Rd RCH/KEW TW9 155 K9
Jocelyns HLWE CM17 29 M7
Jocelyn St PECK SE15 159 P7
Jocketts Hl HHW HP1 35 J6
Jocketts Rd HHW HP1 35 J7
Jockey's Flds FSBYW WC1X 11 P3
Jodane St DEPT SE8 160 E3
Jodies Ct STALE/WH AL4 39 H4
Jodrell Cl ISLW TW7 154 F7
Jodrell Rd BOW E3 140 E3
Jodrell Wy WTHK RM20 166 E4
Joel St NTHWD HA6 93 H10
Johanna St STHWK SE1 * 18 A2
John Adam St CHCR WC2N 11 M9
John Aird Ct BAY/PAD W2 9 K3
John Archer Wy WAND/EARL SW18 179 N2
John Ashby Cl BRXS/STRHM SW2 180 F2
John Austin Cl KUTN/CMB KT2 199 L1
John Bradshaw Rd STHGT/OAK N14 98 E2
John Burns Dr BARK IG11 143 H3
Johnby Cl PEND EN3 80 D3
John Campbell Rd STNW/STAM N16 119 M10
John Carpenter St EMB EC4Y 12 B7
John Cobb Rd WEY KT13 216 B4
John Eliot Cl WAB EN9 45 K8
John Felton Rd BERM/RHTH SE16 19 N2
John Fisher St WCHPL E1 13 N7
John Gooch Dr ENC/FH EN2 79 J5
John Goodchild Wy KUT/HW KT1 199 N3
John Harrison Wy BERM/RHTH SE16 160 C2
GNWCH SE10 161 L2
John Islip St WEST SW1P 17 K7
John Lamb Ct KTN/HRWW/WS HA3 94 D9
John Maurice Cl WALW SE17 18 G5
John McKenna Wk BERM/RHTH SE16 19 P3
John Parker Sq BTSEA SW11 * 157 N9
John Penn St LEW SE13 160 G7
John Perrin Pl KTN/HRWW/WS HA3 115 K5
John Prince's St CAVSQ/HST W1G 10 F5
John Rennie Wk WAP E1W 140 A9
John Roll Wy BERM/RHTH SE16 19 P3
John Ruskin St CMBW SE5 18 E10
John Russell Cl GUW GU2 249 M7
John's Av HDN NW4 116 F2
Johns Cl HART DA3 211 L5
John's Cl ASHF TW15 174 D7
Johnsdale OXTED RH8 261 L5
John Silkin La DEPT SE8 160 C4
Johns La CSHM HP5 33 J8
MRDN SM4 201 M5
John's Ms BMSBY WC1N 11 P2
John Smith Av FUL/PGN SW6 157 J6
John Smith Ms POP/IOD E14 141 J9
Johnson Cl GVW DA11 190 A6
HACK E8 7 N5
Johnson Ct HHS/BOV HP3 35 P8
Johnson Rd CROY/NA CR0 203 L7
HAYES BR2 206 A5
HEST TW5 153 K6
WLSDN NW10 136 A3
Johnsons Av RSEV TN14 228 C6
Johnson's Cl CAR SM5 202 A10
Johnson's Ct FLST/FETLN EC4A 12 B6
Johnsons Dr HPTN TW12 198 B1
Johnson's Pl PIM SW1V 17 H8
Johnson St NWDGN UB2 153 K2
WCHPL E1 140 B8
Johnsons Wy SWCM DA10 189 H2
WLSDN NW10 135 N6
Johnsons Whf RDART DA2 * 166 F10
Johnson Wk CRAWE RH10 283 N10
John Spencer Sq IS N1 6 D2
Johns Pl WCHPL E1 140 A8
John's Rd BH/WHM TN16 244 A6
John's Ter CROY/NA CR0 203 M8
The Johns CHONG CM5 67 P3
Johnston Cl BRXN/ST SW9 158 G7
Johnstone Rd EHAM E6 142 C5
Johnstone Ter CRICK NW2 116 G8
Johnston Rd WFD IG8 101 M6
Johnston Wk GUW GU2 249 M6
John St BMSBY WC1N 11 P2
EN EN1 79 N9
GRAYS RM17 167 P5
HSLW TW3 153 M8
SNWD SE25 203 P4
SRTFD E15 141 L3
Johns Wk CTHM CR3 241 P5
John Tate Rd HERT/BAY SG13 25 N6
John Taylor Ct SL SL1 129 H10
John Trundle Highwalk BARB EC2Y * 12 E3
John Watkin Cl HOR/WEW KT19 219 N5
John Wesley Cl EHAM E6 * 142 C5
John William Cl CDW/CHF RM16 167 J4
KUTN/CMB KT2 * 199 K1
John Williams Cl NWCR SE14 160 C5
John Wilson St WOOL/PLUM SE18 162 D3
John Wooley Cl LEW SE13 * 161 K10
Joiners Arms Yd CMBW SE5 * 159 L7
Joiner's Cl CFSP/GDCR SL9 90 C8
Joiners La CFSP/GDCR SL9 90 B9
Joiner St STHWK SE1 13 H10
Joiners Wy CFSP/GDCR SL9 90 B8
Joinville Pl ADL/WDHM KT15 215 N1
Jolesfield Ct CRAWW RH11 283 J10
Jolive Ct GU GU1 * 268 D1

Jolliffe Rd REDH RH1 ... 258 D2
Jollys La YEAD UB4 ... 133 L7
Jonathan St LBTH SE11 ... 17 N7
Jones Rd CHESW EN7 ... 61 J4
  PLSTW E13 ... 141 N6
Jones Wy SLN SL2 ... 109 J7
Jonquil Cl WGCE AL7 ... 23 L7
Jonson Cl MITCM CR4 ... 202 C4
  YEAD UB4 ... 133 N7
Jordan Cl GSTN WD25 ... 72 C1
  RYLN/HDSTN HA2 ... 113 N8
  SAND/SEL CR2 ... 223 M4
Jordan Rd GFD/PVL UB6 ... 134 C3
Jordans WGCE AL7 ... 23 M4
Jordans Cl CRAWW RH11 ... 283 N5
  DAGE RM10 ... 124 C3
  GU UA10 ... 250 D9
  REDH RH1 ... 276 B5
  STWL/WRAY TW19 ... 175 M3
Jordans La BEAC HP9 ... 89 M4
Jordans Ms WHTN TW2 ... 176 D5
Jordans Rd RKW/CH/CXG WD3 ... 91 K4
Jordans Wy BEAC HP9 ... 89 L7
  RAIN RM13 ... 145 L4
Jordan's Wy LCOL/BKTW AL2 ... 55 N6
Joseph Av ACT W3 ... 136 A4
Joseph Hardcastle Cl NWCR SE14 ... 160 C6
Josephine Av BRXS/STRHM SW2 ... 180 C1
  KWD/TDW/WH KT20 ... 257 J7
Josephine Cl KWD/TDW/WH KT20 ... 257 J7
Joseph Locke Wy ESH/CLAY KT10 ... 197 P9
Joseph Powell Cl BAL SW12 ... 180 D2
Joseph Ray Rd WAN E11 ... 121 K7
Joseph's Rd GU GU1 ... 250 A3
Joseph St BOW E3 ... 140 E7
Joseph Trotter Cl CLKNW EC1R ... 6 B10
Joshua Cl MUSWH N10 ... 98 C8
  SAND/SEL CR2 ... 223 J4
Joshua Wk CHES/WCR EN8 ... 62 F10
Josling Cl GRAYS RM17 ... 167 G5
Joslings Cl SHB W12 ... 118 B4
Joslin Rd PUR RM19 ... 166 B4
Joslyn Cl PEND EN3 ... 80 F4
Joubert St BTSEA SW11 ... 158 A4
Journeys End SLN SL2 ... 129 K7
Jowett St PECK SE15 ... 159 N6
Joyce Av UED N18 ... 99 N9
Joyce Ct WAB EN9 ... 63 J10
Joyce Green La DART DA1 ... 165 N9
  ERITH DA8 ... 165 L2
Joyden's Wood Rd BXLY DA5 ... 186 E7
Joydon Dr CHDH RM6 ... 123 J5
Joydon Dr CRW RM9 ... 124 A9
Joyners Fld HLWS CM18 ... 46 F5
Joy Rd GVE DA12 ... 190 F4
Jubilee Arch WDSR SL4 * ... 149 J7
Jubilee Av CHING E4 ... 101 M7
  LCOL/BKTW AL2 ... 57 J7
  ROMW/RG RM7 ... 124 D3
  WARE SG12 ... 26 E1
  WHTN TW2 ... 176 B4
Jubilee Cl CDALE/KGS NW9 ... 116 A4
  KUT/HW KT1 ... 175 J10
  ROMW/RG RM7 ... 124 C3
  STWL/WRAY TW19 ... 173 M3
  SWCM DA10 ... 189 P7
  WLSDN NW10 ... 136 B4
Jubilee Crs ADL/WDHM KT15 ... 215 N2
  ED N9 ... 99 P2
  GVE DA12 ... 191 H5
Jubilee Dr RSLP HA4 ... 113 L9
Jubilee Gdns STHL UB1 ... 133 P7
  STHWK SE1 ... 11 P10
Jubilee Ri CHEL SW3 * ... 15 P10
Jubilee Ri ABR/ST RM4 ... 247 N10
Jubilee Rd CHEAM SM3 ... 220 C4
  GFD/PVL UB6 ... 134 G3
  ORP BR6 ... 228 B8
  WATN WD24 ... 73 H4
  WTHK RM20 ... 166 G5
Jubilee St WCHPL E1 ... 140 F8
Jubilee Ter BRKHM/BTCW RH3 ... 274
  DORK RH4 ... 272 C1
  FUL/PGN SW6 ... 157 H8
The Jubilee GNWCH SE10 * ... 160 C6
Jubilee Vis ESH/CLAY KT10 * ... 198 B4
Jubilee Wy CRAWE RH10 ... 284 B7
  CHSGTN KT9 ... 199 N10
  DTCH/LGLY SL3 ... 149 N6
  EBED/NFELT TW14 ... 175 H4
  SCUP DA14 ... 185 K5
  WIM/MER SW19 ... 201 L1
Judd St STPAN WC1H ... 5 H10
Jude St CAN/RD E16 ... 140 E8
Judeth Gdns GVE DA12 ... 191 H8
Judge Heath La HYS/HAR UB3 ... 132 D8
Judge's Hi POTB/CUF EN6 ... 60 A5
Judge St WATN WD24 ... 73 H4
Judges' Wk HAMP NW3 ... 117 M8
Judith Av CRW RM5 ... 104 C7
Juer St BTSEA SW11 ... 157 P6
Juglans Rd ORP BR6 ... 227 R8
Jules Thorn Av EN EN1 ... 79 P7
Julia Gdns BARK IG11 ... 143 N4
Juliana Cl EFNCH N2 ... 117 N1
Julian Av ACT W3 ... 135 N9
Julian Cl BAR EN5 ... 77 L7
  WOKN/KNAP GU21 ... 231 H9
  WEY KT13 ... 216 B4
Julian HI HRW HA1 ... 114 D7
Julian Pl POP/IOD E14 ... 160 G6
Julian Rd ORP BR6 ... 227 R5
Julians Cl SEV TN13 ... 265 H3
Julians Wy SEV TN13 ... 265 H3
Julian Tayler Pth FSTH SE23 * ... 182 A5
Julien Rd COUL/CHIP CR5 ... 240 D1
  EA W5 ... 155 H2
Juliette Rd PLSTW E13 ... 141 M4
Juliette Wy SOCK/AV RM15 ... 165 N1
Julius Caesar Wy STAN HA7 ... 95 K4
Julius Nyerere Cl IS N1 * ... 5 P6
Junction Ap BTSEA SW11 ... 157 P9
  LEW SE13 ... 161 H9
Junction Ms BAY/PAD W2 ... 9 N5
Junction Pl BAY/PAD W2 * ... 9 M5
Junction Rd ARCH N19 ... 118 D8
  ASHF TW15 ... 174 D8
  BRW CM14 ... 107 H5
  DORK RH4 ... 272 F2
  EA W5 ... 155 H7
  ED N9 ... 99 P2
  HRW HA1 ... 114 C4
  LTWR GU18 ... 212 A6
  PLSTW E13 ... 141 N5
  ROM RM1 ... 104 C2
  SAND/SEL CR2 ... 223 L3
  TOTM N17 ... 119 P1
Junction Rd East CHDH RM6 ... 123 N5
Junction Rd West CHDH RM6 ... 123 N5
June Cl COUL/CHIP CR5 ... 222 C10
June La REDH RH1 ... 276 F7
Junewood Cl ADL/WDHM KT15 ... 215 J7
Juniper Av SLN SL2 ... 55 J7
Juniper Cl BAR EN5 ... 76 A6
  BRXN/ST SW9 ... 244 B3
  BROX EN10 ... 62 E1
  CHSGTN KT9 ... 219 L6
  GU GU1 ... 249 N5
  OXTED RH8 ... 261 N9
  REIG RH2 ... 275 M2
  RKW/CH/CXG WD3 ... 91 L10
Juniper Ct CHDH RM6 ... 123 L1
  NTHWD HA6 * ... 94 B7
  WOKN/KNAP GU21 ... 231 H9
  RBRW/HUT CM13 ... 107 L3
  RKW/CH/CXG WD3 ... 70 F10

SL SL1 ... 128 D9
SL SL1 ... 149 N1
Juniper Crs CAMTN NW1 ... 4
Juniper Dr CHOB/PIR GU24 ... 230 F1
  SOCK/AV RM15 ... 147 K5
  WAND/EARL SW18 ... 159 M10
Juniper Gdns MTCM CR4 ... 202 D1
  RAD WD7 ... 57 K9
Juniper Ga RKW/CH/CXG WD3 ... 91 K3
Juniper Gn HHN HP1 ... 35 H6
Juniper Gv WAT WD17 ... 73 N4
Juniper La EHAM E6 ... 142 B7
Juniper Rd CRAWW RH11 ... 283 N5
  IL IG1 ... 122 D8
  REIG RH2 ... 275 M2
Juniper St WCHPL E1 * ... 140 D9
Juniper Wy HARH RM3 ... 105 L9
  HYS/HAR UB3 ... 132 L9
Juno Rd HHNE HP2 ... 36 A3
Juno St NWCR SE14 ... 160 C5
Jupiter Dr HHNE HP2 ... 36 A4
Jupiter Wy HOLWY N7 ... 5 P1
Jupp Rd SRTFD E15 ... 141 J2
Jupp Rd West SRTFD E15 ... 141 J3
Jura Cl CRAWW RH11 ... 283 L10
Jurgens Rd PUR RM19 * ... 166 B3
Jury St GVW DA11 ... 190 E12
Justice Wk CHEL SW3 ... 15 N10
Justin Cl BTFD TW8 ... 155 L8
Justin Rd CHING E4 ... 100 E7
Jute La PEND EN3 ... 80 D6
Jutland Cl ARCH N19 ... 118 F6
Jutland Pl EGH TW20 ... 172 F8
Jutland Rd CAT SE6 ... 183 H5
  PLSTW E13 ... 141 M4
Jutsums Av ROMW/RG RM7 ... 124 C4
Jutsums La ROMW/RG RM7 ... 124 C4
Juxon Cl CRAWW RH11 ... 283 J9
  KTN/HRWW/WS HA3 ... 94 A3
Juxon St LBTH SE11 ... 17 P5

## K

Kaduna Cl PIN HA5 ... 113 J3
Kangley Bridge Rd SYD SE26 ... 182 N1
Kaplan Dr WCHMH N21 ... 78 C9
Kara Wy CRICK NW2 ... 116 C9
Karen Cl BRWN CM15 ... 107 H1
  RAIN RM13 ... 145 F4
Karen Ct BMLY BR1 ... 205 L1
  ELTH/MOT SE9 ... 183 P1
Karenza Ct WBLY HA9 * ... 115 H5
Karina Cl CHIG IG7 ... 103 J1
Karma Wy RYLN/HDSTN HA2 ... 113 P6
Kashgar Rd WOOL/PLUM SE18 ... 163 J4
Kashmir Cl ADL/WDHM KT15 ... 215 N3
Kashmir Rd CHARL SE7 ... 162 A6
Kassala Rd BTSEA SW11 ... 158 A7
Kates Cl BAR EN5 ... 76 D9
Katescroft WGCE AL7 ... 23 H9
Katharine St CROY/NA CR0 ... 203 K10
Katherine Cl ADL/WDHM KT15 ... 215 H4
  BERM/RHTH SE16 ... 140 C10
  HHS/BOV HP3 ... 35 N3
Katherine Gdns BARK/HLT IG6 ... 102 F8
  ELTH/MOT SE9 ... 162 A10
Katherine Ms CTHM CR3 ... 241 N5
Katherine Pl ABLGY WD5 ... 55 H8
Katherine Rd EHAM E6 ... 142 A3
Katherine's Wy HLWW/ROY CM19 ... 46 D4
Kathleen Av ACT W3 ... 135 P7
  ALP/SUD HA0 ... 135 K2
Kathleen Rd BTSEA SW11 ... 158 A4
Katrine Sq HHNE HP2 ... 35 N2
Kavanaghs Rd BRW CM14 ... 106 F4
Kavanaghs Ter BRW CM14 ... 106 F4
Kay Av ADL/WDHM KT15 ... 195 P10
Kaye Don Wy WEY KT13 ... 216 B6
Kayemoor Rd BELMT SM2 ... 221 P4
Kays Ter SWFD E18 * ... 101 L10
Kay St BETH E2 ... 7 P7
  SRTFD E15 ... 141 J2
  WELL DA16 ... 163 L7
Kay Wk STALE/WH AL4 ... 39 J5
Kaywood Cl DTCH/LGLY SL3 ... 149 P2
Kean St HOL/ALD WC2B ... 11 N6
Kearton Rd PUR/KEN CR8 ... 241 K5
Keary Rd SWCM DA10 ... 189 L3
Keating Gn CHING E4 ... 100 E7
Keats Av CAN/RD E16 ... 141 N10
  HARH RM3 ... 105 J8
  REDH RH1 ... 258 B8
Keats Cl BORE WD6 ... 75 M8
  CHIG IG7 ... 102 F7
  PEND EN3 ... 80 C9
  STHWK SE1 ... 19 L6
  WAN E11 ... 121 M1
  WIM/MER SW19 ... 179 N9
  YEAD UB4 ... 132 A7
Keats Gv HAMP NW3 ... 117 P9
Keats Pde ED N9 * ... 99 P3
Keats Rd BELV DA17 ... 164 B3
  WELL DA16 ... 163 H7
Keats Wy CROY/NA CR0 ... 204 B6
  GFD/PVL UB6 ... 133 J6
  WDR/YW UB7 ... 132 A3
Keble Cl CRAWE RH10 ... 284 E4
  NTHLT UB5 ... 114 B10
  WPK KT4 ... 200 D10
Keble Pl BARN SW13 ... 156 E5
Keble St TOOT SW17 ... 179 N7
Keble Ter ABLGY WD5 ... 54
Kechill Gdns HAYES BR2 ... 205 M7
Kedleston Dr STMC/STPC BR5 ... 207 J4
Kedleston Wk BETH E2 ... 140
Keeble Cl WOOL/PLUM SE18 * ... 162
Keedonwood Rd BMLY BR1 ... 183 K
Keel Cl BARK IG11 ... 143 N
  BERM/RHTH SE16 ... 140 C10
Keel Dr SL SL1 ... 149 H1
Keeley Rd CROY/NA CR0 ... 203 K9
Keeley St HOL/ALD WC2B ... 11 N6
Keeling Rd ELTH/MOT SE9 ... 184
Keely Cl EBAR EN4 ... 77 N4
Keens La GU GU3 ... 249 J4
Keens Rd CROY/NA CR0 ... 223 K
Keens Yd IS N1 * ... 6 D2
Keens La RGUW GU3 ... 249 L6
Keens Park Rd RGUW GU3 ... 249 L6
Keen's Rd CROY/NA CR0 ... 223 K1
Keen's Yd IS N1 * ... 6 D2
Keepers Ct RGUE GU4 ... 250 F7
Keepers Farm Cl WDSR SL4 ... 149 J8
Keepers Ms TEDD TW11 ... 177 N6
Keepers Wk VW GU25 ... 194 A5
The Keep BKHTH/KID SE3 ... 161 M8
  KUT/CMB KT2 ... 177 L3
Keesey St WALW SE17 ... 159 L6
Keeton's Rd BERM/RHTH SE16 ... 160 A1
Keevil Dr WIM/MER SW19 ... 178 F3
Keighley Cl HOLWY N7 ... 118 F5
Keightley Dr ELTH/MOT SE9 ... 184 F7
Keilder Cl HGDN/ICK UB10 ... 132 B4
Keildon Rd BTSEA SW11 ... 158 B3
Keir Hardie Est CLPT E5 * ... 120 A5
Keir Hardie Wy BARK IG11 ... 143 K2
  YEAD UB4 ... 114
Keith Av EYN DA4 ... 188 A4
Keith Connor Cl VX/NE SW8 * ... 158 C9

Keith Gv SHB W12 ... 156 D1
Keith Park Rd HGDN/ICK UB10 ... 132 C4
Keith Rd BARK IG11 ... 142 G4
  HYS/HAR UB3 ... 152 F2
  WALTH E17 ... 100 E9
Kelbrook Rd BKHTH/KID SE3 ... 162 B8
Kelburn Wy RAIN RM13 ... 145 H5
Kelbys WGCE AL7 ... 23 M4
Kelceda Cl CRICK NW2 ... 116 D7
Kelf Gv HYS/HAR UB3 ... 132 C6
Kelfield Gdns NKENS W10 ... 138 D6
Kelfield Ms NKENS W10 ... 138 D6
Kelland Cl CEND/HSY/T N8 * ... 118 E3
Kelland Rd PLSTW E13 ... 141 M6
Kellaway Rd BKHTH/KID SE3 ... 161 P6
Keller Crs MNPK E12 ... 122 A9
Kellerton Rd LEW SE13 ... 183 K1
Kelling Gdns CROY/NA CR0 ... 203 J7
Kellino St TOOT SW17 ... 180 A7
Kellner Rd THMD SE28 ... 163 J2
Kell St STHWK SE1 ... 18 E3
Kelly Av PECK SE15 ... 159 N7
Kelly Cl BORE WD6 ... 76 A6
  SHPTN TW17 ... 196 F2
  WLSDN NW10 ... 116 A8
Kelly Ms MV/WKIL W9 ... 8
Kelly Rd MLHL NW7 ... 97 H7
Kelly St CAMTN NW1 ... 4
Kelly Wy CHDH RM6 ... 123 P3
Kelman Cl CHES/WCR EN8 ... 62 C7
  CLAP SW4 ... 158 F10
Kelmore Gv EDUL SE22 ... 159 P10
Kelmscott Cl WALTH E17 ... 73 J
  WATW WD18 ... 73 H10
Kelmscott Gdns SHB W12 ... 156 E1
Kelmscott Pl ASHTD KT21 ... 237 H5
Kelmscott Rd BTSEA SW11 ... 179 P1
Kelpatrick Rd SL SL1 ... 128 C8
Kelross Rd HBRY N5 ... 119 J3
Kelsall Cl BKHTH/KID SE3 ... 161 N8
Kelsall Ms RCH/KEW TW9 ... 145 N4
Kelsey La BECK BR3 ... 204 F3
Kelsey Park Av BECK BR3 ... 204 F3
Kelsey Park Rd BECK BR3 ... 204 F3
Kelsey Rd STMC/STPC BR5 ... 207 L2
Kelsey Sq BECK BR3 ... 204 F2
Kelsey St BETH E2 ... 13 P1
Kelsey Wy BECK BR3 ... 204 F3
Kelshall GSTN WD25 ... 73 M2
Kelsie Wy BARK/HLT IG6 ... 103 H1
Kelso Dr GVE DA12 ... 191 J7
Kelso Pl KENS W8 ... 14 C3
Kelso Rd CAR SM5 ... 201 M7
Kelston Rd BARK/HLT IG6 ... 102 E10
Kelvedon Cl KUTN/CMB KT2 ... 177 M9
Kelvedon Gn BRWN CM15 ... 86 A2
Kelvedon Hall La BRW CM14 ... 86 A2
Kelvedon Rd FUL/PGN SW6 ... 157 K6
Kelvedon Wy WFD IG8 ... 102 C7
Kelvin Av LHD/OX KT22 ... 236 E5
  WDGN N22 ... 98 C7
Kelvinbrook E/WMO/HCT KT8 ... 198 A3
Kelvin Cl HOR/WEW KT19 ... 219 M3
Kelvin Crs KTN/HRWW/WS HA3 ... 94 D8
Kelvin Dr TWK TW1 ... 176 G2
Kelvin Gdns CROY/NA CR0 ... 202 F7
  STHL UB1 ... 133 P6
Kelvin Gv CHSGTN KT9 ... 219 J10
  SYD SE26 ... 182 A6
Kelvington Cl CROY/NA CR0 ... 204 A7
Kelvington Rd PECK SE15 ... 182 C4
Kelvin La CRAWE RH10 ... 284 A3
Kelvin Pde ORP BR6 ... 207 H8
Kelvin Rd HBRY N5 ... 119 J3
  TIL RM18 ... 168 B4
  WELL DA16 ... 163 K9
Kelvin Wy CRAWE RH10 ... 284 A3
Kember St IS N1 * ... 5 N1
Kemble Cl POTB/CUF EN6 * ... 59 N9
  WEY KT13 ... 216 E1
Kemble Dr HAYES BR2 ... 222 E3
Kemble Pde POTB/CUF EN6 * ... 59 M9
Kemble Rd CROY/NA CR0 ... 203 J10
  FSTH SE23 ... 182 A6
  TOTM N17 ... 99 P9
Kembleside Rd BH/WHM TN16 ... 243 P4
Kemble St HOL/ALD WC2B ... 11 N6
Kemerton Rd BECK BR3 ... 204 G2
  CMBW SE5 ... 159 H6
  CROY/NA CR0 ... 203 N7
Kemey's St HOM E9 ... 120 D10
Kemishford WOKS/MYFD GU22 ... 231 M9
Kemnal Rd CHST BR7 ... 184 G6
Kempe Cl DTCH/LGLY SL3 ... 150 F3
  STAL AL1 ... 38 B10
Kempe Rd EN EN1 ... 80 A2
  KIL/WHAMP NW6 ... 136 G4
Kemp Gdns CROY/NA CR0 ... 203 K6
Kemplay Rd HAMP NW3 ... 117 N9
Kemp Pl BUSH WD23 ... 73 P1
Kemprow GSTN WD25 ... 74 C1
Kemps Dr NTHWD HA6 ... 92 G8
  POP/IOD E14 ... 140 F9
Kempsford Gdns ECT SW5 ... 14 B8
Kempsford Rd LBTH SE11 ... 18 B6
Kempshott Rd STRHM/NOR SW16 ... 180 F10
Kempson Rd FUL/PGN SW6 ... 157 K7
Kempthorne Rd DEPT SE8 ... 160 D3
Kempthorne St GVW DA11 * ... 190 D
Kempton Av HCH RM12 ... 125 J8
  NTHLT UB5 ... 133 P1
  SUN TW16 ... 176 C9
Kempton Cl ERITH DA8 ... 164 D5
  HGDN/ICK UB10 ... 112 B9
Kempton Ct SUN TW16 ... 176 C9
Kempton Pk SUN TW16 ... 197 J1
Kempton Rd EHAM E6 ... 122 A6
  HPTN TW12 ... 196 F2
Kempton Wk CROY/NA CR0 ... 204 D6
Kempt St WOOL/PLUM SE18 ... 162 G
Kemsing Cl BXLY DA5 ... 185 K
  THHTH CR7 * ... 203 K
Kemsing Rd GNWCH SE10 ... 161 N4
Kemsley Cha BGR/WK TN15 ... 233 K
Kemsley Ct CVW DA11 * ... 190 D
  SWCM DA10 ...
Kemsley Rd BH/WHM TN16 ... 244 A3
Kenbury Cl HGDN/ICK UB10 ... 112 B9
Kenbury Gdns CMBW SE5 ... 158 G
Kenchester Cl VX/NE SW8 ... 158 F
Kencot Wy ERITH DA8 ... 164 A1
Kendal Av ACT W3 ... 135 N

Kendal Av South SAND/SEL CR2 ... 223 K6
Kendal Cl WGCE AL7 ... 23 J
  BRXN/ST SW9 ... 190 C3
  FBAR/BDGN N11 * ... 98 B6
  ISLW TW7 ... 154 F8
  WOOL/PLUM SE18 ... 162 B7
Kendale HHS/BOV HP3 ... 35 P7
Kendale Rd BMLY BR1 ... 183 K
Kendal Gdns NKENS W10 ... 138 D6
  SUT SM1 ... 201 L7
  UED N18 ... 99 L5
Kendal Ms UX/CGN UB8 ... 131 M3
Kendal Pde UED N18 ... 99 L5
Kendal Pl PUT/ROE SW15 ... 179 J3
Kendal Rd WAB EN9 ... 81 H4
  WLSDN NW10 ... 116 D9
Kendal St BAY/PAD W2 ... 9 M7
Kendall Av BECK BR3 ... 204 D2
  SAND/SEL CR2 ... 223 J4
Kendall Av South SAND/SEL CR2 ... 223 K6
Kendall Cl WGCE AL7 ... 23 L7
Kendall Pl MHST W1U ... 10 C1
Kendall Rd BECK BR3 ... 204 D2
  ISLW TW7 ... 154 F8
  WOOL/PLUM SE18 ... 162 B7
Kendalmere Cl MUSWH N10 ... 98 C9
Kender St NWCR SE14 ... 160 B4
Kendoa Rd CLAP SW4 ... 158 E10
Kendon Cl WAN E11 ... 121 N3
Kendor Av HOR/WEW KT19 ... 219 P7
Kendra Hall Rd SAND/SEL CR2 ... 223 J4
Kendrey Gdns WHTN TW2 ... 176 D2
Kendrick Ms SKENS SW7 * ... 15 L5
Kendrick Pl SKENS SW7 * ... 15 L5
Kendrick Rd DTCH/LGLY SL3 ... 149 N2
Kenelm Cl HRW HA1 ... 114 F8
Kenerne Dr BAR EN5 ... 77 H
Kenford Cl GSTN WD25 ... 55 H
Keniham Cl MLHL NW7 ... 97
Kenilford Rd BAL SW12 ... 180 C3
Kenilworth Av COB KT11 ... 218 A10
  RYLN/HDSTN HA2 ... 113 N10
  WALTH E17 ... 100 F10
  WIM/MER SW19 ... 179 L3
Kenilworth Cl BNSTD SM7 ... 239 L
  HHNE HP2 ... 35 P
  SL SL1 ... 149 L2
Kenilworth Crs EN EN1 ... 79 M5
Kenilworth Dr BORE WD6 ... 75 P5
  RKW/CH/CXG WD3 ... 72 C8
  WOT/HER KT12 ... 197 L10
Kenilworth Gdns GDMY/SEVK IG3 ... 123 J
  HCH RM12 ... 124 F
  LOU IG10 ... 82 C10
  OXHEY WD19 ... 93 K6
  STA TW18 ... 173 M8
  UX/CGN UB8 ... 131 N
Kenilworth Rd ASHF TW15 ... 173 N6
  BOW E3 ... 140 D4
  EA W5 ... 135 K10
  EDGW HA8 ... 95 P3
  EW KT17 ... 218 C
  KIL/WHAMP NW6 ... 2
  PGE/AN SE20 ... 183 H
  STMC/STPC BR5 ... 206 F
Kenilworth Ter BELMT SM2 * ... 221 K
Kenley Av CDALE/KGS NW9 ... 96 D
Kenley Cl BXLY DA5 ... 186 B
  CHST BR7 ... 207 H
  EBAR EN4 ... 77 P
  PUR/KEN CR8 ... 241 L
Kenley Gdns HCH RM12 ... 125 L
  THHTH CR7 ... 203 K
Kenley La KUT/HW KT1 ... 199 L
Kenley Rd KUT/HW KT1 ... 199 L
  STHL W16 ... 133
  SUN TW16 ... 197 L
  TWK TW1 ... 176 F
  WIM/MER SW19 ... 201 K
Kenley Wk CHEAM SM3 ... 220 C
  NTGHL W11 ... 8
Kenlor Rd TOOT SW17 ... 179 N
Kenmara Cl CRAWE RH10 ... 284 C
Kenmara Ct CRAWE RH10 ... 284 C
Kenmare Dr MTCM CR4 ... 180 A
  TOTM N17 ... 99 N
Kenmare Gdns PLMGR N13 ... 99 J
Kenmare Rd THHTH CR7 ... 203 H
Kenmere Gdns ALP/SUD HA0 ... 135 M
Kenmere Rd WELL DA16 ... 163 K
Kenmont Gdns WLSDN NW10 ... 136 F
Kenmore Av KTN/HRWW/WS HA3 ... 115 H
Kenmore Cl RCH/KEW TW9 ... 145 P
Kenmore Gdns EDGW HA8 ... 95 N
Kenmore Rd KTN/HRWW/WS HA3 ... 115 J
  PUR/KEN CR8 ... 223 J
Kenmure Rd HACK E8 ... 120 A
Kenmure Yd HACK E8 * ... 120 A
Kennacraig Cl CAN/RD E16 ... 141 M
Kennard Rd FBAR/BDGN N11 ... 98 A
  SRTFD E15 ... 141 J
Kennard St BTSEA SW11 ... 158 E
  CAN/RD E16 ... 142 C
Kennedy Av HOD EN11 ... 44 E
  PEND EN3 ... 80 B
Kennedy Cl CHES/WCR EN8 ... 62 D
  LCOL/BKTW AL2 ... 57 J
  MTCM CR4 ... 202 B
  PIN HA5 ... 93 P
  PLSTW E13 ... 141 L
  SL SL2 ... 129
  STMC/STPC BR5 ... 207 L
Kennedy Gdns SEV TN13 ... 247 K
Kennedy Path W7 * ... 135
Kennedy Rd BARK IG11 ... 143 H
  HNWL W7 ... 134
Kennedy Wk WALW SE17 * ... 19
Kennel Cl LHD/OX KT22 ... 236 B
Kennel La BFOR GU20 ... 210
  HORL RH6 ... 276
  LHD/OX KT22 ... 236
Kennel Wood Crs CROY/NA CR0 ... 225 J
Kennelwood La HAT AL10 ... 40 C
Kennet Cl BTSEA SW11 ... 157 N
  CRAWW RH11 ... 283
  UPMR RM14 ... 126
Kennet Dr YEAD UB4 ... 133 M
Kenneth Av IL IG1 ... 122 C
Kenneth Crs CRICK NW2 ... 116
Kenneth Gdns STAN HA7 ... 94
Kenneth More Rd IL IG1 ... 122 C
Kenneth Rd BNSTD SM7 ... 239
  CHDH RM6 ... 123 P
Kennet Rd DART DA1 ... 184
  ISLW TW7 ... 154
  MV/WKIL W9 ... 8
Kennet Sq MTCM CR4 ... 201 P
Kennet St WAP E1W ... 13
Kennett Ct DTCH/LGLY SL3 ... 150
Kennett Dr YEAD UB4 ... 133 M
Kennett Rd DTCH/LGLY SL3 ... 150
Kennett Wharf La BLKFR EC4V ... 12 F
Kenninghall Rd CLPT E5 ... 120
  UED N18 ... 99
Kenning Rd HOD EN11 ... 44
Kennings Wy LBTH SE11 ... 18
Kenning St BERM/RHTH SE16 ... 140
Kennington La LBTH SE11 ... 17
Kennington Oval LBTH SE11 ... 17
Kennington Park Gdns LBTH SE11 ... 18
Kennington Park Pl LBTH SE11 ... 18
Kennington Park Rd LBTH SE11 ... 18
Kennington Rd LBTH SE11 ... 17
Kenny Dr CAR SM5 ... 222
Kennylands Rd BARK/HLT IG6 ... 103
Kenrick Pl MHST W1U ... 10
Kenrick Sq RDART DA2 ... 188
Kensal Rd NKENS W10 ... 138
Kensington Av MNPK E12 ... 141
  THHTH CR7 * ... 202
  WATW WD18 ... 72
Kensington Church Ct KENS W8 * ... 14 G2

Kensington Church St KENS W8 ... 8 F9
Kensington Church Wk KENS W8 * ... 14 G1
Kensington Ct FBAR/BDGN N11 * ... 98 B6
  STAL AL1 ... 38 F8
Kensington Ct Gdns KENS W8 * ... 15 H3
Kensington Court Ms KENS W8 * ... 15 H3
Kensington Court Pl KENS W8 ... 15 H3
Kensington Ct WFD IG8 ... 102 A10
Kensington Gdns IL IG1 ... 122 C6
Kensington Gardens Sq BAY/PAD W2 ... 8 G6
Kensington Gate KENS W8 ... 15 H2
Kensington High St KENS W8 ... 14 D4
Kensington MI KENS W8 * ... 14
Kensington Palace KENS W8 * ... 8 H10
Kensington Palace Gdns NTGHL W11 ... 8 C8
Kensington Park Gdns NTGHL W11 ... 8 C8
Kensington Park Ms NTGHL W11 ... 8 C6
Kensington Park Rd NTGHL W11 ... 8 C6
Kensington Pl KENS W8 ... 8 B9
Kensington Rd BRWN CM15 ... 86 F10
  KENS W8 ... 15 H2
  NTHLT UB5 ... 133 L5
  ROMW/RG RM7 ... 124 D5
  SKENS SW7 ... 15 K2
Kensington Sq KENS W8 ... 14 G2
Kensington Ter SAND/SEL CR2 ... 223 L4
Kent Av DAGW RM9 ... 144 A6
  WEA W13 ... 135 J5
  WELL DA16 ... 185 M1
Kent Cl BORE WD6 ... 76 A2
  MTCM CR4 ... 202 G2
  ORP BR6 ... 227 N9
  STA TW18 ... 173 M8
  UX/CGN UB8 ... 131 L9
Kent Dr EBAR EN4 ... 78 B4
  HCH RM12 ... 125 L9
  TEDD TW11 ... 176 F10
Kentford Wy NTHLT UB5 ... 133 H5
Kent Gdns RSLP HA4 ... 113 L5
  WEA W13 ... 135 J4
Kent Gate Wy CROY/NA CR0 ... 224 D3
Kent Hatch Rd EDEN TN8 ... 262 F3
  OXTED RH8 ... 261 P6
Kent House La BECK BR3 ... 182 E8
Kent House Rd BECK BR3 ... 182 C10
Kentish La BRKMPK AL9 ... 41 M4
Kentish Rd BELV DA17 ... 164 B2
Kentish Town Rd CAMTN NW1 ... 4 D2
Kentlea Rd THMD SE28 ... 163 N4
Kentmere Rd WOOL/PLUM SE18 ... 163 M6
Kenton Av HRW HA1 ... 114 F4
  STHL UB1 ... 133 L6
  SUN TW16 ... 197 J2
Kenton Gdns KTN/HRWW/WS HA3 ... 115 J2
Kenton La KTN/HRWW/WS HA3 ... 94 G1
Kenton Park Av KTN/HRWW/WS HA3 ... 115 J2
Kenton Park Cl KTN/HRWW/WS HA3 ... 115 J2
Kenton Park Crs KTN/HRWW/WS HA3 ... 115 J2
Kenton Park Pde KTN/HRWW/WS HA3 * ... 115 H2
Kenton Park Rd KTN/HRWW/WS HA3 ... 115 H1
Kenton Rd HOM E9 ... 140 C1
  KTN/HRWW/WS HA3 ... 114 F4
Kentons La WDSR SL4 ... 148 B4
Kenton St STPAN WC1H ... 11 H1
Kent Pas CAMTN NW1 ... 10 A1
Kent Rd BFOR GU20 ... 212 C2
  CHSWK W4 ... 155 P2
  DAGE RM10 ... 124 D3
  E/WMO/HCT KT8 ... 198 A2
  GRAYS RM17 ... 167 J7
  GVW DA11 ... 190 B7
  HART DA3 ... 211 J3
  KUT/HW KT1 ... 199 J2
  RCH/KEW TW9 ... 155 M7
  STMC/STPC BR5 ... 207 M2
  WCHMH N21 ... 99 M3
  WOKN/KNAP GU21 ... 232 A6
  WWKM BR4 ... 204 D9
Kent St BETH E2 ... 7 M7
  PLSTW E13 ... 141 M8
Kent Ter CAMTN NW1 ... 3 P10
Kent Vw SOCK/AV RM15 ... 166 A1
Kent View Gdns GDMY/SEVK IG3 ... 123 K9
Kent Wy SURB KT6 ... 199 K10
Kentwell Cl BROCKY SE4 ... 160 B10
Kentwode Gn BARN SW13 ... 156 E5
Kentyns Rd EDEN TN8 * ... 276 F2
Kenver Av NFNCH/WDSPK N12 ... 97 H5
Kenward Rd ELTH/MOT SE9 ... 183 N4
Kenway CRW RM5 ... 104 B1
  RAIN RM13 ... 145 J6
Ken Wy WBLY HA9 ... 115 N5
Kenway Cl RAIN RM13 ... 145 J6
Kenway Rd ECT SW5 ... 14 C6
Kenwood Av NFNCH/WDSPK N12 ... 97 H4
  RYNPK SW20 ... 200 E2
Kenwood Cl HAMP NW3 ... 117 P4
  WDR/YW UB7 ... 152 C4
Kenwood Dr BECK BR3 ... 205 D2
  RKW/CH/CXG WD3 ... 91
  WOT/HER KT12 ... 217 J7
Kenwood Gdns CLAY IG5 ... 122 B1
  SWFD E18 ... 121 J1
Kenwood Pk WEY KT13 ... 216 E5
Kenwood Rdg PUR/KEN CR8 ... 241 J7
Kenwood Rd ED N9 ... 99 P
  HGT N6 ... 118
Kenworthy Cl CHES/WCR EN8 ... 62
Kenworthy Rd HOM E9 ... 121
Kenwyn Dr CRICK NW2 ... 116
Kenwyn Rd CLAP SW4 ... 158
  DART DA1 ... 171
  RYNPK SW20 ... 200
Kenya Rd HORL RH6 ... 280
Kenyngton Dr SUN TW16 ... 175
Kenyon St FUL/PGN SW6 ... 156
Keogh Rd SRTFD E15 ... 141
Kepler Rd CLAP SW4 ... 158
Keppel Rd DAGW RM9 ... 124
  DORK RH4 ... 254
  EHAM E6 ... 122
Keppel Sp WDSR SL4 ... 171
Keppel St GWRST WC1E ... 11
Kerbela St BETH E2 ... 13
Kerbey St POP/IOD E14 ... 140
Kerdistone Cl POTB/CUF EN6 * ... 59
Kerfield Crs CMBW SE5 ... 159

Kerfield Pl CMBW SE5 ... 159 P10
Kernel Ct GU GU1 ... 249 P10
Kernel St GU GU1 ... 249 P10
Kerria Wy CHOB/PIR GU24 ... 212 B4
Kerri Cl BAR EN5 ... 76 B5
Kerrill Av COUL/CHIP CR5 ... 241 N5
Kerrison Pl EA W5 ... 135 J10
Kerrison Rd BTSEA SW11 ... 157 P9
  EA W5 ... 135 J10
  SRTFD E15 ... 141 J3
Kerry Av SOCK/AV RM15 ... 165 N1
  STAN HA7 ... 95 M1
Kerry Cl PLSTW E13 ... 141 L3
  PLMGR N13 ... 98 G3
  UPMR RM14 ... 126 D6
Kerry Ct STAN HA7 ... 95 M1
Kerry Dr UPMR RM14 ... 126 D6
Kerry Pth NWCR SE14 ... 160 C5
Kerry Rd NWCR SE14 ... 160 C5
Kerry Ter WOKN/KNAP GU21 ... 232 B5
Kersey Dr SAND/SEL CR2 ... 224 A8
Kersey Gdns HARH RM3 ... 105 K4
  ELTH/MOT SE9 ...
Kersfield Rd PUT/ROE SW15 ... 179 K5
Kershaw Cl CDH/CHF RH16 ... 167 L5
  EMPK RM11 ... 125 L2
  WAND/EARL SW18 ... 179 N2
Kershaw Rd DAGE RM10 ... 124 B9
Kersley Ms BTSEA SW11 ... 158 A4
Kersley Rd STNW/STAM N16 ... 119 N8
Kersley St BTSEA SW11 ... 158 A4
Kerstin Cl HYS/HAR UB3 ... 132 G5
Kerswell Cl SEVS/STOTM N15 ... 119 N3
Kerwick Cl HOLWY N7 ... 5 N1
Keslake Rd KIL/WHAMP NW6 ... 136 G4
Kessock Cl TOTM N17 ... 120 A3
Kesters Rd CSHM HP5 ... 51 J8
Kesteven Cl BARK/HLT IG6 ... 103 J7
Keston Av ADL/WDHM KT15 ... 215 K6
  COUL/CHIP CR5 ... 241 H5
  HAYES BR2 ... 225 P4
Keston Cl UED N18 ... 99 L4
  WELL DA16 ... 163 P8
Keston Gdns HAYES BR2 ... 225 P2
Keston Ms WAT WD17 * ... 73 J6
Keston Park Cl HAYES BR2 ... 226 D2
Keston Rd PECK SE15 ... 159 H9
  THHTH CR7 ... 202 G6
  TOTM N17 ... 119 P3
Kestral Av EHAM E6 ... 142 A1
  HNHL SE24 ... 181 J1
  STA TW18 ... 173 A6
Kestrel Cl BARK/HLT IG6 ... 103 L5
  BERK HP4 ... 33 P6
  CDALE/KGS NW9 ... 96 E7
  CRAWW RH11 ... 283 J5
  CSTN WD25 ... 55 M10
  HCH RM12 ... 142 D1
  HOR/WEW KT19 ... 219 M7
  KUTN/CMB KT2 ... 177 J1
  RGUE GU4 ... 250 C8
  WLSDN NW10 ... 116 A10
Kestrel Gn HAT AL10 ... 40 A5
Kestrel Pl NWCR SE14 * ... 160 B9
Kestrel Rd WAB EN9 ... 63 M10
The Kestrels LCOL/BKTW AL2 ... 55 M7
  HYS/HAR UB3 ... 152 E1
  WGCE AL7 ... 23 J3
  WOKN/KNAP GU21 ... 231 N1
Keswick Av EMPK RM11 ... 125 L6
  PUT/ROE SW15 ... 178 A6
  WIM/MER SW19 ... 201 L1
Keswick Cl CRAWW RH11 ... 282 G1
  STAL AL1 ... 38 E9
  SUT SM1 ... 221 P1
Keswick Ct SLN SL2 ... 129 L9
Keswick Dr LTWR GU18 ... 212 A7
  PEND EN3 ... 80 B2
Keswick Gdns PUR RM19 ... 166 C5
  REDBR IG4 ... 122 B3
  RSLP HA4 ... 112 E3
  WBLY HA9 ... 115 N5
Keswick Ms EA W5 ... 135 K10
Keswick Rd BXLYHN DA7 ... 164 B3
  EGH TW20 ... 172 D8
  GT/LBKH KT23 ... 254 B7
  ORP BR6 ... 207 N10
  PUT/ROE SW15 ... 179 J4
  WHTN TW2 ... 176 B2
  WWKM BR4 ... 205 H5
Kettering Rd HARH RM3 ... 105 J8
Kettering St STRHM/NOR SW16 ... 180 F10
Kett Gdns BRXS/STRHM SW2 ... 180 B3
Kettlebaston Rd LEY E10 ... 120 E6
Kettlebury Rd CHONG CM5 ... 67 M4
Kettlewell Cl FBAR/BDGN N11 ... 98 A6
  WOKN/KNAP GU21 ... 232 B1
Kettlewell Ct SWLY BR8 ... 208 C2
Kettlewell HI WOKN/KNAP GU21 ... 232 B1
Kevan Dr RPLY/SEND GU23 ... 251 N5
Kevelioc Rd TOTM N17 ... 99 N8
Kevin Cl HSLWW TW4 ... 153 M6
Kevington Cl STMC/STPC BR5 ... 207 M10
Kevington Dr CHST BR7 ... 207 M10
Kew Br RCH/KEW TW9 ... 155 N6
Kew Bridge Arches CHSWK W4 * ... 155 N6
Kew Bridge Ct BTFD TW8 ... 155 N6
Kew Bridge Rd BTFD TW8 ... 155 N6
Kew Cl UX/CGN UB8 ... 131 J8
Kew Crs CHEAM SM3 ... 201 J10
Kewferry Dr NTHWD HA6 ... 92 A7
Kewferry Rd NTHWD HA6 ... 92 B7
Kew Foot Rd RCH/KEW TW9 ... 155 M7
Kew Gardens Rd RCH/KEW TW9 ... 155 N6
Kew Gn RCH/KEW TW9 ... 155 M5
Kew Meadow Pth RCH/KEW TW9 ... 155 M7
Kew Riverside Pk RCH/KEW TW9 ... 155 N6
Kew Rd RCH/KEW TW9 ... 155 N6
Keybridge Rd VX/NE SW8 * ... 158 F6
Keyes Rd DART DA1 ... 171 N5
  CRICK NW2 ... 116 C1
Key Cl WCHPL E1 ... 140 E6
Keyfield Ter STAL AL1 * ... 38 C5
Keymer Cl BH/WHM TN16 ... 243 N1
Keymer Rd BRXS/STRHM SW2 ... 180 B3
  CRAWW RH11 ... 283 L5
Keynes Cl EFNCH N2 ... 118 A1
Keynsham Av WFD IG8 ... 101 N6
Keynsham Gdns ELTH/MOT SE9 ... 184 B4
Keynsham Rd ELTH/MOT SE9 ... 184 A4
  MRDN SM4 ... 201 M5
Keynton Cl HERT/WAT SG14 ... 24 B2
Keysers Rd BROX EN10 ... 43 H5
Keystone Crs IS N1 ... 5 J6
Keywood Dr SUN TW16 ... 176 D7
Keyworth Cl CLPT E5 ... 120 G2
Keyworth St STHWK SE1 ... 18 E3
Kezia St DEPT SE8 ... 160 A1
Khalsa Av GVE DA12 ... 190 E7
Khama Rd TOOT SW17 ... 179 L7
Khartoum Pl GVE DA12 ... 190 F7
Khartoum Rd IL IG1 ... 122 C1
  PLSTW E13 ... 141 M3
  TOOT SW17 ... 179 L7
Khyber Rd BTSEA SW11 ... 157 N8
Kibes La WARE SG12 ... 26 C2
Kibworth St VX/NE SW8 ... 158 F5
Kidbrooke Down CRAWW RH11 ... 283 L9
Kidbrooke Gdns BKHTH/KID SE3 ... 161 P9
Kidbrooke Gv BKHTH/KID SE3 ... 161 P9
Kidbrooke La ELTH/MOT SE9 ... 162 B10
Kidbrooke Park Cl BKHTH/KID SE3 ... 161 P9
Kidbrooke Park Rd BKHTH/KID SE3 ... 161 P9

BKHTH/KID SE3 ............... 161 N8
Kidbrooke Park Rd
  BKHTH/KID SE3 ............. 161 N7
  LEE/GVPK SE12 ............. 183 N1
Kidbrooke Wy BKHTH/KID SE3.. 161 N8
Kidderminster Pl
  CROY/NA CRO ............... 203 J8
Kidderminster Rd
  CROY/NA CRO ............... 203 J8
  SLN SL2 ................... 128 C9
Kidderpore Av HAMP NW3 .. 117 K9
Kidderpore Gdns HAMP NW3.. 117 K9
Kidd Pl CHARL SE7 .......... 162 B4
Kidworth Cl HOR/WEW KT19.. 207 G6
Kielder Cl BARK/HLT IG6 .... 103 J7
Kier Pk ASC SL5 ............. 192 B3
Kiffen St SDTCH EC2A ....... 13 H1
Kilberry Cl ISLW TW7 ....... 154 C2
Kilbride Ct HHNE HP2 * ..... 36 A1
Kilburn Br KIL/WHAMP NW6 .. 2 F6
Kilburn High Rd
  KIL/WHAMP NW6 ........... 2 C2
Kilburn La NKENS W10 ....... 2 A9
Kilburn Park Rd MV/WKIL W9.. 2 E10
Kilburn Pl KIL/WHAMP NW6 .. 2 F6
Kilburn Priory
  KIL/WHAMP NW6 ........... 2 G6
Kilburn Sq KIL/WHAMP NW6 .. 2 F6
Kilburn V KIL/WHAMP NW6 .. 2 F6
Kilby Cl GSTN WD25 ......... 73 L1
Kilcorral Cl EW KT17 ....... 220 D10
Kildare Cl RSLP HA4 ........ 113 K6
Kildare Gdns BAY/PAD W2 .. 8 F5
Kildare Rd CAN/RD E16 ...... 141 M7
Kildare Ter BAY/PAD W2 .. 8 F5
Kildoran Rd CLAP SW4 ....... 180 F1
Kildowan Rd GDMY/SEVK IG3.. 123 K6
Kilfillan Gdns BERK HP4 .... 33 N6
Kilgour Rd FSTH SE23 ....... 182 D2
Kilkie St FUL/PGN SW6 ...... 157 M8
Killarney Rd WAND/EARL SW18.. 179 M2
Killburns Mill Cl WLGTN SM6.. 202 C9
Killearn Rd CAT SE6 ........ 183 J4
Killester Gdns WPK KT4 ..... 220 E1
Killewarren Wy
  STMC/STPC BR5 ........... 207 N1
Killick St SEV TN13 ........ 246 F2
Killick St IS N1 ........... 5 N7
Killieser Av BRXS/STRHM SW2.. 180 C1
Killip Cl CAN/RD E16 ....... 141 L8
Killowen Av NTHLT UB5 ...... 114 B10
Killowen Cl
  KWD/TDW/WH KT20 ......... 238 G10
Killowen Rd HOM E9 ......... 140 C1
Killyon Rd VX/NE SW8 ....... 158 D9
Kilmaine Rd FUL/PGN SW6 .. 157 H6
Kilmarnock Gdns BCTR RM8 .. 123 M8
Kilmarnock Pk REIG RH2 .... 257 L5
Kilmarnock Rd WOKN WD19 ... 93 L5
Kilmarsh Rd HMSMTH W6 .. 156 F3
Kilmartin Av STRHM/NOR SW16.. 203 H3
Kilmartin Gdns GDMY/SEVK IG3.. 123 K7
Kilmartin Wy HCH RM12 ...... 125 J3
Kilmington Cl RBRW/HUT CM13.. 107 N3
Kilmiston Av SHPTN TW17 .... 196 D6
Kilmorey Gdns TWK TW1 ...... 176 G1
Kilmorey Rd TWK TW1 ........ 154 G10
Kilmorie Rd FSTH SE23 ...... 182 B4
Kiln Av AMS HP6 ............ 69 P4
Kiln Cl BERK HP4 ........... 34 E3
  HYS/HAR UB3 .............. 152 E5
Kilncroft HHS/BOV HP3 .. 36 C8
Kilndown GVE DA12 .......... 190 F9
Kilner St POP/IOD E14 ...... 140 F7
Kilnfield BRWN CM15 ........ 87 J1
  CHONG CM5 ................ 67 N5
  WCCE AL7 ................. 23 J7
Kiln Gnd HHS/BOV HP3 .. 36 B8
Kiln House Cl WARE SG12 .. 26 D1
Kiln La ASC SL5 ............ 192 F5
  BRKHM/BTCW RH3 .......... 273 N1
  CSHM HP5 ................. 51 M7
  EW KT17 .................. 220 B7
  HLWE CM17 ................ 47 M2
  HORL RH6 ................. 280 A2
  RPLY/SEND GU23 ........... 233 L10
  SLN SL2 .................. 109 H6
  WDSR SL4 ................. 170 A9
Kilnmead CRAWE RH10 ........ 283 P6
Kilnmead Cl CRAWE RH10 .. 283 P6
Kiln Mdw RGUW GU3 .. 249 H6
Kiln Ms TOOT SW17 .......... 179 N8
Kiln Pl KTTN NW5 ........... 4 B1
Kiln Rd EPP CM16 ........... 66 B3
  TRING HP23 ............... 32 B4
Kilnside ESH/CLAY KT10 .. 218 F4
Kiln Wy GRAYS RM17 ......... 167 L4
  NTHWD HA6 ................ 92 F7
Kilnwood La HORS RH12 ...... 282 D10
Kilpatrick Wy YEAD UB4 .. 135 M7
Kilravock St NKENS W10 .. 2 A10
Kilross Rd EBED/NFELT TW14.. 174 E4
Kilrue La WOKN/KNAP GU21.. 216 C1
Kilrush Ter WOKN/KNAP GU21.. 232 D2
Kilsha Rd WOT/HER KT12 ..... 197 J6
Kilsmore La CHES/WCR EN8 .. 62 C4
Kilvinton Dr ENC/FH EN2 .. 79 L4
Kilworth Av BRWN CM15 ...... 87 M10
Kilworth Cl WGCE AL7 ....... 23 L7
Kimbell Gdns FUL/PGN SW6 .. 157 H7
Kimber Cl WDSR SL4 ......... 148 B5
Kimber Ct RGUE GU4 * .. 250 C8
Kimberley Av EHAM E6 .. 142 B4
  GNTH/NBYPK IG2 ........... 122 G5
  PECK SE15 ................ 160 A8
  ROMW/RG RM7 ............. 124 C4
Kimberley Cl DTCH/LGLY SL3.. 150 C3
  HORL RH6 ................. 279 P4
Kimberley Ct
  KIL/WHAMP NW6 .. 2 B4
Kimberley Gdns EN1 EN1 ..... 79 N7
  FSBYPK N4 ................ 119 J3
Kimberley Pl PUR/KEN CR8 .. 223 H7
Kimberley Ride COB KT11 .. 218 A3
Kimberley Rd BECK BR3 ...... 204 C2
  BRXN/ST SW9 .............. 158 F5
  CAN/RD E16 ............... 141 L6
  CHING E4 ................. 101 K2
  CROY/NA CRO .............. 203 J6
  KIL/WHAMP NW6 ........... 2 B4
  STRW/RED AL3 ............. 138 A5
  TOTM N17 ................. 99 P10
  WAN E11 .................. 121 J7
Kimberley Wy CHING E4 ...... 101 K2
Kimber Rd WAND/EARL SW18.. 179 L5
Kimbers Dr SL SL1 * ........ 128 C5
Kimble Crs BUSH WD23 ....... 94 B1
Kimble Rd WIM/MER SW19 ..... 179 M10 no
Kimblewick WATW WD18 * .. 72 D10
Kimbolton Cl LEE/GVPK SE12.. 183 L2
Kimbolton Gn BORE WD6 ...... 95 P8
Kimbolton Rw CHEL SW3 * ... 15 P8
Kimmeridge Gdns
  ELTH/MOT SE9 ............. 184 B7
Kimmeridge Rd
  ELTH/MOT SE9 ............. 184 B7
Kimps Wy HHS/BOV HP3 .. 36 B9
Kimpton Av BRWN CM15 ....... 106 C5
Kimpton Cl HHNE HP2 ........ 36 C1
Kimpton Link Est
  CHEAM SM3 * .............. 201 J10
Kimpton Park Wy CHEAM SM3.. 201 J10
Kimpton Pl GSTN WD25 ....... 55 L10
Kimpton Rd CHEAM SM3 ....... 201 J10
  CMBW SE5 ................. 159 J9
Kimptons Cl POTB/CUF EN6.. 58 E5
Kimptons Md POTB/CUF EN6.. 58 E6
Kinburn Dr EGH TW20 ........ 172 B8

Kinburn St BERM/RTHH SE16 *.. 160 C1
Kincaid Rd PECK SE15 ....... 160 A6
Kincardine Gdns
  MV/WKIL W9 * ............. 8 E2
Kinch Gv WBLY HA9 .......... 115 L5
Kincraig Dr SEV TN13 ....... 247 H9
Kinder Cl THMD SE28 ........ 143 M9
Kinderscout HHS/BOV HP3 .. 36 B8
Kindersley Wy ABLGY WD5.. 54 D7
Kinder St WCHPL E1 ......... 140 A8
Kinderton Cl STHGT/OAK N14.. 98 D2
Kinfauns Av EMPK RM11 ...... 125 K4
Kinfauns Rd
  BRXS/STRHM SW2 .......... 181 H5
  GDMY/SEVK IG3 ............ 123 L6
Kingaby Gdns RAIN RM13 ..... 145 H2
King Alfred Av CAT SE6 ..... 182 F7
King Alfred Rd HARH RM3 .. 105 N10
King And Queen Cl
  ELTH/MOT SE9 ............. 184 B7
King Arthur Cl PECK SE15 ... 160 B6
King Arthur Ct
  CHES/WCR EN8 ............. 62 D5
King Charles I Island
  WHALL SW1A ............... 11 L9
King Charles Rd BRWD WD7.. 57 K8
King Charles' Rd BRYLDS KT5.. 199 L5
King Charles St WHALL SW1A.. 17 K1
King Charles Ter WAP E1W *.. 140 B8
King Charles Wk
  WIM/MER SW19 ............. 179 H4
King Croft Rd HARP AL5 ..... 20 C4
Kingcup Cl CROY/NA CRO.. 204 C8
Kingcup Dr CHOB/PIR GU24.. 230 F1
King David La WCHPL E1 .. 140 B9
Kingdon Rd KIL/WHAMP NW6 .. 2 F1
King Edward Av RAIN RM13.. 145 H4
King Edward Dr
  CDW/CHF RM16 ............ 168 B2
  CHSGTN KT9 ............... 199 K10
  GRAYS RM17 ............... 168 B3
King Edward III Ms
  BERM/RTHH SE16 .......... 160 A1
King Edward Pl
  STALE/WH AL4 ............. 21 J2
King Edward Rd BAR EN5 .. 77 K8
  BRW CM14 ................. 107 H4
  CHES/WCR EN8 ............. 62 D9
  LEY E10 .................. 121 H6
  RAD WD7 .................. 57 J7
  RDART DA2 ................ 166 F10
  ROM RM1 .................. 124 C4
  WALTH E17 ................ 120 D1
King Edward's Gdns ACT W3.. 135 M10
King Edward's Gv TEDD TW11.. 176 G9
King Edward's Pl ACT W3 *.. 135 M10
King Edward's Rd RSLP HA4.. 112 F6
  BARK IG11 ................ 142 G3
  ED N9 .................... 100 H4
  HACK E8 .................. 140 A3
  PEND EN3 ................. 80 C4
  WARE SG12 ................ 26 D1
King Edward St
  HHS/BOV HP3 * ........... 35 H10
  STBT EC1A ................ 12 E5
King Edward VII Av WDSR SL4.. 149 K6
King Edward Wk STHWK SE1.. 18 C3
Kingfield Dr
  WOKS/MYFD GU22 .......... 232 C6
Kingfield Gdns
  WOKS/MYFD GU22 .......... 232 C6
Kingfield Rd EA W5 ......... 135 J6
  LHD/OX KT22 .............. 236 G6
Kingfield St POP/IOD E14 .. 161 H3
Kingfisher Cl BROX EN10 .... 44 F6
  CRAWE RH10 ............... 284 B4
  KTN/HRWW/WS HA3 ......... 94 B3
  NTHWD HA6 ................ 92 C9
  RBRW/HUT CM13 ........... 107 M1
  STALE/WH AL4 ............. 21 J2
  STMC/STPC BR5 ........... 207 N4
  THMD SE28 ................ 143 H9
Kingfisher Ct DORK RH4 *.. 272 F1
  RGUE GU4 * ............... 250 C8
Kingfisher Dr HHS/BOV HP3.. 54 A4
  RCHPK/HAM TW10 .......... 177 H7
  REDH RH1 ................. 258 B7
  RGUE GU4 ................. 250 F8
  STA TW18 ................. 173 J7
Kingfisher Gdns
  SAND/SEL CR2 ............. 224 C6
Kingfisher Lure KGLGY WD4 *.. 54 C5
  RKW/CH/CXG WD3 .......... 71 L8
Kingfisher Ms LEW SE13 .. 182 G1
Kingfisher Pl WDGN N22 *.. 98 G10
Kingfisher Rd UPMR RM14.. 126 E6
Kingfisher St EHAM E6 .. 142 H7
Kingfisher Wy BECK BR3 .. 204 C5
  HLWW/ROY CM19 ........... 27 M1
  WLSDN NW10 ............... 118 A10
King Gdns CROY/NA CRO.. 223 J2
King Garth Ms FSTH SE23 .. 182 F5
King George Av BUSH WD23.. 74 A10
  CAN/RD E16 ............... 142 A8
  WOT/HER KT12 ............. 197 L5
King George Cl
  ROMW/RG RM7 ............. 124 D1
  SUN TW16 ................. 174 D9
King George Rd WAB EN9 *.. 63 H10
  WARE SG12 ................ 26 D1
King George's Av WATW WD18.. 72 F9
King George's Dr
  ADL/WDHM KT15 ........... 215 K6
King George Sq
  RCHPK/HAM TW10 .......... 177 J2
King George's Rd BRWN CM15.. 86 G10
King George St GNWCH SE10.. 161 H6
King George VI Av MTCM CR4.. 202 H4
  TIL RM18 ................. 169 L3
Kingham Cl WAND/EARL SW18.. 179 M4
  NTGHL W11 ................ 8 A9
King Harolds Wy BXLYHN DA7.. 146 A6
King Harry La STALW/RED AL3.. 137 H7
King Harry St HHW HP1 *.. 35 N6
King Henry Ms HRW HA1 *.. 114 D6
  ORP BR6 .................. 227 J2
King Henry's Dr CROY/NA CRO.. 225 J7
King Henry's Ms PEND EN3.. 80 F3
King Henry's Reach
  HMSMTH W6 ................ 156 F5
King Henry's Rd HAMP NW3.. 3 N4
  KUT/HW KT1 ............... 199 M1
King Henry St
  STNW/STAM N16 ........... 7 J1
King Henry Ter WAP E1W *.. 140 A9
Kinghorn St STBT EC1A .. 12 E4
King James Av POTB/CUF EN6.. 60 D7
King James Ct STHWK SE1.. 18 D2
King James St STHWK SE1.. 18 D2
King John Ct SDTCH EC2A.. 13 K1
King John's Cl
  STWL/WRAY TW19 .......... 171 P2
King John St WCHPL E1 .. 140 C7
King John's Wk
  ELTH/MOT SE9 ............. 184 B7
Kinglake Est WALW SE17 *.. 19 L7
Kinglake St WALW SE17 ...... 19 L8
Kinglet Cl FSTGT E7 ........ 141 M1
Kingly Ct REGST W1B * .. 11 J7
Kingly St REGST W1B .. 11 J6
Kingpost RGUE GU4 * .. 250 F8
King & Queen Cl
  ELTH/MOT SE9 * ........... 184 B7
King & Queen St WALW SE17.. 19 H7
King & Queen Whf
  BERM/RTHH SE16 * ........ 140 C10
Kingsand Rd LEE/GVPK SE12.. 183 M5

King's Arms Yd LOTH EC2R.. 12 G5
Kingsash Dr YEAD UB4 ....... 133 M3
King's Av BAL SW12 ......... 180 E4
King's Av BF/WBF KT14 .. 215 N8
  BMLY BR1 ................. 183 N6
  CAR SM5 .................. 221 P4
  CHDH RM6 ................. 124 A4
  CLAP SW4 ................. 180 F2
  EA W5 .................... 135 J4
  HHS/BOV HP3 .............. 36 A10
  MUSWH N10 ................ 118 B3
  NWMAL KT3 ................ 200 C4
  REDH RH1 ................. 275 P2
  WATW WD18 * .............. 73 H8
King's Av CFD/PVL UB6 .. 134 A8
  HSLW TW3 ................. 154 A7
  SUN TW16 ................. 174 A7
  WCHMH N21 ................ 99 J2
  WFD IG8 .................. 101 P6
Kingsbridge Av ACT W3 .. 155 L1
Kingsbridge Crs STHL UB1.. 133 N7
Kingsbridge Dr MLHL NW7.. 96 C8
Kingsbridge Rd BARK IG11.. 142 C4
  HARH RM3 ................. 105 M7
  MRDN SM4 ................. 200 A3
  NKENS W10 ................ 136 F8
  NWDGN UB2 ................ 153 N3
  WOT/HER KT12 ............. 197 J2
Kingsbrook LHD/OX KT22 .. 236 F4
Kingsbury Av STALW/RED AL3.. 9 H4
Kingsbury Crs STA TW18 ..... 172 G7
Kingsbury Gn
  CDALE/KGS NW9 * ......... 115 P3
Kingsbury Ms STALW/RED AL3.. 38 A5
Kingsbury Rd
  CDALE/KGS NW9 ........... 115 H4
  IS N1 .................... 7 K1
Kingsbury Ter IS N1 ........ 7 K1
King's Cha E/WMO/HCT KT8.. 198 B3
King's Cha BRW CM14 ........ 107 H4
Kingsclere Cl PUT/ROE SW15.. 178 D3
Kingsclere Pl ENC/FH EN2 *.. 79 K6
Kingscliffe Gdns
  WIM/MER SW19 ............. 179 H4
Kings Cl CSTG HP8 .......... 90 A3
  DART DA1 ................. 164 F10
  HDN NW4 .................. 116 A2
  LEY E10 .................. 120 C5
  NTHWD HA6 ................ 92 G7
  THDIT KT7 ................ 198 F6
  WALTH E17 ................ 101 H10
  WIM/MER SW19 ............. 179 H1
  WOT/HER KT12 ............. 197 J2
King's Cl KGLGY WD4 ........ 53 L7
King's College Rd RSLP HA4.. 112 C4
King's College Rd HAMP NW3.. 3 M3
Kingscote Hl CRAWW RH11.. 283 P11
Kingscote Rd CHSWK W4 .. 156 A4
  CROY/NA CRO .............. 204 A4
  NWMAL KT3 ................ 200 A3
Kingscote St BLKFR EC4V.. 12 C7
Kings Ct HARP AL5 .......... 20 D2
  STBT EC1A ................ 12 E5
King's Ct STHWK SE1 * ...... 18 D1
Kingscourt Rd
  STRHM/NOR SW16 .......... 180 E6
Kingscroft WGCE AL7 ........ 23 L4
Kingscroft Rd BNSTD SM7.. 239 N1
  CRICK NW2 ................ 2 D1
  LHD/OX KT22 .............. 236 G6
King's Cross Br IS N1 * .... 5 K5
King's Cross Rd FSBYW WC1X.. 5 M9
Kings Cross Rd FSBYW WC1X.. 5 M9
Kingsdale Gdns NTGHL W11.. 136 G10
Kingsdale Rd BERK HP4 ...... 33 M6
  PGE/AN SE20 .............. 182 C10
  WOOL/PLUM SE18 .......... 163 J5
Kingsdene
  KWD/TDW/WH KT20 ......... 238 E7
Kingsdon La HLWE CM17 .. 47 M2
Kingsdown Av ACT W3 ........ 136 B9
  SAND/SEL CR2 ............. 223 J6
  WEA W13 .................. 154 C1
Kingsdown Cl
  BERM/RTHH SE16 * ........ 160 A4
  GVE DA12 ................. 191 J4
  NKENS W10 ................ 136 G8
Kingsdowne Ct EA W5 * ...... 135 J4
Kingsdowne Rd SURB KT6 .. 199 K7
Kingsdown Rd ARCH N19 ...... 118 E9
  CHEAM SM3 ................ 221 H4
  EW KT17 .................. 220 E8
  WAN E11 .................. 121 K8
Kingsdown Wy HAYES BR2.. 205 M6
King's Dr BRYLDS KT5 ....... 199 M1
  EDGW HA8 ................. 95 L5
  GVE DA12 ................. 190 G6
  HAYES BR2 ................ 205 H1
  TEDD TW11 ................ 176 A6
  THDIT KT7 ................ 198 F6
  WBLY HA9 ................. 115 H6
The Kings Dr WOT/HER KT12.. 216 G5
Kingsend RSLP HA4 .......... 112 F6
Kings Farm Av
  RCHPK/HAM TW10 .......... 155 M10
Kings Farm Rd
  RKW/CH/CXG WD3 .......... 70 G10
Kingsfield HOD EN11 ........ 44 F1
  WDSR SL4 ................. 148 C7
Kingsfield Av
  RYLN/HDSTN HA2 .......... 114 A3
Kingsfield Ct OXHEY WD19.. 73 L10
Kingsfield Dr PEND EN3 .... 80 C1
Kingsfield Rd HRW HA1 ...... 114 C5
  OXHEY WD19 ............... 93 L1
Kingsfield Ter DART DA1 *.. 187 L2
Kingsfield Wy PEND EN3 .. 80 C1
Kingsford Rd KTTN NW5 * .. 118 A10
Kingsford St KTTN NW5 ...... 118 A10
Kingsford Wy EHAM E6 ....... 142 C7
Kings Gdns IL IG1 .......... 122 C6
  KIL/WHAMP NW6 * ......... 2 E3
  UPMR RM14 ................ 126 D5
Kingsgate CRAWE RH10 ....... 283 P7
  STALW/RED AL3 ........... 38 A8
  WBLY HA9 ................. 115 P8
Kingsgate Av FNCH N3 ....... 117 H1
Kingsgate Cl BXLYHN DA7.. 147 H1
  STMC/STPC BR5 ........... 207 N7
Kingsgate Est IS N1 * ...... 7 K2
Kingsgate Pl KIL/WHAMP NW6.. 2 E3
Kingsgate Rd
  KUT/HW KT1 ............... 199 K1
  KIL/WHAMP NW6 ........... 2 E3
King's Gn LOU IG10 ......... 80 B1
Kingsground ELTH/MOT SE9.. 184 A7
Kings Gv ROM RM1 ........... 125 J4
King's Gv PECK SE15 ........ 160 A6
Kings Hall Ms LEW SE13 * .. 161 M9
King's Hwy WOOL/PLUM SE18.. 163 N6
Kingshill Av
  KTN/HRWW/WS HA3 ......... 114 C2
  NTHLT UB5 ................ 133 J3
  STMC/STPC BR5 ........... 206 B8
  WPK KT4 .................. 201 J10
Kingshill Cl YEAD UB4 * .. 133 N6
Kingshill Dr
  KTN/HRWW/WS HA3 ......... 96 C10
Kingshold Rd HOM E9 .. 139 N1
Kingshill Wy BERK HP4 ...... 33 M7
Kingshurst Rd LEE/GVPK SE12.. 183 M3
Kings Keep HAYES BR2 * .. 205 K3

Kingsland HLWS CM18 ........ 46 F3
  HERT/BAY SG13 ........... 25 P4
Kingsland Gn
  STNW/STAM N16 * ......... 7 K1
Kingsland Pas HACK E8 * .. 7 K8
  HACK E8 .................. 7 L8
Kingsland Rd BETH E2 .. 7 L8
  ROM RM1 .................. 125 H3
  SL SL1 ................... 149 K2
  SNWD SE25 ................ 203 P8
  STALW/RED AL3 ........... 38 A5
  SURB KT6 * ............... 199 H8
  TEDD TW11 ................ 176 C8
  TOTM N17 ................. 99 N9
Kings La BFOR GU20 ......... 212 D2
  EGH TW20 ................. 171 M8
  KGLGY WD4 ................ 53 K7
King's La SUT SM1 .......... 221 N2
Kingslawn Cl PUT/ROE SW15.. 178 C1
Kingslea LHD/OX KT22 ....... 236 F6
Kingsleigh Cl BTFD TW8 *.. 154 B8
Kingsleigh Pl MTCM CR4 .. 202 A3
Kingsleigh Wk HAYES BR2.. 205 L1
Kingsley Av BNSTD SM7 ...... 239 K1
  BORE WD6 ................. 75 L6
  CHES/WCR EN8 ............. 62 A5
  DART DA1 ................. 171 J10
  EA W5 .................... 135 K4
  EFNCH N2 ................. 117 M3
  HORL RH6 ................. 280 A2
  HSLW TW3 ................. 154 B8
  SUT SM1 .................. 221 N1
Kingsley Cl DAGE RM10 ...... 124 C3
  EFNCH N2 ................. 117 M3
Kingsley Ct EDGW HA8 * .. 95 N4
  GPK RM2 .................. 125 J4
  WGCE AL7 ................. 23 J9
Kingsley Dr WPK KT4 ........ 200 C9
Kingsley Flats STHWK SE1 *.. 19 L3
Kingsley Gdns CHING E4 .. 100 F5
  EMPK RM11 ................ 125 L2
Kingsley Ms CHST BR7 ....... 184 G3
  IL IG1 ................... 122 E7
  KENS W8 * ................ 15 H4
  WAP E1W .................. 140 A9
Kingsley Pl HGT N6 ......... 118 B5
Kingsley Rd BARK/HLT IG6.. 102 E6
  CRAWW RH11 ............... 283 J11
  CROY/NA CRO .............. 203 H8
  FSTGT E7 ................. 141 M4
  HORL RH6 ................. 280 A2
  HSLW TW3 ................. 154 B8
  KIL/WHAMP NW6 ........... 2 D5
  LOU IG10 ................. 82 A7
  ORP BR6 .................. 227 J3
  PIN HA5 .................. 113 N2
  PLMGR N13 ................ 99 H5
  RYLN/HDSTN HA2 .......... 114 B9
  WALTH E17 ................ 101 H10
  WIM/MER SW19 ............. 179 K3
Kingsley Wy EFNCH N2 .. 117 M4
Kingsley Wd Dr ELTH/MOT SE9.. 184 C6
Kingslyn Crs NRWD SE19.. 203 M1
Kings Lynn Dr HARH RM3.. 105 N2
Kings MI HMSMTH W6 * .. 156 F3
Kingsman Pde
  WOOL/PLUM SE18 .......... 146 C7
Kingsman St
  WOOL/PLUM SE18 .......... 146 E9
Kingsmead BAR EN5 ......... 77 K8
  BH/WHM TN16 ............. 244 A2
  CHES/WCR EN8 ............. 62 A5
  POTB/CUF EN6 ............. 60 C4
  RCHPK/HAM TW10 .......... 177 L2
  SBW CM21 ................. 29 P2
  STALE/WH AL4 ............. 39 J3
  RYNPK SW20 ............... 200 G3
  WOKN/KNAP GU21 .......... 232 D2
Kingsmead Av
  CDALE/KGS NW9 ........... 116 A5
  ED N9 .................... 100 A5
  MTCM CR4 ................. 202 D3
  ROM RM1 .................. 124 D4
  SUN TW16 ................. 197 K3
  SURB KT6 ................. 199 M9
  WPK KT4 .................. 200 E1
Kingsmead Cl BFN/LL DA15.. 185 K5
  HOR/WEW KT19 ............ 220 A4
  TEDD TW11 ................ 176 C8
Kingsmead Dr NTHLT UB5 .. 133 K4
Kingsmead Rd
  BRXS/STRHM SW2 .......... 181 H5
Kingsmead Wy CLPT E5 ....... 120 D9
Kings Mead Wy CLPT E5 ...... 120 D9
Kingsmere Cl PUT/ROE SW15.. 156 G9
Kingsmere Pk
  CDALE/KGS NW9 ........... 115 P6
Kingsmere Pl
  STNW/STAM N16 * ......... 119 L6
Kingsmere Rd
  WIM/MER SW19 ............. 178 G5
Kings Ms CHIG IG7 * ........ 102 F3
  HHNE HP2 * ............... 35 M5
Kings Ms BMSBY WC1N .. 11 P2
  CLAP SW4 * ............... 180 F1
  CLAP SW4 ................. 180 F1
Kingsmill Gdns DAGW RM9.. 124 B3
Kingsmill Rd DAGW RM9 .. 124 B3
Kingsmill Ter STJWD NW8.. 3 M7
Kingsmoor Rd
  HLWW/ROY CM19 ........... 46 E4
Kingsnympton Pk
  KUTN/CMB KT2 ............. 177 N10
Kings Oak ROMW/RG RM7.. 124 B1
Kingsoak Rd HRW HA1 * .. 114 C5
Kings Orch ELTH/MOT SE9.. 184 B2
King's Paddock HPTN TW12.. 198 B1
Kings Pde CAR SM5 * ........ 201 P10
  SHB W12 * ................ 156 D2
  TOTM N17 * ............... 119 N1
  WLSDN NW10 * ............. 136 G1
Kingspark Ct SWFD E18 .. 121 K1
Kings Pas WAN E11 * ........ 121 J5
King's Pas KUT/HW KT1 * .. 8 D8
Kings Quay WBPTN SW10 *.. 157 H7
King's Reach EMB EC4Y * .. 12 C7
Kings Ride Ga
  RCHPK/HAM TW10 .......... 155 M10
Kings Rd ADL/WDHM KT15.. 215 M10
  BARK IG11 ................ 142 D1
  BELMT SM2 ................ 221 M6
  BRW CM14 ................. 107 H4
  CHEL SW3 ................. 16 A7
  CHES/WCR EN8 ............. 62 A5

  FUL/PGN SW6 .............. 157 L7
  HERT/BAY SG13 ........... 25 P4
  KUTN/CMB KT2 ............. 177 L10
  LCOL/BKTW AL2 ........... 57 H2
  MORT/ESHN SW14 .......... 156 A9
  FLSTW E15 ................ 141 M9
  ROM RM1 .................. 125 H3
  SL SL1 ................... 149 K2
  SNWD SE25 ................ 203 P8
  STALW/RED AL3 ........... 38 A5
  SURB KT6 ................. 199 H8
  TEDD TW11 ................ 176 C8
  TOTM N17 ................. 99 N9
  TWK TW1 .................. 176 G2
  UX/CGN UB8 ............... 131 N5
  WAN E11 .................. 121 K5
  WBPTN SW10 ............... 15 L10
  WIM/MER SW19 ............. 179 K9
King's Scholars' Pas
  PIM SW1V * ............... 16 G4
Kings Shade Wk
  HOR/WEW KT19 * .......... 220 A4
Kings Sq HAT AL10 * ........ 40 A1
King's Rd GU1 .............. 250 A10
Kings Stable St WDSR SL4 .. 149 J6
Kings Stairs Cl
  BERM/RTHH SE16 .......... 160 A1
Kings' Ter CAMTN NW1 * .. 4 G6
Kingsthorpe Rd SYD SE26.. 182 C7
Kingston Av CHEAM SM3 .. 201 H10
  EBED/NFELT TW14 ......... 174 F2
  EHSLY KT24 ............... 252 F2
  LHD/OX KT22 .............. 236 G7
  WDR/YW UB7 ............... 132 A9
Kingston By-Pass
  ESH/CLAY KT10 ........... 198 D10
  RYNPK SW20 ............... 178 C9
Kingston Cl CHDH RM6 ....... 123 P1
  NTHLT UB5 ................ 133 N2
  TEDD TW11 ................ 176 C9
Kingston Ct GVW DA11 * .. 189 N2
Kingston Crs ASHF TW15.. 173 M8
  BECK BR3 ................. 204 E1
Kingston Gdns KUTN/CMB KT2.. 177 M10
Kingston Hall Rd KUT/HW KT1.. 8 F8
Kingston Hill KUTN/CMB KT2.. 177 N9
Kingston Hill Av CHDH RM6.. 123 P1
Kingston Hill Pl
  KUTN/CMB KT2 ............. 177 P7
Kingston House Est
  SURB KT6 * ............... 198 G6
Kingston House Gdns
  LHD/OX KT22 * ............ 236 G7
Kingston La EHSLY KT24 .. 252 B3
  TEDD TW11 ................ 176 C8
  WDR/YW UB7 ............... 132 B1
Kingston Ldg NWMAL KT3 *.. 200 B4
Kingston Pl
  KTN/HRWW/WS HA3 ......... 94 E3
Kingston Ri ADL/WDHM KT15.. 215 K6
Kingston Rd ASHF TW15 .. 173 M8
  BRYLDS KT5 ............... 199 N9
  EBAR EN4 ................. 77 N9
  ED N9 .................... 100 D4
  HOR/WEW KT19 ............ 220 A1
  IL IG1 ................... 122 C9
  KUT/HW KT1 ............... 199 N4
  LHD/OX KT22 .............. 236 F7
  NWDGN UB2 ................ 153 N1
  NWMAL KT3 ................ 200 A4
  PUT/ROE SW15 ............ 178 A4
  ROM RM1 .................. 124 C3
  RYNPK SW20 ............... 200 G3
  STA TW18 ................. 173 K7
  TEDD TW11 ................ 176 E9
  WIM/MER SW19 ............. 179 K10
Kingston Sq NRWD SE19 .. 181 N8
Kingston V PUT/ROE SW15.. 178 A7
Kingstown St CAMTN NW1.. 4 C2
King St ACT W3 ............. 135 N10
  CHERT KT16 ............... 195 K8
  CITYW EC2V ............... 12 F6
  COVGDN WC2E .............. 11 L7
  GNWCH SE10 ............... 161 H5
  HMSMTH W6 ................ 156 D3
  NWDGN UB2 ................ 153 H2
  PLSTW E13 ................ 141 M6
  RCH/KEW TW9 ............. 176 A2
  TOTM N17 ................. 99 N9
  TWK TW1 .................. 176 F2
  WATW WD18 ................ 73 K8
  WHALL SW1A ............... 11 L10
King Street Cloisters
  HMSMTH W6 * .............. 156 E3
King Street Pde TWK TW1 *.. 176 F2
Kings Wk SAND/SEL CR2.. 224 A10
Kings Warren LHD/OX KT22.. 235 M4
Kingswater Pl BTSEA SW11.. 157 N6
Kings Wy CROY/NA CRO.. 222 G2
Kingsway BCTR RM8 ......... 123 J10
  CFSP/GDCR SL9 ........... 50 D1
  HOL/ALD WC2B ............. 11 N6
  HYS/HAR UB3 * ............ 133 H10
  MORT/ESHN SW14 .......... 156 M7
  NFNCH/WDSPK N12 ......... 97 M7
  NWMAL KT3 ................ 200 F4
  PEND EN3 ................. 80 A9
  POTB/CUF EN6 ............. 58 G1
  SLN SL2 .................. 128 G9
  STMC/STPC BR5 ........... 206 G8
  STWL/WRAY TW19 .......... 173 H5
  WBLY HA9 ................. 115 M5
  WOKN/KNAP GU21 .......... 232 D2
Kingsway Crs
  RYLN/HDSTN HA2 .......... 114 B2
Kingsway Ms SLN SL2 ........ 129 H1
Kingsway North Orbital Rd
  GSTN WD25 ................ 55 H10
Kingsway Pde
  STNW/STAM N16 * ......... 119 L6
King's PI CHSWK W4 * ....... 155 P2
  LOU IG10 ................. 80 A1
King's PI STHWK SE1 ........ 18 E2
Kingsway PI CLKNW EC1R *.. 12 B1
Kingsway Ter WEY KT13 ...... 216 B5
The Kingsway EW KT17 ....... 220 C8
Kingswear Rd KTTN NW5 ...... 118 C9
  RSLP HA4 ................. 113 H7

Kingswood Rd EGH TW20 .. 172 A8
Kingswood Rd
  BRXS/STRHM SW2 .......... 180 F2
  CHSWK W4 ................. 155 P2
  GDMY/SEVK IG3 ........... 123 K5
  GSTN WD25 ................ 55 J10
  HAYES BR2 ................ 205 K5
  KWD/TDW/WH KT20 ......... 238 G2
  PGE/AN SE20 .............. 182 B9
  SEV TN13 ................. 246 F7
  WAN E11 .................. 121 K5
  WBLY HA9 ................. 115 M8
  WIM/MER SW19 ............. 179 J1
Kingswood Ter CHSWK W4 .. 155 P2
Kingswood Wy SAND/SEL CR2.. 224 C8
  WLGTN SM6 ................ 222 F2
Kingsworth Cl BECK BR3 .. 204 D5
Kingsworthy Cl KUT/HW KT1.. 199 L2
Kings Yd PUT/ROE SW15 * .. 156 G10
  RKW/CH/CXG WD3 * ........ 91 P2
  SRTFD E15 * .............. 140 F7
Kingthorpe Rd WLSDN NW10.. 136 A2
Kingthorpe Ter
  WLSDN NW10 ............... 136 A2
Kingwell Rd EBAR EN4 ....... 77 N4
Kingweston Cl CRICK NW2.. 117 H8
King William IV Gdns
  PGE/AN SE20 * ........... 182 F8
King William La GNWCH SE10.. 161 H4
King William St CANST EC4R.. 13 H7
King William Wk GNWCH SE10.. 161 H5
Kingwood Rd FUL/PGN SW6.. 157 H6
Kinlet Rd WOOL/PLUM SE18.. 163 J10
Kinloch Dr CDALE/KGS NW9.. 116 B5
Kinloch St HOLWY N7 ........ 118 F8
Kinloss Gdns FNCH N3 .. 117 J1
Kinloss Rd CAR SM5 ......... 201 M7
Kinnaird Av BMLY BR1 ....... 183 L8
  CHSWK W4 ................. 155 P6
Kinnaird Cl BMLY BR1 ....... 183 L8
Kinnaird Wy WFD IG8 ........ 102 C7
Kinnear Rd SHB W12 ......... 156 C1
Kinnersley Mnr REIG RH2 *.. 275 M8
Kinnersley Wk REIG RH2 .. 275 K5
Kinnerton Pl North
  KTBR SW1X * .............. 16 B2
Kinnerton Pl South
  KTBR SW1X * .............. 16 B2
Kinnerton St KTBR SW1X.. 16 C2
Kinnerton Yd KTBR SW1X *.. 16 C2
Kinnoul Rd HMSMTH W6 .. 14 A9
Kinross Av WPK KT4 ......... 200 D3
  ASC SL5 .................. 192 C5
Kinross Cl
  KTN/HRWW/WS HA3 ......... 115 L3
  SUN TW16 ................. 174 C8
Kinross Dr SUN TW16 ........ 174 C8
Kinsale Rd PECK SE15 ....... 159 P9
Kinsella Gdns WIM/MER SW19.. 178 C3
Kintyre Cl STRHM/NOR SW16.. 202 G2
Kinveachy Gdns CHARL SE7.. 162 B4
Kinver Rd SYD SE26 ......... 182 C7
Kipings KWD/TDW/WH KT20.. 238 G3
Kipling Av TIL RM18 ........ 168 E7
Kipling Ct WFD CM14 ........ 106 C6
  CRAWE RH10 ............... 284 D5
Kipling Dr WIM/MER SW19.. 179 N3
Kipling Est STHWK SE1 ...... 19 H2
Kipling Rd BXLYHN DA7 .. 147 H1
  DART DA1 ................. 188 A1
Kipling St STHWK SE1 .. 19 H1
Kipling Wy HARP AL5 ........ 20 E3
Kippings Cl SEV TN13 * .. 246 G10
Kippington Cl SEV TN13 .. 246 G10
Kippington Dr ELTH/MOT SE9.. 184 A7
Kippington Rd SEV TN13 .. 246 G10
Kirby Cl BARK/HLT IG6 .. 103 H7
  HARH RM3 ................. 105 P6
  HOR/WEW KT19 ............ 220 C3
  LOU IG10 ................. 102 A7
  NTHWD HA6 ................ 92 G7
Kirby Gv STHWK SE1 ......... 19 J1
Kirby Rd RDART DA2 ......... 188 B3
  WOKN/KNAP GU21 .......... 231 P7
Kirby St HCIRC EC1N ........ 12 B3
Kirchen Rd WEA W13 ......... 135 H4
Kirkby Cl FBAR/BDGN N11 *.. 98 A7
Kirkcaldy Gn OXHEY WD19.. 93 K4
Kirkdale SYD SE26 .......... 182 B5
Kirkdale Cnr SYD SE26 .. 182 C7
Kirkdale Rd WAN E11 ........ 121 K4
Kirkefields GUW GU2 ........ 249 M1
Kirkfield Cl WEA W13 * ..... 154 G1
Kirkham Rd EHAM E6 ......... 142 B3
Kirkham St WOOL/PLUM SE18.. 163 P7
Kirkland Av
  WOKN/KNAP GU21 .......... 231 M2
Kirkland Cl BFN/LL DA15 .. 185 H2
Kirkland Dr ENC/FH EN2 .. 79 K5
Kirklands WGCW AL8 ......... 23 H1
Kirkland Ter BECK BR3 ...... 183 P8
Kirkland Wk HACK E8 ........ 7 L1
Kirk La WOOL/PLUM SE18.. 162 G5
Kirkleas Rd SURB KT6 ....... 199 K8
Kirklees Rd BCTR RM8 ....... 123 M10
  THHTH CR7 ................ 202 F7
Kirkly Cl SAND/SEL CR2 .. 223 M5
Kirkmichael Rd POP/IOD E14.. 141 M8
Kirk Rd WALTH E17 ......... 120 E4
Kirkside Rd BKHTH/KID SE3.. 161 N8
Kirkstall Av TOTM N17 .. 119 L2
Kirkstall Gdns
  BRXS/STRHM SW2 .......... 180 G5
Kirkstall Rd BRXS/STRHM SW2.. 180 F5
  MRDN SM4 ................. 201 L10
Kirkstead Ct CLPT E5 * ..... 139 H1
Kirkstone Wy BMLY BR1 .. 183 K10
Kirkton Rd SEVS/STOTM N15.. 99 J1
Kirkwall Pl BETH E2 ........ 140 D7
Kirkwall Sp SL SL1 ......... 131 K7
Kirkwood Rd PECK SE15 .. 160 B8
Kirn Rd WEA W13 ............ 135 H4
Kirrane Cl NWMAL KT3 .. 200 C5
Kirsty Cl DORK RH4 ......... 273 H4
Kirtle Rd CSHM HP5 ......... 51 H7
Kirtley Rd SYD SE26 ........ 182 E7
Kirtling St VX/NE SW8 ...... 158 D6
Kirton Cl CHSWK W4 ......... 156 A3
  HCH RM12 ................. 145 K1
Kirton Gdns BETH E2 * ...... 7 M10
Kirton Rd PLSTW E13 ........ 141 P2
Kirton Wk EDGW HA8 ......... 96 E4
Kirwyn Wy CMBW SE5 ......... 159 K6
Kitcat Ter BOW E3 .......... 140 F6
Kitchener Av GVE DA12 .. 190 F7
Kitchener Cl STAL AL1 ...... 38 F7
Kitchener Rd EFNCH N2 .. 117 P1
  FSTGT E7 ................. 141 M3
  THHTH CR7 ................ 203 L3
  TOTM N17 ................. 119 M1
  WALTH E17 ................ 100 G9
Kite Pl BETH E2 * .......... 7 P9
Kites Cl CRAWW RH11 ........ 283 J11
Kite Yd BTSEA SW11 * ....... 158 A7
Kithurst Cl CRAWW RH11.. 283 K9
Kitley Gdns NRWD SE19 .. 203 J4
Kitsbury Rd BERK HP4 ....... 33 N5
Kitsbury Ter BERK HP4 .. 33 N5
Kitsmead CRAWE RH10 .. 285 H3
Kitsmead La VW GU25 ........ 194 D6
Kitson Rd BARN SW13 ........ 156 D7
  CMBW SE5 ................. 159 H7
Kitson Wy HLW CM20 ......... 28 F10
Kittiwake Cl SAND/SEL CR2.. 224 D8
  CRAWW RH11 ............... 282 G10
Kittiwake Pl BELMT SM2 *.. 221 H7
Kittiwake Rd NWDGN UB5.. 133 J5
Kittiwake Wy YEAD UB4 .. 133 L5
Kitt's End Rd BAR EN5 ...... 77 H1
Kiver Rd ARCH N19 .......... 118 E10

Kiwi Ter EHAM E6 ... 142 D5
Klea Av CLAP SW4 ... 180 D2
Knapdale Cl FSTH SE23 ... 182 A5
Knapmill Rd CAT SE6 ... 182 F5
Knapmill Wy CAT SE6 ... 182 F5
Knapp Cl WLSDN NW10 ... 136 N1
Knapp Rd ASHF TW15 ... 174 A4
BOW E3 ... 140 F6
Knapton Ms TOOT SW17 ... 180 B9
Knaresborough Dr
WAND/EARL SW18 ... 179 L4
Knaresborough Pl ECT SW5 * ... 14 C5
Knatchbull Rd CMBW SE5 ... 159 J8
WLSDN NW10 ... 136 A3
Knave Wood Rd
BGR/WK TN15 ... 247 M3
Knebworth Av WALTH E17 ... 100 F9
Knebworth Cl BAR EN5 ... 77 L8
Knebworth Pth WOR/DB6 ... 76 A8
Knebworth Rd
STNW/STAM N16 * ... 119 M9
Knee Hl ABYW SE2 ... 163 H4
Knee Hill Crs ABYW SE2 ... 163 H5
Knella Gn WGCE AL7 ... 23 K5
Knella Rd WGCE AL7 ... 23 J5
Kneller Gdns ISLW TW7 ... 176 C2
Kneller Rd BROCKY SE4 ... 160 D10
NWMAL KT3 ... 200 B9
WHTN TW2 ... 176 B2
Knepp Cl CRAWE RH10 ... 284 D7
Knevett Ter HSLW TW3 ... 153 P10
Knight Cl BCTR RM8 ... 123 M7
Knighten St WAP E1W ... 140 A10
Knighthead Point
POP/IOD E14 * ... 160 F1
Knightland Rd CLPT E5 ... 120 A7
Knighton Cl CRAWE RH10 ... 284 E3
ROMW/RG RM7 ... 124 E4
SAND/SEL CR2 ... 223 J5
WFD IG8 ... 101 N5
Knighton Dr WFD IG8 ... 101 N5
Knighton La BKHH IG9 ... 101 N3
Knighton Park Rd SYD SE26 ... 182 C8
Knighton Rd FSTGT E7 ... 121 H1
REDH RH1 ... 276 B2
ROMW/RG RM7 ... 124 E4
RSEV TN14 ... 246 G3
Knighton-Way La
DEN/HRF UB9 ... 111 L10
Knightrider Ct BLKFR EC4V * ... 12 D7
Knightrider St BLKFR EC4V * ... 12 E7
Knights Av EA W5 ... 155 K1
Knightsbridge SKENS SW7 ... 15 P2
Knightsbridge Crs TW18... 173 L9
Knightsbridge Gdns
ROMW/RG RM7 ... 124 E3
Knightsbridge Gn
KTBR SW1X * ... 16 A2
Knights Chambers ED N9 * ... 99 P4
Knights Cl E/WMO/HCT KT8 ... 197 N5
WDSR SL4 ... 148 C7
Knightscote Cl DEN/HRF UB9 ... 91 N10
Knightsfield WGCW AL8 ... 22 G1
Knights Hl WNWD SE27 ... 181 J8
Knight's Hill Sq WNWD SE27 ... 181 J7
Knights Orch HHW HP1 ... 35 M4
STALW/RED AL3 ... 38 B6
Knight's Pk KUT/HW KT1 ... 199 K3
Knights Pl REDH RH1 ... 258 B9
WDSR SL4 ... 148 D7
Knights Pl WHTN TW2 ... 176 D4
Knights Rdg ORP BR6 ... 227 L2
Knights Rd CAN/RD E16 ... 141 M10
STAN HA7 ... 95 H5
Knights Wk BARK/HLT IG6 ... 104 D1
LBTH SE11 ... 18 C6
Knights Wy BARK/HLT IG6 ... 104 D1
RBRW/HUT CM13... 107 M4
Knightswood
WOKN/KNAP GU21 ... 231 L4
Knightswood Cl EDGW HA8 ... 95 H3
Knightswood Rd RAIN RM13 ... 144 C4
Knightwood Crs NWMAL KT3... 200 B6
Knipp Hl COB KT11 ... 217 N10
Knivet Rd FUL/PGN SW6 ... 14 E10
Knobfield RDKG RH5 ... 270 C9
Knockhall Cha SWCM DA10 ... 189 H1
Knockhall Rd SWCM DA10 ... 189 H2
Knockholt Cl BELMT SM2 ... 221 L6
Knockholt Rd ELTH/MOT SE9 ... 184 A1
RSEV TN14 ... 228 A10
Knole Cl CRAWE RH10 ... 284 E6
CROY/NA CRO * ... 204 A4
Knole La SEV TN13 ... 265 K2
Knole Rd SEV TN13 ... 247 L9
The Knole ELTH/MOT SE9 ... 184 D7
MEO DA13 ... 190 B10
Knole Wy SEV TN13 ... 265 K1
Knole Wd SEV TN13 ... 192 C8
Knoll Crs NTHWD HA6 ... 98 D7
Knoll Dr STHGT/OAK N14 ... 98 G6
Knolles Crs BRKMPK AL9 ... 40 F1
Knoll Gn HHNE HP2 * ... 35 P4
Knollmead BRYLDS KT5 ... 199 J8
Knoll Park Rd CHERT KT16 ... 195 J8
Knoll Ri ORP BR6 ... 207 J8
Knoll Rd BXLY DA5 ... 186 B3
DORK RH4 ... 272 F4
SCUP DA14 ... 186 F4
WAND/EARL SW18 ... 179 L1
Knolls Cl STRHM/NOR SW16... 181 H6
Knolly's Cl STRHM/NOR SW16... 181 J6
Knolly's Rd STRHM/NOR SW16... 181 J6
Knolton Wy SLN SL2 ... 129 N8
Knotley Wy WWKM BR4 ... 204 C9
Knottisford St BETH E2 ... 140 C9
Knottocks Cl BEAC HP9 ... 88 C6
Knottocks Dr BEAC HP9 ... 88 C6
Knottocks End BEAC HP9 ... 88 C6
Knotts Green Ms LEY E10 ... 120 C4
Knotts Green Rd LEY E10 ... 120 C4
Knotts Pl SEV TN13 ... 247 H10
Knowle Av BXLYHN DA7 ... 165 P6
Knowle Cl BRXN/ST SW9 ... 159 K9
CRAWE RH10 ... 285 K2
Knowle Dr CRAWE RH10 ... 285 J2
HARP AL5 ... 20 C4
Knowle Gdns BF/WBF KT14... 215 K8
Knowle Gn STA TW18 ... 173 K8
Knowle Gv VW GU25 ... 193 P7
Knowle Grove Cl VW GU25... 193 P7
Knowle Hl VW GU25 ... 193 N7
Knowle Pk COB KT11 ... 235 M1
Knowle Park Av STA TW18 ... 173 L8
Knowle Rd HAYES BR2 ... 205 P8
WHTN TW2 ... 176 D4
Knowles Cl WDR/YW UB7 ... 131 P10
Knowles Hill Crs LEW SE13 ... 183 J3
The Knowle HOD EN11 ... 44 H
KWD/TDW/WH KT20 * ... 238 G7
Knowl Hl WOKS/MYFD GU22... 232 G5
Knowlton Gn HAYES BR2 ... 205 N8
Knowl Wy BORE WD6 ... 75 K9
Knowsley Av STHL UB1 ... 134 A10
Knowsley Rd BTSEA SW11 ... 158 F1
Knox Rd FSTGT E7 ... 141 M1
GUW GU2 ... 249 G5
Knox St CAMTN NW1 ... 10 A5
Knoyle St NWCR SE14 ... 160 C5
Knutsford Av WATN WD24 ... 73 L7
Kohat Rd WIM/MER SW19 ... 179 L8

Koh-I-Noor Av BUSH WD23 ... 73 P10
Koonowla Cl BH/WHM TN16 ... 244 A5
Kooringa WARL CR6 ... 242 A5
Korda Cl SHPTN TW17 ... 196 A3
Korea Cots COB KT11 * ... 235 L2
Kossuth St GNWCH SE10 ... 161 K4
Kramer Ms ECT SW5 ... 14 F4
Kreedman Wk HACK E8 * ... 119 F10
Kuala Gdns STRHM/NOR SW16... 202 C1
Kydbrook Cl STMC/STPC BR5... 206 F1
Kylemore Cl EHAM E6 ... 142 A4
Kylemore Rd
KIL/WHAMP NW6 ... 2 E3
Kymberley Rd HRW HA1 ... 114 D3
Kyme Rd ROM RM1 ... 124 G4
Kynance Cl HARH RM3 ... 105 K4
Kynance Gdns STAN HA7 ... 95 H9
Kynance Ms SKENS SW7 ... 15 H4
Kynance Pl SKENS SW7 ... 203 K5
Kynaston Cl
KTN/HRWW/WS HA3 ... 94 C8
Kynaston Ct CTHM CR3 ... 259 M1
Kynaston Crs THHTH CR7 ... 203 K5
Kynaston Rd BMLY BR1 ... 183 M8
THHTH CR7 ... 203 K5
Kynaston Wd
KTN/HRWW/WS HA3 ... 94 C8
Kynersley Cl CAR SM5 ... 202 C10
Kyngeshene Gdns GU GU1 ... 268 D1
Kynoch Rd UED N18 ... 100 B6
Kyrle Rd BTSEA SW11 ... 180 B2
Kytes Dr GSTN WD25 ... 55 L9
Kyverdale Rd
STNW/STAM N16 ... 119 N5

L

Laburnham Cl UPMR RM14 ... 126 F3
Laburnham Cl UPMR RM14... 126 F3
Laburnum Av ED N9 ... 99 M3
HCH RM12 ... 125 H7
SUT SM1 ... 201 P10
SWLY BR8 ... 208 E3
TOTM N17 ... 99 L8
WDR/YW UB7 ... 132 A9
Laburnum Cl ALP/SUD HA0... 135 M3
CHES/WCR EN8 ... 62 C1
CHING E4 ... 100 E7
FBAR/BDGN N11 ... 98 A7
GU GU1 ... 249 P7
PECK SE15 ... 160 B6
RBSF CM22 ... 30 D3
Laburnum Ct STAN HA7 ... 95 H5
Laburnum Crs SUN TW16... 197 J1
Laburnum Gdns CROY/NA CRO... 204 C7
Laburnum Gv
CDALE/KGS NW9 ... 115 P5
DTCH/LGLY SL3 ... 150 B5
GVW DA11 ... 190 A3
HSLW TW3 ... 153 N10
LCOL/BKTW AL2 ... 55 P1
NWMAL KT3 ... 200 A4
RSLP HA4 ... 112 E4
SOCK/AV RM15 ... 147 K2
STHL UB1 ... 133 N6
WCHMH N21 ... 99 K5
Laburnum Pl EGH TW20 * ... 171 N9
ELTH/MOT SE9 * ... 184 D1
Laburnum Rd CHERT KT16... 195 K8
EPP CM16 ... 65 M5
EPSOM KT18 ... 220 B9
HOD EN11 ... 44 G1
HYS/HAR UB3 ... 152 G3
MTCM CR4 ... 202 B2
WIM/MER SW19 ... 178 F10
WOKS/MYFD GU22 ... 232 A6
Laburnum St BETH E2 ... 7 K2
Laburnum Wk HCH RM12 ... 125 K10
Laburnum Wy HAYES BR2 ... 206 D7
STWL/WRAY TW19 ... 174 A4
Laceback Cl BFN/LL DA15 ... 185 J3
Lacemaker Ct AMSS HP7 * ... 69 H5
Lacewing Cl PLSTW E13 ... 141 N5
Lacey Av COUL/CHIP CR5 ... 241 H5
Lacey Cl ED N9 ... 99 P3
EGH TW20 ... 172 C10
Lacey Dr BCTR RM8 ... 123 M8
COUL/CHIP CR5 ... 241 H6
EDGW HA8 ... 95 K5
HPTN TW12 ... 197 N1
Lacey Ms BOW E3 ... 140 F4
Laceys Yd CSHM HP5 * ... 7 6
Lackford Rd COUL/CHIP CR5... 240 C4
Lackington St SDTCH EC2A... 13 H3
Lackmore Rd EN EN1 ... 80 B1
Lacock Cl WIM/MER SW19 ... 179 N9
Lacon Rd EDUL SE22 ... 159 P4
Lacrosse Wy
STRHM/NOR SW16 ... 202 E1
Lacy Gn COUL/CHIP CR5 ... 241 H6
Lacy Rd PUT/ROE SW15 ... 156 C10
Ladas Rd WNWD SE27 ... 181 K4
Ladbroke Gdns NTGHL W11... 8 C1
Ladbroke Gv NTGHL W11 ... 8 B6
REDH RH1 ... 258 B9
Ladbroke Ms NTGHL W11 * ... 8 B9
Ladbroke Rd EN EN1 ... 79 N10
EPSOM KT18 ... 220 B9
HORL RH6 ... 280 B2
NTGHL W11 ... 8 B9
REDH RH1 ... 258 B8
Ladbroke Sq NTGHL W11 ... 8 C1
Ladbroke Ter NTGHL W11 * ... 8 C1
Ladbroke Wk NTGHL W11 ... 8 C2
Ladbrook Cl PIN HA5 ... 113 N3
Ladbrooke Cl POTB/CUF EN6... 59 K3
Ladbrooke Dr POTB/CUF EN6... 59 K3
Ladbrooke Rd SL SL1 ... 149 H2
Ladbrook Rd SNWD SE25 ... 203 L3
Ladderstile Ride
KUTN/CMB KT2 ... 177 N8
Ladderswood Wy
WDGN N22 ... 98 D10
Ladds Wy SWLY BR8 ... 208 E4
Ladies Gv STALW/RED AL3 ... 38 A4
Lady Aleford Av STAN HA7 ... 94 G6
Lady Booth Rd KUT/HW KT1... 199 K2
Ladycroft Gdns ORP BR6 ... 226 G3
Ladycroft Rd LEW SE13 ... 160 G9
Ladycroft Wk STAN HA7 ... 95 N8
Ladycroft Wy ORP BR6 ... 226 G3
Ladyday Pl SL SL1 * ... 129 H10
Ladygate Rd RDKG RH5 ... 273 J1
Ladyfields GVW DA11 ... 190 C7
Lady Forsdyke Wy
HOR/WEW KT19 ... 219 M5
Ladygate La RSLP HA4 ... 112 A5
Ladygrove CROY/NA CRO ... 224 D5
Ladygrove Dr RGUE GU4 ... 250 E5
Lady Harewood Wy
HOR/WEW KT19 ... 219 M5
Lady Hay WPK KT4 ... 200 C10
Lady Margaret Rd ASC SL5 ... 192 G3
CRAWW RH11 ... 283 K5
KTTN NW5 ... 120 B10
STHL UB1 ... 133 P5
Ladymead GU GU1 ... 249 P9
Ladymead Cl CRAWE RH10... 284 D10
Lady Meadow KGLGY WD4 ... 54 N3
Ladymere RGUE WLGTN SM6 ... 222 E1
Lady's St John Sq
HERT/WAT SG14 * ... 25 H5
Lady's Cl WATW WD18 ... 73 L8
Ladyship Ter EDUL SE22 * ... 182 A3

Ladyshot HLW CM20 ... 29 K10
Ladysmith Av EHAM E6 ... 142 B4
GNTH/NBYPK IG2 ... 122 G5
Ladysmith Cl MLHL NW7 ... 96 F7
Ladysmith Rd CAN/RD E16 ... 141 L5
ELTH/MOT SE9 ... 184 D2
EN EN1 ... 79 N6
KTN/HRWW/WS HA3 ... 94 E1
STALW/RED AL3 ... 38 C5
TOTM N17 ... 99 P10
Lady Somerset Rd KTTN NW5 ... 118 C9
Ladythorpe Cl
ADL/WDHM KT15 ... 94 C8
Ladywalk RKW/CH/CXG WD3 ... 91 H6
Ladywell Cl BROCKY SE4 ... 160 D2
Ladywell Prospect SBW CM21... 30 A2
Ladywell Rd LEW SE13 ... 182 F1
Ladywell St SRTFD E15 ... 141 L1
Ladywood Cl
RKW/CH/CXG WD3 ... 71 L7
Ladywood Av
WIM/MER SW19 ... 179 J7
Ladywood Rd SURB KT6 ... 199 M9
Lafone Av FELT TW13 ... 175 K4
Lafone St STHWK SE1 ... 19 L1
Lagado Ms BERM/RHTH SE16... 140 G10
Lagger Cl CSTG HP8 ... 89 N4
The Lagger CSTG HP8 ... 89 N4
Laglands Cl REIG RH2 ... 257 M8
Lagley Meadow BERK HP4 * ... 33 M4
Lagonda Av BARK/HLT IG6... 103 J7
Lagonda Wy DART DA1 ... 165 K10
Lagoon Rd STMC/STPC BR5... 207 L5
Laidlaw Dr WCHMH N21 ... 78 G9
Laing Cl BARK/HLT IG6 ... 104 D1
Laing Dean NTHLT UB5 ... 133 K3
Laings Av MTCM CR4 ... 202 A1
Lainlock Pl HSLW TW3 ... 153 K7
Lainson St WAND/EARL SW18... 179 K3
Lairdale Cl DUL SE21 ... 181 K4
Laird Av CDW/CHF RM16 ... 168 A1
Lairs Cl HOLWY N7 ... 5 M1
Laitwood Rd BAL SW12 ... 180 C4
Lake Av BMLY BR1 ... 183 M6
RAIN RM13 ... 145 H6
SL SL1 ... 129 J9
Lake Cl BCTR RM8 ... 123 N8
BF/WBF KT14 ... 215 N8
Lakedale Rd
WOOL/PLUM SE18 ... 163 H4
Lake Dr BUSH WD23 ... 94 B3
Lake End Cl MDHD SL6 ... 128 A3
Lake End Rd MDHD SL6 ... 128 A3
WDSR SL4 ... 148 A2
Lakefield Rd WDGN N22 ... 99 J10
Lakefields Cl RAIN RM13 ... 145 J6
Lake Gdns DAGE RM10 ... 124 B10
RCHPK/HAM TW10 ... 176 G6
WLGTN SM6 ... 202 C10
Lakehall Gdns THHTH CR7 ... 203 J5
Lakehall Rd THHTH CR7 ... 203 J5
Lake House Rd WAN E11 ... 122 A4
Lakehurst Rd HOR/WEW KT19... 220 B2
Lakeland Cl CHIG IG7 ... 103 L5
KTN/HRWW/WS HA3 ... 94 D2
Lake La HORL RH6 ... 280 D3
Lakenheath STHGT/OAK N14... 98 G5
Laker Pl PUT/ROE SW15 ... 157 H10
Lakers Ri BNSTD SM7 ... 239 P2
Lakes Cl RGUE GU4 ... 268 E6
Lakeside BECK BR3 ... 204 G3
ENC/FH EN2 ... 78 E6
HOR/WEW KT19 ... 220 B3
RAIN RM13 ... 145 M4
REDH RH1 ... 258 E6
WEY KT13 ... 196 F9
WLGTN SM6 ... 222 C1
Lakeside Av BARK/HLT IG6... 122 A1
THMD SE28 ... 146 A7
Lakeside Cl BFN/LL DA15 ... 185 M1
CHIG IG7 ... 103 L5
RSLP HA4 ... 112 E2
SNWD SE25 ... 203 P2
WOKN/KNAP GU21 ... 231 L6
Lakeside Crs BRW CM14 ... 107 J4
EBAR EN4 ... 78 A4
HAYES BR2 ... 206 B7
SLN SL2 ... 129 L2
WLSDN NW10 ... 135 J6
Lakeside Dr BRW CM14 ... 107 J4
ESH/CLAY KT10 ... 216 G4
HAYES BR2 ... 206 C7
SLN SL2 ... 129 N3
WLSDN NW10 ... 135 J6
Lakeside Gra WEY KT13 ... 196 D10
Lakeside Pl LCOL/BKTW AL2 ... 57 J3
Lakeside Rd CHES/WCR EN8... 62 D4
PLMGR N13 ... 98 G5
WKENS W14 ... 156 A9
Lake View EDGW HA8 ... 95 L6
POTB/CUF EN6 ... 59 M9
Lake View Est BOW E3 * ... 140 F1
Lakeview Rd WELL DA16 ... 163 H10
WNWD SE27 ... 181 H8
Lake View Ter UED N18 * ... 99 N5
Lakis Cl HAMP NW3 ... 117 H9
Laleham Abbey STA TW18 * ... 196 B2
Laleham Av MLHL NW7 ... 96 A1
Laleham Cl STA TW18 ... 195 L1
Laleham Ct SUT SM1 ... 221 N1
Laleham Reach CHERT KT16... 195 L2
Laleham Rd CAT SE6 ... 160 G10
SHPTN TW17 ... 195 M5
STA TW18 ... 173 H9
Lalor St FUL/PGN SW6 ... 157 J7
Lamarsh Rd BMLY BR1 ... 183 L6
Lamb's Cl ED N9 ... 99 P3
Lamberhurst Cl
STMC/STPC BR5 ... 207 N5
Lamberhurst Rd BCTR RM8... 123 P1
WNWD SE27 ... 181 H7
Lamberhurst Wk
CRAWE RH10 ... 284 B8
Lambert Av RCH/KEW TW9 * ... 150 D2
RCH/KEW TW9 ... 156 D1
Lambert Cl BH/WHM TN16 ... 244 A5
Lambert Ct BUSH WD23 ... 73 H7
Lambert Jones Ms
BARB EC2Y * ... 12 E3
Lambert Rd BNSTD SM7 ... 221 K10
BRXS/STRHM SW2 ... 180 B4
CAN/RD E16 ... 141 L8
NFNCH/WDSPK N12 ... 97 H5
Lambert's Pl CROY/NA CRO... 203 L8
Lambert's Rd BRYLDS KT5... 199 K5
Lambert St IS N1 ... 6 A4

Lambert Wy
NFNCH/WDSPK N12 ... 97 M6
Lambeth Br WEST SW1P ... 17 M5
Lambeth High St STHWK SE1 ... 17 L5
Lambeth Palace Rd
STHWK SE1 ... 17 H5
Lambeth Rd CROY/NA CRO... 203 H8
STHWK SE1 ... 17 L6
Lambeth Wk LBTH SE11 ... 17 P5
PECK SE15 ... 159 N8
Lambkins Ms WALTH E17 ... 121 H2
Lamb La HACK E8 ... 140 A2
Lamble St KTTN NW5 ... 118 B9
Lambley Rd DAGW RM9 ... 143 L1
Lambly Hl VW GU25 ... 194 B3
Lambolle Pl HAMP NW3 ... 3 M1
Lambolle Rd HAMP NW3 ... 3 M1
Lambourn Cha HAMP NW3 ... 3 M1
Lambourn Cl HNWL W7 ... 154 E1
KTTN NW5 ... 118 D9
SAND/SEL CR2 ... 221 J5
Lambourne Av
WIM/MER SW19 ... 179 J7
Lambourne Cl CHIG IG7 ... 103 L4
CRAWE RH10 ... 284 A9
Lambourne Ct UX/CGN UB8 ... 131 L5
Lambourne Dr COB KT11 ... 235 K1
Lambourne Gdns BARK IG11... 143 J7
CHING E4 ... 100 F3
EN EN1 ... 79 P6
HCH RM12 ... 125 L7
Lambourne Gv
BERM/RHTH SE16 ... 160 C4
KUT/HW KT1 ... 199 N1
Lambourne Pl BKHTH/KID SE3... 161 P7
Lambourne Rd BARK IG11 ... 143 H7
CHIG IG7 ... 103 M4
GDMY/SEVK IG3 ... 123 H7
WAN E11 ... 121 P1
Lambourn Rd VX/NE SW8 ... 158 C9
Lambrook Ter FUL/PGN SW6... 157 H6
Lambs Cl ED N9 ... 99 P3
POTB/CUF EN6 ... 60 G5
Lamb's Conduit Pas
FSBYW WC1X ... 11 N3
Lamb's Conduit St
BMSBY WC1N ... 11 N2
Lambscroft Wy
CFSP/GDCR SL9 ... 90 B10
Lambs Green Rd HORS RH12... 282 B10
Lamb's La North RAIN RM13... 145 L4
Lamb's La South RAIN RM13... 145 K6
Lambs Meadow WFD IG8 ... 102 A10
Lambs Ms IS N1 ... 6 C6
Lamb's Pas STLK EC1Y ... 12 G2
Lamb St WCHPL E1 ... 13 L3
Lambs Wk ENC/FH EN2 ... 79 K6
Lambton Av CHES/WCR EN8... 62 C9
Lambton Pl NTGHL W11 ... 8 D7
Lambton Rd ARCH N19 ... 118 F7
RYNPK SW20 ... 200 F1
Lamerock Rd BMLY BR1 ... 183 M8
Lamerton Rd BARK/HLT IG6... 102 F10
Lamerton St DEPT SE8 ... 160 F5
Lamford Cl TOTM N17 ... 99 P5
Lamington St HMSMTH W6... 157 H7
Lamlash St LBTH SE11 ... 18 C5
Lammas Av MTCM CR4 ... 202 B1
Lammas Cl STA TW18 ... 172 E4
Lammas Dr STA TW18 ... 172 G7
Lammas La ESH/CLAY KT10... 217 P1
Lammasmead BROX EN10 ... 43 P2
Lammas Park Gdns EA W5... 135 H10
Lammas Park Rd EA W5 ... 136 A10
Lammas Rd HOM E9 ... 140 G1
LEY E10 ... 120 D7
RCHPK/HAM TW10 ... 176 G10
WATW WD18 ... 72 K9
Lammermoor Rd BAL SW12 *... 180 C3
Lamont Rd WBPTN SW10 ... 15 H10
Lamont Road Pas
WBPTN SW10 ... 15 L10
Lampard Gv STNW/STAM N16... 119 P7
Lampern Sq BETH E2 ... 7 P9
Lampeter Cl HMSMTH W6 ... 14 A10
Lamplighter Cl WCHPL E1 ... 140 E10
Lamplighters Cl WAB EN9 ... 63 M10
Lampmead Rd LEE/GVPK SE12... 161 P9
Lamport Cl WOOL/PLUM SE18... 146 E9
Lampton Av HSLW TW3 ... 153 P7
Lampton House Cl
WIM/MER SW19 ... 178 A8
Lampton Park Rd HSLW TW3... 154 A8
Lampton Rd HEST TW5 ... 154 A6
HSLW TW3 ... 154 A8
Lamsey Rd HHS/BOV HP3 ... 35 N8
Lamson Rd RAIN RM13 ... 144 G6
Lanacre Av CDALE/KGS NW9... 96 E10
Lanadron Cl ISLW TW7 ... 154 A9
Lanark Cl EA W5 ... 135 H1
Lanark Pl MV/WKIL W9 ... 2 E9
Lanark Rd MV/WKIL W9 ... 2 C9
Lanark Sq POP/IOD E14 ... 160 C2
Lanata Wk YEAD UB4 * ... 133 H4
Lanbury Rd PECK SE15 ... 160 C10
Lancashire Ct
MYFR/PKLN W1K ... 10 E7
Lancaster Av BARK IG11 ... 143 H7
EBAR EN4 ... 77 N4
GU GU2 ... 268 C2
MTCM CR4 ... 202 E5
SLN SL2 ... 129 N6
WAN E11 ... 121 M2
WIM/MER SW19 ... 178 A2
WNWD SE27 ... 181 K6
Lancaster Cl ASHF TW15 ... 175 K6
BRW CM15 ... 78 L6
CDALE/KGS NW9 ... 96 E6
CRAWE RH10 ... 284 E6
EGH TW20 ... 172 A7
HAYES BR2 ... 205 L4
KUTN/CMB KT2 ... 177 H1
STWL/WRAY TW19 ... 152 A7
WOKN/KNAP GU21 ... 231 L3
Lancaster Cottages
RCHPK/HAM TW10 * ... 176 A8
Lancaster Ct BAY/PAD W2 ... 8 F8
FUL/PGN SW6 ... 157 K5
WOT/HER KT12 ... 197 J6
Lancaster Dr CRICK NW2 *... 84 C9
HCH RM12 ... 125 N2
HHS/BOV HP3 ... 52 C9
LOU IG10 ... 88 B10
POP/IOD E14 ... 141 N10
Lancaster Gdns
BRYLDS KT5 ... 199 H8
KUTN/CMB KT2 ... 177 H1
WEA W13 ... 135 H6
WIM/MER SW19 ... 178 A2
Lancaster Ga BAY/PAD W2 ... 8 F7
Lancaster Gv HAMP NW3 ... 3 M2
Lancaster House
WOOL/PLUM SE18 * ... 162 G6
Lancaster Ms BAY/PAD W2... 8 F7
RCHPK/HAM TW10 * ... 176 A8
WAND/EARL SW18 ... 179 N3
Lancaster Pk
RCHPK/HAM TW10 ... 176 A8
Lancaster Pl COVGDN WC2E... 11 L8

TPL/STR WC2R ... 11 N7
TWK TW1 ... 155 N9
WIM/MER SW19 ... 178 C8
Langdon Park Rd HGT N6 ... 118 C5
Langdon Pl MORT/ESHN SW14... 155 P8
Langdon Rd EHAM E6 ... 142 D7
HAYES BR2 ... 205 N3
MRDN SM4 ... 201 M5
Langdon Shaw SCUP DA14 ... 186 A1
Langdon Wk MRDN SM4 ... 201 M5
Langdon Wy STHWK SE1 ... 19 P3
Langfield Cl WAB EN9 ... 45 K8
Langford Cl HACK E8 ... 119 M4
SEVS/STOTM N15 ... 119 M4
STALE/WH AL4 ... 39 H4
STJWD NW8 ... 3 K7
Langford Crs EBAR EN4 ... 78 A4
Langford Gn CMBW SE5 ... 159 L4
Langford Pl SCUP DA14 ... 185 K6
STJWD NW8 ... 3 K8
Langford Rd EBAR EN4 ... 78 A4
FUL/PGN SW6 ... 157 L8
WFD IG8 ... 101 P7
Langfords BKHH IG9 ... 102 A3
Langham Cl STALE/WH AL4 ... 39 H4
Langham Ct EMPK RM11 ... 125 L5
RSLP HA4 ... 113 J10
Langham Dene PUR/KEN CR8... 241 K5
Langham Gdns EA W5 ... 135 H3
GDMY/SEVK IG3 ... 123 L4
RCHPK/HAM TW10 ... 176 A7
WCHMH N21 ... 79 H9
WEA W13 ... 135 G9
Langham House Cl
RCHPK/HAM TW10 ... 176 A7
Langham Pde
SEVS/STOTM N15 * ... 119 J7
Langham Park Pl HAYES BR2... 205 L4
Langham Pl CHSWK W4 ... 156 C5
EGH TW20 ... 172 C5
REGST W1B ... 10 E4
SEVS/STOTM N15 ... 119 J7
Langham Rd EDGW HA8 ... 95 P7
RYNPK SW20 ... 200 F1
SEVS/STOTM N15 ... 119 K2
TEDD TW11 ... 176 C7
Langham St REGST W1B ... 10 E4
Langhedge Cl UED N18 ... 99 N7
Langhedge La UED N18 ... 99 N8
Langholm Cl BAL SW12 ... 180 E3
Langholme BUSH WD23 ... 94 B3
Langhorne Dr DAGE RM10 ... 144 B2
Langhorne Rd DAGE RM10 ... 144 B2
Langhurst La CRAWW RH11... 282 D5
Langland Crs STAN HA7 ... 95 J10
Langland Dr PIN HA5 ... 93 M8
Langland Gdns CROY/NA CRO... 204 G1
HAMP NW3 ... 117 H10
Langlands Ri RDART DA2 ... 188 D3
Langlands Ri HOR/WEW KT19... 219 P3
Langler Rd WLSDN NW10 ... 136 F4
Langley Av CRAWW RH11... 283 M5
SURB KT6 ... 199 H7
WPK KT4 ... 200 G7
Langley Broom
DTCH/LGLY SL3 ... 150 C4
Langleybury La KGLGY WD4... 54 C10
RKW/CH/CXG WD3 ... 72 C3
Langley Cl EPSOM KT18 ... 238 A5
GU GU1 ... 249 P9
HARH RM3 ... 105 L8
Langley Ct BECK BR3 * ... 204 G4
CHESW EN7 ... 61 K4
COVGDN WC2E ... 11 L7
Langley Crs DAGW RM9 ... 143 M3
EDGW HA8 ... 95 P4
HYS/HAR UB3 ... 153 H4
KGLGY WD4 ... 54 B6
STALE/WH AL4 ... 38 B4
WAN E11 ... 121 N5
Langley Dr ACT W3 ... 155 N1
BRW CM14 ... 106 F4
CRAWW RH11 ... 283 M5
WAN E11 ... 121 N5
Langley Gdns DAGW RM9 ... 143 M3
STMC/STPC BR5 ... 206 E6
Langley Gn CRAWW RH11 ... 283 J8
Langley Gv NWMAL KT3 ... 185 K9
Langley Hill Cl KGLGY WD4 ... 54 B6
Langley Hill KGLGY WD4 ... 54 B6
Langley La ABLGY WD5 ... 54 A4
VX/NE SW8 ... 17 M9
Langley Lodge La KGLGY WD4... 53 P7
Langley Oaks Av
SAND/SEL CR2 ... 223 J7
Langley Pde CRAWW RH11 *... 283 H6
Langley Pk MLHL NW7 ... 96 B6
Langley Park Rd BELMT SM2... 221 M6
DTCH/LGLY SL3 ... 150 D1
Langley Quay
DTCH/LGLY SL3 ... 150 D1
Langley Rd ABLGY WD5 ... 53 D1
BECK BR3 ... 204 B3
DTCH/LGLY SL3 ... 149 M2
ISLW TW7 ... 154 A8
KGLGY WD4 ... 53 P8
SAND/SEL CR2 ... 224 C7
STA TW18 ... 173 H7
SURB KT6 ... 199 L7
WAT WD17 ... 72 G4
WELL DA16 ... 163 M5
WIM/MER SW19 ... 201 P1
Langley Rw BAR EN5 ... 76 B1
Langley St LSO/SEVD WC2H * ... 11 L6
Langley Vale Rd EPSOM KT18... 238 C9
Langley Wk WAT WD17 ... 72 G4
WOKS/MYFD GU22 ... 229 N9
Langley Whf KGLGY WD4 ... 54 B6
Langley Wd BECK BR3 * ... 205 K6
Langmans Wy
WOKN/KNAP GU21 ... 231 K2
Langmead Dr BUSH WD23 ... 94 C2
Langmead St WNWD SE27 * ... 181 J7
Langport Ct WOT/HER KT12... 197 K6
Langridge Ms HPTN TW12 ... 175 J9
Langroyd Rd TOOT SW17 ... 180 A5
Langshott Cl ADL/WDHM KT15... 215 N8
Langshott HORL RH6 ... 280 D4
Langshott La HORL RH6 ... 280 D3
Langside Av PUT/ROE SW15... 156 G9
Langside Crs STHGT/OAK N14... 98 G4
Langston Hughes Cl
HNHL SE24 * ... 159 N6
Langston Rd LOU IG10 ... 82 G8
Langthorne Crs GRAYS RM17... 167 P3
Langthorne Rd LEW SE13 ... 183 M4
WAN E11 ... 121 P4
Langthorne St FUL/PGN SW6... 157 G5
Langton Av EHAM E6 ... 142 G3
EW KT17 ... 220 E10
TRDG/WHET N20 ... 97 M1
Langton Cl ADL/WDHM KT15... 195 K10
FSBYW WC1X ... 5 P9
WOKN/KNAP GU21 ... 231 L5
Langton Ri EDUL SE22 ... 181 M1
Langton Rd BRXN/ST SW9 ... 159 L5
CRICK NW2 ... 84 B6
E/WMO/HCT KT8 ... 197 N8
HOD EN11 ... 45 H4
KTN/HRWW/WS HA3 ... 94 D7
Langton's Meadow SLN SL2... 129 H1
Langton St WBPTN SW10 ... 15 H10

Langton Vls TOTM N17 * 99 P9
Langton Wy BKHTH/KID SE3 161 M6
CDW/CHF RM16 168 D7
CROY/NA CRO 223 M1
EGH TW20 172 F9
Langtry Rd KIL/WHAMP NW6 2 C6
NTHLT UB5 133 L4
Langtry Wk STJWD NW8 3 K4
Langwood Cha TEDD TW11 177 H9
Langwood Cl ASHTD KT21 237 J5
Langwood Gdns WAT WD17 75 H5
Langworth Dr YEAD UB4 133 J2
Lanhill Rd MV/WKIL W9 8 E1
Lanier Rd LEW SE13 183 H1
Lanigan Dr HSLW TW3 176 A1
Lankaster Gdns EFNCH N2 97 H9
Lankers Dr RYLN/HDSTN HA2 113 N4
Lankton Cl BECK BR3 205 H1
Lannock Rd HYS/HAR UB3 132 G10
Lannoy Rd ELTH/MOT SE9 184 F4
Lanrick Copse BERK 34 B4
Lanrick Rd POP/IOD E14 161 J7
Lanridge Rd ABYW SE2 143 K3
Lansbury Av BARK IG11 111 K4
CHDH RM6 123 P3
EBED/NFELT TW14 175 J2
UED N18 99 L6
Lansbury Cl WLSDN NW10 115 G9
Lansbury Dr YEAD UB4 132 G2
Lansbury Gdns POP/IOD E14 * 141 J8
Lansbury Rd PEND EN3 30 C5
Lansbury Wy UED N18 99 M9
Lanscombe Wk VX/NE SW8 * 158 F6
Lansdell Rd MTCM CR4 202 B2
Lansdown GU GU1 250 D10
Lansdowne Av WOKN/KNAP GU21 231 N5
WOT/HER KT12 197 K8
ORP BR6 206 E9
SL SL1 129 K10
Lansdowne Cl BRYLDS KT5 191 N9
SL SL1 129 K10
TWK TW1 176 E4
Lansdowne Copse WPK KT4 * 200 D1
Lansdowne Ct BROX EN10 * 44 F6
SL SL1 129 K10
WPK KT4 200 D1
Lansdowne Crs NTGHL W11 8 B8
Lansdowne Dr HACK E8 7 J2
Lansdowne Gdns VX/NE SW8 158 F6
Lansdowne Gn VX/NE SW8 158 F6
Lansdowne Gv WLSDN NW10 116 B9
Lansdowne La CHARL SE7 162 A4
Lansdowne Ms CHARL SE7 162 A3
NTGHL W11 8 C10
Lansdowne Pl NRWD SE19 181 J6
STHWK SE1 19 H1
Lansdowne Ri NTGHL W11 8 A9
Lansdowne Rd BMLY BR1 183 M10
CHING E4 100 F3
CROY/NA CRO 203 L8
CSHM HP5 51 K5
FNCH N3 97 J8
GDMY/SEVK IG3 123 J6
HOR/WEW KT19 219 P4
HSLW TW3 154 A9
MUSWH N10 98 D10
NTGHL W11 8 B8
PUR/KEN CR8 223 H8
RYNPK SW20 178 F10
SEV TN13 247 L8
STA TW18 173 L10
STAN HA7 95 H7
SWFD E18 121 M1
TOTM N17 99 H8
UX/CGN UB8 132 C8
WALTH E17 120 F4
WAN E11 121 L7
Lansdowne Sq GVW DA11 191 J7
Lansdowne Ter BMSBY WC1N 11 M2
Lansdowne Wy VX/NE SW8 158 F7
Lansdown Wood Cl WNWD SE27 * 181 J6
Lansdown Pl GVW DA11 190 C4
FSTGT E7 141 P2
SCUP DA14 186 B5
TIL RM18 168 C8
Lansfield Av UED N18 99 P5
Lantern Cl ALP/SUD HA0 115 J3
ORP BR6 206 E9
PUT/ROE SW15 156 D10
Lanterns LOU IG10 82 C5
Lanterns Ct POP/IOD E14 160 F2
Lantern Wy WDR/YW UB7 151 P1
Lanthorn Cl BROX EN10 44 D5
Lant St STHWK SE1 18 E1
Lanvanor Rd PECK SE15 160 B8
Lapford Cl MV/WKIL W9 8 B1
Lapis Cl GVE DA12 191 L4
La Plata Gv BRW CM14 106 C4
Lapse Wood Wk FSTH SE23 182 A4
Lapstone Gdns KTN/HRWW/WS HA3 135 H4
Lapwing Cl ERITH DA8 * 165 H4
HHNE HP2 35 P7
SAND/SEL CR2 224 D6
Lapwing Ct SURB KT6 * 210 C8
Lapwing Pl GSTN WD25 75 N10
Lapwings HART DA3 211 N3
Lapwing Ter FSTGT E7 122 A10
Lapwing Wy ABLGY WD5 59 M1
YEAD UB4 133 L8
Lapworth Cl ORP BR6 207 M9
Lara Cl CHSGTN KT9 219 K14
Larbert Rd STRHM/NOR SW16 202 D1
Larch Av ACT W3 117 H7
ASC SL5 192 C5
GU GU1 249 P7
LCOL/BKTW AL2 55 N6
Larch Cl BAL SW12 180 C5
CHESW EN7 61 N4
DEPT SE8 160 L5
FBAR/BDGN N11 98 E8
KWD/TDW/WH KT20 239 M7
REDH RH1 275 M2
SLN SU2 128 G7
WARL CR6 242 C6
Larch Crs HOR/WEW KT19 219 N3
YEAD UB4 133 K6
Larch Dene ORP BR6 206 F9
Larch Dr CHSWK W4 * 155 N3
Larches Av EN EN1 80 B1
MORT/ESHN SW14 156 A2
The Larches BERK HP4 33 J4
BUSH WD23 76 C7
HGDN/ICK UB10 132 B6
PLMGR N13 99 K4
STALE/WH AL4 21 H3
Larch Gv BFN/LL DA15 185 J4
Larchmoor Pk SLN SU2 128 C5
Larch Ri BERK HP4 33 H4
Larch Rd CRICK NW2 116 F1
LEY E10 120 F7
Larch Tree Wy CROY/NA CRO 205 H10
Larch Wy HAYES BR2 206 D7
Larchwood Av CRW RM5 104 C2
Larchwood Cl BNSTD SM7 241 K6
CRW RM5 104 D2
Larchwood Rd ECH TW20 171 N9
Larchwood Gdns BRWN CM15 104 F1
Larchwood Rd ELTH/MOT SE9 184 F8
HHNE HP2 36 A4
WOKN/KNAP GU21 231 H6
Larcombe Cl CROY/NA CRO 223 N3
Larcom St WALW SE17 18 F7
Larden Rd ACT W3 117 H7
Largewood Av SURB KT6 210 D5
Larissa St WALW SE17 * 19 H7
Larkbere Rd SYD SE26 182 G3
Lark Cl BRW CM14 106 G5

Larken Cl BUSH WD23 94 B2
Larken Dr BUSH WD23 94 B2
Larkfield COB KT11 217 H10
Larkfield Av KTN/HRWW/WS HA3 114 C1
Larkfield Cl HORL RH6 281 H4
Larkfield Rd RCH/KEW TW9 155 N10
SCUP DA14 185 J8
SEV TN13 246 D10
Larkfields GVW DA11 190 B6
Larkhall Cl WALTH E17 * 217 K3
Larkhall La CLAP SW4 158 A4
Larkhall Ri CLAP SW4 158 D9
Larkham Cl FELT TW13 174 F6
Larkhill Ter WOOL/PLUM SE18 * 162 D6
Larkin Cl COUL/CHIP CR5 240 G3
RBRW/HUT CM13 107 P1
Larkings La SLN SU2 129 N3
Larkins Rd HORL RH6 279 N8
Lark Ri CRAWW RH11 283 H6
EHSLY KT24 252 F7
HAT AL10 40 D6
Larksfield HORL RH6 280 C3
Larks Fld HART DA3 211 L4
Larks Fld EN EN1 29 N1
Larks Gv BARK IG11 143 H2
Larkshall Crs CHING E4 101 K5
Larkshall Rd CHING E4 101 K6
Larkspur Cl CDALE/KGS NW9 115 N3
HHW HP1 35 H5
ORP BR6 207 M9
RSLP HA4 113 C5
SOCK/AV RM15 147 N5
Larkspur Gv EDGW HA8 95 P5
Larkspur Wy HOR/WEW KT19 219 P2
RDKG RH5 273 J5
Larks Rdg LCOL/BKTW AL2 55 P2
Larks Ri CSHM HP5 51 J9
Larks Wy WOKN/KNAP GU21 231 H10
Larkswood HLWE CM17 47 M3
Larkswood Cl ERITH DA8 165 N4
Larkswood Ri PIN HA5 113 K2
STALE/WH AL4 39 H1
Larkswood Rd CHING E4 100 F5
Lark Wy CAR SM5 201 P7
Larkway Cl CDALE/KGS NW9 116 A2
Larkwell La HART DA3 211 L4
Larmans Rd PEND EN3 80 B2
Larnach Rd HMSMTH W6 156 G5
Larne Rd RSLP HA4 112 G5
Larner Rd ERITH DA8 164 F6
La Roche Cl DTCH/LGLY SL3 149 P2
Larpent Av PUT/ROE SW15 157 H5
Larsen Dr WAB EN9 63 J10
Larwood Cl EGH/PVL UB6 114 C10
Lascelles Av HRW HA1 114 C5
Lascelles Cl BRWN CM15 86 G9
WAN E11 121 J7
Lascelles Rd DTCH/LGLY SL3 149 N2
Lascott's Rd WDGN N22 98 G7
Lashmere CRAWE RH10 285 L2
Lassa Rd ELTH/MOT SE9 184 B1
Lassell St GNWCH SE10 161 K4
Lasswade Rd CHERT KT16 195 J7
Lastingham Ct STA TW18 175 K9
Latchett Rd SWFD E18 101 N9
Latchford Pl CHIG IG7 103 L5
Latchingdon Gdns WFD IG8 102 B7
Latchmere Cl RCHPK/HAM TW10 177 K8
Latchmere La KUTN/CMB KT2 177 L5
Latchmere Rd BTSEA SW11 158 E2
KUTN/CMB KT2 177 L9
Latchmere St BTSEA SW11 158 A8
Latchmoor Av CFSP/GDCR SL9 110 A2
Latchmoor Gv CFSP/GDCR SL9 110 A2
Latchmoor Wy CFSP/GDCR SL9 110 A2
Lateward Rd BTFD TW8 155 J7
Latham Cl BH/WHM TN16 243 P12
EHAM E6 142 B8
RDART DA2 188 D3
Latham Pl UPMR RM14 126 B5
Latham Rd BXLYHS DA6 186 B1
TWK TW1 176 B5
Latham's Wy CROY/NA CRO 202 G8
Lathkill Cl EN EN1 99 P1
Lathom Rd EHAM E6 142 C2
Latimer Av EHAM E6 142 C3
Latimer Cl AMS HP6 69 N5
CRAWW RH11 283 N4
HHNE HP2 36 C1
PIN HA5 93 K9
WATW WD18 92 F1
WOKS/MYFD GU22 229 K9
WPK KT4 200 E1
Latimer Ct REDH RH1 276 A2
Latimer Dr HCH RM12 125 L8
Latimer Gdns PIN HA5 93 K9
Latimer Pl NKENS W10 139 G1
Latimer Rd BAR EN5 77 L7
CROY/NA CRO * 203 J10
CSHM HP5 51 K10
FSTGT E7 121 P10
NKENS W10 139 G1
RKW/CH/CXG WD3 70 C4
SEVS/STOTM N15 119 M4
TEDD TW11 176 B8
WIM/MER SW19 178 A9
Latimer Wy BEAC HP9 88 B5
Latium Cl STAL AL1 38 C7
Latona Ct VGE DA12 191 J8
Latona Dr VGE DA12 191 K9
La Tourne Gdns ORP BR6 206 F10
Lattimer Pl CHSWK W4 156 B6
Lattimore Rd STAL AL1 38 D7
STALE/WH AL4 21 H3
Latton Cl ESH/CLAY KT10 218 L4
WOT/HER KT12 197 N7
Latton Gn HLWS CM18 47 L10
Latton Hall Cl HLW CM20 29 K10
Latton House HLWS CM18 * 47 L4
Latton St HLW CM20 47 L3
HLWE CM17 47 L2
Latymer Cl WEY KT13 216 D1
Latymer Gdns FNCH N3 * 97 H10
Latymer Rd ED N9 99 N13
Latymer Wy ED N9 99 L3
Laubin Cl TWK TW1 154 G10
Laud Dr CRAWE RH10 284 E10
Lauder Cl NTHLT UB5 133 J4
Lauderdale Dr RCHPK/HAM TW10 177 K8
Lauderdale Pde MV/WKIL W9 * 2 G10
Lauderdale Pl BARB EC2Y * 12 F4
Lauderdale Rd KGLGY WD4 54 D7
MV/WKIL W9 3 H10
Laud St CROY/NA CRO 203 A10
LBTH SE11 17 N7
Laughton Ct BORE WD6 * 77 N1
Laughton Rd NTHLT UB5 133 H4
Launcelot Rd BMLY BR1 183 N1
Launcelot St STHWK SE1 * 18 A2
Launceston CFSP/GDCR SL9 * 110 B9
Launceston Gdns GFD/PVL UB6 115 N6
Launceston Pl KENS W8 14 D2
Launceston Rd GFD/PVL UB6 115 N6
Launch St POP/IOD E14 161 N2
Launders Ga ACT W3 * 155 N1
Launders La RAIN RM13 145 J2
Laundress La STNW/STAM N16 119 G1
Laundry La SUN TW16 196 B2
Laundry Ms FSTH SE23 182 C1
Laundry Rd GU GU1 267 P9
HMSMTH W6 14 A10
Laura Cl EN EN1 79 M9

WAN E11 121 P3
Lauradale Rd EFNCH N2 118 A2
Laura Dr SWLY BR8 187 H8
Laura Pl CLPT E5 120 B9
Laura Ter FSBYPK N4 * 119 J7
Laureate Wy HHW HP1 35 M2
Laurel Av DTCH/LGLY SL3 150 B1
EGH TW20 171 N8
GVE DA12 191 P5
POTB/CUF EN6 59 J8
TWK TW1 176 E4
Laurel Bank CHOB/PIR GU24 * 213 N6
HHS/BOV HP3 35 J10
NFNCH/WDSPK N12 * 97 N5
Laurel Bank Gdns FUL/PGN SW6 157 J8
Laurel Bank Rd ENC/FH EN2 79 K5
Laurel Cl BARK/HLT IG6 102 F7
BFN/LL DA15 185 K6
CRAWE RH10 284 B10
DTCH/LGLY SL3 151 H6
HHW HP1 35 H5
OXHEY WD19 93 L1
RBRW/HUT CM13 87 N9
TOOT SW17 179 P8
Laurel Crs CROY/NA CRO 204 F10
ROMW/RG RM7 124 C5
WOKN/KNAP GU21 231 H10
Laureldene RGUW GU5 248 A10
Laurel Dr OXTED RH8 261 L7
SOCK/AV RM15 147 J6
Laurel Flds POTB/CUF EN6 59 J7
Laurel Gdns BMLY BR1 206 B4
CHING E4 100 C1
HNWL W7 136 A10
HSLWW TW4 153 M10
MLHL NW7 96 A4
Laurel Gv PGE/AN SE20 182 A10
SYD SE26 182 G8
Laurel La WDR/YW UB7 151 P5
Laurel Pk KTN/HRWW/WS HA3 94 B3
Laurel Rd BARN SW13 156 D8
HPTN TW12 176 C1
RYNPK SW20 200 D1
STAL AL1 38 B5
Laurels Cl STALW/RED AL3 38 D1
The Laurels BERK HP4 34 E3
BNSTD SM7 239 J3
BORE WD6 * 75 M5
BRXN/ST SW9 * 159 M3
COB KT11 217 J5
CHESW EN7 61 N3
HART DA2 211 P3
RDART DA2 * 187 K6
Laurel St HACK E8 7 M2
Laurel Vw NFNCH/WDSPK N12 * 97 M4
Laurel Vls HNWL W7 * 154 D1
Laurel Wy SWFD E18 121 L2
TRDG/WHET N20 97 K4
Laurence Ms SHB W12 156 D1
Laurence Pountney Hl CANST EC4R * 12 G7
Laurence Pountney La CANST EC4R 12 G7
Laurie Gv NWCR SE14 160 D7
Laurie Rd HNWL W7 134 D7
Laurier Rd CROY/NA CRO 203 N7
KTTN NW5 118 C2
Lauries Cl HHW HP1 * 34 E8
Laurimel Cl STAN HA7 94 C5
Laurino Pl BUSH WD23 * 94 B3
Lauriston Cl WOKN/KNAP GU21 231 H10
Lauriston Rd HOM E9 140 C2
WIM/MER SW19 178 C10
Lausanne Rd CEND/HSY/T N8 99 H5
PECK SE15 160 B7
Lauser Rd STWL/WRAY TW19 173 M3
Laustan Cl GU GU1 250 F4
Lavant St CRAWW RH11 283 J8
Lavender Av CDALE/KGS NW9 115 P6
MTCM CR4 201 P7
WPK KT4 200 G1
Lavender Cl CAR SM5 222 B1
CHEL SW3 15 M10
CHESW EN7 61 N3
CHING E4 100 F5
COUL/CHIP CR5 * 240 D5
CTHM CR3 259 K4
HART DA3 211 N3
HAYES BR2 206 B6
HLW CM20 29 H10
LHD/OX KT22 237 K7
REDH RH1 276 C6
SOCK/AV RM15 147 K5
Lavender Cots LHD/OX KT22 * 237 K7
Lavender Ct E/WMO/HCT KT8 * 198 A3
Lavender Crs STALW/RED AL3 38 B2
Lavender Dr UX/CGN UB8 131 N3
Lavender Gdns EN EN2 29 N5
HARH RM3 105 J1
KTN/HRWW/WS HA3 94 D7
Lavender Ga LHD/OX KT22 218 A9
Lavender Gv HACK E8 7 M2
MTCM CR4 201 P7
Lavender Hl BTSEA SW11 158 E8
ENC/FH EN2 79 M1
SWLY BR8 208 A3
Lavender Park Rd BF/WBF KT14 215 K9
Lavender Pl IL IG1 123 P9
WHTN TW2 * 176 B2
Lavender Rd BERM/RHTH SE16 140 D10
BTSEA SW11 158 C9
CAR SM5 202 D2
CROY/NA CRO 202 G4
ENC/FH EN2 79 L1
HOR/WEW KT19 219 N3
SUT SM1 221 P1
UX/CGN UB8 132 A7
WOKS/MYFD GU22 229 N7
Lavender Sweep BTSEA SW11 158 E9
Lavender Ter BTSEA SW11 * 157 P9
Lavender Vw WLGTN SM6 222 G3
Lavender Wk BTSEA SW11 158 A10
HHNE HP2 35 N6
Lavengro Rd WNWD SE27 181 N5
Lavenham Rd WAND/EARL SW18 179 J4
Lavernock Rd BXLYHN DA7 164 A8
Laverstock STRHM/NOR SW16 * 119 J8
Laverstoke Gdns PUT/ROE SW15 178 C3
Laverton Ms ECT SW5 15 H5
Laverton Pl ECT SW5 15 H5
Lavidge Rd ELTH/MOT SE9 184 B1
Lavina Gv IS N1 5 N1
Lavington Cl CRAWW RH11 283 H6
HOM E9 140 E1
Lavington Rd CROY/NA CRO 202 G10
WEA W13 135 K5
Lavington St STHWK SE1 * 12 D9
Lavinia Av GSTN WD25 55 K10
Lavrock La RKW/CH/CXG WD3 71 H10
Lawbrook La SHGR GU5 270 A10
Lawdon Gdns CROY/NA CRO 223 J2
Lawford Av RKW/CH/CXG WD3 70 A2
Lawford Cl HCH RM12 125 A6
RKW/CH/CXG WD3 70 A2
Lawford Gdns PUR/KEN CR8 241 J6
DART DA1 168 C8
Lawford Rd CHSWK W4 156 A5
IS N1 6 G2
KTTN NW5 4 E2
Lawford's Hill Rd RGUW GU3 231 H10

Lawkland SLN SU2 129 H5
Lawless St POP/IOD E14 * 140 G9
Lawman Ct RCH/KEW TW9 98 C1
Lawn Av WDR/YW UB7 151 M1
Lawn Cl BMLY BR1 183 N10
DTCH/LGLY SL3 150 B1
EN EN1 99 N1
NWMAL KT3 185 B3
RSLP HA4 112 G8
SWLY BR8 208 D2
Lawn Crs RCH/KEW TW9 155 M8
Lawn Farm Gv CHDH RM6 124 A10
Lawn Gdns HNWL W7 135 D10
Lawn House Cl POP/IOD E14 161 N1
Lawn La VX/NE SW8 17 N8
Lawn Pk SEV TN13 265 J5
Lawn Rd BECK BR3 182 E10
GUW GU2 267 P3
GVW DA11 189 P2
NWMAL KT3 * 118 A10
UX/CGN UB8 131 M2
Lawns Ct WBLY HA9 * 115 M7
Lawns Crs GRAYS RM17 168 A5
Lawnsmead SHGR GU5 268 E3
Lawns Pl GRAYS RM17 * 168 A5
The Lawns BELMT SM2 221 H4
BKHTH/KID SE3 161 L9
BRW CM14 * 107 K6
CHING E4 100 F4
DTCH/LGLY SL3 * 151 H7
HHW HP1 35 H5
NRWD SE19 203 L1
PIN HA5 94 A8
SCUP DA14 186 C3
STALW/RED AL3 38 B5
Lawns Wy CRW RM5 104 D8
Lawnswood BAR EN5 * 77 H9
Lawn Ter BKHTH/KID SE3 161 J9
The Lawn DTCH/LGLY SL3 149 P7
NWDGN UB2 153 P4
Lawn V PIN HA5 93 L10
Lawrance Gdns CHES/WGR EN8 62 C4
Lawrence Rd HERT/BAY SG13 * 24 A6
Lawrence Sq GVW DA11 190 G3
Lawrence Av MLHL NW7 96 A3
MNPK E12 122 D9
NWMAL KT3 200 A6
PLMGR N13 99 J5
WALTH E17 100 C9
WLSDN NW10 136 A3
Lawrence Blds STNW/STAM N16 119 N8
Lawrence Campe Cl TRDG/WHET N20 * 97 N4
Lawrence Cl HMSMTH W6 156 A10
OXHEY WD19 * 93 L4
SEVS/STOTM N15 * 119 M2
SHB W12 136 E9
Lawrence Ct MLHL NW7 * 96 B6
OXHEY WD19 * 93 L4
Lawrence Crs BFOR GU20 212 C3
DAGE RM10 124 C8
EDGW HA8 * 95 N9
Lawrence Dr HGDN/ICK UB10 112 D9
Lawrence Gdns MLHL NW7 96 A3
TIL RM18 168 E6
Lawrence Hl CHING E4 100 F3
Lawrence La CITYW EC2V 12 F6
BRKHM/BTCW RH3 256 G8
Lawrence Moorings SBW CM21 * 30 A1
Lawrence Pde ISLW TW7 * 154 A9
Lawrence Pl IS N1 * 5 M5
Lawrence Rd EA W5 155 K1
EHAM E6 142 B3
ERITH DA8 164 C6
GPK RM2 125 J3
HPTN TW12 175 N10
HSLWW TW4 153 K10
PIN HA5 113 L5
PLSTW E13 141 N3
RCHPK/HAM TW10 176 F7
SEVS/STOTM N15 119 M1
SNWD SE25 203 N4
UED N18 100 A5
WWKM BR4 225 M1
YEAD UB4 132 D4
Lawrence St CAN/RD E16 141 L7
CHEL SW3 15 N10
MLHL NW7 96 C5
Lawrence Wy SL SL1 128 B7
WLSDN NW10 115 J6
Lawrence Yd SEVS/STOTM N15 119 M2
Lawrie Park Av SYD SE26 182 B9
Lawrie Park Crs SYD SE26 182 B9
Lawrie Park Gdns SYD SE26 182 B8
Lawrie Park Rd SYD SE26 182 C10
Laws Cl SNWD SE25 203 L4
Lawson Cl CAN/RD E16 141 P7
IL IG1 122 G10
WIM/MER SW19 178 C6
Lawson Gdns PIN HA5 93 K9
Lawson Rd DART DA1 165 L10
PEND EN3 30 B5
STHL UB1 133 N6
Lawson Ter SHGR GU5 * 268 E10
Lawson Wy ASC SL5 * 192 A6
Law St STHWK SE1 19 H3
Lawton Rd BOW E3 140 G1
EBAR EN4 77 N1
LEY E10 121 H6
LOU IG10 82 G7
Laxcon Cl WLSDN NW10 116 A9
Laxey Rd ORP BR6 227 J3
Laxley Cl CMBW SE5 159 J6
Laxton Gdns REDH RH1 258 F3
Laxton Pl CAMTN NW1 4 D3
Layard Rd BERM/RHTH SE16 160 A3
EN EN1 29 N5
THHTH CR7 203 L2
Layard Sq BERM/RHTH SE16 160 A3
Layborne Av HARH RM3 105 K3
Lay Brook STALE/WH AL4 21 J2
Layburn Crs DTCH/LGLY SL3 150 D3
Laycock St IS N1 6 A1
Layer Gdns ACT W3 136 M9
Layfield Cl HDN NW4 116 A5
Layfield Crs HDN NW4 116 A5
Layfield Rd HDN NW4 116 A5
Layhams Rd HAYES BR2 225 K1
WWKM BR4 225 H4
Layhill HHNE HP2 35 N4
Laymarsh Cl BELV DA17 164 A3
Laymead Cl NTHLT UB5 133 J4
Laystall St FSBYW WC1X * 12 A1
Layters Av CFSP/GDCR SL9 89 P7
Layters Av South CFSP/GDCR SL9 89 P7
Layters Cl CFSP/GDCR SL9 89 P7
Layters Green La CFSP/GDCR SL9 89 N9
Layton Crs CROY/NA CRO 223 H4
Layton Pl RCH/KEW TW9 * 155 M7
Layton Rd BTFD TW8 135 M10
HSLW TW3 176 A1
Layton's La SUN TW16 196 A2
Layzell Wk ELTH/MOT SE9 184 A4
Lazell Gdns BRKHM/BTCW RH3 273 P6
Lazenby Ct COVGDN WC2E * 11 L7
Leabank Cl HRW HA1 114 D8

Leabank Sq HOM E9 140 F1
Leabank Vw SEVS/STOTM N15 119 P4
Leabourne Rd STNW/STAM N16 119 P6
Lea Bridge Rd LEY E10 120 C7
Lea Bushes GSTN WD25 76 A10
Leachcroft CFSP/GDCR SL9 89 N9
Leach Gv LHD/OX KT22 237 H6
Lea Cl BUSH WD23 76 A11
CRAWW RH11 283 J8
WHTN TW2 175 J4
Lea Cots MTCM CR4 * 202 B2
Lea Crs RSLP HA4 112 G9
Leacroft ASC SL5 192 F5
STA TW18 173 L7
Leacroft Av BAL SW12 180 A3
Leacroft Cl PUR/KEN CR8 241 K2
STA TW18 173 L7
WCHMN N21 99 J3
Leacroft Rd IVER SL0 130 C9
Leadale Av CHING E4 100 G8
Leadale Rd STNW/STAM N16 119 P4
Leadbeaters Cl FBAR/BDGN N11 98 A6
Leadenhall Pl BANK EC3V 13 J6
Leadenhall St BANK EC3V 13 J6
Leader Av MNPK E12 122 D10
The Leadings WBLY HA9 116 P8
Leaf Cl NTHWD HA6 92 B8
THDIT KT7 198 D5
Leaf Gv WNWD SE27 181 H4
Leafield Cl STRHM/NOR SW16 181 P9
WOKN/KNAP GU21 231 N4
Leafield La SCUP DA14 186 A7
Leafield Rd RYNPK SW20 201 J3
SUT SM1 210 B6
Leaford Crs WATN WD24 76 A3
Leaforis Rd CHESW EN7 61 P4
Leafy Av KWD/TDW/WH KT20 * 256 G8
Leafy Gv HAYES BR2 225 P2
Leafy Oak Rd LEE/GVPK SE12 183 P7
Leafy Wy CROY/NA CRO 203 N9
Lea Gdns WBLY HA9 115 L10
Leagrave St CLPT E5 120 E8
Lea Gn BRKMPK AL9 * 41 H1
Lea Hall Gdns LEY E10 * 120 F6
Lea Hall Rd LEY E10 120 F6
Leahoe Gdns HERT/BAY SG13 * 25 N6
Leaholme Gdns SL SL1 128 B7
Leaholme Waye RSLP HA4 112 C4
Leahurst Rd LEW SE13 183 J1
Leake St STHWK SE1 17 P1
Lealand Rd SEVS/STOTM N15 119 N3
Leaming Cl MNPK E12 122 B10
Leamington Av BMLY BR1 183 P8
MRDN SM4 201 J4
ORP BR6 227 H1
WALTH E17 120 F3
Leamington Cl BMLY BR1 183 P7
HARH RM3 105 N7
HSLW TW3 176 B1
Leamington Crs RYLN/HDSTN HA2 113 M8
Leamington Gdns GDMY/SEVK IG3 123 J7
Leamington Pk ACT W3 117 H4
Leamington Pl YEAD UB4 132 G6
Leamington Rd HARH RM3 105 N7
NWDGN UB2 153 L3
Leamington Road Vls NTGHL W11 8 D4
Leamore St HMSMTH W6 156 A10
Leamouth Rd EHAM E6 142 B8
POP/IOD E14 141 P8
Leander Dr GVE DA12 191 J7
Leander Gdns GSTN WD25 * 76 A2
Leander Rd BRXS/STRHM SW2 * 180 B2
NTHLT UB5 133 P4
THHTH CR7 202 G5
Leapale La GU GU1 268 A1
Leapale Rd GU GU1 268 A1
Learner Dr RYLN/HDSTN HA2 113 P7
Lea Rd BECK BR3 204 F2
CDW/CHF RM16 168 A5
ENC/FH EN2 79 L5
HOD EN11 45 H1
NWDGN UB2 152 G4
SEV TN13 265 K3
Leas Cl CHSGTN KT9 219 L4
Leas Dr IVER SL0 131 H3
Leas Gn CHST BR7 185 P5
Leaside BRKHM/BTCW RH3 235 P9
HHNE HP2 36 B1
Leaside Av MUSWH N10 98 B1
Leaside Ct HGDN/ICK UB10 132 C5
Leaside Rd CLPT E5 120 E5
Leas La WARL CR6 242 C6
Leasowes Rd LEY E10 120 F5
Leas Rd GU GU1 267 P4
WARL CR6 242 C6
The Leas BUSH WD23 76 B10
HHS/BOV HP3 36 B10
STA TW18 * 173 K7
UPMR RM14 126 D4
Leas Wy LEY E13 * 183 N5
Leaside RW CM14 107 K6
Leasway BRW CM14 107 J4
UPMR RM14 126 D4
Leather Bottle La BELV DA17 164 D4
Leather Cl MTCM CR4 202 B1
Leatherdale St WCHPL E1 140 C5
Leatherhead By-Pass Rd LHD/OX KT22 236 G2
Leatherhead Cl STNW/STAM N16 119 M6
Leatherhead Rd ASHTD KT21 237 L8
CHSGTN KT9 218 G10
GT/LBKH KT23 254 A2
LHD/OX KT22 236 C1
Leather La CLKNW EC1R 12 A2
HCRC EC1N 12 A2
SHGR GU5 270 D5
Leathermarket Ct STHWK SE1 19 J2
Leathermarket St STHWK SE1 19 J2
Leather Rd BERM/RHTH SE16 160 C3
Leathersellers Cl BAR EN5 * 77 H4
Leathes Cl WAP E1W * 140 C8
Leathsale Rd RYLN/HDSTN HA2 114 A8
Leathwaite Rd BTSEA SW11 158 D2
Leathwell Rd DEPT SE8 160 D10
Lea V DART DA1 167 J6
Lea Valley Rd CHING E4 80 D10
Lea Valley Wk BRKMPK AL9 42 A10
BROX EN10 62 F3
CLPT E5 120 A5
HOD EN11 45 J4
PEND EN3 80 A3
STALE/WH AL4 21 H2
WALTH E17 120 A4
Leaveland Cl BECK BR3 204 E4
Leaver Gdns GFD/PVL UB6 133 P1
Leaveden Rd STAN HA7 94 A3
WATN WD24 75 P2
Leavesden Rd STAN HA7 94 A3
WATN WD24 75 P2
Leaves Green Crs HAYES BR2 225 P7
Leaves Green Rd HAYES BR2 225 P7
Leavey Cl WAB EN9 62 A7
Leazes Av CTHM CR3 241 L4
Leazes La CTHM CR3 * 241 L4
Lebanon Av FELT TW13 175 L1
Lebanon Cl WAT WD17 * 74 G1
Lebanon Ct TWK TW1 * 176 C5
Lebanon Dr COB KT11 217 P10
Lebanon Gdns BH/WHM TN16 244 A3

WAND/EARL SW18 179 K2
Lebanon Pk TWK TW1 176 G3
Lebanon Rd CROY/NA CRO 203 N10
WAND/EARL SW18 179 K2
Lebrun Sq BKHTH/KID SE3 161 N10
Lechford Rd HORL RH6 280 A6
Lechmere Ap WFD IG8 101 P10
Lechmere Av CHIG IG7 103 N2
Lechmere Rd CRICK NW2 136 E1
Leckford Rd WAND/EARL SW18 179 M5
Leckhampton Pl BRXS/STRHM SW2 * 181 H3
Leckwith Av ABYW SE2 163 P5
Lecky St SKENS SW7 15 L7
Leconfield Av BARN SW13 156 C9
Leconfield Rd HBRY N5 119 L3
Le Corte Cl KGLGY WD4 54 A5
Lectern La STAL AL1 38 D10
Leda Av PEND EN3 30 D5
Leda Rd WOOL/PLUM SE18 162 C2
Ledborough Ga BEAC HP9 88 B3
Ledborough La BEAC HP9 88 B2
Ledborough Wd BEAC HP9 88 B2
Ledbury Ms North NTGHL W11 * 8 E7
Ledbury Ms West NTGHL W11 * 8 E7
Ledbury Rd CROY/NA CRO 223 K1
NTGHL W11 8 E6
REIG RH2 257 K10
Ledbury St PECK SE15 159 P6
Ledger Cl GU GU1 250 E8
Ledger Dr ADL/WDHM KT15 215 G3
Ledgers Rd WARL CR6 242 F2
Ledger's Rd SL SL1 149 J1
Ledrington Rd NRWD SE19 181 N9
Ledway Dr WBLY HA9 115 N9
Lee Av CHDH RM6 123 P4
Lee Church St LEW SE13 161 K10
Lee Cl HERT/BAY SG13 25 K7
WALTH E17 100 C9
Lee Conservancy Rd HOM E9 120 E10
Leecroft Rd BAR EN5 77 H8
Leeds Cl ORP BR6 207 N9
Leeds Pl FSBYPK N4 * 118 G6
SL SL1 129 K9
Leeds Rd IL IG1 122 G6
SL SL1 129 K9
Lee Farm Cl CSHM HP5 51 M6
Le Fevre Wy POTB/CUF EN6 60 L4
Lee Gardens Av HARH RM11 126 B6
Leegate Cl WOKN/KNAP GU21 231 N3
Lee Gv CHIG IG7 102 E3
Lee High Rd LEW SE13 161 J10
Leeke St FSBYW WC1X 5 N9
Leeland Rd WEA W13 135 F10
Leeland Ter WEA W13 135 F10
Leeland Wy WLSDN NW10 116 B9
Leeming Rd BORE WD6 75 L5
Leemount Cl HDN NW4 * 116 C2
Lee Pk BKHTH/KID SE3 161 L10
Lee Park Wy UED N18 100 C6
Lee Rd BKHTH/KID SE3 161 L9
EN EN1 79 P10
GFD/PVL UB6 135 H5
MLHL NW7 96 C6
WIM/MER SW19 201 L1
Lees Av NTHWD HA6 92 B7
Leeside BAR EN5 77 H9
Leeside Crs GLDGN NW11 117 H4
Leeside Rd TOTM N17 100 E3
Leeson Rd HNHL SE24 * 160 A11
Leesons Hl CHST BR7 205 H10
STMC/STPC BR5 205 J10
Leesons Wy STMC/STPC BR5 205 P5
Lees Pde HGDN/ICK UB10 * 132 C6
The Lees CROY/NA CRO 204 D8
Lees St HACK E8 7 L5
HORL RH6 279 N6
The Lee NTHWD HA6 92 G6
Lee Ter BKHTH/KID SE3 161 H10
Lee Vw ENC/FH EN2 79 J5
Leeward Gdns WIM/MER SW19 179 H9
Leeway DEPT SE8 160 G9
The Leeways CHEAM SM3 * 221 H5
Leewood Cl LEE/GVPK SE12 183 L2
Leewood Pl SWLY BR8 208 B4
Leewood Wy EHSLY KT24 252 A4
Lefevre Wk BOW E3 5 E5
Lefferm St SEVD E13 135 L6
Lefroy Rd SHB W12 156 C1
Left Side STHGT/OAK N14 * 98 E12
Legard Rd HBRY N5 119 H1
Legatt Rd ELTH/MOT SE9 184 A1
Leggatt Rd SRTFD E15 141 H4
Leggatts Cl WATN WD24 72 G2
Leggatts Rd WATN WD24 72 G2
Leggatts Wy WATN WD24 72 H2
Leggatts Wood Av WATN WD24 72 J2
Legge St LEW SE13 183 H1
Leggfield Ter HHW HP1 35 J6
Leghorn Rd WLSDN NW10 116 A2
WOOL/PLUM SE18 162 G4
Legion Cl IS N1 6 B3
Legion Ct MRDN SM4 201 K6
Legion Ter BOW E3 * 140 A11
Legion Wy NFNCH/WDSPK N12 97 P8
Legon Av ROMW/RG RM7 144 A1
Legrace Av HSLWW TW4 153 J10
Leicester Av MTCM CR4 202 G3
Leicester Cl WPK KT4 220 F1
Leicester Gdns GDMY/SEVK IG3 123 H5
GT/LBKH KT23 11 K7
CROY/NA CRO 203 M7
ENFNCH 117 P7
WAN E11 121 N2
WLSDN NW10 136 A2
Leicester Sq LSQ/SEVD WC2H 11 K7
Leigham STRHM/NOR SW16 180 G6
Leigham Cl STRHM/NOR SW16 181 J5
Leigham Court Rd STRHM/NOR SW16 180 G4
Leigham Dr ISLW TW7 153 P6
Leigham Hall Pde STRHM/NOR SW16 * 180 G5
Leigham V STRHM/NOR SW16 181 J5
Leigh Av REDBR IG4 122 G5
Leigh Cl ADL/WDHM KT15 215 J4
NWMAL KT3 200 A2
Leigh Common WGCE AL7 23 H7
Leigh Ct BORE WD6 * 75 P2
RYLN/HDSTN HA2 114 C7
Leigh Crs CROY/NA CRO 205 K10
Leigh Dr HARH RM3 105 N7
Leigh Gdns WLSDN NW10 116 G9
Leigh Hill Rd COB KT11 217 H10
Leigh Hunt Dr STHGT/OAK N14 98 E2
Leigh Jenkins Wy HORL RH6 * 284 D5
Leighlands CRAWE RH10 285 L1
Leigh Orchard Cl STRHM/NOR SW16 180 G6
Leigh Pl FELT TW13 175 L4
RDART DA2 * 187 P8

Leigh Place BELMT SM2 * 221 K4
Leigh Place Rd REIG RH2 274 C5
Leigh Rd BRKHM/BTCW RH3 273 P6
  COB KT11 217 J9
  EHAM E6 142 D2
  GVW DA11 190 B5
  HBRY N5 119 J9
  HSLW TW3 154 C10
  SL1 128 C9
Leigh Rodd OXHEY WD19 93 M4
Leigh Sq WDSR SL4 148 C8
Leigh St STPAN WC1H 11 L1
Leigh Ter STMC/STPC BR5 * 207 L3
The Leigh KUTN/CMB KT2 178 B9
Leighton Av MNPK E12 122 D10
  PIN HA5 113 M1
Leighton Buzzard Rd HHW HP1 35 L1
Leighton Cl EDGW HA8 95 M10
Leighton Crs KTTN NW5 118 D10
Leighton Gdns SAND/SEL CR2 224 A9
  TIL RM18 168 D6
  WLSDN NW10 136 F4
Leighton Gv KTTN NW5 118 D10
Leighton Pl KTTN NW5 118 D10
Leighton Rd EN EN1 79 N9
  KTN/HRWW/WS HA3 94 C10
  KTTN NW5 118 D10
  WEA W13 154 F1
Leighton St CROY/NA CRO 203 J8
Leighton Wy EPSOM KT18 220 A10
Leila Parnell Pl CHARL SE7 161 F6
Leinster Av MORT/ESHN SW14 155 N9
Leinster Gdns BAY/PAD W2 9 J8
Leinster Ms BAY/PAD W2 9 J8
Leinster Pl BAY/PAD W2 9 J8
Leinster Sq BAY/PAD W2 8 F7
Leinster Ter BAY/PAD W2 8 F7
Leisure Sp SL1 SL1 129 K8
Leisure La BF/WBF KT14 * 215 L8
Leisure Wy NFNCH/WDSPK N12 97 N8
Leith Cl CDALE/KGS NW9 116 A6
  SL1 SL1 129 M10
Leithcote Gdns STRHM/NOR SW16 180 G7
Leithcote Pth STRHM/NOR SW16 180 G6
Leith Hl STMC/STPC BR5 207 K1
Leith Hill Rd RDKG RH5 271 M10
Leith Park Rd GVE DA12 190 E6
Leith Rd EW KT17 220 B8
  WDGN N22 99 J8
Leith Towers BELMT SM2 * 221 L4
Leith Vw RDKG RH5 273 N7
Leith Yd KIL/WHAMP NW6 * 2 C1
Lela Av HSLWW TW4 153 H6
Lelitia Cl HACK E8 7 N5
Leman Ct WCHPL E1 13 M6
Lemark Cl STAN HA7 95 J4
Le May Av LEE/GVPK SE12 183 M6
Le May Cl HORL RH6 280 E8
Lemmon Rd GNWCH SE10 161 K5
Lemna Rd WAN E11 121 K5
Lemonfield Dr GSTN WD25 55 M8
Lemonwell Dr ELTH/MOT SE9 184 E1
Lemsford Cl SEVS/STOTM N15 119 J2
Lemsford Ct BORE WD6 75 P8
Lemsford La WGCW AL8 22 E6
  STAL AL1 38 E6
Lemsford Village WGCW AL8 22 C4
Lena Crs ED N9 100 B3
Lena Gdns HMSMTH W6 156 F2
Lena Kennedy Cl CHING E4 101 N3
Lendal Ter CLAP SW4 158 F4
Lenelby Rd SURB KT6 199 M8
Len Freeman Pl FUL/PGN SW6 14 C10
Lenham Rd BXLYHN DA7 164 A5
  BELMT SM2 221 L1
  LEE/GVPK SE12 161 L10
  SUT SM1 221 L1
  THHTH CR7 203 L2
Lenmore Av GRAYS RM17 167 P2
Lennard Av WWKM BR4 205 K9
Lennard Cl WWKM BR4 205 K9
Lennard Rd CROY/NA CRO 203 K8
  HAYES BR2 206 D3
  SEV TN13 246 F6
  SYD SE26 182 B9
Lennard Ter PGE/AN SE20 * 182 C10
Lennon Rd CRICK NW2 116 F10
Lennox Av GVW DA11 190 D2
  ROM RM1 124 C4
Lennox Cl CDW/CHF RM16 167 H3
Lennox Gdns CROY/NA CRO 223 J4
  IL IG1 122 C6
  KTBR SW1X 16 A4
  WLSDN NW10 116 C9
Lennox Gardens Ms KTBR SW1X 16 A5
Lennox Rd FSBYPK N4 118 C2
  GVW DA11 190 C2
  WALTH E17 120 D4
Lennox Rd East GVW DA11 190 D3
Lenor Cl BXLYHS DA6 163 P10
Lensbury Cl CHES/WCR EN8 62 D1
Lensbury Wy ABYW SE2 163 N2
Lens Rd FSTGT E7 141 P2
Lenten Cl SHGR GU5 270 E8
Lent Green La SL1 SL1 128 A6
Lenthall Av GRAYS RM17 167 M1
Lenthall Rd HACK E8 7 M3
  LOU IG10 82 G8
Lenthorp Rd GNWCH SE10 161 L3
Lentmead Rd BMLY BR1 183 L6
Lenton Ri RCH/KEW TW9 155 K9
Lenton St WOOL/PLUM SE18 162 K9
Lenton Ter FSBYPK N4 * 119 H7
Lent Rise Rd MDHD SL6 128 L8
Leof Crs CAT SE6 182 E6
Leominster Rd MRDN SM4 201 M6
Leominster Wk MRDN SM4 201 M6
Leonard Av MRDN SM4 201 M5
  ROMW/RG RM7 124 C6
  RSEV TN14 247 J1
  SWCM DA10 189 K7
Leonard Ct KENS W8 14 E3
Leonard Pl HAYES BR2 * 206 A1
  STNW/STAM N16 119 N9
Leonard Rd CHING E4 101 J5
  ED N9 99 N4
  FSTGT E7 121 N3
  NWDGN UB2 153 L2
  STRHM/NOR SW16 180 C10
Leonardslee Ct CRAWE RH10 * 284 C10
Leonard St CAN/RD E16 142 B10
  SDTCH EC2A 13 H1


Leslie Gdns BELMT SM2 221 K4
Leslie Gv CROY/NA CRO 203 L8
Leslie Grove Pl CROY/NA CRO 203 M8
Leslie Park Rd CROY/NA CRO 203 M8
Leslie Rd CAN/RD E16 141 P8
  CHOB/PIR GU24 213 J6
  DORK RH4 255 J10
  EFNCH N2 117 N1
  WAN E11 121 K6
Lesney Pk ERITH DA8 164 E5
Lesney Park Rd ERITH DA8 164 E5
Lessar Av CLAP SW4 180 D1
Lessingham Av TOOT SW17 180 D1
Lessing St FSTH SE23 182 B1
Lessness Av BXLYHN DA7 163 N7
Lessness Pk BELV DA17 164 A5
Lessness Rd MRDN SM4 201 N6
Lester Av SRTFD E15 141 K6
Lestock Cl SNWD SE25 203 P5
Leswin Pl STNW/STAM N16 119 N8
Leswin Rd STNW/STAM N16 119 N8
Letchfield CSHM HP5 51 N7
Letchfield Gdns WLSDN NW10 136 D5
Letchford Ms WLSDN NW10 * 136 D5
Letchford Ter KTN/HRWW/WS HA3 * 94 A3
Letchmore Rd RAD WD7 74 F2
Letchworth Av EBED/NFELT TW14 174 C3
  OXHEY WD19 93 L6
Letchworth Dr HAYES BR2 205 M5
Letchworth St TOOT SW17 180 A7
Letter Box La SEV TN13 265 K5
Letterstone Rd FUL/PGN SW6 157 J6
Lettice St FUL/PGN SW6 157 J6
Lett Rd SRTFD E15 141 J2
Leucha Rd WALTH E17 120 D3
Levana Cl WIM/MER SW19 179 H4
Levehurst Wy CLAP SW4 158 F8
Leven Cl CHES/WCR EN8 62 C9
  OXHEY WD19 * 93 L6
Levendale Rd FSTH SE23 182 G6
Leven Dr CHES/WCR EN8 62 C9
Leven Rd POP/IOD E14 141 H7
Leven Wy HHW HP2 35 N2
  HYS/HAR UB3 132 F8
Leverett Cl CROY/NA CRO 225 J7
  GSTN WD25 55 H10
Leverholme Gdns ELTH/MOT SE9 184 D7
Leverson St STRHM/NOR SW16 180 D9
Lever Sq CDW/CHF RM16 168 D3
Leverstock Green Rd HHNE HP2 36 B5
Lever St FSBYE EC1V 6 E10
Leverton Pl KTTN NW5 118 D10
Leverton St KTTN NW5 118 D10
Leverton Wy WAB EN9 63 H9
Leveson Rd CDW/CHF RM16 168 E2
Levett Gdns GDMY/SEVK IG3 123 K3
Levett Rd BARK IG11 143 H5
  LHD/OX KT22 236 C6
Levine Gdns BARK IG11 143 N4
Levylsdene GU GU1 250 G10
Lewes Cl CRAWE RH10 284 D9
  GRAYS RM17 167 M5
  NTHLT UB5 133 P1
Leweston Cl WIM/MER SW19 178 C4
Lewes Rd BMLY BR1 206 A2
  HARH RM3 105 K7
  NFNCH/WDSPK N12 97 P6
Leweston Pl STNW/STAM N16 119 N5
Lewes Wy RKW/CH/CXG WD3 72 C5
Lewgars Av CDALE/KGS NW9 115 P4
Lewing Cl ORP BR6 207 H8
Lewin Rd BXLYHS DA6 163 H5
  MORT/ESHN SW14 155 M8
  STRHM/NOR SW16 180 D9
Lewins Rd CFSP/GDCR SL9 110 A1
  EPSOM KT18 219 N10
Lewins Wy SL1 SL1 128 E9
Lewin Ter EBED/NFELT TW14 174 L3
Lewis Av WALTH E17 100 F9
Lewis Cl ADL/WDHM KT15 215 N1
Lewis Crs WLSDN NW10 116 A10
Lewis Gdns EFNCH N2 97 N10
  SEVS/STOTM N15 119 N5
Lewis Gv LEW SE13 161 N10
Lewisham High St LEW SE13 182 C2
Lewisham Hl LEW SE13 161 N10
Lewisham Pk LEW SE13 182 C3
Lewisham Rd LEW SE13 161 N8
Lewisham Wy BROCKY SE4 160 E9
Lewis La CFSP/GDCR SL9 90 B9
Lewis Pl HACK E8 7 N1
Lewis Rd EMPK RM11 125 K4
  MTCM CR4 201 P2
  RCH/KEW TW9 * 177 J1
  SCUP DA14 185 N6
  STHL UB1 153 M1
  SUT SM1 221 L1
  SUT SM1 221 L2
  SWCM DA10 189 K2
  WELL DA16 163 M9
Lewis St CAMTN NW1 4 A1
Lewiston Cl WPK KT4 200 F7
Lexden Dr CHDH RM6 123 L4
Lexden Rd ACT W3 135 N9
  MTCM CR4 202 E4
Lexden Ter WAB EN9 * 63 H10
Lexham Gdns AMS HP6 69 H5
  KENS W8 14 F3
Lexham Ms KENS W8 14 F5
Lexington Cl BORE WD6 75 L1
Lexington Ct POTB/CUF EN6 60 C9
  PUR/KEN CR8 223 K6
Lexington Pl KUT/HW KT1 199 J1
Lexington St SOHO/CST W1F 11 H6
Lexington Wy BAR EN5 76 B5
  UPMR RM14 126 D4
Lexton Gdns BAL SW12 180 G3
Leybourne Av WEA W13 155 H1
Leybourne Pk RCH/KEW TW9 155 N7
Leybourne Rd CRICK NW2 116 B5
  HAYES BR2 205 M5
  UED N18 99 L4
Leybourne St CAMTN NW1 4 C1
Leyburn Cl WALTH E17 121 H2
Leyburn Crs HARH RM3 105 M8
Leyburn Gdns CROY/NA CRO 203 M9
Leyburn Gv UED N18 100 F5
Leyburn House CHARL SE7 * 162 B6
Leyburn Rd HARH RM3 105 M8
  UED N18 100 F5
Leycester Cl BFOR GU20 212 A1
Leycroft Gdns ERITH DA8 165 J1
Leycroft Wy HARP AL5 20 D1
Leydenhatch La SWLY BR8 186 F7
Leyden St WCHPL E1 13 L4
Leydon Cl BERM/RHTH SE16 143 J6
Leyes Rd CAN/RD E16 142 A9
Leyfield WPK KT4 200 C10
Leyhill Cl SWLY BR8 208 C5
Leyland Av EN EN3 80 D2
  STAL AL1 38 B1
Leyland Gdns WFD IG8 105 J7
Leylands La STWL/WRAY TW19 151 H10
Leyland Rd LEE/GVPK SE12 161 K10
Leylang Rd NWCR SE14 160 G8
Leys Av DAGE RM10 144 G6
Leys Cl DAGE RM10 144 G6
  DEN/HRF UB9 91 H6


HRW HA1 114 C2
Leysdown Av BXLYHN DA7 164 D10
Leysdown Rd ELTH/MOT SE9 184 B2
Leysfield Rd SHB W12 156 D1
Leys Gdns EBAR EN4 78 B9
Leyspring Rd WAN E11 121 L6
Leys Rd HHS/BOV HP3 35 J2
Leys Rd East PEND EN3 80 D5
The Leys AMS HP6 68 G1
  EFNCH N2 117 M2
  KTN/HRWW/WS HA3 115 L4
  RAD WD7 74 F3
  STALE/WH AL4 39 J3
  WOT/HER KT12 * 217 M1
Ley St IL IG1 122 E7
Leyswood Dr GNTH/NBYPK IG2 123 H3
Leyton Business Centre LEY E10 123 H3
Leyton Gra LEY E10 121 H4
Leyton Green Rd LEY E10 121 H1
Leyton Park Rd LEY E10 121 K1
Leyton Rd SRTFD E15 121 K10
  WIM/MER SW19 179 M10
Leytonstone Rd SRTFD E15 141 K1
Ley Wk WCCE AL7 23 M5
Leywick St SRTFD E15 141 K4
Leywood Cl AMSS HP7 51 J7
Liardet St NWCR SE14 160 D5
Liberia Rd HBRY N5 6 D1
Liberty Av WIM/MER SW19 201 N1
Liberty Cl HERT/BAY SG13 25 K7
  UED N18 99 N5
  WPK KT4 200 F8
Liberty Hall Rd ADL/WDHM KT15 215 K2
Liberty La ADL/WDHM KT15 215 L2
Liberty Ms WDGN N22 99 J9
  TOOT SW17 160 F10
Liberty St BRXN/ST SW9 158 F6
Liberty Wk AL1 39 H7
Libra Rd BOW E3 140 E3
  PLSTW E13 141 M4
Library Pde WLSDN NW10 * 136 B3
Library St STHWK SE1 18 D2
Library Wy WHTN TW2 176 B3
Lichfield Cl EBAR EN4 78 A7
Lichfield Gdns RCH/KEW TW9 177 K1
Lichfield Gv FNCH N3 97 K9
Lichfield Pl STAL AL1 38 E5
Lichfield Rd BCTR RM8 123 L9
  BOW E3 140 D5
  CRICK NW2 117 H9
  ED N9 99 P3
  EHAM E6 142 A5
  HSLWW TW4 153 H9
  NTHWD HA6 113 H1
  RCH/KEW TW9 * 177 K1
  UPMR RM14 105 N10
  WFD IG8 101 K5
Lichfield Wy BROX EN10 44 E8
  SAND/SEL CR2 224 C6
Lidbury Rd MLHL NW7 97 H7
Lidcote Gdns BRXN/ST SW9 * 158 F8
Liddall Wy WDR/YW UB7 132 A10
Liddell WDSR SL4 148 B9
Liddell Cl KTN/HRWW/WS HA3 115 J1
Liddell Gdns WLSDN NW10 136 F4
Liddell Rd KIL/WHAMP NW6 2 E1
Lidding Rd KTN/HRWW/WS HA3 115 J1
Liddington Hall Dr RGUW GU3 249 K7
Liddington New Rd RGUW GU3 249 K7
Liddington Rd SRTFD E15 141 L3
Liddon Rd BMLY BR1 205 P3
  PLSTW E13 141 L2
Lidfield Rd STNW/STAM N16 119 M3
Lidgate Rd CMBW SE5 158 G6
Lidiard Rd WAND/EARL SW18 179 M5
Lidlington Pl CAMTN NW1 1 F3
Lido Rd GU GU1 250 A9
Lido Sq TOTM N17 99 L10
Lidsey Cl CRAWE RH10 284 D9
Lidstone Cl WOKN/KNAP GU21 231 M5
Lidyard Rd ARCH N19 118 D6
Lieutenant Ellis Wy CHESW EN7 61 N7
Liffler Rd WOOL/PLUM SE18 163 H4
Lifford St PUT/ROE SW15 156 G10
Lightcliffe Rd PLMGR N13 99 H5
Lighter Cl BERM/RHTH SE16 160 A2
Lighterman Ms WCHPL E1 140 C8
Lighterman's Ms POP/IOD E14 160 F1
Lightermans Wy SWCM DA10 * 171 J7
Lightfoot Rd CEND/HSY/T N8 118 A1
Lightley Cl ALP/SUD HA0 135 L1
Lightswood Cl CHESW EN7 61 L1
Lightwater Meadow LTWR GU18 212 A4
Lightwater Rd LTWR GU18 212 A7
Ligonier St BETH E2 13 L1
Lilac Av EN EN1 80 B2
  WOKS/MYFD GU22 232 A6
Lilac Cl BRWN CM15 86 C9
  CHESW EN7 61 P1
  CHING E4 100 F6
Lilac Gdns CROY/NA CRO 204 F10
  EA W5 155 J2
  HYS/HAR UB3 132 F8
  ROMW/RG RM7 124 F6
  SWLY BR8 208 E3
Lilac Pl LBTH SE11 17 N6
  WDR/YW UB7 132 A9
Lilac St SHB W12 156 D6
Lila Wy HARP AL5 20 C5
Liliah Ms HAYES BR2 205 L2
Lilbourne Dr HERT/BAY SG13 25 P4
Lilburne Gdns ELTH/MOT SE9 184 B4
Lilburne Rd ELTH/MOT SE9 184 B1
Lile Crs HNWL W7 134 D7
Lilestone Est STJWD NW8 * 9 N1
Lilford Rd CMBW SE5 158 D8


Limburg Rd BTSEA SW11 157 P10
Lime Av GVW DA11 190 A3
  RBRW/HUT CM13 107 L4
  UPMR RM14 125 P2
  WDR/YW UB7 132 A9
  WDSR SL4 149 L6
  WDSR SL4 170 A4
Limeburner La STP EC4M 12 C5
Limebush Cl ADL/WDHM KT15 215 M5
Lime Cl BRXHI CI9 102 A3
  BMLY BR1 206 B4
  CRAWE RH10 285 J2
  CRAWW RH11 283 M4
  KTN/HRWW/WS HA3 94 F10
  OXHEY WD19 93 H9
  PIN HA5 113 G1
  REIG RH2 275 L3
  RGUE GU4 251 L4
  ROMW/RG RM7 124 D2
  SOCK/AV RM15 147 H5
  WAP E1W 13 M7
Lime Crs SUN TW16 197 K2
Limecroft Cl HOR/WEW KT19 220 A4
Limecroft Rd WOKN/KNAP GU21 230 C3
Limedene Cl PIN HA5 93 L9
Lime Gv ADL/WDHM KT15 215 K1
  BARK/HLT IG6 105 J7
  BLDS AL5 185 J2
  BRWN CM15 87 H4
  CHING E4 100 E7
  GU GU1 249 N6
  HYS/HAR UB3 132 A3
  NWMAL KT3 176 B5
  ORP BR6 206 D9
  RGUE GU4 251 L4
  RSLP HA4 113 J4
  SHB W12 156 F2
  TRDG/WHET N20 97 H2
  WARL CR6 242 D5
  WOKS/MYFD GU22 232 A6
Limeharbour POP/IOD E14 160 G2
Limehouse POP/IOD E14 * 140 F9
Limehouse Cswy POP/IOD E14 * 140 E9
Limehouse Link (Tunnel) POP/IOD E14 140 E8
Lime Kiln Dr CHARL SE7 162 A6
Limekiln Pl NRWD SE19 181 N10
Lime Meadow Av SAND/SEL CR2 223 P9
Lime Pit La SEV TN13 246 D3
Limerick Cl BAL SW12 180 D3
Limerick Gdns UPMR RM14 126 E3
Lime Rd SWLY BR8 208 E3
  STAN HA7 94 G6
  STHGT/OAK N14 98 D10
Limes Av BARN SW13 156 C8
  CAR SM5 202 A8
  CHIG IG7 102 F6
  GLDGN NW11 117 H5
  HORL RH6 280 C6
  MLHL NW7 96 B7
  NFNCH/WDSPK N12 97 M5
  PGE/AN SE20 182 A10
The Limes Av FBAR/BDGN N11 98 C6
Limes Cl ASHF TW15 174 B8
  FBAR/BDGN N11 * 98 D6
Limes Ct HOD EN11 33 H5
Limesdale Gdns EDGW HA8 95 P10
Limes Fld HWW HP1 35 H5
Limes Gdns WAND/EARL SW18 179 K2
Limes Gv LEW SE13 161 N10
Limes Rw BECK BR3 204 G2
  CHES/WCR EN8 62 C8
  CROY/NA CRO 203 L6
  ORP BR6 203 L6 (maybe)
  TWY TW20 172 C8
  WEY KT13 216 B1
Limes Rw ORP BR6 226 F2
The Limes AMS HP6 68 G1
  CMBW SE5 159 M9
  EMPK RM11 125 L2
  EYN DA4 209 N7
  LHD/OX KT22 236 C9
  PUR RM19 165 P4
Lime St CAR SM5 202 A8
  FENCHST EC3M 13 J7
  WALTH E17 120 D4
Lime Street Pas BANK EC3V * 13 J6
Limes Wk EA W5 * 155 J1
  PECK SE15 160 A5
Lime Tree Av ESH/CLAY KT10 198 C5
Limetree Cl BRXS/STRHM SW2 180 A3
Lime Tree Cl GT/LBKH KT23 255 P10
Lime Tree Ct PIN HA5 * 93 P6
Limetree Pl MTCM CR4 202 C1
Lime Tree Pl STAL AL1 38 D7
Lime Tree Rd HEST TW5 154 A7
Limetree Ter WELL DA16 * 164 A4
Lime Tree Wk AMSS HP7 * 69 L5
  BUSH WD23 76 G4
  ENC/FH EN2 79 K4
  RKW/CH/CXG WD3 72 A7
  SEV TN13 265 J1
  VW GU25 36 B6
  WWKM BR4 225 H1
Lime Wk HHNE HP2 111 M10
  HHS/BOV HP3 35 J2
  SRTFD E15 * 141 K3
Limeway Ter DORK RH4 254 F9
Limewood Cl BECK BR3 205 J3
  WALTH E17 120 D2
  WEA W13 134 D7
  WOKN/KNAP GU21 231 J6
Limewood Rd ERITH DA8 164 D6
Limpsfield Av THHTH CR7 202 G5
  WIM/MER SW19 178 G3
Limpsfield Rd SAND/SEL CR2 224 A5
  WARL CR6 242 B2
Linacre Cl PECK SE15 159 K2
Linacre Rd CRICK NW2 136 F4
Lince La DORK RH4 254 A2
Linces Wy WCCE AL7 23 L7
Linchfield Rd DTCH/LGLY SL3 149 H3
Linchmere Pl CRAWW RH11 282 B7
Linchmere Rd LEE/GVPK SE12 183 J5
  STHGT/OAK N14 98 F5
  WHTN TW2 176 E3
Lincoln Av CRAWE RH10 285 H3
  EMPK RM11 125 K4
  ERITH DA8 165 J1
  RYLN/HDSTN HA2 94 C9
  WGCE AL7 23 N4
Lincoln Cl BERK HP4 35 H1
  BORE WD6 76 A1
  ERITH DA8 165 J1
Lincoln Crs EN EN1 79 P6
Lincoln Dr CHES/WCR EN8 62 C8
  OXHEY WD19 93 K3
  RKW/CH/CXG WD3 72 C5
  WOKS/MYFD GU22 233 J1
Lincoln Gn BOW E3 140 E1
Lincoln Green Rd STMC/STPC BR5 207 L3
Lincoln Hatch La SL1 SL1 128 B6
Lincoln Ms KIL/WHAMP NW6 2 A1
  SEVS/STOTM N15 119 K2


Lime Gv GVW DA11 190 A3
  HUT CM13 107 L4
  UPMR RM14 125 P2
  WDR/YW UB7 132 A9
  WDSR SL4 149 L6
  WDSR SL4 170 A4
Lincoln Pk AMSS HP7 69 K5
  ALP/SUD HA0 135 L1
  CFSP/GDCR SL9 90 B9
DORK RH4 255 H10
  EFNCH N2 117 P1
  EN EN1 79 M8
  ERITH DA8 164 G8
  FELT TW13 175 N6
  FSTGT E7 142 A1
  GUW GU2 250 A3
  MTCM CR4 202 F6
  NTHWD HA6 112 G1
  NWMAL KT3 199 N4
  PEND EN3 80 D5
  PLSTW E13 141 N6
  RYLN/HDSTN HA2 113 L7
  SCUP DA14 185 L8
  SNWD SE25 204 A8
  SWFD E18 102 E9
  WPK KT4 200 E9
Lincoln's Cl STALE/WH AL4 39 H1
Lincolns Fld EPP CM16 70 C6
Lincoln's Inn Flds LINN WC2A 11 N5
Lincoln's La BRW CM14 86 B10
The Lincolns MLHL NW7 96 A6
  ST CHEL SW3 16 A9
  WAN E11 121 J9
Lincoln Ter BELMT SM2 * 221 K4
Lincoln Wy EN EN1 79 M8
  RKW/CH/CXG WD3 72 C8
  SL1 128 C9
  SUN TW16 196 F1
Lincombe Rd BMLY BR1 183 N1
Lindal Crs ENC/FH EN2 78 F9
Lindale Cl VW GU25 193 L4
The Lindales TOTM N17 99 P7
Lindal Rd BROCKY SE4 182 B1
Lindbergh Rd GVW DA11 191 K4
Lindbergh Wy WLGTN SM6 222 F5
Lindbury Av COUL/CHIP CR5 241 J3
Linden Av COUL/CHIP CR5 240 C2
  EN EN1 79 P5
  HSLW TW3 176 A1
  RSLP HA4 113 H6
  THHTH CR7 203 J4
  WATW WD18 72 D8
  WBLY HA9 115 L10
  WLSDN NW10 136 E4
Linden Chase Rd SEV TN13 247 J8
Linden Cl ADL/WDHM KT15 215 K7
  CHESW EN7 62 A6
  CRAWE RH10 284 D10
  IVER SL0 130 G5
  KWD/TDW/WH KT20 238 G6
  ORP BR6 207 K2
  PUR RM19 166 A5
  RSLP HA4 113 H6
  STAN HA7 94 G6
  STHGT/OAK N14 99 D10
  TOTM N17 * 99 P7
Linden Cots WIM/MER SW19 * 179 H9
Linden Ct EGH TW20 171 N9
  HARP AL5 20 A3
  LHD/OX KT22 236 C10
Linden Cr GFD/PVL UB6 134 E1
  KUT/HW KT1 199 L2
  WFD IG8 101 H6
  WATN WD24 73 L6
Linden Dr CFSP/GDCR SL9 90 B9
  CTHM CR3 241 K10
  SLN SL2 129 H2
Lindenfield CHST BR7 206 E2
Linden Gdns BAY/PAD W2 8 C8
  CHSWK W4 156 A4
  EN EN1 79 P5
  LHD/OX KT22 237 H7
Linden Gld HHW HP1 35 H5
Linden Gv NWMAL KT3 200 B3
  PECK SE15 160 A5
  TEDD TW11 176 B6
  WARL CR6 242 D4
  WOT/HER KT12 196 D10
Linden Lea DORK RH4 273 H4
  EFNCH N2 117 M3
  GSTN WD25 55 J1
  PIN HA5 93 N8
Linden Leas WWKM BR4 205 K8
Linden Ms BAY/PAD W2 8 C8
  IS N1 6 G1
Linden Pit Pth LHD/OX KT22 236 C10
Linden Pl EHSLY KT24 * 252 F2
  EW KT17 220 B8
  MTCM CR4 201 P4
Linden Ri BRW CM14 107 H2
Linden Rd FBAR/BDGN N11 97 P1
  GU GU1 250 A10
  HPTN TW12 175 H5
  LHD/OX KT22 236 C10
  MUSWH N10 118 C2
  WEY KT13 216 D5
Lindens CI EHSLY KT24 253 J4
Linden Sq DEN/HRF UB9 91 K7
  SEV TN13 246 F8
The Lindens CHSWK W4 156 A7
  CRAWE RH10 285 M1
  CROY/NA CRO 225 P3
  HAT AL10 40 C3
  NFNCH/WDSPK N12 * 97 N6
Linden St ROMW/RG RM7 124 C2
Linden Wk ARCH N19 118 C1
  PUR/KEN CR8 222 B6
Linden Wy PUR/KEN CR8 241 J3
  RPLY/SEND GU23 251 J1
  SHPTN TW17 197 L6
  STHGT/OAK N14 78 D10
  WOKS/MYFD GU22 232 C7
Lindfield Gdns GU GU1 250 A10
  HAMP NW3 117 M10
Lindfield Rd CROY/NA CRO 203 M5
  EA W5 135 N8
  HARH RM3 105 M8
Lindfield St POP/IOD E14 140 G8
Lindhill Cl PEND EN3 80 G1
Lindisfarne Cl GVE DA12 191 H8
Lindisfarne Rd BCTR RM8 123 J8
  RYNPK SW20 178 D8
Lindisfarne Wy... 
Lindley Pl RCH/KEW TW9 155 N7
Lindley Rd GDST RH9 262 D6
  LEY E10 121 K7
  WOT/HER KT12 216 B2
Lindley St WCHPL E1 140 E4
Lindo Cl CSHM HP5 51 J6
Lindore Rd BTSEA SW11 158 D1
Lindores Rd CAR SM5 201 P7
Lindo St PECK SE15 160 B8
Lind Rd SUT SM1 221 M3
Lindrop St FUL/PGN SW6 157 P7
Lindsay Cl CHSGTN KT9 219 L7
  HOR/WEW KT19 219 P10
  STWL/WRAY TW19 151 J7
Lindsay Dr KTN/HRWW/WS HA3 115 K4
  SHPTN TW17 197 M6
Lindsay Pl CHESW EN7 62 A3
Lindsay Rd ADL/WDHM KT15 215 K7
  HPTN TW12 175 K7
  WPK KT4 200 F8
Lindsay Sq PIM SW1V 16 G7
Lindsell Rd GNWCH SE10 (unclear)
Lindsell St GNWCH SE10 161 H7
Lindsey Cl BMLY BR1 206 B1
  MTCM CR4 202 G4


Lindsey Gdns EBED/NFELT TW14 * 174 A2
Lindsey Ms IS N1 6 F1
Lindsey Rd BCTR RM8 123 M8
  DEN/HRF UB9 111 H6
Lindsey St EPP CM16 70 E4
  FARR EC1M 12 D3
Lindsey Wy EMPK RM11 125 K3
Lind St DEPT SE8 160 G8
Lindum Pl STALW/RED AL3 37 N8
Lindum Rd TEDD TW11 177 H10
Lindvale WOKN/KNAP GU21 232 A4
Lindway WNWD SE27 181 J8
Linfield Cl HDN NW4 116 A4
  WOT/HER KT12 217 J2
Linfield Ct HERT/WAT SG14 24 C4
Linfields AMSS HP7 69 P6
Linford Rd RNLW/ROY CM19 46 F5
  WALTH E17 121 H1
Linford St VX/NE SW8 158 D7
Lingards Rd LEW SE13 161 N10
Lingey Cl BFN/LL DA15 185 J2
Lingfield Av KUT/HW KT1 199 K4
  RDART DA2 188 A3
  UPMR RM14 125 P2
Lingfield Cl EN EN1 79 P5
  NTHWD HA6 92 F8
Lingfield Crs ELTH/MOT SE9 162 G10
Lingfield Dr CRAWE RH10 284 F6
Lingfield Gdns COUL/CHIP CR5 241 J5
  ED N9 100 A1
Lingfield Rd GVW DA11 190 C5
  WIM/MER SW19 178 G9
  WPK KT4 200 F10
Lingfield Wy WAT WD17 72 G4
Lingholm Wy BAR EN5 76 G9
Lingmere Cl CHIG IG7 102 F3
Lingmoor Dr GSTN WD25 55 K9
Ling Rd CAN/RD E16 141 M7
  ERITH DA8 164 D5
Lingwell Rd TOOT SW17 179 N6
Lingwood Gdns ISLW TW7 154 B6
Lingwood Rd CLPT E5 119 P5
Linhope St CAMTN NW1 3 P8
Link 10 CRAWE RH10 284 B4
Link Cl HAT AL10 40 E4
Link Dr HAT AL10 40 E4
Linkfield E/WMO/HCT KT8 197 P3
Link Fld HAYES BR2 205 N6
Linkfield WGCE AL7 23 H9
Linkfield Cnr REDH RH1 257 F10
Linkfield Gdns ELTH/MOT SE9 165 (unclear)
Linkfield La REDH RH1 258 A9
Linkfield Rd ISLW TW7 154 A8
  ST REDH RH1 257 F10
Link La WLGTN SM6 222 G5
Linklea Cl CDALE/KGS NW9 96 E7
Link Rd ADL/WDHM KT15 215 P1
  DAGW RM9 144 C6
  DTCH/LGLY SL3 149 P6
  EBED/NFELT TW14 174 G3
  FBAR/BDGN N11 98 B5
  HHW HP1 35 M3
  WATN WD24 73 L6
  WFD IG8 101 L1
Links Brow LHD/OX KT22 236 G9
Links Cl ASHTD KT21 237 H3
Linkscroft Av ASHF TW15 174 C9
Links Dr BORE WD6 75 L7
  RAD WD7 56 F9
  TRDG/WHET N20 97 K2
Links Gdns STRHM/NOR SW16 181 P10
Linkside CHIG IG7 102 F6
  NFNCH/WDSPK N12 97 J7
  NWMAL KT3 200 B2
Linkside Cl ENC/FH EN2 78 G7
Linkside Gdns ENC/FH EN2 78 G7
Links Pl ASHTD KT21 237 J3
Links Rd ACT W3 135 M8
  ASHF TW15 173 M8
  ASHTD KT21 237 J3
  CRICK NW2 116 C7
  WFD IG8 101 H5
  WWKM BR4 205 M7
  WOKN/KNAP GU21 232 A1
Link's Rd EW KT17 220 D9
Links Side ENC/FH EN2 78 G7
Links View N3 97 H1
  RDART DA2 188 A4
  STALW/RED AL3 38 A4
Links View Cl STAN HA7 94 F7
Links View Ct HPTN TW12 * 176 C7
Links View Rd CROY/NA CRO 204 F10
  HPTN TW12 176 B9
Links Wy NTHWD HA6 92 D9
  RKW/CH/CXG WD3 72 D7
  BECK BR3 204 (unclear)
  EHSLY KT24 253 M4
Linkswood Rd SL1 SL1 128 E3
Links Yd WCHPL E1 13 M3
The Link ACT W3 135 N8
  ALP/SUD HA0 135 H6
  CRAWW RH11 283 N6
  CRICK NW2 116 D6
  NTHLT UB5 113 P10
  PEND EN3 80 D5
  PIN HA5 113 K4
  SLN SL2 129 N8
  TEDD TW11 176 B8
Link Wy DEN/HRF UB9 111 K4
  EMPK RM11 125 M6
  RCHPK/HAM TW10 176 E10
  STA TW18 173 J9
Linkway BCTR RM8 123 J7
  FSBYPK N4 119 J6
  GU GU1 249 L10
  HAYES BR2 206 B1
  HORL RH6 280 C8
  NWMAL KT3 200 B4
  PIN HA5 93 H9
  RYNPK SW20 199 K3
Linkway BRW CM14 106 A3
The Linkway BAR EN5 77 K10
  BELMT SM2 221 N5
Linkway Gdns HARP AL5 20 (unclear)
Linley Cl TIL RM18 169 N6
Linley Crs ROMW/RG RM7 124 C1
Linley Rd TOTM N17 99 M10
Linnell Cl GLDGN NW11 117 H4
Linnell Dr GLDGN NW11 117 L4
Linnell Rd CMBW SE5 159 M8
  REDH RH1 276 B1
  UED N18 99 P6
Linnet Cl BUSH WD23 76 A6
  ED N9 100 G2
  SAND/SEL CR2 224 C6
  THMD SE28 145 K8
Linnet Gv RGUE GU4 250 C9
Linnet Ms BAL SW12 180 B3
Linnett Cl CHING E4 101 N4
Linnet Ter CLAY IG5 * 103 P10
Linnet Wy PUR RM19 166 A4
Linom Rd CLAP SW4 158 F10
Linscott Rd CLPT E5 120 F10
Linsdell Rd BARK IG11 143 H2
Linsey Cl HHNE HP2 35 P5
Linsey St BERM/RHTH SE16 159 L1
Linslade Cl HSLWW TW4 175 M1

| Street | Area | Page | Grid |
|---|---|---|---|
| Linslade Rd ORP BR6 | | 227 | K3 |
| Linstead St KIL/WHAMP NW6 | | 2 | E3 |
| Linstead Wy WAND/EARL SW18 | | 179 | H8 |
| Linthorpe Av ALP/SUD HA0 | | 75 | P9 |
| Linthorpe Rd EBAR EN4 | | 135 | H1 |
| STNW/STAM N16 | | 77 | P7 |
| Linton Av BORE WD6 | | 119 | M5 |
| Linton Cl CAR SM5 | | 75 | L6 |
| CHARL SE7 | | 202 | A7 |
| WELL DA16 | | 161 | P4 |
| Linton Ct ROM RM1 | | 148 | C5 |
| Linton Gdns EHAM E6 | | 104 | F10 |
| Linton Gld CROY/NA CR0 | | 142 | B8 |
| Linton Rd BARK IG11 | | 224 | D6 |
| Lintons Cl HOD EN11 | | 142 | F2 |
| Linton's La IS N1 | | 44 | C5 |
| Lintott Ct STWL/WRAY TW19 | | 6 | F6 |
| Linver Rd FUL/PGN SW6 | | 173 | N2 |
| Linwood SBW CM21 * | | 119 | J6 |
| Linwood Cl CMBW SE5 | | 29 | P1 |
| Linwood Crs EN EN1 | | 159 | N8 |
| Linwood Rd HARP AL5 | | 79 | P5 |
| Linzee Rd CEND/HSY/T N8 | | 20 | B4 |
| Lion Av TWK TW1 | | 118 | A2 |
| Lion Cl BROCKY SE4 | | 176 | L4 |
| SHPTN TW17 | | 182 | K7 |
| Lion Ct BORE WD6 | | 195 | H6 |
| Lionel Gdns ELTH/MOT SE9 | | 75 | P5 |
| Lionel Ms NKENS W10 | | 184 | A1 |
| Lionel Rd ELTH/MOT SE9 | | 8 | A5 |
| Lionel Rd North BTFD TW8 | | 184 | A1 |
| Lionel Rd South BTFD TW8 | | 155 | K2 |
| Lion Gate Gdns RCH/KEW TW9 | | 155 | L4 |
| Lion Gate Ms WAND/EARL SW18 | | 155 | L9 |
| Lion Green Rd COUL/CHIP CR5 | | 179 | K3 |
| Lion La CRAWE RH10 | | 240 | E1 |
| Lion Mills BETH E2 * | | 285 | P9 |
| Lion Park Av CHSGTN KT9 | | 7 | P8 |
| Lions Cl BXLYHS DA6 | | 191 | M1 |
| CROY/NA CR0 | | 163 | P10 |
| ED N9 | | 203 | K8 |
| EHAM E6 | | 99 | P3 |
| TWK TW1 | | 142 | C7 |
| Lions Cl LEE/GVPK SE12 | | 176 | L4 |
| Lion Wy BTFD TW8 | | 183 | P6 |
| Liphook Cl HCH RM12 | | 155 | J6 |
| Liphook Crs FSTH SE23 | | 124 | C9 |
| Liphook Rd OXHEY WD19 | | 131 | B6 |
| Lippitts Hl LOU IG10 | | 93 | L5 |
| Lipsham Cl BNSTD SM7 | | 81 | K6 |
| Lipton Cl STHWK SE1 * | | 221 | N9 |
| Lisbon Av WHTN TW2 | | 140 | C8 |
| Lisbon Cl WALTH E17 | | 176 | B5 |
| Lisburne Rd HAMP NW3 | | 100 | A10 |
| Lisford St PECK SE15 | | 118 | H5 |
| Lisgar Ter WKENS W14 | | 159 | N7 |
| Liskeard Cl CHST BR7 | | 14 | C5 |
| Liskeard Gdns BKHTH/KID SE3 | | 184 | F9 |
| Lisle Cl GVE TOOT SW17 | | 161 | M7 |
| Lisle Pl GRAYS RM17 | | 191 | L5 |
| Lisle St LSQ/SEVD WC2H | | 180 | C7 |
| Lismore HBR/BOV HP3 | | 167 | M2 |
| WIM/MER SW19 * | | 11 | K7 |
| Lismore Circ KTTN NW5 | | 36 | D8 |
| Lismore Cl ISLW TW7 | | 179 | J8 |
| Lismore Crs CRAWW RH11 | | 118 | A10 |
| Lismore Pk SLN SL2 | | 154 | F8 |
| Lismore Rd SAND/SEL CR2 | | 283 | N8 |
| TOTM N17 | | 129 | L8 |
| Lismore Wk IS N1 * | | 223 | M5 |
| Lissant Cl SURB KT6 | | 119 | L1 |
| Lissenden Gdns KTTN NW5 | | 199 | H7 |
| Lissoms Rd COUL/CHIP CR5 | | 118 | B9 |
| Lisson Gv STJWD NW8 | | 240 | A6 |
| Lisson St CAMTN NW1 | | 9 | M1 |
| Lister Av HARP RM3 * | | 9 | N3 |
| Lister Cl ACT W3 | | 105 | L10 |
| MTCM CR4 | | 136 | A7 |
| Lister Dr CVW DA11 | | 179 | P10 |
| Lister Gdns UED N18 | | 189 | P4 |
| Lister Rd TIL RM18 | | 99 | K6 |
| WAN E11 | | 168 | D8 |
| Liston Rd CLAP SW4 | | 121 | K6 |
| TOTM N17 | | 158 | D9 |
| Liston Wy WFD IG8 | | 99 | J8 |
| Listowel Cl BRXN/ST SW9 | | 101 | P8 |
| Listowel Rd DAGE RM10 | | 159 | H6 |
| Listria Pk STNW/STAM N16 | | 124 | B8 |
| Litcham Sp SLN SL1 * | | 117 | M7 |
| Litchfield Av MRDN SM4 | | 129 | J8 |
| SRTFD E15 * | | 201 | J7 |
| Litchfield Gdns WLSDN NW10 | | 141 | K1 |
| Litchfield Rd SUT SM1 | | 136 | D1 |
| Litchfield St LSQ/SEVD WC2H | | 221 | M11 |
| Litchfield Wy GLDGN NW11 | | 11 | K7 |
| GUW GU2 | | 117 | M10 |
| Lithgow's Rd HTHAIR TW6 | | 267 | M2 |
| Lithos Rd HAMP NW3 * | | 152 | F10 |
| Little Acre BECK BR3 | | 3 | H1 |
| CRW CM5 | | 104 | B7 |
| Little Acres WARE SG12 | | 204 | F3 |
| GT/LBKH KT23 | | 26 | C3 |
| STALW/RED AL3 | | 235 | N10 |
| Little Albany St CAMTN NW1 | | 38 | C3 |
| Little Argyll St REGST W1B * | | 10 | E1 |
| Little Aston Rd HARP RM3 | | 10 | L2 |
| Little Belhus Cl SOCK/AV RM15 | | 105 | N8 |
| Little Benty WDR/YW UB7 | | 146 | K4 |
| Little Berkhamsted La BRKMPK AL9 | | 151 | N4 |
| Little Birch Cl ADL/WDHM KT15 | | 42 | H4 |
| Little Birches BFN/LL DA15 | | 215 | N5 |
| The Little Boltons WBPTN SW10 | | 185 | H8 |
| Little Bookham St GT/LBKH KT23 | | 15 | H7 |
| Little Bornes DUL SE21 | | 235 | N10 |
| Little Borough BRKHM/BTCW RH3 * | | 181 | M7 |
| Little Brays HLWS CM18 | | 273 | M1 |
| Little Bridge Rd BERK HP4 * | | 47 | K2 |
| Little Britain STBT EC1A | | 34 | A5 |
| Littlebrook Av SLN SL2 | | 12 | D4 |
| Littlebrook Cl CROY/NA CR0 | | 128 | D7 |
| Littlebrook Gdns CHES/WCR EN8 | | 204 | C6 |
| Little Brook Rd HLWW/ROY CM19 | | 62 | G6 |
| Little Brownings FSTH SE23 | | 45 | P1 |
| Little Buntings WDSR SL4 | | 182 | A5 |
| Little Burrow WGCE AL7 | | 148 | B9 |
| Littlebury Rd CLAP SW4 | | 22 | A5 |
| Littlebury Ter BRWN CM15 | | 158 | E9 |
| Little Bushey La BUSH WD23 | | 86 | E5 |
| Little Catherells HHNE HP1 | | 73 | P7 |
| Little Cattins HLWS CM18 * | | 35 | H4 |
| Little Cedars NFNCH/WDSPK N12 | | 46 | C5 |
| Little Chesters KWD/TDW/WH KT20 * | | 97 | M5 |
| Little Chester St KTBR SW1X | | 256 | D1 |
| Little Cloisters WEST SW1P * | | 16 | E3 |
| Little Collins REDH RH1 * | | 17 | L1 |
| Littlecombe Cl PUT/ROE SW15 | | 277 | J10 |
| Little Common STAN HA7 | | 178 | G3 |
| Little Common La REDH RH1 | | 43 | J8 |
| Littlecote Cl WIM/MER SW19 | | 259 | J8 |
| Littlecote Pl PIN HA5 | | 178 | C3 |
| Little Cottage Pl GNWCH SE10 * | | 93 | M9 |
| Little Crabtree CRAWW RH11 | | 160 | G6 |
| | | 283 | M6 |
| Little Cranmore La EHSLY KT24 | | 252 | C4 |
| Littlecroft ELTH/MOT SE9 | | 162 | D9 |
| MEO DA13 | | 190 | B10 |
| Littlecroft Rd EGH TW20 | | 172 | C8 |
| Littledale ABYW SE2 | | 163 | K5 |
| Little Deans Yd WEST SW1P | | 17 | L3 |
| Little Dell WGCW AL8 | | 22 | C3 |
| Little Dimocks BAL SW12 | | 180 | C5 |
| Littledown Rd SLN SL1 | | 129 | L10 |
| Little Dragons LOU IG10 | | 82 | A5 |
| Little Ealing La EAL W5 | | 155 | H3 |
| Little East Fld COUL/CHIP CR5 | | 240 | E7 |
| Little Edward St CAMTN NW1 * | | 4 | F7 |
| Little Elms HYS/HAR UB3 | | 152 | E6 |
| Little Essex St TPL/STR WC2R * | | 12 | C10 |
| Little Ferry Rd TWK TW1 * | | 176 | C4 |
| Littlefield Cl ARCH N19 * | | 118 | D9 |
| KUT/HW KT1 | | 199 | K2 |
| RGUW GU3 | | 249 | J6 |
| Littlefield Rd EDGW HA8 | | 95 | P8 |
| Littlefield Wy RGUW GU3 | | 249 | H6 |
| Littleford La RGUE GU4 | | 269 | K6 |
| Little Foxes HOD EN11 * | | 44 | B5 |
| Little Friday Rd CHING E4 | | 101 | K3 |
| Little Ganett WGCE AL7 * | | 23 | L7 |
| Little Gaynes Gdns UPMR RM14 | | 126 | A9 |
| Little Gaynes La UPMR RM14 | | 125 | P9 |
| Little Gearies BARK/HLT IG6 | | 122 | E2 |
| Little George St WEST SW1P * | | 17 | L2 |
| Little Gerpins Rd RAIN RM13 | | 145 | N3 |
| Little Graylings ABLGY WD5 | | 54 | H7 |
| Little Greencroft CSHM HP5 | | 50 | F5 |
| Little Green St KTTN NW5 | | 195 | H10 |
| RKW/CH/CXG WD3 | | 72 | A7 |
| Little Gregories La EPP CM16 | | 82 | G1 |
| Little Gv BUSH WD23 | | 74 | A8 |
| DORK RH4 * | | 273 | H4 |
| Littlegrove EBAR EN4 | | 77 | P10 |
| Little Grove Av CHESW EN7 | | 61 | M3 |
| Little Grove Fld HLWW/ROY CM19 | | 46 | F1 |
| Little Halliards WOT/HER KT12 * | | 197 | H6 |
| Little Hardings WGCE AL7 | | 23 | M4 |
| Little Hayes KGLGY WD4 | | 54 | B8 |
| Little Heath CHARL SE7 | | 162 | B5 |
| CHDH RM6 | | 123 | L2 |
| Little Heath La BERK HP4 | | 46 | B3 |
| Littleheath La COB KT11 | | 217 | P10 |
| Little Heath La HHW HP1 | | 34 | K7 |
| Little Heath Rd BXLYHN DA7 | | 164 | A7 |
| CHOB/PIR GU24 | | 213 | K5 |
| Little Ilford La MNPK E12 | | 122 | C9 |
| Little Julians HI SEV TN13 | | 265 | H5 |
| Little Kiln GODL GU7 | | 267 | K9 |
| Little Lake WGCE AL7 | | 23 | L8 |
| Little La HARP AL5 | | 20 | B5 |
| Little Laver Rd CHONG CM5 | | 49 | N6 |
| HLWE CM17 | | 31 | M9 |
| Little Ley WGCE AL7 | | 23 | M8 |
| Little London SHGR GU5 | | 269 | P7 |
| Little London UX/CGN UB8 | | 132 | C2 |
| Little Marlborough St REGST W1B * | | 10 | G6 |
| Little Martins BUSH WD23 | | 74 | A8 |
| Littlemead ESH/CLAY KT10 | | 218 | C1 |
| Little Md HAT AL10 | | 40 | E1 |
| WOKN/KNAP GU21 | | 231 | L2 |
| Littlemede ELTH/MOT SE9 | | 184 | C6 |
| Little Mimms HHNE HP2 | | 35 | N5 |
| Littlemoor Rd IL IG1 | | 122 | G8 |
| Littlemore Rd ABYW SE2 | | 163 | K1 |
| Little Moreton Cl BF/WBF KT14 | | 215 | L8 |
| Little Moss La PIN HA5 | | 93 | M10 |
| Little Mundells WGCE AL7 | | 23 | H4 |
| Little Newport St LSQ/SEVD WC2H | | 11 | J7 |
| Little New St FLST/FETLN EC4A | | 12 | B5 |
| Little Oak Cl SHPTN TW17 | | 196 | A4 |
| Little Orch ADL/WDHM KT15 | | 215 | K7 |
| HHNE HP2 | | 36 | B4 |
| WOKN/KNAP GU21 | | 204 | D10 |
| Little Orchard Cl ABLGY WD5 | | 54 | E7 |
| PIN HA5 * | | 93 | M10 |
| Little Orchards EPSOM KT18 | | 220 | B10 |
| Little Orchard Wy RGUE GU4 | | 268 | B7 |
| Little Oxhey La OXHEY WD19 | | 93 | M6 |
| Little Pk FELT TW13 | | 175 | L5 |
| Little Park Gdns ENC/FH EN2 | | 7 | P9 |
| Little Piper's Cl CHESW EN7 | | 61 | J3 |
| Little Platt GUW GU2 | | 249 | J9 |
| Little Pluckett's Wy BKHH IG9 | | 102 | A2 |
| Little Portland St REGST W1B * | | 10 | C3 |
| Littleport Sp SLN SL1 | | 129 | K8 |
| The Little Potters BUSH WD23 | | 94 | C1 |
| Little Pynchons HLWS CM18 | | 35 | N3 |
| Little Queens Rd TEDD TW11 | | 176 | A9 |
| Little Redlands BMLY BR1 | | 206 | B2 |
| Little Reeves Av AMSS HP7 | | 69 | K5 |
| Little Rdg WGCE AL7 * | | 23 | K5 |
| Little Riding WOKS/MYFD GU22 | | 232 | A2 |
| Little Rivers WGCE AL7 | | 23 | K4 |
| Little Roke Av PUR/KEN CR8 | | 35 | P5 |
| Little Roke Rd PUR/KEN CR8 | | 223 | K10 |
| Littlers Cl WIM/MER SW19 | | 223 | K10 |
| Little Russell St NOXST/BSQ WC1A | | 201 | N1 |
| Little St James's St WHALL SW1A | | 11 | L4 |
| Little St Leonards MORT/ESHN SW14 | | 10 | G10 |
| Little Shardeloes AMSS HP7 | | 155 | P9 |
| Little Smith St WEST SW1P | | 48 | F6 |
| Little Somerset St TWRH EC3N | | 17 | L5 |
| Little Spring CSHM HP5 | | 13 | L6 |
| Little Stock Rd CHESW EN7 | | 50 | G4 |
| Little Strd CDALE/KGS NW9 | | 61 | M3 |
| Little Stream Cl NTHWD HA6 | | 96 | H8 |
| Little St GUW GU2 | | 92 | H4 |
| WAB EN9 | | 249 | M6 |
| Little Sutton La DTCH/LGLY SL3 | | 81 | H2 |
| Little Thistle WGCE AL7 | | 150 | E5 |
| Little Thrift STMC/STPC BR5 | | 23 | M9 |
| Little Titchfield St GTPST W1W * | | 206 | F1 |
| Littleton Av CHING E4 | | 10 | C2 |
| Littleton Crs HRW HA1 | | 89 | N10 |
| Littleton La REIG RH2 | | 114 | E7 |
| RGUW GU3 | | 275 | H2 |
| SHPTN TW17 | | 267 | K9 |
| Littleton Rd ASHF TW15 | | 195 | N1 |
| HRW HA1 | | 174 | C2 |
| Littleton St WAND/EARL SW18 | | 61 | E3 |
| Little Trinity La BLKFR EC4V * | | 179 | K5 |
| Little Turnstile HHOL WC1V | | 12 | A5 |
| Littlewade CHSGT GU7 * | | 11 | H4 |
| Little Wk HLWE CM20 * | | 267 | J8 |
| Little Warley Hl Rd RBWL/HUT CM13 | | 23 | J8 |
| Little Warren Cl RGUE GU4 | | 127 | K3 |
| Littlewick Rd WOKN/KNAP GU21 | | 268 | E2 |
| Little Widbury WARE SG12 | | 231 | J2 |
| Little Widbury La WARE SG12 | | 26 | E2 |
| | | 26 | E2 |
| Little Windmill Hl KGLGY WD4 | | 53 | H8 |
| Littlewood LEW SE13 | | 183 | H1 |
| Littlewood Cl WEA W13 | | 247 | K8 |
| Little Woodcote Est WLGTN SM6 * | | 154 | D3 |
| Little Woodcote La CAR SM5 | | 222 | C6 |
| Little Woodlands WDSR SL4 | | 148 | E9 |
| Littleworth Av ESH/CLAY KT10 | | 218 | C1 |
| Littleworth Common Rd ESH/CLAY KT10 * | | 198 | C10 |
| Littleworth La ESH/CLAY KT10 | | 218 | C1 |
| Littleworth Pl ESH/CLAY KT10 | | 218 | C1 |
| Littleworth Rd ESH/CLAY KT10 | | 218 | C1 |
| Little Youngs WGCW AL8 | | 22 | F5 |
| Littlt Halliards WOT/HER KT12 * | | 197 | H6 |
| Livermere Rd HACK E8 | | 7 | L5 |
| Liverpool Gv WALW SE17 | | 18 | G8 |
| Liverpool Rd CAN/RD E16 | | 141 | K7 |
| EA W5 | | 116 | K10 |
| HOLWY N7 | | 6 | A1 |
| KUTN/CMB KT2 | | 177 | M10 |
| LEY E10 | | 121 | H1 |
| SL SL1 | | 128 | G8 |
| STAL AL1 | | 38 | D6 |
| WATW WD18 | | 73 | J9 |
| Livesey Cl KUT/HW KT1 | | 199 | L5 |
| THMD SE28 | | 162 | F2 |
| Livesey Pl PECK SE15 | | 19 | P9 |
| Livingstone Cl CHONG CM5 | | 67 | P5 |
| CRAWE RH10 | | 283 | P9 |
| CTHM CR3 | | 241 | M8 |
| GVE DA12 | | 190 | C8 |
| Livingstone Gdns GVE DA12 | | 190 | C8 |
| Livingstone Rd BTSEA SW11 | | 157 | N9 |
| CRAWE RH10 | | 283 | P9 |
| CTHM CR3 | | 241 | M8 |
| GVE DA12 | | 190 | C8 |
| HSLW TW3 | | 154 | B10 |
| PLMGR N13 | | 98 | F7 |
| STHL UB1 | | 133 | L9 |
| THHTH CR7 | | 205 | L2 |
| WALTH E17 | | 120 | G4 |
| Livingstone Wk HHNE HP2 | | 36 | A1 |
| Lizard St FSBYE EC1V | | 6 | F1 |
| Lizban St BKHTH/KID SE3 | | 161 | N6 |
| Llanbury Cl CFSP/GDCR SL9 | | 90 | B8 |
| Llanelly Rd CRICK NW2 | | 117 | J7 |
| Llanover Rd WBLY HA9 | | 115 | J8 |
| WOOL/PLUM SE18 | | 162 | D6 |
| Llanthony Rd MRDN SM4 | | 201 | N6 |
| Llanvanor Rd CRICK NW2 | | 117 | J7 |
| Llewellyn St BERM/RHTH SE16 | | 19 | P2 |
| Lloyd Av CROY/NA CR0 | | 222 | B10 |
| STRHM/NOR SW16 | | 202 | A9 |
| Lloyd Baker St FSBYW WC1X | | 6 | C4 |
| Lloyd Ct PIN HA5 | | 113 | L3 |
| Lloyd Ms PEND EN3 | | 165 | H6 |
| Lloyd Park Av CROY/NA CR0 | | 223 | N1 |
| Lloyd Rd DAGW RM9 | | 142 | A4 |
| EHAM E6 | | 142 | C3 |
| WALTH E17 | | 120 | C2 |
| WPK KT4 | | 200 | F10 |
| Lloyd's Av FENCHST EC3M * | | 13 | K6 |
| Lloyds Ct CRAWE RH10 * | | 283 | P4 |
| Lloyd's Pl BKHTH/KID SE3 | | 161 | K8 |
| Lloyds Rd EPP CM16 | | 82 | A2 |
| Lloyd's Rw CLKNW EC1R | | 6 | B10 |
| Lloyd St FSBYW WC1X | | 6 | C3 |
| Lloyd Thomas Ct WDGN N22 * | | 98 | D6 |
| Lloyd Vls BROCKY SE4 | | 160 | F8 |
| Loampit Hl LEW SE13 | | 160 | E9 |
| Loampit V LEW SE13 | | 160 | F10 |
| Loanda Cl HACK E8 | | 7 | L5 |
| Loates La WAT WD17 | | 23 | P3 |
| Loats Rd BRXS/STRHM SW2 | | 180 | F2 |
| Lobelia Rd CHOB/PIR GU24 | | 250 | F7 |
| Local Board Rd WAT WD17 | | 73 | L9 |
| Locarno Rd ACT W3 | | 135 | P10 |
| GFD/PVL UB6 | | 134 | B6 |
| Lochaber Rd LEW SE13 | | 156 | F5 |
| Lochaline St HMSMTH W6 | | 156 | F5 |
| Lochan Cl YEAD UB4 | | 133 | M6 |
| Lochinvar Cl SL SL1 | | 148 | C1 |
| Lochinvar St BAL SW12 | | 180 | C3 |
| Lochmere Cl ERITH DA8 | | 165 | H1 |
| Lochnagar St POP/IOD E14 | | 141 | H7 |
| Lockark Cl BERK HP4 | | 33 | L7 |
| Lockesley Dr WOKN/KNAP GU21 | | 231 | N1 |
| Lockesley Est POP/IOD E14 | | 140 | F8 |
| Lockesley Sq SURB KT6 * | | 199 | J6 |
| Lockestone Cl WEY KT13 | | 216 | A3 |
| Locket Rd KTN/HRWW/WS HA3 | | 94 | E10 |
| Locket Road Ms KTN/HRWW/WS HA3 | | 94 | D10 |
| Lockets Cl WDSR SL4 | | 148 | C7 |
| Locke Wy WOKN/KNAP GU21 | | 231 | J2 |
| Lockfield Av PEND EN3 | | 80 | D6 |
| Lockfield Dr WOKN/KNAP GU21 | | 231 | K3 |
| Lockgate Ct HOM E9 | | 120 | L10 |
| Lockhart Cl HOLWY N7 | | 5 | N1 |
| PEND EN3 | | 80 | D6 |
| Lockhart Rd COB KT11 | | 217 | K9 |
| Lockhart St BOW E3 | | 140 | E6 |
| Lockhurst St CLPT E5 | | 138 | D1 |
| Lockington Rd VX/NE SW8 | | 158 | C7 |
| Lock Keepers Cots TOTM N17 * | | 120 | A2 |
| Lock La WOKS/MYFD GU22 | | 233 | L2 |
| Lockley Crs HAT AL10 | | 40 | E2 |
| Lockmead Rd LEW SE13 | | 161 | H9 |
| SEVS/STOTM N15 | | 119 | N4 |
| Lock Rd RCH/KEW TW9 | | 176 | H6 |
| Lock Rd RGUE GU4 | | 250 | A6 |
| RCHPK/HAM TW10 | | 177 | H6 |
| Lock's La MTCM CR4 | | 161 | K6 |
| Locksley Dr WOKN/KNAP GU21 | | 231 | K3 |
| Locksley Est POP/IOD E14 | | 140 | F8 |
| Lockstone Wy WEY KT13 | | 216 | A3 |
| Locks Yd SEV TN13 * | | 265 | K6 |
| Lockton St NTGHL W11 * | | 136 | C6 |
| Lockwell Rd DAGE RM10 | | 124 | A8 |
| Lockwood Cl EBAR EN4 | | 78 | A8 |
| SYD SE26 | | 182 | C7 |
| Lockwood Pth CRAWE RH10 | | 284 | A5 |
| Lockwood Sq BERM/RHTH SE16 | | 19 | N8 |
| Lockwood Wy CHSGTN KT9 | | 219 | H10 |
| WALTH E17 | | 140 | M1 |
| Lockyer Av CHING E4 | | 101 | J4 |
| Lockyer Cl PEND EN3 | | 80 | D6 |
| Lockyer Pth BH/WHM TN16 * | | 262 | F5 |
| Lockyer Rd PUR RM19 | | 166 | G3 |
| Lockyer St STHWK SE1 | | 19 | K3 |
| Locomotive Dr EBED/NFELT TW14 | | 175 | H3 |
| Locton Gdn BOW E3 | | 140 | E1 |
| Loddon Sp SL SL1 | | 129 | K9 |
| Loder Cl WOKN/KNAP GU21 | | 214 | G9 |
| Loder Gdns PECK SE15 | | 160 | B2 |
| Loder St PECK SE15 | | 19 | L9 |
| Lodge Av BCTR RM8 | | 123 | P10 |
| BORE WD6 | | 75 | J4 |
| BH/WHM TN16 | | 244 | F9 |
| BMLY BR1 | | 183 | M5 |
| CROY/NA CR0 | | 202 | G5 |
| DAGW RM9 | | 143 | H5 |
| GPK RM2 | | 125 | H2 |
| Lodge Cl CHIG IG7 | | 103 | K4 |
| COB KT11 | | 235 | N2 |
| CRAWW RH11 | | 283 | M7 |
| EDGW HA8 | | 95 | L7 |
| EGH TW20 | | 172 | A7 |
| HERT/WAT SG14 | | 25 | K3 |
| ISLW TW7 | | 154 | B7 |
| LHD/OX KT22 | | 236 | C2 |
| OXTED RH8 | | 260 | B8 |
| RDKG RH5 | | 273 | H6 |
| SL SL1 | | 149 | H1 |
| UED N18 | | 99 | K6 |
| UX/CGN UB8 | | 131 | M6 |
| WLGTN SM6 | | 202 | B8 |
| Lodge Ct ALP/SUD HA0 | | 115 | K10 |
| Lodge Crs CHES/WCR EN8 | | 62 | C10 |
| ORP BR6 | | 207 | L8 |
| Lodge Dr BRKMPK AL9 | | 40 | C1 |
| PLMGR N13 | | 99 | H5 |
| RKW/CH/CXG WD3 | | 71 | M8 |
| Lodge End CDALE/KGS NW9 | | 56 | C10 |
| RAD WD7 | | 59 | H3 |
| RKW/CH/CXG WD3 | | 72 | E8 |
| Lodge Gdns BECK BR3 | | 204 | E5 |
| Lodge Hall HLWS CM18 | | 35 | P4 |
| Lodge Hl PUR/KEN CR8 | | 241 | H1 |
| REDBR IG4 | | 122 | B2 |
| WELL DA16 | | 163 | L6 |
| Lodgehill Park Cl RYLN/HDSTN HA2 | | 114 | A7 |
| Lodge La BH/WHM TN16 | | 262 | F3 |
| BXLY DA5 | | 185 | N2 |
| CDW/CHF RM16 | | 167 | N2 |
| CROY/NA CR0 | | 224 | C4 |
| CRW RM5 | | 104 | B7 |
| GRAYS RM17 | | 167 | M1 |
| NFNCH/WDSPK N12 | | 97 | M6 |
| RDKG RH5 | | 273 | L10 |
| REDH RH1 | | 258 | B9 |
| REIG RH2 | | 257 | K9 |
| RGUE GU4 | | 250 | D8 |
| ROMW/RG RM7 | | 124 | D4 |
| RPLY/SEND GU23 | | 251 | H2 |
| RSEV TN14 | | 228 | A5 |
| SBW CM21 | | 29 | P1 |
| SEV TN13 | | 246 | E5 |
| STA TW18 | | 173 | J7 |
| STAL AL1 | | 38 | D7 |
| STAN HA7 | | 95 | J5 |
| STHWK SE1 | | 18 | G5 |
| STRHM/NOR SW16 | | 202 | G2 |
| SWCM DA10 | | 189 | H1 |
| SWLY BR8 | | 209 | H4 |
| SWLY BR8 | | 209 | H6 |
| THHTH CR7 | | 203 | H6 |
| TIL RM18 | | 167 | H5 |
| TOOT SW17 | | 180 | A10 |
| TWK TW1 | | 157 | N1 |
| VW GU25 | | 193 | K4 |
| WARE SG12 | | 26 | C3 |
| WBLY HA9 | | 115 | K10 |
| WLCTN SM6 | | 222 | C1 |
| WTHK RM20 | | 167 | J5 |
| The Lodge SHB W12 * | | 156 | G1 |
| Lodge Vls WFD IG8 | | 101 | L8 |
| Lodge Wk WARL CR6 | | 242 | F2 |
| Lodge Wy ASHF TW15 | | 173 | P5 |
| SHPTN TW17 | | 196 | D2 |
| WDSR SL4 | | 148 | A8 |
| Lodore Gdns CDALE/KGS NW9 | | 116 | B3 |
| Lodore Gn HDN/ICK UB10 | | 111 | P9 |
| Lodore St POP/IOD E14 | | 141 | N8 |
| Loewen Rd CDW/CHF RM16 | | 168 | D2 |
| Lofthouse Pl CHSGTN KT9 | | 219 | H3 |
| Loftie St BERM/RHTH SE16 | | 19 | P2 |
| Lofting Rd IS N1 | | 6 | A4 |
| Loftus Rd BARK IG11 | | 142 | F1 |
| SHB W12 | | 136 | E10 |
| Loftus Vls SHB W12 * | | 136 | E10 |
| Logan Cl HSLWW TW4 | | 155 | J10 |
| PEND EN3 | | 80 | E3 |
| Logan Ms ECT SW5 | | 14 | B8 |
| ROM RM1 | | 124 | A4 |
| Logan Pl ECT SW5 | | 14 | B8 |
| Logan Rd ED N9 | | 102 | G1 |
| WBLY HA9 | | 115 | K7 |
| The Logans BAR EN5 | | 76 | G7 |
| Logmore La DORK RH4 | | 272 | D7 |
| Logs Hill CHST BR7 | | 206 | B1 |
| Logs Hill Cl CHST BR7 | | 206 | A1 |
| Loide Gdns STALE/WH AL4 | | 39 | J6 |
| Lois Dr SHPTN TW17 | | 196 | C5 |
| Lolesworth Cl WCHPL E1 | | 13 | L4 |
| Lollards Cl AMS HP6 | | 65 | L6 |
| Lollard St LBTH SE11 | | 17 | N9 |
| Lollesworth La EHSLY KT24 | | 252 | D2 |
| Loman Pth SOCK/AV RM15 | | 146 | E8 |
| Loman St STHWK SE1 | | 18 | E2 |
| Lomas Cl CROY/NA CR0 | | 225 | H4 |
| Lomas Dr HACK E8 | | 7 | M3 |
| Lomas St WCHPL E1 | | 13 | N2 |
| Lombard Av GDMY/SEVK IG3 | | 123 | H6 |
| PEND EN3 | | 80 | D5 |
| Lombard Rd BTSEA SW11 | | 157 | N8 |
| FBAR/BDGN N11 | | 98 | A8 |
| WIM/MER SW19 | | 201 | L2 |
| Lombard St BANK EC3V | | 13 | H6 |
| LEW SE13 | | 183 | H1 |
| UX/CGN UB8 | | 131 | L4 |
| Lombard Wall CHARL SE7 | | 161 | N2 |
| Lombardy Cl HMHL HP2 * | | 36 | F7 |
| WFD IG8 | | 103 | J8 |
| WOKN/KNAP GU21 | | 231 | K3 |
| Lombardy Dr BERK HP4 | | 34 | A6 |
| Lombardy Pl BAY/PAD W2 | | 8 | C8 |
| Lombardy Wy BORE WD6 | | 75 | H1 |
| Lomond Cl ALP/SUD HA0 | | 135 | U2 |
| SEVS/STOTM N15 | | 119 | L3 |
| Lomond Gdns SAND/SEL CR2 | | 224 | D4 |
| Lomond Gv CMBW SE5 | | 159 | L6 |
| Lomond Rd HHNE HP2 | | 36 | A1 |
| Loncin Mead Av ADL/WDHM KT15 | | 215 | M5 |
| Loncroft Rd LOU IG10 | | 82 | G9 |
| Londesborough Rd STNW/STAM N16 | | 119 | M9 |
| London Br CANST EC4R | | 13 | H8 |
| London Bridge St STHWK SE1 | | 13 | H10 |
| London Bridge Wk STHWK SE1 * | | 13 | H9 |
| London City Airport Link CAN/RD E16 | | 141 | L9 |
| Londonderry Pde ERITH DA8 * | | 164 | E6 |
| London End BEAC HP9 | | 88 | G10 |
| London Rd BEAC HP9 | | 182 | K7 |
| London Flds HACK E8 * | | 140 | A2 |
| London Fields East Side HACK E8 | | 140 | A2 |
| London Fields West Side HACK E8 * | | 7 | P3 |
| London La BMLY BR1 | | 183 | L10 |
| London Loop BNSTD SM7 | | 221 | J10 |
| BORE WD6 | | 75 | N10 |
| CROY/NA CR0 | | 224 | D7 |
| EBAR EN4 | | 78 | C3 |
| EN EN1 | | 80 | A3 |
| HAYES BR2 | | 205 | J3 |
| ORP BR6 | | 206 | E8 |
| SAND/SEL CR2 | | 223 | P10 |
| STMC/STPC BR5 | | 206 | D5 |
| WKWM BR4 | | 205 | M10 |
| London Ms BAY/PAD W2 | | 9 | M3 |
| London Rd ABR/ST RM4 | | 84 | D5 |
| ABR/ST RM4 | | 87 | K7 |
| ASC SL5 | | 192 | B5 |
| ASHF TW15 | | 173 | H7 |
| BARK IG11 | | 142 | E2 |
| BECK BR3 | | 88 | E10 |
| BERK HP4 | | 34 | G3 |
| BFOR GU20 | | 192 | B10 |
| BH/WHM TN16 | | 244 | D5 |
| BMLY BR1 | | 183 | M5 |
| BRW CM14 | | 265 | N7 |
| BUSH WD23 | | 202 | B8 |
| CHEAM SM3 | | 200 | G9 |
| CHONG CM5 | | 67 | L10 |
| London Road A1306 SOCK/AV RM15 | | 165 | N1 |
| WTHK RM20 | | 167 | H2 |
| London Road Purfleet PUR RM19 | | 166 | A4 |
| London Rd North REDH RH1 | | 258 | C2 |
| London Rd South REDH RH1 | | 258 | C2 |
| London Rd West REDH RH1 | | 258 | C2 |
| London Rd West AMSS HP7 | | 69 | H6 |
| London Road West Thurrock WTHK RM20 | | 166 | D5 |
| London Stile CHSWK W4 * | | 155 | M4 |
| London Sq BAY/PAD W2 * | | 9 | K1 |
| London Stile POP/IOD E14 | | 154 | M4 |
| London Wd HAYES BR2 | | 226 | D1 |
| Londown La North EW KT17 | | 220 | C6 |
| Londown La South EW KT17 | | 238 | C1 |
| Londown Rd CAT SE6 | | 182 | K7 |
| EW KT17 | | 220 | C6 |
| RGUE GU4 | | 268 | G3 |
| Long Dr ACT W3 | | 136 | B4 |
| GFD/PVL UB6 | | 133 | P4 |
| RSLP HA4 | | 113 | K9 |
| SL SL1 | | 128 | B5 |
| WDR/YW UB7 | | 151 | P1 |
| Long Dyke GU GU1 | | 250 | D2 |
| Long Elmes KTN/HRWW/WS HA3 | | 94 | A9 |
| Long Elms ABLGY WD5 | | 54 | C9 |
| Long Elms Cl ABLGY WD5 | | 54 | C9 |
| Long Fallow LCOL/BKTW AL2 | | 55 | P3 |
| Longfellow Dr AMS HP6 | | 65 | P9 |
| Longfellow Rd WALTH E17 | | 120 | M6 |
| WPK KT4 | | 200 | E8 |
| Longfellow Wy STHWK SE1 * | | 19 | M6 |
| Long Fld CDALE/KGS NW9 | | 96 | B8 |
| Longfield BMLY BR1 | | 183 | N6 |
| HHS/BOV HP3 | | 36 | A10 |
| HLWS CM18 | | 35 | P3 |
| LOU IG10 | | 81 | P7 |
| Longfield Av EA W5 | | 135 | V1 |
| EMPK RM11 | | 124 | G3 |
| HCH RM12 | | 124 | B6 |
| HGT N6 | | 96 | B10 |
| MLHL NW7 | | 96 | A5 |
| PEND EN3 | | 80 | D1 |
| WALTH E17 | | 120 | C2 |
| WBLY HA9 | | 96 | D10 |
| WLGTN SM6 | | 202 | D2 |
| Longfield Crs KWD/TDW/WH KT20 | | 238 | F6 |
| SYD SE26 | | 182 | A5 |
| Longfield Dr AMS HP6 | | 68 | G4 |
| MORT/ESHN SW14 | | 177 | N1 |
| MTCM CR4 | | 201 | P1 |
| Longfield Est STHWK SE1 | | 19 | M5 |
| Longfield La CHESW EN7 | | 61 | N1 |
| Longfield Rd CSHM HP5 | | 50 | E5 |
| DORK RH4 | | 272 | G3 |
| EA W5 | | 135 | H8 |
| HARP AL5 | | 20 | B8 |
| Longfields CHONG CM5 | | 67 | P6 |
| Longfields WAND/EARL SW18 | | 179 | K3 |
| Longford Av EBED/NFELT TW14 | | 174 | A2 |
| STHL UB1 | | 133 | P9 |
| STWL/WRAY TW19 | | 173 | M6 |
| Longford Cl FELT TW13 | | 175 | M6 |
| HPTN TW12 | | 175 | J6 |
| YEAD UB4 | | 133 | L9 |
| Longford Gdns HOR/WEW KT19 | | 219 | H5 |
| SUT SM1 | | 201 | M10 |
| YEAD UB4 | | 133 | L9 |
| Longford Rd WHTN TW2 | | 175 | P4 |
| Longford St CAMTN NW1 | | 10 | F1 |
| Longford Wy STWL/WRAY TW19 | | 173 | P4 |
| Long Furlong Dr SLN SL2 | | 128 | Q6 |
| Long Gore GODL GU7 | | 267 | K9 |
| Long Gro CHIG IG7 | | 103 | N1 |
| Long Gv BEAC HP9 | | 89 | H7 |
| HARP RM3 | | 105 | M10 |
| Long Grove Cl BROX EN10 | | 44 | D5 |
| Long Grove Rd HOR/WEW KT19 | | 219 | J5 |
| PUR/KEN CR8 | | 222 | F7 |
| Longhayes Av CHDH RM6 | | 123 | N1 |
| Longheath Dr GT/LBKH KT23 | | 235 | M10 |
| Longheath Gdns CROY/NA CR0 | | 204 | B5 |
| Longhedge HH CTHM CR3 | | 158 | B9 |
| Longhill Rd CAT SE6 | | 242 | D7 |
| Longhook Gdns NTHLT UB5 | | 183 | H3 |
| Longhope Cl PECK SE15 | | 133 | H4 |
| Longhouse Rd CDW/CHF RM16 | | 19 | K10 |
| Longhurst Rd CROY/NA CR0 | | 168 | E2 |
| EHSLY KT24 | | 204 | A6 |
| LEW SE13 | | 252 | C5 |
| Longland Dr TRDG/WHET N20 | | 183 | K1 |
| Longlands HHNE HP2 | | 97 | L4 |
| Longlands Av COUL/CHIP CR5 | | 36 | A5 |
| Longlands Cl CHES/WCR EN8 | | 222 | B9 |
| Longlands Park Crs BFN/LL DA15 | | 62 | C8 |
| Longlands Rd BFN/LL DA15 | | 185 | H6 |
| WCCE AL7 | | 185 | H6 |
| Long La BXLYHN DA7 | | 23 | J7 |
| CDW/CHF RM16 | | 164 | M1 |
| CROY/NA CR0 | | 168 | B6 |
| FNCH N3 | | 204 | J3 |
| HGDN/ICK UB10 | | 97 | L9 |
| HGDN/ICK UB10 | | 112 | C8 |
| HHS/BOV HP3 | | 132 | B4 |
| RKW/CH/CXG WD3 | | 52 | C7 |
| STBT EC1A | | 90 | G2 |
| STHWK SE1 | | 12 | D3 |
| STWL/WRAY TW19 | | 19 | J1 |
| Longleat Rd EN EN1 | | 174 | A6 |
| Longleat Wy EBED/NFELT TW14 | | 79 | N4 |
| Longleigh La ABYW SE2 | | 174 | D3 |
| WCCE AL7 | | 163 | M5 |
| Longley Av ALP/SUD HA0 | | 23 | M5 |
| Longley Ms CDW/CHF RM16 | | 135 | L3 |
| Longley Rd CROY/NA CR0 | | 168 | C1 |
| HRW HA1 | | 203 | J7 |
| TOOT SW17 | | 114 | C3 |
| Longley St STHWK SE1 | | 179 | P9 |
| Longley Wy CRICK NW2 | | 100 | G7 |
| Long Lodge Dr WOT/HER KT12 | | 116 | F8 |
| Longmans Cl WATW WD18 | | 197 | K3 |
| Long Mark Rd CAN/RD E16 | | 72 | D10 |
| Longmarsh La THMD SE28 | | 142 | A8 |
| Longmarsh Vw EYN DA4 | | 143 | H10 |
| Long Md CDALE/KGS NW9 | | 210 | A1 |
| Longmead CHST BR7 | | 96 | C3 |
| GU GU1 | | 206 | D2 |
| Longmead Cl BRWN CM15 | | 250 | F10 |
| CTHM CR3 | | 241 | M7 |
| Longmead Dr SCUP DA14 | | 185 | N5 |
| Longmeadow GVE DA12 | | 191 | J4 |
| Long Meadow KTTN NW5 | | 5 | J1 |
| RBRW/HUT CM13 | | 107 | P3 |
| Long Meadow Cl WWKM BR4 | | 205 | H7 |
| Longmeadow Rd BFN/LL DA15 | | 185 | H6 |
| Longmead Rd HOR/WEW KT19 | | 220 | B6 |
| HYS/HAR UB3 | | 133 | J9 |
| THDIT KT7 | | 198 | D2 |
| TOOT SW17 | | 180 | B7 |
| Longmere Gdns KWD/TDW/WH KT20 | | 238 | F5 |
| Long Mimms HHNE HP2 | | 35 | P5 |
| Long Moor CHES/WCR EN8 | | 62 | D5 |
| Longmoore St PIM SW1V | | 16 | C7 |
| Longmoor CHES/WCR EN8 | | 62 | D5 |
| Longmore Av BAR EN5 | | 77 | M7 |
| Longmore Cl RKW/CH/CXG WD3 | | 91 | J3 |
| Longmore Gdns WGCE AL7 * | | 23 | J5 |
| Longnor Rd WCHPL E1 | | 141 | H1 |
| Long Pk AMS HP6 | | 69 | H2 |
| Long Park Cl AMS HP6 | | 69 | H2 |
| Long Pond Rd BKHTH/KID SE3 | | 161 | J8 |
| Longport Cl BARK/HLT IG6 | | 103 | K1 |
| Long Reach RPLY/SEND GU23 | | 234 | C10 |
| Long Reach Rd BARK IG11 | | 143 | J6 |
| Long Readings La SLN SL2 | | 128 | B5 |
| Longridge RAD WD7 | | 56 | C10 |
| Longridge Gv WOKS/MYFD GU22 | | 215 | N10 |
| Longridge La STHL UB1 | | 134 | A3 |
| Longridge Rd ECT SW5 | | 14 | C5 |
| Long Ridings AV RBRW/HUT CM13 | | 87 | J3 |
| Long Rdg HLWS CM18 | | 158 | D10 |
| Long Rds WOKS/MYFD GU22 | | 241 | P10 |
| Longshaw Rd CHING E4 | | 101 | J4 |
| Longside CL EGH TW20 | | 194 | H1 |
| Long Spring STALW/RED AL3 | | 38 | D1 |
| Longstaff Crs WAND/EARL SW18 | | 179 | K2 |
| Longstaff Rd WAND/EARL SW18 | | 179 | K2 |
| Longstone Av WLSDN NW10 | | 136 | C2 |
| Longstone Rd IVER SL0 | | 130 | H4 |
| TOOT SW17 | | 180 | C8 |
| Long St BETH E2 | | 7 | L8 |
| WAB EN9 | | 64 | B6 |
| Longthornton Rd STRHM/NOR SW16 | | 202 | D2 |
| Longton Av SYD SE26 | | 181 | P7 |
| Longton Gv SYD SE26 | | 182 | A7 |
| Longtown Cl HARH RM3 | | 105 | K6 |

Longtown Rd HARH RM3 105 K6
Long Vw BERK HP4 33 M3
Longview Wy CRW RM5 104 E9
Longville Rd LBTH SE11 18 C5
Long Wk CSTG HP8 70 B7
EPSOM KT18 238 F5
NWMAL KT3 199 P3
STHWK SE1 19 K3
WDSR SL4 * 171 J1
WOOL/PLUM SE18 162 E5
Longwalk Rd STKPK UB11 132 C10
The Long Wk WDSR SL4 171 J4
Long Wd HLWS CM18 46 G6
Longwood Av DTCH/LGLY SL3 150 E4
Longwood Cl UPMR RM14 126 B10
Longwood Ct WPK KT4 200 D9
Long Wood Dr BEAC HP9 89 L7
Longwood Dr PUT/ROE SW15 178 D2
Longwood Gdns CLAY IG5 122 C2
Longwood La AMSS HP7 69 J5
Longwood Rd
HERT/WAT SG14 24 G4
PUR/KEN CR8 241 L2
Longwood Vw CRAWE RH10 284 B10
Longworth Cl THMD SE28 143 N8
Long Yd BMSBY WC1N 11 N2
The Loning CDALE/KGS NW9 116 C2
PEND EN3 80 B4
Lonsdale HHNE HP2 35 P3
Lonsdale Av EHAM E6 142 A6
ROMW/RG RM7 124 D4
WBLY HA9 115 K10
Lonsdale Cl EHAM E6 142 B6
ELTH/MOT SE9 184 A6
UX/CGN UB8 132 D8
Lonsdale Crs GNTH/NBYPK IG2 122 E4
RDART DA2 188 B5
Lonsdale Dr ENC/FH EN2 78 E8
Lonsdale Dr North
ENC/FH EN2 78 F9
Lonsdale Gdns THHTH CR7 202 G4
Lonsdale Ms NTGHL W11 8 D6
RCH/KEW TW9 * 155 M7
Lonsdale Pl IS N1 6 B4
Lonsdale Rd BARN SW13 156 C6
BXLYHN DA7 164 A8
DORK RH4 272 G1
KIL/WHAMP NW6 2 C7
NTGHL W11 8 C6
NWDGN UB2 153 L2
SNWD SE25 204 A4
WAN E11 121 L5
WEY KT13 216 B4
Lonsdale Sq IS N1 6 B4
Loobert Rd SEVS/STOTM N15 119 M1
Looe Gdns BARK/HLT IG6 122 E1
Loom La RAD WD7 74 E3
Loop Rd CHST BR7 184 F9
EPSOM KT18 237 P2
WAB EN9 62 G8
WOKS/MYFD GU22 232 C6
Lopen Rd UED N18 99 M5
Loppets Rd CRAWE RH10 284 A9
Loraine Cl PEND EN3 80 B9
Loraine Cots HOLWY N7 * 118 G9
Loraine Gdns ASHTD KT21 237 K3
Loraine Rd CHSWK W4 155 N5
HOLWY N7 118 G9
Lord Av CLAY IG5 122 C2
Lord Chancellor Wk
KUTN/CMB KT2 199 P1
Lord Chatham's Ride
RSEV TN14 245 N3
Lord Chatham's Ride
RSEV TN14 245 P4
Lorden Wk BETH E2 7 N10
Lord Hills Rd BAY/PAD W2 9 H3
Lord Holland La
BRXN/ST SW9 * 159 H8
Lord Knyvett Cl
STWL/WRAY TW19 173 N2
Lord Knyvetts Ct
STWL/WRAY TW19 * 173 P2
Lord Mayors Dr SLN SL2 128 E1
Lord Napier Pl HMSMTH W6 156 D4
Lord North St WEST SW1P 17 L4
Lord Roberts Ms
FUL/PGN SW6 * 157 L6
Lordsbury Fld WLGTN SM6 222 D6
Lords Cl DUL SE21 181 K5
FELT TW13 175 M5
RAD WD7 57 K8
Lordsgrove Cl
KWD/TDW/WH KT20 238 E6
Lordship Gv STNW/STAM N16 119 L7
Lordship La EDUL SE22 181 N2
WDGN N22 99 H10
Lordship Pk STNW/STAM N16 119 L7
Lordship Park Ms
STNW/STAM N16 119 K7
Lordship Pl CHEL SW3 15 N10
Lordship Rd CHESW EN7 62 A6
NTHLT UB5 133 M2
STNW/STAM N16 119 L6
Lordship Ter STNW/STAM N16 119 L7
Lordsmead Rd TOTM N17 99 M9
Lords Mill Ct CSHM HP5 51 H8
Lord St CAN/RD E16 142 B10
GVE DA12 190 E3
HOD EN11 44 D3
WAT WD17 73 K7
Lords Vw STJWD NW8 3 N9
Lords Wd WGCE AL7 23 M5
Lordswood Cl RDART DA2 188 D7
Lord Warwick St
WOOL/PLUM SE18 162 C2
Lorenzo St FSBYW WC1X 5 N9
Loretto Gdns
KTN/HRWW/WS HA3 115 K2
Lorian Cl NFNCH/WDSPK N12 97 L5
Lorian Dr REIG RH2 257 M9
Loriners CRAWE RH10 283 N10
Loriners Cl COB KT11 217 H10
Loring Rd BERK HP4 33 P6
ISLW TW7 154 E8
TRDG/WHET N20 97 P3
WDSR SL4 148 E7
Loris Rd HMSMTH W6 156 F2
Lorne Av CROY/NA CR0 204 C7
Lorne Cl SL SL1 148 G2
STJWD NW8 3 P10
Lorne Gdns CROY/NA CR0 204 C7
NTGHL W11 156 G1
WAN E11 121 P2
WOKN/KNAP GU21 231 J5
Lorne Rd BRW CM14 107 H5
FSBYPK N4 118 G6
FSTGT E7 121 N9
KTN/HRWW/WS HA3 94 E10
RCHPK/HAM TW10 177 L1
WALTH E17 120 F3
Lorne Ter FNCH N3 * 97 J10
The Lorne GT/LBKH KT23 253 P2
Lorn Rd BRXN/ST SW9 158 G8
Lorraine Pk
KTN/HRWW/WS HA3 94 D8
Lorrimore Rd WALW SE17 18 D10
Lorrimore Sq WALW SE17 18 D9
Lorton Cl GVE DA12 191 H5
Loseberry Rd ESH/CLAY KT10 218 C2
Loseley Rd GODL GU7 267 K9
Losfield Rd WDSR SL4 148 D7
Lossie Dr IVER SL0 130 E9
Lothair Rd EA W5 155 J1
Lothair Rd North FSBYPK N4 119 J4
Lothair Rd South FSBYPK N4 119 H5
Lothbury LOTH EC2R 12 G5
Lothian Av YEAD UB4 133 J7
Lothian Cl ALP/SUD HA0 114 F9
Lothian Rd BRXN/ST SW9 159 J6
Lothian Wd
KWD/TDW/WH KT20 238 E8
Lothrop St NKENS W10 2 A10
Lots Rd WBPTN SW10 157 M6
Lotus Rd BH/WHM TN16 244 C4
Loubet St TOOT SW17 180 A9
Loudhams Rd AMSS HP7 69 P5
Loudhams Wood La CSTG HP8 70 A6
Loudoun Av BARK/HLT IG6 122 E3
Loudoun Rd STJWD NW8 3 K6
Loudwater Cl SUN TW16 197 H4
Loudwater Dr
RKW/CH/CXG WD3 71 M8
Loudwater Hts
RKW/CH/CXG WD3 71 L7
Loudwater La
RKW/CH/CXG WD3 71 M9
Loudwater Rdg
RKW/CH/CXG WD3 71 M8
Loughborough Pk
BRXN/ST SW9 159 J10
Loughborough Rd
BRXN/ST SW9 159 H8
Loughborough St LBTH SE11 17 P7
Lough Rd HOLWY N7 5 P1
Loughton La EPP CM16 82 G3
Loughton Wy BKHH IG9 102 A2
Louisa Cl HOM E9 140 B2
Louisa St WCHPL E1 140 C7
Louis Cl CHST BR7 184 C7
Louise Bennett Cl
HNHL SE24 * 159 J10
Louise Gdns RAIN RM13 144 F5
Louise Rd SRTFD E15 141 K1
Louise Wk HHS/BOV HP3 52 D4
Louis Flds RGUW GU3 249 H6
Louisville Cl WARE SG12 27 H7
Louisville Rd TOOT SW17 180 B6
Louvaine Rd BTSEA SW11 157 N10
Louvain Rd RDART DA2 188 D3
Louvain Wy GSTN WD25 55 J8
Lovage Ap EHAM E6 142 B7
Lovat Cl CRICK NW2 116 C8
Lovat La FENCHST EC3M 13 J7
Lovatt Cl EDGW HA8 95 N7
Lovatts RKW/CH/CXG WD3 72 B8
Loveday Rd WEA W13 134 G10
Love Green La IVER SL0 130 C7
Lovegrove Dr SLN SL2 128 E6
Lovegrove St STHWK SE1 19 P8
Lovegrove Wk POP/IOD E14 141 H10
Love Hill La DTCH/LGLY SL3 130 D9
Lovejoy La WDSR SL4 148 C8
Lovekyn Cl KUTN/CMB KT2 199 K2
Lovelace Av HAYES BR2 206 D6
Lovelace Cl EHSLY KT24 235 H9
Lovelace Dr
WOKS/MYFD GU22 233 H2
Lovelace Gdns BARK IG11 123 K9
SURB KT6 199 J7
WOT/HER KT12 217 K2
Lovelace Gn ELTH/MOT SE9 162 C9
Lovelace Rd DUL SE21 181 K5
EBAR EN4 97 P1
SURB KT6 199 H7
Lovelace Vls THDIT KT7 * 198 G7
Lovelands La CHOB/PIR GU24 213 H9
KWD/TDW/WH KT20 257 L3
Love La ABLGY WD5 54 G6
BXLY DA5 186 B2
CHEAM SM3 221 H3
CHONG CM5 67 P4
CITYW EC2V 12 F5
GDST RH9 260 B8
IVER SL0 130 G8
KGLGY WD4 53 P5
KWD/TDW/WH KT20 256 C3
MRDN SM4 201 K7
MTCM CR4 201 P3
PIN HA5 113 M1
SNWD SE25 204 A3
SOCK/AV RM15 166 B1
SURB KT6 199 J9
TIL RM18 169 M5
TOTM N17 99 N8
WFD IG8 102 C7
WOOL/PLUM SE18 162 D3
Lovel Av WELL DA16 163 K8
Lovel Cl HHW HP1 35 K6
Lovel End CFSP/GDCR SL9 89 P8
Loveletts CRAWW RH11 283 K8
Lovel Hl WDSR SL4 * 170 A8
Lovelinch Cl PECK SE15 160 B5
Lovel La WDSR SL4 170 A8
Lovell Pl BERM/RHTH SE16 160 D2
Lovell Rd EN EN1 80 A1
RCHPK/HAM TW10 177 H6
STHL UB1 134 A8
Lovells Cl LTWR GU18 212 A6
Lovell Wk RAIN RM13 145 H1
Lovel Md CFSP/GDCR SL9 89 P8
Lovelock Cl PUR/KEN CR8 241 K3
Lovel Rd CFSP/GDCR SL9 89 P8
Loveridge Ms
KIL/WHAMP NW6 2 C2
Loveridge Rd
KIL/WHAMP NW6 2 D2
Lovering Rd CHESW EN7 61 K1
Lover's La SWCM DA10 167 J10
Lovet Rd HLWW/ROY CM19 46 D2
Lovett Dr CAR SM5 201 M7
Lovett Rd DEN/HRF UB9 111 M1
LCOL/BKTW AL2 56 F2
STA TW18 172 E7
Lovetts Pl WAND/EARL SW18 157 M10
Lovett Wy WLSDN NW10 115 P10
Love Wk CMBW SE5 159 L8
Lovibonds Av ORP BR6 206 E10
WDR/YW UB7 132 A8
Lowbell La LCOL/BKTW AL2 57 K3
Lowbrook Rd IL IG1 122 E9
Lowburys DORK RH4 272 F5
Low Cl RDART DA2 188 F1
Lowdell Cl WDR/YW UB7 131 P8
Lowden Rd ED N9 100 A2
HNHL SE24 159 J10
STHL UB1 133 M9
Lowe Av CAN/RD E16 141 M7
Lowe Cl CHIG IG7 103 K6
Lowell St POP/IOD E14 140 D8
Lowen Rd RAIN RM13 144 E4
Lower Addiscombe Rd
CROY/NA CR0 203 L8
Lower Addison Gdns
WKENS W14 14 A2
Lower Adeyfield Rd
HHNE HP2 35 N5
Lower Barn HHS/BOV HP3 36 A9
Lower Barn Rd PUR/KEN CR8 223 K8
Lower Bedfords Rd ROM RM1 105 H7
Lower Belgrave St
BGVA SW1W 16 E4
Lower Bridge Rd REDH RH1 258 A10
Lower Britwell Rd SLN SL2 128 C6
Lower Broad St DAGE RM10 144 B3
Lower Bury La EPP CM16 65 H7
Lower Camden CHST BR7 206 C1
Lower Church St
CROY/NA CR0 * 203 J9
Lower Cippenham La SL SL1 128 E10
Lower Clabdens WARE SG12 26 E2
Lower Clapton Rd HACK E8 120 A10
Lower Clarendon Wk
NKENS W10 8 A6
Lower Common South
PUT/ROE SW15 156 E9
Lower Coombe St
CROY/NA CR0 223 K1
Lower Court Rd
HOR/WEW KT19 219 P7
Lower Crs SLH/COR SS17 169 K2
Lower Cft SWLY BR8 208 G4
Lower Dagnall St
STALW/RED AL3 38 B6
Lower Derby Rd WAT WD17 73 K8
Lower Downs Rd
RYNPK SW20 200 G1
Lower Dr BEAC HP9 88 C6
Lower Dunnymans
BNSTD SM7 221 J10
Lower Edgeborough Rd
GU GU1 268 C1
Lower Emms HHNE HP2 36 D1
Lower Farm Rd EHSLY KT24 235 J10
Lowerfield WGCE AL7 23 K6
Lower Forecourt HORL RH6 280 C8
Lower Gravel Rd HAYES BR2 206 B8
Lower Green Gdns WPK KT4 200 D8
Lower Green Rd
ESH/CLAY KT10 198 A9
Lower Gn West MTCM CR4 201 P3
Lower Grosvenor Pl
BGVA SW1W 16 E3
Lower Grove Rd
RCHPK/HAM TW10 177 L2
Lower Guildford Rd
WOKN/KNAP GU21 231 J5
Lower Hall La CHING E4 100 D6
Lower Hampton Rd
SUN TW16 197 L2
Lower Ham Rd
KUTN/CMB KT2 177 J9
Lower Hatfield Rd
HERT/BAY SG13 42 E1
Lower Higham Rd GVE DA12 191 J4
Lower High St WAT WD17 73 K8
Lower Hill Rd HOR/WEW KT19 219 N8
Lower James St
SOHO/CST W1F * 11 H7
Lower John St SOHO/CST W1F 11 H7
Lower Kenwood Av
ENC/FH EN2 78 F9
Lower Kings Rd BERK HP4 33 N5
KUTN/CMB KT2 177 K10
Lower Lea Crossing
POP/IOD E14 141 K9
Lower Lees Rd SLN SL2 128 F5
Lower Luton Rd
STALE/WH AL4 20 E1
Lower Maidstone Rd
FBAR/BDGN N11 98 D7
Lower Mardyke Av RAIN RM13 144 D4
Lower Marsh STHWK SE1 18 A2
Lower Marsh La BRYLDS KT5 199 L4
Lower Md IVER SL0 130 G5
Lowermead REDH RH1 258 A7
Lower Meadow
CHES/WCR EN8 62 C3
HLWS CM18 47 H5
Lower Merton Ri HAMP NW3 3 N4
Lower Morden La MRDN SM4 200 F6
Lower Mortlake Rd
RCH/KEW TW9 155 K10
Lower Noke Cl HARH RM3 105 M3
Lower Northfield BNSTD SM7 221 J10
Lower Nursery ASC SL5 192 F5
Lower Paddock Rd
OXHEY WD19 73 M10
Lower Park Rd BELV DA17 164 B2
COUL/CHIP CR5 239 P4
FBAR/BDGN N11 98 D6
LOU IG10 82 B9
Lower Paxton Rd STAL AL1 38 D7
Lower Peryers EHSLY KT24 252 F4
Lower Pillory Down CAR SM5 222 B9
Lower Plantation
RKW/CH/CXG WD3 71 M7
Lower Queen's Rd BKHH IG9 102 B3
Lower Range Rd GVE DA12 191 H3
Lower Richmond Rd
PUT/ROE SW15 156 F9
RCH/KEW TW9 155 M9
Lower Riding BEAC HP9 88 A10
Lower Rd BELV DA17 164 C2
BERM/RHTH SE16 160 B1
CFSP/GDCR SL9 110 B1
EHSLY KT24 253 L3
ERITH DA8 164 E3
GVE DA12 191 P5
GVW DA11 167 M10
HHS/BOV HP3 54 B2
LHD/OX KT22 236 C9
LOU IG10 82 D5
PUR/KEN CR8 223 J9
REDH RH1 275 N2
RKW/CH/CXG WD3 70 G8
RYLN/HDSTN HA2 114 C7
STMC/STPC BR5 207 L6
SUT SM1 221 N2
SWLY BR8 187 J10
TIL RM18 168 D9
WARE SG12 26 E5
Lower Robert St CHCR WC2N 11 M8
Lower Sales HHW HP1 35 J7
Lower Sandfields
RPLY/SEND GU23 232 G9
Lower Sand Hills SURB KT6 199 H7
Lower Sawleywood
BNSTD SM7 221 J10
Lower Shott CHESW EN7 61 N2
GT/LBKH KT23 253 P2
Lower Sloane St BGVA SW1W 16 B6
Lower Strd CDALE/KGS NW9 96 C10
Lower St SHGR GU5 270 B5
Lower Sunbury Rd
E/WMO/HCT KT8 197 N2
Lower Swaines EPP CM16 65 H6
Lower Tail OXHEY WD19 93 M4
Lower Teddington Rd
KUT/HW KT1 199 J1
Lower Ter HAMP NW3 117 M8
Lower Thames St MON EC3R 13 J8
Lower Tub BUSH WD23 94 C1
Lower Village Rd ASC SL5 192 B5
Lower Wood Rd
ESH/CLAY KT10 218 F3
Lower Yott HHNE HP2 35 P7
Lowestoft Dr SL SL1 128 B8
Lowestoft Rd WATN WD24 73 J5
Loweswater Cl GSTN WD25 55 K9
WBLY HA9 115 J7
The Lowe CHIG IG7 103 K6
Lowfield SBW CM21 29 P2
Lowfield Heath Rd HORL RH6 279 J9
Lowfield La HOD EN11 44 F3
Lowfield Rd ACT W3 135 P8
KIL/WHAMP NW6 2 E3
Lowfield Wy HORL RH6 279 P10
Low Hall Cl CHING E4 100 F1
Low Hall La WALTH E17 120 D4
Low Hill Rd HLWW/ROY CM19 45 L3
Lowick Rd HRW HA1 114 D2
Lowland Gdns ROMW/RG RM7 124 C4
Lowlands BRKMPK AL9 40 F1
Lowlands Dr
STWL/WRAY TW19 173 N1
Lowlands Rd HRW HA1 114 D5
PIN HA5 113 K5
SOCK/AV RM15 146 B10
Lowman Rd HOLWY N7 118 G9
Lowndes Av CSHM HP5 50 G6
Lowndes Cl KTBR SW1X 16 D4
Lowndes Ct SOHO/CST W1F * 10 G6
Lowndes Ms
STRHM/NOR SW16 180 F5
Lowndes Pl KTBR SW1X * 16 C4
Lowndes Sq KTBR SW1X 16 B2
Lowndes St KTBR SW1X 16 B3
Lowood St WCHPL E1 140 A9
Low Rd BRKMPK AL9 42 A1
Lowry Cl ERITH DA8 164 E3
Lowry Crs MTCM CR4 201 P2
Lowry Rd BCTR RM8 123 L10
Lowshoe La CRW RM5 104 C9
Lowson Gv OXHEY WD19 93 M1
Low Street La TIL RM18 169 J5
Lowswood Cl NTHWD HA6 92 D9
Lowther Cl BORE WD6 75 L9
Lowther Dr ENC/FH EN2 78 F8
Lowther Hl FSTH SE23 182 D3
Lowther Man BARN SW13 * 156 D7
Lowther Rd BARN SW13 156 C7
HOLWY N7 * 119 H10
KUTN/CMB KT2 199 L1
STAN HA7 115 L1
WALTH E17 100 D10
Lowth Rd CMBW SE5 159 K8
Loxford Av EHAM E6 142 A4
Loxford La IL IG1 122 F10
Loxford Rd BARK IG11 142 E1
CTHM CR3 259 N1
Loxford Wy CTHM CR3 259 N1
Loxham Rd CHING E4 100 G8
Loxham St STPAN WC1H * 5 M10
Loxley Cl BF/WBF KT14 215 P10
SYD SE26 182 C8
Loxley Ct WARE SG12 * 26 D2
Loxley Rd BERK HP4 33 K3
HPTN TW12 175 N7
WAND/EARL SW18 179 N4
Loxton Rd FSTH SE23 182 C4
Loxwood Cl
EBED/NFELT TW14 174 E4
STMC/STPC BR5 207 N9
Loxwood Rd TOTM N17 119 M1
Loxwood Wk CRAWW RH11 283 J5
Lubbock Rd CHST BR7 206 D1
Lubbock St NWCR SE14 160 B6
Lucan Dr STA TW18 173 N10
Lucan Pl CHEL SW3 15 N6
Lucan Rd BAR EN5 77 H7
Lucas Av PLSTW E13 141 N3
RYLN/HDSTN HA2 113 P7
Lucas Cl CRAWE RH10 284 C10
Lucas Ct WAB EN9 63 L9
Lucas Crs SWCM DA10 188 G1
Lucas Gdns EFNCH N2 97 M10
Lucas Green Rd
CHOB/PIR GU24 230 C1
Lucas Rd GRAYS RM17 167 M2
PGE/AN SE20 182 B9
Lucas Sq GLDGN NW11 117 K4
Lucas St BROCKY SE4 160 F8
Lucern Cl CHESW EN7 61 M3
Lucerne Cl PLMGR N13 98 F4
WOKS/MYFD GU22 232 B5
Lucerne Dr CRAWE RH10 284 E9
Lucerne Gv WALTH E17 121 J2
Lucerne Ms KENS W8 * 8 F9
Lucerne Rd HBRY N5 119 J9
ORP BR6 207 J8
THHTH CR7 203 J5
Lucerne Wy HARH RM3 105 L7
Lucey Rd BERM/RHTH SE16 19 N4
Lucey Wy BERM/RHTH SE16 19 P4
Lucie Av ASHF TW15 174 C9
Lucien Rd TOOT SW17 180 B7
WIM/MER SW19 179 L5
Lucknow St WOOL/PLUM SE18 163 H6
Lucks Hl HHW HP1 35 H6
Lucorn Cl LEE/GVPK SE12 183 L2
Luctons Av BKHH IG9 101 P2
Luddesdon Rd ERITH DA8 164 B6
Luddington Av VW GU25 194 C2
Ludford Cl CROY/NA CR0 223 J1
Ludgate Broadway
BLKFR EC4V * 12 D6
Ludgate Circ STP EC4M 12 C6
Ludgate Hl STP EC4M 12 C6
Ludgate Sq STP EC4M * 12 D6
Ludham Cl BARK/HLT IG6 102 F9
THMD SE28 143 M8
Ludlow Cl HAYES BR2 * 205 M3
RYLN/HDSTN HA2 113 N9
Ludlow Md OXHEY WD19 93 J4
Ludlow Pl GRAYS RM17 167 N2
Ludlow Rd EA W5 135 H6
FELT TW13 175 H6
GUW GU2 267 N1
Ludlow St FSBYE EC1V * 12 E1
Ludlow Wy EFNCH N2 117 M2
RKW/CH/CXG WD3 72 D8
Ludovick Wk PUT/ROE SW15 156 B10
Ludwick Cl WGCE AL7 * 23 J7
Ludwick Gn WGCE AL7 * 23 J6
Ludwick Wy WGCE AL7 23 J5
Luff Cl WDSR SL4 148 D9
Luffield Rd ABYW SE2 163 L2
Luffman Rd LEE/GVPK SE12 183 N6
Lugard Rd PECK SE15 160 A8
Lugg Ap MNPK E12 122 D8
Luke St SDTCH EC2A 13 J1
Lukin Crs CHING E4 101 J4
Lukin St WCHPL E1 140 B8
Lullarook Cl BH/WHM TN16 243 P2
Lullingstone Av SWLY BR8 208 G3
Lullingstone Cl
STMC/STPC BR5 185 L10
Lullingstone Crs
STMC/STPC BR5 185 K10
Lullingstone La EYN DA4 209 K10
LEW SE13 183 J2
Lullingstone Rd BELV DA17 164 A5
Lullington Garth BMLY BR1 183 K10
BORE WD6 * 75 P9
NFNCH/WDSPK N12 97 J6
Lullington Rd DAGW RM9 143 P2
PGE/AN SE20 181 P10
Lulot Gdns ARCH N19 118 C7
Lulworth Av CHESW EN7 61 J5
HEST TW5 154 A7
WBLY HA9 115 H5
Lulworth Cl CRAWW RH11 283 K10
RYLN/HDSTN HA2 113 N8
Lulworth Crs MTCM CR4 201 P2
Lulworth Dr CRW RM5 104 C6
PIN HA5 113 L5
Lulworth Gdns
RYLN/HDSTN HA2 113 M7
Lulworth Rd ELTH/MOT SE9 184 B5
PECK SE15 * 160 A8
WELL DA16 163 J8
Lulworth Waye YEAD UB4 133 J8
Lumbards WGCE AL7 23 K2
Lumen Rd WBLY HA9 115 J7
Lumley Cl BELV DA17 164 B5
Lumley Gdns CHEAM SM3 221 H2
Lumley Rd CHEAM SM3 221 H3
HORL RH6 280 B4
Lumley St OXSTW W1C 10 D6
Luna Pl STAL AL1 38 F6
Lunar Cl BH/WHM TN16 244 A2
Luna Rd THHTH CR7 203 K3
Lundin Wk OXHEY WD19 * 93 L5
Lundy Cl CRAWW RH11 283 M10
Lundy Dr HYS/HAR UB3 152 F3
Lundy Wk IS N1 6 F2
Lunedale Rd RDART DA2 188 B4
Lunghurst Rd CTHM CR3 242 F7
Lunham Rd NRWD SE19 181 M9
Lupin Cl BRXS/STRHM SW2 181 J5
CROY/NA CR0 204 C8
ROMW/RG RM7 124 E7
WDR/YW UB7 151 N4
Luppits Cl RBRW/HUT CM13 107 M2
Lupton Cl LEE/GVPK SE12 183 N7
Lupton St KTTN NW5 118 D9
Lupus St PIM SW1V 16 F8
Lurgan Av HMSMTH W6 156 G5
Lurline Gdns BTSEA SW11 158 B7
Luscombe Wy VX/NE SW8 158 F6
Lushes Ct LOU IG10 82 E9
Lushes Rd LOU IG10 82 E9
Lushington Dr COB KT11 217 J10
Lushington Rd CAT SE6 182 G8
WLSDN NW10 136 E4
Lushington Ter HACK E8 * 119 P10
Lusted Hall La BH/WHM TN16 243 P6
Lusteds Cl DORK RH4 273 H5
Lutchens Cl EHSLY KT24 253 L3
Luther Cl EDGW HA8 95 P3
Luther King Cl WALTH E17 120 D4
Luther King Rd
HLWW/ROY CM19 46 F1
Luther Ms TEDD TW11 176 E8
Luther Rd TEDD TW11 176 E8
Luthers Cl BRWN CM15 86 D3
Luton Pl GNWCH SE10 161 H6
Luton Rd PLSTW E13 141 M6
SCUP DA14 185 M6
WALTH E17 120 D1
Luton St STJWD NW8 9 M2
Luttrell Av PUT/ROE SW15 178 E1
Lutwyche Rd FSTH SE23 182 E5
Lutyens Cl CRAWW RH11 283 H9
Luxborough La CHIG IG7 102 C5
Luxborough St MHST W1U 10 C3
Luxembourg Ms SRTFD E15 121 K10
Luxemburg Gdns
HMSMTH W6 156 G3
Luxfield Rd ELTH/MOT SE9 184 B4
Luxford Pl SBW CM21 30 A2
Luxford St BERM/RHTH SE16 160 C3
Luxmore St BROCKY SE4 160 E7
Luxor St CMBW SE5 159 K9
Luxted Rd BH/WHM TN16 244 E1
ORP BR6 226 D8
Lyall Av DUL SE21 181 M7
Lyall Ms KTBR SW1X 16 C4
Lyall Ms West KTBR SW1X * 16 C4
Lyall St KTBR SW1X 16 C4
Lyal Rd BOW E3 140 D4
Lycaste Cl STAL AL1 38 E7
Lycett Pl SHB W12 156 D1
Lych Ga GSTN WD25 55 L9
Lych Gate Rd ORP BR6 207 K8
Lych Gate Wk HYS/HAR UB3 132 G9
Lych Wy WOKN/KNAP GU21 232 A2
Lyconby Gdns CROY/NA CR0 204 D7
Lycrome La CSHM HP5 51 J4
Lycrome Rd CSHM HP5 51 K4
Lydd Cl BFN/LL DA15 185 H6
Lydden Gv WAND/EARL SW18 179 L3
Lydden Rd WAND/EARL SW18 179 L3
Lydd Rd BXLYHN DA7 164 A6
Lydeard Rd EHAM E6 142 C2
Lydele Cl WOKN/KNAP GU21 232 C1
Lydford Av SLN SL2 129 J7
Lydford Cl STNW/STAM N16 119 M10
Lydford Rd CRICK NW2 136 G1
MV/WKIL W9 8 D1
SEVS/STOTM N15 119 L3
Lydger Cl WOKS/MYFD GU22 232 E6
Lydhurst Av
BRXS/STRHM SW2 180 G5
Lydia Ms BRKMPK AL9 40 F10
Lydia Rd ERITH DA8 164 G5
Lydney Cl WIM/MER SW19 179 H5
Lydon Rd CLAP SW4 158 D9
Lydsey Cl SLN SL2 128 F5
Lydstep Rd CHST BR7 184 D7
Lye Green Rd CSHM HP5 51 K6
Lye La LCOL/BKTW AL2 55 P6
Lyell Rd WDSR SL4 148 B9
The Lye KWD/TDW/WH KT20 238 F8
Lyfield LHD/OX KT22 218 A10
Lyford Rd WAND/EARL SW18 179 N3
Lyford St WOOL/PLUM SE18 162 B3
Lygarth Cl GT/LBKH KT23 254 C1
Lygean Av WARE SG12 26 D2
Lygon Pl BGVA SW1W * 16 E4
Lyham Cl BRXS/STRHM SW2 180 F2
Lyham Rd BRXS/STRHM SW2 180 F2
Lyle Cl MTCM CR4 202 B7
Lyle Pk SEV TN13 247 J9
Lyles La WGCW AL8 23 H3
Lymbourne Cl BELMT SM2 221 K6
Lymden Gdns REIG RH2 275 L2
Lyme Av BERK HP4 33 J2
Lyme Farm Rd LEE/GVPK SE12 161 M10
Lyme Gv HOM E9 140 B2
Lymer Av NRWD SE19 181 N8
Lyme Regis Rd BNSTD SM7 239 J3
Lyme Rd WELL DA16 163 L7
Lymescote Gdns SUT SM1 201 K9
Lyme St CAMTN NW1 4 G4
Lyme Ter CAMTN NW1 4 G4
Lyminge Cl SCUP DA14 185 J7
Lyminge Gdns
WAND/EARL SW18 179 P4
Lymington Av WDGN N22 99 H10
Lymington Cl
STRHM/NOR SW16 202 E2
Lymington Ct GSTN WD25 * 55 H10
Lymington Dr RSLP HA4 112 E7
Lymington Gdns
HOR/WEW KT19 220 C2
Lymington Rd BCTR RM8 123 N6
KIL/WHAMP NW6 2 G1
Lyminster Cl YEAD UB4 133 M7
Lympstone Gdns PECK SE15 159 P6
Lynbridge Gdns PLMGR N13 99 J5
Lynbrook Cl RAIN RM13 144 E4
Lynbrook Gv PECK SE15 159 M6
Lynceley Gra EPP CM16 65 K5
Lynch Cl UX/CGN UB8 131 M2
Lynchen Cl HEST TW5 153 H7
Lynch Hill La SLN SL2 128 D6
Lynchmere Pl GUW GU2 249 M7
The Lynch HOD EN11 44 G3
UX/CGN UB8 131 M2
Lyncourt BKHTH/KID SE3 * 161 J8
Lyncroft Av PIN HA5 113 L3
Lyncroft Gdns EW KT17 220 C5
HSLW TW3 176 B1
KIL/WHAMP NW6 117 K10
WEA W13 155 H1
Lyndale BRWN CM15 86 E3
CRICK NW2 117 J8
THDIT KT7 * 198 D7
Lyndale Av CRICK NW2 117 J8
Lyndale Cl BKHTH/KID SE3 161 L5
Lyndale Hampton Court Wy
ESH/CLAY KT10 198 D7
Lyndale Rd REDH RH1 258 A7
Lynden Wy SWLY BR8 208 D3
Lyndhurst Av BRYLDS KT5 199 N8
MLHL NW7 96 B7
NFNCH/WDSPK N12 98 A7
PIN HA5 93 J9
STHL UB1 134 A10
STRHM/NOR SW16 202 E2
SUN TW16 197 H3
WHTN TW2 175 N4
Lyndhurst Cl BXLYHN DA7 164 C9
CRAWW RH11 283 N8
CROY/NA CR0 203 N10
HARP AL5 20 B1
ORP BR6 226 E1
WLSDN NW10 116 A8
WOKN/KNAP GU21 232 A1
Lyndhurst Ct BELMT SM2 * 221 K4
Lyndhurst Dr EMPK RM11 125 K6
HARP AL5 20 B1
LEY E10 121 H5
NWMAL KT3 200 B6
SEV TN13 246 F10
Lyndhurst Gdns BARK IG11 143 H1
EN EN1 79 M8
FNCH N3 97 H9
GNTH/NBYPK IG2 122 G4
HAMP NW3 117 N10
PIN HA5 93 J9
Lyndhurst Gv CMBW SE5 159 M8
Lyndhurst Leys HAYES BR2 * 205 J2
Lyndhurst Prior SNWD SE25 * 203 M3
Lyndhurst Ri CHIC IG7 102 D5
Lyndhurst Rd BXLYHN DA7 164 C9
CHING E4 101 H8
COUL/CHIP CR5 240 B2
CSHM HP5 50 G4
GFD/PVL UB6 134 A6
HAMP NW3 117 N10
REIG RH2 275 K3
THHTH CR7 203 H4
UED N18 99 P5
WDGN N22 99 H7
Lyndhurst Sq PECK SE15 159 N7
Lyndhurst Ter HAMP NW3 117 N10
Lyndhurst Wy BELMT SM2 221 K5
CHERT KT16 195 H10
PECK SE15 159 N7
RBRW/HUT CM13 107 P2
Lyndon Av BFN/LL DA15 185 J1
PIN HA5 93 M7
WLGTN SM6 202 B10
Lyndon Md STALE/WH AL4 21 H9
Lyndon Rd BELV DA17 164 B3
Lyndon Yd TOOT SW17 179 L7
Lyndsey Pl CHESW EN7 * 62 A6
Lyndwood Dr WDSR SL4 171 M2
Lyndwood Pde WDSR SL4 * 171 M2
Lyne Cl VW GU25 194 C6
Lyne Crs WALTH E17 100 E9
Lyne Crossing Rd VW GU25 194 D6
Lynegrove Av ASHF TW15 174 D8
Lyneham Wk CLPT E5 * 120 D10
Lyne La CHERT KT16 194 D9
Lyne Rd VW GU25 194 A6
Lynette Av CLAP SW4 180 C2
Lyne Wy HHW HP1 35 J4
Lynford Cl BAR EN5 76 C9
EDGW HA8 95 P9
Lynford Gdns EDGW HA8 95 N4
GDMY/SEVK IG3 123 J7
Lynford Ter ED N9 * 99 N2
Lynhurst Crs HGDN/ICK UB10 132 D2
Lynhurst Rd HGDN/ICK UB10 132 D2
Lynmere Rd WELL DA16 163 L8
Lyn Ms STNW/STAM N16 * 119 N9
Lynmouth Av EN EN1 79 N10
MRDN SM4 200 G7
Lynmouth Dr RSLP HA4 113 J7
Lynmouth Gdns GFD/PVL UB6 134 G3
HEST TW5 153 L7
Lynmouth Ri STMC/STPC BR5 207 L4
Lynmouth Rd EFNCH N2 118 A1
GFD/PVL UB6 134 G3
STNW/STAM N16 119 N6
WALTH E17 120 D4
WGCE AL7 23 J5
Lynn Cl ASHF TW15 174 E8
KTN/HRWW/WS HA3 94 C10
Lynne Cl ORP BR6 227 J3
SAND/SEL CR2 224 B7
Lynnett Rd BCTR RM8 123 N7
Lynne Wk ESH/CLAY KT10 218 B2
Lynne Wy NTHLT UB5 133 L4
Lynn Ms WAN E11 121 K7
Lynn Rd BAL SW12 180 C3
GNTH/NBYPK IG2 122 G5
WAN E11 121 K7
Lynn St ENC/FH EN2 79 L5
Lynn Wk REIG RH2 275 L4
Lynross Cl HARH RM3 105 M10
Lynscott Wy SAND/SEL CR2 223 J5
Lynstead Cl BMLY BR1 205 P2
Lynsted Cl BXLYHS DA6 186 C1
Lynsted Ct BECK BR3 204 D2
Lynsted Gdns ELTH/MOT SE9 162 A10
Lynton Av CDALE/KGS NW9 116 C2
NFNCH/WDSPK N12 97 N5
ROMW/RG RM7 104 C9
STAL AL1 39 H7
STMC/STPC BR5 207 L4
WEA W13 134 F8
Lynton Cl CHSGTN KT9 219 K1
ISLW TW7 154 E10
WLSDN NW10 116 B10
Lynton Crs GNTH/NBYPK IG2 122 E4
Lynton Est STHWK SE1 19 M6
Lynton Gdns EN EN1 99 M1
FBAR/BDGN N11 98 E7
Lynton Md TRDG/WHET N20 97 K4
Lynton Pde CHES/WCR EN8 62 C6
Lynton Rd ACT W3 135 M9
CEND/HSY/T N8 118 E3
CHING E4 100 G6
CROY/NA CR0 203 H6
CSHM HP5 50 G4
GVW DA11 190 D4
KIL/WHAMP NW6 2 D6
NWMAL KT3 200 A5
RYLN/HDSTN HA2 113 M7
STHWK SE1 19 M6
Lynton Rd South GVW DA11 190 D4
Lynton Ter ACT W3 * 135 P8
Lynwood GUW GU2 267 N1
Lynwood Av COUL/CHIP CR5 240 C1
DTCH/LGLY SL3 150 A2
EGH TW20 172 B9
EW KT17 220 C10
Lynwood Cl CRW RM5 104 C7
RYLN/HDSTN HA2 113 M8
SWFD E18 101 P9
WOKN/KNAP GU21 214 G9
Lynwood Crs ASC SL5 192 D6
Lynwood Dr CRW RM5 104 C7
NTHWD HA6 92 F9
WPK KT4 200 D9
Lynwood Gdns CROY/NA CR0 222 G1
STHL UB1 133 N8
Lynwood Gv ORP BR6 207 H7
WCHMH N21 99 H2
Lynwood Hts
RKW/CH/CXG WD3 71 L9
Lynwood Rd EA W5 135 J5
EW KT17 220 C10
REDH RH1 258 B8
THDIT KT7 198 E9
TOOT SW17 180 A6
Lynwood Ter
WIM/MER SW19 * 201 J1
Lynx Hl EHSLY KT24 252 G3
Lyon Meade STAN HA7 95 H9
Lyon Park Av ALP/SUD HA0 135 K1
Lyon Rd HRW HA1 114 E4
ROM RM1 124 G5
WIM/MER SW19 201 M1
WOT/HER KT12 197 M9
Lyons Ct DORK RH4 272 G2
Lyonsdene
KWD/TDW/WH KT20 257 J3
Lyonsdown Av BAR EN5 77 M10
Lyonsdown Rd BAR EN5 77 M9
Lyons Dr GUW GU2 249 M5
Lyons Pl STJWD NW8 9 L2
Lyon St IS N1 5 N4
Lyons Wk WKENS W14 14 A5
Lyon Wy GFD/PVL UB6 134 D3
STALE/WH AL4 39 M6
Lyoth Rd STMC/STPC BR5 206 F9
Lyrical Wy HHW HP1 35 L4
Lyric Cl CRAWE RH10 284 E9
Lyric Dr GFD/PVL UB6 134 A6
Lyric Ms SYD SE26 182 B7
Lyric Rd BARN SW13 156 C7
Lysander CDALE/KGS NW9 * 96 C9
Lysander Cl HHS/BOV HP3 52 C3
Lysander Ct EPP CM16 66 C2
Lysander Gdns SURB KT6 199 L6
Lysander Gv ARCH N19 118 E6
Lysander Ms ARCH N19 * 118 F6
Lysander Rd CROY/NA CR0 222 G3
RSLP HA4 112 E7
Lysander Wy ABLGY WD5 55 H8
ORP BR6 206 F10
WGCE AL7 23 N4
Lys Hill Gdns HERT/WAT SG14 25 J3
Lysias Rd BAL SW12 180 B2
Lysia St FUL/PGN SW6 156 G6
Lysley Pl BRKMPK AL9 59 M3
Lysons Wk PUT/ROE SW15 * 178 D1
Lyster Ms COB KT11 217 K9
Lytchet Rd BMLY BR1 183 M10
Lytchet Wy PEND EN3 80 B5
Lytchgate Cl SAND/SEL CR2 223 M4
Lytcott Dr E/WMO/HCT KT8 197 N3
Lytcott Gv EDUL SE22 181 N1
Lytham Av OXHEY WD19 93 L6
Lytham Cl THMD SE28 143 P8
Lytham St WALW SE17 18 G8
Lyttelton Rd EFNCH N2 117 M3
LEY E10 120 G8
Lyttleton Cl HAMP NW3 3 N4
Lyttleton Rd
CEND/HSY/T N8 * 119 H1
Lytton Av PEND EN3 80 D4
PLMGR N13 99 H3
Lytton Cl EFNCH N2 117 N3
LOU IG10 82 G7
NTHLT UB5 133 N2
Lytton Dr CRAWE RH10 284 E6
Lytton Gdns WGCW AL8 22 G5
WLGTN SM6 222 E1
Lytton Gv PUT/ROE SW15 178 G1

Lytton Pk COB KT11 * 217 N8
Lytton Rd BAR EN5 77 M8
  CDW/CHF RM16 168 D3
  GPK RM2 125 J5
  PIN HA5 93 M8
  WAN E11 121 K5
  WOKS/MYFD GU22 232 E2
Lyttons Wy HOD EN11 26 F10
Lyveden Rd BKHTH/KID SE3 161 N16
  TOOT SW17 179 P9
Lywood Cl
  KWD/TDW/WH KT20 238 F8

**M**

Mabbotts KWD/TDW/WH KT20 238 G7
Mabbutt Cl LCOL/BKTW AL2 55 M6
Mabel Rd SWLY BR8 187 H9
Mabel St WOKN/KNAP GU21 232 A4
Maberley Rd NRWD SE19 181 P10
  BECK BR3 204 C5
Maberley Rd NRWD SE19 203 N1
Mabey's Wk SBW CM21 29 L2
Mabledon Pl CAMTN NW1 5 K10
Mablethorpe Rd
  FUL/PGN SW6 157 H6
Mabley St HOM E9 7 D10
Macaret Cl TRDG/WHET N20 97 L1
Macarthur Cl FSTGT E7 141 M1
  WBLY HA9 116 A3
Macaulay Ter CHARL SE7 * 162 A5
Macaulay Av ESH/CLAY KT10 198 D9
Macaulay Rd CLAP SW4 158 C9
  CTHM CR3 241 M8
  EHAM E6 142 A4
Macbean St WOOL/PLUM SE18 162 D2
Macbeth St HMSMTH W6 156 H4
Macclesfield Br STJWD NW8 3 P7
Macclesfield Rd FSBYE EC1V 6 A5
  SNWD SE25 204 A5
Macclesfield St
  SOHO/SHAV W1D * 11 L7
Macdonald Av DAGE RM10 124 C8
  EMPK RM11 125 M2
Macdonald Cl AMS HP6 69 H1
Macdonald Rd ARCH N19 118 D7
  FBAR/BDGN N11 98 A6
  FSTGT E7 121 M9
  WALTH E17 101 H10
Macdonald Wy EMPK RM11 125 M2
Macduff Rd BTSEA SW11 158 B7
Mace Cl WAP E1W * 140 A10
Mace La RSEV TN14 226 C9
Mace St BETH E2 140 C4
Macer's La BROX EN10 44 H10
Macfarlane La ISLW TW7 154 A4
Macfarlane Rd SHB W12 136 F10
Macgregor Rd CAN/RD E16 141 P7
Machell Rd PECK SE15 160 B9
Macintosh Cl CHESW EC1R * 61 L2
Mackay Rd VX/NE SW8 158 C9
Mackennal St STJWD NW8 3 P8
Mackenzie Cl SHB W12 136 E9
  HOLWY N7 5 N1
Mackenzie Rd BECK BR3 204 C5
Mackenzie Rd SL SL1 149 L1
Mackenzie St GVE DA12 190 C9
Mackie Rd BRXS/STRHM SW2 181 H3
Mackintosh La HOM E9 120 C10
Macklin St HOL/ALD WC2B * 11 M5
Macks Rd BERM/RHTH SE16 19 P5
Mackworth St CAMTN NW1 4 D7
Maclean Rd FSTH SE23 182 D2
Maclean Ter GVE DA12 * 191 J5
Maclennan Av RAIN RM13 145 L4
Macleod Cl GRAYS RM17 168 A3
Macleod House CHARL SE7 * 162 B6
Macleod Rd WCHMH N21 78 F9
Macleod St WALW SE17 18 F8
Maclise Rd WKENS W14 14 A1
Macmahon Cl CHOB/PIR GU24 213 N16
Macmillan Wy TOOT SW17 180 C7
Macoma Rd WOOL/PLUM SE18 162 G5
Macoma Ter WOOL/PLUM SE18 162 G5
Maconochies Rd POP/IOD E14 * 160 C4
Macon Wy UPMR RM14 126 A4
Macquarie Wy POP/IOD E14 160 U3
Macroom Rd MV/WKIL W9 2 D1
Madan Cl BH/WHM TN16 263 H1
Madan Rd BH/WHM TN16 262 G5
Madams Wk EPSOM KT18 220 A10
Mada Rd ORP BR6 206 F10
Maddams St BOW E3 140 G6
Madden Cl SWCM DA10 189 K2
Maddeslield Ct WAD WD7 57 K9
Maddison Cl EFNCH N2 * 97 M10
  TEDD TW11 176 B2
Maddocks Cl SCUP DA14 185 N9
Maddock Wy WALW SE17 18 C10
Maddox Dr CRAWE RH10 284 E8
Maddox La GT/LBKH KT23 235 M10
Maddox Pk GT/LBKH KT23 235 M9
Maddox Rd HHNE HP2 36 U6
  HLW CM20 47 H1
Maddox St CONDST W1S * 10 C7
Madeira Av BMLY BR1 183 J10
Madeira Cl BF/WBF KT14 211 J8
Madeira Crs BF/WBF KT14 211 J9
Madeira Gv WFD IG8 101 P7
Madeira Rd BF/WBF KT14 211 J9
  MTCM CR4 204 A4
  PLMGR N13 99 J5
  STRHM/NOR SW16 180 F8
  WAN E11 121 J1
Madeira Wk EPSOM KT18 220 A10
  REIG RH2 307 N2
  WDSR SL4 149 J7
Madeley Rd EA W5 135 J9
Madeline Gv IL IG1 122 C10
Madeline Rd PGE/AN SE20 181 P10
Madells EPP CM16 65 N11
Madge Gill Wy EHAM E6 142 B3
Madgeways Cl WARE SG12 26 E6
Madgeways La WARE SG12 26 E6
Madinah Rd HACK E8 7 N1
Madison Cl BELMT SM2 221 N6
Madison Crs BXLYHN DA7 163 M6
Madison Gdns BXLYHN DA7 163 M6
Madison Wy SEV TN13 246 C9
Madras Pl HOLWY N7 6 A1
Madras Rd IL IG1 122 C10
Madrid Rd BARN SW13 156 D7
  GUW GU2 249 N8
Madura Rd BRXN/ST SW9 159 J9
Mafeking Av BTFD TW8 155 K5
  EHAM E6 141 N8
  GNTH/NBYPK IG2 122 F4
Mafeking Rd CAN/RD E16 141 H5
  EN EN1 79 N1
  STWL/WRAY TW19 172 A1
  TOTM N17 99 J2
Magazine Pl LHD/OX KT22 236 C9
Magazine Rd CTHM CR3 241 J4
Magdala Av ARCH N19 117 M8
Magdala Rd ISLW TW7 154 H9
  SAND/SEL CR2 223 L4
Magdalen Cl BF/WBF KT14 211 J8
Magdalen Crs BF/WBF KT14 211 P10
Magdalene Gdns EHAM E6 142 D6
Magdalene Rd SHPTN TW17 196 A4

Magdalen Rd
  WAND/EARL SW18 179 M4
Magdelan Gv ORP BR6 227 L1
Magee St LBTH SE11 18 A9
Magellan Bvd CAN/RD E16 142 F9
Magellan Pl POP/IOD E14 160 F9
Magellan Ter CRAWE RH10 * 284 D10
Magna Carta La
  STWL/WRAY TW19 172 A4
Magna Cl HARP AL5 20 C5
Magna Rd EGH TW20 171 N9
Magnaville Rd BUSH WD23 94 D1
Magnet Crs PEND EN3 80 E3
Magnet Rd WBLY HA9 115 J7
  WTHK RM20 167 H5
Magnin Cl HACK E8 * 7 P5
Magnolia Av ABLGY WD5 54 C8
Magnolia Cl HERT/BAY SG13 25 P5
  KUTN/CMB KT2 177 N9
  LCOL/BKTW AL2 56 C2
  SOCK/AV RM15 147 K6
Magnolia Ct HGDN/ICK UB10 * 132 C1
  HORL RH6 * 280 B4
  KTN/HRWW/WS HA3 115 L5
Magnolia Dr BH/WHM TN16 244 A2
  BNSTD SM7 239 J2
Magnolia Gdns EDGW HA8 95 P5
Magnolia Pl CLAP SW4 180 F1
  EA W5 135 J7
  GU GU1 249 P7
Magnolia Rd CHSWK W4 155 N5
Magnolia St WDR/YW UB7 151 N5
Magnolia Wy BRWN CM15 86 B7
  HOR/WEW KT19 219 P2
  RDKG RH5 273 L5
Magnolia Whf CHSWK W4 * 155 N5
Magnum Cl RAIN RM13 145 K6
Magpie Bottom EYN DA4 199 N10
Magpie Cl CDALE/KGS NW9 96 B10
  COUL/CHIP CR5 240 D4
  EN EN1 79 P5
  FSTGT E7 121 L10
Magpie Hall Cl HAYES BR2 206 B6
Magpie Hall La HAYES BR2 206 C6
  HAYES BR2 206 C5
Magpie Hall Rd STAN HA7 94 D3
Magpie La AMSS HP7 88 C1
Magpie Ms GSTN WD25 * 55 K8
Magpie Pl NWCR SE14 * 160 D5
Magpies EPP CM16 * 65 P10
Magpie Wy WCHPL E1 * 140 B7
Maguire Dr RCHPK/HAM TW10 * 176 H7
Maguire St STHWK SE1 19 M1
Mahlon Av RSLP HA4 113 J10
Mahogany Cl
  BERM/RHTH SE16 * 140 D10
Mahon Cl EN EN1 79 N1
Mahonia Cl CHOB/PIR GU24 * 212 E9
Maida Av BAY/PAD W2 9 G1
  CHING E4 100 C1
Maida Rd BELV DA17 146 H8
Maida V MV/WKIL W9 3 H8
Maida Wy CHING E4 100 C1
Maidenbower Dr
  CRAWE RH10 284 D9
Maidenbower La CRAWE RH10 284 C9
Maidenbower Pl CRAWE RH10 284 C9
Maiden Erlegh Av BXLY DA5 185 P4
Maidenhead Av WDSR SL4 148 B6
Maidenhead Rd
  HERT/WAT SG14 * 25 L5
Maidenhead Yd
  HERT/WAT SG14 * 25 L5
Maidenshaw Rd
  HOR/WEW KT19 220 A8
Maidenstone Hl GNWCH SE10 * 161 H7
Maidstone Av CRW RM5 104 D1
Maidstone Buildings Ms
  STHWK SE1 * 12 F10
Maidstone Rd
  FBAR/BDGN N11 98 E7
  SCUP DA14 185 N9
  SCUP DA14 186 A10
  SEV TN13 246 F8
  SWLY BR8 208 C1
Main Av EN EN1 79 N4
  NTHWD HA6 92 D4
Main Barracks
  WOOL/PLUM SE18 * 162 C4
Main Dr CFSP/GDCR SL9 109 P3
  DTCH/LGLY SL3 151 H2
  GFD/PVL UB6 * 133 J8
  WBLY HA9 115 J8
Main Ga TIL RM18 * 168 C8
Mainridge Rd CHST BR7 184 D7
Main Rd BH/WHM TN16 225 P9
  EDEN TN8 262 F10
  EYN DA4 209 M6
  EYN DA4 188 A9
  GPK RM2 105 K10
  ORP BR6 * 227 P5
  RDART DA2 211 H1
  ROM RM1 124 C2
  RSEV TN14 245 P10
  RSEV TN14 245 K4
  SCUP DA14 185 H6
  SWLY BR8 187 H3
  WDSR SL4 148 B6
Main Road Gorse Hl EYN DA4 210 A8
Mainstone Crs
  CHOB/PIR GU24 230 C7
Mainstone Rd CHOB/PIR GU24 230 C7
Main St ADL/WDHM KT15 195 P10
  FELT TW13 175 J7
Maise Webster Cl
  STWL/WRAY TW19 173 N3
Maismore St PECK SE15 19 N10
The Maisonettes SUT SM1 * 221 M1
Maitland Cl BF/WBF KT14 211 K9
  GNWCH SE10 160 G6
  HSLWW TW4 173 P7
  WOT/HER KT12 197 N3
Maitland Park Rd HAMP NW3 4 B1
Maitland Park Vls HAMP NW3 4 B1
Maitland Pl PGE/AN SE20 181 P3
  SRTFD E15 141 J7
Maizecroft HORL RH6 280 E3
Maize St BRWN CM15 86 F9
Majendie Rd
  WOOL/PLUM SE18 162 G4
Major Cl BRXN/ST SW9 159 J9
Major Rd BERM/RHTH SE16 19 P3
  SRTFD E15 121 H10
Major's Farm Rd
  DTCH/LGLY SL3 150 A6
Makepeace Av HGT N6 118 A7
Makepeace Rd NTHLT UB5 133 M1
  WAN E11 121 M2
Makins St CHEL SW3 15 P6
Malabar St POP/IOD E14 160 A1
Malacca Farm RGUE GU4 251 L4
Malam Gdns POP/IOD E14 160 D3
Malan Cl BH/WHM TN16 245 H6
Malbrook Rd PUT/ROE SW15 156 F10
Malcolm Cl PGE/AN SE20 182 B10
Malcolm Crs HDN NW4 95 P4
Malcolm Dr SURB KT6 199 J8
Malcolm Gdns HORL RH6 * 279 N6

Malcolm Pl BETH E2 140 B6
Malcolm Rd COUL/CHIP CR5 240 E1
  HGDN/ICK UB10 112 A9
  PGE/AN SE20 182 B10
  SNWD SE25 203 P6
  WCHPL E1 140 C4
  WIM/MER SW19 179 H9
Malcolms Wy
  STHGT/OAK N14 * 78 D9
Malden Av GFD/PVL UB6 134 D1
  SNWD SE25 203 M5
Malden Crs CAMTN NW1 4 D2
Malden Flds BUSH WD23 74 A5
Malden Green Av WPK KT4 200 C8
Malden Hl NWMAL KT3 200 C3
Malden Hill Gdns NWMAL KT3 200 C2
Malden Pk NWMAL KT3 200 C5
Malden Pl KTTN NW5 118 B10
Malden Rd BORE WD6 75 M7
  CHEAM SM3 201 H5
  KTTN NW5 118 A10
  NWMAL KT3 200 B5
  WAT WD17 73 J6
Maldon Cl CMBW SE5 159 M9
  IS N1 6 E5
Maldon Ct HARP AL5 20 A1
Maldon Rd ACT W3 135 P9
  ED N9 99 N4
  ROMW/RG RM7 124 D5
  WLGTN SM6 222 C2
Malden St GWRST WC1E 11 J2
Maley Av WNWD SE27 181 J5
Malford Gv SWFD E18 121 L1
Malford Ct CRAWE RH10 * 284 D10
Malham Cl FBAR/BDGN N11 98 A7
Malham Rd FSTH SE23 182 C4
Malham Ter UED N18 * 100 A7
Malins Cl BAR EN5 * 76 B9
Malkin Dr BEAC HP9 88 B8
Malkin Wy WATW WD18 * 72 B7
Mallams Ms BRXN/ST SW9 159 H9
Mallard Cl BAR EN5 * 77 N10
  HNWL W7 154 D1
  HORL RH6 280 B2
  KIL/WHAMP NW6 2 F6
  REDH RH1 258 B7
  UPMR RM14 126 C5
  WALTH E17 * 121 J1
Mallard Dr SL SL1 128 C3
Mallard Pl TWK TW1 176 F6
  WDGN N22 98 G10
Mallard Rd ABLGY WD5 55 H7
  SAND/SEL CR2 224 C6
Mallards Ct OXHEY WD19 93 N4
Mallard's Reach WEY KT13 196 F1
Mallards Rd BARK IG11 143 K5
  WFD IG8 101 K8
The Mallards HHS/BOV HP3 35 H10
  STA TW18 195 L2
Mallard Wk BECK BR3 203 J4
  SCUP DA14 186 B4
Mallard Wy CDALE/KGS NW9 115 P5
  GSTN WD25 73 M2
  NTHWD HA6 92 D8
  RBRW/HUT CM13 107 M1
  WLGTN SM6 222 D5
Mall Chambers KENS W8 * 113 K10
Mallet Dr NTHLT UB5 133 J4
Mallet Rd LEW SE13 183 J2
Malling Cl CROY/NA CRO 204 B6
Malling Gdns MRDN SM4 201 M6
Malling Wy HAYES BR2 205 P4
Mallinson Cl HCH RM12 125 K10
Mallinson Rd BTSEA SW11 179 P1
  CROY/NA CRO 202 E10
Mallion Ct WAB EN9 63 L9
Mallord St CHEL SW3 15 M8
Mallory Cl BROCKY SE4 160 D10
  POP/IOD E14 * 140 G6
Mallory Ct LEE/GVPK SE12 183 N3
Mallory Gdns EBAR EN4 98 A1
Mallory St STJWD NW8 9 P2
Mallow Cl CROY/NA CRO 204 C8
  GVE DA11 190 B7
Mallow Crs RGUE GU4 250 E7
Mallow Md MLHL NW7 97 N1
Mallow St FSBYE EC1V 7 H9
Mallows Gn HLWW/ROY CM19 46 D5
The Mallows HGDN/ICK UB10 112 C8
Mall Rd HMSMTH W6 156 F3
Mall Vls HMSMTH W6 * 156 F3
Mallys Pl EYN DA4 210 B1
Malmains Cl BECK BR3 205 J5
Malmains Wy BECK BR3 205 H5
Malmesbury Cl PIN HA5 92 F11
Malmesbury Rd BOW E3 141 K7
  CAN/RD E16 141 K7
  MRDN SM4 201 P8
  SWFD E18 121 H9
Malmesbury Ter CAN/RD E16 141 K7
Malmesbury West Est
  BOW E3 140 E5
Malmes Cft HHS/BOV HP3 36 B8
Malmstone Av REDH RH1 258 C4
Malory Cl BECK BR3 204 B2
Malpas Dr PIN HA5 115 J1
Malpas Rd BROCKY SE4 160 D10
  DAGW RM9 143 P1
  HACK E8 7 N7
  SLN SL2 129 N9

HERT/BAY SG13 * 25 M5
  HHNE HP2 35 N5
  KGLGY WD4 54 A4
  ORP BR6 207 N8
  OXTED RH8 261 L7
  ROM RM1 124 D4
  SHGR GU5 270 C5
  SNWD SE25 203 N2
  STA TW18 173 H7
Malting Wy ISLW TW7 154 A9
Malton Av SL SL1 128 C8
Malton Ms NKENS W10 * 8 A5
  WOOL/PLUM SE18 163 H5
Malton Rd NKENS W10 8 A5
Malton St WOOL/PLUM SE18 163 J10
Maltravers St TPL/STR WC2R 11 P7
Malt St STHWK SE1 19 N5
Malus Cl ADL/WDHM KT15 215 H8
Malus Dr ADL/WDHM KT15 215 J4
Malva Cl WAND/EARL SW18 179 L1
Malvern Av BXLYHN DA7 163 P6
  CHING E4 101 L4
  RYLN/HDSTN HA2 113 M8
Malvern Cl BUSH WD23 74 B10
  CHERT KT16 214 F3
  HAT AL10 40 C3
  HGDN/ICK UB10 112 A9
  MTCM CR4 202 D3
  NKENS W10 8 C5
  STALE/WH AL4 38 C2
  SURB KT6 199 K8
Malvern Dr FELT TW13 175 L8
  GDMY/SEVK IG3 123 J9
  WFD IG8 101 P6
Malvern Gdns CRICK NW2 117 H2
  KTN/HRWW/WS HA3 115 K2
  LOU IG10 82 C10
Malvern Ms KIL/WHAMP NW6 2 E10
Malvern Pl MV/WKIL W9 8 C1
Malvern Rd CEND/HSY/T N8 98 G8
  CRAWW RH11 277 H8
  EHAM E6 142 B3
  EMPK RM11 125 K5
  GUW GU2 249 N8
  HOR/WEW KT19 219 N8
  HPTN TW12 175 J2
  HYS/HAR UB3 152 F6
  KIL/WHAMP NW6 2 E10
  ORP BR6 227 L1
  PEND EN3 80 D5
  SURB KT6 199 K9
  THHTH CR7 203 H4
  TOTM N17 119 P1
  WAN E11 121 K7
Malvern Ter ED N9 99 A5
  IS N1 6 A1
Malvern Wy HHW HP1 35 L4
  RKW/CH/CXG WD3 72 C9
Malvina Av GVE DA12 190 G7
Malwood Rd BAL SW12 180 C2
Malyons Rd LEW SE13 183 H3
  SWLY BR8 187 K1
Malyons Ter LEW SE13 * 183 H3
The Malyons SHPTN TW17 * 196 B6
Managers St POP/IOD E14 * 161 H10
Manan Cl HHS/BOV HP3 35 J9
Manaton Cl PECK SE15 160 A9
Manaton Crs STHL UB1 133 N6
Manbey Gv SRTFD E15 141 K5
Manbey Park Rd SRTFD E15 141 K5
Manbey Rd SRTFD E15 141 K5
Manbey St SRTFD E15 141 K5
Manbre Rd HMSMTH W6 157 H4
Manbrough Av EHAM E6 142 A3
Manchester Ct CAN/RD E16 141 L8
Manchester Dr NKENS W10 8 C5
Manchester Gv POP/IOD E14 161 H9
Manchester Ms MHST W1U * 10 A3
Manchester Rd POP/IOD E14 161 H9
  SEVS/STOTM N15 119 L4
  THHTH CR7 203 N7
Manchester Sq MBLAR W1H * 10 A5
Manchester St MHST W1U 10 A4
Manchester Wy DAGE RM10 124 C9
Manchuria Rd BTSEA SW11 180 A5
Manciple St STHWK SE1 19 J2
Mandalay Rd CLAP SW4 180 C1
Mandarin Wy YEAD UB4 133 J2
Mandela Cl WLSDN NW10 136 G2
Mandela Rd WATN WD24 73 L1
  CAN/RD E16 141 H5
Mandela St BRXN/ST SW9 159 N6
  CAMTN NW1 5 H1
Mandela Wy STHWK SE1 19 K5
Mandelyns BERK HP4 33 K3
Mandeville Cl BROX EN10 43 K5
  GUW GU2 249 M7
  HERT/BAY SG13 25 K8
  WAT WD17 72 G2
  WIM/MER SW19 179 H10
Mandeville Ct CHING E4 100 G5
Mandeville Dr STAL AL1 38 C5
Mandeville Pl MHST W1U * 10 B4
Mandeville Ri WGCW AL8 22 C1
Mandeville Rd HERT/BAY SG13 25 K8
  ISLW TW7 154 F8
  NTHLT UB5 133 N5
  PEND EN3 80 D2
  POTB/CUF EN6 59 M6
  SHPTN TW17 196 B7
  STHGT/OAK N14 98 B2

EMPK RM11 125 K3
  HHS/BOV HP3 35 K3
  HSLWW TW4 153 N2
  NTHLT UB5 133 L2
Manorbrook BKHTH/KID SE3 161 M10
Manor Cha WEY KT13 216 C2
Manor Cl BAR EN5 77 H8
  BERK HP4 33 P5
  CDALE/KGS NW9 115 N2
  DAGE RM10 124 D4
  DART DA1 164 E10
  ENSLY KT24 252 F4
  GVE DA12 191 L5
  HAT AL10 40 C1
  HERT/WAT SG14 24 C1
  HORL RH6 288 A2
  MLHL NW7 96 A4
  ROM RM1 124 D4
  RSLP HA4 112 C6
  SOCK/AV RM15 146 B10
  WARL CR6 242 D3
  WOKS/MYFD GU22 233 J7
  WPK KT4 200 B8
Manor Cottages Ap EFNCH N2 * 97 M10
Manor Ct ACT W3 * 155 M3
  CHES/WCR EN8 62 C7
  DEN/HRF UB9 91 M10
  E/WMO/HCT KT8 * 197 P4
  FELT TW13 * 175 L8
  HRW HA1 * 114 E4
  KUTN/CMB KT2 * 199 M1
  POTB/CUF EN6 * 59 J8
  RAD WD7 74 E3
  SL SL1 128 E10
  WBLY HA9 * 115 K10
  WEY KT13 216 C1
Manor Court Rd HNWL W7 134 D9
Manor Crs BEAC HP9 89 J6
  BF/WBF KT14 216 A9
  BRYLDS KT5 199 M6
  CHOB/PIR GU24 232 B3
  EMPK RM11 125 K3
  GUW GU2 249 M8
  HOR/WEW KT19 219 N8
Manor Cft WDGW HA8 * 95 M7
Manor Croft Pde
  CHES/WCR EN8 * 62 C6
Manorcrofts Rd EGH TW20 172 A9
Manordene Cl THDIT KT7 198 B3
Manordene Rd THMD SE28 143 M6
Manor Dr ADL/WDHM KT15 215 K6
  AMS HP6 68 G2
  BRYLDS KT5 199 N6
  CHOB/PIR GU24 232 B3
  EMPK RM11 125 K3
  EN EN1 80 A1
  ESH/CLAY KT10 198 E10
  FELT TW13 175 E10
  HART DA3 211 L6
  HOR/WEW KT19 220 A8
  SUN TW16 196 A2
  WCHMH N21 77 P9
  WLGTN SM6 222 C1
  WWKM BR4 204 G8
Manor Dr North
  ESH/CLAY KT10 198 C6
  WLGTN SM6 222 C1
Manor Dr South
  ESH/CLAY KT10 218 D1
  WLGTN SM6 222 C1
The Manor Dr WPK KT4 200 B8
Manor Fld GVE DA12 190 H8
Manor Farm ACT W3 * 155 H4
  RGUE GU4 266 B3
Manor Farm Av SHPTN TW17 195 L8
Manor Farm Cl RGUW GU3 248 A8
  WPK KT4 200 B8
Manor Farm Cots WDSR SL4 * 171 H1
Manor Farm Dr CHING E4 101 H4
Manor Farm La EGH TW20 172 A9
Manor Farm Rd ALP/SUD HA0 135 J3
  EN EN1 80 A1
  STRHM/NOR SW16 202 A3
  THHTH CR7 204 G3
Manor Gdns ACT W3 155 J4
  CLAP SW4 158 D8
  GUW GU2 249 M8
  HPTN TW12 175 L10
  RCH/KEW TW9 155 N8
  RGUE GU4 266 B3
  RSLP HA4 113 K4
  SAND/SEL CR2 223 N3
  SUN TW16 196 A2
Manor Ga NTHLT UB5 133 H5
Manorgate Rd KUTN/CMB KT2 199 M1
Manor Green Rd
  HOR/WEW KT19 219 P8
Manor Gv BECK BR3 204 C2
  PECK SE15 160 B5
  RCH/KEW TW9 155 N8
Manor Hall Av HDN NW4 96 A10
Manor Hall Dr HDN NW4 96 B10
Manor Hatch HLWS/HLWX CM18 47 K3
Manor Hatch Cl HLWS/HLWX CM18 47 K3
Manor Hl BNSTD SM7 240 E1
Manor House Ct
  EPSOM KT18 * 219 P9
  SHPTN TW17 196 C7
Manor House Dr
  KIL/WHAMP NW6 136 G2
  NTHWD HA6 92 D8
  WOT/HER KT12 216 C2
Manor House Gdns
  ABLGY WD5 54 C7
Manor House La
  DTCH/LGLY SL3 149 N7
  GT/LBKH KT23 253 N2
Manorhouse La GT/LBKH KT23 253 N2
Manor House Wy ISLW TW7 154 D9
Manor La CFSP/GDCR SL9 108 A3
  FELT TW13 175 J5
  HART DA3 211 J7
  HYS/HAR UB3 152 A6
  KWD/TDW/WH KT20 257 L2
  LEE/GVPK SE12 183 J2
  SUN TW16 196 A2
  SUT SM1 221 N3
Manor Lane Ter LEW SE13 161 K11
Manor Leaze EGH TW20 172 B8
Manor Ldg GUW GU2 249 N8
Manor Ms BROCKY SE4 160 B7
  KIL/WHAMP NW6 2 F1
Manor Mt FSTH SE23 182 B4
Manor Pde HAT AL10 40 C1
  HRW HA1 114 E4
  STNW/STAM N16 119 N6
Manor Pk CHST BR7 206 C6
  LEW SE13 183 J1
  RCH/KEW TW9 155 N8
  STA TW18 172 A9
Manor Park Cl WWKM BR4 204 B9
Manor Park Crs EDGW HA8 96 B1
Manor Park Dr
  RYLN/HDSTN HA2 114 A1

Manor Park Gdns EDGW HA8 96 B1
Manor Park Pde LEW SE13 * 161 K11
Manor Park Rd CHST BR7 206 C6
  EFNCH N2 97 M10
  HART DA3 211 J7
  MNPK E12 122 A6
  SUT SM1 221 N3
  WLSDN NW10 136 G1
  WWKM BR4 204 B9
Manor Pl BORE WD6 75 P7
  CHST BR7 206 D2
  EBED/NFELT TW14 173 K5
  GT/LBKH KT23 253 N2
  MTCM CR4 202 D2
  STA TW18 172 A9
  SUT SM1 221 N3
  WALW SE17 18 E9
Manor Rd ABR/ST RM4 105 H2
  ASHF TW15 157 J9
  BAR EN5 76 B5
  BARK IG11 143 J1
  BECK BR3 204 C1
  BELMT SM2 221 N6
  BH/WHM TN16 244 C4
  BXLY DA5 185 M6
  CAN/RD E16 141 J3
  CHIG IG7 102 F2
  CSHM HP5 50 G5
  DAGE RM10 124 E4
  DART DA1 164 F10
  E/WMO/HCT KT8 198 A3
  ENC/FH EN2 79 M1
  ERITH DA8 164 G5
  GRAYS RM17 168 B5
  GUW GU2 249 N8
  GVE DA12 191 L5
  HAT AL10 40 C1
  HLWE CM17 48 G3
  HOD EN11 44 F1
  HRW HA1 114 F4
  HYS/HAR UB3 133 H8
  IL IG1 57 H2
  LCOL/BKTW AL2 57 H2
  LEY E10 120 F5
  LOU IG10 81 N10
  MTCM CR4 202 D3
  POTB/CUF EN6 59 J7
  RCH/KEW TW9 155 N8
  REDH RH1 258 D9
  REIG RH2 257 J8
  ROM RM1 125 H3
  RPLY/SEND GU23 233 J9
  RSEV TN14 245 N10
  RSLP HA4 112 C6
  RYNPK SW20 201 J2
  SNWD SE25 203 P4
  SRTFD E15 141 K8
  STAL AL1 38 D5
  STALE/WH AL4 39 K1
  STNW/STAM N16 119 M6
  SWCM DA10 189 J2
  TEDD TW11 176 B8
  TIL RM18 168 C8
  TOTM N17 99 P8
  WAB EN9 63 J9
  WAT WD17 73 L5
  WDGN N22 98 A8
  WDSR SL4 148 C9
  WEA W13 134 G4
  WHTN TW2 176 A6
  WLGTN SM6 222 C1
  WOKN/KNAP GU21 231 P2
  WOT/HER KT12 196 E7
  WTHK RM20 167 H5
  WWKM BR4 204 C9
Manor Rd North
  ESH/CLAY KT10 198 D6
  WLGTN SM6 222 C1
Manor Rd South
  ESH/CLAY KT10 198 D7
Manor Royal CRAWE RH10 283 P4
Manorside BAR EN5 77 H8
Manor Sq BCTR RM8 123 P7
Manor St BAR EN5 34 A5
Manor V BTFD TW8 155 H4
Manor Vw FNCH N3 97 H10
  HART DA3 211 M6
Manorville Rd HHS/BOV HP3 35 P3
Manor Vw WEY KT13 216 C2
Manor Wy GRAYS RM17 167 N6
  BECK BR3 204 C2
  BKHTH/KID SE3 161 M10
  BNSTD SM7 240 A2
  BORE WD6 76 A1
  BRW CM14 106 F1
  BXLY DA5 186 B4
  BXLYHN DA7 164 A3
  CDALE/KGS NW9 116 D1
  CHING E4 101 H3
  CHST BR7 205 H5
  CSHM HP5 51 H9
  ECH TW20 172 C9
  EN EN1 79 N1
  HAYES BR2 204 G8
  HRW HA1 113 P1
  MNPK E12 122 A6
  MTCM CR4 202 C2
  PUR/KEN CR8 223 J6
  RAIN RM13 144 G3
  RKW/CH/CXG WD3 72 C2
  RYLN/HDSTN HA2 114 A4
  SAND/SEL CR2 223 L3
  SCWM DA10 167 K10
  TIL RM18 167 K10
  WOKS/MYFD GU22 232 E6
  WPK KT4 200 B8
  BECK BR3 204 C1
  BKHTH/KID SE3 161 M10
  BORE WD6 76 A1
  BRW CM14 106 B4
  BXLY DA5 186 B4
Manor Wood Rd
  PUR/KEN CR8 222 F9
Manresa Rd CHEL SW3 15 N7
Mansard Beeches TOOT SW17 180 B8
Mansard Cl HCH RM12 125 H7
  PIN HA5 113 J1
Mansards The HHW HP1 35 L4
Manse Cl HYS/HAR UB3 152 E5
Mansell Cl CSHM HP5 50 G4
  GUW GU2 249 N5
  SLN SL2 129 N7
Mansell Gv WAT WD17 72 C1
Mansell Rd ACT W3 136 A1
  GFD/PVL UB6 134 A1
Mansell St WCHPL E1 13 N5
Mansell Wy CTHM CR3 241 K8
Mansergh Cl CHARL SE7 162 B6
Manse Rd STNW/STAM N16 119 N8
Manser Rd RAIN RM13 144 F5
Manse Wy SWLY BR8 209 H4
Mansfield SBW CM21 29 K2
Mansfield Av EBAR EN4 78 A4
  RSLP HA4 113 J6
  SEVS/STOTM N15 119 J4
Mansfield Cl ED N9 79 J10
  STMC/STPC BR5 207 N2
  YEAD UB4 132 F2
Mansfield Dr REDH RH1 258 D4
  YEAD UB4 132 F2
Mansfield Gdns HCH RM12 125 J7
  HERT/WAT SG14 25 J3
Mansfield Hl CHING E4 100 C1
Mansfield Ms CAVSQ/HST W1G 10 C3
Mansfield Pl HAMP NW3 3 P1
  IL IG1 122 E8
  SAND/SEL CR2 223 N5
Mansfield Rd ACT W3 135 P7
  BXLYHN DA7 163 P4
  CHING E4 100 G1
  CHSGTN KT9 219 J4
  HAMP NW3 4 B1
  IL IG1 122 B7
  PEND EN3 80 E1
  SAND/SEL CR2 223 N5
  SWFD E18 102 A10
  WALTH E17 119 J1
  WAN E11 121 L2
Mansford St BETH E2 7 N10
Manship Rd MTCM CR4 180 B10
Mansion Cl BRXN/ST SW9 159 N6
Mansion Gdns HAMP NW3 117 J8
Mansion House Pl
  MANHO EC4N 12 G6
Mansion House St
  MANHO EC4N 12 G6
Mansion La IVER SL0 130 F10
Mansion Ms SKENS SW7 15 K6
Manstead Gdns CHDH RM6 123 N8
  RAIN RM13 145 J6
Manston Av NWDGN UB2 153 H3
Manston Cl CHES/WCR EN8 62 B6
  PGE/AN SE20 204 B1
Manstone Rd CRICK NW2 117 M10

| Name | Area | Page | Grid |
|---|---|---|---|
| Manston Gv KUTN/CMB KT2 | | 177 | J8 |
| Manston Rd HLW CM20 | | 47 | H1 |
| RGUE GU4 | | 250 | D6 |
| Manston Wy HTWN ALA | | 145 | J1 |
| WER/HW ALA | | 39 | J7 |
| Manthorpe Rd WOOL/PLUM SE18 | | 162 | F4 |
| Mantilla Rd TOOT SW17 | | 143 | M4 |
| Mantle Rd BROCKY SE4 | | 160 | B9 |
| Mantlet Cl STRHM/NOR SW16 | | 180 | D10 |
| Mantle Wy SRTFD E15 | | 141 | K2 |
| Manton Av HNWL W7 | | 154 | F1 |
| Manton Cl HYS/HAR UB3 | | 132 | E4 |
| Manton Rd ABYW SE2 | | 163 | K3 |
| ENB E2 | | 80 | F3 |
| Manton Ter ADL/WDHM KT15 | | 215 | M1 |
| Mantua St BTSEA SW11 | | 157 | N9 |
| Mantus Cl WCHPL E1 | | 140 | E8 |
| Mantus Rd WCHPL E1 | | 140 | E8 |
| Manus Wy TRDG/WHET N20 | | 97 | H2 |
| Manville Gdns TOOT SW17 | | 180 | C5 |
| Manville Rd TOOT SW17 | | 180 | C5 |
| Manwood Rd BROCKY SE4 | | 160 | B9 |
| Manwood St CAN/RD E16 | | 142 | C10 |
| Manygate La SHPTN TW17 | | 196 | B6 |
| Many Gates BAL SW12 | | 180 | C5 |
| Maori Rd GU GU1 | | 268 | C1 |
| Mapesbury Ms CDALE/KGS NW9 | | 116 | A10 |
| Mapesbury Rd CRICK NW2 | | 2 | A2 |
| Mapeshill Pl CRICK NW2 | | 136 | F1 |
| Mape St BETH E2 | | 140 | A6 |
| Maple Av ACT W3 | | 136 | B10 |
| CHING E4 | | 100 | E7 |
| RYLN/HDSTN HA2 | | 114 | A7 |
| STALW/RED AL3 | | 38 | B2 |
| UPMR RM14 | | 126 | A8 |
| WDR/YW UB7 | | 131 | P9 |
| Maple Cl BARK/HLT IG6 | | 103 | H7 |
| BKHN IG9 | | 103 | A4 |
| BUSH WD23 | | 73 | M6 |
| CLAP SW4 | | 180 | G2 |
| CRAWW RH11 | | 283 | M4 |
| CTHM CR3 | | 241 | N3 |
| FNCH N3 | | 97 | K7 |
| HACK HA9 | | 40 | D5 |
| HCH RM12 | | 125 | J8 |
| HPTN TW12 | | 175 | N9 |
| MTCM CR4 | | 202 | C1 |
| RBRW/HUT CM13 | | 107 | L4 |
| RSLP HA4 | | 113 | J4 |
| STMC/STPC BR5 | | 206 | C5 |
| STNW/STAM N16 | | 119 | P4 |
| SWLY BR8 | | 208 | F2 |
| YEAD UB4 | | 133 | L5 |
| Maple Ct ASHF TW15 | | 174 | E10 |
| THW F20 | | 171 | N9 |
| HACK E8 | | 7 | N1 |
| NWMAL KT3 | | 200 | A3 |
| Maple Crs BFN/LL DA15 | | 185 | J4 |
| SLN SL2 | | 129 | N9 |
| Maplecroft Cl EHAM E6 | | 142 | A4 |
| Maplecroft La UPMR RM14 | | 45 | K7 |
| Mapledale Av CROY/NA CR0 | | 204 | A10 |
| Mapledene Est HACK E8 | | 7 | M3 |
| Mapledene Rd HACK E8 | | 7 | M3 |
| Maple Dr SOCK/AV RM15 | | 147 | N6 |
| Maplefield LCOL/BKTW AL2 | | 56 | A5 |
| Maplefield La CSTG HP8 | | 69 | N7 |
| Maple Gdns ASHF TW15 | | 173 | P5 |
| EDGW HA8 | | 96 | B3 |
| Maple Gn LOU IG10 | | 82 | D6 |
| Maple Gv HHW HP1 | | 35 | H4 |
| Maple Gv BTFD TW8 | | 154 | G6 |
| CDALE/KGS NW9 | | 115 | P5 |
| EA W5 | | 155 | J2 |
| GU GU1 | | 250 | A8 |
| STHL UB1 | | 133 | N1 |
| WAT WD17 | | 73 | H1 |
| WCCE AL7 | | 23 | J2 |
| WOKS/MYFD GU22 | | 232 | B7 |
| Maplehurst LHD/OX KT22 | | 236 | C9 |
| Maplehurst Cl KUT/HW KT1 | | 199 | K4 |
| BH/WHM TN16 | | 244 | A2 |
| Maple Leaf Cl ABLGY WD5 | | 55 | L8 |
| Maple Leaf Dr BFN/LL DA15 | | 185 | J4 |
| Mapleleafe Gdns BARK/HLT IG6 | | 122 | E1 |
| Maple Leaf Sq BERM/RHTH SE16 | | 160 | C1 |
| Maple Lodge Cl RKW/CH/CXG WD3 | | 91 | J5 |
| STRHM/NOR SW16 | | 180 | G8 |
| Maple Ms KIL/WHAMP NW6 | | 2 | C1 |
| Maple Pl BNSTD SM7 | | 220 | G10 |
| FITZ W1T | | 11 | H1 |
| TOTM N17 | | 99 | P8 |
| WDR/YW UB7 | | 131 | P10 |
| Maple Rd ASHTD KT21 | | 237 | J5 |
| CTHM CR3 | | 241 | N10 |
| GRAYS RM17 | | 167 | P5 |
| GVE DA12 | | 190 | D7 |
| PGE/AN SE20 | | 204 | A1 |
| REDH RH1 | | 276 | A4 |
| RPLY/SEND GU23 | | 233 | K10 |
| SURB KT6 | | 199 | J3 |
| WAN E11 | | 121 | K4 |
| Maples PI WAB EN9 | | 133 | K5 |
| Mapleshade Rd BEAC HP9 | | 81 | P1 |
| Maplescombe La EYN DA4 | | 209 | P10 |
| Maple Springs WAB EN9 | | 63 | M9 |
| Maplestead Rd BRXS/STRHM SW2 | | 180 | G3 |
| DAGW RM9 | | 143 | L3 |
| The Maples BNSTD SM7 | | 221 | L9 |
| CHERT KT16 | | 214 | E8 |
| CHESW EC4 | | 61 | M4 |
| ESH/CLAY KT10 | | 218 | F4 |
| HART DA3 | | 211 | N3 |
| HLWW/ROY CM19 | | 46 | K6 |
| KUT/HW KT1 | | 177 | H10 |
| Maple St BETH E2 | | 7 | P8 |
| FITZ W1T | | 10 | E3 |
| ROMW/RG RM7 | | 124 | D2 |
| Maplethorpe Rd THHTH CR7 | | 203 | H4 |
| Mapleton Cl HAYES BR2 | | 205 | M5 |
| Mapleton Crs PEND EN3 | | 80 | B4 |
| Mapleton Rd BH/WHM TN16 | | 179 | L2 |
| CHING E4 | | 101 | H4 |
| EN EN1 | | 80 | A2 |
| WAND/EARL SW18 | | 179 | K2 |
| Maple Tree PI BKHTH/KID SE3 | | 162 | B2 |
| Maple Wk NKENS W10 | | 136 | G6 |
| Maple Wy COUL/CHIP CR5 | | 240 | C7 |
| FELT TW13 | | 175 | H6 |
| Maplewood Gdns BEAC HP9 | | 88 | A10 |
| Maplin Cl WCHMH N21 | | 78 | G2 |
| Maplin Pk DTCH/LGLY SL3 | | 150 | E1 |
| Maplin Rd CAN/RD E16 | | 141 | M8 |
| Maplin St BOW E3 | | 140 | E5 |
| Mapperley Dr WFD IG8 | | 101 | K8 |
| Marabou Cl MNPK E12 | | 122 | B10 |
| Maran Wy ERITHM DA18 | | 147 | J10 |
| Marathon Rd THMD SE28 | | 143 | J10 |
| Marban Rd MV/WKIL W9 | | 2 | C9 |
| Marbeck Cl WDSR SL4 | | 148 | C7 |
| Marble Cl ACT W3 | | 135 | N10 |
| Marble Dr CRICK NW2 | | 116 | G5 |
| Marble Hill Cl TWK TW1 | | 176 | D5 |
| Marble Hill Gdns TWK TW1 | | 176 | D5 |
| Marble Quay WAP E1W | | 13 | M6 |
| Marbles Wy KWD/TDW/WH KT20 | | 238 | G5 |
| Marbrook Ct LEE/GVPK SE12 | | 183 | P6 |
| Marcella Rd BRXN/ST SW9 | | 159 | H8 |
| Marcellina Wy ORP BR6 | | 207 | H2 |
| Marchant Cl MLHL NW7 | | 96 | B7 |
| Marchant Rd WAN E11 | | 121 | J7 |
| Marchant St NWCR SE14 | | 160 | D5 |
| Marchbank Rd WKENS W14 | | 14 | D9 |
| Marchmant Cl HCH RM12 | | 125 | J7 |
| Marchmont Gdns RCHPK/HAM TW10 | | 177 | K1 |
| Marchmont Gn HHNE HP2 | | 35 | N4 |
| Marchmont Rd RCHPK/HAM TW10 | | 177 | L1 |
| WIM/MER SW19 | | 222 | E5 |
| Marchmont St BMSBY WC1N | | 11 | L1 |
| March Rd TWK TW1 | | 216 | B2 |
| WEY KT13 | | 216 | B8 |
| Marchside Cl HEST TW5 | | 153 | L1 |
| Marchwood Cl CMBW SE5 | | 159 | M6 |
| Marchwood Crs EA W5 | | 135 | H8 |
| Marcia Ct SL SL1 | | 128 | E10 |
| Marcia Rd STHWK SE1 | | 19 | K6 |
| Marcilly Rd WAND/EARL SW18 | | 179 | N1 |
| Marconi Gdns BRWN CM15 | | 87 | P9 |
| Marconi Pl FBAR/BDGN N11 | | 98 | C5 |
| Marconi Rd CVW DA11 | | 190 | A6 |
| LEY E10 | | 120 | F6 |
| Marconi Wy STALE/WH AL4 | | 39 | J6 |
| STHL UB1 | | 134 | A8 |
| Marcon Pl HACK E8 | | 7 | P1 |
| Marco Rd HMSMTH W6 | | 156 | F6 |
| Marcus Ct WOKS/MYFD GU22 | | 232 | C4 |
| Marcus Garvey Ms EDUL SE22 | | 182 | A2 |
| Marcus Garvey Wy HNHL SE24 | | 159 | H10 |
| Marcus St SRTFD E15 | | 141 | K8 |
| WAND/EARL SW18 | | 179 | L2 |
| Marcus Ter WAND/EARL SW18 | | 179 | L2 |
| Mardale Dr CDALE/KGS NW9 | | 116 | A3 |
| Mardell Rd CROY/NA CR0 | | 204 | C5 |
| Marden Av HAYES BR2 | | 205 | M6 |
| Marden Crs BXLY DA5 | | 186 | D1 |
| CROY/NA CR0 | | 202 | G6 |
| Marden Rd CROY/NA CR0 | | 202 | G6 |
| ROM RM1 | | 124 | F4 |
| TOTM N17 | | 99 | M10 |
| Marden Sq BERM/RHTH SE16 | | 160 | A2 |
| The Mardens CRAWW RH11 | | 283 | L6 |
| Marder Rd WEA W13 | | 154 | F1 |
| Mardyke Cl RAIN RM13 | | 144 | D4 |
| Mardyke Cl HLW CM20 | | 29 | K9 |
| Mardyke Vw PUR RM19 | | 166 | D2 |
| Marechal Niel Av BFN/LL DA15 | | 184 | G6 |
| Marechal Niel Pde SCUP DA14 | | 184 | C5 |
| Mareschal Rd GUW GU2 | | 267 | P2 |
| Marescroft Rd SLN SL2 | | 128 | D6 |
| Maresfield CROY/NA CR0 | | 203 | M10 |
| Maresfield Gdns HAMP NW3 | | 117 | M10 |
| Mare St HACK E8 | | 140 | A4 |
| Marfield Cl WPK KT4 | | 200 | D8 |
| Marfleet Cl CAR SM5 | | 201 | P9 |
| Marford Rd STALE/WH AL4 | | 21 | L3 |
| WGCW AL8 | | 22 | A5 |
| Margaret Av BRWN CM15 | | 107 | M1 |
| CHING E4 | | 80 | C10 |
| STALW/RED AL3 | | 38 | C4 |
| Margaret Bondfield Av BARK IG11 | | 143 | K2 |
| Margaret Cl ABLGY WD5 | | 54 | G8 |
| GPK RM2 | | 125 | J3 |
| POTB/CUF EN6 | | 59 | M9 |
| STA TW18 | | 37 | M9 |
| WAB EN9 | | 63 | J9 |
| Margaret Dr EMPK RM11 | | 125 | N6 |
| Margaret Gardner Dr ELTH/MOT SE9 | | 184 | C5 |
| Margaret Ingram Cl FUL/PGN SW6 | | 14 | C10 |
| Margaret Lockwood Cl KUT/HW KT1 | | 199 | L4 |
| Margaret Rd BXLY DA5 | | 185 | N2 |
| EBAR EN4 | | 77 | N8 |
| EPP CM16 | | 65 | K5 |
| GU GU1 | | 267 | J3 |
| STNW/STAM N16 | | 119 | N6 |
| Margaret Rutherford Pl BAL SW12 | | 180 | D1 |
| Margaret St REGST W1B | | 10 | F5 |
| Margaretta Ter CHEL SW3 | | 15 | N9 |
| Margaretting Rd MNPK E12 | | 121 | P7 |
| Margaret Wy COUL/CHIP CR5 | | 241 | J3 |
| REDBR IG4 | | 122 | B4 |
| Margate Rd BRXS/STRHM SW2 | | 180 | F1 |
| Margeholes OXHEY WD19 | | 93 | M3 |
| Margery Gv KWD/TDW/WH KT20 | | 257 | H5 |
| Margery La KWD/TDW/WH KT20 | | 257 | H5 |
| Margery Park Rd FSTGT E7 | | 141 | M1 |
| Margery Rd BCTR RM8 | | 123 | N8 |
| Margery St CLKNW EC1R | | 6 | A10 |
| Margery Wd WGCE AL7 | | 23 | K1 |
| Margherita Hl WAB EN9 | | 63 | L10 |
| Margin Dr WIM/MER SW19 | | 178 | D3 |
| Margravine Gdns HMSMTH W6 | | 156 | G4 |
| Margravine Rd HMSMTH W6 | | 156 | G5 |
| Marguerite Vis RYNPK SW20 | | 178 | E10 |
| Marham Gdns MRDN SM4 | | 201 | M6 |
| WAND/EARL SW18 | | 179 | P5 |
| Maria Cl STHWK SE1 | | 19 | P5 |
| Mariam Gdns HCH RM12 | | 125 | M4 |
| Marian Cl CDW/CHF RM16 | | 147 | K10 |
| YEAD UB4 | | 133 | L6 |
| Marian Pl BETH E2 | | 140 | A4 |
| Marian Rd STRHM/NOR SW16 | | 202 | D1 |
| Marian Sq BETH E2 | | 7 | P1 |
| Marian Wy WLSDN NW10 | | 136 | C2 |
| Maria Theresa Cl NWMAL KT3 | | 200 | A5 |
| Maria Ter WCHPL E1 | | 140 | C7 |
| Maricas Av KTN/HRWW/WS HA3 | | 94 | C9 |
| Marie Curie CMBW SE5 | | 159 | N5 |
| Marie Lloyd Wk HACK E8 | | 7 | M2 |
| Marie Manor Wy RDART DA2 | | 188 | B6 |
| Mariette Wy WLGTN SM6 | | 222 | F5 |
| Marigold Aly STHWK SE1 | | 12 | C8 |
| Marigold Cl STHL UB1 | | 133 | M9 |
| Marigold Ct GU GU1 | | 250 | B7 |
| Marigold Pl CHOB/PIR GU24 | | 230 | F1 |
| Marigold Pl HARLW CM17 | | 29 | L7 |
| Marigold Rd TOTM N17 | | 100 | B8 |
| Marigold St BERM/RHTH SE16 | | 160 | A1 |
| Marigold Wy CROY/NA CR0 | | 204 | G8 |
| Marina Ap YEAD UB4 | | 133 | M4 |
| Marina Av NWMAL KT3 | | 200 | E5 |
| Marina Cl CHERT KT16 | | 195 | L8 |
| WELL DA16 | | 163 | H4 |
| Marina Dr CVW DA11 | | 190 | C3 |
| Marina Pl KUT/HW KT1 | | 199 | J1 |
| Marina Wy IVER SL0 | | 131 | K2 |
| SL SL1 | | 128 | C9 |
| TEDD TW11 | | 177 | J10 |
| Marine Ct PUR RM19 | | 165 | N5 |
| Marine Dr BARK IG11 | | 143 | K6 |
| WOOL/PLUM SE18 | | 146 | B8 |
| Marinefield Rd FUL/PGN SW6 | | 157 | L8 |
| Mariner Gdns RCHPK/HAM TW10 | | 176 | C6 |
| Mariner Rd MNPK E12 | | 122 | A8 |
| Mariners Dr RGUW GU3 | | 248 | B6 |
| Mariners Ms POP/IOD E14 | | 161 | J3 |
| Mariners Wk CVW DA11 | | 190 | B3 |
| Mariner Wy HHNE HP2 | | 35 | M5 |
| Marine St BERM/RHTH SE16 | | 19 | N1 |
| Marion Cl SHPTN TW17 | | 196 | C5 |
| Marion Crs STMC/STPC BR5 | | 202 | G8 |
| Marion Gv WFD IG8 | | 101 | K4 |
| Marion Ms DUL SE21 | | 181 | N5 |
| Marion Rd CROY/NA CR0 | | 284 | C10 |
| MLHL NW7 | | 96 | B7 |
| THHTH CR7 | | 203 | K5 |
| Marion Wk HHNE HP2 | | 35 | M5 |
| Marischal Rd LEW SE13 | | 161 | J9 |
| Marisco Cl CDW/CHF RM16 | | 147 | K10 |
| Marish La DEN/HRF UB9 | | 110 | F2 |
| Marish Whf DTCH/LGLY SL3 | | 150 | B1 |
| Maritime Cl RDART DA2 | | 188 | C3 |
| Maritime Ga GVW DA11 | | 190 | B3 |
| Maritime Quay POP/IOD E14 | | 160 | F4 |
| Maritime St BOW E3 | | 140 | E6 |
| Marius Rd TOOT SW17 | | 143 | M4 |
| Marjoram Cl GUW GU2 | | 249 | M6 |
| Marjorams St SRTFD E15 | | 82 | B6 |
| Marjorie Gv BTSEA SW11 | | 158 | A10 |
| Mark Av CHING E4 | | 80 | G10 |
| Mark Cl BXLYHN DA7 | | 163 | P7 |
| HAYES BR2 | | 226 | A1 |
| STHL UB1 | | 133 | P10 |
| Mark Dr CFSP/GDCR SL9 | | 90 | A5 |
| Markedge La COUL/CHIP CR5 | | 240 | A10 |
| REDH RH1 | | 259 | L2 |
| Markenhorn GODL GU7 | | 267 | J10 |
| Markeston Gr OXHEY WD19 | | 93 | L5 |
| Market Chambers ENC/FH EN2 | | 79 | L7 |
| Market Est HOLWY N7 | | 5 | L1 |
| Market Field Rd REDH RH1 | | 258 | A10 |
| Marketfield Wy REDH RH1 | | 258 | A10 |
| Market La DTCH/LGLY SL3 | | 150 | B1 |
| EDGW HA8 | | 96 | F5 |
| Market Link ROM RM1 | | 124 | F2 |
| Market Meadow STMC/STPC BR5 | | 207 | M4 |
| Market Oak La HHS/BOV HP3 | | 36 | B10 |
| Market Pde BMLY BR1 | | 205 | M1 |
| EW KT17 | | 220 | C5 |
| FELT TW13 | | 175 | M5 |
| LEY E10 | | 120 | G4 |
| SCUP DA14 | | 185 | K7 |
| SNWD SE25 | | 203 | P4 |
| STNW/STAM N16 | | 119 | P6 |
| WALTH E17 | | 120 | E1 |
| Market Pl ABR/ST RM4 | | 83 | L7 |
| BERM/RHTH SE16 | | 19 | P5 |
| BTFD TW8 | | 155 | H6 |
| BXLYHS DA6 | | 164 | B10 |
| CFSP/GDCR SL9 | | 90 | A5 |
| DTCH/LGLY SL3 | | 150 | C6 |
| EN EN1 | | 79 | P4 |
| ENC/FH EN2 | | 79 | L7 |
| HERT/WAT SG14 | | 25 | L5 |
| KUT/HW KT1 | | 199 | J2 |
| ROM RM1 | | 124 | F2 |
| STALW/RED AL3 | | 38 | C6 |
| TIL RM18 | | 168 | D8 |
| WAT WD17 | | 73 | K8 |
| Market Rd HOLWY N7 | | 5 | L2 |
| RCH/KEW TW9 | | 157 | N7 |
| Market Sq BH/WHM TN16 | | 262 | F3 |
| ED N9 | | 100 | A9 |
| HLW CM20 | | 28 | C10 |
| Market St EHAM E6 | | 142 | C4 |
| GU GU1 | | 268 | A1 |
| HERT/WAT SG14 | | 25 | L5 |
| HLWE CM17 | | 29 | M7 |
| WATW WD18 | | 73 | H4 |
| WOOL/PLUM SE18 | | 146 | D9 |
| Market Ter BTFD TW8 | | 155 | M6 |
| The Market HNWL W7 | | 135 | L5 |
| PECK SE15 | | 159 | P8 |
| SUT SM1 | | 201 | M8 |
| Market Wk BH/WHM TN16 | | 68 | G6 |
| Market Yard Ms STHWK SE1 | | 19 | L3 |
| Markfield CROY/NA CR0 | | 224 | C6 |
| Markfield Gdns CHING E4 | | 100 | G1 |
| Markfield Rd CTHM CR3 | | 260 | A1 |
| STNW/STAM N16 | | 119 | P2 |
| Mark Hall Moors HLW CM20 | | 29 | L8 |
| Markham Cl BORE WD6 | | 75 | J7 |
| Markham Pl CHEL SW3 | | 16 | A7 |
| Markham Sq CHEL SW3 | | 16 | A7 |
| Markham St CHEL SW3 | | 15 | P7 |
| Markhole Cl HPTN TW12 | | 175 | N10 |
| Markhouse Av WALTH E17 | | 120 | A7 |
| Markhouse Rd WALTH E17 | | 120 | B6 |
| Mark La GVE DA12 | | 191 | N2 |
| MON EC3R | | 13 | L3 |
| Markmanor Av WALTH E17 | | 120 | D5 |
| Mark Oak La LHD/OX KT22 | | 235 | P7 |
| Mark Rd HHNE HP2 | | 36 | B4 |
| Mark's Av CHONG CM5 | | 67 | N3 |
| Marksbury Av RCH/KEW TW9 | | 157 | N8 |
| Marks Rd ROMW/RG RM7 | | 124 | D3 |
| WARL CR6 | | 242 | D4 |
| Marks Sq GVW DA11 | | 190 | C7 |
| Markstone Ter ORP BR6 | | 207 | K2 |
| Mark St REIG RH2 | | 287 | L8 |
| SDTCH EC2A | | 13 | J1 |
| SRTFD E15 | | 141 | K2 |
| Mark Ter RYNPK SW20 | | 178 | F10 |
| Markville Gdns CTHM CR3 | | 259 | P1 |
| Markwade Cl MNPK E12 | | 122 | A6 |
| Mark Wy GODL GU7 | | 266 | D9 |
| SWLY BR8 | | 209 | H5 |
| The Markway SUN TW16 | | 197 | K2 |
| Markwell Cl SYD SE26 | | 182 | A7 |
| Markwell Wk HLWW/ROY CM19 | | 46 | B7 |
| Markyate Rd BCTR RM8 | | 123 | H10 |
| Marland Rd ISLW TW7 | | 154 | C7 |
| Marlands Rd CLAY IG5 | | 122 | F4 |
| Marlborough RDART DA2 | | 188 | C4 |
| Marlborough Av BAY/PAD W2 | | 9 | P3 |
| STAL AL1 | | 38 | G6 |
| STJWD NW8 | | 3 | N8 |
| STHWK SE1 | | 19 | M4 |
| WWKM BR4 | | 204 | B7 |
| Marlborough Cl CDW/CHF RM16 | | 147 | P1 |
| ORP BR6 | | 207 | L1 |
| TRDG/WHET N20 | | 98 | A4 |
| UPMR RM14 | | 126 | D6 |
| WALW SE17 | | 18 | E7 |
| WIM/MER SW19 | | 179 | P7 |
| WOT/HER KT12 | | 197 | L5 |
| Marlborough Crs CHSWK W4 | | 156 | A4 |
| HYS/HAR UB3 | | 152 | E6 |
| SEV TN13 | | 246 | F10 |
| Marlborough Dr BUSH WD23 | | 73 | N8 |
| CLAY IG5 | | 122 | B1 |
| WEY KT13 | | 196 | F10 |
| Marlborough Gdns TRDG/WHET N20 | | 98 | A4 |
| UPMR RM14 | | 126 | A6 |
| Marlborough Ga BAY/PAD W2 | | 9 | M7 |
| Marlborough Gv STHWK SE1 | | 19 | M6 |
| Marlborough HI DORK RH4 | | 272 | G2 |
| HRW HA1 | | 114 | D2 |
| STJWD NW8 | | 3 | M4 |
| Marlborough La CHARL SE7 | | 162 | B6 |
| Marlborough Ms BNSTD SM7 | | 239 | K6 |
| BRXS/STRHM SW2 | | 158 | C10 |
| Marlborough Pde FBAR/BDGN N11 | | 119 | K6 |
| HGDN/ICK UB10 | | 132 | C6 |
| Marlborough Park Av BFN/LL DA15 | | 185 | K4 |
| Marlborough Pl STJWD NW8 | | 3 | J8 |
| Marlborough Rd ARCH N19 | | 118 | F1 |
| ASHF TW15 | | 173 | H7 |
| BCTR RM8 | | 123 | H9 |
| BRWN CM15 | | 86 | F10 |
| CHING E4 | | 100 | G2 |
| CHSWK W4 | | 155 | P4 |
| DTCH/LGLY SL3 | | 150 | A3 |
| EA W5 | | 155 | H3 |
| FELT TW13 | | 175 | L5 |
| FSTGT E7 | | 141 | P3 |
| HAYES BR2 | | 205 | P1 |
| HCDN/ICK UB10 | | 132 | C6 |
| HPTN TW12 | | 175 | P9 |
| HSLWW TW4 | | 175 | N1 |
| SAND/SEL CR2 | | 223 | N1 |
| WAND/EARL SW18 | | 179 | M3 |
| Marlborough Yd ARCH N19 | | 118 | E7 |
| The Marld ASHTD KT21 | | 237 | L4 |
| Marle Gdns WAB EN9 | | 63 | H8 |
| Marler Rd FSTH SE23 | | 182 | E4 |
| Marlescroft Wy LOU IG10 | | 82 | E9 |
| Marley Av BXLYHN DA7 | | 163 | N5 |
| Marley Cl ADL/WDHM KT15 | | 215 | J5 |
| GFD/PVL UB6 | | 133 | P5 |
| SEVS/STOTM N15 | | 119 | J2 |
| Marley Rd BORK RH4 | | 272 | F5 |
| Marley Rd BERM/RHTH SE16 | | 160 | C5 |
| WGCE AL7 | | 23 | K7 |
| Marlin Cl BERK HP4 | | 33 | L4 |
| SUN TW16 | | 174 | F9 |
| Marlin Copse BERK HP4 | | 33 | M6 |
| Marlingdene Cl HPTN TW12 | | 175 | P9 |
| Marlings Cl CHST BR7 | | 207 | H4 |
| CTHM CR3 | | 241 | M5 |
| Marlings Park Av CHST BR7 | | 207 | H4 |
| Marling Wy GVE DA12 | | 191 | H6 |
| Marlins Cl RKW/CH/CXG WD3 | | 71 | H6 |
| SUT SM1 | | 221 | M2 |
| Marlins End BERK HP4 | | 33 | L6 |
| Marlins Meadow WATW SW18 | | 54 | G7 |
| The Marlins NTHWD HA6 | | 92 | G7 |
| Marlins Turn HHW HP1 | | 35 | L3 |
| Marloes Cl ALP/SUD HA0 | | 115 | J9 |
| Marloes Rd KENS W8 | | 14 | G3 |
| Marlow Av PUR RM19 | | 165 | P3 |
| Marlow Cl PGE/AN SE20 | | 204 | A4 |
| Marlow Ct CDALE/KGS NW9 | | 116 | C1 |
| CRAWE RH10 | | 285 | N6 |
| Marlowe Cl BARK/HLT IG6 | | 102 | F9 |
| CHST BR7 | | 184 | G10 |
| Marlowe Gdns ELTH/MOT SE9 | | 184 | A5 |
| Marlowe Rd WALTH E17 | | 121 | H2 |
| Marlowes HHW HP1 | | 35 | L3 |
| Marlowe Sq MTCM CR4 | | 202 | G2 |
| The Marlowes DART DA1 | | 171 | L6 |
| STJWD NW8 | | 3 | J3 |
| Marlowe Wy CROY/NA CR0 | | 222 | G2 |
| Marlow Gdns HYS/HAR UB3 | | 152 | E2 |
| Marlow Rd EHAM E6 | | 142 | G2 |
| PGE/AN SE20 | | 204 | A4 |
| Marlow Wy BERM/RHTH SE16 | | 160 | F1 |
| Marlpit Av COUL/CHIP CR5 | | 240 | F5 |
| Marlpit La COUL/CHIP CR5 | | 240 | F5 |
| Marl Rd WAND/EARL SW18 | | 157 | M10 |
| Marlton St GNWCH SE10 | | 161 | J4 |
| Marlwood Cl BFN/LL DA15 | | 185 | H5 |
| Marlyns Cl RGUE GU4 | | 250 | D1 |
| Marlyns Dr RGUE GU4 | | 250 | D1 |
| Marlyon Rd BARK/HLT IG6 | | 103 | L6 |
| Marmadon Rd WOOL/PLUM SE18 | | 147 | N9 |
| Marmion Ap CHING E4 | | 100 | F5 |
| Marmion Av CHING E4 | | 100 | F5 |
| Marmion Cl CHING E4 | | 100 | E5 |
| Marmion Ms BTSEA SW11 | | 158 | B10 |
| Marmion Pl CHEL SW5 | | 16 | A7 |
| Marmion Rd BTSEA SW11 | | 159 | P7 |
| Marmont Rd PECK SE15 | | 159 | P7 |
| Marmora Rd EDUL SE22 | | 182 | A2 |
| Marmot Rd HSLWW TW4 | | 154 | F9 |
| Marne Av FBAR/BDGN N11 | | 98 | C5 |
| WELL DA16 | | 163 | K3 |
| Marnell Wy HSLWW TW4 | | 153 | N9 |
| Marne St NKENS W10 | | 2 | D10 |
| Marney Rd BTSEA SW11 | | 158 | B10 |
| Marneys Cl EPSOM KT18 | | 237 | M1 |
| Marnfield Crs BRXS/STRHM SW2 | | 180 | A1 |
| Marnham Av CRICK NW2 | | 117 | H9 |
| Marnham Crs GFD/PVL UB6 | | 134 | A4 |
| Marnham Pl ADL/WDHM KT15 | | 215 | K4 |
| Marnham Ri HHW HP1 | | 35 | K4 |
| Marnock Rd BROCKY SE4 | | 182 | A1 |
| Maroon St POP/IOD E14 | | 140 | G7 |
| Maroons Wy CAT SE6 | | 182 | B6 |
| Marquess Rd IS N1 | | 6 | F1 |
| Marquess of North IS N1 | | 6 | E1 |
| Marquis Cl ALP/SUD HA0 | | 135 | L2 |
| Marquis La HARP AL5 | | 20 | C1 |
| Marquis Rd CAMTN NW1 | | 5 | H1 |
| FSBYPK N4 | | 118 | G6 |
| WDGN N22 | | 98 | C8 |
| Marrabon Cl BFN/LL DA15 | | 185 | K4 |
| Marrick Cl PUT/ROE SW15 | | 156 | D10 |
| Married Quarters EDGW HA8 | | 95 | M1 |
| Marrilyne Av PEND EN3 | | 80 | G4 |
| Marriner Ct HYS/HAR UB3 | | 133 | H8 |
| Marriot Rd MUSWH N10 | | 98 | B10 |
| Marriott Cl EBED/NFELT TW14 | | 174 | A2 |
| Marriott Lodge Cl ADL/WDHM KT15 | | 195 | M10 |
| Marriott Rd BAR EN5 | | 76 | C3 |
| FSBYPK N4 | | 118 | C6 |
| SRTFD E15 | | 141 | K3 |
| STMC/STPC BR5 | | 207 | N3 |
| Marriotts CDALE/KGS NW9 | | 116 | C4 |
| Marriotts Wy HHS/BOV HP3 | | 35 | N6 |
| Marriott Ter RKW/CH/CXG WD3 | | 71 | J8 |
| Marr's Bottom AMSS HP7 | | 88 | A3 |
| Marrowells WEY KT13 | | 196 | G6 |
| Marryat Cl HSLWW TW4 | | 153 | N10 |
| Marryat Pl WIM/MER SW19 | | 178 | A1 |
| Marryat Rd EN EN1 | | 80 | A1 |
| WIM/MER SW19 | | 178 | A1 |
| Marryfields Wy CAT SE6 | | 182 | C6 |
| Marsala Rd LEW SE13 | | 161 | H2 |
| Marsden Cl WGCW AL8 | | 22 | C1 |
| Marsden Rd ED N9 | | 100 | D1 |
| PECK SE15 | | 159 | N9 |
| WGCW AL8 | | 22 | C1 |
| Marsden St KTTN NW5 | | 4 | B1 |
| Marsden Wy ORP BR6 | | 227 | K2 |
| Marshall Cl BAL SW12 | | 35 | J5 |
| HSLWW TW4 | | 153 | N9 |
| RYLN/HDSTN HA2 | | 114 | A6 |
| SAND/SEL CR2 | | 223 | N7 |
| WAND/EARL SW18 | | 160 | A8 |
| Marshall Dr YEAD UB4 | | 132 | G2 |
| Marshall Rd LEW SE13 | | 161 | J8 |
| TOTM N17 | | 99 | K8 |
| Marshalls Cl HOR/WEW KT19 | | 238 | A2 |
| STHGT/OAK N14 | | 78 | F9 |
| Marshall's Dr STAL AL1 | | 38 | F3 |
| Marshalls Gv WOOL/PLUM SE18 | | 146 | C9 |
| Marshall's Pl BERM/RHTH SE16 | | 19 | N3 |
| Marshalls Rd ROMW/RG RM7 | | 124 | D2 |
| SUT SM1 | | 221 | N1 |
| Marshall's Rd SUT SM1 | | 221 | M3 |
| Marshall St SOHO/CST W1F | | 11 | H6 |
| Marshalsea Rd STHWK SE1 | | 12 | E9 |
| Marshalswick La STAL AL1 | | 38 | G1 |
| Marsham Cl CHST BR7 | | 184 | E8 |
| Marsham La DEN/HRF UB9 | | 110 | F2 |
| NWDGN UB2 | | 153 | K2 |
| RCHPK/HAM TW10 | | 177 | K2 |
| ROMW/RG RM7 | | 124 | B2 |
| SAND/SEL CR2 | | 223 | K4 |
| SRTFD E15 | | 121 | M1 |
| STAL AL1 | | 38 | D6 |
| SUT SM1 | | 201 | K10 |
| Marsbrook Cl BKHTH/KID SE3 | | 162 | A9 |
| Marsh Av HOR/WEW KT19 | | 220 | B6 |
| MTCM CR4 | | 202 | A2 |
| Marsh Cl CHES/WCR EN8 | | 62 | C4 |
| MLHL NW7 | | 96 | C4 |
| Marsh Ct WIM/MER SW19 | | 179 | P9 |
| WOKN/KNAP GU21 | | 232 | C2 |
| Marsh Dr CDALE/KGS NW9 | | 116 | D6 |
| Marshe Cl POTB/CUF EN6 | | 59 | N8 |
| Marsh Farm Rd WHTN TW2 | | 176 | B6 |
| Marshfield DTCH/LGLY SL3 | | 149 | P7 |
| Marshfield St POP/IOD E14 | | 161 | H2 |
| Marshgate Dr HERT/BAY SG13 | | 25 | M4 |
| Marsh Green Rd DAGE RM10 | | 144 | B8 |
| Marsh HI HOM E9 | | 120 | D9 |
| WAB EN9 | | 63 | K3 |
| Marsh La ADL/WDHM KT15 | | 213 | M2 |
| LEY E10 | | 120 | B7 |
| MLHL NW7 | | 96 | E4 |
| STAN HA7 | | 95 | K3 |
| TOTM N17 | | 100 | C4 |
| WARE SG12 | | 26 | D3 |
| Marshmoor Crs BRKMPK AL9 | | 40 | F8 |
| Marshmoor La BRKMPK AL9 | | 40 | F8 |
| Marsh Rd ALP/SUD HA0 | | 135 | J5 |
| PIN HA5 | | 113 | M2 |
| Marshside Cl ED N9 | | 100 | B2 |
| Marsh St DART DA1 | | 165 | P10 |
| POP/IOD E14 | | 160 | G3 |
| Marsh Ter STMC/STPC BR5 | | 207 | N4 |
| Marsh Wall POP/IOD E14 | | 13 | P8 |
| Marsh Wy RAIN RM13 | | 144 | E8 |
| Marston HOR/WEW KT19 | | 219 | P7 |
| Marston Av CHSGTN KT9 | | 219 | K3 |
| DAGE RM10 | | 124 | B8 |
| Marston Cl CSHM HP5 | | 50 | F1 |
| DAGE RM10 | | 124 | B8 |
| HHS/BOV HP3 | | 36 | A8 |
| KIL/WHAMP NW6 | | 3 | K3 |
| Marston Ct WOT/HER KT12 | | 197 | N7 |
| Marston Rd CLAY IG5 | | 102 | B10 |
| HOD EN11 | | 44 | G2 |
| TEDD TW11 | | 176 | C8 |
| WOKN/KNAP GU21 | | 231 | N3 |
| Marston Wy NRWD SE19 | | 181 | P10 |
| Marsworth Av PIN HA5 | | 93 | L9 |
| Marsworth Cl WATW WD18 | | 72 | F10 |
| YEAD UB4 | | 133 | L5 |
| Martaban Rd STNW/STAM N16 | | 119 | M7 |
| Martello St HACK E8 | | 140 | A2 |
| Martello Ter HACK E8 | | 140 | A2 |
| Martel Pl HACK E8 | | 7 | M1 |
| Marten Ga STALE/WH AL4 | | 38 | C2 |
| Marten Rd WALTH E17 | | 102 | E10 |
| Martens Av BXLYHN DA7 | | 164 | D10 |
| Martens Cl BXLYHN DA7 | | 164 | E10 |
| Martham Cl BARK/HLT IG6 | | 102 | E9 |
| THMD SE28 | | 143 | K10 |
| Martha's Blds FSBYE EC1V | | 12 | G1 |
| Martha St WCHPL E1 | | 140 | B8 |
| Marthorne Crs KTN/HRWW/WS HA3 | | 94 | C10 |
| Martian Av HHNE HP2 | | 36 | A3 |
| Martin Av BXLYHN DA7 | | 164 | F1 |
| Martin Cl CRAWW RH11 | | 283 | N5 |
| ED N9 | | 100 | G3 |
| HGDN/ICK UB10 | | 131 | P4 |
| SAND/SEL CR2 | | 224 | C7 |
| WARL CR6 | | 242 | A2 |
| WDSR SL4 | | 148 | B7 |
| Martin Crs CROY/NA CR0 | | 202 | G8 |
| Martindale IVER SL0 | | 130 | F6 |
| MORT/ESHN SW14 | | 156 | G8 |
| Martindale Av CAN/RD E16 | | 141 | M9 |
| ORP BR6 | | 227 | K2 |
| Martindale Cl RGUE GU4 | | 250 | E1 |
| Martindale Rd BAL SW12 | | 180 | C1 |
| HHW HP1 | | 35 | J5 |
| HSLWW TW4 | | 153 | N9 |
| WOKN/KNAP GU21 | | 231 | L4 |
| Martin Dene BXLYHS DA6 | | 186 | A1 |
| Martin Dr NTHLT UB5 | | 113 | N10 |
| RAIN RM13 | | 145 | J6 |
| RDART DA2 | | 188 | B2 |
| Martineau Cl ESH/CLAY KT10 | | 218 | C1 |
| Martineau Dr DORK RH4 | | 272 | G4 |
| TWK TW1 | | 154 | C10 |
| Martineau Rd HBRY N5 | | 119 | J9 |
| Martinfield WGCE AL7 | | 23 | J1 |
| Martingale Cl SUN TW16 | | 197 | H4 |
| Martingales Cl RCHPK/HAM TW10 | | 177 | J6 |
| Martin Gdns BCTR RM8 | | 123 | M9 |
| Martin Gv MRDN SM4 | | 201 | M3 |
| Martin La CANST EC4R | | 13 | H7 |
| Martini Dr PEND EN3 | | 80 | G1 |
| Martin Ri BXLYHS DA6 | | 186 | A1 |
| Martin Rd BCTR RM8 | | 123 | M9 |
| GUW GU2 | | 249 | K2 |
| SL SL1 | | 149 | K2 |
| SOCK/AV RM15 | | 146 | C10 |
| Martins Cl GU GU1 | | 250 | F9 |
| RAD WD7 | | 74 | D2 |
| STMC/STPC BR5 | | 207 | M3 |
| WWKM BR4 | | 204 | A8 |
| Martins Dr CHES/WCR EN8 | | 62 | D4 |
| HERT/BAY SG13 | | 25 | M5 |
| Martins Mt BAR EN5 | | 76 | C4 |
| Martins Pk SLN SL2 | | 129 | L1 |
| Martin's Pin SLN SL2 | | 129 | L1 |
| The Martins SYD SE26 | | 182 | A8 |
| WBLY HA9 | | 116 | B9 |
| Martinstown Cl EMPK RM11 | | 125 | P4 |
| Martins Wk MUSWH N10 | | 98 | B9 |
| THMD SE28 | | 147 | J5 |
| Martinsyde WOKS/MYFD GU22 | | 232 | G5 |
| Martin Wy MRDN SM4 | | 201 | K2 |
| WOKN/KNAP GU21 | | 231 | L4 |
| Martlesham WGCE AL7 | | 23 | K1 |
| Martlesham Cl HCH RM12 | | 125 | N8 |
| Martlet Gv NTHLT UB5 | | 133 | H6 |
| Martlets CRAWE RH10 | | 285 | P9 |
| The Martlets CRAWE RH10 | | 285 | P9 |
| Martlett Ct HOL/ALD WC2B | | 11 | L6 |
| Martley Dr GNTH/NBYPK IG2 | | 122 | B5 |
| Martock Cl KTN/HRWW/WS HA3 | | 114 | G1 |
| Martock Gdns FBAR/BDGN N11 | | 98 | A9 |
| Marton Cl CAT SE6 | | 182 | E6 |
| Marton Rd STNW/STAM N16 | | 119 | M7 |
| Martys Yd HAMP NW3 | | 117 | J10 |
| Martyr Cl STAL AL1 | | 38 | C10 |
| Martyr Rd GU GU1 | | 268 | A3 |
| Martyrs Av CRAWW RH11 | | 283 | M4 |
| Martyrs La WOKN/KNAP GU21 | | 214 | G10 |
| Marunden Gn SLN SL2 | | 128 | E3 |
| Marvell Av YEAD UB4 | | 132 | G5 |
| Marvels Cl LEE/GVPK SE12 | | 183 | L1 |
| Marvels La LEE/GVPK SE12 | | 183 | L2 |
| Marville Rd FUL/PGN SW6 | | 157 | J6 |
| Marvin St HACK E8 | | 7 | P1 |
| Marwell BH/WHM TN16 | | 262 | E5 |
| Marwell Cl ROM RM1 | | 124 | G4 |
| WWKM BR4 | | 205 | H8 |
| Marwood Cl KGLGY WD4 | | 59 | H1 |
| WELL DA16 | | 163 | N2 |
| Mary Adelaide Cl PUT/ROE SW15 | | 178 | B6 |
| Mary Ann Blds DEPT SE8 | | 160 | F5 |
| Maryat Sq FUL/PGN SW6 | | 157 | H7 |
| Maryatt Av RYLN/HDSTN HA2 | | 114 | A7 |
| Marybank WOOL/PLUM SE18 | | 162 | G3 |
| Mary Cl KTN/HRWW/WS HA3 | | 115 | L2 |
| Mary Datchelor Cl CMBW SE5 | | 159 | L7 |
| Mary Gn STJWD NW8 | | 3 | J5 |
| Maryhill Cl PUR/KEN CR8 | | 241 | K10 |
| Maryland Av MV/WKIL W9 | | 40 | C4 |
| Maryland Pk SRTFD E15 | | 121 | K10 |
| SRTFD E15 | | 121 | J10 |
| THHTH CR7 | | 203 | J1 |
| WDGN N22 | | 99 | H9 |
| Maryland Sq SRTFD E15 | | 121 | K10 |
| Marylands Rd MV/WKIL W9 | | 8 | D1 |
| Maryland St SRTFD E15 | | 121 | J10 |
| Maryland Wk IS N1 | | 6 | E1 |
| Maryland Wy SUN TW16 | | 197 | H2 |
| Mary Lawrenson Pl BKHTH/KID SE3 | | 161 | M6 |
| Marylebone F/O BAY/PAD W2 | | 9 | N4 |
| Marylebone High St CAVSQ/HST W1G | | 10 | D4 |
| Marylebone Ms MHST W1U | | 10 | D4 |
| Marylebone Pas GTPST W1W | | 11 | H5 |
| Marylebone Rd MBLAR W1H | | 9 | P3 |
| Marylee Wy LBTH SE11 | | 17 | P6 |
| Maryon Gv CHARL SE7 | | 162 | B3 |
| Maryon Ms HAMP NW3 | | 117 | M8 |
| Maryon Rd CHARL SE7 | | 162 | B3 |
| Mary Peters Dr GFD/PVL UB6 | | 114 | C10 |
| Mary Pl NTGHL W11 | | 8 | A8 |
| Mary Rd GU GU1 | | 267 | P7 |
| Mary Rose Cl CDW/CHF RM16 | | 167 | H3 |
| DART DA1 | | 166 | B10 |
| HPTN TW12 | | 175 | P9 |
| Maryrose Wy TRDG/WHET N20 | | 97 | N2 |
| Mary Seacole Cl HACK E8 | | 7 | L5 |
| Mary Secole Cl HACK E8 | | 7 | L5 |
| Maryside DTCH/LGLY SL3 | | 150 | B1 |
| Mary's Ter TWK TW1 | | 176 | F5 |
| Mary St CAMTN NW1 | | 4 | F6 |
| Mary Ter CAMTN NW1 | | 4 | E4 |
| Mary Wy OXHEY WD19 | | 93 | K5 |
| Masbro' Rd WKENS W14 | | 156 | G2 |
| Mascalls Gdns BRW CM14 | | 106 | C5 |
| Mascalls La BRW CM14 | | 106 | C5 |
| Mascalls Rd CHARL SE7 | | 162 | B6 |
| Mascotts Cl CRICK NW2 | | 116 | E8 |
| Masefield Av BORE WD6 | | 75 | M5 |
| STAN HA7 | | 94 | E6 |
| STHL UB1 | | 133 | P9 |
| Masefield Crs ERITH DA8 | | 105 | K9 |
| HARH RM3 | | 105 | K9 |
| Masefield Gdns EHAM E6 | | 142 | D6 |
| Masefield La YEAD UB4 | | 133 | J4 |
| Masefield Rd CDW/CHF RM16 | | 168 | B1 |
| CRAWW RH11 | | 283 | H10 |
| DART DA1 | | 188 | A1 |
| GVW DA11 | | 190 | A6 |
| HPTN TW12 | | 175 | P7 |
| Masefield Vw ORP BR6 | | 226 | F10 |
| Masefield Wy STWL/WRAY TW19 | | 174 | A4 |
| Mashie Rd ACT W3 | | 136 | B8 |
| Mashiters HI ROM RM1 | | 104 | E9 |
| Mashiters Wk ROM RM1 | | 124 | F1 |
| Maskall Cl BRXS/STRHM SW2 | | 181 | H1 |
| Maskani Wk STRHM/NOR SW16 | | 179 | M6 |
| Maskelyne Cl BTSEA SW11 | | 158 | D5 |
| Mason Cl BERM/RHTH SE16 | | 19 | P7 |
| BORE WD6 | | 76 | A6 |
| BXLYHN DA7 | | 164 | C9 |
| CAN/RD E16 | | 142 | A6 |
| HPTN TW12 | | 197 | N1 |
| RYNPK SW20 | | 200 | G1 |
| WAB EN9 | | 63 | L10 |
| Mason Dr HARH RM3 | | 115 | M10 |
| Masonic Hall Rd CHERT KT16 | | 195 | H6 |
| Mason Rd CRAWE RH10 | | 285 | P9 |
| SUT SM1 | | 221 | L2 |
| WFD IG8 | | 101 | K5 |
| Mason's Arms Ms CONDST W1S | | 10 | F6 |
| Masons Av CITYW EC2V | | 12 | G5 |
| CROY/NA CR0 | | 203 | K10 |
| KTN/HRWW/WS HA3 | | 114 | D1 |
| Masons Bridge Rd REDH RH1 | | 276 | C5 |
| Masons Ct EW KT17 | | 220 | D8 |
| Masons HI BMLY BR1 | | 205 | M3 |
| HAYES BR2 | | 205 | M3 |
| WOOL/PLUM SE18 | | 146 | G8 |
| Masons Paddock DORK RH4 | | 254 | F10 |
| Masons Pde CHESW EC4 | | 61 | K4 |
| MTCM CR4 | | 202 | A1 |
| Masons Rd EN EN1 | | 80 | A2 |
| HHNE HP2 | | 36 | C5 |
| SL SL1 | | 149 | L3 |
| Mason St WALW SE17 | | 19 | H6 |
| Masons Yd FSBYE EC1V | | 6 | C9 |
| STJS SW1Y | | 11 | H9 |
| Mason Wy WAB EN9 | | 63 | L10 |
| Massetts Rd HORL RH6 | | 280 | A5 |
| Massey Cl FBAR/BDGN N11 | | 98 | B6 |
| Massie Rd HACK E8 | | 7 | N2 |
| Massingberd Wy TOOT SW17 | | 180 | G7 |
| Massinger St WALW SE17 | | 19 | J6 |
| Massingham St WCHPL E1 | | 140 | D6 |
| Masson Av RSLP HA4 | | 133 | K1 |
| Master Cl OXTED RH8 | | 261 | K5 |
| Masterman Rd EHAM E6 | | 142 | B5 |
| Masters Cl STRHM/NOR SW16 | | 179 | M8 |
| Masters Dr BERM/RHTH SE16 | | 160 | A5 |
| Master's St WCHPL E1 | | 140 | C7 |
| Mast House Ter POP/IOD E14 | | 160 | F3 |
| Mastmaker Rd POP/IOD E14 | | 160 | F1 |
| Mast Quay WOOL/PLUM SE18 | | 146 | G8 |
| Maswell Park Crs HSLW TW3 | | 154 | B10 |
| Maswell Park Rd HSLW TW3 | | 176 | A1 |
| Matara Ms WALW SE17 | | 18 | E8 |
| Matcham Rd WAN E11 | | 121 | K8 |
| Matching Fld BRWN CM15 | | 86 | D5 |
| Matching Rd HLWE CM17 | | 29 | N6 |
| RBSF CM22 | | 31 | H4 |
| Matchless Dr WOOL/PLUM SE18 | | 162 | G6 |
| Matfield Cl HAYES BR2 | | 205 | M5 |
| Matfield Rd BELV DA17 | | 147 | K5 |
| Matham Gv EDUL SE22 | | 159 | N10 |
| Matham Rd E/WMO/HCT KT8 | | 198 | C5 |
| Mathecombe Rd SL SL1 | | 148 | E1 |
| Matheson Rd WKENS W14 | | 14 | A2 |
| Mathews Av EHAM E6 | | 142 | D10 |
| Mathews Park Av SRTFD E15 | | 121 | K10 |
| Mathews Yd LSQ/SEVD WC2H | | 11 | L6 |
| Mathias Cl EPSOM KT18 | | 219 | P8 |
| Mathisen Wy DTCH/LGLY SL3 | | 150 | A2 |
| Mathon Ct GU GU1 | | 250 | C10 |
| Matilda Cl NRWD SE19 | | 181 | L10 |
| Matilda Gdns BOW E3 | | 140 | F4 |
| Matilda St IS N1 | | 5 | M6 |
| Matlock Cl BAR EN5 | | 76 | A6 |
| HNHL SE24 | | 159 | H7 |
| Matlock Crs CHEAM SM3 | | 221 | H1 |
| OXHEY WD19 | | 93 | H5 |
| Matlock Gdns CHEAM SM3 | | 221 | H1 |
| HCH RM12 | | 125 | P5 |
| Matlock Pl CHEAM SM3 | | 221 | H1 |

Matlock Rd CTHM CR3 ... 241 M8
LEY E10 ... 121 H4
Matlock St POP/IOD E14 ... 140 D8
Matlock Wy NWMAL KT3 ... 200 A1
Matthew Arnold CI COB KT11 ... 217 H10
STA TW18 ... 173 H4
Matthew CI NKENS W10 * ... 136 C6
Matthew Ct MTCM CR4 ... 202 E6
Matthews Ct ASC SL5 ... 192 C4
Matthew's Gdns CROY/NA CR0 ... 225 J7
Matthews La STA TW18 ... 173 J4
Matthews Rd GFD/PVL UB6 ... 114 C10
Matthew's St BTSEA SW11 * ... 158 A4
Matthey PI CRAWE RH10 ... 284 E4
Matthey Rd REIG RH2 ... 275 K4
Matthias Rd STNW/STAM N16 ... 119 L10
Mattingly Wy PECK SE15 ... 139 N6
Mattison Rd FSBYPK N4 ... 119 H4
Mattock La WEA W13 ... 134 C10
Maud Cashmore Wy WOOL/PLUM SE18 ... 162 C2
Maude CI BEAC HP9 ... 88 F10
Maude Crs WATN WD24 ... 73 J3
Maude Rd BEAC HP9 ... 88 F10
CMBW SE5 ... 159 M8
SWLY BR8 ... 187 H9
WALTH E17 ... 120 D3
Maudesville Cots HNWL W7 ... 134 D10
Maude Ter WALTH E17 ... 120 D2
Maud Gdns BARK IG11 ... 143 J4
PLSTW E13 ... 141 L4
Maud Rd LEY E10 ... 121 L1
PLSTW E13 ... 141 L4
Maudslay Rd ELTH/MOT SE9 ... 162 C19
Maud St CAN/RD E16 ... 141 L1
Maud Wilkes CI KTTN NW5 ... 118 D10
Mauleverer Rd BRXS/STRHM SW2 ... 180 F1
Maundeby Wk THHTH CR7 ... 116 B10
Maunder CI CDW/CHF RM16 ... 167 J3
Maunder Rd HNWL W7 ... 134 D4
Maunds Hatch HLWS CM18 ... 46 C5
Maunsel Pk CRAWE RH10 ... 284 C7
Maunsel St WEST SW1P ... 17 J5
Maurice Av CTHM CR3 ... 241 L8
WDGN N22 ... 99 J10
Maurice Browne CI MLHL NW7 ... 96 C6
Maurice Ct SHB W12 ... 136 B6
Maurice Wk GLDGN NW11 ... 115 J1
Mauritius Rd GNWCH SE10 ... 161 K3
Maury Rd STNW/STAM N16 ... 119 L7
Mauveine Gdns HSLW TW3 ... 153 P10
Mavelstone Rd BMLY BR1 ... 206 A1
Maverton Rd BOW E3 * ... 140 F3
Mavis Av HOR/WEW KT19 ... 220 B2
Mavis CI HOR/WEW KT19 ... 220 B2
Mavis Gv HCH RM12 ... 125 M7
Mawbey Est STHWK SE1 ... 19 N8
Mawbey PI STHWK SE1 ... 19 M8
Mawbey Rd CHERT KT16 ... 214 C6
STHWK SE1 ... 19 N8
Mawbey St VX/NE SW8 ... 158 F6
Mawney CI ROMW/RG RM7 ... 124 C1
Mawney Rd ROMW/RG RM7 ... 124 C10
Mawson CI RYNPK SW20 ... 201 L2
Mawson La CHSWK W4 ... 156 D5
Maxey Gdns DAGW RM9 ... 123 P9
Maxey Rd DAGW RM9 ... 123 P9
WOOL/PLUM SE18 ... 162 F3
Maxfield CI TRDG/WHET N20 * ... 97 M1
Maxilla Wk NKENS W10 * ... 136 C6
Maximfeldt Rd ERITH DA8 ... 164 A6
Maxim Rd ERITH DA8 ... 164 A6
WCHMH N21 ... 79 H10
Maxted CI HEML HP2 * ... 36 D3
Maxted Cnr HNNE HP2 * ... 36 D3
Maxted Pk HRW HA1 ... 114 D5
Maxted Rd HNNE HP2 ... 36 C3
PECK SE15 ... 159 N9
Maxwell CI CROY/NA CR0 ... 202 F4
HYS/HAR UB3 ... 133 H9
RKW/CH/CXG WD3 ... 91 K3
Maxwell Dr BF/WBF KT14 ... 215 M7
Maxwell Gdns ORP BR6 ... 207 J10
Maxwell Ri OXHEY WD19 ... 93 M1
Maxwell Rd ASHF TW15 ... 174 D9
BEAC HP9 ... 88 C3
BORE WD6 ... 75 N7
FUL/PGN SW6 ... 157 L6
NTHWD HA6 ... 92 A9
STAL AL1 ... 38 G7
WDR/YW UB7 ... 151 P3
WELL DA16 ... 163 K10
Maxwell Wy CRAWE RH10 ... 284 B4
Maxwelton Av MLHL NW7 ... 96 A6
Maxwelton CI MLHL NW7 ... 96 A6
Maya CI PECK SE15 ... 159 K8
Mayall Rd HNHL SE24 ... 181 J1
Maya PI FBAR/BDGN N11 ... 98 E6
May Av EFNCH N2 ... 117 M2
STMC/STPC BR5 ... 202 C10
Maybank Av ALP/SUD HA0 ... 114 F10
HCH RM12 ... 125 J8
SWFD E18 ... 101 N10
Maybank Gdns PIN HA5 ... 113 H3
Maybank Rd SWFD E18 ... 101 N9
May Bate Av KUTN/CMB KT2 ... 191 J7
Mayberry PI BRYLDS KT5 ... 199 J3
Maybourne Ri WOKS/MYFD GU22 ... 232 A10
Maybrick Rd EMPK RM11 ... 125 K3
Maybury Av CHES/WCR EN8 ... 62 A4
RDART DA2 ... 188 A4
Maybury CI EN EN1 ... 80 A4
KWD/TDW/WH KT20 ... 239 H5
SL SL1 ... 128 C2
STMC/STPC BR5 ... 201 M6
Maybury Gdns WLSDN NW10 ... 136 D2
Maybury Hill WOKS/MYFD GU22 ... 232 F2
Maybury Ms HGT N6 ... 118 D5
Maybury Rd BARK IG11 ... 143 K4
PLSTW E13 ... 141 P6
WOKN/KNAP GU21 ... 232 D2
Maybury St TOOT SW17 ... 179 P8
Maybush Rd EMPK RM11 ... 125 M5
Maychurch CI STAN HA7 ... 95 M7
May CI CHSGTN KT9 ... 219 L6
STALW/RED AL3 ... 38 C4
Maycock Gv NTHWD HA6 ... 92 D7
Maycroft PIN HA5 ... 93 K9
Maycroft Av GRAYS RM17 ... 168 A4
Maycroft Gdns CHESW EN7 ... 61 M2
Maycroft Rd CHESW EN7 ... 61 M2
Maycross Av MRDN SM4 ... 193 J4
Mayday Gdns BKHTH/KID SE3 ... 162 E2
Mayday Rd THHTH CR7 ... 204 C6
Maydwell Ldg BORE WD6 ... 75 J6
Mayefield Rd THHTH CR7 ... 204 A9
Mayell CI LHD/OX KT22 ... 237 H9
Mayerne Rd ELTH/MOT SE9 ... 162 F4
Mayesbrook Rd BARK IG11 ... 143 J3
Mayes CI CRAWE RH10 ... 284 G10
SWLY BR8 ... 187 K8
WARL CR6 ... 242 C4
Mayesford Rd CHDH RM6 ... 123 M5
Mayeswood Rd LEE/GVPK SE12 ... 183 P7
Mayfair Av BXLYHN DA7 ... 163 N3
CHDH RM6 ... 123 N4
IL IG1 ... 122 C2
WHTN TW2 ... 155 J2
WPK KT4 ... 200 D8
Mayfair CI BECK BR3 ... 204 C4
STALE/WH AL4 ... 38 G1
SURB KT6 ... 199 L8
Mayfair Ct EDGW HA8 ... 95 K8
Mayfair Gdns TOTM N17 ... 99 K7


WFD IG8 ... 101 M8
Mayfair Ms CAMTN NW1 * ... 4 B4
Mayfair PI MYFR/PICC W1J ... 10 F9
Mayfare RKW/CH/CXG WD3 ... 72 A9
Mayfair Ter STHGT/OAK N14 ... 98 A9
Mayfield BXLYHN DA7 ... 164 A9
CRAWE RH10 ... 284 E7
LHD/OX KT22 ... 201 J8
SWCM DA10 ... 189 K2
WCCW AL8 ... 22 F1
Mayfield Av ADL/WDHM KT15 ... 215 G6
CHSWK W4 ... 156 B3
KTN/HRWW/WS HA3 ... 97 M5
NFNCH/WDSPK N12 ... 97 M5
ORP BR6 ... 207 J8
STHGT/OAK N14 ... 98 A9
WEA W13 ... 154 C2
WFD IG8 ... 101 M7
Mayfield CI ADL/WDHM KT15 ... 215 G6
ASHF TW15 ... 174 C9
CLAP SW4 ... 180 L1
HACK E8 ... 7 L2
HGDN/ICK UB10 ... 132 C5
HLWE CM17 ... 30 A7
PGE/AN SE20 ... 204 A1
REDH RH1 ... 276 B6
THDIT KT7 ... 198 C8
WOT/HER KT12 ... 217 H1
Mayfield Crs ED N9 ... 80 A10
THHTH CR7 ... 202 G4
Mayfield Dr PIN HA5 ... 113 N2
WDSR SL4 ... 148 E9
Mayfield Gdns ADL/WDHM KT15 ... 215 L6
BRW CM14 ... 106 C2
HDN NW4 ... 116 C4
HNWL W7 ... 134 C8
STA TW18 ... 173 J10
WOT/HER KT12 ... 217 H1
Mayfield Gn GT/LBKH KT23 ... 253 P5
Mayfield Rd ACT W3 ... 135 N9
BCTR RM8 ... 123 M6
BELMT SM2 ... 221 N3
BELV DA17 ... 164 H4
BMLY BR1 ... 206 B5
CEND/HSY/T N8 ... 118 C4
CHING E4 ... 101 H3
GVW DA11 ... 190 C14
HACK E8 ... 7 L4
PEND EN3 ... 80 C6
PLSTW E13 ... 141 L6
SAND/SEL CR2 ... 223 L5
SHB W12 ... 156 B1
WALTH E17 ... 100 D10
WEY KT13 ... 216 A2
WIM/MER SW19 ... 201 J1
WOT/HER KT12 ... 217 H1
Mayfields CDW/CHF RM16 ... 167 P1
WBLY HA9 ... 96 C10
Mayfields CI WBLY HA9 ... 115 M1
Mayflower Av HEML HP2 ... 35 N6
Mayflower CI BERM/RHTH SE16 ... 160 C5
ERUM/RHTH SE16 ... 160 B1
HERT/WAT SG14 ... 24 F7
RSLP HA4 ... 112 D4
SOCK/AV RM15 ... 147 N6
WAB EN9 ... 45 K9
Mayflower Rd BRXN/ST SW9 ... 158 F9
CDW/CHF RM16 ... 167 H4
LCOL/BKTW AL2 ... 56 A3
Mayflower St BERM/RHTH SE16 ... 160 B1
Mayflower Wy CHONG CM5 * ... 53 L1
SLN SL2 ... 109 H10
Mayfly CI PIN HA5 ... 113 K5
STMC/STPC BR5 ... 201 N4
Mayford CI BAL SW12 ... 180 A4
BECK BR3 ... 204 C3
WOKS/MYFD GU22 ... 232 B4
Mayford Gn WOKS/MYFD GU22 ... 231 P8
Mayford Rd BAL SW12 ... 180 A3
Mayfly Gdns NTHLT UB5 * ... 133 H2
Maygood St IS N1 ... 5 P7
Maygoods CI UX/CGN UB8 ... 131 M7
Maygoods Gn UX/CGN UB8 ... 131 N7
Maygoods La UX/CGN UB8 ... 131 N7
Maygoods Vw UX/CGN UB88 * ... 131 M7
Maygreen Crs EMPK RM11 ... 125 H5
Maygrove Rd KIL/WHAMP NW6 ... 2 D2
Mayhall Av AMS HP6 ... 68 G1
Mayhew CI CHING E4 ... 100 F4
Mayhill Rd BAR EN5 ... 77 H9
CHARL SE7 ... 161 N5
Mayhurst Av WOKS/MYFD GU22 ... 232 F2
Mayhurst Crs WOKS/MYFD GU22 ... 232 F2
Maylands Av HCH RM12 ... 125 M9
HNNE HP2 ... 36 A4
Maylands Dr SCUP DA14 ... 185 N6
UX/CGN UB8 ... 131 N1
Maylands Rd OXHEY WD19 ... 93 K5
Maylands Wy HARH RM3 ... 106 G3
Maylins Dr SBW CM21 * ... 21 J1
Maynard CI CRAWE RH10 ... 285 K11
ERITH DA8 ... 164 C6
FUL/PGN SW6 ... 157 L6
SEVS/STOTM N15 ... 119 M3
Maynard Dr STAL AL1 ... 38 C9
Maynard PI POTB/CUF EN6 ... 60 F3
Maynard Rd HNNE HP2 ... 36 A4
WALTH E17 ... 121 H3
Maynards EMPK RM11 ... 125 M5
Maynards Quay WAP E1W * ... 140 B9
Mayne Av STALW/RED AL3 ... 37 N8
Maynooth Gdns CAR SM5 ... 202 A7
Mayo CI CHES/WCR EN8 ... 62 B4
Mayo Gdns HHW HP1 ... 35 L7
Mayola Rd CLPT E5 * ... 120 D5
Mayow Rd SYD SE26 ... 182 D7
Mayplace Av DART DA1 ... 165 N10
Mayplace CI BXLYHN DA7 ... 164 C9
Mayplace La WOOL/PLUM SE18 ... 162 E5
Mayplace Rd East BXLYHN DA7 ... 164 B10
Mayplace Rd West BXLYHN DA7 ... 164 B10
Maypole Crs BARK/HLT IG6 ... 105 J5
ERITH DA8 ... 165 L5
Maypole Dr CHIG IG7 ... 105 J1
ORP BR6 ... 228 A3
Maypole Rd GVE DA12 ... 191 J4
ORP BR6 ... 228 A3
Mayroyd Av SURB KT6 ... 199 M9
May Rd CHING E4 ... 101 H5
WHTN TW2 ... 176 B4
Mays CI WEY KT13 ... 216 A6
Mays Ct CHCR WC2N * ... 11 J1
Maysfield Rd RPLY/SEND GU23 ... 232 G6
Mays Gn COB KT11 * ... 234 C6
Mays Gv RPLY/SEND GU23 ... 232 G6
May's Hill Rd HAYES BR2 ... 205 K6
May's La BAR EN5 ... 96 E1
Mays Rd TEDD TW11 ... 174 C6
May St WKENS W14 ... 157 N10
Mayswood Gdns DAGE RM10 ... 124 D4
Maythorne Cots LEW SE13 * ... 183 J2
Maythorne CI GNWCH SE10 ... 161 K4
Mayton St HOLWY N7 ... 118 D8
Maytree CI EDGW HA8 ... 95 P4


GU GU1 * ... 249 N7
RAIN RM13 ... 144 F4
Maytree Ct MTCM CR4 ... 202 B3
Maytree Crs WATN WD24 ... 72 G2
Maytrees La STAN HA7 ... 94 E7
Maytree RAD WD7 ... 74 F3
WOKN/KNAP GU21 ... 231 H3
Maytree Wk BRXS/STRHM SW2 * ... 181 H5
Mayville Est STNW/STAM N16 * ... 119 M10
Mayville Rd IL IG1 ... 122 E10
WAN E11 ... 121 K5
Maywater CI SAND/SEL CR2 ... 223 L7
Maywin Dr EMPK RM11 ... 125 N6
Maywood CI BECK BR3 ... 182 G1
Maze HI GNWCH SE10 ... 161 K5
Mazenod Av KIL/WHAMP NW6 ... 2 D1
Maze Rd RCH/KEW TW9 ... 155 M6
McAdam CI HOD EN11 ... 44 F1
McAdam Dr ENC/FH EN2 ... 79 J6
McAlmont Rdg GODL GU7 ... 267 J10
Mc Ardle Wy DTCH/LGLY SL3 ... 150 C6
McAuley CI ELTH/MOT SE9 ... 184 D1
STHWK SE1 ... 18 A3
McAuliffe Dr SL SL1 ... 108 A9
McCall CI CLAP SW4 ... 158 F8
McCall Crs CHARL SE7 ... 162 B4
McCarthy Rd FELT TW13 ... 175 L8
McCoid Wy STHWK SE1 ... 18 E2
McCrone Ms HAMP NW3 * ... 3 M1
McCudden Rd DART DA1 ... 165 N9
McCullum Rd BOW E3 * ... 140 E3
McDermott CI BTSEA SW11 ... 157 P8
McDermott Rd PECK SE15 ... 159 P9
McDonald CI HAT AL10 ... 40 D6
McDonough CI CHSGTN KT9 ... 219 K1
McDougall Ct RCH/KEW TW9 ... 155 M8
McDougall Rd BERK HP4 ... 34 A5
McDowall CI CAN/RD E16 ... 141 M7
McDowall Rd CMBW SE5 ... 159 K7
McEntee Av WALTH E17 ... 100 D9
McEwan Wy SRTFD E15 * ... 141 J3
McGredy CHESW EN7 ... 61 L10
McGregor Rd NTGHL W11 ... 8 C5
McIntosh CI ROM RM1 ... 124 F1
WLGTN SM6 ... 222 F4
McIntosh Rd ROM RM1 ... 124 F1
McKay Rd RYNPK SW20 ... 178 E10
Mc Kellar CI BUSH WD23 ... 94 B3
McKenzie Wy HOR/WEW UB7 ... 219 M6
McKerrell Rd PECK SE15 ... 159 P7
McKillop Wy SCUP DA14 ... 185 M10
McLeod Rd ABYW SE2 ... 162 M3
McLeod's Ms SKENS SW7 ... 15 H4
McMillan CI GVE DA12 ... 190 F7
McMillan St DEPT SE8 ... 160 F6
McNair Rd NWDGN UB2 ... 133 P2
McNeil Rd CMBW SE5 ... 159 L8
McNicol Dr WLSDN NW10 ... 135 P4
McRae La MTCM CR4 ... 202 A7
Mead Av DTCH/LGLY SL3 ... 150 C1
REDH RH1 ... 276 B8
Mead CI CAMTN NW1 * ... 3 P2
CDW/CHF RM16 ... 167 N1
DEN/HRF UB9 ... 111 K1
DTCH/LGLY SL3 ... 150 L1
ECH TW20 ... 172 C9
GPK RM2 ... 105 H10
KTN/HRWW/WS HA3 ... 94 D7
LOU IG10 ... 82 E6
REDH RH1 ... 258 B5
SWLY BR8 ... 209 H5
Mead Ct CDALE/KGS NW9 ... 115 P3
ECH TW20 ... 172 F9
WAB EN9 ... 62 G10
WOKN/KNAP GU21 ... 231 K2
Mead Crs CHING E4 ... 101 H5
GT/LBKH KT23 ... 253 P1
SUT SM1 ... 221 P1
Meadcroft Rd LBTH SE11 ... 18 C14
Meade CI CHSWK W4 ... 155 W4
Mead End ASHTD KT21 ... 237 L2
Meades La CSHM HP5 ... 50 C8
The Meades WEY KT13 * ... 216 E3
Meadfield EDGW HA8 ... 95 N3
Mead Fld RYLN/HDSTN HA2 * ... 113 N8
Meadfield Av DTCH/LGLY SL3 ... 150 D2
Meadfield Rd DTCH/LGLY SL3 ... 150 D2
Meadfoot Rd STRHM/NOR SW16 ... 202 D1
Meadgate Av WFD IG8 ... 102 B6
Meadgate Rd WAB EN9 ... 45 J6
Mead Gv CHDH RM6 ... 123 N1
Mead House La YEAD UB4 ... 132 D2
Meadhurst Av CHERT KT16 ... 174 F9
Meadhurst Rd CHERT KT16 ... 195 L8
Meadlands Dr RCHPK/HAM TW10 ... 177 J5
Mead La CHERT KT16 ... 195 M8
HERT/BAY SG13 ... 25 M4
Meadow Ap CRAWE RH10 ... 285 H2
Meadow Av CROY/NA CR0 ... 204 C6
Meadowbank BKHTH/KID SE3 ... 161 P3
BRYLDS KT5 ... 199 L6
HAMP NW3 ... 4 A1
KGLGY WD4 ... 54 B6
OXHEY WD19 ... 93 K1
WCHMH N21 ... 78 G10
WOT/HER KT12 ... 217 H1
Meadow Bank BXLY DA5 ... 252 C5
HAMP NW3 ... 4 A1
KGLGY WD4 ... 54 B6
OXHEY WD19 ... 93 K1
WCHMH N21 ... 78 G10
Meadowbank CI FUL/PGN SW6 ... 156 F6
Meadowbank Gdns HSLWW TW4 ... 153 W4
Meadowbank Rd CDALE/KGS NW9 ... 116 A5
LTWR GU18 ... 212 B6
Meadowbanks BAR EN5 ... 76 D6
Meadowbrook OXTED RH8 ... 261 H6
Meadowbrook CI DTCH/LGLY SL3 ... 151 N8
Meadowbrook Rd DORK RH4 ... 272 G6
Meadow Bungalows RGUE GU4 ... 268 G6
Meadow CI BARK IG11 ... 143 J2
BRKMPK AL9 ... 40 G10
BXLYHS DA6 ... 186 A1
CAT SE6 ... 182 F5
CHING E4 ... 100 C2
CHST BR7 ... 184 E8
CSHM HP5 * ... 50 C8
ESH/CLAY KT10 ... 198 G10
GODL GU7 ... 267 K10
HERT/BAY SG13 ... 25 M4
HOM E9 ... 120 E10
HSLWW TW4 ... 175 P2
LCOL/BKTW AL2 ... 55 P5
PEND EN3 ... 80 D5
PUR/KEN CR8 ... 241 K1
RAD WD7 ... 57 H6
RCHPK/HAM TW10 ... 177 H4
RSLP HA4 ... 112 G1
RYNPK SW20 ... 200 F4
SEV TN13 ... 247 H9
SLH/COR SS17 ... 169 K2
STALE/WH AL4 ... 39 H5
WDSR SL4 ... 171 K2
WOT/HER KT12 ... 217 H1
Meadow Cots BECK BR3 ... 204 E3
Meadowcote La RBRW/HUT CM13 ... 68 C3
Meadow Ct EPSOM KT18 ... 234 D8
STA TW18 ... 173 H5
Meadowcourt Rd BKHTH/KID SE3 ... 161 L5
Meadow Cft BKHTH/KID SE3 * ... 161 J3


Meadow Cft HAT AL10 ... 40 C4
Meadowcroft STAL AL1 ... 38 F10
Meadowcroft CI CRAWW RH11 ... 283 J8
Meadow Croft CI HORL RH6 ... 280 D7
Meadowcroft CI HORL RH6 * ... 99 J3
Meadowcroft Farm RDART DA2 ... 187 G10
Meadowcroft Rd PLMGR N13 ... 99 G10
BEAC HP9 ... 88 D9
BECK BR3 ... 205 H2
BROX EN10 * ... 44 D8
CHES/WCR EN8 ... 62 B5
DORK RH4 * ... 273 P5
FELT TW13 * ... 174 E1
HART DA3 ... 211 K9
HGDN/ICK UB10 ... 112 B7
OXHEY WD19 ... 93 M4
WEA W13 ... 134 C2
WLGTN SM6 ... 222 E3
WWKM BR4 ... 205 J8
Meadowcross WAB EN9 ... 63 K10
Meadow Dell HAT AL10 ... 40 C4
Meadow Dr AMS HP6 ... 69 K3
HDN NW4 ... 116 B1
MUSWH N10 ... 118 B1
RPLY/SEND GU23 ... 233 J9
Meadowford CI THMD SE28 ... 143 K9
Meadow Gdns EDGW HA8 ... 95 N7
STA TW18 ... 172 G8
Meadow Garth WLSDN NW10 ... 135 P1
Meadow HI COUL/CHIP CR5 ... 222 D9
NWMAL KT3 ... 200 B6
PUR/KEN CR8 ... 222 D9
Meadowlands BAR EN5 ... 76 D6
BGR/WK TN15 ... 247 N6
COB KT11 ... 217 H9
CRAWW RH11 ... 283 M7
OXTED RH8 ... 261 M10
RGUE GU4 ... 251 L6
Meadow La BEAC HP9 ... 88 E9
LEE/GVPK SE12 ... 183 P6
LHD/OX KT22 ... 236 B8
WDSR SL4 ... 148 G5
Meadowlea CI WDR/YW UB7 ... 151 N5
Meadow PI CHSWK W4 * ... 156 B6
VX/NE SW8 ... 158 F6
Meadow Ri COUL/CHIP CR5 ... 222 E9
WOKN/KNAP GU21 ... 231 H3
Meadow Rd ASHF TW15 ... 174 E8
ASHTD KT21 ... 237 K3
BARK IG11 ... 143 J2
BERK HP4 ... 33 N6
BORE WD6 ... 75 N6
BUSH WD23 ... 73 N4
CDW/CHF RM16 ... 147 P10
DTCH/LGLY SL3 ... 150 B2
EPP CM16 ... 65 J5
ESH/CLAY KT10 ... 218 D2
FELT TW13 ... 175 M5
GSTN WD25 ... 55 H10
GVW DA11 ... 189 P4
HAYES BR2 ... 205 K1
HRS/BOV HP3 ... 36 D4
LOU IG10 ... 82 B9
PIN HA5 ... 113 L2
RGUE GU4 ... 250 D6
ROMW/RG RM7 ... 124 D6
STHL UB1 ... 133 N9
SUT SM1 ... 221 P1
VW GU25 ... 193 K5
VX/NE SW8 ... 17 N10
WIM/MER SW19 ... 179 M10
Meadow Road of BERK HP4 ... 33 M5
Meadow Row STHWK SE1 ... 18 E4
Meadows CI LEY E10 ... 130 F7
RBRW/HUT CM13 ... 107 P7
Meadows End SUN TW16 ... 197 H1
Meadowside BEAC HP9 ... 89 L8
BKHTH/KID SE3 ... 161 P10
GSTN WD25 ... 55 J7
GT/LBKH KT23 ... 235 P9
HORL RH6 ... 280 C5
TWK TW1 ... 157 K1
Meadowside Rd BELMT SM2 ... 221 H5
UPMR RM14 ... 126 B10
Meadows Leigh CI WEY KT13 ... 216 D10
Meath Crs BETH E2 ... 140 C5
Meath Green Av HORL RH6 ... 280 A2
Meath Green La HORL RH6 ... 279 P2
Meath Rd IL IG1 ... 122 E10
SRTFD E15 ... 141 L4
Meath St BTSEA SW11 ... 158 C7
Meautys STALW/RED AL3 ... 37 N8
Mecklenburgh PI BMSBY WC1N ... 11 N1
Mecklenburgh Sq BMSBY WC1N ... 11 N1
Mecklenburgh St BMSBY WC1N ... 11 N1
Medburn St CAMTN NW1 ... 5 J7
Medbury Rd GVE DA12 ... 191 J4
Medcalf PI PEND EN3 * ... 80 E3
Medcroft Gdns MORT/ESHN SW14 ... 155 N7
Medebourne CI BKHTH/KID SE3 ... 161 M9
Medebridge Rd CDW/CHF RM16 ... 147 L8
Mede CI STWL/WRAY TW19 ... 172 B7
Medesenge Wy PLMGR N13 ... 99 G10
Medfield St PUT/ROE SW15 ... 178 D3
Medhurst CI BOW E3 ... 140 D4
CHOB/PIR GU24 ... 213 L5
Medhurst Dr BMLY BR1 ... 183 K9
Median Rd CLPT E5 ... 120 B10
Medici CI GDMY/SEVK IG3 ... 123 K4
Medick Ct GRAYS RM17 ... 168 B5
Medina Av ESH/CLAY KT10 ... 198 D10
Medina Rd GRAYS RM17 ... 168 A4
HOLWY N7 ... 118 H8
Medlake Rd EGH TW20 ... 173 H10
Medland CI WLGTN SM6 ... 202 B8
Medlar CI CRAWW RH11 ... 283 M4
GU GU1 * ... 249 P6
NTHLT UB5 ... 133 J1
Medlar Dr SOCK/AV RM15 ... 147 K6
Medlar Rd GRAYS RM17 ... 168 A4
Medlar St CMBW SE5 ... 159 K7
Medley Rd KIL/WHAMP NW6 ... 2 E3
Medman CI UX/CGN UB8 ... 131 M4
Medora Rd BRXS/STRHM SW2 ... 180 A2
ROMW/RG RM7 ... 124 D2
Medow Md RAD WD7 ... 56 E9
Medusa Rd CAT SE6 ... 182 G2
Medway CRAWE RH10 ... 285 K11
DART DA1 ... 165 H9
HHNE HP2 * ... 36 A3
Medway CI CROY/NA CR0 ... 204 B6
IL IG1 ... 122 C6
WAT WD17 ... 21 G3
Medway Dr GFD/PVL UB6 ... 134 D2
Medway Gdns ALP/SUD HA0 ... 114 A7
Medway Ms BOW E3 * ... 140 D3
Medway Pde GFD/PVL UB6 ... 134 D2
Medway Rd BOW E3 ... 140 D3
DART DA1 ... 165 H9
Medway St WEST SW1P ... 17 J4
Medwin St CLAP SW4 ... 158 G10
Medwmin Rd CLAP SW4 * ... 158 G10


MRDN SM4 * ... 201 M1
UPMR RM14 ... 126 D7
UX/CGN UB8 ... 131 P3
WEY KT13 ... 216 D3
Meadway RBRW/HUT CM13 ... 107 P5
The Mead ABR/ST RM4 ... 83 L7
ASHTD KT21 ... 237 K5
BEAC HP9 ... 88 D9
BECK BR3 ... 205 H1
BERK HP4 ... 34 B4
BRYLDS KT5 ... 199 P8
EHSLY KT24 ... 253 M4
ESH/CLAY KT10 ... 218 A5
GDMY/SEVK IG3 ... 123 H9
GLDGN NW11 ... 117 L4
GPK RM2 ... 105 H10
GRAYS RM17 ... 168 A3
HARP AL5 ... 20 D4
HAYES BR2 ... 205 L6
HOR/WEW KT19 ... 219 P8
LHD/OX KT22 ... 218 C10
PEND EN3 ... 80 C2
RSEV TN14 ... 228 A3
RYNPK SW20 ... 200 F4
STA TW18 ... 173 K10
STALE/WH AL4 ... 40 A9
SWGT/OAK N14 ... 98 E3
WARL CR6 ... 242 B2
WFD IG8 ... 101 P6
WGCE AL7 ... 23 J7
WHTN TW2 ... 176 C4
Meadway CI BAR EN5 * ... 77 K7
GLDGN NW11 ... 117 L4
PIN HA5 ... 94 A7
STA TW18 ... 173 J10
Meadway Ct EA W5 * ... 135 P2
Meadway Dr ADL/WDHM KT15 ... 215 M4
WOKN/KNAP GU21 ... 231 P2
Meadway Gdns RSLP HA4 ... 112 E4
Meadway Pk CFSP/GDCR SL9 ... 102 A2
The Meadway BKHH IG9 ... 102 A2
BKHTH/KID SE3 ... 161 J8
HORL RH6 ... 280 D4
ORP BR6 ... 227 L2
POTB/CUF EN6 ... 60 G4
SEV TN13 ... 246 C8
Meaford Wy PGE/AN SE20 ... 182 A10
Meanley Rd MNPK E12 ... 122 B10
Meard St SOHO/CST W1F ... 10 F7
Meare CI KWD/TDW/WH KT20 ... 238 F9
Mears CI STMC/STPC BR5 ... 207 L5
Meath CI STMC/STPC BR5 ... 202 C10
Meath Crs BETH E2 ... 140 C5
Meath Green Av HORL RH6 ... 280 A2
Meath Green La HORL RH6 ... 279 P2
Meath Rd IL IG1 ... 122 E10
SRTFD E15 ... 141 L4
Medlake Rd EGH TW20 ... 173 J8
HORL RH6 ... 280 D4
ORP BR6 ... 227 L2
POTB/CUF EN6 ... 60 G4
SEV TN13 ... 246 C8
Medburn CI CAMTN NW1 ... 5 J7
Medbury Rd GVE DA12 ... 191 J4
Medcalf Rd PEND EN3 ... 80 E3
Medcalf Gdns MORT/ESHN SW14 ... 155 N7
Medebourne CI BKHTH/KID SE3 ... 161 M9
Medeswell PLMGR N13 ... 99 G10
Medesenge Wy PLMGR N13 ... 99 G10
Medfield St PUT/ROE SW15 ... 178 D3
Medhurst CI BOW E3 ... 140 D4
CHOB/PIR GU24 ... 213 L5
Medhurst Dr BMLY BR1 ... 183 K9
Median Rd CLPT E5 ... 120 B10
Medici CI GDMY/SEVK IG3 ... 123 K4
Medina Av ESH/CLAY KT10 ... 198 D10
Medina Rd GRAYS RM17 ... 168 A4
HOLWY N7 ... 118 H8
Medora Rd BRXS/STRHM SW2 ... 180 A2
ROMW/RG RM7 ... 124 D2
Medway St WEST SW1P ... 17 J4
Medwin St CLAP SW4 ... 158 G10
Meeson Rd SRTFD E15 ... 141 L9
Meeson's La GRAYS RM17 ... 168 A4
Meeson St CLPT E5 ... 120 F8
Meeting Aly WAT WD17 * ... 21 G3
Meeting Field Pth HOM E9 * ... 120 F9
Meeting House Aly WAP E1W * ... 140 A9
Meeting House La PECK SE15 ... 159 P7
Megg La KGLGY WD4 ... 50 E4
Mehetabel Rd HOM E9 ... 120 D10
Meister CI IL IG1 ... 122 E9
Melancho CI CHST BR7 ... 204 D1
Melanda CI CHST BR7 ... 184 G1
Melanie CI BXLYHN DA7 ... 163 P9
Melba Wy LEW SE13 ... 161 N9
Melbourne Av PIN HA5 ... 114 E1
WDGN N22 ... 98 B7
WEA W13 ... 154 F2
Melbourne CI ORP BR6 ... 207 H1
STALW/RED AL3 ... 38 A7
WLGTN SM6 ... 222 D2


Melbourne Ct WCCW AL8 ... 22 E6
Melbourne Gdns CHDH RM6 ... 123 P3
Melbourne Gv EDUL SE22 ... 159 M10
Melbourne Ms BRXN/ST SW9 ... 159 H1
CAT SE6 ... 183 H1
Melbourne Rd BUSH WD23 ... 73 N4
EHAM E6 ... 142 C3
IL IG1 ... 122 E6
LEY E10 ... 120 G5
TEDD TW11 ... 177 H9
TIL RM18 ... 168 B7
WIM/MER SW19 ... 201 K1
WLGTN SM6 ... 222 C2
Melbourne Ter EDUL SE22 * ... 159 M10
FUL/PGN SW6 * ... 157 L6
Melbourne Wy EN EN1 ... 79 N10
Melbury Av NWDGN UB2 ... 154 A2
Melbury CI BF/WBF KT14 ... 215 K10
CHERT KT16 ... 195 K7
CHST BR7 ... 184 C5
ESH/CLAY KT10 ... 218 G3
Melbury Ct KENS W8 ... 14 B4
Melbury Dr CMBW SE5 ... 159 M6
Melbury Gdns RYNPK SW20 ... 200 E1
Melbury Rd KTN/HRWW/WS HA3 ... 115 L3
WKENS W14 ... 14 C3
Melbury Ter CAMTN NW1 ... 9 P2
Melcombe Gdns KTN/HRWW/WS HA3 ... 115 L4
Melcombe PI CAMTN NW1 ... 9 L3
Melcombe St CAMTN NW1 ... 9 L2
Meldex CI MLHL NW7 ... 96 F7
Meldon CI FUL/PGN SW6 * ... 157 M7
Meldone CI BRYLDS KT5 ... 199 N6
Meldrum CI OXTED RH8 ... 261 N6
STMC/STPC BR5 ... 202 C1
Meldrum Rd GDMY/SEVK IG3 ... 123 K7
Melfield Gdns CAT SE6 ... 182 G7
Melford Av BARK IG11 ... 143 H1
Melford CI CHSGTN KT9 ... 219 L2
Melford Rd EDUL SE22 ... 181 P4
EHAM E6 ... 142 C6
IL IG1 ... 122 D7
WALTH E17 ... 120 D2
WAN E11 ... 121 K7
Melfort Av THHTH CR7 ... 203 J3
Melfort Rd THHTH CR7 ... 203 J3
Melgund Rd HBRY N5 ... 119 H10
Melina CI HYS/HAR UB3 ... 132 E7
Melina PI STJWD NW8 ... 3 L10
Melina Rd SHB W12 ... 156 E1
The Melings HHNE HP2 ... 36 C1
Melior PI STHWK SE1 ... 19 H1
Melior St STHWK SE1 ... 19 H1
Melksham CI HARH RM3 ... 105 N8
Melksham Dr GDMY/SEVK IG3 ... 105 N8
Melksham Gdns GDMY/SEVK IG3 ... 105 N8
Meller CI CROY/NA CR0 ... 202 F10
Mellifont CI CAR SM5 ... 201 N7
MRDN SM4 ... 201 N7
Melling Dr EN EN1 ... 79 P5
Melling St WOOL/PLUM SE18 ... 163 M6
Mellish CI BARK IG11 ... 143 K5
Mellish Flds HAYES BR2 ... 205 L6
Mellish Gdns WFD IG8 ... 101 M6
Mellish St POP/IOD E14 ... 160 D1
Mellish Wy EMPK RM11 ... 125 K3
Mellitus St SHB W12 ... 136 C6
Mellor CI WOT/HER KT12 ... 197 N7
Mellow La East HGDN/ICK UB10 ... 132 D6
Mellows Rd CLAY IG5 ... 122 C1
WLGTN SM6 ... 222 E2
Mells Crs ELTH/MOT SE9 ... 184 C7
Mell St GNWCH SE10 ... 161 K4
Melody La HBRY N5 ... 119 J10
Melody Rd BH/WHM TN16 ... 243 P4
WAND/EARL SW18 ... 179 M1
Melon PI KENS W8 ... 14 F1
Melon Rd PECK SE15 ... 159 P7
WAN E11 ... 121 K8
Melrose Av BORE WD6 ... 75 P1
CRICK NW2 ... 116 F10
GFD/PVL UB6 ... 134 A4
MTCM CR4 ... 180 C10
POTB/CUF EN6 ... 59 L9
STRHM/NOR SW16 ... 202 A3
WDGN N22 ... 99 J9
WHTN TW2 ... 176 A5
WIM/MER SW19 ... 179 L3
Melrose CI GFD/PVL UB6 ... 134 A4
LEE/GVPK SE12 ... 183 M4
YEAD UB4 ... 133 H7
Melrose Crs ORP BR6 ... 226 G3
Melrose Dr STHL UB1 ... 133 P10
Melrose Gdns EDGW HA8 ... 115 N1
HMSMTH W6 ... 137 K10
NWMAL KT3 ... 200 A3
WOT/HER KT12 ... 217 K2
Melrose PI WAT WD17 ... 72 C4
Melrose Rd BARN SW13 ... 156 E6
BH/WHM TN16 ... 243 P2
COUL/CHIP CR5 ... 240 C1
PIN HA5 ... 113 N2
WAND/EARL SW18 ... 179 J5
WEY KT13 ... 216 B2
WIM/MER SW19 ... 201 K1
Melrose Ter HMSMTH W6 ... 137 K10
WIM/MER SW19 ... 179 K1
Melsa Rd MRDN SM4 ... 193 N4
Melsted Rd HHW HP1 ... 35 L6
Melthorne Dr RSLP HA4 ... 113 K8
Melthorpe Gdns BKHTH/KID SE3 ... 162 A7
Melton CI RSLP HA4 ... 113 K6
Melton Flds HOR/WEW KT19 ... 220 A5
Melton Gdns ROM RM1 ... 124 C5
Melton PI HOR/WEW KT19 ... 220 A5
Melton Rd REDH RH1 ... 258 D6
Melton St CAMTN NW1 ... 5 H10
Melville Av GFD/PVL UB6 ... 114 E10
RYNPK SW20 ... 178 D10
SAND/SEL CR2 ... 223 N4
Melville CI HGDN/ICK UB10 ... 112 B2
Melville Ct DEPT SE8 * ... 160 C3
Melville Gdns PLMGR N13 ... 99 H5
Melville PI IS N1 * ... 6 B1
Melville Rd BARN SW13 ... 156 E4
CRW RM5 ... 104 C8
RAIN RM13 ... 144 A7
SCUP DA14 ... 186 F5
WALTH E17 ... 120 D2
WLSDN NW10 ... 117 H6
Melville Villas Rd ACT W3 * ... 136 A10
Melvin Rd PGE/AN SE20 ... 204 B1
Melvinshaw LHD/OX KT22 ... 237 K3
Melvyn CI CHSHM HP5 ... 50 B2
Memel CI STLK EC1Y * ... 12 E1
Memel St STLK EC1Y * ... 141 N5
Memess Path WOOL/PLUM SE18 ... 146 F6
Memorial CI HEST TW5 ... 143 L5
OXTED RH8 ... 261 L5
Memorial Sq KUT/HW KT1 ... 191 L9
Mendip CI DTCH/LGLY SL3 ... 150 C4
HYS/HAR UB3 ... 152 B1
STALE/WH AL4 ... 39 H1
SYD SE26 ... 182 E6
WPK KT4 ... 200 F3
Mendip Dr CRICK NW2 ... 117 H2
Mendip Houses BETH E2 * ... 140 E1
Mendip Rd BTSEA SW11 ... 158 C8
BUSH WD23 ... 73 N4
BXLYHN DA7 ... 164 F1
EMPK RM11 ... 125 J5
ERITH DA8 ... 164 G7
GNTH/NBYPK IG2 ... 123 H3
Mendlesham WGCE AL7 ... 23 L3

Mendora Rd *FUL/PGN* SW6 ... 157 H6
Mendoza CI *EMPK* RM11 ... 125 H3
Menelik Rd *CRICK* NW2 ... 117 H9
Menlo Gdns *NRWD* SE19 ... 181 L10
Menon Dr *ED* N9 ... 100 A4
Menotti St *BETH* E2 * ... 13 P1
Mentmore CI
*KTN/HRWW/WS* HA3 ... 115 H4
Mentmore Rd *STAL* AL1 ... 38 C8
Mentmore Ter *HACK* E8 ... 140 A2
Meon Ct *KWD/TDW/WH* KT20 ... 238 E8
Meon Rd *ACT* W3 ... 155 P1
Meopham Rd *MTCM* CR4 ... 202 D10
Mepham Crs
*KTN/HRWW/WS* HA3 ... 94 B8
Mepham Gdns
*KTN/HRWW/WS* HA3 ... 94 B8
Mepham St *STHWK* SE1 ... 11 P10
Mera Dr *BXLYHN* DA7 ... 164 B10
Merantum Wy
*WIM/MER* SW19 ... 201 M1
Merbury CI *LEE* SE13 ... 183 H1
*THMD* SE28 ... 142 C10
Merbury Rd *THMD* SE28 ... 142 C10
Merbury St *WOOL/PLUM* SE18 ... 162 E2
Mercator PI *POP/IOD* E14 ... 160 E10
Mercator Rd *LEW* SE13 ... 161 J10
Merceron CI *CRAWE* RH10 ... 284 D10
*THDIT* KT7 ... 198 E12
Merceron Houses *BETH* E2 * ... 140 B5
Merceron St *WCHPL* E1 ... 140 A6
Mercer PI *PIN* HA5 ... 93 K10
Mercers *HHNE* HP2 ... 35 P4
*HLWW/ROY* CM19 ... 46 D4
Mercers CI *CNWCH* SE10 ... 161 L3
Mercers Cots *WCHPL* E1 * ... 140 E6
Mercers Ms *ARCH* N19 ... 118 E8
Mercers PI *HMSMTH* W6 ... 156 F3
Mercers Rw *ARCH* N19 ... 118 E8
Mercer St *LSO/SEVD* WC2H ... 11 L6
Merchant Dr *HERT/BAY* SG13 ... 25 N4
Merchants CI *SNWD* SE25 ... 203 H3
*WOKN/KNAP* GU21 ... 231 H3
Merchant St *BOW* E3 ... 140 E5
Merchiston Rd *CAT* SE6 ... 183 J5
Merchland Rd *ELTH/MOT* SE9 ... 184 F4
Mercia Gv *LEW* SE13 ... 161 H9
Mercia Wy *SL* SL1 ... 128 C10
Mercier Rd *PUT/ROE* SW15 ... 179 H1
Mercury CI *CRAWW* RH11 ... 283 H10
Mercury Gdns *ROM* RM1 ... 124 F2
Mercury Rd *BTFD* TW8 ... 155 H4
Mercury Wk *HWCR* SE14 ... 160 C5
Mercy Ter *LEW* SE13 ... 182 C1
Merebank La *WLGTN* SM6 ... 222 G2
Mere CI *ORP* BR6 ... 206 E9
*WIM/MER* SW19 ... 178 C3
Meredith Av *CRICK* NW2 ... 116 F10
Meredith CI *PIN* HA5 ... 93 J4
Meredith Ms *BROCKY* SE4 ... 160 L10
Meredith Rd *CDW/CHF* RM16 ... 168 D3
Meredith St *CLKNW* EC1R * ... 6 C10
*PLSTW* E13 ... 141 M5
Meredyth Rd *BARN* SW13 ... 156 D8
Mere End *CROY/NA* CR0 ... 204 C7
Merefield Gdns
*KWD/TDW/WH* KT20 ... 238 G5
Mere Rd *KWD/TDW/WH* KT20 ... 238 G10
*SHPTN* TW17 * ... 196 C6
*SL* SL1 ... 149 L2
*WEY* KT13 ... 196 E10
Mereside *ORP* BR6 ... 206 D9
Mereside Pk *ASHF* TW15 * ... 174 D7
Meretone CI *BROCKY* SE4 ... 160 D10
Merevale Crs *MRDN* SM4 ... 201 M6
Mereway Rd *WHTN* TW2 ... 176 C4
Merewood CI *BMLY* BR1 ... 206 D2
Merewood Gdns
*CROY/NA* CR0 ... 204 C7
Merewood Rd *BXLYHN* DA7 ... 164 E10
Mereworth CI *HAYES* BR2 ... 205 L5
Mereworth Dr *CRAWE* RH10 ... 284 E5
*WOOL/PLUM* SE18 ... 162 G6
Meriden CI *BARK/HLT* IG6 ... 102 F9
*BMLY* BR1 ... 184 A10
Meriden Wy *GSTN* WD25 ... 73 M3
*MLHL* NW7 ... 96 A5
Meridian Gv *HORL* RH6 ... 280 D3
Meridian Rd *CHARL* SE7 ... 162 A6
Meridian Sq *SRTFD* E15 ... 141 J10
Meridian Wy *ED* N9 ... 100 C4
*UED* N18 ... 100 B3
*WAB* EN9 ... 62 G10
*WARE* SG12 ... 26 C6
Merifield Gdns *ELTH/MOT* SE9 ... 161 P10
Merleys CI *HART* DA3 ... 211 P3
Merlin CI *WAN* E11 ... 124 A4
Merivale Rd *HRW* HA1 ... 114 B5
*PUT/ROE* SW15 ... 157 H10

Merrivale Ms *WDR/YW* UB7 * ... 131 N10
Merrow Cha *GU* GU1 ... 250 F10
Merrow Common Rd
*RGUE* GU4 ... 250 E5
Merrow Copse *GU* GU1 ... 250 E9
Merrow Ct *MTCM* CR4 * ... 180 E9
Merrow Crs *GU* GU1 ... 250 F9
Merrow Dr *HHW* HP1 ... 35 H5
Merrow PI *RGUE* GU4 ... 250 F5
Merrow Rd *BELMT* SM2 ... 220 G5
Merrows CI *NTHWD* HA6 ... 92 D10
Merrow St *RGUE* GU4 ... 250 G8
*WALW* SE17 ... 18 H9
Merrow Wy *WALW* SE17 ... 18 H9
Merrow Wy *CROY/NA* CR0 ... 235 H5
*GU* GU1 * ... 250 G9
Merrow Woods *GU* GU1 ... 250 E8
Merrydown Rd *CHST* BR7 ... 206 H1
Merryfield Gdns *STAN* HA7 ... 95 H6
Merryfields *STALE/WH* AL4 ... 39 M1
*UX/CGN* UB8 ... 131 N4
Merryfields CI *HART* DA3 ... 211 L4
Merryhill CI WY *CAT* SE6 * ... 182 G3
Merryhill Rd *CHING* E4 ... 101 P1
Merry Hill Mt *BUSH* WD23 ... 94 A3
Merry Hill Rd *BUSH* WD23 ... 93 P1
Merryhills CI *BKHWHM* TW16 ... 244 A2
Merryhills Dr *ENC/FH* EN2 ... 78 F8
Merrylands Rd *CAT* SE16 ... 195 H10
Merrylands Farm
*GT/LBKH* KT23 ... 235 N10
Merrylands Rd *GT/LBKH* KT23 ... 235 N10
Merrymeade Cha *BRWN* CM15 ... 107 J2
Merrymeet *BNSTD* SM7 ... 222 A10
Merryweather Ct
*NWMAL* KT3 * ... 200 B5
Merrywood Gv
*KWD/TDW/WH* KT20 ... 256 C6
Merrywood Pk *REIG* RH2 ... 257 L8
Mersey Av *UPMR* RM14 ... 126 C4
Mersey PI *HHNE* HP2 ... 36 A1
Mersey Rd *WALTH* E17 ... 120 E1
Mersham Dr *CDALE/KGS* NW9 ... 115 M3
Mersham PI *PGE/AN* SE20 ... 204 A1
*THHTH* CR7 ... 203 L2
Mersham Rd *THHTH* CR7 ... 203 L3
Mertham Rd *REDH* RH1 ... 259 H6
Merstham Rd *CHDH* RM6 ... 123 P5
Merstham Rd *BARN* SW13 ... 156 F5
Merten Av *CHSWK* W4 ... 156 C3
*HART* DA3 ... 211 K4
Merton CI *BUSH* WD23 ... 132 C2
*NTHLT* UB5 ... 114 B10
Merton Gdns
*KWD/TDW/WH* KT20 ... 238 G5
*STMC/STPC* BR5 ... 206 E5
Merton Hall Gdns
*RYNPK* SW20 ... 201 H1
Merton Hall Rd
*WIM/MER* SW19 ... 201 H1
Merton High St
*WIM/MER* SW19 ... 179 M10
Merton La *HGT* N6 ... 118 A7
Merton PI *CDW/CHF* RM16 ... 168 D3
*WIM/MER* SW19 * ... 201 N1
Merton Ri *HAMP* NW3 ... 3 M2
Merton Rd *BARK* IG11 ... 145 J2
*ENC/FH* EN2 ... 79 L4
*GDMY/SEVK* IG3 ... 123 J5
*RYLN/HDSTN* HA2 ... 114 B6
*SL* SL1 ... 149 M2
*SNWD* SE25 ... 203 N5
*WALTH* E17 ... 121 K5
*WAND/EARL* SW18 ... 179 K4
*WATW* WD18 ... 73 J8
*WIM/MER* SW19 ... 179 L10
Merton Wy *E/WMO/HCT* KT8 ... 198 A4
*HGDN/ICK* UB10 ... 132 C2
*LHD/OX* KT22 ... 236 F5
Mertoun Ter *MBLAR* W1H * ... 10 A5
Merttins Rd *PECK* SE15 ... 160 C10
Meru CI *KTTN* NW5 ... 118 B9
Mervan Rd *BRXS/STRHM* SW2 ... 159 H10
Mervyn Av *ELTH/MOT* SE9 ... 184 F6
Mervyn Rd *SHPTN* TW17 ... 196 D7
*WEA* W13 ... 154 F2
Merwin Wy *WDSR* SL4 * ... 148 C9
Meryfield CI *BORE* WD6 ... 75 L6
Mesne Wy *RSEV* TN14 ... 228 C8
Messaline Av *ACT* W3 ... 135 P8
Messant CI *HARH* RM3 ... 105 L10
Messenger CI *CRAWW* RH11 ... 283 K5
Messent Rd *ELTH/MOT* SE9 ... 183 P1
Messeter PI *ELTH/MOT* SE9 ... 184 D2
Messina Av *KIL/WHAMP* NW6 ... 2 E4
Metcalf Rd *ASHF* TW15 ... 174 C8
Metcalf Wy *CRAWW* RH11 ... 283 B10
Meteor St *BTSEA* SW11 ... 158 B10
Meteor Wy *WLGTN* SM6 ... 222 F4
Metford Crs *PEND* EN3 ... 80 F4
Methley St *LBTH* SE11 ... 18 B8
Methuen CI *EDGW* HA8 ... 95 M8
Methuen Pk *MUSWH* N10 ... 98 C10
Methuen Rd *BELV* DA17 ... 164 C3
*BXLYHS* DA6 ... 164 A10
*EDGW* HA8 ... 95 M8
Methwold Rd *NKENS* W10 ... 136 G7

Michelsdale Dr *RCH/KEW* TW9. ... 155 K10
Michel Wk *WOOL/PLUM* SE18 ... 162 N4
Michigan CI *MNPK* E12 ... 122 B9
Michigan CI *BROX* EN10 ... 62 D2
Michelham Down
*NFNCH/WDSPK* N12 ... 97 J5
Michols Av *CFSP/GDCR* SL9 ... 90 B6
Mickleham Rd *HHNE* HP2 ... 36 D6
Mickleham Dr *LHD/OX* KT22 ... 253 L2
*ECH* TW20 ... 196 C7
Mickleham Wy *CROY/NA* CR0 ... 225 J4
Micklem Dr *HHW* HP1 ... 35 J5
Micklethwaite Rd
*FUL/PGN* SW6 ... 14 F10
Midcot Wy *BERK* HP4 ... 33 L3
Midcroft *RSLP* HA4 ... 112 F6
*SLN* SL2 ... 128 C6
Mid Cross La *CFSP/GDCR* SL9 ... 90 C6
Middle Boy *ABR/ST* RM4 ... 85 L7
Middle CI *COUL/CHIP* CR5 ... 240 G6
*EW* KT17 ... 220 B8
Middle Dartrey Wk
*WBPTN* SW10 * ... 157 M6
Middle Dene *MLHL* NW7 ... 96 H4
Middle Down *SOTN* WD25 ... 74 A2
Middle Dr *BEAC* HP9 ... 88 C6
Middle Farm CI *EHSLY* KT24 ... 253 L3
Middle Farm PI *EHSLY* KT24 ... 253 L3
Middlefield *HAT* AL10 ... 40 D3
*HORL* RH6 ... 280 D3
*STJWD* NW8 ... 3 L3
*WCCE* AL7 ... 23 H9
Middlefield Av *HOD* EN11 ... 44 F1
Middlefield CI *HOD* EN11 ... 44 F1
*STALE/WH* AL4 ... 39 H3
Middlefield Rd *HOD* EN11 ... 44 F1
Middlefields *CROY/NA* CR0 ... 224 D5
*WEA* W13 ... 134 G2
Middle Furlong *BUSH* WD23 ... 76 A2
Middle Gn *BRWN* CM15 ... 87 H3
*DTCH/LGLY* SL3 ... 130 F9
Middle Green SL *BRYLDS* KT5 ... 199 L6
Middleham Gdns *UED* N18 ... 99 P7
Middleham Rd *UED* N18 ... 99 P7
Middle HI *EGH* TW20 ... 171 P8
Middleknights HI *HHW* HP1 ... 35 H6
Middle La *CEND/HSY/T* N8 ... 247 N7
*CEND/HSY/T* N8 ... 118 F3
*EGH* KT17 ... 220 B8
*HHS/BOV* HP3 ... 35 P4
*TEDD* TW11 ... 176 D7
Middle Lane Ms
*CEND/HSY/T* N8 ... 118 F3
Middlemead CI *GT/LBKH* KT23 ... 235 N4
Middle Meadow *CSTC* HP8 ... 89 N4
Middlemead Rd *GT/LBKH* KT23. ... 235 N4
Middle Ope *WATN* WD24 ... 73 J3
Middle Park Av *ELTH/MOT* SE9 ... 184 A2
Middle Rd *BERK* HP4 ... 35 N5
*DEN/HRF* UB9 ... 110 F5
*EBAR* EN4 ... 77 H10
*LHD/OX* KT22 ... 236 G7
*PLSTW* E13 ... 141 M4
*RBRW/HUT* CM13 ... 107 P5
*RYLN/HDSTN* HA2 ... 114 C7
*STRHM/NOR* SW16 ... 202 D2
*WAB* EN9 ... 62 G8
Middle Rw *NKENS* W10 ... 8 A2
Middlesborough Rd *UED* N18 ... 99 P7
Middlesex CI *STHL* UB1 ... 134 A6
Middlesex Rd *MTCM* CR4 ... 202 F5
Middlesex St *WCHPL* E1 ... 13 K4
Middle St *BRKHM/BTCW* RH3 ... 275 P9
*CROY/NA* CR0 ... 2 D6
*SHGR* GU5 ... 270 B5
*STBT* EC1A ... 12 E3
*WAB* EN9 ... 62 G8
Middle Temple La *EMB* EC4Y ... 11 N6
Middleton Av *CHING* E4 ... 100 G5
*GFD/PVL* UB6 ... 134 C4
*SCUP* DA14 ... 185 M9
Middleton CI *CHING* E4 ... 100 G4
Middleton Dr
*BERM/RHTH* SE16 ... 160 C1
*PIN* HA5 ... 113 H1
Middleton Gdns
*GNTH/NBYPK* IG2 ... 122 E4
Middleton Hall La
*BRWN* CM15 ... 107 K3
Middleton Ms *HOLWY* N7 ... 118 F10
*IS* N1 ... 118 G1
Middleton Rd *BRWN* CM15 ... 107 K2
*CAR* SM5 ... 201 N7
*COB* KT11 ... 235 J5
*GLDGN* NW11 ... 117 J5
*HACK* E8 ... 7 L4
*HOR/WEW* KT19 * ... 220 A6
*HYS/HAR* UB3 ... 132 L7
*NWMAL* KT3 ... 199 P3
*RKW/CH/CXG* WD3 ... 91 K2
Middleton St *BETH* E2 ... 140 A6
Middleton Wy *CRAWW* RH11 ... 161 J10
*LEW* SE13 ... 161 J10
Middle Wk *WOKN/KNAP* GU21 ... 232 B3
Middle Wk *SL* SL1 ... 149 K8
Middleway *GLDGN* NW11 ... 117 J4
Middle Wy *STRHM/NOR* SW16 ... 202 N4
*WATW* WD18 ... 73 K8
The Middle Wy
*KTN/HRWW/WS* HA3 ... 94 E10
Mid Ve *STHWK* SE1 * ... 13 H9
The Midlings *SEV* TN13 ... 264 C5
Middlings Wd *SEV* TN13 ... 264 C5
Midfield Av *BXLYHN* DA7 ... 164 E4
Midfield Wy *STMC/STPC* BR5 ... 207 L4
Midford PI *FITZ* W1T * ... 11 H2
Midgarth CI *LHD/OX* KT22 ... 218 B9
Midgley Rd *CRAWE* RH10 ... 284 A5
Midholm *GLDGN* NW11 ... 117 J2
Midholm *CLDGN* NW11 ... 117 J2
Midholm CI *GLDGN* NW11 ... 117 J2
Midholm Rd *CROY/NA* CR0 ... 204 D10
Mid Holmwood La *RDKG* RH5 ... 272 F4
Midhope CI *WOKS/MYFD* GU22 ... 232 N10
Midhope Rd
*WOKS/MYFD* GU22 ... 232 N10
Midhope St *STPAN* WC1H ... 5 M10
Midhurst Av *CROY/NA* CR0 ... 196 A7
*MUSWH* N10 ... 98 B7
Midhurst CI *CRAWW* RH11 ... 125 K6
*HCH* RM12 ... 125 K6
Midhurst Gdns
*HGDN/ICK* UB10 ... 132 D2
Midhurst HI *BXLYHS* DA6 ... 164 B8
Midhurst Pde *MUSWH* N10 * ... 118 A1
Midhurst Rd *WEA* W13 ... 154 F2
Midland Arches *CRICK* NW2 * ... 116 F6
Midland Crs *HAMP* NW3 ... 3 J1
Midland PI *POP/IOD* E14 * ... 161 N8
Midland Rd *CMTN* NW1 ... 4 G7
*HHNE* HP2 ... 36 B1
*LEY* E10 ... 121 P6
Midland Ter *CRICK* NW2 ... 116 B6
*WLSDN* NW10 ... 136 B6
Mideton Industrial Estate Rd
*GUW* GU2 ... 249 N9

Midstrath Rd *WLSDN* NW10 ... 116 B9
Mid St *REDH* RH1 ... 258 C10
Midsummer Av *HSLWW* TW4 ... 153 N10
Midsummer Wk
*WOKN/KNAP* GU21 ... 232 A2
Midway *CHEAM* SM3 ... 201 J7
*STALW/RED* AL3 ... 38 A9
*WOT/HER* KT12 ... 197 J9
Midway CI *STA* TW18 ... 173 L6
Midwinter CI *WELL* DA16 ... 163 N9
Midwood CI *CRICK* NW2 ... 116 D8
Miena Wy *ASHTD* KT21 ... 223 J4
Mienham Wy *CROY/NA* CR0 ... 225 J4
Mighell Av *REDBR* IG4 ... 122 A9
Milan Rd *STHL* UB1 ... 115 J7
Milborne Gv *WBPTN* SW10 ... 15 K8
Milborne Wy *HOM* E9 ... 140 D1
Milborough Crs
*LEE/GVPK* SE12 ... 183 J7
Milbourne La *ESH/CLAY* KT10 ... 218 B2
Milbrook *ESH/CLAY* KT10 ... 218 B3
Milburn Dr *WDR/YW* UB7 ... 131 P9
Milburn Wk *EPSOM* KT18 ... 238 B11
Milcote St *STHWK* SE1 ... 12 C2
Mildenhall Rd *CLPT* E5 ... 120 B9
*SL* SL1 ... 129 K8
Mildmay Av *IS* N1 ... 7 H1
Mildmay Gv North *IS* N1 ... 119 L10
Mildmay Gv South *IS* N1 ... 119 L10
Mildmay Pk *IS* N1 ... 119 L10
Mildmay Rd *RSEV* TN14 ... 228 G7
*STNW/STAM* N16 ... 7 H1
Mildmay St *IS* N1 ... 7 H1
Mildred Av *BORE* WD6 ... 75 M8
*HYS/HAR* UB3 ... 152 E3
*NTHLT* UB5 ... 114 A6
*WATW* WD18 ... 73 H8
Mildred CI *DART* DA1 ... 171 L2
Mile Cl *WCHPL* E1 ... 140 C9
Mile End Rd *WCHPL* E1 ... 140 C9
The Mile End *WALTH* E17 ... 100 C9
Mile House CI *STAL* AL1 ... 38 F7
Mile House La *STAL* AL1 ... 38 F7
Mile Pth *WOKS/MYFD* GU22 ... 231 N6
Mile Rd *WLGTN* SM6 ... 202 E8
Miles CI *THMD* SE28 ... 143 H10
Miles Dr *THMD* SE28 ... 143 H10
Milespit HI *MLHL* NW7 ... 96 E6
Miles PI *BRYLDS* KT5 * ... 199 L4
Miles Rd *CEND/HSY/T* N8 ... 118 F1
*HOR/WEW* KT19 ... 220 A5
*MTCM* CR4 ... 202 A1
Miles St *VX/NE* SW8 ... 17 L10
Milestone CI *BELMT* SM2 ... 221 N3
*ED* N9 ... 99 N3
*RPLY/SEND* GU23 ... 249 N3
Milestone Rd *PUR/KEN* CR8 ... 222 C10
Milestone Rd *HLWE* CM17 ... 29 N3
*NRWD* SE19 ... 181 N10
Mile Stone Rd *RDART* DA2 ... 187 J8
Miles Wy *TRDG/WHET* N20 ... 97 P3
Milford CI *ABYW* SE2 ... 163 P5
*STALE/WH* AL4 ... 39 J7
Milford Ct *STHL* UB1 * ... 134 B7
Milford Gdns *ALP/SUD* HA0 ... 115 J10
*CROY/NA* CR0 ... 204 B5
*EDGW* HA8 ... 95 M8
Milford Gv *SUT* SM1 ... 209 N2
Milford La *TPL/STR* WC2R ... 11 N7
Milford Ms *STRHM/NOR* SW16 ... 180 F4
Milford Rd *STHL* UB1 ... 133 P9
*WEA* W13 ... 134 G10
Milkhouse Ga *GU* GU1 * ... 268 A6
Milking La *ORP* BR6 ... 226 B8
Milk St *BMLY* BR1 ... 184 A2
*CAN/RD* E16 ... 142 E10
*CITYW* EC2V ... 12 F5
Milkwell Gdns *WFD* IG8 ... 101 N4
Milkwell Yd *CMBW* SE5 ... 159 K7
Milkwood *RGUE* GU4 * ... 268 C7
Mill Bank *DTCH/LGLY* SL3 ... 130 C6
Millais Av *MNPK* E12 ... 122 E4
Millais Crs *HOR/WEW* KT19 ... 220 B2
Millais Gdns *EDGW* HA8 ... 95 M8
Millais PI *TIL* RM18 ... 168 D6
Millais Rd *EN* EN1 ... 79 N9
*NWMAL* KT3 ... 200 B7
*WAN* E11 ... 121 L9
Millais Wy *HOR/WEW* KT19 ... 219 P1
Millan CI *ADL/WDHM* KT15 ... 215 L6
Milland Ct *BORE* WD6 ... 75 P1
Millard CI *STNW/STAM* N16 ... 119 M10
Millard Ter *DENT* RM10 ... 160 K3
Millars Meadow
*BKHTH/KID* SE3 ... 161 L2
Mill Av *UX/CGN* UB8 ... 131 M4
Millbank *WEST* SW1P ... 17 L7
Millbank Est *WEST* SW1P ... 17 L7
The Millbank *CRAWW* RH11 ... 283 J12
Millbank Wy *LEE/GVPK* SE12 ... 183 K4
Millbottom La *RDKG* RH5 ... 273 H5
Millbourne Rd *FELT* TW13 ... 171 P9
Mill Br *BAR* EN5 ... 77 J9
*HERT/WAT* SG14 ... 25 L5
Mill Bridge *BAR* EN5 ... 77 J9
Millbro *SWLY* BR8 ... 187 N3
Millbrook *GU* GU1 ... 268 C2
*WEY* KT13 ... 213 N7
Millbrook Av *ELTH/MOT* SE9 ... 184 C5
Millbrook Gdns *CHDH* RM6 ... 123 P4
*GPK* RM2 ... 124 G2
Millbrook Rd *BRXN/ST* SW9 ... 159 J9
*BUSH* WD23 ... 76 A3
*ED* N9 ... 100 A4
Mill Brook Rd *STMC/STPC* BR5 ... 207 P3
Mill CI *CAR* SM5 ... 202 C10
*CSHM* HP5 ... 64 A3
*DTCH/LGLY* SL3 ... 151 H4
*KUT/HW* KT1 ... 199 M9
*POP/IOD* E14 ... 142 C10
Mill Plat *ISLW* TW7 ... 154 F8
*HGDN/ICK* UB10 ... 112 C9
Mill Pond CI *RSEV* TN14 ... 247 L1
*VX/NE* SW8 ... 158 A8
Millpond Ct *ADL/WDHM* KT15 ... 215 N7
Millpond Est
*BERM/RHTH* SE16 * ... 160 A1
Mill Pond Rd *BFOR* ... 212 A1
Mill Race *WARE* SG12 ... 27 J7
Mill Reach *RGUE* GU4 ... 269 P5
Mill Rdg *EDGW* HA8 ... 95 N3
Mill Rd *CAR RD* E16 ... 141 N10
*CRAWE* RH10 ... 284 C6
*ERITH* DA8 ... 164 D6
*ESH/CLAY* KT10 ... 197 P9
*GVW* DA11 ... 190 B3
*HERT/WAT* SG14 ... 25 J4
*IL* IG1 ... 122 E7
*KWD/TDW/WH* KT20 ... 238 G10
*PUR* RM19 ... 170 C7
*SEV* TN13 ... 266 A9
*SOCK/AV* RM15 ... 170 L5
*WDR/YW* UB7 ... 151 N2
*WHTN* TW2 ... 176 B7
*WIM/MER* SW19 ... 179 N10
Mill Rw *BXLY* DA5 ... 186 F2
*IS* N1 ... 7 K2
Mills CI *HGDN/ICK* UB10 ... 132 D4
Mills Gv *CMTN* NW1 ... 4 B7
Mills Gv *POP/IOD* E14 ... 142 A8
Mill Shaw *OXTED* RH8 ... 261 H6
Millshott CI *WHALL* SW1A * ... 11 H3

*REDH* RH1 ... 277 J10
Miller's Ct *CHSWK* W4 ... 156 C4
Millersdale *HLWW/ROY* CM19 ... 46 E5
Millers Green CI *ENC/FH* EN2 ... 79 M2
Millers La *WDSR* SL4 ... 27 H7
Millers La *CHIG* IG7 ... 103 J2
*REDH* RH1 ... 38 C7
Miller's Ter *HACK* E8 ... 119 N10
Miller St *CAMTN* NW1 ... 4 E7
Miller's Wy *HMSMTH* W6 ... 157 F9
*HERT/WAT* SG14 ... 25 L5
Mill Side *SL* SL1 * ... 133 K8
Millside *CAR* SM5 ... 202 A9
Millstead CI
*KWD/TDW/WH* KT20 ... 238 E9
Mill Stone CI *EYN* DA4 ... 210 B2
Millstone CI *SRTFD* E15 ... 141 J1
Millstone Ms *EYN* DA4 ... 210 B1
Millstream CI *HERT/WAT* SG14 ... 25 L5
*PLMGR* N13 ... 99 H6
Millstream La *SL* SL1 ... 128 D10
Millstream Rd *STHWK* SE1 ... 19 L2
Mill St *BERK* HP4 ... 33 P5
*BH/WHM* TN16 ... 262 G3
*CONDST* W1S ... 10 D7
*DTCH/LGLY* SL3 ... 150 C6
*HHS/BOV* HP3 ... 35 N10
*HLWE* CM17 ... 47 P4
*KUT/HW* KT1 ... 8 C6
*REDH* RH1 ... 275 P7
*SLN* SL2 ... 129 L10
*STHWK* SE1 ... 19 M2
Mills Wy *RBRW/HUT* CM13 ... 107 P2
Millthorne CI
*RKW/CH/CXG* WD3 ... 72 A3
Mill V *HAYES* BR2 ... 205 M3
Mill View CI *EW* KT17 ... 220 C4
Millview CI *REIG* RH2 ... 257 N8
Mill View Gdns *CROY/NA* CR0... ... 204 C10
Millwall Dock Rd *POP/IOD* E14... ... 160 L7
Millwards *HAT* AL10 ... 40 E7
Millway *REIG* RH2 ... 257 N10
Mill Wy *BUSH* WD23 ... 76 M6
*EBED/NFELT* TW14 ... 175 J3
*LHD/OX* KT22 ... 255 L1
*MLHL* NW7 ... 96 B6
*RKW/CH/CXG* WD3 ... 91 J2
Mill Wy
*WCCE* AL7 ... 23 H6
Millway Gdns *NTHLT* UB5 ... 133 N1
Millwell Crs *CHIG* IG7 ... 102 G6
Millwood Rd *HSLW* TW3 ... 176 B1
*STMC/STPC* BR5 ... 207 P2
Mill Yd *WCHPL* E1 ... 13 N7
Milman CI *PIN* HA5 ... 113 J1
Milman Rd *KIL/WHAMP* NW6 ... 136 G4
Milne Ct *CRAWE* RH10 ... 283 H10
Milne Fld *PIN* HA5 ... 93 P6
Milne Gdns *ELTH/MOT* SE9 ... 184 B1
Milne Pk East *CROY/NA* CR0 ... 225 J7
Milne Pk West *CROY/NA* CR0 ... 241 P7
Milner Ct *CTHM* CR3 ... 241 P8
*GSTN* WD25 ... 55 J10
Milner Dr *COB* KT11 ... 217 N8
*WHTN* TW2 ... 176 C3
Milner PI *IS* N1 ... 6 B1
*CAR* SM5 ... 202 B1
Milner Rd *BCTR* RM8 ... 123 N8
*CTHM* CR3 ... 241 P8
*KUT/HW* KT1 ... 199 J3
*MRDN* SM4 ... 201 P5
*SRTFD* E15 ... 141 K5
*THHTH* CR7 ... 203 E3
*WIM/MER* SW19 ... 201 L1
Milner Sq *IS* N1 ... 6 B1
Milner St *CHEL* SW3 ... 16 A5
Milnthorpe Rd *CHSWK* W4 ... 156 A5
Milo Rd *EDUL* SE22 ... 181 N2
Milroy Av *GVW* DA11 ... 190 B5
Milroy Wk *STHWK* SE1 ... 11 P9
Milson Rd *WKENS* W14 ... 115 N1
*WARE* SG12 ... 27 H4
Milton Av *BAR* EN5 ... 76 C6
*CDALE/KGS* NW9 ... 115 N1
*CFSP/GDCR* SL9 ... 110 A2
*CROY/NA* CR0 ... 203 L7
*DORK* RH4 ... 272 C5
*EHAM* E6 ... 142 A2
*GVW* DA12 ... 190 G4
*HGT* N6 ... 118 C6
*HSLW* TW3 ... 176 B7
*SEV* TN13 ... 266 A6
*SUT* SM1 ... 201 N1
*WLSDN* NW10 ... 136 A3
Milton CI *DTCH/LGLY* SL3 ... 150 D9
*EFNCH* N2 ... 117 H2
*RGUW* GU3 ... 248 A8
*STHWK* SE1 ... 19 L4
*SUT* SM1 ... 201 N10
*YEAD* UB4 ... 133 H8
Milton Court *EC2Y* ... 12 G3
Milton Crs *CHONG* CM5 ... 67 N2
Milton Dene *HHNE* HP2 ... 36 C1
Milton Dr *BORE* WD6 ... 75 N8
*SHPTN* TW17 ... 195 P4
Milton Flds *CSTG* HP8 ... 89 N4
Milton Gdns *EPSOM* KT18 ... 220 B10
*STWL/WRAY* TW19 ... 174 A4
Milton Gv *FBAR/BDGN* N11 ... 98 D6
*STNW/STAM* N16 ... 119 L9
Milton Lawns *AMS* HP6 ... 69 J2
Milton Mount Av *CRAWE* RH10. ... 284 D5
Milton Pk *ECH* TW20 ... 172 D5
*HGT* N6 ... 118 C6
Milton PI *GVE* DA12 ... 190 G6
Milton Rd *ACT* W3 ... 136 A10
*BARK* IG11 ... 144 B3
*BRW* CM14 ... 106 C4
*CAR* SM5 ... 284 D6
*CROY/NA* CR0 ... 50 C5
*CSHM* HP5 ... 63 K2
*CTHM* CR3 ... 241 L7
*EGH* TW20 ... 172 C8
*GRAYS* RM17 ... 167 N2
*GVE* DA12 ... 190 E2
*HGDN/ICK* UB10 ... 112 C9
*HNHL* SE24 ... 181 N1
*HNWL* W7 ... 135 K4
*HPTN* TW12 ... 175 P7
*HRW* HA1 ... 114 D2
*MLHL* NW7 ... 96 B6
*MORT/ESHN* SW14 ... 156 A3
*MTCM* CR4 ... 180 B10
*ROM* RM1 ... 124 F3
*SEVS/STOTM* N15 ... 119 J1
*SUT* SM1 ... 201 N1
*SWCM* DA10 ... 189 A2
*WALTH* E17 ... 120 F2
*WARE* SG12 ... 26 C1
*WELL* DA16 ... 163 J1
*WIM/MER* SW19 ... 179 M3
*WLGTN* SM6 ... 192 G10
*WLSDN* NW10 ... 137 H1
Milton St *BARB* EC2Y ... 12 G3
*WATN* WD24 ... 73 N1
Milton Dr *HGDN/ICK* UB10 ... 112 C9
Milverton Gdns
*GDMY/SEVK* IG3 ... 123 J7
Milverton Rd
*KIL/WHAMP* NW6 ... 136 F2
Milverton St *LBTH* SE11 ... 18 B8
Milverton Wy *ELTH/MOT* SE9 ... 184 E6
Milwards *HLWW/ROY* CM19 ... 46 C5
Milward St *WCHPL* E1 ... 140 C8
Mimas Rd *HHNE* HP2 ... 36 A3

| | | | |
|---|---|---|---|
| Mimms Hall Rd *POTB/CUF* EN6 | 58 | G7 |
| Mimms La *RAD* WD7 | 57 | M9 |
| Mimosa La *BRWN* CM15 | 86 | C9 |
| *HARH* RM3 | 105 | K6 |
| *ORP* BR6 | 207 | M9 |
| Mimosa Rd *YEAD* UB4 | 133 | K7 |
| Mimram Rd *HERT/WAT* SG14 | 25 | J6 |
| Mina Av *DTCH/LGLY* SL3 | 150 | A3 |
| Minard Rd *CAT* SE6 | 183 | K3 |
| Mina Rd *WALW* SE17 | 19 | H8 |
| *WIM/MER* SW19 | 201 | L1 |
| Minchenden Crs *STHGT/OAK* N14 | 98 | E4 |
| Minchin Rd *HLW* CM20 | 29 | K10 |
| Mincloth Cl *LHD/OX* KT22 | 236 | F9 |
| Mincing La *CHOB/PIR* GU24 | 213 | L5 |
| *MON* EC3R | 13 | J7 |
| Minden Rd *CHEAM* SM3 | 201 | H9 |
| *PGE/AN* SE20 | 204 | A1 |
| Minehead Rd *RYLN/HDSTN* HA2 | 113 | P8 |
| *STRHM/NOR* SW16 | 180 | C8 |
| Mineral Cl *BAR* EN5 | 76 | F10 |
| Mineral La *CSHM* HP5 | 51 | H8 |
| Mineral St *WOOL/PLUM* SE18 | 163 | H10 |
| Minera Ms *BGVA* SW1W | 16 | B5 |
| *SCUP* DA14 | 185 | H6 |
| *STWL/WRAY* TW19 | 173 | L5 |
| Minerva Cl *BRXN/ST* SW9 | 159 | H6 |
| *KUT/HW* KT1 | 199 | L2 |
| *WLSDN* NW10 | 135 | P6 |
| Minerva St *BETH* E2 | 6 | D2 |
| Minerva Wy *BEAC* HP9 | 88 | F10 |
| Minerva Wy *WLSDN* NW10 | 136 | B4 |
| Minet Av *WLSDN* NW10 | 136 | B4 |
| Minet Dr *HYS/HAR* UB3 | 133 | H10 |
| *WLSDN* NW10 | 136 | B4 |
| Minet Gdns *HYS/HAR* UB3 | 133 | J10 |
| Minford Gdns *WKENS* W14 | 156 | F1 |
| Ming St *POP/IOD* E14 * | 140 | F3 |
| Minimax Cl *EBED/NFELT* TW14 | 175 | H2 |
| The Minims *HAT* AL10 | 40 | D2 |
| Minister Cl *LCOL/BKTW* AL2 | 56 | D4 |
| Ministry Wy *ELTH/MOT* SE9 | 184 | C5 |
| Mink Cl *HSLWW* TW4 | 155 | H4 |
| Minniecroft Rd *SL* SL1 | 128 | A5 |
| Minniedale *BRYLDS* KT5 | 199 | L5 |
| Minnow Wk *WALW* SE17 | 19 | K6 |
| Minoan Dr *HHS/BOV* HP3 | 35 | P10 |
| Minorca Rd *WEY* KT13 | 216 | B3 |
| Minories *TWRH* EC3N | 13 | L4 |
| Minshull Rd *BECK* BR3 | 182 | F10 |
| Minshull St *VX/NE* SW8 * | 158 | E7 |
| Minson Rd *HOM* E9 | 140 | C5 |
| Minstead Gdns *PUT/ROE* SW15 | 178 | C3 |
| Minstead Wy *NWMAL* KT3 | 200 | B6 |
| Minster Av *SUT* SM1 | 201 | K9 |
| Minster Cl *HAT* AL10 | 40 | D6 |
| Minster Ct *EMPK* RM11 | 125 | P7 |
| *MON* EC3R | 13 | J7 |
| Minster Dr *CROY/NA* CR0 | 225 | M1 |
| Minster Gdns *E/WMO/HCT* KT8 | 197 | N4 |
| Minsterley Av *SHPTN* TW17 | 190 | F7 |
| *CRICK* NW2 * | 117 | H10 |
| Minster Rd *BMLY* BR1 | 183 | N10 |
| *CRICK* NW2 | 117 | H10 |
| Minster Wk *CEND/HSY/T* N8 | 118 | F2 |
| Minster Wy *DTCH/LGLY* SL3 | 150 | C1 |
| *EMPK* RM11 | 125 | L5 |
| Minstrel Cl *HHNE* HP1 | 35 | L5 |
| Minstrel Gdns *BRYLDS* KT5 | 199 | L4 |
| Mint Cl *HGDN/ICK* UB10 | 132 | C3 |
| Mint La *PLMGR* N13 | 99 | J4 |
| Minterne Av *NWDGN* UB2 | 153 | P3 |
| Minterne Rd *KTN/HRWW/WS* HA3 | 115 | J1 |
| Mintern Cl *PLMGR* N13 * | 99 | N2 |
| Mintern St *IS* N1 | 7 | H1 |
| Mint La *KWD/TDW/WH* KT20 | 257 | H5 |
| Minton La *HARL* CM17 | 47 | M1 |
| Minton Ms *KIL/WHAMP* NW6 | 3 | L1 |
| Minton Ri *MDHD* SL6 | 128 | H8 |
| Mint Rd *BNSTD* SM7 | 239 | M2 |
| *WLGTN* SM6 | 222 | C2 |
| Mint St *STHWK* SE1 | 18 | E2 |
| Mint Wk *CROY/NA* CR0 | 203 | K10 |
| *WARL* CR6 | 242 | C3 |
| *WOKN/KNAP* GU21 | 231 | K5 |
| Mintwater Cl *EW* KT17 | 220 | D6 |
| Mirabel Rd *FUL/PGN* SW6 | 157 | J5 |
| Mirador Crs *SLN* SL2 | 129 | L2 |
| Miramar Wy *HCH* RM12 | 142 | B7 |
| Miranda Cl *WCHPL* E1 | 140 | D6 |
| Miranda Rd *ARCH* N19 | 118 | D6 |
| Mirfield St *CHARL* SE7 | 162 | A4 |
| Miriam Rd *WOOL/PLUM* SE18 | 163 | H4 |
| Mirren Cl *RYLN/HDSTN* HA2 | 113 | P8 |
| Mirrie La *DEN/HRF* UB9 | 110 | F3 |
| Misbourne Av *CFSP/GDCR* SL9 | 90 | B1 |
| Misbourne Cl *CFSP/GDCR* SL9 | 90 | B1 |
| Misbourne Ct *AMSS* HP7 * | 68 | C7 |
| Misbourne Mdw *DEN/HRF* UB9 | 110 | F6 |
| Misbourne Rd *HGDN/ICK* UB10 | 132 | B4 |
| Miskin Wy *GVE* DA12 | 190 | C9 |
| Missden Dr *HHS/BOV* HP3 | 36 | B1 |
| Missenden Cl *EBED/NFELT* TW14 | 174 | A3 |
| Missenden Gdns *MRDN* SM4 | 201 | M6 |
| *SL* SL1 | 128 | A5 |
| Missenden Rd *CSHM* HP5 | 50 | B8 |
| Mission Gv *WALTH* E17 | 120 | C3 |
| Mission Pl *PECK* SE15 | 159 | F7 |
| Mistletoe Cl *CROY/NA* CR0 | 204 | C8 |
| Mistley Gdns *HORL* RH6 | 279 | N5 |
| Mistley Rd *HLW* CM20 | 29 | K9 |
| Misty's Fld *WOT/HER* KT12 | 197 | N3 |
| Mitali Pas *WCHPL* E1 | 13 | N6 |
| Mitcham La *STRHM/NOR* SW16 | 180 | C8 |
| Mitcham Pk *MTCM* CR4 | 201 | P4 |
| Mitcham Rd *CROY/NA* CR0 | 202 | F6 |
| *EHAM* E6 | 142 | M5 |
| *GDMY/SEVK* IG3 | 123 | K3 |
| *TOOT* SW17 | 180 | A8 |
| Mitchell Av *CVE* DA11 | 190 | A5 |
| Mitchellbrook Wy *WLSDN* NW10 | 136 | A10 |
| Mitchell Cl *ABLGY* WD5 | 55 | H8 |
| *ABYW* SE2 | 146 | D2 |
| *BELV* DA17 | 164 | D2 |
| *HHS/BOV* HP3 | 52 | C5 |
| *RAIN* RM13 | 145 | H1 |
| *SL* SL1 | 148 | F1 |
| *WGCE* AL7 | 23 | M5 |
| Mitchell Rd *ORP* BR6 | 227 | J1 |
| *PLMGR* N13 | 99 | J2 |
| Mitchells Cl *RGUE* GU4 | 268 | B6 |
| Mitchell St *FSBYE* EC1V | 12 | E1 |
| Mitchell Wk *AMS* HP6 | 69 | K4 |
| Mitchell Wy *BMLY* BR1 | 205 | N8 |
| *WLSDN* NW10 | 136 | F1 |
| Mitchison Rd *IS* N1 | 6 | G1 |
| Mitchley Av *PUR/KEN* CR8 | 223 | N9 |
| Mitchley Hl *SAND/SEL* CR2 | 223 | K10 |
| Mitchley Rd *TOTM* N17 | 119 | L2 |
| Mitchley Vw *SAND/SEL* CR2 | 223 | L10 |
| Mitford Rd *ARCH* N19 | 118 | E10 |
| Mitre Cl *HERT/WAT* SG14 * | 25 | J5 |
| Mitre Ct *EBED/NFELT* TW14 | 38 | C10 |
| Mitre Rd *SRTFD* E15 | 140 | C1 |
| *STHWK* SE1 | 18 | B1 |
| Mitre Sq *HDTCH* EC3A | 13 | L3 |
| Mitre St *HDTCH* EC3A | 13 | L3 |
| The Mitre *POP/IOD* E14 | 140 | C9 |
| Mitre Wy *NKENS* W10 | 136 | E7 |

| | | | |
|---|---|---|---|
| *STAL* AL1 | 38 | D8 |
| Mixnams La *CHERT* KT16 | 195 | K3 |
| Mizen Cl *COB* KT11 | 217 | L10 |
| Mizen Wy *COB* KT11 | 235 | L1 |
| Moat Dr *BRWN* CM15 | 87 | H2 |
| *BUSH* WD23 | 74 | A4 |
| *ORP* BR6 | 227 | J3 |
| *SEV* TN13 | 246 | F6 |
| Moat Ct *ASHTD* KT21 | 237 | K3 |
| *ELTH/MOT* SE9 | 184 | C2 |
| Moat Crs *FNCH* N3 | 117 | L1 |
| Moat Cft *WELL* DA16 | 163 | M9 |
| Moat Dr *HRW* HA1 | 114 | A1 |
| *PLSTW* E13 | 141 | P4 |
| *RSLP* HA4 | 112 | F5 |
| *SLN* SL2 | 129 | P7 |
| Moated Farm Dr *ADL/WDHM* KT15 | 215 | M4 |
| Moat Farm Rd *NTHLT* UB5 | 133 | N1 |
| Moatfield Rd *BUSH* WD23 | 74 | A9 |
| Moat La *ERITH* DA8 | 165 | H7 |
| Moat Pl *ACT* W3 | 135 | M8 |
| *BRXN/ST* SW9 | 158 | A9 |
| *DEN/HRF* UB9 | 111 | L9 |
| Moat Side *FELT* TW13 | 175 | K7 |
| *PEND* EN3 | 80 | B8 |
| Moats La *REDH* RH1 | 276 | F6 |
| The Moat *NWMAL* KT3 | 200 | B1 |
| Moat Wk *CRAWE* RH10 | 284 | D6 |
| Moberly Rd *CLAP* SW4 | 180 | E3 |
| Moberly Wy *PUR/KEN* CR8 | 241 | L6 |
| Modbury Gdns *HAMP* NW3 | 4 | B2 |
| Model Cots *MORT/ESHN* SW14 | 155 | P9 |
| *WEA* W13 * | 154 | C1 |
| Model Farm Cl *ELTH/MOT* SE9 | 184 | B6 |
| Moelyn Ms *HRW* HA1 | 114 | F3 |
| Moffat Cl *PLMGR* N13 | 98 | F7 |
| *THHTH* CR7 | 203 | K2 |
| *TOOT* SW17 | 179 | P7 |
| Moffats Cl *BRKMPK* AL9 | 59 | K2 |
| Moffats La *BRKMPK* AL9 | 59 | H3 |
| Mogador Rd *KWD/TDW/WH* KT20 | 257 | H4 |
| Mogden La *ISLW* TW7 | 176 | A1 |
| Mohammad Khan Rd *WAN* E11 * | 121 | L6 |
| Moiety Rd *POP/IOD* E14 | 160 | F1 |
| Moira Cl *TOTM* N17 | 99 | M10 |
| Moira Rd *ELTH/MOT* SE9 | 162 | C10 |
| Moir Cl *SAND/SEL* CR2 | 223 | P5 |
| Molash Rd *STMC/STPC* BR5 | 207 | N4 |
| Mole Abbey Gdns *E/WMO/HCT* KT8 | 197 | P3 |
| Mole Cl *CRAWW* RH11 | 283 | L5 |
| Mole Ct *HOR/WEW* KT19 | 219 | P1 |
| Molember Ct *E/WMO/HCT* KT8 | 198 | D5 |
| Molember Rd *E/WMO/HCT* KT8 | 198 | D5 |
| Mole Rd *LHD/OX* KT22 | 236 | C7 |
| *WOT/HER* KT12 | 217 | L2 |
| Molescroft *ELTH/MOT* SE9 | 184 | F6 |
| Molesey Av *E/WMO/HCT* KT8 | 197 | N4 |
| Molesey Cl *WOT/HER* KT12 | 217 | L1 |
| Molesey Dr *CHEAM* SM3 | 201 | J6 |
| Molesey Park Av *E/WMO/HCT* KT8 | 198 | A5 |
| Molesey Park Cl *E/WMO/HCT* KT8 | 198 | B5 |
| Molesey Park Rd *E/WMO/HCT* KT8 | 198 | A5 |
| Molesey Rd *WOT/HER* KT12 | 217 | L2 |
| Molesford Rd *FUL/PGN* SW6 * | 157 | K7 |
| Molesham Cl *E/WMO/HCT* KT8 | 198 | A3 |
| Molesham Wy *E/WMO/HCT* KT8 | 198 | A4 |
| Moles Hl *LHD/OX* KT22 | 218 | C7 |
| Molesworth *HOD* EN11 | 26 | F9 |
| Molesworth St *LEW* SE13 | 161 | N9 |
| Mole Valley Pl *ASHTD* KT21 | 237 | J5 |
| Molewood Rd *HERT/WAT* SG14 | 25 | J4 |
| Mollands La *SOCK/AV* RM15 | 147 | K6 |
| Mollands La *SOCK/AV* RM15 | 147 | H6 |
| Mollison Av *PEND* EN3 | 80 | D6 |
| Mollison Dr *WLGTN* SM6 | 222 | F4 |
| Mollison Rd *CVE* DA12 | 191 | H8 |
| Mollison Wy *EDGW* HA8 | 95 | L10 |
| Molloy Ct *WOKN/KNAP* GU21 | 232 | D2 |
| Molly Huggins Cl *BAL* SW12 | 180 | D3 |
| Molteno Rd *WAT* WD17 | 73 | H5 |
| Molyneaux Av *HHS/BOV* HP3 | 52 | C5 |
| Molyneux Dr *TOOT* SW17 | 180 | C4 |
| Molyneux Rd *BFOR* GU20 | 212 | B3 |
| *GODL* GU7 | 267 | L6 |
| *WEY* KT13 | 216 | B3 |
| Molyneux's La *MBLAR* W1H * | 9 | J1 |
| Momples Rd *HLW* CM20 | 29 | K10 |
| Monahan Av *PUR/KEN* CR8 | 222 | G8 |
| Monarch Cl *CRAWW* RH11 | 283 | K10 |
| *EBED/NFELT* TW14 | 174 | F3 |
| *RAIN* RM13 | 145 | H4 |
| *TIL* RM18 | 168 | G8 |
| *WWKM* BR4 | 225 | L1 |
| Monarch Dr *CAN/RD* E16 | 142 | A7 |
| Monarch Ms *STRHM/NOR* SW16 | 181 | N8 |
| Monarch Pde *MTCM* CR4 * | 202 | A2 |
| Monarch Pl *BKHH* IG9 | 101 | P3 |
| Monarch Rd *BELV* DA17 | 164 | B2 |
| Monarchs Wy *RSLP* HA4 | 112 | F6 |
| Monarch's Wy *CHES/WCR* EN8 | 62 | D9 |
| Monarch Wk *GNTH/NBYPK* IG2 | 122 | F4 |
| Mona Rd *PECK* SE15 | 160 | B8 |
| Monastery Ct *STALW/RED* AL3 * | 38 | B6 |
| Monastery Gdns *ENC/FH* EN2 | 79 | N1 |
| Mona St *CAN/RD* E16 | 141 | L7 |
| Monaveen Gdns *E/WMO/HCT* KT8 | 198 | A3 |
| Monck's Rw *WAND/EARL* SW18 | 179 | J2 |
| Monck St *WEST* SW1P | 17 | K4 |
| Monclar Rd *CMBW* SE5 | 159 | L10 |
| Moncorvo Cl *SKENS* SW7 | 15 | N2 |
| Moncrieff Cl *EHAM* E6 | 142 | A6 |
| Moncrieff St *PECK* SE15 | 160 | A8 |
| Monday Aly *STNW/STAM* N16 | 119 | K8 |
| Monega Rd *FSTGT* E7 | 141 | P2 |
| *MNPK* E12 | 141 | P2 |
| Money Av *CTHM* CR3 | 241 | L8 |
| Moneyhill Ct *RKW/CH/CXG* WD3 * | 91 | L2 |
| Money Hill Rd *RKW/CH/CXG* WD3 | 91 | M2 |
| Money Hole La *WLYN* AL6 | 23 | M4 |
| Money Rd *WDR/YW* UB7 | 151 | N2 |
| Money Rd *CTHM* CR3 | 241 | L9 |
| Mongers La *EW* KT17 | 220 | C6 |
| Monica Cl *WATN* WD24 | 73 | J4 |
| Monier Rd *BOW* E3 | 140 | A2 |
| Moniva Rd *BECK* BR3 | 182 | B3 |
| Monkchester Cl *LOU* IG10 | 82 | D5 |
| Monk Dr *CAN/RD* E16 | 141 | M9 |
| Monkfrith Av *STHGT/OAK* N14 | 78 | C10 |
| Monkfrith Wy *STHGT/OAK* N14 | 98 | C1 |
| Monkham's Av *WFD* IG8 | 101 | K4 |
| Monkham's Dr *WFD* IG8 | 101 | L4 |
| Monkham's La *WFD* IG8 | 101 | K3 |
| Monks Av *BAR* EN5 | 77 | H7 |
| *E/WMO/HCT* KT8 | 197 | M5 |
| Monksbury *CLAY* IG5 | 142 | F4 |
| Monks Cha *RBRW/HUT* CM15 | 107 | P6 |
| Monks Cl *ABR/ST* RM4 | 87 | H1 |
| *ASC* SL5 | 192 | A6 |
| *BROX* EN10 | 44 | F4 |
| *ENC/FH* EN2 | 79 | L6 |
| *RSLP* HA4 | 113 | L9 |
| *RYLN/HDSTN* HA2 * | 113 | P7 |

| | | | |
|---|---|---|---|
| *STAL* AL1 | 38 | D8 |
| Monksdene Gdns *SUT* SM1 | 201 | M1 |
| Monks Dr *ASC* SL5 | 192 | A6 |
| *ASC* SL5 * | 192 | A6 |
| Monksfield Wy *SLN* SL2 | 128 | F6 |
| Monks Ga *SLN* SL2 | 38 | D8 |
| Monks Gn *RAD* WD7 | 57 | L7 |
| Monks Horton Wy *STAL* AL1 | 38 | F4 |
| Monksmead *BORE* WD6 | 75 | H4 |
| Monks Orchard Rd *BECK* BR3 | 204 | B8 |
| Monks Pk *WBLY* HA9 | 135 | N1 |
| Monks Park Gdns *WBLY* HA9 | 135 | N1 |
| Monks Rd *ENC/FH* EN2 | 79 | J6 |
| *WGCW* AL8 | 22 | G1 |
| Monks Rw *WARE* SG12 * | 26 | C1 |
| Monks Wk *WOOL/PLUM* SE18 | 162 | D3 |
| Monk St *WOOL/PLUM* SE18 | 146 | G9 |
| Monks Wy *BECK* BR3 | 204 | F6 |
| *GLDGN* NW11 | 117 | J2 |
| *STA* TW18 | 173 | N10 |
| *STMC/STPC* BR5 | 206 | F8 |
| Monks Well *SWCM* DA10 | 169 | J10 |
| Monkswell Ct *COUL/CHIP* CR5 | 239 | L10 |
| Monkswick Rd *HLW* CM20 | 29 | H9 |
| Monkswood *WGCW* AL8 | 22 | F1 |
| Monkswood Av *WAB* EN9 | 59 | J9 |
| Monkswood Gdns *BORE* WD6 | 76 | D1 |
| *CLAY* IG5 | 122 | D1 |
| Monk Ter *FSTH* SE23 | 182 | S5 |
| Monkton Rd *WELL* DA16 | 163 | J8 |
| Monkton St *LBTH* SE11 | 18 | B5 |
| Monkville Av *GLDGN* NW11 | 117 | J2 |
| Monkville Pde *GLDGN* NW11 * | 12 | F4 |
| Monkwell Sq *BARB* EC2Y | 12 | F4 |
| Monkwood Cl *ROM* RM1 | 105 | L5 |
| Monmouth Av *KUT/HW* KT1 | 199 | J3 |
| *SWFD* E18 | 102 | D10 |
| Monmouth Cl *CHSWK* W4 | 156 | A2 |
| *MTCM* CR4 | 202 | F2 |
| *WELL* DA16 | 163 | G6 |
| Monmouth Gv *BTFD* TW8 | 155 | K3 |
| Monmouth Pl *BAY/PAD* W2 * | 8 | F6 |
| Monmouth Rd *BAY/PAD* W2 | 8 | F6 |
| *DAGW* RM9 | 124 | A10 |
| *ED* N9 | 100 | A3 |
| *EHAM* E6 | 142 | G5 |
| *HYS/HAR* UB3 | 152 | K5 |
| *WAT* WD17 | 73 | J7 |
| Monmouth St *LSO/SEVD* WC2H | 11 | L6 |
| Monnery Rd *ARCH* N19 | 118 | C3 |
| Monnow Rd *SOCK/AV* RM15 | 146 | B9 |
| *STHWK* SE1 | 19 | N6 |
| Mono La *FELT* TW13 | 175 | L5 |
| Monoux Gv *WALTH* E17 | 100 | K9 |
| Monro Dr *GUW* GU2 | 249 | N1 |
| Monroe Crs *EN* EN1 | 80 | A1 |
| Monroe Dr *MORT/ESHN* SW14 | 177 | N1 |
| Monro Gdns *KTN/HRWW/WS* HA3 | 94 | D9 |
| Monroe Rd *HOR/WEW* KT19 | 219 | M5 |
| Mons Cl *HARP* AL5 | 20 | C5 |
| Monsell Rd *FSBYPK* N4 | 119 | J3 |
| Monson Rd *BROX* EN10 | 44 | E6 |
| *NWCR* SE14 | 160 | C6 |
| *REDH* RH1 | 258 | A3 |
| *WLSDN* NW10 | 136 | D4 |
| Mons Wy *EGH* TW20 | 172 | B6 |
| Mons Wy *HAYES* BR2 | 206 | B6 |
| Montacute Rd *BUSH* WD23 | 94 | D1 |
| *CAT* SE6 | 182 | E3 |
| *CROY/NA* CR0 | 225 | H5 |
| *MRDN* SM4 | 201 | N6 |
| Montagu Crs *UED* N18 | 100 | A5 |
| Montague Av *BROCKY* SE4 | 160 | E10 |
| *HNWL* W7 | 134 | E10 |
| *SAND/SEL* CR2 | 223 | M9 |
| Montagu Gdns *BAR* EN5 | 77 | J8 |
| *UED* N18 | 100 | A5 |
| *WLGTN* SM6 | 222 | E2 |
| Montagu Man *MHST* W1U * | 10 | A2 |
| Montagu Ms North *MBLAR* W1H | 10 | A3 |
| Montagu Ms South *MBLAR* W1H | 10 | A4 |
| Montagu Ms West *MBLAR* W1H | 10 | A4 |
| Montague Pl *MBLAR* W1H | 10 | A3 |
| Montague Rd *DTCH/LGLY* SL3 | 149 | N7 |
| *HDN* NW4 | 116 | A2 |
| *UED* N18 | 100 | A5 |
| Montagu Rw *MHST* W1U | 10 | A3 |
| Montague Sq *PECK* SE15 | 160 | C6 |
| Montague Ter *HAYES* BR2 * | 205 | M4 |
| Montague Waye *NWDGN* UB2 | 153 | N2 |
| Montagu Rd *UED* N18 | 100 | A5 |
| *WLGTN* SM6 | 222 | E2 |
| Montalt Rd *WFD* IG8 | 101 | L6 |
| Montana Cl *SAND/SEL* CR2 | 223 | L6 |
| *SUT* SM1 | 221 | M2 |
| *SYD* SE26 | 182 | D7 |
| Montana Rd *RYNPK* SW20 | 200 | F1 |
| *TOOT* SW17 | 180 | F6 |
| Montbelle Rd *ELTH/MOT* SE9 | 184 | C3 |
| Montbretia Cl *STMC/STPC* BR5 | 207 | M4 |
| Montcalm Cl *HAYES* BR2 | 205 | N7 |
| *YEAD* UB4 | 133 | J5 |
| Montcalm Rd *CHARL* SE7 | 162 | D7 |
| Montclare St *BETH* E2 | 7 | L10 |
| Monteagle Av *BARK* IG11 | 141 | H5 |
| Monteagle Wy *PECK* SE15 | 160 | F1 |
| Montefiore St *VX/NE* SW8 | 158 | D8 |
| Montem La *KUT/HW* KT1 | 191 | J1 |
| Montem Rd *FSTH* SE23 | 162 | B4 |
| *NWMAL* KT3 | 200 | C2 |
| Montem St *FSBYPK* N4 | 118 | N4 |
| Montenotte Rd *CEND/HSY/T* N8 | 118 | B1 |
| Monterey Cl *BXLY* DA5 | 186 | D6 |
| Montesole Ct *PIN* HA5 | 93 | K10 |
| Montesquieu Ter *CAN/RD* E16 * | 141 | L8 |
| Montford Pl *LBTH* SE11 | 17 | M8 |
| Montford Rd *SUN* TW16 | 195 | H4 |
| Montfort Gdns *BARK/HLT* IG6 | 102 | F2 |
| Montfort Pl *WIM/MER* SW19 | 178 | F9 |
| Montfort Ri *REDH* RH1 | 276 | E4 |
| Montgomerie Cl *BERK* HP4 | 33 | M3 |
| Montgomerie Dr *GUW* GU2 | 249 | M5 |

| | | | |
|---|---|---|---|
| Montgomery Ms *FSTH* SE23 | 182 | B3 |
| Montgomery Av | | |
| *ESH/CLAY* KT10 | 198 | D9 |
| *HHNE* HP2 | 36 | B5 |
| Montgomery Cl *BFN/LL* DA15 | 185 | H1 |
| *CRAWE* RH10 | 285 | K7 |
| *HHW* HP1 | 35 | J8 |
| *WDR/YW* UB7 | 23 | K8 |
| Montgomery Crs *HARH* RM3 | 105 | L6 |
| Montgomery Dr *CHES/WCR* EN8 | 62 | D4 |
| Montgomery Gdns *BELMT* SM2 | 221 | N4 |
| Montgomery Pl *SLN* SL2 | 129 | P8 |
| Montgomery Rd *CHSWK* W4 | 155 | L7 |
| *EDGW* HA8 | 95 | L7 |
| *EYN* DA4 | 210 | C1 |
| *RKW/CH/CXG* WD3 | 91 | J3 |
| *STWL/WRAY* TW19 | 172 | F4 |
| *UPMR* RM14 | 126 | E6 |
| *WDR/YW* UB7 | 151 | M5 |
| Montgomery St *POP/IOD* E14 | 140 | F9 |
| Montholme Rd *BTSEA* SW11 | 180 | A2 |
| Monthope Rd *WCHPL* E1 | 13 | N2 |
| Montolieu Gdns *PUT/ROE* SW15 | 178 | E1 |
| Montpelier Av *BXLY* DA5 | 185 | H7 |
| *EA* W5 | 135 | H7 |
| Montpelier Gdns *HGDN/ICK* UB10 | 123 | M5 |
| *CHDH* RM6 | 123 | M5 |
| *EHAM* E6 | 142 | G3 |
| Montpelier Gv *KTTN* NW5 | 118 | D10 |
| Montpelier Ms *SKENS* SW7 | 15 | P3 |
| Montpelier Pl *SKENS* SW7 | 15 | P3 |
| *WCHPL* E1 | 140 | E8 |
| Montpelier Ri *GLDGN* NW11 | 117 | J3 |
| *WBLY* HA9 | 115 | J6 |
| Montpelier Rd *EA* W5 | 135 | M3 |
| *FNCH* N3 | 97 | M9 |
| *PECK* SE15 | 160 | C7 |
| *PUR/KEN* CR8 | 223 | J6 |
| *SUT* SM1 | 221 | M1 |
| Montpelier Rw *BKHTH/KID* SE3 | 161 | L8 |
| *TWK* TW1 | 176 | C3 |
| Montpelier Sq *SKENS* SW7 | 15 | P2 |
| Montpelier St *SKENS* SW7 | 15 | P3 |
| Montpelier Ter *SKENS* SW7 | 15 | P2 |
| Montpelier V *BKHTH/KID* SE3 * | 161 | L8 |
| Montpelier Wk *SKENS* SW7 | 15 | P3 |
| Montpelier Wy *GLDGN* NW11 | 117 | H3 |
| Montrave Rd *PGE/AN* SE20 | 181 | M10 |
| Montreal Pl *HOL/ALD* WC2B | 11 | N7 |
| Montreal Rd *IL* IG1 | 122 | E2 |
| *SEV* TN13 | 246 | F9 |
| *TIL* RM18 | 153 | B6 |
| Montrell Rd *BRXS/STRHM* SW2 | 181 | J2 |
| Montrose Av *BFN/LL* DA15 | 185 | K5 |
| *DTCH/LGLY* SL3 | 149 | P6 |
| *EDGW* HA8 | 96 | A10 |
| *GPK* RM2 | 105 | K10 |
| *KIL/WHAMP* NW6 | 2 | A1 |
| *ROM* RM1 | 105 | H9 |
| *WHTN* TW2 | 176 | A3 |
| *WLSDN* NW10 | 137 | H3 |
| Montrose Cl *ASHF* TW15 | 174 | D9 |
| *WELL* DA16 | 164 | E3 |
| *WFD* IG8 | 101 | H2 |
| *WHTN* TW2 | 176 | A3 |
| Montrose Crs *ALP/SUD* HA0 | 135 | K1 |
| *NFNCH/WDSPK* N12 | 97 | H5 |
| Montrose Gdns *LHD/OX* KT22 | 218 | C4 |
| *MTCM* CR4 | 202 | A8 |
| *SUT* SM1 | 201 | L9 |
| Montrose Pl *KTBR* SW1X | 16 | D2 |
| Montrose Rd *EBED/NFELT* TW14 | 174 | E2 |
| *KTN/HRWW/WS* HA3 | 94 | D10 |
| Montrose Vls *HMSMTH* W6 * | 156 | D4 |
| Montrose Wy *DTCH/LGLY* SL3 | 150 | C10 |
| *FSTH* SE23 | 182 | C4 |
| Montrouge Crs *EW* KT17 | 238 | F2 |
| Montserrat Av *WFD* IG8 | 101 | J8 |
| Montserrat Cl *NRWD* SE19 | 181 | L8 |
| Montserrat Rd *PUT/ROE* SW15 | 178 | B3 |
| Monument Hl *WEY* KT13 | 216 | C1 |
| Monument La *CFSP/GDCR* SL9 | 90 | B7 |
| Monument Rd *WEY* KT13 | 216 | C1 |
| *WOKN/KNAP* GU21 | 214 | D10 |
| Monument St *MON* EC3R | 13 | J7 |
| Monument Wy East *WOKN/KNAP* GU21 | 232 | D2 |
| Monument Wy West *WOKN/KNAP* GU21 | 232 | D2 |
| Monza St *WAP* E1W | 140 | B9 |
| Moodkee St *BERM/RHTH* SE16 | 140 | A8 |
| Moody Rd *PECK* SE15 | 159 | G7 |
| Moody St *WCHPL* E1 | 140 | D1 |
| Moon Ct *LEE/GVPK* SE12 * | 161 | N10 |
| Moon La *BAR* EN5 | 76 | C4 |
| Moon St *IS* N1 | 5 | P1 |
| Moorcroft *EDGW* HA8 | 96 | A10 |
| Moorcroft Gdns *HAYES* BR2 | 206 | C3 |
| Moorcroft La *UX/CGN* UB8 | 132 | B10 |
| Moorcroft Rd *STRHM/NOR* SW16 | 181 | J5 |
| Moordown *WOOL/PLUM* SE18 | 164 | E1 |
| Moore Cl *ADL/WDHM* KT15 | 215 | L6 |
| *MORT/ESHN* SW14 | 155 | N8 |
| *RDART* DA2 | 188 | D3 |
| *WLGTN* SM6 | 223 | J5 |
| Moore Crs *DAGW* RM9 | 143 | G7 |
| Moorefield Rd *TOTM* N17 | 119 | H2 |
| Moore Grove Crs *EGH* TW20 | 172 | B10 |
| Moore Pk Rd *FUL/PGN* SW6 | 157 | L5 |
| Moore Rd *BERK* HP4 | 33 | K8 |
| *NRWD* SE19 | 181 | M8 |
| Moore Wy *BELMT* SM2 | 221 | L8 |
| Moorey Cl *SRTFD* E15 | 140 | D2 |
| Moorfield *RDKG* RH5 | 273 | J10 |
| Moorfield Av *EA* W5 | 135 | K3 |
| Moorfield Point *GU* GU1 | 250 | B6 |
| Moorfield Rd *CHSGTN* KT9 | 236 | B3 |
| *DEN/HRF* UB9 | 111 | J9 |
| *GU* GU1 | 250 | A6 |
| *ORP* BR6 | 207 | N8 |
| *PEND* EN3 | 80 | D1 |
| *UX/CGN* UB8 | 131 | H8 |
| Moorfields *HLWS* CM18 | 46 | A1 |
| Moorfields Highwalk *BARB* EC2Y | 12 | G3 |
| Moor Furlong *SL* SL1 | 131 | H1 |
| Moorgate *LOTH* EC2R | 12 | G4 |
| Moorgate Pl *LOTH* EC2R * | 12 | G5 |
| Moorhall Rd *DEN/HRF* UB9 | 111 | J5 |
| Moor Hall Rd *HLWE* CM17 | 30 | A1 |
| Moorhayes Dr *STA* TW18 | 195 | H3 |
| Moorhen Cl *ERITH* DA8 | 165 | J10 |
| Moorhen Wy *HLWW/ROY* CM19 | 29 | M10 |
| Moorholme *WOKS/MYFD* GU22 | 232 | B6 |
| Moorhouse Rd *BAY/PAD* W2 | 8 | C6 |
| *KTN/HRWW/WS* HA3 | 114 | G1 |
| *OXTED* RH8 | 261 | J9 |
| Moorhurst Av *CHESW* EN7 | 61 | J5 |
| The Moorings *BF/WBF* KT14 | 231 | N1 |
| *BUSH* WD23 | 75 | M8 |
| *CHSWK* W4 * | 155 | M6 |
| *GT/LBKH* KT23 | 253 | P1 |

| | | | |
|---|---|---|---|
| *WDSR* SL4 | 148 | C6 |
| Moorland Cl *CRW* RM5 | 104 | C9 |
| *WHTN* TW2 | 175 | J4 |
| Moorland Rd *BRXN/ST* SW9 | 159 | J10 |
| *CRAWE* RH10 | 285 | K8 |
| *HHW* HP1 | 35 | J8 |
| *WDR/YW* UB7 | 23 | K8 |
| Moorlands *LCOL/BKTW* AL2 * | 56 | D4 |
| *WGCE* AL7 | 23 | K8 |
| Moorlands Av *MLHL* NW7 | 96 | E7 |
| Moorlands Reach *SBW* CM21 * | 30 | A2 |
| The Moorlands *WOKS/MYFD* GU22 | 232 | B8 |
| Moor La *BARB* EC2Y | 13 | G2 |
| *CHSGTN* KT9 | 219 | K11 |
| *RKW/CH/CXG* WD3 | 91 | P3 |
| *STWL/WRAY* TW19 | 172 | F4 |
| *UPMR* RM14 | 126 | H9 |
| *WDR/YW* UB7 | 247 | H6 |
| *WOKS/MYFD* GU22 | 247 | J6 |
| Moor Mead Rd *TWK* TW1 | 176 | B2 |
| Moormede Crs *STA* TW18 | 22 | C8 |
| Moor Mill La *LCOL/BKTW* AL2 | 56 | D5 |
| Moor Pk *HORL* RH6 * | 282 | G8 |
| Moor Park Crs *CRAWW* RH11 | 282 | G8 |
| Moor Park Gdns *KUTN/CMB* KT2 | 178 | B10 |
| Moor Park Rd *NTHWD* HA6 | 92 | D7 |
| Moorpark Dr *BFOR* GU20 | 212 | A2 |
| Moor Rd *CSHM* HP5 | 51 | H9 |
| The Moor *REDH* RH1 | 247 | J6 |
| Moorside *WGCE* AL7 | 23 | K8 |
| Moorside Rd *BMLY* BR1 | 183 | K8 |
| Moorsom Wy *COUL/CHIP* CR5 | 240 | D4 |
| The Moors *REDH* RH1 | 258 | D7 |
| *WGCE* AL7 | 23 | K4 |
| Moorstown Ct *SL* SL1 * | 149 | K1 |
| Moor St *SOHO/SHAV* W1D | 11 | K6 |
| Moors Wk *WGCE* AL7 | 23 | K5 |
| Moorsyde Av *OXHEY* WD19 | 93 | K5 |
| Moor Vw *WATW* WD18 | 93 | H5 |
| Moor Wy *WATW* WD18 | 93 | H1 |
| Moran Cl *LCOL/BKTW* AL2 | 56 | N7 |
| Morant Gdns *CDW/CHF* RH | 104 | C6 |
| Morant Rd *CDW/CHF* RH | 168 | B2 |
| Morants Court Rd *SEV* TN13 | 264 | F2 |
| Morant St *POP/IOD* E14 | 140 | F9 |
| Mora Rd *CRICK* NW2 | 116 | F9 |
| Mora St *FSBYE* EC1V | 6 | F10 |
| Morat St *BRXN/ST* SW9 | 158 | A7 |
| Moravia Cl *BETH* E2 * | 140 | B2 |
| Moravian Pl *WBPTN* SW10 * | 15 | M10 |
| Moravian St *BETH* E2 | 140 | B1 |
| Moray Av *HYS/HAR* UB3 | 132 | E9 |
| Moray Cl *EDGW* HA8 | 95 | N3 |
| *ROM* RM1 * | 105 | L2 |
| Moray Dr *SLN* SL2 | 129 | M8 |
| Moray Ms *HOLWY* N7 | 118 | C7 |
| Moray Rd *HOLWY* N7 | 118 | C7 |
| Moray Wy *ROM* RM1 | 105 | L1 |
| Morcambe Cl *EMPK* RM11 | 125 | P6 |
| *WCHPL* E1 | 14 | E1 |
| Morcambe Gdns *STAN* HA7 | 95 | N5 |
| Morcambe St *POP/IOD* E14 | 19 | L8 |
| *WALW* SE17 | 19 | L8 |
| Mordaunt Gdns *DAGW* RM9 | 143 | J6 |
| Mordaunt Rd *WLSDN* NW10 | 136 | A3 |
| Mordaunt St *BRXN/ST* SW9 | 159 | B9 |
| Morden Cl *KWD/TDW/WH* KT20 | 257 | L2 |
| Morden Ct *MRDN* SM4 | 201 | L4 |
| Morden Court Pde *MRDN* SM4 * | 201 | L3 |
| Morden Gdns *GFD/PVL* UB6 | 114 | E10 |
| *MTCM* CR4 | 201 | N4 |
| Morden Hall Rd *MRDN* SM4 | 201 | L4 |
| Morden Hl *LEW* SE13 | 161 | M9 |
| Morden La *LEW* SE13 | 161 | M8 |
| Morden Rd *BKHTH/KID* SE3 | 161 | L8 |
| *CHDH* RM6 | 124 | A5 |
| *MRDN* SM4 | 201 | L4 |
| *WIM/MER* SW19 | 201 | L2 |
| Morden Rd Ms *BKHTH/KID* SE3 | 161 | L8 |
| Morden St *LEW* SE13 | 161 | L8 |
| Morden Wy *CHEAM* SM3 | 201 | K7 |
| Morden Wharf Rd *GNWCH* SE10 | 141 | K6 |
| Mordon Rd *GDMY/SEVK* IG3 | 123 | J2 |
| Mordred Rd *CAT* SE6 | 183 | H3 |
| Moreau Wk *DTCH/LGLY* SL3 * | 130 | B9 |
| Morecambe Cl *CRAWW* RH11 | 283 | K10 |
| *HCH* RM12 | 125 | J10 |
| *WCHPL* E1 | 14 | E1 |
| Morecambe Gdns *STAN* HA7 | 95 | N5 |
| Morecambe St *POP/IOD* E14 | 19 | L8 |
| *WALW* SE17 | 19 | L8 |
| More Cl *CAN/RD* E16 | 141 | J8 |
| *PUR/KEN* CR8 | 223 | J6 |
| *WKENS* W14 | 156 | G1 |
| Morecote Cl *RGUE* GU4 | 268 | D7 |
| Moree Wy *UED* N18 | 99 | P5 |
| Moreland Cl *CFSP/GDCR* SL9 | 90 | A3 |
| *CRICK* NW2 | 117 | J3 |
| Moreland Cots *BOW* E3 * | 140 | A1 |
| Moreland Dr *CFSP/GDCR* SL9 | 90 | C4 |
| Morelands Av *CDW/CHF* RH | 167 | P3 |
| Moreland St *FSBYE* EC1V | 6 | D8 |
| Moreland Wy *CHING* E4 | 101 | N1 |
| More La *ESH/CLAY* KT10 | 198 | A10 |
| Morel Ct *SEV* TN13 | 246 | F9 |
| Morella Rd *BTSEA* SW11 | 180 | A1 |
| Morello Av *UX/CGN* UB8 | 132 | C7 |
| Morello Cl *SWLY* BR8 | 208 | G4 |
| Morello Dr *DTCH/LGLY* SL3 | 130 | C10 |
| More London Riverside *STHWK* SE1 | 13 | K10 |
| Moremead *WAB* EN9 | 63 | J9 |
| Moremead Rd *CAT* SE6 | 182 | E5 |
| Morena St *CAT* SE6 | 182 | B5 |
| More Rd *GODL* GU7 | 267 | L6 |
| Moresby Av *BRYLDS* KT5 | 199 | N7 |
| Moresby Rd *CLPT* E5 | 138 | D4 |
| Mores La *BRW* CM14 | 86 | D6 |
| Moretaine Rd *ASHF* TW15 | 174 | D7 |
| Moreton Av *ISLW* TW7 | 176 | A5 |
| Moreton Cl *CHESW* EN7 | 62 | A3 |
| *CHSWK* W4 | 62 | A3 |
| *CLPT* E5 | 120 | B8 |
| *MLHL* NW7 | 97 | J5 |
| *SEVS/STOTM* N15 | 119 | H9 |
| *STHGT/OAK* N14 | 222 | C5 |
| Moreton Gdns *WFD* IG8 | 102 | B7 |
| Moreton Pl *PIM* SW1V | 17 | H7 |
| Moreton Rd *SAND/SEL* CR2 | 211 | P9 |
| *WPK* KT4 | 200 | G9 |
| Moreton Ter *PIM* SW1V | 17 | H7 |
| Moreton Terrace Ms North *PIM* SW1V | 17 | H7 |
| Moreton Terrace Ms South *PIM* SW1V | 17 | H7 |
| Moreton St *PIM* SW1V | 17 | H7 |
| Morewood Cl *SEV* TN13 | 246 | C10 |
| Morford Cl *RSLP* HA4 | 113 | H5 |
| Morford Wy *RSLP* HA4 | 113 | J5 |
| Morgan Av *WALTH* E17 | 120 | F2 |
| Morgan Cl *DAGE* RM10 | 144 | B4 |
| Morgan Ct *ASHF* TW15 * | 174 | D7 |
| Morgan Dr *RDART* DA2 | 188 | D10 |
| Morgan Gdns *GSTN* WD25 | 73 | M6 |
| Morgan Rd *BMLY* BR1 | 183 | M6 |
| *HOLWY* N7 | 118 | F10 |
| *NKENS* W10 | 8 | B1 |
| Morgans Cl *HERT/BAY* SG13 | 51 | K3 |
| Morgans La *HYS/HAR* UB3 | 132 | E6 |
| *STHWK* SE1 | 13 | K9 |
| Morgan St *BOW* E3 | 139 | M7 |
| *CAN/RD* E16 | 141 | J6 |
| Morgans Wk *RAIN* RM13 | 145 | K10 |
| Morgan Wy *RAIN* RM13 | 145 | J7 |
| *WFD* IG8 | 102 | G6 |
| Moriarty Cl *BMLY* BR1 | 206 | F4 |
| *HOLWY* N7 | 118 | D9 |
| Moriatry Cl *HOLWY* N7 | 118 | D9 |

| | | | |
|---|---|---|---|
| Morice Rd *HOD* EN11 | 44 | E1 |
| Morie St *WAND/EARL* SW18 | 157 | L10 |
| Morieux Rd *LEY* E10 | 120 | E6 |
| Moring Rd *TOOT* SW17 | 180 | R7 |
| Morkyns Wk *DUL* SE21 * | 181 | M6 |
| Morland Av *CROY/NA* CR0 | 203 | M8 |
| *GLDGN* NW11 | 175 | N8 |
| Morland Cl *GLDGN* NW11 | 28 | F10 |
| *HPTN* TW12 | 175 | H8 |
| *MTCM* CR4 | 201 | P3 |
| Morland Est *HACK* E8 | 7 | P3 |
| Morland Gdns *STHL* UB1 | 134 | A10 |
| *WLSDN* NW10 | 136 | A2 |
| Morland Ms *IS* N1 | 6 | B4 |
| Morland Rd *CROY/NA* CR0 | 203 | N7 |
| *DAGE* RM10 | 144 | B2 |
| *IL* IG1 | 115 | A3 |
| *KTN/HRWW/WS* HA3 | 182 | C10 |
| *PGE/AN* SE20 | 221 | M2 |
| *SUT* SM1 | 221 | M2 |
| *WALTH* E17 | 120 | C3 |
| Morland Wy *CHES/WCR* EN8 | 62 | D4 |
| Morley Av *CHING* E4 | 101 | J8 |
| *UED* N18 | 99 | M9 |
| *WDGN* N22 | 99 | H10 |
| Morley Cl *DTCH/LGLY* SL3 | 150 | C1 |
| *ORP* BR6 | 206 | G9 |
| Morley Crs *EDGW* HA8 | 96 | P5 |
| *RSLP* HA4 | 113 | K2 |
| Morley Crs East *STAN* HA7 | 115 | H1 |
| Morley Crs West *STAN* HA7 | 115 | H1 |
| Morley Gv *HLW* CM20 | 28 | F10 |
| Morley Hl *ENC/FH* EN2 | 79 | L4 |
| Morley Rd *BARK* IG11 | 142 | C5 |
| *CHDH* RM6 | 123 | P5 |
| *CHST* BR7 | 206 | F1 |
| *LEW* SE13 | 161 | H10 |
| *LEY* E10 | 120 | C10 |
| *SAND/SEL* CR2 | 223 | N6 |
| *SRTFD* E15 | 141 | L4 |
| *TWK* TW1 | 177 | J2 |
| Morley Sq *CDW/CHF* RH | 168 | D3 |
| Morley's Rd *RSEV* TN14 | 265 | L9 |
| Morley St *STHWK* SE1 | 18 | B3 |
| Morna Rd *CMBW* SE5 | 159 | K8 |
| Morning La *HOM* E9 | 138 | B1 |
| Morningside Rd *WPK* KT4 | 200 | G10 |
| Mornington Av *ENC/FH* EN2 | 79 | J2 |
| *IL* IG1 | 122 | C5 |
| *WKENS* W14 | 14 | C11 |
| Mornington Cl *BXLY* DA5 | 186 | E4 |
| *WFD* IG8 | 101 | J2 |
| Mornington Crs *CAMTN* NW1 | 4 | F3 |
| *HEST* TW5 | 153 | J7 |
| Mornington Gv *BOW* E3 | 139 | M7 |
| Mornington Ms *CMBW* SE5 | 159 | J7 |
| Mornington Pl *CAMTN* NW1 * | 4 | F3 |
| Mornington Rd *ASHF* TW15 | 174 | D8 |
| *CHING* E4 | 101 | J4 |
| *GFD/PVL* UB6 | 153 | L1 |
| *NWCR* SE14 | 160 | E6 |
| *RAD* WD7 | 56 | F10 |
| *WAN* E11 | 121 | L6 |
| *WFD* IG8 | 101 | L5 |
| Morningtons *HLWW/ROY* CM19 | 46 | A2 |
| Mornington St *CAMTN* NW1 | 4 | F3 |
| Mornington Ter *CAMTN* NW1 | 4 | E2 |
| Mornington Wk *RCHPK/HAM* TW10 | 177 | H7 |
| Morocco St *STHWK* SE1 | 19 | L2 |
| Morpeth Av *BORE* WD6 | 75 | L4 |
| Morpeth Gv *HHNE* HP2 | 35 | P7 |
| Morpeth Gv *HOM* E9 | 140 | C2 |
| Morpeth Rd *HOM* E9 | 140 | C2 |
| Morpeth St *BETH* E2 | 140 | C1 |
| Morpeth Ter *WEST* SW1P | 16 | F4 |
| Morpeth Wk *TOTM* N17 * | 100 | D6 |
| Morrab Gdns *GDMY/SEVK* IG3 | 123 | J2 |
| Morrel Cl *BAR* EN5 | 77 | M7 |
| Morrell's Yd *LBTH* SE11 * | 18 | B7 |
| Morrice Cl *DTCH/LGLY* SL3 | 150 | C3 |
| Morris Av *MNPK* E12 | 122 | C10 |
| Morris Bishop Ter *HGT* N6 * | 90 | C9 |
| Morris Cl *CFSP/GDCR* SL9 | 90 | C3 |
| *CROY/NA* CR0 | 206 | C4 |
| *ORP* BR6 | 207 | H10 |
| Morris Ct *CHING* E4 | 100 | F3 |
| *WAB* EN9 | 63 | L10 |
| Morris Gdns | | |
| *WAND/EARL* SW18 | 179 | K3 |
| Morrish Rd *BRXS/STRHM* SW2 | 180 | F3 |
| Morrison Av *CHING* E4 | 100 | F3 |
| *TOTM* N17 | 99 | M7 |
| Morrison Rd *BARK* IG11 | 143 | M2 |
| *YEAD* UB4 | 133 | J5 |
| Morrison St *BTSEA* SW11 | 159 | J9 |
| Morris Pl *FSBYPK* N4 | 118 | A7 |
| Morris Rd *BCTR* RM8 | 124 | A7 |
| *HARH* RM3 | 105 | J3 |
| *ISLW* TW7 | 176 | A7 |
| *POP/IOD* E14 | 140 | C7 |
| *REDH* RH1 | 276 | F2 |
| *SRTFD* E15 | 121 | K9 |
| Morris St *WCHPL* E1 | 140 | E8 |
| Morriston Cl *OXHEY* WD19 | 93 | K6 |
| Morris Wy *LCOL/BKTW* AL2 | 57 | J2 |
| Morse Cl *DEN/HRF* UB9 * | 91 | M10 |
| *PLSTW* E13 | 141 | M1 |
| Morshead Rd *MV/WKIL* W9 | 2 | D10 |
| Morson Rd *PEND* EN3 | 80 | D10 |
| Morston Cl *KWD/TDW/WH* KT20 | 238 | E6 |
| Mortain Dr *BECK* BR3 | 33 | L3 |
| Morten Gdns *DEN/HRF* UB9 | 111 | K5 |
| Mortens Wd *AMS* HP6 | 67 | L6 |
| Morteyne Rd *TOTM* N17 | 99 | L9 |
| Mortham St *SRTFD* E15 | 141 | K3 |
| Mortimer Cl *BUSH* WD23 | 74 | A10 |
| *CRICK* NW2 | 117 | K7 |
| *STRHM/NOR* SW16 | 180 | E5 |
| Mortimer Crs *KIL/WHAMP* NW6 | 2 | C1 |
| *WPK* KT4 | 200 | G9 |
| Mortimer Dr *EN* EN1 | 79 | P5 |
| Mortimer Ga *CHES/WCR* EN8 | 62 | G2 |
| Mortimer Pl *KIL/WHAMP* NW6 | 2 | C1 |
| Mortimer Rd *DTCH/LGLY* SL3 | 150 | A2 |
| *EHAM* E6 | 142 | E3 |
| *ERITH* DA8 | 164 | E5 |
| *IS* N1 | 7 | K1 |
| *MTCM* CR4 | 202 | A2 |
| *ORP* BR6 | 207 | K9 |
| *WEA* W13 | 135 | H6 |
| *WLSDN* NW10 | 136 | F5 |
| Mortimer Sq *NTGHL* W11 | 10 | F7 |
| Mortimer St *GTPST* W1W | 10 | F5 |
| Mortimer Ter *KTTN* NW5 * | 118 | C10 |
| Mortlake Cl *CROY/NA* CR0 | 222 | G1 |
| Mortlake Dr *MTCM* CR4 | 201 | P1 |
| Mortlake High St *MORT/ESHN* SW14 | 156 | A9 |
| Mortlake Rd *CAN/RD* E16 | 141 | L8 |
| *IL* IG1 | 122 | E5 |
| *RCH/KEW* TW9 | 155 | N6 |
| Morton *KWD/TDW/WH* KT20 * | 257 | H5 |
| Morton Cl *CLAP* SW4 | 158 | G8 |
| *UX/CGN* UB8 | 131 | H2 |
| *WCHPL* E1 | 140 | E8 |
| *WLGTN* SM6 | 223 | K6 |
| Morton Crs *STHGT/OAK* N14 | 98 | E5 |
| Morton Dr *CFSP* | 90 | C3 |
| Morton Gdns *WLGTN* SM6 | 222 | D3 |
| Morton Ms *ECT* SW5 | 14 | D6 |
| Morton Pl *STHWK* SE1 | 17 | P5 |
| Morton Rd *IS* N1 | 6 | E1 |
| *MRDN* SM4 | 201 | P5 |
| *SRTFD* E15 | 141 | L5 |
| *WOKN/KNAP* GU21 | 231 | P1 |
| Morval Rd *BRXS/STRHM* SW2 | 180 | B4 |
| Morvale Cl *BELV* DA17 | 164 | A3 |
| Morven Rd *POTB/CUF* EN6 | 59 | M1 |

Morven Rd TOOT SW17 ... 180 A6
Morville St BOW E3 ... 140 F4
Morwell St RSQ WC1B ... 11 J4
Mosbach Gdns
  RBRW/HUT CM13 ... 107 N3
Moscow Pl BAY/PAD W2 ... 8 A7
Moscow Rd BAY/PAD W2 ... 8 G7
Moselle Av WDGN N22 ... 99 H10
Moselle Cl CEND/HSY/T N8 ... 118 C1
Moselle Pl TOTM N17 ... 99 N8
Moselle Rd BH/WHM TN16 ... 244 B6
Moselle St TOTM N17 ... 99 N8
Mosford Cl HORL RH6 ... 280 A2
Mospey Crs EW KT17 ... 238 C7
Mosquito Wy HAT AL10 ... 40 B3
Moss Bank GRAYS RM17 ... 167 L6
Mossborough Cl
  NFNCH/WDSPK N12 ... 97 L7
Mossbury Rd BTSEA SW11 ... 157 H3
Moss Cl PIN HA5 ... 93 N10
  RKW/CH/CXG WD3 ... 91 N3
  WCHPL E1 ... 13 P5
Mossdown Cl BELV DA17 ... 164 B10
Mossendew Cl DEN/HRF UB9 ... 91 N9
Mossfield COB KT11 ... 217 H9
Mossford Gn BARK/HLT IG6 ... 122 F1
Mossford La BARK/HLT IG6 ... 102 F10
Mossford St BOW E3 ... 140 E6
Moss Gdns FELT TW13 ... 175 H5
  SAND/SEL CR2 ... 224 C4
Moss Gn WCCE AL7 ... 23 H7
Moss Hall Crs
  NFNCH/WDSPK N12 ... 97 L3
Moss Hall Gv
  NFNCH/WDSPK N12 ... 97 L7
Moss La PIN HA5 ... 93 M10
  ROM RM1 ... 124 C4
Mosslea Rd CTHM CR3 ... 241 N2
  HAYES BR2 ... 206 A5
  ORP BR6 ... 206 F10
  PGE/AN SE20 ... 182 B9
Mossop St CHEL SW3 ... 15 P5
Moss Rd DAGE RM10 ... 144 B4
  GSTN WD25 ... 55 J10
  SOCK/AV RM15 ... 147 H7
Moston Cl HYS/HAR UB3 ... 152 G4
Mossville Gdns MRDN SM4 ... 201 J5
Moss Wy RDART DA2 ... 188 C7
Mostyn Av WBLY HA9 ... 115 H3
Mostyn Gdns WLSDN NW10 ... 136 G5
Mostyn Gv BOW E3 ... 140 E4
Mostyn Rd BRXN/ST SW9 ... 159 H3
  BUSH WD23 ... 74 B9
  EDGW HA8 ... 96 A8
  WIM/MER SW19 ... 201 J8
Mostyn Ter REDH RH1 ... 276 B1
Mosul Wy HAYES BR2 ... 206 B6
Mosyer Dr STMC/STPC BR5 ... 207 N9
Motcomb St KTBR SW1X ... 16 C3
Moth Cl WLGTN SM6 ... 222 F6
The Mothers Sq CLPT E5 * ... 120 A9
Motherwell Wy WTHK RM20 ... 166 F7
Moth House
  WOOL/PLUM SE18 * ... 162 B6
Motley Av VX/NE SW8 * ... 158 D8
Motspur Pk NWMAL KT3 ... 200 C6
Mottingham Gdns
  ELTH/MOT SE9 ... 184 A4
Mottingham La
  LEE/GVPK SE12 ... 183 P4
Mottingham Rd ED N9 ... 80 C10
  ELTH/MOT SE9 ... 184 B6
Mottisfont Rd ABYW SE2 ... 163 K2
Motts Hill La
  KWD/TDW/WH KT20 ... 238 D9
Mott St CHING E4 ... 81 K5
Moucheite Rd BH/WHM TN16 ... 225 N8
Moulins Rd HOM E9 ... 138 F3
Moultain Hl SWLY BR8 ... 209 H4
Moulton Av HSLW TW3 ... 135 H5
Moultrie Wy UPMR RM14 ... 126 D4
Moundfield Rd
  STNW/STAM N16 ... 119 P4
Mountacre Cl SYD SE26 ... 181 P5
Mount Adon Pk EDUL SE22 ... 181 P5
Mount Angelus Rd
  PUT/ROE SW15 ... 178 C3
Mount Ararat Rd
  RCHPK/HAM TW10 ... 177 K1
Mount Ash Rd SYD SE26 ... 182 A6
Mount Av CHING E4 ... 100 F4
  CTHM CR3 ... 241 K10
  EA W5 ... 135 J7
  HARH RM3 ... 106 B7
  RBRW/HUT CM13 ... 107 N1
  STHL UB1 ... 133 P8
Mountbatten Cl NRWD SE19 ... 181 M8
  SL1 ... 149 M2
  STAL AL1 ... 38 G3
  WOOL/PLUM SE18 ... 163 H5
Mountbatten Ct BKHH IG9 ... 102 A3
Mountbatten Sq WDSR SL4 * ... 149 H7
Mountbel Rd STAN HA7 ... 94 F10
Mount Cl BMLY BR1 ... 206 B1
  CAR SM5 ... 222 B5
  CRAWE RH10 ... 284 D6
  EA W5 * ... 135 H7
  EBAR EN4 ... 78 B8
  HHW HP1 ... 35 J6
  LHD/OX KT22 ... 236 E9
  PUR/KEN CR8 ... 241 K2
  SEV TN13 ... 246 C2
  SLN SL2 ... 109 H9
  WOKS/MYFD GU22 ... 231 N7
The Mount Cl VW GU25 ... 194 A6
Mountcombe Cl SURB KT6 ... 199 K8
Mount Cots BXLYHS DA6 * ... 165 P10
Mount Ct WWKM BR4 ... 204 B1
  WOOL/PLUM SE18 ... 143 M10
Mount Culver Av SCUP DA14 ... 185 N9
Mount Dr LCOL/BKTW AL2 ... 56 C1
  RYLN/HDSTN HA2 ... 113 N3
  WBLY HA9 ... 115 P7
The Mount Dr REIG RH2 ... 257 M8
Mounteagle Gdns
  STRHM/NOR SW16 ... 180 G6
Mount Echo Av CHING E4 ... 100 G2
Mount Echo Dr CHING E4 ... 100 G2
Mount Ephraim La
  STRHM/NOR SW16 ... 180 E6
Mount Ephraim Rd
  STRHM/NOR SW16 ... 180 E6
Mount Felix WOT/HER KT12 ... 196 A8
Mountfield Cl CAT SE6 ... 183 J5
Mountfield Rd EA W5 ... 135 J8
  EHAM E6 ... 142 D4
  FNCH N3 ... 117 K1
  HHNE HP2 ... 35 P2
Mountfield Ter CAT SE6 ... 183 J5
Mountfield Wy
  STMC/STPC BR5 ... 207 M4
Mountford St WCHPL E1 ... 13 N5
Mountford Ter IS N1 ... 6 A1
Mount Gdns SYD SE26 ... 182 A6
Mount Grace Rd
  POTB/CUF EN6 ... 59 K7
Mount Gv EDGW HA8 ... 95 P4
Mountgrove Rd HBRY N5 ... 119 K8
Mount Harry Rd SEV TN13 ... 247 H3
Mount Hermon Rd
  WOKS/MYFD GU22 ... 232 A5
Mount Hill La CFSP/GDCR SL9 ... 109 H6
Mount Holme THDIT KT7 ... 198 D3
Mounthurst Rd HAYES BR2 ... 205 M7
Mountjoy Cl ABYW SE2 ... 163 L1
Mount La CRAWE RH10 ... 285 P9
Mount Ms HPTN TW12 ... 175 J5
Mount Mills FSBYE EC1V ... 6 D10
Mountnessing La
  BRWN CM15 ... 87 K4

Mountnessing Rd
  BRWN CM15 ... 87 M2
Mount Nod Rd
  STRHM/NOR SW16 ... 180 G6
Mount Nugent CSHM HP5 ... 50 F3
Mount Pde EBAR EN4 * ... 77 P9
Mount Pk CAR SM5 ... 222 B5
Mount Park Av HRW HA1 ... 114 C7
  SAND/SEL CR2 ... 223 J5
Mount Park Crs EA W5 ... 135 J6
Mount Park Rd EA W5 ... 135 J7
  HRW HA1 ... 114 C7
  PIN HA5 ... 113 H3
Mount Pl ACT W3 ... 135 N10
Mount Pleasant ALP/SUD HA0 ... 135 K3
  BH/WHM TN16 ... 244 A3
  DEN/HRF UB9 ... 91 K9
  EBAR EN4 ... 78 A8
  EHSLY KT24 ... 253 N4
  EHSLY KT24 ... 252 C5
  EW KT17 ... 220 C6
  FSBYW WC1X ... 11 J2
  GUW GU2 ... 267 J2
  HERT/BAY SG13 ... 26 B7
  HRW HA1 ... 114 C7
  RDKG RH5 * ... 270 C6
  RSLP HA4 ... 113 K8
  STALW/RED AL3 ... 38 D5
  WEY KT13 ... 196 B10
  WNWD SE27 ... 181 K7
Mount Pleasant Cl
  BRKMPK AL9 ... 40 C7
Mount Pleasant Cots
  EGH TW20 * ... 172 A9
Mount Pleasant Crs
  FSBYW N4 * ... 118 G5
Mount Pleasant Hl CLPT E5 ... 120 A7
Mount Pleasant La
  BRKMPK AL9 ... 40 C7
  LCOL/BKTW AL2 ... 55 N6
Mount Pleasant Pl
  WOOL/PLUM SE18 ... 162 B6
Mount Pleasant Rd CHIG IG7 ... 102 C5
  CRW RM5 ... 104 F3
  CTHM CR3 ... 241 P9
  EA W5 ... 135 H6
  LEW SE13 ... 183 H2
  NWMAL KT3 ... 199 P3
  RSEV TN14 ... 265 J9
  TOTM N17 ... 119 M1
  WALTH E17 ... 100 D10
  WLSDN NW10 ... 136 F2
Mount Pleasant Vls
  FSBYW N4 ... 118 G5
Mount Ri FSTH SE23 ... 182 B5
Mount Rd BCTR RM8 ... 124 A6
  BXLYHS DA6 ... 185 P1
  CHOB/PIR GU24 ... 213 N8
  CHSGTN KT9 ... 219 L1
  CRICK NW2 ... 116 E8
  EBAR EN4 ... 77 N6
  EPP CM16 ... 65 P8
  FELT TW13 ... 175 M4
  HDN NW4 ... 116 D4
  HYS/HAR UB3 ... 133 J5
  MTCM CR4 ... 201 N2
  NRWD SE19 * ... 181 L9
  NWMAL KT3 ... 200 A3
  STALE/WH AL4 ... 21 J2
  WIM/MER SW19 ... 179 K5
  WOKS/MYFD GU22 ... 231 N10
Mount Rw MYFR/PKLN W1K ... 10 B7
Mountsfield Cl
  STWL/WRAY TW19 ... 173 K1
Mountsfield Ct LEW SE13 ... 183 K4
Mountside GUW GU2 ... 267 N3
  KTN/HRWW/WS HA3 ... 114 A3
Mountsorrel HERT/BAY SG13 ... 25 N5
Mounts Pond Rd
  BKHTH/KID SE3 ... 161 J8
The Mount Rd HAMP NW3 * ... 117 M8
Mounts Rd SWCM DA10 ... 188 C3
Mount Stewart Av
  KTN/HRWW/WS HA3 ... 115 J4
Mount Ter WCHPL E1 ... 140 A7
The Mount BMLY BR1 * ... 206 B1
  BRW CM14 ... 104 H4
  BXLYHS DA6 * ... 186 C1
  CHESW EN7 ... 61 L7
  CLPT E5 * ... 120 A7
  COUL/CHIP CR5 ... 240 B10
  CRAWW RH11 ... 282 A4
  ESH/CLAY KT10 ... 217 P3
  EW KT17 ... 220 C6
  GUW GU2 ... 267 N3
  HAMP NW3 ... 117 M8
  HARH RM3 ... 105 K4
  KWD/TDW/WH KT20 ... 257 J2
  LHD/OX KT22 ... 236 D9
  NTHLT UB5 ... 114 A10
  NWMAL KT3 ... 200 C3
  POTB/CUF EN6 ... 59 L6
  RKW/CH/CXG WD3 ... 71 M10
  TRDG/WHET N20 ... 97 H5
  VW GU25 ... 194 A6
  WARL CR6 ... 241 P5
  WBLY HA9 ... 115 N7
  WEY KT13 ... 196 F9
  WOKN/KNAP GU21 ... 232 A4
Mount Vw NWDGN UB2 * ... 153 L3
  ENC/FH EN2 ... 78 G2
  LCOL/BKTW AL2 ... 57 K5
Mountview Cl HAMP NW3 * ... 117 M6
  REDH RH1 ... 275 P7
Mountview Dr REDH RH1 ... 275 P7
Mount View Rd
  CDALE/KGS NW9 ... 116 A2
  CHESW EN7 ... 61 M2
  CHING E4 ... 101 H1
  ESH/CLAY KT10 ... 218 G4
  FSBYPK N4 ... 118 C5
Mountview Rd ORP BR6 ... 207 H8
Mount Vis WNWD SE27 ... 181 J6
Mount Wy CAR SM5 ... 222 B5
Mountway POTB/CUF EN6 ... 59 K6
Mount Wy WCCE AL7 ... 23 J8
Mountwood E/WMO/HCT KT8 ... 198 A3
Mountwood Cl SAND/SEL CR2 ... 224 A6
Mountwood La EPP CM16 ... 66 C5
Movers La BARK IG11 ... 142 C3
Mowatt Cl ARCH N19 ... 118 C6
Mowbray Av BF/WBF KT14 ... 215 P9
Mowbray Crs EGH TW20 ... 172 D8
Mowbray Dr CRAWW RH11 ... 283 J10
Mowbray Gdns DORK RH4 ... 254 C10
  NTHLT UB5 * ... 133 J7
Mowbray Rd BAR EN5 ... 77 M8
  CRICK NW2 ... 2 D3
  EDGW HA8 ... 95 M5
  HLW CM20 ... 29 H9
  NRWD SE19 ... 203 N1
  RCHPK/HAM TW10 ... 177 H6
Mowbrays Cl CRW RM5 ... 104 D1
Mowbrays Rd CRW RM5 ... 104 D10
Mowbrey Gdns LOU IG10 ... 82 F5
Mowlem St BETH E2 ... 128 E10
Mowll St BRXN/ST SW9 ... 159 H6
Moxom Av CHES/WCR EN8 ... 62 C6
Moxon Cl PLSTW E15 ... 141 L4
Moxon St BAR EN5 ... 77 J3
  MHST W1U ... 10 C1
Moye Cl BETH E2 ... 7 P7
Moyers Rd LEY E10 ... 121 H6
Moylan Rd HMSMTH W6 ... 151 J6
Moyne Pl WLSDN NW10 ... 135 M5
Moynihan Dr WCHMN N21 ... 78 G9
Moys Cl CROY/NA CRO ... 202 F6

Moyser Rd STRHM/NOR SW16 ... 180 C8
Mozart Est NKENS W10 ... 2 C10
Mozart St NKENS W10 ... 2 C10
Mucheiney Rd ABYW SE2 ... 201 M6
Muckhatts La EGH TW20 ... 194 B8
Muckingford Rd TIL RM18 ... 168 G5
Mud La HNWL W7 ... 115 K10
Muggeridge Cl SAND/SEL CR2 ... 223 L2
Muggeridge Rd DAGE RM10 ... 124 C9
Muirdown Av
  MORT/ESHN SW14 ... 155 P10
Muir Dr WAND/EARL SW18 ... 179 N1
Muirfield ACT W3 ... 136 B8
Muirfield Cl
  BERM/RHTH SE16 * ... 160 A4
  CRAWW RH11 ... 282 G8
  OXHEY WD19 * ... 93 K6
Muirfield Crs POP/IOD E14 ... 160 C2
Muirfield Gn OXHEY WD19 ... 93 K5
Muirfield Rd OXHEY WD19 ... 93 J5
  WOKN/KNAP GU21 ... 231 M4
Muirkirk Rd CAT SE6 ... 183 H4
Muir Rd CLPT E5 ... 119 P8
Muir St CAN/RD E16 ... 142 C10
Mulberry Av
  STWL/WRAY TW19 ... 173 P4
  WDSR SL4 ... 149 L8
Mulberry Cl BROX EN10 ... 44 E10
  CEND/HSY/T N8 ... 118 F3
  CHING E4 ... 100 F3
  EBAR EN4 ... 77 N8
  GPK RM2 ... 125 J2
  HDN NW4 ... 116 F1
  LCOL/BKTW AL2 ... 56 A6
  NTHLT UB5 ... 133 N4
  STRHM/NOR SW16 ... 180 D7
  WAT WD17 ... 72 C7
  WEY KT13 ... 196 C10
  WOKN/KNAP GU21 ... 214 B10
  WDR/YW UB7 ... 152 A1
Mulberry Dr DTCH/LGLY SL3 ... 150 B4
  PUR RM19 ... 165 N3
Mulberry Gdns HLWE CM17 ... 29 N8
  RAD WD7 ... 57 K9
Mulberry Ga BNSTD SM7 ... 239 J2
Mulberry Gn HLWE CM17 ... 29 N7
Mulberry Hl BRWN CM15 ... 107 L3
Mulberry La CROY/NA CRO ... 203 N8
Mulberry Md HAT AL10 ... 22 B10
Mulberry Ms WDR/YW UB7 ... 152 B2
  WLGTN SM6 ... 223 H6
Mulberry Pde WDR/YW UB7 ... 152 B2
Mulberry Pl ELTH/MOT SE9 ... 162 A10
  HMSMTH W6 ... 156 D4
Mulberry Rd CRAWW RH11 ... 283 L4
  CVW DA11 ... 190 B10
  HACK E8 ... 7 L4
Mulberry St WCHPL E1 ... 13 N5
Mulberry Trees SHPTN TW17 ... 196 F7
Mulberry Wk CHEL SW3 ... 15 M9
Mulberry Wy BARK/HLT IG6 ... 122 F2
  BELV DA17 ... 164 D1
  SWFD E18 ... 101 N10
Mulgrave Rd BELMT SM2 ... 221 J4
  CROY/NA CRO ... 203 L10
  EA W5 ... 135 J5
  HRW HA1 ... 114 E5
  WKENS W14 ... 14 C9
  WLSDN NW10 ... 116 G4
Mulgrave Wy
  WOKN/KNAP GU21 ... 231 M4
Mulholland Cl MTCM CR4 ... 202 C2
Mulkern Rd ARCH N19 ... 118 E6
Mullards Cl MTCM CR4 ... 202 A8
Mullein Ct GRAYS RM17 ... 168 A5
Mullens Rd EGH TW20 ... 172 F8
Muller Rd CLAP SW4 ... 160 G3
Mullet Gdns BETH E2 ... 7 P1
Mulliner Cl EBED/NFELT TW14 ... 156 A9
Mullion Cl
  KTN/HRWW/WS HA3 ... 94 A9
Mullion Wk OXHEY WD19 ... 93 L5
Mull Wk IS N1 * ... 6 F2
Mulready St STJWD NW8 ... 9 N2
Mulready Wk HHS/BOV HP3 ... 35 P10
Multi Wy ACT W3 ... 156 B1
Multon Rd WAND/EARL SW18 ... 179 N3
Mumford Ct CITYW EC2V ... 12 F5
Mumford Mills GNWCH SE10 * ... 160 F6
Mumford Rd HNHL SE24 ... 181 N1
Mumfords La CFSP/GDCR SL9 ... 109 L1
Muncaster Cl ASHF TW15 ... 174 D7
Muncaster Rd ASHF TW15 ... 174 C8
  CLAP SW4 ... 158 A10
Muncies Ms CAT SE6 ... 183 H5
Mundania Rd EDUL SE22 ... 182 A3
Munday Rd CAN/RD E16 ... 141 M8
Munday's Boro Rd RGUW GU3 ... 266 A5
Mundells CHESW EN7 ... 61 P3
  WCCE AL7 ... 23 J4
Munden Gv WATN WD24 ... 73 H4
Munden St WKENS W14 ... 14 A3
Mundesley Cl OXHEY WD19 ... 93 K5
Mundesley Sl SL1 ... 129 K8
Mundford Rd CLPT E5 ... 120 B7
Mundon Gdns IL IG1 ... 122 G6
Mund St WKENS W14 ... 14 B4
Mundy St IS N1 ... 7 L8
Mungo-Park Cl BUSH WD23 * ... 94 B3
Mungo Park Rd GVE DA12 ... 190 D8
  RAIN RM13 ... 145 H1

Murtwell Dr CHIG IG7 ... 102 F7
Musard Rd HMSMTH W6 ... 14 B3
Musbury St WCHPL E1 ... 140 B8
Muscatel Pl CMBW SE5 * ... 159 M7
Muschamp Rd CAR SM5 ... 201 P9
  PECK SE15 ... 159 K6
Muscovy St MON EC3R ... 13 L4
Museum St NOXST/BSQ WC1A ... 11 J4
Musgrave Cl EBAR EN4 ... 77 M5
  CHES/WCR EN8 ... 45 J1
Musgrave Crs FUL/PGN SW6 ... 157 K6
Musgrave Rd ISLW TW7 ... 154 E7
Musjid Rd BTSEA SW11 ... 157 N8
Musk Cl NTHLT UB5 * ... 133 L1
Muskalls Cl CHESW EN7 ... 61 P3
Musleigh Mnr WARE SG12 ... 26 D1
Musley Hl WARE SG12 ... 26 D1
Musley La WARE SG12 ... 26 D1
Musquash Wy HSLWW TW4 ... 153 K8
Mussenden La EYN DA4 ... 210 C6
Mustard Mill Rd STA TW18 ... 22 A7
Muston Rd CLPT E5 ... 120 A7
Muswell Av MUSWH N10 ... 98 C10
Muswell Hl MUSWH N10 ... 118 C1
Muswell Hill Broadway
  MUSWH N10 ... 118 C2
Muswell Hill Pl MUSWH N10 ... 118 C2
Muswell Hill Rd HGT N6 ... 118 B4
Muswell Ms MUSWH N10 ... 118 C2
Muswell Rd MUSWH N10 ... 98 C10
Mutchetts Cl GSTN WD25 ... 55 M9
Mutrix Rd KIL/WHAMP NW6 ... 2 F3
Mutter Rd CLAP SW4 ... 159 L8
Mutton La POTB/CUF EN6 ... 59 L3
Mutton Pl CAMTN NW1 ... 4 B1
Mutton Rw CHONG CM5 ... 67 K8
Muybridge Rd NWMAL KT3 ... 199 P1
Myatt Rd BRXN/ST SW9 ... 159 J7
Myddelton Av EN EN1 ... 79 M4
Myddelton Cl EN EN1 ... 79 N1
Myddelton Gdns WCHMN N21 ... 99 J1
Myddelton Pk
  TRDG/WHET N20 ... 97 N4
Myddelton Pas
  CLKNW EC1R ... 6 B9
Myddelton Rd
  CEND/HSY/T N8 ... 118 F1
Myddelton Sq CLKNW EC1R ... 6 B8
Myddelton St CLKNW EC1R ... 6 C9
Myddleton Av FSBYPK N4 ... 119 J7
Myddleton Pl ELTH/MOT SE9 * ... 162 A10
  HMSMTH W6 ... 156 D4
Myddleton Rd CRAWW RH11 ... 283 L4
  WARE SG12 ... 26 C3
  WDGN N22 ... 98 F8
Myers La NWCR SE14 ... 160 D10
Myerscroft Cl
  NFNCH/WDSPK N12 ... 97 K4
Myers Cl RAD WD7 ... 57 K8
Mygrove Cl RAIN RM13 ... 145 L4
Mygrove Gdns RAIN RM13 ... 145 L4
Mygrove Rd RAIN RM13 ... 145 L4
Myles Ct CHESW EN7 ... 61 K5
Mylius Cl NWCR SE14 ... 160 D10
Mylne Cl CHES/WCR EN8 ... 62 B1
  HMSMTH W6 ... 156 D4
Mylne St IS N1 ... 6 A6
Mylor Cl WOKN/KNAP GU21 ... 214 B10
Mymms Dr BRKMPK AL9 ... 59 K5
Mynchen End BEAC HP9 ... 88 C1
Mynn's Cl EPSOM KT18 ... 219 N10
Myra St ABYW SE2 ... 163 K4
Myrdle St WCHPL E1 ... 13 N1
The Myrke DTCH/LGLY SL3 ... 149 L3
Myrna Cl WIM/MER SW19 ... 179 P10
Myron Pl LEW SE13 ... 161 N1
Myrtle Aly WOOL/PLUM SE18 * ... 162 F7
Myrtle Av EBED/NFELT TW14 ... 174 A1
  RSLP HA4 ... 113 H5
Myrtleberry Cl HACK E8 * ... 7 L2
Myrtle Cl DTCH/LGLY SL3 ... 151 H7
  EBAR EN4 ... 98 A1
  ERITH DA8 ... 164 F6
  LTWR GU18 ... 212 A7
  UX/CGN UB8 ... 132 A7
  WDR/YW UB7 ... 152 A3
Myrtle Cots DORK RH4 * ... 272 F1
  SLN SL2 ... 129 L9
Myrtledene Rd ABYW SE2 ... 163 K6
Myrtle Gdns HNWL W7 ... 134 D10
Myrtle Gv ENC/FH EN2 ... 79 H1
  NWMAL KT3 ... 199 P1
  SOCK/AV RM15 ... 166 B1
Myrtle Pl RDART DA2 ... 188 C4
Myrtle Rd ACT W3 ... 135 P10
  BRW CM14 ... 104 H5
  CROY/NA CRO ... 204 F10
  DORK RH4 ... 272 F1
  EHAM E6 ... 142 A3
  HPTN TW12 ... 175 K7
  HSLW TW3 ... 136 A5
  IL IG1 ... 122 F7
  PLMCR N13 ... 99 P4
  SUT SM1 ... 221 M2
  WALTH E17 ... 120 C5
Myrtleside Cl NTHWD HA6 ... 7 J8
Myrtle Wk IS N1 ... 7 J8
Mysore Rd BTSEA SW11 ... 158 A10
Myton Rd DUL SE21 ... 181 L6

# N

Nadine St CHARL SE7 ... 161 P4
Naffenton Ri LOU IG10 ... 82 A9
Nagle Cl WALTH E17 ... 101 J10
Nag's Head La UPMR RM14 ... 106 B8
  WELL DA16 ... 165 L3
Nag's Head Rd PEND EN3 ... 80 B8
Nailsworth Crs REDH RH1 ... 258 E5
Nailzee Cl CFSP/GDCR SL9 ... 110 B5
Nairn Cl TIL RM18 ... 168 C8
Nairn Gn OXHEY WD19 ... 93 H4
Nairne Gv HNHL SE24 ... 181 L1
Nairn Rd RSLP HA4 ... 133 K1
Nairn St POP/IOD E14 ... 141 H7
Naldera Gdns BKHTH/KID SE3 ... 161 J8
Nallhead Rd FELT TW13 ... 175 K8
Namba Roy Cl
  STRHM/NOR SW16 ... 180 G7
Namton Dr THHTH CR7 ... 202 G4
Nan Clark's La MLHL NW7 ... 96 C3
Nancy Downs OXHEY WD19 ... 93 H4
Nankin St POP/IOD E14 ... 140 M9
Nansen Rd BTSEA SW11 ... 158 B10
Nansen Village
  NFNCH/WDSPK N12 * ... 97 H2
Nant Ct CRICK NW2 * ... 117 H10
Nantes Cl WAND/EARL SW18 ... 157 M10
Nant Rd CRICK NW2 ... 117 H10
Nant St BETH E2 ... 140 A5
Naoroji St FSBYW WC1X ... 6 A8
Napier Av FUL/PGN SW6 ... 157 J9
  POP/IOD E14 ... 160 F4
Napier Cl DEPT SE8 ... 160 B7
  NWCR SE14 * ... 161 H1
  WDR/YW UB7 ... 152 A1
  WKENS W14 ... 14 C3
Napier Ct CTHM CR3 * ... 241 M5
  FUL/PGN SW6 * ... 157 J9
Napier Gdns GU GU1 ... 250 D9
Napier Pl WKENS W14 ... 14 C1
Napier Rd ALP/SUD HA0 ... 135 P1
  ASHF TW15 ... 174 B10
  BELV DA17 ... 164 A2
  BMLY BR1 ... 184 B10
  CRICK NW2 ... 117 H10
  EHAM E6 ... 142 A6
  ENC/FH EN2 ... 80 A4
  HMSMTH W6 ... 14 C3
  HTHAIR TW6 ... 153 J6
  ISLW TW7 ... 154 B10
  SAND/SEL CR2 ... 223 L4
  SEVS/STOTM N15 ... 119 M3
  SNWD SE25 ... 204 B10
  SRTFD E15 ... 141 K4
  TOTM N17 ... 119 M1
  WAN E11 ... 121 K8
  WDR/YW UB7 ... 152 A1
  WKENS W14 ... 14 C4
  WLSDN NW10 ... 136 G5
Napier Ter IS N1 ... 6 C1
Napier Wk ASHF TW15 ... 174 E10
Napier Wy CRAWE RH10 ... 285 N2
Napoleon Rd CLPT E5 ... 120 A8
  TWK TW1 ... 176 C3
Napsbury Av LCOL/BKTW AL2 ... 57 L2
Napsbury La STAL AL1 ... 56 F1
Napton Cl YEAD UB4 ... 133 K3
Narbonne Av CLAP SW4 ... 180 G3
Narboro Ct ROM RM1 ... 125 H4
Narborough Cl
  HGDN/ICK UB10 ... 112 D7
Narborough St FUL/PGN SW6 ... 157 L8
Narcissus Rd
  KIL/WHAMP NW6 ... 117 K10
Narcot La CFSP/GDCR SL9 ... 89 N3
Narcot Rd CSTG HP8 ... 89 M5
Narcot Wy CSTG HP8 ... 89 M6
Narford Rd CLPT E5 ... 119 P8
Narrow Boat Cl THMD SE28 ... 162 G3
Narrow La WARL CR6 ... 242 A5
Narrow St ACT W3 ... 135 N10
  POP/IOD E14 ... 140 D9
Narrow Wy HAYES BR2 ... 206 B9
Nascot Pl WAT WD17 ... 73 J6
Nascot Rd WAT WD17 ... 73 J6
Nascot St SHB W12 ... 136 F8
  WAT WD17 ... 73 J6
Nascot Wood Rd WAT WD17 ... 73 H5
Naseby Cl ISLW TW7 ... 135 P7
  KIL/WHAMP NW6 ... 3 K3
Naseby Ct WOT/HER KT12 * ... 197 K8
Naseby Rd CLAY IG5 ... 102 C9
  DAGE RM10 ... 124 B8
  NRWD SE19 ... 181 L9
Nash Cl BERK HP4 ... 33 M4
  BORE WD6 ... 75 N2
  BRKMPK AL9 ... 40 C9
  SUT SM1 ... 222 A10
Nash Ct GVW DA11 ... 190 E7
Nash Dr REDH RH1 ... 258 A10
Nash Gn BMLY BR1 ... 183 M10
  HGDN/ICK UB10 ... 112 A2
Nash La HAYES BR2 ... 225 J1
Nash Mills La HHS/BOV HP3 ... 35 P9
Nash Rd BROCKY SE4 ... 160 D10
  CHDH RM6 ... 123 N2
  CRAWE RH10 ... 285 H9
  ED N9 ... 81 H3
Nash St CAMTN NW1 ... 4 B8
Nash Wy KTN/HRWW/WS HA3 ... 114 C4
Nasmyth St HMSMTH W6 ... 156 E6
Nassau Rd BARN SW13 ... 156 C7
Nassau St GTPST W1W ... 10 F2
Nassington Rd HAMP NW3 ... 117 N1
Nasturtium Dr
  CHOB/PIR GU24 ... 230 F1
Natalie Cl EBED/NFELT TW14 ... 174 A1
Natalie Ms WHTN TW2 ... 176 C6
Natal Rd FBAR/BDGN N11 ... 98 F6
  IL IG1 ... 122 F9
  STRHM/NOR SW16 ... 180 D8
  THHTH CR7 ... 203 L1
Nathan Cl UPMR RM14 ... 126 D6
Nathaniel Cl WCHPL E1 ... 13 M4
Nathans Rd ALP/SUD HA0 ... 115 K1
Nathan Wy ABYW SE2 ... 163 K1
  THMD SE28 ... 146 F5
National Ter
  BERM/RHTH SE16 * ... 160 A1
Nation Wy CHING E4 ... 101 H2
Natwoke Cl BEAC HP9 ... 88 C6
Naunton Wy HCH RM12 ... 125 L8
Naval Rw POP/IOD E14 ... 141 N9
Navarino Gv HACK E8 ... 7 P1
Navarino Rd HACK E8 ... 7 P1
Navarre Gdns CRW RM5 ... 104 D1
Navarre Rd EHAM E6 ... 142 B4
Navarre St BETH E2 ... 13 L1
Navestock Cl CHING E4 * ... 101 P1
Navestock Crs WFD IG8 ... 101 J10
Navestock Side BRW CM14 ... 88 A10
Navestock Ter WFD IG8 ... 101 K1
Navigator Dr NWDGN UB2 ... 154 C2
Navy St CLAP SW4 ... 158 B9
Nayim Pl HACK E8 ... 7 N1
Naylor Gv PEND EN3 ... 80 C9
Naylor Rd PECK SE15 ... 159 K6
  TRDG/WHET N20 ... 97 M5
Nazareth Ct PECK SE15 ... 160 A8
Nazeingbury Cl WAB EN9 ... 45 L1
Nazeingbury Pde WAB EN9 * ... 45 L1
Nazeing Common WAB EN9 ... 45 P1
Nazeing New Rd BROX EN10 ... 44 F7
Nazrul St BETH E2 ... 7 L8
Neagle Cl BORE WD6 ... 75 P5
Neal Av STHL UB1 ... 133 P2
Neal Cl CFSP/GDCR SL9 ... 110 F6
  NTHWD HA6 ... 93 H9
Neal Ct HERT/WAT SG14 ... 25 K5
  WAB EN9 ... 63 L9
Nealden St BRXN/ST SW9 ... 158 G2
Neale Cl EFNCH N2 ... 117 M1
Neal St LSQ/SEVD WC2H ... 11 J5
  WATW WD18 ... 73 K9
Neal Yd LSQ/SEVD WC2H ... 11 J5
Near Acre CDALE/KGS NW9 ... 96 E6
Neasden Cl WLSDN NW10 ... 116 B10
Neasden La WLSDN NW10 ... 116 C9
Neasham Rd BCTR RM8 ... 123 L10
Neate St CMBW SE5 ... 19 L8
Neath Gdns MRDN SM4 ... 201 N6
Neathouse Pl PIM SW1V ... 16 F7
Neats Acre RSLP HA4 ... 112 G5
Neatscourt Rd EHAM E6 ... 142 A7
Neaves Crs HARH RM3 ... 105 K9
Neb La OXTED RH8 ... 261 H7
Neckinger BERM/RHTH SE16 ... 19 M3
Neckinger Est
  BERM/RHTH SE16 * ... 19 M3
Neckinger St STHWK SE1 ... 19 M2
Nectarine Wy LEW SE13 ... 160 G6
Necton Rd STALE/WH AL4 ... 21 P1
Needham Rd WDSR SL4 ... 148 D7
Needham Rd NTGHL W11 ... 8 B5
Needleman St
  BERM/RHTH SE16 ... 160 A3
Needles Bank GDST RH9 ... 260 A7
Neela Cl HGDN/ICK UB10 ... 132 A1
Neeld Crs HDN NW4 ... 116 A4
  WBLY HA9 ... 115 M10
Neil Wy RKW/CH/CXG WD3 ... 91 J1
Neild Yd LSQ/SEVD WC2H * ... 11 J5
Nelgarde Rd CAT SE6 ... 182 F3
Nella Rd HMSMTH W6 ... 156 G6
Nelldale Rd BERM/RHTH SE16 ... 160 A3
Nello James Gdns
  WNWD SE27 ... 181 N1
Nelmes Cl EMPK RM11 ... 125 M4
Nelmes Crs EMPK RM11 ... 125 M3
Nelmes Rd EMPK RM11 ... 125 M2
Nelmes Wy EMPK RM11 ... 125 M2
Nelson Cl ASC SL5 ... 193 J8
  BH/WHM TN16 ... 224 A3
  CRICK NW2 ... 2 A1
  CROY/NA CRO ... 2 D1
  EBED/NFELT TW14 ... 174 A3
  HAYES BR2 ... 205 N3
  KIL/WHAMP NW6 ... 2 A1
  PECK SE15 ... 159 P6
  ROMW/RG RM7 ... 104 C9
  WOT/HER KT12 ... 197 J8
Nelson Gdns BETH E2 ... 7
  GU GU1 ... 250 D9
  HSLW TW3 ... 175 P2
Nelson Grove Rd
  WIM/MER SW19 ... 201 L1
Nelson La HGDN/ICK UB10 ... 132 C6
Nelson Mandela Cl
  MUSWH N10 ... 98 A10
Nelson Mandela Rd
  BKHTH/KID SE3 ... 161 P9
Nelson Pl IS N1 ... 6 D7
Nelson Rd ASHF TW15 ... 173 P8
  BELV DA17 ... 164 A4
  CEND/HSY/T N8 ... 118 G3
  CHING E4 ... 100 G7
  CTHM CR3 ... 241 P9
  ED N9 ... 81 J3
  GNWCH SE10 ... 160 F4
  GVW DA11 ... 190 C5
  HRW HA1 ... 114 C6
  HTHAIR TW6 ... 152 A2
  NWMAL KT3 ... 200 A5
  PEND EN3 ... 80 C10
  RAIN RM13 ... 144 G4
  SCUP DA14 ... 185 K7
  SEVS/STOTM N15 ... 119 M2
  SOCK/AV RM15 ... 147 H4
  STAN HA7 ... 95 K5
  WAN E11 ... 121 M2
  WDSR SL4 ... 148 E9
  WHTN TW2 ... 175 P2
  WIM/MER SW19 ... 179 K7
Nelsons Rw CLAP SW4 ... 158 E10
Nelson St CAN/RD E16 ... 141 L9
  EHAM E6 ... 142 A2
  HERT/WAT SG14 ... 25 J4
  WCHPL E1 ... 140 B7
Nelson Ter FSBYE EC1V ... 6 D7
Nelson Wk HOR/WEW KT19 ... 219 P8
Nelwyn Av EMPK RM11 ... 125 N3
Nemoure Rd ACT W3 ... 135 P9
Nene Gdns FELT TW13 ... 175 N6
Nene Rd HTHAIR TW6 ... 152 C1
Nepaul Rd BTSEA SW11 ... 157 P8
Nepean St PUT/ROE SW15 ... 178 D2
Neptune Cl CRAWW RH11 ... 283 H8
  RAIN RM13 ... 144 G4
Neptune Ct BORE WD6 * ... 75 M7
Neptune Dr HHNE HP2 ... 35 P5
Neptune Rd HRW HA1 ... 114 C4
  HTHAIR TW6 ... 152 D1
Neptune St BERM/RHTH SE16 ... 160 B2
Nesbit Cl BKHTH/KID SE3 ... 161 K8
Nesbit Rd ELTH/MOT SE9 ... 162 A10
Nesbitts Aly BAR EN5 * ... 77 K3
Nesbitt Sq NRWD SE19 * ... 181 M10
Nesham St WAP E1W ... 13 N9
Ness Rd ERITH DA8 ... 165 L5
Ness St BERM/RHTH SE16 ... 19 N1
Nesta Rd WFD IG8 ... 101 L7
Nestle's Av HYS/HAR UB3 ... 152 G2
Neston Rd WATN WD24 ... 73 K3
Nestor Av WCHMN N21 ... 79 J10
Nethan Dr SOCK/AV RM15 ... 146 B9
Netheravon Rd CHSWK W4 ... 136 C3
Netheravon Rd South
  CHSWK W4 ... 136 D4
Netherbury Rd EA W5 ... 155 J2
Netherby Gdns ENC/FH EN2 ... 78 F4
Netherby Pk WEY KT13 ... 216 F2
Netherby Rd FSTH SE23 ... 181 P5
Nether Cl FNCH N3 ... 97 H4
Nethercote Av
  WOKN/KNAP GU21 ... 231 L3
Nether Ct MLHL NW7 * ... 97 H4
Nethercourt Av FNCH N3 ... 97 H4
Netherfield Gdns BARK IG11 ... 142 G1
Netherfield La WARE SG12 ... 27 J8
Netherfield Rd BAL SW12 ... 160 C2
  NFNCH/WDSPK N12 ... 97 H2
  TOOT SW17 ... 180 A4
Netherford Rd VX/NE SW8 ... 158 D8
Nethergate RBRW/HUT CM13 ... 107 M10
Netherhall Gdns HAMP NW3 ... 117 M10
Netherhall Rd
  HLWW/ROY CM19 ... 45 L3
Netherhall Wy HAMP NW3 ... 3 J1
Netherlands Rd BAR EN5 ... 77 N10
The Netherlands
  COUL/CHIP CR5 ... 240 D5
Netherleigh Cl HGT N6 ... 118 C6
Netherleigh Pk REDH RH1 ... 276 F3
Nether Mt GUW GU2 ... 267 N2
Netherne Ct CTHM CR3 * ... 242 F9
Netherne Dr COUL/CHIP CR5 ... 240 C9
Netherne La COUL/CHIP CR5 ... 240 D9
Netherpark Dr GPK RM2 ... 104 G10
Nether St FNCH N3 ... 97 K8
  NFNCH/WDSPK N12 ... 97 K4
Netherton Rd
  SEVS/STOTM N15 ... 119 L4
  TWK TW1 ... 176 F1
Netherway STALW/RED AL3 ... 37 P2
Netherwood CRAWW RH11 ... 283 K10
Netherwood Pl
  HMSMTH W6 ... 156 C2
Netherwood Rd BEAC HP9 ... 88 C6
  WKENS W14 ... 156 G2
Netherwood St
  KIL/WHAMP NW6 ... 2 D3
Netley Cl CHEAM SM3 ... 220 G4
  CROY/NA CRO ... 225 H4
  SHGR GU5 ... 270 D4
Netley Dr WOT/HER KT12 ... 197 N5
Netley Gdns MRDN SM4 ... 201 N1
Netley Rd BTFD TW8 ... 155 K5
  GNTH/NBYPK IG2 ... 122 G3
  MRDN SM4 ... 201 N6
  WALTH E17 ... 121 J1
Netley St CAMTN NW1 ... 4 C10
Nettlecombe Cl BELMT SM2 ... 221 L7
Nettleden Av WBLY HA9 ... 115 P4
Nettlefold Pl WNWD SE27 ... 181 J6
Nettlestead Cl BECK BR3 ... 183 H10
Nettles Ter GU GU1 * ... 250 F6
Nettleton Rd HGDN/ICK UB10 ... 112 A2
  HTHAIR TW6 ... 153 J6
  NWCR SE14 ... 160 C10
Nettlewood Rd
  STRHM/NOR SW16 ... 180 E5
Neuchatel Rd CAT SE6 ... 182 D5
Nevada Cl NWMAL KT3 ... 199 P1
Nevada St GNWCH SE10 ... 161 H6
Nevern Pl ECT SW5 ... 14 C5
Nevern Rd ECT SW5 ... 14 B6
Nevern Sq ECT SW5 ... 14 B6
Nevil Cl NTHWD HA6 ... 92 F6
Nevill Ct CRAWW RH11 ... 283 K10
Neville Av NWMAL KT3 ... 200 A10
Neville Cl ACT W3 ... 155 P1
  BFN/LL DA15 ... 185 J7
  BNSTD SM7 ... 221 L10
  CAMTN NW1 ... 5 H5
  ESH/CLAY KT10 ... 217 N3
  HSLW TW3 ... 135 J5
  KIL/WHAMP NW6 ... 2 B10
  PECK SE15 ... 159 P6

POTB/CUF EN6 .... 59 J7
SLN SL2 .... 129 L1
WAN E11 .... 121 L8
Neville Cl EFNCH N2 .... 117 M4
Neville Gdns BCTR RM8 .... 123 N8
Neville Gill Cl
WAND/EARL SW18 .... 179 K2
Neville Pl WDGN N22 .... 98 C9
BCTR RM8 .... 123 N7
CROY/NA CR0 .... 203 L7
EA W5 .... 135 K4
FSTGT E7 .... 141 M2
KIL/WHAMP NW6 .... 2 D8
KUT/HW KT1 .... 199 M2
RCHPK/HAM TW10 .... 177 H6
Neville St SKENS SW7 .... 15 L1
Neville Ter SKENS SW7 * .... 15 L7
Neville Wk CAR SM5 .... 201 P7
Nevill Gv WATN WD24 .... 22 C6
Nevill Rd STNW/STAM N16 .... 119 M9
Nevill Wy IG LG10 .... 82 B10
Nevill Wk CAR SM5 .... 201 P7
Nevin Dr CHING E4 .... 127 K8
Nevinson Cl WAND/EARL SW18 .... 179 N2
Nevis Cl ROM RM1 .... 104 F7
Nevis Rd TOOT SW17 .... 180 B5
New Acres Rd THMD SE28 .... 143 H10
Newall Rd HTHAIR TW6 .... 152 D7
New Ar UX/CGN UB8 * .... 131 N3
The New Ar HERT/WAT SG14 * .... 25 L5
Newark Cl RGUE GU4 .... 250 E5
RPLY/SEND GU23 .... 233 J4
Newark Ct WOT/HER KT12 .... 197 K8
Newark Crs WLSDN NW10 .... 135 J4
Newark Gn BORE WD6 .... 76 A7
Newark Knok EHAM E6 .... 142 D8
Newark La RPLY/SEND GU23 .... 233 J6
Newark Rd BFOR GU20 .... 212 A1
CRAWE RH10 .... 284 A5
SAND/SEL CR2 .... 223 L3
Newark St WCHPL E1 .... 140 C7
Newark Wy HDN NW4 .... 116 D1
New Barn Cl WLGTN SM6 .... 222 G3
New Barns Av MTCM CR4 * .... 202
Newbarn La RSEV TN14 .... 244 G2
BEAC HP9 .... 89 K5
New Barn La HART DA3 .... 211 M3
MEO DA13 .... 189 N7
SWLY BR8 .... 208 F1
New Barns Av MTCM CR4 .... 202 C4
New Barns Wy PLSTW E13 .... 141 L6
New Battleridge La
REDH RH1 .... 258 C6
Newberries Av RAD WD7 .... 74 G1
New Berry La WOT/HER KT12 * .... 217 L2
Newberry Rd ERITH DA8 .... 164 G7
Newbery Wy SL SL1 .... 149 J1
Newbiggin Pth OXHEY WD19 .... 95 K5
Newbold Cots WCHPL E1 * .... 140 B8
Newbolt Av CHEAM SM3 .... 220 F2
Newbolt Rd STAN HA7 .... 94 E7
New Bond St CONDST W1S .... 10 F6
MYFR/PICC W1J .... 10 C6
Newborough Av NWMAL KT3 .... 200 A4
New Brent St HDN NW4 .... 116 A3
New Bridge St EMB EC4V .... 12 C6
New Broad St LVPST EC2M .... 13 L4
New Broadway EA W5 .... 135 H9
HGDN/ICK UB10 * .... 132 C6
Newburgh Rd ACT W3 .... 135 P10
GRAYS RM17 .... 168 A4
Newburgh St SOHO/CST W1F .... 10 G7
New Burlington Ms
CONDST W1S .... 10 G7
New Burlington Pl
CONDST W1S .... 10 G7
New Burlington St
CONDST W1S .... 10 G7
Newburn St LBTH SE11 .... 17 P7
Newbury Av PEND EN3 .... 80 E3
Newbury Cl HARH RM3 .... 105 J2
NTHLT UB5 .... 133 N1
HART DA3 .... 188 D3
Newbury Gdns HARH RM3 .... 105 J2
HOR/WEW KT19 .... 220 C1
UPMR RM14 .... 125 N8
Newbury Ms KTTN NW5 .... 4 A3
Newbury Rd CHING E4 .... 101 H1
CRAWE RH10 .... 284 C1
GNTH/NBYPK IG2 .... 72 C4
HARH RM3 .... 105 K6
HAYES BR2 .... 205 M3
HTHAIR TW6 .... 152 A7
Newbury St STBT EC1A .... 12 E3
Newbury Wk HARH RM3 .... 105 L6
Newbury Wy NTHLT UB5 .... 133 M1
New Butt La DEPT SE8 * .... 160 F6
Newby Cl EN EN1 .... 79 M6
Newby Pl POP/IOD E14 .... 141 H9
Newby St VX/NE SW8 .... 159 J10
Newcastle Av BARK/HLT IG6 .... 103 K7
Newcastle Cl
FLST/FETLN EC4A .... 12 C5
Newcastle Pl BAY/PAD W2 .... 9 M4
Newcastle Rw CLKNW EC1R .... 12 B2
New Cswy REIG RH2 .... 275 L3
New Cavendish St
CAVSQ/HST W1G .... 10 D3
GTPST W1W .... 10 D4
New Change STP EC4M .... 12 G6
New Charles St FSBYE EC1V .... 6 E9
New Chilterns AMSS HP7 * .... 69 K5
New Church Rd CMBW SE5 .... 19 H10
Newchurch Rd SLN SL2 .... 128 E7
New City Rd PLSTW E13 .... 141 M5
New Clock Tower Pl
HOLWY N7 .... 5 L1
New Cl FELT TW13 .... 176 D1
WIM/MER SW19 .... 201 M3
New College Ms IS N1 * .... 6 B1
New College Pde HAMP NW3 * .... 3 J1
Newcombe Gdns HSLWW TW4 .... 155 L4
Newcombe Pk ALP/SUD HA0 .... 135 L3
MLHL NW7 .... 96 B6
Newcombe Ri WDR/YW UB7 .... 131 P8
Newcombe St KENS W8 * .... 8
Newcomen Gdns
STRHM/NOR SW16 .... 180 F7
WAN E11 * .... 121 L8
Newcomen Rd BTSEA SW11 .... 157 H3
Newcomen St STHWK SE1 .... 18 G1
Newcome Rd RAD WD7 .... 57 M10
New Compton St
LSQ/SEVD WC2H * .... 11 K6
New Coppice
WOKN/KNAP GU21 .... 231 K5
New Cots BRKMPK AL9 .... 58 F4
DORK RH4 .... 272 G6
REIG RH2 .... 256 G8
New Ct EMB EC4Y * .... 12 A7
NTHLT UB5 .... 114 A10
Newcourt St STJWD NW8 .... 3 N8
New Crane Pl WAP E1W * .... 140 E5
New Crescent Yd
WLSDN NW10 * .... 136 G4
Newcroft Cl UX/CGN UB8 .... 132 A4
New Cross Rd GUW GU2 .... 249 M8
NWCR SE14 .... 160 G6
Newdales Cl ED N9 .... 99 P3
Newdene Av NTHLT UB5 .... 133 J4
Newdigate
STRHM/NOR SW16 * .... 181 P4
Newdigate Gn DEN/HRF UB9 .... 91 N3
Newdigate Rd DEN/HRF UB9 .... 91 N3
HORS RH12 .... 282 A1
Newdigate Rd East
DEN/HRF UB9 .... 91 N3
Newell Ri HHS/BOV HP3 .... 35 P10
Newell St POP/IOD E14 .... 140 E9

New End HAMP NW3 .... 117 M9
New End Sq HAMP NW3 .... 117 N9
New England St
STALW/RED AL3 .... 38 B6
Newenham Rd GT/LBKH KT23 .... 253 P7
Newent Cl CAR SM5 .... 202 A8
PECK SE15 .... 159 M6
New Era Est IS N1 .... 7 J6
New Farm Av HAYES BR2 .... 205 M4
New Farm Dr ABR/ST RM4 .... 83 M7
New Farm La NTHWD HA6 .... 92 F9
New Ferry Ap
WOOL/PLUM SE18 .... 162 D2
New Fetter La
FLST/FETLN EC4A .... 12 B5
Newfield Cl HPTN TW12 .... 197 P1
Newfield La HHNE HP2 .... 36 A6
Newfield Ri CRICK NW2 .... 116 D8
Newfields WGCW AL8 .... 22 G6
Newfield Wy STALE/WH AL4 .... 39 H8
Newford Cl HHNE HP2 .... 36 C5
New Ford Rd CHES/WCR EN8 .... 62 E10
New Forest La CHIG IG7 .... 102 D7
Newgate CROY/NA CR0 .... 203 K8
New Garden Dr WDR/YW UB7 * .... 151 N1
STALE/WH AL4 .... 39 J3
Newgate Cl FELT TW13 .... 175 M5
Newgate St CHING E4 .... 101 K4
STBT EC1A .... 12 D5
Newgatestreet Rd
CHESW EN7 .... 61 J2
Newgate Street Village
HERT/BAY SG13 .... 60 F1
New Globe Wk STHWK SE1 .... 12 E9
New Goulston St WCHPL E1 .... 13 L5
New Green Pl
BRXS/STRHM SW2 .... 181 H3
NRWD SE19 .... 181 M9
New Greens Av
STALW/RED AL3 .... 38 C1
New Hall Cl HHS/BOV HP3 .... 52 D3
New Hall Cl HHS/BOV HP3 .... 52 D3
New Hall Dr HARH RM3 .... 105 M9
Newhall Gdns WOT/HER KT12 .... 197 K9
Newham's Rw STHWK SE1 .... 19 K2
Newham Wy CAN/RD E16 .... 141 L7
EHAM E6 .... 142 B6
Newhaven Cl HYS/HAR UB3 .... 152 C3
Newhaven Crs ASHF TW15 .... 174 E8
Newhaven Gdns
ELTH/MOT SE9 .... 162 A10
Newhaven La PLSTW E13 .... 141 L7
Newhaven Rd SNWD SE25 .... 203 L5
Newhaven Sp SL SL2 * .... 128 C6
New Haw Rd ADL/WDHM KT15 .... 215 M3
New Heston Rd HEST TW5 .... 153 H6
Newhouse Av CHDH RM6 .... 123 N1
Newhouse Cl NWMAL KT3 .... 200 B7
New House Farm La
RGUW GU3 .... 248 C8
Newhouse La CHONG CM5 .... 49 K8
New House La GVW DA11 .... 191 H5
REDH RH1 .... 276 E8
New House Pk STAL AL1 .... 38 F9
Newhouse Rd HHS/BOV HP3 .... 52 D2
Newhouse Wk MRDN SM4 .... 201 M7
Newick Cl BXLY DA5 .... 186 C2
Newick Rd CLPT E5 .... 120 A8
Newing Gn BMLY BR1 .... 184 A10
New Inn La RGUE GU4 .... 250 E7
New Inn Sq SDTCH EC2A * .... 13 K1
New Inn St SDTCH EC2A * .... 13 K1
New Inn Yd SDTCH EC2A .... 13 K1
New Kelvin Av TEDD TW11 .... 176 D9
New Kent Rd STAL AL1 .... 38 E6
WALW SE17 .... 18 F5
King's Ga FUL/PGN SW6 .... 157 K7
New King St DEPT SE8 .... 160 F5
Newland Cl PIN HA5 .... 93 M7
STAL AL1 .... 38 F9
Newland Ct WBLY HA9 .... 115 M7
Newland Dr EN EN1 .... 80 A5
Newland Gdns
HERT/BAY SG13 .... 25 M5
WEA W13 .... 154 F1
Newland Rd CEND/HSY/T N8 .... 118 F1
Newlands Cl UX/CGN UB8 .... 268 C2
Newlands Av RAD WD7 .... 56 A10
THDIT KT7 .... 198 D8
WOKS/MYFD GU22 .... 232 C7
Newlands Cl EDGW HA8 .... 95 K4
HORL RH6 .... 280 A3
NWDGN UB2 .... 153 M4
WOT/HER KT12 .... 217 N1
Newlands Dr DTCH/LGLY SL3 .... 150 C1
Newlands Pk ABLGY WD5 * .... 58 C2
CRAWE RH10 .... 285 M2
SYD SE26 .... 182 B9
Newlands Pl BAR EN5 .... 76 A7
Newlands Quay WAP E1W .... 140 E4
Newlands Rd CRAWW RH11 .... 283 M8
HHW HP1 .... 35 H5
STRHM/NOR SW16 .... 202 F2
WFD IG8 .... 101 L3
The Newlands WLGTN SM6 .... 222 D4
Newland St CAN/RD E16 .... 142 B10
Newland Wy GSTN WD25 .... 55 L9
Newlands Wy CHSGTN KT9 .... 219 G10
POTB/CUF EN6 .... 59 L6
Newlands Woods
CROY/NA CR0 .... 224 C5
New La RGUE GU4 .... 232 C10
New Ling EHAM E6 .... 142 C8
Newling Est BETH E2 * .... 7 M1
New Lodge Dr OXTED RH8 .... 261 L4
New London St MON EC3R * .... 13 K7
New Lydenburg Commercial
Est CHARL SE7 * .... 161 P3
New Lydenburg St CHARL SE7 .... 161 P2
Newlyn Cl LCOL/BKTW AL2 .... 55 M6
ORP BR6 .... 227 J1
UX/CGN UB8 .... 132 B7
Newlyn Gdns
RYLN/HDSTN HA2 .... 113 N5
Newlyn Rd BAR EN5 .... 77 J3
TOTM N17 .... 99 N9
WELL DA16 .... 163 J8
Newman Cl HORS RH12 .... 192 G5
Newman Ct BMLY BR1 * .... 183 N4
Newman Ms WDGN N22 .... 98 G8
CROY/NA CR0 .... 202 C7
HYS/HAR UB3 .... 133 J4
PLSTW E13 .... 141 N5
WALTH E17 .... 120 C3
Newman's Rw LINN WC2A .... 11 N4
Newman St FITZ W1T .... 11 H4
Newmarket Av NTHLT UB5 .... 113 N10
Newmarket Gn
ELTH/MOT SE9 * .... 162 C4
Newmarket Rd CRAWE RH10 .... 284 E4
Newmarket Wy HCH RM12 .... 125 J10
Newmarsh Rd THMD SE28 .... 143 H8
New Mile Rd ASC SL5 .... 192 A2
New Mill Rd STMC/STPC BR5 .... 207 H1
Newminster Ct ENC/FH EN2 * .... 79 J6

Newminster Rd MRDN SM4 .... 201 M6
New Mount St SRTFD E15 .... 141 J7
Newnham Av RSLP HA4 .... 113 K6
Newnham Cl LOU IG10 .... 82 A10
NTHLT UB5 .... 134 B1
THHTH CR7 .... 202 E2
Newnham Gdns NTHLT UB5 .... 134 B1
Newnham Gn WDGN N22 * .... 99 H9
Newnham Pde
CHES/WCR EN8 * .... 62 C6
Newnham Rd CDW/CHF RM16 .... 168 D3
Newnham Wy WDGN N22 .... 98 G9
Newnhams Cl BMLY BR1 .... 206 C3
Newnham Ter STHWK SE1 .... 18 A3
Newnham Wy
KTN/HRWW/WS HA3 .... 115 K3
Newnton Cl RAIN RM13 .... 144 F2
Newnton Cl STNW/STAM N16 .... 119 P3
New Oxford St
NOXST/BSQ WC1A .... 11 K5
New Pde ASHF TW15 * .... 174 A4
DORK RH4 * .... 272 G1
GT/LBKH KT23 * .... 254 B2
RKW/CH/CXG WD3 * .... 72 A10
WDR/YW UB7 * .... 131 P10
New Park Av PLMGR N13 .... 99 K4
New Park Cl NTHLT UB5 .... 133 M1
New Park Dr HHNE HP2 .... 36 A6
New Park Est UED N18 .... 100 B6
New Park Rd ASHF TW15 .... 174 D8
BRXS/STRHM SW2 .... 180 F3
DEN/HRF UB9 .... 91 M9
HERT/BAY SG13 .... 42 D10
New Peachey La UX/CGN UB8 .... 131 N8
Newpiece LOU IG10 .... 82 E7
New Place Gdns REDH RH1 * .... 258 A9
UPMR RM14 .... 126 C7
New Place Sq
BERM/RHTH SE16 * .... 160 A2
New Plaistow Rd SRTFD E15 .... 141 K3
New Pond Pde RSLP HA4 * .... 113 H8
New Pond Rd CODL GU7 .... 267 K6
New Quebec St MBLAR W1H .... 10 A6
New River Av CEND/HSY/T N8 .... 118 C1
WARE SG12 .... 26 C7
New River Crs PLMGR N13 .... 99 J3
New River Wy FSBYPK N4 .... 119 L5
New Rd ABR/ST RM4 .... 83 N10
WOKS/MYFD GU22 .... 233 H2
Newquay Crs
RYLN/HDSTN HA2 .... 113 N3
Newquay Gdns OXHEY WD19 .... 93 J3
Newquay Rd CAT SE6 .... 182 G5
New River Av CEND/HSY/T N8 .... 118 C1

New Street Rd MEO DA13 .... 211 P10
New Street Sq
FLST/FETLN EC4A .... 12 B5
New Swan Yd GVW DA11 * .... 190
New Tank Hill Rd PUR RM19 .... 165 P2
New Trinity Rd EFNCH N2 .... 117 N1
New Union Cl POP/IOD E14 .... 161 H2
New Union St BARB EC2Y .... 12 G4
New Vls TOTM N17 * .... 99 P9
New Wanstead WAN E11 .... 121 M4
New Way La GT/LBKH KT23 .... 48
New Way Rd CDALE/KGS NW9 .... 116 B2
New Wharf Rd IS N1 .... 5 N4
New Wickham La EGH TW20 .... 172 D10
New Wd WGCE AL7 .... 23 M4
Newyears Green La
DEN/HRF UB9 .... 112 A4
New Years La ORP BR6 .... 227 K10
RSEV TN14 .... 245 J2
New Zealand Av
WOT/HER KT12 .... 196 G8
New Zealand Wy RAIN RM13 .... 144 C1
SHB W12 .... 137 J1
Niagara Av EA W5 .... 155 H5
Niagara Cl CHES/WCR EN8 .... 62 C5
IS N1 .... 6 F7
Nibthwaite Rd HRW HA1 .... 114 D3
Nicholas Cl GFD/PVL UB6 .... 134 A1
SOCK/AV RM15 .... 147 H5
WATN WD24 .... 73 J3
Nicholas Gdns EA W5 .... 135 J9
SL SL1 .... 128 D10
WOKS/MYFD GU22 .... 233 H2
Nicholas Ms CHSWK W4 * .... 158 B3
Nicholas Rd BCTR RM8 .... 124 A7
BORE WD6 .... 75 N6
CROY/NA CR0 .... 222 F1
WCHPL E1 .... 140 B6
Nicholas Wy HHNE HP2 .... 36 B6
NTHWD HA6 .... 92 D9
Nicholay Rd ARCH N19 .... 118 E6
Nicholes Rd HSLW TW3 .... 155 H10
Nichol La BMLY BR1 .... 183 M10
Nicholl Rd EPP CM16 .... 81 J2
Nicholls WDSR SL4 .... 148 B9
Nicholls Av UX/CGN UB8 .... 132 B6
Nicholls Fld HLWS CM18 .... 47 L3
Nichollsfield Wk HOLWY N7 .... 118 E10
Nicholls St BETH E2 .... 7 N6
Nichols Cl FSBYPK N4 * .... 119 H6
Nichols Gn EA W5 .... 135 K7
Nicholson Dr BUSH WD23 .... 94 B2
Nicholson Ms EGH TW20 .... 172 G4
Nicholson Rd CROY/NA CR0 .... 203 M4
Nicholson St STHWK SE1 .... 12 C10
Nickelby Cl THMD SE28 .... 143 M8
UX/CGN UB8 * .... 132 B7
Nicol Cl CFSP/GDCR SL9 .... 89 P9
Nicol End CFSP/GDCR SL9 .... 89 P9
Nicoll Pl HDN NW4 .... 116 E4
Nicoll Rd WLSDN NW10 .... 135 H2
Nicoll Wy BORE WD6 .... 76 A9
Nicolson Rd STMC/STPC BR5 .... 202
Nicosia Rd WAND/EARL SW18 .... 179
Nidderdale HHNE HP2 .... 35
Niederwald Rd SYD SE26 .... 182
Nield Rd HYS/HAR UB3 .... 152
Nigel Cl NTHLT UB5 .... 133
Nigel Fisher Wy CHSGTN KT9 .... 219
Nigel Ms IL IG1 .... 122
Nigel Playfair Av HMSMTH W6 .... 156
Nigel Rd FSTGT E7 .... 141
PECK SE15 .... 159
Nigeria Rd CHARL SE7 .... 161
Nightingale Av CHING E4 .... 101
Nightingale Cl ABLGY WD5 .... 58
BH/WHM TN16 .... 243
CAR SM5 .... 202
CHSWK W4 .... 157
COB KT11 .... 253
CRAWW RH11 .... 283
GVW DA11 .... 190
HOR/WEW KT19 .... 219
PIN HA5 .... 113
RAD WD7 .... 74
Nightingale Cnr
STMC/STPC BR5 * .... 207
Nightingale Ct SL SL1 .... 149
SUT SM1 .... 221
Nightingale Crs EHSLY KT24 .... 252
HARH RM3 .... 105
Nightingale Dr
HOR/WEW KT19 .... 219
Nightingale Gv LEW SE13 .... 183
Nightingale La BAL SW12 .... 180
BMLY BR1 .... 205
CEND/HSY/T N8 .... 117
CLAP SW4 .... 180
HORL RH6 .... 280
PLMGR N13 .... 99
RCHPK/HAM TW10 .... 176
SL SL1 .... 149
WAN E11 .... 121
WEY KT13 .... 216
WWCW AL8 .... 22
Nightingale Ms KUT/HW KT1 * .... 199
LBTH SE11 .... 18
Nightingale Pl SKENS SW3 .... 128
Nightingale Pl
RKW/CH/CXG WD3 .... 91

WBPTN SW10 .... 15 N3
WOOL/PLUM SE18 .... 162 D5
Nightingale La BGR/WK TN15 .... 247 L5
BUSH WD23 .... 73 P9
CAR SM5 .... 202 A10
CHESW EN7 .... 61 K1
CLPT E5 .... 120 A8
CSHM HP5 * .... 50 G5
E/WMO/HCT KT8 .... 198 A5
ED N10 .... 100 B1
EHSLY KT24 .... 252 G1
ESH/CLAY KT10 .... 217 N2
GU GU1 .... 250 A10
HNWL W7 .... 134 G10
HPTN TW12 .... 175 P9
RKW/CH/CXG WD3 .... 91 M1
SAND/SEL CR2 .... 224 C5
STMC/STPC BR5 .... 206 F6
WDGN N22 .... 98 F9
WLSDN NW10 .... 136 C4
WOT/HER KT12 * .... 197 K7
Nightingale Shott EGH TW20 .... 173 J7
Nightingale Sq BAL SW12 .... 180 B1
Nightingale St CSTG HP8 .... 90 A2
Nightingale Ter BAL SW12 .... 180 B3
The Nightingales
STWL/WRAY TW19 .... 174 A4
Nightingale V
WOOL/PLUM SE18 .... 162 D5
Nightingale Wk BAL SW12 .... 180 C2
WDSR SL4 .... 149 H9
Nightingale Wy DEN/HRF UB9 .... 91 N3
EHAM E6 .... 141 N8
SEVS/STOTM N15 * .... 119 H7
SWLY BR8 .... 208 F3
Nightingle Av HRW HA1 .... 114 F4
Nile Cl STNW/STAM N16 .... 119 N3
Nile Dr ED N18 .... 100 B3
Nile Rd PLSTW E13 .... 141 N4
Nile St IS N1 .... 6 G9
Nile Ter PECK SE15 .... 19 N9
Nimbus Rd HOR/WEW KT19 .... 220 A6
Nimmo Dr BUSH WD23 .... 94 C1
Nimrod Cl NTHLT UB5 .... 133 L4
STALE/WH AL4 .... 39 H4
Nimrod Dr HAT AL10 .... 40 A5
Nimrod Pas IS N1 * .... 7 M2
Nimrod Rd STRHM/NOR SW16 .... 180 C9
Nina Mackay Cl SRTFD E15 * .... 141 K9
Nine Acre La HAT AL10 .... 40 C5
Nine Acres SL SL1 .... 128 E10
Nine Acres Cl HYS/HAR UB3 .... 152 A2
MNPK E12 .... 122 B10
Nineacres Wy COUL/CHIP CR5 .... 240 F2
Nine Ashes WARE SG12 .... 26 A4
Nine Elms Av UX/CGN UB8 .... 131 N7
Nine Elms Cl EBED/NFELT TW14 .... 174 G4
UX/CGN UB8 .... 131 N7
Nine Elms Gv GVW DA11 .... 190 D3
Nine Elms La VX/NE SW8 .... 17 K10
Ninefields WAB EN9 .... 63 N4
Ninehams Cl CTHM CR3 .... 241 L6
Ninehams Gdns CTHM CR3 .... 241 L6
Ninehams Rd BH/WHM TN16 .... 244 A7
CTHM CR3 .... 241 L7
Ninhams Wd ORP BR6 .... 226 D1
Ninian Rd HHNE HP2 .... 35 P1
Ninnings Av CFSP/GDCR SL9 .... 90 C8
Ninnings Wy CFSP/GDCR SL9 .... 90 C8
Ninth Av HYS/HAR UB3 .... 133 H9
KWD/TDW/WH KT20 * .... 257 J2
Nisbett Wk SCUP DA14 .... 185 L7
Nithdale Rd WOOL/PLUM SE18 .... 163 H6
Nithsdale Gv HGDN/ICK UB10 .... 112 D8
Niton Cl BAR EN5 .... 76 C10
Niton Rd RCH/KEW TW9 .... 155 M9
Niton St FUL/PGN SW6 .... 156 G6
Niven Cl BORE WD6 .... 75 P5
Nixey Cl SL SL1 .... 149 M1
Nizels La RTON TN11 .... 265 N10
No1 St WOOL/PLUM SE18 .... 162 E1
No2 St WOOL/PLUM SE18 .... 162 E1
Noahs Ct CRAWE RH10 * .... 285 P7
Noahs Court Gdns
HEST TW5 .... 25
Noake Mill La HHW HP1 .... 35 K1
Noak Hill Rd ABR/ST RM4 .... 105 L4
HARH RM3 .... 105 L4
Nobel Dr HYS/HAR UB3 .... 152 B6
Nobel Rd UED N18 .... 100 G5
Noble Cl HEST TW5 * .... 153 P7
Noble Cnr HEST TW5 * .... 153 P5
Noble St CITYW EC2V .... 12 F5
Nobles Wy EGH TW20 .... 172 B10
Noel Rd ACT W3 .... 135 H4
EHAM E6 .... 142 B6
IS N1 .... 6 D4
Noel Sq DAGW RM9 .... 79 N4
Noel Ter SOHO/CST W1F * .... 11 H6
Noke Dr REDH RH1 .... 258 E9
Noke La LCOL/BKTW AL2 .... 55 M2
Noke Side LCOL/BKTW AL2 .... 55 P5
The Nokes HHW HP1 .... 35 H2
Nolan Wy CLPT E5 .... 119 P9
Nolton Pl EDGW HA8 .... 95 L3
Nonsuch Cl CHIG IG7 .... 102 E7
Nonsuch Court Av EW KT17 .... 220 E6
Nonsuch Ms CHEAM SM3 .... 220 G5
Nonsuch Wk BELMT SM2 .... 220 D5
The Nook WARE SG12 .... 26 G7
Noons Corner Rd RDKG RH5 .... 274 A9
Norbiton Av KUT/HW KT1 .... 199 M2
Norbiton Common Rd
KUT/HW KT1 .... 199 N2
Norbreck Gdns
WLSDN NW10 * .... 135 M5
Norbroke St SHB W12 .... 136 G9
Norburn St NKENS W10 * .... 8 A1
Norbury Av HSLW TW3 .... 176 A1
STRHM/NOR SW16 .... 202 A2
WATN WD24 .... 22 G1
Norbury Cl STRHM/NOR SW16 .... 202 A2
Norbury Court Rd
STRHM/NOR SW16 .... 202 A2
Norbury Crs
STRHM/NOR SW16 .... 202 B3
Norbury Cross
STRHM/NOR SW16 .... 202 A4
Norbury Gv MLHL NW7 .... 96 B7
Norbury Hl STRHM/NOR SW16 .... 181 P10
Norbury Ri
STRHM/NOR SW16 .... 201 P5
Norbury Rd CHING E4 .... 101 J2
FELT TW13 .... 174 D6
REIG RH2 .... 257 J7
THHTH CR7 .... 202 B5
Norbury Vls KUT/HW KT1 * .... 199 M2
Norcombe Gdns
KTN/HRWW/WS HA3 .... 115 H4
Norcott Cl YEAD UB4 .... 133 J3
Norcott Rd STNW/STAM N16 .... 119 P7
Norcroft Gdns EDUL SE22 .... 181 H1
Norcutt Rd WHTN TW2 .... 176 D4
Norderfeldt Rd ERITH DA8 .... 164 F4
Nordmann Pl SOCK/AV RM15 .... 111 J3
Norelands Dr SL SL1 .... 128 A3
Norfield Rd RDART DA2 .... 186 F7
Norfolk Av PLMGR N13 .... 99 J7
SAND/SEL CR2 .... 223 P6
SEVS/STOTM N15 .... 119 N4
WATN WD24 .... 73 K5
Norfolk Cl EBAR EN4 .... 77 M3
CEND/HSY/T N8 .... 118
PLMGR N13 .... 99 J7
Norfolk Crs BAY/PAD W2 .... 9 M5
BFN/LL DA15 .... 185 H5
Norfolk Farm Cl
WOKS/MYFD GU22 .... 232 F1

Norfolk Farm Rd
WOKS/MYFD GU22 .... 232 G1
Norfolk Gdns BORE WD6 .... 76 A8
BXLYHN DA7 .... 164 A7
WOKN/KNAP GU21 * .... 231 L5
Norfolk House
RKW/CH/CXG WD3 * .... 91 P2
Norfolk House Rd
STRHM/NOR SW16 .... 180 G6
Norfolk La RDKG RH5 .... 272 G8
Norfolk Ms NKENS W10 .... 8 B1
Norfolk Pl BAY/PAD W2 .... 9 M5
CDW/CHF RM16 .... 167 H4
WELL DA16 .... 163 K8
Norfolk Rd BAR EN5 .... 77 K7
BARK IG11 .... 143 H2
DAGE RM10 .... 124 C10
DORK RH4 .... 272 F2
EHAM E6 .... 142 C3
ESH/CLAY KT10 .... 218 D2
FELT TW13 .... 175 K4
GVE DA12 .... 191 M6
HRW HA1 .... 114 A3
PEND EN3 .... 80 A9
RKW/CH/CXG WD3 .... 91 P2
ROMW/RG RM7 .... 124 D4
STJWD NW8 .... 3 M6
THHTH CR7 .... 203 K3
UPMR RM14 .... 125 P8
UX/CGN UB8 .... 131 N1
WALTH E17 .... 101 G10
WIM/MER SW19 .... 179 P10
WLSDN NW10 .... 136 B2
Norfolk Rw STHWK SE1 .... 17 N5
Norfolk Sq BAY/PAD W2 .... 9 M6
Norfolk Square Ms
BAY/PAD W2 .... 9 M6
Norfolk St FSTGT E7 .... 121 M10
Norgrove Pk CFSP/GDCR SL9 .... 110 B2
Norgrove St BAL SW12 .... 180 B4
Norheads La BH/WHM TN16 .... 243 M4
Norhyrst Av SNWD SE25 .... 202 A5
Norland Pl NTGHL W11 .... 8 D10
Norlands Crs CHST BR7 .... 185 H5
Norland Sq NTGHL W11 .... 8 A10
Norlands Ga CHST BR7 .... 206 E1
Norlands La EGH TW20 .... 195 H2
Norley V PUT/ROE SW15 .... 178 D4
Norlington Rd LEY E10 .... 121 L6
Norman Av FFCH E17 .... 120 C8
FELT TW13 .... 175 H6
SAND/SEL CR2 .... 223 K6
STHL UB1 .... 133 J6
TWK TW1 .... 176 C3
WDGN N22 .... 99 H8
Normanby Cl PUT/ROE SW15 .... 179 J1
Normanby Rd WLSDN NW10 .... 116 E10
Normandy Av BAR EN5 .... 76 C7
Normandy Cl CRAWE RH10 .... 284 C9
SYD SE26 .... 182 D6
Normandy Common La
RGUW GU3 .... 248 A7
Normandy Ct HHNE HP2 .... 35 N5
Normandy Dr BERK HP4 .... 33 N4
HYS/HAR UB3 .... 133 G5
Normandy Rd BRXN/ST SW9 .... 159 H7
STALW/RED AL3 .... 38 C5
Normandy Ter CAN/RD E16 .... 141 M8
Normandy Wy ERITH DA8 .... 164 F7
HOD EN11 .... 45 J1
Norman Gv BOW E3 .... 140 G4
Normanhurst
RBRW/HUT CM13 .... 87 P10
Normanhurst Av WELL DA16 .... 163 N7
Normanhurst Cl CRAWE RH10 .... 284 A7
Normanhurst Dr TWK TW1 .... 176 C1
Normanhurst Rd
BRXS/STRHM SW2 .... 180 G5
STMC/STPC BR5 .... 207 L2
WOT/HER KT12 .... 197 L6
Norman Pde SCUP DA14 * .... 185 P6
Norman Rd ASHF TW15 .... 174 C10
BELV DA17 .... 144 C10
BELV DA17 .... 164 B1
EHAM E6 .... 142 C6
EMPK RM11 .... 125 H5
GNWCH SE10 .... 160 G6
IL IG1 .... 122 C10
SEVS/STOTM N15 .... 119 P6
SUT SM1 .... 221 K2
THHTH CR7 .... 202 B3
WAN E11 .... 121 K7
WIM/MER SW19 .... 179 M10
Normans Cl GVW DA11 .... 190 G3
UX/CGN UB8 .... 131 P7
WDGN N22 .... 99 H9
WLSDN NW10 .... 136 A1
Normansfield Av KUT/HW KT1 .... 177 N10
Normansfield Cl BUSH WD23 .... 94 A1
Normanshire Dr CHING E4 .... 100 E1
Normans Md WLSDN NW10 .... 136 A1
Norman's Rd SLN SL2 .... 129 N8
The Normans SLN SL2 .... 129 N8
Norman St FSBYE EC1V .... 6 E10
RSEV TN14 .... 263 P6
Norman Ter
KIL/WHAMP NW6 * .... 117 J10
Normanton Av
WAND/EARL SW18 .... 179 K5
Normanton Pk CHING E4 .... 101 K4
Normanton Rd SAND/SEL CR2 .... 223 M3
Normanton St FSTH SE23 .... 182 C5
Norman Wy ACT W3 .... 135 N7
STHGT/OAK N14 .... 98 F3
Normington Cl
STRHM/NOR SW16 .... 181 H8
Norrels Dr EHSLY KT24 .... 252 G2
Norrels Ride EHSLY KT24 .... 252 G1
Norrice Lea EFNCH N2 .... 117 N3
Norris Cl HOR/WEW KT19 .... 219 P6
LCOL/BKTW AL2 .... 56 C2
Norris Gv BROX EN10 .... 26 D6
Norris La HOD EN11 .... 44 E1
Norris Ri HOD EN11 .... 44 D1
Norris Rd HOD EN11 .... 44 E1
STA TW18 .... 174 A6
Norris St STJS SW1Y .... 11 J8
Norris Wy DART DA1 .... 164 G9
Norroy Rd PUT/ROE SW15 .... 179 H6
Norrys Cl EBAR EN4 .... 78 A4
Norrys Rd EBAR EN4 .... 78 A4
Norseman Cl GDMY/SEVK IG3 .... 123 L6
Norseman Wy GFD/PVL UB6 .... 134 A10
Norstead Pl PUT/ROE SW15 .... 178 D5
Norsted La ORP BR6 .... 227 M10
North Access Rd WALTH E17 .... 120 C4
North Acre CDALE/KGS NW9 .... 97 H7
North Acton Rd WLSDN NW10 .... 136 H4
Northallerton Av SL SL1 .... 129 L10
Northall Rd BXLYHN DA7 .... 164 D8
Northampton Av SL SL1 .... 129 L10
Northampton Gv IS N1 .... 119 L10
Northampton Pk IS N1 .... 6 G1
Northampton Rd
CLKNW EC1R .... 12 B1

CROY/NA CRO 203 P9
PEND EN5 80 D8
**Northampton Rw**
CLKNW EC1R * 12 B1
**Northampton Sq** FSBYE EC1V 6 C10
**Northampton St** IS N1 6 E3
**Northanger Rd**
STRHM/NOR SW16 180 F1
**North Ap** GSTN WD25 55 N10
NTHWD HA6 92 D3
**North Ash Rd** HART DA3 211 L10
**North Audley St**
MYFR/PKLN W1K 10 C7
**North Av** CAR SM5 222 B4
HYS/HAR UB3 133 H9
RAD WD7 57 K8
RCH/KEW TW9 155 N8
RYLN/HDSTN HA2 114 A4
STHL UB1 133 N9
UED N18 99 P5
WEA W13 134 G8
WOT/HER KT12 216 F5
**Northaw Cl** HHNE HP2 36 C1
**Northaw Pl** POTB/CUF EN6 * 59 P2
**Northaw Rd West**
POTB/CUF EN6 60 B8
**North Bank** STJWD NW8 3 N10
**Northbank Rd** WALTH E17 101 H10
**North Barn** BROX EN10 44 G8
**North Birkbeck Rd** WAN E11 121 J8
**Northborough Rd** SLN SL2 128 F6
STRHM/NOR SW16 202 F2
**Northbourne** GODL GU7 267 L9
HAYES BR2 205 M7
**Northbourne Rd** CLAP SW4 158 E10
**Northbrook Dr** NTHWD HA6 92 F9
**Northbrook Rd** BAR EN5 77 H10
CROY/NA CRO 203 L5
IL IG1 122 D7
LEW SE13 183 J1
WDGN N22 98 F7
**Northbrooks**
HLWW/ROY CM19 46 C2
**Northburgh St** FSBYE EC1V 12 D2
**North Burnham Cl** SLN SL1 128 A4
**North Carriage Dr**
BAY/PAD W2 9 H7
**Northchurch La** CSHM HP5 33 H7
**Northchurch Rd** IS N1 13 K2
WBLY HA9 135 N1
**North Circular** PLMGR N13 99 H6
WALTH E17 100 C9
**North Circular Rd** BARK IG11 142 D2
CHING E4 100 C7
EFNCH N2 97 M10
GLDGN NW11 117 N4
IL IG1 122 A4
NFNCH/WDSPK N12 97 P8
REDBR IG4 121 P1
WLSDN NW10 135 L4
**Northcliffe Dr**
TRDG/WHET N20 97 J2
**North Cl** BAR EN5 76 F9
BXLYHS DA6 163 N10
CHIG IG7 103 K6
CRAWE RH10 284 A6
DAGE RM10 144 B3
EBED/NFELT TW14 174 E2
LCOL/BKTW AL2 56 A1
MRDN SM4 201 H4
RDKG RH5 273 H6
WDSR SL4 148 E7
**The North Colonnade**
POP/IOD E14 140 C10
**North Common** WEY KT13 * 216 D1
**North Common Rd** EA W5 135 K9
UX/CGN UB8 111 N10
**Northcote** ADL/WDHM KT15 215 N1
**Northcote Av** BRYLDS KT5 199 M7
EA W5 135 K9
ISLW TW7 176 F1
STHL UB1 133 M9
**Northcote Crs** EHSLY KT24 252 C1
**Northcote Rd** BTSEA SW11 157 P10
CROY/NA CRO 203 L6
EHSLY KT24 252 D1
GVW DA11 190 C4
NWMAL KT3 185 H7
SCUP DA14 185 P8
TWK TW1 176 F1
WALTH E17 120 D2
WLSDN NW10 136 B2
**Northcott Av** WDGN N22 98 F9
**North Countess Rd**
WALTH E17 100 E10
**Northcourt** FITZ W1T * 11 H5
RKW/CH/CXG WD3 91 K2
**North Cray Rd** BXLY DA5 186 B5
SCUP DA14 186 B5
**North Crs** CAN/RD E16 141 J6
FNCH N3 97 J10
GWRST WC1E 11 J3
**Northcroft** SLN SL2 128 C8
**Northcroft Rd** ECH TW20 171 N8
**Northcroft Gdns** EGH TW20 171 N8
**Northcroft Rd** EGH TW20 171 N8
HOR/WEW KT19 220 B4
WEA W13 154 G1
**Northcroft Vis** ECH TW20 171 N8
**North Cross Rd** BARK/HLT IG6 122 F2
EDUL SE22 181 N1
**Northdene** CHIG IG7 102 G6
**North Dene** HSLW TW3 154 A4
MLHL NW7 96 A4
**Northdene Gdns**
SEVS/STOTM N15 119 M4
**North Down** SAND/SEL CR2 223 M7
**Northdown Cl** RSLP HA4 112 G10
**Northdown Ct** CDST RH9 260 B6
**Northdown Gdns**
GNTH/NBYPK IG2 123 H3
**Northdown La** GU GU1 268 B3
**Northdown Rd** BELMT SM2 221 K6
BGR/WK TN15 247 N3
CFSP/GDCR SL9 90 B7
CTHM CR3 260 F1
EMPK RM11 125 J1
HART DA3 211 K2
HAT AL10 40 D7
WELL DA16 163 L8
**North Downs Crs**
CROY/NA CRO 224 G6
**North Downs Rd**
CROY/NA CRO 224 G6
**North Downs St** IS N1 5 N8
**North Downs Wy**
BGR/WK TN15 247 L5
BH/WHM TN16 243 P9
BRKHM/BTCW RH3 256 A8
CTHM CR3 258 G2
GUW GU2 268 A4
OXTED RH8 261 L1
RDKG RH5 253 P10
REDH RH1 258 F2
RGUW GU3 266 C5
RSEV TN14 247 L1
SEV TN13 246 E4
WARL CR6 243 M9
**North End** CROY/NA CRO 203 N8
HAMP NW3 117 M4
HART DA3 211 J1
HARH RM3 105 N3
BKHH IG9 101 P1

**Northend** BRW CM14 107 H6
HHS/BOV HP3 36 C9
**North End Av** HAMP NW3 117 M7
**North End Crs** WKENS W14 14 C6
**North End La** ASC SL5 192 N1
ORP BR6 226 B5
**North End Rd** ERITH DA8 164 G6
**North End Rd** FUL/PGN SW6 157 K6
GLDGN NW11 117 K6
WBLY HA9 115 N8
WKENS W14 14 B6
**North End Wy** HAMP NW3 117 M7
**Northern Av** ED N9 116 B2
**Northernhay Wk** MRDN SM4 201 H4
**Northern Perimeter Road** 152 D7
**Northern Perimeter Road**
**(West)** HTHAIR TW6 151 P7
**Northern Relief Rd** BARK IG11 142 F2
**Northern Rd** SLN SL2 129 J6
**Northey Av** BELMT SM2 220 G6
**North Eyot Gdns**
HMSMTH W6 156 C4
**Northey St** POP/IOD E14 140 D9
**North Farm** LOU IG10 81 P10
**Northfield** HART DA3 211 L3
LTWR GU18 212 A7
RGUE GU4 268 B8
**Northfield Av** PIN HA5 113 L2
STHL UB1 132 G7
**Northfield Cl** BMLY BR1 206 B1
HYS/HAR UB3 152 C2
**Northfield Crs** CHEAM SM3 220 F1
**Northfield Ct** STA TW18 195 L1
**Northfield Farm Ms** COB KT11 217 H9
**Northfield Gdns** DAGW RM9 73 K5
**Northfield Pde**
HYS/HAR UB3 * 152 C2
**Northfield Pk** HYS/HAR UB3 152 C2
**Northfield Rd** WPK KT13 216 C4
**Northfield Recreation Gnd**
EA W5 * 154 G3
**Northfield Rd** BORE WD6 75 N5
CHES/WCR EN8 62 D8
COB KT11 217 H9
DAGW RM9 124 A9
EBAR EN4 77 P7
ED N9 * 116 C1
EHAM E6 142 C1
HEST TW5 153 L5
PEND EN3 80 A10
STA TW18 195 L1
STNW/STAM N16 119 M5
WDSR SL4 148 E5
WEA W13 154 G1
**Northfields** ASHTD KT21 237 K5
EW KT17 220 H1
GRAYS RM17 167 P3
WAND/EARL SW18 157 K10
**North Gdns** WIM/MER SW19 179 N10
**Northga** HLW CM20 28 F10
**Northgate** NTHWD HA6 92 D8
**Northgate Dr** CDALE/KGS NW9 96 B4
**Northgate Pth** BORE WD6 75 L4
**Northgate Pl** CRAWE RH10 283 P6
**Northgate Rd** CRAWE RH10 283 P7
HORL RH6 280 A6
**North Gower St** CAMTN NW1 4 G10
**North Gv** HL SL1 129 K9
**North Gv** CHERT KT16 195 J6
HGT N6 118 B5
HLWS CM18 47 K2
SEVS/STOTM N15 119 L3
**North Hl** HGT N6 118 A4
RKW/CH/CXG WD3 71 H6
**North Hill Av** HGT N6 118 A4
**North Hill Dr** HARH RM3 105 L5
**North Hyde Gdns** 153 H2
HYS/HAR UB3 * 153 H2
**North Hyde La** NWDGN UB2 153 H4
**North Hyde Rd** HYS/HAR UB3 152 F2
**North Hyde Whf**
NWDGN UB2 * 153 H3
**Northiam** NFNCH/WDSPK N12 97 K5
**Northiam St** HACK E8 13 J1
**Northington St** BMSBY WC1N 11 N3
**North Kent Av** GVW DA11 189 P2
**Northlands** POTB/CUF EN6 59 N7
**Northlands Av** ORP BR6 227 H1
**Northlands St** CMBW SE5 159 K8
**North La** TEDD TW11 176 B9
**North Lodge Cl**
PUT/ROE SW15 * 178 G1
**North Lee** EW KT17 * 220 H9
**North Md** CRAWE RH10 283 P5
**Northmead** REDH RH1 257 P7
**North Md** RSLP HA4 113 J10
**Northmead Rd** SLN SL2 128 C8
**North Mews** BMSBY WC1N 11 N2
**North Moors** GU GU1 250 B5
**North Mt** TRDG/WHET N20 * 97 M3
**Northolm** EDGW HA8 96 H5
**Northolme Cl**
CDW/CHF RM16 * 169 L7
**Northolme Gdns** EDGW HA8 95 M9
**Northolme Ri** ORP BR6 207 H9
**Northolme Rd** HBRY N5 119 K9
**Northolt Av** RSLP HA4 113 J10
**Northolt Gdns** GFD/PVL UB6 114 E10
**Northolt Rd** HTHAIR TW6 151 P7
RYLN/HDSTN HA2 114 A9
**Northolt Wy** HCHM RM12 125 K10
**North Orbital Rd**
DEN/HRF UB9 111 J5
LCOL/BKTW AL2 55 M6
**North Orbital Road**
Rd GSTN WD25 55 L9
**North Orbital Road St Albans**
Rd GSTN WD25 55 L9
**Northover** BMLY BR1 183 L8
**North Pde** CHSGTN KT9 219 L2
EDGW HA8 96 B4
STHL UB1 * 133 P8
**North Pk** CFSP/GDCR SL9 110 B1
DTCH/LGLY SL3 150 A2
ELTH/MOT SE9 184 C2
**North Park La** GDST RH9 259 P7
**North Pas** WAND/EARL SW18 179 K1
**North Peckham Est**
PECK SE15 159 N6
**North Pl** HLW CM20 29 N6
MTCM CR4 180 A10
TEDD TW11 176 E9
**Northpoint Cl** SUT SM1 201 M10
**North Pole La** HAYES BR2 225 M3
**North Pole Rd** SHB W12 136 F6
**Northport St** IS N1 7 H6
**Northridge Rd** GVE DA12 190 F6
**Northridge Wy** HHW HP1 35 J7
**North Ri** BAY/PAD W2 * 9 H6
**North Riding** LCOL/BKTW AL2 56 A1
**North Rd** ABR/ST RM4 104 F5
AMS HP6 33 N6
BELV DA17 164 G4
BERK HP4 33 N5
BMLY BR1 205 N1
BRW CM14 107 H2
BTFD TW8 155 N5
CHDH RM6 123 P3
CHES/WCR EN8 62 D5
CRAWE RH10 284 B5
EA W5 155 J2
EBED/NFELT TW14 173 J3
ED N9 100 A2
EDGW HA8 95 N9
GDMY/SEVK IG3 123 H1
GUW GU2 249 N6
HERT/WAT SG14 25 H4
HEST TW5 153 H4
HGT N6 118 B5
HOD EN11 44 H4
HOLWY N7 5 L1
HYS/HAR UB3 133 H6
PUR RM19 166 B3
RCH/KEW TW9 155 N8

REIG RH2 275 J3
RKW/CH/CXG WD3 70 G9
SOCK/AV RM15 147 J2
STHL UB1 133 P9
SURB KT6 199 J6
WDR/YW UB7 152 A2
WIM/MER SW19 179 N9
WOKN/KNAP GU21 232 D2
WOOL/PLUM SE18 163 H3
WOT/HER KT12 217 K2
WWKM BR4 204 C8
**North Road Av** BRW CM14 107 H2
HERT/WAT SG14 25 J3
**North Road Gdns**
HERT/WAT SG14 25 J3
**Northrop Rd** HTHAIR TW6 152 F7
**North Rw** DTCH/LGLY SL3 * 110 B9
MYFR/PKLN W1K 10 B7
**North Several**
BKHTH/KID SE3 * 161 J8
**North Side Wandsworth**
**Common**
WAND/EARL SW18 179 M1
**Northspur Rd** SUT SM1 201 K10
**North Sq** ED N9 100 A3
GLDGN NW11 117 K3
**North Station Ap** REDH RH1 * 276 C2
**Northstead Rd**
BRXS/STRHM SW2 181 H5
**North St** BARK IG11 142 E2
BMLY BR1 205 M1
BXLYHN DA7 164 B10
CAR SM5 222 A1
CLAP SW4 158 C9
CRAWE RH10 285 P9
DORK RH4 272 F2
EGH TW20 172 A8
EMPK RM11 125 L5
GODL GU7 267 K10
GU GU1 268 A1
GVE DA12 190 E3
HDN NW4 116 F3
ISLW TW7 154 F9
LHD/OX KT22 236 F7
PLSTW E15 141 N4
REDH RH1 258 A9
ROM RM1 104 G3
WAB EN9 59 J4
**North Tenter St** WCHPL E1 * 13 M6
**North Ter** SKENS SW7 15 N5
**Northumberland Aly**
FENCHST EC3M * 13 K6
**Northumberland Av**
CHCR WC2N 11 L9
EMPK RM11 125 J4
EN EN1 80 A4
ISLW TW7 154 E7
MNPK E12 121 P6
WELL DA16 163 H10
**Northumberland Cl**
ERITH DA8 164 D6
STWL/WRAY TW19 173 H2
**Northumberland Crs**
EBED/NFELT TW14 174 F2
**Northumberland Gdns**
BMLY BR1 206 D4
ED N9 99 N4
MTCM CR4 202 E5
**Northumberland Gv**
TOTM N17 100 A8
**Northumberland Pk**
ERITH DA8 164 D6
TOTM N17 99 P6
**Northumberland Pl**
BAY/PAD W2 * 8 E5
**Northumberland Rd** BAR EN5 77 M10
EHAM E6 142 B9
MEO DA13 190 C10
RYLN/HDSTN HA2 113 N5
SWLY/COR SS17 169 J1
WALTH E17 120 F5
**Northumberland Wy**
ERITH DA8 164 D7
**Northumbria St** POP/IOD E14 140 A8
**North Verbena Gdns**
HMSMTH W6 156 D4
**North Vw** EA W5 135 H6
IL IG1 113 K5
**Northview** SWLY BR8 208 F2
**North Vw** WIM/MER SW19 178 B8
**North View Av** TIL RM18 168 H3
**North View Crs** EPSOM KT18 238 A5
**Northview Crs** WLSDN NW10 116 C9
**Northview Dr** WFD IG8 102 A10
**Northview Pde** HOLWY N7 * 118 F4
**North View Rd**
CEND/HSY/T N8 118 C1
SEV TN13 247 K7
**North Vis** CAMTN NW1 5 J2
**North Wk** CROY/NA CRO 224 C2
**North Wy** HGDN/ICK UB10 131 P2
PIN HA5 113 K1
CDALE/KGS NW9 95 N4
ED N9 100 B3
FBAR/BDGN N11 98 D7
**Northway** GLDGN NW11 117 L3
GODL GU7 266 G10
GUW GU2 249 N6
MRDN SM4 201 H5
RKW/CH/CXG WD3 91 N1
WCCE AL7 23 J2
WLGTN SM6 222 D1
**Northway Crs** MLHL NW7 96 B5
**Northway Rd** CMBW SE5 159 K9
CROY/NA CRO 203 N6
**Northways Pde** HAMP NW3 * 3 H1
**Northway** GLDGN NW11 117 L3
**North Weald La** KUTN/CMB KT2 177 H8
**North Western Av**
WATN WD24 72 G1
**North Western Avenue Coln**
WATN WD24 73 K2
**North Western Avenue Gade**
**Side** WAT WD17 72 E1
**North Wharf Rd** BAY/PAD W2 9 L4
**Northwick Av**
KTN/HRWW/WS HA3 114 F4
**Northwick Cir**
KTN/HRWW/WS HA3 115 H4
**Northwick Park Rd** HRW HA1 114 F5
**Northwick Rd** ALP/SUD HA0 135 K5
OXHEY WD19 93 K5
**Northwick Ter** STJWD NW8 9 L1
**Northwold Dr** PIN HA5 113 K1
**Northwold Rd**
STNW/STAM N16 119 P7
CLPT E5 119 P7
**Northwood Av** HCH RM12 125 H9
PUR/KEN CR8 223 H9
WOKN/KNAP GU21 231 K6
**Northwood Dr** RDART DA2 188 D2
**Northwood Gdns** CLAY IG5 122 D2
GFD/PVL UB6 114 E10
NFNCH/WDSPK N12 97 H4
**Northwood Hls** NTHWD HA6 * 92 B9
**Northwood Pl** ERITH DA8 164 A10
**Northwood Rd** CAR SM5 222 B3
DEN/HRF UB9 91 P7
EDGW HA8 95 N9
FSTH SE23 182 A5
HGT N6 118 A4
HTHAIR TW6 152 B7
THHTH CR7 203 K2
**Northwood Wy** DEN/HRF UB9 91 N6
NRWD SE19 181 P2
NTHWD HA6 92 C10
**North Woolwich Rd**
CAN/RD E16 141 M10
**North Worple Wy**
MORT/ESHN SW14 156 A9

PIN HA5 113 K1
STHGT/OAK N14 98 D1
SUN TW16 196 F6
SUT SM1 221 M1
THHTH CR7 202 D3
WAB EN9 45 J8
WIM/MER SW19 179 H10
WOKN/KNAP GU21 231 J5
**Norton Cl** BORE WD6 75 M5
CHING E4 100 F6
RGUW GU3 249 L5
**Norton Folgate** WCHPL E1 13 K2
**Norton Gdns**
STRHM/NOR SW16 202 F2
**Norton La** COB KT11 234 G5
**Norton Pk** ASC SL5 192 N5
**Norton Rd** ALP/SUD HA0 135 J1
DAGE RM10 144 E1
LEY E10 120 E6
UX/CGN UB8 131 N5
**Norval Gn** BRXN/ST SW9 * 159 H8
**Norval Rd** ALP/SUD HA0 114 G7
**Norway Dr** SLN SL2 129 N7
**Norway Ga** BERM/RHTH SE16 160 D2
**Norway Pl** POP/IOD E14 140 G8
**Norway St** GNWCH SE10 160 G5
**Norwich Crs** CHDH RM6 123 J4
**Norwich Ms** GDMY/SEVK IG3 123 K1
**Norwich Rd** CRAWE RH10 284 B9
FSTGT E7 121 M10
GFD/PVL UB6 134 A1
NTHWD HA6 112 C1
THHTH CR7 203 K3
**Norwich St** FLST/FETLN EC4A 12 A5
**Norwich Wk** EDGW HA8 95 P8
**Norwood Av** ALP/SUD HA0 135 J1
ROMW/RG RM7 124 E5
**Norwood Cl** CRICK NW2 117 H8
EHSLY KT24 253 M4
HERT/WAT SG14 24 G4
NWDGN UB2 153 J4
WHTN TW2 176 C3
**Norwood Dr** RYLN/HDSTN HA2 113 N4
**Norwood Farm La** COB KT11 217 H7
**Norwood Gdns** NWDGN UB2 153 N3
YEAD UB4 133 K6
**Norwood Green Rd**
NWDGN UB2 153 P3
**Norwood High St** WNWD SE27 181 M2
**Norwood Hl** HORL RH6 278 G4
**Norwood Hill Rd** HORL RH6 279 J6
**Norwood La** IVER SL0 150 B1
**Norwood Park Rd**
WNWD SE27 181 K8
**Norwood Rd** CHES/WCR EN8 62 B4
EHSLY KT24 253 M4
NWDGN UB2 153 M2
WNWD SE27 181 M2
**Notley End** ECH TW20 171 P10
**Notley St** CMBW SE5 159 L6
**Notson Rd** SNWD SE25 203 M4
**Notting Barn Rd** NKENS W10 136 G6
**Nottingham Av** CAN/RD E16 141 P7
**Nottingham Cl** GSTN WD25 55 H10
**Nottingham Ct**
LSQ/SEVD WC2H * 11 L6
**Nottingham Pl** CAMTN NW1 10 C2
**Nottingham Rd** ISLW TW7 154 E8
LEY E10 121 H4
RKW/CH/CXG WD3 90 F2
SAND/SEL CR2 223 K1
TOOT SW17 180 A4
**Nottingham St** MHST W1U 10 C2
**Nottingham Ter** CAMTN NW1 10 C3
**Nova Ms** CHEAM SM3 201 J8
**Novar Cl** ORP BR6 207 J2
**Novar Rd** CROY/NA CRO 203 J8
**Novar Rd** ELTH/MOT SE9 184 F5
**Novello St** FUL/PGN SW6 157 K7
**Novello Wy** BORE WD6 76 A5
**Nowell Rd** BARN SW13 156 D6
**Nower HI** PIN HA5 113 N2
**Nower Rd** DORK RH4 272 F2
**The Nower** BH/WHM TN16 245 J6
**Noyna Rd** TOOT SW17 180 B5
**Nubia Wy** BMLY BR1 183 K7
**Nuding Cl** LEW SE13 160 F9
**Nuffield Cl** SWLY BR8 118 F6
**Nugent Rd** ARCH N19 118 F6
SNWD SE25 203 N3
**Nugents Ct** PIN HA5 * 93 M9
**Nugent's Pk** PIN HA5 93 M9
**Nugent Ter** STJWD NW8 3 H4
**Numbers Farm** KGLGY WD4 * 54 D5
**Nunappleton Wy** OXTED RH8 261 M4
**Nuneaton Rd** DAGW RM9 143 N2
**Nunhead Crs** PECK SE15 160 A9
**Nunhead Gv** PECK SE15 160 A9
**Nunhead La** PECK SE15 160 A9
**Nunnery Cl** STAL AL1 38 C8
**Nunns Rd** ENC/FH EN2 79 K6
**Nunns Wy** GRAYS RM17 168 A3
**Nunsbury Dr** BROX EN10 62 D1
**Nuns La** STAL AL1 38 D10
**Nuns Wk** VW GU25 194 A5
**Nupton Dr** BAR EN5 99 P9
**Nurseries Rd** STALE/WH AL4 21 K4
**Nursery Av** BXLYHN DA7 164 A9
CROY/NA CRO 204 C9
FNCH N3 97 L10
**Nursery Cl** ADL/WDHM KT15 215 M4
AMSS HP7 69 K5
BROCKY SE4 160 K5
CHDH RM6 123 N4
CROY/NA CRO 204 C9
EBED/NFELT TW14 175 J3
EW KT17 220 D5
KWD/TDW/WH KT20 256 D1
ORP BR6 207 H1
OXHEY WD19 93 J2
PEND EN3 80 C2
PUT/ROE SW15 178 G1
RDART DA2 188 D3
SEV TN13 247 K6
SOCK/AV RM15 147 K6
SWLY BR8 208 D2
WFD IG8 102 G7
WOKN/KNAP GU21 231 P2
**Nursery Flds** SBW CM21 19 L5
**Nursery Gdns** CHESW EN7 61 L4
CHST BR7 184 E8
HPTN TW12 175 N7
HSLWW TW4 175 H1
PEND EN3 80 C2
RGUE GU4 268 E5
STA TW18 173 L10
WARE SG12 26 D2
WEY KT13 196 G10
**Nursery Gv** GVE DA12 190 G4
**Nursery Hl** WCCE AL7 23 J1
**Nurserylands** CRAWW RH11 283 K7
**Nursery La** BETH E2 7 L1
DTCH/LGLY SL3 129 N7
FSTGT E7 121 M5
HORL RH6 279 K5
NKENS W10 136 F7
**Nurseryman's Rd**
FBAR/BDGN N11 98 B3
**Nursery Pl** SEV TN13 247 P6
WDSR SL4 171 N1
**Nursery Rd** BROX EN10 * 62 H2
BRXN/ST SW9 158 G10
EFNCH N2 97 H6
GODL GU7 267 L9
HOD EN11 44 D5
HOM E9 140 E1
KWD/TDW/WH KT20 256 D1
LOU IG10 81 K4
MDHD SL6 128 A8
MTCM CR4 201 P3

**Oakapple Cl** SAND/SEL CR2 224 A10
**Oak Av** CEND/HSY/T N8 118 C2
CHOB/PIR GU24 230 F7
CROY/NA CRO 204 F9
EGH TW20 172 F10
ENC/FH EN2 78 G5
HEST TW5 153 H4
HGDN/ICK UB10 112 C7
HPTN TW12 175 M8
LCOL/BKTW AL2 56 A1
WDGN N22 98 A9
**Oakbank** CROY/NA CRO 225 P1
LHD/OX KT22 236 B9
WOKS/MYFD GU22 232 B5
**Oakbank Av** WOT/HER KT12 197 N3
**Oakbank Gv** HNHL SE24 159 K10
**Oakbrook Cl** BMLY BR1 183 N7
**Oak Cl** CRAWE RH10 284 G2
DART DA1 171 H4
GODL GU7 267 K9
HHS/BOV HP3 36 A10
KWD/TDW/WH KT20 255 N6
STHGT/OAK N14 98 C2
WAB EN9 63 J10
**Oakcombe Cl** NWMAL KT3 185 P9
**Oak Cottage Cl** CAT SE6 183 K4
**Oak Cots** HNWL W7 * 154 D1
**Oak Ct** CRAWE RH10 283 N3
**Oak Crs** CAN/RD E16 141 K6
**Oakcroft Cl** BF/WBF KT14 215 J10
PIN HA5 93 H10
**Oakcroft Rd** BF/WBF KT14 215 J10
CHSGTN KT9 219 L1
LEE/GVPK SE12 161 M1
**Oakcroft Vils** CHSGTN KT9 219 L1
**Oakdale** STHGT/OAK N14 98 C2
**Oakdale Av** NTHWD HA6 92 G8
OXHEY WD19 93 A2
**Oakdale Cl** OXHEY WD19 93 A2
**Oakdale Gdns** CHING E4 101 H5
**Oakdale La** EDEN TN8 262 F9
**Oakdale Rd** FSBYPK N4 119 K6
FSTGT E7 141 K2
PECK SE15 159 B9
STRHM/NOR SW16 180 B9
SWFD E18 121 N10
WAN E11 121 J1
WEY KT13 196 F10
**Oakdale Wy** MTCM CR4 202 B7
**Oak Dell** CRAWE RH10 284 D6
**Oakdene** ASC SL5 192 G6
**Oak Dene** EA W5 * 135 J3
**Oakdene** CHST BR7 184 D6
**Oakdene Av** CHST BR7 184 C4
ERITH DA8 164 A10
THDIT KT7 198 B3
**Oakdene Cl**
BRKHM/BTCW RH3 273 P1
HGDNE RH4
**Oakdene Dr** BRYLDS KT5 199 P8
**Oakdene Ms** CHEAM SM3 201 J8

**Oakdene Pk** FNCH N3 97 J3
**Oakdene Rd** RGUW GU3 267 K6
**Oakdene Rd**
BRKHM/BTCW RH3 273 P1
COB KT11 217 J10
GT/LBKH KT23 235 M6
GU GU1 268 B4
HHS/BOV HP3 36 A10
REDH RH1 257 P6
RGUW GU3 267 K6
SEV TN13 247 L5
STMC/STPC BR5 207 H1
WATN WD24 73 J2
**Oakden St** LBTH SE11 18 B5
**Oak Dr** BERK HP4 34 A6
KWD/TDW/WH KT20 255 N6
**Oaken Coppice** ASHTD KT21 237 N6
**Oak End** HLWS CM18 47 J3
**Oak End Dr** IVER SL0 130 F4
**Oaken Dr** ESH/CLAY KT10 218 G3
**Oak End Wy** ADL/WDHM KT15 215 H6
CFSP/GDCR SL9 110 C3
**Oaken Gv** WCCE AL7 23 J1
**Oaken La** ESH/CLAY KT10 218 D1
**Oakenshaw Cl** SURB KT6 199 P6
**Oakeshott Av** HGT N6 118 B7
**Oakey La** STHWK SE1 18 A3
**Oak Farm** BORE WD6 75 P4
**Oakfield** CHING E4 100 G6
**Oak Fld** CSHM HP5 50 G6
**Oakfield** RKW/CH/CXG WD3 91 K1
WOKN/KNAP GU21 231 K2
**Oakfield Av**
KTN/HRWW/WS HA3 114 C1
**Oakfield Cl** NWMAL KT3 200 C5
POTB/CUF EN6 59 J7
RSLP HA4 112 C4
WEY KT13 216 D1
**Oakfield Ct** BORE WD6 75 N8
CAR SM5 221 P7
GFD/PVL UB6 134 C6
UED N18 99 M5
**Oakfield Dr** REIG RH2 257 K8
**Oakfield Gdns** BECK BR3 204 F5
CAR SM5 201 P8
GFD/PVL UB6 134 C6
UED N18 99 M5
**Oakfield La** BORE WD6 75 N8
CROY/NA CRO 203 K8
EHAM E6 142 A3
FNCH N3 97 L9
FSBYPK N4 119 H4
IL IG1 122 F8
PGE/AN SE20 182 A10
STHGT/OAK N14 98 F3
WALTH E17 100 D10
WIM/MER SW19 178 G6
**Oakfields** BF/WBF KT14 215 L10
CRAWE RH10 284 E6
RGUW GU3 249 K8
SEV TN13 265 J2
WOT/HER KT12 197 H8
**Oakfields Rd** GLDGN NW11 117 H4
**Oakford Rd** KTTN NW5 118 D9
**Oak Gdns** CROY/NA CRO 204 F9
EDGW HA8 95 P10
**Oak Gld** EPP CM16 65 N5
NTHWD HA6 92 C9
**Oak Gln** EMPK RM11 125 M1
**Oak Grange Rd** RGUE GU4 251 L5
**Oak Gn** ABLGY WD5 54 F8
**Oak Gv** CRICK NW2 116 C9
HAT AL10 40 C4
HERT/BAY SG13 25 P5
RSLP HA4 113 J6
SUN TW16 175 J10
WWKM BR4 205 H9
**Oak Grove Rd** PGE/AN SE20 204 B1
**Oakhall Dr** SUN TW16 174 G8
**Oak Hall Rd** WAN E11 121 N4
**Oakham Cl** CAT SE6 182 E5
EBAR EN4 78 A2
**Oakham Dr** HAYES BR2 205 M4
**Oakhampton Rd** MLHL NW7 96 C9
**Oakhaven** CRAWE RH10 285 H3
**Oakhill** ESH/CLAY KT10 218 F3
**Oak Hl** EPSOM KT18 238 A2
RGUE GU4 250 F6
SURB KT6 199 K7
WFD IG8 101 J8
**Oakhill Av** HAMP NW3 117 H9
PIN HA5 93 M10
**Oakhill Cha** CRAWE RH10 284 E6
**Oakhill Cl** ASHTD KT21 237 H4
RKW/CH/CXG WD3 91 K1
**Oak Hill Crs** SURB KT6 199 K7
WFD IG8 101 J8
**Oakhill Gdns** WFD IG8 101 K8
**Oak Hill Gdns** WFD IG8 101 K8
**Oak Hill Gv** SURB KT6 199 K6
**Oakhill Pth** SURB KT6 199 K6
**Oak Hill Park Ms** HAMP NW3 117 H8
**Oakhill Pl** PUT/ROE SW15 179 K1
**Oak Hill Rd** SURB KT6 199 K6
ABR/ST RM4 104 F8
RSLP HA4 113 J6
**Oakhill Rd** ASHTD KT21 237 H4
BECK BR3 203 L1
ADL/WDHM KT15 209 J9
ORP BR6 207 J9
PUR RM19 166 A4
REIG RH2 275 L1
RKW/CH/CXG WD3 90 C5
SUT SM1 201 P9
STRHM/NOR SW16 202 A8

THHTH CR7 — 203 H4
WWKM BR4 — 204 G10
Oaklands CI ALP/SUD HA0 — 115 J10
BXLYHS DA6 — 186 A1
CHSGTN KT9 — 219 H1
RGUE GU4 — 268 E2
STMC/STPC BR5 — 207 H6
Oaklands Dr HLWE CM17 — 47 M2
REDH RH1 — 276 C2
SOCK/AV RM15 — 147 H7
WHTN TW2 — 176 B3
Oaklands Gdns PUR/KEN CR8 — 223 K10
Oaklands La BROX EN10 — 46 A2
SHB W12 — 136 D10
Oaklands Pk BAR EN5 — 76 E8
BH/WHM TN16 — 243 P8
STALE/WH AL4 — 39 L4
Oaklands PI CLAP SW4 — 158 E10
Oaklands Rd BMLY BR1 — 183 K10
BXLYHS DA6 — 164 A10
CHSW NW2 — 61 M2
CRICK NW2 — 116 C9
GVW DA11 — 190 C7
HNWL W7 — 154 E1
MORT/ESHN SW14 — 156 A9
RDART DA2 — 188 A4
TRDG/WHET N20 — 97 J1
Oaklands Wy
KWD/TDW/WH KT20 — 238 F8
WLGTN SM6 — 222 D4
Oaklands Wd HAT AL10 — 40 D4
Oakland Wy HOR/WEW KT19 — 220 A3
Oak La EFNCH N2 — 97 N10
EGH TW20 — 171 P6
FBAR/BDGN N11 — 98 E7
ISLW TW7 — 154 D10
POP/IOD E14 — 140 E9
POTB/CUF EN6 — 60 C4
SEV TN13 — 264 C5
TRING HP23 — 32 A7
TWK TW1 — 176 B3
WDSR SL4 — 148 F7
WFD IG8 — 101 L5
WOKS/MYFD GU22 — 232 B5
Oaklawn Rd LHD/OX KT22 — 236 D4
Oak Leaf Cl GUW GU2 — 249 J9
HOR/WEW KT19 — 220 A3
Oakleafe Gdns BARK/HLT IG6 — 122 E1
Oakleigh Av EDGW HA8 — 95 N10
SURB KT6 — 219 N7
TRDG/WHET N20 — 97 N2
Oakleigh Cl EDGW HA8 — 95 P10
OXTED RH8 — 261 K5
Oakleigh Dr
RKW/CH/CXG WD3 — 72 D10
Oakleigh Gdns EDGW HA8 — 95 L6
ORP BR6 — 227 N1
TRDG/WHET N20 — 97 N2
Oakleigh Park Av CHST BR7 — 206 D2
Oakleigh Pk North
TRDG/WHET N20 — 97 N2
Oakleigh Pk South
TRDG/WHET N20 — 97 N2
Oakleigh Ri EPP CM16 — 65 K8
Oakleigh Rd HGDN/ICK UB10 — 132 D2
PIN HA5 — 93 N7
Oakleigh Rd North
TRDG/WHET N20 — 97 N3
Oakleigh Rd South
FBAR/BDGN N11 — 98 B5
Oakleigh Wy MTCM CR4 — 202 C1
SURB KT6 — 199 M8
Oakley Av BARK IG11 — 143 J2
CROY/NA CR0 — 222 F1
EA W5 — 135 M9
Oakley Cl ADL/WDHM KT15 — 215 N1
CHING E4 — 101 H4
EHAM E6 — 142 B8
HNWL W7 — 134 D9
ISLW TW7 — 154 A1
WTHK RM20 — 167 H5
Oakley Ct MTCM CR4 — 202 B7
Oakley Crs FSBYE EC1V * — 6 F10
SL SL1 — 129 K9
Oakley Dell RGUE GU4 — 250 F10
Oakley Dr CAT SE6 — 183 J2
ELTH/MOT SE9 — 184 C4
HARH RM3 — 105 P6
HAYES BR2 — 206 B10
Oakley Gdns BNSTD SM7 — 239 L1
BRKHM/BTCW RH3 — 273 P6
CEND/HSY/T N8 — 118 C3
CHEL SW3 * — 15 P9
Oakley Green Rd WDSR SL4 — 148 A4
Oakley Pk BXLY DA5 — 185 M3
Oakley Pl STHWK SE1 — 19 L8
Oakley Rd HARP AL5 — 20 C7
HAYES BR2 — 206 B10
HOW HA1 — 114 C4
IS N1 — 7 J1
SNWD SE25 — 204 A5
WARL CR6 — 241 P4
Oakley Sq CAMTN NW1 — 5 L3
Oakley St CHEL SW3 — 15 N9
Oakley Yd BETH E2 * — 13 M1
Oak Lodge Av CHIG IG7 — 102 C5
Oak Lodge Cl STAN HA7 — 95 H6
WOT/HER KT12 — 217 K2
Oak Lodge Dr REDH RH1 — 276 B8
WWKM BR4 — 205 H10
Oak Lodge La BH/WHM TN16 — 262 C1
Oaklodge Wy MLHL NW7 — 97 H6
Oak Md GODL GU7 — 267 J8
Oakmead Av HAYES BR2 — 205 M6
Oakmeade PIN HA5 — 93 P7
Oakmead Gdns EDGW HA8 — 96 A5
Oakmead PI MTCM CR4 — 202 A8
Oakmead Rd BAL SW12 — 180 C2
CROY/NA CR0 — 202 E6
Oakmere Av PUR/KEN CR8 — 59 N7
Oakmere Cl POTB/CUF EN6 — 59 N7
Oakmere La POTB/CUF EN6 — 59 N7
Oakmere Rd ABYW SE2 — 163 K5
Oakmoor Wy CHIG IG7 — 103 H6
Oakmore Gdns
STMC/STPC BR5 — 207 M4
Oak Pk BF/WBF KT14 — 215 H4
Oak Park Gdns
WIM/MER SW19 — 160 C4
Oak Piece EPP CM16 — 66 D5
Oak Rdg DORK RH4 — 272 C5
Oak Rd CHOB/PIR GU24 — 212 C5
LCOL/BKTW AL2 — 58 N5

Oak Rw MTCM CR4 — 202 D2
Oakroyd Av POTB/CUF EN6 — 59 M5
Oakroyd Cl POTB/CUF EN6 — 59 M6
Oaks Av CRW RM5 — 104 D10
FELT TW13 * — 175 M5
NRWD SE19 — 181 M8
WPK KT4 — 200 E1
Oaks Cl LHD/OX KT22 — 236 E1
RAD WD7 — 74 E1
Oaksend Cl LHD/OX KT22 — 218 A2
Oaksford Av SYD SE26 — 182 A6
Oaks Gv CHING E4 — 101 K3
Oakshade Rd BMLY BR1 — 183 J1
LHD/OX KT22 — 218 A10
Oakshaw OXTED RH8 — 261 J3
Oakshaw Rd WAND/EARL SW18 — 179 L3
Oakside DEN/HRF UB9 — 131 L1
Oakside La HORL RH6 — 280 D5
Oakside La HORL RH6 — 280 D5
Oaks La CROY/NA CR0 — 204 B10
GNTH/NBYPK IG2 — 123 H2
RDKG RH5 — 272 C9
Oaks Pk BNSTD SM7 * — 222 D10
PUR/KEN CR8 — 223 J10
REIG RH2 — 257 N9
STWL/WRAY TW19 — 173 N1
Oak's Rd WOKN/KNAP GU21 — 232 B3
The Oaks BERK HP4 * — 33 M5
BF/WBF KT14 — 215 K10
BORE WD6 * — 75 M5
CHSGTN KT9 — 219 K4
DORK RH4 * — 272 C5
EPSOM KT18 — 220 B10
FELT TW13 * — 175 M5
HAYES BR2 — 206 D6
MRDN SM4 * — 201 H4
NFNCH/WDSPK N12 — 97 L5
OXHEY WD19 — 93 K2
RDART DA2 — 188 A2
RSLP HA4 — 112 C5
STA TW18 * — 173 J7
SWLY BR8 — 208 F2
WFD IG8 — 101 K8
WOKN/KNAP GU21 * — 232 B3
WOOL/PLUM SE18 — 162 F4
YEAD UB4 — 132 D4
Oaks Tr CAR SM5 — 222 B6
Oaks Wy CAR SM5 — 222 A4
EPSOM KT18 — 238 C5
PUR/KEN CR8 — 223 K10
SURB KT6 — 199 J9
Oakthorpe Rd PLMGR N13 — 99 H4
Oaktree Av PLMGR N13 — 99 H4
Oak Tree Av RDART DA2 — 188 E3
Oak Tree Cl ABLGY WD5 — 59 L6
CHESW EN7 — 61 K4
EA W5 * — 135 H8
HAT AL10 — 40 D3
HERT/BAY SG13 — 26 B8
LOU IG10 — 62 A8
RGUE GU4 — 249 P4
STAN HA7 — 95 H8
VW GU25 — 194 A6
WOKN/KNAP GU21 — 230 C4
Oak Tree Dell CDALE/KGS NW9 — 115 P5
Oak Tree Dr DTCH/LGLY SL3 — 150 C1
EGH TW20 — 171 P8
GU GU1 — 249 P6
TRDG/WHET N20 — 97 M1
Oak Tree Gdns BMLY BR1 — 183 N8
GU GU1 * — 250 D7
Oaktree Gdns HLWE CM17 — 47 N2
Oaktree Garth WGCE AL7 — 23 H6
Oaktree Gv IG1 — 122 C9
Oak Tree Rd STJWD NW8 — 3 M10
WOKN/KNAP GU21 — 230 C4
Oaktree view WATW WD18 — 72 F7
Oakview Cl CHESW EN7 — 61 K3
OXHEY WD19 — 73 K10
Oakview Gv CROY/NA CR0 — 204 D8
Oakview Rd CAT SE6 — 182 C5
Oak Village HAMP NW3 — 118 F4
Oak Vis GLDGN NW11 — 117 J4
Oak Warren SEV TN13 — 265 H5
Oakway BMLY BR1 — 183 H2
HAMP NW3 — 118 A6
Oakway Cl BXLY DA5 — 165 L8
Oakway PI RAD WD7 — 56 F10
Oakways ELTH/MOT SE9 — 184 E5
Oakwell Cl POTB/CUF EN6 — 60 C9
Oak Wd BERK HP4 * — 33 N5
WLGTN SM6 — 222 C5
Oakwood GUW GU2 — 249 N9
GDMY/SEVK IG3 — 123 J7
ORP BR6 — 226 F9
SUT SM1 — 221 K9
WOKN/KNAP GU21 — 230 A4
Oakwood Gdns
GDMY/SEVK IG3 — 123 J7
ORP BR6 — 226 F9
SUT SM1 — 221 K9
WOKN/KNAP GU21 — 230 A4
Oakwood Hill Industrial Est
LOU IG10 — 78 D1
Oakwood La WKENS W14 — 14 A1
Oakwood Ms HLWE CM17 — 29 M7
Oakwood Pde
STHGT/OAK N14 — 78 F10
Oakwood Park Cots
WCHMH N21 * — 78 G10
Oakwood Park Rd
STHGT/OAK N14 — 78 F10
Oakwood PI CROY/NA CR0 — 203 H6
Oakwood Rd CTHM CR3 — 259 H4
HART DA3 — 191 M10
HORL RH6 — 280 D4
LCOL/BKTW AL2 — 58 N5
ORP BR6 — 206 F9
PIN HA5 — 93 J3
REDH RH1 — 259 H4
RYNPK SW20 — 200 D1

VW GU25 — 193 P5
WOKN/KNAP GU21 — 231 K5
Oak yd WAT WD17 * — 73 H8
Oarsman PI E/WMO/HCT KT8 — 198 D4
Oast House Cl
STWL/WRAY TW19 — 172 B3
Oast Rd OXTED RH8 — 261 L4
Oast Wy HART DA3 — 211 K6
Oates Gv HARLW CM19 — 29 K5
Oates Rd CRW RM5 — 104 C6
Oates Wk CRAWE RH10 — 284 A10
Oatfield Rd
KWD/TDW/WH KT20 — 238 E7
ORP BR6 — 207 J8
Oatland Ri WALTH E17 — 100 D3
Oatlands CRAWW RH11 — 283 B8
HORL RH6 — 280 C3
Oatlands Cha WEY KT13 — 196 F10
Oatlands Cl WEY KT13 — 216 D1
Oatlands Dr SL SL1 — 129 N8
WEY KT13 — 216 C1
Oatlands Gn WEY KT13 — 196 E10
Oatlands Mere WEY KT13 — 196 E10
Oatlands Rd
KWD/TDW/WH KT20 — 239 H5
PEND EN3 — 80 B5
Oat La CITYW EC2V — 12 E5
Oatridge Gdns HHNE HP2 — 36 B5
Oban Cl PLSTW E13 — 141 N3
Oban Ct SL SL1 — 149 J1
Oban Rd PLSTW E13 — 141 P5
THHTH CR7 — 203 L4
Oban St POP/IOD E14 — 141 J8
Oberon Cl BORE WD6 — 75 P5
Oberon Wy CRAWW RH11 — 283 H10
SHPTN TW17 — 195 P3
Obelisk Rd EGH TW20 — 172 C2
Oberstein Rd BTSEA SW11 — 157 N10
Oborne CI HNHL SE24 — 181 J1
Observatory Gdns KENS W8 — 14 E1
Observatory Rd
MORT/ESHN SW14 — 155 P10
The Observatory SL SL1 * — 149 M1
Observer Dr WATW WD18 — 72 B1
Occam Rd GUW GU2 — 249 J10
Occupation La EA W5 — 155 J5
WOOL/PLUM SE18 — 162 F4
Occupation Rd WALW SE17 — 18 F9
WATW WD18 — 73 J9
Ocean Est WCHPL E1 — 140 C6
Ocean St WCHPL E1 — 140 C6
Ockendens
WOKS/MYFD GU22 — 232 C4
Ockenden Gdns
WOKS/MYFD GU22 — 232 C4
Ockenden Rd
WOKS/MYFD GU22 — 232 C4
Ockendon Ms IS N1 * — 7 H2
Ockendon Rd IS N1 — 7 H1
UPMR RM14 — 104 F10
Ockham Dr EHSLY KT24 — 234 E10
GFD/PVL UB6 — 134 C2
STMC/STPC BR5 — 185 K10
Ockham Rd North
RPLY/SEND GU23 — 234 D6
Ockham Rd South
RPLY/SEND GU23 — 252 F1
Ockley Ct RGUE GU4 — 250 E5
Ockley Rd CROY/NA CR0 — 202 G7
STRHM/NOR SW16 — 180 F7
Ockleys Md GDST RH9 — 262 C6
Octagon Ar LVPST EC2M * — 13 J4
Octagon Rd WOT/HER KT12 — 216 F6
Octavia Cl MTCM CR4 — 201 P5
Octavia Ct WATW WD24 — 73 K6
Octavia Ms CRICK NW2 * — 136 L1
Octavia Rd ISLW TW7 — 154 E9
Octavia St BTSEA SW11 — 157 P7
Octavia Wy STA TW18 — 173 K9
DEPT SE8 — 160 M8
October PI HDN NW4 * — 116 C1
Octavius St DEPT SE8 — 160 F6
Odard Rd E/WMO/HCT KT8 — 197 P4
Odds Farm Est
FLKWH/TG HP10 * — 108 A5
Odell CI BARK IG11 — 143 J2
Odell Wk LEW SE13 — 160 G9
Odencroft Rd SLN SL2 — 128 F5
Odeon Pde ELTH/MOT SE9 — 162 B10
GFD/PVL UB6 — 134 C1
HOLWY N7 * — 118 F1
ISLW TW7 * — 154 C8
RKW/CH/CXG WD3 — 71 P2
Odessa Rd FSTGT E7 — 121 L9
WLSDN NW10 — 136 D4
Odessa St BERM/RHTH SE16 — 160 C2
Odger St BTSEA SW11 — 158 A4
Odhams Trading Est
WATN WD24 — 73 K2
Odhams Wk LSO/SEVD WC2H * — 11 L1
Odsey Vis FSBYPK N4 * — 119 H4
Odyssey Rd BORE WD6 — 75 N5
Offa Rd STALW/RED AL3 — 38 B6
Offa's Md BOW E3 — 140 B10
Offas Wy STALE/WH AL4 — 21 J3
Offenham Rd ELTH/MOT SE9 — 184 C1
Offerton Rd CLAP SW4 — 158 D9
Offham Slope
NFNCH/WDSPK N12 — 97 J6
Offley PI ISLW TW7 — 154 A8
Offley Rd BRXN/ST SW9 — 159 H6
Offord Cl TOTM N17 — 99 P8
Offord Rd IS N1 — 5 M1
Offord St IS N1 — 5 M1
Ogard Rd HOD EN11 — 45 H1
Ogilby St WOOL/PLUM SE18 — 162 C3
Oglander Rd PECK SE15 — 159 N10
Ogle St GTPST W1W — 10 G3
Oglethorpe Rd DAGE RM10 — 124 A8
Ohio Rd PLSTW E13 — 141 L6
Oil Mill La HMSMTH W6 — 156 F10
Okeburn Rd TOOT SW17 — 180 B8
Okehampton Crs WELL DA16 — 163 P7
Okehampton Rd
WLSDN NW10 — 136 F3
Okehampton Sq HARH RM3 — 105 K7
Olaf St NTGHL W11 — 136 C9
Old Acre BF/WBF KT14 — 215 N10
Oldacre CHOB/PIR GU24 — 212 B8
Old Amersham Rd
CFSP/GDCR SL9 — 110 G6
Old Av BF/WBF KT14 — 214 G10
WEY KT13 — 216 D4
Old Bailey STP EC4M — 11 P4
The Old Bakery ECH TW20 — 172 D8
Old Barn Cl BELMT SM2 — 221 H4
BGR/WK TN15 — 247 P3
Old Barn La CTHM CR3 — 241 N2
RKW/CH/CXG WD3 — 72 A3
Old Barn Rd EPSOM KT18 — 237 P3
Old Barn Wy BXLYHN DA7 — 164 G10
Old Barrack Yd KTBR SW1X * — 16 C1
Old Bellgate Wf
POP/IOD E14 — 160 C2
Old Bells Ct CSHH HP5 — 50 D8
Oldberry Rd EDGW HA8 — 96 A1
Old Bethnal Green Rd
BETH E2 — 7 M10
Old Bexley La BXLY DA5 — 186 A5
Old Bond St CONDST W1S — 10 C7
Oldborough Rd ALP/SUD HA0 — 115 M1
Old Brewery Ms HAMP NW3 * — 117 J2
Old Bridge Cl NTHLT UB5 — 133 P2
Old Bridge St KUT/HW KT1 — 199 P2
Old Brighton Rd South
HORL RH6 — 279 P6
Old Broad St OBST EC2N — 13 H4
Old Bromley Rd BMLY BR1 — 183 J8
Old Brompton Rd ECT SW5 — 14 F5
SKENS SW7 — 15 K7

Old Bldg LINN WC2A — 12 A5
Old Burlington St
CONDST W1S — 10 C7
Oldbury Cl STMC/STPC BR5 — 207 N5
Oldbury Gv BEAC HP9 — 88 C10
Oldbury Pl MHST W1U — 10 B2
EN EN1 — 79 P6
The Old Carriageway
SEV TN13 — 246 D9
Old Castle St WCHPL E1 — 13 L3
Old Cavendish St OXSTW W1C — 10 C4
Old Chapel Rd SWLY BR8 — 208 D7
Old Charlton Rd SHPTN TW17 — 196 D5
Old Char Wharf DORK RH4 — 272 C5
Old Chertsey Rd
CHOB/PIR GU24 — 213 N6
Old Chestnut Av
ESH/CLAY KT10 — 217 P3
Old Chorleywood Rd
RKW/CH/CXG WD3 — 71 N10
Old Church La
CDALE/KGS NW9 — 115 P7
GFD/PVL UB6 — 134 E5
STAN HA7 — 94 C7
Old Church Pth
ESH/CLAY KT10 — 217 P4
Old Church Ri RVMW/RG RM7 — 124 F4
Old Church Rd CHING E4 — 101 M5
WCHPL E1 — 140 F8
Oldchurch Ri ROMW/RG RM7 — 124 E5
Oldchurch Rd ROMW/RG RM7 — 124 E5
Old Church St CHEL SW3 — 15 M9
Old Claygate La
ESH/CLAY KT10 — 218 D3
The Old Coach Rd
HERT/WAT SG14 — 24 A8
Old Common Cl COB KT11 — 217 J8
Old Common Rd COB KT11 — 217 J8
RKW/CH/CXG WD3 — 70 G8
Old Compton St
SOHO/SHAV W1D — 11 J7
Old Cote Dr HEST TW5 — 153 P5
Old Ct ASHTD KT21 — 237 K5
Old Court Fl KENS W8 — 14 C1
Old Court Rd GU GU2 — 267 M1
The Old Crpd BMLY BR1 — 205 N1
Old Crabtree La HHNE HP2 — 35 M7
Old Cross HERT/WAT SG14 — 25 K5
Old Crown RGUE GU4 — 268 F6
Old Crown La BRW CM14 — 86 C6
Old Dairy Ms BAL SW12 — 180 B4
KTTN NW5 — 4 F1
Old Dartford Rd EYN DA4 — 209 N6
Old Dean BRKMPK AL9 * — 22 C3
Old Deer Park Gdns
RCH/KEW TW9 — 155 L9
Old Devonshire Rd BAL SW12 — 180 C3
Old Dock Cl RCH/KEW TW9 — 155 N5
Old Dover Rd BKHTH/KID SE3 — 161 M5
Old Downs HART DA3 — 211 K5
Old Esher Cl WOT/HER KT12 — 217 L2
Old Esher Rd WOT/HER KT12 — 217 L2
Old Farleigh Rd
SAND/SEL CR2 — 224 B6
Old Farm Av BFN/LL DA15 — 184 G4
STHGT/OAK N14 — 98 D1
Old Farm Cl BEAC HP9 — 88 B6
HSLWW TW4 — 153 N6
Old Farm Gdns SWLY BR8 — 208 G3
Old Farmhouse Dr
LHD/OX KT22 — 236 C1
Old Farm La AMSS HP7 — 69 K7
Old Farm Pas HPTN TW12 — 175 N9
Old Farm Rd HPTN TW12 — 175 L1
WDR/YW UB7 — 151 N1
Old Farm Rd East
BFN/LL DA15 — 185 K5
Old Farm Rd West
BFN/LL DA15 — 185 J6
Old Fd EW KT17 — 220 G3
Old Fen Ferry Dr
STWL/WRAY TW19 — 171 P2
Old Field Cl AMS HP6 — 70 P2
Old Fld La GFD/PVL UB6 — 114 D10
Oldfield Cl BMLY BR1 — 206 C4
STAN HA7 — 94 F6
Oldfield Farm Gdns
GFD/PVL UB6 — 134 C3
Oldfield Gdns ASHTD KT21 — 237 J5
Oldfield Gv BERM/RHTH SE16 — 160 C3
Oldfield La North
GFD/PVL UB6 — 134 C1
Oldfield La South
GFD/PVL UB6 — 133 P4
Oldfield Ms HGT N6 — 118 C6
Oldfield Rd ACT W3 — 156 A2
BMLY BR1 — 206 C4
BXLYHN DA7 — 163 P8
HMPTN TW12 * — 175 J5
HNWL W7 — 135 P7
LCOL/BKTW AL2 — 57 J1
STNW/STAM N16 — 119 N8
WIM/MER SW19 — 178 A2
WLSDN NW10 — 136 C2
Oldfields Circ NTHLT UB5 — 134 B1
Oldfields Rd SUT SM1 — 201 K9
Oldfieldwood
WOKS/MYFD GU22 — 232 E5
Old Fishery La HHW HHW11 — 35 J8
Old Fish Street HI
BLKFR EC4V * — 12 E7
Old Fives Ct SL SL1 — 128 A5
Old Fleet La FLST/FETLN EC4A — 12 C5
Old Fold Cl BAR EN5 * — 77 J5
Old Fold La BAR EN5 — 77 J5
Old Fold Vw BAR EN5 — 76 F7
Old Ford Lock BOW E3 * — 140 B7
Old Ford Rd BETH E2 — 7 P8
BOW E3 — 140 D3
Old Forge Crs SHPTN TW17 — 196 C6
Old Forge Ms SHB W12 — 156 F1
Oldforge Rd ARCH N19 — 118 E2
EN EN1 — 79 N4
Old Forge Wy SCUP DA14 — 186 E1
Old Fox Cl CTHM CR3 — 241 P2
Old French Horn La HAT AL10 — 40 C3
Old Gannon Cl NTHWD HA6 — 92 D5
Old Garden Cl STALW/RED AL3 — 38 D2
The Old Gdn SEV TN13 — 246 D9
Old Gloucester St
BMSBY WC1N — 11 M1
Old Grove Cl CHESW EN7 — 61 M1
Old Hall Cl PIN HA5 — 93 M9
Old Hall Dr PIN HA5 — 93 M9
Old Hall Ri WLW CM17 — 29 M6
Oldhall St ACT W3 — 135 N10
Old Harpenden Rd
HAT AL10 — 39 M3
Old Hatch Mnr RSLP HA4 — 112 G5
Old Herns La WGCE AL7 — 23 N7
Old Hertford Rd BRKMPK AL9 — 22 D7
Old Hill CHST BR7 — 206 D1
ORP BR6 — 227 K9
Oldhill St STNW/STAM N16 — 119 P6
Old Homesdale Rd HAYES BR2 — 205 N4
Old Horsham Rd
CRAWW RH11 — 283 C8
Old Hospital Cl BAL SW12 — 180 A4
SWLY BR8 — 208 F1

CONDST W1S — 10 C7
Old House Ct DTCH/LGLY SL3 * — 150 D2
Oldhouse Ct HHNE HP2 — 29 H9
Old House Gdns TWK TW1 — 177 H2
Oldhouse La BFOR GU20 — 212 B5
CHOB/PIR GU24 — 212 F10
Old House La BFOR GU20 — 212 A4
HLWW/ROY CM19 — 46 A4
KGLCY WD4 — 72 B1
Old House Rd HHNE HP2 — 36 A6
Old Howletts La RSLP HA4 — 112 E4
Oldings Cnr BRKMPK AL9 — 22 E10
Old Jamaica Rd
BERM/RHTH SE16 — 19 N3
Old James St PECK SE15 — 160 A9
Old Jewry LOTH EC2R * — 12 G6
Old Kenton La
CDALE/KGS NW9 — 115 N3
Old Kent Rd PECK SE15 — 160 A5
STHWK SE1 — 19 J5
Old Kiln La BRKHM/BTCW RH3 — 273 P8
Old Kingston Rd WPK KT4 — 199 P10
Old Lane Gdns EHSLY KT24 — 234 B8
Old Leys HAT AL10 — 40 D8
Old Library La
HERT/WAT SG14 — 25 K5
Old Lodge Dr BEAC HP9 — 88 C10
Old Lodge La PUR/KEN CR8 — 240 G1
Old Lodge Wy STAN HA7 — 95 H4
Old London Rd EPSOM KT18 — 238 D4
HERT/BAY SG13 — 25 M5
KUTN/CMB KT2 — 199 G2
RDKG RH5 — 255 H6
RSEV TN14 — 245 P1
STAL AL1 — 39 L4
Old Maidstone Rd SCUP DA14 — 186 A10
Old Malden La WPK KT4 — 200 B9
The Old Maltings
HERT/BAY SG13 * — 25 P1
Old Malt Wy
WOKN/KNAP GU21 — 232 A3
Old Manor Cl CRAWW RH11 — 283 K5
Old Manor Dr ISLW TW7 — 176 B2
Old Manor Gdns RGUE GU4 — 268 F6
Old Manor Rd NWDGN UB2 — 153 L3
Old Manor Wy BXLYHN DA7 — 164 G10
CHST BR7 — 184 C8
Old Manor Yd ECT SW5 * — 14 F7
Old Market Sq BETH E2 — 7 L9
Old Martyrs CRAWW RH11 — 283 N4
Old Marylebone Rd
CAMTN NW1 — 9 P4
Old Md CFSP/GDCR SL9 — 90 B7
Old Meadow Cl BERK HP4 — 33 M7
Old Merrow St RGUE GU4 — 250 F7
Old Mill Cl EYN DA4 — 209 M8
Old Mill Ct SWFD E18 — 121 P3
Old Mill Gdns BERK HP4 — 34 A5
Old Mill La REDH RH1 — 258 C4
UX/CGN UB8 — 131 L7
Old Mill Rd DTCH/LGLY SL3 — 150 B1
WOOL/PLUM SE18 — 162 C5
Old Mitre Ct EMB EC4Y * — 12 C4
Old Montague St WCHPL E1 — 13 N3
Old Nazeing Rd BROX EN10 — 44 F7
Old Nichol St BETH E2 — 7 L8
Old North St FSBYW WC1X * — 11 L1
Old Nursery Ct SLN SL2 — 109 H7
Old Nursery Ri ASHF TW15 — 174 C8
Old Oak Av COUL/CHIP CR5 — 239 P5
Old Oak Common La ACT W3 — 136 B5
Old Oak La WLSDN NW10 — 136 C5
Old Oak Rd ACT W3 — 136 D3
Old Oaks Wabb BETH E2 — 69 A8
Old Orch BF/WBF KT14 — 216 A8
HLWS CM18 — 46 G3
PLSTW E13 — 141 P5
Old Orchard Cl EBAR EN4 — 77 N4
UX/CGN UB8 — 132 B8
Old Orchard Ms BERK HP4 — 33 M6
The Old Orch HAMP NW3 * — 118 A2
Old Otford Rd RSEV TN14 — 247 J4
Old Palace Rd CROY/NA CR0 — 203 K10
GUW GU2 — 267 J4
WEY KT13 — 197 H2
Old Palace Yd RCH/KEW TW9 — 177 H1
WHALL SW1A — 17 H3
Old Paradise St LBTH SE11 — 17 L7
Old Park Av BAL SW12 — 180 B3
ENC/FH EN2 — 79 A3
Old Park La MYFR/PKLN W1K — 10 B7
Old Park Ms HEST TW5 — 153 N6
Oldpark Ride CHESW EN7 — 61 J3
Old Park Riding WCHMH N21 — 78 G2
Old Park Rd ABYW SE2 — 163 K4
ENC/FH EN2 — 79 J1
Old Park Rd South
ENC/FH EN2 — 79 K3
Old Park Vw ENC/FH EN2 — 79 A3
Old Parvis Rd BF/WBF KT14 — 215 H5
Old Pearson St GNWCH SE10 — 160 G6
Old Perry St CHST BR7 — 185 H10
GVW DA11 — 190 B5
Old Polhill RSEV TN14 — 246 F1
Old Portsmouth Rd GUW GU2 — 267 J4
Old Post Office La
BKHTH/KID SE3 — 161 J4
Old Pottery Cl REIG RH2 — 275 L2
Old Pound Cl ISLW TW7 — 154 E7
Old Pye St WEST SW1P — 17 J3
Old Quebec St MBLAR W1H — 10 B4
Old Queen St STJSPK SW1H — 17 K2
Old Rectory Cl
KWD/TDW/WH KT20 — 238 D10
Old Rectory Dr HAT AL10 — 40 D4
Old Rectory Gdns EDGW HA8 — 96 A1
STALE/WH AL4 — 21 J2
Old Rectory La DEN/HRF UB9 — 111 H5
EHSLY KT24 — 252 F2
Old Redding
KTN/HRWW/WS HA3 — 94 A6
Old Redstone Dr REDH RH1 — 276 D4
Old Reigate Rd
BRKHM/BTCW RH3 — 273 P8
DORK RH4 — 255 K10
Old Rd ABR/ST RM4 — 103 H1
ADL/WDHM KT15 — 215 J4
BRKHM/BTCW RH3 — 256 C6
DART DA1 — 170 G9
ELTH/MOT SE9 — 185 H1
HARL CM17 — 29 M5
LEW SE13 — 161 N3
PEND EN3 — 80 E6
Old Rd East GVW DA11 — 191 H5
Old Rd West GVW DA11 — 190 C7
Old Royal Free Sq IS N1 * — 6 B1
Old Ruislip Rd NTHLT UB5 — 133 H6
Old St Mary's EHSLY KT24 — 252 F2
Old'sps Ap NTHWD HA6 * — 92 C1
Old Savill's Cots CHIG IG7 * — 103 N2
Old Sax La CRH HP5 — 50 A4
Old School Cl BECK BR3 * — 202 E1
GU GU1 — 250 A10
Old School Crs FSTGT E7 — 141 M1

WIM/MER SW19 — 179 H8
Old School Rd
BRKHM/BTCW RH3 — 273 M3
Old School Ms WEY KT13 — 216 D1
Old School Pl CROY/NA CR0 — 223 H1
WOKS/MYFD GU22 — 232 B7
Old School Sq THDIT KT7 — 198 E6
Old Schools La EW KT17 — 220 C5
Old School Ter CHEAM SM3 * — 220 G1
Old Seacoal La STP EC4M — 12 C3
Old Shire La
RKW/CH/CXG WD3 — 70 E10
WAB EN9 — 63 M10
Old Shire Lane Circular Wk
CSTG HP8 — 90 D3
DEN/HRF UB9 — 90 G10
Old Slade La DTCH/LGLY SL3 — 151 J4
Old Solesbridge La
RKW/CH/CXG WD3 — 71 K7
Old Sopwell Gdns STAL AL1 — 38 D8
Old South Cl PIN HA5 — 93 L8
Old South Lambeth Rd
VX/NE SW8 * — 158 F6
Old Stable Ms HBRY N5 — 119 K8
Old Station Ap LHD/OX KT22 — 236 F7
Old Station Gdns TEDD TW11 * — 176 F9
Old Station La
STWL/WRAY TW19 — 172 C2
Old Station Rd HYS/HAR UB3 — 152 G2
LOU IG10 — 82 B9
The Old Station Yd
WALTH E17 — 121 H2
Oldstead Rd BMLY BR1 — 183 J7
Old Stede Cl ASHTD KT21 — 237 L3
Old St FSBYE EC1V — 12 E1
PLSTW E13 — 141 N4
Old Studio Cl CROY/NA CR0 — 203 J9
The Old Surrey Ms GDST RH9 * — 260 B6
Old Swan Yd CAR SM5 — 222 A4
Old Town CLAP SW4 — 158 D9
CROY/NA CR0 — 203 J10
Old Tramyard
WOOL/PLUM SE18 — 163 H3
Old Tye Av BH/WHM TN16 — 244 B2
Old Uxbridge Rd
RKW/CH/CXG WD3 — 91 H8
Old Waddling La
STALE/WH AL4 — 21 J2
The Old Wk RSEV TN14 — 247 J3
Old Watford Rd
LCOL/BKTW AL2 — 55 M6
Oldway La SL SL1 — 128 B9
Old Westhall Cl WARL CR6 — 242 B5
Old Wharf Wy WEY KT13 — 216 A1
Old Woking Rd BF/WBF KT14 — 215 K8
WOKS/MYFD GU22 — 232 E4
Old Woolwich Rd
GNWCH SE10 — 161 J5
The Old Yard RSEV TN14 — 259 K6
The Old Yews HART DA3 — 211 N3
Old York Rd WAND/EARL SW18 — 179 L1
Oleander Cl ORP BR6 — 226 G2
O'Leary Sq WCHPL E1 — 140 D7
Olga St BOW E3 — 139 K6
Oliphant St NKENS W10 — 2 A9
Olinda Rd STNW/STAM N16 — 119 N4
Oliphant St NKENS W10 * — 2 A9
Olive Rd CRICK NW2 — 116 F9
EA W5 — 155 J2
PLSTW E13 — 141 P5
WIM/MER SW19 * — 179 M10
Oliver Av SNWD SE25 — 203 N5
Oliver Cl ADL/WDHM KT15 — 215 L1
CHSWK W4 — 155 N5
HHS/BOV HP3 — 35 P10
HOD EN11 — 44 G1
LCOL/BKTW AL2 — 58 C3
WTHK RM20 — 166 E6
Oliver Crs EYN DA4 — 209 N7
Oliver Gdns EHAM E6 — 142 B7
Oliver Gv SNWD SE25 — 203 N4
Oliver Ms PECK SE15 — 159 P8
Olive Rd CRICK NW2 — 116 F9
Olivers Wy HERT/BAY SG13 — 26 A8
Oliver's Yd STLK EC1Y * — 13 H1
Olive St ROMW/RG RM7 — 124 C3
Olivia Dr DTCH/LGLY SL3 — 150 C4
Olivia Gdns DEN/HRF UB9 — 91 M9
Olivier Rd CRAWE RH10 — 284 E8
Ollard's Gv LOU IG10 — 82 A8
Olleberrie La
RKW/CH/CXG WD3 — 53 H8
Ollerton Cl BOW E3 * — 140 E3
Ollerton Rd FBAR/BDGN N11 — 98 F6
Ollgar Cl SHB W12 — 136 C10
Olliffe St POP/IOD E14 — 161 K2
Olmar St STHWK SE1 — 19 N9
Olney Rd WALW SE17 — 18 D10
Olron Crs BXLYHS DA6 — 185 H1
Olven Rd WOOL/PLUM SE18 — 162 F6
Olveston Wk CAR SM5 — 201 N6
Olwen Ms PIN HA5 — 93 L10
Olyffe Av WELL DA16 — 163 K8
Olyffe Dr BECK BR3 — 183 M10
Olympia Wy WKENS W14 — 14 B4
Olympic Wy GFD/PVL UB6 — 134 A3
WBLY HA9 — 115 M8
Olympus Gv WDGN N22 — 99 H9
Olympus Sq CLPT E5 * — 120 A3
O'Meara St STHWK SE1 — 12 F10
Omega Cl POP/IOD E14 — 160 E7
Omega Maltings WARE SG12 * — 26 J2
Omega Pl IS N1 — 5 M8
Omega Rd WOKN/KNAP GU21 — 232 E4
Omega St NWCR SE14 — 160 F4
Ommaney Rd NWCR SE14 — 160 F4
Omnibus Wy WALTH E17 — 101 J1
Ondine Rd PECK SE15 — 159 N10
One Pin La SLN SL2 — 109 H3
One Tree Cl FSTH SE23 — 161 K5
One Tree Hill Rd GU GU1 — 268 E2
One Tree La BEAC HP9 — 88 D8
Onequote Wy WOKN/KNAP GU21
Ongar Cl ADL/WDHM KT15 — 215 J3
Ongar Hill ADL/WDHM KT15 — 215 K5
Ongar Pl ADL/WDHM KT15 — 215 K5
Ongar Rd ABR/ST RM4 — 103 J2
ADL/WDHM KT15 — 215 J4
BRW CM14 — 107 J3
FUL/PGN SW6 — 15 K10
Ongar Wy RAIN RM13 — 144 F3
Onra Rd WALTH E17 — 121 J5
Onslow Av BELMT SM2 — 221 M6
RCHPK/HAM TW10 — 177 K7
Onslow Cl CHING E4 — 101 L2
HAT AL10 — 40 C4
Onslow Crs CHST BR7 — 206 A2
WOKS/MYFD GU22 — 232 D7
Onslow Dr SCUP DA14 — 186 E5
Onslow Gdns CHING E4 — 101 L2
SAND/SEL CR2 — 223 P8
SKENS SW7 — 15 J5
SWFD E18 — 121 L4

THDIT KT7 198 D8
WCHMH N21 79 H9
WLGTN SM6 222 D4
Onslow Ms CHERT KT16 195 J6
Onslow Ms East SKENS SW7 * 15 L6
Onslow Ms West SKENS SW7 * 15 L6
Onslow Pde STHCT/OAK N14 * 98 C2
CROY/NA CRO 203 H7
GU GU1 200 C10
RCHPK/HAM TW10 177 K2
WOT/HER KT12 217 H5
Onslow Sq SKENS SW7 15 L6
GU GU1 267 P1
Onslow Wy THDIT KT7 198 D8
WOKS/MYFD GU22 233 J1
Ontario Cl BROX EN10 62 C1
HORL RH6 281 H5
Ontario St STHWK SE1 18 D4
Onyx Ms SRTFD E15 141 K1
Opal Cl CAN/RD E16 142 A8
DTCH/LGLY SL3 129 P6
Opal Ms KIL/WHAMP NW6 2 B1
Opal St LBTH SE11 18 C6
Opecks Cl SLN SL2 129 N6
Opendale Rd SL SL3 128 A7
Openshaw Rd ABYW SE2 163 L3
Openview WAND/EARL SW18 179 M4
Ophir Ter PECK SE15 143 P7
Opossum Wy HSLWW TW4 153 M9
Oppenheim Rd LEW SE13 161 H8
Oppidans Rd HAMP NW3 4 A4
Optima Pk DART DA1 165 N4
Opus Pk GU GU1 250 A6
Oram Pl HHS/BOV HP3 35 N9
Orange Court La ORP BR6 226 D5
Orange Gv CHIG IG7 102 A7
WAN E11 121 K8
Orange Hill Rd EDGW HA8 95 P8
Orange Pl BERM/RHTH SE16 160 B2
Orangery La ELTH/MOT SE9 184 C1
The Orangery
RCHPK/HAM TW10 * 177 H5
Orange Sq LSQ/SEVD WC2H 11 J7
WAP E1W 13 P10
Orange Tree HI ABR/ST RM4 104 E6
Oransay Rd IS N1 6 F2
Oratory La CHEL SW3 * 15 M7
Orbain Rd FUL/PGN SW6 157 H6
Orbel St BTSEA SW11 157 P7
Orbital Crs GSTN WD25 72 C1
Orbital One DART DA1 * 188 A5
Orb St WALW SE17 18 C6
Orchard Av ADL/WDHM KT15 215 G7
ASHF TW15 174 D9
BELV DA17 163 P5
BERK HP4 33 M5
CROY/NA CRO 204 D9
EBED/NFELT TW14 174 E1
FNCH N3 117 K1
GSTN WD25 55 J7
GVW DA11 190 B6
HEST TW5 153 M6
MTCM CR4 202 B8
NWMAL KT3 200 B2
RAIN RM13 145 K6
RBRW/HUT CM13 107 L4
SL SL1 128 C7
STHGT/OAK N14 78 D10
STHL UB1 133 M10
THDIT KT7 198 F8
TRDG/WHET N20 97 N3
WDSR SL4 148 F7
Orchard Cl ALP/SUD HA0 135 K3
ASHF TW15 174 D9
BNSTD SM7 221 L10
BORE WD6 75 L8
BROX EN10 * 44 F6
BUSH WD23 94 C2
BXLYHN DA7 163 P7
CHOB/PIR GU24 212 C9
CRICK NW2 116 D8
DEN/HRF UB9 131 L1
EDGW HA8 95 K7
EGH TW20 172 E8
EHSLY KT24 234 C10
FSTH SE23 182 B2
GU GU1 250 E10
HART DA3 211 N2
HERE/BAY SG13 42 D5
HHNE HP2 36 A4
HOR/WEW KT19 * 219 N5
HORL RH6 280 A3
IS N1 6 F4
LHD/OX KT22 236 D5
NKENS W10 8 B3
POTB/CUF EN6 60 F4
RAD WD7 74 D3
RBSF CM22 30 D3
RGUW GU3 248 A10
RKW/CH/CXG WD3 84 B7
RSEV TN14 112 D5
RSLP HA4 113 K8
RYNPK SW20 200 F4
SOCK/AV RM15 147 H6
STAL AL1 38 C4
THDIT KT7 198 G8
WARE SG12 26 C1
WARE SG12 27 H7
WAT WD17 72 G2
WOKS/MYFD GU22 232 E2
WOT/HER KT12 197 J7
Orchard Cots HYS/HAR UB3 * 152 F1
KUTN/CMB KT2 * 199 M1
Orchard Ct BEAC HP9 89 H7
WLGTN SM6 * 222 D4
WPK KT4 * 200 D8
Orchard Crs EDGW HA8 95 P6
EN EN1 79 N5
Orchard Cft WD CM20 29 K9
Orchard Dr ASHTD KT21 237 J6
BKHH/KID SE3 161 N4
EDGW HA8 95 L6
EPP CM16 83 H2
GRAYS RM17 167 M1
HORL RH6 280 C4
LCOL/BKTW AL2 56 A2
RKW/CH/CXG WD3 70 C5
UX/CGN UB8 131 N6
WAT WD17 72 G1
WOKN/KNAP GU21 232 B1
Orchard End Av AMSS HP7 69 H3
Orchardfield Rd GODL GU7 267 L6
Orchard Gdns CHSGTN KT9 219 J8
EHSLY KT24 253 M4
EPSOM KT18 237 P1
WAB EN9 45 N7
Orchard Ga CDALE/KGS NW9 116 B2
ESH/CLAY KT10 217 M1
NWMAL KT3 200 B1
WFD IG8 101 P5
Orchard Gn CTHM CR3 241 M8
LHD/OX KT22 236 D5
WEY KT13 196 F9
Orchard Gv CROY/NA CRO 204 D7
EDGW HA8 95 M4
KTN/HRWW/WS HA3 115 P3
ORP BR6 207 H9
PGE/AN SE20 181 K7
Orchard HI BFOR GU20 212 C4
LHD/OX KT22 236 D5
WEY KT13 196 F9
Orchard Lea La AMS HP6 69 J4
Orchard Lea MEO DA13 * 189 L7
Orchard Lea Cl
WOKS/MYFD GU22 233 H1

Orchardleigh LHD/OX KT22 236 G8
Orchardleigh Av PEND EN3 80 B6
Orchard Mains
WOKS/MYFD GU22 231 P6
Orchard Md HAT AL10 40 C4
Orchardmede WCHMH N21 79 L10
Orchard Mew
WOKS/KNAP GU21 230 G4
IS N1 7 H4
TOOT SW17 179 M6
The Orchard on The Gn
RKW/CH/CXG WD3 72 A9
Orchard Pde POTB/CUF EN6 * 58 G7
Orchard Pl BWFS/WCR EN8 62 C6
POP/IOD E14 141 K9
STMC/STPC BR5 * 207 M3
TOTM N17 99 H4
UX/CGN UB8 * 131 M7
Orchard Ri CROY/NA CRO 204 D8
KUTN/CMB KT2 199 P1
PIN HA5 112 C1
RCHPK/HAM TW10 * 155 N10
Orchard Ri East BFN/LL DA15 185 H5
Orchard Ri West BFN/LL DA15 185 H5
Orchard Rd BAR EN5 77 H8
BEAC HP9 88 E10
BELV DA17 164 B3
BMLY BR1 205 P3
BTFD TW8 155 H5
CHSGTN KT9 219 K1
CSTG HP8 89 P3
DAGE RM10 144 B5
DORK RH4 272 G5
FELT TW13 175 H4
GUW GU2 267 L3
GVW DA11 189 P5
HCT N6 118 C5
HORL RH6 281 J4
HSLWW TW4 175 H1
HYS/HAR UB3 133 H9
KUT/HW KT1 199 L3
ORP BR6 226 E2
ORP BR6 227 M5
PEND EN3 80 B9
RCH/KEW TW9 155 M9
REIG RH2 257 L10
RGUE GU4 268 B6
RGUW GU3 248 E10
ROMW/RG RM7 104 C10
RSEV TN14 246 C10
SAND/SEL CR2 224 A10
SCUP DA14 185 H7
SEVS/STOTM N15 99 N2
SHCR GU5 270 B5
SOCK/AV RM15 147 H7
SUN TW16 175 J10
SUT SM1 221 L4
SWCM DA10 189 K1
TWK TW1 176 F1
WDSR SL4 171 N3
WELL DA16 163 L9
Orchards Cl BF/WBF KT14 215 K10
Orchardson St STJWD NW8 9 L2
Orchard St CRAWW RH11 283 N1
HHS/BOV HP3 35 N10
MBLAR W1H 10 C5
STALW/RED AL3 38 B7
WALTH E17 120 D2
Orchard Ter EN EN1 * 79 P10
RDART DA2 * 188 A3
WLSDN NW10 * 116 C9
The Orchards BKHTH/KID SE3 161 J8
BNSTD SM7 239 K1
BORE WD6 74 E6
BROX EN10 * 44 F6
CHSWK W4 156 A3
EW KT17 220 C4
GLDGN NW11 117 K3
HSLW TW3 154 D8
KGLGY WD4 54 B5
LTWR GU18 212 A7
RDKG RH5 273 H6
SEV TN13 246 F7
SWLY BR8 208 E2
TRDG/WHET N20 97 L2
VW GU25 194 B5
WCHMH N21 79 L10
WEY KT13 216 C1
WOKN/KNAP GU21 231 N2
WOKS/MYFD GU22 232 B8
Orchard Vw CHERT KT16 195 K6
Orchardville SL SL1 128 A6
Orchard Vls SCUP DA14 * 185 M9
Orchard Wy ADL/WDHM KT15 215 L2
ASHF TW15 174 A5
BGR/WK TN15 247 P3
CHESW EN7 61 K6
CHIG IG7 103 K4
CROY/NA CRO 204 D7
DORK RH4 272 G5
DTCH/LGLY SL3 130 B10
EN EN1 79 M7
ESH/CLAY KT10 218 B3
HHS/BOV HP3 52 D4
KWD/TDW/WH KT20 257 H2
OXTED RH8 261 M9
POTB/CUF EN6 59 L4
RDART DA2 187 L6
REIG RH2 275 L3
SUT SM1 221 N1
RGUW GU3 * 245 J10
RGUW GU3 248 A10

Oriel Gdns CLAY IG5 122 C1
Oriel Rd HOM E9 140 C1
Oriel Wy NTHLT UB5 133 L6
Oriental Cl WOKS/MYFD GU22 232 C3
Oriental Rd ASC SL5 192 C4
CAN/RD E16 142 A10
WOKS/MYFD GU22 232 D3
Orient Cl STAL AL1 38 D8
Orient St LBTH SE11 18 C5
Orient Wy CLPT E5 120 C8
LEY E10 120 F7
Oriel Ct ABLGY WD5 75 H5
Oriole Wy THMD SE28 143 L9
Orion Rd MUSWH N10 98 B7
Orion Wy NTHWD HA6 92 A3
Orissa Rd WOOL/PLUM SE18 145 H4
Orkney St BTSEA SW11 158 A5
Orlando Gdns HOR/WEW KT19 220 A4
Orlando Rd CLAP SW4 158 D9
Orleans Rd NRWD SE19 181 L9
TWK TW1 176 C3
Orlestone Gdns ORP BR6 227 P7
Orleston Ms HOLWY N7 6 B1
Orleston Rd HOLWY N7 6 B1
Orley Farm Rd HRW HA1 114 D8
Orlick Rd GVE DA12 191 L5
Oritons La HORS RH12 282 C3
Ormanton Rd SYD SE26 181 P7
Ormeley Rd BAL SW12 180 C3
Orme Ct BAY/PAD W2 9 J8
Orme Rd KUT/HW KT1 199 N2
SUT SM1 221 L3
Ormerod Gdns MTCM CR4 202 B2
Ormesby Cl THMD SE28 143 N9
Ormesby Dr POTB/CUF EN6 58 C10
Ormesby Wy
KTN/HRWW/WS HA3 115 L4
Orme Sq BAY/PAD W2 9 H8
Orme Square Ga BAY/PAD W2 9 H8
Ormiston Gv SHB W12 136 D5
Ormiston Rd GNWCH SE10 161 M4
Ormond Av HPTN TW12 198 A1
Ormond Cl BMSBY WC1N 11 M3
Ormond Crs HPTN TW12 176 A10
Ormond Dr HPTN TW12 176 A10
Ormonde Av HOR/WEW KT19 220 A5
ORP BR6 206 F9
Ormonde Ga CHEL SW3 16 A8
Ormonde Pl BGVA SW1W 16 B6
WEY KT13 * 216 E3
Ormonde Ri BKHH IG9 101 P7
Ormonde Rd MORT/ESHN SW14 155 N9
NTHWD HA6 92 A5
WOKN/KNAP GU21 231 N2
Ormonde Ter STJWD NW8 * 4 A6
Ormond Rd ARCH N19 118 F6
RCHPK/HAM TW10 177 J1
Ormond Yd STJS SW1Y 11 H9
Ormsby Gdns GFD/PVL UB6 133 P2
Ormsby Pl STNW/STAM N16 119 P9
Ormsby St BETH E2 7 L7
Ormside St PECK SE15 160 C5
Ormskirk Rd OXHEY WD19 93 L5
Ornan Rd HAMP NW3 117 P10
Oronsay HHS/BOV HP3 36 A9
Oronsay Wk IS N1 6 F2
Orphanage Rd WAT WD17 73 K6
Orpheus St CMBW SE5 159 L6
Orpington By-Pass ORP BR6 228 B5
Orpington Gdns UED N18 99 M4
Orpington Rd CHST BR7 207 H3
WCHMH N21 99 J1
Orpin Rd REDH RH1 258 D6
Orpwood Cl HPTN TW12 175 N9
Orsett Heath Crs
CDW/CHF RM16 168 D2
Orsett Ms BAY/PAD W2 * 9 J4
Orsett Rd GRAYS RM17 167 N4
Orsett St LBTH SE11 17 P7
Orsett Ter BAY/PAD W2 * 9 J5
WFD IG8 101 P9
Orsman Rd IS N1 7 J6
Orton Cl STALE/WH AL4 38 E7
Orton Gv EN EN1 79 N5
Orton St WAP E1W 13 N10
Orville Rd BTSEA SW11 157 N8
Orwell Cl WATN WD24 * 73 L7
HYS/HAR UB3 132 D10
Orwell Gdns REIG RH2 275 L4
Orwell Rd PLSTW E13 141 P4

Osier St WCHPL E1 140 G1
Osier Wy BNSTD SM7 221 H10
LEY E10 140 A1
MTCM CR4 202 B5
Oslac Rd CAT SE6 182 G8
Oslo Sq BERM/RHTH SE16 160 D2
Oslow Cl NKENS W10 2 C9
Osman Rd ED N9 99 P4
HMSMTH W6 * 156 F2
Osmond Cl RYLN/HDSTN HA2 114 C6
Osmond Gdns WLGTN SM6 222 D4
Osmund St CRAWE RH10 284 C7
Osney Cl CRAWW RH11 283 M8
Osney Wk CAR SM5 192 J5
Osney Wy GVE DA12 191 J5
Osprey Cl EHAM E6 142 A7
GSTN WD25 55 M10
HAYES BR2 206 B2
SUT SM1 221 J2
WAN E11 121 M2
WDR/YW UB7 151 N1
Osprey Dr EPSOM KT18 238 C10
Osprey Est BERM/RHTH SE16 160 C3
Osprey Gdns SAND/SEL CR2 224 C6
Osprey Ms PEND EN3 80 B3
Osprey Rd WAB EN9 63 M10
Ospringe Cl PGE/AN SE20 182 B10
Ospringe Rd KTTN NW5 118 C2
Osram Rd WBLY HA9 115 J8
Osric Pth IS N1 7 H4
Ossian Rd FSBYPK N4 118 C5
Ossian Ms CHSWK W4 156 C5
Ossington Blds MHST W1U * 10 C3
Ossington Cl BAY/PAD W2 * 9 F8
Ossington St BAY/PAD W2 9 F8
Ossory Rd STHWK SE1 19 N8
Ossulton Pl EFNCH N2 * 117 J5
Ossulton Wy EFNCH N2 117 H5
Ostade Rd BRXS/STRHM SW2 180 A6
Osteley Cl BRXS/STRHM SW2 180 B7
Osteli Crs PEND EN3 80 F4
Osten Ms SKENS SW7 15 H7
Osterberg Rd DART DA1 165 N10
Osterley Av ISLW TW7 154 D1
Osterley Cl STMC/STPC BR5 207 K6
Osterley Crs ISLW TW7 154 A6
Osterley Gdns THHTH CR7 203 K2
Osterley La NWDGN UB2 153 N2
Osterley Park View Rd
HNWL W7 154 D1
Osterley Rd ISLW TW7 154 D1
STNW/STAM N16 119 M9
Oster St STALW/RED AL3 38 B5
Ostlers Dr ASHF TW15 174 D1
Ostliffe Rd PLMGR N13 99 J4
Oswald Cl LHD/OX KT22 236 B5
Oswald Rd LHD/OX KT22 236 B5
STAL AL1 38 D7
STHL UB1 133 M10
Oswald's Md HOM E9 120 D9
Oswald St CLPT E5 120 C8
Oswald Ter CRICK NW2 * 116 F8
Oswald Rd CROY/NA CRO 224 A5
Osward PI ED N9 99 P3
Osward Rd BAL SW12 180 A5
Oswin St LBTH SE11 18 D5
Oswyth Rd CMBW SE5 159 M8
Otford Cl BMLY BR1 206 D3
BXLY DA5 186 C2
PGE/AN SE20 204 B1
Otford Crs BROCKY SE4 182 C2
Otford La RSEV TN14 228 A3
Otford Rd RSEV TN14 247 J6
Othello Cl LBTH SE11 18 C7
Otis St BOW E3 141 H5
Otley Ct FBAR/BDGN N11 * 98 A5
Otley Dr GNTH/NBYPK IG2 122 E4
Otley Rd CAN/RD E16 141 P8
Otley Ter CLPT E5 120 B7
Otley Wy OXHEY WD19 93 J5
Otlinge Rd STMC/STPC BR5 207 N4
Ottawa Ct BROX EN10 62 D1
Ottawa Gdns DAGE RM10 144 E2
Ottawa Rd TIL RM18 168 D3
Ottaway St CLPT E5 119 P8
Otterbourne Rd CHING E4 101 P8
CROY/NA CRO 204 A3
Otterburn Gdns ISLW TW7 154 C6
Otterburn St TOOT SW17 180 A3
Otter Cl CHERT KT16 214 A9
SRTFD E15 141 H3
Otterden St CAT SE6 182 E7
Otterfield Rd WDR/YW UB7 133 N6
Otter Gdns HAT AL10 40 C5
Otteridge Rd WELL DA16 164 E3
Otter Rd GFD/PVL UB6 133 M2
Otters Cl STMC/STPC BR5 207 N4
Otterspool La WATN WD24 73 M4
Otterspool Wy WATN WD24 73 N2
Otto Cl CAT SE6 182 A5
SYD SE26 182 A5
Ottoman Ter WAT WD17 73 K7
Otto St WALW SE17 18 C10
Ottways Av ASHTD KT21 237 J5
Ottways La ASHTD KT21 237 J6
Otway Gdns BUSH WD23 94 E2
Otways Cl POTB/CUF EN6 59 L6
Oulton Cl THMD SE28 143 M8
Oulton Crs BARK IG11 124 G5
POTB/CUF EN6 58 G7
Oulton Rd SEVS/STOTM N15 119 J1
Oulton Wk CRAWE RH10 284 C9
Oulton Wy OXHEY WD19 93 M5
Oundle Av BUSH WD23 94 E1
Ousden Cl CHES/WCR EN8 62 D6
Ousden Dr CHES/WCR EN8 62 D6
Ouseley Rd BAL SW12 180 A4
STWL/WRAY TW19 171 P3
Outdowns EHSLY KT24 253 J6
Outer Cir CAMTN NW1 3 N9
Outfield Rd CFSP/GDCR SL9 90 A6
Outgate Rd WLSDN NW10 136 C2
Outram Pl IS N1 5 M5
WEY KT13 216 D2
Outram Rd CROY/NA CRO 204 B8
EHAM E6 142 A8
WDGN N22 98 A9
Outwich St HDTCH EC3A * 13 K5
Outwood La
KWD/TDW/WH KT20 239 L8
REDH RH1 277 L8
TEDD TW11 176 B8
WDSR SL4 148 H8
WFD IG8 101 N1
WLGTN SM6 239 M7
Oval Gdns GRAYS RM17 167 P5
Oval PI VX/NE SW8 158 A6
Oval Rd CAMTN NW1 4 C1
CROY/NA CRO 204 A9
DAGE RM10 144 D4
Oval Rd North DAGE RM10 144 D6
Oval Rd South DAGE RM10 144 D7
The Oval BETH E2 140 A6
BFN/LL DA15 185 K3
BNSTD SM7 221 K10
BROX EN10 * 44 F6
GODL GU7 267 J10
GUW GU2 267 J2
HART DA3 211 P2
RGUW GU3 248 D7
Ovaltine Dr KGLGY WD4 54 C5
Oval Wy CFSP/GDCR SL9 90 A6
LBTH SE11 17 P8
Ovenden Cl RSEV TN14 245 N6
Ovenden Rd RSEV TN14 245 L4
Overbrook EHSLY KT24 252 F5
Overbrook Wk EDGW HA8 * 95 P2
Overbury Av BECK BR3 184 A1
Overbury Crs CROY/NA CRO 225 J7
Overbury Rd FSBYPK N4 118 E5
Overbury St CLPT E5 120 C9
Overcliffe GVW DA11 190 D4

Overcliff Rd BROCKY SE4 160 F9
GRAYS RM17 168 A5
Overcourt Cl BFN/LL DA15 185 L5
Overdale ASHTD KT21 237 K2
RDKG RH5 273 H1
REDH RH1 259 K9
RSEV TN14 265 J9
Overdale Av NWMAL KT3 199 P2
Overdale Rd CSHM HP5 50 G4
EA W5 155 H2
Overdene Dr CRAWW RH11 283 K7
Overdown Rd CAT SE6 182 F7
Overhill WARL CR6 240 G7
Overhill Cots MTCM CR4 * 202 D2
Overhill Rd EDUL SE22 181 J2
PUR/KEN CR8 223 H5
Overhill Wy BECK BR3 205 J5
Overlea Rd CLPT E5 119 P5
Overlord Cl BROX EN10 44 E6
Overlord Ct LHD/OX KT22 236 C7
Overmead ELTH/MOT SE9 184 C4
SWLY BR8 208 F5
Over Minnis HART DA3 211 L10
Overstand Cl BECK BR3 183 L8
Overstone Gdns CROY/NA CRO 204 F7
Overstone Rd HARP AL5 20 C5
HMSMTH W6 156 F3
Overstream
RKW/CH/CXG WD3 71 L8
Over The Misbourne
CFSP/GDCR SL9 110 D4
Over The Misbourne Rd
DEN/HRF UB9 110 F4
Overthorpe Cl
WOKN/KNAP GU21 231 N3
Overton Cl ISLW TW7 154 E7
WLSDN NW10 135 P1
Overton Ct WAN E11 121 K1
WAN E11 121 N5
Overton Dr CHDH RM6 123 M3
WAN E11 121 N5
Overton Rd ABYW SE2 163 M2
BELMT SM2 221 K3
BRXN/ST SW9 158 C6
LEY E10 120 D6
STHGT/OAK N14 78 F9
Overton's Yd CROY/NA CRO 203 K10
Ovesdon Av RYLN/HDSTN HA2 113 H6
Oveton Wy GT/LBKH KT23 253 P2
Ovett Cl NRWD SE19 181 M2
Ovex Cl POP/IOD E14 161 H2
Ovington Ct
WOKN/KNAP GU21 231 L2
Ovington Gdns CHEL SW3 15 P4
Ovington Ms CHEL SW3 15 P4
Ovington Sq CHEL SW3 15 P4
Ovington St CHEL SW3 15 P4
Owen Cl CROY/NA CRO 203 L6
CRW RM5 104 B2
DTCH/LGLY SL3 150 C4
NTHLT UB5 133 M1
THMD SE28 143 M10
YEAD UB4 133 J5
Owen Gdns WFD IG8 102 B7
Owenite St ABYW SE2 163 L3
Owen Pl LHD/OX KT22 * 236 G8
Owen Rd BFOR GU20 212 C2
PLMGR N13 99 L4
YEAD UB4 133 J5
Owens Ms WAN E11 121 K7
Owen's Rw FSBYE EC1V 6 D8
Owen St FSBYE EC1V 6 D8
Owens Wy FSTH SE23 182 B3
RKW/CH/CXG WD3 72 B9
Owen Wk PGE/AN SE20 181 P7
Owen Wy WLSDN NW10 135 P1
Owgan Cl CMBW SE5 159 L5
Owl Cl SAND/SEL CR2 224 C6
Owlets Hall Cl EMPK RM11 125 N1
Owlsears Cl BEAC HP9 88 C7
Ownstead Gdns
SAND/SEL CR2 223 N6
Ownsted Hl CROY/NA CRO 225 H6
Oxberry Av FUL/PGN SW6 157 H8
Oxdowne Cl COB KT11 218 A10
Oxenden Wood Rd ORP BR6 227 P6
Oxendon St SOHO/SHAV W1D 11 H8
Oxenford St PECK SE15 159 L7
Oxenholme CAMTN NW1 4 G3
Oxenpark Av WBLY HA9 115 K5
Oxestalls Rd DEPT SE8 160 D4
Oxford Av HEST TW5 153 P4
HYS/HAR UB3 152 D8
RYNPK SW20 201 H2
Oxford Cl ASHF TW15 174 D10
CHES/WCR EN8 62 B5
ED N9 100 A3
GPK RM2 125 K3
GVE DA12 191 K4
MTCM CR4 202 D3
Oxford Crs NWMAL KT3 200 B4
MANHO EC4N * 12 G7
Oxford Dr BERM/RHTH SE16 160 A3
RSLP HA4 113 K6
Oxford Gdns CHSWK W4 155 N4
DEN/HRF UB9 111 K8
NKENS W10 136 G3
NTHWD HA6 92 D8
TRDG/WHET N20 97 N3
WCHMH N21 99 K1
Oxford Ga HMSMTH W6 156 G3
Oxford Ms BXLY DA5 186 B4
Oxford Rd CAR SM5 221 P5
ENC/FH EN2 79 K1
HART DA3 211 L10
HRW HA1 114 D4
Oxford Rd East WDSR SL4 149 J7
Oxford Rd North CHSWK W4 155 M4
Oxford Rd South CHSWK W4 155 J4
Oxford Rw SUN TW16 197 K3
Oxford St MHST W1U * 10 C5
SOHO/CST W1F 10 E5
WATW WD18 21 M3
Oxford Wk STHL UB1 133 N10
WEY KT13 * 195 J1
Oxgate Court Pde
CRICK NW2 * 116 E5
Oxgate Gdns CRICK NW2 116 E5
Oxgate La CRICK NW2 116 E4
Oxhawth Crs HAYES BR2 206 F4
Oxhey Av OXHEY WD19 93 M6
Oxhey Dr NTHWD HA6 93 H6
Oxhey La OXHEY WD19 93 M3
Oxhey Ridge Cl NTHWD HA6 93 H6
Oxhey Rd OXHEY WD19 93 M4
Oxleas EHAM E6 142 C4
Oxleas Cl WELL DA16 163 P2

OxleASe Dr HAT AL10 40 E5
Oxleay Rd RYLN/HDSTN HA2 113 P6
Oxleigh Cl NWMAL KT3 200 B3
Oxleys Rd CRICK NW2 116 C2
WAB EN9 63 M9
The Oxleys HLWE CM17 29 N7
Oxlow La DAGW RM9 124 A9
Oxonian St EDUL SE22 159 N10
Oxshott Rd LHD/OX KT22 217 M10
Oxshott Ri COB KT11 235 M1
Oxshott Wy COB KT11 235 M1
Oxted Cl MTCM CR4 201 N3
Oxted Rd GDST RH9 260 B6
Oxtoby Wy STRHM/NOR SW16 202 C1
Oyster Catchers Cl
CAN/RD E16 141 N8
Oysterfields STALW/RED AL3 38 A5
Oyster La BF/WBF KT14 215 N7
Oyster Rw WCHPL E1 140 G8
Ozolins Wy CAN/RD E16 141 N8

**P**

Pablo Neruda HNHL SE24 159 J10
Paceheath Cl CRW RM5 104 E7
Pace PI WCHPL E1 140 A8
Pacific Cl EBED/NFELT TW14 174 A4
SWCM DA10 189 K1
Pacific Rd CAN/RD E16 141 M8
Packet Boat La UX/CGN UB8 131 L8
Packham Cl ORP BR6 207 M10
Packham Rd GVW DA11 190 D8
Packhorse Cl STALE/WH AL4 39 H3
Packhorse La POTB/CUF EN6 58 A7
SEV TN13 246 D2
Packington Sq IS N1 6 E6
Packington St IS N1 6 D5
Packmores Rd ELTH/MOT SE9 184 C1
Padbrook OXTED RH8 261 M5
Padbury CI EBED/NFELT TW14 174 A6
Padbury Ct BETH E2 7 M2
Padcroft Rd WDR/YW UB7 133 N10
Paddenswick Rd HMSMTH W6 156 D2
Paddick Cl HOD EN11 44 E2
Paddington Cl YEAD UB4 133 L6
Paddington Gn BAY/PAD W2 9 L4
Paddington Recreation Gnd
MV/WKIL W9 * 2 G3
Paddington St MHST W1U 10 C3
Paddock Cl BKHTH/KID SE3 161 M9
ERYN DA4 209 L9
NTHLT UB5 133 P6
ORP BR6 226 E1
OXHEY WD19 93 M10
OXTED RH8 261 L3
SYD SE26 182 C7
WARE SG12 28 A3
WPK KT4 200 B8
Paddock Gdns NRWD SE19 181 M9
Paddockhurst Rd
CRAWW RH11 283 K8
Paddock La BAR EN5 76 B3
Paddock Md HLWS CM18 28 C7
Paddock Rd BXLYHS DA6 163 H9
CRICK NW2 116 D8
RSLP HA4 113 L8
Paddocks Cl COB KT11 217 K10
RYLN/HDSTN HA2 114 A9
STMC/STPC BR5 207 N9
Paddocks Md
WOKN/KNAP GU21 231 G2
The Paddocks ABR/ST RM4 84 G10
ADL/WDHM KT15 215 L6
EA W5 * 155 J2
EBAR EN4 78 A7
GT/LBKH KT23 254 A2
HERT/BAY SG13 26 A8
MLHL NW7 * 97 J3
RGUW GU3 248 B10
RKW/CH/CXG WD3 * 84 B3
STALE/WH AL4 * 39 H2
WBLY HA9 * 115 N7
WEY KT13 215 P7
WEY KT13 196 F10
WGCE AL7 23 L4
Paddocks Wy ASHTD KT21 237 K4
CHERT KT16 195 L8
The Paddock BH/WHM TN16 262 F2
BROX EN10 44 F6
CFSP/GDCR SL9 90 B6
CRAWE RH10 284 E6
DORK RH4 272 A3
DTCH/LGLY SL3 149 N7
GU GU1 250 G3
HAT AL10 40 D3
HGDN/ICK UB10 112 C9
VW GU25 194 B6
WDSR SL4 148 B6
WDSR SL4 170 A4
Paddock Wk WARL CR6 242 A5
Paddock Wy CHST BR7 185 L9
RDKG RH5 273 H6
WEY KT13 214 F5
WOKN/KNAP GU21 230 G10
Paddock Wd HARP AL5 20 D4
Padelford La STAN HA7 94 F3
Padfield Rd BRXN/ST SW9 159 F3
Padley Cl CHSGTN KT9 219 L2
Padnall Rd CHDH RM6 123 N1
Padstow Cl DTCH/LGLY SL3 150 B2
ORP BR6 227 J1
Padstow Rd ENC/FH EN2 79 N2
Padstow Wk FELT TW13 174 C5
Padua Rd PGE/AN SE20 204 B2
Pagden St VX/NE SW8 158 C7
Pageant Av CDALE/KGS NW9 96 C10
Pageant Crs
BERM/RHTH SE16 140 E10
Pageant Rd STAL AL1 38 C7
Pageant Wk CROY/NA CRO 203 M10
Page Av WBLY HA9 115 P8
Page Cl DAGW RM9 124 A9
HPTN TW12 175 J8
KTN/HRWW/WS HA3 115 L4
RDART DA2 189 L6
Pages Cl CROY/NA CRO 223 J2
ERITH DA8 164 C6
Page Green Rd
SEVS/STOTM N15 119 P3
Page Green Ter
SEVS/STOTM N15 119 N3
Page Heath La BMLY BR1 206 A3
Page Heath Vls BMLY BR1 206 A3
Page HI WARE SG12 26 A1
Pagehurst Rd CROY/NA CRO 203 P7
Page Meadow MLHL NW7 96 B6
Page Rd EBED/NFELT TW14 174 A2
HERT/BAY SG13 25 P5
Pages Cft HERK HP4 33 M3
Pages Hl MUSWH N10 98 B10
Pages La MUSWH N10 98 A10
UX/CGN UB8 131 M1
Page's Wk STHWK SE1 19 K5
Page's Yd CHSWK W4 156 C5
Paget Av SUT SM1 201 N10
Paget Cl HPTN TW12 176 C7
Paget Gdns CHST BR7 206 C1
Paget La ISLW TW7 154 C8
Paget Pl KUTN/CMB KT2 177 P9
THDIT KT7 198 C10
Paget Ri WOOL/PLUM SE18 145 G6
Paget Rd DTCH/LGLY SL3 150 C3
HGDN/ICK UB10 132 C5
IL IG1 123 P9
STNW/STAM N16 119 L6
Paget St FSBYE EC1V 6 D8

Paget Ter WOOL/PLUM SE18 162 E5
Pagette Gv GRAYS RM17 167 M4
Pagewood Cl CRAWE RH10 284 C8
Pagitts Gv EBAR EN4 77 L5
Paglesfield RBRW/HUT CM13 87 P10
Pagnell St NWCR SE14 160 E6
Pagoda Av RCH/KEW TW9 155 L9
Pagoda Gdns BKHTH/KID SE3 161 J9
Pagoda Gv EPP CM16 181 K5
Paignton Rd RSLP HA4 113 H8
  SEVS/STOTM N15 119 H8
Paines Brook Wy HARH RM3 105 N7
Paines Cl PIN HA5 113 M1
Painesfield Dr CHERT KT16 195 K3
Paine's La PIN HA5 93 M10
Pain's Cl MTCM CR4 202 C1
Pains Hill COB KT11 * 216 L10
  OXTED RH8 261 P8
Pains Hill Pk COB KT11 * 216 C9
Painsthorpe Rd STNW/STAM N16 119 M8
Painters Ash La GVW DA11 190 A6
Painters La PEND EN3 80 D1
Painters Ms BERM/RHTH SE16 19 P5
Painters Rd CAR SM5 201 N8
  WDGN N22 99 H8
Paisley Rd CAR SM5 201 N8
  WDGN N22 99 H8
Pakeman St HOLWY N7 118 C10
Pakenham Cl BAL SW12 129 K5
Pakenham St FSBYW WC1X 5 P10
Pakes Wy EPP CM16 83 H3
Palace Av KENS W8 9 H10
Palace Cl HOM E9 140 E1
  KGLY WD4 54 A6
  SL1 SL1 128 E10
Palace Court Gdns MUSWH N10 118 D1
Palace Dr WEY KT13 196 C10
Palace Gdns BKHH IG9 102 A2
Palace Gardens Ms KENS W8 8 G9
Palace Gardens Ter KENS W8 8 G8
Palace Gn KENS W8 15 J2
Palace Gates Rd WDGN N22 98 F9
  KENS W8 8 G9
Palace Gv BMLY BR1 205 N1
  NRWD SE19 181 N10
Palace Ms FUL/PGN SW6 157 J6
  WALTH E17 120 E2
Palace Pde WALTH E17 120 E2
Palace Rd BCVA SW1W 15 L5
Palace Rd ADL/WDHM KT15 215 L5
  BH/WHM TN16 244 D7
  BMLY BR1 205 N1
  BRXS/STRHM SW2 180 C4
  CEND/HSY/T N8 118 C3
  E/WMO/HCT KT8 198 B3
  FBAR/BDGN N11 98 F8
  KUT/HW KT1 199 J4
  NRWD SE19 181 N10
  RSLP HA4 113 M9
Palace Sq NRWD SE19 181 N10
Palace St WESTW SW1E 16 E5
Palace Vw BMLY BR1 205 N3
  CROY/NA CR0 224 E1
  LEE/GVPK SE12 183 M5
Palace View Rd CHING E4 100 G6
Palamos Rd LEY E10 120 F6
Palatine Av STNW/STAM N16 119 J10
Palatine Rd STNW/STAM N16 119 J10
Palemead Cl FUL/PGN SW6 156 G7
Palermo Rd WLSDN NW10 119 H3
Palestine Gv WIM/MER SW19 201 N1
Palewell Cl STMC/STPC BR5 186 B1
Palewell Common Dr MORT/ESHN SW14 178 A1
Palewell Pk MORT/ESHN SW14 178 A1
Paley Gdns LOU IG10 82 E7
Palfrey Cl STALW/RED AL3 38 C4
Palfrey Pl VX/NE SW8 19 M10
Palgrave Av STHL UB1 133 P9
Palgrave Gdns CAMTN NW1 3 P9
Palgrave Rd SHB W12 156 E4
Palins Wy CDW/CHF RM16 147 M10
Palissy St BETH E2 7 L10
Palladian Circ SWCM DA10 167 H10
Pallant Wy ORP BR6 206 D10
Pallas Rd HHNE HP2 36 A4
Pallet Ct HOD EN11 44 G5
Pallet Wy WOOL/PLUM SE18 162 B6
Pallingham Dr CRAWE RH10 284 D10
Palliser Dr RAIN RM13 111 L6
Palliser Rd CSTG HP8 89 M4
  WKENS W14 14 A7
Pall Ml STJS SW1Y 11 J10
Pall Ml East STJS SW1Y 11 H10
Pall Mall Pl STJS SW1Y 11 H10
Palmar Crs BXLYHN DA7 164 B8
Palmar Rd BXLYHN DA7 164 B8
Palmarsh Rd STMC/STPC BR5 * 207 N4
Palm Av SCUP DA14 185 N9
Palm Cl LEY E10 120 G8
Palmeira Rd BXLYHN DA7 164 A10
  CHEAM SM3 220 F1
  GVE DA12 190 F1
Palmer Av HERT/WAT SG14 153 P2
  HORL RH6 280 A2
  NTHLT UB5 133 M1
  REDH RH1 276 B1
  WWKM BR4 205 J9
Palmer Cl CHERT KT16 214 C3? G5
  HOL/ALD WC2B * 11 M8
  SUN TW16 197 N4
Palmer Crs CHERT KT16 214 G5
  KUT/HW KT1 199 K3
Palmer Gdns BAR EN5 76 B6
Palmer Pl HOLWY N7 119 H10
Palmer Rd BCTR RM8 123 N6
  CRAWE RH10 284 D10
  HERT/WAT SG14 25 L3
  PLSTW E13 141 N6
Palmer's Av GRAYS RM17 167 M4
Palmers Dr GRAYS RM17 167 M4
Palmersfield Rd BNSTD SM7 221 K10
Palmers Gv E/WMO/HCT KT8 197 P4
  WAB EN9 45 L8
Palmers Hl EPP CM16 65 K5
Palmers La BERM E2 80 B5
Palmer's Ldg GUW GU2 267 M1
Palmers Moor La IVER SL0 131 K6
Palmers Orch RSEV TN14 228 G5
Palmers Rd BETH E2 140 C4
  BORE WD6 75 P5
  MORT/ESHN SW14 ? N6
  STRHM/NOR SW16 193 D2
Palmer's Rd FBAR/BDGN N11 98 D8
Palmerston Cl DTCH/LGLY SL3 149 N2
Palmerston Cl REDH RH1 275 P5
  WGCW AL8 22 F5
  WOKN/KNAP GU21 214 D10
Palmerston Crs BKHH IG9 101 N3
Palmerston Crs PLMGR N13 98 G6
  WOOL/PLUM SE18 161 J5
Palmerston Dr STALE/WH AL4 21 J1
Palmerston Gdns WTHK RM20 167 K4
Palmerston Gv WIM/MER SW19 179 K10
Palmerston Rd ACT W3 155 P1
  BKHH IG9 101 N3
  CAR SM5 222 A5
  CROY/NA CR0 203 L5
  FSTGT E7 121 N10
  HSLW TW3 154 D7
  KIL/WHAMP NW6 2 D1
  MORT/ESHN SW14 177 M6
  ORP BR6 226 F1
  WALTH E17 120 M2
  WDGN N22 98 G8
Palmerston Vw POTB/CUF EN6 59 L8
Parkfield Wy HAYES BR2 206 C1
Park Gdns CDALE/KGS NW9 115 N4
  ERITH DA8 164 B13
  KUTN/CMB KT2 177 L8
Park Ga EA W5 135 J7
  EFNCH N2 117 N1
  STWL/WRAY TW19 152 C1
Parkgate Av EBAR EN4 77 M5
Parkgate Cl KUTN/CMB KT2 177 N9
Park Gate Ct HPTN TW12 * 176 B8
  WOKS/MYFD GU22 232 B4
Parkgate Crs EBAR EN4 77 M5
Parkgate Gdns MORT/ESHN SW14 178 A1
Parkgate Ms HGT N6 118 B6
Parkgate Rd BTSEA SW11 157 P6
  REIG RH2 275 L1
  WATN WD24 73 K3
  WLGTN SM6 222 B2
Park Gates HRW HA1 * 114 E6
Park Gn GT/LBKH KT23 235 P10
Park Gv GT/LBKH KT23 235 P10
  BXLYHN DA7 164 D10
  CDALE/KGS NW9 116 A5
  CEND/HSY/T N8 118 H1
Park Grove Rd WAN E11 121 K4
Park Hall Rd DUL SE21 181 L5
  EFNCH N2 117 K2
  REIG RH2 257 K8
Parkham St BTSEA SW11 157 P6
Park HI BMLY BR1 206 B4
  CAR SM5 222 A5
  CLAP SW4 180 E1
  FSTH SE23 182 A5
  HLWE CM17 29 L7
  LOU IG10 82 A9
  RCHPK/HAM TW10 177 L2
Park Hill CI CAR SM5 221 P5
Parkhill CI BH/WHM TN16 244 D7
Park Hill Ri CROY/NA CR0 203 M9
Parkhill Rd CHING E4 101 N1
  HAMP NW3 118 A3
Park Hill Rd HAYES BR2 205 K2
  WLGTN SM6 222 C4
Parkhill Rd BFN/LL DA15 185 H6
  BXLY DA5 186 A3
Park Hill Rd CROY/NA CR0 223 M1
  EW KT17 220 C7
  HHW HP1 35 L6
  HPTN TW12 176 B8
  WLGTN SM6 222 B4
Park House Dr REIG RH2 275 J4
Parkhouse St CMBW SE5 159 L6
Park House Gdns TWK TW1 177 H1
Parkhurst HOR/WEW KT19 219 P6
Parkhurst Gdns BXLY DA5 186 B3
Parkhurst Rd BXLY DA5 186 B3
  FBAR/BDGN N11 97 P8
  GNTH/NBYPK IG2 122 F1
  HOLWY N7 118 D11
  HOLWY N7 * 118 D11
  HORL RH6 281 K6
  HPTN TW12 176 B8
  LEY E10 120 D5
  SUT SM1 221 N2
  WALTH E17 119 M1
  WDGN N22 98 G8
Parkinson Ms WALTH E17 120 D2
Parkland Av DTCH/LGLY SL3 150 A4
  ROM RM1 104 F10
  UPMR RM14 126 A10
Parkland Cl HOD EN11 26 C10
  SEV TN13 265 K5
Parkland Gv ASHF TW15 174 F1
  ISLW TW7 154 E7
Parkland Md BMLY BR1 206 D3
Parkland Rd ASHF TW15 174 F1
  WDGN N22 98 C10
  WFD IG8 101 N8
Parklands ADL/WDHM KT15 215 M2
  BRYLDS KT5 199 P5
  BUSH WD23 74 B10
  CHIC IG7 102 F4
  GT/LBKH KT23 235 P9
  HGT N6 118 C6
  OXTED RH8 261 K7
  RDKG RH5 272 C6
Parklands CI BARN SW13 156 C6
  EBAR EN4 77 N4
  GNTH/NBYPK IG2 122 F1
  MORT/ESHN SW14 177 H1
  STALW/RED AL3 37 P7
Parklands Dr FNCH N3 116 G1
Parklands Pde HEST TW5 * 153 L8
Parklands Pl GU GU1 250 F10
Parklands Rd STRHM/NOR SW16 180 C9
Parkland Wy WPK KT4 200 F4
Park La ASHTD KT21 257 L4
  BEAC HP9 88 G2
  BGR/WK TN15 265 N14
  BROX EN10 44 D6
  BRW CM14 86 C9
  CAR SM5 222 B4
  CHDH RM6 123 N4
  CHEAM SM3 221 H5
  CHES/WCR EN8 62 D10
  COUL/CHIP CR5 240 E7
  CROY/NA CR0 203 P1
  DEN/HRF UB9 91 K9
  DTCH/LGLY SL3 150 A2
  EMPK RM11 125 H5
  HCH RM12 145 J1
  HEST TW5 153 L8
  HHNE HP2 35 P4
  HPTN TW12 176 B8
  MLHL NW7 96 C7
  OXHEY WD19 * 73 H9
  RSEV TN14 227 P2
  SCUP DA14 185 L5
  TOTM N17 99 P10
  WBLY HA9 115 H5
  WDSR SL4 170 E3
  YEAD UB4 132 B5
Park La East REIG RH2 275 L4
Park Lane Paradise CHESW EN7 43 P10
Parkland Av EPSOM KT18 219 N3
Park Lawn Rd WEY KT13 216 D1
Parklea CI CDALE/KGS NW9 96 C7
Parkleigh Rd WIM/MER SW19 201 L2
Park Ley Rd CTHM CR3 242 C6
Parkleys RCHPK/HAM TW10 177 J7
Parkleys Pde RCHPK/HAM TW10 * 177 J7
Park Md BFN/LL DA15 164 B11
Parkmead LOU IG10 82 D7
Put/ROE SW15 178 E2
Parkmead Gdns MLHL NW7 96 C7
Park Meadow BRKMPK AL9 40 F3
  BRWN CM15 87 J4
Parkmead SEE10 161 L4
  GNWCH SE10 161 L4
  NKENS W10 * 10 E1
  RAIN RM13 145 J1
  STWL/WRAY TW19 152 C1
Park Nook Gdns ENC/FH EN2 79 L5
Parkpale La BRKHM/BTCW RH3 273 M5
Park Pde ADL/WDHM KT15 * 155 W?
  HYS/HAR UB3 * 132 F8
  WLSDN NW10 136 C4
Park Piazza LEW SE13 183 J4
Park Pl ACT W3 155 M5
  CAR SM5 222 B5
  EA W5 135 J7
  HPTN TW12 176 B9
  IS N1 7 H5
  LCOL/BKTW AL2 56 C3
  POP/IOD E14 140 F10
  SEV TN13 246 E9
  WBLY HA9 115 L9
Park Place Vis BAY/PAD W2 9 K3
Park Ridings CEND/HSY/T N8 99 H1
Park Ri BERK HP4 33 H1
  HRW/HRWW/WS HA3 94 D9
  LHD/OX KT22 236 F7
Park Rise Cl LHD/OX KT22 236 C7
Park Rise Rd FSTH SE23 182 D4
Park Ri Rd ALP/SUD HA0 135 K1
Park Rd ALP/SUD HA0 135 K1
  AMS HP6 77 J8
  ASHF TW15 174 C8
  BAR EN5 76 C4
  BECK BR3 182 E10
  BMLY BR1 205 N1
  BNSTD SM7 239 L1
  BRW CM14 106 G2
  BRYLDS KT5 199 L6
  BUSH WD23 73 P10
  CDALE/KGS NW9 116 A5
  CEND/HSY/T N8 116 H3
  CHEAM SM3 221 H5
  CHES/WCR EN8 62 C9
  CHST BR7 184 E9
  CHSWK W4 156 A5
  CSHM HP5 50 G7
  CTHM CR3 241 M9
  E/WMO/HCT KT8 198 B4
  EBAR EN4 77 N8
  EFNCH N2 117 N2
  ESH/CLAY KT10 218 A1
  FBAR/BDGN N11 98 E8
  FELT TW13 175 L7
  GU GU1 250 A10
  GVW DA11 190 E5
  HDN NW4 116 A4
  HEST TW5 153 K6
  HNWL W7 135 J5
  HOD EN11 44 F3
  HORL RH6 281 K6
  HPTN TW12 176 B8
  HSLW TW3 176 A1
  IL IG1 122 G8
  KUT/HW KT1 199 H1
  LEY E10 120 F6
  MNPK E12 122 A9
  NWMAL KT3 200 A4
  OXTED RH8 261 L4
  PEND EN3 80 D2
  PLSTW E13 141 P7
  TWK TW1 177 H2
  UED N18 99 L3
  UX/CGN UB8 132 B8
  WELL DA16 164 B3
  WIM/MER SW19 179 N7
  WLGTN SM6 222 C4
  WLSDN NW10 136 B3
  WOKS/MYFD GU22 232 C5
  YEAD UB4 132 C5
Park Rd East ACT W3 155 M5
  HDGN/ICK UB10 131 N4
Park Rd North ACT W3 155 M5
Park Rw GNWCH SE10 161 J5
Park Royal Rd WLSDN NW10 135 P5
Parkshot RCH/KEW TW9 155 K9
  BECK BR3 204 C3
  CDH/CHR HM16 161 L6
  CFSP/GDCR SL9 ? A1
  CHEAM SM3 221 H5
  CHES/WCR EN8 62 D10
  ADL/WDHM KT15 215 H5
  HCH RM12 145 J1
  HEST TW5 153 K6
  HHS/BOV HP3 * 54 G1
  HPTN TW12 176 B8
  MLHL NW7 96 D4
  OXSTW W1C 10 B7
  RCH/KEW TW9 155 J10
  REIG RH2 275 L4
  RGUE GU4 250 G2
  RYLN/HDSTN HA2 114 A4
Park Side BKHH IG9 101 N3
Park Side CRICK NW2 116 D2
  EPP CM16 65 L8
  HYS/HAR UB3 * 132 F8
  SL1 SL1 136 B1? D8
  SOCK/AV RM15 146 C10
Parkside BKHH IG9 101 N3
  CHEAM SM3 221 H5
  SL1 SL1 136 D8
  SOCK/AV RM15 146 C10
  STAN HA7 94 F4
  SWLY BR8 186 E9
  TEDD TW11 176 B2
  WDSR SL4 170 F2
  WLGTN SM6 222 D3
  YEAD UB4 132 C5
Parkside Av BMLY BR1 206 C4
  BROX EN10 44 D5
  BXLYHN DA7 164 G1
  RAIN RM13 111 J9
  WIM/MER SW19 178 E3
Parkside CI EHSLY KT24 * 234 D10
  PGE/AN SE20 182 B10
Parkside Crs BRYLDS KT5 200 B4
  HOLWY N7 119 H10
Parkside Cross BXLYHN DA7 165 N2
Parkside Dr EDGW HA8 94 B8
  WAT WD17 72 E4
Parkside Gdns COUL/CHIP CR5 240 F4
  EBAR EN4 98 A1
  WIM/MER SW19 178 E3
Parkside Ms WARL CR6 242 F7
Parkside Pl EHSLY KT24 * 234 D10
  STA TW18 173 K8
Parkside Rd ASC SL5 192 C9
  BELV DA17 164 C3
  HSLW TW3 176 A1
  NTHWD HA6 72 D3
Parkside St BTSEA SW11 158 B7
Parkside Ter ORP BR6 * 207 K8
  UED N18 99 J10
Parkside BAY/PAD W2 9 P7
Park Sq East CAMTN NW1 10 E1
Park Sq Ms CAMTN NW1 10 E1
Park Sq West CAMTN NW1 10 E1
Parkstead Rd PUT/ROE SW15 178 D1
Park Steps BAY/PAD W2 9 P7
Parkstone Av EMPK RM11 125 M4
  UED N18 98 N6
Parkstone Rd PECK SE15 159 H8
  WALTH E17 121 H1
Park St BERK HP4 33 N4
  BRKMPK AL9 40 F3
  CROY/NA CR0 203 K10
  DTCH/LGLY SL3 150 C2
  LCOL/BKTW AL2 56 C3
  MYFR/PKLN W1K 9 P7
  SL1 SL1 149 L7
  STHWK SE1 12 E9
  TEDD TW11 176 D9
  WDSR SL4 149 J7
Park Street La LCOL/BKTW AL2 56 A5
Park Ter CAR SM5 * 201 P10
  GNWCH SE10 161 J5
  PEND EN3 * 80 C1
  RSEV TN14 * 245 N10
  SWCM DA10 167 M9
  WPK KT4 200 D8
The Park CAR SM5 222 A4
  EA W5 135 J10
  GLDGN NW11 117 L6
  GT/LBKH KT23 253 P1
  HGT N6 118 B5
  SCUP DA14 185 J8
  STAL AL1 38 F4
Parkthorne Cl RYLN/HDSTN HA2 114 A4
Parkthorne Dr RYLN/HDSTN HA2 113 P4
Parkthorne Rd BAL SW12 180 E3
Park Vw ACT W3 135 P7
  ADL/WDHM KT15 215 M2
  BRKMPK AL9 40 F3
  CRAWW RH11 283 M8
  CTHM CR3 241 P9
  EW KT17 220 C9
  GT/LBKH KT23 253 P1
  HOD EN11 44 F4
  HORL RH6 280 B4
  NWMAL KT3 200 C3
  PIN HA5 94 A5
  POTB/CUF EN6 59 M9
  SOCK/AV RM15 146 C10
  WBLY HA9 115 N10
  WDGN N22 98 G1
Parkview ACT W3 135 P7
  WOKS/MYFD GU22 232 C4
Park View Crs FBAR/BDGN N11 98 C5
Park View Dr MTCM CR4 201 N2
Park View Est HBRY N5 * 119 K9
Parkview Gdns CLAY IG5 122 C2
  GRAYS RM17 167 H4
  HDN NW4 116 F3
Parkview Ms RAIN RM13 145 J7
Park View Rd CROY/NA CR0 33 N5
  CRICK NW2 116 C9
  DORK RH4 242 D8
  EA W5 135 K7
  ELTH/MOT SE9 184 E4
  FNCH N3 97 L9
  LHD/OX KT22 236 E6
  PIN HA5 93 J7
  REDH RH1 276 B7
  STHL UB1 133 P10
  TOTM N17 119 P2
  UX/CGN UB8 132 B8
  WELL DA16 164 D4
Parkview V RGUE GU4 250 F7
Park Village East CAMTN NW1 * 4 E1
Park Village West CAMTN NW1 4 E1
Park Vis TOOT SW17 179 P7
Parkville Rd FUL/PGN SW6 157 J6
Park Vis GNWCH SE10 161 J5
Park Vista Apartments CAN/RD E16 * 141 L5
Parkwatts Crs SRTFD E15 141 K9
Park Wy BMPK CM15 107 L2
  CRAWE RH10 284 D5
  E/WMO/HCT KT8 198 A3
  EBED/NFELT TW14 175 J1
  EDGW HA8 95 N9
  ENC/FH EN2 79 H6
  GLDGN NW11 117 H5
  GT/LBKH KT23 235 P9
  RKW/CH/CXG WD3 91 M2
  RSLP HA4 113 M6
Parkway CROY/NA CR0 224 G6
  DORK RH4 272 F1
  ERITH DA18 163 P2
  GDMY/SEVK IG3 123 J8
  GPK RM2 104 G10
  GU GU1 250 B9
  HDGN/ICK UB10 132 B2
  RAIN RM13 145 H1
  RYNPK SW20 200 G4
  SBW CM21 29 F2
  STHGT/OAK N14 98 G3
  WEY KT13 216 D3? E1
  WFD IG8 101 P6
  WGCW AL8 22 B3
Parkway CI WGCW AL8 22 F6
Parkway Gdns WGCW AL8 22 F6
The Parkway HEST TW5 153 H5
  IVER SL0 131 P9
  NWDGN UB2 153 J2
  YEAD UB4 132 E5
Park West Pl BAY/PAD W2 9 N6
Parkwood BECK BR3 182 F10
Parkwood Av ESH/CLAY KT10 198 A4
Parkwood Dr HHW HP1 35 J1
Parkwood Gv SUN TW16 197 N3
Parkwood Ms HGT N6 118 B5
Park Wood Rd BH/WHM TN16 244 B7
  BXLY DA5 186 A3
  ISLW TW7 154 E7
  REDH RH1 258 F9
  WIM/MER SW19 179 J5
Park Works Rd REDH RH1 258 F9
Parlaunt Rd DTCH/LGLY SL3 150 C3
Parley Dr WOKN/KNAP GU21 231 N4
Parliament Ct WCHPL E1 * 13 M2
Parliament Hill Flds KTTN NW5 * 118 B3
Parliament Ms MORT/ESHN SW14 155 P8
Parliament Sq WEST SW1P 17 J3
  HERT/WAT SG14 25 L5
Parliament St WHALL SW1A 17 J3
Parmiter St BETH E2 140 B5
Parndon Mill La HLW CM20 28 B1

Parndon Wood Rd
  HLWW/ROY CM19 ... 46 F6
Parnell Cl ABLGY WD5 ... 54 C6
  CDW/CHF RM16 ... 167 H4
  CRAWE RH10 ... 284 E9
  EDGW HA8 * ... 95 N5
  SHB W12 ... 156 E2
Parnell Gdns WEY KT13 ... 216 A9
Parnell Rd BOW E3 ... 140 E3
Parnel Rd WARE SG12 ... 26 E1
Parnham Av LTWR GU18 ... 212 C7
Parnham St POP/IOD E14 * ... 140 D8
Paroma Rd BELV DA17 ... 164 B2
Parpins KGLGY WD4 * ... 5 J3
Parr Av EW KT17 ... 220 E5
Parr Cl CDW/CHF RM16 ... 167 H3
  ED N9 ... 100 A8
  LHD/OX KT22 ... 236 E6
Parr Crs HHNE HP2 ... 36 C1
Parris Cft HARH RH4 ... 273 H5
Parritt Rd REDH RH1 ... 258 F3
Parrock Av GVE DA12 ... 190 F4
Parrock St GVE DA12 ... 190 E2
Parrotts Cl RKW/CH/CXG WD3 ... 72 B8
Parrotts Fld HOD EN11 ... 44 G2
Parrott's La TRING HP23 ... 32 A6
Parr Rd EHAM E6 ... 142 A3
  STAN HA7 ... 95 J9
Parrs Pl HPTN TW12 ... 175 P10
Parr St IS N1 ... 6 G1
Parry Av EHAM E6 ... 142 C8
Parry Cl EW KT17 ... 220 D4
Parry Dr WEY KT13 ... 216 B6
Parry Gn North
  DTCH/LGLY SL3 ... 150 C3
Parry Gn South
  DTCH/LGLY SL3 ... 150 C3
Parry Rd WOOL/PLUM SE18 ... 162 L3
  SNWD SE25 ... 203 M3
Parry St VX/NE SW8 ... 17 K9
Parsifal Rd KIL/WHAMP NW6 ... 117 K10
Parsloe Rd EPP CM16 ... 88 A6
Parsloes Av DAGW RM9 ... 123 P10
Parsonage Bank EYN DA4 ... 209 N10
Parsonage Cl ABLGY WD5 ... 54 C6
  HYS/HAR UB3 ... 132 C8
  WARL CR6 ... 242 D2
Parsonage Fld BRWN CM15 ... 87 P5
Parsonage Gdns ENC/FH EN2 ... 79 N6
Parsonage La BRKMPK AL9 ... 40 E9
  DORK RH4 ... 272 B3
  ENC/FH EN2 ... 79 N6
  EYN DA4 ... 188 A9
  SCUP DA14 ... 186 A7
  SLN SL2 ... 129 H1
  WDSR SL4 ... 148 F7
Parsonage Leys HLW CM20 ... 47 J1
Parsonage Manorway
  BELV DA17 ... 164 C4
Parsonage Pl AMSS HP7 ... 69 H5
Parsonage Rd BRKMPK AL9 ... 40 E9
  CSTG HP8 ... 89 N4
  EGH TW20 ... 172 A8
  MAN RH13 ... 145 K4
  RKW/CH/CXG WD3 ... 91 N1
  WTHK RM20 ... 167 H5
Parsonage Sq DORK RH4 ... 272 B3
Parsonage St POP/IOD E14 ... 161 N9
Parsons Cl EDGW HA8 ... 95 M4
Parsonsfield Cl BNSTD SM7 ... 238 C5
Parsonsfield Rd BNSTD SM7 ... 238 C6
Parsons Gn FUL/PGN SW6 ... 157 K7
  GU GU1 ... 250 A8
Parsons Green La
  FUL/PGN SW6 ... 157 K7
Parsons Gv EDGW HA8 ... 95 M4
Parsons Md E/WMO/HCT KT8 ... 198 D7
  CROY/NA CRO ... 203 J8
Parsons Md DTCH/LGLY SL3 ... 150 C3
  PLSTW E13 ... 141 P4
Parson's Wood La SLN SL2 ... 129 J2
Parthenia Rd FUL/PGN SW6 ... 157 K7
Partingale La MLHL NW7 ... 96 C6
Partingdale La MLHL NW7 ... 96 C6
Partington Cl ARCH N19 ... 118 C8
Partridge Cl BAR EN5 ... 76 F10
  BUSH WD23 ... 94 B2
  CAN/RD E16 ... 142 A7
  CSHM HP5 ... 51 K4
  STAN HA7 ... 95 K5
Partridge Ct HLWS CM18 ... 47 R6
Partridge Dr ORP BR6 ... 206 F10
Partridge Gn ELTH/MOT SE9 ... 184 D6
Partridge Knoll PUR/KEN CR8 ... 223 J8
Partridge La HORS RH12 ... 282 B3
Partridge Md BNSTD SM7 ... 238 F1
Partridge Rd HLWS CM18 ... 46 H6
  HPTN TW12 ... 175 N9
  SCUP DA14 ... 185 H6
  STALW/RED AL3 ... 38 C2
Partridge Sq EHAM E6 ... 142 H1
The Partridges HHS/BOV HP3 ... 36 B8
Partridge Wy RGUE GU4 ... 250 D8
  WDGN N22 ... 98 F9
Parva Cl HARP AL5 ... 20 C5
Parvills WAB EN9 ... 63 J4
Parvis Rd BF/WBF KT14 ... 215 L8
Pasadena Cl HYS/HAR UB3 ... 133 J9
Pascal St VX/NE SW8 ... 158 E6
Pasfield WAB EN9 ... 63 J9
Pasley Cl WALW SE17 ... 18 D9
Pasquier Rd WALTH E17 ... 120 D1
Passey Pl ELTH/MOT SE9 ... 184 C2
Passfield Dr POP/IOD E14 ... 140 M7
Passmore Gdns
  FBAR/BDGN N11 ... 98 E7
Passmore St BCVA SW1W ... 16 G6
Pastens Rd OXTED RH8 ... 261 P7
Pasteur Cl CDALE/KGS NW9 ... 96 B10
Pasteur Dr HARH RM3 ... 105 L10
Pasteur Gdns IS N1 ... 99 N6
Paston Cl WLGTN SM6 ... 202 D10
Paston Crs LEE/GVPK SE12 ... 183 N3
Paston Rd HHNE HP2 ... 35 N4
Pastoral Wy BRW CM14 ... 106 D1
Pastor St LBTH SE11 ... 18 D5
Pasture Cl ALP/SUD HA0 ... 114 A1
  BUSH WD23 ... 94 B1
Pasture Rd ALP/SUD HA0 ... 114 A1
  CAT SE6 ... 183 K4
  DAGW RM9 ... 124 A1
Pastures HCDN/ICK UB10 ... 132 B1
The Pastures HAT AL10 ... 41 J2
  HHW HP1 ... 35 H5
  LCOL/BKTW AL2 ... 37 P10
  OXHEY WD19 ... 93 J3
  TRDG/WHET N20 ... 96 F1
  WCCE AL7 ... 23 K7
The Pasture CRAWE RH10 ... 284 D7
Patcham Ter VX/NE SW8 ... 158 C7
Patching Cl CRAWW RH11 ... 283 H6
Patching Wy YEAD UB4 ... 114 F5
The Patch SEV TN13 ... 246 F8
Paternoster Cl WAB EN9 ... 63 P3
Paternoster Hl WAB EN9 ... 63 P3
Paternoster Rw ABR/ST RM4 ... 104 M1
  STP EC4M ... 12 E6
Pater St KENS W8 ... 14 E4
Pates Manor Dr
  EBED/NFELT TW14 ... 174 E2
Pathfield Rd STRHM/NOR SW16 ... 180 D9
Pathfields SHGR GU5 ... 270 E8
Path Fld CRAWE RH10 ... 284 D7
Port Short Valley Wy
  HERT/BAY SG13 ... 43 J8
The Path WIM/MER SW19 ... 201 L1

The Pathway OXHEY WD19 ... 93 L2
  RAD WD7 ... 74 L2
  RPLY/SEND GU23 ... 251 L10
Patience Rd BTSEA SW11 ... 157 P8
Patio Cl CLAP SW4 ... 180 E2
Patmore La WOT/HER KT12 ... 216 C5
Patmore Link Rd HHNE HP2 ... 36 D6
Patmore Rd WAB EN9 ... 63 K10
Patmore St VX/NE SW8 ... 158 D7
Patmos Rd BRXN/ST SW9 ... 159 M6
Paton Cl BOW E3 ... 140 F5
Patricia Cl SL SL1 ... 128 D9
Patricia Ct WELL DA16 ... 165 L6
  EMPK RM11 ... 125 M6
Patricia Dr EMPK RM11 ... 125 M6
Patricia Vis TOTM N17 * ... 100 A9
Patrick Gv WAB EN9 ... 62 C9
Patrick Rd PLSTW E13 ... 141 P5
Patrington Cl CRAWW RH11 ... 283 K10
  UX/CGN UB8 ... 131 M5
Patriot Sq BETH E2 ... 140 A4
Patrol Pl CAT SE6 ... 182 C2
Patrons Wy West
  DEN/HRF UB9 ... 111 J4
  EHAM E6 ... 142 D8
Patshull Pl KTTN NW5 ... 4 C1
Patshull Rd KTTN NW5 ... 4 C1
Pattenden Rd CAT SE6 ... 182 E4
Patten Rd WAND/EARL SW18 ... 179 P5
Patterdale Cl BMLY BR1 ... 183 K9
  CRAWW RH11 ... 283 M10
Patterdale Rd PECK SE15 ... 160 B6
  DART DA2 ... 188 B4
Patterson Rd CSHM HP5 ... 50 C4
  NRWD SE19 ... 181 N9
Pattina Wk BERM/RHTH SE16 ... 140 D10
Pattison Rd CRICK NW2 ... 117 K8
Paul Cl CHESW EN7 ... 61 K1
  SRTFD E15 ... 141 K2
Paulet Rd CMBW SE5 ... 159 J8
Paulet Wy WLSDN NW10 * ... 136 B2
Paul Gdns CROY/NA CRO ... 203 N9
Paulhan Rd
  KTN/HRWW/WS HA3 ... 115 J2
Paulin Dr WCHMH N21 ... 99 H1
Pauline Crs WHTN TW2 ... 176 B4
Paulinus Cl STMC/STPC BR5 ... 207 M2
Paul Julius Cl POP/IOD E14 ... 141 J9
Paul Robeson Cl EHAM E6 ... 142 C5
Pauls Ct HOD EN11 * ... 44 F3
Pauls La HOD EN11 * ... 44 F3
Paul's Pl ASHTD KT21 ... 237 N5
Paul St SDTCH EC2A ... 13 J1
  SRTFD E15 ... 141 K3
Paultons Sq CHEL SW3 ... 15 M9
Paultons St CHEL SW3 ... 15 M9
Pauntley St ARCH N19 ... 118 C6
Paveley Dr BTSEA SW11 ... 157 P6
Paveley St STJWD NW8 ... 3 P10
Pavement La CROY/NA CRO ... 203 P8
The Pavement CLAP SW4 ... 158 D10
  EA W5 * ... 155 L6
  REDH RH1 * ... 258 A10
  TEDD TW11 * ... 176 C10
  WAN E11 * ... 121 H6
  WIM/MER SW19 * ... 179 J9
  WNWD SE27 * ... 181 K7
Pavet Cl DAGE RM10 ... 144 C1
Pavilion Cl HLWS CM18 ... 47 R6
Pavilion Ldg
  RYLN/HDSTN HA2 * ... 114 C6
Pavilion Ms FNCH N3 ... 97 K10
Pavilion Pde SHB W12 * ... 136 F6
Pavilion Rd IL IG1 ... 122 C5
  KTBR SW1X ... 16 B2
Pavilion Sq TOOT SW17 ... 179 P6
Pavilion St SHB W12 * ... 136 F6
Pawleyne Cl PGE/AN SE20 ... 182 B10
Pawsey Cl PLSTW E13 ... 141 L7
Pawson's Rd THHTH CR7 ... 203 K6
Pax Cl CRAWW RH11 ... 283 H9
Paxford Rd ALP/SUD HA0 ... 114 C2
Paxman Av AL SL1 ... 149 H2
Paxton Cl RCH/KEW TW9 ... 155 L8
  WOT/HER KT12 ... 197 K7
Paxton Gdns
  WOKN/KNAP GU21 ... 215 H9
Paxton Pl WNWD SE27 ... 181 N7
Paxton Rd BERK HP4 ... 34 B5
  BMLY BR1 ... 183 M10
  CHSWK W4 ... 156 B5
  FSTH SE23 ... 182 A3
  STAL AL1 ... 38 C7
  TOTM N17 ... 99 N8
Paxton Ter PIM SW1V ... 16 F9
Paycock Rd HLWW/ROY CM19 ... 46 D3
Payne Cl BARK IG11 ... 143 H7
  CRAWE RH10 ... 284 E5
Paynell Ct BKHTH/KID SE3 ... 161 K9
Payne Rd BOW E3 ... 140 G6
Paynesfield Av
  MORT/ESHN SW14 ... 156 A9
Paynes Field Cl BERK HP4 ... 33 J3
Paynesfield Rd
  BH/WHM TN16 ... 243 P6
  BUSH WD23 ... 94 E1
Paynes La WAB EN9 ... 45 H10
Payne St DEPT SE8 ... 160 E5
Paynes Wk HMSMTH W6 ... 4 A10
Paynetts Ct WEY KT13 ... 216 E2
Paynes Gdns WFD IG8 ... 101 L7
Peabody Av PIM SW1V * ... 16 F7
Peabody Cl CROY/NA CRO ... 204 B8
  GNWCH SE10 ... 160 G7
  PIM SW1V ... 16 F9
Peabody Cots HNHL SE24 * ... 181 K3
  CMBW SE5 * ... 159 J1
  HMSMTH W6 * ... 156 F4
  HNHL SE24 * ... 181 J3
  NKENS W10 * ... 136 F7
  STHWK SE1 * ... 11 M9
Peabody Hl DUL SE21 ... 181 J4
Peabody Sq IS N1 * ... 6 E5
  CLKNW EC1R * ... 12 B2
Peabody Est BTSEA SW11 ... 157 P10
  CLKNW EC1R * ... 12 B2
  CMBW SE5 * ... 159 L1
  HMSMTH W6 * ... 156 F4
  HNHL SE24 ... 181 J3
  NKENS W10 * ... 136 F7
  STHWK SE1 * ... 11 M9
Peace Cl CHESW EN7 ... 62 A5
  GFD/PVL UB6 ... 134 C3
  SNWD SE25 ... 203 M4
  STHGT/OAK N14 ... 78 C9
Peace Dr WAT WD17 ... 73 H7
Peace Gv WBLY HA9 ... 116 B9
Peacemaker Cl CRAWW RH11 ... 283 H9
Peace St WOOL/PLUM SE18 ... 162 E2
Peaches Cl BELMT SM2 ... 221 H6
Peach Gv WAN E11 ... 121 J6
Peachey La UX/CGN UB8 ... 131 N8
Peach Rd FELT TW13 ... 175 H4
  NKENS W10 ... 136 F6
Peachum Rd BKHTH/KID SE3 ... 161 M9
Peachy Cl EDGW HA8 * ... 95 M7
Peacock Av
  EBED/NFELT TW14 ... 173 L6
Peacock Cl BCTR RM8 ... 123 J5
  CHING E4 ... 101 L1
  EMPK RM11 ... 125 N4
  MLHL NW7 ... 98 A7
Peacock Gdns SAND/SEL CR2 ... 224 D9
Peacocks Centre
  WOKN/KNAP GU21 * ... 10 D5
Peacock Pl IS N1 ... 6 C1
Peacocks CRAWW RH11 ... 283 L9
Peacock St GVE DA12 ... 190 E2
  WALW SE17 ... 18 E7
Peacock Yd WALW SE17 ... 18 E7
Peaketon Av REDBR IG4 ... 122 A6
Peak HI SYD SE26 ... 182 B7

Peak Hill Av SYD SE26 ... 182 B7
Peak Hill Gdns SYD SE26 ... 182 B7
Peaks Hl PUR/KEN CR8 ... 222 F6
Peaks Hill Ri PUR/KEN CR8 ... 222 F6
The Peak SYD SE26 ... 182 B6
Pea Cl BERK HP4 ... 33 J3
  UPMR RM14 ... 146 F2
Peal Gdns WEA W13 ... 134 F5
Peall Rd CROY/NA CRO ... 202 G6
Pearce Av MTCM CR4 ... 202 A2
Pearcefield Av FSTH SE23 ... 182 B4
Pearce Rd CSHM HP5 ... 50 C4
Pearce Cl CDALE/KGS NW9 ... 116 A2
  NWCR SE14 ... 160 B6
Pearcroft Rd WAN E11 ... 121 J7
Pearcroft Rd FUL/PGN SW6 ... 157 L7
Pearse St PECK SE15 ... 15 L7
Pear Tree Av WDR/YW UB7 ... 132 A8
Pear Tree Cl CHSGTN KT9 ... 219 M2
  ADL/WDHM KT15 ... 215 K2
  AMSS HP7 ... 69 L5
  MTCM CR4 ... 201 P2
  SWLY BR8 ... 208 B2
  BEAC HP9 ... 89 H7
Peartree Cl BRWN CM15 ... 87 P4
Pear Tree Cl ERITH DA8 ... 164 E7
Peartree Cl HAYES BR2 ... 204 E9
  SLN SL2 ... 128 D6
Peartree Gdns BCTR RM8 ... 123 H4
  ROMW/RG RM7 ... 104 C10
Pear Tree Hl REDH RH1 ... 276 B9
Peartree La BRWN CM15 ... 87 H3
  WAP E1W * ... 140 E9
  WCCE AL7 ... 23 H6
Pear Tree Md HLWS CM18 ... 47 K4
  ASHF TW15 ... 174 D8
Peartree Rd EN EN1 ... 79 M7
  HHW HP1 ... 35 K5
Peartrees RBRW/HUT CM13 ... 107 P7
The Pear Trees
  FSBYE EC1V * ... 131 N9
Pear Tree St FSBYE EC1V ... 6 E9
Peartree Wk GNWCH SE10 ... 161 H3
Pearwood Cots STAN HA7 * ... 95 H3
Peary Pl BETH E2 ... 140 B5
Peascod St WDSR SL4 ... 149 J7
Peascroft Rd HHS/BOV HP3 ... 36 B4
Peasmead Ter CHING E4 * ... 101 H5
Peatfield Cl BFN/LL DA15 ... 185 H6
Peatmore Av
  WOKS/MYFD GU22 ... 233 K2
Peatmore Cl
  WOKS/MYFD GU22 ... 233 K2
Peatmore Dr CHOB/PIR GU24 ... 230 B7
Pebble Cl KWD/TDW/WH KT20 ... 256 D9
Pebble Hl EHSLY KT24 ... 252 D7
Pebblehill Rd
  BRKHM/BTCW RH3 ... 256 B6
Pebworth Rd HRW HA1 ... 114 F7
Peckarmans Wd SYD SE26 ... 181 M7
Peckett Sq HBRY N5 * ... 119 K9
Peckford Pl BRXN/ST SW9 ... 159 M8
Peckham Gv PECK SE15 ... 159 M6
Peckham High St PECK SE15 ... 159 P7
Peckham Hill St PECK SE15 ... 159 N6
Peckham Park Rd PECK SE15 ... 159 N6
Peckham Rd CMBW SE5 ... 159 M7
Peckham Rye EDUL SE22 ... 159 N9
Peck's Hl WAB EN9 ... 63 L5
Peckwater St KTTN NW5 ... 4 C1
Pedlars End CHONG CM5 ... 49 J7
Pedlars Wk HOLWY N7 ... 118 D3
Pedley Rd BCTR RM8 ... 123 M6
Pedley St WCHPL E1 ... 140 B3
Pednor Bottom CSHM HP5 ... 50 A4
Pednormead End CSHM HP5 ... 50 A6
Pednor Rd CSHM HP5 ... 50 D5
Peek Crs WIM/MER SW19 ... 178 G8
Peeks Brook La HORL RH6 ... 280 F8
Peel Cl CHING E4 ... 101 L1
  ED N9 ... 99 P4
  WDSR SL4 ... 148 B10
Peel Ct SL SL1 * ... 128 C7
Peel Dr CDALE/KGS NW9 ... 116 C1
  CLAY IG5 ... 122 B1
Peel Gv BETH E2 ... 140 B4
Peel Pas KENS W8 * ... 8 E10
Peel Prec KIL/WHAMP NW6 ... 2 D8
Peel Rd KTN/HRWW/WS HA3 ... 115 H6
  ORP BR6 ... 226 F1
  SWFD E18 ... 102 A8
  KENS W8 ... 8 E10
Peel St KENS W8 ... 8 E10
Peel Wy HARH RM3 ... 105 N10
  UX/CGN UB8 ... 131 M5
Peerage Wy EMPK RM11 ... 125 M5
Peeragel Est PEND EN3 * ... 90 G2
Peerless Dr DEN/HRF UB9 ... 111 L2
Peerless St FSBYE EC1V ... 6 G10
Pegamoid Rd UED N18 ... 100 H8
Pegasus Cl STNW/STAM N16 * ... 119 P1
Pegasus Ct BTFD TW8 ... 155 K6
  GVE DA12 ... 190 B1
Pegasus Pl FUL/PGN SW6 * ... 157 K6
  LBTH SE11 ... 18 C10
  STALW/RED AL3 ... 38 C2
Pegasus Rd CROY/NA CRO ... 223 H6
Pegasus Wy FBAR/BDGN N11 ... 98 B7
Pegelm Gdns EMPK RM11 ... 125 N5
Peggotty Wy UX/CGN UB8 ... 131 M8
Pegg Rd HEST TW5 ... 153 P5
Pegler Wy WKENS W14 ... 149 J2
Pegmire La GSTN WD25 ... 75 J5
Pegrams Rd HLWS CM18 ... 46 H5
Peg's La HERT/BAY SG13 ... 43 L7
Pegwell St WOOL/PLUM SE18 ... 163 M3
Pekin Cl POP/IOD E14 * ... 140 L8
Pekin St POP/IOD E14 ... 140 L8
Peldon Av RCH/KEW TW9 ... 154 H8
Peldon Wk IS N1 * ... 6 C1
Pelham Av BARK IG11 ... 143 J3

Pelham Cl CMBW SE5 ... 159 M9
Pelham Cots BXLY DA5 ... 186 C4
Pelham Ct HHNE HP2 ... 36 D6
  WCCE AL7 ... 23 M6
Pelham Crs SKENS SW7 ... 15 N5
Pelham Pl SKENS SW7 ... 15 N5
Pelham Rd BXLYHN DA7 ... 164 B2
  GVW DA11 ... 190 C3
  IL IG1 ... 122 G7
  PGE/AN SE20 ... 182 B2
  SEVS/STOTM N15 ... 119 N2
  SWFD E18 ... 121 N1
  WDGN N22 ... 98 G10
  WIM/MER SW19 ... 178 D3
Pelham Rd South GVW DA11 ... 190 C3
Pelham Cl ESH/CLAY KT10 ... 217 P2
The Pelhams GSTN WD25 ... 75 L1
  RAIN RM13 ... 144 G1
Pelham St SKENS SW7 ... 15 M5
Pelham Wk ESH/CLAY KT10 ... 197 P10
Pelham Wy GFD/LBKH KT23 ... 254 A2
Pelier St WALW SE17 ... 18 F9
Pelinore Rd CAT SE6 ... 183 K5
Pellant Rd FUL/PGN SW6 ... 14 B10
Pellatt Gv WDGN N22 ... 98 G9
Pellatt Rd EDUL SE22 ... 181 M1
  WBLY HA9 ... 115 K7
Pellerin Rd STNW/STAM N16 ... 119 N3
Pelling Hl WDSR SL4 ... 171 K9
Pellings Cl HAYES BR2 ... 205 K3
Pellipar Cl PLMGR N13 ... 99 K10
Pellipar Rd WOOL/PLUM SE18 ... 162 C4
Pellow Cl BAR EN5 ... 77 J10
Pelly Ct EPP CM16 ... 88 C7
Pelly Rd PLSTW E13 ... 141 L4
Pelman Wy HOR/WEW KT19 ... 219 P6
Pelter St BETH E2 ... 7 L9
Pelton Av BELMT SM2 ... 221 L6
Pelton Rd GNWCH SE10 ... 161 K4
Pembar Av WALTH E17 * ... 119 D1
Pemberley Cha HOR/WEW KT19 ... 219 N2
Pemberley Cl HOR/WEW KT19 ... 219 N2
Pemberton Av GPK RM2 ... 125 J1
Pemberton Cl STAL AL1 ... 38 C9
  STWL/WRAY TW19 ... 173 P4
Pemberton Gdns ARCH N19 ... 118 D8
  CHDH RM6 ... 123 P3
  SWLY BR8 ... 208 F3
Pemberton Pl ESH/CLAY KT10 ... 198 B10
  HACK E8 * ... 140 A2
Pemberton Rd
  E/WMO/HCT KT8 ... 198 B4
  FSBYPK N4 ... 119 H4
  SLN SL2 ... 128 D6
Pemberton Rw
  FLST/FETLN EC4A ... 12 C3
Pembley Gn CRAWE RH10 ... 285 M2
Pembrey Wy HCH RM12 ... 145 K1
Pembridge Cha HHS/BOV HP3 ... 52 C4
Pembridge Cl HHS/BOV HP3 ... 52 C4
Pembridge Crs NTGHL W11 ... 8 D7
Pembridge Gdns BAY/PAD W2 ... 8 C7
Pembridge Ms NTGHL W11 ... 8 D7
Pembridge Pl NTGHL W11 ... 8 D6
  WAND/EARL SW18 ... 179 R5
Pembridge Rd NTGHL W11 ... 8 D8
Pembridge Sq BAY/PAD W2 ... 8 C7
Pembridge Vis NTGHL W11 ... 8 C7
Pembroke Av BRYLDS KT5 ... 199 N5
  EN EN1 ... 80 A5
  KTN/HRWW/WS HA3 ... 114 F1
  PIN HA5 ... 111 L5
  WOT/HER KT12 ... 217 L1
Pembroke Cl ASC SL5 ... ...
  BNSTD SM7 ... 239 L3
  BROX EN10 ... 44 D10
  EMPK RM11 ... 125 P2
  ERITH DA8 ... 164 D2
  KTBR SW1X ... 16 C2
Pembroke Gdns DAGE RM10 ... 124 C8
  KENS W8 ... 14 A4
  WOKS/MYFD GU22 ... 232 D4
Pembroke Gardens Cl
  KENS W8 ... 14 A4
Pembroke Ldg STAN HA7 * ... 95 H7
  KENS W8 ... 14 H7
Pembroke Ms KENS W8 * ... 14 C3
  MUSWH N10 ... 97 ...
  SEV TN13 ... 265 ...
Pembroke Pde ERITH DA8 ... 164 D2
Pembroke Pl EDGW HA8 ... 95 M10
  ISLW TW7 ... 154 ...
  KENS W8 ... 14 C3
Pembroke Rd BMLY BR1 ... 205 P2
  CEND/HSY/T N8 ... 118 F2
  CRAWE RH10 ... 284 C7
  EHAM E6 ... 142 C7
  ERITH DA8 ... 164 D2
  CDMY/SEVK IG3 ... 123 K5
  GFD/PVL UB6 ... 134 A6
  KENS W8 ... 14 B4
  MTCM CR4 ... 202 A2
  MUSWH N10 ... 97 ...
  NTHWD HA6 ... 92 A4
  PGE/AN SE20 ... 182 ...
  RSLP HA4 ... 112 F6
  SEV TN13 ... 265 ...
  SNWD SE25 ... 203 M8
  WALTH E17 ... 121 ...
  WBLY HA9 ... 115 ...
  WFD IG8 ... 102 F6
Pembroke Sq KENS W8 ... 14 B3
Pembroke St IS N1 ... 5 J1
Pembroke Studios KENS W8 * ... 14 A3
Pembroke Ter STJWD NW8 * ... 3 L6
Pembroke Vis KENS W8 ... 14 B3
  RCH/KEW TW9 ... 154 H7
Pembroke Wk KENS W8 ... 14 B4
Pembrook Ms BRXN/ST SW9 ... 158 ...
Pembry Cl BRXN/ST SW9 ... 159 M7
Pembury Av WPK KT4 ... 200 E9
Pembury Cl CLPT E5 ... 138 E2
  HAYES BR2 ... 204 E8
Pembury Ct HYS/HAR UB3 ... 152 A2
Pembury Crs SCUP DA14 ... 186 E6
Pembury Pl CLPT E5 ... 138 E2
Pembury Rd BXLYHN DA7 ... 165 K1
  CLPT E5 ... 138 E2
  SNWD SE25 ... 203 P3
  TOTM N17 ... 99 N9
Pemdevon Rd CROY/NA CRO ... 203 H5
Pemerich Cl HYS/HAR UB3 ... 152 A2
Pempath Pl WBLY HA9 ... 115 L7
Penally Pl IS N1 ... 7 H2
Penang St WAP E1W ... 140 A10
Penard Rd NWDGN UB2 ... 153 H2
Penarth St PECK SE15 ... 160 A5
Penates ESH/CLAY KT10 ... 218 ...
Penberth Rd CAT SE6 ... 182 G3
Pencombe Ms NTGHL W11 ... 8 B8
Pencraig Wy PECK SE15 ... 160 A5
Pendall Cl EBAR EN4 ... 77 P4
Penda Rd ERITH DA8 ... 165 ...
Pendarves Rd RYNPK SW20 ... 200 F1
Penda's Md HOM E9 ... 121 J8
Pendell Av HYS/HAR UB3 ... 152 A5
Pendell Rd REDH RH1 ... 275 N4
Pendennis Cl BF/WBF KT14 ... 232 A4
Pendennis Rd GPK RM2 ... 104 G10
  SEVS/STOTM N15 ... 119 K7
  STRHM/NOR SW16 ... 180 F6
  TOTM N17 ... 99 N8
  STMC/STPC BR5 ... 207 N3
Penderel Rd HSLW TW3 ... 175 P1

Penderry Ri CAT SE6 ... 183 J5
Penderyn Wy HOLWY N7 ... 118 E9
Pendle Cl HGDN/ICK UB10 ... 132 C3
Pendle Rd STRHM/NOR SW16 ... 180 C9
Pendlestone Rd WALTH E17 ... 120 C3
Pendleton Cl REDH RH1 ... 276 A4
Pendleton Rd REDH RH1 ... 275 N5
Pendlewood Cl EA W5 ... 135 K3
Pendragon Rd BMLY BR1 ... 183 M6
Pendrell Rd BROCKY SE4 ... 161 N8
Pendrell St WOOL/PLUM SE18 ... 163 L3
Pendula Dr YEAD UB4 ... 133 L3
Pendulum Ms HACK E8 ... 119 N10
Penenden HART DA3 ... 209 K9
Penerley Rd CAT SE6 ... 182 G4
  RAIN RM13 ... 144 G4
Penfold Cl CROY/NA CRO ... 203 H10
Penfold La BXLY DA5 ... 185 M8
Penfold Pl BAY/PAD W2 ... 9 N3
Penfold Rd ED N9 ... 100 G2
Penfold St CMBW SE5 ... 9 M2
Penford Gdns ELTH/MOT SE9 ... 162 A10
Penford St CMBW SE5 ... 159 H9
Pengarth Rd BXLY DA5 ... 185 L3
Penge La PGE/AN SE20 ... 182 B10
Pengelly Cl CHESW EN7 ... 62 A6
Penge Rd PLSTW E13 ... 142 C5
  SNWD SE25 ... 203 P3
Penhale Cl ORP BR6 ... 227 K1
Penhall Rd CHARL SE7 ... 162 A3
Penhill Rd BXLY DA5 ... 185 M5
Penhurst WOKN/KNAP GU21 ... 214 C10
Penhurst Rd BARK/HLT IG6 ... 102 E8
Penifather La GFD/PVL UB6 ... 134 C5
Penington Rd BEAC HP9 ... 108 A1
Peninsular Cl
  EBED/NFELT TW14 ... 174 E2
Peninsular Park Rd
  CHARL SE7 ... 161 M4
Penistone Rd
  STRHM/NOR SW16 ... 181 F10
Penketh Dr HRW HA1 ... 114 C8
Penlow Rd HLWS CM18 ... 46 F4
Penman Cl LCOL/BKTW AL2 ... 55 P3
Penmon Rd ABYW SE2 ... 162 E2
Pennack Rd PECK SE15 ... 19 M10
Pennant Ms KENS W8 ... 14 E5
Pennant Ter WALTH E17 ... 100 E10
Pennard Rd SHB W12 ... 157 H2
The Pennards SUN TW16 ... 197 H3
Penn Av CSHM HP5 ... 50 F6
Penn Cl CRAWW RH11 ... 283 N4
  GFD/PVL UB6 ... 134 A4
  KTN/HRWW/WS HA3 ... 115 J2
  RKW/CH/CXG WD3 ... 70 C10
  UX/CGN UB8 ... 131 N6
Penn Ct CRAWW RH11 ... 283 J7
Penn Dr DEN/HRF UB9 ... 111 J4
Penne Cl RAD WD7 ... 75 F10
Penner Cl WIM/MER SW19 ... 178 H5
Penners Gdns SURB KT6 ... 199 H5
Pennethorne Cl HOM E9 ... 140 E4
Pennethorne Rd PECK SE15 ... 160 A6
Penn Gdns CHST BR7 ... 206 B8
  CRW RM5 ... 104 A8
Penn Gn BEAC HP9 ... 88 C7
Pennine Dr CRICK NW2 ... 116 C2
Pennine La CRICK NW2 ... 117 H7
Pennine Pde CRICK NW2 ... 117 H7
Pennine Wy BXLYHN DA7 ... 165 R4
  GVW DA11 ... 190 B6
  HHNE HP2 ... 36 A3
  HYS/HAR UB3 ... 152 A6
Pennings Av GUW GU2 ... 249 L2
Pennington Cl CRW RM5 ... 104 B2
Pennington Dr WCHMH N21 ... 78 F9
  WEY KT13 ... 196 F10
Pennington Rd
  CFSP/GDCR SL9 ... 90 A8
Pennington St WAP E1W ... 140 A9
Pennington Wy
  LEE/GVPK SE12 ... 183 N10
Penniston Cl TOTM N17 ... 99 K10
Penniwell Cl EDGW HA8 ... 95 L5
Penn La BXLY DA5 ... 185 L2
  RSEV TN14 ... 263 P5
Penn Meadow SLN SL2 ... 129 L3
Penn Rd BEAC HP9 ... 88 B9
  DTCH/LGLY SL3 ... 150 A7
  HOLWY N7 ... 118 F10
  LCOL/BKTW AL2 ... 56 B3
  RKW/CH/CXG WD3 ... 91 J2
  SLN SL2 ... 129 K3
Penn St IS N1 ... 7 H6
Penny Cl RAIN RM13 ... 144 G2
Pennycroft CROY/NA CRO ... 224 D5
Penny Dr RGUW GU3 ... 248 G9
Pennyfield COB KT11 ... 232 ...
Penny Fids GRW CM14 ... 107 H5
Pennyfields POP/IOD E14 ... 140 L8
Penny La SHPTN TW17 ... 196 F7
Pennylets Gn SLN SL2 ... 129 L2
Pennymead HLW CM20 ... 29 K10
Pennymead Dr EHSLY KT24 ... 252 G3
Penny Ms WAND/EARL SW18 ... 179 N5
Pennymoor Wk
  MV/WKIL W9 * ... 8 C1
Penny Rd WLSDN NW10 ... 135 N5
Pennyroyal Av EHAM E6 ... 142 H4
Penpoll Rd HACK E8 ... 140 A1
Penpool La WELL DA16 ... 165 J1
Penrhyn Av WALTH E17 ... 100 F1
Penrhyn Cl CTHM CR3 ... 241 L6
Penrhyn Crs
  MORT/ESHN SW14 ... 155 P10
  WALTH E17 ... 100 F1
Penrhyn Gdns KUT/HW KT1 ... 199 K1
Penrhyn Gv WALTH E17 ... 100 F1
Penrhyn Rd KUT/HW KT1 ... 199 L3
Penrith Cl BECK BR3 ... 204 G1
  PUT/ROE SW15 ... 179 J1
  REIG RH2 ... 257 P9
Penrith Pl WNWD SE27 ... 181 H10
Penrith Rd BARK/HLT IG6 ... 103 J1
  HARH RM3 ... 105 P7
  NWMAL KT3 ... 200 C2
  SEVS/STOTM N15 ... 119 L5
  THHTH CR7 ... 203 K4
  TOTM N17 ... 99 K10
Penrith St STRHM/NOR SW16 ... 180 G10
Penrose Av OXHEY WD19 ... 93 M3
Penrose Gv WALW SE17 ... 18 F9
Penrose Rd LHD/OX KT22 ... 236 B10
Penrose St WALW SE17 ... 18 F9
Penry St STHWK SE1 ... 19 L4
Penryn St CAMTN NW1 ... 5 J5
Pensbury Pl VX/NE SW8 ... 158 D7
Pensbury St VX/NE SW8 ... 158 D7
Penscroft Gdns BORE WD6 ... 76 D3
Pensford Av RCH/KEW TW9 ... 155 P7
Penshurst HLWE CM17 ... 47 L2
Penshurst Av BFN/LL DA15 ... 165 L10
Penshurst Cl CFSP/GDCR SL9 ... 90 A6
  CRAWE RH10 ... 284 A6
Penshurst Gdns EDGW HA8 ... 96 C1
Penshurst Gn HAYES BR2 ... 205 P2
Penshurst Rd BXLYHN DA7 ... 165 J1
  HOM E9 ... 140 ...
  POTB/CUF EN6 ... 60 D4
  THHTH CR7 ... 203 ...
  TOTM N17 ... 99 N8
Penshurst Wy BELMT SM2 ... 221 L7
  STMC/STPC BR5 ... 207 M4
Pensilver Cl EBAR EN4 ... 77 P4

Penson's La CHONG CM5 ... 67 J1
Penstemon Cl FNCH N3 ... 97 K1
Penta Ct BORE WD6 * ... 75 M8
Pentelow Gdns
  EBED/NFELT TW14 ... 173 M4
Pentire Cl UPMR RM14 ... 126 D4
  WOKN/KNAP GU21 ... 214 B10
Pentire Rd WALTH E17 ... 101 K1
Pentland Av EDGW HA8 ... 95 N3
  SHPTN TW17 ... 196 C9
Pentland Cl ED N9 ... 100 B5
  GLDGN NW11 ... 117 H7
Pentland Pl NTHLT UB5 ... 133 M8
Pentland Rd BUSH WD23 ... 94 B10
  KIL/WHAMP NW6 ... 2 D5
  SLN SL2 ... 128 F2
Pentlands Cl MTCM CR4 ... 202 C3
Pentlands St WAND/EARL SW18 ... 179 M7
Pentland Wy HGDN/ICK UB10 ... 112 B3
Pentley Pk WGCW AL8 ... 22 F2
Pentlow St PUT/ROE SW15 ... 157 P5
Pentlow Wy BKHH IG9 ... 102 A2
Pentney Rd BAL SW12 ... 180 A1
  CHING E4 ... 101 J2
  RYNPK SW20 ... 201 H1
Penton Av STA TW18 ... 173 J10
Penton Dr CHES/WCR EN8 ... 62 C5
Penton Gv IS N1 ... 5 K8
Penton Hall Dr STA TW18 ... 195 K1
Penton Pl WALW SE17 ... 18 E8
Penton Ri FSBYW WC1X ... 5 K9
Penton Rd STA TW18 ... 173 J10
Penton St IS N1 ... 5 K7
Pentonville Rd IS N1 ... 5 N6
Pentreath Av GUW GU2 ... 267 L1
Pentrich Av EN EN1 ... 79 N4
Pentridge St PECK SE15 ... 159 N6
Pentstemon Dr SWCM DA10 ... 189 K1
Pentyre Av UED N18 ... 99 L6
Penventon Ct TIL RM18 * ... 168 D8
Penwerris Av ISLW TW7 ... 154 B6
Penwith Rd WAND/EARL SW18 ... 179 L5
Penwith Wk
  WOKS/MYFD GU22 * ... 232 A5
Penwood End
  WOKS/MYFD GU22 ... 231 N7
Penwortham Rd
  SAND/SEL CR2 ... 223 L6
  STRHM/NOR SW16 ... 180 B10
Penylan Pl EDGW HA8 ... 95 M9
Penywern Rd ECT SW5 ... 14 F7
Penzance Cl DEN/HRF UB9 * ... 91 H3
Penzance Gdns HARH RM3 ... 105 P7
Penzance Pl NTGHL W11 ... 8 A9
Penzance Sp SLN SL2 ... 128 G6
Penzance St NTGHL W11 ... 8 A9
Peony Gdns SHB W12 ... 136 D9
Pepler Ms CMBW SE5 ... 19 L8
Pepler Wy SL SL1 ... 128 A5
Peplins Cl BRKMPK AL9 ... 59 H2
Peplins Wy BRKMPK AL9 ... 59 H1
Peploe Rd KIL/WHAMP NW6 ... 136 G1
Peplow Cl WDR/YW UB7 ... 131 N10
Peppard Rd CRAWE RH10 ... 284 E9
Pepper Cl CTHM CR3 ... 259 M1
  EHAM E6 ... 142 J7
Peppercorn Cl THHTH CR7 ... 203 L2
Pepper Hl GVW DA11 ... 189 P6
  WARE SG12 ... 26 E6
Pepperhill La CVW DA11 ... 189 P6
Peppermead Sq LEW SE13 ... 182 G2
Peppermint Cl CROY/NA CRO ... 202 F7
Peppermint Pl WAN E11 * ... 121 K9
Pepper St POP/IOD E14 ... 160 M2
  STHWK SE1 ... 18 F2
Peppett's Gn CSHM HP5 ... 32 C9
Peppie Cl STNW/STAM N16 ... 119 M7
Pepys Cl ASHTD KT21 ... 237 M3
  DTCH/LGLY SL3 ... 150 E3
  GVW DA11 ... 190 A6
  HGDN/ICK UB10 ... 112 C9
  TIL RM18 ... 168 B9
Pepys Crs BAR EN5 ... 76 F7
  CAN/RD E16 ... 141 M7
Pepys Park SE DEPT SE8 ... 160 A3
Pepys Ri ORP BR6 ... 207 J8
Pepys Rd NWCR SE14 ... 160 C7
  RYNPK SW20 ... 200 F2
Pepys St TWRH EC3N ... 13 M7
Perceval Av HAMP NW3 ... 117 J10
Perch St HACK E8 ... 119 L9
Percheron Cl ISLW TW7 ... 154 B9
Percheron Rd BORE WD6 ... 76 A10
Percival Cl LHD/OX KT22 ... 218 A7
Percival Ct TOTM N17 ... 99 N6
Percival Gdns CHDH RM6 ... 123 P4
Percival Rd EMPK RM11 ... 125 K4
  EN EN1 ... 79 N8
  FELT TW13 ... 174 A6
  MORT/ESHN SW14 ... 155 P10
  ORP BR6 ... 206 F10
Percival St FSBYE EC1V ... 6 D8
Percival Wy HOR/WEW KT19 ... 219 P1
Percy Av ASHF TW15 ... 174 C10
Percy Bush Rd WDR/YW UB7 ... 152 A2
Percy Gdns PEND EN3 ... 80 C9
  WPK KT4 ... 200 A4
  YEAD UB4 ... 132 F2
Percy Ms FITZ W1T ... 11 J3
Percy Pl DTCH/LGLY SL3 ... 150 B1
Percy Rd BXLYHN DA7 ... 165 P2
  CAN/RD E16 ... 141 K6
  CDMY/SEVK IG3 ... 123 K2
  GUW GU2 ... 249 N8
  HPTN TW12 ... 175 H10
  ISLW TW7 ... 154 C2
  MTCM CR4 ... 202 A9
  NFNCH/WDSPK N12 ... 97 G2
  PGE/AN SE20 ... 204 ...
  ROMW/RG RM7 ... 104 B8
  SHB W12 ... 156 G1
  SNWD SE25 ... 203 P4
  WAN E11 ... 121 K1
  WATW WD18 ... 73 ...
  WCHMH N21 ... 99 K3
  WHTN TW2 ... 176 B6
Percy St FITZ W1T ... 11 J3
Percy Ter BMLY BR1 ... 206 G8
  CSTG HP8 ... 89 M4
Percy Wy WHTN TW2 ... 176 A6
  SNWD SE25 ... 203 N3
  WLSDN NW10 ... 116 A10
Peregrine Cl WELL DA16 ... 163 M5
Peregrine Gdns CROY/NA CRO ... 204 D1
Peregrine Rd BARK/HLT IG6 ... 103 P2
  SUN TW16 ... 196 A2
  TOTM N17 ... 99 ...
  WAB EN9 ... 63 N1
Peregrin Rd WAB EN9 ... 63 M10
Perham Rd WKENS W14 ... 14 F3
Perham Wy LCOL/BKTW AL2 ... 57 J2
Peridot St EHAM E6 ... 142 H1
Perifield DUL SE21 ... 181 N4
Perimeade Rd GFD/PVL UB6 ... 135 N2
Perimeter Rd East HORL RH6 ... 280 D8
Perimeter Rd North
  HORL RH6 ... 279 N8
Perimeter Rd South
  HORL RH6 ... 283 A10
Periton Rd ELTH/MOT SE9 ... 164 C10
Perivale Gdns GSTN WD25 ... 55 J5
  WEA W13 ... 134 C6
Perivale Village
  GFD/PVL UB6 ... 135 H5
Periwood Crs GFD/PVL UB6 ... 134 G3
Perkin Cl ALP/SUD HA0 ... 114 D10
  HSLW TW3 ... 154 G8
Perkins Cl RDART DA2 * ... 188 H2

Perkin's Rents WEST SW1P. 17 J3
Perkins Rd BARK/HLT IG6. 122 G3
Perkins Sq STHWK SE1. 12 F9
Perleybrooke La WOKN/KNAP GU21. 231 M3
Permain Cl RAD WD7. 57 K9
Perpins Rd ELTH/MOT SE9. 185 N1
Perram Cl BROX EN10. 62 D2
Perran Rd HART DA3. 211 L4
Perran Rd BRXS/STRHM SW2. 181 J5
Perren St KTTN NW5 *. 4 E1
Perrers Rd HMSMTH W6. 156 F2
Perrett Gdns HERT/WAT SG14. 24 F4
Perrin Ct ASHF TW15. 174 A4
Perrin Rd WOKN/KNAP GU21. 232 E1
Perrin Rd ALP/SUD HA0. 114 C9
Perrin's Ct HAMP NW3. 117 M9
Perrin's La HAMP NW3. 117 M9
Perrin's Wk HAMP NW3. 117 M9
Perrior Rd GODL GU7. 267 K10
Perriors Cl CHESW EN7. 61 P5
Perry Av ACT W3. 136 A8
Perry Ct RAIN RM13. 144 E4
 UX/CGN UB8. 132 C3
Perrycroft WDSR SL4. 148 G3
Perryfield HLWE CM17. 31 K9
Perryfield Rd CRAWE RH11. 283 N10
Perryfields Wy SL SL1. 128 A6
Perryfield Wy CDALE/KGS NW9. 116 C4
 RCHPK/HAM TW10. 176 G5
Perry Gdns ED N9. 99 M4
Perry Garth WATW WD18. 133 K3
Perry Gv DART DA1. 165 P10
Perry Hall Cl ORP BR6. 207 K7
Perry Hall Rd ORP BR6. 207 J6
Perry Ri FSTH SE23. 182 D6
Perry Rd DAGW RM9. 144 A7
 HLWS CM18. 46 H4
Perrysfield Rd CHES/WCR EN8. 62 D2
Perrys La ORP BR6. 227 L9
Perry Spring HLWE CM17. 47 N3
Perry St CHST BR7. 185 N3
 DART DA1. 164 F9
 GVW DA11. 190 B4
Perry V FSTH SE23. 182 E5
Perry Wy SOCK/AV RM15. 146 R9
Perrywood WGCW AL8 *. 22 C3
Persant Rd CAT SE6. 183 K6
Perseverance Pl BRXN/ST SW9. 159 H6
Persfield Cl EW KT17. 220 E5
Persfield Ms EW KT17 *. 220 C6
Pershore Cl GNTH/NBYPK IG2. 122 C8
Pershore Gv CAR SM5. 201 N6
Pert Cl MUSWH N10. 98 C3
Perth Av CDALE/KGS NW9. 116 A5
 SL SL1. 129 M10
 YEAD UB4. 133 K6
Perth Cl CRAWW RH11. 283 N4
 NTHLT UB5. 133 N3
 NWMAL KT3. 200 C2
Perth Rd BARK IG11. 142 G4
 BECK BR3. 205 H2
 FSBYPK N4. 119 H6
 GNTH/NBYPK IG2. 122 E4
 LEY E10. 120 D6
 PLSTW E13. 141 M6
 WDGN N22. 99 J9
Perth Ter GNTH/NBYPK IG2. 122 F5
Perwell Av RYLN/HDSTN HA2. 113 N6
Pescot Av HART DA3. 211 M3
Pescot Hi HHW HP1. 35 L4
Petal La HLWE CM17. 29 N10
Petavel Rd TEDD TW11. 176 D9
 WLSDN NW10. 136 E2
Peter Av OXTED RH8. 261 J5
Peterboat Cl CNWCH SE10. 161 K3
Peterborough Av UPMR RM14. 126 D6
Peterborough Ms FUL/PGN SW6. 157 K8
Peterborough Rd CAR SM5. 201 P6
 FUL/PGN SW6. 157 K8
 GUW GU2. 249 K8
 HRW HA1. 114 D6
 LEY E10. 121 H3
Peterborough Vls FUL/PGN SW6. 157 L7
Petergate BTSEA SW11. 157 M10
Peterhead Ms DTCH/LGLY SL3. 150 D4
Peterhill Cl CFSP/GDCR SL9. 90 B4
Peterhouse Pde CRAWE RH10. 284 D4
Peterlee Ct HHNE HP2. 36 A1
Peters Av LCOL/BKTW AL2. 57 H2
Peters Cl BCTR RM8. 123 N4
 STAN HA7. 95 J1
 WELL DA16. 163 H8
Petersfield Cl STALW/RED AL3. 38 D2
Petersfield Av HARH RM3. 105 L3
 SLN SL2. 129 M10
 STA TW18. 173 M8
Petersfield Cl HARH RM3. 105 J3
 UED N18. 99 K6
Petersfield Crs COUL/CHIP CR5. 240 F1
Petersfield Ri PUT/ROE SW15. 178 E1
Petersfield Rd ACT W3. 155 P1
 STA TW18. 173 M8
Petersham Cl BF/WBF KT14. 215 P8
 RCHPK/HAM TW10. 177 J5
 SUT SM1. 221 P4
Petersham Dr STMC/STPC BR5. 207 J2
Petersham La SKENS SW7. 15 J4
Petersham Ms SKENS SW7. 15 J4
Petersham Pl SKENS SW7. 15 J4
Petersham Rd RCHPK/HAM TW10. 177 J5
Petersham Ter CROY/NA CRO *. 202 F10
Peter's Hill BLKFR EC4V. 12 C7
Petersmead Cl KWD/TDW/WH KT20. 238 F10
Peter's Pl BERK HP4 *. 33 L4
Peterstow Cl WIM/MER SW19. 178 H5
Peter St SOHO/CST W1F. 11 H7
Peterswood HLWS CM18. 46 G5
Peterwood Wy CROY/NA CRO. 202 C10
Petherton Rd HBRY N5. 119 K10
Petiver Cl HOM E9 *. 140 A1
Petley Rd HMSMTH W6. 156 H1
Peto Pl CAMTN NW1. 10 F1
Peto St North CAN/RD E16. 141 K9
Petre Rd RBRW/HUT CM13. 127 P4
Petresfield Wy RBRW/HUT CM13. 127 P4
Petridge Rd REDH RH1. 276 A11
Petrie Cl CRICK NW2. 2 B1
Petros Gdns HAMP NW3. 117 K3
 KIL/WHAMP NW6. 117 J3
Petro St South CAN/RD E16. 141 K9
Pett Cl EMPK RM11. 125 J7
Pett Gv STMC/STPC BR5. 207 N8
Petten Gv STMC/STPC BR5. 207 N8
Petters Rd ASHTD KT21. 237 L2

Petticoat La WCHPL E1. 13 K4
Petticoat Sq WCHPL E1. 13 L5
Petticoat Tower WCHPL E1 *. 13 L5
Pettits Bvd ROM RM1. 104 F10
Pettits Cl ROM RM1. 104 F10
Pettits La BRWN CM15. 87 K3
 ROM RM1. 104 F10
Pettits La North ROM RM1. 104 F10
Pettit's Pl DAGE RM10. 124 B10
Pettit's Rd DAGE RM10. 124 B10
Pettiward Cl PUT/ROE SW15. 156 F10
Pettley Gdns ROMW/RG RM7. 124 E3
Pettman Crs THMD SE28. 162 C2
Pettsgrove Av ALP/SUD HA0. 115 H10
Pett St WOOL/PLUM SE18. 162 B10
Petts Wood Rd STMC/STPC BR5. 206 G5
Petty Cross SL SL1. 128 C8
Petty France WESTW SW1E. 17 H3
Pettys Cl CHES/WCR EN8. 62 C4
Petty Wales MON EC3R *. 13 K8
Petworth Cl COUL/CHIP CR5. 240 F5
 NTHLT UB5. 133 N2
Petworth Ct CRAWW RH11. 283 J10
Petworth Gdns HGDN/ICK UB10. 132 D3
 RYNPK SW20. 200 E3
Petworth Rd BXLYHS DA6. 186 B1
 NFNCH/WDSPK N12. 97 P6
Petworth St BTSEA SW11. 157 P7
Petworth Wy HCH RM12. 124 C9
Petyt Pl CHEL SW3. 15 N10
Petyward CHEL SW3. 15 P6
Pevensey Av EN EN1. 79 M6
 FBAR/BDGN N11. 98 E6
Pevensey Cl CRAWE RH10. 284 D8
 ISLW TW7. 154 B4
Pevensey Rd FELT TW13. 175 M4
 SLN SL2. 128 F7
 TOOT SW17. 179 N7
Peverel EHAM E6. 142 D8
Peverel Rd CRAWW RH11. 283 H8
Peveret Cl FBAR/BDGN N11 *. 98 C6
Peveril Dr TEDD TW11. 176 C8
Pewley Bank GU GU1. 268 C4
Pewley Hi GU GU1. 268 B5
Pewley Point GU GU1. 268 C4
Pewley Wy GU GU1. 268 C4
Pewsey Cl CHING E4. 100 F6
Peyton Pl GNWCH SE10. 161 H6
Pharaoh Cl MTCM CR4. 202 A7
Pheasant Cl BERK HP4. 33 H6
 CAN/RD E16. 141 N8
 PUR/KEN CR8. 223 J9
Pheasant Hl CSTG HP8. 89 P3
Pheasant Hi CSHM HP5. 51 J8
Pheasants RKW/CH/CXG WD3. 91 L1
Pheasant Wk LCOL/BKTW AL2. 90 A5
Phelips Rd HLWW/ROY CM19. 46 D6
Phelp St WALW SE17. 18 G10
Phelps Wy HYS/HAR UB3. 152 A1
Phene St CHEL SW3. 15 P9
Philanthropic Rd REDH RH1. 276 B11
Philan Wy CRW RM5. 104 B1
Philbeach Gdns ECT SW5. 14 C7
Philbye Ms SL SL1. 148 L1
Philchurch Pl WCHPL E1. 13 P6
Philimore Cl WOOL/PLUM SE18. 163 H4
Philip Av ROMW/RG RM7. 124 E6
Philip Cl BRWN CM15. 86 G10
Philip Gdns CROY/NA CRO. 204 E9
Philippa Gdns ELTH/MOT SE9. 184 A1
Philip La SEVS/STOTM N15. 119 L2
Philip Rd RAIN RM13. 144 F5
 STA TW18. 173 N9
Philips Cl CAR SM5. 202 B8
Philip St PLSTW E13. 141 M6
Philip Sydney Rd CDW/CHF RM16. 167 J4
Philip Wk PECK SE15. 159 P9
Phillida Rd HARH RM3. 105 P10
Phillimore Gdns KENS W8. 14 E2
 WLSDN NW10. 136 F3
Phillimore Gardens Cl KENS W8. 14 E3
Phillimore Pl KENS W8. 14 E2
 RAD WD7. 74 D1
Phillimore Wk KENS W8. 14 E3
Phillip Av SWLY BR8. 208 E4
Phillippers GSTN WD25. 73 L2
Phillipp St IS N1. 7 K6
Phillips Hatch WOTN/GDN EN11. 268 F9
Philpot La CHOB/PIR GU24. 213 P9
 FENCHST EC3M *. 13 J7
Philpots Cl WDR/YW UB7. 131 N9
Philpot St WCHPL E1 *. 140 C8
Phineas Pett Rd ELTH/MOT SE9. 163 P9
Phipp's Bridge Rd WIM/MER SW19. 201 M2
Phipps Hatch La ENC/FH EN2. 79 M4
Phipps Ms BCVA SW1W. 16 E4
Phipps Rd SL SL1. 128 C7
Phipp St SDTCH EC2A. 13 J1
Phoebe Rd HHNE HP2. 36 A1
Phoebeth Rd LEW SE13. 182 H1
Phoenix Cl HACK E8 *. 7 L5
 HOR/WEW KT19. 219 M8
 NTHWD HA6. 92 G5
 WALTH E17. 100 E10
 WWKM BR4. 205 J9
Phoenix Ct BTFD TW8. 155 K4
 GU GU1. 267 J3
 POP/IOD E14. 160 F3
Phoenix Dr HAYES BR2. 206 A10
Phoenix Pk BTFD TW8 *. 155 J4
Phoenix Pl CAMTN NW1. 11 L1
Phoenix Rd CAMTN NW1. 5 J3
 PGE/AN SE20. 182 B9
Phoenix St LSQ/SEVD WC2H. 11 K6
Phoenix Wy HEST TW5. 153 L6
Phoenix Wharf Rd STHWK SE1. 19 M2
The Phygtle CFSP/GDCR SL9. 90 B2
Phyllis Av NWMAL KT3. 200 G3
Picardy Manorway BELV DA17. 164 C2
Picardy Rd BELV DA17. 164 B3
Picardy St BELV DA17. 164 B2
Piccadilly MYFR/PICC W1J. 10 G9
Piccadilly Ar STJS SW1Y. 10 G8
Piccadilly Circ REGST W1B *. 11 H7
Pickard St FSBYE EC1V. 6 D4
Pickering Av EHAM E6. 142 B9
Pickering Cl HOM E9. 139 H6
Pickering Gdns CROY/NA CRO. 202 F4
 FBAR/BDGN N11. 98 A7
Pickering Pl GU GU2. 249 M8
 WHALL SW1A *. 11 L1
Pickering St IS N1. 6 C1
Pickets Cl BUSH WD23. 94 C1
Pickets St BAL SW12. 180 A3
Pickett Cft STAN HA7. 95 L1
Picketts WGCW AL8. 22 A1
Pickett's Lock La ED N9. 101 H1
Pickford Cl BXLYHN DA7. 165 M7
Pickford Dr DTCH/LGLY SL3. 130 F10
Pickford La BXLYHN DA7. 165 M7
Pickford Rd BXLYHN DA7. 165 M8
Pickfords Whf IS N1. 6 F5
Pickhurst Gn HAYES BR2. 205 K7
Pickhurst La HAYES BR2. 205 L7
 WWKM BR4. 205 K5
Pickhurst Md HAYES BR2. 205 L7

Pickhurst Pk HAYES BR2. 205 K5
Pickhurst Ri WWKM BR4. 205 J8
Pickins Piece DTCH/LGLY SL3. 150 D8
Pickmoss La RSEV TN14. 247 P5
Pickwick Cl HSLWW TW4. 175 H4
Pickwick Gdns GVW DA11. 190 A6
Pickwick Ms UED N18. 99 M6
Pickwick Pl HRW HA1. 114 C9
Pickwick Rd DUL SE21. 181 L5
Pickwick St STHWK SE1. 18 E2
Pickwick Wy CHST BR7. 184 H4
Pickworth Cl VX/NE SW8 *. 158 F6
Picquets Wy BNSTD SM7. 239 J7
Picton Ms WARL CR6. 241 P5
Picton Pl MHST W1U. 10 D6
 SURB KT6. 199 M8
Picton St CMBW SE5. 159 L6
Pied Bull Yd IS N1 *. 5 L1
Piedmont Rd WOOL/PLUM SE18. 162 G4
Field Heath Av UX/CGN UB8. 132 A6
Field Heath Rd UX/CGN UB8. 132 B6
Pier Cl CHEL SW3. 16 C10
Piercing Cl EPP CM16. 82 G1
Pier Four Rd North HORL RH6. 286 A7
Pier Head WAP E1W *. 140 A10
Pierian Spring HHW HP1. 35 L4
Piermont Pl BMLY BR1. 206 F2
Piermont Rd EDUL SE22. 182 A1
Pierrepoint Ar IS N1 *. 6 C2
Pierrepoint Rd ACT W3. 135 N9
Pierrepoint Rw IS N1 *. 6 C2
Pier Rd CAN/RD E16. 162 C1
 EBED/NFELT TW14. 175 J1
 ERITH DA8. 164 F5
 GVW DA11. 190 C2
 SWCM DA10. 166 G10
Pierson Rd WDSR SL4. 148 C8
Pier St POP/IOD E14. 161 H9
Pier Ter WAND/EARL SW18. 157 J1
Pier Wy THMD SE28. 162 G2
Pier Whf GRAYS RM17 *. 167 M6
Pigeonhouse La COUL/CHIP CR5. 257 M1
Pigeon La HPTN TW12. 175 P7
Piggottshill La HARP AL5. 20 B4
Piggotts Orch AMSS HP7. 68 G6
Piggs Cnr GRAYS RM17. 167 P2
Piggy La RKW/CH/CXG WD3. 70 C10
Pigott St POP/IOD E14. 140 M8
Pike Cl BMLY BR1. 183 N6
 HGDN/ICK UB10. 132 A3
Pike La UPMR RM14. 126 E9
Pike Rd MLHL NW7. 96 A5
Pike's End PIN HA5. 113 J2
Pikes Hl EW KT17. 220 B9
Pikes Leap STALE/WH AL4. 21 L1
Pikestone Cl YEAD UB4 *. 133 M6
Pike Wy EPP CM16. 66 S3
Pilgrimage St STHWK SE1. 18 G2
Pilgrims Cl COUL/CHIP CR5. 255 L9
 NTHLT UB5. 114 B10
 WAB EN9. 63 P7
Pilgrims Hi WNWD SE27. 181 K7
Pilgrims La BRWN CM15. 86 B9
 CDW/CHF RM16. 147 H10
 CTHM CR3. 259 K2
 OXTED RH8. 283 P10
Pilgrims La BRW CM14. 86 C8
 CTHM CR3. 258 G2
 HAMP NW3. 117 N9
Pilgrim's Pl ASHF TW15 *. 174 A7
 REIG RH2. 257 K8
Pilgrim's Ri EBAR EN4. 77 N5
Pilgrims' Rd SWCM DA10. 167 K10
Pilgrims Vw SWCM DA10. 167 K10
Pilgrims Wy ARCH N19. 115 J10
 BCR/WKTN15. 247 M2
 CHOB/PIR GU24. 230 F2
 DART DA1. 188 A4
 RDKG RH5. 254 F7
 SHGR GU5. 270 B5
 WBLY HA9. 115 J5
Pilgrims' Wy BH/WHM TN16. 244 E9
 REIG RH2. 257 K8
 RGUE GU4. 271 N4
Pilgrims Wy SAND/SEL CR2. 223 N5
Pilgrims Wy East RSEV TN14. 247 K2
Pilgrims Wy West RSEV TN14. 246 G2
Pilkington Rd ORP BR6. 206 F10
 PECK SE15. 160 A8
Pilkingtons HLWE CM17. 47 N1
Pilot Cl DEPT SE8. 160 E5
Pilots Pl GVE DA12. 191 J4
Pilsden Cl WIM/MER SW19 *. 178 A4
Piltdown Rd OXHEY WD19. 93 H5
Pilton Pl WALW SE17 *. 18 F7
Pimlico Rd BGVA SW1W. 16 C6
Pimlico Wk IS N1. 7 H5
Pinceybrook Rd HLWS CM18. 46 F5
Pinchbeck Rd ORP BR6. 227 N5
Pinchfield RKW/CH/CXG WD3. 90 G6
Pinchin & Johnsons Yd WCHPL E1 *. 13 P7
Pinchin St WCHPL E1. 13 P7
Pincott La EHSLY KT24. 252 C5
Pincott Rd BXLYHS DA6. 186 B1
 WIM/MER SW19. 179 M10
Pincroft Wd HART DA3. 211 H4
Pindar St SDTCH EC2A. 13 J3
Pindock Ms MV/WKIL W9. 9 H2
Pine Apple Ct WESTW SW1E *. 17 H3
Pine Av CHOB/PIR GU24. 230 E7
 GVE DA12. 190 G4
 SRTFD E15. 121 J10
 WWKM BR4. 203 N1
Pine Cl ADL/WDHM KT15. 215 J7
 BERK HP4. 32 B3
 CHES/WCR EN8. 62 B4
 CRAWW RH11. 283 N4
 LEY E10. 120 F7
 PGE/AN SE20. 182 G4
 PUR/KEN CR8. 241 K5
 STAN HA7. 95 H3
 STHGT/OAK N14. 98 D1
 SWLY BR8. 208 G4
 WOKN/KNAP GU21. 211 F5
Pine Coombe CROY/NA CRO. 224 C1
Pinecote Dr ASC SL5. 236 E6
Pine Crs CAR SM5. 221 N7
Pinecrest Gdns ORP BR6. 226 E3
Pinecroft EMPK RM11. 125 P3
 HHS/BOV HP3. 36 A10
Pinecroft Crs BAR EN5. 76 B4
Pine Dean GT/LBKH KT23. 254 A11
Pinefield Cl POP/IOD E14. 160 M3
Pinefields ADL/WDHM KT15 *. 215 L11
 HORL RH6. 286 G4
 RSLP HA4. 94 A7
Pine Gld ORP BR6. 226 C1
Pine Gv BMLY BR1. 184 A5
 BUSH WD23. 75 H6
 FSBYPK N4. 118 D1
 LCOL/BKTW AL2. 55 N5
 TRDG/WHET N20. 96 G2
 WEY KT13. 216 C3
 WIM/MER SW19. 178 A3
Pine Grove Ms WEY KT13 *. 216 D3
Pine Hall Rd BRYLDS KT5. 199 M4
Pine Hill EPSOM KT18. 238 B8
Pinehurst ASC SL5. 192 C5
Pinehurst Av ABLGY WD5. 54 F8
 KWD/TDW/WH KT20. 239 K8
Pinehurst Cl ABLGY WD5. 54 F8
 KWD/TDW/WH KT20. 239 K8
Pinehurst Gdns BF/WBF KT14. 215 M8
Pinelands Cl BKHTH/KID SE3 *. 161 M3
Pinel Cl VW GU25. 194 B4
Pinelees Ct MORT/ESHN SW14 *. 155 P10
Pinemartin Cl CRICK NW2. 116 F7
Pinemeadle La SEV TN13. 247 J9
Pine Pk RGUW GU3. 248 E4
Pine Rdg CAR SM5. 222 B5
Pineridge Cl WEY KT13. 216 F3
Pine Rd CRICK NW2. 116 F4
 WOKS/MYFD GU22. 231 H6
Pines Av EN EN1. 78 B6
Pines Cl AMS HP6. 68 C3
 NTHWD HA6. 32 A5
Pine Shaw CRAWE RH10. 284 D6
Pines Rd BMLY BR1. 206 B3
The Pines BORE WD6. 75 L6
 CDW/CHF RM16. 147 N10
 HHS/BOV HP3. 35 H10
 NRWD SE19. 181 J9
 PUR/KEN CR8. 223 L7
 RSEV TN14. 247 L7
 SUN TW16. 197 H3
 WFD IG8. 101 L4
 WOKN/KNAP GU21. 214 C10
Pinetree Cl CFSP/GDCR SL9. 89 P8
Pine Tree Cl HEST TW5. 153 J7
 HHNE HP2. 35 N5
Pine Tree Hl WOKS/MYFD GU22. 232 G2
Pine Trees STA TW18 *. 173 M8
Pinetrees Cl CRAWE RH10. 285 J2
Pine Trees Dr HGDN/ICK UB10. 111 P9
Pine Tree Wy LEW SE13. 146 H2
Pine View RGUE GU4. 269 J6
Pine Wk BELMT SM2. 221 N7
 BERK HP4. 33 J2
 BNSTD SM7. 240 A2
 BRYLDS KT5. 199 M6
 CAR SM5. 221 N6
 COB KT11. 240 C1
 CTHM CR3. 241 M8
 EHSLY KT24. 264 A2
 GT/LBKH KT23. 254 A1
Pine Wy EGH TW20. 172 A1
Pine Wd SUN TW16. 197 H1
Pinewood WGCE AL7 *. 23 H7
Pinewood Av ADL/WDHM KT15. 215 M5
 BFN/LL DA15. 185 H4
 PIN HA5. 94 A7
 RAIN RM13. 145 J4
 RSEV TN14. 247 L3
 UX/CGN UB8. 132 A8
Pinewood Cl BORE WD6. 76 A5
 CFSP/GDCR SL9. 89 P8
 CROY/NA CRO. 204 D10
 HLWE CM17. 47 N3
 IVER SL0. 130 F2
 NTHWD HA6. 93 J6
 ORP BR6. 206 G6
 PIN HA5. 94 A7
 SLH/CLGW SS17. 169 J6
 STMC/STPC BR5. 207 H4
 WOKN/KNAP GU21. 232 D1
Pinewood Dr ORP BR6. 227 L7
 POTB/CUF EN6. 59 J7
 STA TW18 *. 173 M8
Pinewood Gdns HHS/BOV HP3. 35 P8
Pinewood Gn IVER SL0. 130 F2
Pinewood Gv ADL/WDHM KT15. 215 M6
 WEA W13. 135 H4
Pinewood Ms STWL/WRAY TW19. 173 N2
Pinewood Pk ADL/WDHM KT15. 215 L7
Pinewood Rd ABR/ST RM4. 104 D5
 FELT TW13. 175 N7
 HAYES BR2. 205 M4
 IVER SL0. 130 F2
 VW GU25. 195 L4

RSEV TN14. 247 M7
The Pippins DTCH/LGLY SL3. 130 C10
 GSTN WD25 *. 55 K10
Piquet Rd PGE/AN SE20. 200 E1
Pirbright Crs CROY/NA CRO. 225 H3
Pirbright Rd RGUW GU3. 248 B5
 WAND/EARL SW18. 179 J4
Pirbright Ter CHOB/PIR GU24 *. 230 E7
Pirie Cl CMBW SE5. 141 N10
Pirrip Cl CDW/CHF RM16. 191 J4
Pirton Cl STALE/WH AL4. 39 H1
Pishiobury Dr SBW CM21. 29 N3
Pitcairn Cl ROMW/RG RM7. 124 D3
Pitcairn Rd MTCM CR4. 180 C5
Pitchfont La OXTED RH8. 261 M2
Pitchford St SRTFD E15. 140 C8
Pitch Pond Cl RKW/CH/CXG WD3. 88 A6
Pitchway Rd GU GU3. 250 D10
Pit Farm Rd GU GU1. 250 A10
Pitfield HART DA3. 211 L4
Pitfield St IS N1. 7 J2
Pitfield Wy PEND EN3. 79 P9
 WLSDN NW10. 137 H4
Pitfold Cl LEE/GVPK SE12. 183 M1
Pitfold Rd LEE/GVPK SE12. 183 M1
Pitlake CROY/NA CRO. 203 J9
Pitman St CMBW SE5. 159 K6
Pitsea Pl WCHPL E1. 140 E7
Pitsea St WCHPL E1. 140 E7
Pitsfield WGCW AL8. 22 C2
Pitshanger La EA W5. 135 N2
Pitson Cl ADL/WDHM KT15. 215 N6
Pitstone Cl STALE/WH AL4. 39 H1
Pitt Crs WIM/MER SW19. 179 J2
Pitt Dr STALE/WH AL4. 39 H1
Pittman Gdns IL IG1. 122 F10
Pittman's Fld HLWE CM17. 47 J2
Pitt Pl EW KT17 *. 220 B10
Pitt Rd EW KT17. 220 B10
 ORP BR6. 226 F1
 RYLN/HDSTN HA2. 114 B7
 THHTH CR7. 203 K3
Pitts Head Ms MYFR/PICC W1J. 10 C10
Pittsmead Av HAYES BR2. 205 M7
Pitts Rd SL SL1. 128 F8
Pitt St KENS W8. 14 F1
Pittville Gdns SNWD SE25. 201 P10
Pit Wood Gn KWD/TDW/WH KT20. 238 F6
Pix Farm La HHW HP1. 34 E7
Pixham La DORK RH4. 255 H9
Pixholme Gv DORK RH4. 255 H10
Pixies Hill Crs HHW HP1. 35 J8
Pixies Hill Rd HHW HP1. 35 J8
Pixley St POP/IOD E14. 140 K8
Pixton Wy CROY/NA CRO. 224 D5
Place Farm La BRWN CM15. 86 H5
Place Farm Rd REDH RH1. 259 L5
Placehouse La COUL/CHIP CR5. 240 G5
Plackett Wy SL SL1. 128 C10
Plaines Cl SL SL1. 128 E10
The Plain EPP CM16. 65 L5
Plaistow Gv BMLY BR1. 183 N10
 SRTFD E15. 141 L3
Plaistow La BMLY BR1. 183 M9
Plaistow Park Rd PLSTW E13. 141 L1
Plaistow Rd SRTFD E15. 141 L3
Plaitford Cl RKW/CH/CXG WD3. 91 P3
Plane Av GVW DA11. 190 A3
The Planes CHERT KT16. 195 M4
Plane St SYD SE26. 182 B6
Plane Tree Crs FELT TW13. 175 J7
Plantagenet Cl NWMAL KT3. 200 A4
Plantagenet Gdns CHDH RM6. 123 N5
Plantagenet Pl WAB EN9. 62 G4
Plantagenet Rd BAR EN5. 77 M8
Plantain Gdns WAN E11 *. 122 B2
Plantain Pl STHWK SE1. 18 G1
Plantation Dr STMC/STPC BR5. 207 N8
Plantation La FENCHST EC3M *. 13 J7
Plantation Rd AMS HP6. 69 K3
 ERITH DA8. 165 H7
 SWLY BR8. 187 N9
The Plantation BKHTH/KID SE3 *. 161 M8
Plantation Wy AMS HP6. 69 K3
Plasel Ct WELL DA16 *. 163 N4
Plashet Gdns BRWN CM15. 87 J4
Plashet Gv EHAM E6. 141 N4
Plashet Rd PLSTW E13. 141 L5
Plashets RBSF CM22. 25 J1
The Plashets SEV TN13 *. 266 D6
Plassy Rd CAT SE6. 182 G3
Platford Gn EMPK RM11. 125 M2
Platina St SDTCH EC2A. 7 H7
Plato Rd BRXS/STRHM SW2. 158 F10
Platt Meadow RGUE GU4. 250 D5
Platt's Av HAMP NW3. 117 K8
Platts La HAMP NW3. 117 J7
Platt's Rd PEND EN3. 79 L8
The Platt CAMTN NW1. 5 H1
Platt St CAMTN NW1. 5 H1
Plawsfield Rd BECK BR3. 183 G10
Plaxtol Cl BMLY BR1. 184 B5
Plaxtol Rd ERITH DA8. 164 H4
Playfair St HMSMTH W6. 156 H1
Playfield Av CRW RM5. 104 C4
Playfield Crs EDUL SE22. 181 M1
Playfield Rd EDGW HA8. 96 F5
Playford Rd FSBYPK N4. 118 F10
Playgreen Wy CAT SE6. 182 F7
Playground Cl BECK BR3. 204 C2
Playhouse Ct STHWK SE1 *. 18 E1
Playhouse Sq HLWW/ROY CM19. 46 F1
Playhouse Yd BLKFR EC4V. 12 C6
Plaza Pde ALP/SUD HA0 *. 135 N1
Plaza Wk CDALE/KGS NW9. 115 N9
Pleasance Rd PUT/ROE SW15. 178 A2
 STMC/STPC BR5. 207 H1
The Pleasance PUT/ROE SW15. 156 H10
Pleasant Gv CROY/NA CRO. 204 E10
Pleasant Pl IS N1. 6 E1
 RKW/CH/CXG WD3. 91 H8
 WOT/HER KT12. 217 L7
Pleasant Rd BRKMPK AL9. 40 F1
Pleasant Vw ERITH DA8. 164 C7
Pleasant Wy WLGTN SM6. 202 E9
Pleasure Pit Rd ASHTD KT21. 237 N7
Plender St CAMTN NW1. 4 F1
Pleshey Rd ARCH N19. 117 N1
Plesman Wy WLGTN SM6. 222 F9
Plevna Crs SEVS/STOTM N15. 119 J4
Plevna Rd ED N9. 100 F3
 HPTN TW12. 197 H1
Plevna St POP/IOD E14. 161 M3
Pleydell Av HMSMTH W6. 156 C1
 NRWD SE19. 181 N5
Pleydell Est FSBYE EC1V *. 6 F6
Pleydell Gdns NRWD SE19 *. 181 N5
Pleydell St EMB EC4Y. 12 B6
Plimsoll Cl POP/IOD E14. 140 M8
Plimsoll Rd FSBYPK N4. 119 H9
Plomer Av HOD EN11. 33 J11
Plough Cl CRAWW RH11. 283 J5
 WLSDN NW10. 137 H4
Plough Farm Cl RSLP HA4. 112 B3
 POTB/CUF EN6. 60 A7
Plough La BERK HP4. 34 B2
 COB KT11. 235 N2
 DEN/HRF UB9. 91 H7
 EDUL SE22. 181 M1
 PUR/KEN CR8. 223 H6
 RDKG RH5. 253 P11
 SL SL1. 128 D3
 TEDD TW11. 176 C8
 WIM/MER SW19. 179 M4
 WLGTN SM6. 222 F3
Plough Lane Cl WLGTN SM6. 222 F3
Ploughlees La SL SL1. 129 K5
Ploughmans Cl CAMTN NW1. 5 H1
Ploughmans End ISLW TW7. 176 A1
 WGCE AL7. 23 H5
Plough Pl FLST/FETLN EC4A *. 12 B5
Plough Rd BTSEA SW11. 157 N9
 HOR/WEW KT19. 220 A4
 HORL RH6. 287 K4
Plough St WCHPL E1. 13 N5
Plough Ter BTSEA SW11. 157 N9
Plough Wy BERM/RHTH SE16. 160 C3
Plough Yd SDTCH EC2A. 13 K2
Plover Cl HPH4. 33 P6
 CRAWW RH11. 284 A5
Plover Ct SL SL1 *. 128 C3
Plover Gdns UPMR RM14. 126 E6
Plovers Barron BRWN CM15. 87 J2
Plovers Rd CHOB/PIR GU24. 230 D6
Plover Wy BERM/RHTH SE16. 160 D2
 YEAD UB4. 133 L8
Plowden Blds EMB EC4Y *. 12 A7
Plowman Cl UED N18. 99 L6
Plowman Wy BCTR RM8. 123 M6
Pluto Rd HLWW/ROY CM19. 46 F2
Plough Ri HHNE HP2. 35 P4
Plymouth Dr SEV TN13. 247 K10
Plymouth Rd BMLY BR1. 205 N1
 CAN/RD E16. 141 M7
 CDW/CHF RM16. 167 H4
 SL SL1. 128 C8
Plymouth Whf POP/IOD E14. 161 L3
Plympton Av KIL/WHAMP NW6. 2 C4
Plympton Cl BELV DA17. 163 P2
Plympton Pl ST/JWD NW8. 9 N1
Plympton Rd KIL/WHAMP NW6. 2 C4
Plympton St STJWD NW8. 9 N2
Plymstock Rd WELL DA16. 163 H6
Pocket Hl SEV TN13. 265 H4
Pocklington Cl CDALE/KGS NW9. 96 B10
Pocock Av WDR/YW UB7. 152 A2
Pococks La WDSR SL4. 149 K4
Pocock St STHWK SE1. 18 C1
Podmore Rd WAND/EARL SW18. 157 N10
Poets Cha HHW HP1. 35 L4
Poets Ct HARP AL5. 20 A2
Poets Ga CHESW EN7. 61 L4
Poets Ms HNHL SE24. 181 J1
Poets Rd HBRY N5. 119 L10
Poet's Wy HRW HA1. 114 D2
Pointalls Cl FNCH N3. 97 M10
Point Cl GNWCH SE10. 161 H8
Pointers Cl POP/IOD E14. 160 M8
Pointers Hi DORK RH4. 272 B4
Pointers Rd COB KT11. 234 D2
The Pointers ASHTD KT21. 237 K6
Point Hl GNWCH SE10. 161 H7
Point Pl WBLY HA9. 135 N2
Point Pleasant WAND/EARL SW18. 157 N10
Point Wharf La BTFD TW8. 155 L6
Poland St SOHO/SHAV W1D. 11 H6
Polayn Garth WGCW AL8. 22 F4
Polebrook Rd BKHTH/KID SE3. 161 P3
Polecroft La CAT SE6. 182 C5
Polegate Cots GRAYS RM17 *. 167 N5
Polehanger La HHW HP1. 35 H4
Pole Hill Rd CHING E4. 101 H1
 HGDN/ICK UB10. 132 C6
Polesden Gdns RYNPK SW20. 200 E3
Polesden La RPLY/SEND GU23. 233 J9
Polesden Rd RDKG RH5. 254 A5
Polesden Vw GT/LBKH KT23. 254 A5
Poles Hl CSHM HP5. 50 F5
 RKW/CH/CXG WD3. 53 H9
Poles La CRAWW RH11. 283 N11
Polesteeple Hl BH/WHM TN16. 244 A3
Polesworth Rd DAGW RM9. 144 A4
Polhill RSEV TN14. 246 D1
Police Station Rd WOT/HER KT12. 217 K3
Polish War Memorial Rbt RSLP HA4 *. 133 K1
Pollard Av DEN/HRF UB9. 111 J4
Pollard Cl CAN/RD E16. 141 M9
 CHIG IG7. 103 M5
 HOLWY N7. 118 F10
 WDSR SL4. 171 N1
Pollard Hatch HLWW/ROY CM19. 46 E4
Pollard Rd MRDN SM4. 201 N5
 TRDG/WHET N20. 97 P3
 WOKS/MYFD GU22. 232 E2
Pollards CRAWW RH11. 283 K8
 RKW/CH/CXG WD3. 90 G6
Pollards Cl CHESW EN7. 61 K5
 LOU IG10. 81 P9
Pollards Crs STRHM/NOR SW16. 202 F3
Pollards Hl East STRHM/NOR SW16. 202 G3
Pollards Hl North STRHM/NOR SW16. 202 F3
Pollards Hl South STRHM/NOR SW16. 202 F3
Pollards Hl West STRHM/NOR SW16. 202 F3
Pollards Oak Crs OXTED RH8. 261 M8
Pollards Oak Rd OXTED RH8. 261 M8
Pollard St BETH E2. 7 P7
Pollards Wood Hl OXTED RH8. 261 N8
Pollards Wood Rd OXTED RH8. 261 N7
 STRHM/NOR SW16. 202 F2
Pollen St CONDST W1S. 10 E6
Pollitt Dr STJWD NW8. 9 L1
Pollyhaugh EYN DA4. 209 M10
Polperro Cl ORP BR6. 207 J6
Polperro Ms LBTH SE11. 18 B5
Polsted Rd RGUW GU3. 267 H6
Polsted Rd CAT SE6. 182 L5
Polsten Ms PEND EN3. 85 M1
Polthorne Gv WOOL/PLUM SE18. 162 H5
Polthorne Gv GUW GU2. 267 M4
Polworth Rd STRHM/NOR SW16. 180 A9
The Polygon CLAP SW4 *. 158 D10
Polytechnic St WOOL/PLUM SE18. 162 D5
Pomell Wy WCHPL E1. 13 M5
Pomeroy Cl TWK TW1. 154 C10
Pomeroy Crs WATN WD24. 73 J2
Pomeroy St NWCR SE14. 160 G8
Pomfret Rd CMBW SE5. 159 J4
Pomoja La ARCH N19. 118 F1
Pompadour Cl BRW CM14. 107 H6

| Entry | Page | Grid |
|---|---|---|
| Pond Cl AMSS HP7 | 68 | B10 |
| BKHTH/KID SE3 | 161 | M8 |
| DEN/HRF UB9 | 91 | M10 |
| NFNCH/WDSPK N12 | 97 | P7 |
| WOT/HER KT12 | 217 | H3 |
| Pond Cottage La BECK BR3 | 204 | F8 |
| Pond Cots DUL SE21 | 181 | M4 |
| Pond Cft HAT AL10 | 40 | C3 |
| WGCE AL7 | 23 | H4 |
| Pond Fm Ct HOLWY N7 * | 5 | N3 |
| Pond Farm Cl | | |
| KWD/TDW/WH KT20 | 238 | E10 |
| Pond Farm Cl CLPT E5 * | 120 | B8 |
| Pondfield Crs STALE/WH AL4 | 38 | G3 |
| Pondfield La GVE DA12 | 191 | P10 |
| RBRW/HUT CM13 | 107 | M5 |
| Pondfield Rd DAGE RM10 | 124 | C10 |
| HAYES BR2 | 205 | K8 |
| ORP BR6 | 206 | E10 |
| PUR/KEN CR8 | 241 | J2 |
| Pond Gdn HA4 | 112 | F7 |
| Pond Hill Gdns CHEAM SM3 * | 221 | H3 |
| Pond La CFSP/GDCR SL9 | 89 | N9 |
| SHGR GU5 | 270 | D10 |
| Pond Lees Cl DAGE RM10 | 144 | E2 |
| Pond Md DUL SE21 | 181 | L2 |
| Pond Meadow GUW GU2 | 249 | K10 |
| Pond Park Rd CSHM HP5 | 50 | G5 |
| Pond Piece LHD/OX KT22 | 218 | A9 |
| Pond Pl CHEL SW3 | 15 | N6 |
| Pond Rd BKHTH/KID SE3 | 143 | J2 |
| HHS/BOV HA4 | 58 | B1 |
| SRTFD E15 | 141 | K4 |
| WOKS/MYFD GU22 | 231 | M6 |
| Pondside Av WPK KT4 | 200 | F8 |
| Pondside Cl HYS/HAR UB3 | 152 | E6 |
| Ponds La SHGR GU5 | 269 | P8 |
| The Ponds WEY KT13 | 216 | F3 |
| Pond St HAMP NW3 | 117 | J10 |
| Pond Wk TEDD TW11 | 177 | H9 |
| Pond Wy TEDD TW11 | 177 | M1 |
| Pondwicks AMSS HP7 | 68 | C5 |
| Pondwicks Cl STAL AL1 | 38 | D7 |
| Pondwood Ri ORP BR6 | 207 | H7 |
| Pond Wood Rd CRAWE RH10 | 284 | D5 |
| Ponler St WCHPL E1 | 140 | A8 |
| Ponsard Rd WLSDN NW10 | 136 | F3 |
| Ponsford St HOM E9 | 140 | B1 |
| Ponsonby Pl WEST SW1P | 17 | L7 |
| Ponsonby Rd PUT/ROE SW15 | 178 | E3 |
| Ponsonby Ter WEST SW1P | 17 | L7 |
| Pontefract Rd BMLY BR1 | 183 | M8 |
| Pontoise Cl SEV TN13 | 246 | G8 |
| Ponton Rd VX/NE SW8 | 17 | K10 |
| Pont St KTBR SW1X | 16 | A4 |
| Pont Street Ms KTBR SW1X | 16 | A4 |
| Pony Cha COB KT11 | 217 | N9 |
| Pool Cl BECK BR3 | 182 | F6 |
| E/WMO/HCT KT8 | 197 | M5 |
| Pool Ct CAT SE6 | 182 | F5 |
| Poole Cl RSLP HA4 | 112 | F7 |
| Poole Court Rd HSLWW TW4 | 153 | M8 |
| Poole Rd E/WMO/HCT KT8 | 196 | B5 |
| HOM E9 | 140 | C1 |
| WOKN/KNAP GU21 | 232 | B4 |
| Pooles Blds FSBYW WC1X * | 12 | A2 |
| Pooles La WBPTN SW10 | 157 | N9 |
| Pooles Pk FSBYPK N4 | 119 | H7 |
| Poole St IS N1 | 6 | G5 |
| Poole Wy YEAD UB4 * | 132 | F5 |
| Pooley Av EGH TW20 | 172 | E8 |
| Pooley Dr MORT/ESHN SW14 | 155 | P9 |
| Pooley Green Rd EGH TW20 | 172 | E8 |
| Pooleys La BRKMPK AL9 | 40 | C7 |
| Pool La SL SL1 | 129 | K9 |
| Poolmans Rd WDSR SL4 | 148 | C9 |
| Poolmans St | | |
| BERM/RHTH SE16 | 160 | C1 |
| Pool Rd E/WMO/HCT KT8 | 197 | M5 |
| HRW HA1 | 114 | C5 |
| Poolsford Rd CDALE/KGS NW9 | 45 | H2 |
| Poonah St WCHPL E1 | 140 | B8 |
| Pope Cl EBED/NFELT TW14 | 174 | C4 |
| WIM/MER SW19 * | 179 | N9 |
| Pope Rd HAYES BR2 | 206 | A5 |
| Pope's Av WHTN TW2 | 176 | D5 |
| Popes Cl DTCH/LGLY SL3 | 150 | D5 |
| Popes Dr FNCH N3 | 97 | K3 |
| Popes Gv CROY/NA CR0 | 204 | E10 |
| Popes Gv WHTN TW2 | 176 | D5 |
| Popes La WATN WD24 | 73 | J3 |
| Pope's Rd ABLGY WD5 * | 54 | F7 |
| BRXN/ST SW9 * | 159 | H10 |
| Pope St STHWK SE1 | 19 | K2 |
| Popham Cl FELT TW13 | 175 | M6 |
| Popham Gdns | | |
| RCH/KEW TW9 * | 155 | N9 |
| Popham Rd IS N1 | 6 | D1 |
| Popham St IS N1 | 6 | D5 |
| Popinjays Rw CHEAM SM3 * | 220 | G2 |
| Popis Gdns WARE SG12 | 26 | D1 |
| Poplar Av GVE DA12 | 190 | F7 |
| HAT AL10 | 40 | A4 |
| LHD/OX KT22 | 236 | C8 |
| MTCM CR4 | 202 | A1 |
| NWDGN UB2 | 154 | A1 |
| ORP BR6 | 206 | E9 |
| WDR/YW UB7 | 132 | C3 |
| Poplar Bath St POP/IOD E14 | 140 | E4 |
| Poplar Cl CRAWW RH11 | 283 | M4 |
| CSHM HP5 | 51 | H4 |
| DTCH/LGLY SL3 | 151 | H7 |
| EW KT17 | 238 | E1 |
| HOM E9 | 120 | C10 |
| PIN HA5 | 93 | L9 |
| SOCK/AV RM15 | 147 | J6 |
| Poplar Court Pde TWK TW1 * | 177 | H7 |
| Poplar Crs HOR/WEW KT19 | 219 | P3 |
| Poplar Dr BNSTD SM7 | 220 | C10 |
| RBRW/HUT CM13 | 87 | P10 |
| Poplar Farm Cl | | |
| HOR/WEW KT19 | 219 | P3 |
| Poplar Gdns NWMAL KT3 | 200 | A2 |
| Poplar Gn WOKS/MYFD GU22 | 232 | B5 |
| Poplar Gv FBAR/BDGN N11 | 98 | B7 |
| HMSMTH W6 | 156 | F1 |
| NWMAL KT3 | 200 | A3 |
| WBLY HA9 | 115 | P8 |
| Poplar High St POP/IOD E14 | 140 | G4 |
| Poplar La BECK BR3 | 204 | G5 |
| Poplar Ms SHB W12 | 136 | F10 |
| Poplar Mt BELV DA17 | 164 | C3 |
| Poplar Pl BAY/PAD W2 | 8 | G7 |
| HYS/HAR UB3 | 133 | H9 |
| THMD SE28 | 143 | M9 |
| Poplar Rd ASHF TW15 | 174 | D8 |
| CHEAM SM3 | 201 | J8 |
| DEN/HRF UB9 | 131 | N4 |
| HNHL SE24 | 159 | K10 |
| LHD/OX KT22 | 236 | G8 |
| RGUE GU4 | 268 | B2 |
| WIM/MER SW19 | 201 | K3 |
| Poplar Rd South | | |
| WIM/MER SW19 | 201 | K3 |
| Poplar Rw EPP CM16 | 83 | H3 |
| Poplars WGCE AL7 | 23 | L4 |
| Poplars Cl RSLP HA4 | 55 | J8 |
| HART DA3 | 211 | J8 |
| HAT AL10 | 40 | C4 |
| RSLP HA4 | 112 | F6 |
| Poplar Shaw WAB EN9 | 63 | L9 |
| Poplars Rd WALTH E17 | 120 | G4 |
| The Poplars ASHF/ST RM4 | 85 | L7 |
| BORE WD6 * | 24 | F2 |
| CHESW EN7 | 61 | M2 |
| GVE DA12 | 191 | H7 |
| HHW HP1 | 35 | L7 |
| RDKG RH5 | 278 | B1 |
| STHGT/OAK N14 | 78 | H7 |
| ROMW/RG RM7 | 124 | D2 |
| Poplar Vw WBLY HA9 * | 115 | J7 |
| Poplar Wk CROY/NA CR0 | 203 | K9 |
| CTHM CR3 | 241 | M9 |
| HNHL SE24 | 159 | K10 |
| Poppins Ct FLST/FETLN EC4A * | 12 | C3 |
| Poppleton Rd WAN E11 | 121 | K4 |
| Poppy Cl BELV DA17 | 164 | C2 |
| HHW HP1 | 35 | H5 |
| WLGTN SM6 | 202 | B8 |
| Poppyfields WGCE AL7 | 23 | M5 |
| Poppy Wk CHESW EN7 | 61 | L4 |
| HART DA3 | 211 | L4 |
| Porchester Garden Ms | | |
| BAY/PAD W2 | 9 | H6 |
| Porchester Gdns BAY/PAD W2 * | 9 | H6 |
| Porchester Ga BAY/PAD W2 * | 9 | J8 |
| Porchester Md BECK BR3 | 182 | C9 |
| Porchester Pl BAY/PAD W2 | 9 | M5 |
| Porchester Rd BAY/PAD W2 | 9 | H5 |
| KUT/HW KT1 | 199 | N1 |
| Porchester Sq BAY/PAD W2 | 9 | H5 |
| Porchester Ter North | | |
| BAY/PAD W2 | 9 | H6 |
| Porchester Square Ms | | |
| BAY/PAD W2 | 9 | H5 |
| Porchester Ter BAY/PAD W2 | 9 | J6 |
| Porchfield Cl BELMT SM2 | 221 | L6 |
| GVE DA12 | 190 | F5 |
| Porch Wy TRDG/WHET N20 | 98 | A4 |
| Porcupine Cl ELTH/MOT SE9 | 184 | B5 |
| Porden Rd BRXS/STRHM SW2 | 158 | A10 |
| Porlock Av RYLN/HDSTN HA2 | 114 | B4 |
| Porlock Rd EN EN1 | 99 | N1 |
| Porlock St STHWK SE1 | 19 | H1 |
| Porridge Pot Aly GUW GU2 * | 268 | A2 |
| Porrington Cl CHST BR7 | 206 | C1 |
| Portal Wy ACT W3 | 136 | A7 |
| Portbury Cl PECK SE15 * | 159 | P7 |
| Portchester Ga BAY/PAD W2 * | 9 | J8 |
| Portchester Cl HNHL SE24 | 159 | K10 |
| Portcullis Lodge Rd EN EN1 | 79 | L7 |
| Portelet Rd WCHPL E1 | 140 | C5 |
| Porten Rd WKENS W14 | 167 | H1 |
| Porter Rd EHAM E6 | 142 | C3 |
| Porters Av DAGW RM9 | 143 | L1 |
| Porters Cl BRW CM14 | 106 | F2 |
| Porters Park Dr RAD WD7 | 57 | K8 |
| Porter Sq ARCH N19 | 118 | F6 |
| Porter Sq MHST W1U | 10 | B1 |
| STHWK SE1 | 12 | F9 |
| Porters Wk WAP E1W * | 140 | A9 |
| Porters Wy WDR/YW UB7 | 132 | C3 |
| WDR/YW UB7 | 152 | A2 |
| Porteus Rd BAY/PAD W2 | 9 | K4 |
| Portgate Cl MV/WKIL W9 | 8 | D1 |
| Porthallow Cl ORP BR6 | 227 | J1 |
| Porthcawe Rd SYD SE26 | 182 | D7 |
| Port Hl HERT/WAT SG14 | 25 | K5 |
| Porthkerry Av WELL DA16 | 163 | K10 |
| Portia Wy BOW E3 | 139 | M9 |
| Portinscale Rd PUT/ROE SW15 | 179 | H1 |
| Portland Av BFN/LL DA15 | 185 | K5 |
| GVE DA12 | 190 | E5 |
| NWMAL KT3 | 200 | C7 |
| STNW/STAM N16 | 119 | N6 |
| Portland Cl CHDH RM6 | 123 | P3 |
| SLN SL2 | 130 | A2 |
| WPK KT4 | 200 | E7 |
| Portland Cots CROY/NA CR0 * | 202 | E7 |
| Portland Crs ELTH/MOT SE9 | 184 | B5 |
| FELT TW13 | 174 | A1 |
| GFD/PVL UB6 | 133 | J5 |
| STAN HA7 | 95 | J10 |
| Portland Crs West STAN HA7 * | 115 | J1 |
| Portland Dr CHESW EN7 | 61 | P7 |
| ENC/FH EN2 | 79 | M4 |
| REDH RH1 * | 258 | F6 |
| Portland Gdns CHDH RM6 | 123 | N3 |
| FSBYPK N4 | 119 | H3 |
| Portland Gv VX/NE SW8 | 158 | G7 |
| Portland Ms SOHO/CST W1F * | 11 | H6 |
| Portland Pk GFD/PVL UB6 | 110 | A3 |
| Portland Pl EN EN1 * | 79 | K3 |
| HART DA3 * | 211 | K3 |
| HERT/BAY SG13 * | 26 | E7 |
| REGST W1B * | 10 | E2 |
| SNWD SE25 | 203 | P4 |
| SWCM DA10 * | 167 | H10 |
| Portland Place Flats | | |
| EW KT17 * | 220 | B8 |
| Portland Ri FSBYPK N4 | 119 | H6 |
| Portland Ri ASHF TW15 | 173 | P6 |
| BMLY BR1 | 183 | P7 |
| DORK RH4 | 284 | F2 |
| ELTH/MOT SE9 | 184 | B5 |
| GVW DA11 | 190 | A2 |
| KUT/HW KT1 | 199 | K3 |
| MTCM CR4 | 201 | P2 |
| NTGHL W11 | 8 | A7 |
| NWDGN UB2 | 153 | N2 |
| SEVS/STOTM N15 | 119 | M2 |
| SNWD SE25 | 203 | P4 |
| YEAD UB4 * | 132 | F5 |
| Portland Sq WAP E1W * | 140 | A10 |
| Portland St STALW/RED AL3 | 38 | B6 |
| WALW SE17 | 18 | G8 |
| Portland Ter RCH/KEW TW9 * | 155 | J10 |
| Portley La CTHM CR3 | 241 | N7 |
| Portley Wood Rd CTHM CR3 | 241 | N7 |
| Portman Av MORT/ESHN SW14 | 156 | A9 |
| Portman Cl BXLYHS DA6 | 163 | N9 |
| MBLAR W1H | 10 | A3 |
| WFD IG8 * | 39 | H1 |
| Portman Dr WFD IG8 | 102 | A10 |
| Portman Gdns | | |
| CDALE/KGS NW9 | 116 | A1 |
| HGDN/ICK UB10 | 132 | B2 |
| Portman Ga CAMTN NW1 * | 9 | P2 |
| Portman Ms South | | |
| MBLAR W1H | 10 | B5 |
| Portman Pl BETH E2 | 140 | B5 |
| Portman Rd KUT/HW KT1 | 199 | L2 |
| Portman Sq MBLAR W1H | 10 | B5 |
| Portman St MBLAR W1H | 10 | B5 |
| Portmeadow Wk ABYW SE2 * | 148 | N1 |
| Portmeers Cl WALTH E17 * | 120 | E2 |
| Portmore Gdns CRW RM5 | 104 | B6 |
| Portmore Park Rd WEY KT13 | 216 | B3 |
| Portmore Quays WEY KT13 * | 216 | A3 |
| Portmore Wy WEY KT13 | 196 | B10 |
| Portnall Dr VW GU25 | 193 | K6 |
| Portnall Rd MV/WKIL W9 | 137 | P3 |
| VW GU25 | 193 | L5 |
| Portnalls Cl COUL/CHIP CR5 | 240 | C5 |
| Portnalls Ri COUL/CHIP CR5 | 240 | C5 |
| Portnalls Rd COUL/CHIP CR5 | 240 | C3 |
| Portnoi Cl ROM RM1 | 104 | E10 |
| Portobello Ct NTGHL W11 * | 8 | C6 |
| Portobello Rd NTGHL W11 | 8 | A4 |
| Portpool La FSBYW WC1X | 11 | M2 |
| Portree Cl ED N9 * | 30 | C5 |
| Portree St POP/IOD E14 | 141 | P3 |
| Portsdown EDGW HA8 * | 44 | B9 |
| Portsdown Av GLDGN NW11 | 97 | J4 |
| Portsdown Ms GLDGN NW11 | 97 | J4 |
| Portsea Ms BAY/PAD W2 | 9 | P6 |
| Portsea Pl BAY/PAD W2 | 9 | P6 |
| Portsea Rd TIL RM18 | 158 | F9 |
| Portslade Rd VX/NE SW8 | 158 | G1 |
| Portsmouth Ms CAN/RD E16 | 141 | N6 |
| Portsmouth Rd COB KT11 | 234 | D1 |
| COB KT11 | 216 | D10 |
| KUT/HW KT1 | 199 | J3 |
| PUT/ROE SW15 | 178 | A3 |
| RPLY/SEND GU23 | 233 | K10 |
| THDIT KT7 | 198 | G7 |
| Portsmouth St LINN WC2A | 11 | N5 |
| Portsoken St TWRH EC3N | 13 | M4 |
| Portugal Gdns WHTN TW2 * | 176 | B5 |
| Portugal Rd | | |
| WOKN/KNAP GU21 | 232 | C2 |
| Portugal St LINN WC2A | 11 | P6 |
| Port V HERT/WAT SG14 | 25 | K5 |
| Port Wy CHOB/PIR GU24 | 230 | F5 |
| Portway EW KT17 | 220 | D5 |
| RAIN RM13 | 145 | H3 |
| SRTFD E15 | 141 | M3 |
| Portway Crs EW KT17 | 220 | D5 |
| Portway Gdns | | |
| WOOL/PLUM SE18 | 162 | A7 |
| Postboys Rw COB KT11 * | 217 | H10 |
| Postern Gn ENC/FH EN2 | 79 | H6 |
| The Postern BARB EC2Y * | 12 | F4 |
| Postfield WGCE AL7 | 23 | M2 |
| Post House La GT/LBKH KT23 | 253 | P1 |
| Post La WHTN TW2 | 176 | C4 |
| Post Meadow IVER SL0 | 130 | C5 |
| Postmill Cl CROY/NA CR0 | 204 | B10 |
| Post Office Ap FSTGT E7 | 121 | N10 |
| Post Office La BEAC HP9 | 88 | C8 |
| DTCH/LGLY SL3 | 130 | A8 |
| Post Office Rd HLW CM20 | 28 | F10 |
| Post Office Wk | | |
| HERT/WAT SG14 * | 25 | L5 |
| Post Rd NWDGN UB2 | 154 | A2 |
| Postway Ms IL IG1 | 122 | C8 |
| Postwood Gn HERT/BAY SG13 | 26 | B8 |
| Post Wood Rd WARE SG12 | 26 | E1 |
| Potash Rd HLWE CM17 | 31 | L8 |
| Potier St STHWK SE1 | 19 | H4 |
| Potiphar Pl BRW CM14 | 106 | C5 |
| Potkiln La BEAC HP9 | 109 | H1 |
| Potten End HI HHW HP1 | 35 | H1 |
| Potter Cl MTCM CR4 | 202 | C1 |
| Potterells BRKMPK AL9 | 58 | G1 |
| The Potteries BAR EN5 | 77 | K9 |
| CHERT KT16 | 215 | H3 |
| Potterne Cl WIM/MER SW19 | 178 | C3 |
| Potters Cl CROY/NA CR0 | 204 | D8 |
| LOU IG10 | 82 | B6 |
| PECK SE15 * | 159 | M6 |
| Potters Crouch La | | |
| LCOL/BKTW AL2 | 37 | L10 |
| Potters Fld EN EN1 * | 79 | M4 |
| HLWE CM17 | 47 | N3 |
| STALW/RED AL3 | 38 | D2 |
| Potters Flds STHWK SE1 | 13 | K10 |
| Potters Gv NWMAL KT3 | 199 | P4 |
| Potters Heights Cl PIN HA5 | 93 | J8 |
| Potters La BAR EN5 | 77 | K8 |
| BORE WD6 | 75 | P5 |
| RPLY/SEND GU23 | 233 | N6 |
| STRHM/NOR SW16 * | 180 | A9 |
| Potters Ms BORE WD6 | 75 | J10 |
| Potters Muse SBW CM21 | 29 | P1 |
| Potters Rd FUL/PGN SW6 | 157 | M8 |
| Potter's Rd BAR EN5 | 77 | L8 |
| Potter St HLWE CM17 | 47 | M2 |
| NTHWD HA6 | 93 | J7 |
| Potter Street HI PIN HA5 | 93 | J7 |
| Potters Wy REIG RH2 | 275 | M4 |
| Pottery La NTGHL W11 | 8 | A8 |
| Pottery Rd BTFD TW8 | 155 | K5 |
| BXLY DA5 | 186 | D5 |
| Pottery St | | |
| BERM/RHTH SE16 * | 160 | A1 |
| Pott St BETH E2 | 140 | A5 |
| Pouchen End La HHW HP1 | 34 | G7 |
| Poulcott STWL/WRAY TW19 | 172 | B2 |
| Poulett Gdns TWK TW1 | 176 | B5 |
| Poulett Rd EHAM E6 | 142 | C4 |
| Poulter Pk MRDN SM4 * | 201 | P5 |
| Poulters Wd HAYES BR2 | 226 | A2 |
| Poultney Cl RAD WD7 | 57 | K8 |
| Poulton Av SUT SM1 | 201 | N10 |
| Poultry CITYW EC2V | 12 | G6 |
| Pound Cl HOR/WEW KT19 | 220 | A1 |
| ORP BR6 | 206 | C9 |
| STALE/WH AL4 * | 21 | H9 |
| SURB KT6 | 199 | H8 |
| WAB EN9 | 45 | K9 |
| Pound Ct ASHTD KT21 | 237 | L4 |
| RGUW GU3 | 248 | G8 |
| Pound Court Dr ORP BR6 | 206 | C9 |
| Pound Crs LHD/OX KT22 | 236 | C7 |
| Pound Farm Cl | | |
| ESH/CLAY KT10 | 198 | C8 |
| Pound Fld GSTN WD25 | 72 | C1 |
| GU GU1 | 250 | A10 |
| Poundfield Gdns | | |
| WOKS/MYFD GU22 | 232 | E6 |
| Poundfield Rd LOU IG10 | 82 | D9 |
| Pound Hl RGUW GU3 | 248 | G9 |
| Pound La CSHM HP5 | 32 | E8 |
| HOR/WEW KT19 | 220 | A7 |
| RAD WD7 | 57 | L9 |
| RSEV TN14 | 245 | N1 |
| SEV TN13 | 247 | K10 |
| WLSDN NW10 | 136 | D1 |
| Pound Park Rd CHARL SE7 | 142 | A3 |
| Pound Pl ELTH/MOT SE9 | 184 | D2 |
| Pound Place Cl RGUE GU4 | 268 | C6 |
| Pound Rd BNSTD SM7 | 239 | K3 |
| CHERT KT16 | 195 | K3 |
| Poundwell WGCE AL7 | 23 | K6 |
| Pounsley Rd SEV TN13 | 246 | F7 |
| Pountney Rd BTSEA SW11 | 158 | F2 |
| Poverest Rd STMC/STPC BR5 | 206 | G5 |
| Povey Cross Rd HORL RH6 | 279 | N6 |
| Powderham Ct | | |
| WOKN/KNAP GU21 | 231 | J4 |
| Powder Mill La WHTN TW2 | 175 | N4 |
| Powdermill Ms WAB EN9 | 62 | G4 |
| Powdermill Wy WAB EN9 | 62 | G4 |
| Powell Av RDART DA2 | 188 | D5 |
| Powell Cl EDGW HA8 * | 44 | B2 |
| GUW GU2 | 267 | L2 |
| HORL RH6 | 280 | A6 |
| Powell Gdns DAGE RM10 | 124 | B9 |
| Powell Rd BKHH IG9 | 101 | P1 |
| CLPT E5 | 120 | D8 |
| Powells Cl DORK RH4 | 273 | H5 |
| Powell's Wk CHSWK W4 | 156 | C1 |
| Power Cl GU GU1 | 249 | P9 |
| Power Dr PEND EN3 | 80 | E2 |
| Power Rd CHSWK W4 | 155 | M3 |
| Powerscroft Rd CLPT E5 | 120 | E9 |
| Powis Ct BUSH WD23 * | 94 | C2 |
| POTB/CUF EN6 | 59 | M10 |
| Powis Gdns GLDGN NW11 | 117 | J3 |
| NTGHL W11 | 8 | C5 |
| Powis Ms NTGHL W11 | 8 | C5 |
| Powis Pl BMSBY WC1N | 11 | M2 |
| Powis Rd BOW E3 | 139 | N8 |
| Powis Sq NTGHL W11 | 8 | C5 |
| Powis St WOOL/PLUM SE18 | 126 | G6 |
| Powis Ter NTGHL W11 | 8 | C5 |
| Powle Ter IL IG1 * | 122 | F4 |
| Powlett Pl CAMTN NW1 | 4 | B1 |
| Pownall Gdns HSLW TW3 | 155 | H8 |
| Pownall Rd HACK E8 | 7 | P2 |
| HSLW TW3 | 155 | H8 |
| Pownsett Ter IL IG1 * | 122 | F10 |
| Powster Rd BMLY BR1 | 183 | M5 |
| Powys Cl BXLYHN DA7 | 163 | H7 |
| Powys La PLMGR N13 | 98 | F5 |
| WCHMH N21 | 98 | F2 |
| Poyle La CHOB/PIR GU24 | 212 | B10 |
| Poyle Pk DTCH/LGLY SL3 * | 151 | H9 |
| Poyle Rd DTCH/LGLY SL3 | 151 | H9 |
| GU GU1 | 268 | B2 |
| Poynder Rd TIL RM18 | 168 | E7 |
| Poynders Hl HHNE HP2 | 36 | D7 |
| Poynders Rd CLAP SW4 | 180 | D3 |
| Poynes Rd HORL RH6 | 279 | P2 |
| Poynings Av HARP AL5 | 20 | E3 |
| Poynings Cl ORP BR6 | 206 | G1 |
| Poynings Rd ARCH N19 | 118 | C3 |
| Poynings Wy | | |
| NFNCH/WDSPK N12 | 97 | K6 |
| Poyntell Crs CHST BR7 | 206 | C1 |
| Poynter Rd EN EN1 | 79 | N5 |
| Poynton Rd TOTM N17 | 99 | P10 |
| Poyntz Rd BTSEA SW11 | 158 | F2 |
| Poyser St BETH E2 | 140 | A4 |
| Prae Cl STALW/RED AL3 | 38 | A5 |
| Prae Wd STAL AL1 | 38 | A6 |
| Praed Ms BAY/PAD W2 | 9 | M5 |
| Praed St BAY/PAD W2 | 9 | M5 |
| Praetorian Ct STAL AL1 * | 38 | C7 |
| Pragel St PLSTW E13 | 141 | M4 |
| Pragnell Rd LEE/GVPK SE12 | 183 | N5 |
| Prague Pl BRXS/STRHM SW2 | 180 | F1 |
| Prah Rd FSBYPK N4 | 119 | H2 |
| Prairie Cl ADL/WDHM KT15 | 195 | L10 |
| Prairie Rd ADL/WDHM KT15 | 195 | L9 |
| Prairie St VX/NE SW8 | 158 | A9 |
| Pratts La WOT/HER KT12 | 217 | K6 |
| Pratts Ms CAMTN NW1 | 4 | G6 |
| Pratt St CAMTN NW1 | 4 | G6 |
| Pratt Wk LBTH SE11 | 17 | M7 |
| Prayle Gv CRICK NW2 | 116 | C7 |
| Prebend Gdns HMSMTH W6 | 136 | D10 |
| Prebend St IS N1 | 6 | E6 |
| Precinct Rd HYS/HAR UB3 | 133 | H6 |
| The Precinct SL SL1 * | 128 | A6 |
| The Precinct BROX EN10 * | 44 | E6 |
| ECH TW20 | 172 | D8 |
| GSTN WD25 * | 74 | C1 |
| Premier Av CDW/CHF RM16 | 167 | M4 |
| Premiere Pl POP/IOD E14 | 140 | E4 |
| Premier Pde HORL RH6 * | 280 | C5 |
| Premier Park Rd | | |
| WLSDN NW10 | 135 | N4 |
| Premier Pl WATW WD18 | 72 | C9 |
| Prendergast Rd | | |
| BKHTH/KID SE3 | 161 | K9 |
| Prentis Rd STRHM/NOR SW16 | 179 | P7 |
| Prentiss Ct CHARL SE7 | 142 | C3 |
| Presburg Rd NWMAL KT3 | 200 | B5 |
| Prescelly Pl EDGW HA8 | 95 | J3 |
| Prescott Av STMC/STPC BR5 | 206 | E6 |
| Prescott Cl EMPK RM11 | 125 | J4 |
| Prescott Gn LOU IG10 | 82 | F7 |
| Prescott Pl CLAP SW4 | 158 | A3 |
| Prescott Rd CHES/WCR EN8 | 62 | D3 |
| DTCH/LGLY SL3 | 151 | H8 |
| Presdales Dr WARE SG12 | 26 | C3 |
| Presentation Ms | | |
| BRXS/STRHM SW2 | 180 | A3 |
| Presidents Dr WAP E1W * | 140 | A10 |
| President St FSBYE EC1V * | 6 | E6 |
| Prespa Cl ED N9 * | 31 | H4 |
| Press Rd UX/CGN UB8 | 131 | N2 |
| WLSDN NW10 | 99 | P10 |
| Prestage Wy POP/IOD E14 | 141 | H4 |
| Prestbury Crs BNSTD SM7 | 240 | A2 |
| Prestbury Rd FSTGT E7 | 141 | P2 |
| Prestbury Sq ELTH/MOT SE9 | 184 | C7 |
| Prested Rd BTSEA SW11 | 157 | P10 |
| Preston Av CHING E4 | 101 | J7 |
| Preston Cl STHWK SE1 | 19 | J7 |
| WHTN TW2 | 176 | D6 |
| Preston Ct BAR EN5 * | 77 | K8 |
| WOT/HER KT12 | 197 | K8 |
| Preston Dr BXLYHN DA7 | 163 | N7 |
| HOR/WEW KT19 | 220 | B3 |
| WAN E11 | 121 | H2 |
| Preston Gdns IL IG1 | 122 | B7 |
| PEND EN3 | 80 | D3 |
| WLSDN NW10 | 99 | P10 |
| Preston Hl | | |
| KTN/HRWW/WS HA3 | 115 | L5 |
| Preston La | | |
| KWD/TDW/WH KT20 | 238 | F6 |
| Preston Pl CRICK NW2 | 136 | A3 |
| RCH/KEW TW9 | 155 | N1 |
| Preston Rd | | |
| BKHTH/KID SE3 | 161 | L7 |
| CAN/RD E16 | 141 | P8 |
| KTTN NW5 | 4 | C2 |
| REDH RH1 | 277 | H8 |
| RYNPK SW20 | 200 | C1 |
| SHPTN TW17 | 196 | B5 |
| WAN E11 | 121 | K4 |
| WBLY HA9 | 115 | L4 |
| Prestons Rd WWKM BR4 | 205 | M10 |
| Preston's Rd POP/IOD E14 | 141 | M1 |
| Preston Vis KUT/HW KT1 | 199 | L2 |
| Preston Waye | | |
| KTN/HRWW/WS HA3 | 115 | L6 |
| Prestwich Ter CLAP SW4 | 180 | C3 |
| Prestwick Cl CRAWW RH11 | 282 | C6 |
| NWDGN UB2 | 153 | M4 |
| Prestwick Rd OXHEY WD19 | 93 | M3 |
| Prestwood Av | | |
| KTN/HRWW/WS HA3 | 114 | G2 |
| Prestwood Cl CRAWW RH11 | 283 | L4 |
| KTN/HRWW/WS HA3 | 114 | G2 |
| WOOL/PLUM SE18 * | 163 | P6 |
| Prestwood Gdns | | |
| CROY/NA CR0 | 203 | K7 |
| Prestwood La CRAWW RH11 | 282 | F8 |
| Prestwood Rd IS N1 * | 6 | F8 |
| Pretoria Av WALTH E17 | 119 | J2 |
| Pretoria Cl CHING E4 | 101 | H2 |
| Pretoria Pde BROCKY SE4 * | 161 | N6 |
| Pretoria Rd CAN/RD E16 | 141 | J5 |
| CHERT KT16 | 195 | J8 |
| CHING E4 | 101 | H2 |
| IL IG1 | 122 | C9 |
| LEY E10 | 120 | C5 |
| ROMW/RG RM7 | 124 | D2 |
| STRHM/NOR SW16 | 179 | J9 |
| TOTM N17 | 99 | N7 |
| WATW WD18 | 72 | C8 |
| Pretoria Rd North UED N18 | 99 | N7 |
| Pretty La COUL/CHIP CR5 | 260 | E6 |
| Prevost Rd FBAR/BDGN N11 | 98 | A3 |
| Prey Heath Cl | | |
| WOKS/MYFD GU22 | 231 | P10 |
| Prey Heath Rd | | |
| WOKS/MYFD GU22 | 231 | N10 |
| Price Cl MLHL NW7 | 97 | H7 |
| TOOT SW17 | 179 | H6 |
| Price Rd CROY/NA CR0 | 223 | J4 |
| Prices Ct BTSEA SW11 | 158 | C2 |
| Price's La REIG RH2 | 275 | L8 |
| Prices St STHWK SE1 | 12 | D9 |
| Prickley Wd HAYES BR2 | 205 | K10 |
| Priddy's Yd CROY/NA CR0 * | 2 | C3 |
| Prideaux Pl ACT W3 | 136 | A7 |
| FSBYW WC1X | 5 | N5 |
| Prideaux Rd BRXN/ST SW9 | 158 | A4 |
| Pridham Rd THHTH CR7 | 180 | B9 |
| Priest Croft Cl | | |
| CRAWW RH11 | 282 | D6 |
| Priestfield Rd FSTH SE23 | 182 | B5 |
| Priest Hill Cl HORL RH6 | 280 | C9 |
| Priestlands Park Rd | | |
| BFN/LL DA15 | 185 | J7 |
| Priestley Cl STNW/STAM N16 * | 119 | P5 |
| Priestley Gdns CHDH RM6 | 123 | H5 |
| WOKS/MYFD GU22 | 232 | G4 |
| Priestley Rd GUW GU2 | 267 | J1 |
| MTCM CR4 | 202 | B2 |
| Priestley Wy CRAWE RH10 | 284 | C10 |
| CRICK NW2 | 116 | D10 |
| WALTH E17 | 120 | C1 |
| Priest Osiers BROX EN10 * | 44 | C5 |
| Priest Ct | | |
| RYLN/HDSTN HA2 | 113 | P7 |
| Priests Av ROM RM1 | 104 | D1 |
| Priests Br MORT/ESHN SW14 | 156 | C6 |
| Priests Fld RBRW/HUT CM13 | 107 | P6 |
| Priest's La BRWN CM15 | 107 | K3 |
| Priests Paddock BEAC HP9 | 88 | A4 |
| Prima Rd BRXN/ST SW9 | 159 | H6 |
| Primley La RBSF CM22 | 30 | D2 |
| Primrose Av EN EN1 | 79 | L5 |
| ROMW/RG RM7 | 124 | B1 |
| Primrose Cl BOW E3 | 140 | A1 |
| CAT SE6 | 183 | H8 |
| CRAWW RH11 | 283 | L10 |
| FNCH N3 | 97 | L10 |
| HAT AL10 | 40 | C5 |
| HHW HP1 | 35 | H7 |
| RYLN/HDSTN HA2 | 113 | N10 |
| WLGTN SM6 | 202 | C6 |
| Primrose Dr CHOB/PIR GU24 | 230 | F1 |
| HERT/BAY SG13 | 26 | A5 |
| WDR/YW UB7 | 132 | A3 |
| Primrose Gdns BUSH WD23 | 94 | A1 |
| HAMP NW3 | 3 | P1 |
| RSLP HA4 | 113 | K10 |
| Primrose Gln EMPK RM11 | 125 | J3 |
| Primrose Hl BRW CM14 | 107 | H4 |
| EMB EC4Y | 12 | B6 |
| KGLGY WD4 | 54 | C1 |
| Primrose Hill Studios | | |
| CAMTN NW1 * | 4 | C5 |
| Primrose La CROY/NA CR0 | 204 | B8 |
| GSTN WD25 | 74 | C1 |
| Primrose Ms CAMTN NW1 * | 4 | A4 |
| Primrose Pth CHESW EN7 | 61 | P7 |
| Primrose Pl ISLW TW7 | 154 | E8 |
| Primrose Rd LEY E10 | 120 | C6 |
| SWFD E18 | 102 | E8 |
| WOT/HER KT12 | 217 | H7 |
| Primrose Sq SDTCH EC2A | 13 | J3 |
| Primrose St SDTCH EC2A | 13 | J3 |
| Primrose Wk GVE DA12 | 217 | H2 |
| EW KT17 | 220 | C4 |
| NWCR SE14 | 160 | D6 |
| Primrose Wy ALP/SUD HA0 | 135 | J4 |
| WOKS/MYFD GU22 | 232 | C2 |
| Primula St SHB W12 | 136 | G6 |
| Prince Albert Rd STJWD NW8 | 3 | N9 |
| Prince Albert Sq REDH RH1 | 276 | A5 |
| Prince Albert's Wk WDSR SL4 | 149 | K6 |
| Prince Arthur Ms HAMP NW3 * | 117 | H2 |
| Prince Arthur Rd HAMP NW3 | 117 | H2 |
| Prince Charles Av | | |
| STHGT/OAK N14 * | 78 | F10 |
| Prince Charles Dr HDN NW4 | 116 | A5 |
| Prince Charles Rd | | |
| BKHTH/KID SE3 | 161 | L7 |
| Prince Charles Wy | | |
| WLGTN SM6 | 202 | C9 |
| Prince Consort Cots | | |
| WDSR SL4 | 149 | J8 |
| Prince Consort Dr CHST BR7 | 206 | C1 |
| Prince Consort Rd SKENS SW7 | 15 | L3 |
| Prince Consort's Dr WDSR SL4 | 170 | E2 |
| Prince Edward Rd HOM E9 | 140 | E1 |
| Prince Edward St BERK HP4 | 33 | P6 |
| Prince George Av | | |
| STHGT/OAK N14 | 78 | F10 |
| Prince George Rd | | |
| STNW/STAM N16 | 119 | M9 |
| Prince George's Av | | |
| RYNPK SW20 | 200 | F2 |
| Prince Georges Rd | | |
| WIM/MER SW19 | 201 | N1 |
| Prince Henry Sq CHARL SE7 | 162 | A6 |
| Prince Imperial Rd CHST BR7 | 184 | B7 |
| WOOL/PLUM SE18 | 144 | E10 |
| Prince John Rd ELTH/MOT SE9 | 184 | B1 |
| Princelet St WCHPL E1 | 13 | M3 |
| Prince of Orange La | | |
| GNWCH SE10 * | 161 | H6 |
| Prince of Wales Cl HDN NW4 | 116 | A2 |
| Prince of Wales Dr | | |
| BTSEA SW11 | 157 | P7 |
| Prince of Wales Pas | | |
| CAMTN NW1 * | 4 | G10 |
| Prince of Wales Rd | | |
| BKHTH/KID SE3 | 161 | L7 |
| CAN/RD E16 | 141 | P8 |
| KTTN NW5 | 4 | C2 |
| REDH RH1 | 277 | H8 |
| Prince of Wales Ter | | |
| CHSWK W4 | 156 | B4 |
| KENS W8 | 14 | F2 |
| Prince Regent Ms | | |
| CAMTN NW1 * | 4 | G10 |
| Prince Regent Rd HSLW TW3 | 154 | G8 |
| Prince Rd SNWD SE25 | 203 | M5 |
| Prince Rupert Rd | | |
| ELTH/MOT SE9 | 162 | C10 |
| Princes Av ACT W3 | 155 | P3 |
| CAR SM5 | 222 | A4 |
| CDALE/KGS NW9 | 115 | M2 |
| FNCH N3 | 97 | L9 |
| MUSWH N10 | 118 | B0 |
| PEND EN3 | 80 | D2 |
| STHGT/OAK N14 | 78 | F10 |
| SURB KT6 | 211 | J8 |
| WATW WD18 | 72 | E6 |
| WFD IG8 | 101 | L1 |
| WOT/HER KT12 | 217 | N4 |
| Prince's Av GFD/PVL UB6 | 134 | A4 |
| Princes Cl BERK HP4 | 33 | M3 |
| CDALE/KGS NW9 | 115 | M2 |
| EDGW HA8 | 95 | M6 |
| EPP CM16 | 66 | D1 |
| SAND/SEL CR2 | 242 | A1 |
| SCUP DA14 | 185 | N6 |
| WDSR SL4 | 148 | A4 |
| Prince's Cl HPTN TW12 | 176 | A6 |
| Princes Ct WAP E1W | 140 | A9 |
| WBLY HA9 | 114 | D1 |
| Princes Dr LHD/OX KT22 | 218 | A9 |
| Princesfield Rd WAB EN9 | 63 | N9 |
| Princes Gdns ACT W3 | 135 | P5 |
| EA W5 | 135 | H5 |
| RGUW GU3 * | 249 | K5 |
| SKENS SW7 | 15 | L3 |
| Princes Gate SKENS SW7 | 15 | N2 |
| Princes Gate Ms SKENS SW7 | 15 | N3 |
| Princes Ms BAY/PAD W2 | 8 | F6 |
| HSLW TW3 | 155 | H8 |
| Princes Pde GLDGN NW11 * | 117 | H4 |
| POTB/CUF EN6 * | 59 | J1 |
| Princes Park Av GLDGN NW11 | 97 | H4 |
| HYS/HAR UB3 | 132 | G5 |
| Princes Park Cir HYS/HAR UB3 | 132 | G5 |
| Princes Park Cl HYS/HAR UB3 | 132 | G5 |
| Princes Park Pde | | |
| HYS/HAR UB3 * | 132 | F5 |
| Princes Pl NTGHL W11 | 8 | A8 |
| WAT WD17 | 8 | A8 |
| Princes Plain HAYES BR2 | 206 | F1 |
| Princes Ri LEW SE13 | 161 | H8 |
| Princes Riverside Rd | | |
| BERM/RHTH SE16 | 140 | C10 |
| Princes Rd ASHF TW15 | 174 | A8 |
| BARK/HLT IG6 | 122 | G2 |
| BKHH IG9 | 101 | P3 |
| ECH TW20 | 172 | C9 |
| KUT/HW KT1 | 199 | M1 |
| KUTN/CMB KT2 | 177 | N10 |
| PGE/AN SE20 | 182 | C9 |
| RCHPK/HAM TW10 | 177 | L1 |
| RDART DA2 | 188 | B4 |
| REDH RH1 | 277 | N2 |
| ROM RM1 | 125 | H3 |
| SWLY BR8 | 187 | N9 |
| TEDD TW11 | 175 | P7 |
| UED N18 | 100 | B5 |
| WEA W13 | 135 | H5 |
| Prince's Rd BRW CM14 | 85 | M6 |
| MORT/ESHN SW14 | 156 | A9 |
| REDH RH1 | 276 | B3 |
| TEDD TW11 | 175 | P7 |
| WEY KT13 | 216 | C2 |
| WIM/MER SW19 | 179 | J2 |
| Princess Alice Wy THMD SE28 | 162 | G1 |
| Princess Av TIL RM18 | 169 | M8 |
| Princess Cl SL SL1 | 148 | G9 |
| STALE/WH AL4 | 39 | H7 |
| Princesses Pde DART DA1 * | 186 | C1 |
| Princess Gdns | | |
| WOKS/MYFD GU22 | 232 | G2 |
| Princess Gv BEAC HP9 | 89 | J5 |
| Princess La RSLP HA4 | 112 | F6 |
| Princess Louise Cl | | |
| BAY/PAD W2 | 9 | M3 |
| Princess Margaret Rd | | |
| TIL RM18 | 169 | L3 |
| Princess Mary Cl GUW GU2 | 249 | M1 |
| Princess Mary's Rd | | |
| ADL/WDHM KT15 | 215 | M1 |
| Princess May Rd | | |
| STNW/STAM N16 | 119 | M9 |
| Princess Ms HAMP NW3 | 3 | M1 |
| Princess Pde ORP BR6 * | 206 | D10 |

BARN SW13 — 156 C9
BERK HP4 — 33 P5
CHSWK W4 * — 156 C9
DEN/HRF UB9 — 111 M2
HGT N6 — 66 C3
HPTN TW12 — 197 N1
SNWD SE25 — 203 N4
**Priory St** BOW E3 — 140 C5
WARE SG14 — 173 L8
**Priory Gn** STAL AL1 — 5 N7
**Priory Green Est** IS N1 — 5 N7
**Priory Gv** HARH RM3 — 105 M5
VX/NE SW8 — 158 F7
**Priory HI** ALP/SUD HA0 — 114 F8
**Priory La** E/WMO/HCT KT8 — 197 P4
EVN DA4 — 209 N8
PUT/ROE SW15 — 178 C1
**Priory Leas** ELTH/MOT SE9 * — 184 B4
**Priory Md** BRWN CM15 — 87 H2
RCH ASC SL5 — 192 F7
**Priory Ms** HCH RM12 — 125 J5
STA TW18 — 173 K8
**Priory Pk** BKHTH/KID SE3 — 161 L9
ALP/SUD HA0 — 114 F8
**Priory Pth** HARH RM3 — 105 M4
RCH ASC SL5 — 192 F7
**Priory Rd** BARK IG11 — 142 G2
CEND/HSY/T N8 — 118 C2
CFSP/GDCR SL9 — 109 P1
CHEAM SM3 — 220 G1
CHSGTN KT9 — 199 K10
CHSWK W4 — 156 A4
CROY/NA CR0 — 203 H7
DART DA1 — 165 L10
EHAM E6 — 142 A3
HARH RM3 — 105 M4
HPTN TW12 — 175 N10
HSLW TW3 — 176 B1
KIL/WHAMP NW6 — 2 C4
LOU IG10 — 82 B9
MUSWH N10 — 118 C2
RCH/KEW TW9 — 155 M5
REIG RH2 — 275 K2
SL SL1 — 128 C7
**Priory St** BOW E3 — 140 C5
KIL/WHAMP NW6 — 2 C5
WARE SG12 — 26 E2
**Priory Ter** KIL/WHAMP NW6 — 2 C5
**The Priory** BKHTH/KID SE3 — 161 L9
CROY/NA CR0 * — 203 H10
GDST RH9 — 260 A4
ORP BR6 * — 207 L7
**Priory Vw** BUSH WD23 — 94 C1
**Priory Vls** FBAR/BDGN N11 * — 99 J3
WBPTN SW10 * — 38 D9
**Priory Wk** STAL AL1 — 5 N7
**Priory Wy** CFSP/GDCR SL9 — 109 N6
DTCH/LGLY SL3 — 149 N6
NWDGN UB2 — 153 L2
RYLN/HDSTN HA2 — 114 A2
WDR/YW UB7 — 151 P5
**Pritchard's Rd** BETH E2 — 7 P7
**Pritchett Cl** PEND EN3 — 80 G3
**Priter Rd** BERM/RHTH SE16 — 19 H7
**Private Rd** EN EN1 — 79 L5
**Probert Rd** BRXS/STRHM SW2 — 181 N4
**Probyn Rd** BRXS/STRHM SW2 — 181 J5
**Procter St** GINN WC1R — 11 M4
**Proctor Cl** CRAWE RH10 — 284 D9
MTCM CR4 — 202 B1
**Proctor Gdns** GT/LBKH KT23 — 254 D4
**Proctors Cl** EBED/NFELT TW14 — 175 N6
**Profumo Rd** WOT/HER KT12 — 217 L2
**Progress Wy** CROY/NA CR0 — 202 G9
EN EN1 — 79 N7
WDGN N22 — 117 H1
**Promenade Approach Rd** CHSWK W4 — 156 B6
**Promenade De Verdun** PUR/KEN CR8 — 222 E7
**The Promenade** CHSWK W4 — 156 B7
EDGW HA8 * — 95 M6
**Prospect Cl** BELV DA17 — 164 B3
BUSH WD23 — 94 C1
HSLW TW3 — 153 N7
RSLP HA4 — 113 L3
SYD SE26 — 182 A7
**Prospect Cots** WAND/EARL SW18 — 157 K10
**Prospect Crs** WHTN TW2 — 176 B2
**Prospect Gv** GVE DA12 — 190 C3
**Prospect HI** WALTH E17 — 120 C2
**Prospect La** EGH TW20 — 171 M8
**Prospect Pl** CHSWK W4 — 156 A4
CRAWW RH11 — 283 M7
CRICK NW2 — 117 J8
CRW RM5 — 104 D10
EFNCH N2 — 117 N2
EW KT17 — 228 C6
GRAYS RM17 * — 167 N5
GVE DA12 — 190 C3
HAYES BR2 — 205 N1
RYNPK SW20 — 178 E10
STA TW18 — 173 J8
WAP E1W * — 13 N1
**Prospect Ring** EFNCH N2 — 117 N1
**Prospect Rd** BAR EN5 — 77 K8
CHES/WCR EN8 — 62 B5
EMPK RM11 — 125 N1
SEV TN13 — 247 K9
STAL AL1 — 38 C10
SURB KT6 — 199 H6
WFD IG8 — 101 P6
**Prospect St** BERM/RHTH SE16 — 160 C1
**Prospect V** WOOL/PLUM SE18 — 162 B3
**Prospero Rd** ARCH N19 — 118 C8
**Prossers** WOT/HER KT20 — 237 H10
**Protea Cl** CAN/RD E16 — 141 L6
**Prothero Gdns** HDN NW4 — 116 E3
**Prothero Rd** FUL/PGN SW6 — 157 J5
**Prout Gv** WLSDN NW10 — 116 B9
**Prout Rd** CLPT E5 — 120 A8
**Provence St** IS N1 — 6 E7
**Providence Av** RYLN/HDSTN HA2 — 113 P6
**Providence Ct** HOM E9 * — 140 C3
MYFR/PKLN W1K — 10 B7
**Providence Ct** CRAWE RM5 — 104 A9
IS N1 — 6 B2
WOKS/MYFD GU22 * — 215 K10
**Providence La** HYS/HAR UB3 — 152 E6
**Providence Pl** CRAWE RM5 — 104 A9
IS N1 — 6 B2
WOKS/MYFD GU22 * — 215 K10
**Providence Row Cl** BETH E2 — 140 C5
**Providence Sq** STHWK SE1 * — 19 J1
**Providence Ter** CRAWE RH10 * — 285 P5
**Providence Yd** BETH E2 — 7 N9
**Provost Est** IS N1 — 6 G5
**Provost Rd** HAMP NW3 — 4 B3
**Provost St** FSBYE EC1V — 6 G10
**Prowse Av** BUSH WD23 — 94 G3
**Prowse Pl** CAMTN NW1 — 4 C1
**Prudence La** ORP BR6 — 226 C1
**Pruden Cl** STHGT/OAK N14 * — 98 G2
**Prune HI** EGH TW20 — 172 A10
**Prunus Cl** CHOB/PIR GU24 — 212 D9
**Prusom St** WAP E1W — 140 A10
**Pryor Cl** ABLGY WD5 — 54 G2
**Pucknells Cl** SWLY BR8 — 208 A8
**Puckshill** WOKN/KNAP GU21 — 231 H5
**Pudding La** CHIC IG7 — 83 H10
HHW HP1 — 35 K4
HORL RH6 — 159 K7
MON EC3R — 13 H7
**Pudding Mill La** SRTFD E15 — 140 A7
**Puddingstone Dr** STALE/WH HA4 — 39 H8
**Puddle Dock** BLKFR EC4V — 12 D7
**Puddledock La** BH/WHM TN16 — 263 K8
RDART DA2 — 188 A7
**Puers La** BEAC HP9 — 89 K7
**Puffin Cl** BARK IG11 — 143 L6
BECK BR3 — 204 C5
**Puffin Rd** CRAWW RH11 — 282 C8

**Pulborough Rd** WAND/EARL SW18 — 179 J3
**Pulborough Wy** HSLWW TW4 — 153 L9
**Pulford Rd** SEVS/STOTM N15 — 119 L4
**Pulham Av** BRXN EN10 — 44 D6
EFNCH N2 — 117 M2
**Puller Rd** BAR EN5 — 76 G6
HHW HP1 — 35 K4
**Pulleyns Av** EHAM E6 — 142 H5
**Pulleys Cl** HHW HP1 — 35 J5
**Pulleys La** HHW HP1 — 35 J5
**Pullfields** CSHM HP5 — 50 F6
**Pullman Cl** STAL AL1 — 38 D8
**Pullman Gdns** PUT/ROE SW15 — 178 F2
**Pullman Ms** LEE/GVPK SE12 — 183 N6
**Pullman Pl** ELTH/MOT SE9 — 184 B1
**Pullman Pl** STA TW18 — 173 K8
**Pulpit Cl** CSHM HP5 — 50 F5
**Pulross Rd** BRXN/ST SW9 — 158 E9
**Pulteney Cl** BOW E3 — 140 E3
ISLW TW7 —
**Pulteney Rd** SWFD E18 — 121 N1
**Pulton Pl** FUL/PGN SW6 — 157 K6
**Puma Ct** WCHPL E1 — 13 M3
**Pump Aly** BTFD TW8 — 155 J6
**Pump Cl** NTHLT UB5 — 133 P4
**Pump Ct** EMB EC4Y * — 12 A4
**Pump HI** LOU IG10 — 82 C6
**Pump House Cl** HAYES BR2 — 205 L2
RCH/KEW TW9 — 155 M5
**Pump House Ms** WCHPL E1 — 13 N7
**Pumping Station Rd** CHSWK W4 — 156 B6
**Pumpkin HI** SL SL1 — 128 D1
**Pump La** SL SL1 — 192 D1
EPP CM16 — 51 K9
HYS/HAR UB3 — 153 H1
NWCR SE14 — 160 B6
ORP BR6 — 228 B3
**Punchard Crs** PEND EN3 — 80 G4
**Punch Bowl La** STALW/RED AL3 — 37 H2
CSHM HP5 — 51 H8
HHNE HP2 — 36 E3
**Punchbowl La** RDKG RH5 — 273 P1
**Punchbowl Pk** HHNE HP2 * — 36 E3
**Punch Copse Rd** CRAWE RH10 — 284 A6
**Punch Cft** HART DA3 — 211 K10
**Punderson's Gdns** BETH E2 — 140 A5
**Purbeck Av** NWMAL KT3 — 200 C4
**Purbeck Cl** REDH RH1 — 258 E5
**Purbeck Dr** CRICK NW2 — 116 A8
WOKN/KNAP GU21 — 214 C10
**Purbeck Rd** EMPK RM11 — 125 H5
**Purberry Gv** EW KT17 — 228 C6
**Purbery Shot** EW KT17 * — 220 C6
**Purbrock Av** GSTN WD25 — 73 K2
**Purbrook St** STHWK SE1 * — 19 K3
PUR/KEN CR8 — 223 K10
**Purcell Cl** BORE WD6 — 75 J5
PUR/KEN CR8 — 223 K10
**Purcell Crs** FUL/PGN SW6 — 156 G6
**Purcell Ms** WLSDN NW10 * — 99 H6
**Purcell Rd** CRAWW RH11 — 283 J10
GFD/PVL UB6 — 134 A7
**Purcell St** IS N1 — 7 J1
**Purcers Cross Rd** FUL/PGN SW6 — 157 J7
**Purdom Rd** WCCE AL7 — 23 H8
**Purdy St** BOW E3 — 140 G6
**Purelake Ms** LEW SE13 * — 161 J9
**Purfleet By-Pass** PUR RM19 — 166 A3
**Purfleet Deep Whf** PUR RM19 * — 166 B5
**Purfleet Industrial Access Rd** SOCK/AV RM15 — 165 P2
**Purfleet Rd** SOCK/AV RM15 — 146 A10
**Purford Gn** HLWS CM18 — 47 K2
**Purkis Ct** UX/CGN UB8 — 132 C9
**Purkiss Rd** HERT/BAY SG13 — 25 K8
**Purland Cl** BCTR RM8 — 124 A4
**Purland Rd** THMD SE28 — 163 J2
**Purleigh Av** WFD IG8 — 102 B7
**Purley Av** CRICK NW2 — 117 H7
**Purley Bury Av** PUR/KEN CR8 — 223 K7
**Purley Bury Cl** PUR/KEN CR8 — 223 K7
**Purley Cl** CLAY IG5 — 102 D1
CRAWE RH10 — 284 E10
**Purley Downs Rd** SAND/SEL CR2 — 223 K6
**Purley HI** PUR/KEN CR8 — 223 J8
**Purley Knoll** PUR/KEN CR8 — 222 G7
**Purley Oaks Rd** SAND/SEL CR2 — 223 L6
**Purley Pde** PUR/KEN CR8 * — 223 J6
**Purley Park Rd** PUR/KEN CR8 — 223 J6
**Purley Pl** IS N1 — 6 C1
**Purley Rd** ED N9 — 99 L4
SAND/SEL CR2 — 223 J9
**Purley V** PUR/KEN CR8 — 223 J9
**Purley Wy** CROY/NA CR0 — 202 G9
PUR/KEN CR8 — 223 H6
**Purlieu Wy** EPP CM16 — 83 H1
**Purlings Rd** BUSH WD23 — 74 A9
**Purneys Rd** ELTH/MOT SE9 — 162 A10
**Purrett Rd** WOOL/PLUM SE18 — 163 L4
**Pursers Cross Rd** FUL/PGN SW6 * — 157 J7
**Pursers Ct** SLN SL2 — 129 K2
**Pursers Hollow** SHGR GU5 — 270 E10
**Pursers La** SHGR GU5 — 270 E10
**Pursers Lea** SHGR GU5 — 270 E10
**Pursewardens Cl** WEA W13 — 135 H10
**Pursley Gdns** BORE WD6 — 75 M4
**Pursley Rd** MLHL NW7 — 96 E8
**Purton Ct** SLN SL2 — 129 K2
**Purton La** SLN SL2 — 129 H2
**Purves Rd** WLSDN NW10 — 136 E5
**Putney Br** PUT/ROE SW15 — 157 H9
**Putney Bridge Ap** FUL/PGN SW6 — 157 H9
**Putney Bridge Rd** PUT/ROE SW15 — 157 H10
**Putney Common** PUT/ROE SW15 — 156 F9
**Putney Ex** PUT/ROE SW15 * — 156 G10
**Putney Heath** PUT/ROE SW15 — 178 E3
**Putney Heath La** PUT/ROE SW15 — 178 G2
**Putney High St** PUT/ROE SW15 — 157 H10
**Putney HI** PUT/ROE SW15 — 178 F3
**Putney Park Av** PUT/ROE SW15 — 156 D10
**Putney Park La** PUT/ROE SW15 — 156 E10
**Putney Rd** PEND EN3 — 80 C2
**Puttenham Cl** OXHEY WD19 — 93 K4
**Puttenham Heath Rd** RGUW GU3 — 266 C5
**Puttenham HI** RGUW GU3 — 266 A6
**Puttenham Rd** MFD/CHID GU8 — 266 C10
**Putters Cft** HHNE HP2 — 36 A1
**Puttocks Cl** BRKMPK AL9 — 40 F9
**Puttocks Dr** BRKMPK AL9 — 40 F9
**Pycombe Cnr** NFNCH/WDSPK N12 — 97 J5
**Pycroft Wy** ED N9 — 99 P5
**Pyebush La** BEAC HP9 — 108 F2
**Pye Ct** PTHM CR3 — 241 L8
**Pyecombe Ct** CRAWW RH11 — 283 J10
**Pyenest Rd** HLWW/ROY CM19 — 46 H4
**Pylbrook Rd** SUT SM1 — 201 K10
**Pyle HI** WOKS/MYFD GU22 — 232 A10
**Pylon Wy** CROY/NA CR0 — 202 B8
**Pym Cl** EBAR EN4 — 77 N3
**Pymers Md** DUL SE21 — 181 K4
**Pymmes Brook Trail** EBAR EN4 — 98 A3
**Pymmes Cl** PLMGR N13 — 98 G8
TOTM N17 — 100 A8
**Pymmes Gdns North** ED N9 — 99 N4
**Pymmes Gdns South** ED N9 — 99 N4
**Pymmes Green Rd** FBAR/BDGN N11 — 98 C5
**Pymmes Rd** PLMGR N13 — 98 F7
**Pymms Brook Dr** EBAR EN4 — 77 P8
**Pym Orch** BH/WHM TN16 — 245 M10
**Pym Pl** GRAYS RM17 — 167 M3
**Pynchester Cl** HGDN/ICK UB10 — 112 B7
**Pyne Rd** SURB KT6 — 199 M8
**Pynest Green La** LOU IG10 — 81 M3
**Pynham Cl** ABYW SE2 — 163 K2
**Pynnacles Cl** STAN HA7 — 94 G6
**Pyot Pth** BORE WD6 — 75 M3
**Pyrcroft La** WEY KT13 — 216 C2
**Pyrcroft Rd** CHTK T16 — 195 H7
**Pyrford Common Rd** WOKS/MYFD GU22 — 233 H2
**Pyrford Heath** WOKS/MYFD GU22 — 233 J2
**Pyrford Rd** BF/WBF KT14 — 215 K10
WOKS/MYFD GU22 — 233 L2
**Pyrford Woods Cl** WOKS/MYFD GU22 — 233 J1
**Pyrford Woods Rd** WOKS/MYFD GU22 — 233 H1
**Pyrian Cl** WOKS/MYFD GU22 — 232 C3
**Pyrland Rd** HBRY N5 — 119 L10
RCHPK/HAM TW10 — 177 L2
**Pyrles Gn** LOU IG10 — 82 E6
**Pyrles La** LOU IG10 — 82 E6
**Pyrmont Gv** WNWD SE27 — 181 J6
**Pyrmont Rd** CHSWK W4 — 155 M5
**Pytchley Crs** NRWD SE19 — 181 K9
**Pytchley Rd** EDUL SE22 — 159 M9
**Pytt Fld** HLWE CM17 — 47 L2

## Q

**The Quadrangle** BAY/PAD W2 — 9 N5
GUW GU2 — 267 J3
HNHL SE24 — 181 K1
WBPTN SW10 * — 157 M7
WGCW AL8 — 22 F4
**Quadrant Ar** REGST W1B — 11 H8
**Quadrant Cl** HDN NW4 — 116 E3
**Quadrant Gv** KTTN NW5 — 118 A3
**Quadrant Rd** RCH/KEW TW9 — 155 J10
THHTH CR7 — 203 J4
**The Quadrant** BELMT SM2 — 221 M3
BXLYHN DA7 — 163 N6
EDGW HA8 * — 95 M7
NKENS W10 * — 136 G5
PUR RM19 — 166 B3
RCH/KEW TW9 — 155 M9
RYLN/HDSTN HA2 — 114 C1
RYNPK SW20 — 201 H1
SUT SM1 — 222 A3
STALE/WH AL4 — 38 G3
WEY KT13 — 216 B1
**Quadrant Wy** WEY KT13 — 216 B1
**Quad Rd** WBLY HA9 — 115 J8
**Quaggy Wk** BKHTH/KID SE3 — 161 N10
**Quail Gdns** SAND/SEL CR2 — 224 D6
**Quainton St** WLSDN NW10 — 116 A8
**Quaker Cl** SEV TN13 — 247 L5
**Quaker La** NWDGN UB2 — 153 P2
WAB EN9 — 63 H10
**Quakers Cl** HART DA3 — 211 K3
**Quakers Course** CDALE/KGS NW9 — 96 C3
**Quaker's Hall La** SEV TN13 — 247 K8
**Quakers La** ISLW TW7 — 154 B4
POTB/CUF EN6 — 59 L6
**Quakers Pl** FSTGT E7 — 122 A10
**Quaker St** WCHPL E1 — 13 L2
**Quakers Wk** WCHMH N21 — 79 L10
**Quality Ct** LINN WC2A — 12 A5
**Quality St** REDH RH1 — 258 C4
**Quantock Cl** CRAWW RH11 — 283 L7
DTCH/LGLY SL3 — 150 D4
HYS/HAR UB3 — 152 E6
STALE/WH AL4 — 39 H2
**Quantock Gdns** CRICK NW2 * — 116 G2
**Quantock Ms** PECK SE15 — 159 P8
**Quantock Rd** BXLYHN DA7 — 164 F8
**Quantocks** HHNE HP2 — 36 A3
**Quarles Cl** CRW RM5 — 104 B8
**Quarles Park Rd** CHDH RM6 — 123 J1
**Quarrendon Rd** AMSS HP7 * — 69 J6
**Quarrendon St** FUL/PGN SW6 — 157 K7
**Quarr Rd** CAR SM5 — 201 N6
**Quarry Cl** OXTED RH8 — 261 K6
**Quarry Gdns** LHD/OX KT22 — 237 J7
**Quarry HI** BGR/WK TN15 — 247 L9
GRAYS RM17 — 167 M3
**Quarry Hill Pk** REIG RH2 — 257 M7
**Quarry Park Rd** SUT SM1 — 221 J3
**Quarry Ri** SUT SM1 — 221 J3
**Quarry Rd** OXT DR9 — 260 B4
GODL GU7 — 266 F10
OXTED RH8 — 261 K6
WAND/EARL SW18 — 179 M2
**Quarry St** GU GU1 — 268 C2
**The Quarry** BRKHM/BTCW RH3 — 256 A8
**Quarry Spring** HLW CM20 — 47 K1
**Quarry Springs** HLW CM20 — 47 K1
**Quartermass Cl** HHW HP1 — 35 K5
**Quartermass Rd** HHW HP1 — 35 K5
**Quatre Ports** CHING E4 * — 101 J6
**Quaves Rd** DTCH/LGLY SL3 — 149 N2
**Quay House** POP/IOD E14 * — 160 E1
**Quay La** RDART DA2 — 166 G10
**Quebec Av** BH/WHM TN16 — 262 G6
**Quebec Cl** HORL RH6 — 281 H4
**Quebec Ms** MBLAR W1H — 10 B5
**Quebec Rd** GNTH/NBYPK IG2 — 122 F5
TIL RM18 — 168 D2
YEAD UB4 — 133 K4
**Quebec Wy** BERM/RHTH SE16 — 160 C1
**Queen Adelaide Rd** PGE/AN SE20 — 182 B9
**Queen Alexandra's Wy** HOR/WEW KT19 — 219 M8
**Queen Anne Av** HAYES BR2 — 205 N1
**Queen Anne Dr** ESH/CLAY KT10 — 218 D4
**Queen Anne Ms** CAVSQ/HST W1G — 10 C3
**Queen Anne Rd** HOM E9 — 140 C1
**Queen Annes Av** WHTN TW2 — 176 A4
**Queen Annes Cl** WHTN TW2 — 176 A4
**Queen Anne's Cl** LHD/OX KT22 — 236 C1
**Queen Anne's Gdns** CHSWK W4 — 156 B2
EA W5 — 155 K1
EN EN1 — 79 M10
LHD/OX KT22 — 236 C1
MTCM CR4 — 202 A1
**Queen Anne's Ga** STJSPK SW1H — 17 J2
**Queen Anne's Gv** CHSWK W4 — 156 B2
EA W5 — 155 K1
ED N9 — 99 M10
EN EN1 — 79 M10
**Queen Annes Ms** LHD/OX KT22 — 236 C1
**Queen Anne's Pl** EN EN1 — 79 M10
**Queen Anne's Ride** WDSR SL4 — 171 J1
**Queen Anne's Rd** WDSR SL4 — 149 H10
**Queen Anne St** CAVSQ/HST W1G — 10 C3
**Queen Anne Ter** WAP E1W * — 140 A3
**Queen Bee Ct** HAT AL10 — 40 A2
**Queenborough Gdns** CHST BR7 — 184 G6
**Queenborough Gdns** GNTH/NBYPK IG2 — 122 D2
**Queen Caroline Est** HMSMTH W6 — 156 F4

**Queen Caroline St** HMSMTH W6 — 156 F4
**Queendale Ct** WOKN/KNAP GU21 — 231 L2
**Queen Eleanor's Rd** GUW GU2 — 267 L1
**Queen Elizabeth Av** TIL RM18 — 169 G5
EMB EC4Y * — 12 A7
**Queen Elizabeth College** GNWCH SE10 * — 161 H6
**Queen Elizabeth Ct** WAB EN9 * — 81 J1
**Queen Elizabeth Gdns** MRDN SM4 — 201 K4
**Queen Elizabeth II Br** RDART DA2 — 166 B9
**Queen Elizabeth Rd** KUTN/CMB KT2 — 199 L2
WALTH E17 — 120 D1
**Queen Elizabeth's Cl** STNW/STAM N16 — 119 L7
**Queen Elizabeth's Dr** CROY/NA CR0 — 225 J6
STHGT/OAK N14 — 98 F2
**Queen Elizabeth's Gdns** CROY/NA CR0 — 225 J6
**Queen Elizabeth St** STHWK SE1 — 19 K1
**Queen Elizabeth's Wk** STNW/STAM N16 — 119 L6
WLGTN SM6 — 222 F1
**Queen Elizabeth Wk** BARN SW13 — 156 D7
WDSR SL4 — 149 M8
**Queen Elizabeth Wy** WOKS/MYFD GU22 — 232 C5
**Queenhill Rd** SAND/SEL CR2 — 224 A6
**Queenhythe Crs** RGUE GU4 — 250 A4
**Queenhythe Rd** RGUE GU4 — 250 A4
**Queen Isabella Wy** STBT EC1A — 12 D5
**Queen Margaret's Gv** IS N1 — 119 M10
**Queen Mary Av** ROM RM1 — 124 G4
SURB KT6 — 199 M10
**Queen Mary Cl** ROM RM1 — 124 G4
WOKS/MYFD GU22 — 232 F2
**Queen Mary Rd** NRWD SE19 — 181 J9
SHPTN TW17 — 196 D2
**Queen Mary's Av** CAR SM5 — 222 A4
**Queen Marys Ct** WAB EN9 * — 81 H1
**Queen Mary's Dr** ADL/WDHM KT15 — 215 J6
**Queen Mother Ga** MYFR/PICC W1J — 10 D10
**Queen Mother's Dr** ED/HRF UB9 — 111 J4
**Queens Acre** CHEAM SM3 — 220 G4
WDSR SL4 — 149 J10
**Queens Av** BF/WBF KT14 — 215 N8
FELT TW13 — 175 K7
KTN/HRWW/WS HA3 — 114 C1
MUSWH N10 — 118 B3
TRDG/WHET N20 — 97 N5
**Queen's Av** FNCH N3 — 97 N8
HDN NW4 — 116 F3
HERT/BAY SG13 — 25 L7
HPTN TW12 — 176 A7
HSLW TW3 — 154 A9
KUTN/CMB KT2 — 177 M10
MORT/ESHN SW14 — 156 A9
MTCM CR4 — 201 N3
NWDGN UB2 — 153 L1
NWMAL KT3 — 200 D3
PECK SE15 — 160 B7
STHGT/OAK N14 — 98 C4
WDR/YW UB7 — 132 C1
**Queens Club Gdns** WKENS W14 — 14 B10
**Queens Ct** BELMT SM2 * — 221 K7
SL SL1 * — 129 L8
**Queenscourt** WBLY HA9 — 115 K9
**Queens Crs** WEY KT13 — 216 F2
WOKS/MYFD GU22 — 232 C7
**Queen's Crs** DORK RH4 * — 272 C7
RCHPK/HAM TW10 — 177 L1
STALE/WH AL4 — 38 C1
**Queens Down Rd** CLPT E5 — 120 A4
**Queen's Dr** ABLGY WD5 — 54 C8
**Queens Dr** BRYLDS KT5 — 199 M7
LEY E10 — 120 G5
LHD/OX KT22 — 218 B7
**Queen's Dr** CHES/WCR EN8 — 62 F10
EA W5 — 135 L4
FSBYPK N4 — 119 J3
GODL GU7 — 266 C10
GUW GU2 — 249 L3
RSEV TN14 — 247 K6
THDIT KT7 — 198 B8
**The Queen's Dr** RKW/CH/CXG WD3 — 71 J10
**Queens Elm Sq** CHEL SW3 — 15 L8
**Queens Farm Rd** GVE DA12 — 191 P5
**Queens Gdns** HDN NW4 — 116 F3
RAIN RM13 — 144 A4
RDART DA2 — 188 A4
UPMR RM14 — 126 C4
**Queen's Gdns** BAY/PAD W2 — 9 H5
CHONG CM5 — 45 J4
CRAWE RH10 — 283 P7
CROY/NA CR0 — 203 L4
HAT AL10 — 40 D4
HHNE HP2 — 35 P5
PEND EN3 — 80 B8
**Queens Ga** SKENS SW7 * — 14 F8
EN EN1 — 79 M10
LHD/OX KT22 — 236 D1
MTCM CR4 — 202 A1
**Queen's Ga** SKENS SW7 — 14 F4
**Queens Gate Gdns** PUT/ROE SW15 — 156 G10
**Queen's Gate Gdns** SKENS SW7 — 14 E6
**Queens Gate Ms** SKENS SW7 — 15 L5
**Queen's Gate Ms** SKENS SW7 — 15 L5
**Queen's Gate Pl** SKENS SW7 — 15 L5
**Queen's Gate Place Ms** SKENS SW7 * — 15 L5
**Queen's Gate Ter** SKENS SW7 — 15 L5
**Queens Gv** ABLGY WD5 — 54 C8
STJWD NW8 — 3 N2
**Queen's Gv** STJWD NW8 — 3 N2
**Queen's Grove Rd** CHING E4 — 101 L1
**Queenshill Ldg** ASC SL5 — 192 A3
**Queen's Head St** IS N1 — 6 D1
**Queen's Hill Ri** ASC SL5 — 192 B3
**Queens Keep** TWK TW1 * — 176 F9
**Queensland Av** UED N18 — 99 M5
WIM/MER SW19 — 201 L1
**Queensland Rd** HOLWY N7 — 119 H1
**Queens La** ASHF TW15 — 157 M9
**Queen's La** MUSWH N10 — 118 B4
**Queensmead** STHWK SE1 — 19 N7
**Queensmead** DTCH/LGLY SL3 — 149 N7

**Queensmead** LHD/OX KT22 * — 218 B7
STJWD NW8 — 3 M1
**Queensmead** EW KT17 — 220 E6
**Queensmere Cl** WIM/MER SW19 — 178 G5
**Queensmere Rd** SL SL1 — 149 L1
WIM/MER SW19 — 178 G5
**Queen's Ms** BAY/PAD W2 — 8 F2
**Queensmill Rd** FUL/PGN SW6 — 156 G6
**Queens Pde** CEND/HSY/T N8 * — 119 J2
EA W5 * — 135 L8
FBAR/BDGN N11 * — 98 A6
HDN NW4 * — 116 E3
**Queens Parade Cl** FBAR/BDGN N11 — 98 A6
**Queens Park Gdns** FELT TW13 — 174 G6
**Queens Park Rd** CTHM CR3 — 241 M9
HARH RM3 — 105 L5
**Queens Pl** MRDN SM4 — 201 K4
WAT WD17 — 73 K7
**Queens Prom** KUT/HW KT1 — 199 H3
**Queens Ride** BARN SW13 — 156 E8
RCHPK/HAM TW10 — 177 L2
**Queens Rd** BAR EN5 — 76 C7
BELMT SM2 — 221 K6
BERK HP4 — 33 M4
CHOB/PIR GU24 — 230 D6
CSHM HP5 — 51 H6
EPP CM16 — 66 D1
ERITH DA8 — 164 F5
GVE DA12 — 190 F6
HARP AL5 — 20 A4
HORL RH6 — 280 B4
HYS/HAR UB3 — 132 B5
LOU IG10 — 82 C7
MRDN SM4 — 201 K4
SL SL1 — 129 L9
WARE SG12 — 26 E1
WDR/YW UB7 — 132 A4
WEY KT13 — 216 D2
**Queen's Rd** ASC SL5 — 192 C5
BARK IG11 — 142 F2
BECK BR3 — 203 H2
BKHH IG9 — 101 N3
BMLY BR1 — 205 M2
BRW CM14 — 107 H4
CHES/WCR EN8 — 62 D10
CHST BR7 — 184 E9
CROY/NA CR0 — 203 J6
DTCH/LGLY SL3 — 149 N7
EBAR EN4 — 76 G8
ED N9 — 100 C3
EGH TW20 — 172 C9
EN EN1 — 79 M8
FBAR/BDGN N11 — 98 F6
FELT TW13 — 175 J4
FNCH N3 — 97 M9
GU GU1 — 250 A10
HDN NW4 — 116 F3
HPTN TW12 — 175 N6
HSLW TW3 — 154 A9
KUTN/CMB KT2 — 177 M10
LEY E10 — 120 F5
MORT/ESHN SW14 — 156 A9
NWDGN UB2 — 153 L1
NWMAL KT3 — 200 D3
PECK SE15 — 160 B7
PLSTW E13 — 141 N3
RCHPK/HAM TW10 — 177 J1
THDIT KT7 — 198 B7
TWK TW1 — 176 B9
UED N18 — 99 P10
WALTH E17 — 139 J2
WAT WD17 — 73 K7
WDSR SL4 — 149 J9
WELL DA16 — 164 D3
WIM/MER SW19 — 179 K9
WLSDN NW10 — 119 H4
**Queen's Rd West** PLSTW E13 — 141 M4
**Queen's Rw** WALW SE17 — 18 G9
**Queens Sq** CRAWE RH10 — 283 N7
**The Queen's Sq** HHNE HP2 — 36 A6
**Queens Ter** ISLW TW7 — 154 F10
PLSTW E13 — 141 N3
THDIT KT7 — 198 B8
WCHPL E1 * — 140 B6
**Queen's Ter** ISLW TW7 — 154 F10
**Queens Terrace Cots** HNWL W7 * — 135 L3
**Queensthorpe Ms** SYD SE26 * — 182 C7
**Queensthorpe Rd** SYD SE26 — 182 C7
**Queenstown Gdns** RAIN RM13 — 144 C8
**Queenstown Rd** VX/NE SW8 — 16 G10
**Queen St** BRW CM14 — 107 H6
BXLYHN DA7 — 164 A6
CHERT KT16 — 195 K8
CROY/NA CR0 — 223 K1
ERITH DA8 — 164 E6
EXMO EC3V — 13 H7
GVE DA12 — 190 E2
KGLGY WD4 — 53 K7
MYFR/PICC W1J — 10 E9
ROMW/RG RM7 — 124 D3
SHGR GU5 — 270 D5
STALW/RED AL3 — 38 C1
STP EC4M — 12 E3
TOTM N17 — 99 P7
**Queen Street Pl** CANST EC4R — 12 F7
**Queensville Rd** BAL SW12 — 180 H1
**Queensway** BFN/LL DA15 — 185 K8
CHING E4 — 101 M1
CHONG CM5 — 45 L2
CROY/NA CR0 — 223 K5
ENC/FH EN2 — 79 L5
HHNE HP2 — 35 N6
POTB/CUF EN6 — 59 M6
RDKG RH5 — 271 H10
SUN TW16 — 197 J3
WWKM BR4 — 204 G2
**Queensway North** WOT/HER KT12 — 217 K1
**Queensway South** WOT/HER KT12 — 217 K1
**The Queensway** CFSP/GDCR SL9 — 110 A2
**Queens Well Av** TRDG/WHET N20 — 97 P4
**Queenswood Av** HPTN TW12 — 176 A7
HSLW TW3 — 153 N6
THHTH CR7 — 203 H3
WALTH E17 — 102 A10
WLGTN SM6 — 222 G3
WWKM BR4 — 225 H3
**Queenswood Crs** GSTN WD25 — 51 H9
**Queenswood Gdns** WAN E11 — 121 M8
**Queenswood Pk** FNCH N3 — 97 H2
**Queenswood Rd** BFN/LL DA15 — 185 L7
SYD SE26 — 182 C5
**Queen Victoria Av** ALP/SUD HA0 — 135 J2

**Queen Victoria St** BLKFR EC4V — 12 C7
WDSR SL4 — 149 K6
**Queen Victoria Ter** WAP E1W * — 140 A9
**Queen Victoria Wy** CHOB/PIR GU24 — 230 C5
**Quemerford Rd** HOLWY N7 — 118 G10
**Quendell Wk** HHNE HP2 — 35 P6
**Quendon Dr** WAB EN9 — 63 J1
**Quennell Cl** ASHTD KT21 — 237 L5
**Quennell Wy** RBRW/HUT CM15 — 107 N7
**Quentin Pl** LEW SE13 — 161 K9
**Quentin Rd** LEW SE13 — 161 K9
**Quentins Dr** BH/WHM TN16 — 244 E2
**Quentins Wk** BH/WHM TN16 * — 244 E2
**Quentin Wy** VW GU25 — 193 N4
**Quernmore Cl** BMLY BR1 — 183 M9
**Quernmore Rd** BMLY BR1 — 183 M9
FSBYPK N4 — 119 H4
**Questor** DART DA1 * — 187 N5
**Quex Ms** KIL/WHAMP NW6 — 2 C3
**Quex Rd** KIL/WHAMP NW6 — 2 C3
**Quickbeams** WDGE AL7 — 23 K2
**Quickberry Pl** AMSS HP7 * — 69 H5
**Quickley Brow** RKW/CH/CXG WD3 * — 70 F10
**Quickley La** RKW/CH/CXG WD3 — 70 F10
**Quickley Ri** RKW/CH/CXG WD3 — 70 G10
**Quickly Brow** RKW/CH/CXG WD3 * — 70 E10
**Quickmoor La** KGLGY WD4 — 53 L9
**Quick Rd** CHSWK W4 — 156 B4
**Quicks Rd** WIM/MER SW19 — 179 L10
**Quick St** IS N1 — 6 D6
**Quickswood** HAMP NW3 — 3 P3
**Quickwood Cl** RKW/CH/CXG WD3 — 71 J10
**Quiet Cl** ADL/WDHM KT15 — 215 K1
**Quiet Nook** HAYES BR2 — 206 A10
**Quill Hall La** AMS HP6 — 69 L3
**The Quillot** WOT/HER KT12 — 216 G2
FSBYPK N4 — 135 K5
**Quilp St** STHWK SE1 — 18 E1
**Quilter Cl** STMC/STPC BR5 — 207 N8
**Quilters Pl** ELTH/MOT SE9 — 184 F4
**Quilter St** BETH E2 — 7 N9
WOOL/PLUM SE18 — 163 J4
**Quinbrookes** SLN SL2 — 129 P8
**Quince Cl** ASC SL5 — 192 C4
**Quince Dr** CHOB/PIR GU24 — 230 G1
**Quince Rd** LEW SE13 — 160 G8
**Quinces Cft** HHW HP1 — 35 K4
**Quince Tree Cl** SOCK/AV RM15 — 147 H6
**Quincy Rd** EGH TW20 — 172 D8
**Quinnell Cl** WOOL/PLUM SE18 — 163 J4
**Quinta Dr** BAR EN5 — 76 E9
**Quintin Av** RYNPK SW20 — 201 H1
**Quintin Cl** BECK BR3 — 205 H3
HEST TW5 — 153 J6
WLGTN SM6 — 222 C1
**Quinton Cl** THDIT KT7 — 198 B8
**Quinton St** WAND/EARL SW18 — 179 N5
**Quintrell Cl** WOKN/KNAP GU21 — 231 N5
**Quixley St** POP/IOD E14 — 141 N9
**Quorn Rd** EDUL SE22 — 159 M10

## R

**Raans Rd** AMS HP6 — 69 L4
**Rabbit La** WOT/HER KT12 — 217 H4
**Rabbit Rw** KENS W8 * — 8 F3
**Rabbits Rd** EYN DA4 — 210 E2
MNPK E12 — 122 B9
**Rabies Heath Rd** REDH RH1 — 259 P10
**Rablus Pl** EYN DA4 * — 209 N6
**Rabournmead Dr** NTHLT UB5 — 113 M3
**Raby Rd** NWMAL KT3 — 200 A4
**Raby St** POP/IOD E14 * — 140 G8
**Raccoon Wy** HSLWW TW4 — 153 K8
**Racecourse Rd** HORL RH6 — 280 A8
**Racecourse Wy** HORL RH6 — 280 A8
**Racefield Cl** GVE DA12 — 191 P9
**Rachel Cl** BARK/HLT IG6 — 122 G2
**Rackham Cl** CRAWW RH11 — 283 N9
WELL DA16 — 164 E4
**Rackham Ms** STRHM/NOR SW16 — 180 D9
**Racton Rd** FUL/PGN SW6 — 14 E10
**Radbourne Av** EA W5 — 155 H3
**Radbourne Cl** CLPT E5 — 120 C2
**Radbourne Ct** KTN/HRWW/WS HA3 * — 114 G4
**Radbourne Crs** WALTH E17 — 121 P1
**Radbourne Rd** BAL SW12 — 180 D3
**Radburn Cl** HLWS CM18 — 47 K5
**Radcliffe Av** ENC/FH EN2 — 79 K5
WLSDN NW10 — 136 C4
**Radcliffe Gdns** CAR SM5 — 221 P4
**Radcliffe Rd** CROY/NA CR0 — 203 N9
KTN/HRWW/WS HA3 — 94 F10
STHWK SE1 — 19 K3
WCHMH N21 — 99 J2
**Radcliffe Sq** PUT/ROE SW15 — 178 G2
**Radcliffe Wy** NTHLT UB5 — 133 L5
**Radcot Av** DTCH/LGLY SL3 — 150 E2
**Radcot St** LBTH SE11 — 18 A9
**Raddington Rd** NKENS W10 * — 8 B4
**Radfield Dr** RDART DA2 — 188 B3
**Radfield Wy** BFN/LL DA15 — 185 J6
**Radford Est** WLSDN NW10 — 136 D1
**Radford Rd** LEW SE13 — 183 H2
**Radford Wy** BARK IG11 — 143 H5
**Radius Pk** EBED/NFELT TW14 * — 152 C10
**Radland Rd** CAN/RD E16 — 141 M8
**Rad La** SHGR GU5 — 270 G8
**Radlet Av** SYD SE26 — 182 A5
**Radlett Cl** FSTGT E7 — 141 L1
**Radlett La** RAD WD7 — 57 H7
**Radlett Park Rd** RAD WD7 — 3 N6
**Radlett Pl** STJWD NW8 — 3 N2
**Radlett Rd** GSTN WD25 — 74 B5
LCOL/BKTW AL2 — 56 D5
WAT WD17 — 73 K7
**Radley Av** GDMY/SEVK IG3 — 123 J2
**Radley Cl** EBED/NFELT TW14 — 160 C1
**Radley Ct** BERM/RHTH SE16 — 160 C1
**Radley Gdns** KTN/HRWW/WS HA3 — 115 K2
**Radley Ms** KENS W8 — 14 B3
**Radley's La** SWFD E18 — 101 M10
**Radley Sq** CLPT E5 * — 120 B7
**Radley Ter** CAN/RD E16 * — 141 J7
**Radlix Rd** LEY E10 — 120 F6
**Radnor Av** HRW HA1 — 114 D4
WELL DA16 — 185 H1
**Radnor Cl** CHST BR7 — 185 P2
MTCM CR4 — 202 G5
**Radnor Ct** REDH RH1 — 257 P10
**Radnor Crs** REDBR IG4 — 122 C3
WOOL/PLUM SE18 — 163 P6
**Radnor Gdns** EN EN1 — 79 M4
TWK TW1 — 176 B5
**Radnor Hall** BORE WD6 * — 75 H7
**Radnor Ms** BAY/PAD W2 — 9 L5
**Radnor Pl** BAY/PAD W2 — 9 M5
**Radnor Rd** HRW HA1 — 114 C4
KIL/WHAMP NW6 — 2 A4
PECK SE15 — 159 H6
TWK TW1 — 176 B6
WEY KT13 — 196 B10
**Radnor St** FSBYE EC1V — 6 F9
**Radnor Ter** WKENS W14 — 14 G1
**Radnor Wk** CHEL SW3 — 15 P9

CROY/NA CR0 ....................204 D7
Radnor Wy DTCH/LGLY SL3 ...150 B3
WLSDN NW10 ....................135 N6
Radolphs KWD/TDW/WH KT20 .238 G8
Radstock Av
KTN/HRWW/WS HA3 .............114 F1
Radstock Cl FBAR/BDGN N11 ...98 B6
Radstock St BTSEA SW11 * ......157 N6
WOKS/MYFD ......................232 C4
Raeburn Gdns BAR EN5 ............76 B3
Raeburn Cl GLDGN NW11 .........117 M4
KUT/HW KT1 .....................177 J10
Radstone Ct
WOKS/MYFD GU22 ...............232 C4
Raeburn Cl GLDGN NW11 .........117 M4
Raeburn Rd BFN/LL DA15 ........185 H2
EDGW HA8 ........................114 B2
Radford WD23 ....................132 E4
Raeside Cl BEAC HP9 ..............89 H7
Rafford Wy BMLY BR1 .............205 N2
Ragged Hall La
LCOL/BKTW AL2 ...................37 L10
Ragge Wy BGR/WK TN15 .........247 N6
Ragglesswood CHST BR7 ..........206 D7
Rag Hill Rd HA TN16 ..............244 A7
Raglan Av CHES/WCR EN8 .........62 C10
Raglan Cl HSLWW TW4 .............154 B7
REIC RH2 ........................257 M8
Raglan Cl SAND/SEL CR2 ..........223 J2
Raglan Gdns OXHEY WD19 ..........93 J2
Raglan Rd BELV DA17 .............164 A3
EN EN1 ..........................99 M1
HAYES BR2 .......................205 P4
REIG RH2 ........................257 L8
WALTH E17 .......................121 H3
WOKN/KNAP GU21 ................231 K4
WOOL/PLUM SE18 ...................4 F7
Raglan Ter KTTN NW5 ............247 M4
Raglan Wy WALTH E17 * ..........121 H3
Raglan Wy NTHLT UB5 .............134 B1
Ragley Cl ACT W3 .................155 N7
Rags La CHESW EN7 ...............61 M3
Ragstone Rd SL SL1 ..............149 J7
Ragstones BGR/WK TN15 ..........247 N6
Rahn Rd EPP CM16 .................65 M7
Raider Cl ROMW/RG RM7 .........104 C9
Raikes La RDKG RH5 ..............271 J8
Railey Rd CRAWE RH10 ...........283 P7
Railshead Rd ISLW TW7 ..........154 C10
HNHL SE24 ......................181 H9
Railway Ap CHERT KT16 * ........195 J8
FSBYPK N4 ......................119 H4
HRW HA1 ........................114 E2
STHWK SE1 ........................12 G9
WLCTN SM6 * ....................222 C3
Railway Ar BRXN/ST SW9 ..........159 H10
Railway Ms BERM/RHTH SE16 ......160 B1
Railway Cots BNSTD SM7 * .......221 J10
HMSMTH W6 ......................156 F1
OXTED RH8 ......................261 M9
SRTFD E15 * ....................141 K4
WIM/MER SW19 ...................179 L7
Railway Pl BELV DA17 ...........164 B6
HERT/BAY SG13 * ..................25 M5
Railway Rd CHES/WCR EN8 .........62 E9
TEDD TW11 .......................176 D7
Railway Side BARN SW13 .........156 B9
Railway Station Whf
LEY E10 * ......................120 D6
Railway St CHDH RM6 ............123 M6
GVW DA11 .......................189 M1
HERT/BAY SG13 ...................25 L8
IS N1 .............................5 M8
Railway Ter BH/WHM TN16 ........262 C4
FELT TW13 ......................175 H4
KGLGY WD4 .......................54 B3
LEW SE13 .......................182 C1
SLN SL2 ........................129 L10
STA TW18 .......................172 G8
WALTH E17 ......................101 H3
Railway Vw DTCH/LGLY SL3 .......150 C9
Rainborough Cl WBLY HA9 .........135 H1
Rainbow Av POP/IOD E14 .........160 C4
Rainbow Ct OXHEY WD19 ...........73 K10
WOKN/KNAP GU21 ................231 K2
Rainbow Quay
BERM/RHTH SE16 ................160 C8
Rainbow Rd CDW/CHF RM16 ........167 N8
HLWE CM19 .......................30 F8
PUR RM19 .......................166 D2
Rainbow St CMBW SE5 ............159 N4
Rainer Cl CHES/WCR EN8 ...........62 C5
Raine St WAP E1W ................140 C4
Rainham Cl BTSEA SW11 .........180 A2
ELTH/MOT SE9 ...................185 H2
Rainham Rd RAIN RM13 ...........145 H5
WLSDN NW10 .....................136 F3
Rainham Rd North
DAGE RM10 ......................124 C7
Rainham Rd South
DAGE RM10 ......................144 B1
Rainhill Wy BOW E3 ..............140 F1
Rainsborough Av DEPT SE8 ........160 D3
Rainsford Rd WLSDN NW10 ........135 M5
Rainsford Wy HCH RM12 ..........125 H6
Rainton Rd CHARL SE7 ...........161 M4
Rainville Rd HMSMTH W6 .........156 F5
Raisins Hl PIN HA5 ..............113 J1
Raith Av STHGT/OAK N14 ..........98 E4
YEAD UB4 .......................133 J7
Raleigh Cl ERITH DA8 ...........164 G5
HDN NW4 ........................116 F3
PIN HA5 ........................113 L5
RSLP HA4 .......................112 C7
SL SL1 .........................128 F10
Raleigh Ct CRAWE RH10 ..........284 E9
STA TW18 .......................173 K7
Raleigh Dr BRYLDS KT5 ..........199 P8
ESH/CLAY KT10 ..................218 C2
HORL RH6 .......................281 H4
TRDG/WHET N20 ...................97 P4
Raleigh Gdns
BRXS/STRHM SW2 * ...............180 G2
MTCM CR4 .......................202 A2
Raleigh Ms IS N1 * ...............6 D2
ORP BR6 * ......................227 L7
Raleigh Rd CEND/HSY/T N8 .......119 H7
EN EN1 ..........................79 L8
FELT TW13 ......................174 C5
NWDGN UB2 ......................153 M4
PGE/AN SE20 ....................182 C10
RCH/KEW TW9 ....................155 L9

CHSWK W4 .......................156 A2
WATN WD24 ......................183 L6
Ramney Dr PEND EN3 ..............80 D2
Ramones Ter MTCM CR4 * .........202 A3
Ramornie Cl WOT/HER KT12 .......217 N1
The Ramparts STALW/RED AL3 ......38 C5
Rampart St WCHPL E1 ............140 B8
Ram Pas KUT/HW KT1 .............199 J2
Rampayne St PIM SW1V ............17 J7
Rampton Cl CHING E4 ............100 F4
Ramsay Rd BROX EN10 .............44 D7
Ramsay Gdns HARH RM3 ...........105 J9
Ramsay Rd ACT W3 ...............155 P2
BFOR EN20 ......................212 D2
FSTGT E7 .......................121 L9
Ramsden Rd STAL AL1 .............38 D7
Ramscote La CSHM HP5 ............66 G2
Ramscroft Cl ED N9 .............99 M1
Ramsdale Rd TOOT SW17 .........180 B8
Ramsden Dr CRW RM5 ............104 B8
Ramsden Ga BAL SW12 * ..........180 B3
Ramsden Rd
ERITH DA8 ......................164 G6
FBAR/BDGN N11 ...................98 A6
ORP BR6 ........................207 L5
STMC/STPC BR5 ..................207 M8
Ramsey Cl BRKMPK AL9 ............59 N3
CDALE/KGS NW9 ..................116 C4
GFD/PVL UB6 ....................114 C10
HORL RH6 .......................280 A4
STAL AL1 ........................38 F8
Ramsey Ct SLN SL2 ..............128 C3
Ramsey Lodge Ct STAL AL1 ........38 D5
Ramsey Pl CTHM CR3 .............241 M9
Ramsey Rd THHTH CR7 ............202 G6
Ramsey St BETH E2 ...............13 M1
Ramsey Wk IS N1 .................6 G2
Ramsey Wy STHGT/OAK N14 .........98 D1
Ramsgate Cl CAN/RD E16 .........141 N10
Ramsgate St HACK E8 .............7 J1
Ramsgill Ap GNTH/NBYPK IG2 ......123 J9
Ramsgill Dr GNTH/NBYPK IG2 ......123 J9
Rams Gv CHDH RM6 ...............123 P2
Ramson Ri HNW HP1 ...............35 H7
Ramulis Dr YEAD UB4 ............133 M4
Ramus Wood Av ORP BR6 ..........227 L8
Rancliffe Gdns ELTH/MOT SE9 ....162 B10
Rancliffe Rd EHAM E6 ...........142 A4
Randal Crs REIG RH2 ............275 K2
Randall Av CRICK NW2 ...........116 B7
Randall Cl BTSEA SW11 ..........157 P7
DTCH/LGLY SL3 ..................150 C4
ERITH DA8 ......................164 D5
Randall Dr HCH RM12 ............125 K4
Randall Pl GNWCH SE10 ..........161 H6
Randall Rd LBTH SE11 ............17 M7
LBTH SE11 ......................17 N6
Randalls Crs LHD/OX KT22 .......236 F6
Randalls Pk Av
LHD/OX KT22 ....................236 F7
Randalls Ride HHNE HP2 ..........35 H4
Randalls Rd LHD/OX KT22 ........236 D6
Randalls Wk LCOL/BKTW AL2 .......55 N1
Randell's Rd IS N1 ..............5 M5
Randisbourne Gdns CAT SE6 * ....182 C6
Randle Rd RCHPK/HAM TW10 .......177 H7
Randlesdown Rd CAT SE6 .........182 F7
Randle La RSEV TN14 ............227 N10
Randolf Rd HAYES BR2 ...........206 C9
Randolph Av MV/WKIL W9 ..........2 C8
Randolph Ap CAN/RD E16 .........141 P9
Randolph Cl BXLYHN DA7 .........164 D9
COB KT11 .......................235 P1
KUTN/CMB KT2 * .................177 P2
WOKN/KNAP GU21 ................231 K3
Randolph Crs KIL/WHAMP NW6 ......2 C8
Randolph Gdns
KIL/WHAMP NW6 ...................2 C9
Randolph Ms DTCH/LGLY SL3 ......150 B9
Randolph Ms MV/WKIL W9 ..........9 J7
EW KT17 ........................220 C10
MV/WKIL W9 ......................9 J7
STHL UB1 .......................153 N1
WALTH E17 * ....................120 C3
Randolph St CAMTN NW1 ...........4 G4
Randon Cl RYLN/HDSTN HA2 ........94 A10
Ranelagh WDSR SL4 * .............170 A4
Ranelagh Av BARN SW13 ..........156 D8
Ranelagh Cl EDGW HA8 ............95 N6
Ranelagh Dr EDGW HA8 ............95 N6
TWK TW1 ........................154 C10
Ranelagh Gdns CHSWK W4 * .......155 P6
FUL/PGN SW6 ....................157 H9
GVW DA11 .......................190 C3
IL IG1 .........................122 D6
WAN E11 ........................121 H4
Ranelagh Gv BCVA SW1W ...........16 D7
Ranelagh Pl NWMAL KT3 ..........200 B3
Ranelagh Rd ALP/SUD HA0 ........115 J10
EA W5 ..........................155 J1
EHAM E6 ........................142 D7
HNHE HP2 ........................36 C6
PIM SW1V ........................17 H8
REDH RH1 .......................257 P10
SRTFD E15 ......................141 K4
STHL UB1 .......................153 H1
TOTM N17 .......................119 M1
WAN E11 ........................121 H9
WDGN N22 * .....................98 C9
WLSDN NW10 .....................136 C4
Ranfurly Rd SUT SM1 .............201 N9
Rangefield Rd BMLY BR1 .........183 K8
Rangemoor Rd
SEVS/STOTM N15 .................119 N3
Range Rd GVE DA12 ..............190 G3
Rangers Rd BKHH IG9 ............101 M1
Range Wy SHPTN TW17 ............196 B7
Rangeworth Pl BFN/LL DA15 * ....185 J6
Rangoon St TWRH EC3N * ..........13 N3
Rankin Cl CDALE/KGS NW9 ........116 B1
Ranleigh Gdns BXLYHN DA7 .......164 A6
Ranleigh Wk HARP AL5 ............20 C1
Ranmere St BAL SW12 ............180 C4
Ranmoor Cl HRW HA1 .............114 C2
Ranmoor Gdns HRW HA1 ...........114 C2
Ranmore Av CROY/NA CR0 .........203 N10
Ranmore Cl REDH RH1 ............258 E5
Ranmore Common Rd
RDKG RH5 .......................254 C10
Ranmore Pth STMC/STPC BR5 .....202 K4
Ranmore Pl WEY KT13 * ..........216 D2
Ranmore Rd BELMT SM2 ...........272 A1
DORK RH4 .......................272 F5
RDKG RH5 .......................254 D10
Rannoch Cl EDGW HA8 ............95 N3
Rannoch Rd HMSMTH W6 ...........156 F5
Rannock Av CDALE/KGS NW9 .......116 A5
Ranskill Rd BORE WD6 ...........75 N2
Ransom Cl OXHEY WD19 ............93 K1
Ransom Rd CHARL SE7 ............161 P4
Rant Meadow HHS/BOV HP3 ........36 H1
Ranulf Cl HLWE CM17 ............29 M5
Ranulf Rd CRICK NW2 ............116 C2
Ranwell Cl BOW E3 * .............141 M5
Ranworth Av HOD EN11 ...........26 C9
Ranworth Rd ED N9 ..............99 J3
Ranworth Gdns
POTB/CUF EN6 ...................58 G7
Ranwoth Rd ED N9 ...............100 B3
Ranyard Cl CHSGTN KT9 ..........199 L1
Raphael Av ROM RM1 * ...........105 H1
Raphael Cl KUT/HW KT1 ..........198 G1
RAD WD7 .........................57 K8

Raphael Dr THDIT KT7 ...........198 E8
Raphael Rd GVE DA12 ............190 E2
Raphael St SKENS SW7 ............16 A3
Rapier Cl PUR RM19 .............165 N5
Rapley's Fld CHOB/PIR GU24 .....230 D9
Rapsley La WOKN/KNAP GU21 ......230 G4
Rashleigh Wy EYN DA4 ...........210 B4
Rasper Rd TRDG/WHET N20 .........97 M3
Rastell Av BRXS/STRHM SW2 ......180 E5
Ratcliffe Cl LEE/GVPK SE12 .....183 M3
UX/CGN UB8 .....................224 E4
Ratcliffe Cross St WCHPL E1 * ..140 C8
Ratcliff Rd FSTGT E7 ...........121 P10
Rathbone Market
CAN/RD E16 .....................141 L7
Rathbone Pl FITZ W1T .............11 J4
Rathbone Sq CROY/NA CR0 * ......223 K1
Rathbone St CAN/RD E16 .........141 L7
FITZ W1T ........................11 H4
Rathcoole Av
CEND/HSY/T N8 ..................118 G3
Rathcoole Gdns
CEND/HSY/T N8 ..................118 G3
Rathfern Rd CAT SE6 ............182 K4
Rathgar Av WEA W13 .............134 C10
Rathgar Cl FNCH N3 ..............97 J10
REDH RH1 .......................276 B5
Rathgar Rd BRXN/ST SW9 .........159 J9
Rathlin HHS/BOV HP3 .............36 C8
Rathlin Rd CRAWW RH11 ..........283 J6
Rathmell Dr CLAP SW4 ...........180 C2
Rathmore Rd CHARL SE7 ..........161 N4
GVW DA11 .......................190 D3
Rat's La LOU IG10 ...............81 H4
Rattray Rd BRXS/STRHM SW2 ......159 H10
Ratty's La HOD EN11 .............27 K6
Raul Rd PECK SE15 ..............159 P8
Raveley St KTTN NW5 ............118 D9
Ravel Rd SOCK/AV RM15 ..........146 B3
Ravel Rd SOCK/AV RM15 ..........146 C8
Raven Cl RKW/CH/CXG WD3 .........91 M1
Raven Ct HAT AL10 ..............40 C6
Ravencroft Crs ELTH/MOT SE9 ....184 C6
Ravendale Rd SUN TW16 .........196 C2
Ravenet St BTSEA SW11 ..........158 C7
Ravenfield EGH TW20 ............170 N9
Ravenfield Rd TOOT SW17 .......180 H5
WIM/MER SW19 ...................179 P3
Ravens La CRAWW RH11 ...........283 M5
Ravenoak Wy CHIG IG7 ...........103 H6
Ravenor Park Rd
GFD/PVL UB6 ....................134 A5
Ravens Ait SURB KT6 ............199 H3
Ravensbourne Av HAYES BR2 ......205 J5
STWL/WRAY TW19 .................173 P4
Ravensbourne Gdns
EMPK RM11 ......................124 G1
WEA W13 ........................134 C7
Ravensbourne Pk CAT SE6 ........182 D3
Ravensbourne Pk Crs
CAT SE6 ........................182 E3
TWK TW1 ........................177 H7
Ravensbourne Pl LEW SE13 .......161 P10
Ravensbourne Rd BMLY BR1 .......205 M8
CAT SE6 ........................182 E3
DART DA1 .......................168 E3
GNTH/NBYPK IG2 .................165 H9
TWK TW1 ........................177 H7
Ravensbury Gv MTCM CR4 .........201 M5
Ravensbury La MTCM CR4 .........201 M5
Ravensbury Rd
STMC/STPC BR5 ..................207 L2
WAND/EARL SW18 .................179 L5
Ravensbury Ter
WAND/EARL SW18 .................179 L5
Ravenscar Rd BMLY BR1 ..........183 K7
SURB KT6 .......................211 P1
Ravenscourt CDALE/KGS NW9 ......96 C10
EN EN1 ..........................79 N6
HAYES BR2 ......................205 L2
REDH RH1 .......................258 A9
SUN TW16 .......................196 A10
WOKN/KNAP GU21 ................231 H2
Ravenscourt Av HMSMTH W6 .......156 D7
Ravenscourt Dr DEN/HRF UB9 .....112 C5
HCH RM12 .......................125 N1
Ravenscourt Gdns
HMSMTH W6 ......................156 C7
Ravenscourt Gv HCH RM12 ........125 M7
Ravenscourt Pk HMSMTH W6 .......156 C6
Ravenscourt Pl HMSMTH W6 .......156 D7
Ravenscourt Rd HMSMTH W6 .......156 D7
STMC/STPC BR5 ..................207 K3
Ravenscourt Sq HMSMTH W6 .......156 C6
Ravenscraig Rd
FBAR/BDGN N11 ...................98 C5
Ravenscroft BROX EN10 * ..........44 E6
GSTN WD25 .......................73 N1
Ravenscroft Av GLDGN NW11 ......117 J5
WBLY HA9 .......................115 K6
Ravenscroft Cl CAN/RD E16 ......141 M7
Ravenscroft Cots BAR EN5 * ......77 K10
Ravenscroft Pk BAR EN5 ..........75 P4
Ravenscroft Rd BECK BR3 ........204 B2
CAN/RD E16 .....................141 M7
CHSWK W4 .......................155 P3
PGE/AN SE20 ....................204 B2
WEY KT13 .......................216 D7
Ravenscroft St BETH E2 ...........7 M8
Ravensdale Av
NFNCH/WDSPK N12 ................97 H1
Ravensdale Gdns NRWD SE19 ......181 M5
Ravensdale Rd HSLWW TW4 ........153 N6
STNW/STAM N16 ..................119 N5
Ravensdon St LBTH SE11 ..........17 N9
Ravensfield DAGW RM9 ...........123 N9
Ravensfield Cl DAGW RM9 ........123 N8
Ravens Fld DTCH/LGLY SL3 .......150 A1
Ravenshaw St
KIL/WHAMP NW6 ..................117 J10
Ravenshead Cl SAND/SEL CR2 .....224 B7
Ravenshill CHST BR7 ............206 E1
Ravenshurst Av HDN NW4 .........116 F2
Ravenside Cl UED N18 ...........100 G6
Ravens La BERK HP4 ..............34 A5
Ravenslea Rd BAL SW12 ..........180 A1
Ravensleigh Gdns BMLY BR1 * ....183 M8
Ravensmead CFSP/GDCR SL9 ........90 A3
Ravensmead Rd HAYES BR2 ........183 J10
Ravensmede Wy CHSWK W4 .........156 C1
Ravens Ms LEE/GVPK SE12 * ......183 M1
Ravens Wy LEE/GVPK SE12 ........183 M1
Ravens Wold PUR/KEN CR8 ........241 K1
Ravenswood Av SURB KT6 .........211 N4
WWKM BR4 .......................205 P4
Ravenswood Cl COB KT11 .........235 P5
CRW RM5 ........................104 C6
Ravenswood Ct
KUTN/CMB KT2 ...................177 P9
WOKS/MYFD GU22 * ...............232 C1
Ravenswood Crs
RYLN/HDSTN HA2 .................113 N7
WWKM BR4 .......................205 H8
Ravenswood Gdns ISLW TW7 .......154 A7
Ravenswood Pk NTHWD HA6 .........75 H8
Ravenswood Rd BAL SW12 .........180 C1
CROY/NA CR0 ....................223 J1
WALTH E17 ......................121 J1
Ravensworth Rd
ELTH/MOT SE9 ...................184 C7

SLN SL2 ........................128 F5
NTHLT UB5 ......................133 N3
UPMR RM14 ......................126 E7
Rectory Gn CLAP SW4 ............158 D9
CROY/NA CR0 ....................203 J9
Rectory Gdns BECK BR3 ..........204 E1
Rectory Hl AMSS HP7 .............69 H5
Rectory La AMSS HP7 .............68 G5
ASHTD KT21 .....................237 L4
BERK HP4 ........................33 P5
BF/WBF KT14 ....................215 P4
BFOR EN20 ......................212 B4
BH/WHM TN16 ....................245 M10
BH/WHM TN16 ....................167 H4
BNSTD SM7 ......................240 A1
BRKHM/BTCW RH3 .................256 C8
BUSH WD23 ......................75 P10
CRAWW RH11 .....................283 J5
EDGW HA8 ........................96 C1
GT/LBKH KT23 ...................253 N2
LOU IG10 .......................82 D6
RAD WD7 .........................57 L9
RKW/CH/CXG WD3 .................71 K1
WOOL/PLUM SE18 .................162 G1
Rectory Orch WIM/MER SW19 ......179 H4
Rectory Pk SAND/SEL CR2 .......223 K9
Rectory Park Av NTHLT UB5 ......133 N5
Rectory Pl CHST BR7 * ..........206 F1
WOOL/PLUM SE18 .................162 D3
Rectory Rd BARN SW13 ...........156 D8
BECK BR3 .......................204 F1
COUL/CHIP CR5 ..................257 N1
DAGE RM10 ......................124 B1
GRAYS RM17 .....................168 A3
HAYES BR2 ......................226 A4
HSLWW TW4 ......................153 J8
KWD/TDW/WH KT20 ................256 G9
MNPK E12 .......................122 C10
NWDGN UB2 ......................153 N2
RKW/CH/CXG WD3 .................91 N1
SEVS/STOTM N15 .................119 N7
STNW/STAM N16 ..................119 N7
SUT SM1 ........................201 K10
SWCM DA10 ......................189 K3
TIL RM18 .......................168 G5
WALTH E17 ......................120 C3
WGCW AL8 ........................22 F1
Rectory Sq WCHPL E1 ............140 C7
Rectory Wd HCDN/ICK UB10 .......112 C7
Rectory Wd WARE SG12 ............28 C10
Reculver Ms UED N18 .............99 K4
Reculver Rd BERM/RHTH SE16 .....160 B4
Red Anchor Cl CHEL SW3 * .........15 M10
Redan Pl BAY/PAD W2 ..............8 D7
Redan Rd WKENS W14 .............156 C10
Redan St WKENS W14 .............156 C10
Redan Ter CMBW SE5 .............159 J8
Redbarn Cl PUR/KEN CR8 .........223 J7
Red Barracks Rd
WOOL/PLUM SE18 .................162 C3
Redberry Gv SYD SE26 ...........182 B6
Redbourne Av FNCH N3 ...........97 K9
Redbourne Dr THMD SE28 .........143 M9
Redbourn Rd HHNE HP2 ............35 J2
STALW/RED AL3 ...................37 M4
Redbridge Gdns CMBW SE5 ........159 M6
Redbridge La East REDBR IG4 ....122 A4
Redbridge La West WAN E11 ......122 A10
Redburn St CHEL SW3 ............16 A9
Redbury Cl RAIN RM13 ...........145 H10
Redcar Cl NTHLT UB5 ............114 A10
Redcar Rd HARH RM3 .............105 N6
Redcar St CMBW SE5 .............159 K6
Redcastle Cl WAP E1W ...........140 D9
Red Cedars Rd ORP BR6 ..........207 N1
Redchurch St BETH E2 ............13 N1
WCHPL E1 ........................13 L1
Redcliffe Cl ECT SW5 * ..........14 U8
Redcliffe Gdns IL IG1 ..........122 C6
WBPTN SW10 .....................15 L5
Redcliffe Ms WBPTN SW10 .........15 L5
Redcliffe Pl WBPTN SW10 .........14 G7
Redcliffe Rd WBPTN SW10 .........14 G5
Redcliffe Sq WBPTN SW10 .........14 F5
Redcliffe St WBPTN SW10 .........14 F6
Redclose Av MRDN SM4 ...........201 L5
Redclyffe Rd PLSTW E13 .........141 P3
Redcote Pl DORK RH4 ............255 H5
Red Cottage Ms
DTCH/LGLY SL3 ..................149 P2
Red Ct SL SL1 ..................129 K10
Redcourt WOKS/MYFD GU22 ........232 C1
Redcroft Rd STHL UB1 ...........134 B9
Redcross Wy STHWK SE1 ...........18 F1
Redden Court Rd HARH RM3 .......105 M1
Reddings Av BUSH WD23 ...........74 A9
The Reddings BORE WD6 ..........75 J7
MLHL NW7 ........................97 J4
Reddington Cl SAND/SEL CR2 .....223 J8
Reddington Dr
DTCH/LGLY SL3 ..................150 D2
Reddins Rd PECK SE15 ...........159 P5
Redditch Ct HHNE HP2 * ..........36 A6
Reddons Rd BECK BR3 ............182 D10
Reddown Rd COUL/CHIP CR5 .......240 F6
Reddy Rd ERITH DA8 .............164 J6
Rede Ct WEY KT13 ...............196 C10
Redehall Rd HORL RH6 ...........281 J6
Rede Pl BAY/PAD W2 ..............8 C6
Redfern Av HSLWW TW4 ...........175 P5
Redfern Cl UX/CGN UB8 ..........131 M4
Redfern Gdns CHDH RM6 ..........122 D1
Redfern Rd CAT SE6 .............183 H3
WLSDN NW10 .....................137 H3
Redfield La ECT SW5 * ...........14 C5
Redfield Ms ECT SW5 * ...........14 C5
Redford Av COUL/CHIP CR5 .......240 C5
THHTH CR7 ......................204 F3
WLGTN SM6 ......................222 G5
Redford Cl FELT TW13 ...........174 B5
Redford Rd WDSR SL4 ............148 C5
Redford Wk IS N1 * ..............6 D1
Redgate Dr HAYES BR2 ...........205 N9
Redgate Ter PUT/ROE SW15 .......178 G3
Redgrave Cl CROY/NA CR0 ........203 N4
Redgrave Dr CRAWE RH10 .........284 E8
Redgrave Rd PUT/ROE SW15 .......157 H9
Redgrave Ter BETH E2 * ...........7 P10
Redhall Ct CTHM CR3 ............241 M4
Redhall La RKW/CH/CXG WD3 .......71 P5
Red Hall Ter GNTH/NBYPK IG2 ....135 M9
Redheath Cl GSTN WD25 ..........73 N4
Red Hi CHST BR7 ................185 H10
Redhill Dr EDGW HA8 ............116 C1
Redhill St CAMTN NW1 .............4 F6
Red House Cl BEAC HP9 ...........88 F3
Red House La BXLYHS DA6 ........165 N10
WOT/HER KT12 ...................197 H9
Redhouse Rd BH/WHM TN16 .......243 P9
Red House Rd CROY/NA CR0 ......203 H5
Red House Sq IS N1 * ............6 E1
Redington Gdns HAMP NW3 ........117 J9
Redington Rd HAMP NW3 .........117 H8

HAT AL10 ........................40 E4
NTHLT UB5 ......................133 N3
UPMR RM14 ......................126 E7
Redland Gdns
E/WMO/HCT KT8 * ................197 G8
Redlands COUL/CHIP CR5 .........240 G5
Redlands La RDKG RH5 ...........272 E8
Redlands Rd PEND EN3 ...........80 D5
SEV TN13 .......................256 G10
Redlands Wy
BRXS/STRHM SW2 .................180 A5
Red La ESH/CLAY KT10 ...........218 F3
OXTED RH8 ......................261 N9
RDKG RH5 .......................273 M7
Redleaf Cl BXLYHN DA7 ..........164 A5
LHD/OX KT22 ....................236 D10
Redleaves Av ASHF TW15 .........174 C9
Redlees Cl ISLW TW7 ............154 F10
Red Lion Ct GSTN WD25 ..........74 A3
STMC/STPC BR5 ..................207 M6
WALW SE17 * ....................18 G9
Red Lion Cl FLST/FETLN EC4A * ...12 E1
HSLW TW3 .......................154 A9
Red Lion Crs HLWE CM17 .........47 M5
Red Lion La CHOB/PIR GU24 ......213 K5
HHS/BOV HP3 ....................54 A2
HLWE CM17 ......................47 M3
RKW/CH/CXG WD3 .................71 K1
WOOL/PLUM SE18 .................162 D1
Red Lion Pde PIN HA5 ...........113 M1
Red Lion Pl
WOOL/PLUM SE18 .................162 D3
Red Lion Rd CHOB/PIR GU24 ......213 K5
SURB KT6 .......................199 L8
Red Lion Rw CMBW SE5 ...........18 F10
Red Lion St GINN WC1R ..........11 N1
WAND/EARL SW18 .................179 K1
Red Lion St CSHM HP5 ...........50 C8
GINN WC1R ......................11 N4
Red Lion Yd
MYFR/PKLN W1K * .................10 C7
Red Lodge Cl BXLY DA5 ..........186 A6
Red Lodge Gdns BAR HP4 ..........33 M6
Red Lodge Rd BXLY DA5 .........186 A6
WWKM BR4 .......................205 H8
Redman Cl NTHLT UB5 ............133 J1
Redmans La RSEV TN14 ...........228 G3
Redman's Rd WCHPL E1 ...........140 B7
Redmead La WAP E1W * ............13 N10
Redmead Rd HYS/HAR UB3 ........152 F3
Redmore Rd HMSMTH W6 ...........156 E9
Red Oak Cl ORP BR6 .............206 E10
Red Pl MYFR/PKLN W1K * ..........10 C7
Redpoll Wy ERITH DA18 ..........163 N2
Red Post Hl HNHL SE24 ..........181 L1
Redricks La EPP CM16 ............29 J5
Redriffe Rd PLSTW E13 ..........141 L4
Redriff Rd BERM/RHTH SE16 ......160 C2
ROMW/RG RM7 ....................104 C10
Redroofs Cl BECK BR3 ...........204 C1
Redruth Cl WDGN N22 ............98 G8
Redruth Gdns ESH/CLAY KT10 ....218 C5
Redruth Rd HARH RM3 ...........105 N6
HOM E9 .........................140 B3
Redstart Cl CROY/NA CR0 ........225 J6
EHAM E6 ........................142 H7
NWCR SE14 * ....................160 G8
Redstone Ms REDH RH1 ...........276 B1
Redstone Hollow REDH RH1 .......276 B9
Redstone Mnr REDH RH1 .........258 B10
Redstone Pk REDH RH1 ..........258 B10
Redstone Rd REDH RH1 ..........276 B1
Redstone Rd CEND/HSY/T N8 .....118 G2
Red St GNFD SL3 ................189 L3
Redvers Rd WARL CR6 ............242 C4
WDGN N22 .......................99 H3
Redvers St IS N1 ................7 K9
Redwald Rd CLPT E5 .............120 C9
Redway Dr WHTN TW2 * ...........176 B3
Red Willow HLWW/ROY CM19 .......46 C4
Redwing Cl SAND/SEL CR2 .......224 C7
Redwing Gdns WOT/HER KT12 .....195 P7
Redwing Ms CMBW SE5 ............159 L6
Redwing Rd WLGTN SM6 ..........223 H7
Redwood Cha SOCK/AV RM15 ......147 N6
Redwood Cl BERM/RHTH SE16 .....140 D10
BFN/LL DA15 ....................185 K4
BOW E3 .........................140 F4
CRAWE RH10 .....................283 P5
HCDN/ICK UB10 ..................132 C4
OXHEY WD19 .....................93 K5
PUR/KEN CR8 ....................223 K10
STAL AL1 ........................39 H6
STHGT/OAK N14 ..................98 E6
Redwood Dr ASC SL5 ............192 G6
CRAWW RH11 .....................283 K4
HHS/BOV HP3 ....................35 P8
Redwood Gdns CHIG IG7 ..........103 K6
CHING E4 ........................86 C10
SL SL1 .........................129 J9
Redwood Gv EA W5 ...............155 H2
RGUE GU4 .......................268 F6
Redwood Ms ASHF TW15 * .........174 C9
SL SL1 .........................158 C9
Redwood Mt REIC RH2 ............257 K7
Redwood Pl BEAC HP9 ...........88 C10
Redwood Ri BORE WD6 ...........75 M3
Redwoods ADL/WDHM KT15 .........215 K3
HERT/WAT SG14 ..................25 K4
The Redwoods WDSR SL4 ..........149 J9
Redwood Wy BAR EN5 .............76 A7
Reece Ms SKENS SW7 .............15 L5
Reed Av ORP BR6 ...............207 H10
Reed Cl CAN/RD E16 ............141 M7
IVER SL0 .......................131 H8
LCOL/BKTW AL2 ..................57 J3
LEE/GVPK SE12 ..................183 M1
Reed Ct SWCM DA10 .............167 N10
Reed Dr REDH RH1 ...............276 B3
Reede Gdns DAGE RM10 ...........144 D1
Reede Rd DAGE RM10 .............144 C1
Reede Wy DAGE RM10 .............144 D1
Reedham Cl LCOL/BKTW AL2 .......55 P5
TOTM N17 .......................120 A2
Reedham Park Av
PUR/KEN CR8 ...................241 H2
Reedham St PECK SE15 ...........159 P8
Reedholm Vls
STNW/STAM N16 ..................119 L9
Reedings CRAWW RH11 ............282 D9
Reed Pl BF/WBF KT14 ...........215 H9
BTSEA SW11 .....................157 P10
CLAP SW4 .......................158 C10
SHPTN TW17 .....................196 A6
Reed Pond Wk GPK RM2 ...........105 N10
Reed Rd TOTM N17 ...............99 N10
Reeds Crs WATN WD24 ............73 K6
Reedsfield Cl ASHF TW15 ........174 C5
Reedsfield Rd ASHF TW15 ........174 E5
Reed's Pl CAMTN NW1 .............4 G3
The Reeds WGCE AL7 .............18 B7
Reedworth St LBTH SE11 ..........18 B6
Reenglass Rd STAN HA7 ..........95 N2
Rees Dr STAN HA7 ...............95 P5
Reesland Cl MNPK E12 ..........142 D7
Rees St IS N1 ...................6 F1
Reets Farm Cl
CDALE/KGS NW9 .................116 B4
Reeve Rd REIG RH2 .............275 N4
Reeves Av CDALE/KGS NW9 .......116 A5
Reeves Cnr CROY/NA CR0 .........203 J9
Reeves Ms SWLY BR8 ............208 E3
Reeves Ms MYFR/PKLN W1K ........10 B7
Reeves Rd BOW E3 ..............141 L9
WOOL/PLUM SE18 .................162 G5
Reform Rw TOTM N17 .............99 N10
Reform St BTSEA SW11 ..........158 A8

Regal Cl EA W5 ... 135 J7
WCHPL E1 ... 13 H9
Regal Ct MTCM CR4 ... 202 A3
UED N18 ... 99 N6
Regal Crs WLGTN SM6 ... 202 C10
Regal Dr FBAR/BDGN N11 ... 99 N4
Regalfield Cl GUW GU2 ... 249 M6
Regal La CAMTN NW1 ... 4 D6
Regal Pk PECK SE15 ... 160 B7
WATN N20 ... 73 K4
Regan Cl GUW GU2 ... 249 N5
Regan Wy IS N1 ... 7 J8
Regarder Rd CHIG IG7 ... 103 L6
Regarth Av ROM RM1 ... 124 F4
Regency Cl CHIG IG7 ... 102 F6
LEW5 ... 135 K9
HPTN TW12 ... 181 L4
Regency Ct ADL/WDHM KT15 * ... 215 N1
BRW CM14 ... 107 A8
EN EN1 ... 79 L9
HLWS CM18 ... 47 K4
Regency Crs HDN NW4 ... 96 G10
Regency Dr BF/WBF KT14 ... 2 G7
RSLP HA4 ... 112 F6
Regency Gdns EMPK RM11 ... 125 K5
WOT/HER KT12 ... 157 H5
Regency Lawn KTTN NW5 ... 118 C8
Regency Ms BECK BR3 ... 205 H1
WLSDN NW10 ... 136 D1
Regency Pde HAMP NW3 * ... 4
Regency Pl WEST SW1P * ... 17 J5
Regency St WEST SW1P ... 17 K6
Regency Ter HCT N6 * ... 118 H4
SEVS/STOTM N15 ... 119 M3
SKENS SW7 * ... 15 L7
Regency Wk CROY/NA CR0 ... 204 D6
Regency Wy BXLYHS DA6 ... 163 N9
Regeneration Rd BERM/RHTH SE16 ... 160 C3
Regent Av HGDN/ICK UB10 ... 132 C2
Regent Cl ADL/WDHM KT15 ... 215 N1
CDW/CHF RM16 ... 167 P1
HSLWW TW4 ... 153 J7
KGLGY WD4 ... 54 B5
KTN/HRWW/WS HA3 ... 115 K4
NFNCH/WDSPK N12 ... 97 M6
REDH RH1 ... 258 D5
STALE/WH AL4 ... 23 H6
WCCE AL7 ... 23 H6
Regent Cl GUW GU2 * ... 249 N8
SL SL1 ... 129 K8
Regent Crs REDH RH1 ... 258 A8
Regent Gdns GDMY/SEVK IG3 ... 123 M4
Regent Pde BELMT SM2 * ... 221 M3
STNW/STAM N16 ... 119 N5
Regent Pk CROY/NA CR0 ... 203 N8
WIM/MER SW19 ... 179 M8
EPP CM16 ... 65 J3
HNHL SE24 ... 181 J2
Regents Av PLMGR N13 ... 99 H4
Regents Cl CTHM CR3 ... 241 M4
RAD WD7 ... 56 F10
SAND/SEL CR2 ... 223 M3
YEAD UB4 ... 132 F7
Regents Dr HAYES BR2 ... 226 A2
WFD IG8 ... 102 D7
Regents Ms HORL RH6 ... 280 B4
STJWD NW8 ... 3 K7
Regent's Park Rd CAMTN NW1 ... 4 B5
FNCH N3 ... 117 J1
Regent's Park Ter CAMTN NW1 * ... 4 E5
Regents Pl LOU IG10 ... 102 A1
Regents Plaza KIL/WHAMP NW6 * ... 2 G7
Regent Sq BELV DA17 ... 164 C3
BOW E3 ... 140 G5
STPAN WC1H ... 5 M10
Regent's Rw HACK E8 ... 7 N6
Regent St CHSWK W4 ... 155 M4
REGST W1B ... 10 F5
STJS SW1Y ... 11 J8
WATN ND24 ... 73 J4
WLSDN NW10 ... 136 G5
Regents Wk ASC SL5 ... 192 B6
Regents Whf IS N1 * ... 5 N7
Regent Whf IS N1 * ... 5 N7
Reginald Ms HLWE CM17 ... 29 M10
Reginald Rd DEPT SE8 ... 160 F6
FSTGT E7 ... 141 M2
HARH RM3 ... 105 P9
NTHWD HA6 ... 92 C9
Reginald Sq DEPT SE8 ... 160 F6
Regina Rd FSBYPK N4 ... 118 G6
NWDGN UB2 ... 153 M3
SNWD SE25 ... 205 P8
WEA W13 ... 154 F10
Regina Ter WEA W13 ... 154 F10
Regis Rd KTTN NW5 ... 118 C6
Regnart Blds CAMTN NW1 * ... 5 H10
Reid Av CTHM CR3 ... 241 L7
Reid Cl COUL/CHIP CR5 ... 240 C4
HYS/HAR UB3 ... 132 F8
PIN HA5 ... 113 H1
Reidhaven Rd WOOL/PLUM SE18 ... 163 N8
Reigate Av SUT SM1 ... 201 L8
Reigate Cl CRAWE RH10 ... 284 E4
Reigate HI REIC RH2 ... 257 J7
Reigate Hill Cl REIC RH2 ... 257 K7
Reigate Rd BMLY BR1 ... 183 P5
BRKHM/BTCW RH3 ... 255 M9
DORK RH4 ... 272 A4
EW KT17 ... 220 C6
GDMY/SEVK IG3 ... 123 J3
HORL RH6 ... 279 N5
KWD/TDW/WH KT20 ... 238 C5
LHD/OX KT22 ... 237 H9
REDH RH1 ... 258 D5
REIC RH2 ... 275 M10
REIC RH2 ... 257 M10
Reigate Wy WLGTN SM6 ... 222 F2
Reighton Rd CLPT E5 ... 119 P8
Reinckendorf Av ELTH/MOT SE9 ... 184 F1
Reindeer Cl PLSTW E13 ... 141 H4
Reindorp Cl GUW GU2 ... 250 A2
Reizel Cl STNW/STAM N16 ... 119 N6
Relay Rd SHB W12 ... 136 F7
Relf Rd PECK SE15 ... 159 H10
Reliance Av BRXN/ST SW9 ... 159 H10
Relton Ms SKENS SW7 ... 15 P3
Rembrandt Cl BCVA SW1W ... 16 C7
POP/IOD E14 ... 161 J2
Rembrandt Ct HOR/WEW KT19 ... 220 C3
Rembrandt Dr GVW DA11 ... 190 A6
Rembrandt Rd EDGW HA8 * ... 96 B5
LEW SE13 ... 161 K10
Rembrandt Wy WOT/HER KT12 ... 157 J9
Remington Rd EHAM E6 ... 142 A4
SEVS/STOTM N15 ... 119 L4
Remington St IS N1 ... 6 E6
Remnant St HOL/ALD WC2B ... 11 P1
Remus Cl STNW/STAM N16 ... 38 C10
Remus Rd BOW E3 ... 140 A4
Renaissance Wk GNWCH SE10 ... 161 L2
Rendle Cl CROY/NA CR0 ... 203 N5
Rendlesham Av RAD WD7 ... 74 E3
Rendlesham Cl WARE SG12 ... 26 A1
Rendlesham Pl CLPT E5 ... 119 P9
ENC/FH EN2 ... 79 J1
Rendlesham Wy RKW/CH/CXG WD3 ... 70 F10
Renforth St BERM/RHTH SE16 ... 160 B1
Renfree Wy SHPTN TW17 ... 196 B3
Renfrew Rd HSLWW TW4 ... 153 L8
KUTN/CMB KT2 ... 177 H10
LBTH SE11 ... 18 C7
The Renmans ASHTD KT21 ... 237 L2
Renmuir St TOOT SW17 ... 180 A9

Rennell St LEW SE13 ... 161 H9
Renness Rd WALTH E17 ... 120 D1
Rennets Cl ELTH/MOT SE9 ... 184 G1
Rennets Wood Rd ELTH/MOT SE9 ... 184 G1
Rennie Ct ASHF TW15 ... 173 H6
Rennie Est BERM/RHTH SE16 ... 160 A3
Rennie St STHWK SE1 ... 12 C9
Rennie Ter REDH RH1 ... 276 B11
Rennison Cl CHESW EN7 ... 61 N3
Renown Cl CROY/NA CR0 ... 203 J8
ROMW/RG RM7 ... 104 D3
Rensburg Rd WALTH E17 ... 120 C3
Rensburg Vls WALTH E17 * ... 120 C3
Renshaw Cl BELV DA17 ... 164 A5
Renshaw Dr STMC/STPC BR5 ... 207 N1
Renters Av HDN NW4 ... 116 F4
Renton Cl BRXS/STRHM SW2 * ... 180 C2
Renton Dr STMC/STPC BR5 ... 207 N1
Renwick Rd BARK IG11 ... 143 L6
Repens Wy YEAD UB4 ... 133 L6
Rephidim St STHWK SE1 ... 19 H4
Replingham Rd WAND/EARL SW18 ... 179 J3
Reporton Rd FUL/PGN SW6 ... 157 H7
Repository Rd WOOL/PLUM SE18 ... 162 G5
Repton Av ALP/SUD HA0 ... 115 H9
GPK RM2 ... 125 H1
HYS/HAR UB3 ... 152 A3
Repton Cl CAR SM5 ... 221 P2
Repton Ct BECK BR3 ... 204 G1
GPK RM2 ... 125 H1
Repton Gdns GPK RM2 ... 125 H1
Repton Gn STALW/RED AL3 ... 38 C5
Repton Gv CLAY IG5 ... 102 C9
Repton Pl AMSS HP7 * ... 69 M5
Repton Rd KTN/HRWW/WS HA3 ... 115 L2
ORP BR6 ... 227 K1
Repton St POP/IOD E14 ... 140 D8
Repulse Cl CRW RM5 ... 104 C9
Reservoir Cl SWCM DA10 ... 189 L7
THHTH CR7 ... 203 L3
Reservoir Rd BROCKY SE4 ... 160 B8
RSLP HA4 ... 112 D3
STHGT/OAK N14 ... 78 D9
Resham Cl NWDGN UB2 ... 153 L2
Resolution Wy DEPT SE8 ... 160 F6
Reson Wy HHW HP1 ... 35 L7
Restell Cl BKHTH/KID SE3 ... 161 K5
Restmor Wy CAR SM5 ... 202 B9
Reston Cl BORE WD6 ... 75 M4
Reston Pl KENS W8 ... 15 J2
Restons Crs ELTH/MOT SE9 ... 184 G2
Reston Wy CAN/RD E16 ... 142 A9
Retford Cl BORE WD6 ... 75 M4
HARH RM3 ... 105 N8
Retford Pth HARH RM3 ... 105 P7
Retford Rd HARH RM3 ... 105 P8
Retford St BETH E2 * ... 7 L9
Retingham Wy CHING E4 ... 100 E3
Retreat Cl KTN/HRWW/WS HA3 ... 115 H3
Retreat Pl HOM E9 ... 140 B1
Retreat Rd RCH/KEW TW9 ... 177 J1
The Retreat AMH HP6 ... 70 B5
BRW CM14 ... 106 G2
BRYLDS KT5 ... 199 L6
CDALE/KGS NW9 ... 116 A3
ECH TW20 ... 172 A9
GRAYS RM17 ... 167 N5
MORT/ESHN SW14 ... 156 B9
ORP BR6 ... 227 L3
RBRW/HUT CM13 ... 87 N10
RYLN/HDSTN HA2 ... 113 P5
SEV TN13 * ... 247 K10
THHTH CR7 ... 203 L4
WPK KT4 ... 200 E9
Retreat Wy CHIG IG7 ... 103 L4
Reubens Rd RBRW/HUT CM13 ... 87 N10
Reunion Rw WAP E1W * ... 140 G3
Reveley Sq BERM/RHTH SE16 ... 160 D1
Revell Cl LHD/OX KT22 ... 236 A9
Revell Dr LHD/OX KT22 ... 236 A8
Revell Ri WOOL/PLUM SE18 ... 163 P5
Revell Rd KUT/HW KT1 ... 199 N2
SUT SM1 ... 221 J3
Revelon Rd BROCKY SE4 ... 160 D10
Revels Cl HERT/WAT SG14 ... 25 L3
Revels Rd HERT/WAT SG14 ... 25 L3
Revelstoke Rd WIM/MER SW19 ... 179 H7
Reventlow Rd ELTH/MOT SE9 ... 184 F4
Reverdy Rd STHWK SE1 ... 19 N4
Reverend Cl RYLN/HDSTN HA2 ... 114 A8
Revere Wy HOR/WEW KT19 ... 220 C5
Revesby Cl CHOB/PIR GU24 ... 212 C9
Revesby Rd CAR SM5 ... 201 P6
Review Rd CRICK NW2 ... 116 C7
DAGE RM10 ... 144 C4
Rewell St FUL/PGN SW6 * ... 157 N5
Rewley Rd CAR SM5 ... 201 N6
Rex Av ASHF TW15 ... 174 A7
Rex Pl MYFR/PKLN W1K ... 10 A7
Reydon Av WAN E11 ... 121 P4
Reynard Cl BMLY BR1 ... 206 C3
Reynard Dr NRWD SE19 ... 181 N10
Reynard Pl NWCR SE14 * ... 160 D5
Reynardson Rd TOTM N17 ... 99 K8
Reynard's Wy LCOL/BKTW AL2 ... 55 N5
Reynard Wy HERT/BAY SG13 ... 25 P5
Reynola Gdns CHARL SE7 ... 161 N4
Reynolas Av CHDH RM6 ... 123 M5
CHSGTN KT9 ... 219 K4
MNPK E12 ... 122 D10
Reynolds Cl CAR SM5 ... 202 A8
GLDGN NW11 ... 117 L5
HHW HP1 ... 35 K5
WIM/MER SW19 ... 201 N1
Reynolds Crs STALE/WH AL4 ... 38 C1
Reynolds Dr EDGW HA8 ... 115 L1
Reynolds Pl BKHTH/KID SE3 ... 161 N6
CRAWW RH11 ... 283 M6
RCHPK/HAM TW10 ... 177 L2
Reynolds Rd BEAC HP9 ... 88 D5
CHSWK W4 ... 155 N4
CRAWW RH11 ... 283 M6
NWMAL KT3 ... 200 A4
PECK SE15 ... 182 B1
YEAD UB4 ... 133 K6
Reynolds Wy CROY/NA CR0 ... 223 N1
Reynolds Yd CSHM HP5 ... 50 C4
Rhapsody Crs BRW CM14 ... 106 C6
Rheidol Ms IS N1 ... 6 E5
Rheidol Ter IS N1 ... 6 D6
Rheingold Wy WLGTN SM6 ... 222 F7
Rheola Cl TOTM N17 ... 99 N9
Rhoda St BETH E2 ... 7 L8
Rhodes Av WDGN N22 ... 98 B9
Rhodes Cl EGH TW20 ... 172 F8
Rhodes Ct EGH TW20 * ... 172 F8
Rhodesia Rd BRXN/ST SW9 ... 158 A9
WAN E11 ... 121 P3
Rhodes St HOLWY N7 ... 118 E4
WATN WD24 ... 73 L6
Rhodeswell Rd POP/IOD E14 ... 140 D7
Rhododendron Ride ECH TW20 ... 171 L3
EGH TW20 ... 171 L3
Rhodrons Av CHSGTN KT9 ... 219 K4
Rhondda Gv BOW E3 ... 140 A5
Rhyl Ed CFD/PVL UB6 ... 134 B3
Rhyl St KTTN NW5 ... 4 A1
Rhymes HHW HP1 ... 35 L5
Rhys Av FBAR/BDGN N11 ... 98 C7
Rialto Rd MTCM CR4 ... 202 B1
Ribble Cl WFD IG8 ... 101 J7
Ribblesdale LCOL/BKTW AL2 ... 57 L5
Ribblesdale Av FBAR/BDGN N11 ... 98 A11
NTHLT UB5 ... 134 A1
Ribblesdale Rd CEND/HSY/T N8 ... 118 G2
RDART DA2 ... 188 B4
STRHM/NOR SW16 ... 180 C8

Ribbon Dance Ms CMBW SE5 ... 159 H7
Ribchester Av GFD/PVL UB6 ... 134 E5
Ribston Cl HAYES BR2 ... 206 C8
RAD WD7 ... 57 H3
Rib V HERT/WAT SG14 ... 25 L2
Ricardo Rd WDSR SL4 ... 171 N2
Ricardo St POP/IOD E14 ... 140 G8
Ricards Rd WIM/MER SW19 ... 179 J3
Rice Cl HHNE HP2 ... 36 A5
Rice Pde STMC/STPC BR5 ... 206 A8
Richard Cl WOOL/PLUM SE18 ... 162 B3
Richard House Dr CAN/RD E16 ... 142 A8
Richard Meyjes Rd GUW GU2 ... 267 K4
Richards Av ROMW/RG RM7 ... 124 D3
Richards Cl BUSH WD23 ... 94 C1
HGDN/ICK UB10 ... 132 B3
HAYES BR2 ... 224 A1
HYS/HAR UB3 ... 152 E5
Richards Cots CAR SM5 * ... 222 A4
Richards Fld HOR/WEW KT19 ... 220 A5
Richardson Cl HACK E8 * ... 7 L3
LCOL/BKTW AL2 ... 57 K3
RDART DA2 ... 188 E1
Richardson Gdns DAGE RM10 ... 144 C1
Richardson Pl STALE/WH AL4 ... 39 N8
Richardson Rd SRTFD E15 ... 141 K4
Richardson's Ms FITZ W1T ... 10 G2
Richard's Pl CHEL SW3 ... 15 P5
WALTH E17 ... 120 D4
Richard St WCHPL E1 ... 140 A8
Richards Wy SL SL1 ... 128 E10
Richbell Cl ASHTD KT21 ... 237 J4
Richbell Pl FSBYW WC1N ... 11 N3
Richborne Ter VX/NE SW8 ... 158 G6
Richborough Cl CRAWW RH11 * ... 283 M7
Richborough Rd CRICK NW2 ... 116 C9
Richens Cl HSLW TW3 ... 154 C8
Riches Rd IL IG1 ... 122 F7
Richfield Rd BUSH WD23 ... 94 B1
Richford Ga HMSMTH W6 ... 156 F2
Richford Rd SRTFD E15 ... 141 L3
Richford St HMSMTH W6 ... 156 F1
Richill Ldg WHTN TW2 * ... 175 P2
Richings Pl DTCH/LGLY SL3 ... 151 J2
Richings Wy DTCH/LGLY SL3 ... 151 J2
Richland Av COUL/CHIP CR5 ... 222 B10
Richlands Av EW KT17 ... 220 D1
Richmer Rd ERITH DA8 ... 165 H6
Richmond Av CHING E4 ... 101 N4
EBED/NFELT TW14 ... 174 F2
HGDN/ICK UB10 ... 132 C1
IS N1 ... 5 P5
RYNPK SW20 ... 201 H1
Richmond Br TWK TW1 ... 177 J1
Richmond Blds SOHO/SHAV W1D ... 11 J6
Richmond Cl BH/WHM TN16 ... 243 N5
BORE WD6 ... 76 A5
EPSOM KT18 ... 220 B10
LHD/OX KT22 ... 236 B10
WALTH E17 ... 120 E4
Richmond Crs CHING E4 ... 101 J6
ED N9 ... 99 P2
IS N1 ... 5 P5
SL SL1 ... 129 M10
STA TW18 ... 173 J8
Richmond Dr GVE DA12 ... 191 H5
SHPTN TW17 ... 196 D6
WAT WD17 ... 72 F6
WFD IG8 ... 102 D8
Richmond Gdns HDN NW4 ... 116 D3
KTN/HRWW/WS HA3 ... 94 E8
Richmond Ga RCHPK/HAM TW10 ... 177 L3
Richmond Gn CROY/NA CR0 ... 202 F10
Richmond Gv IS N1 ... 6 C4
Richmond HI RCHPK/HAM TW10 ... 177 K2
Richmond Ms SOHO/SHAV W1D ... 11 J6
Richmond Pde TWK TW1 * ... 177 H2
Richmond Park Rd KUTN/CMB KT2 ... 177 K10
MORT/ESHN SW14 ... 177 P1
Richmond Pl WOOL/PLUM SE18 ... 162 F3
Richmond Rd BAR EN5 ... 77 L9
CHING E4 ... 101 H2
COUL/CHIP CR5 ... 240 C1
CROY/NA CR0 ... 202 F10
EA W5 ... 155 K1
EFNCH N2 * ... 97 M10
FBAR/BDGN N11 ... 98 F7
FSTGT E7 ... 121 N10
GDMY/SEVK IG3 ... 123 J4
HACK E8 * ... 7 L3
IL IG1 ... 122 F8
ISLW TW7 ... 154 F9
KUTN/CMB KT2 ... 177 J8
POTB/CUF EN6 ... 59 M7
ROM RM1 ... 124 C4
RYNPK SW20 ... 200 E1
SEVS/STOTM N15 ... 119 M4
STA TW18 ... 173 J8
THHTH CR7 ... 203 J4
TWK TW1 ... 177 J1
WALTH E17 ... 121 J7
WAN E11 ... 121 M3
Richmond St PLSTW E13 ... 141 M4
Richmond Ter WHALL SW1A ... 17 L1
Richmond Vls WALTH E17 * ... 100 E10
Richmond Wy GT/LBKH KT23 ... 236 A10
RKW/CH/CXG WD3 ... 72 D8
SHB W12 ... 156 G1
WAN E11 ... 121 M7
Richmond Wd ASC SL5 ... 192 C8
Richmount Gdns BKHTH/KID SE3 ... 161 M9
Rich St POP/IOD E14 ... 140 F8
Rickard Cl BRXS/STRHM SW2 ... 181 H4
HDN NW4 ... 116 D2
WDR/YW UB7 ... 151 N2
Rickards Cl SURB KT6 ... 199 K9
Ricketts Hill Rd BH/WHM TN16 ... 244 A4
Rickett St FUL/PGN SW6 ... 14 F7
Rickfield CRAWW RH11 ... 283 K8
Rickfield Cl HAT AL10 ... 40 A2
Rickford Hl RGUW GU3 ... 249 J2
Rickman Crs ADL/WDHM KT15 ... 215 L10
Rickman Hl COUL/CHIP CR5 ... 240 C5
Rickman Hill Rd COUL/CHIP CR5 ... 240 C5
Rickman's La SLN SL2 ... 129 K1
Rickman St WCHPL E1 ... 140 E6
Rickmansworth La CFSP/GDCR SL9 ... 90 B7
Rickmansworth Rd DEN/HRF UB9 ... 91 M9
NTHWD HA6 ... 92 C7
RKW/CH/CXG WD3 ... 72 D8
WATW WD18 ... 72 F6
Rick Roberts Wy SRTFD E15 ... 141 J3
Ricksons La EHSLY KT24 ... 252 E6
Rickthorne Rd ARCH N19 ... 118 E7
Rickwood HORL RH6 ... 280 C9
Rickyard GUW GU2 ... 249 J10
Ridding La GFD/PVL UB6 ... 114 E10
Riddings La HHS/BOV HP3 ... 35 P6
The Riddings CTHM CR3 ... 259 N1
Riddlesdown Av PUR/KEN CR8 ... 223 K8
Riddlesdown Rd PUR/KEN CR8 ... 223 K9

Riddons Rd LEE/GVPK SE12 ... 183 P6
Ride La SHGR GU5 ... 269 N10
Rideout St WOOL/PLUM SE18 ... 162 G3
Ride Rd CFD/PVL UB6 ... 134 E5
Riders Wy GDST RH9 ... 260 B7
The Ride BTFD TW8 ... 154 G4
PEND EN3 ... 80 B7
Ridgdale St BOW E3 ... 140 F4
Ridge Av WCHMN N21 ... 99 K1
Ridgebank SL SL1 ... 128 E9
Ridgebrook Rd BKHTH/KID SE3 ... 161 P10
Ridge Cl BRKHM/BTCW RH3 ... 275 N4
CDALE/KGS NW9 ... 116 A2
HDN NW4 ... 96 G10
THMD SE28 ... 162 C1
WOKS/MYFD GU22 ... 231 N7
Ridge Ct WARL CR6 ... 241 P4
Ridge Crest ENC/FH EN2 ... 78 G5
Ridgecroft Cl BXLY DA5 ... 186 D4
Ridgegate Cl REIG RH2 ... 257 N8
Ridge Gn REDH RH1 ... 276 F8
Ridge Green Cl REDH RH1 ... 276 F8
Ridgehill GLDGN NW11 ... 117 H6
Ridgehurst Av GSTN WD25 ... 54 C9
Ridgelands LHD/OX KT22 ... 236 C10
Ridge La WAT WD17 ... 72 F3
Ridge Langley SAND/SEL CR2 ... 223 P6
Ridge Lea HHW HP1 ... 35 J3
Ridgemead Rd EGH TW20 ... 171 N6
Ridgemount GUW GU2 ... 267 N1
WEY KT13 ... 196 F9
Ridgemount Av COUL/CHIP CR5 ... 240 C3
CROY/NA CR0 ... 204 C9
Ridgemount Cl PGE/AN SE20 ... 182 A10
Ridgemount End CFSP/GDCR SL9 ... 90 B6
Ridgemount Gdns ENC/FH EN2 ... 79 J1
Ridge Mount Rd ASC SL5 ... 192 F8
Ridge Pk PUR/KEN CR8 ... 222 E6
Ridge Rd CEND/HSY/T N8 ... 118 G4
CHEAM SM3 ... 201 J8
CRICK NW2 ... 117 J8
MTCM CR4 ... 180 C10
WCHMN N21 ... 99 L2
Ridgeside CRAWE RH10 ... 284 A7
The Ridges RGUW GU3 ... 267 P5
Ridge St WATN WD24 ... 73 J4
Ridge Ter WCHMN N21 * ... 99 K1
The Ridge BAR EN5 ... 77 J8
BRYLDS KT5 ... 199 M5
BXLY DA5 ... 186 A3
COUL/CHIP CR5 ... 222 F10
CTHM CR3 ... 261 K1
STHWK SE1 * ... 19 L3
EPSOM KT18 ... 237 P4
HAYES BR2 ... 205 L7
HOR/WEW KT19 ... 219 P8
LHD/OX KT22 ... 236 C10
PUR/KEN CR8 ... 222 E6
RAD WD7 ... 57 H1
TWK TW1 ... 176 D5
WOKS/MYFD GU22 ... 231 N7
Ridge Wy CROY/NA CR0 ... 203 J10
DTCH/LGLY SL3 ... 150 B3
FELT TW13 ... 175 M6
RAD WD7 ... 57 H7
Ridgeway BERK HP4 ... 33 L5
BRXN/ST SW9 ... 158 A9
DART DA1 ... 191 P10
ECH TW20 ... 172 B9
GRAYS RM17 ... 167 N7
HCT N6 ... 118 B5
HPTN TW12 ... 175 H9
HTCHE/RSTV SG4 ... 24 ...
WCCE AL7 ... 23 J5
WFD IG8 ... 101 P5
WOKS/MYFD GU22 ... 232 C7
WOT/HER KT12 ... 195 J8
Ridgeway Av EBAR EN4 ... 78 A10
GVE DA12 ... 190 E6
Ridgeway Cl CSHM HP5 ... 50 C4
DORK RH4 ... 272 F4
HHS/BOV HP3 ... 35 H6
LHD/OX KT22 ... 236 C10
WOKN/KNAP GU21 ... 231 J2
Ridgeway Ct REDH RH1 ... 275 P1
Ridgeway Crs ORP BR6 ... 227 H1
Ridgeway Crescent Gdns ORP BR6 ... 227 H1
Ridgeway Dr BMLY BR1 ... 183 N7
DORK RH4 ... 272 F4
Ridgeway East BFN/LL DA15 ... 185 J1
Ridgeway Gdns HGT N6 ... 118 D6
IL IG1 ... 123 H6
WOKN/KNAP GU21 ... 231 J2
Ridgeway North HLWE CM17 ... 47 P1
Ridgeway Pl WIM/MER SW19 ... 178 F7
Ridgeway Rd BRXN/ST SW9 ... 159 ...
DORK RH4 ... 272 F4
ISLW TW7 ... 154 D6
REDBR IG4 ... 121 N1
Ridgeway Rd North ISLW TW7 ... 154 D5
Ridgeways HLWE CM17 ... 47 P3
The Ridgeway ACT W3 ... 155 M2
AMSS HP7 ... 69 K6
CDALE/KGS NW9 ... 116 A2
CHING E4 ... 101 H2
CHOB/PIR GU24 ... 230 B6
CROY/NA CR0 ... 202 C10
ENC/FH EN2 ... 78 D2
FBAR/BDGN N11 ... 98 D7
FSTGT E7 ... 121 N10
GLDGN NW11 ... 117 J7
GPK RM2 ... 125 H2
GU GU1 ... 268 C1
HARH RM3 ... 105 M9
HERT/WAT SG14 ... 24 D2
HORL RH6 ... 280 B7
KTN/HRWW/WS HA3 ... 115 H4
LHD/OX KT22 ... 236 C10
NTHLT UB5 ... 133 K5
POTB/CUF EN6 ... 60 B3
RAD WD7 ... 74 C1
RSLP HA4 ... 112 B3
STALE/WH AL4 ... 39 J2
EW KT17 ... 220 C6
CFD/PVL UB6 ... 114 F10
GVE DA12 ... 191 H7
HGDN/ICK UB10 ... 132 A4
KWD/TDW/WH KT20 ... 238 F7
LCOL/BKTW AL2 ... 56 C1
MLHL NW7 ... 96 H5
PLMGR N13 ... 99 H5
RDART DA2 ... 188 F2
SAND/SEL CR2 ... 224 B5
SEV TN13 ... 265 K4
WAN E11 ... 121 M3
WCHMN N21 ... 99 K1
Ridgeway West BFN/LL DA15 ... 185 J1
Ridgewell Cl DAGE RM10 ... 144 C5
IS N1 ... 6 F2
SYD SE26 ... 182 C11
Ridgmont Rd STAL AL1 ... 38 D7
Ridgmount Gdns GWRST WC1E ... 11 J1
Ridgmount Pl GWRST WC1E ... 11 J1
Ridgmount Rd WAND/EARL SW18 ... 179 L1
Ridgmount St GWRST WC1E ... 11 J1
Ridgway GU GU1 ... 268 D10
WIM/MER SW19 ... 178 F7
The Ridgway BELMT SM2 ... 221 P5
SAND/SEL CR2 ... 223 M6
Ridgway Gdns WIM/MER SW19 ... 178 E7
Ridgway Pl WIM/MER SW19 ... 178 F7
Ridgway Rd BRXN/ST SW9 ... 159 ...
RGUW GU3 ... 250 ...
The Ridings ADL/WDHM KT15 ... 215 H5
ASC SL5 ... 192 B6
ASHTD KT21 ... 237 J5
BAR EN5 ... 77 ...
BRYLDS KT5 ... 199 N4
COB KT11 ... 235 M3
EA W5 ... 135 K3
EBAR EN4 ... 77 ...
EHSLY KT24 ... 252 ...
EPSOM KT18 ... 234 A10
FRY ... 
SUN TW16 ... 195 P2
SWLY BR8 ... 187 N10
TWK TW1 ... 176 D3
Ridings Av WCHMN N21 ... 79 K5
Ridings Cl HGT N6 ... 118 C4
The Ridings BRXN/ST SW2 ... 181 J1
Ridlands Gv OXTED RH8 ... 262 B6
Ridlands La OXTED RH8 ... 262 B6
Ridlands Ri OXTED RH8 ... 262 B6
Ridler Rd EN EN1 ... 79 M4
Ridley Av WEA W13 ... 154 G4
Ridley Cl BARK IG11 ... 143 J2
HARH RM3 ... 105 J9
Ridley Rd FSTGT E7 ... 121 P9
HACK E8 ... 7 M1
WARL CR6 ... 242 B4
WELL DA16 ... 164 E1
WIM/MER SW19 ... 179 L8
WLSDN NW10 ... 136 D3
Ridsdale Rd PGE/AN SE20 ... 204 A1
WOKN/KNAP GU21 ... 231 J6
Riefield Rd ELTH/MOT SE9 ... 162 F10
Riesco Dr CROY/NA CR0 ... 224 B3
Riffel Rd CRICK NW2 ... 116 F10
Riffhams RBRW/HUT CM13 ... 107 N4
Rifle Range La HRW HA1 ... 114 E6
Rifle Pl NTGHL W11 ... 136 C1
Rifle St POP/IOD E14 ... 140 G7
Rigault Rd FUL/PGN SW6 ... 157 H8
Rigby Cl CROY/NA CR0 ... 203 H10
Rigby Gdns CDW/CHF RM16 ... 168 E3
Rigby Ms IL IG1 ... 122 D7
Rigby Pl PEND EN3 ... 80 F3
Rigden St POP/IOD E14 ... 140 G8
Rigeley Rd WLSDN NW10 ... 136 D5
Rigg Ap LEY E10 ... 121 L6
Riggindale Rd STRHM/NOR SW16 ... 180 E8
Right Side STHGT/OAK N14 * ... 98 E2
Riley Rd PEND EN3 ... 80 B4
STHWK SE1 ... 19 L3
Riley St WBPTN SW10 ... 157 N6
Rillside CRAWE RH10 ... 284 B10
Rinaldo Rd BAL SW12 ... 180 C5
Ring Cl BMLY BR1 ... 183 N10
Ringcroft St HOLWY N7 ... 119 H10
Ringers Rd BMLY BR1 ... 205 M3
Ringford Rd WAND/EARL SW18 ... 179 J1
Ringlet Cl CAN/RD E16 ... 141 N7
Ringlewell Cl EN EN1 ... 80 A7
Ringley Av HORL RH6 ... 280 B4
Ringley Park Av REIG RH2 ... 275 N1
Ringley Park Rd REIG RH2 ... 257 M10
Ringmer Av FUL/PGN SW6 ... 157 H7
Ringmer Pl WCHMN N21 ... 79 L9
Ringmer Wy BMLY BR1 ... 206 C5
Ringmore Dr RGUE GU4 ... 250 F7
Ringmore Ri FSTH SE23 ... 162 A4
Ringmore Rd WOT/HER KT12 ... 197 K10
Ring Rd SHB W12 ... 136 F10
Ring Rd North HORL RH6 ... 280 C7
Ring Rd South HORL RH6 ... 280 C7
Ringshall Rd STMC/STPC BR5 ... 207 K3
Ringslade Rd WDGN N22 ... 98 G10
Ringstead Rd CAT SE6 ... 182 C3
SUT SM1 ... 221 N1
Ring Wy FBAR/BDGN N11 ... 98 D7
Ringway NWDGN UB2 ... 153 L4
Ringway Rd LCOL/BKTW AL2 ... 56 A4
Ringwold Cl BECK BR3 ... 182 D10
Ringwood Av CROY/NA CR0 ... 202 F7
EFNCH N2 ... 118 A1
HCH RM12 ... 125 J7
ORP BR6 ... 227 M6
REDH RH1 ... 258 A7
Ringwood Cl CRAWE RH10 ... 283 P9
PIN HA5 * ... 113 K1
Ringwood Gdns PUT/ROE SW15 ... 178 D5
Ringwood Rd WALTH E17 ... 121 J3
Ringwood Wy HPTN TW12 ... 175 P7
WCHMN N21 ... 99 J1
Ripley Av EGH TW20 ... 172 B9
Ripley By-Pass RPLY/SEND GU23 ... 251 H2
Ripley Cl BMLY BR1 ... 206 G7
CROY/NA CR0 ... 225 H3
Ripley Gdns MORT/ESHN SW14 ... 156 A9
SUT SM1 ... 221 N3
Ripley La RGUE GU4 ... 252 A10
Ripley Ms WAN E11 ... 121 K4
Ripley Rd BELV DA17 ... 164 B5
CAN/RD E16 ... 141 P8
ENC/FH EN2 ... 79 K5
GDMY/SEVK IG3 ... 123 H6
HPTN TW12 ... 175 H10
RPLY/SEND GU23 ... 251 M3
Ripleys Market DART DA1 * ... 191 K4
Ripley Vw LOU IG10 ... 80 G3
Ripley Vls EA W5 ... 135 H5
Ripon Cl GUW GU2 ... 249 P2
NTHLT UB5 ... 113 P10
Ripon Gdns CHSGTN KT9 ... 219 J5
IL IG1 ... 122 G5
Ripon Rd ED N9 ... 100 A1
TOTM N17 ... 99 K8
WOOL/PLUM SE18 ... 162 G5
Ripon Wy BORE WD6 ... 75 P9
STALE/WH AL4 ... 39 J2
Rippersley Rd WELL DA16 ... 164 C7
Ripple Rd BARK IG11 ... 142 C7
Rippleside Commercial Est BARK IG11 ... 143 N6
Ripplevale Gv IS N1 ... 5 P1
Rippolson Rd WOOL/PLUM SE18 ... 163 P5
Ripston Rd ASHF TW15 ... 174 B11
Risborough Dr WPK KT4 ... 200 D7
Risborough St STHWK SE1 ... 18 E2
Risdens HLWS CM18 ... 47 P4
Risdon St BERM/RHTH SE16 ... 160 A7
Risebridge Cha ROM RM1 ... 104 D3
Risebridge Rd ROM RM1 ... 104 D5
Risedale Cl HHNE HP2 ... 35 J5
Risedale HI HHS/BOV HP3 ... 36 A8
Risedale Rd BXLYHN DA7 ... 165 P9
HHS/BOV HP3 ... 36 A8
Rise Park Bvd ROM RM1 ... 104 D3
Rise Park Pde ROM RM1 ... 104 C2
The Rise AMSS HP7 ... 69 H5
BORE WD6 ... 75 N2
BKHH IG9 ... 102 E3
BRW CM14 ... 106 D5
BXLY DA5 ... 165 N9
CDALE/KGS NW9 ... 95 G10
DART DA1 ... 190 E3
EDGW HA8 ... 96 C1
EFNCH N2 ... 117 L1
GPK RM2 ... 125 H2
PLSTW E13 ... 141 N3
SAND/SEL CR2 ... 224 B5
SEV TN13 ... 265 K4
WAN E11 ... 121 M3
WCHMN N21 ... 99 K1
Riseway BRWN CM15 ... 107 K4
Rising Hill Cl NTHWD HA6 * ... 92 D3
Risinghill St IS N1 ... 6 A7
Risingholme Cl BUSH WD23 ... 94 A1
KTN/HRWW/WS HA3 ... 94 D9
Risingholme Rd KTN/HRWW/WS HA3 ... 94 D10
Rita Rd VX/NE SW8 ... 158 F6
Ritches Rd SEVS/STOTM N15 ... 119 K3
Ritchie Rd CROY/NA CR0 ... 204 A6
Ritchie St IS N1 ... 6 B7
Ritchings Av WALTH E17 ... 120 D2
Ritcroft Cl HHS/BOV HP3 ... 36 C7
Ritcroft Dr HHS/BOV HP3 ... 36 C7
Ritcroft St HHS/BOV HP3 ... 36 C7
Ritherdon Rd TOOT SW17 ... 180 B5
Ritson Rd HACK E8 ... 7 M1
Ritter St WOOL/PLUM SE18 ... 162 D5
Ritz Ct POTB/CUF EN6 ... 59 K7
Rivaz Pl HOM E9 ... 140 B1
Rivenhall End WCCE AL7 ... 23 H6
Rivenhall Gdns SWFD E18 ... 121 L2
River Av HOD EN11 ... 44 G2
PLMGR N13 ... 99 J4
THDIT KT7 ... 198 F7
Riverbank DORK RH4 ... 272 A2
E/WMO/HCT KT8 ... 198 D3
HHW HP1 ... 35 M2
River Bank THDIT KT7 ... 198 E5
WCHMN N2 ... 99 K1
Riverbank Wy BTFD TW8 ... 154 G5
River Barge Cl POP/IOD E14 ... 161 N1
River Cl CHES/WCR EN8 ... 62 F10
GU GU1 ... 249 P8
NWDGN UB2 ... 154 B1
RAIN RM13 ... 145 J7
RSLP HA4 ... 112 G4
SRTFD E15 ... 141 P4
WAN E11 ... 121 P4
Rivercourt Rd HMSMTH W6 ... 156 E3
River Crane Wy FELT TW13 ... 175 M7
Riverdale Dr WAND/EARL SW18 ... 179 L4
WOKS/MYFD GU22 ... 232 C7
Riverdale Gdns TWK TW1 ... 177 L3
Riverdale Rd BXLY DA5 ... 186 A3
ERITH DA8 ... 165 P4
FELT TW13 ... 175 H7
TWK TW1 ... 177 L2
WOOL/PLUM SE18 ... 163 N4
Riverdene EDGW HA8 ... 95 P5
Riverdene Rd IL IG1 ... 122 D8
River Dr UPMR RM14 ... 126 B4
Riverfield Rd STA TW18 ... 173 J9
River Front EN EN1 ... 79 L7
River Gdns CAR SM5 ... 202 B9
EBED/NFELT TW14 ... 175 ...
River Grove Pk BECK BR3 ... 204 E1
Riverhead Cl WALTH E17 ... 100 C10
Riverhead Dr BELMT SM2 ... 221 L6
River Hl COB KT11 ... 235 J1
Riverholme Dr HOR/WEW KT19 ... 220 A5
River Island Cl LHD/OX KT22 ... 236 C6
River La COB KT11 ... 235 M4
LHD/OX KT22 ... 235 M4
RCHPK/HAM TW10 ... 177 J4
Rivermead BF/WBF KT14 ... 216 A9
KUT/HW KT1 ... 199 J5
Rivermead Cl ADL/WDHM KT15 ... 215 M4
TEDD TW11 ... 176 B10
River Meads WARE SG12 ... 27 H6
River Mdw CAR SM5 ... 202 B6
Rivermill HLWW CM20 ... 28 F9
River Mt WOT/HER KT12 ... 195 N5
River Mount Gdns GUW GU2 ... 267 P5
Rivernook Cl WOT/HER KT12 ... 197 K5
River Pk HHW HP1 ... 35 K8
River Park Gdns HAYES BR2 ... 183 J10
River Park Rd WDGN N22 ... 98 C10
River Park Vw ORP BR6 ... 207 L7
River Pl IS N1 ... 6 E1
River Reach TEDD TW11 ... 177 H9
River Rd BARK IG11 ... 143 H5
BKHH IG9 ... 102 J3
BRW CM14 ... 106 D5
STA TW18 ... 196 A1
WDSR SL4 ... 148 B6
Riversdale GVW DA11 ... 190 B5
Riversdale Rd CRW RM5 ... 104 A3
HBRY N5 ... 118 G3
THDIT KT7 ... 198 B4
Riversdell Cl CHERT KT16 ... 195 K2
Riversend Rd HHS/BOV HP3 ... 35 N1
Riversfield Rd EN EN1 ... 79 N7
Riverside CHARL SE7 ... 142 B11
CHERT KT16 ... 195 K2
DORK RH4 ... 272 A2
EYN DA4 ... 209 L4
GU GU1 ... 
HDN NW4 ... 116 C5
HORL RH6 ... 280 ...
LCOL/BKTW AL2 ... 56 C3
RCH/KEW TW9 ... 
RKW/CH/CXG WD3 ... 
SHGR GU5 ... 268 D10
STA TW18 ... 
Riverside Av E/WMO/HCT KT8 ... 198 A3
LTWR GU18 ... 212 A4
Riverside Cl CHOB/PIR GU24 ... 230 B6
CLPT E5 ... 120 D6
KGLGY WD4 ... 54 A3
KUT/HW KT1 ... 199 H2
STMC/STPC BR5 ... 207 M2
WLGTN SM6 ... 202 C8
Riverside Ct CHING E4 * ... 80 G10
CSHM HP5 * ... 50 ...
HLWW CM20 ... 29 ...
VX/NE SW8 ... 17 ...
Riverside Dr CHSWK W4 ... 156 D5
ESH/CLAY KT10 ... 197 P6
GLDGN NW11 ... 117 J5
MTCM CR4 ... 202 A6
RCHPK/HAM TW10 ... 176 G5
RKW/CH/CXG WD3 ... 72 A5
SHGR GU5 ... 268 D10
STA TW18 ... 
Riverside Gdns ALP/SUD HA0 ... 135 N4
BERK HP4 ... 
ENC/FH EN2 ... 79 K4
HMSMTH W6 ... 156 F4
WOKS/MYFD GU22 ... 232 D7
Riverside Ms CROY/NA CR0 * ... 202 F10
WARE SG12 ... 26 C2
Riverside Pl FBAR/BDGN N11 * ... 99 L1

STWL/WRAY TW19 173 N2
Riverside Av IL IG1 122 E8
OXHEY WD19 73 J10
SCUP DA14 185 P6
SEVS/STOTM N15 119 P4
SRTFD E15 141 M4
STA TW18 173 J10
STWL/WRAY TW19 173 N1
TOOT SW17 179 L7
WOT/HER KT12 217 L1
The Riverside
E/WMO/HCT KT8 198 C3
Riverside Wk SURB KT6 * 199 H6
Riverside Wk ISLW TW7 154 D9
KUT/HW KT1 199 J2
WDSR SL4 149 J6
Riverside Yd TOOT SW17 179 L6
UX/CGN UB8 131 L3
Riversmeet HOD EN11 44 H4
Rivermead MV/WKIL W9 * 25 J6
Riverstone CI
RYLN/HDSTN HA2 114 C7
River St CLKNW EC1R 6 A3
WARE SG12 26 D2
WDSR SL4 149 J6
Riverton CI MV/WKIL W9 2 D10
Riverview GU GU1 * 249 P10
River Vw CDW/CHF RM16 168 D4
ADL/WDHM KT15 215 M2
WGCE AL7 23 H1
Riverview Gdns BARN SW13 118 H5
COB KT11 217 H9
River View Gdns TWK TW1 176 E5
Riverview Pk CAT SE6 182 K5
Riverview Rd CHSWK W4 155 N5
HOR/WEW KT19 219 P1
RDART DA2 188 F1
Riverview Ter PUR RM19 * 166 A4
River Wk DEN/HRF UB9 111 M10
SUN TW16 197 L2
WOT/HER KT12 197 H6
River Wy WHTN TW2 176 A5
GNWCH SE10 161 L2
HLW CM20 29 K6
HOR/WEW KT19 220 A2
LOU IG10 82 D10
Riverway PLMGR N13 99 H6
STA TW18 195 L1
River Whf BELV DA17 * 164 E1
Riverwood La CHST BR7 206 C2
Rivett-Drake CI GUW GU2 249 A10
Rivey CI BF/WBF KT14 215 J10
Rivington Av WFD IG8 102 A10
Rivington Cts MLHL NW7 96 B6
Rivington PI FSBYE EC1V 7 K10
Rivington St SDTCH EC2A 7 K10
Rivington Wk HACK E8 7 N5
Rivulet Rd TOTM N17 99 K8
Rixon CI DTCH/LGLY SL3 130 B8
Rixon St HOLWY N7 119 H8
Rixsen Rd MNPK E12 122 B10
Roach Rd BOW E3 140 F2
Road House Est
WOKS/MYFD GU22 * 232 D6
Roads PI ARCH N19 118 F7
Roakes Av ADL/WDHM KT15 195 N3
Roan St GNWCH SE10 161 N5
Robarts CI PIN HA5 113 J5
Robb Rd STAN HA7 94 F7
Robbs CI HHW HP1 35 K4
Robe End HHW HP1 35 J4
Robert Adam St MHST W1U 10 C5
Roberta St BETH E2 7 N9
Robert Av STAL AL1 38 B10
Robert CI CHIG IG7 103 J6
MV/WKIL W9 9 K2
POTB/CUF EN6 59 H9
WOT/HER KT12 217 J2
Robert Dashwood Wy
WALW SE17 18 E6
Robert Keen CI PECK SE15 159 P7
Robert Lowe CI NWCR SE14 160 H8
Robert Dr BMLY BR1 205 P2
Robert Rd SLN SL2 109 J7
Robertsbridge Rd CAR SM5 201 M7
Roberts CI CHEAM SM3 220 E4
CHES/WCR EN8 62 D6
DAGE RM10 144 B3
ELTH/MOT SE9 184 G4
HARH RM3 105 J9
STMC/STPC BR5 207 M5
STWL/WRAY TW19 173 M2
THHTH CR7 203 L3
WDR/YW UB7 131 P10
Roberts Ct CHSGTN KT9 219 J2
PGE/AN SE20 204 B1
WLSDN NW10 136 G1
Roberts House
WOOL/PLUM SE18 * 162 B6
Roberts La CFSP/GDCR SL9 90 D6
Roberts Ms KTBR SW1X * 16 C4
Robertson CI BROX EN10 62 D2
Robertson Rd BERK HP4 34 B3
Robertson St VX/NE SW8 158 C8
Roberts PI WX/KE EC1R * 12 B1
Robert Sq LEW SE13 161 H10
Roberts St BELV DA17 164 B4
MLHL NW7 97 H6
WALTH E17 100 C9
WATW WD18 73 K9
Robert St CAMTN NW1 4 F10
CHCR WC2N 11 M8
CROY/NA CR0 203 K10
WOOL/PLUM SE18 162 G3
Roberts Wy EGH TW20 171 P10
HAT AL10 40 C5
Roberts Wood Dr
CFSP/GDCR SL9 90 C6
Robeson St BOW E3 140 G4
Robeson Wy BORE WD6 75 P5
Robina CI BXLYHS DA6 163 K10
NTHWD HA6 92 G10
Robin CI ADL/WDHM KT15 215 N2
CRAWW RH11 283 M5
FELT TW13 175 M8
MLHL NW7 96 B4
WARE SG12 27 H8
Robin Gdns REDH RH1 258 E8
Robin Gv BTFD TW8 155 H5
HGT N6 118 B7
KTN/HRWW/WS HA3 115 L4
Robin HI BERK HP4 33 P6
GODL GU7 267 J10
Robinhood CI MTCM CR4 202 D4
Robin Hood Crs
WOKN/KNAP GU21 231 K3
Robin Hood Dr BUSH WD23 73 M5
KTN/HRWW/WS HA3 94 M8
Robin Hood Gdns
POP/IOD E14 * 141 N8
Robin Hood Gn
STMC/STPC BR5 207 N6
Robin Hood La BXLYHS DA6 185 P1
HAT AL10 40 D6
Robinhood La MTCM CR4 202 D4
PUT/ROE SW15 178 B6
RGUE GU4 232 C10
SUT SM1 221 L2
Robin Hood Meadow
HHNE HP2 36 A1
Robin Hood Rd BRWN CM15 106 C1
PUT/ROE SW15 178 B2
WOKN/KNAP GU21 231 K3
Robina Av GVW DA11 190 A3

Robinia CI BARK/HLT IG6 103 H7
PGE/AN SE20 203 P1
Robinia Crs LEY E10 120 C2
Robin La HDN NW4 116 C1
Robin Md WGCE AL7 23 K2
Robins CI LCOL/BKTW AL2 57 K3
UX/CGN UB8 131 M7
Robinsfield HHW HP1 35 K4
Robin's La EPP CM16 82 E7
Robins Nest HI
HERT/BAY SG13 42 D4
Robinson CI CHESW EN7 61 J4
Robinson CI ENC/FH EN2 79 K7
HCH RM12 145 J2
Robins Orch CFSP/GDCR SL9 90 B7
Robins Rd HHS/BOV HP3 36 B8
The Robins BRWN CM15 87 J1
Robinson Crs BUSH WD23 94 B2
DAGE RM10 124 B9
TOOT SW17 179 H9
Robinson's CI WEA W13 134 F7
Robinson St CHEL SW3 16 A9
Robins Wy HHNE HP2 36 B1
Robinsway WOT/HER KT12 217 K1
Robinswood CI BEAC HP9 88 B6
Robinswood Ms HBRY N5 119 J10
Robin Wy GUW GU2 249 N6
POTB/CUF EN6 60 F4
STA TW18 173 J6
STMC/STPC BR5 207 L3
Robin Willis Wy WDSR SL4 171 K9
Robinwood Gv UX/CGN UB8 132 A1
Robinwood PI PUT/ROE SW15 178 A4
Rob Pascoe La DAGW RM9 143 P5
Robsart St BRXN/ST SW9 158 F8
Robson Av WLSDN NW10 136 G2
Robson CI ENC/FH EN2 79 J6
EHAM E6 142 B8
Robsons CI CHES/WCR EN8 62 B5
Robyns Cft GVW DA11 190 B6
Robyns Wy SEV TN13 246 G8
Rocastle Rd BROCKY SE4 182 D1
Rochdale Rd ABYW SE2 163 L4
WALTH E17 120 F5
Rochdale Wy DEPT SE8 160 F6
Rochelle CI BTSEA SW11 157 N10
Rochelle St BETH E2 7 M8
Rochemont Wk HACK E8 * 7 M6
Roche Rd STRHM/NOR SW16 202 F1
Rochester Av BMLY BR1 205 N1
FELT TW13 174 G5
PLSTW E13 141 P5
Rochester CI BFN/LL DA15 185 L2
EN EN1 79 M5
STRHM/NOR SW16 * 180 F10
Rochester Ga
PUT/ROE SW15 178 B2
Rochester High St
PUT/ROE SW15 178 D3
Rochester La
PUT/ROE SW15 178 C6
Rochester V
PUT/ROE SW15 178 C6
Rochester Ms CAMTN NW1 5 H3
EA W5 * 155 H3
Rochester Pde FELT TW13 * 175 H6
Rochester PI CAMTN NW1 4 G1
Rochester Rd CAMTN NW1 4 G1
CAR SM5 222 A1
EGH TW20 172 C8
GVE DA12 191 H4
HCH RM12 145 J2
NTHWD HA6 112 C1
Rochester Rw WEST SW1P 17 N5
Rochester Sq CAMTN NW1 5 H1
Rochester St WEST SW1P 17 N7
Rochester Ter CAMTN NW1 4 G1
Rochester Wk STHWK SE1 * 12 G9
Rochester Way Relief Rd
ELTH/MOT SE9 184 B1
ELTH/MOT SE9 162 A9
ELTH/MOT SE9 162 C9
ELTH/MOT SE9 162 F9
RKW/CH/CXG WD3 72 C9
Roche Wk CAR SM5 201 N6
Rochford Av BRWN CM15 87 M9
CHDH RM6 121 M3
LOU IG10 83 J10
WAB EN9 63 J10
Rochford CI BROX EN10 62 D2
EHAM E6 142 A4
HCH RM12 145 J1
Rochford Gn LOU IG10 82 G1
Rochfords Gdns SLN SL2 129 P10
Rochford Wk HACK E8 * 7 N1
Rochford Wy CROY/NA CR0 202 D4
Rock Av MORT/ESHN SW14 156 A9
Rockbourne Rd FSTH SE23 181 L4
Rockchase Gdns EMPK RM11 125 M4
Rockcliffe Av KGLGY WD4 54 C6
Rock CI MTCM CR4 201 N2
Rockdale Gdns SEV TN13 * 265 J3
Rockdale Pleasance
SEV TN13 * 265 K1
Rockdale Rd SEV TN13 265 J3
Rockells PI EDUL SE22 182 A2
Rockfield CI OXTED RH8 261 J4
Rockfield Rd OXTED RH8 261 L6
Rockford Av GFD/PVL UB6 134 C4
Rock Grove Wy
BERM/RHTH SE16 19 P5
Rockhall Rd CRICK NW2 116 B10
Rockhampton Rd
SAND/SEL CR2 223 M3
STRHM/NOR SW16 181 H7
Rock HI DUL SE21 181 N7
ORP BR6 228 C3
Rockingham Av EMPK RM11 125 J4
Rockingham CI
PUT/ROE SW15 156 C10
UX/CGN UB8 131 M3
Rockingham Ga BUSH WD23 * 74 B10
Rockingham Pde UX/CGN UB8 131 M2
Rockingham Rd UX/CGN UB8 131 L3
Rockingham St STHWK SE1 18 F4
Rockland Rd PUT/ROE SW15 157 H10
Rocklands Dr
KTN/HRWW/WS HA3 94 H10
Rockleigh HERT/WAT SG14 25 K5
Rockleigh Av LEY E10 101 K7
Rockmount Rd NRWD SE19 181 M4
WOOL/PLUM SE18 163 J4
Rockshaw Rd REDH RH1 258 G10
Rocks La BARN SW13 156 D9
Rock St FSBYPK N4 119 H10
Rockware Av GFD/PVL UB6 134 D1
Rockways BAR EN5 76 C10
Rockwell Gdns NRWD SE19 181 M4
Rockwell Rd DAGE RM10 124 D1
Rockwood Gdns UX/CGN UB8 82 F7
Rocliffe St IS N1 6 E5
Rocombe Crs FSTH SE23 182 A3
Rocque La BKHTH/KID SE3 161 J3
Rodborough Rd GLDGN NW11 117 H1
Roden CI HLWE CM17 30 H7
Roden Gdns CROY/NA CR0 204 B3
Rodenhurst Rd CLAP SW4 180 C3
Roden St HOLWY N7 118 F1
IL IG1 122 C10
Rodeo CI ERITH DA8 165 J2
Roderick Rd HAMP NW3 118 B1
Rodgers CI BORE WD6 75 J1
Roding Av WFD IG8 102 G6
Roding Gdns LOU IG10 82 B10
Roding La BKHH IG9 102 B2

CHIG IG7 102 D2
Roding La North WFD IG8 102 B10
Roding La South REDBR IG4 122 A2
Roding Ms WAP E1W 13 P9
Roding Rd CLPT E5 120 C9
EHAM E6 142 E7
LOU IG10 82 C9
Rodings Rw BAR EN5 * 77 H8
The Rodings UPMR RM14 126 A4
Roding Vw BKHH IG9 102 A2
Rodmell CI YEAD UB4 133 K3
Rodmell Slope
NFNCH/WDSPK N12 97 J6
Rodmere St GNWCH SE10 161 K4
Rodney Av STAL AL1 38 K4
Rodney CI CROY/NA CR0 203 J8
NWMAL KT3 200 B5
PIN HA5 113 M5
WOT/HER KT12 197 J8
Rodney Gdns PIN HA5 111 K1
WWKM BR4 215 M1
Rodney PI STHWK SE1 18 F5
WALTH E17 100 D10
WIM/MER SW19 201 M1
Rodney Rd CHONG CM5 67 N5
MTCM CR4 201 P2
NWMAL KT3 200 B5
WALW SE17 18 F6
WAN E11 121 N2
WHTN TW2 175 P3
WOT/HER KT12 197 J9
Rodney St IS N1 5 H7
Rodney Wy DTCH/LGLY SL3 151 H7
GU GU1 250 D9
ROMW/RG RM7 104 C9
Rodona Rd WEY KT13 216 E7
Rodway Rd BMLY BR1 205 N1
PUT/ROE SW15 178 D3
Rodwell CI RSLP HA4 113 K6
Rodwell Rd EDUL SE22 181 L7
Roebuck CI ASHTD KT21 237 K6
FELT TW13 175 J7
REIG RH2 257 K10
Roebuck Gn SL SL1 128 D10
Roebuck La BKHH IG9 101 P2
Roebuck Rd BARK/HLT IG6 103 L7
CHSGTN KT9 219 M2
Roedean Av PEND EN3 80 B5
Roedean CI ORP BR6 206 C2
PEND EN3 80 B5
Roedean Crs PUT/ROE SW15 178 B2
Roe End CDALE/KGS NW9 115 P2
Roefields CI HHS/BOV HP3 35 K10
Roe Gn CDALE/KGS NW9 115 P3
Roe Green CI HAT AL10 40 B4
Roe Green La HAT AL10 40 B4
Roehampton CI GVE DA12 191 H3
PUT/ROE SW15 156 D10
Roehampton Dr CHST BR7 184 F9
Roehampton Ga
PUT/ROE SW15 178 B2
Roehampton High St
PUT/ROE SW15 178 D3
Roehampton La
PUT/ROE SW15 178 D3
Roehampton V
PUT/ROE SW15 178 C6
Roe Hill CI HAT AL10 40 B4
Roehyde Wy HAT AL10 40 B7
Roe La CDALE/KGS NW9 115 N2
Roestock Gdns STALE/WH AL4 40 A3
Roestock La STALE/WH AL4 40 A3
Rofant Rd NTHWD HA6 92 F7
Roffes La CTHM CR3 259 L1
Roffey CI HORL RH6 280 A4
PUR/KEN CR8 241 J2
Roffey's CI CRAWE RH10 285 H1
Roffords WOKN/KNAP GU21 231 N3
Rogers CI CHESW EN7 61 L3
COUL/CHIP CR5 241 J4
Rogers Gdns DAGE RM10 124 B3
Rogers La SLN SL2 129 L3
WARL CR6 242 K4
Rogers Md GDST RH9 260 F9
Rogers Rd CAN/RD E16 141 L8
DAGE RM10 124 B3
GRAYS RM17 167 P3
TOOT SW17 179 H7
Rogers Wk
NFNCH/WDSPK N12 97 L4
Rojack Rd FSTH SE23 182 A1
Rokeby Gdns WFD IG8 102 E3
Rokeby PI RYNPK SW20 178 F9
Rokeby Rd BROCKY SE4 160 C9
Rokeby St SRTFD E15 141 K9
Roke CI KWD/TDW/WH KT20 249 K7
Roke Lodge Rd PUR/KEN CR8 223 K10
Roke Rd PUR/KEN CR8 241 K1
Roker Park Av
HGDN/ICK UB10 111 P9
Rokers La MFD/CHID GU8 266 C10
Rokesby CI WELL DA16 163 P10
Rokesby PI ALP/SUD HA0 115 J10
Rokesly Av CEND/HSY/T N8 118 E5
Roland Gdns SKENS SW7 15 K7
WALW SE17 19 H8
WPK KT4 200 C9
Roles Gv CHDH RM6 121 N2
Rolfe CI BEAC HP9 88 D10
EBAR EN4 77 N3
Rolinsden Wy HAYES BR2 226 A1
Rollason Wy BRW CM14 86 C3
Rollesby Rd CHSGTN KT9 219 M3
Rollesby Wy THMD SE28 143 J5
Rolleston Av STMC/STPC BR5 207 H2
Rolleston CI STMC/STPC BR5 206 G2
Rolleston Rd SAND/SEL CR2 223 M6
Roll Gdns GNTH/NBYPK IG2 122 C2
Rollins St PECK SE15 160 B5
Rollit Crs HSLW TW3 175 P5
Rollit St HOLWY N7 119 H1
Rolls Blds FLST/FETLN EC4A 12 A5
Rollscourt Av HNHL SE24 181 K1
Rolls Park Av CHING E4 101 K6
Rolls Park Rd CHING E4 100 D6
Rolls Rd STHWK SE1 19 L3
Rolls Royce CI WLGTN SM6 222 F4
Rollswood WGCE AL7 23 H8
Rolt St DEPT SE8 160 G6
Rolvenden Gdns BMLY BR1 184 B10
Rolvenden PI TOTM N17 100 D7
Roman Av STA TW18 173 K7
Roman CI ACT W3 155 N1
DEN/HRF UB9 91 K3
EBED/NFELT TW14 175 H3
RAIN RM13 144 F4
Roman Farm Rd GUW GU2 249 J8
Roman Farm Wy GUW GU2 249 J8
Romanfield Rd
BRXS/STRHM SW2 180 A2
Roman Ms KGLGY WD4 54 C6
Romanhurst Av HAYES BR2 205 K9
Romanhurst Gdns HAYES BR2 205 K9
Roman Ri NRWD SE19 181 M2
Roman Rd BETH E2 140 C7

BOW E3 140 E3
BRW CM14 106 C6
CHSWK W4 138 C10
CRICK NW2 116 F3
DORK RH4 272 F4
EHAM E6 142 A6
GVW DA11 189 P6
IL IG1 142 E1
MUSWH N10 98 C8
RAD WD7 74 F1
RDART DA2 188 C3
Romans End STALW/RED AL3 38 B2
Romans Ga THMD SE28 143 K10
Roman St HOD EN11 44 F2
Romans Wy
WOKS/MYFD GU22 233 K1
Roman V HLWE CM17 29 M6
Roman Villa Rd EYN DA4 188 B9
Roman Wk RAD WD7 74 F1
Rom Crs ROMW/RG RM7 124 F5
Romeland BORE WD6 75 J10
STALW/RED AL3 38 B6
WAB EN9 63 H9
Romeland HI STALW/RED AL3 38 B6
Romero CI BRXN/ST SW9 158 E9
Romero Sq BKHTH/KID SE3 161 P10
Romeyn Rd
STRHM/NOR SW16 180 G6
Romford Rd CHIG IG7 103 L5
CHONG CM5 67 M9
SOCK/AV RM15 146 B9
SRTFD E15 141 L1
Romford St WCHPL E1 13 P4
Romilly Dr OXHEY WD19 73 N3
Romilly Rd FSBYPK N4 119 J7
Romilly St SOHO/SHAV W1D 11 K7
Rommany Rd WNWD SE27 181 N5
Romney Cha EMPK RM11 125 K4
Romney CI ASHF TW15 174 D8
CHSGTN KT9 219 K1
GLDGN NW11 117 M6
NWCR SE14 160 B6
RYLN/HDSTN HA2 113 P5
TOTM N17 100 A9
Romney Dr BMLY BR1 184 A10
RYLN/HDSTN HA2 113 P5
Romney Gdns BXLYHN DA7 163 P6
Romney Lock Rd WDSR SL4 149 J6
Romney Rd GNWCH SE10 161 N1
GVW DA11 190 B6
NWMAL KT3 200 A6
WOOL/PLUM SE18 162 F2
YEAD UB4 132 F4
Romney Rw CRICK NW2 * 116 C7
Romney St WEST SW1P 17 K4
Romola Rd HNHL SE24 181 J4
Romsey CI DTCH/LGLY SL3 150 C2
ORP BR6 226 F1
Romsey Dr SLN SL2 109 J8
Romsey Rd DAGW RM9 143 N3
WEA W13 135 H7
Romside PI ROMW/RG RM7 124 E2
Rom Valley Wy
ROMW/RG RM7 124 F4
Ronald Av SRTFD E15 141 K5
Ronald CI BECK BR3 204 C5
Ronald Rd HARH RM3 105 P9
Ronaldsay Sp SL SL1 129 K7
Ronalds Rd BMLY BR1 205 N10
HBRY N5 118 F1
Ronaldstone Rd BFN/LL DA15 185 H2
Rona Rd HAMP NW3 118 B9
Rona Wk IS N1 * 6 G2
Rondu Rd CRICK NW2 117 H1
Ronelean Rd SURB KT6 199 P8
Roneo Cnr ROMW/RG RM7 124 B6
Roneo Link HCH RM12 124 B6
Ronfearn Av STMC/STPC BR5 207 N2
Ron Green Ct ERITH DA8 164 E6
Ron Leighton Wy EHAM E6 142 B8
Ronnelby CI WEY KT13 196 F10
Ronnie La BCTR RM8 123 M7
Ronsons Wy STALE/WH AL4 38 C2
Ronson Wy LHD/OX KT22 234 F8
Ron Todd CI DAGE RM10 144 B5
Ronver Rd LEE/GVPK SE12 183 M6
Rood La FENCHST EC3M 13 H7
Rookby Ct WCHMH N21 99 J3
Rookeries CI FELT TW13 175 J6
Rookery CI LHD/OX KT22 236 D10
Rookery Ct WTHK RM20 166 F5
Rookery Dr CHST BR7 205 N4
DORK RH4 271 P7
Rookery Gdns
STMC/STPC BR5 207 N6
Rookery HI ASHTD KT21 237 M6
REDH RH1 281 J1
Rookery La HAYES BR2 226 C2
GRAYS RM17 168 A4
Rookery Md COUL/CHIP CR5 240 F8
Rookery Rd CLAP SW4 158 D10
ORP BR6 228 C10
STA TW18 173 L7
The Rookery
STRHM/NOR SW16 180 G9
WTHK RM20 166 F5
Rookery Vw GRAYS RM17 168 A4
Rookery Wy CDALE/KGS NW9 115 P3
KWD/TDW/WH KT20 257 K9
Rookesley Rd STMC/STPC BR5 207 P2
Rookfield Av MUSWH N10 118 C1
Rookfield CI MUSWH N10 118 C1
Rooks HI RKW/CH/CXG WD3 71 M8
WGCW AL8 22 F2
Rooksmead Rd SUN TW16 196 B2
Rookstone Rd TOOT SW17 179 J9
Rookwood Av LOU IG10 82 F7
NWMAL KT3 200 D1
WLGTN SM6 222 F3
Rookwood CI GRAYS RM17 167 N3
REDH RH1 258 D5
Rookwood Gdns CHING E4 * 101 H3
Rookwood Rd
STNW/STAM N16 119 P5
Roosevelt Wy DAGE RM10 144 F1
Rootes Dr NKENS W10 136 C10
Roothill La BRKHM/BTCW RH3 273 H10
Ropemaker Rd
BERM/RHTH SE16 143 H6
Ropemaker's Flds
POP/IOD E14 140 G8
Ropemaker St BARB EC2Y 12 G2
Roper La STHWK SE1 19 K2
Ropers Av CHING E4 101 K2
Roper St ELTH/MOT SE9 184 G4
Ropers Wk
BRXS/STRHM SW2 * 180 B1
Ropery St BOW E3 140 E3
Rope St BERM/RHTH SE16 143 J6
Rope Wk SUN TW16 196 D5
Rope Yard Rails
WOOL/PLUM SE18 142 G3
Ropewalk Gdns WCHPL E1 * 13 P5
Ropley St BETH E2 7 N7
Rosa Alba Ms HBRY N5 119 H5
Rosa Av ASHF TW15 174 B5
Rosalind Franklin CI GUW GU2 267 K1

Rosaline Rd FUL/PGN SW6 157 H6
Rosaline Ter FUL/PGN SW6 * 157 H6
Rosamond St SYD SE26 182 A6
Rosamund CI SAND/SEL CR2 223 L9
Rosamund CI CRAWE RH10 284 C9
Rosamun Rd NWDGN UB2 153 H1
Rosary CI HSLW TW3 153 M8
Rosary Ct POTB/CUF EN6 59 N5
Rosary Gdns ASHF TW15 173 K8
BUSH WD23 94 D1
SKENS SW7 15 J5
Rosary Ga BTSEA SW11 158 C10
Rosaville Rd FUL/PGN SW6 157 J6
Roscoe St STLK EC1Y 12 E1
Roscoff CI EDGW HA8 95 N5
Roseacre OXTED RH8 261 M9
Roseacre CI EMPK RM11 125 N6
SHPTN TW17 196 B5
WEA W13 134 G4
Roseacre Gdns RGUE GU4 233 N8
WGCE AL7 23 K2
Roseacre Rd WELL DA16 163 N1
Rose Aly LVPST EC2M 13 K4
STHWK SE1 12 G7
Rose Av GVE DA12 191 H4
MRDN SM4 201 M5
MTCM CR4 202 A5
SWFD E18 102 E10
Rose Bank BRW CM14 107 H5
Rosebank EPSOM KT18 219 N10
PGE/AN SE20 182 A10
WAB EN9 63 K10
Rosebank Av ALP/SUD HA0 114 K10
HCH RM12 125 K10
Rose Bank CI
NFNCH/WDSPK N12 97 P6
Rosebank CI TEDD TW11 176 C2
Rosebank Cots REIG RH2 * 275 L2
Rosebank Est BOW E3 140 B4
Rosebank Gdns ACT W3 136 A8
BOW E3 140 D4
GVW DA11 190 D6
Rosebank Gv WALTH E17 120 C1
Rosebank Rd HNWL W7 154 A5
WALTH E17 120 F4
Rosebank Wy ACT W3 136 C4
Roseberry Ct WAT WD17 * 73 H5
Roseberry Gdns FSBYPK N4 119 J4
ORP BR6 207 N10
UPMR RM14 126 E5
Roseberry PI HACK E8 7 L1
Roseberry St
BERM/RHTH SE16 159 M3
Rosebery Av CEND/HSY/T N8 118 E5
SUT SM1 221 J3
Rosebery Crs
WOKS/MYFD GU22 232 C6
Rosebery Gdns
CEND/HSY/T N8 118 F3
SUT SM1 221 L1
WEA W13 134 F8
Rosebery Ms MUSWH N10 98 C1
Rosebery Pde BUSH WD23 94 A2
Rosebery Pde EW KT17 * 220 C4
Rosebery Rd BUSH WD23 94 A2
CLAP SW4 180 F2
EPSOM KT18 220 A10
GRAYS RM17 167 N3
HSLW TW3 155 H10
KUT/HW KT1 199 N1
MUSWH N10 98 D10
SUT SM1 221 J3
Rosebery Sq WFD IG8 102 G8
Rose Bushes EW KT17 238 D1
Rose Cots HAYES BR2 225 P7
CHESW EN7 61 L1
WCHPL E1 13 L4
Rosecourt Rd CROY/NA CR0 202 A6
Rosecroft Av HAMP NW3 117 H9
BH/WHM TN16 244 C4
Rosecroft Dr CHESW EN7 60 G3
STMC/STPC BR5 207 H3
Rosecroft Gdns WHTN TW2 176 A4
Rosecroft Rd STHL UB1 134 B6
Rosecroft Wk ALP/SUD HA0 115 H10
PIN HA5 93 K10
Rosedale ASHTD KT21 237 H4
Rosedale CI ABYW SE2 142 E10
CRAWW RH11 283 K9
HNWL W7 135 N10
LCOL/BKTW AL2 55 M6
STAN HA7 94 C6
Rosedale Gdns DAGW RM9 143 J2
Rosedale PI DAGW RM9 143 K2
Rosedale Rd DAGW RM9 143 J2
EW KT17 220 D2
FSTGT E7 121 P10
GRAYS RM17 168 A4
RCH/KEW TW9 157 K1
ROM RM1 124 D1
Rosedale Av CROY/NA CR0 202 F7
GFD/PVL UB6 114 C10
MRDN SM4 201 K5
STRHM/NOR SW16 181 M4
Rosedene
LCOL/BKTW AL2 55 P2
Rosedene Av CROY/NA CR0 202 F7
GFD/PVL UB6 114 C10
MRDN SM4 201 K5
STRHM/NOR SW16 181 M4
Rosedene Gdns
GNTH/NBYPK IG2 122 C6
Rosedene Ter LEY E10 120 F8
Rosedew Rd HMSMTH W6 156 G4
Rose Dr CHAM HP5 71 J8
Rose End
NLWDGN UB2 153 H1
Rosefield CI CAR SM5 221 P4
Rosefield Gdns CHERT KT16 214 G4
POP/IOD E14 141 L8
Rosefield Rd STA TW18 173 L8
Rose Garden CI EDGW HA8 95 K7
Rose Gdns EA W5 154 F3
FELT TW13 175 H5
STHL UB1 134 A3
STWL/WRAY TW19 173 J1
WATW WD18 73 H4
Rose Gln CDALE/KGS NW9 115 P3
ROMW/RG RM7 124 F5
Rose HI DORK RH4 272 F2
SUT SM1 201 M8
Rose HI Arch Ms DORK RH4 * 272 F2
WOKN/KNAP GU21 231 P2
Rosehill Av SUT SM1 201 M8
WOKN/KNAP GU21 231 P2
Rosehill CI HOD EN11 44 B5
Rosehill Court Pde
MRDN SM4 * 201 M7
Rosehill Farm Meadow
BNSTD SM7 239 L1
Rosehill Gdns ABLGY WD5 50 G5
SUT SM1 201 M8
Rosehill Pk West SUT SM1 201 M8
Rosehill Rd BH/WHM TN16 243 P5
WAND/EARL SW18 179 M2
Rose Joan Ms
KIL/WHAMP NW6 117 K9
Roseland CI TOTM N17 99 L8
Roselands Av HOD EN11 44 B1
Rose La CHDH RM6 123 P2
RGUE GU4 233 N8
Rose Lawn BUSH WD23 94 C6
Roseleigh Av HBRY N5 119 J9
Roseleigh CI TWK TW1 177 J2
Roselyn Gdns HLW CM20 47 K1
Rosemary Av E/WMO/HCT KT8 197 P3
ED N9 79 L5
ENC/FH EN2 79 L5
FNCH N3 97 L10
HSLWW TW4 153 L8
ROM RM1 124 C1
Rosemary CI CROY/NA CR0 202 P7
OXTED RH8 261 M9
SOCK/AV RM15 147 M5
UX/CGN UB8 132 B7
Rosemary Ct HORL RH6 * 279 P8
Rosemary Crs RGUW GU3 249 L6
Rosemary Dr LCOL/BKTW AL2 56 F2
POP/IOD E14 141 J8
REDBR IG4 122 A3
Rosemary Gdns BCTR RM8 123 K1
CHSGTN KT9 219 K9
Rosemary La HORL RH6 194 C3
HORL RH6 280 C5
HORL RH6 279 N8
MORT/ESHN SW14 155 P9
Rosemary Rd PECK SE15 159 N6
TOOT SW17 179 M6
WELL DA16 163 J10
Rosemary St IS N1 * 6 G1
Rosemead CDALE/KGS NW9 116 C5
POTB/CUF EN6 59 M6
Rose Md POTB/CUF EN6 59 M6
Rosemead Av FELT TW13 174 G5
MTCM CR4 202 D3
WBLY HA9 115 P10
Rosemead CI REDH RH1 275 M2
Rose Meadow
CHOB/PIR GU24 212 F9
Rose Ms UED N18 100 A5
Rosemont Av
NFNCH/WDSPK N12 97 M7
Rosemont Rd ACT W3 135 N9
HAMP NW3 3 J1
NWMAL KT3 199 P3
RCHPK/HAM TW10 177 K2
Rosemoor St CHEL SW3 16 A6
Rosemount Av BF/WBF KT14 215 K9
Rosemount CI WFD IG8 102 K6
Rosemount Dr BMLY BR1 205 H2
Rosemount Rd ALP/SUD HA0 135 K3
WEA W13 134 G4
Rosenau Crs BTSEA SW11 158 A7
Rosenau Rd BTSEA SW11 157 P7
Rosendale Rd DUL SE21 181 K5
Roseneath Av WCHMH N21 99 J3
Roseneath PI
STRHM/NOR SW16 181 N6
Roseneath Rd BTSEA SW11 180 A4
Roseneath Wk EN EN1 79 N1
Rosens Wk EDGW HA8 95 N4
Rosenthal Rd CAT SE6 182 G2
Rosenthorpe Rd PECK SE15 182 B1
Rose Park CI YEAD UB4 133 K7
Roserton St POP/IOD E14 160 F1
The Rosery CROY/NA CR0 204 C6
Roses Cots DORK RH4 * 272 F2
Roses La WDSR SL4 148 C8
The Roses WFD IG8 101 P1
Rose St COVGDN WC2E 11 L7
GUW GU1 189 H4
Rosethorn CI BAL SW12 180 D3
Rosetree PI HPTN TW12 175 H7
Rosetrees GU GU1 268 D1
Rosetta CI VX/NE SW8 158 F6
Rose V HOD EN11 44 A2
Rose Vw BRW CM14 107 H4
Roseveare Rd LEE/GVPK SE12 183 P4
Roseville WCHMH N21 99 H1
Roseville Av HSLW TW3 175 H2
Roseville Rd HYS/HAR UB3 153 J5
Rosevine Rd RYNPK SW20 178 F10
Rose Wk BRYLDS KT5 199 N5
CRAWW RH11 283 L2
SLN SL2 128 G2
STALE/WH AL4 38 B2
WARL CR6 205 P10
The Rose Wk RAD WD7 74 G2
Rosewarne CI
WOKN/KNAP GU21 231 M4
Roseway DUL SE21 181 L2
EDGW HA8 95 P5
Rose Wy LEE/GVPK SE12 183 L5
Rosewell CI PGE/AN SE20 182 A10
Rose Wd WOKS/MYFD GU22 232 D5
Rosewood GFD/PVL UB6 114 F10
HCH RM12 125 H10
Rosewood CI HHW HP1 35 H5
KUTN/CMB KT2 177 M7
SCUP DA14 185 M6
Rosewood Ct BMLY BR1 184 B10
KUTN/CMB KT2 177 M7
ROMW/RG RM7 123 P5
Rosewood Dr ENC/FH EN2 79 H1
SHPTN TW17 196 A7
Rosewood Gdns LEW SE13 161 K9
Rosewood Gv SUT SM1 201 P8
Rosewood Sq SHB W12 137 H7
Rosewood Ter PGE/AN SE20 * 182 B10
Rosher CI SRTFD E15 141 J2
Rosherville Wy GVW DA11 190 C5
Rosina St HOM E9 139 H4
Roskell Rd PUT/ROE SW15 156 G10
Rosken Gv SLN SL2 129 K4
Roslin Rd ACT W3 155 J3
Roslin Wy BMLY BR1 183 P10
Roslyn CI BROX EN10 44 D7
MTCM CR4 201 P1
Roslyn Gdns GPK RM2 104 G10
Roslyn Ms SEVS/STOTM N15 119 J1
Roslyn Rd SEVS/STOTM N15 119 H1
Rosmead Rd NTGHL W11 137 H10
Rosoman PI CLKNW EC1R 12 B1
Rosoman St CLKNW EC1R 6 B9
Ross Av BCTR RM8 124 A5
MLHL NW7 96 C2
Ross CI CRAWE RH10 285 L8
HYS/HAR UB3 152 B3
KTN/HRWW/WS HA3 94 B9
NTHLT UB5 133 L3
Ross Crs GSTN WD25 51 H9
Rossdale SUT SM1 221 P3
Rossdale Dr CDALE/KGS NW9 115 P6
ED N9 80 G9
Rossdale Rd PUT/ROE SW15 156 F10
Rosse Ms BKHTH/KID SE3 161 K2
Rossendale CI ENC/FH EN2 79 J4
Rossendale St CLPT E5 120 D7

Rossendale Wy CAMTN NW1 .... 5 H4
Rossetti Gdns COUL/CHIP CR5 240 C1
Rossetti Ms STJWD NW8 ...... 3 L6
Ross House CHARL SE7 * ..... 162 B6
Rossignol Gdns CAR SM5 ..... 202 B2
Rossindel Rd HSLW TW3 ...... 175 P1
Rossington Av BORE WD6 ..... 75 K4
Rossington Cl CLPT E5 ...... 119 P7
  WAB EN9 ............... 80 A1
Rossington St CLPT E5 ...... 119 P7
Rosslare Rd BAL SW12 ....... 180 C4
  NRWD SE19 ............. 181 K10
Rossiter Flds BAR EN5 ...... 77 H10
Rossiter Ldg GU GU1 * ...... 268 D1
Rossland Cl BXLYHS DA6 ..... 186 B1
Rosslare Cl BH/WHM TN16 .... 262 C4
Rosslyn Av BARN SW13 ....... 156 A9
  BCTR RM8 .............. 124 A5
  CHING E4 .............. 101 L3
  EBAR EN4 .............. 77 P10
  EBED/NFELT TW14 ....... 175 H2
  HARH RM3 .............. 105 J7
Rosslyn Cl HYS/HAR UB3 ..... 132 E7
  SUN TW16 .............. 174 F9
  WWKM BR4 .............. 205 L10
Rosslyn Crs HRW HA1 ........ 132 A4
  WBLY HA9 .............. 115 K8
Rosslyn Hl HAMP NW3 ........ 117 N10
Rosslyn Pk WEY KT13 ........ 216 E1
Rosslyn Park Ms HAMP NW3 ... 117 N10
Rosslyn Rd BARK IG11 ....... 142 C2
  TWK TW1 ............... 177 H2
  WALTH E17 * ........... 121 H2
  WATW WD18 ............. 73 H7
Rossmore Ct CAMTN NW1 * .... 9 P2
  PEND EN3 .............. 80 C8
Rossmore Rd CAMTN NW1 ...... 9 N2
Ross Pde WLGTN SM6 ......... 222 C6
Ross Rd COB KT11 ........... 217 K9
  SNWD SE25 ............. 203 M3
  WHTN TW2 .............. 176 B4
  WLGTN SM6 ............. 222 D5
Ross Wy ELTH/MOT SE9 ....... 164 B9
  NTHWD HA6 ............. 92 C5
Rossway Dr BUSH WD23 ....... 74 B9
Rossway La TRING HP23 ...... 32 F1
Rosswood Gdns WLGTN SM6 .... 222 C3
Rostella Rd TOOT SW17 ...... 179 N2
Rostrevor Av HYS/HAR UB3 ... 132 F10
  SEVS/STOTM N15 ........ 119 V4
Rostrevor Gdns IVER SL0 .... 130 C4
  NWDGN UB2 ............. 153 M4
Rostrevor Rd FUL/PGN SW6 ... 157 J7
  WIM/MER SW19 .......... 179 K8
Roswell Cl CHES/WCR EN8 .... 62 D6
Rotary St STHWK SE1 ........ 18 C3
Rothbury Av RAIN RM13 ...... 145 J7
Rothbury Cots GNWCH SE10 ... 161 K3
Rothbury Pk ISLW TW7 ....... 154 F6
Rothbury Rd HOM E9 ......... 140 E2
Roth Dr RBRW/HUT CM13 ...... 107 N3
Rother Cl GSTN WD25 ........ 55 K10
Rother Crs CRAWW RH11 ...... 283 H9
Rotherfield Rd CAR SM5 ..... 222 B1
  PEND EN3 .............. 80 C3
Rotherfield St IS N1 * ..... 6 E1
Rotherham Wk STHWK SE1 * ... 12 D10
Rotherhill Av
  STRHM/NOR SW16 ........ 180 E9
Rotherhithe New Rd
  BERM/RHTH SE16 ........ 160 A4
Rotherhithe Old Rd
  BERM/RHTH SE16 ........ 160 C3
Rotherhithe St
  BERM/RHTH SE16 ........ 160 A1
Rotherhithe Tnl
  BERM/RHTH SE16 ........ 160 B1
Rothermere Rd CROY/NA CRO .. 222 G6
Rothervale HORL RH6 ........ 280 A2
Rotherwick Hl EA W5 ........ 135 L6
Rotherwick Rd GLDGN NW11 ... 117 K5
Rotherwood Cl RYNPK SW20 ... 201 N1
Rotherwood Rd
  PUT/ROE SW15 .......... 156 G9
Rothery St IS N1 * ......... 6 C1
Rothery Ter BRXN/ST SW9 * .. 159 J6
Rothesay Av GFD/PVL UB6 .... 134 C1
  RCHPK/HAM TW10 ........ 155 N10
  RYNPK SW20 ............ 201 J2
Rothesay Rd SNWD SE25 ...... 203 L4
Rothes Rd DORK RH4 ......... 272 C4
Rothsay Rd FSTGT E7 ........ 141 P2
Rothsay St STHWK SE1 ....... 19 L7
Rothschild Rd CHSWK W4 ..... 155 P5
Rothschild St WNWD SE27 .... 181 J7
Rothwell Gdns DAGW RM9 ..... 143 J4
Rothwell Rd DAGW RM9 ....... 143 H8
Rothwell St CAMTN NW1 ...... 4 B5
Rotten Rw KTBR SW1X ........ 15 J2
Rotterdam Dr POP/IOD E14 ... 161 N1
Rouel Rd BERM/RHTH SE16 .... 19 N4
Rouge La GVE DA12 .......... 190 G4
Roughdown Av HRDN SM4 ...... 201 K6
Roughdown Rd HHS/BOV HP3 ... 35 N9
Roughdown Villas Rd
  HHS/BOV HP3 ........... 35 M9
Roughets La REDH RH1 ....... 259 M5
Roughlands
  WOKS/MYFD GU22 ........ 233 H1
Rough Rew DORK RH4 ......... 272 C6
Rough Rd WOKS/MYFD GU22 .... 231 H8
The Roughs NTHWD HA6 ....... 92 H4
Roughtallys EPP CM16 ....... 66 A3
Roughwood Cl WAT WD17 ...... 72 F4
Roughwood La CSTG HP8 ...... 70 B10
Rounce La CHOB/PIR GU24 .... 212 C9
Round Ash Wy HART DA3 ...... 211 K6
Roundaway Rd CLAY IG5 ...... 60 A8
Roundbush La GSTN WD25 ..... 74 B3
Roundcroft CHESW EN7 ....... 61 N2
Roundel Cl BROCKY SE4 ...... 160 B10
Round Gv CROY/NA CRO ....... 204 C7
Round Gv Cl FSTH SE23 ...... 182 C5
Roundheads End BEAC HP9 .... 38 A5
Roundhedge Wy ENC/FH EN2 ... 78 C4
Round Hl SYD SE26 .......... 182 G5
Roundhill WOKS/MYFD GU22 ... 232 F2
Roundhill Dr ENC/FH EN2 .... 78 C4
  WOKS/MYFD GU22 ........ 232 E4
Roundhills WAB EN9 ......... 63 K10
Roundhill Wy COB KT11 ...... 218 A7
  GUW GU2 ............... 249 L10
The Roundings
  HERT/BAY SG13 ......... 26 A10
Roundin Gdns
  STMC/STPC BR5 ......... 207 L4
Roundmead Av LOU IG10 ...... 62 D7
Roundmead Cl LOU IG10 ...... 62 D7
Roundmoor Dr
  CHES/WCR EN8 .......... 62 D5
Round Oak Rd WEY KT13 ...... 216 H4
Roundtable Rd BMLY BR1 ..... 183 M6
Roundthorn Wy
  WOKN/KNAP GU21 ........ 231 H1
Roundtree Rd ALP/SUD HA0 ... 114 D10
Roundway EGH TW20 .......... 172 H4
Roundways RSLP HA4 ......... 112 C10
The Roundway
  ESH/CLAY KT10 ......... 218 G4
  TOTM N17 .............. 99 H4
  WATW WD18 ............. 73 J7
Roundwood CHST BR7 ......... 206 B5
  KGLGY WD4 ............. 36 B7
Roundwood Av
  RBRW/HUT CM13 ......... 107 N2
  STKPK UB11 ............ 152 A1
Roundwood Cl RSLP HA4 ...... 112 C4
Roundwood Dr WGCW AL8 ...... 22 F1
Roundwood Gv
  RBRW/HUT CM13 ......... 107 N2
Roundwood Lake
  RBRW/HUT CM13 ......... 107 N2

Roundwood Pk
  WLSDN NW10 * .......... 136 D3
Round Wood Rd WLSDN NW10 ... 136 D3
Roundwood Rd WLSDN NW10 .... 136 D1
Roundwood Ter BNSTD SM7 .... 238 G1
Roundwood Vw BNSTD SM7 ..... 238 G1
Roundwood Wy BNSTD SM7 ..... 238 G1
Rounton Rd BOW E3 .......... 140 F6
  WAB EN9 ............... 63 K9
Roupell Rd BRXS/STRHM SW2 .. 180 G4
Roupell St STHWK SE1 ....... 12 B10
Rousden St CAMTN NW1 ....... 4 G2
Rouse Ct CFSP/GDCR SL9 ..... 110 C3
Rouse Gdns DUL SE21 ........ 181 M7
Rous Rd BKHH IG9 ........... 102 B3
Routemaster Cl PLSTW E13 ... 141 N6
Routh Ct EBED/NFELT TW14 ... 174 E4
Routh Rd WAND/EARL SW18 .... 179 P3
Routh St EHAM E6 ........... 144 B10
Rowallan Rd FUL/PGN SW6 .... 157 H6
Rowan Av CHING E4 .......... 100 E7
  EGH TW20 .............. 172 F8
Rowan Cl ALP/SUD HA0 ....... 114 F8
  ASHF TW15 ............. 173 N7
  CRAWE RH10 ............ 284 A7
  EA W5 ................. 155 K1
  GU GU1 ................ 249 N7
  IL IG1 ................ 122 C10
  LCOL/BKTW AL2 ......... 55 J7
  NWMAL KT3 ............. 200 B2
  REIG RH2 .............. 275 M4
  STAL/WH AL4 ........... 39 K6
  STAN HA7 .............. 94 E7
  STRHM/NOR SW16 ........ 202 D1
Rowan Crs STRHM/NOR SW16 ... 202 D1
Rowan Dr BROX EN10 ......... 44 E10
  CDALE/KGS NW9 ......... 116 D10
Rowan Gdns CROY/NA CRO ..... 203 N10
  IVER SL0 .............. 130 C3
Rowan Gn East
  RBRW/HUT CM13 ......... 107 L5
Rowan Gn West
  RBRW/HUT CM13 ......... 107 L5
Rowan Gv COUL/CHIP CR5 ..... 240 C10
  SOCK/AV RM15 .......... 146 B9
Rowanhurst Dr SLN SL2 ...... 109 H10
Rowan Md
  KWD/TDW/WH KT20 ....... 238 E5
Rowan Pl HYS/HAR UB3 ....... 132 A5
Rowan Rd BTFD TW8 .......... 154 C6
  BXLYHN DA7 ............ 164 F6
  HMSMTH W6 ............. 156 H3
  STRHM/NOR SW16 ........ 202 D1
  SWLY BR8 .............. 208 B3
  WDR/YW UB7 ............ 151 N3
Rowans WGCE AL7 ............ 23 J2
The Rowans BROX EN10 ....... 44 B5
  CFSP/GDCR SL9 ......... 109 P1
  HHW HP1 ............... 35 L5
  PLMGR N13 ............. 99 K4
  SOCK/AV RM15 .......... 146 B10
  SUN TW16 .............. 174 C8
  WOKS/MYFD GU22 ........ 232 B4
Rowans Wy LOU IG10 ......... 82 C8
Rowan Ter HMSMTH W6 ........ 156 H3
  PGE/AN SE20 * ......... 203 P1
  WIM/MER SW19 * ........ 179 H10
Rowantree Cl WCHMH N21 ..... 99 L2
Rowantree Ms ENC/FH EN2 .... 79 J6
Rowantree Rd ENC/FH EN2 .... 79 J6
  WCHMH N21 ............. 99 L2
Rowan Wk EFNCH N2 .......... 117 M4
  EMPK RM11 ............. 125 L2
  HAYES BR2 ............. 206 C10
  NKENS W10 * ........... 8 A1
  SBW CM21 .............. 29 P1
Rowan Wy CHDH RM6 .......... 123 M1
  HARP AL5 .............. 20 B3
  SLN SL2 ............... 128 C3
  SOCK/AV RM15 .......... 147 J6
Rowanwood Av BFN/LL DA15 ... 185 K4
Rowbarns Wy EHSLY KT24 ..... 252 G6
Rowben Cl TRDG/WHET N20 .... 97 L2
Rowberry Cl FUL/PGN SW6 .... 156 G6
Rowbury GODL GU7 ........... 267 M3
Rowcroft HHW HP1 ........... 35 H7
Rowcross St STHWK SE1 ...... 19 L7
Rowdell Rd NTHLT UB5 ....... 133 P7
Rowden Pde CHING E4 * ...... 100 F7
Rowden Rd BECK BR3 ......... 183 H4
  CHING E4 .............. 100 C7
  HOR/WEW KT19 .......... 219 P7
Rowditch La BTSEA SW11 ..... 158 H8
Rowdon Av WLSDN NW10 ....... 136 G2
Rowdow La BGR/WK TN15 ...... 229 N10
Rowdowns Rd DAGW RM9 ....... 144 A3
Rowe Gdns BARK IG11 ........ 143 J4
Rowe La HOM E9 ............. 120 E10
Rowena Crs BTSEA SW11 ...... 157 P8
Rowen Wk CSHM HP5 .......... 50 C6
Rowe Wk RYLN/HDSTN HA2 ..... 113 P8
Rowfant Cl CRAWE RH10 ...... 284 F7
Rowfant Rd TOOT SW17 ....... 180 B5
Rowhedge RBRW/HUT CM13 ..... 107 H4
Row Hl ADL/WDHM KT15 ....... 215 P8
Rowhill Rd CLPT E5 ......... 120 A9
  RDART DA2 ............. 186 G9
Rowhurst Av
  ADL/WDHM KT15ADL ...... 215 L3
Rowington Cl BAY/PAD W2 .... 8 G3
Rowland Av
  KTN/HRWW/WS HA3 ....... 113 H1
Rowland Cl CRAWE RH10 ...... 281 H10
  WDSR SL4 .............. 148 C9
Rowland Crs CHIG IG7 ....... 103 H5
Rowland Gv SYD SE26 ........ 182 A6
Rowland Hill Av TOTM N17 ... 99 K8
Rowland Hill St HAMP NW3 ... 117 P10
Rowlands Av PIN HA5 ........ 93 P1
Rowlands Cl CHES/WCR EN8 ... 62 C6
  HGT N6 ................ 118 A4
  MLHL NW7 .............. 96 C5
Rowlandsfields
  CHES/WCR EN8 * ........ 62 C6
Rowlands Rd BCTR RM8 ....... 124 A7
Rowland Wy ASHF TW15 ....... 174 D10
  WIM/MER SW19 .......... 201 N1
Rowlatt Dr STALW/RED AL3 ... 37 P8
Rowley Av BFN/LL DA15 ...... 185 L3
Rowley Cl ALP/SUD HA0 ...... 136 A1
  OXHEY WD19 ............ 73 M10
  WOKS/MYFD GU22 ........ 233 H2
Rowley Gdns CTHM CR3 ....... 241 N6
  FSBYPK N4 ............. 119 K5
Rowley Green Rd BAR EN5 .... 76 B4
Rowley La BAR EN5 .......... 76 A4
  DTCH/LGLY SL3 ......... 150 B4
Rowley Md HERT/BAY SG13 .... 25 M4
Rowley Rd SEVS/STOTM N15 ... 119 K3
Rowley's Rd HERT/BAY SG13 .. 25 N2
Rowley Wk HHW HP1 .......... 36 D1
Rowlheys Pl WDR/YW UB7 ..... 151 N2
Rowlls Rd KUT/HW KT1 ....... 199 L3
Rowmarsh Cl GVW DA11 ....... 190 A10
Rowney Gdns DAGW RM9 ....... 143 J8
  SBW CM21 .............. 29 M3
Rowney Rd DAGW RM9 ......... 143 H8
Rowney Wd SBW CM21 ......... 29 N3
Rowntree Clifford Cl
  PLSTW E13 ............. 141 N6
Rowntree Cl KIL/WHAMP NW6 .. 2 C1
Rowntree Rd WHTN TW2 ....... 176 D4
Rowse Cl SRTFD E15 ......... 141 H9
Rowsley Av HDN NW4 ......... 116 A1
The Rows HLW CM20 * ........ 28 F10

The Row AMSS HP7 * ......... 68 B10
Rowton Rd WOOL/PLUM SE18 ... 162 F6
Row Town ADL/WDHM KT15 ..... 215 N4
Rowzill Rd SWLY BR8 ........ 186 D9
Roxborough Av HRW HA1 ...... 114 C5
  ISLW TW7 .............. 154 A4
Roxborough Pk HRW HA1 ...... 114 D5
Roxborough Rd HRW HA1 ...... 114 C4
Roxbourne Cl NTHLT UB5 ..... 133 L1
Roxburgh Av UPMR RM14 ...... 126 A3
Roxburgh Rd WNWD SE27 ...... 181 J4
Roxburn Wy RSLP HA4 ........ 112 C8
Roxby Pl FUL/PGN SW6 ....... 14 F9
Roxeth Green Av
  RYLN/HDSTN HA2 ........ 114 A10
Roxeth Gn RYLN/HDSTN HA2 ... 114 A9
Roxeth Hl RYLN/HDSTN HA2 ... 114 B9
Roxford Cl SHPTN TW17 ...... 196 F5
Roxley Rd LEW SE13 ......... 182 G2
Roxton Gdns CROY/NA CRO .... 224 E3
Roxwell Cl SL SL1 .......... 128 D10
Roxwell Gdns
  RBRW/HUT CM13 ......... 87 P3
Roxwell Rd BARK IG11 ....... 143 K4
  SHB W12 ............... 156 D1
Roxwell Wy WFD IG8 ......... 101 P8
Roxy Av CHDH RM6 ........... 123 M5
Royal Albert Rd CAN/RD E16 . 142 A4
Royal Ar CONDST W1S * ...... 10 C8
Royal Arsenal West
  WOOL/PLUM SE18 ........ 162 D4
Royal Av CHEL SW3 .......... 16 A7
  WPK KT4 ............... 200 B9
Royal Circ WNWD SE27 ....... 181 H6
Royal Cl DEPT SE8 .......... 160 E5
  GDMY/SEVK IG3 ......... 123 K5
  ORP BR6 ............... 226 E1
  STNW/STAM N16 ......... 119 M6
  WDR/YW UB7 ............ 132 A5
  WIM/MER SW19 .......... 178 C5
  WPK KT4 ............... 200 B9
Royal College St CAMTN NW1 . 4 F1
Royal Connaught Dr
  BUSH WD23 ............. 73 N8
Royal Ct BANK EC3V * ....... 13 L4
  EN EN1 * .............. 79 M10
  HHS/BOV HP3 ........... 35 P9
Royal Crs GNTH/NBYPK IG2 ... 122 C4
  NTGHL W11 ............. 156 C1
  RSLP HA4 .............. 113 M9
Royal Crescent Ms
  NTGHL W11 * ........... 156 C1
Royal Docks Rd EHAM E6 ..... 142 F7
Royal Dr EPSOM KT18 ........ 238 E4
  FBAR/BDGN N11 ......... 98 B6
Royal Earlswood Pk
  REDH RH1 .............. 276 B3
Royal Herbert Pavilions
  WOOL/PLUM SE18 ........ 162 C7
Royal Hill GNWCH SE10 ...... 161 H6
Royal Hospital Rd CHEL SW3 . 16 A9
Royal La WDR/YW UB7 ........ 132 A3
Royal Ms BAL SW12 * ........ 180 C5
Royal Mint Pl WCHPL E1 ..... 13 M7
Royal Mint St WCHPL E1 ..... 13 M7
Royal Naval Pl NWCR SE14 ... 160 B9
Royal Oak Ms TEDD TW11 * ... 176 B8
Royal Oak Pl EDUL SE22 ..... 182 A2
Royal Oak Rd BXLYHN DA6 .... 186 A1
  HACK E8 ............... 140 A1
  WOKN/KNAP GU21 ........ 231 P4
Royal Oak Yd STHWK SE1 ..... 19 J2
Royal Opera Ar STJS SW1Y * . 11 J9
Royal Orchard Cl
  WAND/EARL SW18 ........ 179 H3
Royal Pde BKHTH/KID SE3 .... 161 L8
  CHST BR7 .............. 184 F10
  FUL/PGN SW6 * ......... 157 H6
Royal Pier Rd GVE DA12 ..... 190 B2
Royal Pl GNWCH SE10 ........ 161 H6
Royal Rd CAN/RD E16 ........ 142 A4
  LBTH SE11 ............. 18 C3
  RDART DA2 ............. 187 H8
  SCUP DA14 ............. 185 N6
  TEDD TW11 ............. 176 C8
Royal Route WBLY HA9 ....... 115 L9
Royal St STHWK SE1 ......... 17 P3
Royal Terrace Pier GVE DA12* 190 F2
Royal Victor Pl BOW E3 ..... 140 C4
Royce Cl BROX EN10 ......... 44 E7
Royce Gv WDSR WD25 ......... 54 C10
Royce Rd CRAWE RH10 ........ 284 B2
Roycraft Av BARK IG11 ...... 143 J4
Roycroft Cl
  BRXS/STRHM SW2 ........ 181 J1
  SWFD E18 .............. 101 N1
Roydene Rd
  WOOL/PLUM SE18 ........ 163 K10
Roydon Cl LOU IG10 ......... 102 A1
Roydon Ct WOT/HER KT12 ..... 217 H1
Roydon Rd HLWW/ROY CM19 .... 28 B10
  WARE SG12 ............. 27 J7
Roydon St BTSEA SW11 ....... 159 H1
Roy Gdns GNTH/NBYPK IG2 .... 123 H3
Roy Gv HPTN TW12 ........... 176 A9
Royle Cl CFSP/GDCR SL9 ..... 90 B7
  GPK RM2 ............... 125 J3
Royle Crs WEA W13 .......... 135 H6
Roy Rd NTHWD HA6 ........... 92 G8
Roy Sq POP/IOD E14 ......... 140 D9
Royston Av BF/WBF KT14 ..... 215 P8
  CHING E4 .............. 100 F6
  SUT SM1 ............... 201 N10
  WLGTN SM6 ............. 222 E1
Royston Cl CRAWE RH10 ...... 284 B3
  HEST TW5 * ............ 153 J7
  HEST TW5 .............. 153 J7
  WOT/HER KT12 .......... 197 H7
Royston Gdns IL IG1 ........ 122 A4
Royston Gv PIN HA5 ......... 93 N4
Royston Park Rd PIN HA5 .... 93 N5
Royston Rd BF/WBF KT14 ..... 215 P8
  HARH RM3 .............. 105 K8
  PGE/AN SE20 ........... 204 C1
  RCHPK/HAM TW10 ........ 155 H9
  STAL AL1 .............. 11 B2
The Roystons BRYLDS KT5 .... 199 N5
Royston St BETH E2 ......... 140 B4
Royston Wy SL SL1 .......... 128 C3
Rozel Rd VX/NE SW8 ......... 158 D8
Rubastic Rd NWDGN UB2 ...... 153 K2
Rubens Rd NTHLT UB5 ........ 133 K4
Rubens St CAT SE6 .......... 182 E5
Rubin Pl PEND EN3 .......... 80 F3
Ruby Cl SL SL1 ............. 148 F1
Ruby Ms WALTH E17 * ........ 120 F1
Ruby Rd WALTH E17 .......... 120 F1
Ruby St PECK SE15 .......... 160 A5
  WLSDN NW10 ............ 137 H4
Ruby Triangle PECK SE15 * .. 160 A5
Ruckholt Cl LEY E10 ........ 120 C10
Ruckles Wy AMSS HP7 * ...... 68 C3
Rucklidge Av WLSDN NW10 .... 136 C4
Rudall Crs HAMP NW3 ........ 117 M1
Ruddesley Av NTHLT UB5 ..... 133 L3
Ruddock Cl EDGW HA8 ........ 96 D7
Ruddstreet Cl
  WOOL/PLUM SE18 ........ 162 H10
Ruden Wy EW KT17 ........... 238 G10
Rudge Ri ADL/WDHM KT15 ..... 215 J2
Rudgwick Rd CRAWW RH11 ..... 283 J6
Rudgwick Ter STJWD NW8 * ... 3 M4
Rudland Rd BXLYHN DA7 ...... 164 D3
Rudloe Rd BAL SW12 ......... 180 D3
Rudolf Pl VX/NE SW8 ........ 17 M10
Rudolph Rd BUSH WD23 ....... 73 H1
  KIL/WHAMP NW6 ......... 2 B1
  PLSTW E13 ............. 141 H1
Rudsworth Cl DTCH/LGLY SL3 . 150 B3
Rudyard Gv EDGW HA8 ........ 95 N7

Rue De St Lawrence WAB EN9 . 63 H10
Ruffets Wd GVE DA12 ........ 190 F9
Ruffetts Cl SAND/SEL CR2 ... 224 A4
The Ruffetts SAND/SEL CR2 .. 224 A4
Ruffetts Wy
  KWD/TDW/WH KT20 ....... 239 H4
Ruffle Cl WDR/YW UB7 ....... 151 P1
Rufford Cl
  KTN/HRWW/WS HA3 ....... 114 C4
  WAT WD17 .............. 72 G3
Rufford Rd IS N1 ........... 5 M5
Rufford Street Ms IS N1 * .. 5 M4
Rufus Cl RSLP HA4 .......... 113 L8
Rufus St FSBYE EC1V ........ 7 J7
Rufwood CRAWE RH10 ......... 285 P5
Rugby Av ALP/SUD HA0 ....... 115 N9
  ED N9 ................. 99 N2
  GFD/PVL UB6 ........... 134 C1
Rugby Cl HRW HA1 ........... 114 D2
Rugby Gdns DAGW RM9 ........ 143 M1
Rugby La BELMT SM2 ......... 220 G5
Rugby Rd CDALE/KGS NW9 ..... 115 M2
  CHSWK W4 .............. 156 A1
  DAGW RM9 .............. 143 L2
  TWK TW1 ............... 176 B2
Rugby St BMSBY WC1N ........ 11 N2
Rugby Wy RKW/CH/CXG WD3 .... 73 J2
Ruggles-Brise Rd ASHF TW15 . 173 N8
Rugg St POP/IOD E14 ........ 140 F9
Rugosa Rd CHOB/PIR GU24 .... 212 D9
Ruislip Cl GFD/PVL UB6 ..... 134 A6
Ruislip Rd GFD/PVL UB6 ..... 133 K3
Ruislip Rd East GFD/PVL UB6  134 B6
Ruislip St TOOT SW17 ....... 180 A7
Rumballs Cl HHS/BOV HP3 .... 36 B9
Rumballs Rd HHS/BOV HP3 .... 36 A9
Rumbold Rd FUL/PGN SW6 ..... 157 L6
  HOD EN11 .............. 45 H1
Rum Cl WAP E1W ............. 140 A9
Rumsey Cl HPTN TW12 ........ 175 N9
Rumsey Ms FSBYPK N4 ........ 119 P1
Rumsey Rd BRXN/ST SW9 ...... 158 G9
Rumsley CHESW EN7 .......... 61 P5
Runbury Cir CDALE/KGS NW9 .. 116 A10
Runcie Cl STALE/WH AL4 ..... 38 F2
Runciman Cl ORP BR6 ........ 227 M6
Runcorn Cl TOTM N17 ........ 120 E2
Runcorn Pl NTGHL W11 ....... 8 A8
Rundell Crs HDN NW4 ........ 116 A3
Rundells HLWS CM18 ......... 47 K5
Runes Cl MTCM CR4 .......... 201 N4
Runham Rd HHS/BOV HP3 ...... 35 P8
Runnelfield HRW HA1 ........ 114 D8
Runnemede Rd EGH TW20 ...... 172 C7
Running Waters
  RBRW/HUT CM13 ......... 107 M5
Runnymede WIM/MER SW19 ..... 201 N1
Runnymede Cl WHTN TW2 ...... 176 A2
Runnymede Crs
  STRHM/NOR SW16 ........ 202 E1
Runnymede Gdns
  GFD/PVL UB6 ........... 134 C4
  WHTN TW2 .............. 176 A2
Runnymede Rd WHTN TW2 ...... 176 A2
Runrig Hl AMS HP6 .......... 69 K1
Runsley WGCE AL7 ........... 23 K2
Runtley Wood La RGUE GU4 ... 250 C1
Runway Cl CDALE/KGS NW9 .... 96 C10
The Runway HAT AL10 ........ 40 A2
  RSLP HA4 .............. 113 J10
Rupack St BERM/RHTH SE16 ... 160 F7
Rupert Av WBLY HA9 ......... 115 K10
Rupert Ct E/WMO/HCT KT8 * .. 197 P4
  SOHO/SHAV W1D * ....... 11 J8
Rupert Gdns BRXN/ST SW9 .... 159 J8
Rupert Rd ARCH N19 ......... 118 E8
  CHSWK W4 .............. 156 B2
  KIL/WHAMP NW6 ......... 137 H5
  WDR/YW UB7 ............ 152 B1
Rupert St SOHO/SHAV W1D .... 11 H8
Rural Cl EMPK RM11 ......... 125 J6
Rural V GVW DA11 ........... 190 B3
Rural Wy REDH RH1 .......... 258 B10
  STRHM/NOR SW16 ........ 179 L10
Rusbridge Cl HACK E8 ....... 138 D10
Ruscoe Dr WOKS/MYFD GU22 ... 232 D5
Ruscoe Rd CAN/RD E16 ....... 141 P8
Ruscombe Gdns
  DTCH/LGLY SL3 ......... 149 M6
Ruscombe Wy
  EBED/NFELT TW14 ....... 153 N8
Rusham Park Av EGH TW20 .... 172 C7
Rusham Rd BAL SW12 ......... 179 N1
  EGH TW20 .............. 172 B7
Rushbridge Cl CROY/NA CRO .. 203 K6
Rushbrook Crs WALTH E17 .... 101 H10
Rushbrook Rd ELTH/MOT SE9 .. 184 F1
Rush Cl WARE SG12 .......... 27 H7
Rush Common Ms
  BRXS/STRHM SW2 ........ 180 A3
Rush Cft GODL GU7 * ........ 267 M9
Rushcroft Rd
  BRXS/STRHM SW2 ........ 159 H10
  CHING E4 .............. 100 C4
Rushden Cl NRWD SE19 ....... 181 L10
Rushdene ABYW SE2 .......... 163 M2
Rushdene Av EBAR EN4 ....... 97 P1
Rushdene Cl NTHLT UB5 ...... 133 K4
Rushdene Crs NTHLT UB5 ..... 133 K4
Rushdene Rd BRWN CM15 ...... 107 L3
  PIN HA5 ............... 93 P4
Rushden Gdns CLAY IG5 ...... 122 D1
  MLHL NW7 .............. 96 A3
Rushdon Cl GRAYS RM17 ...... 167 M2
  ROM RM1 ............... 125 K1
Rushen Wk CAR SM5 * ........ 202 A7
Rushes Md HLWS CM18 ........ 47 H3
  UX/CGN UB8 ............ 131 M3
Rushet Rd STMC/STPC BR5 .... 207 H6
Rushett Cl THDIT KT7 ....... 198 D2
Rushett La CHSGTN KT9 ...... 219 J8
Rushett Rd THDIT KT7 ....... 198 E1
Rushetts Pl CRAWW RH11 ..... 283 M1
Rushetts Rd CRAWW RH11 ..... 283 K5
  REIG RH2 .............. 275 P4
Rushey Cl NWMAL KT3 ........ 200 B2
Rushey Gn CAT SE6 .......... 182 A5
Rushey Md BROCKY SE4 ....... 182 A1
Rushfield POTB/CUF EN6 ..... 59 H5
  SBW CM21 .............. 29 P1
Rushford Rd BROCKY SE4 ..... 182 A2
Rush Green Gdns
  ROMW/RG RM7 ........... 124 D6
Rush Green Rd
  ROMW/RG RM7 ........... 124 D6
Rushgrove Av
  CDALE/KGS NW9 ......... 116 C3
Rushgrove Pde
  CDALE/KGS NW9 * ....... 116 C3
Rushgrove St
  WOOL/PLUM SE18 ........ 162 C5
Rush Hill Ms BTSEA SW11 * .. 158 G9
Rush Hill Rd BTSEA SW11 .... 158 G9
Rushleigh Av CHES/WCR EN8 .. 62 C2
Rushley Cl HAYES BR2 ....... 227 J2
Rushmead BETH E2 * ......... 140 A2
  RCHPK/HAM TW10 ........ 176 A5
Rushmead Cl CROY/NA CRO .... 223 J2
Rushmere Av UPMR RM14 ...... 126 A1
Rushmere Ct WPK KT4 ........ 200 E10
Rushmere House
  PUT/ROE SW15 * ........ 178 D7
Rushmere La CSTG HP8 ....... 50 A10
Rushmere Pl RYNPK SW20 ..... 200 C1
Rushmon Gdns WOT/HER KT12 .. 197 J8
Rushmon Pl CHEAM SM3 * ..... 221 H3
Rushmon Vls NWMAL KT3 * .... 200 D2
Rushmoor Cl PIN HA5 ........ 93 G2
  RKW/CH/CXG WD3 ........ 91 J3
Rushmore Cl BMLY BR1 ....... 206 B2
Rushmore Crs CLPT E5 ....... 120 C9
Rushmore Hl ORP BR6 ........ 227 M6
  RSEV TN14 ............. 227 N10
Rushmore Rd CLPT E5 ........ 120 B9
  RSLP HA4 * ............ 113 H8
Rusholme Av DAGE RM10 ...... 124 B8
Rusholme Gv NRWD SE19 ...... 181 M9
Rusholme Rd PUT/ROE SW15 ... 178 G2
Rushout Av
  KTN/HRWW/WS HA3 ....... 114 G4
Rushton Av GSTN WD25 ....... 73 N1
Rushton St IS N1 ........... 7 H1
Rushworth Av
  HDN NW4 * ............. 116 A1
Rushworth Gdns
  HDN NW4 ............... 116 A1
Rushworth Rd REIG RH2 ...... 257 K9
Rushworth St STHWK SE1 ..... 18 D1
Rushymead BCR/WK TN15 ...... 231 K6
Rushy Meadow La CAR SM5 .... 202 A9
Ruskin Av EBED/NFELT TW14 .. 153 P7
  MNPK E12 .............. 142 B1
  RCH/KEW TW9 ........... 155 N6
  UPMR RM14 ............. 126 B5
  WAB EN9 ............... 63 K10
  WELL DA16 ............. 165 H3
Ruskin Cl CHESW EN7 ........ 61 M2
  CRAWE RH10 ............ 285 M3
  GLDGN NW11 ............ 117 H6
Ruskin Dr ORP BR6 .......... 207 H6
  WELL DA16 ............. 165 K4
  WPK KT4 ............... 200 G10
Ruskin Gdns EA W5 .......... 135 J6
  HARH RM3 .............. 105 J9
  KTN/HRWW/WS HA3 ....... 115 L3
Ruskin Gv WELL DA16 ........ 165 K8
Ruskin Pk House CMBW SE5 * . 181 H1
Ruskin Rd BELV DA17 ........ 164 C4
  CAR SM5 ............... 222 B2
  CROY/NA CRO ........... 203 J9
  ISLW TW7 .............. 154 A7
  SEVS/STOTM N15 ........ 119 N6
  STA TW18 .............. 173 J10
  STHL UB1 .............. 133 P3
  TOTM N17 .............. 99 N9
Ruskin Wk ED N9 ............ 99 P3
  HAYES BR2 ............. 206 B6
  HNHE SE24 ............. 162 D5
Rusland Av ORP BR6 ......... 206 C10
Rusland Park Rd HRW HA1 .... 114 D2
Rusper Cl CRICK NW2 ........ 136 F1
  STAN HA7 .............. 95 H5
Rusper Rd DAGW RM9 ......... 143 M1
  WDGN N22 .............. 99 H8
Ruspers Keep CRAWW RH11 .... 283 J6
Russell Av STALW/RED AL3 ... 38 C6
  WDGN N22 .............. 99 J10
Russell Cl BECK BR3 ........ 204 G3
  BKHTH/KID SE3 ......... 161 P6
  BXLYHN DA7 ............ 164 B10
  CHSWK W4 .............. 156 C5
  DART DA1 .............. 165 H9
  KWD/TDW/WH KT20 ....... 256 D1
  NTHWD HA6 ............. 92 B6
  RSLP HA4 .............. 113 J10
  STWL/WRAY TW19 ........ 172 A4
  WAP E1W ............... 140 A9
Russellcroft Rd WGCW AL8 ... 22 F4
Russell Dr STWL/WRAY TW19 .. 172 A4
Russell Gdns GLDGN NW11 .... 117 H5
  RCHPK/HAM TW10 ........ 176 A5
  TRDG/WHET N20 ......... 97 H5
  WDR/YW UB7 ............ 152 B4
  WKENS W14 ............. 14 A3
Russell Gardens Ms
  WKENS W14 * ........... 14 A3
Russell Green Cl PUR/KEN CR8 223 H6
Russell Gv BRXN/ST SW9 ..... 159 H7
  MLHL NW7 .............. 96 B6
Russell Hill PUR/KEN CR8 ... 223 H6
Russell Hill Pl PUR/KEN CR8  223 H6
Russell Hill Rd PUR/KEN CR8  223 H6
Russell Kerr Cl CHSWK W4 * . 155 P6
Russell La TRDG/WHET N20 ... 98 A3
Russell Pde GLDGN NW11 * ... 117 H5
Russell Pl EYN DA4 ......... 209 P1
  HAMP NW3 .............. 117 P10
  HHS/BOV HP3 ........... 35 L9
Russell Rd BKHTH/KID SE3 ... 161 L2
  BUSH WD23 ............. 74 B1
  CEND/HSY/T N8 ......... 118 E4
  CHING E4 .............. 100 E5
  EN EN1 ................ 79 N4
  FSTGT E7 .............. 141 N2
  GVE DA12 .............. 190 B3
  MTCM CR4 .............. 201 P3
  NTHLT UB5 ............. 114 B10
  NTHWD HA6 ............. 92 B7
  SEVS/STOTM N15 ........ 119 H6
  TOTM N17 .............. 99 P3
  TWK TW1 ............... 176 B3
  WALTH E17 ............. 120 G2
  WAN E11 ............... 122 B7
  WDGN N22 .............. 99 J10
  WIM/MER SW19 .......... 179 K10
  WKENS W14 ............. 14 A2
  WOKN/KNAP GU21 ........ 231 P1
Russells KWD/TDW/WH KT20 ... 238 G5
Russells Crs HORL RH6 ...... 280 B5
Russell's Footpath
  STRHM/NOR SW16 ........ 180 A9
Russells Ride CHES/WCR EN8 . 62 C3
Russell Sq BMSBY WC1B ...... 11 L2
Russell St COVGDN WC2E ..... 11 M7
Russell Wy CRAWE RH10 ...... 284 G1
  OXHEY WD19 ............ 93 J1
  SUT SM1 ............... 221 N2
Russell Yd PUT/ROE SW15 .... 157 K9
Russet Cl CHES/WCR EN8 ..... 62 G1
  HGDN/ICK UB10 ......... 132 A5
  HORL RH6 .............. 160 B6
  STWL/WRAY TW19 ........ 172 A4
  WOT/HER KT12 .......... 197 N5
Russet Crs HOLWY N7 * ...... 118 C10
Russet Dr CROY/NA CRO ...... 204 F8
  RAD WD7 ............... 57 K8
Russets Cl CHING E4 ........ 100 E5
Russet Wy STHGT/OAK N14 * .. 78 D8
Russett Cl ORP BR6 ......... 227 L2
Russett Ct CTHM CR3 ........ 282 B1
Russetts Cl WOKN/KNAP GU21 . 232 C1
Russett Wy SWLY BR8 ........ 186 G9
Russett Wd WGCE AL7 ........ 23 N6
Russia Ct CITYW EC2V * ..... 12 G5
Russia Dock Rd
  BERM/RHTH SE16 ........ 140 D10
Russia La BETH E2 .......... 140 B9
Russia Rw CITYW EC2V ....... 12 F6
Russington Rd SHPTN TW17 ... 196 E9
Rusthall Av CHSWK W4 ....... 156 A1
Rusthall Cl CROY/NA CRO .... 204 C10
Rustic Av STRHM/NOR SW16 ... 179 P10
Rustic Pl ALP/SUD HA0 ...... 114 A10
Rustington Wk CHEAM SM3 .... 201 J10
Ruston Av BRYLDS KT5 ....... 199 P7
Ruston Gdns STHGT/OAK N14 * . 78 A9
Ruston Ms NTGHL W11 ........ 8 A6
Ruston Rd WOOL/PLUM SE18 ... 146 D9
Ruston St BOW E3 ........... 140 A4
Rust Sq CMBW SE5 ........... 159 K5
Rutford Rd STRHM/NOR SW16 .. 180 A8
Ruth Cl STAN HA7 ........... 115 L2

Ruthen Cl EPSOM KT18 ....... 219 N10
Rutherford Cl BELMT SM2 .... 221 N5
  BORE WD6 .............. 75 P6
  UX/CGN UB8 ............ 132 A6
  WDSR SL4 .............. 148 E7
Rutherford St WEST SW1P .... 17 H5
Rutherford Wy BUSH WD23 .... 94 C2
  WBLY HA9 .............. 115 M8
Rutherglen Rd ABYW SE2 ..... 163 N6
Rutherwick Cl HORL RH6 ..... 280 C4
Rutherwick Ri COUL/CHIP CR5  240 F3
Rutherwyke Cl EW KT17 ...... 220 D3
Ruthin Cl CDALE/KGS NW9 .... 115 M5
Ruthin Rd BKHTH/KID SE3 .... 161 M5
Ruthven Av CHES/WCR EN8 .... 62 C2
Ruthven St HOM E9 .......... 140 C3
Rutland Ap EMPK RM11 ....... 125 K5
Rutland Av BFN/LL DA15 ..... 185 K3
  SL SL1 ................ 129 H7
Rutland Cl ASHTD KT21 ...... 237 K5
  BXLY DA5 .............. 185 N4
  CHSGTN KT9 ............ 219 L5
  HOR/WEW KT19 .......... 220 A3
  MORT/ESHN SW14 ........ 155 N9
  REDH RH1 .............. 258 A9
  WIM/MER SW19 .......... 179 P9
Rutland Ct CHST BR7 ........ 206 D1
  SKENS SW7 * ........... 15 N3
Rutland Dr EMPK RM11 ....... 125 P3
  MRDN SM4 .............. 201 K7
  RCHPK/HAM TW10 ........ 176 A4
Rutland Gdns BCTR RM8 ...... 123 M10
  CROY/NA CRO ........... 224 A2
  FSBYPK N4 ............. 119 J4
  HNHE SE24 ............. 162 D5
  SKENS SW7 ............. 15 M2
  WEA W13 ............... 134 F7
Rutland Gardens Ms
  SKENS SW7 * ........... 15 M2
Rutland Ga BELV DA17 ....... 164 C4
  HAYES BR2 ............. 207 L2
  SKENS SW7 ............. 15 N2
  SKENS SW7 * ........... 15 N2
Rutland Gate Ms SKENS SW7 * . 15 M2
Rutland Gv HMSMTH W6 ....... 156 G3
Rutland Ms STJWD NW8 ....... 3 H6
Rutland Ms East
  SKENS SW7 * ........... 15 N3
Rutland Ms South
  SKENS SW7 * ........... 15 N3
Rutland Pk CAT SE6 ......... 182 E1
  CRICK NW2 ............. 136 F1
Rutland Pl BUSH WD23 * ..... 94 C2
  FARR EC1M * ........... 12 D3
Rutland Rd FSTGT E7 ........ 142 A2
  HRW HA1 ............... 114 A4
  HYS/HAR UB3 ........... 152 B3
  IL IG1 ................ 122 E9
  SEVS/STOTM N15 ........ 119 P1
  STHL UB1 .............. 133 P6
  WALTH E17 ............. 120 G1
  WAN E11 ............... 122 E9
  WHTN TW2 .............. 176 C5
Rutland St SKENS SW7 ....... 15 N3
Rutland Wk CAT SE6 ......... 182 E5
Rutley Cl WALW SE17 ........ 18 C9
Rutlish Rd WIM/MER SW19 .... 178 A10
Rutson Rd BF/WBF KT14 ...... 232 A1
Rutter Gdns MTCM CR4 ....... 201 N4
Rutts Ter NWCR SE14 ........ 160 G10
The Rutts BUSH WD23 ........ 94 C2
Ruvigny Gdns PUT/ROE SW15 .. 156 G9
Ruxbury Rd CHERT KT16 ...... 194 G6
Ruxley Cl HOR/WEW KT19 ..... 219 N2
  SCUP DA14 ............. 185 N4
Ruxley Crs ESH/CLAY KT10 ... 219 H2
Ruxley La HOR/WEW KT19 ..... 219 N2
Ruxley Ms HOR/WEW KT19 ..... 219 P2
Ruxley Rdg ESH/CLAY KT10 ... 218 F5
Ruxley Towers
  ESH/CLAY KT10 * ....... 218 F4
Ruxton Cl COUL/CHIP CR5 .... 240 D1
  SWLY BR8 .............. 208 F3
Ryan Cl BKHTH/KID SE3 ...... 184 B3
  RSLP HA4 .............. 113 J6
Ryan Ct OXHEY WD19 * ....... 93 M1
Ryan Dr BTFD TW8 ........... 154 F5
Ryan Wy WATN WD24 .......... 73 K5
Ryarsh Crs ORP BR6 ......... 227 H1
Rycroft WDSR SL4 ........... 148 E9
Rycroft La RSEV TN14 ....... 264 F6
Rycroft Wy TOTM N17 ........ 119 N1
Rydal Cl CRICK NW2 ......... 117 H4
  PUR/KEN CR8 ........... 241 K1
Rydal Crs GFD/PVL UB6 ...... 134 C2
Rydal Dr BXLYHN DA7 ........ 164 B5
  WWKM BR4 .............. 205 K10
Rydal Gdns CDALE/KGS NW9 ... 115 N3
  HSLW TW3 .............. 176 A2
  PUT/ROE SW15 .......... 177 H6
  WBLY HA9 .............. 115 H4
Rydal Rd STRHM/NOR SW16 .... 180 D6
Rydal Wy EGH TW20 .......... 172 E10
  PEND EN3 .............. 80 E6
  RSLP HA4 .............. 113 K9
Ryde Heron WOKN/KNAP GU21 * . 231 K3
Rydens Av WOT/HER KT12 ..... 197 K7
Rydens Gv WOT/HER KT12 ..... 197 L7
Rydens Pk WOT/HER KT12 ..... 197 L7
Rydens Rd WOT/HER KT12 ..... 197 H7
Rydens Wy WOKS/MYFD GU22 ... 232 D6
Ryde Pl TWK TW1 ............ 177 K1
Ryder Cl BUSH WD23 ......... 74 A10
  HERT/BAY SG13 ......... 26 A4
  HORL RH6 .............. 160 A2
Ryder Dr BERM/RHTH SE16 .... 160 A9
Ryder Gdns RAIN RM13 ....... 144 C3
Ryder Seed Ms STAL AL1 ..... 11 E4
Ryders Av STALE/WH AL4 ..... 40 B5
Ryder St STJS SW1Y ......... 11 H10
Ryder Yd STJS SW1Y ......... 11 H10
Rydes Av GUW GU2 ........... 249 L2
Ryde's Hill Crs GUW GU2 .... 249 L2
Ryde's Hill Rd GUW GU2 ..... 249 L5
The Ryde BRKMPK AL9 ........ 195 L1
Ryde Vale Rd BAL SW12 ...... 180 D3
Rydings WDSR SL4 ........... 148 E9
Rydons Ms WIM/MER SW19 ..... 178 F10
Rydons La COUL/CHIP CR5 .... 241 K2
Rydon St IS N1 ............. 6 F1
Rydston Cl HOLWY N7 ........ 5 N1
Rye Bank CRAWE RH10 ........ 284 B6
Rye Cl BORE WD6 ............ 76 A1
  BXLY DA5 .............. 169 N9
  LHD/OX KT22 ........... 264 C1
Ryecotes Md DUL SE21 ....... 182 A3
Rye Crs STMC/STPC BR5 ...... 207 P4
Ryecroft GVE DA12 .......... 191 K9
Ryecroft Av CLAY IG5 ....... 121 P1
  WHTN TW2 .............. 176 A3
Ryecroft Crs BAR EN5 ....... 76 A7
Ryecroft Rd LEW SE13 ....... 183 H3
  ORP BR6 ............... 207 L4
  STRHM/NOR SW16 ........ 180 C10
Ryecroft St FUL/PGN SW6 .... 14 D9

STRHM/NOR SW16 181 H9
Ryecroft Rd FUL/PGN SW6 157 L7
Ryedale EDUL SE22 182 A3
Ryedale Ct SEV TN13 246 F7
Ryefield Cl HOD EN11 26 C5
Rye FARL ASHTD KT21 237 J3
Ryefield Crs PIN HA5 * 93 H10
Ryhope Rd FBAR/BDGN N11 93 H10
Rye La LTWR GU18 212 D6
Rye Hill Pk PECK SE15 160 B10
Rye Hill Rd NRWD SE19 181 M8
Ryeland Cl WDR/YW UB7 131 J5
Ryelands CRAWW RH11 283 K8
HORL RH6 280 D3
WCCE AL7 23 J8
Ryelands Cl CTHM CR3 241 M7
Ryelands Ct LHD/OX KT22 236 F4
Ryelands Crs LEE/GVPK SE12 183 P2
Ryelands Pl WEY KT13 159 P8
Rye La PECK SE15 159 P8
RSEV TN14 246 G6
Rye Rd HOD EN11 40 C2
WARE SG12 27 K9
The Rye STHGT/OAK N14 98 D1
Rye Wk PUT/ROE SW15 178 G3
Rye Wy EDGW HA8 95 L7
Ryfold Rd WIM/MER SW19 179 P8
Ryland Cl FELT TW13 174 C7
Rylandes Rd CRICK NW2 116 D8
SAND/SEL CR2 224 A3
Ryland Rd KTTN NW5 4 E1
Rylett Crs SHB W12 156 C1
Rylett Rd SHB W12 156 C1
Rylston Rd FUL/PGN SW6 14 C10
PLMGR N13 99 P4
Rymer Rd CROY/NA CR0 203 M7
Rymer St HNHL SE24 181 J2
Rymill Cl HHS/BOV HP3 52 D4
Rymill St CAN/RD E16 142 D10
Rysbrack St CHEL SW3 16 A3
Rysted La BH/WHM TN16 262 H9
Rythe Cl CHSGTN KT9 219 H4
Rythe Ct THDIT KT7 198 F7
Rythe Rd ESH/CLAY KT10 218 C2
The Rythe ESH/CLAY KT10 218 A6
Ryvers End DTCH/LGLY SL3 150 C2
Ryvers Rd DTCH/LGLY SL3 150 C2
Ryves Cots MTCM CR4 * 202 B2

## S

Sabbarton St CAN/RD E16 141 L8
Sabina Rd CDW/CHF RM16 168 F3
Sabine Rd BTSEA SW11 158 A9
Sabines Rd ABR/ST RM4 85 N7
Sable Cl HSLWW TW4 153 K9
Sable St IS N1 6 D3
Sachfield Dr CDW/CHF RM16 167 L3
Sach Rd CLPT E5 120 A7
Sackville Av HAYES BR2 205 M8
Sackville Cl RYLN/HDSTN HA2 114 C8
SEV TN13 247 J8
Sackville Crs HARH RM3 105 M9
Sackville Est
STRHM/NOR SW16 180 F6
Sackville Gdns IL IG1 122 C6
Sackville Rd BELMT SM2 221 K4
Sackville St CONDST W1S 10 C8
Sacombe Rd HERT/WAT SG14 25 K2
HHW HP1 35 J4
Saddington St GVE DA12 190 E3
Saddlebrook Pk SUN TW16 174 F10
Saddler Rw CRAWE RH10 283 N10
Saddlers Cl BAR EN5 76 E9
PIN HA5 93 P6
Saddlers Hall EYN DA4 * 209 L10
Saddlers Ms KUT/HW KT1 * 199 H1
Saddlers Pk EYN DA4 209 L10
Saddlers Wk KGLGY WD4 * 54 B5
Saddlers Wy EPSOM KT18 238 A5
Saddlescombe Wy
NFNCH/WDSPK N12 97 K6
Sadleir Rd STAL AL1 38 D8
Sadler Cl CHESW EN7 * 61 K3
MTCM CR4 202 A2
Sadlers Cl GU GU1 250 G9
Sadlers Gate Ms
PUT/ROE SW15 156 F9
Sadlers Md HLWS CM18 47 K2
Sadlers Ride E/WMO/HCT KT8 198 B2
Sadlers Wy HERT/WAT SG14 25 H5
Saffron Cl CRAWW RH11 283 K10
CROY/NA CR0 202 F6
DTCH/LGLY SL3 149 N7
GLDGN NW11 117 J3
HOD EN11 44 E2
Saffron Hl HCIRC EC1N 12 B1
Saffron La HHW HP1 35 K5
Saffron Platt GUW GU2 249 M6
Saffron Rd CDW/CHF RM16 167 H3
CRW RM5 104 E10
Saffron St HCIRC EC1N 12 B1
Saffron Wy SURB KT6 199 G8
Sage Cl EHAM E6 142 C7
Sage Ms EDUL SE22 181 N1
Sage St WCHPL E1 140 B9
Sage Wy FSBYW WC1X 5 N10
Sage Yd SURB KT6 199 G8
Saigasso Cl CAN/RD E16 142 A8
Sail Ct LBTH SE11 17 P5
Sainfoin End HHNE HP2 36 B4
Sainfoin Rd TOOT SW17 180 B5
Sainsbury Rd NRWD SE19 181 M8
St Agatha's Dr KUTN/CMB KT2 175 H2
St Agathas Ct CAR SM5 * 202 A8
St Agnells Ct HHNE HP2 36 B2
St Agnells La HHNE HP2 36 A1
St Agnes Cl HOM E9 * 140 B3
St Agnes Pl LBTH SE11 18 B10
St Agnes Well STLK EC1Y 13 H1
St Aidan's Rd EDUL SE22 182 A2
WEA W13 154 C10
St Aidan's Wy GVE DA12 191 H6
St Alban's Av CHSWK W4 156 A2
FELT TW13 174 C7
UPMR RM14 126 D7
WEY KT13 196 B10
St Alban's Av EHAM E6 142 B10
St Alban's Cl RGUW GU3 248 G9
St Albans Crs WDGN N22 99 J8
St Albans Farm
EBED/NFELT TW14 * 175 K3
St Albans Gdns GVE DA12 190 G6
TEDD TW11 * 176 B8
St Albans Gv KENS W8 15 J1
St Albans Gv CAR SM5 201 P7
KENS W8 15 J1
St Albans Hl HHS/BOV HP3 35 P9
St Albans La ABLGY WD5 54 C1
GLDGN NW11 117 K3
St Alban's Ms BAY/PAD W2 9 M3
St Alban's Pl IS N1 6 C2
St Albans Rd BAR EN5 76 E3
CDMY/SEVK IG3 123 J6
GSTN WD25 51 G5
HARP AL5 20 B1
HHNE HP2 35 M7
HHS/BOV HP3 36 B8
KUTN/CMB KT2 175 H7
SUT SM1 221 J3
WALTH E17 57 J2
WAT WD17 73 H3
St Alban's Rd KTTN NW5 118 A8

REIG RH2 257 K8
WFD IG8 101 M8
WLSDN NW10 136 B3
St Albans Rd East HAT AL10 40 F7
St Albans Rd West HAT AL10 39 H4
St Albans St STJS SW1Y 11 J8
WDSR SL4 149 J7
St Albans Ter HMSMTH W6 14 A9
St Alfege Pas GNWCH SE10 161 N1
St Alfege Rd CHARL SE7 162 A5
St Alphage Gdns BARB EC2Y 12 F1
St Alphage Highwalk
BARB EC2Y 12 F4
St Alphage Wk EDGW HA8 95 P10
St Alphege Rd ED N9 100 B1
St Alphonsus Rd CLAP SW4 158 D10
St Amunds Cl CAT SE6 182 F7
St Andrew Ms
HERT/WAT SG14 * 25 K5
St Andrews Av HORL RH6 * 280 C5
St Andrews Av ALP/SUD HA0 114 F9
HCH RM12 124 C10
SLr SL4 148 E8
St Andrews Cl
BERM/RHTH SE16 * 160 A4
CRICK NW2 116 A8
ISLW TW7 154 C7
NFNCH/WDSPK N12 * 97 N5
REIG RH2 275 L1
SHPTN TW17 196 E4
STWL/WRAY TW19 172 B2
WDSR SL4 171 M2
St Andrews Ct WAT WD17 * 73 J1
St Andrew's Ct
WAND/EARL SW18 * 179 M5
St Andrew's Crs WDSR SL4 148 E8
St Andrew's Dr STAN HA7 95 H9
St Andrews Gdns COB KT11 217 K9
St Andrews Ga
WOKS/MYFD GU22 232 C4
St Andrew's Gv
STNW/STAM N16 119 L6
St Andrew's Hl BLKFR EC4V * 12 D6
St Andrew's Meadow
HLWS CM18 47 J3
St Andrews Ms BAL SW12 * 180 E4
BKHTH/KID SE3 161 N6
St Andrew's Ms
STNW/STAM N16 119 M6
St Andrews Pl BRWN CM15 107 J3
St Andrew's Pl CAMTN NW1 * 10 L1
St Andrews Rd CAR SM5 201 P10
CDALE/KGS NW9 115 M7
CRAWW RH11 282 C8
ED N9 100 B1
ROMW/RG RM7 104 C2
SCUP DA14 185 N6
St Andrew's Sq NTGHL W11 * 8 A4
SURB KT6 199 H6
St Andrews Ter
OXHEY WD19 * 93 K6
HERT/WAT SG14 * 25 K5
St Andrews Wk COB KT11 235 J1
St Andrews Wy BOW E3 140 G6
OXTED RH8 262 B7
St Anna Rd BAR EN5 * 76 C7
St Anne's Av
STWL/WRAY TW19 173 N3
St Annes Cl CDW/CHF RM16 * 147 N10
OXHEY WD19 93 K5
St Anne's Ct CHESW EN7 61 N4
HGT N6 118 B8
St Anne's Dr REDH RH1 258 A5
St Anne's Dr North REDH RH1 258 A4
St Annes Gdns WLSDN NW10 135 G5
St Annes Mt REDH RH1 258 B5
St Anne's Pk BROX EN10 44 B6
St Anne's Pas POP/IOD E14 * 140 B8
St Anne's Ri REDH RH1 258 B5
St Anne's Rd CRAWE RH10 284 D3
DEN/HRF UB9 111 M1
LCOL/BKTW AL2 57 J3
St Anne's Rd ALP/SUD HA0 115 J10
BRWN CM15 87 P5
LEY E10 121 K4
St Anne's Rw POP/IOD E14 140 E8
St Anne's Sq POP/IOD E14 140 B8
St Annes Wy REDH RH1 258 A4
St Ann's WOKS/MYFD GU22 232 B4
St Ann's BARK IG11 142 A3
St Ann's Cl CHERT KT16 195 J5
St Ann's Ct HDN NW4 116 A1
St Ann's Gdns HAMP NW3 4 B1
St Ann's Hl WAND/EARL SW18 160 A8
St Ann's Hl REDH RH1 194 H4
St Ann's Park Rd
WAND/EARL SW18 179 N5
St Anns Rd BARN SW13 156 A7
St Ann's Rd BARK IG11 142 A3
CHERT KT16 195 J5
ED N9 99 N3
HRW HA1 114 D4
NTGHL W11 136 C6
SEVS/STOTM N15 119 K3
St Anns Rd STHWP SW1P * 17 J6
St Ann's Ter STJWD NW8 3 M7
St Ann's Vis NTGHL W11 136 C7
St Anns Wy BH/WHM TN16 * 244 E2
CROY/NA CR0 223 J9
St Anselms Rd HYS/HAR UB3 133 J8
St Anthonys Av HHS/BOV HP3 36 C8
WFD IG8 101 N7
St Anthony's Av WFD IG8 101 N7
St Anthony's Cl TOOT SW17 179 N5
St Anthony's Wy
EBED/NFELT TW14 * 152 C10
St Antony's Rd FSTGT E7 141 K4
St Arvans Cl CROY/NA CR0 203 M10
St Asaph Rd BROCKY SE4 160 A11
St Aubins Cl DORK RH4 274 C4
St Aubyn's Av HSLW TW3 153 J8
WIM/MER SW19 179 J3
St Aubyns Cl ORP BR6 207 P10
St Aubyns Gdns ORP BR6 207 P10
St Audreys Av BXLYHN DA7 165 J3
St Audreys Cl HAT AL10 40 G6
St Audreys Gn WCCE AL7 23 J6
St Augusta Ct STALW/RED AL3 38 C4
St Augustine Rd
CDW/CHF RM16 168 E3
St Augustine's Av EA W5 135 H2
HAYES BR2 208 B5
St Augustines Cl BROX EN10 44 E6

St Augustine's Dr BROX EN10 44 E6
St Augustine's Rd BELV DA17 164 A3
CAMTN NW1 5 J3
St Austell Cl EDGW HA8 95 L10
St Awdry's Rd BARK IG11 142 G2
St Barnabas Cl BECK BR3 205 H2
EDUL SE22 159 M10
St Barnabas Gdns
E/WMO/HCT KT8 197 P5
St Barnabas Rd MTCM CR4 180 B10
SUT SM1 221 N2
WALTH E17 120 F4
WFD IG8 101 N9
St Barnabas St BGVA SW1W 16 C7
St Barnabas Ter HOM E9 * 120 C10
St Barnabas Vls VX/NE SW8 158 F7
St Bartholomew's Cl SYD SE26 182 B7
St Bartholomew's Rd
EHAM E6 142 B3
St Benedict's Av GVE DA12 191 H6
St Benets Cl TOOT SW17 179 H5
St Benet's Gv CAR SM5 201 M7
St Benjamins Dr ORP BR6 227 M5
St Bernards CROY/NA CR0 203 M10
St Bernards Cl WNWD SE27 181 L7
St Bernards Rd
DTCH/LGLY SL3 149 P2
St Bernard's Rd EHAM E6 142 A3
St Blaise Av BMLY BR1 205 N2
St Botolph Rd GVW DA11 190 A6
St Botolph's Rd SEV TN13 247 H10
St Botolph St TWRH EC3N 13 L5
St Breladies Cl DRCH RH4 272 F4
St Bride's Av EDGW HA8 95 L9
St Brides Cl ERITHM DA18 163 N1
St Bride St FLST/FETLN EC4A 12 C4
St Catherine's Av BROX EN10 44 F5
St Catherines WEY KT13 * 196 C10
WOKS/MYFD GU22 231 P5
St Catherines Cl CHSGTN KT9 219 J3
TOOT SW17 179 H5
St Catherines Ct FELT TW13 175 H4
St Catherine's Cross
REDH RH1 259 M10
St Catherine's Dr GUW GU2 267 N4
St Catherine's Hl GUW GU2 267 P4
St Catherines Ms CHEL SW3 16 A5
St Catherine's Pk GU GU1 268 C1
St Catherines Rd CHING E4 100 A3
RSLP HA4 112 D3
St Cecilia Rd CDW/CHF RM16 168 E3
St Chads Cl SURB KT6 199 H7
St Chad's Dr GVE DA12 191 H6
St Chad's Gdns CHDH RM6 123 P5
St Chad's Pl FSBYW WC1X 5 M9
St Chad's Rd CHDH RM6 123 P4
St Charles Pl NKENS W10 * 8 A1
WEY KT13 216 B2
St Charles Sq BRW CM14 106 G3
St Christopher Rd
UX/CGN UB8 131 N8
St Christopher's Cl ISLW TW7 154 D7
St Christophers Ct
RKW/CH/CXG WD3 * 70 G8
St Christophers Dr
HYS/HAR UB3 133 J9
St Christopher's Ms
WLGTN SM6 222 D2
St Christopher's Pl MHST W1U * 10 C6
St Clair Cl CLAY IG5 102 C10
OXTED RH8 261 H6
St Clair Dr WPK KT4 200 E10
St Clair Rd PLSTW E13 141 N4
St Clair's Rd CROY/NA CR0 203 M9
St Clare St TWRH EC3N 13 L6
St Clement Cl UX/CGN UB8 131 N8
St Clements Cl WTHK RM20 166 C5
St Clements Ct PUR RM19 165 P3
St Clement's La HLINN W2A 11 P6
St Clement's Wy WTHK RM20 166 E6
St Clements Yd EDUL SE22 * 181 N1
St Cloud Rd WNWD SE27 181 K7
St Columba's Cl GVE DA12 191 H6
St Crispins Cl HAMP NW3 3 P9
St Crispin's Dr STHL UB1 133 N1
St Crispins Wy CHERT KT16 214 F5
St Cross St HCIRC EC1N 12 B1
St Cuthbert's Cl ECH TW20 172 A9
St Cuthberts Gdns PIN HA5 * 93 N8
St Cuthberts Rd CRICK NW2 2 C1
HOD EN11 27 N10
PLMGR N13 99 J7
St Cyprian's St TOOT SW17 180 A7
St David Cl UX/CGN UB8 131 N9
St David's COUL/CHIP CR5 240 G3
St Davids Cl
BERM/RHTH SE16 * 160 A4
WBLY HA9 115 P6
St David's Cl HHS/BOV HP3 36 E8
IVER SL0 130 C3
REIG RH2 257 M9
WWKM BR4 204 B7
St David's Crs GVE DA12 190 G7
St David's Dr BROX EN10 44 E5
EDGW HA8 95 L9
ECH TW20 171 P10
St Davids Ms BOW E3 * 140 D5
St David's Pl HDN NW4 116 A5
St David's Sq POP/IOD E14 160 G4
St Denis Rd WNWD SE27 181 K7
St Deny's Cl
WOKN/KNAP GU21 231 J4
St Dionis Rd FUL/PGN SW6 157 J8
St Donatt's Rd NWCR SE14 161 L2
St Dunstan's Av ACT W3 135 J8
St Dunstan's Cl HYS/HAR UB3 133 K4
St Dunstan's Gdns ACT W3 * 135 J8
St Dunstan's Hl MON EC3R * 13 J5
St Dunstan's La MON EC3R * 13 J5
St Dunstan's Rd FSTGT E7 141 K4
HMSMTH W6 157 H4
HNWL W7 154 A1
HSLWW TW4 153 J8
SNWD SE25 203 H4
WARE SG12 27 K3
St Edith's Rd BGR/WK TN15 247 P7
St Edmunds BERK HP4 33 P6
St Edmund's Av RSLP HA4 113 J2
St Edmunds Cl CRAWW RH11 283 N4
ERITHM DA18 163 N1
TOOT SW17 179 H5
St Edmund's Dr STAN HA7 94 G7
St Edmunds La WHTN TW2 155 J9
St Edmunds Rd DART DA1 168 A2
ED N9 99 H10
IL IG1 123 P4
St Edmund's Ter STJWD NW8 3 P6
St Edwards Cl CROY/NA CR0 223 M9
GLDGN NW11 117 K4
St Edwards Wy ROM RM1 124 D3
St Egberts Wy CHING E4 101 H2

St Elizabeth Dr EPSOM KT18 219 P10
St Elmo Cl SLN SL2 129 J6
St Elmo Crs SLN SL2 129 J6
St Elmo Rd SHB W12 156 F1
St Elmos Cl BERM/RHTH SE16 160 D1
St Erkenwald Ms BARK IG11 142 E3
St Erkenwald Rd BARK IG11 142 E3
St Ervans Rd NKENS W10 * 8 B3
St Etheldreda's Dr HAT AL10 40 F4
St Evroul Ct WARE SG12 26 C1
St Faith's Cl ENC/FH EN2 79 J4
St Faith's Rd DUL SE21 181 J4
St Fidelis' Rd ERITH DA8 148 A8
St Fillans CHDH RM6 123 P5
St Fillans Rd CAT SE6 183 H4
St Francis Cl GVE DA12 191 H7
St Francis Cl ORP BR6 207 H6
OXHEY WD19 93 J2
POTB/CUF EN6 59 M9
St Francis Gdns CRAWE RH10 285 K1
St Francis Wy CDW/CHF RM16 168 F3
EDUL SE22 182 A2
St Francis's Cl OXHEY WD19 93 J2
IL IG1 122 C9
St Gabriel's Cl WAN E11 121 N6
St Gabriel's Rd CRICK NW2 116 C10
St Georges HORL RH6 * 280 C5
St Georges
CDALE/KGS NW9 115 P2
EA W5 155 J1
EMPK RM11 125 N5
FSTGT E7 141 N2
GRAYS RM17 167 P3
HOLWY N7 118 E9
STHL UB1 133 N9
WEY KT13 216 D3
St Georges Circ STHWK SE1 18 D3
St George's Cl GLDGN NW11 117 J4
WDSR SL4 148 D8
WEY KT13 216 D3
St Georges Crs GVE DA12 190 G7
St Georges Dr BAL SW12 * 180 A2
OXHEY WD19 93 J2
St George's Dr
PIM SW1V 16 E6
St George's Est
PIM SW1V 16 E6
St George's Flds BAY/PAD W2 9 P7
St Georges Gdns KTBR SW1X * 16 A3
St George's Gv
TOOT SW17 179 M5
St George's Industrial Est
KUTN/CMB KT2 * 177 J8
St Georges La ASC SL5 192 A3
MON EC3R * 13 J7
St Georges Ms CHSWK W4 * 156 G5
DEPT SE8 160 E5
St George's Pde CAT SE6 * 182 E5
St Georges Pl
ADL/WDHM KT15 215 M1
BMLY BR1 206 C2
CHSWK W4 156 A1
DAGW RM9 123 P10
STMC/STPC BR5 208 B6
SWLY BR8 208 G5
St George's Rd BECK BR3 204 C1
EN EN1 79 N4
FELT TW13 175 J7
FSTGT E7 141 N2
GLDGN NW11 117 J4
HNWL W7 154 C1
IL IG1 122 C5
KUTN/CMB KT2 177 H1
LEY E10 121 H8
MTCM CR4 202 C3
RCH/KEW TW9 155 P7
REDH RH1 276 E6
SCUP DA14 185 M7
SEV TN13 247 J8
St Georges Rd West
BMLY BR1 206 B2
St Georges's Ct STP EC4M * 12 C3
St Georges Sq GVW DA11 190 C7
NWMAL KT3 * 176 C10
St George's Sq FSTGT E7 141 N2
PIM SW1V 17 J7
St George's Square Ms
PIM SW1V 17 J8
St Georges Ter PECK SE15 * 159 P6
St George St CONDST W1S 10 C7
St George's Wy CROY/NA CR0 203 K9
PECK SE15 9 K10
St Gerards Cl CLAP SW4 180 C1
St German's Pl BKHTH/KID SE3 161 M8
St German's Rd FSTH SE23 182 A3
St Giles Av DAGE RM10 144 C2
POTB/CUF EN6 59 J2
St Giles Churchyard
BARB EC2Y * 12 F4
St Giles Cl DAGE RM10 144 C2
HEST TW5 153 M6
ORP BR6 226 G2
St Giles High St
LSQ/SEVD WC2H 11 K5
St Giles Pas LSQ/SEVD WC2H 11 K5
St Giles Rd CMBW SE5 159 N4
St Gothard Rd WNWD SE27 181 M5
St Gregory Cl RSLP HA4 113 K9
St Gregory's Crs GVE DA12 191 H5
St Helena Rd
BERM/RHTH SE16 160 C3
St Helena St FSBYW WC1X * 6 A10
St Helena Ter RCH/KEW TW9 * 177 J1
St Helen's Cl UX/CGN UB8 131 N9
St Helens Ct RAIN RM13 145 H5
St Helens Crs
STRHM/NOR SW16 202 G1
St Helens Gdns NKENS W10 * 8 A2
St Helens Pl LEY E10 120 C7
St Helen's Pl OBST EC2N 13 J3
St Helen's Rd ERITHM DA18 163 N1
HNWL W7 154 B1
St Helens Rd CLVDN CM16 47 M1
IL IG1 123 P4
St Helens Rd REDH RH1 * 258 A4
St Helen's Rd STRHM/NOR SW16 202 G1
WEA W13 134 C10
St Helier Av MRDN SM4 201 P1
St Heliers Av HSLWW TW4 175 J1
St Helier's Rd LEY E10 120 D5
St Hilda's Av ASHF TW15 173 H8
St Hildas Cl CRAWE RH10 284 D4
TOOT SW17 179 H4
St Hilda's Cl KIL/WHAMP NW6 * 2 A4
St Hilda's Rd BARN SW13 156 E5
St Hilda's Wy GVE DA12 191 H7
St Huberts Cl CFSP/GDCR SL9 110 A2
St Huberts La GER/HR SL9 132 A1
St Hughes Cl TOOT SW17 179 H4
St Hugh's Pl PGE/AN SE20 * 204 B2
St Hughes Rd PGE/AN SE20 182 F10
St Ivians Dr GPK RM2 105 L2
St Ives Cl HARH RM3 * 105 M9
St James Av EW KT17 220 C7

SUT SM1 221 K2
TRDG/WHET N20 97 P4
St James' Av CHONG CM5 67 N4
St James Cl EBAR EN4 77 N7
EPSOM KT18 220 B10
STJWD NW8 3 J4
WOKN/KNAP GU21 231 J4
St James' Cl NWMAL KT3 200 C5
RSLP HA4 113 K7
St James Ct ERITH DA8 148 A8
St James Ct WESTW SW1E * 17 H3
St James Gdns ASC SL5 192 E7
St James Gdns ALP/SUD HA0 135 P1
CTHM CR3 241 P8
St James Ms RDART DA2 188 D2
St James Oaks GVW DA11 * 190 D3
St James Rd CAR SM5 201 P10
St James's AV BECK BR3 204 D3
BETH E2 140 B1
GVW DA11 190 D3
St James Rd ED N9 100 A3
PUR/KEN CR8 223 J9
SRTFD E15 121 L10
SURB KT6 199 G8
SUT SM1 221 K3
St James's Av BECK BR3 204 D3
BETH E2 140 B1
GVW DA11 190 D3
St James's Chambers
STJS SW1Y * 11 H9
St James's Cl TOOT SW17 * 180 A5
NWMAL KT3 176 C5
St James's Cots
RCH/KEW TW9 * 177 J1
St James's Ct KUT/HW KT1 * 199 K3
WESTW SW1E 17 H3
St James's Dr BAL SW12 180 A2
St James's Gdns
CAMTN NW1 * 4 C10
NTGHL W11 8 A8
St James's La MUSWH N10 118 C2
St James's Market
STJS SW1Y * 11 J8
St James's Pk CROY/NA CR0 203 K9
St James's Pl WHALL SW1A 10 E9
St James's Rd
BERM/RHTH SE16 19 P7
CROY/NA CR0 203 K9
GVW DA11 190 D3
HPTN TW12 176 B8
KUTN/CMB KT2 175 P10
St James's Rw CHSGTN KT9 219 J3
St James's Sq STJS SW1Y 11 H9
St James's Ter STJWD NW8 * 4 A6
St James St HMSMTH W6 156 G4
WALTH E17 57 H4
St James Ter BAL SW12 * 180 A2
St James's Terrace Ms
STJWD NW8 3 P6
St James Wk CLKNW EC1R 12 C1
DTCH/LGLY SL3 151 H1
St Jerome's Gv UX/CGN UB8 132 D8
St Joan Cl CRAWW RH11 282 D1
St Joans Rd ED N9 100 C10
St John Cl FUL/PGN SW6 157 L6
St Johns Av EW KT17 220 D5
FBAR/BDGN N11 98 A5
HLWE CM17 47 J6
St John's Av BRXN/ST SW9 159 P4
HOM E9 * 120 B10
St John's Church Rd
RDKG RH5 271 N5
St John's Cl BH/WHM TN16 * 244 E2
FUL/PGN SW6 157 K6
LHD/OX KT22 237 H7
POTB/CUF EN6 59 K6
RAIN RM13 145 H2
TRDG/WHET N20 97 M3
UX/CGN UB8 131 K10
WBLY HA9 115 K10
St Johns Cots PGE/AN SE20 * 182 F10
St Johns Ct BKHH IG9 101 N2
ECH TW20 172 A9
STAL AL1 38 G5
St John's Dr WAND/EARL SW18 179 K4
St Johns Gdns NTGHL W11 8 B9
St John's Gv ARCH N19 118 C7
BARN SW13 156 B9
RCH/KEW TW9 155 M9
St John's Hl BTSEA SW11 157 N10
St John's Hl Gv BTSEA SW11 157 N10
St John's Hill Rd
WOKN/KNAP GU21 231 M4
St Johns La ERITH DA8 148 A8
St John's La FARR EC1M 12 D1
St John's Lye
WOKN/KNAP GU21 231 L5
St John's Lye (Festival Path)
WOKN/KNAP GU21 231 L5
St Johns Ms
WOKN/KNAP GU21 231 L5
St John's Ms NTGHL W11 8 A2
St John's Pde SCUP DA14 * 185 M4
St John's Pk BKHTH/KID SE3 161 N6
St John's Pk
STRHM/NOR SW16 202 G1
St John's Pl FARR EC1M 12 D1
St John's Rd BARK IG11 142 G3
BTSEA SW11 157 N10
CAN/RD E16 141 M6
CHING E4 101 J2
CROY/NA CR0 203 J10
DART DA1 190 A6
DORK RH4 272 C7
E/WMO/HCT KT8 197 P5
EHAM E6 142 A3
EPP CM16 79 H2
ERITH DA8 164 A4
FELT TW13 174 G7
GLDGN NW11 117 H4

HHW HP1 35 L8
HRW HA1 114 E4
ISLW TW7 154 A8
KUT/HW KT1 199 H2
LOU IG10 82 C6
LHD/OX KT22 237 H7
NWDGN UB2 153 M2
PGE/AN SE20 182 B10
RCH/KEW TW9 155 K10
RDART DA2 188 B3
REDH RH1 276 A2
SCUP DA14 185 L7
SEV TN13 247 J8
SEVS/STOTM N15 119 M4
SUT SM1 201 K9
UX/CGN UB8 131 L4
WALTH E17 100 C10
WAT WD17 75 J6
WBLY HA9 115 J9
WELL DA16 163 L9
WIM/MER SW19 179 H10
WOKN/KNAP GU21 231 M5
St John's Ter FARR EC1M 12 C2
St John's Wb BERK HP4 25 L5
ENC/FH EN2 79 L4
FSTGT E7 141 N1
NKENS W10 * 8 A1
WOOL/PLUM SE18 162 F5
St John's Terrace Rd
REDH RH1 276 A2
St John's V BROCKY SE4 160 F8
St Johns Vls ARCH N19 * 118 C7
St Johns Wk HLWE CM17 29 M7
St John's Wy ARCH N19 118 C6
CHERT KT16 195 K8
St John's Well Ct BERK HP4 33 N4
St John's Well La BERK HP4 33 N4
St John's Wood High St
STJWD NW8 3 M8
St John's Wood Pk
STJWD NW8 3 L6
St John's Wood Rd
STJWD NW8 9 L1
St John's Wood Ter
STJWD NW8 3 N7
St Josephs Cl NKENS W10 8 A1
ORP BR6 227 J1
St Josephs Dr STHL UB1 133 M10
St Josephs Gv HDN NW4 116 C2
St Josephs Ms BEAC HP9 88 E9
St Joseph's Rd CHES/WCR EN8 62 D7
ED N9 100 A1
St Joseph's St VX/NE SW8 * 158 C7
St Joseph's V FSTH SE23 181 K3
St Jude's Cl EGH TW20 171 P8
St Jude's Rd BETH E2 140 A4
EGH TW20 171 P7
St Jude St STNW/STAM N16 119 N10
St Julian's Cl
STRHM/NOR SW16 181 H7
St Julian's Farm Rd
WNWD SE27 181 H7
St Julian's Rd
KIL/WHAMP NW6 2 D4
St Justin Cl STMC/STPC BR5 207 N3
St Katharines Rd CTHM CR3 259 P5
St Katharine's Wy WAP E1W 13 M9
St Katherines Rd
ERITHM DA18 163 N1
St Katherines Wk
NTGHL W11 * 136 C7
St Katharine's Wy BERK HP4 33 L2
ELTH/MOT SE9 184 G7
St Keverne Rd ELTH/MOT SE9 184 C5
St Kilda Rd ORP BR6 207 J8
WEA W13 154 F1
St Kilda's Rd BRWN CM15 106 C1
HRW HA1 114 D4
STNW/STAM N16 119 L6
St Kitts Ter NRWD SE19 181 M8
St Laurence Cl
STMC/STPC BR5 207 N3
UX/CGN UB8 131 N7
St Laurence Dr BROX EN10 44 D9
St Laurence's Cl
KIL/WHAMP NW6 2 A4
St Lawrence Cl ABLGY WD5 54 F6
EDGW HA8 95 L8
HHS/BOV HP3 52 D5
St Lawrence Cots
POP/IOD E14 141 H10
St Lawrence Dr PIN HA5 113 J3
St Lawrence Rd UPMR RM14 126 B7
St Lawrence St POP/IOD E14 141 H10
St Lawrence Ter NKENS W10 * 8 A1
St Lawrence Wy
BRXN/ST SW9 159 N8
CTHM CR3 241 L9
LCOL/BKTW AL2 55 N6
St Leonards Av
KTN/HRWW/WS HA3 115 J1
St Leonard's Av CHING E4 101 J3
WDSR SL4 148 A2
St Leonards Cl BUSH WD23 73 M8
GRAYS RM17 167 L5
HERT/WAT SG14 25 M3
WELL DA16 163 L9
St Leonard's Cl STALE/WH AL4. 21 H10
St Leonards Crs
STALE/WH AL4 21 H10
St Leonards Dr CRAWE RH10 284 B10
St Leonard's Dr CHING E4 101 J3
St Leonard's Gdns HEST TW5 153 M6
IL IG1 142 C1
St Leonards Ri ORP BR6 227 K1
St Leonard's Rd
EPSOM KT18 238 F5
MORT/ESHN SW14 155 P9
WAB EN9 45 J10
St Leonard's Rd CROY/NA CR0 203 J10
ESH/CLAY KT10 218 E3
HERT/WAT SG14 25 L3
POP/IOD E14 141 M8
THDIT KT7 198 F6
WAN E11 120 E3
WEA W13 135 H9
WLSDN NW10 137 H10
St Leonard's Sq KTTN NW5 4 D2
SURB KT6 199 G5
St Leonard's St BOW E3 140 G5
St Leonard's Ter CHEL SW3 16 A8
St Leonards Wk
DTCH/LGLY SL3 151 J2
STRHM/NOR SW16 180 C10
St Leonards Wy EMPK RM11 125 J7
St Lo Av CHEL SW3 * 15 L3
St Louis Cl POTB/CUF EN6 59 M9
St Louis Rd WNWD SE27 181 M7
St Loy's Rd TOTM N17 100 C9
St Lucia Dr SRTFD E15 141 L3
St Luke Cl UX/CGN UB8 131 N9
St Luke's Av CLAP SW4 158 C10
ENC/FH EN2 79 L4
IL IG1 122 C9
St Lukes Cl RDART DA2 188 G8
SWLY BR8 208 A6
St Lukes Ct WOKN/KNAP GU21 214 F10
St Lukes Ms NTGHL W11 8 B1
St Lukes Pl STAL AL1 * 38 G7
St Luke's Rd CTHM CR3 241 N6
HGDN/ICK UB10 131 P7
St Luke's Sq CAN/RD E16 141 L8

GU GU1 268 C1
St Luke's CI CHEL SW3 15 N7
St Lukes Yd MV/WKIL W9 * 2 C7
St Magnus Ct HHS/BOV HP3 36 C8
St Malo Av ED N9 100 B4
St Margarets BARK IG11 142 C5
KUTN/CMB KT2 * 177 P8
St Margaret's GU GU1 250 C9
St Margarets Av ASHF TW15 174 C7
BFN/LL DA15 184 C6
BH/WHM TN16 * 244 E2
TRDG/WHET N20 97 M2
UX/CGN UB8 131 N7
St Margaret's Av CHEAM SM3 201 H10
RYLN/HDSTN HA2 114 B8
SEVS/STOTM N15 119 J2
St Margarets CI ORP BR6 227 L1
RDART DA2 188 C5
St Margaret's CI BERK HP4 34 A6
IVER SL0 130 C4
St Margarets Crs GVE DA12 191 H6
St Margaret's Dr EPSOM KT18 178 L1
St Margaret's Gv TWK TW1 176 C1
WAN E11 121 L8
WOOL/PLUM SE18 * 162 F5
St Margarets La KENS W8 14 C4
St Margarets Ms
KUTN/CMB KT2 * 177 P8
St Margarets Rd EDGW HA8 95 N6
RSLP HA4 112 E4
WARE SG12 26 F9
St Margaret's Rd BROCKY SE4 160 E10
COUL/CHIP CR5 240 C7
EYN DA4 188 D10
HNWL W7 154 D1
MNPK E12 121 P7
TOTM N17 119 M1
TWK TW1 154 C10
WLSDN NW10 136 H5
St Margaret's Ter
WOOL/PLUM SE18 162 F4
St Margaretes Vw WHNE HP2 * 36 E6
St Marks Av CVW DA11 190 B3
St Marks CI FUL/PGN SW6 157 K7
STALE/WH AL4 39 N8
St Mark's Ct BAR EN5 77 L7
St Marks Crs CAMTN NW1 4 D5
St Marks Ga HOM E9 140 H4
St Mark's Gv WBPTN SW10 * 157 L6
St Mark's HI SURB KT6 199 K6
St Mark's PI DAGE RM10 144 B7
NTGHL W11 * 8 A6
St Mark's Ri HACK E8 13 P2
WIM/MER SW19 * 179 J9
St Mark's Rd EA W5 135 N10
EN EN1 79 N5
HAYES BR2 205 N3
HNWL W7 154 D1
MTCM CR4 204 A2
NKENS W10 136 G8
SNWD SE25 203 P4
TEDD TW11 176 C10
WDSR SL4 149 H8
St Mark's Sq CAMTN NW1 4 C5
St Mark St WCHPL E1 13 M6
St Marks Vls FSBYPK N4 * 118 G7
St Martha's Av
WOKS/MYFD GU22 232 C7
St Marthas Ct RGUE GU4 268 E6
St Martin CI NTHWD HA6 92 E6
St Martins Ap RSLP HA4 112 F5
St Martin's Av EHAM E6 142 G1
EPSOM KT18 220 B10
St Martins CI EHSLY KT24 252 F5
ERITHM DA18 163 K10
OXHEY WD19 93 K5
RBRW/HUT CM13 * 107 P2
St Martin's CI CAMTN NW1 4 C5
EN EN1 80 A5
EW KT17 220 C9
WDR/YW UB7 151 M2
St Martins Ct CHCR WC2N 11 J7
St Martin's Est ASHF TW15 173 P8
St Martins Dr EYN DA4 209 L10
WOT/HER KT12 197 K10
St Martin's La BECK BR3 204 C5
CHCR WC2N 11 L7
St Martin's le Grand
STBT EC1A 12 C2
St Martins Meadow
BH/WHM TN16 245 M9
St Martins Ms DORK RH4 272 F2
St Martin's Ms
WOKS/MYFD GU22 233 K2
St Martins PI CHCR WC2N 11 L8
St Martin's Rd HOD EN11 45 H4
St Martin's Rd BRXN/ST SW9 158 A3
ED N9 100 A3
EFNCH N2 97 N9
St Martin's St
LSQ/SEVD WC2H * 11 K8
St Mary Abbot's Pl KENS W8 14 C4
St Mary Abbots Ter
WKENS W14 14 C4
St Mary At HI MON EC3R * 13 L4
St Mary Av WLGTN SM6 202 B10
St Mary Axe HDTCH EC3A 13 J6
St Marychurch St
BERM/RHTH SE16 160 B1
St Mary Graces Ct WCHPL E1 * 13 M8
St Marys BARK IG11 142 C4
WEY KT13 * 156 B1
St Mary's Ap MNPK E12 122 C10
St Mary's Av BERK HP4 33 J5
BRWN CM15 87 N9
FNCH N3 97 H10
HAYES BR2 205 K3
NTHWD HA6 92 H6
STWL/WRAY TW19 173 N5
TEDD TW11 176 E9
WAN E11 121 L8
St Mary's Church Rd
RSEV TN14 263 P1
St Marys CI GRAYS RM17 193 K8
WATW WD18 * 73 K8
St Mary's CI CHSGTN KT9 219 L4
DEN/HRF UB9 111 J3
EW KT17 220 C4
GRAYS RM17 * 168 A5
CVE DA12 190 F5
LHD/OX KT22 236 C9
OXTED RH8 261 K5
STMC/STPC BR5 207 L2
SUN TW16 197 N4
TOTM N17 119 P9
St Marys Ct HMSMTH W6 * 156 F6
St BH/WHM TN16 * 156 B1
POTB/CUF EN6 59 L8
St Magnus Ctyd WARE SG12 * 26 F9
St Mary's Ctyd HDN NW4 116 B1
St Mary's Est
BERM/RHTH SE16 * 160 B1
St Mary's Gdns LBTH SE11 17 N8
St Marys Gn BH/WHM TN16 243 P4
CHSWK W4 155 N5

IS N1 6 D3
RCH/KEW TW9 155 L10
St Mary's HI ASC SL5 192 B5
St Mary's La HERT/WAT SG14 24 C7
RBRW/HUT CM13 127 N5
UPMR RM14 127 P7
St Mary's Man BAY/PAD W2 * 9 K3
St Mary's Mt CTHM CR3 241 N10
St Mary's Pth IS N1 6 C3
WCHPL E1 13 N5
St Marys PI KENS W8 14 C4
St Marys Rd IL IG1 122 F2
LHD/OX KT22 236 G8
St Mary's Rd ASC SL5 192 A5
BXLY DA5 186 D4
CDW/CHRF RM16 168 A5
CEND/HSY/T N8 118 F2
CHES/WCR EN8 62 B5
DEN/HRF UB9 111 J4
DTCH/LGLY SL3 150 B1
E/WMO/HCT KT8 198 C5
EA W5 155 J1
EBAR EN4 98 A1
ED N9 100 B3
GLDGN NW11 117 H5
HHNE HP2 35 N5
HYS/HAR UB3 132 G9
LEY E10 121 H8
PECK SE15 160 B7
PLSTW E13 141 N4
RDART DA2 188 D1
REIC RH2 275 L1
SAND/SEL CR2 223 L6
SNWD SE25 203 M3
SURB KT6 199 H7
SWLY BR8 208 E4
WATW WD18 * 73 J8
WEY KT13 216 E1
WIM/MER SW19 179 H8
WLSDN NW10 136 B3
WOKN/KNAP GU21 231 P3
WPK KT4 200 B9
St Marys Sq BAY/PAD W2 * 9 K3
St Mary's Ter BORE WD6 * 75 J1
St Mary's Vw
KTN/HRWW/WS HA3 115 H3
WATW WD18 * 73 K8
St Marys Wk STALE/WH AL4 38 G2
St Mary's Wk HYS/HAR UB3 132 C5
LBTH SE11 18 B5
St Marys Wy CHIG IG7 102 D6
GUW GU2 268 A6
HART DA3 211 K3
St Mary's Wy CFSP/GDCR SL9 90 A10
CSHM HP5 50 G8
St Matthew CI UX/CGN UB8 131 N8
St Matthew's Av SURB KT6 199 K8
St Matthews CI RAIN RM13 145 H2
St Matthews Dr BMLY BR1 206 C3
St Matthew's Rd
BRXS/STRHM SW2 180 A1
EA W5 135 N10
REDH RH1 258 A10
St Matthew's Rw BETH E2 7 N10
St Matthew St WEST SW1P * 17 J5
St Matthias CI
CDALE/KGS NW9 116 C3
St Maur Rd FUL/PGN SW6 157 J7
St Meddens CHST BR7 * 184 C10
St Mellion CI THMD SE28 143 N8
St Merryn CI
WOOL/PLUM SE18 162 G6
St Michael's Aly BANK EC3V 13 H6
HHS/BOV HP3 36 C8
St Michael's Av RGUW GU3 249 M5
WBLY HA9 135 M4
St Michaels CI BMLY BR1 206 B3
CAN/RD E16 142 A4
HARP AL5 20 C4
SOCK/AV RM15 146 B9
WRK KT14 200 C9
St Michael's CI
ERITHM DA18 163 K10
FNCH N3 97 J10
HLW CM20 29 H10
NFNCH/WDSPK N12 97 P6
WOT/HER KT12 197 K9
St Michaels Ct GLDGN NW11 * 117 J4
St Michael's Ct SLN SL2 128 C6
St Michaels Crs PIN HA5 113 M4
St Michaels Dr CSTN WD25 55 J9
RSEV TN14 247 L2
St Michaels Gdns NKENS W10 8 A1
St Michael's Gn BEAC HP9 88 D8
St Michael's Ms BCVA SW1W 16 E5
St Michaels Ri WELL DA16 * 163 L7
St Michaels Rd ASHF TW15 174 C7
CDW/CHRF RM16 168 A5
CTHM CR3 241 L6
St Michael's Rd BROX EN10 44 B6
BRXN/ST SW9 158 A3
CRICK NW2 116 F9
CROY/NA CR0 203 K8
WELL DA16 163 H5
WLGTN SM6 222 D5
WOKN/KNAP GU21 214 C10
St Michaels St BAY/PAD W2 9 M3
STALW/RED AL3 38 A6
St Michaels Ter HGT N6 * 118 B5
St Michael St WDGN N22 98 H3
St Michaels Wy
POTB/CUF EN6 59 L6
St Mildreds Ct LOTH EC2R * 12 G6
St Mildreds Rd CAT SE6 183 K3
St Mildred's Rd GU GU1 250 C9
St Monica's Rd
KWD/TDW/WH KT20 239 J7
St Nazaire CI EBF TW20 * 172 F8
St Neots CI BORE WD6 75 M4
St Neot's Rd HARH RM3 105 N8
St Nicholas Av GT/LBKH KT23 254 C5
HCH RM12 125 H8
St Nicholas CI AMSS HP7 35 P5
BORE WD6 75 J10
UX/CGN UB8 131 N8
St Nicholas Crs
WOKS/MYFD GU22 233 K2
St Nicholas Dr SEV TN13 265 J2
SHPTN TW17 196 B7
St Nicholas Glebe TOOT SW17 180 B9
St Nicholas Gn HLWE CM17 29 M10
St Nicholas Gv
RBRW/HUT CM13 107 P6
St Nicholas Mt HHW HP1 * 35 M4
St Nicholas PI LOU IG10 82 D8
St Nicholas Rd SUT SM1 221 L4
THDIT KT7 198 A8
WOOL/PLUM SE18 163 N5
St Nicholas St DEPT SE8 160 E1
St Nicolas La CHST BR7 206 B1
St Ninian's Ct
TRDG/WHET N20 98 A4
St Norbert Rd BROCKY SE4 160 D10
St Normans Wy EW KT17 220 D10
St Olaf's Rd FUL/PGN SW6 157 H6
St Olav's Ct STA TW18 173 L5
St Olave's Est EHAM E6 142 D3
St Olave's Wk
STRHM/NOR SW16 202 E2
St Omer Rdg GU GU1 268 G3
St Omer Rd GU GU1 268 G3
St Onge Pde EN EN1 * 79 L1
St Oswald's PI LBTH SE11 17 L8
St Oswald's Rd
STRHM/NOR SW16 203 H1
St Oswulf St WEST SW1P * 17 K6

St Pancras Gdns
CAMTN NW1 5 K6
St Pancras Station Forecourt
CAMTN NW1 * 4 G3
St Patrick's Gdns CVE DA12 190 G7
St Patrick's Pl CDW/CHRF RM16 168 A5
St Paul UX/CGN UB8 131 N7
St Pauls Av SLN SL2 129 L9
WCHPL E1 13 N5
St Paul's Cl ASC SL5 192 B5
CDW/CHRF RM16 168 A5
CHES/WCR EN8 62 B5
DEN/HRF UB9 111 J4
EA W5 155 L1
HYS/HAR UB3 152 B4
St Paul's CI ADL/WDHM KT15 215 K1
ASHF TW15 174 D8
BORE WD6 75 H3
CAR SM5 201 P7
CHARL SE7 162 A4
CHSGTN KT9 219 J11
EA W5 155 L1
HSLW TW3 153 M8
SOCK/AV RM15 146 B9
St Paul's Cray Rd CHST BR7 206 C1
St Pauls Crs CAMTN NW1 5 K1
HDN NW4 * 116 F2
St Pauls Ms CAMTN NW1 5 K1
DORK RH4 272 G3
St Pauls Pl STAL AL1 38 F6
St Paul's Pl IS N1 6 C1
SOCK/AV RM15 146 B9
St Paul's Ri PLMGR N13 99 J7
RCH/KEW TW9 155 L10
WOKS/MYFD GU22 232 D3
St Paul's Rd BTFD TW8 155 L5
ERITH DA8 164 D6
HHNE HP2 35 P5
IS N1 6 E1
STA TW18 172 D4
THHTH CR7 203 K3
TOTM N17 99 P8
St Pauls Rd East DORK RH4 272 G5
St Pauls Rd West DORK RH4 272 F5
St Pauls Ter WALTH E17 18 D9
St Pauls Vw FNCH N3 97 L8
POP/IOD E14 * 140 E7
St Paul's Wd HI
STMC/STPC BR5 207 H2
St Peter's Av BH/WHM TN16 * 244 E2
St Peter's Av CHONG CM5 67 N2
UED N18 99 P5
WALTH E17 121 K2
St Petersburgh Ms
BAY/PAD W2 8 G1
St Petersburgh Pl
BAY/PAD W2 8 G1
St Peters CI CHST BR7 184 C10
CNTH/NBYPK IG2 123 H2
HAT AL10 40 D3
TOOT SW17 179 P5
St Peter's CI BAR EN5 76 E9
BETH E2 7 P8
BUSH WD23 94 C2
RKW/CH/CXG WD3 91 L3
SL SL1 128 A6
STHL UB1 133 N3
STAL AL1 38 C5
SWCM DA10 189 L1
WDSR SL4 171 M1
WOKS/MYFD GU22 232 D3
St Peter's Gdns WNWD SE27 181 H6
St Peter's Gv HMSMTH W6 156 D3
St Peters Ms FSBYPK N4 119 H3
St Peter's Pl MV/WKIL W9 8 G2
St Peters Rd BRW CM14 106 C3
CRAWW RH11 283 M7
CROY/NA CR0 223 L6
E/WMO/HCT KT8 197 P4
ED N9 100 D7
HMSMTH W6 156 D4
STAL AL1 38 C5
STHL UB1 133 N3
TWK TW1 154 C10
UX/CGN UB8 131 N7
WOKS/MYFD GU22 232 D3
St Peter's Sq BETH E2 7 P8
HMSMTH W6 156 C4
St Peter's St IS N1 6 C1
SAND/SEL CR2 223 L2
STAL AL1 38 C5
St Peter's Ter FUL/PGN SW6 157 H6
St Peters Vls HMSMTH W6 156 C3
St Peters Wy HYS/HAR UB3 152 B4
RKW/CH/CXG WD3 70 B8
St Peter's Wy
ADL/WDHM KT15 195 K10
CHERT KT16 215 K1
EA W5 135 L2
IS N1 7 H1
St Philip's Av WPK KT4 200 F10
St Philip Sq VX/NE SW8 * 157 P2
St Philip's Rd HACK E8 7 M1
St Philip St VX/NE SW8 157 P3
St Philip's Vw IS N1 6 C1
St Pinnock Av STA TW18 195 K4
St Quentin Rd WELL DA16 163 J10
St Quintin Av NKENS W10 136 D7
St Quintin Gdns NKENS W10 136 C7
St Quintin Rd PLSTW E13 141 N5
St Raphael's Wy WLSDN NW10 136 P10
St Regis CI MUSWH N10 98 C10
St Richards Ms CRAWE RH10 284 A7
St Ronans CI EBAR EN4 77 N2
St Ronans Crs WFD IG8 101 N4
St Rule St VX/NE SW8 157 P3
St Saviour's Ct WDGN N22 98 E10
St Saviour's Est STHWK SE1 19 L1
St Saviour's PI GU GU1 * 249 P10
St Saviour's Rd
BRXS/STRHM SW2 180 G1
CROY/NA CR0 203 K6
Saints CI WNWD SE27 181 H7
St Silas Pl KTTN NW5 4 C2
St Simon's Av
PUT/ROE SW15 178 G1
St Stephens Av ASHTD KT21 237 F1
St Stephen's Av SHB W12 156 K1
STALW/RED AL3 38 A6
WALTH E17 121 H1
WEA W13 153 M3
St Stephen's CI
STALW/RED AL3 38 A6
STHL UB1 133 Q7
TEDD TW11 176 A10
WALTH E17 121 H1
St Stephens Crs
RBRW/HUT CM13 107 M5
St Stephen's Crs
BAY/PAD W2 * 8 E5
THHTH CR7 203 H7
St Stephen's Garden Est
NTGHL W11 * 8 E5
St Stephens Gdns
BAY/PAD W2 * 8 E5
TWK TW1 154 E1
St Stephen's Gv LEW SE13 161 H9

St Stephen's HI
STALW/RED AL3 38 B8
St Stephen's Ms BAY/PAD W2 8 F4
St Stephens Pde WHALL SW1A 17 L1
St Stephens Rd BAR EN5 76 D9
EHAM E6 141 P2
HSLW TW3 175 P2
PEND EN3 80 C3
WDR/YW UB7 131 N10
St Stephen's Ter VX/NE SW8 158 A6
St Stephens Ms KIL/WHAMP NW6 * 137 H1
St Stephen's Wk SKENS SW7 15 J5
Saint's Wk CDW/CHRF RM16 168 A5
St Swithin's La MANHO EC4N 12 G7
St Swithuns Rd LEW SE13 * 183 J1
St Teresa WK GUW GU2 268 A9
St Teresa's CI HOM E9 * 121 F9
St Theresa's Rd
EBED/NFELT TW14 152 D10
St Thomas CI SURB KT6 199 L8
St Thomas' Dr PIN HA5 93 M9
St Thomas Gdns IL IG1 * 142 B5
St Thomas PI STALE/WH AL4 21 J3
St Thomas' Rd BELV DA17 164 D1
BRW CM14 107 J8
CAN/RD E16 141 M8
CVW DA11 190 B4
STHGT/OAK N14 98 E1
St Thomas Rd CHSWK W4 155 P6
St Thomas' Rd CVW DA11 190 B4
St Thomas' Dr RGUE GU4 * 251 P7
St Thomas's Gdns HAMP NW3 * 4 C1
St Thomas's Ms GU GU1 268 C2
St Thomas's Pl GRAYS RM17 * 167 P3
HOM E9 140 B2
St Thomas's Rd FSBYPK N4 119 H7
WLSDN NW10 136 B5
St Thomas's Sq HOM E9 140 A2
St Thomas's Wy FUL/PGN SW6 157 J6
St Thomas Wk DTCH/LGLY SL3 150 B6
St Ursula Gv PIN HA5 113 L3
St Ursula Rd STHL UB1 133 P8
St Vincent CI CRAWE RH10 284 E8
WNWD SE27 181 J8
St Vincent Dr STAL AL1 38 E8
St Vincent Rd WHTN TW2 176 B2
WOT/HER KT12 197 J10
St Vincents Cots
WATW WD18 * 73 J8
St Vincents La MLHL NW7 96 E5
St Vincent St MHST W1U 10 D4
St Vincent's Wy
POTB/CUF EN6 59 M10
Salamanca PI LBTH SE11 17 L8
Salamanca Rd STHWK SE1 17 N6
Salamander CI KUTN/CMB KT2 * 176 G9
Salamander Quay
KUT/HW KT1 * 199 J1
Salamons Wy RAIN RM13 144 F7
Salcombe Dr CHDH RM6 124 A4
MRDN SM4 200 D8
Salcombe Gdns MLHL NW7 96 F7
Salcombe Pk LOU IG10 82 A9
Salcombe Rd ASHF TW15 173 P7
STNW/STAM N16 119 K10
WALTH E17 121 J5
Salcombe Wy RSLP HA4 94 B7
Salcot Crs CROY/NA CR0 225 H6
Salcote Rd CVE DA12 191 H8
Salcott Rd BTSEA SW11 179 P1
CROY/NA CR0 202 F10
Salehurst CI
KTN/HRWW/WS HA3 115 K3
Salehurst Rd BROCKY SE4 182 B2
CRAWE RH10 284 F7
Salem PI CROY/NA CR0 203 K10
Salem Rd BAY/PAD W2 8 G1
Sale PI BAY/PAD W2 9 N4
Sale St BETH E2 7 P8
Salford Rd BRXS/STRHM SW2 180 N1
Salhouse CI THMD SE28 143 M8
Salisbury Av BARK IG11 142 D2
FNCH N3 97 H10
SLN SL2 129 H6
STAL AL1 38 C5
SUT SM1 221 J3
SWLY BR8 209 H4
Salisbury CI AMSS HP7 69 H5
POTB/CUF EN6 59 M8
WALW SE17 18 G6
WPK KT4 200 C10
Salisbury Ct EMB EC4Y 12 B6
Salisbury Gdns WDGN N22 98 A1
WIM/MER SW19 * 179 H10
Salisbury Hall Dr HAT AL10 40 A2
Salisbury Pavement
FUL/PGN SW6 * 157 K6
Salisbury PI BF/WBF KT14 215 M7
BRXN/ST SW9 158 C3
Salisbury Prom
CEND/HSY/T N8 * 119 J3
Salisbury Rd BAR EN5 77 H7
BNSTD SM7 239 L1
BXLY DA5 186 B6
CAR SM5 221 K6
CHING E4 100 F4
DAGE RM10 144 C1
DART DA1 191 J1
EHAM E6 141 N4
ED N9 100 D7
EN EN1 79 N4
FELT TW13 153 P5
FSBYPK N4 119 H7
GDMY/SEVK IG3 123 J2
GDST RH9 260 B2
GPK RM2 125 J3
GRAYS RM17 167 P5
HCH RM12 125 K5
HOD EN11 45 H2
HRW HA1 114 C3
HSLWW TW4 153 H7
LEY E10 121 H3
MNPK E12 141 L3
NWDGN UB2 153 M3
NWMAL KT3 200 A3
PEND EN3 80 D1
PIN HA5 113 K1
RCH/KEW TW9 155 K10
RDART DA2 188 E6
SEVS/STOTM N15 119 K1
SNWD SE25 203 N4
UX/CGN UB8 131 L1
WALTH E17 121 H3
WATN WD24 73 H1
WDGN N22 98 E10
WELL DA16 163 P5
WIM/MER SW19 179 H10
WOKS/MYFD GU22 232 A1
Salisbury Sq EMB EC4Y * 12 B6
HERT/WAT SG14 24 A5
Salisbury St ACT W3 155 P1
STJWD NW8 9 M2

Salisbury Ter PECK SE15 160 B9
Salisbury Wk ARCH N19 118 C10
Salix CI GT/LBKH KT23 236 A9
Salix Rd GRAYS RM17 168 A5
Sally Murray CI MNPK E12 122 D9
Salmen Rd PLSTW E13 141 L4
Salmon CI WGCE AL7 23 K2
Salmond CI STAN HA7 94 F7
Salmon La POP/IOD E14 140 D8
Salmon Ms KIL/WHAMP NW6 * 137 H1
Salmon Rd BELV DA17 164 B4
DART DA1 165 N9
Salmons La CTHM CR3 241 M6
Salmons La West CTHM CR3 241 M6
Salmon St CDALE/KGS NW9 115 N6
ED N9 99 P2
Salmon St POP/IOD E14 * 140 C8
Salomons Rd PLSTW E13 141 P7
Salop Rd WALTH E17 120 C4
Saltash CI SUT SM1 221 J1
Saltash Rd BARK/HLT IG6 102 G8
WELL DA16 164 A7
Saltbox HI BH/WHM TN16 225 H9
Saltcote CI DART DA1 190 A1
Saltcoats Rd CHSWK W4 156 B1
Saltcroft CI WBLY HA9 116 N6
Saltdean CI CRAWE RH10 283 N10
Salter CI RYLN/HDSTN HA2 114 A4
Salterford Rd TOOT SW17 180 B9
Salter Rd BERM/RHTH SE16 140 C10
Salters CI BERK HP4 * 34 C1
Salters Gdns WAT WD17 * 73 H3
Salters' Hall Ct MANHO EC4N * 12 G7
Salters HI NRWD SE19 181 L7
Salters Rd NKENS W10 136 C7
WALTH E17 121 J2
Salters Rw IS N1 * 6 G1
Salter St POP/IOD E14 140 F9
WLSDN NW10 136 G5
Salterton Rd HOLWY N7 118 F8
Saltford CI ERITH DA8 164 F6
Salt Hill CI SL SL1 129 H10
Salt Hill Dr UX/CGN UB8 111 K10
Salt Hill Wy SL SL1 129 H10
The Saltings SWCM DA10 189 L1
Saltley CI EHAM E6 141 P8
Saltoun Rd BRXS/STRHM SW2 180 A2
Saltram CI SEVS/STOTM N15 119 N2
Saltram Crs MV/WKIL W9 8 A1
Saltwell St POP/IOD E14 140 F9
Saltwood CI ORP BR6 227 M1
Saltwood Gv WALW SE17 18 G8
Salusbury Rd
KIL/WHAMP NW6 2 B5
Salvador TOOT SW17 179 P4
Salvia Gdns GFD/PVL UB6 134 F3
Salvin Rd PUT/ROE SW15 156 G10
Salway CI WFD IG8 101 N6
Salway PI SRTFD E15 141 J1
Salwey Crs BROX EN10 44 B6
Samantha CI WALTH E17 120 E5
Samantha Ms ABR/ST RM4 104 E3
Samaritan CI CRAWW RH11 283 H9
Sam Bartram CI CHARL SE7 161 P4
Samels Ct HMSMTH W6 156 D4
Samford St STJWD NW8 9 N2
Samira CI WALTH E17 120 D1
Samos Rd PGE/AN SE20 204 A2
Samphire CI CRAWW RH11 283 K10
Samphire St GRAYS RM17 168 B5
Sampleoak La RGUE GU4 269 H7
Sampson Av BAR EN5 76 G9
Sampson CI BELV DA17 164 A3
Sampsons Gn SLN SL2 128 E5
Sampsons HI AMSS HP7 88 D3
Sampson St WAP E1W 13 P10
Samson St PLSTW E13 141 P4
Samuel CI HACK E8 7 M5
NWCR SE14 160 C5
STAN HA7 94 F3
WOOL/PLUM SE18 162 B3
Samuel Gray Gdns
KUTN/CMB KT2 * 176 G9
Samuel Johnson CI
STRHM/NOR SW16 * 180 G5
Samuel Lewis Trust Dwellings
CMBW SE5 * 159 K7
HACK E8 * 119 P9
Samuel Sq STAL AL1 38 C7
Samuel St WOOL/PLUM SE18 162 C5
Sancroft CI CRICK NW2 116 C8
Sancroft Rd
KTN/HRWW/WS HA3 94 E10
Sancroft St LBTH SE11 17 L7
Sanctuary CI DEN/HRF UB9 91 M8
Sanctuary Ms HACK E8 * 7 M2
Sanctuary Rd HTHAIR TW6 171 K8
The Sanctuary BXLY DA5 185 N2
WEST SW1P 17 J3
Sandal Rd EA W5 135 K6
KTTN NW5 5 H2
NWMAL KT3 200 B4
UED N18 99 P6
Sandall CI EA W5 135 K6
Sandal St SRTFD E15 141 K4
Sandalwood Av CHERT KT16 194 G10
Sandalwood CI WCHPL E1 140 A6
Sandalwood Dr RSLP HA4 112 D5
Sandalwood Rd FELT TW13 153 N6
Sanday CI HHS/BOV HP3 36 C8
Sandbach PI
WOOL/PLUM SE18 162 F3
Sandbanks HI RDART DA2 189 H9
Sandbourne Av
WIM/MER SW19 201 L3
Sandbourne Rd NWCR SE14 160 A4
Sandbrook CI MLHL NW7 96 A7
Sandbrook Rd
STNW/STAM N16 119 J8
Sandby Gn ELTH/MOT SE9 162 M8
Sandcliff Rd ERITH DA8 164 B5
Sandcroft CI PLMGR N13 99 J7
Sandcross La REIG RH2 275 H8
Sandell's Av ASHF TW15 174 D7
Sandell St STHWK SE1 17 P2
Sandeman Gdns WARE SG12 26 F7
Sanders CI HPTN TW12 175 H6
LCOL/BKTW AL2 57 H7
Sanders La MLHL NW7 96 F3
Sanderson CI KTTN NW5 * 118 C10
Sanderson Rd UX/CGN UB8 131 H7
Sandersons Av RSEV TN14 247 L3
Sanders Pde
STRHM/NOR SW16 * 180 F9
Sanders Rd HHS/BOV HP3 36 C8
Sandersfield Gdns BNSTD SM7 239 K1
Sanderstead Av BAL SW12 180 C3
Sanderstead CI BAL SW12 180 C3
Sanderstead Court Av
SAND/SEL CR2 223 P6
Sanderstead HI SAND/SEL CR2 223 N8
Sanderstead Rd LEY E10 120 F6
SAND/SEL CR2 223 L6
Sandfield Gdns THHTH CR7 203 J8
Sandfield Pas THHTH CR7 203 K8
Sandfield Rd STAL AL1 38 F6

THHTH CR7 203 J8
Sandfields RPLY/SEND GU23 232 C10
Sandfield Ter GU GU1 268 C4
Sandford Av LOU IG10 82 F7
WDGN N22 99 J3
Sandford CI EHAM E6 142 A5
Sandford Ct BXLYHS DA6 * 165 J6
EHAM E6 142 C5
HAYES BR2 205 N4
Sandford Rd BXLYHS DA6 165 J6
EHAM E6 142 C5
HAYES BR2 205 N3
Sandgate CI ROMW/RG RM7 124 D5
Sandgate La
WAND/EARL SW18 179 P4
Sandgate Rd WELL DA16 163 N6
Sandgate St PECK SE15 160 A5
Sandgates WLGTN SM6 222 E1
Sandhills WLGTN SM6 222 E1
Sandhills Ct VW GU25 194 B5
Sandhills La VW GU25 194 B5
Sandhills Rd REIG RH2 275 K2
Sandhurst Av BRYLDS KT5 199 N4
RYLN/HDSTN HA2 114 A4
Sandhurst CI SAND/SEL CR2 223 M5
Sandhurst Ct HARP AL5 20 C1
Sandhurst Dr GDMY/SEVK IG3 123 J3
Sandhurst Market CAT SE6 * 183 H4
Sandhurst Pde CAT SE6 * 183 H4
Sandhurst Rd BFN/LL DA15 165 H10
BXLY DA5 185 N1
CAT SE6 183 J4
CDALE/KGS NW9 115 M1
ED N9 80 B10
ORP BR6 207 K10
TIL RM18 169 P5
Sandhurst Wy SAND/SEL CR2 223 M4
Sandifer Dr CRICK NW2 116 D1
Sandifield HAT AL10 40 E7
Sandiford Rd CHEAM SM3 201 J9
Sandiland Crs HAYES BR2 205 P10
Sandilands CROY/NA CR0 203 P10
SEV TN13 246 E8
Sandilands Rd FUL/PGN SW6 157 N7
Sandison St PECK SE15 159 N3
Sandland Gv
KWD/TDW/WH KT20 238 D9
Sandlands Rd
KWD/TDW/WH KT20 238 D9
Sandling Ri ELTH/MOT SE9 184 D6
Sandlings CI PECK SE15 160 B1
The Sandlings WDGN N22 99 H10
Sandmartin Wy WLGTN SM6 202 B8
Sandmere CI HHNE HP2 36 B7
Sandmere Rd CLAP SW4 158 G10
Sandon CI ESH/CLAY KT10 198 C1
Sandon PI CHONG CM5 67 H6
Sandon Rd CHES/WCR EN8 62 B6
Sandow Crs HYS/HAR UB3 152 C2
Sandown Av DAGE RM10 144 D1
ESH/CLAY KT10 218 A2
HCH RM12 125 L7
Sandown CI HEST TW5 153 H5
Sandown Ct BELMT SM2 * 221 L8
DAGE RM10 144 C2
SYD SE26 * 182 A6
Sandown Dr CAR SM5 222 B9
Sandown Ga ESH/CLAY KT10 198 B1
Sandown Rd COUL/CHIP CR5 240 B2
ESH/CLAY KT10 218 B1
GVE DA12 190 F9
SLN SL2 128 E7
SNWD SE25 203 P4
WATN WD24 73 K4
Sandown Wy NTHLT UB5 133 M1
Sandpiper CI
BERM/RHTH SE16 160 E1
CRAWW RH11 282 G9
RDART DA2 188 F1
WALTH E17 101 P10
Sandpiper Dr ERITH DA8 165 J6
Sandpiper Rd SAND/SEL CR2 224 C7
SUT SM1 221 J2
The Sandpipers CVE DA12 190 G5
Sandpiper Ter CLAY IG5 * 122 E1
Sandpiper Wy
STMC/STPC BR5 207 N4
Sandpit Hall Rd
CHOB/PIR GU24 213 M8
Sandpit Heath RGUW GU3 249 H5
Sandpit La BRW CM14 106 E2
STAL AL1 39 H4
STALE/WH AL4 39 J4
Sandpit PI CHARL SE7 162 B4
Sandpit Rd BMLY BR1 183 M3
DART DA1 165 K10
REDH RH1 275 P7
WGCE AL7 23 H7
Sandpits Rd CROY/NA CR0 224 C1
RCHPK/HAM TW10 176 A4
Sandra CI HSLW TW3 175 H1
WDGN N22 99 K9
Sandridge CI EBAR EN4 77 P3
HRW HA1 114 D2
Sandridge Pk STALW/RED AL3 38 D1
Sandridge Rd ARCH N19 118 D7
STALW/RED AL3 38 E1
Sandringham Av EN EN1 79 M6
WIM/MER SW19 179 N8
WOKS/MYFD GU22 233 K2
Sandringham CI SL SL1 128 C8
Sandringham Crs
RYLN/HDSTN HA2 113 P8
STALW/RED AL3 38 E1
Sandringham Dr ASHF TW15 173 N7
WELL DA16 163 N5
Sandringham Gdns
BARK/HLT IG6 122 F1
CEND/HSY/T N8 118 E4
E/WMO/HCT KT8 197 N4
HEST TW5 152 C5
NFNCH/WDSPK N12 97 N7
Sandringham Ms EA W5 135 K5
HPTN TW12 * 174 G7
Sandringham Rd BARK IG11 143 H4
BMLY BR1 183 N1
BRWN CM15 86 G5
CRICK NW2 136 A5
FSTGT E7 141 N1
GLDGN NW11 116 E10
HACK E8 7 N1
HTHAIR TW6 173 M6
LEY E10 120 B5
NTHLT UB5 133 N2
THHTH CR7 203 K2
WATN WD24 73 J3
WPK KT4 200 D10
Sandringham Wy
CHES/WCR EN8 62 B10
Sandrock PI CROY/NA CR0 224 C1
Sandrock Rd DORK RH4 272 A4
LEW SE13 160 G11
Sands End La FUL/PGN SW6 157 N7
Sands Farm Dr SL SL1 131 N1
Sandstone La CAN/RD E16 142 A3
Sandstone PI ARCH N19 118 B2
Sandstone Rd LEE/GVPK SE12 183 M2
Sandtoft Rd CHARL SE7 162 B4
Sandway PI STMC/STPC BR5 * 207 M3
Sandway Rd STMC/STPC BR5 207 N3
Sandwell Crs KIL/WHAMP NW6 2 F1
Sandwich St STPAN WC1H 5 H9
Sandwick CI MLHL NW7 96 C5
Sandwood Ms CSHM HP5 50 A6
Sandy Bank Rd CVE DA12 190 G6
Sandy Bury ORP BR6 206 G10

| | | | |
|---|---|---|---|
| Sandy Cl *CRAWE* RH10 | 285 | P5 |
| HERT/WAT SG14 | 25 | J5 |
| WOKS/MYFD GU22 | 232 | E8 |
| Sandycombe Rd | | |
| EBED/NFELT TW14 | 175 | H4 |
| RCH/KEW TW9 | 155 | N8 |
| Sandycoombe Rd *TWK* TW1 | 217 | N9 |
| Sandy Ct *COB* KT11 | 217 | N9 |
| Sandycroft *ABYW* SE2 | 163 | K6 |
| Sandy Cft *EW* KT17 | 220 | H4 |
| Sandycroft Rd *AMS* HP6 | 69 | N5 |
| Sandy Dr *COB* KT11 | 217 | N9 |
| EBED/NFELT TW14 | 174 | F4 |
| Sandy Hill Av | | |
| WOOL/PLUM SE18 | 162 | E4 |
| Sandy Hill La | | |
| WOOL/PLUM SE18 | 162 | E3 |
| Sandy Hill Rd *IL* IG1 | 122 | E9 |
| Sandy Hill Rd *WLGTN* SM6 | 222 | D5 |
| WOOL/PLUM SE18 | 162 | E4 |
| Sandy Holt *COB* KT11 | 217 | M9 |
| Sandy La *ASC* SL5 | 192 | H5 |
| BELMT SM2 | 221 | H5 |
| BH/WHM TN16 | 262 | C1 |
| BRKHM/BTCW RH3 | 256 | B10 |
| BUSH WD23 | 74 | B7 |
| CDW/CHF RM16 | 168 | E5 |
| CHOB/PIR GU24 | 213 | K5 |
| COB KT11 | 218 | A7 |
| COB KT11 | 217 | N8 |
| CRAWE RH10 | 285 | P5 |
| KTN/HRWW/WS HA3 | 115 | L4 |
| KWD/TDW/WH KT20 | 239 | J10 |
| MEO DA13 | 189 | K7 |
| MTCM CR4 | 202 | B1 |
| NTHWD HA6 | 92 | G3 |
| ORP BR6 | 207 | K7 |
| OXTED RH8 | 261 | H5 |
| RCHPK/HAM TW10 | 177 | H5 |
| RDART DA2 | 189 | J6 |
| REDH RH1 | 276 | F1 |
| REIG RH2 | 274 | E1 |
| RGUW GU3 | 248 | C2 |
| RPLY/SEND GU23 | 232 | E10 |
| SCUP DA14 | 185 | N10 |
| SEV TN13 | 247 | K9 |
| SHGR GU5 | 269 | J7 |
| SOCK/AV RM15 | 145 | N2 |
| STMC/STPC BR5 | 207 | N2 |
| TEDD TW11 | 176 | F10 |
| VW GU25 | 194 | B5 |
| WOKS/MYFD GU22 | 232 | E4 |
| WOT/HER KT12 | 197 | J6 |
| WTHK RM20 | 166 | C5 |
| Sandy La North *WLGTN* SM6 | 222 | E4 |
| Sandy La South *WLGTN* SM6 | 222 | D5 |
| Sandy Ldg *PIN* HA5 * | 93 | P7 |
| Sandy Lodge La *NTHWD* HA6 * | 92 | A1 |
| Sandy Lodge La *NTHWD* HA6 | 92 | N3 |
| Sandy Lodge Rd | | |
| RKW/CH/CXG WD3 | 92 | C3 |
| Sandy Lodge Wy *NTHWD* HA6 | 92 | H4 |
| Sandy Md *HOR/WEW* KT19 | 219 | N5 |
| Sandymount Av *STAN* HA7 | 95 | H6 |
| Sandy Ridge *CHST* BR7 | 184 | D9 |
| Sandy Ri *CFSP/GDCR* SL9 | 90 | D9 |
| Sandy Rd *ADL/WDHM* KT15 | 215 | K3 |
| HAMP NW3 | 117 | L2 |
| Sandy's Rw *WCHPL* E1 | 13 | K4 |
| Sandy Wy *COB* KT11 | 217 | P8 |
| CROY/NA CR0 | 204 | E10 |
| WOKS/MYFD GU22 | 232 | F3 |
| WOT/HER KT12 | 196 | C8 |
| Sanford La *STNW/STAM* N16 | 119 | N7 |
| Sanford St *NWCR* SE14 | 160 | C5 |
| Sanford Ter *STNW/STAM* N16 | 119 | N8 |
| Sanger Av *CHSGTN* KT9 | 219 | L8 |
| Sanger Dr *RPLY/SEND* GU23 | 232 | F8 |
| Sangers Dr *HORL* RH6 | 280 | D5 |
| Sangley Rd *CAT* SE6 | 182 | C3 |
| SNWD SE25 | 203 | M4 |
| Sangora Rd *BTSEA* SW11 | 157 | N10 |
| San Juan Dr *CDW/CHF* RM16 | 167 | H3 |
| San Luis Dr *CDW/CHF* RM16 | 167 | J3 |
| San Marcos Dr | | |
| CDW/CHF RM16 | 167 | H3 |
| Sansom St *CMBW* SE5 | 159 | L6 |
| Sans Wk *CLKNW* EC1R * | 59 | H9 |
| Santers La *POTB/CUF* EN6 | 59 | H9 |
| Santiago Wy *CDW/CHF* RM16 | 167 | J4 |
| Santley St *CLAP* SW4 | 158 | F10 |
| Santos Rd *WAND/EARL* SW18 | 179 | K1 |
| Sanway Cl *BF/WBF* KT14 | 215 | P10 |
| Sanway Rd *BF/WBF* KT14 | 215 | P10 |
| Saperton Wk *LBTH* SE11 | 17 | P5 |
| Sapho Pk *GVE* DA12 | 191 | J7 |
| Saphora Cl *ORP* BR6 | 226 | G2 |
| Sappers Cl *SBW* CM21 | 30 | A1 |
| Sapphire Cl *BCTR* RM8 | 73 | K8 |
| Sapphire Rd *DEPT* SE8 | 160 | D3 |
| WLSDN NW10 | 135 | P2 |
| Sappho Cl *WOKN/KNAP* GU21 * | 231 | K2 |
| Saracen Cl *CROY/NA* CR0 | 203 | L6 |
| Saracens Head *HHNE* HP2 | 36 | B5 |
| Saracen's Head Yd | | |
| FENCHST EC3M | 13 | K6 |
| Saracen St *POP/IOD* E14 | 140 | C7 |
| Sara Crs *RDART* DA2 | 166 | F10 |
| Sara Pk *GVE* DA12 | 191 | H7 |
| Saratoga Rd *CLPT* E5 | 120 | B9 |
| Sardinia St *HOL/ALD* WC2B | 11 | N6 |
| Sarel Wy *HORL* RH6 | 280 | D7 |
| Sargeant Cl *UX/CGN* UB8 | 131 | N5 |
| Sarita Cl *KTN/HRWW/WS* HA3 | 94 | C10 |
| Sark Cl *HEST* TW5 | 153 | P6 |
| Sarnesfield Rd *ENC/FH* EN2 * | 79 | L8 |
| Sarratt Av *HHNE* HP2 | 36 | A6 |
| Sarratt La *RKW/CH/CXG* WD3 | 71 | L6 |
| Sarre Av *HCH* RM12 | 150 | B4 |
| Sarre Rd *CRICK* NW2 | 117 | J10 |
| STMC/STPC BR5 | 207 | M5 |
| Sarsby Dr *STWL/WRAY* TW19 | 172 | D5 |
| Sarsen Av *HSLW* TW3 | 153 | N6 |
| Sarsfeld Rd *BAL* SW12 | 180 | A4 |
| Sarsfield Rd *GFD/PVL* UB6 | 134 | D2 |
| Sartor Rd *PECK* SE15 | 160 | C10 |
| Sarum Complex | | |
| UX/CGN UB8 * | 131 | L4 |
| Sarum Gn *WEY* KT13 | 196 | F3 |
| Sarum Pl *HHNE* HP2 | 35 | P2 |
| Sarum Ter *BOW* E3 | 139 | J5 |
| Satanita Cl *CAN/RD* E16 | 142 | A4 |
| Satchell Md *CDALE/KGS* NW9 | 96 | C5 |
| Satchwell Rd *BETH* E2 * | 7 | N8 |
| Satinwood Ct *HHS/BOV* HP3 | 35 | P6 |
| Sattar Ms *STNW/STAM* N16 * | 119 | P8 |
| Saturn Rd *CAT* SE6 | 182 | B3 |
| Saturn Wy *HHNE* HP2 | 36 | A5 |
| Sauls Gn *WAN* E11 | 122 | C6 |
| Sauncey Av *HARP* AL5 | 33 | J5 |
| Saunders Cl *CHES/WCR* EN8 | 62 | C4 |
| CRAWE RH10 * | 284 | C7 |
| GVW DA11 | 190 | F5 |
| POP/IOD E14 * | 140 | C9 |
| Saunders Copse | | |
| WOKS/MYFD GU22 | 231 | M9 |
| Saunders End *AMS* HP6 | 50 | B10 |
| Saunders La | | |
| WOKS/MYFD GU22 | 231 | L10 |
| Saunders Ness Rd | | |
| POP/IOD E14 | 161 | N2 |
| Saunders Rd *HGDN/ICK* UB10 | 112 | G7 |
| WOOL/PLUM SE18 | 163 | N6 |
| Saunders St *LBTH* SE11 | 18 | A6 |
| Saunderton Rd *ALP/SUD* HA0 | 114 | F3 |
| Saunton Av *HYS/HAR* UB3 | 152 | A1 |
| Saunton Rd *HCH* RM12 | 124 | H7 |
| Savage Gdns *EHAM* E6 | 142 | C4 |
| EW EC3N | 13 | M1 |
| Savay Cl *DEN/HRF* UB9 | 111 | K5 |
| Savay La *DEN/HRF* UB9 | 111 | K5 |

| | | | |
|---|---|---|---|
| Savera Cl *NWDGN* UB2 | 153 | K2 |
| Savernake Cl *STAN* HA7 * | 95 | H7 |
| Savernake Rd *ED* N9 | 79 | P10 |
| HAMP NW3 | 118 | A3 |
| Savernake Wk *CRAWE* RH10 | 284 | A10 |
| Savery Dr *SURB* KT6 | 198 | G2 |
| Savile Cl *NWMAL* KT3 | 200 | B5 |
| THDIT KT7 | 198 | B8 |
| Savile Gdns *CROY/NA* CR0 | 203 | N9 |
| Savile Ct *EW* KT17 * | 61 | K1 |
| Savile Row *CONDST* W1S * | 10 | E7 |
| Saville Cl *HOR/WEW* KT19 | 219 | N7 |
| Saville Crs *ASHF* TW15 | 174 | E9 |
| Saville Rd *CAN/RD* E16 | 142 | B10 |
| CHDH RM6 | 124 | A4 |
| CHSWK W4 | 146 | B1 |
| TWK TW1 | 176 | E4 |
| Saville Rw *HAYES* BR2 | 205 | L8 |
| PEND EN3 | 80 | C6 |
| Savill Gdns *RYNPK* SW20 | 200 | D3 |
| Savill Ms *ECH* TW20 | 172 | A9 |
| Savill Rw *WFD* IG8 | 101 | L7 |
| Savona Cl *WIM/MER* SW19 | 178 | G10 |
| Savona St *VX/NE* SW8 | 158 | D6 |
| Savoy Av *HYS/HAR* UB3 | 152 | F4 |
| Savoy Cl *EDGW* HA8 | 91 | N10 |
| EDGW HA8 | 85 | M6 |
| HLWE CM17 | 11 | M8 |
| SRTFD E15 | 140 | C1 |
| Savoy Ct *TPL/STR* WC2R * | 11 | N8 |
| Savoy Hl *TPL/STR* WC2R * | 11 | N7 |
| Savoy Ms *BRXN/ST* SW9 | 158 | F9 |
| STAL AL1 | 38 | C4 |
| Savoy Pde *EN* N1 * | 79 | M7 |
| Savoy Pl *CHCR* WC2N * | 11 | M8 |
| Savoy Rw *TPL/STR* WC2R * | 11 | N7 |
| Savoy St *TPL/STR* WC2R * | 11 | N7 |
| Savoy Steps *TPL/STR* WC2R * | 11 | N7 |
| Savoy St *TPL/STR* WC2R * | 11 | N7 |
| Savoy Wd *HLWW/ROY* CM19 | 46 | D7 |
| Sawbill Cl *YEAD* UB4 | 133 | L7 |
| Sawells *BROX* EN10 | 44 | E7 |
| Sawkins Cl *WIM/MER* SW19 | 178 | C5 |
| Sawley Rd *SHB* W12 | 136 | D10 |
| Sawtry Cl *CAR* SM5 | 201 | N7 |
| Sawtry Wy *BORE* WD6 | 75 | M4 |
| Sawyer Cl *ED* N9 | 99 | P3 |
| Sawyers Cl *DAGE* RM10 | 144 | D1 |
| Sawyers Ct *WDSR* SL4 | 148 | D6 |
| Sawyers Gv *BRWN* CM15 | 107 | J1 |
| Sawyer's Hall La *BRWN* CM15 | 107 | H1 |
| Sawyer's Hl | | |
| RCHPK/HAM TW10 | 177 | L3 |
| Sawyers La *POTB/CUF* EN6 | 58 | G10 |
| Sawyers Lawn *WEA* W13 | 134 | F8 |
| Sawyer St *STHWK* SE1 | 18 | E1 |
| Sawyers Wy *HHNE* HP2 | 36 | A6 |
| Saxby Rd *BRXS/STRHM* SW2 | 161 | P2 |
| Saxham Rd *BARK* IG11 | 143 | H5 |
| Saxley *HORL* RH6 | 280 | D5 |
| Saxlingham Rd *CHING* E4 | 101 | J4 |
| Saxon Av *FELT* TW13 | 175 | M5 |
| Saxonbury Av *SUN* TW16 | 197 | J3 |
| Saxonbury Cl *MTCM* CR4 | 201 | N3 |
| Saxonbury Gdns *SURB* KT6 | 199 | H8 |
| Saxon Cl *AMS* HP6 | 69 | J4 |
| DTCH/LGLY SL3 | 150 | C1 |
| GVW DA11 | 189 | P6 |
| HARH RM3 | 105 | N10 |
| RBRW/HUT CM13 | 109 | N7 |
| RSEV TN14 | 246 | G3 |
| SURB KT6 | 199 | J6 |
| UX/CGN UB8 | 131 | P7 |
| WALTH E17 | 120 | F5 |
| Saxon Ct *BORE* WD6 | 75 | K5 |
| Saxon Dr *ACT* W3 | 135 | N8 |
| Saxonfield Cl | | |
| BRXS/STRHM SW2 | 180 | A3 |
| Saxon Hl *BH/WHM* TN16 * | 262 | C6 |
| Saxon Ms *WAT* WD17 * | 73 | H5 |
| Saxon Rd *ASHF* TW15 | 174 | E9 |
| Schubert Rd *BORE* WD6 | 75 | J10 |
| PUT/ROE SW15 | 179 | J1 |
| Scillonian Rd *GUW* GU2 | 267 | M1 |
| Scinde St *WCHPL* E1 | 13 | L1 |
| Scoble Pl *STNW/STAM* N16 | 119 | N9 |
| Scoles Crs *BRXS/STRHM* SW2 | 181 | H4 |
| Scope Wy *KUT/HW* KT1 | 199 | K4 |
| Scords La *BH/WHM* TN16 | 263 | M8 |
| Scoresby St *STHWK* SE1 | 18 | C2 |
| Scorton Av *GFD/PVL* UB6 | 134 | F4 |
| Scorton Cl *HARH* RM3 | 181 | H4 |
| Scotch Common *WEA* W13 | 134 | F7 |
| Scoter Cl *WFD* IG8 | 101 | N8 |
| Scot Gv *PIN* HA5 | 93 | K3 |
| Scotia Rd *BRXS/STRHM* SW2 | 181 | H3 |

| | | | |
|---|---|---|---|
| Scholefield Rd *ARCH* N19 | 118 | E7 |
| Schonfeld Sq | | |
| STNW/STAM N16 | 119 | L7 |
| Schoolbank Rd *GNWCH* SE10 | 161 | L3 |
| School Cl *BRKMPK* AL9 | 42 | A3 |
| CHOB/PIR GU24 | 230 | D3 |
| CSHM HP5 | 50 | C4 |
| GU GU1 | 250 | A8 |
| School Crs *DART* DA1 | 164 | C10 |
| Schoolfield Rd *WTHK* RM20 | 166 | F5 |
| School Gdns *BERK* HP4 | 34 | E3 |
| School Green La *EPP* CM16 | 66 | D1 |
| School Hl *REDH* RH1 | 258 | D4 |
| School House La *TEDD* TW11 | 176 | C10 |
| Schoolhouse La *WAP* E1W * | 140 | C8 |
| School La *ADL/WDHM* KT15 | 215 | K1 |
| AMSS HP7 | 68 | A8 |
| BEAC HP9 | 89 | J7 |
| BFOR GU20 | 212 | C3 |
| BGR/WK TN15 | 247 | N1 |
| BRKMPK AL9 | 42 | A3 |
| BUSH WD23 | 74 | B7 |
| CFSP/GDCR SL9 | 90 | A10 |
| CHIG IG7 | 103 | J5 |
| CHOB/PIR GU24 | 230 | D8 |
| CHONG CM5 | 48 | E5 |
| DORK RH4 | 272 | C8 |
| EGH TW20 | 172 | C8 |
| EHSLY KT24 | 252 | C5 |
| HART DA3 | 210 | E6 |
| HAT AL10 | 40 | E3 |
| HLW CM20 | 29 | H10 |
| KUT/HW KT1 | 199 | H1 |
| LCOL/BKTW AL2 | 55 | N10 |
| LHD/OX KT22 | 236 | C8 |
| PIN HA5 * | 113 | M2 |
| RBRW/HUT CM13 | 107 | H2 |
| RDART DA2 | 189 | H6 |
| RDKG RH5 | 255 | H5 |
| RGUE GU4 | 251 | P7 |
| RGUW GU3 | 266 | E5 |
| RPLY/SEND GU23 | 234 | C8 |
| SHPTN TW17 | 196 | C6 |
| SLN SL2 | 129 | L9 |
| SLN SL2 | 129 | N2 |
| SURB KT6 | 199 | L8 |
| SWLY BR8 | 187 | J10 |
| WLYN AL6 | 23 | P7 |
| School Md *ABLGY* WD5 | 54 | E8 |
| School Meadow *GUW* GU2 | 249 | K9 |
| School Pas *DEN/HRF* UB9 * | 91 | M10 |
| School Pas *KUT/HW* KT1 | 199 | L1 |
| STHL UB1 | 133 | N10 |
| School Rd *ASC* SL5 | 192 | C5 |
| ASHF TW15 | 174 | C9 |
| BFOR GU20 | 212 | A2 |
| BRWN CM15 | 86 | D3 |
| CHONG CM5 | 66 | G6 |
| DAGE RM10 | 144 | B3 |
| E/WMO/HCT KT8 | 198 | A3 |
| GVE DA12 | 190 | F6 |
| HPTN TW12 | 176 | B9 |
| HSLW TW3 | 154 | B9 |
| KUT/HW KT1 * | 199 | H1 |
| MNPK E12 | 122 | C9 |
| POTB/CUF EN6 | 59 | M6 |
| WDR/YW UB7 | 151 | M4 |
| WLSDN NW10 | 136 | E1 |
| School Road Av *HPTN* TW12 | 176 | B9 |
| School Rnw *HNWL* W7 | 35 | J7 |
| School Sq *GNWCH* SE10 | 161 | L2 |
| School Wy *BCTR* RM8 | 123 | L8 |
| Schoolway | | |
| NFNCH/WDSPK N12 | 97 | N7 |
| Schooner Cl *BARK* IG11 | 143 | L5 |
| BERM/RHTH SE16 | 160 | C1 |
| POP/IOD E14 | 161 | J2 |
| Schooner Ct *RDART* DA2 | 166 | B10 |
| Schroder Ct *ECH* TW20 | 181 | N8 |

| | | | |
|---|---|---|---|
| Scottwell Dr *CDALE/KGS* NW9 | 116 | C3 |
| Scoulding Rd *CAN/RD* E16 | 141 | L8 |
| Scouler St *POP/IOD* E14 | 141 | P8 |
| Scout Ap *WLSDN* NW10 | 99 | M7 |
| Scout Wy *MLHL* NW7 | 96 | A5 |
| Scovell Crs *STHWK* SE1 * | 18 | E3 |
| Scovell Rd *STHWK* SE1 | 18 | E3 |
| Scratchers La *HART* DA3 | 210 | C10 |
| Scrattons Ter *BARK* IG11 | 143 | N4 |
| Scriveners Cl *HHNE* HP2 | 35 | M4 |
| Scriven St *HACK* E8 | 7 | M5 |
| Scrooby St *CAT* SE6 | 182 | C2 |
| Scrubbitts Sq *RAD* WD7 | 74 | F1 |
| Scrubbitts Park Rd *RAD* WD7 | 74 | F1 |
| Scrubs La *WLSDN* NW10 | 136 | D5 |
| Scrutton Cl *BAL* SW12 | 180 | E5 |
| Scrutton St *SDTCH* EC2A | 13 | J1 |
| Scudders Ml *HART* DA3 | 211 | H6 |
| Scutari Rd *EDUL* SE22 | 182 | A1 |
| Scutley La *BFOR* GU20 | 212 | D4 |
| Scylla Crs *HTHAIR* TW6 | 174 | C3 |
| Scylla Rd *HTHAIR* TW6 | 174 | C3 |
| PECK SE15 | 160 | A9 |
| Seaborough Rd | | |
| CDW/CHF RM16 | 168 | F2 |
| Seabright St *BETH* E2 | 140 | A1 |
| Seabrook Dr *WWKM* BR4 | 205 | N1 |
| Seabrooke Ri *GRAYS* RM17 | 167 | N5 |
| Seabrook Gdns | | |
| ROMW/RG RM7 | 124 | B5 |
| Seabrook Rd *BCTR* RM8 | 123 | N8 |
| KGLGY WD4 | 53 | J4 |
| Seaburn Cl *RAIN* RM13 | 144 | F5 |
| Seacole Cl *ACT* W3 | 118 | E10 |
| Seacourt Rd *ABYW* SE2 | 163 | N1 |
| DTCH/LGLY SL3 | 150 | E5 |
| Seacroft Gdns *OXHEY* WD19 | 93 | L4 |
| Seafield Rd *FBAR/BDGN* N11 | 98 | G4 |
| Seaford Cl *RSLP* HA4 | 112 | G7 |
| EN EN1 | 79 | M8 |
| HTHAIR TW6 | 174 | B4 |
| SEVS/STOTM N15 | 119 | L3 |
| WALTH E17 | 120 | C1 |
| WEA W13 | 134 | C10 |
| Seaford St *STPAN* WC1H | 5 | M10 |
| Seaforth Av *NWMAL* KT3 | 200 | F5 |
| Seaforth Crs *HBRY* N5 | 119 | H10 |
| Seaforth Dr *CHES/WCR* EN8 | 62 | C10 |
| Seaforth Gdns | | |
| HOR/WEW KT19 | 220 | C1 |
| WCHMH N21 | 99 | L6 |
| WFD IG8 | 101 | P6 |
| Seaforth Pl *WESTW* SW1E * | 17 | H3 |
| Seager Bldgs *DEPT* SE8 * | 160 | F2 |
| Seager Pl *BOW* E3 | 140 | A4 |
| Seagrave Cl *WCHPL* E1 * | 140 | C7 |
| Seagrave Rd *FUL/PGN* SW6 | 14 | F9 |
| Seagry Rd *WAN* E11 | 121 | M4 |
| Seagull La *CAN/RD* E16 | 141 | M9 |
| Seal Dr *BGR/WK* TN15 | 247 | K10 |
| Seal Hollow Rd *SEV* TN13 | 247 | K10 |
| Sealand Rd *HTHAIR* TW6 | 174 | B4 |
| Sealand Wk *NTHLT* UB5 * | 133 | J6 |
| Seal Rd *RSEV* TN14 | 247 | J3 |
| Seal St *HACK* E8 | 7 | N1 |
| Seaman Cl *LCOL/BKTW* AL2 | 56 | C1 |
| Searches La *ABLGY* WD5 | 53 | P5 |
| Searchwood Ms *WARL* CR6 | 242 | A4 |
| Searchwood Rd *WARL* CR6 | 242 | A4 |
| Searle Hl *REIG* RH2 | 275 | K7 |
| Searles Cl *BTSEA* SW11 | 158 | C4 |
| Searles Dr *EHAM* E6 | 142 | F3 |

| | | | |
|---|---|---|---|
| Seeley Dr *DUL* SE21 | 181 | M7 |
| Seeleys *HLWE* CM17 | 29 | M7 |
| Seeleys Cl *BEAC* HP9 | 88 | C8 |
| Seeleys Rd *BEAC* HP9 | 88 | B7 |
| Seelig Av *CDALE/KGS* NW9 | 116 | C5 |
| Seer Green La *BEAC* HP9 | 89 | K8 |
| Seer Md *BEAC* HP9 | 89 | J7 |
| Seething La *TWRH* EC3N | 13 | K7 |
| Seething Wells La *SURB* KT6 | 199 | H6 |
| Sefton Av | | |
| KTN/HRWW/WS HA3 | 94 | C9 |
| MLHL NW7 | 96 | A6 |
| Sefton Cl *CHOB/PIR* GU24 | 212 | C9 |
| SLN SL2 | 131 | J1 |
| STAL AL1 | 38 | C5 |
| STMC/STPC BR5 | 207 | J4 |
| Sefton Ct *ENC/FH* EN2 * | 79 | J5 |
| WGCW AL8 | 22 | C7 |
| Sefton Paddock *SLN* SL2 | 129 | N2 |
| Sefton Rd *CROY/NA* CR0 | 203 | P8 |
| HOR/WEW KT19 | 220 | A6 |
| STMC/STPC BR5 | 207 | J4 |
| Sefton St *PUT/ROE* SW15 | 156 | F8 |
| Sefton Wy *UX/CGN* UB8 | 131 | M8 |
| Segal Cl *FSTH* SE23 | 163 | L10 |
| Segsbury Gv *BRACK* RG12 | 32 | C5 |
| Sekhon Ter *FELT* TW13 | 175 | P6 |
| Selah Dr *SWLY* BR8 | 186 | G9 |
| Selan Gdns *YEAD* UB4 | 133 | J7 |
| Selbie Av *WLSDN* NW10 | 116 | C10 |
| Selborne Av *BXLY* DA5 | 185 | P4 |
| MNPK E12 | 122 | G9 |
| Selborne Gdns *CFD/PVL* UB6 | 134 | F4 |
| HDN NW4 | 116 | D2 |
| Selborne Rd *CMBW* SE5 | 159 | L8 |
| CROY/NA CR0 | 203 | M10 |
| IL IG1 | 122 | D7 |
| NWMAL KT3 | 200 | B2 |
| SCUP DA14 | 185 | L10 |
| WALTH E17 | 120 | E3 |
| WDGN N22 | 98 | G9 |
| Selborne Wy *WEY* KT13 | 216 | A4 |
| Selbourne Rd *BRW* CM14 | 107 | K4 |
| Selby Cl *CHSGTN* KT9 | 219 | K8 |
| CHST BR7 | 184 | D9 |
| EHAM E6 | 141 | P8 |
| Selby Gdns *STHL* UB1 | 133 | P4 |
| Selby Gn *CAR* SM5 | 201 | P7 |
| Selby Rd *ASHF* TW15 | 174 | F9 |
| CAR SM5 | 194 | G6 |
| EA W5 | 134 | E10 |
| PGE/AN SE20 | 182 | E9 |
| PLSTW E13 | 141 | N7 |
| TOTM N17 | 99 | P4 |
| WAN E11 | 121 | K8 |
| Selby St *WCHPL* E1 | 13 | P1 |
| Selby Wk *WOKN/KNAP* GU21 * | 231 | N4 |
| Selcroft Rd *PUR/KEN* CR8 | 223 | J8 |
| Selden Hl *HHW* HP1 | 35 | L6 |
| Selden Rd *PECK* SE15 | 160 | B8 |
| Sele Mi *HERT/WAT* SG14 | 25 | J5 |
| Sele Rd *HERT/WAT* SG14 | 25 | J5 |
| Selham Cl *CRAWW* RH11 | 283 | K6 |
| Selhurst Cl *WIM/MER* SW19 | 178 | G4 |
| WOKN/KNAP GU21 | 232 | C1 |
| Selhurst New Rd *SNWD* SE25 | 203 | M6 |
| Selhurst Pl *SNWD* SE25 | 203 | M6 |
| Selhurst Rd *ED* N9 | 99 | L4 |
| SNWD SE25 | 203 | M6 |
| Selinas La *BCTR* RM8 | 123 | N4 |
| Selkirk Dr *ERITH* DA8 | 164 | F7 |
| Selkirk Rd *TOOT* SW17 | 179 | P7 |
| WHTN TW2 | 176 | B5 |
| Sellar's Hl *GODL* GU7 | 267 | J10 |
| Sell Cl *CHESW* EN7 | 61 | J1 |
| Sellers Hall Cl *FNCH* N3 | 97 | K8 |
| Sellincourt Rd *TOOT* SW17 | 179 | P8 |
| Sellindge Cl *BECK* BR3 | 182 | E10 |
| Sellons Av *WLSDN* NW10 | 136 | C3 |
| Sells Cl *GU* GU1 | 268 | C2 |

| | | | |
|---|---|---|---|
| Sequoia Gdns *ORP* BR6 | 207 | J7 |
| Sequoia Pk *CRAWW* RH11 | 283 | N9 |
| PIN HA5 | 94 | A7 |
| Serbin Cl *LEY* E10 | 121 | H5 |
| Serenaders La *BRXN/ST* SW9 | 159 | H4 |
| Sergeants Green La *WAB* EN9 | 63 | P9 |
| Sergeants Pl *CTHM* CR3 | 241 | K6 |
| Sergehill La *ABLGY* WD5 | 55 | H2 |
| Serjeant's Inn *EMB* EC4Y * | 12 | B6 |
| Serle St *LINN* WC2A | 11 | P5 |
| Sermon Dr *SWLY* BR8 | 208 | D3 |
| Sermon La *BLKFR* EC4V * | 12 | E6 |
| Serpentine Rd *BAY/PAD* W2 | 9 | P10 |
| SEV TN13 | 247 | K9 |
| Service Rd *HORL* RH6 | 280 | A7 |
| The Service Rd *POTB/CUF* EN6 | 59 | N2 |
| Service Route No 1 | | |
| SRTFD E15 | 141 | J2 |
| Service Route No 2 | | |
| SRTFD E15 | 141 | J2 |
| Service Route No 3 | | |
| SRTFD E15 | 141 | J3 |
| Serviden Dr *BMLY* BR1 | 206 | A1 |
| Setchell Est *STHWK* SE1 * | 19 | L5 |
| Setchell Rd *STHWK* SE1 | 19 | L5 |
| Setchell Wy *STHWK* SE1 | 19 | L5 |
| Seth St *BERM/RHTH* SE16 | 160 | B1 |
| Seton Gdns *DAGW* RM9 | 143 | N3 |
| Settle Rd *HARH* RM3 | 105 | P5 |
| Settles St *WCHPL* E1 | 13 | P4 |
| Settrington Rd *FUL/PGN* SW6 | 157 | L8 |
| Seven Acres *CAR* SM5 | 201 | N9 |
| NTHWD HA6 | 93 | H7 |
| SWLY BR8 | 208 | E3 |
| Seven Arches Ap *WEY* KT13 | 216 | A4 |
| Seven Arches Rd *BRW* CM14 | 107 | K4 |
| Seven Dials *LSQ/SEVD* WC2H * | 11 | J6 |
| Sevenex Pde *WBLY* HA9 * | 115 | K10 |
| Seven Hills Cl *WOT/HER* KT12 | 216 | F5 |
| Seven Hills Rd *IVER* SL0 | 110 | E10 |
| Seven Hills Rd *WOT/HER* KT12 | 216 | F5 |
| Seven Hills Road (South) | | |
| COB KT11 | 216 | F9 |
| Seven Kings Rd | | |
| GDMY/SEVK IG3 | 123 | H6 |
| Seven Kings Wy | | |
| KUTN/CMB KT2 | 199 | J1 |
| Sevenoaks By-Pass | | |
| RSEV TN14 | 264 | F2 |
| Sevenoaks Cl *BELMT* SM2 | 221 | K6 |
| BXLYHN DA7 | 164 | D10 |
| HARH RM3 | 105 | K5 |
| Sevenoaks Rd *BROCKY* SE4 | 182 | C2 |
| ORP BR6 | 227 | J1 |
| ORP BR6 | 227 | J5 |
| RSEV TN14 | 247 | J2 |
| Sevenoaks Wy | | |
| STMC/STPC BR5 | 207 | M2 |
| Seven Seas Rd *HTHAIR* TW6 | 174 | D2 |
| Seven Sisters Rd *HOLWY* N7 | 118 | G8 |
| SEVS/STOTM N15 | 119 | L4 |
| Seven Stars Yd *WCHPL* E1 | 13 | M3 |
| Seventh Av *HYS/HAR* UB3 | 133 | H10 |
| KWD/TDW/WH KT20 | 257 | J2 |
| MNPK E12 | 122 | C9 |
| Severalls Av *CSHM* HP5 | 51 | H6 |
| Severn Av *GPK* RM2 | 105 | L10 |
| Severnake Cl *POP/IOD* E14 | 160 | F3 |
| Severn Crs *DTCH/LGLY* SL3 | 150 | E4 |
| Severn Dr *ENC/FH* EN1 | 79 | N4 |
| ESH/CLAY KT10 | 198 | F9 |
| UPMR RM14 | 126 | C4 |
| WOT/HER KT12 | 197 | L9 |
| Severnmead *HHNE* HP2 | 35 | P5 |
| Severn Rd *CRAWE* RH10 | 284 | B8 |
| SOCK/AV RM15 | 146 | B8 |
| Severns Fld *EPP* CM16 | 65 | K5 |
| Severnvale *LCOL/BKTW* AL2 * | 57 | L3 |
| Severn Wy *GSTN* WD25 | 53 | L10 |
| WLSDN NW10 | 116 | C10 |
| Severus Rd *BTSEA* SW11 | 157 | P10 |
| Seville Ms *IS* N1 | 7 | J4 |
| Seville St *KTBR* SW1X | 16 | F3 |
| Sevington Rd *HDN* NW4 | 116 | E4 |
| Sevington St *MV/WKIL* W9 | 8 | B2 |
| Seward Rd *BECK* BR3 | 182 | G5 |
| HNWL W7 | 154 | F1 |
| Sewardstone Rd *BETH* E2 | 140 | B4 |
| CHING E4 | 88 | C8 |
| WAB EN9 | 63 | H10 |
| Sewardstone Wy *WAB* EN9 | 81 | H2 |
| Seward St *FSBYE* EC1V | 12 | D1 |
| Sewdley St *CLPT* E5 | 120 | C8 |
| Sewell Cl *CDW/CHF* RM16 | 167 | H4 |
| STALE/WH AL4 | 21 | J3 |
| Sewell Harris Cl *HLW* CM20 | 29 | J10 |
| Sewell Rd *ABYW* SE2 | 163 | K1 |
| Sewells *WGCW* AL8 | 23 | H2 |
| Sewell St *PLSTW* E13 | 141 | M5 |
| Sewill Cl *HORL* RH6 | 279 | H8 |
| Sextant Av *POP/IOD* E14 | 161 | J3 |
| Sexton Cl *CHESW* EN7 | 61 | J1 |
| RAIN RM13 | 144 | C3 |
| Sexton Rd *TIL* RM18 | 168 | C7 |
| Seymer Rd *ROM* RM1 | 124 | F1 |
| Seymour Av *CTHM* CR3 | 241 | K9 |
| EW KT17 | 220 | E5 |
| MRDN SM4 | 200 | G7 |
| TOTM N17 | 99 | P9 |
| Seymour Ct *COB* KT11 * | 216 | C8 |
| Seymour Crs *HHNE* HP2 | 35 | P6 |
| Seymour Dr *HAYES* BR2 | 206 | C8 |
| Seymour Gdns *BROCKY* SE4 | 160 | F9 |
| BRYLDS KT5 | 199 | L5 |
| FELT TW13 | 175 | J7 |
| IL IG1 | 122 | C6 |
| RSLP HA4 | 113 | L6 |
| TWK TW1 | 176 | C3 |
| Seymour Ms *EW* KT17 | 220 | E6 |
| MBLAR W1H * | 10 | G5 |
| Seymour Pl *MBLAR* W1H | 10 | F2 |
| SNWD SE25 | 204 | A4 |
| WOKS/MYFD GU22 | 231 | K6 |
| Seymour Rd *GU* GU1 | 248 | D2 |
| STALW/RED AL3 | 38 | D3 |
| TIL RM18 | 168 | C7 |
| WIM/MER SW19 | 178 | A5 |
| Seymours *HLWW/ROY* CM19 | 46 | A7 |
| WOOL/PLUM SE18 | 162 | F12 |
| Seymour Ter *PGE/AN* SE20 | 204 | A1 |
| Seymour Vls *PGE/AN* SE20 | 204 | A1 |
| Seymour Wk *SWCM* DA10 | 189 | K3 |
| WBPTN SW10 | 15 | J9 |
| Seymour Wy *SUN* TW16 | 176 | B9 |
| Seyssel St *POP/IOD* E14 | 161 | N3 |
| Shaa Rd *ACT* W3 | 136 | A9 |
| Shabden Cots | | |
| COUL/CHIP CR5 * | 240 | A7 |
| Shacklands Rd *RSEV* TN14 | 228 | D7 |
| Shackleford Rd | | |
| WOKS/MYFD GU22 | 232 | C8 |
| MFD/CHID GU8 | 266 | C10 |

WOKS/MYFD GU22 232 D6
Shackleton La TEDD TW11 176 D7
Shackleton Cl FSTH SE23 182 A1
Shackleton Rd CRAWE RH10 283 P10
 SL SL1 129 L9
 STHL UB1 133 H9
Shackleton Wy ABLGY WD5 * 55 H8
 WGCE AL7 23 J5
Shacklewood La HACK E8 119 N9
Shacklewell Rd
 STNW/STAM E16 119 N9
Shacklewell Rw HACK E8 119 N9
Shacklewell St BETH E2 13 M1
Shadbolt Av CHING E4 100 B6
Shadbolt Cl WPK KT4 200 C9
Shad Thames STHWK SE1 13 L10
Shadwell Dr NTHLT UB5 133 N6
Shadwell Gdns
 WCHPL E1 * 140 C8
Shadwell Pierhead WAP E1W 140 B9
Shady Bush Cl BUSH WD23 94 B1
Shady La WAT WD17 73 J6
Shaef Wy TEDD TW11 176 F10
Shafter Rd DAGE RM10 144 E1
Shaftesbury LOU IG10 82 A7
Shaftesbury Av BAR EN5 27 M8
 EBED/NFELT TW14 175 H2
 KTN/HRWW/WS HA3 115 H3
 LSQ/SEVD WC2H 11 L5
 NWDGN UB2 153 P3
 PEND EN3 80 D4
 RYLN/HDSTN HA2 114 A6
 SOHO/SHAV W1D 11 J7
Shaftesbury Cir
 RYLN/HDSTN HA2 * 114 B6
Shaftesbury Ct
 RKW/CH/CXG WD3 * 72 D9
Shaftesbury Ct STA TW18 173 N10
Shaftesbury Gdns
 WLSDN NW10 136 B6
Shaftesbury La DART DA1 166 A10
Shaftesbury Ms CLAP SW4 180 L1
 KENS W8 * 14 F4
Shaftesbury Pde
 RYLN/HDSTN HA2 * 114 B6
Shaftesbury Pl BARB EC2Y * 12 F1
Shaftesbury Rd ARCH N19 118 F6
 BECK BR3 204 E2
 CAR SM5 201 J2
 CHING E4 101 J2
 CHOB/PIR GU24 230 E2
 CRAWE RH10 284 E8
 EPP CM16 65 J5
 FSTGT E7 141 P2
 LEY E10 120 F6
 RCH/KEW TW9 155 K9
 ROM RM1 124 G4
 UED N18 99 M7
 WALTH E17 120 C3
 WAT WD17 73 K2
 WOKS/MYFD GU22 232 E3
The Shaftesburys BARK IG11 142 E4
Shaftesbury St IS N1 6 F8
 HMSMTH W6 * 156 C6
Shaftesbury Wy WHTN TW2 176 C6
Shaftesway YEAD UB4 133 H8
Shaftled Wt TOOT SW17 180 A6
Shafto Ms KTBR SW1X 16 A4
Shafton Ms HOM E9 * 140 C3
Shafton Rd HOM E9 140 C3
Shaftsbury Wy KGLGY WD4 52 B3
Shaggy Calf La SLN SL2 129 M9
Shakespeare Av
 EBED/NFELT TW14 175 H2
 FBAR/BDGN N11 98 E4
 TIL RM18 168 E8
 WLSDN NW10 135 P5
 YEAD UB4 133 H8
Shakespeare Crs MNPK E12 142 C2
 WLSDN NW10 135 P5
Shakespeare Dr BORE WD6 75 M8
 KTN/HRWW/WS HA3 115 L4
Shakespeare Gdns EFNCH N2 118 A2
Shakespeare Rd ACT W3 117 K1
 ADL/WDHM KT15 215 N1
 BXLYHN DA7 163 P7
 DART DA1 165 P10
 FNCH N3 97 K9
 HARP AL5 20 A2
 HNHL SE24 181 J1
 HNWL W7 134 E9
 MLHL NW7 96 D5
 ROM RM1 124 G4
 WALTH E17 100 C10
Shakespeare Sq BARK/HLT IG6 102 E7
Shakespeare St WATN WD24 73 M4
Shakespeare Ter
 RCH/KEW TW9 * 155 M9
Shakletons CHONG CM5 67 P4
Shaketons Ms
 STNW/STAM N16 119 M9
Shakspeare Ms
 STNW/STAM N16 119 M9
Shakspeare Wk
 STNW/STAM N16 119 M9
Shalcomb St WBPTN SW10 140 E1
Shalcross Dr CHES/WCR EN8 62 C6
Shaldon Dr MRDN SM4 201 H5
 RSLP HA4 113 K8
Shaldon Rd EDGW HA8 95 K10
Shaldon Wy WOT/HER KT12 197 K10
Shalfleet Dr NKENS W10 136 M9
Shalford Cl ORP BR6 226 F1
Shalford Ct IS N1 6 C7
Shalford Rd RGUE GU4 268 A3
Shalford Rd GU GU1 268 A3
Shalimar Gdns ACT W3 135 P9
Shalimar Rd ACT W3 135 P9
Shallcross Crs HAT AL10 40 C7
Shallons Rd ELTH/MOT SE9 184 G10
Shalstone Rd
 MORT/ESHN SW14 155 N9
Shalston Vls SURB KT6 199 L6
The Shambles GU GU1 268 A2
Shambrook Rd CHESW EN7 61 J1
Shamrock Cl LHD/OX KT22 96 C8
Shamrock Rd CROY/NA CRO 202 G6
 GVE DA12 191 H3
Shamrock St CLAP SW4 158 G8
Shamrock Wy
 STHGT/OAK N14 98 C2
Shandon Rd CLAP SW4 180 C2
Shand St STHWK SE1 13 L2
Shandy St WCHPL E1 140 C7
Shanklin Cl CHESW EN7 61 N5
Shanklin Gdns OXHEY WD19 93 H6
Shanklin Rd CEND/HSY/T N8 117 N8
 SEVS/STOTM N15 119 P2
Shannon Cl CRICK NW2 118 A8
 NWDGN UB2 153 L4
Shannon Gv BRXN/ST SW9 158 G10
Shannon Pl STJWD NW8 3 P7
Shannon Wy BECK BR3 182 G2
 SOCK/AV RM15 146 B8
Shantock Hall La
 HHS/BOV HP3 52 B5
Shantock La HHS/BOV HP3 52 B6
Shap Crs CAR SM5 202 A5
Shaplawd Wy PLMGR N13 98 G6
Shapwick Cl FBAR/BDGN N11 98 A6
Shardcroft Av HNHL SE24 181 J1
Shardeloes Rd BROCKY SE4 181 P1
 NWCR SE14 160 F8
Shard's Sq PECK SE15 160 B5
Shardel Cl THHTH CR7 203 H6
Sharland Rd GVE DA12 191 H8
Sharman Ct SCUP DA14 185 K7
Sharman Rw DTCH/LGLY SL3 150 C4
Sharnbrooke Cl WELL DA16 163 H3
Sharon Cl CRAW RH10 283 B10
 GT/LBKH KT23 235 P10
 HOR/WEW KT19 219 N5
 SURB KT6 199 H9
Sharon Gdns HOM E9 140 F2


Sharon Rd CHSWK W4 156 A1
 PEND EN3 80 D6
Sharpcroft HHNE HP2 35 N4
Sharpecroft HLWW/ROY CM19 46 F1
Sharples La HHW HP1 * 34 E7
Sharples Hall St CAMTN NW1 * 4 F1
Sharps La RSLP HA4 112 E5
Sharpthorne Cl CRAWW RH11 283 J7
 HCH RM12 124 G7
 MNPK E12 142 B1
Shelley Cl BNSTD SM7 238 C1
 CHONG CM5 67 N2
 COUL/CHIP CR5 240 C5
 CRAWE RH10 284 D5
 DTCH/LGLY SL3 150 A4
 EDGW HA8 95 M5
 GFD/PVL UB6 134 C5
 NTHWD HA6 92 C6
 POP/IOD E14 160 A8
 YEAD UB4 133 H7
Shelley Crs HEST TW5 153 K5
 STHL UB1 133 N8
Shelley Dr WELL DA16 163 H7
Shelley Gdns ALP/SUD HA0 115 H7
 WEA W13 135 P2
Shelley Gv LOU IG10 82 C9
Shelley La NTHWD HA6 91 K8
Shelley Ms NHS/BOV HP3 35 N9
Shelley Pl TIL RM18 168 E7
Shelley Rd CSHM HP5 50 C5
 WLSDN NW10 136 A3
Shelleys La RSEV TN14 245 K2
Shellgrove Rd
 STNW/STAM N16 119 M10
Shellness Rd CLPT E5 120 A10
Shell Rd LEW SE13 160 C9
Shellwood Dr RDKG RH5 273 H6
Shellwood Rd BTSEA SW11 158 A6
 REIG RH2 274 A7
Shelly Cl BORE WD6 75 M8
Shelmerdine Cl BOW E3 140 F7
Shelson Av FELT TW13 174 C6
Shelton Av WARL CR6 242 P5
Shelton Cl GUW GU2 249 M5
 WARL CR6 242 B5
Shelton Rd WIM/MER SW19 201 K1
 LSQ/SEVD WC2H 11 L6
Shelvers Gn
 KWD/TDW/WH KT20 238 F7
Shelvers Hl
 KWD/TDW/WH KT20 238 F7
Shelvers Sp
 KWD/TDW/WH KT20 238 F7
Shelvers Wy
 KWD/TDW/WH KT20 238 F7
Shenden Cl SEV TN13 265 K4
Shenden Wy SEV TN13 265 K4
Shenfield Cl COUL/CHIP CR5 240 C5
Shenfield Ct BRWN CM15 107 K3
Shenfield Gdns
 RBRW/HUT CM13 87 N10
Shenfield Rd BRWN CM15 107 K1
 WFD IG8 102 A1
Shenfield St IS N1 7 K8
Shenley Av RSLP HA4 112 G2
Shenleybury RAD WD7 57 K6
Shenleybury Cots RAD WD7 57 L9
Shenley Cl SAND/SEL CR2 223 N6
Shenley Hl RAD WD7 56 G10
Shenley La LCOL/BKTW AL2 56 C1
 WIM/MER SW19 201 J1
Shenley Rd BORE WD6 75 M7
 CROY/NA CR0 159 M7
 HEST TW5 153 M7
 HNHL SE24 181 M1
 RAD WD7 75 J1
Shenstone Cl DART DA1 186 E1
Shenstone Dr SL SL1 128 C6
Shenstone Gdns HARH RM3 105 K9
Shenstone Pk ASC SL5 192 C4
Shepcot Cl WGCE AL7 23 K8
Sheperton BEAC HP9 88 B7
Shepherd Cl ABLGY WD5 54 G6
 CRAWE RH10 283 N10
 FELT TW13 175 M7
Shepherdess Pl IS N1 6 F7
Shepherdess Wk IS N1 6 F7
Shepherd Market
 MYFR/PKLN W1J 10 E7
Shepherd's Bush Gn SHB W12 157 H2
Shepherd's Bush Market
 SHB W12 156 F1
Shepherd's Bush Pl
 SHB W12 * 157 H1
Shepherd's Bush Rd
 HMSMTH W6 156 G1
Shepherds Cl CHDH RM6 123 N1
 ORP BR6 207 H6
 SHPTN TW17 196 C6
 STAN HA7 94 H4
 UX/CGN UB8 * 131 M6
Shepherds Ct HGT N6 118 C4
 HERT/WAT SG14 25 K2
Shepherds Farm
 RKW/CH/CXG WD3 91 K2
Shepherds Gn CHST BR7 184 G10
 HHW HP1 35 H7
Shepherds Hl HARH RM3 105 P10
 HGT N6 118 C4
 REDH RH1 258 F7
Shepherds La BEAC HP9 88 G10
 BFOR GU20 212 F2
 THMD SE28 143 H10
Shepherd's La GUW GU2 249 L7
 HOM E9 120 C10
 RKW/CH/CXG WD3 70 G10
Shepherd's Leas
 ELTH/MOT SE9 * 162 G10
Shepherds Pl
 MYFR/PKLN W1K 10 C7
Shepherds Rd WATW WD18 72 G7
Shepherds Wk BUSH WD23 94 C3
 CRICK NW2 116 D7
 HAMP NW3 119 N10
Shepherds Wy BRKMPK AL9 59 J7
 CSHM HP5 51 J1
 RKW/CH/CXG WD3 91 L1
 SAND/SEL CR2 224 C4
Shepherd's Wy RGUE GU4 268 D5
Shepiston La HYS/HAR UB3 132 E5
Shepley Cl CAR SM5 202 D3
Shepley Dr ASC SL5 193 H5
Shepley Ms PEND EN3 80 G1
Sheppard Cl EN EN1 28 A10
 KUT/HW KT1 199 K4
Sheppard Dr
 BERM/RHTH SE16 159 N4
Sheppards HLWW/ROY CM19 46 C4
Sheppards Cl
 STALW/RED AL3 38 D1
Sheppey Cl CAN/RD E16 141 N8
Shepperton Cl BORE WD6 76 A5
Shepperton Court Dr
 SHPTN TW17 195 K9
Shepperton Marina
 SHPTN TW17 196 A9
Shepperton Rd IS N1 6 F2
 STA TW18 195 N4
 STMC/STPC BR5 201 J1
Shepperton Ter
 TRDG/WHET N20 97 H1
Sheppey Gdns DAGW RM9 143 P4
Sheppey Rd DAGW RM9 143 L5
Sheppey's La KGLGY WD4 52 D1
Sheppeys Wk IS N1 * 6 E1
Shepton Houses BETH E2 * 140 B2
Sherard Rd ELTH/MOT SE9 184 B1


Sherards Orch
 HLWW/ROY CM19 46 A1
Sheraton Cl BORE WD6 75 E3
Sheraton Dr HOR/WEW KT19 219 P9
Sheraton Ms WATW WD18 72 P8
 PEND EN3 80 D4
Sherborne Av NWDGN UB2 153 P5
 PEND EN3 80 D4
Sherborne Cl DTCH/LGLY SL3 151 H7
 EPSOM KT18 238 F3
 YEAD UB4 133 H8
Sherborne Crs CAR SM5 201 P7
Sherborne Gdns
 CDALE/KGS NW9 115 M1
 WEA W13 136 G8
Sherborne Gv BRK/WK TN15 247 P3
Sherborne La MANHO EC4N 13 G2
Sherborne Rd CHEAM SM3 201 K9
 CHSGTN KT9 219 K2
 EBED/NFELT TW14 174 C3
 STMC/STPC BR5 201 J1
Sherborne St IS N1 6 G1
Sherborne Wy RKW/CH/CXG WD3 72 C8
Sherboro Rd
 SEVS/STOTM N15 119 N5
Sherbourne SHGR GU5 269 N5
Sherbourne Dr ASC SL5 193 J5
Sherbourne Gdns
 SHPTN TW17 196 C9
Sherbourne Wk SLN SL2 109 H9
Sherbrooke Cl BXLYHN DA7 164 B10
Sherbrooke Rd FUL/PGN SW6 157 H6
Sherbrooke Ter
 FUL/PGN SW6 * 157 H6
Sherbrook Gdns WCHMN N21 99 H7
Shere Av BELMT SM2 220 F6
Shere Cl CHSGTN KT9 219 J2
 RDKG RH5 273 H6
Sheredan Rd CHING E4 101 K4
Sheredes Dr HOD EN11 44 D1
Shere La SHGR GU5 270 B5
Shere Rd EHSLY KT24 252 D10
 GNTH/NBYPK IG2 122 D3
 RGUE GU4 269 K1
Sherfield Av
 RKW/CH/CXG WD3 91 H4
Sherfield Cl NWMAL KT3 199 N6
Sherfield Gdns PUT/ROE SW15 178 C2
Sherfield Rd GRAYS RM17 167 N5
Sheridan Ct DART DA1 186 C1
 HSLWW TW4 175 M1
Sheridan Crs CHST BR7 206 A2
Sheridan Dr REIG RH2 257 L8
Sheridan Gdns
 KTN/HRWW/WS HA3 115 J4
Sheridan Gra ASC SL5 192 F6
Sheridan Ms WAN E11 121 N4
Sheridan Pl BMLY BR1 184 D8
 HPTN TW12 198 A1
Sheridan Rd BELV DA17 164 B3
 BXLYHN DA7 163 P9
 FSTGT E7 121 L8
 MNPK E12 122 B10
 OXHEY WD19 93 L1
 RCHPK/HAM TW10 177 H6
 SUT SM1 221 P1
 WDSR SL4 148 E7
 WIM/MER SW19 201 J1
Sheridans RD GT/LBKH KT23 254 A8
Sheridan St WCHPL E1 140 C8
Sheridan Ter NTHLT UB5 114 A10
Sheridan Wk CAR SM5 202 C3
 GLDGN NW11 117 K7
Sheridan Wy BECK BR3 204 A9
Sheriff Wy GSTN WD25 55 H9
Sheringham Av MNPK E12 122 D9
 ROMW/RG RM7 124 D4
 STHGT/OAK N14 78 A9
 WHTN TW2 175 M4
Sheringham Dr BARK IG11 123 J10
Sheringham Rd HOLWY N7 5 M1
 PGE/AN SE20 201 A2
Sheringham Wk
 BRKHTH/KID SE3 161 N5
Sherland Ct RAD WD7 * 57 J10
Sherland Rd TWK TW1 176 E6
Sherleys Av ORP BR6 207 H9
Sherlock Ms MHST W1U 10 C3
Shermanbury Cl ERITH DA8 164 D4
Sherman Gdns CHDH RM6 123 N5
Sherman Rd BMLY BR1 184 A4
 SL SL1 129 K7
Shernbroke Rd WAB EN9 63 L10
Shernhall St WALTH E17 121 H3
Sherrard Rd FSTGT E7 141 P1
 MNPK E12 122 A10
Sherrardspark Rd WCCW AL8 22 E3
Sherrards Wy BAR EN5 77 K5
Sherrick Green Rd
 WLSDN NW10 116 A9
Sherriff Cl ESH/CLAY KT10 198 A9
Sherriff Rd KIL/WHAMP NW6 2 D1
Sherringham Av FELT TW13 175 H6
 TOTM N17 99 G9
Sherrin Rd LEY E10 139 N1
Sherry Ms BARK IG11 142 A10
Sherston Ct BRXN/ST SW9 160 B9
 FSBYPK N4 6 D6
Sherwin Wy NWCR SE14 160 C7
Sherwood CDW/CHF RM16 149 N2
 SURB KT6 199 J9
Sherwood Av CHIG IG7 103 K3
 EA W5 * 135 M9
 HAYES BR2 221 M9
 HCH RM12 124 C2
 MHST W1H * 10 A1
 RSLP HA4 94 D5
 STRHM/NOR SW16 181 J10
 YEAD UB4 133 H4
Sherwood Cl BXLY DA5 184 F5
 LHD/OX KT22 236 D2
 WALTH E17 101 J8
 WEA W13 135 P4
Sherwood Ct MBLAR W1H * 10 A1
 SCUP DA14 184 B4
Sherwood Crs BELMT SM2 221 J7
Sherwood Gdns BARK IG11 142 C2
 BERM/RHTH SE16 159 M6
 POP/IOD E14 160 A4
Sherwood House
 RYLN/HDSTN HA2 * 114 B8
Sherwood Park Av
 BFN/LL DA15 185 K5
Sherwood Park Rd
 MTCM CR4 202 G4
 SUT SM1 221 L5
Sherwood Pl HHNE HP2 36 A1
Sherwood Rd BARK/HLT IG6 122 G1
 COUL/CHIP CR5 240 C3
 CROY/NA CR0 202 G6
 HDN NW4 116 C1
 HPTN TW12 176 C7
 RYLN/HDSTN HA2 114 B7
 THHAIR TW6 * 173 P1
 WELL DA16 163 P1
 WIM/MER SW19 179 J10
Sherwood Road (East)
 HTHAIR TW6 173 P1
Sherwood Road (West)
 HTHAIR TW6 173 P1
Sherwood St REGST W1B 10 G7
 TRDG/WHET N20 97 J2
Sherwoods Rd OXHEY WD19 74 D10
Sherwood Ter
 TRDG/WHET N20 97 J2
Sherwood Wk CRAWE RH10 284 F4
 WWKM BR4 204 C5
Shetland Cl BORE WD6 76 B4
 CRAWE RH10 284 F6
Shetland Rd BOW E3 139 L7
Shevon Wy BRWN CM15 106 G2
Shewens Rd WEY KT13 195 J10
Shey Copse
 WOKS/MYFD GU22 232 G4


Shield Dr BTFD TW8 154 F5
Shieldhall St ABYW SE2 163 H3
Shield Rd ASHF TW15 174 A9
Shifford Pth FSTH SE23 182 C6
Shilburn Wy
 WOKN/KNAP GU21 231 M4
Shillibeer Pl MBLAR W1H 9 N4
Shillibeer Wk CHIG IG7 103 J4
Shillingford Cl MLHL NW7 96 F6
Shillingford Rd IS N1 * 6 D5
Shillingford St IS N1 * 6 D5
Shilling Pl HNWL W7 * 134 F10
Shillitoe Av POTB/CUF EN6 58 F5
The Shimmings GU GU1 250 D9
Shinfield St SHB W12 136 F8
Shingle Cl WAB EN9 63 M9
Shinglewell Rd ERITH DA8 164 B10
Shinners Cl SNWD SE25 203 P5
Ship & Mermaid Rw STHWK SE1 13 J1
Ship Hl BH/WHM TN16 243 P7
Shipka Rd BAL SW12 180 C6
Ship La EYN DA4 209 M4
 MORT/ESHN SW14 155 P9
 SOCK/AV RM15 146 A9
 SWLY BR8 209 L1
Shipley Bridge La HORL RH6 280 G10
Shipley Rd CRAWW RH11 283 K7
Shipman Rd CAN/RD E16 141 N8
 FSTH SE23 182 C5
Ship St DEPT SE8 160 F7
Ship Tavern Pas BANK EC3V 13 J7
Shipton Cl BCTR RM8 123 N8
Shipton Rd HGDN/ICK UB10 112 A9
Shipton St BETH E2 7 M9
Shipwright Rd
 BERM/RHTH SE16 160 D1
Shipwright Yd STHWK SE1 * 13 J10
Shirburn Cl FSTH SE23 182 B3
Shirbutt St POP/IOD E14 160 M9
Shirebrook Rd BKHTH/KID SE3 162 A8
Shire Cl BRXS/STRHM SW2 180 B6
Shire Ct EW KT17 220 C4
Shirehall Cl HDN NW4 116 C4
Shirehall Gdns HDN NW4 116 C4
Shirehall La HDN NW4 116 C4
Shirehall Pk HDN NW4 116 C4
Shirehall Rd RDART DA2 187 L8
Shire Horse Wy ISLW TW7 154 E9
Shire La CFSP/GDCR SL9 90 E7
 ORP BR6 227 L1
 ORP BR6 226 C4
 RKW/CH/CXG WD3 70 G9
 TRING HP23 32 B5
Shiremeade BORE WD6 75 L9
Shire Ms WHTN TW2 176 B2
Shire Pde CRAWE RH10 284 E6
 REDH RH1 276 A4
Shires Cl ASHTD KT21 237 J5
The Shires GSTN WD25 55 J7
 RCHPK/HAM TW10 177 K7
Shirland Ms MV/WKIL W9 2 D10
Shirland Rd MV/WKIL W9 2 D10
Shirley Av BELMT SM2 221 J6
 BXLY DA5 185 N3
 COUL/CHIP CR5 241 J5
 CROY/NA CR0 204 B8
 REDH RH1 276 A5
 SUT SM1 221 P1
 WDSR SL4 148 E7
Shirley Church Rd
 CROY/NA CR0 204 C10
Shirley Cl BROX EN10 44 E10
 CHES/WCR EN8 62 B5
 DART DA1 165 K10
 GVE DA12 191 L5
 HSLW TW3 176 B1
 WALTH E17 * 120 C3
Shirley Crs BECK BR3 204 D4
Shirley Dr HSLW TW3 176 B1
Shirley Gdns BARK IG11 143 H1
 HCH RM12 125 K2
 HNWL W7 134 F10
Shirley Gv BTSEA SW11 158 B9
 ED N9 100 D1
Shirley Hills Rd CROY/NA CR0 204 C10
Shirley Oaks Rd CROY/NA CR0 204 C8
Shirley Park Rd CROY/NA CR0 204 B8
Shirley Pl WOKN/KNAP GU21 231 M5
Shirley Rd ABLGY WD5 54 E4
 BFN/LL DA15 185 H8
 CHSWK W4 156 A1
 CROY/NA CR0 204 B8
 EN EN1 28 A4
 SRTFD E15 141 K7
 STAL AL1 38 F7
 WLGTN SM6 222 D9
Shirley Rw SNWD SE25 203 P2
Shirley St CAN/RD E16 141 K8
Shirley Wy CROY/NA CR0 204 E10
Shirlock Rd HAMP NW3 119 N9
Shirwell Cl MLHL NW7 96 C8
Shobden Rd TOTM N17 99 N9
Shobroke Cl CRICK NW2 116 B8
Shoebury Rd EHAM E6 142 C2
Shoe La FLST/FETLN EC4A 12 B5
Sholden Gdns STMC/STPC BR5 207 M5
Sholto Rd HTHAIR TW6 172 C3
Shonks Mill Rd ABR/ST RM4 85 J2
Shooters Av
 KTN/HRWW/WS HA3 115 J4
Shooters Dr WAB EN9 45 M4
 BKHTH/KID SE3 161 N6
Shooters Hill Rd
 BKHTH/KID SE3 161 M7
 CHARL SE7 161 K7
Shooters Rd ENC/FH EN2 79 J6
Shootersway TRING HP23 32 C5
Shootersway La BERK HP4 33 L5
Shoot-Up Hl CRICK NW2 2 B1
Shophouse La SHGR GU5 269 N10
Shoplands WGCW AL8 22 C2
Shop Rd WDSR SL4 148 B6
Shord Hl PUR/KEN CR8 241 L6
Shore Cl EBED/NFELT TW14 175 H3
 HPTN TW12 175 M8
Shoreditch High St
 FSBYE EC1V 7 K10
Shore Gv FELT TW13 175 K5
 SCUP DA14 185 K9
Shoreham Cl CROY/NA CR0 204 B6
 WAND/EARL SW18 179 L2
Shoreham La RSEV TN14 244 B8
 SEV TN13 255 M7
 STMC/STPC BR5 207 N9
Shoreham Pl RSEV TN14 245 J5
Shoreham Road (East)
 HTHAIR TW6 173 P1
Shoreham Road (West)
 HTHAIR TW6 173 P1
Shoreham Wy HAYES BR2 204 A9
Shorncliffe Rd STHWK SE1 19 L4
Shorndean St CAT SE6 183 H3
Shorne Cl BFN/LL DA15 185 K5
 STMC/STPC BR5 201 J1
Shornefield Cl BMLY BR1 205 K1
Shornells Wy ABYW SE2 163 H3
Short Cl CRAWW RH11 283 N4


Shortcroft Rd EW KT17 220 C4
Shortcrofts Rd DAGW RM9 144 A1
Shorter Av BRWN CM15 87 L10
Shorter St TWR EC3N 13 L3
Shortfern SLN SL2 129 P8
Short Gallop CRAWE RH10 * 284 C4
Shortgate NFNCH/WDSPK N12 97 J5
Shortlands HMSMTH W6 156 G3
 HYS/HAR UB3 132 B9
Shortlands Cl BELV DA17 164 A2
 UED N18 99 L4
Shortlands Gdns HAYES BR2 205 J2
Shortlands Gv WGCE AL7 23 J4
Shortlands La HAYES BR2 205 J3
Shortlands Rd HAYES BR2 205 J3
 KUTN/CMB KT2 177 L10
 LEY E10 120 B7
Short La LCOL/BKTW AL2 55 M5
 OXTED RH8 261 N8
 STWL/WRAY TW19 174 A3
Shorts Cft CDALE/KGS NW9 115 N2
Shorts Gdns LSQ/SEVD WC2H 11 L6
Shorts Rd CAR SM5 221 P1
Short St HDN NW4 116 C1
 STHWK SE1 18 B1
Shortway CSHM HP5 50 G5
 ELTH/MOT SE9 183 H5
The Short Wy
 NFNCH/WDSPK N12 97 P7
 WHTN TW2 176 B3
Shortwood Av STA TW18 173 L6
Shotfield WLGTN SM6 222 D7
Shothanger Wy HHS/BOV HP3 52 G1
 HHS/BOV HP3 221 M2
Shottendane Rd
 FUL/PGN SW6 157 K7
Shottery Cl ELTH/MOT SE9 184 B6
Shottfield Av
 MORT/ESHN SW14 155 P9
Shottfield La STALE/WH AL4 21 H9
Shoulder of Mutton Aly
 POP/IOD E14 * 140 D9
Shouldham St MBLAR W1H 9 N4
Showers Wy HYS/HAR UB3 133 H10
Shrapnel Cl WOOL/PLUM SE18 162 E6
Shrapnel Rd ELTH/MOT SE9 162 C9
Shrewsbury Av
 KTN/HRWW/WS HA3 115 K2
 MORT/ESHN SW14 155 P10
Shrewsbury Cl SURB KT6 211 L1
Shrewsbury La
 WOOL/PLUM SE18 162 E7
Shrewsbury Ms BAY/PAD W2 * 2 E7
Shrewsbury Rd BAR EN5 77 J1
 BECK BR3 204 D3
 CAR SM5 201 P7
 FBAR/BDGN N11 98 F5
 FSTGT E7 142 A1
 HTHAIR TW6 174 D2
 REDH RH1 257 P10
Shrewsbury St NKENS W10 136 F6
Shrewton Rd TOOT SW17 * 180 C5
Shrimpton Cl BEAC HP9 88 C3
Shrimpton Rd BEAC HP9 88 C3
Shroffold Rd BMLY BR1 183 K7
 BMLY BR1 183 M6
Shropshire Cl MTCM CR4 202 F4
Shropshire Rd WDGN N22 98 G8
Shroton St CAMTN NW1 9 N2
The Shrubberies CHIG IG7 102 F6
 STAL AL1 * 38 C8
 SWFD E18 101 M10
Shrubbery Gdns WCHMH N21 99 H7
Shrubbery Rd ED N9 100 E4
 EYN DA4 210 C1
 GVE DA12 190 E4
 STHL UB1 133 N10
 STRHM/NOR SW16 181 P7
The Shrubbery HHW HP1 35 H5
 SURB KT6 * 199 K8
 UPMR RM14 126 B8
Shrubbs Hill CHOB/PIR GU24 213 H5
Shrubbs Hill La ASC SL5 193 H6
Shrub Hill Rd HHW HP1 35 L7
Shrubland Gv WPK KT4 200 F10
Shrubland Rd BNSTD SM7 239 J2
 HACK E8 7 N2
 LEY E10 120 F5
 WALTH E17 120 D1
Shrublands BRKMPK AL9 59 J6
 CROY/NA CR0 224 F1
Shrublands Av BERK HP4 33 M5
 CROY/NA CR0 224 F1
Shrublands Cl CHIG IG7 102 F6
 SYD SE26 182 B6
 TRDG/WHET N20 97 J2
Shrublands Dr LTWR GU18 212 A1
The Shrublands POTB/CUF EN6 59 H6
Shrubsall Cl ELTH/MOT SE9 184 H4
Shrubs Rd RKW/CH/CXG WD3 92 A7
Shrubbery Cl IS N1 6 F4
Shuna Wk IS N1 6 H1
Shurland Av EBAR EN4 77 N10
Shurland Gdns PECK SE15 159 N6
Shurlock Av SWLY BR8 209 M1
Shurlock Dr ORP BR6 226 F1
Shuters Sq WKENS W14 14 C3
Shuttle Cl BFN/LL DA15 185 J3
Shuttlemead BXLY DA5 185 H5
Shuttle Rd DART DA1 165 H9
Shuttle St WCHPL E1 13 M5
Shuttleworth Rd BTSEA SW11 157 P6
Sibella Rd CLAP SW4 158 F8
Sibley Av HARP AL5 20 B5
Sibley Cl BMLY BR1 205 P2
 BXLYHS DA6 185 H3
Sibley Gn UX/CGN UB8 132 A5
Sibneys Gn HLWS CM18 47 L5
Sibthorp Rd BRKMPK AL9 40 B10
 LEE/GVPK SE12 183 P10
Sibthorpe Rd LEE/GVPK SE12 183 P10
 MTCM CR4 202 A2
Sibton Rd CAR SM5 201 P7
Sicilian Av NOXST/BSQ WC1A * 11 N3
Sickelfield Cl CHESW EN7 61 N2
Sidbury St FUL/PGN SW6 157 H6
Siddeley Dr HSLWW TW4 175 H3
Siddons La CAMTN NW1 * 10 B1
Siddons Rd CROY/NA CR0 203 H5
 FSTH SE23 182 B5
 TOTM N17 99 N9
Side Rd DEN/HRF UB9 110 C5
 WALTH E17 120 B3
Sideways La HORL RH6 280 B5
Sidford Pl STHWK SE1 17 N3
Sidings Ms HOLWY N7 119 L6
The Sidings BROX EN10 44 E8
 HAT AL10 * 40 C5
 HHNE HP2 * 36 A1
 LOU IG10 82 B10
 SEV TN13 * 246 F6
 WAN E11 * 121 M1
Siding Wy LCOL/BKTW AL2 56 B5
Sidmouth Av ISLW TW7 153 P8
Sidmouth Dr RSLP HA4 113 P10


Sidmouth Rd (continued)

Sidmouth Pde CRICK NW2 * .......... 136 F2
Sidmouth Rd CRICK NW2 .......... 136 F2
  LEY E10 .......... 121 H7
  PECK SE15 .......... 159 N7
  STMC/STPC BR5 .......... 207 L4
  WELL DA16 .......... 163 M6
Sidney Av PLMGR N13 .......... 98 G6
Sidney Cl UX/CGN UB8 .......... 131 M2
Sidney Elson Wy EHAM E6 .......... 142 M4
Sidney Gdns BTFD TW8 .......... 155 J5
  RSEV TN14 .......... 247 G2
Sidney Rd BECK BR3 .......... 204 C2
  BRXN/ST SW9 .......... 158 C8
  EPP CM16 .......... 82 C2
  RYLN/HDSTN HA2 .......... 114 H1
  SNWD SE25 .......... 203 P5
  STA TW18 .......... 173 K7
  TWK TW1 .......... 176 F2
  WDGN N22 .......... 98 G8
  WDSR SL4 .......... 148 B9
  WOT/HER KT12 .......... 197 H7
Sidney Sq WCHPL E1 * .......... 140 B7
Sidney St WCHPL E1 .......... 140 A7
Sidworth St HACK E8 .......... 140 E2
Siebert Rd GNWCH SE3 .......... 164 B7
Siemens Rd WOOL/PLUM SE18 .......... 162 A4
Siena Dr CRAWW RH10 .......... 284 D3
Sienna Cl CHSGTN KT9 .......... 219 J3
Sienna Ter CRICK NW2 * .......... 116 D7
Sierra Dr DAGE RM10 .......... 144 C4
Sigdon Rd HACK E8 .......... 119 F10
The Sigers PIN HA5 .......... 113 J4
Signmakers Yd CAMTN NW1 * .......... 4 F6
Sigrist Sq KUTN/CMB KT2 .......... 199 K1
Silbury Av MTCM CR4 .......... 201 P1
Silbury St IS N1 * .......... 6 D1
Silchester Dr CRAWW RH11 .......... 283 K10
Silecroft Rd BXLYHN DA7 .......... 164 B7
Silesia Blds HACK E8 .......... 140 D1
Silex St STHWK SE1 .......... 18 D2
Silistria Cl WOKN/KNAP GU21 .......... 231 H4
Silk Cl LEE/GVPK SE12 .......... 183 M1
Silkfield Rd CDALE/KGS NW9 .......... 116 B3
Silkham Rd OXTED RH8 .......... 265 J8
Silk Ms KENS SE15 .......... 159 P6
Silk Mill Rd OXHEY WD19 .......... 93 J1
Silk Mills Cl RSEV TN14 .......... 247 K1
Silk Mills Pth LEW SE13 .......... 161 N9
Silkmore La EHSLY KT24 .......... 252 A2
Silkstream Pde EDGW HA8 .......... 95 P5
Silkstream Rd EDGW HA8 .......... 95 P5
Silk St BARB EC2Y .......... 12 F1
Silo Cl GODL GU7 .......... 267 J3
Silo Dr GODL GU7 .......... 267 J3
Silo Rd GODL GU7 .......... 267 J3
Sisoe Rd WDGN N22 .......... 118 C1
Silverbeck Wy STWL/WRAY TW19 .......... 173 K1
  EPP CM16 .......... 65 P3
Silver Birch Av CHING E4 .......... 100 K1
Silver Birch Cl ADL/WDHM KT15 .......... 215 H6
  CAT SE6 .......... 182 E6
  FBAR/BDGN N11 .......... 98 B7
  HGDN/ICK UB10 .......... 111 P9
  THMD SE28 .......... 143 K10
Silver Birches RBRW/HUT CM13 .......... 107 M2
Silver Birch Ms BARK/HLT IG6 * .......... 72 P8
Silvercliffe Gdns EBAR EN4 .......... 77 P8
  KWD/TDW/WH KT20 .......... 239 H10
  NWCR SE14 * .......... 160 D6
Silver Ct WGCE AL7 * .......... 23 K4
Silver Crs CHSWK W4 .......... 155 N3
Silverdale ENC/FH EN2 .......... 78 F8
  HART DA3 .......... 211 L4
  SYD SE26 .......... 182 B7
Silverdale Cl BRKHM/BTCW RH3 .......... 273 N4
  HNWL W7 .......... 134 D10
  NTHLT UB5 .......... 113 K3
  SUT SM1 .......... 221 J1
Silverdale Dr ELTH/MOT SE9 .......... 184 B5
  HCH RM12 .......... 125 J10
  SUN TW16 .......... 197 J2
Silverdale Gdns HYS/HAR UB3 .......... 133 J1
Silverdale Rd BUSH WD23 .......... 73 M9
  BXLYHN DA7 .......... 164 C8
  CHING E4 .......... 101 J2
  HYS/HAR UB3 .......... 133 H1
  STMC/STPC BR5 .......... 206 F4
Silver Dell WATN WD24 .......... 72 C1
Silver Dene PUT/ROE SW15 * .......... 178 F4
Silverfield BROX EN10 .......... 44 E8
Silvergate HOR/WEW KT19 .......... 219 H8
Silverglade CHSGTN KT9 .......... 219 H8
Silverhall St ISLW TW7 .......... 154 F9
Silver Hl BORE WD6 .......... 75 P2
Silverholme Cl KTN/HRWW/WS HA3 .......... 115 K5
Silverlands Cl CHERT KT16 .......... 194 C10
Silver La PUR/KEN CR8 .......... 222 F8
  WWKM BR4 .......... 205 J9
Silverlea Gdns HORL RH6 .......... 280 D5
Silverleigh Rd THHTH CR7 .......... 202 F2
Silverlocke Rd GRAYS RM17 .......... 168 A5
Silvermere Av CRW RM5 .......... 106 C3
Silvermere Dr UED N18 * .......... 100 G6
Silvermere Rd CAT SE6 .......... 182 F2
Silvermere Rw SNWD SE25 * .......... 203 P2
Silver Pl SOHO/CST W1F .......... 11 H5
  LEW SE13 .......... 160 G9
  NKENS W10 .......... 136 G9
Silversmiths Wy WOKN/KNAP GU21 .......... 231 H1
Silver Spring Cl ERITH DA8 .......... 164 G5
Silverstead La BH/WHM TN16 .......... 244 C5
Silversted La BH/WHM TN16 .......... 244 C7
Silverstone Cl REDH RH1 .......... 258 A4
Silverston Wy STAN HA7 .......... 95 K5
Silver St ABR/ST RM4 .......... 83 L1
  CHESW EN7 .......... 61 L6
  EN EN1 .......... 79 L7
  UED N18 .......... 99 L5
  WAB EN9 .......... 59 N8
Silverthorn Dr HHS/BOV HP3 .......... 36 C10
Silverthorne Rd VX/NE SW8 .......... 158 G8
Silverthorn Gdns CHING E4 .......... 100 K1
Silverton Rd HMSMTH W6 .......... 156 G6
Silvertown Wy CAN/RD E16 .......... 141 L9
Silver Tree Cl WOT/HER KT12 .......... 217 H1
Silvertree La GFD/PVL UB6 .......... 134 C5
Silver Trees LCOL/BKTW AL2 .......... 55 N6
Silver Wk BERM/RHTH SE16 .......... 140 K10
Silver Wy WOKN/KNAP GU21 .......... 132 C4
Silverwood Cl BECK BR3 .......... 182 G10
  CROY/NA CRO .......... 213 H1
  NTHWD HA6 .......... 44 B5
  COV/CHF RM16 .......... 147 M9
Silverwood Cl CRAWW RH10 * .......... 285 H1
Silvester Rd EDUL SE22 .......... 181 N10
Silvesters HLWW/ROY CM19 .......... 46 C3
Silvester St STHWK SE1 .......... 18 G2
Silwood Cl ASC SL5 .......... 192 C2
Silwood Estate Regeneration
  Area BERM/RHTH SE16 .......... 160 A1
Silwood Pk ASC SL5 * .......... 192 C2
Silwood St BERM/RHTH SE16 .......... 160 A1
Simmil Rd ESH/CLAY KT10 .......... 218 D3
Simmonds Dr HART DA3 .......... 211 M5

Simmonds Ri HHS/BOV HP3 .......... 35 N8
Simmons Cl BCTR RM8 .......... 123 P8
  TRDG/WHET N20 .......... 97 H2
Simmons Dr BCTR RM8 .......... 123 P8
Simmons Ga ESH/CLAY KT10 .......... 218 B3
Simmons La CHING E4 .......... 100 D7
Simmons Pl CDW/CHF RM16 .......... 147 M10
  STA TW18 .......... 173 H8
Simmons Rd WOOL/PLUM SE18 .......... 162 A4
Simms Cl CAR SM5 .......... 201 P9
Simms Gdns EFNCH N2 .......... 97 M10
Simms Rd STHWK SE1 .......... 19 P6
Simnel Rd LEE/GVPK SE12 .......... 183 N5
Simon Cl NTGHL W11 .......... 8 D7
Simon Dean HHS/BOV HP3 .......... 52 D3
Simonds Rd LEY E10 .......... 120 F7
Simone Cl BMLY BR1 .......... 206 A1
Simone Dr PUR/KEN CR8 .......... 241 K2
Simons Cl CHERT KT16 .......... 214 F5
Simons Wk EGH TW20 .......... 171 P10
  SRTFD E15 .......... 121 J10
Simplemarsh Rd ADL/WDHM KT15 .......... 215 K1
Simplicity La RHWL CM17 .......... 29 N10
Simpson Cl CROY/NA CRO .......... 203 K6
Simpson Dr ACT W3 .......... 136 A9
Simpson Rd HSLWW TW4 .......... 175 N2
  RAIN RM13 .......... 144 A3
  RCHPK/HAM TW10 .......... 177 H7
Simpson's Rd HAYES BR2 .......... 205 M3
  POP/IOD E14 .......... 140 C9
Simpson St BTSEA SW11 .......... 157 P8
Simpsons Wy SL SL1 .......... 129 K10
Simrose Ct WAND/EARL SW18 .......... 179 K1
Sims Cl ROM RM1 .......... 124 C2
Sinclair Cl CRAWE RH10 .......... 284 D9
Sinclair Ct BELMT SM2 .......... 221 L5
Sinclair Gdns WKENS W14 .......... 156 G6
Sinclair Gv GLDGN NW11 .......... 116 C4
Sinclair Rd CHING E4 .......... 100 E6
  WDSR SL4 .......... 149 H9
  WKENS W14 .......... 156 A3
Sinclair Wy RDART DA2 .......... 188 C7
Sinclare Cl EN EN1 .......... 79 N5
Sincots Rd REDH RH1 .......... 258 A10
Sinderby Cl BORE WD6 .......... 75 L5
Singapore Rd WEA W13 .......... 134 F10
Singer St FSBYE EC1V .......... 7 H10
Singles Cross RSEV TN14 .......... 245 N1
Single's Cross La RSEV TN14 .......... 245 M1
Single St BH/WHM TN16 .......... 244 B5
Singleton Cl CROY/NA CRO .......... 203 K7
  HCH RM12 .......... 124 B2
  TOOT SW17 .......... 180 A10
Singleton Rd DAGW RM9 .......... 124 A3
Singleton Scarp NFNCH/WDSPK N12 .......... 97 K3
Singlewell Rd GVW DA11 .......... 190 E7
Singret Pl UX/CGN UB8 .......... 131 M6
Sinnott Rd WALTH E17 .......... 100 D10
Sion Rd TWK TW1 .......... 176 L4
Sipson Cl WDR/YW UB7 .......... 152 C5
Sipson La WDR/YW UB7 .......... 152 C5
Sipson Rd WDR/YW UB7 .......... 152 B6
Sipson Wy WDR/YW UB7 .......... 152 B6
Sir Abraham Dawes Cots PUT/ROE SW15 * .......... 157 H10
Sir Alexander Cl ACT W3 .......... 136 F10
Sir Cyril Black Wy WIM/MER SW19 .......... 179 J10
Sir Francis Wy BRW CM14 .......... 106 C3
Sir Henry Peakes Dr SLN SL2 .......... 128 F1
Sir John Kirk Cl CMBW SE5 .......... 159 K6
Sir John Newsom Wy WGCE AL7 .......... 23 K4
Sir Robert Ms DTCH/LGLY SL3 .......... 150 D4
Sir Thomas More Est CHEL SW3 .......... 15 M10
Sise La MANHO EC4N * .......... 12 G4
Siskin Cl BORE WD6 .......... 75 M8
  BUSH WD23 .......... 73 M8
Sisley Rd BARK IG11 .......... 143 H3
Sispara Gdns WAND/EARL SW18 .......... 179 J2
Sissinghurst Cl BMLY BR1 .......... 183 M4
  CRAWE RH10 .......... 284 E9
Sissinghurst Rd CROY/NA CRO .......... 203 P7
Sister Mabels Wy PECK SE15 * .......... 159 P6
Sisters Av BTSEA SW11 .......... 158 B9
Sistova Rd BAL SW12 .......... 180 C1
Sisulu Pl BRXN/ST SW9 .......... 159 H9
Sitwell Gv STAN HA7 .......... 94 K4
Siverst Cl NTHLT UB5 .......... 134 A1
Siviter Wy DAGE RM10 .......... 144 C2
Siward Rd HAYES BR2 .......... 205 N3
  TOOT SW17 .......... 179 M6
  TOTM N17 .......... 99 J8
Six Acres HHS/BOV HP3 .......... 36 B9
Six Bells La SEV TN13 .......... 265 K2
Sixteenth Av KWD/TDW/WH KT20 * .......... 257 J2
Sixth Av KTN/HRWW/WS HA3 * .......... 73 L1
  HYS/HAR UB3 .......... 133 G10
  KWD/TDW/WH KT20 * .......... 257 J2
  MNPK E12 .......... 122 C9
  NKENS W10 .......... 136 A9
Sixth Cross Rd WHTN TW2 .......... 176 B6
Skardu Rd CRICK NW2 .......... 116 H10
Skarnings Ct WAB EN9 .......... 59 M5
Skeena Hl WAND/EARL SW18 .......... 179 H3
Skeet Hill La STMC/STPC BR5 .......... 208 E6
Skeffington Rd EHAM E6 .......... 142 C1
Skeffington St WOOL/PLUM SE18 .......... 162 F2
Skelbrook St WAND/EARL SW18 .......... 179 L4
Skelgill Rd PUT/ROE SW15 .......... 157 J10
Skelley Rd SRTFD E15 .......... 141 L7
Skelton Cl HACK E8 .......... 7 M1
Skelton Rd FSTGT E7 .......... 141 M1
Skelton's La LEY E10 .......... 120 F5
Skelwith Rd HMSMTH W6 .......... 157 H6
Skenfrith Ho PECK SE15 * .......... 159 L5
Skerne Rd KUTN/CMB KT2 .......... 199 J1
Skerne Wk KUTN/CMB KT2 .......... 199 J1
Sketchley Gdns BERM/RHTH SE16 .......... 160 A5
Sketty Rd EN EN1 .......... 79 N7
Skid Hill La WARL CR6 .......... 243 L1
Skiers St SRTFD E15 .......... 141 K3
Skiffington Cl BRXS/STRHM SW2 .......... 181 H4
Skinner Pl BGVA SW1W * .......... 16 C6
Skinners La ASHTD KT21 .......... 237 J4
  BLKFR EC4V * .......... 12 F7
  HEST TW5 .......... 154 A7
Skinner St CLKNW EC1R .......... 12 L2
Skip La DEN/HRF UB9 .......... 111 H6
Skippers Cl SWCM DA10 .......... 188 B4
Skipsey Av EHAM E6 .......... 142 H3
Skipsea Cl FBAR/BDGN N11 .......... 98 B7
Skipton Cl FBAR/BDGN N11 .......... 98 B7
Skipton Dr HYS/HAR UB3 .......... 133 G4
Skipworth Rd HOM E9 .......... 120 E10
Skylark Rd DEN/HRF UB9 .......... 110 F6
Skylines POP/IOD E14 .......... 140 E10
Skylines Village POP/IOD E14 * .......... 161 N1
Sky Peals Rd WFD IG8 .......... 101 J4
Skyport Dr WDR/YW UB7 .......... 151 N6
Skys Wood Rd STALE/WH AL4 .......... 38 G2

Slacksbury Hatch HLWW/ROY CM19 .......... 46 E1
Sladbrook Rd BKHTH/KID SE3 .......... 162 A9
Slade Cl CHERT KT16 .......... 214 C3
Slade End EPP CM16 .......... 66 H3
Sladedale Rd WOOL/PLUM SE18 .......... 163 H4
Slade Gdns ERITH DA8 .......... 164 G2
Slade Green Rd ERITH DA8 .......... 164 G7
Slade Oak La DEN/HRF UB9 .......... 110 A9
Slade Rd CHERT KT16 .......... 214 C3
Slades Cl ENC/FH EN2 .......... 79 H5
Slades Dr CHST BR7 .......... 184 H7
Slades Gdns ENC/FH EN2 .......... 79 H6
Slades Hl ENC/FH EN2 .......... 79 H6
Slades Ri ENC/FH EN2 .......... 79 H7
The Slade WOOL/PLUM SE18 .......... 163 L10
Slade Wk WALW SE17 .......... 159 L10
Slagrove Pl LEW SE13 .......... 181 H2
Slaidburn St WBPTN SW10 .......... 15 K10
Slaithwaite Rd LEW SE13 .......... 161 H10
Slaney Pl HOLWY N7 .......... 119 H10
Slaney Rd ROM RM1 .......... 124 C3
Slattery Rd FELT TW13 .......... 175 K4
Slaugham Crr CRAWW RH11 .......... 283 J10
Sleaford Gn OXHEY WD19 .......... 93 L4
Sleaford St VX/NE SW8 .......... 158 D6
Sleapcross Gdns STALE/WH AL4 .......... 39 P7
Sleaps Hyde STALE/WH AL4 .......... 39 P7
Sledmere Ct EBED/NFELT TW14 * .......... 174 A7
Sleepers Farm Rd CDW/CHF RM16 .......... 168 E1
Sleets End HHW HP1 .......... 35 L4
Slewins Cl EMPK RM11 .......... 125 K3
Slewins La EMPK RM11 .......... 125 K3
Slievemore Cl CLAP SW4 .......... 158 E9
Slimmons Dr STALE/WH AL4 .......... 38 F2
Slines New Rd CTHM CR3 .......... 242 C6
Slines Oak Rd CTHM CR3 .......... 242 F9
Slingsby Pl LSO/SEVD WC2H .......... 11 L7
Slinfold Pl BKHH IG9 * .......... 101 J4
Slip La BROX EN10 .......... 44 L10
Slippers Hl HHNE HP2 .......... 35 N5
Slippers Pl BERM/RHTH SE16 .......... 140 H2
Slipshatch Rd REIG RH2 .......... 275 J4
Slipshoe St REIG RH2 * .......... 275 J10
The Slip BH/WHM TN16 .......... 262 F6
Sloane Av CHEL SW3 .......... 15 L5
Sloane Court East CHEL SW3 .......... 16 C7
Sloane Ct West CHEL SW3 .......... 16 C7
Sloane Gdns BGVA SW1W .......... 16 B6
  ORP BR6 .......... 206 F10
Sloane Sq BGVA SW1W .......... 16 B5
Sloane St KTBR SW1X .......... 16 B3
Sloane Ter KTBR SW1X .......... 16 B5
Sloansway WCCE AL7 .......... 23 J1
Slocock Hl WOKN/KNAP GU21 .......... 231 P3
Slocum Cl THMD SE28 .......... 143 K9
Slough La BRKHM/BTCW RH3 .......... 256 D9
  CDALE/KGS NW9 .......... 115 P4
  EPSOM KT18 .......... 255 P1
Slough Rd DTCH/LGLY SL3 .......... 149 M4
  IVER SL0 .......... 130 F5
Slowmans Cl LCOL/BKTW AL2 .......... 56 A5
Slyfield Gn GU GU1 .......... 250 A6
Sly St WCHPL E1 * .......... 140 A8
Smaldon Cl WDR/YW UB7 .......... 152 B2
Small Acre HHW HP1 .......... 35 J4
Smallberry Av ISLW TW7 .......... 154 P7
Smallbrook Ms BAY/PAD W2 * .......... 3 L6
Smallcroft WGCE AL7 .......... 23 K4
Smalley Cl STNW/STAM N16 .......... 119 N9
Smallfield Rd HORL RH6 .......... 280 C4
Smallford La STALE/WH AL4 .......... 39 N7
Small Grains HART DA3 .......... 210 G10
Smallmead HORL RH6 .......... 280 C4
Smalls Hill Rd REIG RH2 .......... 274 F10
Smalls Md CRAWW RH11 .......... 285 M7
Smallwood Cl STALE/WH AL4 .......... 39 N7
Smallwood Rd TOOT SW17 .......... 179 N7
Smarden Cl BELV DA17 .......... 163 H2
Smarden Gv ELTH/MOT SE9 .......... 183 M5
Smart Cl HARH RM3 .......... 105 J9
Smart's Heath La WOKS/MYFD GU22 .......... 231 M9
Smart's Heath Rd WOKS/MYFD GU22 .......... 231 M9
Smart's La LOU IG10 .......... 79 L1
Smart's Pl NOXST/BSQ WC1A .......... 11 M5
  UED N18 .......... 99 P6
Smart St BETH E2 * .......... 140 F2
Smeaton Cl WAB EN9 .......... 63 K9
Smeaton Rd PEND EN3 .......... 78 G6
  WAND/EARL SW18 .......... 179 K5
  WFD IG8 .......... 102 G6
Smeaton St WAP E1W .......... 140 A10
Smedley St VX/NE SW8 .......... 158 E8
Smeed Rd BOW E3 .......... 140 F2
Smiles Pl LEW SE13 .......... 161 M8
Smitham Bottom La PUR/KEN CR8 .......... 222 E8
Smitham Downs Rd PUR/KEN CR8 .......... 222 F9
Smithbarn Cl HORL RH6 .......... 280 C4
Smith Cl BERM/RHTH SE16 .......... 140 C10
The Smithers BRKHM/BTCW RH3 .......... 273 N2
Smithfield HHNE HP2 .......... 35 N4
Smithfields HHNE HP2 .......... 35 N4
Smithfield St STBT EC1A .......... 12 D3
Smithies Rd ABYW SE2 .......... 163 L3
Smith's Ct SOHO/SHAV W1D * .......... 11 J7
Smiths La CHESW EN7 .......... 61 L1
  WDSR SL4 .......... 148 D8
Smithson Rd TOTM N17 .......... 99 M8
Smith Sq WEST SW1P .......... 17 J4
Smith St BRYLDS KT5 .......... 199 L6
  CHEL SW3 .......... 15 N8
  WATW WD18 .......... 73 N5
Smith's Yd CROY/NA CRO .......... 2 B6
Smith Ter CHEL SW3 .......... 15 N9
Smithwood Cl WIM/MER SW19 .......... 178 E3
Smithy Cl KWD/TDW/WH KT20 .......... 257 J9
Smithy La KWD/TDW/WH KT20 .......... 257 J10
Smithy's Gn BFOR GU20 .......... 212 C3
Smoke La REIG RH2 .......... 275 L5
Smythe Cl ED N9 .......... 100 E2
Smugglers Wy WAND/EARL SW18 .......... 157 L10
Smugglers Whf RDART DA2 .......... 188 G3
Smug Oak La LCOL/BKTW AL2 .......... 56 L8
Smyrks Rd WALW SE17 .......... 159 N4
Smyrna Rd KIL/WHAMP NW6 .......... 2 A1
Smythe St POP/IOD E14 .......... 140 P1
Snag La ORP BR6 .......... 227 L2
Snakes Hl BRW CM14 .......... 86 B7
Snakes La EBAR EN4 .......... 77 N3
Snakes La East WFD IG8 .......... 101 N10
Snakes La West WFD IG8 .......... 101 J4
Snakey La FELT TW13 .......... 175 J5
Snape Spr SLN SL2 .......... 131 J5
Snaresbrook Dr STAN HA7 .......... 95 N4
Snaresbrook Rd WAN E11 .......... 121 N3
Snarsgate St NKENS W10 .......... 136 B5
Snatts Hl OXTED RH8 .......... 261 L5

Sneath Av GLDGN NW11 .......... 117 J5
Snell Hatch CRAWW RH11 .......... 283 L7
Snellings Av CVW DA11 .......... 190 D5
Snellings Rd WOT/HER KT12 .......... 217 K2
Snells La AMSS HP7 .......... 69 N6
Snells Wood Ct AMSS HP7 .......... 69 N6
Sneyd Rd CRICK NW2 .......... 116 F10
Snipe Cl ERITH DA8 .......... 165 J6
Snowberry Cl SRTFD E15 .......... 121 J1
Snowbury Rd FUL/PGN SW6 .......... 157 N8
Snowcrete Rd DTCH/LGLY SL3 .......... 129 P4
Snowden Av HGDN/ICK UB10 .......... 132 C4
Snowden Cl WDSR SL4 .......... 148 C10
Snowden Crs HYS/HAR UB3 .......... 133 G4
Snowden St SDTCH EC2A .......... 7 K8
Snowdon Rd HTHAIR TW6 .......... 174 D2
Snowdown Cl PGE/AN SE20 * .......... 201 K1
Snowdrop Cl HPTN TW12 .......... 175 P9
Snowdrop Wy CHOB/PIR GU24 .......... 230 F3
Snowerhill Rd BRKHM/BTCW RH3 .......... 274 C4
Snow Hl CRAWE RH10 .......... 285 N2
  CRAWE RH10 .......... 285 N10
Snowhill La CRAWE RH10 .......... 281 N10
Snowsfields STHWK SE1 .......... 19 H1
Snowshill Rd MNPK E12 .......... 122 B10
Snows Paddock BFOR GU20 .......... 192 A4
Snows Ride BFOR GU20 .......... 212 A1
Snowy Fielder Wave ISLW TW7 .......... 154 G8
Soames St PECK SE15 .......... 159 N9
Soames Wk NWMAL KT3 .......... 200 B1
Soane Cl CRAWW RH11 .......... 283 H9
  EA W5 .......... 135 L6
Soaphouse La BTFD TW8 .......... 155 K6
Soham Rd PEND EN3 .......... 79 K10
Soho Sq SOHO/CST W1F .......... 11 J5
Soho St SOHO/SHAV W1D .......... 11 J5
Sojourner-Truth Cl HACK E8 .......... 140 F1
Solander Gdns WCHPL E1 .......... 140 A9
Solar Ct WATW WD18 .......... 72 C10
Solar Wy PEND EN3 .......... 80 E1
Solecote GT/LBKH KT23 .......... 253 P7
Sole Farm Av GT/LBKH KT23 .......... 253 P7
Sole Farm Cl GT/LBKH KT23 .......... 235 N10
Sole Farm Rd GT/LBKH KT23 .......... 253 P7
Solefields Rd SEV TN13 .......... 265 J5
Solent Ri PLSTW E13 .......... 141 K10
Solent Rd KIL/WHAMP NW6 .......... 2 A1
  HTHAIR TW6 .......... 174 A5
Solesbridge Cl RKW/CH/CXG WD3 .......... 71 J7
Solesbridge La RKW/CH/CXG WD3 .......... 71 J7
Solna Av PUT/ROE SW15 .......... 178 F5
Solna Rd WCHMH N21 .......... 99 P5
Solomon Av UED N18 .......... 99 P5
Solomon's Hl RKW/CH/CXG WD3 * .......... 71 J7
Solomon's Pas PECK SE15 .......... 160 A4
Soloms Court Rd BNSTD SM7 .......... 239 P8
Solon New Rd CLAP SW4 .......... 158 F10
Solon Rd BRXS/STRHM SW2 .......... 158 F10
Solway HHNE HP2 .......... 35 M2
Solway Cl HACK E8 * .......... 140 E1
  HSLWW TW4 .......... 153 N10
Solway Rd EDUL SE22 .......... 159 P10
  WDGN N22 .......... 98 G8
Somaford Gv EBAR EN4 .......... 77 N10
Somali Rd CRICK NW2 .......... 117 J9
Somerby Cl BROX EN10 .......... 44 F7
Somerby Rd BARK IG11 .......... 142 G2
Somercoats Cl EBAR EN4 .......... 77 P7
Somerden Rd STMC/STPC BR5 .......... 207 N1
Somerfield Cl KWD/TDW/WH KT20 .......... 239 H5
Somerfield Rd FSBYPK N4 .......... 119 H2
Somerford Cl PIN HA5 .......... 113 H2
Somerford Gv STNW/STAM N16 .......... 119 P9
  TOTM N17 .......... 99 P6
Somerford St BERM/RHTH SE16 .......... 160 C4
Somerford Wy BERM/RHTH SE16 .......... 160 C10
Somerhill Av WELL DA16 .......... 164 H2
Somerhill Rd WELL DA16 .......... 164 H2
Someries Rd HHW HP1 .......... 35 J2
Somerleyton Rd BRXN/ST SW9 .......... 159 H10
Somersby Gdns REDBR IG4 .......... 122 C3
Somers Cl CAMTN NW1 .......... 4 H2
Somers Crs BAY/PAD W2 .......... 3 N6
Somerset Av CHSGTN KT9 .......... 219 J6
  RYNPK SW20 .......... 200 B2
  WELL DA16 .......... 164 B5
Somerset Cl NWMAL KT3 .......... 200 B3
  HOR/WEW KT19 .......... 220 B6
  NFNCH/WDSPK N12 .......... 97 K3
  WFD IG8 .......... 102 C6
  WOT/HER KT12 .......... 217 J2
Somerset Gdns EMPK RM11 .......... 125 P6
  HGT N6 .......... 118 A5
  LEW SE13 .......... 161 J9
  STRHM/NOR SW16 .......... 202 A8
  TEDD TW11 .......... 175 M7
  TOTM N17 * .......... 99 M8
Somerset Rd BAR EN5 .......... 77 H6
  BTFD TW8 .......... 155 K6
  CHSWK W4 .......... 156 A2
  HDN NW4 .......... 116 A1
  HRW HA1 .......... 114 A4
  KUT/HW KT1 .......... 9 F7
  ORP BR6 .......... 207 K1
  REDH RH1 .......... 275 M2
  SLH/COR SS17 .......... 169 K1
  STHL UB1 .......... 133 P7
  TEDD TW11 .......... 175 M7
  TOTM N17 .......... 99 M8
  WALTH E17 .......... 120 D5
  WEA W13 .......... 135 J5
  WIM/MER SW19 .......... 178 A6
Somerset Waye HEST TW5 .......... 153 P5
Somersham Rd BXLYHN DA7 .......... 164 G2
Somers Pl BRXS/STRHM SW2 .......... 181 N7
  REIG RH2 .......... 275 P10
Somers Rd BRXS/STRHM SW2 .......... 181 P7
  PGE/AN SE20 * .......... 201 K10
  REIG RH2 .......... 275 N10
  WALTH E17 .......... 120 B10
  WIM/MER SW19 .......... 178 A7
Somerswey RGUE GU4 .......... 268 F8
Somerton Av RCH/KEW TW9 .......... 156 C8
Somerton Cl PUR/KEN CR8 .......... 241 K2
Somerton Rd CRICK NW2 .......... 116 C10
  PECK SE15 .......... 160 A4
Somertons Cl GUW GU2 .......... 249 N4
Somertrees Av LEE/GVPK SE12 .......... 183 L5
Somervell Rd RYLN/HDSTN HA2 .......... 113 J5
Somerville Av BARN SW13 .......... 156 G9
Somerville Dr CRAWE RH10 .......... 285 M3
Somerville Gdns CHDH RM6 .......... 284 M3

Sondes Place Cots DORK RH4 * .......... 272 E2
Sondes Place Dr DORK RH4 .......... 272 E2
Songhurst Cl CROY/NA CRO .......... 202 G8
Sonia Cl OXHEY WD19 .......... 93 K1
Sonia Gdns HEST TW5 .......... 153 P6
  NFNCH/WDSPK N12 .......... 97 M5
  WLSDN NW10 .......... 116 C9
The Sonnets HHW HP1 .......... 35 L5
Sonning Gdns HPTN TW12 .......... 175 M9
Sonning Rd SNWD SE25 .......... 203 P5
Soothouse Spring STALW/RED AL3 .......... 38 C2
Soper Cl CHING E4 .......... 100 E6
  FSTH SE23 .......... 182 C4
Soper Ms PEND EN3 .......... 80 F4
Soper Sq HLWE CM17 * .......... 29 N10
Sopers Rd POTB/CUF EN6 .......... 60 G5
Sophia Cl HOLWY N7 .......... 5 N1
Sophia Rd CAN/RD E16 .......... 141 N7
  LEY E10 .......... 120 G6
Sophia Sq BERM/RHTH SE16 * .......... 141 L10
Sopwell La STAL AL1 .......... 38 C7
Sopwith Av CHSGTN KT9 .......... 219 K2
Sopwith Cl BH/WHM TN16 .......... 244 A2
  KUTN/CMB KT2 .......... 177 L8
Sopwith Rd HEST TW5 .......... 153 N5
Sopwith Wy KUTN/CMB KT2 .......... 199 K1
  VX/NE SW8 .......... 158 C6
Sorbie Cl WEY KT13 .......... 216 D3
Sorrel Bank CROY/NA CRO .......... 224 D6
Sorrel Cl THMD SE28 .......... 146 H7
Sorrel Gdns EHAM E6 .......... 142 B7
Sorrel La POP/IOD E14 .......... 141 H8
Sorrell Cl BRXN/ST SW9 .......... 159 H8
  NWCR SE14 .......... 160 D6
Sorrel Wy GVW DA11 .......... 190 B7
Sorrento Rd SUT SM1 .......... 201 L10
Sospel Ct SLN SL2 * .......... 131 J1
Sotheby Rd HBRY N5 .......... 119 K9
Sotheran Cl HACK E8 .......... 7 P5
Sotheron Rd WATF WD17 .......... 73 J8
Soudan Rd BTSEA SW11 .......... 158 A7
Souldern Rd WKENS W14 .......... 156 G6
Souldern St WATW WD18 .......... 73 J9
Sounds Ldg SWLY BR8 .......... 208 D6
South Access Rd LEY E10 .......... 120 C5
South Africa Rd SHB W12 .......... 136 E9
South Albert Rd REIG RH2 .......... 257 J9
Southall Ct STHL UB1 .......... 133 L7
Southall La HEST TW5 .......... 153 J5
Southall Wy BRW CM14 .......... 106 E5
Southam Ms RKW/CH/CXG WD3 .......... 72 C10
Southampton Blds LINN WC2A * .......... 12 A4
Southampton Gdns MTCM CR4 .......... 202 F5
Southampton Ms CAN/RD E16 .......... 141 N10
Southampton Pl NOXST/BSQ WC1A .......... 11 L3
Southampton Rd HAMP NW3 .......... 118 A10
  HTHAIR TW6 .......... 174 A2
Southampton Rd East HTHAIR TW6 .......... 174 A2
Southampton Rd West HTHAIR TW6 .......... 174 A2
Southampton Rw RSQ WC1B .......... 11 L3
Southampton St COVGDN WC2E .......... 11 L7
Southampton Wy CMBW SE5 .......... 159 L4
South Audley St MYFR/PKLN W1K .......... 10 D8
South Av CAR SM5 .......... 221 K8
  CHING E4 .......... 100 G1
  EGH TW20 * .......... 172 C1
  RCH/KEW TW9 .......... 155 P6
  STHL UB1 .......... 133 N9
South Avenue Gdns STHL UB1 .......... 133 N9
South Bank BH/WHM TN16 .......... 245 M8
  SURB KT6 .......... 199 K6
Southbank THDIT KT7 .......... 198 C7
South Bank Rd BERK HP4 .......... 33 L3
South Bank Ter SURB KT6 .......... 199 K6
South Birkbeck Rd WAN E11 .......... 121 L8
South Black Lion La HMSMTH W6 .......... 156 D4
South Bolton Gdns WBPTN SW10 * .......... 15 H7
Southborough La HAYES BR2 .......... 206 B2
Southborough Rd BMLY BR1 .......... 206 B3
  HOM E9 .......... 140 E1
  SURB KT6 .......... 199 K8
Southborough Road (The
  Lane) SURB KT6 * .......... 199 K8
Southbourne HAYES BR2 .......... 205 P8
Southbourne Av CDALE/KGS NW9 .......... 95 P10
Southbourne Cl PIN HA5 .......... 113 M5
Southbourne Crs HDN NW4 .......... 116 C1
Southbourne Gdns IL IG1 .......... 122 F10
  LEE/GVPK SE12 .......... 183 M5
  RSLP HA4 .......... 113 H4
Southbridge Pl CROY/NA CRO .......... 223 K1
Southbridge Rd CROY/NA CRO .......... 223 K1
Southbrook SBW CM21 .......... 25 P2
Southbrook Dr CHES/WCR EN8 .......... 62 C4
Southbrook Rd LEE/GVPK SE12 .......... 183 K4
  STRHM/NOR SW16 .......... 202 A10
South Bucks Wy AMSS HP7 .......... 68 B4
Southbury Av EN EN1 .......... 79 P8
Southbury Rd HCH RM12 .......... 125 L10
  EN EN1 .......... 79 N8
South Carriage Dr SKENS SW7 .......... 15 M1
South Chariton Mead La HOD EN11 .......... 45 H4
Southchurch Rd EHAM E6 .......... 142 C4
Southcliffe Dr CFSP/GDCR SL9 .......... 90 B6
South Cl BAR EN5 .......... 76 B3
  BXLYHS DA6 .......... 163 N10
  CRAWE RH10 .......... 284 A6
  DAGE RM10 .......... 144 B3
  HGT N6 .......... 118 C4
  LCOL/BKTW AL2 .......... 56 A1
  PIN HA5 .......... 113 N5
  SL SL1 * .......... 129 L2
  WDR/YW UB7 .......... 152 C5
  WHTN TW2 .......... 175 P6
  MRDN SM4 .......... 201 L6
South Close Gn REDH RH1 .......... 258 C5
The South Colonnade POP/IOD E14 .......... 140 F10
Southcombe St WKENS W14 .......... 14 A2
Southcote WOKN/KNAP GU21 .......... 232 A2
Southcote Av BRYLDS KT5 .......... 199 N6
  FELT TW13 .......... 174 A5
Southcote Rd RSLP HA4 .......... 113 H4
  REDH RH1 .......... 258 D6
  SAND/SEL CR2 .......... 223 P6
  SNWD SE25 .......... 204 A5
  WALTH E17 .......... 120 F2
South Cottage Dr RKW/CH/CXG WD3 .......... 71 J9

South Cottage Gdns RKW/CH/CXG WD3 .......... 71 J9
South Countess Rd WALTH E17 * .......... 120 E1
South Crs CAN/RD E16 .......... 141 J6
  GWRST WC1E * .......... 11 J2
Southcroft EGH TW20 .......... 171 N8
Southcroft Av WELL DA16 .......... 163 N3
  WWKM BR4 .......... 205 H9
Southcroft Rd ORP BR6 .......... 207 N10
  TOOT SW17 .......... 180 B9
South Cross Rd BARK/HLT IG6 .......... 122 G2
South Croxted Rd DUL SE21 .......... 181 L6
Southdale CHIG IG7 .......... 102 G2
Southdean Gdns WIM/MER SW19 .......... 179 J5
South Dene MLHL NW7 .......... 96 A4
Southdene RSEV TN14 .......... 228 A9
Southdown Av HNWL W7 .......... 154 F2
Southdown Ct HAT AL10 .......... 40 D7
Southdown Crs GNTH/NBYPK IG2 .......... 123 H5
  RYLN/HDSTN HA2 .......... 114 B6
Southdown Dr RYNPK SW20 .......... 179 P10
Southdown Rd CAR SM5 .......... 242 E8
  CTHM CR3 .......... 242 E8
  EMPK RM11 .......... 125 J5
  HARP AL5 .......... 20 A2
  HAT AL10 .......... 40 D7
  RYNPK SW20 .......... 200 C1
  WOT/HER KT12 .......... 217 M1
Southdown Vls SEVS/STOTM N15 * .......... 119 J3
South Dr BELMT SM2 .......... 221 H6
  BNSTD SM7 .......... 221 P9
  BRW CM14 .......... 107 J3
  CHOB/PIR GU24 .......... 230 B7
  COUL/CHIP CR5 .......... 240 E1
  GPK RM2 .......... 125 K1
  ORP BR6 .......... 227 H2
  POTB/CUF EN6 .......... 60 F6
  RDKG RH5 .......... 273 H2
  RSLP HA4 .......... 112 F6
  VW GU25 .......... 193 M7
South Ealing Rd EA W5 .......... 155 J1
South Eastern Av ED N9 .......... 100 E4
South Eaton Pl BGVA SW1W .......... 16 D5
South Eden Park Rd BECK BR3 .......... 204 C5
South Edwardes Sq KENS W8 * .......... 14 D4
South End CROY/NA CRO .......... 223 K1
  GT/LBKH KT23 .......... 254 A2
  KENS W8 .......... 14 A1
Southend Arterial Rd EMPK RM11 .......... 125 M1
  GPK RM2 .......... 105 L10
  RBRW/HUT CM13 .......... 107 M2
  UPMR RM14 .......... 126 D3
Southend Cl ELTH/MOT SE9 .......... 184 E2
Southend Crs ELTH/MOT SE9 .......... 184 D2
Southend La SYD SE26 .......... 182 B2
  WAB EN9 .......... 63 N10
Southend Rd BECK BR3 .......... 204 F1
  CLAY IG5 .......... 122 E2
  EHAM E6 .......... 142 C2
  GRAYS RM17 .......... 167 P3
  WALTH E17 .......... 120 E1
Southend Road (North
  Circular) WALTH E17 .......... 101 J7
South End Rw KENS W8 .......... 14 A1
Southerland Cl WEY KT13 .......... 216 D1
Southern Av EBED/NFELT TW14 .......... 175 H4
  REDH RH1 .......... 276 B7
  SNWD SE25 .......... 203 N3
Southern Down FELT TW13 * .......... 175 K4
Southern Dr LOU IG10 .......... 82 C10
Southerngate Wy NWCR SE14 .......... 160 D6
Southern Gv BOW E3 .......... 140 G5
Southernhay LOU IG10 .......... 82 A9
Southern Perimeter Rd HTHAIR TW6 .......... 174 D1
Southern Rd EFNCH N2 .......... 117 J1
  PLSTW E13 .......... 141 L4
Southern Rw NKENS W10 .......... 136 A9
Southern St IS N1 .......... 5 N7
Southern Ter HOD EN11 * .......... 26 C10
Southern Wy CNWCH SE10 .......... 161 K3
  HLWE CM17 .......... 47 M3
  ROMW/RG RM7 .......... 124 A3
Southernwood Cl HHNE HP2 .......... 36 B5
Southerton Rd HMSMTH W6 .......... 156 F7
Southey Rd BRXN/ST SW9 .......... 158 F6
  SEVS/STOTM N15 .......... 119 M3
  WIM/MER SW19 .......... 178 A3
Southey St PGE/AN SE20 .......... 182 G10
Southey Wk TIL RM18 .......... 168 F7
Southfield BAR EN5 .......... 76 C2
  WGCE AL7 .......... 23 K4
Southfield Cl WATN WD24 .......... 73 K4
  UX/CGN UB8 .......... 132 B6
Southfield Gdns SL SL1 .......... 130 A1
  TWK TW1 .......... 176 A2
Southfield Pk RYLN/HDSTN HA2 .......... 114 B4
Southfield Pl WEY KT13 .......... 216 C4
Southfield Rd CHES/WCR EN8 .......... 62 D8
  CHST BR7 .......... 185 N7
  CHSWK W4 .......... 156 A1
  HOD EN11 .......... 44 F1
  PEND EN3 .......... 80 A3
Southfields E/WMO/HCT KT8 .......... 198 B3
  HDN NW4 .......... 116 A1
Southfields Av ASHF TW15 .......... 174 A2
Southfields Ct WAND/EARL SW18 .......... 179 J5
Southfields Ms WAND/EARL SW18 * .......... 179 J5
Southfields Pas WAND/EARL SW18 .......... 179 J5
Southfields Rd CTHM CR3 .......... 242 F10
  WAND/EARL SW18 .......... 179 J5
Southfleet Av HART DA3 .......... 211 N2
Southfleet Rd GVW DA11 .......... 190 C4
  ORP BR6 .......... 207 N10
  RDART DA2 .......... 189 M7
  SWCM DA10 .......... 189 M3
South Gdns WIM/MER SW19 .......... 179 N10
South Ga HLWC CM20 .......... 20 C6
Southgate Av CRAWE RH10 .......... 285 M10
  FELT TW13 .......... 174 A2
Southgate Gv IS N1 * .......... 7 H1
Southgate Pde CRAWE RH10 * .......... 285 M10
Southgate Rd IS N1 .......... 7 H1
  POTB/CUF EN6 .......... 59 M1
South Gipsy Rd WELL DA16 .......... 165 H10
South Gn SL SL1 * .......... 130 C10
South Gv HGT N6 .......... 118 A5
  SEVS/STOTM N15 * .......... 119 J10
  WALTH E17 * .......... 120 D2
South Hall Cl EYN DA4 .......... 209 N4
South Hall Dr RAIN RM13 .......... 145 J7
South Hl CHST BR7 .......... 184 G2
  GU GU1 .......... 268 A2
  NTHWD HA6 .......... 92 B7
South Hill Av RYLN/HDSTN HA2 .......... 114 B8
South Hill Gv HRW HA1 .......... 114 E9
South Hill Park Gdns HAMP NW3 * .......... 117 P9

**Column 1**

South Hill Rd GVE DA12 190 E4
HAYES BR2 205 K3
HHW HP1 35 M5
Southholme Cl NRWD SE19 203 M1
Southill La PIN HA5 113 H2
Southill Rd CHST BR7 184 B10
Southill St POP/IOD E14 140 G8
South Island Pl BRXN/ST SW9 158 C6
South Kensington Station Ar SKENS SW7 15 M5
South Kent Av GVW DA11 189 P2
South Lambeth Pl VX/NE SW8 17 M9
South Lambeth Rd VX/NE SW8 17 M9
Southland Rd WOOL/PLUM SE18 163 J6
ORP BR6 227 H1
Southlands Av HORL RH6 280 B3
ORP BR6 227 H1
Southlands Cl COUL/CHIP CR5 240 G4
Southlands Dr WIM/MER SW19 178 G5
Southlands La OXTED RH8 266 G11
Southlands Rd DEN/HRF UB9 111 J10
HAYES BR2 205 A4
IVER SL0 131 H1
Southland Ter PUR RM19 * 166 A4
South La KUT/HW KT1 199 J3
NWMAL KT3 200 A4
South La West NWMAL KT3 200 A4
Southlea Rd WDSR SL4 149 M9
South Ley WLCCE AL7 23 H8
South Lodge Av MTCM CR4 202 F4
South Lodge Crs ENC/FH EN2 7 J8
South Lodge Dr STHGT/OAK N14 78 E8
South Lodge Rd WOT/HER KT12 216 C6
South Mall ED N9 * 96 C5
HOR/WEW KT19 220 C4
REDH RH1 * 258 A7
Southmead Crs CHES/WCR EN8 62 D1
South Meadow La WDSR SL4 149 H6
Southmead Rd WIM/MER SW19 179 H4
South Molton La MYFR/PKLN W1K 10 C6
South Molton Rd CAN/RD E16 141 M8
South Molton St MYFR/PKLN W1K 10 E6
Southmont Rd ESH/CLAY KT10 198 D8
Southmoor Wy HOM E9 140 E1
South Mt TRDG/WHET N20 * 97 M3
South Norwood HI SNWD SE25 203 H4
South Oak Rd STRHM/NOR SW16 180 C7
Southold Ri ELTH/MOT SE9 184 C6
Southolm St BTSEA SW11 158 C7
South Ordnance Rd PEND EN3 80 F3
Southover BMLY BR1 184 B5
NFNCH/WDSPK N12 97 K5
South Pde CHEL SW3 15 M7
CHSWK W4 138 A4
EDGW HA8 95 M10
HORL RH6 * 280 A3
REDH RH1 * 258 D4
WLGTN SM6 * 222 D3
SEV TN13 265 J1
South Park Av RKW/CH/CXG WD3 71 J9
South Park Crs CAT SE6 183 K4
CFSP/GDCR SL9 110 C3
IL IG1 122 G8
South Park Dr CFSP/GDCR SL9 110 B2
CDMY/SEVK IG3 122 G1
South Park Gdns BERK HP4 33 N4
South Park Hill Rd SAND/SEL CR2 223 L2
South Park La REDH RH1 277 P8
South Park Ms FUL/PGN SW6 157 L9
South Park Rd IL IG1 122 G9
WIM/MER SW19 179 L9
South Park Ter IL IG1 122 G8
South Park Vw CFSP/GDCR SL9 110 C2
South Park Wy RSLP HA4 133 K3
South Pier Rd HORL RH6 280 D6
South Pl BRYLDS KT5 199 L7
EN EN1 29 K8
LVPST EC2M 13 H4
PEND EN3 80 B9
South Place Ms LVPST EC2M 13 H4
Southport Rd WOOL/PLUM SE18 162 G3
South Rdg WEY KT13 216 C6
Southridge Pl RYNPK SW20 178 G10
South Riding LCOL/BKTW AL2 75 N6
South Rw BLKHTH/KID SE3 * 9 P7
CAR SM5 221 P5
South Rd AMS HP6 69 H2
CHDH RM6 123 M3
CHOB/PIR GU24 230 E2
EA W5 135 J9
ED N9 99 P2
EDGW HA8 95 N9
EGH TW20 171 P9
ERITH DA8 164 G5
FELT TW13 175 L8
FSTH SE23 182 C5
HGDN/ICK UB10 132 A2
HLW CM20 29 K8
HPTN TW12 175 J9
REIG RH2 275 L1
RKW/CH/CXG WD3 70 F9
SOCK/AV RM15 147 N4
STHL UB1 133 N10
WDR/YW UB7 152 B2
WEY KT13 216 C8
WHTN TW2 176 C6
WIM/MER SW19 179 N9
WOKN/KNAP GU21 231 J5
South Rw BKHTH/KID SE3 161 K8
DTCH/LGLY SL3 * 110 B3
Southsea Av WATW WD18 73 H8
Southsea Rd KUT/HW KT1 199 K4
South Sea St BERM/RHTH SE16 160 E2
Southside CHERT KT16 195 K8
South Side CFSP/GDCR SL9 110 A1
HMSMTH W6 156 C1
SEVS/STOTM N15 * 119 N5
Southside Common WIM/MER SW19 178 G9
Southspring BFN/LL DA15 184 G5
South Sq GINN WC1R 12 A4
GLDGN NW11 117 J6
South Station Ap REDH RH1 276 G2
South St BMLY BR1 205 K8
BRW CM14 107 H4
DORK RH4 272 F2
EMPK RM11 125 H4
EPSOM KT18 220 A9
GVE DA12 190 E3
HERT/WAT SG14 25 L5
ISLW TW7 154 C8
MYFR/PKLN W1K 10 D7
PEND EN3 80 D5
RAIN RM13 144 D4
ROM RM1 124 A4
STA TW18 173 J8
WARE SG12 26 C1
South V HRW HA1 114 E5
South V HRW HA1 181 N1
Southvale Rd BKHTH/KID SE3 * 161 K8

**Column 2**

South Vale Rd SURB KT6 199 K9
Southview SWLY BR8 208 G4
South Vw BMLY BR1 205 P2
HOR/WEW KT19 219 M6
WDSR SL4 * 149 H4
Southview Av TIL RM18 168 D7
Southview Av WLSDN NW10 116 C10
South View Cl BXLY DA5 186 A2
CHESW EN7 61 M2
Southview Cl CRAWE RH10 285 M10
Southview Cl SWLY BR8 209 H4
TOOT SW17 161 M9
South View Crs NRWD SE19 * 181 K10
WOKS/MYFD UB22 232 B4
Southview Crs GNTH/NBYPK IG2 122 A5
Southview Dr SWFD E18 121 N1
South View Dr UPMR RM14 125 P8
Southview Gdns WLGTN SM6 222 D4
South View Hts WTHK RH20 * 167 H5
South View Rd CEND/HSY/T N8 118 C1
CFSP/GDCR SL9 110 A2
LOU IG10 82 C10
PIN HA5 93 J7
ASHTD KT21 237 L5
Southview Rd WARL CR6 241 P5
South View Rd WTHK RM20 167 H5
Southviews WLGTN SM6 * 202 E10
South Vis CAMTN NW1 5 K2
Southville VX/NE SW8 158 E7
Southville Cl EBED/NFELT TW14 174 F3
HOR/WEW KT19 220 A5
Southville Crs EBED/NFELT TW14 174 F4
Southville Rd EBED/NFELT TW14 174 F4
THDIT KT7 198 F7
South Wk REIG RH2 * 257 L10
WWKM BR4 205 K10
Southwark Bridge Rd STHWK SE1 18 D3
Southwark Park Est BERM/RHTH SE16 * 160 A3
Southwark Park Rd BERM/RHTH SE16 19 M5
Southwark Pl BMLY BR1 206 C3
Southwark St STHWK SE1 18 B1
Southwater Cl BECK BR3 182 C10
CRAWW RH11 285 K7
POP/IOD E14 140 E8
Southway CLDGN NW11 117 L4
GUW GU2 249 K10
PUR RM19 166 D2
RYNPK SW20 200 G4
TRDG/WHET N20 97 K3
WLGTN SM6 222 E4
South Wy ABLGY WD5 54 E9
CAR SM5 221 N6
CHING E4 80 C3
CROY/NA CR0 204 D10
ED N9 100 B3
FBAR/BDGN N11 98 D7
HAT AL10 40 D8
Southway HAYES BR2 205 M7
South Wy KGLGY WD4 113 P2
RYLN/HDSTN HA2 93 M7
WAB EN9 81 H2
WBLY HA9 115 M10
Southway Cl SHB W12 156 E1
Southway Pk GUW GU2 249 M8
Southways Pk CRAWW RH11 * 285 N2
South Weald Dr WAB EN9 63 J3
South Weald Rd BRW CM14 106 F4
Southwell Av NTHLT UB5 133 P4
Southwell Cl CDW/CHF RM16 167 H4
Southwell Gdns SKENS SW7 15 H3
Southwell Grove Rd WAN E11 121 K7
Southwell Pl CMBW SE5 159 K9
CROY/NA CR0 203 H6
KTN/HRWW/WS HA3 95 J2
South Western Rd TWK TW1 176 F2
South West India Dock Entrance POP/IOD E14 161 N1
Southwest Rd WAN E11 121 J6
South Wharf Rd BAY/PAD W2 9 J3
Southwick Ms BAY/PAD W2 * 9 M5
Southwick Pl BAY/PAD W2 9 N5
Southwick St BAY/PAD W2 9 N4
Southwick Yd BAY/PAD W2 * 9 N5
Southwold Dr BARK IG11 123 K10
Southwold Rd BXLY DA5 186 C2
CLPT E5 120 A7
WATN WD24 73 K3
Southwold Sp DTCH/LGLY SL3 150 F1
Southwood Av CHERT KT16 214 F4
COUL/CHIP CR5 240 G3
HGT N6 118 C5
KUTN/CMB KT2 199 P3
WOKN/KNAP GU21 231 J4
Southwood Cl BMLY BR1 206 C4
WPK KT4 201 K1
Southwood Dr BRYLDS KT5 199 P7
Southwood Gdns ESH/CLAY KT10 198 F10
GNTH/NBYPK IG2 122 A2
Southwood La HGT N6 118 B5
Southwood Lawn Rd HGT N6 * 118 B5
Southwood Rd ELTH/MOT SE9 184 E5
THMD SE28 143 L10
South Worple Wy MORT/ESHN SW14 156 A9
Southy Ms CAN/RD E16 141 M10
Sovereign Cl EA W5 135 V1
PUR/KEN CR8 222 G6
RSLP HA4 112 F6
WAP E1W 140 A3
Sovereign Ct E/WMO/HCT KT8 197 N4
HLWW/ROY CM19 46 N
Sovereign Crs BERM/RHTH SE16 140 D9
Sovereign Gv ALP/SUD HA0 115 J8
Sovereign Hts DTCH/LGLY SL3 150 D5
Sovereign Ms BETH E2 7 L1
EBAR EN4 78 A7
Sovereign Pk HHNE HP2 * 36 C4
STALE/WH AL4 39 J7
WLSDN NW10 * 135 N6
Sovereign Pl HRW HA1 114 K3
Sovereign Rd BARK IG11 143 M5
Sowerby Cl ELTH/MOT SE9 184 C1
Sowrey Av RAIN RM13 144 A1
Space Wave EBED/NFELT TW14 175 J4
Spackmans Wy SL SL1 149 H2
Spa Dr EPSOM KT18 219 M10
Spafield St CLKNW EC1R 12 A1
Spa Green Est CLKNW EC1R * 6 B7
Spa Hl NRWD SE19 203 H1
Spalding Cl EDGW HA8 96 B8
Spalding Rd HDN NW4 116 C3
TOOT SW17 180 C8
Spalt Cl RBRW/HUT CM13 107 M3
Spanby Rd BOW E3 140 F6
Spaniards Cl GLDGN NW11 117 M6
Spaniards End HAMP NW3 117 M4
Spaniards Rd HAMP NW3 117 M4
Spanish Pl MHST W1U * 10 C4
Spanish Rd WAND/EARL SW18 179 N3
Sparepenie Hi LOU IG10 82 G6
Sparepenny La EYN DA4 209 H4
Sparkbridge Rd HRW HA1 114 D2
Sparkes Cl HAYES BR2 205 M2
Sparke Ter CAN/RD E16 * 141 H8
Sparkford Gdns FBAR/BDGN N11 98 B6
Sparks Cl ACT W3 136 A8
BCTR RM8 123 M7
HPTN TW12 175 M5

**Column 3**

Sparrow Cl HPTN TW12 175 M9
Sparrow Dr STMC/STPC BR5 206 F8
Sparrow Farm Dr EBED/NFELT TW14 175 M3
Sparrow Farm Rd EW KT17 220 D1
Sparrow Gn DAGE RM10 124 C8
Sparrow Rw CHOB/PIR GU24 212 G3
Sparrows Herne BUSH WD23 94 A1
Sparrows La ELTH/MOT SE9 184 F3
Sparrow's La HLWE CM17 31 M5
Sparrows Md REDH RH1 258 B6
Sparrows Wk BUSH WD23 * 94 B1
Sparrows Wick BUSH WD23 * 94 A1
Sparrowswick Ride STALW/RED AL3 38 B1
Sparrow Wk GSTN WD25 73 H1
Sparsholt Rd ARCH N19 118 C9
BARK IG11 143 H3
Spartan Cl WLGTN SM6 222 F4
Sparta St GNWCH SE10 161 H7
Sparvell Rd WOKN/KNAP GU21 230 C5
Speakers Ct CROY/NA CR0 * 203 L8
Spearman St WOOL/PLUM SE18 * 162 D5
Spear Ms ECT SW5 14 A6
Spears Rd ARCH N19 118 F6
Speart La HEST TW5 153 M4
Spectrum Pl WAL SE17 18 G8
Spedan Cl HAMP NW3 117 L8
Speedbird Wy WDR/YW UB7 151 L6
Speedgate Hl HART DA3 210 P9
Speedwell Cl HHW HP1 * 35 H7
RGUE GU4 250 F7
Speedwell St DEPT SE8 160 F6
Speedy Pl STPAN WC1H 5 L10
Speer Rd THDIT KT7 198 F5
Speirs Cl NWMAL KT3 200 C6
Spekehill ELTH/MOT SE9 184 F4
Speke Rd THNTH CR7 203 L2
Speldhurst Cl HAYES BR2 205 L5
Speldhurst Rd CHSWK W4 156 A2
HOM E9 140 C2
Spellbrook Wk IS N1 * 6 G1
Spelman St WCHPL E1 13 N5
Spelthorne Gv SUN TW16 174 D10
Spelthorne La ASHF TW15 174 D10
Spence Av BF/WBF KT14 215 P10
Spence Cl BERM/RHTH SE16 160 L1
Spencer Av CHESW EN7 61 M4
HYS/HAR UB3 133 J6
Spencer Cl EPSOM KT18 238 B5
FNCH N3 97 H1
ORP BR6 207 H9
UX/CGN UB8 131 M5
WFD IG8 101 P6
WLSDN NW10 135 L5
WOKN/KNAP GU21 214 G6
Spencer Dr EFNCH N2 117 H4
Spencer Gdns EGH TW20 172 A8
MORT/ESHN SW14 177 P1
Spencer Ga STAL AL1 38 D1
Spencer Hill Rd WIM/MER SW19 179 H9
Spencer House SURB KT6 * 199 K5
Spencer Ms CLAP SW4 158 F7
HMSMTH W6 14 A9
STAL AL1 38 D1
Spencer Pk WAND/EARL SW18 179 N1
Spencer Pl CROY/NA CR0 203 L7
IS N1 6 C3
STALE/WH AL4 39 J7
WEST SW1P 17 H4
Spencer Ri KTTN NW5 118 C9
Spencer Rd ACT W3 135 P10
ALP/SUD HA0 115 H7
BMLY BR1 183 L10
BTSEA SW11 157 N10
CEND/HSY/T N8 118 C3
CHSWK W4 155 P5
COB KT11 235 J1
DTCH/LGLY SL3 150 C2
E/WMO/HCT KT8 198 B2
EHAM E6 142 A3
FBAR/BDGN N11 98 C5
GDMY/SEVK IG3 123 J4
ISLW TW7 154 C7
MTCM CR4 202 A7
RAIN RM13 144 E5
RYNPK SW20 200 E1
SAND/SEL CR2 223 P6
TOTM N17 99 P9
WALTH E17 101 H10
WHTN TW2 176 D6
Spencer St CLKNW EC1V 6 C8
NWDGN UB2 152 C2
STALW/RED AL3 38 D1
Spencer Wk HHW HP1 35 K3
REDH RH1 276 B5
WCHPL E1 140 C4
Spenser Av WEY KT13 216 B5
Spenser Crs UPMR RM14 126 A5
Spenser Gv STNW/STAM N16 119 M9
Spenser Ms DUL SE21 181 L4
Spenser Rd HNHL SE24 158 B10
Spenser St WESTW SW1E 17 H3
Spensley Wk STNW/STAM N16 119 L9
Speranza St WOOL/PLUM SE18 163 J4
Sperling Rd TOTM N17 99 N10
Spert St POP/IOD E14 140 G9
Speyhawk Pl POTB/CUF EN6 59 L6
Speyside STHGT/OAK N14 78 D10
Spey St POP/IOD E14 141 N7
Spey Wy ROM RM1 104 F8
Spezia Rd WLSDN NW10 136 D4
Spiceall RGUW GU3 266 C6
Spicer Cl BRXN/ST SW9 159 J8
WOT/HER KT12 197 K6
Spicersfield CHESW EN7 61 P5
Spicers Fld LHD/OX KT22 218 G5
Spicer St STALW/RED AL3 38 B6
Spices Yd CROY/NA CR0 223 K1
Spielman Rd DART DA1 171 M1
Spiers Wy HORL RH6 280 C6
Spigurnell Rd TOTM N17 99 P1
Spikes Bridge Rd STHL UB1 133 M8
Spillbutters BRWN CM15 86 D1
Spilsby Rd HARH RM3 105 L8
Spindle Cl WOOL/PLUM SE18 162 B5
Spindles TIL RM18 168 D6
Spindle Wy CRAWE RH10 283 M6
Spindlewood Gdns CROY/NA CR0 223 M1
Spindlewoods KWD/TDW/WH KT20 238 E6
Spindrift Av POP/IOD E14 160 G3
Spinel Cl WOOL/PLUM SE18 163 N4
Spingate Cl HCH RM12 125 L6
Spinnaker Cl BARK IG11 143 N3
Spinnells Rd RYLN/HDSTN HA2 113 L3
Spinners Wk WDSR SL4 149 H7
Spinney Cl ASC SL5 262 B2
BECK BR3 183 K6
COB KT11 217 M7
CRAWW RH11 283 H10
NWMAL KT3 200 C3
RAIN RM13 144 A4
WDR/YW UB7 131 N7
WPK KT4 200 G7
Spinneycroft LHD/OX KT22 236 C7
Spinney Dr EBED/NFELT TW14 174 A3
Spinney Gdns DAGW RM9 123 P10

**Column 4**

NRWD SE19 181 N8
Spinney Hl ADL/WDHM KT15 215 J2
Spinney La WDSR SL4 170 A4
Spinney Oak BMLY BR1 206 B2
CHERT KT16 214 C5
Spinney Pl AMSS HP? * 69 H5
Spinneys Dr STALW/RED AL3 * 38 A6
Spinney St HERT/BAY SG13 25 P5
The Spinney ALP/SUD HA0 114 F8
ASC SL5 192 D5
STALE/WH AL4 39 NL
STJWD NW8 3 J2
SYD SE26 182 A8
TEDD TW11 176 B8
BARK SW13 * 156 E5
BEAC HP9 88 D10
BERK HP4 33 L6
BROX EN10 44 E5
CFSP/GDCR SL9 110 A6
CHEAM SM3 220 F1
CHONG CM5 67 N6
CSHM HP5 51 J5
EPSOM KT18 238 E5
GT/LBKH KT23 236 A10
HERT/BAY SG13 25 P5
HLW CM20 29 K10
HORL RH6 280 B2
LHD/OX KT22 218 A9
POTB/CUF EN6 59 N7
PUR/KEN CR8 223 J7
RBRW/HUT CM13 107 P4
RPLY/SEND GU23 251 M3
STAN HA7 95 K5
STRHM/NOR SW16 180 D6
SUN TW16 197 H1
SWLY BR8 208 F2
WAT WD17 73 M1
WCHMH N21 99 H1
WCCE AL8 23 H6
Spinney Wy RSEV TN14 226 G7
The Spinning Wk SHGR GU5 270 B5
Spinning Wheel Md HLWS CM18 47 K8
Spire Cl GVE DA12 190 E4
Spire Pl WARL CR6 242 D4
Spirit Quay WAP E1W 13 P9
Spital Heath DORK RH4 273 H1
Spital La RBRW/HUT CM14 106 C4
Spital Sq WCHPL E1 13 L3
Spital St DART DA1 171 H5
WCHPL E1 13 N3
Spital Yd WCHPL E1 * 13 L3
Spitfire Cl DTCH/LGLY SL3 150 D4
Spitfire Est HEST TW5 * 153 K4
Spitfire House WOOL/PLUM SE18 * 162 B6
SYD SE26 182 B7
Spitfire Wy HEST TW5 133 P10
Spode Wk KIL/WHAMP NW6 * 117 L10
Spondon Rd SEVS/STOTM N15 119 P2
Spook Hl RDKG RH5 272 C7
Spoonbill Wy YEAD UB4 133 L7
Spooners Dr LCOL/BKTW AL2 56 B3
Spooner Wk WLGTN SM6 222 E2
Sportsbank St CAT SE6 183 H3
Sportsfield Ap BEAC HP9 * 89 J6
Sportsman Pl BETH E2 7 N6
Spottons Gv TOTM N17 99 M9
Spout Hl CROY/NA CR0 224 F2
Spout La EDEN TN8 262 F10
STWL/WRAY TW19 173 K1
Spout La North STWL/WRAY TW19 151 L10
Spratt Hall Rd WAN E11 121 M4
Spratts La CHERT KT16 215 H3
Spray St WOOL/PLUM SE18 162 G5
Spreighton Rd E/WMO/HCT KT8 198 A4
Sprimont Pl CHEL SW3 16 A7
Springall St PECK SE15 160 A6
Springate Fld DTCH/LGLY SL3 150 B1
Spring Av EGH TW20 172 B9
Springbank WCHMH N21 78 G10
Springbank Rd LEW SE13 183 J5
Springbank Wk CAMTN NW1 5 K2
Spring Bottom La REDH RH1 259 H1
Springbourne Ct BECK BR3 183 L9
Spring Bridge Rd EA W5 135 L9
Spring Cl BAR EN5 77 J6
BCTR RM8 123 N5
BORE WD6 75 M6
CRAWW RH11 283 M8
DEN/HRF UB9 91 N7
Springclose La CHEAM SM3 221 H4
Spring Copse CRAWE RH10 285 N4
Springcopse Rd REIG RH2 275 N4
Spring Cnr FELT TW13 175 H6
Spring Cots SURB KT6 * 199 K4
Spring Court Rd ENC/FH EN2 79 H1
Springcroft AMST DA2 211 M6
Springcroft Av EFNCH N2 117 N4
Spring Crofts BUSH WD23 73 P1
Spring Cross HART DA3 211 L10
Spring Dr PIN HA5 113 H4
Springett Cl RAIN RM13 145 N1
Springfarm Cl RAIN RM13 145 L2
Springfield BUSH WD23 94 C2
CLPT E5 120 A5
EPP CM16 65 J8
LTWR GU18 212 B7
OXTED RH8 261 J4
Springfield Av HPTN TW12 176 A9
MUSWH N10 118 D1
RYNPK SW20 201 J3
SWLY BR8 208 G4
Springfield Cl CHONG CM5 67 N1
NFNCH/WDSPK N12 97 N5
POTB/CUF EN6 59 J8
RKW/CH/CXG WD3 72 C9
STAN HA7 95 H6
WDSR SL4 149 L8
WOKN/KNAP GU21 231 N3
Springfield Dr GNTH/NBYPK IG2 122 A5
LHD/OX KT22 236 D5
Springfield Gdns BMLY BR1 206 C2
CDALE/KGS NW9 116 A3
CHING E4 101 N1
RSLP HA4 113 J5
UPMR RM14 126 A3
WFD IG8 101 H1
WWKM BR4 204 G4
Springfield Gv CHARL SE7 161 N5
SUN TW16 197 H1
Springfield La KIL/WHAMP NW6 2 F6
WEY KT13 216 C2
Springfield Mdw WEY KT13 216 C1
Springfield Pde Ms PLMGR N13 99 H5
Springfield Pl NWMAL KT3 199 P3
Springfield Rd ASHF TW15 174 N4
BMLY BR1 206 C2
BXLYHN N16 164 C1
CDW/CHF RM16 168 B1
ISLW TW7 98 F1
MUSWH N10 98 F1
ORP BR6 227 L3
CHES/WCR EN8 62 B5
CHING E4 101 N1
CRAWW RH11 283 K8
CSHM HP5 51 J5
DTCH/LGLY SL3 150 D4
EHAM E6 142 C2
EW KT17 220 F6

**Column 5**

FBAR/BDGN N11 98 D6
GSTN WD25 55 J9
GU GU1 268 B1
HHNE HP2 36 A5
HNWL W7 134 D10
HRW HA1 114 D4
KUT/HW KT1 199 K4
SEVS/STOTM N15 119 P2
SRTFD E15 * 141 K5
STAL AL1 38 F7
STALE/WH AL4 39 J9
STJWD NW8 3 J2
SWD SE26 182 A8
TEDD TW11 176 B8
THHTH CR7 203 K1
WALTH E17 120 E4
WDSR SL4 148 G8
WELL DA16 163 L9
WHTN TW2 175 P4
WIM/MER SW19 179 J8
WLGTN SM6 222 C2
Springfields AMS HP6 133 H3
BROX EN10 44 E5
WAB EN9 63 K10
WGCW AL8 22 E7
Springfields Cl CHERT KT16 195 L8
Springfield Wk KIL/WHAMP NW6 2 G6
ORP BR6 227 L3
Spring Gdns ASC SL5 192 D5
BH/WHM TN16 243 P4
CRAWE RH10 285 K2
HBRY N5 119 K10
HCH RM12 125 J9
ORP BR6 227 L3
ROMW/RG RM7 124 D3
WFD IG8 101 P8
WHALL SW1A 11 L9
WLGTN SM6 222 D2
Spring Gn CHSWK W4 156 C3
GODL GU7 267 K9
GVE DA12 190 E4
HPTN TW12 198 A1
LHD/OX KT22 236 A9
LOU IG10 82 A10
MTCM CR4 202 B3
Springhall La HERT/BAY SG13 26 E9
Springhall Rd SBW CM21 29 H1
Springhaven Cl GU GU1 250 D10
Springhead Rd ERITH DA8 164 N3
Springhill Cl CMBW SE5 159 L9
Spring Hills HLW CM20 29 J6
Springholm Cl BH/WHM TN16 243 P4
Springhurst Cl CROY/NA CR0 224 E1
Spring La STAN HA7 94 A5
Spring La CLPT E5 120 A6
HHW HP1 * 35 K5
MUSWH N10 118 B1
OXTED RH8 261 J7
Springmead Cl ORP BR6 227 L3
Spring Ms MRDN SM4 201 N8
Spring Park Av CROY/NA CR0 204 D9
Spring Park Dr BECK BR3 205 H5
Springpark Rd FSBYPK N4 119 K6
Spring Park Rd CROY/NA CR0 204 C9
Spring Pl BARK IG11 142 C4
KTTN NW5 118 B10
Spring Plat CRAWE RH10 284 D7
Spring Plat Ct CRAWE RH10 * 284 E7
Springpond Rd DAGW RM9 123 P10
Springrice Rd LEW SE13 183 H2
Spring Ri EGH TW20 172 B9
Spring Rd FELT TW13 174 D6
Spring Shaw Rd STMC/STPC BR5 207 K1
The Springs BROX EN10 44 E10
HERT/BAY SG13 25 N4
Spring St BAY/PAD W2 9 L6
EW KT17 220 E6
Spring Tide Cl PECK SE15 * 159 P7
Spring Ter RCH/KEW TW9 164 C10
SWCM DA10 189 J5
Springvale Av BTFD TW8 136 A8
Springvale Ct GT/LBKH KT23 254 A2
Spring Vale Cl SWLY BR8 186 C10
Springvale Ter WKENS W14 156 G2
Springvale Wy STMC/STPC BR5 207 M3
Spring Villa Rd EDGW HA8 95 M6
Spring Vis WEY KT13 * 134 C10
Spring Wk BROX EN10 44 B7
WCHPL E1 13 N3

**Column 6**

WOKN/KNAP GU21 230 C4
Squadrons Ap HCH RM12 145 K1
Square St HLWE CM17 29 M10
The Square BH/WHM TN16 243 P6
BROX EN10 44 D9
CAR SM5 222 B2
CRAWE RH10 283 N7
GUW GU2 267 G3
HHW HP1 * 35 N6
HMSMTH W6 156 F4
IL IG1 122 D5
RCH/KEW TW9 29 P1
SBW CM21 29 P1
SEV TN13 246 F9
STKPK UB11 132 E10
SWLY BR8 208 E3
WATN WD24 73 J5
WDR/YW UB7 151 L2
WFD IG8 101 M6
Squarey St TOOT SW17 179 M6
Squerryes Mede BH/WHM TN16 262 F3
The Squerryes CTHM CR3 241 M7
Squire Gdns STJWD NW8 3 L10
Squires Bridge Rd SHPTN TW17 196 A4
Squires Cl CRAWE RH10 285 P5
Squires Ct WIM/MER SW19 179 K7
Squires Fld SWLY BR8 209 H1
Squire's La FNCH N3 97 L9
Squire's Mt HAMP NW3 117 N8
Squires Rd SHPTN TW17 196 A4
Squires Wy RDART DA2 188 B8
Squires Wood Dr CHST BR7 184 C10
Squirrel Cha HHW HP1 35 H5
Squirrel Cl CRAWW RH11 283 L4
HSLWW TW4 153 K9
Squirrel Dr WDSR SL4 170 A5
Squirrel La WDSR SL4 170 A5
Squirrel Ms WEA W13 * 134 F9
Squirrel's Cha SCDW/CHF RM16 168 D2
Squirrels Cl CODL GU7 267 K8
HDGN/ICK IG10 132 B2
NFNCH/WDSPK N12 97 M5
Squirrels Gn GT/LBKH KT23 235 P9
WPK KT4 200 C10
Squirrel's Heath Av GPK RM2 125 J1
Squirrels Heath La EMPK RM11 125 L2
GPK RM2 125 K1
Squirrels Heath Rd HARH RM3 105 M10
The Squirrels BUSH WD23 74 C10
HERT/BAY SG13 25 P5
LEW SE13 161 J9
PIN HA5 113 N1
Squirrel's Wy EPSOM KT18 238 A1
Squirrel Wd BF/WBF KT14 215 N1
Squirries St BETH E2 7 P9
Stable Cl CRAWE RH10 284 E10
EPSOM KT18 238 B5
KUTN/CMB KT2 175 P10
NTHLT UB5 133 P4
Stable Ms BEAC HP9 89 J8
BXLY DA5 186 C5
Stable Ms REIG RH2 257 K10
TWK TW1 176 E4
WNWD SE27 181 K8
Stables End ORP BR6 226 G4
The Stables Market CAMTN NW1 * 4 E4
Stables Ms BRKMPK AL9 * 59 N4
The Stables COB KT11 217 N10
Stable Wk LBTH SE11 18 A9
Stable Wk NKENS W10 136 F8
Stable Yard Rd WHALL SW1A 5 S7
Stacey Av UED N18 100 B5
Stacey Cl GVE DA12 191 H8
LEY E10 121 J3
Stacey St HOLWY N7 119 H8
LSO/SEVD WC2H 11 K6
Stackfield HLW CM20 28 A3
Stackfield Rd CRAWW RH11 283 K8
Stackhouse St KTBR SW1X 16 A3
Stacklands WGCW AL8 22 E7
Stack La HART DA3 211 L9
Stack Rd HART DA3 210 C4
Stacy Pth CMBW SE5 * 159 M6
Staddon Cl BECK BR3 204 D4
Staddon Ct BECK BR3 204 D4
Stadium Rd HDN NW4 116 B5
WOOL/PLUM SE18 162 C6
Stadium St WBPTN SW10 157 J8
Stadium Wy HLWW/ROY CM19 28 C10
WBLY HA9 115 L9
Staffa Rd LEY E10 120 G7
Stafford Av CLAY IG5 102 D10
EMPK RM11 125 H2
SLN SL2 129 H6
Stafford Cl CDW/CHF RM16 168 B3
CHEAM SM3 221 H4
CHES/WCR EN8 62 A5
CTHM CR3 241 N9
EDGW HA8 2 E10
MDHD SL6 128 A8
RDART DA2 188 E1
SLH/COR SL9 169 K2
STHGT/OAK N14 78 D9
WALTH E17 120 G1
Stafford Cross CROY/NA CR0 222 G4
Stafford Dr BROX EN10 44 F6
Stafford Gdns CROY/NA CR0 222 G4
Stafford Lake WOKN/KNAP GU21 230 A6
Stafford Pl RCHPK/HAM TW10 177 L3
WESTW SW1E 17 G3
Stafford Ri CTHM CR3 241 P9
Stafford Rd BOW E3 139 P4
CRAWW RH11 283 K4
CROY/NA CR0 223 H1
CTHM CR3 241 N9
FSTGT E7 141 K6
HRW HA1 94 B9
KIL/WHAMP NW6 2 C4
NWMAL KT3 199 P3
RSLP HA4 112 G9
SCUP DA14 185 M6
WLGTN SM6 222 D6
Staffords HLWE CM17 31 P7
Staffordshire St PECK SE15 159 P7
Staffords Pl HORL RH6 280 E5
Stafford St CONDST W1S * 10 F7
CONDST W1S * 10 E8
Stafford Ter KENS W8 14 A3
Stag Cl EDGW HA8 96 B6
Stagbury Av COUL/CHIP CR5 239 P5
Stagbury Cl COUL/CHIP CR5 239 P5
Stagbury House COUL/CHIP CR5 239 P5
Stag Green Av BRKMPK AL9 59 M1
Stag La BKHH IG9 101 K1
CDALE/KGS NW9 96 B10
EDGW HA8 96 B6
PUT/ROE SW15 178 C8
RKW/CH/CXG WD3 70 F10
Stag Leys ASHTD KT21 237 L6
Stag Leys Cl BNSTD SM7 240 A4
Stags Wy ISLW TW7 154 C6
Stainash Crs STA TW18 173 L8
Stainash Pde STA TW18 * 173 L8
Stainbank Rd MTCM CR4 202 C3
Stainby Cl WDR/YW UB7 132 B2
Stainby Rd BORE WD6 75 J3
Stainer St STHWK SE1 15 H1
Staines Av CHEAM SM3 200 G10
Staines By-Pass STA TW18 173 H6
Staines La CHERT KT16 195 H4
Staines Lane Cl CHERT KT16 195 H5

| | | | |
|---|---|---|---|
| Staines Rd CHERT KT16 | 195 | H6 |
| EBED/NFELT TW14 * | 175 | L1 |
| EBED/NFELT TW14 | 174 | A7 |
| IL IG1 | 122 | G9 |
| STA TW18 | 195 | J2 |
| STWL/WRAY TW19 | 172 | B3 |
| WHTN TW2 | 176 | B6 |
| Staines Rd East SUN TW16 | 175 | H10 |
| Staines Rd West ASHF TW15 | 194 | D10 |
| Stainford Cl ASHF TW15 | 174 | E8 |
| Stainforth Rd | | |
| CNTH/NBYPK IG2 | 122 | G5 |
| WALTH E17 | 120 | F2 |
| Staining La CITYW EC2V | 12 | C4 |
| Stainmore Cl CHST BR7 | 206 | G1 |
| Stainsbury St BETH E2 | 140 | E1 |
| Stainsby Pl POP/IOD E14 | 140 | F8 |
| Stainsby Rd POP/IOD E14 | 140 | F8 |
| Stains Cl CHES/WCR EN8 | 62 | D4 |
| Stainton Rd CAT SE6 | 183 | J5 |
| PEND EN3 | 80 | B5 |
| Stainton Wk | | |
| WOKN/KNAP GU21 * | 231 | H5 |
| Stairfoot La SEV TN13 | 246 | F8 |
| Staiths Wy | | |
| KWD/TDW/WH KT20 | 238 | C6 |
| Stakers Ct HARP AL5 | 20 | A2 |
| Stakescorner Rd RGUW GU3 | 267 | M8 |
| Stalbridge St CAMTN NW1 | 9 | P3 |
| Stalham St BERM/RHTH SE16 | 141 | H2 |
| Stalham Wy BARK/HLT IG6 | 102 | A3 |
| Stambourne Wy NRWD SE19 | 181 | M10 |
| WWKM BR4 | 205 | H10 |
| Stambourne Woodland Wk | | |
| NRWD SE19 | 181 | M10 |
| Stamford Brook Av | | |
| HMSMTH W6 | 156 | C2 |
| Stamford Brook Gdns | | |
| HMSMTH W6 * | 156 | C2 |
| Stamford Brook Rd | | |
| HMSMTH W6 | 156 | C2 |
| Stamford Cl HAMP NW3 * | 117 | M8 |
| KTN/HRWW/WS HA3 | 94 | D8 |
| POTB/CUF EN6 | 59 | N8 |
| SEVS/STOTM N15 | 119 | P3 |
| STHL UB1 | 133 | P9 |
| Stamford Cots WBPTN SW10 * | 157 | L6 |
| Stamford Dr HAYES BR2 | 205 | L4 |
| Stamford Gdns DAGW RM9 | 143 | M2 |
| Stamford Green Rd | | |
| EPSOM KT18 | 219 | N9 |
| Stamford Gv East | | |
| STNW/STAM N16 | 119 | P6 |
| Stamford Gv West | | |
| STNW/STAM N16 | 119 | P6 |
| Stamford Hl STNW/STAM N16 | 119 | P6 |
| Stamford Rd DAGW RM9 | 143 | L2 |
| EHAM E6 | 142 | B3 |
| IS N1 | 7 | K3 |
| SEVS/STOTM N15 | 119 | P3 |
| WAT WD17 | 73 | J6 |
| WOT/HER KT12 | 197 | L10 |
| Stamford St STHWK SE1 | 12 | A1 |
| Stamp Pl BETH E2 | 7 | L8 |
| Stanborough HACK E8 * | 7 | L1 |
| Stanborough Av BORE WD6 | 75 | M4 |
| WGCW AL8 | 22 | F6 |
| Stanborough Cl HPTN TW12 | 175 | N9 |
| WGCW AL8 | 22 | F6 |
| Stanborough Gn WGCW AL8 | 22 | F7 |
| Stanborough Ms WGCW AL8 | 22 | F7 |
| Stanborough Pas HACK E8 * | 7 | L1 |
| Stanborough Rd HSLW TW3 | 154 | C9 |
| WGCW AL8 | 22 | E8 |
| Stanbridge Pl WCHMN N21 | 99 | J3 |
| Stanbridge Rd PUT/ROE SW15 | 156 | F9 |
| Stanbrook Rd ABYW SE2 | 163 | L1 |
| GVW DA11 | 190 | C4 |
| Stanbury Av WAT WD17 | 72 | F3 |
| Stanbury Ct HAMP NW3 | 4 | C3 |
| Stanbury Rd PECK SE15 | 160 | A7 |
| Stancroft CDALE/KGS NW9 | 116 | E2 |
| Standale Gv RSLP HA4 | 112 | D3 |
| Standard Pl SDTCH EC2A * | 7 | K10 |
| Standard Rd BELV DA17 | 164 | B4 |
| BXLYHS DA6 | 163 | P10 |
| HSLWW TW4 | 153 | N6 |
| ORP BR6 | 226 | D6 |
| PEND EN3 | 80 | D4 |
| WLSDN NW10 | 155 | P6 |
| Standen Av HCH RM12 | 125 | L8 |
| Standen Rd WAND/EARL SW18 | 179 | K3 |
| Standfield ABLGY WD5 | 54 | F7 |
| Standfield Rd DAGE RM10 | 124 | B10 |
| Standingford | | |
| HLWW/ROY CM19 | 46 | B6 |
| Standinghall La CRAWE RH10 | 285 | H9 |
| Standish Rd HMSMTH W6 | 156 | D3 |
| Standring Ri HHS/BOV HP3 | 35 | J7 |
| Stane Cl WIM/MER SW19 | 179 | L10 |
| Stane Gv VX/NE SW8 | 158 | G8 |
| Stane Wy ABLGY WD5 | 220 | D6 |
| WOOL/PLUM SE18 | 162 | A6 |
| Stanfields Ct HLW CM20 | 29 | L1 |
| Stanford Cl HPTN TW12 | 175 | N9 |
| ROMW/RG RM7 | 124 | C4 |
| RSLP HA4 | 112 | C4 |
| WFD IG8 | 102 | B4 |
| Stanford Ct WAB EN9 | 63 | M9 |
| Stanford Gdns SOCK/AV RM15 | 146 | D10 |
| Stanford Pl WALW SE17 | 19 | L6 |
| Stanford Rivers Rd | | |
| CHONG CM5 | 67 | P7 |
| Stanford Rd CDW/CHF RM16 | 168 | B1 |
| FBAR/BDGN N11 | 98 | A4 |
| KENS W8 | 15 | H4 |
| STRHM/NOR SW16 | 202 | A8 |
| The Stanfords EW KT17 | 220 | C8 |
| Stanford St PIM SW1V | 17 | N7 |
| Stanford Wy | | |
| STRHM/NOR SW16 | 202 | A8 |
| Stangate Crs BORE WD6 | 76 | B3 |
| Stangate Gdns STAN HA7 | 94 | G5 |
| Stanger Rd SNWD SE25 | 203 | P4 |
| Stanham Pl DART DA1 | 165 | H10 |
| Stan Hl HORL RH6 | 278 | F7 |
| Stanhope Av FNCH N3 | 117 | J1 |
| HAYES BR2 | 205 | M8 |
| KTN/HRWW/WS HA3 | 94 | D9 |
| Stanhope Cl | | |
| BERM/RHTH SE16 * | 141 | J7 |
| Stanhope Gdns BCTR RM8 | 124 | A8 |
| FSBYPK N4 | 119 | H4 |
| HGT N6 | 118 | C6 |
| IL IG1 | 122 | C6 |
| MLHL NW7 | 96 | F6 |
| SKENS SW7 | 15 | K5 |
| Stanhope Ga MYFR/PAD W2 | 10 | D9 |
| Stanhope Gv BECK BR3 | 204 | E5 |
| Stanhope Heath | | |
| STWL/WRAY TW19 | 173 | M2 |
| Stanhope Ms East SKENS SW7 | 15 | K5 |
| Stanhope Ms South | | |
| SKENS SW7 | 15 | K6 |
| Stanhope Ms West | | |
| SKENS SW7 | 15 | K5 |
| Stanhope Pde CAMTN NW1 * | 4 | F7 |
| Stanhope Park Rd | | |
| GFD/PVL UB6 | 134 | B4 |
| Stanhope Pl BAY/PAD W2 | 10 | A6 |
| Stanhope Rd BAR EN5 | 76 | C7 |
| BCTR RM8 | 124 | A7 |
| BFN/LL DA15 | 163 | P9 |
| BXLYHN DA7 | 163 | P8 |
| CAR SM5 | 222 | B4 |
| CHES/WCR EN8 | 62 | D9 |
| CROY/NA CRO | 203 | M10 |
| GFD/PVL UB6 | 134 | B7 |
| HGT N6 | 118 | D4 |
| NFNCH/WDSPK N12 | 97 | M6 |
| RAIN RM13 | 145 | J1 |
| STAL AL1 | 11 | J5 |
| SWCM DA10 | 189 | L2 |
| WALTH E17 | 120 | G3 |

| | | | |
|---|---|---|---|
| Stanhope Rw | | |
| MYFR/PICC W1J * | 10 | E10 |
| Stanhopes OXTED RH8 | 261 | N1 |
| Stanhope St CAMTN NW1 | 4 | E1 |
| Stanhope Wy SEV TN13 | 246 | E8 |
| WHTN TW2 * | 176 | B3 |
| Stanier Cl WKENS W14 | 14 | D8 |
| Stanier Cl CRAWE RH10 | 284 | C8 |
| WKENS W14 | 14 | D8 |
| Stanlake Rd SHB W12 | 136 | F10 |
| Stanlake Vis SHB W12 | 136 | F10 |
| Stanley Av ALP/SUD HA0 | 135 | K2 |
| BARK IG11 | 143 | K3 |
| BCTR RM8 | 124 | A6 |
| BECK BR3 | 205 | H3 |
| CSHM HP5 | 50 | C7 |
| GFD/PVL UB6 | 134 | B3 |
| GPK RM2 | 125 | H2 |
| LCOL/BKTW AL2 | 55 | P1 |
| NWMAL KT3 | 200 | D5 |
| Stanley Cl ALP/SUD HA0 | 135 | K2 |
| COUL/CHIP CR5 | 240 | G3 |
| CRAWE RH10 | 283 | P9 |
| ELTH/MOT SE9 | 184 | F4 |
| GPK RM2 | 125 | H2 |
| RDART DA2 | 188 | D1 |
| UX/CGN UB8 | 131 | N4 |
| VX/NE SW8 | 17 | N10 |
| Stanley Cots SLN SL2 | 129 | L10 |
| Stanley Crs GVE DA12 | 190 | G8 |
| NTGHL W11 | 8 | C7 |
| Stanleycroft Cl ISLW TW7 | 154 | A7 |
| Stanley Dr HAT AL10 | 40 | E6 |
| Stanley Gdns ACT W3 | 156 | A1 |
| BORE WD6 | 75 | K5 |
| CRICK NW2 | 82 | B10 |
| MTCM CR4 * | 180 | B9 |
| SAND/SEL CR2 | 223 | P8 |
| WLGTN SM6 | 222 | D3 |
| WOT/HER KT12 | 217 | K2 |
| Stanley Gardens Rd | | |
| TEDD TW11 | 176 | D8 |
| Stanley Gn East | | |
| DTCH/LGLY SL3 | 150 | C3 |
| Stanley Gn West | | |
| DTCH/LGLY SL3 | 150 | C3 |
| Stanley Gv CROY/NA CRO | 203 | H3 |
| VX/NE SW8 | 158 | B9 |
| Stanley Hl AMSS HP7 | 69 | K6 |
| CHOB/PIR GU24 | 230 | B8 |
| Stanley Hill Av AMSS HP7 | 69 | J5 |
| Stanley Park Rd CAR SM5 | 222 | B6 |
| Stanley Pas CAMTN NW1 * | 5 | K8 |
| Stanley Pl CHONG CM5 | 67 | P5 |
| Stanley Rd ACT W3 | 155 | P2 |
| ASHF TW15 | 173 | P8 |
| BELMT SM2 | 221 | L8 |
| CAR SM5 | 222 | A5 |
| CHING E4 | 101 | H4 |
| CROY/NA CRO | 203 | H7 |
| ED N9 | 99 | N2 |
| EFNCH N2 | 117 | N2 |
| EN EN1 | 79 | M7 |
| FBAR/BDGN N11 | 98 | E7 |
| GRAYS RM17 | 167 | N4 |
| GVW DA11 | 190 | B5 |
| HAYES BR2 | 205 | P3 |
| HCH RM12 | 125 | K1 |
| HRT/BAY SG13 | 25 | M6 |
| HSLW TW3 | 154 | B10 |
| IL IG1 | 122 | G7 |
| MNPK E12 | 122 | B10 |
| MORT/ESHN SW14 | 155 | N10 |
| MRDN SM4 | 201 | K4 |
| MUSWH N10 | 98 | B8 |
| NTHWD HA6 | 93 | H9 |
| ORP BR6 | 207 | J8 |
| RYLN/HDSTN HA2 | 114 | D7 |
| SCUP DA14 | 185 | K6 |
| SEVS/STOTM N15 | 119 | J2 |
| STHL UB1 | 133 | M4 |
| SWCM DA10 | 189 | L2 |
| SWFD E18 | 101 | L9 |
| TEDD TW11 | 175 | N8 |
| WALTH E17 | 120 | C4 |
| WAT WD17 | 73 | K7 |
| WBLY HA9 | 135 | L2 |
| WHTN TW2 | 176 | C6 |
| WIM/MER SW19 | 179 | K10 |
| WOKN/KNAP GU21 | 232 | C3 |
| Stanley Sq CAR SM5 | 222 | B9 |
| Stanley St CTHM CR3 | 241 | K8 |
| DEPT SE8 | 160 | E6 |
| Stanley Ter ARCH N19 * | 118 | F7 |
| BXLYHS DA6 * | 164 | B10 |
| Stanley Wy STMC/STPC BR5 | 207 | L5 |
| Stanmer St BTSEA SW11 | 17 | K8 |
| Stanmore Cha STALE/WH AL4 | 39 | J7 |
| Stanmore Gdns | | |
| RCH/KEW TW9 | 155 | M7 |
| SUT SM1 | 201 | M10 |
| Stanmore HI STAN HA7 | 95 | G1 |
| Stanmore Rd BELV DA17 | 164 | D3 |
| RCH/KEW TW9 | 155 | L9 |
| SEVS/STOTM N15 | 119 | J2 |
| WAN E11 | 121 | L6 |
| WATN WD24 | 73 | J5 |
| Stanmore St IS N1 | 5 | N5 |
| Stanmore Ter BECK BR3 | 204 | E7 |
| Stanmore Wy LOU IG10 | 82 | D5 |
| Stanmount Rd | | |
| LCOL/BKTW AL2 * | 55 | P1 |
| Stannard Ms HACK E8 * | 7 | N1 |
| Stannard Rd HACK E8 * | 7 | N1 |
| Stannary Pl LBTH SE11 | 18 | B8 |
| Stannary St LBTH SE11 | 18 | B9 |
| Stannet Wy WLGTN SM6 | 222 | D1 |
| Stansbury Sq NKENS W10 | 2 | D1 |
| Stansfeld Rd CAN/RD E16 | 142 | A8 |
| Stansfield Rd BRXN/ST SW9 | 158 | A9 |
| HSLWW TW4 | 153 | J8 |
| Stansgate Rd DAGE RM10 | 124 | B7 |
| Stanstead Cl CTHM CR3 | 241 | M10 |
| HAYES BR2 | 205 | L5 |
| Stanstead Dr HOD EN11 | 44 | C1 |
| Stanstead Gv CAT SE6 | 182 | E4 |
| Stanstead Pl AMSS HP7 * | 69 | G4 |
| Stanstead Rd CTHM CR3 | 259 | L2 |
| FSTH SE23 | 182 | C4 |
| HRT/BAY SG13 | 25 | N4 |
| HOD EN11 | 44 | G1 |
| WAN E11 | 121 | N3 |
| WARE SG12 | 33 | G1 |
| Stansted Cl HCH RM12 | 145 | J1 |
| Stansted Crs BXLY DA5 | 184 | G7 |
| Stanswood Gdns CMBW SE5 | 159 | N6 |
| Stanthorpe Cl | | |
| STRHM/NOR SW16 * | 180 | D7 |
| Stanthorpe Rd | | |
| STRHM/NOR SW16 | 180 | D7 |
| Stanton Av TEDD TW11 | 176 | D9 |
| Stanton Cl HOR/WEW KT19 | 219 | N2 |
| STALE/WH AL4 | 39 | J2 |
| STMC/STPC BR5 | 207 | M7 |
| Stanton Rd BARN SW13 | 156 | C8 |
| CROY/NA CRO | 203 | K7 |
| RYNPK SW20 | 200 | G2 |
| Stanton St PECK SE15 | 159 | P7 |
| Stanton Whf SHGR GU5 | 268 | D10 |
| Stanton Wy DTCH/LGLY SL3 | 150 | B3 |
| SYD SE26 | 182 | G7 |
| Stanway Cl CHIG IG7 | 103 | H5 |
| Stanway Cots CHERT KT16 * | 195 | K2 |
| Stanway Gdns ACT W3 | 135 | M10 |
| EDGW HA8 | 96 | E7 |
| Stanway Rd WAB EN9 | 63 | M9 |

| | | | |
|---|---|---|---|
| Stanway St IS N1 | 7 | K7 |
| Stanwell Cl STWL/WRAY TW19 | 173 | N2 |
| Stanwell Gdns | | |
| STWL/WRAY TW19 | 173 | N2 |
| Stanwell Moor Rd STA TW18 | 151 | L5 |
| Stanwell New Rd STA TW18 | 173 | L7 |
| Stanwell Pl | | |
| STWL/WRAY TW19 | 173 | M2 |
| Stanwell Rd ASHF TW15 | 173 | P8 |
| DTCH/LGLY SL3 | 150 | A9 |
| Stanwick Rd WKENS W14 | 14 | C6 |
| Stanworth St STHWK SE1 | 19 | L2 |
| Stanwyck Gdns HARH RM3 | 105 | J6 |
| Stapenhill Rd ALP/SUD HA0 | 114 | Q8 |
| Staple Cl BXLY DA5 | 186 | E6 |
| Staple Inn HHOL WC1V | 12 | A4 |
| Staple La RGUE GU4 | 251 | P9 |
| SHGR GU5 | 251 | P9 |
| Staplefield Cl | | |
| BRXS/STRHM SW2 * | 180 | A3 |
| PIN HA5 | 93 | M8 |
| Stapleford WGCE AL7 | 23 | M5 |
| Stapleford Av | | |
| GNTH/NBYPK IG2 | 123 | H3 |
| Stapleford Cl CHING E4 | 101 | H4 |
| KUT/HW KT1 | 199 | M2 |
| WIM/MER SW19 | 179 | H3 |
| Stapleford Gdns CRW RM5 | 104 | B7 |
| Stapleford Rd ABR/ST RM4 | 84 | C8 |
| ALP/SUD HA0 | 135 | J2 |
| Stapleford Wy BARK IG11 | 143 | H3 |
| Staplehurst Cl REIG RH2 | 275 | M4 |
| Staplehurst Rd CAR SM5 | 221 | P4 |
| LEW SE13 | 183 | J1 |
| REIG RH2 | 275 | M4 |
| Staple La RGUE GU4 | | |
| Staplehurst | | |
| Staples Cl BERM/RHTH SE16 | 140 | D10 |
| Staple St STHWK SE1 | 19 | H2 |
| Stapleton Crs RAIN RM13 | 145 | H1 |
| Stapleton Gdns CROY/NA CRO | 223 | G3 |
| Stapleton Hall Rd FSBYPK N4 | 118 | G5 |
| Stapleton Vis | | |
| STNW/STAM N16 * | 119 | M9 |
| Stapley Rd BELV DA17 | 164 | A6 |
| STALW/RED AL3 | 38 | C5 |
| Stapylton Av SWCM DA10 | 188 | G2 |
| Stapylton Rd BAR EN5 | 76 | B4 |
| Starboard Av SWCM DA10 | 188 | G2 |
| Starboard Wy POP/IOD E14 | 160 | F2 |
| Starbuck Cl ELTH/MOT SE9 | 184 | D3 |
| Starch House La | | |
| BARK/HLT IG6 | 103 | J3 |
| Starcross St CAMTN NW1 | 5 | H10 |
| Starfield Rd SHB W12 | 156 | E1 |
| Star & Garter HI | | |
| RCHPK/HAM TW10 | 177 | K4 |
| Star Hill Rd RSEV TN14 | 246 | D4 |
| Star Holme Ct WARE SG12 | 26 | D2 |
| Starkey Cl CHESW EN7 | 61 | K1 |
| Star La COUL/CHIP CR5 | 241 | K6 |
| EPP CM16 | 65 | K6 |
| STMC/STPC BR5 | 208 | A3 |
| Starlight Wy STALE/WH AL4 | 39 | H8 |
| Starling Cl BKHH IG9 | 101 | M2 |
| PIN HA5 | 93 | M3 |
| HART DA3 | 211 | N3 |
| PIN HA5 | 113 | K1 |
| Starling La POTB/CUF EN6 | 60 | G1 |
| Starling Pl GSTN WD25 | 55 | K8 |
| Starling Rd CROY/NA CRO | 204 | D6 |
| Starmans Cl DAGW RM9 | 143 | P5 |
| Star Rd WAP E1W | 13 | M8 |
| HGDN/ICK UB10 | 132 | D6 |
| ISLW TW7 | 154 | C8 |
| WKENS W14 | 14 | C9 |
| Starrock La COUL/CHIP CR5 | 240 | B6 |
| Starrock Rd COUL/CHIP CR5 | 240 | C5 |
| Star St BAY/PAD W2 | 9 | M5 |
| WARE SG12 | 26 | D2 |
| Starts Cl ORP BR6 | 226 | A6 |
| Starts Hill Av ORP BR6 | 226 | B2 |
| Starts Hill Rd ORP BR6 | 226 | A1 |
| Starveall Cl WDR/YW UB7 | 132 | A2 |
| Starwood Cl BF/WBF KT14 | 215 | M7 |
| Starwood Ct DTCH/LGLY SL3 | 149 | P2 |
| Star Yd LINN WC2A | 12 | A1 |
| State Farm Av ORP BR6 | 226 | E1 |
| Staten Gdns TWK TW1 | 176 | E1 |
| Statham Gv STNW/STAM N16 | 119 | M9 |
| UED N18 | 99 | M6 |
| Station Ap ALP/SUD HA0 | 134 | G1 |
| BAR EN5 | 77 | M8 |
| BECK BR3 | 204 | A1 |
| BELMT SM2 | 221 | H4 |
| BF/WBF KT14 | 215 | K8 |
| BKHH IG9 | 102 | A5 |
| BKHTH/KID SE3 | 161 | N9 |
| BXLYHN DA7 | 164 | D1 |
| BXLYHN DA7 | 163 | P8 |
| CAMTN NW1 * | 10 | C2 |
| CFSP/GDCR SL9 | 110 | A3 |
| CHES/WCR EN8 * | 62 | D10 |
| CHST BR7 | 206 | D1 |
| CHST BR7 | 184 | B9 |
| COUL/CHIP CR5 | 240 | A4 |
| CROY/NA CRO * | 203 | L9 |
| CTHM CR3 | 241 | P3 |
| DEN/HRF UB9 | 110 | A5 |
| DORK RH4 | 272 | E1 |
| DTCH/LGLY SL3 | 150 | D1 |
| EA W5 | 135 | L8 |
| EDGW HA8 | 96 | D2 |
| EGH TW20 | 172 | B8 |
| EPP CM16 | 65 | K7 |
| ESH/CLAY KT10 | 218 | C2 |
| EYN DA4 | 209 | L10 |
| EYN DA4 | 210 | A2 |
| FBAR/BDGN N11 | 98 | A6 |
| FNCH N3 | 97 | K3 |
| GDDL GU7 | 267 | L10 |
| GPK RM2 | 125 | J2 |
| GVW DA11 | 189 | N9 |
| HARH RM3 | 105 | K5 |
| HARP AL5 | 20 | A6 |
| HART DA3 | 211 | K2 |
| HAYES BR2 | 205 | P5 |
| HDN NW4 | 116 | D4 |
| HERT WAT SG14 | 51 | J3 |
| HHS/BOV HP3 | 35 | M7 |
| HHW HP1 | 35 | N1 |
| HOLWY N7 | 118 | D7 |
| HPTN TW12 | 175 | L5 |
| HRW HA1 | 114 | E4 |
| HSLW TW3 | 154 | A10 |
| IL IG1 | 122 | F7 |
| KGLGY WD4 | 53 | J1 |
| KUT/HW KT1 | 8 | E8 |
| LCOL/BKTW AL2 | 55 | P1 |
| LEW SE13 | 183 | J1 |
| LHD/OX KT22 | 236 | F5 |
| LOU IG10 | 81 | L2 |
| MED DA13 | 189 | J7 |
| MLHL NW7 | 96 | F2 |
| MNPK E12 | 122 | A9 |
| NWMAL KT3 | 200 | D5 |
| ORP BR6 | 207 | J9 |
| ORP BR6 | 225 | J1 |
| OXHEY WD19 | 91 | M2 |
| PIN HA5 | 113 | M1 |
| PUR/KEN CR8 * | 223 | H7 |
| RAD WD7 | 74 | F1 |
| RCH/KEW TW9 | 155 | M7 |
| RKW/CH/CXG WD3 | 70 | F9 |
| RSEV TN14 | 247 | K2 |
| RSLP HA4 | 112 | F6 |
| SAND/SEL CR2 | 223 | P5 |
| SHPTN TW17 | 196 | A4 |
| STA TW18 | 195 | K1 |
| STMC/STPC BR5 | 207 | K4 |
| STRHM/NOR SW16 | 180 | D9 |
| SUN TW16 | 197 | H1 |
| SURB KT6 | 191 | N10 |
| SWFD E18 | 101 | N10 |
| SWLY BR8 | 208 | B7 |
| SYD SE26 | 182 | G5 |
| VW GU25 | 235 | N6 |
| WALTH E17 | 120 | C5 |
| WAN E11 | 104 | F10 |
| WAT WD18 | 72 | B6 |
| WDR/YW UB7 | 131 | P10 |

| | | | |
|---|---|---|---|
| WELL DA16 | 163 | J8 |
| WEY KT13 | 216 | B3 |
| WFD IG8 * | 101 | P7 |
| WLSDN NW10 | 136 | C5 |
| WOKS/MYFD GU22 | 232 | C3 |
| Station Ap East REDH RH1 | 276 | A2 |
| Station Approach Rd | | |
| CHSWK W4 | 155 | P6 |
| HORL RH6 | 280 | C7 |
| KWD/TDW/WH KT20 | 238 | C10 |
| TIL RM18 | 158 | D6 |
| TIL RM18 | 171 | K8 |
| TOTM N17 | 119 | P7 |
| TWK TW1 | 176 | B7 |
| UPMR RM14 | 126 | E4 |
| UX/CGN UB8 | 131 | M6 |
| WALTH E17 | 120 | D4 |
| WAT WD17 | 73 | J6 |
| WCHMN N21 | 99 | J2 |
| WDGN N22 | 98 | E9 |
| WDR/YW UB7 | 151 | P2 |
| WIM/MER SW19 | 179 | L2 |
| WLSDN NW10 | 136 | C5 |
| Station Ar | | |
| GU GU1 | 267 | P5 |
| Station Wy BKHH IG9 | 102 | A5 |
| CHEAM SM3 | 221 | H4 |
| CRAWE RH10 | 283 | D8 |
| ESH/CLAY KT10 | 218 | D3 |
| STAL AL1 | 38 | C6 |
| Station Yd ASHF TW15 * | 174 | A7 |
| KWD/TDW/WH KT20 | 239 | J8 |
| PUR/KEN CR8 * | 223 | J7 |
| RSLP HA4 * | 112 | E7 |
| STHL UB1 | 133 | N1 |
| TWK TW1 | 176 | B7 |
| Staunton Rd KUTN/CMB KT2 | 177 | L10 |
| SLN SL2 | 129 | J7 |
| Staunton St DEPT SE8 | 141 | P9 |
| Staveley Cl HOLWY N7 * | 118 | E9 |
| PECK SE15 | 160 | B7 |
| Staveley Ct STAL AL1 | 38 | G7 |
| Staveley Gdns CHSWK W4 | 156 | A6 |
| Staveley Rd ASHF TW15 | 174 | D3 |
| CHSWK W4 | 155 | P5 |
| Staveley | | |
| WOKN/KNAP GU21 | 231 | K3 |
| Staverton Rd CRICK NW2 | 81 | P4 |
| EMPK RM11 | 125 | L4 |
| Stave Yard Rd | | |
| BERM/RHTH SE16 | 141 | J6 |
| Stavordale Rd CAR SM5 | 201 | P8 |
| HBRY N5 | 118 | J9 |
| Stayne End VW GU25 | 193 | N6 |
| Stayner's Rd WCHPL E1 | 13 | J1 |
| Stayton Rd SUT SM1 | 201 | K10 |
| Steadfast Rd KUT/HW KT1 | 199 | J1 |
| Stead St WALW SE17 | 18 | G6 |
| Steam Farm La | | |
| EBED/NFELT TW14 | 152 | G10 |
| Stean St HACK E8 | 7 | L5 |
| Stebbing Wy BARK IG11 | 143 | K4 |
| Stebondale St POP/IOD E14 | 161 | H4 |
| Stedly SCUP DA14 * | 185 | K7 |
| Stedman Cl BXLY DA5 | 187 | H2 |
| HGDN/ICK UB10 | 112 | B8 |
| Steed Cl EMPK RM11 | 125 | J7 |
| Steedman St WALW SE17 | 18 | E6 |
| Steeds Rd MUSWH N10 | 98 | A8 |
| Steeds Wy LOU IG10 | 82 | B7 |
| Steel Ap BARK IG11 | 143 | L5 |
| Steele Av RDART DA2 | 188 | F1 |
| Steele Rd CHSWK W4 | 155 | P2 |
| ISLW TW7 | 154 | F10 |
| TOTM N17 | 119 | M4 |
| WAN E11 | 121 | K9 |
| WLSDN NW10 | 135 | P4 |
| Steele's Ms South HAMP NW3 | 4 | B2 |
| Steele's Rd HAMP NW3 | 4 | A2 |
| Steeles Studios HAMP NW3 * | 4 | A2 |
| Steel's La LHD/OX KT22 | 218 | B10 |
| WCHPL E1 | 140 | D8 |
| Steep Cl ORP BR6 | 227 | J3 |
| Steep Hl CHOB/PIR GU24 | 213 | H4 |
| CROY/NA CRO | 224 | B5 |
| STRHM/NOR SW16 | 180 | D5 |
| Steeplands BUSH WD23 | 94 | A1 |
| Steeple Cl FUL/PGN SW6 | 157 | H9 |
| WIM/MER SW19 | 178 | C10 |
| Steeple Heights Dr | | |
| BH/WHM TW16 | | |
| Steeple Point ASC SL5 | 244 | A3 |
| Steeplestone Cl UED N18 | 99 | K6 |
| Steeple Wk IS N1 * | 6 | F5 |
| Steeple Wy BRWN CM15 | 86 | G2 |
| Steerforth St | | |
| WAND/EARL SW18 | 179 | L5 |
| Steering Cl ED N9 | 100 | B2 |
| Steers Md MTCM CR4 | 180 | B8 |
| Steers Wy BERM/RHTH SE16 | 160 | D1 |
| Stella Cl UX/CGN UB8 | 132 | C7 |
| Stella Rd TOOT SW17 | 180 | A9 |
| Stelling Rd ERITH DA8 | 164 | B6 |
| Stellman Cl CLPT E5 | 119 | P9 |
| Stembridge Rd PGE/AN SE20 | 204 | A4 |
| Sten Cl PEND EN3 | 80 | F3 |
| Stenning Av SLH/COR SS17 | 169 | L1 |
| Stepbridge Pth | | |
| WOKN/KNAP GU21 | 232 | A3 |
| Stepgates CHERT KT16 | 195 | L7 |
| Stepgates Cl CHERT KT16 | 195 | L7 |
| Stephan Cl HACK E8 | 7 | M3 |
| Stephen Av RAIN RM13 | 145 | H1 |
| Stephen Cl CRAWW RH11 | 283 | G6 |
| EGH TW20 | 172 | F9 |
| ORP BR6 | 207 | H10 |
| Stephendale Rd | | |
| FUL/PGN SW6 | 157 | L9 |
| Stephen Ms FITZ W1T | 11 | J1 |
| Stephen Pl CLAP SW4 | 158 | D9 |
| Stephens Cl HARH RM3 | 105 | K6 |
| Stephenson Av TIL RM18 | 168 | D7 |
| Stephenson Cl | | |
| WELL DA16 | 163 | J8 |
| Stephenson Ct SL SL1 * | 149 | L1 |
| Stephenson Dr WDSR SL4 | 148 | G1 |
| Stephenson Pl CRAWE RH10 | 284 | C7 |
| Stephenson Rd GUW GU2 | 249 | H9 |
| HNWL W7 | 135 | P3 |
| WALTH E17 | 120 | G3 |
| WHTN TW2 | 175 | P5 |
| Stephenson St CAN/RD E16 | 141 | N5 |
| WLSDN NW10 | 137 | H2 |
| Stephenson Wy BUSH WD23 | 91 | H1 |
| CAMTN NW1 | 11 | H1 |
| CRAWE RH10 | 284 | C7 |
| WATN WD24 | 73 | J5 |
| Stephen's Rd SRTFD E15 | 141 | H8 |
| Stephen St FITZ W1T | 11 | J3 |
| Stepney Cswy WCHPL E1 | 140 | E8 |
| Stepney Gn WCHPL E1 | 140 | E7 |
| Stepney High St WCHPL E1 | 140 | F7 |
| Stepney Wy WCHPL E1 | 140 | C7 |
| The Steps EHSLY KT24 * | 253 | L5 |
| Sterling Av PIN HA5 | 113 | L5 |
| EDGW HA8 | 95 | J10 |
| WLSDN NW10 | 136 | D2 |
| Sterling Cl WLSDN NW10 | 136 | D2 |
| Sterling Gdns NWCR SE14 | 160 | D5 |

| | | | |
|---|---|---|---|
| Sterling Pk CRAWE RH10 * | 284 | C2 |
| Sterling Pl EA W5 | 155 | K3 |
| WEY KT13 | 216 | F1 |
| Sterling Rd ENC/FH EN2 | 79 | L5 |
| Sterling Wy (North Circular) | | |
| UED N18 | 99 | G6 |
| Stern Cl BARK IG11 | 143 | M4 |
| Sterndale Rd WKENS W14 * | 156 | C2 |
| Sterne St SHB W12 | 156 | G1 |
| Sternhall La PECK SE15 | 159 | P9 |
| Sternhold Av | | |
| BRXS/STRHM SW2 | 180 | A5 |
| Sterry Dr DAGE RM10 | 124 | B10 |
| Sterry Dr HOR/WEW KT19 | 220 | B3 |
| THDIT KT7 | 198 | D6 |
| Sterry Gdns DAGE RM10 | 124 | B10 |
| Sterry Rd BARK IG11 | 143 | J3 |
| Sterry St STHWK SE1 | 18 | G2 |
| Steucers La FSTH SE23 | 182 | G4 |
| Steve Biko Ct CAT SE6 | 182 | A7 |
| Steve Biko La CAT SE6 | 182 | C4 |
| Steve Biko Rd HOLWY N7 | 119 | H6 |
| Steve Biko Wy HSLW TW3 | 153 | P7 |
| Stevedale Rd WELL DA16 | 164 | D3 |
| Stevedore St WAP E1W | 140 | A10 |
| Stevenage Crs BORE WD6 | 75 | K2 |
| Stevenage Ri HHNE HP2 | 36 | A2 |
| Stevenage Rd EHAM E6 | 142 | D4 |
| FUL/PGN SW6 | 156 | G7 |
| Stevens Av HOM E9 | 140 | C1 |
| Stevens Cl BECK BR3 | 182 | F9 |
| BXLY DA5 | 186 | E7 |
| EW KT17 | 220 | B8 |
| HPTN TW12 | 175 | H9 |
| PIN HA5 | 113 | K3 |
| POTB/CUF EN6 | 58 | G8 |
| RDART DA2 | 188 | B2 |
| Stevens Gn BUSH WD23 | 94 | B2 |
| Stevens La ESH/CLAY KT10 | 218 | G6 |
| Stevenson Cl BAR EN5 | 77 | N10 |
| ERITH DA8 | 165 | A4 |
| Stevens Crs | | |
| BERM/RHTH SE16 | 19 | P7 |
| Stevenson Rd SLN SL2 | 109 | J7 |
| Stevens Rd PUR/KEN CR8 | 223 | L1 |
| Stevens Rd BCTR RM8 | 123 | L7 |
| Stevens St CHIG IG7 | 19 | K3 |
| Stevens St STHWK SE1 | 19 | K3 |
| Stevention Rd WLSDN NW10 | 136 | C9 |
| Steward Cl CHES/WCR EN8 | 62 | D4 |
| Stewards Cl EPP CM16 | 65 | K9 |
| Stewards Green Rd EPP CM16 | 65 | L9 |
| Stewart KWD/TDW/WH KT20 | 238 | G7 |
| Stewart Av SHPTN TW17 | 196 | B5 |
| SL SL1 | 129 | L7 |
| UPMR RM14 | 126 | A8 |
| Stewart Cl ABLGY WD5 | 54 | D5 |
| CDALE/KGS NW9 | 115 | P4 |
| CHST BR7 | 184 | E8 |
| HPTN TW12 | 175 | M9 |
| WOKN/KNAP GU21 | 231 | L3 |
| Stewart Quay HYS/HAR UB3 | 152 | F1 |
| Stewart Rd HARP AL5 | 20 | A1 |
| SRTFD E15 | 121 | J9 |
| Stewartsby Cl UED N18 | 99 | K6 |
| Stewarts Dr SLN SL2 | 108 | G10 |
| Stewart's Gv CHEL SW3 | 15 | M7 |
| Stewart's Rd VX/NE SW8 | 158 | D7 |
| Stewart St POP/IOD E14 | 161 | H1 |
| Stew La BLKFR EC4V | 12 | E7 |
| Steyne Rd ACT W3 | 135 | N10 |
| Steyning Cl CRAWE RH10 | 283 | P5 |
| PUR/KEN CR8 | 241 | J2 |
| Steyning Gv ELTH/MOT SE9 | 184 | C7 |
| Steynings Wy | | |
| NFNCH/WDSPK N12 | 97 | K5 |
| Steyning Wy HSLWW TW4 | 153 | K10 |
| Steyton Rd BXLY DA5 | 185 | P5 |
| Stickland Rd BELV DA17 | 164 | B3 |
| Stickleton Cl GFD/PVL UB6 | 134 | A5 |
| Stifford Clays Rd | | |
| CDW/CHF RM16 | 147 | L10 |
| Stifford Hl CDW/CHF RM16 | 147 | J10 |
| SOCK/AV RM15 | 147 | L10 |
| Stifford Rd SOCK/AV RM15 | 146 | C10 |
| Stile Cft HLWS CM18 | 47 | K5 |
| Stilecroft Gdns ALP/SUD HA0 | 114 | G8 |
| Stile Hall Gdns CHSWK W4 | 155 | M4 |
| Stile Pth SUN TW16 | 197 | H3 |
| Stile Rd DTCH/LGLY SL3 | 150 | A3 |
| Stiles Cl ERITH DA8 | 164 | C4 |
| HAYES BR2 | 205 | C6 |
| Stillingfleet Rd BARN SW13 | 156 | E4 |
| Stillington St WEST SW1P | 17 | M5 |
| Stillness Rd FSTH SE23 | 182 | D2 |
| Stilton Pth BORE WD6 | 75 | M4 |
| Stilwell Dr UX/CGN UB8 | 132 | A6 |
| Stipularis Dr YEAD UB4 | 133 | H3 |
| Stirling Av PIN HA5 | 113 | L5 |
| SHPTN TW17 | 196 | F3 |
| WLGTN SM6 | 222 | F4 |
| Stirling Cl BNSTD SM7 | 239 | J3 |
| CRAWE RH10 | 284 | C2 |
| RAIN RM13 | 145 | J5 |
| SCUP DA14 | 185 | H7 |
| STRHM/NOR SW16 | 202 | D1 |
| UX/CGN UB8 | 131 | M5 |
| WDSR SL4 | 148 | G1 |
| Stirling Cr DART CR3 | 227 | L2 |
| ORP BR6 | 227 | K2 |
| Stirling Gv HSLW TW3 | 154 | C8 |
| Stirling Rd ACT W3 | 155 | H3 |
| BRXN/ST SW9 | 158 | F8 |
| GUW GU2 | 249 | G10 |
| HYS/HAR UB3 | 133 | J9 |
| KTN/HRWW/WS HA3 | 114 | F1 |
| PLSTW E13 | 141 | M4 |
| SL SL1 | 131 | F7 |
| TOTM N17 | 119 | D1 |
| WALTH E17 | 120 | D9 |
| WDGN N22 | 99 | J9 |
| WHTN TW2 | 175 | P5 |
| Stirling Wk BRYLDS KT5 | 199 | N6 |
| NWMAL KT3 | 199 | P4 |
| Stirling Wy ABLGY WD5 | 55 | H6 |
| BORE WD6 | 76 | A10 |
| CROY/NA CRO | 202 | G7 |
| WGCE AL7 | 23 | P5 |
| Stirrup Wy CRAWE RH10 | 284 | D6 |
| Stites Hill Rd COUL/CHIP CR5 | 241 | J6 |
| St Ives Pl RYLN/HDSTN HA2 | 113 | N8 |
| St John's St SL1 | | |
| St Martin-in-the-Fields | | |
| CHCR WC2N * | 11 | L8 |
| Stoat Cl HERT/BAY SG13 | 25 | P1 |
| Stoats Nest Rd | | |
| COUL/CHIP CR5 | 240 | F1 |
| Stoats West Village | | |
| COUL/CHIP CR5 | 240 | F1 |
| Stockbreach Cl HAT AL10 | 40 | A3 |
| Stockbreach Rd HAT AL10 | 40 | A3 |
| Stockbridge Cl CHESW EN7 | 61 | M2 |
| Stockbury Rd CROY/NA CRO | 204 | B6 |
| Stockdale Rd WDSR SL4 | 148 | G3 |
| Stockdove Wy GFD/PVL UB6 | 134 | C3 |
| Stocker Gdns DAGW RM9 | 143 | M2 |
| Stockers Farm Rd | | |
| RKW/CH/CXG WD3 | 91 | M4 |
| Stockers La | | |
| WOKS/MYFD GU22 | 232 | C6 |
| Stockfield HORL RH6 | 280 | C2 |
| Stockfield Av HOD EN11 | 44 | F1 |
| Stockfield Rd ESH/CLAY KT10 | 218 | D2 |
| STRHM/NOR SW16 | 180 | A5 |
| Stockford Av MLHL NW7 | 96 | C6 |
| Stockhams Cl SAND/SEL CR2 | 223 | L6 |
| Stockholm Rd | | |
| BERM/RHTH SE16 | 160 | B4 |
| Stockholm Wy WAP E1W * | 139 | P4 |
| Stockhurst Cl PUT/ROE SW15 | 156 | G9 |
| Stockingswater La PEND EN3 | 80 | D7 |
| Stockland Rd ROMW/RG RM7 | 124 | E4 |

Stockley Cl WDR/YW UB7 152 C1
Stockley Farm Rd
WDR/YW UB7 152 C2
Stockley Rd UX/CGN UB8 132 B8
WDR/YW UB7 152 C2
Stock Orchard Crs
HOLWY N7 * 118 G9
Stock Orchard St HOLWY N7 118 G10
Stockport Rd
RKW/CH/CXG WD3 90 F1
STRHM/NOR SW16 202 E1
Stocks Cl HORL RH6 280 C5
Stocksfield BRWN CM15 86 E3
Stocksfield Rd WALTH E17 * 121 H1
Stocks La BRWN CM15 86 E3
Stocks Meadow HHNE HP2 36 B5
Stocks Pl HGDN/ICK UB10 132 B3
POP/IOD E14 140 E9
Stock St PLSTW E13 141 M4
Stockton Cl BAR EN5 77 M8
Stockton Gdns MLHL NW7 96 A4
TOTM N17 99 K8
Stockton Rd REIG RH2 275 K3
TOTM N17 99 K8
UED N18 99 P7
Stockwell Av BRXN/ST SW9 158 G9
Stockwell Cl BMLY BR1 205 N2
CHESW EN7 61 P4
Stockwell Gdns BRXN/ST SW9 158 G7
Stockwell Gn BRXN/ST SW9 158 G8
Stockwell La BRXN/ST SW9 158 G8
CHESW EN7 62 A4
Stockwell Park Crs
BRXN/ST SW9 158 G8
Stockwell Park Rd
BRXN/ST SW9 158 G7
Stockwell Park Wk
BRXN/ST SW9 158 G9
Stockwell Rd BRXN/ST SW9 158 G8
Stockwell St GNWCH SE10 161 H5
Stockwell Ter BRXN/ST SW9 158 G7
Stocton Cl GU GU1 249 P9
Stocton Rd GU GU1 249 P9
Stodart Rd PGE/AN SE20 204 B1
Stofield Gdns ELTH/MOT SE9 184 A6
Stoford Cl WIM/MER SW19 179 H4
Stoke Av BARK/HLT IG6 103 K7
Stoke Cl COB KT11 235 N2
Stoke Common Rd SLN SL2 109 M9
Stoke Cots LHD/OX KT22 * 236 C7
Stoke Court Dr SLN SL2 129 K3
Stoke Flds GU GU1 250 A10
Stoke Gdns SL SL1 129 K10
Stoke Gn SLN SL2 129 M6
Stoke Gv GU GU1 250 A10
Stoke Ms GU GU1 268 A1
Stoke Mill Cl GU GU1 250 A8
Stokenchurch St
FUL/PGN SW6 157 L7
Stoke Newington Church St
STNW/STAM N16 119 L8
Stoke Newington Common
STNW/STAM N16 119 N7
Stoke Newington High St
STNW/STAM N16 119 N8
Stoke Newington Rd HACK E8 119 N10
Stoke Park Av SLN SL2 129 H5
Stoke Park Ct GU GU1 * 250 A10
Stoke Pl WLSDN NW10 136 C5
Stoke Poges La SL SL1 129 K10
Stoke Ridings
KWD/TDW/WH KT20 * 238 G9
Stoke Rd COB KT11 235 M2
GU GU1 250 A9
KUTN/CMB KT2 177 P10
RAIN RM13 145 L4
SLN SL2 129 L8
WOT/HER KT12 197 K10
Stokesay SLN SL2 129 M8
Stokesby Rd CHSGTN KT9 219 L3
Stokes Cl CRAWE RH10 284 D10
Stokesheath Rd LHD/OX KT22 218 B7
Stokesley St SHB W12 136 C8
Stokes Ridings
KWD/TDW/WH KT20 238 G9
Stokes Rd CROY/NA CR0 204 C6
EHAM E6 142 B6
Stoke Wd SLN SL2 109 L9
Stoll Cl CRICK NW2 116 F8
Stompond La WOT/HER KT12 197 H9
Stomp Rd SL SL1 128 A7
Stonard Rd BCTR RM8 123 L10
PLMGR N13 99 H4
Stonards Hl EPP CM16 65 M7
LOU IG10 82 C10
Stondon Pk FSTH SE23 182 D2
Stonebanks WOT/HER KT12 197 H7
Stonebridge Fld WDSR SL4 148 G4
Stonebridge Flds RGUE GU4 268 A7
Stonebridge Pk WLSDN NW10 136 A2
Stonebridge Rd GVW DA11 189 N1
SEVS/STOTM N15 119 M3
Stonebridge Wy WBLY HA9 135 N1
Stonebridge Whf RGUE GU4 268 A7
Stone Blds LINN WC2A 11 P4
Stone Castle Dr RDART DA2 188 F2
Stonechat Sq EHAM E6 142 B7
Stone Cl BCTR RM8 124 A7
CLAP SW4 158 D8
WDR/YW UB7 132 A10
Stonecot Cl CHEAM SM3 201 H8
Stonecot Hl CHEAM SM3 201 H8
Stone Ct CRAWE RH10 284 E8
Stonecourt Cl HORL RH6 280 D4
Stone Crs EBED/NFELT TW14 174 G3
Stonecroft AMS HP6 68 B1
Stonecroft Av IVER SL0 131 H8
Stonecroft Cl BAR EN5 76 E8
Stonecroft Rd ERITH DA8 164 D6
Stonecroft Wy CROY/NA CR0 202 F7
Stonecrop Cl CDALE/KGS NW9 116 A1
CRAWW RH11 283 K10
Stonecrop Rd RGUE GU4 250 F8
Stonecross STAL AL1 38 D5
Stonecross Rd HAT AL10 40 E2
Stonecutter St
FLST/FETLN EC4A 12 C5
Stonefield Cl BXLYHN DA7 164 B9
CRAWE RH10 283 N8
RSLP HA4 113 M10
Stonefield St IS N1 6 B5
Stonefield Wy CHARL SE7 162 A6
RSLP HA4 113 L10
Stonegate Cl STMC/STPC BR5 207 M3
Stone Gv EDGW HA8 95 K5
Stonegrove Gdns EDGW HA8 95 K6
Stonehall Av IL IG1 122 B4
Stone Hall Gdns KENS W8 * 14 G4
Stone Hall Pl KENS W8 * 14 G4
Stone Hall Rd WCHMH N21 98 G1
Stoneham Rd
FBAR/BDGN N11 98 D6
Stonehill Cl GT/LBKH KT23 253 P1
MORT/ESHN SW14 178 A1
Stonehill Crs CHERT KT16 214 B3
Stonehill Ga ASC SL5 * 192 C6
Stonehill Rd CHERT KT16 214 A4
CHSWK W4 155 M4
MORT/ESHN SW14 177 P1
Stonehills WGCW AL8 22 G5
Stonehills Ct DUL SE21 181 M6
Stonehill Woods Pk
SCUP DA14 * 186 C9
Stonehorse Rd PEND EN3 80 B9
Stone House Ct LVPST EC2M 13 K5
Stone House Gdns
CTHM CR3 259 M1
Stonehouse La PUR RM19 166 D4
RSEV TN14 227 N5
Stonehouse Rd RSEV TN14 227 N5
Stoneings La RSEV TN14 245 J4
Stonelea Rd HHS/BOV HP3 36 A9
Stoneleigh Av EN EN1 80 A4
WPK KT4 200 D10
Stoneleigh Broadway
EW KT17 220 D2
Stoneleigh Cl CHES/WCR EN8 62 C9
Stoneleigh Crs
HOR/WEW KT19 220 D2
Stoneleigh Dr HOD EN11 26 G10
Stoneleigh Pk WEY KT13 216 D3
Stoneleigh Park Av
CROY/NA CR0 204 C6
Stoneleigh Park Rd
HOR/WEW KT19 220 C3
Stoneleigh Pl NTGHL W11 136 G9
Stoneleigh Rd BMLY BR1 206 E3
CAR SM5 201 P7
CLAY IG5 122 B1
OXTED RH8 262 B6
TOTM N17 99 N10
Stoneleigh St NTGHL W11 136 G9
Stoneleigh Ter ARCH N19 118 C7
Stonell's Rd TOOT SW17 179 M6
Stonely Crs SWCM DA10 167 H10
Stonemasons Cl
SEVS/STOTM N15 * 119 L2
Stoneness Rd WTHK RM20 166 G5
Stonenest St FSBYPK N4 118 G6
Stone Park Av BECK BR3 204 F4
Stone Pl WPK KT4 200 D9
Stone Place Rd RDART DA2 188 D1
Stoners Cl HORL RH6 279 N7
Stones Cross Rd SWLY BR8 208 D5
Stones End St STHWK SE1 18 E2
Stones La DORK RH4 272 B3
Stone's Rd EW KT17 220 B7
Stone St GVW DA11 190 E2
Stoneswood Rd OXTED RH8 261 N6
Stonewall EHAM E6 142 D7
Stonewood RDART DA2 189 H6
Stonewood Rd ERITH DA8 164 F4
Stoney Aly WOOL/PLUM SE18 162 D8
Stoneyard La POP/IOD E14 140 G9
Stoney Brook GUW GU2 249 K9
Stoney Cl BERK HP4 33 L3
Stoney Cft COUL/CHIP CR5 240 D8
Stoneycroft HHW HP1 35 K6
WGCE AL7 23 K4
Stoneycroft Cl LEE/GVPK SE12 183 L3
Stoneycroft Rd WFD IG8 102 B7
Stoneydown WALTH E17 120 D2
Stoneydown Av WALTH E17 120 D2
Stoneyfield CFSP/GDCR SL9 109 P6
Stoneyfield Rd
COUL/CHIP CR5 240 G3
Stoneyfields Gdns EDGW HA8 95 P5
Stoneyfields La EDGW HA8 95 P6
Stoney Gv CSHM HP5 51 J6
Stoneyland Ct EGH TW20 172 C8
Stoneylands Rd EGH TW20 172 C8
Stoney La CSHM HP5 32 E8
HDTCH EC3A 13 K5
HHS/BOV HP3 52 E3
HHW HP1 34 E9
KGLGY WD4 53 H6
NRWD SE19 181 N9
SLN SL2 128 F3
Stoney Meade SL SL1 128 G10
Stoney St STHWK SE1 12 G9
Stonhouse St CLAP SW4 158 D9
Stonnell's Rd BTSEA SW11 180 A1
Stonny Cft ASHTD KT21 237 L3
Stonor Rd WKENS W14 14 C6
Stonycroft Cl PEND EN3 80 D6
Stony Hl ESH/CLAY KT10 217 N4
Stony La CHONG CM5 49 J9
CSHM HP5 70 B3
Stony Pth LOU IG10 82 C5
Stonyshotts WAB EN9 63 K10
Stony Wd HLWS CM18 46 G2
Stopes St PECK SE15 159 N6
Stopford Rd PLSTW E13 141 M3
WALW SE17 * 18 D8
Stopham Rd CRAWE RH10 284 D10
Store Rd CAN/RD E16 162 D1
Storers Quay POP/IOD E14 161 J3
Store St GWRST WC1E 11 J4
SRTFD E15 121 J10
Storey Rd HGT N6 118 A4
WALTH E17 120 E2
Storey's Ga STJSPK SW1H 17 K2
Storey St HHS/BOV HP3 35 N10
Stories Ms CMBW SE5 * 159 M8
Stories Rd CMBW SE5 159 M9
Stork Rd FSTGT E7 141 L1
Storksmead Rd EDGW HA8 96 B8
Storks Rd BERM/RHTH SE16 19 P4
Stormont Rd BTSEA SW11 158 B10
HGT N6 118 A5
Stormont Wy CHSGTN KT9 219 H2
Stormount Dr HYS/HAR UB3 152 D1
Stornaway Rd DTCH/LGLY SL3 150 F3
Stornaway Strd GVE DA12 191 J7
Stornoway HHS/BOV HP3 36 C8
Storrington Rd CROY/NA CR0 203 N8
Storr's La RGUW GU3 231 H10
Stortford Rd HOD EN11 44 G2
Stort Mi HLW CM20 29 L5
Stort Valley Wy CHONG CM5 48 E6
HLWW/ROY CM19 27 M10
HLWW/ROY CM19 45 M2
SBW CM21 29 N4
Story St IS N1 5 N4
Stothard St WCHPL E1 140 B6
Stott Cl WAND/EARL SW18 179 N2
Stoughton Av CHEAM SM3 220 G2
Stoughton Cl LBTH SE11 17 P6
PUT/ROE SW15 178 D4
Stoughton Rd GUW GU2 249 M7
Stour Av NWDGN UB2 153 P2
Stourcliffe St MBLAR W1H 10 A6
Stour Cl HAYES BR2 225 P1
SL SL1 148 G2
Stourhead Cl WIM/MER SW19 178 G3
Stourhead Gdns RYNPK SW20 200 D3
Stour Rd BOW E3 140 F2
CDW/CHF RM16 168 D4
DAGE RM10 124 B7
DART DA1 165 H9
Stourton Av FELT TW13 175 N7
Stour Wy UPMR RM14 126 D4
Stovell Rd WDSR SL4 148 G6
Stowage DEPT SE8 160 G5
The Stowage DEPT SE8 160 F5
Stow Crs WALTH E17 100 D9
Stowe Crs RSLP HA4 112 C4
Stowe Gdns ED N9 99 N2
Stowell Av CROY/NA CR0 225 J6
Stowe Rd ORP BR6 227 L1
SHB W12 156 E1
SL SL1 128 D9
The Stow HLW CM20 29 J9
Stowting Rd ORP BR6 227 H1
Stox Md KTN/HRWW/WS HA3 94 C9
Stracey Rd WLSDN NW10 136 A3
Strachan Pl RYNPK SW20 178 F9
Stradbroke Dr CHIG IG7 102 E7
Stradbroke Gv BKHH IG9 102 A2
CLAY IG5 122 B1
Stradbroke Pk CHIG IG7 102 E7
Stradbroke Rd HBRY N5 119 K9
Stradbrook Cl
RYLN/HDSTN HA2 113 N8
Stradella Rd HNHL SE24 181 K2
Strafford Cl POTB/CUF EN6 59 K8
Strafford Ga POTB/CUF EN6 59 K8
Strafford Rd ACT W3 155 P1
BAR EN5 77 H7
HSLW TW3 153 N9
TWK TW1 176 F3
Strafford St POP/IOD E14 160 F1
Strahan Rd BOW E3 140 D4
Straight Rd HARH RM3 105 J6
WDSR SL4 171 N2
Straightsmouth GNWCH SE10 161 H6
The Straight NWDGN UB2 153 L1
Strait Rd EHAM E6 142 B9
The Straits WAB EN9 62 G8
Straker's Rd EDUL SE22 160 A10
Strand CHCR WC2N 11 M8
Strandburgh Pl HHS/BOV HP3 36 C8
Strand Cl CRAWE RH10 284 E9
EPSOM KT18 238 A5
Strand Dr RCH/KEW TW9 155 M6
Strandfield Cl
WOOL/PLUM SE18 163 H4
Strand-On-The-Green
CHSWK W4 155 M5
Strand Pl UED N18 99 M5
Strangeways WAT WD17 72 F2
Strangways Ter WKENS W14 14 C3
Stranraer Gdns SL SL1 129 K10
Stranraer Wy IS N1 5 N4
Strasburg Rd BTSEA SW11 158 B7
Stratfield Dr BROX EN10 44 D5
Stratfield Park Cl
WCHMH N21 99 J1
Stratfield Rd BORE WD6 75 L7
SL SL1 149 M1
Stratford Av HGDN/ICK UB10 132 A4
Stratford Cl BARK IG11 143 K2
DAGE RM10 144 D2
SLN SL2 128 C6
Stratford Ct NWMAL KT3 200 A4
Stratford Gv PUT/ROE SW15 156 G10
Stratford House Av BMLY BR1 206 B3
Stratford Pl OXSTW W1C 10 E6
Stratford Rd HTHAIR TW6 174 C2
KENS W8 14 F4
NWDGN UB2 153 M3
PLSTW E13 141 M3
THHTH CR7 203 H4
WAT WD17 73 H6
YEAD UB4 133 J6
Stratford Studios KENS W8 14 F4
Stratford Vls CAMTN NW1 5 H3
Stratford Wy HHS/BOV HP3 35 L9
LCOL/BKTW AL2 55 N5
WAT WD17 72 G6
Strathan Cl WAND/EARL SW18 179 H2
Strathaven Rd LEE/GVPK SE12 183 N2
Strathblaine Rd BTSEA SW11 179 N1
Strathbrook Rd
STRHM/NOR SW16 180 G10
Strathcona Av GT/LBKH KT23 253 M4
Strathcona Gdns
WOKN/KNAP GU21 231 H5
Strathcona Rd WBLY HA9 115 J7
Strathdale STRHM/NOR SW16 180 G8
Strathdon Dr TOOT SW17 179 N6
Strathearn Av HYS/HAR UB3 152 G6
WHTN TW2 176 B4
Strathearn Cots
TRDG/WHET N20 * 97 K4
Strathearn Pl BAY/PAD W2 9 N7
Strathearn Rd SUT SM1 221 K2
WIM/MER SW19 179 K8
Stratheden Rd
BKHTH/KID SE3 161 M7
Strathfield Gdns BARK IG11 142 G1
Strathleven Rd
BRXS/STRHM SW2 180 F1
Strathmore TIL RM18 169 M3
Strathmore Cl CTHM CR3 241 M7
Strathmore Gdns EDGW HA8 95 N10
FNCH N3 97 L9
HCH RM12 124 G6
Strathmore Rd CRAWW RH11 283 K4
CROY/NA CR0 203 K7
TEDD TW11 176 D7
WIM/MER SW19 179 K6
Strathnairn St STHWK SE1 19 P6
Strathray Gdns HAMP NW3 3 N2
Strath Ter BTSEA SW11 157 P10
Strathville Rd
WAND/EARL SW18 179 K5
Strathyre Av
STRHM/NOR SW16 203 H3
Stratton Av ENC/FH EN2 79 L3
WLGTN SM6 222 E5
Stratton Chase Dr CSTG HP8 89 M3
Stratton Cl BXLYHN DA7 163 P9
EDGW HA8 95 L7
HSLW TW3 153 N7
WIM/MER SW19 201 J2
WOT/HER KT12 * 197 K8
Strattondale St POP/IOD E14 161 H2
Stratton Dr BARK IG11 123 H10
Stratton Gdns STHL UB1 133 N8
Stratton Pl AMSS HP7 * 69 L5
Stratton Rd BEAC HP9 88 A9
BXLYHN DA7 163 P9
HARH RM3 105 P6
SUN TW16 196 G2
WIM/MER SW19 201 K2
Stratton St MYFR/PICC W1J 10 F9
Stratton Ter BH/WHM TN16 262 F3
Stratton Wk HARH RM3 105 P6
Strauss Rd CHSWK W4 * 156 A1
Strawberry Cl CHOB/PIR GU24 230 C7
Strawberry Crs
LCOL/BKTW AL2 56 G2
Strawberry Fld HAT AL10 40 D7
Strawberry Flds
CHOB/PIR GU24 230 F1
ORP BR6 226 E2
SWLY BR8 208 F2
WARE SG12 26 A1
Strawberry Hill Rd TWK TW1 176 E6
Strawberry La CAR SM5 202 A10
Strawberry Ri CHOB/PIR GU24 230 F1
Strawberry Ter MUSWH N10 * 98 A9
Strawberry V EFNCH N2 97 N9
TWK TW1 176 E6
Straw Cl CTHM CR3 241 K9
Strawfields WGCE AL7 23 L4
Strawmead HAT AL10 40 E2
Strawson Ct HORL RH6 280 A3
Strayfield Rd ENC/FH EN2 79 H2
Streakes Field Rd CRICK NW2 116 D7
Stream Banks RGUW GU3 248 G9
Stream Cl BF/WBF KT14 215 N8
Streamdale ABYW SE2 163 L5
Stream La EDGW HA8 95 N7
Streamline Ms EDUL SE22 182 A4
Streamside SL SL1 128 E10
Streamside Cl ED N9 99 N2
HAYES BR2 205 M4
Stream Wy BELV DA17 164 B5
Streatfeild Av EHAM E6 142 C3
Streatfield Rd
KTN/HRWW/WS HA3 115 H1
Streatham Cl
STRHM/NOR SW16 * 180 F5
Streatham Common
STRHM/NOR SW16 * 180 E10
Streatham Common North
STRHM/NOR SW16 180 G8
Streatham Common South
STRHM/NOR SW16 180 F9
Streatham Ct
STRHM/NOR SW16 180 F6
Streatham Gn
STRHM/NOR SW16 * 180 F7
Streatham High Rd
STRHM/NOR SW16 180 F10
Streatham Hl
BRXS/STRHM SW2 180 F4
Streatham Pl
BRXS/STRHM SW2 180 F3
Streatham Rd MTCM CR4 202 B1
Streatham St
NOXST/BSQ WC1A 11 L5
Streatham V
STRHM/NOR SW16 180 D10
Streathbourne Rd TOOT SW17 180 B5
Streatleigh Pde
STRHM/NOR SW16 * 180 F5
Streatley Pl HAMP NW3 117 N9
Streatley Rd KIL/WHAMP NW6 2 C4
Streeters La WLGTN SM6 202 E10
Streetfield Ms BKHTH/KID SE3 161 M8
Street Hl CRAWE RH10 284 F8
Streets Heath CHOB/PIR GU24 212 E7
The Street ASHTD KT21 237 L4
BRKHM/BTCW RH3 256 A10
EHSLY KT24 252 C4
EHSLY KT24 253 L3
EYN DA4 210 A4
GVE DA12 191 P8
HORL RH6 279 H8
KGLGY WD4 53 K7
LHD/OX KT22 236 C8
MFD/CHID GU8 266 C10
RBSF CM22 30 E3
RGUE GU4 251 K8
RGUE GU4 268 B5
RGUW GU3 266 A5
SHGR GU5 268 D10
Streimer Rd SRTFD E15 141 H4
Strelley Wy ACT W3 136 B9
Stretton Rd CROY/NA CR0 203 M7
RCHPK/HAM TW10 177 H5
Stretton Wy BORE WD6 75 K4
Strickland Av DART DA1 165 N10
Strickland Cl CRAWW RH11 283 H8
Strickland Rw
WAND/EARL SW18 179 N3
Strickland St DEPT SE8 160 F8
Strickland Wy ORP BR6 227 J1
Stride Rd PLSTW E13 141 L4
Strimon Cl ED N9 100 B3
Stringer's Av RGUE GU4 250 A4
Stringhams Copse
RPLY/SEND GU23 233 J10
Stripling Wy WATW WD18 73 H10
Strode Cl MUSWH N10 98 B8
Strode Rd FSTGT E7 121 M9
FUL/PGN SW6 156 G6
TOTM N17 99 M10
WLSDN NW10 136 D1
Strodes College La EGH TW20 172 C8
Strode's Crs STA TW18 173 M8
Strode St EGH TW20 172 D7
Stroma Cl HHS/BOV HP3 36 D8
Stroma Ct SL SL1 128 C9
Strond Green Gdns
CROY/NA CR0 204 B7
Strond Green Wy
CROY/NA CR0 204 B7
Strone Rd FSTGT E7 141 P1
MNPK E12 142 A1
Strone Wy YEAD UB4 133 M6
Strongbow Crs ELTH/MOT SE9 184 C1
Strongbow Rd ELTH/MOT SE9 184 C1
Strongbridge Cl
RYLN/HDSTN HA2 113 P6
Stronsa Rd SHB W12 156 C1
Stronsay Cl HHS/BOV HP3 36 D8
Strood Av ROMW/RG RM7 124 E6
Strood La WDSR SL4 170 B9
Stroud Cl WDSR SL4 148 C9
Stroud Crs PUT/ROE SW15 178 C6
Stroude Rd VW GU25 194 B4
Stroudes Cl WPK KT4 200 C7
Stroud Fld NTHLT UB5 133 M1
Stroud Ga RYLN/HDSTN HA2 114 A9
Stroud Green Rd FSBYPK N4 118 G6
Stroud Green Wy
CROY/NA CR0 204 A7
Stroudley Cl CRAWE RH10 284 C8
Stroud Rd SNWD SE25 203 P6
WIM/MER SW19 179 K6
Strouds Cl CHDH RM6 123 L3
Stroudwater Pk WEY KT13 216 C3
Stroud Wy ASHF TW15 174 C9
Strout's Pl BETH E2 7 L9
Strudgate Cl CRAWE RH10 284 C9
Strutton Gnd STJSPK SW1H 17 J3
Struttons Av GVW DA11 190 C5
Strype St WCHPL E1 13 L4
Stuart Av CDALE/KGS NW9 116 D5
EA W5 155 L1
HAYES BR2 205 M8
RYLN/HDSTN HA2 113 N8
WOT/HER KT12 197 K8
Stuart Cl BRWN CM15 86 G9
CRAWE RH10 284 D8
HGDN/ICK UB10 132 B1
SWLY BR8 186 G10
WDSR SL4 148 E8
Stuart Ct AMS HP6 * 69 J4
BORE WD6 75 J10
Stuart Crs CROY/NA CR0 204 E10
HYS/HAR UB3 132 D8
REIG RH2 275 K3
WDGN N22 98 G9
Stuart Evans Cl WELL DA16 163 M9
Stuart Gv TEDD TW11 176 D8
Stuart Mantle Wy ERITH DA8 164 E6
Stuart Pl MTCM CR4 202 A1
Stuart Rd ACT W3 135 P10
BARK IG11 143 J3
EBAR EN4 97 P1
GRAYS RM17 167 N4
GVW DA11 190 D2
KIL/WHAMP NW6 2 E10
KTN/HRWW/WS HA3 114 E1
PECK SE15 160 B10
RCHPK/HAM TW10 176 G5
REIG RH2 275 K3
THHTH CR7 203 K4
WARL CR6 242 A6
WELL DA16 163 L7
WIM/MER SW19 179 K6
Stuarts Cl HHS/BOV HP3 35 N8
Stuart Wy CHESW EN7 62 A7
STA TW18 173 L9
VW GU25 193 M4
WDSR SL4 148 D8
Stubbers La UPMR RM14 146 D1
Stubbs Cl CDALE/KGS NW9 115 P3
DORK RH4 273 H4
Stubbs Dr BERM/RHTH SE16 160 A4
Stubbs End Cl AMS HP6 69 K3
Stubbs Hl ORP BR6 227 M9
Stubbs La KWD/TDW/WH KT20 257 J4
Stubbs Wy WIM/MER SW19 201 N1
Stubbs Wd AMS HP6 69 K2
Stubs Hl DORK RH4 273 H4
Stucley Pl CAMTN NW1 4 F4
Stucley Rd HEST TW5 154 B6
Studdridge St FUL/PGN SW6 157 K8
Studd St IS N1 6 C5
Stud Gn GSTN WD25 55 H8
Studholme Ct HAMP NW3 * 117 K9
Studholme St PECK SE15 160 A6
Studio Ms HDN NW4 116 F2
Studio Pl KTBR SW1X 16 B2
Studios Rd SHPTN TW17 196 A3
The Studios BUSH WD23 73 P10
Studio Wy BORE WD6 75 P5
Studland Cl BFN/LL DA15 185 J6
Studland Rd BF/WBF KT14 216 A9
HNWL W7 134 C8
KUTN/CMB KT2 177 K9
SYD SE26 182 C8
Studland St HMSMTH W6 156 E3
Studley Av CHING E4 101 J8
Studley Cl CLPT E5 120 D10
Studley Ct SCUP DA14 185 L8
Studley Crs HART DA3 211 P2
Studley Dr REDBR IG4 122 A4
Studley Grange Rd HNWL W7 154 D2
Studley Rd CLAP SW4 158 F7
DAGW RM9 143 N2
FSTGT E7 141 N1
Stukeley Rd FSTGT E7 141 N2
Stukeley St HOL/ALD WC2B 11 M5
Stumblets CRAWE RH10 284 D6
Stumps Hill La BECK BR3 182 F9
Sturdy Rd PECK SE15 160 A8
Sturge Av WALTH E17 100 G9
Sturgeon Rd WALW SE17 18 E8
Sturges Fld CHST BR7 184 G10
Sturgess Av HDN NW4 116 E5
Sturge St STHWK SE1 18 E2
Sturla Cl HERT/WAT SG14 25 J4
Sturlas Wy CHES/WCR EN8 62 C9
Sturmer Cl STALE/WH AL4 39 H7
Sturmer Wy HOLWY N7 118 G10
Sturminster Cl YEAD UB4 133 K8
Sturrock Cl SEVS/STOTM N15 119 L2
Sturry St POP/IOD E14 140 G8
Sturt Ct RGUE GU4 250 E8
Sturt's La KWD/TDW/WH KT20 256 C3
Sturt St IS N1 6 F8
Stutfield St WCHPL E1 13 P6
Stychens Cl REDH RH1 259 K9
Stychens La REDH RH1 259 K9
Stylecroft Rd CSTG HP8 90 A3
Styles End GT/LBKH KT23 254 A3
Styles Gdns BRXN/ST SW9 159 J9
Styles Wy BECK BR3 205 H4
Styventon Pl CHERT KT16 195 J7
Subrosa Dr REDH RH1 258 C6
Subrosa Pk REDH RH1 * 258 C6
Succomb's Hl CTHM CR3 242 A6
Succombs Pl WARL CR6 242 A5
Sudbourne Rd
BRXS/STRHM SW2 180 F1
Sudbrooke Rd BAL SW12 180 A2
Sudbrook Gdns
RCHPK/HAM TW10 177 K6
Sudbrook La
RCHPK/HAM TW10 177 K4
Sudbury EHAM E6 142 D8
Sudbury Av ALP/SUD HA0 115 H8
Sudbury Court Dr HRW HA1 114 F8
Sudbury Court Rd HRW HA1 114 F8
Sudbury Crs ALP/SUD HA0 114 G10
BMLY BR1 183 M8
Sudbury Cft ALP/SUD HA0 114 E9
Sudbury Gdns CROY/NA CR0 223 M1
Sudbury Heights Av
GFD/PVL UB6 114 E10
Sudbury Hl HRW HA1 114 E8
Sudbury Hill Cl ALP/SUD HA0 114 E8
Sudbury Rd BARK IG11 123 J10
Sudeley St IS N1 6 D8
Sudicamps Ct WAB EN9 63 M9
Sudlow Rd WAND/EARL SW18 157 K10
Sudrey St STHWK SE1 18 E2
Suez Av GFD/PVL UB6 134 E4
Suez Rd PEND EN3 80 D8
Suffield Cl SAND/SEL CR2 224 C8
Suffield Rd CHING E4 100 G4
PGE/AN SE20 204 B2
SEVS/STOTM N15 * 119 N3
Suffolk Cl BORE WD6 76 A9
HORL RH6 280 B5
LCOL/BKTW AL2 57 H1
SL SL1 128 D8
Suffolk Dr RGUE GU4 250 E5
Suffolk La CANST EC4R 12 G7
Suffolk Park Rd WALTH E17 120 D2
Suffolk Rd BARK IG11 142 G2
BARN SW13 156 C6
DAGE RM10 124 C10
GDMY/SEVK IG3 123 H4
GVE DA12 190 G2
PEND EN3 80 A9
PLSTW E13 141 L5
POTB/CUF EN6 59 H8
RYLN/HDSTN HA2 113 N4
SCUP DA14 185 M9
SEVS/STOTM N15 119 L4
SNWD SE25 203 N4
WLSDN NW10 136 B2
WPK KT4 200 C9
Suffolk St FSTGT E7 121 M10
STJS SW1Y 11 K9
Suffolk Vls
WAND/EARL SW18 * 179 K3
Suffolk Wy EMPK RM11 125 P2
SEV TN13 265 K1
Sugar House La SRTFD E15 141 H4
Sugar La HHW HP1 34 E8
Sugar Loaf Wk BETH E2 * 140 B5
Sugden Rd BTSEA SW11 158 B9
THDIT KT7 198 F8
Sugden Wy BARK IG11 143 J4
Sulgrave Gdns HMSMTH W6 156 F1
Sulgrave Rd HMSMTH W6 156 F1
Sulina Rd BRXS/STRHM SW2 180 F3
Sulivan Ct FUL/PGN SW6 157 K8
Sulivan Rd FUL/PGN SW6 157 K9
Sullington Hl CRAWW RH11 283 N9
Sullivan Av CAN/RD E16 142 A7
Sullivan Cl BTSEA SW11 157 P9
E/WMO/HCT KT8 197 P3
YEAD UB4 133 K7
Sullivan Crs DEN/HRF UB9 91 N10
Sullivan Dr CRAWW RH11 283 H10
Sullivan Rd LBTH SE11 18 B5
TIL RM18 168 D7
Sullivans Reach
WOT/HER KT12 196 G7
Sullivan Wy BORE WD6 75 H10
Sultan Rd WAN E11 121 N2
Sultan St BECK BR3 204 C2
CMBW SE5 159 K6
Sumatra Rd KIL/WHAMP NW6 2 E1
Sumburgh Rd BAL SW12 180 B2
Sumburgh Wy SL SL1 129 K7
Summer Av E/WMO/HCT KT8 198 D5
Summer Cl BF/WBF KT14 216 A10
Summer Ct HHNE HP2 35 N4
Summer Crossing THDIT KT7 198 E5
Summer Dl WGCW AL8 22 G1
Summerene Cl
STRHM/NOR SW16 180 D10
Summerfield ASHTD KT21 237 J5
HAT AL10 40 D7
Summerfield Av
KIL/WHAMP NW6 2 B7
NFNCH/WDSPK N12 97 P7
Summerfield Cl
LCOL/BKTW AL2 57 H2
Summerfield La SURB KT6 199 J9
Summerfield Pl
CHERT KT16 * 214 G3
Summerfield Rd EA W5 134 G6
GSTN WD25 73 H1
LOU IG10 82 A10
Summerfields Cl
ADL/WDHM KT15 215 J2
Summer Gdns
E/WMO/HCT KT8 198 D5
Summer Gv BORE WD6 75 J10
Summerhayes Cl
WOKN/KNAP GU21 214 B10
Summerhays COB KT11 217 L9
Summer Hl BORE WD6 75 M9
CHST BR7 206 D2
Summerhill Cl ORP BR6 227 H1
Summerhill Ct STAL AL1 * 38 E5
Summerhill Gv EN EN1 79 M10
Summerhill Rd
SEVS/STOTM N15 119 L2
Summerhill Wy MTCM CR4 202 B1
Summerhouse Av HEST TW5 153 M7
Summerhouse Dr BXLY DA5 186 E7
RDART DA2 186 E8
Summerhouse La
DEN/HRF UB9 91 K8
GSTN WD25 74 B5
WDR/YW UB7 151 N5
Summerhouse Rd
STNW/STAM N16 119 M7
Summerhouse Wy
ABLGY WD5 54 G6
Summerland Gdns
MUSWH N10 118 C1
Summerlands Av ACT W3 135 P9
Summer La GODL GU7 266 F9
Summerlay Cl
KWD/TDW/WH KT20 239 H7
Summerlea SL SL1 128 G10
Summerleas Cl HHNE HP2 35 P6
Summerlee Av EFNCH N2 118 A2
Summerlee Gdns EFNCH N2 118 A2
Summerleigh WEY KT13 * 216 E3
Summerley St
WAND/EARL SW18 179 L5
Summerly Av REIG RH2 257 K9
Summer Pl WATW WD18 * 72 G10
Summer Rd E/WMO/HCT KT8 198 C5
Summersbury Dr RGUE GU4 268 B8
Summersbury Hall
RGUE GU4 * 268 B8
Summersby Rd HGT N6 118 C4
Summers Cl BELMT SM2 221 K4
WBLY HA9 115 N6
WEY KT13 216 B7
Summerskille Cl ED N9 100 A3
Summersland Rd
STALE/WH AL4 39 H2
Summers La
NFNCH/WDSPK N12 97 N8
Summers Rd SL SL1 128 B5
Summer's Rd GODL GU7 267 L10
Summers Rw
NFNCH/WDSPK N12 97 P7
Summers St CLKNW EC1R 12 A2
Summerstown TOOT SW17 179 M6
Summersvere Cl CRAWE RH10 284 B4
Summers Wy
LCOL/BKTW AL2 * 57 K3
Summers Wd BORE WD6 * 75 N8
Summerswood Cl
PUR/KEN CR8 241 L2
Summerswood La BORE WD6 76 B1
Summerton Wy THMD SE28 143 N9
Summer Trees SUN TW16 197 J1
Summerville Gdns SUT SM1 221 J3
Summerwood Rd ISLW TW7 176 E2
Summit Av CDALE/KGS NW9 116 A3
Summit Cl CDALE/KGS NW9 116 A2
EDGW HA8 95 M8
STHGT/OAK N14 98 D3
Summit Dr WFD IG8 102 A10
Summit Est STNW/STAM N16 * 119 P5
Summit Rd NTHLT UB5 133 P2
POTB/CUF EN6 59 H6
WALTH E17 120 G2
The Summit LOU IG10 82 C5
Summit Wy NRWD SE19 181 M10
STHGT/OAK N14 98 C3
Sumner Av PECK SE15 * 159 N7
Sumner Cl LHD/OX KT22 236 C10
ORP BR6 226 F1
Sumner Gdns CROY/NA CR0 203 H8
Sumner Pl ADL/WDHM KT15 215 K2
SKENS SW7 15 M6
Sumner Place Ms SKENS SW7 15 M6
Sumner Rd CROY/NA CR0 203 J8
HRW HA1 114 B5
PECK SE15 19 M10
Sumner Rd South
CROY/NA CR0 203 H8
Sumners Farm Cl
HLWW/ROY CM19 46 D6
Sumner St STHWK SE1 12 E9
Summit Pl WEY KT13 216 B4
Sumpter Cl HAMP NW3 3 K2
Sumpter Yd STAL AL1 38 C7
Sunbeam Crs NKENS W10 136 F6
Sunbeam Rd WLSDN NW10 135 P6
Sunbury Av MLHL NW7 96 A6
MORT/ESHN SW14 156 A10
Sunbury Cl WOT/HER KT12 197 H6
Sunbury Ct BAR EN5 * 77 H8
SUN TW16 197 L2
WDSR SL4 149 J5
Sunbury Court Rd SUN TW16 197 K2
Sunbury Gdns MLHL NW7 96 A6
Sunbury La BTSEA SW11 157 N7
WOT/HER KT12 197 H6
Sunbury Rd CHEAM SM3 200 G10
FELT TW13 174 G6
WDSR SL4 149 J5
Sunbury St WOOL/PLUM SE18 162 C2
Sunbury Wy FELT TW13 175 K8
Sun Cl WDSR SL4 149 J5
Sun Ct ERITH DA8 164 G8
Suncroft Pl SYD SE26 182 B6
Sundale Av SAND/SEL CR2 224 B6
Sundeala Cl SUN TW16 175 H10
Sunderland Av STAL AL1 38 F5
Sunderland Gv GSTN WD25 54 G10
Sunderland Mt FSTH SE23 * 182 C5
Sunderland Rd EA W5 155 J2
FSTH SE23 182 C4
Sunderland Ter BAY/PAD W2 8 G5
Sunderland Wy MNPK E12 122 A7
Sundew Av SHB W12 136 D9
Sundew Cl LTWR GU18 212 C7
Sundew Ct ALP/SUD HA0 * 135 K4
Sundew Rd HHW HP1 35 H8
Sundial Av SNWD SE25 203 N2
Sundon Crs VW GU25 193 N5
Sundorne Rd CHARL SE7 161 N4
Sundown Av SAND/SEL CR2 223 N7
Sundown Rd ASHF TW15 174 D8
Sundridge Av BMLY BR1 206 A1
WELL DA16 162 G8
Sundridge Hl RSEV TN14 245 M4
Sundridge La RSEV TN14 245 L3
Sundridge Pde BMLY BR1 * 183 N10
Sundridge Pl CROY/NA CR0 203 P8
Sundridge Rd CROY/NA CR0 203 N8
RSEV TN14 246 B6
WOKS/MYFD GU22 232 D5
Sunfields Pl BKHTH/KID SE3 161 N6
Sunflower Wy HARH RM3 105 L9
Sun Hl HART DA3 210 F9
WOKN/KNAP GU21 231 M3
Sun in Sands Rbt
BKHTH/KID SE3 161 N6
Sunken Rd CROY/NA CR0 224 B2
Sunkist Wy WLGTN SM6 222 F5
Sunland Av BXLYHS DA6 163 P10
Sun La BKHTH/KID SE3 161 N6
GVE DA12 190 F5
HARP AL5 20 A1
Sunleigh Rd ALP/SUD HA0 135 K3
Sunley Gdns GFD/PVL UB6 134 F4
Sunlight Cl WIM/MER SW19 * 179 M9
Sunlight Sq BETH E2 140 A5
Sunmead Cl LHD/OX KT22 236 E8
Sunmead Pde LHD/OX KT22 * 236 F8
Sunmead Rd HHNE HP2 35 N4
SUN TW16 197 H3
Sunna Gdns SUN TW16 197 J2
Sunning Av ASC SL5 192 D7
Sunningdale STHGT/OAK N14 98 E6
Sunningdale Av ACT W3 136 B9
BARK IG11 142 G3
FELT TW13 175 M5
RAIN RM13 145 J6
RSLP HA4 113 K6
Sunningdale Cl
BERM/RHTH SE16 * 160 A4
STAN HA7 94 F8
SURB KT6 199 K9
THMD SE28 143 P8
Sunningdale Ct CRAWE RH10 283 N9
Sunningdale Gdns
CDALE/KGS NW9 115 P3
KENS W8 14 F4
Sunningdale Ldg EDGW HA8 * 95 L6
Sunningdale Ms WGCE AL7 * 23 J1
Sunningdale Pk ASC SL5 * 192 E5
Sunningdale Rd BMLY BR1 206 B4
RAIN RM13 145 H2
SUT SM1 201 J10
Sunningfield Rd HDN NW4 116 E1
Sunningfields Crs HDN NW4 96 E10
Sunninghill GVW DA11 190 B5
Sunninghill Cl ASC SL5 192 C4
Sunninghill Ct ACT W3 * 155 P1
Sunninghill Pk ASC SL5 * 192 C2
Sunninghill Rd ASC SL5 192 C5
LEW SE13 160 G8
WDSR SL4 170 C8
Sunnings La UPMR RM14 146 C3
Sunningvale Av
BH/WHM TN16 243 P3
Sunningvale Cl BH/WHM TN16 244 A2
Sunny Av CRAWE RH10 285 P5
Sunny Bank EPSOM KT18 237 P2
SNWD SE25 203 P3
WARL CR6 242 D3
Sunnybank Rd POTB/CUF EN6 59 K9

**Column 1**

Sunny Crs *WLSDN* NW10 — 135 P2
Sunny Cft *HLWS* CM18 — 47 J4
Sunnycroft Gdns *UPMR* RM14 — 126 F3
Sunnycroft Rd *HSLW* TW3 — 154 A8
　*SNWD* SE25 — 203 H4
　*STHL* UB1 — 133 P7
Sunnydale *ORP* BR6 — 206 D9
Sunnydale Gdns *MLHL* NW7 — 96 F3
Sunnydale Rd *LEE/GVPK* SE12 — 185 J1
Sunnydell *LCOL/BKTW* AL2 — 56 H7
Sunnydene Av *CHING* E4 — 101 J4
　*RSLP* HA4 — 113 H6
Sunnydene Gdns *HARH* RM3 — 105 N8
Sunnydene Gdns
　*ALP/SUD* HA0 — 135 H1
Sunnydene Rd *PUR/KEN* CR8 — 223 J9
Sunnyfield *BRKMPK* AL9 — 40 G1
　*MLHL* NW7 — 96 C5
Sunny Gardens Rd *HDN* NW4 — 116 F1
Sunnyhill *CLPT* E5 — 120 D9
　*HOR/WEW* KT19 — 220 B5
　*CRAWE* RH10 — 285 P5
Sunnyhill Rd *HHW* HP1 — 35 L6
　*RKW/CH/CXG* WD3 — 90 F7
　*STRHM/NOR* SW16 — 180 F7
Sunnyhurst Cl *SUT* SM1 — 201 K10
Sunnymead *CRAWW* RH11 — 283 N10
Sunnymead Av *MTCM* CR4 — 202 E5
Sunnymead Rd *CDALE/KGS* NW9 — 116 A5
　*PUT/ROE* SW15 — 178 G3
Sunnymede *CHIG* IG7 — 103 L4
Sunnymede Av *CAR* SM5 — 221 N7
　*CSHM* HP5 — 51 K4
　*HOR/WEW* KT19 — 220 B5
Sunnymede Dr *BARK/HLT* IG6 — 122 F2
Sunny Ms *CRW* CM14 — 104 D8
Sunny Nook Gdns
　*SAND/SEL* CR2 — 223 L3
Sunny Pl *HDN* NW4 — 116 F2
Sunny Ri *CTHM* CR3 — 241 L10
The Sunny Rd *PEND* EN3 — 80 C5
Sunnyside *CAT* SE6 — 182 E3
　*CRICK* NW2 — 82 A1
　*WAB* EN9 — 45 L8
　*WOKN/KNAP* GU21 — 230 C5
　*WOT/HER* KT12 — 197 K5
Sunnyside Dr *CHING* E4 — 101 H1
Sunnyside Gdns *UPMR* RM14 — 126 B8
Sunnyside Pl *WIM/MER* SW19 — 179 H5
Sunnyside Rd *ARCH* N19 — 118 E5
　*CSHM* HP5 — 50 G6
　*EA* W5 — 135 J10
　*EPP* CM16 — 65 J8
　*IL* IG1 — 122 F8
　*LEY* E10 — 120 F6
　*TEDD* TW11 — 176 C7
Sunnyside Rd East *ED* N9 — 99 N4
Sunnyside Rd North *ED* N9 — 99 N4
Sunnyside Rd South *ED* N9 — 99 N4
Sunny Vw *CDALE/KGS* NW9 — 116 A3
Sunny Wy *NFNCH/WDSPK* N12 — 97 P8
Sun Pas *BERM/RHTH* SE16 — 19 N3
Sunray Av *BRYLDS* KT5 — 199 N9
　*HAYES* BR2 — 206 B6
　*HNHL* SE24 — 159 L10
　*WDR/YW* UB7 — 133 N1
Sunrise Av *HCH* RM12 — 125 K8
Sunrise Cl *FELT* TW13 — 175 N6
Sunrise Crs *HHS/BOV* HP3 — 35 N9
Sun Rd *SWCM* DA10 — 189 L2
　*WKENS* SW14 — 14 C8
Sunset Av *CHING* E4 — 100 G2
　*WFD* IG8 — 101 M6
Sunset Cl *ERITH* DA8 — 165 J6
Sunset Dr *ABR/ST* RM4 — 105 J6
Sunset Gdns *SNWD* SE25 — 203 M2
Sunset Rd *HNHL* SE24 — 159 K10
　*WIM/MER* SW19 — 178 E9
Sunset Vw *BAR* EN5 — 77 H6
Sunshine Wy *MTCM* CR4 — 202 A2
Sun Sq *HHW* HP1 — 35 N5
Sun St *SBW* CM21 — 30 A2
　*SDTCH* EC2A — 13 H3
　*WAB* EN9 — 45 M7
Sun Street Pas *LVPST* EC2M — 13 J4
Superior Dr *ORP* BR6 — 227 J3
Surbiton Ct *SURB* KT6 — 199 J6
Surbiton Court Ms *SURB* KT6 — 199 J6
Surbiton Crs *KUT/HW* KT1 — 199 K4
Surbiton Hall Cl *KUT/HW* KT1 — 199 K4
Surbiton Hill Pk *BRYLDS* KT5 — 199 K4
Surbiton Hill Rd *SURB* KT6 — 199 K4
Surlingham Cl *THMD* SE28 — 143 N9
Surly Hall Wk *WDSR* SL4 — 46 E2
Surma Cl *WCHPL* E1 — 13 P1
Surman Crs *RBRW/HUT* CM13 — 107 P1
Surmans Cl *DAGW* RM9 — 143 J5
Surrendale Pl *MV/WKIL* W9 — 8 F2
Surrey Av *SLN* SL2 — 129 K9
Surrey Canal Rd *PECK* SE15 — 160 B5
Surrey Ct *FNCH* N3 — 117 H1
Surrey Crs *CHSWK* W4 — 155 M4
Surrey Dr *EMPK* RM11 — 125 P3
Surrey Gdns *EHSLY* KT24 — 234 C9
　*FSBYPK* N4 — 119 K4
Surrey Gv *SUT* SM1 — 201 N1
　*WALW* SE17 — 19 J8
Surrey Hills Av
　*KWD/TDW/WH* KT20 — 255 P6
Surrey La *BTSEA* SW11 — 157 P2
Surrey Ms *WNWD* SE27 — 181 M7
Surrey Mt *FSTH* SE23 — 182 A4
Surrey Quays Rd
　*BERM/RHTH* SE16 — 160 B2
Surrey Rd *BARK* IG11 — 143 H2
　*DAGE* RM10 — 124 C10
　*HRW* HA1 — 114 B4
　*PECK* SE15 — 182 C1
　*WWKM* BR4 — 204 C8
Surrey Rw *STHWK* SE1 — 18 C1
Surrey Sq *WALW* SE17 — 19 J7
Surrey St *CROY/NA* CR0 — 203 K10
　*PLSTW* E13 — 141 N3
　*TPL/STR* WC2R — 11 P7
Surrey Ter *WALW* SE17 — 19 K6
Surrey Water Rd
　*BERM/RHTH* SE16 — 140 C10
Surridge Cl *RAIN* RM13 — 145 K5
Surridge Gdns *NRWD* SE19 — 181 P3
Surr St *HOLWY* N7 — 118 F10
Sury Basin *KUTN/CMB* KT2 — 199 L3
Susan Cl *ROMW/RG* RM7 — 124 D1
Susannah St *POP/IOD* E14 — 140 G8
Susan Wd *CHST* BR7 — 206 D1
Sussex Av *HARH* RM3 — 105 N8
　*ISLW* TW7 — 154 C10
Sussex Border Pth
　*CRAWE* RH10 — 285 L3
　*HORL* RH6 — 276 F7
　*HORL* RH6 — 279 M7
　*HORS* RH12 — 282 A4
Sussex Cl *ARCH* N19 — 118 E1
　*CSTG* HP8 — 89 N3
　*NWMAL* KT3 — 200 B4
　*REDBR* IG4 — 122 C4
　*REIG* RH2 — 275 N1
　*SL* SL1 — 149 K1
　*TWK* TW1 — 176 C2
　*WOKN/KNAP* GU21 — 231 H3
Sussex Crs *NTHLT* UB5 — 133 N5
Sussex Ga *HGT* N6 — 118 C5
Sussex Gdns *CHSGTN* KT9 — 219 J3
　*FSBYPK* N4 — 119 K5
　*HDN* NW4 — 118 A3
Sussex Ms *BAY/PAD* W2 — 9 M7
Sussex Ms East *BAY/PAD* W2 — 9 M7
Sussex Ms West *BAY/PAD* W2 — 9 M7

**Column 2**

Swallowdale La *HHNE* HP2 — 36 B3
Swallow Dr *NTHLT* UB5 — 133 P4
　*WLSDN* NW10 — 136 A1
Swallow End *WCCE* AL7 — 23 J5
Swallowfield *EGH* TW20 — 155 P10
Swallowfield Rd *CHARL* SE7 — 161 N4
Swallow Flds *IVER* SL0 — 130 C6
Swallowfields *WCCE* AL7 — 23 J5
Swallowfield Wy
　*HYS/HAR* UB3 — 152 E1
Swallow La *ABLGY* WD5 — 40 D6
　*STRHM/NOR* SW16 — 180 D6
Swallow Oaks *ABLGY* WD5 — 54 G7
Swallow Pk *HHNE* HP2 — 36 B3
Swallow Ri *WOKN/KNAP* GU21 — 231 H3
Swallow St *EHAM* E6 — 142 B7
　*IVER* SL0 — 130 C7
Swallowtail Cl
　*STMC/STPC* BR5 — 207 N4
Swallowtail Wk *BERK* HP4 — 33 L2
Swanage Rd *CHING* E4 — 101 H8
　*WAND/EARL* SW18 — 179 M2
Swanage Waye *YEAD* UB4 — 133 K8
Swan Av *EHAM* E6 — 142 B7
Swanbourne Dr *HCH* RM12 — 125 L9
Swanbridge Rd *BXLYHN* DA7 — 164 B5
Swan Cl *CROY/NA* CR0 — 205 M7
　*CSHM* HP5 — 50 C3
　*FELT* TW13 — 175 M7
　*RKW/CH/CXG* WD3 — 91 N1
　*STMC/STPC* BR5 — 207 K3
　*WALTH* E17 — 100 D9
Swan Ct *GU* GU1 — 250 A8
　*HHW* HP1 — 35 M7
Swandon Wy *WAND/EARL* SW18 — 157 L10
Swan Dr *CDALE/KGS* NW9 — 96 B10
Swanfield Rd *CHES/WCR* EN8 — 62 D9
Swanfield St *BETH* E2 — 7 L8
Swanhill *WCCE* AL7 — 23 K2
Swan Island *TWK* TW1 — 176 F6
Swan La *CANST* EC4R — 12 G8
　*GU* GU1 — 268 A1
　*HORL* RH6 — 279 J8
　*LOU* IG10 — 101 P1
　*TRDG/WHET* N20 — 97 M4
Swanley Bar La
　*POTB/CUF* EN6 — 59 L5
Swanley La *POTB/CUF* EN6 — 59 L5
Swanley Rd *WELL* DA16 — 163 M1
Swanley Village Rd *SWLY* BR8 — 208 G3
Swan Md *HHS/BOV* HP3 — 54 A1
　*STHWK* SE1 — 19 J4
Swan Ms *BRXN/ST* SW9 — 158 G8
Swan Mill Gdns *DORK* RH4 — 255 H10
Swanns Meadow
　*GT/LBKH* KT23 — 253 P2
Swan Pas *WCHPL* E1 — 13 M8
Swan & Pike Rd *PEND* EN3 — 80 F4
Swan Pl *BARN* SW13 — 156 C8
　*BH/WHM* TN16 — 262 C3
Swan Rd *BERM/RHTH* SE16 — 160 B1
　*CHES/WCR* EN8 — 62 C10
　*FELT* TW13 — 175 M7
　*IVER* SL0 — 131 J8
　*WDR/YW* UB7 — 151 N1
　*WOOL/PLUM* SE18 — 162 A2
Swans Cl *STALE/WH* AL4 — 39 A5
Swanscombe Rd *CHSWK* W4 — 156 B4
Swanscombe St *SWCM* DA10 — 189 L2
Swansea Cl *CRW* RM5 — 104 E8
Swansea Rd *HTHAIR* TW6 — 174 D2
　*PEND* EN3 — 80 B8
Swanshope *LOU* IG10 — 89 M7
Swanston Path *OXHEY* WD19 — 33 M8
Swan St *ISLW* TW7 — 154 G9
　*STHWK* SE1 — 18 F3
The Swansway *WEY* KT13 — 196 B10
Swanton Gdns
　*WIM/MER* SW19 — 178 G4
Swanton Rd *ERITH* DA8 — 164 B8
　*SHPTN* TW17 — 196 F7
Swan Wy *PEND* EN3 — 80 C6
Swanwick Cl *PUT/ROE* SW15 — 178 C10
Swanworth La *RDKG* RH5 — 273 H3
Swan Yd *IS* N1 — 6 C2
Swanzy Rd *RSEV* TN14 — 247 K6
Sward Rd *STMC/STPC* BR5 — 207 M6
Swaton Rd *BOW* E3 — 140 F6
Swaylands Rd *BELV* DA17 — 164 B5
Swaynesland Rd *EDEN* TN8 — 262 C10
Swayne's La *GU* GU1 — 251 H10
Swaythling Cl *UED* N18 — 100 A5
Sweden Ga *BERM/RHTH* SE16 — 160 D3
Sweeney Crs *STHWK* SE1 — 19 M2
Sweeps Ditch Cl *STA* TW18 — 195 K1
Sweeps La *ECH* TW20 — 172 C9
　*STMC/STPC* BR5 — 207 N5
Sweet Briar *HHW* HP1 — 35 K5
Sweetbriar Cl *HHW* HP1 — 35 K5
Sweet Briar Gn *ED* N9 — 100 C2
Sweet Briar Gv *ED* N9 — 99 N4
Sweet Briar Wk *UED* N18 — 99 N5
Sweetcroft La
　*HGDN/ICK* UB10 — 132 A2
Sweet La *SHGR* GU5 — 270 E9
Sweetmans Av *PIN* HA5 — 113 L1
Sweets Wy *TRDG/WHET* N20 — 97 N3
Swete St *PLSTW* E13 — 141 M4
Sweyne Rd *SWCM* DA10 — 189 K2
Sweyn Pl *BKHTH/KID* SE3 — 161 M8
Swievelands Rd
　*BH/WHM* TN16 — 243 N5
Swift Cl *HYS/HAR* UB3 — 132 A8
　*RYLN/HDSTN* HA2 — 114 A7
　*THMD* SE28 — 143 L8
　*UPMR* RM14 — 126 D6
　*WALTH* E17 — 100 D8
Swiftfields *WCCE* AL7 — 23 M6
Swift La *FELT* TW13 — 175 L7
Swift Rd *FELT* TW13 — 175 K7
　*FUL/PGN* SW6 — 157 K7
Swiftsden Wy *BMLY* BR1 — 183 K9
Swift St *FUL/PGN* SW6 — 157 K7
Swiller's La *GVE* GU24 — 191 P8
Swinbrook Rd *NKENS* W10 — 8 A2
Swinburne Crs *CROY/NA* CR0 — 204 B6
Swinburne Gdns *TIL* RM18 — 168 G8
Swinburne Rd
　*PUT/ROE* SW15 — 156 D10
Swinderby Rd *ALP/SUD* HA0 — 135 L10
Swindon Cl *GDMY/SEVK* IG3 — 123 J2
　*HARH* RM3 — 105 N4
Swindon La *HARH* RM3 — 105 N4
Swindon Rd *HTHAIR* TW6 — 174 D2
Swindon St *SHB* W12 — 137 J8
Swinfield Cl *FELT* TW13 — 175 M7
Swinford Gdns *BRXN/ST* SW9 — 159 H9
Swingate La *WOOL/PLUM* SE18 — 163 N9
Swing Gate La *BERK* HP4 — 34 A8
Swinnerton St *HOM* E9 — 121 J9
Swinton Cl *WBLY* HA9 — 116 C5
Swinton Pl *FSBYW* WC1X — 5 N7
Swinton St *FSBYW* WC1X — 5 N7
Swires Shaw *HAYES* BR2 — 226 A1
Swiss Av *WATW* WD18 — 72 A4
Swiss Cl *WATW* WD18 — 72 A4

**Column 3**

Swithland Gdns
　*ELTH/MOT* SE9 — 184 C10
Sword Cl *BROX* EN10 — 44 C6
Swyncombe Av *EA* W5 — 154 C3
Swynford Gdns *HDN* NW4 — 116 D2
Sybil Ms *FSBYPK* N4 — 119 J4
Sybil Phoenix Cl *DEPT* SE8 — 140 F7
Sybourn St *WALTH* E17 — 120 D7
Sycamore Ap
　*RKW/CH/CXG* WD3 — 72 D9
Sycamore Av *BFN/LL* DA15 — 185 J2
　*BOW* E3 — 140 B2
　*EA* W5 — 155 P2
　*HAT* AL10 — 40 D5
　*HYS/HAR* UB3 — 132 F9
　*UPMR* RM14 — 125 P9
Sycamore Cl *ACT* W3 — 136 B10
　*AMS* HP6 — 69 J3
　*BUSH* WD23 — 73 M6
　*CAR* SM5 — 222 A1
　*CHESW* EN7 — 61 N3
　*CRAWW* RH11 — 283 M5
　*EBAR* EN4 — 77 N10
　*FELT* TW13 — 175 H6
　*GSTN* WD25 — 73 J1
　*LHD/OX* KT22 — 236 E8
　*NTHLT* UB5 — 133 M3
　*SAND/SEL* CR2 — 223 M2
　*TIL* RM18 — 168 D7
　*WDR/YW* UB7 — 132 A9
Sycamore Ct *WEY* KT13 — 196 B2
Sycamore Dene *CSHM* HP5 — 51 J4
Sycamore Dr *BRW* CM14 — 107 H2
Sycamore Fld
　*HLWW/ROY* CM19 — 46 D5
　*SHB* W12 — 156 F1
Sycamore Gdns *MTCM* CR4 — 201 N2
　*SHB* W12 — 156 F1
Sycamore Gv *CDALE/KGS* NW9 — 115 P5
　*NWMAL* KT3 — 200 B3
　*PGE/AN* SE20 — 181 P6
Sycamore Hl *FBAR/BDGN* N11 — 98 B7
Sycamore Ms *CLAP* SW4 — 158 F2
　*ERITH* DA8 — 164 E4
Sycamore Pl *AMS* HP6 — 69 H3
　*BMLY* BR1 — 184 E5
Sycamore Ri *BERK* HP4 — 34 A6
　*BNSTD* SM7 — 220 C10
　*CSTG* HP8 — 89 M4
Sycamore Rd *AMS* HP6 — 69 H3
　*GU* GU1 — 250 A10
　*RKW/CH/CXG* WD3 — 72 D9
　*WIM/MER* SW19 — 178 D9
Sycamores *GT/LBKH* KT23 — 258 B10
　*HHS/BOV* HP3 — 35 J3
　*RAD* WD7 — 58 N5
Sycamore St *FSBYE* EC1V — 12 E2
Sycamore Wk *NKENS* W10 — 8 A1
　*TEDD* TW11 — 176 A6
Sycamore Wy *SOCK/AV* RM15 — 147 J6
　*THHTH* CR7 — 203 L4
　*WDGN* N22 — 98 C8
Sydcote *DUL* SE21 — 181 K5
Sydenham Av *SYD* SE26 — 182 A8
　*BH/WHM* TN16 — 262 C3
Sydenham Cl *ROM* RM1 — 124 G2
Sydenham Cots
　*LEE/GVPK* SE12 — 183 P5
Sydenham Hl *FSTH* SE23 — 182 A5
　*SYD* SE26 — 181 P6
Sydenham Park Rd *SYD* SE26 — 182 B5
Sydenham Pk *SYD* SE26 — 182 A5
Sydenham Rd *CROY/NA* CR0 — 203 K9
　*GU* GU1 — 268 A2
　*SYD* SE26 — 182 C8
Sydenham Station Ap
　*SYD* SE26 — 182 C7
Sydmons Ct *FSTH* SE23 — 182 B3
Sydney Av *PUR/KEN* CR8 — 222 G8
Sydney Chapman Wy
　*BAR* EN5 — 77 J2
Sydney Cl *SKENS* SW7 — 15 M6
Sydney Gv *ASHF* TW15 — 157 H3
　*HDN* NW4 — 116 F3
　*SL* SL1 — 129 H8
Sydney Ms *CHEL* SW3 — 15 M6
Sydney Pl *SKENS* SW7 — 15 M6
Sydney Rd *ABYW* SE2 — 142 G6
　*BAR* EN5 — 77 J2
　*BFN/LL* DA15 — 185 H7
　*BXLYHS* DA6 — 163 N10
　*CEND/HSY/T* N8 — 119 H2
　*EBED/NFELT* TW14 — 173 N1
　*ENC/FH* EN2 — 79 L1
　*GU* GU1 — 268 C1
　*MUSWH* N10 — 98 B9
　*RCH/KEW* TW9 — 155 N10
　*RYNPK* SW20 — 200 G2
　*SCUP* DA14 — 185 H7
　*SUT* SM1 — 221 K1
　*TEDD* TW11 — 176 A6
　*TIL* RM18 — 168 D8
　*WAN* E11 — 121 N4
　*WATW* WD18 — 72 F9
　*WFD* IG8 — 101 M5
Sydney St *CHEL* SW3 — 15 N7
Sydney Ter *ESH/CLAY* KT10 — 218 C7
Syke Cluan *DTCH/LGLY* SL3 — 151 H1
Syke Ings *DTCH/LGLY* SL3 — 151 H2
Sykes Rd *SL* SL1 — 128 C8
Sylvana Cl *HGDN/ICK* UB10 — 132 A3
Sylvan Av *CHDH* RM6 — 123 P5
　*EMPK* RM11 — 125 M3
　*MLHL* NW7 — 96 B7
　*WDGN* N22 — 99 H7
Sylvan Cl *HHS/BOV* HP3 — 36 B7
　*OXTED* RH8 — 261 N1
　*SAND/SEL* CR2 — 224 A6
　*WOKS/MYFD* GU22 — 232 E4
Sylvan Ct *CRAWW* RH11 — 283 J9
Sylvandale *WGCE* AL7 — 23 M6
Sylvan Gdns *SURB* KT6 — 199 J7
Sylvan Gv *CRICK* NW2 — 82 A1
　*PECK* SE15 — 140 B10
Sylvan Hl *NRWD* SE19 — 203 M1
Sylvan Ms *SWCM* DA10 — 189 M2
Sylvan Rd *CRAWE* RH10 — 284 B9
　*FSTGT* E7 — 141 M1
　*IL* IG1 — 122 F7
　*NRWD* SE19 — 203 M1
　*WALTH* E17 — 120 D2
　*WAN* E11 — 121 M1
Sylvan Ter *PECK* SE15 — 140 B10
Sylvan Wy *BCTR* RM8 — 123 H2
　*CHIG* IG7 — 103 N1
　*REDH* RH1 — 276 F8
　*WCCE* AL7 — 23 M6
　*WWKM* BR4 — 204 G3
Sylverdale Rd *CROY/NA* CR0 — 203 J10
　*PUR/KEN* CR8 — 223 J5
Sylvester Av *CHST* BR7 — 184 D10
Sylvester Path *HACK* E8 — 7 P1
Sylvester Rd *ALP/SUD* HA0 — 135 L10
　*EFNCH* N2 — 97 H3
　*HACK* E8 — 7 P1
　*WALTH* E17 — 120 C2
Sylvestres *RSEV* TN14 — 246 C3
Sylvestrus Cl *KUT/HW* KT1 — 159 P9
Sylvia Av *PIN* HA5 — 95 M7
　*BRW* CM14 — 107 J4
Sylvia Ct *WBLY* HA9 — 136 C4
Sylvia Gdns *WBLY* HA9 — 136 C4

**Column 4**

Symons St *CHEL* SW3 — 16 B6
Symphony Cl *EDGW* NW8 — 95 M8
Symphony Ms *NKENS* W10 — 2 B7
Syon Gate Wy *BTFD* TW8 — 154 F6
Syon La *ISLW* TW7 — 154 F6
Syon Pk *ISLW* TW7 — 154 F6
Syon Park Gdns *ISLW* TW7 — 154 G6
Syracuse Av *RAIN* RM13 — 145 L5
Sythwood *WOKN/KNAP* GU21 — 231 N3
Szabo Crs *RGUW* GU3 — 248 A10

# T

Tabard Garden Est
　*STHWK* SE1 — 18 G1
Tabard St *STHWK* SE1 — 18 G1
Tabarin Wy *EW* KT17 — 238 F2
Tabernacle Av *PLSTW* E13 — 141 M6
Tabernacle St *SDTCH* EC2A — 13 H2
Tableer Av *CLAP* SW4 — 180 D1
Tabley Rd *HOLWY* N7 — 118 F3
Tabor Gdns *CHEAM* SM3 — 221 H3
Tabor Gv *WIM/MER* SW19 — 179 H10
Tabor Rd *HMSMTH* W6 — 156 G10
Tabrums Wy *UPMR* RM14 — 126 D5
Tachbrook Rd
　*EBED/NFELT* TW14 — 174 C3
　*NWDGN* UB2 — 132 L3
　*UX/CGN* UB8 — 131 N8
Tachbrook St *PIM* SW1V — 17 H6
Tack Ms *BROCKY* SE4 — 160 F9
Tadema Rd *WBPTN* SW10 — 157 M7
Tadlows Cl *UPMR* RM14 — 126 A10
Tadmor Cl *SUN* TW16 — 195 J4
Tadmor St *SHB* W12 — 136 G10
Tadorne Rd
　*KWD/TDW/WH* KT20 — 238 F7
Tadworth Av *NWMAL* KT3 — 200 C4
Tadworth Cl
　*KWD/TDW/WH* KT20 — 238 G8
Tadworth Pde *HCH* RM12 — 125 J9
Tadworth Rd *CRICK* NW2 — 81 J8
Tadworth St
　*KWD/TDW/WH* KT20 — 238 F9
Taeping St *POP/IOD* E14 — 160 G3
Taffy's How *MTCM* CR4 — 201 P3
Tait Ct *BOW* E3 — 140 E3
Tait Rd *CROY/NA* CR0 — 203 M7
Tait St *WCHPL* E1 — 140 E1
Takeley Cl *CRW* RM5 — 104 E10
　*WAB* EN9 — 63 H3
Talacre Rd *KTTN* NW5 — 4 D1
Talbot Av *DTCH/LGLY* SL3 — 150 C2
　*OXHEY* WD19 — 33 M8
Talbot Cl *REIG* RH2 — 275 L1
　*SEVS/STOTM* N15 — 119 N2
Talbot Ct *BANK* EC3V — 13 G7
　*HHS/BOV* HP3 — 35 N8
Talbot Gdns *HDN* NW4 — 116 C3
Talbot Pl *BKHTH/KID* SE3 — 161 H8
　*DTCH/LGLY* SL3 — 149 P7
Talbot Rd *ALP/SUD* HA0 — 115 J10
　*ASHF* TW15 — 175 N8
　*BAY/PAD* W2 — 8 F5
　*CAR* SM5 — 222 B2
　*DAGW* RM9 — 144 A2
　*EDUL* SE22 — 159 M10
　*EHAM* E6 — 142 B1
　*FSTGT* E7 — 121 M9
　*HGT* N6 — 118 B4
　*HRW* HA1 — 95 J10
　*ISLW* TW7 — 154 F10
　*KTN/HRWW/WS* HA3 — 94 E10
　*NTGHL* W11 — 8 F5
　*NWDGN* UB2 — 152 A2
　*RKW/CH/CXG* WD3 — 91 P2
　*SEVS/STOTM* N15 — 119 N2
　*THHTH* CR7 — 203 L4
　*WDGN* N22 — 98 D10
　*WEA* W13 — 135 F4
Talbot Sq *BAY/PAD* W2 — 9 L6
Talbot Wk *NTGHL* W11 — 8 F5
　*WLSDN* NW10 — 137 H5
Talbot Yd *STHWK* SE1 — 12 G10
Talbrook *BRW* CM14 — 106 E4
Talcott Pth
　*BRXS/STRHM* SW2 — 181 H1
Talehangers Cl *BXLYHS* DA6 — 163 N10
Taleworth Cl *ASHTD* KT21 — 237 J6
Taleworth Pk *ASHTD* KT21 — 237 J5
Taleworth Rd *ASHTD* KT21 — 237 J5
Talfourd Pl *PECK* SE15 — 159 N7
Talfourd Rd *PECK* SE15 — 159 M7
Talfourd Wy *REDH* RH1 — 276 A3
Talgarth Rd *HMSMTH* W6 — 14 A4
Talgarth Wk *CDALE/KGS* NW9 — 116 B3
Talisman Cl *GDMY/SEVK* IG3 — 123 L1
Talisman Sq *SYD* SE26 — 181 P7
Talisman Wy *EW* KT17 — 238 F2
　*WBLY* HA9 — 116 C10
Tallack Cl *KTN/HRWW/WS* HA3 — 94 D4
Tallack Rd *LEY* E10 — 120 B5
Tall Elms Cl *HAYES* BR2 — 205 P1
Talleyrand Cl *EYN* DA4 — 188 A8
Tallis Cl *CAN/RD* E16 — 141 K5
Tallis Gv *CHARL* SE7 — 161 N5
Tallis St *EMB* EC4Y — 11 P7
Tallis Vw *WLSDN* NW10 — 136 A1
Tallis Wy *BORE* WD6 — 75 J1
Tall Oaks *AMS* HP6 — 69 J3
Tallon Rd *HWWL* W7 — 107 J4
Tall Trees *DTCH/LGLY* SL3 — 151 P2
　*STRHM/NOR* SW16 — 202 A3
Tall Trees Cl *EMPK* RM11 — 125 P2
Talma Gdns *WHTN* TW2 — 155 N10
Talmage Cl *FSTH* SE23 — 182 A3
Talman Cl *CRAWW* RH11 — 283 J9
Talma Rd *BRXS/STRHM* SW2 — 142 A6
Talus Cl *PUR* RM19 — 166 C3
Talwin St *BOW* E3 — 140 G5
Tamar Cl *BOW* E3 — 140 B10
Tamar Dr *SOCK/AV* RM15 — 146 F2
Tamar Gn *HHNE* HP2 — 36 A3
Tamarind Cl *GUW* GU2 — 249 M5
Tamarind Yd *WAP* E1W — 13 N5
Tamarisk Rd *SOCK/AV* RM15 — 146 F2
Tamarisk Sq *SHB* W12 — 136 G10
Tamarisk Wy *SL* SL1 — 148 G1
Tamar St *CHARL* SE7 — 142 E10
Tamar Wy *DTCH/LGLY* SL3 — 151 H2
Tamberlayne Gdns *WOKS/MYFD* GU22 — 232 A3
Tamesis Gdns *WPK* KT4 — 200 B10
Tamesis St *GU* GU1 — 251 M6
Tamian Wy *HSLWW* TW4 — 153 K10
Tamworth Av *WFD* IG8 — 101 M6
Tamworth La *MTCM* CR4 — 202 C1
Tamworth Pk *MTCM* CR4 — 202 C3
Tamworth Pl *CROY/NA* CR0 — 203 K9
Tamworth Rd *CROY/NA* CR0 — 203 K9
　*HERT/BAY* SG13 — 25 N4
Tamworth St *FUL/PGN* SW6 — 14 A10

**Column 5 / 6**

Tanfield Av *CRICK* NW2 — 116 C9
Tanfield Ct *CHESW* EN7 — 61 P3
Tanfield Rd *CROY/NA* CR0 — 223 K1
Tangent Link *HARH* RM3 — 105 L9
Tangier La *DTCH/LGLY* SL3 — 105 L9
Tangier Rd *GU* GU1 — 268 G2
　*RCHPK/HAM* TW10 — 155 M10
Tangier Wd
　*KWD/TDW/WH* KT20 — 239 H3
Tangle Tree Cl *FNCH* N3 — 97 L10
Tanglewood Cl *CHERT* KT16 — 193 N10
　*CROY/NA* CR0 — 204 B10
　*STAN* HA7 — 94 C1
　*WOKS/MYFD* GU22 — 232 C2
Tanglewood Ride *CHOB/PIR* GU24 — 212 C8
Tanglewood Wy *FELT* TW13 — 175 D3
Tangley Gv *PUT/ROE* SW15 — 178 C3
Tangley La *RGUW* GU3 — 249 L6
Tangley Park Rd *HPTN* TW12 — 175 N8
Tanglyn Av *SHPTN* TW17 — 196 B5
Tangmere Crs *HCH* RM12 — 145 J1
Tangmere Gdns *NTHLT* UB5 — 133 G4
Tangmere Gv *KUTN/CMB* KT2 — 177 J8
Tangmere Rd *CRAWW* RH11 — 283 J7
Tangmere Wy
　*CDALE/KGS* NW9 — 96 B10
Tanhouse Fld *KTTN* NW5 — 118 C4
Tan House La *BRW* CM14 — 85 P7
Tanhouse Rd *OXTED* RH8 — 261 J8
Tankerfield Pl *STALW/RED* AL3 — 38 B6
Tankerton Houses
　*STPAN* WC1H — 5 M3
Tankerton Rd *SURB* KT6 — 199 L9
Tankerton St *STPAN* WC1H — 5 L9
Tankerton Ter *CROY/NA* CR0 — 202 F7
Tankerville Rd
　*STRHM/NOR* SW16 — 180 G10
Tank Hill Rd *PUR* RM19 — 165 P2
　*SOCK/AV* RM15 — 165 P2
Tank La *PUR* RM19 — 166 A3
Tankridge Rd *CRICK* NW2 — 116 E7
The Tanneries *WCHPL* E1 — 140 E6
Tanners Cl *STALW/RED* AL3 — 25 K1
　*WOT/HER* KT12 — 197 J6
Tanners Ct *HERT/BAY* SG13 — 25 K1
Tanners Dean *LHD/OX* KT22 — 237 H8
Tanners End La *UED* N18 — 99 H5
Tannersfield *RGUE* GU4 — 268 B8
Tanners HI *ABLGY* WD5 — 54 C7
Tanner's HI *BRKHM/BTCW* RH3 — 273 N2
　*DEPT* SE8 — 160 F7
Tanners Meadow
　*BRKHM/BTCW* RH3 — 273 N4
Tanners Ms *DEPT* SE8 — 160 E7
Tanner St *BARK* IG11 — 142 F1
　*STHWK* SE1 — 19 K3
Tanners Wood La *ABLGY* WD5 — 54 F8
Tannery Cl *CROY/NA* CR0 — 204 C5
　*DAGE* RM10 — 124 C8
Tannery La *RPLY/SEND* GU23 — 233 H8
　*SHGR* GU5 — 268 F8
The Tannery *REDH* RH1 — 257 F10
Tannington Ter *HBRY* N5 — 119 H8
Tannsfeld Rd *SYD* SE26 — 182 C8
Tannsfield Dr *HHNE* HP2 — 36 A4
Tannsmore Cl *HHNE* HP2 — 36 A4
Tansley Cl *HOLWY* N7 — 118 E10
Tanswell St *STHWK* SE1 — 18 A2
Tansy Cl *EHAM* E6 — 142 B8
　*HARH* RM3 — 105 M7
　*RGUE* GU4 — 250 F8
Tant Av *CAN/RD* E16 — 141 P8
Tantony Gv *CHDH* RM6 — 123 N1
Tanworth Cl *NTHWD* HA6 — 92 D7
Tanworth Gdns *PIN* HA5 — 93 J10
Tanyard La *BXLY* DA5 — 186 B3
Tanyard Wy *HORL* RH6 — 280 C3
Tan Yard La *BXLY* DA5 — 186 B3
Tanys Dell *HLWE* CM20 — 29 N3
Tanza Rd *HAMP* NW3 — 118 A9
Tapestry Cl *BELMT* SM2 — 221 L4
Taplow Ct *MTCM* CR4 — 201 P4
Taplow Rd *PLMGR* N13 — 99 P3
Taplow St *IS* N1 — 6 F8
Tapner's Rd
　*BRKHM/BTCW* RH3 — 274 C6
Tappesfield Rd *PECK* SE15 — 160 B3
Tapp St *WCHPL* E1 — 140 A6
Tapster St *BAR* EN5 — 77 J2
Tara Ms *CEND/HSY/T* N8 — 118 F4
Taransay Rd *IS* N1 — 6 C1
Taransey *HHS/BOV* HP3 — 36 C8
Tara Ter *BROCKY* SE4 — 160 C5
Tarbay La *WDSR* SL4 — 148 A8
Tarbert Rd *EDUL* SE22 — 181 M1
Tarbert Wk *WCHPL* E1 — 140 F4
Target Cl *EBED/NFELT* TW14 — 174 F2
Tarham Cl *HORL* RH6 — 276 A6
Tariff Rd *UED* N18 — 99 P7
Tarleton Gdns *FSTH* SE23 — 182 A6
Tarling Cl *SCUP* DA14 — 185 L6
Tarling Rd *CAN/RD* E16 — 141 H8
　*EFNCH* N2 — 97 H1
Tarling St *WCHPL* E1 — 140 E9
Tarmac Wy *WDR/YW* UB7 — 151 L6
Tarnbank *ENC/FH* EN2 — 78 F7
Tarn St *STHWK* SE1 — 18 E3
Tarnwood Pk *ELTH/MOT* SE9 — 184 F6
Tarnworth Rd *HARH* RM3 — 105 P6
Tarpan Wy *BROX* EN10 — 62 D2
Tarquin Ho *SYD* SE26 — 181 M8
Tarragon Cl *NWCR* SE14 — 160 G4
Tarragon Dr *GUW* GU2 — 249 M5
Tarragon Gv *SYD* SE26 — 182 C8
Tarrant Dr *HARP* AL5 — 20 A2
Tarrant Pl *MBLAR* W1H — 9 N2
Tarrington Cl
　*STRHM/NOR* SW16 — 180 E7
Tartar Hill Rd *COB* KT11 — 217 K9
Tartar Rd *COB* KT11 — 217 K9
Tarver Rd *WALW* SE17 — 19 D8
Tarves Wy *GNWCH* SE10 — 160 G6
Tash Pl *FBAR/BDGN* N11 — 98 C6
Tasker Cl *HYS/HAR* UB3 — 152 B6
Tasker Rd *CDW/CHF* RM16 — 168 G2
　*HAMP* NW3 — 118 A10
Tasmania Ter *UED* N18 — 99 H5
Tasman Rd *BRXN/ST* SW9 — 158 F9
Tasso Rd *HMSMTH* W6 — 14 B4
Tate Cl *LHD/OX* KT22 — 237 H9
Tate Gdns *BUSH* WD23 — 89 N1
Tate Rd *CAN/RD* E16 — 142 C10
　*CFSP/GDCR* SL9 — 90 C8
　*SUT* SM1 — 221 L3
Tates Orch *HART* DA3 — 211 N1
Tatham Pl *STJWD* NW8 — 3 M3
Tatnell Rd *FSTH* SE23 — 182 C2
Tatsfield Av *WAB* EN9 — 45 J2
Tatsfield La *BH/WHM* TN16 — 263 M2
Tattenham Cnr Rd
　*EPSOM* KT18 — 238 C3
Tattenham Crs *EPSOM* KT18 — 238 D3
Tattenham Gv *EPSOM* KT18 — 238 E4
Tattenham Wy
　*KWD/TDW/WH* KT20 — 239 H3
Tattersall Cl *ELTH/MOT* SE9 — 184 B1
Tattle HI *HERT/WAT* SG14 — 24 B1
Tatton Crs *CLPT* E5 — 120 E10
Tatton St *HLWE* CM17 — 29 M10
Tatum St *WALW* SE17 — 19 H6
Tauber Cl *BORE* WD6 — 75 L8

Tauheed Cl *FSBYPK* N4 — 119 K7
Taunton Av *CTHM* CR3 — 241 N9
 *HSLW* TW3 — 154 B8
 *RYNPK* SW20 — 200 G2
Taunton Cl *BARK/HLT* IG6 — 103 J7
 *BXLYHN* DA7 — 164 E6
 *CHEAM* SM3 — 201 K8
 *CRAWE* RH10 — 284 C7
 *ENC/FH* EN2 — 79 M10
Taunton La *COUL/CHIP* CR5 — 241 H5
Taunton Ms *CAMTN* NW1 — 10 C1
Taunton Ms *CAMTN* NW1 — 10 B1
Taunton Rd *GFD/PVL* UB6 — 134 C1
 *GVW* DA11 — 189 M1
 *HARH* RM3 — 105 K5
 *LEE/GVPK* SE12 — 183 K1
Taunton V *GVE* DA12 — 190 C6
Taunton Wy *STAN* HA7 — 95 K10
Tavern Cl *CAR* SM5 — 201 P7
Taverners *HHNE* HP2 — 35 P4
Taverners Cl *NTGHL* W11 — 8
Taverner Sq *HBRY* N5 — 119 K3
Taverners Wy *CHING* E4 — 101 K2
 *HOD* EN11 — 44 F3
Tavistock Av *GFD/PVL* UB6 — 134 F4
 *MLHL* NW7 — 96 C8
 *STAL* AL1 — 38 B9
 *WALTH* E17 — 120 C1
Tavistock Cl *HARH* RM3 — 105 L9
 *POTB/CUF* EN6 — 59 N7
 *STA* TW18 — 173 N10
 *STAL* AL1 — 38 C9
 *STNW/STAM* N16 * — 119 M10
Tavistock Crs *COVGDN* WC2E * — 11 M7
 *NTGHL* W11 — 8
Tavistock Gdns *GDMY/SEVK* IG3 — 123 H9
Tavistock Gv *CROY/NA* CR0 — 203 L7
 *EDGW* HA8 — 36 L9
 *FSBYPK* N4 — 119 L4
 *HAYES* BR2 — 205 L4
 *HGDN/ICK* UB10 — 112 C10
 *NTGHL* W11 — 8
Tavistock Ms *NTGHL* W11 * — 8
Tavistock Pl *STHGT/OAK* N14 * — 11
 *STPAN* WC1H — 11
Tavistock Rd *CAR* SM5 — 201 N8
 *CROY/NA* CR0 — 203 L8
 *EDGW* HA8 — 36 L9
 *FSBYPK* N4 — 119 L4
 *HAYES* BR2 — 205 L4
 *HGDN/ICK* UB10 — 112 C10
 *NTGHL* W11 — 8
 *SRTFD* E15 — 141 L7
 *SWFD* E18 — 121 M1
 *WATN* WD24 — 73 L3
 *WDR/YW* UB7 — 131 N10
 *WLSDN* NW10 — 99 J1
Tavistock Sq *STPAN* WC1H — 11 K1
Tavistock St *COVGDN* WC2E — 11 L1
Tavistock Ter *ARCH* N19 — 118 C8
Taviton St *STPAN* WC1H — 11 J1
Tavy Br *ABYW* SE2 — 163 L3
Tavy Cl *LBTH* SE11 — 18 B7
Tawney Common *EPP* CM16 — 66 B8
Tawney La *ABR/ST* RM4 — 84 D5
 *EPP* CM16 — 66 D8
Tawny Rd *THMD* SE28 — 143 L9
Tawneys Rd *HLWS* CM18 — 47 J3
Tawny Cl *FELT* TW13 — 175 H6
 *WEA* W13 — 134 G10
Tawny Wy *BERM/RHTH* SE16 — 160 C3
Tayben Av *WHTN* TW2 — 176 D2
Taybridge Rd *BTSEA* SW11 — 158 B9
Tayburn Cl *POP/IOD* E14 — 141 N8
Tayfield Cl *HGDN/ICK* UB10 — 112 D8
Tayles Hill Dr *EW* KT17 — 229
Taylifers *HLWW/ROY* CM19 — 46 D6
Taylor Av *RCH/KEW* TW9 — 155 N6
Taylor Cl *CRW* RM5 — 104 B8
 *DEPT* SE8 — 160 L5
 *HOR/WEW* KT19 — 219 M7
 *HPTN* TW12 — 176 C7
 *HSLW* TW3 — 154 B7
 *ORP* BR6 — 227 J1
 *STALE/WH* AL4 — 38 F2
Taylor Dr *ASHTD* KT21 — 237 J3
 *MTCM* CR4 — 179 P10
 *WLGTN* SM6 — 222 C2
Taylors Av *HOD* EN11 — 44 F4
Taylor's Blds *WOOL/PLUM* SE18 — 162 E3
Taylor's Cl *SCUP* DA14 — 185 J7
Taylor's Ct *FELT* TW13 — 175 J4
Taylor's Gn *ACT* W3 * — 136 B8
Taylor's La *BAR* EN5 — 77 J5
 *SYD* SE26 — 182 A7
 *WLSDN* NW10 — 136 B2
Taylors Md *MLHL* NW7 — 96 D6
Taylor Rd *CSHM* HP5 — 51 J3
Taylor Wk *CRAWW* RH11 * — 283 M7
Taymount Ri *FSTH* SE23 — 182 B5
Taynton Dr *REDH* RH1 — 258 E6
Tayport Cl *IS* N1 — 5 N4
Tayside Dr *EDGW* HA8 — 95 N4
Taywood Rd *NTHLT* UB5 — 133 M6
Teak Cl *BERM/RHTH* SE16 — 140 D10
Teal Av *STMC/STPC* BR5 — 207 N4
Teal Cl *CAN/RD* E16 — 142 A7
 *PEND* EN3 — 30 C3
 *SAND/SEL* CR2 — 224 C7
Teal Ct *DORK* RH4 * — 272 F1
Teal Dr *NTHWD* HA6 — 32 D8
Teale St *BETH* E2 — 7 P7
Tealing Dr *HOR/WEW* KT19 — 220 H1
Teal Pl *SUT* SM1 — 221 J2
Teal Wy *HHS/BOV* HP3 — 54 A1
Teasel Cl *CRAWW* RH11 — 283 L10
 *CROY/NA* CR0 — 204 C6
Teasel Crs *THMD* SE28 — 143 H10
Teasel Wy *SRTFD* E15 — 141 K5
Teazle Md *EPP* CM16 — 65 L1
Teazlewood Pk *LHD/OX* KT22 — 216 F1
Tebworth Rd *TOTM* N17 — 99 N8
Technology Pk *CDALE/KGS* NW9 * — 116 A1
Tedder Cl *CHSGTN* KT9 — 219 H4
 *HGDN/ICK* UB10 — 132 A2
 *RSLP* HA4 — 113 H10
Tedder Rd *HHNE* HP2 — 36 B5
 *SAND/SEL* CR2 — 224 B7
Teddington Pk *TEDD* TW11 — 176 B7
Teddington Park Rd *TEDD* TW11 — 176 A6
Tedworth Gdns *CHEL* SW3 — 16 A8
Tedworth Sq *CHEL* SW3 — 16 A8
Tees Av *GFD/PVL* UB6 — 134 D4
Teesdale Av *ISLW* TW7 — 154 B6
Teesdale Cl *BETH* E2 — 7 P8
Teesdale Gdns *ISLW* TW7 — 154 A7
 *SNWD* SE25 — 203 M2
Teesdale Rd *RDART* DA2 — 188 B4
 *STHL* UB2 — 132 E7
 *WAN* E11 — 121 L4
Teesdale St *BETH* E2 — 140 A4
Teesdale Yd *BETH* E2 * — 7 P8
Tees Dr *HARH* RM3 — 105 K8
Tee Side *HERT/BAY* SG13 — 26 A4
The Tee *ACT* W3 — 136 B8
Teevan Cl *CROY/NA* CR0 — 203 P7
Teevan Rd *CROY/NA* CR0 — 203 P6
Tegg's La *WOKS/MYFD* GU22 — 233 J2
Teignmouth Cl *CLAP* SW4 — 158 A1
 *EDGW* HA8 — 95 L10
Teignmouth Gdns *GFD/PVL* UB6 — 134 F4
 *WELL* DA16 — 163 M8
Telcote Wy *RSLP* HA4 * — 113 K5

Telegraph HI *HAMP* NW3 — 117 L8
Telegraph La *ESH/CLAY* KT10 — 218 E1
Telegraph Ms *GDMY/SEVK* IG3 — 123 J6
Telegraph Pas *BRXS/STRHM* SW2 — 180 F3
Telegraph PI *POP/IOD* E14 — 160 G3
Telegraph Rd *PUT/ROE* SW15 — 176 F3
Telegraph Tr *WLGTN* SM6 — 222 B8
Telephone PI *WKENS* W14 — 14 C4
Telferscot Rd *BAL* SW12 — 180 E4
Telford Cl *GSTN* WD25 — 73 L1
Telford Ct *GU* GU1 — 268 C1
Telford Dr *SL* SL1 — 128 F10
Telford PI *CRAWE* RH10 — 283 P8
Telford Rd *CDALE/KGS* NW9 — 116 C4
 *ELTH/MOT* SE9 — 184 C5
 *LCOL/BKTW* AL2 — 57 H7
 *NKENS* W10 — 8 A3
 *STHL* UB1 — 114 B7
 *WHTN* TW2 — 175 P3
Telford Road North Circular Rd *FBAR/BDGN* N11 — 98 D6
Telfords Yd *WAP* E1W — 13 N4
Telford Ter *PIM* SW1V — 16 G9
Telford Wy *ACT* W3 — 136 B7
 *YEAD* UB4 — 133 M7
Telham Ct *CRAWW* RH11 * — 283 J10
Telham Rd *EHAM* E6 — 142 D4
Telison Av *WLSDN* NW10 — 136 A2
Telscombe Cl *ORP* BR6 — 207 H9
Telston La *RSEV* TN14 — 246 F3
Temeraire PI *BTFD* TW8 — 155 L4
Temeraire St *BERM/RHTH* SE16 — 160 B1
Tempelhof Av *HDN* NW4 — 116 F5
Temperance St *STALW/RED* AL3 — 38 B6
Temperley Rd *BAL* SW12 — 180 B3
Tempest Av *POTB/CUF* EN6 — 59 M8
Tempest Md *EPP* CM16 — 66 C3
Tempest Rd *EGH* TW20 — 172 F4
Tempest Wy *RAIN* RM13 — 145 H1
Templar Dr *GVW* DA11 — 190 B2
 *THMD* SE28 — 143 N8
Templar PI *HPTN* TW12 — 175 P10
Templars Av *GLDGN* NW11 — 117 J4
Templars Ct *DART* DA1 * — 187 P1
Templars Crs *FNCH* N3 — 97 K10
Templars Dr *KTN/HRWW/WS* HA3 — 94 C7
Templar St *CMBW* SE5 — 158 J8
Temple Av *BCTR* RM8 — 124 B6
 *CROY/NA* CR0 — 204 G10
 *EMB* EC4Y — 12 A4
 *TRDG/WHET* N20 — 97 N10
Temple Bank *HLW* CM20 — 29 L6
Temple Bar Rd *WOKN/KNAP* GU21 — 231 L5
Temple Cl *CHESW* EN7 — 61 P7
 *CRAWE* RH10 — 284 E8
 *FNCH* N3 — 97 J10
 *THMD* SE28 — 162 F2
 *WAN* E11 — 121 K5
 *WAT* WD17 — 72 G6
Templecombe Ms *WOKS/MYFD* GU22 * — 232 E2
Templecombe Rd *HOM* E9 — 140 B3
Templecombe Wy *MRDN* SM4 — 201 H5
Temple Ct *POTB/CUF* EN6 — 58 G7
Templedene Av *STA* TW18 — 173 L10
Temple Dwellings *BETH* E2 * — 140 A4
Temple Field Ct *ADL/WDHM* KT15 — 215 L3
Temple Flds *HERT/WAT* SG14 — 25 J3
Temple Fortune HI *GLDGN* NW11 — 117 K3
Temple Fortune La *GLDGN* NW11 — 117 J4
Temple Gdns *BCTR* RM8 — 123 P1
 *GLDGN* NW11 — 117 J4
 *RKW/CH/CXG* WD3 — 92 C4
 *STA* TW18 — 195 J1
 *WCHMH* N21 — 99 J3
Temple Gv *ENC/FH* EN2 — 79 J7
 *GLDGN* NW11 — 117 K4
Temple La *EMB* EC4Y — 12 B6
Temple Mead *HLWE* CM17 — 47 P2
Temple Mead Cl *STAN* HA7 — 95 J5
Templeman Cl *PUR/KEN* CR8 — 241 H2
Templeman Rd *HNWL* W7 — 134 E7
Temple Md *HHNE* HP2 — 35 N5
 *HLWW/ROY* CM19 — 45 N1
Templemead Cl *ACT* W3 — 136 B8
Temple Mead Cl *STAN* HA7 — 94 G7
Temple Mills La *LEY* E10 — 120 G9
Templepan La *RKW/CH/CXG* WD3 — 71 P3
Temple Pde *BAR* EN5 * — 97 N1
Temple Pk *UX/CGN* UB8 — 132 B5
Temple PI *TPL/STR* WC2R — 11 P7
Temple Rd *BH/WHM* TN16 — 168 D3
 *CEND/HSY/T* N8 — 118 G2
 *CHSWK* W4 — 155 P2
 *CRICK* NW2 — 99 K10
 *CROY/NA* CR0 — 223 L1
 *EA* W5 — 155 J2
 *EHAM* E6 — 142 B3
 *HOR/WEW* KT19 — 220 D3
 *HSLW* TW3 — 154 A10
 *RCH/KEW* TW9 — 155 L8
 *SUT* SM1 — 201 N10
 *WEA* W13 — 134 G10
Temple Sheen Rd *MORT/ESHN* SW14 — 155 P10
Temple St *BETH* E2 — 140 A4
Temple Ter *WDGN* N22 * — 99 H10
Templeton Cl *CHING* E4 — 100 F5
Templeton Cl *NRWD* SE19 — 203 L1
 *STNW/STAM* N16 * — 119 M10
Templeton PI *ECT* SW5 — 14 F6
Templeton Rd *FSBYPK* N4 — 119 H1
Temple Vw *SLN* SL2 — 109 H10
Temple Wy *SLN* SL2 — 201 N10
Templewood *WEA* W13 — 134 G7
Templewood Av *HAMP* NW3 — 117 H9
Templewood Gdns *HAMP* NW3 — 117 H9
Templewood La *SLN* SL2 — 109 H10
Temple Yd *BETH* E2 * — 7 P8
Tenacre *WOKN/KNAP* GU21 — 231 K9
Tenbury Cl *FSTGT* E7 — 122 A1
Tenbury Ct *BAL* SW12 — 179 P3
Tenby Av *KTN/HRWW/WS* HA3 — 94 E8
Tenby Cl *CHDH* RM6 — 123 P4
 *SEVS/STOTM* N15 — 119 N2
Tenby Dr *ASC* SL5 — 192 C5
Tenby Gdns *NTHLT* UB5 — 114 A5
Tenby Rd *CHDH* RM6 — 123 P4
 *EDGW* HA8 — 96 A4
 *PEND* EN3 — 30 G3
 *WALTH* E17 — 120 B5
 *WELL* DA16 — 163 N1
Tenby Wy *WOKS/MYFD* GU22 — 232 G2
Tenchleys La *OXTED* RH8 — 262 A7
Tench St *WAP* E1W * — 160 A1
Tenda Rd *STHWK* SE1 — 160 A3
Tendring Rd *HLWS* CM18 — 46 G1
Tendring Wy *CHDH* RM6 — 123 M3
Tenham Av *BRXS/STRHM* SW2 — 180 B3
Tenison Wy *STHWK* SE1 — 12 A10
Tennand Cl *CHESW* EN7 — 61 P1

Tenniel Cl *BAY/PAD* W2 — 9 J6
Tennis Av *BORE* WD6 — 75 N9
Tennison Av *BORE* WD6 — 75 N9
Tennison Cl *COUL/CHIP* CR5 — 241 L8
Tennison Rd *SNWD* SE25 — 203 N4
Tennis St *STHWK* SE1 — 18 G1
Tenniswood Rd *EN* EN1 — 79 M5
 *GRAYS* RM17 — 167 N2
 *MNPK* E12 — 142 E2
 *NWMAL* KT3 — 200 E5
 *TWK* TW1 — 176 E4
 *WAB* EN9 — 63 K10
Tennyson Cl *RCHPK/HAM* TW10 — 176 D7
 *FELT* TW13 — 177 J10
 *PEND* EN3 — 80 C9
 *WELL* DA16 — 163 P1
Tennyson Rd *ADL/WDHM* KT15 — 215 P1
 *ASHF* TW15 — 173 P8
 *HARH* RM3 — 105 K8
 *HNWL* W7 — 134 E7
 *KIL/WHAMP* NW6 — 2 C1
 *LCOL/BKTW* AL2 — 55 P2
 *LEY* E10 — 120 C6
 *MLHL* NW7 — 96 C6
 *PGE/AN* SE20 — 182 G10
 *RBRW/HUT* CM13 — 107 P1
 *SRTFD* E15 — 141 K2
 *WALTH* E17 — 120 E4
 *WIM/MER* SW19 — 179 M9
Tennyson St *VX/NE* SW8 — 158 C8
Tennyson Wk *GVW* DA11 — 190 A6
 *TIL* RM18 — 168 B8
Tennyson Wy *HCH* RM12 — 124 C6
Tensing Rd *STHL* UB2 — 132 E8
Tensing Rd *NWDGN* UB2 — 153 P2
Tentelow La *NWDGN* UB2 — 154 A2
Tenterden Cl *ELTH/MOT* SE9 — 184 C7
 *HDN* NW4 — 116 C1
Tenterden Dr *HDN* NW4 — 116 C1
Tenterden Gdns *CROY/NA* CR0 — 203 P7
 *HDN* NW4 — 116 C1
Tenterden Rd *BCTR* RM8 — 124 A7
 *CROY/NA* CR0 — 203 P7
 *TOTM* N17 — 99 N8
Tenterden St *CONDST* W1S — 10 F6
Tenter Gnd *WCHPL* E1 — 13 L4
Tenth Av *KWD/TDW/WH* KT20 * — 257 J2
Tent Peg La *STMC/STPC* BR5 — 206 F5
Tent St *WCHPL* E1 — 140 A6
Tenzing Rd *HHNE* HP2 — 36 B6
Tercel Pth *CHIG* IG7 — 103 L5
Teredo St *BERM/RHTH* SE16 — 160 F2
Terence Cl *GVE* DA12 — 191 J5
Teresa Gdns *CHES/WCR* EN8 — 62 B10
Terling Cl *WAN* E11 — 121 L8
Terling Rd *BCTR* RM8 — 124 B6
The Terlings *BRW* CM14 — 106 F4
Terling Wk *IS* N1 * — 6 E1
Terminus PI *BGVA* SW1W — 16 F4
Terminus St *HLW* CM20 — 28 G10
Tern Gdns *UPMR* RM14 — 126 D6
Tern Rd *CRAWW* RH11 — 282 C6
Terrace Gdns *BARN* SW13 — 156 C9
 *WAT* WD17 — 73 J6
Terrace Rd *HOM* E9 — 140 C2
 *PLSTW* E13 — 141 M3
 *WOT/HER* KT12 — 197 J6
The Terraces *RDART* DA2 — 188 B3
Terrace St *GVE* DA12 — 190 E2
The Terrace *ADL/WDHM* KT15 — 215 P2
 *ASC* SL5 — 192 C5
 *BARN* SW13 — 156 A8
 *BETH* E2 — 140 B5
 *CHING* E4 — 101 K4
 *DEPT* SE8 — 160 E5
 *EFNCH* N2 * — 117 H2
 *FNCH* N3 * — 97 J10
 *GVE* DA12 — 190 E2
 *KIL/WHAMP* NW6 — 2 A1
 *SEV* TN13 — 246 E8
 *WOKS/MYFD* GU22 — 232 E2
Terrace Wk *DAGW* RM9 — 123 P10
Terrac St *RCH/KEW* TW9 — 155 L10
Terrapin Rd *TOOT* SW17 — 180 G5
Terretts PI *IS* N1 * — 6 C1
Terrick Rd *WDGN* N22 — 98 F9
Terrick St *SHB* W12 — 137 J6
Terrilands *PIN* HA5 — 113 N1
Terront Rd *SEVS/STOTM* N15 — 119 K5
Terry Pl *UX/CGN* UB8 * — 131 M7
Tessa Sanderson Wy *GFD/PVL* UB6 — 114 C10
Testard Rd *GUW* GU2 — 267 J5
Testers Cl *OXTED* RH8 — 261 N7
Testerton Rd *NTGHL* W11 * — 136 G1
Testerton Wk *NTGHL* W11 * — 136 G1
Testwood Rd *WDSR* SL4 — 148 C7
Tetbury Pl *IS* N1 — 6 B1
Tetcott Rd *WBPTN* SW10 — 157 M6
Tetherdown *MUSWH* N10 — 118 B1
Tethys Rd *HHNE* HP2 — 36 A3
Tetty Wy *BMLY* BR1 — 205 M2
Teversham La *VX/NE* SW8 — 158 F7
Teviot Av *SOCK/AV* RM15 — 146 A4
Teviot Cl *GUW* GU2 — 249 M7
 *WELL* DA16 — 163 L1
Teviot St *POP/IOD* E14 — 141 N7
Tewin Cl *SLN* SL2 — 110 E5
Tewin Rd *HNHL* SE24 * — 33 J4
Tewin Wk *WGCE* AL7 — 23 J4
Tewin Rd *HHNE* HP2 — 36 C6
 *WGCE* AL7 — 23 J4
Tewkesbury Av *FSTH* SE23 — 182 A4
 *PIN* HA5 — 113 M3
Tewkesbury Cl *BF/WBF* KT14 — 215 N7
 *LOU* IG10 — 82 B10
Tewkesbury Gdns *CDALE/KGS* NW9 — 115 N1
Tewkesbury Rd *CAR* SM5 — 201 N8
 *SEVS/STOTM* N15 — 119 L5
 *WEA* W13 — 134 F10
Tewkesbury Ter *FBAR/BDGN* N11 — 98 D7
Tewson Rd *WOOL/PLUM* SE18 — 163 N4
Teynham Av *EN* EN1 — 79 M1
Teynham Gn *HAYES* BR2 — 205 M5
Teynham Rd *RDART* DA2 — 188 B4
Teynton Ter *TOTM* N17 — 99 K9
Thackeray Av *TIL* RM18 — 168 E7
Thackeray Cl *ISLW* TW7 — 154 F8
 *UX/CGN* UB8 — 132 C8
 *WIM/MER* SW19 — 178 D10
Thackeray Dr *CHDH* RM6 — 123 L5
Thackeray Ms *HACK* E8 — 7 N1
Thackeray Rd *EHAM* E6 — 142 A4
 *VX/NE* SW8 — 158 C8
Thackeray St *KENS* W8 — 15 H3
Thakeham Cl *SYD* SE26 — 182 A8
Thalia Cl *GNWCH* SE10 — 161 J1
Thal Massing Cl *RBRW/HUT* CM13 — 107 N3
Thame Cl *HNHL* SE24 — 159 H4
Thame Rd *BERM/RHTH* SE16 — 160 C1
Thames Av *CHERT* KT16 — 193 J3
 *DAGW* RM9 — 144 C6
 *GFD/PVL* UB6 — 134 E4
 *HHNE* HP2 — 36 A1
 *WBPTN* SW10 — 157 M7
 *WPK* KT4 — 200 G6
Thames Bank *MORT/ESHN* SW14 — 155 P6
Thamesbank PI *THMD* SE28 — 143 M8
Thames Cir *POP/IOD* E14 — 160 D5
Thames Cl *CHERT* KT16 — 195 J2
 *HPTN* TW12 — 198 A3
 *RAIN* RM13 — 145 J4

Thames Crs *CHSWK* W4 — 156 B6
Thamesdale *LCOL/BKTW* AL2 — 57 L3
Thames Down Link *BRYLDS* KT5 — 199 P5
 *EPSOM* KT18 — 219 L8
 *RDKG* RH5 — 255 H8
Thames Eyot *TWK* TW1 * — 176 D4
Thamesfield Ms *SHPTN* TW17 — 196 D4
Thamesgate Cl *RCHPK/HAM* TW10 — 176 D7
Thames Lock *WEY* KT13 * — 196 B9
Thames Mdw *WDSR* SL4 — 148 C7
 *WOT/HER* KT12 — 197 H6
Thames Meadow *E/WMO/HCT* KT8 — 197 P3
Thamesmere Dr *THMD* SE28 — 143 K9
Thames PI *PUT/ROE* SW15 — 156 G9
Thamespoint *TEDD* TW11 * — 177 J10
Thames Quay *WBPTN* SW10 * — 157 M7
Thames Reach *KUT/HW* KT1 * — 199 J1
Thames Rd *BARK* IG11 — 143 K5
 *CAN/RD* E16 — 142 A10
 *CHSWK* W4 — 155 M5
 *DART* DA1 — 165 H9
 *DTCH/LGLY* SL3 — 150 A3
 *WDSR* SL4 * — 148 B6
Thames Side *KUT/HW* KT1 — 199 J1
 *STA* TW18 — 195 K1
 *WDSR* SL4 — 149 J6
Thames St *GNWCH* SE10 — 160 G5
 *KUT/HW* KT1 — 199 J2
 *STA* TW18 — 173 J8
 *SUN* TW16 — 197 J3
 *WDSR* SL4 — 149 J7
 *WEY* KT13 — 216 C1
 *WOT/HER* KT12 — 196 G7
Thamesvale Cl *HSLW* TW3 — 153 P8
Thames Vw *CDW/CHF* RM16 — 168 C4
Thames Village *CHSWK* W4 — 155 P7
Thamley *PUR* RM19 — 165 P3
Thanescroft Gdns *CROY/NA* CR0 — 203 M10
Thanet Dr *HAYES* BR2 — 206 A10
Thanet PI *CROY/NA* CR0 — 223 K1
Thanet Rd *BXLY* DA5 — 186 B3
 *ERITH* DA8 — 164 F6
Thanet St *STPAN* WC1H — 5 L10
Thane VIs *HOLWY* N7 — 118 G10
Thanet Cl *GVE* DA12 — 190 C8
Tharp Rd *WLGTN* SM6 — 222 E3
Thatcham Gdns *TRDG/WHET* N20 — 97 M1
Thatcher Cl *WDR/YW* UB7 * — 151 P1
 *CRAWE* RH10 — 283 N10
Thatchers Cft *HHNE* HP2 — 35 P2
Thatchers Cl *RGUW* GU3 — 249 J5
Thatchers La *RGUW* GU3 — 249 J4
Thatchers Wy *ISLW* TW7 — 176 C1
Thatches Gv *CHDH* RM6 — 123 P1
Thaxted Rd *BKHH* IG9 — 102 B1
 *ELTH/MOT* SE9 — 184 F1
Thaxted Wy *WAB* EN9 — 63 J9
Thaxton Rd *WKENS* W14 — 14 D9
Thayers Farm Rd *BECK* BR3 — 183 H5
Thayer St *MHST* W1U — 10 D5
Thaynesfield *POTB/CUF* EN6 — 59 N1
Theatre Sq *SRTFD* E15 — 141 J1
Theatre St *BTSEA* SW11 — 158 A9
Theberton St *IS* N1 — 6 B1
The Beverley *MRDN* SM4 — 200 G8
The Bridge School *IS* N1 * — 6 F1
The Courtyard *HAYES* BR2 — 226 B3
 *CHOB/PIR* GU24 — 230 C9
The Green *WIM/MER* SW19 — 178 G8
The Laurels *LCOL/BKTW* AL2 — 55 P4
Thela Av *WARE* SG12 — 27 J7
Theleway Cl *HOD* EN11 — 26 C1
Thellusson Wy *RKW/CH/CXG* WD3 — 91 K1
Thelma Cl *GVE* DA12 — 191 J8
Thelma Gv *TEDD* TW11 — 176 B9
Thelusson Ct *RAD* WD7 — 74 F1
Theobald Crs *KTN/HRWW/WS* HA3 — 94 C9
Theobald Rd *CROY/NA* CR0 — 203 H8
 *WALTH* E17 — 139 J3
Theobalds Av *GRAYS* RM17 — 167 P4
Theobald's Cl *POTB/CUF* EN6 — 59 P3
Theobald's Rd *GINN* WC1R — 11 N3
 *POTB/CUF* EN6 — 60 F6
Theobalds Park Rd *ENC/FH* EN2 — 79 J1
Theobald St *BORE* WD6 — 75 P6
 *STHWK* SE1 — 19 H4
Theodora Wy *PIN* HA5 — 112 G1
Theodore Rd *LEW* SE13 — 183 K5
Thepps Cl *REDH* RH1 — 276 D8
Therapia La *CROY/NA* CR0 — 202 E7
Therapia Rd *EDUL* SE22 — 182 B2
Theresa Rd *HMSMTH* W6 — 137 H9
Theresa's Wk *SAND/SEL* CR2 — 223 L5
Therfield Rd *STALW/RED* AL3 — 38 D3
Thermopylae Ga *POP/IOD* E14 — 160 F5
Thessaly Rd *VX/NE* SW8 — 158 C7
Thetford Cl *PLMGR* N13 — 99 H6
Thetford Rd *ASHF* TW15 — 173 H7
 *DAGW* RM9 — 143 P7
 *NWMAL* KT3 — 200 B5
Thetis Ter *RCH/KEW* TW9 * — 155 N6
Thicket Crs *SUT* SM1 — 221 N1
Thicket Gv *DAGW* RM9 — 143 M1
 *PGE/AN* SE20 — 181 G10
Thicket Rd *PGE/AN* SE20 — 181 P10
 *SUT* SM1 — 221 N1
Thicket Ter *PGE/AN* SE20 * — 181 G10
The Thicket *WDR/YW* UB7 — 133 L5
Thickthorne La *STA* TW18 — 173 M10
Thieves La *HERT/WAT* SG14 — 25 M8
Third Av *BOW* E3 — 140 A10
 *CHDH* RM6 — 123 M4
 *DAGE* RM10 — 144 D5
 *EN* EN1 — 80 B9
 *GNTH/NBYPK* IG2 — 123 P8
 *HYS/HAR* UB3 — 133 J5
 *HLWW/ROY* CM19 — 46 C2
 *KWD/TDW/WH* KT20 * — 257 J2
 *MNPK* E12 — 122 F8
 *NKENS* W10 — 8 B1
 *PEND* EN3 — 30 F9

 *PLSTW* E13 — 141 M5
 *WALTH* E17 — 120 J7
 *WBLY* HA9 — 115 J7
 *WTHM* RM20 — 166 F5
Third Cl *E/WMO/HCT* KT8 — 198 C3
Third Crs *SL* SL1 — 129 H7
Third Cross Rd *WHTN* TW2 — 176 C5
Thirkleby Cl *SL* SL1 — 129 H10
Thirleby Rd *EDGW* HA8 — 96 A9
 *WEST* SW1P — 17 H4
Thirlmere Av *GFD/PVL* UB6 — 135 L1
Thirlmere Gdns *NTHWD* HA6 — 32 C8
 *WBLY* HA9 — 115 H5
Thirlmere Ri *BMLY* BR1 — 183 L9
Thirlmere Rd *BXLYHN* DA7 — 164 D8
 *BRXS/STRHM* SW16 — 180 E7
 *MUSWH* N10 — 98 C9
Thirsk Cl *NTHLT* UB5 — 133 P4
Thirsk Rd *BORE* WD6 — 75 M4
 *BTSEA* SW11 — 158 B9
 *MTCM* CR4 — 180 B10
 *SNWD* SE25 — 203 L4
Thirteenth Av *KWD/TDW/WH* KT20 * — 257 J2
Thisilefield Cl *BXLY* DA5 — 185 N4
Thistlebrook *ABYW* SE2 — 163 M2
Thistle Cl *HHW* HP1 — 35 L7
Thistlecroft *HHW* HP1 — 35 L7
Thistlecroft Gdns *STAN* HA7 — 95 N7
Thistlecroft Rd *WOT/HER* KT12 — 217 K1
Thistledene *BF/WBF* KT14 — 215 J9
Thistledene Av *CRW* RM5 — 104 C6
 *RYLN/HDSTN* HA2 — 113 M8
Thistle Gv *WBPTN* SW10 — 15 K8
 *WGCE* AL7 — 23 M8
Thistlemead *CHST* BR7 — 206 E2
Thistle Md *CLPT* E5 — 82 D7
Thistle Rd *GVE* DA12 — 191 H3
The Thistles *HRW* HA1 * — 35 L5
Thistlewaite Rd *CLPT* E5 — 120 A8
Thistle Wy *HORL* RH6 — 281 K5
Thistlewood Cl *HOLWY* N7 — 118 C7
Thistlewood Crs *CROY/NA* CR0 — 225 J8
Thistley Cl *COUL/CHIP* CR5 — 240 C8
 *NFNCH/WDSPK* N12 — 97 P5
Thoby La *BRWN* CM15 — 87 M3
Thomas A Beckett Cl *HRW* HA1 — 114 C3
Thomas Baines Rd *BTSEA* SW11 — 157 N9
Thomas Bata Av *TIL* RM18 — 169 L3
Thomas Cl *BRWN* CM15 — 107 K3
Thomas Cribb Ms *EHAM* E6 — 142 C8
Thomas Dean Rd *SYD* SE26 * — 182 G7
Thomas Dinwiddy Rd *LEE/GVPK* SE12 — 183 N6
Thomas Doyle St *STHWK* SE1 — 18 C3
Thomas Dr *GPK* RM2 — 125 K2
Thomas' La *CAT* SE6 — 182 C3
Thomas Moore Wy *EFNCH* N2 — 117 M1
Thomas More Sq *WAP* E1W — 13 N8
Thomas More St *WAP* E1W — 13 N8
Thomas North Ter *CAN/RD* E16 — 141 L7
Thomas PI *KENS* W8 * — 14 G4
Thomas Rd *POP/IOD* E14 — 140 C8
Thomas Rochford Wy *CHES/WCR* EN8 — 63
Thomas St *WOOL/PLUM* SE18 — 162 D3
Thomas Wall Cl *SUT* SM1 — 221 L2
Thompkins La *SLN* SL2 — 128 E2
Thompson Av *DAGW* RM9 — 124 A8
 *RCH/KEW* TW9 — 155 N9
Thompson Cl *CHEAM* SM3 — 201 K8
 *DTCH/LGLY* SL3 — 150 D5
 *IL* IG1 — 122 E9
Thompson Rd *DAGW* RM9 — 124 A8
 *EDUL* SE22 — 181 N2
 *HGDN/ICK* UB10 — 131 P2
 *HSLW* TW3 — 154 A10
Thompson's Av *CMBW* SE5 — 158 K6
Thompson's La *CHOB/PIR* GU24 — 230 C9
Thomson's La *CHOB/PIR* GU24 — 213 J5
Thomson Av *RKW/CH/CXG* WD3 — 91 K1
Thomson Crs *CROY/NA* CR0 — 203 H8
Thomson Rd *KTN/HRWW/WS* HA3 — 114 D1
Thong La *GVE* DA12 — 191 D1
Thorburn Sq *STHWK* SE1 — 19 L4
Thorburn Wy *WIM/MER* SW19 — 179 N4
Thoresby St *IS* N1 — 6 F7
Thorkhill Gdns *THDIT* KT7 — 198 B3
Thorkhill Rd *THDIT* KT7 — 198 C3
Thorley Cl *BF/WBF* KT14 — 215 K10
Thorley Gdns *WOKS/MYFD* GU22 — 215 K10
Thornaby Gdns *UED* N18 — 99 J7
Thornash Cl *WOKN/KNAP* GU21 — 231 P1
Thornash Rd *WOKN/KNAP* GU21 — 231 P1
Thornash Wy *WOKN/KNAP* GU21 — 231 P1
Thorn Av *BUSH* WD23 — 94 B2
Thornbank Cl *STA* TW18 — 172 B8
Thornbury Wy *GU* GU1 — 250 F2
Thornbridge Rd *IVER* SL0 — 130 F3
Thornbrook *EPP* CM16 — 65 N1
Thornbury *HARP* AL5 — 20
Thornbury Av *ISLW* TW7 — 154 C6
Thornbury Cl *HOD* EN11 — 26 C9
 *STNW/STAM* N16 — 119 M10
Thornbury Gdns *BORE* WD6 — 75 P8
Thornbury Rd *CLAP* SW4 — 180 P2
 *ISLW* TW7 — 154 C6
Thornbury Sq *HGT* N6 — 118 C6
Thornby Rd *CLPT* E5 — 120 E8
Thorncliffe Rd *CLAP* SW4 — 159 N10
 *NWDGN* UB2 — 153 N4
Thorn Cl *HAYES* BR2 — 206 D6
 *NTHLT* UB5 — 133 N5
Thorncombe Rd *EDUL* SE22 — 181 L4
Thorncroft Cl *COUL/CHIP* CR5 — 241 H7
Thorncroft Rd *SUT* SM1 — 221 L2
Thorncroft St *VX/NE* SW8 — 158 E6
Thorndales *BRW* CM14 — 107 J5
Thorndean St *WAND/EARL* SW18 — 179 M4
Thorndene Av *RBRW/HUT* CM13 — 107 J3
Thorndike Av *NTHLT* UB5 — 133 H5
Thorndike Cl *WBPTN* SW10 — 157 M6
Thorndike Rd *IS* N1 — 6 F1
Thorndike St *PIM* SW1V * — 17 J7
Thorndon Ap *RBRW/HUT* CM13 — 107 M4
Thorndon Cl *STMC/STPC* BR5 — 184 A10
Thorndon Ct *RBRW/HUT* CM13 — 107 N7
Thorndon Gdns *HOR/WEW* KT19 — 220 B1
Thorndon Ga *RBRW/HUT* CM13 — 107 N7
Thorndon Rd *STMC/STPC* BR5 — 207 J2

Thorndown La *BFOR* GU20 — 212 C4
Thorn Dr *DTCH/LGLY* SL3 — 130 B8
Thorndyke Cl *CRAWE* RH10 — 284 E8
Thorndyke Ct *PIN* HA5 — 93 N8
Thorne Cl *ASHF* TW15 — 174 D10
 *CAN/RD* E16 — 141 M8
 *ERITH* DA8 — 164 C5
 *ESH/CLAY* KT10 — 218 C4
 *HHW* HP1 — 35
 *WAN* E11 — 121 K9
Thornelee Gdns *CROY/NA* CR0 — 223 J2
Thorne Rd *VX/NE* SW8 — 158 F6
Thorne's Cl *BECK* BR3 — 205 A4
Thorne St *BARN* SW13 — 156 B9
Thorney Crs *BTSEA* SW11 — 157 N6
Thorneycroft Cl *WOT/HER* KT12 — 197 K6
Thorneycroft Dr *PEND* EN3 — 80 H4
Thorney Hedge Rd *CHSWK* W4 — 155 N3
Thorney La North *IVER* SL0 — 131 J8
Thorney La South *WDR/YW* UB7 — 151 J1
Thorney Mill Rd *WDR/YW* UB7 — 151 J2
Thorney St *WEST* SW1P — 17 J5
Thornfield Av *MLHL* NW7 — 97 H9
Thornfield Pde *MLHL* NW7 * — 97 H8
Thornfield Rd *LEW* SE13 — 183 H1
Thornford Rd *LEW* SE13 — 183 H1
Thorngate Rd *MV/WKIL* W9 — 2
Thorngrove Rd *PLSTW* E13 — 141 N3
Thornham Gv *SRTFD* E15 — 121 J5
Thornham St *GNWCH* SE10 — 160 G5
Thornhaugh St *STPAN* WC1H — 11 K3
Thornhill Av *SURB* KT6 — 66 D2
 *WOOL/PLUM* SE18 — 163 H6
Thornhill Bridge Whf *IS* N1 — 5 N6
Thornhill Cl *AMSS* HP7 — 68 F6
Thornhill Gdns *BARK* IG11 — 143 H5
 *LEY* E10 — 120 G7
Thornhill Gv *IS* N1 — 6 A4
Thornhill Rd *CROY/NA* CR0 — 203 L6
 *HGDN/ICK* UB10 — 112 B9
 *IL* IG1 — 6 A3
 *LEY* E10 — 120 G7
 *NTHWD* HA6 — 92 D5
 *SURB* KT6 — 199 K9
Thornhill Sq *IS* N1 — 6 A4
Thornhill Wy *SHPTN* TW17 — 196 B5
Thorn La *RAIN* RM13 — 145 L4
Thorniaw Rd *WNWD* SE27 — 181 H7
Thornleas Pl *EHSLY* KT24 — 252 F1
Thornley Cl *TOTM* N17 — 99 P8
Thornley Dr *RYLN/HDSTN* HA2 — 114 B7
Thorn Md *HHNE* HP2 — 35 N6
Thornridge *BRW* CM14 — 106 C1
Thornsbeach Rd *CAT* SE6 — 183 H4
Thornsett Pl *PGE/AN* SE20 — 204 A4
Thornsett Rd *PGE/AN* SE20 * — 204 A4
 *WAND/EARL* SW18 — 179 L5
Thornsett Ter *PGE/AN* SE20 * — 204 A4
Thorn's Meadow *BH/WHM* TN16 — 245 M9
Thornton Av *BRXS/STRHM* SW2 — 180 E4
 *CHSWK* W4 — 156 B3
 *CROY/NA* CR0 — 202 G6
 *WDR/YW* UB7 — 152 A2
Thornton Cl *GUW* GU2 — 249 M7
 *HORL* RH6 — 279 P4
 *WDR/YW* UB7 — 152 A2
Thornton Dene *BECK* BR3 — 204 F2
Thornton Gdns *BAL* SW12 — 180 G4
Thornton HI *WIM/MER* SW19 — 178 H10
Thornton Hl *HORL* RH6 — 279 P4
Thornton PI *MBLAR* W1H — 10 A3
Thornton Rd *BAL* SW12 — 77 H7
 *BAR* EN5 — 77 H7
 *BELV* DA17 — 164 C3
 *BMLY* BR1 — 183 M8
 *CAR* SM5 — 201 N8
 *CROY/NA* CR0 — 202 C6
 *IL* IG1 — 122 E9
 *MORT/ESHN* SW14 — 156 A9
 *POTB/CUF* EN6 — 59 M6
 *THHTH* CR7 — 203 H5
 *UED* N18 — 100 B4
 *WAN* E11 — 121 J7
 *WIM/MER* SW19 — 178 H10
Thornton Rw *THHTH* CR7 — 203 H5
Thorntons Farm Av *ROMW/RG* RM7 — 124 D7
Thornton Side *BRXN/ST* SW9 — 258 C7
Thornton St *HERT/WAT* SG14 — 25 J5
 *STALW/RED* AL3 — 38 B5
Thornton Wy *GLDGN* NW11 — 117 L3
Thorntree Rd *CHARL* SE7 — 162 A4
Thornville Gv *MTCM* CR4 — 201 M2
Thornville St *DEPT* SE8 — 160 G9
Thornwood Cl *SWFD* E18 — 101 N10
 *LEW* SE13 — 183 K1
Thorogood Gdns *SRTFD* E15 — 121 K10
Thorogood Wy *RAIN* RM13 — 144 A10
Thorold Cl *SAND/SEL* CR2 — 224 C6
Thorold Rd *IL* IG1 — 122 B7
 *WDGN* N22 — 98 F8
The Thoroughfare *KWD/TDW/WH* KT20 — 238 D10
Thorparch Rd *VX/NE* SW8 — 158 D7
Thorpebank Rd *SHB* W12 — 136 D10
Thorpe By-Pass *EGH* TW20 — 193 N2
Thorpe Cl *CROY/NA* CR0 — 225 H7
 *EMPK* RM11 — 125 L4
 *NKENS* W10 — 8 A4
 *ORP* BR6 — 207 H9
 *SYD* SE26 * — 182 C7
Thorpe Ct *TOOT* SW17 — 179 P7
Thorpe Crs *OXHEY* WD19 — 33 J3
 *WALTH* E17 — 101 J10
Thorpedale Gdns *GNTH/NBYPK* IG2 — 122 D2
Thorpedale Rd *FSBYPK* N4 — 118 F2
Thorpefield Cl *STALE/WH* AL4 — 39 J3
Thorpe Hall Rd *WALTH* E17 — 101 N10
Thorpe La *EGH* TW20 — 194 C1
Thorpe Pk *CHERT* KT16 * — 195 H3
Thorpe Rd *BARK* IG11 — 124 C9
 *CHERT* KT16 — 194 C5
 *EHAM* E6 — 142 B1
 *FSTGT* E7 — 121 M8
 *KUTN/CMB* KT2 — 176 C9
 *SEVS/STOTM* N15 — 119 K4
 *STA* TW18 — 194 E1
 *STAL* AL1 — 10 E4
 *THHTH* CR7 — 101 G2
Thorpeside Cl *STA* TW18 — 195 H2
Thorpewood Av *SYD* SE26 — 182 A4
Thorpland Av *HGDN/ICK* UB10 — 112 C2
Thorsden Cl *WOKS/MYFD* GU22 — 232 B5
Thorsden Ct *WOKS/MYFD* GU22 * — 232 B5
Thorsden Wy *NRWD* SE19 * — 181 M9
Thorverton Rd *CRICK* NW2 — 99 L10
Thrale Rd *STRHM/NOR* SW16 — 180 D8
Thrale St *STHWK* SE1 — 12 F10
Thrasher Cl *HACK* E8 * — 7 N3
Thrawl St *WCHPL* E1 — 13 M3
Threadneedle St *LOTH* EC2R — 13 H6
Three Arches Pk *REDH* RH1 * — 276 B4
Three Arch Rd *REDH* RH1 — 276 B4
Three Bridges Rd — 283 P7
Three Castles Pth *ASC* SL5 — 192 C1
Three Cherry Trees La *HHNE* HP2 — 36 C2

**Column 1**

Three Close La *BERK* HP4 ........ 33 H3
Three Colts La *BETH* E2 .......... 140 A6
Three Colt St *POP/IOD* E14 * .... 140 B4
Three Corners *BXLYHN* DA7 ...... 164 C8
  HHS/BOV HP3 * .................... 36 B8
Three Forests Wy
  ABR/ST RM4 ...................... 103 P2
  CHIG IG7 ......................... 102 G3
  EPP CM16 ......................... 84 C2
  HLWW/ROY CM19 .................. 27 M10
  RBSF CM22 ........................ 31 P1
Three Gates *GU* GU4 ............. 250 F9
Three Gates Rd *HART* DA3 ....... 210 F7
Three Households Rd
  HLWW/ROY CM19 .................. 46 C8
Three Kings Yd
  MYFR/PKLN W1K * ................. 10 C7
Three Meadows Ms
  KTN/HRWW/WS HA3 ................ 94 A9
Three Mill La *BOW* E3 ........... 141 E9
Three Oak La *STHWK* SE1 ........ 19 L1
Three Oaks Cl *HGDN/ICK* UB10 .. 112 A8
Three Pears Rd *GU* GU1 ......... 251 H9
Three Valleys Wy *BUSH* WD23 .... 73 L3
Threshers Pl *NTGHL* W11 ......... 8 A7
Threshold Wy *CHOB/PIR* GU24 ... 214 B8
Thriftwood *SYD* SE26 ............ 182 B6
Thrift Farm La *BORE* WD6 ....... 75 P6
Thrift Gn *RBRW/HUT* CM13 ...... 35 N4
Thrifts Md *EPP* CM16 ............ 107 M4
Thrift La *RSEV* TN14 ............ 244 G3
Thrigby Rd *CHSGTN* KT9 ......... 219 L3
Throckmorton Rd
  CAN/RD E16 ....................... 141 M10
Throgmorton Av *OBST* EC2N ..... 13 H5
Throgmorton St *OBST* EC2N ..... 13 H4
Throstle Pl *GSTN* WD25 * ........ 55 K8
Throwley Cl *ABYW* SE2 .......... 163 N10
Throwley Rd *SUT* SM1 ........... 221 L2
Throwley Wy *SUT* SM1 ........... 221 L1
Thrums *WATN* WD24 ............. 73 J3
Thrupp Cl *MTCM* CR4 ........... 202 C12
Thrupps Av *WOT/HER* KT12 ...... 217 L12
Thrupps La *WOT/HER* KT12 ...... 217 L12
Thrush Av *HAT* AL10 ............ 40 D6
Thrush Gn *RKW/CH/CXG* WD3 .... 91 M11
  RYLN/HDSTN HA2 .................. 59 P4
Thrush St *WALW* SE17 .......... 18 E7
Thumbswood *WCCE* AL7 ......... 23 K8
Thundercourt *WARE* SG12 ....... 26 C1
Thunderer Rd *DAGW* RM9 ....... 143 P6
Thundridge Cl *WCCE* AL7 ........ 23 L6
Thurbarn Rd *CAT* SE6 ........... 182 D10
Thurgood Rd *HOD* EN11 ......... 44 F1
Thurland Rd
  BERM/RHTH SE16 ................. 19 N3
Thurlby Rd *WFD* IG8 ............. 102 C4
Thurlby Rd *ALP/SUD* HA0 ........ 135 J1
  WNWD SE27 ....................... 181 H7
Thurleigh Av *BAL* SW12 ......... 180 B5
Thurleigh Rd *BAL* SW12 ......... 180 A6
Thurleston Av *MRDN* SM4 ....... 201 H5
Thurlestone Av
  GDMY/SEVK IG3 ................... 123 J9
  NFNCH/WDSPK N12 ............... 98 A1
Thurlestone Cl *SHPTN* TW17 * .. 196 B9
Thurlestone Pde
  SHPTN TW17 * .................... 196 D6
Thurloe Cl *SKENS* SW7 ......... 15 L5
Thurloe Gdns *ROM* RM1 ........ 124 F4
Thurloe Pl *SKENS* SW7 ......... 15 M5
Thurloe Place Ms
  SKENS SW7 * ..................... 15 M5
Thurloe Sq *SKENS* SW7 ......... 15 M5
Thurloe St *SKENS* SW7 ......... 15 L5
Thurloe Wk *GRAYS* RM17 ....... 167 M2
Thurlow Cl *CHING* E4 ........... 101 P2
Thurlow Gdns *ALP/SUD* HA0 * ... 115 J10
  BARK/HLT IG6 ..................... 72 F1
Thurlow Hl *DUL* SE21 ........... 181 K5
Thurlow Park Rd *DUL* SE21 ..... 181 J5
Thurlow Rd *HAMP* NW3 ......... 117 N10
  HNWL W7 .......................... 154 F1
Thurlow St *WALW* SE17 ......... 19 J8
Thurlow Ter *KTTN* NW5 ......... 118 A10
Thurlow Wk *WALW* SE17 ........ 19 J7
Thurlston Rd *RSLP* HA4 ......... 113 H8
Thurlton Ct *WOKN/KNAP* GU21 .. 232 B2
Thurnham Wy
  KWD/TDW/WH* KT20 .............. 238 G6
Thurrock Park Wy *TIL* RM18 .... 168 A4
Thursby Rd *WOKN/KNAP* GU21 .. 231 M4
Thursland Rd *SCUP* DA14 ....... 185 P8
Thursley Crs *CROY/NA* CR0 ..... 225 J4
Thursley Gdns
  WIM/MER SW19 ................... 178 G5
Thursley Rd *ELTH/MOT* SE9 ..... 184 C2
Thurso Cl *HARH* RM3 ........... 106 A7
Thurso St *TOOT* SW17 .......... 179 N7
Thurstans *HLWW/ROY* CM19 .... 46 E6
Thurston Rd *DEPT* SE8 ......... 160 G8
  SL SL1 ............................ 129 JB
  STHL UB1 ......................... 133 N8
Thurtle Rd *BETH* E2 ............ 7 M6
Thwaite Cl *ERITH* DA8 .......... 164 D5
Thyer Cl *ORP* BR6 .............. 226 F1
Thyme Ct *RGUE* GU4 ........... 250 E3
Thyra Gv *NFNCH/WDSPK* N12 .. 97 L7
Tibbatts Rd *BOW* E3 ........... 140 G6
Tibbenham Pl *CAT* SE6 ......... 182 F5
Tibberton Sq *IS* N1 ............. 6 F4
Tibbets Cl *WIM/MER* SW19 ..... 178 G5
Tibbenham Pl *CAT* SE6 ......... 182 F5
Tibbet's Ride *PUT/ROE* SW15 .. 178 G3
Tibbles Cl *GSTN* WD25 ......... 73 M1
Tibbs Hill Rd *ABLGY* WD5 ...... 54 E1
Tiber Cl *BOW* E3 ............... 140 F3
Tiber Gdns *IS* N1 .............. 5 M6
Ticehurst Cl *CRAWE* RH10 ..... 284 F12
  STMC/STPC BR5 ................... 185 K10
Ticehurst Rd *FSTH* SE23 ....... 182 D5
Tichborne *RKW/CH/CXG* WD3 ... 90 C6
Tichmarsh *HOR/WEW* KT19 .... 219 P6
Tickenhall Dr *HLWE* CM17 ...... 47 N1
Tickford Cl *ABYW* SE2 ......... 163 M9
Tidal Basin Rd *CAN/RD* E16 .... 141 J4
Tidenham Gdns *CROY/NA* CR0.. 204 F10
  PUT/ROE SW15 ................... 159 J8
Tideway Cl *RCHPK/HAM* TW10 .. 176 G7
Tidford Rd *WELL* DA16 ......... 163 JB
Tidworth Rd *BOW* E3 ........... 140 F1
Tidy's La *EPP* CM16 ............ 85 H3
Tiepigs La *WWKM* BR4 .......... 205 N3
Tierney Rd *BRXS/STRHM* SW2 .. 181 H1
Tierney Ter
  BRXS/STRHM SW2 ................. 180 F4
Tiger La *HAYES* BR2 ............ 205 N4
Tiger Moth Wy *HAT* AL10 ...... 40 A5
Tiger Wy *CLPT* E5 .............. 120 A9
Tigres Cl *ED* N9 ................ 100 B3
Tilbrook Rd *BKHTH/KID* SE3 .... 161 P3
Tilburstow Hill Rd *GDST* RH9 .. 260 H8
Tilbury Cl *PECK* SE15 .......... 159 N6
  PIN HA5 * ......................... 93 N6
  STMC/STPC BR5 ................... 207 L2
Tilbury Md *HLWS* CM18 ......... 47 N5
Tilbury Rd *EHAM* E6 ............ 131 P2
  LEY E10 ........................... 121 H5
Tilbury Wk *DTCH/LGLY* SL3 ..... 136 C7
Tiledesey Rd *PUT/ROE* SW15 ... 178 G2
Tilecroft *WCCW* AL8 ............ 22 C2
Tile Farm Rd *ORP* BR6 ......... 206 G10
Tilegate Rd *CHONG* CM5 ....... 48 C5
Tilehouse Cl *BORE* WD6 ....... 75 P4
Tilehouse La *DEN/HRF* UB9 .... 111 H4

**Column 2**

  RKW/CH/CXG WD3 ................. 91 H9
Tilehouse Rd *RGUE* GU4 ........ 268 B4
Tilehouse Wy *DEN/HRF* UB9 .... 111 J3
Tilehurst La *RDKG* RH5 ......... 273 K5
Tilehurst Rd *CHEAM* SM3 ....... 221 H2
  WAND/EARL SW18 ................. 179 N4
Tilekiln Cl *CHESW* EN7 .......... 61 N5
Tile Kiln Cl *HHS/BOV* HP3 ....... 36 C7
Tile Kiln Crs *HHS/BOV* HP3 ...... 36 C7
Tile Kiln La *BXLY* DA5 ........... 186 D5
  DEN/HRF UB9 ...................... 112 C5
  HGT N6 ............................ 118 C6
Tilers Cl *REDH* RH1 ............ 258 D6
Tiler's Wy *REIG* RH2 ............ 275 M4
Tileyard Rd *HOLWY* N7 .......... 5 L3
Tilford Av *CROY/NA* CR0 ........ 225 H4
Tilford Gdns *WIM/MER* SW19 ... 178 G4
Tilgate Dr *CRAWE* RH10 * ....... 259 K9
Tilgate Pde *CRAWE* RH10 * ..... 283 P10
Tilgate Pl *CRAWE* RH10 ......... 283 P10
Tilgate Wy *CRAWE* RH10 ........ 283 P10
Tilia Cl *SUT* SM1 .............. 221 J2
Tilia Rd *CLPT* E5 ............... 120 A9
Tilia Wk *BRXN/ST* SW9 ......... 159 J4
Till Av *EYN* DA4 ............... 209 N1
Tillett Cl *WLSDN* NW10 ......... 135 P1
Tillett Wy *BETH* E2 ............. 7 N9
Tilley La *EPSOM* KT18 .......... 237 P9
Tilley Rd *FELT* TW13 ........... 175 H4
Tillingbourne Gdns *FNCH* N3 ... 117 J1
Tillingbourne Gn
  STMC/STPC BR5 ................... 207 K4
Tillingbourne Rd *RGUE* GU4 .... 268 B6
Tillingbourne Wy *FNCH* N3 ...... 117 J2
Tillingdown Hl *CTHM* CR3 ....... 242 A8
Tillingdown La *CTHM* CR3 ....... 242 A10
Tillingham Ct *WAB* EN9 ......... 63 M9
Tillingham Wy
  NFNCH/WDSPK N12 ............... 97 K5
Tilling Rd *CRICK* NW2 .......... 116 E6
Tilling Wy *WBLY* HA9 ........... 115 J8
Tillman St *WCHPL* E1 ........... 140 A8
Tilloch St *IS* N1 * .............. 5 N1
Tillotson Cl *CRAWE* RH10 ....... 284 E8
Tillotson Rd *ED* N9 ............ 99 N3
  IL IG1 ............................ 122 D5
  KTN/HRWW/WS HA3 .............. 94 A8
Tillwicks Rd *HLWS* CM18 ....... 47 J2
Tilly's La *STA* TW18 ........... 173 H7
Tilmans Md *EYN* DA4 ........... 209 N1
Tilney Ct *LHD/OX* KT22 ......... 236 F6
Tilney Gdns *IS* N1 ............. 6 G2
Tilney Rd *DAGW* RM9 ........... 144 A11
  NWDGN UB2 ....................... 153 K5
Tilney St *MYFR/PKLN* W1K ...... 10 B9
Tilson Cl *CMBW* SE5 ........... 159 M6
Tilson Gdns *BRXS/STRHM* SW2.. 180 F5
Tilson Rd *TOTM* N17 ........... 99 P9
Tilston Cl *WAN* E11 ............ 121 L8
Tilstone Cl *STA* TW18 .......... 148 C3
Tilstone Cl *WDSR* SL4 .......... 148 D5
Tilsworth Rd *BEAC* HP9 ......... 88 B10
Tilsworth Wk *STALE/WH* AL4 ... 39 H1
Tilt Cl *COB* KT11 .............. 235 M2
Tithams Corner Rd *GODL* GU7 .. 267 N9
Tithams Gn *GODL* GU7 .......... 267 N10
Tilt Meadow *COB* KT11 ......... 14 B10
Tilton St *FUL/PGN* SW6 ........ 14 B10
Tilt Rd *COB* KT11 .............. 235 K1
Tilt Vw *COB* KT11 * ............ 235 K1
The Tiltwood *ACT* W3 .......... 135 P9
Tilt Yard Ap *ELTH/MOT* SE9 .... 184 C2
Timber Cl *CHST* BR7 ........... 206 D2
  CT/LBKH KT23 ..................... 254 B5
  WOKS/MYFD GU22 ................. 233 J1
  WCCE AL7 .......................... 23 J2
Timbercroft *HOR/WEW* KT19 ... 220 B1
Timbercroft La
  WOOL/PLUM SE18 ................. 163 H5
Timberdene Av *BARK/HLT* IG6 .. 102 F9
Timberham Farm Rd
  HORL RH6 ......................... 279 N7
Timberling Gdns
  SAND/SEL CR2 ..................... 223 L6
Timber Mill Wy *CLAP* SW4 ..... 158 E10
Timber Orch *HERT/WAT* SG14 .. 25 H1
Timber Pond Rd
  BERM/RHTH SE16 ................. 160 C1
Timberridge
  RKW/CH/CXG WD3 ................ 71 M4
Timberslip Dr *WLGTN* SM6 ..... 222 E6
The Timbers *CHEAM* SM3 ...... 220 G5
Timber St *FSBYE* EC1V * ....... 12 E1
Timbertop Rd *BH/WHM* TN16 .. 243 P4
Timberwharf Rd
  SEVS/STOTM N15 ................. 119 P4
Timberwood *SLN* SL2 .......... 110 A8
Time Sq *HACK* E8 * ............ 119 N10
Times Sq *SUT* SM1 * ........... 221 L2
Timperley Ct *BIL* BR1 * ........ 206 C4
Timothy Cl *BXLYHS* DA6 ........ 185 J11
  CLAP SW4 ......................... 181 H1
Timperley Gdns *REDH* RH1 ..... 257 P9
Timplings Rw *HHW* HP1 ........ 35 L4
Timsway *STA* TW18 ............ 173 J8
Tindale Cl *SAND/SEL* CR2 ...... 223 L7
Tindall Cl *HARH* RM3 .......... 105 N10
Tindalls Ms *MCH* RM12 ........ 132 D6
Tindal St *BRXN/ST* SW9 ........ 159 J4
Tine Rd *CHIG* IG7 ............. 103 H6
Tinkers La *TRING* HP23 ......... 32 F5
Tinniswood Cl *HBRY* N5 ........ 119 H10
Tinsey Cl *EGH* TW20 ........... 173 N7
Tinsley Cl *CRAWE* RH10 ........ 284 D4
  SNWD SE25 ........................ 203 A3
Tinsley Gn *CRAWE* RH10 ....... 284 C2
Tinsley La *CRAWE* RH10 ........ 284 C2
Tinsley La North *CRAWE* RH10 .. 284 C1
Tinsley La South *CRAWE* RH10 .. 284 C2
Tinsley Rd *WCHPL* E1 .......... 140 G8
Tintagel Cl *EW* KT17 ........... 220 C10
  HHNE HP2 ......................... 35 N1
Tintagel Crs *EDUL* SE22 ........ 159 N10
Tintagel Dr *STAN* HA7 .......... 94 A3
Tintagel Gdns *RYLN/HDSTN* HA2. 113 P9
  WOKS/MYFD GU22 ................. 232 D2
Tintells La *EHSLY* KT24 ........ 252 C4
Tintern Av *CDALE/KGS* NW9 .... 115 N1
Tintern Cl *PUT/ROE* SW15 ...... 178 G3
  SL SL1 ............................ 149 H2
  WIM/MER SW19 .................... 179 M10
Tintern Gdns *STHGT/OAK* N14 .. 98 J4
Tintern Rd *CAR* SM5 ........... 201 N8
  CRAWW RH11 ...................... 283 J12
  WDGN N22 ......................... 99 K9
Tintern St *CLAP* SW4 .......... 181 J1
Tintern Wy *RYLN/HDSTN* HA2 ... 114 F10
Tinto Rd *CAN/RD* E16 .......... 141 K4
Tinwell Ms *BORE* WD6 ......... 76 A3
Tinworth St *LBTH* SE11 ........ 17 M7
Tippendell La *LCOL/BKTW* AL2.. 55 H7
Tippetts Cl *ENC/FH* EN2 ....... 77 H6
Tips Cross Md *BRWN* CM15 .... 86 G5
Tipthorpe Rd *BTSEA* SW11 ..... 158 F9
Tipton Dr *CROY/NA* CR0 ........ 224 A3
Tiptree Cl *CHING* E4 ........... 101 N4
  EMPK RM11 ........................ 125 J2
Tiptree Crs *CLAY* IG5 .......... 102 C3
Tiptree Dr *ENC/FH* EN2 ........ 78 B2
Tiptree Rd *RSLP* HA4 .......... 113 H8
Tisdall Pl *WALW* SE17 .......... 19 J7
Titan Ct *BTFD* TW8 * .......... 155 L7

**Column 3**

Titan Rd *GRAYS* RM17 ......... 167 M4
  HHNE HP2 ......................... 36 A3
Titchborne Rw *BAY/PAD* W2 .... 9 J3
Titchfield Rd *CAR* SM5 ......... 201 N8
  PEND EN3 ......................... 80 D1
  STJWD NW8 ........................ 3 P1
Titchwell Rd
  WAND/EARL SW18 ................. 179 N3
Tite Hi *EGH* TW20 ............. 172 A4
Tite St *CHEL* SW3 .............. 16 A9
Tithe Barn Cl *KUTN/CMB* KT2 .. 199 L1
  STAL AL1 .......................... 38 B9
Tithe Barn Wy *NTHLT* UB5 ..... 133 J4
Tithe Cl *MLHL* NW7 ............ 96 D9
  VW GU25 ........................... 194 A6
  WOT/HER KT12 .................... 197 J6
  YEAD UB4 .......................... 132 C2
Tithe Farm Av
  RYLN/HDSTN HA2 ................. 113 P8
Tithe Farm Cl
  RYLN/HDSTN HA2 ................. 113 P8
Tithelands *HLWW/ROY* CM19 ... 46 C4
Tithe La *STWL/WRAY* TW19 .... 172 C2
Tithepit Shaw La *WARL* CR6 .... 242 A11
The Tithe *CRAWW* RH11 ....... 283 K4
Tithe Wk *MLHL* NW7 ........... 96 D9
Titian Av *BUSH* WD23 .......... 94 D1
Titlarks Hill Rd *ASC* SL5 ....... 192 C8
Titley Cl *CHING* E4 ............ 100 F6
Titmus Cl *CRAWE* RH10 ........ 284 D3
Titmus Dr *CRAWE* RH10 ........ 284 D3
Titmuss Av *THMD* SE28 ........ 143 J9
Titmuss St *SHB* W12 * ......... 156 F1
Titness Pk *ASC* SL5 * .......... 192 F3
Titsey Hl *WARL* CR6 ........... 243 L11
Titsey Rd *OXTED* RH8 ......... 261 N3
Tiverton Av *CLAY* IG5 .......... 122 D1
Tiverton Cl *CROY/NA* CR0 ...... 203 N7
Tiverton Cl *HARP* AL5 .......... 20 C1
Tiverton Dr *ELTH/MOT* SE9 .... 184 G5
Tiverton Rd *ALP/SUD* HA0 ...... 135 J3
  EDGW HA8 ......................... 96 A5
  HSLW TW3 ......................... 135 H11
  POTB/CUF EN6 .................... 59 N7
  RSLP HA4 .......................... 113 H8
  SEVS/STOTM N15 .................. 119 L4
  UED N18 ........................... 99 M6
  WLSDN NW10 ...................... 136 G3
Tiverton St *STHWK* SE1 ........ 18 E4
Tiverton Wy *CHSGTN* KT9 ...... 219 H10
  MLHL NW7 ......................... 96 C8
Tivoli Gdns *WOOL/PLUM* SE18 .. 162 B3
Tivoli Rd *CEND/HSY/T* N8 ...... 118 N3
  HSLWW TW4 ....................... 153 M10
  WNWD SE27 ........................ 181 K8
Toad La *HSLWW* TW4 .......... 153 N10
Tobago St *POP/IOD* E14 ........ 160 F1
Tobermory Cl *DTCH/LGLY* SL3 .. 150 B3
Tobin Cl *HAMP* NW3 ........... 3 N1
  HOR/WEW KT19 .................... 219 N7
Toby La *WCHPL* E1 ............. 140 D6
Toby Wy *SURB* KT6 ............ 199 P4
Tockley Rd *SL* SL1 ............. 128 K5
Toddbrook *HLWW/ROY* CM19 .. 46 E2
Todd Cl *RAIN* RM13 ............ 145 L6
Todds Cl *HORL* RH6 ............ 279 H11
Toft Av *GRAYS* RM17 ........... 168 A3
Toftwood Cl *CRAWE* RH10 ..... 284 D8
Tokenhouse Yd *LOTH* EC2R ..... 12 G5
Token Rd *PUT/ROE* SW15 ...... 157 N10
Tokyngton Av *WBLY* HA9 ....... 135 M1
Toland Sq *PUT/ROE* SW15 ..... 178 D1
Tolcarne Dr *PIN* HA5 * ......... 93 J1
Toley Av *KTN/HRWW/WS* HA3 .. 115 K5
Tolhurst Dr *NKENS* W10 ....... 2 C1
Tollbridge Cl *NKENS* W10 ...... 8 B1
Tolldene Cl *WOKN/KNAP* GU21 . 231 N5
Tollers La *COUL/CHIP* CR5 ...... 240 G5
Toilesbury Gdns *BARK/HLT* IG6. 122 C1
Toilet St *WCHPL* E1 ............ 140 C6
Tollgate *GU* GU1 ............... 250 G9
Tollgate Av *REDH* RH1 ......... 276 A5
Tollgate Cl *RKW/CH/CXG* WD3 .. 71 J3
Tollgate Dr *DUL* SE21 .......... 181 M5
  YEAD UB4 .......................... 133 L9
Tollgate Gdns
  KIL/WHAMP NW6 ................... 2 G1
Tollgate Rd *BRKMPK* AL9 ...... 58 D7
  CAN/RD E16 ....................... 141 P7
  CHES/WCR EN8 .................... 80 C1
  DORK RH4 ......................... 272 G5
  EHAM E6 ........................... 142 B7
  REDH RH1 .......................... 276 A7
  STALE/WH AL4 ..................... 40 B10
Tollhouse La *WLGTN* SM6 ....... 222 D5
Tollhouse Wy *ARCH* N19 ....... 118 C7
Tollington Pk *FSBYPK* N4 ....... 118 C7
Tollington Pl *FSBYPK* N4 ....... 118 C7
Tollington Rd *HOLWY* N7 ....... 118 F8
Tollington Wy *HOLWY* N7 ...... 118 F8
Tolpit End *HHW* HP1 .......... 35 J4
Tolmers Av *POTB/CUF* EN6 .... 60 F4
Tolmers Gdns *POTB/CUF* EN6 .. 60 F4
Tolmers Ms *POTB/CUF* EN6 .... 60 E4
Tolmers Sq *CAMTN* NW1 * ..... 11 H1
Tolpits Cl *WATW* WD18 ........ 72 C9
Tolpits La *WATW* WD18 ........ 92 D1
Tolpuddle Av *PLSTW* E13 ....... 141 P3
Tolpuddle St *IS* N1 ............ 6 A2
Tolsford Rd *HACK* E8 .......... 120 A3
Tolson Rd *ISLW* TW7 ........... 154 F9
Tolvaddon Cl
  WOKN/KNAP GU21 ................. 231 M3
Tolverne Rd *RYNPK* SW20 ...... 200 F1
Tolworth Broadway
  SURB KT6 ......................... 199 M8
Tolworth Cl *SURB* KT6 ......... 199 N8
Tolworth Gdns *CHDH* RM6 ..... 123 N3
Tolworth Park Rd *SURB* KT6 ... 199 M9
Tolworth Ri North (Kingston
  By-Pass) *BRYLDS* KT5 ........... 199 P7
Tolworth Ri South
  BRYLDS KT5 ....................... 199 P7
Tolworth Rd *SURB* KT6 ........ 199 M9
Tolworth Underpass (Kingston
  By-Pass) *SURB* KT6 ............. 199 M10
Tom Cribb Rd *THMD* SE28 ..... 142 G2
Tom Groves Cl *SRTFD* E15 .... 121 J10
Tom Hood Cl *SRTFD* E15 ....... 121 J10
Tom Jenkinson Rd
  CAN/RD E16 ....................... 141 M10
Tomkins Cl *BORE* WD6 ......... 75 K5
Tomkyns La *UPMR* RM14 ...... 105 P12
Tomlin Cl *HOR/WEW* KT19 ..... 220 A7
Tomlin Rd *SLN* SL2 ............ 110 A7
Tomlin's Gv *BOW* E3 ........... 140 E5
Tomlinscote Wy *FRIM* GU16 ... 231 K12
Tomlins Orch *BARK* IG11 ...... 142 D7
Tomlins Rd *POP/IOD* E14 ...... 141 M9
Tom Nolan Cl *SRTFD* E15 ..... 141 K4
Tomlinson Cl *BETH* E2 * ........ 7 P7
  CHSWK W4 .......................... 155 N4
Tomlins Orch *BARK* IG11 ...... 142 D7
Tompion St *FSBYE* EC1V ........ 12 D1
Tom's La *KGLGY* WD4 .......... 53 K7
Tom Smith Cl *GNWCH* SE10 ... 161 K1
Tomswood Hl *BARK/HLT* IG6 ... 102 D3
Tomswood Rd *CHIG* IG7 ....... 102 D4
Tonbridge By-Pass
  BGR/WK TN15 ..................... 265 M9
Tonbridge Cl *BNSTD* SM7 ...... 222 A10
Tonbridge Crs
  KTN/HRWW/WS HA3 .............. 115 K2
Tonbridge Rd
  E/WMO/HCT KT8 .................. 197 N4
  HARH RM3 ......................... 105 N3
  SEV TN13 .......................... 265 K3
Tonbridge St *STPAN* WC1H ..... 5 L10

**Column 4**

Tonfield Rd *CHEAM* SM3 ........ 201 J8
Tonge Cl *BECK* BR3 ............. 204 F5
PGE/AN SE20 * .................... 182 A10
Tonsley Hl *WAND/EARL* SW18 .. 179 L1
Tonsley Pl *WAND/EARL* SW18 .. 179 L1
Tonsley Rd *WAND/EARL* SW18 .. 179 L1
Tonsley St *WAND/EARL* SW18 .. 179 L1
Tonstall Rd *HOR/WEW* KT19 ... 220 A6
MTCM CR4 .......................... 202 B2
Tooke Cl *PIN* HA5 .............. 93 M9
Tookey Cl *KTN/HRWW/WS* HA3 . 115 M9
Took's Ct *FLST/FETLN* EC4A ... 11 K3
Tooley St *GWW* DA11 ........... 190 A3
STHWK SE1 .......................... 19 L1
Toorack Rd
KTN/HRWW/WS HA3 ................ 94 C10
Toot Hill Rd *CHONG* CM5 ....... 66 G6
Tooting Bec Gdns
STRHM/NOR SW16 ................... 180 E7
Tooting Gv *TOOT* SW17 ......... 179 H9
Tooting High St *TOOT* SW17 ... 179 P9
Tootswood Rd *HAYES* BR2 ...... 205 K5
Tooveys Mill Cl *KGLGY* WD4 .... 54 A5
Topaz Cl *SL* SL1 ............... 128 C10
Topcliffe Dr *ORP* BR6 .......... 226 G4
Top Dartford Rd *SWLY* BR8 .... 187 H9
Topham Sq *TOTM* N17 .......... 99 K9
Topham St *CLKNW* EC1R * ...... 12 A1
Top House Ri *CHING* E4 ........ 101 N1
Topiary Sq *RCH/KEW* TW9 ..... 155 L9
The Topiary *ASHTD* KT21 ....... 237 K6
Topland Rd *CFSP/GDCR* SL9 ... 90 A3
Toplands Av *SOCK/AV* RM15 ... 146 A10
Topley St *ELTH/MOT* SE9 ....... 161 P10
Topmast Point *POP/IOD* E14 * . 160 F1
Top Pk *BECK* BR3 .............. 205 K5
CFSP/GDCR SL9 ..................... 109 P4
Topping La *UX/CGN* UB8 ........ 131 N5
Topsfield Cl *CEND/HSY/T* N8 .. 118 F5
Topsfield Pde
CEND/HSY/T N8 * .................. 118 F3
Topsfield Rd *CEND/HSY/T* N8 .. 118 F5
Topsham Rd *TOOT* SW17 ....... 180 A6
Topstreet Wy *HARP* AL5 ........ 20 B3
Torbay Cl *KIL/WHAMP* NW6 .... 2 C4
Torbay Rd *CAMTN* NW1 * ...... 4 B3
RYLN/HDSTN HA2 .................... 113 M7
Torbay St *CAMTN* NW1 * ....... 4 B3
Torbitt Wy *CANTN/NBYPK* IG2 . 123 J3
Torbridge Cl *EDGW* HA8 ........ 95 K8
Torcross Dr *FSTH* SE23 ......... 182 B5
Torcross Rd *RSLP* HA4 ......... 113 G3
Tor Gdns *KENS* W8 ............. 14 C1
Tor Gv *THMD* SE28 ............. 143 H10
Torin Ct *EGH* TW20 ............ 171 P8
Torkildsen Wy *HLW* CM20 ...... 28 C9
Tor La *WEY* KT13 .............. 230 F11
Tormead Cl *SUT* SM1 .......... 221 K3
Tormead Rd *GU* GU1 ........... 250 C10
Tormount Rd
WOOL/PLUM SE18 ................... 163 H5
Toronto Av *MNPK* E12 ......... 122 C9
Toronto Dr *HORL* RH6 .......... 281 H5
Toronto Rd *IL* IG1 ............. 122 E6
TIL RM18 ............................ 168 D8
Torquay Gdns *REDBR* IG4 ...... 122 A2
Torquay Sp *SLN* SL2 ........... 128 G5
Torquay St *BAY/PAD* W2 ....... 9 M2
Torrance Cl *EMPK* RM11 ....... 125 K6
Torrens Rd *BRXS/STRHM* SW2 . 180 A3
SRTFD E15 .......................... 141 L1
Torrens Sq *SRTFD* E15 ......... 141 L1
Torrens St *FSBYE* EC1V ......... 6 C5
Torrens Wk *GVE* DA12 .......... 191 H4
Torres Sq *POP/IOD* E14 ........ 160 F4
Torrey Dr *BRXN/ST* SW9 ........ 159 H8
Torriano Av *KTTN* NW5 ......... 118 D10
Torriano Cots *KTTN* NW5 ....... 118 D10
Torriano Ms *KTTN* NW5 ......... 118 D10
Torridge Gdns *PECK* SE15 ...... 160 B10
Torridge Rd *DTCH/LGLY* SL3 ... 150 C5
THHTH CR7 .......................... 203 J5
Torridon Cl *WOKN/KNAP* GU21 . 231 N5
Torridon Rd *CAT* SE6 ........... 183 J4
Torrington Av
NFNCH/WDSPK N12 .................. 97 N5
Torrington Cl *ESH/CLAY* KT10 .. 218 D3
Torrington Gv *GU* GU1 .......... 82 F9
POTB/CUF EN6 ...................... 59 N9
RYLN/HDSTN HA2 .................... 114 A9
Torrington Gdns
FBAR/BDGN N11 ..................... 98 D7
GFD/PVL UB6 ........................ 135 H3
LOU IG10 ............................ 82 F9
Torrington Gv
NFNCH/WDSPK N12 .................. 97 N5
Torrington Pk
NFNCH/WDSPK N12 .................. 97 N5
Torrington Pl *BSTSEA* SW11 * .. 11 J3
WAP E1W ............................ 13 N9
Torrington Rd *BCTR* RM8 ....... 124 A4
BERK HP4 ........................... 33 N5
ESH/CLAY KT10 ..................... 218 D3
GFD/PVL UB6 ....................... 135 H3
RSLP HA4 ........................... 113 N10
Torrington Sq *CROY/NA* CR0 ... 203 L7
STPAN WC1H ........................ 11 K2
Torrs Rd *WELL* DA16 ........... 163 M8
Torr Rd *PGE/AN* SE20 .......... 182 G10
Tortoiseshell Wy *BERK* HP4 .... 33 L5
Torver Rd *HRW* HA1 ............ 114 D2
Torwood Cl *BERK* HP4 .......... 33 L5
Torwood La *CTHM* CR3 ......... 241 N6
Torworth Rd *BORE* WD6 ........ 75 M5
Tothill St *STJSPK* SW1H ........ 17 J2
Totnes Rd *WELL* DA16 ......... 163 H6
Totnes Vls *FBAR/BDGN* N11 * .. 98 D6
Totnes Wk *EFNCH* N2 .......... 117 H2
Tottan Ter *WCHPL* E1 .......... 140 C8
Tottenhall Rd *PLMGR* N13 ...... 99 H7
Tottenham Court Rd *FITZ* W1T . 11 G4
Tottenham Gn East
SEVS/STOTM N15 ................... 119 N10
Tottenham Green East South
Side *SEVS/STOTM* N15 .......... 119 N10
Tottenham La *CEND/HSY/T* N8 . 118 F5
Tottenham Ms *FITZ* W1T * ...... 11 H3
Tottenham Rd *IS* N1 ............ 7 J2
Tottenham St *FITZ* W1T ........ 11 H3
Totterdown St *TOOT* SW17 ..... 180 A7
Totteridge Common
TRDG/WHET N20 .................... 96 G2
Totteridge La
TRDG/WHET N20 .................... 97 H2
Totteridge Village
TRDG/WHET N20 .................... 96 G1
Totternhoe Cl
KTN/HRWW/WS HA3 ................ 115 H3
Totton Rd *THHTH* CR7 .......... 203 J4
Toucan Cl *WLSDN* NW10 ....... 135 M4
Toulmin Dr *STALW/RED* AL3 ... 38 B2
Toulon St *CMBW* SE5 .......... 159 K6
Tournay Rd *FUL/PGN* SW6 ..... 157 J5
Toussaint Wk
BERM/RHTH SE16 ................... 19 N5
Tovey Av *HOD* EN11 ............ 44 F1
Tovey Cl *LCOL/BKTW* AL2 ...... 57 J2
WAB EN9 ............................ 45 K9
Tovil Cl *PGE/AN* SE20 .......... 200 G3
Towcester Rd *BOW* E3 .......... 140 G6
Tower Br Wap F1 ................. 19 P1
Tower Br Wap E1W * ............. 140 A5
Tower Bridge Ap *TWRH* EC3N .. 19 N4
Tower Bridge Ms
ALP/SUD HA0 ....................... 114 D9
Tower Bridge Rd *STHWK* SE1 .. 19 N4
Tower Blds *WAP* E1W * .......... 140 A5
Tower Cl *BRKHTH/KID* SE3 ..... 161 L2

**Column 5**

HAMP NW3 ........................... 117 N10
ORP BR6 ............................ 207 J9
PGE/AN SE20 ....................... 182 A10
WOKN/KNAP GU21 .................. 232 A3
Tower Ct *BRW* CM14 ........... 106 C5
LSQ/SEVD WC2H * ................. 11 L5
Tower Gdns *ESH/CLAY* KT10 ... 218 F4
Tower Gardens Rd *TOTM* N17 .. 99 P8
Towergate Cl *UX/CGN* UB8 ..... 111 P10
Tower Gv *WEY* KT13 ............ 196 B10
Tower Hamlets Rd *FSTGT* E7 .. 121 P2
WALTH E17 .......................... 101 L12
Towerhill *SHGR* GU5 ............ 270 D6
Tower Hl *STALE/WH* AL4 ........ 21 L6
Tower Hi Ri *SHGR* GU5 ......... 270 D6
Tower Hl *BRW* CM14 ........... 107 H5
DORK RH4 ........................... 272 C4
KGLGY WD4 ......................... 53 H5
Tower La *WBLY* HA9 ............ 115 J8
WALTH E17 .......................... 120 F2
Tower Ms *CLPT* E5 ............. 120 D9
WALTH E17 .......................... 120 F2
Tower Ri *RCH/KEW* TW9 ........ 155 K9
Tower Rd *AMSS* HP7 ............ 68 B5
BELV DA17 .......................... 164 C5
BXLYHN DA7 ......................... 164 C10
EPP CM16 ........................... 65 H6
KWD/TDW/WH KT20 ................ 238 F10
ORP BR6 ............................ 207 J9
TWK TW1 ............................ 176 C5
WARE SG12 .......................... 26 D1
WLSDN NW10 ....................... 136 D2
Tower Royal *MANHO* EC4N * ... 12 F7
Towers Av *HGDN/ICK* UB10 .... 132 D5
Towers Ct *HGDN/ICK* UB10 .... 132 D5
Towers Pl *RCH/KEW* TW9 ....... 177 K1
Towers Rd *PIN* HA5 ............ 93 M9
HHNE HP2 ........................... 35 P5
Towers Rd *GRAYS* RM17 ........ 167 M1
The Towers *PUR/KEN* CR8 ...... 241 K11
Tower St *HERT/WAT* SG14 ..... 25 K3
LSQ/SEVD WC2H * .................. 11 L6
Towers Wk *WEY* KT13 ......... 216 C3
Towers Wd *EYN* DA4 ........... 210 C1
Tower Ter *WDGN* N22 .......... 98 G10
Tower Vw *BUSH* WD23 .......... 94 D1
CROY/NA CR0 ....................... 204 D8
Towfield Rd *FELT* TW13 ........ 175 N5
Town Barn Rd *CRAWE* RH10 ... 283 M7
Town Cl *CSHM* HP5 ............. 50 C8
Towncourt Crs
STMC/STPC BR5 .................... 206 F5
Towncourt La *STMC/STPC* BR5.. 206 F5
Towncourt Pth *FSBYPK* N4 ..... 119 K6
Townend Cl *CRAWE* RH10 ...... 241 H6
Town End Pde *KUT/HW* KT1 * . 199 J3
Towney Md *NTHLT* UB5 ......... 133 N4
Town Farm Wy
STWL/WRAY TW19 .................. 173 N3
Townfield *CSHM* HP5 ........... 50 G8
RKW/CH/CXG WD3 .................. 91 M1
Townfield Cnr *GVE* DA12 ....... 190 F4
Town Field La *CSTG* HP8 ....... 89 P4
Townfield Rd *DORK* RH4 ....... 272 F3
HYS/HAR UB3 ....................... 132 G10
Town Flds *HAT* AL10 ........... 40 D3
Townfield Sq *HYS/HAR* UB3 ... 132 G10
Town Field Wy *ISLW* TW7 ...... 154 F8
Towngate *COB* KT11 ........... 235 M1
Town Hall Approach Rd
SEVS/STOTM N15 ................... 119 N2
Town Hall Ar *BERK* HP4 ........ 33 P5
Townhall Av *CHSWK* W4 ........ 156 A4
Town Hall Pde
BRXS/STRHM SW2 * ................ 158 G10
Town Hall Rd *BTSEA* SW11 ..... 158 A9
Townholm Crs *HNWL* W7 ....... 154 E2
Town La *STWL/WRAY* TW19 .... 173 N2
Townley Ct *SRTFD* E15 ......... 141 L1
Townley Rd *BXLYHS* DA6 ....... 185 H3
EDUL SE22 .......................... 159 M7
Townley St *WALW* SE17 ........ 18 G7
Town Md *CRAWW* RH11 ........ 283 N6
REDH RH1 ........................... 259 L9
Town Meadow *BTFD* TW8 ...... 155 J6
Townmead Rd *FUL/PGN* SW6.... 158 B9
RCH/KEW TW9 ....................... 155 N9
Town Mead Rd *WAB* EN9 ....... 63 J10
Town Pier Sq *GVW* DA11 ....... 190 C2
Town Quay *BARK* IG11 .......... 142 C8
STAL TW18 * ........................ 173 H9
Town Rd *ED* N9 ................ 100 A3
Townsend *HHNE* HP2 ........... 35 P1
Townsend Av *STAL* AL1 ......... 38 D3
STHGT/OAK N14 .................... 98 G6
Townsend Dr *STALW/RED* AL3 . 38 C2
Townsend La *CDALE/KGS* NW9 . 96 F12
WOKS/MYFD GU22 .................. 232 F2
Townsend Ms
WAND/EARL SW18 ................... 179 M5
Townsend Rd *ASHF* TW15 ...... 173 H9
CSHM HP5 ........................... 50 G6
SEVS/STOTM N15 ................... 119 N2
STHL UB1 ........................... 133 H1
STJWD NW8 ......................... 3 N2
Townsend St *HERT/BAY* SG13 .. 25 M5
Townsend Yd *HGT* N6 .......... 118 B6
Townsend Cl *SCUP* DA14 ...... 185 L9
Townsend St *STJWD* NW8 ..... 3 N2
Townshend Rd *CHST* BR7 ...... 184 D8
RCH/KEW TW9 ....................... 155 L9
STJWD NW8 ......................... 3 N2
Townshend Ter
RCH/KEW TW9 ....................... 155 L9
Townson Av *NTHLT* UB5 ........ 133 H4
Townson Wy *NTHLT* UB5 ....... 133 H4
Town Square *DEN/HRF* UB9 * .. 110 B5
Town Sq *GVW* DA11 ............ 190 C2
Town Tree Rd *ASHF* TW15 ..... 174 B8
Town Whf *ISLW* TW7 * ......... 154 G9
Towpath Rd *UED* N18 .......... 100 G7
Towpath Wy *CROY/NA* CR0 .... 203 N6
Towton Rd *WNWD* SE27 ........ 181 M5
Toynbec Cl *RYNPK* SW20 ...... 201 N1
Toynbee Rd *RYNPK* SW20 ..... 201 H1
Toynbee St *WCHPL* E1 ......... 13 N2
Toy's Hl *RSEV* TN16 ............ 245 P8
Tracery The *BNSTD* SM7 ....... 239 L1
Tracey Av *CRICK* NW2 .......... 116 G1
Tracious Cl *WOKN/KNAP* GU21. 231 N2
Tracy Av *DTCH/LGLY* SL3 ....... 150 C4
Tracyes Rd *HLWS* CM18 ........ 47 L5
Trade Cl *PLMGR* N13 .......... 99 G5
Trader Rd *EHAM* E6 ............ 142 E5
Tradescant Rd *VX/NE* SW8 ..... 158 F6
Trading Estate Rd
WLSDN NW10 ........................ 135 P6
Trafalgar Av *BROX* EN10 ....... 44 F2
PECK SE15 .......................... 19 M8
TOTM N17 ........................... 99 M7
WPK KT4 ............................ 200 G8
Trafalgar Cl
BERM/RHTH SE16 * ................. 141 P8
Trafalgar Dr *WOT/HER* KT12 .. 197 H10
Trafalgar Gdns *CRAWE* RH10 .. 284 C4
WCHPL E1 ........................... 140 D7
Trafalgar Gv *GNWCH* SE10 .... 161 L1
Trafalgar Pl *UED* N18 .......... 99 M9
WAN E11 ............................ 121 H2
Trafalgar Rd *GNWCH* SE10 .... 161 L1
RAIN RM13 .......................... 144 G2

**Column 6**

WHTN TW2 * ......................... 176 C5
WIM/MER SW19 ..................... 179 L10
Trafalgar Sq *STJS* SW1Y * ...... 11 K9
Trafalgar St *WALW* SE17 ....... 18 G7
Trafalgar Wy *CROY/NA* CR0 .... 202 G9
POP/IOD E14 ........................ 141 N9
Trafford Cl *BARK/HLT* IG6 ...... 103 J7
RAD WD7 ............................ 57 K8
Trafford Rd *THHTH* CR7 ........ 202 G5
Trahorn Cl *WCHPL* E1 * ........ 13 N2
Tramway Av *ED* N9 ............. 100 A1
PGE/AN SE20 ........................ 204 B1
Tramway Pth *MTCM* CR4 ....... 201 P4
Tranby Ms *HOM* E9 ............. 120 C10
Tranley Ms *HAMP* NW3 ......... 117 P9
Tranmere Rd *ED* N9 ............ 99 N1
WAND/EARL SW18 ................... 179 M5
WHTN TW2 ........................... 176 B5
Tranquil Dl *BRKHM/BTCW* RH3. 256 G9
Tranquil Pas *BKHTH/KID* SE3 * . 161 J2
Tranquil Ri *ERITH* DA8 ......... 164 F14
Tranquil V *BKHTH/KID* SE3 ..... 161 J2
Transept St *CAMTN* NW1 ....... 9 N4
Transmere Rd
STMC/STPC BR5 .................... 206 F6
Transom Cl *BERM/RHTH* SE16.. 160 C4
Transom Sq *POP/IOD* E14 ...... 160 G4
Transport Av *BTFD* TW8 ....... 154 F4
Tranton Rd *BERM/RHTH* SE16 . 160 A3
Trapp's Ct *CSHM* HP5 .......... 51 H5
Trapp's La *CSHM* HP5 .......... 51 H5
Traps Hl *LOU* IG10 ............. 82 C8
Traps La *NWMAL* KT3 ........... 200 B2
Trapstyle Rd *WARE* SG12 ...... 25 P1
Trasher Md *DORK* RH4 ......... 273 H8
Travellers Cl *BRKMPK* AL9 ..... 40 F9
Travellers La *HAT* AL10 ........ 41 D6
Travellers Site *CHING* E4 * .... 100 B3
Travellers Wy *HSLWW* TW4 .... 153 K8
Travers Cl *WALTH* E17 .......... 100 G9
Travers Rd *HOLWY* N7 ......... 119 H9
Travic Rd *SLN* SL2 ............. 128 C5
Travis Ct *SLN* SL2 ............. 128 C5
Treacher's Cl *CSHM* HP5 ....... 50 B3
Treacy Cl *BUSH* WD23 .......... 94 B3
Treadgold St *NTGHL* W11 ...... 8 A7
Treadway St *BETH* E2 .......... 140 A4
Treadwell Rd *EPSOM* KT18 .... 238 B2
Treaty St *IS* N1 ............... 5 N6
Trebble Rd *SWCM* DA10 ....... 189 N2
Trebeck St *MYFR/PICC* W1J ... 10 D9
Trebellan Dr *HHNE* HP2 ........ 36 A5
Trebovir Rd *ECT* SW5 .......... 14 B6
Treby St *BOW* E3 .............. 140 E6
Trecastle Wy *HOLWY* N7 ....... 118 D8
Tredegar Rd *BOW* E3 .......... 140 E4
FBAR/BDGN N11 .................... 98 E8
Tredegar Sq *BOW* E3 .......... 140 D5
Tredegar Ter *BOW* E3 .......... 140 D5
Trederwen Rd *HACK* E8 ........ 7 P5
Tredown Rd *SYD* SE26 ......... 182 E8
Tredwell Cl *HAYES* BR2 ......... 206 A4
Tredwell Rd *WNWD* SE27 ...... 181 J7
Treebourne Rd
BH/WHM TN16 ...................... 243 P3
Treebys Av *RGUE* GU4 ......... 250 A4
Tree Cl *ABR/ST* RM4 ........... 83 L7
RCHPK/HAM TW10 .................. 177 J4
Treen Av *BARN* SW13 .......... 273 H5
Tree Rd *CAN/RD* E16 ........... 141 P8
Treeside Cl *WDR/YW* UB7 ...... 151 N3
Tree Top Ms *DAGE* RM10 ...... 144 E1
Treetops *GVW* DA11 ........... 191 J4
BGR/WK TN15 ....................... 247 P3
Tree Tops *BRWN* CM15 ........ 107 H2
CTHM CR3 ........................... 241 P4
Treetops Cl *ABYW* SE2 ........ 163 P4
NTHWD HA6 ......................... 92 B2
Treetops Vw *LOU* IG10 ......... 82 A9
Tree View Cl *NRWD* SE19 ...... 203 M1
Tree View Ct *REIG* RH2 * ...... 257 N10
Treewall Gdns *BMLY* BR1 ...... 183 N6
Treeway *REIG* RH2 ............. 257 L7
Trefgarne Rd *DAGE* RM10 ..... 124 B8
Trefoil Rd *WAND/EARL* SW18.. 179 M1
Trefusis Wk *WAT* WD17 ........ 72 E5
Tregaron Av *CEND/HSY/T* N8 .. 118 F5
Tregaron Gdns *NWMAL* KT3 ... 200 B2
Tregarthen Pl *LHD/OX* KT22 .. 237 H7
Tregarth Pl *WOKN/KNAP* GU21. 231 L3
Tregarvon Rd *BTSEA* SW11 .... 158 B10
Tregelles Rd *HOD* EN11 ........ 44 F1
Tregenna Av
RYLN/HDSTN HA2 .................... 113 P9
Tregenna Cl *STHGT/OAK* N14 .. 98 B9
Tregony Rd *ORP* BR6 ........... 227 J1
Trego Rd *HOM* E9 .............. 140 C2
Tregothnan Rd *BRXN/ST* SW9 . 158 P9
Tregunter Rd *WBPTN* SW10 ... 15 J3
Trehaven Pde *REIG* RH2 ....... 275 L5
Treheam Gdns *RICH* IG2 ....... 122 G8
Treherne Ct *BRXN/ST* SW9 * .. 142 J5
Trehurst St *CLPT* E5 ........... 120 D10
Trelawn Cl *CHERT* KT16 ....... 214 F4
Trelawney Av *DTCH/LGLY* SL3 . 150 B2
Trelawney Est *HOM* E9 ........ 120 E1
Trelawney Rd *BARK/HLT* IG6 .. 103 J7
Trelawn Rd *BRXS/STRHM* SW2. 142 B11
LEY E10 ............................. 121 H1
Trellis Sq *BOW* E3 ............. 140 C5
Treloar Gdns *NRWD* SE19 ..... 181 L9
Trelwney Est *HOM* E9 ......... 120 E1
Tremadoc Rd *CLAP* SW4 ....... 158 E10
Tremaine Cl *BROCKY* SE4 ...... 160 D11
Tremaine Gv *HHNE* HP2 ........ 35 P2
Tremaine Rd *PGE/AN* SE20 .... 202 E3
Trematon Pl *TEDD* TW11 ...... 177 H10
Trematon Wy *UED* N18 ........ 99 M7
Tremlett Gv *ARCH* N19 ........ 118 C2
Tremlett Ms *ARCH* N19 ........ 118 C2
Trenance *WOKN/KNAP* GU21 .. 231 M3
Trenance Gdns
GDMY/SEVK IG3 .................... 123 K8
Trenchard Av *RSLP* HA4 ....... 113 J8
Trenchard Cl *CDALE/KGS* NW9. 96 B10
STAN HA7 ........................... 94 G7
WOT/HER KT12 ...................... 217 K2
Trenchard Ct *MRDN* SM4 ...... 201 L6
Trenchard St *GNWCH* SE10 ... 161 J1
Trenchold St *VX/NE* SW8 ...... 158 C5
Trenches La *DTCH/LGLY* SL3 .. 130 D10
Trench Cl *ORP* BR6 ............. 227 J1
Trenham Dr *WARL* CR6 ......... 242 B2
Trenholme Cl *PGE/AN* SE20 ... 182 A10
Trenholme Ter *PGE/AN* SE20 .. 182 A10
Trenmar Gdns *WLSDN* NW10 .. 136 E5
Trent Av *EA* W5 ............... 155 J3
UPMR RM14 ......................... 104 G10
Trentbridge Cl *BARK/HLT* IG6 . 103 K7
Trent Gdns *STHGT/OAK* N14 ... 78 C10
Trentham Crs *STJWD* NW8 * ... 9 K1
Trentham Dr
WOKS/MYFD GU22 .................. 232 D7
Trentham Rd *REDH* RH1 ........ 275 A2
Trentham St
WAND/EARL SW18 .................... 179 K6
Trent Pk *EBAR* EN4 ............ 78 A6
Trent Rd *BKHH* IG9 ............ 102 G5
DTCH/LGLY SL3 ..................... 150 C5
Trent Wy *WPK* KT4 ............. 200 G8
YEAD UB4 ........................... 132 F5
Trentwood Side *ENC/FH* EN2 .. 79 G3
Treport St *WAND/EARL* SW18.. 179 L5
Tresco Cl *BMLY* BR1 ........... 183 N6
Tresco Gdns *GDMY/SEVK* IG3 . 123 M9
Tresco Rd *PECK* SE15 .......... 160 A4
Tresham Crs *STJWD* NW8 ...... 9 N1
Tresham Rd *BARK* IG11 ........ 143 H7

Tresilian Av WCHMH N21 ..... 78 C9
Tresillian Wy
 WOKN/KNAP GU21 .... 231 M3
Tressel CI IS N1 ..... 6 D4
Tresillian Crs BROCKY SE4 .... 160 C6
Tresillian Rd BROCKY SE4 .... 160 F9
Tresta Wy WOKN/KNAP GU21 .... 231 M1
Trestis CI YEAD UB4 .... 133 L6
Treswell Rd DAGW RM9 .... 143 P9
Tretawn Gdns MLHL NW7 .... 96 B5
Tretawn Pk MLHL NW7 .... 96 B5
Trevalga Wy HHNE HP2 .... 35 M9
Trevanion Rd WKENS W14 .... 14 B7
Treve Av HRW HA1 .... 114 B5
Trevellance Wy GSTN WD25 .... 55 G9
Trevelyan Av MNPK E12 .... 122 C9
Trevelyan CI DART DA1 .... 165 N10
Trevelyan Crs
 KTN/HRWW/WS HA3 .... 115 J5
Trevelyan Gdns
 WLSDN NW10 .... 136 F3
Trevelyan PI STAL AL1 .... 38 D1
Trevelyan Rd SRTFD E15 .... 121 K9
 TOOT SW17 .... 180 A9
Trevelyan Wy BERK HP4 .... 33 J6
Trevera Ct CHES/WCR EN8 .... 62 D9
 HOD EN11 * .... 44 F2
Trevereux HI OXTED RH8 .... 262 D8
Treveris St STHWK SE1 .... 2 D10
Treverton St NKENS W10 .... 136 G6
Treville St PUT/ROE SW15 .... 178 E3
Treviso Rd FSTH SE23 .... 182 C5
Trevithick CI
 EBED/NFELT TW14 .... 174 G4
Trevithick St DEPT SE8 .... 165 N10
Trevone Gdns PIN HA5 .... 113 M4
Trevor CI EBAR EN4 .... 77 N10
 HAYES BR2 .... 205 M7
 ISLW TW7 .... 158 C3
 KTN/HRWW/WS HA3 .... 94 E8
 NTHLT UB5 .... 133 K4
Trevor Crs RSLP HA4 .... 112 C9
Trevor Gdns EDGW HA8 .... 96 A9
 NTHLT UB5 .... 133 K4
Trevor PI SKENS SW7 .... 15 P2
Trevor Rd EDGW HA8 .... 96 A9
 HYS/HAR UB3 .... 152 F1
 WFD IG8 .... 101 M8
 WIM/MER SW19 .... 179 H10
Trevor Sq SKENS SW7 .... 15 P2
Trevor St SKENS SW7 .... 15 P2
Trevose Av BF/WBF KT14 .... 215 J10
Trevose Rd WALTH E17 .... 101 J9
Trevose Wy OXHEY WD19 .... 93 K4
Trewarden Av IVER SL0 .... 88 G9
Trewenna Dr CHSGTN KT9 .... 219 J2
 POTB/CUF EN6 .... 59 N8
Trewince Rd RYNPK SW20 .... 200 F1
Trewint St WAND/EARL SW18 .... 179 M5
Trewsbury Rd SYD SE26 .... 182 C8
Treyford CI CRAWW RH11 .... 283 Q11
Triandra Wy YEAD UB4 .... 133 L6
Triangle Pas EBAR EN4 * .... 77 M8
Triangle PI CLAP SW4 .... 181 E10
Triangle Rd HACK E8 .... 140 E4
The Triangle BFN/LL DA15 * .... 185 K3
 HACK E8 .... 7 M1
 KUT/HW KT1 .... 199 P7
 WOKN/KNAP GU21 .... 231 H4
Triangle Wy ACT W3 .... 155 M2
Trident Av HAT AL10 * .... 40 B3
Trident St GSTN WD25 .... 54 C10
Trident St BERM/RHTH SE16 .... 160 F3
Trident Wy NWDGN UB2 .... 153 J2
Trigg's CI WOKS/MYFD GU22 .... 232 A5
Trigg's La WOKS/MYFD GU22 .... 231 P5
Trilby Rd FSTH SE23 .... 182 C5
Trim St NWCR SE14 .... 144 F10
Trinder Rd ARCH N19 .... 118 F6
 BAR EN5 .... 76 F9
Trindles Rd REDH RH1 .... 276 G2
Tring Av EA W5 .... 135 L10
 STHL UB1 .... 133 N8
 WBLY HA9 .... 135 K1
Tring CI GNTH/NBYPK IG2 .... 122 F3
 HARH RM3 .... 105 M5
Tringham CI CHERT KT16 .... 214 C9
 WOKN/KNAP GU21 .... 231 H4
Tring Rd BERK HP4 .... 33 H2
Trinidad Gdns DAGE RM10 .... 144 D4
Trinidad St POP/IOD E14 .... 140 G2
Trinity Av EFNCH N2 .... 117 N1
 EN EN1 .... 30 C5
Trinity Buoy Whf
 POP/IOD E14 * .... 141 J7
Trinity Church Rd BARN SW13 .... 156 B5
Trinity Church La STHWK SE1 .... 18 F3
Trinity Churchyard GU GU1 * .... 268 A2
Trinity CI CLAP SW4 .... 158 G10
 CRAWE RH10 .... 284 D5
 HACK E8 .... 7 M1
 HAYES BR2 .... 206 B4
 HSLWW TW4 .... 153 M10
 LEW SE13 .... 161 L10
 NTHWD HA6 .... 92 F7
 SAND/SEL CR2 .... 223 N6
 STWL/WRAY TW19 .... 151 K2
 WAN E11 .... 121 K7
Trinity Ct ELTH/MOT SE9 .... 184 G2
 RKW/CH/CXG WD3 .... 91 H7
Trinity Ct ASC SL5 .... 192 F5
 TOOT SW17 .... 180 A5
Trinity Dr UX/CGN UB8 .... 132 D8
Trinity Est DEPT SE8 .... 160 E4
Trinity Gdns BRXN/ST SW9 .... 158 G10
 CAN/RD E16 .... 121 L7
Trinity Gv GNWCH SE10 .... 161 H6
 HERT/WAT SG14 .... 25 K4
Trinity Hall CI WATN WD24 .... 73 H6
Trinity La CHES/WCR EN8 .... 62 D1
Trinity Ms HHNE HP2 .... 36 A1
 PGE/AN SE20 .... 204 A2
Trinity Pde HSLW TW3 * .... 154 A9
Trinity Pk CHING E4 .... 100 G7
Trinity PI BXLYHS DA6 .... 149 H6
Trinity RI BRXS/STRHM SW2 .... 181 J3
Trinity Rd BARK/HLT IG6 .... 122 F1
 EFNCH N2 .... 117 N1
 GVE DA12 .... 191 J9
 HERT/BAY SG13 .... 26 B3
 RCH/KEW TW9 .... 155 L9
 STHL UB1 .... 133 M10
 WAND/EARL SW18 .... 179 L1
 WARE SG12 .... 26 D1
 WDGN N22 .... 98 F8
Trinity Sq TWRH EC3N .... 13 N3
Trinity St CAN/RD E16 .... 141 J7
 ENC/FH EN2 .... 79 K6
 STHWK SE1 * .... 18 F2
Trinity Wk HERT/BAY SG13 .... 26 B3
Trinity Wy ACT W3 .... 136 E9
 CHING E4 .... 100 E7
Trio PI STHWK SE1 .... 18 E2
Tripton Rd NLWS CM18 .... 47 L9
Tristan Gdns BUSH WD23 * .... 73 M8
Tristan Sq BKHTH/KID SE3 .... 161 L3
Tristram CI WALTH E17 .... 121 J1
Tristram Dr ED N9 .... 99 N4
Tristram Rd BMLY BR1 .... 183 L10
Trist Wy CRAWW RH11 .... 283 K5
Triton Sq CAMTN NW1 .... 4 A8
Triton Av CROY/NA CR0 .... 222 F4
Tritton Rd DUL SE21 .... 181 P1
Trittons KWD/TDW/WH KT20 .... 238 F7
Triumph CI CDW/CHF RM16 .... 167 N2
 HYS/HAR UB3 .... 152 B7
Triumph Rd EHAM E6 .... 142 C8
Trivett CI RDART DA2 .... 188 F1


Trodd's La RGUE GU4 .... 269 J1
Trojan Wy CROY/NA CR0 .... 202 G10
Trolling Down HI RDART DA2 .... 188 A5
Troon CI BERM/RHTH SE16 * .... 160 A4
 CRAWW RH11 .... 282 D10
 THMD SE28 .... 143 N8
Troon St WCHPL E1 .... 140 D8
Troopers Dr HARH RM3 .... 105 L5
Trosley Av GVW DA11 .... 190 E6
Trosley Rd BELV DA17 .... 164 B5
Trossachs Rd EDUL SE22 .... 181 M1
Trothy Rd STHWK SE1 .... 19 L5
Trotsworth Av VW GU25 .... 194 A4
Trotters Bottom BAR EN5 .... 76 B3
Trotters Gap WARE SG12 .... 27 K7
Trotters La CHOB/PIR GU24 .... 213 G6
Trotters Rd HLWS CM18 .... 47 K3
Trotter Wy HOR/WEW KT19 .... 219 M6
Trotton CI CRAWE RH10 .... 284 D10
Trott Rd MUSWH N10 .... 98 B8
Trotts La WHTN TW16 .... 262 F5
Trott St BTSEA SW11 .... 157 N7
Trotwood CHIG IG7 .... 102 G6
Troughton Rd CHARL SE7 .... 161 N4
Troutbeck PI SLN SL2 .... 129 M9
Troutbeck Rd NWCR SE14 .... 160 D7
Trout La WDR/YW UB7 .... 131 M9
Trout Ri RKW/CH/CXG WD3 .... 71 L7
Trout Rd WDR/YW UB7 .... 131 M9
Troutstream Wy
 RKW/CH/CXG WD3 .... 71 L8
Trouville Rd CLAP SW4 .... 180 D2
Trowbridge CI HARH RM3 .... 105 L2
 HOM E9 .... 140 A1
Trowers Wy REDH RH1 .... 258 F3
Trowley Ri ABLGY WD5 .... 54 F7
Trowlock Av TEDD TW11 .... 177 H9
Trowlock Wy TEDD TW11 .... 177 H9
Troy Ct KENS W8 .... 14 E3
Troy Rd NRWD SE19 .... 181 L9
Troy Town PECK SE15 .... 159 P9
Trubshaw Rd NWDGN UB2 .... 153 P2
Trueman CI EDGW HA8 * .... 95 N8
Trueman Rd PUR/KEN CR8 .... 241 L6
Truesdale Dr DEN/HRF UB9 .... 111 M2
Trulock Rd TOTM N17 .... 99 N8
Truman's Rd STNW/STAM N16 .... 119 M10
Trumpers Wy HNWL W7 .... 154 A2
Trumper Wy SL SL1 .... 128 E10
Trumpington Dr STAL AL1 .... 38 C9
Trumpington Rd FSTGT E7 .... 121 L9
Trumps Green Av VW GU25 .... 194 A6
Trumps Green Rd VW GU25 .... 193 P8
Trumps Green Rd VW GU25 .... 194 B6
Trumps Mill La VW GU25 .... 194 C6
Trundlers Wy BUSH WD23 .... 94 F1
Trundle St STHWK SE1 .... 18 E1
Trundley's Rd DEPT SE8 .... 160 C5
Trundley's Ter DEPT SE8 .... 160 C3
Trunley Heath Rd SHGR GU5 .... 267 M9
Truro Gdns IL IG1 .... 122 A5
Truro Rd GVE DA12 .... 190 G6
 WALTH E17 .... 120 C2
 WDGN N22 .... 98 F8
Truro St KTTN NW5 .... 4 C1
Truro Wy YEAD UB4 .... 132 G5
Truesdale Rd EHAM E6 .... 142 C8
Truslove Rd WNWD SE27 .... 181 H8
Truss Hill Rd ASC SL5 .... 192 B5
Trussley Rd HMSMTH W6 .... 156 F2
Trustees CI DEN/HRF UB9 .... 111 H6
Trustons Gdns EMPK RM11 .... 125 H5
Trust Rd CHES/WCR EN8 .... 62 D10
Tryfan CI REDBR IG4 .... 122 A3
Tryon Crs HOM E9 .... 140 B3
Trys HI CHERT KT16 .... 194 C9
Trystings CI ESH/CLAY KT10 .... 218 F5
Tuam Rd WOOL/PLUM SE18 .... 162 G5
Tubbenden CI ORP BR6 .... 207 H9
Tubbenden Dr ORP BR6 .... 226 G1
Tubbenden La ORP BR6 .... 226 G1
Tubbenden La South ORP BR6 .... 226 G2
Tubbs Cft WCCE AL7 .... 23 L6
Tubbs Rd WLSDN NW10 .... 136 C4
Tubs Hill Pde SEV TN13 * .... 247 H10
Tubwell Rd SLN SL2 .... 129 N5
Tucker Dr WATW WD18 * .... 73 K9
Tuckey Gv RPLY/SEND GU23 .... 233 J10
Tuck Rd RAIN RM13 .... 145 H1
Tudor Av CHESW EN7 .... 62 A1
 GPK RM2 .... 125 H1
 HPTN TW12 .... 175 P9
 WAT WD24 .... 73 L3
 WPK KT4 .... 200 E10
Tudor CI ASHF TW15 .... 173 N7
 BNSTD SM7 .... 239 L4
 BRWN CM15 .... 87 L10
 BRXS/STRHM SW2 .... 180 A5
 CDALE/KGS NW9 .... 115 P7
 CHEAM SM3 .... 220 G2
 CHESW EN7 .... 62 A7
 CHIG IG7 .... 102 D5
 CHSGTN KT9 .... 219 K2
 CHST BR7 .... 206 C1
 COB KT11 .... 217 N9
 COUL/CHIP CR5 .... 241 H4
 CRAWE RH10 .... 284 B6
 GT/LBKH KT23 .... 235 P10
 GVW DA11 .... 190 B4
 HAMP NW3 .... 3 M1
 HAT AL10 .... 40 B7
 HGT N6 .... 118 D5
 HORL RH6 .... 281 J4
 MLHL NW7 .... 96 D7
 PIN HA5 .... 113 H5
 SAND/SEL CR2 .... 242 A11
 WARE SG12 .... 28 A3
 WFD IG8 .... 101 N6
 WLGTN SM6 .... 222 G6
 WOKS/MYFD GU22 .... 232 D5
Tudor Ct BORE WD6 .... 69 Q4
 ELTH/MOT SE9 * .... 162 B10
 SWLY BR8 .... 208 D7
 WALTH E17 .... 120 E5
Tudor Ct North WBLY HA9 .... 115 M10
Tudor Ct South WBLY HA9 .... 115 M10
Tudor Crs BARK/HLT IG6 .... 102 F2
 ENC/FH EN2 .... 79 K5
 RSEV TN14 .... 247 K5
Tudor Dr GPK RM2 .... 124 G1
 KUTN/CMB KT2 .... 177 H4
 MRDN SM4 .... 200 G6
 RSEV TN14 .... 247 K2
 WATN WD24 .... 73 L4
 WOT/HER KT12 .... 197 L6
Tudor Est WLSDN NW10 * .... 135 M4
Tudor Gdns ACT W3 .... 135 M8
 BARN SW13 .... 156 A9
 CDALE/KGS NW9 .... 115 P7
 GPK RM2 .... 125 H1
 SL SL1 .... 130 A8
 TWK TW1 .... 176 A4
 UPMR RM14 .... 126 C1
 WWKM BR4 .... 214 A10
Tudor Gv HOM E9 .... 140 A3
Tudor La WSR SL4 .... 171 P3
Tudor Manor Gdns
 GSTN WD25 .... 55 L8
Tudor Ms WLSDN NW10 * .... 136 C4
Tudor Orch EYN DA4 * .... 33 N3
Tudor Pde ELTH/MOT SE9 * .... 162 B10
 ROM RM1 * .... 104 C6
Tudor Rd BAR EN5 .... 77 H4
 BECK BR3 .... 204 F4
 DTCH/LGLY SL3 .... 149 H1
 EDGW HA8 .... 95 M4
 GDMY/SEVK IG3 .... 124 C1


BARK IG11 .... 143 J2
BECK BR3 .... 205 H3
CHING E4 .... 100 G9
ED N9 .... 100 A1
GODL GU7 .... 267 K10
HACK E8 .... 140 A3
HPTN TW12 .... 175 P10
HSLW TW3 .... 154 C10
HYS/HAR UB3 .... 133 N9
KTN/HRWW/WS HA3 .... 94 A10
KUTN/CMB KT2 .... 177 M10
NRWD SE19 .... 181 N10
PIN HA5 .... 93 K10
PLSTW E13 .... 141 M9
SNWD SE25 .... 204 A5
STALE/WH AL4 .... 21 K1
STALW/RED AL3 .... 38 D2
WAN E11 .... 133 J1
Tudor Vis CHESW EN7 .... 61 M5
Tudor Wk LHD/OX KT22 .... 236 F6
 WARE SG12 .... 26 C2
 WAT WD24 .... 73 L3
 WAY KT15 .... 196 C10
Tudor Wy ACT W3 .... 155 M1
 HERT/WAT SG14 .... 25 H5
 HGDN/ICK UB10 .... 132 B1
 RKW/CH/CXG WD3 .... 91 K2
 STHGT/OAK N14 .... 98 G1
 STMC/STPC BR5 .... 206 G6
 WAB EN9 .... 63 J9
 WDR/YW UB7 .... 148 D2
 WOKN/KNAP GU21 .... 231 H4
Tudway Rd BKHTH/KID SE3 .... 161 P10
Tuffnell Park Rd HOLWY N7 .... 118 C9
Tufter Rd CHIG IG7 .... 103 M5
Tufton Gdns E/WMO/HCT KT8 .... 198 A2
Tufton Rd CHING E4 .... 100 F5
Tufton St WEST SW1P .... 17 J4
Tugboat St THMD SE28 .... 163 H1
Tugela Rd CROY/NA CR0 .... 203 L6
Tugela St CAT SE6 .... 182 C5
Tugmutton CI ORP BR6 .... 226 E1
Tugswood CI COUL/CHIP CR5 .... 240 E7
Tugwood CI COUL/CHIP CR5 .... 240 E7
Tulip CI BRWN CM15 .... 86 C9
 CROY/NA CR0 .... 204 C8
 EHAM E6 .... 142 B7
 HARH RM3 .... 105 K7
 HPTN TW12 .... 175 P9
 NWDGN UB2 .... 154 B1
Tulip Gdns CHING E4 * .... 101 J4
 IL IG1 .... 142 E1
Tulip Wy WDR/YW UB7 .... 151 N3
Tull St CAR SM5 .... 202 D3
Tuise CI BECK BR3 .... 205 H5
Tulse HI BRXS/STRHM SW2 .... 181 H3
Tulsemere Rd WNWD SE27 .... 181 K5
Tulyar CI KWD/TDW/WH KT20 .... 238 C5
Tumber St HLWS CM18 .... 47 K2
Tumbler St HLWS CM18 .... 47 K2
Tumblewood Rd BNSTD SM7 .... 239 H2
Tumbling Bay WOT/HER KT12 .... 197 H6
Tumbling Bay Weir
 WARE SG12 * .... 26 E1
Tummons Gdns SNWD SE25 .... 203 M2
Tuncombe Rd UED N18 .... 99 M5
Tunfield Rd HOD EN11 .... 26 C10
Tunis Rd SHB W12 .... 136 F10
Tunley Rd TOOT SW17 .... 180 B5
 WLSDN NW10 .... 136 G1
Tunmarsh La PLSTW E13 .... 141 N1
Tunmers End CFSP/GDCR SL9 .... 89 P3
Tunnan Leys EHAM E6 .... 142 D8
Tunnel Av GNWCH SE10 .... 161 H1
 GNWCH SE10 .... 146 E10
Tunnel Gdns FBAR/BDGN N11 .... 98 B8
Tunnel Link Rd HTHAIR TW6 .... 174 B1
Tunnel Rd BERM/RHTH SE16 .... 160 B1
 HORL RH6 .... 280 D7
Tunnel Rd East WDR/YW UB7 .... 152 C6
Tunnel Rd West WDR/YW UB7 .... 152 B7
Tunnel Wood CI WAT WD17 .... 72 G3
Tunnel Wood Rd WAT WD17 .... 72 G3
Tunnmeade CRAWW RH11 .... 282 A11
Tunstall Av BARK/HLT IG6 .... 103 K1
Tunstall CI ORP BR6 .... 227 H4
Tunstall Rd BRXN/ST SW9 .... 158 C10
 CROY/NA CR0 .... 203 M4
Tunstock Wy BELV DA17 .... 163 P2
Tunworth CI CDALE/KGS NW9 .... 115 P4
Tunworth Crs PUT/ROE SW15 .... 176 D6
Tupelo Rd LEY E10 .... 120 C7
Tuppy St THMD SE28 .... 162 F2
Tupwood CI CTHM CR3 .... 259 P7
Tupwood La CTHM CR3 .... 259 P6
Tupwood Scrubbs Rd
 CTHM CR3 .... 241 P6
Turene CI WAND/EARL SW18 .... 157 M10
Turfhouse La CHOB/PIR GU24 .... 213 K5
Turin Rd ED N9 .... 100 B1
Turin St BETH E2 .... 7 N9
Turkey Oak CI NRWD SE19 .... 203 M1
Turkey St EN EN1 .... 79 P2
Turks CI UX/CGN UB8 .... 132 B5
Turks Rw CHEL SW3 .... 16 E7
Turle Rd FSBYPK N4 .... 118 C2
 STRHM/NOR SW16 .... 202 F2
Turlewray CI FSBYPK N4 .... 118 C6
Turley CI SRTFD E15 .... 141 K3
Turmore Dl WCCW AL8 .... 22 F6
Turnagain La
 FLST/FETLN EC4A * .... 12 C5
Turnage Rd BCTR RM8 .... 124 A6
Turnant Rd TOTM N17 .... 99 K9
Turnberry CI
 BERM/RHTH SE16 * .... 160 A4
 HDN NW4 .... 96 C10
Turnberry Ct OXHEY WD19 * .... 93 K4
Turnberry Dr LCOL/BKTW AL2 .... 55 M6
Turnberry Wy ORP BR6 .... 206 G8
Turnbury CI THMD SE28 .... 143 N8
Turnchapel Ms CLAP SW4 .... 158 C10
Turner Av BH/WHM TN16 .... 225 P6
 MTCM CR4 .... 202 A1
 SEVS/STOTM N15 .... 119 M2
 WHTN TW2 .... 176 A5
Turner CI ALP/SUD HA0 .... 115 J10
 BRXN/ST SW9 .... 159 J7
 GLDGN NW11 .... 117 L4
 RGUE GU4 .... 268 C1
Turner Ct CMBW SE5 * .... 159 L10
Turner Dr GLDGN NW11 .... 117 L4
Turner Ms SUT SM1 .... 221 L4
Turner Rd BUSH WD23 .... 74 B8
 DTCH/LGLY SL3 .... 149 H1
 EDGW HA8 .... 95 K4
 NWMAL KT3 .... 200 A7
 RDART DA2 .... 188 C6
 WALTH E17 .... 121 H2
 WLSDN NW10 * .... 135 M8
Turners CI CHING CM5 .... 56 A2
 STA TW18 .... 173 L8
 TRDG/WHET N20 .... 98 A4
Turners Gdns SEV TN13 .... 265 K6
Turners HI HHNE HP2 .... 35 P7
Turner's HI CHES/WCR EN8 .... 62 C5
Turners Hill Rd CRAWE RH10 .... 284 F1
Turners La WOT/HER KT12 .... 217 K12
Turners Meadow Wy
 BECK BR3 .... 204 B1
Turner's Oak Shaw HART DA3 .... 149 L9
Turners PI EYN DA4 .... 210 B1
Turner's Rd BOW E3 .... 140 C7
Turner St CAN/RD E16 .... 141 J7


WCHPL E1 .... 140 A7
Turners Wk CSHM HP5 .... 51 H6
Turners Wd GLDGN NW11 .... 117 N6
Turnerville Rd WKENS W14 .... 14 C1
Turney Rd DUL SE21 .... 181 K3
Turneys Orch
 RKW/CH/CXG WD3 .... 70 G9
Tuners CI HCH RM12 .... 125 K10
Turnfield Rd BROX EN10 * .... 62 D2
Turnford Vls BROX EN10 * .... 62 D2
Turnham CI GUW GU2 .... 267 P4
Turnham Green Ter
 CHSWK W4 .... 156 B3
Turnham Rd BROCKY SE4 .... 182 D1
Turnmill St FARR EC1M .... 12 D1
Turnoak Av WOKS/MYFD GU22 .... 232 B6
Turnoak La WOKS/MYFD GU22 .... 232 B6
Turnpike CI DEPT SE8 .... 160 E6
Turnpike Dr ORP BR6 .... 227 M5
Turnpike La CEND/HSY/T N8 .... 118 F1
 HGDN/ICK UB10 .... 131 P5
 SUT SM1 .... 222 A4
 TIL RM18 .... 169 N6
Turnpike Link CROY/NA CR0 .... 3 M2
Turnpike Ms CEND/HSY/T N8 * .... 119 H1
Turnpike Pde
 SEVS/STOTM N15 * .... 119 J1
Turnpike PI CRAWW RH11 .... 283 N5
Turnpike Wy ISLW TW7 .... 154 F7
Turnstone CI CDALE/KGS NW9 .... 115 J5
 PLSTW E13 .... 141 N2
 SAND/SEL CR2 .... 224 D6
Turnstone HART DA3 .... 211 M3
Turnstone CI
 CDALE/KGS NW9 .... 96 B10
 HGDN/ICK UB10 .... 112 C10
 PLSTW E13 .... 141 M2
 SAND/SEL CR2 .... 224 D6
Turp Av CDW/CHF RM16 .... 167 P1
Turpentine La PIM SW1V .... 16 F7
Turpin Av CRW RM5 .... 104 B8
Turpin CI PEND EN3 .... 80 F3
Turpington CI HAYES BR2 .... 206 B5
Turpington La HAYES BR2 .... 206 A6
Turpin Rd EBED/NFELT TW14 .... 174 A2
Turpins CI HERT/WAT SG14 .... 24 G5
Turpins Ri BFOR GU20 .... 212 A1
Turpins Yd CRICK NW2 * .... 137 J2
Turpin Wy WLGTN SM6 .... 222 C6
Turquand St WALW SE17 .... 18 F6
Turret Gv CLAP SW4 .... 158 D9
Turton Rd ALP/SUD HA0 .... 115 K10
Turton Wy SL SL1 .... 149 J2
Turville St BETH E2 .... 7 N9
Tuscan Rd WOOL/PLUM SE18 .... 162 G9
Tuscany Gdns CRAWE RH10 .... 283 P5
Tushmore Av CRAWE RH10 .... 283 P4
Tushmore Crs CRAWE RH10 * .... 283 P5
Tushmore La CRAWE RH10 .... 283 P5
Tushmore Rd CRAWE RH10 .... 283 P5
Tuskar St GNWCH SE10 .... 161 K4
Tussauds CI
 RKW/CH/CXG WD3 .... 72 B9
Tussock CI CRAWW RH11 .... 283 K9
Tuxford CI BORE WD6 .... 75 J1
 CRAWE RH10 * .... 284 D9
Tweed TIL RM18 .... 169 M3
Tweeddale Gv HGDN/ICK UB10 .... 112 D8
Tweeddale Rd CAR SM5 .... 201 N8
Tweed La BRKHM/BTCW RH3 .... 255 P6
Tweedmouth Rd PLSTW E13 .... 141 N1
Tweed Rd DTCH/LGLY SL3 .... 150 E5
Tweed Wy ROM RM1 .... 104 E3
Tweedy Rd BMLY BR1 .... 205 M1
Tweenways CSHM HP5 .... 51 J6
Twelve Acre CI GT/LBKH KT23 .... 235 N10
Twelve Acres WGCE AL7 .... 23 H7
Twelve Av
 KWD/TDW/WH KT20 * .... 257 J2
Twelvetrees Crs BOW E3 .... 140 H6
Twentyman CI WFD IG8 .... 101 H6
Twickenham Br TWK TW1 .... 177 H1
Twickenham CI CROY/NA CR0 .... 202 G10
Twickenham Gdns
 GFD/PVL UB6 .... 114 C10
 KTN/HRWW/WS HA3 .... 94 D8
Twickenham Rd FELT TW13 .... 175 M7
 ISLW TW7 .... 154 E10
 TEDD TW11 .... 176 F7
 WAN E11 .... 121 J3
Twig Folly CI BETH E2 .... 140 C4
Twig Folly Whf BETH E2 * .... 140 C4
Twigg CI ERITH DA8 .... 164 F6
Twilley St WAND/EARL SW18 .... 179 L3
Twinches La SL SL1 .... 128 C4
Twine Ct WCHPL E1 .... 140 F8
Twinehan CI
 NFNCH/WDSPK N12 .... 97 K5
Twine Ter BOW E3 * .... 140 H6
Twining Av WHTN TW2 .... 176 A5
Twinn Rd MLHL NW7 .... 97 H1
Twinoaks COB KT11 .... 217 P9
Twin Tumps Wy THMD SE28 .... 143 K9
Twisden Rd KTTN NW5 .... 118 B5
The Twitten CRAWW RH11 .... 283 N9
Twitton La RSEV TN14 .... 246 F1
Twitton Mdw RSEV TN14 .... 246 F1
Two Acres WCCE AL7 .... 23 J8
Two Beeches HHNE HP2 .... 36 A5
Two Dells La CSHM HP5 .... 50 A3
Two Gates La CSHM HP5 .... 52 C10
Two Mile Dr SL SL1 .... 148 D1
Two Ponds La BERK HP4 .... 33 H5
Two Waters Rd HHS/BOV HP3 .... 35 N9
Twybridge Wy WLSDN NW10 .... 136 G5
Twycross Ms GNWCH SE10 .... 161 K3
Twycross Rd GODL GU7 .... 267 J10
Twyford Abbey Rd
 WLSDN NW10 .... 135 L5
Twyford Av ACT W3 .... 135 M10
 EFNCH N2 .... 117 M1
Twyford Crs ACT W3 .... 135 M10
Twyford Rd CAR SM5 .... 202 A7
 HRW HA2 .... 114 C5
 IL IG1 .... 142 C10
 RYLN/HDSTN HA2 .... 114 A3
 STALE/WH AL4 .... 39 J1
Twyford St IS N1 .... 5 L1
Twyne CI CRAWW RH11 .... 283 J9
Twyner CI HORL RH6 .... 280 H5
Twynersh Av CHERT KT16 .... 195 H4
Tyas Rd CAN/RD E16 .... 141 L6
Tybenham Rd
 WIM/MER SW19 .... 201 N1
Tyberry Rd PEND EN3 .... 80 D1
Tyburn La HRW HA1 .... 114 E6
Tyburn Wy MBLAR W1H .... 9 L6
Tycehurst HI LOU IG10 .... 80 B7
Tychbourne Dr RGUE GU4 .... 250 H10
Tydcombe Rd WARL CR6 .... 242 F6
Tye Green Village
 HLWS CM18 .... 47 J4
Tye La ORP BR6 .... 226 F5
Tyers Ga STHWK SE1 .... 19 J1
Tyers St LBTH SE11 .... 17 L7
Tyers Ter LBTH SE11 .... 17 L8
Tyeshurst CI ABYW SE2 .... 163 H5
Tyfield CI CHES/WCR EN8 .... 62 D2
Tylecroft Rd
 STRHM/NOR SW16 .... 202 F2
Tyle Gn HHNE HP2 .... 36 A1
Tylehurst Gdns IL IG1 .... 142 C1
Tyle PI WDSR SL4 .... 171 N3


Tyler CI BETH E2 .... 7 L7
Tyler Gdns ADL/WDHM KT15 .... 215 M1
Tyler Rd CRAWE RH10 .... 283 N10
 NWDGN UB2 .... 153 L2
Tylers CI GDST RH9 .... 260 E6
 KGLGY WD5 .... 54 A5
Tylers Crs HCH RM12 .... 125 K10
Tylersfield ABLGY WD5 .... 55 H7
Tylers Ga KTN/HRWW/WS HA3 .... 115 M1
Tylers Green Rd SWLY BR8 .... 208 D6
Tylers Hill Rd CSHM HP5 .... 51 J8
Tyler St GNWCH SE10 .... 161 K4
 GNWCH SE10 * .... 161 K4
Tyler Wy BRW CM14 .... 106 C2
Tylney Av NRWD SE19 .... 181 P4
Tylney CI CHIG IG7 * .... 103 J6
Tylney Cft HLWW/ROY CM19 .... 46 E6
Tylney Rd BMLY BR1 .... 206 A2
 FSTGT E7 .... 121 P9
Tynan CI EBED/NFELT TW14 .... 175 M4
Tyndale La IS N1 .... 6 C3
Tyndale Ms SL SL1 .... 148 C3
Tyndale Ter IS N1 .... 6 C2
Tyndall Rd LEY E10 .... 121 H7
 WELL DA16 .... 163 J9
Tyne CI CRAWE RH10 .... 284 D9
 UPMR RM14 .... 126 C4
Tynedale LCOL/BKTW AL2 .... 57 L3
Tynedale CI RDART DA2 .... 188 C4
Tynedale Rd
 BRKHM/BTCW RH3 .... 273 N4
Tyne Gdns SOCK/AV RM15 .... 149 M6
Tyneham CI BTSEA SW11 * .... 158 B9
Tyneham Rd BTSEA SW11 .... 158 B9
Tynemouth CI EHAM E6 .... 142 E8
Tynemouth Dr EN EN1 .... 79 P4
Tynemouth Rd MTCM CR4 .... 180 B10
 SEVS/STOTM N15 .... 119 N2
 WOOL/PLUM SE18 .... 147 M3
Tynemouth St FUL/PGN SW6 .... 157 M8
Tynemouth Ter
 SEVS/STOTM N15 * .... 119 N2
Tyne St WCHPL E1 .... 13 N1
Tynsdale Rd WLSDN NW10 .... 136 B2
Type St BETH E2 .... 140 C4
Tyrrell Av WELL DA16 .... 163 P6
Tyrawley Rd FUL/PGN SW6 .... 157 L7
Tyre La CDALE/KGS NW9 .... 116 C2
Tyrell Gdns WDSR SL4 .... 148 C9
Tyrell CI HRW HA1 .... 114 E8
Tyrell Ri BRWN CM15 * .... 107 H6
Tyrells PI GU GU1 * .... 268 C1
Tyrone Rd EHAM E6 .... 142 C4
Tyron Wy SCUP DA14 .... 185 P1
Tyrrell Av WELL DA16 .... 163 P6
Tyrrell Rd EDUL SE22 * .... 159 P10
Tyrrells PI GRAYS RM17 .... 168 A4
Tyrwhitt Av BRYLDS KT5 .... 203 N2
Tyrwhitt Rd BROCKY SE4 .... 160 F9
Tysea HI ABR/ST RM4 .... 104 C1
Tysea Rd HLWS CM18 .... 47 J8
Tysoe Av PEND EN3 .... 80 E2
Tysoe St FSBYW WC1X .... 6 A10
Tyson Gdns FSTH SE23 * .... 182 B3
Tyson Rd FSTH SE23 .... 182 B3
Tyssen PI SOCK/AV RM15 .... 147 M4
Tyssen Rd STNW/STAM N16 .... 119 N8
Tyssen St HACK E8 .... 7 N1
 IS N1 .... 7 K7
Tytherbarns La
 RPLY/SEND GU23 .... 251 K2
Tytherton Rd ARCH N19 .... 118 E2
Tyttenhanger Gn
 STALE/WH AL4 .... 39 J9

---

# U

Uamvar St POP/IOD E14 .... 140 G7
Uckfield Gv MTCM CR4 .... 202 B1
Uckfield Rd PEND EN3 .... 80 C3
Udall Gdns CRW RM5 .... 104 B7
Udall St WEST SW1P .... 17 H6
Udney Park Rd TEDD TW11 .... 176 B9
Uffington Rd WLSDN NW10 .... 136 D3
 WNWD SE27 .... 181 H7
Ufford CI KTN/HRWW/WS HA3 .... 94 A8
Ufford Rd
 KTN/HRWW/WS HA3 .... 94 A8
Ufford St STHWK SE1 .... 18 B1
Ufton Gv IS N1 .... 7 J1
Ufton Rd IS N1 .... 7 J1
Uhura Sq STNW/STAM N16 * .... 119 M9
Ullathorne Rd
 STRHM/NOR SW16 .... 180 D7
Ulleswater Rd
 STHGT/OAK N14 .... 98 F5
Ulleswater Vls
 STHGT/OAK N14 * .... 98 F5
Ullin St POP/IOD E14 .... 141 H7
Ullswater CI BMLY BR1 .... 183 K9
 LTWR GU18 .... 212 A10
 PUT/ROE SW15 .... 178 A7
 YEAD UB4 .... 132 F2
Ullswater Crs COUL/CHIP CR5 .... 240 A7
 PUT/ROE SW15 .... 178 A7
Ullswater Rd BARN SW13 .... 156 D6
 HHS/BOV HP3 .... 35 P8
 LTWR GU18 .... 212 A6
 WNWD SE27 .... 181 J5
Ullswater Wy HCH RM12 .... 125 H10
Ulster Ct CTHM CR3 * .... 242 H9
Ulster Gdns PLMGR N13 .... 99 K3
Ulster PI CAMTN NW1 .... 3 P10
Ulundi Rd BKHTH/KID SE3 .... 161 N5
Ulva Rd PUT/ROE SW15 .... 178 G3
Ulverscroft Rd EDUL SE22 .... 181 H5
Ulverston CI STAL AL1 .... 38 C6
Ulverston Rd WALTH E17 .... 101 N9
Ulwyn Av BF/WBF KT14 .... 215 P9
Ulysses Rd KIL/WHAMP NW6 .... 137 J3
Umberston St WCHPL E1 .... 140 A9
Umberville Wy SLN SL2 .... 128 E6
Umbria St PUT/ROE SW15 .... 178 D4
Umfreville Rd FSBYPK N4 .... 118 G5
Underacres CI HHNE HP2 .... 36 A5
Undercliff Rd LEW SE13 .... 160 G11
Underhill BAR EN5 .... 77 K6
Underhill Park Rd REIG RH2 .... 257 K7
Underhill Rd DAGW RM9 .... 124 A6
 EDUL SE22 .... 159 J9
Underhill St CAMTN NW1 .... 4 B1
Underne Av STHGT/OAK N14 .... 98 C1
Undershaft BANK EC3A .... 13 K3
Undershaw Rd BMLY BR1 .... 183 N6
Underwood CROY/NA CR0 .... 206 C11
Underwood Rd CHING E4 .... 101 N2
 CTHM CR3 .... 259 P6
 WCHPL E1 .... 7 P10
 WFD IG8 .... 102 B4
Underwood Rw IS N1 .... 6 F7
Underwood St IS N1 .... 6 F7
The Underwood
 ELTH/MOT SE9 .... 184 C5
Undine Rd POP/IOD E14 .... 160 G3
Undine St TOOT SW17 .... 180 E8
Uneeda Dr GFD/PVL UB6 .... 134 C1
Unicorn Ms BSTGT RM14 .... 125 J12
Union CI WAN E11 .... 121 N9
Union Ct CLPT E5 * .... 120 B2
Union Dr WCHPL E1 .... 140 E6
Union Gv VX/NE SW8 .... 158 D6
Union Rd IS N1 .... 6 E5


Union Gv VX/NE SW8 .... 158 E6
Union Pk GNWCH SE10 .... 161 L4
Union Rd ALP/SUD HA0 .... 135 K4
 CLAP SW4 .... 158 E8
 CROY/NA CR0 .... 203 K3
 FBAR/BDGN N11 .... 98 E7
 HAYES BR2 .... 206 A5
 NTHLT UB5 .... 133 P4
 NWMAL KT3 .... 6 E6
 KUT/HW KT1 .... 177 H6
 STHWK SE1 .... 12 D10
Union Wk BETH E2 .... 7 L9
Union St BAR EN5 .... 76 H6
 KUT/HW KT1 .... 177 H6
 STHWK SE1 .... 12 D10
Unity CI CROY/NA CR0 .... 224 C5
 NRWD SE19 .... 181 K8
 WLSDN NW10 .... 136 D1
Unity Ms CAMTN NW1 .... 5 J7
Unity Rd PEND EN3 .... 80 B5
Unity Wy WOOL/PLUM SE18 .... 162 A2
University CI BUSH WD23 .... 73 P8
 MLHL NW7 .... 96 C8
University Gdns BXLY DA5 .... 186 C10
University PI ERITH DA8 .... 164 C6
University St FITZ W1T .... 11 H2
University Wy CAN/RD E16 .... 142 D9
 DART DA1 .... 165 N9
Unstead La SHGR GU5 .... 267 P10
Unwin Av EBED/NFELT TW14 .... 174 C11
Unwin CI PECK SE15 .... 19 N10
Unwin Rd ISLW TW7 .... 154 D9
 SKENS SW7 .... 15 M3
Upbrook Ms BAY/PAD W2 .... 9 K6
Upcerne Rd WBPTN SW10 .... 157 N6
Up Cnr CSHM HP5 .... 89 N3
Upcroft WDSR SL4 .... 148 C9
Upcroft Av EDGW HA8 .... 96 C3
Updale CI POTB/CUF EN6 .... 59 H9
Updale Rd SCUP DA14 .... 186 A7
Updown Hi BFOR GU20 .... 212 C3
Upfield CROY/NA CR0 .... 204 A9
 HORL RH6 .... 280 D6
Upfield CI HORL RH6 .... 280 D7
Upfield Rd HNWL W7 .... 134 E6
Upfolds Gn RGUE GU4 .... 250 F6
Uphall Rd IL IG1 .... 142 C10
Upham Park Rd CHSWK W4 .... 156 C3
Uphill Dr CDALE/KGS NW9 .... 115 P3
 MLHL NW7 .... 96 B5
Uphill Gv MLHL NW7 .... 96 B4
Uphill Rd MLHL NW7 .... 96 B4
Upland Av CSHM HP5 .... 50 G4
Upland Court Rd HARH RM3 .... 105 N10
Upland Dr BRKMPK AL9 .... 59 L1
Upland Ms EDUL SE22 .... 159 J7
Upland Rd BELMT SM2 .... 221 N4
 BXLYHN DA7 .... 164 A9
 CTHM CR3 .... 242 F6
 EDUL SE22 .... 181 P3
 PLSTW E13 .... 141 M6
 SAND/SEL CR2 .... 223 L2
Uplands ASHTD KT21 .... 237 J6
 BECK BR3 .... 204 F2
 RKW/CH/CXG WD3 .... 72 A10
 WARE SG12 .... 26 F1
 WGCW AL8 .... 22 F1
Uplands CI CFSP/GDCR SL9 .... 110 B6
 MORT/ESHN SW14 .... 177 N1
 WOOL/PLUM SE18 .... 162 G9
Uplands Dr LHD/OX KT22 .... 237 H6
Uplands Park Rd ENC/FH EN2 .... 79 H6
Uplands Rd CEND/HSY/T N8 .... 118 F6
 CHDH RM6 .... 123 N1
 EBAR EN4 .... 98 A1
 ORP BR6 .... 207 L8
 PUR/KEN CR8 .... 241 K3
 WFD IG8 .... 102 B8
The Uplands CFSP/GDCR SL9 .... 110 B6
 LCOL/BKTW AL2 .... 55 M6
 LOU IG10 .... 80 C7
 RSLP HA4 .... 113 H6
Uplands Wy SEV TN13 .... 246 G9
 WCHMH N21 .... 79 H9
Upland Wy EPSOM KT18 .... 238 F4
Upminster Rd HCH RM12 .... 125 N7
Upminster Rd North
 RAIN RM13 .... 145 K5
Upminster Rd South
 RAIN RM13 .... 145 H6
Upney CI HCH RM12 .... 125 K10
Upney La BARK IG11 .... 143 J2
Upper Av BNSTD SM7 .... 239 J9
Upparrk Dr GNTH/NBYPK IG2 .... 122 F4
Upper Abbey Rd BELV DA17 .... 164 A3
Upper Ashlyns Rd BERK HP4 .... 33 N6
Upper Austin Lodge Rd
 EYN DA4 .... 229 L2
Upper Bank St POP/IOD E14 .... 140 G10
Upper Bardsey Wk IS N1 * .... 6 F1
Upper Barn HHS/BOV HP3 .... 36 A7
Upper Belgrave St KTBR SW1X .... 16 D3
Upper Belmont Rd CSHM HP5 .... 50 G4
Upper Berenger Wk
 WBPTN SW10 * .... 157 N6
Upper Berkeley St
 MBLAR W1H .... 10 A6
Upper Beulah Hi NRWD SE19 .... 202 E2
Upper Blantyre Wk
 WBPTN SW10 * .... 157 N6
Upper Bourne End La
 HHW HP1 .... 52 E1
Upper Brentwood Rd
 GPK RM2 .... 125 K2
Upper Bridge Rd REDH RH1 .... 257 P10
Upper Brighton Rd SURB KT6 .... 199 J6
Upper Brockley Rd
 BROCKY SE4 .... 160 E8
Upper Brook St
 MYFR/PKLN W1K .... 10 C7
Upper Butts BTFD TW8 .... 155 P6
Upper Caldy Wk IS N1 * .... 6 F1
Upper Camelford Wk
 NTGHL W11 * .... 8 A1
Upper Cavendish Av FNCH N3 .... 117 K1
Upper Cheyne Rw CHEL SW3 .... 15 N10
Upper Clabdens WARE SG12 .... 26 E2
Upper Clapton Rd CLPT E5 .... 120 A7
Upper Clarendon Wk
 NTGHL W11 * .... 8 B1
Upper Cornsland BRW CM14 .... 107 H4
Upper Court Rd CTHM CR3 .... 242 F9
 HOR/WEW KT19 .... 219 P7
Upper Culver St STAL AL1 .... 38 C6
Upper Dagnall St
 STALW/RED AL3 * .... 38 C6
Upper Dartrey Wk
 WBPTN SW10 * .... 157 M6
Upper Dengie Wk IS N1 * .... 6 E1
Upper Dunnymans
 BNSTD SM7 * .... 221 J10
Upper Edgeborough Rd
 GU GU1 .... 268 C1
Upper Elmers End Rd
 BECK BR3 .... 204 C4
Upper Fairfield Rd
 LHD/OX KT22 .... 236 G7
Upper Farm Rd
 E/WMO/HCT KT8 .... 197 N4
Upper Fosters HDN NW4 * .... 23 A4
Upper Forecourt HORL RH6 .... 280 C8
Upper George St CSHM HP5 * .... 51 H6
Upper Gladstone Rd
 CSHM HP5 * .... 51 H6
Upper Gn West MTCM CR4 .... 202 A2
Upper Green East MTCM CR4 .... 202 A2
Upper Grosvenor St
 MYFR/PKLN W1K .... 10 C8
Upper Grotto Rd TWK TW1 .... 176 E5
Upper Gn Sthwk .... 12 H7
Upper Grove Rd BELV DA17 .... 164 A6


Union Gv VX/NE SW8 .... 158 E8
Union Pk GNWCH SE10 .... 161 L4
Union Rd ALP/SUD HA0 .... 135 L4
 CLAP SW4 .... 158 E8
 CROY/NA CR0 .... 203 K3
 FBAR/BDGN N11 .... 98 E7
 HAYES BR2 .... 206 A5
 NTHLT UB5 .... 133 P4
Union Sq IS N1 .... 6 F3
Union St BAR EN5 .... 76 H5
 KUT/HW KT1 .... 177 H6
 STHWK SE1 .... 12 D10
Union Wk BETH E2 .... 7 L9
Unity CI CROY/NA CR0 .... 224 C5
 NRWD SE19 .... 181 K8
 WLSDN NW10 .... 136 D1
Unity Ms CAMTN NW1 .... 5 J7
Unity Rd PEND EN3 .... 80 B5
Unity Ter HRW HA2 .... 114 C7
Unity Wy WOOL/PLUM SE18 .... 162 A2
University CI BUSH WD23 .... 73 P8
 MLHL NW7 .... 96 C8
University Gdns BXLY DA5 .... 186 C10
University PI ERITH DA8 .... 164 C6
University Rd WIM/MER SW19 .... 179 N8
University St FITZ W1T .... 11 H2
University Wy CAN/RD E16 .... 142 D9
 DART DA1 .... 165 N9
Unstead La SHGR GU5 .... 267 P10
Unwin Av EBED/NFELT TW14 .... 174 C11
Unwin CI PECK SE15 .... 19 N10
Unwin Rd ISLW TW7 .... 154 D9
 SKENS SW7 .... 15 M3
Upbrook Ms BAY/PAD W2 .... 9 K6
Upcerne Rd WBPTN SW10 .... 157 N6

Upper Guildown Rd GUW GU2.... 267 N3
Upper Gulland Wk IS N1.... 6 F2
Upper Halliford Rd
 SHPTN TW17.... 196 F3
Upper Ham Rd
 RCHPK/HAM TW10.... 177 J1
Upper Handa Wk IS N1 *.... 6 F1
Upper Harestone CTHM CR3.... 259 N5
Upper Harley St CAMTN NW1.... 10 D2
Upper Hawkwell Wk IS N1 *.... 6 F2
Upper Heath Rd STAL AL1.... 38 E4
Upper High St EW KT17.... 220 B9
Upper Hwy KGLGY WD4.... 54 D8
Upper Hill Ri
 RKW/CH/CXG WD3.... 71 L10
Upper Hitch OXHEY WD19.... 93 M2
Upper Holly Hill Rd BELV DA17.... 164 C4
Upper Hook HLWS CM18.... 47 J3
Upper John St SOHO/CST W1F *.... 11 H7
Upper Kiln DORK RH4 *.... 273 H4
Upper Lattimore Rd STAL AL1.... 38 D6
Upper Lees Rd SLN SL2.... 128 F5
Upper Lismore Wk IS N1 *.... 6 F1
Upper Ldg KENS W8 *.... 9 H10
Upper Lodge Wy
 COUL/CHIP CR5.... 240 E8
Upper Ml HMSMTH W6.... 156 D4
Upper Manor Rd GODL GU7.... 267 K10
Upper Marlborough Rd
 STAL AL1.... 38 D6
Upper Marsh STHWK SE1 *.... 17 P3
Upper Marsh La HOD EN11.... 44 F4
Upper Meadow CSHM HP5.... 50 C4
Upper Mealines HLWS CM18.... 47 K4
Upper Montagu St
 MBLAR W1H.... 10 A3
Upper Mulgrave Rd
 BELMT SM2.... 38 D6
Upper North St POP/IOD E14.... 140 F7
Upper Nursery ASC SL5.... 192 F5
Upper Paddock Rd
 OXHEY WD19.... 73 M10
Upper Pk HLW CM20.... 28 C10
 LOU IG10.... 82 A9
Upper Park Rd BELV DA17.... 164 C3
 BMLY BR1.... 205 N1
 FBAR/BDGN N11.... 98 C6
 HAMP NW3.... 4 A1
 KUTN/CMB KT2.... 177 M9
Upper Pth DORK RH4 *.... 273 H4
Upper Phillimore Gdns
 KENS W8.... 14 C2
Upper Pillory Down CAR SM5.... 222 B9
Upper Pines BNSTD SM7.... 240 A3
Upper Rainham Rd HCH RM12.... 124 C4
Upper Ramsey Wk IS N1 *.... 6 G1
Upper Rawreth Wk IS N1 *.... 6 F5
Upper Richmond Rd
 PUT/ROE SW15.... 156 E10
Upper Richmond Rd West
 RCHPK/HAM TW10.... 155 M10
Upper Riding BEAC HP9.... 36 B2
Upper Rd DEN/HRF UB9.... 110 C5
 PLSTW E13.... 141 M5
 WLGTN SM6.... 222 F2
Upper Rose HI DORK RH4.... 272 F6
Upper Ryle BRW CM14.... 106 G1
Upper St Martin's La
 LSQ/SEVD WC2H *.... 11 L6
Upper Sales HHW HP1.... 35 J7
Upper Sawleywood
 BNSTD SM7.... 221 J10
Upper Selsdon Rd
 SAND/SEL CR2.... 223 N5
Upper Sheppey Wk IS N1 *.... 6 G1
Upper Sheridan Rd BELV DA17.... 164 C3
Upper Shirley Rd
 CROY/NA CR0.... 204 B10
Upper Shot WGCE AL7.... 23 K4
Upper Shott CHESW EN7.... 61 N2
Upper Sq ISLW TW7.... 154 F7
Upper Stanford Rd
 CHOB/PIR GU24.... 248 E1
Upper Station Rd RAD WD7.... 74 F1
Upper Stonefield
 HLWW/ROY CM19.... 46 E1
Upper St IS N1.... 6 B2
 SHGR GU5.... 270 A4
Upper Sunbury Rd
 HPTN TW12.... 197 N1
Upper Sutton La HEST TW5.... 153 P7
Upper Swaines EPP CM16.... 65 J6
Upper Tachbrook St
 PIM SW1V.... 16 G5
Upper Tail OXHEY WD19.... 93 M4
Upper Talbot Wk NTGHL W11 *.... 8 B6
Upper Teddington Rd
 KUT/HW KT1.... 199 N1
Upper Ter HAMP NW3.... 117 M8
Upper Thames St BLKFR EC4V *.... 12 C6
Upper Tollington Pk
 FSBYPK N4.... 119 N6
Upperton Rd GUW GU2.... 267 P5
 SCUP DA14.... 185 J8
Upperton Rd East PLSTW E13.... 141 N5
Upperton Rd West PLSTW E13.... 141 M5
Upper Tooting Pk TOOT SW17.... 180 A5
Upper Tooting Rd TOOT SW17.... 180 A7
Upper Town Rd STHL UB1.... 134 A6
Upper Tulse HI
 BRXS/STRHM SW2.... 180 G3
Upper Vernon Rd SUT SM1.... 221 N2
Upper Village Rd ASC SL5.... 192 B5
Upper Wk VW GU25.... 194 B4
Upper Walthamstow Rd
 WALTH E17.... 121 J2
Upper West St REIG RH2.... 257 J10
Upper Whistler Wk
 WBPTN SW10 *.... 157 M6
Upper Wickham La
 WELL DA16.... 163 G8
Upper Wimpole St
 CAVSQ/HST W1G.... 10 D3
Upper Woburn Pl
 STPAN WC1H.... 11 K1
Upper Woodcote Village
 PUR/KEN CR8.... 222 E9
Uppingham Av STAN HA7.... 115 H1
Upsdell Av PLMGR N13.... 99 H7
Upshire Rd WAB EN9.... 63 L8
Upshot La WOKS/MYFD GU22.... 233 J7
Upstall St CMBW SE5.... 159 J7
Upton WOKN/KNAP GU21.... 231 N10
Upton Av FSTGT E7.... 141 M2
 STALW/RED AL3.... 11 P4
Upton CI BXLY DA5.... 186 A2
 CRICK NW2.... 117 H8
 GLDGN NW11.... 116 G8
 LCOL/BKTW AL2.... 56 C1
 SL SL1.... 149 L2
Upton Court Rd
 DTCH/LGLY SL3.... 149 N3
Upton Dene BELMT SM2.... 221 L4
Upton Gdns
 KTN/HRWW/WS HA3.... 115 H4
Upton La FSTGT E7.... 141 N1
Upton Lea Pde SLN SL2 *.... 129 N9
Upton Lodge CI BUSH WD23.... 94 B1
Upton Pk SL SL1.... 149 N2
Upton Park Rd FSTGT E7.... 141 N2
Upton Rd BXLYHS DA6.... 163 H6
 HSLW TW3.... 153 K7
 SL SL1.... 149 N1
 THHTH CR7.... 203 L1
 UED N18.... 99 P6
 WATW WD18.... 18 A1
 WOOL/PLUM SE18.... 162 F5
Upton Rd South BXLY DA5.... 186 A3
Upway GFD/PVL UB6.... 134 A5
 NFNCH/WDSPK N12.... 97 N3
Uranus Rd HHNE HP2.... 19 J6
Urban Av HCH RM12.... 125 J5
Urban Ms FSBYPK N4.... 119 J5
Urlwin St CMBW SE5.... 18 C4

Urlwin Wk BRXN/ST SW9.... 159 H7
Urmston Dr WIM/MER SW19.... 179 H4
Ursula Ms FSBYPK N4.... 119 J6
Ursula St BTSEA SW11.... 157 P7
Urswick Rd DAGW RM9.... 143 P6
 CLPT E5.... 120 B10
 DAGW RM9.... 143 P6
Usborne Ms VX/NE SW8 *.... 158 C6
Usher Rd BOW E3.... 140 L4
Usherwood CI
 KWD/TDW/WH KT20.... 255 P7
Usk Rd BTSEA SW11.... 157 M10
 SOCK/AV RM15.... 146 B7
Usk St BETH E2.... 140 C5
Uvedale CI CROY/NA CR0.... 225 J7
Uvedale Crs CROY/NA CR0.... 225 J7
Uvedale Rd DAGE RM10.... 124 B8
 ENC/FH EN2.... 79 L9
 OXTED RH8.... 261 L5
Uverdale Rd DTCH/LGLY SL3.... 149 H5
Uxbridge Rd DTCH/LGLY SL3 *
 EA W5.... 135 K9
 FELT TW13.... 175 L5
 HCDN/ICK UB10.... 132 B5
 HNWL W7.... 134 D1
 HPTN TW12.... 176 A8
 KUT/HW KT1.... 199 J4
 RKW/CH/CXG WD3.... 91 K3
 SHB W12.... 136 D9
 SL SL1.... 149 M1
 SLN SL2.... 129 H9
 STHL UB1.... 133 P10
 YEAD UB4.... 133 H8
Uxbridge Road (Harrow Weald)
 KTN/HRWW/WS HA3.... 94 B3
 STAN HA7.... 94 F6
Uxbridge Road (Hatch End)
 PIN HA5.... 93 M9
Uxbridge Road High St
 STHL UB1.... 133 N10
Uxbridge Road (Pinner)
 PIN HA5.... 93 L10
Uxbridge Road (Stanmore)
 STAN HA7.... 94 E7
Uxbridge Road The Broadway
 YEAD UB4.... 133 L9
Uxbridge St KENS W8.... 8 E8
Uxendon Crs WBLY HA9.... 115 K6
Uxendon HI WBLY HA9.... 115 L6

# V

Vache La CSTG HP8.... 89 P3
Vache Ms CSTG HP8 *.... 90 A1
Vaillant Rd WEY KT13.... 216 D1
Valance Av CHING E4.... 101 L2
Valan Leas HAYES BR2.... 205 K3
Vale Av BORE WD6.... 75 N9
Vale CI BRWN CM15.... 86 E9
 CFSP/GDCR SL9.... 90 A9
 COUL/CHIP CR5.... 222 F10
 EFNCH N2.... 118 A1
 EPSOM KT18.... 238 B5
 MV/WKIL W9.... 3 J10
 ORP BR6.... 226 D1
 TWK TW1 *.... 176 F6
 WEY KT13.... 196 E10
Vale Cots PUT/ROE SW15 *.... 178 B6
Vale Ct ACT W3 *.... 136 C10
 STALE/WH AL4.... 38 B1
 WEY KT13.... 196 E10
Vale Crs PUT/ROE SW15.... 178 A8
Vale Cft ESH/CLAY KT10.... 218 E4
 PIN HA5.... 113 M3
Vale Dr BAR EN5.... 77 J4
Vale End EDUL SE22.... 159 N10
Vale Farm Rd
 WOKN/KNAP GU21.... 232 B3
Vale Gv ACT W3.... 136 A10
 FSBYPK N4.... 119 K5
 SL SL1.... 149 K2
Vale La ACT W3.... 135 M7
Valence Av BCTR RM8.... 123 N4
Valence Circ BCTR RM8.... 123 N4
Valence Dr CHESW EN7.... 61 N4
Valence Rd ERITH DA8.... 164 E6
Valence Wood Rd BCTR RM8.... 123 N4
Valencia Rd STAN HA7.... 95 H5
Valency CI NTHWD HA6.... 92 G5
Valentia PI BRXN/ST SW9.... 158 B5
Valentine Av BXLY DA5.... 185 P5
Valentine PI STHWK SE1.... 18 C1
Valentine Rd HOM E9 *.... 140 C1
 KTN/HRWW/WS HA3.... 114 A8
Valentines Rd IL IG1.... 122 E6
Valentines Wy ROMW/RG RM7.... 124 F7
Valentine Wy CSTG HP8.... 90 A4
Vale of Health HAMP NW3.... 117 M8
Valerian Wy SRTFD E15.... 141 K5
Vale Ri CSHM HP5.... 51 H4
 GLDGN NW11.... 117 J6
Vale Rd BMLY BR1.... 206 D2
 BUSH WD23.... 93 M9
 CSHM HP5.... 32 C10
 ESH/CLAY KT10.... 218 C5
 FSBYPK N4.... 119 K5
 FSTGT E7.... 141 N1
 MTCM CR4.... 180 D9
 SUN TW16.... 196 A5
 SUT SM1.... 221 N1
 WDSR SL4.... 148 E6
 WEY KT13.... 196 E10
Vale Rw HBRY N5.... 119 J8
Vale Royal HOLWY N7.... 5 M4
Valeside HERT/WAT SG14.... 25 H4
Vale St DUL SE21.... 181 L6
Valeswood Rd BMLY BR1.... 183 P4
Vale Ter FSBYPK N4.... 119 N5
The Vale ACT W3.... 136 A10
 BRW CM14.... 107 H2
 CFSP/GDCR SL9.... 90 A9
 CHEL SW3.... 15 J9
 COUL/CHIP CR5.... 222 F10
 CRICK NW2.... 116 F5
 CROY/NA CR0.... 204 C9
 EBED/NFELT TW14.... 175 J2
 GLDGN NW11.... 116 D8
 HEST TW5.... 153 M5
 MUSWH N10.... 98 B2
 RSLP HA4.... 113 H9
 SHB W12.... 136 C10
 STHGT/OAK N14.... 98 F1
 SUN TW16 *.... 195 P4
 WFD IG8.... 101 M4
Valetta Gv PLSTW E13.... 141 M5
Valetta Rd ACT W3.... 156 B1
Valette St HACK E8 *.... 7 J1
Valiant CI NTHLT UB5.... 133 L5
 ROMW/RG RM7.... 124 D1
Valiant Wy EHAM E6.... 142 A7
Vallance Rd BETH E2.... 7 P3
 WCHPL E1.... 20 B1
Valley Av NFNCH/WDSPK N12.... 97 J10
Valley CI HERT/BAY SG13.... 25 N5
 LOU IG10.... 82 A5
 PIN HA5.... 93 H10
 WAB EN9.... 63 H8
 WARE SG12.... 26 A1
Valley Ct CTHM CR3.... 241 P9
Valley Dr CDALE/KGS NW9.... 115 N3
 GVE DA12.... 191 P9
Valley End DTCH/LGLY SL3.... 129 H3
Valleyfield Rd
 STRHM/NOR SW16.... 180 A9
Valley Fields Crs ENC/FH EN2.... 79 H6

Valley Gdns ALP/SUD HA0.... 135 L2
 SWCM DA10.... 188 C6
 WIM/MER SW19.... 179 N10
The Valley Gn WGCW AL8.... 22 F4
Valley Gv CHARL SE7.... 161 P6
Valley HI LOU IG10.... 102 A3
Valley Mushroom Farm
 BH/WHM TN16.... 244 A6
Valley Pk WATW WD18.... 92 G5
Valley Rd BELV DA17.... 164 B4
 ERITH DA8.... 164 D3
 HART DA3.... 210 G10
 HAYES BR2.... 205 K2
 HGDN/ICK UB10.... 131 P4
 PUR/KEN CR8.... 241 L1
 RKW/CH/CXG WD3.... 71 K9
 STALW/RED AL3.... 38 D2
 STMC/STPC BR5.... 184 C5
 STRHM/NOR SW16.... 180 A7
Valley Side CHING E4.... 100 F2
Valleyside HHW HP1.... 35 J6
Valley Vw BAR EN5.... 77 H10
 BH/WHM TN16.... 243 P4
 CHESW EN7.... 61 K4
 CSHM HP5.... 50 F5
 SWCM DA10.... 188 C6
Valley View Gdns
 KENH/WIL N21.... 119 J1 *
Valley View Ter EYN DA4 *.... 209 M8
Valley Wk CROY/NA CR0.... 204 B9
 RKW/CH/CXG WD3.... 72 D9
Valliere Rd WLSDN NW10.... 136 D5
Valliers Wood Rd
 BFN/LL DA15.... 184 G1
Vallis Wy CHSGTN KT9.... 219 J1
 WEA W13.... 115 J6
Valmar Rd CMBW SE5.... 159 K7
Valnay St TOOT SW17.... 180 A8
Valognes Av WALTH E17.... 100 D9
Valonia Gdns
 WAND/EARL SW18.... 179 J2
Vambery Rd
 WOOL/PLUM SE18.... 162 F5
Vanbrough Crs NTHLT UB5.... 133 H1
Vanbrugh CI CAN/RD E16.... 141 N6
Vanbrugh Dr WOT/HER KT12.... 197 N2
Vanbrugh Flds
 BKHTH/KID SE3.... 161 L5
Vanbrugh HI GNWCH SE10.... 161 L4
Vanbrugh Pk BKHTH/KID SE3.... 161 L6
Vanbrugh Park Rd
 BKHTH/KID SE3.... 161 L5
Vanbrugh Park Rd West
 BKHTH/KID SE3.... 161 L6
Vanbrugh Rd CHSWK W4.... 156 B1
Vanbrugh Ter BKHTH/KID SE3.... 161 L6
Vanburgh CI CAN/RD E16.... 142 A7
 ORP BR6.... 227 H1
Vancouver CI HOR/WEW KT19.... 219 P3
 ORP BR6.... 227 K1
Vancouver Dr CRAWW RH11.... 283 N4
Vancouver Man EDGW HA8 *.... 95 N9
Vancouver Rd BROX EN10.... 62 C1
 EDGW HA8.... 95 N9
 FSTH SE23.... 182 D5
 RCHPK/HAM TW10.... 177 H7
 YEAD UB4.... 133 J6
Vanda Crs STAL AL1.... 38 C7
Vanderbilt Rd
 WAND/EARL SW18.... 179 L4
Vanderbilt Vls SHB W12 *.... 156 C1
Vanderville Gdns EFNCH N2.... 97 M10
Vandome CI CAN/RD E16.... 141 N8
Vandon St STJSPK SW1H.... 17 H3
Van Dyck Av NWMAL KT3.... 200 A7
Vandyke CI PUT/ROE SW15.... 178 F1
Vandyke Cross ELTH/MOT SE9.... 184 B1
Vandy St SDTCH EC2A.... 13 J1
Vane CI HAMP NW3.... 117 N10
 KTN/HRWW/WS HA3.... 115 L4
Vanessa CI BELV DA17.... 164 B4
Vanessa Wk GVE DA12.... 191 M8
Vanessa Wy BXLY DA5.... 186 E6
Van Gogh CI ISLW TW7.... 154 F9
Vanguard CDALE/KGS NW9 *.... 96 B8
Vanguard CI CAN/RD E16.... 141 M7
 CROY/NA CR0.... 203 J8
 ROMW/RG RM7.... 124 C1
Vanguard Wy CROY/NA CR0.... 223 N1
 CTHM CR3.... 242 A5
 EDEN TN8.... 262 D10
 HTHAIR TW6.... 152 F8
 OXTED RH8.... 261 L1
Vanoc Gdns BMLY BR1.... 183 M7
Vanquish Wk GVE DA12.... 191 J6
Vansittart Est WDSR SL4 *.... 149 H1
Vansittart Rd FSTGT E7.... 121 M9
Vansittart St NWCR SE14.... 160 D6
Vanston PI FUL/PGN SW6.... 157 K6
Vantage PI KENS W8 *.... 14 F4
Vantorts CI SBW CM21.... 29 P1
Vantorts Rd SBW CM21.... 29 P1
Vantorts Rd TOOT SW17.... 180 A8
Vapery La CHOB/PIR GU24.... 250 C7
Varcoe Rd BERM/RHTH SE16.... 159 N4
Vardens Rd BTSEA SW11.... 157 N10
Varden St WCHPL E1.... 140 C8
Varden CI ACT W3.... 136 A8
Vardy Dr TWK TW1.... 154 C10
Varley Rd CAN/RD E16.... 141 N8
Varley Wy MTCM CR4.... 201 N2
Varna Rd FUL/PGN SW6.... 157 H6
 HPTN TW12.... 198 A1
Varndell St CAMTN NW1.... 4 C9
Varney CI CHESW EN7.... 61 P3
 HHW HP1.... 35 J6
Varney Rd HHW HP1.... 35 J6
Varsity Dr TWK TW1.... 154 C10
Varsity Rw MORT/ESHN SW14.... 155 P8
Vartry Rd SEVS/STOTM N15.... 119 M4
Vassall Rd BRXN/ST SW9.... 159 H4
Vaughan Av BERM/RHTH SE16.... 19 M4
 HCH RM12.... 125 L1
 HDN NW4.... 116 D3
 HMSMTH W6.... 156 A4
Vaughan Est BETH E2 *.... 7 P3
Vaughan Gdns EYN DA4.... 209 M1
 IL IG1.... 122 A5
 WDSR SL4.... 148 A4
Vaughan Rd CMBW SE5.... 159 K8
 HARP AL5.... 20 A3
 HRW HA1.... 114 B5
 SRTFD E15.... 141 L1
 THDIT KT7.... 198 D10
 WELL DA16.... 163 P1
Vaughan St BERM/RHTH SE16.... 160 B1
Vaughan Wy DORK RH4 *.... 272 E7
 SLN SL2.... 128 F4
 WAP E1W.... 20 B6
Vaughan Williams CI
 DEPT SE8.... 160 F6
Vaughan Williams Wy
 BRW CM14.... 106 B1
Vaux Crs WOT/HER KT12.... 217 J3
Vauxhall Br STHWK SE1.... 17 J7
Vauxhall Bridge Rd PIM SW1V.... 16 F5
Vauxhall CI GVE DA11.... 190 C3
Vauxhall Gdns SAND/SEL CR2.... 223 M6
Vauxhall Gv VX/NE SW8.... 17 M9

Vauxhall Rd HHNE HP2.... 36 B6
Vauxhall St LBTH SE11.... 17 M7
 LBTH SE11.... 17 N7
Vawdrey CI WCHPL E1.... 140 E6
Veals Md MTCM CR4.... 201 P1
Vectis Rd TOOT SW17.... 180 C9
Veda Rd LEW SE13.... 160 F10
Vega Crs NTHWD HA6.... 92 G5
Vega Rd BUSH WD23.... 93 M9
Veitch CI EBED/NFELT TW14.... 174 C3
Veldene Wy RYLN/HDSTN HA2.... 113 P9
Velizy Av HLW CM20.... 28 C10
Vellacott CI PUR RM19.... 166 C4
Vellum Dr CAR SM5.... 202 B10
Velocity Wy PEND EN3.... 80 E3
Venables CI DAGE RM10.... 124 C3
Venables St STJWD NW8.... 9 M1
Vencourt PI HMSMTH W6.... 156 D3
Venetia Rd EA W5.... 135 K8
 FSBYPK N4.... 119 K5
Venetian Rd CMBW SE5.... 158 G7
Venetia Rd EA W5.... 135 K8
Ventnor Av STAN HA7.... 94 G9
Ventnor Dr TRDG/WHET N20.... 97 H1
Ventnor Gdns BARK IG11.... 142 F1
Ventnor Rd BELMT SM2.... 221 L4
 NWCR SE14.... 160 C6
Ventnor Ter
 SEVS/STOTM N15 *.... 119 P2
Venton CI WOKN/KNAP GU21.... 231 N5
Ventura Pk LCOL/BKTW AL2.... 56 C9
Venture CI BXLY DA5.... 185 P5
Venue SE POP/IOD E14.... 141 L9
Venus CI SLN SL2.... 128 E6
Venus Ms MTCM CR4.... 201 P3
Venus Rd WOOL/PLUM SE18.... 146 E8
Vera Av WCHMH N21.... 79 H9
Vera Ct OXHEY WD19.... 93 L1
Vera Lynn CI FSTGT E7.... 121 M9
Vera Rd FUL/PGN SW6.... 157 H7
Verbena CI CAN/RD E16.... 141 K6
 SOCK/AV RM15.... 147 K6
Verbena Gdns HMSMTH W6.... 156 C3
Ver-colne Valley Wk
 HHS/BOV HP3.... 52 A4
 STALW/RED AL3.... 38 A6
 WAT WD17.... 73 L7
Verdant La CAT SE6.... 183 K4
Verdayne Av CROY/NA CR0.... 204 C8
Verdayne Gdns WARL CR6.... 242 B2
Verderers Rd CHIG IG7.... 103 K6
Verdon Rd BARN SW13.... 156 D6
Verdun Rd WOOL/PLUM SE18.... 146 K5
Vereker Dr SUN TW16.... 197 H5
Vereker Rd WKENS W14.... 14 B8
Vere Rd LOU IG10.... 82 F8
Vere St CAVSQ/HST W1G.... 10 E6
Verity CI NTGHL W11.... 8 A6
Vermont CI ENC/FH EN2.... 79 J8
Vermont Rd NRWD SE19.... 181 L9
 SUT SM1.... 201 L10
 WAND/EARL SW18.... 179 L2
Verney Gdns DAGW RM9.... 123 P9
Verney Rd BERM/RHTH SE16.... 159 N5
 DAGW RM9.... 123 P9
Verney St WLSDN NW10.... 116 D6
Verney Wy BERM/RHTH SE16.... 159 N5
Vernham Rd
 WOOL/PLUM SE18.... 162 F5
Vernon Av MNPK E12.... 122 C9
 PEND EN3.... 80 D1
 RYNPK SW20.... 200 F3
 WFD IG8.... 101 M3
Vernon CI CHERT KT16.... 214 C3
 HOR/WEW KT19.... 219 P3
 STMC/STPC BR5.... 207 L3
 STWL/WRAY TW19.... 173 P4
Vernon Crs EBAR EN4.... 78 B9
Vernon Dr CTHM CR3.... 241 N4
 DEN/HRF UB9.... 91 M9
 STAN HA7.... 94 F9
Vernon Ms FSBYW WC1X *.... 5 P9
Vernon PI FSBYW WC1X.... 11 L2
Vernon Ri FSBYW WC1X.... 5 P7
Vernon Rd BOW E3.... 140 C10
 BUSH WD23.... 93 M9
 CEND/HSY/T N8 *.... 119 H1
 FELT TW13.... 174 D5
 GDMY/SEVK IG3.... 123 K6
 MORT/ESHN SW14.... 156 B7
 SRTFD E15.... 141 K2
 SUT SM1.... 221 P3
 WALTH E17.... 121 H1
 WAN E11.... 121 K6
Vernon's CI STAL AL1.... 38 D7
Vernon Sq FSBYW WC1X.... 5 P7
Vernon St WKENS W14.... 14 B4
Vernon Wk
 KWD/TDW/WH KT20.... 238 G6
Vernon Yd NTGHL W11 *.... 8 C7
Veroan Rd BXLYHN DA7.... 163 P8
Verona CI UX/CGN UB8.... 131 M6
Verona Ct CHSWK W4 *.... 156 B4
Verona Dr SURB KT6.... 199 H5
Verona Gdns GVE DA12.... 191 H7
Veronica CI HARH RM3.... 105 K8
Veronica Gdns
 STRHM/NOR SW16.... 202 D1
Veronica Rd TOOT SW17.... 181 C6
Veronique Gdns BARK/HLT IG6.... 122 C5
Verralls WOKS/MYFD GU22.... 233 H5
Verran Rd BAL SW12 *.... 180 A2
Versailles Rd PGE/AN SE20.... 181 P10
Verulam Av PUR/KEN CR8.... 222 D6
 WALTH E17.... 120 G2
Verulam CI WGCE AL7.... 23 J5
Verulam Ct CDALE/KGS NW9 *.... 116 D5
Verulam Pde GFD/PVL UB6.... 133 P6
 STALW/RED AL3.... 38 B2
Verulam Rd GFD/PVL UB6.... 133 L5
 STALW/RED AL3.... 12 A5
Verulam St FSBYW WC1X.... 11 N1
Verwood Dr EBAR EN4.... 78 C4
Verwood Rd
 RYLN/HDSTN HA2.... 94 B10
Veryan WOKN/KNAP GU21.... 231 M5
Veryan CI STMC/STPC BR5.... 184 D9
Vesta Av STAL AL1.... 38 B9
Vesta Rd BROCKY SE4.... 160 B8
 HHNE HP2.... 36 A4
Vestris Rd FSTH SE23.... 182 A3
Vestry Ms CMBW SE5.... 159 L7
Vestry Rd CMBW SE5.... 159 L7
 RSEV TN14.... 247 L2
 WALTH E17.... 121 K1
Vestry St IS N1.... 7 H6
Vevey Rd BRW CM14.... 107 H2
Vexil PI PUR RM19.... 166 C2
Veysey CI HHW HP1.... 35 M6
Viaduct PI BETH E2 *.... 140 C5
Viaduct Rd WARE SG12.... 26 E2
Viaduct St BETH E2.... 140 C5
The Viaduct MUSWH N10 *.... 118 C2
 WAN E11 *.... 121 L1
Viaduct Wy WGCE AL7.... 23 J2

Vian Av PEND EN3.... 80 D1
Vian St LEW SE13.... 160 G9
Via Romana GVE DA12.... 191 L4
Vibart Gdns BRXS/STRHM SW2.... 180 A1
Vibart Wk IS N1 *.... 5 M5
Vibia CI STWL/WRAY TW19.... 173 P4
Viburnum CI CHOB/PIR GU24.... 212 N3
Vicarage Av CHARL SE7.... 161 P1
Vicarage CI EBED/NFELT TW14.... 174 C2
 ERITH DA8.... 164 A6
 HFBR HP4.... 34 C3
 KWD/TDW/WH KT20.... 239 H10
 NTHLT UB5.... 133 K5
 POTB/CUF EN6.... 59 H8
 RSLP HA4.... 112 E5
 STAL AL1.... 38 B9
 WPK KT4.... 200 G9
Vicarage Ct BECK BR3 *.... 204 D3
 EGH TW20.... 172 E8
Vicarage Crs BTSEA SW11.... 157 N8
 EGH TW20.... 172 E8
Vicarage Dr BARK IG11.... 142 F2
 BECK BR3.... 204 F1
 MORT/ESHN SW14.... 156 B7
Vicarage Farm Rd
 HSLWW TW4.... 153 M8
Vicarage Gdns BERK HP4.... 34 C3
 KENS W8.... 14 C1
 MTCM CR4.... 201 P3
Vicarage Gate Ms
 KWD/TDW/WH KT20.... 239 H10
Vicarage Gn CMBE SE5.... 159 L7
Vicarage HI WOT/HER KT12.... 197 K6
Vicarage La CHIC IG7.... 102 G4
 EHAM E6.... 142 A2
 EPP CM16.... 48 C10
 GVE DA12.... 191 K5
 HHS/BOV HP3.... 52 E2
 HORL RH6.... 295 K1
 IL IG1.... 122 C6
 KGLGY WD4.... 54 A5
 LHD/OX KT22.... 236 C6
 SEV TN13.... 265 J1
 SLN SL2.... 129 N10
 SLN SL2.... 129 H1
 STA TW18.... 173 H6
 SURB KT6.... 199 N2
 SUT SM1.... 221 N2
 SWFD E18.... 102 F2
 TEDD TW11.... 176 F3
 TWK TW1.... 176 F3
 UED N18.... 99 N5
Vicarage Md
 WOKN/KNAP GU21.... 231 J3
Vicarage Pde
 SEVS/STOTM N15 *.... 119 K2
Vicarage Pk
 WOOL/PLUM SE18.... 162 F4
Vicarage Rd BERK HP4.... 34 D2
 BXLY DA5.... 186 C4
 CRAWE RH10.... 285 N9
 CROY/NA CR0.... 203 H10
 DAGE RM10.... 144 C2
 EGH TW20.... 172 E8
 EPP CM16.... 65 M5
 HCH RM12.... 125 H6
 HDN NW4.... 116 A4
 KUT/HW KT1.... 199 H1
 LEY E10.... 120 C6
 MORT/ESHN SW14.... 156 A7
 SRTFD E15.... 141 L2
 STA TW18.... 173 H6
 STAL AL1.... 38 D6
 WDSR SL4.... 149 J7
Vicarage Sq GRAYS RM17.... 167 M5
Vicarage Wk BTSEA SW11 *.... 157 N7
 DTCH/LGLY SL3.... 150 A2
 RYLN/HDSTN HA2.... 113 P5
Vicarage Wy HLW CM20.... 28 C10
 RYLN/HDSTN HA2.... 94 B10
 WLSDN NW10.... 115 H9
Vicars Bridge CI ALP/SUD HA0.... 135 K4
Vicar's CI EN EN1.... 80 A4
 HOM E9.... 140 D3
 SRTFD E15.... 141 N3
Vicars HI LEW SE13.... 160 G10
Vicar's Moor La WCHMH N21.... 99 H1
Vicars Oak Rd NRWD SE19.... 181 M9
Vicar's Rd KTTN NW5.... 118 C10
Vicents Wk DORK RH4 *.... 272 F2
Viceroy CI EFNCH N2 *.... 117 P2
Viceroy Pde EFNCH N2 *.... 117 P2
Viceroy Rd VX/NE SW8.... 158 A7
Vickers CI WLGTN SM6.... 223 J5
Vickers Dr North WEY KT13.... 215 P9
Vickers Dr South WEY KT13.... 215 P10
Vickers Rd ERITH DA8.... 164 E4
Victor Ap HCH RM12.... 125 L1
Victor Gdns HCH RM12.... 125 L1
Victoria Ar WESTW SW1E *.... 16 F4
Victoria Av BECK BR3.... 183 J10
 CRW RM5.... 104 C1
 E/WMO/HCT KT8.... 197 P4
 EBAR EN4.... 78 A4
 HORL RH6.... 280 C5
 HRW HA1.... 114 A2
 HYS/HAR UB3.... 132 A4
 RKW/CH/CXG WD3.... 91 N1
Victoria CI CDW/CHF RM16.... 169 P1
 E/WMO/HCT KT8.... 197 N3
 EBAR EN4.... 78 A4
 HORL RH6.... 280 D5
 HRW HA1.... 114 D4
 HYS/HAR UB3.... 132 A4
 RYLN/HDSTN HA2.... 113 P5
 WEY KT13.... 196 G10
Victoria Cottages
 RCH/KEW TW9 *.... 155 N9
 WCHPL E1 *.... 140 E7
Victoria Ct RGUE GU4 *.... 268 B6
 WBLY HA9.... 114 G5
Victoria Crs IVER SL0.... 131 K9
 NRWD SE19.... 181 L9
 SEVS/STOTM N15.... 119 M3
 WIM/MER SW19.... 179 J4
Victoria Dock Rd CAN/RD E16.... 141 L8
Victoria Dr RYLN/HDSTN HA2.... 113 P5
 WIM/MER SW19.... 179 H5
Victoria Embankment
 CHCR WC2N *.... 11 M7
Victoria Embankment Gdns
 CHCR WC2N *.... 11 L8
Victoria Gdns BH/WHM TN16.... 243 P1
 HEST TW5.... 153 M5
 NTGHL W11.... 8 D9
Victoria Ga BAY/PAD W2.... 9 N7
Victoria Gv KENS W8.... 14 G3
 TRDG/WHET N20 *.... 97 M3
Victoria Grove Ms
 BAY/PAD W2 *.... 8 G8
Victoria Hill Rd SWLY BR8.... 208 D1
Victoria La BAR EN5.... 77 H4
 HYS/HAR UB3.... 132 A5
Victoria Ms CRAWW RH11.... 283 N9
 HEST TW5.... 153 M5
 KIL/WHAMP NW6.... 2 C7
 WAND/EARL SW18.... 179 M4

Victoria Pde RCH/KEW TW9 *.... 155 M7
Victoria Park Rd HOM E9.... 140 B3
Victoria Park Sq BETH E2.... 140 C5
Victoria Park Studios
 HOM E9 *.... 140 B1
Victoria Pas WATW WD18 *.... 73 K8
 RCH/KEW TW9.... 155 M8
Victoria PI EW KT17.... 220 B8
 RCH/KEW TW9.... 177 J1
Victoria Rd ACT W3.... 136 A4
 ADL/WDHM KT15.... 215 N1
 ASC SL5.... 192 A5
 BARK IG11.... 142 E1
 BERK HP4.... 33 P5
 BFN/LL DA15.... 185 J3
 BKHH IG9.... 102 A3
 BRW CM14.... 107 H5
 BUSH WD23.... 93 J2
 BXLYHS DA6.... 164 B10
 CHING E4.... 101 K2
 CHST BR7.... 184 D8
 COUL/CHIP CR5.... 240 E1
 CRAWW RH11.... 283 N6
 CSHM HP5.... 51 H4
 DAGE RM10.... 124 D10
 EA W5.... 135 H4
 EBAR EN4.... 77 N4
 EN N9.... 99 H4
 ERITH DA8.... 164 F5
 FELT TW13.... 175 J4
 FSBYPK N4.... 119 J5
 GU GU1.... 250 B10
 GVW DA11.... 190 C4
 HARP AL5.... 20 A2
 HAYES BR2.... 206 A5
 HDN NW4.... 116 A2
 HORL RH6.... 280 D6
 KENS W8.... 15 H3
 KIL/WHAMP NW6.... 2 C7
 KUT/HW KT1.... 199 L2
 MLHL NW7.... 96 C6
 MORT/ESHN SW14.... 156 B7
 MTCM CR4.... 179 P10
 NWDGN UB2.... 152 N2
 PLSTW E13.... 141 M4
 REDH RH1.... 276 B1
 ROM RM1.... 124 E3
 RSLP HA4.... 113 J9
 SEV TN13.... 265 J1
 SEVS/STOTM N15 *.... 119 P2
 SLN SL2.... 129 N10
 SLN SL2.... 129 H1
 STA TW18.... 173 H6
 SURB KT6.... 199 N2
 SUT SM1.... 221 N2
 SWFD E18.... 102 F2
 TEDD TW11.... 176 F3
 TWK TW1.... 176 E6
 UED N18.... 99 M5
 UX/CGN UB8.... 131 M2
 WAB EN9.... 63 H10
 WALTH E17.... 101 H10
 WAN E11.... 121 J9
 WATN WD24.... 73 J4
 WDGN N22.... 98 G9
 WDSR SL4.... 148 E4
 WEY KT13.... 196 E10
 WIM/MER SW19.... 179 P10
 WLSDN NW10.... 136 D2
Victoria Road Ms
 WIM/MER SW19 *.... 179 N10
Victory Wy BERM/RHTH SE16.... 160 D1
 HEST TW5.... 153 N4
 RDART DA2.... 188 G6
 ROMW/RG RM7.... 104 C10
Vienna CI WFD IG8.... 102 A10
Viersen CI BH/WHM TN16.... 243 P4
 CHIG IG7.... 103 P1
 HGT N6.... 118 A5
 HRW HA1.... 114 D4
View Crs CEND/HSY/T N8.... 118 E3
Viewfield CI
 KTN/HRWW/WS HA3.... 115 K5
Viewfield Rd BFN/LL DA15.... 185 M4
 WAND/EARL SW18.... 179 J2
Viewland Rd
 WOOL/PLUM SE18.... 163 J4
Viewlands Av BH/WHM TN16.... 245 H6
View Rd HGT N6.... 118 A5
 POTB/CUF EN6.... 59 M8
The View ABYW SE2.... 163 P4
Viga Rd WCHMH N21.... 99 H4
Vigerons Wy WOKN/KNAP GU21.... 231 N1
Viggory La WOKN/KNAP GU21.... 231 N1
Vigilant CI SYD SE26.... 182 B6
Vigilant Wy GVE DA12.... 191 J6
Vignoles Rd ROMW/RG RM7.... 124 C5
Vigors Cft HAT AL10.... 40 C5
Vigo St CONDST W1S.... 10 G8
Viking CI BOW E3.... 140 D4
Viking Gdns EHAM E6.... 142 B7
Viking PI LEY E10.... 120 B6
Viking Rd GVW DA11.... 190 D8
 STHL UB1.... 133 M9
Viking Wy BRWN CM15.... 86 G10
 ERITH DA8.... 163 P2
Vilia CI GVE DA12.... 191 L5
Villacourt Rd
 WOOL/PLUM SE18.... 163 K6
Village Ar CHING E4 *.... 101 N1
Village CI CHING E4.... 101 M1
 HAMP NW3 *.... 117 N10
 HOD EN11.... 45 J1
 WEY KT13.... 196 E10
Village Gdns EW KT17.... 220 C10
Village Green Av
 BH/WHM TN16.... 244 D5
Village Green Rd DART DA1.... 165 H10
Village Green Wy
 BH/WHM TN16.... 244 D5

| Name | Ref | Page | Grid |
|---|---|---|---|
| Village La SLN SL2 | | 109 | J6 |
| Village Ms ASC SL5 | | 192 | B4 |
| CDALE/KGS NW9 * | | 96 | A7 |
| Village Mt HAMP NW3 * | | 117 | N9 |
| Village Park Cl EN EN1 | | 79 | N10 |
| Village Rd AMSS HP7 | | 68 | E10 |
| DEN/HRF UB9 | | 111 | K6 |
| EGH TW20 | | 194 | H9 |
| EN EN1 | | 79 | L10 |
| FNCH N3 | | 97 | H10 |
| WDSR SL4 | | 148 | A3 |
| The Village CHARL SE7 | | 161 | P5 |
| HAMP NW3 * | | 117 | M7 |
| WDSR SL4 * | | 170 | C5 |
| Village Rw BELMT SM2 | | 221 | K4 |
| Village Wy AMSS HP7 | | 100 | A6 |
| ASHF TW15 | | 174 | A1 |
| BARK/HLT IG6 | | 122 | F1 |
| BECK BR3 | | 204 | F4 |
| DUL SE21 | | 181 | L2 |
| PIN HA5 | | 113 | M5 |
| SAND/SEL CR2 | | 223 | P8 |
| WLSDN NW10 | | | |
| Village Wy East PIN HA5 | | 113 | N5 |
| Villa Rd BRXN/ST SW9 | | 119 | H9 |
| Villas Rd WOOL/PLUM SE18 | | 162 | F3 |
| Villa St WALW SE17 | | 19 | H8 |
| Villiers Av BRYLDS KT5 | | 199 | L5 |
| WHTN TW2 | | 175 | N4 |
| Villiers Cl BRYLDS KT5 | | 199 | L4 |
| LEY E10 | | | |
| Villiers Crs STALE/WH AL4 | | 39 | J5 |
| Villiers Gv BELMT SM2 | | 220 | C5 |
| Villiers Rd BECK BR3 | | 204 | C2 |
| CRICK NW2 | | 136 | D1 |
| ISLW TW7 | | 154 | D8 |
| KUT/HW KT1 | | 199 | L8 |
| OXHEY WD19 | | 73 | M10 |
| SLN SL2 | | 129 | J7 |
| STHL UB1 | | 133 | N10 |
| Villiers St CHCR WC2N | | 11 | M9 |
| HERT/BAY SG13 | | 25 | M5 |
| The Villiers WEY KT13 * | | 216 | E3 |
| Villier St UX/CGN UB8 | | 131 | N5 |
| Vimy Cl HSLWW TW4 | | 171 | N1 |
| Vincam Cl WHTN TW2 | | 175 | P5 |
| Vincennes Est WNWD SE27 * | | 181 | J1 |
| CAR SM5 | | 221 | N7 |
| Vincent Av BRYLDS KT5 | | 199 | N8 |
| Vincent Cl BAR EN5 | | 77 | N7 |
| BARK/HLT IG6 | | 141 | J2 |
| BFN/LL DA15 | | 185 | H4 |
| CHERT KT16 | | 195 | H7 |
| CHES/WCR EN8 | | 62 | D4 |
| ESH/CLAY KT10 | | 198 | A10 |
| HAYES BR2 | | 205 | N4 |
| LHD/OX KT22 | | 236 | A9 |
| WDR/YW UB7 | | 152 | B5 |
| Vincent Dr DORK RH4 | | 272 | F2 |
| HGDN/ICK UB10 | | 132 | A3 |
| SHPTN TW17 | | 196 | F5 |
| Vincent Gdns CRICK NW2 | | 116 | C8 |
| Vincent La DORK RH4 | | 272 | F2 |
| Vincent Pde FSBYPK N4 * | | 55 | N1 |
| Vincent Rd ACT W3 | | 155 | P2 |
| ALP/SUD HA0 | | 135 | L2 |
| CHERT KT16 | | 195 | H7 |
| CHING E4 | | 101 | J7 |
| COB KT11 | | 235 | M2 |
| COUL/CHIP CR5 | | 240 | D2 |
| CROY/NA CRO | | 203 | M7 |
| DAGW RM9 | | 143 | P7 |
| DORK RH4 | | 272 | F2 |
| HSLWW TW4 | | 153 | L9 |
| ISLW TW7 | | 154 | C7 |
| KUT/HW KT1 | | 199 | M3 |
| RAIN RM13 | | 145 | K6 |
| SEVS/STOTM N15 | | 119 | K2 |
| WDGN N22 | | 99 | H10 |
| WOOL/PLUM SE18 | | 162 | C3 |
| Vincent Rw HPTN TW12 | | 176 | B9 |
| Vincents Cl BERM/RHTH SE16 | | 160 | D1 |
| COUL/CHIP CR5 | | 240 | A4 |
| Vincent Sq BH/WHM TN16 | | 225 | P7 |
| WDGN N22 | | 99 | H10 |
| WEST SW1P | | 17 | H5 |
| Vincent Ter CAN/RD E16 | | 141 | M7 |
| WEST SW1P | | 17 | H5 |
| Vincent Vls SEVS/STOTM N15 * | | 119 | K2 |
| Vincent Wk DORK RH4 * | | 272 | F2 |
| Vincenzo Cl BRKMPK AL9 | | 40 | F9 |
| Vince St FSBYE EC1V | | 7 | H10 |
| Vine Av SEV TN13 | | 247 | J10 |
| Vine Cl BRYLDS KT5 | | 199 | L6 |
| CLPT E5 | | 119 | P9 |
| RGUW GU3 | | 249 | J2 |
| STWL/WRAY TW19 | | 173 | K1 |
| SUT SM1 | | 209 | M10 |
| WDR/YW UB7 | | 152 | B3 |
| WWAL AL8 | | 23 | J2 |
| Vine Cots HNWL W7 * | | 134 | D10 |
| WCHPL E1 * | | | |
| Vine Ct KTN/HRWW/WS HA3 | | 115 | N4 |
| WCHPL E1 * | | 13 | P4 |
| Vine Court Rd SEV TN13 | | 247 | K10 |
| Vine Gdns IL IG1 | | 122 | F10 |
| Vinegar St WAP E1W | | 140 | A10 |
| Vinegar Yd STHWK SE1 | | 19 | J1 |
| Vine Gv HGDN/ICK UB10 | | 132 | A2 |
| HLW CM20 | | 28 | C6 |
| Vine Hi HSLW TW3 | | 154 | A10 |
| Vine Pl HSLW TW3 | | 154 | A10 |
| Vineries Cl WDR/YW UB7 | | 152 | D4 |
| The Vineries CAT SE6 | | 182 | F4 |
| EN EN1 | | 79 | N4 |
| STHGT/OAK N14 | | 78 | D10 |
| Vine Rd BARN SW13 | | 156 | C9 |
| E/WMO/HCT KT8 | | 198 | A3 |
| ORP BR6 | | 227 | J3 |
| SLN SL2 | | 129 | L1 |
| SRTFD E15 | | 141 | L2 |
| Vine Rw RCHPK/HAM TW10 * | | 177 | J1 |
| Vine St BRXS/STRHM SW2 | | 159 | H4 |
| BRXN/ST SW9 | | | |
| Vine Sq WKENS W14 | | 19 | H8 |
| Vine St MYFR/PICC W1J | | 11 | H8 |
| ROMW/RG RM7 | | 13 | L6 |
| TWRH EC3N | | 13 | L6 |
| UX/CGN UB8 | | 131 | M7 |
| Vine Street Br FARR EC1M | | 12 | B2 |
| The Vine SEV TN13 | | 247 | K10 |
| Vineway BRW CM14 | | 107 | P4 |
| Vine Yd STHWK SE1 | | 19 | J1 |
| Vineyard Av MLHL NW7 | | 97 | H8 |
| Vineyard Cl CAT SE6 | | 182 | F4 |
| KUT/HW KT1 | | 199 | L3 |
| Vineyard Gv FNCH N3 | | 97 | M10 |
| Vineyard Hill Rd WIM/MER SW19 | | 179 | H1 |
| The Vineyard RCHPK/HAM TW10 | | 177 | J1 |
| SUN TW16 * | | 197 | H5 |
| WARE SG12 | | 26 | F1 |
| WCCW AL8 | | 23 | H5 |
| Vineyard Wk CLKNW EC1R * | | 12 | A1 |
| Vineyard Pth MORT/ESHN SW14 | | 138 | A6 |
| Vineyard Rd FELT TW13 | | 175 | H6 |
| Vineyards Rd POTB/CUF EN6 | | 60 | C5 |
| The Vineyards RCHPK/HAM TW10 | | 177 | J1 |
| SUN TW16 * | | 197 | H5 |
| WARE SG12 | | 26 | F1 |
| WCCW AL8 | | 23 | H5 |
| Vineyard Wk CLKNW EC1R * | | 12 | A1 |
| Viney Bank CROY/NA CRO | | 224 | G9 |
| Viney Rd LEW SE13 | | 140 | C9 |
| Vining St BRXS/STRHM SW2 | | 159 | H4 |
| Vinlake Av HGDN/ICK UB10 | | 111 | P2 |
| Vinries Bank MLHL NW7 | | 96 | E3 |
| Vinson Cl ORP BR6 | | 207 | K8 |
| Vintage Ms CHING E4 * | | 101 | P1 |
| Vintry Ms WALTH E17 | | 120 | F3 |
| Viola Av ABYW SE2 | | 130 | A4 |
| EBED/NFELT TW14 | | 175 | F3 |
| STWL/WRAY TW19 | | 173 | P4 |
| Viola Cl SOCK/AV RM15 | | 147 | H5 |
| Viola Sq SHB W12 | | 136 | C9 |
| Violet Av ENC/FH EN2 | | 79 | L4 |
| UX/CGN UB8 | | 132 | A7 |
| Violet Cl CAN/RD E16 | | 141 | K6 |
| CHEAM SM3 | | 201 | N8 |
| DEPT SE8 | | 160 | B5 |
| WLGTN SM6 | | 202 | B8 |
| Violet Gdns CROY/NA CRO | | 223 | J8 |
| Violet Hi STJWD NW8 | | 3 | J8 |
| Violet La SAND/SEL CR2 | | 223 | J2 |
| Violet Rd BOW E3 | | 140 | C6 |
| SWFD E18 | | 120 | N10 |
| WALTH E17 | | 120 | F4 |
| Violet St BETH E2 | | 140 | A4 |
| Violet Ter UX/CGN UB8 | | 132 | B7 |
| Virgil Dr BROX EN10 | | 44 | E9 |
| Virgil St STHWK SE1 | | 17 | P3 |
| Virginia Av VW GU25 | | 193 | P5 |
| Virginia Cl ASHTD KT21 | | 241 | J6 |
| CRW RM5 | | 104 | D3 |
| HAYES BR2 | | 205 | K3 |
| STA TW18 | | 195 | M3 |
| WEY KT13 | | 216 | D3 |
| Virginia Dr VW GU25 | | 193 | P4 |
| Virginia Gdns BARK/HLT IG6 | | 102 | G10 |
| Virginia Pk VW GU25 | | 194 | B4 |
| Virginia Pl COB KT11 | | 217 | H10 |
| Virginia Rd BETH E2 | | 7 | L10 |
| THHTH CR7 | | 203 | J1 |
| Virginia St WCHPL E1 | | 13 | P8 |
| Viscount Cl FBAR/BDGN N11 | | 98 | C6 |
| Viscount Dr EHAM E6 | | 142 | C7 |
| Viscount Gdns BF/WBF KT14 | | 215 | P8 |
| Viscount Rd STWL/WRAY TW19 | | 173 | L5 |
| Viscount Wy HTHAIR TW6 | | 173 | N3 |
| Vista Av PEND EN3 | | 80 | C6 |
| Vista Dr REDBR IG4 | | 122 | A3 |
| The Vista CHING E4 | | 101 | P1 |
| ELTH/MOT SE9 | | 184 | A2 |
| Vista Wy KTN/HRWW/WS HA3 | | 115 | K4 |
| Viveash Cl HYS/HAR UB3 | | 152 | C2 |
| Vivian Av HDN NW4 | | 116 | E3 |
| WBLY HA9 | | 135 | N1 |
| Vivian Cl OXHEY WD19 | | 93 | H3 |
| Vivian Gdns OXHEY WD19 | | 93 | H3 |
| WBLY HA9 | | 115 | M10 |
| Vivian Rd BOW E3 | | 140 | C6 |
| Vivian Sq PECK SE15 | | 160 | A9 |
| Vivian Wy EFNCH N2 | | 117 | H3 |
| Vivien Cl CHSGTN KT9 | | 219 | K4 |
| Vivienne Cl CRAWW RH11 | | 283 | N4 |
| TWK TW1 | | 177 | J2 |
| Vixen Cl HAT AL10 | | 40 | F7 |
| Vixen Dr HERT/BAY SG13 | | 25 | P5 |
| Vixen Ms HACK E8 * | | 7 | L1 |
| Voce Rd WOOL/PLUM SE18 | | 162 | G6 |
| Voewood Cl NWMAL KT3 | | 200 | C5 |
| Vogan Cl REIG RH2 | | 275 | L3 |
| Voltaire Rd CLAP SW4 | | 158 | F9 |
| Volt Av WLSDN NW10 | | 136 | A5 |
| Volta Wy CROY/NA CRO | | 202 | G8 |
| Voluntary Pl WAN E11 | | 121 | N1 |
| Vorley Rd ARCH N19 | | 118 | D7 |
| Voss St BETH E2 | | 7 | P10 |
| Voss Wy STRHM/NOR SW16 | | 180 | F9 |
| Voyagers Cl THMD SE28 | | 142 | M8 |
| Vulcan Cl EHAM E6 | | 142 | D8 |
| Vulcan Ga ENC/FH EN2 | | 79 | H4 |
| Vulcan Rd BROCKY SE4 | | 160 | C8 |
| Vulcan Ter BROCKY SE4 | | 160 | B8 |
| Vulcan Wy CROY/NA CRO | | 225 | K6 |
| HOLWY N7 | | 5 | P1 |
| WLGTN SM6 | | 222 | F8 |
| Vyner Rd ACT W3 | | 136 | A9 |
| Vyner St BETH E2 | | 140 | A4 |
| Vyners Wy HGDN/ICK UB10 | | 112 | B10 |
| The Vyne BXLYHN DA7 | | 164 | C9 |
| Vyse Cl BAR EN5 | | 76 | F8 |

## W

| Wacketts CHESW EN7 | | 61 | P3 |
| Wadard Ter SWLY BR8 * | | 209 | K5 |
| Wadbrook St KUT/HW KT1 | | 199 | L3 |
| Wadding St WALW SE17 | | 18 | G6 |
| Waddington Av COUL/CHIP CR5 | | 241 | H5 |
| Waddington Cl COUL/CHIP CR5 | | 241 | J5 |
| CRAWW RH11 | | 283 | K10 |
| EN EN1 | | 79 | M8 |
| Waddington Rd SRTFD E15 | | 121 | J10 |
| STALW/RED AL3 | | 38 | C6 |
| Waddington St SRTFD E15 | | 141 | J1 |
| Waddington Wy NRWD SE19 | | 203 | K1 |
| Waddling La STALE/WH AL4 | | 21 | J2 |
| Waddon Cl CROY/NA CRO | | 223 | H1 |
| Waddon Court Rd CROY/NA CRO | | 223 | H1 |
| Waddon Marsh Wy CROY/NA CRO | | 202 | G8 |
| Waddon New Rd CROY/NA CRO | | 203 | J10 |
| Waddon Park Av CROY/NA CRO | | 223 | H1 |
| Waddon Wy CROY/NA CRO | | 223 | H5 |
| Wade Av STMC/STPC BR5 | | 207 | N7 |
| Wade Dr SL SL1 | | 130 | F2 |
| Wade's Gv WCHMH N21 | | 99 | H1 |
| Wade's Hi WCHMH N21 | | 99 | H10 |
| Wade's La TEDD TW11 | | 176 | B7 |
| Wadesmill Rd HERT/WAT SG14 | | 25 | L2 |
| Wadeson St BETH E2 | | 140 | A1 |
| Wade's Pl POP/IOD E14 | | 140 | G9 |
| The Wades HAT AL10 | | 40 | D7 |
| Wadeville Av CHDH RM6 | | 123 | P4 |
| Wadeville Cl BELV DA17 | | 164 | B4 |
| Wadham Av WALTH E17 | | 100 | C8 |
| Wadham Cl CRAWE RH10 | | 284 | D6 |
| SHPTN TW17 | | 196 | D9 |
| Wadham Gdns GFD/PVL UB6 | | 134 | C1 |
| HAMP NW3 | | 3 | N4 |
| Wadham Rd ABLGY WD5 | | 54 | G2 |
| CHING E4 | | 101 | H9 |
| PUT/ROE SW15 | | 157 | H10 |
| WALTH E17 | | 100 | G9 |
| Wadhurst Cl PGE/AN SE20 | | 204 | A3 |
| Wadhurst Rd CHSWK W4 | | 138 | A7 |
| VX/NE SW8 | | 157 | P10 (?) |
| Wadley Cl HNHE HP2 | | 8 | A2 |
| Wadley Rd WAN E11 | | 121 | M1 |
| Wadsworth Cl GFD/PVL UB6 | | 135 | H4 |
| PEND EN3 | | 80 | E5 |
| Wadsworth Rd GFD/PVL UB6 | | 134 | G4 |
| Wager St BOW E3 | | 140 | D5 |
| Waggon Cl GUW GU2 | | 249 | H5 |
| Waggoners Wy WARE SG12 | | 26 | C1 |
| Waggon Rd BAR EN5 | | 77 | K1 |
| Waghorn Rd KTN/HRWW/WS HA3 | | 115 | P1 |
| PLSTW E13 | | 141 | N1 |
| Waghorn St PECK SE15 | | 159 | P9 |
| Wagner St PECK SE15 | | 160 | B6 |
| Wagon Wy RKW/CH/CXG WD3 | | 71 | M8 |
| Wagstaff Gdns DAGW RM9 | | 143 | N2 |
| Wagtail Cl CDALE/KGS NW9 | | 96 | C5 |
| EN EN1 | | 80 | A5 |
| Wagtail Gdns SAND/SEL CR2 | | 224 | G6 |
| Wagtail Wk BECK BR3 | | 204 | A3 |
| Wagtail Wy STMC/STPC BR5 | | 207 | N4 |
| Waight Cl HAT AL10 | | 40 | B2 |
| Waights Ct KUT/HW KT1 | | 199 | K1 |
| Wain Cl POTB/CUF EN6 | | 59 | L1 |
| Wainfleet Av CRW RM5 | | 104 | D10 |
| Wainford Cl WIM/MER SW19 | | 178 | C4 |
| Wainwright Gv ISLW TW7 | | 154 | C10 |

| Wainwrights CRAWE RH10 | | 283 | N10 |
| Waite Davies Rd LEE/GVPK SE12 | | 183 | L3 |
| Waite St STP SE4M | | 12 | C6 |
| Waithman St STP SE4M | | | |
| Wake Cl GUW GU2 | | 249 | N5 |
| Wakefield Cl BF/WBF KT14 | | 215 | P8 |
| Wakefield Crs SLN SL2 | | 129 | L2 |
| Wakefield Gdns IL IG1 | | 122 | B4 |
| NRWD SE19 | | 181 | M10 |
| Wakefield Ms STPAN WC1H | | 5 | L5 |
| Wakefield Rd FBAR/BDGN N11 | | 98 | E6 |
| RCHPK/HAM TW10 | | 176 | G1 |
| SEVS/STOTM N15 | | 119 | N3 |
| SWCM DA10 | | 189 | H1 |
| Wakefield St BMSBY WC1N | | 11 | M1 |
| EHAM E6 | | 142 | A4 |
| GVW DA11 * | | 190 | C2 |
| STPAN WC1H | | 5 | M6 |
| UED N18 | | 99 | P6 |
| Wakehams Wk CHES/WCR EN8 * | | 62 | D7 |
| Wakehams Green Dr | | | |
| CRAWE RH10 | | 284 | E1 |
| Wakehurst Dr CRAWE RH10 | | 283 | N10 |
| Wakehurst Rd BTSEA SW11 | | 179 | P1 |
| Wakeling La ALP/SUD HA0 | | 135 | J3 |
| Wakeling Rd HNWL W7 | | 134 | E7 |
| Wakeling St POP/IOD E14 | | 140 | G8 |
| Wakely Cl BH/WHM TN16 | | 243 | P4 |
| Wakemans Hill Av | | | |
| CDALE/KGS NW9 | | 116 | A3 |
| Wakerfield Cl EMPK RM11 | | 125 | N3 |
| Wakering Rd BARK IG11 | | 142 | F1 |
| Wakerly Cl EHAM E6 | | 142 | C8 |
| Wakley St FSBYE EC1V | | 6 | C9 |
| Walberswick St VX/NE SW8 | | 158 | F1 |
| Walbrook MANHO EC4N | | 12 | G7 |
| Walburgh St WCHPL E1 | | 140 | C8 |
| Walburton Rd PUR/KEN CR8 | | 222 | D9 |
| Walcorde Av WALW SE17 | | 18 | F6 |
| Walcot Rd PEND EN3 | | 80 | G6 |
| Walcot Sq LBTH SE11 | | 18 | B5 |
| Walcott St WEST SW1P * | | 17 | H5 |
| Waldeck Gv WNWD SE27 | | 181 | J6 |
| Waldeck Rd CHSWK W4 | | 155 | M5 |
| MORT/ESHN SW14 | | 155 | M5 |
| SEVS/STOTM N15 | | 119 | J1 |
| WEA W13 | | 134 | G8 |
| Waldegrave Gdns TWK TW1 | | 176 | C5 |
| UPMR RM14 | | 126 | A1 |
| Waldegrave Pk HARP AL5 | | 20 | C2 |
| TWK TW1 | | 176 | C6 |
| Waldegrave Rd BCTR RM8 | | 123 | M8 |
| BMLY BR1 | | 206 | G3 |
| CEND/HSY/T N8 | | 119 | H1 |
| EA W5 | | 135 | L4 |
| NRWD SE19 | | 181 | N10 |
| TWK TW1 | | 176 | C6 |
| Waldegrove CROY/NA CRO | | 203 | N10 |
| Waldemar Av FUL/PGN SW6 | | 157 | H6 |
| WEA W13 | | 135 | H10 |
| Waldemar Rd WIM/MER SW19 | | 179 | K8 |
| Walden Av CHST BR7 | | 184 | G10 |
| PLMGR N13 | | 99 | K3 |
| RAIN RM13 | | 144 | A2 |
| Walden Cl BELV DA17 | | 164 | A4 |
| Walden Gdns THHTH CR7 | | 202 | G4 |
| Waldenhurst Rd | | | |
| STMC/STPC BR5 | | 207 | N7 |
| Walden Pde CHST BR7 * | | 184 | C9 |
| Walden Pl WGCW AL8 | | 22 | G3 |
| Walden Rd CHST BR7 | | 184 | G10 |
| EMPK RM11 | | 125 | L4 |
| TOTM N17 | | 99 | L9 |
| WGCW AL8 | | 22 | G3 |
| Waldens Cl STMC/STPC BR5 | | 207 | N7 |
| Waldenshaw Rd FSTH SE23 | | 182 | E6 |
| Waldens Park Rd | | | |
| WOKN/KNAP GU21 | | 231 | P3 |
| Waldens Rd STMC/STPC BR5 | | 207 | P6 |
| WOKN/KNAP GU21 | | 231 | P4 |
| Walden St WCHPL E1 | | 140 | A8 |
| Walden Wy BARK/HLT IG6 * | | 103 | H8 |
| EMPK RM11 | | 125 | L4 |
| MLHL NW7 | | 96 | G4 |
| Waldo Cl CLAP SW4 | | 180 | D1 |
| Waldon Til SL SL1 | | 169 | L3 |
| Waldo Pl MTCM CR4 | | 179 | P10 |
| Waldorf Cl SAND/SEL CR2 | | 223 | J5 |
| Waldo Rd BMLY BR1 | | 205 | P3 |
| WLSDN NW10 | | 136 | D5 |
| Waldram Crs FSTH SE23 | | 182 | E6 |
| Waldram Park Rd FSTH SE23 | | 182 | G6 |
| Waldram Pl FSTH SE23 | | 182 | E6 |
| Waldrist Wy ERITHM DA18 | | 164 | A1 |
| Waldron Gdns HAYES BR2 | | 205 | J3 |
| Waldronhyrst CROY/NA CRO | | 223 | J1 |
| Waldron Ms CHEL SW3 | | 15 | M9 |
| Waldron Rd RYLN/HDSTN HA2 | | 114 | B10 |
| WAND/EARL SW18 | | 179 | M4 |
| The Waldrons CROY/NA CRO | | 223 | K1 |
| OXTED RH8 | | 261 | L7 |
| Waldron's Yd RYLN/HDSTN HA2 | | 114 | C7 |
| Waldstock Rd THMD SE28 | | 143 | K9 |
| Waleran Cl STAN HA7 | | 94 | F7 |
| Walerand Rd LEW SE13 | | 161 | M8 |
| Wales Av CAR SM5 | | 221 | P2 |
| Wales Cl PECK SE15 | | 160 | A6 |
| Wales Farm Rd ACT W3 | | 136 | A7 |
| Waleton Acres WLGTN SM6 * | | 222 | D7 |
| Waley St WCHPL E1 | | 140 | E7 |
| Walfield Av TRDG/WHET N20 | | 97 | H1 |
| Walford Rd RDKG RH5 | | 272 | C6 |
| STNW/STAM N16 | | 119 | M9 |
| UX/CGN UB8 | | 131 | M4 |
| Walfords Cl HLWE CM17 | | 29 | M8 |
| Walfrey Gdns DAGW RM9 | | 143 | P2 |
| Walham Green Ct FUL/PGN SW6 * | | 157 | L6 |
| Walham Gv FUL/PGN SW6 | | 157 | K5 |
| Walham Ri WIM/MER SW19 | | 179 | K6 |
| Walham Yd FUL/PGN SW6 | | 157 | D5 (?) |
| Walkden Rd CHST BR7 | | 184 | D7 |
| Walker Cl DART DA1 | | 164 | C9 |
| EBED/NFELT TW14 | | 174 | A3 |
| FBAR/BDGN N11 | | 98 | D5 |
| HNWL W7 | | 134 | D1 |
| HPTN TW12 | | 175 | P8 |
| WALTH E17 | | 100 | D9 |
| Walker Crs DTCH/LGLY SL3 | | 150 | C4 |
| Walker Gv HAT AL10 | | 40 | A3 |
| Walker Rd CRAWE RH10 | | 284 | C9 |
| Walkers Cl HARP AL5 | | 20 | D1 |
| Walkers Ct HARP AL5 * | | 20 | D1 |
| SOHO/CST W1F * | | 11 | J7 |
| Walkerscroft Md DUL SE21 | | 181 | L6 |
| DUL SE21 | | | |
| Walker's Pl PUT/ROE SW15 | | 156 | G10 |
| Walkers Rd HARP AL5 | | 20 | D1 |
| Walkfield Dr EPSOM KT18 | | 238 | C5 |
| The Walk EFNCH N2 | | 117 | N1 |
| The Walk PEND EN3 | | 80 | D3 |
| PLMGR N13 * | | 99 | K3 |
| POTB/CUF EN6 | | 59 | N3 |
| WDSR SL4 | | 148 | B3 |
| Walkley Rd DART DA1 | | 171 | J1 |
| Walkwood End BEAC HP9 | | 88 | B3 |
| Walkwood Ri BEAC HP9 | | 88 | B4 |
| Wallace Cl HGDN/ICK UB10 | | 131 | N1 |
| RGUW GU3 | | 249 | H1 |
| SHPTN TW17 | | 196 | F6 |
| THMD SE28 | | 143 | L9 |
| Wallace Crs CAR SM5 | | 210 | C10 |
| Wallace Flds EW KT17 | | 220 | C10 |
| Wallace Rd IS N1 | | 6 | F1 |
| Wallace Sq COUL/CHIP CR5 | | 240 | E6 |
| Wallace Wy ARCH N19 | | 118 | D7 |

| Wallace Wy ROM RM1 | | 104 | E8 |
| Wallaga La CRAWE RH10 | | 285 | K7 |
| Wallasey Crs HGDN/ICK UB10 | | 112 | B7 |
| Wallbutton Rd BROCKY SE4 | | 160 | C8 |
| Wallcote Av CRICK NW2 | | 116 | C10 |
| Walled Garden Cl BECK BR3 | | 204 | G4 |
| The Walled Gdn BRKHM/BTCW RH3 | | 274 | A1 |
| KWD/TDW/WH KT20 | | 238 | C2 |
| WLYN AL6 * | | 23 | K1 |
| Wall End Rd EHAM E6 | | 142 | D7 |
| Wallenger Av GPK RM2 | | 125 | J1 |
| Wallenger Dr NTHWD HA6 | | 93 | H9 |
| Waller Dr NTHWD HA6 | | 113 | N5 |
| Waller La CAR SM5 | | 211 | K9 |
| Waller Rd BEAC HP9 | | 88 | E9 |
| NWCR SE14 | | 160 | C7 |
| Wallers Cl DAGW RM9 | | 143 | P3 |
| Wallers Hoppet LOU IG10 | | 82 | C5 |
| Wallflower St SHB W12 | | 136 | C5 |
| Wallgrave Rd ECT SW5 | | 14 | F5 |
| Wallhouse Rd ERITH DA8 | | 165 | K6 |
| Wallingford Av NKENS W10 | | 136 | G7 |
| Wallingford Rd UX/CGN UB8 | | 131 | L4 |
| Wallingford Wk STAL AL1 | | 38 | C9 |
| Wallington Cl RSLP HA4 | | 112 | D4 |
| Wallington Rd CSHM HP5 | | 50 | G4 |
| Wallis Cl BTSEA SW11 | | 157 | N9 |
| EMPK RM11 | | 125 | K6 |
| Wallis Ct CRAWE RH10 * | | 284 | D8 |
| Wallis Ms LHD/OX KT22 * | | 236 | F8 |
| Wallis Pk GVW DA11 | | 189 | N1 |
| Wallis Rd HOM E9 | | 140 | E1 |
| STHL UB1 | | 134 | A8 |
| Wallman Pl WDGN N22 | | 98 | C9 |
| Wallorton Gdns MORT/ESHN SW14 | | 156 | A10 |
| Wallside BARB EC2Y * | | 12 | F2 |
| Wall St IS N1 | | 7 | H2 |
| Wallwood Rd WAN E11 | | 121 | J1 |
| Wallwood St POP/IOD E14 | | 140 | L7 |
| Walmar Cl EBAR EN4 | | 77 | N1 |
| Walmer Cl CHING E4 | | 101 | L1 |
| ORP BR6 | | 226 | G1 |
| ROMW/RG RM7 | | 104 | C10 |
| Walmer Pl MBLAR W1H * | | 10 | A3 |
| Walmer Rd NTGHL W11 | | 8 | A8 |
| Walmer St CAMTN NW1 | | 10 | A3 (?) |
| Walmar Ter WOOL/PLUM SE18 | | 162 | F7 |
| Walmgate Rd GFD/PVL UB6 | | 134 | G1 |
| Walmington Fold NFNCH/WDSPK N12 | | 97 | K7 |
| Walm La CRICK NW2 | | 116 | C10 |
| Walney Wk IS N1 | | 6 | F1 |
| Walnut Av WDR/YW UB7 | | 152 | B2 |
| Walnut Cl BARK/HLT IG6 | | 122 | F2 |
| CAR SM5 | | 222 | A2 |
| DEPT SE8 | | 160 | E5 |
| EPSOM KT18 | | 238 | C7 |
| EYN DA4 | | 199 | L7 (?) |
| HYS/HAR UB3 | | 132 | F9 |
| LCOL/BKTW AL2 | | 56 | A3 |
| Walnut Ct BARK/HLT IG6 | | 122 | F2 |
| WOKN/KNAP GU21 | | 232 | C1 |
| Walnut Gdns SRTFD E15 | | 121 | L3 |
| Walnut Gn BUSH WD23 | | 73 | N6 |
| Walnut Gv EN EN1 | | 79 | L9 |
| HHNE HP2 | | 35 | H6 |
| HLW CM20 | | 28 | H8 (?) |
| WGCE AL7 | | 23 | H8 |
| Walnut La CRAWW RH11 | | 283 | L4 |
| Walnut Ms BELMT SM2 | | 221 | M4 |
| Walnut Rd LEY E10 | | 120 | F7 |
| Walnut Tree Av DART DA1 * | | 171 | P3 |
| WIM/MER SW19 | | 179 | H4 |
| Walnut Tree Cl BARN SW13 | | 156 | C7 |
| BH/WHM TN16 | | 262 | G2 |
| BNSTD SM7 | | 220 | C10 (?) |
| CHES/WCR EN8 | | 62 | C7 |
| GU GU1 | | 249 | P10 (?) |
| HOD EN11 | | 79 | N6 (?) |
| Walnut Tree Gdns GODL GU7 | | 267 | K10 |
| Walnut Tree La BF/WBF KT14 | | 215 | P8 |
| Walnut Tree Pk GU GU1 * | | 249 | P10 (?) |
| Walnut Tree Pl RPLY/SEND GU23 | | 232 | C9 |
| Walnut Tree Rd BCTR RM8 | | 123 | P4 |
| BTFD TW8 | | 155 | K5 |
| ERITH DA8 | | 164 | F4 |
| GNWCH SE10 | | 161 | N4 |
| HEST TW5 | | 153 | N5 |
| SHPTN TW17 | | 196 | D4 |
| Walnut Tree Wk LBTH SE11 | | 18 | A5 |
| WARE SG12 | | 26 | C2 |
| Walnut Wy BKHH IG9 | | 102 | A2 |
| RSLP HA4 | | 133 | K1 |
| SWLY BR8 | | 208 | E2 |
| Walpole Av COUL/CHIP CR5 | | 240 | A5 |
| RCH/KEW TW9 | | 155 | N7 |
| Walpole Cl PIN HA5 | | 94 | B6 |
| WEA W13 | | 155 | H1 |
| Walpole Crs TEDD TW11 | | 176 | B6 |
| Walpole Gdns CHSWK W4 | | 155 | P4 |
| WHTN TW2 | | 176 | B6 |
| Walpole Ms STJWD NW8 | | 3 | J1 |
| WIM/MER SW19 | | 179 | N5 |
| Walpole Pk EA W5 | | 135 | K8 |
| WEY KT13 | | 216 | B7 |
| Walpole Pl TEDD TW11 | | 176 | B6 |
| WOOL/PLUM SE18 | | 143 | H10 (?) |
| Walpole Rd CROY/NA CRO | | 2 | E4 |
| E/WMO/HCT KT8 | | 197 | P4 |
| EHAM E6 | | 141 | H2 |
| HAYES BR2 | | 206 | A5 |
| SURB KT6 | | 199 | L7 |
| SWFD E18 | | 121 | J4 |
| TEDD TW11 | | 176 | B6 |
| TOTM N17 | | 99 | K10 |
| WALTH E17 | | 120 | C3 |
| WDSR SL4 | | 170 | D5 |
| WIM/MER SW19 | | 179 | N5 |
| Walpole St CHEL SW3 | | 16 | A7 |
| Walrond Av WBLY HA9 | | 115 | M5 |
| Walrus Rd HTHAIR TW6 | | 151 | N9 |
| Walsham Cl STNW/STAM N16 | | 119 | P6 |
| THMD SE28 | | 143 | N8 |
| Walsham Rd EBED/NFELT TW14 | | 175 | J3 |
| NWCR SE14 | | 160 | C4 |
| Walsh Crs CROY/NA CRO | | 225 | M9 |
| Walshford Wy BORE WD6 | | 74 | D1 |
| Walsingham CDALE/KGS NW9 | | 96 | A3 |
| Walsingham Gdns HOR/WEW KT19 | | 220 | B1 |
| Walsingham Pk CHST BR7 | | 206 | C2 |
| Walsingham Pl BTSEA SW11 | | 180 | A2 |
| Walsingham Rd CLPT E5 | | 119 | P8 |
| CROY/NA CRO | | 225 | M9 |
| ENC/FH EN2 | | 79 | L9 |
| MTCM CR4 | | 194 | B3 |
| STMC/STPC BR5 | | 207 | P5 |
| WEA W13 * | | 135 | P10 |
| Walsingham Wy LCOL/BKTW AL2 | | 57 | H7 |
| Walter Mead Cl CHONG CM5 | | 67 | P3 |
| Walter Rodney Cl MNPK E12 | | 122 | E5 |
| Walters Cl CHESW EN7 | | 61 | L1 |
| HYS/HAR UB3 | | 132 | F8 |
| Walters Md ASHTD KT21 | | 237 | J7 |
| Walters Rd PEND EN3 | | 80 | D3 |
| SNWD SE25 | | 202 | G3 |
| Walter St BETH E2 | | 140 | C2 |
| KUTN/CMB KT2 * | | 177 | L10 |
| Walter Ter WCHPL E1 | | 140 | D8 |
| Walterton Rd MV/WKIL W9 | | 8 | B2 |

| Walter Wk EDGW HA8 | | 95 | P7 |
| Waltham Av CDALE/KGS NW9 | | 115 | M4 |
| GUW GU2 | | 249 | N7 |
| HYS/HAR UB3 | | 152 | A2 |
| Waltham Cl BF/WBF KT14 | | 215 | P8 |
| DART DA1 | | 172 | A1 |
| Waltham Dr EDGW HA8 | | 95 | M10 |
| Waltham Gdns PEND EN3 | | 80 | B2 |
| Waltham Ga CHES/WCR EN8 | | 62 | D2 |
| Waltham Park Wy CHING E4 * | | 101 | P7 |
| Waltham Rd CAR SM5 | | 193 | N10 |
| CTHM CR3 | | 242 | A8 |
| NWDGN UB2 | | 153 | M2 |
| WAB EN9 | | 63 | K2 |
| WFD IG8 | | 102 | F8 |
| Walthamstow Av CHING E4 | | 101 | K4 (?) |
| Walthamstow Avenue (North Circular) CHING E4 | | 100 | D6 |
| Waltham Wy CHING E4 | | 100 | E4 |
| Waltheof Av TOTM N17 | | 99 | L9 |
| Waltheof Gdns TOTM N17 | | 99 | L9 |
| Walton Av CHEAM SM3 | | 209 | J10 |
| NWMAL KT3 | | 200 | D3 |
| RYLN/HDSTN HA2 | | 113 | N9 |
| WBLY HA9 | | 115 | N8 |
| Walton Br SHPTN TW17 | | 196 | F7 |
| Walton Bridge Rd SHPTN TW17 | | 196 | F7 |
| Walton Cl CRICK NW2 | | 116 | A6 |
| HRW HA1 | | 114 | C2 |
| VX/NE SW8 | | 158 | F6 |
| Walton Dr HRW HA1 | | 114 | C2 |
| WLSDN NW10 | | 136 | A1 |
| Walton Gdns ACT W3 | | 135 | N7 |
| FELT TW13 | | 174 | G7 |
| RBRW/HUT CM13 | | 87 | P9 |
| WAB EN9 | | 62 | G9 |
| WBLY HA9 | | 115 | K7 |
| Walton Gn CROY/NA CRO | | 224 | G5 |
| Walton Heath CRAWE RH10 | | 284 | E5 |
| Walton La SLN SL2 | | 128 | E4 |
| WEY KT13 | | 196 | D9 |
| Walton Pk WOT/HER KT12 | | 197 | L9 |
| Walton Park La WOT/HER KT12 | | 197 | L9 |
| Walton Pl CHEL SW3 | | 16 | A3 |
| Walton Rd BUSH WD23 | | 73 | L8 |
| CRW RM5 | | 104 | A8 |
| E/WMO/HCT KT8 | | 197 | P4 |
| EPSOM KT18 | | 237 | P7 |
| HOD EN11 | | 44 | C1 |
| HRW HA1 | | 114 | C2 |
| MNPK E12 | | 122 | E7 |
| SEVS/STOTM N15 * | | 119 | N2 |
| WOKN/KNAP GU21 | | 232 | E1 |
| WOT/HER KT12 | | 197 | L5 |
| Walton St CHEL SW3 | | 15 | P5 |
| ENC/FH EN2 | | 79 | L6 |
| KWD/TDW/WH KT20 | | 238 | D10 |
| STAL AL1 | | 26 | C3 |
| Walton Ter WOKN/KNAP GU21 | | 232 | E1 |
| Walton Vis IS N1 * | | 7 | K4 |
| Walton Wy ACT W3 | | 135 | N7 |
| MTCM CR4 | | 202 | A1 |
| Walt Whitman Cl HNHL SE24 * | | 159 | P10 |
| Walverns Cl OXHEY WD19 | | 73 | K10 |
| Walworth Pl WALW SE17 | | 18 | E8 |
| Walworth Rd STHWK SE1 | | 18 | E5 |
| Walwyn Av BMLY BR1 | | 206 | A3 |
| Wambrook Cl RBRW/HUT CM13 | | 107 | P3 |
| Wamborough Dr PUT/ROE SW15 | | 178 | E4 |
| Wanborough Hi RGUW GU3 | | 266 | B3 |
| Wanderer Dr BARK IG11 | | 143 | K3 |
| Wander Whf KGLGY WD4 | | 54 | C5 |
| Wandle Bank CROY/NA CRO | | 202 | F10 |
| WIM/MER SW19 | | 179 | N9 |
| Wandle Cl CRAWE RH10 | | 284 | D8 |
| Wandle Court Gdns CROY/NA CRO | | 202 | F10 |
| Wandle Rd CROY/NA CRO | | 202 | E10 |
| CROY/NA CRO | | 202 | G10 |
| MRDN SM4 | | 201 | N5 |
| TOOT SW17 | | 179 | P5 |
| WLGTN SM6 | | 202 | C9 |
| Wandle Side WLGTN SM6 | | 202 | C10 |
| CROY/NA CRO | | 202 | F10 |
| Wandle Wy MTCM CR4 | | 202 | A2 |
| WAND/EARL SW18 | | 179 | L6 |
| Wandsworth Br WAND/EARL SW18 | | 157 | M9 |
| Wandsworth Bridge Rd FUL/PGN SW6 | | 157 | L7 |
| Wandsworth Common West Side WAND/EARL SW18 | | 179 | M1 |
| Wandsworth High St WAND/EARL SW18 | | 157 | L9 |
| Wandsworth Rd VX/NE SW8 | | 17 | K9 |
| Wangey Rd CHDH RM6 | | 123 | N5 |
| Wanless Rd HNHL SE24 | | 159 | N9 |
| Wanley Rd CMBW SE5 | | 159 | L10 |
| Wanlip Rd PLSTW E13 | | 141 | N6 |
| Wannions Cl CSHM HP5 | | 51 | M6 |
| Wannock Gdns BARK/HLT IG6 | | 102 | E10 |
| Wansbeck Rd HOM E9 | | 140 | E2 |
| Wansdown Pl FUL/PGN SW6 | | 157 | L5 |
| Wansey St WALW SE17 | | 18 | E6 |
| Wansford Cl BRW CM14 | | 106 | E4 |
| Wansford Gn WOKN/KNAP GU21 * | | 231 | L3 |
| Wansford Pk BORE WD6 | | 76 | A3 |
| Wansford Rd WFD IG8 | | 101 | P9 |
| Wanstead Cl BMLY BR1 | | 205 | A7 (?) |
| HAYES BR2 | | 206 | A7 |
| Wanstead La IL IG1 | | 122 | A7 |
| Wanstead Park Av MNPK E12 | | 122 | A5 |
| Wanstead Park Rd IL IG1 | | 122 | A6 |
| Wanstead Pl WAN E11 | | 121 | M4 |
| Wanstead Rd BMLY BR1 | | 205 | P1 |
| Wansunt Rd BXLY DA5 | | 186 | D4 |
| Wantage Cl CRAWE RH10 | | 285 | J3 |
| Wantage Rd LEE/GVPK SE12 | | 183 | L1 |
| The Waplings KWD/TDW/WH KT20 * | | 258 | E10 |
| Wapping Dock St WAP E1W * | | 140 | A10 |
| Wapping High St WAP E1W | | 25 | P10 (?) |
| Wapping La WAP E1W | | 140 | A9 |
| Wapping Wall WAP E1W | | 140 | C9 |
| Wapseys La SLN SL2 | | 109 | K5 |
| Wapseys Wd CFSP/GDCR SL9 * | | 91 | H3 |
| Warbank La KUTN/CMB KT2 | | 178 | C10 |
| Warbank Cl CROY/NA CRO | | 225 | N7 |
| Warbeck Rd SHB W12 | | 136 | G10 |
| Warberry Rd WDGN N22 | | 98 | G10 |
| Warblers Cl EYN DA4 | | 181 | N4 (?) |
| Warblers Gn COB KT11 | | 217 | N10 |
| Warboys Ap KUTN/CMB KT2 | | 177 | N9 |
| Warboys Crs CHING E4 | | 101 | N1 |
| Warboys Rd KUTN/CMB KT2 | | 177 | N9 |
| Warburton Cl IS N1 | | 7 | J1 |
| KTN/HRWW/WS HA3 | | 94 | D7 |
| Warburton Rd HACK E8 | | 140 | A3 |
| WHTN TW2 | | 176 | A4 |
| Warburton St HACK E8 | | 140 | A3 |
| Warburton Ter WALTH E17 | | 101 | J10 |
| War Coppice Rd CTHM CR3 | | 259 | P3 |
| Wardalls Gv NWCR SE14 | | 160 | B6 |
| Ward Av GRAYS RM17 | | 167 | M1 |
| Ward Cl CHESW EN7 | | 61 | P3 |
| ERITH DA8 | | 166 | A5 (?) |
| IVER SL0 | | 131 | H3 |
| SAND/SEL CR2 | | 223 | M2 |
| Wardell Cl MLHL NW7 | | 96 | G5 |
| Wardell Fld CDALE/KGS NW9 | | 96 | D6 |
| Warden Av CRW RM5 | | 104 | D8 |
| RYLN/HDSTN HA2 | | 113 | M6 |

| Warden Rd KTTN NW5 | | 4 | D1 |
| Wardens Gv STHWK SE1 | | 12 | E10 |
| Ward Gdns SL SL1 | | 128 | D9 |
| Ward Hatch HLW CM20 | | 29 | L8 |
| Ward La WAND EARL SW18 | | 179 | L3 (?) |
| Wardle Av CRE | | 242 | B2 (?) |
| Wardley St WAND/EARL SW18 | | 179 | L3 |
| Wardo Av FUL/PGN SW6 | | 157 | H7 |
| Wardour Ms SOHO/CST W1F | | 11 | J5 |
| Wardour St SOHO/CST W1F | | 11 | H5 |
| Ward Rd ARCH N19 | | 118 | C8 |
| SRTFD E15 | | 141 | J3 |
| Wardrobe Pl BLKFR EC4V * | | 12 | D6 |
| The Wardrobe RCH/KEW TW9 * | | 177 | J1 |
| Ward Royal WDSR SL4 * | | 149 | H7 |
| Ward Royal Pde WDSR SL4 * | | 149 | H7 |
| Wards Dr RKW/CH/CXG WD3 | | 71 | J2 |
| Wards La EGH TW20 | | 174 | E6 |
| Wards Pl EGH TW20 | | 172 | F9 (?) |
| Wards Rd GNTH/NBYPK IG2 | | 122 | G2 |
| Wards Wharf Ap CAN/RD E16 | | 162 | A1 |
| Wareham Cl HSLW TW3 | | 153 | P10 |
| Warehame's La HERT/WAT SG14 | | 25 | K6 |
| Waremead Rd GNTH/NBYPK IG2 | | 122 | E3 |
| Warenford Wy BORE WD6 | | 75 | M5 |
| Warenne Hts REDH RH1 | | 275 | N2 |
| Warenne Rd LHD/OX KT22 | | 236 | B8 |
| Ware Park Rd HERT/WAT SG14 | | 25 | L1 |
| Warepoint Dr THMD SE28 | | 162 | C1 |
| Warescot Rd HERT/BAY SG13 | | 25 | M5 |
| HOD EN11 | | 44 | C2 |
| Warescot Cl BRWN CM15 | | 106 | C1 |
| Warescot Rd BRWN CM15 | | 106 | C1 |
| Wareside Cl WGCE AL7 | | 23 | L6 |
| Warfield Rd EBED/NFELT TW14 | | 174 | F3 |
| HPTN TW12 | | 198 | A1 |
| WLSDN NW10 | | 136 | G5 |
| Wargrave Av SEVS/STOTM N15 | | 119 | N4 |
| Wargrave Rd RYLN/HDSTN HA2 | | 114 | B8 |
| Warham Rd FSBYPK N4 | | 54 | G10 (?) |
| KTN/HRWW/WS HA3 | | 94 | E10 |
| RSEV TN14 | | 247 | J2 (?) |
| SAND/SEL CR2 | | 223 | K2 |
| Warham St CMBW SE5 | | 159 | J6 |
| Waring Cl ORP BR6 | | 227 | J3 |
| Waring Dr ORP BR6 | | 227 | J3 |
| Waring Rd SCUP DA14 | | 186 | E3 |
| Waring St WNWD SE27 | | 181 | K7 |
| Warkworth Gdns ISLW TW7 | | 154 | F6 |
| Warkworth Rd TOTM N17 | | 99 | J6 |
| Warland Rd WOOL/PLUM SE18 | | 162 | A1 (?) |
| Warley Av BCTR RM8 | | 124 | A5 |
| YEAD UB4 | | 133 | K5 |
| Warley Gap RBRW/HUT CM13 | | 106 | G8 |
| Warley Hi RBRW/HUT CM13 | | 107 | N6 |
| Warley Mt BRW CM14 | | 107 | H5 |
| Warley Rd ED N9 | | 101 | D10 (?) |
| RBRW/HUT CM13 | | 101 | N8 (?) |
| WFD IG8 | | 101 | P8 |
| YEAD UB4 | | 133 | H8 |
| Warley St BETH E2 | | 140 | C2 |
| RBRW/HUT CM13 | | 107 | L10 |
| Warlingham Rd THHTH CR7 | | 203 | J4 |
| Warlock Rd MV/WKIL W9 | | 8 | A1 |
| Warlow Cl HOLWY N7 * | | 118 | F9 |
| Warmark Rd HHW HP1 | | 35 | H4 |
| Warming Cl CLPT E5 | | 119 | P9 |
| Warmington Rd HNHL SE24 | | 181 | K2 |
| Warmington St PLSTW E13 | | 141 | M6 |
| Warminster Gdns SNWD SE25 | | 203 | P2 |
| Warminster Rd SNWD SE25 | | 202 | C4 |
| Warminster Wy MTCM CR4 | | 180 | B9 |
| Warndon St BERM/RHTH SE16 | | 160 | B3 |
| Warneford Pl OXHEY WD19 | | 73 | M10 |
| Warneford Rd KTN/HRWW/WS HA3 | | 115 | J1 |
| Warneford St HOM E9 | | 140 | A3 |
| Warner Av CHEAM SM3 | | 201 | H9 |
| Warner Cl CDALE/KGS NW9 | | 116 | C5 |
| EBAR EN4 | | 77 | P4 |
| HPTN TW12 | | 175 | N8 |
| HYS/HAR UB3 | | 152 | D1 |
| SL SL1 | | 128 | D10 |
| SRTFD E15 | | 121 | K10 |
| Warner Pl BETH E2 | | 7 | P8 |
| Warner Rd BMLY BR1 | | 183 | L10 |
| CEND/HSY/T N8 | | 118 | C2 |
| CMBW SE5 | | 159 | K7 |
| WALTH E17 | | 119 | F1 (?) |
| WARE SG12 | | 26 | C3 |
| Warners Av HOD EN11 | | 64 | A1 |
| Warners End Rd HHW HP1 | | 35 | H4 |
| Warners La SHGR GU5 | | 269 | P7 |
| Warner St CLKNW EC1R | | 12 | A2 |
| Warner Ter POP/IOD E14 * | | 140 | G7 |
| Warner Yd CLKNW EC1R | | 12 | A2 |
| Warnford Rd ORP BR6 | | 227 | J3 |
| Warnham Court Rd CAR SM5 | | 222 | A6 |
| Warnham Rd CRAWE RH10 | | 284 | B9 |
| NFNCH/WDSPK N12 | | 97 | P3 |
| Warple Ms ACT W3 | | 156 | B1 |
| Warple Wy ACT W3 | | 156 | B1 |
| Warren Av BELMT SM2 | | 220 | F8 (?) |
| BMLY BR1 | | 183 | K10 |
| ORP BR6 | | 227 | J4 |
| RCHPK/HAM TW10 | | 177 | N1 |
| SAND/SEL CR2 | | 224 | C4 |
| WAN E11 | | 121 | J2 |
| Warren Cl BXLYHS DA6 | | 186 | B1 |
| DTCH/LGLY SL3 | | 150 | D3 |
| ED N9 | | 101 | L1 |
| ESH/CLAY KT10 | | 218 | B2 |
| HAT AL10 | | 40 | A3 |
| WBLY HA9 | | 115 | J7 |
| YEAD UB4 | | 133 | H8 |
| Warren Ct CHARL SE7 * | | 161 | P4 |
| CHIG IG7 | | 103 | J1 |
| SEV TN13 | | 265 | K1 |
| Warren Crs ED N9 | | 99 | N1 |
| Warren Cutting KUTN/CMB KT2 | | 178 | A10 |
| Warren Dr GFD/PVL UB6 | | 134 | B3 |
| Warren Dr North BRYLDS KT5 | | 199 | P8 |
| Warren Dr South BRYLDS KT5 | | 199 | P8 |
| The Warren Dr WAN E11 | | 121 | P5 |
| Warreners La WEY KT13 | | 216 | E8 |
| Warren Flds PIN HA5 * | | 94 | B5 |
| IVER SL0 | | 130 | F2 |
| Warren Flds STAN HA7 * | | 95 | K2 |
| Warrenfield Cl CHESW EN7 | | 61 | N3 |
| Warren Gdns ORP BR6 | | 227 | K2 |
| Warren Gv BORE WD6 | | 76 | A3 |
| Warren Hi EPSOM KT18 | | 238 | B7 |
| LOU IG10 | | 81 | P5 |
| Warren Hts CDW/CHF M16 | | 167 | K3 (?) |
| Warren La BRWN CM15 | | 86 | D5 |
| CDW/CHF M16 | | 167 | J3 (?) |

| Entry | Ref | Pg | Grid |
|---|---|---|---|
| LHD/OX KT22 | | 218 | B8 |
| OXTED RH8 | | 261 | M10 |
| STAN HA7 | | 94 | F3 |
| WOKS/MYFD GU22 | | 233 | K4 |
| WOOL/PLUM SE18 | | 162 | E2 |
| Warren Lane Ga | | | |
| WOOL/PLUM SE18 | | 162 | E2 |
| Warren Lodge Dr | | | |
| KWD/TDW/WH KT20 | | 239 | H10 |
| Warren Md BNSTD SM7 | | 238 | F7 |
| Warren Ms W1T * | | 10 | G2 |
| Warren Rd | | | |
| BRKHM/BTCW RH3 | | 273 | P7 |
| Warrenne Wy REIG RH2 | | 257 | K10 |
| Warren Pde SLN SL3 | | 129 | P10 |
| Warren Pk KUTN/CMB KT2 | | 177 | N9 |
| KWD/TDW/WH KT20 | | 255 | P7 |
| WARL CR6 | | 242 | C4 |
| Warren Park Rd | | | |
| HERT/WAT SG14 | | 25 | K4 |
| SUT SM1 | | 221 | N11 |
| Warren Pl HERT/WAT SG14 * | | 25 | L4 |
| Warren Pond Rd CHING E4 | | 101 | L2 |
| Warren Ri KUTN/CMB KT2 | | 200 | A9 |
| Warren Rd ADL/WDHM KT15 | | 215 | K6 |
| ASHF TW15 | | 174 | F10 |
| BARK/HLT IG6 | | 122 | G3 |
| BNSTD SM7 | | 220 | F10 |
| BUSH WD23 | | 94 | B2 |
| BXLYHS DA6 | | 186 | B6 |
| CHING E4 | | 101 | H3 |
| CRICK NW2 | | 116 | C7 |
| CROY/NA CR0 | | 245 | J4 |
| CODL GU7 | | 267 | K10 |
| GU GU1 | | 268 | C5 |
| HAYES BR2 | | 205 | M9 |
| HGDN/ICK UB10 | | 111 | P9 |
| KUTN/CMB KT2 | | 177 | P9 |
| LEY E10 | | 121 | H8 |
| MEO DA13 | | 189 | N8 |
| ORP BR6 | | 227 | J2 |
| ORP BR6 | | 227 | N4 |
| PUR/KEN CR8 | | 223 | J8 |
| REIG RH2 | | 257 | L9 |
| SCUP DA14 | | 185 | M6 |
| STAL AL1 | | 38 | D1 |
| WAN E11 | | 121 | P4 |
| WHTN SW2 | | 176 | C2 |
| WIM/MER SW19 | | 179 | P9 |
| Warrens Shawe La EDGW HA8 | | 95 | N3 |
| The Warrens HART SG13 | | 211 | L6 |
| Warren St FITZ W1T | | 10 | C1 |
| Warren Ter CDW/CHF RM16 * | | 147 | L1 |
| HERT/WAT SG14 | | 25 | L5 |
| The Warren ASHTD KT21 | | 237 | L5 |
| BELMT SM2 | | 221 | N5 |
| CFSP/GDCR SL9 | | 90 | C8 |
| CSHM HP5 | | 50 | D4 |
| EHSLY KT24 | | 252 | C6 |
| GVE DA12 | | 190 | G7 |
| HEST TW5 | | 153 | N6 |
| KGLGY WD4 | | 54 | A5 |
| KWD/TDW/WH KT20 | | 239 | H9 |
| LHD/OX KT22 | | 218 | B8 |
| MNPK E12 | | 122 | B9 |
| RAD WD7 | | 56 | F9 |
| WPK KT4 | | 220 | A1 |
| YEAD UB4 | | 133 | H8 |
| Warren Vw GVE DA12 | | 191 | H8 |
| Warren Wy EDGW HA8 | | 95 | N4 |
| WEY KT13 | | 216 | D3 |
| Warren Wood Cl HAYES BR2 | | 205 | M9 |
| Warriner Av GVE DA12 | | 191 | F8 |
| Warriner Dr ED N9 | | 99 | F3 |
| Warrington Av SL SL1 | | 129 | H8 |
| Warrington Cl CRAWW RH11 | | 283 | H10 |
| Warrington Crs MV/WKIL W9 | | 9 | J2 |
| Warrington Gdns EMPK RM11 | | 125 | K4 |
| MV/WKIL W9 | | 9 | J2 |
| Warrington Pl POP/IOD E14 * | | 141 | H10 |
| Warrington Rd BCTR RM8 | | 123 | N7 |
| CROY/NA CR0 | | 203 | J10 |
| HRW HA1 | | 114 | C3 |
| RCHPK/HAM TW10 | | 177 | J1 |
| Warrington Sq WDSR SL4 | | 171 | N5 |
| Warrington Sq BCTR RM8 | | 123 | N7 |
| Warrior Av GVE DA12 | | 190 | F7 |
| Warrior Sq MNPK E12 | | 122 | F9 |
| Warsaw Cl RSLP HA4 | | 133 | J1 |
| Warspite Rd | | | |
| WOOL/PLUM SE18 | | 162 | B2 |
| Warton Rd SRTFD E15 | | 141 | N10 |
| Warwall EHAM E6 | | 142 | E8 |
| Warwick Av EDGW HA8 | | 95 | N4 |
| ECH TW20 | | 194 | F1 |
| MV/WKIL W9 | | 9 | H2 |
| POTB/CUF EN6 | | 60 | C3 |
| RYLN/HDSTN HA2 | | 113 | N9 |
| SLN SL2 | | 129 | H6 |
| STA TW18 | | 173 | H8 |
| Warwick Cl BUSH WD23 | | 94 | D1 |
| BXLY DA5 | | 186 | A3 |
| EBAR EN4 | | 77 | N9 |
| EMER RM11 | | 125 | N2 |
| HERT/WAT SG13 | | 25 | K7 |
| HPTN TW12 | | 176 | B10 |
| ORP BR6 | | 227 | K10 |
| POTB/CUF EN6 | | 60 | E3 |
| RDKG RH5 | | 272 | E4 |
| Warwick Crs BAY/PAD W2 | | 9 | J3 |
| YEAD UB4 | | 132 | C6 |
| Warwick Deeping CHERT KT16 | | 214 | F2 |
| Warwick Dene EA W5 | | 135 | K10 |
| Warwick Dr CHES/WCR EN8 | | 62 | C1 |
| PUT/ROE SW15 | | 156 | E9 |
| Warwick Gdns ASHTD KT21 | | 237 | J3 |
| FSBYPK N4 | | 119 | J1 |
| GPK RM2 | | 125 | K1 |
| IL IG1 | | 123 | P2 |
| THDIT KT7 | | 198 | E6 |
| THHTH CR7 * | | 203 | H4 |
| WKENS W14 | | 14 | C4 |
| Warwick Gv BRYLDS KT5 | | 199 | L7 |
| CLPT E5 | | 120 | A6 |
| Warwick House St STJS SW1Y | | 11 | K9 |
| Warwick La RAIN RM13 | | 111 | N11 |
| STP EC4M * | | 12 | D5 |
| UPMR RM14 | | 146 | A4 |
| WOKN/KNAP GU21 | | 231 | M5 |
| Warwick Ms | | | |
| RKW/CH/CXG WD3 | | 72 | B10 |
| Warwick Pde | | | |
| KTN/HRWW/WS HA3 * | | 94 | G10 |
| Warwick Pl NORE WD6 | | 76 | A7 |
| BERM W14 | | 36 | B2 |
| EA W5 | | 155 | J1 |
| GVW DA11 | | 9 | J1 |
| MV/WKIL W9 | | 9 | J3 |
| THDIT KT7 * | | 198 | F6 |
| UX/CGN UB8 | | 131 | M2 |
| Warwick Pl North PIM SW1V * | | 16 | E7 |
| Warwick Rd ASHF TW15 | | 173 | P8 |
| BAR EN5 | | 77 | L8 |
| BEAC HP9 | | 48 | A7 |
| BORE WD6 | | 76 | A7 |
| CHING E4 | | 100 | F6 |
| COUL/CHIP CR5 | | 222 | D10 |
| EA W5 | | 135 | K10 |
| ECT SW5 | | 14 | E6 |
| FBAR/BDGN N11 | | 98 | E7 |
| HSLWW TW4 | | 153 | H9 |
| KENS W8 | | 111 | J1 |
| KUTN/CMB KT2 | | 199 | N1 |
| MNPK E12 | | 122 | B10 |
| NWDGN UB2 | | 153 | N2 |
| NWMAL KT3 | | 199 | P3 |
| PEND EN3 | | 105 | H4 |
| REDH RH1 | | 258 | E3 |
| SCUP DA14 | | 185 | L8 |
| SRTFD E15 | | 141 | L1 |
| STAL AL1 | | 38 | E4 |
| SUT SM1 | | 221 | N2 |
| THDIT KT7 | | 198 | E5 |
| THHTH CR7 | | 203 | H3 |
| UED N18 | | 99 | M5 |
| WALTH E17 | | 100 | F3 |
| WAN E11 | | 121 | N3 |
| WDR/YW UB7 | | 131 | P10 |
| WELL DA16 | | 165 | N9 |
| WHTN TW2 | | 176 | D4 |
| Warwick Square Ms | | | |
| PIM SW1V | | 16 | E6 |
| Warwick Sq EARL SW1V * GU U1 | | 268 | E3 |
| PIM SW1V | | 16 | E6 |
| STP EC4M * | | 12 | D5 |
| Warwick Ter WALTH E17 * | | 121 | J7 |
| WOOL/PLUM SE18 | | 162 | G5 |
| Warwick Vls ECH TW20 * | | 194 | F1 |
| Warwick Wy PIM SW1V | | 16 | F7 |
| RKW/CH/CXG WD3 | | 72 | D8 |
| Warwick Wold Rd REDH RH1 | | 259 | H5 |
| Warwick Yd STLK EC1Y * | | 12 | F2 |
| MNPK E12 | | 122 | B9 |
| Washington Av HHNE HP2 | | 35 | P1 |
| REIG RH2 | | 257 | K8 |
| Washington Cl BOW E3 | | 140 | G5 |
| WDSR SL4 | | 148 | D9 |
| Washington Rd BARN SW13 | | 156 | D6 |
| CRAWW RH11 | | 283 | H10 |
| EHAM E6 | | 141 | P2 |
| KUT/HW KT1 | | 199 | M2 |
| SWFD E18 | | 101 | L10 |
| WPK KT4 | | 200 | F1 |
| Wash La BAR EN5 | | 76 | F1 |
| POTB/CUF EN6 | | 58 | E9 |
| Washneys Rd ORP BR6 | | 227 | K9 |
| Washpond La WARL CR6 | | 243 | F4 |
| Washponds Cots WARL CR6 | | 243 | H4 |
| The Wash HERT/WAT SG14 | | 25 | L5 |
| Wasp Green La REDH RH1 | | 277 | J10 |
| Wassand Cl CRAWE RH10 | | 284 | D7 |
| Wastdale Rd FSTH SE23 | | 182 | C4 |
| Watchfield Ct CHSWK W4 * | | 155 | P4 |
| Watchlytes WGCE AL7 | | 23 | M5 |
| Watchmead WGCE AL7 | | 23 | K5 |
| The Watch | | | |
| NFNCH/WDSPK N12 * | | 97 | M5 |
| Watcombe Rd SNWD SE25 | | 204 | A5 |
| Waterbank Rd CAT SE6 | | 182 | G6 |
| Waterbeach WGCE AL7 | | 23 | M5 |
| Waterbeach Cl SL SL1 | | 129 | J8 |
| Waterbeach Rd DAGW RM9 | | 143 | M1 |
| SL SL1 | | 129 | J8 |
| Waterbourne Wy | | | |
| PUR/KEN CR8 | | 223 | L10 |
| Water Brook La HDN NW4 | | 116 | F3 |
| Watercress Dr RSEV TN14 | | 247 | K6 |
| Watercress Pl IS N1 | | 7 | K4 |
| Watercress Rd CHESW EN7 | | 61 | L2 |
| Watercress Wy | | | |
| WOKN/KNAP GU21 | | 231 | N3 |
| Watercroft Rd RSEV TN14 | | 228 | A6 |
| Waterdale HERT/BAY SG13 | | 25 | K7 |
| Waterdale Rd ABYW SE2 | | 165 | K5 |
| Waterdales GVW DA11 | | 190 | A4 |
| Waterden Cl GU GU1 | | 268 | C3 |
| Waterden Rd GU GU1 | | 268 | B3 |
| Water End Rd BORE WD6 | | 75 | L6 |
| Waterend La STALE/WH AL4 | | 21 | P3 |
| WLYN AL6 | | 22 | C2 |
| Water End Rd BERK HP4 | | 34 | E3 |
| Waterer Gdns | | | |
| KWD/TDW/WH KT20 | | 239 | H4 |
| Waterer Ri WLGTN SM6 | | 222 | E3 |
| Waterfall Cl HOD EN11 | | 44 | A2 |
| VW GU25 | | 193 | L3 |
| Waterfall Rd FBAR/BDGN N11 | | 98 | C5 |
| WIM/MER SW19 | | 179 | N9 |
| Waterfall Ter TOOT SW17 | | 179 | P9 |
| Waterfield | | | |
| KWD/TDW/WH KT20 | | 238 | G6 |
| Waterfield Cl BELV DA17 | | 164 | B2 |
| THMD SE28 | | 143 | L6 |
| Waterfield Cots | | | |
| MORT/ESHN SW14 * | | 155 | N10 |
| Waterfield Dr WARL CR6 | | 242 | A5 |
| Waterfield Gdns CRAWW RH11 | | 283 | H10 |
| SNWD SE25 | | 203 | M4 |
| Waterfield Gn | | | |
| KWD/TDW/WH KT20 | | 238 | G6 |
| Waterfields LHD/OX KT22 | | 236 | G5 |
| Waterfields Wy BUSH WD23 | | 73 | L8 |
| Waterford Cl COB KT11 | | 217 | H7 |
| Waterford Common | | | |
| HERT/WAT SG14 | | 25 | J1 |
| Waterford Gn WGCE AL7 | | 23 | L5 |
| Waterford Gn FUL/PGN SW6 | | 157 | L6 |
| Waterford Rd FUL/PGN SW6 | | 14 | B10 |
| WTHK RM20 | | 166 | F2 |
| Waterfront WTHK RM20 * | | 166 | F2 |
| The Waterfront BORE WD6 | | 74 | D3 |
| Water Gdns STAN HA7 * | | 94 | G7 |
| The Water Gdns BAY/PAD W2 | | 9 | N5 |
| Watergate EMB EC4Y * | | 12 | C7 |
| Watergate St DEPT SE8 | | 160 | G5 |
| The Watergate OXHEY WD19 | | 93 | L3 |
| Waterhall Av CHING E4 | | 101 | K5 |
| Waterhall Cl WALTH E17 | | 100 | G9 |
| Waterhead Cl ERITH DA8 | | 164 | F6 |
| Waterhouse Cl HAMP NW3 | | 117 | N10 |
| Waterhouse La | | | |
| KWD/TDW/WH KT20 | | 239 | H7 |
| PUR/KEN CR8 | | 241 | K5 |
| REDH RH1 | | 259 | L8 |
| STHWK SE1 | | 11 | P9 |
| SUT SM1 | | 221 | N2 |
| UX/CGN UB8 | | 131 | N5 |
| Waterloo Gv GVE DA12 | | 190 | G7 |
| Waterloo Ter IS N1 | | 6 | C1 |
| WEY KT13 * | | 216 | B1 |
| Waterloow Rd ARCH N19 | | 118 | D6 |
| Waterloo Rd | | | |
| KUTN/CMB KT2 * | | 177 | K10 |
| Waterman Ct OXHEY WD19 | | 73 | J10 |
| Waterman St | | | |
| PUT/ROE SW15 | | 156 | G9 |
| Watermans Cl | | | |
| KUTN/CMB KT2 * | | 177 | K10 |
| Watermans Ms EA W5 * | | 135 | L4 |
| Watermans Sq PGE/AN SE20 | | 182 | E10 |
| Watermans Wy EPP CM16 | | 66 | B3 |
| SWCM DA10 | | 166 | G10 |
| Watermans Wy WAP E1W | | 140 | A10 |
| Watermark Wy | | | |
| HERT/BAY SG13 * | | 25 | N5 |
| Watermead | | | |
| EBED/NFELT TW14 | | 174 | F4 |
| WOKN/KNAP GU21 | | 230 | E8 |
| Watermead La CAR SM5 | | 202 | A6 |
| Water Meadow | | | |
| LCOL/BKTW AL2 * | | 56 | C4 |
| Watermeadow La | | | |
| FUL/PGN SW6 | | 157 | M8 |
| Watermead La CAR SM5 | | 202 | A6 |
| Watermead Rd CAT SE6 | | 183 | H7 |
| Watermead Wy TOTM N17 | | 100 | A9 |
| Watermeadow Sq PGE/AN SE20 * | | 182 | D10 |
| Water Ms PECK SE15 | | 160 | B10 |
| Watermill Cl BH/WHM TN16 | | 245 | L10 |
| RCHPK/HAM TW10 | | 176 | D6 |
| Watermill La HERT/WAT SG14 | | 25 | L2 |
| UED N18 | | 99 | M6 |
| Water Mill Wy EYN DA4 | | 210 | A2 |
| FELT TW13 | | 175 | H7 |
| Watermint Quay | | | |
| STNW/STAM N16 | | 119 | P5 |
| Waterperry La | | | |
| CHOB/PIR GU24 | | 213 | L6 |
| Water Rd ALP/SUD HA0 | | 135 | L3 |
| Water Rw WARE SG12 * | | 26 | C2 |
| Waters Dr RKW/CH/CXG WD3 | | 91 | P7 |
| STA TW18 | | 173 | J7 |
| Waters Edge HOR/WEW KT19 | | 219 | N1 |
| Water's Edge FUL/PGN SW6 * | | 156 | G7 |
| Watersfield Wy EDGW HA8 | | 95 | J8 |
| Waterside CSHM HP5 | | 51 | H8 |
| HORL RH6 | | 280 | B2 |
| KGLGY WD4 | | 54 | A5 |
| LCOL/BKTW AL2 * | | 57 | L7 |
| RAD WD7 | | 56 | G10 |
| UX/CGN UB8 | | 131 | M7 |
| WALTH E17 | | 120 | B4 |
| WGCE AL7 | | 23 | K3 |
| Waterside Av BECK BR3 | | 204 | C5 |
| Waterside Cl BARK IG11 | | 123 | K9 |
| BERM/RHTH SE16 | | 19 | P2 |
| BOW E3 | | 140 | E3 |
| CRAWW RH11 | | 283 | H9 |
| HARH RM3 | | 105 | P8 |
| NTHLT UB5 | | 133 | N5 |
| SURB KT6 | | 199 | K9 |
| THMD SE28 | | 143 | J10 |
| Waterside Ct KGLGY WD4 | | 54 | C5 |
| LEW SE13 * | | 161 | J10 |
| Waterside Dr DTCH/LGLY SL3 | | 150 | C1 |
| WOT/HER KT12 | | 197 | L7 |
| Waterside Ms DEN/HRF UB9 | | 91 | K7 |
| GU GU1 | | 249 | P8 |
| Waterside Pl CAMTN NW1 * | | 4 | D1 |
| Waterside Rd GU GU1 | | 250 | A7 |
| NWDGN UB2 | | 153 | P2 |
| Waterside Wy TOOT SW17 | | 179 | M7 |
| WOKN/KNAP GU21 | | 231 | N4 |
| Waterslade REDH RH1 | | 257 | P2 |
| Watersmeet | | | |
| HLWW/ROY CM19 | | 46 | C5 |
| Watersmeet Cl RGUE GU4 | | 250 | D5 |
| Watersmeet Wy THMD SE28 | | 143 | N8 |
| Waterson Rd CDW/CHF RM16 | | 168 | D3 |
| Waterson St BETH E2 | | 7 | K1 |
| Watersplash Cl | | | |
| KUT/HW KT1 | | 199 | K3 |
| Watersplash La ASC SL5 | | 192 | D1 |
| Watersplash Rd SHPTN TW17 | | 196 | B7 |
| Waters Rd CAT SE6 | | 183 | K6 |
| KUT/HW KT1 | | 199 | N2 |
| Waters Sq KUT/HW KT1 | | 199 | N3 |
| Waterstone Wy RDART DA2 | | 188 | D2 |
| Water St TPL/STR WC2R | | 12 | A7 |
| Watertown Gv GVE DA12 | | 191 | H3 |
| Water Tower Cl UX/CGN UB8 | | 111 | P10 |
| Water Tower Hi CROY/NA CR0 | | 223 | L1 |
| Water Tower Pl IS N1 | | 6 | A1 |
| Water Tower Rd BRW CM14 | | 107 | H6 |
| Waterway Av LEW SE13 | | 160 | G9 |
| Waterway Rd LHD/OX KT22 | | 236 | F9 |
| Waterworks Cots RSEV TN14 | | 247 | K6 |
| Waterworks La CLPT E5 | | 120 | C7 |
| Watling Vw STAL AL1 | | 38 | B9 |
| Watney Rd PUR/KEN CR8 | | 222 | B9 |
| Watney Market WCHPL E1 * | | 140 | D1 |
| Watney St WCHPL E1 | | 140 | D1 |
| Watneys Rd CROY/NA CR0 | | 202 | B2 |
| Watson Av CHEAM SM3 | | 201 | J8 |
| EHAM E6 | | 142 | G7 |
| STALW/RED AL3 | | 38 | C1 |
| Watson Cl STNW/STAM N16 | | 119 | L10 |
| WIM/MER SW19 | | 179 | P7 |
| WTHK RM20 | | 166 | F7 |
| Watson Rd DORK RH4 | | 272 | B5 |
| Watson's Ms CAMTN NW1 | | 9 | N2 |
| Watson's Rd WDGN N22 | | 98 | C9 |
| Watsons Rd WDGN N22 | | 98 | C9 |
| Watson's Wk STAL AL1 | | 38 | D7 |
| Watsons St DEPT SE8 | | 160 | C5 |
| Watson St LEY E10 | | 121 | K5 |
| Wattendon Rd PUR/KEN CR8 | | 241 | J2 |
| Wattisfield Rd CLPT E5 | | 120 | B2 |
| Wattleton Rd BEAC HP9 | | 48 | B7 |
| Watton Rd WARE SG12 | | 26 | B1 |
| Watt's Cl KWD/TDW/WH KT20 | | 238 | G8 |
| Watts Crs PUR RM19 | | 166 | B3 |
| Watts Gv BOW E3 | | 140 | F4 |
| Watt's La KWD/TDW/WH KT20 | | 238 | G8 |
| CHST BR7 | | 206 | F1 |
| Watts Lea WOKN/KNAP GU21 | | 231 | M1 |
| Watts Md KWD/TDW/WH KT20 | | 238 | G8 |
| Watts Rd THDIT KT7 | | 198 | F7 |
| Watts St PECK SE15 | | 159 | F7 |
| WAP E1W | | 140 | A10 |
| Wat Tyler Rd GNWCH SE10 | | 161 | H8 |
| Wauchope Rd ARCH N19 | | 118 | E1 |
| Wavell Cl CHESW EN7 | | 62 | D3 |
| Wavell Cl BKHTH/KID SE3 | | 161 | L5 |
| Wavell Dr BFN/LL DA15 | | 185 | H2 |
| Wavell Gdns SLN SL2 | | 128 | E5 |
| Wavel Ms KIL/WHAMP NW6 * | | 2 | F2 |
| Wavel Pl SYD SE26 | | 181 | N7 |
| Wavendon Av CHSWK W4 | | 156 | A4 |
| Wavendon Rd CHSWK W4 | | 156 | A4 |
| Waveney HHNE HP2 | | 35 | P2 |
| Waveney Av PECK SE15 | | 160 | A10 |
| Waveney Cl WAP E1W | | 13 | P9 |
| Waveney Wk BRYLDS KT5 | | 199 | N6 |
| CHING E4 | | 100 | E5 |
| PUR/KEN CR8 | | 241 | M2 |
| SUT SM1 | | 201 | L9 |
| WBLY HA9 | | 97 | H11 |
| WHTN TW2 | | 176 | C1 |
| Waverley Cl E/WMO/HCT KT8 | | 197 | N4 |
| HAYES BR2 | | 205 | A5 |
| HYS/HAR UB3 | | 152 | E3 |
| Waverley Ct WOKS/MYFD GU22 | | 232 | B4 |
| Waverley Crs HARH RM3 | | 105 | K7 |
| WOOL/PLUM SE18 | | 162 | G5 |
| Waverley Dr CHERT KT16 | | 194 | G10 |
| VW GU25 | | 193 | N4 |
| Waverley Gdns BARK IG11 | | 143 | H4 |
| BARK/HLT IG6 | | 102 | F10 |
| CDW/CHF RM16 | | 167 | M1 |
| EHAM E6 | | 142 | B7 |
| NTHWD HA6 | | 93 | H9 |
| Waverley Gv FNCH N3 | | 116 | C1 |
| Waverley Pl FSBYPK N4 * | | 119 | H1 |
| LHD/OX KT22 * | | 236 | C8 |
| STJWD NW8 | | 3 | L7 |
| Waverley Rd CEND/HSY/T N8 | | 118 | C4 |
| COB KT11 | | 218 | A10 |
| ENC/FH EN2 | | 79 | M1 |
| EW KT17 | | 220 | E2 |
| RAIN RM13 | | 145 | J5 |
| RYLN/HDSTN HA2 | | 113 | M7 |
| SL SL1 | | 129 | M7 |
| SNWD SE25 | | 204 | A4 |
| STALW/RED AL3 | | 38 | B4 |
| STHL UB1 | | 133 | P9 |
| SWFD E18 | | 101 | P9 |
| TOTM N17 | | 100 | C7 |
| WALTH E17 | | 121 | H1 |
| WEY KT13 | | 216 | B2 |
| WOOL/PLUM SE18 | | 162 | F4 |
| Waverton Rd WAND/EARL SW18 | | 179 | N1 |
| Waverton St MYFR/PKLN W1K | | 10 | B8 |
| Wavertree Rd BRXS/STRHM SW2 | | 180 | A2 |
| SWFD E18 | | 101 | M10 |
| Waxlow Crs STHL UB1 | | 134 | A6 |
| Waxlow Rd WLSDN NW10 | | 135 | N4 |
| Waxlow Wy NTHLT UB5 | | 133 | M6 |
| Waxwell La PIN HA5 | | 93 | L1 |
| Wayborne Gv RSLP HA4 | | 112 | D4 |
| Waycross Rd UPMR RM14 | | 126 | D4 |
| Waye Av HEST TW5 | | 153 | H5 |
| Wayfarer Rd HTHAIR TW6 | | 151 | L9 |
| Wayfarers Pk BERK HP4 | | 33 | L5 |
| Wayfaring Gn GRAYS RH17 | | 167 | L4 |
| Wayford St BTSEA SW11 | | 157 | P8 |
| Wayland Av HACK E8 | | 119 | F10 |
| Waylands HYS/HAR UB3 | | 132 | C7 |
| STWL/WRAY TW19 | | 172 | B2 |
| SWLY BR8 | | 208 | G4 |
| Waylands Cl RSEV TN14 | | 245 | P1 |
| Waylett Pl ALP/SUD HA0 | | 115 | J9 |
| WNWD SE27 | | 181 | J6 |
| Wayne Cl ORP BR6 | | 227 | N3 |
| Waynefleet Pl ESH/CLAY KT10 | | 197 | P9 |
| Waynflete Tower Av | | | |
| ESH/CLAY KT10 | | 197 | N10 |
| Waynflete Sq NKENS W10 | | 136 | G9 |
| Waynflete St WAND/EARL SW18 | | 179 | M5 |
| Wayre St HLWE CM17 | | 29 | M7 |
| Wayside CRAWW RH11 | | 283 | H9 |
| CROY/NA CR0 | | 224 | G3 |
| GLDGN NW11 | | 117 | H6 |
| MORT/ESHN SW14 | | 155 | P10 |
| POTB/CUF EN6 | | 59 | K6 |
| WDR/YW UB7 | | 57 | J9 |
| Wayside Av BUSH WD23 | | 74 | C10 |
| HCH RM12 | | 125 | L1 |
| Wayside Cl ROM RM1 | | 124 | C1 |
| Wayside Ct TWK TW1 | | 177 | N2 |
| Wayside Gdns CFSP/GDCR SL9 | | 90 | A6 |
| DAGE RM10 | | 124 | B10 |
| Wayside Gv ELTH/MOT SE9 | | 184 | F1 |
| WBLY HA9 | | 97 | H11 |
| GNTH/NBYPK IG2 | | 122 | D4 |
| The Wayside HHS/BOV HP3 | | 36 | A5 |
| The Way REIG RH2 | | 257 | N9 |
| Wayville Rd DART DA1 | | 188 | A3 |
| Way Volante GVE DA12 | | 191 | H7 |
| Weald Bri EPP CM16 | | 48 | G2 |
| Weald Bridge Rd EPP CM16 | | 48 | F1 |
| Weald Cl BERM/RHTH SE16 | | 160 | A4 |
| BRW CM14 | | 106 | G5 |
| Weald Hall La EPP CM16 | | 65 | M1 |
| Weald Hall La KTN/HRWW/WS HA3 | | 94 | C5 |
| Weald La KTN/HRWW/WS HA3 | | 94 | C6 |
| Weald Park Wy BRW CM14 | | 106 | D4 |
| Weald Ri KTN/HRWW/WS HA3 | | 94 | B8 |
| Weald Rd BRW CM14 | | 105 | P5 |
| UX/CGN UB8 | | 131 | P2 |
| Weald Sq CLPT E5 * | | 120 | A7 |
| Wealdstone Rd CHEAM SM3 | | 201 | J8 |
| The Weald CHST BR7 | | 184 | G4 |
| Wealdway GVW DA11 | | 190 | B6 |
| Weald Wy CTHM CR3 | | 259 | M3 |
| REIG RH2 | | 275 | M4 |
| ROMW/RG RM7 | | 124 | C1 |
| YEAD UB4 | | 132 | F5 |
| Weald End CHING E4 | | 101 | A8 |
| Weald Cl PUR/KEN CR8 | | 222 | D9 |
| Weald Gn CSTN WD25 | | 55 | J8 |
| Weardale Av RDART DA2 | | 188 | B5 |
| Weardale Gdns ENC/FH EN2 | | 79 | N5 |
| Weardale Rd LEW SE13 | | 161 | J10 |
| Wear Pl BETH E2 | | 140 | A2 |
| Wearside Rd LEW SE13 | | 160 | G10 |
| Weasdale Ct WOKN/KNAP GU21 | | 231 | M1 |
| Weatherall Cl ADL/WDHM KT15 | | 215 | L2 |
| Weatherhill Cl HORL RH6 | | 280 | C4 |
| Weatherhill Rd HORL RH6 | | 281 | H4 |
| Weatherley Cl BOW E3 | | 140 | E4 |
| Weaver Cl CRAWW RH11 | | 283 | H10 |
| CROY/NA CR0 | | 224 | G3 |
| EHAM E6 | | 142 | C6 |
| Weavers Cl GVW DA11 | | 190 | C4 |
| ISLW TW7 | | 154 | C10 |
| Weavers La RSEV TN14 | | 247 | K7 |
| Weavers St STHWK SE1 | | 19 | L2 |
| Weavers Ter FUL/PGN SW6 * | | 14 | A10 |
| Weaver St WCHPL E1 | | 13 | N2 |
| Weavers Wy CAMTN NW1 | | 5 | J5 |
| Weaver Wk WNWD SE27 | | 181 | J12 |
| Webb Cl DTCH/LGLY SL3 | | 150 | A3 |
| NKENS W10 | | 136 | B3 |
| Webber Cl BORE WD6 | | 75 | J10 |
| ERITH DA8 | | 165 | L8 |
| Webber Rw STHWK SE1 | | 18 | B2 |
| Webber St STHWK SE1 | | 18 | B2 |
| Webb Est CLPT E5 * | | 119 | P5 |
| Webb Pl WLSDN NW10 | | 136 | C5 |
| Webb Rd BKHTH/KID SE3 | | 161 | L5 |
| Webbs Rd BTSEA SW11 | | 179 | P1 |
| Webbs Meadow SEV TN13 | | 265 | K1 |
| Webb St STHWK SE1 | | 19 | J4 |
| Webster Cl HCH RM12 | | 125 | L1 |
| WAB EN9 | | 63 | M9 |
| Webster Gdns EA W5 | | 135 | K6 |
| Websters Cl WOKS/MYFD GU22 | | 231 | M6 |
| Weddell Rd CRAWE RH10 | | 284 | A10 |
| Wedderburn Rd BARK IG11 | | 143 | J2 |
| HAMP NW3 | | 117 | N10 |
| Wedgewood Cl EPP CM16 | | 65 | J6 |
| NTHWD HA6 * | | 92 | C6 |
| Wedgewood Dr HLWE CM17 | | 47 | N2 |
| Wedgewood Pl COB KT11 | | 217 | H9 |
| Wedgewoods BH/WHM TN16 * | | 243 | F7 |
| Wedgwood Wk KIL/WHAMP NW6 * | | 117 | L10 |
| Wedgwood Wy NRWD SE19 | | 181 | K10 |
| Wedhey HLWW/ROY CM19 | | 46 | F1 |
| Wedlake Cl EMPK RM11 | | 125 | N6 |
| Wedlake St NKENS W10 * | | 8 | B1 |
| Wedmore Av CLAY IG5 | | 102 | C9 |
| Wedmore Gdns ARCH N19 | | 118 | E8 |
| Wedmore Ms ARCH N19 | | 118 | E9 |
| Wedmore Rd GFD/PVL UB6 | | 134 | C5 |
| Wedmore St ARCH N19 | | 118 | E9 |
| Wednesbury Gdns HARH RM3 | | 105 | N8 |
| Wednesbury Rd HARH RM3 | | 105 | N8 |
| Weech Rd KIL/WHAMP NW6 | | 117 | K9 |
| Weedington Rd KTTN NW5 | | 118 | A7 |
| Weedon Cl CFSP/GDCR SL9 | | 89 | N9 |
| ENC/FH EN2 | | 80 | A1 |
| EW KT17 | | 220 | E2 |
| Weedon La AMS HP6 | | 68 | A5 |
| Weekes Dr SL SL1 | | 128 | G10 |
| Weekley Sq BTSEA SW11 * | | 157 | N9 |
| Weigall Rd LEE/GVPK SE12 | | 161 | M10 |
| Weighbridge Rd ADL/WDHM KT15 | | 215 | L5 |
| Weighhouse St MYFR/PKLN W1K | | 10 | D7 |
| Weighton Rd KTN/HRWW/WS HA3 | | 94 | C9 |
| PGE/AN SE20 | | 204 | A2 |
| Weihurst Gdns SUT SM1 | | 221 | N2 |
| Weimar St PUT/ROE SW15 | | 157 | M2 |
| Weirbrook CRAWE RH10 | | 284 | B10 |
| Weirdale Av TRDG/WHET N20 | | 98 | A3 |
| Weird Wd HART DA3 | | 211 | P5 |
| Weir Hall Av UED N18 | | 99 | H4 |
| Weir Hall Gdns UED N18 | | 99 | H4 |
| Weir Hall Rd UED N18 | | 99 | H4 |
| Weir Pl STA TW18 | | 195 | H11 |
| Weir Rd BAL SW12 | | 180 | A7 |
| BXLY DA5 | | 186 | C3 |
| CHERT KT16 | | 195 | H7 |
| WIM/MER SW19 | | 179 | L6 |
| WOT/HER KT12 | | 196 | C8 |
| Weirs Pas CAMTN NW1 | | 5 | G5 |
| Weiss Rd PUT/ROE SW15 | | 157 | H11 |
| Welbeck Av BFN/LL DA15 | | 185 | H4 |
| BMLY BR1 | | 183 | M4 |
| HYS/HAR UB3 | | 132 | D7 |
| Welbeck Cl BORE WD6 | | 75 | M7 |
| EW KT17 | | 220 | E4 |
| NWMAL KT3 | | 200 | C3 |
| Welbeck Rd CAR SM5 | | 201 | P7 |
| EBAR EN4 | | 77 | N10 |
| EHAM E6 | | 142 | A5 |
| RYLN/HDSTN HA2 | | 114 | A6 |
| SUT SM1 | | 201 | P7 |
| Welbeck Vls WCHMH N21 * | | 99 | H1 |
| Welbeck Wy CAVSQ/HST W1G | | 10 | C4 |
| Welby Ct PLSTW E13 | | 141 | P4 |
| Welby St CMBW SE5 | | 159 | J7 |
| Welch Pl PIN HA5 | | 93 | K9 |
| Welclose St STALW/RED AL3 | | 38 | B6 |
| Welcomes Cots CTHM CR3 * | | 242 | F4 |
| Welcomes Rd PUR/KEN CR8 | | 241 | K8 |
| Welden SLN SL2 | | 129 | K8 |
| Welders La CFSP/GDCR SL9 | | 89 | L8 |
| Weldon Cl RSLP HA4 | | 133 | K4 |
| Weldon Dr E/WMO/HCT KT8 | | 197 | L8 |
| Weld Pl FBAR/BDGN N11 | | 98 | C6 |
| Welfare Rd SRTFD E15 | | 141 | K7 |
| Welford Cl CLPT E5 | | 120 | C8 |
| Welford Pl WIM/MER SW19 | | 178 | C8 |
| Welham Cl BORE WD6 | | 75 | H7 |
| Welham Rd BRKMPK AL9 | | 40 | F10 |
| Welhouse Rd CAR SM5 | | 201 | P6 |
| Welkin Gn HHNE HP2 | | 36 | B1 |
| Wellacre Rd KTN/HRWW/WS HA3 | | 114 | C4 |
| Welland Cl BFN/LL DA15 | | 185 | L5 |
| Welland Dr DTCH/LGLY SL3 | | 150 | L1 |
| Welland Gdns GFD/PVL UB6 | | 134 | C4 |
| Welland Ms WAP E1W | | 13 | P9 |
| Wellands Cl BMLY BR1 | | 206 | F1 |
| Welland St GNWCH SE10 | | 161 | H5 |
| Well Ap BAR EN5 | | 76 | A4 |
| Wellbrook Dr CRAWE RH10 | | 284 | B10 |
| Wellbury Ter HHNE HP2 | | 36 | B1 |
| Wellby Cl ED N9 | | 90 | D9 |
| Well Cl RSLP HA4 | | 113 | M6 |
| Wellclose Sq WCHPL E1 | | 13 | N7 |
| Wellclose St WCHPL E1 | | 13 | N7 |
| Well Cottage Cl WAN E11 | | 122 | A3 |
| Well Cft HHW HP1 | | 35 | M5 |
| Wellcroft WGCE AL7 | | 23 | K7 |
| Wellcroft SL SL1 | | 128 | G10 |
| WGCE AL7 | | 23 | K6 |
| Welldon Crs HRW HA1 | | 114 | D4 |
| Well End Rd BORE WD6 | | 75 | P3 |
| Wellen Ri HHS/BOV HP3 | | 35 | P9 |
| Weller Cl AMS HP6 | | 69 | K3 |
| CRAWE RH10 | | 284 | E8 |
| Weller Ms HAYES BR2 | | 205 | N6 |
| Weller Pl ORP BR6 | | 227 | P7 |
| Wellers Cl BH/WHM TN16 | | 262 | F5 |
| Weller St STHWK SE1 | | 18 | E1 |
| Wellesford Cl BNSTD SM7 | | 239 | J3 |
| Wellesley HLWW/ROY CM19 | | 46 | D6 |
| Wellesley Av DTCH/LGLY SL3 | | 151 | J2 |
| HMSMTH W6 | | 156 | G2 |
| NTHWD HA6 | | 92 | C6 |
| Wellesley Cl CHARL SE7 * | | 161 | N4 |
| Wellesley Court Rd CROY/NA CR0 * | | 203 | L9 |
| Wellesley Crs POTB/CUF EN6 | | 59 | H9 |
| WHTN TW2 | | 176 | D5 |
| Wellesley Gv CROY/NA CR0 | | 203 | L9 |
| Wellesley Pde WHTN TW2 * | | 176 | D6 |
| Wellesley Park Ms ENC/FH EN2 * | | 79 | J6 |
| Wellesley Pl KTTN NW5 | | 118 | B10 |
| Wellesley Rd BELMT SM2 | | 221 | N6 |
| BRW CM14 | | 107 | H2 |
| CHSWK W4 | | 155 | N6 |
| CROY/NA CR0 | | 203 | K8 |
| HRW HA1 | | 114 | D3 |
| IL IG1 | | 122 | E7 |
| KTTN NW5 | | 118 | B10 |
| SL SL1 | | 149 | M1 |
| WALTH E17 | | 120 | F4 |
| WAN E11 | | 121 | P5 |
| WHTN TW2 | | 176 | D6 |
| Wellesley St WCHPL E1 | | 140 | C7 |
| Wellesley Ter IS N1 | | 6 | F9 |
| Welley Rd STWL/WRAY TW19 | | 150 | D10 |
| STWL/WRAY TW19 | | 172 | B1 |
| Well Farm Rd CTHM CR5 | | 241 | P5 |
| Wellfield Av MUSWH N10 | | 118 | C1 |
| Wellfield Cl HAT AL10 | | 40 | D3 |
| Wellfield Gdns CAR SM5 | | 221 | P5 |
| Wellfield Rd HAT AL10 | | 40 | D2 |
| STRHM/NOR SW16 | | 180 | F7 |
| Wellfields LOU IG10 | | 82 | G7 |
| Wellfit St HNHL SE24 | | 159 | J4 |
| Wellgarth GFD/PVL UB6 | | 134 | G1 |
| Wellgarth Rd GLDGN NW11 | | 117 | G6 |
| Well Gv TRDG/WHET N20 | | 97 | M2 |
| Well Hall Pde ELTH/MOT SE9 * | | 162 | G10 |
| Well Hall Rd ELTH/MOT SE9 | | 162 | G10 |
| Well Hi ORP BR6 | | 228 | C4 |
| Well Hill La ORP BR6 | | 228 | C5 |
| Wellhouse La BAR EN5 | | 76 | A4 |
| BRKHM/BTCW RH3 | | 273 | P4 |
| Wellhurst Cl ORP BR6 | | 227 | P7 |
| Welling High St WELL DA16 | | 165 | J9 |
| Wellington Av BFN/LL DA15 | | 185 | K5 |
| CHING E4 | | 101 | K4 |
| ED N9 | | 100 | F4 |
| HSLW TW3 | | 175 | P1 |
| PIN HA5 | | 93 | P7 |
| SEVS/STOTM N15 | | 119 | P2 |
| VW GU25 | | 193 | N6 |
| WPK KT4 | | 200 | G9 |
| Wellington Cl CRAWE RH10 | | 284 | F4 |
| DAGE RM10 | | 144 | D2 |
| NWCR SE14 | | 160 | C2 |
| OXHEY WD19 | | 73 | L10 |
| WOT/HER KT12 | | 196 | G8 |
| Wellington Crs NWMAL KT3 | | 199 | P2 |
| Wellington Dr DAGE RM10 | | 144 | D2 |
| PUR/KEN CR8 | | 222 | G6 |
| WGCE AL7 | | 23 | M5 |
| Wellington Gdns CHARL SE7 | | 161 | P4 |
| WHTN TW2 | | 176 | C7 |
| Wellington Hi CHIG IG7 | | 84 | G11 |
| Wellington Hl LOU IG10 | | 81 | N4 |
| Wellingtonia Av ABR/ST RM4 | | 104 | F4 |
| Wellington Ms CHARL SE7 | | 161 | P5 |
| EDUL SE22 | | 159 | P10 |
| HOLWY N7 | | 118 | E5 |
| STRHM/NOR SW16 | | 180 | E6 |
| Wellington Pde BFN/LL DA15 * | | 185 | K1 |
| Wellington Park Est CRICK NW2 * | | 115 | D7 |
| Wellington Pas WAN E11 * | | 121 | M3 |
| Wellington Pl BROX EN10 * | | 44 | B9 |
| BRW CM14 | | 107 | H6 |
| COB KT11 | | 217 | P3 |
| EFNCH N2 | | 117 | H7 |
| CODL GU7 | | 267 | K10 |
| STJWD NW8 | | 3 | M9 |
| Wellington Rd ASHF TW15 | | 173 | H7 |
| BELV DA17 | | 164 | A4 |
| BXLY DA5 | | 186 | B2 |
| CROY/NA CR0 | | 203 | J7 |
| CHES/WCR EN8 | | 241 | K8 |
| EA W5 | | 155 | H3 |
| EBED/NFELT TW14 | | 174 | A1 |
| EHAM E6 | | 142 | A8 |
| EN EN1 | | 99 | M1 |
| EPP CM16 | | 66 | D4 |
| FSTGT E7 | | 121 | L3 |
| HAYES BR2 | | 205 | N4 |
| HPTN TW12 | | 176 | C7 |
| KTN/HRWW/WS HA3 | | 114 | D1 |
| LCOL/BKTW AL2 | | 57 | J6 |
| LEY E10 | | 120 | G6 |
| NKENS W10 | | 136 | C5 |
| PIN HA5 | | 93 | M3 |
| STAL AL1 | | 38 | G7 |
| STJWD NW8 | | 3 | K6 |
| STMC/STPC BR5 | | 207 | L2 |
| TIL RM18 | | 168 | B8 |
| UX/CGN UB8 | | 131 | M3 |
| WALTH E17 | | 121 | H1 |
| WAN E11 | | 121 | M3 |
| WAT WD17 | | 73 | J4 |
| WIM/MER SW19 | | 179 | K5 |
| Wellington Rd North HSLWW TW4 | | 153 | P6 |
| Wellington Rd South HSLWW TW4 | | 175 | P1 |
| Wellington Rw BETH E2 | | 7 | M9 |
| Wellington Sq CHEL SW3 | | 15 | N8 |
| IS N1 | | 5 | K1 |
| Wellington St COVGDN WC2E | | 11 | M7 |
| GVE DA12 | | 191 | J7 |
| HERT/WAT SG14 | | 25 | J4 |
| SL SL1 | | 149 | H1 |
| WOOL/PLUM SE18 | | 162 | D3 |
| Wellington Ter BAY/PAD W2 | | 9 | H7 |
| CEND/HSY/T N8 * | | 119 | H8 |
| HRW HA1 | | 114 | C5 |
| WAP E1W * | | 140 | C4 |
| WOKN/KNAP GU21 | | 231 | K4 |
| Wellington Wy BOW E3 | | 140 | A2 |
| HORL RH6 | | 280 | A10 |
| WEY KT13 | | 216 | B5 |
| Wellington Wy ELTH/MOT SE9 | | 162 | G8 |
| Well La BRWN CM15 | | 86 | C6 |
| CDW/CHF RM16 | | 147 | N10 |
| HLW CM20 | | 46 | C2 |
| HLWW/ROY CM19 | | 46 | D5 |
| MORT/ESHN SW14 | | 155 | P10 |
| WOKN/KNAP GU21 | | 231 | H7 |
| Wellmeade Dr SEV TN13 | | 265 | J5 |
| Wellmeadow Rd CAT SE6 | | 183 | H3 |
| HNWL W7 | | 154 | C4 |

Well Pth WOKN/KNAP GU21... 231 P5
Well Rd BAR EN5... 76 F9
HAMP NW3... 117 N8
POTB/CUF EN6... 59 P5
RSEV TN14... 247 K3
Wellacre Rd KTN/HRWW/WS HA3... 115 J5
Wells Cl BH/WHM TN16... 262 F9
CHESW... 61 K1
GT/LBKH KT23... 236 A10
NTHLT UB5... 133 H4
SAND/SEL CR2... 223 M2
STALW/RED AL3... 38 C5
WDSR SL4... 148 F6
Wells Dr CDALE/KGS NW9... 116 A6
Wellsfield BUSH WD23... 73
Wells Gdns IL IG1... 122 B5
RAIN RM13... 144 G1
Wells House Rd WLSDN NW10... 136 F3
Wellside Gdns
MORT/ESHN SW14... 155 P10
Wells La ASC SL5... 192 A3
RGUW GU3... 248 B5
Wells Ms FITZ W1T *... 11 H4
Wellsmoor Gdns BMLY BR1... 206 F3
Wells Park Rd SYD SE26... 181 P6
Wells Pl CMBW SE5... 159 M6
REDH RH1... 258 C6
WAND/EARL SW18... 178 E6
Wellspring Crs WBLY HA9... 115 N9
Wells Ri STJWD NW8... 4 A2
RGUE GU4... 250 F7
SHB W12... 156 F1
Wells Sq FSBYW WC1X... 5 N10
ST GPFST W1W... 10 C4
Wellstead Av ED N9... 100 B1
Wellstead Rd EHAM E6... 142 D4
Wells Ter FSBYPK N4... 119 H7
The Wells STHGT/OAK N14... 98 E2
Wellstones WAT WD17 *... 73 J8
Well St HOM E9... 140 B2
SRTFD E15... 141 K1
Wells Wy CMBW SE5... 19 H10
Weltje Rd HMSMTH W6... 156 F1
Welton Rd WOOL/PLUM SE18... 163 H6
Welwyn Av EBED/NFELT TW14... 174 C2
Welwyn Cl CRAWW RH11... 283 H10
Welwyn Ct HHNE HP2... 36 A2
Welwyn Rd HERT/WAT SG14... 24 F4
Welwyn St BETH E2... 140 B5
Welwyn Wy YEAD UB4... 132 F6
Wembley Hill Rd WBLY HA9... 115 L10
Wembley Park Dr WBLY HA9... 115 L9
Wembley Rd HPTN TW12... 197 P1
Wembley Wy WBLY HA9... 135 N9
Wemborough Rd STAN HA7... 94 G9
Wembury Ms HGT N6... 118 C5
Wembury Rd HGT N6... 118 C5
Wemyss Rd BKHTH/KID SE3... 161 L8
Wendela Cl WOKS/MYFD GU22... 232 C2
Wendela Ct HRW HA1... 114 D8
Wendell Rd SHB W12... 156 C1
Wendley Dr ADL/WDHM KT15... 215 J6
Wendling Rd SUT SM1... 201 N8
Wendon St BOW E3... 140 E2
Wendover Cl HARP AL5... 20 C7
STALE/WL AL4... 8 H1
YEAD UB4... 133 L8
Wendover Dr NWMAL KT3... 200 D4
Wendover Gdns
RBRW/HUT CM13... 107 N3
Wendover Pl STA TW18... 172 G8
Wendover Rd ELTH/MOT SE9... 162 A9
HAYES BR2... 205 N4
SL SL1... 128 A7
STA TW18... 172 G8
WLSDN NW10... 136 C4
Wendover Wy BUSH WD23 *... 74 B1
HCH RM12... 125 K10
ORP BR6... 207 K6
WELL DA16... 185 K1
Wendon Cl
WOKN/KNAP GU21 *... 231 M4
The Wend COUL/CHIP CR5... 222 F4
Wendy Cl EN EN1... 79 N10
Wendy Crs GUW GU2... 249 M8
Wendy Wy ALP/SUD HA0... 135 K3
Wenham Pl HAT AL10... 40 D3
Wengeo La WARE SG12... 26 A1
Wenham Dr CRAWW RH11... 283 M10
HHNE HP2... 36 A2
Wenlack Cl DEN/HRF UB9... 111 K8
Wenlock Ct CRAWW RH11... 283 K9
Wenlock Edge DORK RH4 *... 273 H4
Wenlock Gdns HDN NW4 *... 116 D2
Wenlock Rd EDGW HA8... 95 H6
IS N1... 6 F3
Wenlock St IS N1... 6 F3
Wennington Rd BOW E3... 140 C4
RAIN RM13... 145 J1
Wensley Av WFD IG8... 101 M8
Wensley Cl CRW RM5... 104 B6
ELTH/MOT SE9... 184 C1
FBAR/BDGN N11... 98 B7
Wensleydale CRAWW RH11... 283 M10
HHNE HP2... 36
Wensleydale Av CLAY IG5... 102 B10
Wensleydale Gdns
HPTN TW12... 176 A10
Wensleydale Rd HPTN TW12... 197 P1
Wensley Rd UED N18... 100 A7
Wensum Wy
RKW/CH/CXG WD3... 91 N2
Wentbridge Pth BORE WD6... 75 M4
Wentland Cl CAT SE6... 183 J5
Wentland Rd CAT SE6... 183 J5
Wentworth Av BORE WD6... 75 K8
FNCH N3... 97 K8
SLN SL2... 128 F5
Wentworth Cl ASHF TW15... 174 C7
FNCH N3... 97 L8
GVW DA11... 190 C8
HAYES BR2 *... 205 M9
MRDN SM4... 201 M9
ORP BR6... 227 H2
POTB/CUF EN6... 59 K7
RPLY/SEND GU23... 232 G1
SURB KT6... 199 J9
THMD SE28... 143 N8
WAT WD17... 72 G4
Wentworth Crs HYS/HAR UB3... 152 A3
PECK SE15... 159 P6
Wentworth Dene WEY KT13... 216 C2
Wentworth Dr CRAWE RH10... 93 L8
OXHEY WD19... 31 K3
PIN HA5... 113 H5
VW GU25... 195 L4
Wentworth Gdns PLMGR N13... 99 J1
Wentworth Hl WBLY HA9... 115 N9
Wentworth Ms BOW E3... 140 D6
Wentworth Pk FNCH N3... 97 L8
Wentworth Pl CDW/CHF RM16... 168 A2
CSHM HP5 *... 5
STAN HA7 *... 94 G7
Wentworth Rd BAR EN5... 76 C5
CROY/NA CR0... 204 D9
GLDGN NW11... 117 J4
HNWL W7... 135 H7
HRT/BAY SG13... 24 G3
MNPK E12... 141 J9
NWDGN UB2... 153 K3

UPMR RM14... 126 D7
Westbush Cl HOD EN11... 26 A10
Westcar La WOT/HER KT12... 217 J3
West Carriage Dr
BAY/PAD W2... 15 M1
West Central St
LSQ/SEVD WC2H... 11 L5
West Chantry
KTN/HRWW/WS HA3... 94 A9
Westchester Dr HDN NW4... 116 A9
Westcliffe Vis KUT/HW KT1 *... 199 L2
West Cl ASHF TW15... 173 P7
BAR EN5... 76 E9
EBAR EN4... 78 B8
ED N9... 99 N4
GFD/PVL UB6... 134 B4
HOD EN11... 44 F1
RAIN RM13... 145 J6
WBLY HA9... 115 L6
Western Ter HMSMTH W6 *... 156 D4
HOD EN11 *... 26 C10
Western Vw HYS/HAR UB3... 152 C1
Westcombe Dr BAR EN5... 77 K9
Westcombe Lodge Dr
YEAD UB4... 132 C7
Westcombe Park Rd
BKHTH/KID SE3... 161 M6
BKHTH/KID SE3... 161 M6
West Common
CFSP/GDCR SL9... 110 A3
HARP AL5... 20 C5
West Common Gv HARP AL5... 20 A5
HAYES BR2... 205 N1
West Common Rd HAYES BR2... 225 N1
UX/CGN UB8... 111 N10
Westcoombe Av RYNPK SW20... 200 C1
Westcote Rd STRHM/NOR SW16... 180 C8
Westcott Cl BMLY BR1... 206 B5
CROY/NA CR0... 224 C5
SEVS/STOTM N15... 119 N4
Westcott Crs HNWL W7... 134 D7
Westcott House
POP/IOD E14 *... 140 F9
Westcott Rd DORK RH4... 272 F9
WALW SE17... 18 D9
Westcott St DORK RH4... 272 A5
Westcott Wy BELMT SM2... 220 F6
West Ct ALP/SUD HA0... 115 H7
West Crescent Rd GVE DA12 *... 190 E2
West Crs WDSR SL4... 148 E7
Westcroft SLN SL2... 128 C6
Westcroft Cl CRICK NW2... 117 H9
PEND EN3... 80 B4
Westcroft Gdns MRDN SM4... 201 J3
Westcroft Park Dr WFD IG8... 102 B7
Westcroft Rd CAR SM5... 222 B1
CROY/NA CR0... 224 C5
Westcroft Sq HMSMTH W6... 156 D1
Westcroft Wy CRICK NW2... 117 H9
West Cromwell Rd
WKENS W14... 14 D7
Westdean Av LEE/GVPK SE12... 183 N4
Westdean Cl
WAND/EARL SW18... 179 L2
Westdean La CSHM HP5... 50 B4
Westdene WOT/HER KT12... 217 J2
West Dene Dr HARH RM3... 105 L6
West Down GT/LBKH KT23... 254 A3
Westdown Rd CAT SE6... 182 F3
SRTFD E15... 121 H9
West Drayton Park Av
WDR/YW UB7... 151 P2
West Drayton Rd UX/CGN UB8... 132 C7
UX/CGN UB8... 132 C8
West Dr ADL/WDHM KT15... 215 J5
ASC SL5... 193 J5
BELMT SM2... 220 E6
CAR SM5... 221 N6
GSTN WD25... 73 J8
KTN/HRWW/WS HA3... 94 C7
KWD/TDW/WH KT20... 238 G4
STRHM/NOR SW16... 180 C7
VW GU25... 193 K7
West Drive Gdns
KTN/HRWW/WS HA3... 94 C7
West Eaton Pl BGVA SW1W... 16 C5
West Eaton Place Ms
KTBR SW1X... 16 C5
West Ella Rd WLSDN NW10... 136 B2
West End Av LEY E10... 121 H4
PIN HA5... 113 L2
West End Cl WLSDN NW10... 135 P2
West End La BAR EN5... 76 G3
BRKMPK AL9... 41 M4
HYS/HAR UB3... 152 D6
KIL/WHAMP NW6... 2 C1
PIN HA5... 113 L2
SLN SL2... 129 K3
West End Rd BROX EN10... 43 N9
NTHLT UB5... 133 J4
RSLP HA4... 112 G8
STHL UB1... 133 M10
Westerdale HHNE HP2... 35 P5
Westerdale Rd GNWCH SE10... 161 L4
Westerfield Rd
SEVS/STOTM N15 *... 119 N3
Westerfolds Cl
WOKS/MYFD GU22... 232 F5
Westergate ABYW SE2... 163 P5
Westerham Av ED N9... 99 L4
Westerham Cl
ADL/WDHM KT15 *... 215 M5
BELMT SM2 *... 221 K6
Westerham Dr BFN/LL DA15... 185 M2
Westerham Hl BH/WHM TN16... 263 K1
Westerham Rd BH/WHM TN16... 263 N1
HAYES BR2... 226 A3
LEY E10... 120 C4
OXTED RH8... 261 L5
RSEV TN14... 246 D10
WARL CR6... 241 N9
Westerley Crs SYD SE26... 182 E8
Westerman ADL/WDHM KT15... 215 M5
Western Av BRW CM14... 107 H2
CHERT KT16... 195 K3
CHOB/PIR GU24... 230 F7
DAGE RM10... 144 D1
DEN/HRF UB9... 111 N9
EA W5... 135 K5
EGH TW20... 194 E3
EPP CM16... 65 J3
GFD/PVL UB6... 134 B3
GLDGN NW11... 116 C4
NTHLT UB5... 134 A3
HDN/ICK UB10... 112 A10
RSLP HA4... 133 J2
WTHK RM20 *... 166 F3
Western Ct BFN/LL DA15 *... 185 J4
Western Cross Cl SWCM DA10... 189 Q7
Western Dr SHPTN TW17... 196 E9
Western Gdns BRW CM14... 107 H3
EA W5... 135 N4
Western Gtwy CAN/RD E16... 141 M9
WIM/MER SW19... 178 A3
Western Man BAR EN5 *... 77 L5
Western Pde BAR EN5... 77 N5
West India Av POP/IOD E14... 140 F10

HGDN/ICK UB10 *... 132 C1
Western Perimeter Rd
HTHAIR TW6... 151 L9
Western Pl BERM/RHTH SE16... 160 A7
DORK RH4 *... 272 F2
Western Rd BRW CM14... 107 H3
BRXN/ST SW9... 159 H5
EA W5... 135 J9
EFNCH N2... 118 A1
MTCM CR4... 201 P1
NWDGN UB2... 153 K3
ROM RM1... 124 F3
SUT SM1... 221 K2
WAB EN9... 45 K8
WALTH E17... 121 L2
WDGN N22... 98 C10
WLSDN NW10... 135 P6
Western Ter HMSMTH W6 *... 156 D4
HOD EN11 *... 26 C10
Western Vw HYS/HAR UB3... 152 C1
Westernville Gdns
GNTH/NBYPK IG2... 122 F5
Western Wy BAR EN5... 77 K10
THMD SE28... 162 G2
West Farm Av ASHTD KT21... 237 H4
West Farm Cl ASHTD KT21... 237 H5
West Farm Dr ASHTD KT21... 237 J5
Westferry Circ POP/IOD E14... 140 F10
Westferry Rd POP/IOD E14... 160 F2
Westfield AMS HP6... 68 B1
BRKMPK AL9... 41 K9
HLWS CM18... 47 K9
RDKG RH5... 270 F9
Westfield Av SAND/SEL CR2... 223 J10
WATN WD24... 73 L4
WOKS/MYFD GU22... 232 B7
Westfield Cl CDALE/KGS NW9... 115 P1
CHES/WCR EN8... 62 C1
GVE DA12... 190 F9
PEND EN3... 80 D7
SUT SM1... 221 J1
WBPTN SW10... 157 M6
Westfield Common
WOKS/MYFD GU22... 232 B8
Westfield Dr GT/LBKH KT23... 236 A8
KTN/HRWW/WS HA3... 115 J3
Westfield Gdns CHDH RM6... 123 M4
KTN/HRWW/WS HA3... 115 J2
Westfield Gv
WOKS/MYFD GU22... 232 B6
Westfield Pde
ADL/WDHM KT15 *... 215 N8
Westfield Pk PIN HA5... 93 N8
Westfield Park Dr WFD IG8... 102 B7
Westfields BARN SW13... 156 A5
STALW/RED AL3... 37 P8
Westfields Av BARN SW13... 156 B9
Westfields Rd ACT W3... 135 N4
Westfield St
WOOL/PLUM SE18... 161 H9
Westfield Wy RSLP HA4... 112 F8
WCHPL E1... 140 D5
WOKS/MYFD GU22... 232 B7
West Flexford La RGUW GU3... 266 C11
West Gdns EW KT17... 120 G2
TOOT SW17... 179 P9
WAP E1W... 140 A9
West Ga EA W5... 135 K5
HLW CM20... 46 F1
Westgate Crs SL SL1... 128 E9
Westgate Est
EBED/NFELT TW14 *... 174 C4
West Gate Ms BECK BR3 *... 205 H1
Westgate Rd BECK BR3... 205 H4
SNWD SE25... 204 A4
Westgate St HACK E8... 140 A3
Westgate Ter WBPTN SW10... 15 H8
Westglade
KTN/HRWW/WS HA3... 115 J3
West Green Dr CRAWW RH11... 283 M7
West Green Pl GFD/PVL UB6... 134 C1
West Green Rd
SEVS/STOTM N15... 119 J2
West Gv GNWCH SE10... 161 H7
WFD IG8... 102 A9
West Halkin St KTBR SW1X... 16 C3
West Hall BF/WBF KT14... 215 M10
West Hallowes ELTH/MOT SE9... 184 H4
West Hall Pk WARL CR6... 242 B5
Westhall Pk WARL CR6... 242 B5
Westhall Rd WARL CR6... 241 P4
West Ham La SRTFD E15... 141 J7
West Hampstead Ms
KIL/WHAMP NW6... 2 C1
West Harding St
FLST/FETLN EC4A *... 12 B5
Westharold SWLY BR8... 208 E3
West Hatch Mnr RSLP HA4... 112 G6
Westhay Gdns
MORT/ESHN SW14... 177 N1
West Heath CHOB/PIR GU24... 230 C9
West Heath Av GLDGN NW11... 117 K6
West Heath Cl DART DA1 *... 186 G2
HAMP NW3... 117 H4
West Heath Dr GLDGN NW11... 117 K7
West Heath Gdns HAMP NW3... 117 H4
West Heath La SEV TN13... 265 H4
West Heath Rd ABYW SE2... 163 N5
HAMP NW3... 117 H3
West Hi BH/WEW KT19... 219 P9
ORP BR6... 226 F8
PUT/ROE SW15... 179 H2
RYLN/HDSTN HA2... 114 B7
SAND/SEL CR2... 223 K5
WAND/EARL SW18... 178 A4
WIM/MER SW19... 178 A3
West Hill Bank OXTED RH8... 261 J7
West Hill Ct HGT N6 *... 118 B7
West Hill Dr DART DA1... 170 G9
WOKS/MYFD GU22... 232 A5
West Hill Pk HGT N6 *... 117 P7
West Hill Rd RDKG RH5... 270 B10
West Hill Wy TRDG/WHET N20... 97 H1
Westholm GLDGN NW11... 117 H3
West Holme ERITH DA8... 164 G3
Westholme ORP BR6... 207 H1
Westholme Gdns RSLP HA4... 113 H6
Westhorne Av ELTH/MOT SE9... 183 M2
LEE/GVPK SE12... 183 M1
Westhorpe Gdns HDN NW4... 116 A2
Westhorpe Rd PUT/ROE SW15... 156 G9

West India Dock Rd
POP/IOD E14... 140 G9
West Kent Av GVW DA11... 189 P2
Westlake Cl PLMGR N13... 99 H4
YEAD UB4... 133 J5
Westland Av BRW CM14... 107 H3
Westland Cl GSTN WD25... 59 M6
STWL/WRAY TW19 *... 173 P2
Westland Dr BRKMPK AL9... 59 J9
HAYES BR2... 205 L9
Westland Pl FSBYE EC1V *... 6 E6
Westland Rd WAT WD17 *... 73 J6
Westlands Av SL SL1... 128 B8
Westlands Cl HYS/HAR UB3... 153 H3
SL SL1... 128 B8
Westlands Ter BAL SW12... 180 E5
Westland Vw CDW/CHF RM16... 147 M10
West La BERM/RHTH SE16... 160 A7
RDKG RH5... 271 L5
Westlea Av GSTN WD25... 73 M3
Westlea Rd BROX EN10... 44 E9
HNWL W7... 154 F2
Westleas HORL RH6... 279 P2
Westlees Cl RDKG RH5... 273 H5
Westleigh Av COUL/CHIP CR5... 240 B2
PUT/ROE SW15... 178 F1
Westleigh Dr BMLY BR1... 206 B2
Westleigh Gdns EDGW HA8... 95 M8
West Links ALP/SUD HA0... 135 J5
Westlinton Cl MLHL NW7... 97 H7
West Lodge Av ACT W3... 135 M10
West Lodge Ct ACT W3 *... 135 M10
Westlyn Cl RAIN RM13... 145 K5
Westly Wd WGCE AL7... 23 K4
Westmacott Dr
EBED/NFELT TW14... 174 G3
West Malling Cl HCH RM12... 125 J10
Westmead HOR/WEW KT19... 220 B5
PUT/ROE SW15... 178 F6
Westmead Cl WGCE AL7... 23 L8
West Md HOR/WEW KT19... 220 B5
RSLP HA4... 113 K9
Westmead Cr SL SL1... 148 G5
Westmead Rd SUT SM1... 221 N2
Westmeade CHESW EN7... 61 M2
Westmede CHIG IG7... 116 B10
Westmere Dr MLHL NW7... 96 A4
Westmede BARK/HLT IG6... 102 F7
Westmead Rd BKHT/KID SE3... 276 B6
West Mersea Cl CAN/RD E16... 141 N10
West Ms PIM SW1V... 16 F6
SEVS/STOTM N15... 119 R3
West Mi GVW DA11... 190 C8
Westminster Av THHTH CR7... 203 J2
Westminster Br WHALL SW1A... 17 M2
Westminster Bridge Rd
WHALL SW1A... 17 M2
Westminster Cl
EBED/NFELT TW14... 175 H4
TEDD TW11... 176 A9
Westminster Ct HARP AL5 *... 20 B4
STAL AL1... 38 B8
WOKS/MYFD GU22 *... 232 B7
Westminster Dr PLMGR N13... 98 F4
Westminster Gdns BARK IG11... 143 K9
BARK/HLT IG6... 102 G10
CHING E4... 101 K2
Westminster Ldg STAL AL1 *... 38 B8
Westmoat Cl BECK BR3... 183 N10
Westmont Rd ESH/CLAY KT10... 216 G9
Westmoor Gdns PEND EN3... 80 D6
Westmoor Rd PEND EN3... 80 D6
Westmoor St CHARL SE7... 162 A3
Westmoreland Av
EMPK RM11... 125 K3
WELL DA16... 163 H9
Westmoreland Dr BELMT SM2... 221 L5
Westmoreland Pl BMLY BR1 *... 205 M3
EA W5 *... 135 J7
PIM SW1V... 16 F8
Westmoreland Rd BARN SW13... 156 F1
CMBW SE5... 18 E9
HAYES BR2... 205 M1
KTN/HRWW/WS HA3... 114 B2
WALW SE17... 18 E9
Westmoreland St
CAVSQ/HST W1G *... 10 B2
Westmoreland Ter
PGE/AN SE20 *... 182 A10
PIM SW1V... 16 F8
Westmore Rd BH/WHM TN16... 243 P6
Westmorland Cl
HOR/WEW KT19... 220 B6
MNPK E12... 122 A7
TWK TW1... 176 G2
Westmorland Rd HRW HA1... 114 A3
WALTH E17... 120 F2
Westmorland Wy MTCM CR4... 202 F4
Westmount Rd ELTH/MOT SE9... 162 E9
West Oak BECK BR3... 205 J1
Westoe Rd ED N9... 99 J4
Weston Av ADL/WDHM KT15... 215 K1
E/WMO/HCT KT8... 197 M4
THDIT KT7... 198 A8
Weston Cl COUL/CHIP CR5... 240 G6
POTB/CUF EN6... 59 J8
RBRW/HUT CM13... 107 H2
Weston Ct FBAR/BDGN N11 *... 98 C7
Weston Dr CALE... 183 L10
STAN HA7... 94 G9
Weston Gdns ISLW TW7... 154 C7
WOKS/MYFD GU22... 233 H2
Weston Gn DAGW RM9... 123 P9
THDIT KT7... 198 D9
Weston Green Rd
ESH/CLAY KT10... 198 C8
Weston Gv BMLY BR1... 183 L10
HORL RH6... 280 C6
Weston Lea EHSLY KT24... 272 E6
Weston Pk CEND/HSY/T N8... 118 F6
KUT/HW KT1... 198 D9
THDIT KT7... 198 D9
Weston Park Cl THDIT KT7 *... 198 D9
Weston Ri FSBYW WC1X... 5 N9
Weston Rd BMLY BR1... 205 L1
CHSWK W4... 155 P2
DAGW RM9... 123 P9
ENC/FH EN2... 79 L6
EW KT17... 220 B7
GUW GU2... 248 D3
SL SL1... 128 C7
THDIT KT7... 198 D9
Weston St STHWK SE1... 19 H3
Westonville Rd SHB W12... 156 F1
Weston Wy WOKS/MYFD GU22... 233 H2
Westover Cl BELMT SM2... 221 L9
Westover Hl HAMP NW3... 117 H3
Westover Rd
WAND/EARL SW18... 179 M2
Westow Hl NRWD SE19... 180 F10
RYLN/HDSTN HA2... 114 A5
West Palace Gdns WEY KT13... 196 C10
West Pk ELTH/MOT SE9... 184 B5
West Pk Av RCH/KEW TW9... 155 N7
West Pk Cl CHDH RM6... 123 P2
HEST TW5... 153 N5
West Pk Rd RCH/KEW TW9... 155 P7
STHL UB1... 134 D6
Westpole Av EBAR EN4... 78 G5

West Pl EPP CM16... 47 L10
NWDGN UB2 *... 154 A3
WIM/MER SW19... 178 A9
West Point Sl SL1... 128 C10
Westpole Av EBAR EN4... 78 G5
Westport Rd PLSTW E13... 142 C3
Westport St WCHPL E1... 140 G4
West Poultry Av FARR EC1M *... 12 C4
West Quarters SHB W12... 136 D8
West Quay YEAD UB4... 133 M7
Westray HHS/BOV HP3... 36 B8
Westridge Cl CSHM HP5... 50 E6
HHW HP1... 35 J6
West Ridge Gdns
GFD/PVL UB6... 134 B4
West Ri BAY/PAD W2 *... 9 N7
West Rd BKHTH HP4... 33 M4
CHDH RM6... 123 P4
CHEL SW3... 16 E9
CHSGTN KT9... 219 H7
CLAP SW4... 180 C1
EA W5... 135 K7
EBAR EN4... 98 A2
EBED/NFELT TW14... 174 A5
GU GU1... 268 B1
HDN NW4... 29 K7
KUTN/CMB KT2... 199 P3
REIG RH2... 275 L1
ROMW/RG RM7... 124 C5
SOCK/AV RM15... 146 G3
SRTFD E15... 141 L5
TOTM N17... 100 A8
WDR/YW UB7... 152 A2
WEY KT13... 216 C4
Westrow Dr BARK IG11... 143 J1
Westrow Gdns
GDMY/SEVK IG3... 123 J7
West Shaw HART DA3... 211 J3
West Sheen V RCH/KEW TW9... 155 L10
West Side BROX EN10... 62 D1
HDN NW4... 96 E10
West Side Common
WIM/MER SW19... 178 B9
West Smithfield STBT EC1A... 13 L5
West Spur Rd UX/CGN UB8... 131 N5
West St HLW CM20 *... 28 F10
LBTH SE11... 18 C4
West St BETH E2... 140 A4
BMLY BR1... 183 L3
BXLYHN DA7... 164 A10
CAR SM5... 202 A10
CRAWW RH11... 283 N8
CROY/NA CR0... 223 K1
DORK RH4... 272 F2
EPSOM KT18... 219 P9
ERITH DA8... 164 E3
EW KT17... 220 B6
GRAYS RM17... 167 M5
GVW DA11... 190 D2
HERT/BAY SG13... 25 K6
HOR/WEW KT19... 219 P9
HRW HA1... 114 C6
LSQ/SEVD WC2H... 11 K6
REIG RH2... 257 J10
SUT SM1... 221 L2
WALTH E17... 120 C3
WAN E11... 121 K8
WARE SG12... 26 C2
WAT WD17... 73 J6
WOKN/KNAP GU21... 232 C3
West Street Pl CROY/NA CR0 *... 223 K1
West Temple Sheen
MORT/ESHN SW14... 177 N1
West Tenter St WCHPL E1... 13 M6
West Ter BFN/LL DA15 *... 185 H4
West Thurrock Wy
WTHK RM20... 166 F3
West Towers PIN HA5... 113 L4
West Valley Rd HHS/BOV HP3... 35 M10
West Vw CSHM HP5... 51 J5
EBED/NFELT TW14... 174 D4
HAT AL10... 40 D2
West View HNWL W7... 134 D8
West Vw LOU IG10... 82 C7
West View Av CTHM CR3... 241 N4
West View Cl NKENS W10... 15 K6
West View Ct BORE WD6 *... 75 J4
West View Dr WFD IG8... 102 A10
West View Rd RAIN RM13 *... 145 K5
REDH RH1... 275 P3
WLSDN NW10... 135 L5
Westview Ct BORE WD6... 75 J10
Westview Crs ED N9... 99 M1
Westview Dr WFD IG8... 102 A10
West View Rd RAIN RM13 *... 145 K5
Westview Ri HHNE HP2... 35 N5
West View Rd STALW/RED AL3... 9 P4
SWLY BR8... 208 G6
WARL CR6... 242 A5
Westville Rd SHB W12... 156 D1
THDIT KT7... 198 F2
West Wk EBAR EN4... 98 B2
HYS/HAR UB3... 133 H10
Westward Ho GU GU1... 249 K3
Westward Rd CHING E4... 100 E6
Westward Wy
KTN/HRWW/WS HA3... 115 K4
West Warwick Pl PIM SW1V *... 16 F6
West Wy CRAWE RH10... 284 D6
BRW CM14... 106 F4
CAR SM5... 221 N6
CROY/NA CR0... 204 D9
EDGW HA8... 96 B1
HARP AL5... 20 B1
HEST TW5... 153 P5
PEND EN3... 80 C3
PIN HA5... 113 L1
RKW/CH/CXG WD3... 112 C6
RSLP HA4... 113 J2
SHPTN TW17... 196 E6
UED N18... 99 L4
WLSDN NW10... 135 H9
WWKM BR4... 205 J6
Westway BAY/PAD W2... 9 J2
CRAWE RH10... 285 H2
CTHM CR3... 241 L8
GUW GU2... 249 K6
HORL RH6... 280 C6
RYNPK SW20... 200 D7
West Wy STMC/STPC BR5... 206 G3
Westway Cl RYNPK SW20... 200 C4
West Way Gdns CROY/NA CR0... 204 C9
Westways REDH RH1... 258 G3
HOR/WEW KT19... 220 C1
Westwell Cl STMC/STPC BR5... 202 C1
Westwell Rd
STRHM/NOR SW16... 180 F9
Westwood Ap
STRHM/NOR SW16... 180 F9
Westwick Cl HMSMTH W6... 156 C1
Westwick Gdns HMSMTH W6... 156 C1
HSLWW TW4... 153 P9
Westwick Pl GSTN WD25... 55 K10
Westwood Av HHNE HP2... 36 A2
NRWD SE19... 181 L5
WHTN TW2... 176 C1
Westwood Cl AMS HP6... 68 B7
BMLY BR1... 184 C6
ESH/CLAY KT10... 198 B10
POTB/CUF EN6... 59 K4
RSLP HA4... 112 F2
Westwood Dr AMS HP6... 68 B7
Westwood Gdns BARN SW13... 156 A5
Westwood La WELL DA16... 164 A5
Westwood Pk FSTH SE23... 181 P4
Westwood Pl SYD SE26 *... 181 P8
Westwood Rd BARN SW13... 156 A5

| | | |
|---|---|---|
| BFOR GU20 | 212 | C2 |
| COUL/CHIP CR5 | 240 | E4 |
| GDMY/SEVK IG3 | 123 | J8 |
| MEO DA13 | 189 | N8 |
| West Woodside BXLY DA5 | 185 | H4 |
| Westwood Wy SEVT TN13 | 246 | G8 |
| Wetheral Ms STAN HA7 | 94 | D3 |
| Wetherby Cl NTHLT UB5 | 134 | A4 |
| Wetherby Gdns ECT SW5 | 15 | L5 |
| Wetherby Ms ECT SW5 | 15 | H7 |
| Wetherby Pl SKENS SW7 | 15 | L5 |
| Wetherby Rd BORE WD6 | 75 | K5 |
| ENC/FH EN2 | 79 | K5 |
| Wetherby Wy CHSGTN KT9 | 219 | K6 |
| Wethered St WALTH E17 | 120 | E5 |
| Wetherell Rd HOM E9 | 140 | C5 |
| Wetherly Cl HLWE CM17 | 29 | M8 |
| Wettern Cl SAND/SEL CR2 | 223 | M6 |
| Wetton Pl EGH TW20 | 172 | C8 |
| Wexfenne Gdns | | |
| WOKS/MYFD GU22 | 233 | L2 |
| Wexford Rd BAL SW12 | 180 | A3 |
| Wexham Park La | | |
| DTCH/LGLY SL3 | 129 | P6 |
| Wexham Pl SLN SL2 | 129 | N4 |
| Wexham Rd SLN SL1 | 149 | M1 |
| Wexham St SLN SL2 | 129 | N6 |
| Wexham Woods | | |
| DTCH/LGLY SL3 | 129 | P7 |
| Wey Av CHERT KT16 | 195 | K3 |
| Weybank RPLY/SEND GU23 | 233 | P2 |
| Weybarton BF/WBF KT14 | 216 | A4 |
| Weybourne Cl HARP AL5 | 20 | C1 |
| Weybourne Pl SAND/SEL CR2 | 223 | L6 |
| Weybourne St | | |
| WAND/EARL SW18 | 179 | M5 |
| Weybridge Ct | | |
| BERM/RHTH SE16 * | 160 | A4 |
| Weybridge Pk WEY KT13 | 216 | B3 |
| Weybridge Rd | | |
| ADL/WDHM KT15 | 215 | P1 |
| THHTH CR7 | 203 | H4 |
| Weybrook Dr RGUE GU4 | 250 | C5 |
| Wey Cl ADL/WDHM KT15 | 215 | N5 |
| HOR/WEW KT19 | 219 | P1 |
| Wey Ct ADL/WDHM KT15 | 215 | N5 |
| Weydown Cl RGUW GU3 | 249 | L5 |
| WIM/MER SW19 | 179 | L4 |
| Weydown La RGUW GU3 | 249 | M5 |
| Weyhill Rd WCHPL E1 | 13 | N5 |
| Weylands Pk WEY KT13 | 216 | E3 |
| Wey La CSHM HP5 | 50 | C8 |
| Weylea Av RGUE GU4 | 250 | D7 |
| Weyland Rd BCTR RM8 | 124 | A4 |
| Wey Manor Rd | | |
| ADL/WDHM KT15 | 215 | N5 |
| Weyman Rd BKHTH/KID SE3 | 161 | P7 |
| Weymead Cl CHERT KT16 | 195 | M8 |
| Weymouth Av EA W5 | 155 | H1 |
| MLHL NW7 | 96 | B5 |
| Weymouth Cl EHAM E6 | 142 | A4 |
| Weymouth Ct BELMT SM2 * | 221 | L4 |
| Weymouth Dr CDW/CHF RM16 | 167 | J4 |
| Weymouth Ms | | |
| CAVSQ/HST W1G | 10 | E5 |
| Weymouth Rd HAYED UB4 | 132 | F5 |
| Weymouth St | | |
| CAVSQ/HST W1G | 10 | D3 |
| HHS/BOV HP3 | 35 | N10 |
| Weymouth Ter BETH E2 | 7 | L2 |
| Weymouth Vls FSBYPK N4 * | 118 | C2 |
| Weymouth Wk STAN HA7 | 94 | D3 |
| Wey Rd WEY KT13 | 196 | A10 |
| Weyside Cl BF/WBF KT14 | 216 | A4 |
| Weyside Gdns GU GU1 | 249 | N8 |
| Weyside Rd GU GU1 | 249 | N9 |
| Wey - South Pth GUW GU2 | 268 | A5 |
| Wey View Ct GU GU1 * | 267 | K1 |
| Whadcoat St FSBYPK N4 | 119 | H7 |
| Whalebone Av CHDH RM6 | 124 | A4 |
| Whalebone Gv CHDH RM6 | 124 | A4 |
| Whalebone La North | | |
| CHDH RM6 | 123 | P2 |
| CRW RM5 | 103 | P8 |
| Whalebone La South | | |
| BCTR RM8 | 124 | A5 |
| Whaley Rd SRTFD E15 * | 141 | K4 |
| Whaley Rd POTB/CUF EN6 | 59 | M9 |
| Wharfdale Cl FBAR/BDGN N11 | 98 | B7 |
| Wharfdale Rd IS N1 | 5 | H4 |
| Wharfedale HHNE HP2 | 35 | P3 |
| Wharfedale Gdns THHTH CR7 | 202 | C2 |
| Wharfedale Rd RDART DA2 | 188 | B4 |
| Wharfedale St WBPTN SW10 | 14 | C8 |
| Wharf La POP/IOD E14 | 140 | C8 |
| RKW/CH/CXG WD3 | 91 | P1 |
| RPLY/SEND GU23 | 232 | F9 |
| TWK TW1 | 176 | F4 |
| Wharf Pl BETH E2 | 7 | J10 |
| Wharf Rd BROX EN10 | 44 | E10 |
| BRW CM14 | 107 | H4 |
| CAMTN NW1 | 5 | H4 |
| GRAYS RM17 | 167 | L5 |
| GU GU1 | 249 | P10 |
| GVE DA12 | 191 | K2 |
| HHW HP1 | 35 | L8 |
| PEND EN3 | 80 | D10 |
| SRTFD E15 | 141 | J3 |
| STWL/WRAY TW19 | 173 | J8 |
| Wharf Rd South GRAYS RM17 | 167 | L5 |
| Wharfside Cl ERITH DA8 | 164 | G4 |
| Wharfside Rd POP/IOD E14 | 141 | K8 |
| Wharf St CAN/RD E16 | 141 | K7 |
| Wharf Ter PUT/ROE SW15 | 157 | H9 |
| The Wharf RDART DA2 | 166 | G10 |
| Wharf Wy KGLGY WD4 | 54 | D9 |
| Wharley Hook HLWS HLWH | 48 | A7 |
| Wharncliffe Dr STHL UB1 | 134 | E7 |
| Wharncliffe Gdns SNWD SE25 | 203 | M2 |
| Wharncliffe Rd SNWD SE25 | 203 | L2 |
| Wharton Cl WLSDN NW10 | 136 | B1 |
| Wharton Cots FSBYW WC1X * | 5 | J6 |
| Wharton Rd BMLY BR1 | 205 | N1 |
| Wharton St FSBYW WC1X * | 5 | J6 |
| Whateley Rd EDUL SE22 | 181 | N1 |
| PGE/AN SE20 | 182 | G1 |
| Whately Cl GUW GU2 | 249 | N5 |
| Whatley Av RYNPK SW20 | 200 | G3 |
| Whatman Rd FSTH SE23 | 182 | C3 |
| Whatmore Cl | | |
| STWL/WRAY TW19 | 173 | K2 |
| Wheastone Rd NKENS W10 * | 8 | A7 |
| Wheatash Rd | | |
| ADL/WDHM KT15 | 195 | N8 |
| Wheatbarn WCCE AL7 | 23 | J2 |
| The Wheatbutts WDSR SL4 | 148 | A4 |
| Wheat Cl STALE/WH AL4 | 38 | F2 |
| Wheatcroft CHESW EN7 | 62 | A4 |
| Wheatfield HAT AL10 | 40 | E1 |
| Wheatfields HLWE CM17 | 29 | N5 |
| PEND EN3 | 80 | D5 |
| Wheatfield Wy HORL RH6 | 280 | D5 |
| KUT/HW KT1 | 199 | N1 |
| Wheathampstead Rd | | |
| HARP AL5 | 20 | C1 |
| Wheathill Rd PGE/AN SE20 | 204 | A4 |
| Wheat Knoll PUR/KEN CR8 | 241 | M6 |
| Wheatlands HEST TW5 | 153 | P5 |
| Wheatlands Rd | | |
| DTCH/LGLY SL3 | 149 | N2 |
| TOOT SW17 | 180 | B6 |
| Wheatley Cl EMPK RM11 | 125 | J2 |
| HDN NW4 | 96 | D10 |
| RDART DA2 | 188 | B4 |
| SBW CM21 | 29 | M2 |
| WGCE AL7 | 23 | J4 |
| Wheatley Crs HYS/HAR UB3 | 133 | H9 |
| Wheatley Gdns ED N9 | 99 | M3 |
| Wheatley Rd ISLW TW7 | 154 | G8 |

| | | |
|---|---|---|
| WGCE AL7 | 23 | J6 |
| Wheatley's Stable WH AL4 | 39 | H4 |
| Wheatfoot Ter BMLY BR1 | 183 | L6 |
| Wheatley St CAVSQ/HST W1G | 10 | D4 |
| Wheatley Terrace Rd | | |
| ERITH DA8 | 164 | C5 |
| Wheatsheaf Cl CFSP/GDCR SL9 | 90 | B7 |
| Wheatsheaf Cl CHERT KT16 | 214 | C3 |
| NTHLT UB5 | 113 | M10 |
| Wheat Sheaf Cl POP/IOD E14 | 160 | F3 |
| Wheatsheaf Cl | | |
| WOKN/KNAP GU21 | 232 | C1 |
| RSEV TN14 | 228 | A5 |
| Wheatsheaf Hl RSEV TN14 | 264 | A7 |
| Wheatsheaf La FUL/PGN SW6 | 156 | F6 |
| STA TW18 | 173 | J10 |
| VX/NE SW8 | 158 | F6 |
| Wheatsheaf Pde WDSR SL4 * | 171 | M1 |
| Wheatsheaf Rd ROM RM1 | 124 | C4 |
| WARE SG12 | 28 | A1 |
| Wheatsheaf Ter | | |
| FUL/PGN SW6 | 157 | J6 |
| Wheatstone Cl CRAWE RH10 | 284 | C2 |
| DTCH/LGLY SL3 | 149 | M2 |
| WIM/MER SW19 | 201 | N1 |
| Wheatstone Rd ERITH DA8 | 164 | C5 |
| NKENS W10 | 8 | C8 |
| Wheeler Av OXTED RH8 | 261 | L1 |
| Wheeler Gdns IS N1 | 5 | M5 |
| Wheeler La WCHPL E1 | 13 | L1 |
| Wheeler Pl HAYES BR2 | 205 | N4 |
| Wheeler Rd CRAWE RH10 | 284 | C9 |
| Wheelers EPP CM16 | 65 | J5 |
| Wheelers Cl WAB EN9 | 45 | K8 |
| Wheelers Cross BARK IG11 | 142 | C4 |
| Wheelers Dr RSLP HA4 | 112 | D4 |
| Wheelers Orch | | |
| CFSP/GDCR SL9 | 90 | B7 |
| Wheel Farm Dr DAGE RM10 | 124 | D8 |
| Wheelock Cl ERITH DA8 | 164 | G4 |
| Wheelright Cl BUSH WD23 | 74 | A10 |
| Wheelwrights Pl | | |
| DTCH/LGLY SL3 | 150 | F6 |
| Wheelwright St HOLWY N7 | 5 | M1 |
| Whelan Wy WLGTN SM6 | 202 | F1 |
| Wheler St WCHPL E1 | 13 | L2 |
| Whellock Rd CHSWK W4 | 156 | B6 |
| Whenman Av BXLY DA5 | 186 | D5 |
| Wherwell Rd GUW GU2 | 267 | P2 |
| Whetstone Cl | | |
| TRDG/WHET N20 | 97 | J3 |
| Whetstone Pk LINN WC2A | 11 | L1 |
| Whetstone Rd BKHTH/KID SE3 | 161 | P8 |
| Whewell Rd ARCH N19 | 118 | F7 |
| Whichcote St STHWK SE1 * | 12 | A10 |
| Whichert Cl BEAC HP9 | 88 | B5 |
| Whichcote Dr DEPT SE8 | 160 | F8 |
| Whidborne St STPAN WC1H | 5 | M10 |
| Whielden Ga AMSS HP7 | 68 | C9 |
| Whielden Hts AMSS HP7 | 68 | C9 |
| Whielden La AMSS HP7 | 68 | B9 |
| Whielden St AMSS HP7 | 68 | C9 |
| Whimbrel Cl SAND/SEL CR2 * | 223 | L7 |
| Whimbrel Wy YEAD UB4 | 133 | L8 |
| Whinchat Rd THMD SE28 | 146 | B2 |
| Whinfell Cl STRHM/NOR SW16 | 180 | E8 |
| Whinfell Wy GVE DA12 | 191 | J7 |
| Whinshill Ct ASC SL5 | 192 | F6 |
| Whinyates Rd ELTH/MOCT SE9 | 144 | D9 |
| Whipley Cl RGUE GU4 | 250 | E5 |
| Whippendell Cl | | |
| STMC/STPC BR5 | 207 | L1 |
| Whippendell Rd WATW WD18 * | 7 | F9 |
| Whippendell Wy | | |
| STMC/STPC BR5 | 207 | L1 |
| Whips Cross Rd WAN E11 | 121 | K3 |
| Whiskin St CLKNW EC1R | 6 | C10 |
| Whisper Wd | | |
| RKW/CH/CXG WD3 | 71 | L7 |
| Whistler Cl CRAWE RH10 | 284 | A10 |
| Whistler Gdns EDGW HA8 | 95 | L10 |
| Whistlers Av BTSEA SW11 * | 157 | N6 |
| Whistlers Wy WBPTN SW10 * | 15 | J9 |
| Whistler St HBRY N5 | 118 | F2 |
| Whistler Wk WBPTN SW10 * | 15 | M6 |
| Whiston Rd BETH E2 | 7 | L1 |
| Whitacre Ms LBTH SE11 | 18 | A4 |
| Whitakers Vly LOU IG10 | 82 | C5 |
| Whitbread Cl TOTM N17 | 99 | N8 |
| Whitbread Rd BROCKY SE4 | 160 | D10 |
| Whitburn Rd LEW SE13 | 182 | C1 |
| Whitby Av WLSDN NW10 | 135 | N5 |
| Whitby Cl BH/WHM TN16 | 243 | N10 |
| RDART DA2 | 187 | N1 |
| Whitby Gdns CDALE/KGS NW9 | 115 | M1 |
| SUT SM1 | 201 | N9 |
| Whitby Pde RSLP HA4 * | 113 | K2 |
| Whitby Rd RSLP HA4 | 113 | K2 |
| RYLN/HDSTN HA2 | 114 | B8 |
| SL SL1 | 129 | H9 |
| SUT SM1 | 201 | N9 |
| WOOL/PLUM SE18 | 162 | C5 |
| Whitby St WCHPL E1 | 13 | L1 |
| Whitcher Cl NWCR SE14 | 160 | D5 |
| Whitcher Pl KTTN NW5 | 4 | D1 |
| Whitchurch Av EDGW HA8 | 95 | L7 |
| Whitchurch Cl EDGW HA8 | 95 | L7 |
| Whitchurch Gdns EDGW HA8 | 95 | L7 |
| Whitchurch Pde EDGW HA8 * | 95 | M7 |
| Whitchurch Rd HARH RM3 | 105 | P5 |
| NKENS W10 | 136 | C9 |
| Whitcomb St | | |
| SOHO/SHAV W1D | 11 | J7 |
| Whitcome Ms RCH/KEW TW9 | 155 | N7 |
| Whiteadder Wy | | |
| POP/IOD E14 | 160 | G3 |
| Whitear Wk SRTFD E15 | 141 | J3 |
| White Av CVW DA11 | 190 | C6 |
| Whitebarn La DAGE RM10 | 144 | B3 |
| Whitebeam Av HAYES BR2 | 206 | D1 |
| Whitebeam Cl BGR/WK TN15 | 247 | P5 |
| CHESW EN7 | 61 | M2 |
| VX/NE SW8 * | 158 | A5 |
| Whitebeam Dr REIG RH2 | 275 | L3 |
| SOCK/AV RM15 | 147 | N5 |
| Whitebeams HAT AL10 | 40 | A1 |
| LCOL/BKTW AL2 | 56 | A4 |
| White Beam Wy | | |
| KWD/TDW/WH KT20 | 238 | D2 |
| White Bear Yd CLKNW EC1R * | 6 | A12 |
| Whiteberry Rd RDKG RH5 | 272 | A10 |
| White Bridge Cl | | |
| EBED/NFELT TW14 | 174 | G2 |
| White Bushes REDH RH1 | 276 | B6 |
| Whitechapel High St | | |
| TWRH EC3N | 13 | L5 |
| Whitechapel Rd WCHPL E1 | 13 | M3 |
| White Church La WCHPL E1 | 13 | M4 |
| White City Cl SHB W12 | 136 | G10 |
| White City Rd SHB W12 | 136 | G9 |
| White Cl SL SL1 | 129 | L10 |
| White Conduit St IS N1 | 5 | N3 |
| Whitecote Rd STHL UB1 | 134 | B8 |
| White Craig Cl PIN HA5 | 93 | P4 |
| Whitecroft STAL AL1 | 38 | F5 |
| SWLY BR8 | 208 | F2 |
| Whitecroft Cl BECK BR3 | 205 | J4 |
| Whitecroft Wy BECK BR3 | 205 | J4 |
| Whitecross Pl SDTCH EC2A * | 13 | H1 |
| Whitecross St STLK EC1Y | 12 | F1 |
| Whitefield Av CRICK NW2 | 116 | F7 |
| PUR/KEN CR8 | 241 | L9 |
| Whitefield Cl PUT/ROE SW15 | 179 | H1 |
| STMC/STPC BR5 | 207 | M1 |
| Whitefields Rd CHESW EN7 | 62 | B1 |

| | | |
|---|---|---|
| CHES/WCR EN8 | 62 | B4 |
| Whitefoot La BMLY BR1 | 183 | J7 |
| Whitefoot Ter BMLY BR1 | 183 | L6 |
| Whiteford Rd SLN SL2 | 129 | K7 |
| White Friars SEV TN13 | 265 | H3 |
| Whitefriars Av | | |
| KTN/HRWW/WS HA3 | 94 | D10 |
| Whitefriars Dr | | |
| KTN/HRWW/WS HA3 | 94 | D10 |
| Whitefriars St EMB EC4Y | 12 | A4 |
| White Gdns DAGE RM10 | 144 | B1 |
| White Gate Gdns | | |
| KTN/HRWW/WS HA3 | 94 | D10 |
| White Gates HCH RM12 | 125 | K7 |
| White Gates THDIT KT7 | 198 | F7 |
| Whitegates | | |
| WOKS/MYFD GU22 | 232 | C6 |
| Whitegates Cl | | |
| RKW/CH/CXG WD3 | 72 | B8 |
| Whitegate Wy | | |
| KWD/TDW/WH KT20 | 238 | G6 |
| Whitehall La BKHH IG9 | 101 | M3 |
| EGH TW20 | 172 | C10 |
| ERITH DA8 | 164 | G8 |
| GRAYS RM17 | 167 | P4 |
| REIG RH2 | 275 | J4 |
| STWL/WRAY TW19 | 172 | C3 |
| VW GU25 | 194 | C1 |
| Whitehall Pk ARCH N19 | 118 | D6 |
| Whitehall Park Rd CHSWK W4 | 155 | N6 |
| Whitehall Pl WLGTN SM6 * | 222 | E1 |
| White Hart Av | | |
| WOOL/PLUM SE18 | 163 | J2 |
| White Hart Cl CSTG HP8 | 89 | M4 |
| SEV TN13 | 265 | K4 |
| White Hart Dr HHNE HP2 | 36 | A7 |
| White Hart La BARN SW13 | 156 | A6 |
| RGUW GU3 | 248 | F9 |
| ROMW/RG RM7 | 104 | B3 |
| WDGN N22 | 99 | H9 |
| White Hart Meadow | | |
| BEAC HP9 | 88 | D10 |
| White Hart Pde | | |
| RPLY/SEND GU23 | 233 | H9 |
| White Hart Pde SEV TN13 * | 246 | F8 |
| White Hart Rd HHNE HP2 | 36 | B7 |
| ORP BR6 | 207 | K7 |
| SL SL1 | 149 | J2 |
| WOOL/PLUM SE18 | 163 | H3 |
| White Hart Rw CHERT KT16 * | 195 | K4 |
| White Hart St LBTH SE11 | 18 | B8 |
| White Hart Ter TOTM N17 * | 99 | N8 |
| White Hart Wd SEV TN13 | 265 | K5 |
| White Hart Yd GVW DA11 | 190 | E2 |
| STHWK SE1 | 12 | G10 |
| Whitehaven CHESW EN7 * | 61 | M4 |
| SL SL1 | 129 | L9 |
| Whitehaven Cl HAYES BR2 | 204 | B2 |
| Whitehaven St STJWD NW8 | 9 | K1 |
| Whiteheads Gv CHEL SW3 | 15 | N5 |
| White Heart Av UX/CGN UB8 | 132 | D7 |
| Whiteheath Av RSLP HA4 | 112 | D5 |
| White Hedge Dr | | |
| STALW/RED AL3 | 38 | B4 |
| White Hermitage WDSR SL4 * | 171 | P1 |
| White Hern CHES/WCR EN8 | 62 | B4 |
| White Heron Ms TEDD TW11 * | 176 | F8 |
| Whitehall BERK HP4 | 34 | A4 |
| White Hl BERK HP4 | 33 | P10 |
| BFOR GU20 | 212 | A1 |
| COUL/CHIP CR5 | 239 | N9 |
| CSHM HP5 | 51 | H8 |
| DEN/HRF UB9 | 92 | B7 |
| HHW HP1 | 35 | J7 |
| SAND/SEL CR2 | 223 | L6 |
| WLYN AL6 | 22 | C1 |
| White Hill Cl CSHM HP5 | 51 | H6 |
| Whitehill La BGR/WK TN15 | 247 | H6 |
| REDH RH1 | 259 | L3 |
| RPLY/SEND GU23 | 234 | C6 |
| Whitehill Rd CDW/CHF RM16 | 190 | F6 |
| VW GU25 | 194 | B3 |
| Whitehills Rd LOU IG10 | 82 | G7 |
| Whitehorn Rd HOR/YW UB7 | 132 | A10 |
| White Horse Dr EPSOM KT18 | 219 | P10 |
| White Horse Hl CHST BR7 | 184 | D7 |
| White Horse Hl CHST BR7 | 203 | M4 |
| White Horse La | | |
| LCOL/BKTW AL2 | 57 | J2 |
| RPLY/SEND GU23 | 233 | M7 |
| WCHPL E1 | 140 | C6 |
| White Horse Rd EHAM E6 | 142 | C4 |
| WCHPL E1 | 140 | D8 |
| WDSR SL4 | 148 | C8 |
| Whitehorse Rd CROY/NA CR0 | 203 | K7 |
| THHTH CR7 | 203 | K7 |
| White Horse St MYFR/PICC W1J | 10 | F10 |
| Whitehouse Av BORE WD6 | 75 | N8 |
| White House Cl | | |
| CFSP/GDCR SL9 | 90 | A7 |
| Whitehouse Dr GU GU1 | 250 | E10 |
| White House Dr STAN HA7 | 95 | H3 |
| White House La ENC/FH EN2 | 79 | K5 |
| RGUE GU4 | 250 | G4 |
| White House Rd RSEV TN14 | 264 | D5 |
| White Ledges WEA W13 | 135 | H4 |
| Whiteledge Rd PLSTW E13 | 141 | L4 |
| Whiteley WDSR SL4 | 148 | D5 |
| Whiteley Rd NRWD SE19 | 181 | P5 |
| Whiteleys Pde | | |
| HGDN/ICK UB10 * | 132 | D6 |
| White Lilies Island WDSR SL4 | 148 | G6 |

| | | |
|---|---|---|
| PECK SE15 * | 160 | B5 |
| White Lion Hl BLKFR EC4V | 12 | D7 |
| White Lion Ms AMSS HP7 | 69 | M5 |
| White Lion Rd AMSS HP7 | 69 | M5 |
| HHS/BOV HP3 | 35 | N10 |
| White Lion Sq HAT AL10 | 40 | D3 |
| White Lion St IS N1 | 5 | N3 |
| White Lion Wk GU GU1 | 268 | A1 |
| White Lion Wy SLN SL2 | 51 | H8 |
| White Ldg NRWD SE19 | 181 | J10 |
| White Lodge Cl BELMT SM2 | 221 | N4 |
| EFNCH N2 | 117 | N4 |
| ISLW TW7 | 154 | F8 |
| SEV TN13 | 247 | J9 |
| White Lodge Gdns REDH RH1 | 276 | B8 |
| The White Ldg BAR EN5 * | 77 | H7 |
| White Lyon Ct STBT EC1A | 12 | E3 |
| White lyons Rd BRW CM14 | 107 | H4 |
| Whitemore Rd GU GU1 | 250 | A6 |
| White Oak Dr BECK BR3 | 184 | A10 |
| White Oak Gdns BFN/LL DA15 | 185 | J3 |
| Whiteoaks BNSTD SM7 | 221 | L9 |
| Whiteoaks Av GNTH/NBYPK IG2 | 123 | H4 |
| Whites Cl SWCM DA10 | 189 | G7 |
| White's Grounds STHWK SE1 * | 19 | L1 |
| Whites Grounds Est | | |
| STHWK SE1 * | 19 | K1 |
| White Shack La | | |
| RKW/CH/CXG WD3 | 72 | A3 |
| Whites La DTCH/LGLY SL3 | 149 | N8 |
| Whites Meadow BMLY BR1 * | 206 | D4 |
| White's Rw WCHPL E1 | 13 | L4 |
| White's Sq CLAP SW4 | 158 | L10 |
| Whitestile Rd BTFD TW8 | 155 | K5 |
| Whitestone La HAMP NW3 | 117 | M8 |
| Whitestone Wk HAMP NW3 * | 117 | M8 |
| White St STHL UB1 | 153 | L1 |
| White Stubbs La BROX EN10 | 43 | L4 |
| Whitethorn WGCE AL7 | 23 | K6 |
| Whitethorn Av | | |
| COUL/CHIP CR5 | 240 | B1 |
| WDR/YW UB7 | 131 | P9 |
| Whitethorn Gdns | | |
| CROY/NA CR0 | 204 | A9 |
| EMPK RM11 | 125 | K4 |
| ENC/FH EN2 | 79 | J3 |
| Whitethorn St BOW E3 | 140 | A3 |
| White Tower Wy WCHPL E1 | 140 | D7 |
| Whitewaits HLW CM20 | 29 | H10 |
| White Wy NTHLT UB5 | 134 | B1 |
| Whitewebbs La ENC/FH EN2 | 79 | M1 |
| Whitewebbs Pk ENC/FH EN2 | 79 | P1 |
| Whitewebbs Rd ENC/FH EN2 | 79 | J2 |
| Whitewebbs Wy | | |
| STMC/STPC BR5 | 207 | J1 |
| Whitewood Cots | | |
| BH/WHM TN16 | 243 | P6 |
| Whitewood Rd BERK HP4 | 34 | B3 |
| Whitfield Cl GUW GU2 | 249 | M7 |
| Whitfield Pl FITZ W1T * | 10 | G2 |
| Whitfield Rd BXLYHN DA7 | 164 | A6 |
| EHAM E6 | 141 | P2 |
| GNWCH SE10 | 161 | J2 |
| Whitfield St FITZ W1T | 11 | H5 |
| Whitford Gdns MTCM CR4 | 202 | A3 |
| Whitgift Av SAND/SEL CR2 | 223 | K2 |
| Whitgift St CROY/NA CR0 | 203 | K10 |
| LBTH SE11 | 17 | N6 |
| Whit Hern Ct CHES/WCR EN8 * | 62 | A6 |
| Whitings Rd BAR EN5 | 76 | F9 |
| Whitings Wy EHAM E6 | 142 | A7 |
| Whitland Rd CAR SM5 | 202 | A9 |
| Whitley Cl STWL/WRAY TW19 | 152 | G10 |
| Whitley Rd HOD EN11 | 44 | B3 |
| TOTM N17 | 99 | N8 |
| Whitlock Dr WIM/MER SW19 | 179 | H3 |
| Whitman Rd WCHPL E1 | 139 | L8 |
| Whitmead Cl SAND/SEL CR2 | 223 | L4 |
| Whitmoor La RGUE GU4 | 250 | C2 |
| Whitmore Av CDW/CHF RM16 | 147 | N10 |
| Whitmore Cl FBAR/BDGN N11 | 98 | C6 |
| Whitmore Gdns WLSDN NW10 | 136 | F2 |
| Whitmore Rd BECK BR3 | 204 | E3 |
| HNWL W7 | 135 | L7 |
| IS N1 | 7 | J6 |
| Whitmores Cl EPSOM KT18 * | 237 | P6 |
| Whitmore Wd HHNE HP2 | 36 | C5 |
| Whitmore Wy HORL RH6 | 259 | P5 |
| Whitnell Wy PUT/ROE SW15 * | 178 | F1 |
| Whitney Av REDBR IG4 | 122 | F2 |
| Whitney Rd LEY E10 | 120 | F5 |
| Whitney Wk SCUP DA14 | 186 | G5 |
| Whitstable Cl BECK BR3 | 184 | B10 |
| RSLP HA4 | 113 | K3 |
| Whitstable Pl CROY/NA CR0 | 223 | J2 |
| Whitstone La BECK BR3 | 204 | B4 |
| Whittaker Av RCH/KEW TW9 * | 201 | J10 |
| Whittaker Rd CHEAM SM3 | 201 | J10 |
| EHAM E6 | 141 | P2 |
| Whittaker St BGVA SW1W | 16 | C6 |
| Whittaker Wy STHWK SE1 | 159 | M3 |
| Whittell Gdns SYD SE26 | 182 | B6 |
| Whittenham Cl SLN SL2 | 129 | M10 |
| Whittingstall Rd | | |
| FUL/PGN SW6 | 157 | J7 |
| HOD EN11 | 44 | D1 |
| Whittington Av BANK EC3V | 13 | J4 |
| YEAD UB4 | 132 | G2 |
| Whittington Ms | | |
| NFNCH/WDSPK N12 | 97 | H2 |
| Whittington Rd CRAWE RH10 | 283 | P10 |
| WDGN N22 | 98 | E6 |
| Whittington Wy PIN HA5 | 113 | N3 |
| Whittlebury Cl CAR SM5 | 222 | A4 |
| Whittle Cl GSTN WD25 | 54 | G10 |
| STHL UB1 | 134 | A5 |
| WALTH E17 | 120 | B1 |
| Whittle Pkwy SL SL1 | 155 | N6 |
| Whittle Rd HEST TW5 | 153 | L6 |
| HSLWW TW4 | 154 | A1 |
| Whittlesea Rd | | |
| KTN/HRWW/WS HA3 | 94 | B10 |
| Whittlesey St STHWK SE1 * | 12 | B10 |
| Whitton Av East GFD/PVL UB6 | 114 | A10 |
| Whitton Av West NTHLT UB5 | 115 | A10 |
| Whitton Cl GFD/PVL UB6 | 134 | C1 |
| Whitton Dene HSLW TW3 | 175 | J1 |
| ISLW TW7 | 154 | G9 |
| Whitton Manor Rd ISLW TW7 | 176 | A2 |
| Whitton Rd HSLW TW3 | 176 | A1 |
| WHTN TW2 | 176 | A2 |
| Whitton Waye HSLW TW3 | 175 | H2 |
| Whitwell Rd GSTN WD25 | 73 | L1 |
| PLSTW E13 | 141 | P2 |
| Whitworth Crs PEND EN3 | 80 | C2 |
| Whitworth Rd CRAWW RH11 | 283 | N10 |
| SNWD SE25 | 203 | J1 |
| WOOL/PLUM SE18 | 162 | G4 |
| Whopshott Av | | |
| WOKN/KNAP GU21 | 231 | P2 |
| Whopshott Cl | | |
| WOKN/KNAP GU21 | 231 | N2 |

| | | |
|---|---|---|
| Whopshott Dr | | |
| WOKN/KNAP GU21 | 231 | P2 |
| Whorlton Rd PECK SE15 | 159 | P9 |
| Whybridge Cl RAIN RM13 | 148 | A1 |
| Whybrow Gdns BERK HP4 | 34 | B3 |
| Whymark Av WDGN N22 | 119 | H1 |
| Whytebeam Vw BH/WHM TN16 | 241 | N4 |
| Whytecliffe Rd North | | |
| PUR/KEN CR8 | 241 | J7 |
| Whytecliffe Rd South | | |
| PUR/KEN CR8 | 241 | J7 |
| Whytecroft HEST TW5 | 153 | L6 |
| Whyteleafe Hl CTHM CR3 | 241 | M5 |
| Whyteleafe Rd CTHM CR3 | 241 | N1 |
| Whytewille Rd FSTCT E7 | 141 | N1 |
| Wichling Cl STMC/STPC BR5 | 207 | N8 |
| Wick Av STALE/WH AL4 | 21 | J3 |
| Wickenden Rd SEV TN13 | 247 | K8 |
| Wickers Meadow | | |
| RSEV TN14 | 246 | G5 |
| Wickersley Rd BTSEA SW11 | 158 | A8 |
| Wickers Oake NRWD SE19 | 181 | P5 |
| Wicket St LBTH SE11 | 18 | B6 |
| Wicket Rd GFD/PVL UB6 | 134 | F5 |
| Wickets End MRDN SM4 * | 57 | K9 |
| The Wickets ASHF TW15 | 173 | P7 |
| The Wicket CROY/NA CR0 | 224 | F2 |
| Wickford Dr HARH RM3 | 105 | N6 |
| Wickford St WCHPL E1 | 140 | C1 |
| Wickford Wy WALTH E17 | 120 | C2 |
| Wickham Av CHEAM SM3 | 201 | G3 |
| CROY/NA CR0 | 204 | D9 |
| Wickham Cha WWKM BR4 | 204 | A9 |
| Wickham Cl DEN/HRF UB9 | 91 | N9 |
| HNWL W7 * | 135 | K7 |
| NWMAL KT3 | 200 | D3 |
| EGH TW20 | 172 | D10 |
| Wickham Ct BECK BR3 | 204 | C3 |
| Wickham Court Rd WWKM BR4 | 205 | H9 |
| Wickham Crs WWKM BR4 | 204 | A9 |
| Wickham Fld RSEV TN14 | 246 | G2 |
| Wickham Gdns BROCKY SE4 | 160 | E9 |
| Wickham La ABYW SE2 | 163 | K5 |
| EGH TW20 | 172 | D10 |
| Wickham Ms BROCKY SE4 | 160 | E9 |
| Wickham Rd BECK BR3 | 204 | C3 |
| BROCKY SE4 | 160 | E9 |
| CDW/CHF RM16 | 168 | F1 |
| CHING E4 | 101 | H8 |
| CROY/NA CR0 | 204 | D9 |
| KTN/HRWW/WS HA3 | 94 | C10 |
| Wickham St LBTH SE11 | 17 | M7 |
| WELL DA16 | 163 | K7 |
| WELL DA16 | 163 | K8 |
| Wickhams Wy HART HA3 | 211 | L5 |
| Wickham Whf WARE SG12 * | 28 | B2 |
| Wick La BOW E3 | 139 | N1 |
| EGH TW20 | 171 | L9 |
| Wickliffe Av FNCH N3 | 97 | H10 |
| Wickliffe Gdns WBLY HA9 | 115 | M7 |
| Wicklow St FSBYW WC1X | 5 | L9 |
| Wick Rd EGH TW20 | 171 | N10 |
| HOM E9 | 140 | C1 |
| TEDD TW11 | 176 | E8 |
| TRING HP23 | 32 | B1 |
| Wicks Cl LEE/GVPK SE12 | 184 | E3 |
| Wicksteed Cl BXLY DA5 | 186 | E6 |
| The Wick HERT/WAT SG14 | 25 | J3 |
| Wickwood St CMBW SE5 | 159 | J8 |
| Widbrook BRWN CM15 | 87 | H2 |
| Widbury Gdns WARE SG12 | 28 | B2 |
| Widbury Hl WARE SG12 | 28 | C2 |
| Widdenham Rd HOLWY N7 | 118 | F9 |
| Widdecombe Av | | |
| RYLN/HDSTN HA2 | 113 | P7 |
| Widdin St SRTFD E15 | 141 | K2 |
| Widecombe Cl HARH RM3 | 105 | L9 |
| Widecombe Gdns REDBR IG4 | 122 | F2 |
| Widecombe Rd | | |
| ELTH/MOT SE9 | 184 | B6 |
| Widecombe Wy EFNCH N2 | 117 | H3 |
| Widecroft Rd IVER SL0 | 131 | H4 |
| Widegate St WCHPL E1 | 13 | K3 |
| Widenham Cl PIN HA5 | 93 | G2 |
| Widewater Pl DEN/HRF UB9 * | 111 | J1 |
| Wide Wy MTCM CR4 | 202 | G1 |
| Widford Rd WARE SG12 | 28 | C1 |
| WGCE AL7 | 23 | J4 |
| Widgeon Cl CAN/RD E16 | 141 | N9 |
| Widgeon Rd ERITH DA8 | 165 | J6 |
| Widgeon Wy GSTN WD25 | 73 | M1 |
| Widley Rd MV/WKIL W9 | 2 | A2 |
| Widmore Dr HHNE HP2 | 36 | B1 |
| Widmore Lodge Rd BMLY BR1 | 205 | H4 |
| Widmore Rd BMLY BR1 | 205 | K4 |
| UX/CGN UB8 | 132 | C7 |
| Widworthy Hayes | | |
| BRWN CM15 | 87 | H3 |
| Wieland Rd NTHWD HA6 | 93 | H8 |
| Wigeon Wy YEAD UB4 | 133 | L8 |
| Wiggenhall Rd WATW WD18 | 7 | F7 |
| Wiggie La REDH RH1 | 258 | G8 |
| Wiggins La RCHPK/HAM TW10 | 177 | H5 |
| Wiggins Md CDALE/KGS NW9 | 95 | P6 |
| Wigginton Av WBLY HA9 | 135 | M2 |
| Wigginton Bottom | | |
| TRING HP23 | 32 | C1 |
| Wightman Rd | | |
| CEND/HSY/T N8 | 118 | C1 |
| Wigley Bush La BRW CM14 | 106 | D3 |
| Wigley Rd FELT TW13 | 175 | L4 |
| Wigmore Pl MHST W1U | 10 | D4 |
| Wigmore Rd CAR SM5 | 202 | A7 |
| Wigmore St MHST W1U | 10 | C4 |
| Wigram Rd WAN E11 | 122 | B1 |
| Wigram Sq WALTH E17 | 121 | H1 |
| Wigston Cl UED N18 | 98 | B5 |
| Wigston Rd PLSTW E13 | 141 | K3 |
| Wigton Gdns STAN HA7 | 96 | A6 |
| Wigton Pl LBTH SE11 | 18 | B8 |
| Wigton Rd HARH RM3 | 105 | N2 |
| WALTH E17 | 101 | H10 |
| Wigton Wy HARH RM3 | 105 | N2 |
| Wilberforce Ms CLAP SW4 | 158 | E10 |
| Wilberforce Rd | | |
| CDALE/KGS NW9 | 116 | A4 |
| FSBYPK N4 | 119 | H2 |
| WIM/MER SW19 | 178 | D3 |
| Wilberforce Wy GVE DA12 | 191 | L9 |
| WIM/MER SW19 | 178 | C3 |
| Wilbury Av BELMT SM2 | 221 | J8 |
| Wilbury Rd WOKN/KNAP GU21 | 232 | B5 |
| Wilbury Wy UED N18 | 99 | J1 |
| Wilby Ms NTGHL W11 | 8 | E10 |
| Wilcon Wy GSTN WD25 | 55 | L10 |
| Wilcot Av OXHEY WD19 | 74 | D4 |
| Wilcot Cl OXHEY WD19 | 74 | D4 |
| Wilcox Cl CHOB/PIR GU24 | 230 | G2 |
| VX/NE SW8 | 158 | F6 |
| Wilcox Gdns SHPTN TW17 | 183 | D4 |
| Wilcox Rd SUT SM1 | 221 | M1 |
| TEDD TW11 | 176 | A6 |
| VX/NE SW8 | 158 | F6 |

| | | |
|---|---|---|
| Wilder Cl RSLP HA4 | 113 | J1 |
| Wilderness Av BGR/WK TN15 | 247 | M8 |
| Wilderness Ms CLAP SW4 | 158 | C10 |
| Wilderness Rd CHST BR7 | 184 | G8 |
| GUW GU2 | 267 | L1 |
| OXTED RH8 | 261 | K6 |
| The Wilderness BERK HP4 | 33 | M5 |
| E/WMO/HCT KT8 | 198 | B5 |
| HPTN TW12 | 176 | B2 |
| Wilde Rd ERITH DA8 | 164 | C6 |
| Wilders Cl WOKN/KNAP GU21 | 231 | N7 |
| Wilderton Rd | | |
| STNW/STAM N16 | 119 | M5 |
| Wildfell Rd CAT SE6 | 182 | G3 |
| Wildfield Cl RGUW GU3 | 248 | B7 |
| Wild Goose Dr NWCR SE14 | 160 | B7 |
| Wildgreen North | | |
| DTCH/LGLY SL3 | 150 | D3 |
| Wildgreen South | | |
| DTCH/LGLY SL3 | 150 | D3 |
| Wild Hatch GLDGN NW11 | 117 | K4 |
| Wildhill Rd BRKMPK AL9 | 41 | J7 |
| Wild Oaks SEV TN13 | 247 | H5 |
| Wildoak La NTHWD HA6 | 92 | E7 |
| Wildwood Av LCOL/BKTW AL2 | 55 | N6 |
| Wildwood Cl EHSLY KT24 | 252 | G1 |
| LEE/GVPK SE12 | 183 | L3 |
| WOKS/MYFD GU22 | 233 | J1 |
| Wildwood Ct PUR/KEN CR8 | 241 | L1 |
| Wildwood Gv HAMP NW3 | 117 | M6 |
| Wildwood Ri GLDGN NW11 | 117 | L4 |
| Wildwood Rd GLDGN NW11 | 117 | L4 |
| Wildwood Ter HAMP NW3 | 117 | L6 |
| Wiley Gv FBN/LL EN2 * | 79 | L7 |
| NTHWD HA6 | 92 | B3 |
| Wilford Rd DTCH/LGLY SL3 | 150 | B3 |
| Wilfred Av RAIN RM13 | 148 | C6 |
| Wilfred Owen Cl | | |
| WIM/MER SW19 | 179 | M9 |
| Wilfred St WEY KT13 | 216 | C3 |
| WOKN/KNAP GU21 | 232 | B5 |
| Wilfrid Gdns ACT W3 | 135 | P7 |
| Wilhelmina Av COUL/CHIP CR5 | 240 | D5 |
| Wilkes Rd BTFD TW8 | 155 | K5 |
| Wilkes St WCHPL E1 | 13 | M5 |
| Wilkins Cl HYS/HAR UB3 | 152 | G4 |
| MTCM CR4 | 201 | P1 |
| Wilkin's Green La HAT AL10 | 39 | P5 |
| Wilkins Green Ter | | |
| STALE/WH AL4 * | 39 | N6 |
| Wilkins Gv CWCW AL8 | 22 | C6 |
| Wilkinson Cl CHESW EN7 | 61 | K2 |
| HGDN/ICK UB10 | 132 | C3 |
| Wilkinson Rd CAN/RD E16 | 142 | B9 |
| Wilkinson St VX/NE SW8 | 158 | C6 |
| Wilkinson Wy CHSWK W4 | 156 | A1 |
| HHS/BOV HP3 | 36 | N10 |
| Wilkin St KTTN NW5 | 4 | C1 |
| Wilkin Street Ms KTTN NW5 | 4 | E1 |
| Wilks Gdns CROY/NA CR0 | 204 | D9 |
| Wilks Pl IS N1 | 7 | K8 |
| Willan Rd TOTM N17 | 99 | L10 |
| Willan Wall CAN/RD E16 | 141 | L8 |
| Willard St VX/NE SW8 | 158 | C9 |
| Willats Cl CHERT KT16 * | 195 | J6 |
| Willcocks Cl CHSGTN KT9 | 219 | K10 |
| Willcott Rd ACT W3 | 135 | N10 |
| Will Crooks Gdns | | |
| ELTH/MOT SE9 | 162 | A10 |
| Willenhall Rd WLSDN NW10 | 135 | N4 |
| Willenhall Av BAR EN5 | 77 | M10 |
| Willenhall Dr HYS/HAR UB3 | 132 | F9 |
| Willenhall Rd | | |
| WOOL/PLUM SE18 | 162 | G4 |
| Willersley Av BFN/LL DA15 | 185 | J4 |
| ORP BR6 | 206 | G10 |
| Willersley Cl BFN/LL DA15 | 185 | J4 |
| Willesden La KIL/WHAMP NW6 | 2 | B1 |
| Willes Rd KTTN NW5 | 4 | E1 |
| Willett Cl NTHLT UB5 | 133 | K1 |
| STMC/STPC BR5 | 207 | H6 |
| Willett Rd THHTH CR7 | 203 | H3 |
| Willetts La DEN/HRF UB9 | 111 | J4 |
| Willett Wy STMC/STPC BR5 | 206 | G5 |
| Willey Broom La CTHM CR3 | 259 | H1 |
| Willey Farm La CTHM CR3 | 259 | K2 |
| Willey La CTHM CR3 | 259 | L1 |
| William Ash Cl DAGW RM9 | 143 | L1 |
| William Barefoot Dr | | |
| ELTH/MOT SE9 | 184 | D5 |
| ELTH/MOT SE9 | 184 | D7 |
| William Booth Rd | | |
| PGE/AN SE20 | 202 | E1 |
| William Carey Wy HRW HA1 | 114 | D4 |
| William Cl CRW RM5 | 104 | D1 |
| EFNCH N2 | 97 | N10 |
| LEW SE13 | 161 | H9 |
| NWDGN UB2 | 154 | B1 |
| William Covell Cl | | |
| ENC/FH EN2 | 78 | G4 |
| William Dr STAN HA7 | 94 | F1 |
| William Ellis Cl WDSR SL4 | 171 | M1 |
| William Ellis Wy | | |
| BERM/RHTH SE16 * | 19 | P4 |
| William Evans Rd | | |
| HOR/WEW KT19 | 219 | M7 |
| William Evelyn Ct RDKG RH5 * | 271 | N5 |
| William Foster La WELL DA16 | 163 | K3 |
| William Gdns HORL RH6 | 281 | H4 |
| PUT/ROE SW15 | 178 | E2 |
| William Guy Gdns BOW E3 | 140 | C5 |
| William Hartley Yd | | |
| DTCH/LGLY SL3 | 129 | N6 |
| William Hunter Wy BRW CM14 | 107 | H3 |
| William Margrie Cl | | |
| PECK SE15 * | 159 | P8 |
| William Morley Cl EHAM E6 | 142 | A3 |
| William Morris Cl WALTH E17 | 120 | C1 |
| William Morris Wy | | |
| FUL/PGN SW6 | 157 | M9 |
| Wilmount Ct CSHM HP5 * | 50 | C4 |
| William Pl BOW E3 | 139 | P1 |
| William Petty Wy | | |
| STMC/STPC BR5 | 207 | M8 |
| William Rd CAMTN NW1 | 4 | E10 |
| CTHM CR3 | 241 | L8 |
| SUT SM1 | 221 | M2 |
| WIM/MER SW19 | 178 | B3 |
| Williams Av WALTH E17 | 101 | H10 |
| Williams Blds WCHPL E1 * | 140 | D5 |
| Williams Cl CEND/HSY/T N8 * | 118 | B1 |
| FUL/PGN SW6 | 157 | H6 |
| Williamson Cl GNWCH SE10 | 161 | L1 |
| Williamson Rd FSBYPK N4 | 119 | J4 |
| Williamson St HOLWY N7 | 118 | D1 |
| Williamson Wy MLHL NW7 | 97 | H1 |
| RKW/CH/CXG WD3 | 91 | K2 |
| Williams Sq BERM/RHTH SE16 | 140 | D10 |
| Williams Ter CROY/NA CR0 | 223 | H5 |
| Williams St BARK IG11 | 142 | E2 |
| BERK HP4 | 34 | A5 |
| BUSH WD23 | 75 | C1 |
| CAR SM5 | 222 | A10 |
| GRAYS RM17 | 167 | N5 |
| GVE DA12 | 191 | K8 |
| KTBR SW1X | 16 | B2 |
| LEY E10 | 120 | E7 |
| TOTM N17 | 99 | H6 |
| WDSR SL4 | 149 | G1 |
| Williams Wy CRAWE RH10 | 284 | C7 |

| Street | Page | Grid |
|---|---|---|
| RAD WD7 | 74 | G1 |
| RDART DA2 | 186 | E5 |
| Willfield Wy GLDGN NW11 | 117 | G10 |
| Willingale Ct EPP CM16 | 83 | H3 |
| Willingale Rd LOU IG10 | 42 | F7 |
| Willingdon Rd WDGN N22 | 99 | J10 |
| Willinghall Cl WAB EN9 | 63 | J8 |
| Willingham Cl KTTN NW5 | 118 | D10 |
| Willingham Ter KTTN NW5 | 118 | D10 |
| Willis Av BELMT SM2 | 221 | P3 |
| Willis Cl EPSOM KT18 | 219 | N10 |
| Willis Rd CROY/NA CRO | 203 | K4 |
| ERITH DA8 | 168 | D3 |
| STRTFD E15 | 141 | L8 |
| Willmore End WIM/MER SW19 | 201 | L2 |
| Willoners SLN SL2 | 128 | F2 |
| Willoughby Av CROY/NA CRO | 222 | G1 |
| Willoughby Cl BROX EN10 | 44 | D7 |
| Willoughby Gv TOTM N17 | 100 | A8 |
| Willoughby La TOTM N17 | 100 | A8 |
| Willoughby Ms TOTM N17 | 100 | A8 |
| Willoughby Park Rd TOTM N17 | 100 | A8 |
| Willoughby Rd CEND/HSY/T N8 | 119 | H1 |
| DTCH/LGLY SL3 | 150 | H1 |
| HAMP NW3 | 117 | N9 |
| KUTN/CMB KT2 | 199 | L1 |
| TWK TW1 | 117 | N9 |
| Willoughby Wy CHARL SE7 | 161 | N3 |
| Willow Av BARN SW13 | 156 | C8 |
| BFN/LL DA15 | 148 | B5 |
| DEN/HRF UB9 | 131 | M1 |
| SWLY BR8 | 208 | G4 |
| WDR/YW UB7 | 132 | A9 |
| Willow Bank RCHPK/HAM TW10 | 176 | C6 |
| WOKS/MYFD GU22 | 232 | B8 |
| Willowbank Gdns KWD/TDW/WH KT20 | 238 | E8 |
| Willow Brean RDR RH6 | 279 | P5 |
| Willow Bridge Rd IS N1 | 6 | E2 |
| Willowbrook HPTN TW12 | 176 | A8 |
| WDSR SL4 | 136 | A4 |
| Willowbrook Est PECK SE15 * | 159 | N6 |
| Willowbrook Rd NWDGN UB2 | 153 | N3 |
| PECK SE15 | 19 | M10 |
| STWL/WRAY TW19 | 173 | P4 |
| Willow Ct LCOL/BKTW AL2 | 57 | J4 |
| The Willow Centre MTCM CR4 | 202 | A5 |
| Willow Cha CSHM HP5 | 50 | F4 |
| Willow Cl ADL/WDHM KT15 | 255 | J4 |
| BORE WD6 | 102 | A4 |
| BRWN CM15 | 86 | B3 |
| BTFD TW8 | 155 | H5 |
| BXLY DA5 | 186 | A2 |
| CAT SE6 | 183 | L4 |
| CFSP/GDCR SL9 | 90 | B10 |
| CHERT KT16 | 195 | H9 |
| CHESW EN7 | 61 | M2 |
| CRAWW RH10 | 283 | P5 |
| DTCH/LGLY SL3 | 150 | C5 |
| HAYES BR2 | 206 | C5 |
| HCH RM12 | 125 | J8 |
| RBRW/HUT CM13 | 87 | N10 |
| STMC/STPC BR5 | 207 | L6 |
| Willow Cnr HORL RH6 * | 279 | J7 |
| Willow Ct HORL RH6 * | 280 | C1 |
| STAN HA7 * | 95 | J8 |
| Willowcourt Av KTN/HRWW/WS HA3 | 114 | C3 |
| Willow Crs STAL AL1 | 39 | H6 |
| Willow Crs East DEN/HRF UB9 | 111 | M10 |
| Willow Crs West DEN/HRF UB9 | 111 | M10 |
| Willow Dene BUSH WD23 | 94 | D1 |
| PIN HA5 | 93 | L10 |
| Willowdene BRWN CM15 | 86 | B9 |
| CHES/WCR EN8 | 62 | D3 |
| HGT N6 * | 118 | A5 |
| Willowdene Cl WHTN TW2 | 176 | A5 |
| Willowdene Ct BRW CM14 | 107 | H5 |
| Willow Dr BAR EN5 | 77 | H8 |
| Willow Edge KGLGY WD4 * | 46 | B10 |
| Willow End NTHWD HA6 | 93 | H7 |
| SURB KT6 | 199 | K8 |
| TRDG/WHET N20 | 97 | K3 |
| Willowfield HLWS CM18 | 46 | G2 |
| Willowfields Cl WOOL/PLUM SE18 | 163 | N4 |
| Willow Gdns HSLW TW3 * | 153 | P7 |
| Willow Gn CHOB/PIR GU24 | 273 | P3 |
| CHST BR7 | 184 | D9 |
| RSLP HA4 | 112 | G7 |
| Willow Gv CHST BR7 | 184 | B3 |
| RSLP HA4 | 113 | J8 |
| WOOL/PLUM SE18 | 162 | C5 |
| Willowhayne Dr WOT/HER KT12 * | 187 | J7 |
| Willowhayne Gdns WPK KT4 * | 220 | G1 |
| Willow La AMSS HP7 | 69 | L7 |
| GU GU1 | 250 | D9 |
| MTCM CR4 | 202 | A5 |
| WATW WD18 | 73 | H9 |
| WOOL/PLUM SE18 | 162 | C5 |
| Willowmead CHIG IG7 * | 103 | K4 |
| Willowmead Cl EA W5 * | 135 | N1 |
| WOKN/KNAP GU21 | 232 | A2 |
| Willowmere ESH/CLAY KT10 | 218 | A1 |
| Willow Mt CROY/NA CRO * | 223 | N1 |
| Willow Pk RSEV TN14 | 246 | G3 |
| Willow Rd CHING E4 | 101 | P1 |
| WDSR SL4 | 149 | H5 |
| WEST SW1P | 8 | B9 |
| Willow Rdg CRAWE RH10 | 285 | P10 |
| Willow Rd CHDH RM6 | 123 | P4 |
| DTCH/LGLY SL3 | 151 | H8 |
| EA W5 | 155 | K1 |
| EN EN1 | 79 | M6 |
| ERITH DA8 | 165 | H7 |
| GODL GU7 | 267 | L9 |
| HAMP NW3 | 117 | N9 |
| NWMAL KT3 | 199 | P4 |
| REDH RH1 | 275 | N9 |
| WLGTN SM6 | 222 | C6 |
| Willows Av MRDN SM4 | 201 | L5 |
| Willows Cl PIN HA5 | 95 | H6 |
| Willowside LCOL/BKTW AL2 | 57 | K3 |
| Willows Pth EPSOM KT18 | 233 | N6 |
| Willow Ter WLSDN NW10 * | 136 | C4 |
| The Willows AMS HP6 | 68 | C1 |
| BECK BR3 * | 204 | A1 |
| BF/WBF KT14 | 215 | P9 |
| BORE WD6 * | 77 | M5 |
| EBAR EN4 | 77 | H10 |
| ESH/CLAY KT10 | 218 | A1 |
| GRAYS RM17 | 168 | A5 |
| LTWR GU18 * | 263 | B7 |
| OXHEY WD19 | 93 | J1 |
| RGUE GU4 * | 250 | G8 |
| RGUW GU3 * | 249 | K3 |
| RKW/CH/CXG WD3 | 89 | L8 |
| STAL AL1 | 38 | B9 |
| WARE SG12 * | 26 | D1 |
| WEY KT13 * | 213 | B10 |
| Willow St CHING E4 | 101 | N1 |
| ROMW/RG RM7 | 105 | J2 |
| SDTCH EC2A | 13 | L4 |
| Willow Tree Cl NTHLT UB5 | 133 | N3 |
| WAND/EARL SW18 | 179 | L4 |
| Willow Tree La YEAD UB4 | 133 | L6 |
| YEAD UB4 | 133 | K6 |
| Willowtree Cl HGDN/ICK UB10 | 112 | D8 |
| Willow Tree La YEAD UB4 | 133 | K6 |
| Willow Tree Rd YEAD UB4 | 133 | L7 |
| Willow Tree Wk BMLY BR1 | 184 | B5 |
| Willowtree Wy THHTH CR7 | 203 | J5 |
| Willow V CHST BR7 | 184 | D9 |
| LHD/OX KT22 | 236 | A9 |
| SHB W12 | 136 | D10 |
| Willow Vw WARE SG12 * | 26 | D5 |
| WIM/MER SW19 | 201 | N1 |
| Willow Wk CHEAM SM3 | 201 | J10 |
| CHERT KT16 | 195 | L7 |
| DART DA1 * | 187 | M1 |
| ECH TW20 * | 173 | J8 |
| KWD/TDW/WH KT20 | 255 | N6 |
| ORP BR6 | 206 | F10 |
| REDH RH1 | 276 | C2 |
| SEVS/STOTM N15 | 119 | L4 |
| SHGR GU5 | 270 | B5 |
| STHWK SE1 | 19 | K5 |
| UPMR RM14 | 126 | D6 |
| WALTH E17 | 120 | D3 |
| WCHMH N21 | 78 | G10 |
| Willow Wy ALP/SUD HA0 * | 114 | F8 |
| BF/WBF KT14 | 215 | M7 |
| FNCH N3 | 97 | L8 |
| GDST RH9 | 260 | H10 |
| GU GU1 * | 249 | N6 |
| HARH RM3 | 106 | A7 |
| HAT AL10 | 40 | C7 |
| HHW HP1 | 35 | L4 |
| HOR/WEW KT19 | 220 | A3 |
| LCOL/BKTW AL2 | 55 | P3 |
| NTGHL W11 | 136 | G9 |
| POTB/CUF EN6 | 59 | L9 |
| RAD WD7 | 74 | D2 |
| SUN TW16 | 197 | H4 |
| SYD SE26 | 182 | A6 |
| WHTN TW2 | 176 | A5 |
| WOKS/MYFD GU22 | 232 | B6 |
| Willow Wood Cl SL SL1 | 128 | A4 |
| Willow Wood Cl SNWD SE25 | 203 | M6 |
| Willow Wren Whf NWDGN UB2 * | 153 | L7 |
| Will Rd KTTN NW5 | 4 | E1 |
| Willrose Crs ABYW SE2 | 163 | L4 |
| Wills Crs HSLW TW3 | 176 | A2 |
| Wills Gv MLHL NW7 | 96 | D6 |
| Willson Rd ECH TW20 | 171 | N8 |
| Willman Gv HACK E8 * | 7 | P3 |
| Wilmar Cl UX/CGN UB8 | 131 | N2 |
| YEAD UB4 | 132 | E6 |
| Wilmar Wy BGR/WK TN15 | 247 | N6 |
| Wilmer Cl KUTN/CMB KT2 | 177 | L8 |
| Wilmer Crs KUTN/CMB KT2 | 177 | L8 |
| Wilmer Gdns IS N1 | 7 | J6 |
| Wilmerhatch La EPSOM KT18 | 237 | N3 |
| Wilmer Lea Cl SRTFD E15 | 141 | H2 |
| Wilmer Pl STNW/STAM N16 | 119 | N7 |
| Wilmer Wy FBAR/BDGN N11 | 98 | E6 |
| ORP BR6 | 207 | N8 |
| Wilmington Av CHSWK W4 | 156 | A6 |
| ORP BR6 | 207 | N8 |
| Wilmington Gdns BARK IG11 | 142 | C2 |
| Wilmington Sq FSBYW WC1X | 6 | A10 |
| Wilmington St FSBYW WC1X | 6 | A10 |
| Wilmot Cl PECK SE15 * | 159 | H6 |
| Wilmot Cots RBRW/HUT CM13 | 239 | L1 |
| Wilmot Gn RBRW/HUT CM13 | 107 | H7 |
| Wilmot Pl CAMTN NW1 * | 4 | G1 |
| HNWL W7 | 134 | D10 |
| Wilmot Rd CAR SM5 | 222 | A2 |
| LEY E10 | 120 | G7 |
| PUR/KEN CR8 | 223 | H8 |
| SL SL1 | 148 | A5 |
| TOTM N17 | 119 | J1 |
| Wilmots Cl REIG RH2 | 257 | M9 |
| Wilmot's La HORL RH6 | 281 | M3 |
| REDH RH1 | 277 | L10 |
| Wilmot St BETH E2 | 140 | A6 |
| Wilmot Wy BNSTD SM7 | 221 | K10 |
| Wimbledon Hill Rd WIM/MER SW19 | 179 | H9 |
| Wimbledon Park Rd WIM/MER SW19 | 179 | H6 |
| Wimbledon Park Side PUT/ROE SW15 | 178 | E4 |
| Wimbolt St BETH E2 | 7 | N9 |
| Wimborne Av NWDGN UB2 | 153 | P5 |
| REDH RH1 | 276 | A5 |
| STMC/STPC BR5 | 207 | J3 |
| YEAD UB4 | 133 | J8 |
| Wimborne Cl BKHH IG9 | 103 | P5 |
| EW KT17 | 220 | B9 |
| LEE/GVPK SE12 | 165 | H4 |
| SEVK CM21 | 29 | N1 |
| WPK KT4 * | 200 | F8 |
| Wimborne Dr EDGW HA8 | 115 | M1 |
| PIN HA5 | 113 | L5 |
| Wimborne Gdns WEA W13 | 134 | G8 |
| Wimborne Gv WAT WD17 | 72 | G3 |
| Wimborne Rd ED N9 | 99 | J3 |
| TOTM N17 | 99 | M10 |
| Wimborne Wy BECK BR3 | 204 | C3 |
| Wimbourne Ct IS N1 | 6 | F1 |
| Wimbourne St IS N1 | 6 | F1 |
| Wimpole Cl HAYES BR2 | 205 | P4 |
| KUT/HW KT1 | 199 | L2 |
| Wimpole Ms CAVSQ/HST W1G | 10 | E3 |
| Wimpole Rd WDR/YW UB7 | 131 | N10 |
| Wimpole St CAVSQ/HST W1G | 10 | E4 |
| Wimshurst Cl CROY/NA CRO | 202 | F8 |
| Winans Wk BRXN/ST SW9 | 159 | H8 |
| Wincanton Crs NTHLT UB5 | 113 | P10 |
| Wincanton Gdns BARK/HLT IG6 | 122 | C1 |
| Wincanton Rd HARH RM3 | 105 | L4 |
| WAND/EARL SW18 | 179 | J3 |
| Winchcomb Gdns ELTH/MOT SE9 | 146 | A9 |
| Winchcombe Rd CAR SM5 | 201 | N9 |
| Winchdells HHS/BOV HP3 | 36 | A9 |
| Winchelsea Av BXLYHN DA7 | 164 | A6 |
| Winchelsea Cl PUT/ROE SW15 | 178 | C1 |
| Winchelsea Rd FSTGT E7 | 121 | M9 |
| TOTM N17 | 119 | M1 |
| WLSDN NW10 | 136 | A3 |
| Winchendon Rd FUL/PGN SW6 | 157 | J6 |
| TEDD TW11 | 176 | C7 |
| Winchester Av CDALE/KGS NW9 | 115 | L1 |
| HEST TW5 | 153 | N5 |
| KIL/WHAMP NW6 | 2 | B5 |
| UPMR RM14 | 125 | P7 |
| Winchester Crs GVE DA12 | 190 | E6 |
| Winchester Dr PIN HA5 | 113 | L3 |
| Winchester Ms WPK KT4 * | 201 | J1 |
| Winchester Pk HAYES BR2 | 205 | J5 |
| Winchester Pl HACK E8 * | 7 | P1 |
| HGT N6 | 118 | A6 |
| Winchester Rd BXLYHN DA7 | 147 | J5 |
| CHING E4 | 101 | N8 |
| ED N9 | 99 | N2 |
| FELT TW13 | 175 | N6 |
| HAMP NW3 | 3 | M1 |
| HAYES BR2 | 205 | J5 |
| HGT N6 | 118 | A6 |
| IL IG1 | 122 | C8 |
| KTN/HRWW/WS HA3 | 115 | K2 |
| ORP BR6 | 227 | N1 |
| TWK TW1 | 176 | C7 |
| WOT/HER KT12 | 197 | J6 |
| Winchester Sq STHWK SE1 | 12 | G9 |
| Winchester St ACT W3 | 135 | P10 |
| PIM SW1V | 16 | F7 |
| Winchester Wk STHWK SE1 | 12 | G9 |
| Winchet Wk CROY/NA CRO | 72 | C9 |
| Winchfield Cl KTN/HRWW/WS HA3 | 115 | H4 |
| Winchfield Rd SYD SE26 | 182 | D8 |
| Winchfield Wy RKW/CH/CXG WD3 | 91 | M1 |
| Winchilsea Crs E/WMO/HCT KT8 | 198 | B2 |
| Winchmore Hill Rd STHGT/OAK N14 | 98 | E2 |
| Winchmore Vls WCHMH N21 * | 98 | C1 |
| Winchstone Cl SHPTN TW17 | 196 | A4 |
| Winch Vw EPP CM16 | 65 | L5 |
| Winckley Cl KTN/HRWW/WS HA3 | 115 | K2 |
| Wincott St LBTH SE11 | 18 | D6 |
| Wincrofts Dr ELTH/MOT SE9 | 162 | G4 |
| Windall Cl NRWD SE19 | 203 | P1 |
| Windborough Rd CAR SM5 | 222 | B4 |
| Windermere Av FNCH N3 | 97 | K10 |
| HCH RM12 | 125 | H10 |
| KIL/WHAMP NW6 | 2 | B6 |
| RSLP HA4 | 113 | K5 |
| STAL AL1 | 38 | C10 |
| WBLY HA9 | 115 | H6 |
| WIM/MER SW19 | 201 | L3 |
| Windermere Gdns REDBR IG4 | 121 | P3 |
| Windermere Gv WBLY HA9 * | 114 | G5 |
| Windermere Hall EDGW HA8 * | 95 | L6 |
| Windermere Rd ARCH N19 * | 118 | C1 |
| BXLYHN DA7 | 164 | B1 |
| COUL/CHIP CR5 | 240 | F1 |
| CROY/NA CRO | 203 | N8 |
| EA W5 | 155 | H2 |
| EMPK RM11 | 125 | K5 |
| MUSWH N10 | 98 | B10 |
| PUT/ROE SW15 | 177 | P9 |
| STHL UB1 | 133 | J8 |
| STRHM/NOR SW16 | 202 | D1 |
| Windermere Wy REIG RH2 | 257 | N5 |
| SL SL1 | 128 | B3 |
| WDR/YW UB7 | 131 | P5 |
| Winders Rd BTSEA SW11 | 157 | J8 |
| Windfield Cl SYD SE26 | 182 | D7 |
| UPMR RM14 | 125 | P7 |
| WAB EN9 | 63 | K10 |
| WDSR SL4 | 148 | B8 |
| Windmill Dr CLAP SW4 * | 179 | K2 |
| CRICK NW2 | 82 | B7 |
| KES BR2 | 216 | A3 |
| LHD/OX KT22 | 236 | A9 |
| REIG RH2 | 257 | N8 |
| RKW/CH/CXG WD3 | 72 | A10 |
| Windmill End EW KT17 | 220 | B10 |
| Windmill Fld BFOR GU20 | 212 | C3 |
| WARE SG12 | 26 | C3 |
| Windmill Flds ENC/FH EN2 | 79 | H6 |
| Windmill Gdns ENC/FH EN2 | 79 | J7 |
| Windmill Gv CROY/NA CRO | 203 | J7 |
| Windmill HI AMSS HP7 | 51 | J7 |
| HAMP NW3 * | 117 | M8 |
| KGLGY WD4 | 53 | J8 |
| RSLP HA4 | 112 | G5 |
| Windmill La BAR EN5 | 76 | C10 |
| BUSH WD23 | 94 | D2 |
| CHES/WCR EN8 | 62 | D6 |
| EW KT17 | 220 | C7 |
| GFD/PVL UB6 | 134 | A2 |
| IL IG1 | 122 | E10 |
| SCUP DA14 | 185 | M8 |
| SRTFD E15 | 141 | J1 |
| SURB KT6 | 198 | D7 |
| Windmill Ms CHSWK W4 * | 156 | B3 |
| Windmill Pas CHSWK W4 * | 156 | B3 |
| Windmill Ri KUTN/CMB KT2 | 177 | L9 |
| Windmill Rd BRXS/STRHM SW2 | 180 | F2 |
| BTFD TW8 | 155 | N6 |
| CHSWK W4 | 156 | B3 |
| CROY/NA CRO | 203 | K7 |
| DTCH/LGLY SL3 | 110 | A10 |
| ELTH/MOT SE9 | 146 | G7 |
| HNWL W7 | 135 | K5 |
| HPTN TW12 | 176 | A8 |
| MTCM CR4 | 202 | D5 |
| RSEV TN14 | 265 | J9 |
| SL SL1 | 129 | J10 |
| SUN TW16 | 196 | F5 |
| UED N9 | 99 | L5 |
| WAND/EARL SW18 | 179 | N2 |
| WIM/MER SW19 | 178 | E8 |
| Windmill Rd West SUN TW16 | 196 | F6 |
| Windmill Rw LBTH SE11 | 18 | A8 |
| Windmill Shott EN EN1 * | 79 | P5 |
| Windmill St BUSH WD23 | 94 | E2 |
| FITZ W1T | 11 | J4 |
| GVE DA12 | 190 | E3 |
| Windmill Ter SHPTN TW17 * | 196 | E7 |
| Windmill Wk STHWK SE1 * | 12 | B2 |
| Windmore Av CDALE/KGS NW9 | 96 | C9 |
| Windmore Cl ALP/SUD HA0 | 114 | A4 |
| Windover Av CDALE/KGS NW9 | 115 | K3 |
| Windridge Cl STALW/WH AL4 | 39 | H2 |
| Windrose Cl BERM/RHTH SE16 | 160 | C1 |
| Windrush NWMAL KT3 | 183 | N5 |
| Windrush Av DTCH/LGLY SL3 | 150 | C2 |
| Windrush Cl BTSEA SW11 * | 157 | P4 |
| CHSWK W4 * | 155 | P6 |
| HACK E8 | 8 | P4 |
| UX/CGN UB8 | 131 | L6 |
| Windrush La FSTH SE23 | 182 | A4 |
| Windrush Rd WLSDN NW10 | 136 | F2 |
| Windrushes CTHM CR3 | 259 | P7 |
| Windrush Sq BRXS/STRHM SW2 * | 160 | A9 |
| Windsock Wy HTHAIR TW6 | 151 | L8 |
| Windsor Av CDW/CHF RM16 | 167 | N1 |
| CHEAM SM3 | 201 | H10 |
| E/WMO/HCT KT8 | 197 | P5 |
| EDGW HA8 | 96 | C5 |
| HGDN/ICK UB10 | 132 | C2 |
| NWMAL KT3 | 199 | P5 |
| SUT SM1 | 201 | J10 |
| UX/CGN UB8 | 113 | J10 |
| WALTH E17 | 100 | D10 |
| WIM/MER SW19 | 201 | N1 |
| Windsor Br WDSR SL4 | 149 | J6 |
| Windsor Cl CHESW EN7 | 61 | P6 |
| CHST BR7 | 184 | B4 |
| FNCH N3 | 97 | H1 |
| GUW GU2 | 267 | J3 |
| HHNE HP2 | 35 | P8 |
| HHS/BOV HP3 | 52 | D4 |
| NTHWD HA6 | 113 | J6 |
| RYLN/HDSTN HA2 | 113 | P9 |
| SL SL1 | 128 | B8 |
| WNWD SE27 | 181 | H1 |
| Windsor Ct AMS HP6 * | 68 | D5 |
| NTHLT UB5 * | 113 | N10 |
| PIN HA5 * | 113 | L1 |
| STHGT/OAK N14 * | 98 | D1 |
| Windsor Court Rd CHOB/PIR GU24 | 213 | K5 |
| PLMGR N13 | 98 | G1 |
| Windsor Crs RYLN/HDSTN HA2 | 113 | P10 |
| WBLY HA9 | 115 | H4 |
| Windsor Dr ASHF TW15 | 173 | H9 |
| BAR EN5 | 78 | A10 |
| DART DA1 | 187 | L2 |
| HERT/WAT SG14 | 24 | A4 |
| ORP BR6 | 227 | K3 |
| Windsor End BEAC HP9 | 108 | E1 |
| Windsor Gdns CROY/NA CRO | 202 | G1 |
| HYS/HAR UB3 | 152 | E2 |
| MV/WKIL W9 | 8 | E2 |
| Windsor Great Pk ASC SL5 * | 210 | E10 |
| Windsor La SL SL1 | 128 | B8 |
| Windsor Ms CAT SE6 | 183 | M1 |
| Windsor Park Rd HYS/HAR UB3 | 152 | C1 |
| Windsor Pl CHERT KT16 * | 195 | K6 |
| ERITH DA8 * | 148 | C9 |
| WDR/YW UB7 * | 132 | D1 |
| Windsor Rd ASC SL5 | 170 | A10 |
| BAR EN5 | 76 | C10 |
| BCTR RM8 | 123 | P7 |
| BXLYHS DA6 | 86 | P10 |
| CFSP/GDCR SL9 | 109 | P4 |
| CHING E4 | 100 | C4 |
| CHOB/PIR GU24 | 213 | K5 |
| CRICK NW2 | 100 | D4 |
| CSHM HP5 | 50 | C4 |
| DTCH/LGLY SL3 | 149 | K4 |
| EA W5 | 135 | K5 |
| EBAR EN4 | 77 | P4 |
| EMPK RM11 | 125 | L4 |
| FSTGT E7 | 121 | K1 |
| FSTH SE23 | 182 | B6 |
| GVE DA12 | 190 | E7 |
| HOLWY N7 | 118 | F10 |
| HSLWW TW4 | 153 | J8 |
| IL IG1 | 122 | C9 |
| KTN/HRWW/WS HA3 | 94 | B9 |
| KUTN/CMB KT2 | 177 | K7 |
| LEY E10 | 120 | G7 |
| NWDGN UB2 | 153 | J6 |
| PEND EN3 | 80 | E3 |
| RCH/KEW TW9 | 155 | N5 |
| RDART DA2 | 188 | F3 |
| SL SL1 | 149 | K2 |
| STWL/WRAY TW19 | 173 | N5 |
| SUN TW16 | 176 | F7 |
| TEDD TW11 | 175 | N6 |
| TOTM N17 | 100 | D5 |
| WAN E11 | 121 | H4 |
| WATN WD24 | 73 | J5 |
| WDGN N22 | 97 | P9 |
| WDSR SL4 | 148 | B8 |
| WDSR SL4 | 170 | B1 |
| WPK KT4 | 200 | E9 |
| The Windsors BKHH IG9 | 103 | L2 |
| Windsor St CHERT KT16 | 195 | K6 |
| IS N1 | 6 | D1 |
| UX/CGN UB8 | 131 | L3 |
| Windsor Ter IS N1 | 7 | H7 |
| Windsor Wk CMBW SE5 | 159 | H7 |
| WEY KT13 | 213 | K4 |
| Windsor Wy RYLN/HDSTN HA2 | 113 | N3 |
| RKW/CH/CXG WD3 | 91 | K1 |
| WKENS W14 | 19 | H1 |
| WOKS/MYFD GU22 | 232 | G7 |
| Windsor Wd WAB EN9 * | 63 | K9 |
| Windspoint Dr PECK SE15 | 160 | A5 |
| Windstock Cl BERM/RHTH SE16 | 160 | E2 |
| Windus Rd STNW/STAM N16 | 119 | N5 |
| Windward Cl PEND EN3 | 80 | C1 |
| Windycroft Cl PUR/KEN CR8 | 222 | E9 |
| Windy HI RBRW/HUT CM13 | 107 | P2 |
| Windy Rdg BMLY BR1 | 184 | D5 |
| Windy Ridge Cl WIM/MER SW19 | 178 | G8 |
| Wine Cl WAP E1W | 140 | G9 |
| Wine Office Ct FLST/FETLN EC4A | 12 | B5 |
| Winern Glebe BF/WBF KT14 | 215 | N3 |
| Winery La KUT/HW KT1 | 199 | L3 |
| Winey Cl CHSGTN KT9 | 219 | H4 |
| Winford Dr BROX EN10 | 44 | E8 |
| Winforton St GNWCH SE10 | 161 | H7 |
| Winfrith Rd WAND/EARL SW18 | 179 | M3 |
| Wingate Crs CROY/NA CRO | 202 | F6 |
| Wingate Rd HMSMTH W6 | 156 | F6 |
| IL IG1 | 122 | C10 |
| Wingate Wy STAL AL1 | 38 | F7 |
| Wingfield GRAYS RM17 | 167 | L6 |
| Wingfield Cl ADL/WDHM KT15 | 215 | L6 |
| RBRW/HUT CM13 | 107 | M4 |
| Wingfield Ms PECK SE15 | 159 | P9 |
| Wingfield Rd GVW DA11 | 190 | E3 |
| KUTN/CMB KT2 | 177 | L9 |
| SRTFD E15 | 121 | K10 |
| WALTH E17 | 120 | G3 |
| Wingfield St PECK SE15 | 159 | P9 |
| Wingfield Wy RSLP HA4 | 133 | J1 |
| Wingford Rd BRXS/STRHM SW2 | 180 | F2 |
| Wingletye La EMPK RM11 | 125 | N6 |
| Wingmore Rd HNHL SE24 | 160 | A9 |
| Wingrave Crs BRW CM14 | 106 | D5 |
| Wingrave Rd HMSMTH W6 | 157 | H5 |
| Wingrove Dr PUR RM19 | 166 | A4 |
| Wingrove Rd CAT SE6 | 183 | K5 |
| Wings Cl SUT SM1 | 221 | K1 |
| Wingway BRW CM14 | 107 | H2 |
| Winifred Av HCH RM12 | 125 | J9 |
| Winifred Cl BAR EN5 | 76 | C10 |
| Winifred Pl NFNCH/WDSPK N12 | 97 | M6 |
| Winifred Rd BCTR RM8 | 123 | P7 |
| COUL/CHIP CR5 | 240 | B2 |
| ERITH DA8 | 164 | F4 |
| HHS/BOV HP3 | 35 | N10 |
| HPTN TW12 | 175 | N7 |
| WIM/MER SW19 | 201 | K1 |
| Winifred St CAN/RD E16 | 142 | C10 |
| Winifred Ter EN EN1 * | 99 | N1 |
| Winkers Cl CFSP/GDCR SL9 | 90 | C9 |
| Winkers La CFSP/GDCR SL9 | 90 | C9 |
| Winkfield Pln WDGN N22 | 99 | H9 |
| Winkfield Rd WDGN N22 | 99 | H9 |
| Winkley St BETH E2 | 140 | C6 |
| Winkworth Cots WCHPL E1 * | 140 | A6 |
| Winkworth Pl BNSTD SM7 | 221 | H10 |
| Winkworth Rd BNSTD SM7 | 221 | H10 |
| Winlaton Rd BMLY BR1 | 183 | J7 |
| Winmill Rd BCTR RM8 | 124 | A8 |
| Winn Common Rd WOOL/PLUM SE18 | 163 | H5 |
| Winnett St SOHO/SHAV W1D * | 11 | L9 |
| Winnings Wy WOKN/KNAP GU21 | 231 | N4 |
| Winnington Cl EFNCH N2 | 117 | H4 |
| Winnington Rd EFNCH N2 | 117 | H5 |
| PEND EN3 | 80 | E3 |
| Winnington Wy WOKN/KNAP GU21 | 231 | N4 |
| Winnipeg Dr ORP BR6 | 227 | J3 |
| Winnock Rd WDR/YW UB7 | 131 | N10 |
| Winns Av WALTH E17 | 120 | C4 |
| Winns Ms SEVS/STOTM N15 | 119 | M4 |
| Winns Ter WALTH E17 | 100 | F10 |
| Winsbeach WALTH E17 | 121 | K1 |
| Winscombe Crs EA W5 | 135 | J6 |
| Winscombe St KTTN NW5 | 118 | C8 |
| Winscombe Wy STAN HA7 | 94 | F6 |
| Winsford Rd CAT SE6 | 182 | E4 |
| Winsford Ter UED N9 * | 99 | L5 |
| Winsham Gv BTSEA SW11 | 180 | B1 |
| Winslade Rd BRXS/STRHM SW2 | 180 | F1 |
| Winslade Wy CAT SE6 * | 183 | L1 |
| Winsland Ms BAY/PAD W2 * | 9 | K5 |
| Winsland St BAY/PAD W2 | 9 | J5 |
| Winsley St GTPST W1W | 11 | J6 |
| Winslow CDEN/HRF UB9 | 132 | A3 |
| Winslow Cl PIN HA5 | 113 | J4 |
| WLSDN NW10 | 99 | H8 |
| Winslow Gv CHING E4 | 102 | E1 |
| Winslow Rd HMSMTH W6 | 157 | H5 |
| Winslow Wy FELT TW13 | 175 | L4 |
| WOT/HER KT12 | 197 | K10 |
| Winsor Ter EHAM E6 | 142 | A5 |
| Winstanley Cl COB KT11 | 217 | H10 |
| Winstanley Rd BTSEA SW11 | 157 | N10 |
| Winstead Gdns DAGE RM10 | 124 | D10 |
| Winston Av CDALE/KGS NW9 | 115 | L5 |
| Winston Churchill Wy CHES/WCR EN8 | 62 | B7 |
| Winston Cl KTN/HRWW/WS HA3 | 94 | B9 |
| RDART DA2 | 188 | A2 |
| ROMW/RG RM7 | 124 | C2 |
| Winston Ct KTN/HRWW/WS HA3 | 94 | A8 |
| Winston Dr COB KT11 | 235 | M2 |
| Winston Rd STNW/STAM N16 | 119 | M1 |
| Winston Wy BERK HP4 | 33 | L5 |
| IL IG1 | 122 | C9 |
| POTB/CUF EN6 | 59 | J2 |
| WOKS/MYFD GU22 | 232 | G6 |
| Winstre Rd BORE WD6 | 75 | M5 |
| Winter Av EHAM E6 | 142 | A1 |
| Winterborne Av ORP BR6 | 206 | G3 |
| Winterbourne Gv WEY KT13 | 213 | K5 |
| Winterbourne Rd BCTR RM8 | 123 | N6 |
| CAT SE6 | 182 | E6 |
| THHTH CR7 | 203 | H3 |
| Winter Box Wk RCHPK/HAM TW10 | 176 | E6 |
| Winterbrook Rd HNHL SE24 | 181 | K2 |
| Winterburn Cl FBAR/BDGN N11 | 98 | A6 |
| Winterdown Gdns ESH/CLAY KT10 | 217 | N3 |
| Winterdown Rd ESH/CLAY KT10 | 217 | N3 |
| Winterfold CRAWE RH10 | 284 | H3 |
| Winterfold Cl WIM/MER SW19 | 178 | B4 |
| Wintergarden Crs RDART DA2 | 188 | F3 |
| Winter Gdns CRAWW RH11 | 282 | E6 |
| Winters Crt GVE DA12 | 190 | F9 |
| Winterscroft Rd HOD EN11 | 44 | B1 |
| Wintersells Rd BF/WBF KT14 | 194 | B10 |
| Winterstoke Gdns MLHL NW7 | 97 | H5 |
| Winterstoke Rd CAT SE6 | 183 | H6 |
| Winterton Pl WBPTN SW10 * | 15 | K9 |
| Winterwell Rd BRXS/STRHM SW2 | 160 | A9 |
| Winthorpe Gdns BORE WD6 | 75 | P2 |
| Winthorpe Rd PUT/ROE SW15 | 157 | K10 |
| Winthrop St WCHPL E1 | 140 | C1 |
| Winton Ap RKW/CH/CXG WD3 | 72 | D9 |
| Winton Av FBAR/BDGN N11 | 98 | B1 |
| Winton Cl ED N9 | 101 | H9 |
| Winton Crs RKW/CH/CXG WD3 | 72 | D9 |
| Winton Dr CHES/WCR EN8 | 62 | D3 |
| RKW/CH/CXG WD3 | 72 | D9 |
| Winton Gdns EDGW HA8 | 95 | L8 |
| Winton Rd ORP BR6 | 226 | E1 |
| WARE SG12 | 26 | E2 |
| The Wintons BUSH WD23 | 94 | C2 |
| Winton Ter STAL AL1 * | 38 | D7 |
| Winvale SL SL1 | 149 | K2 |
| Winwood SLN SL2 | 129 | M8 |
| Wireless Rd BH/WHM TN16 | 244 | A1 |
| Wirral Wood Cl CHST BR7 | 184 | D9 |
| Wisbeach Rd CROY/NA CRO | 202 | E5 |
| Wisborough Ct CRAWW RH11 | 283 | J10 |
| Wisborough Rd SAND/SEL CR2 | 223 | N5 |
| Wisdom Dr HERT/BAY SG13 | 25 | M5 |
| Wisdons Cl DAGE RM10 | 124 | D7 |
| Wise La MLHL NW7 | 96 | D7 |
| WDR/YW UB7 | 132 | A3 |
| Wiseman Rd LEY E10 * | 120 | F7 |
| Wisemans Gdns SBW CM21 | 29 | M2 |
| Wise Rd SRTFD E15 | 141 | J3 |
| Wiseton Rd TOOT SW17 | 179 | H3 |
| Wishart Rd BKHTH/KID SE3 | 162 | A7 |
| Wishaw Wk FBAR/BDGN N11 * | 97 | P7 |
| Wishbone Wy WOKN/KNAP GU21 | 231 | L2 |
| Wisley La RPLY/SEND GU23 | 253 | P2 |
| Wisley Rd BTSEA SW11 | 180 | A1 |
| STMC/STPC BR5 | 185 | K10 |
| Wistaria Cl BRWN CM15 | 86 | C9 |
| ORP BR6 | 206 | D1 |
| Wistaria Dr LCOL/BKTW AL2 | 56 | G2 |
| Wisteria Cl IL IG1 | 122 | C10 |
| MLHL NW7 | 96 | C7 |
| Wisteria Gdns SWLY BR8 | 208 | E2 |
| Wisteria Rd LEW SE13 | 161 | J10 |
| Wistlea Crs STALE/WH AL4 | 39 | J2 |
| Wiston Ct CRAWW RH11 | 283 | J10 |
| Witanhurst La HGT N6 | 118 | B6 |
| Witan St BETH E2 | 140 | A5 |
| Witches La SEV TN13 | 246 | E9 |
| Witchford Wcce AL7 | 23 | N5 |
| Witham Cl LOU IG10 | 82 | B10 |
| Witham Rd DAGE RM10 | 124 | B10 |
| GPK RM2 | 125 | J3 |
| ISLW TW7 | 154 | C7 |
| PGE/AN SE20 | 182 | G4 |
| WEA W13 | 134 | F10 |
| Withens Cl STMC/STPC BR5 * | 207 | M4 |
| Witherby Cl CROY/NA CRO | 223 | M2 |
| Wither Dl HORL RH6 | 279 | P3 |
| The Witherings EMPK RM11 | 125 | M3 |
| Witherington Rd HBRY N5 * | 118 | E1 |
| Withers Md CDALE/KGS NW9 | 96 | C9 |
| Witherston Wy ELTH/MOT SE9 | 165 | H5 |
| Withey Brook HORL RH6 | 279 | N6 |
| Withey Cl WDSR SL4 | 148 | G2 |
| Withey Mdw STA TW18 | 173 | J9 |
| Withey Mdw HORL RH6 | 279 | N6 |
| Withies La RGUW GU3 | 267 | H7 |
| The Withies LHD/OX KT22 | 236 | D6 |
| WOKN/KNAP GU21 | 231 | K3 |
| Withybed Cnr KWD/TDW/WH KT20 | 238 | E9 |
| Withy Cl LTWR GU18 | 263 | B6 |
| Withycombe Rd WIM/MER SW19 | 178 | G3 |
| Withy La RSLP HA4 | 93 | H10 |
| Withy Md CHING E4 | 102 | E10 |
| Withypitts CRAWE RH10 | 285 | P10 |
| Withypitts East CRAWE RH10 | 285 | P10 |
| Witley Cl LCOL/BKTW AL2 | 56 | A4 |
| Witley Crs CROY/NA CRO | 225 | H3 |
| Witley Gdns NWDGN UB2 | 153 | N3 |
| Witley Rd ARCH N19 | 118 | D7 |
| Witney Cl HGDN/ICK UB10 | 112 | A9 |
| PIN HA5 | 93 | N7 |
| Witney Pth FSTH SE23 | 182 | G4 |
| Wittenham Wy CHING E4 | 102 | E10 |
| Wittering Cl KUTN/CMB KT2 | 177 | J8 |
| Wittersham Rd BMLY BR1 | 183 | L5 |
| Wivenhoe Cl PECK SE15 | 159 | P9 |
| Wivenhoe Ct HSLW TW3 | 153 | L8 |
| Wivenhoe Rd BARK IG11 | 143 | K4 |
| Wix HI EHSLY KT24 | 252 | C6 |
| Wix Rd DAGW RM9 | 143 | N8 |
| Wixs La CLAP SW4 | 159 | L10 |
| Woburn Av EPP CM16 | 83 | H3 |
| Woburn Cl BUSH WD23 | 74 | B10 |
| THMD SE28 | 146 | B6 |
| WIM/MER SW19 | 179 | M9 |
| Woburn Pk ADL/WDHM KT15 * | 195 | M10 |
| Woburn Rd CAR SM5 | 202 | B8 |
| CROY/NA CRO | 2 | D4 |
| Woburn Sq STPAN WC1H | 11 | K2 |
| Wodeham Gdns WCHPL E1 | 13 | M9 |
| Wodehouse Av CMBW SE5 | 159 | M7 |
| Wodehouse Rd DART DA1 | 168 | D10 |
| Wodeland Av GUW GU2 | 267 | K2 |
| Woffington Cl TEDD TW11 | 177 | H10 |
| Woking Cl PUT/ROE SW15 | 176 | D2 |
| Woking Rd RGUE GU4 | 249 | P5 |
| Wold Cl CRAWW RH11 | 283 | J10 |
| Woldham Rd HAYES BR2 | 205 | P4 |
| Woldhurstlea Cl CRAWW RH11 | 283 | K9 |
| Woldingham Rd CTHM CR3 | 242 | C5 |
| WARL CR6 | 242 | A6 |
| Wolds Dr ORP BR6 | 226 | E1 |
| The Wold CTHM CR3 | 242 | B3 |
| Wolfe Cl HAYES BR2 | 205 | M6 |
| Wolfe Crs BERM/RHTH SE16 | 160 | G1 |
| CHARL SE7 | 161 | N3 |
| Wolfendale Cl REDH RH1 | 258 | D5 |
| Wolferton Rd WNWD SE27 | 181 | J7 |
| Wolf La WDSR SL4 | 148 | B3 |
| Wolfram Cl LEW SE13 | 183 | K1 |
| Wolfs HI OXTED RH8 | 261 | M7 |
| Wolfs Rd OXTED RH8 | 261 | N6 |
| Wolftencroft Cl BTSEA SW11 | 157 | N9 |
| Wollaston Cl STHWK SE1 | 18 | D5 |
| Wolmer Cl EDGW HA8 | 96 | B8 |
| Wolmer Gdns EDGW HA8 | 95 | M4 |
| Wolseley WAND/EARL SW18 | 179 | K5 |
| Wolseley Gdns CEND/HSY/T N8 | 118 | P4 |
| WAND/EARL SW18 | 179 | N5 |
| Wolseley Rd CEND/HSY/T N8 | 118 | P4 |
| FSTGT E7 | 141 | J1 |
| KTN/HRWW/WS HA3 | 114 | D1 |
| MTCM CR4 | 202 | B7 |
| ROMW/RG RM7 | 124 | D2 |
| WDGN N22 | 99 | H8 |
| Wolseley St STHWK SE1 | 19 | M2 |
| Wolsey Av CHESW EN7 | 61 | N2 |
| EHAM E6 | 142 | G3 |
| THDIT KT7 | 198 | B7 |
| WALTH E17 | 119 | N1 |
| Wolsey Cl HSLW TW3 | 154 | B10 |
| KUTN/CMB KT2 | 177 | N1 |
| NWDGN UB2 | 153 | H1 |
| RYNPK SW20 | 178 | G10 |
| WPK KT4 | 220 | E1 |
| Wolsey Crs CROY/NA CRO | 224 | G7 |
| MRDN SM4 | 201 | J7 |
| Wolsey Gdns BARK/HLT IG6 | 122 | F2 |
| Wolsey Gv EDGW HA8 | 96 | D2 |
| ESH/CLAY KT10 | 218 | A1 |
| Wolsey Ms KTTN NW5 | 4 | F1 |

| Entry | Page | Grid |
|---|---|---|
| Wolsey Rd ASHF TW15 | 173 | P7 |
| E/WMO/HCT KT8 | 198 | C1 |
| EN N1 | 80 | A6 |
| ESH/CLAY KT10 | 218 | A1 |
| HHW HP1 | 35 | N7 |
| HPTN TW12 | 176 | A9 |
| IS N1 | 119 | L10 |
| NTHWD HA6 | 92 | D3 |
| SUN TW16 | 174 | G10 |
| Wolsey St WCHPL E1 * | 140 | B7 |
| Wolsey Wk WOKN/KNAP GU21 | 232 | B6 |
| Wolsey Wy CHSGTN KT9 | 219 | M2 |
| Wolstan Cl DEN/HRF UB9 | 111 | K8 |
| Wolstonbury NFNCH/WDSPK N12 | 97 | G3 |
| Wolstonbury Cl CRAWW RH11 * | 283 | M10 |
| Wolvens La RDKG RH5 | 271 | P6 |
| Wolvercote Rd ABYW SE2 | 163 | N1 |
| Wolverley St BETH E2 * | 140 | A5 |
| Wolverton Av KUTN/CMB KT2 | 199 | M1 |
| Wolverton Cl HORL RH6 | 280 | A6 |
| Wolverton Gdns EA W5 | 135 | L9 |
| HMSMTH W6 | 156 | G3 |
| HORL RH6 | 280 | A5 |
| Wolverton Rd STAN HA7 | 94 | G7 |
| Wolverton Wy STHGT/OAK N14 | 78 | D9 |
| Wolves La WDGN N22 | 99 | H3 |
| Wombwell Gdns GVW DA11 | 190 | B5 |
| Womersley Rd CEND/HSY/T N8 | 118 | C4 |
| Wonersh Common Rd SHGR GU5 | 268 | E10 |
| Wonersh Wy BELMT SM2 | 220 | G5 |
| Wonford Cl KUTN/CMB KT2 | 200 | D3 |
| KWD/TDW/WH KT20 | 256 | D2 |
| Wonham La BRKHM/BTCW RH3 | 274 | C1 |
| Wonham Wy SHGR GU5 | 270 | E8 |
| Wonnacott PEND EN3 | 80 | C3 |
| Wontford Rd PUR/KEN CR8 | 241 | H1 |
| Wontner Cl IS N1 | 6 | E4 |
| Wontner Rd BAL SW12 | 180 | A5 |
| Wooburn Cl UX/CGN UB8 | 132 | C6 |
| Wooburn Common Rd SL SL1 | 108 | A7 |
| Woodall Rd PEND EN3 | 80 | C9 |
| Woodall Rd CHSGTN KT9 | 219 | H4 |
| Woodbank RKW/CH/CXG WD3 | 71 | M10 |
| Woodbank Av CFSP/GDCR SL9 | 110 | A4 |
| Woodbank Dr CSTG HP8 | 90 | A1 |
| Woodbank Rd BMLY BR1 | 183 | L6 |
| Woodbastwick Rd SYD SE26 | 182 | C9 |
| Woodberry Av RYLN/HDSTN HA2 | 114 | B2 |
| WCHMH N21 | 99 | H3 |
| Woodberry Cl MLHL NW7 | 96 | G8 |
| SUN TW16 | 175 | H9 |
| Woodberry Crs MUSWH N10 | 118 | C5 |
| Woodberry Down EPP CM16 | 65 | K5 |
| FSBYPK N4 | 119 | K6 |
| Woodberry Gdns NFNCH/WDSPK N12 | 97 | M7 |
| Woodberry Gv BXLY DA5 | 186 | G6 |
| FSBYPK N4 | 119 | K5 |
| NFNCH/WDSPK N12 | 97 | M7 |
| Woodberry Wy CHING E4 | 101 | N1 |
| NFNCH/WDSPK N12 | 97 | M7 |
| Woodbine Cl HLWW/ROY CM19 | 46 | E1 |
| WHTN TW2 | 176 | C5 |
| Woodbine Gv ENC/FH EN2 | 79 | L4 |
| PGE/AN SE20 | 182 | A10 |
| Woodbine La WPK KT4 | 200 | E10 |
| Woodbine Pl WAN E11 | 121 | M4 |
| Woodbine Rd BFN/LL DA15 | 185 | H4 |
| Woodbines Av KUT/HW KT1 | 199 | J5 |
| Woodbine Ter HOM E9 * | 140 | E1 |
| Woodborough Rd PUT/ROE SW15 | 156 | C10 |
| Woodbourne Av STRHM/NOR SW16 | 180 | C6 |
| Woodbourne Dr ESH/CLAY KT10 | 218 | E3 |
| Woodbourne Gdns WLGTN SM6 | 222 | C4 |
| Woodbridge Av LHD/OX KT22 | 236 | F4 |
| Woodbridge Cl HARH RM3 | 105 | L4 |
| HOLWY N7 | 118 | C2 |
| Woodbridge Gv HI GUW GU2 | 249 | N9 |
| Woodbridge Hill Gdns GUW GU2 | 249 | N8 |
| Woodbridge La HARH RM3 | 105 | L4 |
| Woodbridge Mdw GU1 | 249 | N6 |
| Woodbridge Rd BARK IG11 | 123 | J10 |
| GU GU1 | 249 | P10 |
| Woodbrook Gdns WAB EN9 | 63 | P3 |
| Woodbrook Rd ABYW SE2 | 163 | K5 |
| Woodburn Cl HDN NW4 | 116 | C3 |
| Woodbury Cl BH/WHM TN16 | 244 | C4 |
| CROY/NA CR0 | 3 | N1 |
| WAN E11 | 121 | N2 |
| Woodbury Dr BELMT SM2 | 221 | M6 |
| Woodbury Gdns LEE/GVPK SE12 | 183 | N6 |
| Woodbury Hl LOU IG10 | 82 | H6 |
| Woodbury Park Rd WEA W13 | 134 | C6 |
| Woodbury Rd WALTH E17 | 120 | C8 |
| Woodbury St TOOT SW17 | 179 | P8 |
| Woodby Dr ASC SL5 | 192 | G7 |
| Woodchester Sq BAY/PAD W2 | 8 | B3 |
| Woodchurch Cl SCUP DA14 | 184 | H4 |
| Woodchurch Dr BMLY BR1 | 184 | A10 |
| Woodchurch Rd KIL/WHAMP NW6 | 2 | F1 |
| Wood Cl BETH E2 | 13 | N1 |
| CDALE/KGS NW9 | 116 | A5 |
| HAT AL10 | 40 | E4 |
| HRW HA1 | 114 | C5 |
| REDH RH1 | 276 | A1 |
| WDSR SL4 | 149 | H10 |
| Woodcliffe Dr CHST BR7 | 206 | D2 |
| Woodcock Cl STWL/WRAY TW19 | 151 | L10 |
| Woodcock Dell Av KTN/HRWW/WS HA3 | 115 | H5 |
| Woodcock Dr CHOB/PIR GU24 | 213 | H6 |
| Woodcock Hl KTN/HRWW/WS HA3 | 115 | H4 |
| RKW/CH/CXG WD3 | 91 | P6 |
| Woodcockhill STALE/WH AL4 | 21 | P1 |
| Woodcock La CHOB/PIR GU24 | 212 | G4 |
| Woodcocks CAN/RD E16 | 141 | P7 |
| Woodcombe Crs FSTH SE23 | 162 | B3 |
| Wood Common HAT AL10 | 40 | E1 |
| Woodcot Cl PEND EN3 | 80 | B10 |
| Woodcote GUW GU2 | 267 | N4 |
| HORL RH6 | 280 | C5 |
| Woodcote Av HCH RM12 | 125 | H9 |
| MLHL NW7 | 96 | F4 |
| THHTH CR7 | 208 | C1 |
| WLGTN SM6 | 222 | C5 |
| Woodcote Cl CHES/WCR EN8 | 62 | B6 |
| EPSOM KT18 | 220 | A10 |
| KUTN/CMB KT2 | 177 | L1 |
| Woodcote Dr ORP BR6 | 206 | G7 |
| PUR/KEN CR8 | 222 | F9 |
| Woodcote End EPSOM KT18 | 238 | B10 |
| Woodcote Green Rd EPSOM KT18 | 237 | P10 |
| Woodcote Grove Rd COUL/CHIP CR5 | 240 | E6 |
| Woodcote House Ct EPSOM KT18 * | 238 | A10 |
| Woodcote Hurst EPSOM KT18 | 237 | P10 |
| Woodcote La PUR/KEN CR8 | 222 | E7 |
| WLGTN SM6 | 222 | D7 |
| Woodcote Park Av PUR/KEN CR8 | 222 | D7 |
| Woodcote Park Rd EPSOM KT18 | 237 | P2 |
| Woodcote Pl WNWD SE27 * | 181 | J8 |
| Woodcote Rd EPSOM KT18 | 238 | A1 |
| WAN E11 | 121 | M5 |
| WLGTN SM6 | 222 | C3 |
| Woodcote Side EPSOM KT18 | 237 | N1 |
| Woodcote Valley Rd PUR/KEN CR8 | 222 | E9 |
| Wood Crs HHS/BOV HP3 | 35 | N4 |
| Woodcrest BELMT SM2 * | 221 | M4 |
| Woodcrest Wk REIG RH2 | 257 | P8 |
| Woodcroft GFD/PVL UB6 | 134 | F1 |
| HLWS CM18 | 46 | F1 |
| NTHLT UB5 | 114 | B1 |
| WCHMH N21 | 98 | G2 |
| Woodcroft Av MLHL NW7 | 96 | G6 |
| STAN HA7 | 94 | F9 |
| WARE SG12 | 27 | M7 |
| Woodcroft Crs HGDN/ICK UB10 | 132 | C3 |
| Woodcroft Ms DEPT SE8 | 160 | D3 |
| Woodcroft Rd CRAWW RH11 | 282 | C9 |
| CSHM HP5 | 51 | L3 |
| THHTH CR7 | 203 | J5 |
| Woodcutter Pl LCOL/BKTW AL2 | 56 | B3 |
| Woodcutters Av CWTH RG45 | 167 | P1 |
| Woodcutters Cl EMPK RM11 | 125 | L2 |
| Wood Dene PECK SE15 * | 160 | A7 |
| SEV TN13 | 264 | C8 |
| Woodedge Cl CHING E4 | 101 | L2 |
| Wooden Bridge Ter WNWD SE27 * | 181 | J6 |
| Woodend ESH/CLAY KT10 | 198 | B9 |
| LHD/OX KT22 | 255 | H1 |
| NRWD SE19 | 181 | K9 |
| SUT SM1 | 201 | N1 |
| Wood End SWLY BR8 | 208 | D4 |
| Wood End Av RYLN/HDSTN HA2 | 114 | A9 |
| Woodend Cl CRAWE RH10 | 284 | B5 |
| ENC/FH EN2 | 36 | D5 |
| HHNE HP2 | 35 | P2 |
| Wood End Cl NTHLT UB5 | 114 | D4 |
| Woodend Gdns ENC/FH EN2 | 78 | A4 |
| Wood End Gdns NTHLT UB5 | 114 | B10 |
| Wood End Gn YEAD UB4 | 132 | G7 |
| Wood End Green Rd HYS/HAR UB3 | 132 | E7 |
| Wood End La NTHLT UB5 | 134 | A1 |
| Woodend Pk COB KT11 | 235 | L1 |
| Wood End Rd HRW HA1 | 114 | C9 |
| Wood End Rd WALTH E17 | 101 | H10 |
| The Wood End WLGTN SM6 | 222 | C5 |
| Wood End Wy NTHLT UB5 | 114 | B10 |
| Wooder Gdns FSTGT E7 | 121 | P5 |
| Wooderson Cl SNWD SE25 | 203 | M4 |
| Woodfall Av BAR EN5 | 77 | J9 |
| Woodfall Dr DART DA1 | 164 | C10 |
| Woodfall Rd FSBYPK N4 | 119 | H6 |
| Woodfall St CHEL SW3 | 16 | A8 |
| Wood Fld HAMP NW3 * | 35 | N6 |
| Woodfarrs CMBW SE5 | 159 | L10 |
| Woodfield ASHTD KT21 | 237 | J3 |
| Wood Fld HAMP NW3 * | 118 | J10 |
| Woodfield Av ALP/SUD HA0 | 115 | H8 |
| CAR SM5 | 222 | B7 |
| CDALE/KGS NW9 | 116 | B2 |
| EA W5 | 135 | H6 |
| GVW DA11 | 190 | G4 |
| NTHWD HA6 | 92 | F5 |
| STRHM/NOR SW16 | 180 | E6 |
| Woodfield Cl ASHTD KT21 | 237 | J3 |
| COUL/CHIP CR5 | 240 | D5 |
| CRAWE RH10 | 283 | P6 |
| EN EN1 | 79 | M8 |
| NRWD SE19 | 181 | K10 |
| REDH RH1 | 257 | P9 |
| Woodfield Crs EA W5 | 135 | J6 |
| Woodfield Dr EBAR EN4 | 98 | C2 |
| CPK RM2 | 125 | M2 |
| HHS/BOV HP3 | 36 | E8 |
| Woodfield Gdns HHS/BOV HP3 | 36 | B9 |
| NWMAL KT3 | 200 | C5 |
| Woodfield Gv STRHM/NOR SW16 | 180 | D6 |
| Woodfield Hl COUL/CHIP CR5 | 240 | D6 |
| Woodfield La ASHTD KT21 | 237 | J2 |
| BRKMPK AL9 | 41 | P9 |
| STRHM/NOR SW16 | 180 | D6 |
| Woodfield Pk AMS HP6 * | 36 | C3 |
| Woodfield Pl BKHH IG9 | 94 | C1 |
| Woodfield Rd ASHTD KT21 | 237 | J3 |
| CRAWE RH10 | 284 | A5 |
| EA W5 | 135 | H6 |
| HSLWW TW4 | 153 | J8 |
| MV/WKIL W9 | 8 | A1 |
| RAD WD7 | 74 | F2 |
| THDIT KT7 | 198 | E3 |
| WCCE AL7 | 23 | J5 |
| Woodfields SEV TN13 | 246 | E9 |
| WOTH/WD18 * | 73 | K8 |
| The Woodfields SAND/SEL CR2 | 223 | N7 |
| Woodfield Wy FBAR/BDGN N11 | 98 | A4 |
| HCH RM12 | 125 | L6 |
| REDH RH1 | 257 | P9 |
| STALE/WH AL4 | 39 | H5 |
| The Woodfines EMPK RM11 | 125 | L4 |
| Woodford Av CNTH/NBYPK IG2 | 122 | D2 |
| Woodford Bridge Rd REDBR IG4 | 122 | A1 |
| Woodford Ct WAB EN9 | 63 | M9 |
| Woodford Crs PIN HA5 | 93 | J10 |
| Woodford New Rd WALTH E17 | 121 | K1 |
| Woodford Pl WBLY HA9 | 115 | K4 |
| Woodford Rd FSTGT E7 | 121 | N9 |
| SWFD E18 | 121 | M2 |
| WAT WD17 | 73 | J4 |
| Woodford Wy SLN SL2 | 128 | F5 |
| Woodgate GSTN WD25 | 55 | J9 |
| Woodgate Av CHSGTN KT9 | 219 | J2 |
| Woodgate Crs NTHWD HA6 | 93 | H7 |
| Woodgate Dr STRHM/NOR SW16 | 180 | D10 |
| Woodgavil BNSTD SM7 | 239 | L7 |
| Woodget Cl EHAM E6 | 142 | H8 |
| Woodgrange Av EN EN1 | 79 | P10 |
| EA W5 | 135 | L6 |
| KTN/HRWW/WS HA3 | 115 | H3 |
| NFNCH/WDSPK N12 | 98 | A10 |
| Woodgrange Cl KTN/HRWW/WS HA3 | 115 | J3 |
| Woodgrange Gdns EN EN1 | 79 | P10 |
| Woodgrange Rd FSTGT E7 | 121 | N10 |
| Woodgrange Ter EN EN1 * | 79 | P10 |
| Woodgreen Rd WAB EN9 | 63 | N9 |
| Woodhall Av DUL SE21 | 181 | N6 |
| PIN HA5 | 93 | L7 |
| Woodhall Ga PIN HA5 | 93 | L8 |
| Woodhall La ASC SL5 | 192 | D9 |
| HHNE HP2 | 35 | M1 |
| OXHEY WD19 | 93 | L4 |
| RAD WD7 | 75 | K1 |
| WCCE AL7 | 23 | H7 |
| Woodham La ADL/WDHM KT15 | 215 | H6 |
| WOKN/KNAP GU21 | 214 | E9 |
| Woodham Park Rd ADL/WDHM KT15 | 215 | J6 |
| Woodham Park Wy ADL/WDHM KT15 | 215 | J7 |
| Woodham Ri WOKN/KNAP GU21 | 232 | D1 |
| Woodham Rd CAT SE6 | 183 | H6 |
| WOKN/KNAP GU21 | 232 | B1 |
| Woodham Wave WARE SG12 | 27 | H7 |
| Woodham Waye WOKN/KNAP GU21 | 214 | E10 |
| Woodhatch Cl EHAM E6 | 142 | H7 |
| Woodhatch Rd REDH RH1 | 276 | A5 |
| REIG RH2 | 275 | N4 |
| Woodhatch Spinney COUL/CHIP CR5 | 240 | F2 |
| Woodhaven Gdns BARK/HLT IG6 | 122 | F2 |
| Woodhaw EGH TW20 | 172 | E7 |
| Woodhayes HORL RH6 | 280 | C3 |
| Woodhayes Rd WIM/MER SW19 | 178 | F9 |
| Woodhead Dr ORP BR6 | 207 | H10 |
| Woodhead Rd WLSDN NW10 | 116 | B10 |
| Woodhill WOOL/PLUM SE18 | 47 | H4 |
| Woodhill Crs KTN/HRWW/WS HA3 | 115 | J4 |
| Woodhouse Cl EDUL SE22 | 159 | P10 |
| GFD/PVL UB6 | 134 | E4 |
| HYS/HAR UB3 | 152 | F2 |
| Woodhouse Eaves NTHWD HA6 | 93 | H6 |
| Woodhouse Gv FSTGT E7 | 142 | B1 |
| Woodhouse La BROX EN10 | 48 | N7 |
| Woodhouse Rd NFNCH/WDSPK N12 | 97 | M7 |
| WAN E11 | 121 | L8 |
| Woodhurst Av GSTN WD25 | 73 | L1 |
| STMC/STPC BR5 | 185 | J3 |
| Woodhurst Dr DEN/HRF UB9 | 111 | J3 |
| Woodhurst La OXTED RH8 | 261 | K7 |
| Woodhurst Pk OXTED RH8 | 261 | K6 |
| Woodhurst Rd ABYW SE2 | 163 | K4 |
| ACT W3 | 135 | P10 |
| Woodhyrst Gdns PUR/KEN CR8 | 241 | H1 |
| Wooding Gv HLWW/ROY CM19 | 46 | E1 |
| Woodington Cl ELTH/MOT SE9 | 164 | F1 |
| Woodknoll Dr CHST BR7 | 206 | C1 |
| Woodland Ap GFD/PVL UB6 | 134 | F1 |
| Woodland Av HART DA3 | 211 | L5 |
| HHW HP1 | 35 | L7 |
| HRBR/HUT CM13 | 87 | P9 |
| SL SL1 | 129 | J9 |
| WDSR SL4 | 148 | E10 |
| Woodland Cl CDALE/KGS NW9 | 115 | P4 |
| EHSLY KT24 | 252 | G5 |
| HART DA3 | 211 | P3 |
| HGDN/ICK UB10 | 112 | C7 |
| HHW HP1 | 35 | L7 |
| HOR/WEW KT19 | 220 | B5 |
| RBRW/HUT CM13 | 87 | P9 |
| WEY KT13 * | 216 | E1 |
| WFD IG8 | 101 | H4 |
| Woodland Ct GLDGN NW11 * | 117 | H3 |
| OXTED RH8 | 261 | J4 |
| STALW/RED AL3 | 58 | E2 |
| Woodland Crs BERM/RHTH SE16 | 160 | C1 |
| GNWCH SE10 | 161 | K5 |
| Woodland Dr COB KT11 | 217 | N7 |
| EHSLY KT24 | 252 | A5 |
| STALE/WH AL4 | 21 | N5 |
| WAT WD17 | 72 | C5 |
| Woodland Gdns ISLW TW7 | 154 | D9 |
| MUSWH N10 | 118 | C3 |
| SAND/SEL CR2 | 224 | B7 |
| Woodland Gld SLN SL2 | 109 | J8 |
| Woodland Gra DTCH/LGLY SL3 | 151 | H3 |
| Woodland Gv CROY/NA CR0 | 3 | H4 |
| EPP CM16 | 65 | K4 |
| GNWCH SE10 | 161 | K4 |
| WEY KT13 | 216 | D1 |
| Woodland HI NRWD SE19 | 181 | M9 |
| Woodland La RKW/CH/CXG WD3 | 70 | G7 |
| Woodland Ms STRHM/NOR SW16 | 180 | F6 |
| Woodland Mt HERT/BAY SG13 | 35 | N5 |
| Woodland PI HHW HP1 * | 35 | L7 |
| RKW/CH/CXG WD3 | 90 | H4 |
| Woodland Ri BGR/WK TN15 | 247 | M9 |
| GFD/PVL UB6 | 134 | F1 |
| MUSWH N10 | 118 | C4 |
| OXTED RH8 | 261 | K6 |
| WELL DA16 | 148 | D4 |
| Woodland Rd CHING E4 | 101 | H2 |
| FBAR/BDGN N11 | 98 | B6 |
| HERT/BAY SG13 | 26 | B4 |
| LOU IG10 | 82 | B7 |
| NRWD SE19 | 181 | M8 |
| RKW/CH/CXG WD3 | 90 | H4 |
| THHTH CR7 | 203 | H4 |
| Woodlands ADL/WDHM KT15 | 195 | P10 |
| ASHTD KT21 | 237 | L3 |
| BRKMPK AL9 | 59 | L3 |
| BXLYHS DA6 | 186 | C1 |
| CFSP/GDCR SL9 | 110 | C6 |
| CRAWE RH10 | 284 | E5 |
| GLDGN NW11 | 117 | H3 |
| HORL RH6 | 280 | D3 |
| LCOL/BKTW AL2 | 56 | B3 |
| RAD WD7 | 56 | F10 |
| RYLN/HDSTN HA2 | 114 | A6 |
| SLN SL2 | 109 | J8 |
| WOKS/MYFD GU22 | 232 | A4 |
| Woodlands Gdns EPSOM KT18 | 238 | F3 |
| WALTH E17 * | 121 | K2 |
| Woodlands Gld BEAC HP9 | 88 | B7 |
| Woodlands Gv COUL/CHIP CR5 | 240 | C3 |
| ISLW TW7 | 154 | B8 |
| Woodlands HI BEAC HP9 | 108 | A4 |
| Woodlands La BFOR GU20 | 212 | E4 |
| Woodlands Ms CROY/NA CR0 | 224 | D5 |
| Woodlands Pde ASHF TW15 | 174 | D9 |
| Woodlands Pk ADL/WDHM KT15 | 215 | J2 |
| BXLY DA5 | 186 | D7 |
| GU GU1 | 250 | E9 |
| KWD/TDW/WH KT20 | 255 | N7 |
| WOKN/KNAP GU21 | 214 | F9 |
| Woodlands Park Rd GNWCH SE10 | 161 | K5 |
| SEVS/STOTM N15 | 119 | K3 |
| Woodlands Ri SWLY BR8 | 208 | G2 |
| Woodlands Rd BARN SW13 | 156 | A6 |
| BF/WBF KT14 | 215 | J10 |
| BMLY BR1 | 206 | C2 |
| BUSH WD23 | 73 | M8 |
| DA7 | 163 | P9 |
| ED N9 | 100 | F2 |
| EN EN1 | 79 | L4 |
| EPSOM KT18 | 237 | M1 |
| GT/LBKH KT23 | 253 | N4 |
| GU GU1 | 250 | A6 |
| HARH RM3 | 105 | P9 |
| HRW HA1 | 114 | E3 |
| IL IG1 | 122 | F8 |
| ISLW TW7 | 154 | A7 |
| LHD/OX KT22 | 236 | C4 |
| ORP BR6 | 227 | L3 |
| ROM RM1 | 124 | C1 |
| STHL UB1 | 133 | L10 |
| SURB KT6 | 199 | J7 |
| VW GU25 | 195 | P4 |
| WALTH E17 | 121 | H1 |
| WAN E11 | 121 | K7 |
| Woodlands Rd East VW GU25 | 193 | P3 |
| Woodlands Rd West VW GU25 | 193 | P3 |
| Woodlands St LEW SE13 | 183 | J5 |
| The Woodlands AMS HP6 | 36 | C3 |
| BRXN/ST SW9 * | 159 | J6 |
| ESH/CLAY KT10 | 198 | B9 |
| HORL RH6 | 281 | J4 |
| HRW HA1 * | 114 | D7 |
| ISLW TW7 | 154 | A7 |
| LEW SE13 | 183 | J3 |
| NRWD SE19 | 181 | K10 |
| ORP BR6 | 227 | L3 |
| STAN HA7 * | 94 | G4 |
| STHGT/OAK N14 | 98 | C7 |
| WLGTN SM6 | 222 | C8 |
| Woodland St HACK E8 * | 7 | L1 |
| Woodlands Wy ASHTD KT21 | 237 | M2 |
| KWD/TDW/WH KT20 | 255 | N6 |
| PUT/ROE SW15 | 179 | H4 |
| Woodland Ter CHARL SE7 | 162 | B3 |
| Woodland Vw CHSM HP5 | 51 | H4 |
| GODL GU7 | 267 | K8 |
| Woodland Wk HAMP NW3 | 117 | P10 |
| HOR/WEW KT19 | 219 | N8 |
| Wood La BCTR RM8 | 123 | P8 |
| CDALE/KGS NW9 | 116 | A5 |
| CTHM CR3 | 241 | L10 |
| DAGW RM9 | 123 | P8 |
| HCH RM12 | 124 | C4 |
| HGT N6 | 118 | A3 |
| HHNE HP2 | 35 | L2 |
| ISLW TW7 | 154 | D9 |
| IVER SL0 | 131 | J2 |
| KWD/TDW/WH KT20 | 239 | L10 |
| MUSWH N10 | 118 | C3 |
| RDART DA2 | 188 | C7 |
| RSEV TN14 | 243 | P10 |
| SEV TN13 | 247 | H9 |
| SNWD SE25 | 204 | A6 |
| SUT SM1 | 201 | J1 |
| WDGN N22 | 99 | H8 |
| WDSR SL4 | 147 | K3 |
| WFD IG8 | 101 | M5 |
| Wood La End HHNE HP2 | 36 | C5 |
| Woodlawn Cl PUT/ROE SW15 | 179 | J1 |
| Woodlawn Crs WHTN TW2 | 176 | D9 |
| Woodlawn Dr FELT TW13 | 154 | D5 |
| Woodlawn Rd FUL/PGN SW6 | 156 | G6 |
| Woodlea Dr HAYES BR2 | 205 | K5 |
| Woodlea Gv NTHWD HA6 | 92 | D7 |
| Woodlea Rd STNW/STAM N16 | 119 | M9 |
| Woodlee Cl VW GU25 | 193 | P2 |
| Woodleigh Gdns STRHM/NOR SW16 | 180 | E6 |
| Woodley Cl TOOT SW17 | 180 | A10 |
| Woodley La AMSS HP7 * | 36 | C3 |
| Woodley Hl CSHM HP5 | 51 | J10 |
| Woodley La SUT SM1 | 201 | J2 |
| Woodley Rd ORP BR6 | 207 | N9 |
| WARE SG12 | 26 | E1 |
| Wood Lodge Gdns BMLY BR1 | 184 | B10 |
| Wood Lodge Gv SEV TN13 * | 247 | K8 |
| Wood Lodge La WWKM BR4 | 205 | H10 |
| Woodmancote Gdns BF/WBF KT14 | 215 | K9 |
| Woodmancourt GODL GU7 | 267 | K8 |
| Woodman La CHING E4 | 81 | J9 |
| Woodman Ms RCH/KEW TW9 | 155 | P6 |
| Woodman Pth BARK/HLT IG6 | 103 | J4 |
| Woodman Rd BARK/HLT IG6 | 103 | H4 |
| BRW CM14 | 107 | H6 |
| COUL/CHIP CR5 | 240 | D3 |
| HHS/BOV HP3 | 35 | P8 |
| Woodmans GV WLSDN NW10 | 116 | C10 |
| Woodmansterne La BNSTD SM7 | 239 | N1 |
| Woodmansterne Rd CAR SM5 | 221 | P8 |
| COUL/CHIP CR5 | 240 | C5 |
| STRHM/NOR SW16 | 180 | D10 |
| Woodmansterne St BNSTD SM7 | 239 | P1 |
| Woodman St CAN/RD E16 | 142 | F4 |
| Wood Md TOTM N17 * | 100 | F2 |
| Wood Meads EPP CM16 | 65 | K5 |
| Woodmere ELTH/MOT SE9 | 164 | F4 |
| Woodmere Av CROY/NA CR0 | 204 | C10 |
| WATN WD24 | 72 | D2 |
| Woodmere Cl BTSEA SW11 | 158 | A1 |
| CROY/NA CR0 | 204 | D10 |
| Woodmere Gdns CROY/NA CR0 | 204 | C10 |
| Woodmere Wy BECK BR3 | 205 | H5 |
| Woodmill Rd CLPT E5 | 120 | B7 |
| YEAD UB4 | 132 | C7 |
| Woodstock Gra EA W5 * | 135 | K10 |
| Woodstock Gv GODL GU7 | 267 | K10 |
| SHB W12 | 156 | G1 |
| Woodstock La North SURB KT6 | 199 | H8 |
| Woodstock La South ESH/CLAY KT10 | 218 | G2 |
| Woodstock Ms CAVSO/HST W1G | 10 | D4 |
| Woodstock Ri CHEAM SM3 | 201 | J8 |
| Woodstock Rd ALP/SUD HA0 | 135 | L2 |
| BROX EN10 | 44 | D5 |
| BUSH WD23 | 94 | B1 |
| CAR SM5 | 222 | B2 |
| CHSWK W4 | 156 | B3 |
| COUL/CHIP CR5 | 240 | C2 |
| CROY/NA CR0 | 203 | L10 |
| FSBYPK N4 | 119 | H6 |
| FSTGT E7 | 141 | P2 |
| GLDGN NW11 | 117 | J5 |
| WALTH E17 | 101 | J10 |
| Woodstock Rd North STAL AL1 | 38 | G4 |
| Woodstock Rd South STAL AL1 | 38 | G4 |
| Woodstock St CAN/RD E16 | 141 | G8 |
| OXSTW W1C | 10 | B6 |
| Woodstock Ter POP/IOD E14 | 140 | C9 |
| Woodstock Wy MTCM CR4 | 202 | G2 |
| Woodstone Av EW KT17 | 220 | D2 |
| Wood St BAR EN5 | 76 | F8 |
| CAN/RD E16 | 141 | N9 |
| CHSWK W4 | 156 | B4 |
| CITYW EC2V | 12 | F5 |
| GRAYS RM17 | 167 | P5 |
| KUT/HW KT1 | 199 | J1 |
| MTCM CR4 | 202 | B7 |
| REDH RH1 | 258 | D5 |
| SWLY BR8 | 209 | K1 |
| WALTH E17 | 121 | H1 |
| Woodsway LHD/OX KT22 | 218 | G10 |
| Woodsyre SYD SE26 | 181 | N7 |
| Wood Ter CRICK NW2 * | 116 | C7 |
| Woodthorpe Rd ASHF TW15 | 173 | N8 |
| PUT/ROE SW15 | 156 | E10 |
| Woodtree Cl HDN NW4 | 96 | F10 |
| Wood V FSTH SE23 | 182 | A4 |
| HAT AL10 | 40 | E4 |
| Woodvale Av SNWD SE25 | 203 | N3 |
| Woodvale Pk STAL AL1 | 38 | G6 |
| Woodvale Wy GLDGN NW11 | 116 | C8 |
| Wood Vw HHW HP1 | 35 | L4 |
| POTB/CUF EN6 | 60 | F3 |
| CDW/CHF RM16 | 168 | B5 |
| Woodview CHSGTN KT9 | 219 | H7 |
| RDART DA2 | 188 | F9 |
| SLN SL2 * | 128 | E2 |
| Woodview Av CHING E4 | 101 | M5 |
| Woodview Cl ASHTD KT21 | 237 | L9 |
| ORP BR6 | 206 | F9 |
| PUT/ROE SW15 | 178 | A7 |
| SAND/SEL CR2 | 224 | A10 |
| Woodview Rd SWLY BR8 | 208 | D2 |
| Woodville Cl LEE/GVPK SE12 | 183 | M1 |
| TEDD TW11 | 176 | F7 |
| Woodville Cots GVE DA12 * | 191 | H2 |
| Woodville Court Ms WAT WD17 * | 73 | H6 |
| Woodville Gdns BARK/HLT | 122 | E1 |
| EA W5 | 135 | K4 |
| RSLP HA4 | 112 | D5 |
| SURB KT6 * | 199 | J7 |
| Woodville Gv WELL DA16 * | 163 | K9 |
| Woodville Pl GVW DA11 | 190 | E3 |
| HERT/WAT SG14 | 25 | J3 |
| Woodville Rd BAR EN5 | 77 | L7 |
| EA W5 | 135 | K8 |
| GLDGN NW11 | 117 | H5 |
| KIL/WHAMP NW6 | 2 | C2 |
| LHD/OX KT22 | 236 | C6 |
| MRDN SM4 | 201 | K4 |
| RCHPK/HAM TW10 | 176 | C6 |
| STNW/STAM N16 | 119 | M10 |
| SWFD E18 | 101 | N10 |
| WALTH E17 | 121 | H2 |
| WAN E11 | 121 | L4 |
| Woodville St WOOL/PLUM SE18 | 146 | A7 |
| Woodwards RKW/CH/CXG WD3 | 90 | C6 |
| Woodyard Cl KTTN NW5 | 118 | B10 |
| Woodyard La DUL SE21 | 181 | M3 |
| The Woodyard EPP CM16 | 65 | M4 |
| Woodyates Rd LEE/GVPK SE12 | 183 | M2 |
| Woodyers Cl SHGR GU5 | 268 | E10 |
| Woolacombe Rd BKHTH/KID SE3 | 162 | E1 |
| Woolacombe Wy HYS/HAR UB3 | 151 | P2 |
| Woolborough Cl CRAWE RH10 | 284 | A4 |
| Woolborough La CRAWE RH10 | 284 | C4 |
| Woolborough Rd CRAWE RH10 | 283 | N6 |
| Wooler St WALW SE17 | 18 | G8 |
| Woolf Cl THMD SE28 | 146 | B10 |
| Woolf Ms STPAN WC1H | 11 | L1 |
| Woolhampton Wy CHIG IG7 | 103 | L4 |
| Woolhams CTHM CR3 | 259 | N2 |
| Woollam Crs STALW/RED AL3 | 38 | B2 |
| Woollard St WAB EN9 | 63 | M5 |
| Woollaston Rd FSBYPK N4 | 119 | J4 |
| Woollett Cl DART DA1 | 165 | H10 |
| Woolmans Cl BROX EN10 | 44 | E8 |
| Woolmead Av CDALE/KGS NW9 | 116 | D5 |
| Woolmer Cl BORE WD6 | 75 | H4 |
| Woolmer Dr HHNE HP2 | 36 | D6 |
| Woolmer Gdns UED N18 | 99 | P3 |
| Woolmer Rd UED N18 | 99 | P3 |
| Woolmore St POP/IOD E14 | 141 | N9 |
| Woolneigh St FUL/PGN SW6 | 157 | P3 |
| Woolridge Cl EBED/NFELT TW14 | 174 | A4 |
| Woolridge Wy HOM E9 * | 140 | E2 |
| Wool Rd RYNPK SW20 | 178 | F9 |
| Woolstaplers Wy BERM/RHTH SE16 | 139 | N9 |
| Woolston Cl WALTH E17 | 100 | C10 |
| Woolstone Rd FSTH SE23 | 182 | G5 |
| Woolwich Church St WOOL/PLUM SE18 | 162 | A5 |
| Woolwich Common WOOL/PLUM SE18 | 162 | A10 |
| Woolwich Foot Tnl CAN/RD E16 | 162 | D1 |
| Woolwich High St WOOL/PLUM SE18 | 162 | G10 |
| Woolwich Manorway CAN/RD E16 | 162 | E1 |
| Woolwich Manor Wy EHAM E6 | 142 | G5 |

Woolwich New Rd
WOOL/PLUM SE18 162 D4
Woolwich Rd ABYW SE2 163 N5
BELV DA17 164 A4
BXLYHN DA7 164 B9
CHARL SE7 161 P3
GNWCH SE10 161 M4
Wooster Gdns POP/IOD E14 141 J8
Wooster Rd BEAC HP9 88 B7
Wootton Cl EMPK RM11 125 L3
EPSOM KT18 238 B2
Wootton Dr HHNE HP2 36 A1
Wootton Gv FNCH N3 97 K9
Wootton St STHWK SE1 18 B1
Worbeck Rd PGE/AN SE20 204 A2
Worcester Av TOTM N17 99 P8
UPMR RM14 126 E6
Worcester Cl CRICK NW2 116 D8
CROY/NA CR0 204 E9
MEO DA13 190 C10
MTCM CR4 202 B2
SWCM DA10 166 G10
Worcester Ct WOT/HER KT12 197 K9
Worcester Crs MLHL NW7 96 B4
WFD IG8 101 P5
Worcester Dr ASHF TW15 174 C9
CHSWK W4 156 B2
Worcester Gdns GFD/PVL UB6 134 B1
IL IG1 122 B5
SL SL1 149 J1
WPK KT4 200 B10
Worcester Ms
KIL/WHAMP NW6 3 H1
Worcester Park Rd WPK KT4 199 P10
Worcester Rd BELMT SM2 221 K4
GUW GU2 249 L8
HAT AL10 40 C3
MNPK E12 122 C8
REIG RH2 257 K9
UX/CGN UB8 131 M7
WALTH E17 100 C10
WIM/MER SW19 179 J8
Worcesters Av EN EN1 79 P4
Wordsworth Av GFD/PVL UB6 134 C4
MNPK E12 142 B2
PUR/KEN CR8 241 L1
SWFD E18 121 L1
Wordsworth Cl CRAWE RH10 284 C5
HARH RM3 105 K9
TIL RM18 168 F8
Wordsworth Ct HAT AL10 * 40 D3
Wordsworth Dr CHEAM SM3 220 F1
Wordsworth Gdns BORE WD6 75 M9
Wordsworth Md REDH RH1 258 C8
Wordsworth Pde
CEND/HSY/T N8 * 119 J2
Wordsworth Pl HAMP NW3 118 A10
Wordsworth Rd
ADL/WDHM KT15 215 N1
HPTN TW12 175 N7
PGE/AN SE20 182 C10
SLN SL2 128 C6
STHWK SE1 19 L6
STNW/STAM N16 119 M9
WELL DA16 163 H7
WLGTN SM6 222 D3
Wordsworth Wk
GLDGN NW11 117 J2
Wordsworth Wy DART DA1 165 P10
WDR/YW UB7 151 P3
Worfield St BTSEA SW11 157 P6
Worgan St BERM/RHTH SE16 160 C2
LBTH SE11 17 N7
Works Rd ADL/WDHM KT15 215 L5
Worland Rd SRTFD E15 141 K2
Worlds End EPSOM KT18 * 238 A2
World's End COB KT11 217 H10
Worlds End Est
WBPTN SW10 * 157 N6
Worlds End La ORP BR6 227 K4
World's End La WCHMH N21 78 G9
Worlds End Pas
WBPTN SW10 * 157 N6
Worley Pl BEAC HP9 89 J6
Worley Rd STALW/RED AL3 38 B5
Worleys Dr ORP BR6 226 G1
Worlidge St HMSMTH W6 156 F4
Worlingham Rd EDUL SE22 159 N10
Wormholt Rd SHB W12 136 D10
Wormholt Ter SHB W12 * 136 D10
Wormley Ct WAB EN9 63 M9
Wormley Lodge Cl BROX EN10 44 E9
Wormwood St OBST EC2N 13 J5
Wormyngford Ct WAB EN9 63 M9
Wornington Green Est
NKENS W10 8 A3
Wornington Rd NKENS W10 8 A2
Woronzow Rd STJWD NW8 3 M6
Worple Av ISLW TW7 176 F1
STA TW18 173 L9
WIM/MER SW19 178 G10
Worple Cl RYLN/HDSTN HA2 113 N6
Worple Rd EPSOM KT18 220 B10
ISLW TW7 154 F10
LHD/OX KT22 236 G9
RYNPK SW20 200 F2
STA TW18 173 L10
Worple Road Ms
WIM/MER SW19 179 J9
Worplesdon Rd RGUW GU3 249 L5
Worple St MORT/ESHN SW14 156 A9
The Worple STWL/WRAY TW19 172 C2
Worple Wy RCHPK/HAM TW10 177 K1
RYLN/HDSTN HA2 113 N6
Worrin Cl BRWN CM15 107 L2
Worrin Rd BRWN CM15 107 L3
Worsfold Cl RPLY/SEND GU23 232 E9
Worships Hl SEV TN13 246 F8
Worship St SDTCH EC2A 13 H2
Worslade Rd TOOT SW17 179 N7
Worsley Bridge Rd SYD SE26 182 E8
Worsley Gv CLPT E5 119 P9
Worsley Rd WAN E11 121 K9
Worsopp Dr CLAP SW4 180 D1
Worsted Gn REDH RH1 258 E5
Worth Cl ORP BR6 227 H1
Worthfield Cl HOR/WEW KT19 220 A4
Worth Gv WALW SE17 18 G8
Worthing Cl GRAYS RM17 167 K5
SRTFD E15 141 K3
Worthing Rd HEST TW5 153 N5
Worthington Cl MTCM CR4 202 C4
Worthington Rd SURB KT6 199 L8
Worth Park Av CRAWE RH10 284 D6
Worth Rd CRAWE RH10 284 D7
Worth Wy CRAWE RH10 284 D8
Wortley Rd CROY/NA CR0 203 H7
EHAM E6 142 A2
Worton Gdns ISLW TW7 154 C8
Worton Rd ISLW TW7 154 E9
Worton Wy ISLW TW7 154 C8
Wotton Dr RDKG RH5 271 M6
Wotton Gn STMC/STPC BR5 207 N4
Wotton Rd CRICK NW2 116 F9
DEPT SE8 160 E5
Wotton Wy BELMT SM2 220 F6
Wouldham Rd CAN/RD E16 141 L8
GRAYS RM17 167 K5
Wouldham Ter
STMC/STPC BR5 * 207 L3
Wrabness Wy STA TW18 195 L1
Wragby Rd WAN E11 * 121 K8
Wrampling Pl ED N9 99 P2
Wrangley Ct WAB EN9 63 M9
Wray Av CLAY IG5 122 D1
Wray Cl EMPK RM11 125 L5
Wray Common Rd REIG RH2 257 M9
Wray Crs FSBYPK N4 118 F7
Wrayfield Av REIG RH2 257 M9
Wrayfield Rd CHEAM SM3 200 G10
Wraylands Dr REIG RH2 257 N8
Wray La REIG RH2 257 M6
Wraymead Pl REIG RH2 * 257 L9
Wray Mill Pk REIG RH2 257 N8
Wray Park Rd REIG RH2 257 L9
Wray Rd BELMT SM2 221 J5
Wraysbury Cl HSLWW TW4 175 M1
Wraysbury Dr WDR/YW UB7 131 N9
Wraysbury Gdns STA TW18 173 H7
Wraysbury Rd
STWL/WRAY TW19 172 E5
Wrays Wy YEAD UB4 132 F7
Wrekin Rd WOOL/PLUM SE18 162 F6
Wren Av CRICK NW2 116 F9
NWDGN UB2 153 N3
Wren Cl CAN/RD E16 141 L8
ED N9 100 C2
HTHAIR TW6 151 L9
SAND/SEL CR2 224 C6
STMC/STPC BR5 207 N3
Wren Ct CRAWE RH10 * 283 P10
Wren Crs ADL/WDHM KT15 215 N2
BUSH WD23 94 B2
Wren Dr WAB EN9 63 M10
WDR/YW UB7 151 N1
Wren Gdns DAGW RM9 123 N10
HCH RM12 124 G6
Wren Ms LEW SE13 * 161 K10
Wren Pl BRW CM14 107 J4
Wren Rd CMBW SE5 159 L7
DAGW RM9 123 N10
SCUP DA14 185 M6
Wren's Av ASHF TW15 174 D8
Wrens Cft GVW DA11 190 B7
Wrensfield HHW HP1 35 K7
Wren's Hl LHD/OX KT22 236 B1
The Wrens HLWW/ROY CM19 46 E1
Wren St FSBYW WC1X 11 P1
Wren Ter LOU IG10 * 82 D6
Wrentham Av WLSDN NW10 136 G4
Wrenthorpe Rd BMLY BR1 183 K7
Wren Wk TIL RM18 168 E6
Wren Wd WGCE AL7 23 L4
Wrenwood Wy PIN HA5 113 J2
Wrexham Rd BOW E3 140 F4
HARH RM3 105 L5
Wricklemarsh Rd
BKHTH/KID SE3 161 N8
Wrigglesworth St NWCR SE14 160 C6
Wright WDSR SL4 148 B9
Wright Cl LEW SE13 161 J10
STALE/WH AL4 21 J4
Wright Gdns SHPTN TW17 196 B5
Wright Rd HEST TW5 153 K6
Wrights Aly WIM/MER SW19 178 F9
Wrightsbridge Rd BRW CM14 105 N2
Wrights Cl DAGE RM10 124 C9
Wrights La BRWN CM15 87 J2
Wright's La KENS W8 14 G3
Wrights Pl WLSDN NW10 * 135 P1
Wrights Rd SNWD SE25 203 M3
Wright's Rd BOW E3 140 E4
Wright's Rw WLGTN SM6 222 C1
Wrigley Cl CHING E4 * 101 J6
Wriotsley Wy
ADL/WDHM KT15 215 K3
Wrotham Rd BAR EN5 77 H6
CAMTN NW1 5 H4
MEO DA13 190 D10
WEA W13 135 H10
WELL DA16 163 M7
Wroths Pth LOU IG10 82 C5
Wrottesley Rd WLSDN NW10 136 D4
WOOL/PLUM SE18 162 F5
Wroughton Rd BTSEA SW11 180 A2
Wroughton Ter HDN NW4 * 116 E2
Wroxall Rd DAGW RM9 143 M1
Wroxham Av HHS/BOV HP3 35 N8
Wroxham Gdns ENC/FH EN2 79 H1
FBAR/BDGN N11 98 D8
POTB/CUF EN6 58 G7
Wroxham Rd THMD SE28 143 N9
Wroxham Wk CRAWE RH10 284 C9
Wroxham Wy BARK/HLT IG6 102 E9
Wroxton Rd PECK SE15 160 A8
Wrythe Gn CAR SM5 202 A10
Wrythe Green Rd CAR SM5 202 A10
Wrythe La CAR SM5 201 N8
Wulfstan St SHB W12 136 C8
Wulstan Pk POTB/CUF EN6 59 M8
Wyatt Cl BUSH WD23 94 D1
FELT TW13 175 L4
YEAD UB4 133 H7
Wyatt Dr BARN SW13 156 E5
Wyatt Park Rd
BRXS/STRHM SW2 180 G5
Wyatt Rd DART DA1 164 G9
FSTGT E7 141 M1
HBRY N5 119 K8
STA TW18 173 K8
WDSR SL4 148 C9
Wyatt's Cl RKW/CH/CXG WD3 71 K7
Wyatt's Green Rd
BRWN CM15 87 J2
Wyatt's La WALTH E17 121 H1
Wyatt's Rd RKW/CH/CXG WD3 71 J8
Wybert St CAMTN NW1 10 F1
Wyborne Wy WLSDN NW10 135 P2
Wyburn Av BAR EN5 77 J7
Wychcombe Studios
HAMP NW3 * 4 A2
Wyche Gv SAND/SEL CR2 223 K4
Wych Elm HLW CM20 28 F10
Wych Elm Cl EMPK RM11 125 P4
KUTN/CMB KT2 177 L10
Wych Elm Ri GU GU1 268 B3
Wych Elm Rd EMPK RM11 125 P4
Wychelm Rd LTWR GU18 212 B7
Wych Elms LCOL/BKTW AL2 56 A4
Wycherley Cl BKHTH/KID SE3 161 L6
Wycherley Crs BAR EN5 77 L10
Wychford Dr SBW CM21 29 M2
Wych Hl WOKS/MYFD GU22 231 P5
Wych Hill La
WOKS/MYFD GU22 232 A5
Wych Hill Pk
WOKS/MYFD GU22 232 A5
Wych Hill Ri
WOKS/MYFD GU22 231 P5
Wychwood Av EDGW HA8 95 J7
THHTH CR7 203 J3
Wychwood Cl EDGW HA8 95 J7
SUN TW16 175 H9
Wychwood End HGT N6 118 D5
Wychwood Gdns CLAY IG5 122 C2
Wychwood Wy NTHWD HA6 92 G8
Wycliffe Cl CHES/WCR EN8 62 C5
WELL DA16 163 J7
Wycliffe Rd BTSEA SW11 158 B8
WIM/MER SW19 179 L9
Wycliffe Rw GVW DA11 190 C4
Wyclif St FSBYE EC1V 6 C10
Wycombe End BEAC HP9 108 C1
Wycombe Gdns GLDGN NW11 117 J7
Wycombe Pl STAL AL1 38 G3
WAND/EARL SW18 179 M2
Wycombe Rd ALP/SUD HA0 135 M3
GNTH/NBYPK IG2 122 C3
TOTM N17 99 P9
Wycombe Sq KENS W8 8 D10
Wycombe Wy STALE/WH AL4 38 G3
Wyddial Gn WGCE AL7 23 L5
Wydell Cl MRDN SM4 200 F6
Wydenhurst Rd CROY/NA CR0 203 P7
Wydeville Manor Rd
LEE/GVPK SE12 183 N7
Wyecliffe Gdns REDH RH1 258 D6
Wye Cl ASHF TW15 174 C7
ORP BR6 207 J7
RSLP HA4 112 D4
Wyedale LCOL/BKTW AL2 57 L3
Wyemead Crs CHING E4 101 K3
Wye Rd GVE DA12 190 G5
Wye St BTSEA SW11 157 N9
The Wye HHNE HP2 36 B1
Wyeth's Ms EW KT17 220 C9
Wyeth's Rd EW KT17 220 C9
Wyevale Cl NTHWD HA6 113 H1
Wyfields CLAY IG5 102 E9
Wyfold Rd FUL/PGN SW6 157 H7
Wyke Cl ISLW TW7 154 E5
Wyke Gdns HNWL W7 154 E2
Wykeham Av DAGW RM9 143 M1
EMPK RM11 125 L4
Wykeham Cl GVE DA12 191 H9
WDR/YW UB7 152 B5
Wykeham Gn DAGW RM9 143 M1
Wykeham Hl WBLY HA9 115 L6
Wykeham Ri TRDG/WHET N20 97 H2
Wykeham Rd GU GU1 250 G9
HDN NW4 116 F3
KTN/HRWW/WS HA3 114 G2
Wykeridge Cl CSHM HP5 50 G3
Wyke Rd BOW E3 140 F2
RYNPK SW20 200 F2
Wylands Rd DTCH/LGLY SL3 150 D4
Wylchin Cl PIN HA5 112 G2
Wyldes Cl GLDGN NW11 117 M6
Wyldewood ASC SL5 192 C6
Wyldfield Gdns ED N9 99 N3
Wyld Wy WBLY HA9 135 N1
Wyldwood Cl HLWE CM17 29 M5
Wyleu St FSTH SE23 182 D3
Wylie Rd NWDGN UB2 153 P2
Wyllen Cl WCHPL E1 140 B6
Wyllyotts Pl POTB/CUF EN6 59 J8
Wylo Dr BAR EN5 76 C10
Wymark Cl RAIN RM13 144 G4
Wymering Rd MV/WKIL W9 2 F10
Wymers Cl SL SL1 128 A4
Wymond St PUT/ROE SW15 156 F9
Wynan Rd POP/IOD E14 160 G4
Wynaud Ct WDGN N22 98 G7
Wyncham Av BFN/LL DA15 185 H4
Wynches Farm Dr
STALE/WH AL4 39 J5
Wynchgate
KTN/HRWW/WS HA3 94 D8
STHGT/OAK N14 98 F1
Wynchlands Crs
STALE/WH AL4 39 J6
Wyncote Wy SAND/SEL CR2 224 C5
Wyncroft Cl BMLY BR1 206 C3
Wyndale Av CDALE/KGS NW9 115 M4
Wyndcliff Rd CHARL SE7 161 N5
Wyndcroft Cl ENC/FH EN2 79 J7
Wyndham Av COB KT11 217 H9
Wyndham Cl BELMT SM2 221 K4
ORP BR6 206 F8
Wyndham Crs HSLWW TW4 175 N2
KTTN NW5 118 D8
SL SL1 128 A4
Wyndham Est CMBW SE5 159 K6
Wyndham Ms MBLAR W1H 10 A4
Wyndham Pl MBLAR W1H 10 A4
Wyndham Rd CMBW SE5 159 K6
EBAR EN4 98 A2
EHAM E6 142 A2
KUTN/CMB KT2 177 L10
WEA W13 154 G2
WOKN/KNAP GU21 231 N4
Wyndhams End WGCE AL7 23 J9
Wyndham St CAMTN NW1 10 A3
Wyndham Yd MBLAR W1H * 10 A4
Wyndhurst Cl SAND/SEL CR2 223 J4
Wyneham Rd HNHL SE24 181 L1
Wynell Rd FSTH SE23 182 C6
Wynford Gv STMC/STPC BR5 207 L3
Wynford Pl BELV DA17 164 B5
Wynford Rd IS N1 5 N7
Wynford Wy ELTH/MOT SE9 184 C6
Wyngrave Pl BEAC HP9 88 B6
Wynlea Cl CRAWE RH10 285 P5
Wynlie Gdns PIN HA5 93 J10
Wynn Bridge Cl WFD IG8 102 A9
Wynndale Rd SWFD E18 101 N9
Wynne Rd BRXN/ST SW9 159 H8
Wynn's Av BFN/LL DA15 185 K1
Wynnstay Gdns KENS W8 14 F3
Wynnstow Pk OXTED RH8 261 L7
Wynnswick Rd BEAC HP9 89 H6
Wynsham Wy BFOR GU20 212 A2
Wynter St BTSEA SW11 157 M10
Wynton Gdns SNWD SE25 203 M5
Wynton Gv WOT/HER KT12 197 H10
Wynton Pl ACT W3 135 N8
Wynyard Ter LBTH SE11 17 P7
Wynyatt St FSBYE EC1V 6 C9
Wyre Gv EDGW HA8 95 N4
HYS/HAR UB3 153 H3
Wyresdale Crs GFD/PVL UB6 134 E5
Wysemead HORL RH6 280 D3
Wyteleaf Cl RSLP HA4 112 D4
Wythburn Pl MBLAR W1H 10 A6
Wythenshawe Rd DAGE RM10 124 B8
Wythes Cl BMLY BR1 206 C2
Wythes Rd CAN/RD E16 142 B10
Wythfield Rd ELTH/MOT SE9 184 C2
Wyton WGCE AL7 23 N5
Wyvenhoe Rd
RYLN/HDSTN HA2 114 B8
Wyvern Cl ORP BR6 207 L10
Wyvern Est NWMAL KT3 * 200 D3
Wyvern Pl ADL/WDHM KT15 * 215 L1
Wyvern Rd PUR/KEN CR8 223 H6
Wyvern Wy UX/CGN UB8 131 L3
Wyvil Rd VX/NE SW8 158 F6
Wyvis St POP/IOD E14 140 G7


## Y


Yabsley St POP/IOD E14 141 H10
Yaffle Rd WEY KT13 216 D6
Yalding Gv STMC/STPC BR5 207 N4
Yalding Rd BERM/RHTH SE16 19 N4
Yale Cl HSLWW TW4 175 N1
Yale Wy HCH RM12 125 H9
Yarborough Rd
WIM/MER SW19 201 N1
Yarbridge Cl BELMT SM2 * 221 L6
Yardley Cl CHING E4 80 G9
REIG RH2 257 L8
Yardley La CHING E4 80 G9
Yardley St FSBYW WC1X 6 A10
Yard Md EGH TW20 172 D6
Yarm Cl LHD/OX KT22 237 H9
Yarm Court Rd LHD/OX KT22 237 H9
Yarmouth Cl CRAWE RH10 284 B9
Yarmouth Crs TOTM N17 120 A3
Yarmouth Pl MYFR/PICC W1J 10 E10
Yarmouth Rd SL SL1 129 H8
WATN WD24 73 J4
Yarm Wy LHD/OX KT22 237 H9
Yarnton Wy ABYW SE2 163 M1
ERITHM DA18 164 A2
Yarrow Crs EHAM E6 142 B7
Yarrowside AMSS HP7 69 N6
Yateley St WOOL/PLUM SE18 162 A2
Yattendon Rd HORL RH6 280 C4
Yeading Av RYLN/HDSTN HA2 113 M7
Yeading Fk YEAD UB4 133 K7
Yeading Gdns YEAD UB4 133 J7
Yeading La YEAD UB4 133 J8
Yeames Cl WEA W13 134 F8
Yearling Cl WARE SG12 26 E4
Yeate St IS N1 6 G4
Yeatman Rd HGT N6 118 A4
Yeats Cl HNWL W7 134 E9
LEW SE13 * 161 J8
REDH RH1 275 M3
WLSDN NW10 136 B1
Ye Cnr OXHEY WD19 73 L10
Yeend Cl E/WMO/HCT KT8 197 P4
Yeldham Rd HMSMTH W6 156 G4
Yeldham Vls HMSMTH W6 * 156 G4
Yellowcress Dr
CHOB/PIR GU24 230 F2
Yellowpine Wy CHIG IG7 103 L5
Yelverton Cl HARH RM3 105 K9
Yelverton Rd BTSEA SW11 157 N8
Yenston Cl MRDN SM4 201 K6
Yeoman Cl EHAM E6 142 E9
Yeoman Dr STWL/WRAY TW19 173 P4
Yeoman Rd NTHLT UB5 133 M2
Yeomanry Cl EW KT17 220 C8
Yeomans Acre RSLP HA4 113 H4
Yeoman's Mdw SEV TN13 265 H2
Yeoman's Rw CHEL SW3 15 P4
Yeomans Ter
WOKN/KNAP GU21 * 231 J3
Yeoman St BERM/RHTH SE16 160 D3
Yeomans Wy PEND EN3 * 80 A6
Yeoman's Yd WCHPL E1 13 M7
Yeoman Wy REDH RH1 276 C5
Yeomen Wy BARK/HLT IG6 102 F7
Yeo St BOW E3 140 G7
Yeoveney Cl
STWL/WRAY TW19 172 G5
Yeovil Cl ORP BR6 207 H9
Yeovil Rd SL SL1 128 D7
Yeovilton Pl KUTN/CMB KT2 177 J8
Yerbury Rd ARCH N19 118 E8
Yester Dr CHST BR7 184 B10
Yester Pk CHST BR7 184 C10
Yester Rd CHST BR7 184 C10
Yevele Wy EMPK RM11 125 M5
Yew Av WDR/YW UB7 131 P9
Yewbank Cl PUR/KEN CR8 241 L1
Yew Cl BKHH IG9 102 A3
CHESW EN7 * 61 M3
Yewdale Cl BMLY BR1 183 K9
Yewfield Rd WLSDN NW10 136 C1
Yew Gv CRICK NW2 116 G9
WGCE AL7 23 M6
Yewlands HOD EN11 44 F4
SBW CM21 29 P2
Yewlands Cl BNSTD SM7 239 L1
Yewlands Dr HOD EN11 44 F4
Yew Pl WEY KT13 * 196 G10
Yews Av EN EN1 80 A2
The Yews ASHF TW15 * 174 C7
BF/WBF KT14 * 215 P8
Yew Tree Bottom Rd EW KT17 238 E3
Yewtree Cl MUSWH N10 98 D9
RYLN/HDSTN HA2 114 A2
Yew Tree Cl WCHMH N21 99 H1
WPK KT4 200 B8
BEAC HP9 88 E10
COUL/CHIP CR5 240 A5
CSHM HP5 51 M6
HORL RH6 280 B2
LEW SE13 161 H9
RBRW/HUT CM13 87 N10
SEV TN13 246 E9
WELL DA16 163 K7
Yew Tree Ct BORE WD6 75 J10
Yew Tree Dr CTHM CR3 259 N1
GU GU1 249 N5
HHS/BOV HP3 52 E4
Yewtree End LCOL/BKTW AL2 56 A3
Yew Tree Gdns CHDH RM6 123 P3
EPSOM KT18 237 P1
ROMW/RG RM7 124 E3
Yew Tree La REIG RH2 257 L7
Yew Tree Rd BECK BR3 204 E3
DORK RH4 254 F10
DTCH/LGLY SL3 149 M2
HGDN/ICK UB10 132 A3
HORL RH6 279 H8
SHB W12 136 C9
Yewtrees EGH TW20 194 F3
Yew Trees SHPTN TW17 196 A4
Yew Tree Wk EHSLY KT24 253 L3
HSLWW TW4 175 N1
PUR/KEN CR8 223 K6
Yew Wk HOD EN11 44 F4
HRW HA1 114 D6
Yoakley Rd STNW/STAM N16 119 M7
Yoke Cl HOLWY N7 5 M1
Yolande Gdns ELTH/MOT SE9 184 B1
Yonge Pk HOLWY N7 119 H8
York Av BFN/LL DA15 185 H5
HNWL W7 134 D10
HYS/HAR UB3 132 D8
MORT/ESHN SW14 177 P1
SL SL1 129 J8
STAN HA7 94 G9
WDSR SL4 148 G8
York Br CAMTN NW1 10 C1
York Blds CHCR WC2N 11 M8
York Cl BF/WBF KT14 215 P8
BRWN CM15 107 L1
CMBW SE5 * 159 K8
EHAM E6 142 C8
HNWL W7 134 D10
KGLGY WD4 54 B5
MRDN SM4 201 L4
STA TW18 173 P9
York Crs BORE WD6 76 A6
LOU IG10 82 B7
Yorke Gdns REIG RH2 257 K9
Yorke Ga CTHM CR3 241 L8
WAT WD17 73 H6
Yorke Rd REIG RH2 257 K9
RKW/CH/CXG WD3 72 B10
Yorkes HLWS CM18 47 J3
York Gdns WOT/HER KT12 197 L9
York Ga CAMTN NW1 10 D2
STHGT/OAK N14 98 F1
York Gv PECK SE15 160 B7
York Hl LOU IG10 82 B7
WNWD SE27 181 J6
York House Pl KENS W8 14 G1
Yorkland Av WELL DA16 163 J10
York Ms IL IG1 122 D7
KTTN NW5 118 C10
York Pde BTFD TW8 * 155 J4
CDALE/KGS NW9 * 116 D4
York Pl BTSEA SW11 157 M9
IL IG1 122 D7
York Ri KTTN NW5 118 C8
ORP BR6 207 H8
York Rd ACT W3 135 P8
BAR EN5 77 M9
BELMT SM2 221 K5
BF/WBF KT14 215 N8
BH/WHM TN16 243 N5
BRWN CM15 107 L1
BTFD TW8 155 J4
BTSEA SW11 157 M10
CHES/WCR EN8 62 D10
CHING E4 100 F6
CROY/NA CR0 203 H7
EA W5 155 H2
EPP CM16 66 B3
FBAR/BDGN N11 98 E7
FSTGT E7 141 M1
GU GU1 268 A1
GVW DA11 190 A3
HSLW TW3 154 A9
IL IG1 122 D8
KUTN/CMB KT2 177 L10
LEY E10 121 H8
NTHWD HA6 93 H10
RAIN RM13 144 E2
RCHPK/HAM TW10 177 L1
SAND/SEL CR2 224 C6
STAL AL1 38 E5
STHWK SE1 17 P1
TEDD TW11 176 D7
UED N18 100 A6
UX/CGN UB8 131 N2
WALTH E17 120 C3
WATW WD18 73 K9
WCHMH N21 99 L1
WDSR SL4 148 G8
WEY KT13 216 D2
WIM/MER SW19 179 L9
WOKS/MYFD GU22 232 A5
Yorkshire Cl STNW/STAM N16 119 M8
Yorkshire Gdns UED N18 100 A6
Yorkshire Grey Yd
GINN WC1R * 11 N4
Yorkshire Rd MTCM CR4 202 F5
POP/IOD E14 140 D8
York Sq POP/IOD E14 140 D8
York St MBLAR W1H 10 A4
MHST W1U 10 B3
MTCM CR4 202 B7
York Street Chambers
MHST W1U * 10 B3
York Ter ENC/FH EN2 79 K4
ERITH DA8 164 D7
York Ter East CAMTN NW1 10 D2
York Ter West CAMTN NW1 10 C2
Yorkton St BETH E2 7 N7
York Wy CHSGTN KT9 219 J4
FELT TW13 175 N6
GSTN WD25 73 L2
HHNE HP2 35 P7
HOLWY N7 5 L2
TRDG/WHET N20 98 A4
York Way Ct IS N1 5 M6
York Way Est HOLWY N7 5 L2
Youngfield Rd HHW HP1 35 J5
Youngmans Cl ENC/FH EN2 79 K5
Young Rd CAN/RD E16 141 P8
Youngs Ms HERT/WAT SG14 25 K5
Youngs Ri WGCW AL8 22 E5
Youngs Rd GNTH/NBYPK IG2 122 G3
Young St KENS W8 14 G2
LHD/OX KT22 236 E10
Youngstroat La
CHOB/PIR GU24 214 B6
Yoxley Ap GNTH/NBYPK IG2 122 F4
Yoxley Dr GNTH/NBYPK IG2 122 F4
Yukon Rd BAL SW12 180 C3
BROX EN10 62 D1
Yule Cl LCOL/BKTW AL2 55 N6
Yunus Khan Cl WALTH E17 120 F3


## Z


Zambezie Dr ED N9 100 B4
Zambra Wy BGR/WK TN15 247 N6
Zampa Rd BERM/RHTH SE16 160 B4
Zander Ct BETH E2 7 P9
Zangwill Rd BKHTH/KID SE3 162 A7
Zealand Av WDR/YW UB7 151 N6
Zealand Rd BOW E3 140 D4
Zelah Rd STMC/STPC BR5 207 L7
Zennor Rd BAL SW12 180 D4
Zenoria St EDUL SE22 159 N10
Zermatt Rd THHTH CR7 203 K4
Zetland St POP/IOD E14 141 H7
Zig Zag Rd PUR/KEN CR8 241 K2
RDKG RH5 255 H6
Zinnia Dr CHOB/PIR GU24 230 F2
Zion Pl GVE DA12 190 E3
THHTH CR7 203 L4
Zion Rd THHTH CR7 203 L4
Zoar St STHWK SE1 12 E9
Zoffany St ARCH N19 118 E7


## Index - featured places


02 Centre
KIL/WHAMP NW6 3 J1
2 Willow Road (NT)
HAMP NW3 117 P9
30 St Mary Axe
HDTCH EC3A 13 K6
41 Hotel
BGVA SW1W 16 F3
51 Buckingham Gate (Hotel)
WESTW SW1E 17 H3
7/7 Memorial
MYFR/PKLN W1K 10 C10
Aarotya Medical Centre
SEVS/STOTM N15 119 K2
Abbey Business Centre
VX/NE SW8 158 D7
Abbey Christian School for the English Language
STJWD NW8 3 K8
The Abbey Clinic
BELV DA17 164 A4
Abbey College London
BAY/PAD W2 8 F6
Abbey Gateway
STALW/RED AL3 38 B6
Abbey Industrial Estate
ALP/SUD HA0 135 L3
MTCM CR4 202 A5
Abbeylands School
ADL/WDHM KT15 215 K2
Abbey Lane Commercial Estate
SRTFD E15 141 J4
Abbey Mead Industrial Park
WAB EN9 62 G10
Abbey Medical Centre
STJWD NW8 3 H6
Abbey Mills
WIM/MER SW19 201 M1
Abbey Park Industrial Estate
BARK EC2Y 142 E4
Abbey Primary School
ABYW SE2 163 M2
MRDN SM4 201 K7
STALW/RED AL3 38 B7
Abbey Road ⊖
SRTFD E15 141 J4
Abbey Road Health Centre
SRTFD E15 141 K3
Abbey Road Studios
STJWD NW8 3 K8
Abbey Sports Centre
BARK EC2Y 142 F3
Abbey Trading Estate
SYD SE26 182 D8
Abbey View Golf Club
STALW/RED AL3 38 A7
Abbey Wharf Industrial Estate
BARK EC2Y 142 G5
Abbey Wood ⇌
ABYW SE2 163 M2
Abbey Wood School
ABYW SE2 163 K2
Abbotsbury Primary School
MRDN SM4 201 K5
Abbotsfield School
HGDN/ICK UB10 132 C4
Abbots Hill School
HHS/BOV HP3 54 C1
Abbots Hospital
GU GU1 268 A1
Abbots Langley Primary School
ABLGY WD5 54 F5
Abbotsweld Primary School
HLWS CM18 46 G3
Abbotswood Medical Centre
ABLGY WD5 55 H8
Abbs Cross School & Arts College
HCH RM12 125 J8
ABC Cinema
GVE DA12 190 E2
PUT/ROE SW15 157 H9
Abercorn Place School
CAMTN NW1 9 P3
Abercorn School
MBLAR W1H 10 A4
STJWD NW8 3 K8
Aberdeen Wharf
WAP E1W 140 A10
Aberdour School
KWD/TDW/WH KT20 239 J4
Aberglen Industrial Estate
HYS/HAR UB3 152 E1
Abingdon House School
KENS W8 14 F3
Abinger Common First School
RDKG RH5 271 L8
Abney Park Cemetery
STNW/STAM N16 119 M7
Aboyne Lodge Primary School
STALW/RED AL3 38 C5
Abridge Golf & Country Club
ABR/ST RM4 84 A3
Acacia Business Centre
WAN E11 121 K8
The Academy at Peckham
PECK SE15 159 N7
The Academy of Contemporary Music
GUW GU2 267 P1
The Academy School
HAMP NW3 117 N9
Acland Burghley School
KTTN NW5 118 C9
Acorn Industrial Park
DART DA1 187 H1
Acorn Medical Centre
HGDN/ICK UB10 132 B3
TWK TW1 176 F4
Acorns CE School
REIG RH2 274 D6
The Acorns First School
BRKHM/BTCW RH3 256 A10
Acorn Trading Centre
WTHK RM20 167 K5
Acre Road Health Clinic
KUTN/CMB KT2 177 L10
ACS Egham International School
EGH TW20 193 P1
ACS Hillingdon International School
HGDN/ICK UB10 132 A3
Activity World
HAT AL10 40 E1
Acton Business Centre
WLSDN NW10 136 A6
Acton Central ⊖
ACT W3 136 A10
Acton Central Industrial Estate
ACT W3 135 N9
Acton Health Centre
ACT W3 135 P10
Acton High School
ACT W3 155 M1
Acton Hospital
ACT W3 155 M1
Acton Lane Medical Centre
CHSWK W4 155 P1
Acton Main Line ⇌
ACT W3 135 P8
Acton Park Industrial Estate
ACT W3 156 A1
Acton Superbowl
ACT W3 135 M7
Acton Swimming Baths
ACT W3 135 P10
Acton Town ⊖
ACT W3 155 M1
Acton & West London College
ACT W3 135 N10
Acumen (Anglo School)
NRWD SE19 203 M1
Adams Bridge Business Centre
WBLY HA9 115 N10
Adamsrill Primary School
SYD SE26 182 D6
Adath Yisroel Cemetery
EN EN1 79 N5
Addey & Stanhope School
NWCR SE14 160 E7
Addington Business Centre
CROY/NA CR0 225 K6
Addington Court Golf Club
CROY/NA CR0 224 E5
Addington Golf Club
CROY/NA CR0 224 E1
Addington High School
CROY/NA CR0 225 K8
Addington Palace Golf Club
CROY/NA CR0 224 D3
Addington Village ⊖
CROY/NA CR0 224 F3
Addiscombe ⊖
CROY/NA CR0 203 P8
Addiscombe CC
CROY/NA CR0 203 P10
Addison Primary School
WKENS W14 156 G2
Addlestone ⇌
ADL/WDHM KT15 215 N1
Addlestone Cemetery
ADL/WDHM KT15 195 K9
Adelphi Theatre
COVGDN WC2E 11 M8
Adeyfield School
HHNE HP2 36 B6
Adler Industrial Estate
HYS/HAR UB3 152 E1
Admiral Hyson Industrial Estate
STHWK SE1 160 A3
Admiralty Arch
STJS SW1Y 11 K9
The Adult College of Barking & Dagenham
BARK EC2Y 143 H1
Aerodrome Hotel
CROY/NA CR0 223 H3
Africa Centre
COVGDN WC2E 11 M7
Aga Khan University
CAN/RD E16 141 L7
RSQ WC1B 11 K4
Agency of Jewish Education
HDN NW4 116 G2
Agnew's
CONDST W1S 10 G9

Agora Shopping Centre PECK SE15 159 P8
AHA International London Centre BMSBY WC1N 11 P3
Ainslie Wood Primary School CHING E4 100 G6
Airbase Unity Elementary School RSLP HA4 112 D7
Airbus Coach Station HTHAIR TW6 152 A9
Air Call Business Centre CDALE/KGS NW9 116 A1
Airedale Physiotherapy Clinic CHSWK W4 156 C4
Airlinks Golf Club NWDGN UB2 153 K3
Air Links Industrial Estate HEST TW5 153 K4
Airport Gate Business Centre WDR/YW UB7 152 A6
Airport Industrial Estate BH/WHM TN16 244 A1
Akiva School FNCH N3 97 K10
Aksaray Sports Club STNW/STAM N16 119 L9
Alban Arena Cinema STAL AL1 38 C6
Alban Wood Primary School GSTN WD25 55 J9
Albany Centre & Theatre DEPT SE8 160 E6
Albany Clinic
BFN/LL DA15 185 K7
WIM/MER SW19 179 L10
Albany Park ⇌ SCUP DA14 185 N5
Albany Park Canoe & Sailing Club KUTN/CMB KT2 177 J9
Albany School (Grant Maintained) PEND EN3 80 C4
The Albany School HCH RM12 125 J7
Albemarle Primary School WIM/MER SW19 179 H5
Albert Memorial SKENS SW7 15 L1
Albion College RSQ WC1B 11 L4
Albion Health Centre WCHPL E1 140 A7
Albion J & I School BERM/RHTH SE16 160 B1
Albion Street Health Centre BERM/RHTH SE16 160 B1
Albright Industrial Estate RAIN RM13 144 G7
Alchemea IS N1 6 D5
The Alchemy Gallery CLKNW EC1R 12 A1
Aldenham Country Park BORE WD6 74 G9
Aldenham Golf & Country Club GSTN WD25 74 A4
Aldenham Preparatory School BORE WD6 74 E6
Alderbrook Primary School BAL SW12 180 C3
Aldersbrook County Secondary School MNPK E12 121 P6
Aldersbrook Primary School MNPK E12 121 N6
The Alderton Primary School LOU IG10 82 D9
Alderwood Primary School ELTH/MOT SE9 184 G2
Aldgate ⊖ TWRH EC3N 13 L6
Aldgate Bus Station HDTCH EC3A 13 L5
Aldgate East ⊖ WCHPL E1 13 M5
Aldro School MFD/CHID DA13 266 B10
Aldwickbury Park Golf Club HARP AL5 20 D2
Aldwickbury School HARP AL5 20 D3
Aldwych Theatre HOL/ALD WC2B 11 N6
Alexander Barracks CHOB/PIR GU24 230 A7
Alexander First School WDSR SL4 148 B9
Alexander McLeod Primary School ABYW SE2 163 L4
Alexandra Avenue Clinic RYLN/HDSTN HA2 113 N7
Alexandra Business Centre PEND EN3 80 C8
Alexandra Infant School
KUTN/CMB KT2 177 M10
PGE/AN SE20 182 C10
Alexandra Junior School
HSLW TW3 154 A8
SYD SE26 182 C9
Alexandra Palace WDGN N22 118 E1
Alexandra Palace Ice Rink WDGN N22 98 E10
Alexandra Park School FBAR/BDGN N11 98 D8
Alexandra Primary School WDGN N22 98 G10
Alexandra School RYLN/HDSTN HA2 113 N7
Al Falah Boys School CLPT E5 120 A8
Alfred Salter Primary School BERM/RHTH SE16 160 C1
Alfreds Way Industrial Estate BARK EC2Y 143 K3
Alfriston Special School BEAC HP9 88 B5
Al-Khair Primary & Secondary School CROY/NA CR0 203 L8
Allenby Primary School STHL UB1 133 P8
Allen Edwards Primary School CLAP SW4 158 F7
The All England Lawn Tennis & Croquet Club WIM/MER SW19 178 G6
Alleyns Junior School EDUL SE22 181 M1
Allfarthing JMI School WAND/EARL SW18 179 M2
All Nations Christian College WARE SG12 26 G4
All Saints ⊖ POP/IOD E14 141 H8
All Saints Benhilton CE Primary School SUT SM1 201 L10
All Saints Catholic School & Technology College BCTR RM8 124 B6
All Saints CE Infant School LHD/OX KT22 236 F5
All Saints CE Junior School NRWD SE19 203 M1
All Saints CE Primary School
BKHTH/KID SE3 161 K8
CAR SM5 222 B2
CRICK NW2 117 J8
FUL/PGN SW6 157 H8
PUT/ROE SW15 156 F9
TRDG/WHET N20 97 N3
WIM/MER SW19 179 M10
All Souls CE Primary School GTPST W1W 10 G4
Allum Lane Cemetery BORE WD6 75 K9
Allum Medical Centre WAN E11 121 J5
Alma J & I School BERM/RHTH SE16 19 N5
Alma Primary School PEND EN3 80 D9
Almeida Theatre IS N1 6 C4
Al-Noor Primary School GDMY/SEVK IG3 123 L6
Alperton ⊖ ALP/SUD HA0 135 J3
Alperton Cemetery ALP/SUD HA0 135 J3
Alperton Community School ALP/SUD HA0 135 K2
Alperton High School ALP/SUD HA0 135 J3
Alperton Sports Ground ALP/SUD HA0 135 J4
Alpha Business Centre WALTH E17 120 E3
Alpha Business Park BRKMPK AL9 40 F9
Alpha Preparatory School HRW HA1 114 D3
Alpine Business Centre EHAM E6 142 D7
Al-Risaala Boys Secondary School BAL SW12 180 C4
Al Sadiq & Al-Zahra High School KIL/WHAMP NW6 2 A5
Alscot Road Industrial Estate STHWK SE1 19 M5
Altmore Infant School EHAM E6 142 C2
The Alton School PUT/ROE SW15 178 C3
Ambler Primary School FSBYPK N4 119 J8
Ambleside Junior School WOT/HER KT12 197 K8
Ambresbury Banks Fort EPP CM16 64 E10
Ambulance Centre STRHM/NOR SW16 180 G6
AMC Business Centre WLSDN NW10 135 N5
The American Community School COB KT11 217 L6
American Intercontinental University MHST W1U 10 D4
Amersham ⇌ ⊖ AMS HP6 69 H4
Amersham & Chiltern RFC AMS HP6 68 F2
Amersham General Hospital AMSS HP7 68 F7
Amersham Hill CC AMS HP6 69 K4
The Amersham School AMSS HP7 69 K6
Amersham Town FC AMSS HP7 68 F5
Amersham & Wycombe College
AMSS HP7 69 L5
CSHM HP5 51 J3
AMF Bowling
CRAWW RH11 283 N7
LEW SE13 161 H9
Amherst School SEV TN13 246 F9
Amida Golf FELT TW13 175 P6
Ampere Way ⊖ CROY/NA CR0 202 G8
Ampthill Square Medical Centre CAMTN NW1 5 H8
Amwell View Special School WARE SG12 26 G7
Anchorage Point Industrial Estate CHARL SE7 161 P2
Anchor Bay Industrial Estate ERITH DA8 164 G6
Anchor Retail Park WCHPL E1 140 B6
Andaz Hotel LVPST EC2M 13 J4
Andover Medical Centre HOLWY N7 118 G8
The Andrew Ewing Primary School HEST TW5 153 N6
Andrews Lane J & I School CHESW EN7 62 A4
Anerley ⇌ ⊖ PGE/AN SE20 203 P1
Anerley School NRWD SE19 203 P1
Angel ⊖ IS N1 6 C7
Angel Centre DART DA1 187 M2
Angel Road ⇌ UED N18 100 B6
Angerstein Business Park GNWCH SE10 161 M3
Anglesea Centre GVW DA11 190 E2
Anglian Industrial Estate BARK EC2Y 143 J6
Animal Cemetery REDBR IG4 122 A1
Annemount School EFNCH N2 117 M4
Annunciation RC Infant School EDGW HA8 96 A9
The Annunciation RC Junior School MLHL NW7 96 A7
Anson Primary School CRICK NW2 116 G10
Anthony Roper Primary School EYN DA4 209 M9
Apex Hotel MON EC3R 13 K7
Apex Industrial Estate WLSDN NW10 136 C6
Apex Primary School IL IG1 122 D6
Apex Retail Park FELT TW13 175 N6
Apollo Theatre SOHO/SHAV W1D 11 J7
Apollo Victoria Theatre PIM SW1V 16 G4
Apostolic Nuncio WIM/MER SW19 178 F6
Applecroft JMI School WGCW AL8 22 E5
Applegarth Primary School CROY/NA CR0 224 G3
Apsley ⇌ HHS/BOV HP3 53 P1
Apsley House, The Wellington Museum KTBR SW1X 16 C1
Apsley Mills Retail Park HHS/BOV HP3 35 P10
Aquarius Business Park CRICK NW2 116 D6
Aquarius Golf Club EDUL SE22 182 B1
Aragon Primary School MRDN SM4 201 H7
Arbour Vale Special School Sports College SLN SL2 129 M8
Arcadia Shopping Centre EA W5 135 J9
Arcadia University BAY/PAD W2 8 G8
The Archbishop Lanfranc School CROY/NA CR0 202 F6
Archbishop Sumners CE Primary School LBTH SE11 18 B6
Archbishop Tenisons CE School CROY/NA CR0 203 N10
Archbishop Tenison's School VX/NE SW8 17 P10
Archdale Business Centre RYLN/HDSTN HA2 114 B7
Archdeacon Cambridge's CE Primary School WHTN TW2 176 D5
Arches Business Centre NWDGN UB2 153 N1
Arches Leisure Centre GNWCH SE10 161 J5
Archgate Business Centre NFNCH/WDSPK N12 97 M5
Architecture Association School of Architecture RSQ WC1B 11 J4
Archway ⊖ ARCH N19 118 D7
Archway Business Centre ARCH N19 118 E8
Archway Leisure Centre ARCH N19 118 D7
Archway Theatre HORL RH6 280 B5
Ardleigh Green Primary School EMPK RM11 125 L1
Ardmore House Hotel STAL AL1 38 E5
Arena ⊖ SNWD SE25 204 B5
Arena Essex PUR RM19 166 F1
Arena Estate FSBYPK N4 119 J4
Argent Centre Industrial Estate HYS/HAR UB3 153 H1
Argyle Primary School STPAN WC1H 5 M10
Arkley Golf Club BAR EN5 76 C9
Arklow Trading Estate NWCR SE14 160 D5
Armourers & Braziers' Hall LOTH EC2R 12 G4
Army Training Regiment CHOB/PIR GU24 230 B7
Arndale Health Centre WAND/EARL SW18 179 K2
Arnett Hills Primary School RKW/CH/CXG WD3 71 K10
Arnhem Wharf Primary School POP/IOD E14 160 E2
Arnold House School STJWD NW8 3 L7
Arnos Grove ⊖ FBAR/BDGN N11 98 D5
Arnos Pool FBAR/BDGN N11 98 E6
Arsenal ⊖ HBRY N5 119 H8
Arsenal FC (Emirates Stadium) HOLWY N7 119 H9
Artsdepot NFNCH/WDSPK N12 97 M6
The Arts Educational School CHSWK W4 156 B3
Arts Theatre LSQ/SEVD WC2H 11 K7
Ashburnham Primary School WBPTN SW10 157 N6
Ashburton Community School CROY/NA CR0 204 A7
Ashburton Primary School CROY/NA CR0 204 A6
Ashby Mill BRXS/STRHM SW2 180 F2
Ashby Mill School CLAP SW4 180 F1
The Ashcombe School DORK RH4 254 G10
Ashcroft Technology Academy PUT/ROE SW15 179 J1
Asheridge Road Industrial Estate CSHM HP5 50 F5
Ashfield Junior School BUSH WD23 94 A1
Ashford ⇌ ASHF TW15 174 A6
Ashford Cemetery STWL/WRAY TW19 174 A5
Ashford CE Primary School ASHF TW15 174 C9
Ashford Clinic ASHF TW15 173 P6
Ashford Hospital STWL/WRAY TW19 173 P5
Ashford Industrial Estate ASHF TW15 174 D7
Ashford Manor Golf Club ASHF TW15 174 A9
Ashford Park Primary School ASHF TW15 173 M7
Ashford Sports Club
ASHF TW15 173 N7
STWL/WRAY TW19 174 A4
Ashgrove College WALTH E17 120 F1
Ashgrove Trading Estate BMLY BR1 183 J9
Ash Industrial Estate HLWW/ROY CM19 46 C2
Ashleigh Commercial Estate CHARL SE7 161 P3
Ashley Centre Shopping Precinct EPSOM KT18 220 A9
Ashley Primary School WOT/HER KT12 197 H8
Ashlyns School BERK HP4 33 P7
Ashmead Primary School BROCKY SE4 160 F8
Ashmole Centre STHGT/OAK N14 98 D2
Ashmole Primary School VX/NE SW8 17 P10
Ashmole School STHGT/OAK N14 98 D2
Ashmount Primary School ARCH N19 118 E5
Ashtead ⇌ ASHTD KT21 237 J3
Ashtead Clinic ASHTD KT21 237 K3
Ashtead Common National Nature Reserve ASHTD KT21 237 J2
Ashtead CC ASHTD KT21 237 K3
Ashtead Hospital ASHTD KT21 237 K6
Ashton House School ISLW TW7 154 C7
Ashton Playing Fields Track WFD IG8 102 B7
Aspen House School LBTH SE11 18 C10
Aspen House Secondary & Primary School BRXS/STRHM SW2 180 F4
Asquith Court School
HPTN TW12 198 A1
KTN/HRWW/WS HA3 114 G4
Asquith School PEND EN3 80 B8
Assembly Rooms SURB KT6 199 K4
Associated Newspapers Offices BERM/RHTH SE16 160 C2
Assunah School TOTM N17 99 N10
Astley Cooper School HHNE HP2 36 B1
The Astolat Industrial Estate RGUW GU3 267 P8
Aston Clinic NWMAL KT3 200 B4
Aston House School EA W5 135 J8
Astra Business Centre REDH RH1 276 B10
Asylum Medical Centre CEND/HSY/T N8 119 H1
Athelney Primary School CAT SE6 182 F6
Athelstan House School HPTN TW12 197 P1
Athenaeum Hotel MYFR/PICC W1J 10 E10
Athena Medical Centre CLPT E5 120 B9
Atherton Leisure Centre SRTFD E15 141 L1
Athlone House Hospital HGT N6 118 A6
Athlon Industrial Estate ALP/SUD HA0 135 J4
Atkinson Morley Hospital RYNPK SW20 178 E10
Atlantic House (Richmond American International University) KENS W8 15 J3
Atlas Business Centre CRICK NW2 116 E7
Atlas Medical Centre HORL RH6 280 B8
Atlas Transport Estate BTSEA SW11 157 M8
Attlee Youth & Community Centre WCHPL E1 13 M4
Atwood Primary School SAND/SEL CR2 223 P10
Audley Primary School CTHM CR3 241 M7
Auriol Junior School HOR/WEW KT19 220 C1
Austin Lodge Golf Club EYN DA4 229 M5
Australia House HOL/ALD WC2B 11 P6
Aveley FC SOCK/AV RM15 146 B9
Aveley Medical Centre SOCK/AV RM15 147 H6
Aveley Primary School SOCK/AV RM15 146 D10
Aveley School (School House) SOCK/AV RM15 146 D10
Avenue House Museum FNCH N3 97 J10
Avenue House School WEA W13 134 G8
Avenue Industrial Estate
CHING E4 100 E7
HARH RM3 105 L10
Avenue Medical Centre SLN SL2 128 F5
Avenue Pre-Preparatory School HGT N6 118 C5
Avenue Primary School MNPK E12 122 B9
The Avenue Primary School BELMT SM2 221 K6
Avenue Road ⊖ BECK BR3 204 C2
Avery Hill Park ELTH/MOT SE9 184 F2
Avondale Park Primary School NTGHL W11 8 A8
Avon House School WFD IG8 101 M5
Avon Trading Estate WKENS W14 14 D6
Axis Business Centre SRTFD E15 140 G3
Aycliffe Drive Primary School HHNE HP2 35 P2
Aylands School PEND EN3 80 B2
The Aylesham Centre PECK SE15 159 P7
Ayloff Primary School HCH RM12 125 J9
Aylward First & Middle Schools STAN HA7 95 J6
Aysgarth Medical Centre IVER SL0 130 G4
Azhar Academy FSTGT E7 141 M1
B6 Sixth Form College CLPT E5 120 A8
BAA Heathrow Visitor Centre HTHAIR TW6 152 C7
Babington House School CHST BR7 184 C9
BackCare Clinic WPK KT4 200 D8
Bacon's College BERM/RHTH SE16 140 D10
Baden Powell House SKENS SW7 15 K5
Baglioni Hotel KENS W8 15 J2
Bakers Hall MON EC3R 13 K8
Baker Street ⊖ CAMTN NW1 10 B2
Balaam Leisure Centre PLSTW E13 141 M6
Bales College NKENS W10 136 G5
Balfour Business Centre NWDGN UB2 153 L2
Balfour Medical Centre GRAYS RM17 167 P3
Balgowan Primary School BECK BR3 204 D2
Balham ⇌ ⊖ BAL SW12 180 C4
Balham Girls Preparatory Secondary School TOOT SW17 180 A6
Balham Health Centre BAL SW12 180 C5
Balham Leisure Centre TOOT SW17 180 B5
Balmoral Trading Estate BARK EC2Y 143 J6
Baltic Exchange HDTCH EC3A 13 K5
Bancrofts School WFD IG8 101 M4
Bandon Hill Cemetery WLGTN SM6 222 E2
Bandon Hill Primary School WLGTN SM6 222 E3
Bangabandhu Primary School BETH E2 140 B5
Bank ⊖ ⊖ LOTH EC2R 12 G6
Bank of England Extension CITYW EC2V 12 E6
Bank of England (& Museum) LOTH EC2R 12 G6
Bankside Gallery STHWK SE1 12 D8
Bankside Jetty STHWK SE1 12 E8
Bankside Park Industrial Estate BARK EC2Y 143 K5
Bannister Stadium KTN/HRWW/WS HA3 94 B7
Bannockburn Primary School WOOL/PLUM SE18 163 J3
The Banqueting House, Whitehall WHALL SW1A 11 L10
Banstead ⇌ BNSTD SM7 221 H10
Banstead Athletic FC KWD/TDW/WH KT20 238 F6
Banstead Clinic BNSTD SM7 239 K1
Banstead County Junior School BNSTD SM7 239 J2
Banstead Downs Golf Club BELMT SM2 221 K7
Banstead Infant School BNSTD SM7 239 J1
Banstead Sports Centre KWD/TDW/WH KT20 238 F6
Banstead Village Clinic BNSTD SM7 239 L1
Barbara Castle Health Centre HLWW/ROY CM19 46 D5
Barbara Speake Theatre School ACT W3 136 B9
Barber Surgeons' Hall BARB EC2Y 12 F4
Barbican ⊖ FARR EC1M 12 D3
Barbican Cinema BARB EC2Y 12 E3
Barbican Exhibition Halls BARB EC2Y 12 F3
The Barbican BARB EC2Y 12 E3
Barbican Theatre BARB EC2Y 12 F3
Barclay Primary School LEY E10 121 J4
Barham Primary School ALP/SUD HA0 135 H1
Baring Primary School LEE/GVPK SE12 183 M3
Baring Road Medical Centre BMLY BR1 183 M5
Barkantine Clinic POP/IOD E14 160 F1
Barking ⇌ ⊖ ⊖ BARK EC2Y 142 F2
Barking Abbey Comprehensive School (Lower) IL IG1 122 G10
Barking Abbey Comprehensive School (Upper) BARK EC2Y 143 J1
Barking Abbey Industrial Estate BARK EC2Y 142 E3
Barking Abbey Leisure Centre BARK EC2Y 143 K1
Barking Abbey School BARK EC2Y 143 J1
Barking College ROMW/RG RM7 124 E7
Barking FC BCTR RM8 123 L10
Barking Hospital BARK EC2Y 143 J2
Barking Industrial Park BARK EC2Y 143 J3
Barking RUFC DAGW RM9 143 N3
Barkingside ⊖ BARK/HLT IG6 122 G2
Barkingside Cemetery BARK/HLT IG6 122 E1
Barkingside FC BARK/HLT IG6 122 G2
Barlby Primary School NKENS W10 136 G6
Barley Lane Primary School GDMY/SEVK IG3 123 K5
Barnabas Medical Centre NTHLT UB5 134 B1
Barn Croft Primary School WALTH E17 120 D4
Barnehurst ⇌ BXLYHN DA7 164 D8
Barnehurst Primary School ERITH DA8 164 D7
Barnehurst Public Golf Club BXLYHN DA7 164 E9
Barn Elms Athletics Track BARN SW13 156 E8
Barn Elms Sports Centre BARN SW13 156 F7
Barn Elms Water Sports Centre PUT/ROE SW15 156 F8
Barnes ⇌ BARN SW13 156 D9
Barnes Bridge ⇌ BARN SW13 156 B8
Barnes Cray Primary School DART DA1 165 H10
Barnes Hospital MORT/ESHN SW14 156 B9
Barnes Primary School BARN SW13 156 B9
Barnes Sports Club BARN SW13 156 C7
Barnet College
BAR EN5 77 J8
CDALE/KGS NW9 96 C9
EBAR EN4 98 A2
FBAR/BDGN N11 98 A4
HDN NW4 116 D4
NFNCH/WDSPK N12 97 M6
Barnet Copthall Pool HDN NW4 96 E8
Barnet Copthall Stadium HDN NW4 96 F9
Barnet FC (Underhill) BAR EN5 77 K9
Barnet General Hospital BAR EN5 76 G8
Barnet Health Centre BAR EN5 77 K9
Barnet Hill JMI School BAR EN5 77 J9
Barnet Hospital Chest Clinic BAR EN5 76 G8
Barnet Museum BAR EN5 77 H8
Barnet Trading Estate BAR EN5 77 J7
Barnett Wood Infant School ASHTD KT21 237 J3
Barnfield Primary School EDGW HA8 95 P9
Barnhill Community High School YEAD UB4 133 J5
Barn Hotel RSLP HA4 112 F7
Barnsbury Complex IS N1 6 A3
Barnsbury Primary School WOKS/MYFD GU22 232 A7
Barnsbury School for Girls IS N1 6 A2
Barn Theatre WGCW AL8 22 F5
Barnwood County First School GUW GU2 249 K9
Barons Court ⊖ HMSMTH W6 156 G4
Barons Court Theatre WKENS W14 14 B7
Barratt Industrial Park BOW E3 141 H6
Barrett Industrial Park STHL UB1 133 P10
Barrett Way Industrial Estate RYLN/HDSTN HA2 114 C1
Barrington Primary School WELL DA16 163 N8
Barrow Hedges Primary School CAR SM5 221 P4
Barrow Hill Junior School STJWD NW8 3 N8
Barton House Health Centre STNW/STAM N16 119 L8
Barwell Business Park CHSGTN KT9 219 J4
Bassett House School NKENS W10 136 G8
Baston School HAYES BR2 205 N9
Bat & Ball ⇌ RSEV TN14 247 K7
Batchwood Golf Club STALW/RED AL3 38 A3
Batchwood School STALW/RED AL3 38 C3
Bates Industrial Estate HARH RM3 105 P8
Bath Factory Estate HNHL SE24 181 K2
Battersea Arts Centre (BAC) BTSEA SW11 158 A9
Battersea Business Centre BTSEA SW11 158 B9
Battersea Dogs' Home VX/NE SW8 158 C6
Battersea Park ⇌ BTSEA SW11 158 C6
Battersea Power Station (disused) VX/NE SW8 16 F10
Battersea Sports Centre BTSEA SW11 157 N9
Battersea Technology College BTSEA SW11 158 A7
Battersea Tutorial College TOOT SW17 180 B5
Bayford ⇌ HERT/BAY SG13 43 H4
Bayford Primary School HERT/BAY SG13 42 G4
Bayhurst Wood Country Park DEN/HRF UB9 112 A3
Baylis Business Centre SL SL1 129 J9
Baylis Court School SL SL1 129 J7
Bayswater ⊖ BAY/PAD W2 8 G7
BBC Broadcasting House REGST W1B 10 F4
BBC Media Village SHB W12 136 F9
BBC Studios MV/WKIL W9 8 G1
BBC Television Centre SHB W12 136 F9
BBC Worldwide SHB W12 136 F8
Beacon Hill Industrial Estate PUR RM19 166 A4
Beacon Hill School SOCK/AV RM15 146 F7
Beacon School BNSTD SM7 239 H3
The Beacon School AMS HP6 68 G1
Beaconsfield ⇌ BEAC HP9 88 D8
Beaconsfield CC BEAC HP9 88 E10
Beaconsfield Golf Club BEAC HP9 89 H9
Beaconsfield High School BEAC HP9 88 C10
Beaconsfield RFC BEAC HP9 108 E1
Beaconsfield School BEAC HP9 88 D10
Beaconsfield School of Lawn Tennis BEAC HP9 88 D8
Beales Hotel HAT AL10 40 B3
Beal High School REDBR IG4 122 B1
Beam Primary School DAGE RM10 144 D4
Bean Primary School RDART DA2 189 H6
Beatrice Tate School BETH E2 140 A5
Beatrix Potter Primary School WAND/EARL SW18 179 M4
Beauclerc Infant School SUN TW19 197 K3
The Beaufort Hotel CHEL SW3 16 A4
Beaufort Primary School WOKN/KNAP GU21 231 L2
Beaumont Primary School
LEY E10 120 G5
PUR/KEN CR8 222 G10
Beaumont School STALE/WH AL4 39 J5
Beaver College BAY/PAD W2 8 G8
The Beavers Community Primary School HSLWW TW4 153 K9
Beaverwood School for Girls CHST BR7 185 H9
Beckenham Business Centre BECK BR3 182 D9
Beckenham Crematorium BECK BR3 204 B3
Beckenham CC BECK BR3 182 G10
Beckenham Hill ⇌ CAT SE6 183 H8
Beckenham Hospital BECK BR3 204 E2
Beckenham Junction ⇌ ⊖ BECK BR3 204 F1
Beckenham Leisure Centre BECK BR3 204 D1
Beckenham Place Park Golf Course BECK BR3 182 G9
Beckenham RFC BECK BR3 204 D4
Beckenham Road ⊖ BECK BR3 204 C1
Beckenham School of Art BECK BR3 204 D5
Beckenham Theatre Centre BECK BR3 204 G2
Beckenham Town FC BECK BR3 204 F5
Becket Sports Centre DART DA1 187 K2
Beckford Primary School KIL/WHAMP NW6 117 J10
Beckmead School BECK BR3 204 F8
The Beck Theatre HYS/HAR UB3 132 G8
Beckton ⊖ EHAM E6 142 D7
Beckton Park ⊖ EHAM E6 142 C9
Beckton Ski Centre EHAM E6 142 D6
Beckton Triangle Retail Park EHAM E6 142 E5
Becontree ⊖ DAGW RM9 143 M1
Becontree Day Hospital BCTR RM8 123 P7
Becontree Primary School BCTR RM8 123 L8
Bective House Clinic PUT/ROE SW15 157 J10
Beddington Infants School WLGTN SM6 202 D10

Beddington Lane ⊖ CROY/NA CR0 202 D6
Beddington Medical Centre CROY/NA CR0 222 F1
Beddington Park Primary School CROY/NA CR0 202 E10
Beddington Trading Estate CROY/NA CR0 202 F8
Bedelsford School KUT/HW KT1 199 K3
Bedensfield Clinic SCUP DA14 185 P8
Bedfont Cemetery EBED/NFELT TW14 174 D4
Bedfont Health Clinic EBED/NFELT TW14 174 F3
Bedfont Industrial Park ASHF TW15 174 E6
Bedfont J & I School EBED/NFELT TW14 174 F2
Bedfont Lakes Country Park EBED/NFELT TW14 174 D5
Bedfont Lakes Office Park EBED/NFELT TW14 174 D4
The Bedford Arms Hotel RKW/CH/CXG WD3 70 E4
Bedford Hotel RSQ WC1B 11 M3
Bedington Infant School WLGTN SM6 222 D1
Bedmond JMI School ABLGY WD5 54 G4
Bedonwell Clinic ABYW SE2 163 P5
Bedonwell Medical Centre BELV DA17 164 A4
Bedonwell Primary School BXLYHN DA7 163 P5
Beechcroft Farm Industrial Estate BGR/WK TN15 211 J10
Beechfield JMI School WATN WD24 73 H3
Beech House School SAND/SEL CR2 223 N6
Beech Hyde Primary School STALE/WH AL4 21 J4
Beecholme Primary School MTCM CR4 202 C1
Beechwood School SLN SL2 128 G5
STRHM/NOR SW16 180 F6
Beehive Preparatory School REDBR IG4 122 C2
The Beehive School ARCH N19 118 E5
Beis Hamedrash Elyon GLDGN NW11 117 H5
Beis Malka Girls School STNW/STAM N16 119 N6
Beis Rochel D'Satmar Girls School STNW/STAM N16 119 M5
Beis Yaakov Primary School CDALE/KGS NW9 116 A1
Bekonscot Model Village & Railway BEAC HP9 88 C8
Belcon Industrial Estate HOD EN11 45 H3
Belfry Shopping Centre REDH RH1 258 A9
Belgrave Walk ⊖ MTCM CR4 201 N4
Belhus Chase Specialist College SOCK/AV RM15 146 C9
Belhus Golf Club & Leisure Centre SOCK/AV RM15 146 D8
Belhus Woods Country Park SOCK/AV RM15 146 C5
Bellamy's Wharf BERM/RHTH SE16 140 C10
Bellenden Primary School PECK SE15 159 P9
Bellenden Road Business Centre PECK SE15 159 N8
Bellenden Road Retail Park PECK SE15 159 N7
Bellerbys College DEPT SE8 160 G5
Bellerby Theatre GU GU1 268 A1
Belleville Primary School BTSEA SW11 180 A1
Belle Vue Cinema WLSDN NW10 136 E2
Bell Farm Junior School WOT/HER KT12 217 K1
Bell Industrial Estate CHSWK W4 155 P3
Bellingham ⇌ CAT SE6 182 G6
Bellingham Trading Estate CAT SE6 182 G6
Bell Lane Combined School AMS HP6 69 N4
Bell Lane JMI School HDN NW4 116 G2
Belmont ⇌ BELMT SM2 221 L6
Belmont Bowling Club STRHM/NOR SW16 180 F6
Belmont First School KTN/HRWW/WS HA3 94 E10
Belmont Infant School TOTM N17 119 K1
Belmont Medical Centre UX/CGN UB8 131 N2
Belmont (Mill Hill Preparatory School) MLHL NW7 96 D4
Belmont Park School LEY E10 121 H4
Belmont Primary School CHSWK W4 156 A3
ERITH DA8 164 B6
Belmore Primary School YEAD UB4 133 J5
Belsize Park ⊖ HAMP NW3 117 P10
Belswains Infant School HHS/BOV HP3 36 A10
Belvedere ⇌ BELV DA17 164 C2
Belvedere Day Hospital WLSDN NW10 136 D3
Belvedere Industrial Estate BELV DA17 144 E10
Belvedere Link Business Park ERITH DA8 164 D2
Belvedere Primary School BELV DA17 164 C3
Belvue Business Centre NTHLT UB5 134 A2
Belvue School NTHLT UB5 133 P3
Benedict House Preparatory School BFN/LL DA15 185 J7
Benedict Primary School MTCM CR4 201 N3
Bengeo Primary School HERT/WAT SG14 25 K2
Ben Jonson Primary School WCHPL E1 140 D6
Bensham Manor School THHTH CR7 203 K5
Benson Primary School CROY/NA CR0 204 D10
Bentalls Shopping Centre KUT/HW KT1 199 J2
Benthal Primary School STNW/STAM N16 119 P8
Bentley Golf Club BRWN CM15 86 D5
The Bentley Kempinski Hotel SKENS SW7 15 J6
Bentley St Pauls CE Primary School BRWN CM15 86 C6
Bentley Street Industrial Estate GVE DA12 190 F2
Bentley Wood Girls School STAN HA7 94 E6
Bentworth Primary School SHB W12 136 E8
Ben Uri Gallery, London Jewish Museum of Art STJWD NW8 3 H6
Benyon Primary School SOCK/AV RM15 147 H4
Beormund School STHWK SE1 18 G2
Berger Primary School HOM E9 140 C1
Berkeley Clinic RKW/CH/CXG WD3 91 M2
The Berkeley Hotel KTBR SW1X 16 C1
Berkeley Primary School HEST TW5 153 L5
Berkhamsted ⇌ BERK HP4 33 P4
Berkhamsted Castle BERK HP4 34 A4
Berkhamsted Collegiate Preparatory School BERK HP4 33 N5
Berkhamsted Collegiate School (Castle Campus) BERK HP4 33 P5
Berkhamsted FC BERK HP4 33 N4
Berkhamsted Golf Club BERK HP4 34 B2
Berkhamsted Health Centre BERK HP4 33 M4
Berkhamsted School House BERK HP4 33 P5
Berkhamsted Tennis Club BERK HP4 33 N4
Berlitz School of Languages HHOL WC1V 11 P4
Bermondsey ⊖ ⊖ BERM/RHTH SE16 19 P3
Bermondsey Town Hall STHWK SE1 19 L4
Bermondsey Trading Estate BERM/RHTH SE16 160 B3
Bernards Heath Infant School STAL AL1 38 E4
Bernards Heath Junior School STALW/RED AL3 38 D3
Berrygrove Primary School GSTN WD25 73 L1
Berrylands ⇌ BRYLDS KT5 199 N4
Berrymede Infant School ACT W3 155 N1
Berrymede Junior School ACT W3 155 N1
Bertram House School TOOT SW17 180 B5
Bessemer Grange J & I School HNHL SE24 181 L1
Bessemer Park Industrial Estate BRXN/ST SW9 159 J10
Best Western Bromley Court Hotel BMLY BR1 183 K9
Best Western Cumberland Hotel HRW HA1 114 E4
Best Western Donnington Manor Hotel SEV TN13 246 E4
Best Western Gatwick Moat House Hotel HORL RH6 279 P6
Best Western Homestead Court Hotel WGCE AL7 23 J7
Best Western Lodge Hotel PUT/ROE SW15 179 J1
Best Western Manor Hotel GVE DA12 190 G9
Best Western Master Robert Hotel HEST TW5 153 N7
Best Western Mostyn Hotel MBLAR W1H 10 B6
Best Western Phoenix Hotel BAY/PAD W2 8 G7
Best Western Reigate Manor Hotel REIG RH2 257 K7
Best Western the Watermill Hotel HHW HP1 34 F8
Best Western Weald Park Hotel, Golf & Country Club BRW CM14 85 P8
Best Western White House Hotel WATW WD18 73 H8
Beta Health Clinic HHW HP1 35 N6
Betchworth ⇌ BRKHM/BTCW RH3 256 A8
Betchworth Park Golf Club DORK RH4 273 K1
Bethlem Royal Hospital BECK BR3 204 F7
Bethnal Green ⇌ WCHPL E1 140 A6
Bethnal Green ⊖ BETH E2 140 B5
Bethnal Green Technology College BETH E2 7 M10
Beths Grammar School for Boys BXLY DA5 186 B2
The Betty Layward School STNW/STAM N16 119 L8
Beulah Infant School THHTH CR7 203 K2
Beverley School NWMAL KT3 200 D5
Beverley Trading Estate MRDN SM4 200 G7
Bevington Primary School NKENS W10 8 B3
Bewbush Community Primary School CRAWW RH11 283 J10
Bewbush Medical Centre CRAWW RH11 283 H10
Bewhurst County First School CRAWW RH11 283 J10
Bexley ⇌ BXLY DA5 186 B4
Bexley College BELV DA17 164 D3
Bexley CC BXLY DA5 186 B4
Bexley Grammar School WELL DA16 163 L10
Bexleyheath ⇌ BXLYHN DA7 163 P8
Bexleyheath Cemetery BXLYHN DA7 164 A9
Bexleyheath Centre BXLYHS DA6 163 P10
Bexleyheath Golf Club BXLYHS DA6 185 P1
Bexleyheath Marriott Hotel BXLYHS DA6 164 C10
Bexleyheath School BXLYHN DA7 164 A9
Bexleyheath Superbowl BXLYHS DA6 164 A10
Bexley RFC BXLY DA5 186 B3
BFI London IMAX Cinema STHWK SE1 11 P10
The Bharani Medical Centre SL SL1 128 C8
Bickerly School of Dance HAYES BR2 206 B5
Bickley ⇌ BMLY BR1 206 B3
Bickley Park CC BMLY BR1 206 B2
Bickley Park Pre-Preparatory School BMLY BR1 206 B3
Bickley Park Preparatory School BMLY BR1 206 A3
Big Ben WHALL SW1A 17 M2
Biggin Hill Airport BH/WHM TN16 225 P8
Biggin Hill Business Park BH/WHM TN16 244 A1
Biggin Hill Primary School BH/WHM TN16 244 B2
Bigham's Park Farm HHW HP1 35 H1
Bigland Green Primary School WCHPL E1 140 A8
Billingsgate Fish Market POP/IOD E14 140 G10
Bingham Hotel TWK TW1 177 J2
Binscombe Medical Centre GODL GU7 267 J9
Bircherley Green Shopping Centre HERT/WAT SG14 25 L5
Birchmere Business Park THMD SE28 163 K1
Birchwood Avenue Primary School HAT AL10 40 D2
Birchwood Industrial Area BRKMPK AL9 40 F1
Birchwood Leisure Centre HAT AL10 40 E1
Birchwood Park Golf Club RDART DA2 186 D10
Bird College SCUP DA14 185 K6
Birkbeck ⇌ ⊖ BECK BR3 204 B2
Birkbeck College GWRST WC1E 11 K2
RSQ WC1B 11 K4
Birkbeck Primary School SCUP DA14 185 L6
Bishop Challoner Catholic Collegiate School WCHPL E1 140 B9
Bishop Challoner Girls School WCHPL E1 13 P7
Bishop Challoner School HAYES BR2 205 J2
Bishop David Brown School WOKN/KNAP GU21 214 G9
Bishop Douglass RC School EFNCH N2 97 M10
Bishop Gilpin Primary School WIM/MER SW19 179 J8
Bishophalt School UX/CGN UB8 132 A5
Bishop John Robinson CE Primary School THMD SE28 143 M9
Bishop Justus CE (Secondary) School HAYES BR2 206 B7
Bishop Perrin CE Primary School WHTN TW2 176 A3
Bishop Ramsey CE School (Upper) RSLP HA4 113 H5
Bishop Ramsey CE School RSLP HA4 112 G5
Bishopsgate Institute LVPST EC2M 13 K4
Bishopsgate School EGH TW20 171 M6
Bishops Hatfield Girls School HAT AL10 40 D4
Bishops Wood Hospital NTHWD HA6 92 C7
Bishop Thomas Grant School STRHM/NOR SW16 180 G8
Bishop Wand CE Secondary School SUN TW19 196 G2
Bishop Winnington-Ingram CE Primary School RSLP HA4 112 E5
Bisley CE Primary School CHOB/PIR GU24 230 F2
Bittacy Business Centre MLHL NW7 97 H7
Blackburn Trading Estate STWL/WRAY TW19 174 A2
Blackfen Medical Centre BFN/LL DA15 185 J1
Blackfen School for Girls BFN/LL DA15 185 L2
Blackfriars ⇌ BLKFR EC4V 12 C8
Blackfriars Millennium Pier EMB EC4Y 12 B7
Blackfriars Pier BLKFR EC4V 12 D8
Blackheath ⇌ BKHTH/KID SE3 161 L9
Blackheath Bluecoat School BKHTH/KID SE3 161 N6
Blackheath Business Estate GNWCH SE10 161 H7
The Blackheath Clinic BKHTH/KID SE3 161 M10
Blackheath High School GDST BKHTH/KID SE3 161 L8
Blackheath High Senior School BKHTH/KID SE3 161 M6
Blackheath Hospital BKHTH/KID SE3 161 L9
Blackheath Preparatory School BKHTH/KID SE3 161 M7
Blackheath RFC (The Rectory Field) BKHTH/KID SE3 161 N6
Blackhorse Lane ⊖ CROY/NA CR0 203 P7
Blackhorse Road ⊖ ⊖ WALTH E17 120 C2
Black Park Country Park IVER SL0 130 D4
Blackshots Leisure Centre CDW/CHF RM16 168 A1
Blackwall ⊖ POP/IOD E14 141 H9
Blackwall Trading Estate POP/IOD E14 141 J7
Blair Peach Primary School STHL UB1 133 L10
Blake College GTPST W1W 10 G3
Blake Hall (non-operational) ⇌ CHONG CM5 67 H3
Blanche Nevile School HGT N6 118 A4
MUSWH N10 118 B1
Blenheim Business Centre MTCM CR4 202 A1
Blenheim High School HOR/WEW KT19 220 A6
Blenheim Primary School ORP BR6 207 N9
Blenheim Shopping Centre PGE/AN SE20 182 B10
Blessed Dominic RC Primary School CDALE/KGS NW9 96 B10
Blessed Sacrament RC Primary School IS N1 5 M6
Bletchingley Golf Club REDH RH1 259 L9
Blood Transfusion Centre EDGW HA8 95 N8
Bloomfield Clinic Guys STHWK SE1 19 H1
Bloomsbury International NOXST/BSQ WC1A 11 M4
Bloomsbury Theatre GWRST WC1E 11 J1
Blossom House School RYNPK SW20 178 F10
Blossoms Inn Medical Centre BLKFR EC4V 12 F7
Blue Gate Fields Infant School WCHPL E1 140 B9
The Blue School ISLW TW7 154 F9
Bluewater Shopping Centre RDART DA2 188 E3
Blyth's Wharf POP/IOD E14 140 D9
BMI Medical Centre CAVSQ/HST W1G 10 D4
Bnois Jerusalem Girls School STNW/STAM N16 119 L5
The Bob Hope Theatre ELTH/MOT SE9 184 C2
The Bobsleigh Hotel HHS/BOV HP3 52 E2
Bocketts Farm Park LHD/OX KT22 254 E1
Bodywise Natural Health Centre BETH E2 140 B5
Boleyn Cinema EHAM E6 142 A4
Bolingbroke Hospital BTSEA SW11 179 P1
Bolingbroke Primary School BTSEA SW11 157 N7
Bond First School MTCM CR4 202 A2
Bond Primary School MTCM CR4 202 A2
Bond Street ⊖ OXSTW W1C 10 D6
Bonner Primary School BETH E2 140 C4
Bonneville Primary School CLAP SW4 180 D2
Bonnington Hotel RSQ WC1B 11 M3
Bonnygate Primary School SOCK/AV RM15 146 G7
Bonny Grove Specific Learning Difficulties Base CHESW EN7 61 P6
Bon Secours Hospital BEAC HP9 88 E9
Bonus Pastor Catholic College BMLY BR1 183 J7
Bookham ⇌ GT/LBKH KT23 235 N9
Bookham Grange Hotel GT/LBKH KT23 235 M9
Bookham Industrial Estate GT/LBKH KT23 235 N9
Boomes Industrial Estate RAIN RM13 144 G6
Booster Cushion Theatre WDGN N22 98 G10
Borehamwood FC BORE WD6 75 N6
Borehamwood Industrial Park BORE WD6 76 A6
Borers Business Park CRAWE RH10 285 K2
Borough ⊖ STHWK SE1 18 F2
Borough Cemetery HSLWW TW4 175 P3
Borough Market STHWK SE1 12 G9
Borthwick Wharf DEPT SE8 160 F4
Bosch Broadwater Park Business Estate DEN/HRF UB9 111 K4
Boston Business Park HNWL W7 154 D2
Boston Manor ⊖ HNWL W7 154 F3
Botany Bay CC ENC/FH EN2 78 E2
Botwell RC Primary School HYS/HAR UB3 152 G1
Boulevard 25 Retail Park BORE WD6 75 M7
Boundary Business Centre WOKN/KNAP GU21 232 D1
Boundary Business Park MTCM CR4 201 N2
Bounds Green ⊖ FBAR/BDGN N11 98 E8
Bounds Green Health Centre FBAR/BDGN N11 98 E8
Bounds Green Industrial Estate FBAR/BDGN N11 98 C7
Bounds Green Infant School FBAR/BDGN N11 98 E8
Bourne Business Park ADL/WDHM KT15 195 M9
Bourne CP School RSLP HA4 113 K10
Bourne Hall Health Centre EW KT17 220 C5
Bournehall J & I School BUSH WD23 73 P9
Bourne Hall Museum EW KT17 220 C5
Bourne Road Industrial Park DART DA1 186 E1
Bourneside Sports Club STHGT/OAK N14 98 F2
Bousfield Primary School ECT SW5 15 J7
Boutcher CE Primary School STHWK SE1 19 L4
Bovingdon Primary School HHS/BOV HP3 52 E3
Bowater House SKENS SW7 16 A2
Bow Church ⊖ BOW E3 140 F5
Bowden House Clinic HRW HA1 114 D7
Bower Hill Industrial Estate EPP CM16 65 K8
Bower Park School ROM RM1 104 F7
Bowes Park ⇌ WDGN N22 98 F8
Bowes Primary School FBAR/BDGN N11 98 E6
Bowes Road Clinic FBAR/BDGN N11 98 D6
Bow Junior & Youth Centre BOW E3 140 E7
Ealing Conservative Bowling Club EA W5 135 H9
Bowman Trading Estate CDALE/KGS NW9 115 M1
Bow Road ⊖ BOW E3 140 F5
Bow Secondary School BOW E3 140 F4
Bow Triangle Business Centre BOW E3 140 F6
Boxgrove Primary School ABYW SE2 163 M2
GU GU1 250 E9
Box Hill Country Park (NT) KWD/TDW/WH KT20 255 K8
Box Hill School RDKG RH5 254 G3
Box Hill & Westhumble ⇌ RDKG RH5 254 G7
Boxmoor Golf Club HHS/BOV HP3 35 H10
Boxmoor Primary School HHW HP1 35 K7
Boyd School UPMR RM14 126 D7
BPP Law School HHOL WC1V 11 N4
Brackenbury Health Centre HMSMTH W6 156 E2
Brackenbury Primary School HMSMTH W6 156 E2
Bracken Industrial Estate BARK/HLT IG6 103 J8
Bracton Centre RDART DA2 186 G5
Bradbourne School SEV TN13 247 H7
Brady Primary School RAIN RM13 145 K7
Brady Recreation Centre WCHPL E1 13 N3
Braeside Senior School BKHH IG9 101 N2
Braincroft Primary School CRICK NW2 116 C8
Braintree Road Industrial Estate RSLP HA4 113 J9
Bramah's Tea & Coffee Museum STHWK SE1 12 F10
Brambletye Junior School REDH RH1 276 B2
The Bramley Business Centre SHGR GU5 268 C10
Bramley Golf Club SHGR GU5 268 B10
Bramley School KWD/TDW/WH KT20 256 D1
Brampton College HDN NW4 116 F2
Brampton Manor School EHAM E6 142 A6
Brampton Primary School BXLYHN DA7 163 N8
EHAM E6 142 B5
Brandlehow Primary School PUT/ROE SW15 157 J10
Branfil Primary School UPMR RM14 125 P8
Branollys Health Centre PLSTW E13 141 M6
Breakspear Crematorium RSLP HA4 112 D3
Breakspeare School ABLGY WD5 54 F7
Breakspear Junior School HGDN/ICK UB10 112 B7
Breaside Preparatory School BMLY BR1 205 P1
Brecknock Primary School HOLWY N7 5 K1
Bredinghurst School PECK SE15 160 B10
Brent Adult College WLSDN NW10 136 A3
Brent Arts Council CRICK NW2 116 D8
Brent Child & Family Clinic WLSDN NW10 116 C10
Brent Cross ⊖ GLDGN NW11 116 G5
Brent Cross Shopping Centre HDN NW4 116 F5
Brentfield Medical Centre WLSDN NW10 136 A1
Brentfield Primary School WLSDN NW10 136 A1
Brentford ⇌ BTFD TW8 155 J5
Brentford Business Centre BTFD TW8 155 H6
Brentford FC (Griffin Park) BTFD TW8 155 J5
Brentford Fountain Leisure Centre BTFD TW8 155 L4
Brentford Health Centre BTFD TW8 155 H5
Brentford School for Girls BTFD TW8 155 J5
Brent Knoll School FSTH SE23 182 C6
Brent Park Industrial Estate NWDGN UB2 153 J2
The Brent Primary School RDART DA2 188 B3
Brentside First School HNWL W7 134 D7
Brentside High School HNWL W7 134 D6
Brentside Primary School HNWL W7 134 D6
Brent Trading Estate WLSDN NW10 116 B10
Brent Valley Golf Club HNWL W7 134 D9
Brentwaters Business Park BTFD TW8 155 H6
Brentwood ⇌ BRW CM14 107 H4
Brentwood Academy of Health & Beauty BRWN CM15 107 J3
Brentwood Chiropody Surgery BRW CM14 107 J3
The Brentwood Clinic BRWN CM15 107 J2
Brentwood Community Hospital BRWN CM15 107 K2
Brentwood County High School BRW CM14 107 J4
Brentwood IT Learning Centre BRW CM14 107 H3
Brentwood Park Ski & Snowboard Centre RBRW/HUT CM13 107 H8
Brentwood Pre-Preparatory School BRWN CM15 107 K2
Brentwood RFC BRW CM14 107 K5
Brentwood School BRWN CM15 107 J3
Brentwood Sports Ground BRWN CM15 107 J2
Brentwood Theatre BRWN CM15 107 J2
Brentwood Ursuline Convent High School BRW CM14 107 J4
Brettenham Primary School ED N9 99 P5
Brewers' Hall CITYW EC2V 12 F4
Brewery Industrial Estate IS N1 6 E8
Brewery Mews Business Centre ISLW TW7 154 E9
The Brewery ROMW/RG RM7 124 F4
Brian Johnston Centre BGR/WK TN15 247 N8
Brickendon Grange Golf Club HERT/BAY SG13 43 J5
Bricket Wood ⇌ LCOL/BKTW AL2 56 A7
Bricket Wood Sports Centre LCOL/BKTW AL2 56 A7
Brickfields Industrial Estate HHNE HP2 36 C2
Brick Lane Music Hall CAN/RD E16 142 A10
Brick Lane Music House WCHPL E1 13 M2
Bricklayer Arms Industrial Estate STHWK SE1 19 L6
The Bridewell Theatre EMB EC4Y 12 C6
The Bridge Academy BETH E2 7 L6
The Bridge Business Centre NWDGN UB2 153 P1
Bridgegate Business Centre WGCE AL7 23 J4
Bridge Industrial Estate HORL RH6 280 C4
Bridge Lane Theatre BTSEA SW11 157 P7
The Bridge Leisure Centre SYD SE26 182 E8
Bridge Medical Centre CRAWE RH10 284 B6
Bridge Park Business & Leisure Centre WLSDN NW10 135 N2
The Bridge School ARCH N19 118 D7
HOLWY N7 5 K1
Bridge View Industrial Estate WTHK RM20 166 F5
Bridgewater School BERK HP4 33 M3
Brigham Young University BAY/PAD W2 8 G8
Bright Sparks Montessori School WKENS W14 156 G1
The Brigidine School WDSR SL4 149 J9
Brigstock Medical Centre THHTH CR7 203 J5
Brimsdown ⇌ PEND EN3 80 D6
Brimsdown Industrial Estate PEND EN3 80 B6
Brimsdown Infant School PEND EN3 80 C7
Brindishe Primary School LEE/GVPK SE12 183 L1
Britain & London Visitor Centre STJS SW1Y 11 J9
Britannia Business Centre CHES/WCR EN8 62 E10
CRICK NW2 116 G9
Britannia Industrial Estate DTCH/LGLY SL3 151 H8
Britannia Leisure Centre IS N1 7 H6
Britannia Sports Ground WALTH E17 100 F8
Britannia Village Primary School CAN/RD E16 141 N10
British Air Transport Association (BATA) Medical Centre TIL RM18 169 M3
British Airways Museum HTHAIR TW6 152 F10
The British American Drama Academy CAMTN NW1 4 D6
SRTFD E15 141 J4
British Cartoon Centre BMSBY WC1N 11 M2
British Dental Association CAVSQ/HST W1G 10 E4
The British Hernia Centre HDN NW4 116 E3
British Library CAMTN NW1 5 K9
British Library Newspaper Library CDALE/KGS NW9 116 B1
British Medical Association STPAN WC1H 11 K1
British Museum RSQ WC1B 11 L4
British Telecom Tower GTPST W1W 10 G3
British Transport Police GUW GU2 267 N1
BRIT School for Performing Arts CROY/NA CR0 203 L6
Brittania Business Park CHES/WCR EN8 62 E10
Brittons School Technology College RAIN RM13 144 G2
Britwell Health Clinic SLN SL2 128 F5
Brixton ⇌ ⊖ BRXN/ST SW9 159 H10
Brixton Academy BRXN/ST SW9 159 H9
Brixton Recreation Centre BRXN/ST SW9 159 H9
Broadfield Primary School HHNE HP2 36 A6
Broadfields Primary School EDGW HA8 95 M3
HLW CM20 29 H10
Broadford Park Business Centre RGUE GU4 268 A7
Broadford Primary School HARH RM3 105 L7
Broadgate LVPST EC2M 13 H3
Broadgate Ice Arena LVPST EC2M 13 H4
Broadhurst School KIL/WHAMP NW6 3 J3
Broadmead J & I School CROY/NA CR0 203 L6
The Broadmere Primary School WOKN/KNAP GU21 214 G9
Broadreach College THMD SE28 163 J2
Broadwalk Shopping Centre EDGW HA8 95 M7
Broadwater Farm Primary School TOTM N17 99 L10
Broadwater Park Golf Club GODL GU7 267 M10
Broadwater Primary School TOOT SW17 179 N7
Broadwater School GODL GU7 267 M9
Broadway Clinic EDGW HA8 95 N9
Broadway Retail Park CRICK NW2 116 G9
Broadway Shopping Centre HMSMTH W6 156 F4
Broadway Square BXLYHS DA6 164 B10
Broadway Squash & Fitness Centre HMSMTH W6 156 G3
Brockenhurst Hotel ASC SL5 192 A6
Brockham School BRKHM/BTCW RH3 273 N2
Brocklebank Health Centre WAND/EARL SW18 179 L3
Brocklebank Industrial Estate GNWCH SE10 161 M3
Brockley ⇌ ⊖ BROCKY SE4 160 E9
Brockley Cross Business Centre BROCKY SE4 160 D9
Brockley Primary School BROCKY SE4 182 E1
Brockwell Lido HNHL SE24 181 J2
Broke Hill Golf Club RSEV TN14 228 A5
Bromet Primary School OXHEY WD19 93 L1
Bromley by Bow ⊖ BOW E3 140 G5
Bromley Cemetery BMLY BR1 183 L10

Bromley Civic Centre *BMLY* BR1 205 N2
Bromley College of Further & Higher Education *BMLY* BR1 205 M1; *HAYES* BR2 206 A6
Bromley FC *HAYES* BR2 205 N5
Bromley Golf Club *HAYES* BR2 206 B7
Bromley High School GDST *BMLY* BR1 206 D4
Bromley Industrial Centre *BMLY* BR1 206 A3
Bromley Mall Indoor Market *BMLY* BR1 205 M2
Bromley Museum *ORP* BR6 207 L7
Bromley North *BMLY* BR1 205 M1
Bromley Road Infant School *BECK* BR3 204 G1
Bromley Road Retail Park *CAT* SE6 182 G5
Bromley Ski Centre *STMC/STPC* BR5 207 N1
Bromley South *BMLY* BR1 205 N3
Bromley Tennis Centre *ORP* BR6 206 G10
Bromley Wendover Lawn Tennis Club *HAYES* BR2 205 N4
Brompton Cemetery *WBPTN* SW10 15 H10
Brompton Medical Centre *ECT* SW5 15 H7
Brompton Oratory *SKENS* SW7 15 N4
Brompton Park Crescent Leisure Centre *FUL/PGN* SW6 14 G10
Bromyard Leisure Centre *ACT* W3 136 B10
Brondesbury *KIL/WHAMP* NW6 2 C3
Brondesbury College for Boys *KIL/WHAMP* NW6 136 G2
Brondesbury Park *KIL/WHAMP* NW6 2 A5
Brook Business Centre *IVER* SL0 131 K4
Brook Community Primary School *HACK* E8 119 P10
Brooke Trading Estate *ROM* RM1 124 G5
Brook Farm Industrial Estate *ABR/ST* RM4 104 E1
Brookfield House School *WFD* IG8 101 K7
Brookfield Primary School *CHEAM* SM3 201 H8; *HGT* N6 118 C7
Brookfield Retail Park *CHES/WCR* EN8 62 C3
Brook House FC *YEAD* UB4 132 G5
Brook Industrial Estate *YEAD* UB4 133 L10
Brook Industrial Park *STMC/STPC* BR5 207 M4
Brookland Infant School *CHES/WCR* EN8 62 D4
Brookland Junior School *GLDGN* NW11 117 L2
Brooklands Airfield (disused) *WEY* KT13 216 A6
Brooklands Business Park *WEY* KT13 216 B6
Brooklands College *WEY* KT13 216 B3
Brooklands Industrial Estate *WEY* KT13 215 P6
Brooklands Museum *WEY* KT13 216 B5
Brooklands Primary School *BKHTH/KID* SE3 161 M9
Brooklands School *REIG* RH2 257 L8
Brook Lane Business Centre *BTFD* TW8 155 J4
Brookmans Park *BRKMPK* AL9 58 G2
Brookmans Park Golf Club *BRKMPK* AL9 59 K1
Brookmans Park Primary School *BRKMPK* AL9 59 H2
Brookmarsh Trading Estate *DEPT* SE8 160 G6
Brookmead Industrial Estate *CROY/NA* CR0 202 D6
The Brook School *CRAWE* RH10 284 D10
Brookside Primary School *HARH* RM3 105 M6; *YEAD* UB4 133 K5
Brookweald CC *BRW* CM14 106 D2
Brookwood *CHOB/PIR* GU24 230 F7
Brookwood Cemetery *CHOB/PIR* GU24 230 G8
Brookwood CP School *CHOB/PIR* GU24 230 F6
Brookwood Military Cemetery *CHOB/PIR* GU24 230 F7
Broomfield House School *RCH/KEW* TW9 155 L7
Broomfield School *FBAR/BDGN* N11 98 E6
Broomsleigh Business Park *SYD* SE26 182 E8
Broomwood Hall Lower School *BAL* SW12 180 A2; *STRHM/NOR* SW16 180 E6
Brownlow Medical Centre *FBAR/BDGN* N11 98 F6
Brown's Hotel *MYFR/PICC* W1J 10 F8
Brown's School *ORP* BR6 228 A2
Broxbourne *BROX* EN10 44 F6
Broxbourne Business Centre *CHES/WCR* EN8 62 C2
Broxbourne Primary School *BROX* EN10 44 F7
Broxbourne Sailing Club *WAB* EN9 45 J6
The Broxbourne School *BROX* EN10 44 D8
Broxbourne Sports Club *BROX* EN10 44 E7
Broxbourne Woods National Nature Reserve *BROX* EN10 43 L6
Bruce Castle Museum *TOTM* N17 99 M9
Bruce Grove *TOTM* N17 99 N10
Bruce Grove Primary School *TOTM* N17 99 N10
Brunei Gallery *STPAN* WC1H 11 K2
Brunel Bus Station *SL* SL1 129 L10
Brunel Engine House *BERM/RHTH* SE16 160 B1
Brunel HSBC Education Trust Academy *UX/CGN* UB8 131 P5
Brunel University *GLDGN* NW11 116 G4; *ISLW* TW7 154 D6; *TWK* TW1 154 G10
Brunel University (Osterley Campus) Track *ISLW* TW7 154 D6
Brunel University (Runnymede Campus) *EGH* TW20 172 A6
Brunswick Health Centre *FBAR/BDGN* N11 98 B3
Brunswick Housing & Shopping Centre *BMSBY* WC1N 11 M1
Brunswick Industrial Park *FBAR/BDGN* N11 98 C5
Brunswick Medical Centre *BMSBY* WC1N 11 L1
Brunswick Park JMI School *STHGT/OAK* N14 98 B2
Brunswick Park Primary School *CMBW* SE5 159 L6
Brushwood Junior School *CSHM* HP5 51 K5
BT Centre *STBT* EC1A 12 E5
Buckhurst Hill *BKHH* IG9 102 A3
Buckhurst Hill FC *BKHH* IG9 102 B2
Buckhurst Hill Primary School *BKHH* IG9 102 B3
Buckingham College Preparatory School *PIN* HA5 113 N5
Buckingham Palace *WHALL* SW1A 16 G2
Buckingham Primary School *HPTN* TW12 175 N8
Buckingham Road Cemetery *IL* IG1 122 G7
Buckinghamshire Golf Club *DEN/HRF* UB9 111 M7
Buckland Primary School *STA* TW18 173 M10
Bucks Chilterns University College *CSTG* HP8 90 D3
Building Centre *GWRST* WC1E 11 J4
Bullers Wood School *CHST* BR7 206 C1
Bullsbridge Industrial Estate *NWDGN* UB2 153 J3
The Bull Theatre *BAR* EN5 77 J8
Buncefield Oil Refinery *HHNE* HP2 36 E3
BUPA Roding Hospital *REDBR* IG4 122 A1
Burbage School *IS* N1 7 J7
Burdett Coutts CE Primary School *WEST* SW1P 17 J4
Burgess Business Park *CMBW* SE5 159 L6
Burgess Park Tennis Centre *CMBW* SE5 18 F10
Burghwood Clinic *BNSTD* SM7 239 J2
Burhill Golf Club *WOT/HER* KT12 217 H5
Burhill Infant School *WOT/HER* KT12 217 L3
Burleigh Primary School *CHES/WCR* EN8 62 C6
Burlington Danes School *SHB* W12 136 E8
Burlington Infant School *NWMAL* KT3 200 C4
Burney Street Clinic *GNWCH* SE10 161 H6
Burnham *SL* SL1 128 C8
Burnham Abbey *MDHD* SL6 128 A10
Burnham Beeches Golf Club *SL* SL1 128 C3
Burnham Beeches Hotel *SL* SL1 128 C4
Burnham Beeches National Nature Reserve *SLN* SL2 108 F10
Burnham FC *SL* SL1 128 A5
Burnham Grammar School *SL* SL1 128 C6
Burnham Health Centre *SL* SL1 128 A5
Burnham Trading Estate *DART* DA1 165 L10
Burnham Upper School *SL* SL1 128 A6
Burnhill Business Centre *BECK* BR3 204 F2
Burnley Road Clinic *WLSDN* NW10 116 D10
Burns Hotel *ECT* SW5 14 G6
Burnside Industrial Estate *BARK/HLT* IG6 103 L6
Burnt Ash Primary School *BMLY* BR1 183 M8
Burntmill Industrial Estate *HLW* CM20 28 F8
Burnt Mill School *HLW* CM20 29 H9
Burnt Oak *EDGW* HA8 95 P9
Burnt Oak Junior School *BFN/LL* DA15 185 K4
Burntwood School *TOOT* SW17 179 N5
Burpham Foundation Primary School *RGUE* GU4 250 D6
Bursted Wood Primary School *BXLYHN* DA7 164 C8
Burstow Business Centre *HORL* RH6 281 J2
Burstow Lodge Business Centre *HORL* RH6 280 C6
Burstow Primary School *HORL* RH6 281 H4
Burvale Cemetery *WOT/HER* KT12 217 H3
Burwell Industrial Estate *LEY* E10 120 D6
Burwood Park School & College *WOT/HER* KT12 216 G3
Burwood School *ORP* BR6 207 N9
Burys Court School *REIG* RH2 274 F6
Bushey *OXHEY* WD19 73 L10
Bushey Golf & Country Club *BUSH* WD23 73 P10
Bushey Grove Leisure Centre *BUSH* WD23 73 N8
Bushey Hall Golf Club *BUSH* WD23 73 M7
Bushey Hall School *BUSH* WD23 73 N10
Bushey Hall Swimming Pool *BUSH* WD23 73 N9
Bushey Health Centre *BUSH* WD23 73 N10
Bushey Heath Primary School *BUSH* WD23 94 C2
Bushey Jewish Cemetery *BUSH* WD23 74 A7
Bushey Manor Junior School *BUSH* WD23 73 N9
Bushey Meads School *BUSH* WD23 74 B9
Bushey Museum & Art Gallery *BUSH* WD23 73 P10
Bushey & Oxhey Infant School *BUSH* WD23 73 M9
Bush Hall Hotel *BRKMPK* AL9 40 G1
Bush Hill Park *EN* EN1 79 N10
Bush Hill Park Golf Club *WCHMH* N21 79 K9
Bush Hill Park Medical Centre *EN* EN1 79 N10
Bush Hill Park Primary School *EN* EN1 79 P9
BBC Bush House *HOL/ALD* WC2B 11 N6
Bush Industrial Estate *ARCH* N19 118 D8; *WLSDN* NW10 136 A6
Bushy Hill Junior School *GU* GU1 250 G9
The Business Academy Bexley *ERITH* DA18 163 P1
The Business Centre *CEND/HSY/T* N8 98 F10; *HARH* RM3 105 L8; *IL* IG1 122 E7
The Business Design Centre *IS* N1 6 B6
Business Park 5 *LHD/OX* KT22 236 F6
Business Training & Solutions *CDALE/KGS* NW9 96 C9
The Business Village *SLN* SL2 129 N10
Bute House Preparatory School for Girls *HMSMTH* W6 156 F3
Butlers Court County First & Middle School *BEAC* HP9 88 D10
Butlers Wharf *STHWK* SE1 13 M10
Butler's Wharf Business Centre *STHWK* SE1 19 M1
Butler's Wharf Pier *STHWK* SE1 13 M10
Butterfly Sports Club *ELTH/MOT* SE9 184 E2
Buxlow Preparatory School *WBLY* HA9 115 K8
Buzzard Creek Industrial Estate *BARK* IG11 143 J7
Byam Shaw School of Art *ARCH* N19 118 D7
Byfleet & New Haw *ADL/WDHM* KT15 215 N6
Byfleet Business Centre *BF/WBF* KT14 215 N7
Byfleet CP School *BF/WBF* KT14 215 N7
Byfleet Industrial Estate *BF/WBF* KT14 215 N7; *WATW* WD18 92 D2
Bygrove Prim School *POP/IOD* E14 140 G8
Byron Court Primary School *ALP/SUD* HA0 115 H7
Byron Primary School *COUL/CHIP* CR5 240 F3
Cabot Place *POP/IOD* E14 140 F10
The Cadogan Hotel *KTBR* SW1X 16 B4
Cadogan Pier *CHEL* SW3 15 P10
Calcot Medical Centre *CFSP/GDCR* SL9 90 A9
Caldicott School *SLN* SL2 128 G2
Caledonian Market *STHWK* SE1 19 K3
Caledonian Road *HOLWY* N7 5 M1
Caledonian Road & Barnsbury *HOLWY* N7 5 P3
Cally Pool *IS* N1 5 N5
Calverton Primary School *CAN/RD* E16 142 A8
Calvi House Pre-Preparatory School *COB* KT11 216 F9
Cambell Primary School *DAGW* RM9 143 N2
Camberwell Business Centre *CMBW* SE5 159 L6
Camberwell College of Arts *CMBW* SE5 159 M7
Camberwell Leisure Centre *CMBW* SE5 159 L7
Camberwell New Cemetery *PECK* SE15 182 C2
Camberwell Trading Estate *CMBW* SE5 159 J8
Cambridge Heath *BETH* E2 140 A4
Cambridge Park Bowling & Sports Club *TWK* TW1 177 H2
Cambridge School *HMSMTH* W6 156 E3
Cambridge Theatre *LSQ/SEVD* WC2H 11 L6
Camden Arts Centre *HAMP* NW3 117 L10
Camden House Clinic *BKHTH/KID* SE3 161 K8
Camden Junior School *CAR* SM5 222 A1
Camden Market *CAMTN* NW1 4 D4
Camden Mews Day Hospital *CAMTN* NW1 5 H3
Camden People's Theatre *CAMTN* NW1 4 G10
Camden Road *CAMTN* NW1 4 G3
Camden School for Girls *KTTN* NW5 5 H2
Camden Theatre *CAMTN* NW1 4 G7
Camden Town *CAMTN* NW1 4 F5
Camden Town Hall & St Pancras Library *CAMTN* NW1 5 L9
Camelot Primary School *PECK* SE15 160 A6
Cameron House School *CHEL* SW3 15 M9
Campanile Hotel *RDART* DA2 166 C9
Camperdown House *WCHPL* E1 13 M6
Camphill Industrial Estate *BF/WBF* KT14 215 L7
Campion House College *ISLW* TW7 154 C6
Campion School *EMPK* RM11 125 N2
Camp Primary School *STAL* AL1 38 G7
Campsbourne School *CEND/HSY/T* N8 118 F1
Campus West Cinema *WGCW* AL8 22 G4
Campus West Leisure Centre *WGCW* AL8 22 F4
Canada House *STJS* SW1Y 11 K9
Canada House Business Centre *RSLP* HA4 113 K6
Canada Place *POP/IOD* E14 140 F10
Canada Square *POP/IOD* E14 140 G10
Canada Water *BERM/RHTH* SE16 160 B2
Canada Water Retail Park *BERM/RHTH* SE16 160 C2
Canada Wharf Museum *BERM/RHTH* SE16 140 E10
Canal Cafe Theatre *BAY/PAD* W2 9 H3
Canal Industrial Park *GVE* DA12 190 G2
Canary Riverside *BERM/RHTH* SE16 140 E10
Canary Wharf *POP/IOD* E14 140 F10
Canary Wharf Pier *POP/IOD* E14 140 E10
Canberra Primary School *SHB* W12 136 E9
Canbury 2000 Business Park *KUTN/CMB* KT2 199 K1
Canbury Business Centre *KUTN/CMB* KT2 199 K1
Canbury Medical Centre *KUTN/CMB* KT2 199 L1
Canbury School *KUTN/CMB* KT2 177 N9
Cann Hall Primary School *WAN* E11 121 L8
The Canning School *ECT* SW5 14 G5; *KENS* W8 14 E3
Canning Town *POP/IOD* E14 141 K8
Cannizaro House Hotel *WIM/MER* SW19 178 F9
Cannon Hill Clinic *STHGT/OAK* N14 98 F4
Cannon Lane First School *PIN* HA5 113 L4
Cannon Sports Club *CANST* EC4R 12 F7
Cannon Street *CANST* EC4R 12 G8
Cannon Trading Estate *WBLY* HA9 115 N9
Cannon Wharf Business Centre *DEPT* SE8 160 D3
Canon Barnett Primary School *WCHPL* E1 13 M5
Canonbury *HBRY* N5 119 K10
Canonbury Business Centre *IS* N1 6 F5
Canonbury Primary School *IS* N1 6 C2
Canon Palmer RC High School *IL* IG1 123 H6
Canons Brook Golf Club *HLWW/ROY* CM19 28 D10
Canons High School *EDGW* HA8 95 L10
The Canons Leisure Centre *MTCM* CR4 202 A4
Canons Park *EDGW* HA8 95 K8
Canterbury Industrial Estate *NWCR* SE14 160 C5
Cantium Retail Park *STHWK* SE1 19 N9
Capel Manor Primary School *EN* EN1 80 A1
Capital Business Centre *ALP/SUD* HA0 135 J4; *MTCM* CR4 202 A5; *SAND/SEL* CR2 223 L3; *WATN* WD24 73 L2
Capital City Academy *WLSDN* NW10 136 E3
The Capital Hotel *CHEL* SW3 16 A2
Capital Industrial Estate *BELV* DA17 144 D10; *BELV* DA17 164 C3
Capital Radio *LSQ/SEVD* WC2H 11 K8
Capital Wharf *WAP* E1W 13 P10
Capitol Industrial Park *CDALE/KGS* NW9 115 P1
Caplan Estate *MTCM* CR4 202 D1
Capswood Business Centre *CFSP/GDCR* SL9 110 F6
Cardiff Road Industrial Estate *WATW* WD18 73 J10
Cardinal Hinsley College *WLSDN* NW10 136 D3
Cardinal Newman Catholic Primary School *WOT/HER* KT12 197 L10
Cardinal Pole RC School *HOM* E9 140 D1
Cardinal Pole RC Secondary Lower School *HOM* E9 140 C2
Cardinal Road Infant School *FELT* TW13 175 J4
The Cardinal Vaughan Memorial School *WKENS* W14 14 A1
Cardinal Wiseman RC School (Technology & Art College) *GFD/PVL* UB6 134 B7
Cardwell Primary School *WOOL/PLUM* SE18 162 C3
Carew Manor School *WLGTN* SM6 202 E10
Cargo Terminal *HORL* RH6 279 N8
Carlisle Infant School *HPTN* TW12 176 A9
Carlton House *STJS* SW1Y 11 J10
The Carlton Mitre Hotel *E/WMO/HCT* KT8 198 D3
Carlton Primary School *KTTN* NW5 118 B10
Carlton Vale Infant School *MV/WKIL* W9 2 D9
Carlyle Business Centre *CHERT* KT16 195 J7
Carlyle's House (NT) *CHEL* SW3 15 N10
Carnwath Road Industrial Estate *FUL/PGN* SW6 157 L9
Carpenders Park *OXHEY* WD19 93 L4
Carpenders Park Cemetery *OXHEY* WD19 93 N5
Carpenters' Hall *OBST* EC2N 13 H4
Carpenters Primary School *SRTFD* E15 141 H3
Carrier Business Park *CRAWE* RH10 284 C6
Carshalton *CAR* SM5 221 P1
Carshalton AFC *SUT* SM1 201 P10
Carshalton Beeches *CAR* SM5 222 A3
Carshalton College *CAR* SM5 202 A10
Carshalton High School for Boys *CAR* SM5 201 N9
Carshalton High School for Girls *CAR* SM5 201 P10
Carshalton War Memorial Hospital *CAR* SM5 222 A2
Carterhatch Infant School *EN* EN1 80 A5
The Cartoon Museum *RSQ* WC1B 11 L4
Caryl Thomas Clinic *HRW* HA1 114 D2
Cascades Leisure Centre *GVE* DA12 191 K7
The Cassel Hospital *RCHPK/HAM* TW10 177 J7
Cassidy Medical Centre *FUL/PGN* SW6 157 K6
Cassiobury J & I Schools *WAT* WD17 72 F5
Castilion Primary School *THMD* SE28 143 M8
Castle Bar Park *HNWL* W7 134 E7
Castlebar School *HNWL* W7 134 E7
Castlebar Special School *WEA* W13 134 F7
Castlecombe Primary School *ELTH/MOT* SE9 184 B8
Castle Hall Theatre & Civic Centre *HERT/WAT* SG14 25 K5
Castle Hill Primary School *CROY/NA* CR0 225 H3
Castle Industrial Estate *WALW* SE17 18 E5
Castle Montessori School *BERK* HP4 34 A5
Castleview Combined School *DTCH/LGLY* SL3 150 A3
Casualty Plus Clinic *BTFD* TW8 155 H4
Caterham *CTHM* CR3 241 P9
The Caterham Dene Hospital *CTHM* CR3 241 N9
Caterham High School *CLAY* IG5 102 C10
Caterham Preparatory School *CTHM* CR3 259 N2
Caterham School *CTHM* CR3 259 N2
Catford *CAT* SE6 182 F3
Catford Bridge *CAT* SE6 182 F3
Catford Cricket & Sports Club *CAT* SE6 182 G4
Catford Cyphers CC *CAT* SE6 182 E5
Catford High School *CAT* SE6 183 J6
Catford Trading Estate *CAT* SE6 182 G5
Catford Wanderers Sports Club *CAT* SE6 183 H7
Cathall Leisure Centre *WAN* E11 121 J8
Cathedral of St Mary & St Helen *BRWN* CM15 107 J3
The Cathedral School of St Saviour & St Mary Overy *STHWK* SE1 18 F1
Cator Park School for Girls *BECK* BR3 182 D10
Cavendish College *FITZ* W1T 11 J3
Cavendish Hotel *STJS* SW1Y 11 H9
Cavendish Primary School *CHSWK* W4 156 B6
Cavendish School *BERM/RHTH* SE16 160 B3
The Cavendish School *CAMTN* NW1 4 E5
Cavendish Special School *HNWL* W7 134 E8
The Cavendish Sports College *HHW* HP1 35 L5
Caxton Hall *STJSPK* SW1H 17 J3
Caxton Trading Estate *HYS/HAR* UB3 152 F1
Cayley Primary School *WCHPL* E1 140 D7
Cecil Park Clinic *PIN* HA5 113 M2
Cecil Road Primary School *GVW* DA11 190 C4
Cecil Sharpe House *CAMTN* NW1 4 D5
The Cedar School *FSTGT* E7 141 P1
Cedars Manor School *KTN/HRWW/WS* HA3 94 B9
The Cedars Primary School *HEST* TW5 153 H6
Cedar Way Industrial Estate *CAMTN* NW1 5 J4
Cenotaph *WHALL* SW1A 17 L1
Centaurs Business Centre *ISLW* TW7 154 F5
Centaurs RFC *ISLW* TW7 154 E5
Central Business Centre *WLSDN* NW10 116 B10
Centrale *CROY/NA* CR0 203 K9
Centrale Shopping Centre *CROY/NA* CR0 203 K9
Central Foundation Boys School *SDTCH* EC2A 13 H1
Central Foundation Girls School (Lower) *BOW* E3 140 D5
Central Foundation Girls School (Upper) *BOW* E3 140 E5
Central Hall *STJSPK* SW1H 17 K2
Central Hendon Clinic *HDN* NW4 116 E2
Central London Golf Club *TOOT* SW17 179 N5
Central London Markets *STBT* EC1A 12 C4
Central Medical Centre *MRDN* SM4 201 M4
Central Middlesex Hospital *WLSDN* NW10 135 P5
Central Park Arena *DART* DA1 187 M4
Central Park Pool *HARH* RM3 105 M6
Central Park Primary School *EHAM* E6 142 A4
Central Primary School *WAT* WD17 73 K8
Central St Martins College of Art & Design *RSQ* WC1B 11 N4
Central School of Ballet *CLKNW* EC1R 12 B2
Central School of Fashion *GTPST* W1W 10 G4
Central School of Speech & Drama *HAMP* NW3 3 L3
Central Square Shopping Centre *WBLY* HA9 135 K1
Central Sussex College *CRAWE* RH10 283 P7
Centre Court Shopping Centre *WIM/MER* SW19 179 J9
The Centre Performing Arts College *CHARL* SE7 162 A2
Centre Point *LSQ/SEVD* WC2H 11 K5
Chace Community School *EN* EN1 79 M5
Chadwell Heath *CHDH* RM6 123 N5
The Chadwell Heath Foundation School *CHDH* RM6 123 L4
Chadwell Heath Industrial Park *BCTR* RM8 123 P6
Chadwell Heath Leisure Centre *CHDH* RM6 123 N4
Chadwell Infant & Primary School *CHDH* RM6 123 M5
Chadwell Road Cemetery *GRAYS* RM17 168 A3
Chadwell St Mary Cemetery *CDW/CHF* RM16 168 D3
Chadwell St Mary Primary School *CDW/CHF* RM16 168 D3
Chadwell Springs Golf Club *WARE* SG12 26 B3
Chaffinch Business Park *BECK* BR3 204 C3
Chafford Hundred *WTHK* RM20 166 G3
Chafford Hundred Primary School *CDW/CHF* RM16 167 H4
Chafford School *RAIN* RM13 145 K7
Chafford Sports Complex *RAIN* RM13 145 K7
Chailey Industrial Estate *HYS/HAR* UB3 153 H1
Chalcot School *CAMTN* NW1 4 E3
Chalfont & Latimer *AMSS* HP7 69 P5
Chalfont Leisure Centre *CFSP/GDCR* SL9 89 P9
Chalfont St Giles Infant School *CSTG* HP8 89 N4
Chalfont St Giles Junior School *CSTG* HP8 89 N4
Chalfont St Peter FC *CFSP/GDCR* SL9 90 A8
Chalfont St Peter Infant School *CFSP/GDCR* SL9 89 P8
Chalfont St Peter Junior School *CFSP/GDCR* SL9 90 A8
The Chalfonts Community College *CFSP/GDCR* SL9 89 P8
Chalfonts & Gerrards Cross Health Clinic *CFSP/GDCR* SL9 90 A9
Chalgrove Primary School *FNCH* N3 117 H1
Chalk Farm *HAMP* NW3 4 C3
Chalkhill Primary School *WBLY* HA9 115 N8
Chalk Lane Hotel *EPSOM* KT18 238 A1
The Chamberlain Hotel *TWRH* EC3N 13 L7
Chambersbury JMI School *HHS/BOV* HP3 36 C9
Chambers Business Park *WDR/YW* UB7 152 B5
Chambers Wharf *BERM/RHTH* SE16 19 P1
Chancellors School *BRKMPK* AL9 59 K1
Chancery Court Hotel *HOL* WC1V 11 N4
Chancery Lane *FSBYW* WC1X 12 A4
Chandlers Field Primary School *E/WMO/HCT* KT8 197 P5
Chandos Business Centre *WLGTN* SM6 222 D3
Channelsea Business Centre *SRTFD* E15 141 J4
Channing School *HGT* N6 118 C6
Chantry Primary School *GVE* DA12 190 F2
Chantry School *WDR/YW* UB7 131 P8
The Chantry *GVE* DA12 190 F2
Chapel End Infant School *WALTH* E17 100 G10
Chapel End Junior School *WALTH* E17 100 G9
Chapel High Shopping Centre *BRW* CM14 107 H3
Chapman Park Industrial Estate *WLSDN* NW10 136 C1
Charing Cross *CHCR* WC2N 11 L9
Charing Cross Hospital *HMSMTH* W6 156 G5
Charing Cross Hotel *CHCR* WC2N 11 L8
Charles Darwin School *BH/WHM* TN16 244 C1
The Charles Dickens Museum *BMSBY* WC1N 11 N2
Charles Dickens Primary School *STHWK* SE1 18 E2
Charles Edward Brooke School (Lower School) *CMBW* SE5 159 J7
Charles Edward Brooke School (Upper School) *BRXN/ST* SW9 159 J7
Charlotte Sharman Primary School *LBTH* SE11 18 C4
Charlotte Turner Primary School *DEPT* SE8 160 F5
Charlton *CHARL* SE7 161 P4
Charlton Athletic FC (The Valley) *CHARL* SE7 161 P4
Charlton Cemetery *CHARL* SE7 162 B5
Charlton Health & Fitness Centre *CHARL* SE7 161 P4
Charlton House *CHARL* SE7 162 A5
Charlton Manor Junior School *CHARL* SE7 162 A6
Charlton RFC *ELTH/MOT* SE9 184 E3
Charlton School *CHARL* SE7 162 B5
Charlwood Place *HORL* RH6 279 H7
Charlwood Village Infant School *HORL* RH6 279 J8
Charrington Bowl *SURB* KT6 199 N9
Charrville Primary School *YEAD* UB4 132 F4
Charter Clinic *CHEL* SW3 16 A8
Charterhouse *FARR* EC1M 12 D2
Charterhouse School Students Residences *GODL* GU7 266 G10
Charteris Road Sports Centre *HAMP* NW3 117 P10; *KIL/WHAMP* NW6 2 D6
Charter Nightingale Hospital & Counselling Centre *CAMTN* NW1 9 P3
The Charter School *HNHL* SE24 181 L1
Charters School *ASC* SL5 192 C7
Chartridge Combined School *CSHM* HP5 50 B3
Chartridge Park Golf Club *CSHM* HP5 50 C4

Chartwell Business Centre BMLY BR1 206 A3
Chartwell (NT) BH/WHM TN16 263 J7
Chase Bridge Primary School WHTN TW2 176 D2
Chase Farm Hospital ENC/FH EN2 79 H4
Chase Lane Primary School CHING E4 100 E5
Chase Road Trading Estate WLSDN NW10 136 A6
Chase Side Primary School ENC/FH EN2 79 K6
Chaseville Clinic WCHMH N21 78 G10
Chater Infant School WATW WD18 73 H8
Chater Junior School WATW WD18 73 H8
Chatsworth Infant School BFN/LL DA15 185 K4
Chatsworth J & I School HSLW TW3 154 B10
Chaucer Clinic NWDGN UB2 154 C1
Chaulden Infant School HHW HP1 35 H7
Chaulden Junior School HHW HP1 35 J7
The Chauncy School WARE SG12 26 A1
Cheam BELMT SM2 221 J4
Cheam Common J & I School WPK KT4 200 E9
Cheam Fields Primary School CHEAM SM3 221 H2
Cheam High School CHEAM SM3 221 H1
Cheam Leisure Centre CHEAM SM3 220 G1
Cheam Park Farm Junior School CHEAM SM3 201 H10
Cheam Sports Club CHEAM SM3 221 H4
Cheapside CE Primary School ASC SL5 192 D1
Chelsea Bridge Business Centre VX/NE SW8 158 C6
Chelsea Centre & Theatre WBPTN SW10 157 M6
Chelsea Cinema CHEL SW3 15 P8
Chelsea College of Art & Design CHEL SW3 15 N8
WEST SW1P 17 K7
Chelsea FC (Stamford Bridge) FUL/PGN SW6 157 L6
Chelsea Fields Industrial Estate WIM/MER SW19 201 N1
Chelsea Group of Children WBPTN SW10 157 M6
Chelsea Independent College FUL/PGN SW6 157 L6
Chelsea Leisure Centre CHEL SW3 15 P8
Chelsea Old Town Hall CHEL SW3 15 P8
Chelsea Physic Garden CHEL SW3 16 A9
Chelsea & Westminster Hospital WBPTN SW10 15 K10
Chelsea Wharf WBPTN SW10 157 N6
Chelsfield ORP BR6 227 L2
Chelsfield Lakes Golf Centre ORP BR6 227 P4
Chelsfield Park Hospital ORP BR6 228 A2
Chelsfield Primary School ORP BR6 227 P2
Chenies CC RKW/CH/CXG WD3 70 F5
Chenies Combined School RKW/CH/CXG WD3 70 D4
Chenies Manor House RKW/CH/CXG WD3 70 E4
Chennestone Community School SUN TW19 197 J2
Cherington House Health Centre HNWL W7 134 E10
Cherry Garden Pier BERM/RHTH SE16 160 A1
Cherry Garden School BERM/RHTH SE16 19 P5
Cherry Lane Primary School WDR/YW UB7 152 A3
Cherry Lodge Golf Club BH/WHM TN16 244 D3
Cherry Orchard Primary School CHARL SE7 161 P6
Cherry Tree Primary School WATN WD24 73 H2
Chertsey CHERT KT16 195 J8
Chertsey Business Centre CHERT KT16 195 K7
Chertsey C & CC Site CHERT KT16 195 M7
Chertsey Cemetery CHERT KT16 195 K8
Chertsey Hall CHERT KT16 195 K7
Chertsey Museum CHERT KT16 195 K6
Chertsey Recreation Centre CHERT KT16 195 H8
Chertsey Town FC CHERT KT16 195 J6
Chesham CSHM HP5 51 H7
Chesham Bois CE Combined School AMS HP6 69 K1
Chesham Cemetery CSHM HP5 50 G5
Chesham Community Hospital CSHM HP5 51 H8
Chesham Health Centre CSHM HP5 50 G8
Chesham High School CSHM HP5 51 J6
Chesham Leisure Centre CSHM HP5 51 J7
Chesham & Ley Hill Golf Club CSHM HP5 51 P7
Chesham Park Community College CSHM HP5 50 F6
Chesham Preparatory School CSHM HP5 51 M3
Chesham United FC CSHM HP5 50 G9
Cheshunt CHES/WCR EN8 62 E6
Cheshunt Cemetery CHESW EN7 61 P7
Cheshunt Community Hospital CHES/WCR EN8 62 D7
Cheshunt FC CHES/WCR EN8 62 B8
Cheshunt Marriott Hotel BROX EN10 62 C2
Cheshunt Park Golf Club CHESW EN7 62 A3
Cheshunt School CHESW EN7 62 B6
Chessington CC CHSGTN KT9 219 H4
Chessington Community College & Sports Centre CHSGTN KT9 219 J4
Chessington Golf Club CHSGTN KT9 219 J4
Chessington North CHSGTN KT9 219 K2
Chessington South CHSGTN KT9 219 J4
Chessington World of Adventures CHSGTN KT9 219 H6
The Chesterfield Mayfair Hotel MYFR/PICC W1J 10 E9
Chesterfield Primary School PEND EN3 80 D3
Chesterton Primary School BTSEA SW11 158 B7
Chestnut Grove School BAL SW12 180 B4
Chestnut Lane First School AMS HP6 69 K2
Chestnuts Primary School SEVS/STOTM N15 119 K3
Chevening Cross RSEV TN14 246 B6
Chevening Primary School SEV TN13 246 C8
Cheyne Centre CHEL SW3 15 N10
Chicken Shed Theatre STHGT/OAK N14 78 B9
Chigwell CHIG IG7 102 E5
Chigwell Cemetery CHIG IG7 102 G5
Chigwell Golf Club CHIG IG7 102 D6
Chigwell Primary School CHIG IG7 102 F3
Chigwell Row Infants School CHIG IG7 103 M3
Chigwell School CHIG IG7 102 F3
Childerditch Industrial Park RBRW/HUT CM13 127 L1
Childeric Primary School NWCR SE14 160 D6
Childs Hill Clinic CRICK NW2 117 J7
Childs Hill Primary School CRICK NW2 117 H8
Childs Welfare Clinic BCTR RM8 123 M10
Chiltern Business Village UX/CGN UB8 131 L4
Chiltern Open Air Museum CSTG HP8 90 D3
The Chiltern Pools AMS HP6 69 J4
The Chilterns Crematorium AMSS HP7 68 E7
Chiltonian Industrial Estate LEE/GVPK SE12 183 L2
Chilworth RGUE GU4 269 H6
Chilworth CE Infant School RGUE GU4 268 G6
The Chimes Shopping Centre UX/CGN UB8 131 N2
Chimnocks Wharf POP/IOD E14 140 D9
Chingford CHING E4 101 K1
Chingford CE Infant School CHING E4 101 J2
Chingford CE Junior School CHING E4 101 J2
Chingford Foundation School CHING E4 100 G2
Chingford Hall Primary School CHING E4 100 E7
Chingford Health Centre CHING E4 100 F5
Chingford Industrial Centre CHING E4 100 D6
Chingford Mount Cemetery CHING E4 100 G4
Chingford RFC CHING E4 100 F2
Chinthurst School KWD/TDW/WH KT20 238 F9
Chipping Ongar Primary School CHONG CM5 67 N6
Chipstead COUL/CHIP CR5 240 A4
Chipstead Golf Club COUL/CHIP CR5 240 A4
Chipstead RFC COUL/CHIP CR5 240 A7
Chipstead Valley Primary School COUL/CHIP CR5 240 B2
Chisenhale Primary School BOW E3 140 D4
Chislehurst BMLY BR1 206 D2
Chislehurst Caves CHST BR7 206 D1
Chislehurst Cemetery CHST BR7 185 H8
Chislehurst Golf Club CHST BR7 184 E10
Chislehurst Natural Health Centre CHST BR7 184 E9
Chislehurst & Sidcup Grammar School BFN/LL DA15 185 L5
Chiswick CHSWK W4 155 P6
Chiswick & Bedford Park Preparatory School CHSWK W4 156 B3
Chiswick Business Park CHSWK W4 155 N3
Chiswick Community School CHSWK W4 156 A6
Chiswick House CHSWK W4 156 A5
Chiswick Moran Hotel CHSWK W4 155 N4
Chiswick Park CHSWK W4 155 P3
Chobham Common National Nature Reserve CHOB/PIR GU24 193 H10
Chobham FC CHOB/PIR GU24 213 L8
Chobham Golf Club WOKN/KNAP GU21 231 J1
Chobham RFC CHOB/PIR GU24 213 K6
Chobham St Lawrence CE Primary School CHOB/PIR GU24 213 K7
Cholesbury Camp Hillfort TRING HP23 32 B6
Chorleywood RKW/CH/CXG WD3 70 F8
Chorleywood Golf Club RKW/CH/CXG WD3 70 G8
Chorleywood Health Centre RKW/CH/CXG WD3 70 F8
Chorleywood Lawn Cemetery RKW/CH/CXG WD3 71 J7
Chorleywood Primary School RKW/CH/CXG WD3 70 F10
Chorleywood Road Cemetery RKW/CH/CXG WD3 91 N1
Chrisp Street Health Centre POP/IOD E14 140 G8
Christ Church Bentinck CE Primary School CAMTN NW1 9 N3
Christ Church Brondesbury CE J & I School KIL/WHAMP NW6 2 C4
Christchurch CE Infant School VW GU25 193 M3
Christ Church CE Junior School EA W5 135 J9
Christ Church Cemetery BRW CM14 107 H5
Christ Church CE Primary School BAR EN5 76 G6
BRXN/ST SW9 159 H7
BRXS/STRHM SW2 180 G4
BRYLDS KT5 199 M6
BTSEA SW11 157 P9
CHEL SW3 15 P9
FSTH SE23 182 C5
RKW/CH/CXG WD3 71 J8
WOOL/PLUM SE18 162 D7
Christchurch CE Primary School HAMP NW3 117 N8
Christchurch CE Primary School WCHPL E1 13 M4
Christchurch Industrial Centre STHWK SE1 12 C9
Christchurch Junior School CHERT KT16 214 G3
Christ Church Malden CE Primary School NWMAL KT3 200 B3
Christ Church Primary School ERITH DA8 164 E5
NWMAL KT3 200 A3
PUR/KEN CR8 223 J6
WARE SG12 26 D2
Christ Church School CAMTN NW1 4 F8
Christian Meeting Hall BECK BR3 204 F1
Christopher Hatton Primary School FSBYW WC1X 12 A2
Christopher Hotel WDSR SL4 149 J6
Christopher Place Shopping Centre STALW/RED AL3 38 C6
Christs College Finchley FNCH N3 117 L1
Christ's College Guildford GU GU1 249 P7
Christs College School EFNCH N2 117 L1
Christ's College Ski Club GUW GU2 249 N7
Christs School RCHPK/HAM TW10 177 L1
Christ the King RC Primary School FSBYPK N4 118 G6
Christ the King Sixth Form College LEW SE13 161 J9
Chrysalis Theatre BAL SW12 180 B4
Chrysanthemum Clinic CHSWK W4 155 P6
Chrysolyte Independent Christian School STHWK SE1 19 H3
Church Down Adult School LEE/GVPK SE12 183 M5
Church End Medical Centre WLSDN NW10 136 B1
Church Farm House Museum HDN NW4 116 E1
Church Farm Swimming Pool EBAR EN4 98 A2
Churchfield Primary School ED N9 99 N2
Churchfields J & I School SWFD E18 101 M9
Churchfields Primary School BECK BR3 204 C3
Churchgate CE Primary School HLWE CM17 29 P8
Church Hill Primary School EBAR EN4 98 A1
Church House WEST SW1P 17 K3
Churchill Business Park BH/WHM TN16 262 G2
Churchill CE Primary School BH/WHM TN16 262 F1
Churchill Clinic STHWK SE1 18 B3
Churchill College RYNPK SW20 200 F2
Churchill Gardens Primary School PIM SW1V 16 G8
Churchill Museum & Cabinet War Rooms STJSPK SW1H 17 K1
Churchill Theatre BMLY BR1 205 M2
Church Lane School UPMR RM14 126 G10
Church Langley Primary School HLWE CM17 47 M1
Churchmead School DTCH/LGLY SL3 149 N6
Church Stairs BERM/RHTH SE16 160 A1
Church Street CROY/NA CR0 203 K9
Church Street Industrial Estate WARE SG12 26 C1
Church Trading Estate ERITH DA8 165 H6
Church Wood RSPB Reserve SLN SL2 109 K6
Cineworld BXLYHS DA6 164 C10
CHEL SW3 15 M9
CRAWE RH10 283 N6
CRICK NW2 116 E6
EA W5 135 J9
EN EN1 79 P8
FELT TW13 175 J5
HLW CM20 29 J7
HMSMTH W6 156 E3
SL SL1 149 L1
SOHO/SHAV W1D 11 J8
WBPTN SW10 15 K8
WDGN N22 99 H10
Cippenham Infants School SL SL1 128 C9
Cippenham Junior School SL SL1 128 C9
Cippenham Medical Centre SL SL1 148 F1
Citigroup Tower POP/IOD E14 140 G10
City Business Centre BERM/RHTH SE16 160 B1
The City Business Centre CRAWW RH11 283 N3
City Business College FSBYE EC1V 6 D10
City Central Estate FSBYE EC1V 6 E10
City College of Higher Education IS N1 7 H9
City & Guilds of London Art School LBTH SE11 18 B8
City Health Centre FSBYE EC1V 12 G1
City & Islington College FSBYE EC1V 6 F10
HBRY N5 6 B1
IS N1 6 G5
STLK EC1Y 12 G2
City & Islington Sixth Form College FSBYE EC1V 6 C8
City Literary College HHOL WC1V 11 M5
City of East London College WCHPL E1 13 P5
City of London Academy STHWK SE1 19 P7
The City of London Academy Islington IS N1 6 E6
The City of London Academy EDUL SE22 181 P1
City of London Business College SEVS/STOTM N15 119 M3
SEVS/STOTM N15 119 P3
City of London Cemetery MNPK E12 122 B7
City of London Club OBST EC2N 13 J5
City of London College WCHPL E1 13 N5
City of London Crematorium MNPK E12 122 B8
City of London Freemens School ASHTD KT21 237 N5
City of London School BLKFR EC4V 12 D7
City of London School for Girls BARB EC2Y 12 E3
City of London School Sports Ground LEE/GVPK SE12 183 P5
City of Westminster Cemetery HNWL W7 134 E10
City of Westminster College BAY/PAD W2 9 L3
MV/WKIL W9 2 D10
MV/WKIL W9 2 F10
City of Westminster Vehicle Pound MYFR/PKLN W1K 10 B8
City Thameslink FLST/FETLN EC4A 12 C5
City University CLKNW EC1R 6 C10
STBT EC1A 12 E4
City University Business School BARB EC2Y 12 F3
Civic Centre & Woodville Halls GVW DA11 190 E3
Civic Hall Cinema HOD EN11 44 E4
Civil Service Sports Ground CHSWK W4 156 B7
LEE/GVPK SE12 183 P2
Clandon RGUE GU4 251 L5
Clandon CE Infant School RGUE GU4 251 K7
Clandon Park (NT) RGUE GU4 251 K8
Clandon Regis Golf Club RGUE GU4 251 L7
Clapham Common CLAP SW4 158 D10
Clapham Common Clinic CLAP SW4 158 E10
Clapham High Street CLAP SW4 158 E9
Clapham Junction BTSEA SW11 157 P10
Clapham Manor Primary School CLAP SW4 158 D9
Clapham Manor Street Public Baths CLAP SW4 158 E9
Clapham North CLAP SW4 158 F9
Clapham North Business Centre CLAP SW4 158 E9
Clapham Picture House CLAP SW4 158 D10
Clapham South CLAP SW4 180 C2
Clapton CLPT E5 120 A7
Clapton Girls Technology College CLPT E5 120 B9
Clara Grant Primary School BOW E3 140 F6
Clare House Primary School BECK BR3 205 H2
Claremont Clinic FSTGT E7 121 P10
Claremont Fan Court School ESH/CLAY KT10 218 A3
Claremont High School KTN/HRWW/WS HA3 115 K3
Claremont Landscape Garden (NT) ESH/CLAY KT10 217 P4
Claremont Primary School CRICK NW2 116 G7
Claremont Way Industrial Estate CRICK NW2 116 F6
Clarence House WHALL SW1A 17 H1
Clarendon Primary School ASHF TW15 174 A6
Clarendon Special School HPTN TW12 176 A9
Claridge's Hotel MYFR/PKLN W1K 10 E7
Claverings Industrial Estate ED N9 100 B3
Claycots Primary School SLN SL2 128 F6
Claygate ESH/CLAY KT10 218 C3
Claygate Primary School ESH/CLAY KT10 218 D4
Clayhall Clinic CLAY IG5 122 B1
Clayponds Hospital BTFD TW8 155 K3
Cleeve Park School SCUP DA14 185 M6
Clementine Churchill Hospital HRW HA1 114 D8
Cleopatra's Needle CHCR WC2N 11 N9
Clerkenwell Heritage Centre FARR EC1M 12 C2
Clerkenwell Parochial CE Primary School CLKNW EC1R 6 A10
Cleveland Primary School IL IG1 122 E9
Cleves Junior School WEY KT13 216 G1
Cleves Primary School EHAM E6 142 A3
Clewer Green CE First School WDSR SL4 148 E9
C & L Golf & Country Club NTHLT UB5 133 J2
Clifton Hill School CTHM CR3 241 L10
Clifton Lodge School EA W5 135 H9
Clifton Primary School NWDGN UB2 153 M3
Clink Exhibition STHWK SE1 12 G9
Clissold Leisure Centre STNW/STAM N16 119 L8
Clissold Park Natural Health Centre STNW/STAM N16 119 M7
C & L Leisure Centre RSLP HA4 133 J2
Clock House BECK BR3 204 D2
Clockhouse Industrial Estate EBED/NFELT TW14 174 C4
Clockhouse Primary School CRW RM5 104 C7
Clock Museum CITYW EC2V 12 F5
Cloisters Business Centre VX/NE SW8 158 C6
Clore Gallery WEST SW1P 17 L6
Clore Shalom School RAD WD7 57 K6
Clore Tikva School BARK/HLT IG6 102 F10
Clothworkers' Hall FENCHST EC3M 13 K7
Clouster's Green WAP E1W 13 N9
Coach Museum WDSR SL4 149 K7
Coalhouse Fort TIL RM18 169 P7
Coates Way JMI School GSTN WD25 55 M9
Cobbold Estate WLSDN NW10 136 C1
Cobham Bus Museum COB KT11 216 D8
The Cobham Health Centre COB KT11 217 J9
Cobham RFC COB KT11 217 L8
Cobham & Stoke D'Abernon COB KT11 235 M3
Cobourg Primary School CMBW SE5 19 L9
Cochrane Theatre GINN WC1R 11 N4
Cockfosters EBAR EN4 78 B8
Cockfosters Sports Ground EBAR EN4 78 A7
The Cockpit Theatre STJWD NW8 9 N2
Coldharbour Industrial Estate CMBW SE5 159 K8
Coldharbour Leisure Centre ELTH/MOT SE9 184 C5
Coldharbour Sports Ground ELTH/MOT SE9 184 D5
Colebrooke Primary School IS N1 6 C7
Colegrave School SRTFD E15 121 J10
Coleraine Park Primary School TOTM N17 100 A9
Coleridge Primary School HGT N6 118 E5
Coleshill CE First School AMSS HP7 68 E10
Coleshill CC AMSS HP7 68 F9
Colfe's Preparatory School LEE/GVPK SE12 183 M2
Colfe's Senior School LEE/GVPK SE12 183 M2
Colham Manor Primary School UX/CGN UB8 132 B8
Colindale CDALE/KGS NW9 116 B1
Colindale Business Park CDALE/KGS NW9 115 P1
Colindale Hospital CDALE/KGS NW9 116 B1
Colindale Primary School CDALE/KGS NW9 116 C2
Coliseum Theatre CHCR WC2N 11 L8
College Fields Business Centre WIM/MER SW19 201 P1
College of Arms BLKFR EC4V 12 E6
College of Business & Technology FSTGT E7 121 M10
College of Central London SDTCH EC2A 13 J1
College of Fuel Technology HGT N6 118 B4
The College of Law FITZ W1T 11 J4
LINN WC2A 12 A5
RGUW GU3 267 P4
College of North East London CEND/HSY/T N8 119 H2
SEVS/STOTM N15 119 N2
WDGN N22 98 D9
College of North West London KIL/WHAMP NW6 2 E5
WBLY HA9 115 M8
WLSDN NW10 116 C10
College of Organists FLST/FETLN EC4A 12 B4
College of Osteopathy BORE WD6 75 N7
College of Teachers EPP CM16 82 G2
College Park School BAY/PAD W2 8 F6
Collett Special School HHW HP1 35 M5
Collier Row Clinic CRW RM5 104 C9
Collier Row FC CRW RM5 104 A9
Collier's Wood WIM/MER SW19 179 N10
Collingwood Business Centre ARCH N19 118 F8
Collingwood Preparatory School WLGTN SM6 222 C2
The Collingwood Suite Conference Centre WGCW AL8 22 F7
Collins Method School CRICK NW2 136 F1
Collis Primary School TEDD TW11 176 G9
Colnbrook CE Primary School DTCH/LGLY SL3 150 G7
Colnbrook School OXHEY WD19 93 K3
Colnbrook Sports Club DTCH/LGLY SL3 151 J7
Colne Bridge Retail Park WAT WD17 73 L9
Colne Valley Retail Park WAT WD17 73 L9
Colney Fields Shopping Park LCOL/BKTW AL2 57 L4
Colney Heath JMI School STALE/WH AL4 39 P8
Coln Industrial Estate DTCH/LGLY SL3 151 J6
Coloma Convent Girls School CROY/NA CR0 204 C10
Colonial Business Park WATN WD24 73 K5
Colonnades Leisure Park CROY/NA CR0 223 H3
The Colonnades Shopping Centre BGVA SW1W 16 E5
Colours Sports Club SUT SM1 221 M2
Columbia Primary School BETH E2 7 M9
Colvestone Primary School HACK E8 119 N10
Colville Primary School NTGHL W11 8 C6
Colyers Lane Medical Centre ERITH DA8 164 E7
Combe Bank Senior School RSEV TN14 245 P9
Comber Grove Primary School CMBW SE5 159 K6
Combermere Barracks WDSR SL4 148 G9
Comedy Theatre STJS SW1Y 11 J8
Comeille House Trading Estate DEPT SE8 160 D4
Comfort Hotel ENC/FH EN2 79 J6
Comfort Inn HYS/HAR UB3 152 F4
Commonside School HLWS CM18 47 J5
Commonswood JMI School WGCE AL7 23 L8
Commonwealth Institute WKENS W14 14 D3
Community Arts Centre GNWCH SE10 160 G6
Community Care Centre ENC/FH EN2 79 L5
Community Centre (Island History Trust) POP/IOD E14 161 H3
Community College & School GNWCH SE10 161 H6
The Community College HACK E8 140 A3
The Community Drug & Alcohol Team HLW CM20 28 F10
Community Mental Health Centre GSTN WD25 55 K10
HHNE HP2 35 N5
Compass Theatre HGDN/ICK UB10 112 D8
Complementary Health Centre LEE/GVPK SE12 183 K2
Compton Leisure Centre NTHLT UB5 133 M3
The Compton School NFNCH/WDSPK N12 97 P7
Compton Sports Centre NFNCH/WDSPK N12 97 P7
Concord Business Centre ACT W3 135 N7
Concorde Business Park BH/WHM TN16 244 A1
Conductive Education Centre MUSWH N10 118 C1
Conduit House GNWCH SE10 161 J6
Coney Hill School HAYES BR2 205 L9
Connaught Business Centre CDALE/KGS NW9 116 C3
CROY/NA CR0 222 G3
MTCM CR4 202 A5
The Connaught Hotel MYFR/PKLN W1K 10 D8
Connaught House School BAY/PAD W2 9 P6
Connaught School for Girls WAN E11 121 K6
Connections Business Park RSEV TN14 247 J6
Consort Clinic PECK SE15 160 A9
Consulate General of Monaco SKENS SW7 15 L5
Consulate General of the Republic of Guinea Bissau KENS W8 15 J3
Consulate of Burkina Faso BTSEA SW11 157 M9
Consulate of Chile CAVSQ/HST W1G 10 E2
Consulate of Colombia GTPST W1W 10 G5
Consulate of Eritrea IS N1 6 B7
Consulate of Guinea MYFR/PKLN W1K 10 C8
Consulate of Panama MYFR/PICC W1J 10 E10
Convent of Jesus & Mary Infant School CRICK NW2 136 F1
Convent of Jesus & Mary Language College WLSDN NW10 136 C3
Convent of St John the Baptist WDSR SL4 148 F8
Convoy's Wharf DEPT SE8 160 E4
Conway Medical Centre WOOL/PLUM SE18 162 G4
Conway Primary School WOOL/PLUM SE18 163 H3
Coombe Girls School NWMAL KT3 200 A2
Coombe Hill Golf Club KUTN/CMB KT2 178 A10
Coombe Hill J & I School NWMAL KT3 200 A1
Coombe Lane CROY/NA CR0 224 B2
Coombe Wood Golf Club KUTN/CMB KT2 177 N10
Coopersale Hall School EPP CM16 65 L10
Coopersale & Theydon Garnon CE School EPP CM16 65 N5
Coopers Company & Coburn School UPMR RM14 126 C8
Coopers' Hall LVPST EC2M 13 K4
Coopers Lane Primary School LEE/GVPK SE12 183 M5
Coopers Technology College CHST BR7 206 F1
Copenhagen Primary School IS N1 5 M6
Copland Specialist Science College WBLY HA9 115 L10
Coppermill Primary School WALTH E17 120 C3
Coppetts Wood Hospital MUSWH N10 98 A9
Coppetts Wood Primary School MUSWH N10 98 B9
Coppice Primary School CHIG IG7 103 K6
Copthall School MLHL NW7 96 E8
The Copthorne Business Centre CRAWE RH10 285 J2
Copthorne CE Junior School CRAWE RH10 285 J2
Copthorne Fairway Infant School CRAWE RH10 285 J2
Copthorne Golf Club CRAWE RH10 285 K2
Copthorne Hotel CRAWE RH10 285 H3
SL SL1 149 H1
Copthorne Hotel & Resort Effingham Park CRAWE RH10 285 N1
Copthorne Junior School CRAWE RH10 285 J2
Copthorne Preparatory School CRAWE RH10 285 M2
Copthorne Squash Club CRAWE RH10 285 H3
Copthorne Tara Hotel KENS W8 14 G3
Corbets Tey School UPMR RM14 126 A10
Cordwainers College HACK E8 140 B2
Corinium Industrial Estate AMS HP6 69 L4
Corinthian Casuals FC SURB KT6 199 M10
Corinthian Sports Club HART DA3 211 J6
Corner House Hotel HORL RH6 280 A5
Cornfield School REDH RH1 276 A5

Coronet Cinema
NTGHL W11 8 E9
SEVS/STOTM N15 119 J1
Corpus Christi RC Primary School
BRXS/STRHM SW2 180 G1
Corus Hotel
BAY/PAD W2 9 L7
BORE WD6 95 K1
Cosmopolitan College
IS N1 5 N8
Coston Primary School
GFD/PVL UB6 134 B5
Coteford Infant School
PIN HA5 113 H3
Coulsdon CE Primary School
COUL/CHIP CR5 240 G4
The Coulsdon Eye Clinic
COUL/CHIP CR5 240 D1
Coulsdon Manor Hotel
COUL/CHIP CR5 240 G2
Coulsdon Sixth Form College
COUL/CHIP CR5 241 H5
Countess Anne Primary School
HAT AL10 40 E3
County Mall Shopping Centre
CRAWE RH10 283 P7
County Oak Retail Park
CRAWW RH11 283 N3
Courtauld Institute of Art
TPL/STR WC2R 11 P8
Court Farm Industrial Estate
STWL/WRAY TW19 174 A2
Courtfield Medical Centre
ECT SW5 15 H6
Courtland JMI School
MLHL NW7 96 B3
Courtwood Primary School
CROY/NA CR0 224 E6
Covent Garden ⊖
COVGDN WC2E 11 L7
Covent Garden Flower Market
VX/NE SW8 17 K10
Covent Garden Medical Centre
LSQ/SEVD WC2H 11 L6
Coward Industrial Estate
CDW/CHF RM16 168 E4
Cowley Business Park
UX/CGN UB8 131 M5
Cowley Hill Primary School
BORE WD6 75 N5
Cowley Mill Industrial Estate
IVER SL0 131 K4
Cowley St Laurence CE Primary School
UX/CGN UB8 131 M7
Coworth Flexlands School
CHOB/PIR GU24 213 L7
CP House Business Centre
BUSH WD23 73 N5
Crabtree Junior School
HARP AL5 20 B2
Crafts Council
IS N1 6 B8
Craggy Island Climbing Centre
GU GU1 250 B6
Crampton Primary School
WALW SE17 18 D6
Cranborne Industrial Estate
POTB/CUF EN6 59 H6
Cranborne Primary School
POTB/CUF EN6 59 H7
Cranbourne JMI School
HOD EN11 26 G10
Cranbrook College
IL IG1 122 D7
Cranbrook Primary School
IL IG1 122 C5
Crane Park Island Nature Reserve
WHTN TW2 175 N5
Cranford Community College
HEST TW5 153 J5
Cranford Infant School
HSLWW TW4 153 H8
Cranford Junior School
HSLWW TW4 153 J8
Cranford Park Junior School
HYS/HAR UB3 152 G3
Cranford Park Primary School
HYS/HAR UB3 152 G1
Cranham Health Centre
UPMR RM14 126 D5
Cranleigh Gardens Industrial Estate
STHL UB1 133 N7
Cranmer Primary School
MTCM CR4 202 A4
Cranmore School
EHSLY KT24 252 D5
The Craven Clinic
HMSMTH W6 156 E3
Craven Park Medical Centre
WLSDN NW10 136 A3
Crawford Primary School
CMBW SE5 159 K7
Crawley ⇌
CRAWE RH10 283 P8
Crawley College Annexe
CRAWW RH11 283 M6
Crawley Down Health Centre
CRAWE RH10 285 P5
Crawley Health Clinic
CRAWE RH10 283 P7
Crawley Hospital
CRAWW RH11 283 M7
The Crawley Lawn Tennis Club
CRAWE RH10 284 C5
Crawley Museum (Goffs Park House)
CRAWW RH11 283 L8
Crawley RFC
CRAWW RH11 283 K3
Crayfield Industrial Park
STMC/STPC BR5 207 M2
Crayfields Business Park
STMC/STPC BR5 207 M1
Crayford ⇌
DART DA1 186 F2
Crayford Commercial Centre
DART DA1 186 F1
Crayford Industrial Estate
DART DA1 186 G1
Crayford Leisure Centre & Greyhound Stadium
DART DA1 186 F2
Crayford Medical Centre
DART DA1 186 G1
Craylands Primary School
SWCM DA10 189 J1
Crayside Industrial Estate
DART DA1 165 H9
Cray Valley Golf Club
STMC/STPC BR5 207 P1
Creekmouth Industrial Estate
BARK EC2Y 143 J6
Creek Road Health Centre
DEPT SE8 160 F5
Creek Road Industrial Estate
DEPT SE8 160 G5
Crescent Hotel
HRW HA1 114 D4
Creswick Primary School
WGCE AL7 22 G8
Crewe House
MYFR/PICC W1J 10 E9
Crews Hill ⇌
ENC/FH EN2 60 G10
Crews Hill Golf Club
ENC/FH EN2 60 G10
Cricket Green School
MTCM CR4 201 P3
Cricklefield Stadium
IL IG1 123 H7
Cricklewood ⇌
CRICK NW2 116 G8
Cricklewood Trading Estate
CRICK NW2 117 H8
Crispin Industrial Centre
UED N18 100 B6
Criterion Theatre
MYFR/PICC W1J 11 H8
Crockenhill Cemetery
SWLY BR8 208 E6
Crockenhill Primary School
SWLY BR8 208 D6
Crockham Hill CE Primary School
EDEN TN8 262 F9
Crofton Leisure Centre
BROCKY SE4 182 F2
Crofton Park ⇌
BROCKY SE4 182 E1
Croham Hurst Golf Club
SAND/SEL CR2 223 N3
Cromer Road Primary School
BAR EN5 77 L7
Cromwell Business Centre
BARK EC2Y 143 H5
Cromwell Hospital
ECT SW5 14 G5
Cromwell Medical Centre
CHESW EN7 62 A6
Crook Log Primary School
BXLYHS DA6 163 N10
Crook Log Sports Centre
WELL DA16 163 N9
Crosby Hall
CHEL SW3 15 M10
Crossharbour ⊖
POP/IOD E14 160 G2
Crossways Academy
BROCKY SE4 160 D8
Crouch End Art School
CEND/HSY/T N8 118 F3
Crouch End Health Centre
CEND/HSY/T N8 118 F3
Crouch Hill ⊖
FSBYPK N4 118 G5
Crouch Hill Recreation Centre
CEND/HSY/T N8 118 F5
Crouch Industrial Estate
LHD/OX KT22 236 F5
Crowland Primary School
SEVS/STOTM N15 119 P3
Crowlands Primary School
ROMW/RG RM7 124 D4
Crown Business Centre
WDR/YW UB7 132 A10
Crown Business Estate
CSHM HP5 51 H6
Crown Close Business Centre
BOW E3 140 F3
Crowndale Health Centre
CAMTN NW1 5 H7
Crowne Plaza
CAN/RD E16 141 M9
EA W5 135 K5
WDR/YW UB7 152 B3
Crowne Plaza Hotel
CRAWW RH11 283 N5
Crownfield Primary School
ROMW/RG RM7 104 B10
Crown Lane Clinic
STHGT/OAK N14 98 D2
Crown Lane Primary School
WNWD SE27 181 K7
Crown Moran Hotel
CRICK NW2 116 G9
Crown Prosecution Service
STAL AL1 38 C6
Crown Trading Centre
HYS/HAR UB3 152 F1
Crown Woods School
ELTH/MOT SE9 184 F1
Croxley ⊖
RKW/CH/CXG WD3 72 C10
Croydon Airport Industrial Estate
CROY/NA CR0 223 H4
Croydon Bowling Club
SAND/SEL CR2 223 K2
Croydon Cemetery
CROY/NA CR0 202 G5
Croydon Clocktower Cinema
CROY/NA CR0 203 K10
Croydon College
CROY/NA CR0 203 L10
Croydon Crematorium
THHTH CR7 202 F5
Croydon Fairfield Halls Cinema
CROY/NA CR0 203 L10
Croydon FC
SNWD SE25 204 B5
Croydon High Junior School GDST
SAND/SEL CR2 224 A7
Croydon Road Industrial Estate
BECK BR3 204 B4
Croydon Sports Arena
SNWD SE25 204 B5
Crusader Industrial Estate
FSBYPK N4 119 K4
Crystal Palace ⇌ ⊖
PGE/AN SE20 181 P9
Crystal Palace FC (Selhurst Park)
SNWD SE25 203 M4
Crystal Palace FC Soccer & Sports Centre
BRXN/ST SW9 158 G9
Crystal Palace Museum
NRWD SE19 181 N9
Cuaco Sports Ground
BECK BR3 182 F9
Cubitt Town Infants School
POP/IOD E14 161 H2
Cuddington Cemetery
WPK KT4 200 E9
Cuddington CP School
WPK KT4 200 C10
Cuddington Croft Primary School
BELMT SM2 220 G5
Cuddington Golf Club
BNSTD SM7 221 H9
Cudham CE Primary School
BH/WHM TN16 244 D2
Cuffley ⇌
POTB/CUF EN6 60 G5
Cuffley School
POTB/CUF EN6 60 G6
Culloden Primary School
POP/IOD E14 141 J8
Culvers House Primary School
MTCM CR4 202 B8
Cumberland Business Park
WLSDN NW10 135 N5
The Cumberland Hotel
FITZ W1T 11 J5
OXSTW W1C 10 B6
Cumberland Park Industrial Estate
WLSDN NW10 136 D5
The Cumming Museum
WALW SE17 18 E6
Cumnor House School
SAND/SEL CR2 223 J5
Cunningham Hill J & I School
STAL AL1 38 F8
Curwen Primary School
PLSTW E13 141 M4
Curzon CE Primary School
AMSS HP7 68 A8
Curzon Mayfair Cinema
MYFR/PICC W1J 10 E10
Curzon Soho Cinema
SOHO/SHAV W1D 11 K7
Custom House
GVE DA12 190 F2
MON EC3R 13 J8
Custom House for ExCeL ⊖
CAN/RD E16 141 N9
Cutlers' Hall
STP EC4M 12 D5
Cutty Sark ⊖
GNWCH SE10 161 H5
Cutty Sark Clipper Ship
GNWCH SE10 161 H5
Cygnet Clinic Beckton
EHAM E6 142 E7
Cygnet Leisure Centre
GVW DA11 190 B4
Cygnus Business Centre
WLSDN NW10 116 C10
Cypress Infant School
SNWD SE25 203 M2
Cypress Junior School
SNWD SE25 203 M2
Cyprus ⊖
CAN/RD E16 142 D9
Cyprus College of Art
WNWD SE27 181 J7
Cyril Jackson Primary School
POP/IOD E14 140 E9
Dacorum Athletics Track
HHNE HP2 36 A8
Dacorum Education Support Centre
HHNE HP2 36 B6
Dacre Industrial Estate
CHES/WCR EN8 62 E5
Dagenham Chest Clinic
BCTR RM8 124 A8
Dagenham Civic Centre
DAGE RM10 124 C7
Dagenham Dock ⇌
DAGW RM9 144 A4
Dagenham East ⊖
DAGE RM10 144 D1
Dagenham Heathway ⊖
DAGW RM9 144 A1
Dagenham Priory Comprehensive School & Performing Arts College
DAGE RM10 144 C2
Dagenham & Redbridge FC
DAGE RM10 124 C10
Dagenham Superbowl
DAGE RM10 144 C4
Dagenham Swimming Pool
DAGE RM10 124 B7
Daiglen School
BKHH IG9 101 P2
Daily Telegraph Newspaper Offices
POP/IOD E14 160 F2
Dair House School
SLN SL2 128 G3
Dairy Meadow Primary School
NWDGN UB2 153 N2
D'Albiac House
HTHAIR TW6 152 B8
Dali Universe
STHWK SE1 17 N1
Dallington School
FSBYE EC1V 12 D1
Dalmain Primary School
FSTH SE23 182 D4
Dalston Junction ⊖
HACK E8 7 L2
Dalston Kingsland ⊖
HACK E8 7 L1
Dame Alice Owens School
POTB/CUF EN6 59 H9
Dame Tipping CE Primary School
ABR/ST RM4 104 E4
Damilola Taylor Centre
PECK SE15 159 N6
Danegrove Primary School
EBAR EN4 77 P10
Danesfield Manor School
WOT/HER KT12 197 J9
Danes Hill Pre-Preparatory School
LHD/OX KT22 218 B9
Danes Hill School
LHD/OX KT22 218 C10
Danetree School
HOR/WEW KT19 219 P4
Danson House
BXLYHS DA6 163 M10
Danson Primary School
WELL DA16 163 L10
Danson Watersports Centre
BXLYHS DA6 185 M1
Dapdune Wharf (NT)
GU GU1 249 P10
Darell Primary School
RCH/KEW TW9 155 M9
Darenth Country Park
RDART DA2 188 C5
Darenth Primary School
RDART DA2 188 E9
Darenth Rest Cemetery
RDART DA2 188 C5
Darenth Valley Golf Club
RSEV TN14 229 H8
Darent Industrial Park
ERITH DA8 165 L4
Darent Valley Hospital
RDART DA2 188 C4
Darley Dene Infant School
ADL/WDHM KT15 215 M2
Darrick Wood Primary School
ORP BR6 226 E1
Darrick Wood School
ORP BR6 206 E10
Darrick Wood Sports Centre
ORP BR6 206 F10
Darrick Wood Swimming Pool
ORP BR6 206 E10
Dartford ⇌
DART DA1 187 M1
Dartford Adult Education Centre
DART DA1 187 K3
Dartford FC
RDART DA2 188 A4
Dartford Golf Club
DART DA1 187 J5
Dartford Grammar School for Boys
DART DA1 187 K2
Dartford Grammar School for Girls
DART DA1 187 K3
Dartford Hospital School
HART DA3 211 M3
Dartford Museum & Library
DART DA1 187 M3
Dartford Natural Health Centre
DART DA1 187 M3
Dartford Technology College
DART DA1 187 K3
Dartford Tunnel
WTHK RM20 166 C7
Dartford West Health Centre
DART DA1 187 K2
Darwin Centre
SKENS SW7 15 L4
Darwin Leisure Centre
BH/WHM TN16 244 C2
Dashes Recreation Centre
HLW CM20 29 H10
Datapoint Business Centre
BOW E3 141 J6
Datchet ⇌
DTCH/LGLY SL3 149 N7
Datchet Golf Club
DTCH/LGLY SL3 149 M6
Datchet Parish Council Cemetery
DTCH/LGLY SL3 150 A6
Datchet St Marys Primary School
DTCH/LGLY SL3 149 N6
Datchet Sports Club
DTCH/LGLY SL3 149 N6
Daubeney Primary School
CLPT E5 120 D9
Davenant Foundation School
LOU IG10 82 F4
Davenies School
BEAC HP9 88 D9
The David Beckham Academy
GNWCH SE10 161 L1
David Game College
KENS W8 8 E9
David Livingstone Primary School
THHTH CR7 203 K1
David Lloyd Leisure
BKHH IG9 102 C2
NFNCH/WDSPK N12 97 N8
David Lloyd Leisure Centre
SKENS SW7 15 H5
David Lloyd Sports Centre
EN EN1 79 P6
David Lloyd Tennis Centre
SCUP DA14 185 M8
Davidson Primary School
CROY/NA CR0 203 N7
Davies Laing & Dick College
BAY/PAD W2 8 G8
Davies Lane Primary School
WAN E11 121 L7
Davies's College
STHWK SE1 18 G1
Dawlish Primary School
LEY E10 121 H7
Dawnay CP School
GT/LBKH KT23 253 P1
Days Hotel
BAY/PAD W2 9 M6
MLHL NW7 95 P3
RSLP HA4 113 K10
STHWK SE1 18 A4
Days Hotel London South Ruislip
RSLP HA4 113 K9
Days Inn
PIM SW1V 17 H7
POTB/CUF EN6 58 F10
Days Lane Primary School
BFN/LL DA15 185 J2
Dean College of London
HOLWY N7 118 G8
Deanesfield Primary School
RSLP HA4 113 L9
Deansbrook Infant School
MLHL NW7 95 P7
Deansfield Primary School
ELTH/MOT SE9 162 D9
Deans Trading Estate
RAIN RM13 145 L6
Debden ⊖
LOU IG10 82 F8
Debden Park High School
LOU IG10 82 G7
Debden Sports Club
LOU IG10 82 F9
De Bohun Primary School
STHGT/OAK N14 78 C9
Dedworth Clinic
WDSR SL4 148 D7
Dedworth County Middle School
WDSR SL4 148 D7
Dedworth Green First School
WDSR SL4 148 D8
De Havilland Aircraft Heritage Centre & Mosquito Aircraft Museum
LCOL/BKTW AL2 57 N5
De Havilland Primary School
HAT AL10 40 D6
Delrow School
GSTN WD25 74 B5
Delta Wharf
GNWCH SE10 161 J1
Denbies Wine Estate
RDKG RH5 254 G8
Deneholm Primary School
CDW/CHF RM16 167 P1
Dene House Hospital
WDSR SL4 149 H9
Denham ⇌
DEN/HRF UB9 111 K5
Denham Aerodrome
DEN/HRF UB9 111 H3
Denham Country Park
DEN/HRF UB9 111 L7
Denham Golf Club
DEN/HRF UB9 110 G4
Denham Golf Course ⇌
DEN/HRF UB9 110 G5
Denham Village Infant School
DEN/HRF UB9 111 J7
Denmark Hill ⇌ ⊖
CMBW SE5 159 L9
Denmead School
HPTN TW12 175 P10
Denvale Trade Centre
STMC/STPC BR5 207 L5
Denver Industrial Estate
RAIN RM13 144 G8
Department for Environment, Food & Rural Affairs
CHCR WC2N 11 L9
Department for Transport
WEST SW1P 17 K5
Department of Art & Design (London Metropolitan University)
WCHPL E1 13 M5
Department of Economics (London Metropolitan University)
TWRH EC3N 13 L6
Department of Education
STJSPK SW1H 17 K2
Department of Health
WHALL SW1A 17 L1
Department of Trade & Industry
STJSPK SW1H 17 K3
Deptford ⇌
DEPT SE8 160 F6
Deptford Bridge ⊖
DEPT SE8 160 F7
Deptford Business Centre
NWCR SE14 160 C4
Deptford Green School
NWCR SE14 160 E6
Deptford Park Business Centre
DEPT SE8 160 D4
Deptford Park Primary School
DEPT SE8 160 D4
Deptford Trading Estate
DEPT SE8 160 D4
De Rougemont Manor Hotel
RBRW/HUT CM13 106 F10
Dersingham Infant School
MNPK E12 122 C10
Derwentwater Primary School
ACT W3 135 P10
Design Centre Chelsea Harbour
FUL/PGN SW6 157 M7
Design Museum
STHWK SE1 13 M10
De Stafford College
CTHM CR3 241 N7
Deutsche Schule
RCHPK/HAM TW10 177 J4
De Vere Theobalds Park Hotel
CHESW EN7 61 P9
Devonshire Hospital
MHST W1U 10 D3
Devonshire House Preparatory School
HAMP NW3 117 M10
Devonshire Primary School
BELMT SM2 221 M4
Devons Road ⊖
BOW E3 140 G6
Dewhurst St Mary JMI School
CHES/WCR EN8 62 A5
Diamond College
SOHO/SHAV W1D 11 K5
Diana Fountain
E/WMO/HCT KT8 198 E2
Diana Princess of Wales Memorial Fountain
BAY/PAD W2 9 M10
Diane Matthews Clinic
ROMW/RG RM7 124 E2
Dilkes Primary School
SOCK/AV RM15 146 E8
Dilloway Industrial Estate
NWDGN UB2 153 M1
Discovery Business Park
BERM/RHTH SE16 19 P4
Discovery Primary School
THMD SE28 143 J10
The District Cemetery
HAT AL10 40 D8
Divine Saviour RC Primary School
ABLGY WD5 54 E8
Docklands Medical Centre
POP/IOD E14 160 F3
Docklands Sailing & Watersports Centre
POP/IOD E14 160 F2
Dockley Road Industrial Estate
BERM/RHTH SE16 19 N4
Dockmaster's House
POP/IOD E14 140 F9
Dock Offices
BERM/RHTH SE16 160 B2
Dockwell's Industrial Estate
EBED/NFELT TW14 175 J1
Dockyard Industrial Estate
WOOL/PLUM SE18 162 B2
Doddinghurst Infant School
BRWN CM15 86 G3
Doddinghurst Junior School
BRWN CM15 86 G3
Dog Kennel Hill Primary School
EDUL SE22 159 M9
Dokal Industrial Estate
NWDGN UB2 153 M1
Dollis Hill ⊖
WLSDN NW10 116 D10
Dollis Infant School
MLHL NW7 96 F8
The Dolphin Leisure Centre
ROM RM1 124 G2
Dolphin School
BTSEA SW11 179 P1
The Dominie
BTSEA SW11 158 A7
Dominion Business Park
ED N9 100 C3
Dominion Theatre
RSQ WC1B 11 K5
Dominoes Health Centre
GRAYS RM17 167 M5
Donhead (Wimbledon College Preparatory School)
WIM/MER SW19 178 G10
Donmar Warehouse Theatre
LSQ/SEVD WC2H 11 L6
Donnington Primary School
WLSDN NW10 136 E2
Donyngs Recreation Centre
REDH RH1 257 P9
Doods Brow School
REDH RH1 258 G9
The Dorchester Hotel
MYFR/PKLN W1K 10 D9
Dorchester Primary School
WPK KT4 200 F8
Dorking ⇌
DORK RH4 255 H10
The Dorking Business Park
DORK RH4 272 F1
Dorking Cemetery
DORK RH4 255 H10
Dorking (Deepdene) ⇌
DORK RH4 255 H10
Dorking FC (Meadowbank)
DORK RH4 272 F1
Dorking General Hospital
DORK RH4 272 F3
Dorking Golf Club
RDKG RH5 273 H3
Dorking Halls
DORK RH4 273 H1
Dorking Lawn Tennis & Squash Club
DORK RH4 272 F4
Dorking Museum
DORK RH4 272 F2
Dorking RFC
BRKHM/BTCW RH3 255 N10
Dorking Sports Centre
DORK RH4 273 H1
Dorking West ⇌
DORK RH4 272 E1
Dorma Trading Park
LEY E10 120 C6
Dormers Wells High School
STHL UB1 133 P8
Dormers Wells Junior School
STHL UB1 134 A9
Dormers Wells Leisure Centre
STHL UB1 134 A8
Dormers Wells Medical Centre
STHL UB1 133 P8
Dorothy Barley Primary School
BCTR RM8 123 L10
Dorset Road Infant School
ELTH/MOT SE9 184 B5
Dorset Square Hotel
CAMTN NW1 10 A3
Dorton College of Further Education
BGR/WK TN15 247 M8
Dorton House School
BGR/WK TN15 247 N8
The Douay Martyrs RC School
HGDN/ICK UB10 112 C9
Douglas Bader Foundation
PUT/ROE SW15 178 D2
Dover Road Primary School
GVW DA11 190 B4
Dovers Corner Industrial Estate
RAIN RM13 144 G5
Dovers Green School
REIG RH2 275 M4
Downderry Primary School
BMLY BR1 183 K7
Downe Manor Primary School
NTHLT UB5 133 J5
Downe Primary School
ORP BR6 226 D7
Downfield Primary School
CHES/WCR EN8 62 D7
Down Hall Country House Hotel
RBSF CM22 31 H4
Downham Health Centre
BMLY BR1 183 K7
Downhills Primary School
TOTM N17 119 L2
Down House
ORP BR6 226 D8
Downsell Primary School
SRTFD E15 121 J9
Downsend School - Ashtead Lodge
ASHTD KT21 237 K4
Downsend School Epsom Lodge
EW KT17 220 C9
Downsend School Leatherhead Lodge
LHD/OX KT22 237 H6
Downshall Primary School
GNTH/NBYPK IG2 123 H5
The Downs Primary School
HLW CM20 46 G1
Downsview Primary School
NRWD SE19 181 K10
SWLY BR8 209 H3
Downsview School
CLPT E5 120 A9
Downs Way CP School
OXTED RH8 261 K3
Drapers Hall
LOTH EC2R 13 H5
Drapers Sports Ground
SRTFD E15 121 H9
The Draycott Hotel
CHEL SW3 16 B5
Drayton Green ⇌
HNWL W7 134 E9
Drayton Green Primary School
WEA W13 134 F9
Drayton House School
GU GU1 268 C1
Drayton Manor High School
HNWL W7 134 E9
Drayton Park ⇌
HOLWY N7 119 H10
Drayton Park Primary School
HBRY N5 119 H10
DRCA Business Centre
BTSEA SW11 158 B7
Dr Challoners Grammar School
AMS HP6 69 H4
Dr Challoners High School
AMSS HP7 69 N6
Drew Primary School
CAN/RD E16 142 B10
Drift Golf Club
EHSLY KT24 234 F9
The Drill Hall
GWRST WC1E 11 J3
Driving Test Centre
CRAWW RH11 283 N8
The Drizen School
EDGW HA8 95 M8
Dr Johnson's House
FLST/FETLN EC4A 12 B5
Dropmore Infant School
SL SL1 108 B8
Dr Tripletts CE J & I School
HYS/HAR UB3 132 G8
Drury Way Industrial Estate
WLSDN NW10 116 A9
Duchess Theatre
COVGDN WC2E 11 N7
Duff Miller College
SKENS SW7 15 K5
Duke of York Column
STJS SW1Y 11 K10
Duke of York Theatre
CHCR WC2N 11 L8
Dukes Hotel
WHALL SW1A 10 G10
Dulverton Primary School
ELTH/MOT SE9 184 G5
Dulwich College
DUL SE21 181 M4
Dulwich College Track
DUL SE21 181 M5
Dulwich Hamlet FC
EDUL SE22 159 M10
Dulwich Hamlet Junior School
HNHL SE24 181 L2
Dulwich Hospital
EDUL SE22 159 M10
Dulwich Leisure Centre
EDUL SE22 159 P10
Dulwich Medical Centre
EDUL SE22 181 P1
Dulwich Picture Gallery
DUL SE21 181 M3
Dulwich & Sydenham Hill Golf Club
DUL SE21 181 P5
Dulwich Village CE Infant School
DUL SE21 181 M2
Dunbar Wharf
POP/IOD E14 140 E9
Duncombe Primary School
ARCH N19 118 F6
Duncombe School
HERT/WAT SG14 25 K4
Dundee Wharf
POP/IOD E14 140 E9
Dundonald Primary School
WIM/MER SW19 179 J10
Dundonald Road ⊖
WIM/MER SW19 179 J10
Dunningford Primary School
HCH RM12 124 G10
Dunottar School
REIG RH2 275 N1
Dunraven School
STRHM/NOR SW16 180 G6
Dunton Green ⇌
SEV TN13 246 G5
Dunton Green Primary School
SEV TN13 246 F6
Duppas Junior School
CROY/NA CR0 223 J2
Durand Primary School
BRXN/ST SW9 158 G7
Durands Wharf
BERM/RHTH SE16 160 E1
Durants School
PEND EN3 80 B5
Durdans Park Primary School
STHL UB1 133 N7
Durston House School
EA W5 135 J8
Dycorts School
HARH RM3 105 P5
Dysart School
KUTN/CMB KT2 177 J7
SURB KT6 199 K7
Eaglesfield School
WOOL/PLUM SE18 162 D7
Eagle Trading Estate
MTCM CR4 202 A6
Ealdham Primary School
ELTH/MOT SE9 161 P10
Ealing Abbey
EA W5 135 H8
Ealing Abbey Scriptorium
WEA W13 135 H8
Ealing Broadway ⇌ ⊖
EA W5 135 J9
The Ealing Broadway Centre
EA W5 135 J9
Ealing Central Sports Ground
GFD/PVL UB6 134 F4
Ealing Civic Centre
EA W5 135 H9
Ealing College Upper School
WEA W13 134 G8
Ealing Common ⊖
EA W5 135 L10
Ealing CC
EA W5 135 K8
Ealing Film Studios
EA W5 135 H10
Ealing Golf Club
GFD/PVL UB6 134 G5
Ealing Hammersmith & West London College
WKENS W14 14 A7
Ealing Hospital
NWDGN UB2 154 C1
Ealing Independent College
EA W5 135 H9
Ealing Northern Sports Centre
GFD/PVL UB6 114 C9
Ealing Park Health Centre
EA W5 155 J3
Ealing Road Trading Estate
BTFD TW8 155 J4
Ealing Snooker Club
WEA W13 134 G10
Ealing Sports Centre
EA W5 135 K9
Ealing & West London College
EA W5 135 H10
Eardley Primary School
STRHM/NOR SW16 180 D9
Earlham Primary School
FSTGT E7 121 L10
WDGN N22 98 G8
Earl's Court ⊖
ECT SW5 14 F7

Earl's Court Exhibition Centre
ECT SW5 14 E8
Earlsfield
WAND/EARL SW18 179 M4
Earlsfield Primary School
WAND/EARL SW18 179 M5
Earlsmead First & Middle School
RYLN/HDSTN HA2 113 N9
Earlsmead Primary School
SEVS/STOTM N15 119 N2
Earlswood
REDH RH1 276 A2
Earlswood Infant School
REDH RH1 276 B1
Earth Galleries
SKENS SW7 15 M4
East Acton
SHB W12 136 C8
East Acton Primary School
ACT W3 136 B9
East Barking Centre
BCTR RM8 123 M10
East Barnet Health Centre
EBAR EN4 77 N9
East Barnet School
EBAR EN4 77 N7
EBAR EN4 78 A10
East Beckton District Centre
EHAM E6 142 C8
East Berkshire College
WDSR SL4 149 H8
Eastbrook Comprehensive School
DAGE RM10 124 D9
Eastbrook End Cemetery
LOU IG10 82 A8
ROMW/RG RM7 124 F8
Eastbrookend Country Park
ROMW/RG RM7 124 E9
Eastbury Comprehensive School
BARK EC2Y 143 J3
Eastbury Farm JMI School
NTHWD HA6 92 G5
Eastbury Primary School
BARK EC2Y 143 J2
Eastcote
RSLP HA4 113 K5
Eastcote CC
PIN HA5 113 J3
Eastcote Health Centre
PIN HA5 113 K5
Eastcote Industrial Estate
RSLP HA4 113 K5
Eastcote Lane Cemetery
RYLN/HDSTN HA2 114 A8
Eastcote Primary School
WELL DA16 162 G9
Eastcourt Independent School
GDMY/SEVK IG3 123 K6
East Croydon
CROY/NA CR0 203 L9
East Dulwich
EDUL SE22 159 M10
East End Computing & Business College
WCHPL E1 140 A8
Eastern Business Park
HTHAIR TW6 152 G8
Eastfield Primary School
PEND EN3 80 C4
East Finchley
EFNCH N2 117 P2
East Finchley Cemetery
EFNCH N2 117 L1
East Finchley Medical Centre
EFNCH N2 117 P2
East Finchley School of English
EFNCH N2 117 P1
Eastgate Business Park
LEY E10 120 D6
East Greenwich Christ Church CE Primary School
GNWCH SE10 161 K3
East Ham
EHAM E6 142 B2
East Ham Industrial Estate
EHAM E6 142 A7
East Ham Jewish Cemetery
EHAM E6 142 B5
East Ham Leisure Centre
EHAM E6 142 C3
East Ham Memorial Hospital
EHAM E6 142 A2
East Ham Nature Reserve
EHAM E6 142 C6
East Hill Cemetery
DART DA1 187 P3
East India
POP/IOD E14 141 J9
Eastlea Community Centre
CAN/RD E16 141 L6
Eastlea Community School
CAN/RD E16 141 K6
East London Business College
WAN E11 121 K6
East London Cemetery
PLSTW E13 141 L5
East London Crematorium
SRTFD E15 141 L5
East London RFC
EHAM E6 142 C7
East London RUFC
SRTFD E15 141 L4
Eastman Dental Hospital
FSBYW WC1X 11 N1
East Molesey CC
E/WMO/HCT KT8 198 B3
East Putney
PUT/ROE SW15 179 H1
East Sheen Cemetery
RCHPK/HAM TW10 177 M1
East Sheen Primary School
MORT/ESHN SW14 156 B10
East Surrey College
REDH RH1 258 B7
East Surrey Hospital
REDH RH1 276 C4
East Surrey Museum
CTHM CR3 241 N10
East Thamesmead Business Park
ERITHM DA18 164 A1
East Tilbury
SLH/COR SS17 169 L3
East Tilbury Infant School
TIL RM18 169 L3
East Wickham Primary School
WELL DA16 163 J7
Eastwick Infant School
GT/LBKH KT23 236 A10
Eastwick Junior School
GT/LBKH KT23 236 A10
Eaton Manor RFC
WAN E11 121 P3
Eaton Square Preparatory School
BGVA SW1W 16 E5
Eaton Square School
PIM SW1V 16 G6
Ebbisham County Infants School
EPSOM KT18 219 P10
Ebbisham Sports Club
HOR/WEW KT19 219 P8
Ebbsfleet Industrial Estate
GVW DA11 189 M1
Ebbsfleet International
SWCM DA10 189 M2
Ecclesbourne Primary School
THHTH CR7 203 K5
Echelford Primary School
ASHF TW15 174 C8
Eclipse Estate
HOR/WEW KT19 219 P9
Eden College
STHWK SE1 18 D3
Edenham High School
CROY/NA CR0 204 D7
Eden High School
FUL/PGN SW6 157 J7
Eden Medical Centre
WKENS W14 14 D6
Eden Park
BECK BR3 204 F5
Edenvale Child Health Clinic
MTCM CR4 180 B10
Eden Walk Shopping Centre
KUT/HW KT1 199 K2
Edes Business Park
WLGTN SM6 202 B9
Edgebury Primary School
CHST BR7 184 F7
Edge Business Centre
CRICK NW2 116 E7
Edge Grove School
GSTN WD25 74 B3
Edgware
EDGW HA8 95 N7
Edgwarebury Cemetery
EDGW HA8 95 M3
Edgware Clinic
EDGW HA8 95 M7
Edgware College
KIL/WHAMP NW6 3 J2
Edgware Community Hospital
EDGW HA8 95 N8
Edgware FC & Wealdstone FC
EDGW HA8 95 M8
Edgware Infant School
EDGW HA8 95 M7
Edgware Jewish Primary School
EDGW HA8 95 N6
Edgware Junior School
EDGW HA8 95 N7
Edgware Road
BAY/PAD W2 9 M4
Edinburgh Primary School
WALTH E17 120 E3
Edith Neville Primary School
CAMTN NW1 5 J8
Edmonton Cemetery
WCHMH N21 99 L3
Edmonton Green
ED N9 99 P3
Edmonton Green Shopping Centre
ED N9 100 A3
Edmonton Leisure Centre
ED N9 99 P4
Edmonton Lower School
ED N9 99 M2
Edmonton Upper School
EN EN1 99 N1
Edmund Waller Primary School
NWCR SE14 160 C8
Education Centre
UX/CGN UB8 131 M1
WOOL/PLUM SE18 162 E4
Edward Betham CE Primary School
GFD/PVL UB6 134 C5
Edward Pauling School
FELT TW13 174 F5
Edward Wilson Primary School
BAY/PAD W2 8 G3
Edwin Lambert School
EMPK RM11 125 H4
Effingham Community Sports Centre
EHSLY KT24 253 M3
Effingham CC
EHSLY KT24 235 J10
Effingham Golf Club
EHSLY KT24 253 L4
Effingham Junction
EHSLY KT24 235 H9
Effingham Park Golf Club
CRAWE RH10 285 N1
Effra Road Retail Park
BRXS/STRHM SW2 181 H1
The Egerton House Hotel
CHEL SW3 15 P4
Egerton Rothesay Preparatory School
BERK HP4 33 N5
Egerton Rothesay School
BERK HP4 33 L5
Egham
EGH TW20 172 D8
Egham Business Village
EGH TW20 194 F2
Egham CC
EGH TW20 172 E9
Egham Sports Centre
EGH TW20 172 E9
Egham Town FC
EGH TW20 172 F9
Eglinton Junior School
WOOL/PLUM SE18 162 D5
Eglinton Primary School
WOOL/PLUM SE18 162 D6
Elangeni Junior School
AMS HP6 69 K2
Elbourne Trading Estate
BELV DA17 164 C2
Eldenwall Industrial Estate
BCTR RM8 123 P6
Eldon Infants School
ED N9 100 A2
Eldon Junior School
ED N9 100 B2
Eleanor Estate
CHES/WCR EN8 62 E10
Eleanor Palmer Primary School
KTTN NW5 118 D9
Eleanor Smith Special School
PLSTW E13 141 M4
Electrical Trades Union College
ESH/CLAY KT10 217 P1
Electric Cinema
NTGHL W11 8 C6
The Electric Theatre
GU GU1 267 P1
Electron Trade Centre
STMC/STPC BR5 207 L4
Elephant & Castle
WALW SE17 18 E5
Elephant & Castle
STHWK SE1 18 D4
Elephant & Castle Leisure Centre
LBTH SE11 18 D5
Elephant & Castle Shopping Centre
STHWK SE1 18 D4
Elers Clinic
HYS/HAR UB3 152 E3
Elfrida Primary School
CAT SE6 182 G7
Eliot Bank Primary School
FSTH SE23 182 A5
Elizabeth Garrett Anderson Hospital
CAMTN NW1 5 K10
Elizabeth Selby Infant School
BETH E2 7 P9
Elizabeth Trading Estate
NWCR SE14 160 C5
Ellen Wilkinson Primary School
CAN/RD E16 142 A7
Ellen Wilkinson School for Girls
ACT W3 135 L8
Ellern Mede School
TRDG/WHET N20 96 G2
Ellerslie Square Industrial Estate
BRXS/STRHM SW2 158 F10
Ellingham Primary School
CHSGTN KT9 219 J4
Elliswick Lawn Tennis Club
HARP AL5 20 A1
Elmbridge Leisure Centre
WOT/HER KT12 197 J5
Elmbridge Museum
WEY KT13 216 B1
Elm Court School
WNWD SE27 181 J5
Elmers End
BECK BR3 204 C4
The Elmgreen School
WNWD SE27 181 J5
Elmgrove Middle School
KTN/HRWW/WS HA3 114 F2
Elmhurst Primary School
FSTGT E7 141 N2
Elmhurst School
SAND/SEL CR2 223 L2
Elm Lea Trading Estate
TOTM N17 99 P8
Elm Park
HCH RM12 125 H9
The Elms Football & Tennis Club
STAN HA7 94 G6
The Elms Health Centre
POTB/CUF EN6 59 M7
Elms Industrial Estate
HARH RM3 106 A8
The Elmsleigh Centre Shopping Precinct
STA TW18 173 J7
Elmstead Woods
CHST BR7 184 B9
Elmtree Infant School
CSHM HP5 50 G6
Elmwood J & I School
CROY/NA CR0 203 J7
Elm Wood Primary School
DUL SE21 181 L6
Elsdale Street Health Centre
HOM E9 140 B2
Elsley Primary School
WBLY HA9 135 L1
Elsley School
BTSEA SW11 158 B9
Elstree Aerodrome
BORE WD6 74 E7
Elstree & Borehamwood
BORE WD6 75 L8
Elstree Golf & Country Club
BORE WD6 75 J7
Elstree Studios
BORE WD6 75 M7
Elstree Way Clinic
BORE WD6 75 N6
Eltham
ELTH/MOT SE9 162 C10
Eltham Bus Station
ELTH/MOT SE9 184 C1
Eltham CE Primary School
ELTH/MOT SE9 184 C1
Eltham College Junior School
ELTH/MOT SE9 184 A4
Eltham College Senior School
ELTH/MOT SE9 184 A5
Eltham Crematorium
ELTH/MOT SE9 162 G10
Eltham Green School
ELTH/MOT SE9 184 A2
Eltham Health Clinic
ELTH/MOT SE9 184 B1
Eltham Health & Fitness Centre
ELTH/MOT SE9 184 D2
Eltham Hill Technology College
ELTH/MOT SE9 184 B2
Eltham Palace
ELTH/MOT SE9 184 B3
Eltham Pools
ELTH/MOT SE9 184 B1
Eltham Warren Golf Club
ELTH/MOT SE9 184 E1
Elthorne Park High School
HNWL W7 154 E2
Elthorne Sports Centre
HNWL W7 154 E2
Elverson Road
LEW SE13 160 G8
Elystan Business Centre
YEAD UB4 133 K9
Emanuel School
BTSEA SW11 179 N1
Embankment
CHCR WC2N 11 M9
Embankment Pier
CHCR WC2N 11 N9
Embassy of Afghanistan
SKENS SW7 15 L2
Embassy of Albania
BGVA SW1W 16 F4
Embassy of Algeria
NTGHL W11 8 B10
Embassy of Angola
MYFR/PKLN W1K 10 C8
Embassy of Argentina
MYFR/PKLN W1K 10 E7
Embassy of Armenia
KENS W8 14 G3
Embassy of Austria
KTBR SW1X 16 C3
Embassy of Bahrain
SKENS SW7 15 J4
Embassy of Belarus
KENS W8 15 H2
Embassy of Belgium
KTBR SW1X 16 D4
Embassy of Bolivia
BGVA SW1W 16 D4
Embassy of Bosnia-Herzegovina
CAVSQ/HST W1G 10 F5
Embassy of Brazil
MYFR/PKLN W1K 10 C7
Embassy of Bulgaria
SKENS SW7 15 K3
Embassy of Cameroon
NTGHL W11 8 B10
Embassy of China
CAVSQ/HST W1G 10 E3
Embassy of Costa Rica
BAY/PAD W2 9 K7
Embassy of Cote d'Ivoire
KTBR SW1X 16 D3
Embassy of Croatia
GTPST W1W 10 F2
Embassy of Cuba
LSQ/SEVD WC2H 11 L5
Embassy of Democratic Republic of the Congo
KTBR SW1X 16 B4
Embassy of Denmark
KTBR SW1X 16 A3
Embassy of Dominican Republic
BAY/PAD W2 9 H6
Embassy of Ecuador
KTBR SW1X 16 A3
Embassy of Egypt
MYFR/PICC W1J 10 E9
Embassy of Estonia
SKENS SW7 15 K2
Embassy of Ethiopia
SKENS SW7 15 M2
Embassy of Finland
KTBR SW1X 16 C3
Embassy of France
KTBR SW1X 16 B1
Embassy of Gabon
SKENS SW7 15 K4
Embassy of Georgia
KENS W8 14 G2
Embassy of Germany
KTBR SW1X 16 C3
Embassy of Ghana
HGT N6 118 C6
Embassy of Greece
NTGHL W11 8 C10
Embassy of Guatemala
WBPTN SW10 15 J9
Embassy of Honduras
MBLAR W1H 10 B3
Embassy of Hungary
KTBR SW1X 16 D4
Embassy of Iceland
KTBR SW1X 16 C5
Embassy of Indonesia
MYFR/PKLN W1K 10 D8
Embassy of Iran
SKENS SW7 15 M2
Embassy of Iraq
SKENS SW7 15 K3
Embassy of Ireland
KTBR SW1X 16 E2
Embassy of Israel
KENS W8 15 H1
Embassy of Italy
MYFR/PKLN W1K 10 D7
Embassy of Japan
MYFR/PICC W1J 10 F10
Embassy of Jordan
KENS W8 14 E2
Embassy of Korea
WESTW SW1E 17 H3
Embassy of Krygyzstan
MBLAR W1H 10 A4
Embassy of Kuwait
KTBR SW1X 16 B1
Embassy of Latvia
CAMTN NW1 10 C2
Embassy of Lebanon
KENS W8 8 G9
Embassy of Liberia
BAY/PAD W2 8 F7
Embassy of Lithuania
MBLAR W1H 10 A4
Embassy of Luxembourg
KTBR SW1X 16 C2
Embassy of Mexico
MYFR/PICC W1J 10 E10
Embassy of Mongolia
KENS W8 15 H2
Embassy of Morocco
SKENS SW7 15 J5
Embassy of Mozambique
FITZ W1T 10 G2
Embassy of Myanmar
MYFR/PICC W1J 10 E9
Embassy of Nepal
KENS W8 8 G9
Embassy of Netherlands
SKENS SW7 15 K2
Embassy of Norway
KTBR SW1X 16 D3
Embassy of Paraguay
SKENS SW7 15 H4
Embassy of Peru
KTBR SW1X 16 B3
Embassy of Philippines
KENS W8 8 G10
Embassy of Poland
CAVSQ/HST W1G 10 E3
Embassy of Portugal
KTBR SW1X 16 C2
Embassy of Qatar
MYFR/PKLN W1K 10 D9
Embassy of Romania
KENS W8 14 G1
Embassy of Russian Federation
KENS W8 8 G10
Embassy of Saudi Arabia
MYFR/PICC W1J 10 E9
Embassy of Senegal
CRICK NW2 136 F2
Embassy of Slovak Republic
KENS W8 8 G9
Embassy of Slovenia
MHST W1U 10 E5
Embassy of Spain
KTBR SW1X 16 D3
Embassy of Sudan
WHALL SW1A 10 G10
Embassy of Sweden
MBLAR W1H 10 A4
Embassy of Switzerland
MBLAR W1H 10 A4
Embassy of Syria
KTBR SW1X 16 C2
Embassy of Thailand
SKENS SW7 15 K4
Embassy of the Holy See
WIM/MER SW19 178 F6
Embassy of the United States
MYFR/PKLN W1K 10 C7
Embassy of Tunisia
SKENS SW7 15 M2
Embassy of Turkey
KTBR SW1X 16 D2
Embassy of Turkmenistan
FITZ W1T 11 H4
Embassy of Ukraine
NTGHL W11 8 B10
Embassy of United Arab Emirates
BAY/PAD W2 15 M1
Embassy of Uruguay
SKENS SW7 15 P3
Embassy of Uzbekistan
NTGHL W11 8 C10
Embassy of Venezuela
SKENS SW7 15 M4
Embassy of Vietnam
KENS W8 15 H3
Embassy of Yemen
SKENS SW7 15 L5
Emberhurst School
ESH/CLAY KT10 198 C7
Ember Sports Club
ESH/CLAY KT10 198 B8
Embroidery World Business Centre
WFD IG8 102 A10
EMD Walthamstow Cinema
WALTH E17 120 F2
Emerson Park
EMPK RM11 125 M5
Emerson Park School
EMPK RM11 126 A5
Emery Theatre
POP/IOD E14 140 G8
Emmanuel CE Primary School
KIL/WHAMP NW6 117 K10
Emmetts Garden (NT)
RSEV TN14 263 N5
Empire Cinema
LSQ/SEVD WC2H 11 K7
The Endeavour School
BRWN CM15 107 L3
Endsleigh Industrial Estate
NWDGN UB2 153 M3
Enfield Business Centre
PEND EN3 80 B6
Enfield CC
EN EN1 79 M8
Enfield Chace Lower School
ENC/FH EN2 79 M4
Enfield Chase
ENC/FH EN2 79 K7
Enfield College
PEND EN3 80 B7
Enfield County School
ENC/FH EN2 79 L7
Enfield Crematorium
EN EN1 80 A3
Enfield FC
ED N9 100 B3
Enfield Golf Club
ENC/FH EN2 79 J8
Enfield Grammar School (Upper)
ENC/FH EN2 79 L7
Enfield Town
EN EN1 79 L8
Engayne Primary School
UPMR RM14 126 D4
Englefield Green Cemetery
EGH TW20 171 P9
Englefield Green Infant School
EGH TW20 171 P8
English Martyrs RC Primary School
WALW SE17 18 G6
WCHPL E1 13 M6
Ensham Secondary School
TOOT SW17 180 A8
Enterprise Business Park
POP/IOD E14 160 G1
Enterprise Industrial Estate
BERM/RHTH SE16 160 B4
Epping
EPP CM16 65 K7
Epping Cemetery
EPP CM16 64 G6
Epping County Infant School
EPP CM16 65 H5
Epping Forest College
LOU IG10 82 E8
Epping Forest District Museum
WAB EN9 63 H9
Epping Forest Field Centre
LOU IG10 81 P4
Epping Golf Course
EPP CM16 65 L9
Epping House School
HERT/BAY SG13 42 D7
Epping Junior School
EPP CM16 65 J6
Epping Ongar Railway
CHONG CM5 67 M3
EPP CM16 65 L6
EPP CM16 66 E3
Epping Sports Centre
EPP CM16 65 J7
Epping Upland CE Primary School
EPP CM16 46 E10
Epsom
HOR/WEW KT19 220 A9
Epsom Bowls
EPSOM KT18 220 B10
Epsom Business Park
EW KT17 220 B7
Epsom Cemetery
EPSOM KT18 238 B2
Epsom College
EW KT17 220 D10
Epsom Downs
EW KT17 238 D2
Epsom Downs Primary School
EPSOM KT18 238 F5
Epsom Downs Racecourse
EPSOM KT18 238 C3
Epsom & Ewell High School
HOR/WEW KT19 219 P3
Epsom General Hospital
EPSOM KT18 237 P1
Epsom Golf Club
EW KT17 238 D1
Epsom Health Clinic
EPSOM KT18 220 B9
Epsom Primary School
HOR/WEW KT19 220 A7
Epsom Sports Club
EPSOM KT18 238 A1
Eric Liddell Sports Centre
ELTH/MOT SE9 184 A5
Eridge House Preparatory School
FUL/PGN SW6 157 J8
Erith
ERITH DA8 164 E4
Erith & District Hospital
ERITH DA8 164 E5
Erith Health Centre
ERITH DA8 164 F5
Erith Library & Museum
ERITH DA8 164 F4
Erith Playhouse
ERITH DA8 164 G4
Erith School
ERITH DA8 164 D6
Erith School Community Sports Centre
ERITH DA8 164 D6
Erith Small Business Centre
ERITH DA8 164 G5
Erith Sports Centre
ERITH DA8 164 F5
Erith Stadium
ERITH DA8 164 F5
Ernest Bevin College
TOOT SW17 179 P6
Eros
MYFR/PICC W1J 11 J8
Esher
ESH/CLAY KT10 198 C9
Esher CE High School
ESH/CLAY KT10 197 P10
Esher Church Primary School
ESH/CLAY KT10 218 B3
Esher College
THDIT KT7 198 D7
Esher RFC
WOT/HER KT12 197 M9
Essendene Lodge School
CTHM CR3 241 N8
Essendine Primary School
KIL/WHAMP NW6 2 F10
Essendon Primary School
BRKMPK AL9 42 A3
The Essex Nuffield Hospital
BRWN CM15 107 K2
Essex Primary School
MNPK E12 142 B1
Ethelburga GM School
BTSEA SW11 157 P7
Eton College
WDSR SL4 149 J4
Eton College Rowing Lake
WDSR SL4 148 B5
Eton End PNEU School
DTCH/LGLY SL3 149 M5
Eton Porny CE First School
WDSR SL4 149 J5
Eton Wick CE First School
WDSR SL4 148 F4
Eton Wick FC
WDSR SL4 148 E4
Euro Business Centre
SRTFD E15 141 L3
Euro Freightliner Terminal
WLSDN NW10 136 B5
Eurolink Business Centre
BRXS/STRHM SW2 159 H10
Europa Trading Estate
ERITH DA8 164 E4
WTHK RM20 167 J4
European Business Centre
CDALE/KGS NW9 116 A1
European Business School London
CAMTN NW1 10 C1
European College of Business Management
SDTCH EC2A 13 J1
European Language School
WDSR SL4 148 G8
European School of Economics
KTBR SW1X 16 D2
European Vocational College
HDTCH EC3A 13 K6
Euro Way School
CEND/HSY/T N8 119 H1
Euro Way School London
FSBYPK N4 119 J5
Euston
CAMTN NW1 5 J10
Euston Centre University of Westminster
CAMTN NW1 10 F1
Euston Square
CAMTN NW1 11 H1
Euston Tower
CAMTN NW1 10 G1
Evans Business Centre
CRICK NW2 116 D8
Eveline Day School
TOOT SW17 180 A5
Eveline Lowe Primary School
STHWK SE1 19 N8
Evendine College
SOHO/SHAV W1D 11 J5
Everest Sports Club
CHES/WCR EN8 62 A5
Eversley College
SBW CM21 29 N1
Eversley Medical Centre
CROY/NA CR0 203 H6
Eversley Primary School
WCHMH N21 78 F9
Everyman Belsize Park
HAMP NW3 117 P10
Everyman Cinema
HAMP NW3 117 M9
Evolution House, Kew Gardens
RCH/KEW TW9 155 K8
Ewell Athletics Track
HOR/WEW KT19 220 A3
Ewell Castle Junior School
EW KT17 220 C5
Ewell Castle School
EW KT17 220 D5
Ewell East
EW KT17 220 E6
Ewell Grove Infant School
EW KT17 220 C5
Ewell West
HOR/WEW KT19 220 B5
EW Fact/Emile Woolf Colleges
HOLWY N7 5 M1
ExCeL Exhibition Centre
CAN/RD E16 141 N9
Excelsior College
UED N18 99 M7
Exchange Square
SDTCH EC2A 13 J3
The Exchange
IL IG1 122 E7
Executive Medical & Occupational Health Centre
CROY/NA CR0 203 L10
Executive Park Industrial Estate
STAL AL1 38 G6
Exhibition Halls
WBLY HA9 115 M9
Express by Holiday Inn
CAN/RD E16 141 L8
CHING E4 100 F8
CRAWE RH10 284 B7
CROY/NA CR0 203 K9
GNTH/NBYPK IG2 122 G4
HHS/BOV HP3 53 P1
HMSMTH W6 156 E3
PIM SW1V 17 H7
SDTCH EC2A 7 J10
STHWK SE1 12 D9
WAND/EARL SW18 157 L10
WAP E1W 140 C9
WIM/MER SW19 179 N10
The Eye Clinic
NOXST/BSQ WC1A 11 K5
Eynsford
EYN DA4 229 L1
Eynsford Castle
EYN DA4 209 M9
Eynsford CC
EYN DA4 209 M9
Faculty of Engineering & Science (University of Westminster)
FITZ W1T 11 H3
Fairacres Industrial Estate
WDSR SL4 148 B8
Fairbrook Medical Centre
BORE WD6 75 N6
Faircharm Trading Estate
DEPT SE8 160 G6
IS N1 6 E7
Fairchildes Primary School
CROY/NA CR0 225 K8
The Faircross Complementary Medical Centre
BARK EC2Y 143 H1
Fairfield Clinic
BKHH IG9 101 N2
Fair Field Junior School
RAD WD7 74 D2
Fairfield Medical Centre
GT/LBKH KT23 254 A2
Fairfield Pool & Leisure Centre
DART DA1 187 M3
Fairfields Primary School
CHESW EN7 61 P3
Fairfield Trade Park
KUT/HW KT1 199 L3
Fairholme Primary School
EBED/NFELT TW14 174 E4
Fairlawn Primary School
FSTH SE23 182 B3
Fairley House School
PIM SW1V 17 J6
Fairlop
BARK/HLT IG6 103 H9
Fairlop Primary School
BARK/HLT IG6 102 F9
Fairoaks Airport
CHOB/PIR GU24 214 C7
Fairview Industrial Centre
RAIN RM13 144 E8
Fairview Industrial Estate
AMS HP6 69 L4
HYS/HAR UB3 152 G1
OXTED RH8 261 M9
Fairview Medical Centre
STRHM/NOR SW16 202 F1
Fairway Primary School
MLHL NW7 96 A3
Fairways Business Park
LEY E10 120 D7
Falconbrook Primary School
BTSEA SW11 157 N8
Falcon Business Centre
BTSEA SW11 157 P10
Falconer Special School
BUSH WD23 73 N9
Falcon Park Industrial Estate
WLSDN NW10 116 B10
The Falcons Preparatory School for Boys
RCH/KEW TW9 155 J9
The Falcons School for Girls
EA W5 135 L10
Falconwood
ELTH/MOT SE9 162 G9
Falkner House School
SKENS SW7 15 K7
Family Records Centre
FSBYW WC1X 6 A10
Fanmakers' Hall
LVPST EC2M 13 J4
The Fan Museum
GNWCH SE10 161 H6
Faraday Building
BLKFR EC4V 12 D6
Farleigh Court Golf Club
WARL CR6 224 F8
Farleigh Rovers FC
WARL CR6 242 E2
Farm Lane Trading Estate
FUL/PGN SW6 14 E10
Farnborough Primary School
ORP BR6 226 G2
Farncombe
GODL GU7 267 L10
Farncombe CC
GODL GU7 267 L10
Farncombe CE Infant School
GODL GU7 267 K10
Farnell House Medical Centre
HSLW TW3 154 A7
Farnham Common Infant School
SLN SL2 108 G9
Farnham Common Junior School
SLN SL2 109 H9
Farnham Common Middle School
SLN SL2 109 H9

Farnham Green Primary School GDMY/SEVK IG3 123 K4
Farnham Park Golf Club SLN SL2 129 K3
Farnham Road Hospital GUW GU2 267 N2
Farnham Royal CE Combined School SLN SL2 129 H5
Farnham Royal CC SLN SL2 129 H5
Farningham Road ⇌ EYN DA4 209 P2
Farningham Woods (Nature Reserve) SWLY BR8 209 L4
Farringdon ⇌ ⊖ FARR EC1M 12 B3
Farrington & Stratford House School CHST BR7 184 G10
Fawbert & Barnard Infant School SBW CM21 29 P1
Fawbert & Barnards (UNDL) Primary School HLWE CM17 29 M8
Fawkham CE Primary School HART DA3 210 F8
Fawkham Manor Hospital HART DA3 211 H8
Featherstone Industrial Estate NWDGN UB2 153 M1
Featherstone Primary School NWDGN UB2 153 L3
Featherstone Road Health Clinic NWDGN UB2 153 M2
Federation St Elpheges RC School WLGTN SM6 222 F3
Felnex Trading Estate WLGTN SM6 202 B9
Feltham ⇌ FELT TW13 175 J4
Feltham Airparcs Leisure Centre FELT TW13 175 L5
Feltham Athletics Arena EBED/NFELT TW14 175 H3
Felthambrook Industrial Estate FELT TW13 175 J6
Feltham Cemetery FELT TW13 174 G6
Feltham Community College FELT TW13 175 K5
Feltham Hill Infant School FELT TW13 174 G6
Feltham Hill Junior School FELT TW13 174 G6
Feltham & Hounslow Borough FC EBED/NFELT TW14 175 H3
Feltham Superbowl FELT TW13 175 J5
Feltonfleet School COB KT11 216 F9
Fenchurch Street ⇌ FENCHST EC3M 13 K7
Fenstanton J & I School BRXS/STRHM SW2 181 H4
Fenton House (NT) HAMP NW3 117 M8
Ferrier Industrial Estate WAND/EARL SW18 157 L10
Ferry Island Retail Park TOTM N17 119 N1
Ferry Lane Industrial Estate RAIN RM13 145 H7
WALTH E17 120 B1
Ferry Lane Primary School TOTM N17 120 A2
Festival Pier STHWK SE1 11 P9
Fetcham Social & Sports Club LHD/OX KT22 236 D7
Fetcham Village Infant School LHD/OX KT22 236 C8
Fiddlebridge Industrial Centre HAT AL10 40 D3
Field End J & I Schools RSLP HA4 113 L7
Field Infant School WATW WD18 73 K9
Fielding Primary School WEA W13 154 G2
Field Junior School WATW WD18 73 K9
Fieldway ⊖ CROY/NA CR0 224 G4
Film House Cinema RCH/KEW TW9 177 J1
Financial Times STHWK SE1 12 F9
Financial Times Newspaper Offices POP/IOD E14 141 H8
Finchley Catholic High School NFNCH/WDSPK N12 97 M4
Finchley Central ⊖ FNCH N3 97 K9
Finchley CC FNCH N3 97 L10
Finchley Golf Club MLHL NW7 97 J7
Finchley Industrial Centre NFNCH/WDSPK N12 97 M5
Finchley Lawn Tennis Club FNCH N3 97 J7
Finchley Lido Leisure Centre NFNCH/WDSPK N12 97 N8
Finchley Memorial Hospital NFNCH/WDSPK N12 97 M8
Finchley Road ⊖ KIL/WHAMP NW6 3 K2
Finchley Road & Frognal ⊖ KIL/WHAMP NW6 117 L10
Finchley Youth Theatre EFNCH N2 117 P1
Finsbury Circus Medical Centre LVPST EC2M 13 H4
Finsbury Health Centre CLKNW EC1R 12 A1
Finsbury Leisure Centre FSBYE EC1V 6 F10
Finsbury Park ⇌ ⊖ FSBYPK N4 119 H7
Finsbury Park Track FSBYPK N4 119 J5
Finton House School TOOT SW17 180 A5
Fircroft Primary School TOOT SW17 180 A5
Fire Brigade HQ STHWK SE1 17 N5
Fire Brigade Museum STHWK SE1 18 E1
Firepower Royal Artillery Museum WOOL/PLUM SE18 162 E2
Firs Farm Primary School PLMGR N13 99 L4
First Quarter Business Park HOR/WEW KT19 220 A7
Fisher Athletic FC BERM/RHTH SE16 140 C10
Fisher Industrial Estate WATW WD18 73 K9
Fishmonger's Hall CANST EC4R 12 G8
Fitness Unlimited Leisure Centre BOW E3 140 F4
Fitzrovia Medical Centre FITZ W1T 10 G2
Fitzroy Nuffield Hospital MBLAR W1H 10 A5
Five Bridges LBTH SE11 17 P8
Five Elms Primary School DAGW RM9 124 A8
Five Ways Business Centre FELT TW13 175 J6
Flamstead End Primary School CHESW EN7 61 P3
Flamsteed House Museum GNWCH SE10 161 J6
Flaxman Sports Centre CMBW SE5 159 K8
Fleecefield Primary School ED N9 99 P5
Fleetdown Junior School RDART DA2 188 B5
Fleet Primary School HAMP NW3 118 A10
Fleetville Infant School STAL AL1 38 F6
Fleetville Junior School STAL AL1 38 F6
Fleetway Business Park GFD/PVL UB6 134 G4
Fleetway Sports Club GVE DA12 190 F4
Fleming Lab Museum BAY/PAD W2 9 M5
Flora Gardens Primary School HMSMTH W6 156 E3
Florence Nightingale Health Centre HLWE CM17 47 M1
Florence Nightingale Museum STHWK SE1 17 N2
Flutters Leisure Centre FUL/PGN SW6 157 K6
Follys End Christian High School SNWD SE25 203 M6
Follys End Christian School SAND/SEL CR2 223 M1
Fondu Sports Club PUR RM19 166 B3
Fontigarry Farm Business Park REIG RH2 275 M9
The Foot Clinic WIM/MER SW19 179 H9
The Foot Health Centre COUL/CHIP CR5 240 E1
Fordbridge Medical Centre ASHF TW15 174 A7
The Ford College CONDST W1S 10 F6
Fordgate Business Park BELV DA17 164 D1
Ford Industrial Park DAGW RM9 144 C5
Fordview Industrial Estate RAIN RM13 144 E5
Forelander Trading Estate CHERT KT16 195 M8
Foreign & Commonwealth Office WHALL SW1A 17 K1
Foreland Medical Centre NTGHL W11 8 A7
Forest Business Park LEY E10 120 C5
Forestdale Primary School CROY/NA CR0 224 D5
Foresters Primary School WLGTN SM6 222 E3
Forest Gate ⇌ FSTGT E7 121 M10
Forest Gate Community School FSTGT E7 121 M10
Forest Hill ⇌ ⊖ FSTH SE23 182 B5
Forest Hill Business Centre FSTH SE23 182 B5
Forest Hill Industrial Estate FSTH SE23 182 B5
Forest Hill Pools SYD SE26 182 B5
Forest Hill School FSTH SE23 182 C6
Forest House Business Centre WAN E11 121 L5
Forest Industrial Park BARK/HLT IG6 103 H8
Forest Medical Centre LOU IG10 82 B9
Forest Park Cemetery & Crematorium BARK/HLT IG6 103 M6
Forest Preparatory School WALTH E17 121 K2
Forest Road Medical Centre WALTH E17 120 E1
Forest Trading Estate WALTH E17 120 C1
Forge Close Clinic HAYES BR2 205 M8
Forge Lane Primary School FELT TW13 175 M9
Forge Wood Industrial Estate CRAWE RH10 284 C3
The Former Health Centre CHARL SE7 162 A3
Forres CP School HOD EN11 26 G10
Forster Park Primary School CAT SE6 183 K6
Fortismere School EFNCH N2 98 A10
Fortune Theatre HOL/ALD WC2B 11 M6
Forty Hall ENC/FH EN2 79 N3
Forty Hill CE Primary School ENC/FH EN2 79 P3
The Forum EDGW HA8 95 M7
Forum Theatre HAT AL10 40 C3
Fossdene Primary School CHARL SE7 161 N4
Foster's Primary School WELL DA16 163 M9
Foulds School BAR EN5 76 G7
The Foundling Museum BMSBY WC1N 11 M1
The Fountain Studios WBLY HA9 115 M8
Fountayne Business Centre SEVS/STOTM N15 119 P2
Fountayne Road Health Centre STNW/STAM N16 119 P7
Four Seasons Hotel BERM/RHTH SE16 140 E10
MYFR/PKLN W1K 16 E1
Four Swannes Primary School CHES/WCR EN8 62 D9
Foxfield Primary School WOOL/PLUM SE18 162 F4
Foxhills Resort CHERT KT16 214 C1
Fox Primary School KENS W8 8 E10
Frances Bardsley School for Girls ROM RM1 125 H3
Francis Bacon School STAL AL1 38 G9
Franciscan Primary School TOOT SW17 180 B7
Francis Combe School GSTN WD25 55 K8
Francis Holland School BGVA SW1W 16 D6
CAMTN NW1 10 A2
Frank Barnes Primary School STJWD NW8 3 M4
Franklin Industrial Estate PGE/AN SE20 204 B1
Frederick Bremer Secondary School WALTH E17 101 H10
Freehold Industrial Centre HSLWW TW4 175 K1
Freemantles School CHERT KT16 195 H7
Free Trade Wharf WAP E1W 140 C9
Freezywater St Georges CE Primary School PEND EN3 80 B2
Freightliners City Farm HOLWY N7 6 A1
The French Institute SKENS SW7 15 L5
Fresh Wharf Estate BARK EC2Y 142 E3
Freuchen Medical Centre WLSDN NW10 136 C4
Freud Museum HAMP NW3 3 K1
Friars Primary Foundation School STHWK SE1 18 C1
The Friary Centre GU GU1 267 P1
Friends House CAMTN NW1 5 J10
Friern Barnet School FBAR/BDGN N11 98 A6
Friern Bridge Retail Park FBAR/BDGN N11 98 C7
Frithsden Vineyard HHW HP1 34 E1
Frithwood Primary School NTHWD HA6 92 G7
Frogmore House WDSR SL4 149 L9
Frogmore Industrial Estate HBRY N5 119 K9
HYS/HAR UB3 152 F1
WLSDN NW10 135 P5
Frogmore Road Industrial Estate HHS/BOV HP3 35 N9
Fryent Country Park KTN/HRWW/WS HA3 115 M5
Fryent Medical Centre CDALE/KGS NW9 115 P5
Fryent Primary School CDALE/KGS NW9 115 P5
Fulham Broadway ⊖ FUL/PGN SW6 157 K6
Fulham Cemetery FUL/PGN SW6 156 G6
Fulham Clinic FUL/PGN SW6 14 B10
WKENS W14 14 D9
Fulham Cross Girls Secondary School FUL/PGN SW6 156 G6
Fulham FC (Craven Cottage) PUT/ROE SW15 156 F7
Fulham Medical Centre FUL/PGN SW6 157 L6
Fulham Palace FUL/PGN SW6 156 G8
Fulham Pools FUL/PGN SW6 14 B10
Fulham Pre-Preparatory School FUL/PGN SW6 157 H8
Fulham Primary School FUL/PGN SW6 14 E10
Fullbrook School ADL/WDHM KT15 215 K7
Fuller Smith & Turner Sports Club CHSWK W4 156 B7
Fullwell Cross Health Centre BARK/HLT IG6 102 F10
Fullwell Cross Swimming Pool & Recreation Centre BARK/HLT IG6 102 F10
Fullwood Primary School BARK/HLT IG6 122 F2
Fulmer Infant School DTCH/LGLY SL3 110 B9
Fulwell ⇌ WHTN TW2 176 C7
Fulwell Golf Club HPTN TW12 176 C7
Furness Primary School WLSDN NW10 136 D4
Furness School SWLY BR8 186 G9
Furness Swanley FC SWLY BR8 208 E5
Furzedown Primary School TOOT SW17 180 C9
Furze Field Leisure Centre POTB/CUF EN6 59 H7
Furzefield Primary School REDH RH1 258 E4
Furze Infant School CHDH RM6 123 P4
Future Business College CONDST W1S 10 F6
Gade Valley JMI School HHW HP1 35 L5
Gaflac Sports Ground Pavilion SUN TW16 197 H1
Gainsborough Clinic PLMGR N13 99 G5
Gainsborough Primary School HOM E9 140 E1
SRTFD E15 141 K5
Galleria Shopping Centre HAT AL10 40 C4
Galley Hill Industrial Estate SWCM DA10 189 K1
Galley Hill Primary School HHW HP1 35 K4
Galliard Primary School ED N9 79 P10
Gallions Mount Primary School WOOL/PLUM SE18 163 J4
Gallions Primary School EHAM E6 142 E8
Gallions Reach ⊖ EHAM E6 142 E9
Gallions Reach Shopping Park EHAM E6 142 E7
Gants Hill ⊖ GNTH/NBYPK IG2 122 D4
Gants Hill Medical Centre GNTH/NBYPK IG2 122 D4
Garden Court Business Centre WCGE AL7 23 J5
Gardener Industrial Estate SYD SE26 182 D8
Garden Fields JMI School STALW/RED AL3 38 C3
Garden House School BGVA SW1W 16 C7
Garden of Rest Cemetery CFSP/GDCR SL9 90 C8
Garden Primary School MTCM CR4 202 E3
Gardens of the Rose (Royal National Rose) LCOL/BKTW AL2 55 N2
Garden Suburb Infant School GLDGN NW11 117 J3
Garfield Primary School FBAR/BDGN N11 98 C6
WIM/MER SW19 179 M9
Garratt Park Secondary Special School WAND/EARL SW18 179 M6
Garrick Industrial Centre CDALE/KGS NW9 116 C3
Garrick Theatre LSQ/SEVD WC2H 11 L8
Garston ⇌ GSTN WD25 73 M1
Garston Clinic WATN WD24 73 J2
Garston JMI School GSTN WD25 73 L1
Garston Manor Special School GSTN WD25 55 K8
Garston Medical Centre GSTN WD25 73 K2
Garth Primary School MRDN SM4 201 N5
The Garth Road Industrial Centre MRDN SM4 200 F7
Gascoigne Primary School BARK EC2Y 142 F3
Gate Cinema KENS W8 8 E9
Gatehouse School BETH E2 140 C4
The Gatehouse Theatre HGT N6 118 B5
The Gate Theatre NTGHL W11 8 E9
Gateway EHAM E6 142 E6
The Gateway Academy CDW/CHF RM16 168 D5
Gateway Business Centre SYD SE26 182 D9
WOOL/PLUM SE18 162 F2
Gateway Industrial Estate WLSDN NW10 136 C5
Gateway Primary School RDART DA2 188 A2
Gatton Park Business Centre REDH RH1 258 C6
Gatton School TOOT SW17 179 P7
Gatwick Airport ⇌ HORL RH6 280 C8
Gatwick Airport HORL RH6 280 A8
Gatwick Gate Industrial Estate HORL RH6 279 P10
Gatwick Industrial Estate HORL RH6 279 J9
Gatwick Manor Golf Club CRAWE RH10 283 P2
Gatwick Medical Centre HORL RH6 280 C8
Gatwick North Terminal HORL RH6 279 P7
Gatwick Park Hospital HORL RH6 279 P5
Gatwick South Terminal HORL RH6 280 B8
Gatwick Worth Hotel CRAWE RH10 284 G6
Gayhurst Primary School HACK E8 7 P3
Gayhurst School CFSP/GDCR SL9 109 P2
Gaynes School Language College UPMR RM14 126 B9
Gazelda Industrial Estate WAT WD17 73 K9
Gearies Infant School GNTH/NBYPK IG2 122 D3
Gearies Junior School GNTH/NBYPK IG2 122 E3
Geffrye Museum BETH E2 7 K8
Gemini Business Estate NWCR SE14 160 C4
General Medical Clinics WCHPL E1 13 L3
Genesis Business Park WOKN/KNAP GU21 232 F1
Genesis Cinema WCHPL E1 140 B6
Geoffrey Chaucer Technology College STHWK SE1 18 G4
The Geoffrey Lloyd Foulkes Clinic IL IG1 122 D7
Geoffrey Whitworth Theatre DART DA1 165 H10
George Abbot School GU GU1 250 D8
George Eliot Junior School STJWD NW8 3 K5
George Elliot Infant School STJWD NW8 3 K5
George Greens School POP/IOD E14 161 H4
George Mitchell School LEY E10 120 G6
George Spicer Primary School EN EN1 79 N7
George Street ⊖ CROY/NA CR0 203 K9
George Street Primary School HHNE HP2 35 N5
George Tomlinson Primary School WAN E11 121 K6
Germal College FSBYPK N4 119 H6
Gerrards Cross ⇌ CFSP/GDCR SL9 110 B3
The Gerrards Cross CE School CFSP/GDCR SL9 110 B5
Gerrards Cross Golf Club CFSP/GDCR SL9 110 C1
Gerrards Cross Sports Centre CFSP/GDCR SL9 110 A5
Ghyll Manor Hotel HORS RH12 282 A5
Gibbs Green Special School WKENS W14 14 D7
Gibson Business Centre TOTM N17 99 N7
The Gibson Business Centre TOTM N17 99 N8
Gidea Park ⇌ GPK RM2 125 J2
Gidea Park College GPK RM2 125 H1
Gidea Park Primary School GPK RM2 124 G2
Gidea Park Sports Ground GPK RM2 105 K10
The Gielgud Theatre SOHO/CST W1F 11 J7
Giffin Business Centre DEPT SE8 160 F6
Gifford Primary School NTHLT UB5 133 N4
Gilbert Collection TPL/STR WC2R 11 P7
Gilbert Colvin Primary School CLAY IG5 102 D9
Gilbert Scott Primary School SAND/SEL CR2 224 D4
Gillespie Primary School HBRY N5 119 J8
Gipsy Hill ⇌ NRWD SE19 181 M8
Girdlers' Hall CITYW EC2V 12 F4
The Glade Business Centre WTHK RM20 166 E4
Glade Primary School CLAY IG5 102 C9
The Glades Shopping Centre BMLY BR1 205 M2
Gladstone Medical Centre CRICK NW2 116 C9
Gladstone Park Primary School WLSDN NW10 116 D10
The Gladys Aylward School UED N18 99 L5
Glaziers/Scientific Instrument Makers Hall STHWK SE1 12 G9
Glebe First & Middle School KTN/HRWW/WS HA3 115 J2
Glebe Primary School HGDN/ICK UB10 112 E9
Glebe School WWKM BR4 205 J8
Gleen Lecky Health Centre PUT/ROE SW15 156 G10
Glenbrook Primary School CLAP SW4 180 E2
Glencairn Sports Club FBAR/BDGN N11 98 D8
Glenesk School EHSLY KT24 252 E1
Glenham College IL IG1 122 E7
Glenlyn Medical Centre E/WMO/HCT KT8 198 B5
Glenthorne High Specialist Arts CHEAM SM3 201 K8
Globe Academy STHWK SE1 18 G4
Globe Industrial Estate GRAYS RM17 167 P5
Globe Primary School BETH E2 140 B5
Globe Wharf BERM/RHTH SE16 140 C9
Gloucester Primary School PECK SE15 19 L10
Gloucester Road ⊖ SKENS SW7 15 J5
Glyn Technology School EW KT17 220 C7
Goal Farm Golf Club CHOB/PIR GU24 230 C7
Godalming Leisure Centre GODL GU7 267 M10
Godolphin Infant School SL SL1 129 H7
Godolphin Junior School SL SL1 129 J7
Godolphin & Latymer School HMSMTH W6 156 E3
Godstone Farm GDST RH9 260 B9
Godstone Village School GDST RH9 260 A8
Godwin Junior School FSTGT E7 121 N9
Goethe Institute SKENS SW7 15 M3
Goffs Oak JMI School CHESW EN7 61 J4
Goffs School CHESW EN7 61 P5
Goldbeaters Primary School EDGW HA8 96 A9
Golden Hinde Educational Trust STHWK SE1 12 G8
Golders Green ⊖ GLDGN NW11 117 K5
Golders Green Crematorium GLDGN NW11 117 K5
Golders Green Health Centre GLDGN NW11 117 L6
Golders Hill Health Centre GLDGN NW11 117 M4
Golders Hill School GLDGN NW11 117 K5
Goldhawk Industrial Estate SHB W12 156 E2
Goldhawk Road ⊖ SHB W12 156 F1
Goldings Hill Clinic LOU IG10 82 D6
Goldsmiths College Sports Ground SCUP DA14 186 A6
Goldsmiths Hall STBT EC1A 12 E5
Goldsmiths University of London DEPT SE8 160 F5
LEW SE13 161 K10
NWCR SE14 160 D7
Goldsworth CP School WOKN/KNAP GU21 231 P4
Goldsworth Park Health Centre WOKN/KNAP GU21 231 M3
Goldsworth Park Trading Estate WOKN/KNAP GU21 231 M2
Goldsworth Road Industrial Estate WOKN/KNAP GU21 232 A3
Golf Driving Range REDH RH1 276 B3
Gomshall ⇌ SHGR GU5 270 F5
Gomshall Mill SHGR GU5 270 D5
Gonville Primary School THHTH CR7 202 G5
Goodge St ⊖ FITZ W1T 11 H3
Gooding Health Centre HOLWY N7 5 L1
Goodmayes ⇌ GDMY/SEVK IG3 123 K6
Goodmayes Retail Park CHDH RM6 123 L5
Goodrich J & I School EDUL SE22 181 P2
Goodrington School EMPK RM11 125 L4
Good Shepherd RC Primary School BMLY BR1 183 L7
CROY/NA CR0 224 G4
The Good Shepherd RC Primary School SHB W12 156 C1
Goodwyn School MLHL NW7 96 D6
Goose Green Primary School EDUL SE22 159 N10
Goose Green Trading Estate EDUL SE22 159 P10
Gordonbrock Primary School BROCKY SE4 182 F1
Gordon Hill ⇌ ENC/FH EN2 79 J5
Gordon Hospital WEST SW1P 17 J6
Gordon House Health Centre WEA W13 134 G10
Gordon Infant School IL IG1 122 G8
Gordon Primary School ELTH/MOT SE9 162 C10
Gordons School CHOB/PIR GU24 212 D8
Goresbrook Leisure Centre DAGW RM9 143 N3
Goresbrook Sports Centre DAGW RM9 143 N3
Gorhambury STALW/RED AL3 37 K5
Gorhambury (Remains) STALW/RED AL3 37 J5
The Goring Hotel BGVA SW1W 16 F3
Gorringe Park Primary School MTCM CR4 202 B1
Gosai Cinema WEA W13 134 G10
Gosbury Hill Health Centre CHSCTN KT9 219 K1
Gosden House School SHGR GU5 268 B9
Gosford Primary School REDBR IG4 122 C3
Gosling Ski & Board Centre WGCW AL8 22 F8
Gosling Sports Park WGCW AL8 22 F7
Gospel Oak ⊖ HAMP NW3 118 B9
Gossops Green Clinic CRAWW RH11 283 J9
Gossops Green Community Primary School CRAWW RH11 283 K8
Gove Farm Retail Park CHDH RM6 123 M5
Government Offices WHALL SW1A 11 L9
Gower House School CDALE/KGS NW9 115 P7
Grace Business Centre MTCM CR4 202 A6
Grace Theatre at the Latchmere BTSEA SW11 158 A8
Graduate School of Management TOTM N17 99 N9
Grafton Primary School BCTR RM8 123 P7
HOLWY N7 118 F8
Grahame Park Health Centre CDALE/KGS NW9 96 B9
Grahame Park J & I School CDALE/KGS NW9 96 B9
Granard Business Centre MLHL NW7 96 B7
Granard Primary School PUT/ROE SW15 178 E2
Granby Sports Club CHST BR7 184 B8
Grand Avenue Primary School BRYLDS KT5 199 P6
Grande Vitesse Industrial Centre STHWK SE1 12 D10
Grand Union Industrial Estate WLSDN NW10 135 N5
The Grange City Hotel TWRH EC3N 13 L7
The Grange Community Infant School ADL/WDHM KT15 215 J6
Grange First School RYLN/HDSTN HA2 114 A6
Grange Hill ⊖ CHIG IG7 102 G5
The Grange Museum CRICK NW2 116 C9
Grange Park ⇌ WCHMH N21 79 J9
Grange Park Clinic YEAD UB4 132 G6
Grange Park Junior School YEAD UB4 132 G6
Grange Park Preparatory School WCHMH N21 79 J10
Grange Park Primary School WCHMH N21 79 H8
Grange Primary School CAN/RD E16 141 L6
EA W5 155 J1
STHWK SE1 19 J4
Grange Whitehall Hotel RSQ WC1B 11 L4
Grangewood Independent School FSTGT E7 142 A2
Grangewood School PIN HA5 113 H3
Granton Primary School STRHM/NOR SW16 180 D10
Granville Road Industrial Estate CRICK NW2 117 J7
The Granville School SEV TN13 247 H9
Grasmere Primary School STNW/STAM N16 119 L9
Grasshoppers RFC ISLW TW7 154 E5
Grassroots School HPTN TW12 197 P1
Grasvenor Avenue Infant School BAR EN5 77 K10
Gravel Hill ⊖ CROY/NA CR0 224 D4
Gravel Hill Primary School BXLYHS DA6 186 C1
Graveney School TOOT SW17 180 C9
Gravesend ⇌ GVW DA11 190 D2
Gravesend Cemetery GVW DA11 190 D4
Gravesend CC GVW DA11 190 D3
Gravesend Grammar School GVE DA12 190 G3
Gravesend Museum GVW DA11 190 E2
Gravesend & Northfleet FC GVW DA11 189 M1
Gravesend & North Kent Hospital GVW DA11 190 D2
Gravesend Rowing Club GVE DA12 190 F2
Gravesend Yacht Club GVE DA12 190 G2
Graves Yard Industrial Estate WELL DA16 163 K8
Grays ⇌ GRAYS RM17 167 M5
Grays Athletic FC GRAYS RM17 167 N5
Grays Business Centre GRAYS RM17 167 P2
Grays Convent School GRAYS RM17 167 N3
Grays Farm Primary School STMC/STPC BR5 207 L1
Grays Health Centre GRAYS RM17 167 M4
The Grays School GRAYS RM17 167 N2
Grazebrook Primary School STNW/STAM N16 119 M7
Great Bookham County Infant School GT/LBKH KT23 253 P2
Great Cambridge Industrial Estate EN EN1 80 A9
Great Chapel Street Medical Centre SOHO/SHAV W1D 11 J5
Great Cockrow Steam Railway Centre CHERT KT16 194 G8
Greater London Authority Headquarters (City Hall) STHWK SE1 13 K10
Greatham Road Industrial Estate BUSH WD23 73 M8
Great Jubilee Wharf WAP E1W 140 B10
Greatness Park Cemetery RSEV TN14 247 L7
Great Ormond Street Hospital for Children BMSBY WC1N 11 M2
Great Portland Street ⊖ GTPST W1W 10 F2
Great Scotland Yard WHALL SW1A 11 L9
Great Stony School CHONG CM5 67 P3
Great Western Industrial Park NWDGN UB2 154 A1
Great West Trading Estate BTFD TW8 154 G5
Great Wood Country Park POTB/CUF EN6 60 B2
Grebe House Wildlife Centre & Gardens STALW/RED AL3 38 A6
Greek School of London ACT W3 135 N9
Greenacre School for Girls BNSTD SM7 221 L9
Greenacres Primary School ELTH/MOT SE9 184 D5
Green Business Centre EGH TW20 172 F7

The Green CE Primary School *TOTM* N17 ... 119 N1
Green Dragon Primary School *BTFD* TW8 ... 155 K4
Green End Business Centre *RKW/CH/CXG* WD3 ... 71 K3
Greenfield Medical Centre *CRICK* NW2 ... 117 H8
Greenfield School *WOKS/MYFD* GU22 ... 232 B5
Greenfields Junior School *SHB* W12 ... 136 C9
Greenfields Primary School *OXHEY* WD19 ... 93 K6
Greenfields Special School *MUSWH* N10 ... 98 A9
Greenford ⇌ ⊖ *GFD/PVL* UB6 ... 134 C3
Greenford Avenue Medical Centre *HNWL* W7 ... 134 D7
Greenford Green Clinic *GFD/PVL* UB6 ... 114 D10
Greenford High School *STHL* UB1 ... 133 P5
Greenford Industrial Estate *GFD/PVL* UB6 ... 134 A3
Greenford Park Cemetery Greenford Park Cemetery *GFD/PVL* UB6 ... 134 A7
Greenford Road Medical Centre *GFD/PVL* UB6 ... 134 C4
Greenford Sports Centre *STHL* UB1 ... 133 P5
Greengate Medical Centre *PLSTW* E13 ... 141 N5
Greengrove College *STHGT/OAK* N14 ... 98 F3
Greenheath Business Centre *BETH* E2 ... 140 A5
Greenhill College *HRW* HA1 ... 114 E3
Greenhill Park Medical Centre *WLSDN* NW10 ... 136 B3
Greenhithe For Bluewater ⇌ *RDART* DA2 ... 188 G1
Greenhithe Health Clinic *SWCM* DA10 ... 188 G1
Greenland Pier *BERM/RHTH* SE16 ... 160 E2
Green Lane Business Park *ELTH/MOT* SE9 ... 184 D5
Green Lane Primary School *WPK* KT4 ... 200 E7
Green Lanes Primary School *HAT* AL10 ... 22 C10
Greenleaf Primary School *WALTH* E17 ... 120 E1
The Green Man Hotel *HLWE* CM17 ... 29 N7
Greenmead Primary School *PUT/ROE* SW15 ... 178 E1
Green Park ⊖ *MYFR/PICC* W1J ... 10 F10
The Green School *ISLW* TW7 ... 154 F6
Greenshaw High School *SUT* SM1 ... 201 M9
Greenshields Industrial Estate *CAN/RD* E16 ... 141 M10
Greenside Primary School *SHB* W12 ... 156 D1
Greenslade Primary School *WOOL/PLUM* SE18 ... 162 G5
Green Street Green Primary School *ORP* BR6 ... 227 J3
Greenvale Primary School *SAND/SEL* CR2 ... 224 C7
Greenvale School *FSTH* SE23 ... 182 D6
Greenway First School *BERK* HP4 ... 33 L5
Greenwich ⇌ ⊖ *GNWCH* SE10 ... 160 G6
Greenwich Centre Business Park *DEPT* SE8 ... 160 G6
Greenwich Cinema *GNWCH* SE10 ... 161 H6
Greenwich Community College *WOOL/PLUM* SE18 ... 162 E3
Greenwich Industrial Estate *CHARL* SE7 ... 161 N3
*GNWCH* SE10 ... 160 G6
Greenwich Natural Health Centre *GNWCH* SE10 ... 161 H6
Greenwich Odeon Cinema *GNWCH* SE10 ... 161 L3
Greenwich Pier *GNWCH* SE10 ... 161 H4
Greenwich School of Management *GNWCH* SE10 ... 161 H6
Greenwich Theatre & Art Gallery *GNWCH* SE10 ... 161 J6
Greenwood Park Leisure Centre *LCOL/BKTW* AL2 ... 56 A1
Greenwood Primary School *NTHLT* UB5 ... 114 B10
Greenwood Theatre *STHWK* SE1 ... 19 H1
Green Wrythe Primary School *CAR* SM5 ... 201 N6
Gresham College *HCIRC* EC1N ... 12 A4
Gresham Primary School *SAND/SEL* CR2 ... 223 N8
Gresham Way Industrial Estate *WIM/MER* SW19 ... 179 L6
Greville Primary School *ASHTD* KT21 ... 237 L3
Grey Coat Hospital School for Girls *WEST* SW1P ... 17 J4
The Greycoat Hospital *WEST* SW1P ... 17 J6
Grey Court School *RCHPK/HAM* TW10 ... 177 J6
Griffen Manor School *WOOL/PLUM* SE18 ... 163 H7
Grimsdyke First & Middle School *PIN* HA5 ... 93 N7
Grims Dyke Golf Club *PIN* HA5 ... 93 P6
Grim's Dyke Hotel *KTN/HRWW/WS* HA3 ... 94 B5
Grinling Gibbons Primary School *DEPT* SE8 ... 160 E5
Grist Memorial Sports Club *E/WMO/HCT* KT8 ... 198 D5
Grocers' Hall *CITYW* EC2V ... 12 G6
Grosvenor House Hotel *MYFR/PKLN* W1K ... 10 C8
Grove Health Centre *KENS* W8 ... 8 F9
The Grove Health Centre *SHB* W12 ... 156 E1
Grovehill Medical Centre *HHNE* HP2 ... 36 A2
The Grove Hotel *RKW/CH/CXG* WD3 ... 72 D3
Grove House (Froebel College) *PUT/ROE* SW15 ... 178 C2
Grove House Primary School for Deaf Children *WNWD* SE27 ... 181 J5
The Grove Infant School *HARP* AL5 ... 20 C3
The Grove Junior School *HARP* AL5 ... 20 C3
Grovelands Business Centre *HHNE* HP2 ... 36 D4
Grovelands Priory Hospital *STHGT/OAK* N14 ... 98 F2
Grovelands School *WOT/HER* KT12 ... 197 J6
Grove Medical Centre *DEPT* SE8 ... 160 D3
The Grove Medical Centre *ARCH* N19 ... 118 E7
Grove Park ⇌ *BMLY* BR1 ... 183 M6
Grove Park Cemetery *LEE/GVPK* SE12 ... 184 A7
Grove Park Industrial Estate *CDALE/KGS* NW9 ... 116 A2
Grove Park Primary School *CHSWK* W4 ... 155 P5
Grove Park School *CDALE/KGS* NW9 ... 115 P2
Grove Primary School *CHDH* RM6 ... 123 L3
Grove Road Primary School *HSLW* TW3 ... 153 P10
The Groves Medical Centre *NWMAL* KT3 ... 200 B3
Grove Village Medical Centre *EBED/NFELT* TW14 ... 174 F4
Grundy Park Leisure Centre *CHES/WCR* EN8 ... 62 D6
The Gryphon Industrial Park *STALW/RED* AL3 ... 38 E2
Guardian Angels RC Primary School *BOW* E3 ... 140 D6
Guardian Business Centre *HARH* RM3 ... 105 L8
Guardian Newspapers *POP/IOD* E14 ... 160 G1
Guards' Chapel & Museum *STJSPK* SW1H ... 17 H2
Guards Polo Club *EGH* TW20 ... 193 J1
Guildford ⇌ *GUW* GU2 ... 267 P1
Guildford Adult & Community Learning Centre *GU* GU1 ... 268 B2
Guildford Castle *GU* GU1 ... 268 A2
Guildford Cathedral *GUW* GU2 ... 249 N10
Guildford College (Merrist Wood Campus) *RGUW* GU3 ... 249 H4
Guildford College of Further & Higher Education *GU* GU1 ... 250 A9
Guildford County School *GUW* GU2 ... 267 N2
Guildford Crematorium *GODL* GU7 ... 267 N9
Guildford Cricket Ground (Surrey CCC) *GU* GU1 ... 249 P10
Guildford Golf Club *GU* GU1 ... 250 F10
Guildford Grove Primary School *GUW* GU2 ... 249 K10
Guildford High School *GU* GU1 ... 250 B10
Guildford Hockey & CC *GU* GU1 ... 249 P10
Guildford House Gallery *GU* GU1 ... 268 A2
Guildford Industrial Estate *GUW* GU2 ... 249 M9
Guildford Lido *GU* GU1 ... 250 A9
Guildford Museum *GU* GU1 ... 268 A2
The Guildford Nuffield Hospital *GUW* GU2 ... 249 K10
Guildford Rowing Club *GU* GU1 ... 268 A3
Guildford Spectrum *GU* GU1 ... 250 B9
Guildford Spectrum Athletics Stadium *GU* GU1 ... 250 B8
Guilford School of Acting *GUW* GU2 ... 267 P2
Gumley House Convent School *ISLW* TW7 ... 154 F9
Gunnersbury ⊖ ⊖ *CHSWK* W4 ... 155 N4
Gunnersbury Catholic School *BTFD* TW8 ... 155 H4
Gunnersbury Cemetery *BTFD* TW8 ... 155 M3
Gunnersbury Park Museum *ACT* W3 ... 155 M2
Gunpowder Park *WAB* EN9 ... 81 H2
Gurnell Leisure Centre *WEA* W13 ... 134 E5
Guru Gobind Singh Khalsa College *CHIG* IG7 ... 102 C2
Guru Nanak Medical Centre *STHL* UB1 ... 133 L10
Guru Nanak Sikh Primary School *YEAD* UB4 ... 133 K10
Guru Nanak Sikh Secondary School *YEAD* UB4 ... 133 K10
Guru Nanak Sports Club *GVE* DA12 ... 190 F3
Guy's Hospital *STHWK* SE1 ... 13 H10
Guys Kings & Thomas Medical School (Kings College London) *STHWK* SE1 ... 12 E9
Gwyn Jones Primary School *WAN* E11 ... 121 J5
GX Superbowl *EHAM* E6 ... 142 D7
Gypsy Moth IV *GNWCH* SE10 ... 161 H5
Haberdasher Askes Pre-Preparatory School *LCOL/BKTW* AL2 ... 56 A4
Haberdashers Askes Hatcham College *NWCR* SE14 ... 160 C8
Haberdashers Askes Knights Academy *BMLY* BR1 ... 183 M7
The Haberdashers Askes School *BORE* WD6 ... 74 G7
Haberdashers' Hall *STBT* EC1A ... 12 C4
Haberdashers RUFC *BORE* WD6 ... 75 L6
Hackbridge ⇌ *WLGTN* SM6 ... 202 C9
Hackbridge Primary School *WLGTN* SM6 ... 202 B8
Hackney Business Centre *HACK* E8 ... 140 A1
Hackney Central ⇌ *HACK* E8 ... 140 A1
Hackney City Farm *BETH* E2 ... 7 N8
Hackney Community College *IS* N1 ... 7 J8
Hackney Downs ⇌ *HACK* E8 ... 119 P10
Hackney Empire Variety Theatre *HACK* E8 ... 140 A1
Hackney Free & Parochial CE School *HOM* E9 ... 140 B1
The Hackney Museum *HACK* E8 ... 140 A1
Hackney Sports Centre *HOM* E9 ... 120 F9
Hackney Wick ⊖ *HOM* E9 ... 140 F1
Hacton Primary School *HCH* RM12 ... 125 M9
Hadley Wood ⇌ *EBAR* EN4 ... 77 M4
Hadley Wood Golf Club *EBAR* EN4 ... 77 P5
Hadley Wood Primary School *EBAR* EN4 ... 77 M4
The Haelan Clinic *CEND/HSY/T* N8 ... 118 F4
Haggerston ⊖ *HACK* E8 ... 7 L4
Haggerston School *BETH* E2 ... 7 M7
Haggerston Swimming Pool *BETH* E2 ... 7 M6
Hague Primary School *BETH* E2 ... 140 A6
Haileybury College *HERT/BAY* SG13 ... 26 C9
Haileybury College Track *HERT/BAY* SG13 ... 26 C9
Hailey Hall Special School *HERT/BAY* SG13 ... 26 E9
Hailey Road Business Park *ERITHM* DA18 ... 164 B1
Haimo Primary School *ELTH/MOT* SE9 ... 184 A1
Hainault ⊖ *BARK/HLT* IG6 ... 102 G8
Hainault Business Park *BARK/HLT* IG6 ... 103 M6
Hainault Forest Country Park *CHIG* IG7 ... 103 N4
Hainault Forest Golf Complex *CHIG* IG7 ... 103 N7
Hainault Forest High School & the Learning Centre *BARK/HLT* IG6 ... 103 K6
Hakim Qureshi Clinic *NWDGN* UB2 ... 153 M2
The Hale Clinic *CAMTN* NW1 ... 10 F2
Half Moon Theatre *WCHPL* E1 ... 140 C6
Haling Manor High School *SAND/SEL* CR2 ... 223 J4
The Halkin Hotel *KTBR* SW1X ... 16 D2
Halley Primary School *POP/IOD* E14 ... 140 D7
Hallfield Clinic *BAY/PAD* W2 ... 9 J6
Hallfield Infant School *BAY/PAD* W2 ... 9 H6
Halliford Health Clinic *SHPTN* TW17 ... 196 F4
Halliford School *SHPTN* TW17 ... 196 D7
Hallmark Trading Estate *WBLY* HA9 ... 115 P9
Hall Mead School *UPMR* RM14 ... 126 C5
Hall Place & Gardens *BXLY* DA5 ... 186 D2
The Hall Pre-Preparatory School *NTHWD* HA6 ... 92 E7
Halls Business Centre *HYS/HAR* UB3 ... 153 H2
The Hall School *HAMP* NW3 ... 3 M2
Hall School Wimbledon *RYNPK* SW20 ... 200 G1
Hall School Wimbledon Junior Department *PUT/ROE* SW15 ... 178 D6
Hallsville Primary School *CAN/RD* E16 ... 141 M8
Halstead Place School *RSEV* TN14 ... 227 P8
Halstead Preparatory School *WOKN/KNAP* GU21 ... 232 C1
Halstead Primary School *RSEV* TN14 ... 228 A9
Halstow Primary School *GNWCH* SE10 ... 161 L4
Hambledon Clinic *CMBW* SE5 ... 159 L9
Hambrough Primary School *STHL* UB1 ... 133 M10
Hamer Indoor Market *BOW* E3 ... 140 E4
Ham Health Clinic *RCHPK/HAM* TW10 ... 177 H6
Ham House & Garden (NT) *RCHPK/HAM* TW10 ... 177 H4
Hamilton Road Industrial Estate *WNWD* SE27 ... 181 L7
Ham Lands Nature Reserve *RCHPK/HAM* TW10 ... 176 G7
Hamlet International Industrial Estate *ERITH* DA8 ... 164 E4
Hammersmith ⊖ *HMSMTH* W6 ... 156 F3
Hammersmith Apollo *HMSMTH* W6 ... 156 F4
Hammersmith Cemetery *HMSMTH* W6 ... 14 A8
Hammersmith Hospital *SHB* W12 ... 136 D8
Hammersmith Industrial Estate *HMSMTH* W6 ... 156 F5
Hammersmith New Cemetery *RCH/KEW* TW9 ... 155 N8
Hammersmith Physio & Sports Injury Clinic *HMSMTH* W6 ... 156 F3
The Hammond JMI School *HHNE* HP2 ... 36 A2
Hampden Gurney School *MBLAR* W1H ... 9 P5
Ham & Petersham CC *RCHPK/HAM* TW10 ... 177 J7
The Hampshire School *SKENS* SW7 ... 15 N2
Hampstead ⊖ *HAMP* NW3 ... 117 M9
Hampstead Cemetery *CRICK* NW2 ... 117 J9
Hampstead College of Fine Art & Humanities *HAMP* NW3 ... 3 P2
Hampstead Golf Club *GLDGN* NW11 ... 117 M5
Hampstead Heath ⊖ *HAMP* NW3 ... 117 P9
Hampstead Medical Centre *HAMP* NW3 ... 117 M9
Hampstead Parochial CE School *HAMP* NW3 ... 117 M9
Hampstead School *CRICK* NW2 ... 117 H9
The Hampstead School of Art *HAMP* NW3 ... 117 K9
Hampstead School of English *KIL/WHAMP* NW6 ... 117 K9
Hampstead Theatre *HAMP* NW3 ... 3 L3
Hampton ⇌ *HPTN* TW12 ... 197 P1
Hampton Cemetery *HPTN* TW12 ... 175 P10
Hampton Community College *HPTN* TW12 ... 175 P8
Hampton Court ⇌ *E/WMO/HCT* KT8 ... 198 D4
Hampton Court House School *E/WMO/HCT* KT8 ... 198 D2
Hampton Court Palace *E/WMO/HCT* KT8 ... 198 E3
Hampton Court Palace Golf Club *SURB* KT6 ... 199 H5
Hampton Farm Industrial Estate *FELT* TW13 ... 175 M6
Hampton FC *HPTN* TW12 ... 198 A1
Hampton Hill Junior School *HPTN* TW12 ... 176 B8
Hampton Infant School *HPTN* TW12 ... 175 N10
Hampton Junior School *HPTN* TW12 ... 197 P1
The Hampton Medical Centre *HPTN* TW12 ... 175 P10
Hampton Open Air Pool *HPTN* TW12 ... 176 B10
Hampton Road Industrial Park *CROY/NA* CR0 ... 203 K6
Hampton School *HPTN* TW12 ... 175 P8
Hampton Wick ⇌ *KUT/HW* KT1 ... 199 J1
Hampton Wick Infants School *TEDD* TW11 ... 177 H10
Hamsey Green Infant School *WARL* CR6 ... 242 A2
Hamsey Green Junior School *WARL* CR6 ... 242 A2
Handel's House *MYFR/PKLN* W1K ... 10 E7
Handsworth Health Clinic *CHING* E4 ... 101 J7
Hanger Lane ⊖ *EA* W5 ... 135 L5
Hanover Primary School *IS* N1 ... 6 D7
Hanover Trading Estate *HOLWY* N7 ... 118 F10
Hanover West Industrial Estate *WLSDN* NW10 ... 135 P5
Hanwell ⇌ *HNWL* W7 ... 134 D9
Hanworth Business Park *CHERT* KT16 ... 195 J8
Hanworth Trading Estate *FELT* TW13 ... 175 M6
Happy Valley Industrial Estate *KGLGY* WD4 ... 54 C4
Harbinger Primary School *POP/IOD* E14 ... 160 F3
Harborough School *ARCH* N19 ... 118 E7
The Harefield Academy *DEN/HRF* UB9 ... 91 N9
Harefield CC *DEN/HRF* UB9 ... 91 M10
Harefield Health Centre *DEN/HRF* UB9 ... 91 M9
Harefield Hospital *DEN/HRF* UB9 ... 91 M9
Harefield Infant School *DEN/HRF* UB9 ... 91 L10
Harefield Junior School *DEN/HRF* UB9 ... 91 M9
Harefield Manor Hotel *ROM* RM1 ... 124 G2
Harefield Road Industrial Estate *RKW/CH/CXG* WD3 ... 91 P5
Harenc School *SCUP* DA14 ... 185 M8
Haresfoot School *BERK* HP4 ... 33 N8
Haresfoot Senior School *BERK* HP4 ... 34 D3
Hare Street Primary School *HLWW/ROY* CM19 ... 46 F1
Harewood Down Golf Club *CSTG* HP8 ... 69 N8
Hargrave Park Primary School *ARCH* N19 ... 118 D7
Haringey Arts Council *ED* N9 ... 99 P3
Haringey Community Health Clinic *SEVS/STOTM* N15 ... 119 N2
Haringey Sixth Form Centre *TOTM* N17 ... 99 N8
Harkness Industrial Estate *BORE* WD6 ... 75 M8
The Harlequin Shopping Centre *WAT* WD17 ... 73 K8
Harlequins RFC & Harlequins RL (The Stoop) *WHTN* TW2 ... 176 D3
Harlesden ⊖ ⊖ *WLSDN* NW10 ... 136 A4
Harlesden Primary School *WLSDN* NW10 ... 136 B4
Harley Medical Centre *CAVSQ/HST* W1G ... 10 F5
The Harley Medical Centre *CANST* EC4R ... 12 F7
Harley Street Clinic *CAVSQ/HST* W1G ... 10 E4
The Harley Street Clinic *CAVSQ/HST* W1G ... 10 E3
Harlington Community School *HYS/HAR* UB3 ... 152 E3
Harlowbury Primary School *HLWE* CM17 ... 29 N7
Harlow Business Park *HLWW/ROY* CM19 ... 46 B1
Harlow College *HLW* CM20 ... 29 H10
*HLW* CM20 ... 46 F1
Harlow Mill ⇌ *HLW* CM20 ... 29 L6
Harlow Museum (Passmores House) *HLWS* CM18 ... 46 F2
Harlow RFC *HLW* CM20 ... 28 E9
Harlow Town ⇌ *HLW* CM20 ... 28 G8
Harlow Town FC *HLWW/ROY* CM19 ... 28 B10
Harlyn Primary School *PIN* HA5 ... 113 J1
Harold Court Primary School *HARH* RM3 ... 105 P8
The Harold Macmillan Medical Centre *HRW* HA1 ... 114 C5
Harold Wood ⇌ *HARH* RM3 ... 105 N9
Harold Wood Clinic *HARH* RM3 ... 105 N10
Harold Wood JMI School *HARH* RM3 ... 125 P1
Harp Business Centre *CRICK* NW2 ... 116 D7
Harpenden ⇌ *HARP* AL5 ... 20 A2
Harpenden Common Golf Club *HARP* AL5 ... 20 A5
Harpenden House Hotel *HARP* AL5 ... 20 A3
Harpenden Memorial Hospital *HARP* AL5 ... 20 A1
Harperbury Hospital *RAD* WD7 ... 57 H7
Harringay ⇌ *FSBYPK* N4 ... 119 H4
Harringay Green Lanes ⊖ *FSBYPK* N4 ... 119 J4
Harrington Hill Primary School *CLPT* E5 ... 120 A6
Harrington Road ⊖ *SNWD* SE25 ... 204 B3
Harris Academy Bermondsey *STHWK* SE1 ... 19 M5
Harris Academy Falconwood *WELL* DA16 ... 162 G10
Harris Academy Merton School *STRHM/NOR* SW16 ... 202 E3
Harris Academy South Norwood *SNWD* SE25 ... 203 N3
Harris City Academy Crystal Palace *NRWD* SE19 ... 203 N1
Harris Girls Academy *EDUL* SE22 ... 182 B1
Harrodian School *BARN* SW13 ... 156 C6
Harrods Store *CHEL* SW3 ... 16 A3
Harrovian Business Village *HRW* HA1 ... 114 C5
Harrow Arts Centre *PIN* HA5 ... 93 P8
Harrow Borough FC *RYLN/HDSTN* HA2 ... 113 P9
Harrow Cemetery *HRW* HA1 ... 114 C4
Harrow College *HRW* HA1 ... 114 D5
*KTN/HRWW/WS* HA3 ... 94 D7
Harrow CC *HRW* HA1 ... 114 D9
Harrow Driving Cycling & Road Safety Centre *KTN/HRWW/WS* HA3 ... 114 F1
Harrow Heritage Museum *RYLN/HDSTN* HA2 ... 114 B1
Harrow High School *HRW* HA1 ... 114 F4
Harrow Leisure Centre *KTN/HRWW/WS* HA3 ... 114 E1
Harrow-on-the-Hill ⇌ ⊖ *HRW* HA1 ... 114 D4
Harrow RFC *STAN* HA7 ... 94 G4
Harrow Road Health Centre *BAY/PAD* W2 ... 8 F3
Harrow School *RYLN/HDSTN* HA2 ... 114 D7
Harrow Town CC *RYLN/HDSTN* HA2 ... 113 P6
Harrow Weald Cemetery *KTN/HRWW/WS* HA3 ... 94 D7
Harrow & Wealdstone ⇌ ⊖ ⊖ *HRW* HA1 ... 114 D2
Harry Gosling Primary School *WCHPL* E1 ... 13 P6
Harte & Garter Hotel *WDSR* SL4 ... 149 J7
Hartham Pool *HERT/WAT* SG14 ... 25 L4
Hartley Primary School *EHAM* E6 ... 142 B3
*HART* DA3 ... 211 K5
Hartsbourne Primary School *BUSH* WD23 ... 94 C3
Hartspring Industrial Park *BUSH* WD23 ... 73 P6
Hartspring Sports Centre *BUSH* WD23 ... 73 P6
The Hartswood Clinic *RBRW/HUT* CM13 ... 106 G7
Hartswood Golf Club *BRW* CM14 ... 107 K5
Harven School of English *WOKS/MYFD* GU22 ... 232 C3
Harvey Centre *HLW* CM20 ... 46 G1
Harvey Road Primary School *RKW/CH/CXG* WD3 ... 72 B10
Harvington School *EA* W5 ... 135 H8
Harwood Equestrian Centre *UPMR* RM14 ... 146 A1
Harwood Hill JMI School *WGCW* AL8 ... 23 H1
Haseltine Primary School *SYD* SE26 ... 182 E7
Haslemere Business Centre *EN* EN1 ... 80 A8
Haslemere Industrial Estate *EBED/NFELT* TW14 ... 175 H1
*HLWW/ROY* CM19 ... 46 D2
*WAND/EARL* SW18 ... 179 L5
*WGCE* AL7 ... 23 J4
Haslemere Primary School *MTCM* CR4 ... 201 N2
Hasmonean High School Boys Site *HDN* NW4 ... 96 G10
Hasmonean High School Girls Site *MLHL* NW7 ... 96 D9
Hasmonean Primary School *HDN* NW4 ... 116 G3
Haste Hill Golf Club *NTHWD* HA6 ... 92 F10
Hastings Clinic *BRXS/STRHM* SW2 ... 180 C1
Hastingwood Business Centre *HLWE* CM17 ... 47 M3
Hastingwood Trading Estate *UED* N18 ... 100 D7
Hatcham Mews Business Centre *NWCR* SE14 ... 160 C6
Hatch End ⊖ *PIN* HA5 ... 93 P8
Hatch End High School *KTN/HRWW/WS* HA3 ... 94 A8
Hatch End Swimming Pool *PIN* HA5 ... 93 P8
Hatchlands Park (NT) *RGUE* GU4 ... 252 A6
Hatfield ⇌ *BRKMPK* AL9 ... 40 F3
Hatfield Business Park *HAT* AL10 ... 40 A1
Hatfield House, Park & Gardens *BRKMPK* AL9 ... 40 G4
Hatfield House Tennis Club *BRKMPK* AL9 ... 40 G4
Hatfield Hyde Cemetery *WGCE* AL7 ... 23 H8
Hatfield Leisure Centre *HAT* AL10 ... 40 E6
Hatfield London Country Club *BRKMPK* AL9 ... 42 A5
Hatfield Primary School *MRDN* SM4 ... 201 H6
Hatfield Road Cemetery *STAL* AL1 ... 38 F6
Hatfield Swim Centre *HAT* AL10 ... 40 D3
Hatton Cross ⊖ *HTHAIR* TW6 ... 152 G10
Hatton School *WFD* IG8 ... 122 A1
Havelock Primary School *NWDGN* UB2 ... 153 N2
Havenbury Industrial Estate *DORK* RH4 ... 272 F1
Haven Green Clinic *EA* W5 ... 135 J8
Havering College *HARH* RM3 ... 105 N5
Havering College of Further & Higher Education *EMPK* RM11 ... 125 J5
*EMPK* RM11 ... 125 M2
Havering Country Park *ABR/ST* RM4 ... 104 E5
Havering CC *ABR/ST* RM4 ... 84 G6
Havering Sixth Form College *EMPK* RM11 ... 125 N6
Haverstock School *HAMP* NW3 ... 4 C3
Hawes Down Clinic *WWKM* BR4 ... 205 J9
Hawes Down Primary School *WWKM* BR4 ... 205 J8
Hawkedale GM School *SUN* TW16 ... 196 G3
The Hawker Centre *KUTN/CMB* KT2 ... 177 J8
Hawkesdown House School *KENS* W8 ... 8 F10
Hawkins Clinic *EW* KT17 ... 238 F1
*PUT/ROE* SW15 ... 156 G10
*RYNPK* SW20 ... 200 C1
Hawksmoor Primary School *THMD* SE28 ... 143 L9
Hawley Infant School *CAMTN* NW1 ... 4 F4
Hawridge & Cholesbury CE Combined School *CSHM* HP5 ... 32 D7
The Hawthorns School *REDH* RH1 ... 259 J7
The Hawth Theatre & Conference Complex *CRAWE* RH10 ... 284 A8
Haydon School *PIN* HA5 ... 113 H1
Haydons Road ⇌ *WIM/MER* SW19 ... 179 M8
Hayes ⇌ *HAYES* BR2 ... 205 L8
Hayes Bridge Middle School *STHL* UB1 ... 153 M1
Hayes Bridge Retail Park *YEAD* UB4 ... 133 K9
Hayes CC *HYS/HAR* UB3 ... 132 G8
Hayes FC *HYS/HAR* UB3 ... 132 G9
Hayes Grove Priory Hospital *HAYES* BR2 ... 205 M9
Hayes & Harlington ⇌ *HYS/HAR* UB3 ... 152 G2
The Hayes Manor School *HYS/HAR* UB3 ... 132 E8
Hayes Park J & I School *YEAD* UB4 ... 132 G6
Hayes Pool *HYS/HAR* UB3 ... 132 G10
Hayes Primary School *HAYES* BR2 ... 205 N8
The Hayes Primary School *PUR/KEN* CR8 ... 241 J2
Hayes School *HAYES* BR2 ... 205 N9
Hayes Social & Sports Club *HYS/HAR* UB3 ... 132 G9
Hayes Stadium Sports Centre *HYS/HAR* UB3 ... 132 E8
Hay Lane School *CDALE/KGS* NW9 ... 115 P2
Haymerle School *PECK* SE15 ... 19 N10
Hays Galleria *STHWK* SE1 ... 13 J9
Hayward Gallery *STHWK* SE1 ... 11 P10
Haywood Grove School *HHNE* HP2 ... 36 B2
Hazelbury Junior School *ED* N9 ... 99 M4
Hazeldene Medical Centre *WBLY* HA9 ... 135 N1
Hazelwick School *CRAWE* RH10 ... 284 B5
Hazelwood Infant School *PLMGR* N13 ... 99 J5
Hazelwood Junior School *PLMGR* N13 ... 99 H5
Hazelwood School *OXTED* RH8 ... 261 M7
Headstart Montessori School *TOOT* SW17 ... 179 M6
Headstone Lane ⊖ *RYLN/HDSTN* HA2 ... 94 A9
Health & Vitality Osteopathic Clinic *HOR/WEW* KT19 ... 220 A2
The Heart Hospital *CAVSQ/HST* W1G ... 10 D4
Heathbrook Primary School *VX/NE* SW8 ... 158 D8
Heath Business Centre *HSLW* TW3 ... 154 B10
*REDH* RH1 ... 276 C10
Heathcote Medical Centre *KWD/TDW/WH* KT20 ... 238 G8
Heathcote School *CHING* E4 ... 101 K3
Heathermount the Learning Centre *ASC* SL5 ... 192 C6
Heatherton House School *AMS* HP6 ... 69 H2
Heathfield College *HAYES* BR2 ... 225 P3
Heathfield House School *CHSWK* W4 ... 155 P4
Heathfield Primary School *WHTN* TW2 ... 175 P4
Heathfield School *PIN* HA5 ... 113 L5
Heath House Preparatory School *BKHTH/KID* SE3 ... 161 L8
The Heathland School *HSLW* TW4 ... 175 N2
Heathlands Special School *STALW/RED* AL3 ... 38 D3
Heath Lane Cemetery *HHW* HP1 ... 35 L7
Heathmere Primary School *PUT/ROE* SW15 ... 178 D4
Heathrow Airport Central Bus & Coach Station *HTHAIR* TW6 ... 152 B9
Heathrow Airport Terminal 4 *HTHAIR* TW6 ... 174 C1
Heathrow Airport Terminal 5 *HTHAIR* TW6 ... 151 M9
Heathrow Airport (Terminals 1 & 3) *HTHAIR* TW6 ... 152 C8
Heathrow Air Traffic Control Tower *HTHAIR* TW6 ... 152 C9
Heathrow International Trading Estate *HSLWW* TW4 ... 153 J9
Heathrow Medical Centre *HYS/HAR* UB3 ... 152 E4
Heathrow Primary School *WDR/YW* UB7 ... 152 A5
Heathrow Terminal 4 ⇌ ⊖ *HTHAIR* TW6 ... 174 D2
Heathrow Terminal 5 ⇌ ⊖ *HTHAIR* TW6 ... 151 M9
Heathrow Terminals 1 & 3 ⇌ ⊖ *HTHAIR* TW6 ... 174 D1
Heathrow Viewing Area *HTHAIR* TW6 ... 152 C9
Heathrow World Cargo Centre *HTHAIR* TW6 ... 174 A1
Heathside Preparatory School *HAMP* NW3 ... 117 M9
Heathside Preparatory School (Lower) *HAMP* NW3 ... 117 M9
Heathside Preparatory School (Upper) *HAMP* NW3 ... 117 M9
Heathside School *WEY* KT13 ... 216 A2
Heathway Industrial Estate *DAGE* RM10 ... 124 C9
Heathway Medical Centre *DAGW* RM9 ... 124 A9
Heavers Farm Primary School *SNWD* SE25 ... 203 N5
Heber Primary School *EDUL* SE22 ... 181 N2
Heckford Street Business Centre *WAP* E1W ... 140 C9
Hedges & Butler Estate *SRTFD* E15 ... 141 H4
Hedgewood School *YEAD* UB4 ... 132 F5
Helena Road Clinic *WLSDN* NW10 ... 116 E9

Heliport Industrial Estate BTSEA SW11 157 N8
Helston Court Business Centre WIM/MER SW19 178 E8
Hemel Hempstead ⇌ HHS/BOV HP3 35 K9
Hemel Hempstead (Camelot) RFC HHW HP1 35 J8
Hemel Hempstead General Hospital HHNE HP2 35 N7
Hemel Hempstead RLFC HHNE HP2 36 A3
Hemel Hempstead School HHW HP1 35 M7
Hemel Hempstead Silver Blades Ice Rink HHNE HP2 36 A7
Hemel Hempstead Sports Centre HHW HP1 35 M8
Hemel Hempstead Town CC HHW HP1 35 M8
Hemel Hempstead United FC HHNE HP2 36 C6
Hemel Ski Centre HHS/BOV HP3 35 P8
Henderson Hospital BELMT SM2 221 K5
Hendon ⇌ HDN NW4 116 D4
Hendon Cemetery MLHL NW7 96 G9
Hendon Central ⊖ HDN NW4 116 E3
Hendon Crematorium MLHL NW7 96 G8
Hendon FC CRICK NW2 116 G7
Hendon Golf Club MLHL NW7 96 F8
Hendon Hall Hotel HDN NW4 116 F1
Hendon Preparatory School HDN NW4 116 G1
Hendon School HDN NW4 116 G3
Hendon Secretarial College HDN NW4 116 E3
Hendon Youth Sports Centre CRICK NW2 116 G5
Henrietta Barnett School GLDGN NW11 117 L3
Henry Cavendish Primary School BAL SW12 180 D4
Henry Compton School FUL/PGN SW6 156 G7
Henry Fawcett Primary School LBTH SE11 18 A9
Henry Green Primary School BCTR RM8 123 N6
Henry Maynard J & I School WALTH E17 121 H3
Henwick Primary School ELTH/MOT SE9 162 A9
Herbert Morrison Primary School VX/NE SW8 158 F6
The Hereward County School LOU IG10 82 F5
Hereward House School HAMP NW3 3 N2
Herington House School RBRW/HUT CM13 87 N10
Heritage Close Shopping Centre STALW/RED AL3 38 C6
Heritage House Special School CSHM HP5 51 J6
Her Majestys' Theatre STJS SW1Y 11 K9
Hermitage County First School WOKN/KNAP GU21 231 K5
Hermitage Primary School UX/CGN UB8 131 N2
WAP E1W 13 N9
The Hermitage School WOKN/KNAP GU21 231 K5
Hermitage Stairs WAP E1W 13 N10
Herne Hill ⇌ HNHL SE24 181 J1
Herne Hill School HNHL SE24 181 K1
Herne Hill Stadium (Cycle Centre) HNHL SE24 181 L2
Heron Industrial Estate SRTFD E15 140 G4
Heron Quays ⊖ POP/IOD E14 140 F10
Heronsgate Primary School THMD SE28 162 G2
Heron Trading Estate ACT W3 135 N7
Herringham Primary School CDW/CHF RM16 168 E2
Herschel Grammar School SL SL1 129 H8
Hersham ⇌ WOT/HER KT12 197 M10
Hersham Trading Estate WOT/HER KT12 197 M9
Hertford C & CC Site HERT/BAY SG13 25 N7
Hertford Cemetery HERT/WAT SG14 25 H4
Hertford Corn Exchange HERT/WAT SG14 25 L5
Hertford County Hospital HERT/WAT SG14 25 J5
Hertford East ⇌ HERT/WAT SG14 25 L4
Hertford Heath Primary School HERT/BAY SG13 26 A8
Hertford Museum HERT/WAT SG14 25 L5
Hertford North ⇌ HERT/WAT SG14 25 J5
Hertford Regional College BROX EN10 62 E1
WARE SG12 26 C3
Hertford St Andrew Primary School HERT/WAT SG14 24 G4
Hertfordshire Business Centre LCOL/BKTW AL2 57 J2
Hertfordshire Country Club WGCE AL7 22 F8
Hertford Town FC HERT/BAY SG13 25 J6
Hertingfordbury Cowper Primary School HERT/WAT SG14 24 D7
Hertsmere Jewish Primary School RAD WD7 75 H4
Hertswood School & Sports Centre BORE WD6 75 P5
Heston Community School HEST TW5 153 P6
Heston Community Sports Hall HEST TW5 153 P6
Heston Industrial Mall HEST TW5 153 N6
Heston Infant School HEST TW5 153 P6
Heston Junior School HEST TW5 153 P6
Heston Park CC HEST TW5 153 N5
Heston Swimming Baths HEST TW5 153 N5
Hextable Community Primary School SWLY BR8 186 G9
Heythrop College KENS W8 14 G3
Higgs Industrial Estate HNHL SE24 159 J9
Highams Lodge Business Centre WALTH E17 120 C1
Highams Park ⇌ CHING E4 101 H7
Highams Park Primary School CHING E4 101 J7
High Barnet ⊖ BAR EN5 77 K8
High Beeches Primary School HARP AL5 20 C3
High Beech Golf Club LOU IG10 81 N3
High Beech VC Primary School LOU IG10 81 M5
Highbridge Industrial Estate UX/CGN UB8 131 M1
Highbridge Retail Park WAB EN9 62 G10
Highbury Fields School HBRY N5 119 J9
Highbury Grove School HBRY N5 119 K10
Highbury & Islington ⇌ ⊖ ⊖ HOLWY N7 6 B1
Highbury Park Clinic HBRY N5 119 J8
Highbury Pool HBRY N5 6 C1
Highbury Quadrant Primary School HBRY N5 119 K9
Highbury Square Development HBRY N5 119 J8
Highclere Hotel ASC SL5 192 C5
High Commission of Angola MHST W1U 10 B4
High Commission of Antigua & Barbuda MHST W1U 10 C5
High Commission of Bahamas MYFR/PICC W1J 10 D9
High Commission of Bangladesh SKENS SW7 15 K3
High Commission of Barbados FITZ W1T 11 J5
High Commission of Belize CAVSQ/HST W1G 10 F5
High Commission of Botswana OXSTW W1C 10 E6
High Commission of Brunei KTBR SW1X 16 C3
High Commission of Canada MYFR/PKLN W1K 10 D7
High Commission of Cyprus MYFR/PKLN W1K 10 C7
High Commission of Dominica ECT SW5 15 H6
High Commission of Fiji SKENS SW7 15 J2
High Commission of Guyana BAY/PAD W2 8 G8
High Commission of Jamaica SKENS SW7 15 L2
High Commission of Kenya CAVSQ/HST W1G 10 E3
High Commission of Lesotho KTBR SW1X 16 C3
High Commission of Malawi MYFR/PKLN W1K 10 E7
High Commission of Malaysia KTBR SW1X 16 D2
High Commission of Maldives MHST W1U 10 C3
High Commission of Malta CONDST W1S 11 H8
High Commission of Mauritius SKENS SW7 15 K4
High Commission of Namibia CAVSQ/HST W1G 10 F4
High Commission of New Zealand STJS SW1Y 11 J9
High Commission of Nigeria CHCR WC2N 11 L9
EMB EC4Y 12 B6
High Commission of Pakistan KTBR SW1X 16 B3
High Commission of Papua New Guinea STJS SW1Y 11 H9
High Commission of St Vincent & the Grenadines KENS W8 15 H2
High Commission of Seychelles MHST W1U 10 B3
High Commission of Sierra Leone REGST W1B 10 G5
High Commission of Singapore KTBR SW1X 16 B2
High Commission of South Africa CHCR WC2N 11 J9
High Commission of Sri Lanka BAY/PAD W2 9 M7
High Commission of Swaziland WESTW SW1E 16 G3
High Commission of The Gambia KENS W8 15 H2
High Commission of Tonga MBLAR W1H 9 P4
High Commission of Trinidad & Tobago KTBR SW1X 16 C3
High Commission of Uganda CHCR WC2N 11 K9
High Commission of Zambia KENS W8 15 J2
High Commission of Zimbabwe CHCR WC2N 11 L8
High Cross Centre SEVS/STOTM N15 119 P2
High Elms Country Park ORP BR6 226 F4
High Elms Golf Club ORP BR6 226 F4
Highfield Infant School HAYES BR2 205 L4
Highfield Junior School HAYES BR2 205 K4
Highfield Primary School WCHMH N21 99 J2
Highfield School HGDN/ICK UB10 132 C5
WAND/EARL SW18 179 P3
High Firs Primary School SWLY BR8 208 G4
Highgate ⊖ HGT N6 118 C4
Highgate Cemetery HGT N6 118 B6
Highgate Golf Club EFNCH N2 117 P4
Highgate Junior School HGT N6 118 A5
Highgate Private Hospital HGT N6 118 A4
Highgate School HGT N6 118 A5
Highgate Wood School MUSWH N10 118 D3
Highgrove Pool RSLP HA4 113 H5
Highlands J & I School IL IG1 122 C6
Highlands Primary School IL IG1 122 B6
High March School BEAC HP9 88 C7
Highshore School PECK SE15 159 N7
High Street Business Park CHES/WCR EN8 62 D8
High Street Kensington ⊖ KENS W8 14 G2
High View Primary School BTSEA SW11 157 N10
Highview Primary School WLGTN SM6 222 F2
The Highway Primary School ORP BR6 227 M2
The Highway Trading Centre WAP E1W 140 C9
High Wood Hospital BRW CM14 106 G2
Highwood Primary School BUSH WD23 73 M5
High Wych Primary School SBW CM21 29 K2
Hillbrook Primary School TOOT SW17 180 A7
Hill Crest London School CROY/NA CR0 203 N8
Hillcroft Primary School CTHM CR3 241 M9
Hillcross Primary School MRDN SM4 201 J4
Hilldene Primary School HARH RM3 105 K7
Hille Business Centre WATN WD24 73 J5
Hill Farm Industrial Estate GSTN WD25 54 G9
Hillgrove Business Park WAB EN9 45 H8
Hillhouse CE VC Primary School WAB EN9 63 L9
Hill House International Junior School KTBR SW1X 16 B4
Hill House School CHEL SW3 15 P9
KTBR SW1X 16 A4
Hillingdon ⊖ HGDN/ICK UB10 132 C1
Hillingdon Borough FC RSLP HA4 112 C3
Hillingdon Cemetery UX/CGN UB8 131 P5
Hillingdon Hospital UX/CGN UB8 132 A7
Hillingdon Manor School UX/CGN UB8 132 C7
Hillingdon Primary School HGDN/ICK UB10 132 B5
Hill Mead Infant School BRXN/ST SW9 159 J10
Hillmead Primary School BRXN/ST SW9 159 J10
Hill School BH/WHM TN16 244 E9
Hills Grove Primary School WELL DA16 163 M6
Hillside Infant School NTHWD HA6 93 H8
Hillside Primary School STMC/STPC BR5 207 M7
Hill Top First School WDSR SL4 148 D9
Hilltop Primary School CRAWW RH11 283 M9
Hillyfield Primary School WALTH E17 120 D1
Hilly Fields Medical Centre BROCKY SE4 182 F1
Hilton Docklands Pier BERM/RHTH SE16 140 E10
The Hiltongrove Business Centre WALTH E17 120 F2
Hinchley Wood ⇌ ESH/CLAY KT10 198 E10
Hinchley Wood Primary School ESH/CLAY KT10 198 F9
Hinchley Wood School & Sixth Form Centre ESH/CLAY KT10 198 F9
Hinley Clinic LBTH SE11 18 B6
Hispaniola WHALL SW1A 11 M10
Hitherfield Primary School STRHM/NOR SW16 181 H5
Hither Green ⇌ LEW SE13 183 K2
Hither Green Cemetery CAT SE6 183 L5
Hither Green Primary School LEW SE13 183 J2
HM Customs & Excise HTHAIR TW6 152 C7
HM Prison BRXS/STRHM SW2 180 F2
CHOB/PIR GU24 230 E3
HHS/BOV HP3 52 C2
HOLWY N7 5 N2
HOLWY N7 118 F9
RPLY/SEND GU23 251 M3
SHB W12 136 D8
THMD SE28 163 H2
WAND/EARL SW18 179 N3
HM Prisons BELMT SM2 221 M8
HMS Belfast STHWK SE1 13 K9
HMS President EMB EC4Y 12 B7
HM Young Offenders Institution FELT TW13 174 E6
Hobbayne First & Middle School HNWL W7 134 E8
Hobbayne Primary School HNWL W7 134 D8
Hobbs Hill Wood Primary School HHS/BOV HP3 36 C8
Hobletts Manor Junior School HHNE HP2 36 B5
Hockley Industrial Centre REDH RH1 276 A1
Hoddesdon Health Centre HOD EN11 44 F4
Hoddesdon Industrial Estate HOD EN11 45 H2
Hoddesdon Lawn Tennis Club HOD EN11 44 E3
Hoebridge Golf Centre WOKS/MYFD GU22 232 F5
Hoe Bridge School WOKS/MYFD GU22 232 E5
Hogan Business Centre WOKN/KNAP GU21 232 B3
Hogarth Business Park CHSWK W4 156 B5
Hogarth Industrial Estate WLSDN NW10 136 D6
Hogarth Primary School BRWN CM15 107 K3
Hogarth's House CHSWK W4 156 A5
Holbeach Primary School CAT SE6 182 F3
Holborn ⊖ HHOL WC1V 11 M5
Holborn College WOOL/PLUM SE18 162 A3
Holborn College Independent School HMSMTH W6 156 F4
Holborn Medical Centre BMSBY WC1N 11 N2
Holborn Town Hall HHOL WC1V 11 M5
Holdbrook Primary School CHES/WCR EN8 62 E10
Holiday Inn BORE WD6 76 B7
BRW CM14 106 D5
BTFD TW8 155 H6
BXLY DA5 186 C2
CAMTN NW1 4 E4
CHSGTN KT9 219 H5
FSBYW WC1X 5 P10
GUW GU2 267 L1
HHNE HP2 36 E6
HORL RH6 279 P5
HYS/HAR UB3 152 E7
SHPTN TW17 196 G6
SUT SM1 221 L2
WDR/YW UB7 152 B7
WOKN/KNAP GU21 232 C2
Holland House KENS W8 14 D2
Holland House School EDGW HA8 95 M5
Holland Park ⊖ NTGHL W11 8 C10
Holland Park Pre-Preparatory School WKENS W14 14 C4
Holland Park School KENS W8 8 D10
Holland Park Theatre KENS W8 14 D2
Holland Street Clinic KENS W8 14 F2
Hollickwood JMI School MUSWH N10 98 C8
Hollies Way Industrial Estate POTB/CUF EN6 59 L7
Holloway Road ⊖ HOLWY N7 118 G10
Holloway School HOLWY N7 118 E10
Hollybush Business Centre HORL RH6 284 G1
Hollybush Primary School HERT/WAT SG14 25 H5
Hollydale Primary School PECK SE15 160 B8
The Hollyfield School SURB KT6 199 K5
Holly House Private Hospital BKHH IG9 101 N3
Holly Industrial Park WATN WD24 73 K5
Hollymount Primary School RYNPK SW20 200 F1
Holly Park JMI School FBAR/BDGN N11 98 B6
Holly Trees Junior School BRW CM14 106 G5
Holly Trees Primary School BRW CM14 107 H5
Hollywood Bowl BERM/RHTH SE16 160 C2
CRAWE RH10 283 N6
Holmesdale School REIG RH2 257 L8
The Holme CAMTN NW1 4 B10
Holmethorpe Industrial Estate REDH RH1 258 C7
Holmleigh Primary School STNW/STAM N16 119 N6
Holmshill School BORE WD6 75 P6
Holtsmere End Junior School HHNE HP2 36 C1
Holwell J & I School WGCE AL7 23 H6
Holocaust Memorial Garden KTBR SW1X 16 B1
The Holy Cross Catholic Girls School NWMAL KT3 200 A4
Holy Cross Preparatory School KUTN/CMB KT2 177 P10
Holy Cross RC Primary School CAT SE6 183 H4
HLWS CM18 47 K3
SOCK/AV RM15 146 G9
Holy Family Catholic School DTCH/LGLY SL3 150 C4
Holy Family RC Primary School ADL/WDHM KT15 215 K3
BKHTH/KID SE3 161 N10
POP/IOD E14 140 F9
Holy Family Technology College WALTH E17 120 G2
Holy Ghost RC Primary School BAL SW12 180 A3
Holy Innocents Catholic Primary School ORP BR6 207 J10
Holy Rood Catholic Primary School WAT WD17 72 E2
Holy Trinity CE Junior School GU GU1 268 C2
WLGTN SM6 222 D1
Holy Trinity CE Primary School ASC SL5 192 F6
BRXS/STRHM SW2 180 G3
CHOB/PIR GU24 212 F8
DART DA1 187 K1
EFNCH N2 117 N1
GVE DA12 190 F3
HAMP NW3 3 K2
KTBR SW1X 16 C5
NTHWD HA6 92 D7
RCHPK/HAM TW10 155 M10
SYD SE26 182 D7
The Holy Trinity CE School CRAWW RH11 283 K9
Holy Trinity College BMLY BR1 205 P1
Holy Trinity in St Silas CAMTN NW1 4 E3
Holy Trinity Lamorbey CE Primary School BFN/LL DA15 185 K4
Holy Trinity Primary School CHES/WCR EN8 62 C8
HACK E8 7 L2
WIM/MER SW19 179 K9
Holy Trinity School CHEL SW3 16 B5
Holywell School WATW WD18 72 G10
Home Farm Industrial Estate WARE SG12 27 L6
Homefield Preparatory School SUT SM1 221 K2
Home Office WEST SW1P 17 K4
Home Park Golf Club GDST RH9 281 P3
Home Park Industrial Estate KGLGY WD4 54 C7
Homers First School WDSR SL4 148 C7
Homerswood J & I School WGCW AL8 22 G1
Homerton ⊖ HOM E9 140 C1
Homerton University Hospital HOM E9 120 C10
Homoeopathic Health Centre PLSTW E13 141 M6
The Homoeopathic Health Centre MLHL NW7 96 C6
Honeypot Business Centre STAN HA7 95 K9
Honeypot Lane Centre STAN HA7 95 J9
Honeypot Medical Centre STAN HA7 95 K10
Honeywell Primary School BTSEA SW11 180 A2
Honilands Primary School EN EN1 80 A2
Honor Oak Crematorium FSTH SE23 182 C1
Honor Oak Gallery FSTH SE23 182 C2
Honor Oak Health Centre BROCKY SE4 160 D10
Honor Oak Park ⇌ ⊖ FSTH SE23 182 C2
Honourable Artillery Company STLK EC1Y 12 G2
Hook Lane Primary School WELL DA16 163 K9
Hook Rise South Industrial Park CHSGTN KT9 199 L10
Hopewell School BARK EC2Y 142 G1
Horizon Business Centre ED N9 100 C3
Horizon Industrial Estate PECK SE15 19 N10
Horizon Primary School SWLY BR8 208 F2
Horizon School STNW/STAM N16 119 M9
Horley ⇌ HORL RH6 280 C5
Horley Adult Education Centre HORL RH6 279 P4
Horley Anderson Centre HORL RH6 279 P4
Horley Health Centre HORL RH6 280 B4
Horley Infant School HORL RH6 280 B4
Horley Lawn Tennis Club HORL RH6 280 A4
Hornchurch ⊖ HCH RM12 125 L8
Hornchurch Cemetery HCH RM12 125 M7
Hornchurch Clinic EMPK RM11 125 M6
Hornchurch Country Park HCH RM12 145 K1
Hornchurch Sports Centre EMPK RM11 125 K7
Hornchurch Stadium UPMR RM14 125 P7
Horndon Industrial Park RBRW/HUT CM13 127 N4
The Horniman Museum & Gardens FSTH SE23 182 A4
Horniman Primary School FSTH SE23 182 A4
Horn Park Primary School LEE/GVPK SE12 183 N3
Hornsby House School BAL SW12 180 B4
Hornsey ⇌ CEND/HSY/T N8 118 G2
Hornsey Central Hospital CEND/HSY/T N8 118 D3
Hornsey Rise Health Centre ARCH N19 118 E5
Hornsey Secondary School for Girls CEND/HSY/T N8 118 G3
Horn Stairs BERM/RHTH SE16 140 E10
Horse Guards Parade WHALL SW1A 11 K10
Horsell CE Junior School WOKN/KNAP GU21 231 P2
Horsell Cemetery WOKN/KNAP GU21 232 A2
Horsell Village School WOKN/KNAP GU21 232 A2
Horsenden Hill Golf Club GFD/PVL UB6 134 G1
Horsenden Primary School GFD/PVL UB6 134 D1
Horseshoe Business Park LCOL/BKTW AL2 56 A6
Horsley ⇌ EHSLY KT24 252 F1
Horsley C & CC Site EHSLY KT24 234 D10
Horsley Sports Club EHSLY KT24 252 G3
Horton Country Park HOR/WEW KT19 219 M5
Horton Hospital HOR/WEW KT19 219 P7
Horton Industrial Park WDR/YW UB7 132 A10
Horton Kirby CE Primary School EYN DA4 210 B3
Horton Kirby Trading Estate EYN DA4 210 B2
Horton Park Golf & Country Club HOR/WEW KT19 219 P4
Horton Trading Estate DTCH/LGLY SL3 150 E9
Hortus Cemetery NWDGN UB2 153 N1
Hospital of St John & St Elizabeth STJWD NW8 3 L8
The Hotel Russell RSQ WC1B 11 L2
Hotham Primary School PUT/ROE SW15 156 G10
Hot Shots Ten Pin Bowling HHNE HP2 36 A7
Hotspur Industrial Estate TOTM N17 100 A7
Houndsfield Primary School ED N9 99 P1
Hounslow ⇌ HSLW TW3 154 B10
Hounslow Business Park HSLW TW3 153 P10
Hounslow CC HSLW TW3 153 N8
Hounslow Cemetery HSLWW TW4 175 N3
Hounslow Central ⊖ HSLW TW3 154 A8
Hounslow East ⊖ HSLW TW3 154 B8
Hounslow Heath Golf Club HSLWW TW4 175 L1
Hounslow Heath Infant School HSLWW TW4 153 M9
Hounslow Heath Junior School HSLWW TW4 153 M9
Hounslow Manor School HSLW TW3 154 A9
Hounslow Manor Sports Hall HSLW TW3 154 A9
Hounslow Town Primary School HSLW TW3 154 B9
Hounslow West ⊖ HSLWW TW4 153 M8
House of Detention CLKNW EC1R 12 B1
House of St Barnabus SOHO/SHAV W1D 11 J6
Houses of Parliament WHALL SW1A 17 M2
Houston Business Park YEAD UB4 133 K10
Howard Business Park WAB EN9 63 J10
The Howard Centre WGCW AL8 22 G5
Howard Industrial Estate CSHM HP5 51 H5
Howard of Effingham School EHSLY KT24 253 L3
Howard Primary School SAND/SEL CR2 223 K1
Howbury Centre ERITH DA8 165 H6
Howe Dell Primary School HAT AL10 40 E4
Howland Quay BERM/RHTH SE16 160 C2
How Wood ⇌ LCOL/BKTW AL2 56 B4
How Wood Primary School LCOL/BKTW AL2 56 B3
Hoxton ⊖ BETH E2 7 L8
Hoxton Hall Community Theatre IS N1 7 J7
HQS Wellington (Master Mariners) TPL/STR WC2R 12 A8
HSBC Group Management Training College LCOL/BKTW AL2 56 B7
HSBC Sports Club BECK BR3 182 D9
HSBC Tower POP/IOD E14 140 G10
Hubbinet Industrial Estate ROMW/RG RM7 124 D1
Hugh Myddelton Primary School CLKNW EC1R 6 B10
The Humana Wellington Hospital STJWD NW8 3 M9
Humber Trading Estate CRICK NW2 116 E7
Hunsdon Primary School WARE SG12 28 A2
Huntercombe Manor Hospital MDHD SL6 128 B9
Hunterian Museum LINN WC2A 11 P5
Hunters Hall Primary School DAGE RM10 124 C10
Hunter Street Health Centre STPAN WC1H 11 L1
Huntsman Sports Club BKHTH/KID SE3 161 M10
Hurlingham Business Park FUL/PGN SW6 157 K9
Hurlingham House FUL/PGN SW6 157 K9
Hurlingham Private School PUT/ROE SW15 157 J10
Huron University RSQ WC1B 11 L3
Hurricane Trading Centre CDALE/KGS NW9 96 C9
Hurst Drive Primary School CHES/WCR EN8 62 B10
Hurst Green ⇌ OXTED RH8 261 L8
Hurst Green School OXTED RH8 261 M8
Hurst Lodge School ASC SL5 192 A8
Hurstmere School BFN/LL DA15 185 L4
Hurst Park Primary School E/WMO/HCT KT8 197 P3
Hurst Primary School BXLY DA5 185 N4
Hurtmore Golf Club GODL GU7 266 E10
Hyatt Carlton Tower Hotel KTBR SW1X 16 B4
Hyatt Regency, The Churchill MBLAR W1H 10 B5
Hyde Heath Infant School AMS HP6 50 B10
The Hyde Industrial Estate CDALE/KGS NW9 116 C3
Hyde Park Corner ⊖ KTBR SW1X 16 C1
The Hyde School CDALE/KGS NW9 116 C3
Hyland Business Centre REDH RH1 258 A10
Hyland House School WALTH E17 101 J10
Hyleford Leavers Unit School BARK/HLT IG6 102 G10
Hythe Road Industrial Estate WLSDN NW10 136 D6
The Hythe School STA TW18 172 G8
Ian Mikardo High School BOW E3 140 G5
Ibis Hotel CAMTN NW1 5 H10
CAN/RD E16 141 N9
CRAWE RH10 283 P2
FUL/PGN SW6 14 E9
GNWCH SE10 161 H5
HYS/HAR UB3 152 F7
POP/IOD E14 141 H9
SRTFD E15 141 K1
WBLY HA9 115 M10
WTHK RM20 166 E5
Ibstock Place School PUT/ROE SW15 178 B2
ICA Cinema STJS SW1Y 11 K9
Ickburgh School CLPT E5 120 A8
Ickenham ⊖ HGDN/ICK UB10 112 D9
Ickenham Clinic HGDN/ICK UB10 112 D8
Ide Hill CE Aided Primary School RSEV TN14 263 P7
Ifield ⇌ CRAWW RH11 283 K7
Ifield Community College CRAWW RH11 283 K6
Ifield Golf & Country Club CRAWW RH11 282 G7
Ifield School GVE DA12 190 F8
Ihlara Sport FC HBRY N5 119 K9
Ilderton Primary School PECK SE15 160 B5
Ilford ⇌ IL IG1 122 D8
Ilford County High School BARK/HLT IG6 102 F10
Ilford Golf Club IL IG1 122 C6
Ilford Jewish Primary School BARK/HLT IG6 122 G1
Ilford Medical Centre IL IG1 122 E8
Ilford Preparatory School GDMY/SEVK IG3 123 J6
Ilford Retail Park IL IG1 122 F7
Ilford Swimming Pool IL IG1 122 G7
Ilford Ursuline High School IL IG1 122 E7
Ilford Ursuline Preparatory School IL IG1 122 E7
Iman Zakaria Academy FSTGT E7 121 N10
Imber Court Trading Estate E/WMO/HCT KT8 198 C6
Immanuel CE Primary School STRHM/NOR SW16 180 F9
Immanuel College BUSH WD23 94 D1
Immanuel School ROM RM1 104 F7
Imperial College PUT/ROE SW15 156 G8
SKENS SW7 15 L3
SKENS SW7 15 L8
Imperial College Athletic Ground HYS/HAR UB3 152 D5
Imperial College of London SKENS SW7 15 L2
Imperial College of Science FUL/PGN SW6 14 E9
Imperial College of Science & Technology SKENS SW7 15 M2
Imperial College of Science Technology & Medicine ASC SL5 192 E3
SKENS SW7 15 K3

Imperial College School of Medicine
PIM SW1V 17 J6
Imperial Retail Park
GVW DA11 190 D2
Imperial Trading Estate
RAIN RM13 145 K6
Imperial War Museum
STHWK SE1 18 B4
Imperial War Museum Annexe
LBTH SE11 18 B4
Imperial Wharf ⇌ ⊖
FUL/PGN SW6 157 M7
Inchbald School of Design
BGVA SW1W 16 D5
PIM SW1V 16 G6
Independent Industrial Estate
WDR/YW UB7 132 A10
Independent Jewish School
HDN NW4 116 G3
India House
HOL/ALD WC2B 11 N7
Industrial Health Clinic
UX/CGN UB8 131 L5
The Infirmary Royal Hospital
CHEL SW3 16 C8
Ingrave Johnstone CE Primary School
RBRW/HUT CM13 107 P7
Innellan House School
PIN HA5 113 M1
Innholders Hall
CANST EC4R 12 G7
Innkeeper's Lodge
BEAC HP9 88 D10
BECK BR3 204 F6
BORE WD6 75 P6
CHEAM SM3 201 K8
DTCH/LGLY SL3 150 C4
LCOL/BKTW AL2 57 K3
NTHLT UB5 133 P1
REDH RH1 258 B10
SAND/SEL CR2 223 K5
STHGT/OAK N14 98 F3
WAN E11 121 M2
WDSR SL4 171 M1
WEY KT13 196 F10
WFD IG8 102 C7
WOKN/KNAP GU21 232 B2
WOT/HER KT12 197 H10
Innova Business Park
PEND EN3 80 E2
Inns of Court & Chancery
TPL/STR WC2R 12 A6
Inns of Court Law School
GINN WC1R 11 P3
Institute of Cancer Research
ECT SW5 15 K7
Institute of Education University of London
RSQ WC1B 11 K2
Instituto Espanol Canada Blanch
NKENS W10 8 B4
Intercontinental Hotel
MYFR/PICC W1J 16 D1
International Community School
CAMTN NW1 10 C2
International Medical Centre
ECT SW5 14 F6
International School of Business Studies (ISBS)
PIN HA5 113 P5
International School of London
ACT W3 155 M3
International Trading Estate
NWDGN UB2 153 J2
International University
BUSH WD23 73 N8
Invicta Industrial Estate
SRTFD E15 141 H5
Invicta Primary School
BKHTH/KID SE3 161 M5
Invicta Sports Club
DART DA1 187 L1
Inwood Business Centre
HSLW TW3 154 A10
IQRA Independent School
BRXN/ST SW9 159 H9
Ironmonger Row Baths
FSBYE EC1V 6 E10
Ironmongers Hall
STBT EC1A 12 E4
Islamia Primary School
KIL/WHAMP NW6 2 B5
Islamic College
WCHPL E1 13 P5
Islamic College for Advanced Studies
WLSDN NW10 136 E2
The Islamic Grammar School
WAND/EARL SW18 179 J3
Islamic Shaksiyah Foundation School
WALTH E17 120 D3
Island Clinic
POP/IOD E14 161 H1
Island Gardens ⊖
POP/IOD E14 161 H3
Isleworth ⇌
ISLW TW7 154 E8
Isleworth Cemetery
ISLW TW7 154 F8
Isleworth Recreation Centre
ISLW TW7 154 E10
Isleworth & Syon School for Boys
ISLW TW7 154 D6
Isleworth Town Primary School
ISLW TW7 154 E8
Islington Arts & Media School
FSBYPK N4 118 G6
Islington Business Centre
IS N1 6 F5
Islington Crematorium
MUSWH N10 98 A9
Islington Green Medical Centre
IS N1 6 C5
Islington Tennis Centre
HOLWY N7 5 M2
Islington Town Hall
IS N1 6 C3
Ismaili Centre
SKENS SW7 15 M5
Italia Conti Academy of Theatre Arts
BRXN/ST SW9 158 F9
FARR EC1M 12 E2
Italian Hospital
PIM SW1V 16 G5
Iver ⇌
DTCH/LGLY SL3 151 J1
Iver Golf & Leisure Centre
IVER SL0 130 E10
Iver Heath Health Centre
IVER SL0 130 G4
Iver Heath Infant School
IVER SL0 130 G5
Iver Heath Primary School
IVER SL0 130 G4
Iver Village Infant School
IVER SL0 131 J8
Iver Village Junior School
IVER SL0 131 H8
Ivybridge Primary School
TWK TW1 176 E2
Ivybridge Retail Park
ISLW TW7 176 E1
Ivy Chimneys Primary School
EPP CM16 65 J8
Ivydale Primary School
PECK SE15 160 C10
Jack & Jill School
HPTN TW12 175 P9
WHTN TW2 176 D5
Jack Taylor School
STJWD NW8 3 J5
Jack Tizard School
FUL/PGN SW6 156 G7
SHB W12 136 F9
Jacques Prevert School
HMSMTH W6 156 G3
James Allens Preparatory Girls School
HNHL SE24 181 L1
James Dixon Primary School
PGE/AN SE20 203 P1
James Elliman School
SLN SL2 129 K8
James Oglethorpe Primary School
UPMR RM14 126 E7
Jamestown Mental Health Centre
HAMP NW3 4 A3
James Wolfe Primary School
GNWCH SE10 160 G6
Jamiatul Ummah School
WCHPL E1 140 A8
Janet Adegoke Leisure Centre
SHB W12 136 D9
The Japanese School
ACT W3 135 M9
Japan Green Medical Centre
ACT W3 135 N10
Jenner Health Centre
FSTH SE23 182 D4
Jenny Hammond Primary School
WAN E11 121 K9
Jermyn Street Theatre
MYFR/PICC W1J 11 H8
Jerounds Junior School
HLWW/ROY CM19 46 E4
Jessop Primary School
HNHL SE24 159 J10
Jewel Tower
WEST SW1P 17 L3
Jewish Cemetery
GLDGN NW11 117 K4
RAIN RM13 145 M5
Jewish Community Theatre
HNHL SE24 159 L9
Jewish Free School
KTN/HRWW/WS HA3 115 M4
KTTN NW5 5 H1
The Jewish Museum
CAMTN NW1 4 E6
FNCH N3 97 L10
Johanna Primary School
STHWK SE1 18 A2
John Ball Primary School
BKHTH/KID SE3 161 K8
John Betts Primary School
HMSMTH W6 156 D2
John Bramston Primary School
BARK/HLT IG6 103 K7
John Burns Primary School
BTSEA SW11 158 B8
John Chilton School
NTHLT UB5 133 M2
John Dixon Clinic
BERM/RHTH SE16 160 A2
John Donne Primary School
PECK SE15 160 A7
John F Kennedy RC School
HHW HP1 35 J5
John F Kennedy School
CAN/RD E16 142 A7
John F Kennedy Special School
SRTFD E15 141 K3
John Keble CE Primary School
WLSDN NW10 136 C4
John Kelly Girls Technology College
CRICK NW2 116 C8
The John Loughborough School
TOTM N17 99 N10
John Lyon School
RYLN/HDSTN HA2 114 C6
John Nightingale School
E/WMO/HCT KT8 197 N3
John Paul II RC School
WIM/MER SW19 178 G3
John Penrose School
DEN/HRF UB9 91 N9
John Penrose Sports Centre
DEN/HRF UB9 91 N9
John Perryn Primary School
ACT W3 136 B8
John Perry Primary School
DAGE RM10 144 E1
John Roan Lower School
BKHTH/KID SE3 161 L6
John Roan School
BKHTH/KID SE3 161 K6
John Ruskin College
SAND/SEL CR2 224 D4
John Ruskin Primary School
WALW SE17 18 E9
John Scott Health Centre
FSBYPK N4 119 K6
John Scurr Primary School
WCHPL E1 140 B6
John Smith House
WALW SE17 18 E6
Johnsons Industrial Estate
HYS/HAR UB3 153 H2
John Stainer Primary School
BROCKY SE4 160 D9
The John Warner School
HOD EN11 26 G10
Jordans School
BEAC HP9 89 K7
The Jo Richardson Community School
DAGW RM9 143 N3
Joseph Clarke Special School
CHING E4 101 J7
Joseph Hood Primary School
RYNPK SW20 201 H2
Joseph Lancaster Primary School
STHWK SE1 18 F4
Joydens Wood Infant School
RDART DA2 186 F7
Joydens Wood Junior School
BXLY DA5 186 F7
Jubilee Centre
STALW/RED AL3 38 C5
Jubilee Country Park
BMLY BR1 206 E4
Jubilee Hall Clinic
CRAWE RH10 284 B7
Jubilee Market
COVGDN WC2E 11 M7
Jubilee Primary School
BRXS/STRHM SW2 181 H2
THMD SE28 143 M9
Jubilee Sports Centre
NKENS W10 2 B10
Jubilee Sports Ground
CHING E4 101 J5
Julians Primary School
STRHM/NOR SW16 181 H7
Jumeirah Carlton Tower Hotel
KTBR SW1X 16 B3
Jumeirah Lowndes Hotel
KTBR SW1X 16 B3
Juno Way Industrial Estate
NWCR SE14 160 C5
Jurys Clifton-Ford Hotel
MHST W1U 10 D4
Jurys Great Russell Street
NOXST/BSQ WC1B 11 K5
Jurys Inn
CROY/NA CR0 203 K9
Jurys Inn Chelsea
FUL/PGN SW6 157 M7
Jurys Inn Hotel
HTHAIR TW6 152 G9
Jurys Inn Islington
IS N1 6 A8
Jurys Kensington Hotel
SKENS SW7 15 L6
JVC Business Park
CRICK NW2 116 D6
Kaizen Primary School
PLSTW E13 141 N6
Kangley Business Centre
SYD SE26 182 E8
Katella Trading Estate
BARK EC2Y 143 H5
Katherine Road Medical Centre
FSTGT E7 141 P1
Katherines Primary School
HLWW/ROY CM19 46 C3
Keats House
HAMP NW3 117 N9
Keats House Health Centre
HLWS CM18 47 J4
Keble Preparatory School
WCHMH N21 99 H1
Keir Hardie Primary School
CAN/RD E16 141 M7
Keith Davis Cue Sports Club
DAGW RM9 143 N2
Kelmscott Community Centre
WALTH E17 120 E4
Kelmscott Leisure Centre
WALTH E17 120 E4
Kelmscott School
WALTH E17 120 E4
Kelrose Swimming Pool Centre
RBRW/HUT CM13 127 K3
Kelsey Park Sports College
BECK BR3 204 F3
Kelvedon Hatch C & CC Site
BRWN CM15 86 E6
Kelvedon Hatch Primary School
BRWN CM15 86 D2
Kelvedon Hatch Secret Nuclear Bunker
BRW CM14 86 B2
Kelvin Business Centre
CRAWE RH10 284 A4
Kelvin Industrial Estate
GFD/PVL UB6 134 A3
Kemnal Technology College
STMC/STPC BR5 185 L10
Kempton Park ⇌
SUN TW16 175 J10
Kempton Park Racecourse
SUN TW16 175 J10
Kemsing Down Nature Reserve
BGR/WK TN15 247 P2
Ken Barrington Centre
LBTH SE11 17 P10
Kender Primary School
NWCR SE14 160 B7
Kenilworth Primary School
BORE WD6 76 A7
Kenley ⇌
PUR/KEN CR8 223 L10
Kenley Primary School
PUR/KEN CR8 241 M2
Kenley Sports Club
PUR/KEN CR8 223 K10
Kenmont Primary School
WLSDN NW10 136 D5
Kenmore Park First School
KTN/HRWW/WS HA3 115 J1
Kenneth More Theatre
IL IG1 122 F8
Kennington ⊖
LBTH SE11 18 C7
Kenningtons Primary School
SOCK/AV RM15 146 B8
Kensal Green ⊖ ⊖
WLSDN NW10 136 F5
Kensal Green Cemetery
WLSDN NW10 136 E5
Kensal Rise ⊖
WLSDN NW10 136 F4
Kensal Rise Primary School
KIL/WHAMP NW6 136 G4
Kensington & Chelsea Town Hall
KENS W8 14 F2
Kensington Avenue Primary School
THHTH CR7 203 H1
Kensington Business Centre
SKENS SW7 15 P3
Kensington & Chelsea College
CHEL SW3 15 M9
KENS W8 14 E1
NKENS W10 8 B3
The Kensington Clinic
KENS W8 14 G4
Kensington House Hotel
KENS W8 15 J2
Kensington Leisure Centre
NTGHL W11 136 G9
Kensington Market
KENS W8 14 G2
Kensington (Olympia) ⇌ ⊖ ⊖
WKENS W14 14 A4
Kensington Palace State Apartments & Royal Ceremonial Dress Collection
KENS W8 9 H10
Kensington Park School
REGST W1B 10 F3
Kensington Preparatory School
FUL/PGN SW6 157 J7
Kensington Primary School
MNPK E12 142 C1
Kensington School of Business
HCIRC EC1N 12 B3
Kensington Wharf
WBPTN SW10 157 N6
Kensit Memorial College
FNCH N3 97 H10
Kent House ⇌
BECK BR3 204 D1
Kentish Town ⇌ ⊖
KTTN NW5 118 D10
Kentish Town CE Primary School
KTTN NW5 118 D10
Kentish Town Health Centre
KTTN NW5 4 G2
Kentish Town Industrial Estate
KTTN NW5 118 C10
Kentish Town Sports Centre
KTTN NW5 4 D1
Kentish Town West ⊖
KTTN NW5 4 D2
Kent Kraft Industrial Estate
SWCM DA10 189 L1
Kenton ⊖
KTN/HRWW/WS HA3 114 G4
Kenton CC
KTN/HRWW/WS HA3 115 H2
Kenton Clinic
KTN/HRWW/WS HA3 115 K3
Kent Park Industrial Estate
PECK SE15 160 A5
Kenwood House
HAMP NW3 117 P6
Kenyngton Manor Primary School
SUN TW16 175 H8
The Kerem School
EFNCH N2 117 N3
Kestner Industrial Estate
RDART DA2 166 F10
Keston CE Primary School
HAYES BR2 226 A2
Keston Primary School
COUL/CHIP CR5 241 H5
Kew Bridge ⇌
BTFD TW8 155 L4
Kew Bridge Steam Museum
BTFD TW8 155 L4
Kew College
RCH/KEW TW9 155 M6
Kew Gardens ⊖ ⊖
RCH/KEW TW9 155 M7
Kew Palace
RCH/KEW TW9 155 K6
Kew Retail Park
RCH/KEW TW9 155 N7
Kew Riverside Primary School
RCH/KEW TW9 155 N8
Keyplan & Roxburghe College
FITZ W1T 11 H2
Keys Meadow Primary School
PEND EN3 80 E2
PEND EN3 80 F4
Keyworth Primary School
WALW SE17 18 C8
Khalsa College London
HRW HA1 114 E4
Khalsa Primary School
SLN SL2 129 M8
Kidbrooke ⇌
BKHTH/KID SE3 161 P9
Kidbrooke Park Primary School
BKHTH/KID SE3 161 P8
Kidbrooke School
BKHTH/KID SE3 162 A8
Kilburn ⊖
CRICK NW2 2 C2
Kilburn High Road ⊖
KIL/WHAMP NW6 2 F6
Kilburn Park ⊖
KIL/WHAMP NW6 2 F7
Kilburn Park Junior School
KIL/WHAMP NW6 2 E8
Killick Street Medical Centre
IS N1 5 N7
Killigrew Primary School
LCOL/BKTW AL2 56 A1
Kilmorie Primary School
FSTH SE23 182 D5
Kiln Park Business Centre
EW KT17 220 B7
Kimberley Industrial Estate
WALTH E17 100 E8
Kimpton Industrial Estate
CHEAM SM3 201 J9
Kinetic Business Centre
BORE WD6 75 L7
King Alfred School
GLDGN NW11 117 L6
King Athelstan Primary School
KUT/HW KT1 199 L3
Kingdom Hall of Jehovah's Witnesses
ORP BR6 207 J9
King Edward Court Shopping Centre
WDSR SL4 149 J7
King Edwards Road Clinic
RSLP HA4 112 E6
King Edward VII Hospital
WDSR SL4 149 H9
King Edward VII Hospital for Officers
MHST W1U 10 D3
King Fahad Academy
ACT W3 136 B9
King Fahad Academy (Girls Upper School)
EA W5 155 H3
Kingfield School
WOKS/MYFD GU22 232 D6
The Kingfisher Medical Centre
DEPT SE8 160 E5
The Kingfisher Sports Centre
KUT/HW KT1 199 K2
King George Hospital
GNTH/NBYPK IG2 123 K3
King George V ⊖
CAN/RD E16 142 D10
King George VI Youth Hostel
KENS W8 14 D1
Kingham Industrial Estate
WLSDN NW10 136 A5
King Harold School
WAB EN9 63 K9
King Henry's Drive ⊖
CROY/NA CR0 224 G5
King Henry VIII Mound
RCHPK/HAM TW10 177 K4
King & Queen Wharf
BERM/RHTH SE16 140 C9
Kings Arms Hotel
BH/WHM TN16 262 G3
Kings Avenue Medical Centre
STHL UB1 134 B8
Kings Avenue School
CLAP SW4 180 F1
Kingsbury ⊖
CDALE/KGS NW9 115 M3
Kingsbury Green Primary School
CDALE/KGS NW9 115 N3
Kingsbury High School
CDALE/KGS NW9 115 N2
Kingsbury Hospital
CDALE/KGS NW9 115 M2
Kingsbury Trading Estate
CDALE/KGS NW9 115 P4
Kingsbury Watermill Museum & Waffle House
STALW/RED AL3 38 A6
Kings College for Arts & Technology
GUW GU2 249 K10
Kings College (Hampstead Campus)
HAMP NW3 117 K9
King's College Hospital
CMBW SE5 159 K9
Kings College London
HOL/ALD WC2B 11 M6
STHWK SE1 12 C9
WEST SW1P 17 H5
Kings College London - Humanities
TPL/STR WC2R 11 N7
Kings College London - Law
TPL/STR WC2R 11 P7
Kings College London (Waterloo Campus)
STHWK SE1 12 A10
Kings College School
WIM/MER SW19 178 F9
Kings College School of Medicine & Dentistry
CMBW SE5 159 L8
DUL SE21 181 L2
Kings College Sports Ground
RSLP HA4 112 F4
Kingscote Pre-Preparatory School
CFSP/GDCR SL9 110 B1
Kings Court First School
WDSR SL4 171 M3
Kingscroft School
STA TW18 173 K9
King's Cross ⇌ ⊖
CAMTN NW1 5 L8
King's Cross St Pancras ⊖
CAMTN NW1 5 L9
Kingsdale School
DUL SE21 181 M6
Kings Estate
HCH RM12 125 H9
Kings Farm Primary School
GVE DA12 190 F7
Kingsfield Business Centre
REDH RH1 276 B1
Kingsford Community School
PLSTW E13 141 P6
Kingsgate Business Centre
KUTN/CMB KT2 199 K1
Kingsgate Primary School
KIL/WHAMP NW6 2 E3
Kings Hall Leisure Centre
CLPT E5 120 B10
Kings Head Theatre
IS N1 6 C5
Kingshill Cemetery
BERK HP4 33 N7
Kings House School
RCHPK/HAM TW10 177 L1
Kingsland College of Business Studies
SRTFD E15 141 J4
Kingsland Health Centre
IS N1 7 K3
Kingsland Shopping Centre
HACK E8 7 L1
Kings Langley ⇌
KGLGY WD4 54 D6
Kings Langley Primary School
KGLGY WD4 54 A4
Kings Langley School
KGLGY WD4 53 P4
Kingsley Primary School
CROY/NA CR0 202 G8
Kings Mall Shopping Centre
HMSMTH W6 156 F3
Kingsmeadow Athletics Centre
KUT/HW KT1 199 M3
Kingsmead Primary School
CLPT E5 120 D9
Kingsmead School
EN EN1 79 P7
Kingsmoor Primary School
HLWW/ROY CM19 46 F5
Kingsmoor Recreation Centre
HLWW/ROY CM19 46 E5
The Kings Oak Private Hospital
ENC/FH EN2 79 H4
King Solomon High School
BARK/HLT IG6 102 G10
Kings Park Industrial Estate
KGLGY WD4 54 C5
Kings Private Clinic
GDMY/SEVK IG3 123 J6
MHST W1U 10 C3
Kings School of English
BECK BR3 204 E2
Kings Stairs
BERM/RHTH SE16 160 A1
Kingston ⇌
KUTN/CMB KT2 199 K1
Kingston Business Centre
CHSGTN KT9 199 K10
Kingston Cemetery
KUT/HW KT1 199 L3
Kingston College of Further Education
KUT/HW KT1 199 K3
Kingston College Theatre
KUT/HW KT1 199 J3
Kingston Crematorium
KUT/HW KT1 199 M3
Kingston Grammar School
KUT/HW KT1 199 L2
Kingston Hospital
KUTN/CMB KT2 199 M1
Kingstonian FC
NWMAL KT3 199 N3
Kingston University
KUT/HW KT1 199 K4
KUTN/CMB KT2 178 A10
PUT/ROE SW15 178 C5
King Street College
HMSMTH W6 156 F3
Kingsway Business Park
HPTN TW12 197 N1
Kingsway College
CAMTN NW1 10 G1
KTTN NW5 4 E1
STPAN WC1H 5 N10
Kingsway Infant School
GSTN WD25 55 H10
Kingsway Junior School
GSTN WD25 55 H10
Kingswey Business Park
WOKN/KNAP GU21 214 F10
Kingswood ⇌
KWD/TDW/WH KT20 239 J7
Kingswood Golf Club
KWD/TDW/WH KT20 239 K10
Kingswood House School
HOR/WEW KT19 219 N9
Kingswood Primary School
KWD/TDW/WH KT20 257 J4
WNWD SE27 181 L7
Kings Wood School
HARH RM3 105 P5
Kisharon School
GLDGN NW11 117 J4
K+K Hotel George
ECT SW5 14 F6
KLC School of Design
WBPTN SW10 157 M7
Knaphill Junior School
WOKN/KNAP GU21 231 H4
Knaphill Lower School
WOKN/KNAP GU21 230 G4
Knightsbridge ⊖
CHEL SW3 15 P3
Knightsbridge Barracks
SKENS SW7 15 P2
Knightsbridge Medical Centre
KTBR SW1X 16 B3
Knightsbridge School
KTBR SW1X 16 A4
Knockhall Community Primary School
SWCM DA10 189 H1
Knockholt ⇌
RSEV TN14 227 P5
Knole House (NT)
BGR/WK TN15 265 L2
Knole Park Golf Club
BGR/WK TN15 247 L10
Knollmead Primary School
BRYLDS KT5 199 P9
Knowledge Point School
HOLWY N7 5 N2
Knowle Park Infant School
STA TW18 173 K8
Knowl Hill School
CHOB/PIR GU24 230 D8
Knutsford School
WATN WD24 73 L4
Kobi Nazrul Primary School
WCHPL E1 13 P5
KP Estate
RAIN RM13 144 F9
Krishna-Avanti Primary School
EDGW HA8 95 M9
Kubrick Business Estate
FSTGT E7 121 N9
Laban Centre for Movement & Dance
DEPT SE8 160 G6
Laburnum Health Centre
DAGE RM10 124 B7
Ladbroke Grove ⊖
NTGHL W11 8 A5
Ladbroke Primary School
POTB/CUF EN6 59 L8
Lady Bankes Junior School
RSLP HA4 113 H7
Lady Boswells CE Primary School
SEV TN13 265 K1
The Lady Eleanor Holles School
HPTN TW12 176 A8
Lady Margaret Primary School
STHL UB1 133 N7
Lady Margaret School
FUL/PGN SW6 157 K7
Ladymead Retail Centre
GU GU1 249 P9
Ladywell ⇌
LEW SE13 182 G1
Ladywell Arena
LEW SE13 182 G2
Ladywell Cemetery
BROCKY SE4 182 E1
Ladywell Leisure Centre
LEW SE13 183 H1
Laharna Trading Estate
WATN WD24 73 K4
Laine Theatre Arts
EW KT17 220 B9
Laings Sports Ground
BAR EN5 76 B8
Lake Business Centre
TOTM N17 99 P7
Laker Industrial Estate
BECK BR3 182 E8
Lakeside Industrial Estate
DTCH/LGLY SL3 151 H6
Lakeside Retail Park
WTHK RM20 166 F3
Lakeside Shopping Centre
WTHK RM20 166 G3
Lakeside Special School
WGCW AL8 22 E7
Laleham CE Primary School
STA TW18 195 M2
Laleham Golf Club
CHERT KT16 195 L4
Laleham Lea Preparatory School
PUR/KEN CR8 222 F6
Lambeth Academy
CLAP SW4 180 D1
Lambeth Cemetery
TOOT SW17 179 M8
Lambeth College
BRXS/STRHM SW2 180 G1
CLAP SW4 180 D1
STHWK SE1 13 K10
STRHM/NOR SW16 180 F5
VX/NE SW8 158 E7
Lambeth Crematorium
TOOT SW17 179 M7
Lambeth Hospital
BRXN/ST SW9 158 F9
Lambeth North ⊖
STHWK SE1 18 A3
Lambeth Palace
STHWK SE1 17 N4
Lambourne Golf Club
SL SL1 128 A1
Lambourne Primary School
ABR/ST RM4 83 L8
Lambs Court
POP/IOD E14 140 D9
Lammas School
LEY E10 120 E6
Lamont Business Centre
CROY/NA CR0 202 F7
Lamorbey Swimming Centre
BFN/LL DA15 185 K5
Lampton School
HSLW TW3 153 P7
The Lanark Medical Centre
MV/WKIL W9 3 H9
Lancaster Gate ⊖
BAY/PAD W2 9 L7
Lancaster House
WHALL SW1A 16 G1
Lancasterian Primary School
TOTM N17 99 M9
Lancaster Road Industrial Estate
EBAR EN4 77 N9
Lancelot Medical Centre
ALP/SUD HA0 115 J10
The Landmark Hotel
CAMTN NW1 10 A3
The Lanesborough Hotel
KTBR SW1X 16 C1
Lanesborough School
GU GU1 250 E10
Lanford Obesity Clinic
ED N9 100 A1
Langafel CE Primary School
HART DA3 211 M3
Langbourne Primary School
DUL SE21 181 M6
Langdon Down Centre
TEDD TW11 177 H10
Langdon Park ⊖
POP/IOD E14 140 G7
Langdon Park School
POP/IOD E14 140 G8
Langdon School
EHAM E6 142 E4
Langford Primary School
FUL/PGN SW6 157 L8
Langham Hotel
CAVSQ/HST W1G 10 F5
Langhedge Lane Industrial Estate
UED N18 99 N7
Langley ⇌
DTCH/LGLY SL3 150 D1
Langley Academy
DTCH/LGLY SL3 150 B2
Langley Business Centre
DTCH/LGLY SL3 150 D1
Langley Business Park
DTCH/LGLY SL3 150 C1
Langley Grammar School
DTCH/LGLY SL3 150 C3
Langley Green Primary School
CRAWW RH11 283 M5
Langley Health Centre
DTCH/LGLY SL3 150 D4
Langley Manor School
DTCH/LGLY SL3 130 B10
Langley Park Country Park
DTCH/LGLY SL3 130 D6
Langley Park Girls School & Sports Centre
BECK BR3 204 G5
Langley Park Golf Club
BECK BR3 205 J6
Langley Park School for Boys
BECK BR3 204 G6
Langshott County Infant School
HORL RH6 280 D4
Langshott Manor Hotel
HORL RH6 280 E2
Langthorne Health Centre
WAN E11 121 J8
Langthorne Hospital
WAN E11 121 J9
Langtons J & I School
EMPK RM11 125 M6
The Lansbury Estate
WOKN/KNAP GU21 231 J4
Lansbury Lawrence Primary School
POP/IOD E14 140 G8
Lansdowne College
BAY/PAD W2 8 G8
Lansdowne Primary School
TIL RM18 168 C8
Lansdowne School
BRXN/ST SW9 158 G9
Larchwood Primary School
BRWN CM15 86 F10
La Retraite RC Girls School
BAL SW12 180 D3
Lark Hall Primary School
CLAP SW4 158 E8
Larkshall Business Centre
CHING E4 101 J3
Larkswood Primary School
CHING E4 100 G5
Larmenier & Sacred Catholic Primary School
HMSMTH W6 156 G3
La Sainte Union Catholic Secondary School
HGT N6 118 B8
La Sainte Union Convent School
KTTN NW5 118 C8
La Salette RC Primary School
RAIN RM13 145 H5
Latchmere Leisure Centre
BTSEA SW11 158 A8
Latchmere Primary School
KUTN/CMB KT2 177 L9
Lathom Junior School
EHAM E6 142 B2
Latimer Road ⊖
NTGHL W11 136 G9

Latton Bush Business Centre
 HLWS CM18.........................47 J4
Latymer All Saints CE
 Primary School
 ED N9...............................99 N3
The Latymer
 Preparatory School
 HMSMTH W6......................156 D4
The Latymer School
 ED N9...............................99 M3
Latymer Upper School
 HMSMTH W6......................156 D3
Laughton Cemetery
 LOU IG10............................82 C7
Launcelot Primary School
 BMLY BR1..........................183 M7
Laurance Haines School
 WATW WD18........................73 H10
Laurel Clinic
 EA W5..............................155 H3
Lauriston Primary School
 HOM E9............................140 C3
Lavender Primary School
 ENC/FH EN2.........................79 L4
Lawdale Junior School
 BETH E2..............................7 P9
Lawn Primary School
 GVW DA11.........................189 P2
Lawrence Trading Estate
 GNWCH SE10......................161 K3
 GRAYS RM17......................167 P3
Lawrence University
 SKENS SW7..........................15 K6
Lawrence Wharf
 BERM/RHTH SE16................140 C10
Laycock Primary School
 IS N1.................................6 B2
Lazards Sports Club
 SUN TW16.........................197 J3
Leadenhall Market
 BANK EC3V...........................13 J6
Leah Manning Centre
 HLW CM20...........................28 G9
Lea Junior School
 SLN SL2...........................129 N3
Lea Park Trading Estate
 LEY E10.............................120 E6
Lea Road Industrial Park
 CHES/WCR EN8.....................62 F10
Leaside Business Centre
 PEND EN3............................80 E6
Leatherhead ≥
 LHD/OX KT22.....................236 F7
Leatherhead Business Park
 LHD/OX KT22.....................236 G5
Leatherhead Clinic
 LHD/OX KT22.....................237 H7
Leatherhead CC
 LHD/OX KT22.....................236 F9
Leatherhead & Dorking
 Gymnastics Club
 LHD/OX KT22.....................236 F7
Leatherhead FC
 LHD/OX KT22.....................236 F8
Leatherhead Golf Club
 LHD/OX KT22.....................236 F2
Leatherhead Hospital
 LHD/OX KT22.....................237 H8
Leatherhead Industrial Estate
 LHD/OX KT22.....................236 F7
Leatherhead Institute
 LHD/OX KT22.....................236 G7
Leatherhead Leisure Centre &
 Water Park
 LHD/OX KT22.....................236 F9
Leatherhead Museum
 LHD/OX KT22.....................236 F7
Leatherhead Trinity School
 LHD/OX KT22.....................236 G6
Leathermarket Gardens
 STHWK SE1..........................19 J2
Leathersellers Sports Ground
 LEE/GVPK SE12...................183 P3
Leathers Hall
 HDTCH EC3A........................13 J5
Lea Valley High School
 EN EN1...............................80 E1
Lea Valley Primary School
 TOTM N17............................99 P8
Lea Valley Trading Estate
 UED N18...........................100 B5
 UED N18...........................100 C1
Leavesden Green JMI School
 GSTN WD25...........................55 H10
Leavesden Hospital
 ABLGY WD5.........................55 H7
Lebanon Road ⊖
 CROY/NA CRO......................203 M9
L'Ecoles Des Petits School
 FUL/PGN SW6......................157 L8
Lee ≥
 LEE/GVPK SE12...................183 M2
Lee Manor Primary School
 LEW SE13..........................183 N2
Leeside Court
 BERM/RHTH SE16................140 C10
Leeside Trading Estate
 TOTM N17..........................100 B1
Leesons Primary School
 STMC/STPC BR5...................207 K3
Lee Valley Camping &
 Caravan Park
 ED N9..............................100 D2
Lee Valley Campsite
 CHING E4............................80 G6
Lee Valley Caravan Park
 HOD EN11............................45 H5
Lee Valley Ice Centre
 LEY E10.............................120 C7
Lee Valley Leisure Complex,
 Athletics Centre & Golf Club
 ED N9..............................100 D1
Lee Valley Park
 WAB EN9.............................62 G4
Lee Valley Park Farms
 WAB EN9.............................63 H4
Lee Valley Watersports Centre
 CHING E4...........................100 D7
Legoland Windsor
 WDSR SL4..........................170 C1
Leicester Square ⊖
 LSQ/SEVD WC2H.....................11 K7
Leigh Close Industrial Estate
 NWMAL KT3.........................200 A4
Leigh Technology Academy
 DART DA1..........................187 P4
Leighton House Museum
 WKENS W14...........................14 C1
Leisurezone
 HLW CM20............................46 C1
Lena Gardens Primary School
 HMSMTH W6.......................156 F2
Lent Rise Combined School
 SL SL1.............................128 A7
Leopold Primary School
 WLSDN NW10.......................136 C2
Leopold Street Clinic
 BOW E3............................139 K4
Lesnes Abbey
 BELV DA17.........................163 N5
Lesnes Abbey (remains of)
 BELV DA17.........................163 L5
Lessness Heath
 Primary School
 BELV DA17.........................164 B4
The Leverton Infant School
 WAB EN9.............................63 L10
The Leverton Junior School
 WAB EN9.............................63 L10
The Levin Hotel
 KTBR SW1X...........................16 A3

Lewin Mead Community Mental
 Health Centre
 STRHM/NOR SW16................180 E9
Lewis Clinic
 CAR SM5............................222 B1
Lewisham ≥ ⊖
 DEPT SE8...........................160 G8
Lewisham Bridge
 Primary School
 LEW SE13..........................160 G9
Lewisham Business Centre
 NWCR SE14.........................160 G5
Lewisham Centre
 LEW SE13..........................161 H10
Lewisham College
 BROCKY SE4........................160 F8
Lewisham Crematorium
 CAT SE6...........................183 L5
Lewisham Lions Centre
 BERM/RHTH SE16................160 C8
Ley Hill CC
 CSHM HP5............................51 P7
Ley Hill School
 CSHM HP5............................51 N6
Ley Park Primary School
 BROX EN10...........................44 E8
The Leys Primary School
 DAGE RM10.........................144 D2
Leyton ⊖
 WAN E11...........................121 H8
Leyton Business Centre
 LEY E10............................120 E7
Leyton Cross
 RDART DA2.........................187 H5
Leyton FC
 LEY E10............................120 E6
Leyton Industrial Village
 LEY E10............................120 C5
Leyton Leisure Centre
 LEY E10............................120 C5
Leyton Midland Road ⊖
 LEY E10............................121 H6
Leyton Orient FC
 (Matchroom Stadium)
 LEY E10............................120 C8
Leyton Sixth Form College
 LEY E10............................121 J4
Leytonstone ⊖
 WAN E11...........................121 K6
Leytonstone High Road ⊖
 WAN E11...........................121 K7
Leytonstone School
 WAN E11...........................121 K7
Leyton Youth Sports Ground
 LEY E10............................120 C6
The Liberty City Clinic
 SDTCH EC2A.........................13 J1
Liberty II Centre
 ROM RM1...........................124 F2
Liberty Middle School
 MTCM CR4..........................201 P2
The Liberty
 ROM RM1...........................124 F3
Library & Community Centre
 BTSEA SW11........................157 N3
Library & Council Building
 CRAWE RH10.......................283 P7
Light Industrial Estate
 WDSR SL4..........................170 A5
L'Ile Aux Enfants
 KTTN NW5...........................118 B10
Lilian Baylis School
 VX/NE SW8...........................17 N9
Lilian Baylis Technology School
 VX/NE SW8...........................17 N9
Lillian Baylis School
 LBTH SE11...........................17 P6
Lillian Baylis Theatre
 CLKNW EC1R..........................6 C1
Lillian Bishop School of English
 SKENS SW7..........................15 L5
Limehouse ≥ ⊖
 WCHPL E1..........................140 D8
Limehouse Hole Stairs
 BERM/RHTH SE16................140 E10
Limes Business Centre
 HORL RH6..........................279 J9
Limes Farm Primary School
 CHIG IG7...........................102 C7
The Limes Medical Centre
 EPP CM16............................65 L5
 EPP CM16............................66 C2
Lime Trees Park Golf Club
 NTHLT UB5.........................133 K3
Lime Walk JMI School
 HHS/BOV HP3........................36 A8
Limpsfield CE Infant School
 OXTED RH8.........................261 N5
Limpsfield Chart Golf Club
 OXTED RH8.........................261 P5
Limpsfield Grange School
 OXTED RH8.........................261 M3
Limpsfield Lawn Tennis Club
 OXTED RH8.........................261 M4
Lincoln Road Clinic
 EN EN1..............................79 P9
Lincoln's Inn
 LINN WC2A...........................11 P5
Linden Bridge School
 WPK KT4...........................200 B10
Linden Lodge School
 WIM/MER SW19.....................179 H4
Linden Bennett School
 FELT TW13..........................175 L8
Linford Christie Stadium
 SHB W12...........................136 D7
The Link Day Primary School
 CROY/NA CRO......................222 F1
The Link Secondary School
 CROY/NA CRO......................222 G1
Links Primary School
 TOOT SW17.........................180 B9
Linley House School
 BRYLDS KT5........................199 L6
Linley Sambourne House
 KENS W8............................14 E2
Linnet House Clinic
 STJWD NW8.........................3 N8
Linton Mead Primary School
 THMD SE28.........................143 L9
Lionel Road Primary School
 BTFD TW8..........................155 K3
Liongate Hotel
 E/WMO/HCT KT8....................198 E3
Lion House School
 PUT/ROE SW15.....................156 C10
Lion Retail Park
 WOKS/MYFD GU22..................232 E2
Lismarrine Industrial Park
 BORE WD6...........................74 C10
Lisson Grove Health Centre
 STJWD NW8............................9 N1
Lister Community School
 PLSTW E13.........................141 N4
The Lister Hospital
 BGVA SW1W.........................16 E8
Lister House Clinic
 CAVSQ/HST W1G.....................10 E5
Lister House Surgery
 HAT AL10...........................40 D3
Lister Medical Centre
 HLWW/ROY CM19.....................46 F4
Littlebrook Business Centre
 DART DA1..........................166 B9
Little Chalfont Golf Club
 AMS HP6............................70 B6
Little Chalfont Primary School
 AMS HP6............................70 B4
Little Danson Welfare Clinic
 WELL DA16.........................163 K10
Little Davids School
 CROY/NA CRO......................224 G3
Littledown Special School
 SENS SL1..........................129 L9
Little Green Junior School
 RKW/CH/CXG WD3....................72 B7

Little Hands Theatre
 HACK E8...........................116 F2
Little Hay Golf Complex
 HHS/BOV HP3........................34 F10
Little Heath Primary School
 CHDH RM6...........................59 M6
Little Heath School
 CHDH RM6..........................123 L2
Little Ilford School
 MNPK E12..........................122 C10
Little Parndon Primary School
 HLW CM20............................28 E10
Little Reddings Primary School
 BUSH WD23..........................74 A9
Little St Helens School
 NTHWD HA6...........................92 F7
Little Spring Primary School
 CSHM HP5............................50 G4
Little Stanmore First &
 Middle School
 EDGW HA8............................95 K9
Little Thurrock Primary School
 GRAYS RM17........................168 A2
Littleton CE Infant School
 SHPTN TW17........................196 B3
Little Venice Medical Centre
 MV/WKIL W9..........................9 K2
Little Wandsworth School
 TOOT SW17.........................180 B5
Liverpool Street ≥
 LVPST EC2M..........................13 J3
Liverpool Street ⊖
 LVPST EC2M..........................13 J4
Livesey Museum
 for Children
 PECK SE15...........................19 P10
Livingstone Hospital
 DART DA1..........................187 N3
Livingstone Primary School
 EBAR EN4............................77 N7
The Livity School
 BRXS/STRHM SW2...................180 F1
Lloyd Park ⊖
 CROY/NA CRO......................223 N1
Lloyd Park Centre
 WALTH E17.........................100 F10
Lloyd's
 FENCHST EC3M.......................13 J4
Lloyds Register CC
 DUL SE21..........................181 L4
Lochinver House School
 POTB/CUF EN6.......................59 L1
Lockers Park School
 HHW HP1............................35 L6
Locks View Court
 POP/IOD E14........................140 D9
Lockwood Industrial Park
 TOTM N17..........................120 A1
Lodge School
 PUR/KEN CR8.......................222 E8
Lodge Sun Sports Club
 WAT WD17............................72 F5
Log Church
 CHONG CM5..........................50 B7
Lombard Business Centre
 CROY/NA CRO.......................202 G7
Lombard Business Park
 CROY/NA CRO.......................202 G7
 WAND/EARL SW18....................179 N2
 WIM/MER SW19.....................201 M2
Lombard Trading Estate
 CHARL SE7.........................161 N3
Lombardy Retail Park
 HYS/HAR UB3.......................133 J9
London Academy
 EDGW HA8............................95 L5
London Academy of
 Music & Dramatic Art
 CAVSQ/HST W1G......................10 E4
London Allergy Clinic
 CAVSQ/HST W1G......................10 E4
London Bridge ≥ ⊖
 STHWK SE1..........................13 H10
London Bridge City Pier
 STHWK SE1..........................13 J9
London Bridge Hospital
 STHWK SE1..........................13 H9
London Bridge Hotel
 STHWK SE1..........................12 C10
London Bridge Sports Centre
 CANST EC4R.........................12 G8
London Brookes College
 HDN NW4...........................116 E2
London Business School
 CAMTN NW1..........................10 A1
London Butterfly House
 BTFD TW8..........................155 H7
The London Canal Museum
 IS N1...............................5 M7
London Capital College
 CAMTN NW1...........................4 C5
London Centre of
 Contemporary Music
 STHWK SE1..........................12 F10
London Chest Hospital
 BETH E2...........................140 B4
London Chinese Dance School
 CAN/RD E16........................141 J7
 REGST W1B..........................10 F3
London City Airport ⊖
 CAN/RD E16........................142 B10
London City Airport
 CAN/RD E16........................142 B10
London City College (English
 Language Institute) & Schiller
 International University
 STHWK SE1..........................11 P10
London City Mission
 STHWK SE1...........................19 K1
The London Clinic
 CAVSQ/HST W1G......................10 D2
London College of Business &
 Computer Services
 CLAP SW4..........................158 E10
London College of
 Business & Computing
 BETH E2...........................140 A4
London College
 of Communication
 LBTH SE11...........................18 C4
London College of Fashion
 CAVSQ/HST W1G......................10 F5
 MHST W1U............................10 B3
 SDTCH EC2A.........................13 K1
London College of
 Further Education
 LBTH SE11...........................18 C6
London College of
 Higher Education
 CLAP SW4..........................158 C9
London College of International
 Business Studies
 HHOL WC1V...........................11 M4
London College of Science
 & Technology
 GDMY/SEVK IG3.....................123 K6
London Colney JMI School
 LCOL/BKTW AL2......................57 J2
London Colney Nature Reserve
 LCOL/BKTW AL2......................57 K4
London Commodity Exchange
 WAP E1W.............................13 M8
London Contemporary
 Dance School
 CAMTN NW1...........................4 G5
London Cornish RFC
 PUT/ROE SW15.....................178 C6
The London Dungeon
 STHWK SE1..........................13 H10
London Esthetique
 POP/IOD E14.......................141 K8
London Eye ⊖
 STHWK SE1...........................17 N1
London Eye Clinic
 CAVSQ/HST W1G......................10 E4

London Fields ≥
 HACK E8...........................140 A2
London Fields Lido
 HACK E8...........................140 A2
London Fields Primary School
 HACK E8...........................140 A3
London Film Academy
 FUL/PGN SW6.......................157 K6
London Film School
 LSQ/SEVD WC2H.......................11 L6
London Financial
 Training College
 FSBYPK N4.........................119 J3
London Foot Hospital
 FITZ W1T............................10 C2
London Gender Clinic
 HDN NW4...........................116 E4
London Group Business Park
 CRICK NW2.........................116 C6
London Heart Clinic
 CAVSQ/HST W1G......................10 C4
The London Industrial Estate
 EHAM E6...........................142 D7
London Industrial Park
 EHAM E6...........................142 E7
London International College
 POP/IOD E14.......................141 K8
 SOHO/SHAV W1D......................11 H5
London International
 Cruise Terminal
 TIL RM18..........................168 D10
The London & International
 School of Acting
 MV/WKIL W9..........................8 D2
London Irish RFC
 SUN TW16..........................197 H1
The London Irish Youth Theatre
 HGT N6............................118 C6
London Islamic School
 / Madrasah
 WCHPL E1..........................140 A8
London Jewish Girls High School
 HDN NW4...........................116 F3
London Ladies & Girls FC
 CAT SE6...........................182 G8
London Lane Clinic
 BMLY BR1..........................183 L10
London Lighthouse
 NTCHL W11...........................8 B5
London Living Theatre
 SYD SE26..........................182 C7
The London Make-up Academy
 UED N18...........................100 A6
London Marriott Hotel
 HAMP NW3............................3 M4
 MYFR/PKLN W1K......................10 D7
 OXSTW W1C..........................10 C6
 STHWK SE1...........................17 N1
London Marriott West India
 Quay Hotel
 POP/IOD E14.......................140 F9
London Metrocity College
 BOW E3............................140 F5
London Metropolitan University
 HBRY N5...........................119 K10
 HOLWY N7..........................118 G10
 LVPST EC2M..........................13 H4
 WCHPL E1............................13 L5
 WCHPL E1............................13 P5
London Natural
 Therapy School
 POP/IOD E14.......................141 K9
 SOHO/CST W1F.......................11 H7
London Nautical School
 STHWK SE1..........................12 B9
London Open College
 FSBYE EC1V...........................6 D9
London Oratory School
 FUL/PGN SW6.......................157 K6
London Road ≥
 GU GU1............................250 B10
London Road Cemetery
 BRW CM14..........................106 G3
 STAL AL1...........................39 H10
London Road Medical Centre
 CROY/NA CRO.......................203 H6
LPR Sports Club
 BARK/HLT IG6......................103 J9
LSE Sports Club
 NWMAL KT3.........................200 A6
Lubavitch Boys Primary School
 CLPT E5...........................119 N5
Lubavitch House School
 (Senior Girls)
 STNW/STAM N16.....................119 M5
Lucas Vale Primary School
 DEPT SE8..........................160 F7
Lullingstone Castle
 EYN DA4...........................229 K2
Lullingstone Park Golf Club
 ORP BR6...........................228 E1
Lullingstone & Preston Hill
 Country Park
 ORP BR6...........................228 G1
Lullingstone Roman Villa
 EYN DA4...........................209 J10
Lutomer House Business Centre
 POP/IOD E14.......................140 C10
Lux Cinema
 IS N1...............................7 J10
Lycee Francais
 SKENS SW7..........................15 L5
Lycee Francais
 Charles De Gaulle
 BTSEA SW11........................158 C10
The Lyceum Theatre
 COVGDN WC2E.........................11 N7
Lynch Hill School
 SLN SL2...........................128 E5
Lyndean Industrial Estate
 ABYW SE2..........................163 M2
Lyndhurst House
 Preparatory School
 HAMP NW3..........................117 N10
Lyndhurst Middle School
 BORE WD6............................75 L5
Lyndhurst Primary School
 CMBW SE5..........................159 L8
Lyne & Longcross CE
 Infant School
 CHERT KT16........................194 E9
Lynton Preparatory School
 EW KT17...........................220 C7
Lyon Business Park
 BARK IG11.........................143 H4
Lyon Park Infant School
 ALP/SUD HA0........................135 L2
Lyonsdown School
 BAR EN5............................77 M9
Lyons Industrial Estate
 CHERT KT16........................193 L8
Lyoncross School
 UX/CGN UB8.........................131 N8
Lyric Theatre
 SOHO/SHAV W1D......................11 J7
Lyric Theatre Hammersmith
 HMSMTH W6.........................156 F3

Longley Trading Estate
 CRAWE RH10........................283 P8
Longmead Business Centre
 HOR/WEW KT19.....................220 A7
Longmead Industrial Estate
 HOR/WEW KT19.....................220 A7
Longmead Primary School
 WDR/YW UB7........................151 N2
Longshaw Primary School
 CHING E4..........................101 J4
Longwood Business Park
 SUN TW16..........................196 G5
Longwood School
 BUSH WD23..........................73 M8
Lord Chancellors Department
 WEST SW1P..........................17 K4
Lord Lister Health Centre
 TOTM N17...........................99 M10
Lord's Tour & MCC Museum
 STJWD NW8............................3 L10
Lord Williamson School
 NKENS W10............................8 A3
Loreto College
 STAL AL1............................38 D6
Lorimar Business Centre
 RAIN RM13.........................144 F8
Loseley Fields Primary School
 GODL GU7..........................267 K8
Loseley Park
 RGUW GU3..........................267 L6
Loughborough Junction ≥
 CMBW SE5..........................159 J8
Loughborough Primary School
 CMBW SE5..........................159 J8
Loughton ⊖
 LOU IG10............................82 B9
Loughton CC
 LOU IG10............................82 C7
Loughton Golf Club
 LOU IG10............................82 E5
Loughton Hall Clinic
 LOU IG10............................82 B7
Loughton Health Centre
 LOU IG10............................82 B7
Loughton Mental Health Centre
 LOU IG10............................82 B9
Lovelace Primary School
 CHSGTN KT9........................219 H2
Lovell's Wharf
 GNWCH SE10........................161 J4
Lower Clapton Health Centre
 CLPT E5...........................120 B10
Lower Place Business Centre
 WLSDN NW10........................135 P4
Lowewood Museum
 HOD EN11............................44 F4
Lowfield Heath Industrial Estate
 HORL RH6..........................279 P10
Lowfield Heath Windmill
 HORL RH6..........................278 F9
Lowfield Medical Centre
 DART DA1..........................187 M3
Lowfield Sports Ground
 BOW E3............................139 M4
Lowfield Sports Ground
 BARN SW13.........................156 D5
Low Hall Sports Ground
 LEY E10...........................120 C4
Loxford School of Science
 & Technology
 IL IG1............................122 G10
Loyola Preparatory School
 BKHH IG9...........................101 P2
LPR Sports Club
 BARK/HLT IG6......................103 J9
LSE Sports Club
 NWMAL KT3.........................200 A6
Lubavitch Boys Primary School
 CLPT E5...........................119 N5
Lubavitch House School
 (Senior Girls)
 STNW/STAM N16.....................119 M5
Lucas Vale Primary School
 DEPT SE8..........................160 F7
Lullingstone Castle
 EYN DA4...........................229 K2
Lullingstone Park Golf Club
 ORP BR6...........................228 E1
Lullingstone & Preston Hill
 Country Park
 ORP BR6...........................228 G1
Lullingstone Roman Villa
 EYN DA4...........................209 J10
Lutomer House Business Centre
 POP/IOD E14.......................140 C10
Lux Cinema
 IS N1...............................7 J10
Lycee Francais
 SKENS SW7..........................15 L5
Lycee Francais
 Charles De Gaulle
 BTSEA SW11........................158 C10
The Lyceum Theatre
 COVGDN WC2E.........................11 N7
Lynch Hill School
 SLN SL2...........................128 E5
Lyndean Industrial Estate
 ABYW SE2..........................163 M2
Lyndhurst House
 Preparatory School
 HAMP NW3..........................117 N10
Lyndhurst Middle School
 BORE WD6............................75 L5
Lyndhurst Primary School
 CMBW SE5..........................159 L8
Lyne & Longcross CE
 Infant School
 CHERT KT16........................194 E9
Lynton Preparatory School
 EW KT17...........................220 C7
Lyon Business Park
 BARK IG11.........................143 H4
Lyon Park Infant School
 ALP/SUD HA0........................135 L2
Lyonsdown School
 BAR EN5............................77 M9
Lyons Industrial Estate
 CHERT KT16........................193 L8
Lyoncross School
 UX/CGN UB8.........................131 N8
Lyric Theatre
 SOHO/SHAV W1D......................11 J7
Lyric Theatre Hammersmith
 HMSMTH W6.........................156 F3

Maida Vale ⊖
 MV/WKIL W9...........................3 H10
Maida Vale Medical Centre
 MV/WKIL W9...........................2 G10
Maidenbower First &
 Middle School
 CRAWE RH10........................284 D9
Maidenbower Junior School
 CRAWE RH10........................284 E9
Malcolm Primary School
 PGE/AN SE20.......................182 B10
The Malden Centre
 NWMAL KT3.........................200 C4
Malden Golf Club
 NWMAL KT3.........................200 B2
Malden Manor ≥
 NWMAL KT3.........................200 B5
Malden Manor Primary School
 NWMAL KT3.........................200 B7
Malden Parochial
 Primary School
 WPK KT4...........................200 B8
Malden Road Baths
 CHEAM SM3.........................220 G1
Malham Road Industrial Estate
 FSTH SE23.........................182 C4
The Mall Bexleyheath
 BXLYHS DA6........................164 B10
Mall Galleries
 STJS SW1Y..........................11 K9
The Mall
 WHTN TW2..........................176 C6
Malmaison Charterhouse
 Square Hotel
 FARR EC1M...........................12 D3
Malmesbury Primary School
 BOW E3............................140 C5
 MRDN SM4..........................201 M7
Malorees Junior School
 KIL/WHAMP NW6....................136 G2
Maltings Arts Theatre
 STAL AL1............................38 C6
The Maltings Industrial Estate
 SBW CM21............................30 A1
 WARE SG12...........................27 J7
The Maltings Shopping Centre
 STAL AL1............................38 C6
Maltmans Green School
 CFSP/GDCR SL9.....................109 P1
Malvern Way Infant School
 RKW/CH/CXG WD3....................72 D9
Manby Lodge Infant School
 WEY KT13..........................216 C1
Mandarin Oriental Hotel
 KTBR SW1X...........................16 B1
Mandeville Health Centre
 STAL AL1............................38 C9
The Mandeville Hotel
 MHST W1U............................10 C5
Mandeville Primary School
 CLPT E5...........................120 B1
 STAL AL1............................38 C9
Mandeville Special School
 NTHLT UB5.........................133 N1
Manford Industrial Estate
 ERITH DA8.........................165 J5
Manford Primary School
 CHIG IG7..........................103 J6
Manford Way Health Centre
 BARK/HLT IG6......................103 J7
Manor Brook Medical Centre
 BKHTH/KID SE3.....................161 N10
The Manor Community
 Primary School
 SWCM DA10.........................189 L9
Manorcroft Primary School
 EGH TW20..........................172 D9
Manor Drive Health Centre
 WPK KT4...........................200 C8
Manorfield Primary School
 HORL RH6..........................280 A4
 POP/IOD E14.......................140 C7
Manor Green Primary School
 CRAWW RH11........................283 N3
The Manor Hotel
 RAIN RM13.........................145 N4
Manor House ⊖
 FSBYPK N4.........................119 K6
Manor House School
 GT/LBKH KT23......................253 M6
Manor Infant School
 BARK EC2Y.........................143 J1
Manor Lodge School
 RAD WD7............................57 P2
Manor Mead School
 SHPTN TW17........................196 C5
Manor Oak Primary School
 STMC/STPC BR5.....................207 N5
Manor of Groves Golf Club
 SBW CM21............................29 J1
Manor of Groves Hotel
 SBW CM21............................29 J1
Manor Park ≥
 MNPK E12..........................122 A9
Manor Park Cemetery
 FSTGT E7..........................122 A9
Manor Park Crematorium
 FSTGT E7..........................121 P9
Manor Park Medical Centre
 SLN SL2...........................129 J7
Manor Park Methodist School
 MNPK E12..........................122 B9
Manor Park Primary School
 SUT SM1...........................221 N2
Manor Place Industrial Estate
 BORE WD6............................75 P7
Manor Primary School
 SRTFD E15.........................141 K4
The Manor Primary School
 ROM RM1...........................124 G3
Manoridge Primary School
 FNCH N3............................97 L9
Manor Special School
 WLSDN NW10........................136 G4
Manor Way Business Centre
 RAIN RM13.........................144 E7
Manor Way Industrial Estate
 GRAYS RM17........................167 P6
Mansfield Infant College
 IL IG1............................122 D7
Mansion House ⊖
 STP EC4M............................12 F6
Manzoori Clinic
 SWLY BR8..........................186 G10
Maple Cross Industrial Estate
 RKW/CH/CXG WD3....................91 H5
Maple Cross JMI School
 RKW/CH/CXG WD3....................90 G6
Mapledown School
 CRICK NW2.........................116 C5
Maple Grove Business Centre
 HSLWW TW4.........................153 K10
Maple Grove Primary School
 HHNE HP2...........................36 A1
Maple House Independant
 Montessori School
 THHTH CR7.........................203 J3
Maple Industrial Estate
 FELT TW13.........................175 H6
Maple Primary School
 STAL AL1............................38 D5I
Maple River Industrial Estate
 HLW CM20............................29 L6
Maples Business Centre
 IS N1..............................6 B5I
Marble Arch ⊖
 MBLAR W1H...........................10 B7
Marble Arch ⊕
 OXSTW W1C..........................10 B7
Marble Hill House
 TWK TW1...........................177 H3
Marden Lodge Primary School
 CTHM CR3..........................242 A6
Margaret Roper Catholic
 Primary School
 PUR/KEN CR8.......................223 H6

Margaret Wix JMI School STALW/RED AL3 38 B2
Maria Fidelis Convent School CAMTN NW1 5 H10
Maria Montessori Childrens House HAMP NW3 117 N10
Marillac Hospital RBRW/HUT CM13 107 J7
Mariner Business Centre CROY/NA CR0 222 G2
Marion Richardson Primary School WCHPL E1 140 C8
Marion Vian Primary School BECK BR3 204 C5
Marish Infant School DTCH/LGLY SL3 150 C2
The Marist Preparatory School ASC SL5 192 C4
The Marist RC Primary School BF/WBF KT14 215 J9
Marist Senior School ASC SL5 192 C4
Maritime Greenwich College DEPT SE8 160 F6
Maritime Industrial Estate CHARL SE7 161 N3
Maritime Museum GNWCH SE10 161 K3
Marjorie McClure School CHST BR7 206 F1
The Marjory Kinnon School EBED/NFELT TW14 174 F1
The Market COVGDN WC2E 11 M7
Market Trading Estate NWDGN UB2 153 J3
Mark Hall Community School & Sports College HLWE CM17 29 M8
Mark Hall Cycle Museum HLW CM20 29 L8
Marks Gate Junior School CHDH RM6 123 P1
Marlborough CC DUL SE21 181 P4
Marlborough Day Hospital STJWD NW8 3 J7
Marlborough First & Middle School HRW HA1 114 D2
Marlborough House STJS SW1Y 11 H10
Marlborough Primary School
CHEL SW3 15 P6
ISLW TW7 154 F7
Marlborough School
BFN/LL DA15 185 K4
STAL AL1 38 B9
Marlborough Trading Estate RCH/KEW TW9 155 N7
Marlin Montessori School BERK HP4 33 N5
Marlowe Business Centre NWCR SE14 160 D6
Marlowes Health Centre HHW HP1 35 M6
Marlowes Shopping Centre HHW HP1 35 M7
Marner Primary School BOW E3 140 G6
Marriott Hotel
DTCH/LGLY SL3 150 C4
ECT SW5 14 G5
HYS/HAR UB3 152 E6
KIL/WHAMP NW6 2 G7
MBLAR W1H 9 P5
Marshalls Park School ROM RM1 104 F10
Marshfields CE School CHERT KT16 215 H3
Marsh Gate Business Centre SRTFD E15 141 H4
Marshgate Primary School RCHPK/HAM TW10 177 L1
Marshgate Trading Estate HERT/BAY SG13 25 M4
Marsh Green School DAGW RM9 144 B4
Marsh View Industrial Estate RAIN RM13 145 N5
Martan College HOL/ALD WC2B 11 M5
Martin Baker Sports Ground DEN/HRF UB9 111 J5
Martinbridge Industrial Estate EN EN1 79 P9
Martindale Industrial Estate EN EN1 79 M9
Martinfield Business Centre WGCE AL7 23 J4
Martin Primary School EFNCH N2 117 P2
Marvels Lane Primary School LEE/GVPK SE12 183 P7
Marygreen Manor Hotel BRW CM14 106 E5
Maryland ⇌ SRTFD E15 121 K10
Maryland Industrial Estate SRTFD E15 121 K10
Maryland Primary School SRTFD E15 121 K10
Marylebone ⇌ ⊖ CAMTN NW1 9 P2
Marylebone Health Centre CAMTN NW1 10 D2
Marymount International School KUTN/CMB KT2 177 P10
Mary Wallace Theatre TWK TW1 176 F4
Maswell Park Health Centre HSLW TW3 176 B1
Matching Green CE Primary School HLWE CM17 31 L9
Mathilda Marks Kennedy Primary School MLHL NW7 96 A6
Matrix Business Centre DART DA1 187 M1
The Matthew Arnold School STA TW18 173 M9
Maudlin's Green WAP E1W 13 M9
The Maudsley Hospital CMBW SE5 159 L8
Maughan Library (Kings College) LINN WC2A 12 A5
Maunds Wood CP School HLWS CM18 46 C5
Mawbrey Brough Health Centre VX/NE SW8 158 F6
The Mawney School ROMW/RG RM7 124 E3
May Avenue Industrial Estate GVW DA11 190 C4
Maybury Business Centre WOKS/MYFD GU22 232 D3
Maybury Infant School WOKN/KNAP GU21 232 C2
Mayday University Hospital THHTH CR7 203 J6
Mayesbrook Park Arena BARK EC2Y 123 K10
Mayespark Primary School GDMY/SEVK IG3 123 K8
Mayfield Infant School CHES/WCR EN8 62 D3
Mayfield Primary School HNWL W7 134 C8
Mayfield School PIN HA5 113 M1
Mayflower Primary School POP/IOD E14 140 F8
Maylands Golf Club HARH RM3 106 A6
Mayplace Primary School BXLYHN DA7 164 E10
Maypole Primary School RDART DA2 186 F6
Maytime School IL IG1 122 D8
Mayville J & P School WAN E11 121 K8
Maze Hill ⇌ GNWCH SE10 161 K5
McKay Trading Estate
DTCH/LGLY SL3 151 H8
NKENS W10 8 A1
McMillan Clinic HYS/HAR UB3 132 D9
MDQ Majidiah School WCHPL E1 140 A9
The Mead Business Centre HERT/BAY SG13 25 M4
Mead Industrial Park HLW CM20 29 J7
The Mead Infant School WPK KT4 200 C10
Meadlands Primary School RCHPK/HAM TW10 177 H7
Meadowbrook Industrial Centre CRAWE RH10 284 B4
Meadowcroft County Infant School CHERT KT16 195 J10
Meadowgate School BROCKY SE4 160 C9
Meadow High School UX/CGN UB8 131 P7
Meadowside Leisure Centre BKHTH/KID SE3 161 P10
The Meadow Special School STMC/STPC BR5 185 K10
Meadow Wood School BUSH WD23 74 B9
Mead Primary School HARH RM3 105 N7
Mead Road Infant School CHST BR7 184 F9
The Mead School HLWS CM18 47 H3
Meath Green Infant School HORL RH6 280 A2
Meath Green Junior School HORL RH6 280 A2
Meath School CHERT KT16 214 G4
The Medical Centre
CRAWW RH11 283 J9
EHSLY KT24 252 F2
WAT WD17 73 J6
Medical Express Clinic CAVSQ/HST W1G 10 E3
Mednurs Clinic SEVS/STOTM N15 119 L4
Megabowl KUTN/CMB KT2 199 K2
Melcombe Primary School HMSMTH W6 156 G5
Melia White House Hotel CAMTN NW1 10 F1
Mellish Industrial Estate WOOL/PLUM SE18 162 A2
Mellow Lane School HGDN/ICK UB10 132 D6
Melrose Special School MTCM CR4 201 P3
Memorial Hospital WOOL/PLUM SE18 162 D8
Menorah Grammar School
EDGW HA8 95 P8
GLDGN NW11 117 H5
Menorah High School for Girls CRICK NW2 116 C8
Menorah Primary School GLDGN NW11 117 H5
Menzies Chequers Hotel HORL RH6 280 B2
MERC Education WOOL/PLUM SE18 162 E2
Mercers College WARE SG12 26 C2
Mercers' Hall CITYW EC2V 12 F6
The Merchant Taylors Hall BANK EC3V 13 H6
Merchant Taylors School NTHWD HA6 92 F2
Mercure Burford Bridge Hotel RDKG RH5 255 H7
Mercure Castle Hotel WDSR SL4 149 J7
Mercure London City Bankside Hotel STHWK SE1 12 E10
Mercure Thames Lodge STA TW18 173 H8
Mercure White Horse Hotel DORK RH4 272 G2
Meridian Clinic BRXN/ST SW9 158 G9
Meridian Locality Mental Health Centre CHARL SE7 161 P5
Meridian Primary School GNWCH SE10 161 J4
Meridian Sports Club CHARL SE7 162 B6
Meridian Trading Estate CHARL SE7 161 N3
Merlin Primary School BMLY BR1 183 M6
Merlin School PUT/ROE SW15 178 G1
Mermaid Theatre BLKFR EC4V 12 D7
Merrielands Retail Park DAGW RM9 144 A3
Merrist Wood Golf Club RGUW GU3 249 H5
Merrow Business Centre RGUE GU4 250 G7
Merrow CE Infant School RGUE GU4 250 G8
Merry Hill Infant School BUSH WD23 94 A1
Merryhills Clinic ENC/FH EN2 78 G7
Merryhills Primary School ENC/FH EN2 78 G8
Merstham ⇌ REDH RH1 258 D4
Merstham Primary School REDH RH1 258 D4
Merton Abbey Primary School WIM/MER SW19 201 L1
Merton Adult College RYNPK SW20 201 H3
Merton College MRDN SM4 201 J6
Merton Court Preparatory School SCUP DA14 185 M7
Merton Industrial Park WIM/MER SW19 201 M1
Merton Park ⊖ WIM/MER SW19 201 K1
Merton Park Primary School WIM/MER SW19 201 J2
Merton Road Industrial Estate WAND/EARL SW18 179 K3
Meryfield Primary School BORE WD6 75 L5
The Method Studio FSBYW WC1X 11 N3
Metro Business Centre SYD SE26 182 E9
The Metro Golf Centre HDN NW4 96 F9
Metro Industrial Centre ISLW TW7 154 D8
Metropolis Centre BORE WD6 75 M7
Metropolitan Business Centre HACK E8 7 K4
Metropolitan Hospital STHWK SE1 18 B3
The Metropolitan Hotel MYFR/PKLN W1K 10 E10
Metropolitan Police Bushey Sports Ground BUSH WD23 73 P7
Metropolitan Police FC E/WMO/HCT KT8 198 C6
Metropolitan Police Hayes Sports Club HAYES BR2 205 L9
Metropolitan Police (Hendon) Track CDALE/KGS NW9 116 C1
Metropolitan Police Training School, Hendon CDALE/KGS NW9 116 C1
Metropolitan Tabernacle STHWK SE1 18 D5
Metro Trading Centre WBLY HA9 115 N9
Michael Faraday Primary School WALW SE17 19 H8
Michael Manley Industrial Estate VX/NE SW8 158 D7
Michael Sobell Sinai School KTN/HRWW/WS HA3 115 M4
The Michael Tippett School LBTH SE11 18 B6
Micklem JMI School HHW HP1 35 K5
Midas Business Centre DAGE RM10 124 B9
Midas Industrial Estate
DAGE RM10 124 B9
UX/CGN UB8 131 L4
Middlegreen Trading Estate DTCH/LGLY SL3 150 A1
Middle Park Primary School ELTH/MOT SE9 184 A3
Middle Row Primary School NKENS W10 8 A1
Middlesex Business Centre NWDGN UB2 153 P1
Middlesex CCC (Lord's Cricket Ground) STJWD NW8 3 M9
Middlesex Hospital Medical School FITZ W1T 11 H3
Middlesex Hospital Nurses Home GTPST W1W 10 G3
Middlesex Hospital School of Physiotherapy FITZ W1T 11 H3
Middlesex Hospital Sports Ground CHST BR7 185 J8
Middlesex School of Complementary Medicine STAN HA7 95 K9
Middlesex University
ARCH N19 118 D6
GLDGN NW11 117 L6
PEND EN3 80 C9
WDGN N22 98 F10
Middlesex University (Cat Hill Campus) EBAR EN4 78 B10
Middlesex University (Enfield Campus) PEND EN3 80 A9
Middlesex University (Hendon Campus) HDN NW4 116 E2
Middlesex University (Trent Park Campus) EBAR EN4 78 D6
Middleton Special School WARE SG12 26 C4
Mid Essex Adult Community College RBRW/HUT CM13 87 N10
Midfield Primary School STMC/STPC BR5 185 K10
Mid Kent Golf Club GVW DA11 190 E6
Midleton Industrial Estate GUW GU2 249 N9
Midway Mission Hospital BETH E2 7 L10
Milbourne Lodge Junior School ESH/CLAY KT10 218 B2
Milbourne Lodge School ESH/CLAY KT10 218 C3
Mile End ⊖ BOW E3 140 E6
Mile End & Bow Business Centre WCHPL E1 140 A7
Mile End Hospital WCHPL E1 140 C5
Mile End Stadium POP/IOD E14 140 F7
Milehams Industrial Estate PUR RM19 165 P2
Miles Coverdale Primary School SHB W12 156 F1
Milestone Hotel KENS W8 15 H2
Milestone School HART DA3 211 L8
Military Barracks WOOL/PLUM SE18 162 D4
Millbank Millennium Pier WEST SW1P 17 L6
Millbank Primary School WEST SW1P 17 K6
Millbank Tower WEST SW1P 17 L6
Millbarn Medical Centre BEAC HP9 88 E10
Millbrook School CHES/WCR EN8 62 D5
Millennium Arena BTSEA SW11 158 B6
Millennium Bailey's Hotel SKENS SW7 15 J5
Millennium Balloon STHWK SE1 13 K10
Millennium & Copthorne Hotels at Chelsea FC FUL/PGN SW6 157 L6
Millennium Dance 2000 Theatre School HAMP NW3 117 P10
Millennium Gloucester Hotel ECT SW5 15 H6
Millennium Harbour POP/IOD E14 160 E1
Millennium Hotel KTBR SW1X 16 B2
Millennium Hotel London Mayfair MYFR/PKLN W1K 10 D8
Millennium Primary School GNWCH SE10 161 L2
Millennium Quay DEPT SE8 160 G5
Millennium Wharf POP/IOD E14 161 J2
Mill Farm Business Park HSLWW TW4 175 M3
Millfields Primary School CLPT E5 120 B9
Millfield Theatre UED N18 99 L5
Mill Green Business Park MTCM CR4 202 A7
Mill Green Golf Club WGCE AL7 23 J10
Mill Hill Broadway ⇌ MLHL NW7 96 B7
Mill Hill Cemetery MLHL NW7 96 F7
Mill Hill County High School MLHL NW7 96 B3
The Mill Hill CC MLHL NW7 96 F4
Mill Hill East ⊖ MLHL NW7 96 G8
Mill Hill Golf Club MLHL NW7 96 B3
Mill Hill Industrial Estate MLHL NW7 96 C7
Mill Hill School MLHL NW7 96 E5
Mill Lane Medical Centre KIL/WHAMP NW6 117 K10
Mill Lane Trading Estate CROY/NA CR0 202 G10
Mill Mead J & I School HERT/WAT SG14 25 K5
The Mill Primary School CRAWW RH11 283 K7
Mill River Trading Estate PEND EN3 80 D8
Millside Industrial Estate DART DA1 165 L10
Mill Street Clinic STHWK SE1 19 M1
Mill Studio Business Centre WARE SG12 26 D2
Mill Trading Estate WLSDN NW10 135 N4
The Mill Trading Estate WLSDN NW10 135 P5
Millwall FC (The New Den) BERM/RHTH SE16 160 B4
Milmead Industrial Centre TOTM N17 100 A10
Milton Mount Primary School CRAWE RH10 284 C5
Milton Natural Health Centre HGT N6 118 D5
Milton Road Business Park GVE DA12 190 F3
Milton's Cottage CSTG HP8 89 N4
Minet Clinic HYS/HAR UB3 133 H10
Minet J & I Schools HYS/HAR UB3 133 J10
Ministry of Defence WHALL SW1A 11 L10
Mint Business Park CAN/RD E16 141 M7
Mirravale Trading Estate CHDH RM6 123 P5
Mission Grove Primary School WALTH E17 120 E3
Mitcham ⊖ MTCM CR4 201 P4
Mitcham CC MTCM CR4 201 P4
Mitcham Eastfields ⇌ MTCM CR4 202 B2
Mitcham Golf Club MTCM CR4 202 B5
Mitcham Industrial Estate MTCM CR4 202 B1
Mitcham Junction ⇌ ⊖ MTCM CR4 202 B5
Mitcham Vale High School STRHM/NOR SW16 202 D2
Mitchell Brook Primary School WLSDN NW10 136 A1
Mitre Bridge Industrial Park NKENS W10 136 E6
Mitre House Hotel BAY/PAD W2 9 L6
Moatbridge School ELTH/MOT SE9 184 A2
The Moat School FUL/PGN SW6 157 H8
Moberly Sports & Education Centre WLSDN NW10 136 G5
Mole Business Park LHD/OX KT22 236 F7
Molesey Cemetery E/WMO/HCT KT8 197 P3
Molesey Hospital E/WMO/HCT KT8 197 P5
Mollison Drive Health Centre WLGTN SM6 222 F4
Monega Primary School MNPK E12 122 A10
Monken Hadley CE Primary School BAR EN5 77 K5
Monkfrith Primary School EBAR EN4 98 B1
Monks Hill Sports Centre SAND/SEL CR2 224 C4
Monksmead School BORE WD6 75 P7
Monks Orchard Primary School CROY/NA CR0 204 C5
Monro Industrial Estate CHES/WCR EN8 62 D10
The Montague on the Gardens Hotel RSQ WC1B 11 L3
Montbelle Primary School ELTH/MOT SE9 184 D7
The Montcalm-Hotel Nikko MBLAR W1H 10 B6
Monteagle Primary School DAGW RM9 143 L3
Montem Primary School
HOLWY N7 118 G8
SL SL1 148 G1
Montem Sports Centre SL SL1 149 J1
Montpelier Primary School EA W5 135 J7
Monument ⊖ MANHO EC4N 13 H7
Monument Bridge East Industrial Estate WOKN/KNAP GU21 232 E1
The Monument CANST EC4R 13 H7
Moorcroft School UX/CGN UB8 132 A8
Moore Place Golf Club ESH/CLAY KT10 217 P2
Moorfields Eye Hospital FSBYE EC1V 6 G10
Moorgate ⇌ ⊖ BARB EC2Y 12 G4
Moor House School OXTED RH8 261 L8
Moor Lane Junior School CHSGTN KT9 219 L2
Moor Park ⊖ NTHWD HA6 92 E4
Moor Park Golf Club RKW/CH/CXG WD3 92 C4
Moor Park Industrial Estate WATW WD18 92 D1
Mora Primary School CRICK NW2 116 F9
Morden ⊖ WIM/MER SW19 201 L3
Morden Cemetery MRDN SM4 200 F6
Morden College Homes BKHTH/KID SE3 161 M8
Morden First School MRDN SM4 201 K5
Morden Hall Medical Centre WIM/MER SW19 201 L3
Morden Hall Park (NT) MRDN SM4 201 M4
Morden Mount Primary School LEW SE13 160 G8
Morden Park Pool MRDN SM4 201 J5
Morden Road ⊖ WIM/MER SW19 201 L2
Morden Road Clinic WIM/MER SW19 201 L3
Morden South ⇌ MRDN SM4 201 K5
Moreland Primary School FSBYE EC1V 6 D9
Moreton Bay Industrial Estate GPK RM2 105 L10
Moreton CE Primary School CHONG CM5 49 K6
Moreton Industrial Estate SWLY BR8 209 J4
Morgans JMI School HERT/BAY SG13 25 L7
Moriah Jewish Day School PIN HA5 113 M6
Morley College STHWK SE1 18 B3
Morningside Primary School HOM E9 140 B1
Mornington Crescent ⊖ CAMTN NW1 4 G7
Mornington Sports & Fitness Centre CAMTN NW1 4 F5
Morpeth School BETH E2 140 B5
Mortimer Road Clinic WLSDN NW10 136 F5
Mortimer School STRHM/NOR SW16 180 E5
Mortlake ⇌ MORT/ESHN SW14 155 P9
Mortlake Cemetery MORT/ESHN SW14 156 B9
Mortlake Crematorium RCH/KEW TW9 155 N8
Moselle School TOTM N17 99 M10
Moselle Special School TOTM N17 99 L10
Mosiah Foundation Supplementary School STNW/STAM N16 119 M6
Mossbourne Community Academy HACK E8 119 P9
Mossford Green Primary School BARK/HLT IG6 102 F10
Moss Hall Junior School FNCH N3 97 L7
The Mother & Baby Clinic HOM E9 140 B1
Motspur Park ⇌ NWMAL KT3 200 E5
Mottingham ⇌ ELTH/MOT SE9 184 C4
Mottingham Community Health Clinic ELTH/MOT SE9 184 B7
Mottingham Primary School ELTH/MOT SE9 184 C6
Mount Alvernia Hospital GU GU1 268 B2
Mount Carmel RC Primary School EA W5 155 H2
Mount Carmel RC Technical College for Girls ARCH N19 118 E6
Mount Cemetery GUW GU2 267 N3
Mount Grace School POTB/CUF EN6 59 L6
The Mount Infant School NWMAL KT3 199 N3
Mount Medical Centre FELT TW13 175 M5
Mount Pleasant Lane J & I School LCOL/BKTW AL2 55 M7
Mount School MLHL NW7 96 E6
Mount Stewart Infant School KTN/HRWW/WS HA3 115 J4
Mount Vernon Hospital NTHWD HA6 92 C6
The Movieum of London STHWK SE1 17 N1
Mowat Industrial Estate WATN WD24 73 K4
Mowlem Primary School BETH E2 140 B4
Mowlem Trading Estate TOTM N17 100 B8
MPR Eurotots School KIL/WHAMP NW6 136 G2
MS Business Centre PIN HA5 113 L1
MSP Business Centre WBLY HA9 115 N9
Mudchute ⊖ POP/IOD E14 160 G3
Mudchute City Farm POP/IOD E14 161 H3
Mudlands Estate RAIN RM13 144 F5
Mulberry Business Centre BERM/RHTH SE16 160 C1
Mulberry House School CRICK NW2 117 H10
Mulberry Primary School TOTM N17 99 N10
Mulberry School for Girls WCHPL E1 140 A8
Mulgrave Primary School WOOL/PLUM SE18 162 D3
Munroe Centre STHWK SE1 19 H1
Murky Puddle Theatre NWMAL KT3 200 C3
Murray Business Centre STMC/STPC BR5 207 L3
Muschamp Primary School CAR SM5 201 P9
Museum in Docklands POP/IOD E14 140 F9
Museum of Domestic Design & Architecture EBAR EN4 78 A9
Museum of Fulham Palace FUL/PGN SW6 156 G8
Museum of Garden History STHWK SE1 17 M4
Museum of London BARB EC2Y 12 E4
Museum of London Archaeology IS N1 6 F6
Museum of Richmond TWK TW1 177 J1
Museum of St Albans STAL AL1 38 D6
Museum of the Artillery in the Rotunda CHARL SE7 162 B4
Museum of the Order of St John FARR EC1M 12 D2
Musical Museum BTFD TW8 155 K5
Muswell Hill Bowling Club MUSWH N10 118 B1
Muswell Hill Golf Club MUSWH N10 98 C9
Muswell Hill Primary School MUSWH N10 118 C1
Myatt Garden Primary School BROCKY SE4 160 E8
Myatts Field Clinic BRXN/ST SW9 159 J7
N1 Shopping Centre IS N1 6 B7
Nagi Business Centre ALP/SUD HA0 135 J4
Nags Head Shopping Centre HOLWY N7 118 F8
Naima Jewish Preparatory School KIL/WHAMP NW6 2 G7
Nancy Rueben Primary School HDN NW4 116 G2
Nascot Wood Infant School WAT WD17 73 H4
Nash College of Further Education WWKM BR4 205 L10
Nash Mills Primary School HHS/BOV HP3 54 A1
The National Archives RCH/KEW TW9 155 M6
National Army Museum CHEL SW3 16 B9
National College of Government ASC SL5 192 E5
National Film Theatre STHWK SE1 11 P9
National Film & TV School BEAC HP9 88 D9
National Gallery LSQ/SEVD WC2H 11 K8
National Hospital for Neurology & Neurosurgery RSQ WC1B 11 L2
National Maritime Museum GNWCH SE10 161 J5
National Physical Laboratory TEDD TW11 176 D9
National Portrait Gallery LSQ/SEVD WC2H 11 K8
National Sports Centre NRWD SE19 181 P9
National Temperance Hospital CAMTN NW1 4 G9
National Tennis Centre PUT/ROE SW15 178 B1
National Youth Theatre Great Britain HOLWY N7 118 F8
The Natural History Museum SKENS SW7 15 L4
Natural Therapy Clinic TOOT SW17 180 C8
Natwest Sports Club BECK BR3 182 E9
Navigation College CANST EC4R 12 F7
Nazeing CP School WAB EN9 45 K9
Nazeing Glass Industrial Estate BROX EN10 45 H7
Nazeing Golf Club WAB EN9 45 P10
Nazeing Park School WAB EN9 45 P8
Neasden ⊖ WLSDN NW10 116 B10
Negus Sixth Form Centre WOOL/PLUM SE18 162 G5
Nelmes Primary School EMPK RM11 125 N2
Nelson Dock Museum BERM/RHTH SE16 140 E10
Nelson Hospital RYNPK SW20 201 J2
Nelson Primary School
EHAM E6 142 D4
WHTN TW2 176 A2
Nelson's Column STJS SW1Y 11 K9
Nelson Trading Estate WIM/MER SW19 201 L1
Neo Clinic PIM SW1V 16 G5
New Addington ⊖ CROY/NA CR0 225 H6
New Addington Pools & Fitness Centre CROY/NA CR0 225 H6
The New Ambassadors Theatre LSQ/SEVD WC2H 11 K6
New Ash Green Primary School HART DA3 211 L9
New Atlas Wharf POP/IOD E14 160 E2
The New Aylesbury Medical Centre WALW SE17 19 H7
New Barnet ⇌ BAR EN5 77 M9
The New Beacon School SEV TN13 264 G3
New Beckenham ⇌ BECK BR3 182 D10
Newberries Primary School RAD WD7 75 H1
New Brentford Cemetery HSLW TW3 153 N8
Newbridge School CHDH RM6 123 L3
Newbury Park ⊖ GNTH/NBYPK IG2 122 G4
Newbury Park Health Centre GNTH/NBYPK IG2 122 G4
The New Business Centre WLSDN NW10 136 C5
New Caledonian Wharf BERM/RHTH SE16 160 E2
New Chiswick Pool CHSWK W4 156 B6
New City Primary School PLSTW E13 141 P5
The New College WDSR SL4 149 H6
New Connaught Rooms HOL/ALD WC2B 11 M6
New Covent Garden Market VX/NE SW8 158 E6
New Crane Wharf WAP E1W 140 B10
New Cross ⇌ ⊖ NWCR SE14 160 E6
New Cross Gate ⇌ ⊖ NWCR SE14 160 D6
New Cross Sports Arena NWCR SE14 160 D6
New Elgiva Theatre CSHM HP5 50 G7
New Eltham ⇌ ELTH/MOT SE9 184 E4
New End Primary School HAMP NW3 117 M9
New End Theatre HAMP NW3 117 M8
New England Industrial Estate
BARK EC2Y 142 F4
HOD EN11 45 H2
Newfield Primary School WLSDN NW10 136 C2
Newham City Farm CAN/RD E16 142 A8
Newham College of Further Education
EHAM E6 142 C4
SRTFD E15 141 K2
Newham General Hospital PLSTW E13 141 P6
Newham Leisure Centre PLSTW E13 141 P7
Newham Medical Centre PLSTW E13 141 P4
Newham Sixth Form College PLSTW E13 141 N6
Newham Training & Education Centre SRTFD E15 141 K1
New Haw Therapy Clinic ADL/WDHM KT15 215 L6

New Hope Christian School EDUL SE22 159 N10
New Horizons Computer Learning Centre FSBYE EC1V 6 G10
Newington Court Business Centre STHWK SE1 18 E4
Newington Green Primary School STNW/STAM N16 119 M10
Newington Industrial Estate WALW SE17 18 D6
New Kings Primary School FUL/PGN SW6 157 J8
Newland House School TWK TW1 176 E7
New London Theatre LSQ/SEVD WC2H 11 M5
New Malden ⇌ NWMAL KT3 200 B3
New Monument School WOKS/MYFD GU22 232 F1
Newnham Junior School RSLP HA4 113 K6
New North Community School IS N1 6 G3
Newport School LEY E10 121 H7
New River Sports Centre WDGN N22 99 J8
New River Trading Estate CHES/WCR EN8 62 C2
New River Village CEND/HSY/T N8 118 G1
New Rush Hall School IL IG1 122 F7
New School FUL/PGN SW6 157 J7
The New School at West Heath SEV TN13 265 J5
New Scotland Yard STJSPK SW1H 17 J3
News International WAP E1W 13 P8
News International Offices WAP E1W 140 A9
New Southgate ⇌ FBAR/BDGN N11 98 B6
New Southgate Cemetery FBAR/BDGN N11 98 C4
New Southgate Crematorium FBAR/BDGN N11 98 C4
New Southgate Industrial Estate FBAR/BDGN N11 98 D6
New Southgate Pain Clinic & Medical Centre FBAR/BDGN N11 98 D6
New Spitalfields Market LEY E10 120 F9
Newstead Wood School for Girls ORP BR6 206 C10
Newton Farm First & Middle School RYLN/HDSTN HA2 113 N7
Newton Industrial Estate CHDH RM6 123 N2
Newton Medical Centre BAY/PAD W2 8 G5
Newton Preparatory School VX/NE SW8 158 C6
Newtons Primary School RAIN RM13 144 E4
Newtown School CSHM HP5 51 H5
New Victoria Hospital KUTN/CMB KT2 200 B1
New Victoria Theatre WOKN/KNAP GU21 232 B3
New Woodlands School BMLY BR1 183 K7
New Zealand Golf Club ADL/WDHM KT15 215 H8
Next Generation Fitness Club HAT AL10 40 B3
Nextstep CHES/WCR EN8 62 D10
N H Harrington Hall Hotel SKENS SW7 15 J6
Nicholas Breakspear RC School STALE/WH AL4 39 K7
Nightingale Clinic PLSTW E13 141 P4
Nightingale Primary School
CLPT E5 119 P8
SWFD E18 121 P2
WDGN N22 98 G9
WOOL/PLUM SE18 162 E5
Nightingale School TOOT SW17 179 P5
Nizels Golf & Leisure Club RTON TN11 265 M10
Noak Hill School ABR/ST RM4 105 M3
Noam Primary School NFNCH/WDSPK N12 97 L6
Noel Coward Theatre CHCR WC2N 11 L7
Noel Park Primary School WDGN N22 99 J10
The Noke by Thistle LCOL/BKTW AL2 55 N3
Nomad Theatre EHSLY KT24 252 G4
Nonsuch High School for Girls CHEAM SM3 220 G4
Nonsuch Industrial Estate HOR/WEW KT19 220 B7
Nonsuch Park Hotel EW KT17 220 F2
Nonsuch Primary School EW KT17 220 E2
Noor Ul Islam Primary School LEY E10 121 H7
Norbiton ⇌ KUTN/CMB KT2 199 M1
Norbury ⇌ STRHM/NOR SW16 202 C1
Norbury Business & Enterprise College STRHM/NOR SW16 203 H1
Norbury Complementary Therapy Clinic STRHM/NOR SW16 202 C1
Norbury First & Middle School HRW HA1 114 D3
Norbury Health Centre STRHM/NOR SW16 202 C2
Norbury Manor Primary School STRHM/NOR SW16 202 F1
Norbury Trading Estate STRHM/NOR SW16 202 C2
Norland Place School NTGHL W11 8 A10
Norlington School LEY E10 121 J6
Norman Booth Leisure Centre HLWE CM17 29 N8
Normand Croft Community School WKENS W14 14 D9
Normandy Primary School BXLYHN DA7 164 E7
Normanhurst School CHING E4 101 J1
Norman Park Athletics Track HAYES BR2 205 N6
Norman Shaw Building (MP's Offices) WHALL SW1A 17 L1
North Acton ⊖ WLSDN NW10 136 A6
North Acton Business Park ACT W3 136 A8
Northaw Primary School POTB/CUF EN6 60 B5
North Beckton Primary School EHAM E6 142 C6
North Bridge House Preparatory School CAMTN NW1 4 E6
North Bridge House School HAMP NW3 3 K1
Northbrook CE School LEE/GVPK SE12 183 K1
Northbury Primary School BARK EC2Y 142 E1
Northchurch CC BERK HP4 33 J2
North Clinic BMLY BR1 205 M1
North Croydon Medical Centre THHTH CR7 203 J6
North Downs Business Park SEV TN13 246 D2
North Downs Golf Club CTHM CR3 260 F1
North Dulwich ⇌ HNHL SE24 181 L1
North Ealing ⊖ ACT W3 135 L8
North Ealing Primary School WEA W13 134 G6
North East Surrey College of Technology EW KT17 220 D7
North East Surrey Crematorium NWMAL KT3 200 F6
Northend Primary School ERITH DA8 164 G7
North End Trading Estate ERITH DA8 164 F6
North Feltham Trading Estate EBED/NFELT TW14 153 J10
Northfields ⊖ WEA W13 155 H2
Northfields Industrial Estate ALP/SUD HA0 135 M3
Northfields Prospect Business Centre PUT/ROE SW15 157 J10
Northfleet ⇌ GVW DA11 189 M2
Northfleet Cemetery GVW DA11 189 P4
Northfleet Industrial Estate GVW DA11 167 L10
Northfleet School for Girls GVW DA11 190 A5
Northfleet Technology College GVW DA11 190 A4
Northgate Business Centre EN EN1 80 A7
Northgate Clinic CDALE/KGS NW9 116 B4
Northgate Industrial Park CRW RM5 104 A10
Northgate Primary School CRAWE RH10 283 P5
North Greenwich ⊖ GNWCH SE10 161 K1
North Harringay Primary School CEND/HSY/T N8 119 H2
North Harrow ⊖ RYLN/HDSTN HA2 113 P3
North Havering College of Adult Education ROM RM1 124 F2
North Holmwood CC RDKG RH5 273 H7
North London College SEVS/STOTM N15 119 N1
North London Collegiate School EDGW HA8 95 K7
The North London Hospice NFNCH/WDSPK N12 97 L4
North London International School (Diploma Centre) NFNCH/WDSPK N12 97 P6
North London International School (Lower School) NFNCH/WDSPK N12 97 L4
North London International School (Upper School) FBAR/BDGN N11 98 A6
North London Nuffield Hospital ENC/FH EN2 79 H6
North London School of Physiotherapy ARCH N19 118 D6
North London Tutorial College HDN NW4 116 F4
North Middlesex Golf Club NFNCH/WDSPK N12 97 N4
North Middlesex Hospital UED N18 99 M6
North Mymms CC BRKMPK AL9 58 D4
Northolt ⊖ NTHLT UB5 133 P2
Northolt Aerodrome RSLP HA4 133 H1
Northolt High School NTHLT UB5 133 N1
Northolt Park ⇌ RYLN/HDSTN HA2 114 A9
Northolt Primary School NTHLT UB5 133 L2
Northolt Road Clinic RYLN/HDSTN HA2 114 B8
Northolt Swimarama NTHLT UB5 133 P1
North Orbital Trading Estate STAL AL1 38 F10
North Peckham Civic Centre STHWK SE1 19 P9
North Pole Depot WLSDN NW10 136 C6
North Primary School STHL UB1 133 N9
North Sheen ⇌ RCH/KEW TW9 155 M10
Northside Primary School NFNCH/WDSPK N12 97 M6
The North Street Health Centre CLAP SW4 158 D9
Northumberland Heath Medical Centre ERITH DA8 164 E6
Northumberland Heath Primary School ERITH DA8 164 C6
Northumberland Park ⇌ TOTM N17 100 A9
Northumberland Park Industrial Estate TOTM N17 100 A7
Northumberland Park School TOTM N17 99 P8
Northview Primary School WLSDN NW10 116 B9
North Watford Cemetery GSTN WD25 73 H1
North Watford Health Clinic GSTN WD25 55 L10
Northway School MLHL NW7 96 A3
North Weald ⇌ EPP CM16 66 C3
North Weald Airfield EPP CM16 66 A2
North Weald Golf Club EPP CM16 48 B9
North Wembley ⊖ ⇌ ALP/SUD HA0 115 J8
North & West Essex Adult Community College HLW CM20 28 F9
North West Kent College
GVE DA12 191 J4
RDART DA2 187 J5
North West London Jewish Primary School CRICK NW2 2 A3
North West London Medical Centre MV/WKIL W9 3 J8
North Westminster Community Secondary School MV/WKIL W9 8 F1
North Weylands Industrial Estate WOT/HER KT12 197 M9
Northwick Park ⊖ KTN/HRWW/WS HA3 114 G5
Northwick Park Hospital & Clinical Research Centre HRW HA1 114 G5
Northwold Primary School CLPT E5 119 P7
Northwood ⊖ NTHWD HA6 92 F8
Northwood Cemetery NTHWD HA6 92 C10
Northwood College NTHWD HA6 92 E8
Northwood FC NTHWD HA6 92 C10
Northwood Golf Club NTHWD HA6 92 E8
Northwood Hills ⊖ NTHWD HA6 93 H10
Northwood & Pinner Community Hospital NTHWD HA6 93 H9
Northwood Preparatory School RKW/CH/CXG WD3 92 D3
Northwood Primary School ERITHM DA18 163 P2
Northwood School NTHWD HA6 93 J9
Northwood Sports Centre NTHWD HA6 93 J9
Norwegian/British Monument BAY/PAD W2 9 N9
The Norwegian School WIM/MER SW19 178 F10
Norwood Green Infant School NWDGN UB2 153 M4
Norwood Green Junior School NWDGN UB2 153 M4
Norwood Heights Shopping Centre NRWD SE19 181 M9
Norwood Junction ⇌ ⊖ SNWD SE25 203 P4
Norwood School NRWD SE19 181 K8
Notre Dame Preparatory School COB KT11 216 G7
Notre Dame RC Girls School STHWK SE1 18 C3
Notre Dame RC Primary School WOOL/PLUM SE18 162 E5
Notre Dame University LSQ/SEVD WC2H 11 K8
Notting Hill & Ealing High School WEA W13 134 G7
Notting Hill Gate ⊖ NTGHL W11 8 E9
Notting Hill Preparatory School NTGHL W11 8 B5
Novello Theatre
ASC SL5 192 C5
HOL/ALD WC2B 11 N7
Novotel
CAMTN NW1 5 K9
CAN/RD E16 141 N9
GNWCH SE10 160 G6
STHWK SE1 12 F10
STHWK SE1 17 N5
TWRH EC3N 13 K7
WDR/YW UB7 152 B3
Novotel London West HMSMTH W6 156 G4
Nower Hill High School PIN HA5 113 P2
NTGB Sports Ground EHAM E6 142 D1
Nugent Shopping Park STMC/STPC BR5 207 L4
Number 10 Bowling ROM RM1 124 F3
Nunhead ⇌ PECK SE15 160 B9
Nutfield ⇌ REDH RH1 276 F2
Nutfield Cemetery REDH RH1 258 E9
Nutfield Church CE Primary School REDH RH1 276 G1
Nutfield Priory Hotel REDH RH1 258 D10
Nutley Dean Business Park HORL RH6 279 H1
NutriLife Clinic MHST W1U 10 C3
The O2 POP/IOD E14 141 J10
Oakdale Infant School SWFD E18 101 N10
Oakdale Junior School SWFD E18 101 P10
Oak Farm Clinic HGDN/ICK UB10 132 C3
Oak Farm Infant School HGDN/ICK UB10 132 C3
Oakfield First School WDSR SL4 148 G8
Oakfield Junior School LHD/OX KT22 236 C9
Oakfield Preparatory School DUL SE21 181 L5
Oakfield Primary School DART DA1 187 L5
Oakfield Road Industrial Estate PGE/AN SE20 182 A10
Oakfield School WOKS/MYFD GU22 233 J1
Oakfields Montessori School UPMR RM14 146 B1
Oak Heights Independent School HSLW TW3 154 A9
Oak Hill Health Centre SURB KT6 199 K6
Oakhyrst Grange School CTHM CR3 259 L2
Oakington Manor School WBLY HA9 115 N10
Oakland CP School EBAR EN4 78 A10
Oakland Park Golf Club CSTG HP8 89 L5
Oaklands College
BORE WD6 75 P6
HARP AL5 20 A2
HAT AL10 40 D4
STAL AL1 38 D6
STALE/WH AL4 39 K5
WGCW AL8 22 G4
Oaklands Infant School BH/WHM TN16 243 P2
Oaklands Junior School BH/WHM TN16 243 P2
Oaklands Primary School HNWL W7 154 E1
Oaklands School
ISLW TW7 154 C9
LOU IG10 82 A9
Oak Lane Cemetery TWK TW1 176 F3
Oak Lane Medical Centre TWK TW1 176 G3
Oakleigh Park ⇌ TRDG/WHET N20 97 N1
Oakleigh School TRDG/WHET N20 97 P4
Oakley Green Cemetery WDSR SL4 148 A6
Oak Lodge JMI School WWKM BR4 204 G7
Oak Lodge Medical Centre EDGW HA8 95 N8
Oak Lodge School
BAL SW12 180 A3
EFNCH N2 117 M1
Oakmere Primary School POTB/CUF EN6 59 N8
The Oaks Industrial Estate HLW CM20 29 J8
Oaks Park High School GNTH/NBYPK IG2 122 G3
The Oaks Primary School CRAWE RH10 284 A10
Oaks Sports Centre CAR SM5 222 A7
Oakthorpe Primary School UED N18 99 K6
Oak Tree Clinic WOKN/KNAP GU21 231 J4
Oak Tree Medical Centre GDMY/SEVK IG3 123 H7
Oak View Primary School HAT AL10 40 E5
Oakwood ⊖ STHGT/OAK N14 78 D8
Oakwood Business Park WLSDN NW10 136 A5
Oakwood Estate HLW CM20 29 K7
Oakwood Hill Industrial Estate LOU IG10 82 E9
Oakwood Independent School PUR/KEN CR8 223 J9
Oakwood Industrial Park CRAWE RH10 284 B4
Oakwood JMI School STALE/WH AL4 39 H5
Oakwood Medical Centre STHGT/OAK N14 78 D9
Oakwood School
BXLYHN DA7 164 E10
HORL RH6 280 C4
Oakwood Sports Centre HORL RH6 280 D4
Oasis Academy PEND EN3 80 E3
Oasis Academy Coulsdon COUL/CHIP CR5 241 J6
Oasis Academy Enfield PEND EN3 80 E2
Oasis Sports Centre LSQ/SEVD WC2H 11 L5
Oast House Centre STA TW18 173 J7
Oatlands Park Hotel WEY KT13 196 D10
Oatlands School WEY KT13 216 E1
The Observatory Shopping Centre SL SL1 149 M1
Ockendon ⇌ SOCK/AV RM15 146 G5
Ockendon School SOCK/AV RM15 146 F7
Odds Farm Park Rare Breeds Centre FLKWH/TG HP10 108 A5
Odeon Cinema
BAR EN5 77 K9
BAY/PAD W2 10 A6
BECK BR3 204 F2
BERM/RHTH SE16 160 C2
CAMTN NW1 4 F5
CFSP/GDCR SL9 110 B3
ED N9 100 C1
ELTH/MOT SE9 162 B10
ESH/CLAY KT10 218 A1
EW KT17 220 B9
FITZ W1T 11 J4
HAMP NW3 3 L4
HAT AL10 40 C3
HAYES BR2 205 M2
HHNE HP2 36 A7
HOLWY N7 118 F8
KENS W8 14 E4
KUT/HW KT1 199 K2
MUSWH N10 118 B2
RCH/KEW TW9 177 J1
ROM RM1 124 G3
STJS SW1Y 11 J8
STRHM/NOR SW16 180 F6
SWFD E18 101 M10
UX/CGN UB8 131 N3
WIM/MER SW19 179 K10
Odeon Covent Garden Cinema LSQ/SEVD WC2H 11 K6
Odeon Multiplex Cinema GU GU1 267 P1
Odeon Wardour Street Cinema SOHO/SHAV W1D 11 J7
Odessa Infant School FSTGT E7 121 M10
Odhams Industrial Estate WATN WD24 73 K3
Odhams Trading Estate WATN WD24 73 K2
Odyssey Business Park RSLP HA4 113 J10
Old Abbotstonians RFC YEAD UB4 132 E4
Old Actonians Sports Club EA W5 155 L1
Old Admiralty STJS SW1Y 11 K10
Old Bancroftians FC BKHH IG9 102 A5
Old Barnes Cemetery BARN SW13 156 E8
Old Barn Theatre CRAWW RH11 283 J5
Old Beckenhamian RFC WWKM BR4 205 J10
Old Bellgate Wharf POP/IOD E14 160 E2
Old Bexley Business Park BXLY DA5 186 C3
Old Bexley CE Primary School BXLY DA5 186 A4
The Old Brickworks Business Centre HARH RM3 105 P8
Old Brockleians Sports Ground LEE/GVPK SE12 183 P2
Old Bromlians CC HAYES BR2 205 N5
Old Cemetery EDUL SE22 182 A2
Old Chigwellians Sports Club CHIG IG7 102 E2
Old Colfeian Sports Club LEE/GVPK SE12 183 M1
The Old Cottage Hospital EW KT17 220 C9
Old Curiosity Shop LINN WC2A 11 N5
Old Elthamians Sports Club CHST BR7 185 H9
Oldfield House Special School HPTN TW12 197 N1
Oldfield Primary School GFD/PVL UB6 134 C4
Oldfields Trading Estate SUT SM1 201 K10
Old Fold Manor Golf Club BAR EN5 77 H5
Old Ford Primary School BOW E3 140 E4
Old Guildfordians RFC GU GU1 250 C9
The Old Guild Theatre GVW DA11 190 A4
Old Harlow Health Centre HLWE CM17 29 M7
Oldhill Medical Centre STNW/STAM N16 119 N6
Old Jamaica Business Estate BERM/RHTH SE16 19 M3
Old Lyonian Sports Ground RYLN/HDSTN HA2 114 B3
Old Merchant Taylors Sports Club RKW/CH/CXG WD3 72 C8
Old Millhillians Sports Ground RYLN/HDSTN HA2 93 P9
Old Oak Primary School SHB W12 136 C8
Old Operating Theatre & Herb Garret Museum STHWK SE1 12 G10
Old Owens Sports Ground TRDG/WHET N20 97 N2
Old Palace Primary School BOW E3 140 G5
Old Palace School CROY/NA CR0 203 J10
Old Royal Naval College GNWCH SE10 161 J4
Old Royal Observatory Greenwich GNWCH SE10 161 J6
Old St Patricks School WCHPL E1 13 N2
Old Spitalfields Market Hall WCHPL E1 13 L3
Old Street ⇌ ⊖ FSBYE EC1V 6 G10
Old Sun Wharf POP/IOD E14 140 D9
Old Tiffinians Sports Ground E/WMO/HCT KT8 198 D5
Old Town Hall CHERT KT16 195 K7
Old Treasury WHALL SW1A 17 L1
Old Verulamiums RFC LCOL/BKTW AL2 57 H1
Old Vicarage School RCHPK/HAM TW10 177 K2
Old Vic Theatre STHWK SE1 18 B1
Old War Office WHALL SW1A 11 L10
Old Wilsonians Sports Club WWKM BR4 205 K8
Old Windsor Church Road Cemetery WDSR SL4 171 N1
Old Windsor Crimp Hill Cemetery WDSR SL4 171 L3
Olga Primary School BOW E3 140 D4
Oliver Business Park WLSDN NW10 135 P4
Oliver Goldsmith Primary School
CDALE/KGS NW9 116 A3
CMBW SE5 159 N7
Oliver House Preparatory School CLAP SW4 180 C2
Olympia WKENS W14 14 B4
Olympia Industrial Estate WDGN N22 98 G10
Olympic Industrial Estate WBLY HA9 115 N9
Olympic Retail Park WBLY HA9 115 M9
Olympic site (under development) SRTFD E15 140 G2
Olympic Trading Estate WBLY HA9 115 N9
One Aldwych Hotel COVGDN WC2E 11 N7
The One Stanley Medical Centre ALP/SUD HA0 135 K2
Ongar ⇌ CHONG CM5 67 N4
Ongar & District Sports Club CHONG CM5 67 P4
Ongar Health Centre CHONG CM5 67 P4
Ongar Leisure Centre CHONG CM5 67 P2
Ongar Place Infant School ADL/WDHM KT15 215 K3
Ongar War Memorial Hospital CHONG CM5 67 P2
On Sai Clinic ECT SW5 14 G6
Onslow Infant School GUW GU2 267 L2
Onslow St Audreys School HAT AL10 40 E4
The Open University
FSBYW WC1X 5 N9
HAMP NW3 117 K9
Ophaboom Theatre WLSDN NW10 136 E4
Optima Business Park HOD EN11 45 H2
Optimax Laser Eye Clinic HAMP NW3 3 K2
Orange Tree Theatre RCH/KEW TW9 155 K10
Orchard Business Centre
BECK BR3 182 E8
REDH RH1 276 B9
The Orchard Health Centre BARK EC2Y 142 F4
Orchard Hill College WLGTN SM6 222 C3
Orchard House Industrial Estate CSHM HP5 51 H8
Orchard House School CHSWK W4 156 A3
Orchard J & I School HOM E9 140 B2
The Orchard Junior School HSLWW TW4 153 P10
Orchard Primary School
SCUP DA14 185 L8
WATN WD24 72 G2
The Orchard School
BRXS/STRHM SW2 180 G4
E/WMO/HCT KT8 198 C5
Orchards Community Infant School REIG RH2 275 K3
Orchard Shopping Centre DART DA1 187 M2
The Orchard Theatre DART DA1 187 M2
Orchard Way Primary School CROY/NA CR0 204 D7
Oriel High School CRAWE RH10 283 N7
Oriel Primary School FELT TW13 175 M6
Orient Industrial Park LEY E10 120 F7
Orion Business Centre NWCR SE14 160 C4
The Orion Primary School CDALE/KGS NW9 96 B9
Orleans House Gallery TWK TW1 176 G4
Orleans Infant School TWK TW1 176 G3
Orley Farm School HRW HA1 114 C8
Orpington ⇌ ORP BR6 207 H9
Orpington College of Further Education ORP BR6 207 K8
The Orpington Halls ORP BR6 207 K9
Orpington Hospital ORP BR6 227 J1
Orpington Mental Health Centre ORP BR6 207 J10
Orpington Priory ORP BR6 207 L7
Orpington Retail Park STMC/STPC BR5 207 M4
Orpington Superbowl ORP BR6 207 K8
Orpington Trade Centre STMC/STPC BR5 207 L3
Osidge JMI School STHGT/OAK N14 98 D2
Osier Industrial Estate WAND/EARL SW18 157 K10
Osmani Primary School WCHPL E1 13 P2
Osterley ⊖ ISLW TW7 154 C6
Osterley Park & House (NT) ISLW TW7 154 B5
Osterley RFC NWDGN UB2 154 A2
Otford ⇌ RSEV TN14 247 K2
Otford Primary School RSEV TN14 247 H2
Our Lady Immaculate RC Primary School BRYLDS KT5 199 N8
Our Lady of Dolours RC Primary School BAY/PAD W2 8 G3
Our Lady of Grace RC Junior School CRICK NW2 116 E8
Our Lady of Grace RC Primary School CHARL SE7 161 N5
Our Lady of Hartley RC Primary School HART DA3 211 L5
Our Lady of Lourdes RC Primary School
FBAR/BDGN N11 98 C6
NFNCH/WDSPK N12 97 M8
WAN E11 121 L4
WLSDN NW10 135 P3
Our Lady of Muswell RC Primary School MUSWH N10 98 B10
Our Lady of Peace Infant School SL SL1 128 B7
Our Lady of Peace Junior School SL SL1 128 B7
Our Lady of the Rosary RC Prim School STA TW18 173 K9
Our Lady of the Rosary RC School ELTH/MOT SE9 185 H2
Our Lady of the Sacred Heart School HOLWY N7 5 P1
Our Lady of the Visitation RC Primary School GFD/PVL UB6 134 B6
Our Lady of Victories RC Primary School
PUT/ROE SW15 156 G10
SKENS SW7 15 K6
Our Lady Queen of Heaven CP School CRAWW RH11 283 L5
Our Lady Queen of Heaven RC Primary School PUT/ROE SW15 178 G3
Our Lady RC Primary School
CAMTN NW1 5 H5
POP/IOD E14 140 E8
Our Lady & St Johns RC Primary School BTFD TW8 155 H4
Our Lady & St Joseph Primary School IS N1 7 J2
Our Lady & St Philip Neri Infants School FSTH SE23 182 C6
Our Lady & St Philip Neri RC Primary School SYD SE26 182 D7
Our Ladys Catholic Primary School
AMS HP6 68 G1
DART DA1 187 L2
Our Ladys RC Primary School WGCE AL7 23 H7
Outwood Windmill REDH RH1 277 L9
Oval ⊖ LBTH SE11 18 A10
Oval Business Centre LBTH SE11 17 P8
Oval House Theatre LBTH SE11 18 A10
Oval Primary School CROY/NA CR0 203 M8
Overton Grange School BELMT SM2 221 L5
Oxford Circus ⊖ REGST W1B 10 F5
Oxford Gardens Primary School NKENS W10 136 G8
Oxford House College SOHO/SHAV W1D 11 J5
Oxhey Park Golf Centre OXHEY WD19 93 L2
Oxhey Wood Primary School OXHEY WD19 93 K5
Oxo Tower Wharf STHWK SE1 12 B8
Oxshott ⇌ LHD/OX KT22 218 B9
Oxshott Village Sports Club LHD/OX KT22 218 B10
Oxted ⇌ OXTED RH8 261 K5
Oxted Health Centre OXTED RH8 261 L5
Oxted & Limpsfield Hospital OXTED RH8 261 J4
Oxted School OXTED RH8 261 L4
Pachesham Park Golf Centre LHD/OX KT22 236 D4
Paddington ⇌ ⊖ BAY/PAD W2 9 L5
Paddington Academy MV/WKIL W9 8 F2
Paddington Bowling & Sports Club MV/WKIL W9 8 G1
Paddington Community Hospital MV/WKIL W9 8 E3
Paddington Green Primary School BAY/PAD W2 9 L2
Paddington Old Cemetery KIL/WHAMP NW6 2 C6
Paddington Recreation Ground Athletics Track KIL/WHAMP NW6 2 F9
Paddock Primary School BTSEA SW11 158 B10
Paddock School PUT/ROE SW15 156 C10
Paines Lane Cemetery PIN HA5 113 M1
Pain Relief Clinic HDN NW4 116 E4
Painshill Park COB KT11 217 H10
Painters Ash Primary School GVW DA11 190 A6

Paint Pots Montessori School WBPTN SW10 15 K10
Pakeman Primary School HOLWY N7 118 G8
Palace Gardens Shopping Centre ENC/FH EN2 79 L7
Palace of Westminster WHALL SW1A 17 M2
Palace Theatre SOHO/SHAV W1D 11 K7
WAT WD17 73 J7
Palladium Theatre SOHO/CST W1F 10 G6
Palmer's College GRAYS RM17 168 B3
Palmers Green ⇌ PLMGR N13 98 G5
Palmers Green High School WCHMH N21 99 H3
Palmerston Business Centre SUT SM1 221 M2
Palm House, Kew Gardens RCH/KEW TW9 155 L7
Panorama Pier STHWK SE1 12 E8
Panshanger Aerodrome WGCE AL7 23 P5
Panshanger Golf & Squash Complex WGCE AL7 23 M3
Panshanger JMI School WGCE AL7 23 K4
Papillon House KWD/TDW/WH KT20 256 B5
Paradise Swimming Pools MLHL NW7 96 B6
Paradise Wildlife Park BROX EN10 43 N7
Paramount Industrial Estate WATN WD24 73 K4
Paray House School FUL/PGN SW6 157 J8
Parayhouse School WBPTN SW10 157 M6
Parchmore Medical Centre THHTH CR7 203 K3
Pardes House & Beis Yaakov School FNCH N3 97 J10
Parent Infant Clinic HAMP NW3 117 M10
Parish CE Primary School BMLY BR1 183 M10
Park Avenue Clinic WAT WD17 73 H6
Park Business Centre KIL/WHAMP NW6 2 E10
Parker Industrial Centre RDART DA2 188 B3
Parkes Hotel CHEL SW3 15 P3
Parkfield Industrial Estate BTSEA SW11 158 B8
Parkfield JMI School HDN NW4 116 E5
Parkfield Medical Centre POTB/CUF EN6 59 L8
Parkgate House School CLAP SW4 158 B10
Parkgate Infant School WATN WD24 73 K3
Parkgate Junior School WATN WD24 73 K3
Park Hall Trading Estate WNWD SE27 181 K6
Park High School STAN HA7 95 J10
Park Hill Junior School CROY/NA CR0 203 L10
Parkhill Primary School CLAY IG5 122 C1
Park Hill School KUTN/CMB KT2 177 M10
Park House Medical Centre KIL/WHAMP NW6 2 B7
Park House RFC HAYES BR2 205 P9
Park Industrial Estate LCOL/BKTW AL2 56 D3
Parklands Primary School ROM RM1 124 E1
Park Lane Primary School WBLY HA9 115 K9
Park Medical Centre BERM/RHTH SE16 160 C3
Park Mews Small Business Centre HNHL SE24 181 K2
Park Plaza County Hall Hotel STHWK SE1 17 P1
Park Primary School SRTFD E15 141 L2
Park Road Clinic CEND/HSY/T N8 118 E3
Park Road Industrial Estate SWLY BR8 208 G3
Park Road Swimming Centre CEND/HSY/T N8 118 E3
Park Royal ⊖ EA W5 135 M6
Park Royal Business Centre WLSDN NW10 136 A6
Park School WOKS/MYFD GU22 232 D3
Park School for Girls IL IG1 122 D7
Parkside Business Estate DEPT SE8 160 E5
Parkside Clinic NTGHL W11 8 B5
Parkside Health NTGHL W11 8 B6
Parkside Hospital WIM/MER SW19 178 G6
Parkside Primary School BORE WD6 75 L4
Parkside School COB KT11 235 P4
Park Street ⇌ LCOL/BKTW AL2 56 C2
Park Street CE Primary School LCOL/BKTW AL2 56 C3
Park View Academy SEVS/STOTM N15 119 K2
Park Walk Primary School WBPTN SW10 15 L10
Parkway Primary School ERITHM DA18 163 P2
Parkway Trading Estate HEST TW5 153 K5
Park Wood Golf Club BH/WHM TN16 244 B8
Parkwood Hall School SWLY BR8 209 J3
Parkwood Primary School FSBYPK N4 119 J7
Parlaunt Park Combined School DTCH/LGLY SL3 150 E2
Parliament Hill Fields Athletics Track HAMP NW3 118 A9
Parliament Hill Lido HAMP NW3 118 B9
Parliament Hill School KTTN NW5 118 B9
Parmiter Industrial Centre BETH E2 140 A4
Parmiters School GSTN WD25 55 K7
Parndon Wood Cemetery HLWW/ROY CM19 46 F7
Parndon Wood Crematorium HLWW/ROY CM19 46 F7
Parndon Wood Nature Reserve HLWS CM18 46 G7
Parnells Sports Ground KTN/HRWW/WS HA3 115 L4
Parsloes Primary School DAGW RM9 144 A1
Parsonage Farm Primary School RAIN RM13 145 K5
Parsons Green ⊖ FUL/PGN SW6 157 K7
Parsons Green Health Clinic FUL/PGN SW6 157 K7
Pascals College BECK BR3 204 F2
Passmores School & Technology College HLWS CM18 46 G3
Passport Language Schools BMLY BR1 205 N1
Pastoria Hotel LSQ/SEVD WC2H 11 K8
Patent Office FLST/FETLN EC4A 12 A4
The Patrick Doody Clinic & Health Centre WIM/MER SW19 179 K10
Pattinson Clinic RCH/KEW TW9 177 J1
The Paul Robeson Theatre HSLW TW3 154 A9
Pauls Theatre School EMPK RM11 125 L5
Pavilion Barclays Sports Ground EA W5 135 K7
The Pavilion Leisure Centre BMLY BR1 205 M2
Pavilion Restaurant RCH/KEW TW9 155 K8
Pavilions Shopping Centre UX/CGN UB8 131 M2
Paxton Primary School NRWD SE19 181 N9
Payne Clinic EW KT17 220 D9
PCMS London SRTFD E15 141 J4
PDSA Hospital REDBR IG4 122 A1
Peace Pagoda CHEL SW3 16 B10
Peacock Cinema WOKN/KNAP GU21 232 B3
Peacock Estate TOTM N17 99 N7
Peacock Industrial Estate TOTM N17 99 N8
The Peacocks Shopping Centre WOKN/KNAP GU21 232 B3
The Peacock Theatre HOL/ALD WC2B 11 N6
Peall Road Industrial Estate CROY/NA CR0 202 G6
Pear Tree Mead Primary School HLWS CM18 47 K4
Peasantry Welcome Centre TEDD TW11 198 E1
Peaslake School SHGR GU5 270 F10
Peckham Park Primary School PECK SE15 159 P6
The Peckham Pulse Health & Leisure Centre PECK SE15 159 P7
Peckham Rye ⇌ ⊖ PECK SE15 159 P8
Pedham Place Industrial Estate SWLY BR8 209 H5
Peerglow Industrial Estate WATW WD18 92 C1
Pelham Primary School BXLYHN DA7 164 B9
WIM/MER SW19 179 K10
Pembridge Hall Preparatory School for Girls BAY/PAD W2 8 F7
Pendragon School BMLY BR1 183 M6
Penge East ⇌ SYD SE26 182 B9
Penge West ⇌ ⊖ PGE/AN SE20 182 A10
Peniel Academy BRWN CM15 86 D4
Penn Wood School SLN SL2 129 J6
Pentavia Retail Park MLHL NW7 96 C8
Penwortham Primary School STRHM/NOR SW16 180 C9
Percival David Foundation of Chinese Art STPAN WC1H 11 K1
Perivale ⊖ GFD/PVL UB6 134 F4
Perivale Industrial Park GFD/PVL UB6 134 F4
Perivale New Business Centre GFD/PVL UB6 135 H4
Perivale Park Athletics Track GFD/PVL UB6 134 D5
Perivale Park Golf Course GFD/PVL UB6 134 D5
Perrin Road Clinic ALP/SUD HA0 114 G9
Perry Hall Primary School ORP BR6 207 J6
Perrymount Primary School FSTH SE23 182 C5
Perrywood Business Park REDH RH1 276 C8
Perth Trading Estate SL SL1 128 G7
The Petchy Academy HACK E8 119 N10
Peterborough Primary School FUL/PGN SW6 157 K8
Peterborough & St Margaret's School STAN HA7 94 D4
Peter Hills School BERM/RHTH SE16 140 C10
Peter James Business Centre HYS/HAR UB3 153 H1
Peterley Business Centre BETH E2 140 A4
Peter Pan Statue BAY/PAD W2 9 L9
The Petersham Hotel RCHPK/HAM TW10 177 K3
Peterswood Infant School HLWS CM18 46 G5
Petrie Museum of Egyptian Archaeology FITZ W1T 11 H2
Petts Hill Primary School NTHLT UB5 114 A10
Petts Wood ⇌ STMC/STPC BR5 206 F5
Pewley Down Infant School GU GU1 268 B2
Pewterers' Hall CITYW EC2V 12 F4
Phipps Bridge ⊖ WIM/MER SW19 201 M3
Phoenix Academy ED N9 100 A2
Phoenix Business Centre CSHM HP5 50 G6
POP/IOD E14 140 F7
Phoenix Cinema EFNCH N2 117 P2
Phoenix College MRDN SM4 201 L5
Phoenix High School SHB W12 136 D9
Phoenix Industrial Estate HRW HA1 114 E2
Phoenix Leisure Centre CAT SE6 182 G3
Phoenix School HAMP NW3 3 K2
Phoenix Secondary & Primary School BOW E3 140 E5
Phoenix Theatre LSQ/SEVD WC2H 11 K6
Phoenix Trading Estate GFD/PVL UB6 135 H3
Physical Energy Statue BAY/PAD W2 9 L10
Piccadilly Circus ⊖ MYFR/PICC W1J 11 J8
Piccadilly Theatre SOHO/SHAV W1D 11 J7
Pickford Lane Medical Centre BXLYHN DA7 163 P7
Pickhurst Infant School WWKM BR4 205 K6
Pickhurst Junior School WWKM BR4 205 L6
Picture House Cinema SRTFD E15 141 J1
Pield Heath School UX/CGN UB8 131 P6
Pilgrims Way J & I School PECK SE15 160 B5
Pilot Industrial Centre WLSDN NW10 136 B6
Pilton Estate CROY/NA CR0 203 J9
Pimlico ⊖ PIM SW1V 17 J7
Pimlico Academy PIM SW1V 17 H8
The Pines Trading Estate RGUW GU3 249 K8
Pine Trees Business Park STA TW18 173 H8
Pinewood Film Studios IVER SL0 130 E2
The Pinewood Hotel DTCH/LGLY SL3 130 B7
Pinewood Primary School CRW RM5 104 C6
Pinewood Special School WARE SG12 26 C4
Pinkwell Primary School HYS/HAR UB3 152 D3
Pinnacles Cricket & Squash Club SUT SM1 221 K3
Pinner ⊖ PIN HA5 113 M2
Pinner Hill Golf Club PIN HA5 93 J7
Pinner Medical Centre PIN HA5 113 M2
Pinner New Cemetery PIN HA5 113 P1
Pinner Park Primary School PIN HA5 114 A1
Pinner View Medical Centre HRW HA1 114 B3
Pinner Wood School PIN HA5 93 K9
Pioneers Industrial Park CROY/NA CR0 202 F8
Pippins School ASHF TW15 174 A7
DTCH/LGLY SL3 151 J7
Pirbright Camp CHOB/PIR GU24 230 A6
Pirbright Primary School CHOB/PIR GU24 230 D8
Pitfarm Lawn Tennis Club GU GU1 250 D10
Pitshanger Manor Museum EA W5 135 H10
Pitwood Park Industrial Estate KWD/TDW/WH KT20 238 G6
Pixham School DORK RH4 255 H10
Pixies Hill Primary School HHW HP1 35 J7
Plaisterers Hall STBT EC1A 12 E4
Plaistow ⊖ SRTFD E15 141 L4
Plaistow Hospital PLSTW E13 141 N4
Plaistow Primary School PLSTW E13 141 N4
Plantation House Medical Centre LOTH EC2R 13 H5
Plashet Jewish Cemetery MNPK E12 142 A1
Plashet Road Medical Centre FSTGT E7 141 N2
Plashet School EHAM E6 142 B2
Players Theatre CHCR WC2N 11 M9
Playgolf Northwick Park HRW HA1 114 F6
Playhouse HLW CM20 46 F1
Playhouse Cinema EPSOM KT18 220 A10
The Playhouse CHCR WC2N 11 M9
Playhouse Theatre EPSOM KT18 219 P9
Plaza Business Centre PEND EN3 80 E6
Plaza Cinema OXTED RH8 261 K5
Plough Industrial Estate LHD/OX KT22 236 F6
Plumcroft Primary School WOOL/PLUM SE18 162 F5
Plumstead ⇌ WOOL/PLUM SE18 162 G3
Plumstead Cemetery ABYW SE2 163 L6
Plumstead Leisure Centre WOOL/PLUM SE18 163 J4
Plumstead Manor School WOOL/PLUM SE18 162 G4
The Pointer School BKHTH/KID SE3 161 M7
Polesden Lacey Infant School GT/LBKH KT23 254 B3
Polesden Lacey (NT) RDKG RH5 254 A6
Police Cadet School WAN E11 121 M6
The Polish Institute & Sikorski Museum SKENS SW7 15 M2
Polish War Memorial RSLP HA4 133 J1
Polka Theatre for Children WIM/MER SW19 179 L9
Polygon Business Centre DTCH/LGLY SL3 151 J8
Ponders End ⇌ PEND EN3 80 D9
Ponders End Industrial Estate PEND EN3 80 E8
Pond Meadow School GUW GU2 249 K9
Ponsbourne Park Hotel HERT/BAY SG13 42 F9
Ponsbourne St Marys Primary School HERT/BAY SG13 42 F10
Ponsbourne Tunnel HERT/BAY SG13 42 G10
HERT/BAY SG13 43 H5
Pontoon Dock ⊖ CAN/RD E16 141 P10
Pooles Park Primary School FSBYPK N4 118 G7
Pools on the Park RCH/KEW TW9 155 J10
Pope John Primary School SHB W12 136 E9
Pope Paul RC Primary School POTB/CUF EN6 59 J9
Pop In Business Centre WBLY HA9 115 N10
Poplar ⊖ POP/IOD E14 140 G9
Poplar Business Park POP/IOD E14 160 F1
Poplar Primary School WIM/MER SW19 201 K3
Pop Up Theatre CLKNW EC1R 6 B8
Porchester Leisure Centre BAY/PAD W2 8 C5
Portcullis House WHALL SW1A 17 M2
Porters Park Golf Club RAD WD7 57 H10
Portico City Learning Centre CLPT E5 120 B9
Portland Business Centre DTCH/LGLY SL3 149 N7
The Portland Hospital REGST W1B 10 F2
Portland House Medical Centre GFD/PVL UB6 134 A6
Portland Medical Centre SNWD SE25 204 A5
Portland Place School REGST W1B 10 F3
The Portman Clinic HAMP NW3 3 L1
Portobello Medical Centre NTGHL W11 8 B6
Portway Primary School SRTFD E15 141 M3
Potten End First School BERK HP4 34 E3
Potterells Medical Centre BRKMPK AL9 58 G1
Potters Bar ⇌ POTB/CUF EN6 59 K8
Potters Bar CC POTB/CUF EN6 59 L8
Potters Bar FC POTB/CUF EN6 59 L8
Potters Bar Golf Club POTB/CUF EN6 59 K7
Potter Street Primary School HLWE CM17 47 L3
Pound Hill Infant School CRAWE RH10 284 D6
Pound Hill Junior School CRAWE RH10 284 D6
Pound Park Nursery School CHARL SE7 162 A4
The Pountney Clinic HSLW TW3 153 P9
Poverest Primary School STMC/STPC BR5 207 K5
Powell Corderoy Primary School DORK RH4 272 E3
Powergate Business Park WLSDN NW10 136 A5
Power Industrial Estate ERITH DA8 164 G7
Prae Wood Primary School STALW/RED AL3 37 P7
Pratts Bottom Primary School ORP BR6 227 M7
Premier Cinema DORK RH4 273 H1
PECK SE15 159 P8
Prendergast Ladywell Fields College BROCKY SE4 182 F2
Prendergast School BROCKY SE4 160 F10
Presdales School WARE SG12 26 C3
Preston Manor School WBLY HA9 115 L7
Preston Medical Centre WBLY HA9 115 K8
Preston Park Primary School WBLY HA9 115 J6
Preston Road ⊖ WBLY HA9 115 K6
Priestmead Middle School KTN/HRWW/WS HA3 114 G1
Primrose Hill School CAMTN NW1 4 D5
Primrose Montessori School HBRY N5 119 K8
Prince Charles Cinema LSQ/SEVD WC2H 11 K7
Prince Edward Theatre SOHO/SHAV W1D 11 J6
Prince of Wales Primary School PEND EN3 80 E3
Prince of Wales Theatre STJS SW1Y 11 J8
Prince Regent ⊖ CAN/RD E16 141 P9
Princes College NOXST/BSQ WC1A 11 L5
Princes Court Business Centre WAP E1W 140 A9
Princes Park Stadium DART DA1 187 P4
Princes Plain Primary School HAYES BR2 206 B7
Princess Alexandra Hospital HLW CM20 28 E10
Princess Avenue School MUSWH N10 118 C1
Princess Frederica CE J & I School WLSDN NW10 136 E4
Princess Grace Hospital MHST W1U 10 C2
Princess Louise Hospital NKENS W10 136 F7
Princess Margaret Hospital WDSR SL4 149 J8
Princess May Primary School STNW/STAM N16 119 M10
Princess of Wales Conservatory RCH/KEW TW9 155 L6
The Princess Royal Distribution Centre WLSDN NW10 135 N3
The Princess Royal University Hospital ORP BR6 206 D10
Prins Willem-Alexander School WOKS/MYFD GU22 232 F5
Priors Field School GODL GU7 266 E8
Prior Weston Primary School STLK EC1Y 12 F2
Priory CE Primary School WIM/MER SW19 179 L8
The Priory CE VA School DORK RH4 272 E3
The Priory Leisure Centre STMC/STPC BR5 207 M8
Priory Preparatory School BNSTD SM7 239 K1
Priory Retail Park WIM/MER SW19 179 N10
Priory School SL SL1 128 C7
STMC/STPC BR5 207 M8
Priory Shopping Centre DART DA1 187 L2
Priory Special School SNWD SE25 203 N4
Privy Council STJS SW1Y 11 J10
Privy Council Office WHALL SW1A 11 L10
Progress Business Centre SL SL1 128 C8
Progress Business Park CROY/NA CR0 202 G9
Pronto Trading Estate YEAD UB4 132 F7
Prospect Business Park LOU IG10 82 G8
Prospect House School PUT/ROE SW15 178 G3
Prospect Industrial Estate CSHM HP5 51 H8
Proud Gallery CHCR WC2N 11 L8
Providence Road School WDR/YW UB7 131 P10
Providence Square STHWK SE1 19 N1
Provident Industrial Estate HYS/HAR UB3 153 H1
PS Tattershall Castle WHALL SW1A 11 M10
Pudding Mill Lane ⊖ SRTFD E15 140 G3
Pumphouse Educational Museum BERM/RHTH SE16 140 D10
Pump House Theatre WATW WD18 73 K9
Pump Lane Industrial Estate HYS/HAR UB3 153 J1
The Purcell School HRW HA1 114 C8
Purdy Hicks Gallery STHWK SE1 12 C9
Purfleet ⇌ PUR RM19 165 P4
Purfleet Industrial Park SOCK/AV RM15 145 N10
Purfleet Primary School PUR RM19 165 P3
Purford Green Infant School HLWS CM18 47 K3
Purford Green Junior School HLWS CM18 47 K2
Purley ⇌ PUR/KEN CR8 223 J7
Purley Community Health Clinic PUR/KEN CR8 223 H7
Purley & District War Memorial Hospital PUR/KEN CR8 223 H7
Purley Downs Golf Club SAND/SEL CR2 223 L7
Purley John Fisher RFC COUL/CHIP CR5 241 H6
Purley Oaks ⇌ SAND/SEL CR2 223 L5
Purley Oaks Primary School SAND/SEL CR2 223 L4
Purley Secretarial & Language College PUR/KEN CR8 223 H7
Purley Shopping Centre & Pool PUR/KEN CR8 223 H7
Purley Sports Club PUR/KEN CR8 222 E6
Pursuit Centre WAP E1W 140 B9
Putney ⇌ PUT/ROE SW15 156 G10
Putney Animal Hospital PUT/ROE SW15 156 G10
Putney Arts Theatre PUT/ROE SW15 156 G10
Putney Bridge ⊖ FUL/PGN SW6 157 H9
Putney Exchange Shopping Centre PUT/ROE SW15 156 G10
Putney High School PUT/ROE SW15 178 G1
Putney Leisure Centre PUT/ROE SW15 156 F10
Putney Lower Common Cemetery BARN SW13 156 E8
Putneymead Medical Centre PUT/ROE SW15 156 F10
Putney Park School PUT/ROE SW15 156 E10
Putney School of Art PUT/ROE SW15 157 H10
Putney Town Social & Bowls Club PUT/ROE SW15 156 F8
Putney Vale Cemetery PUT/ROE SW15 178 D5
Putney Vale Crematorium PUT/ROE SW15 178 D5
Puttenham CE Infant School RGUW GU3 266 A5
Puttenham Golf Club RGUW GU3 266 C5
Pylon Trading Estate CAN/RD E16 141 J6
Pyrcroft Primary School CHERT KT16 195 H6
Pyrford CE Primary School WOKS/MYFD GU22 233 J2
Pyrford Golf Club WOKS/MYFD GU22 233 L3
Quadrant Business Park KIL/WHAMP NW6 2 B5
Quality Hotel DTCH/LGLY SL3 150 E5
HRW HA1 114 C4
STAL AL1 38 E8
WBLY HA9 115 M9
Quarry Hill Infant School GRAYS RM17 167 N4
Quarry Hill Junior School GRAYS RM17 167 N4
Quarryside Business Park REDH RH1 258 C6
Quebec House (NT) BH/WHM TN16 262 G2
Quebec Industrial Estate BERM/RHTH SE16 160 D1
The Queen Anne Royal Free First School WDSR SL4 149 J9
Queen Charlotte's & Chelsea Hospital SHB W12 136 E8
Queen Charlotte's Cottage, Kew Gardens RCH/KEW TW9 155 J8
Queen Eleanor's CE Junior School GUW GU2 267 L1
Queen Elizabeth College KENS W8 14 E1
Queen Elizabeth Conference Centre WEST SW1P 17 K2
Queen Elizabeth Hall STHWK SE1 11 N9
Queen Elizabeth Hospital WOOL/PLUM SE18 162 C5
Queen Elizabeth II Hospital WGCE AL7 23 K9
Queen Elizabeth II School MV/WKIL W9 8 D2
Queen Elizabeth Leisure Centre BAR EN5 77 J8
Queen Elizabeth Museum CHING E4 101 L1
Queen Elizabeths Boys School BAR EN5 76 G7
Queen Elizabeth's Foundation Training College LHD/OX KT22 236 C3
Queen Elizabeths Girls School BAR EN5 77 J8
Queen Elizabeth Stadium EN EN1 79 N6
Queenhithe Stairs BLKFR EC4V 12 E8
Queen Mary College WCHPL E1 140 C6
Queen Mary's Hospital HAMP NW3 117 M8
Queen Marys Hospital SCUP DA14 185 K8
Queen Mary's Hospital for Children SUT SM1 201 M8
Queen Mary's University Hospital PUT/ROE SW15 178 D2
Queen Mary & Westfield College SWFD E18 101 M9
Queen Mother Sports Centre PIM SW1V 16 G5
Queensbridge Primary School HACK E8 7 M4
Queensbridge Sports Centre HACK E8 7 M3
Queen's Building HTHAIR TW6 152 C9
Queensbury ⊖ STAN HA7 115 L1
Queens Business & Secretarial College SKENS SW7 15 L5
The Queens CE Primary School RCH/KEW TW9 155 L6
Queen's Club WKENS W14 14 A8
Queens College London CAVSQ/HST W1G 10 E4
Queens College Preparatory School CAVSQ/HST W1G 10 E3
The Queen's Gallery BGVA SW1W 16 F2
Queensgate Centre HLW CM20 29 H7
Queens Gate School SKENS SW7 15 L5
Queens Hospital ROMW/RG RM7 124 F5
The Queens House GNWCH SE10 161 J5
Queens Ice Rink & Bowl BAY/PAD W2 9 H8
Queens Manor Primary School FUL/PGN SW6 156 F6
Queensmead School RSLP HA4 113 L9
Queensmead Sports Centre RSLP HA4 113 L10
Queens Medical Centre RCHPK/HAM TW10 177 L1
Queensmere Shopping Centre SL SL1 149 L1
Queensmill School FUL/PGN SW6 157 K8
Queen's Park ⇌ KIL/WHAMP NW6 2 C8
Queens Park Community School WLSDN NW10 136 F3
Queens Park Health Centre NKENS W10 2 B9
Queens Park Primary School NKENS W10 8 B1
Queens Park Rangers FC (Loftus Road Stadium) SHB W12 136 E10
Queen's Road Cemetery CROY/NA CR0 203 K6
Queen's Road Peckham ⇌ ⊖ PECK SE15 160 A7
Queens School BUSH WD23 73 N7
Queens Schools WDSR SL4 149 H5
Queens Sports Centre GODL GU7 266 G10
Queens Theatre EMPK RM11 125 L5
SOHO/SHAV W1D 11 J7
Queenstown Road Battersea ⇌ VX/NE SW8 158 C7
Queensway ⊖ BAY/PAD W2 9 H8
Queensway Business Centre PEND EN3 80 B8
Queensway Health Centre HAT AL10 40 E3
Queenswell J & I School TRDG/WHET N20 97 N3
Queenswood School BRKMPK AL9 59 N4
Queen Victoria Memorial WHALL SW1A 16 G2
The Questors Theatre EA W5 135 H9
Quintin Kynaston School Technology College STJWD NW8 3 K6
Quwwat UL Islam Girl's School FSTGT E7 141 M1
Rabbsfarm Primary School WDR/YW UB7 131 N8
Racecourse Yacht Basin WDSR SL4 148 E6
Radcliffe College SOHO/SHAV W1D 10 G6
Radisson Edwardian Berkshire Hotel OXSTW W1C 10 E6
Radisson Edwardian Grafton Hotel CAMTN NW1 10 G1
Radisson Edwardian Hampshire Hotel LSQ/SEVD WC2H 11 K8
Radisson Edwardian Hotel HYS/HAR UB3 152 D6
Radisson Edwardian Kenilworth Hotel RSQ WC1B 11 K4
Radisson Edwardian Marlborough Hotel NOXST/BSQ WC1A 11 K5
Radisson Edwardian Mayfair Hotel MYFR/PICC W1J 10 F8
Radisson Edwardian Mountbatten Hotel LSQ/SEVD WC2H 11 L6
Radisson Edwardian Vanderbilt Hotel SKENS SW7 15 K5
Radisson SAS Portman Hotel MBLAR W1H 10 B5
Radlett ⇌ RAD WD7 74 F1
Radlett CC RAD WD7 74 G3
Radlett Lodge School RAD WD7 57 H8
Radlett Preparatory School RAD WD7 75 H4
RAF Uxbridge HGDN/ICK UB10 131 P3
RAF West Ruislip (University of Maryland) HGDN/ICK UB10 112 D7
Raglan Infant School EN EN1 79 M10
Raglan Junior School EN EN1 99 M1
Raglan Primary School HAYES BR2 205 P4
Railton Road Clinic HNHL SE24 181 J1
Rainbow Industrial Estate RYNPK SW20 200 E2
WDR/YW UB7 131 N9
Rainbow Leisure Centre EW KT17 220 B8
Rainbow Natural Health Centre REDH RH1 276 A1
Rainbow Quay BERM/RHTH SE16 160 D2

**Rainbow School for Autistic Children**
*WAND/EARL* SW18 179 M5
**Raines Foundation School**
*BETH* E2 140 A5
**Rainham ⇌**
*RAIN* RM13 144 G6
**Rainham Cemetery**
*RAIN* RM13 145 K5
**Rainham Hall (NT)**
*RAIN* RM13 145 H6
**Rainham Marshes RSPB Reserve**
*RAIN* RM13 145 J9
**Rainham Trading Estate**
*RAIN* RM13 144 F5
**Rainham Village Primary School**
*RAIN* RM13 145 H6
**The Raleigh School**
*EHSLY* KT24 252 D1
**Ramac Industrial Estate**
*CHARL* SE7 161 M4
**Ramada Encore Hotel**
*ACT* W3 136 A7
**Ramada Hotel**
*BAY/PAD* W2 8 G8
*CRAWE* RH10 284 B5
*EA* W5 135 L9
*EHSLY* KT24 252 G5
*GSTN* WD25 74 B7
*HAT* AL10 40 B4
**Rambert School**
*TWK* TW1 176 G1
**Randal Cremer Primary School**
*BETH* E2 7 L7
**Randalls Park Crematorium**
*LHD/OX* KT22 236 D6
**Randolph Medical Centre**
*DTCH/LGLY* SL3 149 N6
**Ranelagh Gardens (site of Chelsea Flower Show)**
*BGVA* SW1W 16 D8
**Ranelagh Primary School**
*SRTFD* E15 141 K4
**Rangefield Primary School**
*BMLY* BR1 183 K8
**Ransomes Dock Business Centre**
*BTSEA* SW11 157 P6
**Raphael Independent School**
*EMPK* RM11 125 H4
**The Rathbone Education Centre**
*CAN/RD* E16 141 L7
**Rathbow Clinic**
*BAY/PAD* W2 9 M2
**Rathfern Primary School**
*FSTH* SE23 182 E4
**Ravenor Primary School**
*GFD/PVL* UB6 133 P5
**Ravensbourne ⇌**
*BECK* BR3 183 H10
**Ravensbourne College of Design & Communication**
*CHST* BR7 184 D8
**Ravensbourne School**
*HARH* RM3 105 L9
**The Ravensbourne School**
*HAYES* BR2 205 N4
**Ravenscourt Park ⊖**
*HMSMTH* W6 156 D3
**Ravenscourt Park Preparatory School**
*HMSMTH* W6 156 D3
**Ravenscroft Medical Centre**
*GLDGN* NW11 117 J5
**Ravenscroft Primary School**
*CAN/RD* E16 141 M6
**Ravenscroft School**
*TRDG/WHET* N20 97 J1
**Ravenside Retail Park**
*UED* N18 100 C7
**Ravens Lawn Tennis Club**
*NFNCH/WDSPK* N12 97 N5
**Ravensquay Business Centre**
*STMC/STPC* BR5 207 L5
**Ravenstone Preparatory School**
*SKENS* SW7 15 K4
**Ravenstone Primary School**
*BAL* SW12 180 B4
**Ravenswood Industrial Estate**
*WALTH* E17 121 H2
**Ravens Wood School**
*HAYES* BR2 206 A10
**Ray Lodge Primary School**
*WFD* IG8 102 A7
**Raynehurst Community Primary School**
*GVE* DA12 191 J6
**Rayners Lane ⊖**
*RYLN/HDSTN* HA2 113 N6
**Raynes Park ⇌**
*RYNPK* SW20 200 F2
**Raynes Park High School**
*RYNPK* SW20 200 E3
**Raynes Park Sports Ground**
*RYNPK* SW20 200 D2
**Raynes Park Vale FC**
*RYNPK* SW20 200 G5
**Raynham Primary School**
*UED* N18 99 P6
**Reay Primary School**
*BRXN/ST* SW9 159 H6
**Records Office**
*CLKNW* EC1R 12 B1
**Rectory Business Centre**
*SCUP* DA14 185 L7
**Rectory Road ⇌**
*STNW/STAM* N16 119 P8
**Redbridge ⊖**
*REDBR* IG4 122 A4
**Redbridge College**
*CHDH* RM6 123 L3
**Redbridge Drama Centre**
*SWFD* E18 101 M9
**Redbridge Museum**
*IL* IG1 122 E8
**Redbridge Primary School**
*REDBR* IG4 122 B3
**Redbridge Sports Centre**
*BARK/HLT* IG6 102 G9
**Redburn Industrial Estate**
*PEND* EN3 80 C10
**Redcliffe School**
*WBPTN* SW10 15 J9
**Redden Court School**
*HARH* RM3 125 N1
**Reddiford School**
*PIN* HA5 113 M2
**Reddings Primary School**
*HHS/BOV* HP3 36 B8
**Redford Lodge Psychiatric Hospital**
*ED* N9 99 P3
**Red Gates School**
*CROY/NA* CR0 223 H2
**Redhill ⇌**
*REDH* RH1 258 B9
**Redhill Aerodrome**
*REDH* RH1 276 F5
**Redhill Business Centre**
*REDH* RH1 258 A9
**Redhill College**
*REDH* RH1 276 C1
**Redhill FC**
*REDH* RH1 276 A4
**Redhill Lawn Tennis Club**
*REDH* RH1 258 A8
**Redhill Primary School**
*CHST* BR7 184 E9
**Redhill & Reigate Golf Club**
*REDH* RH1 275 N3
**Red House (NT)**
*BXLYHS* DA6 163 P10
**Redlands Primary School**
*WCHPL* E1 140 B7
**Redlibbets Golf Club**
*BGR/WK* TN15 211 J9
**Red Lion Business Park**
*SURB* KT6 199 L9
**Redriff Primary School**
*BERM/RHTH* SE16 160 D1
**Red Rose Trading Estate**
*EBAR* EN4 77 N9
**Redstone Cemetery**
*REDH* RH1 276 C1
**Reedham ⇌**
*PUR/KEN* CR8 222 G9
**Reedham Park School**
*PUR/KEN* CR8 223 H10
**Reed Place Business Park**
*SHPTN* TW17 196 A8
**Reeds School**
*COB* KT11 217 P8
**Reeves Corner ⊖**
*CROY/NA* CR0 203 J9
**Regal International College**
*ALP/SUD* HA0 115 K10
**Regent Business Centre**
*HYS/HAR* UB3 153 J1
**Regent Clinic**
*CAVSQ/HST* W1G 10 E4
**Regent College London**
*PIN* HA5 113 N5
**Regent's Park ⊖**
*CAMTN* NW1 10 E2
**Regent's Park Barracks**
*CAMTN* NW1 4 E8
**Regent's Park Clinic**
*CAMTN* NW1 10 A1
**Regent's Park Medical Centre**
*CAMTN* NW1 4 F9
**Regent's Park Open Air Theatre**
*CAMTN* NW1 4 C10
**Regent's Park Track**
*STJWD* NW8 4 A7
**Regina Coeli RC Primary School**
*SAND/SEL* CR2 223 J4
**Reigate ⇌**
*REIG* RH2 257 K9
**Reigate College**
*REIG* RH2 257 L9
**Reigate Day Hospital**
*REDH* RH1 257 N10
**Reigate Grammar School**
*REIG* RH2 257 M10
**Reigate Heath Golf Club**
*REIG* RH2 256 F10
**Reigate Hill Golf Club**
*REIG* RH2 258 B4
**Reigate Parish Infant School**
*REIG* RH2 257 M10
**Reigate Priory Junior School**
*REIG* RH2 257 K10
**Reigate Priory Museum**
*REIG* RH2 257 K10
**Reigate St Marys Preparatory & Choir School**
*REIG* RH2 257 L10
**Reigate School**
*REIG* RH2 275 M3
**Renaissance Hotel**
*HTHAIR* TW6 152 C7
**Renoir Cinema**
*BMSBY* WC1N 11 M1
**Renwick Industrial Estate**
*BARK* EC2Y 143 L4
**The Retail Business Centre**
*EW* KT17 220 C6
**Rewards Centre**
*HSLW* TW3 154 B9
**Reynard Mills Trading Estate**
*BTFD* TW8 155 H4
**Reynolds Health & Fitness**
*RDART* DA2 186 F5
**Reynolds Sports Centre**
*ACT* W3 155 M1
**Rhoda McGaw Theatre & Cinema**
*WOKN/KNAP* GU21 232 B3
**Rhodes Avenue Primary School**
*WDGN* N22 98 D9
**Rhodes Farm Clinic**
*MLHL* NW7 96 F5
**RHS Garden Wisley**
*RPLY/SEND* GU23 234 A4
**Rhyl Primary School**
*KTTN* NW5 4 C1
**RIBA Library Drawings & Manuscript Collection**
*MBLAR* W1H 10 B5
**Ricards Lodge High School**
*WIM/MER* SW19 179 J7
**Richard Alibon Primary School**
*DAGE* RM10 124 B10
**Richard Atkins Primary School**
*BRXS/STRHM* SW2 180 F3
**Richard Cloudesley School**
*STLK* EC1Y 12 E2
**Richard Cobden Primary School**
*CAMTN* NW1 5 H6
**Richard Hale School**
*HERT/BAY* SG13 25 L6
**Richdales Institute**
*ALP/SUD* HA0 135 J3
**Rich Industrial Estate**
*STHWK* SE1 19 K4
**Richings Park Golf Club**
*DTCH/LGLY* SL3 150 G3
**Richings Park Sports Club**
*WDR/YW* UB7 151 J2
**Richmond ⇌ ⊖ ⊖**
*RCH/KEW* TW9 155 K10
**Richmond Adult & Community College**
*RCH/KEW* TW9 155 J10
**Richmond American International University**
*KENS* W8 14 G2
*RCHPK/HAM* TW10 177 K2
**The Richmond Clinic**
*RCH/KEW* TW9 155 L10
**Richmond Community College**
*TWK* TW1 176 E4
**Richmond FC**
*RCH/KEW* TW9 155 J10
**Richmond Gate Hotel**
*RCHPK/HAM* TW10 177 K3
**The Richmond Golf Club**
*RCHPK/HAM* TW10 177 K5
**The Richmond Green Medical Centre**
*RCH/KEW* TW9 177 J1
**Richmond Hill Hotel**
*RCHPK/HAM* TW10 177 K3
**Richmond House School**
*HPTN* TW12 175 N8
**Richmond Park Golf Club**
*PUT/ROE* SW15 178 B3
**Richmond Park National Nature Reserve**
*RCHPK/HAM* TW10 178 B5
**Richmond Road Medical Centre**
*KUTN/CMB* KT2 177 K10
**Richmond Theatre**
*RCH/KEW* TW9 155 J10
**Richmond upon Thames College**
*WHTN* TW2 176 D3
**Rickmansworth ⇌ ⊖**
*RKW/CH/CXG* WD3 91 N1
**Rickmansworth Park Primary School**
*RKW/CH/CXG* WD3 91 P1
**Rickmansworth PNEU School**
*RKW/CH/CXG* WD3 71 M10
**Rickmansworth Public Golf Club**
*RKW/CH/CXG* WD3 92 A3
**Rickmansworth School**
*RKW/CH/CXG* WD3 72 A10
**Rickmansworth Sports Club**
*RKW/CH/CXG* WD3 71 P10
**Riddlesdown ⇌**
*PUR/KEN* CR8 223 K8
**Riddlesdown High School**
*PUR/KEN* CR8 223 M10
**Ridge House Clinic**
*WCHMH* N21 99 L1
**Ridgeway Hotel**
*CHING* E4 100 G3
**Ridgeway Primary School**
*SAND/SEL* CR2 223 M5
**Rio Cinema**
*HACK* E8 119 N10
**Ripley Arts Centre**
*BMLY* BR1 206 A1
**Ripley CE Infant School**
*RPLY/SEND* GU23 233 L7
**Ripley Court School**
*RPLY/SEND* GU23 233 M7
**Ripley CC**
*RPLY/SEND* GU23 233 M7
**Ripple Infant School**
*BARK* EC2Y 143 H3
**Rippleside Cemetery**
*BARK* EC2Y 143 K3
**Risebridge Golf Club**
*ROM* RM1 104 G8
**Rise Park Primary School**
*ROM* RM1 104 E9
**Risley Avenue Primary School**
*TOTM* N17 99 M9
**The Ritz Hotel**
*WHALL* SW1A 10 G9
**Ritzy Cinema**
*BRXN/ST* SW9 159 H10
**Riverbank Park Plaza Hotel**
*STHWK* SE1 17 N6
**River Brent Business Park**
*HNWL* W7 154 D2
**Riverdene Industrial Estate**
*WOT/HER* KT12 217 L2
**River Gardens Business Centre**
*EBED/NFELT* TW14 153 J10
**River House Montessori School**
*POP/IOD* E14 140 F10
**River Lee Country Park**
*WAB* EN9 44 G10
*WAB* EN9 62 G5
**Riverley Primary School**
*LEY* E10 120 F6
**River Mole Business Park**
*ESH/CLAY* KT10 197 P8
**River Park Industrial Estate**
*BERK* HP4 33 M4
**River Place Health Centre**
*IS* N1 6 E4
**River Road Business Park**
*BARK* EC2Y 143 H5
**Riversdale Primary School**
*WAND/EARL* SW18 179 K4
**Riverside Business Centre**
*WAND/EARL* SW18 179 L4
**The Riverside Business Centre**
*GU* GU1 249 P10
**Riverside Business Park**
*WIM/MER* SW19 201 M1
**Riverside Community Health Care**
*WKENS* W14 156 G2
**Riverside Golf Club**
*THMD* SE28 143 P8
**Riverside Industrial Estate**
*BARK* EC2Y 143 K5
*DART* DA1 187 M1
*LCOL/BKTW* AL2 57 K3
**Riverside Primary School**
*BERM/RHTH* SE16 19 P2
**Riverside Quarter**
*WAND/EARL* SW18 157 K10
**Riverside Retail Park**
*RSEV* TN14 247 K5
**Riverside School**
*STMC/STPC* BR5 207 M2
**Riverside Shopping Centre**
*HHW* HP1 35 M7
**Riverside Studios Cinema**
*HMSMTH* W6 156 F4
**Riverside Swimming Centre**
*ERITH* DA8 164 F4
**Riverside Wandle Trading Estate**
*MTCM* CR4 202 A7
**Riverston School**
*LEE/GVPK* SE12 183 M1
**Riverview C E Primary School**
*HOR/WEW* KT19 219 P1
**Riverview Clinic**
*GVE* DA12 191 J8
**Riverview Junior School**
*GVE* DA12 191 H7
**Riverway Industrial Estate**
*RGUW* GU3 267 P9
**The RJ Mitchell Primary School**
*HCH* RM12 145 J1
**RNLI Lifeboat Station**
*TWRH* EC3N 13 K9
**Roan Industrial Estate**
*MTCM* CR4 201 P1
**Robert Blair Primary School**
*HOLWY* N7 5 M2
**Robert Browning Primary School**
*WALW* SE17 18 F7
**Robertswood Combined School**
*CFSP/GDCR* SL9 90 C8
**Robin Hood Infant School**
*SUT* SM1 221 K2
**Robin Hood Junior School**
*SUT* SM1 221 L2
**Robin Hood Lane Health Centre**
*SUT* SM1 221 K2
**Robin Hood Primary School**
*KUTN/CMB* KT2 178 A8
**Robinsfield Infant School**
*STJWD* NW8 3 M7
**The Roche School**
*WAND/EARL* SW18 179 K1
**Rockliffe Manor Primary School**
*WOOL/PLUM* SE18 163 J5
**Rockmount Primary School**
*NRWD* SE19 181 K9
**Rockware Business Centre**
*GFD/PVL* UB6 134 C3
**The Rockwell Hotel**
*ECT* SW5 14 G5
**Rodd Estate**
*SHPTN* TW17 196 D5
**Roding Lane Cemetery**
*WFD* IG8 102 B9
**Roding Primary School**
*BCTR* RM8 123 M9
*WFD* IG8 102 B8
**Roding Valley ⊖**
*BKHH* IG9 102 A5
**Roding Valley High School**
*LOU* IG10 82 B9
*LOU* IG10 82 E8
**Roebuck Hotel**
*WARE* SG12 26 B1
**Roebuck Road Trading Estate**
*BARK/HLT* IG6 103 L7
**Roe Green Junior School**
*CDALE/KGS* NW9 115 N2
**Roehampton Church School**
*PUT/ROE* SW15 178 E3
**The Roehampton Priory Hospital**
*PUT/ROE* SW15 156 C10
**Roehampton Recreation Centre**
*PUT/ROE* SW15 178 C3
**Roehampton University (Digby Stuart College)**
*PUT/ROE* SW15 178 C1
**Roehampton University (Froebel College)**
*PUT/ROE* SW15 178 C2
**Roehampton University (Southlands College)**
*PUT/ROE* SW15 178 C1
**Roehampton University (Whitelands College)**
*PUT/ROE* SW15 178 C3
**Roger Ascham Primary School**
*WALTH* E17 100 E9
**Roger Bannister Sports Ground**
*KTN/HRWW/WS* HA3 94 B7
**Rokeby School**
*KUTN/CMB* KT2 177 P10
*SRTFD* E15 141 J2
**Roke Primary School**
*PUR/KEN* CR8 223 K10
**Roker Park Golf Club**
*RGUW* GU3 249 J5
**Rokesly Junior School**
*CEND/HSY/T* N8 118 F3
**Roman Bath**
*TPL/STR* WC2R 11 P7
**Roman Industrial Estate**
*CROY/NA* CR0 203 M7
**Roman Road Primary School**
*EHAM* E6 142 A6
**Roman Theatre of Verulamium**
*STALW/RED* AL3 37 P6
**Romford ⇌**
*ROM* RM1 124 F4
**Romford Cemetery**
*ROMW/RG* RM7 124 D5
**Romford Clinic**
*ROM* RM1 124 G2
**Romford Golf Club**
*GPK* RM2 125 H1
**Romford Ice Arena**
*ROMW/RG* RM7 124 F5
**Romford IT Learning Centre**
*ROM* RM1 124 F3
**Romford Shopping Hall**
*ROM* RM1 124 F2
**Ronald Rose Primary School**
*PUT/ROE* SW15 178 G3
**Rood Lane Medical Centre**
*FENCHST* EC3M 13 J7
**Rooks Heath College for Business & Enterprise**
*RYLN/HDSTN* HA2 113 P8
**Roosevelt Memorial**
*MYFR/PKLN* W1K 10 D7
**Ropery Business Park**
*CHARL* SE7 161 P3
**Rosary Priory High School**
*BUSH* WD23 74 D10
**Rosary RC Infant School**
*HEST* TW5 153 N5
**Rosary RC Primary School**
*HAMP* NW3 117 P10
**Rosebery Industrial Park**
*TOTM* N17 100 A10
**Rosebery School**
*EPSOM* KT18 219 P10
**Rose Bruford College**
*BFN/LL* DA15 185 L4
**Rosedale Clinic**
*CHESW* EN7 61 P4
**Rosedale College**
*HYS/HAR* UB3 132 E8
**Roseland JMI School**
*HOD* EN11 26 E10
**Roselands Clinic**
*NWMAL* KT3 199 P4
**Rose McAndrew Clinic**
*BRXN/ST* SW9 158 G8
**Rosemead Preparatory School**
*DUL* SE21 181 K5
**Rosendale Primary School**
*DUL* SE21 181 K3
**Rose of Kingston (Kingston Theatre)**
*KUT/HW* KT1 199 J2
**Rose Theatre Exhibition**
*STHWK* SE1 12 E9
**Rosetta Primary School**
*CAN/RD* E16 141 N7
**Rosewood Medical Centre**
*HCH* RM12 125 J10
**Rosherville CE Primary School**
*GVW* DA11 190 B2
**Rosh Pinah Primary School**
*EDGW* HA8 95 N3
**Rosslyn Park RFC**
*PUT/ROE* SW15 156 C10
**Rotherfield Primary School**
*IS* N1 6 F5
**Rotherhithe ⊖**
*BERM/RHTH* SE16 160 B1
**Rotherhithe Civic Centre**
*BERM/RHTH* SE16 160 B1
**Rotherhithe Primary School**
*BERM/RHTH* SE16 160 B3
**The Rotunda**
*KUT/HW* KT1 199 K2
**The Roundhouse Theatre**
*CAMTN* NW1 4 C3
**Roundshaw J & I School**
*WLGTN* SM6 222 F4
**Rowan Preparatory School**
*ESH/CLAY* KT10 218 E4
**Rowans Primary School**
*WGCE* AL7 23 K2
**Rowans School**
*RYNPK* SW20 178 D10
**Rowfant Business Centre**
*CRAWE* RH10 285 M7
**Rowhill Grange Hotel**
*RDART* DA2 187 H8
**Rowhill School**
*RDART* DA2 187 K7
**Rowley Industrial Park**
*ACT* W3 155 N2
**Roxbourne First School**
*RYLN/HDSTN* HA2 113 M7
**Roxbourne Medical Centre**
*RYLN/HDSTN* HA2 114 A7
**Roxeth First & Middle School**
*RYLN/HDSTN* HA2 114 C7
**Roxeth Mead School**
*RYLN/HDSTN* HA2 114 C7
**Roxwell Trading Park**
*LEY* E10 120 D5
**Royal Academy of Arts**
*MYFR/PICC* W1J 10 G8
**Royal Academy of Dance**
*BTSEA* SW11 157 P7
**Royal Academy of Dramatic Art**
*GWRST* WC1E 11 J3
**Royal Academy of Music**
*CAMTN* NW1 10 D2
**Royal Adelaide Hotel**
*WDSR* SL4 149 J8
**Royal Air Force Museum London**
*CDALE/KGS* NW9 96 D10
**Royal Albert ⊖**
*CAN/RD* E16 142 B9
**Royal Albert Hall**
*SKENS* SW7 15 L2
**The Royal Alexandra & Albert School**
*REIG* RH2 257 P5
**Royal Arsenal**
*WOOL/PLUM* SE18 162 E2
**The Royal Ballet School**
*RCHPK/HAM* TW10 178 A4
**Royal Ballet Upper School**
*COVGDN* WC2E 11 M6
**The Royal Berkshire Hotel**
*ASC* SL5 192 F3
**Royal Blackheath Golf Club**
*ELTH/MOT* SE9 184 C3
**Royal Botanic Gardens, Kew**
*BTFD* TW8 155 K6
**Royal Botanic Gardens Kew School**
*RCH/KEW* TW9 155 L6
**Royal Brompton Hospital**
*CHEL* SW3 15 N7
**Royal Chace Hotel**
*ENC/FH* EN2 78 G4
**Royal College of Anaesthetists**
*RSQ* WC1B 11 L3
**Royal College of Art**
*SKENS* SW7 15 K2
*SKENS* SW7 15 K4
**Royal College of Art Sculpture School**
*BTSEA* SW11 157 P6
**Royal College of Music**
*SHB* W12 156 D2
*SKENS* SW7 15 L3
**Royal College of Nursing**
*CAMTN* NW1 11 H1
*IS* N1 6 C6
**Royal College of Obstetricians & Gynaecologists**
*CAMTN* NW1 10 A1
**Royal College of Ophthalmologists**
*CAMTN* NW1 10 C2
**Royal College of Paediatrics & Child Health**
*GTPST* W1W 10 F3
**The Royal College of Pathology**
*STJS* SW1Y 11 J10
**Royal College of Physicians**
*CAMTN* NW1 10 E1
**Royal College of Surgeons**
*LINN* WC2A 11 P5
**Royal College of Veterinary Surgeons**
*WEST* SW1P 17 L5
**Royal Courts of Justice**
*LINN* WC2A 11 P6
**Royal Court Theatre**
*BGVA* SW1W 16 C6
**Royal Court Young Peoples Theatre**
*NKENS* W10 8 B4
**The Royal Docks Community School**
*CAN/RD* E16 141 P8
**Royal Docks Medical Centre**
*EHAM* E6 142 D8
**Royal Epping Forest Golf Club**
*CHING* E4 101 K1
**Royal Exchange**
*BANK* EC3V 13 H6
**Royal Festival Hall**
*STHWK* SE1 11 N10
**The Royal First School (Crown Aided)**
*WDSR* SL4 171 H8
**Royal Free Hospital**
*HAMP* NW3 117 P10
**Royal Garden Hotel**
*KENS* W8 15 H1
**Royal Geographical Society**
*SKENS* SW7 15 L2
**Royal Grammar School**
*GU* GU1 268 B1
**Royal Gunpowder Mills**
*WAB* EN9 62 G8
**Royal Holloway**
*EGH* TW20 172 A9
**Royal Holloway University of London**
*EGH* TW20 194 A1
**Royal Holloway University of London (Hall of Residence)**
*EGH* TW20 172 A7
**The Royal Horseguards Hotel**
*WHALL* SW1A 11 M10
**Royal Horticultural Society New Hall**
*WEST* SW1P 17 J4
**Royal Horticultural Society Old Hall**
*WEST* SW1P 17 J5
**Royal Hospital**
*RCH/KEW* TW9 155 K9
**Royal Hospital Chelsea**
*CHEL* SW3 16 C9
**Royal Hospital for Neuro-disability**
*PUT/ROE* SW15 179 H2
**Royal Hospital & Home**
*PUT/ROE* SW15 178 E3
**Royal Hospital Museum**
*CHEL* SW3 16 C8
**Royal Institute of British Architects**
*REGST* W1B 10 F3
**Royal Institution's Faraday Museum**
*MYFR/PICC* W1J 10 F8
**The Royal Kent CE Primary School**
*LHD/OX* KT22 218 B10
**Royal Lancaster Hotel**
*BAY/PAD* W2 9 M8
**The Royal Landscape**
*EGH* TW20 171 L9
**Royal Liberty School**
*GPK* RM2 125 K1
**The Royal London Estate**
*TOTM* N17 100 A8
**Royal London Homeopathic Hospital**
*BMSBY* WC1N 11 M3
**Royal Marsden Hospital**
*BELMT* SM2 221 M6
*CHEL* SW3 15 M7
**Royal Masonic School for Girls**
*RKW/CH/CXG* WD3 71 N9
**Royal Mews**
*WDSR* SL4 149 K7
**The Royal Mews**
*BGVA* SW1W 16 F3
**Royal Mid-Surrey Golf Club**
*RCH/KEW* TW9 155 J9
**Royal Military School of Music**
*WHTN* TW2 176 C2
**Royal Mint Court**
*TWRH* EC3N 13 M8
**Royal National Orthopaedic Hospital**
*GTPST* W1W 10 F2
*STAN* HA7 94 G2
**Royal National Theatre**
*STHWK* SE1 12 A9
**Royal National Throat Nose & Ear Hospital**
*FSBYW* WC1X 5 N9
**Royal Oak ⊖**
*BAY/PAD* W2 9 H4
**Royal Opera House**
*COVGDN* WC2E 11 M6
**Royal Park Primary School**
*SCUP* DA14 185 P6
**Royal Russell Preparatory School**
*CROY/NA* CR0 224 A3
**The Royal School**
*HAMP* NW3 117 N9
**Royal Society of Arts**
*CHCR* WC2N 11 M8
**Royal Society of Medicine**
*CAVSQ/HST* W1G 10 E5
**Royal Surrey County Hospital**
*GUW* GU2 249 K10
**Royal Terrace Pier**
*GVE* DA12 190 F1
**Royal Veterinary College**
*BRKMPK* AL9 58 G4
*CAMTN* NW1 5 J6
**Royal Victoria ⊖**
*CAN/RD* E16 141 M9
**Royal Victoria Docks Watersports Centre**
*CAN/RD* E16 141 M9
**Royal Wimbledon Golf Club**
*WIM/MER* SW19 178 E8
**Royal Windsor Racecourse**
*WDSR* SL4 148 F5
**Roydon ⇌**
*HLWW/ROY* CM19 27 M9
**Roydonbury Industrial Estate**
*HLWW/ROY* CM19 46 C1
**Roydon CP School**
*HLWW/ROY* CM19 45 N1
**Royston Primary School**
*PGE/AN* SE20 204 C1
**RSPCA Animal Hospital**
*FSBYPK* N4 118 G7
**Rudolf Steiner School**
*KGLGY* WD4 53 P5
**Rudolph Steiner Hall**
*CAMTN* NW1 10 A1
**Rufus Business Centre**
*WIM/MER* SW19 179 L5
**Ruislip ⊖**
*RSLP* HA4 112 F7
**Ruislip Gardens ⊖**
*RSLP* HA4 113 H9
**Ruislip Gardens Primary School**
*RSLP* HA4 112 F9
**Ruislip Golf Club**
*HGDN/ICK* UB10 112 D7
**Ruislip High School**
*RSLP* HA4 113 H8
**Ruislip Manor ⊖**
*RSLP* HA4 113 H6
**Ruislip Manor FC**
*RSLP* HA4 112 G7
**Ruislip RFC**
*RSLP* HA4 112 F7
**Ruislip Woods National Nature Reserve**
*NTHWD* HA6 112 D1
*RSLP* HA4 112 F3
**Runnymede**
*WDSR* SL4 171 P4
**Runnymede Hospital**
*CHERT* KT16 194 G10
**Runnymede Hotel & Spa**
*EGH* TW20 172 E6
**Runnymede (NT)**
*EGH* TW20 172 B6
**Rushcroft School**
*CHING* E4 100 G8
**Rushey Green Primary School**
*CAT* SE6 182 G4
**Rush Green Primary School**
*ROMW/RG* RM7 124 E6
**Rushmore Primary School**
*CLPT* E5 120 B9
**Ruskin House School**
*HNHL* SE24 181 K1
**Russell Clinic**
*STALW/RED* AL3 38 C6
**Russell House School**
*RSEV* TN14 247 J1
**The Russell JMI School**
*RCHPK/HAM* TW10 177 J5
**The Russell School**
*RCHPK/HAM* TW10 177 J4
*RKW/CH/CXG* WD3 70 E8
**Russell Square ⊖**
*STPAN* WC1H 11 L2
**Russet House School**
*EN* EN1 80 A5
**Rutherford Way Industrial Estate**
*CRAWE* RH10 284 B2
**Rutlish School**
*RYNPK* SW20 201 J2
**Ruxley Corner Industrial Estate**
*SCUP* DA14 185 N9
**Ruxley Park Golf Centre**
*STMC/STPC* BR5 207 N1
**Rydens School**
*WOT/HER* KT12 197 K10
**The Ryde Primary School**
*BRKMPK* AL9 40 F1
**Rydes Hill Preparatory School**
*RGUW* GU3 249 L8
**Rydon Business Centre**
*LHD/OX* KT22 236 F6
**Ryebrook Business Park**
*LHD/OX* KT22 236 F6
**Ryefield Primary School**
*HGDN/ICK* UB10 132 E3
**Rye House ⇌**
*HOD* EN11 45 H1
**Rye House Stadium**
*HOD* EN11 45 J1
**Ryelands Primary School**
*SNWD* SE25 204 A5
**Rye Meads RSPB Reserve**
*HOD* EN11 27 J10
**Rye Oak Primary School**
*PECK* SE15 160 A9
**Rye Park Industrial Estate**
*HOD* EN11 45 H1
**Ryvers School**
*DTCH/LGLY* SL3 150 A2
**Saatchi Gallery**
*CHEL* SW3 16 B7
**Sacred Heart Catholic Primary School**
*PUT/ROE* SW15 178 D1
**Sacred Heart High School**
*HMSMTH* W6 156 F3
**Sacred Heart Language College**
*KTN/HRWW/WS* HA3 94 D10
**Sacred Heart of Mary Girls School**
*UPMR* RM14 126 A7
**Sacred Heart RC Infant School**
*BTSEA* SW11 157 P8
**Sacred Heart RC JMI School**
*TRDG/WHET* N20 97 P3
**Sacred Heart RC Primary School**
*NWMAL* KT3 200 D4
*OXHEY* WD19 73 N10
*RSLP* HA4 112 F7
*TEDD* TW11 176 G10
*WARE* SG12 26 B2
**Sacred Heart RC School**
*CMBW* SE5 159 K7
**Sacred Heart School**
*HOLWY* N7 118 G10
**Saddlers Hall**
*CITYW* EC2V 12 F5
**Sadler's Wells Theatre**
*CLKNW* EC1R 6 B9
**Safari Cinema**
*CROY/NA* CR0 203 J8
**Safari Cinema & Bingo**
*HRW* HA1 114 E3
**Saffron Green Primary School**
*BORE* WD6 76 A8
**Sai Medical Centre**
*POP/IOD* E14 141 H9
**St Adrians RC Primary School**
*STAL* AL1 38 B9
**St Agathas RC Primary School**
*KUTN/CMB* KT2 177 L9
**St Agnes RC Primary School**
*BOW* E3 140 F5
*CRICK* NW2 117 H8
**St Aidans Primary School**
*FSBYPK* N4 119 H5
**St Aidans RC Primary School**
*IL* IG1 122 G6
**St Albans ⇌**
*STAL* AL1 38 E6
**St Albans Abbey ⇌**
*STAL* AL1 38 C8
**St Alban & St Stephen Infant School**
*STAL* AL1 38 E7
**St Alban & St Stephen RC JM School**
*STAL* AL1 38 F6
**St Albans Cathedral**
*STALW/RED* AL3 38 B6
**St Albans CE Primary School**
*HCIRC* EC1N 12 A3
**St Albans City FC**
*STAL* AL1 38 E5
**St Albans City Hospital**
*STALW/RED* AL3 38 B4
**St Albans Girls School**
*STALW/RED* AL3 38 D2
**St Albans Health Clinic**
*HGT* N6 118 B8

St Albans High School for Girls
STAL AL1 38 D5
St Albans Lawn Tennis Club
STALE/WH AL4 39 H4
St Albans Musical Museum
LCOL/BKTW AL2 56 A4
St Albans Music School
STALW/RED AL3 38 C3
St Albans Organ Museum
STAL AL1 38 G7
St Albans Primary School
HLW CM20 29 J9
St Albans Principal Health Centre
STAL AL1 38 C6
St Albans RC Aided Primary School
E/WMO/HCT KT8 198 A5
St Albans RC Church & School Presbytery
HCH RM12 125 H10
St Albans RC JMI School
HCH RM12 145 J2
St Albans Retail Park
STAL AL1 38 C8
St Albans Road Infant School
DART DA1 187 N2
St Albans School
STALW/RED AL3 38 B6
St Albert the Great RC Primary School
HHS/BOV HP3 36 B7
St Alfege with St Peter CE Primary School
GNWCH SE10 161 H5
St Aloysius College
HGT N6 118 D6
St Aloysius RC Infant School
CAMTN NW1 5 J9
St Aloysius RC Junior School
CAMTN NW1 5 H8
St Andrew & St Francis CE JMI School
CRICK NW2 136 D1
St Andrews Arts Centre
GVW DA11 190 E2
St Andrews Catholic School
LHD/OX KT22 237 H6
St Andrews CE J & I School
UX/CGN UB8 131 N3
St Andrews CE JMI School
TRDG/WHET N20 97 J3
St Andrews CE Primary School
CRAWE RH10 284 B8
EN EN1 79 L6
EPP CM16 66 D1
STHGT/OAK N14 98 D1
St Andrews CE VA High School
CROY/NA CR0 203 J10
St Andrews Greek School
CAMTN NW1 4 F2
St Andrews Primary School
BRXN/ST SW9 158 G8
COB KT11 217 K9
IS N1 5 P5
WARE SG12 27 J7
St Andrews School
RYLN/HDSTN HA2 114 A3
WLSDN NW10 136 E2
St Andrew's School
WOKN/KNAP GU21 232 A2
St Angelas Ursuline School
FSTGT E7 141 N1
St Annes Catholic High School for Girls
ENC/FH EN2 79 L8
St Annes Catholic High School
PLMGR N13 99 H5
St Annes Catholic Primary School
BNSTD SM7 239 K2
CHERT KT16 195 K8
St Annes CE Primary School
WAND/EARL SW18 179 L1
St Annes CP School
STWL/WRAY TW19 173 P3
St Annes RC Primary School
VX/NE SW8 17 N9
WCHPL E1 13 N2
St Anne's Special School
MRDN SM4 201 K5
St Anne's Trading Estate
POP/IOD E14 140 E8
St Anns CE Primary School
SEVS/STOTM N15 119 L3
St Ann's General Hospital
FSBYPK N4 119 K3
St Anns Heath Junior School
VW GU25 194 C5
St Anns School
HNWL W7 134 D10
St Ann's Shopping Centre
HRW HA1 114 D4
St Anselms RC Primary School
DART DA1 187 N1
HRW HA1 114 D5
NWDGN UB2 153 N2
TOOT SW17 180 B6
St Anthonys Hospital
WPK KT4 200 G8
St Anthonys RC Primary School
EDUL SE22 181 P2
PGE/AN SE20 204 A1
SLN SL2 129 H5
WATW WD18 72 F9
St Anthony's School (Junior House)
HAMP NW3 117 N10
St Anthony's School (Senior House)
HAMP NW3 117 M10
St Antonys RC Primary School
FSTGT E7 141 M2
WFD IG8 101 M5
St Aubyns School
WFD IG8 101 L8
St Augustines CE High School
KIL/WHAMP NW6 2 F8
St Augustines Primary School
BELV DA17 164 A2
KIL/WHAMP NW6 2 F7
St Augustines Priory School
EA W5 135 K7
St Augustines RC Infant School
GNTH/NBYPK IG2 122 E3
St Augustines RC Primary School
CAT SE6 182 G8
GNTH/NBYPK IG2 122 E3
HOD EN11 44 G4
WKENS W14 14 B10
St Barnabas CE Primary School
BGVA SW1W 16 D7
St Barnabas & St Philip's CE Primary School
KENS W8 14 E4
St Bartholomews CE Primary School
SYD SE26 182 B7
St Bartholomews Hospital
STBT EC1A 12 D4
SWLY BR8 208 G3
St Bartholomews Medical School
FARR EC1M 12 D2
St Bartholomews RC Primary School
SWLY BR8 208 F3
St Bartholomews & Royal London School of Medicine
FARR EC1M 12 E3
St Bartholomew's the Great
STBT EC1A 12 D4
St Barts Hospital Sports Ground
CHST BR7 184 G9
St Barts & the Royal London Hospital
WCHPL E1 140 A7
St Bedes CE Junior School
RPLY/SEND GU23 232 G10
St Bedes RC Infant School
BAL SW12 180 E4
St Bedes RC Primary School
CHDH RM6 123 M3
St Bedes School
REDH RH1 257 P7
St Benedicts Junior School
EA W5 135 H7
St Benedicts School
EA W5 135 J7
St Bernadette Catholic Junior School
BAL SW12 180 D3
St Bernadette RC Primary School
LCOL/BKTW AL2 57 J3
St Bernadettes RC Primary School
HGDN/ICK UB10 132 C3
KTN/HRWW/WS HA3 115 L2
St Bernards Catholic Grammar School
SL SL1 149 P1
St Bernards Preparatory School
SL SL1 149 N1
St Bonaventures School
FSTGT E7 141 M2
St Boniface RC Primary School
TOOT SW17 180 A8
St Botolphs CE Primary School
GVW DA11 190 A3
St Catherine of Sienna RC Primary School
GSTN WD25 55 L8
St Catherines Hoddeson CE Primary School
HOD EN11 44 G3
St Catherine's Hospice
CRAWE RH10 283 N9
St Catherines Preparatory School
SHGR GU5 268 C10
St Catherine's Primary School
REDH RH1 259 L9
St Catherines Primary School
WARE SG12 26 A1
St Catherines RC Girls School
BXLYHS DA6 186 C1
St Catherines RC J & I School
WDR/YW UB7 151 N1
St Catherines RC School
BAR EN5 77 J8
St Catherines School
TWK TW1 176 E5
St Cecilias CE School
WAND/EARL SW18 179 J3
St Cecilias RC Primary School
WPK KT4 200 G9
St Chads RC Primary School
SNWD SE25 203 M5
St Charles Borromeo RC Primary School
WEY KT13 196 B10
St Charles Hospital
NKENS W10 136 G7
St Charles Primary School
NKENS W10 136 G7
St Christinas RC Preparatory School
STJWD NW8 3 P7
St Christophers School
BECK BR3 205 H2
EPSOM KT18 220 B10
HAMP NW3 117 N10
WBLY HA9 115 L8
St Clare Business Park
HPTN TW12 176 B9
St Clement Danes CE Primary School
HOL/ALD WC2B 11 N6
St Clement Danes School
RKW/CH/CXG WD3 70 G6
St Clement & St James CE Primary School
NTGHL W11 8 A9
St Clements Hospital
BOW E3 140 E5
St Clements Junior School
CHES/WCR EN8 62 D3
St Clements Primary School
EW KT17 220 C5
St Columbas Preparatory School
STALW/RED AL3 38 A8
St Columbas RC Boys School
BXLYHS DA6 186 C1
St Cross RC Primary School
HOD EN11 44 F5
St Cuthbert Mayne RC Primary School
HHW HP1 35 L5
St Cuthberts CE Primary School
EGH TW20 171 P10
St Cuthbert with St Mattias CE Primary School
ECT SW5 14 F7
St Cyprians Greek Orthodox Primary School
THHTH CR7 203 K2
St Davids College
WWKM BR4 204 G7
St Davids Health Centre
STWL/WRAY TW19 173 N3
St Davids School
ASHF TW15 174 A6
PUR/KEN CR8 222 G7
St Dominic RC Primary School
HARP AL5 20 A3
St Dominics RC Primary School
HAMP NW3 118 A10
HOM E9 140 D1
St Dominics Sixth Form College
HRW HA1 114 D7
St Dunstans Catholic Primary School
WOKS/MYFD GU22 232 D3
St Dunstans CE Primary School
CHEAM SM3 221 H3
St Dunstans College
CAT SE6 182 E4
St Ebba's Hospital
HOR/WEW KT19 219 P5
St Edmunds RC Primary School
ED N9 100 A2
POP/IOD E14 160 F3
WHTN TW2 176 A3
St Edwards Catholic First School
WDSR SL4 148 F7
St Edwards CE Comprehensive School
CHDH RM6 124 B4
St Edwards CE Primary School
ROM RM1 124 E2
St Edwards RC JMI School
STJWD NW8 9 N2
St Edwards Royal Free Ecumenical School
WDSR SL4 148 F7
St Elizabeths RC Primary School
BETH E2 140 B4
RCHPK/HAM TW10 177 L2
St Ethelberts Catholic Primary School
SLN SL2 129 M8
St Eugene de Mazenod RC Primary School
KIL/WHAMP NW6 2 F4
St Faiths CE School
WAND/EARL SW18 179 L1
St Fidelis Catholic Primary School
ERITH DA8 164 D5
St Francesca Cabrini Primary School
FSTH SE23 182 B2
St Francis Catholic School
CTHM CR3 241 N7
St Francis de Sales RC J & I School
TOTM N17 99 N8
St Francis of Assisi Primary School
CRAWE RH10 283 P8
NKENS W10 136 G9
St Francis RC Primary School
PECK SE15 19 P10
SRTFD E15 121 K10
St Francis, Westborough Primary School
GUW GU2 249 L9
St Francis Xavier College
BAL SW12 180 C2
St Gabriels CE Primary School
PIM SW1V 16 G8
St Georges Business Park
WEY KT13 216 B5
St George's Cathedral
STHWK SE1 18 B3
St Georges CE Infant School
AMSS HP7 69 K4
St Georges Centre
GVW DA11 190 E2
St Georges CE Primary School
BMLY BR1 205 P2
CMBW SE5 159 M6
VX/NE SW8 158 D7
St Georges CE School
GVW DA11 190 D5
St George's Chapel
WDSR SL4 149 J6
St George's College
ADL/WDHM KT15 195 N10
St Georges College
HOLWY N7 119 H8
St George's College Track
ADL/WDHM KT15 195 N9
St Georges Elizabethan Theatre
HOLWY N7 118 E9
St Georges Hanover Square CE Primary School
MYFR/PKLN W1K 10 D8
St George's Hill Golf Club
WEY KT13 216 D7
St Georges Hospital
HCH RM12 125 L9
TOOT SW17 179 P8
St Georges Industrial Estate
AMSS HP7 69 L4
KUTN/CMB KT2 177 J8
PLMGR N13 99 J8
St Georges Medical Centre
HDN NW4 116 E1
St Georges Pre-Preparatory School
WDSR SL4 149 J6
St Georges RC Primary School
ENC/FH EN2 79 L6
HRW HA1 114 E8
St Georges RC School
MV/WKIL W9 3 H8
St Georges School
ASC SL5 192 A4
St Georges School Technology College
HARP AL5 20 A1
St Georges Shopping Centre & Cinema
HRW HA1 114 C4
St Georges University of London
TOOT SW17 179 N8
St George the Martyr CE Primary School
BMSBY WC1N 11 N2
St George Wharf
VX/NE SW8 17 L9
St Gildas RC Junior School
CEND/HSY/T N8 118 F5
St Giles CE (Aided) Infant School
ASHTD KT21 237 L4
St Giles College London Central
RSQ WC1B 11 M3
St Giles Primary School
POTB/CUF EN6 58 D8
St Giles School
SAND/SEL CR2 223 J3
St Gregorys High School
KTN/HRWW/WS HA3 115 J3
St Gregorys RC Primary School
EA W5 135 H6
St Helens Catholic Infant School
WALTH E17 121 H3
St Helens Catholic Junior School
BRWN CM15 107 J1
St Helens College
HGDN/ICK UB10 132 B2
St Helens Primary School
STALE/WH AL4 21 J3
St Helens RC Primary School
BRXN/ST SW9 159 H9
CAN/RD E16 141 L6
St Helens School
NTHWD HA6 92 F7
St Helier ⇌
MRDN SM4 201 K6
St Helier Hospital
CAR SM5 201 M8
St Hildas School
BUSH WD23 94 A1
St Hugh of Lincoln RCP School
WOKN/KNAP GU21 231 J5
St Ignatius College
ENC/FH EN2 79 P3
St Ignatius RC Primary School
SEVS/STOTM N15 119 M4
SUN TW16 197 H1
St James CE J & I School
BERM/RHTH SE16 19 N3
St James CE Primary School
HLWS CM18 46 G5
MUSWH N10 118 B2
NWCR SE14 160 D7
PEND EN3 80 B6
WEY KT13 196 D10
St James CE Junior School
FSTGT E7 121 L10
St James Independent School for Girls
NTGHL W11 8 E7
WKENS W14 14 C5
St James Independent School for Senior Boys
TWK TW1 176 F5
St James Independent Schools for Juniors
WKENS W14 14 B5
St James & Lucie Clayton College
SKENS SW7 15 H6
St James Medical Centre
CROY/NA CR0 203 L7
St James RC Primary School
HAYES BR2 206 E5
WHTN TW2 176 D6
St James Street ⇌
WALTH E17 120 D3
St James's Health Centre
WALTH E17 120 D3
St James's Palace
WHALL SW1A 11 H10
St James's Park ⊖
STJSPK SW1H 17 J3
St James the Great RC Primary School
PECK SE15 159 N7
THHTH CR7 203 J2
St Joachims RC Primary School
CAN/RD E16 141 P8
St Joan of Arc RC Primary School
HBRY N5 119 J9
St Joan of Arc RC School
RKW/CH/CXG WD3 91 P1
St John Fisher RC First & Middle School
PIN HA5 113 P2
St John Fisher RC Primary School
ERITHM DA18 163 P2
GFD/PVL UB6 135 H5
LOU IG10 82 F6
RYNPK SW20 200 F5
STALE/WH AL4 39 H3
St John of Jerusalem CE Primary School
HOM E9 140 B2
St Johns ⇌
DEPT SE8 160 F8
St Johns & St James CE School
UED N18 99 N6
St Johns Angell Town CE Primary School
BRXN/ST SW9 159 H8
St Johns Beaumont School
WDSR SL4 171 N5
St John's CE Community Primary School
DORK RH4 272 G5
St Johns CE J & I (Mixed) School
WGCW AL8 22 C6
St Johns CE Primary School
BETH E2 140 B4
BKHH IG9 101 N2
CROY/NA CR0 204 C10
CTHM CR3 260 A2
ENC/FH EN2 79 J2
FBAR/BDGN N11 98 A5
KUT/HW KT1 199 K3
PGE/AN SE20 182 B10
SEV TN13 247 L9
TRDG/WHET N20 97 M3
WLYN AL6 23 J1
St Johns CE School
CDALE/KGS NW9 116 B3
St John's CE Walham Green Primary School
FUL/PGN SW6 157 H7
St Johns Church of England School
STAN HA7 94 F5
St John's Concert Hall
WEST SW1P 17 L4
St Johns CP School
WOKN/KNAP GU21 231 K4
St Johns Highbury Vale CE Primary School
HBRY N5 119 J9
St John's Hospital Day Centre
BTSEA SW11 157 N10
St Johns Infant School
RAD WD7 74 E1
St John's Lodge
CAMTN NW1 4 C9
St Johns Preparatory School
POTB/CUF EN6 59 P10
St Johns Primary School
REDH RH1 275 P2
WEA W13 134 F9
St Johns RC Comprehensive School
GVE DA12 190 G4
St Johns RC Primary School
BERM/RHTH SE16 160 D1
GVE DA12 190 G4
RKW/CH/CXG WD3 91 L2
St Johns RC Special School
WFD IG8 102 D6
St Johns & St Clements CE J & I School
PECK SE15 159 P9
St Johns School
EPP CM16 65 H6
LHD/OX KT22 236 G7
NTHWD HA6 93 J7
St Johns Senior School
ENC/FH EN2 79 H5
St Johns Upper Holloway CE Primary School
ARCH N19 118 D7
St Johns Walworth CE Primary School
WALW SE17 18 E6
St Johns Way Medical Centre
ARCH N19 118 E6
St John's Wood ⊖
STJWD NW8 3 L7
St Johns Wood Pre-Preparatory School
STJWD NW8 3 N9
St John the Baptist CE Junior School
KUT/HW KT1 177 J10
St John the Baptist CE Primary School
BMLY BR1 183 H7
St John the Baptist Primary School
WARE SG12 26 F6
St John the Baptist School
WOKS/MYFD GU22 232 D5
St John the Baptist VA CE Primary School
IS N1 7 J8
St John the Divine CE Primary School
CMBW SE5 159 J6
St John the Evangelist RC Primary School
IS N1 6 C7
St John Vianney RC Primary School
SEVS/STOTM N15 119 J2
St Joseph's Annexe
ABYW SE2 163 M5
St Josephs Catholic High School
SLN SL2 129 M8
St Josephs Catholic Infant School
LEY E10 120 E6
St Josephs Catholic Junior School
CMBW SE5 159 K6
St Josephs Catholic Primary School
BMLY BR1 183 P10
DAGW RM9 124 A9
EPSOM KT18 219 P10
REDH RH1 257 P9
St Josephs CE Combined School
CFSP/GDCR SL9 109 P1
St Josephs College
STRHM/NOR SW16 181 J9
St Josephs Convent Preparatory School
GVE DA12 190 F5
St Josephs Convent School
WAN E11 121 M4
St Josephs in the Park
HERT/WAT SG14 25 H7
St Joseph's Primary School
HERT/WAT SG14 25 H4
St Josephs Primary School
WAND/EARL SW18 179 K1
St Joseph's RC College
MLHL NW7 96 C5
St Josephs RC First & Middle School
KTN/HRWW/WS HA3 94 F10
St Josephs RC Infant School
NRWD SE19 181 K9
St Josephs RC J & I School
HDN NW4 116 E2
St Josephs RC JMI School
CHES/WCR EN8 62 D9
St Josephs RC Junior School
LEY E10 120 F6
NRWD SE19 181 K9
WBLY HA9 115 L10
St Josephs RC Primary School
ARCH N19 118 C6
BARK EC2Y 142 F3
BERM/RHTH SE16 19 N2
CHEL SW3 16 A6
DART DA1 164 E10
DEPT SE8 160 F6
DORK RH4 272 F2
GNWCH SE10 161 K4
HNWL W7 134 D10
HOL/ALD WC2B 11 M5
KUT/HW KT1 199 K2
MV/WKIL W9 9 J1
OXHEY WD19 93 J4
STHWK SE1 18 F1
WLSDN NW10 136 B2
St Josephs RC School
GVW DA11 190 A3
St Josephs School
UPMR RM14 126 A7
St Joseph the Worker RC Primary School
RBRW/HUT CM13 87 P10
St Judes CE Junior School
EGH TW20 171 P9
St Judes CE Primary School
HNHL SE24 181 J2
STHWK SE1 18 C4
St Judes & St Pauls CE Primary School
IS N1 7 J1
St Katharine Pier
WAP E1W 13 M9
St Katharines Knockholt CE Primary School
RSEV TN14 245 L3
St Katherine
TPL/STR WC2R 11 P8
St Lawrence Business Centre
FELT TW13 175 J5
St Lawrence Catholic School
FELT TW13 175 J5
St Lawrence CE School
WAB EN9 63 L9
St Lawrence Junior School
E/WMO/HCT KT8 198 C3
St Lawrence Primary School
EHSLY KT24 253 L3
St Lawrence University
BMSBY WC1N 11 P2
St Leonards CE Primary School
STRHM/NOR SW16 180 E8
St Leonards Hospital
IS N1 7 K7
St Lukes Catholic Primary School
HLWW/ROY CM19 46 F3
St Luke's Catholic Sixth Form College
SCUP DA14 185 J8
St Luke's Cemetery
HAT AL10 40 E3
St Lukes Cemetery
HAYES BR2 206 C6
St Lukes CE Primary School
CAN/RD E16 141 L8
FSBYE EC1V 6 F10
KUTN/CMB KT2 199 L1
MV/WKIL W9 2 D8
POP/IOD E14 161 J3
WNWD SE27 181 K8
St Luke's Health Centre
CAN/RD E16 141 L8
St Lukes Hospital for the Clergy
FITZ W1T 10 G2
St Lukes School
THHTH CR7 203 H4
St Lukes Special School
LOU IG10 82 D8
St Lukes Woodside Hospital
MUSWH N10 118 B2
St Margaret Clitherow RC Primary School
THMD SE28 143 L10
St Margaret's ⇌
TWK TW1 176 G2
St Margarets ⇌
WARE SG12 27 H7
St Margarets Business Centre
TWK TW1 176 F3
St Margarets CE Primary School
CRAWW RH11 283 L6
WOOL/PLUM SE18 162 F5
St Margarets Clitherow RC Primary School
WBLY HA9 115 P8
St Margarets Hospital
EPP CM16 65 L5
St Margarets Primary School
BARK EC2Y 142 E3
St Margarets School
BUSH WD23 93 P1
HAMP NW3 117 L9
St Margaret's School
KWD/TDW/WH KT20 238 G7
St Marks Catholic School
HSLW TW3 153 N9
St Marks CE Academy
MTCM CR4 202 C2
St Marks CE Primary School
ARCH N19 118 F7
HAYES BR2 205 M3
LBTH SE11 17 P9
SNWD SE25 203 P4
St Marks Industrial Estate
CAN/RD E16 142 A10
St Marks Primary School
HNWL W7 154 D1
MTCM CR4 202 A2
St Marks West Essex Catholic School
HLWS CM18 47 H1
St Marthas Junior School
BAR EN5 77 H7
St Marthas Senior School
EBAR EN4 77 K5
St Martin-in-the-Fields
CHCR WC2N 11 L8
St Martin in the Fields High School
BRXS/STRHM SW2 181 J4
St Martin of Porres RC Primary School
FBAR/BDGN N11 98 D7
St Martins CE Junior School
EPSOM KT18 238 A1
St Martins CE Primary School
DORK RH4 272 E1
St Martins Hospital
MYFR/PKLN W1K 10 C7
St Martins House Business Centre
EHSLY KT24 252 F5
St Martins Medical Centre
RSLP HA4 112 F5
St Martins School
MLHL NW7 96 B6
RBRW/HUT CM13 107 P2
St Martins School of Art
SOHO/SHAV W1D 11 K6
St Martins Theatre
LSQ/SEVD WC2H 11 K7
St Martins Walk Shopping Centre
DORK RH4 272 G1
St Mary Abbots CE Primary School
KENS W8 14 G2
St Mary Abbots Church Hall
KENS W8 14 G1
St Mary & All Saints CE Primary School
BEAC HP9 88 D9
St Mary Cray ⇌
STMC/STPC BR5 207 K4
St Mary Cray Cemetery
STMC/STPC BR5 207 N4
The St Marylebone CE School
MHST W1U 10 D3
St Marylebone Crematorium
FNCH N3 117 L1
St Mary Magdalene CE Primary School
MV/WKIL W9 8 G2
WOOL/PLUM SE18 162 C3
St Mary Magdalen RC Junior School
CRICK NW2 136 E1
St Mary Magdalens Catholic Primary School
BROCKY SE4 160 D10
St Mary Magdalens Primary School
MORT/ESHN SW14 156 A9
St Mary of the Angels RC Primary School
NTGHL W11 8 E5
St Marys Abbey
MLHL NW7 96 D4
St Mary & St Michael Primary School
WCHPL E1 140 B8
St Mary & St Peters CE Primary School
TEDD TW11 176 D8
St Marys Bryanston Square CE Primary School
MBLAR W1H 9 P3
St Marys Catholic Primary School
CHING E4 101 J2
HCH RM12 125 H6
St Marys CE Combined School
AMSS HP7 68 G5
St Marys CE Infant School
LHD/OX KT22 237 H8
St Marys CE Junior School
CEND/HSY/T N8 118 F2
OXTED RH8 261 K4
STWL/WRAY TW19 173 P2
St Mary's Cemetery
AMSS HP7 68 G6
BTSEA SW11 179 P1
St Marys CE Primary School
BF/WBF KT14 215 P9
BRWN CM15 87 L10
CHSGTN KT9 219 K3
EBAR EN4 77 P10
FNCH N3 97 J9
IS N1 6 D4
LEW SE13 182 G1
PUT/ROE SW15 156 G9
SL SL1 149 M2
STNW/STAM N16 119 L7
SWLY BR8 208 F4
TWK TW1 176 F3
WALTH E17 120 G2
WLSDN NW10 136 B1
St Mary's CE School
HDN NW4 116 E1
St Marys First School
BERK HP4 33 K3
St Marys Greek Cathedral
WDGN N22 98 G9
St Marys Hare Park School
GPK RM2 125 K1
St Marys High School
CHESW EN7 62 A6
CROY/NA CR0 203 K8
St Marys Hospital
BAY/PAD W2 9 M5
St Marys Hospital Medical School
BAY/PAD W2 9 M5
St Marys Infant School
CAR SM5 221 P1
St Mary's Junior School
TWK TW1 176 G3
St Marys Kilburn Primary School
KIL/WHAMP NW6 2 F5
St Marys Primary School
BRKMPK AL9 40 E9
WKENS W14 156 G2
St Marys RC Infant School
CAR SM5 222 A2
St Marys RC J & I School
CROY/NA CR0 203 L8
St Marys RC Junior School
FSBYPK N4 119 L3
WALTH E17 121 H1
St Marys RC Primary School
BECK BR3 183 H10
CHSWK W4 156 B4
CLAP SW4 180 D1
ELTH/MOT SE9 184 D1
ISLW TW7 154 F9
KIL/WHAMP NW6 2 E7
NKENS W10 8 A2
PEND EN3 80 C8
TIL RM18 168 C8
UX/CGN UB8 131 M3
VX/NE SW8 158 C7
WIM/MER SW19 179 K10
St Marys & St Johns CE Primary School
HDN NW4 116 E3
St Marys School
CEND/HSY/T N8 118 G3
CFSP/GDCR SL9 110 B2
HAMP NW3 117 M10
St Marys School Ascot
ASC SL5 192 A7
St Marys Tutorial College
GUW GU2 267 P3
St Mary's Western Eye Hospital
MBLAR W1H 10 A3
St Matthew Academy
LEW SE13 161 J9
St Matthews CE (Aided) Infant School
COB KT11 235 J4
St Matthews CE Primary School
PEND EN3 80 B9
REDH RH1 258 A8
RYNPK SW20 200 D1
SURB KT6 199 K7
WDR/YW UB7 131 P10
St Matthias CE Primary School
BETH E2 13 M1
STNW/STAM N16 119 M10
St Meryl JMI School
OXHEY WD19 93 M4
St Michael & All Angels CE Academy
CMBW SE5 159 J6
St Michael at Bowes Junior School
PLMGR N13 99 H7
St Michaels & St Martins RC Primary School
HSLWW TW4 153 N9
St Michaels Catholic Grammar School
NFNCH/WDSPK N12 97 L6
St Michaels CE First School
RDKG RH5 255 H3
St Michaels CE Primary School
ASC SL5 192 C5
CAMTN NW1 4 G5
ENC/FH EN2 79 K5
HGT N6 118 B5
WAND/EARL SW18 179 J3
WDGN N22 98 G9
WELL DA16 163 M7
St Michaels CE VA Primary School
STALW/RED AL3 38 A6
St Michael's Manor Hotel
STALW/RED AL3 38 A6
St Michaels RC Primary School
EHAM E6 142 C4
St Michaels RC School
ASHF TW15 174 B8
GSTN WD25 55 K8
St Michaels RC Secondary School
BERM/RHTH SE16 19 N2
St Michaels Sydenham CE Primary School
SYD SE26 182 D7
The St Michael Steiner School
WAND/EARL SW18 179 K1
St Monica's RC Primary School
IS N1 7 J9
St Monicas RC Primary School
STHGT/OAK N14 98 F4
St Nicholas Centre
SUT SM1 221 L2

St Nicholas CE Primary School
*SHPTN* TW17 196 C6
St Nicholas Preparatory School
*SKENS* SW7 15 M2
St Nicholas School
*BORE* WD6 75 K10
*CDALE/KGS* NW9 115 P7
*CHST* BR7 184 F10
*HLWE* CM17 30 A8
*PUR/KEN* CR8 223 H10
*REDH* RH1 258 E5
St Nicolas CE Infant School
*GUW* GU2 267 P2
St Olaves Grammar School
*ORP* BR6 207 L10
St Olaves Preparatory School
*ELTH/MOT* SE9 184 E5
St Pancras Hospital
*CAMTN* NW1 5 J6
St Pancras International ⇌ ⊖
*CAMTN* NW1 5 L8
St Pancras International Youth Hostel
*CAMTN* NW1 5 K9
St Pancras & Islington Cemetery
*EFNCH* N2 97 P9
St Patricks Church School
*STHWK* SE1 12 A10
St Patricks Infants School
*WAP* E1W 140 A10
St Patricks International School
*SOHO/SHAV* W1D 11 H5
St Patricks RC JMI School
*ROMW/RG* RM7 104 C9
St Patricks RC Primary School
*WALTH* E17 120 D2
*WOOL/PLUM* SE18 162 C3
St Paulinus CE Primary School
*DART* DA1 164 F10
St Paul's ⊖
*STP* EC4M 12 E5
St Pauls & All Hallows Infant School
*TOTM* N17 99 P8
St Pauls & All Hallows Junior School
*TOTM* N17 99 P8
St Paul's Cathedral
*STP* EC4M 12 E6
St Paul's Cathedral School
*STP* EC4M 12 E6
St Pauls Catholic College
*SUN* TW16 197 H1
St Pauls CE Primary School
*KGLGY* WD4 54 C10
*ADL/WDHM* KT15 215 K1
*BTFD* TW8 155 J5
*CHSGTN* KT9 219 K1
St Paul's CE Primary School
*DORK* RH4 272 G2
St Pauls CE Primary School
*FBAR/BDGN* N11 98 B6
*HAMP* NW3 3 P4
*MLHL* NW7 96 E5
*SWLY* BR8 209 J1
*WALW* SE17 18 D8
*WCHMH* N21 99 J1
*WCHPL* E1 13 P7
St Pauls CE Junior School
*KUTN/CMB* KT2 177 M10
St Pauls Cray CE Primary School
*STMC/STPC* BR5 207 M3
St Pauls Cray Health Clinic
*STMC/STPC* BR5 207 K2
St Pauls Girls School
*HMSMTH* W6 156 G3
St Paul's Primary School
*HMSMTH* W6 156 F4
St Pauls Primary School
*KGLGY* WD4 53 K7
St Pauls RC Primary School
*CHESW* EN7 62 A3
*THDIT* KT7 198 D7
*WDGN* N22 98 G10
St Pauls RC School
*ABYW* SE2 163 K5
St Pauls Road Medical Centre
*IS* N1 6 D1
St Pauls School
*BARN* SW13 156 E4
St Pauls Steiner School
*IS* N1 6 G1
St Pauls Way Community School
*BOW* E3 140 F7
St Pauls with St Lukes CE Primary School
*BOW* E3 140 E7
St Pauls with St Michaels CE School
*HACK* E8 7 P5
St Peter Chanel RC Primary School
*SCUP* DA14 185 M8
St Peter & Paul CE Infant School
*CTHM* CR3 259 H1
St Peter & Paul RC Primary School
*STMC/STPC* BR5 207 H2
St Peter & St Pauls Primary School
*FSBYE* EC1V 12 C1
St Peters Catholic Comprehensive School
*GU* GU1 250 F9
St Peters Catholic Primary School
*ROM* RM1 124 E1
St Peters CE Combined School
*SL* SL1 128 A5
St Peters CE Middle School
*WDSR* SL4 171 L2
St Peters CE Primary School
*BRW* CM14 106 C3
*HMSMTH* W6 156 D4
*MV/WKIL* W9 8 E2
*OXTED* RH8 260 F9
*WALW* SE17 18 G8
*WAP* E1W 140 B10
St Peter's Church
*KTBR* SW1X 16 E3
St Peters Eaton Square CE Primary School
*BGVA* SW1W 16 E4
St Peters Hospital
*CHERT* KT16 194 G10
St Peter's Hospital
*COVGDN* WC2E 11 M7
St Peters JMI School
*STAL* AL1 38 D7
St Peters Primary School
*RKW/CH/CXG* WD3 91 L2
*SAND/SEL* CR2 223 L3
St Peters RC Primary School
*DAGW* RM9 144 A3
*LHD/OX* KT22 237 H6
*WOOL/PLUM* SE18 162 E4
St Philip Howard Catholic Primary School
*HAT* AL10 40 E4
St Philips School
*CHSGTN* KT9 219 J3
*SKENS* SW7 15 K6
St Phillips Infant School
*SYD* SE26 182 A7
St Philomenas Catholic High School
*CAR* SM5 221 P2
St Philomenas RC Primary School
*STMC/STPC* BR5 207 M7
St Quintins Health Centre
*NKENS* W10 136 F7
St Raphaels Hospice
*WPK* KT4 200 G9
St Raphaels RC Primary School
*NTHLT* UB5 133 J4
St Raphaels Way Medical Centre
*WLSDN* NW10 115 P10
St Richards with St Andrews CE Primary School
*RCHPK/HAM* TW10 176 G6
St Robert Southwell RC Primary School
*CDALE/KGS* NW9 115 P4
St Roses RC Infant School
*HHW* HP1 35 K8
SS Andrews & Marks CE Junior School
*SURB* KT6 199 J5
St Saviour & St Olaves School
*STHWK* SE1 19 H4
St Saviours CE Primary School
*HNHL* SE24 159 K9
*MV/WKIL* W9 9 H2
*POP/IOD* E14 140 G7
*WALTH* E17 120 E5
St Saviours CE Infant School
*EA* W5 135 J10
St Saviours RC Primary School
*LEW* SE13 161 H10
St Scholasticas RC Primary School
*CLPT* E5 119 P8
SS Mary & Pancras CE Primary School
*CAMTN* NW1 5 J8
SS Peter & Paul RC Primary School
*MTCM* CR4 202 A4
SS Peter & Pauls RC Primary School
*IL* IG1 122 G8
St Stephens CE Junior School
*TWK* TW1 176 F2
St Stephens CE Primary School
*BAY/PAD* W2 8 F4
*DEPT* SE8 160 F8
*SHB* W12 136 E10
St Stephens CE School
*VX/NE* SW8 158 F6
St Stephens Primary School
*EHAM* E6 141 P2
St Stephens RC Primary School
*WELL* DA16 163 K9
St Swithun Wells RC Primary School
*RSLP* HA4 113 K8
St Teresa RC First & Middle School
*KTN/HRWW/WS* HA3 94 B9
St Teresa RC Primary School
*BCTR* RM8 123 M9
St Teresas Preparatory School
*EHSLY* KT24 253 L4
St Teresa's RC Primary School
*BORE* WD6 75 N6
St Teresas School
*RDKG* RH5 253 L8
St Theresas RC Primary School
*FNCH* N3 117 K1
St Thomas a' Becket RC Primary School
*ABYW* SE2 163 K2
St Thomas Becket RC Primary School
*SNWD* SE25 203 P6
St Thomas CE Primary School
*NKENS* W10 8 A2
St Thomas Childrens Day Hospital
*LBTH* SE11 17 P7
St Thomas' Hospital
*STHWK* SE1 17 N3
St Thomas More RC Primary School
*BERK* HP4 33 M5
*BXLYHN* DA7 164 A8
*ELTH/MOT* SE9 162 B9
St Thomas More RC School
*CHEL* SW3 16 A5
*ELTH/MOT* SE9 184 D2
*WDGN* N22 99 H8
St Thomas of Canterbury
*MTCM* CR4 202 B3
St Thomas of Canterbury CE Junior School
*BRWN* CM15 107 J1
St Thomas of Canterbury Infant School
*BRWN* CM15 107 J1
St Thomas of Canterbury RC Primary School
*GRAYS* RM17 167 N3
*FUL/PGN* SW6 157 J6
St Thomas of Caterbury Catholic Primary School
*GU* GU1 250 E10
St Thomas Primary School
*SEV* TN13 265 J1
St Thomas the Apostle College
*PECK* SE15 160 B7
St Ursulas Catholic Infant School
*HARH* RM3 105 J7
St Ursulas Convent School
*GNWCH* SE10 161 J6
St Vincent de Paul RC Primary School
*WEST* SW1P 16 G4
St Vincents Catholic Primary School
*ELTH/MOT* SE9 184 B7
St Vincents Hospital
*PIN* HA5 112 F1
St Vincents RC Primary School
*BCTR* RM8 123 M7
St Vincent's RC Primary School
*MHST* W1U 10 C4
St Vincents RC Primary School
*MLHL* NW7 96 E5
St Walter & St John Sports Ground
*TOOT* SW17 179 P4
St Wilfrids RC School
*CRAWW* RH11 283 L8
St William of York Primary School
*FSTH* SE23 182 D3
St Winefrides Catholic Primary School
*MNPK* E12 122 C10
St Winifreds Catholic Junior School
*LEE/GVPK* SE12 183 L2
St Winifreds RC Infant School
*LEW* SE13 183 K1
Salcombe Preparatory School (Infants)
*STHGT/OAK* N14 78 C10
Salcombe Preparatory School (Juniors)
*STHGT/OAK* N14 98 C1
Salesian College
*CHERT* KT16 195 K8
Salesian RC School
*CHERT* KT16 195 H9
Salfords ⇌
*REDH* RH1 276 C8
Salfords Industrial Estate
*REDH* RH1 276 B9
Salfords Primary School
*REDH* RH1 276 B6
Salisbury Infant School
*HAT* AL10 40 E2
Salisbury Lawn Tennis Club
*STAL* AL1 38 G5
Salisbury Primary School
*MNPK* E12 122 A10
Salisbury School
*ED* N9 100 B2
Salters' Hall
*BARB* EC2Y 12 F4
Salusbury Primary School
*KIL/WHAMP* NW6 2 C6
Salvatorian College
*KTN/HRWW/WS* HA3 94 C10
Samuel Jones Industrial Estate
*PECK* SE15 159 M6
Samuel Rhodes School
*IS* N1 6 A5
Sandcross Junior School
*REIG* RH2 275 J3
Sanders Draper School
*HCH* RM12 125 L9
Sanderstead ⇌
*SAND/SEL* CR2 223 L5
Sanderstead Junior School
*SAND/SEL* CR2 223 L5
Sandfield CP School
*GU* GU1 268 A1
Sandgate Trading Estate
*BERM/RHTH* SE16 160 A4
Sandhurst Primary School
*CAT* SE6 183 K3
Sandilands ⊖
*CROY/NA* CR0 203 N9
Sandown Grandstand & Exhibition Centre
*ESH/CLAY* KT10 198 A10
Sandown Industrial Park
*ESH/CLAY* KT10 197 P9
Sandown Park Racecourse
*ESH/CLAY* KT10 198 A10
Sandown Road Industrial Estate
*WATN* WD24 73 K3
Sandown Sports Club & Dry Ski Slope
*ESH/CLAY* KT10 198 A10
Sandridge Gate Business Centre
*STALE/WH* AL4 20 G10
*STALE/WH* AL4 38 E2
Sandridge School
*STALE/WH* AL4 21 J9
Sandridge Youth Club & Sports Centre
*STALW/RED* AL3 20 G10
Sandringham Primary School
*FSTGT* E7 141 P1
Sandringham School
*STALE/WH* AL4 38 G2
Sandy Lodge Golf Club
*NTHWD* HA6 92 E3
Sapcote Trading Centre
*WLSDN* NW10 116 C10
Saracen Industrial Area
*HHNE* HP2 36 B4
Sarah Bonnell School
*SRTFD* E15 141 K1
Sarbir Industrial Park
*HLW* CM20 29 M6
Sarratt School
*RKW/CH/CXG* WD3 71 K2
Sarum Hall School
*HAMP* NW3 3 P3
Satellite Business Village
*CRAWE* RH10 283 P3
Satmer Trust School
*STNW/STAM* N16 119 P7
Savoy Pier
*TPL/STR* WC2R 11 N8
The Savoy
*TPL/STR* WC2R 11 M8
Savoy Theatre
*TPL/STR* WC2R 11 N8
Sawbridge Health Clinic
*SBW* CM21 29 P1
Sawyers Hall College of Science & Technology
*BRWN* CM15 107 H1
Saxeway Business Centre
*CSHM* HP5 50 D4
Saxon Business Centre
*WIM/MER* SW19 201 M2
Saxon CP School
*SHPTN* TW17 196 A5
Sayer Clinic
*CROY/NA* CR0 222 G1
Sayer Clinics
*MBLAR* W1H 10 B6
Sayes Court Junior School
*ADL/WDHM* KT15 215 L2
Scargill Infant School
*RAIN* RM13 145 H2
Scargill Junior School
*RAIN* RM13 145 H1
Scarsdale Place Medical Centre
*KENS* W8 14 G3
School of Oriental & African Studies
*GWRST* WC1E 11 K2
Schomberg House
*STJS* SW1Y 11 H10
Schooling Licensed Conveyancers
*GRAYS* RM17 167 N4
School of Architecture & Design (London Metropolitan University)
*HOLWY* N7 6 B1
School of English
*GLDGN* NW11 117 K6
School of Islamic Republic Iran
*KIL/WHAMP* NW6 2 E8
School of Oriental & African Studies
*STPAN* WC1H 11 K2
The School of Pharmacy
*BMSBY* WC1N 11 M1
The School of St David & St Katharine
*CEND/HSY/T* N8 118 F2
Science Museum
*SKENS* SW7 15 M4
Science Museum IMAX Cinema
*SKENS* SW7 15 L4
The Science Museum Library
*SKENS* SW7 15 L3
Scott's Grotto
*WARE* SG12 26 C3
Scotts Park Primary School
*BMLY* BR1 205 P1
Scotts Primary School
*HCH* RM12 125 K10
Scott Wilkie Primary School
*CAN/RD* E16 141 P8
The Screen at Reigate
*REIG* RH2 257 K10
Screen Cinema
*WOT/HER* KT12 197 H8
Screen on Baker Street Cinema
*MHST* W1U 10 B3
Screen on the Green Cinema
*IS* N1 6 C6
Seal CE Primary School
*BGR/WK* TN15 247 N6
Sealife London Aquarium
*WHALL* SW1A 17 N2
Seaton House School
*BELMT* SM2 221 N6
Sebright Primary School
*BETH* E2 7 N7
Secombe Centre
*SUT* SM1 221 L3
Sedgehill School
*CAT* SE6 182 G8
Sedgewick Centre
*WCHPL* E1 13 M5
Sedleys CE Primary School
*MEO* DA13 189 M8
Seer Green ⇌
*BEAC* HP9 89 H8
Seer Green CE Combined School
*BEAC* HP9 89 H7
Sefton Park School
*SLN* SL2 129 N2
Selborne Primary School
*GFD/PVL* UB6 134 E4
The Sele School
*HERT/WAT* SG14 24 G5
The Selfridge Hotel
*MBLAR* W1H 10 D6
Selhurst ⇌
*SNWD* SE25 203 M5
The Selhurst Medical Centre
*SNWD* SE25 203 M6
Sellincourt School
*TOOT* SW17 179 P9
Selsdon Community Centre
*SAND/SEL* CR2 224 A6
Selsdon High School
*SAND/SEL* CR2 224 C4
Selsdon Nature Reserve
*CROY/NA* CR0 224 D7
Selsdon Primary School
*SAND/SEL* CR2 224 B5
Selsdon Road Industrial Estate
*SAND/SEL* CR2 223 L4
Selwyn Primary School
*CHING* E4 101 H8
*PLSTW* E13 141 M3
Semaphore Tower
*COB* KT11 234 E3
Send CE First School
*RPLY/SEND* GU23 232 G10
Send CC
*RPLY/SEND* GU23 232 E10
Sergeant Industrial Estate
*WAND/EARL* SW18 179 L2
Serpentine Gallery
*BAY/PAD* W2 9 M10
Serpentine Lido & Cafe
*SKENS* SW7 15 N1
Servite RC Primary School
*WBPTN* SW10 15 J9
Seven Islands Leisure Centre
*BERM/RHTH* SE16 160 B2
Seven Kings ⇌
*GDMY/SEVK* IG3 123 H6
Seven Kings Health Centre
*GDMY/SEVK* IG3 123 H6
Seven Kings High School
*GNTH/NBYPK* IG2 122 G5
Seven Mills Primary School
*POP/IOD* E14 160 F1
Sevenoaks ⇌
*SEV* TN13 247 H10
Sevenoaks Business Centre
*RSEV* TN14 247 K7
Sevenoaks CC
*SEV* TN13 247 J10
Sevenoaks Hospital
*SEV* TN13 247 K7
Sevenoaks Library & Museum
*SEV* TN13 265 K1
Sevenoaks Primary School
*SEV* TN13 247 J8
Sevenoaks RFC
*SEV* TN13 265 K1
Sevenoaks School
*SEV* TN13 265 K2
Sevenoaks School Track
*SEV* TN13 265 K2
Sevenoaks Swimming Centre
*SEV* TN13 265 K1
Sevenoaks Way Industrial Estate
*STMC/STPC* BR5 207 M3
Seven Sisters ⇌ ⊖
*SEVS/STOTM* N15 119 M3
Seven Sisters Primary School
*SEVS/STOTM* N15 119 L3
Seymour Gardens Medical Centre
*IL* IG1 122 C6
Seymour Leisure Centre
*MBLAR* W1H 10 A4
Shaare Zedek Medical Centre
*GLDGN* NW11 117 J4
Shacklewell Primary School
*HACK* E8 119 N9
Shadwell ⊖ ⊖
*WCHPL* E1 140 A8
Shadwell Dock Stairs
*WAP* E1W 140 C9
Shaftesbury High School
*KTN/HRWW/WS* HA3 94 A9
Shaftesbury Hospital
*LSQ/SEVD* WC2H 11 L6
Shaftesbury Medical Centre
*RYLN/HDSTN* HA2 114 B6
Shaftesbury Park Primary School
*BTSEA* SW11 158 B9
Shaftesbury Primary School
*FSTGT* E7 141 P2
Shaftesbury Theatre
*LSQ/SEVD* WC2H 11 L5
Shahjalal Medical Centre
*WCHPL* E1 13 P6
Shakespeare Business Centre
*BRXN/ST* SW9 159 J9
Shakespeare Industrial Estate
*WATN* WD24 73 H4
Shakespeare's Globe Theatre & Exhibition
*STHWK* SE1 12 E9
Shalford ⇌
*RGUE* GU4 268 B6
Shalford Infant School
*RGUE* GU4 268 B6
Shalford Mill (NT)
*RGUE* GU4 268 B5
The Shamrock Sports Club
*ACT* W3 135 P8
Shannon Corner Retail Park
*NWMAL* KT3 200 D4
Shapla Primary School
*WCHPL* E1 13 N7
Sharp Sports Centre
*EDGW* HA8 95 M7
Shawcroft School
*STMC/STPC* BR5 207 P5
Shawley Primary School
*EPSOM* KT18 238 F4
Shaw Primary School
*SOCK/AV* RM15 146 G8
Shears Green Primary School
*GVW* DA11 190 C6
Sheeji Medical Centre
*SL* SL1 129 J9
Sheen Lane Health Centre
*MORT/ESHN* SW14 155 P9
Sheen Lawn Tennis & Squash Club
*MORT/ESHN* SW14 177 P1
Sheen Mount Primary School
*RCHPK/HAM* TW10 177 N1
Sheen Sports Centre
*MORT/ESHN* SW14 156 B10
Sheepcot Medical Centre
*GSTN* WD25 55 K10
Sheering CE Primary School
*RBSF* CM22 30 E2
Shell Centre
*STHWK* SE1 11 P10
Shelley Primary School
*CHONG* CM5 67 N2
Shelley School
*CLAP* SW4 158 D9
Shendish Manor Golf Club
*HHS/BOV* HP3 53 N2
Shene School
*MORT/ESHN* SW14 156 B10
Shenfield ⇌
*RBRW/HUT* CM13 107 M1
Shenfield CC
*BRWN* CM15 87 L10
Shenfield High School
*BRWN* CM15 87 M9
Shenfield Sports Centre
*BRWN* CM15 87 M9
Shenley Primary School
*RAD* WD7 57 L9
Shenstone School
*DART* DA1 186 E1
Shenval Industrial Estate
*HLW* CM20 29 K7
Shepherd Primary School
*RKW/CH/CXG* WD3 91 K2
Shepherd's Bush ⇌ ⊖ ⊖
*SHB* W12 156 G1
Shepherd's Bush CC
*ACT* W3 136 B9
Shepherd's Bush Empire
*SHB* W12 156 F1
Shepherd's Bush Market ⊖
*SHB* W12 136 F10
Shepherds Lane Cemetery
*BEAC* HP9 88 E10
Shepperton ⇌
*SHPTN* TW17 196 D5
Shepperton Business Park
*SHPTN* TW17 196 D5
Shepperton Health Centre
*SHPTN* TW17 196 C5
Shepperton Studios
*SHPTN* TW17 196 A3
Sheraton Belgravia Hotel
*KTBR* SW1X 16 C4
Sheraton Business Centre
*GFD/PVL* UB6 135 H4
Sheraton Park Tower Hotel
*KTBR* SW1X 16 B1
Sheraton Skyline Hotel
*HYS/HAR* UB3 152 E6
Shere CE Infant School
*SHGR* GU5 270 B5
Sheredes School
*HOD* EN11 44 E4
Sheringdale Primary School
*WAND/EARL* SW18 179 J4
Sheringham Junior School
*MNPK* E12 122 C9
Sherington Primary School
*CHARL* SE7 161 N5
Sherlock Holmes Hotel
*MHST* W1U 10 B3
Sherlock Holmes Museum
*CAMTN* NW1 10 B2
Sherwood Park Primary School
*BFN/LL* DA15 185 L2
Sherwood Park School
*WLGTN* SM6 202 E10
Sherwood School
*MTCM* CR4 202 D4
The Ship Hotel
*WEY* KT13 196 C10
Shire Horse Centre
*CSTG* HP8 90 D4
The Shire London
*BAR* EN5 76 F4
Shirley Clinic
*CROY/NA* CR0 204 B8
Shirley High School
*CROY/NA* CR0 204 C10
Shirley Oaks Hospital
*CROY/NA* CR0 204 B7
Shirley Park Golf Club
*CROY/NA* CR0 204 A9
Shirley Wanderers RFC
*WWKM* BR4 225 H1
Shirley Windmill
*CROY/NA* CR0 204 B10
Shooters Hill Golf Club
*WOOL/PLUM* SE18 162 F7
Shooters Hill Post 16 Campus
*WOOL/PLUM* SE18 162 D6
Shooting Star House (Childrens Hospice)
*HPTN* TW12 175 N9
Shopping City
*WDGN* N22 98 G10
Shore Business Centre
*HOM* E9 140 B2
Shoreditch Comprehensive School
*IS* N1 7 K8
Shoreditch High Street ⊖
*WCHPL* E1 13 L2
Shoreham ⇌
*RSEV* TN14 229 H7
Shoreham CP School
*RSEV* TN14 228 G7
Shorne CE Primary School
*GVE* DA12 191 P8
Shortlands ⇌
*HAYES* BR2 205 K2
Shortwood Infant School
*STA* TW18 173 L6
Shotfield Health Clinic
*WLGTN* SM6 222 C3
Showcase Bluewater Cinema
*RDART* DA2 188 E4
Showcase Cinema
*WDGN* N22 99 H10
Showcase Newham Cinema
*BARK* EC2Y 142 F5
Shrewsbury House School
*SURB* KT6 199 J9
Shrewsbury Road Health Centre
*FSTGT* E7 142 A2
Sidcup ⇌
*BFN/LL* DA15 185 K5
Sidcup Cemetery
*BXLY* DA5 185 N5
Sidcup Golf Club
*BFN/LL* DA15 185 K5
Sidcup Health Centre
*SCUP* DA14 185 K6
Sidcup Sports Club
*SCUP* DA14 185 J7
Sidney Russell School
*DAGW* RM9 123 P9
Silicon Business Centre
*GFD/PVL* UB6 135 H4
Silverdale Industrial Estate
*HYS/HAR* UB3 153 H1
Silverglade Business Park
*CHSGTN* KT9 219 H8
Silver Industrial Estate
*TOTM* N17 99 N10
Silvermere Golf Club
*COB* KT11 216 C9
Silver Street ⇌
*UED* N18 99 N5
Silver Street Cemetery
*CHESW* EN7 61 L6
Silver Street Medical Centre
*UED* N18 99 M5
Silver Wing Industrial Estate
*CROY/NA* CR0 222 G3
Simon Balle School
*HERT/BAY* SG13 25 M6
Simon Marks Jewish Primary School
*STNW/STAM* N16 119 N6
Simpson Health Centre
*BEAC* HP9 88 B8
Singlegate Primary School
*WIM/MER* SW19 179 N10
Singlewell Primary School
*GVE* DA12 190 G9
Sion College
*EMB* EC4Y 12 B7
Sion Manning RC Girls School
*NKENS* W10 136 G7
Sir Christopher Wren's House Hotel
*WDSR* SL4 149 H6
Sir Francis Drake Primary School
*DEPT* SE8 160 D4
Sir Frederic Osborn School
*WGCE* AL7 23 L4
Sir George Monoux College
*WALTH* E17 100 G10
Sir James Altham Swimming Pool
*OXHEY* WD19 93 M6
Sir James Barrie School
*VX/NE* SW8 158 D7
Sir John Cass Foundation School
*HDTCH* EC3A 13 K6
Sir John Cass Found/ Redcoat School
*WCHPL* E1 140 C7
Sir John Heron Primary School
*MNPK* E12 122 C9
Sir John Lillie Primary School
*FUL/PGN* SW6 14 B10
Sir John Newsom School
*WGCE* AL7 23 H7
Sir John Soane's Museum
*LINN* WC2A 11 N5
Sir Thomas Abney Primary School
*STNW/STAM* N16 119 L5
Sir Thomas Lipton Memorial Hospital
*STHGT/OAK* N14 98 C1
Sir William Burrough Primary School
*POP/IOD* E14 140 D8
Sir William Perkins School
*CHERT* KT16 195 H8
Site of Greenwich Hospital
*GNWCH* SE10 161 L4
Six Bridges Trading Estate
*STHWK* SE1 19 P8
Skidmore Clinic
*RKW/CH/CXG* WD3 91 P2
Skillion Business Park
*BARK* IG11 143 J5
Skinners Company Lower Girls School
*CLPT* E5 120 A6
Skinners Company School for Girls
*STNW/STAM* N16 119 M5
Sky Business Park
*EGH* TW20 194 F2
Skywood JMI School
*STALE/WH* AL4 39 H3
Slade Green ⇌
*ERITH* DA8 165 H7
Slade Green FC
*ERITH* DA8 165 J7
Slade Green Primary School
*ERITH* DA8 165 H6
Slade School of Fine Art
*STPAN* WC1H 5 K10
Sleaford Industrial Estate
*VX/NE* SW8 158 D6
Sloane Hospital
*BECK* BR3 205 J1
Sloane Square ⊖
*BGVA* SW1W 16 C6
Slough ⇌
*SL* SL1 129 L10
Slough Cemetery
*SL* SL1 129 L8
Slough Community Mental Health Centre
*DTCH/LGLY* SL3 150 D3
Slough Crematorium
*SLN* SL2 129 L8
Slough & Eton CE School
*SL* SL1 149 J2
Slough Grammar School
*SL* SL1 149 N2
Slough Ice Arena
*SL* SL1 149 J1
Slough Indoor Tennis Centre
*SL* SL1 129 J10
Slough Islamic Primary School
*SLN* SL2 129 M9
Slough Museum
*SL* SL1 149 M1
Slough RFC
*DTCH/LGLY* SL3 149 N4
Slough Sports Club
*SL* SL1 149 K2
Slough Town FC
*SLN* SL2 129 M7
Slough Trading Estate
*SL* SL1 128 F7
Slyfield Industrial Estate
*GU* GU1 250 A5
Smallberry Green Primary School
*ISLW* TW7 154 F8
Smallwood Primary School
*TOOT* SW17 179 N7
SMA Medical Centre
*LEY* E10 120 G5
Smitham ⇌
*COUL/CHIP* CR5 240 F1
Smitham Primary School
*COUL/CHIP* CR5 240 D2
Smithy Street School
*WCHPL* E1 140 B7
Smug Oak Green Business Centre
*LCOL/BKTW* AL2 56 A5
Snaresbrook ⊖
*WAN* E11 121 M3
Snaresbrook College Preparatory School
*SWFD* E18 101 M10
Snaresbrook Primary School
*SWFD* E18 121 M2
Snowhill Business Centre
*CRAWE* RH10 285 P1
Snowsfields Primary School
*STHWK* SE1 19 J1
Sobell Leisure Centre
*HOLWY* N7 118 G8
Sobell Medical Centre
*HOLWY* N7 119 H9
Sofitel Hotel
*HORL* RH6 280 A7
Sofitel St James Hotel
*STJS* SW1Y 11 J9
Soho Parish CE Primary School
*SOHO/CST* W1F 11 J7
Solefield School
*SEV* TN13 265 K3
Somerset House
*COVGDN* WC2E 11 N7
Somers Heath Primary School
*SOCK/AV* RM15 146 F9
Somers Town Community Sports Centre
*CAMTN* NW1 5 H8
Sopwell House Hotel, Country Club & Spa
*STAL* AL1 38 E10
Sorsby Health Centre
*CLPT* E5 120 C9
South Acton ⊖
*ACT* W3 155 P2
Southall ⇌
*STHL* UB1 153 N1
Southall & West London College
*STHL* UB1 153 M1
Southbank Business Centre
*VX/NE* SW8 17 K10
Southbank International School Kensington
*NTGHL* W11 8 D8
Southbank International School Westminster
*BAY/PAD* W2 8 F8
South Bank University
*STHWK* SE1 18 C3
South Bermondsey ⇌
*BERM/RHTH* SE16 160 B4
Southborough Primary School
*HAYES* BR2 206 D5
Southborough School
*SURB* KT6 199 K10
Southbury ⇌
*EN* EN1 80 A8
Southbury Primary School
*PEND* EN3 80 A8
South Camden Community School
*CAMTN* NW1 5 H7
South Chelsea College
*BRXN/ST* SW9 158 G10
South Croydon ⇌
*SAND/SEL* CR2 223 L2
South Croydon Medical Centre
*SAND/SEL* CR2 223 K4

South Croydon Sports Club
*CROY/NA* CRO ............223 M2
Southdown Industrial Estate
*HARP* AL5 ..............20 B3
South Ealing
*EA* W5 ................155 J2
South Ealing Cemetery
*EA* W5 ................155 J3
South Eastern University
*HOLWY* N7 ..............118 C8
Southern Clinic
*REIG* RH2 .............275 M1
Southern Road Primary School
*PLSTW* E13 ............141 N4
Southern Valley Golf Club
*GVE* DA12 .............191 K7
South Essex Crematorium
*UPMR* RM14 ............126 C10
Southfield First & Middle School
*CHSWK* W4 .............156 B1
Southfield Medical Centre
*CHSWK* W4 .............156 A1
Southfields
*WAND/EARL* SW18 .......179 J4
Southfield School
*HAT* AL10 .............40 E8
The Southfields Clinic
*WAND/EARL* SW18 .......179 K2
Southfields Community College
*WAND/EARL* SW18 .......179 K4
Southfields Park Primary School
*HOR/WEW* KT19 .........219 N6
Southgate
*STHGT/OAK* N14 ........98 E2
Southgate Cemetery
*STHGT/OAK* N14 ........98 D3
Southgate College
*STHGT/OAK* N14 ........98 D3
Southgate Compton CC
*EBAR* EN4 ............78 A8
Southgate Leisure Centre
*STHGT/OAK* N14 ........98 E1
Southgate Primary School
*CRAWE* RH10 ...........283 N9
Southgate Road Medical Centre
*IS* N1 ...............7 H3
Southgate School
*EBAR* EN4 ............78 C9
South Greenford ⇌
*GFD/PVL* UB6 ..........134 D5
South Grove Primary School
*WALTH* E17 ............120 D4
South Hampstead ⇌
*KIL/WHAMP* NW6 ........3 K4
South Hampstead CC
*CRICK* NW2 ............136 F2
South Hampstead High School
*HAMP* NW3 ............3 L2
South Haringey Infant School
*FSBYPK* N4 ...........119 J3
South Harrow ⊖
*RYLN/HDSTN* HA2 .......114 B8
South Herts Golf Club
*TRDG/WHET* N20 ........97 K2
South Hill JMI School
*HHW* HP1 .............35 M7
South Kensington ⊖
*SKENS* SW7 ...........15 M5
South Kenton ⊖
*ALP/SUD* HA0 ..........115 H6
Southlake Primary School
*ABYW* SE2 ............163 N1
South Lewisham Health Centre
*CAT* SE6 .............183 H7
South London Crematorium
*MTCM* CR4 ............202 D2
South London Gallery
*CMBW* SE5 ............159 M7
The South London Natural
  Health Centre
*CLAP* SW4 ............158 D10
South London Tamil School
*CROY/NA* CRO ..........203 K7
South London Theatre
*WNWD* SE27 ...........181 K6
Southmead Primary School
*WIM/MER* SW19 ........179 H4
South Merton ⇌
*RYNPK* SW20 ..........201 J3
South Norwood Country Park
*SNWD* SE25 ...........204 B4
South Norwood Hill
  Medical Centre
*SNWD* SE25 ...........203 M2
South Norwood Medical Centre
*SNWD* SE25 ...........203 M4
South Norwood Pools &
  Fitness Centre
*SNWD* SE25 ...........203 P5
South Norwood Primary School
*SNWD* SE25 ...........203 P5
South Nutfield CC
*REDH* RH1 ............276 C2
South Park Business Centre
*IL* IG1 ..............123 H7
South Park Clinic
*IL* IG1 ..............122 C9
South Park Hotel
*SAND/SEL* CR2 .........223 M1
South Park Primary School
*GDMY/SEVK* IG3 ........123 H8
South Quay ⇌
*POP/IOD* E14 .........160 C1
South Quay Plaza
*POP/IOD* E14 .........160 C1
South Rise Primary School
*WOOL/PLUM* SE18 .......162 C4
South Ruislip ⇌⊖
*RSLP* HA4 ............113 K9
Southside Industrial Estate
*VX/NE* SW8 ...........158 D6
Southside Shopping Centre
*WAND/EARL* SW18 .......179 L2
South Thames College
*PUT/ROE* SW15 ........178 C2
*PUT/ROE* SW15 ........178 C1
*TOOT* SW17 ...........179 P8
*WAND/EARL* SW18 .......179 L1
South Tottenham ⇌
*SEVS/STOTM* N15 .......119 N3
Southville Infant School
*EBED/NFELT* TW14 .....174 C4
Southwark ⊖
*STHWK* SE1 ...........12 C10
Southwark Bridge Stairs
*BLKFR* EC4V ..........12 E8
Southwark Cathedral
*STHWK* SE1 ...........12 C9
Southwark College
*BERM/RHTH* SE16 .......160 A2
*CMBW* SE5 ............159 M6
*STHWK* SE1 ...........18 B1
*STHWK* SE1 ...........15 K3
Southwark Park Primary School
*BERM/RHTH* SE16 .......160 A3
Southwark Park Sports Centre
*BERM/RHTH* SE16 .......160 B3
Southwark Sports Ground
*DUL* SE21 ............181 N4
South West
  Middlesex Crematorium
*FELT* TW13 ...........175 M4
South Wimbledon ⊖
*WIM/MER* SW19 ........179 L10
Southwold Primary School
*CLPT* E5 .............120 B7
South Woodford ⊖
*SWFD* E18 ............101 M10
South Woodford Health Centre
*SWFD* E18 ............101 M9
Southwood Hospital
*HGT* N6 ..............118 B5
Southwood Primary School
*DACW* RM9 ............123 P9
Sovereign Business Centre
*PEND* EN3 ............80 E7

The Space Arts Centre Cinema
*DEPT* SE8 ............160 E3
Sparrow Farm Community
  Junior School
*EW* KT17 .............220 E2
Sparrow Farm Infant School
*EBED/NFELT* TW14 .....175 K3
Sparrow Farm Junior School
*EBED/NFELT* TW14 .....175 K3
Spa School
*STHWK* SE1 ...........19 N6
Speakers Corner
*BAY/PAD* W2 ..........10 B7
The Speech Centre
*CAMTN* NW1 ...........5 K9
Speedway Industrial Estate
*HYS/HAR* UB3 .........152 E1
Speke's Monument
*BAY/PAD* W2 ..........9 K9
Spelthorne Clinic
*ASHF* TW15 ...........174 E9
Spelthorne Infant School
*ASHF* TW15 ...........174 E9
Spelthorne Leisure Centre
*STA* TW18 ............173 K8
Spelthorne Sports Club
*ASHF* TW15 ...........174 E10
Spencer House
*WHALL* SW1A ..........10 C10
Sphere Industrial Estate
*STAL* AL1 ............38 F7
The Spinney Infant School
*HLW* CM20 ............29 K10
The Spinney Junior School
*HLW* CM20 ............29 K10
The Spires Shopping Centre
*BAR* EN5 .............77 H7
Spitalfields Community Farm
*BETH* E2 .............13 N1
Spitalfields Health Centre
*WCHPL* E1 ............13 M1
Spitfire Business Park
*CROY/NA* CRO .........223 H3
Splashworld Swimming Centre
*BXLYHS* DA6 ..........163 M10
Sports Arena
*STALW/RED* AL3 .......38 A7
Springfield Christian School
*CAT* SE6 .............182 E6
Springfield Community
  Primary School
*SEVS/STOTM* N15 ......119 P4
Springfield Hospital
*TOOT* SW17 ..........179 P6
Springfield Primary School
*SUN* TW16 ...........196 F1
*VX/NE* SW8 ..........158 E6
Spring Grove Primary School
*ISLW* TW7 ...........154 C8
Springhallow School
*HNWL* W7 ............134 B8
Springmead JMI School
*WCCE* AL7 ...........23 M4
Spring Park Primary School
*CROY/NA* CRO .........204 F10
Springvale Retail Park
*STMC/STPC* BR5 .......207 M3
Springwell Infant School
*HEST* TW5 ...........153 M6
Springwell Junior School
*HEST* TW5 ...........153 M6
Sprint Industrial Estate
*BF/WBF* KT14 .........215 N7
Squerryes Court
*BH/WHM* TN16 .........262 F4
Squirrels Heath Infant School
*GPK* RM2 ............125 J3
Squirrels Heath Junior School
*GPK* RM2 ............125 J3
Squirrels Trading Estate
*HYS/HAR* UB3 .........152 C2
The Stables Gallery & Art Centre
*CRICK* NW2 ...........136 D9
Stadium Business Centre
*WBLY* HA9 ...........115 N6
Stadium Industrial Estate
*WBLY* HA9 ...........115 N10
Stadium Retail Park
*WBLY* HA9 ...........115 M8
Stafford Cross Business Park
*CROY/NA* CRO .........222 G2
The Stafford Hotel
*WHALL* SW1A ..........10 C10
Stafford Industrial Estate
*EMPK* RM11 ..........125 L1
Stag Lane First School
*CDALE/KGS* NW9 .......95 M10
Stag Lane Medical Centre
*CDALE/KGS* NW9 .......115 P1
Stags School
*STALW/RED* AL3 .......38 D2
Stag Theatre
*SEV* TN13 ...........265 J1
Staines ⇌
*STA* TW18 ...........173 K8
Staines Cemetery
*STA* TW18 ...........173 M6
Staines County Court
*STA* TW18 ...........173 K8
Staines Preparatory School
*STA* TW18 ...........173 K8
Staines RFC
*FELT* TW13 ..........175 H8
Staines Town FC
*STA* TW18 ...........173 K10
Stamford Brook ⊖
*CHSWK* W4 ...........156 C3
Stamford Clinic
*HMSMTH* W6 ..........156 D3
Stamford Green CP
*HOR/WEW* KT19 .......219 N8
Stamford Hill ⇌
*SEVS/STOTM* N15 .....119 N4
Stamford Hill Primary School
*SEVS/STOTM* N15 .....119 L4
Stanborough Primary School
*GSTN* WD25 ..........73 K1
Stanborough School
*GSTN* WD25 ..........73 J1
*WGCW* AL8 ...........22 E7
Stanburn First School
*STAN* HA7 ...........95 H8
Standard Industrial Estate
*CAN/RD* E16 ..........95 M1
Stamford Green School
*STRHM/NOR* SW16 .....202 E1
Stanhill Court Hotel
*HORL* RH6 ...........278 F6
Stanhope Primary School
*GFD/PVL* UB6 ........134 B6
Stanley Hill Cemetery
*AMSS* HP7 ...........69 K6
Stanley Infant School
*TEDD* TW11 ..........176 D7
Stanley Park High School
*CAR* SM5 ............222 B3
Stanley Park Primary School
*CAR* SM5 ............222 A4
Stanmore ⊖
*STAN* HA7 ...........95 J5
Stanmore College
*STAN* HA7 ...........94 C7
Stanmore Golf Club
*STAN* HA7 ...........94 G8
Stanton Square
  Industrial Estate
*SYD* SE26 ...........182 E7
Stanwell Burial Ground
*STWL/WRAY* TW19 .....173 M3
Stapleford Abbotts Golf Club
*ABR/ST* RM4 .........105 H1
Stapleford Abbotts
  Primary School
*ABR/ST* RM4 .........84 C9
Staple Inn Buildings
*HHOL* WC1V ..........12 A4

Staples Corner Business Park
*CRICK* NW2 ..........116 D6
Staples Road J & I School
*LOU* IG10 ...........82 B7
Staple Tye Shopping Centre
*HLWS* CM18 ..........46 C4
Star Business Centre
*RAIN* RM13 ..........144 E7
Star Business Centre
*RDKST* RH5 ..........273 H4
Starksfield Primary School
*ED* N9 ..............99 M2
Star Lane ⇌
*CAN/RD* E16 .........141 K6
Star Primary School
*CAN/RD* E16 .........141 K6
Stationers Hall
*STP* EC4M ...........12 D6
Stationery Office
*HOL/ALD* WC2B .......11 N5
Stebon Primary School
*POP/IOD* E14 ........140 E7
Stepgates Community School
*CHERT* KT16 .........195 J5
Stephen Hawking Primary
  Special School
*POP/IOD* E14 ........140 D8
Stepney Day Hospital
*WCHPL* E1 ...........140 B8
Stepney Green ⊖
*WCHPL* E1 ...........140 C6
Stepney Greencoat CE
  Primary School
*POP/IOD* E14 ........140 E8
Stepney Green College
*WCHPL* E1 ...........140 C7
Sterling Industrial Estate
*DAGE* RM10 ..........124 C9
Sterling Way Clinic
*UED* N18 ............99 N6
Stewards School
*HLWS* CM18 ..........46 F5
Stewart Fleming Primary School
*PGE/AN* SE20 ........204 B3
Stewart Headlam Primary School
*WCHPL* E1 ...........140 A6
Stifford Clays Health Centre
*CDW/CHF* RM16 .......147 N3
Stifford Clays Primary School
*CDW/CHF* RM16 .......147 N10
Stifford Primary School
*GRAYS* RM17 .........167 K4
Stillness Primary School
*FSTH* SE23 ..........182 D2
Stirling Industrial Centre
*BORE* WD6 ...........76 A9
Stirling Retail Park
*BORE* WD6 ...........76 A10
Stirling Way Industrial Estates
*CROY/NA* CRO ........202 F7
Stockley Academy
*WDR/YW* UB7 .........132 A8
Stockley Park Business Centre
*STKPK* UB11 .........132 D10
Stockley Park Golf Club
*STKPK* UB11 .........132 D9
Stockwell ⊖
*CLAP* SW4 ...........158 F8
Stockwell Lodge Medical Centre
*CHESW* EN7 ..........61 P3
Stockwell Park School
*BRXN/ST* SW9 ........158 F3
Stockwell Primary School
*BRXN/ST* SW9 ........158 G3
Stoke Cemetery
*GUW* GU2 ............249 N7
Stoke Green CC
*SLN* SL2 ............129 N6
Stoke Hill CP School
*GU* GU1 .............249 P7
Stoke Newington ⇌
*STNW/STAM* N16 ......119 N7
Stoke Park Golf Club
*SLN* SL2 ............129 J5
Stoke Poges School
*SLN* SL2 ............129 L2
Stompond Lane Track
*WOT/HER* KT12 .......197 H9
Stonebridge Park ⊖ ⇌
*ALP/SUD* HA0 ........135 M2
The Stonebridge Primary School
  (London Welsh School)
*WLSDN* NW10 .........135 P3
Stonebridge Shopping Centre
*WLSDN* NW10 .........136 A3
Stone Cemetery
*RDART* DA2 ..........188 D3
Stone Crossing ⇌
*RDART* DA2 ..........188 D1
Stonehill Business Centre
*UED* N18 ............100 C7
Stonehill Business Park
*UED* N18 ............100 C6
Stone House Hospital
*RDART* DA2 ..........188 B2
Stone Lake Retail Park
*CHARL* SE7 ..........161 P3
Stoneleigh ⇌
*HOR/WEW* KT19 .......220 C2
Stoneleigh First School
*EW* KT17 ............220 E1
Stoneydown Park
  Primary School
*WALTH* E17 ..........120 D2
Stony Dean Special School
*AMSS* HP7 ...........69 L5
Stormont School
*POTB/CUF* EN6 .......59 M7
Stoughton County Junior School
*GUW* GU2 ............249 N7
Stowford College
*BELMT* SM2 ..........221 M4
Strand on the Green J & I School
*CHSWK* W4 ...........155 M5
Strand Palace Hotel
*COVGDN* WC2E ........11 M7
Stratford College
*SRTFD* E15 ..........141 K2
Stratford High Street ⊖
*SRTFD* E15 ..........141 J2
Stratford International ⇌⊖
*SRTFD* E15 ..........141 H1
Stratford ⇌⊖
*SRTFD* E15 ..........141 H1
Stratford School
*FSTGT* E7 ...........141 H1
Stratford Shopping Centre
*SRTFD* E15 ..........141 J2
Strathmore School
*RCHPK/HAM* TW10 .....177 J7
Strawberry Fields School
*NTGHL* W11 ..........8 F6
Strawberry Hill ⇌
*WHTN* TW2 ...........176 D6
Strawberry Hill Golf Club
*WHTN* TW2 ...........176 D5
Streatham ⇌
*STRHM/NOR* SW16 .....180 E8
Streatham Cemetery
*TOOT* SW17 ..........179 P6
Streatham & Clapham
  High School
*STRHM/NOR* SW16 .....180 D6
Streatham Common ⇌
*STRHM/NOR* SW16 .....180 G4
Streatham & Croydon RFC
*THHTH* CR7 ..........203 H5
Streatham Hill ⇌
*STRHM/NOR* SW16 .....180 F5
Streatham Ice Rink
*STRHM/NOR* SW16 .....180 E8
Streatham Leisure Centre
*STRHM/NOR* SW16 .....180 F5
Streatham Modern School
*STRHM/NOR* SW16 .....180 F9

Streatham Park Cemetery
*MTCM* CR4 ...........202 D2
Streatham Swimming Pool
*STRHM/NOR* SW16 .....180 F8
Streatham Vale Sports Club
*STRHM/NOR* SW16 .....180 D10
Streatham Wells Primary School
*BRXS/STRHM* SW2 .....180 G5
Streete Court School
*GDST* RH9 ...........260 D6
Strodes College
*EGH* TW20 ...........172 C8
Stroud Green Primary School
*FSBYPK* N4 ..........119 H6
Stroud Wood Business Centre
*LCOL/BKTW* AL2 ......56 D3
Stubbers (Outdoor
  Pursuits Centre)
*UPMR* RM14 ..........146 E1
Studholme Medical Centre
*STA* TW18 ...........174 A7
The Study Preparatory School
*WIM/MER* SW19 .......178 C8
The Study School
*NWMAL* KT3 ..........200 B5
Sturt Priory Hospital
*KWD/TDW/WH* KT20 ....256 D2
Sudbourne Primary School
*BRXS/STRHM* SW2 .....180 G1
Sudbury Court Sports Club
*ALP/SUD* HA0 ........115 H8
Sudbury Golf Club
*GFD/PVL* UB6 ........134 D1
Sudbury & Harrow Road ⇌
*ALP/SUD* HA0 ........114 C10
Sudbury Hill ⊖
*HRW* HA1 ............114 D9
Sudbury Primary School
*ALP/SUD* HA0 ........114 C9
Sudbury Town ⊖
*GFD/PVL* UB6 ........134 C1
Suffolks Primary School
*EN* EN1 .............80 A6
Sullivan Primary School
*FUL/PGN* SW6 ........157 K8
Summerside JMI School
*NFNCH/WDSPK* N12 ....97 N7
Summerswood Primary School
*BORE* WD6 ...........75 N8
Summit Business Park
*SUN* TW16 ...........175 H10
Summers Community
  Recreation Centre
*HLWW/ROY* CM19 ......46 D5
Swanley ⇌
*SWLY* BR8 ...........208 E4
Swanley Business Centre
*SWLY* BR8 ...........208 E3
Swanscombe ⇌
*SWCM* DA10 ..........189 L1
Swanscombe Business Centre
*SWCM* DA10 ..........189 K1
Swanscombe Cemetery
*SWCM* DA10 ..........189 K2
Swansmere School
*WOT/HER* KT12 .......197 K8
Swan Valley
  Community School
*SWCM* DA10 ..........189 L3
Swan Wharf Business Centre
*UX/CGN* UB8 .........131 M4
Swedish School
*BARN* SW13 ..........156 D5
*NWDGN* UB2 ..........153 N2
Swimming Pool
*HERT/WAT* SG14 ......25 L3
Swing Gate First School
*BERK* HP4 ...........34 A6
Swiss Cottage ⊖
*KIL/WHAMP* NW6 ......3 L3
Swiss Cottage Hotel
*HAMP* NW3 ...........3 M5
Swiss Cottage Leisure Centre
*HAMP* NW3 ...........3 M4
Swiss Cottage School
*STJWD* NW8 ..........3 M4
Swissotel The Howard
*TPL/STR* WC2R .......11 P7
Sybil Elgar School
*EA* W5 ..............135 K9
*NWDGN* UB2 ..........153 N2
Sybourn Infant School
*LEY* E10 ............120 D6
The Sybourn Junior School
*WALTH* E17 ..........120 E5
Sydenham ⇌
*SYD* SE26 ...........182 B8
Sydenham Girls School
*SYD* SE26 ...........182 A6
Sydenham High Junior School
*SYD* SE26 ...........182 A7
Sydenham High School
  Sports Ground
*CAT* SE6 ............182 F8
Sydenham High Senior School
*SYD* SE26 ...........182 A8
Sydenham Hill ⇌
*DUL* SE21 ...........181 M6
The Sydney Russell School
*DACW* RM9 ...........123 N10
Syon House
*BTFD* TW8 ...........155 H7
Syon Lane ⇌
*ISLW* TW7 ...........154 F6
Syon Park
*BTFD* TW8 ...........155 H8
Syracuse University
*NTCHL* W11 ..........8 C8
Sythwood Primary School
*WOKN/KNAP* GU21 .....231 N2

Sutton Cemetery
*CHEAM* SM3 ..........201 J9
Sutton Civic Centre
*SUT* SM1 ............221 L2
Sutton College of Learning
  for Adults
*SUT* SM1 ............221 L2
Sutton Common ⇌
*SUT* SM1 ............201 K9
Sutton General Hospital
*SUT* SM1 ............221 L6
Sutton Grammar School for Boys
*SUT* SM1 ............221 M2
Sutton Green Golf Club
*WOKS/MYFD* GU22 .....232 B8
Sutton High Junior School
*SUT* SM1 ............221 L3
Sutton High
  School for Girls GDST
*SUT* SM1 ............221 K3
Sutton House
*HACK* E8 ............120 B10
Suttons Business Park
*RAIN* RM13 ..........144 E5
Suttons JMI School
*RCH* RM12 ...........125 L9
Suttons Manor Clinic
*ABR/ST* RM4 .........84 F5
Sutton Superbowl
*SUT* SM1 ............221 L2
Sutton United FC
*SUT* SM1 ............221 K1
Sutton West Centre
*SUT* SM1 ............221 K2
Swaffield Primary School
*WAND/EARL* SW18 .....179 M2
Swakeleys School
*HGDN/ICK* UB10 ......132 C4
Swallow Dell Primary School
*WGCE* AL7 ...........23 K6
Swaminarayan School
*WLSDN* NW10 .........136 A1

Tattenham Corner ⇌
*EPSOM* KT18 .........238 D4
Tattenham Health Centre
*EPSOM* KT18 .........238 E4
Tavistock Clinic
*HAMP* NW3 ...........3 L2
TAVR Centre
*KUT/HW* KT1 .........199 J4
Tavy Clinic
*ABYW* SE2 ...........163 N3
Tawhid Boys School
*STNW/STAM* N16 ......119 N7
Taylor Trading Estate
*HERT/BAY* SG13 ......26 A4
Tayyibah Girls School
*STNW/STAM* N16 ......119 P6
Teardrop Industrial Park
*SWLY* BR8 ...........209 K5
TechnClass
*HARH* RM3 ...........105 P9
Teddington ⇌
*TEDD* TW11 ..........176 F9
Teddington Business Park
*TEDD* TW11 ..........176 E8
Teddington Cemetery
*TEDD* TW11 ..........176 D7
Teddington Clinic
*TEDD* TW11 ..........176 D9
Teddington Memorial Hospital
*TEDD* TW11 ..........176 D9
Teddington Pool & Fitness Centre
*TEDD* TW11 ..........176 F8
Teddington School
*TEDD* TW11 ..........177 J9
The Teddington Theatre Club
*E/WMO/HCT* KT8 ......198 C5
Teikyo School
*SLN* SL2 ............130 A2
Telferscot Primary School
*BAL* SW12 ...........180 D4
Temperate House, Kew Gardens
*RCH/KEW* TW9 ........155 L8
Temple ⊖
*TPL/STR* WC2R .......12 A7
Temple Court Business Centre
*WOKN/KNAP* GU21 .....232 C3
Temple Grove Hatcham School
*NWCR* SE14 .........160 C6
Temple Hill Primary School
*DART* DA1 ...........187 P1
Temple of Bacchus
*CMBW* SE5 ..........159 K8
Temple of Mithras
*MANHO* EC4N .........12 G6
Templewood Primary School
*WGCW* AL8 ...........22 F3
Tenby Road Clinic
*EDGW* HA8 ...........95 L10
Tenterden Sports Ground
*KTN/HRWW/WS* HA3 ....115 K5
Terence McMillan Stadium
*PLSTW* E13 ..........141 P6
Tetherdown Primary School
*MUSWH* N10 ..........118 B2
Tewin Bury Farm Hotel
*WLYN* AL6 ...........23 M2
Tewin Cowper Primary School
*WLYN* AL6 ...........23 P1
Tewin Road Business Centre
*WGCE* AL7 ...........23 H4
Tewin Water School
*WLYN* AL6 ...........23 K1
Thames Barrier
*CAN/RD* E16 .........162 A1
Thames Barrier Information &
  Learning Centre
*CHARL* SE7 ..........162 A2
Thames Christian College
*BTSEA* SW11 .........157 N9
Thames Ditton ⇌
*THDIT* KT7 ..........198 C2
Thames Ditton & Esher Golf Club
*ESH/CLAY* KT10 ......198 C9
Thames Ditton Infant School
*THDIT* KT7 ..........198 E6
Thames Ditton Junior School
*THDIT* KT7 ..........198 E7
Thames Gateway Park
*DACW* RM9 ...........144 A5
Thames House
*WEST* SW1P ..........17 L5
Thameside Industrial Estate
*CAN/RD* E16 .........142 A10
Thameside Infant School
*GRAYS* RM17 .........167 P5
Thameside Theatre
*GRAYS* RM17 .........167 M4
Thames Industrial Park
*TIL* RM18 ...........169 M3
Thamesmead Leisure Centre
*THMD* SE28 ..........143 L9
Thamesmead School
*SHPTN* TW17 .........196 E6
Thamesmead Shopping Centre
*THMD* SE28 ..........143 K9
Thames Valley Athletics Centre
*WDSR* SL4 ..........149 K4
Thames Valley Community
  Infant School
*SL* SL1 .............149 H1
Thames Valley Cultural Centre
*WDSR* SL4 ..........149 J7
The Thames Valley
  Nuffield Hospital
*DTCH/LGLY* SL3 ......129 P3
Thames Valley University
*EA* W5 ..............135 K9
*SL* SL1 .............129 K10
Thamesview Business Centre
*RAIN* RM13 ..........144 F7
Thames View Clinic
*BARK* EC2Y ..........143 J4
Thames View J & I School
*BARK* EC2Y ..........143 K4
Thamesview School
*GVE* DA12 ...........191 J6
Thames Water Tower
*NTGHL* W11 ..........156 G1
Theatre de l'Ange Fou
  International School of
  Corporeal Mime
*ARCH* N19 ...........118 F6
Theatre for Mankind
*FSBYPK* N4 ..........118 G6
Theatre Magenta
*LHD/OX* KT22 ........236 F5
Theatre Museum Library
  & Archive
*COVGDN* WC2E ........11 M7
Theatre of the Dispossessed
*WIM/MER* SW19 .......178 G4
The Theatre on the Hill
*CTHM* CR3 ..........241 M4
Theatre Royal
*HOL/ALD* WC2B .......11 M6
*SRTFD* E15 ..........141 J1
*WDSR* SL4 ..........149 J6
Theatre Royal Haymarket
*STJS* SW1Y ..........11 K8
Theobalds Grove ⇌
*CHES/WCR* EN8 .......62 C8
Theobalds Park C & C Site
*CHESW* EN7 ..........61 P10
Theodore McLeary
  Primary School
*EDUL* SE22 ..........159 N10
Therapia Lane ⇌
*CROY/NA* CRO ........202 F7
Therapia Trading Estate
*CROY/NA* CRO ........202 E7
Therfield School
*LHD/OX* KT22 ........236 F5
Theydon Bois ⊖
*EPP* CM16 ...........83 J2
Theydon Bois Cemetery
*EPP* CM16 ...........83 K4

Theydon Bois Golf Club EPP CM16 64 G10
Theydon Bois Primary School EPP CM16 83 H2
Thistlebrook Industrial Estate ABYW SE2 163 M2
Thistle Hotel
BAY/PAD W2 9 K8
BCVA SW1W 16 F4
CAMTN NW1 5 H10
FITZ W1T 11 H5
FSBYE EC1V 6 E10
NOXST/BSQ WC1A 11 L4
WDR/YW UB7 151 M7
WESTW SW1E 16 F4
Thistle Marble Arch Hotel MBLAR W1H 10 B6
Thistle Piccadilly Hotel SOHO/SHAV W1D 11 K8
Thomas Arnold Primary School DAGW RM9 144 A2
Thomas Buxton Infant School WCHPL E1 13 N2
The Thomas Coram Middle School BERK HP4 34 A7
Thomas Fairchild Primary School IS N1 6 G7
Thomas Francis Academy BRXN/ST SW9 159 J10
Thomas Gamuel Primary School WALTH E17 120 F4
Thomas Harding Junior School CSHM HP5 50 G8
Thomas Jones Primary School NTGHL W11 8 A6
Thomas Knyvett College ASHF TW15 173 P6
Thomas London Independent Day School KENS W8 15 H3
Thomas More Catholic School PUR/KEN CR8 222 G6
The Thomas Rivers Medical Centre SBW CM21 29 M2
Thomas Road Industrial Estate POP/IOD E14 140 F7
Thomas's Fulham FUL/PGN SW6 157 L9
Thomas's Preparatory School
BTSEA SW11 157 N7
BTSEA SW11 180 A1
Thomas Tallis School BKHTH/KID SE3 161 N9
Thomas Willingale Primary School LOU IG10 82 F7
Thorncroft Manor LHD/OX KT22 236 F9
Thorndon North Country Park RBRW/HUT CM13 107 L6
Thorndon Park Golf Club RBRW/HUT CM13 107 N7
Thorndon South Country Park RBRW/HUT CM13 107 M8
Thorney Park Golf Club WDR/YW UB7 151 L1
Thornhill Primary School IS N1 6 A4
Thornton Heath ⇌ THHTH CR7 203 K4
Thornton Heath Health Centre THHTH CR7 203 K4
Thornton Heath Pools & Fitness Centre THHTH CR7 203 K4
Thornton Road Industrial Estate CROY/NA CR0 202 F6
Thorntree Primary School CHARL SE7 162 A4
Thorpe CE Infant School EGH TW20 194 F3
Thorpe Cemetery EGH TW20 194 F2
Thorpe CC EGH TW20 194 C4
Thorpe Hall Primary School WALTH E17 101 H9
Thorpe House School CFSP/GDCR SL9 110 B2
Thorpe Industrial Park EGH TW20 194 G1
Thorpe Lea Primary School EGH TW20 172 G9
Thorpe Park CHERT KT16 195 J4
Three Bridges ⇌ CRAWE RH10 284 C7
Three Bridges Business Centre NWDGN UB2 154 B1
Three Bridges Community Centre CRAWE RH10 284 B7
Three Bridges CC CRAWE RH10 284 B7
Three Bridges FC CRAWE RH10 284 B7
Three Bridges First School CRAWE RH10 284 B6
Three Bridges Junior School CRAWE RH10 284 A7
Three Bridges Primary School NWDGN UB2 154 A2
Three Mills Heritage Centre BOW E3 141 H5
Thurrock Athletics Stadium CDW/CHF RM16 168 A1
Thurrock & Basildon College CDW/CHF RM16 168 C3
Thurrock Business Centre WTHK RM20 166 E5
Thurston Industrial Estate LEW SE13 160 G9
Tibetan Buddhist Centre WALW SE17 18 E7
Tidemill Primary School DEPT SE8 160 F6
Tideway Industrial Estate VX/NE SW8 17 H10
Tiffin Girls School KUTN/CMB KT2 177 K9
Tiffin School & Sports Centre KUTN/CMB KT2 199 L2
Tilbury Fort TIL RM18 168 F10
Tilbury/Gravesend Passenger Ferry TIL RM18 168 E10
Tilbury Industrial Park TIL RM18 169 L4
Tilbury Leisure Centre
TIL RM18 168 D8
TIL RM18 168 E8
Tilbury Manor Junior School TIL RM18 168 E6
Tilbury Town ⇌ TIL RM18 168 C8
Tilehouse Combined School DEN/HRF UB9 111 H4
Tiller Centre (Swimming Baths) POP/IOD E14 160 F2
Tiller Leisure Centre POP/IOD E14 160 F2
Tillingbourne Junior School RGUE GU4 268 E7
Timbercroft Primary School WOOL/PLUM SE18 163 H6
Timbers Clinic KTN/HRWW/WS HA3 94 C7
Timebridge Youth & Community Centre CROY/NA CR0 224 G2
Times Square Shopping Centre SUT SM1 221 L2
Titan Industrial Estate GRAYS RM17 167 M3
Tithe Barn Museum UPMR RM14 126 B5
Tiverton Primary School SEVS/STOTM N15 119 L4
Tobacco Dock WAP E1W 140 A9
Tokyngton Community Centre WBLY HA9 115 N10
Toldos School STNW/STAM N16 119 L6
Tollgate Primary School PLSTW E13 141 P6
Tolworth ⇌ BRYLDS KT5 199 N9
Tolworth CP School SURB KT6 199 L8
Tolworth Girls School SURB KT6 199 L10
Tolworth Recreation Centre SURB KT6 199 L10
Tom Hood School WAN E11 121 L8
Tomo Industrial Estate UX/CGN UB8 131 M8
Toot Hill Golf Club CHONG CM5 66 G7
Tooting ⇌ TOOT SW17 180 A9
Tooting Bec ⊖ TOOT SW17 180 B6
Tooting Bec Athletics Track TOOT SW17 180 C7
Tooting Broadway ⊖ TOOT SW17 179 P8
Tooting Leisure Centre TOOT SW17 179 N7
Tooting & Mitcham United FC MTCM CR4 202 B1
Top Meadow Golf Club UPMR RM14 147 J1
Torah Temimah Primary School CRICK NW2 116 E9
Torah Vodaas GLDGN NW11 117 J7
Tormead School GU GU1 250 C10
Torriano Junior School KTTN NW5 118 D10
Torridon Primary School CAT SE6 183 J5
Torrington Clinic NFNCH/WDSPK N12 97 M6
Torrington Park Health Centre NFNCH/WDSPK N12 97 M5
Total Health Clinic SHB W12 156 E1
Tottenham Cemetery TOTM N17 99 M8
Tottenham Court Road ⊖ SOHO/SHAV W1D 11 J5
Tottenham Green Leisure Centre SEVS/STOTM N15 119 M2
Tottenham Hale ⇌ ⊖ TOTM N17 120 A1
Tottenham Hale Retail Park SEVS/STOTM N15 119 P2
Tottenham Hotspur FC (White Hart Lane) TOTM N17 99 N8
Tottenham Park Cemetery ED N9 100 A4
Tottenham Sports Centre TOTM N17 99 N9
Totteridge CC TRDG/WHET N20 97 K3
Totteridge & Whetstone ⊖ TRDG/WHET N20 97 L3
Tower 42 OBST EC2N 13 J5
The Tower Bridge Exhibition STHWK SE1 13 L10
Tower Bridge Primary School STHWK SE1 19 L1
Tower Bridge Wharf WAP E1W 13 N10
Tower Gateway ⊖ TWRH EC3N 13 L7
Tower Hamlets College
BETH E2 7 N10
POP/IOD E14 140 G9
WCHPL E1 140 B7
Tower Hill ⊖ TWRH EC3N 13 L8
The Tower Hotel WAP E1W 13 M9
Tower Industrial Estate SNWD SE25 203 P4
Tower Millennium Pier TWRH EC3N 13 K9
Tower of London TWRH EC3N 13 L8
Tower Retail Park DART DA1 186 G1
Towers Business Park WBLY HA9 115 N9
Towers Infant School EMPK RM11 125 K5
Towers Junior School EMPK RM11 125 K5
Tower Stairs MON EC3R 13 J8
Town Farm Primary School STWL/WRAY TW19 173 N3
Townley Grammar School for Girls BXLYHS DA6 186 A2
Townmead Business Centre FUL/PGN SW6 157 M8
Town Medical Centre SEV TN13 265 J1
Townsend CE School STALW/RED AL3 38 B1
Townsend Industrial Estate WLSDN NW10 135 P3
Townsend Primary School WALW SE17 19 H5
Toynbee Hall & Curtain Theatre WCHPL E1 13 L4
Trade Union Congress NOXST/BSQ WC1A 11 K5
Traditions Golf Club WOKS/MYFD GU22 233 K1
Trafalgar Business Centre BARK EC2Y 143 J6
Trafalgar Infant & Junior School WHTN TW2 176 C5
Trafalgar Infant School WHTN TW2 176 C4
Trafalgar Square STJS SW1Y 11 K9
Trafalgar Trading Estate PEND EN3 80 E8
Tramshed Theatre WOOL/PLUM SE18 162 E3
Trans Atlantic College BETH E2 7 K7
Transport for London Lost Property Office CAMTN NW1 10 B2
Transport House WEST SW1P 17 L4
Travellers Lane Industrial Estate HAT AL10 40 E8
Travelodge
ACT W3 135 M6
BTFD TW8 155 K5
BTSEA SW11 157 M9
CAMTN NW1 9 P3
CAN/RD E16 142 A10
CHES/WCR EN8 62 B9
DORK RH4 273 H1
EPP CM16 48 F10
FELT TW13 175 H4
FSBYW WC1X 5 P9
GUW GU2 249 N9
HAT AL10 40 C3
HEST TW5 153 K5
HHNE HP2 35 N7
HLW CM20 28 G8
HORL RH6 279 P10
IL IG1 122 E8
KUTN/CMB KT2 199 K2
LHD/OX KT22 236 F8
LSQ/SEVD WC2H 11 L5
POP/IOD E14 141 J8
PUR RM19 166 E2
RDART DA2 188 D1
REDBR IG4 122 C4
SL SL1 149 K1
STA TW18 173 H7
STPAN WC1H 5 M9
SUN TW16 175 H10
SURB KT6 199 N8
WCHPL E1 13 L5
WLSDN NW10 135 M4
Travelodge Croydon Central CROY/NA CR0 203 L9
Travelodge Watford Central WATW WD18 73 J8
Travelodge Windsor Central WDSR SL4 149 H7
Treasury WHALL SW1A 17 L2
The Treaty Centre HSLW TW3 154 A9
Treehouse School MUSWH N10 118 B2
The Treehouse School BMSBY WC1N 11 N1
Treetops Special School GRAYS RM17 167 N3
Trent CE Primary School EBAR EN4 78 A8
Trent Country Park EBAR EN4 78 B6
Trent Park Cemetery EBAR EN4 78 B7
Trent Park Golf Club STHGT/OAK N14 78 D8
Trevelyan Middle School
WDSR SL4 148 F8
WDSR SL4 149 H10
Trevor Roberts School HAMP NW3 3 M3
Tricor Business Park CHES/WCR EN8 62 D10
Tricor Trading Estate CHES/WCR EN8 62 D10
Tricycle Cinema KIL/WHAMP NW6 2 D4
Tricycle Theatre KIL/WHAMP NW6 2 D3
Trident Business Centre TOOT SW17 180 A8
Trident Industrial Estate
DTCH/LGLY SL3 151 H9
HOD EN11 45 H2
Trinity Business Centre BERM/RHTH SE16 160 E1
Trinity Catholic Lower High School WFD IG8 101 M5
Trinity College Centre PECK SE15 159 M6
Trinity College of Music
GNWCH SE10 161 H5
MHST W1U 10 D4
Trinity Hospital GNWCH SE10 161 J4
Trinity House TWRH EC3N 13 K7
Trinity RC High School (Upper) WFD IG8 101 M5
Trinity St Marys Primary School BAL SW12 180 B4
Trinity St Stephen CE First School WDSR SL4 149 H7
Trinity School
CROY/NA CR0 204 B9
DAGE RM10 124 B8
Trinity School Belvedere BELV DA17 164 D3
Trinity Trading Estate HYS/HAR UB3 153 H2
Tripcock Point Development Site THMD SE28 143 J9
Triumph Trading Estate TOTM N17 99 P7
Trocadero SOHO/SHAV W1D 11 J8
Trojan Business Centre WLSDN NW10 136 C1
Troy Industrial Estate HRW HA1 114 E3
True Buddha School IS N1 5 N6
Trumps Green Infant School VW GU25 194 A6
TS Queen Mary TPL/STR WC2R 11 N8
TTMH Belz Day School STNW/STAM N16 119 P5
Tubbenden J & I Schools ORP BR6 226 G1
Tudor Court Primary School CDW/CHF RM16 167 L1
Tudor Enterprise Park KTN/HRWW/WS HA3 114 C1
Tudor Lodge Health Centre WIM/MER SW19 178 G4
Tudor Lodge Hotel PIN HA5 113 J4
Tudor Lodge School PUR/KEN CR8 222 F6
Tudor Primary School
FNCH N3 97 M9
HHS/BOV HP3 35 P8
STHL UB1 133 M9
Tudors Business Centre KWD/TDW/WH KT20 239 J8
Tufnell Park ⊖ KTTN NW5 118 C9
Tufnell Park Primary School HOLWY N7 118 E9
Tuke School PECK SE15 160 A7
Tulse Hill ⇌ WNWD SE27 181 J5
Tunnel Avenue Trading Estate GNWCH SE10 161 J1
Tunnel Industrial Estate
WTHK RM20 166 E3
WTHK RM20 166 E5
Turin Grove School ED N9 100 B1
Turkey Street ⇌ PEND EN3 80 B3
Turners Hill CE Primary School CRAWE RH10 285 P10
Turney School DUL SE21 181 K3
Turnford School CHES/WCR EN8 62 D4
Turnham Green ⊖ CHSWK W4 156 B3
Turnham Primary School BROCKY SE4 160 D10
Turnpike Lane ⊖ SEVS/STOTM N15 119 J1
Turtle Key Arts Centre FUL/PGN SW6 14 F10
Tutorial College of West London STHL UB1 133 P10
Tweeddale Primary School CAR SM5 201 N7
Twenty Nevern Square Hotel ECT SW5 14 F6
Twickenham ⇌ TWK TW1 176 F3
Twickenham Cemetery WHTN TW2 176 A4
Twickenham Park Health Centre TWK TW1 177 H2
Twickenham Preparatory School HPTN TW12 198 A1
Twickenham Stadium ISLW TW7 176 D2
Twickenham Trading Estate TWK TW1 176 E2
Two Bridges Business Park SAND/SEL CR2 223 L3
Two Rivers Retail Park STA TW18 173 H7
Two Waters JMI School HHS/BOV HP3 53 N1
Twyford CE High School ACT W3 135 M10
Twyford Sports Centre ACT W3 135 N10
Tyburn Infant School STJWD NW8 9 M1
Tynemouth Road Health Centre SEVS/STOTM N15 119 N2
The Type Museum BRXN/ST SW9 158 G7
Tyrrells Wood Golf Club LHD/OX KT22 237 L10
Tyssen Primary School STNW/STAM N16 119 P6
UCI Cinema
BAY/PAD W2 9 H6
SUT SM1 221 L2
WTHK RM20 166 E3
UCI Empire Cinema LSQ/SEVD WC2H 11 K8
UK Passport Office PIM SW1V 16 F5
The Ullswater Business Park COUL/CHIP CR5 240 F2
Ullswater Trading Estate COUL/CHIP CR5 240 F2
Underhill Infant School BAR EN5 77 H9
Unicorn Primary School BECK BR3 204 G5
Unicorn School RCH/KEW TW9 155 L7
Unicorn Theatre STHWK SE1 19 K1
Union Business Park UX/CGN UB8 131 M2
United Medical & Dental Schools STHWK SE1 17 N3
Unity College KTTN NW5 118 C9
Unity Trading Estate WFD IG8 122 A1
University Church of Christ the King STPAN WC1H 11 J2
University College for the Creative Arts at Epsom EPSOM KT18 220 A10
University College Hospital
CAMTN NW1 11 H1
HAMP NW3 3 M2
University College London
FITZ W1T 11 H3
GWRST WC1E 11 J2
STPAN WC1H 11 J1
University College London, Astor College FITZ W1T 11 H3
University College London Medical School FITZ W1T 10 G3
University College London Obstetrics Hospital GWRST WC1E 11 H2
University College School HAMP NW3 117 M9
University Hospital Lewisham LEW SE13 182 G1
University of California WHALL SW1A 10 G10
University of East London
BARK EC2Y 123 K9
CAN/RD E16 142 D9
PLSTW E13 141 N5
SRTFD E15 141 J3
University of Greenwich
DART DA1 187 N5
GNWCH SE10 161 J4
WOOL/PLUM SE18 162 D3
University of Greenwich (Mansion Site) ELTH/MOT SE9 184 F2
University of Greenwich School of Health RDART DA2 188 A2
University of Greenwich (Southwood Site) ELTH/MOT SE9 184 F3
University of Greenwich Sports Ground
ELTH/MOT SE9 162 B10
ELTH/MOT SE9 184 F3
University of Hertfordshire
HAT AL10 40 D3
STAL AL1 38 E8
University of Hertfordshire (Bayfordbury Observatory) HERT/BAY SG13 25 J10
University of Hertfordshire (College Lane Campus) HAT AL10 40 C6
University of Hertfordshire (de Havilland Campus) HAT AL10 40 A4
University of Hertfordshire (Faculty of Law) STAL AL1 38 D5
University of Hertfordshire (Fielder Centre) HAT AL10 40 A1
University of London
BAY/PAD W2 9 L6
BMSBY WC1N 11 M2
CLKNW EC1R 12 B1
ENC/FH EN2 79 P2
FITZ W1T 11 J5
MBLAR W1H 9 P5
STHWK SE1 12 G10
STPAN WC1H 11 K1
University of London Athletics Ground NWMAL KT3 200 D5
The University of Surrey GUW GU2 249 M10
University of the Arts London MYFR/PKLN W1K 10 E6
University of Westminster
CAMTN NW1 10 G1
CAVSQ/HST W1G 10 F5
CHSWK W4 155 P7
GTPST W1W 10 F3
HRW HA1 114 F5
University of Westminster, Environment MHST W1U 10 C3
University Vandals RFC SHPTN TW17 196 D7
Uphall Primary School IL IG1 122 E10
Upland Primary School BXLYHN DA7 164 A9
Uplands Business Park WALTH E17 100 C10
Upminster ⇌ ⊖ UPMR RM14 126 B7
Upminster Bridge ⊖ HCH RM12 125 P7
Upminster Cemetery UPMR RM14 126 C10
Upminster Golf Club UPMR RM14 126 B5
Upminster Primary School UPMR RM14 126 B8
Upminster Trading Park UPMR RM14 127 J5
Upney ⊖ BARK EC2Y 143 J2
Upper Clapton RFC EPP CM16 47 L10
Upper Halliford ⇌ SHPTN TW17 196 F2
Upper Holloway ⊖ ARCH N19 118 E7
Upper Montagu Street Clinic CAMTN NW1 10 A3
Upper Tooting Independent High School TOOT SW17 179 P5
Upper Warlingham ⇌ WARL CR6 241 P4
Upshire Primary School WAB EN9 63 N9
Upton Cross Primary School PLSTW E13 141 N3
Upton Day Hospital BXLYHS DA6 163 P10
Upton Hospital SL SL1 149 L2
Upton House School WDSR SL4 149 H8
Upton Lane Medical Centre FSTGT E7 141 N1
Upton Park ⊖ PLSTW E13 141 P3
Upton Primary School BXLY DA5 185 P1
Upton Road School BXLYHS DA6 185 P1
The Urdang Academy LSQ/SEVD WC2H 11 L6
Ursuline High School RYNPK SW20 178 G10
Ursuline Preparatory School RYNPK SW20 178 G10
Uxbridge ⊖ UX/CGN UB8 131 N2
Uxbridge CC UX/CGN UB8 131 P1
Uxbridge Cemetery UX/CGN UB8 132 A5
Uxbridge College
HYS/HAR UB3 133 H9
NTGHL W11 8 B5
UX/CGN UB8 131 P1
Uxbridge FC WDR/YW UB7 132 B9
Uxbridge Golf Club HGDN/ICK UB10 111 P7
Uxbridge Health Centre UX/CGN UB8 131 N2
Uxbridge High School
HGDN/ICK UB10 131 P4
UX/CGN UB8 131 N4
Uxbridge Industrial Estate UX/CGN UB8 131 L4
Uxbridge Swimming Pool UX/CGN UB8 131 P1
Uxendon Manor JMI School KTN/HRWW/WS HA3 115 K3
Vale Farm Sports Centre ALP/SUD HA0 114 G9
Vale Industrial Estate WATW WD18 92 D2
The Vale Medical Centre FSTH SE23 182 D5
Valence House Museum & Library BCTR RM8 123 N7
Valence Primary School BCTR RM8 123 N7
Valence School BH/WHM TN16 263 J2
Valentine High School GNTH/NBYPK IG2 122 D4
Valentines High Lower School GNTH/NBYPK IG2 122 E3
Vale Primary School EPSOM KT18 238 A5
Vale Resource Base TOTM N17 99 M9
The Vale School SKENS SW7 15 J4
Vallance Road School WCHPL E1 13 N2
Valley End CC CHOB/PIR GU24 212 F4
Valley End CE Infant School CHOB/PIR GU24 212 F3
The Valley Gardens EGH TW20 193 K2
Valley Link Business Centre PEND EN3 80 D10
Valley Link Business Estate PEND EN3 80 D10
Valley Primary School HAYES BR2 205 L2
Valmar Trading Estate CMBW SE5 159 K7
V & A Museum of Childhood BETH E2 140 B5
Vanbrugh Theatre GWRST WC1E 11 J2
Vanguard Trading Estate SRTFD E15 141 H3
Vaudeville Theatre COVGDN WC2E 11 M7
Vaughan First & Middle School RYLN/HDSTN HA2 114 B4
Vauxhall ⇌ ⊖ VX/NE SW8 17 M8
Vauxhall Primary School LBTH SE11 17 N7
Venus School of Therapies LOU IG10 82 A9
Vernon House Special School WLSDN NW10 115 P10
Verulam Golf Club STAL AL1 38 E8
Verulam Industrial Estate STAL AL1 38 E8
Verulamium Museum STALW/RED AL3 38 A6
Verulam School STAL AL1 38 F5
Vestry Hall MTCM CR4 202 A3
Vestry House Museum WALTH E17 120 G2
Vestry Industrial Estate RSEV TN14 247 J5
Vicarage Fields Health Clinic BARK EC2Y 142 F2
The Vicarage Field Shopping Centre BARK EC2Y 142 F2
Vicarage Primary School EHAM E6 142 C5
Vicarage Road Cemetery WATW WD18 73 H8
Vicars Green Primary School GFD/PVL UB6 135 H4
V I Components Industrial Park ERITH DA8 164 F4
Victoria ⇌ ⊖ PIM SW1V 16 F5
Victoria & Albert Museum SKENS SW7 15 M4
Victoria Barracks WDSR SL4 149 J7
Victoria Business Centre WELL DA16 163 K8
Victoria Bus Station PIM SW1V 16 F4
Victoria CE First School BERK HP4 33 P5
Victoria Chiropractic Clinic SKENS SW7 16 A2
Victoria Clinic WOKN/KNAP GU21 232 C2
Victoria Coach Station BGVA SW1W 16 E6
Victoria Hall FNCH N3 97 J9
Victoria Industrial Estate ACT W3 136 A7
Victoria Industrial Park DART DA1 187 L1
Victoria Junior School FELT TW13 175 J4
Victoria Medical Centre PIM SW1V 17 H6
Victoria Palace Theatre BGVA SW1W 16 F4
Victoria Park Industrial Centre HOM E9 140 E2
Victoria Park Plaza Hotel PIM SW1V 16 G5
Victoria Place Shopping Centre BGVA SW1W 16 F5
Victoria Rail/Air Terminal PIM SW1V 16 F5
Victoria Retail Park RSLP HA4 113 L10
Victoria Square Business Area STAL AL1 38 E7
Victoria Wharf POP/IOD E14 140 D9
Victoria Wharf Industrial Estate DEPT SE8 160 D4
Victor Seymour Infant School CAR SM5 202 A10
Victory Business Centre ISLW TW7 154 E10
Victory Day School THHTH CR7 203 K4
Victory Primary School WALW SE17 18 F5
Viking Business Centre ROMW/RG RM7 124 D5
Viking Primary School NTHLT UB5 133 L5
Village Infant School DAGE RM10 144 B2
The Village Medical Centre SL SL1 128 C10
The Village School HAMP NW3 4 B1
Village Shopping Centre SL SL1 149 L
Villiers High School STHL UB1 133 P10
The Vine Clinic KUTN/CMB KT2 177 K9
Vine Medical Centre E/WMO/HCT KT8 198 B3
The Vines School BTSEA SW11 158 B10
The Vineyard Primary School RCHPK/HAM TW10 177 K2
Vinopolis, City of Wine STHWK SE1 12 F9
Vinters' Hall BLKFR EC4V 12 F7
V I P Trading Estate CHARL SE7 161 P3
Virginia Primary School BETH E2 7 L10
Virginia Water ⇌ VW GU25 194 B5
Virgo Fidelis Convent Schools NRWD SE19 181 K9
Visage School of Hair & Beauty ELTH/MOT SE9 184 D2
Viscount Industrial Estate DTCH/LGLY SL3 151 H9
Vision College of Technology HOM E9 140 F
Vita et Pax School STHGT/OAK N14 78 C9
Vittoria Primary School IS N1 5 P6
Voyager Business Estate BERM/RHTH SE16 19 N3
Vue Cinema
ACT W3 135 M6
CROY/NA CR0 202 G9
DAGW RM9 143 P3
FUL/PGN SW6 157 K6
GSTN WD25 55 K9
HAMP NW3 3 J1
HRW HA1 114 D4
LSQ/SEVD WC2H 11 K7
NFNCH/WDSPK N12 97 N8
ROMW/RG RM7 124 F3
SHB W12 156 G1
STA TW18 173 H7
WTHK RM20 166 F2
Vulcan Business Centre CROY/NA CR0 225 K5
Vyners School HGDN/ICK UB10 112 A9
Waddon ⇌ CROY/NA CR0 223 H1
Waddon Clinic CROY/NA CR0 223 H2
Waddon Infant School CROY/NA CR0 223 H2
Waddon Marsh ⊖ CROY/NA CR0 203 H9
Wadham Lodge Sports Centre WALTH E17 100 G9
Wadsworth Business Centre GFD/PVL UB6 135 H4
The Waldegrave Clinic TEDD TW11 176 E8
Waldegrave Girls School WHTN TW2 176 C6
Waldo Industrial Estate BMLY BR1 205 P3
Waldorf School of South West London BAL SW12 180 D5
Waldron Health Centre & Surgery NWCR SE14 160 E6
Walker Primary School STHGT/OAK N14 98 E3
The Wallace Centre DEPT SE8 160 G5
The Wallace Collection MHST W1U 10 C5
Wallace Fields County Infant School EW KT17 220 D9
Wallace Fields Junior School EW KT17 220 D8
Wallbrook Business Centre HSLWW TW4 153 J9
Wallington ⇌ WLGTN SM6 222 C
Wallington County Grammar School WLGTN SM6 202 C1
Wallington High School for Girls WLGTN SM6 222 C5
Walmer Road Clinic NTGHL W11 8 A
Walm Lane Clinic CRICK NW2 116 G1
Walnuts Leisure Centre ORP BR6 207 K8
Walnuts Shopping Centre ORP BR6 207 K8
Walnut Tree Walk Primary School LBTH SE11 18 A
Waltham Abbey Cemetery WAB EN9 63 H10
Waltham Abbey Gatehouse & Bridge WAB EN9 63 H
Waltham Abbey Jewish Cemetery WAB EN9 81 N

Waltham Abbey Marriott Hotel WAB EN9 63 L10
Waltham Abbey Swimming Pool WAB EN9 81 J1
Waltham Cross CHES/WCR EN8 62 D10
Waltham Forest College WALTH E17 120 B1
WALTH E17 120 C1
Waltham Forest Pool & Track WALTH E17 100 G10
Waltham Forest Theatre WALTH E17 120 E1
Waltham Holy Cross Infant School WAB EN9 63 J9
Walthamstow Academy WALTH E17 100 E9
Walthamstow Business Centre WALTH E17 101 H10
Walthamstow Central WALTH E17 120 F3
Walthamstow Hall Junior School SEV TN13 247 J8
Walthamstow Hall Senior School SEV TN13 247 K9
Walthamstow Marsh Nature Reserve CLPT E5 120 A5
Walthamstow Queens Road WALTH E17 120 F3
Walthamstow School for Girls WALTH E17 120 C2
Walton Business Centre WOT/HER KT12 197 J7
Walton Casuals FC WOT/HER KT12 197 J5
Walton Cemetery WOT/HER KT12 197 H7
Walton Community Hospital WOT/HER KT12 197 J9
Walton Heath Golf Club Shop KWD/TDW/WH KT20 256 E1
Walton & Hersham FC WOT/HER KT12 197 H9
Walton Leigh School WOT/HER KT12 216 F1
Walton-on-Thames WOT/HER KT12 197 H10
Walton-on-Thames CC WOT/HER KT12 196 G8
Walton on the Hill CE Junior School KWD/TDW/WH KT20 256 D1
Walton on the Hill Primary School KWD/TDW/WH KT20 238 E10
Walton Swimming Pool WOT/HER KT12 197 J8
Walworth Academy STHWK SE1 19 K8
Walworth Lower Secondary School WALW SE17 19 H7
Walworth Town Hall WALW SE17 18 E6
Wanborough RGUW GU3 248 A10
Wandle Park CROY/NA CR0 203 H9
Wandle Recreation Centre WAND/EARL SW18 179 L2
Wandle Trading Estate MTCM CR4 202 A7
Wandle Valley School CAR SM5 201 P7
Wandsworth Adult College BTSEA SW11 158 B7
TOOT SW17 179 P5
Wandsworth Cemetery WAND/EARL SW18 179 M4
Wandsworth Common TOOT SW17 179 P3
Wandsworth Road VX/NE SW8 158 D8
Wandsworth Town WAND/EARL SW18 157 L10
Wandsworth Trading Estate WAND/EARL SW18 179 L3
Wansfell College EPP CM16 82 G1
Wanstead WAN E11 121 N4
Wanstead CC WAN E11 121 N5
Wanstead CE Primary School WAN E11 121 M3
Wanstead Golf Club WAN E11 121 P5
Wanstead High School WAN E11 121 P4
Wanstead Hospital WAN E11 121 N2
Wanstead Leisure Centre WAN E11 121 P4
Wanstead Park FSTGT E7 121 N9
Wapping WAP E1W 140 B10
Wapping Pier Head WAP E1W 13 P10
Wapping Wharf WAP E1W 140 B10
Ware WARE SG12 26 D2
Warley Hill Business Park RBRW/HUT CM13 107 H7
Warley Hospital BRW CM14 106 G6
Warley Lodge Hospital RBRW/HUT CM13 107 J9
Warley Park Golf Club RBRW/HUT CM13 107 J10
Warley Primary School BRW CM14 107 H6
Warlingham Park School WARL CR6 242 F2
Warlingham RFC & John Fisher Sports Club WARL CR6 242 A2
Warlingham School WARL CR6 242 A2
Warlingham Sports Club WARL CR6 242 C3
Warlingham Village Primary School WARL CR6 242 C3
War Memorial Sports Ground SUT SM1 221 P1
Warnford Industrial Estate HYS/HAR UB3 152 F1
Warren Comprehensive School CHDH RM6 124 A3
Warren Dell Primary School OXHEY WD19 93 K4
Warrender School RSLP HA4 112 G5
Warren Junior School CHDH RM6 124 A3
Warren Mead Infant School BNSTD SM7 238 F1
Warren Mead Junior School BNSTD SM7 238 G1
The Warren Medical Centre YEAD UB4 133 J8
Warren Primary School CDW/CHF RM16 167 H2
Warren Road Primary School ORP BR6 227 J1
Warren Sports Centre CHDH RM6 124 A3
Warren Street CAMTN NW1 10 C1
Warwick Avenue MV/WKIL W9 9 J2
Warwick Dubbing Theatre SOHO/CST W1F 11 J6
Warwick Estate BAY/PAD W2 9 H4
Warwick Leadlay Gallery GNWCH SE10 161 H5
Warwick Quadrant & Harlequin Theatre, Cinema & Library REDH RH1 258 B9
Warwick School for Boys WALTH E17 121 H2
The Warwick School REDH RH1 258 C9
The Washington Mayfair Hotel MYFR/PICC W1J 10 F9
Watchlytes School WGCE AL7 23 L5
Waterfield First School CRAWW RH11 283 H9
Waterfields Retail Park WAT WD17 73 L8
Waterfront Leisure Centre WOOL/PLUM SE18 162 D2
Water Gardens Shopping Centre HLW CM20 46 C1
Watergate School CAT SE6 182 G8
LEW SE13 160 G10
Water Lane Primary School HLWW/ROY CM19 46 D5
Waterloo STHWK SE1 18 A1
Waterloo East STHWK SE1 12 B10
Waterloo Health Centre STHWK SE1 18 A2
Waterloo School of English NOXST/BSQ WC1A 11 L4
Watermans Arts, Cinema & Theatre Centre BTFD TW8 155 K5
Watermans Business Park STA TW18 173 H7
The Watermans Hall MON EC3R 13 J8
Watermeads High School MRDN SM4 201 N6
Watermill Business Centre PEND EN3 80 E6
Water Rats Theatre STPAN WC1H 5 M9
Waterside Business Centre ISLW TW7 154 G10
Waterside Combined School CSHM HP5 51 J9
Waterside Industrial Estate HOD EN11 45 J4
Waterside Primary School WOOL/PLUM SE18 162 C4
The Waterside Trading Centre HNWL W7 154 D2
Waterside Trading Estate ADL/WDHM KT15 215 P1
Watersmeet Centre RKW/CH/CXG WD3 91 P1
Watersports Centre STNW/STAM N16 119 K6
Waterways Business Centre PEND EN3 80 E4
Waterways Heritage Museum RKW/CH/CXG WD3 91 P2
Watford WATW WD18 72 G7
Watford Arches Retail Park WAT WD17 73 K9
Watford Business Centre WAT WD17 73 J7
Watford FC & Saracens RFC (Vicarage Road Stadium) WATW WD18 73 J9
Watford General Hospital WATW WD18 73 J9
Watford Grammar School for Boys WATW WD18 72 G8
Watford Grammar School for Girls WATW WD18 73 K9
Watford High Street WATW WD18 73 K8
Watford Junction WAT WD17 73 K6
Watford Museum WATW WD18 73 K9
Watford North WATN WD24 73 K3
Watford Sports & Leisure Centre GSTN WD25 55 K9
Watling Boys' Club EDGW HA8 95 M8
Watling Clinic EDGW HA8 96 A8
Watling Medical Centre EDGW HA8 95 P9
Watling Street Burial Ground RDART DA2 188 A3
Watling View Special School STAL AL1 38 C10
Wattenden Primary School PUR/KEN CR8 241 J3
The Watts Cemetery RGUW GU3 266 G6
The Watts Gallery RGUW GU3 266 G6
Wavelengths Leisure Pool & Library DEPT SE8 160 F6
Waverley Industrial Estate HRW HA1 114 C1
Waverley Lower Secondary School EDUL SE22 182 A1
Waverley School PEND EN3 80 B8
Waxchandlers' Hall CITYW EC2V 12 F5
Weald Community Primary School RSEV TN14 265 J9
Weald Country Park BRW CM14 106 D1
Weald Middle School KTN/HRWW/WS HA3 94 E8
Wealdstone Cemetery KTN/HRWW/WS HA3 114 F1
Webber Douglas Academy of Dramatic Art SKENS SW7 15 K6
Webster Graduate Studies Center CAMTN NW1 10 B1
Welbeck Clinic CRICK NW2 117 K8
Welbourne Primary School SEVS/STOTM N15 119 P2
Welham Green BRKMPK AL9 40 G9
Wellcome Institute CAMTN NW1 11 J1
Welldon Park Middle School RYLN/HDSTN HA2 114 B9
Wellesley Road CROY/NA CR0 203 K9
Welling WELL DA16 163 K8
The Welling Clinic WELL DA16 163 K8
Welling Medical Centre WELL DA16 163 J10
Welling School WELL DA16 163 L7
Wellington Arch MYFR/PICC W1J 16 D1
Wellington Barracks WESTW SW1E 17 H2
Wellington Primary School BOW E3 140 F5
CHING E4 100 G3
HSLW TW3 153 N8
Welling United FC WELL DA16 163 M9
Wells Park School CHIG IG7 103 J5
Wells Primary School WFD IG8 101 N5
Welwyn Garden City WGCW AL8 23 H4
Welwyn Garden City CC WGCW AL8 22 G1
Welwyn Garden City Football & Social Club WGCE AL7 23 L3
Welwyn Garden City Golf Club WGCW AL8 22 E5
Welwyn RFC WGCW AL8 22 F6
Welwyn Viaduct WGCW AL8 23 H1
Wembley Arena WBLY HA9 115 M9
Wembley Central WBLY HA9 115 K10
Wembley Commercial Centre WBLY HA9 115 J7
Wembley Conference Centre WBLY HA9 115 L9
Wembley FC ALP/SUD HA0 114 G9
Wembley High Technology College ALP/SUD HA0 115 H8
Wembley Hospital ALP/SUD HA0 135 J1
Wembley Park WBLY HA9 115 M8
Wembley Park Business Centre WBLY HA9 115 N8
Wembley Primary School WBLY HA9 115 K8
Wembley Stadium WBLY HA9 115 M9
Wembley Stadium WBLY HA9 115 M10
Wembley Stadium Industrial Estate WBLY HA9 115 M8
WBLY HA9 115 P8
Wendell Park Primary School SHB W12 156 C1
Wennington Hall Farm Business Centre RAIN RM13 145 M8
The Wenta Business Centre WATN WD24 73 L3
Wentworth Golf Club VW GU25 193 M5
Wentworth Tutorial College GLDGN NW11 116 G4
The Wernher Collection at Ranger's House GNWCH SE10 161 J7
Wesley's Chapel, House & Museum STLK EC1Y 12 G1
Wessex Gardens Primary School GLDGN NW11 117 H6
West 12 Shopping & Leisure Centre SHB W12 156 G1
West Acton ACT W3 135 M8
West Acton Primary School ACT W3 135 N8
West Ashtead Primary School ASHTD KT21 237 J6
West Beckton Health Centre CAN/RD E16 141 P7
Westbourne Green Sports Complex BAY/PAD W2 8 F4
Westbourne Park NTGHL W11 8 D3
Westbourne Primary School SUT SM1 201 K10
Westbridge College BTSEA SW11 157 P7
West Brompton ECT SW5 14 F8
Westbrooke School WELL DA16 163 N9
Westbrook Hay Preparatory School HHW HP1 34 G9
The Westbury Hotel CONDST W1S 10 F7
Westbury Medical Centre WDGN N22 99 K10
West Byfleet BF/WBF KT14 215 K8
West Byfleet Golf Club BF/WBF KT14 215 J9
West Byfleet J & I School BF/WBF KT14 215 L8
West Byfleet Physiotherapy Clinic BF/WBF KT14 215 K8
Westcombe Park BKHTH/KID SE3 161 M4
Westcott CE First School DORK RH4 272 B3
Westcourt Primary School GVE DA12 191 H5
Westcroft Leisure Centre CAR SM5 222 B1
West Croydon CROY/NA CR0 203 J8
West Dene School PUR/KEN CR8 222 G9
West Drayton WDR/YW UB7 131 P10
West Drayton Cemetery WDR/YW UB7 151 P2
West Drayton CC WDR/YW UB7 151 M3
West Drayton Primary School WDR/YW UB7 151 P1
West Dulwich DUL SE21 181 L4
West Ealing WEA W13 134 G9
West Ealing Business Centre WEA W13 134 F9
West End Sports & Social Club ESH/CLAY KT10 217 N3
Westerham Golf Club BH/WHM TN16 263 K1
Western Avenue Business Park ACT W3 135 N6
Western Cemetery CHESW EN7 61 P10
Western House Hospital WARE SG12 26 C1
Western House Primary School SL SL1 128 E9
Western International Market NWDGN UB2 153 J3
Western Trading Estate WLSDN NW10 135 P6
West Essex Golf Club CHING E4 81 K8
West Ewell Infant School HOR/WEW KT19 220 A2
Westferry POP/IOD E14 140 E9
Westfield Community Primary School HOD EN11 44 E2
Westfield Community Technical College WATW WD18 72 G9
Westfield First School BERK HP4 33 L4
Westfield London SHB W12 136 F10
Westfield Primary School WOKS/MYFD GU22 232 B7
Westfields Primary School BARN SW13 156 C8
Westfield Stratford City development SRTFD E15 141 H1
West Finchley FNCH N3 97 L7
Westgate Primary School DART DA1 187 L3
Westgate Retail Park SL SL1 128 F9
Westgate School SL SL1 128 F10
West Green Primary School CRAWW RH11 283 M7
SEVS/STOTM N15 119 K2
West Grove Primary School STHGT/OAK N14 98 E1
West Ham SRTFD E15 141 K5
West Ham Church Primary School SRTFD E15 141 L3
West Ham Lane Clinic SRTFD E15 141 K3
West Hampstead KIL/WHAMP NW6 2 F2
West Hampstead KIL/WHAMP NW6 2 G2
West Hampstead Clinic KIL/WHAMP NW6 2 F3
West Hampstead Thameslink KIL/WHAMP NW6 2 E1
West Ham United FC (Upton Park) PLSTW E13 142 A4
West Harrow HRW HA1 114 B4
West Hatch High School WFD IG8 102 C6
West Hendon Clinic CDALE/KGS NW9 116 C4
West Herts Business Centre BORE WD6 75 N7
West Herts Cemetery GSTN WD25 55 L7
West Herts College WAT WD17 73 H4
West Herts College (Dacorum Campus) HHW HP1 35 M5
West Herts College (Leggatts Campus) WATN WD24 73 H2
West Herts College (Watford Campus) WAT WD17 73 H6
West Herts Crematorium GSTN WD25 55 L7
West Herts Golf Club RKW/CH/CXG WD3 72 E7
West Hill Golf Club CHOB/PIR GU24 230 G7
West Hill Primary School DART DA1 187 K2
WAND/EARL SW18 179 K1
West Hill School LHD/OX KT22 236 F4
West Horndon RBRW/HUT CM13 127 P4
West India Pier POP/IOD E14 160 E1
West India Quay POP/IOD E14 140 F9
West India Shopping Centre POP/IOD E14 140 F10
West Kensington WKENS W14 14 C7
West Kent Golf Club ORP BR6 226 B8
Westland Heliport BTSEA SW11 157 N9
West Lea School ED N9 99 M4
West Lodge Middle School PIN HA5 113 L2
West Lodge Park Hotel EBAR EN4 78 A4
West Lodge Preparatory School BFN/LL DA15 185 J6
West London Academy NTHLT UB5 133 L3
West London Academy Primary NTHLT UB5 133 L2
West London Tamil School WLSDN NW10 136 C4
West Mead Clinic RSLP HA4 113 K8
West Middlesex Golf Club STHL UB1 134 B9
West Middlesex University Hospital ISLW TW7 154 F8
Westminster WHALL SW1A 17 M2
Westminster Abbey WEST SW1P 17 L3
Westminster Abbey Choir School WEST SW1P 17 K3
Westminster Academy BAY/PAD W2 8 F4
Westminster Bridge Park Plaza Hotel STHWK SE1 17 N2
Westminster Business Square LBTH SE11 17 N8
Westminster Cathedral WESTW SW1E 16 G4
Westminster Cathedral Choir School WEST SW1P 17 H4
Westminster Cathedral RC Primary School PIM SW1V 17 K7
Westminster City Hall WESTW SW1E 17 H4
Westminster City School WESTW SW1E 17 H3
Westminster Hall WHALL SW1A 17 M2
Westminster Industrial Estate WOOL/PLUM SE18 162 A2
Westminster Kingsway College CAMTN NW1 4 G10
WEST SW1P 17 H5
Westminster Lodge Leisure Sports Centre STAL AL1 38 B8
Westminster Natural Health Centre PIM SW1V 16 G6
Westminster Pier WHALL SW1A 17 M2
Westminster School WEST SW1P 17 L3
Westminster Theatre WESTW SW1E 16 G3
Westminster Under School WEST SW1P 17 J6
Westmoor Community Clinic PUT/ROE SW15 178 D3
West Norwood WNWD SE27 181 J7
West Norwood Clinic WNWD SE27 181 K5
West Norwood Crematorium WNWD SE27 181 K6
West One Shopping Centre MYFR/PKLN W1K 10 D6
Weston Green School THDIT KT7 198 D8
Weston Park Clinic CEND/HSY/T N8 118 F3
Weston Park Primary School CEND/HSY/T N8 118 G3
West Park Hospital EPSOM KT18 219 K8
Westpoint Trading Estate ACT W3 135 N7
West Ramp Coach Park HTHAIR TW6 152 B7
West Ruislip RSLP HA4 112 D7
West Silvertown CAN/RD E16 141 M10
West Sutton SUT SM1 221 K1
West Thames College ISLW TW7 154 D7
West Thamesmead Business Park THMD SE28 163 J2
West Thornton Primary School CROY/NA CR0 202 G7
West Thurrock Primary School WTHK RM20 166 F5
West Twyford Primary School WLSDN NW10 135 M4
Westward Preparatory School WOT/HER KT12 197 J9
Westway Business Centre BAY/PAD W2 8 G4
The Westway Clinic REDH RH1 257 P9
Westway Sports Centre NKENS W10 136 G8
West Wickham WWKM BR4 205 H7
West Wickham Swimming Baths WWKM BR4 205 H8
West Wimbledon Primary School RYNPK SW20 200 E3
Westwood Language College for Girls NRWD SE19 181 K10
Westwood Primary School WELL DA16 163 H10
Westwood School BUSH WD23 94 C3
Wetherby Preparatory School BAY/PAD W2 8 F7
Wexham Court Primary School SLN SL2 129 P7
Wexham Park Golf Club DTCH/LGLY SL3 129 P4
Wexham Park Hospital DTCH/LGLY SL3 129 P6
Wexham School Sports College SLN SL2 129 N7
Weybridge WEY KT13 216 C3
Weybridge Business Park ADL/WDHM KT15 215 P1
Weybridge Cemetery WEY KT13 216 A2
Weybridge CC WEY KT13 196 F9
Weybridge Hospital WEY KT13 216 B1
Weyfield Primary School GU GU1 250 A7
Wey House School SHGR GU5 268 B9
Wey Retail Park BF/WBF KT14 215 P8
Whaddon House Clinic CMBW SE5 159 M9
Wheatcroft School HERT/BAY SG13 25 P4
Wheatfields Junior School STALE/WH AL4 38 G2
Whelpley Hill Park CSHM HP5 52 A2
Whipps Cross Hospital LEY E10 121 J4
Whitchurch Middle School STAN HA7 95 H8
White Bridge Primary School LOU IG10 102 B1
Whitechapel WCHPL E1 140 A7
Whitechapel Art Gallery WCHPL E1 13 M5
White City SHB W12 136 F9
Whitefield School CRICK NW2 116 G5
Whitefield School & Leisure Centre WALTH E17 101 J9
Whitefriars First & Middle School KTN/HRWW/WS HA3 94 D10
Whitefriars Trading Estate KTN/HRWW/WS HA3 94 C10
Whitehall Estate HLWW/ROY CM19 46 B2
Whitehall Infant School UX/CGN UB8 131 M4
Whitehall Theatre WHALL SW1A 11 K9
White Hart Lane TOTM N17 99 N8
Whiteheath Infant School RSLP HA4 112 C4
Whiteheath Junior School RSLP HA4 112 D4
Whitehill Primary School GVE DA12 190 F6
White Horse Hotel HERT/WAT SG14 24 G6
Whitehorse Manor Primary School THHTH CR7 203 L5
The White House Preparatory School BAL SW12 180 E4
Whiteleys Shopping Centre BAY/PAD W2 8 G6
White Lodge Centre CHERT KT16 194 G9
Whiterose Trading Estate EBAR EN4 97 P1
The Whitewebbs Museum of Transport & Industry ENC/FH EN2 79 J1
Whitewebbs Park Golf Club ENC/FH EN2 79 L3
Whitgift Almshouses CROY/NA CR0 203 K9
Whitgift School SAND/SEL CR2 223 K2
Whitgift Shopping Centre CROY/NA CR0 203 K9
Whitings Hill Primary School BAR EN5 76 F9
Whitmore High School RYLN/HDSTN HA2 114 B6
Whitmore Primary School IS N1 7 H7
Whittingham Community Primary School WALTH E17 100 D9
Whittington Hospital ARCH N19 118 C7
Whitton WHTN TW2 176 B3
Whitton Health Centre WHTN TW2 176 B4
Whitton Health Clinic WHTN TW2 176 A4
Whitton School WHTN TW2 176 A5
Whitton Sports & Fitness Centre WHTN TW2 176 A5
Whybridge Infant School RAIN RM13 145 H3
Whybridge Junior School RAIN RM13 144 G3
Whyteleafe CTHM CR3 241 N3
Whyteleafe Business Village CTHM CR3 241 N3
Whyteleafe FC CTHM CR3 241 N5
Whyteleafe School CTHM CR3 241 N4
Whyteleafe South CTHM CR3 241 N5
Wickham Theatre WWKM BR4 205 J10
Widewater Business Centre DEN/HRF UB9 111 M3
Wide Way Health Clinic MTCM CR4 202 E3
Widmore Centre BMLY BR1 205 P2
Wigmore Hall CAVSQ/HST W1G 10 E5
Wigram House (University of Westminster) WEST SW1P 17 J4
Wilberforce Primary School NKENS W10 2 B9
Wilbury Primary School UED N18 99 L6
Wilderness Golf Club BGR/WK TN15 247 P8
Wilderness School SEV TN13 247 M7
Wilderness Sports Centre SEV TN13 247 M7
Willesden Centre for Health & Care WLSDN NW10 136 D2
Willesden Green CRICK NW2 136 F1
Willesden Junction WLSDN NW10 136 C4
Willesden Medical Centre CRICK NW2 136 E1
Willesden New Cemetery WLSDN NW10 136 C2
Willesden Sports Centre WLSDN NW10 136 E3
Willesden Sports Stadium WLSDN NW10 136 E3
William Bellamy J & I School DAGE RM10 124 B7
William Byrd School HYS/HAR UB3 152 D5
William Davies Primary School FSTGT E7 142 A1
William Edwards School CDW/CHF RM16 147 P9
William Ellis School KTTN NW5 118 B8
William Ellis Sports Ground EDGW HA8 95 M9
William Ford CE Junior School DAGE RM10 144 B2
William Hogarth School CHSWK W4 156 B5
William Morris Academy HMSMTH W6 156 G4
William Morris Gallery WALTH E17 120 F1
William Morris Primary School MTCM CR4 202 E3
William Morris School WALTH E17 100 D9
William Patten Primary School STNW/STAM N16 119 N7
William Penn Leisure Centre RKW/CH/CXG WD3 91 J2
William Torbitt J & I School GNTH/NBYPK IG2 123 H3
William Tyndale Primary School IS N1 6 D3
Willington School WIM/MER SW19 179 J9
Willow Brook Primary LEY E10 120 F6
Willow Business Centre MTCM CR4 202 A5
Willow Business Park SYD SE26 182 B6
Willowfield Adult Education Centre WALTH E17 120 C1
Willowfield School WALTH E17 120 D1
The Willows Clinic CHST BR7 184 D9
The Willows School YEAD UB4 133 L6
Willow Tree Primary School NTHLT UB5 133 M1
Wilmington Entreprise College RDART DA2 187 H6
Wilmington Grammar School for Boys RDART DA2 187 J6
Wilmington Grammar School for Girls RDART DA2 187 J5
Wilmington Primary School RDART DA2 187 J6
Wilson's School WLGTN SM6 222 F3
Wilton's Music Hall WCHPL E1 13 N7
Wimbledon WIM/MER SW19 179 J9
Wimbledon Chase RYNPK SW20 201 H2
Wimbledon Chase Primary School RYNPK SW20 201 H1
Wimbledon Common Golf Club WIM/MER SW19 178 E8
Wimbledon Common Pre-Preparatory School WIM/MER SW19 178 G10
Wimbledon (Gap Road) Cemetery WIM/MER SW19 179 L7
Wimbledon High School WIM/MER SW19 179 H9
Wimbledon House School WIM/MER SW19 201 J1
Wimbledon Lawn Tennis Museum WIM/MER SW19 179 H6
Wimbledon Park WIM/MER SW19 179 K6
Wimbledon Park Athletics Track WIM/MER SW19 179 J5
Wimbledon Park Golf Club WIM/MER SW19 179 J6
Wimbledon Park Primary School WIM/MER SW19 179 K5
Wimbledon Recreation Centre WIM/MER SW19 179 L9
Wimbledon RFC RYNPK SW20 178 C10
Wimbledon School of Art WIM/MER SW19 201 H1
Wimbledon Squash & Badminton Club WIM/MER SW19 179 H10
Wimbledon Stadium WIM/MER SW19 179 L7
Wimbledon Stadium Business Centre WIM/MER SW19 179 L6
Wimbledon Theatre WIM/MER SW19 179 K10
Wimbledon Windmill WIM/MER SW19 178 F6
Winchcombe Business Centre PECK SE15 19 K10
Winchmore Hill WCHMH N21 99 J1
Winchmore Hill CC AMSS HP7 68 A10

Winchmore Hill Clinic *WCHMH* N21 ...99 J2
Winchmore Hill CC *WCHMH* N21 ...99 K2
Winchmore School *WCHMH* N21 ...99 K3
Windermere JMI Primary School *STAL* AL1 ...38 G8
Windermere Golf Club *CHOB/PIR* GU24 ...212 D7
Windmill Business Centre *NWDGN* UB2 ...134 B10
Windmill Trading Estate *MTCM* CR4 ...202 D5; *SUN* TW16 ...196 E1
Windrush Primary School *THMD* SE28 ...143 L10
Windsor Arts Centre *WDSR* SL4 ...149 H8
The Windsor Boys School *WDSR* SL4 ...148 G7
Windsor Business Centre *WDSR* SL4 ...148 G6
Windsor Castle *WDSR* SL4 ...149 K6
Windsor Cemetery *WDSR* SL4 ...148 G9
Windsor Coach Park *WDSR* SL4 ...149 H6
Windsor Cricket & Rugby Clubs *WDSR* SL4 ...149 K5
Windsor English Language Centre *WDSR* SL4 ...149 H8
Windsor & Eton Central ≥ *WDSR* SL4 ...149 H7
Windsor & Eton FC *WDSR* SL4 ...148 G10
Windsor & Eton Riverside ≥ *WDSR* SL4 ...149 J6
Windsor Girls School *WDSR* SL4 ...148 F9
Windsor Industrial Estate *HERT/BAY* SG13 ...26 A3
Windsor Lawn Tennis Club *WDSR* SL4 ...148 G7
Windsor Leisure Centre *WDSR* SL4 ...148 G6
Winfield House *CAMTN* NW1 ...3 P9
Wingate & Finchley FC *NFNCH/WDSPK* N12 ...97 N8
Wingate Trading Estate *TOTM* N17 ...99 N8
Wingfield Primary School *BKHTH/KID* SE3 ...161 M9
Winns Primary School *WALTH* E17 ...100 E10
Winsor Primary School *EHAM* E6 ...142 D8
Winston Churchill's Britain at War Experience *STHWK* SE1 ...13 H10
The Winston Churchill School *WOKN/KNAP* GU21 ...231 K4
Winston House Preparatory School *SWFD* E18 ...101 M9
Winston Way Primary School *IL* IG1 ...122 D8
Winterbourne Infant School *THHTH* CR7 ...203 H4

Winton Primary School *IS* N1 ...5 N8
Wishmore Cross School *WOKS/MYFD* GU24 ...213 K6
Witley Industrial Estate *NWDGN* UB2 ...153 N3
Woking ≥ *WOKN/KNAP* GU21 ...232 C3
Woking Athletics Track *WOKN/KNAP* GU21 ...214 F9
Woking Business Park *WOKN/KNAP* GU21 ...232 E1
Woking College *WOKS/MYFD* GU22 ...232 D6
Woking Community Hospital *WOKS/MYFD* GU22 ...232 C4
Woking FC *WOKS/MYFD* GU22 ...232 C6
Woking Golf Club *WOKS/MYFD* GU22 ...231 M6
Woking High School *WOKN/KNAP* GU21 ...232 A1
Woking & Horsell CC *WOKN/KNAP* GU21 ...232 A3
Woking Hospice *WOKS/MYFD* GU22 ...232 B4
Woking Leisure Centre & Pool *WOKS/MYFD* GU22 ...232 C5
Woking Nuffield Hospital *WOKN/KNAP* GU21 ...214 B10
Woking St John's Crematorium *WOKN/KNAP* GU21 ...231 K5
Woldingham ≥ *CTHM* CR3 ...242 C8
Woldingham Golf Club *CTHM* CR3 ...242 C6
Woldingham School *CTHM* CR3 ...260 D1
Wolf Fields Primary School *NWDGN* UB2 ...153 N3
Wolfson Hillel Primary School *STHGT/OAK* N14 ...78 E10
Wolfson Medical Centre *RYNPK* SW20 ...178 D10
Wolsey Business Park *WATW* WD18 ...92 E1
Wolsey Junior School *CROY/NA* CR0 ...225 J4
Wolsey Place Shopping Centre *WOKN/KNAP* GU21 ...232 N3
The Women's Library *WCHPL* E1 ...13 L5
Wonersh Cemetery *SHGR* GU5 ...268 C9
Woodacre Special School *SOCK/AV* RM15 ...146 E7
The Woodberry Clinic *MUSWH* N10 ...118 C1
Woodberry Down Centre *FSBYPK* N4 ...119 K6
Woodberry Down Community Primary *FSBYPK* N4 ...119 K5
Woodbridge Business Park *GU* GU1 ...249 P6
Woodbridge High School & Language College *WFD* IG8 ...101 K5
Woodcock Hill Cemetery *RKW/CH/CXG* WD3 ...91 N5
Woodcote High School *PUR/KEN* CR8 ...222 E9

Woodcote House School *BFOR* GU20 ...212 A2
Woodcote Park Golf Club *COUL/CHIP* CR5 ...222 D10
Woodcotes Primary School *COUL/CHIP* CR5 ...222 E10
Woodcroft Primary School *EDGW* HA8 ...96 A8
Woodcroft School *LOU* IG10 ...82 C5
Wood End J & I Schools *GFD/PVL* UB6 ...114 C10
Wood End Park Junior School *UX/CGN* UB8 ...132 D9
Woodfield School *CDALE/KGS* NW9 ...116 B6; *REDH* RH1 ...258 F5
Woodfield Special School *HHS/BOV* HP3 ...36 D8
Woodford ⊖ *WFD* IG8 ...101 N7
Woodford County High School for Girls *WFD* IG8 ...101 L7
Woodford Golf Club *WFD* IG8 ...101 L6
Woodford Green Preparatory School *WFD* IG8 ...101 M7
Woodford Green Primary School *WFD* IG8 ...101 L6
Woodford Trading Estate *WFD* IG8 ...101 P10
Woodgrange Infant School *FSTGT* E7 ...121 N9
Woodgrange Park ⊖ *FSTGT* E7 ...122 A10
Woodgrange Park Cemetery *MNPK* E12 ...122 A10
Wood Green ⊖ *WDGN* N22 ...99 H10
Wood Green Health Centre *WDGN* N22 ...98 C9
Wood Green Old Boys FC *WDGN* N22 ...99 H8
Woodhall School *OXHEY* WD19 ...93 M5
Woodhill Primary School *CHARL* SE7 ...162 B3
Woodhouse College *NFNCH/WDSPK* N12 ...97 N7
Woodlands First & Middle School *KTN/HRWW/WS* HA3 ...94 B8
Woodlands J & I School *IL* IG1 ...122 C9
Woodlands Medical Centre *LEW* SE13 ...183 J2
Woodlands Park Hotel *COB* KT11 ...236 B3
Woodlands Preparatory School *RBRW/HUT* CM13 ...127 J2
Woodlands Primary School *BORE* WD6 ...75 N8
Woodlands School *LHD/OX* KT22 ...237 H8
Wood Lane ⊖ *SHB* W12 ...136 F9
Wood Lane Medical Centre *RSLP* HA4 ...112 F6
Wood Lane School *FUL/PGN* SW6 ...157 M7
Wood Lane Sports Centre *BCTR* RM8 ...124 C6

Woodlea Primary School *CTHM* CR3 ...242 E8
Woodman Road Cemetery *BRW* CM14 ...107 J6
Woodmansterne Primary School *COUL/CHIP* CR5 ...240 C2
Woodmansterne Primary School *BNSTD* SM7 ...222 A10; *STRHM/NOR* SW16 ...202 E1
Woodmansterne Sports Club *BNSTD* SM7 ...239 P1
Woodridge Primary School *NFNCH/WDSPK* N12 ...97 K4
Woodside ⊖ *SNWD* SE25 ...204 A6
Woodside Health Centre *SNWD* SE25 ...204 A5
Woodside High School *WDGN* N22 ...99 J8
Woodside Infant School *CROY/NA* CR0 ...203 P7
Woodside Junior School *AMS* HP6 ...69 K4
Woodside Park ⊖ *NFNCH/WDSPK* N12 ...97 K5
Woodside Park Golf Club *NFNCH/WDSPK* N12 ...97 K5
Woodside Park International School *NFNCH/WDSPK* N12 ...97 L5
Woodside Primary School *CDW/CHF* RM16 ...168 C2; *CHESW* EN7 ...61 K5; *WALTH* E17 ...121 H1
Woodside School *BELV* DA17 ...164 C3
Woodside Stadium *GSTN* WD25 ...55 K9
Wood Street ≥ *WALTH* E17 ...121 J2
Wood Street County Infant School *RGUW* GU3 ...249 H8
Woodwells Cemetery *HHNE* HP2 ...36 E5
Wood Wharf *POP/IOD* E14 ...140 C10
Wood Wharf Business Park *POP/IOD* E14 ...161 H1
Woolmore Primary School *POP/IOD* E14 ...141 H9
Woolston Manor Golf Club *CHIG* IG7 ...82 G9
Woolwich Arsenal ≥ ⊖ *WOOL/PLUM* SE18 ...162 E3
Woolwich Cemetery *WOOL/PLUM* SE18 ...163 J6
Woolwich Dockyard ≥ *WOOL/PLUM* SE18 ...162 C3
Woolwich Polytechnic School *THMD* SE28 ...143 K10
Worcester Park ≥ *WPK* KT4 ...200 D8
Worcesters Primary School *ENC/FH* EN2 ...29 N4
World Business Centre Heathrow *HTHAIR* TW6 ...152 D7
World End *TIL* RM18 ...168 E10
World Rugby Museum & Twickenham Stadium Tours *WHTN* TW2 ...176 D2

Worlds End Place *WBPTN* SW10 ...157 M6
World Spiritual University *WLSDN* NW10 ...136 D2
World University Service *STLK* EC1Y ...12 C2
Wormholt Park Primary School *SHB* W12 ...136 D9
Wormley Primary School *BROX* EN10 ...44 D9
Worple Primary School *ISLW* TW7 ...154 F10
Worplesdon ≥ *WOKS/MYFD* GU22 ...231 N10
Worplesdon CP School *RGUW* GU3 ...249 J6
Worplesdon Golf Club *WOKS/MYFD* GU22 ...231 K8
Worsley Bridge Junior School *BECK* BR3 ...182 F10
Worton Hall Industrial Estate *ISLW* TW7 ...154 D10
Wray Common County Middle School *REIG* RH2 ...257 N9
Wray Common Primary School *REIG* RH2 ...257 N9
Wraysbury ≥ *STWL/WRAY* TW19 ...172 C2
Wraysbury Medical Centre *STWL/WRAY* TW19 ...172 C2
Wraysbury Primary School *STWL/WRAY* TW19 ...172 B2
Wren Academy *NFNCH/WDSPK* N12 ...97 N6
Wrencote House *CROY/NA* CR0 ...203 K10
Wrotham Road Health Clinic *GVW* DA11 ...190 E4
Wrotham Road Primary School *GVW* DA11 ...190 E3
The Wroxham School *POTB/CUF* EN6 ...58 F7
Wyborne Primary School *ELTH/MOT* SE9 ...184 E4
Wyke Green Golf Club *ISLW* TW7 ...154 E5
Wykeham Primary School *HCH* RM12 ...125 H6; *WLSDN* NW10 ...116 A8
The Wyllyotts Centre Cinema *POTB/CUF* EN6 ...59 J8
Wyndham Grand Hotel *WBPTN* SW10 ...157 M7
Wyndhams Theatre *CHCR* WC2N ...11 K7
Wyvil Primary School *VX/NE* SW8 ...158 F6
Yale University Press *HAMP* NW3 ...117 P9
Yardley Primary School *CHING* E4 ...80 C10
Yattendon School *HORL* RH6 ...280 B3
Yavneh College *BORE* WD6 ...75 N8
Yeading FC *YEAD* UB4 ...133 K10
Yeading Junior School *YEAD* UB4 ...133 K7
Yeading Medical Centre *NTHLT* UB5 ...133 K5

Yeading Primary School *YEAD* UB4 ...133 K7
Yehudi Menuhin School *COB* KT11 ...235 P5
Ye Olde Fighting Cocks Inn *STALW/RED* AL3 ...38 A7
Yerbury Primary School *ARCH* N19 ...118 E8
Yeshivo Horomo Talmudical College *STNW/STAM* N16 ...119 L6
Yesodey Hatorah Jewish Boys School *SEVS/STOTM* N15 ...119 N5
Yesodey Hatorah School For Girls *STNW/STAM* N16 ...119 N5
Yetev Lev Day School for Boys *STNW/STAM* N16 ...119 P6
Yewtree Primary School *HHNE* HP2 ...35 P4
Ylewsley Health Centre *WDR/YW* UB7 ...131 P10
YMCA Community & Sports Centre *REDH* RH1 ...276 B3
YMCA Leisure Centre *RSQ* WC1B ...11 K5
York Clinic *STHWK* SE1 ...12 C10; *WOKN/KNAP* GU21 ...232 B3
Yorke Mead Primary School *RKW/CH/CXG* WD3 ...72 B9
York Hall *BETH* E2 ...140 A4
York House Medical Centre *WOKS/MYFD* GU22 ...232 C4
York House School *RKW/CH/CXG* WD3 ...72 A4
York Road Junior School & Language Unit *DART* DA1 ...187 J1
York Water Gate *CHCR* WC2N ...11 M9
Young England RFC *IS* N1 ...6 A6
Young Actors Theatre *VX/NE* SW8 ...17 M10; *VX/NE* SW8 ...158 C6
Young Vic Theatre *STHWK* SE1 ...18 B1
Yvonne Arnaud Theatre *GUW* GU2 ...268 C2
Zennor Road Industrial Estate *BAL* SW12 ...180 D4
Zephyr Business Centre *SEVS/STOTM* N15 ...119 M2
The Zetter Hotel *FARR* EC1M ...12 C2
Ziam Trading Estate *CLPT* E5 ...120 B6
Zobel College *SEV* TN13 ...247 J10
ZSL London Zoo *CAMTN* NW1 ...4 C7

## Acknowledgements

Schools address data provided by Education Direct.

Petrol station information supplied by Johnsons.

Garden centre information provided by:

Garden Centre Association · Britains best garden centres

Wyevale Garden Centres

The boundary of the London Congestion Charging Zone and Low Emission Zone supplied by Transport for London

The statement on the front cover of this atlas is sourced, selected and quoted from a reader comment and feedback form received in 2004

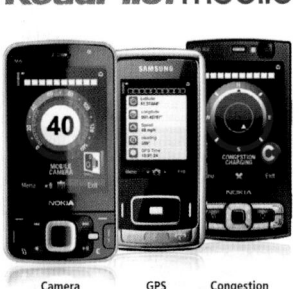

# AA Travel Guides
## The world at your fingertips

**Notes**

**Notes**

**Notes**

# AA Street by Street

# QUESTIONNAIRE

**Dear Atlas User**
**Your comments, opinions and recommendations are very important to us.**
**So please help us to improve our street atlases by taking a few minutes to**
**complete this simple questionnaire.**

You do not need a stamp (unless posted outside the UK). If you do not want to remove this page from your street atlas, then photocopy it or write your answers on a plain sheet of paper.

**Send to: Marketing Assistant, AA Publishing, 14th Floor Fanum House,**
**Freepost SCE 4598, Basingstoke RG21 4GY**

## ABOUT THE ATLAS...

**Please state which city / town / county you bought:**

_____

**Where did you buy the atlas?** (City, Town, County)

_____

**For what purpose?** (please tick all applicable)

**To use in your local area** ☐   **To use on business or at work** ☐

**Visiting a strange place** ☐   **In the car** ☐   **On foot** ☐

**Other** (please state)

_____

_____

**Have you ever used any street atlases other than AA Street by Street?**

**Yes** ☐   **No** ☐

**If so, which ones?**

_____

**Is there any aspect of our street atlases that could be improved?**
(Please continue on a separate sheet if necessary)

_____

_____

_____

_____

GSA040w

continued overleaf

**Please list the features you found most useful:**

_____
_____
_____

**Please list the features you found least useful:**

_____
_____
_____

## LOCAL KNOWLEDGE...

**Local knowledge is invaluable. Whilst every attempt has been made to make the information contained in this atlas as accurate as possible, should you notice any inaccuracies, please detail them below (if necessary, use a blank piece of paper) or e-mail us at _streetbystreet@theAA.com_**

_____
_____
_____

## ABOUT YOU...

**Name (Mr/Mrs/Ms)**
**Address**
                                        Postcode
**Daytime tel no**
**E-mail address**

**Which age group are you in?**

**Under 25** ☐   **25-34** ☐   **35-44** ☐   **45-54** ☐   **55-64** ☐   **65+** ☐

**Are you an AA member?**   YES ☐   NO ☐

**Do you have Internet access?**   YES ☐   NO ☐

_____

Thank you for taking the time to complete this questionnaire. Please send it to us as soon as possible, and remember, you do not need a stamp (unless posted outside the UK).

We may use information we hold about you to, telephone or email you about other products and services offered by the AA, we do NOT disclose this information to third parties.

Please tick here if you do not wish to hear about products and services from the AA. ☐

GSA040w